W9-ARU-010

1981

BRITANNICA BOOK OF THE YEAR

1981
BRITANNICA BOOK OF THE YEAR

ENCYCLOPÆDIA BRITANNICA, INC.

CHICAGO, TORONTO, LONDON, GENEVA, SYDNEY, TOKYO, MANILA, SEOUL

Library of Congress Catalog Card Number: 38–12082
International Standard Book Number: 0–85229–381-X
International Standard Serial Number: 0068–1156

BRITANNICA BOOK OF THE YEAR

(Trademark Reg. U.S. Pat. Off.)
Printed in U.S.A.

THE UNIVERSITY OF CHICAGO

The Britannica Book of the Year is published with the editorial advice of the faculties of the University of Chicago.

CONTENTS

Frontispiece photograph on page 153 by James Mason—Black Star

SPECIAL REPORTS

DANGER SIGNALS FROM THE ARC OF CRISIS

by R. W. Bradnock and K. S. McLachlan

HENRI BUREAU—SYGMA

With a suddenness that has severely jolted the international community, instability and uncertainty have spread across Asia Minor and Southwest Asia. The so-called northern tier states, Turkey, Iran, Afghanistan, and Pakistan, have been profoundly destabilized by ethnic and religious conflict within their borders, and this conflict has already brought intervention by the big powers in its wake.

There are grave risks that the underlying tensions within this arc of crisis will prove contagious. Neighbouring oil-exporting states in the Persian Gulf, notably Iraq, have already been drawn into active involvement, but the threat of major upheaval extends well beyond the immediate area, to the Indian Ocean and the Indian subcontinent. The Iranian revolution that reached a climax in February 1979 signaled a clear warning that there was a danger of prolonged turbulence in the strategically vital region stretching from Turkey to Pakistan, designated by Zbigniew Brzezinski, national security adviser to U.S. Pres. Jimmy Carter, as the "arc of crisis."

Yet the situation was scarcely new. Historically the region has been one of endemic instability, and it was only during the 1970s that there appeared to be growing maturity and credible signs of authority.

That this authority was more apparent than real was demonstrated by the events that followed the exile of the shah of Iran in January 1979. His departure removed the chief prop to stable government in the region, and governmental authority which had seemed secure was shown to have been built on foundations of sand. In all four states, enforced modernization by rulers with scarcely any claim to democratic legitimacy had failed to win the acceptance of societies still cast in a traditional mold.

International pacts and agreements, whether within the region (such as the Regional Cooperation for Development among Turkey, Iran, and Pakistan) or beyond it (the Central Treaty Organization, or CENTO), never proved effective vehicles for either joint economic development or mutual defense. Indeed, the four states have little in common, even in respect of Islam. Iran has a predominantly Shiʿah population and now a Shiʿah government. Pakistan is officially a Sunni state, though it has a significant Shiʿah minority. Turkey has long been officially secular, and Afghanistan has a government ideologically opposed to Islam though grudgingly tolerant of its practice.

Internal Problems. The rise of nation-states during the 20th century and the crystallization of firm frontiers has divided ethnic, linguistic, and religious groups who formerly migrated freely across the borderlands. In an area of poor and marginal environments, pastoral nomadism was one of the few possible economic responses. Containment and control of these peripheral areas of tribal occupation proved precarious, even during periods of strong central government. As the erosion of central authority accelerated in the late 1970s, so cohesive tribal organizations in the border regions were reestablished. At times they were expressed in traditional forms, as when tribal hierarchies reemerged in place of government structures. Occasionally, they were manifested in modern political form as a party system claiming formalized regional autonomy.

The convulsions that have shaken these four Islamic countries have potentially different implications for each one's future internal structure. They also have unpredictable though profound implications for the future relationships of these countries with each other and with their neighbours.

Iran. In Iran the decline of central government authority was accompanied by revolts in those areas where specific ethnic groups of Sunni Muslim faith inhabited coherent territories on the geographic fringes of the country. For the most part these groups reacted in self-defense against the rampant Shiʿah Muslim nationalism of the Khomeini government. Regional movements for autonomy sprang up in Kurdestan, Baluchistan, Khuzestan, and the Turkmen Sahra of the eastern Caspian plain. De facto autonomy was seized less dramatically but just as effectively by a number of tribal groups in the inaccessible mountain zones of the Zagros, including the Qashqa'i and the Bakhtiari. The arm of the new civil administration based in Teheran simply failed to penetrate these areas.

The most destabilizing elements of the revolt against the alliance between Shiʿah Islam and Iranian nationalism came from those groups, such as the Kurds, the Arabs, and the Baluch, whose lands spread across political frontiers. While none of them claimed total autonomy, they did articulate specific demands for regional self-administration, including rights to linguistic and religious freedom. Two main factors have given strength to the Kurdish revolt and have precluded a settlement with Teheran. First, the Kurds worked within the framework of the Kurdish Democratic Party. This unity implied a pan-Kurdish movement. Second, the Kurds proposed a federal and democratic political structure for Iran. Arab, Baluch, and Turkmen groups presented similar programs. These had to be taken seriously, because all the tribal or party organizations could draw support, both intellectual and military, from related and sympathetic groups outside Iran's borders.

The Islamic republican regime in Teheran was

Keith S. McLachlan is senior lecturer and Robert W. Bradnock is lecturer in geography with special reference to South Asia at the School of Oriental and African Studies, University of London.

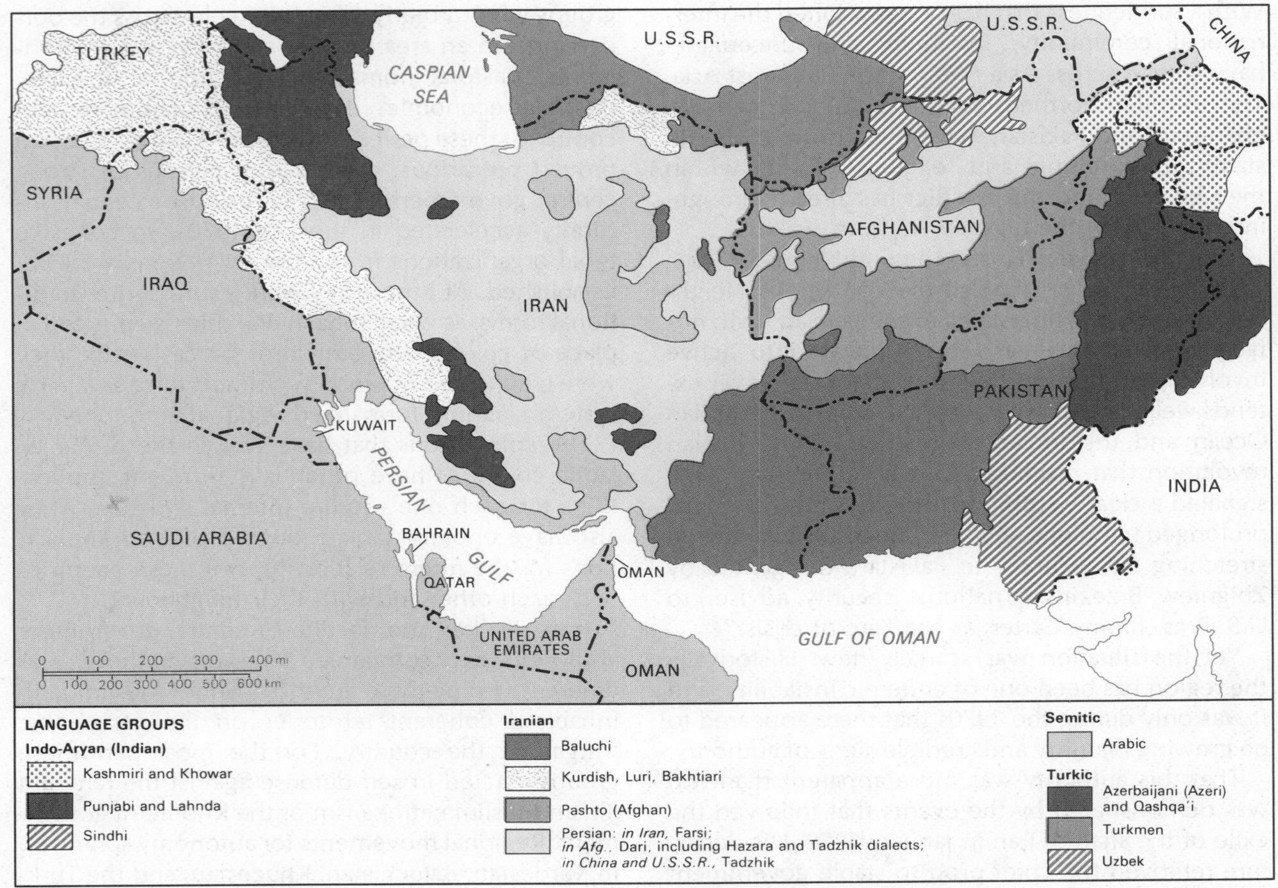

The Iranian revolution peaked in February 1979, leaving in its wake a prolonged upheaval in the region stretching from Turkey to Pakistan. This area was designated by Zbigniew Brzezinski, national security adviser to U.S. Pres. Jimmy Carter, as the "arc of crisis."

profoundly hostile to the various claims for provincial autonomy. It did not wish to give up any power, to permit deviations from the Shiʿah line of the Ayatollah Ruhollah Khomeini, or to allow, in the provinces, an unfettered democracy that might prove attractive to the Iranian heartland. The Iranian government declared a holy war against the Kurds and designated them as traitors. Few concessions to the Kurds or the other minorities were likely to be made by the government, despite the military weakness of the Iranian Army and the Islamic Militia. Continuing warfare appeared inevitable as the minorities pressed their demands, ensuring political dislocation within the country and opportunities for involvement in Iranian affairs by outside interests. Thus Iraqi backing of Kurdish and Arab movements with arms and logistical support contributed to the war beginning in September 1980.

The alienation of almost half the geographic area of the country from the central government had severe economic side effects. Among the most serious were loss of agricultural output from the rainfed lands of the west lying within Kurdestan; disruption of the southern oil fields and the main Gulf ports by guerrilla and military action; failure of the important cotton-growing area in the Turkmen region; and diversion of funds and personnel away from development of the vital productive sectors of the economy.

Turkey. Although Turkey's internal problems in 1980 were less severe than those of Iran, the difference was only a matter of degree. Economic failure had precipitated a political crisis that threatened civil war, leading to a military coup in September 1980. The rapid rise in energy prices after 1973 hit Turkey particularly hard, and by 1980 the country's total foreign exchange earnings were scarcely large enough to cover its import bill for petroleum. Turkey's balance of payments deteriorated, leading to shortages of goods and accelerating inflation.

To obtain help from international financial institutions such as the International Monetary Fund, Turkey was forced to embark on an economic stabilization program that included large devaluations of the Turkish lira and a sharp reduction in public-sector indebtedness. These measures increased domestic economic distress. A growing number of workers, estimated at three million, were unemployed, with the highest concentrations in urban areas. After 1974 there had been a growing exodus of peasant families from the land, concentration of a rapidly expanding population in the western provinces, and unrestrained proliferation of urban slum districts. At the same time, employment opportunities were declining.

Political polarization in Turkish society grew apace from 1974. Democracy continued to exist but ceased to work. Legislation needed to run the state was rarely passed. On the streets and in the university campuses, right- and left-wing factions fought a bloody war that resulted in more than a thousand deaths in the first half of 1980 alone. From the 1960s, the left wing had gained strength as a result of poor management of the economy and the many strains in a rapidly changing traditional society. Governments tacitly supported anti-left-wing activities, including violence, and a pattern of extralegal and extraparliamentary confrontation between extreme left and right established itself. Insecurity was made worse by sharp economic contrasts between a relatively prosperous and urbanized west and a backward and neglected east, the former europeanized, the latter conservative and mainly attached to its Islamic or Turkish nationalist legacy.

Violence in political life was exacerbated by the Kurdish problem. There are some seven million Kurds in Turkey, mainly in 18 provinces of the southeast. They represent approximately 15–16% of the total population and have kept their ethnic and linguistic identity despite oppression by the majority group. As Kurdish nationalism spread in Iraq and, particularly, in Iran after 1979, Turkey's Kurds were encouraged to seek concessions from and recognition by the central authorities. After years of neglect, the Kurds had good reason to feel they had little to lose except their poverty and subservience if they joined the general Kurdish movement.

Demonstrators in Tabriz, Iran, wave a torn photograph of the Ayatollah Ruhollah Khomeini during continued outbursts of violence in January.

WIDE WORLD

ABBAS—GAMMA/LIAISON

Despite a military takeover in September, the Turkish government was unable to end the fighting between right- and left-wing factions.

The aggregate effect of these factors—Turkey's economic difficulties; the political cleavages between Communist left and fascist right, Muslim fundamentalism and secular political parties in the Kemalist tradition, Turkish elites and Kurdish nationalists; the geographic division separating Anatolian east from Mediterranean west—was an internal security problem of mammoth proportions. By 1980 the situation had hardened to such an extent that no immediate solutions were apparent. Despite the military coup of September, further chaos and insecurity appeared to threaten this western wing of the arc of crisis.

Afghanistan. Of the four states in the crescent of crisis, Afghanistan had been least touched by the forces of modernization and least effectively brought under any form of central governmental authority. Virtually accepting Soviet hegemony in 1973, Pres. Mohammad Daud Khan led Afghanistan away from its earlier balancing act between the superpowers and attempted to assert his own central authority over the country. Subsequent attempts to distance himself from the Soviet Union contributed to his ultimate downfall, and the succession of puppet regimes, first under Nur Mohammad Taraki and then, from December 1979, under Babrak Karmal (*see* BIOGRAPHIES), pursued an ever more vigorous pro-Soviet Communist line. Alone in the region, the Afghan government of 1980 was attempting to undermine the role of religion and to assert a secular, Marxist ideology throughout the country.

What may have seemed a difficult situation to the Soviets at the end of 1979, when they invaded Afghanistan in force to quash rebel tribesmen battling the Kabul government, appeared almost insoluble as 1980 drew to a close. Far from being brief and effective, the Soviet armed presence turned out to be protracted and was seemingly unable to cope with continuing unrest and armed resistance. Unlike its neighbours, Afghanistan had never really known a powerful and effective central government. Always a marchland, it is still occupied by tribal groups, fiercely independent of each other, practicing a nomadic pastoralism for which the politics of settled agricultural or urban society has no relevance, and clinging to their Islamic faith and group identity with extraordinary tenacity. For them the new Islamic movements to east and west had no particular significance. Their struggle, unlike that in Iran, had become a fight against an invader.

Yet while the problems facing the Soviet Army appeared enormous and the base of popular support for the Communist regime seemed to become ever narrower, the implications of Soviet dominance in the country remained profound. Unable to fight a united battle or to agree on a civilian government in peacetime, Afghanistan appeared certain to remain a battleground of warring interests in the immediate future. For the global powers it remained a crucial piece of the southwest Asian jigsaw. The question of who controlled it was of fundamental significance for Iran, for the Persian Gulf, for Pakistan, and ultimately for India. Internally it remained the space in which nomadic tribes attempted to assert their own control and the right to retain their own patterns of living. At the end of 1980 it seemed there could be no winners, only losers.

Pakistan. The rise of a new Islamic self-awareness and power in the western countries of the crescent of crisis was reflected in the political changes that overtook Pakistan after 1977, but the reflection was distorted by Pakistan's unique historical, cultural, and economic background.

Born out of the partition of British India in 1947, with Islam as its sole raison d'être, Pakistan has always regarded the Islamic faith as the touchstone of its national identity. In its 30-year history, religion has repeatedly proved to be the only significant factor contributing to the national integration of an otherwise extremely diverse country. In 1971 even that was insufficient to contain the regional and cultural pressures that led to the secession of Bangladesh (former East Pakistan) and the emergence of Pakistan in its present form.

Yet despite the fundamental role of Islam throughout Pakistan's history, the replacement of Zulfikar Ali Bhutto's government by that of Gen. Mohammad Zia-ul-Haq in the coup of 1977 represented a real break with the established pattern of Pakistani government. In contrast to all his predecessors in power, General Zia asserted that Pakistan

Islamic guerrilla fighters in Afghanistan downed their weapons for a brief moment of prayer before a skirmish with Soviet troops in September 1980.

RICHARD EMICA—SIPA PRESS/BLACK STAR

SHELDON—CONTACT

Thousands of Afghan refugees poured into Pakistan border towns during the Soviet invasion of Afghanistan. The United Nations High Commissioner for Refugees estimated the current total at more than one million.

was to abandon the pursuit of Western-style economic and political goals and embark on the process of transforming its society into one based entirely on Islamic principles. The preceding 30 years were seen by the new government as a period of apostasy, and the secularization of government, encouraged by all major Pakistani leaders from Mohammad Ali Jinnah through Mohammad Ayub Khan to Bhutto, was looked on with contempt.

In part, the reversion to Islam was a possible option for General Zia because of the political and economic failures of previous governments. The tribal and ethnic minorities of the west and northwest had never become wholeheartedly integrated into the national polity. Democratic politics had frequently been betrayed by party factionalism and the assertion of regional or pressure-group self-interest. Ideologically defined groups fought with each other and among themselves. The dismemberment of Pakistan in 1971 was significant not merely in itself but also as an omen of what the country's future might be: subjection to India in the east and ultimately to the Soviet Union in the north; possible further defection of tribes such as the Pashtun and Baluchis in the west; and continued failure to provide the economic growth that alone could sustain the drive to some form of secular westernization.

In this context, it is perhaps no surprise that General Zia should have seen a call for a return to the "true principles" of Islam as the proper path for his new government. Such a call might be perceived as resolving some of Pakistan's major and apparently insoluble problems. Failure to meet the expectations aroused by the much proclaimed programs of development could be deflected by the assertion that these goals themselves were inappropriate for an Islamic state. At the same time, while traditional sources of economic and military aid—the U.S. and Western Europe—might be discouraged by the new political trends, the newly rich Arab oil states could now be wooed on quite a different footing. This newfound unity with major countries in the Muslim world might itself be seen as a protection from possible interference in Pakistan's internal affairs by either India or the Soviet Union.

Despite the support which General Zia obtained from the Arab world, the political future of Pakistan remained far from clear. The Soviet presence in Afghanistan was matched by strong pro-Soviet political forces inside Pakistan. The strength of Zia's own position was still far from secure. And, while disaffection in Baluchistan quieted during 1980, it remained near the surface.

Through 1980 General Zia continued his struggle to find ways of neutralizing political opposition internally while retaining some credibility externally. Signs that a continued Soviet presence in Afghanistan would force a reassessment of his broad strategy of external relations surfaced at several points. Outwardly, the civil situation in Pakistan remained calm throughout the year, but 1980 might well prove a turning point in Pakistan's history.

The Spillover Effects: the U.S.S.R. Unfortunately, the minorities problem that was wracking the region was not confined to the northern tier states themselves. Spillover effects were many and serious. In 1980 the U.S.S.R. had a Muslim population of some 50 million, mainly concentrated in Azarbaijan, Turkmeniya, Uzbekistan, Kazakhstan, Kirgiziya, and Tadzhikistan adjacent to the Soviet Union's southern border. Although Islam is by no means a dominant force in these territories, neither is it dead, despite many years of Communist control and official discouragement.

With the Muslim states showing a more rapid rate of population growth than other areas of the Soviet Union, the proportion of Muslims could rise from the current 20% to 40% or more by the year 2000. The Russian leadership could not contemplate with equanimity a revitalization of Islamic sentiment stimulated by the ayatollahs in Iran. This was vividly attested to by the rapid withdrawal of Soviet troops of Central Asian origin after the initial invasion of Afghanistan.

The Arab States of the Gulf. The full impact of the Iranian revolution had yet to be felt. There were many indications that problems arising from the upheaval in Iran could damage the prospects for long-term stability in the region. Small but influential communities of Iranians existed in most of the Arab states around the Persian Gulf. Some were trading groups established for generations; others comprised recent immigrant labour. Their sympathies lay with Ayatollah Khomeini and the Iranian revolution, and there was a not unreasonable fear in the minds of the indigenous Arab populations that the Iranians among them represented a fifth column that was actively engaged in subverting the established order.

Iranian religious emissaries active in these communities have been expelled in recent months, the most notable example being Ahmed Abbas Muhri, who was expelled from Kuwait in September 1979. Bahrain and the United Arab Emirates were equally affected, and the former was particularly at risk since Iranian claims to sovereignty over Bahrain had been resurrected by Ayatollah Rouhani, a senior Iranian cleric. During a tour of the Gulf in April 1980, the then Iranian foreign minister, Sadegh Ghotbzadeh, suggested that all Arab states in the area were formerly under the aegis of Iran and could still be deemed to be so. Continuing vigorous calls by the Iranian hierarchy to export the revolution to adjacent regions, including one by Ayatollah Khomeini's nominated successor, Ayatollah Hussein Ali Montazeri, in February 1980, did little to diminish Arab apprehensions.

However, the main threat to the Arab world arising from the Iranian revolution was not so much political as religious. Iran had gained little from its political campaign for the reversion of Bahrain to Iranian control or from its militant retention of the islands of Abu Musa and the Tunbs, seized by the shah's regime in 1971. Its appeal to Shiʿah communities in the Arab world was much more insidious and effective. Iraq's Arab population is almost equally divided between Shiʿah and Sunni Islam (the Kurds are mainly Sunni), with approximately 5.8 million Shiʿah concentrated in the south of the country. Scattered among the other states of the Persian Gulf and the Arabian Peninsula are a further 2 million–3 million Shiʿah, many of whom are Arab rather than immigrant Iranian. Shiʿah majorities exist in Bahrain and Yemen (Sanʿaʾ; North Yemen). Elsewhere in the Arab world, there is a large minority of Shiʿah in Lebanon, while Shiʿah communities in Syria exert a virtual stranglehold on the government. In all, there are approximately 85 million–90 million Shiʿah in the world. Most significantly, there are appreciable Shiʿah groups in all the oil-exporting states of the Middle East.

The appeal of the Iranian revolution to the Shiʿah elsewhere in the region arises not simply from the historical cleavages between the two main branches of Islam, although these go back to AD 661 and the assassination of Ali, son-in-law of the Prophet Muhammad. Nor is Shiʿah exultation over the rise to preeminence of their leaders in Iran the main ingredient. Most Shiʿah minorities are resentful over the poor treatment that has been afforded them by ruling Sunni elites.

Nowhere is this more true than in Iraq, where the Shiʿah have good reason to feel oppressed and neglected, but this is also perceived to be the case in countries as different as Lebanon and Saudi Arabia. In Lebanon the Shiʿah occupy the least fertile land and have the fewest privileges in education and commerce. In Saudi Arabia the Shiʿah are scarcely represented in government at any level, have benefited least of any indigenous group from oil wealth, and are found largely among the labouring rather than the proprietor classes.

Social and economic resentments compound religious differences and open up a receptive audience to the revolutionary spirit engendered in Iran. This is inevitable, regardless of whether or not the Iranian religious authorities seek to export their revolution as a conscious policy. And, as the Shiʿah hierarchy consolidated its position in Teheran, the likelihood of an official drive to spread Khomeini's doctrines throughout the Shiʿah world would be enhanced and the threat to the internal stability of Arab states with Shiʿah minorities increased. Shiʿah riots occurred in the Eastern Province of Saudi Arabia in December 1979; sectarian assassinations affected Shiʿah and Sunni communities in Lebanon throughout 1980; and there were riots in Shiʿah areas of Iraq in December 1979.

JOHN STATHATOS—CAMERA PRESS/PHOTO TRENDS

Members of the Kurdish Democratic Party staged a demonstration in Mahabad, northern Iran, near the Iraqi border, demanding linguistic and religious freedom.

It is a measure of Shiʿah importance in the current situation that the presumed deaths of two Shiʿah leaders, the Imam Moussa Sadr of Lebanon and Mohammed Baqr as-Sadr in Iraq, were at the heart of Irano-Arab conflicts and have led to Shiʿah militancy within the respective communities. In the case of several Arab regimes, the rise of stiff Shiʿah opposition could exacerbate their existing political instability, which derives mainly from their lack of popular mandate and legitimacy. Among the Arab states in the Gulf, only Iraq had made significant conciliatory gestures to its Shiʿah population by way of general elections and specific improvements in living standards. Indeed, Iraqi fears of Iranian interference in its affairs were acute enough to encourage what was in many ways a preemptive military strike against Iran in September 1980. Equally, in the eastern part of the region, the Shiʿah minority in Pakistan forced a significant change in government policy regarding imposition of the *zakat* tax (roughly analogous to a tithe), and the Sunni-dominated government was forced into an awareness of the importance of the Shiʿah.

The Western Countries. For the West and, indeed, for all those countries that draw substantial proportions of their oil supplies from the Persian Gulf states, the effects of the crisis in Iran and the Middle East have already been apparent in erratic oil supplies and uncertain pricing of petroleum on the international market. Other problems loom for the oil industry. The Persian Gulf contributed one-third of world oil production and accounted for two-thirds of the oil entering international trade in 1979. The crucial importance of the area's oil has tended to grow rather than diminish over time. Thus the possibility that the Iranian revolution might be exported represents a double threat to the West: such an eventuality would bring political chaos to neighbouring oil-exporting states and it would disrupt vital oil production.

Just as alarming would be a drop in oil production in the Arab states as the oil exporters attempted to placate Iran by trimming output or as Arab governments opted for the Iranian model of oil conservation. From 1979 Kuwait clearly chose to minimize its oil output and to eschew rapid domestic growth through industrialization. It is not impossible that, encouraged by the Iranian experience in oil pricing during 1979 and 1980, Kuwait could reduce its production from the 1979 level of 1,945,000 bbl per day to a level of 500,000 bbl. Reductions in output in Kuwait or any other Arab state would cause further disarray in the international oil market and open the way for a new price explosion.

The U.S. purchased one quarter of its oil imports from the Persian Gulf area in 1979, representing approximately 12% of its entire consumption. Its interests in the region go far deeper than oil supply, however. In defining the "arc of crisis," Brzezinski had strategic considerations strongly in mind. In this context, the danger signal transmitted from the northern tier countries was that Afghanistan had already fallen to the U.S.S.R. and other countries might slide the same way. The U.S. had to respond to the regional problems and the individual crises within each state by shoring up its own political and military position and supporting its local allies.

In view of the bitter differences between the U.S. and Iran over the seizure of the U.S. embassy in late 1979 and the holding of diplomatic personnel as hostages, the position of the U.S. in Iran remained extremely weak. At the same time, the U.S.

position in Afghanistan was entirely undermined by the Soviet invasion. Pakistan, wary of accepting U.S. aid, edged toward an uneasy neutrality, rejecting a U.S. offer of arms as too small to be of value and emphasizing its commitment to the nonaligned bloc. The U.S. also made moves to reach an accommodation with Turkey and to assist its economic and political recovery. To the south of the crescent of crisis, it sought to create a set of staging posts and bases that would enable it to bring its military power to bear should this be required. Arrangements were made for the use of the former Soviet base at Berbera in Somalia. Facilities in Egypt and Oman were also available to U.S. forces, and the existing U.S. base on the island of Diego Garcia was expanded to provide further underpinning for the U.S. position in the Indian Ocean.

Perhaps the greatest threat to world stability arising from the crises of 1979–80 lay in a paradox. On the one hand, the weakness of the four countries of the arc invited intervention by the great powers. On the other hand, for a number of reasons, neither the U.S. nor the U.S.S.R. was able to improve its position or to protect its vital economic interests. By February 1979 the eclipse of U.S. influence in Iran appeared to open the way for the Soviet Union, which had long felt the need to draw its strategically placed neighbour into its sphere of control. In fact, however, the U.S.S.R. had less political sway, less commercial access, and less reason for satisfaction than had been the case during the shah's regime. In Turkey, too, the U.S.S.R. had been unable to profit from the sharp decline in U.S. involvement and Turkey's desperate economic plight.

While control of Afghanistan might give the U.S.S.R. a long-term advantage in its relations with Pakistan, in the short term those relations worsened dramatically. In Afghanistan itself, the outright invasion of a country that was already an economic satellite and political client put the U.S.S.R. under great odium. Furthermore, at least in the short term, the area of real Soviet influence was reduced rather than increased as large parts of the country slipped into rebellion. At the end of 1980, the Soviet-supported government in Kabul controlled only the lowlands and the towns.

For the U.S. the situation was little better. The main political and economic patron of Turkish, Iranian, and Pakistani regimes in the recent past, the U.S. by 1980 was alienated to a greater or lesser degree from all three states. From being a serious competitor for the favours of the Afghan government in the period prior to 1973, the U.S. had become an insignificant political and economic factor well before the coup that brought the Marxists to power in 1978. The promotion by the U.S. government of a settlement of the Palestine problem through the Camp David accords, marked as it was by insensitivity to Muslim sentiment concerning both the future of the Palestinian refugees and the status of Jerusalem, damaged U.S. credibility in the eyes of Islamic nations, including both the northern tier countries and the Arab states, especially Saudi Arabia. Failure of the U.S. to secure the speedy release of the hostages in Iran, and particularly the disastrous outcome of its military expedition to free them in April 1980, further eroded its strength and influence in the region.

Throughout 1980 the two superpowers struggled to restore their positions and reimpose stability. In doing so, they converted local difficulties into international problems and raised the spectre of a major superpower clash in the area. Since instability appeared to have reasserted itself as the political hallmark of the region, the potential for conflict with worldwide implications seemed certain to persist. It was this danger that constituted the most threatening outcome of the turmoil in the crescent of crisis.

Conclusion. The outside world tended to view the deterioration in economic conditions and political security in the northern tier states purely in terms of its international impact. Danger signals were read largely as threats to the world's oil supply or as warnings of a slide by the superpowers into conflict. Within the countries of the region, the causes of and effects flowing from their domestic crises were matters of more concern than the international implications. But the two aspects of the crisis were inseparable.

There were few remedies that promised immediate relief, and the passage of time appeared to be worsening the situation. In Iran oil resources needed to support continuing large-scale exports were running down. In Turkey overseas indebtedness had become chronic and a burden on the future. In Pakistan the rate of economic growth had dipped seriously below the rate of population increase. In Afghanistan destruction of the agricultural base by military action and an exodus from the land were eroding one of the few bases for productive economic life.

In most cases, economic failures were matched by political chaos. There was a growing tendency toward national disintegration as minority ethnic and religious groups, resentful of national regimes that failed to hear their cultural voices and respond to their economic aspirations, laid claim to autonomy. With the resurgence of powerful traditional forces and the emergence of so many problems without easy solution, it could be many years before the crescent of crisis ceased to pose a threat to regional and international stability.

THE MEDIA AND THE THIRD WORLD: A FAIR SHAKE?

by Rosemary Righter

Ever since the first messenger was killed for bringing bad news, politicians have held in precarious balance the state's need for information and their natural distaste for criticism. Information shapes our world and will shape it more comprehensively still as the age of the computer advances. Much of that information comes as news and commentary: reality sifted, selected, and interpreted by the press. In Western societies, although the sparring between government and press continues, it has slowly become accepted that an open, democratic society requires a freely informed public if it is to function effectively. After World War II, the Universal Declaration of Human Rights enshrined that recognition as a universal principle. Freedom "to seek, receive and impart information and ideas through any media and regardless of frontiers" was formally listed as an essential individual right.

Inevitably, this doctrine of the "free flow of information," recent and imperfectly respected as it is, has been exercised most conspicuously by the international press, based in those Western countries where the concept developed. Equally inevitably, it has come under attack from a number of political leaders of third world countries. In the 1970s these leaders began to allege that the doctrine served as a convenient mantle for "cultural imperialism," enabling the rich countries to perpetuate an inegalitarian world order and to impose their views, their cultures, and their market economies on the vulnerable societies of the less developed world.

When, in 1976, the nonaligned governments issued their call for a New World Information Order as "an integral part of the overall struggle for political, economic and social independence," few in the West noticed. Those who did were united in viewing it as a serious threat to the free flow of information. They were right in one important respect: the call for a new "balance" involved not only the pattern of news flows but the content of news. At UNESCO, in 1974, the new majority formed by the emerging states had dismissed the principle of the "free flow of information" as outmoded, "belonging to the 19th century." For some it was not only outmoded but a fraud, practiced on them by the handful of countries whose news agencies, networks, and newspapers set the international agenda in terms of their own interests.

The Third World's Grievances. Since 1976 demands for the establishment of a "new order" have multiplied in almost every international forum, above all at UNESCO and the United Nations itself. There the question of communications—and their control—is rapidly becoming one of the most intractable areas of disagreement between the less developed countries and the West.

Two basic claims underlie the third world challenge. The first, which must be taken very seriously, is that the news and views of less developed countries should be enabled to reach the outside world directly. The facts are clear enough. Although more than 100 national news agencies exist, around 80% of the international news circulated worldwide is supplied by only four: Reuters, the Associated Press, United Press International, and Agence France-Presse. Many third world leaders feel that their affairs are sparsely and poorly reported by these agencies. To remedy the situation, they are seeking to build up their own media to serve national audiences and to compete for attention in the international marketplace.

It is the second claim that makes the issue politically explosive. This is that the role of the media must be altered radically. At home, the press must be used for the general good (as governments perceive it), as a tool for mobilizing the masses for development and the task of nation building, and as an instrument for propagation of the national ideology. It is not only the Western press which is under attack; the model of a free press itself is being rejected as alien and undesirable.

Such an approach goes well beyond the more familiar arguments of national leaders that their so-

---

Rosemary Righter is development correspondent of The Sunday Times, *London. She is the author of* Whose News?: Politics, the Press and the Third World *and co-author of* The Exploding Cities.

cieties are too vulnerable to permit an independent press to function freely. And it leads naturally to the effort, at the international level, to establish controls on the activities of the "transnational" media and on the flow of news across frontiers.

News and Economics. From the outset, the attack on the information structure has been explicitly linked with the campaign, launched in 1974, for a New International Economic Order. The demand for a fairer share of the world's resources which that campaign embodies has been accompanied by outspoken distrust of Western financial power and economic prescriptions; as negotiations have stalled, it has been marked by growing bitterness. To the extent that the economic struggle sought to break the chain of dominance forged by the industrialized West, it was bound, eventually, to focus on the press. Western reporting of third world affairs is widely held responsible for the miserly attitude to trade, aid, and financial reforms taken by Western leaders. Above all, it is blamed for public indifference to the issues at stake.

However quixotic the belief that Western publics, given better information, would rush to lobby their governments in favour of a new economic order, there is force in the charge that the international media fail to report and explain pressures for change. Parochialism, of course, is not confined to the Western press. Worldwide, newspapers allocate only a quarter of their space to foreign news. Television and radio tend to be hemmed in still more tightly by the pressure of time and by editors' perceptions of market tastes.

The news agencies merely offer the basic ingredients for this thin diet. But because they claim to provide an international service, they bear the brunt of the third world's offensive. At one extreme, they stand accused of deliberate manipulation of the news in the service of vested interests. More moderate critics charge that they lack objectivity—the very basis of their claim to credibility—because they select news in terms of their main markets, judge events through Western eyes, and therefore subject the less developed world to an unrelenting one-way flow of Western ideas and preoccupations. Their third world coverage concentrates on calamity and political turmoil, neglecting or treating only superficially the struggles against poverty, hunger, and illiteracy which are the constants of development.

There is another side to the coin. National censorship all too frequently sees to it that publics are not "swamped" by alien (or embarrassing) news. In fact, the agencies provide far more stories about economic and social development than the press of the less developed countries cares to use. And, in a sense, the agencies are being criticized for failing to do what they have never attempted. On combined budgets of less than $400 million, the "Big Four" cannot cover the globe.

But if this is so, the justification for third world access to the international news flow is all the greater. The exchange of news may well be an essential precondition for better North-South understanding. The key question is: what news? Western editors are not merely obstructive or fanciful when they fear they are being asked to accept propaganda, to deceive their publics in the name of some larger good. The "new information order," as it is being promoted, is more likely to produce a "guided" press in the service of a kind of cultural nationalism than a richer and more diverse flow of news. The end result may be national monopolies established in the name of the struggle against international monopoly. In the list of demands that make up the call for a new information order, the missing ingredient is the very concept of press freedom.

A Rising Debate. Yet the complaints are not just the invention of tinpot dictatorships, nor are the proposals mere international rhetoric. They are becoming institutionalized and embedded in international politics.

The first moves toward the "new news" originated in UNESCO, the body of the UN committed by its constitution to promote "the free flow of ideas by word and image." In 1970 UNESCO turned its focus of attention away from technical assistance to the media, emphasizing instead the content of news and the role of the media in society. It announced a major international communications program, with the express purpose of assisting governments to use the media more effectively for development purposes. This change in policy was largely ignored by Western governments.

They were finally alerted, in 1976, by three events: the call for a New World Information Order issued by the nonaligned nations; the first of a series of UNESCO intergovernmental conferences on communications policy, held in Latin America; and a UNESCO "declaration" on the media, which came before its General Conference that autumn.

The declaration was something of a fluke. It arose not out of UNESCO's communications program but from a Byelorussian proposal of 1972 aimed at bringing pressure on foreign broadcasters beaming programs to the Soviet Union and Eastern Europe. But because of its timing, what began as a narrow East-West quarrel rapidly developed into a symbol of North-South disagreement on the media's role. The 1976 draft, in the name of such worthy goals as the promotion of peace and the fight against apartheid, imposed duties on the media and required states to use their power to see that the media con-

ALAIN NOGUES—SYGMA

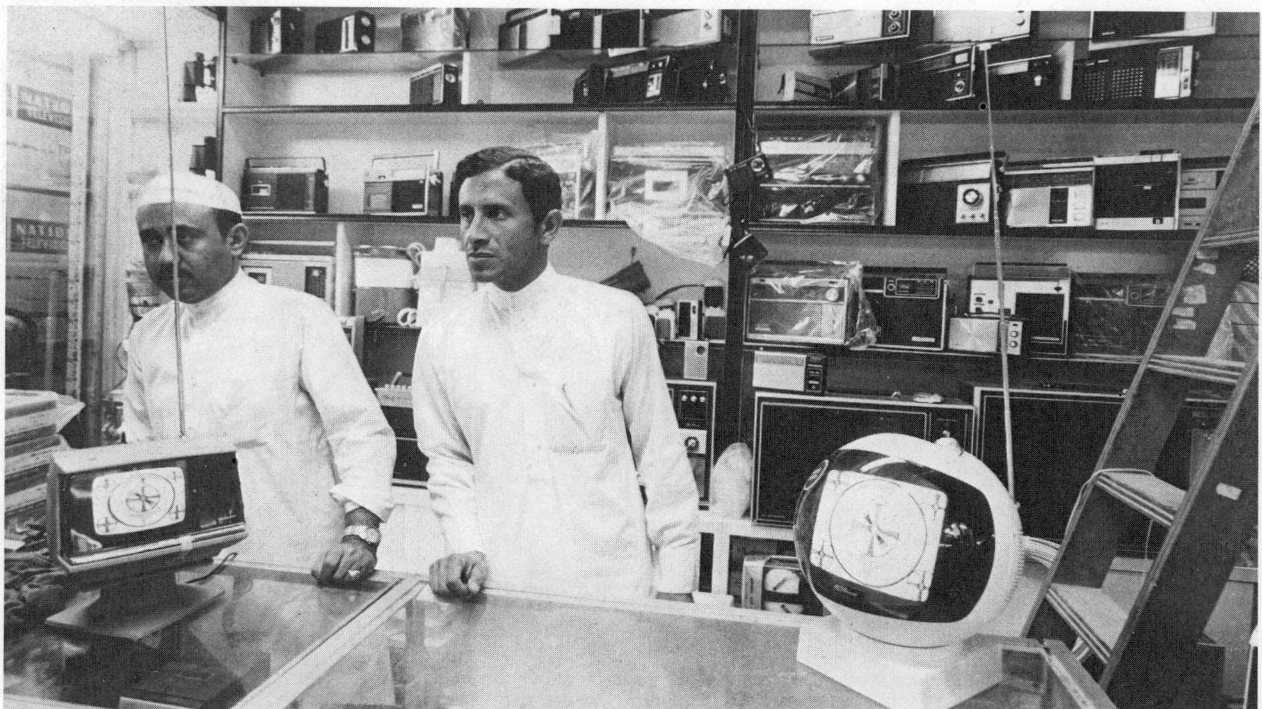

"Many third world leaders feel that their affairs are sparsely and poorly reported. . . . they are seeking to build up their own media to serve national audiences and to compete for attention in the international marketplace."

formed. The key paragraph said that "States are responsible, in the international sphere, for all mass media under their jurisdiction."

The proposed declaration challenged Western assumptions in two ways. It advocated the setting of international standards for and state control of the media; and its existence forced debate on Western governments, which do not believe that questions of news content and news values belong on the intergovernmental agenda at all. The declaration thus came to symbolize the growing pressures against the free-flow principle. In the confrontation that resulted, genuine grievances became obscured by the rhetoric of freedom versus sovereignty.

At the 1978 General Conference of UNESCO, to the surprise of most observers, the challenge of the declaration was deflected by the negotiation of a new text that switched the whole focus of the original, eliminating all references to state control and emphasizing human rights, diversity of news sources, the free flow of information, and access to news sources. The result was widely interpreted as a victory for the West.

So, in a sense, it was, although the final document was little more than an exercise in squaring the circle. In Western eyes, the fact that the basic issues were not addressed was an advantage, since it avoided the pretense that a UN resolution could reconcile the fundamental conflict between those who view the press as an instrument of state power and those who see it as a guarantee against the abuse of power. But to win agreement on the new text, Western negotiators assured the third world nations that their aspirations for "a new, more just and more effective world information and communication order" would be taken seriously, and they promised aid for communications development. A little time was thereby purchased.

The phrasing of the assurance, which took days to negotiate, was deliberate. By now, the proponents of a New World Information Order had formulated some of its key elements in such a way that Western negotiators believed acceptance of the slogan meant, by implication, acquiescence in the concept of state control of the media. The most explicit formulation had come from Mustapha Masmoudi, who as Tunisia's secretary of state for information had chaired the nonaligned governments' information group in 1976. By 1978, as Tunisia's representative at UNESCO, he had become the chief negotiator for the third world voting group. Some months before the General Conference, UNESCO had provided him with "nonaligned experts" (coming, it turned out, from Cuba, Vietnam, and East Germany) to assist him in setting out the goals of the "new order."

Masmoudi's paper began by redefining communication as "a social goal and a cultural product and not as a material commodity." Each nation

ASLAK AARHUS—GAMMA/LIAISON

"[Western press coverage of the third world] concentrates on calamity and political turmoil, neglecting or treating only superficially the struggles against poverty, hunger, and illiteracy which are the constants of development."

"should choose its information in accordance with its own realities and requirements" and should have power to regulate the collection, processing, and transmission of news across national frontiers. "Abuses" of the right of access to information should be prevented and, to that end, "appropriate criteria" should be devised to ensure that news selection was "truly objective." In the same way, "the right of those receiving information" (the public) should be regulated "to ensure free and balanced flow of information." The new "news" would, of course, be "an essential corollary of the New International Economic Order."

The MacBride Report. Masmoudi had a target audience. At the height of the confrontation over the media declaration in 1976, the director general of UNESCO, Amadou Mahtar M'Bow, was invited by the General Conference to conduct a survey of communications problems. His response was to set up an independent International Commission for the Study of Communication Problems, to report to him in 1980. The 16 members, including Masmoudi, met eight times over two years under the presidency of Sean MacBride, Irish statesman, lawyer, holder of both the Nobel and Lenin peace prizes—a man with a rooted belief in the power of the media and the possibility of channeling that power in the cause of world peace.

Nothing escaped the MacBride Commission's purview. It was to look at the totality of communications, considered, M'Bow suggested, as a "sociocultural problem" with "political, ideological and philosophical" dimensions. But its mandate was not entirely open-ended. The members were to seek ways of establishing a new information order and, while they were at it, to consider how the media could be better used for objectives ranging from education to "safeguarding peace."

Born in controversy, the commission could not have been expected to resolve the dichotomy between two approaches to information, but the report that finally surfaced in 1980 was a hybrid that actually sharpened the controversy. Voluminous, indigestible, and ambiguous as it was, it could not obscure the internal contradiction between its professions of respect for the principle of freedom and the didactic and paternalistic character of many of its recommendations. MacBride replied to Western critics by pointing to the pieties scattered throughout its 500 pages, to its condemnation of censorship and its insistence on free access to news sources for journalists. But where it proposed action, the report betrayed a passion to regulate which impinged directly on the practices of free reporting.

Journalists, it said, must be free; at the same time, they should promote friendly relations between states, foster cultural identity, enhance the dignity of nations and peoples, respect national sovereignty, and support just causes such as disarmament and liberation movements. Governments, it said, should formulate "comprehensive communications policies . . . linked to overall social, cultural, economic and political goals." Communication was to become "an instrument for creating awareness of national priorities."

According to MacBride, the commission was concerned "that freedom of information as a doctrine has sometimes been 'misapplied' or 'narrowly interpreted.'" One aspect of the report's proposed remedy was that "effective legal measures" should "circumscribe the action of transnationals [including news organizations] by requiring them to comply with specific criteria and conditions defined by national legislation and development policies." Who was to decide whether or not a news report so conformed? The recommendation constituted an open invitation to governments.

In a report that was intended to be interpreted and used, what mattered was not so much the quality of its analysis as the hostages it offered to governments and to UNESCO, whose future strategies it was intended to influence. To governments, which by nature love the idea of centralized planning, the report offered encouragement in harnessing news to the service of national policy. To UNESCO, it suggested that the policy of helping governments to do this should be strengthened. Further, it encouraged UNESCO, as an intergovernmental body, to continue concerning itself with international standard setting and with the content of news. Characteristic of the MacBride Report's ambiguity was its failure to define what a New World Information Order actually meant. But on balance, its proposals for reform were weighted in favour of the many forces, at both the national and the international level, that aimed to limit the public's freedom of choice in the name of the public good.

Belgrade, 1980. With such ammunition, it was perhaps inevitable that the next UNESCO General Conference, in Belgrade, Yugos., should mark the watershed between the uneasy truce that followed agreement on the 1978 declaration and the next stage of the campaign for a New World Information Order. The détente had been fragile anyway. Western promises of assistance to third world communications had, with limited exceptions, remained promises, although efforts had been made by at least some of the international media to improve the quality of their third world reporting.

Western hopes before Belgrade had been that pressures for a "new order" could be rechanneled. But the heart of the essential, never articulated, bargain was that the West was prepared to help build up the third world's media if its leaders would refrain from seeking to define the New World Information Order. That bargain fell apart at Belgrade. A small group of less developed countries, led by Iraq, Cuba, Tunisia, and Venezuela, pressed toward a definition. They insisted on including a statement of principles in a resolution on the MacBride Report, and Venezuela pushed through a resolution asking the UNESCO secretariat to prepare a fuller definition of the "new order" with a view to producing another declaration. In fact, a secret text had already been prepared, calling for regulation of international news agencies and for the right of states to use the media for propaganda and to take measures to "protect" themselves against reporting that was deemed "irresponsible," "distorted," or likely to harm national interests.

By the end of the conference the West—again unprepared and without a positive strategy—had agreed to accept a central role for UNESCO in communications; had agreed to the new international program; had been forced to accept increases in UNESCO's budget; had accepted defeat when they tried to divert funds from communications research to technical projects; and had concurred, without a vote being taken, on the MacBride resolution, which included a number of "basic considerations." Strikingly absent from these considerations were references to the free flow of information and ideas or to freedom from censorship and government control. Only Switzerland, the U.K., West Germany, and the U.S. resisted compromise, and only the U.K. maintained its opposition to the end. The net result was that a "New World Information Order" would now be defined by politicians. News-as-instrument was coming of age.

Shaping the New Order. The technological revolution in communications looming in the 1980s meant that changes in news flows and news structures were inevitable. The world was moving toward a "new order" of some kind. It was in this context that international moves to regulate the media were most disturbing. It was natural for Western governments to hope to avoid ideological debate, but the chief lesson of the 1970s was that absentees have no influence.

If, in the 1980s, governments moved further toward shaping their national media to official ideologies (as had already happened in revolutionary Iran), the "new order" threatened to bring with it a positive manipulation of the media that went far beyond mere censorship. Much more was at stake than the fortunes of the Western press. At issue was the ability of citizens, in less developed countries as in the West, to make their opinions heard and to choose on the basis of knowledge. This fundamental right of access, which so much of the rhetoric obscured or ignored, was imperiled as the decade began by a mistrust of Western values and life-styles that made freedom itself a suspect word, synonymous with entrenched privilege.

CALENDAR OF EVENTS OF 1981

JANUARY

1 *New Year's Day*
6 *Epiphany*
8 *Battle of New Orleans (1815)*
13 *Birth of Horatio Alger (1832)*
15 *Molière Day*
18 *Traditional birth date of the Prophet Muhammad*
19 *Birth of Robert E. Lee (1807)*
20 *Presidential Inauguration Day*
22 *Birth of Francis Bacon (1561)*
26 *Australia Day; Republic Day in India*
27 *Birth of Mozart (1756); Vietnam War Cease-fire (1973)*
30 *Birth of Franklin D. Roosevelt (1882)*

8 **The Battle of New Orleans.** On Jan. 8, 1815, American forces under Andrew Jackson defeated the British in the Battle of New Orleans. The victory made Jackson a national hero and helped him to be elected president in 1828 and again in 1832. New Orleans was the last battle of the War of 1812; as a matter of fact, the war had been over for more than two weeks when the battle was fought. U.S. and British representatives meeting in Ghent, Belg., signed a treaty on Dec. 24, 1814, but the news didn't cross the Atlantic until several weeks later. Had news of the treaty arrived before the British attacked, there would never have been a Battle of New Orleans and Jackson might never have been elected the seventh president of the United States. There were those, however, who apparently were not properly impressed by Jackson's victory at New Orleans. On March 31, 1815, a judge of the United States District Court of that city fined Jackson $1,000 for contempt because his defense of the city had included a declaration of martial law. Twenty-nine years later, on Jan. 8, 1844, the House of Representatives voted to return the money to Jackson with interest at 6%.

20 **Inauguration Day in the U.S.** Ronald Reagan was scheduled to become the 40th president of the United States on this date. In so doing, he would perpetuate several long-standing traditions. He would ride down Pennsylvania Avenue at the head of the inaugural parade, deliver an inaugural address, preside at several inaugural balls around the city of Washington, and, of course, take the presidential oath of office. The oath, always administered by the chief justice of the United States, reads as follows: "I do solemnly swear (or affirm) that I will faithfully execute the office of President of the United States, and will, to the best of my Ability, preserve, protect, and defend the Constitution of the United States." Reagan would be the first professional actor and the first man born in Illinois to occupy the presidency. He would also be the oldest man ever to assume the presidency. Reagan was born Feb. 6, 1911. On Inauguration Day Reagan would be 69 years and 349 days old. When William Henry Harrison assumed office in 1841 he was 68 years and 23 days old.

27 **Vietnam War Cease-Fire.** The longest and least popular war in the history of the U.S. ended on this date in 1973 when the U.S., North Vietnam, South Vietnam, and the Viet Cong signed an "Agreement on Ending the War and Restoring Peace in Vietnam" in Paris. The U.S. had been involved in the war since defeated French forces departed under terms of the 1954 Geneva agreement.

FEBRUARY

2 *Candlemas Day; Ground Hog Day*
4 *Birth of Charles Lindbergh (1902)*
5 *Chinese New Year*
6 *Birth of Aaron Burr (1756); Waitangi Day in New Zealand*
7 *Birth of Sir Thomas More (1477)*
11 *National Foundation Day in Japan (660 BC); Independence of Vatican City (1929)*
14 *St. Valentine's Day*
19 *Birth of Copernicus (1473)*
24 *Gregorian Calendar Day (1582)*

2 **Candlemas.** This Christian feast day can trace its origins back to the Roman Feast of Lights in which participants carried lighted torches in a ritual of springtime rebirth. As taken over by the Christian Church, Candlemas commemorates two events that occurred together: the Presentation of the Christ Child in the Temple and the Purification of the Blessed Virgin Mary. The feast carried greater significance before the Reformation than it does today, but the Roman Catholic, Eastern Orthodox, and Anglican churches continue the observance by blessing all the candles that will be used on their altars during the year.

5 **Chinese New Year.** The Chinese New Year always falls between January 21 and February 19; or, in Zodiac terms, on the first new moon after the sun has left the sign of Capricorn and entered Aquarius. The highly complex Chinese calendar dates back to the 27th century BC. Associated with it are 12 animals: rat, ox, tiger, hare, dragon, serpent, horse, ram, monkey, rooster, dog, and boar; and five elements: earth, metal, fire, water, and wood. During the Han dynasty (202 BC–AD 220), 60-year cycles were developed, and each year was designated by combining the 12 animals and five elements. In practice, though, the Chinese use only the name of the animal. The year 1981 is the year 4679, the Year of the Rooster.

MARCH

4 *Ash Wednesday*
6 *Birth of Michelangelo (1475)*
14 *Birth of Albert Einstein (1879)*
15 *Ides of March*
17 *St. Patrick's Day*
20 *Jewish feast of Purim*
21 *Vernal equinox in the Northern Hemisphere; autumnal equinox in the Southern Hemisphere*
25 *Independence Day in Greece*
26 *Birth of Robert Frost (1874)*
30 *Birth of Francisco José de Goya (1746); birth of Vincent van Gogh (1853)*
31 *Birth of René Descartes (1596)*

4 **Ash Wednesday.** Ash Wednesday begins the season of Lent, the penitential period of the 40 days (excluding Sundays) immediately preceding Easter. The number 40 has long been important in religions. Moses and Elijah stayed 40 days in the wilderness; the Jews searched 40 years for the Promised Land; Jonah allowed the city of Ninevah 40 days to repent. But the most credible explanation for the 40 days of Lent seems to be the 40-day fast of Christ in the desert. The custom of marking the forehead with ashes on Ash Wednesday is believed to have originated during the papacy of Gregory the Great, who was pope from 590 to 604. Originally, only those doing public penance received ashes. As time went on, ashes were distributed to everyone. Ash Wednesday is observed by Roman Catholics, Anglicans, and certain other Christian denominations.

6 **Birth of Michelangelo.** The great artist of the Renaissance was born at Caprese in Tuscany, Italy, on March 6, 1475, and died in Rome on Feb. 18, 1564, just three weeks short of his 90th birthday. Like many other geniuses, Michelangelo was barely into his teens when his artistic talents began to attract attention, and when he was 23 he was commissioned by a French cardinal to create the "Pieta." In the spring of 1499 the "Pieta" was installed in St. Peter's in Rome, where visitors have been spellbound by it ever since. Among Michelangelo's other masterpieces are the marble statue of "David" in Florence, the ceiling frescoes in the Sistine Chapel at the Vatican, the statue of "Moses" for the monument to Pope Julius II, the statues of the Medici monument, and "The Last Judgment," the huge fresco on the wall behind the main altar of the Sistine Chapel.

15 **The Ides of March.** Credit Shakespeare with educating the world to the significance of the Ides. Had the immortal bard not written *Julius Caesar,* few persons would know today that the great Roman leader died on the 15th of this month. In the play Caesar is warned to

"Beware the Ides of March." (Every month of the Roman calendar had an Ides. In March, May, July, and October it fell on the 15th; in other months on the 13th.) Brutus was one of the leading parties to Caesar's assassination. He was the subject of the most famous dying gasp in history: "Et tu, Brute."

APRIL

1 *April Fool's Day*
2 *Birth of Hans Christian Andersen (1805); Pony Express begins (1860)*
4 *Founding of NATO (1949)*
6 *Founding of the Mormon Church (1830)*
9 *Bataan Day in the Philippines*
13 *Birth of Thomas Jefferson (1743)*
14 *Pan American Day*
18 *San Francisco Earthquake and Fire (1906)*
19 *Easter Sunday; Passover*
20 *Boston Marathon*
22 *Earth Day*
26 *Daylight Savings Time begins in the U.S.; Orthodox Easter Sunday*

9 **Bataan Day.** Following the Japanese invasion of the Philippines in December 1941, an estimated 7,000-10,000 Filipinos and U.S. troops died during a forced march to an internment camp in April 1942. The march of some 70,000 began at the southern end of the Bataan Peninsula and ended, for those who survived, 88 km (55 mi) away at San Fernando. There the prisoners were loaded onto railroad cars and taken to the internment camp.

19 **Passover.** For Jews, Passover is one of the most solemn and complex holidays of the year. The observance dates back to the time of the Exodus (*c.* 1300 BC) when the Jews fled Egypt. Certain elements of the feast day are possibly even older. The 12th chapter of the book of Exodus contains the original observances. On the tenth day of the lunar month of Nisan (now mid-March to mid-April), each household was to select a lamb, inspect it carefully to make sure it was perfect, then on the 14th day slaughter it. The blood was to be smeared on the doorposts and lintel of each house; the meat was to be roasted whole and eaten, along with unleavened bread and bitter herbs. That night an angel of the Lord would travel throughout Egypt and execute judgment by slaying the firstborn of each household. But if the household was marked with the sacrificial blood, it would be spared or "passed over." Passover continues to be a memorial to the Exodus, but has also become a day of thanks, spiritual renewal, and family and communal solidarity.

20 **The Boston Marathon.** According to tradition, the first marathon was run by a Greek soldier in 490 BC to announce the victory of the Greeks over the Persians. He ran from Marathon to Athens, a distance of 25 mi (40 km). As a footrace, the marathon dates back only to 1896, the year the Olympics were revived in Athens; the Boston version was run for the first time the following year. In the early years of marathon running, there was no standard distance; the length of the course varied between 24 and 27 mi. Finally, in 1924, the Olympic marathon distance was standardized at exactly 26 mi 385 yd—the distance between the royal residence at Windsor Castle and the royal box in the stadium at London used in the 1908 Games. For competitors in the Boston Marathon, it means running from Hopkinton, Mass., to Prudential Center in downtown Boston.

MAY

1 *Law Day in the U.S.*
4 *Observance of Constitution Memorial Day in Japan*
5 *Cinco de Mayo in Mexico*
7 *Observance of Independence Day in Israel; sinking of the Lusitania (1915)*
8 *VE Day (1945)*
10 *Mother's Day in the U.S.*
14 *Independence of Paraguay (1811)*
20 *Birth of Honoré de Balzac (1799)*
22 *National Heroes Day in Sri Lanka*
24 *Indianapolis 500 auto race*
25 *Memorial Day in the U.S.*
28 *Ascension Day*
29 *Birth of Charles II of Great Britain (1630)*

10 **Mother's Day.** The origin of Mother's Day in the U.S. and other countries probably dates back to 18th- and 19th-century England and the custom of "mothering." It was a day when young men and women who had moved away would return to their ancestral homes with gifts of cakes and flowers for their mothers. Credit for originating Mother's Day in the U.S. belongs to Anna M. Jarvis (1864–1948), who was greatly devoted to her own mother, Anna Reeves Jarvis, and felt that a special day should be set aside to honour all mothers. Accordingly, in 1907, on the second anniversary of her mother's death, Miss Jarvis started a letter-writing campaign to bring about a national observance in honour of mothers. In May 1908 Miss Jarvis organized church services in honour of her mother in Grafton, W.Va., and in Philadelphia where the family had lived. Official recognition soon followed. In 1910 the governor of West Virginia issued an official proclamation of Mother's Day. By 1911 observances in honour of mothers were held in every state of the union. The Mother's Day International Association was incorporated on Dec. 12, 1912. Finally, in May 1914, Pres. Woodrow Wilson made the national observance of Mother's Day official with a presidential proclamation. It has been observed on the second Sunday of May ever since.

JUNE

3 *Derby in Epsom Downs, Surrey, England*
5 *Baptism of Adam Smith (1723)*
6 *Dragon Boat Festival in China; Anniversary of D-Day (1944)*
8 *Death of Muhammad (632)*
11 *Kamehameha Day in Hawaii*
13 *Queen's "official" birthday in Great Britain*
15 *Magna Carta Day (1215)*
18 *Battle of Waterloo (1815)*
21 *Summer solstice in the Northern Hemisphere; Winter solstice in the Southern Hemisphere; Father's Day in the U.S.*
25 *Custer's defeat at the Little Bighorn (1876)*
27 *Birth of Helen Keller (1880)*

6 **D-Day.** World War II in Europe ended with Germany's unconditional surrender on May 8, 1945. Yet the allied victory over Hitler's Nazis and the other Axis powers might never have been won at all had it not been for Operation Overlord or D-Day, the daring landing at Normany on June 6, 1944. It was carried out by the largest invasion fleet in history, involving 4,000 ships and several thousand smaller craft. They carried more than 150,000 troops to the now-famous stretch of French coast between Cherbourg and Le Havre. Ten thousand American, British, French, and Canadian soldiers were killed or wounded during the assault, but the invasion succeeded in breaking the Nazi stranglehold on Europe.

11 **Kamehameha Day.** The most important holiday in Hawaii honours the islands' greatest leader, King Kamehameha I. When Kamehameha became the leader of part of the island of Hawaii in 1782, he launched a campaign to consolidate the islands. By virtue of his political skill and military might, Kamehameha united all but two of the islands under his rule. The exceptions were Kauai and Niihau, both of which were added peacefully in 1810. During his reign, Kamehameha organized the government, checked oppression, encouraged industry, and thwarted Russian designs on the islands.

15 **Magna Carta.** When the English barons forced King John to sign Magna Carta they established the basis for constitutional liberties that have prevailed ever since in England. Until that time, the king had simply assumed many powers, and had fallen into the habit of exercising them arbitrarily. To protect themselves against such encroachments of royal authority, the barons met at Stamford during Easter week of 1215 and drew up a charter. They sent it to John for his approval, but he refused to sign it. The barons reacted by renouncing their allegiance to John on May 5 and marching on London. When they captured the city, John capitulated. Magna Carta contains the first detailed definition of the

relationship between the barons and the king. It sought to regularize the judicial system, abolish arbitrary abuses of feudal tenures, protect commerce, and standardize weights and measures. Clause 39 of the charter contains the historic basis for English civil liberties: "no freeman shall be arrested or imprisoned or disseized [dispossessed] or outlawed or exiled or in any way victimized, neither will we attack him or send anyone to attack him, except by the lawful judgment of his peers or by the law of the land."

JULY

1 *Dominion Day in Canada*
2 *Declaration of Independence Resolution (1776)*
3 *First Day of Ramadan*
4 *Independence Day in the U.S.*
10 *Birth of Marcel Proust (1871)*
11 *Birth of John Quincy Adams (1767)*
14 *Bastille Day in France*
16 *British Open golf championship begins; partial eclipse of the Moon*
20 *First human landing on the Moon (1969)*
26 *Beginning of the Salzburg Festival*
28 *14th Amendment Ratification*
30 *Total eclipse of the Sun*

3 **First Day of Ramadan.** The holy month of Ramadan marks a month-long period of prayer and fasting during which Muslims commemorate God's revelation to Muhammad. The revelation was communicated to the Prophet by the Angel Gabriel on *laylat al-qadr* or "Night of the Decree," which is traditionally identified with the 27th of Ramadan. During Ramadan, the ninth month of the Islamic calendar, Muslims are expected to abstain from food, drink, and sexual intercourse from sunrise to sunset. The last day of Ramadan coincides with July 31, 1981, in the Western calendar.

16 **British Open.** The game of golf can be dated back to the 14th or 15th century in Scotland, where it became so popular that the Scottish Parliament feared the people would lose their proficiency at the more important skill of shooting arrows at the country's enemies. As a consequence of this concern, Parliament in 1457 passed a law prohibiting golf. The Scots largely ignored the prohibition, however, and by the early part of the 16th century King James IV himself was playing the game. The British Open has been played since 1860. That year the winner was Willie Park, who won the tournament a total of four times: in 1860, 1863, 1866, and 1875. In the years 1896-1914, the redoubtable Harry Vardon won it six times. The only five-time winner was Peter Thomson, who won it first in 1954 and for the fifth time in 1965.

20 **Moon Day.** Neil Armstrong became the first human to set foot on the Moon, an act that was viewed all over the world by a television audience estimated at 600 million. Those who watched the historic event heard Armstrong say, as he stepped onto the lunar surface: "That's one small step for a man, one giant leap for mankind." Accompanying him in the lunar module "Eagle" was Air Force Col. Edwin E. ("Buzz") Aldrin, Jr., who joined Armstrong on the Moon's surface about 20 minutes later. The third member of the team was Air Force Lieut. Col. Michael Collins, who remained in the command module "Columbia." He circled the moon while Armstrong and Aldrin took pictures, gathered soil and rock samples, and performed various scientific tests. They spent a total of 21½ hours on the Moon's surface, over two hours outside the capsule. Then they lifted off the Moon in the "Eagle" and rejoined Collins for the return journey to Earth. The mission had begun on July 16 at 9:32 AM Eastern Daylight Time (EDT) when a Saturn V launch rocket roared off the pad at Cape Kennedy in Florida. It ended at 12:50 PM EDT, July 24, when the "Columbia" splashed down in the Pacific Ocean.

AUGUST

1 *Birth of Francis Scott Key (1779)*
2 *Islamic Feast of Id al-fitr*
3 *Columbus embarks for the New World (1492)*
6 *Hiroshima Peace Day*
12 *Assassination of King Philip of Pokanket (1676)*
15 *Assumption of the Virgin Mary; birth of Sir Walter Scott (1771)*
17 *First Balloon Crossing of the Atlantic (1978)*
18 *Birth of Meriwether Lewis (1774)*
19 *Birth of Orville Wright (1871)*
20 *Birth of Eliel Saarinen (1873)*
23 *Sacco and Vanzetti Memorial Day (1927)*
26 *Women's Equality Day*

3 **Columbus Embarks for the New World.** On this date in 1492 Columbus and his crew sailed out of Palos in southern Spain seeking a westerly route to the Indies. On October 12 the voyagers landed on Watling Island in the Bahamas, now known as San Salvador. Columbus made three more voyages to the New World and discovered many more islands, but he never set foot on the North American mainland.

23 **Execution of Sacco and Vanzetti.** One of the most celebrated murder trials of this century resulted in the conviction and eventual execution of Nicola Sacco, a shoe worker, and Bartolomeo Vanzetti, a fish peddler. Both men had immigrated to the U.S. from Italy in 1908; both were anarchists. On May 5, 1920, they were arrested for the April 20 murders of a paymaster and a security guard in South Braintree, Mass. After the two were convicted, many throughout the country felt they had been found guilty for their radical beliefs rather than for the murders. Attempts to secure a retrial failed, even though a convicted murderer confessed that he had taken part in the crime with members of the Joe Morelli gang. Sacco and Vanzetti were sentenced to death on April 9, 1927; they were executed on August 23 amid vigorous worldwide protest.

SEPTEMBER

2 *Great Fire of London begins (1666)*
3 *World War II Declaration (1939)*
4 *Founding of Los Angeles (1781)*
7 *Labor Day in the U.S.*
15 *Mexican Independence Days begin*
18 *Creation of the U.S. Army Air Service (1914)*
23 *Autumnal equinox in the Northern Hemisphere; vernal equinox in the Southern Hemisphere; Nathan Hale Day*
25 *Balboa discovers the Pacific; Native American Day*
28 *Birth of Confucius (551 BC)*
29 *Rosh Hashana (Jewish year 5742)*

22 **Nathan Hale Day.** Nathan Hale was born in Coventry, Conn., on June 6, 1755, and became a schoolteacher shortly after his graduation from Yale University in 1773. When the Revolutionary War broke out in 1775, Hale joined a Connecticut regiment, served at the siege of Boston, and won a commission as a captain. It is believed that Hale was a member of a daring band that captured a British provision sloop from under the very guns of a man-of-war. His next adventure, however, cost him his life. Disguised as a Dutch schoolteacher in order to obtain military information from behind British lines, Hale was caught and hanged as a spy. Shortly before his death he is supposed to have uttered the immortal words, "I only regret that I have but one life to lose for my country." Hale was executed without benefit of a trial. At the time of his death he was barely 20 years old. In memory of Hale's heroic act, the governor of Connecticut annually proclaims September 22 as Nathan Hale Day.

23 **Autumnal Equinox.** This is the first day of fall in the Northern Hemisphere or, more scientifically, the exact moment when the centre of the Sun appears to pass directly over the celestial equator in its apparent path southward. Actually the Sun's apparent movement is a result of the changing declination of the Earth's axis as it orbits the Sun. The autumnal equinox always occurs on or about September 21. In 1981 it will occur at precisely 3:05 AM, Greenwich Mean Time, on September 23. In the Southern Hemisphere it will be the first day of Spring.

25 Native American Day. Efforts to establish a national day in honour of Native Americans date back to 1912 and to Arthur C. Parker, a noted anthropologist and archaeologist. Parker, who was part Seneca, advocated that a day be set aside to honour American Indians. Two years later, Red Fox James, a member of the Blackfoot tribe, won the support of 24 state governors for a day in honour of Indians and presented their endorsements at the White House. The following year the Society of American Indians directed its president, the Rev. Sherman Coolidge, to call upon the country to observe the second Sunday in May as a day in honour of Native Americans. The first state observance of American Indian Day (now Native American Day) took place on May 13, 1916, in New York. There is still no national day of observance in honour of Native Americans, although a number of states have set aside the fourth Friday in September or the second Saturday in May.

OCTOBER

- **1** *Founding of the People's Republic of China (1949)*
- **2** *Birth of Mahatma Gandhi (1869)*
- **8** *Yom Kippur*
- **9** *Chicago Fire (1871)*
- **12** *Columbus Day; Thanksgiving Day in Canada*
- **16** *John Brown's Raid (1859)*
- **18** *Alaska Day*
- **19** *Bicentennial of American victory at Yorktown (1781)*
- **22** *Cuban Missile Crisis (1962)*
- **23** *Swallows depart from San Juan Capistrano*
- **24** *United Nations Day*
- **28** *Founding of Harvard University (1636)*
- **29** *Stock market collapse (1929)*
- **31** *Halloween*

23 Swallows Depart from Capistrano. The little California mission town of San Juan Capistrano has been famous for the punctuality of its swallows since Spanish colonial times. The legendary little birds are supposed to arrive on March 19 (St. Joseph's Day) and leave for their winter home in Argentina on October 23 (the date of St. John's death). Quite often they do just that, but sometimes they do not. Weather and feeding conditions are usually responsible when the birds do not conform to schedule. They nest all over town, but one of their favourite places is the San Juan Capistrano mission, built in 1776 by Fra Junípero Serra and named for St. John of Capistrano, a crusader.

29 Stock Market Crashes. In 1929 more than 16 million shares of stock were sold, causing the collapse of the stock market and triggering the Great Depression of the 1930s. Ever since then Oct. 29, 1929, has been known as "Black Tuesday." But like many other momentous events, it really didn't happen on a single day. Prices dropped sharply in early September, so some date the actual "crash" on the 24th when panic selling started. On that date, "Black Thursday," nearly 13 million shares of stock changed hands, touching off a panic that reached its peak five days later on the 29th.

NOVEMBER

- **1** *All Saint's Day; Reformation Sunday*
- **2** *All Soul's Day*
- **5** *Guy Fawkes Day in the U.K.*
- **10** *Birth of Martin Luther (1483)*
- **11** *Armistice Day (1918)*
- **18** *Birth of Ignacy (Jan) Paderewski (1860)*
- **19** *Gettysburg Address (1863)*
- **21** *Birth of Voltaire (1694)*
- **22** *Assassination of Pres. John F. Kennedy (1963)*
- **26** *Thanksgiving Day in the U.S.*
- **30** *Birth of Samuel Clemens (Mark Twain; 1835)*

1 Reformation Sunday. Protestants trace their religious lineage to Oct. 31, 1517, the day Martin Luther nailed his Ninety-five Theses to the door of the church in Wittenberg, Germany, thereby setting in motion a chain of events that contributed to the Protestant Reformation. Luther's Theses consisted of a list of grievances against the Roman Catholic Church under Pope Leo X. Perhaps the best remembered, and the one that angered Luther the most, was the sale of indulgences. According to church doctrine, when a priest granted one of the faithful an indulgence, that person's sins were forgiven by God. As an ordained priest and a teacher of philosophy and theology at the University of Wittenberg, Luther became incensed at the widespread practice within the church of offering indulgences for sale. Pope Leo X himself abused the practice of granting indulgences by selling them to finance an addition to St. Peter's Basilica in Rome. Luther expected the people of Wittenberg to oppose him when he published the theses; instead they gave him their enthusiastic support, and it wasn't long before Luther's Ninety-five Theses were being read all over Germany. The rebellious young priest was branded a heretic and excommunicated, but with the help of powerful German princes he became the acknowledged leader of the Reformation. Most Protestant churches observe Reformation Sunday on the Sunday nearest October 31.

19 The Gettysburg Address. "Four score and seven years ago our fathers brought forth on this continent a new nation, conceived in liberty, and dedicated to the proposition that all men are created equal." So begins the famous Gettysburg Address of Pres. Abraham Lincoln, 16th president of the U.S. Ironically, it almost went unnoticed when the grim, gangling Kentuckian delivered it on the battlefield at Gettysburg, Pa., on Nov. 19, 1863. Lincoln was not the main speaker at the consecration of the Civil War cemetery. That honour had fallen to Edward Everett, a noted orator, who spoke for nearly two hours. When Lincoln rose to speak, many in the crowd were distracted by a photographer. Less than three minutes later Lincoln had finished, having little effect on most of those who had heard him. Most major newspapers ignored Lincoln's speech altogether and two—the *Chicago Times* and *The Times* of London—criticized it as dull.

DECEMBER

- **2** *The Monroe Doctrine (1823)*
- **7** *Japanese attack Pearl Harbor (1941)*
- **9** *Birth of John Milton (1608)*
- **10** *Human Rights Day*
- **17** *First powered flight by the Wright Brothers (1903)*
- **20** *Louisiana Purchase (1803)*
- **21** *Hanukka*
- **25** *Christmas*
- **26** *Boxing Day*
- **29** *Massacre at Wounded Knee (1890)*

2 Monroe Doctrine. In his message to the U.S. Congress on Dec. 2, 1823, Pres. James Monroe stated that ". . . the American continents, by the free and independent condition which they have assumed and maintain, are henceforth not to be considered as subjects for future colonization by any European powers." Monroe also declared "we could not view any interposition for the purpose of oppressing them [former colonies of European powers], or controlling in any other manner their destiny, by any European power in any other light than as the manifestation of an unfriendly disposition toward the United States." The doctrine was occasioned by the prevalent feeling that Russia posed a threat to what is now Alaska and that the European powers were reluctant to recognize the sovereignty of the new republics in Central and South America. Though he did not mention the Monroe Doctrine by name, Pres. John F. Kennedy invoked its spirit when he demanded the removal of Soviet missiles from Cuba in 1962.

10 Human Rights Day. On Dec. 10, 1948, the United Nations General Assembly adopted the Universal Declaration of Human Rights, 30 articles setting forth the basic rights and freedoms of individuals. One of the chief authors of the document was Eleanor Roosevelt, who had been chairman of the UN Commission on Human Rights (1946-51). The day is observed by most member countries of the UN. In the U.S., observances continue throughout Human Rights Week, which runs from December 10 to December 17 and includes the anniversary of the U.S. Bill of Rights on December 15.

JANUARY

2 *U.K. steelworkers strike*

More than 100,000 unionized steelworkers went on strike for higher wages at the government-owned British Steel Corporation. Prime Minister Margaret Thatcher said substantial pay increases could not be justified until the iron and steel plants became more productive, efficient, and profitable. The strike was not expected to create an immediate crisis because private steel mills continued to operate and because industrial manufacturers carried relatively large inventories.

UN agency halts food to Cambodia

The UN World Food Program announced that no more emergency food would be shipped to Cambodia during January because only a few hundred tons of the 30,000 tons already ashore had been distributed to those in need. The International Red Cross and the UN Children's Fund (UNICEF), however, planned to continue shipments even though storage space was at a premium in the capital city of Phnom Penh and the port city of Kompong Som.

3 *Turmoil in El Salvador continues*

El Salvador's coalition government collapsed when dozens of high-ranking officials resigned their posts. The number included 10 of the 11 Cabinet ministers and two civilians from the five-man ruling junta. The political instability was attributed to the government's failure to come to terms with the leftists. On January 8 Salvador Samoyoa, until recently the minister of education, announced that he would join the Popular Liberation Forces, leftist guerrillas who on January 3 seized five radio stations in the capital city of San Salvador and on January 4 attacked the main headquarters of the National Guard.

4 *Carter embargoes U.S. grain to U.S.S.R.*

Pres. Jimmy Carter announced that U.S. grain sales to the U.S.S.R. would be limited in 1980 to the eight million metric tons sanctioned by a 1976 trade agreement. The 17 million additional tons on order by the Soviet Union would not be sold, Carter said, because the Soviet Union had initiated "an extremely serious threat to peace" by sending its military forces into Afghanistan on Dec. 27, 1979. Carter also cut off shipments of high technology equipment, curtailed Soviet fishing rights in U.S. waters, postponed the opening of new consulates, and deferred new economic and cultural exchanges. On January 7 Vice-Pres. Walter Mondale announced that the U.S. government would assist its farmers by purchasing the grain originally destined for the U.S.S.R. On January 12 representatives of Argentina, Australia, Canada, and the European Community met with U.S. officials in Washington, D.C., and agreed not to weaken the U.S. position by increasing their exports of wheat and corn to the Soviet Union.

Mauritanian head of state ousted

Mauritania's head of state, Lieut. Col. Mohamed Mahmoud Ould Louly, was removed from office and replaced by Lieut. Col. Mohamed Khouna Ould Haidalla, the premier. Other officials were also deposed. The ruling junta, known as the Military Committee for National Salvation, said the changes were made to rid the country "of all those who do not work with resolution and determination for the goal of national liberation."

6 *Indira Gandhi's Congress (I) Party wins Indian election*

In national elections held on January 3 and 6, Indira Gandhi's Congress (I) Party captured 350 of the 542 seats in the Lok Sabha, India's lower house of Parliament. The victory meant that Gandhi would again assume the powers of prime minister. The Janata Party, which controlled 295 seats when it came to power in March 1977, suffered a staggering defeat. It won only 31 seats in the new Parliament and, like all the other defeated parties, failed to win the minimum 50 seats needed to qualify as the official opposition party.

7 *Waldheim reports to UN on Iran*

UN Secretary-General Kurt Waldheim briefed the UN Security Council behind closed doors on his recent trip to Iran. He reported that Iran's Revolutionary Council was not "prepared to respond to the call of the international community for the release of the [U.S.] hostages." During his three-day stay in Iran, Waldheim was not permitted to meet Ayatollah Ruhollah Khomeini or visit the 50 U.S. hostages held by militants in the U.S. embassy in Teheran. At a news conference held in New York City on January 4, Waldheim remarked that the "situation is evidently more grave and serious than people believe."

9 *Raiders of Grand Mosque executed*

Saudi Arabia publicly beheaded 63 persons, all said to have been involved in the November 1979 raid on Islam's most sacred shrine, the Grand Mosque at Mecca. The Islamic court that convicted the 63 of murder acquitted 28 others. The criminals included 41 from Saudi Arabia, 10 from Egypt, 6 from Yemen (Aden), and 3 from Kuwait; the remaining 3 came from Yemen (San 'a'), Sudan, and Iraq.

NATO to use Turkish bases

Under terms of a new agreement reached by officials representing the U.S. and Turkey, two dozen military bases in Turkey would be made available to NATO forces. The bases would be controlled by the Turkish Army and special permission

Indira Gandhi received congratulations after she was reelected as prime minister of India. Mrs. Gandhi had been absent from that position since her party's defeat in 1977.

LAURENT MAOUS—GAMMA/LIAISON

would be needed for the U.S. to use the bases for its own "purposes." The pact also stipulated that the U.S. would provide Turkey with $2.5 billion in military and economic aid during the next five years. Formal ratification of the treaty was expected within two months.

11 *Castro takes over key ministries*

Cuban Pres. Fidel Castro Ruz assumed personal control of the Ministries of Defense, Interior, Public Health, and Culture; he also appointed trusted aides to head the Ministries of Industry, Economy, Communications, and Transportation. The shakeup was related to a growing economic crisis in Cuba. About 25% of the country's tobacco crop harvested in 1979 had been destroyed by rust and a fungous disease was threatening to destroy a quarter of the 1980 sugar crop. Both commodities rank high as currency-earning exports.

13 *U.S.S.R. vetoes anti-Iranian motion*

The Soviet Union vetoed a proposed UN Security Council resolution, sponsored by the U.S., that called for sanctions against Iran because it continued to hold U.S. hostages in Teheran. During the voting East Germany sided with the Soviet Union, Bangladesh and Mexico abstained, and China took no stand. The other ten members of the Council supported the resolution. The U.S. plan included a cutoff of all exports, except food and medicine, to Iran and the termination of all loans and credits.

14 *UN condemns U.S.S.R. aggression*

The UN General Assembly overwhelmingly approved a resolution demanding "the immediate, unconditional and total withdrawal of the foreign troops" now in Afghanistan. Even though the General Assembly was acting in direct response to the Soviet invasion of Afghanistan on Dec. 27, 1979, the resolution did not mention the U.S.S.R. by name. The vote was 104–18 in favour of the resolution; 18 nations abstained and 12 were officially absent. An attempt by the UN Security Council to pass a similar resolution on January 7 was thwarted by a Soviet veto.

Black leaders register parties for Zimbabwe election

Ten black parties were officially registered to compete for the 80 seats reserved for blacks in the national legislature of a new government. Joshua Nkomo, leader of the Zimbabwe African People's Union, chose the name Patriotic Front. The name formerly signified a guerrilla coalition that included Nkomo's followers and those of Robert Mugabe, who led the Zimbabwe African National Union. After years in exile, both Nkomo (on January 13) and Mugabe (on January 27) returned to Zimbabwe Rhodesia and were greeted by huge crowds of supporters.

UPI

The United Nations Security Council voted in January for the withdrawal of foreign troops in Afghanistan. The Soviet Union vetoed the resolution.

18 *Japanese accused as Soviet spies*

Yukihisa Miyanaga, a retired army general, and two former subordinates were arrested in Tokyo on charges of spying for the U.S.S.R. All three allegedly passed "highly sensitive military secrets" to Soviet agents while serving in the intelligence division of Japan's Self-Defense Force. Shigeto Nakana, army chief of staff, accepted responsibility for the breach of security and resigned his post on January 28. A short time later, Prime Minister Masayoshi Ohira replaced the director general of Japan's Defense Agency and noted that the agency would no longer be given access to intelligence reports compiled by Japan's overseas military attachés.

22 *Sakharov exiled to Gorky*

Andrey D. Sakharov, an internationally respected champion of human rights, was exiled with his wife to the Soviet city of Gorky. At the same time the Presidium of the Supreme Soviet stripped the 58-year-old physicist and winner of the 1975 Nobel Peace Prize of all his Soviet honours. Sakharov was accused of persistently engaging in subversive activities against the U.S.S.R. and of calling upon "imperialist states" to interfere in the internal affairs of the Soviet Union. He had urged worldwide pressure on the U.S.S.R. to force it to withdraw its troops from Afghanistan. He also publicly supported a boycott of the Summer Olympic Games in Moscow.

23 *Carter says U.S. will protect Persian Gulf area*

President Carter, in his annual state of the union message before a joint session of Congress, warned the Soviet Union: "An attempt by any outside force to gain control of the Persian Gulf region will be regarded as an assault on the vital interests of the United States of America. And such an assault will be repelled by any means necessary, including military force."

25 *Bani-Sadr wins Iranian election*

Iranian Finance Minister Abolhassan Bani-Sadr was elected the first president of the Islamic Republic of Iran, with 75% of the popular vote. He defeated six other official candidates. According to Iran's new constitution, the president serves a four-year term and has authority to appoint the prime minister and sign treaties. Ayatollah Khomeini, however, retains the right to dismiss the president.

Seoul demonstrators sentenced

A military court in Seoul, South Korea, sentenced 17 persons to prison for involvement in a demonstration that took place in the nation's capital on Nov. 24, 1979. The protest, which violated a martial law decree, was directed against the nation's constitution and the choice of Choi Kyu Hah to replace the late Park Chung Hee as president. Former president Yun Po Sun's two-year sentence was suspended, presumably because he was 83 years old. A 77-year-old Quaker, sentenced to a one-year term, was also spared incarceration. Other sentences ranged from one to four years.

29 *Canadians help U.S. diplomats escape from Iran*

U.S. and Canadian officials publicly acknowledged that six U.S. citizens, all employed at the U.S. embassy in Teheran, had been spirited out of Iran on January 28 using Canadian diplomatic passports stamped with forged Iranian exit visas.

The four Canadians who supplied the false documents represented the last members of the Canadian mission in Iran; they departed with the Americans. The six U.S. citizens—four men and two women—had avoided capture on Nov. 4, 1979, by slipping out a back door at the U.S. embassy while Iranian militants were taking 50 of their fellow countrymen hostage. The following day the six made their way to the Canadian embassy.

Islamic conference condemns invasion of Afghanistan

An emergency session of the Conference of Islamic States, which convened in Islamabad, Pakistan, condemned "Soviet military aggression against the Afghan people" and demanded that all Soviet troops be withdrawn immediately. The foreign ministers also suspended Afghanistan from their organization and asked that their respective governments sever diplomatic relations with it. Egypt did not attend the conference because it was at odds with most Islamic states over its peace treaty with Israel. Six additional nations refused to send representatives: Afghanistan, Guinea-Bissau, Yemen (Aden), Syria, Uganda, and Upper Volta.

31 *Guatemalan Indians die in fire after seizing Spanish embassy*

Thirty-nine Quiche Indians who invaded the Spanish embassy in Guatemala City lost their lives when fire swept through the building. The Spanish ambassador, who had been taken hostage by the Indians, was only slightly injured, but two former high-ranking Guatemalan officials reportedly died in the blaze. The one Indian survivor was kidnapped from his hospital bed the following day and murdered. Some claimed the fire was inadvertently started by police when they stormed the embassy. Others said the Indians, who hoped the invasion would force the government to release some of their imprisoned colleagues, set the fire accidentally. On February 1 Spain suspended diplomatic relations with Guatemala, demanding to know why the police had been allowed to assault the embassy after Spain had made repeated requests for restraint.

Queen Juliana to abdicate

Queen Juliana of The Netherlands, citing her age as the reason, unexpectedly announced that she would abdicate on her 71st birthday. Her oldest daughter, 42-year-old Beatrix, would assume the throne on April 30.

FEBRUARY

2 *U.S. congressmen accused of bribery*

During its prime time evening news program, NBC reported that for two years agents of the FBI had been gathering evidence of corruption against certain members of the U.S. Congress. Posing as Arab businessmen, FBI agents were reportedly able to obtain promises of special treatment from U.S. government officials in exchange for money. Some of the secret meetings were recorded and videotaped. The FBI operation was code-named Abscam ("Abdul Enterprises Ltd.-scam"). Three days later a U.S. senator from New Jersey was accused of illegal involvement in licensing a gambling casino. On February 8 a federal judge revealed another FBI investigation, this one code-named Brilab ("bribery-labour"). The governor-elect and the lieutenant governor of Louisiana as well as the speaker of the Texas House of Representatives were all accused of accepting bribes in an insurance kickback scheme. The FBI agents posed as insurance company representatives. They then offered money to the officials to secure insurance contracts covering city and state employees.

4 *Millions of illegal aliens in U.S.*

In a report prepared for the Select Commission on Immigration and Refugee Policy of the U.S. Congress and the White House, the U.S. Census Bureau estimated that there were no more than six million illegal aliens living in the U.S. at any one time. The report further stated that the number might be as low as 3.5 million. Mexicans, who comprise the largest segment of illegal residents, were estimated to number between 1.5 million and 3 million. The U.S. Immigration and Naturalization Service had earlier estimated that as many as 12 million illegal aliens were in the U.S.

French embassy and consulate in Libya wrecked

Libyans wrecked and burned the French embassy in Tripoli and wreaked havoc in the French consulate in Benghazi. France claimed the attacks were organized by the Libyan government, apparently because it objected to French support of Tunisia. France ordered its ambassador and other diplomats to leave Libya and requested Libyan government officials to leave France.

5 *Militants seize Spanish embassy in El Salvador*

About 50 armed members of the Popular League of February 28 took control of the Spanish embassy in San Salvador. The Spanish ambassador was among those taken hostage. The militants demanded the release of 13 imprisoned comrades and a visit by the Organization of American States to investigate violations of human rights. The siege ended on February 18, one day after the government freed 11 of the militants' colleagues. The taking of the Spanish embassy was but one of many such incidents disrupting the country. On February 5 the Revolutionary Salvadoran Student Movement occupied the Ministry of Education and took hostages. After leaving the building on February 12, they staged a demonstration during which three persons were killed by police gunfire. That same day police stormed the headquarters of the Christian Democratic Party, which had been invaded by militants on January 29. By the time the police assault was over, 7 persons had been killed and 23 wounded.

7 *New Zealand closes Iran embassy*

The New Zealand government announced the closure of its embassy in Teheran. After the embassy was broken into the previous day and important items were stolen, New Zealand said it had failed to receive satisfactory guarantees of protection from Iran.

9 *UN conference on development aid fails to reach accord*

The United Nations Industrial Development Organization ended a three-week conference in New Delhi, India, after voting 83–22 in favour of a resolution calling for the establishment of a huge fund to aid less developed nations. Industrialized Western nations, however, refused to accept either the original plan, which called for a fund of $300 billion to be created by the year 2000, or the more modest proposal submitted by India. In rejecting the proposals, the U.S. delegate noted that the World Bank and the International Monetary Fund were already working to achieve the very goals discussed during the conference; in addition, he said that the suggested method of administering the fund was unacceptable.

10 *Famine averted in Cambodia*

James Grant, executive director of the UN Children's Fund (UNICEF), reported that food shipments had averted famine in Cambodia, at least for the next few months.

11 *Marcos admits election fraud*

In an address before the National Assembly, Philippine Pres. Ferdinand Marcos admitted that his party, the New Society Movement, had engaged in fraud and terrorism to win the municipal elections held on January 30. He then accused the opposition of using similar tactics. Two leading members of Marcos's party, after charging that the government made use of "guns, goons, and gold" to preserve its political power, sought membership in the opposition Nacionalista Party. One of the two had been replaced as information minister on February 4. On February 12 four political groups announced they would join forces to oppose Marcos and martial law.

14 *China shuffles military commands*

In a major reorganization of China's armed forces, 6 of the country's 11 regional military commanders were replaced and hundreds of other officers were replaced or reassigned. The shakeup, which was said to be part of China's plan to modernize its defense forces, also included the appointment of a new navy commander. In addition, four new members were named to the Military Affairs Commission, which supervises the armed forces.

17 *Waldheim selects commission to visit Iran*

UN Secretary-General Kurt Waldheim named a five-man commission to visit Iran to discuss its grievances; it was hoped that the visit would lead to the release of the U.S. hostages held in Teheran. The group included H. W. Jayawardene, a lawyer and brother of Sri Lanka's president; Louis-Edmond Pettiti, a French judge on the European Court of Human Rights; Andrés Aguilar Mawdsley, Venezuela's representative to the UN; Adib Daoudy, adviser to Syrian Pres. Hafez al-Assad; and Mohammed Bedjaoui, an Algerian member of the UN International Law Commission.

Indira Gandhi dissolves nine state assemblies

Indian Prime Minister Indira Gandhi dissolved nine state assemblies and placed them under the control of the central government until new elections could be held in March. Gandhi's Congress (I) Party, which controlled only 7 of India's 22 states, hoped that new elections would give it control over more local assemblies. Former prime minister Charan Singh characterized Gandhi's tactics as "fascism . . . on the prowl."

Fighting in Lebanon continues

According to reports emanating from northern Lebanon, at least 60 villagers in Qnat were killed during a six-day artillery duel between Christian Falangists and Syrian troops. A rival Christian group led by former president Suleiman Franjieh also battled the Falangists. Several days earlier in southern Lebanon Palestinians and Israeli-supported Christians exchanged artillery fire. The United Nations Interim Force in Lebanon (UNIFIL) described the situation as very serious.

18 *Trudeau regains power in Canada*

Pierre Elliott Trudeau was in effect reelected prime minister of Canada when the Liberal Party that he headed won 44% of the popular vote and 147 seats in the 282-seat House of Commons. Trudeau replaced Joe Clark, who assumed office on June 4, 1979. Clark's Progressive Conservatives won 33% of the vote and 103 seats in the lower house. The New Democratic Party increased its representation by securing 32 seats. The Social Credit Party, which helped topple Clark's government, lost all of its five seats. One seat in Quebec remained vacant because of the death of a candidate; it would be filled in a special election. Trudeau was sworn in on March 3.

Poland gets new premier

Edward Babiuch became Poland's new premier when he replaced Piotr Jaroszewicz as chairman of the Council of Ministers. Jaroszewicz was one of four members of the Politburo who lost their positions during the eighth congress of the ruling Polish United Workers' Party. The country's troubled economy dominated discussions during the four-day meeting, which ended on February 15.

Pierre Trudeau (left) was jubilant after the February 18 elections returned him to power as prime minister of Canada. At right is Liberal Party president Alastair Graham.

CANADIAN PRESS

19 *EC offers neutrality plan for Afghanistan*

The nine foreign ministers of the European Community issued a statement in Rome guaranteeing Afghanistan's neutrality if the U.S.S.R. agreed to withdraw its troops from that country. The proposal had been submitted by Lord Carrington of Great Britain. On February 28 the British Foreign Office formally presented the plan to the Soviet ambassador in London. Early indications that the U.S.S.R. would reject the proposal were substantiated on March 14 when Soviet Foreign Minister Andrey Gromyko said Moscow would not accept any plan that affected the sovereignty of the Afghan government.

21 *Violence spreads in Afghanistan following strike in capital*

Shopkeepers, workers, and local government officials began a general strike in Kabul, the capital of Afghanistan, to protest the presence of Soviet troops in the country. At least 300 civilians reportedly died in the violence that followed; an unknown number of Soviet and Afghan soldiers also lost their lives. On February 22 Soviet and Afghan troops were placed under a joint command and martial law was imposed on Kabul. On February 24, for the first time, the official Soviet newspaper *Pravda* acknowledged that the rebels were offering serious resistance, not only in Kabul but in other major cities as well. The Soviet news agency Tass reported that "foreign agents and mercenaries" were mainly responsible for the upheaval. On February 26 numerous Shi'ah Muslims were arrested along with others suspected of having fomented the trouble.

25 *Government ousted in Suriname*

The government of Prime Minister Henck Arron was toppled in Suriname by army sergeants who led a pre-dawn coup. Arron had led the country since November 1975, when the tiny South American republic gained independence from The Netherlands.

26 *Egypt and Israel establish new ties*

In simultaneous ceremonies in Cairo and Jerusalem, Egypt and Israel formally exchanged ambassadors. The event was another step in the process of gradually normalizing relations between the two countries. The new Egyptian envoy, however, was careful to note that his presence in Jerusalem, the residence of Israel's president, in no way implied recognition of that city as Israel's capital.

27 *Diplomats seized in Colombia*

About 25 armed men and women, all members of the leftist M-19 Movement, seized control of the Dominican Republic embassy in Bogotá, Colombia. A number of diplomats were taken hostage shortly after they arrived for a reception commemorating the independence of the Dominican Republic. Five persons were reportedly wounded by gunfire during the takeover. The guerrillas demanded a ransom of $50 million, the release of more than 300 leftists accused of terrorism, and the publication of a manifesto.

29 *China rehabilitates Liu Shaoqi*

The 11th Central Committee of China's Communist Party approved the rehabilitation of the late Liu Shaoqi (Liu Shao-ch'i), who died on Nov. 12, 1969, in political disgrace. The fact of his death was not generally known until several years after the event. Liu, whose views differed from those of the late Chairman Mao Zedong (Mao Tse-tung), was expelled from the Communist Party in 1968 by the eighth Central Committee and ousted as president (head of state) of the People's Republic. At that time he was branded a "renegade, traitor, and scab." A special memorial service for Liu was held in Beijing's (Peking's) Great Hall of the People on May 17, 1980. Party Chairman Hua Guofeng (Hua Kuo-feng) presided while Vice-Premier Deng Xiaoping (Teng Hsiao-p'ing) delivered the eulogy. He described Liu as "a great Marxist and proletarian revolutionary."

South Korea restores rights to political activists

South Korean Pres. Choi Kyu Hah granted amnesty to 687 political dissidents who had lost their civil rights after being arrested for violating presidential decrees. Choi expressed the hope that his action would lead to national reconciliation. Among those whose civil rights were restored were former president Yun Po Sun and Kim Dae Jung, a former leader of the opposition New Democratic Party (NDP). Kim immediately charged that the NDP had "failed to take a grip on the political situation" after the assassination of Pres. Park Chung Hee in 1979 because Kim Young Sam, the current leader of the NDP, was "intent on promoting his presidential . . . campaign."

MARCH

1 *U.S. casts vote against Israel in Security Council*

All 15 members of the UN Security Council, including the U.S., approved a resolution calling on Israel to dismantle its settlements in the West Bank and Gaza Strip. Both regions were occupied by Israel during the 1967 war. Donald F. McHenry, speaking for the U.S., declared: "We regard settlements in the occupied territories as illegal under international law, and we consider them to be an obstacle to the successful outcome to the current negotiations, which are aimed at a comprehensive, just and lasting peace in the Middle East." The Israeli delegate insisted that the settlements provided vital military security for his country. On March 3 President Carter declared that the U.S. vote had been cast in error. While conceding that the U.S. opposed such settlements, he argued that their removal was subject to negotiations related to Palestinian autonomy. On the question of Jerusalem, also mentioned by the Security Council, Carter reiterated the U.S. position: the city "should be undivided with free access to the holy places for all faiths and . . . its status should be determined in the negotiations for a comprehensive peace settlement."

New Tunisian prime minister named

Tunisian Pres. Habib Bourguiba named Mohamed Mzali interim prime minister after Hedi Nouira, prime minister since 1970, suffered a stroke. Nouira had been viewed as the most likely successor to the president, who was in ill health, and the one best qualified to meet challenges from neighbouring Libya.

2 *Japan adopts a plan to shore up its faltering yen*

The Japanese government announced a plan to bolster the yen on international currency markets. On Oct. 31, 1979, the yen stood at a postwar high of 176.08 yen for one U.S. dollar; on March 1, 1980, the rate had fallen to 249.80 yen per dollar. Japan sought and received promises of cooperation from Switzerland, the U.S., and West Germany to help stabilize the market. The three countries said they were prepared to establish a $5 billion foreign exchange facility with the Bank of Japan; the money could then be used when necessary to support the yen by stabilizing its exchange rate.

4 *Mugabe leads his party to victory in Zimbabwe Rhodesia election*

Robert Mugabe, for six years the leader of the Zimbabwe African National Union (ZANU) guerrillas, was declared winner of a national election that was a prelude to the formal establishment of black rule in Zimbabwe Rhodesia and its recognition as an independent nation. Mugabe's ZANU-Patriotic Front won 62.9% of the popular vote and 57 of the 80 seats reserved for blacks in a future 100-seat Parliament. Twenty of the remaining seats went to supporters of Joshua Nkomo and three to followers of Bishop Abel Muzorewa. In a plea for reconciliation and national unity, Mugabe declared that "there is a place for everybody in this country."

5 *Pakistan declines U.S. aid*

Pakistani Foreign Minister Agha Shahi said that the U.S. offer of $400 million in aid was unacceptable. He explained that talks between the two countries, which intensified after the Soviet invasion of neighbouring Afghanistan in December 1979, had failed because the U.S. commitment to Pakistan's security was too weak and the "quantum of the aid package" too small. The U.S. and Pakistan were also at odds over a nuclear facility being built near Islamabad. The U.S. was concerned that the plant was being constructed to produce enriched uranium for nuclear weapons. Pakistan repeatedly insisted that it had a right to build and test a "peaceful nuclear device."

6 *Pak Hung Ju executed in Korea*

Col. Pak Hung Ju, one of seven men sentenced to death for complicity in the assassination of South Korean Pres. Park Chung Hee in October 1979, was executed by firing squad. Pak was the chief bodyguard of Kim Jae Kyu, who planned and carried out the murder while serving as head of the Korean Central Intelligence Agency.

10 *UN commission rebuffed in Iran*

Ayatollah Ruhollah Khomeini ended all hope that the UN special commission of inquiry would succeed in its mission to Iran when he announced that the panel would not be allowed to see all the U.S. hostages being held in Teheran until after it issued a report "on the crimes of the deposed shah and on interventions of the invading United States in Teheran." Khomeini also stated that contact with the hostages would be limited to questioning. UN Secretary-General Kurt Waldheim immediately announced that a report would not be issued until the panel completed the second part of its dual mandate; namely, interviews with each of the hostages and steps toward their release. Unable to carry out this part of its mission, the five-man UN commission departed Iran the following day.

11 *Somare ousted in Papua New Guinea*

Michael T. Somare, prime minister of Papua New Guinea since it gained independence from Australia in September 1975, was removed from office by a parliamentary vote of no confidence. He was replaced by Sir Julius Chan, leader of the opposition People's Progress Party.

MONTES—GAMMA/LIAISON

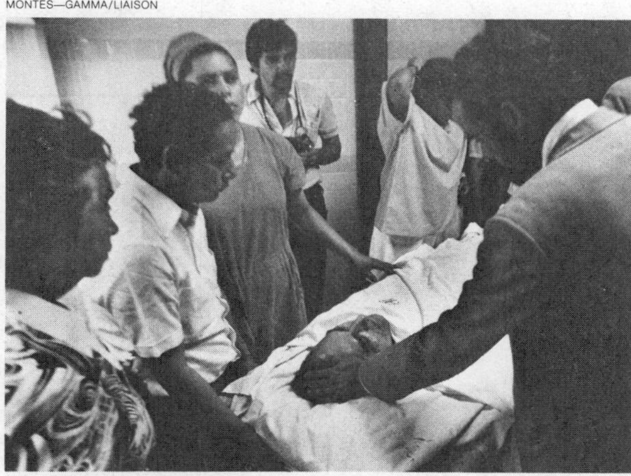

Archbishop Oscar Arnulfo Romero, an outspoken opponent of the political violence that racked El Salvador, was shot and killed as he celebrated mass in a chapel outside San Salvador on March 24.

12 *Iranians continue to enter U.S.*

The U.S. Immigration and Naturalization Service reported that more than 11,000 Iranian students, businessmen, visitors, and permanent residents had legally entered the U.S. since Iranian militants took U.S. diplomats hostage in Teheran on Nov. 4, 1979. During that same period, about 12,700 Iranians left the U.S. for various reasons.

13 *Ford Motor Co. acquitted by jury*

A jury in Winamac, Ind., found the Ford Motor Co. not guilty of reckless homicide in a case involving the deaths of three teenage girls. All three were killed in August 1978 when the Pinto subcompact in which they were riding burst into flames after it was struck from behind by a van. The prosecution claimed Ford knew of a design defect in the Pinto but failed to correct it. Ford's defense attorneys contended that other small cars, and even larger ones, also could not have withstood the impact of such a crash without spilling a large quantity of fuel. Two hospital employees testified that the driver of the Pinto told them before she died that the Pinto was not moving when it was struck by the van. This bolstered Ford's contention that the closing speed at the time of the crash was approximately 80 kph (50 mph), substantially greater than that estimated by the prosecution.

14 *Iran begins electing Majlis*

Iran completed the first round of elections for its new 270-member Majlis (parliament). On March 26, however, the ruling Revolutionary Council indefinitely postponed the second round, scheduled for April 4, because of charges of fraud and irregularities in the first round. The mullah-dominated Islamic Republican Party was the principal target of criticism. Pres. Abolhassan Bani-Sadr had promised on March 16 that "the many complaints of cheating" would be investigated and the election results voided if such action seemed justified.

15 *China issues guidelines to party*

The Chinese Communist Party issued a new set of principles "for internal party political life." Among other things, officials were henceforth forbidden to use "their position and power to seek preferment for family or relatives with regard to such matters as enrollment in schools, transferring from one school to another, promotions, employment, and travel abroad." The new guidelines also facilitate the dismissal, retirement, and transfer of officials, who have traditionally held their posts indefinitely unless they fell into political disfavour.

17 *Carter signs 1980 Refugee Act*

President Carter signed into law the Refugee Act of 1980, which had earlier been approved by the U.S. Senate and House of Representatives. The legislation extended the definition of refugees to include persons from every part of the world and it increased the number of refugees and immigrants allowed to enter the U.S. each year from 290,000 to 320,000.

19 *Cambodian refugees killed in camp*

According to Thai sources, rival factions of the National Liberation Movement of Cambodia engaged in bloody fighting inside a refugee camp near the Cambodia-Thailand border. At least 46 persons were reported killed, many of them civilians. The trouble was linked to personal animosities and an effort to replace the camp commander.

Italian premier resigns

Faced with a no confidence vote in Parliament, Italian Premier Francesco Cossiga resigned after announcing that Italy needed a stable government. Cossiga's Christian Democrats had functioned with the active support of the Liberals and Social Democrats and abstention by the Socialists. When the latter announced they would vote with the Communists, Cossiga resigned.

21 *Australia wool strike ends*

Faced with a government threat to close down the wool industry because nonstriking union members were financing strikes in Melbourne and Sydney, the secretary of the Storemen and Packers Union agreed to terms ending an 11-week strike by Australian wool handlers. The settlement included weekly pay increases ranging from about U.S. $3 to $4.65.

23 *Deposed shah leaves Panama*

The deposed shah of Iran, Mohammad Reza Pahlavi, left Panama with his family and flew to Cairo where he was offered permanent asylum by Egyptian Pres. Anwar as-Sadat. Though Iran was reportedly about to request the Panamanian government to extradite the shah, U.S. diplomats doubted that Panama would have honoured the petition.

24 *Archbishop Romero assassinated*

Roman Catholic Archbishop Oscar Arnulfo Romero y Galdamez was shot and killed while saying mass in a small chapel in San Salvador. One of El Salvador's most respected defenders of human rights and a champion of the poor, Romero frequently made public pleas for an end to the violence that was devastating his country. During the funeral service on March 30, about 30 persons were killed when bombs and sniper fire triggered a stampede among the 75,000 mourners.

Chad death toll exceeds 700

Westerners fleeing N'Djamena, the capital of Chad, estimated that more than 700 persons had been killed during several days of intense fighting between troops loyal to Pres. Goukouni Oueddei and those who supported Hissen Habré. In August 1979 the rivals had agreed to end hostilities and form a coalition government headed by Oueddei.

27 *Mt. St. Helens volcano erupts*

After a week-long series of earthquakes and moderate emissions of smoke and ash, Mt. St. Helens erupted for the first time since 1857. Volcanic ash was hurled some 4,500 m (about 14,500 ft) into the air and descended on a wide area of southwestern Washington state and on parts of neighbouring Oregon. Seismologists predicted that further eruptions would almost certainly follow in the near future.

28 *Hungary ends party congress*

The Hungarian Socialist Workers' Party ended its 12th congress after hearing Janos Kadar, the party's first secretary, pledge continued loyalty to the U.S.S.R. Kadar also called for improved economic performance because inflation-adjusted incomes had risen only 9% since 1975. The 1979 rate of inflation was estimated at between 15 and 20%.

APRIL

1 *U.K. steel strike ends*

A 13-week strike against the state-owned British Steel Corporation ended when union leaders accepted a 15.5% pay increase. The figure included an 11% national component and an additional 4.5% tied to productivity. Pensions and vacations were also improved but many workers were not satisfied with the settlement.

Brazilian metalworkers strike

Little more than a year after they had struck for higher wages, a quarter of a million metalworkers in the towns of Sorocaba and Taubate and in the industrial suburbs of São Paulo, Brazil's largest city, went on strike to enforce their demands for a further 15% increase in wages. Their leader, Luis Ignacio de Silva, also demanded that the workweek be reduced from 48 to 40 hours. The government threatened to declare the strike illegal and to bar the labour leaders from ever holding such positions in the future. On April 7 workers in Sorocaba and Taubate accepted a court-ordered settlement, but some 200,000 in the São Paulo area refused to return to work. On April 18 violence erupted between the police and 40,000 metalworkers who had decided at a meeting to continue the strike. On April 19 de Silva and 16 others were arrested.

2 *Prime rate reaches 20%*

Many major U.S. banks increased their prime lending rate to an unprecedented 20%. The figure represented the interest paid by top-rated corporations for borrowing money; all other commercial bank loans were fixed at even higher rates because there was at least some possibility of eventual default by the borrowers.

4 *FALN terrorists arrested*

Police arrested 11 members of the FALN, a terrorist organization advocating independence for Puerto Rico. The police in Evanston, Ill., were first called to investigate suspicious-looking joggers who were making repeated trips to a van which, it turned out, contained a large number of firearms. Among those taken into custody was Carlos Torres, the FBI's most wanted fugitive. He was the chief suspect in 11 bombings that had been attributed to the FALN since 1974.

6 *Cubans pour into Peruvian embassy seeking asylum*

Thousands of Cubans flooded the Peruvian embassy compound in Havana seeking political refuge and guarantees of safe passage out of the country. Before the onrush, which began on April 4, 25 Cubans had already found safety in the Peruvian embassy, 15 in the Venezuelan embassy, and one in the embassy of Argentina. On April 7 Pres. Fidel Castro visited the Peruvian embassy to assure the refugees they would be allowed to emigrate if other countries were willing to accept them. On April 10 a spokesman for the U.S. Department of State said the U.S. would accept "a fair share" of the Cubans but expected Latin-American countries to lead the way. During the preceding 15 months, the U.S. had accepted about 9,500 Cuban exiles and, according to one estimate, about 800,000 had been received since Castro came to power in 1959.

WERNER GARTUNG—GAMMA/LIAISON

A coup in Liberia, led by Army Master Sgt. Samuel Doe, resulted in hasty trials and executions for most of the former government officials.

Refugees from Ethiopia create immense problems in Somalia

Two members of the U.S. Congress toured a refugee camp in Somalia, then declared that the refugee problem there was even greater than that in Cambodia. According to one estimate, 1.3 million ethnic Somalis were living in 21 camps under squalid conditions. The refugees had fled the Ogaden region of Ethiopia, where fierce fighting continued over attempts to make the territory part of Somalia.

7 *U.S. severs relations with Iran*

The U.S. government formally severed diplomatic relations with Iran and ordered all Iranian diplomats to leave the U.S. by midnight the following day. An additional 250 Iranian military trainees were told to depart before midnight April 11. Other Iranians with valid U.S. visas would be permitted to stay; however, visas already issued but not yet used were canceled.

Japan sets up defense committee

The Japanese Diet (parliament) created a committee on defense, the first such body since World War II. Though the group was authorized only to discuss questions related to defense, its establishment was considered a potentially significant departure from past Japanese policy. While all major political parties supported the new committee, the leader of the opposition Democratic Socialist Party expressed special satisfaction, saying that his party had been demanding this commitment for seven years.

9 *Belgian prime minister resigns*

King Baudouin I of Belgium accepted the resignation of Prime Minister Wilfried Martens after he failed for a second time to push through a constitutional change that would have established three administrative regions based on linguistic differences: Wallonia, Flanders, and Brussels. Eight members of Martens's own party defected during the voting because they felt the Flemish minority in Brussels would not be sufficiently protected.

11 *Libyans slain in London*

Two political opponents of Libyan leader Muammar al-Qaddafi were assassinated in London, the first on April 11 and the second on April 25. Two Libyan students were arrested after the first incident and charged with murder. On April 26 Qaddafi publicly warned Libyan exiles to return home or be "liquidated." The U.S. had earlier ordered two Libyan diplomats out of the country for threatening anti-Qaddafi Libyan students.

12 *Liberian president slain in coup*

Liberian Pres. William R. Tolbert, Jr., and 27 others were slain in a coup led by 28-year-old Army Master Sgt. Samuel K. Doe, who then took over the government. Doe, who accused Tolbert of corruption and failure to work for the welfare of the common people, promised to respect free enterprise and private property. He also said that members of Tolbert's administration would be tried on charges of treason and corruption.

13 *Haitians seek refuge in Florida*

Four small boats carrying 326 Haitian refugees arrived in Florida, the largest one-day total ever recorded. During March about 1,300 Haitians had sailed to Florida to avoid harsh poverty and alleged political oppression. U.S. immigration officials reported that some 12,000 Haitians had already settled in the Florida area, but leaders of the Haitian community there suggested that 30,000 would be a more accurate figure.

15 *OECD bolsters Turkish economy*

The Turkish government of Prime Minister Suleyman Demirel received a promise of $1,160,000,000 in aid from 16 nations that met in Paris under the auspices of the Organization for Economic Cooperation and Development. The U.S. and West Germany each pledged $295 million, the other countries less. Turkey had already adopted strong austerity policies to combat its high inflation and unemployment rates and its critical shortage of foreign exchange.

18 *Zimbabwe becomes independent*

Zimbabwe Rhodesia, formerly the colony of Southern Rhodesia, became the independent nation of Zimbabwe in a midnight ceremony presided over by Prince Charles of Great Britain. After the Rev. Canaan Banana received the charter of independence that ended 90 years of white rule, he was sworn in as president. Robert Mugabe, who then took the oath of office as prime minister, declared: "The wrongs of the past must now stand forgiven and forgotten." UN Secretary-General Kurt Waldheim was present, as were representatives of more than 100 nations.

Taiwan concludes sedition trial

A Taipei military court found eight persons guilty of sedition for their part in a Dec. 10, 1979, demonstration that escalated into a riot. During the trial the defendants admitted organizing the Kaohsiung demonstration but denied any intent to overthrow the government or promote independence for Taiwan. Shih Ming-te, manager of the banned periodical *Formosa,* was sentenced to life imprisonment. The others, all of whom had connections with the magazine, received prison sentences of 12 or 14 years.

19 *Japan rejects Iran's oil price*

Following talks with representatives of the National Iranian Oil Company, Japanese oil industry executives announced they would not pay the $35-per-barrel price demanded by Iran. Japan was importing about 500,000 bbl of Iranian oil each day, which made it Iran's best customer, but Iranian oil accounted for only about 10% of Japan's total imports. Japan, moreover, had a stockpile of 415.8 million bbl of oil that, if used to replace its Iranian imports, would last more than two years. In addition, several oil-exporting nations had signified a willingness to replace the Iranian shortfall. Iran, on the other hand, depended heavily on its oil exports, which had fallen to about 1.5 million bbl per day, some 4 million bbl less than the level maintained during the reign of the deposed shah.

21 *South Yemen gets new president*

According to reports from the People's Democratic Republic of Yemen (Aden; South Yemen), Abd-al Fattah Ismail resigned as chairman of the Presidential Council and as secretary-general of the ruling Socialist Party; he was replaced by Prime Minister Ali Nasir Muhammad Husani. In March 1979 the Yemen Arab Republic (San'a'; North Yemen) and South Yemen had signed an agreement, sponsored by the Arab League Council, in which they undertook to end their fighting by uniting their countries. Some outside observers speculated that Ismail's apparent willingness to enter negotiations may actually have led to his ouster by Husani, who reportedly wanted to delay talks until South Yemen agents were able to infiltrate the smaller but much more populous North Yemen.

25 *U.S. rescue mission in Iran fails*

The Carter administration issued an early morning bulletin that read in part: "The President has ordered the cancellation of an operation in Iran that was under way to prepare for a rescue of our hostages. The mission was terminated because of equipment failure. During the subsequent withdrawal, there was a collision between our aircraft on the ground at a remote desert location. There were no military hostilities but the President deeply regrets that eight American crewmen of the two aircraft were killed and others were injured in the accident. . . .The President accepts full responsibility for the decision to attempt the rescue." In a nationally televised address that evening, Carter provided few other details. It was later revealed that the mission was scrubbed after three of the eight RH-53 helicopters that were to carry out the rescue developed mechanical problems. The servicemen died in an explosion that occurred when one of the six C-130 transport planes used during the mission was struck by a helicopter as it was preparing to take off.

Swedish strikes cripple nation

Sweden's airports and Stockholm's subways were shut down when 14,000 public-sector workers went on strike for higher wages and management locked out an additional 12,000 employees. On May 1 the employers' association locked out 770,000 more workers because the country's principal labour union refused to call off the wildcat strikes and would not sanction overtime work. The impasse quickly affected nearly one million workers and brought much of Sweden's transportation and industry to a standstill. The

Charred debris marked the tragic outcome of the secret U.S. mission to rescue embassy personnel being held hostage by Iran. Eight U.S. crewmen died in the unsuccessful operation.

WIDE WORLD

employers' association estimated that the work stoppage was costing at least $120 million a day in lost production. On May 2 Prime Minister Thorbjörn Fälldin said his government did not intend to enter the conflict.

27 *Bogotá terrorists end seizure of Dominican embassy*

Sixteen members of the M-19 Movement peacefully ended their 61-day occupation of the Dominican Republic embassy in Bogotá, Colombia, by flying out of the country on a Cuban airliner. The plane also carried 12 hostages: the papal nuncio, six ambassadors, and five lower-level diplomats from various countries. The end came after two nongovernmental negotiators reportedly turned over a $2.5 million ransom to the terrorists and gave guarantees of safe passage out of the country. After the escape plane landed in Havana, all hostages were released unharmed.

28 *Carter accepts Vance resignation*

President Carter formally accepted the resignation of U.S. Secretary of State Cyrus R. Vance, who had asked to be relieved of his duties on April 21. Vance took the step because he vigorously opposed the use of military force to secure the release of the U.S. hostages held in Teheran. In his letter to Carter, Vance remarked: "You would not be well served in the coming weeks and months by a Secretary of State who could not offer you the public backing you need on an issue and decision of such extraordinary importance—no matter how firm I remain in my support on other issues, as I do, or how loyal I am to you as our leader." In defense of his decision Carter said: "There is a deeper failure than that of incomplete success. That is the failure to attempt a worthy effort—a failure to try."

30 *Iran's London embassy attacked*

Six Arabic-speaking Iranians from Khuzestan Province seized the Iranian embassy in London, then threatened to blow up the building together with the hostages unless their demands were met. They insisted that 91 Arabs allegedly held as political prisoners in Khuzestan be released and that the province be granted a measure of autonomy. On May 5 British commandos stormed the embassy after the terrorists killed a hostage. During the assault, three terrorists were killed and two captured and the embassy was completely destroyed by fire. The body of a second hostage was later found, but 19 were rescued unharmed.

MAY

2 *Pope John Paul II visits Africa*

Pope John Paul II began an 11-day, 17,900-km (11,200-mi) tour of Africa that included stops in Zaire, the Congo, Kenya, Ghana, Upper Volta, and the Ivory Coast. The pope spoke frequently of the need to bring African cultural values and beliefs into line with basic Roman Catholic teachings. In Zaire the pontiff urged Catholics to adhere to the doctrines of monogamy, chastity, and clerical celibacy. He also used the occasion to tell priests: "Leave political responsibility to those who are entrusted with it . . . . Your domain of action, and it is vast, is that of faith and morals." At the open-air mass in Kinshasa on May 4, John Paul consecrated seven new bishops. The ceremony, however, was preceded by a tragedy; seven women and two children were trampled to death in the crowd.

4 *Yugoslav President Tito dies*

President Tito of Yugoslavia died in a Ljubljana hospital, where he had been hospitalized since January. Stevan Doronjski replaced Tito as chairman of the League of Communists and Vice-Pres. Lazar Kolisevski, a Macedonian, became interim president of the State Presidency. This eight-member body represented all of Yugoslavia's six republics and two autonomous provinces. On May 15, according to schedule, Kolisevski was replaced by Cvijetin Mijatovic, a Serb, who would hold the post for one year.

Yugoslav officials and representatives of other nations attended the state funeral of President Tito in Belgrade in May.

A. KELER—SYGMA

5 *Cuban refugees stream into U.S.*

On a day that saw 3,500 Cubans arrive in Key West, Fla., President Carter said the U.S. would welcome all such refugees with "an open heart and open arms." At the same time the U.S. sought to arrange a more orderly migration of these people and warned boat owners that they would be subject to heavy fines if they ferried aliens illegally to U.S. shores. On May 6 several hundred National Guard troops were dispatched to Key West to quell disorders that erupted in the temporary, overcrowded quarters holding the new arrivals. On May 14 Carter announced plans to reduce the unrestricted flow of Cubans by first screening those seeking asylum. Those with close relatives in the U.S. and those classified as bona fide political prisoners would be given special consideration. On May 21, with an estimated 67,000 Cubans already in the U.S. and some 23,000 resettled, the Carter administration said the Cubans would be treated as applicants for asylum, not as refugees. As such, they would have no automatic claim to government funds.

8 *Muskie becomes secretary of state*

Edmund Muskie was sworn in as U.S. secretary of state, one day after being confirmed by the Senate, which approved the appointment by a vote of 94–2. The procedure was expedited so Muskie could

TONI SICA—GAMMA/LIAISON

During a meeting in Stockholm a spokesman for Swedish metalworkers at Atlas Copco urged his fellow strikers to fight.

attend a NATO meeting in Brussels the following week.

Benigno Aquino leaves P.I. for U.S.

Benigno S. Aquino, Jr., a former senator and longtime critic of Philippine Pres. Ferdinand Marcos, was released from prison and allowed to fly to the U.S. for a heart-bypass operation. He had been incarcerated for seven and a half years. Before leaving Manila, Aquino told reporters he expected to return in about three weeks.

11 *Swedish strikers accept pact*

About one-quarter of Sweden's workers prepared to return to work after government-appointed mediators worked out a wage settlement acceptable to both labour and management. Prime Minister Thorbjörn Fälldin first assured the employers' association that a planned freeze on prices would not be implemented. Management then ended its lockout and workers ended their strike. The pact was expected to increase the employers' wage costs by 10% or more.

Brazilian metalworkers end strike

Tens of thousands of Brazilian metalworkers who had been on strike since April 1 returned to work, though many were still disgruntled. On May 19 the government released Luis Ignacio de Silva and other labour leaders arrested on April 19. Some interpreted the move as an attempt to placate the workers.

13 *Prominent Indonesians express grave concerns to Parliament*

A group of 50 prominent Indonesians, some of who were highly respected elder statesmen, sent a "statement of concern" to Parliament over statements made by President Suharto. The document created considerable excitement, and attempts were made to suppress it. The signatories expressed dismay at some of the statements made by Suharto in a speech delivered in Sumatra on March 27 before ABRI (armed forces) commanders and in a second speech in West Java three weeks later. In Sumatra Suharto included nationalism and religion on his list of discredited philosophies; in Java he castigated housewives and students for spreading rumours, including one that his wife was taking commissions related to government contracts. In essence, the 50 accused Suharto of distorting the state ideology (*Pancasila:* belief in God, nationalism, human rights, social justice, and democracy) to attack his enemies. They were also disturbed by the statement that ABRI would support the government-controlled Golkar Party in the 1982 election; a contrary pledge had been given by Defense Minister Gen. Mohammad Jusuf.

16 *Japanese government falls*

The Japanese government fell when 69 members of Prime Minister Masayoshi Ohira's factious Liberal-Democratic Party abstained in a vote of no confidence. The vote, which came as a great surprise to many, was 243–187. The lower house of the Diet (parliament) was dissolved on May 19 and elections were scheduled for June 22. On that date half of the membership of the upper House of Councillors would also face election in the first such simultaneous election since 1945.

Muskie meets Gromyko in Vienna

U.S. Secretary of State Edmund Muskie held a three-hour meeting with Soviet Foreign Minister Andrey Gromyko in Vienna. Both were in the Austrian capital to attend a celebration commemorating the 25th anniversary of Austria's liberation from Allied occupation. The meeting was held in private and was the first high-level contact between the two nations since the Soviet invasion of Afghanistan in December 1979. A few hours before meeting Gromyko, Muskie declared that "the principles of neutrality, of independence and territorial integrity . . . are today being violated." He then added that "an act of aggression anywhere threatens security everywhere."

17 *Racial riots rock Miami area*

Racial riots erupted in Miami, Fla., hours after an all-white jury acquitted four former Dade County policemen charged with murder in the fatal beating of Arthur McDuffie. The 33-year-old black insurance executive died in December 1979, four days after being apprehended for a traffic violation. During the three-day riot at least 14 persons were killed, more than 300 injured, and nearly 1,000 arrested. Among the dead were three whites who were dragged from their car and beaten; several blacks said to be looting were shot and killed. Property damage, mostly from arson and looting, was estimated at $100 million.

Pollution of Mediterranean curbed

Practically all nations bordering the Mediterranean Sea signed, or were expected soon to sign, an antipollution pact sponsored by the United Nations Environment Program. The agreement was also endorsed by the European Economic Community. The eventual cost was expected to be at least $10 billion.

18 *Tensions mount in South Korea*

Total martial law was imposed on South Korea in the wake of growing antigovernment demonstrations in the capital and five other cities. Two days later the Cabinet headed by Shin Hyon Hwak, prime minister since Dec. 10, 1979, resigned "for failure to maintain domestic calm." It was replaced by a Cabinet led by Park Choong Hoon, but Gen. Lee Hui Sung held power as martial law commander. Under martial law, universities were closed, labour strikes and political rallies forbidden, and "slanderous statements" against the late president Park Chung Hee or Pres. Choi Kyu Hah prohibited. Among those arrested were Kim Jong Pil, a former prime minister and leader of the Democratic Republican Party; Kim Young Sam, head of the opposition New Democratic Party; and Kim Dae Jung, whose political stronghold was the city of Kwangju. The demonstrators were demanding constitutional reforms and free elections.

Mt. St. Helens in Washington state erupts again

Mt. St. Helens in Washington state erupted with devastating violence while being monitored by scientists who arrived in large numbers after the initial blast in March. The complex geologic phenomenon began with a sudden horrendous explosion that caused extensive damage to the environment and claimed the lives of at least 34 persons.

Peru holds national elections

Fernando Belaúnde Terry, ousted from the presidency in an October 1968 military coup, was reelected president of Peru with 43% of the popular vote. Armando Villanueva del Campo, one of 14 other candidates, represented the Alianza Popular Revolucionaria Americana (APRA); he received 27% of the vote. In the 60-seat

Senate and in the 180-seat Chamber of Deputies, Belaúnde's party failed to gain absolute majorities. Peru's current president, Gen. Francisco Morales Bermúdez, was expected to return the country to civilian rule on July 28, as promised.

20 *Quebec voters reject separatism*

Quebec voters turned out in large numbers to defeat a referendum calling for association with but basic independence from the rest of Canada. The proposal carried in only 14 of the province's 110 electoral districts. Prime Minister Pierre Elliott Trudeau remarked that "we must not delay in rebuilding our house." The next day he announced that talks would soon get under way with provincial and territorial leaders to rewrite Canada's constitution.

21 *Rioters in Kwangju generate crisis in South Korea*

Antigovernment elements in Kwangju, South Korea, took control of the city to reinforce earlier demands that led to violent confrontations in major cities and the imposition of martial law on May 18. Seizing arms and military vehicles, they paraded through Kwangju shouting for the downfall of Gen. Chun Doo Hwan, head of the Korean Central Intelligence Agency, and the release of Kim Dae Jung, who on May 22 was formally accused of plotting to overthrow the government. After negotiations failed, troops were ordered to retake the city on May 27. Four days later the Martial Law Command reported that 170 persons had died in Kwangju, 144 of them civilians. Estimates by the Associated Press and other sources were much higher.

22 *Islamic states end conference*

The Conference of Islamic States ended a six-day meeting in Islamabad, Pakistan, after adopting a series of resolutions. One called for negotiations to secure the "immediate, total, and unconditional withdrawal of all Soviet troops" from Afghanistan. Another condemned the U.S. for its "recent military aggression" against Iran; *i.e.*, for its attempt to rescue the U.S. hostages held in Iran.

24 *Park Chung Hee's assassin hanged*

Kim Jae Kyu, who assassinated Pres. Park Chung Hee while serving as head of the Korean Central Intelligence Agency, was hanged with four accomplices. An appeal of the verdict was denied by the Supreme Court on May 19.

25 *Weizman resigns defense post*

Ezer Weizman resigned his post as defense minister in the Cabinet of Israeli Prime Minister Menachem Begin. Though Weizman had publicly asserted several times that Begin's settlements policy was jeopardizing negotiations for Palestinian autonomy, he continued to work for the government until confronted with cuts in the military defense budget. Weizman had little hope of winning a fight with the finance minister because many party members had deserted him after his April 16 call for new elections. Begin, later accused Weizman of "maddening ambition."

28 *Iran's new Majlis convenes*

Iran's new Majlis convened for the first time even though 29 seats still remained vacant in the 270-seat legislature. The formation of the Majlis was delayed until the votes were tallied from the second round of elections that took place on May 9. The hard-line Islamic Republican Party and its supporters held about 130 seats. During the two-hour first session, Pres. Abolhassan Bani-Sadr declared that Iran's economy was in a sorry state. Messages from Ayatollah Ruhollah Khomeini and from the militants holding the U.S. hostages were also read.

31 *South Korea sets up special security committee*

Gen. Chun Doo Hwan became chairman of South Korea's newly created Special Committee for National Security Measures. Fifteen of its 25 members were military officers. The committee would help coordinate the work of the martial law administration and the State Council, Pres. Choi Kyu Hah's civilian Cabinet. The government also established a Standing Committee to "deliberate and coordinate" matters falling within the jurisdiction of those entrusted with the nation's security. On June 2 General Chun resigned as head of the Korean Central Intelligence Agency. In another development announced that same day, the constitutional committee was authorized to draft a new charter within two months so it could be submitted to a national referendum before September 20.

Congress (I) Party wins state assembly elections in India

Prime Minister Indira Gandhi's Congress (I) Party won control of eight of the nine state assemblies that she had dissolved on February 17.

JUNE

1 *Cuban refugees riot in Arkansas*

About 300 Cuban refugees, frustrated by what they considered unjustified delays in being released from the Ft. Chaffee relocation centre in Arkansas where they were awaiting processing, attacked military guards with bottles, then leaped over a barrier and attempted to escape. Later in the day another attempt to gain freedom was made, but the refugees were driven back by police and soldiers using tear gas and billy clubs. During the rioting, 40 persons were injured and four buildings burned to the ground. Possible violence had been foreshadowed earlier in the week when some 1,000 of the 18,000 refugees held a rally to protest their continued detention.

Chinese premier ends Japan visit

Premier Hua Guofeng (Hua Kuo-feng), the first Chinese head of government ever to visit neighbouring Japan, returned to Beijing (Peking) after a series of meetings with Japanese Prime Minister Masayoshi Ohira. The two discussed such international problems as the Soviet invasion of Afghanistan, Iran's holding of U.S. hostages, North Korea's assessment of political changes in South Korea, Japan's military posture, and the future role of the Association of the Southeast Asian Nations (ASEAN).

2 *Arab mayors maimed by bombs*

Two West Bank Arab mayors, both staunch supporters of the Palestine Liberation Organization (PLO), were severely maimed by bombs that destroyed their cars. A third mayor escaped injury when Israeli military officials warned him not to approach his vehicle. In a fourth city, seven persons were injured by a hand-thrown grenade. Israeli Prime Minister Menachem Begin called the attacks "crimes of the gravest type" and promised there would be a "most intensive investigation" of the incidents. It was widely assumed that Israeli extremists had carried out the attacks.

Thatcher accepts EC proposal

British Prime Minister Margaret Thatcher approved a proposal, worked out by the foreign ministers of the European Community (EC), that would reduce Britain's 1980 budget contribution to $865 million from an estimated $2.5 billion. Britain had complained that it was required to make the largest net contribution to the EC budget, even though it was the third poorest nation of the group. This was so because much of the EC's budget was used to subsidize inefficient agricultural producers on the continent, indirectly penalizing Britain, which imported large quantities of food and thus did not qualify for aid. The accord, which embraced budget adjustments through 1982, would not take effect until ratified by the other EC members.

3 *Cuban refugees in U.S. exceed 100,000*

With the arrival of 4,496 new Cuban refugees in the U.S., the total since April 21 reached 101,476. On June 7 President Carter ordered the U.S. Department of Justice to expel any refugee who had committed "serious crimes" in Cuba and to prosecute or deport those found responsible for the rioting at Ft. Chaffee, Arkansas, on June 1. Federal officials had already determined that about 700 Cubans were either guilty of past serious crimes or were mentally deficient. Of that number, some 450 were classified as "hardened criminals." About 100 others were suspected of instigating the Ft. Chaffee riots. On June 30 U.S. authorities revealed that 1,395 Cubans had records of serious crimes and were being held in U.S. prisons. The 9,417 Cubans who had convictions for petty crimes and the 5,516 who had been arrested in Cuba for political crimes were not being held.

7 *Lebanese prime minister resigns*

Lebanese Prime Minister Selim al-Hoss, unable to control violent clashes among Lebanon's military factions, resigned together with his Cabinet. Pres. Elias Sarkis agreed not to accept Hoss's resignation before consulting on a possible successor. After weeks of fruitless meetings with political leaders, Sarkis asked Takieddin as-Solh on July 20 to try to form a government. Solh had been prime minister from July 1973 to October 1974.

8 *Violence continues to plague northeastern India*

Tribals in India's Tripura State, a panhandle jutting into the eastern border of Bangladesh, massacred at least 378 immigrants from Bangladesh in the village of Mandai in another episode of sporadic violence. The event was part of a continuing struggle by inhabitants of northeastern India to maintain their ethnic identity by either gaining total independence or obtaining some degree of autonomy from the central government. The trouble in Tripura reportedly started when the Tripura Upajan Suba Samiti, a tribal political organization, called for a market boycott and tribal policemen left their posts. The state government had to ask New Delhi to send paramilitary forces to quell the rioting. The tribals, once a majority in Tripura, deeply resented the presence of hundreds of thousands of Bengali refugees in their area. They were also incensed that the Bengalis had been allowed to take over some of the best land because they supported the central government.

10 *Khomeini says Iran faces chaos*

Ayatollah Ruhollah Khomeini warned fellow Iranians that internal political strife was driving the country toward chaos. He also remarked that choosing a prime minister and resolving the U.S. hostage situation were the principal obstacles to national stability. Pres. Abolhassan Bani-Sadr and his moderate supporters faced powerful opposition from the fundamentalist Islamic Republican Party. It controlled the Majlis and seemed disinclined to compromise, despite Khomeini's pleas for a united effort to solve the country's serious economic and social problems.

12 *Prime Minister Ohira dies*

Japanese Prime Minister Masayoshi Ohira died unexpectedly of a heart attack in a Tokyo hospital, ten days before national elections for both houses of the Diet (parliament). Masayoshi Ito, chief Cabinet secretary, automatically became acting prime minister. Later that day the Cabinet resigned, as required by the constitution, but it would continue to function in a caretaker capacity until after the elections. Ito and other prominent members of Ohira's Liberal-Democratic Party called on all disputing factions within the party to set differences aside and work together to assure a party victory in the June 22 elections.

13 *EC supports Palestinian goals*

The nine member nations of the European Community issued a declaration on the Middle East at the end of a two-day conference in Venice, Italy. Sections of the document endorsed the suggestion that the Palestine Liberation Organization be "associated with" negotiations to end the Israeli-Arab conflict and called on Israel to "put an end to the territorial occupation" of the West Bank and Gaza Strip. The declaration also expressed opposition to "any unilateral initiative" by Israel to change the current status of Jerusalem, the eastern portion of which had been occupied by Israel after the 1967 war. There were indications that Israel intended to declare all of Jerusalem the nation's undivided capital.

Auto workers strike in U.S.S.R.

Western news media reported they had learned from unofficial Soviet sources that more than 250,000 auto workers in the U.S.S.R. had staged separate two-day walkouts in early May. The rumoured strikes occurred at two of the nation's largest automobile factories, in Gorky and Togliatti, and involved more Soviet workers than any other strike in modern

Rioting Cuban refugees took to the main street of Ft. Chaffee, Arkansas, to demand quicker release from the refugee camp.

UPI

JUNE

FRANCOIS LOCHON—GAMMA/LIAISON

Pope John Paul II was taken on a grand tour during his visit to Brazil beginning in June.

times. Although the cause of the strikes was not certain, the workers reportedly took action to protest protracted shortages of meat and dairy products. Observers attributed the shortages to a poor 1979 grain harvest, to the U.S. grain embargo, and to stockpiling for the Moscow Olympic Games in July.

U.K. expels Libyan diplomat

The British Foreign Office ordered Musa Kusa, the head of the Libyan diplomatic mission in London, to leave the country for publicly approving the planned assassination of two more Libyans living in England (two Libyans had been killed in April). On June 12 Kusa told a reporter for *The Times* that two former Libyan government employees were marked for death because they had misappropriated funds. Libyan leader Muammar al-Qaddafi, however, had earlier indicated that steps would be taken to stifle criticism voiced by dissident Libyans living abroad.

18 *Prominent South Koreans accused*

South Korea's Martial Law Command (MLC), headed by Gen. Lee Hui Sung, announced that former prime minister Kim Jong Pil and eight other officials, all accused of corruption, had agreed to donate their personal fortunes to the state and to leave politics in exchange for immunity from prosecution. Kim was said to have acquired some $36 million illegally. The MLC said that confiscated properties and money would go into national welfare funds. Two days later more than 300 agents of the Korean Central Intelligence Agency were removed from their posts for being corrupt, inept, or abusive in exercising their authority.

22 *Liberal-Democrats win Japanese national election*

The Liberal-Democratic Party was returned to power in Japan with solid majorities in both houses of the Diet (parliament). The previous government, headed by the late prime minister Masayoshi Ohira, had held only a slight working majority with the support of independents. Voting for the lower 511-seat House of Representatives gave the Liberal-Democrats 284 seats, an increase of 26, and the Socialist Party 107 seats, the same number it had held in the previous Diet. The Komeito suffered a severe setback when its representation dropped from 58 to 33 seats. The Democratic Socialist Party won 32 seats, a loss of 4, and the Communist Party lost 12 seats for a new total of 29. The Liberal Club won 12 seats, an increase of 8; other minor parties more than doubled their previous representation to 14. Voting results for the 252-seat upper House of Councillors showed: Liberal-Democrats 135; Socialists 47; Komeito 26; Communists 12; Democratic Socialists 12; others 19. One seat remained vacant.

23 *Venice economic conference ends*

The leaders of Canada, France, Italy, Great Britain, Japan, the United States, and West Germany ended their two-day economic summit conference in Venice, Italy. All viewed inflation as their "immediate top priority." They also pledged to reduce their dependence on imported oil by developing alternative fuels and expressed concern that escalating oil prices would drive less developed nations "into ever-increasing indebtedness and put at risk the whole basis of their economic growth and social progress unless something can be done to help them."

24 *IMF looks at world economies*

The International Monetary Fund, which monitors economic performance in 140 countries, issued a report entitled *World Economic Outlook*. According to the report, there would be a sharp drop in the growth of world trade, increased inflation, a worldwide slowdown in production, and a worsening of the current U.S. recession, making it the nation's second worst since World War II. Less developed nations would be the most adversely affected because rising oil prices would depress world markets and weaken demand for raw materials supplied by such countries. As a consequence, some poor nations would be unable to repay debts. The report noted that the external public debt of less developed countries that had no oil reserves stood at $250 billion at the end of 1979, more than 300% greater than it was at the end of 1973.

26 *France develops own neutron bomb*

French Pres. Valéry Giscard d'Estaing announced the successful testing of a prototype neutron bomb that could go into production in several years, or somewhat later if modifications were made. The controversial bomb is designed to kill military personnel by intense radiation, without extensive material damage to the surrounding area. Advocates of the weapon say it would neutralize the Warsaw Pact's numerical superiority in tanks. President Carter, however, deferred production of the U.S. neutron bomb in 1978, saying a final decision would depend on the Soviet Union's buildup of conventional weapons.

29 *Bolivians vote for president*

Early returns indicated that former Bolivian president Hernán Siles Zuazo had defeated other presidential candidates in the Bolivian election but had failed to win the 50% of the popular vote needed to obtain the presidency. It appeared, therefore, that the newly elected Congress would have to choose a president after it convened on August 4. Though Siles had won a similar plurality of the popular vote in the July 1979 election, the Congress named Walter Guevara Arze president in August, but he was ousted in a military coup the following November. His successor, Col. Alberto Natusch Busch, was replaced some two weeks later by Lydia Gueiler Tejada.

30 *Pope begins visit to Brazil*

Pope John Paul II began the first ever papal visit to Brazil, which has the world's largest Roman Catholic population. During his 12-day pilgrimage, the pontiff visited Brasília, Belo Horizonte, Rio de Janeiro, São Paulo, Aparecida do Norte, São José dos Campos, Pôrto Alegre, Curitiba, Salvador, Recife, Teresina, Belém, Fortaleza, and Manaus. In public speeches John Paul reaffirmed the church's commitment to political and social justice and endorsed the work of the clergy toward this end, provided it avoided class violence and conformed to Christian, not Marxist, principles. In Rio de Janeiro the pope said the church wished to play no part in partisan politics but would speak out "to summon consciences, guard people and their liberty, and demand the necessary remedies."

Supreme Court approves limits on abortion funding

The U.S. Supreme Court, in a 5–4 decision, overruled two federal district court judges who held that Medicaid funds (jointly funded by the federal government and the states) must be used to pay for abortions sought by poor women. In effect, the court upheld the Hyde amendment, which prohibits the use of Medicaid funds for abortions except in cases that result from rape or incest or where the life of the woman is endangered. The court did not deny the constitutional right to abortions; it merely ruled that federal and state governments had no constitutional obligation to pay for the procedure.

JULY

2 *U.K. unveils plan for home rule in Northern Ireland*

The British government released a plan that would restore a degree of home rule to Northern Ireland which, because of prolonged sectarian violence, had been ruled directly from London since March 1972. The proposal suggested a single-chamber legislature elected by proportional representation. Executive power would either be shared in direct proportion to election percentages or would be granted to the majority party. The latter type of executive would be supplemented by a Council of the Assembly, which would provide equal representation for those who opposed the executive. London would continue to have responsibility for law and order, international relations, and finance.

4 *Zimbabwe moves to cut South African diplomatic ties*

The South African diplomatic mission in Salisbury was ordered closed down by Robert Mugabe, prime minister of Zimbabwe, who charged that the mission was involved in the recruiting of 5,000 troops to be used to "destabilize" black African governments. South Africa, in response, announced on July 8 the withdrawal of all senior diplomats from Zimbabwe. South Africa denied any subversive intent behind the recruitments, but admitted that the mission had processed applications filed by white former Rhodesian military personnel who wished to join South Africa's armed forces.

OAU meets in Sierra Leone

The Organization of African Unity (OAU) ended its 17th annual summit conference in Freetown, Sierra Leone, on a note of discord. Mozambique and Zimbabwe both denounced Morocco for continuing to fight the Polisario Front for control of what was formerly the Spanish Sahara. When the Polisario Front requested admission to the OAU as the Saharan Arab Democratic Republic, it was reported that at least eight dissenting nations, including Morocco, threatened to leave the organization if admission was granted, even though a majority of the members favoured admission. A committee was then formed to continue discussions.

5 *U.S. airlifts arms to Thailand*

The U.S. began airlifting arms to Bangkok to enhance the military capability of Thai forces stationed along the Cambodian border. The U.S. decision was taken following incursions into Thailand in late June by Vietnamese troops who controlled Cambodia.

UPI

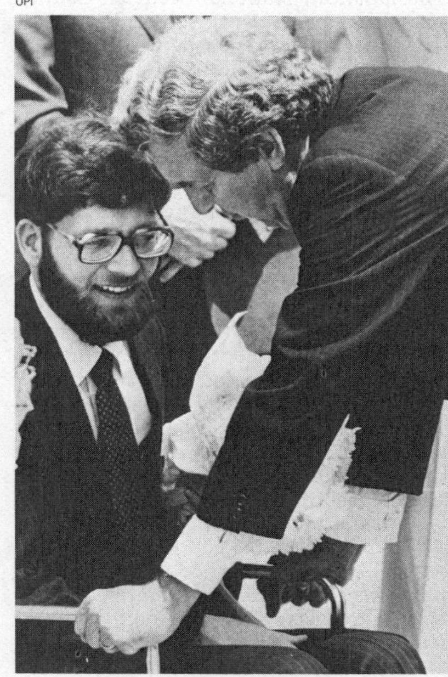

Richard Queen, an American hostage held by the Iranians, was greeted by U.S. Secretary of State Edmund Muskie after Queen was released and arrived in Washington, D.C., in July.

8 *Falangists defeat rival forces*

In two days of intense fighting in and around Beirut, Christian militia of the Falangist Party of Lebanon decisively defeated the militia of the National Liberal Party (NLP), a rival Christian organization. With the capture or surrender of vital NLP strongholds, the Falangists seemed to have won a definitive victory. Two days later a Falangist spokesman remarked that Lebanon would now be freed of Palestinians because "there is one command, one view of the future."

U.S. rejects Saudi arms request

A bipartisan group of 68 U.S. senators sent a letter to President Carter saying they would not approve the sale of special F-15 jet fighter equipment to Saudi Arabia because Saudi planes would then have an offensive capability that could be used to threaten Israel. The Saudi ambassador to the U.S. denounced the decision because, he said, it inhibited his country's ability to defend itself against threats from "all directions." He also noted that similar equipment could be purchased elsewhere.

9 *South Korea purges top officials*

South Korea's Special Committee for National Security Measures announced that 232 high-ranking government officials had either resigned under pressure or had been dismissed from their posts as part of a "purification drive." Six days later 4,760 lower-level public officials were discharged "to help restore public confidence in officialdom by decisively rooting out malpractices and irregularities." On July 19 the Martial Law Command reported that 3 former Cabinet ministers and 14 incumbent legislators had been taken into custody. All would be investigated for political irregularities and corrupt practices. On July 22 the government announced that an additional 1,819 officials of various state-financed organizations and affiliated agencies had been fired. Of this number, 39 were presidents or vice-presidents and 128 were members of boards of directors.

10 *Military coup in Iran fails*

The Iranian government announced it had foiled a military coup. The alleged conspiracy reportedly involved armoured division and air force officers and resulted in the immediate arrest of more than 300 persons. The plot was said to have included the bombing of Ayatollah Ruhollah Khomeini's residence in Qom and the office of Pres. Abolhassan Bani-Sadr in Teheran. Former prime minister Shahpur Bakhtiar was accused of masterminding the plot from his exile in Paris. On July 31, 11 persons were executed by firing squad after being convicted of involvement in the abortive coup. Their deaths raised to 36 the number of those put to death for participating in the conspiracy.

11 *Iran releases ailing U.S. hostage*

Richard I. Queen, a 28-year-old U.S. vice-consul and one of 53 hostages held by the Iranian government, was unexpectedly released because of a serious but undiagnosed ailment. He was flown to Zürich, Switz., then to a U.S. Air Force hospital in Wiesbaden, West Germany, where doctors said he was suffering from multiple sclerosis.

13 *President of Botswana dies*

Sir Seretse Khama, the 59-year-old president of the southern African republic of Botswana, died of cancer in the capital city of Gaborone. He had been president since Botswana gained independence from Great Britain in 1966. On July 18 the National Assembly elected Vice-Pres. Quett Masire to the presidency.

14 *Billy Carter registers as foreign agent of Libya*

President Carter's brother Billy registered with the U.S. Department of Justice as an agent of the Libyan government. He had been charged with violating the Foreign

Agents Registration Act because he had not reported services performed for Libya since 1978. Billy Carter said he had received a loan of $220,000 from the Libyan government in 1980, but his lawyers acknowledged there was no precise schedule for repayment. On July 24 the U.S. Senate set up a special panel to investigate the matter. The next day U.S. Attorney General Benjamin Civiletti, contradicting previous statements, admitted he had spoken to the president about the matter more than a month earlier. On July 30 the president acknowledged he and his brother had discussed classified State Department cables dealing with Libya.

17 *Suzuki chosen as Ohira's successor*

Zenko Suzuki was elected prime minister of Japan by a decisive margin in both houses of the Diet (parliament). In the lower House of Representatives, he received 291 votes; his closest rival, Socialist Ichio Asukata, received 106. In the upper House of Councillors, Suzuki defeated Asukata 134–49. Suzuki, a dark-horse candidate to succeed the late Masayoshi Ohira as leader of the Liberal-Democratic Party, was elected to that post on July 15; his elevation to the prime ministership was then assured.

Military seizes power in Bolivia

Army Gen. Luis García Meza Tejada led a military coup to prevent the Bolivian Congress from electing Hernán Siles Zuazo president on August 4. Siles, a leftist, had finished first in the June election but had fallen short of receiving an absolute majority of the popular vote. After the coup, García Meza, who had the support of the navy and air force commanders, disbanded Congress and declared the country a military zone. Strong opposition to the coup quickly surfaced in many parts of the country.

18 *Murders lead to Kingston curfew*

The Jamaican National Security Council placed sections of Kingston under curfew in an attempt to curb night violence by armed gangs. During the first half of July alone about 70 persons had been slain by gunmen.

19 *Olympic Games open in Moscow*

The Games of the XXII Olympiad opened in Moscow after months of heated controversy. The U.S. had called for a boycott of the Games to protest the Soviet invasion of Afghanistan in December 1979. Of the 65 nations that did not participate, more than half supported the U.S. stand; the rest stayed away because they could not afford the cost or could not field world-class athletes. Canada, China, Japan, Kenya, and West Germany were among the nations that backed the U.S. position and refused to be represented. Ultimately, 6,000 athletes from 81 nations joined the Games, about 4,000 fewer than had originally been expected. The competitions were witnessed by roughly 150,000 foreign tourists, about one-half the number that would have been present under ordinary circumstances.

24 *U.S. oil imports drop 14%*

The American Petroleum Institute reported that the U.S. imported 14% less crude oil during the first half of 1980 than it did during the first six months of 1979. Energy Secretary Charles W. Duncan, Jr., attributed the decline to conservation, higher prices, and reduced demand stemming from the economic recession currently affecting the country.

The Olympics were held in Moscow from July 19 until August 3.

SIMON—GAMMA/LIAISON

26 *Bani-Sadr picks prime minister*

Iranian Pres. Abolhassan Bani-Sadr selected Mostafa Mir-Salim as the first prime minister of the Iranian Islamic Republic. The choice was a compromise to placate the Islamic Republican Party (IRP), but the Majlis (parliament), which was dominated by the IRP, rejected the nomination.

27 *Deposed shah of Iran dies*

The deposed shah of Iran, Mohammad Reza Pahlavi, died in an Egyptian military hospital in Cairo. He had been suffering from lymphatic cancer for about seven years. At the state funeral on July 29, Egyptian Pres. Anwar as-Sadat led the procession. The only other world figures in attendance were former U.S. president Richard M. Nixon and Constantine II, the exiled king of Greece.

Police jail Iranian demonstrators

Nearly 200 pro-Khomeini demonstrators were arrested in Washington, D.C., after clashing with fellow Iranian counter-demonstrators, U.S. citizens, and the police. On August 4 many of those being held finally agreed to reveal their identities to federal authorities. The next evening all but one male demonstrator were released; he was charged with assaulting a police officer.

28 *Peru returns to democracy*

The presidential inauguration of Fernando Belaúnde Terry ended 12 years of military rule in Peru. The event, applauded worldwide, was attended by representatives of some 100 nations. At Belaúnde's request, however, Argentina's president did not attend because Argentine intelligence agents, assisted by Peruvian army authorities, had reportedly violated Peru's sovereignty by kidnapping three Argentines living in Peru.

30 *Israel makes undivided Jerusalem its national capital*

The Israeli Knesset (parliament) passed a law formally making all of Jerusalem the nation's capital. The vote was 69–15, with 3 abstentions. The new law formalized a claim that was first made in 1967 when Israeli troops occupied Arab East Jerusalem as a result of war. Most countries having diplomatic relations with Israel, however, had long recognized the special status of Jerusalem and maintained their embassies in Tel Aviv-Yafo rather than in Jerusalem. The action taken by the Knesset, therefore, was widely criticized because it presumably meant that Israel was not prepared to negotiate the future status of the holy city with the Arabs.

U.K. proposes three citizenships

The British government published a White Paper calling for the establishment of three classes of citizenship. The first, British Citizenship, would apply to persons "connected with the United Kingdom itself" and would include the vast majority of those now holding U.K. citizenship. The second type, Citizenship of the British Dependent Territories, would include such important areas as the Crown Colony of Hong Kong. The third classification, British Overseas Citizens, would cover British overseas citizens who do not fit into either of the other two categories and do not have the right of free entry into the U.K. In time, the right of abode in the U.K. would be restricted to those belonging to the first category. In addition, the new plan, if adopted, would grant citizenship through mothers (as well as fathers) to some children born abroad. Critics charged that the three-category plan would discriminate against nonwhites and would provide no protection to persons in the third category. If circumstances turned the latter into refugees, they would be worse off than persons who were legally stateless and thus fell under UN protection.

AUGUST

2 *Bomb blast in Bologna kills 76*

A bomb planted in a waiting room at the central train station in Bologna, Italy, killed 76 persons outright and injured about 200 others. Investigators believed neofascist terrorists were responsible. The explosive charge, which was equivalent to about 40 kg (88 lb) of dynamite, caused the entire ceiling of one wing of the station to collapse. On August 6 French police in Nice arrested an Italian right-wing extremist who was suspected of complicity in the crime. On August 27 police in Rome arrested an additional 22 persons, all connected in some way with right-wing activities.

Registration of U.S. youth ends

The two-week period during which all U.S. males born in 1960 and 1961 were required to register for a possible future military draft came to an end. The process involved no inductions or classification of those who signed up. On September 4 the director of the Selective Service System announced that 93% of those required to register had complied with the proclamation signed by President Carter on July 2. Antidraft groups, however, disputed this claim.

5 *U.S. adopts new war strategy*

U.S. government officials revealed that President Carter had endorsed a new targeting strategy to be used in the event of a nuclear war with the Soviet Union. In place of all-out retaliation against Soviet cities and industrial centres, the U.S. would concentrate on the country's ability to wage war by attacking its military installations and command posts.

Belgians get regional autonomy

The Belgian Parliament voted 156–19 to grant limited autonomy to the country's two principal linguistic regions. Dutch-speaking Flanders and French-speaking Wallonia would each have its own assembly and executive with authority over public health, cultural affairs, and city projects. The central government would continue to bear the major responsibility in such areas as education, finance, and law enforcement. Parliament postponed a decision on the Brussels area because of its special problems. The area lies in a Dutch-speaking region, but a majority of the residents speak French.

BOCCON-GIBO—SIPA PRESS/BLACK STAR

Lech Walesa, leader of the striking Polish workers, was hailed when the Polish government capitulated to the workers' demands.

6 *Zimbabwe Cabinet official arrested and charged with murder*

Edgar Z. Tekere, secretary-general of the ruling Zimbabwe African National Union Patriotic Front party and a member of Prime Minister Robert Mugabe's Cabinet, was arrested and charged with the murder of a white farmer on August 4. Six of Tekere's accomplices were also arrested. Mugabe, who was reportedly consulted before the arrests were made, informed Parliament that he would not interfere in the case.

11 *Iranian prime minister chosen*

The Iranian Majlis (parliament) approved the selection of Mohammad Ali Raja'i as prime minister. In secret balloting, the former minister of education received 153 votes; there were 24 negative votes and 19 abstentions. Earlier, Pres. Abolhassan Bani-Sadr had nominated others, but none had been found acceptable.

China removes Mao's images

The Central Committee of the Chinese Communist Party published a directive calling for the removal of most public portraits, statues, slogans, and poems of the late chairman Mao Zedong (Mao Tse-tung). Images of Mao had already begun to disappear in Beijing (Peking) some two weeks earlier. The committee defended its action on the grounds that "inappropriate commemoration" of Mao "fosters the incorrect view that history is created by individuals." Portraits of Stalin, Marx, Engels, and Lenin were also ordered removed from Tian An Men (T'ien An Men) Square in the nation's capital.

13 *President ousted in Suriname*

Johan Ferrier, president of the small South American republic of Suriname since it gained independence from The Netherlands in 1975, was overthrown in a military coup. He was replaced by Prime Minister Hendrick R. Chin A Sen.

14 *Polish workers defy government*

Labour unrest in Poland reached crisis proportions after 17,000 workers went on strike and seized the Lenin Shipyard in Gdansk. Within a few days 120,000 workers in northern Poland had joined the strike. They then formed a central committee to consolidate their various demands and strengthen their bargaining position with the government. When negotiations, token concessions, and threats coupled with arrests failed to undermine the resolve of the strikers, the government reversed its previous position and reluctantly agreed to negotiate directly with representatives of the strikers. The next day, August 24, Edward Babiuch was ousted as chairman of the Council of Ministers (premier); three other members of the Politburo and 11 other top officials were also dismissed. On August 26, after tens of thousands of workers in other parts of Poland had joined the strike, Deputy Premier Mieczyslaw Jagielski agreed to most of the workers' demands, but not to the establishment of trade unions independent of the Communist Party. On August 31 the government finally granted workers the right to strike and form independent trade unions. Within a few days most of the strikers had returned to work, including some 200,000 coal miners who had gone on strike in Silesia on August 29.

18 *Japan to cut back oil imports and increase defense spending*

Japanese Prime Minister Zenko Suzuki, in his first major policy speech since assuming office, outlined some of the principal goals of his administration. Lamenting Japan's worrisome reliance on imported oil, he declared that Japan would try to reduce its dependence on foreign energy from the current 72% to 50% by 1985. This could be accomplished, he said, by using alternative sources of energy such as coal and nuclear power. The prime minister also affirmed his support for the U.S.-Japanese security treaty and pledged that Japan would assume ever greater responsibility for its own defense through "steady and significant increases" in its military budget.

20 *U.S. reveals "Stealth" aircraft*

The U.S. revealed that it had developed an airplane that could avoid detection by radar. The so-called Stealth aircraft is reportedly coated with a special material that diffuses radar waves and is so shaped that the conventional sharp corners of a plane, which made the craft especially vulnerable to radar detection, have been substantially modified. The revelation upset those who believed the announcement was tantamount to the disclosure of top military secrets to help bolster President Carter's presidential campaign by showing he had not neglected defense.

Security Council urges nations not to recognize Jerusalem

The UN Security Council approved a resolution urging all nations to disregard Israel's declaration that the entire city of Jerusalem is its undivided capital. The vote was 14–0; the U.S., which abstained because the resolution was "flawed," maintained that the status of Jerusalem was a matter to be negotiated, not decided by a single nation. The resolution also called on nations that maintain embassies in Jerusalem to remove them.

21 *Soviet sub disabled near Japan*

A Soviet nuclear submarine caught fire and surfaced in international waters some 160 km (100 mi) east of Okinawa. A British tanker permitted Soviet officers to radio for help, but the Soviets, apparently unwilling to risk the possible disclosure of military secrets, would accept no further aid from the British or from Japanese crews in the area. Initially the U.S.S.R. defied Japan by having its sub towed into Japanese waters without first giving assurances that there was no radiation leakage from the ship's nuclear reactor and that no nuclear weapons were aboard. On August 24 the Soviet Union complied with Japan's request by stating that the disabled sub posed no danger.

BRIAN F. ALPERT—KEYSTONE

Zimbabwe Prime Minister Robert Mugabe addressed the UN General Assembly in August.

Somalia-U.S. arms pact signed

The U.S. and Somalia signed an agreement that bolstered Somalia's defense capabilities and facilitated U.S. military access to the Indian Ocean and the Persian Gulf. In return for $25 million in military aid in 1981 and additional aid later, the U.S. naval and air forces would be permitted to use airfields and port facilities at Mogadishu and Berbera. Somalia, moreover, pledged not to use U.S. military equipment outside its own borders and promised not to involve itself again in the Ogaden region of Ethiopia, where ethnic Somalis had been fighting for independence.

22 *Billy Carter testifies before Senate subcommittee*

Billy Carter, the president's brother, concluded two days of testimony before a Senate subcommittee investigating Carter's dealings with Libya. During the course of the questioning, Carter said he had never interceded on Libya's behalf with any U.S. official, though he conceded he had been invited to Libya because he was related to the president. The panel was generally severely critical of Carter for accepting a $220,000 loan from a government that had "engaged in terrorism and assassination." Sen. Patrick Leahy (Vt.) reflected the convictions of other members of the panel when he told Carter that his dealings with Libya had damaged both the president and the nation.

25 *Zimbabwe joins United Nations*

The newly created African nation of Zimbabwe was admitted to the United Nations as its 153rd member. Prime Minister Robert Mugabe was present when his country's delegation was seated with other nations in the General Assembly.

27 *Chun Doo Hwan elected president*

South Korea's National Conference for Unification elected Chun Doo Hwan president. The 48-year-old former army general, who immediately assumed full powers of his office, replaced South Korea's fourth president, Choi Kyu Hah, who resigned on August 16 to establish "the precedent of peaceful transfer of power." During the formal inauguration ceremony on September 1, Chun promised to lift martial law as soon as there was "no longer any danger of disturbances." He also pledged that a referendum on a revised constitution would be held no later than October. On September 2 the new president appointed a 20-member Cabinet, which included both civilians and military personnel. Nam Duck Woo, who had been finance minister during the presidency of Park Chung Hee, was named prime minister.

French Navy keeps port open

The French government used Navy tugboats armed with water cannons and tear gas to prevent striking fishermen from blockading the country's largest oil tanker terminal at Fos in southern France. In an effort to gain subsidies to cover increased costs for diesel fuel and to protect the jobs of crews manning fishing trawlers, the fishermen had intermittently blockaded other ports during the previous two weeks and had attempted to close the port of Antifer, an important oil terminal in northern France. Some 7,000 British tourists had been stranded in Cherbourg before the fishermen let them depart on August 19.

29 *Anti-Marcos foes in P.I. unite*

Seventy-two leaders of eight different political groups in the Philippines announced the signing of a document called Covenant for Freedom. The statement called for an end to exploitation and injustice and for the establishment of "a new order based on social justice." The signatories, most of whom were members of the defunct Congress, pledged to use peaceful means to end martial law and restore democracy to the country. On August 22 a series of bombings had damaged a number of government offices and businesses in the Manila area. A militant group calling itself the April 6 Liberation Movement took responsibility for the violence. The group issued a statement in which it condemned martial law and vowed that violence would henceforth be used "as the ultimate weapon against a repressive regime which has refused to listen to reason."

31 *Abscam trial ends in convictions*

Rep. Michael O. Myers of Pennsylvania and three co-defendants became the first persons convicted of bribery and conspiracy in a case arising from the FBI's "Abscam" investigation. Videotapes introduced by government prosecutors showed Myers accepting $50,000 in cash from an undercover agent in exchange for a promise to introduce special immigration legislation that would permit certain Arab sheikhs to reside in the U.S. The sheikhs were actually undercover FBI agents.

SEPTEMBER

1 *Syria and Libya announce merger*

After secret negotiations between Libyan and Syrian representatives, the Libyan leader Col. Muammar al-Qaddafi publicly proposed the merger of the two nations so they could oppose Israel more effectively. In a message of acceptance, Syrian Pres. Hafez al-Assad told Qaddafi that unity was "the only way to safeguard Arab integrity and rights." Though details of the merger were still to be worked out, a formal agreement uniting the two nations was signed on September 10. In 1973 Libya had signed a similar agreement with Egypt, but nothing materialized. The following year Qaddafi tried to unite Libya with Tunisia, but that plan also failed.

4 *Saudis nationalize Aramco*

The head of Saudi Arabia's national oil company confirmed that his country had completed the takeover of the Arabian American Oil Co. (Aramco). At one time all of Aramco's assets were owned by four U.S. oil companies: Exxon Corp., Mobil Oil Corp., Texaco Inc., and Standard Oil Co. (Calif.). In 1973 Saudi Arabia purchased 25% of Aramco's Saudi Arabian facilities and in 1974 an additional 35% interest. When the remaining 40% was bought for $1.5 billion during the second quarter of 1980, Aramco became in effect a service company selling Saudi crude on world markets.

Queensland coal strike ends

Australian coal miners in Queensland ended a ten-week strike that had been called to protest government taxes on housing provided by the mining companies. The workers considered the housing as essential, especially in remote areas; the government feared the precedent would spread to other industries and severely affect tax revenues. Miners finally accepted a compromise whereby taxes would be levied on the housing, but not until 1989 for most workers and for some not until 2020. During the strike Japanese steel mills were directly affected because Australian coal exports were down by more than five million metric tons.

6 *Gierek loses party post in Poland*

Edward Gierek, secretary of the Polish Communist Party, was replaced by 53-year-old Stanislaw Kania. On September 5 Gierek was officially reported to have been hospitalized for a serious heart ailment. He had not appeared in public since the political shakeup in late August. Kania, whose previous responsibilities included supervision of various security forces and relations with the Roman Catholic Church, was believed to have counseled moderation during the recent confrontation between the government and Poland's striking workers.

7 *China changes its top leadership and suppresses the "four bigs"*

China's National People's Congress, which had been in session since August 30, approved a number of changes in the nation's leadership that were meant to serve as guidelines for years to come. As expected, Premier Hua Guofeng's (Hua Kuo-feng's) resignation was accepted and Zhao Ziyang (Chao Tzu-yang), who as governor of Sichuan (Szechwan) Province had dramatically improved the region's economy, was named in his place. Deng Xiaoping (Teng Hsiao-p'ing) and six other elderly vice-premiers all resigned to make room for three younger men. Hua and Deng, however, remained chairman and vice-chairman, respectively, of the Chinese Communist Party. In addition, five vice-chairmen of the Standing Committee of the Congress were replaced. The Congress also set up a committee to revise the constitution and it adopted a resolution that called for the immediate deletion of the "four bigs" from the constitution. These were specific types of freedoms that had evolved during the Cultural Revolution to carry out "struggle through reasoning." The "four bigs" were: great contending, broad airing of views, large-character posters, and great debates. Other important decisions taken by the Congress involved Chinese citizenship, taxes, and the legal age for marriage.

11 *Chileans approve new constitution*

By a margin of more than two to one, Chilean voters indicated their approval of a new constitution that would permit Gen. Augusto Pinochet Ugarte to retain the presidency until 1989. After the results of the voting were made known, a spokesman for the U.S. Department of State decried "the repeated government intimidation" of those who opposed the new constitution. "We do not believe," he said, "that the plebiscite in its substance or process gave meaningful choices to the voters." Pinochet, who before the election promised not to seek a second term, had suspended the 1926 constitution after seizing power in 1973.

12 *Khomeini sets conditions for release of U.S. hostages*

Ayatollah Ruhollah Khomeini announced four conditions that the U.S. had to meet to secure the release of 52 of its citizens held hostage in Iran since Nov. 4, 1979. It had to cancel all claims against Iran; turn over to Iran all property of the late shah; release Iran's frozen assets; and promise not to interfere politically or militarily in Iran. On September 15 Ayatollah Hasheimi Rafsanjani, speaker of the Majlis (parliament), said Khomeini had inadvertently failed to include among the conditions a U.S. apology for its past involvement in Iranian affairs.

Military stages coup in Turkey

Gen. Kenan Evren, chief of staff of Turkey's armed forces, led a bloodless coup and took over control of the government. Parliament was dissolved and the constitution suspended. The military, which claimed it had acted to prevent civil war, had earlier warned that political violence and other unsolved problems were pushing Turkey toward disaster. On September 18 Evren was sworn in as head of state. Two days later the National Security Council chose retired Adm. Bulent Ulusu to be the country's prime minister. As a step toward reorganizing local administrations, Turkey's 1,700 mayors and their city councils were summarily dismissed on September 26.

More bombings rock Manila

The April 6 Liberation Movement took credit for another series of bombings in the Manila area; this time one person was killed and 60 were injured. The targets included shopping centres and government ministries. In a message sent to the news media, the terrorists claimed that the government agencies had become "tools of the Marcos dictatorship" and that the shopping centres were controlled "by the dictator's relatives and friends." The group also reaffirmed its determination to fight for freedom and democracy.

17 *Somoza assassinated in Paraguay*

Anastasio Somoza Debayle, president of Nicaragua for 23 years before he was forced to flee the country in July 1979, was assassinated in Asunción, Paraguay. His driver and a financial adviser were also slain when gunmen, prepositioned around the designated ambush site, fired machine guns and a bazooka into the former president's car.

Kim Dae Jung sentenced to death

Kim Dae Jung, former leader of the opposition New Democratic Party, was sentenced to hang after being found guilty of sedition by a military court in Seoul, South Korea. Twenty-three other defendants were given prison terms. All had the right of appeal, first to a military court and then, if necessary, to the nation's Supreme Court.

Polish unions form national body

The leaders of Poland's new independent labour unions, meeting in Gdansk, agreed to form a national federation that would take into account differences among the participating groups. All the unions would adopt the same bylaws and would register as a single group, but the national commission would function principally as an advisory and consultative body. On September 24 the union organization registered under the name Solidarity with a Warsaw court.

Party politics disrupts Uganda

Paulo Muwanga, chairman of Uganda's governing Military Commission, announced that all members of the Cabinet who did not belong to the Uganda People's Congress (UPC) party would be dismissed if they did not resign. The move gave the UPC, which was headed by former president Milton Obote, effective control of all the country's governing agencies. The other political parties responded by boycotting the National Consultative Council, an interim legislative body that was scheduled to be replaced through elections on September 30.

OWEN FRANKEN—SYGMA

Nicaraguan refugees followed the coffin of former dictator Anastasio Somoza during his funeral in Miami, Florida, in September.

18 *Cuba returns hijackers to U.S.*

The Cuban government, having issued a stern warning the previous day to potential hijackers, arrested two Cubans the moment they landed in Havana aboard a Delta Air Lines jet they had hijacked in South Carolina. They were immediately returned to the U.S., where they faced charges of air piracy. The two had arrived in the U.S. during the spring with tens of thousands of other Cubans seeking asylum. Since August 10 there had been 11 other successful hijackings by Cuban refugees who were attempting to return to their native land.

19 *Fuel explosion rocks Titan 2 missile site in Arkansas*

A fuel explosion at an underground Titan 2 nuclear missile silo near Damascus, Ark., killed one person and injured 21 others. The blast hurled the Titan's nuclear warhead about 225 m (750 ft), but initial reports indicated there were no radiation leaks and no significant damage to the ten-megaton warhead. A military spokesman explained that the detonation mechanism had not been activated because of fail-safe devices. The explosion was triggered by an Air Force maintenance technician who accidentally dropped a 1.5-kg (3-lb) wrench socket. The part fell 21 m (71 ft) and ruptured the missile's first-stage fuel tank. When toxic vapours began to fill the chamber, the maintenance crew was forced to retreat. About six and a half hours later the fuel exploded. An automatic sprinkler had poured tons of water into the silo but the water did not reach either the fuel tank or an engine that had caught fire. On September 22 the warhead was removed to the Little Rock Air Force Base after technicians had disarmed the detonator in "a very delicate operation."

22 *Iraq and Iran conflict escalates into major warfare*

Fighting between Iraq and Iran reached new intensity when Iraqi aircraft attacked ten Iranian airfields and an oil refinery at Kermanshah. The next day Iraqi planes launched additional sorties, setting oil and gas tanks ablaze at the Abadan oil refinery. On land, Iraqi troops crossed the Iranian border at several points and moved against strategically important centres. Rival naval forces also engaged in battle, principally in the Shatt al-Arab, a vital waterway separating the two countries. Iranian jets retaliated with strikes deep into Iraq, hitting the Iraqi capital of Baghdad as well as oil installations at Kirkuk and Mosul and petrochemical complexes in the Basra and Zubair areas. Iran also attacked Kharg Island, a major Iraqi oil terminal in the Persian Gulf.

26 *Bombing in Munich kills 12*

A bomb explosion at the entrance to the site of Munich's annual Oktoberfest killed 12 persons and injured more than 200 others. West German police speculated that 21-year-old Gundolf Köhler, a member of an outlaw organization known as the Defense Sports Group, had planted the bomb shortly before he was killed when the explosive detonated prematurely. Karl-Heinz Hoffmann, leader of the banned group, and five companions were arrested, but all six were released for lack of evidence.

Jewish centres in Paris attacked

Unidentified gunmen in Paris machine-gunned a Jewish synagogue, school, day-care centre, and a memorial dedicated to Jews who had been deported during World War II. Two days later a similar attack was made against another synagogue. No injuries were reported in the incidents. Police tended to discount claims from anonymous callers who said they were members of a group called the National European Fascists, which carried out the attacks. Jewish leaders complained that they had repeatedly asked for police protection, but none had been provided because, according to officials, there was insufficient manpower to satisfy such requests.

27 *Zia's mediation efforts fail*

Pakistani Pres. Mohammad Zia ul-Haq arrived in Teheran hoping to persuade Iranian leaders, and later Iraqi leaders in Baghdad, to end their warring and settle their differences through peaceful negotiations. Zia's mission, sponsored by the Conference of Islamic States, ended in failure. In a report to members of the conference on October 1, Zia said Iran refused to bow to Iraq's demands, which included a discussion of claims to territory occupied by Iran.

30 *Saudis get U.S. radar aircraft*

The U.S. government sent four Air Force radar command planes to Saudi Arabia to help the country better protect its eastern oil fields from possible Iranian attacks. At the same time the U.S. affirmed its neutrality in the Iran-Iraq conflict and declared that the planes were solely for defensive purposes. Saudi Arabia had reportedly also requested Hawk antiaircraft missiles and other equipment, but the U.S. was said to have refused.

OCTOBER

2 *Taiwan and U.S. representatives get diplomatic privileges*

The American Institute in Taiwan and the Coordination Council for North American Affairs, which is staffed by personnel from Taiwan, signed an agreement in Washington, D.C., granting members of each organization "nondiplomatic immunity." The agreement of necessity was endorsed by the Republic of China in Taiwan and by the U.S. Though neither organization was officially a government agency, the People's Republic of China denounced the arrangement as being "unacceptable."

5 *Helmut Schmidt wins reelection*

West Germany's ruling coalition of Social Democrats (SPD) and Free Democrats (FDP) increased its majority in the Bundestag (lower house of Parliament) from a modest 10 seats to a substantial 45. The victory guaranteed Helmut Schmidt four more years as federal chancellor. The SDP gained 4 seats by increasing its total to 218. Though the FDP gained a significant 14 seats, raising its total from 39 to 53, the chairman of the party said the FDP would not demand more than the four Cabinet posts it already held.

10 *Algeria struck by earthquakes*

El Asnam, a city of 125,000 inhabitants in northern Algeria, was hit by two devastating earthquakes that reduced most of its buildings to rubble. The first quake, which registered 7.7 on the Richter scale, occurred shortly after noon. The second, about four hours later, registered 6.5. There were widely conflicting reports about the number of fatalities, but the final death toll amounted to more than 4,000 persons.

13 *UN General Assembly supports ousted Cambodian government*

The UN General Assembly voted 74–35, with 32 abstentions, against a resolution that would have ousted the UN representative of the Pol Pot regime that ruled Cambodia before it was overthrown by guerrillas backed by invading Vietnamese troops. Tommy T. B. Koh of Singapore expressed the sentiments of the majority when he denounced the "gross and extensive violations of the human rights" of Cambodians under Pol Pot's regime. He warned, however, that approval of the resolution would mean the eventual recognition of the current government in Phnom Penh headed by Heng Samrin, which "is nothing more than a puppet, installed by the Vietnamese and kept in office by 200,000 Vietnamese troops."

14 *Striking federal employees in Canada return to work*

Most of Canada's 47,000 striking federal government clerks ended their 15-day walkout after the government granted wage increases amounting to about 25% over a two-year period. The government, however, refused to grant cost-of-living increases and a shorter workweek. Some other workers faced possible prosecution because they took part in sympathy strikes in support of the clerks. Customs officials, food inspectors, and other clerical workers were also among those who had refused to work. Clerks involved in the processing of pension checks and others whose jobs were considered essential by the Public Service Staff Relations Board remained on their jobs.

15 *French president visits China*

French Pres. Valéry Giscard d'Estaing arrived in China for a one-week visit, during which he was scheduled to meet Communist Party Chairman Hua Guofeng (Hua Kuo-feng), Vice-Chairman Deng Xiaoping (Teng Hsiao-p'ing), and Premier Zhao Ziyang (Chao Tzu-yang). On October 17 it was announced that China would purchase two 900-Mw nuclear atomic reactors from France at an approximate cost of $950 million each.

Fiat strike settlement reported

A tentative settlement was reported between the Fiat auto manufacturing company and striking workers at its plants in Turin, Italy. The original dispute involved the planned dismissal of 14,500 employees. The union reportedly was willing to accept 23,000 layoffs, provided the workers received about 90% of their normal wages in unemployment compensation and a promise that they would be rehired in 1983 if they had not found other jobs in the meantime. The strike, which had shut down the plants for more than a month, cost Fiat about $580 million in lost production and the work force about $70 million in lost wages.

16 *Sri Lanka Parliament ousts former prime minister*

The Sri Lanka Parliament voted 139–18 to expel former prime minister Sirimavo Bandaranaike from Parliament and to revoke her civil rights for seven years. Though she was forbidden to run for office or take active part in political campaigns, she retained her post as nominal head of the Sri Lanka Freedom Party. A special commission had found Bandaranaike guilty of abusing her power while serving as head of government.

China sets off nuclear blast

China detonated a nuclear device in the atmosphere for the first time since December 1978. The blast, which occurred at the Lop Nor test site in northwestern China, was considerably smaller than the November 1976 explosion, which was estimated to have equaled approximately four million tons of TNT.

18 *Australians retain Malcolm Fraser*

Australian Prime Minister Malcolm Fraser was returned to power for a second time when a coalition of his Liberal Party and the National Country Party retained their majority in the lower house of Par-

UPI

U.S. citizens released from Cuban jails returned home on October 27.

liament. The opposition Labor Party made significant gains in the national elections, but not enough to take over control of the government.

19 *Convention of U.S. travel agents bombed in Manila*

A convention of the American Society of Travel Agents was aborted in Manila when 20 persons were injured by a bomb that exploded shortly after Philippine Pres. Ferdinand Marcos had addressed the 5,000 delegates. The April 6 Liberation Movement, which claimed responsibility for this and a series of earlier attacks, had warned several agents in advance to cancel the convention or accept responsibility "for lives lost during a time of upheaval in our nation." On October 20 Marcos ordered the arrest of 30 persons, most of whom were currently living in the U.S.

20 *Greece rejoins NATO forces*

NATO's Defense Planning Committee unanimously approved Greece's return to the alliance's integrated military organization. President Carter noted that the bilateral decision culminated "very long and detailed negotiations between Greece, Turkey, and other members of NATO." Greece had withdrawn its forces from NATO in 1974 as a protest after Turkey, also a NATO member, sent combat forces into Cyprus and took control of the northern section of the island.

21 *Soviets admit crop failures*

In an address before a plenary session of the Communist Party Central Committee, Soviet Pres. Leonid Brezhnev explained that two consecutive poor grain harvests had created food shortages of serious dimensions. As a consequence, he said, some cities and industrial centres were not receiving adequate meat and milk. He attributed the crop failures to adverse weather and to farm equipment that was poorly designed and often in short supply. Brezhnev also noted the problems posed by a chronic housing shortage and a lack of durable, high quality consumer goods.

22 *South Korean voters approve new constitution*

South Korean voters overwhelmingly approved a referendum sanctioning certain fundamental changes in their country's constitution. Pres. Chun Doo Hwan had promised such a referendum during his inaugural address on September 1. The new charter limits the president to one seven-year term. It also guarantees human rights, reinstates habeas corpus, and outlaws torture of prisoners. In addition, the new constitution restricts presidential powers by giving the National Assembly the right to nullify emergency decrees and no longer permits the chief executive to appoint one-third of the National Assembly. Although all previously existing political parties were abolished, the new charter provided for the organization of new political groups, which could commence political activities no later than three months prior to the first presidential election.

Lebanese prime minister named

Lebanese Pres. Elias Sarkis appointed former minister of justice Shafiq al-Wazzan prime minister. He replaced Selim al-Hoss, who had stayed on as caretaker after submitting his resignation on June 7. On October 25 Wazzan named a 22-member Cabinet, which included five ministers who had held office in the previous administration.

23 *Soviet Premier Kosygin resigns*

Aleksey N. Kosygin, chairman of the Council of Ministers (premier), resigned as head of the Soviet government . The 76-year-old leader, who had been in ill health for some time, was replaced by his first deputy, 75-year-old Nikolay A. Tikhonov, a Ukrainian industrial planner. Kosygin and Soviet Pres. Leonid Brezhnev had assumed positions of power in the Soviet Union when Nikita Khrushchev was ousted in 1964.

Hong Kong limits new refugees

In an effort to stem the flood of illegal immigrants into Hong Kong, Sir Murray MacLehose, governor of the British crown colony, announced a drastic change of policy, effective immediately. The measure had the approval of Hong Kong's Legislative Council (parliament). The new rules permitted authorities to arrest and repatriate all illegal aliens who failed to register as citizens before midnight on October 26. Previously, Chinese who managed to cross the border into Hong Kong without being apprehended by border guards could legally register as permanent residents of Hong Kong after making contact with relatives or friends and finding housing accommodations.

Screen actors in U.S. end strike

Some 60,000 members of the Screen Actors Guild and the American Federation of Television and Radio Artists ended their 94-day strike by accepting a new contract that called for a 32.5% increase in minimum salaries over a three-year period and a 4.5% share in gross revenues derived from original programs that were made for pay television or for videodiscs and video cassettes. During the strike, which was the longest in the industry's history, most new programs broadcast by the three major U.S. networks were live shows or those that had been finished before the strike began. The walkout also indirectly affected some 40,000 technicians, secretaries, and drivers. About 5,000 members of the musicians' union were still negotiating and were expected to sign new contracts in the near future.

24 *Solidarity gets legal status*

The president of a three-judge Warsaw court announced that Solidarity, Poland's new independent federation of trade unions, had been granted legal status. But he also declared that the federation's charter had been amended to include a statement that the Polish Communist Party played a "leading role" in national affairs and that socialism was the foundation of Polish society. Other changes were also made, but representatives of Solidarity did not consider them vital. Objecting to the assertion of the Communist Party's supremacy in his union's nonpolitical charter, Lech Walesa, leader of Solidarity, pledged to appeal the case to the Supreme Court. On November 10 the court averted a nationwide strike by ruling that the party supremacy clause need not be included in the federation's charter.

OWEN FRANKEN—SYGMA

Jamaicans, happy about the election results, cheered the victory of Edward Seaga as new prime minister.

27 *Cuba frees 30 U.S. prisoners*

The Cuban government pardoned and released 30 U.S. prisoners in what was generally regarded as a gesture of goodwill by Cuban Pres. Fidel Castro. Five of the 30 were arrested when their plane landed in Miami, Fla.; four faced charges of plane hijacking and one a charge of violating his parole. Three other Americans, who faced serious charges if they returned to the U.S., preferred to remain in Cuba.

28 *Saudi Arabia cuts ties to Libya*

Saudi Arabia severed diplomatic relations with Libya following a series of speeches by Libyan leader Col. Muammar al-Qaddafi. Qaddafi had criticized Saudi Arabia's acceptance of four radar surveillance planes from the U.S. in October. The Libyan leader also told all Muslims that they should forgo the annual religious pilgrimage to Mecca because all of Saudi Arabia, including Islam's most sacred shrines, was "under U.S. occupation." Saudi Arabia viewed Qaddafi's remarks as a slur on their guardianship of the Islamic holy places.

29 *Beijing bombing kills nine*

A bomb explosion inside the main Beijing (Peking) railway terminal killed 9 persons and injured 81 others. China's offical Xinhua (Hsinhua) News Agency reported that "an unknown person" was responsible. Police suspected that the person who carried the bomb into the station died when the bomb exploded, possibly prematurely.

30 *Manley defeated in Jamaica*

Jamaican Prime Minister Michael Manley, leader of the People's National Party, ended his eight-year tenure as head of the government when the Jamaica Labour Party, led by Edward Seaga, captured 51 of 60 seats in the House of Representatives. Manley's defeat, in what was perhaps the most important election in the nation's history, was an emphatic repudiation of his socialist policies and the special ties he had fostered with Cuba. At his swearing-in on November 1, Seaga said the Bank of Jamaica had run out of foreign exchange on October 29, but he expressed hope that the nation's economy would begin to stabilize after Jamaica obtained a $180 million from the International Monetary Fund.

31 *Iraq captures Iranian oil minister*

Mohammad Jawad Baqir Tunguyan, Iran's minister of petroleum, was captured by Iraqi troops near Abadan, an important Iranian oil refining centre under Iraqi siege. The deputy oil minister and several other government officials were also taken. When Iran denounced the captures as a violation of international law, Iraq replied that the men were prisoners of war, not hostages. Moreover, Iran itself had violated international law, Iraq said, when it seized U.S. citizens as hostages in November 1979.

NOVEMBER

2 *Iranian Majlis approves terms for release of U.S. hostages*

The Iranian Majlis (parliament) approved conditions for the release of 52 U.S. hostages. They were essentially the same terms as those announced by Ayatollah Ruhollah Khomeini on September 12, but the action moved the long impasse one step closer to a final resolution.

4 *Reagan wins U.S. presidency*

Ronald Reagan, a conservative Republican and former governor of California, soundly defeated incumbent Democratic Pres. Jimmy Carter in the presidential election. The margin of Reagan's victory was unexpected. He received more than 43.2 million votes, while Carter got a bit more than 34.9 million. John Anderson, a Republican running as an independent, received about 5,580,000 votes. More astonishing still was Reagan's electoral vote count. His 489 to 49 margin represented all but six states and the District of Columbia. The election also gave Republicans control of the U.S. Senate for the first time since 1956. Democrats lost 33 seats in the House of Representatives but retained their majority. The Republicans also picked up an additional four governorships, for a new total of 23, and won control of five additional chambers in state legislatures; in 1981 Republicans would control both legislative chambers in 14 states. Liberal Democrats suffered an especially severe defeat in the Senate. Among those who lost their seats were such prominent politicians as George McGovern of South Dakota, Birch Bayh of Indiana, Frank Church of Idaho, John Culver of Iowa, Gaylord Nelson of Wisconsin, Warren Magnuson of Washington, and John Durkin of New Hampshire. Edward Kennedy of Massachusetts did not have to run for reelection, but the Republican victory meant he would have to turn over the chairmanship of the Judiciary Committee to Strom Thurmond, a conservative from South Carolina. The House also lost a surprising number of well-known Democratic congressmen, including majority whip John Brademas of Indiana; Al Ullman of Oregon, chairman of the Ways and Means Committee; and Harold Johnson of California, chairman of the Public Works Committee.

Iraq warns Iran to negotiate

Iraqi Pres. Saddam Hussein, in an address delivered before the country's National Assembly, warned Iran that Iraq might broaden its claims if its call for a cease-fire and peace talks fell on deaf ears. The following day Ayatollah Ruhollah Khomeini reiterated Iran's determination to continue fighting as long as Iraqi soldiers occupied Iranian territory. The two countries had signed a border agreement in 1975, but Iraq was now demanding sovereignty over the vital Shatt al-Arab waterway, three small islands of Abu Musa and Greater and Lesser Tunb at the mouth of the Persian Gulf, and a section of land along the Iraqi-Iranian border.

6 *Islamic states hold conference*

Representatives of 23 Islamic states concluded a three-day meeting in Ankara, Turkey; the conference had been convened mainly to strengthen economic bonds among Islamic nations. In their first such conference, the delegates approved a ten-point program that called for greater cooperation in such areas as science, technology, industry, agriculture, communications, health, and finance. Representatives of the Palestine Liberation Organization, eight international organizations, and the Turkish-controlled section of Cyprus also participated in the discussions.

MICHAEL EVANS—SYGMA

Ronald Reagan, winner of the 1980 U.S. presidential election, and his wife, Nancy, showed victory smiles on election night.

7 *Nyerere names new Cabinet*

Tanzanian Pres. Julius Nyerere named a new Cabinet following his reelection to a fourth five-year term on October 26. Cleopa David Msuya was named prime minister, and Ahmed Salim Salim was given the post of foreign minister.

8 *Ghotbzadeh arrested and released*

Sadegh Ghotbzadeh, former Iranian foreign minister, was arrested on orders issued by the Teheran public prosecutor. Ghotbzadeh charged that the state broadcasting system, which he once headed, was falling under the control of Islamic fundamentalists who had no legitimate authority to determine the content of its broadcasts. On November 10 Ayatollah Ruhollah Khomeini ordered Ghotbzadeh's release.

Israeli Labour Party supports Jordanian-Palestinian state

Members of Israel's Labour Party created an uproar in some quarters when it announced its support for a Jordanian-Palestinian state that would extend beyond Jordan into the West Bank and include the Gaza Strip. Palestinians would constitute a majority in the proposed state. When Israel Galilee, a Labour Party official, was asked if his party was prepared to recognize Yasir Arafat, leader of the PLO, as head of such a state, he replied: "It wouldn't enter my mind to dictate to the proposed state who shall head it." On December 18 former defense minister Shimon Peres was reconfirmed as chairman of the Labour Party, which hoped to gain control of the government by winning the 1981 parliamentary elections.

10 *U.S. envoys arrive in Algeria to negotiate hostage issue*

Warren Christopher, U.S. deputy secretary of state, arrived in Algeria with a team of U.S. government officials. He carried the U.S. response to demands the Iranian Majlis had made for the release of 52 U.S. hostages. The U.S. delegates reportedly explained the constitutional limitations placed on presidential powers and other pertinent points of U.S. law before departing Algiers on November 11. The next day Algeria, which was acting as an intermediary, delivered their secret response to Iranian officials in Teheran.

U.K. Labour Party elects leader

Michael Foot, a British MP for 30 years, was elected by his Labour Party colleagues to lead their party. After defeating Denis Healey in the runoff election, Foot took over the post vacated in October by former prime minister James Callaghan. Foot was known to support broad government welfare programs, the nationalization of vital industries, and nuclear disarmament.

ITC rejects auto imports limits

The U.S. International Trade Commission ruled that there was not sufficient justification for placing restrictions on automobile and light truck imports into the U.S., despite the serious financial problems plaguing U.S. automobile manufacturers. Most members of the ITC agreed with foreign competitors that oil prices, the economic recession, and a change in consumer demand were the principal reasons U.S. automakers now found themselves in serious difficulties.

12 *Voyager 1 flies past Saturn*

The U.S. unmanned spacecraft Voyager 1 came within 125,000 km (77,000 mi) of the planet Saturn. Though Pioneer 11 had flown by Saturn in 1979, Voyager 1 gathered much more detailed and spectacular data. Among other discoveries, the Voyager 1 flight revealed that Saturn has far more rings than anyone had suspected, some of which were eccentric. One ring appeared to be made up of two braided strands of particles, a phenomenon that baffled scientists. Voyager 1 also came within 4,000 km (2,500 mi) of Titan, Saturn's largest moon. The three new moons that Voyager photographed increased the known number to 15.

South Korea bans 835 politicians

The Political Renovation Committee of South Korea released the names of 811 politicians forbidden to engage in political activities until the end of June 1988. The purge was undertaken to establish "a new political atmosphere with the start of the Fifth Republic." The list included 210 members of the defunct National Assembly and 254 officials of recently abolished political parties. Three days later 24 other names were added to the list. On November 25 the South Korean government announced that 268 of the 586 politicians who had filed appeals had been cleared and reinstated.

14 *Polish labour leader meets Kania*

Lech Walesa, head of Solidarity, Poland's independent federation of trade unions, met for 90 minutes with Communist Party leader Stanislaw Kania. The two men reportedly discussed the role of Solidarity in solving the serious economic and political problems plaguing the nation. The next day Walesa addressed workers at a Warsaw steel mill and called for an end to wildcat strikes.

Guinea-Bissau president ousted

Luis de Almeida Cabral, president of the small African nation of Guinea-Bissau since independence in 1974, was ousted from power by Premier João Bernardo Vieira. The black socialist opposed Cabral's plan to unite Guinea-Bissau with its sister republic, Cape Verde. The matter had strong racial overtones because, unlike Guinea-Bissau, Cape Verde has a large mixed-blood population.

15 *John Paul II visits West Germany*

Pope John Paul II arrived in Cologne, West Germany, to begin a five-day religious pilgrimage aimed at strengthening the Roman Catholic Church and improving relations with Protestant churches. It was the first papal visit to Germany since 1782. In a meeting with Protestant church leaders, the pontiff quoted Martin Luther several times and expressed a willingness to study ways to reconcile doctrinal differ-

JET PROPULSION LABORATORY/NASA

The rings around the planet Saturn were dramatically captured in photos taken by the U.S. spacecraft Voyager 1 on November 6.

ences between the Catholic and Lutheran churches. In Munich young Catholics read a statement challenging Catholic teaching on such matters as sexual behaviour and the role of women in the church.

20 *China puts Mao's widow and nine others on trial*

The long-awaited trial of Jiang Qing (Chiang Ch'ing), leader of the gang of four and widow of the late Chinese Communist Party chairman Mao Zedong (Mao Tse-tung), and nine of her associates got under way in Beijing (Peking). Five of the ten defendants were former high-ranking military officers. The four major crimes listed in the indictments were: framing and persecuting party and state leaders and plotting to overthrow the political power of the dictatorship of the proletariat; persecuting and suppressing large numbers of cadres and ordinary people; plotting to assassinate Chairman Mao and stage an armed counterrevolutionary coup d'etat; and planning an armed rebellion in Shanghai. The trial was the final repudiation of the leftist leaders who had struggled for control of the government.

23 *Severe earthquake hits Italy*

An earthquake measuring 6.9 on the Richter scale wreaked immense damage in dozens of cities, towns, and villages in southern Italy. The hardest hit provinces were Naples, Salerno, Potenza, and Avellino. More than 3,000 persons were reported killed. Rescue operations were severely hampered in some places because of their remoteness and a shortage of heavy equipment to remove the rubble.

24 *Tobago chooses its first parliament*

The Democratic Action Congress party won 8 of the 12 seats in Tobago's first parliamentary election. The group favoured substantial autonomy from Trinidad, a relatively rich island that had dominated Tobago since 1889. The new parliament, which was sanctioned by Trinidad, would give the smaller island control of its own internal affairs. The two Caribbean islands had formed one nation after Great Britain granted them independence in 1962.

25 *Coup in Upper Volta succeeds*

The government of Sangoulé Lamizana, president of Upper Volta, one of the world's poorest nations, was overthrown in a military coup led by Col. Saye Zerbo. Lamizana had seized power in 1966, but in 1978 was elected president of Upper Volta. Zerbo said that the coup had been launched because of the country's deteriorating economic and political climate.

27 *Arabs end summit conference*

The Arab League concluded a three-day summit conference in Amman, Jordan, despite a boycott by Algeria, Lebanon, Libya, Yemen (Aden), Syria, and the Palestine Liberation Organization. Syria had asked for a postponement because it felt "internal conflicts among Arab countries," including divided loyalties in the Iran-Iraq war, should first be resolved.

28 *Haiti arrests 200 as agitators*

Haitian police began to round up about 200 persons whose criticism of the government was labeled Communist-inspired agitation. It was the largest roundup of the government's critics since Jean-Claude Duvalier assumed the presidency in 1971. Those arrested included a large number of journalists as well as politicians, teachers, students, and human rights activists.

DECEMBER

2 *U.S., EEC, and NATO warn the U.S.S.R. against an invasion of Poland*

President Carter, speaking through his press secretary, sternly warned the U.S.S.R. that relations between the two countries would be seriously affected by a Soviet invasion of Poland. The same day all nine members of the European Economic Community expressed similar views by urging compliance with the UN Charter and the Helsinki accords, which protect nations from outside interference in their internal affairs. On December 12 the foreign ministers of NATO informed the Soviets that an invasion of Poland would put an end to East-West détente.

4 *UNESCO reports on illiteracy*

UNESCO issued a report on the extent of illiteracy around the world. According to the study, one-third of the world's population can neither read nor write. In Africa two-thirds of the people are uneducated and in non-Soviet Asia about one-half of the population. The UNESCO report estimated that the total number of illiterates throughout the world would increase by 70 million during the next decade but that the overall percentage would decrease by several percentage points. It also expected India to have the largest number of uneducated at the turn of the century.

Portugal's premier dies in crash

Portuguese Premier Francisco Sá Carneiro was killed in a plane crash near Lisbon. Eight others, including the defense min-

DECEMBER

ister, also lost their lives. During his year in office, Sá Carneiro had moved Portugal toward greater democracy through broad economic and constitutional reforms. His death apparently weakened the Democratic Alliance coalition so severely that its candidate lost the presidential election on December 7 to incumbent Gen. António Ramalho Eanes, who, supported by Socialists, Communists, and independents, was reelected.

5 *Warsaw Pact discusses Poland*

Members of the Warsaw Pact convened in Moscow to discuss the sericus problems faced by Poland and to decide what position the Pact should take to meet the crisis facing one of its members. Before disbanding, the Soviet Union and its six Eastern European allies expressed confidence that Poland would be able to overcome its difficulties without damaging its socialist system of government. At least for the moment the fear that Poland would be invaded by Soviet forces seemed to have subsided.

6 *Taiwan voters choose lawmakers*

For the first time since 1977, voters in Taiwan went to the polls to select members for the Legislative Yuan and for the National Assembly. The ruling Kuomintang's (KMT's) candidates captured 57 of the 70 contested seats in the legislature, giving it more than 92% of the body's 360 seats. The KMT also won 63 of the 76 contested seats in the National Assembly. That body's main responsibilities are to elect or recall the president and vice-president, amend the constitution, or vote on constitutional amendments.

8 *Tekere freed after conviction*

Edgar Z. Tekere, head of Zimbabwe's manpower, planning, and development ministry, was freed by a Salisbury court even though he had been found guilty of murdering a white farmer in early August. The decision to set Tekere and one of his aides free was based on a 1975 law that protected government officials from criminal charges resulting from antiterrorist activities.

10 *Leonid Brezhnev proposes peace plan for Persian Gulf area*

Soviet Pres. Leonid Brezhnev, in an address before the Indian Parliament, proposed a "doctrine of peace and security" for the Persian Gulf area. Simply stated, it called upon all major powers to pledge not to "use or threaten to use force against the countries of the Persian Gulf area and not to interfere in their internal affairs." The next day the U.S. rejected the proposal saying there could be no long-term security in the region as long as Soviet troops remained in Afghanistan.

Jordan and Syria ease tensions

Mounting tension between Jordan and Syria began to abate when both countries agreed to begin withdrawing troops from the border separating their two countries. The differences between the two nations were highlighted in late November when Syria dispatched tanks and troops to the border area. Jordan quickly responded and began to step up preparations for war. Though both are Arab nations, Syria refused to support Iraq in its war with Iran because of long-standing enmities.

Soviet Premier Aleksey Kosygin was buried with full military honours in December in Moscow.

UPI

FALN suspects indicted

A federal grand jury in Chicago indicted 11 persons on charges of terrorism connected with more than a score of bombings that took place in the Chicago area beginning in June 1975. All were suspected of being members of the FALN, a Puerto Rican organization seeking to gain independence for their country through violent means. Only one of those indicted was still at liberty.

12 *Italian magistrate kidnapped*

Members of the Red Brigades, a terrorist organization responsible for numerous acts of violence throughout Italy, kidnapped Giovanni D'Urso, a director general in the Ministry of Justice. The section that he headed was responsible for the disposition and care of terrorists. The kidnappers made several telephone calls to demand that a maximum security prison on the island of Asinara be closed down.

Polish churchmen warn dissidents

After a two-day meeting presided over by Stefan Cardinal Wyszynski, Poland's Roman Catholic bishops cautioned dissidents that extremism could destroy "the freedom and statehood of the fatherland." Two days later a pastoral letter expressing similar thoughts was read during Sunday church services. Fear persisted that the Soviet Union might invade Poland if continued unrest was perceived as a threat to Poland's Communist government. On December 14 hundreds of self-employed farmers met in Warsaw to organize a trade union. The government had earlier indicated that such farmers had no right to organize a union because they were not working for wages. On December 16, in an unusual display of goodwill, government officials attended the unveiling of a 43-m (140-ft) steel monument that had been erected in Gdansk to honour 28 shipyard workers who had been killed in 1970 during disturbances. The local Communist Party leader told the crowd that because "the lessons of the past have been learned" the recent labour troubles had "ended in agreement rather than bloodshed."

13 *Obote again Uganda's president*

Uganda's state electoral commission announced that the Uganda People's Congress had won a majority of seats in the parliamentary elections and that Milton Obote would, as a consequence, become president of Uganda for a second time. The four-party race, however, had been so tainted by charges of fraud, intimidation, and unfair tactics that the Democratic Party demanded new elections supervised by an independent commission.

16 *Libyan troops control Chad capital*

Libyan troops, at the request of Goukouni Oueddei, president of Chad, used heavy artillery and aircraft to drive troops loyal to Premier Hissen Habré out of the nation's capital. Though Libya had sent several thousand troops into Chad as early as June, they were not asked to interfere actively in the civil war until December 12. After fleeing to Cameroon, Habré signed, "with reservations," a cease-fire agreement worked out by the Organization of African Unity.

18 *Aleksey N. Kosygin dies in Moscow*

Aleksey N. Kosygin, chairman of the Soviet Union's Council of Ministers for 16 years, died in Moscow. The 76-year-old leader had been forced by ill health to relinquish the premiership in late October. Kosygin's elaborate state funeral in Red Square was attended by Pres. Leonid Brezhnev and other top Soviet leaders. As a sign of honour, the ashes of the former head of government were placed in the wall of the Kremlin.

19 *U.S. prime rate hits record 21.5%*

Most large U.S. banks raised their prime interest rate, the interest they charged on loans to preferred corporate customers, to an all-time high of 21.5%. Despite the unprecedented levels that interest rates had reached during the year, demands for loans had continued at a high level.

21 *Iran demands $24 billion before it will release U.S. hostages*

The Iranian minister of state for executive affairs declared during a news conference in Teheran that "it is very easy" for the U.S. to meet Iran's latest demands for the release of 52 American hostages. Iran was asking the U.S. to turn over $24 billion in all. About $10 billion of that sum, to be deposited in the Central Bank of Algeria, represented identified frozen Iranian assets. An additional $4 billion would be a guarantee against unidentified assets. The final $10 billion would serve as a bond until the former shah's property in the U.S. could be identified and recovered. The statement also seemed to indicate that Iran sought to be absolved of all responsibility connected with lawsuits that might be brought against it by companies or individuals. U.S. Secretary of State Edmund Muskie described the Iranian demands as "unreasonable."

25 *Iraq expands war in Iran*

Iraqi Pres. Saddam Hussein announced that Iraqi forces had moved into Iran's Kurdistan province the previous week. The multipronged offensive extended the war to almost the entire border area of the two countries.

26 *Algerian envoy visits hostages*

Abdelkarim Gheraieb, the Algerian ambassador to Iran, announced that he had visited all 52 U.S. hostages in Teheran and found "the conditions of their present existence satisfactory." The ambassador and an official from the Algerian Foreign Ministry were reportedly allowed the visit to counter rumours that some of the hostages were in jail and others in poor health. The papal nuncio had said he saw only about half the hostages when he and other clergymen visited the captives on Christmas Day. The Teheran government also sent satellite-beamed film clips of some hostages to the U.S.

WIDE WORLD

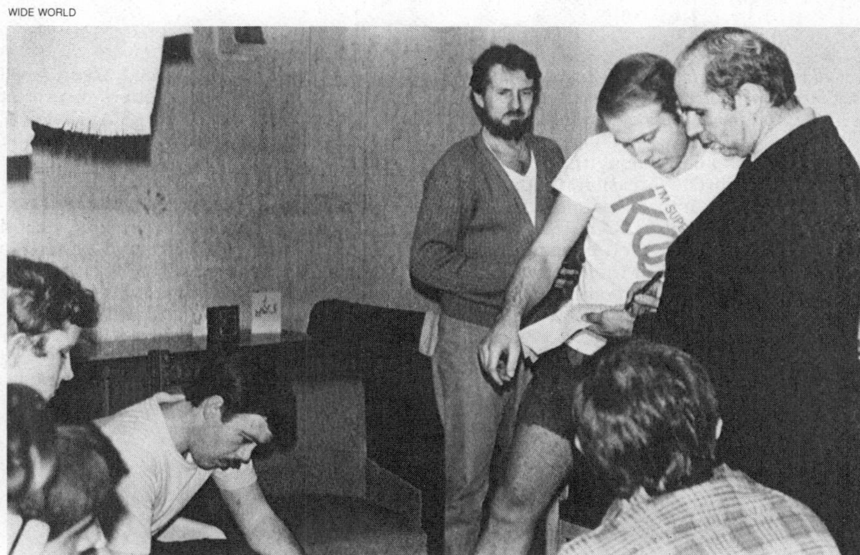

The Algerian ambassador to Iran, Abdelkarim Gheraieb, conferred with U.S. hostages when he visited with them on December 26.

27 *Afghans in Iran stage protest*

Some 5,000 Afghans marked the first anniversary of the Soviet invasion of their country by attacking the Soviet embassy in Teheran, Iran. During the violence some Afghans climbed over the embassy walls and smashed windows until they were driven off by Iranian security guards. The crowd then moved to the Afghan embassy to vent its anger. Two days later, in Kabul, the capital of Afghanistan, anti-Soviet and antigovernment demonstrators hurled rocks at vehicles until Soviet tanks and soldiers took control of the streets.

28 *Mexico to end fishing accords with U.S. government*

Mexico announced that it was about to give formal notice to the U.S. that it would terminate all existing fishing agreements between the two countries. The decision followed several years of unsuccessful negotiations to determine each country's fishing rights. In July, after Mexico had arrested six San Diego (Calif.)-based tuna seiners for fishing in Mexican waters, the U.S. embargoed Mexican tuna imports. Though the accords affected various types of fishing, by far the most important and most lucrative was tuna. Mexico was determined to vastly improve its fishing industry.

29 *China concludes historic trials*

The most important criminal trials in modern Chinese history ended in Beijing (Peking), but no sentences were expected to be announced until late January at the earliest. All ten defendants had been prosecuted for serious crimes that were viewed as an attempt to seize control of the government. Jiang Qing (Chiang Ch'ing), the 67-year-old widow of party chairman Mao Zedong (Mao Tse-tung) and the central figure of the proceedings, had defiantly challenged the court to sentence her to death "in front of one million people in Tian An Men [T'ien An Men] Square." Throughout the trial, Jiang insisted she had never acted except on the orders of her husband. Only one of the other defendants refused to cooperate with the court. The five former military commanders on trial were stigmatized as members of the "Lin clique," a reference to the late Lin Biao (Lin Piao), who had been minister of defense. Lin died in a 1971 plane crash while reportedly attempting to escape to the Soviet Union.

31 *U.S. census figures announced*

The U.S. Census Bureau publicized statistics on the 1980 population survey, which is required by law every ten years. The total population of the country was put at 226,504,825—an 11.4% increase over the 1970 figure. The comparative statistics required that 17 congressional seats be transferred from states in the Northeast and Midwest regions of the country to states in the South and West that had increased their populations during the preceding decade. New York lost five seats; Illinois, Ohio, and Pennsylvania, two each; six other states lost one seat each. Florida gained four seats; Texas, three; and California, two; eight other states gained one seat each.

UNUSUAL BUT NOTEWORTHY EVENTS OF 1980

Not all the news events of 1980 made prominent headlines. Among items reported less breathlessly in the worldwide press were the following:

Aetna Life & Casualty thought April Fools' Day an appropriate occasion to publish some of the most unusual claims it had received during the 1970s. One fellow who couldn't sleep because of buzzing mosquitoes got out of bed in the middle of the night and gave his bedroom a thorough spraying. The next morning he discovered he had used an aerosol can of red enamel.

Big Ben, perhaps the most renowned of London's many famous landmarks, was the subject of a BBC overseas broadcast on April 1. Foreigners who wrote letters of protest had probably never heard of April Fools' jokes. The Big Ben clock wasn't really going digital.

Leo Wollman, a Brooklyn, N.Y., psychiatrist, studied 3,000 fast-food customers and decided that those who eat hot dogs tend to be outgoing, aggressive, and ambitious. Those who eat hamburgers are generally quieter, more introverted, and more conservative. Wollman also views hamburger eaters as potential executives because they are "used to making decisions—well done, rare, ketchup, or mustard."

UPI

Chicken-man Ted Giannoulas gained national renown as the mascot of the San Diego Padres baseball team. Flapping his wings, wiggling his tail, leaping through the air, rolling on the ground, and threatening to bite off the heads of umpires, he won everyone's heart. But not, apparently, the hearts of his sponsors at radio station KGB. He was fired by the station after he began to moonlight in his costume at other events, and another man was given his outfit. Giannoulas, unfazed, devised a new chicken-man costume and was promptly brought to court by KGB for wearing a costume "substantially similar" to its own. The case finally went before Superior Court Judge Raúl Rosado, who ruled that Giannoulas could continue to perform in his by-then nationally known suit. Discounting an ancient Roman proverb that clothes made the man, Rosado felt that the man, not the outfit, made the act.

Tombstones can be expensive in more ways than one, as Bernard Gladsky of Baltimore, Md., found out in February. When his father died in 1977, he commissioned Kirby L. Smith to carve the tombstone inscription. It read: "Stanley J. Gladsky, 1895–1977, abused, robbed and starved by his beloved daughter." Gloria Kovatch charged her brother with libel and sued for $500,000. Gladsky insisted that the engraving was done in jest, but added his sister had once sent their father to the hospital on a bus while he was suffering from malnutrition and dehydration. A Superior Court jury awarded Kovatch $2,000.

Irma Loyear left the cleaning service business to enroll in the art department of the University of Wisconsin at Superior. When she was elected homecoming queen, other female students were understandably disappointed. But the crowd at the coronation ceremony thought she was terrific. They jumped up and shouted "Irma! Irma!" as the 76-year-old beauty smiled.

A Greyhound bus driver, flagged down in April by the California highway patrol, protested a citation for speeding on the grounds that he could not keep to his schedule while observing the 55 mph (88 kph) speed limit. After angrily signing the ticket, the driver informed the unsympathetic officer that the officer had "just bought a bus full of people." With that he walked away, leaving all 42 passengers sitting in the driverless bus.

Brazil's program for reducing its dependence on OPEC oil includes the use of sugarcane alcohol as automotive fuel. The same sugarcane alcohol provides the kick in Brazil's rumlike *cachaca,* a potent and popular drink. Small wonder, therefore, that some Brazilians began to drink the fuel. Government officials figured out a way to make the fuel undrinkable; it planned to poison the alcohol with a small quantity of regular gasoline.

Violence in sports is not always limited to the players. That fact bothered the European Football Union so much it felt something dramatic had to be done to prevent a repeat of the spectator violence that followed West Ham United's loss in London to the Madrid Castilla soccer team of Spain. The rematch several weeks later was played in London's 40,000-seat Upton Park stadium. But no roars greeted hometown goals. Only officials and reporters were allowed to witness the game, which the English team won 5–1.

When textile workers at the Darlington Manufacturing Plant in South Carolina voted for union representation, the owners shut down the plant "for economic reasons." The matter went all the way to the Supreme Court before both sides agreed to a settlement. Milliken & Co. offered $5 million in back pay, and the workers accepted. Some would receive as little as $50, others as much as $36,000. Money belonging to workers who had died would go to their beneficiaries. Everyone seemed relieved to have the matter finally settled. It had, after all, been in litigation for 24 years.

Mary Ellen Wolfe of Illinois suffers from rheumatoid arthritis, so she has a special appreciation of the importance of medical research. When she wrote an Ohio medical school to say she wished to will her body upon her death to the college, she received a totally unexpected reply. The chairman of the anatomy department sent an authorization form and informed Wolfe that "budgetary stringencies oblige the college to request a modest $60 fee of each donor." She was also told that she would have to arrange to have her cadaver shipped to the school herself. Wolfe's reaction was equivalent to telling the director to drop dead.

Canceling credit cards can sometimes have startling repercussions, as Larry and Bonnie Dallas of St. Louis, Mo., found out in mid-July. Just when they thought they had managed to close their Visa account, they received 101 new cards in the mail. Like certain salesmen, computers apparently are not always willing to take "no" for an answer.

Nancy Ann Ermert couldn't understand how any court could have convicted her of welfare fraud. In mid-December the Washington state Supreme Court concurred and ordered a Superior Court decision reversed. Ermert, who began to receive public assistance in 1971, bought a new compact car in 1975 using borrowed money and $1,400 from a savings account. That's when her troubles began. She was charged with fraud for not fully reporting her resources to the government. In reversing Ermert's conviction, the state Supreme Court agreed that the money in the savings account was neither unreported income nor resources because every cent of it had been saved from welfare checks.

Sotheby's, the famous London auction house, sent one of its experts on Oriental art to the home of an elderly couple to see what antiques would be acceptable for auction. The man was clearly startled when he spotted a red and white Chinese bottle in the bedroom that had been converted into a lamp. The foot-high bottle was a rare 14th-century creation that Sotheby's auctioned off in 90 seconds for $672,800.

When A. James Manchin, West Virginia's secretary of state, heard about the case of Mary Marvich, he wondered aloud if lunatics had taken over the U.S. Department of Immigration and Naturalization. Marvich had been told that her application for citizenship could not be approved until she supplied the name of the ship that carried her to the U.S. But Marvich claimed she could not remember. Little wonder, since the 107-year-old woman had emigrated from the Balkans in 1894.

David Berkowitz, the notorious "Son of Sam" killer, was sentenced to 315 years in prison for killing six persons in New York City in 1977. After the Bureau of Disability Determination certified that Berkowitz was unable to hold a job because of "a mental impairment," he began to receive $300 a month from the Social Security Administration. From his prison cell in Attica, N.Y., Berkowitz said he had faked insanity during his trial and now wanted to be declared legally sane so he could personally manage his own finances.

JIM WILSON—NEWSWEEK

Before taking her life in San Francisco, one of Mary Murphy's last decisions concerned her faithful ten-year-old dog. Fearing Sido would be lonely without her, Murphy stipulated in her will that the mutt be put to sleep. When this news became public, the Society for the Prevention of Cruelty to Animals (SPCA) took the matter to court. After noting that "even stray and abandoned dogs have rights," the judge ruled that Sido could live out her remaining years with the head of the local SPCA.

A November issue of the *Journal of the American Medical Association* carried a report on an unusual side effect of silicone implants used to enlarge the breasts. The topic had been raised by an airline stewardess who had undergone such surgery. According to Dr. Charles C. Fullett, implants inserted at sea level would expand to twice their normal size at 5,500 m (18,000 ft) and to three times their size at 9,150 m (30,000 ft) if the airplane lost its cabin pressure.

Elizabeth N. Brown of Mount Juliet, Tenn., was awarded $2,000 in September because she has nightmares of giant Coca-Cola bottles chasing her and then exploding. Brown testified that the nightmares began in 1977, after an incident in which she picked up a 900-g (32-oz) bottle of Coke that exploded in her hand.

A first-class counterfeiter will spend countless hours trying to duplicate authentic government currency. A 26-year-old man in Hamilton, Mont., had no such ambition. He took a genuine $20 bill, changed the figure to $22, substituted a drawing of a cigar-smoking man in a Panama hat for the engraved likeness of Andrew Jackson, and photocopied it on rag-bond paper. He also used the name Alaska Jack for that of the U.S. treasurer. A cashier at the court of Judge Herbert Kester accepted the bill as payment for a $20 traffic fine. No one was saying whether or not the cashier gave the jokester $2 in change.

Sex discrimination can be financially rewarding, as in the case of two California men who went to dinner at the Ojai Valley Inn in 1976. Both were refused seats unless they wore staff-supplied neckties with their leisure suits. The men finally complied under protest, then sued the restaurant for sex discrimination. Only males, they noted, were obliged to wear the ties. A Superior Court judge dismissed the case, but a higher court reversed the ruling. After listening to testimony, a jury awarded Robert Hales $13,000 and Irving Losner, whose stay in the hotel had been much briefer, $5,000 in damages. However unhappy the men might have been about the neckties, they were certainly delighted with their suits.

Miss Piggy's film debut as an eyelash-fluttering temptress trying to win the love of Kermit the Frog was a smashing success. Bruce Collin, a Cincinnati, Ohio, businessman, was so taken with her stunning performance in *The Muppet Movie* that he helped launch a campaign to have the superstar nominated for an Oscar as best actress of the year. Collin was not at all surprised when 38,000 movie fans sent letters praising Miss Piggy for her sensitive interpretation of a very difficult role. Apprised of this development, Miss Piggy wrote to Collin to say: "I feel I am but a humble actress/singer and I do not believe it is my place to comment on this wise, perceptive, discerning and tasteful Oscar campaign."

Legionnaire's disease terrified a lot of people until it was finally identified by medical sleuths. Early in the year flight attendants aboard Eastern Airlines planes flying between New York and Florida got another scare. Some 95 attendants reported 170 cases of "red sweat," mysterious red spots on the skin that seemed to exude a bloodlike liquid. Eastern ordered its flight supervisors to board flights to look for clues. The National Institute for Occupational Safety and Health also sent representatives to help. On March 19 Eastern Airlines happily reported that the ominous red spots were nothing more than tiny flecks of red ink that came from letters stenciled on the rubber life vests used by the attendants who demonstrated their use before takeoff.

Bob Amparan, principal of Memorial Junior High School in San Diego, Calif., says it makes sense—financial as well as academic—to pay truant students to attend class each day. During the previous year, Amparan's school lost $9 per day for each unauthorized absence. All told, the school was denied $132,000 in state funds because its absence rate was close to 9%. Amparan thinks students will stop playing hookey if they have a 25-cents-a-day incentive to attend class. The money would take the form of credits that could be redeemed for milk, fresh fruit, and school-related items.

John Storms, a traffic officer in Tulsa, Okla., said he had checked the books to be sure Mary Glynn Boudreaux had set a new record for "points of impact from one single incident." In mid-December she vented her rage against a boyfriend by staging her own personal demolition derby near Tulsa's downtown business district. All told, she rammed her car into 18 vehicles, 5 street signs, and 2 fences. One target was absolutely irresistible: a postal jeep waiting for a green light.

Western observers, getting their first peek at the actual proceedings of Chinese divorce courts, were afforded a rare glimpse of the human comedy and tragedy in that formerly closed society. When Yao Yitian, a 52-year-old editor, began to recite a litany of abuses he had endured during 18 years of married life, the spectators were quite reserved. He testified that domestic tensions had become so great that the mere sound of his wife's voice made him wince in pain. But the spectators started smiling when his shrewish wife, Chen Zhengyu, who was vehemently contesting the divorce, sought to bolster her case on Marxist principles. She reminded the judge that the late Chairman Mao Zedong had often insisted that in a socialist society there could be no progress without strife.

Winning a million dollars in the Massachusetts state lottery should be a thrilling experience. But the very first winner of the Big Money Game didn't even smile when his name was announced during a live television broadcast. He was already dead. In another drawing in September the winning ticket belonged to Wilfred Madelle, Jr. He didn't attend the drawing either, but a lottery spokesman said Madelle will get the money. Not immediately, but after he leaves the Worcester County House of Correction, where he has been doing time for breaking and entering. He regrets the breaking, but he's happy about entering. The lottery, that is.

William Wilcox, a movie projectionist in Illinois, was so determined to have his unborn son named after him that he took the matter to court. His estranged wife was equally insistent that their son would not be named William Earl Wilcox IV. Circuit Court Judge Robert C. Buckley made some preliminary rulings, and then continued the case. Before the couple returned to court, Tammi Wilcox gave birth to a lovely daughter.

Diplomatic immunity is rooted in solid principles, but flagrant violations of the privilege can be infuriating. In 1967 the Soviet embassy in Canada asked Wallace Edwards's firm to print a magazine to be sold at the Expo 67 exhibition in Montreal. After he completed the job, Soviet officials refused to pay the $26,000 bill. When asked to help, Canadian government officials shied away from a confrontation with the Soviets, claiming that all embassy personnel have immunity. But Edwards wanted his money and finally found a law firm willing to tackle the issue and Canada's bureaucracy. Lawyer Ron Manes felt "that if a country descends into the commercial arena to participate in our capitalist system, it must play by the same rules as everyone else and pay its just debts." In October Edwards won his first battle. The Toronto sheriff ordered the Soviet freighter "Stanislavsky" seized. Then Soviet embassy bank accounts in Ottawa were frozen by court order. Only then did the Soviet officials agree to pay the debt and an additional $10,000 in interest. They also handed over a supply of caviar and vodka and footed the bill for Edwards's victory celebration at the Royal York Hotel. "You've got to have a little fun in life," Edwards remarked, as he patted his 36,000 Canadian one-dollar bills.

WIDE WORLD

When android C3PO won a leading role in *Star Wars,* his silicon-chip brain had not been programmed to include swinging a rhythmical baton. But that had to change when John Williams, who composed the prizewinning score of the blockbuster movie, was named to succeed Arthur Fiedler as conductor of the Boston Pops. On opening night, C3PO moved to the podium and without batting an electronic eyelash conducted the 100-member orchestra in a moving rendition of the movie's theme song.

Fur lovers, beware. The *Johannesburg Star,* a South African newspaper, announced in April that hundreds of women who thought they had bought expensive seal, mink, or ermine coats might actually be wearing garments of doctored rat fur. What's more, a spokesman for one of the Johannesburg fashion houses said the fact is well known by those whose business it is to know such things.

Tahitian kiir is not only a potent drink; it's also very expensive. A French woman, well aware of these facts, was somewhat unnerved when the waitress returned with so much *kiir* it threatened to slosh over the edge of a large drinking glass. When the woman complained that she couldn't drink that much *kiir,* the unperturbed waitress simply flung most of it into the bushes and asked, "Is that enough?"

Texas criminal law stipulates that any person convicted of three felonies must receive a life sentence. William James Rummel argued that in his case such a sentence constituted a "grossly disproportionate" punishment; as such, it violated the U.S. constitutional provision against cruel and unusual punishment. Rummel was convicted and served time for an $80 credit card fraud and for the forging of a $28.36 check. He then accepted a $120.75 check after falsely promising to repair an air conditioner. The third felony led to his life sentence. In March the U.S. Supreme Court ruled 5–4 that the Texas law did not violate the U.S. Constitution. Justice William Rehnquist explained that states have a valid interest in imposing such a sentence on those "who by repeated criminal acts have shown that they are simply incapable of conforming to the norms of society. . . ." In Texas, prisoners serving life sentences are eligible for parole after 12 years.

Undecided voters were beset on every side during the U.S. presidential election, but none perhaps so persistently as Reagan Carter, the owner of a welding shop in Beaumont, Texas. He honestly could not decide which candidate he preferred. But with a name like his, it's not surprising that employees right next door couldn't give him much sympathy. They worked for the Nixon Ford Motor Co.

Joseph Kamoo, a Swiss inventor, applied for a patent for a technological improvement of Muslim prayer rugs. Since Muslims perform their daily prayers facing Mecca, it is important, but sometimes difficult, to know how to line up the rectangular mat in the proper direction. Kamoo's rug has a map and compass that permit believers to align their rugs properly no matter where they are. The rug map is simply rotated around the compass until the needle points to the city where the believer happens to be. When that is done, the rug is facing Mecca.

American pollsters spend huge sums of money and countless hours trying to predict the outcome of the U.S. presidential election. In gauging public opinion these experts generally count themselves lucky if they come to within three percentage points of the actual vote count. Perhaps Nepali astrologers know something American pollsters don't. About a score of the kingdom's astrologers reached a consensus on April 21 that a national referendum would carry with 55% of the vote. Eleven days later the referendum was endorsed by 54.79% of the voters.

When 260 squatters refused to leave a luxury apartment building in Amsterdam, a judge issued an order for their removal. The defiant squatters, however, swore they would not be evicted without a struggle. A huge crowd was on hand to witness the showdown. Some 2,000 policemen arrived with dogs, horses, water cannons, armoured personnel carriers, and army sharpshooters positioned in cages on hydraulic platforms. The first serious problems came when the angry crowd began to attack the police with cobblestones, bags of paint, and homemade firebombs. They were finally subdued by tear gas. The police then moved forward to assault the building. To their chagrin, they found only one squatter in the building. He was armed with a bouquet of flowers.

Occupational hazards vary from job to job, but in the U.S. neither mining nor police work heads the list of most dangerous professions. Miners have an on-the-job death rate of 56 per 100,000, while police officers have a rate of 35 per 100,000. But, according to a study conducted by the International Association of Fire Fighters, an average 68 out of 100,000 fire fighters die in the performance of their duties.

When he retired from the U.S. Army, Vietnam veteran James Tobin signed up as a civilian pilot with his old employer. His first assignment was to fly a load of light weapons from the Picatinny Arsenal in Dover, N.J., to the Aberdeen Proving Grounds in Maryland. The plane was traveling 320 kph (200 mph) at 2,745 m (9,000 ft) when a flashing light indicated a rear door of the U-21 Beechcraft was not properly closed. Leaving his co-pilot at the controls, Tobin went to investigate. The moment he touched the latch he was sucked through the open door and somersaulted into space. Incredibly, one of his feet was firmly caught by a holding line attached to the door. When the co-pilot saw Tobin dangling in midair, he made a very careful emergency landing. Tobin went to the hospital with a broken right arm, possibly pondering the old saying that no one really ever knows what to expect on the first day of a new job.

Cosmetic firms, usually in fierce competition for new fragrances, showed no interest at all in Arthur F. Isbell's patented aroma. Though two small bottles of chemicals have to be mixed to produce the smell, that inconvenience was not the real problem. They simply didn't think the aroma would sell. Hunters and wildlife photographers, on the other hand, think it's great. Human odours, which alert animals to danger, seem to be effectively masked by Isbell's artificial skunk bouquet.

Edwin Robinson was struck by lightning in June and lived to tell an incredible tale. After a truck accident in February 1971, he began to lose his sight and hearing. More than eight years later, during a midsummer thunderstorm in Maine, he picked up his aluminum cane and went outside in search of his pet chicken. That's when it happened. A bolt of lightning knocked him unconscious. Twenty minutes later he awoke, got to his feet, and realized that something wonderful had occurred. His head was "clear as a bell." For the first time in almost a decade Robinson no longer felt what seemed to be a tight band around his head. As his eyesight and hearing—and even the hair on his head which he had lost over the years—began to come back to him, the 62-year-old former truck driver hoped he could travel to Virginia to see his four grandchildren.

Students at Yale University, harassed by upcoming midterm examinations, decided to filch a highly revered moose head from the university's Ezra Stiles College. They then fashioned a crude ransom note addressed to the president of Yale. It read, "Dear Bart: We have your moose. Cancel midterms or we'll eat him. The Moose Liberation Army." President A. Bartlett Giamatti, unintimidated by such tactics, contemptuously responded: "Let them eat mousse."

Political conventions can be humbling, even for those only peripherally involved. When Walter Cronkite and his wife boarded a plane for the Republican Party convention in Detroit, a flight attendant asked their names. The most recognizable face in TV newscasting smilingly replied, "Walter and Betsy." But the attendant wanted the last name, too, and even asked how it was spelled. Giggling with embarrassment, the stewardess apologized for not immediately recognizing the famous face and name. She then proceeded to ask the couple why they were going to Detroit.

Robert Kornbach was driving with his wife and sister-in-law on New York's Cross Island Expressway when he decided to pull over and let his wife, Maureen, take the wheel. All three switched places. Robert slid over to the passenger's seat. His sister-in-law, Elizabeth, moved to the back seat, and Maureen took over the driving duties. Some time later the Kornbachs panicked. Their six-week-old son was not in the car. In the process of moving to the back seat, Elizabeth had set Brian on the roof of the car and presumed Robert would pick up the baby and hold him in the front seat. But Robert had not gotten out of the car. A tollbooth attendant frantically reached the New York City police, who soon reported that Brian had been found and was none the worse for his harrowing experience.

Sally Lippman was very grateful when a friend suggested that a visit to a New York disco might help relieve the loneliness she felt after the death of her husband. Sally went and loved it. In time she met and fell in love with 28-year-old Yiannis Touzos. When they decided to get married in June, disco habitués hoped that would not end 80-year-old "Disco Sally's" nights out on the town.

A healthy big toe is worth $8,657.50, according to calculations worked out by an arbitrator for the Illinois Industrial Commission. Members of the Cook County Board, none of them a known expert on big toes, must have thought the figure was just about right because they approved an award of $3,463 as compensation to a former assistant state's attorney who sustained a 40% injury to his big toe while hurrying to answer a phone.

Presidential invitations are hard to come by, especially if you happen to be the owner of Eddie's Standard Service Station. So when Edward Finkelstein received a White House invitation, he jumped at the chance to visit the nation's capital. He didn't get much from the special briefing for several hundred VIP's, but he had lunch with Missouri Sen. Thomas Eagleton. Finkelstein said he enjoyed every minute of it and felt just fine when other senators passed by and patted him on the shoulder—even though "they didn't know me from Adam." Actually, they didn't know him from another Finkelstein named Edward who should have received the invitation. But the St. Louis, Mo., publisher had only one listing in the phone book, so the White House chose the Finkelstein with two: one a residence, the other an office. The latter was Eddie's gas station.

Pacific Southwest Airlines flights from Los Angeles to San Francisco are as uneventful as a bus ride across town. Habitual air travelers, therefore, merely smiled indulgently when the pilot identified the Golden Gate Bridge. It was in fact the San Mateo Bridge. Moments later those smiling eyes opened wide in wonderment. The flight attendant had just advised the passengers to extinguish their seatbelts and fasten their cigarettes.

Weary travelers stranded at airports for long hours may soon be blessing Grant Russell for inventing the Sleep-a-Matic. The chairlike contraption opens into a 1.8-m (6-ft) daybed when quarters are inserted into the coin slot. A high-pitched tone rouses the sleeper when the selected number of 15-minute periods has elapsed. Russell seems to have thought of everything—except, perhaps, how to dislodge bone-weary travelers who simply ignore the buzzing or continue to sleep on despite the noise.

Two hours after being shot in the abdomen, 24-year-old Margarette Maddox of Chicago gave birth to a 4-lb 4-oz baby boy. When doctors at Michael Reese Hospital examined the newborn infant, they found bullet fragments in the child's elbow and thigh. After surgery, the child was reported doing well.

DISASTERS OF 1980

The loss of life and property from disasters in 1980 included the following:

AVIATION

January 21, Near Lashkarak, Iran. An Iran Air Boeing 727, engulfed in dense fog, crashed in the Elburz Mountains; all 128 persons aboard were killed.

February 22, Near Agra, India. An Indian Air Force plane carrying 47 persons, including 31 paratroopers, 12 jump instructors, and 4 crew members, caught fire on takeoff and crashed; although two persons survived the crash, one died shortly after.

March 14, Southern Turkey. A U.S. Air Force C-130 Hercules transport plane, returning to Incirlik, crashed in the Taurus Mountains; all 18 persons aboard were killed and later identified as U.S. citizens.

March 14, Warsaw, Poland. A Polish IL-62 jetliner attempting to make an emergency landing on a foam-covered runway crashed nearly 3 km (2 mi) short of the airport. The crash, in which all 87 persons aboard, including 22 U.S. amateur boxers and officials, were killed, was attributed to a faulty engine.

April 12, Near Florianópolis, Brazil. A Transbrasil Boeing 727 smashed into a wooded hillside during a tropical rainstorm while approaching the airport; of the 58 persons aboard only 4 survived the crash, which was the country's worst air disaster in 20 years.

April 25, Santa Cruz de Tenerife, Canary Islands. A chartered British Boeing 727 airliner crashed on the slope of the 3,718-m (12,198-ft) Teide Peak, a snowcapped volcanic mountain; all 146 persons aboard, including 138 British vacationers and 8 crew members, were killed.

April 27, Bangkok, Thailand. A Thai twin-engine Hawker Siddeley 748 turboprop airliner crashed short of the runway when it was struck by a bolt of lightning; of the 57 persons aboard, 40 were killed and 11 were injured.

May 28, Los Palmas, Canary Islands. A Spanish Air Force C-130 Hercules transport plane crashed into a mountain during heavy fog and rain; the ten military personnel aboard were believed dead.

June 12, Near Valley, Neb. An Air Wisconsin twin-engine turboprop airplane slammed into a muddy soybean field during an intense thunderstorm; 12 of the 15 persons aboard were killed.

June 18, Near Aspen, Colo. Two airplanes, a Cessna 182 and a Cessna 310, crashed over Maroon Pass in the central Rocky Mountains; authorities believe the two light airplanes may have collided before crashing in the pass. Ten persons were found dead.

June 28, Tyrrhenian Sea. An Italian DC-9 jetliner traveling from Bologna to Palermo on the island of Sicily plunged into the Tyrrhenian Sea; all 81 persons aboard were killed.

July 7, Alma-Ata, Kazakhstan, U.S.S.R. A Soviet airliner with 163 persons aboard crashed while taking off from the republic's capital, Alma-Ata; reliable sources reported that all aboard died in the second worst air disaster in the country's history.

August 19, Riyadh, Saudi Arabia. A flaming Lockheed L-1011 TriStar jumbo jetliner returned to make an emergency landing at Riyadh airport when the pilot realized the airplane was on fire; despite efforts by rescue workers, all 301 persons aboard the aircraft lost their lives. The death toll made the disaster the second worst single plane crash in aviation history. An official report said poisonous gas was responsible for the deaths but the cause of the fire was unknown.

August 26, Jakarta, Indon. An Indonesian Viscount turboprop plane crashed in marshy ground some 32 km (20 mi) short of the airport; all 31 persons aboard were found dead.

September 7, Tidjikdja, Mauritania. A twin-engine military aircraft crashed during unfavourable weather conditions in central Mauritania; all nine persons aboard, including a member of the governing Military Committee, were killed.

September 12, Off the coast of The Bahamas. A chartered DC-3 airplane making a "casino flight" from Palm Beach, Fla., to The Bahamas plummeted into the Atlantic Ocean during a fierce storm; all 34 persons aboard were killed.

September 14, Near Medina, Saudi Arabia. A Saudi Arabian Air Force C-130 Hercules transport plane carrying 89 persons burst into flames and crashed into the desert while approaching Medina airport; there were no survivors.

November 13, Cairo, Egypt. A U.S. Air Force C-141 transport plane that was attempting to land equipment for the joint exercises by the U.S. Rapid Deployment Force and the Egyptian military crashed while making its approach to the airport; 13 servicemen lost their lives.

November 19, Seoul, South Korea. A Korean Airlines Boeing 747 jet crash-landed and burst into flames at Kimpo International Airport after the pilot reported difficulty operating the controls; 13 of the 226 persons aboard were killed.

November 24, Colombia. A DC-3 Colombian customs plane crashed near the Panamanian border; all 15 persons aboard were killed.

December 4, Near Lisbon, Port. A Cessna C-421 airplane carrying Portuguese Premier Francisco Sá Carneiro to a political rally crashed into a house shortly after takeoff; all seven persons aboard the aircraft died, and one person on the ground was killed by a wing that snapped off the plane. Officials ruled out the possibility of sabotage.

December 5, Tanzania. An airplane carrying eight UN officials crashed in Tanzania; the pilot, an unidentified passenger, and all of the UN officials aboard were killed.

December 21, Colombia. A Colombian jetliner crashed in the Guajira Desert minutes after takeoff from Ríohacha, after a bomb exploded in a rear restroom; all 70 persons aboard were killed.

FIRES AND EXPLOSIONS

January 1, Chapais, Que. A fast-burning fire, fueled by spruce and pine bough decorations, trapped New Year's Eve revelers inside a crowded club; 46 persons died in the blaze.

April 13, Aracaju, Brazil. An explosion in a fireworks factory in northeastern Brazil claimed the lives of ten persons.

May 9, Chutto Ado, Pak. A fire, apparently started when an electric pole fell during a storm, killed 18 persons in a blaze that completely destroyed the village.

May 20, Kingston, Jamaica. A fast-burning fire leveled a wooden two-story home for elderly women and trapped many inside. In the worst fire in the history of Jamaica, 144 women were known dead and 11 others were missing.

July 24, Queens, N.Y. An explosion in a metal factory was triggered by a spark from a welder's torch that ignited lacquer vapour in the basement of the factory. The blast left 11 persons dead and 4 others in critical condition.

July 26, Bradley Beach, N.J. A four-story wood and stucco hotel caught fire on the ground floor and became a blazing inferno when the main staircase served as a wind tunnel to fuel the fire; 23 persons, some elderly and retarded, were trapped in their rooms and succumbed to the intense heat. Seventeen others escaped.

August 2, Bologna, Italy. A bomb explosion at a train station crushed a restaurant, two crowded waiting rooms, and a train platform, and claimed the lives of 76 persons and injured some 200 others. The blast, linked to right-wing terrorists, was the worst terrorist incident in the history of Italy.

August 8, Western Ireland. A raging fire, possibly caused by an incendiary bomb, ripped through the 40-room Central Hotel on Donegal Bay; ten persons, including five children, were killed and eight others were injured.

August 14, Iraq. An electrical fire in a theatre in a suburb of

Twenty-two members of the U.S. Olympic boxing team were among 87 persons killed near the Warsaw airport in Poland when a Polish Airlines jetliner crashed on March 14.

UPI

KEYSTONE

A fire in the MGM Grand Hotel in Las Vegas, Nevada, in November killed 84 people. Many others were rescued by helicopters from the roof of the building.

Baghdad sent panicking patrons to the exits; although the fire was relatively minor, 59 persons were killed in the stampede.

August 16, London, England. An early morning fire at two adjoining social clubs killed 37 persons who were trapped in by locked doors; Scotland Yard believed the blaze was started by a homemade gasoline bomb.

August 18, Deh-Bozoorg, Iran. A dynamite explosion occurred when the explosives stored in a private home were inadvertently ignited by a spark from a welder's tool; at least 90 villagers were killed when they attempted to extinguish the fire and some 40 others were injured.

October 4, Off the coast of Saudi Arabia. A blowout on an offshore oil rig in the Persian Gulf suffocated 19 persons who inhaled toxic gas as a result of the blast.

October 23, Ortuella, Spain. An explosion in one of three units of an elementary school leveled the structure and killed 3 adults and 61 children; the blast was caused either by a faulty basement boiler that was being repaired at the time of the mishap or by a propane tank outside the building.

October 28, Chicago, Ill. A fire ripped through a two-story structure on the city's South Side and claimed the lives of ten persons, eight of them children; the building had been cited for numerous building code violations.

October 31, Gorna Grupa, Poland. A fire that engulfed the third floor of a mental hospital claimed the lives of 50 persons, some of whom were believed to have been trampled as they raced down corridors; 260 other patients were rescued, 29 of them injured.

November 16, Bangkok, Thailand. An explosion in an army munitions factory occurred when a worker inadvertently connected the wrong fuse in a rocket; the explosion detonated some 5,000 other rockets which triggered a two-and-a-half-hour blaze and destroyed a four-block area. Thirty-eight persons were killed and some 350 others were injured.

November 20, Kawaji, Japan. A fire that was believed started by a smoldering cigarette left near an oxygen cylinder destroyed the Kawaji Prince Hotel; 44 persons succumbed in the blaze.

November 24, Near Ankara, Turkey. A liquefied gas explosion at an engagement party set off a series of blasts that collapsed dining rooms and killed at least 97 persons; most of the victims were children and women, including the bride-to-be.

Late November, Southern California. Fires that were fueled by hurricane-force winds charred more than 34,400 ha (85,000 ac) in San Bernardino, Riverside, Orange, San Diego, and Los Angeles counties in southern California. The fires, which were attributed to a combination of arson, dry vegetation, and the seasonal Santa Ana winds, claimed 4 lives and destroyed over 400 homes.

November 21, Las Vegas, Nev. A fast-burning fire that ripped through the first and second floors of the luxurious 26-story MGM Grand Hotel killed 84 persons, most of whom died from carbon monoxide poisoning. Many of the 3,500 others trapped on the upper floors were rescued from the roof by helicopters, a few jumped to their deaths, and others crashed windows trying to escape the deadly fumes. The origin of the fire was uncertain, but the disaster was magnified because no fire alarm was sounded and the sprinkler system did not function. It was the second most deadly hotel fire in U.S. history.

December 4, Near White Plains, N.Y. A blazing fire at the three-story convention centre at the Stouffer's Inn killed 26 persons, most of them corporate executives, and injured at least a dozen others, some of whom jumped three stories to escape the fire; it was the worst fire in Westchester County's history.

December 18, Salt Lake City, Utah. A four-alarm fire in an apartment building claimed the lives of 12 Vietnamese refugees; the family was unable to escape because their back door had been nailed shut after a burglary one month earlier.

December 31, Nairobi, Kenya. A terrorist bomb exploded in the Norfolk Hotel on New Year's Eve just as revelers were sitting down in the dining room; at least 13 persons were known dead, 85 were injured, and 10 others were missing.

MARINE

January 28, Off the coast of Florida. The 55-m (180-ft) Coast Guard tender "Blackthorn" collided with the 178-m (585-ft) tanker "Capricorn" in Tampa Bay and sank; 26 crewmen aboard the "Blackthorn" lost their lives.

January 31, Japan Sea. The 5,130-ton freighter "Hatsufuji" capsized and sank in the Japan Sea; 2 crewmen drowned, 1 survived, and 20 others were missing and presumed dead.

February 7, South Africa. A small lobster boat carrying 30 fishermen sank off the southwest coast of the country; all aboard were missing and presumed drowned.

April 22, Central Philippines. The interisland ferry "Don Juan" collided with an oil tanker 16 km (10 mi) east of the island of Maestre de Campo; 96 persons were known dead of the nearly 1,000 passengers and crew aboard the ferry.

Early May, Gujarat State, India. A boat carrying wedding party revelers capsized while crossing a river in western India; some 50 persons were believed drowned.

May 17, Near Havana, Cuba. A small boat, the Miami-based "Olo Yumi," carrying 52 Cuban refugees capsized in rough seas; although the boat was equipped with life jackets the passengers apparently did not know how to use them. Fourteen persons were drowned and 38 others were rescued.

July 28, Near Dacca, Bangladesh. A passenger launch carrying 300 persons collided with another vessel and capsized in the Padma River; 50 persons were missing and feared drowned.

August 22, Near Ciudad del Carmen, Mexico. A run-down ferryboat loaded with a bus, passenger cars, and several cargo trucks sank off the coast of Ciudad del Carmen; at least 50 persons drowned.

September 6, Santo Domingo, Dominican Republic. Twenty-two stowaways concealed in the ballast tanks of a Panamanian freighter were found dead, some drowned, others suffocated; 12 others were rescued.

October 5, North Pacific Ocean. Two Japanese fishing boats were lost at sea in stormy Pacific waters; 11 crew members from the "Genei Maru No. 61" and 14 others from the "Tora Maru No. 28" were believed drowned.

October 21, Negros Oriental Province, Phil. A motorboat capsized on a swollen river in the central Philippines; nine persons were known dead and two others were missing.

Late October, Atlantic Ocean. After leaving Philadelphia, Pa., on October 24, the 152-m (500-ft) freighter "Poet" disappeared without a trace; the 34 crewmen aboard were presumed dead.

MINING

March 27, South Africa. A cable supporting an elevator cage snapped and sent 31 coal miners plummeting more than 1,500 m (5,000 ft) down a shaft at Vaal Reef's mine, the world's largest and deepest gold mine; the impact of the crash flattened the cage and killed all aboard.

November 7, Near Madison, W.Va. A methane gas explosion in a coal mine claimed the lives of five miners who were working in an isolated section of the mine.

November 29, Northern Romania. A gas explosion in the Livezeni coal mine in the Jiu Valley claimed the lives of 49 miners and injured 26 others.

MISCELLANEOUS

Early January, Brazil. A polio outbreak in Brazil claimed the lives of at least 25 children; the southern states of Santa Catarina and Paraná were most seriously affected.

Early January, Java, Indon. Eighteen persons died of food poisoning after eating fermented soybean cakes; about 100 others were hospitalized.

January 20, Sincelejo, Colombia. Eight bleacher sections surrounding the largest bullring in Colombia collapsed under the weight of some 3,000 spectators; authorities attributed the collapse to both the large crowd and the heavy rains that apparently softened the ground which held wooden support beams. At least 165 persons were known dead, and another 500 were injured, many of them trampled or impaled on splintered beams.

March 4, Lagos, Nigeria. When the door of a van in which 68 prisoners were being transported was opened, 47 prisoners were found suffocated and 7 others were unconscious; the fate of the other 14 prisoners was undisclosed.

March 27, Off the coast of Norway. A five-legged floating oil-field platform overturned in gale-force winds in the North Sea, in what was the worst disaster in the history of offshore oil operations; 123 of the 212 men aboard were drowned when one of the anchored legs gave way and caused the platform to overturn.

April 19, Sikkim State, India. A makeshift movie theatre collapsed as a result of a landslide; 17 soldiers were killed and 30 others were injured.

April–May, Mozambique. An outbreak of cholera claimed the lives of 10 persons near the capital city of Maputo; 200 cases of the disease had been recorded in the country.

May 4, Kinshasa, Zaire. Nine persons, including 7 women and 2 children, were trampled to death when a huge crowd of people, estimated at 1.5 million, pushed forward to attend a mass celebrated by Pope John Paul II; 72 others were injured.

Mid-June, Near Lushoto, Tanzania. An outbreak of bubonic plague in a village with a population of 1,400 people killed 12 persons.

Summer, Madhya Pradesh State, India. An epidemic of cholera swept through Madhya Pradesh and killed 390 persons.

A devastating series of earthquakes in southern Italy in November demolished several villages, leaving an estimated 3,000 dead and 310,000 homeless.

UPI

August 29, Maseru, Lesotho. More than 12 persons were trampled to death when a crowd rioted outside a concert hall; one witness said the crowd panicked when police fired tear gas canisters.

September–October, Northern India. An epidemic of encephalitis, a viral disease spread by mosquitoes, caused the deaths of at least 400 persons in India.

NATURAL

January 1, Azores Islands. An earthquake measuring 6.9 on the Richter scale struck the Portuguese ten-island chain, killing at least 56 persons and injuring 400 others; hardest hit was Terceira Island, where 70% of the buildings in the capital, including several historic monuments, were destroyed.

Early January, Northwestern U.S. A winter storm that crippled Oregon and Washington left 13 persons dead.

January, Bihar State, India. A cold wave claimed the lives of at least 79 poor persons who lacked the required food and clothing to withstand temperatures as low as 2° C (36° F).

January, Mascarene Islands. Cyclone Hyacinthe battered the volcanic island of Réunion, a French overseas département located in the western Indian Ocean; at least 20 persons died as a result of the storm.

February, California, Arizona, and Mexico. A nine-day rainstorm blasted Mexico, Arizona, and southern California, where flooding prompted huge mudslides; damage in the affected areas was estimated at half a billion dollars and a total of 36 persons lost their lives.

February 10, Chile. An intense five-hour thunderstorm claimed the lives of ten persons in Chile; one person in Santiago was electrocuted when a high tension power cable broke, and nine others in the city of Talca drowned in flash floods.

March 2, Eastern U.S. A crippling snowstorm that left hundreds of motorists stranded and dumped more than 30 cm (12 in) of snow on Norfolk, Va., contributed to the deaths of at least 36 persons, including 13 in North Carolina, 6 in Ohio, 5 in Missouri, 3 in South Carolina, 3 in Tennessee, 2 in Pennsylvania, and 1 each in Kentucky, Virginia, Maryland, and Florida.

March 27–28, Turkey. Heavy rainfall, which triggered landslides and floods, pummeled the village of Ayvazhaci in central Kayseri Province and lashed Konya Province and the region of Kahramanmaras in the southwest; at least 75 persons were feared dead.

Early April, Central Peru. Heavy rains triggered mud-and-rock slides and caused severe flooding; at least 90 persons were missing and believed dead and some 400 others were stranded and left homeless.

Early April, Fiji. Raging Cyclone Wally caused landslides and floods that killed at least 13 persons and left thousands of others homeless.

April 2, Northeastern Syria. A four-minute storm claimed the lives of 10 persons and injured at least 12 others.

May 13, Kalamazoo, Mich. Devastating tornadoes ripped through downtown Kalamazoo and left a trail of death and destruction; 5 persons were killed and at least 65 others were treated at hospitals.

May 18, Toutle, Wash. The eruption of Mt. St. Helens ripped more than 400 m (1,300 ft) from the top of the 2,950-m (9,677-ft) volcano, which spewed tons of mud, volcanic rocks, and ash; 34 persons were known dead and 53 others were missing and believed buried under debris.

June–August, U.S. A blistering heat wave scorched the nation with temperatures soaring above 38° C (100° F) nearly every day in Texas; hardest hit were Houston and Dallas. The Midwest and Eastern sections of the U.S. were also affected; Missouri experienced the highest death toll in the nation with 311 deaths. The nationwide death toll was officially put at 1,265 persons, most of them poor and elderly who could not afford the expense of air conditioning.

Early July, Gujarat State, India. Weeklong rains in western India caused rampant flooding that cut off villages and made thousands of persons homeless when 37 dams overflowed their banks; 11 persons lost their lives in the floodwaters.

July 23, Northern Vietnam. Typhoon Joe rampaged through the country killing more than 130 persons, destroying newly planted rice fields, and affecting some three million people who lost their homes to violent winds and severe flooding.

July 29, Western Nepal. A severe earthquake measuring 6.5 on the Richter scale jolted the country; hardest hit were the far western districts of Darchula and Baitadi. At least 87 persons were killed, 5,600 were injured, and some 35,000 others were left homeless.

July–August, India. Devastating monsoon floods in six states in India ravaged 19,400 sq km (7,500 sq mi) of the country; property damage was estimated at more than $131 million and at least 600 people were known dead.

Early August, Barbados, St. Lucia, Haiti, Dominican Republic, Jamaica, Cuba, and the U.S. Ferocious Hurricane Allen, the second strongest Atlantic hurricane of the century, battered the Caribbean with winds of 280 kph (175 mph) and gusts of 315 kph (195 mph);

hardest hit was Haiti, where at least 220 persons died and the citrus crop was annihilated. Citizens of Texas, Florida, and Alabama were braced for the storm and many had evacuated the areas of Corpus Christi and Brownsville, in Texas, but the storm lost much of its intensity over Mexico. The cumulative death toll was put at more than 270.

August, Central China. The swollen Dongting (Tung-t'ing) Lake (China's second largest freshwater lake), which is fed by the Chang Jiang (Yangtze River; the country's longest river), overflowed and flooded two provincial cities; thousands of persons were feared dead in the lake districts.

August 14, Japan. A rockfall that sent a dozen rocks measuring more than one metre (three feet) in diameter down Mt. Fuji, Japan's highest peak, struck and killed 12 mountain climbers; more than 30 others were injured.

August 20, Pakistan. Lightning struck and killed 10 persons in a mountainous district some 320 km (200 m) north of Islamabad.

August 24, Jammu and Kashmir State, India. Three earth tremors in northern India killed 13 persons and injured 40 others in the state of Jammu and Kashmir.

August–September, West Bengal State, India. Seasonal monsoon rains which caused heavy flooding and triggered landslides contributed to the deaths of nearly 1,500 people in the state.

September 1–3, Arandas, Mexico. Heavy rains caused a dam above the small town of Arandas to burst and release a flood of water that swept away 50 homes and killed at least 24 people. Swollen by the intense rainfall, the Colorado River rose by 3 m (10 ft) in eight hours, flooding the town; at least 100 people were reported dead or missing.

September 11, Korea. Typhoon Orchid triggered landslides on the southeastern coast of the country; 7 persons were killed and over 100 fishermen were lost at sea.

September 15–16, Central Vietnam. Raging Typhoon Ruth wreaked further damage on Vietnam, which was still reeling from the ravages of Typhoon Joe in July; 164 persons were known dead, tens of thousands of buildings were destroyed, and rice fields were inundated.

Mid-September, Orissa State, India. Several days of torrential rain caused widespread flash floods and burst a dam that inundated two towns with 3 m (10 ft) of water; at least 300,000 persons were marooned and some 200 others were drowned.

Mid-September, Caracas, Venezuela. A week of heavy rain caused the Guaire River to overflow its banks and paralyze the capital city; at least 20 persons were drowned or buried in huge mudslides, and highways leading to the international airport and the vital port city of La Guaira were blocked by landslides.

September, Bangladesh. Flooding in 12 northwestern districts of Bangladesh killed a total of 655 persons.

Late September, Maharashtra State, India. A killer cyclone claimed the lives of at least 12 persons and injured 25 others.

October, Thailand. Relentless monsoon flooding inundated 44 of the country's 72 provinces; 28 persons were killed in the floods and heavy damage to crops and housing was reported.

October 10, El Asnam, Alg. A powerful earthquake measuring 7.7 on the Richter scale reduced 80% of El Asnam to rubble in only 30 seconds; although early estimates put the death toll as high as 20,000, a report in November revealed that 4,000 persons died, 60,000 were injured, and some 300,000 others were left homeless.

October 12, Jammu and Kashmir State, India. Violent hailstorms in the state of Jammu and Kashmir claimed the lives of 28 persons.

October 24, Southern Mexico. A severe earthquake measuring 6.5 on the Richter scale crumbled brick and adobe buildings and killed at least 29 persons; hundreds of others were injured when a public market building collapsed in Huajuápan de León.

November 23–24, Southern Italy. A series of major earthquakes peaking at 6.9 on the Richter scale rocked the cities of Naples, Salerno, Avellino, and Potenza, jolted a total of 179 communities, killed an estimated 3,000 people, and left some 310,000 others homeless. Although the initial destruction was believed minimal, later reports confirmed that the magnitude of the disaster was overwhelming and that most of the victims died in remote villages. Many people were thought buried (in some cases alive) beneath the rubble, but the aftershocks and the unavailability of adequate help thwarted rescue attempts.

December 15, Naples, Italy. A wing of a 400-year-old Bourbon palace, used as a home for the aged, collapsed as a result of damage suffered during the earthquakes on November 23–24; eight patients and one hospital worker were killed.

December 19, Central Iran. Two earthquakes, one measuring 5.7 and the other measuring 5.9 on the Richter scale, struck Iran and killed 26 persons; the quakes fractured the gold dome of the Massoumeh shrine in the holy city of Qom and shook nearby villages.

RAILROADS

January 22, China. An explosion aboard a train destroyed a railroad car and left more than 20 persons injured or dead at a railroad station in China; as a result of the blast, the sixth in 1980, passengers were prohibited from carrying combustibles or firecrackers.

February 4, Near Gualanday, Colombia. A locomotive slammed into a bus after the signal device apparently failed to operate; 10 persons were killed and at least 25 others were injured.

June 2, Near Borlänge, Sweden. A head-on collision between two trains, one empty and one carrying 250 passengers, resulted in the deaths of 12 persons, 7 of them children; the accident was attributed to a damaged signal system.

June 30, Near Sofiok, Hung. A train crashed into a bus that entered a flashing railroad crossing and dragged it 800 m (2,600 ft) before stopping; 19 persons were killed and 16 others were injured.

July 15, Torralba del Moral, Spain. A packed express train smashed into a freight train when the engineer of the express failed to stop at an inoperative signal; 16 persons were killed when the first four coaches were hurled down a 200-m (650-ft) embankment.

August 1, Buttevant, County Cork, Ireland. An express train derailed and crashed after it apparently hit a faulty switch that steered the locomotive to a side track but left passenger cars on the main track; 17 persons were killed and 40 others were injured in the wreckage.

August 19, Near Torun, Poland. A freight train and a crowded passenger train collided head-on when the freight train missed a stop signal and went barreling down the wrong track; at least 62 persons were killed and 50 others were injured in Poland's worst rail disaster to date.

November 21, Near Vibo Valentia, Italy. A bizarre train crash occurred after a freight train lost 28 of its 41 cars and a southbound passenger train traveling at about 160 kph (100 mph) struck the uncoupled cars; the impact of this crash hurled several boxcars onto an adjacent track, where a northbound train, traveling at approximately the same speed, slammed into them. Twenty-eight persons were killed and 100 others were injured.

TRAFFIC

January 2, Yugoslavia. A bus traveling in central Yugoslavia plunged off a road into the swirling waters of the Neretva River; at least 20 persons were feared drowned.

February 23, Near Cacocum, Cuba. A bus traveling to the Cristino Naranjo sugar mill overturned on a curve and caught on fire; ten persons were killed and nine others were seriously injured.

April 7, Near Culiacán, Mexico. A bus traveling from Tijuana to Mexico City careened off the right side of a narrow bridge while attempting to pass a truck and landed in a shallow ditch; 48 persons were killed and 36 others were injured.

May 9, Tampa Bay, Fla. A bus, several cars, and a pickup truck plunged 43 m (140 ft) into Tampa Bay after a ship struck the Sunshine Skyway Bridge during a blinding rainstorm and tore away more than 305 m (1,000 ft) of the span; the driver of the pickup truck survived, but 35 other persons were killed, most of them from the bus.

May 21, Near Dapoli, India. A bus traveling to Bombay turned over and caught fire; 30 passengers burned to death and 41 others were seriously injured.

May 21, Karnataka State, India. A bus plunged into the Khushavathi River some 400 km (250 mi) north of the capital city of Bangalore; 19 persons were killed and 40 others were injured.

May 28, Near Swift Current, Sask. A bus carrying members of a Canadian Pacific rail crew was sideswiped by a car and then flipped over in front of an oncoming tanker truck; 22 persons died in the blazing wreckage.

June 5, Jasper, Ark. A chartered bus traveling along a dangerous highway on Jasper Mountain in the Ozarks went out of control, slid down a 15-m (50-ft) embankment, and smashed into a thicket of trees; 20 Texan tourists were killed and 13 others were injured, some seriously.

June 7, Maguzulu, South Africa. A speeding freight train slammed into the side of a bus loaded with shoppers at an unguarded crossroad; at least 45 persons were killed and dozens of others were injured.

June 7, Orkney, South Africa. A truck crashed into the rear of a tractor-towed flatbed trailer about 200 km (125 mi) west of Johannesburg; 17 persons were killed and 13 others were seriously injured.

June 15, Near Sukabumi, Java, Indon. A bus slid off a road and caught fire on the island of Java; 21 persons were killed.

August 3, Near Rio de Janeiro, Brazil. A collision between a bus and a truck on a highway northeast of Rio de Janeiro killed 28 persons. There was only one survivor, a passenger from the bus.

September 21, Near Lahore, Pak. A crowded bus fell into an irrigation canal; the plunge killed 50 persons and seriously injured 6 others.

October 15, Near Oaxaca, Mexico. An overcrowded bus plunged to the bottom of the 230-m (750-ft) El Basurero gorge; 23 persons were killed and 18 others were injured in the crash.

December 13, Near Guzmán, Mexico. A trailer truck collided head-on with a bus filled with Roman Catholic pilgrims traveling to a shrine in Jalisco to commemorate the 449th anniversary of the miracle of the Virgin of Guadalupe; 37 persons were killed and 18 others were injured in the crash.

FERMENT IN CENTRAL AMERICA

by Peter Calvert

MICHEL PHILIPPOT—SYGMA

Central America was in ferment in 1980. In Nicaragua the year-old Government of National Reconstruction struggled to maintain the unity forged in the revolution against the Somoza dictatorship. El Salvador's moderate military junta found itself increasingly helpless in the face of terror from both the right and the left. Fearing contagion, Guatemala's military regime became ever more repressive, while Honduras began tentative steps toward a return to civilian government. Even democratic and prosperous Costa Rica was experiencing economic difficulties. Meanwhile, the U.S. looked on nervously, unsure of which way the tide was running. Long dismissed as a cluster of banana republics firmly under U.S. control, Central America was a relative newcomer among the world's hot spots. But the sources of the current unrest reached back to the region's independence movement and beyond.

Central America is the term given in geography to the land bridge connecting North and South America, a volcanic region formed by the collision of continental plates. In politics it has a more restricted meaning, referring to the countries between the southern frontier of Mexico and the Isthmus of Panama, specifically the five countries of Guatemala, El Salvador, Honduras, Nicaragua, and Costa Rica. Panama, which because of its past history is classified as a South American country, has so much in common with the Central American republics that it is normally considered together with them.

Common Colonial Heritage. All this area lay within that part of the world claimed by Spain under its agreement with Portugal in 1494, and the five countries of Central America proper once formed the captaincy general of Guatemala, with its capital at Antigua (Guatemala). This, in turn, was a subordinate unit of the viceroyalty of New Spain, with its capital at Mexico City. When Mexico became independent in 1821, it took the provinces of Central America with it. After the short-lived episode of the Mexican Empire, the provinces seceded from Mexico to become a separate Central American republic.

Peter Calvert is reader in politics at the University of Southampton and the author of Latin America; Mexico; The Mexicans; *and* Emiliano Zapata.

The enlightened and imaginative government of the republic proved too liberal for the taste of many of its citizens. In 1838 an insurrection led by an illiterate mule driver from Guatemala, Rafael Carrera, began the disintegration of Central America into the five countries in existence today. Since then, almost every generation has seen an attempt to reunify Central America, but none has gotten further than the moment of formal establishment before being destroyed by a revolt in one or another of the states. Nevertheless, the tradition that the five states were once one country and ought to be once again, coupled with the fact that they are relatively small by the standard of the mainland Americas, has meant that writers have tended to treat them together, emphasizing what they have in common rather than what separates them.

What they have in common is their relatively small size, their common Spanish colonial heritage, predominantly rural economies dominated in each case by the production of food crops and one or two tropical export crops (coffee in El Salvador and Costa Rica, coffee and cotton in Guatemala, bananas in Honduras), an unusual degree of vulnerability to natural catastrophes such as earthquakes and hurricanes, and a 19th-century history of dictatorship and political turmoil. But even such generalizations can be misleading unless seen in perspective.

Take, for example, the question of size. It is true that the Central American countries are relatively small by American standards; however, compared with many ancient or historic nations and many current member states of the United Nations, they are not. Guatemala, for example, is roughly the same size as mainland Greece, and El Salvador, the smallest of the mainland states, is only slightly smaller than Belgium. Moreover, one of the consequences of disunification—and one of the factors that has made reunification so difficult—has been the tendency to emphasize those factors that keep the countries apart. Hence, during their relatively long independent existence of nearly a century and a half, the states have become less and less like one another.

U.S. and Other Influences. In the 19th century, an age dominated in world politics by sea power,

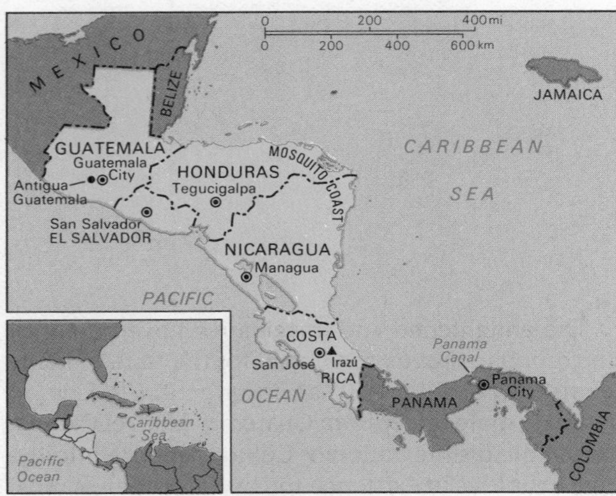

The nations of Central America

Central America was seen by the great powers less as a land bridge than as an obstacle to travel. For the Spaniards it had always been both: an essential link in the chain of communication that ran from Spain to Cuba, onward to the Isthmus, and from there southward to Callao, Lima, and the southern continent. With the rise of the United States, and particularly after its acquisition of California, a new power developed an interest in the strategic route across the Isthmus. The Spanish-American War (1898) brought an urgent awareness of its importance to the U.S. public. But it was not until the early 20th century that politics and technology were brought together to make the dream of an interoceanic canal a reality.

The separation of Panama from Colombia (1903), and the treaty that gave the U.S. unfettered control of the canal, also gave the U.S. a vital strategic interest in Central America and its political stability. Disturbances in the area immediately to the north of the canal carried the risk that European powers might intervene there, with unpredictable consequences for the defense of the Canal Zone, now under virtual U.S. sovereignty.

The collapse of Spanish authority in the region had left one mainland colony in British hands: Belize, then rather misleadingly known as British Honduras. In the middle years of the 19th century it had seemed for a time that British influence would be extended into the Mosquito Coast of Honduras itself, but any moves in this direction were ended voluntarily by Britain in 1860. In the early 20th century German influence in Guatemala was strong but was not seen in the U.S. as a strategic threat. Instead, interest focused on disturbances in Nicaragua, which offered the only serious alternative site for an isthmian canal. In 1910 a change of government there brought Nicaragua clearly within the U.S. sphere of influence, just as World War I decisively put a stop to any lingering possibilities of European expansion within the Americas.

By 1920 the U.S. was unquestionably the dominant power in the area, and soon afterward its control over Nicaragua was reinforced by military occupation. Contingents of U.S. Marines had already occupied nearby Haiti and the Dominican Republic in the course of the war. It was the height of irony that U.S. withdrawal from Nicaragua in the era of Pres. Franklin D. Roosevelt's Good Neighbor Policy was to have consequences for the Nicaraguans at least as undesirable as the occupation itself. Control of the Nicaraguan National Guard that had been formed by the U.S. to keep peace fell into the hands of the elder Anastasio Somoza. This enabled him to take power in 1936 and to found the dynasty that retained political control of the country, the largest in Central America, down to 1979.

Regional Divergences. By this time, the political and social fortunes of the Central American states had begun to diverge sharply. Costa Rica, immediately to the south of Nicaragua, had had a series of liberal and enlightened presidents going back to the 1880s. Supported by a relatively well-to-do population of medium landowners, they had introduced mass education, abolished the death penalty, and laid the foundations for a democratic government that became the strongest in the region and at times one of the strongest in the Americas. After World War II there were fears of a return to a more authoritarian form of rule, but the revolution of 1948, led by José ("Pepe") Figueres, reestablished competitive party government. Furthermore, it destroyed the basis of the militarism so endemic in the region by accomplishing the drastic step of abolishing the armed forces.

In the three northern states, the 1930s saw the emergence of conservative dictatorships, accompanied by the first steps toward economic modernization. In El Salvador control of the economy remained in local hands, in the persons of the members of a tightly knit oligarchy (the so-called 14 families). At the other end of the scale, in Honduras, modernization took the form of an "enclave economy" on the northern coast, where the big banana plantations of the United Fruit Co. were virtually autonomous. The bulk of the Honduran people were only indirectly affected by the changes going on around them.

These very dissimilar countries were the first to leap to the support of the U.S. after the Japanese attack on Pearl Harbor in 1941. Small and poor, they were of only modest assistance in the global conflict, although their strategic significance for the U.S. remained. But their adherence to the Allied cause

PERRY KRETZ—STERN/BLACK STAR

Soldiers searched a family outside their home in the mountains of Nicaragua after it was reported that a group of rebels were seen there.

was to have far-reaching consequences. The presence of U.S. forces during the war and the dissemination of the ideals of the Allies created a desire for change that was all the more keenly felt because it had come relatively late. At the end of the war, peaceful revolutions in Guatemala and El Salvador ended the dictatorships there. In these and other Central American countries, the tension between the ideals of democratic government and the actuality brought the first stirrings of the unrest that has become the dominant political fact of Central America in recent years.

Roots of Unrest. The factors leading to this unrest can be viewed on two levels, economic and political. The fundamental economic problems are those of most small, underdeveloped economies in a world of big enterprise, with producers dependent on the whims of the world market and the great majority of the people existing, as their ancestors have for centuries, at or near a subsistence level. And in an area prone to natural disasters, subsistence is something that can be put in hazard at any moment—as by the eruption of Mt. Irazú in Costa Rica in 1963, the Managua (Nicaragua) earthquake of 1972, or the hurricane in Honduras in 1974. Central Americans are often described as fatalistic. They really have no option, when their weak and underfinanced governments have no spare capacity to meet a crisis without outside help which may or may not materialize.

The fundamental political problem is the traditional weakness of government, jealously fostered by those who fear strong rule, interrupted by the recurrent establishment of dictatorship as a method of achieving some movement. Yet, in a very real sense, both the fear of strong government and the urge to establish dictatorships are irrelevant. The most important changes in the daily lives of Central Americans during this century have taken place without reference to either. Improvements in medicine, transport, and communications, rural electrification, the spread of the sewing machine and the bicycle—all have been beyond the control of the region's governments. Paradoxically, the spread of such innovations has tended to increase, rather than decrease, the already existing contrasts between rich and poor.

There is also the problem of militarism. With the sole exception of Costa Rica, the armed forces of Central America have remained strong, to the extent that they have preempted the effective growth of political parties and organs of civilian participation, such as trade unions. Further, the armies are locked into a tradition that makes them fearful of cooperation with neighbouring states. Each sees the others as rivals and as convenient scapegoats for its own failures. The most striking example of this has been the long-standing Guatemalan claim to Belize, which was revived in the 1930s and which has blocked that colony's advance to full independence for more than a decade. Understandably, the citizens of Belize are unwilling to risk finding themselves under the control of an alien dictatorship. Accordingly, they have sought guarantees of safety, which Britain has not been able, and the U.S. has not been willing, to provide.

Because the change and ferment after World War II occurred during a period of U.S. hegemony in the region, the U.S. has been unable to avoid involvement in the troubles that have ensued. In the immediate postwar period, it was the target of unrealizable expectations. In the more recent period, it has been blamed on all sides for every political and economic shortcoming.

The Cuban Model. It has been noted that the first wave of unrest in the postwar period resulted directly from the impact of the ideas of the Allies, the Atlantic Charter, and the UN Declaration of Human Rights. The emergence of democracy was stifled by military officers of limited imagination. Most notable was the case of Guatemala (1954), where a right-wing revolt, aided by the Republican administration in Washington, effectively forestalled the possibility of a land reform that could have broadened the basis of ownership.

This incident was crucial in the radicalization of those who created the second wave of unrest in the area, this time centred on the Cuban revolution of 1959. Though the Cuban government does not appear to have assisted revolutionary movements in the mainland states directly, there can be no doubt of the effect of its example and its encouragement. Throughout the region, left-wing elements had been affected in some degree by the heady optimism of the early days. In Guatemala itself, not one but three guerrilla movements emerged seeking to emulate the Cuban example.

U.S. efforts to isolate Cuba after the "missile crisis" of 1962 received powerful support from the military regimes that had seized power in the area. In El Salvador in 1960 and in Guatemala and Honduras in 1963, military juntas had taken over in an effort to forestall what they saw as a threat to themselves and to their social and institutional position. Ironically, however, it was not until after U.S. interest had been diverted by the war in Vietnam and the problems of superpower rivalry that the local political elites found themselves with a virtually free hand. They took advantage of it to crack down ruthlessly, not only on armed dissent but on every sign of political opposition. Beginning between 1967 and 1973 in Guatemala, armed right-wing gangs appeared, bent on eliminating enemies of the government. They were subsequently imitated in El Salvador, where their activities culminated in 1980 with the assassination at mass of the outspoken Archbishop Oscar Romero of San Salvador.

The emergence of the new, independent states of the Commonwealth Caribbean actually helped to foster a rapprochement between the U.S. and Cuba itself. At the same time, the crisis in mainland Central America, where right-wing governments were now firmly entrenched, grew and spread. One special grievance was eliminated. In 1968 a left-wing military regime emerged in Panama dedicated to renegotiating the terms of the U.S. presence in the Canal Zone. Ten years later, climaxing the most successful diplomatic action of Pres. Jimmy Carter's administration, the U.S. Senate ratified an agreement transferring the Canal Zone back to Panama.

Meanwhile, the situation in Nicaragua had reached the breaking point. Exasperated beyond belief by the ruthless self-seeking of the Somoza regime, which had not stopped short even at profiting from the Managua earthquake, the citizens formed a coalition of all social groups and interests to overthrow the dictatorship. Months of fighting followed in city and countryside against the still-loyal forces of the National Guard before Somoza's regime was finally toppled in 1979. This event, and the expectation of real far-reaching social change under the new provisional government, in turn played a major part in bringing the crisis in El Salvador to a head. Certainly Somoza's fall marks the most important change in the political balance of the region in the last 36 years.

Elusive Unity. The future of the area in general, and of El Salvador in particular, is also closely bound up with the future of the most recent attempt to unify the region: the Central American Common Market (CACM), formed in 1960. Because the economies involved are very similar and the opportunities for diversification and trade are limited, the organization enjoyed only partial economic success during its first seven years. Nevertheless, in political terms, it did offer hope for better cooperation for the future.

Unfortunately, anger in El Salvador over the treatment of Salvadorans seeking work in Honduras, along with Honduran irritation over the pressure of Salvadoran immigration, led to the outbreak in 1969 of the "Soccer War," so called because feelings had been exacerbated by an international soccer match between the two nations. Despite the small size of the forces involved and the brief duration of the war—it lasted less than two weeks—some 2,000 people were killed. Honduras broke off all trade with El Salvador and seceded from the CACM, disrupting the delicate trade balance between the interlocked economies of the five nations and crippling the hopes for regional cooperation that the organization had begun to engender. Not until October 1980 was a peace treaty signed between the two countries.

It seems, therefore, that the future of Central America must be sought in diversity rather than in unity. This does not preclude restoration of the CACM. On the contrary, the organization could only benefit from increased diversity among its members. But, as so often before in Central America, politics has proved to be most powerful where most locally based, and generalizations about the future are likely to prove even more misleading than those about the past.

FOUNDATION FOR SURVIVAL

The desperate need for cooperation between North and South nations

by Brij Khindaria

The bone-jarring shocks dealt to the Western industrialized market economies in recent years have raised the spectre of a chain of periodic global recessions that could make the 1930s crash look like a storm in a teacup.

This may sound exaggerated, but it is the considered view of an alarming number of specialists. It has been voiced in such respected institutions as the International Monetary Fund (IMF), the World Bank, and the Organization for Economic Cooperation and Development. It is also the opinion of the Independent Commission on International Development Issues—known as the Brandt Commission from the name of its head, former West German chancellor Willy Brandt. In its 1980 report, "North-South: A Program for Survival," the prestigious independent panel paints an apocalyptic picture: "The world community faces much greater dangers than at any time since World War II. It is clear that the world economy is now functioning so badly that it damages both the immediate and longer-run interests of all nations."

Why has such a gloomy view taken hold among so many moderate and sober thinkers? At a time when humanity has such an unprecedented fund of knowledge and resources, why do economic crises proliferate, and why do people die of hunger, poor sanitation, or simple ignorance? There are no easy answers, but it is obvious that the economic crises of the West and the state of the world's less developed nations are intimately related.

Even a cursory analysis of the various stalemates in current international economic negotiations raises warning flags about likely economic upheavals if nations persist in beggar-thy-neighbour rivalry. These deadlocked negotiations are not only between poorer and richer nations ("South" and "North") but also between Western market economies and centrally planned economies and within those two groupings. The need is for boldness and enterprise—bold actions that break with tradition where necessary—to sustain the global economy by bringing equity to the world's three billion people in 120 underprivileged nations without damaging the richer Western and Eastern economies. In the words of the Brandt Commission: "The North-South debate is often described as if the rich nations were being asked to make sacrifices in response to the demands of the poor. We reject this view. The world is now a fragile and interlocking system, whether for its people, ecology or its resources. The world can become stronger by becoming a just and humane society. If it fails in this it will move towards its own destruction."

A World Economy on Its Knees. What has brought the world economy to its knees? Some of the answers lie in three crippling blows dealt to it in recent years, and especially in 1979 and 1980.

The worst was the realization that the leading industrial nations no longer know how to manage their internal economic affairs. Inflation and unemployment continue to spiral, spending on wages, salaries, and social welfare is reaching crippling proportions, unit costs of industrial outputs are rising, and severe jitters characterize foreign markets and foreign exchanges. Almost every government is reduced to patching up problems with stopgap measures. In this volatile environment, business and industry face extraordinary uncertainties and investment risks.

The effects of this drift in economic management were sharply aggravated by the oil price rises of 1979 and 1980. The oil price increases of 1973–74 were neutralized by subsequent gradual drops in real prices because of recession, inflation, and energy savings, but 1979's doubling of the real price for oil more than made up for lost ground. At the same time, there were growing fears of turmoil in the Gulf area, forestalling all Western efforts to bring some predictability to the pricing and supply policies of oil exporters.

Turmoil in the Third World. The second blow came from the growing inability of regimes in less developed countries, whatever their political colour, to maintain domestic law and order and industrial peace. With the overwhelming majority of their populations living in grinding poverty, third world governments cannot allow their people to think that

---

A writer on North-South relations and correspondent of the Financial Times *(London), Brij Khindaria is a specialist in the work of international organizations and the role of private enterprise in economic development.*

BRUNO BARBEY—MAGNUM

Western industrialized nations sell 40% of their exports to less developed countries.

their nation's resources are being exploited by foreign companies or governments. Within every less developed country lurks an ayatollah eager to wreak vengeance on governments seen to collude with foreign exploiters. As a result, Western governments and transnational corporations can no longer rely on sympathetic local regimes to protect their economic interests.

Internal social and economic tensions have also increased the risks of political instability in less developed countries, and the future seems bleaker still. UN agencies predict that less developed countries will contain at least 800 million destitute people and more than one billion unemployed by the year 2000. Clearly, the Western industrialized nations, which together sell 40% of their exports to less developed countries, stand to lose heavily from third world misery—even if by some miracle they manage to put their own economic houses in order.

The third blow for the global economy was the heightened tension between the Western allies, led by the U.S., and the Soviet bloc, especially following the Soviet occupation of Afghanistan in late 1979. As a result, the world is becoming an unsafe place for any less developed country wishing to play one bloc against the other to gain economic concessions. Each superpower is more willing to twist arms to get support, and neither hesitates to gain influence by encouraging destabilization of unsympathetic governments. Such interference can only lessen the ability of weak and mismanaged states to solve their economic problems. Again, the real loser is the world economy.

The North-South Dialogue. Given this background of strife, and uncertainty, how can the world's economic, social, and political systems be saved? Clearly, all parties must talk and keep talking, instead of retreating into autarchy and confrontation.

Many eminent world personalities, experts, and institutions have made suggestions for keeping international economic tensions within manageable proportions, and many of these suggestions have found their way into what has come to be known as the North-South dialogue. The North includes all the world's industrialized nations—both market and centrally planned economies. The South includes all the less developed countries, which in formal negotiations use the label Group of 77 (although the Group contains 119 states). The North-South talks are less a dialogue than a series of uncoordinated but formal negotiations on a bewildering variety of subjects—monetary, financial, and trade relations, the use of science and technology for development, food, health, education, transport, communication, and environmental issues.

Although it failed to produce a real breakthrough, 1980 was an active year in North-South negotiations. The most important event was a special session of the UN General Assembly held in New York City from August 25 to September 13. The session had two main aims. One was to establish a program for "global negotiations" on all problems in economic relations between less developed and industrialized countries. The other was to decide the shape of the International Development Strategy for the Third UN Development Decade (1980–90). Another significant conference was a joint meeting of the International Monetary Fund and the World Bank held in Washington, D.C., from September 29 to October 4. The meeting laid the foundation for substantive policy changes by the two institutions, both of which have become important forces for development in the past decade.

THE SPECIAL SESSION. The special session was a disappointment for all participants. It failed to decide on the topics for global negotiations, the forums where the negotiations should be held, how they should be organized, and how quickly they should be completed. Nor was the International Development Strategy approved, although substantive negotiations on it were completed.

The main reason for the failure was timing. In mid-1979, when the decision was taken to convene the special session, it appeared that the price of oil would continue to rise in real terms. The top priority of Western diplomats was to get OPEC (the Organization of Petroleum Exporting Countries) to talk, if not about pricing policies, at least about oil supplies. They had already scored some success in persuading several oil-importing less developed countries to think again about giving OPEC automatic diplomatic support. But recession in the West dashed third world hopes of gaining economic concessions, and third world solidarity again became a powerful slogan. This was especially true as OPEC steadfastly refused to discuss energy unless the West pledged to begin negotiations on all the South's economic demands.

An oil glut began to appear in the spring of 1980, and by the time the special session took place, OPEC had temporarily lost much of its ability to frighten the West. The West is understandably reluctant to demonstrate any unnecessary flexibility toward the South. Fulfillment of the South's demands would change the world's trade and monetary structures so fundamentally that the Western nations would lose control over the decision-making process. Hence, the Western attitude at the special session was one of slow-moving caution.

The key third world demand for more say in running the world's economy is a legitimate one, but placing a large part of economic decision-making power in the hands of 120 disparate and, in many cases, unstable nations carries incalculable dangers. The stability of the world economy depends heavily on Western economic health. Until economic links among the less developed countries become much stronger and more self-sustaining, every blow to the West is a blow to the less developed nations as well.

THE GLOBAL NEGOTIATIONS. At the special session India, speaking for the Group of 77, said the global negotiations should deal with all the "major issues in the fields of raw materials, energy, trade, development, money, and finance." The detailed agenda suggested by the Group of 77 ran to four pages and covered almost every imaginable issue. In contrast, the West suggested an agenda dealing only with food security, energy, and trade problems, including financing of balance of payments deficits. But the session never got around to discussing the agenda. It became deadlocked over how the global negotiations should be conducted.

Less developed countries want a powerful central body to initiate and monitor negotiations on various themes held in forums of its choice, including existing UN specialized agencies. The separate sets of talks would be closely coordinated, and the central body would hold final negotiations to reach a balanced package deal. Industrialized countries want to reduce any central body's role to a minimum and to hold decentralized negotiations in various specialized agencies without attempting to draw all the strands into a package.

The Group of 77's position is based on the disputable belief that simultaneous negotiation of such complex and disparate themes is feasible and that some kind of grand package deal can be achieved. It reflects the Group's eagerness to get as much as possible from the industrialized countries in return for any OPEC concessions on energy issues. With equal conceptual fuzziness, the industrialized countries want to limit the negotiations to the ills that most threaten their own economies or that they—rather than the third world—believe to be important for third world development.

THE INTERNATIONAL DEVELOPMENT STRATEGY. The International Development Strategy for the Third UN Development Decade, starting on Jan. 1, 1981, fell far short of third world objectives, mainly because Western governments felt they could not make long-term commitments while recession and economic distress prevailed at home.

The Strategy, which is not obligatory, sets modest goals. Industrialized countries are asked to raise official development assistance from the current average annual level of about 0.36% of gross national product (GNP) to 0.7% by 1985 and 1% by 1990. (The target in the 1970s Strategy, 0.7%, was surpassed by a few countries, although the average level for the 1970s was 0.31%.)

The goal for the less developed countries as a whole is to achieve an average yearly growth rate of 7% of gross domestic product (GDP). (The target in the previous Strategy was 6% and the rate actually achieved was 5.5%, although the poorer countries managed only 3.2%.) Exports should be increased by at least 7.5% each year and imports by at least 8%. (The 1970s target was 7% for both exports and imports; in actuality, exports rose by only 4.5% per year while imports increased by 9%.) The savings target is set at 24% of GDP per year by 1990 (compared with a 1970s target of 20% and actual savings of 21.5% in 1980). The target for growth of agricultural production is 4% per year, while that for manufacturing output is 9% (compared with targets of 4 and 8% in the 1970s and actual rates of 2.9 and 6.8%, respectively).

Issues Under Debate. Energy remains the most difficult problem for all oil-importing countries, less developed and developed, but it has never been discussed substantively at any North-South negotiation. Apart from its own problems with OPEC, the West has been trying to get OPEC to contribute more toward third world development. In fact OPEC has been more generous than the West in percentage terms, although the proportion fell from a 1975 peak of 2.7% of GNP to 1.28%, or $4.7 billion, in 1979. This was still small compared with the $27 billion increase in the poor countries' 1979 oil bill, however, and third world indebtedness (because of higher oil bills, more expensive manufactured imports from the West, and falling commodity prices) is an urgent problem.

FOREIGN DEBT. The foreign debt of oil-importing less developed countries stands at about $300 billion, compared with $114 billion in 1973. Many countries are so deeply in debt that interest payments and service charges alone swallow half their yearly export earnings. The less developed countries have had current account deficits averaging $30 billion, or 4% of their combined GNP, for six years running, and commercial banks are seriously concerned about the risk of default.

A major challenge facing the banking system is finding ways to relend to needy countries the $100 billion–$120 billion oil exporters are expected to place on world capital markets annually during the 1980s. The difficulty lies not in finding borrowers but in setting terms that do not slow their economic growth. The IMF, which lends to cover balance of payments deficits, is facing mounting third world criticism for placing onerous conditions on loans. Both the IMF and the World Bank are increasing their lending capabilities. The World Bank also has an energy development fund of $27 billion.

ENERGY. The energy outlook for less developed countries is bleak. According to World Bank estimates, their oil import bill rose from $7 billion in 1973 to $67 billion in 1980 and is expected to reach $124 billion in 1985 and $230 billion by 1990. The real energy crunch has not yet come. It will take shape in the 1980s when increasing industrialization in the third world gives rise to a much larger demand for commercial energy. To make more oil available to the third world at sensible prices, industrialized countries may have to make considerable changes in their life-styles.

If oil is beyond their reach, less developed countries may have to turn massively to nuclear energy. This conjures up a nightmare of dangers, ranging from poor security standards and unsafe waste disposal to uncontrollable proliferation of nuclear weapons.

FOOD. The UN Food and Agriculture Organization estimates that food aid must be increased to 18 million tons by 1985 from the current 10 million-ton level if widespread starvation is to be prevented. Less developed countries now buy 50 million tons of cereals each year, or two-thirds of total world imports, making them a force to be reckoned with for the cereal traders of the U.S., Canada, and Australia. Third world and Eastern European needs have converted food into a weapon, but it is double-edged. Thus the U.S. banned cereal exports to the Soviet Union as punishment for the Afghanistan invasion, but a drop in foreign demand means less income for North America's farmers.

TRADE. To help the poorer nations, both the European Economic Community and the U.S. have

A UN agency estimates that food aid to less developed countries will have to be increased by 80% by 1985 if malnutrition and starvation are to be alleviated.

UPI

elaborate schemes involving very low import duties on thousands of third world products. However, imports of third world-made manufactured goods are still discouraged by most Western nations because they compete with ailing domestic industries. This is the biggest problem in North-South trade.

The third world believes there is ample evidence to show that more people in industrialized countries have lost their jobs because of technological advances than because of cheap imports. Furthermore, one U.S. worker in 20 is employed because of trade with less developed countries. The third world also sells far fewer manufactured goods than it buys. Between 1970 and 1977, less developed country imports of such goods rose from $32 billion to $141 billion, while exports increased from $6 billion to $30.9 billion.

RAW MATERIALS. Raw materials account for almost all the exports of 19 less developed countries and for more than 85% of the exports of 76 others. Only seven less developed countries can claim that raw materials make up less than half their exports. So there is severe pressure on third world governments to seek better prices and to gain more control over raw material resources. Oil, copper, and bauxite have already been nationalized in most countries, and the UN Conference on Trade and Development (UNCTAD) is currently conducting negotiations to improve producers' incomes through international commodity arrangements for at least 18 major raw materials.

INDUSTRY AND TECHNOLOGY. The UN Industrial Development Organization estimates that official development assistance (ODA) must total at least $400 billion between now and the year 2000 if less developed countries are to obtain a 25% share of world manufacturing output, instead of the current 10%. Although it will be difficult to attain, the ODA figure constitutes less than 10% of total investment needed. Private investors find many less developed countries unattractive because of restrictive legislation, poor infrastructure, lack of skilled workers, and lack of legal protection for their technology. Yet without such help, third world markets will not become wealthy enough to buy more Western-made goods.

TRANSNATIONAL CORPORATIONS. The six countries that supply almost three-quarters of the third world's manufactured exports (South Korea, Hong Kong, Mexico, Singapore, Yugoslavia, and India) succeeded partly because of help from transnational corporations. Most less developed countries remain mistrustful of transnationals, however, because their power rivals that of many governments and because they are controlled from abroad. According to the UN Centre on Transnational Corporations, such companies now control almost one-third of all world production; in 1976 total sales of their foreign affiliates, at about $830 billion, nearly equaled the GNP of all oil-importing less developed countries. The UN is currently preparing an International Code of Conduct for Transnational Corporations.

ECONOMIC AND TECHNICAL COOPERATION. Less developed countries plan to hold several economic negotiations among themselves during the 1980s. The experience of the past decade has been that they have much to learn from one another, and they also wish to take advantage of each other's markets. Successful cooperation will help them gain bargaining power and correct historical distortions whereby many of them have better links with the West than with their neighbours.

Cooperation for Survival. How much money would make a difference in development? The Brandt Commission makes the following points: (1) One half of 1% of a year's total world military spending would pay for all the farm equipment needed to make the world's poorest countries self-sufficient in food by 1990. (2) Half a day's military expenditure would finance eradication of malaria in less developed countries. Even less could end onchocerciasis (river blindness), which debilitates millions in Africa. (3) The cost of one tank would provide 1,000 classrooms for 30,000 children. It could also protect 100,000 tons of rice from destruction by pests. (4) The price of one warplane could pay for 40,000 village pharmacies.

The third world already has more power than the industrialized countries are willing to admit. It lies in the teeming masses of human beings still living in misery, although their countries are crammed with natural resources and unexploited wealth. They are waiting to get their most basic human right—dignity—and their patience is wearing thin.

The Brandt Commission suggests some emergency measures to solve the most urgent problems. It calls for a summit of some 25 world political leaders to revive the faltering North-South dialogue and it suggests levying a tax on trade or air travel or arms transfers to ensure funds for development. To those who say that such an international tax would be unworkable, the commission replies that the same thing was said of the national income tax.

The financial and technical means to feed, clothe, and house all the world's people are available, but do we have the political will, intellectual genius, and humanitarian drive to do so?

Economic cooperation today is no longer a matter of philanthropy, or even of interdependence and mutual interest. It means our survival and that of the environment in which we live. Only bold moves can put the doomsday forecasters out of business.

PEOPLE OF THE YEAR

BIOGRAPHIES

The following is a selected list of men and women who influenced events significantly in 1980.

Abboud, A(lbert) Robert

The year 1980 was a bad one for the U.S. economy; many people lost their jobs. One of the most prominent of them was A. Robert Abboud, fired in April from his position as chairman of First Chicago Corp., parent company of the First National Bank of Chicago. Since Abboud's 1979 salary had been $263,985, his sufferings were primarily psychological. By August he had found employment as president and chief operating officer of Occidental Petroleum Corp., among the nation's largest industrial firms.

Abboud was dismissed from First National after the bank's earnings declined sharply. The nation's ninth largest bank, First National listed assets of $29.8 billion. According to his critics, Abboud had believed that interest rates, already high in 1979, would soon decline. Therefore, during the final months of 1979 he made many loans at fixed rates. When the interest rate rose steeply during the first months of 1980, reaching an unprecedented 20% at one point, those loans became unprofitable. Meanwhile, many savers withdrew their funds from First National to purchase higher yielding instruments. The bank had to borrow heavily in the expensive short-term money market, and profits fell.

Abboud's personality also appears to have caused his firing. His enemies called him "abrasive," claiming that he had a ferocious temper and blaming him for more than 200 executive-level resignations during his tenure as chairman. He delegated badly, they said, and created chaos.

In August Abboud provided a quite different version of events at the bank. When he had taken over in 1975, he said, First National was close to bankruptcy as a result of irresponsible loan policies. He wrote off the irrecoverable loans, clamped down on credit, and engineered what he called "the biggest turnaround in banking history."

Of Lebanese descent, A(lbert) Robert Abboud was born in Boston on May 29, 1929. After graduating from Harvard University in 1951, he served with the U.S. Marine Corps during the Korean War. He returned to Harvard for law and business degrees and then joined First National of Chicago as a management trainee. In ten years he rose to head its International Division. After serving as vice-president, Abboud became chairman in 1975.

(VICTOR M. CASSIDY)

Anderson, John Bayard

A major surprise in the 1980 campaign was John B. Anderson's strong showing in the early Republican primaries, which led to his independent candidacy for president.

Anderson started the long campaign as a respected but little-known ten-term congressman from Rockford, Ill., where he was born on Feb. 15, 1922. A conservative at the start of his political career, he stood out from the pack by taking liberal positions unpopular with the conservative constituency other GOP hopefuls were trying to attract. But he gained support from young people, independents, Democrats, and moderate Republicans. Many Democrats crossed over to vote for Anderson in the "open" primaries, enabling him to finish a strong second in Vermont, Massachusetts, and Illinois.

UPI

This encouraged Anderson to become an independent candidate, though he failed to win a single primary. Unlike previous independent or third-party candidates, he had no single issue to use as a rallying point. His "national unity" campaign was based on the idea that he offered a respectable alternative for those who could not accept Ronald Reagan or Jimmy Carter. Patrick Lucey, a Democrat and former Wisconsin governor, became Anderson's vice-presidential running mate.

Despite opposition from the Democrats, who feared he would take votes away from Carter, Anderson fought his way onto the ballot in all 50 states. The polls showed him at about 15% in early September and threatening to hurt Carter in the Midwest and Northeast. The League of Women Voters invited Anderson to participate in the first presidential debate in Baltimore, Md., which Carter avoided because of Anderson's presence.

Thereafter, Anderson's support began to decline as voters became convinced that he could not win. The campaign went heavily into debt and almost collapsed when Anderson was not included in the second and final presidential debate in late October. On election day, Anderson pulled 5.5 million votes, or 6.5% of the national total, which qualified him to receive $4 million in federal funds. Reagan overwhelmed Carter, and the so-called "Anderson factor" proved to be of little consequence. However, in the 20th century, only Theodore Roosevelt (1912), Robert La Follette (1924), and George Wallace (1968) had won higher popular vote percentages as independent or third-party candidates.

(HAL BRUNO)

Ballesteros, Severiano

In common with many fine Spanish golfers, Severiano Ballesteros entered the game as a caddie, at Santander in northern Spain. Born at Pedrena, near Santander, on April 9, 1957, he was one of four golfing brothers who were nephews of Ramón Sota, a professional golfer. Ballesteros turned professional in 1974 at the age of 17. Within a year it was clear that he had exceptional talent. In 1976 he led the European Order of Merit and delighted huge crowds at Birkdale by tying for second with Jack Nicklaus behind Johnny Miller in the British Open championship.

The power and flair of his golf, fearless play, and striking looks made Ballesteros the most exciting young golfer to emerge since Nicklaus was a similar age. He and Manuel Pinero won the World Cup for Spain in 1976, and he and Antonio Garrido repeated the feat the following year. During 1977 and 1978 Ballesteros remained the leading money winner in Europe and won tournaments in ten or more countries. These included Japan, Britain, New Zealand, and, most notably, the Greater Greensboro Open in the U.S., but he was not tempted to compete regularly on the U.S. circuit.

Ballesteros's career reached its first great peak when he won the 1979 British Open at Lytham, with Ben Crenshaw and Nicklaus three strokes behind, and became the youngest champion of the century. His victory was based on well-nigh uninhibited attack. Immense drives were unleashed, rarely finding fairways, but the rough was so trampled by the crowds that even the wildest shots were not costly, and his short game and putting were superb for their skill and confidence.

Many Americans claimed that he would have been nowhere on a course in the U.S. This was probably true, but he showed that he had the control and judgment to adapt his game at Augusta, Ga., in April 1980 with one of the most commanding victories in the history of the Masters. None of the established U.S. golfers was in sight of catching him. His driving was rarely wild, and his approach shots and putting were almost faultless.

At that time Ballesteros's horizons seemed limitless, but unfortunately he mistook his starting time for the second round of the 1980 U.S. Open and was disqualified. This was a setback, and later he did not excel in the British Open. In five years, however, he had won £230,000 official money in Europe. (P. A. WARD-THOMAS)

Bani-Sadr, Abolhassan

JACQUES HAILLOT—CAMERA PRESS

Abolhassan Bani-Sadr was elected first president of the Islamic Republic of Iran on Jan. 25, 1980, with 75% of the popular vote. The nation's religious leader, Ayatollah Ruhollah Khomeini, administered the oath of office on February 4. Two days later Khomeini appointed Bani-Sadr chairman of the Revolutionary Council, Iran's policy-making body. As president of the republic Bani-Sadr was appointed commander in chief of the armed forces on February 19.

Bani-Sadr's presidency was an uphill struggle against enemies in the clergy seeking to reduce him to a figurehead and also against inexperienced departmental executives. He was forced to accept Mohammad Ali Raja'i (*q.v.*), not a man of his choice, as prime minister on August 11, and soon the two men were at odds, the president refusing to accept one-third of the prime minister's Cabinet nominations. A climax was reached on October 31, when Bani-Sadr wrote Khomeini a letter (first published in Stockholm on December 8) complaining that his incompetent ministers were a greater danger than Iraq's aggression (begun on September 22) and that their rivalries should be stopped before Iran lost both the war and the revolution; the president also noted that he had warned of the worsening economy and of the need to reorganize the armed forces, without avail. Some indignant members of the Majlis (parliament) on December 16 demanded his punishment for revealing "military secrets."

Bani-Sadr was born on March 22, 1933, at Hamaden, a village near Abadan, the younger son of Ayatollah Seyed Nasrollah Bani-Sadr. He studied theology and economics at the University of Teheran and spent four years at the Institute of Social Research. He was a leader of the antishah student movement in the early 1960s and was imprisoned twice for political activities. Wounded in the unsuccessful uprising of June 1963, he emigrated to France, where he continued his studies and also taught at the Sorbonne in Paris. A fervent Islamic nationalist and revolutionary economist, he began to publish the results of his studies in the early 1970s.

Bani-Sadr joined Khomeini's entourage during the latter's exile in France, and the two returned to Iran together on Feb. 1, 1979. Bani-Sadr was appointed deputy minister of economy and finance in Mehdi Bazargan's government in July 1979 and became full minister in November of that year. In August and September 1980 the president was fortunate to escape injury in two helicopter crashes near the Iraq frontier. (K. M. SMOGORZEWSKI)

Beatrix, Queen

In a broadcast to the Dutch nation on Jan. 31, 1980, Queen Juliana of The Netherlands, who had reigned since September 1948, announced her intention to abdicate in favour of her eldest daughter, Crown Princess Beatrix. Three months later, on April 30, Beatrix was crowned queen at a special session of both houses of Parliament.

Beatrix Wilhelmina Armgard, princess of Orange-Nassau and of Lippe-Biesterfeld, was born at Soestdijk Palace in Baarn on Jan. 31, 1938, the first child of the then Crown Princess Juliana and Prince Bernhard of Lippe-Biesterfeld. After the outbreak of World War II, the royal family in May 1940 took refuge in England. Princess Juliana and her daughters Beatrix and Irene then went to Ottawa, where they stayed throughout the war.

After the German surrender the family returned to The Netherlands in August 1945. Beatrix enrolled in 1956 as a student at the State University of Leiden. She attended lectures and tutorials in sociology, jurisprudence, economics, parliamentary history, and current international affairs, and was graduated in 1961.

On June 28, 1965, Queen Juliana and Prince Bernhard announced the engagement of Beatrix to a West German diplomat, Claus von Amsberg. The following November Parliament passed a bill authorizing the marriage—a procedure necessitated by a provision in the constitution that excluded from the succession all members of the ruling dynasty and their descendants who married without the consent of Parliament. Princess Beatrix's choice of a former member of Hitler's army displeased many Dutch people, but within a short time von Amsberg succeeded in winning the sympathy of a great number of them. Although the marriage ceremony in Amsterdam on March 10, 1966, was accompanied by widespread and violent demonstrations, these were mainly directed against prevailing political and social conditions and probably only to a lesser degree reflected opposition to the marriage. There were also some antimonarchist demonstrations during Beatrix's coronation, but when the couple later toured The Netherlands, they were received everywhere with great enthusiasm.

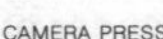

CAMERA PRESS

Queen Beatrix and Prince Claus had three children: Prince Willem-Alexander Claus George Ferdinand (born April 27, 1967); Prince Johan Friso Bernhard Christiaan David (born Sept. 25, 1968); and Prince Constantijn Christof Frederik Aschwin (born Oct. 11, 1969). (DICK BOONSTRA)

Beckwith, Charles A.

He is something of a mystery to the country he serves, as is the U.S. Army unit he commands. The unit, formed in 1977 and called "Blue Light," is an elite antiterrorist outfit based at Ft. Bragg, North Carolina. Its commander is Col. Charles A. Beckwith, a tough, gravel-voiced combat veteran, who in 1980 led an attempt to rescue the Americans being held hostage at the U.S. embassy in Teheran, Iran.

For much of his career Beckwith specialized in commando operations and "special warfare," assignments that made him a rather shadowy figure in the army hierarchy. When journalists tried to find out something about him in the wake of the rescue attempt in Iran, the Army's records department would provide only the following: Born Jan. 22, 1929. Attended college. Commissioned 1952. Assignment "classified." Serial number 258–364046.

Despite such secrecy some details of Beckwith's career have surfaced. He entered the Army in 1953 and was an early volunteer for the Special Forces. As a major in Vietnam in the 1960s, he became commander of the "Delta Project," several hundred Indochinese troops under the direction of the Special Forces. On one operation with the unit, Beckwith was seriously wounded; he impressed a field surgeon with his toughness when he sat up in his litter and demanded immediate trauma treatment because, he said, "I'm bleeding to death."

"He was right," the surgeon was quoted as saying later. "A few more minutes and he would have been dead."

After his service in Vietnam, Beckwith was assigned to the Special Warfare School at Ft. Bragg and was named commander of Blue Light. When the attempt to free the hostages was made in April, Beckwith was the assault commander. With about 90 of his Blue Light troops, he helicoptered at night to a spot in the Iranian desert, from which the next phase of the assault on Teheran was to have been launched.

But then things started to go wrong. Three of the eight RH–53 Sea Stallion helicopters developed mechanical problems. One chopper collided on the ground with a C–130 cargo plane, which exploded in flames. Eight men were killed and five injured, and the hostages remained hostages. But criticism of the operation did not seem to touch on Beckwith himself, and he faded back into his customary obscurity.

(STANLEY W. CLOUD)

Beheshti, Ayatollah Mohammad Hossein

The strong man of the Islamic Republic of Iran in 1980 was Ayatollah ("Gift of God," a religious term of honour) Mohammad Hossein Beheshti. A member of Iran's Islamic Revolutionary Council given power on Feb. 3, 1979, by Ayatollah Ruhollah Khomeini shortly after his return from France, Beheshti was appointed the council's "first secretary." In the Majlis (parliament) inaugurated on May 28, 1980, he led the Islamic Republican Party (IRP), the religiously oriented party which, with its supporters, formed the most important and most cohesive group in that body.

Of the total of 270 seats in the Majlis, some 225 were filled as of November 1980. About 70 of the deputies were card-carrying members of the IRP, and another 60 usually followed its lead. The other principal group consisted of some 50 deputies, including former nationalist supporters of Mehdi Bazargan, a pupil of the Iranian leader Mohammad Mosaddeg and prime minister in 1979, and followers of Pres. Abolhassan Bani-Sadr (*q.v.*). The remaining 40-odd deputies were either Mujaheddin (Islamic socialists), Fedayin (secular Marxists), or members of the Tudeh ("Masses") Party—Communists faithful to Soviet orders who, provisionally, were supporting the ayatollahs. Since Ayatollah Hashemi Rafsanjani, the speaker of the Majlis, was effectively the number two man in the IRP, Behesti had no serious difficulty defeating his rivals.

Born in 1929, Beheshti was tall and vigorous, with a heavy pepper-and-salt beard and a hawk nose. Reputed to be a cunning manipulator behind the scenes, he was a good public speaker and behaved in a magisterial manner when dealing with both equals and subordinates. In the 1960s he served as a mullah to Iranian Muslim students in West Germany, and he could speak German and English fluently.

(K. M. SMOGORZEWSKI)

Belaúnde Terry, Fernando

Winner of two consecutive elections, Fernando Belaúnde Terry returned in 1980 to the presidency of Peru after a 12-year hiatus. His first victory, in 1963, had been supported by the military, but five years later a junta forced him from office and into exile. After ten years spent teaching in the U.S., he returned to Lima in 1978. When elections were scheduled for 1980, Belaúnde joined a 12-man field, won 43% of the vote, and took the oath of office on July 28.

He took over a government that had been brought by two military juntas to the brink of chaos. The first, led by Gen. Juan Velasco Alvarado, had pursued some of Belaúnde's own policies and distributed hacienda land among one-third of the nation's peasants. But agricultural production soon plummeted, and country people swarmed to the cities. Velasco nationalized the Exxon Corp. subsidiary International Petroleum Co. and gave workers part ownership of many industries. These and other measures eventually led to runaway inflation, unmanageable short-term foreign debt, and huge losses by state companies and farm cooperatives.

Another coup expelled Velasco in 1975, and the new junta hired able civilians to clean up the economic mess. New exploitation of Amazon jungle oil fields brought petroleum independence and fueled the export trade. A government austerity program reduced inflation but also cut consumer income and strangled employment rates.

During his second campaign Belaúnde repeated many of his earlier pledges. He promised to attract foreign investment, increase agricultural production, and accelerate industrial output in order to create one million new jobs.

Belaúnde was born in Lima on Oct. 7, 1912. His great-grandfather had been president of Peru and his grandfather finance minister. His father, ambassador to both Chile and Mexico, had also served as prime minister. Belaúnde was serving in the Chamber of Deputies when his father's government was overthrown in 1948. Eight years later he founded the Popular Action party and became a national leader in his own right.

(PHILIP KOPPER)

Benn, Tony

In the turmoil that divided Britain's Labour Party in 1980, Tony Benn emerged as the acknowledged if still unofficial and unelected leader of the party's radical populist left. He did not contest the election for a new leader of the parliamentary Labour Party after the resignation of James Callaghan. His reason was that he had been instrumental in persuading the Labour Party conference in October to abandon the traditional practice of having the new leader elected by Labour members of Parliament in favour of a new electoral college system that would give a voice to grass-roots party activists and trade unionists. Benn preferred to wait for the electoral college system to be set up. In a challenge for the leadership, he could expect greater support from the grass roots than from his fellow MP's. Those fellow MP's, in fact, failed to reelect him to the "shadow cabinet" in December.

During the 1970s he had become the most influential of left-wing thinkers in the Labour Party. He set out his ideas in a book called *Arguments for Socialism*, published in 1979. In his view, Britain's consensus-based, Keynesian, managed welfare state economy had collapsed. The "democratic socialism" he offered would involve a large measure of public investment, public expenditure, and public ownership combined with self-management in the workplace and open (as opposed to secretive) government. He regarded this as "a home-grown British product," distinct from both capitalism and Communism.

Benn, a fierce critic of the British class system, came from a prosperous middle-class family himself. His father was a Liberal and then a Labour MP who ended up in the House of Lords as Viscount Stansgate. Benn inherited the peerage on his death and waged a long fight to rid himself of a title that disqualified him from sitting in the House of Commons. Later he also shed the names with which he was christened, Anthony Wedgwood, to become plain Tony Benn, and withdrew his entry from *Who's Who* (which disclosed a private school and Oxford University education).

Born on April 3, 1925, Benn was the youngest MP when first elected to Parliament in 1950. He was a Cabinet minister in the Labour governments of 1966–70 and 1975–79 and had been a member of the Labour Party's national executive committee for more than 20 years.

(HARFORD THOMAS)

Blake, Eubie

To say that Eubie Blake has had a remarkable career would be an understatement; it would be far closer to the truth to say that he has had *several* remarkable careers. He has worked at various times over the years as a pianist, singer, composer, vaudeville performer, musical director, recording artist, concert and jazz-festival performer, record-company founder, and talk-show

KATHERINE YOUNG

guest. No less remarkable was the fact that Blake in 1980 at the age of 97 was still active musically, playing the piano a number of hours each day in his Brooklyn, N.Y., home and even performing occasionally in public.

James Hubert Blake was born on Feb. 7, 1883, in Baltimore, Md., the son of former slaves. He demonstrated an early talent for music, and his formal instruction in piano and organ included rigorous training in the classics. But the young Blake developed a passion for ragtime, which his mother considered indecent music and forbade him to play at home. So he went elsewhere to perform, making his first public appearance at one of Baltimore's notorious sporting houses at the age of 15.

In 1915 he formed a prolific and long-standing partnership with singer/lyricist Noble Sissle. After touring the vaudeville circuit for a number of years, the pair scored a triumph in 1921 with *Shuffle Along*, the first Broadway musical to be composed, produced, directed, and performed solely by blacks. They followed this success with *Elsie* in 1923 and *Chocolate Dandies* the next year. Their compositions included such favourites as "Love Will Find a Way" and "I'm Just Wild About Harry." Blake also scored the music for *Blackbirds of 1930*, which starred the famous black performer Ethel Waters.

From the 1930s to the 1950s Blake experienced diminishing popularity, but he and his music returned to prominence with the release of several recordings during the 1950s and 1960s. He then launched a series of appearances that included concerts and jazz festivals throughout the U.S. and Europe. He crowned this revival of interest in his music with a triumphant return to Broadway with *Eubie!*, a show based on *Shuffle Along* that opened to popular and critical acclaim in 1978. (BASCO ESZEKI)

Brett, George

In a race for the division championship that provoked yawns, George Brett was opening mouths in amazement. The Kansas City Royals' third baseman was ringing baseball's chimes with a startling .400 batting average as September 1980 began, a time when fans otherwise would have looked at the Royals' 20-game lead in the American League's West Division and left wake-up calls for October. Nobody had batted .400 that late in a season since Ted Williams finished at .406 in 1941. Williams is still the last .400 hitter for a full season, but Brett's average did not fall below that mark until September 20 and his .390 finish was the best in 39 years.

"Brett is probably the best player in the game today," according to Minnesota Twins manager Gene Mauch.

Brett also drove in 118 runs in 117 games; scored 87 runs; hit 33 doubles, 9 triples, and 24 home runs; led the league with a .664 slugging percentage; and won the American League's most valuable player award. His streak of 30 games with at least one hit was the longest of the year. After seven full seasons he had become the only player besides Ty Cobb to lead the American League three times in both hits and triples. Although the left-handed hitter lacked exceptional speed, his .294 average in 1978 was his only dip below .300 since 1975.

Brett was born May 15, 1953, in Glendale, W.Va., and grew up in Hermosa Beach, Calif. He is the youngest of four sons, all of whom played professional baseball. Brett was 14 when his brother Ken pitched for Boston in the 1967 World Series. They were together in 1980 when Ken pitched for Kansas City.

The exclamation point on Brett's astonishing season was a decisive three-run home run in the third game of the American League championship series against the New York Yankees, whom Kansas City beat three games to zero. Brett holds a league record with six home runs in championship series, but previous important homers had not kept New York from winning series against the Royals in 1976, 1977, and 1978.

Brett started only 113 of Kansas City's 162 regular-season games, but the injuries that sidelined him also illustrated his value. The Royals had a won-lost record of 74–39 when Brett started and 23–26 when he did not. During the World Series, which Kansas City lost to Philadelphia, Brett needed hemorrhoid surgery. (KEVIN M. LAMB)

Bush, George

Some conservatives were unhappy when Ronald Reagan (*q.v.*) chose George Bush to be his vice-presidential running mate on the 1980 Republican ticket, but Bush's appeal to middle-of-the-road voters helped create the Reagan landslide.

The polls did not give Bush much chance in May 1979, when he announced that he would be among those challenging Reagan for the GOP nomination. He had held many top government jobs and was well known in party circles, but he was relatively unknown to the general public. He worked long and hard to build name identification. He also recruited an excellent campaign organization, which enabled him to upset Reagan in the Iowa precinct caucuses and become an instant "front-runner." But that ended abruptly when Reagan came back to win the New Hampshire primary.

Bush stayed in the race long after the other challengers quit. He won major primaries in Pennsylvania and Michigan, demonstrating that he could attract voters in the vital northern industrial states. He was a logical choice to balance the ticket, but his opposition had angered Reagan while his moderate stance on many issues antago-

BILL HARRISON—SPECTRUM

nized the GOP right wing. But after Reagan's unsuccessful attempt to get former president Gerald Ford to be his running mate, the shocked Detroit convention learned that Bush had been chosen.

Bush was born June 12, 1924, in Milton, Mass., the son of Prescott Bush, a wealthy investment banker and U.S. senator. After graduation from Yale University, he began selling oil-drilling equipment in Texas and later founded his own company. He became involved in Texas politics and served two terms in Congress (1967–71) between unsuccessful tries for the Senate. Pres. Richard Nixon appointed Bush ambassador to the UN. In 1974 he became Republican national chairman, helping the embattled GOP survive Watergate. Ford named Bush to head the first U.S. liaison office in Beijing (Peking) and then to be director of the Central Intelligence Agency. (HAL BRUNO)

Carter, Billy

It began, perhaps, as just another sibling rivalry: the younger brother—unappreciated, resentful—taking his revenge on the prim, proper, and overachieving firstborn. But in this case, the older brother, Jimmy Carter, was president of the United States. From the day Jimmy Carter was elected in 1976, it was clear that brother Billy would be a problem. While Jimmy was trying to live down the redneck image of the white Southerner, Billy appeared to revel in it.

Things might have remained at that relatively harmless level except that Billy Carter became involved with a foreign government—the regime of Libya's Muammar al-Qaddafi—whose relations with the U.S. were, at best, strained. In 1978 Billy Carter became Libya's most prominent American apologist. However, the case did not achieve the status of a major political issue until July 14, 1980, when papers were filed in federal court revealing that Billy Carter had agreed "under protest" to register as a Libyan agent and admitted receiving $220,000 from Qaddafi's government. (Billy claimed the money was a "loan" and that he had only a business relationship with Libya as an oil broker for a U.S. firm, Charter Oil Co.) Questions immediately arose about the extent of the president's knowledge of Billy's activities and whether they had affected U.S. foreign policy.

After a series of public hearings, a subcommittee of the Senate Judiciary Committee concluded that while Libya had sought out Billy in hopes of influencing the U.S., that hope soon faded. The subcommittee's report, which was also critical of the president's and the administration's handling of the case, said: "[Billy Carter's] conduct was contrary to the interests of . . . the United States and merits severe criticism."

William Alton Carter III was born March 29, 1937, in Plains, Ga. In 1979, in the midst of his dealings with Libya, he entered an alcoholic rehabilitation centre in California. Neither that experience nor the furor over his Libya connection seemed to dampen his determination to remain independent of his brother. For his part, the president was tolerant and stoic, but when he was defeated for reelection on November 4, some observers thought the voters, in some measure, had responded to the antics of his younger brother. (STANLEY W. CLOUD)

Carter, Jimmy

James Earl Carter, Jr., the once-obscure Georgia politician whose skillful use of the "trust" issue in 1976 helped him win election as the 39th president of the United States, went down to swift and overwhelming defeat in 1980. Seeking reelection to a second term, Democrat Carter was beaten by his Republican opponent, Ronald Reagan (*q.v.*), in an electoral vote landslide.

In some important respects Carter was defeated by a mirror image of himself. Like Carter four years earlier, Reagan hammered away in his campaign at bureaucratic inefficiency and waste, portraying himself as an untainted outsider who would come to Washington to clean up the mess, defeat the twin economic devils of unemployment and inflation, and restore faith in the U.S. at home and abroad.

UPI

Faced with such an opponent, Carter again appealed to the voters' trust, suggesting repeatedly that Reagan was too "dangerous" a man to have a finger on the nuclear trigger. In the end, however, it seemed clear that Reagan's easygoing manner—which he put to especially good use a week before the election when the two candidates were televised in their only face-to-face debate—was reassuring even to many Democrats.

Carter's defeat apparently ended a remarkable chapter in U.S. political history. The rise of this Plains, Ga., peanut farmer first to the governorship of his state and then to the presidency captured the imagination of a nation and proved Carter's intelligence, determination, and ambition.

Yet, as president, he seemed to lack something crucial. Despite his more or less successful attempts to push through, for example, a national energy policy, significant environmental legislation, and civil service reform—and despite his dramatic role as catalyst for the historic Camp David peace agreement between Israel and Egypt—Carter never seemed able to build a solid constituency or harness the national will. The storming of the U.S. embassy in Teheran by Islamic radicals one year to the day before the 1980 election and the holding of U.S. hostages there caused many to question Carter's ability to employ power effectively. Moreover, the fact that most of the hostages were still in captivity on election day undoubtedly underscored Reagan's portrayal of Carter as weak and uncertain. (STANLEY W. CLOUD)

Chan, Sir Julius

Sir Julius Chan became prime minister of Papua New Guinea in March 1980, shortly after he was knighted. Ignoring the hint that knighthood implied retirement from active politics, he defeated on the floor of Parliament his old colleague, Michael T. Somare (who had led Papua New Guinea since its independence five years earlier).

Chan had served his political apprenticeship in colonial Papua New Guinea. He was first elected to the old Legislative Council in 1968, when the territory was totally under Australian control. He had no trace of xenophobia, however. His education by Roman Catholic Marist brothers at Ashgrove, Queensland, gave him a sympathetic concern for his nearest ally's viewpoint. His sympathy was reinforced by the need to keep Western investors interested in Papua New Guinea and its nearest neighbour, Indonesia, at arm's length.

Chan's accession to national leadership marked the end of a shrewd campaign that began when he brought the People's Progress Party into a government coalition with Somare's Pangu Party at the time of independence and became deputy prime minister. He soon withdrew from the coalition, however, feeling that he was not given a sufficient role in government and that, despite his well-known financial expertise, his advice was too often disregarded. On becoming prime minister he followed a policy of consultation with his ministers and included, in his Cabinet, radicals like John Kaputin, Somare's minister of planning and development, as well as conservatives. His first policy statements recognized the problems of Papua New Guinea's strategic location and ethnic pluralism. He was also at pains to emphasize the stability of democratic institutions and continuity in government policy and administration under his new regime.

Chan was born on Aug. 29, 1939, on Tanga Island in the northern islands of Papua New Guinea, of mixed Chinese and Papua New Guinea extraction. His family had plantation, shipping, and trading interests. He characterized his takeover as a "friendly and constitutional change of government at a time when our country needs new leaders and new ideas to keep moving ahead." (A. R. G. GRIFFITHS)

Charles, Mary Eugenia

"I don't believe in women's liberation because in Dominica women are the strongest part of society. We don't have to put up a fight for recognition." So said the Caribbean's first female prime minister, Eugenia Charles, after her Freedom Party's landslide victory in Dominica's first post-independence election on July 21.

Her remarks were typical of her strong-willed and determined approach to life and to politics. Her first involvement in active politics came in 1968, when she and a broad-based group known as "Freedom Fighters" came together to oppose legislation curtailing freedom of the press. Eventually the group formed itself into the Dominica Freedom Party and, initially against her wishes, Eugenia Charles became party leader. Politically, she was most commonly described as a conservative, but in reality she was probably more of a centrist. She favoured social welfare programs and limited state intervention but clearly opposed the more left-wing regional interpretations of socialism.

She was a strict constitutionalist and a skilled debater in Parliament. She provoked much anger when, as leader of the opposition, she spoke courageously against the government's excesses and especially its business dealings in 1979 with the South African government. But behind such resoluteness was a quiet individual who apparently enjoyed "cooking and being with friends."

Eugenia Charles was born in Pointe Michel, Dominica, in 1919 and was educated locally and in Grenada. She graduated in law from the University of Toronto, was called to the bar at the Inner Temple, London, and studied juvenile delinquency at the London School of Economics. She was elected to the then House of Assembly in 1970. From 1975 she served as leader of the opposition. In addition to her political activities, she was a director of the Fort Young Hotel and Dominica Cooperative Bank and had a busy legal practice. Unmarried, she lived with her 104-year-old father, reputedly the oldest man in the Caribbean. (DAVID A. JESSOP)

Chun Doo Hwan

For almost ten months after the October 1979 assassination of South Korea's long-time president Park Chung Hee, government leadership in the country remained in a state of flux. By August 1980, however, it became clear that a relatively obscure offi-

KIMCHON-KIL—CAMERA PRESS

cer, Lieut. Gen. Chun Doo Hwan, was working his way to the top in ways identical to those Park himself had used two decades earlier.

First, he took charge of the investigation when his mentor was shot dead and arrested all suspects, including his own nominal superior, Army Chief of Staff Gen. Chung Seung Hwa. Then, heading a group of younger officers, he took control of the military in a coup. He was also promoted to full general. Like Park he let a figurehead, Pres. Choi Kyu Hah, stay in office for almost a year while he himself remained chairman of a special committee wielding all power. On August 27, five days after formally retiring from the Army, Chun was elected president of the country.

Chun was born Jan. 18, 1931, as the sixth of nine children in a rural family in Naechonri in southeastern Korea. His father, a farmer of modest means, was said to have given intensive tutoring to his children in Confucian ideals. After graduation from the Taegu technical high school in 1951, in the middle of the Korean War, Chun entered the Korean Military Academy. He was in the first class to receive the full four-year course of instruction. He emerged an infantry officer and, after four years in front-line rifle units, joined the Special Forces in the U.S.

Quick promotions marked his subsequent career. He commanded the White House Division in Vietnam and was at different times chief of the Capital Garrison Command in Seoul, commander of the famed 1st Airborne Special Forces Group and later of the 1st Infantry Division, and, from March 1979, commanding general of the Defense Security Command. The post was to prove the springboard to political power.

Chun, respected in Korean military circles for his professional competence and reputation for honesty, was a nationalist steeped in his country's traditional virtues. A soccer enthusiast, he captained the Military Academy team. In 1958 he married Lee Soon Ja, daughter of Brig. Gen. Lee Kyu Dong, then chief of staff of the Military Academy. (T. J. S. GEORGE)

Church, Sam, Jr.

When Sam Church, Jr., was a boy, homes in the West Virginia coal country boasted pictures of three heroes: Jesus, Franklin D. Roosevelt, and John L. Lewis. The president of the United Mine Workers, Lewis had improved the miner's lot and made the UMW a power in national economic and political affairs. Stepping down after four decades as president, he was succeeded by a protégé, W. A. "Tony" Boyle, who was found guilty of the murder of a reform candidate for the presidency after a disputed election between the two men.

The U.S. Department of Labor supervised new elections, and reform candidate Arnold Miller won the top job in 1972. But he proved to be an inept administrator and negotiator who was unable to keep wildcat strikes from closing unionized mines. The UMW lost members, influence, and effectiveness. Then Miller suffered his second heart attack in late 1979 and resigned. He was succeeded on Nov. 16, 1979, by Sam Church, Jr., his vice-president and executive assistant, who was the son of a disabled miner and for eight years a miner himself.

At the first national union convention Church chaired, the membership gave him several votes of confidence. He won the right to name his own vice-president, and his proposal to double union dues was approved. The rank and file were clearly willing to trade some local autonomy for better national representation and effective leadership.

Early in 1980 Church began hiring the first of 100 new organizers to rebuild union membership. He also began amassing a strike fund worthy of the name. With new contracts in the offing, he meant to go to the bargaining table with the wherewithal to call strikes selectively. Observers expected him "to play off company against company" in the time-honoured Lewis tradition.

Forbes and other business journals cautiously applauded his election, believing he would restore discipline and end the wildcat strikes. Church says he enjoys management's respect because "I don't throw them the curves and I don't consider them the enemy. . . . Both the union and the industry have a job to do and that is to produce coal."

Born on Sept. 20, 1936, in Matewah, W.Va., Church attended college briefly and then went to work in a Baltimore, Md., sugar warehouse. He went to the mines in 1965 and held a series of local union jobs before being called to union headquarters in 1975. (PHILIP KOPPER)

Cook, Betty

As 1980 drew to a close, a 58-year-old Californian tidied up the Newport Beach marine-engine and powerboat ship, kissed the grandchildren goodbye, and then headed for Australia to defend the world ocean racing title. World champion in 1977 and 1979, Betty Cook also won U.S. titles in 1978 and 1979. Like the hairy-chested men who once dominated this notoriously expensive sport, she has set records, been knocked unconscious, and broken more than one rib while driving a powerboat in weather battleships avoid. But as she finished packing, she confessed she'd be playing catch-up ball in Australia. That was because she spent so much time in 1980 at something besides piloting upward of 1,500 horsepower through and over rough seas in the neighbourhood of 145 kph (90 mph).

Cook, who did postgraduate work at Massachusetts Institute of Technology three decades earlier, was close to launching a prototype boat with a revolutionary stern-drive and inboard-engine package. Nearly 75% lighter than conventional systems, her surprisingly efficient model uses less gas and horsepower to deliver the same high speeds and performance. The secret, she said in an interview, lies in the fact that the vertically trimmable propeller operates two-thirds out of the water.

Growing up in Glens Falls, N.Y., Cook started ballet at the age of five to please her mother and also played sandlot baseball to her father's delight. After earning a political science degree at Boston University, she moved to studies at MIT, married another student, put him through school and took a back seat while raising two boys.

In 1974, having tired of serving as hostess while her husband, Paul, raced powerboats, she entered a 96-km (60-mi) race with him as crewman and won four trophies. She was on her way toward international competition. By 1980 she was racing two boats, a twin-engined catamaran and a monohull, both called "Kaama" (after an antelope encountered in a crossword puzzle) and both crewed by a throttleman and navigator. (PHILIP KOPPER)

Craig, Jim

Jim Craig was giving one last tug on the nation's heartstrings. The United States had just defeated Finland 4–2, winning its first Olympic gold medal in ice hockey since 1960. Craig's teammates were a pantomime of pandemonium on television sets throughout his country. But Craig was at the side of the rink, scanning the stands, and the words millions of Americans saw on his lips were, "Where's my father?"

For weeks, strangers asked Craig if he had found his father. "That impressed me," he said. "People really cared." In a country so cool toward ice hockey that its professional National Hockey League does not have a network television contract, people rallied for two weeks around the amateur stickhandlers who helped them forget about the embarrassment of Iranians holding American hostages and the danger of the Soviet troops in Afghanistan. Indeed, the gold-medal victory against Finland February 24 was somewhat of an anticlimax after the U.S. team had defeated the Soviet Union 4–3 two nights before.

In that victory goalie Craig made 36 saves against the same players who had consistently beaten NHL all-star teams. As he did so often, he shut out his opponents in the final period, when the U.S was overcoming a 3–2 deficit.

It was the youngest U.S. Olympic hockey team ever. Craig, born May 31, 1957, in North Easton, Mass., had just finished college. His Boston University team had been national champion in 1978, and he had been an all-American as a senior in 1979, completing his college career with a three-year record of 55 wins, 6 losses, and 3 ties. But for two weeks in February, the rest of the country knew little of Craig's past record. It knew him as an outstanding hockey player and a loving son who greeted his father after games and who missed his mother. She had died three years earlier. Toward the end of the Finland game, Craig was thinking about how proud she would have been. So when it ended, he had to make eye contact with his father.

That done, he joined his teammates at centre ice, accepted the gold medal, and unwound by dancing on the Lake Placid, N.Y., rink, kissing his medal, and waving his index finger. Within a week he was playing for the NHL Atlanta Flames in their first home sellout of the season, and on June 2 he was traded to his hometown Boston Bruins. (KEVIN M. LAMB)

Doe, Samuel Kanyon

Master Sgt. Samuel Doe became Liberia's head of state in April 1980 after leading an attack by enlisted men on the Executive Mansion and killing Pres. William R. Tolbert, Jr. (*see* OBITUARIES); 13 prominent personalities identified with Tolbert were later summarily tried and executed. The coup by underprivileged soldiers extinguished the country's century-old Americo-Liberian political system.

Doe's action was inspired by political developments after the Easter riots of 1979 over a substantial increase in the price of rice, the country's staple food. The Army was used to put down the demonstrations, which they did with great violence. Doe and a few of his co-conspirators were unhappy about their role in suppressing the demonstrations and subsequently made contact with the two radical groups opposed to the Tolbert regime, the Movement for Justice in Africa (MOJA) and the People's Progressive Party (PPP). Doe himself visited the prisons where those arrested in the demonstrations were being held. He also began to attend classes at the Marcus Garvey Institute, where most of the teaching was done by MOJA sympathizers.

WERNER GARTUNG—CAMERA PRESS

After the coup Doe set up a People's Redemption Council composed of himself and 14 other low-ranking soldiers. At the same time they established a Cabinet made up of MOJA and PPP members, as well as a few ministers from the Tolbert regime. The killing of President Tolbert and the public executions alienated most African countries, but relations gradually thawed after Doe agreed not to continue liquidating members of the former government. While leftist in outlook, Doe's regime announced that it did not intend to sever Liberia's traditionally close links with the U.S.

Samuel Doe, unknown before his dramatic coup, was 28 years old when he emerged from the obscurity of the barracks. A member of the Krahn tribe, which provided the soldiers who engaged in the assault on the Executive Mansion, he enlisted in the Army after completing the 11th grade. Major grievances of the enlisted men were their low pay and poor housing conditions; one of Doe's first actions after taking power was to triple the basic pay for soldiers. (COLIN LEGUM)

Fallaci, Oriana

"On every professional experience I leave some of my soul." These are the words of Oriana Fallaci, an Italian-born journalist best-known for her provocative interviews of political leaders. Fallaci made news in 1979 when she interviewed the Ayatollah Ruhollah Khomeini, Iran's leader. Fallaci was one of the few Western journalists whom Khomeini would consent to meet because several years earlier she had published a devastating interview with the shah of Iran which the shah had banned from that nation's press.

Fallaci spoke with Khomeini at his home in Qom, Iran, for three hours. She wore a Muslim chador, or floor-length veil, during most of the conversation in deference to Khomeini's strict religious views. At one point, however, when the Iranian leader said that she was not obligated to wear Islamic dress, Fallaci suddenly cast off the veil, calling it a "stupid medieval rag." He got up and left the room, but saw her again the next day. Overall, the encounter was a draw. Fallaci was impressed with Khomeini's dignity and charisma; she concluded that the world press had misrepresented him. But she did draw blood with questions about Iran's many executions.

Oriana Fallaci never planned to become a journalist. Of Spanish and Italian descent, she was born on June 29, 1930, in Florence, Italy. During World War II she joined the anti-Fascist resistance, helping downed Allied fliers to flee Italy through its partisan underground. When the war ended, she decided to study medicine and took a part-time reporting job with a local newspaper to make ends meet. She soon discovered that she preferred journalism, becoming in time special correspondent for *Europeo*, an Italian magazine.

Fallaci did her first major interviews with celebrities—entertainers, film stars, and popular novelists. Always thoroughly prepared, she would carry a tape recorder and notebook and would begin each conversation with a provocative question. She often goaded her subjects into startling revelations. Though some have protested that Fallaci rearranges interview materials to reflect her personal impressions of her subjects, producing, in effect, highly personal statements, she replies that she is as much a creative writer as a reporter.

(VICTOR M. CASSIDY)

Falwell, Jerry

A new force appeared on the U.S. political scene in 1980 as fundamentalist Protestant ministers successfully organized their followers as political activists for conservative causes and candidates. These politicized evangelicals claimed credit for the election of Ronald Reagan (*q.v.*) as president of the U.S. and the defeat of liberal senators and congressmen across the country. While their claims may be exaggerated, most of the liberals targeted by the loose alliance of conservative political action committees and fundamentalist religious groups were defeated.

Their most notable success came in Alabama, where Republican Jeremiah Denton was elected to the U.S. Senate and Rep. John H. Buchanan, Jr., himself a conservative Baptist minister, was beaten in the Republican primary because he was not far enough to the right to satisfy the evangelicals. In Oklahoma Don Nickles won an upset victory in the Republican primary and was elected to the Senate with strong fundamentalist support.

Best known of these religious groups is Moral Majority Inc., founded and led by the Rev. Jerry Falwell, minister of the Thomas Road Baptist Church in Lynchburg, Va. Born in Lynchburg in 1933, Falwell was an outstanding high-school student and athlete. He graduated from a Bible college in Missouri in 1956 and then returned to Lynchburg to found his own independent Baptist church, in an abandoned soft drink-bottling factory. Six months later his first religious program appeared on local television. By 1980 his "Old Time Gospel Hour" was carried by almost 700 television and radio stations and was heard by some 18 million people each week. His church claimed 17,000 members, more than one-quarter of Lynchburg's population.

Falwell's religious-political crusade focused on what were described as "family issues." The Moral Majority opposed abortion, homosexual rights, and the Equal Rights Amendment and supported school prayer, increased defense spending, and a strong anti-Communist foreign policy. Falwell viewed the issues as more important than individual candidates and personally avoided making a formal endorsement of anyone, though he publicly announced that he would vote for Reagan.

(HAL BRUNO)

Finnbogadóttir, Vigdís

The choice of Vigdís Finnbogadóttir as Iceland's first woman president came as no surprise in a country where women's rights had gained much in influence in recent years. She ran against three male candidates in the presidential election of June 30, 1980, and succeeded in gaining a narrow plurality of votes, 33.6%, over her nearest rival with 32.1%. She took office on August 1 for a period of four years.

Finnbogadóttir was born on April 15, 1930, the daughter of a professor of civil engineering. Her mother was for many years in the forefront of the Icelandic wom-

ICELANDIC EMBASSY, LONDON

en's movement as head of the Nurses Association. After graduating from a local college in Reykjavik in 1949, she studied French literature and drama at the University of Grenoble and at the Sorbonne in France. Subsequently she studied in Denmark and Sweden and at the University of Iceland. For many years she taught French in local Reykjavik colleges, working as a tourist guide in summer.

In 1972 Finnbogadóttir became the director of the Reykjavik Theatre Company, a small group known locally for its theatrical excellence and ability to tackle difficult works and give unknown playwrights a chance. The company enjoyed success under her leadership and introduced many Icelandic works to the stage. It was in this post that she became nationally known as a cultural spokeswoman, an important factor in her subsequent election as president. She also gave French lessons on television, which made her face known throughout the nation.

The presidential campaign was one not of issues but of personalities. Although the presidential race was nonpolitical, Finnbogadóttir apparently enjoyed greater support from the political left and, above all, from women. She projected herself during the campaign with warmth, wit, and much grace, unflinchingly responding to questions about her private life (she was divorced), her health, her political views, and her nine-year-old adopted daughter. The presidency was a largely powerless post, as in most parliamentary democracies, but Vigdís (she preferred to be called by her first name) saw it as one through which national unity and cultural heritage could and should be fostered.

(BJÖRN MATTHÍASSON)

Foot, Michael

In November 1980, at the age of 67, Michael Foot became leader of Britain's Labour Party following the retirement of James Callaghan. His choice by a majority vote of Labour members of Parliament, with 139 votes to 129 for Denis Healey, was in many ways a surprising outcome of some months of divisive internal conflict within the party. A late entrant in the contest, only persuaded to run by the insistence of his friends, Foot himself said he had never expected to become party leader.

A long and active political career in the Labour Party began for Foot when at the age of 21 (he was born in Plymouth, England, on July 23, 1913) he left the Liberals, with whom his family had strong links, to express his revulsion against the mass unemployment of the mid-1930s. From 1945, apart from a break between 1955 and 1960, he was a member of Parliament. In 1974 he established himself as a leading member of Prime Minister Harold Wilson's Cabinet team, first as secretary of state for employment in charge of complex and controversial trade union legislation and then, from 1976 to 1979, as leader of the House of Commons, a role that required him to hold the parliamentary party together. It was this experience that led him to the party leadership.

Meanwhile, in his first 40 years in the party Foot had won a reputation as a wild and wayward rebel of the left. This image did less than justice to his place in the rich tradition of dissent in British politics. As a writer and journalist, Foot was in the line of political pamphleteers reaching back to William Cobbett, John Wilkes, and Jonathan Swift. He was the author of a two-volume biography of Aneurin Bevan, his close friend and mentor, and was involved in the left-wing Labour weekly *Tribune* from the time of its founding in the 1930s until he joined the Cabinet.

Foot was a gifted speaker, whether in Parliament, on the platform, or in front of the television camera, one of the very few orators in contemporary British politics who could rouse an audience by the passion, conviction, and wit of his argument. Upon his election as party leader, he promised to launch "a hurricane of national protest" against unemployment and to bring the arms race back into the centre of political debate.

(HARFORD THOMAS)

Forlani, Arnaldo

Italy's premier at the end of 1980 was Arnaldo Forlani, a Christian Democrat politician who had risen steadily through the party ranks in large part because of the patronage and friendship of Amintore Fanfani, a veteran party leader who in 1980 was president of the Senate. Forlani in October succeeded Francesco Cossiga at the head of Italy's 40th government since the end of World War II. He inherited an unstable political situation that was compounded by the breaking of a major scandal involving a government minister and some prominent public figures alleged to have helped defraud Italy of millions of dollars during the 1970s. He also had to deal with the much-criticized relief operation following the disastrous earthquake in southern Italy in November 1980 and a new bout of terrorism by the left-wing Red Brigades.

Forlani's unflamboyant style and his unflappable manner stood him in good stead in dealing with this series of challenges, and the fact that he had always stood slightly apart from the factionalism that divides the Christian Democrats helped him to survive some hectic months. Forlani was born in Pesaro on Italy's Adriatic coast on Dec. 8, 1925. He obtained a degree in law and then gained extensive political experience at the local level before embarking on a career at Christian Democrat headquarters in Rome in the 1950s.

Elected to the national Chamber of Deputies in 1958, Forlani received his first junior ministerial post in 1968. He then served as Christian Democrat Party leader from 1969 to '73. In 1974 he was appointed defense minister by Premier Aldo Moro, who was later murdered by the Red Brigades. A brief experience as minister in charge of relations with the UN led to his appointment for three years as Italy's foreign minister, a post exercised with diligence but without distinction.

(DAVID DOUGLAS WILLEY)

Fox, Terry

On the eve of the operation that removed his right leg because of bone cancer, Terry Fox read an article about a U.S marathon runner who had only one leg. Then and there, he was determined to run across Canada to help people who suffered from cancer. In October 1977 Fox asked the Canadian Cancer Society to sponsor what he called his "Marathon of Hope." His objective was to raise $1 million for cancer research. He did not wish to do this for fame or for financial gain, but instead to set a good example. As he told the Society, "The people in cancer clinics all over the world need people who believe in miracles. . . . I believe in miracles. I have to."

Terrence Stanley Fox of Port Coquitlam, B.C., was born in Winnipeg, Man., on July 28, 1958. At the time that he had his operation for removal of his right leg, he was a student at Simon Fraser University in British Columbia. After 14 months of training to learn how to use his artificial limb, he proclaimed himself ready for his marathon.

On April 12, 1980, Fox dipped his artificial limb into the Atlantic Ocean at St. John's, Newfoundland, and then began his cross-Canada run. Accompanying him was his friend Doug Alward, who drove a van supplied by Ford Canada. The War Amputees Association kept Fox's three artificial limbs in repair during his run and paid to have two new legs made. Jogging an average of 42 km (26 mi) a day, he received an enthusiastic welcome in every community through which he passed. Donations and pledges poured in from as far away as Cape Town, South Africa. Early in September, however, Fox was forced to stop his marathon at Thunder Bay, Ont., after running 5,375 km (3,339 mi), because it was discovered that cancer had spread to his lungs.

Fox had run slightly more than halfway to his goal and had collected nearly $2 million in donations. Although he was no longer running, his marathon continued. On Sept. 9, 1980, the CTV television network in Canada organized a four-hour telethon. This program sent the total donations skyrocketing to $12 million.

Fox became a Canadian folk hero. The government of British Columbia presented him with the province's highest honour, the Order of the Dogwood. Canadian Press named him Canadian of the Year, the first nonpolitician in 15 years to receive the award, and on September 19 he became the youngest Companion of the Order of Canada.

(DIANE LOIS WAY)

Gandhi, Indira Priyadarshini

In January 1980 Indira Gandhi marched back to power and took office for the fourth time as prime minister of India. But even in the 33 months that she had been out of power, the country's politics had revolved around her. The collapse of the Janata Party government was as much due to her strategy as to the contradictions and feuds among its components. The incapacity of the caretaker government of Charan Singh and his Lok Dal Party made people long for a "government that works," and in the January general elections the country entrusted itself to the hand that would govern. In her victory statement Mrs. Gandhi called for an end to "mutual recrimination and vindictiveness." Unlike the Janata government, she did not set up inquiry commissions against her opponents, but she got the president to dissolve assemblies in states that had Janata or Lok Dal governments. In subsequent elections her Congress (Indira) Party won handsomely.

The popular impression was that the mandate was not only for Indira Gandhi but also for her younger son Sanjay Gandhi (*see* OBITUARIES). At least half the new legislators were of the youth wing of the Congress Party. This created problems in running the party as well as in forming the Cabinet. Many of Indira Gandhi's old colleagues in government had cast their lot with the opposition. Some came back during and after the elections, but there was a reluctance to reward them with office in preference to those who had stood by her in her ordeals.

Sanjay Gandhi's death in a plane crash in June introduced new uncertainties in the party. Indira Gandhi chose to tread warily. Persistent economic trouble, the unresolved crisis in Assam, and the eruption of religious and caste riots gave an opportunity to the opposition to accuse her of indecisiveness and nonperformance. But public opinion polls and the result of 15 by-elections to various state assemblies held in November, of which Congress won 10, showed that her popular support was solid.

Indira Gandhi was born in Allahabad on Nov. 19, 1917, the only child of Jawaharlal Nehru, India's first prime minister. Educated mainly in Europe, in 1942 she married a lawyer, Feroze Gandhi (d. 1960), by whom she had two sons. Elected president of the Congress Party in 1959, she was minister for information and broadcasting from 1964 until 1966, when she first became prime minister. (H.Y. SHARADA PRASAD)

García, Matías William

The United States is a nation of immigrants, people who came to escape persecution or to find opportunity. Many of these new citizens follow a typical pattern. They arrive poor and uneducated. They encounter discrimination and often must take the worst jobs. After a few years they learn English and may begin to prosper. Their children become Americans.

Communist Cuba provided the U.S. with large numbers of immigrants in 1980. Some of these people were permitted to fly out. Others fled in boats, sailing 145 km (90 mi) to the coast of Florida. So many came that they overwhelmed the U.S. Immigration and Naturalization Service. They were housed in military camps while officials struggled to settle them permanently. It soon became apparent that Cuba had deliberately sent a number of undesirables along with the other refugees. Some new arrivals had psychiatric problems, while others had criminal records. There were riots in refugee camps and even a murder.

Matías William García, who was appointed commissioner of the Immigration and Naturalization Service in July 1980, stated that the service needs "a new policy and a new direction." He planned a reorganization to cope with the backlog of work resulting from the Cuban refugees, to improve administrative procedures, and to raise employee morale.

Thoroughly familiar with the problems of Spanish-speaking Americans, García was born on Nov. 7, 1927, in San Antonio, Texas, of Mexican descent. In 1951 he received a law degree from St. Mary's University in San Antonio. Until the late 1960s he practiced as a trial lawyer. At that time he became politically active as an advocate of the Mexican-American minority in Texas by challenging the validity of equal employment practices at a U.S. Air Force base near San Antonio. From 1972 to 1980 he was a Texas state representative, aggressively speaking in the legislature on behalf of Hispanics. (VICTOR M. CASSIDY)

García Meza Tejada, Luis

"There will be no electoral adventures in this country." So speaking, Gen. Luis García Meza installed himself as president of Bolivia after a military coup on July 17, 1980. This army officer led a three-man junta, consisting of himself, Gen. Waldo Bernal, commander of the Air Force, and Rear Adm. Ramiro Terrazas, the Navy commander. García Meza's Government of National Reconstruction came to power in the 189th coup in Bolivia's 155 years of independence. The new president promised to transform his country into "a modern and industrial society." Bolivia at present is one of the poorest and most backward nations in Latin America.

The junta forced Pres. Lydia Gueiler Tejada, then the only woman leader in Latin America, to resign. Twenty soldiers, armed with automatic weapons, had burst into a room in the Quemado Palace where she was meeting with her Cabinet. A few days after García Meza took power, dissident tin miners and peasants stormed an army barracks, but they were beaten back after a five-hour battle. There were numerous arrests throughout the country, and foreign journalists were detained. By the end of 1980 it appeared that the junta had consolidated its position at the head of the country.

The coup was a setback for democracy in Bolivia. The U.S. reacted by stopping all but humanitarian aid. In November 1979 the Bolivian Congress had asked Gueiler Tejada to run the country until a successor could be chosen in a popular election. When the election, which took place on June 29, 1980, failed to produce a clear winner, it was decided that Congress would choose the president on August 4. The military, whose presidential candidate had placed third in the national balloting, anticipated that Hernán Siles Zuazo, a leftist, would be elected and acted to prevent him from taking office. It claimed that the popular elections were "fraudulent" and that Siles was a Communist.

Little is known about General García Meza. At the time of the coup he led the 6th Division of the Bolivian Army. (VICTOR M. CASSIDY)

Gemayel, Bashir

Younger son of Pierre Gemayel, who had founded Lebanon's right-wing Christian Falangist Party, Bashir Gemayel emerged in 1980 as the leader of the party's Maronite wing. In two days of battles ended on July 8, the Maronite Falangists overran the headquarters of the Falangist Party's main rival, the National Liberal Party, leaving 75 dead. The victory marked the effective takeover of power by 29-year-old Bashir Gemayel from his 75-year-old father.

Bashir Gemayel, born in Bickfawa in the mountains behind Beirut, was thought of as the military chief of the party, representing its hard-liners. His more moderate elder brother, Amin, represented the Metn region in Parliament from 1970 and attempted to work within the framework of the Lebanese government for improvements to Falangist-held areas; Bashir, on the other hand, favoured the partition of Lebanon. By 1980 Falangist supremacy in the Christian Maronite heartland east and north of Beirut almost represented an alternative government within the nation.

The Maronite community had been split for more than two years by a bitter feud between the Falangists and former president Suleiman Franjieh, during which Franjieh's son Tony was killed in June 1978. The party's military wing, led by Bashir Gemayel, was behind this feud but, more seriously for the future of Lebanon as a political entity, Gemayel was also a prime instigator of tacit collaboration between the military wing and Israel. This alliance sprang from the military wing's opposition to the continuing Syrian presence in Lebanon's Christian areas. Pierre Gemayel had formerly promoted rapprochement with Syria, and the eclipse of his father by Bashir Gemayel seemed to portend the breakup of centralized government in Lebanon. Resigning Prime Minister Selim al-Hoss warned on July 9 that there was a disturbing tendency in Lebanon toward "party hegemony" in all aspects of life. Political leaders ignored his plea to cooperate so that the Army could be deployed countrywide to restore the legitimacy of the central authorities. (JOHN WHELAN)

Griffith, Darrell

Darrell Griffith could leap four feet, toes to floor, on a single bound, but he did not seem to be able to keep his University of Louisville team from landing in a heap. As a freshman Griffith had promised to lead his college team to a national basketball championship. As a junior he watched from the bench as his team was upset in the national tournament for the third consecutive year. It was there that he decided that in building his playing style around fancy dunk shots he had made the frosting but forgotten the cake.

"I knew I was going to have to be able to do more than just jump if I wanted to be a complete player," Griffith said. So before his senior season he dribbled basketballs through an obstacle course of 12 chairs for three hours a night. As the only senior starter on Louisville's team, Griffith was better than ever in 1979–80, averaging 22.9 points, 4.8 rebounds, and 3.8 assists per game. He won two player of the year awards and made virtually every All-America team. He also led Louisville to the 1980 national championship on March 24.

In the championship game Louisville trailed the University of California at Los Angeles (UCLA) 50–45 with 6 min 28 sec to play. Within slightly more than four minutes, Griffith was responsible for a total of 11 points, giving Louisville a 56–54 lead it never lost in winning 59–54. UCLA coach Larry Brown called him "the greatest player in the country."

UCLA had tried guarding Griffith with three different people. The University of Iowa had tried four in the semifinal game, when Griffith scored 34 points. "I've guarded other guys who could leap high before," said Bob Hansen of Iowa, "but all of them could come down." After the season the Utah Jazz made Griffith the second choice in the professional National Basketball Association's draft of college players.

Griffith was born in Louisville, Ky., June 16, 1958, and began practicing dunk shots ten years later. He ran toward a netless basket in the alley behind his home and scaled a garage door to stuff the ball through the hoop. He was eight when he started shooting balls at that basket and throwing wadded-up socks at the light fixture in his room when he could not go outdoors.

(KEVIN M. LAMB)

Hagman, Larry

Question: What combines Texas oil, Hollywood soap, Byzantine intrigue, a $700,000-a-week price tag, 300 million addicts worldwide, and the seven deadly sins? Answer: "Dallas," a television serial that triumphed over everything but the Super Bowl in the U.S. TV ratings game and attracted more than half of Great Britain's population for one episode alone.

This slick multigenerational family saga features more skullduggery than the Old Testament as it strobes the sexual and corporate misdoings of more than 30 characters —all of them variously related by blood, marriage, venery, venality, vanity, vengeance, vendetta, and other vices. In the eye of this maelstrom oil baron J. R. Ewing, Jr., boozes, bribes, and debauches his way through some of the fastest paced scripts ever to haul prime time's winged chariot across the purple stage.

J. R. is played by Larry Hagman, whom critics say fits the part "like an iron whip in a velvet glove." He's "an overstuffed Iago in a Stetson hat" and has "a barracuda smile." Born in Weatherford, Texas, in 1931 to musical-comedy star Mary Martin and a Texas lawyer-politician, Hagman turned misfit after his parents' divorce. After a year of college he dropped out and joined his mother in *South Pacific* during its London run. After managing USO tours for the Air Force, he acted in New York City both on and off Broadway. He then moved to California, where he appeared in many movies and television shows. They included "I Dream of Jeannie," which featured him as an Air Force officer whose private and professional lives were alternately sandbagged and saved by the gorgeous genie he found in a bottle while marooned on a desert island. It ran on television for years.

According to Hagman, his character of J. R. Ewing in "Dallas" resembles some of the live oilmen, cattlemen, and politicians he met while chauffeuring his father, then a state senate candidate, around Texas. "My character is milk toast compared with some of those people," Hagman says. "Fratricide, patricide, brothers and sisters shooting each other. It was unbelievable." In the 1980 season's final episode he got shot, lying at death's door all summer while millions of fans waited—longer than expected because of an actors' strike—to find out who dun it.

(PHILIP KOPPER)

Haidalla, Mohamed Khouna Ould

In a palace revolution on Jan. 4, 1980, Mauritania's premier, Lieut. Col. Mohamed Ould Haidalla, seized power from his colleague Lieut. Col. Mohamed Mahmoud Ould Louly, replacing him as head of state and of the Military Committee for National Salvation. Three days later he combined the functions of head of state and premier, retaining also the post of defense minister, which he had held in the previous Cabinet formed in June 1979. In June 1980 Haidalla expressed his support for recognition of the Saharan Arab Democratic Republic (Western Sahara—the former Spanish Sahara—divided between Mauritania and Morocco in 1976) by the Organization of African Unity, and in September he welcomed a delegation of the Saharan Polisario Front to Nouakchott. On July 5 he officially abolished slavery.

As premier in succession to Lieut. Col. Ahmed Ould Bouceif, who died in a plane crash off Dakar, Senegal, in May 1979, Haidalla was considered to be at the same time a progressive, a fervent nationalist, and the supporter of a form of rapprochement with Algeria, where he went on an official visit in October 1980. When Louly took over as head of state in June 1979, replacing Col. Mustafa Ould Salek, Haidalla was already seen as the "strong man" of the military government, and he played a crucial role in the reestablishment of diplomatic relations between Algiers and Nouakchott in August 1979. Visiting France in September of the same year, he strove to win increased support for Mauritania's independence and sovereignty.

Born in Western Sahara in 1940, Haidalla was of Sahrawi origin and belonged to a Regueibat tribe of the Bir-Enzeram region, north of Nouadhibou (formerly Port-Étienne). After secondary school in Rosso in the south of the country, he joined the Army in 1962 and attended military training courses in France at Saint-Cyr and Saint-Maixent. He served in different parts of Mauritania, notably in Bir Moghrein where he was appointed chief of general staff following the coup on July 10, 1978, which overthrew the civilian regime of Pres. Moktar Ould Daddah.

(PHILIPPE DECRAENE)

Haughey, Charles J.

For the Republic of Ireland, 1980 was the year of Charles J. Haughey. In December 1979, after 25 years in active politics, he succeeded Jack Lynch as prime minister and leader of the ruling Fianna Fail party in a closely fought contest with Lynch's deputy, George Colley. From that moment he was determined to dominate party and government. An ardent Irish nationalist, he stressed his government's aim of achieving a united Ireland by peaceful means and appealed to the British government to encourage such unity. Fianna Fail's comfortable victory in a November by-election in County Donegal was seen as an important token of confidence in Haughey's leadership.

Born at Castlebar, County Mayo, on Sept. 16, 1925, Haughey was the son of an army officer and was himself a commissioned officer in a branch of the Defence Force during 1947–57. He was educated at University College, Dublin, and at the King's Inns, where he read law before qualifying as a chartered accountant. After two unsuccessful efforts, in 1954 and 1956, he gained a seat in Parliament in the general election of 1957, which brought Fianna Fail back to power after a period of coalition government. He was parliamentary secretary (1960–61) to the minister for justice and, after the 1961 general election, was himself minister for justice for three years before being promoted to the major responsibility of agriculture. He held this post until 1966 when, on the change of leadership from Sean Lemass to Jack Lynch, he became minister for finance.

In 1970 Haughey was implicated in a plot to import arms for use in Northern Ireland. Lynch dismissed him from the government, and he was charged with related offenses, including conspiracy. He was found not guilty and, in the wake of the verdict, challenged the party leader, but unsuccessfully. After five years as a backbench member, he was brought back to prominence by Lynch, and he acted as Lynch's health spokesman during the period in opposition between 1975 and 1977. On the party's return to power, he was appointed minister for health and social welfare.

(MAVIS ARNOLD)

Hawley, Sandy

When Sandy Hawley was a child, he liked to ride the hobbyhorse in the local five-and-dime store. Thus began a lifetime career of riding horses. On Sept. 1, 1980, Hawley won his 4,000th race, the 11th jockey in Thoroughbred racing history to reach that mark and the first to do so in only 12 seasons of racing. Hawley, whose mounts have earned over $2 million each year since 1973, has been considered a top jockey in Canada —and, in fact, in all North America—almost since his career began.

It was Hawley's uncle who suggested that Sandy would make a good jockey because of his small size, 5 ft 2 in tall and 110 lb. Sandford Desmond Hawley, who was born in Oshawa, Ont., on April 16, 1949, was always a good athlete in school. When he was 15, his uncle got him a job with Duke Campbell, a Canadian horse trainer who boarded his horses at E. P. Taylor's National Stud Farm (now Windfields Farm) in Oshawa. The first Thoroughbred that Hawley petted bit him; the first he rode bolted.

Undeterred, he quickly established a rapport with horses. In his first full season of riding (1969) he was Canada's leading jockey. In 1973 Hawley set a record of 515 victories in one season and was acknowledged to be the top jockey in Canada and North America. In that same year, and again in 1976, Hawley won the Lou Marsh Trophy as Canada's best athlete. He was the second jockey to be made a Companion of the Order of Canada (1976); the first to be so honoured was Ron Turcotte.

In 1976 Hawley became the youngest jockey to achieve 3,000 victories. He also received in that year the Eclipse Award, North America's highest honour for a jockey, and the George Woolf Memorial Jockey Award for the rider who reflects credit on racing, his profession, and himself.

Although he resided in Ontario until 1979, Hawley began riding at the large California racetracks in 1974. Because he spent so much of the racing season there, Hawley moved to Arcadia, Calif., in 1979. He was injured in a race at the Santa Anita track in Arcadia in January 1980 and missed much of the racing season before scoring his 4,000th win. (DIANE LOIS WAY)

Hayden, William George

William Hayden, who succeeded Gough Whitlam as leader of the Australian Labor Party in 1977, narrowly failed in October 1980 to overturn Australia's conservative coalition government, which all pre-election opinion polls had predicted he would do. As Labor leader, he had the almost impossible task of holding together an amalgam of trade unionists, Fabian socialists, blue-collar radicals, social reformers, and left-wing intellectuals. By organizing his election campaign around a triumvirate of political figures, he managed to maintain party unity and come within range of defeating the conservatives. But when Labor lost the 1980 election, and Hayden failed to become prime minister of Australia, he became dispensable as party leader.

Hayden had mounted a carefully programmed series of personal appearances. He projected a likable, modest, low-profile, self-effacing image, and he expected to win votes from those who disapproved of his authoritarian-strong-man rival, Malcolm Fraser, leader of the Liberal Country Party government that had held office for five years. Some party members worried that Hayden had overdone the humble-origins, "struggle from the log cabin" image; in particular, they criticized his reminiscence that his earliest childhood memory was of being awakened by the crash of a body on the front verandah as his father came home drunk yet again. Whether his effort was good enough to keep him in control of a party that had never been charitable to losers remained to be seen.

Born Jan. 23, 1933, Hayden left school to join the public service, read Kafka, Brecht, Sartre, and Moravia at night, was conscripted as a national serviceman, and subsequently served in the police force. He first entered the House of Representatives as a member for Oxley in 1961.

(A. R. G. GRIFFITHS)

Hayes, Denis Allen

While many individuals and groups have worked outside the U.S. government structure to effect policy changes, few have ever gone on to become part of the so-called Establishment themselves. An important exception is Denis Hayes, an environmental activist and longtime critic of U.S. environmental and energy policies, who on July 26, 1979, was appointed director of the Department of Energy's Solar Energy Research Institute (SERI) at Golden, Colo.

The appointment of Hayes to this position met with mixed reaction. Those opposed argued that he lacked the necessary experience for the job—that majoring in history at Stanford University and organizing the first Earth Day in 1970 and Sun Day in 1978 hardly qualified him to direct SERI. They also felt that Hayes's relative youth—he was 34 when he was appointed—and his stance as an avowed solar advocate might prohibit the kind of dispassionate objectivity that his position required. Hayes's supporters, on the other hand, cited his experience in such responsible positions as trustee of Stanford University (1971–72), director of the Illinois State Energy Office (1974–75), and senior researcher with the Worldwatch Institute (1975–79). They also pointed out that Hayes had written a well-researched book on the prospects for solar energy, *Rays of Hope*.

Living up to his reputation as an aggressive and dynamic administrator, Hayes during his first year as director set SERI on a new and controversial course. The institute still invests, in his words, "in some fairly speculative research enterprises, which is a traditional role for government. In addition, though, we are trying to get products out of the laboratory and into the marketplace, something that government has had virtually no successful experience with."

Denis Allen Hayes was born on Aug. 29, 1944, in Wisconsin Rapids, Wis. He received an associate degree from Clark College, Vancouver, Wash., and a bachelor's degree from Stanford. In 1969 he founded and served as national coordinator of Environmental Action, Inc., the group responsible for organizing the first Earth Day.

(BASCO ESZEKI)

Heiden, Eric Arthur

In the 1980 Winter Olympic Games, Eric Arthur Heiden took a sport that involves going in circles to a level of dizzying heights. By his performance he aroused interest in speed skating, a demanding exercise that previously had stirred fewer hearts in the U.S. than mud wrestling and tug-o'-war. The pride of Madison, Wis., was on the covers of three national magazines in the same week as he became the first skater in Olympic history to win gold medals in every one of the five events.

Heiden was not an overnight phenomenon. He and his younger sister, Beth, had been the darlings of U.S. speed skating since 1977. Eric was just 18 then and became the first world champion since 1891 from the United States, which had only one speed-skating rink (at West Allis, Wis.) until another was built at Lake Placid, N.Y., for the Olympics. Subsequently, he won three world championships and four world sprint championships. "And nobody knew. Nobody cared," Heiden said. Most U.S. sports fans prefer their competition man-against-man, and Heiden competed man-against-clock, circling an oval in a monotonous rhythm that an untrained eye found no more entertaining than watching a second hand sweep.

To make those eyes pop, Heiden had to make time stand still. He won the 1,000-m Olympic race by more time than separated the second- and ninth-place finishers. His winning margin in the 1,500 m was the same as the margin between number two and number seven. In his fifth victory on February 23, Heiden set a world record in the 10,000 m and won by the equivalent of 100 m. His closest call was in the 5,000 m, when he turned a 4.47-sec deficit after 1,400 m into a 1-sec lead at 4,200.

"There is no excitement to skating now," said Frode Rønning of Norway. "The medals can be delivered before the race. He is the greatest speed skater there has ever been, without a doubt. A lot of us are going to keep on skating next year because Eric is giving up."

All along, Heiden called the publicity surrounding his quest "the Great Whoopee," refusing to capitalize commercially on his Olympic success. He tried for a fourth world championship in Heerenveen, Neth., but, probably affected by a post-Olympic letdown, he won only one of the four races to finish second overall. His future plans included returning to college and possibly a career in medicine. For most of 1980, however, he was engaged in competitive bicycle racing and in promoting the sport of cycling. (KEVIN M. LAMB)

Hunt, (Nelson) Bunker

Bunker Hunt lost money in 1980—something he rarely does. He lost so much and in such an extraordinary way that his failure caused a brief financial panic late in March. Hunt and his brother W. Herbert had been speculating in silver bullion and silver futures contracts (those that promise delivery of a commodity at a specified price and time). They started this in 1973 after concluding that they needed investments that were safer than foreign oil. Because silver consumption substantially exceeded production each year, the brothers foresaw a long-term silver price rise and began to purchase large quantities of the metal at $2 and $3 per troy ounce.

By January 1980 the Hunts, in association with Arab investors, were reputed to own more than 120 million oz of silver bullion and futures contracts, a substantial fraction of the world's annual production. By that time silver had risen to $52.50 per troy ounce. The brothers acquired their holdings by buying on margin (paying only a small fraction of the cost of the future in cash and borrowing the balance) and by reinvesting their profits from a steadily rising market in further purchases which drove the price still higher.

Silver prices collapsed when the Commodity Futures Trading Commission, a U.S. government agency, forced the Chicago Board of Trade and the New York Commodity Exchange to raise margin requirements (the fraction of a commodity future's cost payable in cash) for silver and to limit the number of futures contracts that any individual could hold. In so doing, the commission was attempting to lessen the rate of inflation. Its actions depressed the price of silver, causing the Hunts's brokers to withdraw credit and require cash. When the brothers were unable to meet these demands, their paper empire collapsed. In May the Hunts obtained a $1.1 billion loan from a consortium of 13 banks to help put their affairs in order.

Bunker Hunt would suffer few privations in spite of his 1980 losses. Born on Feb. 22, 1926, in El Dorado, Ark., he was the second of 14 children that H. L. Hunt sired by three wives. The elder Hunt, a legendary oilman, started with a $5,000 inheritance and built a fortune of more than $2 billion by the time of his death in 1974.

(VICTOR M. CASSIDY)

Hu Yaobang

Hu Yaobang (Hu Yao-pang) became one of China's most influential leaders when, in February 1980, he was appointed general secretary of the Chinese Communist Party and was elected to the Politburo's Standing Committee, the inner circle of the ruling body. A close associate of Vice-Chairman Deng Xiaoping (Teng Hsiao-p'ing) since the early 1940s, Hu became one of a small group of relatively young but tested officials selected to carry out China's program of modernization and ensure a smooth transition of authority. Hu, who directs party affairs on a day-to-day basis, is known for his moderate views, pragmatic policies, and organizational ability. In his new post he has been mobilizing party workers for the modernization drive that Premier Zhao Ziyang (Chao Tzu-yang) is pushing forward as the government's chief executive.

Born into a poor peasant family in Hunan Province in 1915, Hu received little formal education. He joined the Communist Party in 1933, three years after being accepted into the Young Communist League. A veteran of the historic Long March (1934–35), he worked closely with Deng in the 1930s and served as political commissar under Deng in the 2nd Field Army during the war against Japan. In the late 1940s, he and Deng moved into Sichuan (Szechwan) Province when their army took over the area from Nationalist forces. Hu remained there until 1952, then followed Deng to Beijing (Peking), where he became head of the Young Communist League. After the Cultural Revolution was launched in 1966, both Hu and Deng were twice purged and twice rehabilitated. After his second rehabilitation in 1977, Hu became director of the party's organization department and soon afterward was made a member of the Politburo, secretary-general, and propaganda chief.

A self-taught party veteran, Hu is known for his simple way of life. In recent years, he has played a significant role in strengthening party discipline, determining China's new political stance, drawing up a program for economic development, enhancing the status of intellectuals, and downgrading outmoded Maoist ideology in favour of a policy to "seek truth through practice." Such policies have revived critical judgment and fostered the artistic, scientific, and technological advances that are so essential to China's drive toward modernization.

(WINSTON L. Y. YANG)

Ito, Ritsu

There was something eerie about the headline: Ritsu Ito was reported to be alive and well in China. The news meant nothing to younger Japanese, but their parents remembered, or seemed to remember, that Ito was a high-ranking Japanese Communist who vanished some 30 years earlier without a trace.

Ritsu Ito was born in Gifu Prefecture in 1913. He was studying at the First National Higher School (later Tokyo University) when he and other members of the Communist Youth League were arrested in 1933. After promising to forsake Communism, he was released. Ito was arrested a second time in 1939 in a roundup of known Communists. No one knows for sure what transpired while he was in police custody, but he reportedly gave an important tip to the savage "thought police" (*tokko*) of prewar Japan, which later led to the arrest of Richard Sorge, a German who spied for the U.S.S.R. during World War II. Posing as a journalist, Sorge operated as a secret agent for the Comintern, Far East. His assignment included gathering information on top-level decisions taken by the Japanese government. Sorge proved his worth. He secretly cabled Soviet authorities the exact date that Germany would attack the Soviet Union and, at a later date, was able to notify Moscow that a large number of Japanese troops had been transferred from Manchuria. This information permitted Stalin to redeploy some of his Siberian forces against Hitler. Sorge and his aide, Hidemi Ozaki, were arrested in October 1941 and executed in 1944. In Beijing (Peking) Ito neither affirmed nor denied involvement in the Sorge case. He simply told a member of the Japanese embassy: "I made a mistake in 1941."

After World War II, Ito was the reliable right-hand man of Kyuichi Tokuda, the powerful secretary-general of the Japanese Communist Party (JCP). When the Korean War erupted in 1950, Ito backed local party hard-liners who advocated violence, but he and other radicals had to go underground when Gen. Douglas MacArthur, commander of the Allied occupation forces in Japan, ordered the "Red Purge." In September 1951 Ito and Tokuda disappeared so quietly that not even their own families knew what had happened to them. After Ito returned to Japan on Sept. 3, 1980, he was taken to a hospital where he met his Communist wife and sons. The head of the JCP, Kenji Miyamoto, shrugged off Ito's reappearance as unimportant. But when and if Ito decides to tell his story, he may disclose information that could profoundly affect the future of the JCP.

(TAKAO TOKUOKA)

Julien, Claude Norbert

Claude Julien became heir to an imposing journalistic legacy in 1980 when he was elected as the paper's editor by his colleagues on the staff of the influential Parisian daily *Le Monde*. He would succeed Jacques Fauvet, whose mandate was to expire on Dec. 31, 1982.

The success story of *Le Monde* began on Dec. 11, 1944, when Gen. Charles de Gaulle's provisional government entrusted the task of creating a prestige newspaper to replace *Le Temps* (which had collaborated during the German occupation) to Hubert Beuve-Méry, a 40-year-old former diplomatic correspondent. The paper's print order rose from 140,000 copies in 1944 to about 600,000 in 1980, when its daily readership was put at 1.5 million. Politically independent but leftward leaning, *Le Monde* in 1980 was the target of government-initiated legal proceedings, charged with undermining the independence and authority of French justice.

The team of almost 200 journalists on the paper gained its independence in 1951 when it set up an editorial group that rapidly acquired a 40% holding in the *Le Monde* limited company and a minority veto on all decisions. The other shareholders—managers and administrators—agreed to leave the choice of editor to the editorial group provided that its choice won 60% of the vote. At first in 1980 no one managed to achieve this magic figure. But after several votes Julien collected the 62.8% of the 752 shares present or represented in the election. Considered by his colleagues a man of the left, he owed his success to the high standards, serious approach, competence and skill that he demonstrated throughout the campaign. But the decision still had to be ratified by the *Le Monde* limited company.

Julien was born at Saint-Rome-de-Cernon, Aveyron, on May 17, 1925. His education was partly in the U.S., at the University of Notre Dame in South Bend, Ind. He joined the staff of *La Vie Catholique* (1949–50) and then became editor in chief of *La Dépêche Marocaine* in Tangiers (1950–51). He moved in 1951 to the foreign desk of *Le Monde* and took charge of it in 1969. In 1973 he became editor in chief of *Le Monde Diplomatique*, a monthly published by the group.

(JEAN KNECHT)

Kania, Stanislaw

Quite unexpectedly, on Sept. 6, 1980, Poland learned that Edward Gierek, leader of the Polish United Workers' (Communist) Party (PUWP) since Dec. 20, 1970, had been hospitalized following a heart attack. The party's Central Committee had released him from his post of first secretary and had unanimously called Stanislaw Kania to that position. Kania had been a full member of the Politburo since December 1975, but he was barely known to the Polish public. He immediately received a congratulatory telegram from Soviet Pres. Leonid Brezhnev, who described him as "standing firmly on the position of proletarian internationalism."

Kania told the Central Committee that the wave of strikes rolling across Poland was directed not against the role of the party and its foreign policy but against the party's serious mistakes in economic matters and against "distortions in public life." He developed his policies in detail in his report presented to the Central Committee on October 6. Repeating his attachment to "democratic centralism" (*i.e.,* Communist Party predominance), he avoided mentioning "proletarian internationalism" (*i.e.,* undisputed Soviet leadership of the "socialist camp"). On October 21 Kania met the Polish primate, Stefan Cardinal Wyszynski, in Warsaw to discuss problems of internal

CAMERA PRESS

peace and development. On October 30 he visited Moscow, and on November 14 he received strike leader Lech Walesa (*q.v.*). Kania appeared to wish to cooperate with the new independent trade union, and in this he was supported by the "liberal" wing of the party.

Son of a smallholder, Kania was born on March 8, 1927, at Wrocanka, a village near Krosno. He joined the anti-Nazi resistance movement in 1944 and the Communist Party in April 1945. After helping its Rzeszow provincial organization create a party youth movement, he was sent to the party school, graduating in 1952. He was made an alternate member of the Central Committee in 1964, a full member of that body in 1968, and a full member of the Politburo in 1975.

(K. M. SMOGORZEWSKI)

Karmal, Babrak

Ten months after his installation as Afghanistan's president by the Soviet armed forces on Dec. 27, 1979, Babrak Karmal was greeted on Oct. 16, 1980, at the Kremlin with the pomp and circumstance befitting the head of an allied power. That same morning Soviet Pres. Leonid Brezhnev and Karmal discussed Soviet-Afghan relations, and in the afternoon they signed a statement setting out the range of their talks and the points on which they agreed. Speaking at the state banquet for Karmal, Brezhnev proclaimed with ringing defiance that "the revolutionary process in Afghanistan is irreversible" and that "the support and solidarity of the Soviet Union" were on the side of the Afghans and their government. In his reply, Karmal alleged that "if it had not been for the Soviet Union there would be no Afghanistan. . . ."

UPI

Babrak Karmal was born in 1929 near Kabul and graduated from Kabul University in 1961. After Nur Mohammad Taraki founded the opposition Khalq ("Masses") Party in 1963, Karmal joined it, but following the overthrow of the monarchy in July 1973 he split the opposition by founding a rival Parcham ("Flag") Party. In 1977, under Soviet pressure, the two factions reunited to form the People's Democratic Party (PDP), with Taraki as leader and Karmal and Hafizullah Amin as his deputies. In April 1978, with Soviet help, the PDP overthrew Pres. Mohammad Daud, and a People's Republic of Afghanistan was formed with Taraki as president of the Revolutionary Council and prime minister. Karmal was his deputy, and Amin was foreign minister.

In March 1979 Amin became prime minister, while Taraki continued as president of the Revolutionary Council. The new premier had Karmal sent to Prague as ambassador. Considering Amin's anti-Islamic policy to be dangerous in the existing situation, the Kremlin advised Taraki to dismiss him. On September 16, however, Taraki was killed. The Kremlin now decided that a full-scale invasion of Afghanistan was unavoidable. On December 27 the Soviet Army entered Kabul, Amin was executed, and Karmal was recalled from Prague and made both president of the Revolutionary Council and prime minister of Afghanistan.

(K. M. SMOGORZEWSKI)

King, Stephen

"I like to scare people, I really do," says the young author who has terrified 22 million of them—assuming at least one reader finished each printed copy of his six published novels. Stephen King, in person a "tall, pudgy, bearlike," and basically amiable man, has been riding a wave of popularity since *Carrie* was published in 1974. According to the *New York Times Magazine,* he is a gentle nonconformist who lives quietly in a tiny Maine town and interrupts work to pick up his kids from nursery school. According to horror cultists, he is King of the Bizarre.

"I write about ordinary people caught up in extraordinary circumstances," he says, but this ordinariness is tinged with the psychic and the supernatural. *Carrie* concerns a high school girl who ignites her classmates at the senior prom by pyrokinesis. In *The Shining,* a boy sees murders in the past while his father, caretaker of a snowbound resort hotel in the Rockies, goes homicidally mad. *The Stand* constructs a thermonuclear Armageddon between the normally human and satanic survivors of a chemical warfare plague that accidentally sweeps the world. *Firestarter,* a best-seller in 1980, focuses on an eight-year-old girl who incinerates objects just by looking at them.

In his own view, King is the beneficiary of a popular craving for catharsis—an inevitable phenomenon in hard times. During the depression of the '30s, "people went to the movies for the same reason they go to the movies now—either to laugh or to get scared out of their minds." (Two of his novels have lit up box offices from coast to coast, *Carrie* and *The Shining,* which Stanley Kubrick made with Jack Nicholson in 1980.) King goes on to describe a theory of "luridical" positivism. Horror fans, he believes, seek a kind of humane affirmation in scary fictions that present an outsider who threatens normal people, then is vanquished in the end. (By contrast, he says, science fiction celebrates the alien, the outsider, as heroic.)

The novelist was born in Portland, Me., on Sept. 21, 1947, and was raised in small towns by his mother after her husband deserted the family. He graduated from the University of Maine and taught English locally for $6,000 a year before writing *Carrie,* which earned a $2,500 advance. Published in paperback, it sold four million copies before becoming the film that made Sissy Spacek (*q.v.*) a star.

(PHILIP KOPPER)

Lansing, Sherry Lee

Hollywood has known powerful women—and not only the "box-office bombshells," from Jean Harlow to Bo Derek. Performers like Gloria Swanson and Marilyn Monroe consorted with statesmen. Barbra Streisand and Goldie Hawn became sometime producers and directors. "Superagent" Sue Mengers was said to have at least as much influence as any executive in putting film "packages" together. But none ever quite held the title that bespoke her power. When Sherry Lansing took over as president of 20th Century-Fox in January 1980, she became the first to have the actual clout and the executive accoutrements.

She was the daughter of a lucky and aggressive woman who fled Europe with the Nazis at her heels before World War II, settled in Chicago, and supported herself as a realtor. Sherry Lee Lansing, born July 31, 1944, attended a school for gifted children and was graduated summa cum laude from Northwestern University's speech school in 1966. Her first job was teaching math in the riot-torn Watts section of Los Angeles. Burned out emotionally after three years, she turned to modeling, appeared in TV ad campaigns for Max Factor and Alberto-Culver, and then tried her hand at acting. She was featured in two films. "I wasn't interested in being an actress at first," she recalls, "but when I walked onto that set I started to become obsessed with film."

After taking courses at UCLA and USC, she started reading scripts as a freelance at $5 an hour, became a story analyst at Universal, and then accepted Daniel Melnick's offer to be story editor at MGM. Promoted to the vice-presidency for creative affairs, she left MGM to take a similar job at Columbia when Melnick moved there. Before her ultimate promotion, she had had "total control" of only two films, but both were critical and commercial successes: *Kramer vs. Kramer* and *The China Syndrome.*

TONY KORODY—SYGMA

Known as hard working, efficient, and personable, she evidently meant to be a no-frills executive. At Fox, she was the fifth president in a decade, succeeding Richard Zanuck and Alan Ladd, Jr. Some insiders predicted she would be kept under the thumbs of the parent corporation's officers, but no one quibbled about her reported $300,000 salary and possible bonuses totaling $1 million. One wag suggested that "Hollywood has a new story line: Girl meets Boy, Girl works for Boy, Girl replaces Boy at the top." (PHILIP KOPPER)

Lieberman, Nancy

Nancy Lieberman has taken the stereotype of a female basketball player to the baseline and destroyed it. In the 1980 New York Pro Summer League, the 5-ft 10-in, 146-lb guard was the only woman in a league dominated by professional stars, but former National Basketball Association scoring leader Nate Archibald said, "She's not a woman out there. She's a player."

Lieberman came along at just the right time for an aggressive player to yank women's basketball out of the sewing room and into the showroom. When she entered high school, girls' teams had just recently begun playing basketball with boys' rules instead of using a half-court version. College teams had not recruited women heavily until Lieberman started touring campuses. She chose Old Dominion University in Norfolk, Va. Her school won national championships in 1979 and 1980, with Lieberman averaging more than 20 points a game in her junior and senior years.

The Women's Professional Basketball League hoped she would do the same for its box offices when Dallas made her the first choice in its draft of college players. The league was struggling financially—several of its franchises had drowned in red ink—and it needed a star with the name recognition of Lieberman.

The national attention began in 1975 when, shortly before her 17th birthday on July 1, Lieberman became the youngest player ever to make the U.S. Olympic women's basketball team, which finished second in the 1976 Games. People began to notice then how much Lieberman played like the best men in the game, dribbling with her head up and the ball protected, passing behind her back to unguarded teammates, lifting her elbows to wedge into place for a rebound.

She had learned by playing against boys on the playgrounds, first in her Far Rockaway, N.Y., hometown and later in nearby New York City's Harlem ghetto. Her mother was not entirely sure that basketball was a properly dainty hobby for her daughter to be pursuing, and she once punctured the ball with a screwdriver. But she knew there was no stopping her daughter the day she flat out told her that basketball was for boys. Nancy stuck out her chin, assuming the posture of a guard about to make a charge, and told her mother, "Yeah? Then I'll make history." (KEVIN M. LAMB)

Lini, the Rev. Walter Hadye

Father Walter Lini became prime minister of the new republic of Vanuatu (formerly the Anglo-French condominium of the New Hebrides) on July 30, 1980. He had been the condominium's chief minister since elections in November 1979, when his Vanuaaku Party won 62% of the vote and 26 of the 39 seats in the Representative Assembly.

Lini was born on Pentecost Island in 1942. After obtaining a basic education in the New Hebrides, he went to St. Peter's Theological College in the Solomon Islands and St. John's Theological College in Auckland, N.Z., before returning to the New Hebrides as an Anglican priest. In June 1971 Lini and two teacher friends formed the New Hebridean Culture Association, which was primarily concerned with the effect of Western influences on traditional lifestyles. The association soon evolved into the New Hebrides National Party (later known as the Vanuaaku Party).

In 1974 Lini was granted leave to work for the Vanuaaku Party which, under his leadership, narrowly won the general election of 1975 but boycotted the 1977 election as a protest against delays in moving toward independence. The Vanuaaku Party then formed a "people's provisional government" which controlled large sections of the country and encouraged its supporters to withhold taxes. After a change in French policy had made independence an early prospect, the Vanuaaku Party agreed to join with its Francophone rivals in the formation of a government of national unity.

For a few weeks either side of independence, Lini had to deal with secessionist movements on the islands of Espíritu Santo and Tanna, whose chief leader was Jimmy Stevens (*q.v.*). The situation served to emphasize all the weaknesses and frustrations inherent in condominium rule. Lini was firm in dealing with the metropolitan powers, adroit in canvassing support from his Pacific neighbours, and successful (with the aid of troops from Papua New Guinea) in maintaining the territorial integrity of Vanuatu. (BARRIE MACDONALD)

McGraw, Tug

Tug McGraw left the pitcher's mound pounding his chest with one hand and punching the sky with his other, reviving himself just in time to celebrate. In the last two games of major league baseball's 1980 World Series he loaded the bases before dramatically striking out the last batter. "Tug belongs to Hollywood," said Kansas City Royals outfielder José Cardenal, McGraw's last-out victim in the fifth game. After the sixth game the World Series championship belonged to McGraw's Philadelphia Phillies for the first time in their 98 years of existence, four games to two.

Frank Edwin McGraw, Jr., has been a spirited sort since he was born Aug. 30, 1944, in Martinez, Calif. His parents nicknamed him "Tug" as an infant because of what he did while his mother nursed him. As the New York Mets' best relief pitcher he rallied the team around his slogan "You Gotta Believe" in 1973, when they charged from last place to first in the season's final month and won the National League championship series before losing the World Series, four games to three. His role was similar at Philadelphia, where the acrimonious clubhouse screamed out for someone to make the game fun. "The criticism used to bounce around that place like marbles in a bathtub," McGraw said.

McGraw was not above criticism in 1979 when the left-hander's 5.14 earned run average was the worst of his career. The team had loaded itself with expensive players and promptly dropped out of sight in the National League East Division's pennant race, which it had won the previous three years. But in 1980 the Phillies began winning games in late innings, when McGraw appeared in most of his 57 games. He won 5, lost 4, and saved 20. With a 1.47 earned run average, he allowed fewer than two earned runs per nine innings for the third time since his first full season in 1969 and fewer than three for the seventh time.

McGraw has been called "Scroogie" because the cornerstone of his success has been a screwball, a pitch that breaks in the opposite direction from a curve ball. But what keeps batters off balance is his variety of pitches, which include an assortment of fast balls that McGraw has taken the trouble to name. His Peggy Lee, he says, makes batters ask, "Is that all there is?"

McGraw pitched in all five championship series games against Houston and in four of the six World Series games. In the World Series he allowed one run in eight innings, saved two games, and won another. (KEVIN M. LAMB)

MacGregor, Ian

To rescue Britain's ailing and virtually bankrupt nationalized steel industry, the British government picked a 67-year-old Scotsman, Ian MacGregor, who had been working in the U.S. metal industry for 35 years and had become a highly successful U.S. businessman. It was a controversial appointment, defended by Britain's secretary of state for industry, Sir Keith Joseph, on the grounds that Ian MacGregor was "the best man available in the world."

He was also one of the most expensive. Having built up the U.S. metals business Amax, he had become a partner in the investment bankers Lazard Frères. To detach him from Lazard Frères for a three-year contract with the British Steel Corporation

(BSC), the British government agreed to pay to Lazard Frères £225,000 for each of the three years plus £1,150,000 if he succeeded in putting BSC back on its feet. As chairman of BSC, MacGregor would draw an official salary of £48,500 (his income in the U.S. was said to be around $1 million). The terms of his appointment, described as "an unprecedented transfer fee," caused an uproar in Parliament.

Born in Scotland on Sept. 21, 1912, MacGregor took a degree in metallurgy at the University of Glasgow. During World War II he went with a British mission to the U.S. as an expert on tank design and settled there, though with a Welsh wife and a holiday home in Scotland he had kept up his British connections. On taking up the chairmanship of BSC in July 1980, he avoided personal publicity. He brought with him a reputation for making cool, well-thought-out decisions.

MacGregor took over at a time when the recession had created worldwide overcapacity in steel and when British steel production had fallen by one-third from the previous year and was losing more than £500 million annually. To meet this situation, he planned a reorganization that would decentralize the corporation, allow greater local autonomy, and eliminate the chronically unprofitable operations in the business. (HARFORD THOMAS)

McHenry, Donald F.

On Aug. 15, 1979, Andrew Young, who had been president-elect Jimmy Carter's first appointment following the 1976 election, resigned as U.S. ambassador to the UN. Young handed in his resignation after admitting that he had held an unauthorized meeting with a representative of the Palestine Liberation Organization—a contact that violated U.S. policy.

As Young's successor, Carter chose Donald F. McHenry, who had been Young's deputy. While Young and McHenry share certain basic political attitudes, their personalities could hardly be more dissimilar. Where Young tends to a certain flamboyance of style and rhetoric, McHenry is a quiet professional, a diplomat with a diplomat's patience. Born in St. Louis, Mo., on Oct. 13, 1936, McHenry grew up in the poor black neighbourhoods of East St. Louis, Ill. He graduated from Illinois State and earned a master's degree from Southern Illinois University at Carbondale. He joined the State Department in 1963 as a junior officer at the Office of UN Political Affairs. Ten years later he left government service, following the U.S. invasion of Cambodia and then-president Richard Nixon's decision to make Henry Kissinger secretary of state.

With Carter's election, McHenry returned to the State Department and the UN. He was given a number of delicate and highly visible assignments, including acting as a U.S. troubleshooter in South West Africa/Namibia and Angola. After becoming ambassador, he pressed the U.S. case against the Soviet invasion of Afghanistan before the Security Council and helped push through a General Assembly resolution condemning the Soviet action.

Despite his solid reputation as a professional, McHenry was unable to avoid controversy. In March 1980 the vote he cast for a UN resolution opposing Israel's policy of creating Jewish settlements in the West Bank raised a storm of protest in the U.S. and Israel. The administration was on record as opposing the policy but, out of consideration for Israeli sensibilities, had never before voted in favour of such a resolution. In the aftermath, Carter blamed poor communications within the administration for the "mistake." However that may have been, some critics charged that McHenry's vote was in keeping with his personal attitude. (STANLEY W. CLOUD)

Maillet, Antonine

In 1979 Antonine Maillet became the first non-European to win France's prestigious literary award the Prix Goncourt. Her winning novel, *Pelagie la Charrette,* was the second of her works to be entered in this competition. The first time that Maillet was a candidate for this award, which she called "the Stanley Cup of literature," her novel *Les Cordes-des-Bois* lost the prize by one vote (1977).

Born on May 10, 1929, in Buctouche, New Brunswick, Maillet grew up in a French Canadian milieu. Both her parents were schoolteachers, and they imbued her with a sense of her Acadian ancestry. The Acadians were settlers in the former French colony that comprised the Maritime Provinces of Canada and parts of Quebec and New England. In 1755 the British had deported many of them to other areas. Maillet's first book, *Pointe-aux-Coques,* was an account of this deportation. Published in 1958, it won the Champlain Prize in 1960. *Pelagie la Charrette* told the tale of an Acadian family deported to Georgia and its ten-year trek to return to its homeland.

A writer since the age of 20, Maillet dealt in all her works with Acadian culture and identity. Although by 1980 she had written 17 books, including novels, short stories, and plays, she was not well known, even in Canada. In all her works she used the Acadian French she learned in childhood, which may have limited her reading audience to some extent. She is best known in French Canada for a one-character play, *La Sagouine* ("The Washerwoman"), which won the La Presse Literary Award in 1976.

Maillet entered a convent in 1951 because she saw this as one way to achieve her goal of becoming a teacher of literature. Eventually, she did teach creative writing at the University of Quebec and the University of Montreal. She left the convent in the mid-1960s and settled in Montreal in 1970. For the past few years Maillet has devoted full time to writing. Her novel *Don l'Orignal* won the Canadian Governor General's Award for French Language Literature in 1972. Also in 1972, Maillet was the first woman to win the City of Montreal Grand Prize for Literature for her novel *Mariagélas.* The Canadian government made her an Officer of the Order of Canada in 1976. (DIANE LOIS WAY)

Marriner, Neville

Only with the birth in London in 1959 of the Academy of St. Martin in the Fields (ASM) chamber ensemble under the direction of a dashing young violinist-conductor, Neville Marriner, did works such as Bach's *Brandenburg Concertos* and Vivaldi's *The Four Seasons* take on for the first time in more than a century the kind of sparkle and polish their composers surely intended. Gone, under Marriner's inspired stewardship, was the opaque, unornamented turgidity of 19th-century baroque performing style. Instead, everything was light and shade, the crisp virtuosity of ASM members yielding a fresh sophistication captivating in its transparency.

Such was the great success, critical and public, enjoyed by the ASM that Marriner's name within a short time became a watchword among the cognoscenti. Then, encouraged by Pierre Monteux to study conducting, Marriner turned to the larger symphonic forms. He subsequently conducted major symphony orchestras throughout the world, and for the 1979–80 season took up the music directorship of the Minnesota Symphony in succession to Stanislav Skrowaczewski.

Marriner was born in Lincoln, England, on April 15, 1924, into a family in which "music was . . . what television is for most people today." He studied at London's Royal College of Music (RCM)—with an interval of military service during 1941–43—and later at the Paris Conservatory. His early career was as a violinist; he played with a number of small ensembles before gaining his first orchestral experience with the London Philharmonia and then joining the London Symphony Orchestra (LSO) to lead its second violin section. Meanwhile, he taught briefly at Eton College and in 1950 became a professor at the RCM. It was during this time with the LSO that he turned to conducting, and subsequently his violin playing was reserved for private occasions.

In 1969 Marriner became music director and conductor of the Los Angeles Chamber Orchestra, with which he made a highly successful tour of Europe in 1974. In the summer of 1979 the ASM was resident orchestra at the Aix-en-Provence Festival in France, where Marriner directed it in concerts and in a new production of *The Marriage of Figaro.* In addition to his Minnesota directorship, he served as music director of the Detroit Symphony's Meadow Brook Festival. (MOZELLE A. MOSHANSKY)

Masire, Quett Ketumile Jonny

The natural choice as successor to Botswana's Pres. Sir Seretse Khama, who died in July 1980 (*see* OBITUARIES), was Quett Masire. In 1962 the two men had cooperated closely in forming the Botswana Democratic Party (BDP), which had ruled the country since its independence in 1966. When Sir Seretse became prime minister of the then British protectorate of Bechuanaland in 1965, Masire became deputy prime minister; after Bechuanaland became the republic of Botswana a year later, he was made Seretse's vice-president and finance minister. In 1967 he was made minister of development planning, a post well suited to his energy and enthusiasm for tackling difficult problems head-on.

Masire was born on July 23, 1925, at Kanye, the capital of his Bangwaketse tribe. He became a teacher and then went into journalism, becoming a reporter on *The African Echo* and later editor of *Therisanyo.* Combining journalism with politics, he served first on his tribal council and subsequently on the legislative and executive councils under the British administration. However, his real political mark was made as the hardworking secretary-general of the BDP. For a time in 1969 his promising political career received a setback when he was defeated in his home constituency by the former Bangwaketse chief, but after spending some years as a nominated member of Parliament, he made a strong comeback and regained his seat in the 1974 elections.

A short, well-built, lively man, called the "pocket Hercules" of Botswana, Masire enjoyed taking on tough political opponents and the even tougher economic problems which beset the vast, arid stretch of country that embraces the Kalahari Desert. Like the late Sir Seretse, he was a passionate enemy of South Africa's system of racial separation. Masire strongly believed in the ideals of a nonracial society and favoured political moderation. In addition to being president of Botswana, he was the chairman of a new grouping of nine states in southern Africa (Botswana, Zambia, Zimbabwe, Angola, Malawi, Tanzania, Mozambique, Lesotho, and Swaziland) that were committed to lessening their economic dependence on South Africa. (COLIN LEGUM)

Messner, Reinhold

Long the ultimate goal in man's struggle to surmount nature's most formidable obstacles, Mt. Everest was in 1980 scaled for the first time by a solo climber. The Chinese Mountaineering Association reported that 35-year-old Reinhold Messner of Italy reached the 8,848-m (29,028-ft) summit at 3:20 PM on August 20, having made the ascent entirely alone and without using oxygen. It was Messner's second ascent of Everest; the first time had been in 1978 with Peter Habeler of Austria—also a record as it was the first ascent made without oxygen.

Messner's Everest exploits crowned an impressive series of Himalayan climbs, all on peaks topping 8,000 m and all without oxygen. In 1970 he traversed Nanga Parbat with his brother Günther, who was killed during the descent, Reinhold himself being badly frostbitten; in 1972 he made a solo ascent of Manaslu; in 1975 he and Peter Habeler made the first ascent of the northwest face of Gasherbrum I (Hidden Peak); in 1978 he again climbed Nanga Parbat, reaching the summit alone by a new route; and in 1979 he led a team of six in an Alpine-style ascent of K2—the world's second highest peak (8,611 m).

Messner was born in South Tirol, Italy, in 1944. He attended college in Bolzano and then became a schoolteacher. Later he started a successful Alpine climbing school and then began earning a livelihood by lecturing and writing books on mountaineering. Messner was introduced to climbing as a small boy by his father, and from the age of 13 he climbed difficult routes in the Eastern Alps with his brothers Helmut and Günther. He was also influenced by the Tirolean mountaineer Sepp Mayerl and became widely known for his bold solo and winter Alpine climbs. Later he climbed in the world's highest ranges, in the Andes, the Hindu Kush, New Guinea, East Africa, and Alaska, but his Himalayan exploits in particular established him in the very front rank of world mountaineers.

In his successful 1980 attack on Everest, Messner set out from the Tibetan side, following the north col-northeast ridge route taken by British climbers George Mallory and Andrew Irvine, who disappeared on the mountain in 1924, and by an ill-fated Soviet expedition of 1952. His solo climb began from a small base camp at the foot of the ridge. (JOHN NEILL)

Mondale, Walter Frederick

It is the nature of the office of vice-president of the United States that the fortunes of its occupants rise and fall with the fortunes of the person who happens to be president at the same time. Thus, in 1976 Vice-President-elect Walter F. ("Fritz") Mondale joined President-elect Jimmy Carter (*q.v.*) in victory. Four years later they went down to defeat as the incumbent Democrats were overwhelmed by the Republican ticket headed by Ronald Reagan and George Bush (*qq.v.*).

Carter had chosen Mondale as his running mate after a long talent search in 1976. From their first meeting the two men achieved a rapport which, by all accounts, lasted through their term in office. At the beginning of that term Carter had pledged that Mondale would play a more significant role in the administration than any other vice-president in U.S. history. On the basis of the record they compiled in office, it seems at least arguable that the pledge was kept, even though the historical standard by which their performance is measured is notoriously low.

In many ways, Mondale was Carter's opposite: a northerner from Minnesota (where he had been a protégé of Hubert H. Humphrey); a former U.S. senator; a certified member of the Democratic Party's establishment; a man whose own presidential hopes died aborning in 1974 when he dropped out of the race, acknowledging that he did not have a taste for the kind of nonstop campaigning necessary to capture the presidency. Still, despite their differences (or perhaps in part because of them), Mondale and Carter worked closely and well together. Mondale functioned both as a key adviser to Carter and as an important political operative.

Undoubtedly, there were disagreements. It was known, for example, that the vice-president did not agree with the president's conservative approach to the abortion issue; Mondale was also reported to have been chagrined at the often insensitive way Carter's staff, if not Carter himself, dealt with Mondale's former colleagues in the Congress. Such disagreements, however, did not appear to undermine Mondale's position as a loyal and self-effacing member of the Carter team.

What the future might hold for Mondale was unclear. Turning 53 on Jan. 5, 1981, he clearly had a chance for the Democratic presidential nomination in 1984. But whether he would campaign for it remained unknown. (STANLEY W. CLOUD)

Mugabe, Robert

Robert Mugabe became prime minister of the new republic of Zimbabwe in April 1980 after his Zimbabwe African National Union (ZANU) won a clear majority in elections held to determine the future of the country formerly known as Rhodesia. Although he had been widely portrayed as a revolutionary Marxist and a tough guerrilla leader, Mugabe surprised his critics by displaying a spirit of forgiveness and tolerance toward his black and white opponents after gaining power. He included a number of his defeated black opponents in his government, as well as two white ministers, one of whom had been a Rhodesian Front leader in Ian Smith's former white supremacist regime. While Mugabe took his country into the nonaligned camp, he made it clear that he would look largely to the Western community for economic and technical aid. His tolerance and calm approach to the bristling problems inherited after a long and bitter war were decisive in preventing the chaos that many had predicted would be the fate of Rhodesia if the guerrillas of the Patriotic Front ever came to power.

Born in Kutama on Feb. 21, 1924, Mugabe was the son of a labourer. Educated by Roman Catholics, he became a teacher but soon showed his militant temperament when he threatened to "box the ears" of the then prime minister, R. S. Garfield Todd, when the government made deductions from the meagre wages of teachers. (He nominated Todd as a senator in his new Parliament.) He continued hiseducation in South Africa at the University for Fort Hare, a nursery for black nationalism. During 1956–60 he taught in Ghana.

Returning home, Mugabe joined Joshua Nkomo in the African nationalist movement. In 1963, however, he helped the Rev. Ndabaningi Sithole form ZANU, a breakaway from Nkomo's Zimbabwe African People's Union (ZAPU). Arrested in 1964, Mugabe was held in detention until 1974. He used this time to study law by correspondence and gained degrees from the University of London. After being released, he went into exile and established himself as an effective political leader of ZANU's military forces based in Mozambique. Mugabe cooperated with his old political rival, Nkomo, within the Patriotic Front uniting ZANU and ZAPU during the Lancaster House negotiations in London which ended the war in Rhodesia. After the agreement, however, his party decided to end its alliance with ZAPU in order to fight the elections on its own. (COLIN LEGUM)

Murjani, Mohan

So-called designer jeans, the hottest pants to warm the cockles of retailers' fiscal hearts since bloomers, made more than one fortune in 1980. Gilding the most ostentatiously proletarian of garments with their upper-crust names, Gloria Vanderbilt, Calvin Klein, Jordache, and Sasson—the Big Four in the U.S.—raised sales by 50% over the previous year. Observers, such as *Newsweek*'s business reporter, found it notable that designer jeans might command 10% of the $5 billion international jeans market before the bubble burst.

One of the richest rags stories in all this involved a 34-year-old Indian named Mohan ("Mike") Murjani. With a little help from a friend in the form of Ms. Vanderbilt, American heiress, designer, and fashion plate, he had boosted his family's Hong

Kong textile and clothing business to the $500 million mark. Son of a Hong Kong immigrant, educated in England and Massachusetts, Murjani took over his father's business—mostly 99-cent blouses—in 1967. "I realized we must expand," he says. He steered the company into worsteds, acrylics, and knitwear and even acquired a bicycle firm, but the oil crisis of 1973–74 and the resultant recession prompted a cutback. Three years later, as he searched for a way to recoup, Murjani wandered into a department store that sold jeans in bulk. "I thought: What if these jeans were exciting, had a big name attached, were in fact a classy, perfect fit."

His plan involved "three things that matter: the product, the name, and the marketing." The *New York Times* put it slightly differently: "The marketing of Vanderbilt jeans is a tribute to promotion, advertising and respectable hype." According to *India Today*, Murjani turned down several nominal collaborators, including Princess Lee Radziwill. "He chose Vanderbilt for the status. 'What we were trying to tell buyers was . . . Jeans are not a cowboy affair, jeans are glamorous.' " According to this source, Murjani hired the heiress to lend her name to the pants and her face to a massive ad campaign. In that respect he was just joining the competition, which got so sizzling that U.S. TV networks banned some commercials as too suggestive.

In 1980 Murjani had a good number of factories in Hong Kong and nearby Maçao employing thousands of people—who turned out only half of his wares. Having become the largest clothing exporter in the colony, he was laying plans to market his own threads with his name alone.

(PHILIP KOPPER)

Muskie, Edmund Sixtus

When Cyrus Vance suddenly resigned as U.S. secretary of state in April 1980 to protest the ill-fated attempt to rescue the U.S. hostages in Iran, Pres. Jimmy Carter surprised Washington by giving the job to Sen. Edmund S. Muskie of Maine. It was seen as a masterful political stroke that removed from contention one of the few Democrats who might be a compromise presidential candidate should the Democratic convention become deadlocked between Carter and Ted Kennedy. The appointment also generated some badly needed support from the party's mainstream which viewed Muskie as the type of experienced leader who should have been on the Carter team from the beginning.

UPI

Knowing Muskie's pride and famous temper, Washington insiders also saw it as a setback for Zbigniew Brzezinski, the president's national security adviser, who frequently had outmaneuvered Vance in the ongoing rivalry between the National Security Council and the State Department. But five months later there were rumours that a frustrated and angry Muskie was ready to quit because of his inability to control the State Department bureaucracy and Brzezinski's continuing influence over foreign policy. Both Carter and Muskie denied the reports.

But it all became academic when Carter lost the election to Ronald Reagan. With a dozen leading Democratic senators going down to defeat as well, the party was left desperately short of leaders with Muskie's experience and stature. Born March 28, 1914, in Rumford, Maine, he had served six years in the Maine House of Representatives before being elected governor in 1954 and U.S. senator four years later. In 1968 he became nationally known as Hubert Humphrey's vice-presidential running mate. His excellent performance in that losing cause made him a favourite for the 1972 Democratic presidential nomination, but a combination of poor organization, fatigue, and the famous Muskie temper lost it in the early primaries.

In his fourth term and 22nd year in the Senate, Muskie was a powerful and respected figure when Carter named him to the Cabinet. As the first and only chairman of the Budget Committee, he had forced the committees to work within their budget and spending targets. It was uncertain what Muskie would do after a lifetime in office, but Republicans as well as Democrats agreed that the Senate would miss him.

(HAL BRUNO)

Noguchi, Isamu

"His great strength is that he does not belong." Thus Calvin Tomkins summed up a *New Yorker* profile on Isamu Noguchi at a time when three major galleries, including the Whitney Museum of American Art, simultaneously were celebrating his work. Genetically Occidental and Oriental, artistically surrealistic, naturalistic, and traditional, Noguchi has been described as the "preeminent American sculptor." Yet other critics regard him as Japanese like his father, a poet and professor of English, or as pan-national like his mother, a woman of Scots-Irish and U.S. Indian descent.

Born in Los Angeles on Nov. 17, 1904, Noguchi was reared in Japan. Returning to the United States, he was apprenticed to sculptor Gutzon Borglum, who told him to quit sculpting. Noguchi was then taken in by Romanian sculptor Constantin Brancusi, from whom he learned the art by example because neither spoke the other's language. Noguchi later designed dance sets for Martha Graham, New York City playgrounds for parks commissioner Robert Moses, and gardens for UNESCO headquarters in Paris and for the *Reader's Digest* building in Tokyo.

The materials and forms of Noguchi's work are as varied as his credits: huge steel fountains; featherweight lamps made of mulberry paper; table-sized stone "landscapes" like "The Wave," which looks like a crystal bubble of Swedish granite; such structures as the 12-story aluminum "Detroit Pylon"; interior furniture.

Art critics despair at fitting his works into conventional cubbyholes, just as museum directors despair at finding floors strong enough to support his largest polished stones. "There is, in any case, no reason to feel frustrated because we cannot find a skeleton key to Noguchi's oeuvre," an *Art in America* critic mused. "He spreads himself willfully, not to say in spite of himself, all over the place, and in so doing produces an art whose frequent appearance of simplicity is only the mask for a diversity of motives issuing from a highly convoluted expressive temperament."

(PHILIP KOPPER)

Obote, Milton

In December 1980 Apollo Milton Obote became the first African leader to regain his presidency through an electoral process after having been deposed by a military coup. He had been overthrown as president of Uganda by Gen. Idi Amin in January 1971. Obote spent the next eight years in exile in neighbouring Tanzania as the guest of his friend Pres. Julius Nyerere. He used the time to establish a new core for his former ruling Uganda People's Congress (UPC) and to sustain his army in exile, numbering about 700 men. These two elements played a leading role in helping the Tanzanian Army to overthrow Amin in early 1979 and provided the foundation on which Obote was able to build the electoral organization that enabled him to defeat his Democratic Party opponents.

Milton Obote (he does not use the name Apollo) was born Dec. 28, 1925, in the village of Akokoro in the Lango district in central Uganda, the third of nine children of a peasant family. After completing secondary school, he entered the East African university college of Makerere but was expelled for his political activities before he could graduate. When the colonial government prevented the militant young nationalist student from accepting scholarships offered to him in the U.S. and West Germany, he crossed the border into Kenya in 1950 to work as a labourer on the sugar plantations and to acquire experience in trade unionism. He joined the party of Kenyan leader Jomo Kenyatta, the Kenya African Union, and became involved in the independence struggle of that country.

Obote returned to Uganda in 1957 and was at once nominated by his district to represent it in the colonial Legislative Council. A year later he was elected to the new legislature as a member of the Uganda National Congress, which he soon left to form the UPC. In 1962 he led his party to victory in the elections immediately prior to Uganda's independence.

A conflict between Obote's ruling party and the ruling Kabaka of Buganda, which led to the defeat and exile of the Kabaka, left deep tensions between it and the people of Buganda (a large district of Uganda). Obote narrowly escaped two attempts to assassinate him. However, by 1967 he felt sufficiently strong to present a new constitution, based on a multiparty parliamentary system, and proposed to campaign for election. He was overthrown by Amin before the new elections could take place.

(COLIN LEGUM)

Ovett, Steve

In 42 races since May 1977, Steve Ovett lost only once at 1,500 m or at one mile, but that loss came about in the most important 1,500-m race of his life, the finals at the 1980 Olympic Games in Moscow. Having won the Moscow Olympic 800-m title in a major upset over arch-rival Sebastian Coe on July 26, Ovett ended up bronze medalist in the 1,500-m final six days later, as Coe (3 min 38.4 sec) ran the last 600 m in 79.2 sec to win over East Germany's Jurgen Straub (3 min 38.8 sec). But world records at 1,500 m (3 min 31.36 sec in Koblenz, West Germany, on August 27) and one mile (3 min 48.8 sec in Oslo on July 1) gained Ovett the nod as Britain's outstanding athlete of 1980.

Ovett was born in Brighton on Oct. 9, 1955. He won the English Schools Junior Boys 400 m in a record 51.8 sec in 1970, and his career has been marked with success ever since that sunny day at Solihull. In 1973 he won the European junior (under 20) 800-m title in 1 min 47.5 sec and ran his first four-minute mile. In 1975 he outclassed a tough field to take the Europa Cup two-lap title. Having won the British trials at both 800 m and 1,500 m, Ovett traveled to Montreal in 1976 for the Olympic Games. Demoralized by his lane 8 draw in the 800-m final, he took fifth place as Alberto Juantorena (Cuba) ran a world-record 1 min 43.50 sec. Ovett won his 1,500-m heat two days later, but was shut out of a place in the final.

In 1977 Ovett began his campaign to become the world's best miler, and he succeeded almost effortlessly, defeating Olympic champion John Walker (3 min 54.7 sec) in London in June and winning the World Cup 1,500-m title in Düsseldorf, West Germany, in 3 min 34.45 sec. In 1978 he devastated the 1,500-m field in 3 min 35.6 sec at the European championships in Czechoslovakia. Overshadowed by the exploits of Coe throughout most of 1979, Ovett showed his form with late-season marks of 3 min 49.57 sec (mile) in London in August and 3 min 32.11 sec for 1,500 m in Brussels in September, missing Coe's world records by a hairbreadth. He also ran 800 m in 1 min 44.91 sec and 1,000 m in a U.K. record of 2 min 15.91 sec.

(DAVID COCKSEDGE)

Pavarotti, Luciano

"He's the biggest turn-on in opera today," said one observer. Though he sings classical music only, Luciano Pavarotti has acquired a popular following. His recordings of opera and other serious works sell in unusual numbers. He can fill any opera or concert house in the world. Wherever he goes, fans mob him.

Pavarotti has an exceptionally pure and supple tenor voice. He sings with perfect focus and, over the years, has grown from a rather wooden performer into a passionate and convincing one. Though his voice is not unusually large, he has always been a disciplined technician who can sing the most difficult music with apparent ease.

"Everybody sings" is Pavarotti's description of Modena, Italy, where he was born on Oct. 12, 1935. His father, Fernando, a baker, occasionally sang tenor roles in local productions. The Pavarotti household often attended operas and concerts. As a youth Pavarotti studied music and played many sports, becoming especially good at soccer. Today he plays tennis twice each week.

Though Pavarotti considered a performing career at an early age, his family recommended that he find a more secure livelihood. He became an elementary-school teacher in 1955 and worked in that profession for two years. When he decided to study music full time, he moved from Modena to Mantua and sold insurance to support himself.

Pavarotti's operatic career began in 1961 with a tour of small Italian opera houses. Four years later his big break came. Richard Bonynge, a conductor, heard him perform and hired him to tour Australia with Bonynge's soprano wife, Joan Sutherland. Pavarotti won wide acclaim for his performance in Donizetti's *The Daughter of the Regiment,* an opera that includes a tenor aria with nine high C's. Well-received debuts at the world's major opera houses and concert tours of Europe and North America followed. Pavarotti slowly expanded his repertoire to include many leading Italian operatic roles.

(VICTOR M. CASSIDY)

Poniatowski, Prince Michel Casimir

The friend, confidant, and most trusted aide of Valéry Giscard d'Estaing, manager of the campaign that had brought Giscard to the presidency of France in 1974, Prince Michel Poniatowski was in 1980 involved in a cause célèbre known as "the de Broglie affair." By turns minister of state, minister of the interior, president of the National Federation of Independent Republicans, honorary president of the Republican Party, and Giscard's personal envoy abroad with the rank of ambassador, Poniatowski was in 1980 a member of the council of the Union pour la Démocratie Française and president of the Commission for Development and Cooperation of the European Parliament. He was famous both for his witty sallies and for his liability to controversy.

The de Broglie affair had begun on Dec. 24, 1976, when Prince Jean de Broglie, former minister and negotiator of the Algerian War settlement, was shot and killed in Paris. Over the succeeding months and years the case brewed into a scandal involving business, politics, and a host of shady deals. Jean de Broglie had been engaged in a variety of activities in a number of different firms. At the time of his death he had debts amounting to Fr 12 million. A founder, with Giscard and Raymond Marcellin, of the Independent Republicans and the reputed bankroller of the party, he died a victim of enemies who decided to eliminate him when he became a liability.

In 1980 the Socialist Party, with the support of the Communists, set forth a motion that Poniatowski, minister of the interior at the time of de Broglie's murder, should appear before the High Court of Justice accused of "failure to assist a person who knew himself to be in danger." Poniatowski brought a libel action against the Socialist and Communist parties and affirmed before the parliamentary commission appointed to examine the motion that "he was never in receipt of preliminary information concerning a plan to assassinate Jean de Broglie." At the year's end the commission had not yet decided whether or not Poniatowski should be made to stand trial.

Born in Paris on May 16, 1922, Poniatowski numbered a marshal of France, an Austrian field marshal, and a king of Poland among his forebears. After graduating in law, he attended the École Nationale d'Administration and in 1948 joined the Ministry of Finance, where from 1959 he was closely associated with Giscard.

(JEAN KNECHT)

Prem Tinsulanond

Over the years military prime ministers have become commonplace in Thailand, and so there were no raised eyebrows when one general passed the job to another early in 1980. However, there were notable differences this time: Kriangsak Chamanand was the first military leader to leave the premiership voluntarily, and Prem Tinsulanond was the first to assume the post with such obvious hesitation that he instantly became known as the "reluctant prime minister."

The change of guard followed a loss of support in Parliament suffered by Kriangsak as a result of mounting economic problems and a rising crime wave. On March 3, three days after Kriangsak resigned, the two houses of Parliament met in joint session and elected General Prem as the new prime minister. Prem received 399 votes, while the only other serious contender, former prime minister Kukrit Pramoj, got 80. Kriangsak himself backed the winner.

A career military officer, Prem was born on Aug. 26, 1920, in the southern province of Songkhla. After school in Bangkok, he graduated from the Chulachomklao Royal Military Academy in 1941 and became a cavalry man. His training included a stint at the U.S. Army Cavalry School, Fort Knox, Kentucky. It was after his appointment as commander of the 2nd Army in 1974 that he achieved national recognition as one of the country's most capable field officers with a reputation for incorruptibility.

Never directly involved in the political infighting that seemed continuous in Bangkok, Prem was recognized in political circles as a traditionalist and firm royalist. In 1977 he joined Kriangsak's Cabinet as deputy minister of the interior. His major concern in that post was to formulate programs to assist villagers as part of the government's intensified efforts to combat Communist subversion in rural areas. Two years later he was promoted to defense minister while concurrently holding the post of Army commander in chief. A bachelor, Prem was fond of saying that he was married to the Army.

(T. J. S. GEORGE)

Raja'i, Mohammad Ali

Mohammad Ali Raja'i, a former teacher of mathematics and a leading member of the clergy-dominated Islamic Republican Party (IRP), was elected by the Majlis (parliament) on Aug. 11, 1980, as the second prime minister of the Islamic Republic of Iran. For more than nine months following the resignation of Mehdi Bazargan, Iran had had no prime minister. Three candidates for the post proposed by Pres. Abolhassan Bani-Sadr (*q.v.*) were rejected by the IRP, and Raja'i became prime minister against the advice of the president. He soon came in conflict with Bani-Sadr over his choice of ministers; only two-thirds of those originally put forward by Raja'i were included in the Cabinet approved by the Majlis on September 10.

Born in 1933 in Kazvin, about 160 km (100 mi) northwest of Teheran, Raja'i enlisted in the Iranian Air Force at the age of 16. In 1960 he obtained his teacher's diploma. He joined the Iranian Liberation Movement in 1960 and was imprisoned three times for his political activities. He became a member of the Central Committee of the Association of Islamic Teachers and headed the Ministry of Education in the first post-revolutionary Cabinet.

Six weeks after Raja'i became prime minister, Iraq launched its attack against Iran. According to Teheran radio, he replied to an offer of Soviet military assistance by telling the Soviet ambassador that "Iran is not ready to exchange its independence for Soviet aid." In New York City in October to address the UN Security Council, Raja'i declared that "a fair settlement can be found only if the aggressor is conquered and punished; this is our final position." While in New York City, he told reporters that a decision on the U.S. hostages was "not far away" but alluded to some "obstacles to a solution" and declined to meet any U.S. officials before returning to Teheran.

(K. M. SMOGORZEWSKI)

Rallis, Georgios

When in May 1980 the Greek Parliament elected Konstantinos Karamanlis president of the republic, Georgios Rallis, his foreign minister and longtime associate, was chosen by the ruling New Democracy Party to succeed him as party leader and prime minister. The vote in the party's parliamentary caucus was 88 for Rallis against 84 votes for his sole adversary, Defense Minister Evangelos Averoff-Tossizza, a favourite of the party's right wing. Rallis's political moderation and candour guaranteed that the party would abide by Karamanlis's middle-of-the-road policies, and this tipped the scales in his favour.

After taking over, Rallis called for a mild climate in government–opposition relations, easing the strain of polarization that was rapidly setting in on the Greek political scene. He readjusted Karamanlis's strict anti-inflationary practices to give economic growth greater impetus, and he settled the outstanding problem of Greece's military reintegration in NATO after an estrangement lasting six years.

Born in Athens on Dec. 26, 1918, Rallis hailed from a long and distinguished line of Greek politicians, blemished only by his father's service as Nazi-sponsored prime minister in the last phase of the German occupation of Greece during World War II. After graduating in 1939 from the law school of Athens University, Rallis joined the Army as a reserve officer and saw action on the Albanian front in 1940–41. Although he was never associated with his father's wartime record, it was not until 1950 that he went into politics, being elected to Parliament thereafter under the banner of the main right-wing party in its different mutations—Populist Party, Greek Rally, and Karamanlis's National Radical Union, which he helped found in 1955.

Rallis served in several Cabinet posts but being a staunch anti-Communist quit the party with others after disagreeing over the reform of the electoral law, which, he then prophesied, would bolster the extreme left. Although his prophecy was vindicated, he rejoined Karamanlis in 1961 and was reelected. Minister of public order in the Cabinet toppled by the 1967 military coup, Rallis was subsequently arrested repeatedly for his antiregime activity. With the collapse of the dictatorship in 1974, he joined the first national unity government under Karamanlis, and when the New Democracy Party won a landslide victory he became Karamanlis's closest Cabinet aide.

(MARIO MODIANO)

Rather, Dan

After becoming television's first "anchorman" at the 1952 political conventions, Walter Cronkite covered every major news event and countless minor ones for three decades. As on-camera managing editor of the "CBS Evening News," he rose to unrivaled esteem; one pollster found him to be the most respected man in America. But he moaned, "I'm not a newsman anymore, I'm just a personality." Having covered every presidential inauguration from Harry Truman's to Jimmy Carter's, he decided to step down after one more. CBS executives piously said nobody would ever "replace" him, but the question remained: "Who would succeed Cronkite?"

After months of secret negotiations, Dan Rather answered that he would. But this was not just a matter of being chosen for the job. Rather had already turned down offers for the top newsman job at ABC and NBC in order to remain at CBS with a contract that would earn him at least $1 million a year for five years.

Born in Wharton, Texas, on Oct. 31, 1931, the son of a waitress and an oil pipeline labourer, Rather studied at Sam Houston State Teachers College in Huntsville, Texas. After graduation he went to work for the *Houston Chronicle* but soon left print journalism for radio station KTRH, the Houston affiliate of CBS. There he climbed the ladder from writer to reporter to news director before switching to the network's local television outlet as director of news and public affairs.

He first gained national attention when happenstance put him in the right place at the right time—marooned with a TV crew on Galveston Island during a killer hurricane in 1961. His unruffled performance won him a job covering civil rights for CBS, and two years later he happened to be in Dallas when Pres. John F. Kennedy was assassinated. He not only covered that shattering story and its aftershocks but also skillfully coordinated nonstop coverage for days. He became CBS's White House correspondent in 1964 and then was sent abroad to assignments in London and Vietnam. In 1966 he returned to his White House post, where his aggressive questioning often incurred the ire of Richard Nixon's administration. In 1975 Rather was named a co-anchorman of CBS's popular television news show "60 Minutes."

(PHILIP KOPPER)

Reagan, Ronald Wilson

On Nov. 4, 1980, Ronald W. Reagan was elected the 40th president of the United States, in a landslide that produced a nationwide Republican victory. The former governor of California received 51% of the popular vote to 41% for Pres. Jimmy Carter, 7% for independent John Anderson, and 1% for minor candidates. Reagan carried 44 of the 50 states, overwhelming Carter 489 to 49 in electoral votes.

At the age of 69, Reagan was the oldest man to become president, though his age never became an issue in the campaign. Born in Tampico, Ill., on Feb. 6, 1911, he was graduated from Eureka College in Illinois. After graduation he became a radio sports announcer, first in Davenport and then in Des Moines, Iowa. In 1937 he began a long career as a motion-picture actor. Among his most notable films were *Knute Rockne—All American* (1940), *Kings Row* (1942), and *The Hasty Heart* (1950). From 1947 to 1952 and from 1959 to 1960 he served as president of the Screen Actors Guild.

When his movie career declined, Reagan became a traveling spokesman for General Electric Co. as well as host of "General Electric Theater" on television. During that time he changed from a Democrat to a conservative Republican and campaigned for Barry Goldwater for president in 1964.

Reagan's success as a political speaker led to his decision to run for governor of California as a Republican in 1966. He won and was reelected in 1970, serving in that office until 1974. He made a halfhearted bid for the Republican presidential nomination in 1968 and seriously attempted to take it away from Pres. Gerald Ford in 1976.

The 1980 Reagan campaign got off to a shaky start when he was upset by George Bush (*q.v.*) in the Iowa precinct caucuses. But Reagan quickly came back to win the New Hampshire primary and never again was seriously threatened for the nomina-

STEVE MELTZER—WEST STOCK INC./AUTHENTICATED NEWS INTERNATIONAL tion. At the July convention in Detroit he chose Bush to balance the ticket over objections from his conservative supporters, who felt that Bush was a "moderate."

But that was exactly what Reagan wanted, and throughout the campaign he moderated his own conservative positions on many issues in order to attract the independent and Democratic voters he needed to win. In his acceptance speech and during the televised debates, Reagan quoted Franklin D. Roosevelt and made a special effort to convince Democrats that he was not a right-wing ideologue.

While Reagan attacked the Carter administration's record, Carter painted Reagan as a simplistic and dangerous right-winger whose policies might lead the country into war or a depression. This strategy was partly successful until the Carter-Reagan televised debate on October 28 in Cleveland, during which Reagan skillfully refuted the charges.

(HAL BRUNO)

Rodgers, Bill

Bill Rodgers, both a Man o' War and a Midas of long-distance running, won his fourth Boston Marathon in 1980 to become the first racer in more than half a century to win that race three times in a row. Few records stand for 50 years in any modern sport, even the event named for the lonely feat of an army messenger who died in 490 BC bringing news to Athens of the Greek victory over the Persians at Marathon. Of course, the modern races have little in common with the ancient heroics that cost the Greek soldier his life. What began as solitary ordeal has become a lemming chase that in 1980 was marred by skulduggery.

At Boston, for instance, more than 5,300 runners officially entered the event, which was swelled by a few thousand also-rans who had not qualified to enter. The first woman to cross the finish line, Rosie Ruiz, claimed laurels for her victory. But it soon became clear that she had run only the last few miles of the course. Her dubious win threatened to eclipse Rodgers's considerable achievement.

Other events also clouded the year for Rodgers. Seeking his fifth win in the newer and larger New York (City) Marathon (which has no entrance requirements), he fell and lost. Perhaps even worse, he did not even get a shot at the prize he may have wanted most, a gold medal in the Olympic Games. That was because Pres. Jimmy Carter ordered a U.S. boycott of the Summer Olympics in Moscow to protest the Soviet invasion of Afghanistan. For Rodgers, at 32, the 1980 Games were quite possibly the last in which he could seriously compete.

Nonetheless, he continued to excel in long-distance running, in part because of what doctors considered a nearly perfect physique for the sport—light frame and long legs. Those attributes helped but could not fully explain his remarkable success on the international circuit, including ten marathon wins in under 2 hr 12 min. In an era when other runners studied physiology and physics and practiced fad diets, Rodgers simply trained hard, running an average of 130 mi a week.

Born in 1948 and raised in Newington, Conn., Rodgers began running track in high school as a miler. Not until after graduation from Wesleyan University did he enter marathon competition, winning his first Boston race in 1975.

(PHILIP KOPPER)

Rogers, Kenny

The recipient of the 1980 Grammy for best male country vocalist (awarded by the National Academy of Recording Arts and Sciences) is not only a survivor in a business dependent on fickle fans and changing styles but a good subject for nostalgia buffs. Kenny Rogers began his career with the Bobby Doyle Jazz Trio and later was a member of The New Christy Minstrels folk singers and The First Edition pop/rock group.

Rogers's ability to adapt and assimilate various musical genres is a key factor in his continuing success, but the common denominator in his style is the influence of country music. His soft, yet grainy voice has always reflected the country sound of his Texas childhood. Equally important is that he recognizes what he does best, the country story-ballad. One of the biggest hits for The First Edition was "Ruby Don't Take Your Love to Town," written by country singer Mel Tillis.

After The First Edition broke up in 1975, Rogers enjoyed steady but modest success as a solo country artist. Then in 1977 his career skyrocketed. His recording of "Lucille" hit number one early in the year and won him a Grammy, four Academy of Country Music (ACM) awards, and the Country Music Association's award for male vocalist of the year. Between 1977 and mid-1979 he had sold more than five million records, collected two platinum and five gold solo albums, and recorded two gold duet albums with Dottie West. As well as receiving more awards, including the 1979 ACM entertainer of the year, he has been host on the Johnny Carson "Tonight" show, emceed two television specials of his own, and starred in a made-for-TV movie based on his recording of "The Gambler."

Born in 1938, Rogers grew up with six other children in what he refers to as a Houston tenement. His father's family enjoyed playing musical instruments and, after briefly attending college in Houston, he decided to try to make his living with music. By 1980 he was performing in more than 200 sold-out concerts a year.

(JULIE KUNKLER)

Ryan, Claude

In the May 20, 1980, referendum in the province of Quebec, voters were asked to choose whether they wished their province to remain part of the Canadian confederation or to separate but retain an economic union with Canada. This latter condition was referred to by the Quebec government as "sovereignty association." The provincial leader of the forces favouring retention of the confederation was the head of the Quebec Liberal Party, Claude Ryan. The fact that the federalist view won the referendum on May 20 was in great measure due to the efforts of Ryan, who oversaw every detail of the campaign.

A newcomer to the political arena, Ryan was elected as leader of the Quebec Liberals in April 1978, and he spent the next year rebuilding the party. He was first elected to political office on April 30, 1979, when he won a seat representing Argenteuil in the Quebec National Assembly. He was not uninitiated to the world of politics, however. As publisher of the influential Montreal daily newspaper *Le Devoir*, Ryan commented publicly upon and advised privately the political leaders of Quebec. His report on Canadian constitutional reform, *A New Canadian Federation*, was published in January 1980. This answer to the Parti Québécois' proposal for sovereignty association was the culmination of 17 years of preparation. The paper called for greater decentralization of power and major change in the structure of the federal government.

Born Jan. 26, 1925, in Montreal, Claude Ryan was educated at College St. Croix in Montreal (1937–44), at the School of Social Service, University of Montreal (1944–46), and at the Pontifical Gregorian University in Rome (1951–52). From 1945 to 1962, he served as the general secretary of L'Action Catholique Canadien in Montreal. This organization is a Roman Catholic movement of lay people who encourage spirituality among the laity.

In 1962 Ryan accepted a position as editorial writer with *Le Devoir*, and he became known for his depth and thoroughness. He received the Human Relations Award of the Canadian Council of Christians and Jews in 1966 and was elected to the Canadian News Hall of Fame in 1968.

(DIANE LOIS WAY)

Salnikov, Vladimir

The young man had put Soviet swimming on the world map in the late 1970s. Before him, said Sergey Vaitsekhovsky, senior coach of the Soviet national swimming team, "not a single Soviet swimmer won at major contests, to say nothing about approaching world records." But he surpassed himself at the 1980 Moscow Olympic Games. On July 22 Vladimir Salnikov won the 1,500-m freestyle in a world record time of 14 min 58.27 sec, more than 4 sec faster than Brian Goodell's previous record of 15 min 2.40 sec set at the Montreal Olympic Games in 1976. On July 24 Salnikov won his second Olympic gold medal in the 400-m freestyle in 3 min 51.31 sec. Of Salnikov's 1,500-m performance, John Hennessy, *The Times* of London correspondent who witnessed it, wrote, "He was well ahead at the finish and no doubt could have clipped a few more seconds off his time had he been extended."

Leading up to his 1980 Olympic triumphs, Salnikov was European 1,500-m champion in 1977, world champion in the 400-m and 1,500-m freestyle in 1978, and winner of all his races in a brilliant 1979 season, setting new world records for the 400-m (3 min 51.40 sec, later surpassed) and 800-m (7 min 56.49 sec) freestyle.

Salnikov was born in Leningrad on May 21, 1960, the son of a sea captain. He began swimming at the age of six and quickly drew the attention of coaches from the Ekran Juvenile Sport School in Leningrad, one of the leading swimming centres of the U.S.S.R. Salnikov then devoted almost all his spare time to training sessions in the school's swimming pool. However, regular training and frequent trips to contests did not affect his studies. He finished secondary school with good marks and was admitted into the Leningrad Lesgaft Institute of Physical Culture, where he was a second-year student in 1980. (R. M. GOODWIN)

Samaranch, Juan Antonio

At the 83rd session of the International Olympic Committee (IOC), held in Moscow in July 1980 immediately prior to the opening of the Games of the XXII Olympiad, Juan Antonio Samaranch of Spain was elected to succeed Lord Killanin of Ireland as the IOC's president. He thus inherited what might well be considered one of the year's most thankless tasks.

Indeed, Samaranch was taking over as head of the worldwide Olympic movement at a crucial time. Along with politically inspired boycotts of the Olympic Games, which again occurred in 1980, there were many other pressures on the Olympic movement, not the least of which were nationalism and commercialism. It remained to be seen whether Samaranch would make an effective stand against these pressures and whether the Olympic movement would still be a force for goodwill among the young people of the world when his presidency of the IOC ended.

Samaranch, born in Barcelona on July 17, 1920, the son of an industrialist, was a graduate of the Higher Institute of Business Studies in Barcelona. Under the Franco regime he became the municipal councillor responsible for sports in the city, was a national delegate for physical education and sports (1967–71), and served as president of the Barcelona Diputación, or prefecture (1973–77). In 1977 he was appointed Spanish ambassador to the U.S.S.R.

Samaranch's sporting career had been more distinguished in administration than on the field of play. He was president of the Spanish Skating Federation and chief government representative to the Spanish teams at the Winter Olympics in 1956 and the Summer Olympics in 1960 and 1964. A member of the Spanish Olympic Committee from 1953 and its president (1967–71), he became a member of the IOC in 1966. There he fulfilled a variety of functions, including that of president of the IOC Press Commission. Those who worked with him described him as an adequate chairman who listened to other people's ideas but seldom put forward any of his own.

(CHRIS BRASHER)

Sauvé, Jeanne

The first order of business when the 32nd Canadian Parliament convened on April 14, 1980, was the election of the first woman speaker of the House, the Hon. Jeanne Sauvé. Competent, conscientious, and pragmatic, Sauvé studied her House of Commons catechism for an hour a day to prepare herself for the job.

This was the fourth time in her eight years in Parliament that Sauvé had had to acclimatize herself to a new position. After she was elected in 1972 to represent the riding of Ahuntsic (Montreal), she was made the minister of state for science and technology, becoming the first Quebec woman to serve in the federal Cabinet. She also served in the Cabinet as minister of the environment (1974) and as minister of communications (1975–79). On Nov. 29, 1978, she assumed the position of adviser to the secretary of state for external affairs. In this role she was responsible for advising on relations with the French-speaking world. Sauvé was reelected as the member of Parliament for the riding of Laval-des-Rapides in 1979.

Born on April 26, 1922, in Prud'Homme, Sask., the former Jeanne Mathilde Benoit grew up in Ottawa. From 1942 to 1947 she served as the national president of Jeunesse Étudiante Catholique Internationale, a Roman Catholic students' organization. She studied economics in London (1948–50) and was granted a diploma in French civilization by the University of Paris in 1951. After a year working for UNESCO in Paris, she returned to Canada and began a career as a journalist and broadcaster. From 1952 to 1972 she worked for the Canadian Broadcasting Corporation and La Société Radio Canada. In 1972 she was one of the founders of the Institute of Political Research, a government-sponsored agency formed to advise the federal Cabinet.

It was but one step from adviser to the Cabinet to elected member of the Cabinet. She had married the Hon. Maurice Sauvé, who was himself a member of Parliament from 1962 to 1968 and forestry minister in the Cabinet of Lester Pearson from 1964 to 1968. During her years in the House of Commons, Jeanne Sauvé was both popular and powerful. When Prime Minister Pierre Trudeau *(q.v.)* proposed her for the office of speaker, she believed that she had been chosen partly because of her sex.

(DIANE LOIS WAY)

Schmidt, Helmut

West Germany's federal chancellor, Helmut Schmidt, was reelected by the Bundestag, the federal parliament, on Nov. 5, 1980, for a further four-year term. A month earlier, his Social Democratic Party (SPD) and its Free Democratic coalition partner had won the federal election with a greatly increased majority. Schmidt, who since first becoming chancellor in May 1974 had acquired the reputation of an effective crisis manager, was easily the most esteemed politician in the country—and one of the most influential of Western Europe's leaders.

BRIAN F. ALPERT—KEYSTONE

In a statement to the Bundestag on January 17, Schmidt said that the primary international task was to prevent an escalation of crises and to defuse them. "We know that the federal republic is not a big power," he added, "but we are involved within the scope of our possibilities—and these are not insignificant." However, the chancellor had to put up with a good deal of criticism from the U.S. and from the opposition in West Germany to the effect that he was soft in his approach to the Soviet Union. Schmidt visited Moscow at the beginning of July for talks with Soviet Pres. Leonid Brezhnev and afterward said he felt sure that Moscow "clearly recognizes that the problem of Afghanistan will have to be resolved by a political solution." He claimed that, together with his friend Pres. Valéry Giscard d'Estaing of France, he had helped get the superpowers talking again after a dangerous break in the East-West dialogue.

Born in Hamburg on Dec. 23, 1918, Schmidt was the son of a grammar-school teacher. During World War II he served with an armoured division on the eastern front and later took part in the Ardennes offensive. He joined the SPD immediately after the war, studied economics in Hamburg, and during 1949–53 worked in the city administration. Elected to the Bundestag in 1953, he gave up his seat in 1961 and returned to Hamburg as senator (minister) for internal affairs. In 1965 he was called back to Bonn by the party leadership, becoming defense minister (1969–72), minister of economics and finance (July–December 1972), then minister of finance until he succeeded Willy Brandt as chancellor. (NORMAN CROSSLAND)

Seaga, Edward Philip George

Edward Seaga, who took office as Jamaica's prime minister on Nov. 1, 1980, was both by personality and by politics almost the exact opposite of his predecessor, Michael Manley. While Manley had the charisma and oratorical skills that kept audiences spellbound, Seaga, though certainly capable of holding his own at public meetings, was much more of a private person. This had the effect on both Jamaicans and outsiders of making him appear calculating, uncompromising, and lacking in warmth. But in reality he was a caring man of ideas, with a strong resolve to carry through what he believed to be right. Though unsmiling in public and a disciplinarian within the Jamaica Labour Party (JLP), he was more relaxed in private.

Seaga was pro-Western, pro-free enterprise, and generally to the right of centre in terms of Caribbean politics. His support of big business, Western models of development, and International Monetary Fund (IMF) assistance for Jamaica earned him the largely unwarranted reputation of not being concerned about the poor. Both his personal and public life belied this; unlike many JLP parliamentarians, he had a clear understanding of the poor, having spent several months living and working in rural communities while undertaking research. His constituency incorporated an area that, as minister of development, he had transformed from a slum into a model of rehabilitation.

WIDE WORLD

The son of a Lebanese immigrant to Jamaica, Seaga was born in Boston, Mass., in 1930. He was educated at Wolmer's Boys School (Kingston), Harvard University, and the University of the West Indies, where he studied child development, revival cults, and faith healing. In 1959, while working as a financial consultant and university lecturer, he entered the upper house of the Jamaican Legislative Council as its youngest member ever. He was elected to Parliament and was appointed minister of development and welfare. In 1967 he became minister of finance and planning and developed a reputation as something of a financial wizard. When the People's National Party won the 1972 election, the then JLP leader, Hugh Shearer, stepped down. Seaga was appointed to succeed him and, despite criticism, remained party leader when the JLP suffered its second consecutive defeat in 1976. (DAVID A. JESSOP)

Sembene, Ousmane

Although Ousmane Sembene was widely revered as the father of the African cinema, in 1980 his most recent film, *Ceddo*, remained banned in his native Senegal. Made in 1977, *Ceddo* was an ambitious, panoramic account of aspects of African religions. Although ostensibly banned because of a legalistic quibble over the "incorrect" transcription of its Wolof-language title, in fact its criticism of the role of Islam in precolonial days probably rendered it politically unacceptable to a government heavily reliant upon Muslim support.

Sembene was born in 1923 in Ziguinchor in southern Senegal and spent his early years as a fisherman on the Casamance coast. He studied at the École de Céramique at Marsassoum and then moved to Dakar, where he found work as a bricklayer, plumber, and apprentice mechanic until he was drafted into the French Army in 1939. In 1942, during World War II, he joined the Free French forces and landed in France for the first time in 1944. After demobilization he remained in France, working as a docker in Marseille, and became a militant trade unionist.

Had he made no films, Sembene would still have enjoyed an international reputation as a leading African writer. He taught himself to read and write in French and in 1956 published his first novel, *Le Docker noir*, based on his experiences in Marseille. Among the works that followed were *O pays, mon beau peuple!* (1957), *Les Bouts de bois de dieu* (1960), *Voltaïque* (1962), *L'Harmattan* (1964), and *Xala* (1974), which also provided the subject of one of his best films. About 1960 Sembene became interested in motion pictures, particularly as a medium of education and propaganda in his own country. Failing to get a film apprenticeship or education in France, he accepted an invitation to go to the Moscow Film School. Returning to Africa, he made three short subjects, all reflecting a strong social commitment, and in 1967 a feature film, *Le Noir de...*, the first ever produced by an African filmmaker. It described the virtual enslavement of an illiterate girl from Dakar employed as a servant by a French family.

With *Mandabi* ("The Money Order"), a comedy of daily life and corruption in Dakar, Sembene in 1968 took the revolutionary decision to film not in French but in the Wolof language. All his subsequent films were in Wolof. (DAVID ROBINSON)

Shaffer, Peter

British playwright Peter Shaffer won his greatest theatrical triumph in 1980. His drama *Amadeus*, premiered at London's National Theatre in the autumn of 1979, won several top honours in 1980: the Best Play Award given by the London daily newspaper *The Evening Standard* and *Plays and Players* magazine's Best New Play of the Year Award. Also, for the best performance of the year, the Variety Club of Great Britain Award was given to Paul Scofield in the leading role of Salieri, the Austrian composer and contemporary of Mozart whose rivalry with the younger man of genius provided the framework for the most controversial drama of the season.

Amadeus was highly praised as one of the finest plays of its day by every critic except one. The exception was James Fenton of *The Sunday Times*, who vilified it but provided the National Theatre with a useful quote in its advertisements: "the play James Fenton loves to hate."

Most of Shaffer's plays were performed by the National Theatre. His psychological drama *Equus* (1973), about the mutilation of a stableful of horses by a deranged stable lad, also won accolades in its time, was widely staged throughout the world, and made an absorbing film.

Born in Liverpool on May 15, 1926, and educated at St. Paul's School in London and Trinity College, Cambridge, Shaffer—after completing his national service in the coal mines—worked in the New York City Public Library and for a London music publisher. He was also music critic of a London weekly for a year, but after the success of his first acclaimed play, *Five Finger Exercise* (1958), he devoted all his time to writing dramas and comedies, television plays, film scripts, and thrillers, the last in collaboration with his twin brother, Anthony. The epic *The Royal Hunt of the Sun* (1964) dealt with the search of the Spanish conquistador Francisco Pizarro for the Inca god Atahuallpa. He wrote *The Battle of Shrivings* (1970) for John Gielgud, who had made Shaffer's name by directing *Five Finger Exercise. Amadeus*, directed by Peter Hall, opened at New York City's Broadhurst Theatre in December 1980. (OSSIA TRILLING)

Shamir, Yitzhak

Yitzhak Shamir was appointed Israel's minister of foreign affairs in March 1980 following the resignation of Moshe Dayan in October 1979. Prime Minister Menachem Begin had himself assumed responsibility for foreign affairs during the interim before inviting his close associate to take over the portfolio. A loyal member of the Begin team, Shamir was a man of few words who held clear and firm opinions, though his essential toughness was overlaid with an easy charm. He was known to be a strong supporter of the right of Jews to settle in Israeli-occupied Arab territories and was regarded as a possible successor to Begin.

Born in 1915 in Ruzinoy, eastern Poland, Shamir joined the Beitar Zionist youth movement as a young man and studied law in Warsaw. He emigrated to Palestine in 1935 and enrolled as a student at the Hebrew University in Jerusalem. There he joined the Irgun Zvai Leumi (IZL) underground movement, and in 1940, following a split in the IZL on questions of policy, he joined the Israel Freedom Fighters (IFF), later known as the Stern Group after its founder, Abraham Stern. The IZL and the IFF operated independently and often in opposition to the mainstream of Jewish resistance in Palestine, represented by the Haganah.

Following the death of Stern, Shamir played a central part in reorganizing the Sternist Central Committee, together with Israel Scheib-Eldad and the late Nathan Yellin-Mor. Shamir was arrested by the British mandate authorities in 1941 and 1946. After his second escape from internment in Eritrea, he made his way to France where he was granted asylum. He returned to Israel in May 1948 and served in important positions in the civil service until 1965. After engaging in private commerce for a time, he joined Begin's Herut movement in 1970 and was appointed to head the movement's immigration department and, later, the organization department. In March 1975 he was elected chairman of the Executive. First elected to the Knesset in 1973, he became its speaker after Begin's electoral victory in 1977. (JON KIMCHE)

Shimada, Yoko

The filming of "Shogun" was in deep trouble five weeks into production. Despite scores of interviews, no one had been found to play the role of Mariko, the beautiful samurai lady who combined gentleness and sensitivity with a will of steel. Then Yoko Shimada was given an audition. "There was never any doubt," said producer and screenwriter Eric Bercovici. He had found his "Japanese Scarlett O'Hara." Shimada was strikingly beautiful, stood 5-ft 6-in tall, was model-thin, and spoke English.

Yoko Shimada was born on May 17, 1953, in Kumamoto Prefecture. She enrolled in the Wakagusa private drama academy while in junior high school and was rated well above average in her mastery of English. In 1971 she was chosen over 12,000 other aspirants for a role in the TV movie "Hyoten" ("Freezing Point"). Thereafter, she was cast as the traditional pure and innocent heroine of romantic stories. But when Shimada firmly resisted, directors gave in and offered her more varied roles. After ten feature films and some two dozen television shows in Japan, Shimada reached what she has called "the turning point in a lackluster career." She was offered the part of Mariko in the U.S.-produced 12-hour miniseries "Shogun." The 27-year-old actress had been named Japan's best TV actress in 1975 and had made occasional visits to the U.S. to study English with an American woman. But for her, "the toughest part of 'Shogun' was learning English all over again." For others, the toughest part would have been finding sufficient courage to perform before 125 million Americans. Shimada also shared the burden of bringing a knowledge of feudal Japan to an audience that knew next to nothing about the subject and probably had never seen a Japanese movie. One measure of Shimada's success was suggested by those who thought "Shogun" lacked its earlier vitality after Mariko gave her life to save her lover, English pilot John Blackthorne (played by Richard Chamberlain).

With "Shogun" completed, Shimada fulfilled commitments in Japan, then returned to the U.S. to film *Little Champion.* She has also signed to act in *The Foxes* and *Comeback,* for each of which she will reportedly earn half a million dollars. In addition, she has an $800,000 contract for three U.S. television commercials. "Shogun" does indeed seem to have been a turning point in what Shimada hopes will be an exciting international film career. (KAY K. TATEISHI)

Sipe, Brian

Maybe losing a football game to Brian Sipe would be easier to take if he stood 6 ft 4 in and threw nothing but perfect spirals. The way the Cleveland Browns quarterback does win games, an opponent has to reach under his coat and pull out a bloody hand before he realizes he has been stabbed.

"Resourceful," they call him. For some reason a scrambler who's barely 6 ft tall inspires creative superlatives for doing the same things for which hulking first-round draft choices get called simply "great." "Efficient" is another term, as is "feisty."

"I think those are terms people apply to things they don't understand," Sipe says. "I have the feeling, when people describe my play that way, that they'd also like to include 'lucky' but they're afraid to say it. I'm sure we'll throw for 300 yards some days and teams will leave the stadium not sure how we beat them."

The way the Cleveland Browns did win in 1980 was usually by passing and usually by a touchdown or less. The Browns had 12 of their 16 games decided by that margin and won 9 of them. Their 11–5 record ended Pittsburgh's eight-year string of championships in the Central Division of the National Football League's American Conference.

Sipe hurled the Browns to the top with the NFL's best-passer rating and the uncommon combination of many big plays and few bad ones. His 30 touchdown passes trailed the league leader by one; his 14 interceptions in 554 attempts was the league's lowest rate. He also became the third NFL passer ever to gain more than 4,000 yd, and 60.8% of his passes were complete. At the season's end he was named the league's most valuable player. "He's totally dependable in stress situations," said Sipe's coach, Sam Rutigliano.

The confidence that Sipe displayed in 1980 had to be rebuilt after his first two NFL seasons, which he spent on the Browns' supplemental roster, ineligible to play. He had been just a 13th-round draft choice in 1972. Scouts had said he was too small, even though he had been the national collegiate passing champion for San Diego State, in the city where he was born Aug. 8, 1949. But in 1976 the Browns' regular quarterback was injured, and Sipe became their starter. In 1978 Rutigliano became their coach and said he would let Sipe throw on any down, from anywhere. (KEVIN M. LAMB)

Spacek, Sissy

If Monday's child is fair of face and Tuesday's tot is full of grace, perhaps a Christmas baby comes with gifts to personify everything in Santa's stocking from lumps of coal to sugarplums. Sissy Spacek, born in a small Texas town on Dec. 25, 1949, was variously a squirrel hunter, frog gigger, rodeo rider, drum majorette, Spanish Club officer, and homecoming queen. Starting out with a mail-order guitar, she studied with a local preacher and then gave lessons herself at 50 cents an hour. But before she could even get a part in her high-school play, her brother was stricken with leukemia and she was packed off to visit cousins Rip Torn and Geraldine Page in New York City.

They introduced her to show business, and she aimed at wowing the world as a rock singer before enrolling in Lee Strasberg's Theatrical Studio—and discovering that she knew everything the "Method" master had to teach. Between modeling stints, bubble-gum commercials, and nightclub singing jobs, she auditioned for movies and won a featured role in *Prime Cut,* a morbid white-slavery saga that the public ignored. In one critic's view it bombed because Spacek's sensitive performance "made too many people feel guilty."

Next she appeared as the passive-romantic-sadistic tagalong to Martin Sheen's teenage psychopathic murderer in *Badlands* and then as a waif in the homespun television serial "The Waltons." Her first major recognition came in the title role in *Carrie,* a terrifying film adaptation of a horror novel by Stephen King (*q.v.*). She played a miserable teenager who repays various tormentors by destroying them via telekinesis. In this as in previous performances, she won favourable reviews and the attention of her peers.

In 1980 Spacek won her second motion picture Academy Award nomination for portraying country music star Loretta Lynn in *Coal Miner's Daughter*. Aging 22 years in the film, she grows from barefoot urchin to the epitome of Nashville chic. Roger Angell applauded in *The New Yorker* "her ability to convince us so easily that she is a young-looking 14-year-old at the beginning, and a bewigged, decked-out, 40ish celebrity-star, and a mother of six, at its end." (PHILIP KOPPER)

Stevens, Jimmy Moli

Beginning in the 1960s, Jimmy Stevens led the first widespread protest against colonialism in the New Hebrides, an Anglo-French condominium that achieved independence as Vanuatu on July 30, 1980. Born of mixed European-Islander descent on June 15, 1927, Stevens was a man of limited education but of charismatic personality, with the ability to articulate the grievances of ordinary villagers. In the early 1960s he joined a small group of Espíritu Santo islanders opposing the encroachment of a cattle industry into "dark bush land." They called their movement Nagriamel (after two plants, nagaria and namele), and by 1970 it had a large following (Stevens claimed 10,000). Nagriamel rejected colonial control over New Hebridean land, championed "custom," and repudiated many of the highly suspect land sales of the early colonial period.

In the 1970s the anticolonial initiative passed from Stevens to the Vanuaaku Party under Walter Lini (*q.v.*). Stevens found himself heading a regional movement that was increasingly allied with pro-French and pro-settler groups opposed to decolonization and to the anglophone groups that dominated the new government. He was encouraged (and funded) by them and also by U.S. business interests that had invested heavily and speculatively in land. For example, the Phoenix Foundation, a group of libertarian U.S. businessmen hoping for a tax haven and a free hand in commercial development, backed Stevens and provided a constitution for his Vemarana (after a traditional Santo name) secessionist government launched on the eve of Vanuatu's independence. French settlers imported arms through New Caledonia and drilled Stevens's force of bow-and-arrow-wielding tribesmen.

As the nationalist leadership passed to the younger educated elite, Stevens managed to hold the support of local villagers. But in doing so he mortgaged their interests to foreigners whose aims were incompatible with those of Nagriamel. It was the price that had to be paid for a defiant gesture in defense of local identity. But within a month of independence, Vanefo village, Stevens's headquarters, fell to Papua New Guinea troops called in by the new Vanuatu government. Stevens was arrested and put on trial and on November 21 was sentenced to 14½ years' imprisonment. (BARRIE MACDONALD)

Stevens, Siaka Probyn

The long and checkered political career of Pres. Siaka Stevens of Sierra Leone was crowned by his election as chairman for 1980–81 of the Organization of African Unity. He presided over the OAU's 1980 summit meeting in Freetown in July. Another highly successful event of the year for Stevens was his five-day official visit to Britain in November, which resulted in a £3.5 million capital aid grant from the U.K. to Sierra Leone for investment in various development projects.

Born in Moyamba in the southern province of Sierra Leone on Aug. 24, 1905, Stevens completed his secondary schooling at the Albert Academy in Freetown. He worked as a policeman, railwayman, and miner before devoting himself to labour politics. He helped to found the United Mineworkers' Union in 1943 and served as its general secretary for 15 years. In 1947 he studied unionism at Ruskin College, Oxford, and with the British Trades Union Congress. On his return home in 1948 he made his mark as a militant labour leader. He was elected to the colonial legislature in 1951 and after the granting of internal self-government in 1952 became his country's first minister of lands, mines, and labour. He was prominent in forming the Sierra Leone People's Party, which eventually took his country to independence. In 1958 he became the deputy leader of the People's National Party and two years later formed another party, the All People's Congress (APC).

After independence in April 1961 Stevens led the parliamentary opposition and also served as mayor of Freetown. When his APC won the 1967 general elections, he became prime minister but was promptly ousted by an army coup and went into exile. After a second military coup in 1968 he returned to become prime minister once again. Three years later, when Sierra Leone became a republic, he was elected president. After being returned for a new term of office in 1976, he won support for his plan to turn Sierra Leone into a single-party state, for which the necessary legislation was passed in 1978. In foreign affairs he played an important role in building bridges between his radical French-speaking neighbour, Guinea, and the formerly conservative English-speaking Liberia. (COLIN LEGUM)

Stirling, James Frazer

An unusual honour for an architect still in his prime is to receive the Gold Medal for Architecture of the Royal Institute of British Architects, but this award was bestowed upon James Stirling in 1980. Best known for his three "red" buildings of the 1960s, major monuments of a style later termed "brutalist," he was a powerful spokesman for the generation of architects who entered practice after World War II. Typically, his work emphasized the importance of materials, especially in his use of hard technological surfaces of brilliant red brick, glass, tiles, metal, and plastic. His buildings stand in sculptural isolation from their landscapes in their uncompromising geometrical organization, their different parts clearly articulated as form and texture contrast and curves and angles collide, defined by bright strident colours and hard shiny surfaces.

Stirling was born in Glasgow on April 22, 1926, and educated in Liverpool, receiving his architectural training at the University of Liverpool's School of Architecture (1945–50). He began practice in the early 1950s in London and from 1956 to 1963 was in partnership with James Gowan. His early projects consisted of housing. His work always showed a concern for social usage and a sense of community, and he was one of the first to advocate the type of low-rise mass housing that found favour in Britain after the failure of high-rises as a solution to low-cost housing problems. His first major "red" building was the Engineering Department building for Leicester University (1959–63). Two variations on this theme followed: the History Faculty Library for Cambridge University (1964–67) and the Florey Building at Queen's College, Oxford (1966–71). In these three works Stirling integrated the industrial ethic with architectural form in a new way. The Leicester building arguably had the greatest impact on architects of any postwar building. With its hard red brick and tile and its glass and industrial framing, it was a radical departure.

Stirling's Olivetti Training School at Haslemere, Surrey (1969–72), exhibited a change of emphasis toward a greater manipulation of space and the use of newer materials. Later works were less "hard" and technological, revealing an increasing interplay of shapes, spaces, and symbols. (SANDRA MILLIKIN)

Streep, Meryl

Few were surprised when Meryl Streep won the Academy Award as best supporting actress in April 1980. She had portrayed the mother in *Kramer vs. Kramer*, a film about a woman who abandons her self-absorbed husband and her child to seek independence. She returns 18 months later to demand custody of the boy after the father, following a painful period of self-examination, has established a relationship with his son. The film confounds traditional expectations. The father, initially insensitive, slowly transforms himself into an affectionate parent. The mother, understandably desperate to escape at first, returns as a kind of villain but wins the sympathy of the audience during a courtroom scene near the end of the film. Both Meryl Streep and Dustin Hoffman, the two stars of the film, won Academy Awards for their intense and convincing portrayals of two people facing particularly contemporary problems.

Meryl Streep could "have made it to the screen on looks alone," wrote one critic. Though undeniably beautiful, she has succeeded as an artist in a wide variety of stage and film roles. Born in Summit, N.J., in 1949, Streep was an unattractive child with a good singing voice. She performed in musicals in high school. After obtaining a drama degree from Vassar College in Poughkeepsie, N.Y., she performed on stage in Vermont for a time and then won a three-year scholarship to the Yale University School of Drama. From there she went to New York City and a series of classical stage roles. She appeared in plays by Shakespeare, Chekhov, Brecht, Arthur Miller, and Tennessee Williams. Her films included *The Seduction of Joe Tynan, The Deer Hunter*, and *Kramer vs. Kramer*.

(VICTOR M. CASSIDY)

Suzuki, Zenko

Zenko Suzuki was virtually unknown at home and abroad when he was elected prime minister of Japan on July 17, 1980. Masayoshi Ohira, his predecessor, had been forced in mid-May to call new elections when factious members of his own Liberal-Democratic Party (LDP) withheld their support in a crucial parliamentary vote of no confidence. Ohira died unexpectedly ten days before the election, which the LDP won overwhelmingly. Then a three-week battle for succession was on. When supporters of the three main candidates refused to compromise, party leaders Takeo Fukuda and Kakuei Tanaka, both former prime ministers, swung their support to dark horse Suzuki. Though he had never served as party secretary-general or held any of the key portfolios, Suzuki, a loyal and longtime party workhorse, was elected party president, assuring him the prime ministership.

Suzuki was born on Jan. 11, 1911, in Yamada Town, Iwate Prefecture. Because his fisherman father could afford nothing better, Suzuki attended Imperial Fisheries Institute (now Tokyo University of Fisheries), then joined the Japan Fisheries Association. In 1947, "burning with humanitarianism," he won a seat in the lower house of the Diet (parliament) as a Socialist. Realizing he had little hope of getting government funds to aid constituents recovering from two devastating 1948 typhoons, he switched to the conservative Liberal Party (forerunner of the LDP) and won reelection 12 times. His gifts as a mediator in Japan's complex political world also brought him the chairmanship of the LDP executive council a record ten times.

It comes as no surprise, therefore, that Prime Minister Suzuki has adopted the slogan "politics of harmony." He is continuing Ohira's foreign policy of moderate internationalism and is working closely with the U.S., other Western nations, and China. In matters of finance, trade, and defense he has been cautious. If recent polls are to be trusted, excessive caution may contain the seeds of Suzuki's eventual downfall. Numerous voters apparently feel he has not been aggressive enough in facing controversial issues, such as debating a revision of the postwar constitution and solving the dilemma of visiting Yasukuni Shrine, which honours Japan's war dead. An official visit would be an implicit endorsement of Shinto as a state religion, a status it no longer enjoys. One newspaper editorial urged Suzuki to speak out more clearly on his political beliefs. The prime minister doubtless heard the message; time will tell if he feels he must also heed it.

(KAY K. TATEISHI)

Taylor, Kenneth

A man who enjoyed reading cloak-and-dagger novels, Ambassador Kenneth Taylor authored his own "Canadian Caper" in Iran. After the U.S. embassy in Teheran was seized by militants on Nov. 4, 1979, Taylor, the Canadian ambassador to Iran, found himself host to six members of the U.S. embassy staff who had escaped capture. After hiding them for more than three months, Taylor helped engineer their escape from the country. While Iranians were preoccupied with their presidential election, the Canadian embassy was closed and the Americans, supplied with Canadian passports, were spirited out of the country as part of the Canadian entourage.

Although he insisted that his was not an individual effort and that he had had the advice of others in engineering the escape, Taylor became a hero for the U.S. The U.S. Congress awarded him a specially struck gold medal. For six months Taylor and his wife crisscrossed the United States, making speeches, shaking hands, and receiving awards. The American Academy of Achievement presented him with its Gold Plate Award; the state of California with its Medal of Merit; and the Detroit-Windsor Border Area with the International Freedom Festival Award.

Born in Calgary, Alta., on Oct. 5, 1934, Taylor received a B.A. degree from the University of Toronto in 1957 and an M.A. degree in business administration from the University of California at Berkeley in 1959. After graduation in 1959 Taylor joined the Canadian Foreign Service's Trade Commissioner Service, for which he served in several posts, both in Canada and abroad, until 1977. His first posting with the Canadian Department of External Affairs took place in 1977, when he was made ambassador to Iran. He was chosen for this post because he had the skills and experience to promote sales of Canadian-made pulp and paper equipment and thermal power plant parts.

Canadians were also proud of Taylor's Iranian success. The Canadian government made him an Officer of the Order of Canada, and Laurentian University in Sudbury, Ont., gave him an honorary degree. The citizens of New York City, who had given Taylor the key to their city in 1980, were delighted when in July 1980 he was appointed the Canadian consul general in New York and the commissioner to Bermuda. (DIANE LOIS WAY)

Thatcher, Margaret Hilda

In her second year as Britain's first woman prime minister, Margaret Thatcher reinforced her claim to the nickname "the iron lady." There were to be no reversals of policy, none of the so-called U-turns which had characterized the governments of the 1970s. Committed to a monetarist policy of squeezing inflation out of the economy by cutting government expenditure and holding down the money supply by high interest rates, she had said in 1979 that things would get worse before they got better.

Get worse they did, with unemployment over two million, inflation rising from 10 to 20% in the government's first year and falling only slowly in the later months of 1980, sky-high interest rates, and a surge of bankruptcies. But Thatcher did not flinch from the consequences of the monetarist remedy. She resisted pressures from business to lower interest rates, and she persisted with a crusade against government and public-sector expenditure regardless of mounting protests from within her own Conservative Party. In one sector she could claim some success—there was a decline in the level of wage increases as trade unions came to see that there was a limit to the employers' capacity to pay.

Thatcher's abrasive, hawkish style was also seen in her conduct of foreign affairs. She secured a substantial refund of British contributions to the European Economic Community, though at the cost of some ill feeling among her fellow heads of state. She echoed the hard-line attitudes of the U.S. toward the Soviet Union, and she brought the U.K. into the nuclear arms race with decisions to provide bases in Britain for cruise missiles and to spend £5 billion on a new generation of nuclear submarines. She was coldly unsympathetic to the Brandt Commission's proposals to move ahead with aid for the third world.

Margaret Thatcher was born on Oct. 13, 1925, the daughter of a successful grocer who became the mayor of the small market town of Grantham, Lincolnshire. After studying science at the University of Oxford, she worked for a time as a research chemist. But politics was her first interest, and in 1959 she was elected to Parliament. A member of the Cabinet (as minister of education and science) in Edward Heath's government of 1970–74, she was elected leader of the Conservative Party after the defeat of the Heath government in the 1974 general election. (HARFORD THOMAS)

Thompson, Daley Francis

The 1980 Olympic Games decathlon champion, Daley Thompson, was never reluctant to come forward. Before the Moscow Games he said: "I don't even think about the possibility of not winning—it never occurs to me. I really am that confident." An engaging, articulate young man who was given much television and press coverage, Thompson earned the tag of the "Muhammad Ali of track."

The brash 22-year-old justified his confidence with a briefly held world record score (8,622 points) for the tough ten-event test at Götzis, Austria, in May 1980. In Moscow Thompson ran, jumped, hurdled, and threw his way to the Olympic decathlon title, running up 8,495 points; his chief rival, Guido Kratschmer (West Germany), the current world record holder (8,649), did not compete because of West Germany's Olympic boycott.

Born in London on July 30, 1958, the son of a Nigerian father and a Scottish mother, Thompson completed his first decathlon at 16 in Cwmbran, Wales, in 1975 and won it with 6,685 points, a record total for his age. He then trained under coach Bruce Longden at Crawley, West Sussex, for the 1976 Olympic Games where he finished 18th. Later, Thompson raised the U.K. record to 7,905 and then ran up 7,921 in May 1977 at Götzis. In 1977 he amassed 8,190 in Madrid and won the European junior title at Donetsk, Ukraine. Thompson boosted the U.K. record to 8,238 points in 1978 and gained world acclaim when he took the Commonwealth title at Edmonton, Alta., in 1978 with 8,467 points (later invalidated because of wind assistance). In the 1978 European championships at Prague he lost to A. Grebenyuk of the U.S.S.R., though his 8,289 was a U.K. record till May 1980.

In the 1980 Olympic decathlon Thompson's marks for the ten events were: 100 m, 10.62 sec; 400 m, 48.01 sec; 1,500 m, 4 min 39.90 sec; 110-m hurdles, 14.47 sec; high jump, 2.08 m; pole vault, 4.70 m; long jump, 8.00 m; shot put, 15.18 m; discus, 42.24 m; and javelin, 64.16 m.

(DAVID COCKSEDGE)

Thorn, Gaston

After a long and varied career both as a politician in his native Luxembourg and as an international statesman, Gaston Thorn in June 1980 was designated as next president of the Commission of the European Community. He would take office in January 1981, succeeding Roy Jenkins of the U.K. Meanwhile, he resigned as Luxembourg's foreign minister and as president of the European Community's Council of Ministers.

Born in Luxembourg on Sept. 3, 1928, Thorn was educated there (where as a schoolboy during World War II he took part in anti-Nazi activities) and also in France and in Switzerland. He qualified as a doctor of law and was appointed to the Luxembourg bar. During the 1950s he took an active part in local politics, becoming a Luxembourg City municipal councillor and then mayor of Luxembourg (1961–63). Meanwhile, he had joined the liberal Democratic Party and in 1959 became a member of Parliament and, soon afterward, of the European Parliament. In 1961 he was named the Democratic Party's chairman.

Thorn had extensive ministerial experience. Following the 1968 general election he became foreign minister and minister for trade in the Christian Socialist-Democratic coalition. His personal popularity—he was as much at ease among soccer fans as with fellow statesmen—contributed to his party's success in the 1974 election, which ended 50 years of Christian Socialist domination in Luxembourg politics. He then served as prime minister in a coalition with the Workers' Socialist Party. He also took responsibility for the portfolios of foreign affairs and foreign trade, economy, and the middle classes, retaining these responsibilities after the 1979 election in a new Christian Socialist-Liberal coalition headed by Pierre Werner.

In September 1975 Thorn was elected president of the 30th UN General Assembly, and the following year he was chosen to head the newly formed Federation of Liberal and Democratic Parties within the European Community. Multilingual, living at the crossroads of the Germanic and Latin civilizations of Europe, he was a firm believer in the need for European unity. However, his appointment as president of the Commission had been preceded by some disagreement, and it was known that he had not been the favoured candidate of France's Pres. Valéry Giscard d'Estaing.

(JOHN PALMER)

Tikhonov, Nikolay Aleksandrovich

Nobody was surprised when on Oct. 23, 1980, Pres. Leonid Brezhnev informed the Supreme Soviet of the U.S.S.R. that Aleksey Kosygin (*see* OBITUARIES) had written to announce his resignation from the premiership and then proposed the election of Nikolay Tikhonov in his place; the Supreme Soviet unanimously accepted the proposal. For in November 1979 Tikhonov, first deputy premier of the Soviet government, had been elected a full member of the party's ruling Politburo, a move paving his way to still higher promotion.

On Nov. 6, 1980, shortly after his appointment as premier, Tikhonov delivered the traditional speech celebrating the 63rd anniversary of the October Revolution. He pointed out that the national income for only five days was now equal to the national income total for the whole of 1928, on the eve of the first five-year plan period.

Tikhonov was born on May 14, 1905, in

Kharkov, Ukraine, the son of a Russian, not Ukrainian, worker. He began his career as an engine driver's assistant on the railways but subsequently graduated from the Dnepropetrovsk Metallurgical Institute and obtained a doctorate in engineering science. From 1930 he worked as an engineer, as head of a production shop, and then as director of a plant at Dnepropetrovsk. At that time Brezhnev served in that city as secretary of the Communist Party's regional committee. As the two men became friends, Brezhnev advised Tikhonov to join the party, which he did in 1940.

During World War II and afterward, Tikhonov held many leading posts in the Soviet Ministry of Ferrous Metallurgy. From 1957 to 1960, at the peak of Pres. Nikita Khrushchev's reforming zeal, he was chairman of the short-lived Dnepropetrovsk Economic Council. In 1963 he became a vice-chairman of the State Planning Committee (Gosplan), a post carrying the rank of minister. In 1965, one year after Brezhnev became the party's leader, Tikhonov was appointed a deputy premier of the Soviet Council of Ministers. Observers ruled out Tikhonov as a contender for the party leadership in the event of Brezhnev's resignation or death.

(K. M. SMOGORZEWSKI)

Toyoda, Eiji

In Arthur Hailey's novel *Wheels,* a Detroit auto engineer sneers at a Japanese import and remarks: "Wherever [quality] is going . . . it ain't gone to Japan . . . at least not to the plant that produced this clunker." In October 1980 Hailey wrote to the editor of a Tokyo newspaper that he now had "the greatest respect for Japanese cars and the evidence is that my wife has a Toyota Corolla; it is our second Toyota and the original . . . is still in excellent condition."

Eiji Toyoda (also pronounced Toyota), the 67-year-old president of the Toyota Motor Co., must have chuckled contentedly when he read those words. In June 1980 his company finished the fiscal year with a profit of $638 million on sales of $14,712,000,000. Toyota exports to the U.S. were up 27.3% over the previous year and increased overall an astonishing 39.3%.

Eiji Toyoda was born in Aichi Prefecture on Sept. 12, 1913. He graduated from the University of Tokyo's department of engineering in 1936, then joined the Toyota Automatic Weaving Machine Manufacturing Co. The company was founded by Sakichi Toyoda, Eiji's uncle, whose invention became the basis of the future Toyoda industrial empire. Just one year later Eiji Toyoda was transferred to the Toyota Motor Co., which had just been set up by Sakichi's son, Kiichiro. In 1945 Eiji became chief of management production and technology, then director of the company. After a series of other promotions, he became president of Toyota Motor Co. in 1967, replacing his cousin Kiichiro. The highly successful 1,000-cc Toyota Corolla had just gone on the market; one future buyer would be Arthur Hailey.

Eiji Toyoda is currently edging toward a joint venture with Ford Motor Co., but he describes the process as equivalent to climbing Mt. Everest. A basic agreement, reached in July 1980, stipulated that "if and when" Toyota decides to produce automobiles in the U.S., it will utilize Ford's idle plants. Douglas Fraser, president of the United Auto Workers, is also urging Toyota to absorb some of the unemployed U.S. auto workers by building its own assembly line in the U.S. As Eiji Toyoda nears retirement, he says his hobby is strolling among his 43,900 factory workers watching them manufacture cars that are known the world over for good mileage, durability, and cheap repairs.

(TAKAO TOKUOKA)

Trudeau, Pierre Elliott

After his Liberal Party had been swept from power in Canada in a general election in May 1979, Prime Minister Pierre Trudeau assured the Canadian people that he would soon retire from political life. But when the government of Prime Minister Joe Clark was brought down on a vote on the government budget in December 1979, he reconsidered his decision. In the election on Feb. 18, 1980, his party was returned to power with a clear majority in the Canadian House of Commons, and on March 3 Trudeau again became prime minister.

Trudeau was first elected to the House of Commons in 1965 to represent the riding of Mount Royal (Montreal) and was soon appointed parliamentary secretary to Prime Minister Lester Pearson. After a year as Canada's minister of justice and attorney general (1967–68), Trudeau was elected leader of the Liberal Party of Canada. He was sworn in as prime minister on April 20, 1968. In his 11 years in that position (1968–79), Trudeau introduced policies and programs designed to strengthen Canadian unity, increase social justice for all Canadians, and bring stability and peace to international relations.

Born Oct. 18, 1919, in Montreal, Trudeau earned a degree in law from the University of Montreal. After receiving a master of arts degree in political economy from Harvard University, he took postgraduate courses in law, economics, and political science at the École des Sciences Politiques in Paris and the London School of Economics. From 1951 to 1961 he practiced law in Quebec Province, specializing in labour law and civil liberties cases. During this period he wrote extensively on reform in politics and on the theory and practice of federalism. He was co-founder of the monthly review *Cité Libre,* one of the most influential forces for reform in Quebec during the 1950s and '60s. He also was an associate professor of law at the University of Montreal from 1961 to 1965.

Of primary importance to Trudeau, once he regained power in 1980, was the reform of Canada's constitution. In 1978 he had introduced a bill in the House of Commons proposing a set of changes in the constitution, including the incorporation of a charter of rights and freedoms in the document, in particular, minority language rights. Trudeau also wanted the constitution to define more clearly the division of legislative powers between the federal and provincial governments. The British North America Act, Canada's current constitution, was enacted by the British Parliament in 1867 and had remained under the control of the U.K. Trudeau's first order of business when the Canadian Parliament met in October 1980 was to begin a process to bring the act under Canadian control.

(DIANE LOIS WAY)

Ulusu, Bulent

If Adm. Bulent Ulusu had not retired from the command of the Turkish Navy in August 1980, he would have been a member of the National Security Council that took over the country's government on September 12. As it was, his fellow commanders appointed him prime minister. Had there been no military coup, Admiral Ulusu would have become Turkish ambassador in Rome. He had learned Italian some 20 years earlier when he had served for two years in the NATO naval headquarters in Malta.

Because of its links with Istanbul, the old imperial Ottoman capital, and also because of the abiding influence of British naval officers, who had advised the Ottoman Navy for decades before World War I, the Turkish Navy was considered the most gentlemanly of the nation's three military services, and it had often provided the republic with statesmen and diplomats of poise and savoir-faire. Bulent Ulusu followed that tradition. When he was chairman of the Turkish Naval Trust, he was described by a leading journalist as "a courteous man, with whom it is a pleasure to work, with an unequalled understanding of teamwork and high ability as a coordinator." Coordinating ability was precisely the quality required of him by his colleagues of the National Security Council, who saw him as their chief executive, presiding over a team of technicians charged with the task of putting Turkey to rights after the country had been brought to the verge of civil war and bankruptcy by the excesses of political passions. For many Turks too, Admiral Ulusu symbolized the hope of calm after a storm. Certainly there was a world of difference between his infrequent matter-of-fact statements and the impassioned rhetoric of the politicians whom he replaced.

Born in Istanbul in 1923, Ulusu was educated at the naval academy and later at the naval staff college. A career of steady promotion took him through subordinate commands to the top job of commander in chief of the Navy in 1977. By that time he had forged links with the leaders of the other services, with whom he worked while a member of the Supreme Military Council.

(ANDREW MANGO)

Walesa, Lech

After mid-August 1980, Lech Walesa was recognized at home and abroad as a charismatic leader of millions of Polish workers organized in the independent self-governing trade union Solidarity.

Listening on August 14 to protests at the huge Gdansk shipyard caused by an increase in food prices and the dismissal of another union activist, Walesa—then unemployed—climbed over the wall and appealed to 17,000 workers to strike. A strike committee headed by Walesa was elected to negotiate with management. Three days later the strikers' demands were conceded, but when strikers in other Gdansk enterprises asked Walesa to continue his strike out of solidarity, he immediately agreed. An Interfactory Strike

BOOK OF THE YEAR

ALAIN NOGUES—SYGMA

Committee uniting the enterprises of the Gdansk-Sopot-Gdynia area was formed, and a general strike was proclaimed.

The workers of the Baltic seaboard had learned a lesson from December 1970, when their street demonstrations were fired upon leaving some 20 dead. In 1980 they occupied the plants and closed the gates. On August 31 Walesa and Mieczyslaw Jagielski, Poland's first deputy premier, signed an agreement conceding the right of workers to organize freely and independently. On December 16, at Gdansk, the creator and leader of Solidarity lit the flame at a monument erected to the memory of the workers killed by the militiamen ten years earlier. In the presence of dignitaries of state and church and 200,000 people, Walesa pleaded forcefully for national reconciliation: "No one should undertake action which might threaten Poland's freedom and sovereignty."

Lech Walesa, son of a carpenter, was born on Sept. 29, 1943, at Popowo near Wloclawek. He received only primary and technical education and in 1967 began work as an electrician at the Gdansk shipyard. Having witnessed the 1970 tragedy, he decided to struggle for really free trade unions. In 1976 Walesa, then delegate to the official trade union at the shipyard, drew up a list of workers' grievances, but the management dismissed him. In January 1979 he was fired from an electrical engineering plant for taking part in a demonstration.

A short man with a splendid mustache and a round face alive with nervous energy, Walesa showed himself to be a skilled negotiator. Asked by a French reporter about the source of his moral strength, he replied, "I am a Christian. . . . Without (God) I would be a nobody."

(K. M. SMOGORZEWSKI)

Warren, Robert Penn

With the publication at age 75 of his 13th volume of poetry, *Being Here,* Robert Penn Warren added another work to a literary output that has earned him the title of "the most distinguished man of letters still at work in the U.S. today." Though best known for the 1946 novel that won him the Pulitzer Prize, *All the King's Men,* based on the life of Louisiana demagogue Huey Long, Warren also made important contributions as a poet, essayist, and teacher.

Warren was born on April 24, 1905, in Kentucky, in a tobacco-farming region that forms the background for many of his novels. He grew seriously interested in literature while attending Vanderbilt University in Tennessee, where he fell in with the leading members of the Fugitives, a group of poets who emerged as one of the driving forces behind the Southern literary renaissance. In 1935 he helped to found the *Southern Review,* one of the leading literary journals of the U.S. during its seven years of existence. He collaborated with Cleanth Brooks to write *Understanding Poetry* (1938), the first of several widely used textbooks in which he introduced the methods of the New Criticism into U.S. colleges and universities.

Warren's own creative potential began to emerge with the publication of his first book of poems, *Thirty-Six Poems,* in 1935 and his first novel, *Night Rider,* in 1939, after which the stream never stopped. His finest novels are all firmly based on real historical incidents and personages, out of which Warren invents the painful moral dilemmas that confront his characters. Using a rich and powerful style, he describes in tones of tragic irony the individual's attempt to define himself and find a line of acceptable conduct in the face of a hostile and degrading environment. The search is often unsuccessful and may end in violence and death rather than ennoblement. Warren's preoccupation with the full range of human character and his emphasis on moral seeking mark him as one of the last remaining giants of the literary tradition that produced an older figure to whom he is sometimes compared, William Faulkner. (PAUL MENDELSON)

Weld, Philip

Phil Weld, a retired newspaper publisher from Dollivers Neck, Gloucester, Mass., broke two records in 1980: he won the 12th Royal Western-Observer Singlehanded Transatlantic Race in the best-ever solo sailing time from Great Britain to the U.S. of 17 days 23 hr 12 min (Plymouth to Newport, R.I.); and, at 65, he was the oldest competitor to have won the race since its inauguration in 1960. His trimaran "Moxie" was entered in the Pen Duick class for the largest yachts (overall length of from 44 ft to 56 ft). Weld, born Dec. 11, 1914, in New York City, is an ecologist passionately interested in man's best use of the elements. As a yachtsman he is a fervent multihull enthusiast and loves singlehanded racing. Three times winner of the Newport-Bermuda race, he finished third in the French Route du Rhum in 1978. He took part in the 1972 Singlehanded Transatlantic Race in the trimaran "Trumpeter" but because of problems with the boat only completed the course after 39 days 13 hr 25 min, placing 27th out of 38 finishers.

He then built a 60-ft trimaran called "Gulf Streamer," in which he took part in the 1974 Observer Round Britain Race and finished third. In this same boat he was entered for the 1976 Singlehanded Transatlantic Race, but on his way to Plymouth the boat capsized and Weld survived four days on the upturned hull before being rescued. "Gulf Streamer" was lost, and with typical wry humour he named his next boat "Rogue Wave." With Briton David Cooksey, he sailed it in the 1978 Round Britain Race to finish third overall, after leading the fleet with only 100 mi to go.

In his latest boat, "Moxie," Weld invested some of the proceeds of the sale of his newspapers in Newburyport and Beverly to Dow Jones and Co. It had been built by another competitor, Walter Greene, especially for the 1980 race, using Dick Newick's latest design ideas.

Wenzel, Hanni and Andreas

"The mouse that roared" aptly described how the tiny principality of Liechtenstein produced in 1980 both the men's and women's skiing World Cup winners—brother and sister Andreas and Hanni Wenzel from Planken, a village with 200 residents on a plateau overlooking the Rhine River. Furthermore, in the 1980 Winter Olympics at Lake Placid, N.Y., Hanni won two gold medals, for the slalom and giant slalom, and a silver in the downhill. Her brother completed a unique family record by adding a silver in the men's giant slalom. In the Olympic events collectively, Hanni won the women's overall title and Andy was the men's runner-up; these were also the concurrently decided world championship combined rankings recognized by the International Ski Federation.

Each thus proved to be a consistent and versatile three-event skier. Andreas finished respectably high in all three types of race in the 1980 World Cup competition, while Hanni did exceptionally well. En route to winning the overall award, she won five giant slaloms, two slaloms, and two combined events. She ended victor in the giant slalom, runner-up in the slalom, and third in the downhill. During the season's 24 World Cup races she failed to finish only once and was placed 19 times among the top five. Her lowest place in the seven downhill races was seventh. Her giant slalom victory at Mégève, France, by 5.02 sec was the second biggest winning race margin in the history of the World Cup, bettered only by Marie-Theres Nadig's 5.5 sec at Furano, Japan, in 1979.

Hanni, who first raced internationally in 1973, also won the World Cup in 1978, was runner-up in 1975 and 1979, and finished third in 1974. Her career total of World Cup race victories was 22 at the end of the 1979–80 season. She was named 1980 "skier of the year" by *Ski Racing* magazine.

Hanni was born on Dec. 14, 1956, and her brother, Andreas, on March 18, 1958. A younger sister, Petra, born on Nov. 20, 1961, also became an international ski racer.

(HOWARD BASS)

Williams, John

Arthur Fiedler, commercially America's most successful orchestral conductor and arguably the greatest popularizer of ensemble music since Sousa, personified the Boston Pops Orchestra for half a century. His death in 1979 left the Boston Symphony (the Pops' parent organization) bereft and seriously concerned about the future, since Fiedler's concerts had provided a third of its earnings. Choosing a successor, in *Newsweek*'s view, was tantamount to electing a new pope. A six-month search found a fitting maestro in John Williams, a Hollywood conductor and composer with almost as many film scores to his credit as Fiedler had encores in his repertoire.

Born Feb. 8, 1932, in Queens, N.Y., Williams moved to California as an adolescent when his father, a jazz drummer and orchestra percussionist, began working for movie companies. He studied music briefly at UCLA, then joined the Air Force and arranged pieces for service bands. After a year at the Juilliard School in New York, he returned to California, where he continued his private studies and began working in the film studios.

NIK WHEELER—BLACK STAR

Williams seemed to have no short suits when it came to contriving cinematic scores. By the time he had written more than 50 of them, his oeuvre included such varied vehicles as *Dracula, Gidget Goes to Rome,* and *Towering Inferno*. He won his first Oscar for adapting the stage musical *Fiddler on the Roof* for the screen. His second was for *Jaws,* which owed much of its suspense to the score. (Once the shark's theme was established, Williams would reintroduce it before the shark, one of its victims, or some red herring appeared.) In 1977 he was nominated twice for Academy Awards; his *Star Wars* beat out *Close Encounters of the Third Kind.* For *Superman* he contrived a planet Krypton theme that according to *High Fidelity* magazine was a "single tonic-dominant brass motif—an apparent inversion" of the benevolent aliens' theme in *Close Encounters.*

His film work aside, Williams enjoyed a substantial reputation as a conductor and composer—notably of two symphonies and a violin concerto. At the Pops, he said, he would hire more young soloists, experiment with electronic and mixed-media pieces, and offer more film music. As a guest conductor, he once had *Star Wars* robot C3PO share the podium.

(PHILIP KOPPER)

Yourcenar, Marguerite

On March 6, 1980, by 20 votes to 12, the French Academy elected Marguerite Yourcenar as its first woman member since it was founded in 1635. While most felt that the revolution was long overdue, conservative academicians fought hard to prevent it, making a last stand on the issue of the candidate's nationality. Belgian by birth, she acquired U.S. citizenship in 1947 and lived in Maine. But Alain Peyrefitte, justice minister and himself an academician, granted her dual nationality on the grounds of her "evident cultural links" with France.

After that, even the most fervent male chauvinist must have found Yourcenar's claim hard to deny. Marguerite de Crayencour, born June 8, 1903, in Brussels of a French father and Belgian mother, had created a body of work that, despite its cosmopolitan outlook, manifestly belonged to the French cultural tradition and was remarkable for its qualities of style and intellect. To such writers, immortality may come more easily than popular acclaim, but in 1951 *Mémoires d'Hadrien* (*Memoirs of Hadrian,* 1954), her brilliant excursion into the world of imperial Rome, achieved immediate success. It was an imaginative tour de force, a historical novel that convincingly penetrated the mind of its 2nd-century hero, revealing him as a man haunted by the impermanence of human culture and thus oddly close to the sensibility of our own time.

The personality of Hadrian had fascinated her long before the novel appeared, and the book's concerns were central to all her work. In 1968, with *L'Oeuvre au noir,* she set in northern Europe during the 16th century an imaginary figure who, like Hadrian, ultimately transcended the age to which he belonged.

In 1973, with *Souvenirs pieux,* she began a unique "family autobiography," which won over some earlier critics of her work. In recent years she gained many awards, among them the Grand Prix national des Lettres and the Grand Prix de la Litterature de l'Académie française. Austere, dedicated to her craft, she was likened to the 19th-century novelist Gustave Flaubert, who also adopted the viewpoint of someone of the opposite sex for his masterpiece *Madame Bovary*. In one thing, however, she succeeded where Flaubert failed: inconceivable though it would have been in his day, she was elected to the French Academy.

(ROBIN BUSS)

Zhao Ziyang

Zhao Ziyang (Chao Tzu-yang) became premier of China in September 1980, succeeding Hua Guofeng (Hua Kuo-feng), who remained chairman of China's Communist Party. Zhao's elevation followed his election to full membership in the Politburo in 1979 and his appointment as vice-premier earlier in 1980. It was his years as governor of Sichuan (Szechwan) Province and party first secretary (1975–80) that brought Zhao to the forefront. During that time he was remarkably successful in reviving the province's economy, which had been badly damaged by the disasters of the Cultural Revolution. As China's chief administrator, Zhao now has the formidable task of implementing the Four Modernizations: agriculture, industry, national defense, and science and technology.

RICHARD MELLOUL—SYGMA

Born into a landlord family in Henan (Honan) Province in 1919, Zhao joined the Young Communist League in 1932 and became a member of the Chinese Communist Party in 1938. During World War II he served in local party organizations in northern China. After the establishment of the People's Republic in 1949, he was moved to Guangdong (Kwangtung) Province, where he became provincial first party secretary in 1965. Purged in 1967 during the Cultural Revolution, he was later rehabilitated and sent in 1975 to Sichuan, China's most populous province, where through bold and flexible programs he increased industrial output and raised agricultural production. These results were achieved through such innovative policies as rewarding workers on the basis of work rather than need and providing incentives based on free enterprise and market forces rather than on rigid quotas established by central authorities. In addition, factory managers were given much greater autonomy and peasants were allowed to benefit from individual initiative. For such achievements as raising Sichuan's industrial output by 81% in three years, Zhao was made a Politburo alternate in 1977 and a full member in 1979.

An economic experimenter, Zhao has advocated "any structure, system, policy, or measure" that might stimulate the forces of production. He has also redefined Communism as "state ownership of the means of production and paying workers according to their work." All these changes are in harmony with the pragmatism of Vice-Chairman Deng Xiaoping (Teng Hsiao-p'ing) and have become guiding principles for China's future economic development. Zhao is perhaps the most important member of a new team of energetic, fairly young leaders entrusted to carry out the transformation of China into a stable and prosperous superpower during the coming decades.

(WINSTON L. Y. YANG)

NOBEL PRIZES

In 1980 U.S. citizens won prizes in five of the six Nobel categories. The Prize for Peace, however, went to an Argentine dissident, Adolfo Pérez Esquivel. Another 1980 laureate was Czeslaw Milosz, the first author writing in Polish to win the Prize for Literature. The Prize for Economics went to Lawrence R. Klein of the Wharton School at the University of Pennsylvania. Nobel Prizes in the physical and medical sciences were all shared. James W. Cronin of the University of Chicago and Val L. Fitch of Princeton University divided the Prize for Physics for their discoveries of exceptions to long-accepted rules describing the behaviour of subatomic particles. The Prize for Chemistry, celebrating investigations into the structure and function of DNA, went to Paul Berg of Stanford University, Walter Gilbert of Harvard University, and Frederick Sanger, a member of the British Medical Research Council. The Prize for Medicine or Physiology was shared by Jean Dausset of the University of Paris; George Snell, a scientist emeritus at the Jackson Laboratory in Bar Harbor, Maine; and Baruj Benacerraf, a Venezuelan working at Harvard University. All three performed groundbreaking work in immunogenetics. In 1980 the honorarium accompanying each prize amounted to $212,000.

Prize for Peace

"The prize is not for me but for my organization and for the cause of human rights and justice in Latin America," Adolfo Pérez Esquivel said when news of the award reached him in his Buenos Aires office. "I accept this prize in the name of Latin America and its workers, in the name of its campesinos and its priests who are working diligently for the peace and rights of all." Pérez has worked most conspicuously for political have-nots, the disenfranchised and brutally repressed people of Argentina in particular. His Nobel citation placed his work in this perspective: "In the early 1970s Argentina experienced a form of civil war in which extreme terrorist organizations created an atmosphere of insecurity and fear by their murders, bomb attacks, abductions and blackmail. The military regime that was subsequently set up has itself made use of extreme violence. Thousands of persons have vanished without trace, and in many cases we know that they have been brutally treated and put to death. All this has been carried out under cover of complete silence, without the semblance of legal procedure. This has disrupted the lives of men and women who have nothing in common with terrorism. Pérez Esquivel is among those Argentines who have shone a light in the darkness. He champions a solution of Argentina's grievous problems that dispenses with the use of violence, and is the spokesman of a revival of respect of human rights."

Pérez, the son of a fisherman, became an architect and sculptor, and for many years was professor of sculpture at the Argentine National School of Fine Arts. Barely a decade ago he joined an organization that

DIEGO GOLDBERG—SYGMA

Adolfo Pérez Esquivel

soon developed an agenda embracing the full spectrum of human concerns. In 1971 he joined the group that was organizing artisans' cooperatives. Within a year it was working for disarmament, nuclear nonproliferation, and social reforms generally. During a 1974 conference in Colombia, Pérez was elected secretary-general of Service for Peace and Justice in Latin America.

In Argentina victims of repression are called *desaparecidos*, people who have simply disappeared. The Organization of American States concluded that thousands of these people "may be presumed dead." Pérez himself suffered at the hands of the military junta that overthrew Isabel Perón's regime in 1976. Going to a police station in 1977 to renew his passport, he was detained and then held in La Plata prison for 14 months without being charged. He was tortured in ways he declines to discuss.

The government had little to say about his new celebrity. For days it maintained an official silence, then declared that its policies were necessary to protect "values cherished by all the West" and said Pérez was the dupe of terrorist groups. He replied: "I have never supported terrorism. . . . We have denounced the killing of generals, colonels, and innocent relatives of military officials. We have no connections with political parties of any sort. . . ."

The 48-year-old laureate says: "You cannot talk solely of human rights in terms of torture and imprisonment and killing. True, this is the gravest aspect. But we must also look at the case of the peasant who has no land and is dying of hunger." Pérez's organization thus endorses agrarian reforms and the organization of urban workers. The Buenos Aires magazine *Gente* mused that the Peace Prize had lost stature with its selection of Pérez, whose award creates a novel embarrassment for the government. Under Argentine law, winners of Nobel Prizes receive life pensions of $5,000 a month. If Pérez ever receives his due, he plans to use those funds, as well as the Nobel stipend, to pursue his goal of persuading his government and others to change their method of governing.

Prize for Economics

When Lawrence R. Klein became odds-on favourite to head President-elect Jimmy Carter's economic brain trust, a colleague predicted that the University of Pennsylvania professor would not take the job. He was then building a computer model of the world's economy, a tool designed to project the influence of discrete factors in one nation (*i.e.,* a new British income tax or an Iranian oil price hike) on businesses and whole economies elsewhere. "That's the project that will guarantee him a Nobel Prize," the associate accurately prophesied in 1976. It was Klein who applied the theories of econometrics—the study of dynamic and interdependent cause-and-effect relationships among disparate economic elements—to examine real-world problems and forecast short-term changes in local or international economic conditions.

Working first with Arthur Goldberger, Klein used Keynesian theories and new statistical methods to forecast the development of business fluctuations and to study the effects of economic-political measures such as tax or tariff policies. "The basic structure of a Klein model," *New York Times* economics analyst Leonard Silk explains, is "an interlocking set of equations that needed to be solved simultaneously to determine the output of the entire economic system. The individual equations were estimated by empirical analysis of past relationships among economic variables" such as the effects of agricultural shortages on manufacturing. "For instance, one equation in the model would specify that the future level of consumption is a definable function" of consumers' changing income, which in turn depends in part on government tax policies. "A second equation would seek to predict business investments in new plants and equipment by making it a function of past profits," which depend in part on consumer activity.

Part of the beauty of Klein's models is their flexibility. New information can be fed to his high-speed computers as it becomes available and old speculations can be updated with newly observed data. Further, his system could test marketplace theories. During the 1950s his models were used for short-term forecasts in the U.S. His much more sophisticated Wharton Econometric Forecasting Model is now used, as the Nobel committee noted, to forecast fluctuations in gross national product, exports, investments, and consumption. The model also projects how taxes, public spending programs, and rising import costs affect facets of a national economy or how one element can alter the international economic climate.

By the 1970s, Klein's so-called LINK Project could analyze the diffusion of business fluctuations between different countries and make forecasts of international trade and capital movements. It also enabled

WIDE WORLD

Lawrence Klein

economists to study the economic effects of political measures in one country on other countries, as well as on itself. "Thanks to Mr. Klein's contributions," the Nobel committee said, "the building of econometric models has attained a widespread, not to say, universal use" in capitalist, socialist, and third world nations. His work has benefited private interests as well as governments.

Born in Omaha, Neb., on Sept. 14, 1920, Klein graduated from the University of California at Berkeley in 1942, then earned a doctorate at the Massachusetts Institute of Technology, where he studied with Paul A. Samuelson (who won the Nobel Prize for Economics in 1970). Klein is Benjamin Franklin professor of economics and finance at the Wharton School, University of Pennsylvania, where he has taught for 22 years.

Prize for Literature

The winner of the 1980 Nobel Prize for Literature has published poems, novels, essays, autobiography, and criticism. A respected scholar at the University of California at Berkeley, Czeslaw Milosz has edited volumes of Eastern European verse and translated many poets—Shakespeare, Milton, Eliot, Baudelaire, Whitman, and Sandburg among them—into his native Polish. He has also translated the Psalms into Polish, a task that required him to add Hebrew to the other languages he already commanded: English, Greek, Latin, French, and Russian.

"His writing is many-voiced and dramatic, insistent and provocative," the Nobel citation reads in part. "He is an author of great importance—captivating and arresting.... The world that Milosz depicts in his poetry, prose and essays is the world in which man lives after having been driven out of paradise."

Born in Vilna, Russian Lithuania, on June 30, 1911, Milosz moved to Russia proper where his father worked as a civil engineer. After World War I the family returned to their hometown, which had become Wilno, then part of Poland. He graduated from college and at 21 published his first book of verse, *Poem of the Frozen Times.* By then he was both a socialist and a leader of the Catastrophist group of poets. When Nazi Germany invaded Poland to trigger World War II, Milosz joined the Resistance, continued to write clandestinely, and became a war hero as well. After the war his collection *Rescue* became one of the first books published in Communist Poland and the new government further rewarded him with an appointment to the foreign service. After serving as cultural attaché in Washington, D.C., and as first secretary for cultural affairs in Paris, he sought political asylum in France in 1951. "I have rejected the new faith," he then declared, "because the practice of the lie is one of its principal commandments and 'social realism' [the officially approved literary style] is nothing more than a different name for a lie." A decade later he immigrated to the U.S. where he became a naturalized citizen.

Chosen over several internationally popular nominees such as Graham Greene, Günter Grass, and Norman Mailer, Milosz enjoys only a modest following among the reading public—except in Poland, where his books still circulate clandestinely. Works that are available in English include: *Postwar Polish Poetry,* an anthology of his translations; *The Captive Mind,* an essay on Communist society and politics; *Native Realm: A Search for Self-Definition,* an autobiography; *History of Polish Literature; Selected Poems,* introduced by poet Kenneth Rexroth; and *Bells in Winter,* a collection of later poems. Joseph Brodsky, an exiled Russian poet teaching in New York City and an authority on Slavic literature, has called Milosz "perhaps the greatest poet of our time." (PHILIP KOPPER)

Prize for Chemistry

Paul Berg of Stanford University won half the prize in recognition of "his fundamental studies of the biochemistry of nucleic acids, with particular regard to recombinant DNA," a citation that Berg prefers to interpret as an acknowledgment of the merits of an entire body of work rather than of a single achievement. The other half of the prize was divided between Walter Gilbert of Harvard University and Frederick Sanger of the University of Cambridge for independently developing ways of finding the order in which the individual links are present in the chainlike molecules of nucleic acids. Sanger, who won the Nobel Prize for Chemistry in 1958, is the fourth person to win a prize a second time.

Berg, born in New York City in 1926, graduated from Pennsylvania State College in 1948 and received a Ph.D. in biochemistry from Western Reserve University in 1952. He held research fellowships in Copenhagen and at Washington University in St. Louis before joining the faculty of the latter in 1955. In 1959 he moved to Stanford, where he was named Willson professor of biochemistry in 1970.

During the 1960s Berg investigated stages in the process by which bacterial genes direct the production of proteins. He studied the copying of DNA onto a molecule of RNA and the conversion of amino acids into the reactive forms that line up with the RNA for assembly into protein molecules.

Around 1968 he began to study the biologic activity of isolated genes in higher organisms. It appeared feasible to take DNA molecules apart and put the pieces back together in new combinations. He pioneered in gene splicing—patching a fragment of DNA from a chosen species into the DNA of a plasmid or a virus that can enter animal or bacterial cells and exert its effects there. This method has been used to prepare DNA's that bring about the formation of human insulin and other rare proteins in bacteria.

Faced with the chance that organisms containing modified DNA's might become the agents of dangerous infections, Berg and others called for the deferment of these experiments and for the convocation of an international meeting to consider the problem. At a conference in 1975, scientists from 17 nations classified experiments on recombinant DNA and recommended safeguards for each category. Since then the restrictions have been relaxed as the hazards have proved less serious than had been feared.

Sanger was born in 1918 in Rendcombe, Gloucestershire, England. He received his bachelor's degree from St. John's College of the University of Cambridge in 1939 and his doctorate in chemistry from that university in 1943. He has remained at Cambridge, first as a research fellow in the university's department of biochemistry, then as a member of the staff of the Medical Research Council. Between 1943 and 1955 he and his collaborators worked out procedures—now used all over the world—for determining the order in which amino acids are linked in proteins. Sanger then switched his attention to the structure of nucleic acids, long-chain molecules like proteins but made up of four kinds of links called nucleotides. Sanger devised methods of building up "nested sets" of short chains of nucleotides complementary to overlapping stretches of DNA. The members of these sets are related as are the letters in the sequences ABC, ABCD, ABCDE, ABCDEF, and so on. Knowing the length of each segment and the identity of its last member, Sanger can reconstruct the whole string of nucleotides in the original DNA.

Gilbert was born in Boston in 1932 and earned bachelor's and master's degrees at

Paul Berg

UPI

Harvard in 1953 and 1954. He continued his education at the University of Cambridge, concentrating in mathematics and physics and obtaining his Ph.D. in 1957. He joined the Harvard faculty as a theoretical physicist but within a few years redirected his efforts into molecular genetics. He was named American Cancer Society professor of molecular biology in 1972.

Gilbert, with Allan Maxam, developed a method of determining nucleotide sequences of DNA's by finding conditions in which chemical reagents cleave the chains only at the positions occupied by a selected one of the four nucleotides. The lengths of the fragments produced by these procedures, like those built up by Sanger's, are measured by the same analytical techniques.

Prize for Physics

James Cronin of the University of Chicago and Val Fitch of Princeton University won the Physics Prize for performing an experiment in 1964 that implies that reversing the direction of time would not precisely reverse the course of certain reactions of subatomic particles.

The principle of time-reversal invariance (designated *T*) states that particle interactions should be indifferent to the direction of time; charge conjugation (*C*) provides that sets of charged particles should interact the same way if all the charges were interchanged; and parity conservation (*P*) holds that natural processes do not distinguish between right- and left-handed behaviour. These three symmetries were once thought to govern all the laws of physics, but in 1956 T. D. Lee and C. N. Yang suggested, correctly, that *P* does not apply to certain processes. Physicists abandoned the view that *C*, *P*, and *T* are independently true but saved the overall concept by proposing that any *P* violation must be offset by an equal *C* violation.

Cronin, Fitch, James Christenson, and René Turlay refined earlier measurements of the behaviour of neutral K mesons, uncharged particles formed in large accelerators. One kind of these K mesons decays quickly to two pi mesons, but the other decays slowly to three pi mesons; both processes obey combined *CP* symmetry. The four scientists, using a very sensitive detector, found events in which long-lived K mesons decay to two, instead of three, pi mesons. This demonstration of *CP* violations forced another revision of the *CPT* relation: when *CP* symmetry is violated, *T* symmetry must also fail.

James Cronin

FRANK MCMAHON

Commentators speculate that Cronin and Fitch were not honoured sooner because their finding has only recently been incorporated in cosmology. Earlier theories had foundered because *T*-inviolability implies that the matter and antimatter formed in a symmetrical big bang should have annihilated one another.

Cronin, born in Chicago in 1931, graduated from Southern Methodist University at Dallas, Texas, in 1951, and returned to Chicago for postgraduate training, receiving his Ph.D. from the university in 1955. He then joined the staff of the Brookhaven National Laboratory and in 1958 was appointed to the Princeton faculty. In 1971 he moved to the University of Chicago.

Fitch was born in Merriman, Neb., in 1923 and switched his interest from chemistry to physics when, as a member of the U.S. Army, he was sent to Los Alamos, N.M., to work on the Manhattan Project. He graduated from McGill University in Montreal with a bachelor's degree in electrical engineering in 1948 and was awarded a Ph.D. in physics by Columbia University in 1954. He then joined the faculty of Princeton, where he was named Cyrus Fogg Brackett professor of physics in 1976.

Prize for Physiology or Medicine

The prize for 1980 was divided equally among George Snell of the Jackson Laboratory, Bar Harbor, Maine; Jean Dausset of the University of Paris; and Baruj Benacerraf of the Harvard Medical School, Boston. Their contributions underlie much of present knowledge of the hereditary qualities that determine the transplantability of tissue between individuals and that affect the susceptibility of persons to an important group of diseases.

Snell, who was born in Bradford (now part of Haverhill), Mass., in 1903, graduated from Dartmouth College in 1926 and earned an Sc.D. in genetics from Harvard in 1930. He joined the Jackson Laboratory in 1935 and in 1944 began to study how heredity affects the outcome of tissue transplantation. The laboratory's founder, Clarence C. Little, had proved that tumours grafted from one mouse to another usually survive if the mice belong to the same genetic strain but, after weeks or months, are rejected if the mice are of different strains. Snell, in years of breeding and grafting experiments, confirmed and extended these results by developing 69 distinct inbred strains of mice, in which he detected 11 genetic loci associated with tissue compatibility. Each strain, requiring about 15 generations to establish, was genetically identical to one older strain except that it would accept skin grafts from only one other strain.

In 1937 Peter Gorer, in England, had reported that after a mouse had received an incompatible graft, its blood serum agglutinated the red blood cells of the donor. Gorer's test gave reliable results within three days after transplantation. Gorer concluded that the recipient's immune system develops antibodies that not only attack the graft but also evoke the specific blood reaction. He also identified a genetic locus controlling the antibodies. Together, Gorer and Snell later showed that the most important of the gene loci found by Snell coincided with the one pinpointed by Gorer. This locus, now called the major histocompatibility complex, contains several genes, each of which can exist in 20 to 30 forms.

Dausset, who was born in 1916 in Toulouse, France, received his medical degree from the University of Paris in 1945. After the war he attended the Harvard Medical School, then returned to France as laboratory director of the national blood transfusion centre. In 1952 he found that blood serums from patients who had received many transfusions caused the leukocytes and platelets, but not the red cells, in the blood of other individuals to agglutinate. These human antigens are controlled by a single genetic locus like the major histocompatibility complex found by Gorer and Snell in mice. The finding that these antigens are detectable in most human tissues made it possible to use Dausset's tests to predict the compatibility of various tissues available for grafting.

The confusion evolving as independent research teams developed different ways of identifying human antigens was resolved after 1965, when Dausset (then an associate professor at the University of Paris) and two other scientists offered a novel proposal, later found valid, concerning the organization of the human gene complex. Tissue matching has now become indispensable in bringing together suitable donors and recipients of transplants of skin, kidneys, and other organs.

Benacerraf was born in Caracas, Venezuela, in 1920. He graduated from Columbia University in 1942 and received a medical degree from the Medical College of Virginia in 1945. He went to France in 1950 as director of research at the National Centre for Scientific Research at the Broussais Hospital in Paris. In 1956 he joined the New York University Medical School and worked for a time with Gerald Edelman on the structure of antibodies. Troubled by the inhomogeneity of the antibodies available, Benacerraf quit Edelman's project and sought more uniform specimens by immunizing experimental animals with synthetic antigens, soon finding that antibody formation depends strongly on both the genetic strain of the animal and the chemical structure of the antigen.

Benacerraf moved to the National Institutes of Health in Bethesda, Md., in 1968 and was named Fabyan professor of comparative pathology at the Harvard Medical School in 1970. He and other scientists have shown that the genes controlling the responses to his antigens are located in the major histocompatibility complexes of the animals; those in humans also are associated with several heredity-linked diseases in which the immune system produces antibodies that attack the individual's own tissues. Benacerraf's findings have been valuable in guiding studies of these disorders, which include psoriasis, Graves' disease, and Reiter's disease.

(JOHN V. KILLHEFFER)

OBITUARIES

The following is a selected list of prominent men and women who died during 1980.

Adamson, Joy (Joy-Friederike Victoria Gessner), Austrian-born naturalist, artist, and author (b. Jan. 20, 1910, Troppau, Silesia, Austria-Hungary—d. Jan. 3, 1980, Shaba National Reserve, Kenya), won international renown with her African wildlife books, especially those describing how she and her game-warden husband reared a lion cub, Elsa, to maturity and eventually returned it to its natural habitat. *Born Free* (1960), *Living Free* (1961), and *Forever Free* (1962), all best-sellers that were developed into films, were followed by *Elsa and Her Cubs* (1965) and *The Story of Elsa* (1966). Other books included *The Peoples of Kenya* (1967), *The Spotted Sphinx* (a study of cheetahs, 1969), and an autobiography, *The Searching Spirit* (1978). Educated in Vienna, Joy-Friederike Gessner lived in Kenya from 1937. She was a gifted artist, and many of her paintings of Kenyan flora and fauna and tribal life are on permanent exhibition in the National Museum and State House, Nairobi.

MARION KAPLAN—CAMERA PRESS

Ahlers, Conrad, West German journalist (b. Nov. 8, 1922, Hamburg, Germany—d. Dec. 18, 1980, Bonn, West Germany), precipitated (1962) a political crisis (the "*Spiegel* affair") in West Germany with an article he wrote as an editor of the weekly newsmagazine *Der Spiegel.* The piece allegedly revealed military secrets, and Ahlers and other staff members were arrested. After various irregularities in the judicial procedures, all charges were dropped. Defense Minister Franz-Josef Strauss, who had Ahlers arrested before a warrant had been issued, was forced to resign, and public confidence in the Christian Democratic-Free Democratic coalition headed by Chancellor Konrad Adenauer was severely shaken. When Willy Brandt became chancellor in 1969, he appointed Ahlers government spokesman, a post that he held until 1972, when he was elected to the Bundestag (lower house of Parliament) as a Social Democrat. In 1980 Ahlers, who had begun his journalistic career with the German service of the BBC in London, became head of Deutsche Welle, West Germany's foreign broadcasting service.

Allon, Yigal, Israeli soldier and politician (b. Oct. 10, 1918, Kfar Tabor, Palestine—d. Feb. 29, 1980, Afula, Israel), was best known as the architect of the Allon Plan, a peace initiative that he formulated after Israel captured Arab territory in the 1967 Six-Day War. The plan proposed restoring most of the West Bank territory to Jordan while retaining Israeli paramilitary settlements along the Jordan River. The plan was never adopted. Allon was one of the first recruits of the Palmach, the Haganah's commando strike force, which smuggled Jewish survivors from Europe into Palestine in defiance of British restrictions on immigration. During World War II he fought as a volunteer alongside British soldiers against the Vichy-French in Lebanon and Syria. Israel proclaimed independence on May 15, 1948, and the Haganah, a Zionist military organization representing the majority of the Jews in Palestine after World War I, surfaced as the Israeli Army. As commander of the Palmach, Allon fought major battles against the Arabs on various fronts; pursuing Egyptian forces from the Negev into Sinai, he captured many prisoners of war including Gamal Abdel Nasser, then a junior officer. Allon's refusal to place the Palmach under the Haganah's command earned him the enmity of David Ben-Gurion, the first Israeli prime minister. Allon entered politics in 1955 when he was first elected to the Knesset (parliament) as representative of his own Ahdut Ha Avoda. He served in the Cabinets of David Ben-Gurion, Levi Eshkol, and Golda Meir, holding several ministerial positions. His unexpected death occurred while Allon was seriously being considered for the leadership of the Labour Party.

Amalrik, Andrey Alekseyevich, Soviet-born historian and playwright (b. 1938, Moscow, U.S.S.R.—d. Nov. 11, 1980, near Guadalajara, Spain), one of the most consistent and courageous Soviet dissidents, served two terms in Siberia and was imprisoned in a labour camp before being granted an exit visa in 1976. Amalrik first came into conflict with the authorities as a student; his university thesis was rejected because it contravened official teaching on early Russian history. Two years later, in 1965, he was sentenced to exile in Siberia for "parasitism"; he described his experiences in a book (*Involuntary Journey to Siberia*) published outside the U.S.S.R. His strength lay both in his ability to see the ludicrous side of Soviet life and in his appeals to rights theoretically granted under the Soviet constitution. This, and the publication abroad in 1969 of his well-argued essay *Will the Soviet Union Survive Until 1984?,* were especially provoking to the authorities, and he was sentenced in 1970 to three years in a labour camp. In July 1973 he was sentenced to a further three years; this was commuted to exile in Siberia. Amalrik was released in May 1975, returned to Moscow, but was subject to continual harassment by the authorities. The following year he reluctantly accepted an exit visa and went into exile in The Netherlands, eventually settling in France where he continued to campaign for human rights. He died in a car crash while traveling to meetings associated with the review conference of the Helsinki Final Act.

Amendola, Giorgio, Italian politician (b. Nov. 21, 1907, Rome, Italy—d. June 5, 1980, Rome), was a veteran member of the Italian Communist Party. Though lacking the conciliatory abilities which would have taken him to the highest office in the party, he was among its most popular and respected leaders. His father was a prominent Liberal, murdered by the Fascists in 1926, three years before Giorgio joined the Communists. He studied law, spent two years in jail for his opposition to Mussolini, and in 1937 took over the leadership of the exiled Italian Communist Party in France. He returned secretly to Italy in 1943 and in the following year was arrested by the Germans, but he was released when they failed to identify him. He served briefly in the postwar government and in 1948 was elected parliamentary deputy for Naples, a seat he held for the rest of his life. Amendola was also elected to the Politburo and other party organs but was not identified with any faction in the party. His sometimes unorthodox views probably deprived him of any key position in the leadership. He was a member of the Italian delegation to the European Parliament and a committed European, though he remained loyal to the U.S.S.R. and to traditional concepts of party discipline.

Andersch, Alfred, German-born writer (b. Feb. 4, 1914, Munich, Germany—d. Feb. 21, 1980, Berzona, Tessin, Switz.), was a dominant figure in post-World War II West German literature and helped found Gruppe 47, a movement that also included Heinrich Böll and Günter Grass. Rebelling against the nationalism of his father, an army officer, he was imprisoned in Dachau in 1933 for his Communist activities. In 1944 Andersch was sent to fight on the Italian front, but he deserted and was taken prisoner by U.S. forces. Poet, essayist, and novelist, he is remembered particularly for his last novel, *Winterspelt* (1974), and for his work as a radio producer, which allowed him to promote young writers and play an active part in German cultural life. He moved to Switzerland in the late 1950s and later took Swiss nationality. His last book, *Der Vater eines Mörders,* was published posthumously in 1980.

Ardrey, Robert, U.S. writer (b. Oct. 16, 1908, Chicago, Ill.—d. Jan. 14, 1980, Kalk Bay, South Africa), stirred debate among anthropology experts with his controversial theory on the evolution of human behaviour, which was set forth in such books as *The Territorial Imperative, African Genesis, The Social Contract,* and *The Hunting Hypothesis.* Ardrey, who theorized that humans displayed aggressive behaviour because they had "risen from the ape," concluded that humans inherited the drive to defend territory, possess power, and initiate war. His critics, however, argued that human aggressiveness was environmental in origin and thus a learned response. Before becoming a self-trained anthropologist, Ardrey enjoyed a career begun in the 1930s as a playwright and wrote *Star Spangled, Casey Jones, Thunder Rock,* and *Shadow of Heroes.* He also wrote scripts for films, including those for *Khartoum, Madame Bovary,* and *The Three Musketeers.*

Arkell, the Rev. A(nthony) J(ohn), British historian and egyptologist (b. July 29, 1898, Hinxhill, Kent, England—d. Feb. 26, 1980, Chelmsford, Essex, England), was an outstanding colonial administrator who combined a passion for the past with a humanitarian concern for the peoples of modern Africa. After service with the Royal Flying Corps, he joined the Sudan Political Service in 1920 and set about abolishing the illegal slave trade between that country and Ethiopia. He established villages for the freed slaves who called themselves "the Sons of Arkell." He wrote a history of Darfur Province, was appointed commissioner for archaeology and anthropology for the Sudan government in 1938, and undertook several valuable digs that opened up the previously unknown field of Sudanese prehistory. In 1948 Arkell became curator at University College, University of London, where he reorganized and cataloged the Flinders Petrie Collection of Egyptian Antiquities and wrote his authoritative *History of the Sudan* (1955; 2nd ed., rev., 1961). Arkell was a reader in Egyptian archaeology at University College until his retirement in 1963, when he was ordained.

Armitage, John, British editor (b. Sept. 25, 1910, Lincoln, England—d. Feb. 1, 1980, Letchworth, England), was the London editor of *Encyclopædia Britannica* from 1949 to 1967, undertaking the major part of its first extensive revision after World War II. An educationalist of wide and generous sympathies, he wrote *To Christian England* (1942) and *Our Children's Education* (1960) and was chairman of the Liberal Party's education advisory committee (1948–56). An authority on books and printing, he built up a flourishing bookshop and book business in Letchworth. Educated at Bedford School and Emmanuel College, Cambridge, Armitage was assistant editor (1937–39) and editor (1939–54) of *The Fortnightly*, and after World War II he joined *The Times Educational Supplement* (1946–49). He had an abiding interest in sports and was an outstanding rugby fives player (British amateur champion in 1938). Armitage wrote *A History of Ball Games and Rugby Fives* (1934) for the "Lonsdale Library," contributed to the *Oxford Companion to Sports and Games*, and in 1977 published *Man at Play*, an attractive history of Western games and sports.

Armstrong of Sanderstead, William Armstrong, Baron, British administrator (b. March 3, 1915, Stirling, Scotland—d. July 12, 1980, Oxford, England), was head of Britain's Home Civil Service from 1968 to 1974, a period of controversy over relations between the government and its civil service advisers. He studied at Oxford and joined the Board of Education in 1938. From 1949 to 1953 he was principal secretary to three chancellors of the Exchequer and in 1962 was made a joint permanent secretary at the Treasury. During the next six years he was involved in the government's far-reaching reorganization of the economic ministries. Armstrong played a still more controversial role as head of the civil service under the Heath government in the early 1970s. He was closely involved with the government in its prices and incomes policy and in its subsequent confrontation with the trade unions; though in theory apolitical, he was accused of publicly taking sides in the dispute. He was also criticized for accepting, immediately after his retirement, the chairmanship of the Midland Bank, despite a general rule that civil servants should not go directly to such appointments. He was knighted in 1963 and made a life peer in 1975.

Aronson, Boris, Russian-born stage designer (b. Oct. 15, 1899, Kiev, Russia—d. Nov. 16, 1980, near Nyack, N.Y.), was the master creator of scores of stunning backgrounds for Broadway theatre productions and the winner of six Tony awards for his superb settings for *The Rose Tattoo, Pacific Overtures, Cabaret, Zorba, Company,* and *Follies*. Without really understanding how he was able to achieve such perfection, Aronson continued to surprise and delight audiences with the originality of his designs. Other Broadway productions for which he designed sets included *Fiddler on the Roof, The Diary of Anne Frank, The Crucible, A Little Night Music,* and *The Price*. He also worked his magic at the Group Theatre, where he completed sets for *Awake and Sing!, Paradise Lost,* and *Gentle People*. His credits also included sets for the operas *Mourning Becomes Electra* and *Fidelio* and for the ballet *The Nutcracker* (1976) featuring Mikhail Baryshnikov.

Ballantrae, Bernard Edward Fergusson, Baron, British Army officer (b. May 6, 1911—d. Nov. 28, 1980, London, England), served under Orde Wingate in Burma during World War II and described Wingate's guerrilla campaigns in *Beyond the Chindwin* (1945) and *The Wild Green Earth* (1946). In a varied career as soldier, writer, and public servant, he was also governor-general of New Zealand (1962–67), lord high commissioner of the General Assembly of the Church of Scotland (1973–74), and chairman of the British Council (1972–76). Ballantrae combined a love of literature with a dedication to the Army, which he joined in 1931 as an officer in the Black Watch. He served in Palestine during the troubled 1930s and also, less successfully, during the years following World War II. He was transferred to other commands, including intelligence work, until his retirement in 1958. His literary works included a biography of Earl Wavell, a novel, poetry, travel books, and an autobiography, *The Trumpet in the Hall* (1970). Ballantrae was made a life peer in 1972 and Knight of the Thistle in 1974.

Ballinger, (Violet) Margaret Livingstone, South African politician (b. Jan. 11, 1894, Glasgow, Scotland—d. Feb. 7, 1980, South Africa), was a tireless worker for black rights and in 1954 became the first national chairman of the Liberal Party of South Africa. After studies in Port Elizabeth, at Rhodes University, Grahamstown, South Africa, and at Somerville College, University of Oxford, she was appointed lecturer in history at the University of the Witwatersrand, Johannesburg, South Africa. With her husband, William Ballinger, she published studies of Swaziland, Bechuanaland, and Basutoland and, after her election to Parliament in 1937, undertook a courageous struggle against racial discrimination and for the improvement of conditions among the black majority. She left Parliament in 1960 after the abolition of Bantu representation and became an associate fellow of Nuffield College, University of Oxford. She was actively involved in many aspects of welfare, including the Margaret Ballinger Home for crippled African children, and she received the Royal African Society medal and honorary doctorates from Rhodes University and the University of Cape Town, Rondebosch, South Africa. In 1969 she published *From Union to Apartheid*.

Barnett, Lady Isobel, British television personality (b. June 30, 1918—d. Oct. 20, 1980, Leicestershire, England), became a household name in the early days of British television through her appearances on the panel game "What's My Line?" Barnett later appeared on such radio and television programs as "Many a Slip" and "Any Questions?" Her charm and intelligence made her an ideal participant in the quiz and panel games at which she excelled. Barnett wrote an autobiography, *My Life Line* (1956), and was at one time a doctor and justice of the peace. Her death, by her own hand, came four days after she was convicted of shoplifting.

Barthes, Roland Gérard, French semiotician and critic (b. Nov. 12, 1915, Cherbourg, France—d. March 26, 1980, Paris, France), made important contributions to the study of sign systems and in 1976 became the first person to hold the chair of literary semiology at the Collège de France. Barthes studied at the University of Paris until his academic career was interrupted by tuberculosis. After a period with the Centre National de la Recherche Scientifique during World War II, he taught at the universities of Bucharest and Alexandria before being appointed in 1960 to the École Pratique des Hautes Études. His somewhat unorthodox career and his homosexuality distanced him from French bourgeois society, on whose symbols and attitudes he turned a critical and ironic eye in *Mythologies* (1957). In this work, as in his literary criticism, he drew on Marxism, psychoanalysis, and the structuralist linguistics of Ferdinand de Saussure to examine the sign systems underlying all manifestations of human culture. Central to them is language, the arbitrary constructs of which he studied in *Le Degré zéro de l'écriture* (1953; *Writing Degree Zero*, 1967). In his contributions to the periodical *Tel Quel* he helped to establish the theoretical basis for the "new novel," and by the 1960s, with structuralism the fashionable intellectual doctrine, he was the subject of bitter attacks from traditional academics after the publication of *Sur Racine* (1963). His style, always stimulating though sometimes eccentric and needlessly obscure, was widely imitated and parodied. To some, such discoveries as the rapprochement between Sade, Fourier, and Loyola were brilliant insights; to others, they remained perverse contrivances. But by the late 1970s Barthes's intellectual stature was virtually unchallenged, and his *Fragments d'un discours amoureux* (1977) found a wide audience for a characteristic expression of his highly individual talent.

Bastyan, Sir Edric Montague, British Army officer (b. April 5, 1903, Dorset, England—d. Oct. 7, 1980, Adelaide, Australia), was in charge of administration for the Allied land forces in Southeast Asia during World War II and held other important staff posts before being appointed governor of South Australia in 1961. Bastyan trained at Sandhurst and served in several regiments, mainly in the administrative staff, before war broke out. During the postwar period he held major appointments in the British Army of the Rhine, as chief of staff (1949–50), Eastern Command, and as director of staff duties at the War Office (1950–52). From 1957 until his retirement in 1960 he was commander of the British forces in Hong Kong. He was a popular governor in South Australia and later served as governor of Tasmania (1968–74). He was knighted in 1962.

Bates, L(ucius) C(hristopher), U.S. newspaper publisher (b. 1901?, Mississippi—d. Aug. 22, 1980, Little Rock, Ark.), was the publisher of the *Arkansas State Press*, a weekly pro-civil rights newspaper, and a prominent black leader who initiated the historic 1957 desegregation of Central High School in Little Rock, Ark. Gov. Orval Faubus called out the state's National Guard in a final attempt to thwart integration, but Bates and his wife, Daisy, ushered nine black students into the school with the aid of federal troops. Thereafter Bates's home was the target of attacks by segregationists who hurled stones, bottles, and bombs. His newspaper was also boycotted by advertisers, and Bates closed the paper in 1959. During the 1960s, however, Bates and Faubus joined forces: realizing that federal aid was crucial to the state, Faubus asked Bates to recommend qualified blacks to work in federally funded state agencies. Bates also served as field secretary of the NAACP.

Beadle, Sir (Thomas) Hugh (William), Rhodesian lawyer (b. Feb. 6, 1905, Salisbury, Rhodesia—d. Dec. 14, 1980, Johannesburg, South Africa), as chief justice of Rhodesia (1961–77) ruled in 1968 that Prime Minister Ian Smith's 1965 unilateral declaration of independence for Rhodesia was valid because Rhodesia was a country in effective and firm control of its territory. After graduating in law from Cape Town University, Beadle became a Rhodes scholar at Queen's College, Oxford, and practiced as an advocate in Southern Rhodesia (1930–39). He entered the Southern Rhodesian Parliament in 1939 and was parliamentary secretary to Prime Minister Sir Godfrey Huggins (1940–46). He was minister of justice, of internal affairs, of health, and of education. He then served as a judge of Southern Rhodesia's High Court from 1950 to 1961, when he was appointed chief justice. In 1966 he accompanied Smith on his HMS "Tiger" negotiations with British Prime Minister Harold Wilson. Beadle was knighted in 1961.

Beaton, Sir Cecil Walter Hardy, British photographer, writer, and designer (b. Jan. 14, 1904, London, England—d. Jan. 18, 1980, Broad Chalke, near Salisbury, England), was a man whose striking personality and original approach to photographic portraiture went hand-in-hand with his single-minded climb up the ladder of success. From his Cambridge days in the early 1920s, his charm induced society beauties to sit for him, and the freshness of his work then drew in the famous, to be

DMITRI KASTERINE—CAMERA PRESS

depicted in settings of luxury and sometimes of bizarre beauty. In New York in 1929 and 1930 Beaton was commissioned by *Vogue* and by Condé Nast, who for some years gave him a contract for exclusive photography. In 1930 Beaton published *The Book of Beauty*—the first of more than 30 books that were mostly photographic or autobiographical. His diaries recounted many encounters with the famous, including his improbable courtship of Greta Garbo. In 1930 he held in London the first of many photographic, painting, and stage design exhibitions that culminated in an exhibition of his photographs in the National Portrait Gallery, London, in 1968. He also photographed the wedding (1937) of Mrs. Wallis Simpson and the duke of Windsor in France. During World War II Beaton worked for the Ministry of Information and won wide acclaim for his wartime photographs of the siege of Britain, published in *Winged Squadrons*. In 1956 he achieved new fame as designer of the costumes for the musical *My Fair Lady*, which won him the Nieman-Marcus fashion award. He also designed sets and costumes for Oscar Wilde's *Lady Windermere's Fan*. Knighted in 1972, Beaton spent his declining years at his house near Salisbury. His collection of hats and a pressed rose plucked from a vase by Greta Garbo at their first meeting (1932) were among the memorabilia auctioned by Christie's for £400,000 after Beaton's death.

Bennett, Sir Thomas Penberthy, British architect (b. Aug. 14, 1887, London, England—d. Jan. 29, 1980, London), established a reputation as a teacher of architecture, with designs of numerous well-known buildings in London, and as an administrator of Britain's pioneering "New Towns" projects. Bennett headed the Northern Polytechnic School of Architecture, Surveying, and Building (1920–28) and during World War II was director of works and controller of temporary housing at the Ministry of Works. After the war he became chairman of Crawley New Town (1947–60) and of Stevenage New Town Development Corporation (1951–53). A fellow of the Royal Society of Arts and the Royal Institute of British Architects, he was knighted in 1946. Bennett's designs included theatres, cinemas, apartment houses, banks, department stores, office buildings, chapels, and synagogues.

Berling, Zygmunt, Polish Army officer (b. April 27, 1896, Limanowa, Austria-Hungary—d. July 11, 1980, Warsaw, Poland), was in command of an infantry regiment in Wilno (Vilnius) when (1939) he was made a prisoner of war by the Soviet Army which invaded Poland in accordance with the German-Soviet secret treaty of 1939. The Soviet Army captured 230,670 Polish soldiers, confined some 9,400 officers in three camps, and collected 448 others at Gryazovets camp. The remaining soldiers were classified as unfit for any collaboration with the U.S.S.R. and were massacred in April 1940. Berling was one of the 448 survivors. Though German-Soviet relations were officially friendly at that time, Lavrenty Beria, head of the Soviet intelligence services, suggested that Berling organize a Polish division to fight the Germans. Unaware of the tragic fate of his fellow officers, Berling welcomed the opportunity. In October 1943, the 1st Polish Division, under General Berling, distinguished itself at Lenino (U.S.S.R.). In July 1944 a Polish army joined the 1st Belorussian Army Group under Marshal K. K. Rokossovsky. At the end of July, Rokossovsky's army group approached the Vistula River near Warsaw. On August 1 the Polish Home Army in German-occupied Poland began an uprising. Stalin ordered Rokossovsky to stop his offensive. Rokossovsky obeyed but Berling, who was convinced that an alliance with the U.S.S.R. was in Poland's interest, sent hundreds of soldiers across the Vistula. A bridgehead was established but Berling had acted against Stalin's order. By Jan. 17, 1945, when Soviet forces entered Warsaw, Berling had been relieved of his command. He was pensioned in 1953.

Bitar, Salah ad-Din, Syrian politician (b. 1912, Damascus, Syria—d. July 21, 1980, Paris, France), was premier of Syria four times during the 1960s and a prominent theoretician of Arab democratic nationalism. Bitar, who founded (with Michel Aflak) the Ba'ath Party, later criticized the policies of both wings of the party as editor in chief of the journal *Al Ahaa al-Arabi* ("Arab Renaissance"); in 1966 he clashed with younger members of the party who felt he was too conservative. Bitar was forced into exile after being ousted as premier. Earlier he served as minister of state when Egypt and Syria were temporarily merged to form the United Arab Republic. During the last ten years of his life, Bitar lived in exile in Paris where he reportedly associated with other exiles. He was assassinated outside the building where he edited his magazine. The Syrian government denied reports that he was "marked for murder" because of his opposition to Pres. Hafez al-Assad.

Blackburne, Sir Kenneth William, British colonial administrator (b. Dec. 12, 1907, Bristol, England—d. Nov. 4, 1980, Douglas, Isle of Man), served as governor-general of Jamaica from 1962, when the island became independent, until his retirement in 1963. Earlier, Blackburne was captain general and governor in chief (1957–62). At a crucial time in Jamaica's history, both because of local political issues and because of the increasing Jamaican immigration to the U.K., Blackburne brought to his task a wide experience of colonial administration and a specialized knowledge of the Caribbean. He joined the Colonial Service in 1930 and served in Nigeria, Palestine, and The Gambia before his appointment in 1943 as administrative secretary to the comptroller for development and welfare in the West Indies. As director of information services (1947–50) at the Colonial Office in London, he was particularly concerned with improving understanding in Britain of the peoples of the colonial territories. He was governor of the Leeward Islands (1950–56) before succeeding Sir Hugh Foot in Jamaica. Blackburne was knighted in 1952.

Blanshard, Paul, U.S. writer, polemicist, and lawyer (b. Aug. 27, 1892, Fredericksburg, Ohio—d. Jan. 27, 1980, St. Petersburg, Fla.), created a national furor with the publication of *American Freedom and Catholic Power* (1949), the first in a series of controversial books that severely attacked the Roman Catholic Church. For nearly two decades Blanshard plagued the church with such best-sellers as *Communism, Democracy, and Catholic Power* (1951), *The Irish and Catholic Power* (1953), and *Religion and the Schools* (1963). In the last named his harsh criticism of the church's "un-American" involvement in the affairs of state education was said to have contributed to the establishment of federal bans on prayer in public schools and on aid to religiously affiliated schools. Blanshard, who was a Congregationalist minister before espousing atheism, first voiced his criticism when he became a Vatican correspondent for *The Nation*. He was the twin brother of Brand Blanshard, a noted philosopher.

Bonham, John ("BONZO"), British rock musician (b. May 31, 1947, Redditch, Worcestershire, England—d. Sept. 25, 1980, Windsor, England), was the heavy-handed drummer with the Led Zeppelin rock band, which he joined when it was formed in 1968. Bonham's aggressive drumming provided the rhythmical base for the group's music and contributed largely to the success of the band, which gained an international reputation as pioneers of "acid rock." During the late '60s and early '70s the group made many successful tours in Europe and the U.S. Bonham's career started with the group Band of Joy, which also included Robert Plant, Led Zeppelin's lead singer. Led Zeppelin made few public appearances after 1977, but it toured Europe shortly before Bonham's death.

Borg Olivier, George, Maltese politician (b. July 5, 1911, Valletta, Malta—d. Oct. 29, 1980, Sliema, Malta), led the Maltese Nationalist Party from 1950 to 1976, twice served as the island's prime minister, and was its leader at the time Malta gained independence from Britain in 1964. His political philosophy was based on a moderate, pro-Western stance, and he campaigned throughout his career for Malta to retain its links with Britain and NATO, in opposition to his main political rival, Labour Party leader Dom Mintoff. Trained as a lawyer, Borg Olivier served on the Council of Government (1939–47) and in 1947 was elected to the Legislative Assembly created by the post-World War II constitution. He was minister of works and of education under Enrico Mizzi, whom he succeeded (1950) as Nationalist Party leader and prime minister. In 1955, after the failure of the coalition government, Mintoff was elected and stayed in power until his resignation provoked the constitutional crisis of 1958–62. In 1962 the Nationalists were returned to power with Borg Olivier again prime minister. After endorsement by referendum of the independence constitution, the island became independent on Sept. 21, 1964. Borg Olivier believed that the country's economy as well as its defense interests were best served by strong links with Britain, but the economic benefits of this policy were eroded by British defense cuts. In 1971 Mintoff won the election, and in 1974 he declared Malta a republic. Borg Olivier retired in 1976 but remained a member of Parliament.

Boun Oum na Champassak, Prince, Laotian political figure (b. Dec. 11, 1911, Champassak, Laos—d. March 17, 1980, near Paris, France), was one of the leading representatives of the Laotian right until forced to flee to France in 1975. Educated in Saigon, he took part in the resistance movement against the Japanese during World War II and supported France following the war. After an independence agreement was signed in 1949, Boun Oum served as prime minister of Laos from 1949 to 1950 (and later from 1960 to 1962). Despite the 14-nation 1954 Geneva Conference agreement stating that Laos was to be a unified, independent buffer state, the deeply divided country continued to be torn apart by three factions. The civil war among pro-Western (led by Boun Oum), Communist (Pathet Lao, led by Souphanouvong), and neutralist (led by Souvanna Phouma) forces was halted in 1962 when the three reaffirmed that Laos was a neutral state. Boun Oum rejoined the government four years later as minister of religion, serving until 1972, and retained the honorary title of inspector general of the realm until the Pathet Lao gained full control of Laos in 1975. The Lao People's Democratic Republic condemned Boun Oum to death in absentia.

Boussac, Marcel, French textile industrialist (b. April 17, 1889, Châteauroux, France—d. March 21, 1980, Château de Mivoisin, France), was dubbed France's "King of Cotton" because of his vast textile holdings throughout the country. Boussac opened (1909) his first business in Paris and made a fortune during World War I as a producer of cotton shirts for the forces and of special cotton cloth used to cover aircraft wings. After 1918 he bought textile mills in France and in Poland. At the end of World War II he launched the young couturier Christian Dior and, at the height of his racing reputation in the 1950s, owned some 300 racehorses. In 1951 Boussac became a press baron after obtaining control of the right-wing Paris newspaper *L'Aurore* and the only racing daily in France, *Paris-Turf*. The opening of French frontiers to cheap textiles in the late 1950s signaled the collapse of his empire. Repeated attempts to salvage the group failed. In 1978 he sold his newspapers, what was left of his textile holdings, and his racing stables. The buyers of his empire paid him Fr 700 million, an annuity of Fr 2 million, and the lifelong use of his house in Paris, his villa at Deauville, and the Château de Mivoisin.

Boustead, Sir (John Edmund) Hugh, British soldier (b. April 14, 1895, Ceylon—d. April 3, 1980, Dubai, United Arab Emirates), enjoyed an unusually adventurous career, which he recounted in his 1971 autobiography, *The Wind of Morning*. A cadet at the Royal Naval College, Dartmouth, Devon, he deserted his ship at Cape Town in 1914 and joined the South African Brigade to serve on the Western

Front during World War I. He was commissioned in the field after being wounded at Arras and was awarded the Military Cross, having also been pardoned for deserting ship. In 1919 his brigade served with Gen. A. I. Denikin in south Russia. Boustead went to Worcester College, Oxford, to learn Russian but then served in the eastern Mediterranean. From 1924 to 1929 he served in the Sudan Defense Force's Camel Corps, commanding it in 1931 after general-staff service in Egypt. In 1935 he left the Army for the Sudan Political Service. Boustead rejoined the Army during World War II and fought against the Italians in Ethiopia; he was awarded the Distinguished Service Order in 1941 and was knighted in 1965. After the war he served various Arab rulers and became British political agent in Abu Dhabi (1961–65). After a lecture tour in the U.S., Colonel Boustead finally retired from military service in 1965. He then went to Tangier but returned to Arabia, where he managed the stud horses of the sheikh of Abu Dhabi.

Boyd, Julian Parks, U.S. historian (b. Nov. 3, 1903, Converse, S.C.—d. May 28, 1980, Princeton, N.J.), was a librarian at Princeton University during the 1940s when he undertook one of the most ambitious and massive ventures in the history of publishing, *The Papers of Thomas Jefferson*. In the course of over 30 years of scholarly immersion in the documents of Jefferson, Boyd published 19 of the projected 60 volumes, which include Jefferson's letters, speeches, manuscripts, and reports. Boyd later joined Princeton University's history faculty and was recognized as an expert on 18th-century American history. Other distinguished works included *Anglo-American Union: Joseph Galloway's Plans to Preserve the British Empire, 1774–1788* (1941) and *The Declaration of Independence: The Evolution of the Text as Shown in Facsimiles of Various Drafts by Its Author* (1943).

Brosio, Manlio, Italian diplomat (b. July 10, 1897, Turin, Italy—d. March 14, 1980, Turin), was secretary-general of the North Atlantic Treaty Organization (NATO) from 1964 to 1971. Brosio opposed Fascism as a member of the Liberal Party, and after Mussolini's fall in 1943 he joined the clandestine resistance to German occupation. During the postwar coalition governments of Bonomi and De Gasperi, he was secretary of the Liberal Party until his appointment as ambassador to Moscow in 1946. He then served successively as ambassador to London, Washington, and Paris. As NATO secretary-general he was profoundly concerned by France's decision to withdraw its forces from the organization and faced additional problems when the U.S.S.R. invaded Czechoslovakia. In 1972 he was elected senator for Turin.

Browne, E(lliot) Martin, British actor, producer, and theatrical director (b. Jan. 29, 1900, Zeals, Wiltshire, England—d. April 27, 1980, London, England), was a major influence on poetic and religious drama and the director of T. S. Eliot's plays for more than 25 years. Browne first directed Eliot's *The Rock,* then *Murder in the Cathedral* for the Canterbury Festival, and later his four modern poetic dramas. During World War II Browne formed the Pilgrim Players and in the postwar years continued to encourage poetic drama by producing works by such new writers as Christopher Fry. For ten years Browne was director of the British Drama League and was involved in many productions as an actor as well as a director. Browne also worked as a visiting professor in the U.S., lecturing extensively on religious drama and giving recitals of Shakespeare, T. S. Eliot, and medieval mystery plays. As a young man he had worked in the U.S. as a professional actor.

Bullard, Sir Edward Crisp, British scientist (b. Sept. 21, 1907, Norwich, England—d. April 3, 1980, La Jolla, Calif.), pursued an outstanding academic career as a geophysicist before becoming an adviser to the U.S. government on nuclear power. During World War II his team developed degaussing techniques to protect naval vessels from magnetic mines. Bullard's work in marine geophysics was fundamental to the development of the science, and he made original contributions in such areas as seismic measurement, the study of the Earth's magnetic field, the dating of rocks, and the use of computers in geophysics. Bullard was professor of physics at the University of Toronto (1946–49) and director of Britain's National Physical Laboratory (1950–55) before going to Cambridge, where he was professor of geophysics from 1964 until his retirement in 1974. He then moved to the U.S., having been professor at the University of California at San Diego since 1963. He was knighted in 1953 and received many honours including the Sedgwick (1936) and Vetlesen (1968) prizes and the Royal Society's Royal Medal (1975).

Burhop, Eric Henry Stoneley, Australian-born nuclear physicist (b. Jan. 31, 1911, Hobart, Tasmania—d. Jan. 22, 1980, London, England), was professor of physics at University College in London (1960–78) and made important contributions to the study of elementary particle physics, particularly in connection with K-meson and neutrino research. He collaborated in the Manhattan Project (to develop an atomic bomb) at Berkeley, Calif., during World War II. Burhop was a prominent campaigner for nuclear arms control, East-West détente, and the advancement of international scientific cooperation through membership in the Pugwash movement (of which he was a founder) and as president of the World Federation of Scientific Workers. A graduate of Melbourne and Cambridge universities, Burhop worked (1933–35) at the Cavendish Laboratory, Cambridge, under Lord Rutherford, returning to Australia as a research physicist and lecturer at Melbourne (1935–45). In 1945 he joined University College, London, and was reader in physics there from 1950 until becoming professor in 1960. A fellow of the Royal Society from 1963, he was awarded the Joliot-Curie Medal of the World Peace Council in 1966 and a Lenin Peace Prize in 1972. His publications included *The Challenge of Atomic Energy* (1951), *The Auger Effect* (1953), and (with H. S. W. Massey) *Electronic and Ionic Impact Phenomena* (1953). He edited *High Energy Physics* (vol. i–iv, 1967–69).

Burpee, David, U.S. horticulturist (b. April 5, 1893, Philadelphia, Pa.—d. June 24, 1980, Doylestown, Pa.), was the purveyor of a vast array of flower and vegetable seeds featured in a mail-order catalog that became a traditional "rite of spring" for U.S. gardeners. After the death of his father in 1915, Burpee, with virtually no training in horticulture, assumed leadership of the W. Atlee Burpee Co., the world's largest mail-order seed company. His preference for the marigold above all other flowers sparked his unsuccessful campaign (1959) to have it designated the national flower and his offer of a $10,000 prize to anyone who could develop a white marigold. Twenty-one years later an Iowa widow collected the money. Burpee also developed the first ruffled sweet peas, the first hybrid zinnias, the first odourless marigolds, and the stunning red-and-gold marigold, the first commercial seed producing a hybrid flower. The Burpee Co. distributed some four million catalogs annually and offered new listings of hybrid flowers and vegetables with each publication. As part of a unique merchandising idea, each year Burpee named a new flower after a well-known personality such as Pearl Buck, Kate Smith, and Helen Hayes. In 1970 Burpee, who served as head of the company for 55 years, sold it to General Foods Corp., which sold the business to ITT in 1979.

Busch, Ernst, East German actor and singer (b. Jan. 22, 1900, Kiel, Germany—d. June 8, 1980, East Berlin, East Germany), was the leading interpreter of roles created by the dramatist Bertolt Brecht. Busch came from a working-class family, joined the Communist Party, and took up acting professionally when he lost his job with Krupp. He moved to Berlin in 1925 and three years later played in Brecht's *Threepenny Opera*. He also gained wide recognition as a singer, interpreting songs by Brecht and the composer Kurt Weill. He left Germany when the Nazis took power in 1933 and lived in various European countries and the U.S.S.R. before fighting as a member of the International Brigade in the Spanish Civil War. Imprisoned during World War II, he was condemned to death by the Gestapo but was later reprieved; he was severely tortured before his release in 1945. Returning to East Berlin, he played with the Deutsches Theater and with Brecht's Berliner Ensemble, where he gave memorable performances in *Mother Courage, The Mother, The Caucasian Chalk Circle,* and *Galileo.* After he retired in 1961, he continued his career as a singer and remained one of the most respected figures in East German theatre.

Butlin, Sir William ("Billy") Edmund, British businessman (b. Sept. 29, 1899, South Africa—d. June 12, 1980, Jersey, Channel Islands), founded (1935) his first holiday camp at Skegness, which provided seaside vacations at reasonable cost and organized entertainment for the whole family. In its heyday, during the mid-1950s, Butlin's Ltd. provided some 600,000 vacations a year. The company's name was a byword for a type of chalet-based holiday camp that demanded no personal initiative from its customers, who allowed themselves to be entertained from morning to night. Butlin's biography was the classic story of a self-made man. His parents moved from South Africa to Canada, and at the age of 14 he started work in a department store. He served with the Canadian Army in World War I and following his return, with £10 in his pocket, worked his way to England. There he joined his uncle's traveling fun fair, eventually setting up his own carnival booth. In 1935 he recognized the need to provide a complete "entertainment package" for working-class vacationers. His two camps, which were an immediate success, were taken over by the armed forces during World War II, and he was appointed director general of hostels to the Ministry of Supply. He was knighted Sir Billy in 1964. When Butlin retired in 1968, his numerous resorts had attained immense popularity.

Byrd, Henry Roeland (Roy Byrd), U.S. blues pianist (b. Dec. 19, 1918, Bogalusa, La.—d. Jan. 30, 1980, New Orleans, La.), originated a unique piano style that combined the elements of blues, New Orleans marching music, and Caribbean rhythms and thereby laid the foundation for the evolution of rock 'n' roll. As a young boy living in New Orleans, Byrd learned music basics from his mother. He constructed his own instruments and played and danced in the streets for tips. But when he found an old discarded piano, Byrd patched it up and mastered it under the tutelage of such barrelhouse pianists as Sullivan Rock and Kid Stormy Weather. Although his recordings of the 1950s and '60s, including "Go to the Mardi Gras," "Big Chief," and "Mardi Gras in New Orleans," gained local popularity and were heard yearly during the Mardi Gras festivities, it was Fats Domino, Huey Smith, and Allen Toussaint who achieved stardom by adopting his style. It was not until the 1970s that "Professor Longhair," as Byrd was known to his fans, attained recognition. After producing the record album *Live on the Queen Mary* with Paul McCartney, Byrd and his professional band, the Blues Scholars, were a smash success on tours of Europe and the U.S.

Caetano, Marcello José das Neves Alves, Portuguese lawyer and politician (b. Aug. 17, 1906, Lisbon, Port.—d. Oct. 26, 1980, Rio de Janeiro, Brazil), was premier of Portugal (1968–74) succeeding António de Oliveira Salazar, the dictator who had ruled the country for 36 years. An academic lawyer, he obtained his doctorate in 1931 and was appointed professor of law at Lisbon University two years later. Meanwhile, he had joined Salazar's National Union group, helped draft the country's new constitution, and in 1940 became head of the national youth movement. By 1955 he was in the key post of minister of the presidency and, despite his occasional disputes with Salazar, wholeheartedly supported the latter's right-wing policies. When Salazar resigned because of illness, Caetano was a natural successor, but he proved less able to pursue a policy of single-minded opposition to the independence of Portugal's African colonies. Though no less hostile than Salazar to African nationalism, he was more sensitive to international opinion and had to face growing economic difficulties at home, in a country impoverished by its colonial wars. However, any changes he might have contemplated in colonial and domestic policies were preempted by the 1974 military coup under Gen. António de Spínola. Caetano went to Brazil, where he became head of the Institute of Comparative Law in Rio de Janeiro.

Carpentier y Valmont, Alejo, Cuban writer (b. Dec. 26, 1904, Havana, Cuba—d. April 24, 1980, Paris, France), was the leading Cuban novelist of his generation and a major influence on Latin-American literature. The son of a Frenchman, he studied music and architecture at the University of Havana before becoming a journalist. In 1928 he fled to Paris to escape imprisonment for his opposition to the Machado regime and during the next decade was strongly influenced by surrealism. Carpentier returned to Cuba in 1939 but turned away from European influences and began to search for the roots of Latin-American history. In 1949 he published *El reino de este mundo* (*The Kingdom of this World*, 1957), an imaginative evocation of the Haitian ruler Henri Christophe. He was appointed professor of the history of music at the National Conservatory but spent much of his time in Europe until the 1959 revolution. He then was appointed to several leading posts, including that of cultural attaché at Cuba's Paris embassy. In 1962 he published *El siglo de las luces* (*Explosion in a Cathedral*, 1963), another historical novel on the theme of revolution. Carpentier's other novels included *Los pasos perdidos* (1953; *The Lost Steps*, 1956), considered to be his masterpiece, and *El acoso* (1956). He also wrote on the history of music and was the librettist for several operas.

Champion, Gower, U.S. Broadway musical director and choreographer (b. June 22, 1921, Geneva, Ill.—d. Aug. 25, 1980, New York, N.Y.), climaxed his career with *42nd Street*, the Broadway musical that opened to rave reviews the night of his death. The winner of seven Tony awards, Champion directed and choreographed such magnificent musicals as *Hello Dolly!, Lend an Ear, Bye Bye Birdie, Carnival, I Do! I Do!,* and *Irene.* Earlier Champion achieved audience approval as a dancer with his first wife, Marge. Together they appeared on the original Sid Caesar-Imogene Coca television show, "The Admiral Revue," and in such films as *Mr. Music, Showboat, Three for the Show,* and *Jupiter's Daughter.* The couple also appeared on the variety shows of Ed Sullivan, Perry Como, Steve Allen, and Dinah Shore. Champion's successful Broadway debut with *Bye Bye Birdie* in 1960 confirmed his career as a musical director-choreographer. After experiencing several lean years, Champion concentrated his efforts on the production of *42nd Street* even though he was suffering from a rare fatal blood disease known as Waldenström's macroglobulinemia.

Chekova, Olga, Russian-born film actress (b. April 26, 1897, Aleksandropol, Russia—d. March 9, 1980, near Munich, West Germany), appeared in more than 100 films in a career spanning some five decades of cinema history and was chosen actress of the state in 1938 by Germany's Nazi regime. After studying art and painting in St. Petersburg (now Leningrad), Chekova emigrated (1921) to Germany and appeared in many films directed by Fritz Murnau, including *A Doll's House, Peer Gynt,* and *Bel Ami.* She resumed her career after World War II but in the 1960s abandoned acting to run a cosmetics firm. Besides starring in a West German television series in 1971, Chekova retained her link with the cinema by managing a film studio.

Cheney, Sheldon Warren, U.S. theatre critic and art historian (b. June 29, 1886, Berkeley, Calif.—d. Oct. 10, 1980, Berkeley), penned profound writings on the Modernist movement in U.S. drama in such discerning works as *The New Movement in the Theatre* (1914), *A Primer of Modern Art* (1924), *Expressionism in Art* (1934), and *The Story of Modern Art* (1941). His most ambitious work, *The Theatre: Three Thousand Years of Drama, Acting, and Stagecraft* (1929), was heralded as the first definitive history of the theatre. Cheney's definition of the Modernist movement was embraced by such theatre giants as playwright Eugene O'Neill and set designer Robert Edmond Jones. In 1916 Cheney founded *Theatre Arts Magazine,* which became a monthly international review and permanent record of events in the theatre. He also served (1916–21) as editor of the magazine, which ceased publication in 1964. His interest in architecture found expression in the critically acclaimed *The New World Architecture* (1930). Cheney spent his final years compiling his notes and articles which he bequeathed to his alma mater, the University of California at Berkeley.

Chervenkov, Vulko, Bulgarian Communist leader (b. Aug. 24, 1900, Zlatitsa, Bulg.—d. Oct. 21, 1980, Sofia, Bulg.), joined the Bulgarian Workers' Party in 1919 and was (1920–25) a member of the Central Committee of the Communist Youth League. In 1923 Chervenkov took part in an unsuccessful Communist uprising and in 1925 fled to Moscow. There he studied at the Marx-Lenin School where he later served as director. In 1941, shortly after the German aggression against the U.S.S.R., he was appointed director of the Khristo Botev radio station, which broadcast to Bulgaria. In September 1944 Georgi Dimitrov, head of the Comintern and Chervenkov's brother-in-law, sent him to Bulgaria where he was elected a member of the Central Committee of the Bulgarian Communist Party (BCP). He became secretary-general of the party in 1949 and in 1950 was named premier. His position was seriously weakened after the death of Stalin in 1953 and became precarious with Khrushchev's denunciation (1956) of the Stalin personality cult. On April 17, 1956, Chervenkov was replaced as premier, but for five years he remained in office as one of the deputy premiers. In 1962 he was expelled from the BCP, but he was silently rehabilitated seven years later.

Clurman, Harold Edgar, U.S. theatre director and critic (b. Sept. 18, 1901, New York, N.Y.—d. Sept. 9, 1980, New York), contributed to the excellence of the theatre as a founder (1931) of the Group Theatre, an experimental company that served as a forum for playwrights Clifford Odets, Irwin Shaw, and William Saroyan and nurtured such actors as Lee Strasberg, John Garfield, Lee J. Cobb, and Stella Adler. The Group Theatre also introduced the Stanislavsky method of dramatic training, which emphasized realism and encouraged actors to rely on their inner impulses. After briefly working as an actor, the versatile Clurman directed a number of plays there, most notably *Awake and Sing!* (1935), and enhanced his reputation with *Member of the Wedding* (1950), *Tiger at the Gates* (1955), and the farcical *Waltz of the Toreadors* (1957). Clurman's deep immersion in the theatre prompted him to become a drama critic for *The New Republic* and *The Nation.* His writing also extended to books: Clurman published *On Directing* (1972), *The Divine Pastime* (1974), and his memoirs, *All People Are Famous* (1974).

Cochran, Jacqueline, U.S. aviator (b. 1910?, Pensacola, Fla.—d. Aug. 9, 1980, Indio, Calif.), was a determined and independent woman who earned her flying wings at the age of 22 and held more speed, distance, and altitude records than any other flyer during her career as a crack pilot. In 1935 Cochran became the first woman to enter the Bendix Transcontinental Air Race and won the Bendix Trophy in 1938. She served as a captain in the British Air Force Auxiliary. After the Japanese attacked Pearl Harbor, she instructed U.S. women on how to fly transport planes. In 1943 Cochran was named director of the Women's Air Force Service Pilots, with responsibility for training 1,200 women. In 1953 she broke the world speed records for both men and women in a Sabre jet on 100-km (652.552 mph), 500-km (590.321 mph), and 15-km (675.471 mph) courses. In the same year she became the first woman to fly faster than the speed of sound. Cochran broke her own speed records for 100 km and 500 km in 1961, and in 1960 she became the first woman to fly at Mach 2 (twice the speed of sound). Orphaned in infancy, Cochran was brought up in poverty by foster parents. In her autobiography, *The Stars at Noon* (1954), she explained her life as a rise "from sawdust to stardust." She retired from the Air Force Reserve in 1970 with the rank of colonel.

Coghill, Nevill Henry Kendal Aylmer, British Chaucerian scholar (b. April 19, 1899, Skibbereen, County Cork, Ireland—d. Nov. 6, 1980, Cheltenham, England), was Merton professor of English literature at the University of Oxford (1957–66) and the translator of Chaucer's *Canterbury Tales* into modern verse. He studied at Exeter College, Oxford, where he became a research fellow in 1924 and official fellow and librarian in 1925. A popular lecturer, he established his reputation as a scholar with his studies on *Piers Plowman* and published *The Poet Chaucer* (1949) and *Shakespeare's Professional Skills* (1964). Though sometimes scorned by his fellow academics, his Penguin Classics versions of Chaucer (*The Canterbury Tales,* 1951; *Troilus and Criseyde,* 1971) conveyed the vigour of the medieval works and did much to ensure that they remained a living part of English culture. His musical version of *The Canterbury Tales,* written with Martin Starkie, ran for five years in London and was later seen on Broadway and in Australia. He also helped found the Oxford University Dramatic Society, gave Richard Burton his first major part in one of his plays, and in 1966 directed Burton and Elizabeth Taylor in a production of Marlowe's *Dr. Faustus.* He was made a member of the Royal Society of Literature in 1950.

Cole, Dame Margaret Isabel, British writer and educationist (b. 1893, Cambridge, England—d. May 7, 1980, Goring-on-Thames, England), graduated from Girton College, Cambridge, before joining the Fabian (later Labour) Research Department (LRD), where she met and married (1918) the Socialist economist G. D. H. Cole. Having left the LRD in 1925 because of its Communist leanings, Cole organized conferences and acted as secretary to the New Fabian Bureau (1935–39) and to a renewed Fabian Society (1939–53) while lecturing in London and Cambridge. The research she inspired bore fruit in the legislation of the 1945–51 Labour government, some of whose leading Cabinet members had been her associates. Cole was also a member of various London County Council (LCC) education committees and was an LCC alderman (1952–65). She was made president of the Fabian Society in 1963 and a Dame of the British Empire in 1970. Her work included *Twelve Studies in Soviet Russia* (1932), *The Webbs and Their Work* (ed., 1949), and *Diaries of Beatrice Webb* (ed., 1952 and 1956); she wrote *Beatrice Webb: A Memoir* (1945), an autobiography, *Growing Up into Revolution* (1949), and *The Life of G. D. H. Cole* (1971).

Colean, Miles Lanier, U.S. government official (b. Aug. 4, 1898, Peoria, Ill.—d. Sept. 16, 1980, Washington, D.C.), helped draft the legislation that created (1934) the Federal Housing Administration (FHA), a U.S. government agency designed to restore lender confidence in mortgage loans, broaden housing demand, and stimulate construction. After graduating from Columbia University with a degree in architecture, Colean worked for such architectural firms as R. H. Dana in New York City (1922–24) and Holabird and Root in Chicago (1925–29); he was also a partner of Cowles, Colean in Chicago (1929–34). In Washington he served as technical director (1934–37) and then assistant administrator (1937–40) of the FHA. Besides advising presidents Dwight D. Eisenhower and Richard M. Nixon, Colean wrote an impressive list of books including *Can America Build Houses?, American Housing: Problems and Prospects, The Federal Land Bank System,* and *Renewing Our Cities,* in which he coined the term "urban renewal."

Coleraine, Richard Kidston Law, 1ST BARON, British politician (b. Feb. 27, 1901, Helensburgh, Scotland

—d. Nov. 15, 1980, London, England), served as minister of state at the Foreign Office during World War II and later as minister of education. The son of Bonar Law, U.K. prime minister from October 1922 to May 1923, he opposed appeasement of Hitler in the years leading up to the war and joined the wartime coalition government, first at the War Office and then at the Foreign Office. He had previously worked as a journalist in Britain and in the U.S., where he was on the staff of the *New York Herald-Tribune* and the *Philadelphia Public Ledger*. He was elected a Conservative member of Parliament in 1931. An able minister, primarily concerned with measures for the postwar relief of Europe, he was appointed to the Ministry of Education in 1945. But he lost his seat in South-West Hull in the general election that year. Later he returned to Parliament in a by-election but devoted himself increasingly to his business interests, which included chairmanship of several companies. He was raised to the peerage in 1954 and became an active member of the House of Lords.

Connell, Amyas Douglas, New Zealand-born architect (b. 1901, New Zealand—d. April 19, 1980, London, England), was a pioneer of the modern movement in domestic architecture during the 1930s. The house at Amersham, Buckinghamshire, called High and Over (designed in 1929), shocked traditionalists with its bold geometric outline. After training at the University of London, Connell went into partnership with Basil Ward and Colin Lucas; during the 1930s the trio, influenced by the ideas of Le Corbusier, became leading designers of private houses. After World War II Connell went to Kenya, where he designed many public buildings. He became an associate of the Royal Institute of British Architects in 1937 and a fellow in 1964.

Connelly, Marc(us Cook), U.S. playwright (b. Dec. 13, 1890, McKeesport, Pa.—d. Dec. 21, 1980, New York, N.Y.), was the Pulitzer Prize-winning author of *The Green Pastures* (1930), a delightful play based on Roark Bradford's sketches of *Ol' Man Adam an' His Chillun*. The semimusical play, for which Connelly gained enduring renown, was a black folk-version of the Old Testament. On Feb. 26, 1930, *The Green Pastures* finally made its Broadway debut after several producers turned it down because they felt it might offend blacks. The play grossed $3 million in its first five years. In 1917 Connelly joined the *Morning Telegraph* in New York City as a reporter for theatre news. While working the theatre beat, he met George S. Kaufman, who worked for the drama section of the *New York Times*. They collaborated on a series of plays that included *Dulcy* (1921), starring Joan Fontaine; *To the Ladies* (1922), starring Helen Hayes; *Merton of the Movies* (1922), a satire on Hollywood; and *Be Yourself* (1924), the last of their joint efforts. Connelly was a member of the Round Table at the Algonquin Hotel, a prominent group of literary personalities. A charming raconteur, Connelly displayed his wit in *Voices Offstage: A Book of Memoirs* (1968). Shortly before his death, he was asked if conversation at the Algonquin was still as scintillating as in the 1920s; he replied, "Mine is."

Courtneidge, Dame Cicely, British actress (b. April 1, 1893, Sydney, Australia—d. April 26, 1980, London, England), played musical comedy and revue, both in a celebrated partnership with her husband, Jack Hulbert, and as a highly talented and much loved comedienne in her own right. The daughter of actor Robert Courtneidge, she made her first stage appearance in 1901 and married Hulbert in 1918. By the 1930s they were well-established figures in revue and the variety theatre and had made several films together. After World War II she starred in Ivor Novello's *Gay's the Word*, then turned increasingly toward the nonmusical theatre, gaining notable successes in *Dear Octopus* and *Move Over Mrs. Markham*. In 1974, after more than 70 years on the stage and nearly 60 years of marriage, she played opposite her husband in *Breath of Spring*. Her autobiography, *Cicely*, appeared in 1953. She was made a DBE in 1972.

Culshaw, John Royds, British record producer (b. May 28, 1924, Southport, Lancashire, England—d. April 27, 1980, London, England), publicized and shaped the recording of classical music during the long-playing and stereo record eras. His recording of the complete cycle of Wagner's *Ring*, with Georg Solti conducting, was a milestone in stereo technique and won eight Grand Prix des Disques. He joined the Decca Record Co. in 1946 and became manager of its classical division in 1956. He encouraged many leading artists to take advantage of new developments in the field, notably Benjamin Britten, whom Culshaw persuaded to conduct recordings of his main works. As head of music programs at BBC Television from 1967 to 1975, Culshaw again turned to Britten, first as conductor of a televised performance of *Peter Grimes* and then to commission the opera *Owen Wingrave*. Culshaw lectured extensively and published several works, including a biography of Rachmaninoff in 1949. He was awarded the OBE in 1966.

Curran, Sir Charles John, British broadcasting administrator (b. Oct. 13, 1921, Dublin, Ireland—d. Jan. 9, 1980, Barnet, Hertfordshire, England), was director general of the British Broadcasting Corporation (BBC) from 1969 to 1977 and president of the European Broadcasting Union from 1973 to 1978. A graduate of Magdalene College, Cambridge, Curran served in the Indian Army during World War II and joined the BBC in 1947 as a producer of informative talks. After a period as BBC representative in Canada (1956–59), he was the corporation's secretary (1963–66) and director of external services (1967–69) before succeeding Sir Hugh Greene as director general. During his term as chief executive Curran successfully preserved the BBC's independent status in the face of strong political pressures and mounting financial constraints. He was knighted in 1974 and in 1978 became managing director and chief executive of Visnews, an international television news agency. He described his years at the BBC in *A Seamless Robe* (1979).

Dagover, Lil (MARTA-MARIA LILLITS), German actress (b. Sept. 30, 1897, Pati, Java—d. Jan. 30, 1980, Munich, West Germany), starred in the classic silent film *The Cabinet of Dr. Caligari* (1919) and went on to make more than 100 films in Europe and the U.S. During the 1920s she worked for leading directors including Fritz Lang in Germany and Julien Duvivier in France. But Dagover's career was sidetracked by her acquiescence with the Nazi regime, which made her a state actress for her performances in such films as *Kreutzer Sonata* (1936). After World War II Dagover continued to make films and appear on television. She also resumed a stage career, with much-acclaimed performances in *Gigi* and *The Mad Woman of Chaillot*. She came out of retirement to act in Maximilian Schell's *Tales from the Vienna Woods* (1979).

Day, Dorothy, U.S. social worker (b. Nov. 8, 1897, New York, N.Y.—d. Nov. 29, 1980, New York), was a vital force in the Roman Catholic Church as the founder (with Peter Maurin in 1933) of the *Catholic Worker*, a monthly tabloid that expressed a new social philosophy. The ensuing Catholic Worker Movement preached personal reform, radical agrarianism, absolute pacifism, and the personal practice of the principles expressed by Jesus in the Sermon on the Mount. Before World War II, Day and members of the movement instituted their program by establishing hospitality houses for the needy; a total of 35 houses were opened across the U.S. Several communitarian farms were also established for the poor. Although the movement waned during the war and many hospitality houses disappeared, Day's tireless commitment to social justice remained fervent. Day, who earlier wrote for Marxist publications and was a member of the Socialist Party and the International Workers of the World, converted to Catholicism because she wanted her child (by a common-law marriage) to be baptized a Catholic. In her autobiography, *The Long Loneliness* (1952), Day revealed that her religious conversion was a choice between God and man and that she was most occupied with "the conflict of flesh and spirit." During the later years of her life Day spent most of her time opposing the Vietnam War and nuclear proliferation.

Dean, William Ralph ("DIXIE"), British association football (soccer) player (b. 1907, Birkenhead, England—d. March 1, 1980, Merseyside, England), was a great centre forward who tallied 473 goals in 502 matches between 1924 and 1939 and scored a record 60 goals in one season (1927–28). He also scored three or more goals in a match a record 37 times. Dean first worked as a railway apprentice but at 16 turned to professional soccer and at 17 played for the Tranmere Rovers. In the 1924–25 season he scored 27 goals in 27 matches. Transferred to Everton (1925–38), Dean lifted that club to success by scoring a record 349 goals in 399 games. He then played (1938–39) a final major season for Notts County. An outstanding feature of his game was his powerful and accurate heading.

Dilhorne, Reginald Edward Manningham-Buller, 1ST VISCOUNT, British lawyer and politician (b. Aug. 1, 1905—d. Sept. 7, 1980, Knoydart, Inverness-shire, Scotland), held the highest legal offices in Britain, serving as solicitor general (1951–54), attorney general (1954–62), and lord chancellor (1962–64). During and after World War II, he also served as a Conservative member of Parliament. He opposed the abolition of the death penalty, changes in the laws relating to homosexuality, and the relaxing of laws on abortion. He similarly favoured limiting the rights of accused people and the reform of trial procedure. He was educated at Eton and Oxford before being called to the bar by the Inner Temple in 1927. As attorney general, he was an eloquent prosecutor in the sensational murder trial of John Bodkin Adams (who was acquitted) but later, in the House of Commons, he had to defend his decision to prosecute Adams. In 1963 he led the inquiry into security aspects of the Profumo affair and in the same year was involved in a controversy with Labour leader Harold Wilson, who had alleged that the judiciary was being improperly influenced by the government. Dilhorne was created a viscount in 1964 and became Conservative deputy leader in the House of Lords in 1965.

Diop, Alioune, Senegalese publisher (b. 1910, Saint-Louis, Senegal—d. May 2, 1980, Paris, France), founded the journal *Présence Africaine* in 1947 and made it a leading voice of black African opinion during a crucial period in the continent's history. French-educated and a Catholic, he served as Senegalese representative in the French Senate from 1946 to 1948 and came into contact with leading French and Francophone African intellectuals. But *Présence Africaine* was faithfully open to the full range of African cultures and ideologies and reflected the excitement and uncertainties of a period when many African countries were seeking independence. In 1956 Diop organized in Paris the first World Congress of Black Writers and Artists, which was attended by Senegal's poet-president Léopold Senghor, French poet and playwright Aimé Césaire, and U.S. writer Richard Wright. Diop later served as secretary-general of the Festival of Black Arts.

Dönitz, Karl, German naval officer (b. Sept. 16, 1891, Grünau, Berlin, Germany—d. Dec. 24, 1980, Aumühle, West Germany), was commander in chief of the German Navy (1943–45) and Adolf Hitler's successor as head of the Third Reich. The son of a Prussian civil servant, Dönitz entered the German Navy in 1910 and during World War I became a U-boat commander. After the war he continued his naval career first as commander of a torpedo boat and later of the cruiser "Emden." The London Naval Agreement of 1935 permitted Germany to build a fleet of 70 U-boats, and Hitler appointed Dönitz to take charge of this project. Because of the shortage of materials and the priority Hitler gave to the Luftwaffe, Germany had only 25 U-boats capable of service in the Atlantic at the outbreak of World War II. By the end of the war, however, around 1,000 U-boats had been built and placed in service, more than half of which were destroyed by the Allies. Out of 39,000 men who served aboard German U-boats, 27,082 perished. In January 1943 Hitler dismissed Grand Admiral Erich Raeder as commander in chief of the German Navy and appointed Grand Admiral Dönitz in his stead—thus replacing the builder of capital ships with the enthusiastic submariner—but the Battle of the Atlantic was finally won by the Allies. Hitler developed a very high regard for Dönitz and appointed him, rather than Hermann Göring, as his successor. On May 1, 1945, Dönitz announced Hitler's suicide and he ruled the remnants of the Third Reich from Flensburg until he was arrested by the Allied Control Commission on May 22. He was put on trial at Nürnberg for his part in the "conspiracy against the peace," was sentenced to ten years' imprisonment in Spandau jail, and was released in 1956.

Dornberger, Walter Robert, German-born guided-missile and space-vehicle engineer (b. Sept. 6, 1895, Giessen, Hessen, Germany—d. June 26, 1980, Baden-Württemberg, West Germany), managed the development of the German V-2 rocket and Wasserfall missiles during World War II. A professional army officer, he graduated from the School of Technology in Charlottenberg (now Technical University of Berlin) with a B.A. in 1927 and an M.A. in 1930. In the same year, he returned to duty as a captain with the German Army in the ballistics branch of its ordnance department, where he became interested in developing the rocket, a weapon not specifically forbidden by the Versailles Treaty. Dornberger was instrumental in establishing a rocket-testing facility in Kummersdorf, near Berlin, and began recruiting a team of civilian engineers and scientists to staff it. He principally drew on the ranks of the Deutsche Verein für Raumschiffahrt, a group of young space enthusiasts who were developing liquid-propelled rockets in Berlin. Among the most notable of these were Wernher von Braun, Arthur Rudolph, and Klaus Riedel. As the scope of their activities increased, they established a larger rocket development and test facility, the famous centre at Peenemünde (now in East Germany) on the Baltic coast. There, the Dornberger-Braun team developed the V-2 rocket that bombed Belgium, France, and England during World War II. At the end of World War II, Maj. Gen. Dornberger was imprisoned in England for two years. After his release he moved to the U.S. and was a consultant for the U.S. Air Force at Wright-Patterson Field, in Dayton, Ohio; he later served as technical assistant to the president, a vice-president, and chief scientist of the Bell Aircraft Corp. in Buffalo, N.Y. At Bell, he was involved in the design of the Rascal air-to-surface missile and Project Dyna-Soar. Dornberger, the author of *V-2* (1954), retired in 1965.

Douglas, Helen Gahagan, U.S. actress and congressional representative (b. Nov. 25, 1900, Boonton, N.J.—d. June 28, 1980, New York, N.Y.), starred on Broadway in *Dreams for Sale* (1922), sang opera in Europe, and then returned to the Broadway footlights and married (1931) Melvyn Douglas, her leading man in *Tonight or Never*. Douglas became interested in politics after her marriage and championed liberal causes in California. In 1940 she became a Democratic national committeewoman and in 1944 was elected representative of California's 14th congressional district. Douglas was propelled into the national spotlight in 1950 when she ran for the Senate against Richard M. Nixon. Although never accused of being a Communist, Douglas was made to appear as one because of her liberal views. Douglas lost the race and never ran for public office again. During the 1950s she occasionally returned to the stage and supported liberal Democratic politicians.

Douglas, William O(rville), U.S. Supreme Court justice (b. Oct. 16, 1898, Maine, Minn.—d. Jan. 19, 1980, Washington, D.C.), served on the U.S. Supreme Court from April 17, 1939, to Nov. 12, 1975, longer than any other justice in the history of the tribunal. Douglas, who vigorously defended civil rights and the individual's right to privacy, also maintained that the protection of free speech is "essential to the very existence of a democracy." He was instrumental in deciding such landmark cases as the 1966 Miranda decision, which guaranteed rights such as that to legal counsel during police interrogation, and *Griswold* v. *Connecticut* (1965), which struck down a state law barring the use of contraceptives. As a champion of the First Amendment, he argued in the Pentagon Papers case of 1971 that "secrecy in government is fundamentally undemocratic, perpetuating bureaucratic errors. Open debate and discussion of public issues are vital to our national health." Douglas often stood alone in his liberal court opinions—he filed more than 500 arguments in dissent and seemed more concerned with reaffirming his convictions than with winning over his colleagues. His position on the court provided Douglas with countless opportunities to promote his belief that the U.S. Constitution was designed "to keep the Government off the backs of the people." Before his appointment to the court by Pres. Franklin D. Roosevelt, Douglas attended (1922–25) the Columbia University School of Law in New York City, where he was graduated second in his class. After briefly working for a Wall Street law firm and teaching at Columbia, he joined the faculty of Yale University, where he demonstrated his expertise in financial law. He then joined the Securities and Exchange Commission and became its chairman in 1937. Having survived several attempted impeachments during his tenure, Douglas continued to work even after suffering a debilitating stroke in 1974, but he reluctantly retired in 1975 because of ill health.

WIDE WORLD

Durante, Jimmy (James Francis Durante), U.S. comedian (b. Feb. 10, 1893, New York, N.Y.—d. Jan. 29, 1980, Santa Monica, Calif.), was a much-loved entertainer whose honky-tonk piano playing, loud raspy voice, and comedy antics made him a magical success. Hilarity predictably broke out when "the great Schnozzola" (so-called because of his large nose) strutted across the stage sporting his battered hat and sat down at the piano to bang out the nonsensical "Inka Dinka Doo." With such classic lines as "Everybody's gettin' into de act," "I got a million of 'em," and "Am I mortified," Durante delighted radio, television, nightclub, and theatre audiences for more than 60 years. Although Durante's father hoped his son would become a concert pianist, Durante started performing in 1910; among his early performances was one with Eddie Cantor, then a singing waiter. He next teamed up with singer Eddie Jackson and dancer Lou Clayton in a vaudeville act that attracted huge crowds to the Club Durant and the Palace. After a highly successful run on Broadway in such shows as *The New Yorkers* (1930), *Strike Me Pink* (1933), and *Jumbo* (1935), Durante turned to Hollywood. From 1930 to 1951 he appeared in 32 motion pictures but achieved his greatest applause as a showstopper in nightclubs. Durante starred on his own television show from 1950 to 1956 but doubted the durability of his popularity and returned to the nightclub circuit in the 1960s. His last two films were *Jumbo* (1962) and *It's a Mad, Mad, Mad, Mad World* (1963). The sentimental Durante, who fervently ended his routine with the curious line "Goodnight, Mrs. Calabash, wherever you are," ended his career following a stroke in 1972.

UPI

Ebert, Carl (Anton Charles), German-born opera director (b. Feb. 20, 1887, Berlin, Germany—d. May 14, 1980, Santa Monica, Calif.), as artistic director and producer of the Glyndebourne Festival Opera from 1935 to 1959, established new standards of production in British opera. Ebert started his career as an actor in 1909 and went on to direct the Darmstadt State Theatre before turning to opera and becoming (1931) general manager of the Berlin City Opera. Under the Nazi regime Ebert left Germany and in 1935 made his debut as a director at Glyndebourne with a brilliant production of *Figaro*. From then until his retirement in 1959 Ebert was responsible for some of the festival's most original works, integrating music and stagecraft in productions that showed an unerring sense of pace and timing. His contribution to British music did not end there; he was associated with the Sussex Mozart festivals and with the Edinburgh Festival and from 1965 to 1977 was director of productions at the Scottish Opera Company. During World War II Ebert worked in the U.S. and after the war served (1946–54) as professor and head of the opera department at the University of Southern California and director (1950–54) of the Guild Opera Company, both in Los Angeles. He played a significant role in reestablishing opera in West Germany during the postwar years and returned to the Berlin City Opera as director (1954–61).

Emmet of Amberley, Evelyn Violet Elizabeth Emmet, Baroness, British politician (b. March 18, 1899, Cairo, Egypt—d. Oct. 10, 1980, Amberley Castle, West Sussex, England), was Conservative member of Parliament for East Grinstead (1955–64) and chairman of the National Union of the Conservative Party (1955–56). After obtaining her degree at Lady Margaret Hall, Oxford, she traveled extensively in Europe and during World War I served as secretary to her father, Lord Rennell of Rodd, Britain's ambassador in Rome. Between the wars she pursued a career in local government and served as a justice of the peace. Emmet became a member of the executive of the National Union of the Conservative Party in 1948. In 1952, though not yet a member of Parliament, she was appointed British delegate to the UN. On her retirement from the House of Commons she was created a life peer and in 1968 became deputy chairman of committees in the House of Lords. From 1974 to 1977 she was also a member of the select committee of the House of Lords European Economic Community committee.

Emney, Fred, British actor (b. Feb. 12, 1900, London, England—d. Dec. 25, 1980, Bognor Regis, West Sussex, England), sported loud tweed suits, a monocle, and a cigar while regaling audiences with his subtle humour. The son of an eminent comedian, Emney appeared as a page boy in 1915 and as a squire in the Drury Lane pantomime *Puss in Boots* (1916). After touring in musical comedy, he left for the U.S. where, from 1920 to 1931, he appeared in vaudeville. In Britain he played a rear admiral in A. Pinero's *The Schoolmistress* and Lord Gorgeous in the pantomime *Goody Two Shoes* at the London Palladium. From 1935 to 1938 Emney was a resident comedian with Leslie Henson and Richard Hearne at the Gaity Theatre in London. His other credits included *Big Top* (1942), *It's Time to Dance* (1943), *Big Boy* (1945), *Blue for a Boy* (1950), *Happy as a King* (1953), and *When We Are Married* (1970).

Erim, Nihat, Turkish politician (b. 1912, Kandira, Turkey—d. July 19, 1980, Istanbul, Turkey), was prime minister of Turkey from 1971 to 1972, heading a coalition government while the country was under martial law. Trained as a lawyer in Istanbul and Paris, he taught at the University of Ankara until his appointment in 1942 as legal adviser to the Ministry of Foreign Affairs. He became a member of Parliament in 1945 and served as minister of public works and deputy prime minister from 1948 to 1950. A member of the Republican People's Party, he agreed in 1971 to lead a government independent of party loyalties at a difficult time in the country's affairs. Erim imposed strict policies of law and order and acceded to U.S. requests to ban poppy cultivation in an attempt to halt the drug traffic. His recent identification with right-wing policies may have provided the motive for his assassination.

Etchebaster, Pierre, French real tennis player (b. May 1894, France—d. March 24, 1980, Saint-Jean-de-Luz, France), dominated real tennis as world champion from 1928 to 1954. Etchebaster started as a player of pelota, the game of his native Basque region, before taking up real tennis, the ancestor of lawn tennis known in France as *jeu de paume*. By 1926 he was a challenger for the world championship, which he won in 1928 against G. F. Covey. From then until his retirement he successfully defended his title, showing mastery of tactics, technical supremacy, and amazing resilience, so that in his last defense, against James Dear in New York, he outlasted a younger man in the three-day contest.

Evans, Bill (William John Evans), U.S. pianist-composer (b. Aug. 16, 1929, Plainfield, N.J.—d. Sept. 15, 1980, New York, N.Y.), was an innovative jazz virtuoso who played with the Miles Davis group that produced the classic jazz recording *Kind of Blue*. The album, which introduced a variety of scales and modes as the basis for improvisation, discarded the traditional harmonic structures. Evans, who then formed his own trio, received Grammy awards for *Conversations with Myself* (1963), *Live at Montreaux* (1968), *Alone* (1970), and two for *The Bill Evans Album* (1971). The latter won Grammys for best jazz performance by a soloist and for best jazz performance by a group.

Fabbri, Diego, Italian playwright (b. July 2, 1911, Forli, Italy—d. Aug. 14, 1980, Riccione, Italy), wrote plays for stage and television, which often carried religious themes that brought him into conflict with the Roman Catholic Church. He wrote for the theatre while working toward a doctorate in law (1936). Fabbri established his literary reputation during the post-World War II years with such plays as *Il Seduttore* (1951) and *La Bugiarda* (1956). The latter, a very successful work, was performed outside Italy, as were *Processo a Gesù* (1953) and *Figli d'Arte* (1959; directed by Luchino Visconti and winner of a prize at the Paris Théâtre des Nations). His later plays, mainly written for television, also dealt with problems of faith and individual conscience.

Farago, Ladislas, Hungarian-born writer (b. Sept. 21, 1906, Csurgo, Hung.—d. Oct. 15, 1980, New York, N.Y.), was the author of an impressive array of war and espionage books that included *Burn After Reading, The Broken Seal, The Game of the Foxes, The Tenth Fleet,* and *Strictly from Hungary*. He also worked on *Behind Closed Doors* (with Rear Adm. Ellis M. Zacharias) and wrote *Patton: Ordeal and Triumph,* a colourful biography of Gen. George S. Patton. The book was the basis for the blockbuster motion picture *Patton* (1970), which won seven Academy Awards including best picture. In 1972 Farago made headlines in the *London Daily Express* when he announced that Martin Bormann, Hitler's ruthless deputy during World War II, was alive and living as an Argentine businessman. Farago's allegations were discredited when a picture, supposedly of Bormann, was identified as that of a schoolteacher and when West German officials declared (1973) that Bormann's skeleton had been unearthed in 1972. Nonetheless, Farago stood by his story and reported his findings in *Aftermath* (1974).

Farrell, Edelmiro J., Argentine politician (b. Aug. 12, 1887, Avellaneda, Arg.—d. Oct. 31, 1980, Buenos Aires, Arg.), was an army general who became minister of war and then vice-president under Gen. Pedro Pablo Ramírez. When the latter resigned under pressure, Farrell became president of Argentina. In that capacity (1944–46), Farrell took a historic step when, under pressure from the U.S., he declared war on Germany and Japan during World War II. On June 4, 1946, Juan D. Perón, Farrell's labour minister, was elected president and Farrell retired from public life.

Fernandez, Royes, U.S. dancer (b. July 15, 1929, New Orleans, La.—d. March 3, 1980, New York, N.Y.), was a principal dancer (1950–53 and 1957–72) with the American Ballet Theatre and gained renown for his leading roles in *Giselle, La Sylphide, Swan Lake,* and *Les Sylphides*. Fernandez, who partnered such prima ballerinas as Alicia Markova and Margot Fonteyn, captivated audiences with his classical style and technical virtuosity. He also made notable performances in such modern ballets as *Lilac Garden, Études,* and *Theme and Variations*. After his last appearance (1972) with the American Ballet Theatre, Fernandez became professor of dance at the College of the Arts at the State University of New York. He was also an instructor at the Ballet Theatre School.

Fernández-Miranda y Hevia, Torcuato, Spanish jurist and politician (b. Nov. 10, 1915, Asturias, Spain—d. June 19, 1980, London, England), was a leading figure in the Falangist movement under Gen. Francisco Franco but surprised many of his extremist supporters by becoming the man chiefly responsible for the constitutional changes that led to a more democratic regime after Franco's death. While at the University of Oviedo he became chairman of the Catholic Law Students' Society, and in 1936 he had to go into hiding before joining Franco's army during the Civil War. After Franco took power, Fernández-Miranda completed his studies and lectured in law in Oviedo and Madrid. He was appointed to a post in the Ministry of Education and in 1962 became secretary-general of Spain's only legal political organization, the Movimiento. He joined the Cabinet of Premier Luis Carrero Blanco and was a leading opponent of political reform. He was acting premier for a few days in 1973 after Carrero Blanco's assassination. When Prince Juan Carlos became king after Franco's death in 1975, Fernández-Miranda was appointed president of the Cortes (parliament). Essentially a pragmatist, he recognized the need for democratic changes and tried to ensure that the fundamental restructuring of the system took place constitutionally. In 1978, however, he resigned from the Union of the Democratic Centre because he disapproved of the liberal constitution voted in that year.

Ferranti, Sir Vincent Ziani de, British electrical engineer and industrialist (b. Feb. 16, 1893—d. May 20, 1980, Macclesfield, Cheshire, England), took over his father's company in 1930 and eventually built Ferranti Ltd. into a leading international electronics concern specializing in television, radar, and defense electronics. He was managing director to 1958 and then chairman (1958–63). During World War II Ferranti was released from the Army to direct the firm's war work. During the years that followed, his company, which employed over 20,000 people in Canada, Scotland, and England, worked extensively with computers and defense electronics in a joint venture with Victoria University of Manchester. Ferranti was knighted in 1948 and served as president of the Institution of Electrical Engineers (1946–47) and as chairman of the international executive council of the World Power Conference (1950–62).

Finletter, Thomas Knight, U.S. government official (b. Nov. 11, 1893, Philadelphia, Pa.—d. April 24, 1980, New York, N.Y.), was principal author of a persuasive 1948 report entitled "Survival in the Air Age," which led to the rapid expansion of the U.S. Air Force. This report warned that the Soviet Union would reach air parity with the U.S. by 1952 and strongly advocated improving military preparedness by increasing the Air Force to 95 wings at a cost of $18 billion. Subsequently the Air Force, created in 1947, tripled in size. An avowed proponent of world peace, Finletter advocated military disarmament and favoured U.S. military strength "purely as a deterrent and countermeasure." A corporate lawyer by profession, he frequently interrupted his practice to hold government posts. Before World War II he became (1941) a special assistant to Secretary of State Cordell Hull; in 1945 he was a consultant to the U.S. delegation to the conference that drew up the UN Charter in San Francisco; and after the war he headed a task force on the future of American air power. During the Korean War Finletter was named (1950) the second secretary of the Air Force by Pres. Harry S. Truman, and a decade later he was again drafted, this time by Pres. John F. Kennedy, to become (1961) permanent representative to the North Atlantic Treaty Organization.

Fogarty, Anne Whitney, U.S. fashion designer (b. Feb. 2, 1919, Pittsburgh, Pa.—d. Jan. 15, 1980, New York, N.Y.), was the creator of an ultrafeminine shirtwaist dress that featured a tiny waist and a bouffant ballerina skirt, supported by as many as a dozen petticoats. This style, which was introduced in the early 1950s, revolutionized junior fashions and became known as the young "American look." Fogarty worked as a model and designed dresses for Youth Guild before joining (1950) Margot Dresses, where she popularized her shirtwaist dresses of printed cotton, denim, and linen. She then designed (1958–62) an exclusive women's collection for Saks Fifth Avenue stores, and later, with Leonard Sunshine, she designed collections on Seventh Avenue, including dresses for Tricia Nixon. Shortly before her death, Fogarty completed a line of spring-into-summer sportswear and dresses.

Fontanet, Joseph, French politician (b. Feb. 9, 1921, Frontenex, Savoie, France—d. Feb. 2, 1980, Paris, France), was a leading member of the Gaullist Mouvement Républicain Populaire (MRP), which he served as secretary-general from 1963 to 1967. He joined the MRP when it was founded by Gen. Charles de Gaulle after the Liberation. Fontanet was elected a deputy in 1950 and from 1969 to 1974 was successively minister of labour and minister of education before retiring from politics. In the latter post he introduced measures designed to give schools more freedom in organizing their timetables. He was awarded the Legion of Honour and in 1978 joined the Société d'Études et de Réalisations pour les Équipements Collectifs. Fontanet was shot and killed by an unknown assailant.

Fouché, Jacobus Johannes, South African politician (b. June 6, 1898, Wepener, Orange Free State—d. Sept. 23, 1980, Cape Town, South Africa), was president of South Africa from 1968 to 1974 and known to his Afrikaner supporters as "Oom Jim" ("Uncle Jim"). A dedicated Afrikaner nationalist, he became a Nationalist Party member of Parliament in 1941. As minister of defense (1959–66) he had to deal with the UN embargo on arms supplies and his failure in this respect led to his replacement by P. W. Botha. Fouché continued to exercise a considerable influence in white South African political affairs, however, and held minor ministerial posts until his appointment as president of the republic.

Fox, Virgil Keel, U.S. organist (b. May 3, 1912, Princeton, Ill.—d. Oct. 25, 1980, West Palm Beach, Fla.), justified his belief that church, classical, and even rock music could successfully be played on the large modern organ. Fox demonstrated the versatility of the instrument as the accomplished organist at Riverside Church in New York City for 19 years and as the flamboyant star of light-rock concerts, for which he wore iridescent jackets and rhinestone-studded shoes. Fox, who was invited to play the best organs in the world, maintained a grueling schedule that included some 70 concerts a year. The richness of his playing technique could also be heard on more than 40 recordings. The son of parents deeply entrenched in a musical tradition, Fox began playing the piano at an early age. At first he resisted organ lessons because he felt that the music sounded monotonous, but his progress was remarkable. At age 10 he became a church organist; at 14 he played before an audience of 3,000; at 17 he was chosen winner of the National Federation of Music Clubs contest; and at 19 he won a full scholarship to the Peabody Conservatory of Music in Baltimore, Md., and made his professional debut in New York City.

Frank, Otto, German-born merchant (b. May 12, 1889, Frankfurt am Main, Germany—d. Aug. 20, 1980, Basel, Switz.), was the father of Anne Frank whose diary, published after her death in 1945, became world famous. Frank, decorated for bravery as a German officer in World War I, escaped with his family from the Nazi anti-Jewish persecutions in Germany before the outbreak of World War II. Living in Amsterdam, he and his family went into hiding in 1942 to avoid deportation from The Netherlands, which was occupied by Germany in 1940. They were discovered and arrested in 1944 and sent to Auschwitz, where they were separated. Anne and her elder sister were moved to Bergen-Belsen, where they both died of typhus early in 1945. Their mother died in Auschwitz, but Frank was freed by the Soviets on Jan. 27, 1945. Returning to Amsterdam, he recovered the diary that Anne had kept while in hiding and, although reluctant, was persuaded to publish it in 1947. It was later translated into numerous languages, dramatized, and filmed. Frank, who moved to Switzerland in the 1950s, turned over all the proceeds to the Anne Frank Foundation in Amsterdam.

Friedman, Elizebeth Smith, U.S. cryptographer (b. Aug. 26, 1892, Huntington, Ind.—d. Oct. 31, 1980, Plainfield, N.J.), used her expertise in deciphering codes to aid the U.S. government during both World Wars I and II and to solve international crimes, especially drug and liquor smuggling cases. Friedman began working as a cryptanalyst in 1916 at the Riverbank Laboratories in Geneva, Ill.; the U.S. government acquired the centre in 1917 for a military cryptography training school. Besides rendering her services to the War Department (1921–22), Navy Department (1923), Treasury Department (1924–42), and International Monetary Fund (1946–49), Friedman became enmeshed in such cases as the Doll Woman case (1944), in which her testimony convicted an antique doll dealer, Velvalee Dickinson, of spying for the Japanese government. She also cracked (1937) a complicated Chinese code for the Canadian government; the breakthrough led to the arrest and conviction of a gang of five opium smugglers. Together with her husband, William (also a cryptographer), Friedman wrote *The Shakespearean Ciphers Examined,* which refuted the notion that Sir Francis Bacon had written the sonnets and plays attributed to William Shakespeare. After retirement, Friedman spent her time writing, researching, and compiling a bibliography of her husband's work.

Froman, Jane, U.S. singer and actress (b. Nov. 10, 1907, University City, Mo.—d. April 22, 1980, Columbia, Mo.), was a popular singer with the Paul Whiteman Band and appeared in such notable Broadway musicals as *Ziegfeld Follies* (1934), *Keep Off the Grass* (1940), and *Laugh, Town, Laugh* (1942) before suffering severe injuries in a near fatal 1943 airplane crash. Froman and a group of USO entertainers were aboard the plane when it crashed into the Tagus River in Lisbon. Froman underwent over 30 operations to correct paralyzing leg and arm injuries. Her undying optimism, heroic comeback, and subsequent marriage to the pilot who, despite a broken back, managed to save her inspired the romantic motion picture *With a Song in My Heart* (1952), starring Susan Hayward. Froman, who made her singing comeback in *Artists and Models* (1943) before she could even walk again, rallied the support of her fans when she sang such tearjerkers as "I'll Walk Alone." Her marriage to the pilot later ended in divorce.

Fromm, Erich, German-born psychoanalyst and social philosopher (b. March 23, 1900, Frankfurt am Main, Germany—d. March 18, 1980, Muralto, Switz.), incorporated an awareness of the profound effect of economic and social factors on human behaviour into his concept of Freudian psychoanalysis, thus modifying the orthodox Freudian emphasis on unconscious drives. Fromm, who was trained in psychoanalysis at the University of Munich (1923–24) and at the Psychoanalytic Institute in Berlin, was an orthodox Freudian until he introduced a confrontational technique that was in direct opposition to the Freudian ideal of the analyst's role as passive and noncommittal. This practice was one of Fromm's major contributions to psychoanalysis and is now widely used by practitioners. Fromm became a giant in the field of psychology through his 20 books, which reflected his broad interests in such subjects as the nature of man, religion, ethics, and love. After leaving Nazi Germany in 1934, Fromm lectured (1934–41) at Columbia University in New York City, where his views became increasingly controversial. In *Escape from Freedom* (1941) Fromm recounted his theories on the alienation of human beings in a technological society; in *The Sane Society* (1955) he called for international harmony in the nuclear age; and in *The Art of Loving* (1956), a classic among college students in the 1960s, he suggested that "love is the only sane and satisfactory answer to the problem of human existence." Other notable works included *Man for Himself* (1947), *Zen Buddhism and Psychoanalysis* (1960), *Marx's Concept of Man* (1961), and *The Revolution of Hope* (1968). He also served on the faculties of Bennington (Vt.) College; Universidad Nacional Autónoma de México (National Autonomous University), Mexico City; Michigan State University, East Lansing; and New York University, New York City.

MICHIGAN STATE UNIVERSITY

Galíndez, Víctor, Argentine boxer (b. 1949?, Argentina—d. Oct. 26, 1980, De Mayo, Arg.), held the title of light-heavyweight champion of the World Boxing Association from 1974 to 1978 and again in 1979. After knocking out Len Hutchins in 1974 to gain the crown, Galíndez defended his title ten times before losing to Mike Rossman on Sept. 15, 1978. Six months later, however, Galíndez regained his title in a brutal rematch with Rossman, who was forced to quit in the tenth round because of a broken hand. Galíndez retired from boxing in 1980 after sustaining two successive knockouts: one by Marvin Johnson, the other by Jesse Burnett. Galíndez's interests quickly turned to auto racing. He was killed with his teammate, Nito Lizeviche, when, after finishing one lap of the De Mayo auto race, the two abandoned their car and were struck by another driver.

Gandhi, Sanjay, Indian politician (b. Dec. 14, 1946, India—d. June 23, 1980, New Delhi, India), was the son of Congress (I) Party leader and prime minister Indira Gandhi and was a controversial figure who seemed destined to become a major force in Indian politics. Heir apparent of India's leading political family, he went on from unremarkable studies at a prestigious private school to an uncompleted apprenticeship with Rolls-Royce in England. He returned to India and opened a car factory near Delhi, but the enterprise failed. In 1975, when his mother used her power as prime minister to declare a state of emergency, Sanjay began to play an increasing role behind the scenes. He was widely thought to be a powerful but nega-

KEYSTONE

tive influence on his mother's policies. His campaigns for birth control and slum clearance aroused hostility, mainly because of the harsh methods he used to implement them. But his ruthless and willful approach was combined with undoubted political acumen, and he was responsible for many of the electoral gains of his mother's Congress (I) Party and his own Youth Congress early in 1980. There were serious doubts, however, about his respect for democratic institutions and the use he would make of the power he seemed certain to acquire. Gandhi died when the light aircraft in which he was flying crashed.

Gary, Romain (ROMAIN KACEW), French novelist (b. May 8, 1914, Vilnius, Russia—d. Dec. 2, 1980, Paris, France), won the Goncourt Prize in 1956 for *Les Racines du ciel* (*The Roots of Heaven*), a novel about man's destruction of his natural environment. Some 20 other works expressed the outlook of a rather solitary man who felt deeply concerned by the great events and follies of his time. Gary and his mother, a Russian Jewish actress, settled during the 1920s in France, where he studied law before joining (1940) Gen. Charles de Gaulle in London. Already trained as an aviator, he served with the Free French Forces in Europe and North Africa, earning the Croix de Guerre and Compagnon de la Libération. Gary unconditionally admired de Gaulle, the leader who refused to capitulate to the great powers. From 1945 to 1960 Gary was with the diplomatic service, becoming French consul general in Los Angeles, where he also worked on some of his best-known novels, including *The Roots of Heaven;* he later served on the staff of the minister of information. His novels, some written first in English, include *L'Éducation européenne* (1945), *Clair de femme* (1977), and *Les Cerfs-volants* (1980). One of his plays, *Lady L,* was made into a film starring Sophia Loren. His second marriage, in 1963 to the actress Jean Seberg, was dissolved in 1970. Gary blamed her suicide in 1979 on the U.S. Federal Bureau of Investigation, which spread falsehoods to discredit her radical views. In a note to his publisher, Gary denied that his own suicide was motivated by hers.

Genevoix, Maurice Charles Louis, French writer (b. Nov. 29, 1890, Décize, France—d. Sept. 8, 1980, Alsudia-Cansades, Spain), embarked on a successful writing career after sustaining a severe wound during World War I and receiving a 100% disability pension. Before the war he won a place at the elitist École Normale Supérieure, and after the war became the most famous among the *écrivains-combattants* of World War I. His first book, *Sous Verdun* (1916), was followed by four more wartime books collected later as *Ceux de'14.* In 1925 he published *Raboliot,* the story of a gamekeeper; for this book he won the Prix Goncourt. Genevoix also traveled and published books on Canada, Mexico, Central America, and Africa. In 1946 he was elected a member of the French Academy and in 1958 he was appointed its permanent secretary. Genevoix retired from this post in 1973 and started a new career in broadcasting. Shortly before his death he published his memoirs, *30,000 Jours.*

Gero, Erno (ERNO SINGER), Hungarian Communist leader (b. July 8, 1898, Budapest, Hung.—d. March 12, 1980, Budapest), was named (July 18, 1956) first secretary of the Hungarian Workers' (Communist) Party and served as the country's last Stalinist leader before the 1956 rebellion. After his pro-Soviet broadcast on Oct. 23, 1956, large crowds gathered to protest the oppression of the Hungarian people by the Hungarian and Soviet regimes. Gero, who was unable to crush the rebellion, called in Soviet troops who fired on the demonstrators. He was replaced (October 25) as first secretary by Janos Kadar, who was then installed as premier (November 4) by the Soviets. Although Gero was initially believed to have been killed by rebels in Budapest, he escaped into exile. In 1944 he had become a member of the Politburo, and he served as minister in many Communist governments. He was the driving force behind rapid industrialization, demanding in 1950 that Hungary be made a "country of iron and steel."

Gillott, Jacky, British novelist and broadcaster (b. 1939?, Lytham Saint Anne's, Lancashire, England —d. Sept. 19, 1980, Somerset, England), was one of Britain's first woman television reporters and the author of such widely acclaimed novels as *Salvage* (1968), *The Head Case* (1979), and *Intimate Relations* (1980). After graduating from University College in London, she joined a provincial newspaper before starting a new career with Independent Television News. She continued to work in broadcasting and journalism, presenting the British Broadcasting Corporation's "Kaleidoscope" program on the arts.

Gil Robles y Quinones, José Maria, Spanish politician (b. Nov. 27, 1898, Salamanca, Spain—d. Sept. 14, 1980, Madrid, Spain), was a prominent leader of the Catholic centre-right during the 1930s. Gil Robles was graduated as a doctor of law from the University of Madrid and continued his studies at the Sorbonne in Paris and at Heidelberg, Germany. In 1929 he was appointed to a chair of law at the University of Salamanca. At the time of the fall of the monarchy in 1931 he founded Acción Nacional (later Acción Popular), which gained five seats in the Constituent Cortes (parliament), an assembly dominated by left-wing parties. Convinced that a moderate centre party, loyal to the republic but with a Christian Democratic base, was indispensable to protect Spain against Communism and Fascism, Gil Robles founded the Confederación Española de Derechas Autónomas (CEDA). During the elections of November 1933, CEDA won 115 seats. Therefore neither the left nor the right could form a government without CEDA. But the president of the republic, Niceto Alcalá Zamora, fearing an armed revolt of the left, called not on Gil Robles but on Alejandro Lerroux, leader of a smaller Radical Party, to form a government which CEDA agreed to support. Gil Robles was called a "Fascist" by the left and a "traitor" by the right. A new general election held in February 1936 resulted in a Frente Popular majority in the Cortes. A few days before the Civil War began on July 18, Gil Robles escaped assassination by taking refuge in France and later in Portugal. He did not side with Gen. Francisco Franco and only returned to Spain in 1953 to resume his law practice. In 1962 he took part with Salvador de Madariaga at the congress of the European Movement in Munich, West Germany, to plead that Spain's association with the EEC should be conditional upon its observance of democratic principles. As a result, he was exiled for another two years. When Franco died in 1975, Gil Robles gave up the leadership of the Christian Democratic movement. The party's principal sector merged with Adolfo Suárez's Unión del Centro Democrático, which obtained 34.3% of the votes at a general election in June 1977.

Giri, Varahagari Venkata, Indian politician (b. Aug. 10, 1894, Berhampur, Orissa, India—d. June 24, 1980, Madras, India), was president of India from 1969 to 1974 and a close ally of Prime Minister Indira Gandhi. The son of a lawyer, he studied law at the National University in Dublin, where he became involved in the nationalist Sinn Fein movement before being expelled in 1916. When Giri returned to India, he joined the independence movement of Mohandas Gandhi and was imprisoned in 1922. After his release he helped organize the railwaymen's trade union, which he built up into a major political force. Giri was elected to the Legislative Assembly in Madras in 1937 and was India's high commissioner in Ceylon (now Sri Lanka) from 1947 to 1951 before joining Jawaharlal Nehru's government as labour minister (1952–54). After his resignation over a controversial pay award to bank employees, he spent ten years as a provincial governor. In 1967 Giri was elected vice-president as a member of the Congress Party. He campaigned for the presidency two years later as an independent, and the Congress Party split over Indira Gandhi's support for him. During his presidency (1969–74) Giri worked closely with Gandhi on such measures as restrictions on private wealth and the nationalization of banks.

Gordon-Walker, Patrick Chrestien Gordon Walker, BARON (b. April 7, 1907, Worthing, England—d. Dec. 2, 1980, London, England), was foreign secretary (1964–65) in Harold Wilson's Labour government. He was elected to Parliament in 1945 for Smethwick and two years later appointed under-secretary of state for Commonwealth relations. Gordon-Walker skillfully handled negotiations with India at the time of its emergence as a republic and was appointed Commonwealth secretary, serving from 1950 to 1951. He was criticized at that time for apparently giving in to South African pressure in opposing the tribal chieftaincy of Seretse Khama (*q.v.*) in Bechuanaland (later Botswana) because of Khama's marriage to a white woman. He became "shadow" foreign secretary while Labour was in opposition and was dramatically defeated in the 1964 election. Despite Gordon-Walker's defeat, Wilson appointed him foreign secretary. After three successful months (October 1964–January 1965) in the post, he ran for the supposedly "safe" Labour seat at Leyton, but was defeated. He resigned his post and was sent on a fact-finding mission to Southeast Asia. He was finally elected at Leyton with a handsome majority in 1966 and served briefly as secretary of state for education and science. In 1974 he was made a life peer, then spent a year as a member of the European Parliament.

Gorman, Patrick Emmet, U.S. labour leader (b. Nov. 27, 1892, Louisville, Ky.—d. Sept. 3, 1980, Chicago, Ill.), served from 1923 to 1942 as president of the Amalgamated Meat Cutters and Butcher Workmen of North America. Gorman began working in 1911 moving beef and hog carcasses. When he was elected (1912) a union business agent, he earned his high school diploma in night school and eventually received a law degree from the University of Louisville. Gorman served as vice-president of the union during the recession of 1920–21 when workers lost their jobs, had their pay reduced three times, and took part in a violent 13-week strike that claimed 31 lives. With the membership at fewer than 7,500, Gorman rebuilt the union; he was elected general vice-president in 1923 and then became president of the international union. He was named (1976) chairman of the board of the union which became the largest affiliate of the AFL-CIO when it merged (1979) with the Retail Clerks International Union to become the United Food and Commercial Workers Union with a membership of 1.3 million in the United States and Canada.

Griffin, John Howard, U.S. author (b. June 16, 1920, Dallas, Texas—d. Sept. 9, 1980, Fort Worth, Texas), temporarily altered the pigment of his skin in order to experience firsthand the life of a black man in the South; he described his adventures in the gripping best-seller *Black like Me* (1961). The book, which detailed countless incidents of hatred, suspicion, and hostility toward Griffin, who appeared to be a black, sold more than a million copies and later became a motion picture. During a ten-year period of blindness, which ended before he traveled in the southern states in 1957, Griffin published two spiritual novels: *Devil Ride Outside* (1952) and *Nuni* (1956). His last book, *A Time To Be Human,* was published in 1977.

Griffith, Hugh (Emrys), Welsh actor (b. May 30, 1912, Anglesey, Wales—d. May 14, 1980, London, England), won an Oscar for his supporting role in *Ben Hur* (1959) and brought energy and ebullience to such character parts as Squire Western in *Tom Jones* (1963) and Professor Welch in *Lucky Jim* (1957). Though in films his comedy had a savage bite that raised it above the level of slapstick, it was on stage that he was able to exhibit the full range of his talent. After World War II Griffith joined the Shakespeare Memorial Company (now the Royal Shakespeare Company) and appeared in many notable productions, including *Love's Labour's Lost, Dr. Faustus,* and *The Caucasian Chalk Circle.* He played King Lear in 1949 and Falstaff in 1964, the latter perhaps his most memorable performance. He also won acclaim for his roles in Jean Anouilh's *The Waltz of the Toreadors* in 1956 and the New York production of *Look Homeward, Angel* in the following year. Griffith, who began his career as a bank clerk, was made an honorary doctor of literature of the University of Wales in 1965.

Guilloux, Louis, French novelist (b. Jan. 15, 1899, St.-Brieuc, France—d. Oct. 14, 1980, St.-Brieuc), portrayed the social struggles of the people of his native Brittany in novels that gave a harsh, disillusioned picture of the desolate lives of working men who sometimes achieved tragic grandeur. It was a life that he knew well: his father was a cobbler and an active socialist. Guilloux won a scholarship to attend secondary school and worked in various jobs before entering journalism in Paris in 1919. His first novel, *La Maison du peuple,* appeared in 1927. He published three other novels before writing his masterpiece, *Le Sang noir* (1935; *Bitter Victory,* 1938). Set in Guilloux's hometown during World War I, it has as its central character an idealist embittered by experience, driven by his sense of the absurdity of existence to a point beyond hope or despair. Guilloux's own left-wing ideals were severely tested by a visit to the Soviet Union with André Gide in 1936, but his hostility to Fascism forced him into hiding in World War II. He won the Prix Populiste in 1942 with *Le Pain des rêves* and was awarded the Grand Prix National des Lettres in 1967 and the Grand Prix de Littérature de l'Académie Française in 1973.

Guston, Philip, Canadian-born painter (b. June 27, 1913, Montreal, Que.—d. June 7, 1980, Woodstock, N.Y.), was a prominent member of the group of Abstract Expressionist painters that included Jackson Pollock, Willem de Kooning, and Franz Kline. Their Action painting (spontaneous, energetic brushstrokes or dropping or throwing paint on a canvas with a brush) represented a more instinctive and personal expression than the work of the 20th-century Realist painters. Guston, who first met Pollock when the two attended a Los Angeles high school, studied at an art school for only three months in 1930 before he began painting murals in the U.S. and in Mexico. He joined (1935) Pollock in New York, where he worked in the mural section of the Works Progress Administration's Federal Art Project. After this assignment he returned to easel painting and in the 1940s gained critical acclaim for his representational paintings, especially those depicting the figurative images of children. In the 1950s Guston joined the Abstract Expressionist movement and won recognition with a series of "White Paintings," including "Dial" (1956), "The Clock" (1957), and "The Tale" (1961). His departure from the strong colours of the Abstract Expressionist painters to a pale rose colour and his tendency to arrange brushstrokes in lyrical vertical and horizontal directions reminded critics of Impressionism. Guston thereafter became known as an Abstract Impressionist to distinguish him from the Action painters. After 1962 the gray and black colours that predominated in his canvases created a dark, brooding atmosphere. His early figurative style reemerged but in the form of sombre images resembling disembodied heads and phantom children. Trained observers generally felt that his figurations were less sensuous and refined than his earlier abstractions. Guston's honours included a first prize at the Carnegie International Exhibition (1945), Guggenheim fellowships (1947, 1968), and the Rome Prize Fellowship of the American Academy in Rome (1948).

Guttmann, Sir Ludwig, German-born British neurosurgeon (b. July 3, 1899, Tost, Silesia, Germany [now Poland]—d. March 18, 1980, Aylesbury, England), was (1944–66) the first director of the internationally famous National Spinal Injuries Centre, Stoke Mandeville Hospital, near Aylesbury. In 1948 he founded the annual Stoke Mandeville Games for the Paralysed, which inspired the international paraplegic games held since 1952. Guttmann received his training at Freiburg and Breslau (now Wroclaw, Poland) universities. In 1933 he was elected director of the neurology and neurosurgery department of the Jewish Hospital at Breslau and there helped fellow Jews to flee abroad. He went to England with his family in 1939 to take up a research appointment at the University of Oxford. At Stoke Mandeville, Guttmann and his staff trained many doctors to head similar units in other countries; he also lectured and advised on paraplegic treatment and rehabilitation in more than 30 countries. After retiring in 1966 he raised funds for the Stoke Mandeville Sports Centre for the Paralysed and Other Disabled and became its director in 1969. He was founder president (1961–69) of the International Medical Society of Paraplegia and edited its journal, *Paraplegia,* from 1963. He was also president of the British (1962) and International (1966) sports associations for the Disabled. A fellow of the Royal College of Surgeons (1961) and of the Royal College of Physicians (1962), he was made a fellow of the Royal Society in 1976. He was knighted in 1966 and received honours from many countries, including (1954) the first Rehabilitation Medal of the World Veterans Association. Guttmann was also the author of a standard textbook on neurology.

Hall, Paul, U.S. union leader (b. Aug. 21, 1914, near Birmingham, Ala.—d. June 22, 1980, New York, N.Y.), was enlisted by Harry Lundeberg to help organize a seaman's union and, with 500 other men, founded (1938) the Seafarers International Union (SIU), which countered the growing influence of the Communists. In the 1940s and '50s, Hall again displayed his leadership and determination by fighting racketeers who threatened to infiltrate the SIU. He was named a vice-president of the union in 1948, and when Lundeberg died in 1957, Hall became president of both the SIU and the AFL-CIO Maritime Trades Department. As the dynamic president of the SIU, Hall cooperated with the New York State Crime Commission in efforts to block mob penetration into the locals. He was also a vice-president of the AFL-CIO and a founder (1979) of the Labor for Carter Committee.

Haskell, Arnold Lionel, British ballet critic (b. July 19, 1903, London, England—d. Nov. 14, 1980, Bath, England), directed the Royal Ballet School from 1947 to 1964 and became the first ballet critic appointed by a British newspaper when he joined the *Daily Telegraph* in 1935. Haskell described his enthusiasm for ballet as "balletomania" and used the term as the title of his most important book, which was published in 1934. He studied law, but while he was convalescing in Paris, his early love for dance was rekindled when he met some leading Russian dancers. He married Vera Saitsova and in 1936 founded the Royal Ballet Benevolent Fund. In 1950 he was made chevalier of the Légion d'Honneur and in 1954 CBE. His writings include a study of the sculptor Jacob Epstein, a popular paperback introduction to ballet, and two volumes of autobiography. He was part-author of the article on ballet in *Encyclopædia Britannica.*

Hatta, Mohammad, Indonesian politician (b. Aug. 12, 1902, Bukittinggi, Sumatra, Netherlands East Indies—d. March 14, 1980, Jakarta, Indon.), was prime minister (1948–50) of Indonesia before serving as vice-president (1950–56). Earlier Hatta was one of the architects of his country's independence from The Netherlands (proclaimed in 1945 and recognized by The Netherlands in 1949). Active from his days as an economics student in the struggle against Dutch rule, he was arrested, exiled, and then imprisoned (1935–42). Freed by the Japanese, Hatta joined Sukarno as a leader of the independence movement. He resigned from the vice-presidency in 1956 because of Sukarno's economic policies and growing Communist influence in the regime. He devoted his retirement to lecturing at Indonesian universities and writing his political testament, *Portrait of a Patriot* (1972). After Sukarno's ouster in 1967, Hatta opposed many aspects of the new regime established by President Suharto. In 1970 he participated in a government commission on corruption and in 1976 signed a manifesto against the regime, which was used by others in a plot to overthrow Suharto.

Haymes, Dick, U.S. singer (b. Sept. 13, 1918, Buenos Aires, Arg.—d. March 28, 1980, Los Angeles, Calif.), basked in the limelight as a top soloist with the swing-era bands of Tommy Dorsey, Harry James, Bunny Berigan, and Benny Goodman before his career was ravaged by alcoholism, six divorces, bankruptcy, and deportation proceedings. In his heyday Haymes, a creamy-voiced baritone, was ranked with Frank Sinatra and became famous for his renditions of such songs as "Little White Lies" and "It Might as Well Be Spring." He also appeared in 35 films, including *Billy Rose's Diamond Horseshoe, One Touch of Venus,* and *State Fair* opposite Jeanne Crain. Among his wives were Rita Hayworth, Joanne Dru, Fran Jeffries, and Nora Eddington.

Hays, Paul R., U.S. judge (b. April 2, 1903, Des Moines, Iowa—d. Feb. 13, 1980, Tucson, Ariz.), was appointed (1961) a judge of the U.S. Court of Appeals for the 2nd circuit by Pres. John F. Kennedy and was a member (1971) of a tribunal that ruled on the Pentagon Papers case. Hays extended a restraining order against publication by the *New York Times* of a secret Pentagon study (known as the Pentagon Papers) outlining the origins of the Vietnam war. He then voted with the majority when the court ruled 5–3 to delay publication of portions of the documents until secret hearings could determine whether circulation of the papers would be detrimental to national security. Later the Supreme Court approved the right of publication. Hays also wrote the majority opinion in a 2–1 ruling that declared that the Swedish film *I Am Curious—Yellow* was not obscene. While studying at Columbia University, Hays was an instructor (1926–32) there in Latin and Greek. After briefly working with the law firm of Cravath, de Gersdorff, Swaine & Wood in New York City, he returned to his alma mater, where he taught law from 1936 to 1971. In 1974 he became senior member of the Court of Appeals. Hays discussed his role as a labour arbitrator and impartial chairman of various companies in such books as *Cases and Materials on Civil Procedure* (1947) and *Labor Arbitration: A Dissenting View* (1966).

Hendy, Sir Philip Anstiss, British art historian (b. Sept. 27, 1900, Carlisle, England—d. Sept. 6, 1980, Oxford, England), was director of the National Gallery, London, from 1946 to 1967. His achievements during this period included supervising the return of paintings that had been hidden in Wales for safekeeping during World War II and planning for the gallery's postwar revival and expansion. He was also a scholar, noted for publishing works on the modern painter Matthew Smith and on Piero della Francesca, as well as many articles, catalogs, and guides. After a period at the Wallace Collection in London, he went to Boston to catalog the paintings in the Isabella Stewart Gardner Museum. Hendy later served (1930–33) as curator of paintings at the Boston Museum of Fine Arts. After his return to Britain he was appointed director of the City Art Gallery in Leeds and named Slade professor at Oxford. As director of the National Gallery he was involved in controversies over the cleaning of pictures and in 1961 over security after the theft of a Goya portrait of the duke of Wellington. Hendy was much respected for his work in reorganizing the gallery's collections, his encouragement of scientific restoration, and his supervision of recataloging. Knighted in 1950, he was adviser (1968–71) to the Israel Museum, Jerusalem, and president of the International Council of Museums (1959–65).

Hitchcock, Sir Alfred Joseph, British-born motion-picture director (b. Aug. 13, 1899, London, England —d. April 29, 1980, Los Angeles, Calif.), shocked, jolted, and terrified motion-picture audiences and then relieved the mounting tension with touches of humour in a succession of thrillers that earned him the undisputed title "master of suspense." An expert in film technique, Hitchcock relied on silence and visual imagery rather than dialogue to increase apprehension in plots that exploited childhood phobias, guilt, suspicion, delusion, violence, and sexual obsession. In some of his most spine-tingling scenes, Cary Grant was pursued by a cropduster plane in a deserted field in *North by Northwest* (1959); Janet Leigh was murdered in the shower by knife-wielding Anthony Perkins in *Psycho* (1960); and Tippi Hedren was totally unaware of a flock of menacing birds gathering behind her on a jungle gym in *The Birds* (1963). In 1925 Hitchcock launched his directing career in Britain with *The Pleasure Garden* and in 1929 he directed *Blackmail,* the first successful British sound picture. Later he turned out such classics as *The Man Who Knew Too Much* (1934), *The Thirty-Nine Steps* (1935), and *The Lady Vanishes* (1938) before establishing his reputation in Hollywood with the haunting *Rebecca* (1940), which won an Academy Award for best picture. One of the most widely known directors in the history of film, Hitchcock perpetuated his own popularity by making cameo appearances in every one of his films and by displaying the unique line drawing he made of his distinctive profile, which opened his television series in the 1950s and '60s. Many of his masterpieces dealt with the theme of the "wronged man" pursued and stalked by both villains and the police on trains, in lifeboats, in theatres, and at such exotic places as the United Nations, the top of the Statue of Liberty, and across the carved faces on Mt. Rushmore. During more than 50 years of moviemaking, Hitchcock directed 54 films, including such enduring works as *Notorious* (1946), *Strangers on a Train* (1951), *Dial M for Murder* (1954), *Rear Window* (1954), *Vertigo* (1958), *Torn Curtain* (1966), and *Frenzy* (1972). His last film, *Family Plot,* appeared in 1976. His artistic influence was also evident in the works of such leading film directors as François Truffaut, Claude Chabrol, Eric Rohmer, Lindsay Anderson, and Peter Bogdanovich. Hitchcock, who was a noted practical joker, delighted in charting his own imaginary death. In the perfect scene he would devour a splendid meal and then be killed by "a smashing blonde." Hitchcock received one of his greatest tributes when he was knighted by Queen Elizabeth II in early 1980.

AGIP/PICTORIAL PARADE

Howard, Elston Gene, U.S. baseball player (b. Feb. 23, 1929, St. Louis, Mo.—d. Dec. 14, 1980, New York, N.Y.), as an all-around player (1955–68) for the New York Yankees, excelled as an outfielder, first baseman, and catcher and was named the American League's most valuable player in 1963 after batting .287 with 28 home runs and 85 runs batted in. The first black to play for the team, Howard was a backup catcher for Yogi Berra until manager Casey Stengel recognized the magnitude of Howard's versatility and put him in the lineup as an outfielder. As one of the Yankees' most consistent hitters, he averaged .274 with 167 home runs over 14 seasons. He became the team's starting catcher in 1961 after batting .348 and hitting 21 home runs. His other laurels included the Babe Ruth Award as the outstanding player in the 1958 World Series, two Gold Glove Awards for fielding (1963, 1964), and a place on the American League All-Star team nine times. In 1967 he was traded to the Boston Red Sox but retired as a player after one season with a .241 batting average. In 1968 he returned to the Yankee fold as the first black coach in the American League, a position he held until 1979. In 1980 Howard was an administrative assistant to George Steinbrenner, the Yankee's principal owner.

UPI

Hurstfield, Joel, British historian (b. Nov. 4, 1911—d. Nov. 29, 1980, California), was Astor professor of English history at the University of London (1962–79) and a noted authority on the 16th century. The title of his book *Freedom, Corruption and Government in Elizabethan England* (1973) summarized his central viewpoint on the period. An expert on many aspects of Tudor life, he produced such detailed studies as *The Queen's Wards* (1958) and the broad surveys that appear in contributions to *Encyclopædia Britannica.* He studied at University College, London, and lectured at University College, Southampton, until 1940. The subsequent break in his academic career allowed him to pursue his interest in contemporary political administration. His study on the control of raw materials became part of the official history of World War II. In 1946 he was appointed lecturer at the University of London where he was public orator (1967–71). He also made several visits to lecture or carry out research in the U.S. and, after his retirement in 1979, became senior research associate at the Huntington Library in California. His other major works included *Elizabeth I and the Unity of England* (1960) and *The Elizabethan Nation* (1964).

Iturbi, José, Spanish-born pianist (b. Nov. 28, 1895, Valencia, Spain—d. June 28, 1980, Hollywood, Calif.), was a gifted musician who won renown as a virtuoso pianist, accomplished conductor, and motion-picture actor. Iturbi, who began performing professionally at age seven, was graduated with honours from the Paris Conservatory in 1912. He was named (1919) head of the piano department at the Geneva Conservatory and in 1923 began touring Europe and South America playing Spanish music. In 1929 he made his U.S. debut and received rave reviews from the critics; his 1930 U.S. tour was even more exhilarating: he gave 77 concerts. While in Mexico in 1933, Iturbi first exhibited his conducting ability. Three years later he was chosen to lead the Rochester (N.Y.) Philharmonic Orchestra, a position he held until 1944. He often delighted audiences by appearing in a dual role as conductor and pianist. His flamboyant personality attracted the motion-picture industry, which signed Iturbi to a series of films in the 1940s. Playing classical, jazz, and popular music, he appeared (usually as himself) in such films as *Thousands Cheer, Anchors Aweigh,* and *Music for Millions.* He also wrote a number of musical compositions in the Spanish style, most notably *Pequeña danza española.* Iturbi, who prided himself on being different from other classical musicians, also enjoyed flying, boxing, and motorcycle riding.

Iwaszkiewicz, Jaroslaw, Polish poet, novelist, essayist, and playwright (b. Feb. 20, 1894, Kalnik, Ukraine—d. March 2, 1980, Stawisko, Poland), was a highly gifted and prolific writer whose works, including *The Maidens of Wilko, Mother Joan of the Angels,* and *Fame and Glory,* were translated into several languages and made into films. Iwaszkiewicz studied law at the University of Kiev and at the same time (1912) attended the Music Conservatory. He settled in Warsaw in 1918 and published (1923) his first novel, *Hilary, Son of a Bookkeeper,* in France. In 1953 he served as a chairman of the Polish Committee to Defend Peace and was a nonparty member of the Sejm (parliament). He twice presided (1945–49 and 1959–72) over the Polish Writers' Union and was named (1955) editor in chief of *Tworczosc* ("Creation"), an intellectual literary monthly. Iwaszkiewicz also translated works by Chekhov, Tolstoy, Kierkegaard, and Shakespeare.

Jacques, Hattie (Josephine Edwina), British actress (b. Feb. 7, 1924, Kent, England—d. Oct. 6, 1980, London, England), brought a note of charm and pathos to slapstick comedy roles by making audiences laugh with her at her ample figure and schoolgirl voice. Her regular appearances in the film series *Carry On,* her association with the leading radio and television comedians of her time, and her occasional stage appearances established her as one of the best-loved personalities in British entertainment. Jacques started her career in pantomime, but she became better known as Sophie Tuckshop in the radio series "Itma," and as partner to Tony Hancock in his radio and television series with Eric Sykes, Jacques gave a remarkable impression of elegance and used the expressive qualities of her voice and face to full advantage. On stage, she was associated particularly with the Players' Theatre, where she made her acting debut in 1944, and with St. Martin's Theatre and the London Palladium.

Janssen, David (David Harold Meyer), U.S. actor (b. March 27, 1931, Naponee, Neb.—d. Feb. 13, 1980, Malibu, Calif.), intrigued television audiences as the elusive Dr. Richard Kimble, who, unjustly accused of murdering his wife, spent four TV seasons dodging police while searching for the only person who could prove his innocence—a one-armed man—in the television series "The Fugitive" (1963–67). The final episode of the series was seen by 30 million addicted viewers. Janssen, who portrayed a tough, terse, but likable character with the highest of morals, earlier starred in "Richard Diamond, Private Detective" from 1957 to 1960 and from 1974 to 1976 starred in "Harry O." He also starred in a number of motion pictures, the most notable being *The Green Berets* and *The Shoes of the Fisherman,* both in 1968.

Journiac, René, French jurist and administrator (b. May 11, 1921, Saint-Martin-Vésubie, Alpes-Maritimes, France—d. Feb. 6, 1980, near Yaoundé, Cameroon), was Pres. Valéry Giscard d'Estaing's principal adviser on African affairs. A member of the Resistance during World War II, he studied law and served as a magistrate in Cameroon before joining the staff of future president Georges Pompidou. In 1967 he was appointed to the General Secretariat for African Affairs, where Jacques Foccart wielded enormous influence in formulating and administering France's policy toward its former African territories. The secretariat was suppressed by President Giscard, perhaps because of Foccart's Gaullist sympathies, and Journiac took over in 1974 as the president's confidential adviser. He was known to have been actively involved in negotiations over France's involvement in Chad, including the release of Françoise Claustre (the ethnologist held hostage during 1974–77 by rebel forces in that country), and in arranging the deposition of Emperor Bokassa I of the Central African Empire in 1979. Journiac died in a plane crash while on his way to Gabon for talks with Pres. Omar Bongo.

Kaempfert, Berthold, West German composer (b. Oct. 16, 1923, Hamburg, Germany—d. June 22, 1980, Majorca, Spain), achieved international success with the love song "Strangers in the Night," made popular by Frank Sinatra. Kaempfert trained at the Hamburg Music Academy and served with a naval band during World War II. Captured in 1945, he formed a prisoner-of-war band and after his release embarked on a career as bandleader and arranger and composer of popular melodies. His band's undemanding sound provided easy listening on the British forces' radio network and in U.S. Army clubs, but it was not until he recorded "Wonderland by Night" in 1961 that he gained his first major success. This was followed by "Spanish Eyes" and "Strangers in the Night," which sold more than ten million copies; other hits included "African Night," "Swinging Safari," and "Blue Midnight." Kaempfert later settled (1966) in Switzerland.

Kapwepwe, Simon Mwansa, Zambian politician (b. April 12, 1922, Chinsali, Northern Rhodesia [now Zambia]—d. Jan. 26, 1980, Zambia), was his country's foreign minister (1964–67) and vice-president (1967–70). He was closely associated with Pres. Kenneth Kaunda from the early days of black nationalism in the British protectorate of Northern Rhodesia and after that area gained independence in 1964. Both belonged to the Bemba tribe in the north of the country and became teachers before entering nationalist politics, first within the African National Congress and then, from 1958, in their breakaway Zambia African National Congress. In 1960 both joined the newly formed United National Independence Party (UNIP), which under Kaunda's leadership won a large majority in preindependence elections in 1964. Kapwepwe's growing opposition to Kaunda's policies became apparent in 1969 when he tendered (but at Kaunda's request withdrew) his resignation from the vice-presidency. However, in October 1970 he was replaced as vice-president, though he retained the local government portfolio he had assumed that January. In August 1971 he resigned from the government and formed the United Progressive Party (UPP) to "stamp out . . . capitalism, tribalism, and sectionalism." The UPP was banned in February 1972, and Kapwepwe was placed under detention until January 1973. In 1977 he rejoined the UNIP, the sole legal party since the early 1970s, but his intended candidacy in the 1978 presidential election was disqualified by UNIP's national council.

Katanyan, Vasily Abgarovich, Soviet literary historian (b. April 28, 1902, Moscow, Russia—d. Feb. 15, 1980, Moscow, U.S.S.R.), was an authority on the poet Vladimir Mayakovsky and in 1952 married Lili Brik, the poet's former mistress. Of Armenian origin, Katanyan grew up in Tiflis (now Tbilisi) before returning to Moscow, where he became a figure in a glittering circle of writers and artists that included Mayakovsky and Osip Brik, Lili's husband. He published criticism and wrote for film and theatre, including the script of a 1963 film version of *Anna Karenina.* But Katanyan's life work was the massive biography of Mayakovsky, which he revised shortly before his own death. When Lili Brik died in 1978, he survived as one of the last representatives of a golden age in Soviet letters that had all but come to an end with Mayakovsky's suicide in 1930 and the Stalinist purges, in which Katanyan's own brother was executed.

Kautner, Helmut, West German film director, actor, and scriptwriter (b. March 25, 1908, Düsseldorf, Germany—d. April 20, 1980, Castellina, Italy), was the leading German director of the postwar period and almost the only one then known outside his own country. His success was partly due to his noncollaboration with the Nazi regime and Joseph Goebbels's criticism of Kautner's film *Romanze in Moll* (1943) as decadent and "defeatist." Kautner began as a cabaret singer before becoming an actor and film scriptwriter. He directed his first film in 1939 and managed to evade pressure from the Ministry of Propaganda during the war years. Allowed to resume work by the British authorities after the war, Kautner made *In jenen Tagen* (1947) and other films on the Nazi era, including *The Last Bridge* (1953) and *The Devil's General* (1955), which established his international reputation. During a brief period in Hollywood (1957) he produced two mediocre films, *The Wonderful Years* and *A Stranger in My Arms.* His later work in Germany failed to revive his reputation, though *Der Reste ist Schweigen* (1959), a version of *Hamlet* set in contemporary Germany, was perhaps unjustly neglected. Kautner last directed in 1970.

Khama, Sir Seretse, Botswanan politician (b. July 1, 1921, Serowe, Bechuanaland—d. July 13, 1980, Gaberone, Botswana), became the first president of Botswana when the former Bechuanaland protectorate gained independence from Britain in 1966. Born into tribal chieftaincy, he studied in South Africa and then went to Britain, where he read law at Oxford. There, he met his future wife, Ruth Williams; their mixed marriage caused controversy both in Bechuanaland, where the tribal chiefs opposed it, and in Britain, where the government tried to block the marriage. At home Khama won popular support, but Britain exiled him until he renounced his chieftaincy in 1956. He founded the Democratic Party in 1962 and became prime minister in 1965 after a landslide victory at the polls. After negotiations on independence, he became president of the Republic of Botswana in 1966 and was granted a knighthood by Queen Elizabeth II. A moderate, he faced a difficult situation in his relations with white minority governments in South Africa and Rhodesia and with the guerrilla armies opposing the Rhodesian regime. Though he refused to compromise on the principle of majority rule, his primary concern was the prosperity of his country, which he sought by diversifying its economy. He also achieved free universal education and stuck firmly to his ideals of democracy and multiracialism.

Klindt-Jensen, Ole, Danish archaeologist (b. March 31, 1918, Næstved, Denmark—d. June 13, 1980, Moesgård, Århus, Denmark), became professor (1961) of Nordic archaeology and European prehistory at the University of Århus and head of the university's Archaeological Institute and Museum at Moesgård. He enjoyed an international reputation among archaeologists and was secretary-general of the International Union of Prehistoric and Protohistoric Sciences. He published a *History of Scandinavian Archaeology* in 1975.

Kokoschka, Oskar, Austrian painter (b. March 1, 1886, Pöchlarn, Austria—d. Feb. 22, 1980, Villeneuve, Switz.), was the foremost Expressionist painter of portraits and landscapes of the 20th century, using tense, writhing lines to express the anguished presence of the human character and large, vibrantly coloured compositions to evoke the beauty of landscape. At 18 Kokoschka won a scholarship to the School of Arts and Crafts in Vienna and later became an instructor there. But he rejected the prevailing emphasis on the decorative arts and taught himself to paint in oils instead. Along with his quickly developing modernist style of painting, he wrote several early Expressionist plays, which provoked such scandal that he was dismissed from his teaching post. In 1912 he began a love affair with Alma Mahler (widow of Gustav Mahler), and during the next few years he painted his greatest portraits, achieving a psychological intensity and a sinuous handling of paint that was remarkable among artists of the time. Kokoschka

KEYSTONE

fought in World War I and suffered a severe head injury in 1916. Settling in Dresden, Germany, after his recovery, he did his great panoramic views of cities and landscapes in the following years. His style in this genre became less tortured and more expansive and colourful, though it retained a sense of sweep and imaginative suggestion. He settled in Prague, Czech., in 1934 to avoid the Nazi infiltration of Austria but was forced to flee to England in 1938 when that country was invaded by Hitler. His works had already been condemned as "degenerate" by the Nazis and removed from German museums. He poked fun at this hostility toward his work by painting a self-portrait entitled "Self-Portrait of a Degenerate Artist." He spent his last years in Switzerland and Austria, painting watercolours of flowers and composing his memoirs.

Kostelanetz, Andre, Russian-born conductor (b. Dec. 22, 1901, St. Petersburg [now Leningrad], Russia—d. Jan. 13, 1980, Port-au-Prince, Haiti), attracted record-breaking audiences with arrangements of popular and semiclassical numbers and unique medleys of symphonic works. Kostelanetz first gained recognition as the conductor of the Columbia Broadcasting System symphony orchestra, which highlighted the 1930s radio program the "Chesterfield Hour." His celebrity status was further enhanced when he married opera star Lily Pons in 1938. As a pioneer in the art of recording classical music, Kostelanetz devised special microphone techniques that contributed to what came to be known as the "Kostelanetz sound"; his records sold an astronomical 52 million copies. As the eminent maestro (1952–79) of the New York Philharmonic and as its longest serving conductor over consecutive seasons, Kostelanetz directed the best-attended concert in history with an audience of 200,000 people in New York City's Central Park. His "Promenade" series (1963–78) of concerts with the Philharmonic featured symphonic music, dance, mime, narration, and folksinging. While performing with the world's leading ensembles in the U.S., Europe, Israel, and Japan, Kostelanetz revived forgotten music and popularized the new works that he commissioned from such major U.S. composers as Aaron Copland and Virgil Thomson. Kostelanetz, who displayed an efficient conducting style, was sometimes chided for making classical music "too popular" in an effort to attract the masses. He characteristically defended his first priority and concluded: "Criticism is upsetting, but if what I do expands the meaning of music in terms of attendance, that's all that really matters."

Kosygin, Aleksey Nikolayevich, Soviet statesman (b. Feb. 20, 1904, St. Petersburg [now Leningrad], Russia—d. Dec. 18, 1980, Moscow, U.S.S.R.), was head of the government of the U.S.S.R. from Oct. 15, 1964, to Oct. 23, 1980. He volunteered (1919) for the Red Army during the Civil War; later he joined the Communist Party (1927). Having graduated from the Leningrad Textile Institute, he became director of a Leningrad textile plant in 1937 and chairman of the Leningrad city council (*i.e.*, mayor) in 1938. After serving as people's commissar for the textile industry (1939–40), Kosygin was a deputy chairman of the Council of People's Commissars (1940–46) and of its successor body, the Council of Ministers (1946–53). (Except for two periods of political turmoil in mid-1953 and late 1956–mid-1957, Kosygin retained this post until 1960.) During World War II he played an important role in organizing the evacuation of much of the country's industry to the east, out of the path of the invading German armies. As a highly qualified engineer and technologist, he made his career not as party *aparatchik* but as an economic administrator. During the Nikita Khrushchev era, Kosygin held a number of ministerial posts dealing with light industry and economic planning. In 1960 he became one of the two first deputy chairmen of the Council of Ministers under Khrushchev and succeeded him as chairman (premier) in October 1964.

UPI

Kosygin's career within the party structure was slow and checkered. He was elected to the Central Committee in 1939, became a candidate (nonvoting) member of the Politburo in 1946 and a full member of this key body in 1948. When the Politburo was (temporarily) reorganized as the Presidium of the Central Committee, he was demoted (1952) to candidate membership and finally dropped in March 1953 following Stalin's death. He was readmitted to candidate membership in 1957 and to full membership in 1960.

During the first six years of his premiership, Kosygin used his intelligence and common sense to improve the functioning of the national economy. Well aware of his country's needs, he exercised a moderating influence within the Soviet leadership. Through his many official visits abroad, his imposing figure and mournful face became widely known to the outside world. After 1970, however, Kosygin's role was more and more overshadowed by the power of Leonid Brezhnev, general secretary of the party and later also state president. Kosygin was forced by ill health to retire in October 1980.

Langley, Noel A., South African novelist and playwright (b. Dec. 25, 1911, Durban, South Africa—d. Nov. 4, 1980, Desert Hot Springs, Calif.), was the author of witty comedies and the creator of many successful film scripts, including *The Wizard of Oz, Trio, Tom Brown's Schooldays,* and *The Search for Bridey Murphy.* Langley's career started in 1934 when he staged two plays in London. His versatility, ability to work rapidly, and well-crafted scripts gained him recognition in Hollywood after he had written *Maytime* (1936), a romantic musical starring Jeannette Macdonald and Nelson Eddy. His stage plays included melodrama, musical productions, historical drama, and light comedy. Among his novels were *Cage Me a Peacock* (1935), which he later adapted as a stage musical, *There's a Porpoise Close Behind Us* (1936), and *An Elegance of Rebels* (1960).

Laurie, John, Scottish actor (b. March 25, 1897, Dumfries, Scotland—d. June 23, 1980, Chalfont St. Peter, England), had a distinguished career as a Shakespearean actor before playing "Private Fraser," the Scottish mortician in BBC Television's comedy series "Dad's Army." His first London appearance was in 1922 at the Old Vic, where he later starred in most of the leading Shakespearean roles, including Hamlet and Macbeth. At Stratford he appeared as Richard III and Othello. He played King Lear in Australia in 1959 and appeared as Gloucester at the Aldwych Theatre in 1964 in a production of *King Lear* that later toured Europe and the U.S. His films included *Henry V, Hamlet, Fanny by Gaslight,* and *Uncle Silas.* Laurie also appeared as John the Baptist in the radio production of Dorothy L. Sayers's *The Man Born to Be King.*

Laye, Camara, African writer (b. 1928, Kouroussa, French Guinea—d. Feb. 4, 1980, Senegal), wrote novels in French that gave a remarkable insight into the African sensibility and bore witness to the passing of traditional African society. The son of a Malinke goldsmith, he was trained in Conakry and in France as an engineer. While studying in Paris, he worked for eight months in an automobile factory. His first novel, *L'Enfant noir* (1953; *The Dark Child,* 1955), explored the tribal world of his childhood but was criticized by some Africans on the grounds that it concentrated too heavily on indigenous customs and beliefs. It was followed by an allegorical work, *Le Regard du roi* (1954; *The Radiance of the King,* 1956), a novel of considerable energy and feeling and, though written in French, distinctly African in style. In 1955 he returned to Guinea and entered politics but ten years later was obliged to leave for Senegal, where he became a university lecturer. He also published *Dramouss* (1966; *A Dream of Africa,* 1968), once more investigating African psychology and the fast-disappearing world of his childhood.

Léger, Jules, Canadian diplomat (b. April 4, 1913, St. Anicet, Que.—d. Nov. 22, 1980, Ottawa, Ont.), was a career diplomat for 35 years before becoming Canada's 21st governor-general on Jan. 14, 1974. Léger, who suffered a massive stroke less than six months after taking office, relearned English and French, and when he was unable to speak had his wife deliver his speeches. During his tenure, Léger introduced a new informality to the office by having parties for thousands of children at his home. He also supervised the transfer from Britain of the power to sign treaties and accredit diplomats abroad. Undaunted by his illness, Léger remained in office for his full five-year term. Earlier, Léger enjoyed a diverse diplomatic career as ambassador to Mexico (1953–54), Italy (1962–64), France (1964–68), Belgium and Luxembourg (1973–74), and the North Atlantic Council and the Organization for European Cooperation in Paris (1958–62).

Lennon, John (Winston), British musician and songwriter (b. Oct. 9, 1940, Liverpool, England—d. Dec. 8, 1980, New York, N.Y.), founded the Beatles, Britain's most successful rock group, and, with Paul McCartney, wrote its most memorable songs. The most complex personality among the four Beatles and their intellectual leader, Lennon steered them from the image-forming days of Beatlemania in the early 1960s, through experimentation with drugs and Eastern mysticism, to a more politically committed stance at the end of the

FRED WARD—BLACK STAR

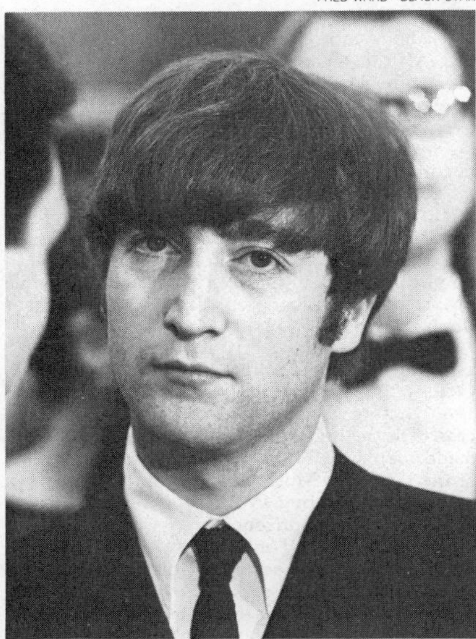

decade. His need to seek other outlets for his talents led to the group's final dissolution in 1970. After several years of political activism, Lennon withdrew into virtual seclusion with his Japanese wife, Yoko Ono, and it was a cruel twist of fate that he was gunned down outside his luxury apartment at the Dakota only months after his return to the music scene.

Lennon's father left when his son was three years old, and the boy was brought up by an aunt in a working-class district of Liverpool. He had an undistinguished school career and formed his first pop group, the Quarrymen, shortly before entering Liverpool College of Art. In 1958 Paul McCartney joined his group, which later became the Silver Beatles and finally the Beatles with George Harrison and Ringo Starr. Through their songs the group transformed rock-style music into a sophisticated form and generated new excitement for rock-and-roll. In 1962 the four Beatles, all from working-class backgrounds in Liverpool, excited audiences at Liverpool's Cavern Club, singing Lennon and McCartney's songs. With the help of manager Brian Epstein, the Beatles soon captured the British audience, and when "I Want to Hold Your Hand" was released (1964) in the U.S. and the group appeared on the "Ed Sullivan Show," Beatlemania was born. The Beatles, with their lively rhythms and their "dishmop" hairstyles, personified the '60s: they were British, they were working-class, and they belonged to a generation setting new trends in fashion and behaviour. The group maintained an unbeaten record of number-one smash hits from 1964 to 1967. The classic album *Sgt. Pepper's Lonely Hearts Club Band* (1967) included such mind-expanding songs as "Lucy in the Sky with Diamonds" and "A Day in the Life" and gave the Beatles widespread recognition as serious artists.

By this time, however, Lennon's public statements and a highly publicized relationship with avant-garde film producer Yoko Ono had increasingly distinguished him from the rest of the group. Lennon and McCartney's songwriting became more of an individual effort: Lennon's forceful and complex style clashed with McCartney's wistful tunes. Together Lennon and Ono began to create a new identity apart from the Beatles. They shocked fans by appearing nude on the album cover of *Two Virgins* and gained even greater attention by staging a honeymoon "bed-in" for peace. Lennon's personal vision inspired such songs as "Give Peace a Chance" and later the haunting "Imagine." The Beatles disbanded in 1970 after the release of the album *Abbey Road.* Lennon went through an intense period of self-discovery and during this time released his most impressive solo album, *Plastic Ono Band,* which was followed by several joint albums with his wife. In 1975 Lennon disappeared from the public eye to become a "househusband" and care for his son Sean. In 1980 he recorded his last album, *Double Fantasy,* which celebrated a dialogue of love with Yoko Ono and included the hit "Starting Over." The Sunday after Lennon was killed, thousands of mourners around the world, at the request of his widow, paid a ten-minute "silent tribute" to him at precisely 2:00 PM New York time.

Lesage, Jean, Canadian politician (b. June 10, 1912, Montreal, Que.—d. Dec. 11, 1980, near Quebec, Que.), as premier of Quebec from 1960 to 1966 was the architect of the "Quiet Revolution," a sweeping period of reform that vastly increased the role of the provincial government. Under the new political structure, the province took control of the schools, nationalized hydroelectric power, implemented spending controls, introduced a provincial pension plan, and modernized the civil service. Lesage's Cabinet, which was called *l'équipe de tonnerre* ("the team of thunder"), included such diverse personalities as René Lévesque, who was to become leader of the separatist Parti Québécois, and Claude Wagner, a conservative champion of law and order. Lesage served as his own finance minister and minister of federal-provincial affairs. After earning a law degree from Laval University in Quebec, Lesage served (1939–44) as a crown attorney before his election (1945) to Canada's House of Commons. When Lesage was elected leader of the provincial Liberal Party in 1958, he resigned his national post. In the 1960 provincial elections he staged a stunning upset over the Union Nationale, which had been in power for 16 years. When the Union Nationale returned to power in 1966, Lesage became leader of the opposition until his retirement in 1970.

Lesser, Sol, U.S. motion-picture producer (b. Feb. 17, 1890, Spokane, Wash.—d. Sept. 19, 1980, Hollywood, Calif.), produced a series of 19 immensely popular "Tarzan" movies featuring Johnny Weissmuller in the title role. Other credits included such classics as *Oliver Twist* (1922), *Stage Door Canteen* (1945), and his Academy Award-winning documentary, *Kon-Tiki* (1951). His profits from *Stage Door Canteen* were so great that Lesser donated $1.5 million to the American Theatre Wing; he retired at the age of 36 to embark on a two-year round-the-world cruise but became bored after two months. He returned to Hollywood's marquee lights and purchased a small theatre that evolved into a chain in California known as Principal Theatres. Lesser was also responsible for the idea behind guest star appearances at theatres, previewing movies, and an audience film-rating system. The last-named gave birth to the G, PG, R, and X ratings for movies. Lesser remained active in later years teaching cinematography at the University of Southern California, where he received a master's degree in film education at the age of 86.

Levene, Sam (SAMUEL LEVINE), U.S. actor (b. Aug. 28, 1905, Russia—d. late December 1980, New York, N.Y.), enjoyed more than 50 years on Broadway and wowed audiences as Nathan Detroit, the crap-game operator in the Broadway musical *Guys and Dolls.* Levene, an accomplished character actor who created legendary comic roles, usually appeared as a gruff but likable fellow whose tough exterior shielded an inner softness. He also gave noteworthy performances as Patsy in *Three Men on a Horse;* as the theatrical agent Finkelstein in *Dinner at Eight;* as Sidney Black in *Light Up the Sky;* and as Al Lewis, a retired vaudevillian, in *The Sunshine Boys.* He appeared in more than 100 other films, notably *Shadow of the Thin Man, Crossfire, The Babe Ruth Story, And Justice for All, The Last Embrace,* and *The Champ.* Levene, who was found dead in his apartment by his son on December 28, died of a heart attack some days earlier.

Levenson, Sam(uel), U.S. entertainer (b. Dec. 28, 1911, New York, N.Y.—d. Aug. 27, 1980, New York), was a high school Spanish teacher whose amusing classroom anecdotes about his poor but happy childhood in Brooklyn became the basis for a highly successful nightclub act and for such humorous best-sellers as *Everything but Money, Sex and the Single Child,* and *You Don't Have To Be In Who's Who To Know What's What.* His clever monologues, which were laced with touches of matzo-barrel philosophy, were sometimes sprinkled with serious observations about child rearing and morality. The youngest of eight children, Levenson consistently elicited appreciative laughter with such remarks as "Our menu at mealtime offered two choices—take it or leave it." After guest appearances on television shows with Ed Sullivan, Milton Berle, and Jack Benny, he starred (1951) in his own show, "The Sam Levenson Show." For three years (1951–54) he was a regular panelist on the television program "This Is Show Business," and he appeared on several other television shows.

Libby, Willard Frank, U.S. chemist (b. Dec. 17, 1908, Grand Valley, Colo.—d. Sept. 8, 1980, Los Angeles, Calif.), was awarded the 1960 Nobel Prize for Chemistry for developing a radioactive carbon technique that dated material derived from once-living organisms, including human remains and artifacts, as old as 50,000 years. His "atomic clock" measured small amounts of radioactivity in organic or carbon-containing materials and identified older objects as those with less radioactivity. This system proved to be an invaluable tool for archaeologists, anthropologists, and Earth scientists, who were able to pinpoint the final period of the North American Ice Age to 10,000 years ago (rather than the previously believed 25,000 years ago) using the technique. After receiving his Ph.D. (1933) from the University of California at Berkeley, Libby taught chemistry at his alma mater. When World War II broke out, he joined the Manhattan Project at Columbia University, where (1941–45) his laboratory team was responsible for developing a technique to separate uranium isotopes, a process vital to the creation of the atomic bomb. From 1945 to 1959 Libby worked at the Institute for Nuclear Studies at the University of Chicago, where he conducted his prizewinning carbon-14 research and proved that tritium, hydrogen's heaviest isotope, was produced by cosmic radiation. As the first chemist to serve on the Atomic Energy Commission (now the Nuclear Regulatory Commission), Libby headed Pres. Dwight D. Eisenhower's "Atoms for Peace" project and conducted studies on the effects of radioactive fallout. In 1959 he joined the University of California at Los Angeles, where he remained until his death.

UPI

Lloyd, Norman, U.S. composer and teacher (b. Nov. 8, 1909, Pottsville, Pa.—d. July 31, 1980, Greenwich, Conn.), as director of education (1946–49) of the Juilliard School of Music introduced the Literature and Materials of Music, a new approach to teaching musical theory. The method relied more on classroom interaction with composers and choreographers than on textbook instruction. From 1965 to 1972 Lloyd was a director of the Rockefeller Foundation and designed its arts program. Earlier, during the 1930s, he collaborated with choreographers at Bennington College in Vermont, where they worked on the scoring of such dances as *Panorama* for Martha Graham, *Lament* for Doris Humphrey, and *La Malinche* for José Limón. Lloyd also wrote three textbooks, was co-author of *The Complete Sightsinger,* and provided the musical arrangements in *The Fireside Book of Favorite American Songs* and *The Fireside Book of Folk Songs.*

Longo, Luigi, Italian Communist leader (b. March 15, 1900, Fubine Monferrato, Piedmont, Italy—d. Oct. 16, 1980, Rome, Italy), succeeded Palmiro Togliatti as general secretary of the Italian Communist Party (PCI) in 1964 and remained leader of the party until his retirement in 1972. A founder-member of the PCI, he struggled against Italian Fascism until Mussolini's ban on political parties forced him into exile. He gained valuable organizing experience during the Spanish Civil War but was arrested in France in 1939 and sent back to Italy, where he was imprisoned. Released in 1943, he became deputy commander of the Italian partisan military corps, winning the U.S. Bronze Star for his contribution to the Allied war effort. After the war, he was made deputy secretary of the PCI. Knowing his loyalty to the Soviet Union, many were surprised when he was chosen to succeed Togliatti as leader of the strongest and most independent of the European Communist parties. But he showed a firm commitment to the "Italian road to socialism" and took sole responsibility for his party's firm denunciation of the Soviet intervention in Czechoslovakia in 1968. After his retirement, he became party president and continued to support the diversity of roads to socialism. He expressed misgivings, however, concerning the policy of "historic compromise" with non-Communist political parties that was pursued by his successor, Enrico Berlinguer.

Longworth, Alice Lee Roosevelt, U.S. socialite (b. Feb. 12, 1884, New York, N.Y.—d. Feb. 20, 1980, Washington, D.C.), prided herself on being for some 80 years the nation's most charming barbed-tongued critic of prominent politicians. "Princess Alice" became an instant celebrity when, at age 17, she moved into the White House after her father, Theodore Roosevelt, was elected U.S. president. The irrepressible and irreverent young lady so exasperated her father that he once confided to a friend that he could run the country or try to control his daughter; he certainly could not do both. In 1906 Alice married Nicholas Longworth, who was later elected speaker of the House of Representatives. Though widowed in 1931, Alice Longworth continued to find politics fascinating and politi-

UPI

cians inviting targets for ridicule. To her, Warren G. Harding was "a slob"; Calvin Coolidge looked like he "had been weaned on a pickle"; and presidential candidate Thomas E. Dewey resembled "a groom on a wedding cake." Longworth's outrageous attitude was eloquently advertised on a needlepoint pillow in her sitting room. It invited guests who could find nothing good to say about anyone to sit by her.

Lowenstein, Allard K., U.S. political activist (b. Jan. 16, 1929, Newark, N.J.—d. March 14, 1980, New York), was the man who stymied Lyndon B. Johnson's hopes for reelection in 1968 by persuading Eugene McCarthy to run against the president on a "peace" platform opposing the war in Vietnam. Although McCarthy lost, his race was so impressive that Johnson finally withdrew. Earlier, Lowenstein taught at Stanford University and supported the civil rights movement of the 1960s. From 1968 to 1970 he served in Congress as a Democratic representative from Long Island's 5th district but failed to win reelection in six other tries. In 1977 Lowenstein was named a U.S. representative to the UN Commission on Human Rights and later in the year became a U.S. representative on the UN Trusteeship Council. Lowenstein was shot to death in his law office at Rockefeller Center in New York City; Dennis Sweeney, who worked with Lowenstein during the civil rights movement, was taken into police custody and indicted on a charge of second-degree murder.

McConachy, Clark, New Zealand billiards player (b. April 18, 1895, Glenorchy, N.Z.—d. April 1980, Auckland, N.Z.), was world professional billiards champion (1951–68) and, with Australian Walter Lindrum and Englishmen Joe Davis and Tom Newman, made up the "big four." The foursome ironically dampened public interest in billiards because they could score long sequences of nursery cannons (caroms) to run up enormous breaks. McConachy compiled a record of 466 consecutive cannons in 1932; his highest break was 1,943. He entered the world championship in 1922 but was held off by the other three until he defeated John Barrie in London in 1951. At 73 and suffering from Parkinson's disease, he was narrowly beaten by challenger Rex Williams in 1968. Also a formidable snooker player, he was beaten by Joe Davis in the world professional championship final in 1932.

McCormack, John William, U.S. politician (b. Dec. 21, 1891, Boston, Mass.—d. Nov. 22, 1980, Dedham, Mass.), rose from the poverty of his youth to become speaker of the U.S. House of Representatives (1962–70). As the breadwinner of the family, armed with only a grammar school diploma, McCormack earned four dollars a week as an office boy in a law firm. By studying on his own he passed the bar examinations at age 21, although he never attended high school. His firm loyalty to the Democratic Party won him election as a delegate to the Massachusetts constitutional convention at the age of 25; he then served for two years in the Massachusetts House of Representatives and three years in the Senate. After losing his 1926 bid to become a member of the U.S. House, McCormack won in 1928 and for the next 42 years remained a permanent fixture in Congress. His strong party allegiance cemented his friendship with two powerful Texas Democrats, John Nance Garner and Sam Rayburn, and with very little seniority, McCormack was appointed to the Ways and Means Committee. Although he was approached on several occasions to run for mayor of Boston or for the U.S. Senate, McCormack always declined, saying "I have loved the House." During his tenure, McCormack earned a reputation as a skillful debater who opposed Communism, defended the war in Vietnam, and backed such social legislation as civil rights bills, antipoverty programs, housing laws, Social Security, job safety regulations, and wage-and-hour laws. Shortly before McCormack's retirement in 1970 he came under fire when two of his closest associates, Martin Sweig and Nathan Voloshen, were indicted for influence peddling. He was the first House speaker in more than a century to retire voluntarily.

UPI

McDonnell, James Smith, Jr., U.S. aerospace executive (b. April 9, 1899, Denver, Colo.—d. Aug. 22, 1980, St. Louis, Mo.), was founder (1939) and chairman (1939–67) of McDonnell Aircraft Co. before engineering the largest aerospace merger in

UPI

history. After the 1967 merger of his company with the failing Douglas Aircraft Co., McDonnell Douglas Corp. became one of the largest manufacturers of military aircraft in the U.S. McDonnell, who held a master's degree in aeronautical engineering, first designed (1928) the Doodlebug, a small monoplane for private pilots. His new firm prospered from military contracts secured during World War II, and in 1946 McDonnell sold the U.S. Navy the FH-1 Phantom, the world's first carrier-based jet fighter. He later enhanced his reputation as a supplier of jet fighters with a succession of Phantoms, Banshees, Demons, and Voodoos. McDonnell began work on a manned orbital craft a year before the National Aeronautics and Space Administration awarded his company the contract (1959) to produce Mercury, which carried the first U.S. astronaut into orbit. In 1961 he won the contract to assemble the Gemini capsule—the first two-man spacecraft. Although the company reported sales of $5.3 billion in 1979 with backlog orders of $10.8 billion, McDonnell Douglas Corp. was plagued in the late 1970s and 1980 with lawsuits and the loss of contracts after several of its DC-10s were involved in crashes. An energetic worker, McDonnell retired as chairman a month before his death.

McEwen, Sir John, Australian politician (b. March 29, 1900, Chiltern, Victoria, Australia—d. Nov. 21, 1980, Melbourne, Australia), was leader of the Country Party from 1958 to 1971 and prime minister of Australia for two months in the interim following the death of Harold Holt in December 1967. After leaving school at age 13, McEwen was a farmer before entering politics in 1934 as a member of the Victoria state Parliament. McEwen rapidly advanced to membership in the federal Parliament and to the post of minister of the interior. In 1940 he was successively external affairs minister and air minister. Three years later he became deputy leader of the Country Party. Although his party remained a minority in government, he was for many years (1958–71) deputy prime minister and held the vital ministerial portfolios of commerce and agriculture (1949–56) and trade (1956–63); in the latter post he was recognized as a statesman of great ability and integrity. He was also a noted opponent of British entry into the European Economic Community.

McKelway, St. Clair, U.S. writer (b. Feb. 13, 1905, Charlotte, N.C.—d. Jan. 10, 1980, New York, N.Y.), as a respected writer for *The New Yorker* magazine painstakingly garnered biographical information that highlighted his succinct and witty profiles on such figures as Father Divine, founder of the Peace Mission Movement, dancer Bill Robinson, and journalist Walter Winchell (written with A. J. Liebling). McKelway's style, which many readers found refreshing, was so distinctive that it was impossible for others to duplicate it. Some of his stories were expanded into books, including *Gossip: The Life and Times of Walter Winchell* (1940), *True Tales from the Annals of Crime and Rascality* (1954), *The Edinburgh Caper* (1962), and *The Big Little Man from Brooklyn* (1969). Before joining (1933) *The New Yorker,* McKelway was an accomplished journalist working for the *New York World, New York Herald Tribune,* the *Chicago Tribune,* and the *Bangkok Daily Mail* in Thailand. In a typical example of his capricious nature, McKelway agreed to take the position of managing editor at *The New Yorker* for only three years (1936–39) because he preferred to do his bookkeeping in units of three. He also suffered from bouts of manic depression, which he later poked fun at in some of his writings.

MacKenzie, Rachel, U.S. editor (b. Dec. 2, 1909, Shortsville, N.Y.—d. March 28, 1980, New York, N.Y.), earned the admiration of scores of prominent writers for the skill with which she edited copy as fiction editor (1956–79) of *The New Yorker* magazine. MacKenzie, who nurtured the careers of such literary giants as Isaac Bashevis Singer and Saul Bellow, both Nobel laureates, also showered encouragement on authors Philip Roth, Bernard Malamud, Penelope Mortimer, and Noel Perrin. MacKenzie, an accomplished author in her own right, published *Risk* (1971) and *The Wine of Astonishment* (1974). Before joining *The New Yorker* she taught literature at the College of Wooster in Ohio, at Radcliffe and Tufts in Massachusetts, and at the Bread Loaf Writers' Conference in Vermont.

McLuhan, (Herbert) Marshall, Canadian communications theorist (b. July 21, 1911, Edmonton, Alta. —d. Dec. 31, 1980, Toronto, Ont.), was a leading social theorist and the first to examine the complex ways in which the media affect customs, thinking, and perception in modern civilization. His aphorism "the medium is the message" summarized his belief that the way in which information is received (whether via books, radio, television, etc.) has a greater impact than the information itself. McLuhan, who was a professor (1946–63) and director (1963–80) of the Centre for Culture and Technology at the University of Toronto, became an electronic age oracle during the 1960s with his difficult but insightful books: *The Mechanical Bride* (1951), *The Gutenberg Galaxy* (1962), *Understanding Media* (1964), *The Medium Is the Massage* (1967), and *War and Peace in the Global Village* (1968). McLuhan received numerous Canadian and international honours and in 1970 was made a Companion of the Order of Canada. Although many of his ideas were perplexing, others were quickly adopted, including the terms "hot" and "cool" medium; books, phonographs, and films were characterized as hot, allowing less participation than television, telephones, and tape recorders, which were cool. McLuhan's theory of communications postulated that primitive man lived in an "Eden" because communication involved face-to-face conversation, touch, smell, sight, and sound. But when the printing press was invented, man began acquiring information in isolation through books and began thinking in a linear, sequential fashion. With the birth of the electronic age, however, McLuhan visualized a return to Eden, with all people united by electronics and interacting in a "global village." "McLuhanism," a term that refers to his prophetic observations, is now an official entry in the *Oxford English Dictionary*.

McQueen, Steve (Terrence Stephen McQueen), U.S. actor (b. March 24, 1930, Indianapolis, Ind.—d. Nov. 7, 1980, Juarez, Mexico), became a top box-office attraction as the macho loner whose independence and rebellious encounters with authority made him a silent hero to his fans. His cool blue eyes, sand-blond hair, and youthful features belied his tough-guy attitude and projected an effortless sex appeal on the screen. Demand for motion pictures in which he starred became so overwhelming that McQueen could command $5 million for each film. The laconic McQueen best expressed his personality, though, behind the wheel of a speeding car or flying through the air on a motorcycle, stunts that horrified movie producers who feared for his safety. His first television role, as the friendless bounty hunter in "Wanted—Dead or Alive," set the stage for the remote characters he

UPI

played in such motion pictures as *The Cincinnati Kid* (1965) and *The Sand Pebbles* (1966), for which he received an Oscar nomination. McQueen vaulted to stardom after appearing as a tough gunslinger in *The Magnificent Seven* (1960), and he perpetuated this image in *The Great Escape* and the thrill-packed *Bullitt* (1968), which displayed his daredevil driving down the sloping streets of San Francisco. Nearly every one of his films became a hit, including *The Getaway, Love with the Proper Stranger, The Reivers, Pappillon, The Thomas Crown Affair, Junior Bonner,* and the racing adventures *Le Mans* and *On Any Sunday*. After appearing in *The Towering Inferno* (1974), McQueen made only two other films: *Tom Horn* and *The Hunter*. In 1976, in a surprising role reversal, he portrayed the main character in Henrik Ibsen's *An Enemy of the People,* a film never released to the general public. McQueen, who died of a heart attack after surgery to remove a tumour, had been under treatment for mesothelioma, a rare form of cancer.

McWilliams, Carey, U.S. editor (b. Dec. 13, 1905, Steamboat Springs, Colo.—d. June 27, 1980, New York, N.Y.), crusaded for the civil rights of minorities and the oppressed in scores of books and served for two decades (1955–75) as the outspoken editor of the liberal magazine *The Nation*. McWilliams, who practiced law in California from 1927 to 1938, was the state's commissioner of immigration and housing from 1938 to 1942. His association with *The Nation* began in 1945 when he became a contributing editor; he successively served as associate editor (1951–52), editorial director (1952–55), and, finally, editor. His writings include *Factories in the Field: The Story of Migratory Farm Labor in California* (1939), *Prejudice: Japanese-Americans, Symbols of Racial Intolerance* (1944), and *Anti-Semitism in America* (1948).

Mallalieu, Sir (Joseph Percival) William, British politician (b. June 18, 1908, Delph, Yorkshire, England—d. March 13, 1980, Boarstall, Buckinghamshire, England), was successively minister of defense (Royal Navy), minister of state at the Board of Trade, and minister of state at the Ministry of Technology in Harold Wilson's Labour government of 1964–70. Educated at Oxford and Chicago universities (president of the Oxford Union in 1930), he entered journalism and in World War II served in the Royal Navy, first as ordinary seaman and later as lieutenant. During 1945–50 he sat in the House of Commons as Labour member for Huddersfield and from 1950 to 1979 for Huddersfield East. Mallalieu was parliamentary secretary to the minister of food from 1946 to 1949, but his first major appointment was that of undersecretary of state for defense (Royal Navy) in 1964. He published several volumes of reminiscences, including *Very Ordinary Seaman* (1944) and *Extraordinary Seaman* (1957), and while Labour was in opposition he was a frequent broadcaster. He was knighted in 1979.

Manning, Olivia (Mrs. R. D. Smith), British novelist (b. 1915, Portsmouth, England—d. July 23, 1980, Ryde, Isle of Wight), traveled with her husband during World War II in Eastern Europe and North Africa and drew on those experiences while writing the *Balkan Trilogy: The Great Fortune* (1960), *The Spoilt City* (1962), and *Friends and Heroes* (1965). The novels, evoking the sense of isolation and the tragicomic atmosphere of the time, were greatly admired by critics and fellow writers, who often felt the trilogy had not obtained the public success it deserved. Trained as an artist, Manning published her first novel, *The Wind Changes,* in 1937 and two years later married Reginald Smith. Her travels formed the basis not only of *The Balkan Trilogy* but of the best of her other work, including *School for Love* (1951), *Artist Among the Missing* (1949), and *The Danger Tree* (1977). She was made CBE in 1976.

Mantovani (Annunzio Paolo Mantovani), Italian-born British conductor (b. Nov. 15, 1905, Venice, Italy—d. March 29, 1980, Royal Tunbridge Wells, England), was destined for fame when he discovered the "tumbling strings" effect that became the hallmark of his music. Among the more than 100 million Mantovani records sold were such Gold Disc titles as "Charmaine," "Wyoming," and "Lovely Lady." While many other light orchestras were being driven out of business by rock 'n' roll and succeeding trends in popular music, Mantovani swept on with relentless inevitability. The son of a violinist at the Covent Garden Opera, he showed an early talent for the instrument and was giving recitals of classical music by the age of 16. But Mantovani found that his real talent lay in popular music and, after a successful period with the Hotel Metropole orchestra, he formed his own band. At a time when the "palm court" sound was in demand, the orchestra prospered, but it was not until, with the help of arranger Ronnie Binge, Mantovani developed its distinctive strings that he achieved great popularity. From then on, huge international record sales and a weekly radio program installed the undemanding Mantovani sound in millions of homes.

Margai, Sir Albert (Michael), West African politician (b. Oct. 10, 1910, Bonthe, Sierra Leone—d. Dec. 18, 1980, Washington, D.C.), was prime minister of Sierra Leone from April 29, 1964, until March 21, 1967, when he was ousted by a military coup. He was called to the bar by the Middle Temple, London, in 1947 and returned to Sierra Leone to practice law and serve in local government. Together with his elder brother, Sir Milton Margai, he formed the Sierra Leone People's Party. He was then elected by the Protectorate Assembly to a seat in the Legislative Council. Margai held ministerial portfolios in education, local government, and social welfare. In 1957 he broke away from his brother and founded the People's National Party with Siaka Stevens. He was reconciled with his brother in 1960 and was made minister of finance. After Sir Milton died, Margai succeeded him as prime minister in 1964 and was knighted in 1965. His focus on a one-party state with an executive president and his promulgation of such a constitution led to his overthrow by the Army, which set up a National Reformation Council.

Mar Ignatius Yacoub III, patriarch of Antioch and All the East (b. 1912, Bartella, Iraq—d. June 26, 1980, Damascus, Syria), as leader of the Syrian Orthodox Church (with followers in the Middle East and India) combined scholarship and dedication with an active commitment to the ecumenical movement. He studied in the seminary of Mar Mattai, took his monastic vows in Homs, Syria, and went to India as secretary to the patriarchal legate and later, after his ordination as deacon and priest, as dean of the theological faculty in Malabar. In 1950 he became bishop of the diocese of Beirut and Damascus and in 1957 was elected patriarch. He reunited the divided Indian church and founded two new dioceses in Western Europe. A noted writer and scholar, he was also a spokesman for the Arab cause who protested strongly against the Israeli occupation of Jerusalem and expressed regret at the tragedy of the Lebanese civil war. In 1979 he visited Britain to meet the archbishop of Canterbury and in 1980 went to Rome for discussions with Pope John Paul II.

Marini, Marino, Italian sculptor (b. Feb. 27, 1901, Pistoia, Italy—d. Aug. 6, 1980, Viareggio, Italy), blended elements of archaic Greek, Etruscan, and Gothic sculpture in his works and was particularly well known for a series of horses and riders. After attending the Florence Academy of Fine Arts he became an art teacher and eventually professor of sculpture at the Brera Academy, Milan (1940–70). Marini's distinctive style was slow to emerge and was first apparent in his monumental "Pomona" figure, dating from 1941. He also created some striking portrait busts, including those of Igor Stravinsky, Henry Moore, Marc Chagall, and Henry Miller. The Marino Marini Museum, which he presented to the city of Milan in 1974, displays an extensive range of his work.

Marquard, Richard ("Rube"), U.S. baseball player (b. Oct. 9, 1889, Cleveland, Ohio—d. June 1, 1980, Baltimore, Md.), was a colourful personality who won 19 consecutive games as a left-handed pitcher for the 1912 New York Giants, a modern baseball record never equaled. When Marquard was acquired (1908) from a minor league team for a record $11,000, he was dubbed the "$11,000 Beauty," but after he won only 9 games and lost 18 in his first three seasons, his nickname became the "$11,000 Lemon." In 1913 he teamed up with singer Blossom Seeley in a vaudeville act and became involved in a marital scandal when the couple was pursued by Seeley's husband along the East Coast. Later she obtained a divorce and married Marquard, but the marriage ended in divorce in 1920. During his 18 years (1908–25) in the major leagues, Marquard played with the Giants, the Brooklyn Dodgers, the Cincinnati Reds, and the Boston Braves. His lifetime record included 205 wins and 177 losses, and he participated in five World Series, three with the Giants and two with the Dodgers. The peak of his career, however, was with the Giants; in 1911 he won 25 games, in 1912 he scored 27 victories, and in 1913 he accumulated 24 wins. Marquard pitched and coached in the minor leagues during the early 1930s and then worked as a pari-mutuel clerk at racetracks.

Martenot, Maurice Louis Eugène, French musician (b. Oct. 14, 1898, Paris, France—d. Oct. 8, 1980, Paris), was the inventor of the Ondes Martenot, an electronic instrument that supplied colour and tone to orchestral compositions. Martenot first demonstrated the device at the Paris Opéra in 1928. Leading composers such as Varese, Boulez, Jolivet, Honegger, Milhaud, and Messiaen appreciated the capacity of the new instrument. Martenot and his sister Ginette scheduled a world tour of demonstration concerts, and Martenot wrote studies on the instrument's use. He studied at the Paris Conservatoire and later taught there. He also established his own institution, the École d'Art Martenot at Neuilly.

Martinez, Maria, U.S. potter (b. April 5, 1887, San Ildefonso Pueblo, N.M.—d. July 20, 1980, San Ildefonso Pueblo), revitalized the ancient Indian art of pottery making with her husband, Julian, and became so skilled that she turned out perfectly shaped and balanced pottery without the use of a potter's wheel. Her lustrous black-on-black ware, which is displayed in major museums of the world, is coveted by collectors who sometimes pay up to $15,000 for her magnificent pots. Even after her husband died in 1943 Martinez continued her work until her retirement in 1970. She was the recipient of numerous awards and honours, including one from the American Ceramic Society.

Meany, (William) George, U.S. labour leader (b. Aug. 16, 1894, New York, N.Y.—d. Jan. 10, 1980, Washington, D.C.), was the powerful and crusty president (1955–79) of the 13.6 million-member American Federation of Labor-Congress of Industrial Organizations (AFL-CIO) and the eloquent self-appointed spokesman for all U.S. labour. Distinguished by his obstreperous rhetoric, downturned mouth, half-closed eyelids, and conspicuous cigar, Meany authoritatively accomplished his number one job of "holding the boys together." Following in his father's footsteps, Meany was a plumber before becoming secretary-treasurer of the New York Building Trades Council in 1923. He became president of the New York State Federation of Labor in 1934 and later served (1940–52) as secretary-treasurer of the national AFL before becoming its president in 1952. Meany's greatest accomplishment was the 1955 merger of two competitive and dissimilar organizations: the AFL, which organized crafts, and the CIO, which organized workers by industry. As president of the unified AFL-CIO, Meany never hesitated to promote his conservative views: he criticized a succession of presidents from Franklin D. Roosevelt to Jimmy Carter for their economic and foreign policies; he adamantly opposed Communism and helped lead (1977) the U.S. out of the International Labour Organization when it refused to criticize repressive labour policies in Communist countries; and he hawkishly supported U.S. involvement in the war in Vietnam when it was not in vogue to do so. In 1957 he expelled the Teamsters Union from the AFL-CIO on the grounds that its leaders, notably Dave Beck and Jimmy Hoffa, were corrupt, but critics asserted that Meany took action only when the public was aroused. Meany was also taken to task for his foot-dragging on racial integration, but he supported a provision for equal job opportunities that was included in the Civil Rights Act of 1964. His later disputes with Walter Reuther, former CIO president and president of the United Auto Workers (UAW), resulted in the withdrawal (1968) of the UAW from the AFL-CIO. Decreased membership in the federation and Meany's advancing age began to threaten his job. But Meany refused to be bullied. In a typical confrontation with one of his harshest critics, he dropped his cane in front of machinists' union leader William W. Winpisinger. As Winpisinger bent over to pick it up Meany humiliated his adversary by saying, "Wimp, if you had any class you would have had a wheelchair here for me." On Nov. 15, 1979, the nation's grand old man of organized labour retired after 12 successive terms as AFL-CIO president.

Mercer, David, British dramatist (b. June 27, 1928, Wakefield, Yorkshire, England—d. Aug. 8, 1980, Haifa, Israel), used a highly individual talent to create works for the theatre, films, and television. His complex leading characters were at odds with the world and apt to express themselves in bursts of sustained rhetoric, but these depictions sometimes received harsh treatment from the critics. The son of a railwayman, he left school at 14 but returned to take a degree at the University of Durham. In 1962 his television play "A Suitable Case for Treatment" won a British Screenwriters' Guild award and the film version, *Morgan!*, won the British Film Academy award in 1966 for best screenplay. His other notable television plays included "A Climate of Fear" (1962) and "Let's Murder Vivaldi" (1968). His first stage play, *The Governor's Lady* (1960), was followed by *Ride a Cock Horse* (1965), *Belcher's Luck* (1966), *After Haggerty* (1970), and *Duck Song* (1974), all performed by the Royal Shakespeare Company. In 1978 he won the French Film Academy's award for his screenplay *Providence* (1977), directed by Alain Resnais.

Milestone, Lewis (LEWIS MILSTEIN), Russian-born director (b. Sept. 30, 1895, Chisinau, Russia—d. Sept. 25, 1980, Los Angeles, Calif.), was a maverick filmmaker whose Academy Award directing triumphs included *Two Arabian Knights* (1927), a war comedy, and *All Quiet on the Western Front* (1930), a moving drama about the ruinous emotional and physical effects of war. Milestone, who made some 30 films during a 40-year career, directed numerous other war films, notably *A Walk in the Sun, Pork Chop Hill,* and *The North Star;* other features included *The Front Page, Of Mice and Men,* and the 1962 remake of *Mutiny on the Bounty,* starring Marlon Brando. His earlier films featured leading stars of the era, including Joan Crawford in *Rain* (1932), Al Jolson in *Hallelujah I'm a Bum* (1933), John Gilbert in *The Captain Hates the Sea* (1934), and Bing Crosby and Ethel Merman headlining *Anything Goes* (1936). After working as a movie cutter, assistant director, and screenwriter, Milestone made his directing debut with *Seven Sinners* (1925) and thereafter worked for any studio willing to meet his contract demands.

Miller, Henry (Valentine), U.S. writer (b. Dec. 26, 1891, New York, N.Y.—d. June 7, 1980, Pacific Palisades, Calif.), transcended a literary barrier when he chronicled the intimate details of his life in Paris in the sexually explicit *Tropic of Cancer* (published in France in 1934). The book was released in the U.S. in 1964 after the Supreme Court ruled that it could not constitutionally be banned as obscene. Miller, who felt that his greatest contribution to American literature was to establish the importance of life, also published the candid, quasi-autobiographical *Tropic of Capricorn* and *The Rosy Crucifixion* trilogy: *Sexus, Plexus,* and *Nexus.* His reputation as a writer of merit was further enhanced by *The Colossus of Maroussi* (1941), a travel book touting the importance of Greece, and *The Air-Conditioned Nightmare* and *Sunday After the War,* two books dealing with the mechanization, commercialization, and general deterioration of the U.S. as a society. Besides exploring Bohemian sexuality, Miller also took on the role of philosopher as the hero-narrator. In his final years Miller quietly painted scores of watercolours at his home in Pacific Palisades.

UPI

Mohammad Ali, Chaudhri, Pakistani politician (b. July 1905, Jullundur, India—d. Dec. 1, 1980, Karachi, Pakistan), was prime minister of Pakistan from 1955 to 1956 and played an important role in breaking up the old Indian Empire and in forming the new state. He was educated at Punjab University, where he lectured on chemistry before joining the civil service. He worked in the accounts department of the (British) government of India, was appointed private secretary to the minister of finance, and during World War II was a leading member of the Supply Department. In 1947, after independence for India and the creation of the separate state of Pakistan, he became secretary-general to the government of Pakistan and was finance minister before his appointment as prime minister. He oversaw the ratification of the new constitution and, by what came to be known as the "Mohammad Ali formula," settled the division of powers between West and East Pakistan. It proved a controversial solution and the constitution was abrogated in 1958. During the military dictatorship of Mohammad Ayub Khan, Mohammad Ali led his Muslim League Party in opposition to the regime. He also wrote a key study on *The Emergence of Pakistan.*

Mohammad Reza Pahlavi, former ruler of Iran (b. Oct. 26, 1919, Teheran, Iran—d. July 27, 1980, Cairo, Egypt), was the eldest son of Reza Pahlavi, an army officer who in 1925 abolished the decaying Qajar dynasty and proclaimed himself shah-in-shah ("king of kings"). The young Mohammad, having completed his preliminary studies in 1931 in Teheran, was sent to Switzerland to continue his education. Returning to Teheran in 1936, he entered the Officers' Training College and received a commission in the Army. On Sept. 16, 1941, his pro-German father abdicated in his favour under Soviet and British pressure.

The new shah-in-shah began his reign under difficult conditions, with Soviet and British (and later, U.S.) troops occupying large areas of the country. After World War II the shah adopted a pro-Western foreign policy, but he lacked the experience and authority to dominate such groups as the Shi'ah religious leaders, Communist agitators, and rich landlords. In April 1951 the shah appointed as prime minister Mohammad Mosaddeq, a nationalist leader who immediately pushed an oil nationalization act through the Majlis (parliament). Mosaddeq's quest for power led to strained relations with the shah. In 1953, fearing assassination, the shah fled to Rome while a military coup overthrew Mosaddeq. After returning to Teheran, in 1954 the shah took steps to revive the oil industry. During the next two decades oil revenues were used to transform Iran into a developing industrial and military power able to dominate and stabilize southwestern Asia.

He divorced Princess Fawzia of Egypt in 1948 and Soraya Esfandiari in 1958 because neither had produced an heir to the throne. He then married (December 1959) Farah Diba, who gave birth to Crown Prince Reza in October 1960. The coronation of the shah and the empress Farah took place in 1967. In October 1971, in the presence of some

UPI

3,000 international guests, including 69 heads of state or their representatives, Mohammad Reza laid a wreath at the tomb of Cyrus the Great, the founder of the Persian Empire. The ostentatious ceremony was meant to signify Iran's new role and power in the Persian Gulf area.

Supported by a powerful army and an energetic secret police (Savak), the shah rode roughshod over Muslim conservatives and sternly suppressed opposition to his centralist planning. The quadrupling of the price of oil in 1973 enabled the shah to speed up the pace of industrialization, but the increasing misuse of the new wealth by his government and the large sums spent on weaponry left many citizens alienated and dissatisfied. In 1978 a revolution was instigated by two strange allies: the Islamic fundamentalists and the Communists of the underground Tudeh ("Masses") Party. The explosion caught the shah off guard. Declining to use force against massed demonstrators bellowing "death to the tyrant," he left the country with his consort on Jan. 16, 1979. Deeply disappointed with the West, he took refuge first in Egypt, then in Morocco, and subsequently in The Bahamas and Mexico, where he was found to be suffering from cancer. The U.S. government, which had refused the shah's request for asylum, admitted him for specialized medical treatment in New York City. On December 15 the shah flew to Panama and for three months found sanctuary on the island of Contadora. When the Iranian revolutionary government requested his extradition, the shah accepted (March 1980) an invitation from Pres. Anwar as-Sadat to reside in Egypt.

Moraes, Vinicius de, Brazilian lyricist, author, and government official (b. Oct. 19, 1913, Rio de Janeiro, Brazil—d. July 9, 1980, Rio de Janeiro), catapulted to stardom with the international favourite bossa nova song "The Girl from Ipanema," which he co-wrote with composer Antonio Carlos Jobim. The song became popular during the 1960s and helped to make the Brazilian bossa nova dance the rage around the world. A prominent poet in Brazil, Moraes wrote *O Caminho para a Distância* (1933), *Forma e Exegese* (1946), and *Poemas, Sonetas e Baladas* (1946). His diplomatic career began in 1943 when he joined the Ministry of Foreign Affairs. Moraes served as vice-consul (1947–50) in Los Angeles and consul (1958–60) in Montevideo, Uruguay, before being dismissed in 1969 by Brazil's military regime, which gained power in 1964. In his nightclub performances Moraes frequently poked fun at his dismissal, which apparently resulted from his "vagabond ways," including nine marriages. He was also the co-author of the musical drama *Orfeu da Conceição,* which served as the basis for *Black Orpheus,* the winner of the Academy Award for best foreign film for 1959. Moraes's musical works were compiled in 18 original albums and in four anthologies.

Morris, Margaret, British dancer and dance teacher (b. April 17, 1891, London, England—d. Feb. 29, 1980, Glasgow, Scotland), pioneered modern dance in Britain and developed a system of notation using abstract symbols. While dancing and acting, Morris met Isadora Duncan's brother Raymond. Morris incorporated Isadora's "Greek positions" into her ballets of 1910, into her production of Gluck's *Orpheus* at the Savoy Theatre, London, and into her performance of Maeterlinck's *The Blue Bird* at the Haymarket Theatre. She later opened a school and toured with her own company. Morris applied her techniques to help physically and mentally handicapped children and developed special exercises for athletes and pregnant women. By World War II Margaret Morris Movement centres had been established internationally, but the war closed her British centres except the one in Glasgow. There she founded the Celtic Ballet, which, in the 1960s, became the Scottish National Ballet. But when her husband, the Scottish painter J. D. Ferguson, and her principal dancer died in 1961, she closed her London and Glasgow dance schools. The Morris Movement classes, however, continued to flourish, and Morris herself trained dancers for the 1972 Glasgow production of *Hair.*

Mosley, Sir Oswald Ernald, British politician (b. Nov. 16, 1896, London, England—d. Dec. 3, 1980, Orsay, France), was the founder (1932) and leader of the British Union of Fascists (BUF) from 1932 to 1940 and head of the Union Movement, which he founded in 1948. The two groups distributed anti-Semitic propaganda, staged hostile demonstrations in Jewish sections of East London, and emblazoned Nazi insignia on their uniforms. After serving (1918–31, with the exception of one two-year period) in the House of Commons as a Conservative, an independent, and then a Labour Party member, Mosley formed the socialist New Party but was defeated for reelection to Parliament despite his powerful orations. After a trip to Fascist Italy, Mosley returned to England and founded the BUF, becoming a British imitator of Hitler and Mussolini. But, unlike the continental Fascist leaders, Mosley, with his open advocacy of totalitarianism, failed to win popular support in his native land. His pro-German agitations constituted a danger to national security with the start of World War II, and in 1940 Mosley was interned without a trial. He was released in 1943 because of poor health. After the death of his first wife, Lady Cynthia Curzon, in 1933, Mosley married (1936) Diana Mitford, daughter of the 2nd Baron Redesdale, a prewar defender of Nazi Germany. After the war, Mosley reorganized the BUF as the Union Movement, but the party faded away in a few years' time. In 1957 he published his autobiography, *Mosley: The Facts.*

Muñoz Marín, Luis, Puerto Rican politician (b. Feb. 18, 1898, San Juan, P.R.—d. April 30, 1980, San Juan), who, while serving (1948–64) as the first elected governor of Puerto Rico, introduced Operation Bootstrap, an ingenious and highly successful program that brought economic stability to an island of poverty-stricken people. Operation Bootstrap granted tax exemptions of 10 to 16 years to U.S. companies willing to open branch factories on the island. As a result unemployment dipped, roads were built, and urban developments were constructed in sugarcane fields. The son of the publisher and patriot Luis Muñoz Rivera, Muñoz Marín was educated in the U.S. and during the 1920s lived in New York, where he pursued a literary career. He returned to his homeland in 1931, when the island had been devastated by two hurricanes that destroyed the sugarcane, coffee, and tobacco harvests and caused widespread suffering. Elected to the Puerto Rican Senate in 1932, Muñoz Marín, who was expelled from the Liberal Party in 1937 because he advocated complete independence from the U.S., founded (1938) the Popular Democratic Party, which won its first Senate victory in 1940. Muñoz Marín served as president of the Senate from 1940 to 1948. When the U.S.-appointed governor Rexford G. Tugwell took office, Muñoz Marín reversed his position on U.S. independence and worked with Tugwell to improve the island's condition. After the U.S. gave Puerto Rico the right to elect its own governor, Muñoz Marín was elected to four successive four-year terms beginning in 1948. He was instrumental in persuading the U.S. to change Puerto Rico's status to that of a commonwealth (1952). In 1964 he refused to run for a fifth term but returned to the Senate.

Nenni, Pietro Sandro, Italian politician (b. Feb. 9, 1891, Faenza, Italy—d. Jan. 1, 1980, Rome, Italy), was leader of the Italian Socialist Party (PSI), twice foreign minister, and several times deputy premier. The son of a peasant, he first became a journalist. When Italy invaded Libya in September 1911, Nenni organized a strike against the campaign. He was jailed for his activities and met Benito Mussolini in prison. He joined the PSI in 1921. In 1922, when Mussolini came to power, Nenni, an ardent anti-Fascist, attacked him in the newspaper *Avanti,* of which he was chief editor. In 1925 he was arrested for publishing a booklet on the Fascists' murder of Socialist leader Giacomo Matteotti, and in the following year he fled to Paris. During the Spanish Civil War Nenni was political commissar of the Garibaldi Brigade. In 1940 he was arrested in Vichy France by the German Gestapo, taken back to Italy in 1943, and interned on the island of Ponza by Mussolini. In August of the same year he was released by order of Marshal Pietro Badoglio. Nenni was then elected secretary-general of the PSI and in 1945 became vice-premier in the government of Feruccio Parri. Elected to the Constituent Assembly in 1946, he became vice-premier again in Christian Democrat Alcide De Gasperi's coalition government. In 1946 Nenni was named foreign minister, but in January 1947 the PSI split and Nenni, heading the party's left wing, made an alliance with the Communists. For almost a decade the alliance opposed Christian Democrat governments. In 1952 Nenni received the Stalin Peace Prize from the Soviet Union, but after the Soviet invasion of Hungary in November 1956 he repudiated the prize and broke with the Communists. In 1963 he finally brought the PSI back into a full-fledged coalition with the Christian Democrats under Aldo Moro. He served as foreign minister in 1968–69 and was vice-premier in three successive Cabinets. Nenni was made a life senator in 1971 and in June 1979 was elected president of the Senate.

Nielsen, Arthur Charles, U.S. market research engineer and business executive (b. Sept. 5, 1897, Chicago, Ill.—d. June 1, 1980, Chicago), was the founder (1923) and chairman (1957–75) of the lucrative A. C. Nielsen Co., the largest market-research concern in the world. The firm, which was financed with the backing of Nielsen's fraternity brothers, eventually established a business foothold by analyzing retail food and drug sales, which still remains the company's largest and most profitable operation. Nielsen Co. entered the radio program rating field in 1942 but became best known to the general public for its television rating service, which from 1950 has gauged the popularity of television shows with random weekly samplings of 1,170 U.S. households. The three major U.S. television networks have used Nielsen's results to determine which programs will be offered to an audience comprising some 73 million households.

Ohira, Masayoshi, Japanese politician (b. March 12, 1910, Toyohama, Kagawa Prefecture, Japan—d. June 12, 1980, Tokyo, Japan), was selected party leader of the feuding Liberal-Democratic Party (LDP) in November 1978, a political victory that assured his formal election as prime minister of Japan on Dec. 7, 1978. Ohira, aptly nicknamed "the Bull," was the son of a poor farmer who died when the boy was 16. In addition to working on the farm, Ohira completed high school and passed entrance examinations for the elite Tokyo University of Commerce (now Hitotsubashi University). After graduation (1936) he joined the Ministry of Finance and in 1949 was appointed private secretary to Finance Minister Hayato Ikeda. In 1952 he

WOLF MORRISON—KEYSTONE

won the first of ten successive elections to the House of Representatives. When Ikeda became prime minister in 1960, he named Ohira chief Cabinet secretary. As foreign minister (1962–64) Ohira prepared the way for restoration of relations with South Korea. In the Cabinet of Kakuei Tanaka, Ohira also served as foreign minister (1972–74); he was the co-architect of rapprochement with the People's Republic of China. He was finance minister from 1974 to 1976, secretary-general of the LDP from 1976 to 1978, and with the backing of Tanaka (who remained influential despite his ouster as prime minister in 1974 because of his involvement in the Lockheed scandal) succeeded Takeo Fukuda as prime minister in 1978. During his tenure as prime minister Ohira had to submit his programs for the approval of his coalition government. On May 16, 1980, Ohira's government fell when fellow members of the LDP failed to support him on a vote of no confidence. New elections were scheduled for June 22—just ten days after Ohira unexpectedly died of a heart attack.

Okun, Arthur Melvin, U.S. economist (b. Nov. 28, 1928, Jersey City, N.J.—d. March 23, 1980, Washington, D.C.), was a liberal economist who was a staff economist (1961–62) and member (1964–68) of the nation's Council of Economic Advisers (CEA) and then presided (1968–69) as its chairman under Pres. Lyndon B. Johnson. A firm advocate of Keynesian economic theories, Okun believed that fiscal policy (the raising and spending of revenue) was a better means of controlling the economy than federal monetary policy (controlling the supply of money). Thus, when the country faced recession in the mid–1960s, the CEA advised the president to lower taxes to stimulate consumer spending. During Okun's tenure as president of the CEA, the federal government created a huge budget deficit by borrowing money to finance the war in Vietnam. On the CEA's recommendation, Congress passed a 10% tax surcharge in June 1968. After leaving the CEA, Okun became (1969) a senior fellow at the Brookings Institution, where he forecast and analyzed trends in the economy. Earlier, he was the architect of the widely used "Okun's Law," which stipulated that for every 3% rise in the rate of economic growth above the economy's long-term potential growth rate, unemployment would decrease 1%. But during the turbulent 1970s when stagflation (a stagnating economy with inflation) afflicted the country, the rule no longer held true. For the remainder of his life Okun attempted to find ways to stifle inflation while avoiding recession. He also formulated the universal definition for recession: two consecutive quarters of negative gross national product growth. Okun's many books included *The Political Economy of Prosperity* and *Equality and Efficiency: The Big Tradeoff.* At the time of his death he was working on a volume dealing with stagflation, tentatively titled *Prices and Quantities in Cyclical Fluctuations.*

Owen, Johnny, British boxer (b. 1956, Merthyr Tydfil, Wales—d. Nov. 3, 1980, Los Angeles, Calif.), won the British, European, and Commonwealth bantamweight titles before dying of brain injuries sustained in a challenge bout with world champion Lupe Pintor of Mexico. Though apparently of fragile build, he was an athlete of great skill and total dedication who had lost only one of his 26 professional bouts. In fact, most commentators put him ahead of Pintor at the time of his fatal knockout. Owen gained the British title in 1977, the Commonwealth title the following year, and in 1980 defeated European champion Juan Rodríguez. In June he successfully defended his British and Commonwealth titles against Johnny Feeney.

Owens, Jesse (JAMES CLEVELAND OWENS), U.S. athlete (b. Sept. 12, 1913, Danville, Ala.—d. March 31, 1980, Tucson, Ariz.), demonstrated that he was one of the most sensational track and field stars of all time when he captured four gold medals at the 1936 Olympic Games in Berlin and thereby crushed Adolf Hitler's dream of using the Olympics to prove Aryan supremacy. In the 100-m dash (10.3 sec) Owens tied the Olympic record; in the 200-m dash (20.7 sec) and in the running broad jump (now referred to as the long jump; 26 ft 5¼ in [8.06 m]) he broke both Olympic and listed world records; and as a member of the world-record-breaking U.S. 400-m relay team (39.8 sec) he ran as the all-important anchor man. His times in the 100-m dash and the 200-m dash were so stupendous that they would have claimed Olympic gold medals as late as 1960 and 1964, respectively. Earlier Owens attended Ohio State University, where he exhibited a mark of excellence by breaking five world records and tying another in 45 minutes of competition. After his stunning Olympic victory Owens was virtually forgotten. He was forced to take a job as a playground janitor and ended his amateur career when he accepted money to race against cars, horses, and dogs. Owens's accomplishments were officially recognized in 1976 when Pres. Gerald R. Ford awarded him the Presidential Medal of Freedom and in 1979 when Pres. Jimmy Carter presented him with a Living Legacy Award. In the later years of his life Owens headed a lucrative public relations firm and traveled some 200,000 mi a year as an inspirational public speaker. The U.S. "Ambassador to Sports" died of lung cancer.

CULVER PICTURES

Paasio, Rafael, Finnish politician (b. June 6, 1903, Uskela, Fin.—d. March 17, 1980, Turku, Fin.), was twice Finland's prime minister, heading a coalition government from 1966 to 1968 and a Social Democratic minority government from February to September 1972. A typographer and journalist, Paasio was editor in chief (1942–66) of *Turun Päivälehti,* a Social Democratic newspaper, and a member of the municipal council of Turku from 1945. He was a member of Parliament from 1948 to 1975 and from 1949 to 1966 was chairman of its Foreign Affairs Committee. He succeeded Vaino Tanner as chairman (1963–75) of the Social Democratic Party, which under his leadership became Finland's largest party. As prime minister Paasio sought to stabilize the country's economy and to reassure the Soviet Union of Finland's reliability as a neighbour.

Pal, George, Hungarian-born film producer and director (b. Feb. 1, 1908, Cegled, Hung.—d. May 2, 1980, Beverly Hills, Calif.), achieved cinematic excellence with both his ingenious animated cartoons and his spectacular science fiction films, which won numerous Academy Awards for their striking special effects. While in Europe, Pal developed the "Puppetoons," highly sophisticated wire-jointed puppets with wooden heads. They were specially designed to be adjusted for pose and expression between the takes of stop-motion photography. He introduced his Puppetoon series in the U.S. in 1940 and earned recognition with *Jasper Goes Hunting* (1944) and *Jasper's Close Shave* (1945). Before turning to feature-length science fiction films, Pal was honoured with a special Academy Award in 1943 "for the development of novel methods and techniques" in animated films. Pal made seven films that received Academy Awards (five for elaborate special effects): *Destination Moon, When Worlds Collide, The War of the Worlds, Tom Thumb, The Time Machine, The Wonderful World of the Brothers Grimm,* and *Faces of Dr. Lao.*

Paleckis, Justas, Lithuanian pro-Soviet agent (b. 1898, Telsiai, Lithuania—d. Jan. 26, 1980, Moscow, U.S.S.R.), was appointed head of the puppet government of Soviet Lithuania by Soviet High Commissar Vladimir G. Dekanozov on June 18, 1940, three days after the Soviet Army invaded Lithuania. Paleckis immediately dissolved the Seimas (parliament) and staged a July 14 election featuring only pro-Soviet candidates. On July 21 the new Seimas voted unanimously for a resolution requesting the U.S.S.R. to annex Lithuania. On August 3 the Supreme Soviet of the U.S.S.R. granted the request. On June 22, 1941, however, when Hitler invaded the U.S.S.R., Paleckis fled to Moscow. When the Soviet Army reoccupied Lithuania, he was appointed chairman of the Presidium of the Supreme Soviet of Lithuania. From 1966 to 1970 he was also chairman of the Soviet of Nationalities, part of the Supreme Soviet of the U.S.S.R.

Parrot, André, French archaeologist (b. Feb. 15, 1901, Désandans, Doubs, France—d. Aug. 24, 1980, Paris, France), excavated and identified the site of the ancient Semitic city of Mari, in modern Syria, previously known only from references in Babylonian texts. Parrot, a Protestant theologian, began excavations in 1933 at Tall Hariri and, from a temple dedication, was able to identify it as Mari. Still more exciting discoveries followed in 1935, when workers began to uncover Zimrilim's palace. The site revealed earlier buildings, dating from around 3500 BC, and thousands of tablets with cuneiform inscriptions of the 19th and 18th centuries BC. Parrot also worked on sites in Lebanon and Iraq. In 1946 he was appointed chief curator of French national museums and undertook a major reorganization of Near Eastern antiquities in the Louvre. He became general inspector of museums in 1965 and from 1968 to 1972 was the first director of the Louvre. A member of the Académie des Inscriptions et Belles-Lettres, he wrote several books and edited *Cahiers d'archéologie biblique.*

Patterson, William Allan, U.S. airline executive (b. Oct. 1, 1899, Honolulu, Hawaii—d. June 13, 1980, Glenview, Ill.), played a dramatic role in shaping the history of aviation as the pioneering first president (1934–63) of United Airlines, which became the world's largest commercial air carrier. In 1929 Patterson persuaded Philip G. Johnson (president of the Boeing Airplane Co. and Boeing Air Transport) and W. E. Boeing (chairman of the Boeing companies and the United Aircraft and Transport Corp.) to purchase Pacific Air Transport. Pacific and Boeing merged to form United Airlines with Patterson as general manager and later as president. United flights eventually spanned the nation from coast to coast and were the first to carry female flight attendants and have pilots who were guaranteed a monthly salary regardless of their hours in the air. Patterson was also instrumental in helping the Douglas Aircraft Co. develop the DC-4, the first airliner equipped solely for passengers. After retiring as president in 1963, Patterson was elected chairman of the board. He held the position until 1966, when he was named director emeritus and honorary chairman of both United Airlines and its parent company, UAL Inc.

Payne, the Rev. Ernest Alexander, British Baptist clergyman (b. Feb. 19, 1902, London, England—d. Jan. 14, 1980, London), was an influential supporter of ecumenism and joint president (1968–75) of the World Council of Churches (WCC). Payne was also chairman (1962–71) of the executive committee of the British Council of Churches, of which he became first honorary life president in 1978. As a student at Regent's Park College, London, Payne was greatly influenced by the renowned Baptist theologian Henry Wheeler Robinson. Payne later became Robinson's colleague when the college relocated at Oxford, where he was senior tutor (1940–51) and university lecturer in comparative religion and the history of modern missions (1946–51). During 1951–67 he was general secretary of the Baptist Union of Great Britain and Ireland, of which he became vice-president (1976–77) and president (1977–78); he was also vice-president (1965–70) of the Baptist World Alliance. Payne's commitment to ecumenism intensified when in 1954 the second assembly of the WCC, meeting at Evanston, Ill., elected him vice-chairman of the council's central committee, a post he retained until his election to the joint presidency in 1968. Among his many publications were *The Free Church Tradition in the Life of England* (1944), *Henry Wheeler Robinson* (1946), and *Out of Great Tribulation: Baptists in the Soviet Union* (1974). He was made a Companion of Honour in 1968.

Pettersson, Allan Gustaf, Swedish composer (b. Sept. 19, 1911, Uppsala, Sweden—d. July 1980, Stockholm, Sweden), claimed to be Sweden's only proletarian composer as the creator of "Barefoot Songs," which reflected the hardships of life for the poor in Sweden's pre-welfare state. The son of a poor blacksmith, Pettersson was accepted into the Swedish Royal Academy of Music at age 19. He studied under Karl-Birger Blomdahl during World War II and later in Paris with Arthur Honegger and René Leibowitz. During the two decades following his return (1953) to Sweden, he produced 15 symphonies. Pettersson's first work, a sonata for piano and violin, was completed in 1943 and his last, a concerto written for violinist Ida Haendel, was premiered in Stockholm in 1980. He was appointed to the board of the Royal Academy of Music in 1970 and in 1979 received the title of professor.

Piaget, Jean, Swiss psychologist (b. Aug. 9, 1896, Neuchâtel, Switz.—d. Sept. 16, 1980, Geneva, Switz.), was thought by many to have been the major figure in 20th-century developmental psychology and was the first to make a systematic study of the acquisition of understanding in children. His massive output, including *Le Langage et la pensée chez l'enfant* (1923; *The Language and Thought of the Child,* 1926), *Le Jugement et le raisonnement chez l'enfant* (1924; *Judgment and Reasoning in the Child,* 1928), *La Représentation du monde chez l'enfant* (1926; *The Child's Conception of the World,* 1929), and *La Construction du réel chez l'enfant* (1937; *The Construction of Reality in the Child,* 1954), influenced generations of teachers, educators, and child psychologists throughout the world, offering them a framework, based on observation, to categorize the different and successive stages in the development of human intelligence. He created a new awareness of the preadolescent years as crucial in intellectual life

A.S.L./PICTORIAL PARADE

and revolutionized classroom techniques, notably in the teaching of mathematics, and the perceptions teachers had of their roles in the classroom. Piaget, who published his first scientific article at the age of 11 and was an accomplished zoologist by 15, received a doctorate in natural sciences at the University of Neuchâtel in 1918. His interest soon turned toward psychology and, in particular, the intelligence tests devised by Alfred Binet. From 1921 to 1925 he worked at the J. J. Rousseau Institute in Geneva and was professor of philosophy at Neuchâtel (1926–29). He then served as professor of child psychology and the history of scientific thought at the University of Geneva. His work on children was sometimes criticized because it was based on small samples, in particular his own children, rather than on much broader observations. It was Piaget's close study of individuals, however, that allowed him to enter the child's conceptual universe and postulate its evolution through four precise stages. In 1955 he founded the International Centre of Genetic Epistemology in Geneva, which he continued to direct after his retirement in 1971; he was also a co-director of the Education Department of UNESCO.

Pignedoli, Sergio Cardinal, Italian prelate of the Roman Catholic Church (b. June 4, 1910, Reggio nell'Emilia, Italy—d. June 15, 1980, Reggio nell'Emilia), was head of the Vatican Secretariat for Non-Christians and was expected by many to become pope after the death of Paul VI in 1978. In the two conclaves Pignedoli was passed over in favour of John Paul I and then John Paul II. Ordained at 23, he became chaplain to the Italian Navy during World War II. He served as nuncio in Latin America, became auxiliary to Archbishop Giovanni Montini (the future Paul VI) in Milan, and then became apostolic delegate to western Africa and Canada. In 1966 Paul VI sent him to Vietnam in the hope of finding a solution to the conflict and of improving relations with the Buddhists. In 1967 he became secretary of the Sacred Congregation for the Evangelization of the Peoples, and he was made a cardinal in 1973. His career was clouded by an incident at the 1976 meeting between Muslims and Christians in Tripoli, Libya; he signed a statement containing two paragraphs condemning Zionism that the Vatican had not approved. Pignedoli continued to improve Vatican relations with other faiths and won affection for his warm personality and his appreciation of the diversity of cultural traditions in the church.

Popovic, Cvetko, Yugoslav teacher (b. 1896, Bosnia—d. June 7, 1980, Sarajevo, Yugos.), was a member of the Young Bosnians, the nationalist group responsible for the killing of Austrian Archduke Franz Ferdinand at Sarajevo on June 28, 1914. The assassination, carried out by Gavrilo Princip, led to the declaration of war a month later by Austria-Hungary against Serbia and triggered the outbreak of World War I. The Young Bosnians thus achieved their aim of collapsing the Austro-Hungarian Empire. Popovic, only 18 at the time of the shooting, fled from Sarajevo but was arrested shortly afterward and served four years' hard labour. After his release in 1918 he became a teacher, then joined the staff of the Sarajevo ethnographic museum.

Porter, Katherine Anne, U.S. writer (b. May 15, 1890, Indian Creek, Texas—d. Sept. 18, 1980, Silver Spring, Md.), as master of the short and long story, exhibited her skillful style with an array of characters enfolded in a rich and complex texture. The depth with which she developed her characters was alien to the short story and was usually achieved only in the novel. A near fatal bout with influenza inspired Porter to write the absorbing "Pale Horse, Pale Rider" (1939), which chronicled an ill-fated romance that ends when the young man dies during the influenza epidemic of 1919. The title of the story was taken from a verse in Revelation that reads: ". . . behold a pale horse: and his name that sat on him was Death." In this and in "Noon Wine" and "Old Mortality," Porter introduced the spirited and independent Miranda, who, like characters in her other stories, experiences self-deception and self-betrayal. Such works as "Flowering Judas," "The Jilting of Granny Weatherall," and "The Leaning Tower" were spiced with autobiographical information and reflected Porter's upbringing in Texas and Louisiana convents, her job as a newspaperwoman in Chicago, and her trips to Mexico and Germany. Fame and fortune, however, eluded Porter until she published her only novel, *Ship of Fools* (1962). The book, which received mixed reviews, was an international best-seller and was made into a star-studded motion picture. In 1966 her *Collected Stories* won both the Pulitzer Prize and the National Book Award for fiction.

Raft, George (GEORGE RANFT), U.S. actor (b. Sept. 27, 1895, New York, N.Y.—d. Nov. 24, 1980, Hollywood, Calif.), portrayed an imperturbable tough guy in a highly successful motion-picture career that sometimes paralleled his offscreen association with gangsters. As a testimony to his coolness, Raft nonchalantly flipped a coin as he was being gunned down by a gangster in a classic scene from *Scarface* (1932). Although his acting was never highly touted, Raft's soft voice, slicked-back hair, and chiseled features shadowed beneath a fedora made him a natural for the role of a gangster. He was also convincing as a convict and played in such prison dramas as *Each Dawn I Die* and *Invisible Stripes*. A wayward youth at the age of 13, Raft hustled in dance halls and billiard parlours before attempting to become a ballplayer and prizefighter. He garnered better success as a dancer in clubs and earned his first film role in *Queen of the Night Clubs* (1929). During his 50-year film career, Raft appeared in *Souls at Sea, Night After Night, They Drive by Night, Manpower, Johnny Angel, Some Like It Hot,* and *Ocean's Eleven*. His links to organized crime were confirmed when he testified before a New York federal grand jury investigating Mafia financial transactions in 1966. In 1967 he was refused entrance to England as an undesirable. During the last years of his life Raft, who was once one of Hollywood's highest paid stars, was plagued by money problems. He appeared in television commercials and served as a goodwill ambassador for the Riviera Hotel in Las Vegas, Nev.

Reed, Stanley Forman, U.S. Supreme Court justice (b. Dec. 31, 1884, Minerva, Ky.—d. April 3, 1980, Huntington, N.Y.), was (1938–57) the Supreme Court justice whose early decisions both reflected and strengthened the liberal philosophy of the New Deal policies of Pres. Franklin D. Roosevelt. Because his decisions moved toward the centre as his career progressed, Reed was generally considered a moderate. Reed wrote more than 300 opinions, including a majority opinion in 1946 dismissing contempt convictions against the *Miami* (Fla.) *Herald* and its editor for the publication of two editorials and a cartoon. In 1949 Reed dissented from the majority when he voted against an Alabama state "literacy" statute that attempted to ban black voters from the polls. In the same year he testified as a character witness on behalf of Alger Hiss, a U.S. State Department official accused of involvement in a Communist spy ring and later convicted of perjury. Reed concurred with the majority in 1951, upholding the conviction of 11 Communist leaders for violating the Smith Act; in 1952 he voted against the majority ruling that Pres. Harry S. Truman exceeded his power when he seized the steel companies. Selected by Pres. Dwight D. Eisenhower to head the newly created Civil Rights Commission (1957), Reed declined because he feared that the presence of a former Supreme Court justice on an investigatory and advisory commission might lessen public respect for the impartiality of the judiciary. Earlier in his career Reed served (1912–16) with the Kentucky legislature and was solicitor general in the administration of Pres. Herbert Hoover. He retired (1957) from the Supreme Court at the age of 72.

Reeves, the Right Rev. (Richard) Ambrose, Anglican prelate (b. Dec. 6, 1899, Norwich, England—d. Dec. 23, 1980, Shoreham-by-Sea, East Sussex, England), was bishop of Johannesburg, South Africa (1949–61), and a strong opponent of apartheid. He was active in the Student Christian Movement (SCM) while an undergraduate at Sidney Sussex College in Cambridge, and he also attended the College of the Resurrection, Mirfield. His work as rector of bombed-out St. Nicholas Church in Liverpool (1942–49) marked him as an Anglo-Catholic who could cooperate with other religious traditions and thereby rebuild a Christian community. As bishop of Johannesburg he strove to build up parishes and missions and help Africans in an area of industrial change. He was so vigorously outspoken against apartheid and critical of the South African government, especially after the Sharpeville shooting of March 1960, that he was deported from the country and resigned his see. He was general secretary of the SCM (1962–65) and was named president of the Anti-Apartheid Movement in 1970. His biography, *Ambrose Reeves,* by J. S. Peart-Binns, was published in 1973.

Reksten, Hilmar, Norwegian shipowner (b. Oct. 29, 1897, Bergen, Norway—d. July 1, 1980, Bergen), built up one of the world's largest supertanker fleets during the 1950s and '60s and based his most profitable operations on short-term charter contracts after the closure of the Suez Canal in 1967. The son of a ship's engineer, Reksten was graduated from commercial high schools in Bergen and Cologne, Germany. After five years in a shipping office, in 1929 he bought his first ship, which was 14 years old and weighed 2,000 tons. He owned six ships when World War II broke out but lost them all during the war. Reksten worked for the London-based Norwegian Shipping and Trade Mission, and after the war he diversified his shipping interests. He concentrated on tankers after the 1956 Suez crisis and headed the Great Norwegian Spitsbergen Coal Co., exploiting Svalbard's coal resources, until 1962. Following the collapse of the tanker market as a result of the 1973 oil crisis, Reksten came into conflict with the Aker shipbuilding group over canceled orders and with the Norwegian government over alleged tax evasion and currency violations totaling some $200 million. He was acquitted of most of the charges, but after his death his estate was declared bankrupt to facilitate a search for assets transferred abroad.

Renaldo, Duncan (RENAULT RENALDO DUNCAN), Romanian-born actor (b. April 23, 1904, Romania —d. Sept. 3, 1980, Santa Barbara, Calif.), was the indomitable leading character in the popular television series "The Cisco Kid" (1951–56). He and his sidekick, Pancho (Leo Carillo), corralled outlaws in the old West without ever killing them. Renaldo also starred in the films *The Bridge of San Luis Rey* (1929) and *Trader Horn* (1931) but was best remembered for his 156 television episodes as the Cisco Kid and for the many feature films he made playing that role. Although Renaldo was jailed (1934–36) for falsifying his birthplace in order to obtain a U.S. passport, he was pardoned by Pres. Franklin D. Roosevelt. He then returned to Hollywood and made several Westerns with Roy Rogers and Gene Autry.

Rhine, J(oseph) B(anks), U.S. psychologist (b. Sept. 29, 1895, Waterloo, Pa.—d. Feb. 20, 1980, Hillsborough, N.C.), was credited with coining the term extrasensory perception (ESP) in the course of researching such phenomena as mental telepathy, precognition, and clairvoyance. Rhine initially studied to be a botanist but became fascinated with "psychic occurrences." With psychologist William McDougall he helped to establish in 1930 the Parapsychology Laboratory at Duke University, Durham, N.C. There Rhine held some 90,000 experiments using a wide variety of human subjects. In 1934 his book *Extra-Sensory Perception* created a sensation with the general public but was greeted with skepticism by the scientific community. His *New Frontiers of the Mind* (1937) further explained his experiments. Rhine left Duke in 1965 and formed his own research centre, the Foundation for Research on the Nature of Man.

Robert, Paul Charles Jules, French lexicographer (b. Oct. 19, 1910, Orléansville [El Asnam], Algeria—d. Aug. 10, 1980, Mougins, France), followed Émile Littré and Pierre Larousse in creating a French dictionary that became a household name. Unlike its predecessors, "Le Grand Robert" (*Dictionnaire alphabétique et analogique de la langue française,* 7 vol., 1951–70) was based on the principle of cross-referencing to create a network of etymological, semantic, or syntactical analogies, so that the user could pursue "the many threads which simple logic weaves among words." Robert studied law before publishing the first installment of his work, which won an award from the French Academy. This allowed him to continue with a small team of assistants. Robert published a one-volume edition, *Petit Robert,* followed by *Micro-Robert* (1971) and a French-English dictionary (1979). He also published an anthology, *Divertissement sur l'amour* (1951) and a two-volume autobiography (1979–80).

Roberts, Rachel, Welsh actress (b. Sept. 20, 1927, Llanelly, Wales—d. Nov. 26, 1980, Los Angeles, Calif.), won British Film Academy awards for her performances in *Saturday Night and Sunday Morning* (1960) and *This Sporting Life* (1963), two films on working-class themes that introduced a new note of realism into the British cinema. In 1979 she was named best supporting actress for her role in *Yanks*. She studied at the Royal Academy of Dramatic Art and acted in classic roles at the Old Vic, in Stratford, and at the Bristol Old Vic. But some of her most outstanding theatrical performances were in modern parts, in the musical *Maggie May* in 1964, in *Alpha Beta* in 1972, and in John Osborne's *The End of Me Old Cigar* in 1975. Her other films included *Picnic at Hanging Rock, O Lucky Man,* and *Murder on the Orient Express.* After her first marriage, to Alan Dobie, was dissolved in 1960, she married Rex Harrison in 1962; they were divorced in 1971.

Romero y Galdames, Oscar Arnulfo, Salvadoran archbishop (b. Aug. 15, 1917, Ciudad Barrios, El Salvador—d. March 24, 1980, San Salvador, El Salvador), fearlessly condemned the violent activities of government armed forces, right-wing groups, and leftist guerrillas involved in El Salvador's intense civil conflict. Romero, a champion of the poor and a strong advocate of human rights, was nominated for the 1979 Nobel Peace Prize by a number of U.S. congressmen and 118 members of the British Parliament. Although Romero was considered a conservative before his appointment as archbishop in 1977, he courageously denounced the regime of dictator Gen. Carlos Humberto Romero (no relation) and the brutal activities of the National Guard. He also refused to support the military-civilian junta that replaced the deposed Romero and suffered the anguish of repeated threats to his life. In February 1980 a bomb destroyed the archdiocese's radio station. Before his assassination at the hands of an unknown assailant, Romero had declared: "I am prepared to offer my blood for the redemption and resurrection of El Salvador. If God accepts the sacrifice, I hope it will be a seed of liberty and a sign of hope."

Rukeyser, Muriel, U.S. poet (b. Dec. 15, 1913, New York, N.Y.—d. Feb. 12, 1980, New York), voiced her opposition to social injustice in a series of poems published over a span of more than four decades. As literary editor of the *Student Review* of Vassar College, Poughkeepsie, N.Y., Rukeyser traveled to Alabama in the early 1930s and covered the Scottsboro trial in which nine black youths were accused of raping two white girls. She recounted her experience in a poem entitled "The Trial" and thereafter became an ardent champion of those she viewed as underdogs and oppressed. Her dramatic lyrical verse and heavy use of symbolism are masterfully evidenced in such works as *Theory of Flight* (1935), *The Soul and Body of John Brown* (1940), *The Green Wave* (1948), *Waterlily Fire* (1962), *Breaking Open* (1973), and *The Gates* (1976). Other subjects explored in her poetry included the 1936 Spanish counter-Olympics, the Spanish Civil War, the slow death of coal miners afflicted with silicosis, and the fate of Kurdish Socialists executed in Iran in 1979. *The Collected Poems of Muriel Rukeyser* was published in 1978.

Sá Carneiro, Francisco, Portuguese politician (b. July 19, 1934, Oporto, Portugal—d. Dec. 4, 1980, near Lisbon, Portugal), was premier of the right-wing coalition government voted into power at Portugal's December 1979 general election. A lawyer by profession, Sá Carneiro was elected to the National Assembly in 1969 but resigned in 1973. After a military coup in April 1974, he founded the Partido Popular Democrático (PPD) and represented it as minister without portfolio in the government of Adélino da Palma Carlos during Gen. António de Spínola's presidency (May–July 1974). At the 1975 elections for the Constituent Assembly the PPD emerged as the second strongest party, securing 80 seats. The Socialists won 116 seats and the Communists 30. That distribution was more or less repeated at the election to the National Assembly held in April 1976. In the following general election of December 1979 Sá Carneiro changed the name of his party to Partido Social Democrático and formed with the Centre Democrats and Monarchists an Alianca Democrática. His party won 128 seats in the 250-member Assembly; the Socialists obtained 74 and the Communists 44. Sá Carneiro then became premier, succeeding a government of technocrats headed by Senhora María de Lurdes Pintassilgo. One year later, in a light-plane crash near Lisbon, Sá Carneiro was killed together with a female companion of several years, Danish-born Snu Abecassis.

Sanders, "Colonel" Harland, U.S. business executive (b. Sept. 9, 1890, near Henryville, Ind.—d. Dec. 16, 1980, Shelbyville, Ky.), was a dapper self-styled Southern gentleman whose white hair, white goatee, white double-breasted suits, and black string ties became a trademark in 48 countries for Kentucky Fried Chicken. Sanders, who quit school in seventh grade, held a variety of jobs before opening (1929) Sanders' Cafe in the rear of a service station. The cafe, which offered family-style dinners, soon gained a large clientele and in the mid-1930s Sanders received his honorary colonel's title. He perfected his recipe for "finger lickin' good chicken" in 1939 by using a secret blend of 11 spices and a pressure cooker to seal in flavour and moisture. After selling his restaurant, Sanders took to the road armed with his recipe but signed up only five restaurants in two years. By 1964, however, there were more than 600 franchises in the U.S. and Canada and Sanders was making $300,000 a year. In the same year Sanders signed

UPI

most of his fast-food empire over to John Brown of Kentucky and Jack Massey of Tennessee, providing he received $2 million, a lifetime salary of $40,000 a year, and a seat on the board of directors. In 1971 the company, which boasted 3,500 franchises and $700 million a year in business, was acquired by Heublein Corp. Sanders remained active as an official ambassador for the company even as a nonagenarian.

Santamaría Cuadrado, Haydée, Cuban revolutionary (b. 1927?—d. July 28, 1980, Havana, Cuba), became one of the most prominent women in Cuba after fighting beside Fidel Castro during the abortive 1953 coup that provided the name for Castro's 26th of July Movement. Santamaría's brother and fiancé were both tortured to death after the attack on the Moncada army barracks, and she was captured and subjected to brutal interrogations and a seven-month prison term. After her release, Santamaría worked in Cuba's underground before joining Castro's guerrillas at his Sierra Maestra camp. Castro finally came to power in 1959 and Santamaría became (1965) one of five women in the 100-member Central Committee of the Cuban Communist Party. In 1976 she became a member of the Council of State. At the time of her death she was serving as director of Cuba's cultural centre and state publishing house. Santamaría took her own life.

Sartre, Jean-Paul, French philosopher and writer (b. June 21, 1905, Paris, France—d. April 15, 1980, Paris), had an unrivaled influence on the intellectual life of France after World War II with his philosophical theory of Existentialism. He wove together contemporary ideas with the theories of Kierkegaard, Heidegger, Husserl, Marx, and Freud, among others. His theory, which was developed in his first major philosophical treatise, *L'Être et le néant* (1943; *Being and Nothingness,* 1956), portrayed man in a godless universe, condemned to freedom by the fact that his existence precedes the meaning he chooses to give it. While this freedom is defined by circumstances and limited by that of others, man cannot evade it except by deliberate choice. The theme of human consciousness in a hostile world had already been explored in Sartre's first novel, *La Nausée* (1938; *Nausea,* 1949), written while he was a teacher. The war interrupted his academic career, and Sartre was taken prisoner in 1940. Released the following year, he returned to Paris, where he became active in the Resistance. In 1945 he founded the review *Les Temps modernes* with his lifelong companion, Simone de Beauvoir. During the next few years he published *Les Chemins de la liberté,* in which problems of individual liberty are played out against the background of prewar society. The novels include *L'Âge de raison* (1945; *The Age of Reason,* 1947), *Le Sursis* (1945; *The Reprieve,* 1947), and *La Mort dans l'âme* (1949; *Iron in the Soul* [U.S. title, *Troubled Sleep*], 1950). During the same period he reached a new audience for his philosophical concepts in such plays as *Huis-clos* (1945; *In Camera* [U.S. title, *No Exit*], 1946), *Les Mains sales* (1948; *Crime passionel* [U.S. title, *Dirty Hands*], 1949), *Le Diable et le bon dieu* (1951; *Lucifer and the Lord,* 1953), and *Les Séquestrés d'Altona* (1960; *Loser Wins* [U.S. title, *The Condemned of Altona*], 1960). Their sustained rhetoric and passionate debate on moral predicaments established him as the leading dramatist of ideas in the contemporary French theatre. His growing conviction that Marxism was the fundamental theory against which others must be measured was the starting point for another major philosophical work, *Critique de la raison dialectique* (1960; *Critique of Dialectical Reason,* 1976). Sartre published *Les Mots* (*The Words*), an intellectual autobiography, in 1964; he refused the Nobel Prize in the same year. His advocacy of political action, which contributed to the social consciousness of his generation, never wavered—from his support for Algerian independence in 1954 and his condemnation of the Soviet invasion of Hungary to his support of the 1968 student revolt. Often in conflict with the authorities, in his later years he lent his name to numerous leftist publications. His monumental biography of the novelist Gustave Flaubert, *L'Idiot de la famille,* absorbed the final productive years of his life: the first two volumes appeared in 1971 and the third in 1972. In 1974 his increasing blindness forced him to abandon both writing and active political life.

AGIP/PICTORIAL PARADE

Schary, Dore (Isidore), U.S. motion-picture producer and playwright (b. Aug. 31, 1905, Newark, N.J.—d. July 7, 1980, New York, N.Y.), oversaw the production of more than 300 films as the "boy wonder of Hollywood" during the 1940s and '50s and was one of the few Hollywood executives to vocalize his opposition to the McCarthy era blacklist. As a writer (1936–41) for MGM, Schary won an Academy Award for the original screenplay of *Boys Town,* and as executive producer (1941–43) he released many successful films including *Joe Smith, American* and *Lassie, Come Home.* For the next few years, after leaving MGM, he worked for David O. Selznick's Vanguard Productions as producer, but in 1947 Schary joined RKO, where he turned out such films as *Crossfire,* a progressive drama attacking anti-Semitism. When Howard Hughes took over RKO, Schary returned to MGM as vice-president in charge of production, where he supervised or personally produced about 250 movies. Films produced by Schary included *Battleground, Designing Woman,* and *Bad Day at Black Rock.* In 1956 Schary was dismissed from MGM. He then wrote and produced the highly successful play *Sunrise at Campobello* (1957), depicting Franklin Delano Roosevelt after he was stricken with polio. Schary's autobiography, *Heyday,* was published in 1979.

Schlabrendorff, Fabian von, West German lawyer (b. July 1, 1907, Halle, Germany—d. Sept. 3, 1980, Wiesbaden, West Germany), was one of the group of German officers who plotted to kill Adolf Hitler during World War II. As assistant adjutant on Hitler's general staff, he delivered (March 1943) a parcel containing a time bomb to the plane flying Hitler to East Prussia. The bomb failed to explode but Schlabrendorff was able to recover the parcel unopened. The following year he was also involved in preparations for Col. Claus von Stauffenberg's abortive assassination attempt on July 20 and was arrested. Schlabrendorff was acquitted by the Nazi People's Court but was personally sentenced to death by SS leader Heinrich Himmler; he was awaiting execution when the war ended. In 1967 he was appointed a judge of the Federal Constitutional Court, West Germany's highest court, and served until his retirement in 1975. He recounted his experiences in a book, *Offiziere Gegen Hitler* (*The Secret War Against Hitler*).

Sellers, Peter Richard Henry, British comedian and film actor (b. Sept. 8, 1925, Southsea, England—d. July 24, 1980, London, England), won international fame as the star of film comedies after helping to create a new style in British humour through his contribution to the radio series "The Goon Show." He came from a theatrical family and began his career with the World War II British forces' group ENSA. In 1951 he and Spike Milligan formed "The Goon Show" team whose zany humour, ad-libbing, and exploitation of the medium marked a

CAMERA PRESS

new era in radio comedy. Here, as in his early films and recordings, Sellers relied mainly on his outstanding gift for vocal mimicry; but his face was as adaptable as his voice, and his portrayal of a trade unionist in the film *I'm All Right Jack* showed for the first time the extent of his ability to become the characters he played. By the 1960s he was an established star, making such films as *The Millionairess, The Waltz of the Toreadors, Mr. Topaze,* and *I Love You Alice B. Toklas.* In these, as in lesser vehicles for his talents, he showed a genius that overcame the limitations of his material: his timing was superb and his feel for the telling detail that evoked character was uncanny. It was this accuracy of observation rather than the humour of his scripts that delighted his audiences and, like many great comic actors, he excelled in pathos and in hinting at the tragic dimension behind the comedy. In 1964 the original *Pink Panther* opened, in which Sellers played the part of a bungling French detective, Inspector Clouseau. During the 1970s he returned to this character three times in the series of *Pink Panther* films and, despite their immense success, it seemed to some critics that he was often sacrificing his finest talents to repetitive farce. But his recent film, *Being There,* won critical acclaim for his portrayal of a simple-minded gardener. His other films included *The Mouse that Roared,* in which he played three roles, *Heavens Above, Lolita,* and *What's New Pussycat?*

Shelley, Norman, British actor (b. Feb. 15, 1903, London, Eng.—d. Aug. 22, 1980, London), was a versatile actor who, after making his first radio broadcast in 1926, worked for more than 50 years in radio. Shelley exploited his extraordinary gift for mimicry in a wide range of roles, notably in plays by Shakespeare and Jean Anouilh, and in soap operas and in the *Children's Hour.* His most memorable performance was a 1940 radio impersonation for American listeners of Winston Churchill declaring before Parliament that Britain would never surrender to Germany. Only many years later was it publicly known that the recorded voice was not Churchill's. Shelley started work as a Shakespearean actor during the 1920s, playing alongside many leading figures in the British theatre; he later appeared in a variety of classical and modern dramas. Principally a character actor, he found his true vocation in radio, adapting his voice to Shakespearean verse, everyday speech, or the gruff tones of Dennis the Dachshund in the much-loved children's program "Toytown."

Sherrill, the Rt. Rev. Henry Knox, U.S. Episcopal bishop (b. Nov. 6, 1890, Brooklyn, N.Y.—d. May 11, 1980, Boxford, Mass.), was presiding bishop of the Episcopal Church from 1946 to 1958 and a vocal promoter of worldwide Christian unity and cooperation. Because he strongly supported ecumenism, Sherrill was chosen first president of the National Council of Churches, a post he held for two years. He also served (1954–61) as one of the six presidents of the World Council of Churches, which he helped found. Sherrill began his ministry in 1914 as a curate at Trinity parish in Boston. During World War I he was an army chaplain in Europe and in 1923 was named rector at Trinity parish. In 1930, at the age of 39, he had the distinction of being named bishop of Massachusetts. Even after he stepped down as presiding bishop, Sherrill remained active in church affairs; in 1966 he was one of 85 church leaders who urged Pope Paul VI to approve artificial methods of contraception.

Shukairy, Ahmed Assad, Palestinian nationalist (b. 1908, Acre, Palestine—d. Feb. 26, 1980, Amman, Jordan), led the Palestine Liberation Organization (PLO) from 1964 to 1967. Graduated from the American University of Beirut, Lebanon, and the Jerusalem Law School, he became an official of the Arab League and a delegate for both Syria and Saudi Arabia at the United Nations. As the PLO's first president he was a leading spokesman for the Palestinian cause during the mid-1960s and was active as a propagandist and negotiator with Arab governments and international organizations. After the 1967 Arab-Israeli war there was a new militancy among Palestinian groups, and Shukairy was thought by some to be ineffectual. Accused of failure in coordinating the activities of the guerrilla groups, he resigned and virtually disappeared from active political life.

Simonin, Albert Charles, French writer (b. April 18, 1905, Paris, France—d. Feb. 15, 1980, Paris), brilliantly exploited the language of the Parisian underworld in tough, fast-talking thrillers that rivaled those of the leading American practitioners of the genre. The authenticity of Simonin's work was derived from childhood experiences in La Chapelle district of Paris. He left school at 12 and assumed a variety of jobs, including chimney-sweep, jeweler, and taxi driver. The last of these inspired *Voilà Taxi* (1935), his first book, written in the slang that became his hallmark. Simonin took up journalism and wrote popular fiction under various pseudonyms before achieving popular and critical success in 1953 with *Touchez pas au grisbi,* which gained the Prix des Deux-Magots and was filmed with Jean Gabin in the leading role. Its sequel, *Le Cave se rebiffe,* was equally successful and was followed by a dictionary of French argot, *Le petit Simonin illustré* (1957). Simonin also wrote film scripts and in 1977 published the first volume of his autobiography, *Confessions d'un enfant de la Chapelle,* which won the Prix Saint-Simon.

Simpson, William Hood, U.S. Army officer (b. May 19, 1888, Weatherford, Texas—d. Aug. 15, 1980, San Antonio, Texas), was an expert tactician who commanded the 9th Army when it thrust into the heart of Germany during World War II and became, on April 12, 1945, the first Allied army to cross the Elbe River. As head of the 9th Army, Simpson led 13 divisions with some 341,000 men through France, Belgium, and The Netherlands in an assault on Germany's western fortifications, the Siegfried Line or West Wall. After the successful attack, the Army awaited the permission of Gen. Dwight D. Eisenhower to march into Berlin, but it was ordered to hold its position on the Elbe while the Soviet Army took the city. After graduating from West Point in 1909, Simpson served under Gen. John J. Pershing in the 1916 Mexican Punitive Expedition, which attempted to capture Pancho (Francisco) Villa, who had executed 16 U.S. citizens. Besides distinguishing himself at the Command and General Staff School at Ft. Leavenworth and at the Army War College in Washington, D.C., Simpson served with the 33rd Division in France during World War I, becoming divisional chief of staff. In 1943 he was named commander of the 4th Army and in 1944 he took command of the 8th Army (redesignated the 9th Army in order to avoid confusion with the British 8th Army when the two units were in France). After his retirement (1946), Simpson was active in banking and civic affairs; he received the rank of four-star general in 1954 when Congress enacted special legislation to promote 11 World War II generals.

Sjöberg, Alf, Swedish film and theatre director (b. June 21, 1903, Stockholm, Sweden—d. April 17, 1980, Stockholm), was first and foremost a man of the theatre, but was best known outside Sweden for his films, particularly *Frenzy* (1944), and for his version of August Strindberg's *Miss Julie,* which won the Grand Prix at the 1951 Cannes Film Festival. A pupil at Stockholm's Royal Dramatic Theatre from 1923, Sjöberg made his directing debut there in 1930. During the 1930s he visited Paris and Moscow and was greatly influenced by the Russian producer and director Vsevolod Meyerhold. Sjöberg directed some 150 productions for the Royal Dramatic Theatre, including plays by Shakespeare, Ibsen, Strindberg, and Brecht. He also introduced dramatists such as Jean-Paul Sartre, T. S. Eliot, Witold Gombrowicz, Eugène Ionesco, and Fernando Arrabal to the Swedish stage. The first of his 18 films was *The Strongest One* (1929), a silent semidocumentary about seal hunters in the Greenland Sea.

Smythe, Conn (CONSTANTINE FALKLAND KARRYS SMYTHE), Canadian sports executive (b. Feb. 2, 1895, Toronto, Ont.—d. Nov. 18, 1980, Caledon, Ont.), was an astute businessman who built a hockey empire from the profits of a sand-and-gravel business. Smythe, who played a formidable role in the history of Canadian hockey, purchased the Toronto St. Pats franchise in 1928 but changed the name to the more patriotic Toronto Maple Leafs. Abiding by his tough standards, which often included more aggressive playing on the ice, the Maple Leafs won seven Stanley Cup championships. Smythe's promotional acumen filled Maple Leaf Gardens with fans who responded to his newspaper advertisement, "If you're tired of seeing the kind of hockey the Boston Bruins are playing, come to the Garden tonight and see a real hockey club, the Toronto Maple Leafs." During the Depression, Smythe erected (1931) the multimillion-dollar arena Maple Leaf Gardens by paying trade unions with shares in the team. After his induction (1958) into hockey's Hall of Fame, in 1961 Smythe sold the franchise to a group led by his son, Stafford. After his formal retirement from hockey (although he never stopped giving advice), Smythe built a championship Thoroughbred racing stable. His horses won 147 stakes races, including the prestigious Queen's Plate three times and the Canadian Oaks three times. In 1976, his most lucrative year, the stable's purse money totaled more than $500,000.

Snow, C(harles) P(ercy) Snow, BARON, British novelist (b. Oct. 15, 1905, Leicester, England—d. July

UPI

1, 1980, London, England), came to find government interaction with the scientific community more fascinating than science itself and described it in novels that combined craftsmanship and psychological insight. A scientist by training and a novelist by profession, he deplored the gap between the "two cultures." During the 1960s Snow was a widely respected pundit whose public career reached its climax in 1964, when he was appointed undersecretary at the Ministry of Technology and made a life peer. He rose from a relatively humble background to become a fellow of Christ's College, Cambridge, and conduct research in crystallography. He published his first novel, *Death Under Sail,* in 1932 and eight years later began his 11-volume *Strangers and Brothers* series. It portrayed, in near-documentary style, the largely masculine worlds of university politics (*The Masters,* 1951), scientific research (*The New Men,* 1954), and, in a phrase that was to stand for the inner workings of central government, *Corridors of Power* (1964). Snow was a government adviser during World War II and later a civil service commissioner and a director of English Electric Co. Ltd.

Somoza Debayle, Anastasio, Nicaraguan politician (b. Dec. 5, 1925, Léon, Nicaragua—d. Sept. 17, 1980, Asunción, Paraguay), assumed (1967) the presidency of Nicaragua after both his father (1933–56) and brother (1957–63) had served as presidents in a succession that created a Somoza dynasty lasting 45 years. From 1963 to 1967 the country was ruled by puppets of Somoza, who then won office in a general election that many believed was rigged. He stepped down from office in 1972 to allow the rewriting of the constitution, but when a devastating earthquake rocked Managua in December 1972, Somoza appointed himself president of an emergency committee with absolute power to administer financial and material aid from other countries. Somoza returned to office in 1974 under the new constitution, which permitted him to rule until 1981. But his administration was bombarded with accusations: the U.S. made charges of human rights violations, and the 1978 murder of Pedro Joaquím Chamorro, a prominent newspaper editor and foe of the regime, was said to have been sanctioned by Somoza. This latter charge sparked demands for Somoza's resignation. The Sandinista National Liberation Front led a

WIDE WORLD

bloody insurrection that claimed 10,000 lives in September 1978 and a total of 50,000 before Somoza was forced to resign on July 17, 1979. Somoza, who reportedly got $100 million out of the country, fled first to Miami, Fla., then to The Bahamas, and finally to Paraguay. He was gunned down in the capital city of Asunción by a barrage of machine-gun and bazooka fire.

Spychalski, Marian, Polish Communist leader (b. Dec. 6, 1906, Lodz, Poland—d. June 7, 1980, Warsaw, Poland), was an architect who joined the underground Communist Party of Poland in 1931. During World War II he was prominent in the resistance movement against the Germans. In 1945 he was appointed first deputy minister of national defense but in 1949 he was dismissed from the government and from the Central Committee of the Communist Party, and in 1950 he was imprisoned for "Titoist deviations." Spychalski was rehabilitated in 1956 and succeeded Marshal K. K. Rokossowski as minister of defense. In 1959 Spychalski was elected a member of the Politburo. Two years later he graduated from the General Staff Academy and in 1963 Wladyslaw Gomulka made him marshal of Poland. In 1968 he left the Army and was elected chairman of the Council of State. When Gomulka was forced to resign (1970) as first secretary of the Polish United Workers' Party, Spychalski also resigned.

Stein, William H(oward), U.S. biochemist (b. June 25, 1911, New York, N.Y.—d. Feb. 2, 1980, New York), was co-winner with his associate, Stanford Moore, and Christian B. Anfinsen of the 1972 Nobel Prize for Chemistry for making fundamental contributions to enzyme chemistry. Together with his colleagues, Stein deciphered the molecular structure of the digestive enzyme ribonuclease, a complex protein consisting of a single chain of 124 amino acids. This accomplishment, which was basic to the progress of medical research, represented a landmark in the field of chemistry because it raised hope that damaged or defective enzymes, which can cause mental retardation or early death, might be repaired through chemical means. Stein, who earned (1938) a Ph.D. from Columbia University in New York City, joined the staff of Rockefeller Institute, New York City, in 1938 and became a professor in 1952. He served as editor (1968–71) of the *Journal of Biological Chemistry,* the leading journal in its field. Since 1969 he had been confined to a wheelchair with polyneuritis, a rare paralyzing disease.

Stewart, Donald Ogden, U.S. playwright and screenwriter (b. Nov. 30, 1894, Columbus, Ohio—d. Aug. 2, 1980, London, England), was the Oscar-winning author of the screenplay for *The Philadelphia Story* and for such other films as *Holiday, The Prisoner of Zenda, The Barretts of Wimpole Street, Keeper of the Flame,* and *Life with Father.* Before his prolific career as a screenwriter, Stewart worked at *Vanity Fair* magazine. There he produced a parody of Scott Fitzgerald that launched his career as a satirical playwright. Some of his most clever works included *A Parody Outline of History* (1921) and *Aunt Polly's Story of Mankind,* a satire on the middle class. During the McCarthy purges of the 1950s, Stewart was blacklisted in Hollywood. He moved to London, where he established permanent residence.

Stewart, Ella Winter, Australian-born journalist (b. 1898, Melbourne, Australia—d. Aug. 5, 1980, London, England), devoted her life to radical causes, to the peace movement, and to support for struggling writers and artists. After her parents moved to London in 1910, she attended the London School of Economics and in 1924 met her first husband, the U.S. journalist Lincoln Steffens, at the Versailles Peace Conference. Two years later they settled in California and in 1930, increasingly committed to Socialism, she visited the Soviet Union. *Red Virtue* (1931) was one result of this experience. During the 1930s she was active in U.S. and international left-wing causes, playing an important role in the anti-Fascist struggle. After Steffens's death in 1936 she married writer Donald Ogden Stewart. Her visit to the U.S.S.R. during World War II inspired *I Saw the Russian People* (1945). The Stewarts left the U.S. during the McCarthy era and settled in Britain to continue their work for the peace movement. They visited Ghana in 1964 and organized an exhibition of African art on their return to London. Stewart published her autobiography, *And Not to Yield,* in 1963. Her death came only three days after that of her husband.

Still, Clyfford, U.S. painter (b. Nov. 30, 1904, Grandin, N.C.—d. June 23, 1980, Baltimore, Md.), was regarded as an Abstract Expressionist but viewed himself as the creator of a new frontier in art. His paintings were derived from two symbolic images: an upright man symbolizing a free individual and the dualities of the Sun and Earth. During the 1930s he painted distorted, angular, and bony figures of men and bloated, pregnant figures of women with the American West as a backdrop. After a brief respite (1941–43), Still returned to his easel but began abstracting his images: by 1947 all references to figures and landscapes had evolved into ragged, shredded lines and open colour fields. About this time, like other Abstract Expressionists, he began working on very large canvases to effect a sense of immediacy and limitlessness. Still was uncompromisingly antitraditionalist, so much so that he eliminated referential titles to his paintings and even painted for a time (1948–49) almost exclusively in black. In the 1950s, however, he returned to the use of colour and produced an open lyricism not found in his earlier works. A few months before his death, Still was honoured with the largest one-man exhibition ever held for a living artist by the Metropolitan Museum of Art in New York City.

Summerskill, Edith Clara Summerskill, Baroness, British politician (b. April 19, 1901, London, England—d. Feb. 4, 1980, London), as a practicing physician was known during most of her parliamentary career as Dr. Edith Summerskill and was minister of national insurance in the Labour government of 1950–51. She championed such causes as equal rights and equal pay for women, birth control and availability of painless childbirth methods, and a wife's fair share of her husband's property (secured with the Married Women's Property Act, 1964). Her negative views on boxing as physically damaging were expressed in *The Ignoble Art* (1956). She qualified as a doctor in 1924; in 1938 she was elected to Parliament for West Fulham (after 1955 for Warrington) and sat in the House of Commons continuously until created a life peer in 1961.

In Clement Attlee's Labour government of 1945–50 Summerskill served as parliamentary secretary to the Ministry of Food with great efficiency at a time when rationing was still in force. In her brief term as minister of national insurance she worked to improve state insurance plans and workers' compensation. She was also a member of Labour's shadow cabinet until 1957 and was chairman of the Labour Party in 1954–55. Among her publications were *Letters to My Daughter* (1957) and *A Woman's World* (1967). She was made a member of the Privy Council in 1949 and a Companion of Honour in 1966.

Sutherland, Graham Vivian, British artist (b. Aug. 24, 1903, London, England—d. Feb. 17, 1980, London), by the time of his death was internationally preeminent among British painters. Romantic in the pastoral tradition of Samuel Palmer, he evolved a personal style that combined naturalism and abstraction in tender, tragic, and also cruelly strident images; his portraiture too evoked presences of unusual power. His forms included Welsh hills, spiky thorns, and seashore waste searingly vivid in colour. Sutherland attended Goldsmiths' College School of Art in London and first attracted attention as a landscape etcher, being elected a member of the Royal Society of Painter-Etchers and Engravers in 1926. Landscape poster design for the Shell-Mex petroleum company came in 1930 and, with Henry Moore as a colleague, he taught at the Chelsea School of Art. His first exhibition of paintings was held in London in 1938. During World War II he was an official war artist and depicted the rubble and wrenched metal of bombed streets. His "Crucifixion" (1946) for St. Matthew's Church in Northampton exemplified his "thorn" pictures. The immense tapestry of "Christ in Glory" woven to his design was hung behind the altar of the new cathedral at Coventry in 1962. There was hardly an art capital in the world that did not exhibit his work. His masterly portraits of Somerset Maugham, Helena Rubinstein, Lord Beaverbrook, and Sir Winston Churchill (the latter was disliked and destroyed by the Churchill family), remarkable for their character and force, belong broadly to the 1950s. Sutherland was a trustee (1948–54) of the Tate Gallery, London, and the recipient of many honorary distinctions. In 1960 he was awarded the Order of Merit. In 1976 the Graham Sutherland Gallery was opened at Picton Castle, Pembrokeshire.

Sutherland, Dame Lucy Stuart, British historian (b. June 21, 1903, Australia—d. Aug. 20, 1980, Oxford, England), was widely admired as a scholar and as an outstanding educational administrator while principal (1945–71) of Lady Margaret Hall, University of Oxford. Educated at the University of Witwatersrand, South Africa, and at Somerville College, Oxford, she specialized in the study of the City of London, publishing *A London Merchant, 1695–1774* (1933) and *The East India Company in Eighteenth Century Politics* (1952). During World War II she was assistant secretary at the Board of Trade and subsequently exercised her administrative skills as principal of Lady Margaret Hall and as chairman of many committees and government commissions. She was made CBE in 1947, a fellow of the British Academy in 1954, and DBE in 1969. She also became the first woman pro-vice-chancellor (1960–69) of the University of Oxford. She edited the second volume of *The Correspondence of Edmund Burke* (1960), published jointly by the universities of Cambridge and Chicago.

Sutton, Willie (William Francis Sutton, Jr.), U.S. crime figure (b. June 30, 1901, Brooklyn, N.Y.—d. Nov. 2, 1980, Spring Hill, Fla.), repeatedly captured headlines as a notorious bank robber and as a cunning prison escape artist. Sutton, who began a life of crime at age nine, robbed his first bank in 1927. Before his final capture in 1952, he had spent 33 years in prison, 4 years on parole, and 6 years in hiding. In 1930 Sutton impersonated a Western Union messenger in a $48,000 bank hold-up. Thereafter he assumed an ingenious array of disguises that included a bank guard, policeman, window washer, a mover, and a striped-pants diplomat and earned the nickname "Willie the Actor." His irresistible compulsion to rob banks was satisfied with the utmost precision and planning, but he never used violence. Sutton studied the duties and schedules of bank personnel, and before the bank was even open for business he had escaped with the booty after greeting each employee at gunpoint. By his own estimate he had netted $2 million from his bank robberies alone. When the authorities finally apprehended him, Sutton was jailed, but he frustrated the law by escaping in 1932 and 1948 from two "escape-proof" cells. In 1952 Sutton was recognized on the New York subway, caught by police, and incarcerated until 1969. After his release Sutton chronicled his feats in *Where the Money Was,* which revealed that he robbed banks simply because he "loved it." Sutton spent the last two years of his life living quietly in Florida with his sister.

Symonette, Sir Roland Theodore, Bahamian politician (b. Dec. 16, 1898, The Current, Eleuthera, Bahama Islands—d. March 13, 1980, Nassau, The Bahamas), as leader of the mainly white United Bahamian Party (UBP) became the first prime minister of The Bahamas in 1964, when internal self-government was introduced. From 1955 to 1964 Symonette had been leader of the government in the House of Assembly. Educated at a day school on Eleuthera Island, Symonette became a shipyard owner and contractor for the construction of roads, wharves, and harbours in The Bahamas. He was one of the "Bay Street Boys," a financier group that opened up The Bahamas to tourism and investment, particularly from the U.S., with gambling casinos as an important adjunct. This policy aroused resentment among the black population, whose Progressive Liberal Party was to form the next government in 1967. Symonette became a member of the House of Assembly in 1935 and of the UBP Executive Council in 1949. He was knighted in 1959 and was leader of the opposition party in the House of Assembly from 1967 until he resigned his parliamentary seat in 1977.

Talmon, Jacob Leib, Israeli historian (b. June 14, 1916, Rypin, Poland—d. June 16, 1980, Jerusalem, Israel), was professor of modern history at the Hebrew University of Jerusalem and a noted moderate in Arab-Israeli relations. His reputation was founded on his work *The Origins of Totalitarian Democracy,* for which he was awarded the Israel Prize for Social Sciences in 1956. He studied in Jerusalem and Paris and at the London School of Economics. A member of the Israel Academy of Sciences and Humanities and one of the nation's most respected scholars, he pleaded for a more open policy toward the Arab world and opposed the establishment of new settlements in the occupied territories. His other publications included *Israel Among the Nations, The Age of Violence,* and *The Unique and the Universal.*

Tatarkiewicz, Wladyslaw, Polish philosopher (b. April 4, 1886, Warsaw, Russian Empire—d. April 3, 1980, Warsaw, Poland), was professor of philosophy principally at the University of Warsaw and the eminent author of *A History of Philosophy* (3 vol., 6th ed. 1968), his most important scholarly work. He also published some 140 other works, including *History of Aesthetics* (3 vol., 1962–67) and a popular series of books on the human condition: *Concentration and Dream, On Happiness,* and *On Perfection.* Tatarkiewicz, who earned a Ph.D. at Marburg University in Germany in 1910, was fluent in seven languages and became a member of the Polish Academy of Sciences in 1956. He also contributed a chapter on "Eighteenth Century Polish Art" for *The Cambridge History of Poland* (1941).

Thomas, William Miles Webster Thomas, BARON, British engineer and industrialist (b. March 2, 1897, Ruabon, Wales—d. Feb. 8, 1980, London, England), was engaged (1924) by W. R. Morris (later Lord Nuffield) as sales promotion adviser at Morris Motors Ltd. By 1940 he was managing director and vice-chairman of the company, which was at the height of its prosperity. He left Morris Motors in 1947 to serve as chairman of the Southern Rhodesia Development Co-ordinating Commission and from 1948 to 1951 was director of the Colonial Development Corporation. From 1949 to 1956 he was chairman of British Overseas Airways Corporation (BOAC), which prospered until three of its pioneer De Havilland Comet jets had serious accidents. After leaving BOAC, Thomas became chairman of Monsanto Chemicals Ltd. (1956–63). He was president (1965–72) and chairman (1965–70) of the National Savings Committee and chairman of Britannia Airways Ltd. Thomas was knighted in 1943 and made a life peer in 1971. His autobiography, *Out on a Wing,* appeared in 1964.

Tito (JOSIP BROZ), Yugoslav statesman (b. May 7 [official birthday, May 25], 1892, Kumrovec, Croatia—d. May 4, 1980, Ljubljana, Yugos.), became head of the Yugoslav state in 1943 and then served (1953–80) as the country's first elected president. Tito was the first head of a Communist state to defy the Soviet Union, insisting on Yugoslavia's right to set its own political course. He also played a leading role in establishing the nonaligned nations movement. Tito was inducted (1913) into the Austro-Hungarian Army and was wounded at the Bukovina front, where he was captured by the Russians in March 1915. In 1918 he joined the Red Army and became a Communist. In 1920 he returned home to what was now a new country, the Kingdom of Serbs, Croats, and Slovenes. He joined the Communist Party there and was sentenced (1928) to five years' imprisonment for subversive activities. After his release Tito worked in Moscow for the Comintern, then went (1936) to Zagreb and to Paris to recruit volunteers to fight for the Republicans in the Spanish Civil War. In 1937, after a long climb in the party hierarchy, he became secretary-general of the Communist Party of Yugoslavia. Shortly before World War II he visited Moscow and in 1940 secretly convened the Yugoslavian Communist fifth party congress, which adhered to a Comintern directive to keep Yugoslavia out of the war between Nazi Germany and the Western democracies.

CAMERA PRESS

In April 1941 Germany, Italy, and Bulgaria invaded and partitioned Yugoslavia. After Germany attacked the U.S.S.R. (June 22), Moscow ordered Tito to begin armed resistance against the German and Italian invaders. As commander in chief of the Partisan units, he began military operations in Serbia and built up a guerrilla organization that numbered 250,000 troops by 1943. Tito grew increasingly independent of Moscow. A rival Yugoslavian underground resistance organization, the Chetniks of Col. Draza Mihajlovic, hoped for a restoration of the kingdom under the exiled Serbian dynasty that had previously governed the country. Tito and Mihajlovic met twice in 1941, but reached no agreement because Tito wanted the Serbian-dominated kingdom transformed into a federal socialist state. Britain initially supported Mihajlovic, but then turned to Tito because his Partisans were fighting the German forces much more effectively than the Chetniks. By 1944, having wrested physical control of large parts of Yugoslavia from the Germans, Tito traveled to Moscow, where he met Stalin for the first time; he later met Churchill in Italy.

Once Tito was installed in Belgrade (Oct. 20, 1944), he started organizing Yugoslavia into a federal state ruled by a totalitarian Communist regime. In the summer of 1948 a Soviet attempt to overthrow him failed, and a historic split between Belgrade and Moscow followed on June 28, when Yugoslavia was expelled from the Cominform. Stalin tried to isolate Yugoslavia by instituting an economic blockade, inciting border incidents, and by threatening the country with military invasion. But by then Tito's government was firmly established with its own people, and Tito was elected president in January 1953. After Stalin's death, the Soviet attitude toward Yugoslavia became more conciliatory. In 1961 Tito was host to the first conference of 25 nonaligned nations, and he was still a leading member of the organization in 1980. A decade before his death, Tito planned for a collective leadership to succeed him.

Tolbert, William Richard, Jr., West African politician (b. May 13, 1913, Bensonville, Liberia—d. April 12, 1980, Monrovia, Liberia), was president of Liberia from 1971 to 1980. When Tolbert came to power he attempted to stamp out the corruption and inefficiency that had grown under his predecessor, Pres. William Tubman, and to reinvigorate the economy. But in time corruption seeped back, and the economic climate of 1980 was against him. The March arrest of opposition leaders who had called for a general strike sparked a coup led by Master Sgt. Samuel Doe (*see* BIOGRAPHIES). Tolbert was shot at once and his older brother Frank was also later executed.

Tolbert served as vice-president for 20 years (1951–71) while Tubman ruled the country. Tolbert was also Liberia's leading Baptist and the president (1965–70) of the Baptist World Alliance. He graduated from Liberia College and entered politics in the early 1940s. In 1943 he was elected to the House of Representatives where Tubman singled him out for the vice-presidency.

Ton Duc Thang, Vietnamese politician (b. Aug. 19, 1888, Long Xuyen Province, French Indochina—d. March 30, 1980, Hanoi, Vietnam), became president of North Vietnam following the death of Ho Chi Minh in 1969 and from 1976 was president of the reunited Socialist Republic of Vietnam. Educated in French schools in Saigon, he was an active anticolonialist before World War I and was forced to escape to France, where he joined the French Navy. He was discharged in 1919 after being involved in a mutiny protesting Western intervention in the Soviet Union. He returned to southern Vietnam in 1920 and joined the Revolutionary League of the Youth of Vietnam, founded in 1925 by Ho Chi Minh. From 1929 to 1945 he was imprisoned for sedition and complicity to murder and after his release rapidly rose to become a leading member of the Vietnamese Communist Party. He was vice-president of North Vietnam from 1960 and, although prevented by age from playing an active role in government, was a highly respected president.

Travers, Ben, British playwright (b. Nov. 12, 1886, London, England—d. Dec. 18, 1980, London), was one of Britain's most successful comic playwrights of the 20th century. Famed for his sequence of Aldwych farces (1925–33), Travers amused audiences with his comedy *The Bed Before Yesterday* in

1975. As a young man working for his father's wholesale grocery business in Malaya, he was deeply influenced by the plays of A. W. Pinero. After World War I he wrote light novels before making his theatrical debut with *The Dipper* (1922). After its success he became the house dramatist for the Aldwych Theatre and worked with farceurs such as Tom Walls, Ralph Lynn, and Robertson Hare. The first of his Aldwych plays was *A Cuckoo in the Nest* (1925), followed by *Rookery Nook* (1926), *Thark* (1927), *Plunder* (1928), *Banana Ridge* (1928), and *A Night Like This* (1930). Travers wrote two volumes of autobiography, *Vale of Laughter* (1957) and *A-Sitting on a Gate* (1978).

Tynan, Kenneth Peacock, British drama critic and director (b. April 2, 1927, Birmingham, England—d. July 26, 1980, Santa Monica, Calif.), applied his devastating wit to the unmasking of pretentiousness and vapidity in the British post-World War II theatre and brought equal enthusiasm to the task of encouraging new forms of drama. As drama critic of *The Observer* (1954–63), he hailed the arrival of the "Angry Young Men," helped open the British stage to the works of continental dramatists like Brecht and Beckett, and laboured to create a climate in which socially committed and experimental drama could flourish. Something of a dandy, he had a brilliant career at Oxford and in 1950 opened his campaign against the superficiality of contemporary drama with a critical survey entitled *He That Plays the King.* For more than a decade he wielded enormous influence, but by the early 1960s, with most of his battles won, he had begun to seek new outlets for his energy and talents. He worked as a script editor for Ealing Films, contributed to *The New Yorker,* and was involved with television. His appointment as literary manager of the National Theatre in 1963 opened new prospects for him, and he played an important part in encouraging experimentation in the company. But the post's official status was restricting, and he had to produce independently Rolf Hochhuth's controversial play *Soldiers* and his own erotic revue, *Oh, Calcutta!,* which he presented in New York in 1969 and in London the following year.

Valli, Romolo, Italian actor (b. Feb. 7, 1925, Reggio nell'Emilia, Italy—d. Feb. 1, 1980, Rome, Italy), appeared in leading stage roles and won many awards for his work in films by such renowned directors as Luchino Visconti, Bernardo Bertolucci, and Vittorio De Sica. Valli was also well known as a theatre manager and founded the Compagnia dei Giovani with his friend Giorgio de Lullo and others in 1954. His first major success came in the early 1950s at the Piccolo Teatro in Milan, and he went on to star in works by classical and modern dramatists. He toured in London and Paris and managed the Festival of Two Worlds in Spoleto (1972–78). His many films included Bertolucci's *1900,* De Sica's *The Garden of the Finzi-Continis,* and Visconti's *Il Gattopardo* and *Death in Venice.* He was appearing in a new play with his company I Giovani del Teatro Elisio when he died in an automobile accident.

Van, Bobby (Robert King), U.S. entertainer (b. Dec. 6, 1930, New York, N.Y.—d. July 31, 1980, Los Angeles, Calif.), sang and danced on Broadway and won a Tony nomination for his portrayal of Billy Early in the 1971 revival of *No, No, Nanette.* Van, who began his career as a bandleader and trumpet player at resorts in the Catskill Mountains, was welcomed on Broadway when he demonstrated his lithe and breezy dance routines. He appeared in such musicals as *On Your Toes, Doctor Jazz,* and *Red, White, and Blue* and later appeared in such motion pictures as *The Affairs of Dobie Gillis, Small Town Girl,* and *Kiss Me Kate.* Van, who sported a perpetual grin, appeared on numerous television variety shows and was the lively host of such television game shows as "The Fun Factory."

Van Vleck, John H(asbrouck), U.S. physicist (b. March 13, 1899, Middletown, Conn.—d. Oct. 27, 1980, Cambridge, Mass.), shared the 1977 Nobel Prize for Physics with Philip W. Anderson and Sir Nevill F. Mott for their independent but closely related contributions to the understanding of the behaviour of electrons in magnetic, noncrystalline solid materials. Van Vleck, who dedicated most of his career to the study of magnetism in the structure of atoms, was informally recognized as "the father of modern magnetism." He published his scholarly *The Theory of Electric and Magnetic Susceptibilities* in 1932, and in 1934 became an associate professor at Harvard University. From 1945 to 1949 he was chairman of Harvard's physics department and from 1951 to 1969 he was Hollis professor of mathematics and natural philosophy, the oldest endowed chair in the U.S. Although the trio's discoveries did not lead directly to practical applications, their research work served as a foundation for such electronic devices as tape recorders, office copying machines, lasers, high-speed computers, and solar energy converters. Van Vleck retired from his chair at Harvard in 1969.

Viktoria Luise, Dowager Duchess of Brunswick and Lüneburg, Princess, member of the German imperial family (b. Sept. 13, 1892, Marmor Palace, near Berlin, Germany—d. Dec. 11, 1980, Braunschweig, West Germany), was the only daughter and last surviving child of Emperor William II (the Kaiser) and a great-granddaughter of Queen Victoria of England. In 1913 Princess Viktoria was married to Ernest Augustus, duke of Brunswick and Lüneburg, the great-grandson of the duke of Cumberland, son of George III of England. The wedding, attended by most of the crowned heads of Europe, took place shortly before the outbreak of World War I. Viktoria wrote three volumes of autobiography; a one-volume English version, *The Kaiser's Daughter,* was published in 1977.

Vysotsky, Vladimir, Soviet actor and poet (b. 1938, U.S.S.R.—d. July 24, 1980, Moscow, U.S.S.R.), was a foremost member of Yury Lyubimov's Taganka Theatre company and an immensely popular folksinger. His ballads, sung to his own guitar accompaniment, reflected the ups and downs of everyday life experienced by ordinary Soviet men and women. Though his songs sometimes carried a note of protest, Vysotsky was not a dissident in the generally accepted sense. After an unsettled youth, he graduated (1964) from the Moscow Art Theatre Drama School and joined the Taganka company when it was formed the following year. He appeared in films and in plays by Brecht, Mayakovsky, Chekhov, and Shakespeare. Vysotsky's third marriage was to the Soviet-born French actress Marina Vlady.

Wagner, Winifred Williams, British-born German cultural figure (b. June 23, 1897, Hastings, England—d. March 5, 1980, Überlingen, West Germany), directed the Bayreuth Festival of Wagner's operatic works from 1930 to 1944 and gained notoriety for her friendship with Adolf Hitler. As a child, Winifred Williams was adopted by the musician Charles Klindworth and educated in Berlin. There she met and married Richard Wagner's son, Siegfried, and when both he and his mother, Cosima, died in 1930, she took over the Wagner festival, which was in progress at the time. Some years earlier she had met Hitler and developed a close friendship with him; she supported the Nazi regime and in a 1975 television interview reaffirmed her admiration for its leader. She did, however, use her influence to protect Jewish musicians and singers, though actively supporting the association of Wagner's name with nationalistic and anti-Semitic attitudes. After World War II she was tried and given a suspended jail sentence and was fined. When the Bayreuth Festival was revived in 1951, it was on the condition that she should not be associated with it. Her sons Wieland and Wolfgang successively took over direction of the festival and maintained the ban imposed on their mother.

Wallenberg, Jacob, Swedish banker and financier (b. Sept. 27, 1892, Stockholm, Sweden—d. Aug. 2, 1980, Stockholm), was the patriarch of a financial dynasty that had large holdings in some of Sweden's most important industrial concerns, including Saab-Scania, Asea, LM Ericsson, Atlas Copco, and Swedish Match. The source of the Wallenbergs' power was the family bank, Stockholm Enskilda Bank. But following a merger in 1971 they no longer had full control over the newly established Skandinaviska Enskilda Banken. During World War II Wallenberg arranged trade deals with Germany on behalf of the Swedish government and after the war he took part in financial negotiations with other Scandinavian countries and Britain.

Walsh, Raoul, U.S. actor and film director (b. March 11, 1892, New York, N.Y.—d. Dec. 31, 1980, Hollywood, Calif.), played John Wilkes Booth in *Birth of a Nation* (1915) and starred as the Mexican revolutionary Pancho Villa in *The Life of Villa* before mastering the technical art of filmmaking under D. W. Griffith. After directing *The Regeneration* (1916), Walsh made over 100 films, including the silent classics *What Price Glory?, Sadie Thompson,* and *The Thief of Bagdad* and such sound films as *Klondike Annie, High Sierra, They Died with Their Boots On, Manpower, Gentleman Jim, White Heat, The Naked and the Dead,* and his last, *A Distant Trumpet* (1964). His best films were fast-paced action and adventure stories, set in the old West, the gangster underworld, or in war. He also directed many historical adventures. A 1929 eye injury that required Walsh to wear a distinctive patch over his right eye ended his acting career. In his later years he was totally blind.

Walsh, Stella (Stanislawa Walasiewicz), Polish-born track star (b. April 3, 1911, Wierzchownia—d. Dec. 4, 1980, Cleveland, Ohio), competed for her native Poland in two Olympics, setting a world record of 11.9 sec in 1932 when she won a gold medal in the 100-m dash; four years later she earned a silver medal competing in the same event. During her 40-year track career Walsh captured some 40 U.S. championships. In 1930 she became the first woman to run the 100-yd dash in less than 11 sec. Walsh was fatally shot outside a discount store, where she was shopping for streamers to welcome the Olympic women's basketball team from Poland.

Ward of North Tyneside, Irene Mary Bewick Ward, Baroness, British politician (b. Feb. 23, 1895, London, England—d. April 26, 1980, London), was an occasionally rebellious Conservative member of the British Parliament for 38 years and the longest serving woman member of the House of Commons in history. During her tenure, Ward was the fearless champion of old-age pensioners and the nursing services and upheld the interests of the shipbuilding and fishing industries in northeast England. She entered the House of Commons in 1931 as member for Wallsend-on-Tyne but was defeated in 1945. She returned in 1950 for Tynemouth, which she represented until her elevation to the House of Lords in 1974. Ward was made a Dame of the British Empire in 1955 and a Companion of Honour in 1973. In the 1930s she was in Britain's delegation to the League of Nations, and during World War II served the Ministry of Labour. After the war she secured the passage of bills in Parliament to improve the lot of old people in institutions and demanded better pay and conditions for nurses and midwives.

Wendel, Heinrich, West German theatrical designer (b. March 9, 1915, Bremen, Germany—d. May 1980, Düsseldorf, West Germany), pioneered new techniques in stage design with the Wuppertal theatre company from 1953 to 1964 and then with the Deutsche Oper am Rhein, Düsseldorf. He trained in Bremen, Berlin, and Hamburg and during World War II worked for theatres in Wuppertal and Nürnberg before being appointed (1945) head of design in the Württemberg state theatres. A versatile designer, he brought an original approach to work in drama, ballet, and opera. He made particularly novel use of photography and projection in his designs for the 1965 production of Monteverdi's *L'Incoronazione di Poppea,* the 1968 production of Schoenberg's *Moses und Aron,* and the 1971 production of Zimmermann's *The Soldiers.* Wendel's influence on German opera and ballet was at its height during his period in Wuppertal; his work at numerous foreign festivals ensured his international reputation.

West, Mae, U.S. actress (b. Aug. 17, 1893, Brooklyn, N.Y.—d. Nov. 22, 1980, Los Angeles, Calif.), was a blond bombshell who reigned for nearly 50 years as a Hollywood sex goddess with her sultry glances, sauntering strut, and throaty salutations generously laced with racy double entendres. Her legendary hourglass figure was bedecked with skintight gowns and draped with diamonds. In her heyday during the 1930s and '40s, West both shocked and delighted audiences with such comical one-liners as "I'm not good and tired, just tired"; "It's better to be looked over than over-looked"; and "Between two evils I always pick the one I never tried before." Her natural affinity for comedy made her a sensation on the Broadway stage; she first appeared (1911) in *Á la Broadway and Hello, Paris* to rave reviews and then starred with Al Jolson in *Vera Violetta.* After *A Winsome Widow,* West returned to vaudeville and became accustomed to spicing up her prepared scripts. Censors protested when she introduced the outrageous shimmy dance on Broadway. When she turned her hand to playwriting, she again raised their ire with *Sex* (for which she was arrested, fined $500, and sentenced to ten days in prison), *The Pleasure Man* (raided after the first performance and closed after the second), and *The Constant Sinner* (stopped by police in Washington but permitted to play to packed houses in New York for over a year). Her most famous role, though, was as "Diamond Lil," a bad girl with a good heart. Following her first motion picture, *Night After Night* (1932) with George Raft, West appeared again as Diamond Lil in *She Done Him Wrong* (1933) with Cary Grant. Her other films included *I'm No Angel, Go West Young Man, My Little Chickadee* (with W. C. Fields), and *The Heat's On.* Besides recording three albums, *The Fabulous Mae West, Way Out West,* and *Wild Christmas,* West wrote the autobiographical *Goodness Had Nothing to Do With It.* In 1970 she made a cameo appearance in *Myra Breckinridge* and in 1977 her final film, *Sextette,* was released. Britain's Royal Air Force contributed to West's immortality by naming an inflatable life jacket after her.

White, Antonia, British writer (b. March 31, 1899, London, England—d. April 10, 1980, Daneshill, Sussex, England), made her mark with her first novel, *Frost in May* (1933), a study of a girl at a convent school. White drafted the book when she was 15 and published it after she had lost the Roman Catholic faith she was to recover later in life. Her lifetime output of fiction, small but distinguished, was deeply rooted in personal experience. After her schooling at the Convent of the Sacred Heart in Roehampton, St. Paul's Girls' School in London, and the Academy of Dramatic Arts, she was involved in advertising and journalism. White became a newspaper fashion editor (1934–39) and during World War II worked for the BBC (1940–43) and for the Political Intelligence Department of the Foreign Office (1943–45). She then resumed creative writing with *The Lost Traveller* (1950), *The Sugar House* (1952), and *Beyond the Glass* (1954). White also became a prolific translator of French, winning the Denyse Clairouin Prize in 1950. Her more than 30 translations include major works by Guy de Maupassant, Colette, and Voltaire. In 1965 she published *The Hound and the Falcon,* an exchange of letters with a fellow Catholic seeking his way back to the faith, that recounts her own return to Catholicism.

Wilder, Alec (ALEXANDER LAFAYETTE CHEW WILDER), U.S. composer (b. Feb. 16, 1907, Rochester, N.Y.—d. Dec. 24, 1980, Gainesville, Fla.), had an eclectic musical career as the composer of popular music during the 1930s and '40s; a blend of popular and classical music during the 1940s; and chamber music during the 1950s. Although Wilder produced hundreds of popular songs, his most memorable compositions were for Frank Sinatra and Bing Crosby, including "I'll Be Around," "It's So Peaceful in the Country," and "While We're Young." His conviction that "the best of popular music is really great melody writing" was explored in his 1972 book *American Popular Song* (with James T. Maher), but his uniqueness was downgraded by critics who regarded his music as "frivolous."

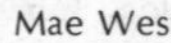

Mae West

RAY JONES—UNIVERSAL PICTURES

Wilhelmina (WILHELMINA BEHMENBURG COOPER), Dutch-born fashion model and businesswoman (b. 1940?, The Netherlands—d. March 1, 1980, Greenwich, Conn.), epitomized the haute monde look of the 1950s and 1960s with her stunning 5-ft 11-in matchstick figure, large brown eyes, high hollow cheekbones, and stacked brown hair. Wilhelmina, who graced nearly 300 covers of major U.S. and European magazines, was featured on the cover of *Vogue* a record 28 times. In 1967, at the height of her career as one of the nation's most photographed beauties, she opened her own modeling agency. Wilhelmina Models Inc. in early 1980 reportedly rivaled in size and billings Eileen and Jerry Ford's modeling agency. Wilhelmina was particularly pleased when her photo appeared on the cover of *Fortune* magazine's Dec. 3, 1979, issue; she had become one of the few women ever to appear on the cover alone. After a short illness, she succumbed to lung cancer.

Yahya Khan, Agha Mohammad, Pakistani politician (b. Feb. 4, 1917, Chakwal, India—d. Aug. 9, 1980, Rawalpindi, Pakistan), was a professional soldier who became commander in chief of the Pakistani armed forces in 1966 and served as president of Pakistan from 1969 to 1971. As head of the armed forces, Yahya Khan succeeded Pres. Mohammad Ayub Khan when the latter resigned his office in March 1969. In 1971 a serious conflict erupted between the central government and the Awami Party of East Pakistan, led by Sheikh Mujibur Rahman. The East Pakistani leader demanded autonomy for his half of the geographically divided nation, and Yahya Khan responded by ordering the Army to suppress the Awami Party. The brutality with which his orders were carried out, and the resulting influx of millions of East Pakistani refugees into India, led to the Indian invasion of East Pakistan and the rout of its West Pakistani occupiers. East Pakistan became the independent state of Bangladesh, and with its loss Yahya Khan resigned (Dec. 20, 1971). After five years under house arrest, he was released and lived quietly out of the public eye.

Yalin-Mor, Nathan (NATHAN FRIEDMAN-YELLIN), Israeli journalist and political figure (b. June 28, 1913, Grodno, Russia—d. Feb. 18, 1980, Tel Aviv, Israel), was one of the three leaders who succeeded Abraham Stern at the head of the terrorist Stern Group during the period of the British mandate in Palestine. The group was responsible for attacks on British forces. Shortly before Israel achieved full independence, Yalin-Mor was arrested and charged with the murder (1948) of UN mediator Count Folke Bernadotte. Although Yalin-Mor was acquitted of murder, he was convicted of engaging in underground activities and sentenced to eight years' imprisonment. However, he was released from jail under an amnesty and served a term in the Israeli Knesset (parliament). Switching political orientation, he became a member of left-wing organizations, advocating a conciliatory line in Arab–Israeli relations. Yalin-Mor took a pro-Soviet stance on several international issues.

Zepler, Eric Ernest, German-born physicist (b. Jan. 27, 1898, Westphalia, Germany—d. May 13, 1980, Southampton, England), made notable advances in the theory of radio design and was a pioneer of electronics education. During World War II radios built from his designs were used by both the German and British air forces. Zepler studied in Berlin, Bonn, and Würzburg, then went to work for Telefunken in 1925. Ten years later he fled Nazi Germany and joined the Marconi company in England. There he began the analytical work that resulted in his 1943 book, *The Technique of Radio Design,* for many years the standard textbook on the subject. In 1949 the first chair of electronics in Britain was created for him at the University of Southampton, where he instituted the diploma in electronics that, with his other educational work, helped establish electronics as a separate discipline. In 1963 he moved into the field of acoustics, conducting research on hearing and the detection of sound. Zepler was an international chess master and published several books on the game.

THE GLOBAL VIEWS OF PRESIDENT SADAT

by Anwar as-Sadat

ROBERT AZZI—MAGNUM

Since the time I was very young, my great interest was in politics. Even as a boy in secondary school in Cairo and on vacation at home, in my own village of Mit Abul-Kum, in the heart of the Nile Delta, I started reading newspapers and books on current affairs and recording what I read. In fact, my hobby was politics. At that time Mussolini was in Italy. I saw his pictures and read about how he would change his facial expressions when he made public addresses, variously taking a pose of strength, or aggression, so that people might look at him and read power and strength in his very features. I was fascinated by this. I stood before the mirror at home and tried to imitate this commanding expression, but for me the results were very disappointing. All that happened was that the muscles of my face got very tired. It hurt.

Later on, I was reading Machiavelli. I suppose everyone who has any interest in politics has read him and what he says about the art of political maneuvering. It is a classic source of teaching for diplomats and statesmen. Of course, I was fascinated by parts of this book. But when I thought of putting his teaching into practice, I felt that I would only be cheating myself. I felt awkward inside, just the way my face had hurt when I tried to project the soul of the "new Roman Empire" by imitating Mussolini's gestures.

Politics is only one aspect of life. It is just like everything else we do. For the politician, as with the lawyer, the doctor, or the farmer, there are certain ethics which must be upheld, ethics which impose limits on any efforts to make a success or to have influence in this life. To have any real influence one must be true to his inner self—at work, at home, at school, or in the Ministry of Foreign Affairs. When I reach peace with myself, I find that I am strongest. But at those moments when I have not found this inner peace, I am very weak. At those times I try to avoid doing anything until this sense of inner peace returns.

I first felt that inner peace in my village of Mit Abul-Kum, where I still have my living roots, deep in the soil of that Nile community. But I really found this peace in Cell 54, a bare damp room in Cairo Central Prison, where I spent 18 months for revolutionary activity. I was in solitary, where I could not read or write or listen to the radio. Suffering builds up a human being and gives him self-knowledge. It made me know God and his love. Thus I learned in Cell 54 to value that inner success which helps a man to be true to himself.

Democracy is not merely laws and provisions; it is a mode of daily life. Democracy is essentially a matter of ethics, and in a democracy we must stand ready for a daily test of ethics. When we call now for measures to ensure ethical democratic practice, this is not a cunning device to impose ties and restrictions or a relinquishing of democracy. Rather our call comes from a profound and sincere belief that a free society bears the responsibility of protecting itself. I will fight for democracy and ethics whatever position I hold, so that on the day ordained by God I can give an account of my performance with an easy conscience, at peace with myself.

I have often said that the new Egypt, indeed any country, should be a state founded on faith and science. I did not intend this as a slogan whose glitter would attract the masses but as a genuine appeal linked to the roots of democracy and freedom. Science is the emancipation of the human mind to accomplish good and achieve progress for the sake of man, free of bonds and chains. Faith is a commitment to principles, values, and ethics upheld by religions which before and after the advent of divine religions have unceasingly toiled to liberate human dignity.

Religion was never a bond. God in his glory favoured man by enabling him to think, released his capacities and created him in his own image. The U.S. Declaration of Independence, which followed the British Bill of Rights, states that the natural rights of man bestowed on him by God are the rights to life, to freedom, and to the pursuit of happiness. Hence, freedom is a natural right, but its practice depends on the consent and agreement of the community. Otherwise chaos prevails.

Let me illustrate this point about faith. I have been asked about it many times. I remember a reporter in London in 1975, who questioned most intently on this. Go back for a moment to 1972 and the early part of 1973, when everyone in the world thought that the Arabs were of low significance, either militarily or politically or in any other way. The fabulous victory of Israel in 1967 and the dimensions of the Arab defeat had confirmed that impression. At that time in Egypt I was planning the October war against Israel. I had turned to war only after my peace initiative had failed. That was in February 1971, when I offered to conclude a peace treaty with Israel. After that there was no alternative to war. Sometimes one has to swallow a bitter pill so that he may regain his health. After my 1971 initiative failed, it was clear to me that Egypt was a hopeless case unless we proved that we were fit to live, that we could fight, that we were not a dead body.

In October 1973 Henry Kissinger was in the State Department [as U.S. secretary of state]. Henry told me later that he had called Abba Eban, the foreign minister of Israel, who was roving about the United States collecting money. Kissinger at that time was the diplomatic star of the whole world. He had real-

A Visit with President Sadat

by Frank Gibney

At 62, Anwar as-Sadat is a rare phenomenon among late 20th-century statesmen: a man who knows his own mind, keeps his own counsel, and acts on his own hunches. He is also one of the world's few remaining political leaders to whom that much abused word "charisma" might be justly applied. It did not always seem so. Like Harry Truman, Konrad Adenauer, and a few celebrated others, Sadat was a late bloomer, politically speaking. For almost two decades he played a courteous second fiddle to his old friend Gamal Abdel Nasser. In the end Sadat was the only member of the original revolutionary officers' group not to be purged by Egypt's moody dictator. As a result, since the Egyptian revolution of 1952, Sadat has been able to observe the workings of Egypt's government and its problems from a variety of vantage points: as Cabinet minister, secretary-general of the Islamic Conference, speaker of the National Assembly, editor of the government newspaper *al-Gomhouria*, and, finally, as vice-president.

A Revolutionary Presidency. When Sadat succeeded to Egypt's presidency in 1970, few people would have taken bets on his political longevity. Egypt was still suffering in every way from the disastrous defeat by Israel in 1967. The economy was in ruins. A power struggle for the ultimate succession was going on among Nasser's other old subordinates, several of them agents of the Soviet Union. But Sadat acted with surprising swiftness. On the one hand he removed political troublemakers from office. On the other he repealed the repressive edicts of the Nasser era, which had kept Egyptians in a state of fear and economic stagnation. In 1972, to the world's surprise, he denounced the one-sided treaty of alliance with the U.S.S.R. and in one week sent 17,000 Soviet military and political advisers packing.

Equally surprising was Sadat's sudden "October war" against Israel in 1973, which, as noted in his autobiography, *In Search of Identity*, he contends was, paradoxically, a necessary prelude to any kind of lasting peace in the Middle East. After the ensuing cease-fire, when later peace measures seemed to be faltering, he startled everyone again, his own people included, by his unprecedented visit to Jerusalem in 1977, when he addressed Israel's Knesset in a personal effort to break the deadlock in negotiations. U.S. Pres. Jimmy Carter's Camp David accords between Egypt and Israel were the outgrowth of Sadat's initiative.

There are still many problems involved with consummating the peace between Egypt and Israel, and Egypt's fellow Arab nations continue their formal boycott as an indication of their displeasure with Sadat. At home, however, his popularity continued. He received a striking vote of confidence in the 1979 elections. Although Egypt's staggering economic problems are by no means solved, new oil revenues and advances in both the agricultural and industrial sectors have for several years given the nation a healthy growth rate of 7 to 9%. An "open door" policy encourages foreign investment in the country, and an economy which under Nasser had approached Soviet state-controlled totalitarianism is moving quickly in the direction of free enterprise and association with the West.

The author of these changes is a tireless propagandist for them—constantly explaining, exhorting, and admonishing as he makes his unending round of parliamentary meetings and talks with foreign leaders and prays at the mosques of Egypt's countryside. He is able to do so much because of intense self-discipline and the bulwark of a very private, family-centred life. He and his wife Jehan, a strikingly handsome woman with a magnetic presence of her own, live simply (but well) either at one of their houses outside of Cairo or, in the summer, at their beach villa at al-Mansurah outside of Alexandria. They spend a great deal of time with children and grandchildren. Sadat exercises regularly by walking at least one hour a day. Almost every evening he looks at one film: his only recreation. He spends a great deal of time by himself, thinking and planning.

A visit to Sadat is a memorable experience. There is a magnetism about him that communicates itself in the confines of a drawing room as surely as it does in his constant public appearances, where his power as an orator plays no small part in his success. He received me in the rambling, comfortable house at the Qanater, some ten miles up the Nile River from Cairo.

As always impeccably tailored, with a dark blue suit and a large Windsor knot in his tie, he was missing only the pipe that he smokes almost continually. That was because on Thursdays, the day we met, he fasts—abstaining from food and tobacco from dawn to sunset, in the Muslim tradition.

Sadat is gifted with an innate sense of theatre. In a sense almost every conversation is a performance. His English is at once expressive and explicit. He often impatiently searches for words in the middle of a sentence. He is a learner, as well read in Western history and literature as in his own. His talk is peppered with references ranging from the Magna Carta to Franklin D. Roosevelt, and he entertains German visitors with quotations from *Faust*. (He learned German in a Cairo prison.) He is an enthusiast with a sense of history.

Sadat's own confidence of success comes from his conviction that he has at last made Egypt a government of institutions. He has certainly done much in that direction. Only time will tell whether the machinery of government that Sadat has rebuilt can govern on its own, without dependence on the transitory charisma of a single leader.

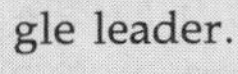

Frank Gibney, Vice-Chairman of the Britannica Board of Editors, was the founding president of TBS-Britannica, Tokyo ized détente between the two superpowers, he had made the first of his mysterious voyages to China. Now he wanted to do something in the Middle East. So he called Eban and said, "Why don't you be generous? You are the victorious side. Why don't you take some initiatives on your side to get peace?" That was on Thursday, the fourth of October.

Eban answered him: "Why don't you recognize the fact that you know nothing about the Arabs. We know everything about the Arabs. Ours is the only way to teach them and deal with them—let me tell you that. Why should we make peace now, when the Arabs will not be important for 50 years."

Forty-eight hours later the war started. When Kissinger woke Nixon to tell him, they both believed that the Israelis would crush our bones. Most of the world believed it. Most of the Arabs believed it. Of course the Israelis believed it. So when they telephoned Kissinger after war broke out, they told him: "It's only a matter of 48 hours." Two days later they talked to Kissinger again and told him: "Give us another 48 hours. We need time because it was Yom Kippur and we didn't completely mobilize, but we don't need any armaments or munitions."

Another 48 hours passed. Then it was Moshe Dayan who called Kissinger on the telephone. He said, "S.O.S. Please, Mr. Kissinger, send us 400 tanks." Kissinger called Golda Meir to confirm this and she said, "Yes, it was a decision by the Cabinet."

Remember that scenario. They had lost 400 tanks on the Egyptian front and one-third of their Air Force. And do you know what Kissinger told me he said? "Mrs. Meir," he told her, "we shall send you the 400 tanks. But whatever happens after that, you have lost the war. Be prepared for that." And this was at a time when everyone in the world was convinced that any Arab force starting a war would be crushed. I answer by recalling the reporter's question in London about faith and science. For my actions in 1973 came from a conviction given me by faith. I knew at the beginning what the computers would tell me, if I relied on science only. If I were to feed the computers with the information on the balance of power between us, the characteristics of the Israeli armament and the characteristics of our armament, the computer would tell me: "Don't even think of starting any action against Israel or you will be crushed." I knew that, but I took my decision because I had faith in our course of action. The computer alone would have advised me either to stalemate or commit suicide. But I knew both the limits and the possibilities of what God gives us in our life. So I took this action. I took it out of my inner conviction that it was the only thing to do. And before taking this course I discussed it with all our commanders—not just the chief of staff but all of them, including many low-ranking officers, so they would know what was to happen. For we had a problem there. Not only did the lower commanders not know what was about to happen, but they all had a complex about the Israelis, rather like the complex about Vietnam in America. And this complex I had to attack.

The October war of 1973 was for us in Egypt a historic transformation—from despair to hope, from complete lack of self-confidence to the regaining of that confidence. After the cease-fire we initiated an ambitious program of building and reconstruction despite the economic crises which beset us. Our economy at that time was below zero because of the burdens and responsibilities of constant military preparation. Despite these obstacles we succeeded in restoring our economic path from total isolation to an open-door policy.

And since that time we have worked wholeheartedly for peace. My peace initiative when I visited Jerusalem in 1977 was not a television show or an offer of surrender, as some adolescents in the Arab world alleged. It was a unique and historic event that challenged in one confident plunge a fearful block of spite, bitterness, and bad feelings which had piled up and multiplied over a period of 30 years. Let that October war be the last of the wars.

Without that initiative the Camp David summit would never have materialized. And without the persistence and wisdom of President Carter we would never have found a path leading to a real and lasting peace.

Yet other Arabs came out with statements saying: "Alas, the Camp David agreements have not restored Jerusalem to us nor have they established a Palestinian state." They attacked the agreements and tried to boycott us.

To them I say: Should not the people concerned sit down to talk at issue with someone, do you just let it go—or do you sit down and discuss it with the side concerned? Regrettably many of our Arab brothers can never face up to responsibility. They weep over Arab solidarity, but Moscow Radio draws up their slogans for them. Their uncompromising position is a splendid thing for Israel's hawks.

Ninety percent of the Israeli people are for peace. I told the Israeli people when I visited there that the exercise by the Palestinians of their right to self-determination poses no threat to Israel or its security. Indeed it is the only sure way to peaceful and harmonious coexistence. By contrast, the policy of building Israeli settlements in Arab-occupied territories is a serious obstacle to peace. It is unfounded, ill-conceived, and illegal. In the Egyptian-Israeli peace treaty we set a model for security arrangements that protect the legitimate interests of all par-

RICHARD MELLOUL—SYGMA

ties concerned. Such measures are applicable to other fronts as well.

Here, in fact, was a radical difference between Menachem Begin [prime minister of Israel] and myself. Begin believed that signing a peace agreement concluded the whole affair. I replied that this was only the premise of the arduous stage of entrenching and assuring peace.

We do not accept Israeli sovereignty over Arab Jerusalem. When I spoke to the Knesset in the heart of Israel in 1977, I said that Arab Jerusalem must become Arab again. Eight hundred million Muslims do not accept Israeli sovereignty over Arab Jerusalem. This is a fact. Yet to those dwarfs who criticize us in Arab countries, I say again: I will continue to sit down with the Israelis and talk to these issues and work to reduce our disagreements, in the interests of peace.

There are those, like the insane Khomeini in Iran, who want to say that Islam is opposed to peace. Is Islam against peace, when the very greetings exchanged among Muslims are those of peace? God Almighty is Faith and omnipotent Peace. Life hereafter is peace. Believers should choose peace. This is Islam. This is the faith of our Egyptian people.

Let us review the recent history of Egypt by decades. The '50s was our time of glorious victory. We had our July 23 Revolution in 1952. We nationalized the Suez Canal. We became a nonaligned power. We witnessed the Iraqi revolution and the fall of the Baghdad Pact, despite its support by America, Britain, and the West. We thought our victory complete.

Yet the '60s became our time of defeat. We had to cope with the effects of the Israeli victory of 1967. And in our economy with crass stupidity we had copied the Soviet Union's pattern of socialism. Our socialism was coloured with Marxism. Where free enterprise was regarded as "odious capitalism," naturally individual effort came to a standstill. This resulted in the passivity of the people from which we still suffer.

The '70s marked the end of our suffering. In 1975 we reopened the Suez Canal. We began to develop the oil of Sinai and the Red Sea—without this source of energy our country would have gone bankrupt. We could see the end of our suffering, but we had to work to create the conditions for the '80s. Now in the '80s we shall reap the fruits of our suffering and our hard work. We are just starting to do this.

In this decade of the '80s, 80% of Sinai will have been returned to us. It is rich in minerals. We have the new oil that has been discovered. In 1975 we still imported oil. We are now exporters rather than importers. We now have an income of $2 billion a year from our oil sales; by 1985 we hope this figure will be $12 billion. This year, 1981, I shall be opening the Suez Canal for the third time. The first was the original opening by the khedive Ismail in 1869. Then I reopened it in 1975 after it had been closed for eight years. Now we have the third opening. It is a completely new canal. We worked silently for five years, widening and deepening that canal. I have already opened the tunnel under the canal to Sinai after six years of work. This project is a masterpiece, one of the wonders of the world.

We live most of us in this narrow Nile Valley, occupying only 4% of Egypt's total land area. We have lived on this narrow 4% when we were a population of 17 million, then 20 million, then 30 million, now 42 million. There is rich soil elsewhere in Egypt, and we are reclaiming it, notably in the New Valley. Let us be grateful to God for the potential provided us. Yet we are truly racing against time.

The public sector, the state, cannot do this alone. We need modern agricultural companies using modern technology. But according to past concepts of socialism in this country, the land had to be parceled into state farms. God be praised, this era is over. In the past debates were held over whether owning five lorries [trucks] would amount to capitalism, with the result that no one bought any. In the past, when the government was expected to meet every need, people's attitudes were negative. That belongs to a dead era of impoverishing socialism. Now we have an open-door policy for our economy —and democratic socialism.

Yet we all must continue to face the problems of foreign intervention. The Soviet invasion of Afghanistan was not unexpected. I had been cautioning against such developments all along. For throughout the '70s you Americans really suffered from your Vietnam complex. It was this which gave the Soviets their freedom of action. In Africa and the Middle East they have built three belts of security for themselves. They built them right under your nose. You gave them the opportunities. The first belt stretches from Angola to Mozambique. The second belt runs from Afghanistan through the anarchy of Iran, then South Yemen, Ethiopia, and finally Libya. The third belt is now under construction. Libya and Syria are starting a union together. The Soviet Union has already signed a treaty with Syria. This would be automatic in the case of Libya. Look at the map. These three belts are clearly seen. They threaten us. We are a small country. But if the Soviets try to consolidate these belts, I shall fight.

If you in America do not again take up your responsibilities, as the first superpower of the world and the one which supports peace, all of us are doomed. We shall see the Soviet Union in the Persian Gulf as well as in the Mediterranean. We shall see them putting their puppets everywhere. And we know what it means to be a puppet of the Soviet Union. They foreclose people's dreams. They cancel out all logic. For they themselves are robots. It is only the heads of the party who can act. They do everything.

In the "people's democracies" there is no orderly transfer of power. There are only coups. See how Stalin came after Lenin. Then there was Malenkov for only a few months—and where is he now? Khrushchev came and ousted him. Then Brezhnev took over. But he will be ousted in the same way.

Yet we still have the upper hand. The forces of peace can win. Despite all these puppets, all these countries that depend on the Soviets, they are despised and hated. They are despised and hated in the Arab world because they do not have the support of the people. I have dealt with the Soviet Union for a long time. I know that if you check them, they will pull back. In 1972 I abrogated Egypt's treaty with the Soviet Union, because they violated it. We had 17,000 of them here in Egypt, but in 1972 in one week I ordered them out.

For three years I have told the Americans this. I have said to the United States and the Western European nations that I will give them facilities to defend their position in the Persian Gulf. For the collapse of the oil facilities there could mean the collapse of Western civilization. Without this oil the factories will stop. Look at all your tanks in NATO. Without oil they are scarecrows. But we are ready to give the United States every facility to reach the Gulf states, to protect their interests.

When I was in Washington, someone in your Congress asked how much money it would cost to build a base on the Red Sea. He asked if I wanted an American base there and I said we would not. Why should we have *your* bases there? It could bring on hate for you and for me. If Johnson or Dulles had asked me this question, I would have told them, "Go to hell." Your use of *our* facilities, however, is different. This we give you on a basis of partnership —air, naval, and military facilities. But America should drop the Dulles mentality for the '70s and the '50s and cease thinking of "bases."

Of course to share our facilities with you and to cooperate in other economic matters is not only in your interest. It is in our interest. To whom will we send our oil, if not the West? Who will give us the know-how to rebuild our countries? Who will in the end share with us the nuclear energy to replace oil, if Western civilization collapses?

The Soviet Union will not give us these things. I worked with the Soviets for almost 20 years. They may have the technology to build airplanes and reach the Moon, but they have no technology for the consumer. They have new technology in the military field only. It is not deep-rooted. We have had Soviet factories here. We have now hundreds of Soviet factories which were built for us by the Soviet Union and quickly became out of date, because the Soviets have no technology at all, apart from the military.

In the '80s there must be a new peaceful order in the world. And I have a hunch that we in Egypt can participate in it. To protect this order the United

States must accept its responsibilities. You Americans did not ask me for facilities to reach the hostages in Iran. But one day I came and said that I was ready to give the United States such facilities. I remain ready to offer any facilities that will help you reach the Gulf states. For the face of the United States has changed for us from that of the policeman, who represented imperialism and colonialism, to that of the peacemaker.

We should have a new order in the international economy. As I told Henry Kissinger, long before the prices of oil rose so high, why don't we call the producers and the consumers of oil together. Let us sit down together and agree upon what we need to build up our countries. Let us regulate oil prices and also commodity and food prices. To whom can the oil-producing countries send their oil? Who will give them the know-how they need, if the West collapses?

If it is God's will, I hope I may help make this contribution. Let us agree, producers and consumers on a certain level, on certain ratios, we can become one family. Because all of us need each other.

That is the dream I have for the '80s. Let us hope the day will come when I can tell the whole world about my idea. Let us hope for the time when, instead of having confrontation, we have *complementations*.

When I first came to power in 1970, I had to stand by myself. Our people had been taught unfortunately to be totally dependent on their leader. This was indeed their custom. When they become confident of their leader, they give him freedom of action to the extent that they ultimately become totally dependent on him. That was the situation after Nasser's death.

Gamel Abdel Nasser and I had been friends since we were 19. We were young cadets and officers together. When I was sent to jail for the first time in 1942, he took charge of the Free Officers group which I had started. I was in jail for six years. I was released in time to take part in our July 23rd Revolution in 1952. It was I who gave the ultimatum to the king in Alexandria, asking him to leave. When this revolution actually took place, the dream I had had since my childhood was realized.

We had three foes to fight against in our revolution: the king, foreign colonialism, and our own irresponsible party system, which had become dissolute and hopelessly corrupt. Four years later, in 1956, the British evacuated this country and at last ended the shameful era when the secretary for oriental affairs at their embassy in Cairo was the real ruler of Egypt, fawned upon by the pashas and the party leaders.

Yet for all our successes in achieving independence, the revolution failed to establish sound democratic practice. A one-party system was set up, which turned into a totalitarian regime under the name of socialism. Nasser regarded everyone with suspicion. Anxiety gnawed continually at his heart. It was only natural, therefore, that he bequeathed a legacy of suspicion to his colleagues and to everybody. The hate that prevailed in Egypt for 18 years before I assumed the presidency was a destructive force. We still suffer from its consequences.

KARL SCHUMACHER—THE WHITE HOUSE

Israeli Prime Minister Menachem Begin (left) and Egyptian Pres. Anwar as-Sadat shared pleasantries before resuming their discussions on peace at Camp David, Maryland.

But Nasser was my friend. I never quarreled with him but stood by him alike in victory and defeat. In the months before he died, we spent many hours together in his home and at my house near the Pyramids. "Anwar," he told me, "look to the succession of power." At that time we had just seen two surprise changes in international politics. Prime Minister [Edward] Heath in England had called an election suddenly and, to his surprise, lost. In Lebanon, according to the constitution left them by the French, they had had another election and Suleiman Franjieh won it by one vote—he was one of the bad ones. We made comparisons with Egypt. I joked with Nasser. "Gamal," I said, "what will your successor do—this poor man who will have to succeed you. What will he do in place of this giant?"

We both laughed. I was not even considered. For I had already had two heart attacks. It was clear that I would not succeed him and, indeed, would probably die before him.

Events turned out otherwise, and I did succeed him. But if we had not been close friends and not spent so much time together that last year, I would have missed many details. In particular there was our relationship with the Soviet Union. The Soviets would have denied facts or asserted things that never happened between them and Nasser. But I knew everything.

Politically and economically Nasser had left me a pitiable legacy. We had no real relations with any country except the Soviet Union. Many of our own people in the political leadership were Soviet agents. Economically we were almost bankrupt thanks to the Yemeni expedition, the Israeli defeat of 1967, and the Marxist application of socialism. We had had socialist slogans in place of social democracy. Two months after I came to power, I abolished the state sequestration of private property. In May 1971 I ordered the detention centres closed and I put an end to arbitrary arrests. I ordered the Ministry of the Interior to burn the recorded tapes of individuals' private conversations. This was a symbol of the restoration to the people of their long-lost freedom.

All this was not easy. The Soviets tried to create havoc for me. They left me not one moment of peace in those first months. So I had to use lots of power in the first stages. For some years I was—I can say without boasting—the sole guarantor of the country's security. But now everything is changing. With the help of my aides, my friends, and the cadres whom I have trained we have now built a state of *institutions*. So I could retire at this moment. I should like to remain another year or two to achieve with my political party what I have achieved with my aides. But if I were compelled to retire now, by illness or by death, I would not be sorry. They could now carry on.

The vice-president and the acting prime minister know every small detail in the workings of this country—inside and out. We have developed a sense of teamwork. We now have a pension and retirement system, which protects our people against disease or disablement and helps their survivors after death. We have a clear view before us.

All this took me ten years to do. Our very constitutional referendum was in my opinion a turning point in our democratic course. When the majority decided to join the National Democratic Party, the political party I deemed it my duty to establish, they were attracted by tangible achievements. They were attracted by our May 15 revolution which eliminated corrupt centres of power; by the expelling of the Soviet military experts from Egypt; by the October victory; by the peace initiative.

I stepped into the political arena to establish a genuine democracy that would achieve in tangible realities, not merely in words, man's freedom, his dignity and prosperity. For the same purpose I welcomed the establishment of an opposition party. We call for a patriotic honest opposition, to say "no" when it finds fault with our decisions, to help the majority redress any deviation in its course, but by resorting to proof and not defamation, to facts and not to rumours like the deceitful parties of the past. For no man is above the law. We are all responsible to the people.

This could have taken 50 years or it might not have been achieved in my lifetime. In a lifetime of a nation, what are 20, 30, or 50 years? But all this took ten years, and I am proud of it.

Politicians are replaced. Why not? This is life. Our good friend President Carter was defeated by the vote of the American people. That is democracy. The will of the people must always be respected.

There are two species of people who do not always realize this: artists and politicians. They both want to stay on stage. The artist stays on the stage and won't leave it until the audience throws eggs at him. The politician waits in the limelight until the people in the streets throw stones. A wise politician knows when to leave. Take the case of my friend Walter Cronkite. When he came to interview me a year ago, he had already decided on his retirement, but he didn't tell me. "You rogue," I joked with him later, "why didn't you tell me then." But I admire a man who can decide on his retirement at the climax of his success.

For my part, my only will to the Egyptian people is: keep what I have created with you: the spirit of the Egyptian family. We have been a family for 7,000 years. Whenever the spirit of the family is neglected, we lose our direction and face a miserable end. Whenever we stick to the family tradition, we shall succeed. This is the tradition of this soil. Family ties, family values, family tradition.

Egypt is now one of the happiest countries in the world. We are not self-supporting. We are still suffering from certain difficulties, from lack of services and in various other ways. But because we struggle against the difficulties we are happy. The more you struggle to succeed, the more you take out of life. God Almighty has taught us that Allah changes not the condition of a folk until they change what is in their hearts.

I have brought this country back to realize what is the mainstream of our culture: the Egyptian family and its ties. For that I am a most happy man.

AMERICAN INGENUITY—DOES IT STILL THRIVE?

by Neil P. Ruzic

The pursuit of ingenuity in the United States is faltering. Fewer new technological enterprises have been started in recent years, and national productivity actually decreased for the first time in 1980. But if Yankee ingenuity is not entirely well, it is still very much alive. The U.S. still produces more Nobel laureates each year than the rest of the world combined. It continues to lead the world in computers, communications, space technology, electronics—where it was first to develop the transistor, integrated circuits, and microminiaturized circuits—chemicals, construction, agriculture, and medicine. It also leads in the exciting new fields of biological innovation, including that of recombinant DNA or "genetic engineering."

Meanwhile, social innovation takes its usual back seat to both physical and biological technologies. But that is a commentary more on humanity in general than a divergence between Americans and other nationals in comparative degrees of ingenuity.

Energy. While physicists struggle with diverse methods of controlling the ultimate power source—nuclear fusion—engineers are at work on fuel cells, hydromagnetic power, the extraction of oil from shale, new catalysts, synthetic fuels, and a variety of methods for harnessing the wind and Sun.

Giant commercial sailing ships are returning to the oceans owing to increases in diesel fuel costs. These new cargo vessels are wind-assisted diesel-powered craft, saving 10 to 40% of a typical fuel bill. Under computer control, sails and engines work together to keep a ship cruising at a constant 12 knots. Instead of tacking to catch the wind, as did the old clipper ships, the new vessels use wind power whenever possible to reduce engine load; but the engine never stops completely, and the ships travel in straight paths. In most designs the sails are set in winds up to 40 knots, folding up within two or three minutes in heavier winds.

The design pioneered by Dynaship Corp. of Palo Alto, Calif., sets or furls the sails with power rollers located inside hollow masts. The rollers and rotation of the mast itself are controlled automatically from the bridge—no seamen climbing yardarms here. The first new U.S. sail-freighter was scheduled to be the 450-ton "Patricia A." Four sails ranging from 16 to 50 ft in width will assist the 170-ft freighter across the Caribbean starting in April 1981.

The U.S. National Aeronautics and Space Administration (NASA), which has an active program to transfer ingenious ideas from the space program to private use, built the world's largest wind-turbine generator at Boone, N.C. At wind speeds of 25 mph on a tower high over the Smoky Mountains, its 200-ft rotor produces 2,000 kw, enough to power several hundred homes.

Meanwhile, private U.S. inventors developed two ingenious methods to speed up the wind for wind turbines. Since the power in the wind is proportionate to the cube of its velocity but only to the square of the rotor diameter, it pays to increase wind speed and use smaller, faster rotors. One method, devised by Alfred Weisbrich of Windsor, Conn., employs a stack of hollow toroids at the top of a building, silo, or tower. Each toroid is shaped something like an automobile wheel without the tire. The ambient wind is entrained and accelerated around the channel formed by the flanges of each "wheel." Two wind turbines are placed there, mounted on a circular track, to keep the rotors headed into the wind.

The other wind augmenter, pioneered by Pas Sforza of Huntington, N.Y., uses a delta wing to build up vortices of air. The delta wing, in the shape of an isosceles triangle, is inclined about 22° to the ground. On a stationary surface, such as a large roof, vortices strong enough to be termed miniature tornadoes are created toward the base of the triangle even when the wind is moderate. In a typical design twin rotors are placed at these focal points, where they turn in opposite directions atop the delta roof. Both the toroidal arrangement and the delta wing increase wind velocity by more than 50%, resulting in about a fourfold increase in electrical or mechanical power.

Among the many designs for generating solar power are saltwater ponds used as heat exchangers.

Neil P. Ruzic, founder of Industrial Research, Oceanology, *and other magazines, is president of Island for Science Inc., Beverly Shores, Indiana. He is the author of eight books on the practical applications of science and holds the first U.S. patent for a device to be used exclusively on the Moon.*

As the Sun's radiation heats the pond, the salt dissolves, making the heated water heavier and keeping it at the bottom. A top layer of fresh water remains relatively cool through evaporation and a cooling system. Southern California Edison Co. planned to employ this design in a station that would generate 5,000 kw by mid-1981.

Transportation. A significant breakthrough in the application of solar power to aviation occurred when the "Solar Riser" flew for the first time on April 29, 1979. Designed by Larry Mauro of Santa Clara, Calif., the craft was fitted with 500 solar cells, a helicopter battery, and a small electric motor.

While solar cells have a long climb on the efficiency scale ahead of them, the dream of efficient electric automobiles for long distances is at hand. The breakthrough was the successful laboratory testing of a new battery at Lawrence Livermore National Laboratory. The battery uses air, water, and aluminum plates. Instead of being recharged, it is refueled periodically with tap water. Recharging consists of replacing the aluminum plates, which are consumed in operation. This would have to be done every 1,000 to 3,000 mi, depending on their thickness. The Livermore engineers were working on a design that would allow the plates to be replaced in 15 minutes.

Most electric cars are powered by batteries that have to be recharged overnight after driving about 150 mi. The new aluminum-air battery, weighing just under 1,000 lb, would allow long-distance driving. A five-passenger electric car moving at 55 mph would stop to "refuel" (with about six gallons of water) approximately every 250 mi.

Meanwhile, at Garrett-AiResearch in Torrance, Calif., flywheels were being adapted to electric cars to give them improved acceleration and start-stop capabilities. A car sponsored by the U.S. Department of Energy featured a unique continuously variable transmission and all-fibreglass chassis.

Transportation research inches forward every day with progress made in high-strength plastics, hovercraft, hydrofoils, fast submarines, automobiles with computer-controlled injection for greater fuel economy and fewer pollutants, wheelless 300-mph rail cars, and vertical (and short-)-takeoff-and-landing aircraft. Air buses, of which the Boeing 747 was the first, were being designed to carry 1,000 or more passengers.

Ocean Exploitation. The need for desalination in freshwater-poor regions like the Caribbean is obvious. But the scarcity of fresh water is becoming worldwide. The United States is expected to require 29,000,000,000 gal of desalinated water a day by the year 2000.

Reverse osmosis and vacuum stills are in use today, but more cost-effective methods are needed. One ingenious idea for a solar still, developed by Philip Youngner at St. Cloud (Minn.) State University, boils water at 150° F (65° C) at reduced pressure. The water is heated in a solar pond and then passes through an intricate piping system that creates a vacuum in a vertical pipe by the falling motion of entrapped air bubbles in the water. A specially designed bellows pump lifts the distilled water to a heat exchanger, where it is cooled by indirect contact with ambient ocean water. Energy for the pumps is expended only when the distillation unit is being started. Afterward, no energy is required other than the warmth of the solar pond. The result is distilled water projected at less than $2 per 1,000 gal, a remarkable improvement over conventional desalinators.

Many designs for seafarms are being proposed. One grows shrimp in a symbiotic relationship with seaweed. The seaweed adds to the water oxygen that the shrimp require while using the shrimp metabolites and carbon dioxide as nutrients. Seaweed is grown for its gels of carrageenan and agar, used as additives in some 10,000 food products as thickeners, emulsifiers, and stabilizers. Not only does the seaweed contribute oxygen to the system but it also provides shade, hiding places, and a portion of their diet to the shrimp. By growing two crops in the same structures at the same time, profitability of the seafarm is approximately doubled.

The oceans also are being exploited for the nodules found on the seafloor that are rich in manganese and nickel; for ocean thermal energy conversion, in which the difference in temperature between the cold bottom layers and warm surface is used to produce electricity and distilled water as a by-product; and for growing food crops on land by gradual adaption to salt water. With some 80% of the Earth's animal life living in the oceans, pharmacologists are entering the sea in diving masks to search for new drugs. Anticancer substances from sea invertebrates, antibiotics from sponges and coelenterates, immunosuppressive activity in tunicates, and prostaglandins from the common sea whip are among the examples of marine drugs.

New ocean devices worthy of mention include underwater robots and a new compact seawater hydraulic motor. The motor, developed by Westinghouse Electric Corp., uses seawater as the working fluid rather than oil, thereby eliminating pollution and fire hazards. The motor can be used under water for such purposes as drilling holes in the seabed for installing dock pilings.

Space and Communications. NASA was finding more and more uses for its Landsat remote-sensing satellites, which acquire voluminous data about fea-

WIDE WORLD

Voyager 1 spacecraft (artist's concept) transmitted photographs of Saturn to the Jet Propulsion Laboratory in Pasadena, California, in November. This new technique, cable television, picturephones, and electrical transmission of newspapers are a few examples of American ingenuity at work.

tures on the Earth's surface from orbital altitudes above 500 mi. The satellite's exceptional utility results from its sensitive onboard detectors, which pick up energy emitted from features on the land. Landsats make agricultural inventories, prospect for new oil and mineral resources, monitor pollution, and improve the accuracy of maps.

Bell Laboratories introduced designs for sending electronic mail and other information as packets of digital data by using narrow microwave beams from satellites. Xerox completed technical specifications for "Ethernet," a communications network that would link machines made by various manufacturers in different offices.

Cable television, picturephones, interoffice communications, and the electrical transmission of newspapers are examples of American ingenuity at work. Mobile radiotelephones soon will be widespread following the recent innovation by AT&T of using a series of low-power transmitters, each serving a limited area or "cell," instead of relying on a single powerful radio transmitter to link local mobile-home users with regular telephone lines. The new system permits a number of mobile-phone conversations on the same channel at the same time, but through different cells, without interference. As a vehicle travels from one cell to another, its calls are handed off automatically to the new cell. A computer assigns channels in such a way that the low-power transmissions do not overlap.

Computers and Robots. Probably the prime beneficiary of the U.S.'s early lead in space technology has been the computer. The great scientific discoveries of the past two decades, in antibiotics and contraceptives, in pulsars and astrophysics, in the chemistry of new materials, in the fundamental knowledge that, in turn, spurs tomorrow's progress —all would have proceeded, if at all, on a much lower level of awareness without space-stimulated computer technology.

Computers take over more jobs daily. Approximately 200,000 microcomputers, called "microprocessors," already have been sold for home use. They could become as standard as the telephone. They can answer personal correspondence, cross-index journals, keep a log of people talked to on the phone, dim and brighten living room lights, open and close the drapes, balance the checkbook, keep track of investments, update the Christmas card list, collate menus, play electronic games, report on the seepage of water in the basement, and lock the front door at night.

Computerized robots today work the assembly lines in many of the nation's automobile and aircraft factories. Rows of sleek, smoothly articulated arms swing out, surround a car, dip forward with pneumatic air bursts, and weld metal to metal. At McDonnell Douglas in St. Louis, Mo., some two dozen acres of milling machines noisily grind grooves, slots, and intricate patterns in airframe parts to a tolerance of 0.0025 in. All those machines work virtually alone, watchdogged by master computer-robots that make decisions.

Construction. Housing developments might be built better and more economically if they were prefabricated at a factory at the development site. In this regard Leon Blachura of Clarkston, Mich., obtained a patent for a "house leveler." He envisions newly built houses being carried and lifted into place by big cranes, set down on prepared foundations, and leveled by jacks built into perimeter frames. A developer might start by placing houses farthest out, working in toward the factory along semifinished roads. When all houses were completed, the factory could be converted into a community building.

NASA developed a flat electrical wire for spacecraft that is now being used along baseboards and under carpets in wiring homes and offices. Because it is very thin, the wire can be mounted on the surface of walls and floors instead of inside them. One version of the wire is so thin it can be completely hidden by paint. Installation costs are reduced significantly by using such wire, especially in remodeling projects.

Also derived from space technology is an improved inorganic paint for coastal bridges that are subject to extreme corrosion from seawater spray. Zinc-rich coatings with both organic and inorganic binders have been tried in the past. But organic paints do not last as long and require a finish coat, while inorganics normally are more difficult to apply but require only one coat. The unique inorganic zinc-dust coating developed by NASA for painting spacecraft gantries is formulated with a potassium silicate water-base binder loaded with zinc particles to provide uniform coverage in a single coat. One gallon of the paint covers 375 sq ft, almost double the usual coverage for inorganic paints. And the paint is expected to last about twice as long. It is being tested on the Golden Gate Bridge.

Also affecting construction, a "glue revolution" is under way in the United States. Nuts and bolts, nails, and rivets are being replaced by synthetic superadhesives—epoxies, silicones, cyanoacrylates, anaerobics, and hotmelts—emerging from the nation's prolific polymer chemical laboratories. Half the shoes made in the U.S. are put together with these new adhesives. They stick fenders to hoods and hold helicopter rotors together.

Safety. "Firefly," a lightweight, portable fire-fighting module designed for combating shipboard or dockside fires, is being manufactured by Aviation Power Supply Inc. of Burbank, Calif. It can be mounted on a light truck for use by local fire departments or transported by helicopter to hard-to-reach fire scenes such as forests, high-rise buildings, or offshore oil rigs. Within a compact package it has everything needed for fire fighting: its own pump, which delivers 2,000 gal of water per minute; a fast-starting gas turbine; hoses; monitors; nozzles; protective suits; and other equipment.

A patent was granted to D. G. Dalziel of Lake Forest, Ill., for a telescoping and pivoting arm to swing out from under the belly of a helicopter. The craft thus could reach places otherwise inaccessible, such as alongside tall buildings or mountain overhangs. Harnesses, cages, or life vests could be attached along the arm to reach endangered people.

Among the many security devices being developed to fight crime is one produced by Sentry Products Inc. of Santa Clara, Calif., called SCAN, for Silent Communications Alarm Network. It is a signaling device that looks like a pen and emits a silent, ultrasonic, alert signal. The signal activates a series of receivers interconnected with a constantly monitored master console in, for example, a school principal's office. An outbreak of violence in a high school triggered the development of SCAN.

Defense. Among the few ingenious but nonclassified recent devices for military defense is the radar-foiling airplane appropriately called "Stealth." Rather than a single invention, Stealth is a series of design improvements. The smaller a plane, the less surface it presents to radar, and so Stealth aircraft are small. Because engine pods and other projections and sharp angles reflect radar well, Stealth is ultra-streamlined. Since radar picks up metals easily, Stealth is made of a nonmetallic composite of graphite, epoxy resins, and asbestos filaments that absorb and diffuse radar waves. The design also insulates hot engine parts to shield them from infrared or heat-seeking missiles. The exhaust nozzles are bent at odd angles to disperse the fumes so as to confuse heat sensors. Finally, computerized devices send out confusing radar signals.

Recombinant DNA. By far the hottest field in biology is "genetic engineering" or "gene splicing," achieved by recombinant DNA (deoxyribonucleic acid) technology. In this process a gene from the DNA of one organism is combined with the DNA of another. For example, the DNA for making a desired product is inserted into the DNA of a laboratory strain of a common bacterium. The bacterium, following directions from the new DNA, then produces the new product.

U.S. biologists are applying this technology in several ways. For instance, instead of crossbreeding to improve crop plants, they are performing gene-splicing experiments that can have several desired effects. These include increasing food yield, reducing water requirements, speeding growth so that two crops can be raised in a single season, and developing bacteria capable of nitrogen fixation in order to eliminate the need for fertilizer. To grow fuel, genes are being recombined to produce alcohol from vegetables without recourse to the low efficiency of fermentation. Nonrenewable raw materials can become renewable through recombinant DNA techniques for the manufacture of plastics and organic chemicals. Gene splicing offers potential solutions for tranforming the genes responsible for toxic wastes into harmless or useful materials.

Most successes so far have been for treating disease. For example, insulin—which when derived from cattle causes allergic responses in 20% of diabetics using it—has been produced that is identical to that made by the human body. Human "interferons," natural defense products made by the body in reponse to viral infections, also are under investigation, and synthetic versions of these substances are being developed by means of recombinant DNA technology.

Antiviral Drugs. Researchers are out to kill viruses that cause everything from the common cold to some kinds of cancer. One of the most promising approaches concerns "immunopotentiators," which increase natural defense mechanisms.

For instance, Newport Pharmaceuticals International Inc. of Newport Beach, Calif., developed a new drug called "Isoprinosine." It enhances cellular immunity, potentiates the antiviral action of interferon in the body, and inhibits the growth of viruses in a cell by blocking the translation of viral messenger-RNA (ribonucleic acid) on the host cell.

Health Devices. One of the most effective spinoffs from the U.S. space effort is the cardiac pacemaker that can be charged, an outgrowth of miniaturized solid-state circuitry developed for spacecraft. Some 30,000 pacemakers are implanted in the chests of heart patients each year. These pacemakers formerly had to be removed surgically every couple of years for recharging. Now they are rechargeable through the skin by inductance. Once a week the patient simply wears a charger vest for an hour to recharge his pacemaker. Because recharging can be done frequently, only one cell is required and the size of the pacemaker is half its former thickness, weighing only two ounces.

Also introduced recently was an advanced cardiac pacing system that allows a physician to reprogram a patient's implanted pacer without surgery. Called "Programalith" and made by Pacesetter Systems Inc. of Sylmar, Calif., the system has a two-way communications capability, permitting the device to be fine tuned to the patient's changing needs. The device uses technologies originally designed to send coded instructions to unmanned satellites and to receive messages back from them.

Other examples of ingenuity in medicine and health care include an improved physician's portable "black bag," consisting of an electronic vital signs monitor, electrocardiogram recorder, and equipment for minor surgery, along with the usual stethoscope and drugs. O. A. Battista, president of Research Services Corp. of Fort Worth, Texas, patented "Landel" disposable contact lenses, wound and burn dressings, bioassimilable bone dressings, and high-foam dental creams in which millions of tiny bubbles trap bacteria and food particles so that they can be flushed away efficiently.

Stimulants of Innovation. Turning toward social innovations, Battista is starting an "Olympiad of knowledge." Similar to the Olympic Games of sports, his proposed annual knowledge competition would encourage and recognize competitive achievements of human minds and discover solutions to society's problems.

The annual IR-100 competition, started by Neil Ruzic, gives recognition to the developers of the 100 most significant new technical products of the year. The products themselves are on display each year for a month at the Museum of Science and Industry in Chicago.

Ruzic's "Island for Science" is a subtropical island base established to work out practical ideas for improvement in near-ocean living conditions. U.S. innovators associated with the new facility include those described earlier working on augmented windmill systems, shrimp and seaweed mariculture, solar desalination, and marine pharmaceuticals.

Economics. Often working independently and surreptitiously, many Americans have established an "underground economy" in the face of high inflation and taxation. It consists of barter arrangements between professionals, nonrecorded tips, under-the-table cash payments for services, and black-market activities—all designed to elude the tax collector. While nothing to be proud of, it is an example of ingenuity that cannot be ignored. Economists estimate that this subterranean economy in the U.S. is as large as 27% of the gross national product. That would approximate $700 billion.

Legal economic innovations include the variable-rate mortgage to help the beleaguered home buyer: interest rates are tied to an index of lenders' cost of money. An affiliate of the First Boston Corp. developed a novel way for corporations to issue bonds in a fast-fluctuating market. Securities are sold to investors on a trial plan. Instead of putting down the full purchase price for a bond, an investor pays only 25% of that price. After six months or so he or she has the option of completing the purchase or losing the down payment.

Work sharing has proliferated among companies hit by decreased production. About 2.2 million workers in 1980 shared work schedules with coworkers. For instance, at Pan American Airways flight attendants fly one month and then are laid off one month but retain their seniority.

Peace. Satellites that make inspection possible render treaties between nations more meaningful. Another suggestion in the interest of peace is to turn the entire armed services of the United States into a combination defense force and peace corps. With peace—and defense—as its mission, the military would continue its armed presence but in times of relative peace would "wage peace" on other countries that invited it to do so. Following a "declaration of peace" on a country, the U.S. would pursue its objectives there with all the men, machines, money, and fervour formerly expended only for war.

If American ingenuity can devise nuclear and thermonuclear bombs, it can and should be harnessed—fast—toward peace on Earth.

ARTICLES FROM THE 1981 PRINTING OF THE BRITANNICA

Wars have many woeful effects. It seems odd to say it, but one woeful effect of wars is the trouble they cause for encyclopaedists. This is particularly true when a war ends with a realignment or reorganization of countries.

Such a war was the Vietnam war; that part of it, to be more precise, in which the United States was engaged—the part covering the years 1954–73. (The first part of the Vietnam war, involving Vietnamese rebels and their French colonial masters, ended with the Battle of Dien Bien Phu, in 1954.)

One result of Dien Bien Phu was a "temporary" partition of Vietnam, at the 17th parallel of latitude; this was supposed to last only until "free elections" were held in 1956. The elections were never held. Instead, the next phase of the war erupted; the United States saw much of its world hegemony as well as its self-respect go down in that conflict, and the whole thing ended in ignominy in 1973.

Except it wasn't over then, either. Within two years South Vietnam was swallowed up by the victorious North, and a new version of the old country came into existence.

Clearly an entirely new article in Britannica, to replace two obviously antique articles, was needed. It was commissioned in 1979 and will appear in the 1981 printing. Major parts of it are preprinted here.

VIETNAM, SOCIALIST REPUBLIC OF

The Socialist Republic of Vietnam (Cong Hoa Xa Hoi Chu Nghia Viet Nam) is the 16th most populous nation in the world, and the third most populous Communist state, with a total population estimated in 1979 to be about 52,000,000. Covering an area of 127,200 square miles (329,600 square kilometres), the country is bordered by the People's Republic of China on the north, Laos and Cambodia (Kampuchea) on the west, and the Gulf of Thailand and the South China Sea on the south and east. The national capital of Hanoi is located in the north. The largest city, Saigon, officially renamed Ho Chi Minh City in 1976, is located in the south.

On September 2, 1945, following the Japanese surrender that ended World War II, the Democratic Republic of Vietnam was proclaimed in Hanoi. The return of the French, however, precipitated the First Indochina War, which came to a close with the Geneva Accords of 1954. This agreement provided for the temporary military partition of Vietnam at the 17th parallel and promised nationwide elections in July 1956 (the elections were never held). The two political entities that emerged were the Democratic Republic of Vietnam, better known as North Vietnam, and the Republic of Vietnam, usually referred to as South Vietnam. By the late 1950s, insurgency supported by North Vietnam began to spread in South Vietnam, and it intensified considerably following the toppling of the government and the assassination of President Ngo Dinh Diem in 1963. In March 1965, U.S. Marines landed at Da Nang, marking the beginning of direct U.S. military involvement in the conflict; about the same time, North Vietnamese troops began infiltrating the south. A cease-fire agreement signed in Paris in January 1973 technically ended the war and provided for the withdrawal of the last U.S. forces. The cease-fire was not honoured, however, and an offensive by North Vietnamese armed forces in South Vietnam early in 1975 brought about the collapse of the Saigon government on April 30. The Provisional Revolutionary Government of South Vietnam, which was created by the Communists in 1969, emerged in May 1975 as the official ruling body of the south for a year. Negotiations between delegations from the north and south resulted in elections on April 25, 1976, of a new National Assembly for the whole country. This National Assembly convened for the first time in Hanoi on June 24; on July 2 it proclaimed the reunification of the country.

THE LANDSCAPE

Relief. Vietnam encompasses 127,200 square miles (329,600 square kilometres). Its principal physiographic features are the Chaîne Annamitique (Annamite Chain or Cordillera; Truong Son), extending from north to south in central Vietnam and dominating the interior, and two extensive alluvial deltas formed by the Red River (Song Hong) in the north and the Mekong River (Song Cuu Long) in the south. Between these two deltas is a long, relatively narrow coastal plain.

Northern Vietnam. From north to south, the uplands of northern Vietnam can be divided into two distinct regions—the region north of the Red River and the massif that extends south of the Red River into neighbouring Laos. The Red River forms a deep, relatively wide valley that runs in a straight northwest–southeast direction for much of its 130 miles (210 kilometres) from the border with the People's Republic of China to the edge of the delta. North of the Red River, the relief is moderate with two essential regions. One region has heights characterized by a northwest–southeast trend such as are found between the Red River and the Song Lo (Clear River); appended to this is a marked depression from Cao Bang to the sea. The second region is characterized by mountains in its eastern portion that form arcs convex to the east and southeast. This region also contains a sub-area of wide terraces, extensive alluvial plains, and low hills; it extends from the Red River delta along the Lo, Chay, Chu, Thuong, Luc Nam, and Ky Cung rivers.

Compared with the area north of the Red River, the vast massif extending southwest across Laos to the Mekong River is of considerably higher elevation and is overlain with poor soils. Among its outstanding topographical features is the Fan Si Pan chain, the highest peaks of which are Mount Fan Si Pan (10,312 feet [3,143 metres]) and Pou Luong (9,796 feet [2,986 metres]). It is a crystalline formation with few plains. South of the Black River are the Ta P'ing, Son La, and Moc Chau plateaus, which are separated by deep valleys. Below the northern uplands is the Red River delta. Roughly triangular in shape, the 4,250-square mile (11,000-square kilometre) delta extends 150 miles (240 kilometres) inland and measures 75 miles (120 kilometres) along the Gulf of Tonkin.

The Red River delta

The Red River delta can be divided into four sub-regions. The northwest section has the highest and most broken terrain, and its extensive natural levees invite settlement despite frequent flooding. The low-lying eastern portion of the delta has bench marks of less than seven feet (two metres) elevation in the vicinity of Bac Ninh. Rivers running through this area form small valleys only slightly lower than the general surface level, so they are subject to flooding by unusually high tides. The third and fourth sub-regions are the poorly drained lowlands to the west and the coastal area, which is marked by the remains of former beach ridges left by continuous deltaic aggradation.

Central Vietnam. In central Vietnam, the Chaîne Annamitique runs parallel to the coast, with several peaks rising more than 6,000 feet (1,830 metres). Several spurs jut into the South China Sea, forming compartments isolated from one another. One such spur dissects the coastal plain at Mui Ron (previously called the Gate of Annam) and another rises at the Hai Van pass (the Col des Nuages), just north of Da Nang. Communication across the main chain in central Vietnam is difficult. Located at Lao Bao inland from Quang Tri, is the chief pass, the Ai Lao, which provided an ancient invasion route between the coastal plain and the interior. The southern portion of the Chaîne Annamitique has two identifiable regions. One consists of mountain plateaus of approximately 1,700 feet (518 metres) in elevation that have experienced little erosion, as in the vicinity of Lac Giao (former Ban Me Thuot). The second region is characterized by heavily eroded plateaus; in the vicinity of Pleiku, the plateau is about 2,500 feet (760 metres) above sea level and in the Da Lat area, about 4,900 feet (1,500 metres) in elevation.

The Mekong River delta

Southern Vietnam. South of the mountain range there is an identifiable terrace region that gives way to the Mekong River delta. The terrace region includes the alluvial plains along the Saigon and Dong Nai rivers. The lowlands of southern Vietnam are dominated by alluvial plains, the most extensive of which is the Mekong River delta, covering an area of 15,600 square miles (40,400 square kilometres). Smaller deltaic plains also occur along the south-central coast of the South China Sea.

Soils. In northern Vietnam, the heavy seasonal rains wash away rich humus from the highlands, leaving slow-dissolving alumina and iron oxides that give the soil its characteristic reddish colour. The soils of Red River delta vary; some are fertile and suitable to intense cultivation, while others lack soluble bases. Nonetheless, the delta soils are in good condition, without any lateritic tendencies, and are easily worked. The diking of the Red River to prevent flooding deprives the delta's paddy fields of enriching silts, necessitating the use of chemical fertilizers.

A 1961 soil survey in southern Vietnam (below the 17th parallel) has identified 25 soil associations, but certain soil types predominate. Among these are red and yellow podzolic soils (soils that are heavily leached in their upper layers, with a resulting accumulation of materials in the lower layers), which occupy 43 percent of the land area, and latosols (reddish-brown leached tropical soils), which comprise some 12 percent. These soil types dominate the central highlands. Alluvial soils account for about 27 percent of the land in the south and are concentrated in the Mekong River delta, as are peat and muck soils. Gray podzolic soils are found in parts of the central highlands and in old terraces along the Mekong River, while regurs (rich black loams) and latosols occur in both the central highlands and the terrace zone. Along the coast of central Vietnam are regosols (soft, undeveloped soils) and non-calcic brown soils.

Vegetation and animal life. *Vegetation.* The vegetation of Vietnam is rich and diversified because of the great range of climate, topography, and soils and the varying effects of human habitation. The forests of Vietnam can be divided into two broad categories: evergreen forests, which include the conifers, and deciduous forests. There are more than 1,500 species of woody plants in Vietnam, varying in size from small shrubs to large trees and ranging from hardwoods such as ebony and teak to palms, mangroves, and bamboos. There are also numerous species of woody vines, or lianas, and herbaceous plants. In the aggregate, the dense and open forests, savannas, brushland, and bamboo cover approximately 40 percent of the total area of Vietnam.

In most areas the forests are mixed, containing a large number of species within an area of a square mile. Rain forests are relatively limited and pure stands are few. The nearest to pure forest types are the pines—the three-needled *Pinus khasya* and two-needled *P. merkusii* found in the uplands—and the mangrove forests of the coastal swamps. In the mountainous regions there are subtropical species such as varieties of *Quercus*, *Castanopsis*, *Pinus*, and *Podocarpus*. Brushwood, bamboo, weeds, and tall grasses invade cutover forests and grow around settlements and along arterial highways and railroads. Between the cutover areas and the upland forests are other mixtures of forest types.

Permanent cultivation covers large areas of the Vietnam lowlands and smaller portions of the highlands. Much of this acreage is in wet rice, the staple of the Vietnamese diet. Plantations of banana, other fruit trees, coconut, and sugarcane are found in the Mekong River delta, while tea and coffee are grown in the central highlands. Extensive rubber estates occur in the central highlands and the terrace region. Fields, groves, and kitchen gardens throughout Vietnam contain a wide variety of fruit (banana, orange, mango, jackfruit, and coconut) trees and vegetables. Kapok trees are found in many villages, and the Vietnamese cultivate areca palms and betel peppers for their nuts and leaves.

Animal life. The most common domesticated animals in Vietnam are water buffalo, cattle, dogs, cats, pigs, goats, ducks, and chickens. Wild game in the central highlands includes elephants and tapirs; of the varieties of rhinoceroses (*Rhinoceros sondaicus* and *Didermocerus sumatrensis*), none has been seen since the early 1940s. Also found in the forests are big cats, including tigers, leopards, ounces (*Leo uncia*), and clouded leopards (*Leo nebulosa*); several kinds of wild oxen, including gaurs and koupreys; and various types of bears, among them the black bear and honey bear. Deer are plentiful; they include the small musk deer and barking deer. Other common wild animals are wild boars, porcupines, jackals, otters, mongooses, hares, skunks, and squirrels, including flying squirrels. In the highland villages, traps are placed near granaries to catch rats, which are roasted and eaten.

There are many different kinds of small wild cats and three types of civets—Malagasy civets, binturongs, and palm civets. Primates such as the langur, macaque, gibbon, and rhesus monkey live in the forests. Crocodiles are found on the edges of some lakes and along river banks; other reptiles include several kinds of lizards, pythons, and cobras. Of the wide variety of land and water birds, 586 species have been identified in southern Vietnam alone.

Traditional regions. Diverse cultural traditions, geographical variations, and the events of history have created distinct traditional regions. The general topographical dichotomy of highland and lowland regions also has ethnolinguistic significance; the lowlands generally have been occupied by ethnic Vietnamese, while the highlands have been the home of numerous smaller ethnic groups that differ culturally and linguistically from the Vietnamese. The highland peoples can be divided into the northern ethnic groups, with affinities to peoples in southern China, and the southern highland populations, with ties to the Mon-Khmer and Austronesian peoples of Cambodia, Indonesia, and elsewhere in Southeast Asia. A north–south variation also evolved among the ethnic Vietnamese as they expanded from the Red River delta along the coastal plain into the Mekong River delta. After the mid-19th century, Vietnam was divided by the French into Tonkin in the north, Annam in the centre, and Cochinchina in the south. The Vietnamese themselves have long made a distinction among the north (*bac ky*), with Hanoi as its cultural centre; the centre (*trung ky*), with the traditional royal capital of Hue; and the south (*nam ky*), with Saigon (now Ho Chi Minh City) as its urban centre.

Highland and lowland dichotomy

PEOPLE AND POPULATION

Settlement patterns. *Rural communities.* Topography has strongly influenced human settlement in Vietnam. In the Red River delta a number of distinct settlement patterns can be identified, the most common of which is the "relief" village associated with topographical features such as levees, hillsides, or beach ridges. Levee settlements, usually located along river banks, often abut each other and form one elongated settlement, while clusters of farmsteads at the base of a hill may cover the hill if it is low. Most villages are enclosed by a bamboo hedge or earthen wall.

"Relief" villages

Lowland Vietnamese villages on the coastal plain in central Vietnam are characteristically close-knit, small clusters of farmsteads near a watercourse. Fishing villages normally are situated in a sheltered inlet. Vietnamese villages in the Mekong River delta are less varied than those in the Red River delta. Settlements are strung out along the rivers, canals, and streams and major roads. On the deltaic plain, most settlements are loose-knit clusters of farmsteads, although some farmsteads are scattered about the paddy fields.

In some Vietnamese settlements, particularly those in northern and central Vietnam, geomantic principles determine the internal orientation of houses and village buildings such as the *dinh*, the communal meeting hall and sanctuary for the cult of the guardian spirit, and the village Buddhist pagoda. In central Vietnam, houses and the *dinh* traditionally face the sea.

The physical pattern of settlements of the Cham and Khmer minorities closely resembles that of the Vietnamese settlements. Among the highland ethnic groups, settlement patterns vary considerably. Permanent and shifting (slash-and-burn) fields are within walking distance of the village, kitchen gardens are invariably found close to the farmstead, and good water sources are nearby. Internal arrangement of the settlement may not have any particular orientation or it may be dictated by practical considerations or ideational principles. Most groups in the northern highlands have no particular patterns for their settlements. In the central highlands, however, the Sedang prefer not to have the morning sun strike the main entrance of a house, and the Mnong Chil build their dwellings facing away from the prevailing winds. In the same region, many Jarai longhouses have a north–south orientation because of wind and rain patterns; the main entrance always faces south so that the sun may dry the rice, cotton, and other things they place on the veranda. The Katu orient their settlements around a stake to which sacrificial animals are tied and build their communal men's houses (where rituals and gatherings of the leaders take place) facing away from the rising sun.

For the most part, highland people prefer to build their houses on pilings. Exceptions occur among the Hmong (Miao, Meo), Mien (Yao), Stieng, and some Mnong groups. Floor plans for houses vary from group to group depending on whether or not a house will be occupied by an extended family and whether there are cultural prescriptions for certain parts of the house. In the central highlands, for example, the Rhadé trace descent through the female line and husbands live with their wives after marriage; their longhouses, therefore, are arranged with compartments for the women of the family and their husbands and children.

Urban settlement. Vietnam's traditional major cities are Hanoi, Hue, and Saigon (Ho Chi Minh City). Archaeological research in the vicinity of Hanoi has revealed traces of the ancient citadel of Co Loa, which dates to the 3rd century BC. Throughout Vietnamese history the Hanoi area has been a place of importance and the site of several early capitals. Hanoi served as the French colonial capital from 1902 until 1954, and the city retains the charming architecture that is part of that heritage. Hanoi also has long been a centre of trade and industry for northern Vietnam; the city's outport of Haiphong was developed by the French in the late 19th century as a trade and banking centre.

The imperial past is rooted in Hue. The Nguyen family controlled central and southern Vietnam from Hue after 1687, and Emperor Gia Long established his capital there in 1802. Located on the Song Huong (Perfume River), Hue was intended to be the physical and administrative centre of the kingdom and was laid out in the early 19th century according to geomantic principles. The heart of the city is the imperial citadel of Dai Noi ("Great Within"), modelled on the Manchu palace in Peking. Hue was the intellectual and religious heart of Vietnam, and its economic functions were ancillary. Many of the traditions of the mandarins (senior public officials) have been preserved in Hue, and until vast destruction occurred during the Tet Offensive of 1968, traditional Vietnamese architecture was much in evidence.

The city of Hue

Saigon, renamed Ho Chi Minh City in 1976, was built largely by the French on a plan devised by Théodore Lebrun, an adviser to Gia Long. As the administrative capital and principal port of the French province of Cochinchina, its riverfront was dominated by the port and commercial establishments. A French-provincial style of life prevailed in the city and its architecture recalled towns and cities in southern France. With the establishment of Hanoi as the capital of the Socialist Republic of Vietnam in 1976, Saigon lost its administrative functions as the capital of South Vietnam. The city of Cholon, adjoining Saigon, was a major centre for the ethnic Chinese until 1978, when large private enterprises were abolished and vast numbers of Chinese left the country.

Ethnolinguistic groups. Vietnam has one of the most complex ethnolinguistic patterns in Asia. The great tradition of China is represented by the ethnic Vietnamese, who were Sinicized during the 1,000 years of Chinese rule. Since the 10th century the Vietnamese have carried this tradition from the Red River delta southward along the coastal plain to the Mekong River delta. Chinese influence permeates all levels of the Vietnamese language, one of the Mon-Khmer languages of the Austro-Asiatic language family.

Indian influence is found among the Cham and Khmer minorities. The Cham, whose language belongs to the Austronesian language family, are remnants of a once large population that formed the majority in the Indianized kingdom of Champa, which existed in what is now central Vietnam from the 2nd century AD until its absorption by the Vietnamese between the 15th and 17th centuries. Cham populations remain in the south central coastal plain, where they cling to many customs of the Brahmins (the highest Hindu caste), and in a small pocket of the Mekong River delta close to the Cambodian border, where they have adopted Islām. The Khmer, whose language is one of the Mon-Khmer languages, are scattered throughout the Mekong River delta. They are descendants of a population that was once part of the Khmer Empire, spectacular traces of which are to be seen in the ruins of Angkor in neighbouring Cambodia.

Cham and Khmer minorities

Other minorities include the ethnic groups that inhabit the highlands. In the central highlands are people less advanced than the lowlanders and, while their cultures vary considerably, they still share many characteristics derived from a way of life oriented around kin groups and small communities. Known collectively by the French as the Montagnards ("Highlanders"), they have affinities with other Southeast Asians. Those who speak languages of Austronesian stock include the Rhadé, Jarai, Chru, and Roglai; they have linguistic ties with the Cham, Malay, and Indonesians. Other Montagnards—such as the Bru, Pacoh, Katu, Cua, Hre, Rengao, Sedang, Bahnar, Mnong Maa, and Stieng—speak languages of Mon-Khmer stock, affiliating them with the Cambodians (Khmer). Unlike the lowlanders, the Montagnards historically remained aloof from Chinese and Indian influences, but between the end of the 19th century and 1954 they were exposed to French influence. French missionaries and administrators provided roman script for some of the Montagnard languages and additional orthographies have been devised since. A desire to preserve their own cultural identities has given rise to intense ethnonationalism among the Montagnards. This is the principal ideology that has sustained the United Struggle Front for the Oppressed Races (known by its French acronym, FULRO), which has been active since the mid-1960s.

The Montagnards

The various groups in northern Vietnam have ethnolinguistic affiliations with peoples in southern China. They include the tribal Tai (Thai) groups—the Tai Dam (Black Tai), Tai Khao (White Tai), Nung, and Tay (Tho)—who are generally found in the upland valleys. Representing the largest of the highland ethnolinguistic groups, they speak Tai languages. At higher elevations are scattered the Hmong and Mien, whose languages are of the Sino-Tibetan language family.

The tribal Tais

Before the establishment of the Socialist Republic of Vietnam in 1976, most of the ethnic minorities in the highlands of North Vietnam were grouped in the autonomous regions of Tay Bac and Viet Bac. There were indications that the minorities in these zones had little actual autonomy, and that the policy of the Hanoi government was to assimilate them into the Vietnamese cultural sphere. When the unification of North and South Vietnam took place, the two autonomous regions in the north were abolished and autonomy was not given to the groups in the central highlands. Rather, it was announced that the minorities were to be given a "new culture," and implementation of a program to move massive numbers of ethnic Vietnamese from the lowlands into "new economic zones" in the mountain region was begun.

Religious groups. Beliefs and values of Taoism and Confucianism shape the Vietnamese view of the universal order, the cult of the ancestors is ubiquitous, and the Mahāyāna (Greater Vehicle) tradition of Buddhism is widespread. Animist beliefs are held by many tribal peoples. During the 1920s, the syncretic religion of Cao Dai appeared, and in 1939 the Hoa Hao sect, which claims to be a "pure Buddhism," spread through parts of the Mekong River delta. Before 1975, estimates of the numbers of religious adherents were kept in South Vietnam. Active practitioners of Buddhism were estimated to have been about 5,000,000, and the Hoa Hao claimed 1,500,000. Government sources reported 750,000 adherents of Cao Dai, although leaders of the sect claimed 3,000,000 members when all eight branches of the movement were included.

Roman Catholicism was first introduced among the Vietnamese in the 17th century, and it spread widely following the French conquest in the mid-19th century. The heaviest concentrations of Roman Catholics in Vietnam were initially in the north where, in 1954, their estimated number was 1,200,000; about 65 percent of them fled to the south after the partition of the country in that year. In South Vietnam, Roman Catholicism claimed 1,560,000 adherents in 1966.

Roman Catholicism and Protestantism

In 1959 all foreign clergy were expelled from North Vietnam, leaving only native priests. Though the 1960 constitution guaranteed freedom of religion, the North Vietnamese government tried to supplant organized religion with its own "scientific materialism" and to gain control over the existing faiths by sponsoring patriotic religious organizations. These included the Unified Buddhist Church; the Patriotic Catholic Church, whose clergy and members have renounced allegiance to the pope; the Viet Nam Cao Dai Union; and the Viet Nam Protestant Church.

Protestantism came to Vietnam with a mission in the Mekong River delta in 1911, and it spread primarily among small segments of the urban population in the central and southern regions. Congregations grew in Saigon, in the Mekong River delta towns, and in the highland centres of Da Lat, Ban Me Thuot, and Pleiku. By 1975, the Protestant community was reported to have had 200,000 members. Following the Communist conquest of South Vietnam in 1975, all foreign Christian clergy were expelled from the south.

Demography. Demographic figures for Vietnam are for the most part estimates; the disruptions and dislocations of war rendered it extremely difficult to conduct a census in North or South Vietnam. Furthermore, no accurate figures on civilian and military war dead were available. In 1974, North Vietnam's population was estimated at 23,787,375 and South Vietnam's at 23,614,653, for a total of 47,402,028. The 1979 estimates for Vietnam ranged between 50,000,000 and 52,600,000. The population growth rate was estimated to be about three percent annually. In 1977, the fertility rate was reported to be almost six per thousand, with 41 percent of the women being of reproductive age. For the period of 1975–80, the United Nations estimated a crude birth rate of almost 41 per thousand, while the crude death rate was estimated at almost 18 per thousand; in 1960 these rates were almost 42 and about 20 per thousand, respectively. Concerning age structure, 41 percent of the population was 14 years old or younger, 55 percent was between 15 and 64 years of age, and 4 percent was 65 or older.

Ethnic minorities form significant segments of the population in certain areas. Until their emigration in 1978, the ethnic Chinese, who were primarily urban, numbered about 1,500,000. In the northern highlands adjacent to the Chinese border, there were estimated to be 350,000 Hmong and close to 2,000,000 Tai-speaking peoples, including 470,000 Nung and 740,000 Tay (Tho); the remainder are largely Black Tai and White Tai. Estimates for the southern minorities predate 1975. The highland ethnic groups numbered between 800,000 and 1,000,000 while the Khmer minority numbered between 500,000 and 700,000 and the Cham population was about 57,000.

One effect of the war was a displacement of the rural population to the cities, especially in the south. It has been estimated that the urban population of South Vietnam grew from 13 percent in 1950 to more than 24 percent in 1970. In 1964 the greater Saigon area was reported to have 1,371,000 residents; by 1973, the population of the metropolitan area was estimated to be 3,806,000—an increase of more than 150 percent. In 1976 the Saigon population was 3,460,500, while Hanoi had about 1,443,500 residents; Haiphong, 1,190,900; Da Nang, 492,000; Nha Trang, 216,000; Qui Nhon, 214,000; and Hue, 209,000.

For all of Vietnam, the urban population rose from about 13 percent in 1960 to 17 percent in 1975. Between 1960 and 1970 the urban population grew annually at the rate of four percent; between 1970 and 1975 the growth rate increased slightly. For a variety of reasons, the government launched a program in 1976 to resettle large segments of the urban population in rural "new economic zones." The announced plan called for the resettlement of 10,000,000 people over 20 years, 4,000,000 of them to clear an additional 2,500,000 acres (1,000,000 hectares) of land by 1980. In mid-1978 it was reported that 1,330,000 people had been resettled in the new areas. The ultimate goal was to regroup some 160,000 rural settlements into 15,000 or 20,000 residential agglomerations, making services more economical and releasing 1,000,000 acres (800,000 hectares) for cultivation.

The resettlement plan

Emigration problems

The demography of Vietnam also has been affected by emigration. In 1954, almost 1,000,000 refugees fled from North Vietnam, which has not permitted emigration since then. With the collapse of the South Vietnamese government in 1975, more than 220,000 South Vietnamese fled the country, most of them going to the United States and France. In 1978 an estimated 160,000 ethnic Chinese left Vietnam for the People's Republic of China, which claimed to have accepted 260,000, a small number of them ethnic Vietnamese, from Vietnam by 1979. In addition, more than 300,000 refugees, many of them ethnic Chinese, arrived by boat in other Asian countries by 1979. The number of refugees who perished is unknown, but estimates of the total number who fled Vietnam between 1975 and 1979 run as high as 1,000,000.

THE NATIONAL ECONOMY

Vietnam has a definite economic potential. Its population is literate and energetic, and it has a number of natural resources. Its geographic position puts it within easy reach of all the other countries of the region. Vietnam's varied topography lends itself to a wide range of agricultural and industrial exploitation, and its long coastline provides excellent harbours and access to marine resources. In addition to vast areas of cultivable land, there are good soils supporting valuable forests and there are deposits of minerals (including coal) and possibly of crude oil and natural gas. A potential for the generation of hydroelectric power exists. Economic development by 1980, however, was seriously constrained by a number of social, political, economic, and military factors.

Economic integration

The reunification of Vietnam required the integration of the society and economy of the south into the socialist framework determined for the new nation by the north. During the period of separation between 1954 and 1975, there were three layers to the Vietnamese economy: the bottom layer was based on the cultivation of rice; the middle layer was dominated by mining in the north and rubber estates in the south; and the third layer was a wartime creation with large-scale Soviet and Chinese aid in the north and substantial U.S. aid in the south. The socialist economy of North Vietnam developed one of the most impressive industrial systems in Southeast Asia, although living standards remained low because of basic inefficiencies, the decision during the war years to disperse industry in the face of U.S. bombing, and the need to maintain a large military complex. The economy of South Vietnam was based largely on free enterprise, with less industry but a more important agricultural sector and a higher standard of living than in the north.

Since reunification in 1976, the task of developing the economy has been rendered difficult by the disruptions and destruction of 30 years of war, the need to integrate the two divergent economies, and other factors. In the north, collective ownership accounted for 90 percent of the means of production. State ownership in the south, however, affected only a relatively small part of the economy, in 1976 covering 70 percent of the total industrial output, but leaving the greater part of agriculture, trade, and transport in private hands. The stated intention of the unified government was to extend full socialization to the south on the pattern already established in the north.

Originally it was announced that the two economies would be gradually integrated during the period of the five-year plan of 1976–80, reflecting an awareness of the need to establish socialist institutions in the south while economic transformation was taking place. Despite the lack of socialist political development in the south by 1977, however, it was decided to accelerate the pace of economic integration. The second plenum of the Vietnam Communist Party Central Committee held in July of that year announced an "unprecedented development" in agriculture that was to include collectivization. The program of agricultural reform, however, ran into serious barriers. In the rich Mekong River delta, the government had to deal not with large landlords, but with their former tenants, who had become individual proprietors. The majority of the southern farmers in the late 1970s were middle-income peasants who owned enough land and implements to farm successfully without relying on outside labour. With their skill and experience in farm management, they were the central figures in the rural economy of the south. The poor comprised approximately 30 to 40 percent of the peasantry in the Mekong River delta, whereas they had been in the majority in the north.

The southern farmers

The organizations designed to manage the transition of the rural economy in the south were cooperative management committees, called Village or Hamlet Production Committees. Their main task was to attract middle-income peasants into the cooperatives. At a government-sponsored meeting held in January 1978, it was reported that two-thirds of the peasants in the south were not yet participating in any form of collective labour, and details of an accelerated cooperativization program were announced.

Paddy production diminished after 1976 because of adverse weather and shortages of chemical fertilizers, pesticides, gasoline, credit, and spare parts for irrigation pumps (all of which are particularly important in the farming of the high-yield rice varieties adopted during the 1960s). Other factors were the southern farmers' reaction against collectivization and their unwillingness to produce a surplus for the markets while money and consumer goods were in short supply.

Socialization of commerce

The government's move to socialize the commercial sector by abolishing major private enterprises in the south was more successful than the attempt to collectivize agriculture. In November 1977 the government announced that capitalist enterprises in the south had not fully utilized their capacities and that more than 1,000,000 persons "were engaged in nonproductive commercial activities." On March 23, 1978, the government ordered the suppression of "bourgeois trade" and froze the goods and assets of some 30,000 businesses in Saigon alone. These businesses were to be replaced by a "fine socialist trade network," but the 4,000 state shops were clearly inadequate and shortages and serious inflation occurred. On May 6, 1978, a new currency was issued, ending the two separate currencies that had been used after 1975.

The government's moves against the private commercial sector, which mainly affected the ethnic Chinese, and deteriorating political relations with China precipitated the flight of ethnic Chinese from Vietnam in 1978. This serious loss of economic talent was compounded by the regime's policy of placing anyone associated with the former South Vietnamese government or the U.S. mission in jails or re-education centres. The resettlement program, which affected vast numbers of people including highly trained and educated individuals, also resulted in a loss of human resources. The large military organization maintained by the Vietnamese after 1975 and the war in 1979 with Cambodia (Kampuchea) further strained the national budget and diverted large numbers of personnel from the reconstruction of war-damaged roads, railway lines, dikes, irrigation projects, and bridges.

Resources. *Mineral resources.* Rich mineral deposits are a major source of wealth. In the provinces of Hanoi, there are large reserves of anthracite coal. Two percent of the world's supply of raw phosphates and one percent of its high-grade chromite come from Vietnam. There are also significant deposits of tin, antimony, bauxite, gold, iron ore, lead, tungsten, zinc, and lime.

In 1978, Vietnam signed an agreement with a West German firm to explore offshore oil deposits. Under the agreement, an area off the Mekong delta coast was given to the company for exploration. Similar agreements were signed with Italian and Canadian companies, and Norwegian and French government aid projects involved seismic surveys and drilling off Vung Tau, a beach resort near Saigon.

Biological resources. Forests are potentially a major natural resource. The total area under forest cover is 52,000,000 acres (21,000,000 hectares). In the absence of an accurate national forest inventory, it is difficult to estimate forest potential. It is known, however, that logging operations in large areas of dense forest would generally yield less than 40 cubic yards (30 cubic metres) of marketable timber per hectare.

Fish and shellfish from Vietnam's coastal waters and the plains of the Mekong and Bassac rivers are a major resource and the second most important food staple after rice.

Sources of national income. *Agriculture.* Agriculture is by far the most important economic sector in Vietnam. It is estimated that about 70 percent of the population earns its income from farming. In addition, agriculture is the main source of raw materials for the processing industries and a major contributor to exports. Of the nation's 80,000,000 acres (32,000,000 hectares) of land, only 12,000,000–15,000,000 acres are cultivated, however, or less than 0.3 acre (0.12 hectare) per person, one of the lowest such ratios in the world. The primary agricultural areas are the two large river deltas and the southern terrace region; the Red River delta has more than 1,700,000 acres of cultivated land, the Mekong River delta has 5,000,000 acres, and the terrace region has almost 2,000,000 acres. The strip of coastal land between the deltas is a region of low productivity; the central highlands area also is of low productivity, but has a significant agricultural potential.

Rice production

Rice is the most important crop, grown on about 75 percent of the cropped land, principally in the Red River and Mekong River deltas. In the late 1970s, the rice yield accounted for more than half of the total agricultural output. Drying and storage facilities were generally inadequate and there are additional losses due to industrial purposes (such as the production of alcohol) and seed requirements. Assuming a milling yield of 60 percent of the original crop—losses here due to obsolete equipment and the wide range of paddy varieties—from 6,500,000 to 7,500,000 tons, or 280 to 330 pounds (130 to 150 kilograms) per capita, of milled rice were produced in 1976. With average annual consumption estimated at 350 to 400 pounds (160 to 180 kilograms) per capita and a total rice demand of 7,000,000–8,000,000 tons, the deficit in 1976 amounted to about 500,000 tons. Part of this deficit was covered by subsidiary food crops such as maize (corn), sweet potatoes, and manioc (cassava), and the rest was covered by imports or reduced consumption. Bad weather, pests, and other factors (including a strong probability of deliberate low yields by some Mekong delta farmers) combined in 1978 to bring rice production to a low level of 220 pounds (100 kilograms) per person, roughly doubling the deficit and requiring massive imports and aid.

As of early 1980, the food situation remained precarious because neither the 1979 production target nor the 1979–80 cereal import requirements had yet been met. In fact, a significant decrease in local food production was expected because of the severe drought that affected the November-December planting of the winter-spring (secondary) rice crop in the northern provinces. By mid-March 1980, about 92 percent of the total planned area had been sown and transplanted in winter-spring (secondary) rice.

Agriculture is basically labour intensive in Vietnam, but whether the resettlement of millions of people in the "new economic zones" would significantly affect rice production during the 1980s was uncertain. Many of the new zones are located in areas not amenable to paddy farming and, although mechanization was expected to be increasingly important, by 1980 it had been concentrated more on irrigation schemes than on the acquisition of farm machinery. Of the estimated 29,000 tractors in Vietnam in 1977, one-third were idle because of the lack of spare parts and fuel. The greater part of the plowing was still done by water buffalo, which numbered more than 2,200,000 in the 1970s.

Industrial crops

Industrial crops include rubber, tea, coffee, fruit trees, sugarcane, tobacco, and jute. Located in the south, the rubber industry was seriously disrupted by the war. In 1975, the rubber estates were nationalized and a rehabilitation program was launched. In 1978, output was estimated at about 50,000 tons. Tea is grown on about 50,000 acres (20,000 hectares), with annual production at about 11,000 tons. Coffee production has been diminishing as the disease of leaf rust (caused by the fungus *Hemileia vastatrix*) and the parasitic berry borer (*Stephanoderes hamjei*) forced abandonment of Arabica coffee. Robusta and Chari coffee production in 1977 was around 5,500 tons. In 1976, fruit trees were planted on about 320,000 acres (130,000 hectares), bananas on 136,000 acres, and pineapples on 162,000 acres. Citrus fruits (oranges, limes, and grapefruit) were also important. In 1977 it was estimated that sugarcane was grown on 160,000 acres, with an annual production of around 1,400,000 tons. That same year the area under jute was estimated at 67,000 acres, with an annual production of 34,000 tons. There was only one factory producing jute bags, with an annual capacity of 3,000 tons, the balance was processed by small village shops.

An increase of agricultural production was of major importance to the government. In 1979 a full 40 percent of the national budget was set aside for a development plan that called for the extension of cultivated areas by the resettlement of 10,000,000 people by the year 2000 (see *Demography* above).

Fishing. After rice, fish is the most important staple food, and the estimated annual production in 1977 was 800,000 tons, a substantial contribution to Vietnam's food economy and protein supply. The export of seafoods such as lobsters, prawns, shrimp, and crabs is an excellent potential source of foreign exchange, but production methods are inefficient. Government officials have reported that refugees who left the country by sea took more than 5,000 fishing boats, seriously hampering plans to increase production. About 100,000 fishermen and fish farmers were engaged in the late 1970s in inland fisheries, the most important of which were located on the plains of the Mekong and Bassac rivers. The principal fish farmed are species of tilapia, carp, catfish, and snakehead.

Forestry. The Ministry of Forestry estimated timber extraction at 2,100,000 cubic yards (1,600,000 cubic metres) in 1976. There is little modernization of forest industries. About 350 brickkilns produce charcoal in mangrove areas, and there are a number of furniture and pulp and paper factories, as well as wooden handicraft centres. In the south, most timber has been used for reconstruction.

Manufacturing. At the end of the Vietnam War, industries in the southern and northern parts of the country faced different difficulties. Wartime destruction of the industrial plant had not been great in the south, but the supply of imported raw materials and spare parts had been seriously disrupted. Industries that relied on local raw materials resumed operations quickly, but they experienced problems of unreliable supplies and poor logistics. The task of adequate maintenance, repair, and replacement of industrial machinery was complicated by the heterogeneity of equipment that had been purchased from different countries. These problems resulted in a post-war utilization of the southern industrial capacity of about 50 percent.

Northern industrial development

In the north, there was a period of intense reconstruction of industry from 1973 to 1975. Notable industries not completely rebuilt by 1975 were large and capital-intensive, including the Gia Lam railroad workshops in Hanoi, the Viet Tri chemical combine, the Nam Dinh textile mill, and the Haiphong shipyard and cement plant. Despite the reconstruction progress, there has been serious underutilization of industrial capacity, as well as unsatisfactory levels of production and a deterioration in the quality of output. Industry has been plagued by old equipment that is subject to frequent breakdowns, inadequate protection of equipment against the weather, insufficient maintenance of tools and materials, and inadequate standards and guidelines for the use of equipment.

Energy. The production of electricity remained insufficient by 1980, although great increases over the production capacity of the 1960s had been achieved. Coal-burning plants were the primary source of electricity, most of which was utilized for purposes of industry and irrigation.

Foreign trade. Since 1976, Vietnam has suffered an unfavourable balance of payments, with the value of imports greatly exceeding that of exports. Vietnam's major trading partners are the Soviet Union and Japan; the government joined the Council for Mutual Economic Assistance (Comecon) as a full partner in 1978.

Major exports are coal, rubber, light industrial products, handicrafts, fish, and processed agricultural products. The total value of these exports, and especially of coal, was adversely affected by the refugee exodus and the war in Cambodia and political conflict with China in the late 1970s.

Imports are directed toward food, agriculture (20 percent of investment expenditure), and industry, power, and railways (40 to 50 percent of investment expenditure). The volume of imports of raw materials, fuels, fertilizers, and insecticides was expected to grow at the same rate (10 to 15 percent by 1980) as the projected expansion of related economic activities. The government clearly intended to restrict imports of consumer goods—apart from food grains and other essential foodstuffs—as long as foreign exchange remained scarce.

Foreign aid. In 1977, the International Monetary Fund lent U.S. $36,000,000 to Vietnam for "reconstruction of the economy." The Vietnam government assumed South Vietnam's membership in the World Bank, and in 1978 that institution approved its first loan to Vietnam, a sum of U.S. $60,000,000 for improved water management southwest of Saigon. The World Bank loan was not implemented by 1980, however. Loans from Denmark, The Netherlands, Kuwait, and the Organization of Petroleum Exporting Countries (OPEC) were received. After protracted negotiations, Hanoi agreed to pay the debt owed to Japan by the former Saigon government, and in return it received a promise of a loan for the purchase of non-military goods. After Vietnam became a full member of Comecon in 1978, that organization promised to support numerous projects abandoned by China. Loans that had been approved for South Vietnam by the Asian Development Bank were to be implemented in 1980, but no new loans were approved. The United Nations Development Program projects in agriculture, forestry and fisheries; natural resources development; social security and other social services; and transport and communications were implemented in 1979.

Labour. The end of the war in 1975 left an estimated 3,500,000 persons, a large number of them former military personnel, unemployed in the south, while in the north a large armed force was maintained and the government claimed to have achieved full employment. By 1977, the number of unemployed had been reduced by half, largely by the resettlement program. In 1960, an estimated 81 percent of the labour force was engaged in agriculture and 5 percent in industry; by 1979, the percentage in agriculture had dropped to 70 percent, while that in industry had risen to 8 percent. Between 1960 and 1979, the percentage of those in service industries had risen from 14 to 22 percent. The average annual growth of the labour force for the period of 1960–70 was 1.0 percent; it rose between 1970 and 1978 to 1.7 percent. In 1978, the total labour force in Vietnam was reported to be about 21,470,000. The general mobilization of March 1979 undoubtedly favourably affected the labour market by reducing the number of unemployed, but that program and the flight of refugees also removed skilled workers from the economic sector.

Trade unions

The Vietnam General Confederation of Trade Unions, an instrument of the Communist Party, is the only legal labour organization. North Vietnam had adopted the Soviet-style "single manager system" in industry, giving factory administrators a wide margin of latitude in factory management and placing a heavy burden on labour unions to exercise political leadership among the workers. The South Vietnam Federation of Trade Unions, founded in 1961, carried on the Communist Party's struggle against the trade unions sponsored by the Saigon government; in 1976, the Federation merged with the General Confederation of Trade Unions.

Economic problems and prospects. The growth rate of Vietnam's gross national product has declined since the annual rate of nine percent was achieved in 1976. Within two years the economy's growth rate had dropped below the annual rate of population increase of about three percent, suggesting a decline in per capita income during 1978. The situation was further complicated by substantial budget deficits, with expenditures exceeding receipts by as much as one third. The deficit was financed by foreign aid receipts and loans from the state bank.

Total credit outstanding, like income and the rate of increase of the money supply, was growing, but at a decreasing rate after 1976. Continued growth in the money supply is probably partly intended to offset the effect on the southern economy of the currency conversion of May 1978. Much of the southern money supply was eliminated by the change to a single Vietnamese currency because the amount of new currency issued was limited and the use of commercial credit was virtually abolished. Even so, prices outside the state-owned sector rose sharply, and barter and the use of gold as a medium of exchange increased, particularly in rural areas.

Economic output in the south, especially of rice, fell significantly and much of the service sector of the southern economy was eliminated. The southern economy, therefore, experienced a severe contraction that was likely to persist; investments that would normally counteract this trend were not made, and the ethnic Chinese, who were the primary source of investment, had fled. The drop in southern income also curtailed the region's ability to purchase northern industrial products.

Economic controls

Because Vietnam severely restricted foreign trade and exchange, the conversion of income estimates into foreign currency terms was less meaningful than it is for most countries. Income in the north in the late 1970s was more evenly distributed than in the south because wages were established by the state. Transportation to and from work, education, medicine, and health services were free. Although housing was relatively poor, it was provided to all workers in state-owned enterprises at a charge of one percent of salary. Price controls and rationing were also used throughout Vietnam to influence the level and distribution of personal income. Food was rationed and food prices on the free market, where the bulk of transactions occurred in the south, were at least two or three times the level of controlled prices. Many industrial consumer goods, such as cloth, were also rationed. In the north, most of the working population outside the state-owned sector were employed in cooperatives, the greater part of them agricultural. The relatively high level of consumption that existed in the south before 1975 fell significantly with the end of U.S. foreign aid and imports. Markets for the remaining "luxury" goods thrived outside the official sector in places such as Saigon.

TRANSPORTATION

The geography of Vietnam has rendered transportation between the north and south difficult. Except for air and sea communications, traffic has been limited to the narrow coastal corridor. The two large deltas, where most of the population is concentrated, have good internal transportation systems based on vast networks of navigable inland waterways, roads, and cart trails. Air travel, which was highly developed in the south, declined in that region after 1975. During the late 1970s, the government attempted to nationalize truck and bus services in the south. In the north, nearly 30 percent of the Chinese- and Soviet-made trucks were out of service in 1978 because of shortages of spare parts. Heavy floods in 1978 damaged roads and bridges and repairs were rendered difficult because of the diversion of military labour to the war in Cambodia and along the Chinese border. In 1978, work was begun on the expansion of the port of Haiphong and a new major port facility on the Red River near Hanoi.

Roads. The war years brought about the major development of roads in the north and the south. In the south, the emphasis was on the construction and improvement of major arterial highways, while in the north priority was given to the construction of secondary roads. By the mid-1970s the two networks included a total of 41,000 miles (66,000 kilometres) of roads, 13,000 miles in the south and 28,000 in the north.

Railroads. During the war years, the 1,640 miles (2,640 kilometres) of railroads in Vietnam were subjected to aerial bombing attacks in the north and sabotage in the south, resulting in extensive destruction. More than 400 bridges, 40 of them major ones, were destroyed, and stations, warehouses, railroad yards, and other facilities were destroyed or rendered inoperable. The government launched a comprehensive reconstruction program and, in 1976, the trans-Vietnam railroad between Hanoi and Saigon began operations for the first time in 30 years. That year the railroad transported 6,000,000 tons of freight and 30,000,000 passengers. The government planned to expand the railroad system by 1985 to a rail network of 1,860 miles and a stock of more than 500 locomotives, 1,200 passenger cars, and 12,000 freight cars, which would at least quintuple the transport volume of 1976. In 1978 it was reported that Comecon agreed to modernize the Hanoi–Saigon railway track, making it broad gauge, and an agreement was signed with India for the purchase of equipment and cars.

Waterways. There is an extensive network of navigable rivers and canals in the Red River delta (3,700 miles, or 6,000 kilometres) and the Mekong River delta (3,000 miles, or 4,800 kilometres). Maintenance work to avoid silting has been hampered by wartime damage to dredging equipment and by general deterioration. Most coastal and ocean shipping is centred in the northern port of Haiphong and the southern port of Saigon. The ports of Hon Gai and Cam Pha are used mainly as export stations for coal, while Vinh and Da Nang serve as transit ports for Laos. The war brought considerable improvements to port facilities at Cam Ranh, Nha Trang, and Qui Nhon.

Port facilities

Air Traffic. The U.S. military presence in the south during the war years resulted in the construction of more than 100 airfields, a number far in excess of likely future requirements. By 1977, seven airports and about 6,200 miles (10,000 kilometres) of air corridors were in operation. Noi Bai, the new airport at Hanoi, was opened to international traffic in 1978; it is intended to function as the hub of aviation for all of Vietnam. Soviet, East German, Chinese, and Laotian aircraft began using the new facility, but the lack of facilities at Noi Bai led to a decision by Air France to land at Saigon's Tan Son Nhut airport. In 1978, Vietnam agreed to open the air route across the central part of the country to international airlines, except those based in the U.S., South Korea, and Taiwan.

ADMINISTRATION AND SOCIAL CONDITIONS

Administration. *Structure of the central government.* The elections of April 25, 1976, produced a new unicameral National Assembly of 492 members (243 from the south and 249 from the north), the major task of which was to establish a single national government for the unified nation. The principle of universal suffrage for those 18 years of age or older determined the electorate. On June 24 the assembly met for the first time, and on July 2 it exercised its first prerogatives, creating the Socialist Republic of Vietnam and electing the nation's president, two vice presidents, and cabinet, and the members of the Standing Committee of the National Assembly. The primary task of the Standing Committee was to draft a new constitution, which was published in August 1979 and was to be implemented in stages. Because of internal and external crises, however, the North Vietnamese constitution of January 1, 1960, remained in effect. The 1960 document describes Vietnam as a "people's democratic state, based on the alliance between the workers and the peasants, and led by the working class." Most basic civil rights are guaranteed, but they are also carefully circumscribed by the wide latitude that the Vietnamese Communist Party and the state enjoy in interpreting them and by the stipulation that "the state forbids any person to use democratic freedoms to the detriment of the interests of the state and of the people." The 1960 constitution also guarantees a wide range of "social rights," including the rights to a job, an education, and "material assistance in old age in the case of illness or disability." The 1960 constitution, like that of 1946, stresses the multi-ethnic character of Vietnam, and it declares that autonomous zones for the minorities "may be established"; those zones that had been established in the north, however, were abolished in 1976.

The 1960 constitution

The National Assembly is the supreme organ of the government. The Council of Ministers is comprised of the prime minister and deputy prime ministers, all of whom are named by the National Assembly, and the heads of government ministries and various state organizations. The Council coordinates and directs the activities of the ministries and the various state organizations at the level of the central government and supervises the activities of administrative committees at the level of local government.

Each ministry is headed by a minister, who is assisted by several vice ministers. Responsibilities of the ministries usually are defined along narrow functional lines; there are, for example, numerous economic ministries concerned with subsectors such as grains and food products, marine products, afforestation, water conservancy, light industry, engineering and metals, power and coal, and construction. Larger ministries tend to be relatively self-sufficient, with their own colleges, training institutions, and health, social, and cultural facilities. There are also a number of commissions under the Council of Ministers, including the State Planning Commission, headed by a deputy prime minister; the State Bank, headed by a director general with ministerial rank; and the Central Agriculture Commission. Under the prime minister's office are a number of general departments that have a lower status in the administration than ministries. The more important departments are headed by ministers. Committees under the prime minister's office are also formed to supervise projects, such as the Da River hydroelectric project, that involve more than one ministry.

Regional and local government. The traditional administrative units of local government in Vietnam have been the provinces, districts, and villages. Following reunification in 1976, local administration was reorganized into 35 provinces and 3 municipalities (Hanoi, Haiphong, and Saigon) on the provincial level. There are about 500 districts, each with an average population of around 100,000. At either the provincial or district level, the highest government authority is an elected People's Council, the actual work of which is carried out by administrative committees appointed by the councils. After 1976, an effort was made to upgrade the responsibilities of the districts; growth of agricultural cooperatives, for example, was expected to place more economic management in the sphere of district administration. Village administration is represented by village people's councils.

The political process. The most important political institution in Vietnam is the Vietnamese Communist Party (Dang Cong san Viet Nam), founded in 1976 from the Vietnamese Workers' Party (Lao Dong) of North Vietnam. Any citizen of the age of 18 or over who "has engaged in labour and not been an exploiter" is eligible to join. At the fourth party congress in 1976 it was reported that membership numbered 1,553,500, or just more than three percent of the total population; of this total 273,000 party members were in the south, representing about one percent of the population of that region. In the late 1970s there was a concentrated effort to recruit party members from the Ho Chi Minh Communist Youth League, whose membership consisted of about 30 percent of all youths between the ages of 15 and 30 in the north and about 10 percent of that age group in the south.

The Vietnamese Communist Party

Effective authority within the Vietnamese Communist Party lies with the Politburo's 14 voting members and 3 alternates and the Central Committee's 101 full members and 32 alternates. Of the two bodies, however, the Politburo has more political power. It is not known precisely how decisions are made within the Politburo, but it appears that they result from a process of compromise among its senior members. The secretary general of the Vietnamese Communist Party presides over the party's Secretariat, which is elected by the Central Committee. The Secretariat directs the tasks of the party organization and the coordination of party and state bureaucracies in carrying out the resolutions of the Central Committee and the Politburo; it also has responsibility for implementing party resolutions.

Justice. The judicial system consists of the courts and the People's Organs of Control. The National Assembly supervises the work of the Supreme People's Court, which is the highest court of appeal and the court of first instance for special cases (such as those involving treason). This court in turn supervises the judicial work of local People's Courts, which are responsible to their corresponding People's Councils. The People's Courts function at all levels of government except the village level, where the village administrative committee functions as a primary court.

People's Organs of Control

The People's Organs of Control act as watchdogs for the state; they monitor the performance of government agencies, maintain vast powers of surveillance, and act as prosecutors before the People's Courts. The People's Supreme Organ of Control is responsible only to the Standing Committee of the National Assembly.

The armed forces. Until a general mobilization was ordered in March 1979, it was estimated that Vietnam's active military personnel totalled 615,000; the total subsequently rose to an estimated 1,023,000. Military forces included the army, paramilitary regional and provincial forces, the militia, and the reserves. There are separate military commands in Hanoi, Haiphong, and Saigon.

Social services. *Educational services.* Because of their Confucianist traditions, education has always been important to the Vietnamese. Rural education in the south was badly disrupted during the war years, and all religious and private schools were nationalized after 1975. The government appeared in the late 1970s to be achieving its goals in education and reformed the educational system in 1979. Twelve years of schooling were provided free to everyone. The educational system was divided into three levels; after the first nine years of schooling, students would be selected to continue into higher education or to attend technical or vocational training institutions. In the 1977–78 school year, some 11,400,000 general education students (4,700,000 of them in the south) were enrolled in all three levels, representing an increase of about nine percent over the previous year's enrollment. There also were 125,000 students in the 268 vocational schools and 134,000 students in the nation's 63 universities and colleges.

In 1978 the government claimed that illiteracy had been abolished in the south, as it already had been in the north. Emphasis was placed on training in science and technology, although a lack of equipment hindered the program, and several thousand students were sent to study languages and technology abroad. While most of the students sent to other countries went to the Soviet Union and eastern Europe, some studied in France, Great Britain, and Australia.

Health. Before unification, health services were underdeveloped in the rural areas of South Vietnam, but were well developed in North Vietnam. Between 1960 and 1975, for example, the North Vietnamese health program reduced the number of cases of poliomyelitis from 3.1 to 0.7 per 100,000 inhabitants, of typhoid from 17.6 to 0.5, and of diphtheria from 16.4 to 3.2. On the basis of the number of persons X-rayed, tuberculosis was reduced by half.

Between 1975 and 1977 there was a general increase in health facilities and personnel (physicians, assistant physicians, nurses, and midwives) throughout Vietnam. Health facilities included hospitals, health centres, leprosy centres, sanatoriums, and village health and maternity centres.

CULTURAL LIFE AND INSTITUTIONS

Fine arts. Chinese influence permeates all aspects of traditional Vietnamese culture, and it is strongly manifest in language, art, architecture, music, theatre, literature, and poetry. Deeply rooted in the Vietnamese oral tradition, poetry was highly regarded by the educated class centred in the royal courts, and it was expressed in Chinese form and style. By the 14th century, however, a demotic script called *chu nom* ("southern characters") came into use among the Vietnamese literati, permitting the emergence of an explicitly Vietnamese "tale in the southern script" (*truyen nom*) that, during the 17th and 18th centuries, evolved into the form of a long narrative poem. This art form reached its culmination in the best known of Vietnamese poems, *Kim Van Kieu* ("The Tale of Kieu") by Nguyen Du (1765–1820). Further evolution of this literary tradition was arrested by the French conquest and the imposition of French culture on the Vietnamese elite. Despite this and later influences from the outside, poetry has retained its importance in the Vietnamese artistic tradition. Vietnamese poetry is now written in a romanized script based on the first Latin script for the tonal language devised by Father Alexandre de Rhodes, a Jesuit priest from Avignon.

Importance of poetry

Traditional Chinese opera, called *hat tuong* in the north and *hat boi* in the south, is popular among the Vietnamese, as is the more indigenous *cai luong*, a satirical musical comedy. The theatre is strictly controlled and all actors and other performers are unionized employees of the state. Painting has failed to flourish among the Vietnamese; it has been bound for centuries first by rigid traditional Chinese forms, then by a style imitative of French Impressionism, and now by the tenets of Socialist Realism. High quality lacquer ware, however, continues to be produced.

Folk arts. Folk traditions flourish among the peoples of the central highlands, who continue to produce most of the things they need. Precious hardwood is used for carving crossbows and figures, most of which are destined for tombs. Among the Rhadé, a mountain tribal group living mainly in Dac Lac province, hardwood is used extensively in the construction of longhouses built on pilings. Among the highlanders, women weave blankets, blouses, skirts, and loincloths, while the men weave baskets and mats. They have a wide variety of musical instruments, but gongs are the most common. Dancing is found among only a few groups. The Cham and Khmer minorities have retained some folk arts, but as they become more assimilated into Vietnamese culture, their own traditions fade.

Press and broadcasting. The Vietnamese press and all broadcasting facilities are strictly controlled and operated by the government, the Vietnamese Communist Party, or subordinate organizations. *Nhan Dan*, with a circulation of 200,000, is the official Vietnamese Communist Party newspaper; it is published in Hanoi. Other newspapers published in the capital are *Thu Do Hanoi* (30,000), *Thoi Moi* (30,000), and the biweekly *Nhan Dan Nong Thong* (21,000). *Lao Dong* (72,000) is the weekly trade union publication, and *Quan Doi Nhan Dan* is the army organ. Of the 30 Vietnamese-language newspapers that were published in the south before 1975, only *Tin Sang* remains; *Giai Phong* began publication in Saigon in 1975. The government maintains the Vietnam News Agency in Hanoi. Foreign news agencies with offices in Hanoi include *Agence France-Presse*, Czechoslovak News Agency (Četkea), and Novosti Press Agency and TASS of the Soviet Union.

The government-controlled Voice of Vietnam broadcasts over the two networks from Hanoi. Liberated Radio Saigon began transmittal in the south in May 1975. Television was introduced into South Vietnam in 1966 and into North Vietnam in 1970. In the late 1970s there were reported to be 2,600,000 radio receivers and 2,000,000 television receivers in the country; there were 47,000 telephones, most of them in the south.

(GERALD C. HICKEY)

There is no better way to recapture the dolorous experience of the eastern Mediterranean during the 1970s than to compare the new Britannica article on Beirut, prepared for the 1981 edition, with the one it replaced, which first appeared in 1974.

The old article, after recounting the long history of the city itself, went on to record the many delights of modern Beirut. We read of the high-rise apartments; the fashionable department stores; the luxurious hotels; the diversity and quality of the educational facilities, making Beirut "an ebullient centre of learning and culture"; the recreational areas, where "those with leisure are able to enjoy the rare scenic delights of the coast or to picnic in the shade of the pine or olive groves on the outskirts of the city's southern fringe."

After the civil war that raged through the mid-1970s, almost all of this is gone. True, Beirut, even after the destruction of so many buildings and institutions, is still remarkably alive. If today's Beirut is no longer the hub of the Arab Middle East, no other city has taken its place. But despite the bustling activity among the ruins, the overall impression is of desolation. Beirut the beautiful, once the jewel of the eastern Mediterranean, has become a woeful symbol of man's passion and cruelty.

BEIRUT

Beirut (Arabic, Bayrūt; French spelling, Beyrouth) is the capital, largest city, and main port of the Republic of Lebanon. It occupies a metropolitan area of approximately 26 square miles (67 square kilometres) on the Mediterranean coast, at the foot of Mt. Lebanon. It comprises two hills, al-Ashrafīyah (East Beirut) and al-Muṣayṭibah (West Beirut), that protrude into the sea as a roughly triangular peninsula; in the immediate hinterland lies a narrow coastal plain (al-Sāḥil) that extends from the mouth of the Nahr al-Kalb (Dog River) in the north to that of the Nahr al-Dāmūr (Damur River) in the south.

The resident population of Beirut in 1980 probably exceeded 1,000,000 (no dependable figures were available), and was more or less evenly divided between Muslims and Christians. The overwhelming majority in both religious groups was ethnically Arab, and included Palestinian refugees, Syrian residents, and others. The most important ethnic minority was the Christian Armenians; there was also a Kurdish ethnic minority among the Muslims. East Beirut was almost solidly Christian, West Beirut was predominantly Muslim, and a number of mixed neighbourhoods (notably in the district of Ra's Bayrūt) were cosmopolitan in character. The Jewish community, which had been concentrated in the neighbourhood of Wādī Abū Jamīl, was reckoned at less than 2,000. The larger Christian communities were the Maronites and the Greek Orthodox; the Christian minorities, apart from the Armenians, included Greek Catholics, Protestants, Roman Catholics, and others. Originally, the Sunnīs were the dominant Muslim community, but Shīʿī Muslims began moving into the city in increasing numbers from the 1960s. Small numbers of Druzes lived in parts of West Beirut.

Ethnic and religious groups

History. The antiquity of Beirut is indicated by its name, derived from the Canaanite name of Beʾerōt (Wells), referring to the underground water table which is still tapped by the local inhabitants for general use. Although the city is mentioned in Egyptian records of the second millennium BC, it did not gain prominence until it was granted the status of a Roman colony, the Colonia Julia Augusta Felix Berytus, in 14 BC. The original town was located in the valley between the hills of al-Ashrafīyah and al-Muṣayṭibah. Its suburbs were also fashionable residential areas under the Romans, who constructed an aqueduct to augment the city's water supply. Between the 3rd and 6th centuries AD, Beirut was famous for its school of law. The Roman city was destroyed by a succession of earthquakes, culminating in the earthquake and tidal wave of AD 551. When the Muslim conquerors occupied Beirut in 635, it was still mostly in ruins.

Arab and Christian rule. Reconstructed on a small scale by the Muslims, Beirut reemerged as a small, walled garrison town administered from Baalbek as part of the *jund* (Muslim province) of Damascus. Until the 9th or 10th century, it remained commercially of no significance, and was notable mainly for the careers of two eminent local jurists, al-Awzāʿī (died 774) and al-Makḥūl (died 933). A return of maritime commerce to the Mediterranean in the 10th century revived the importance of the town, particularly after Syria passed under the rule of the Fāṭimid caliphs of Egypt in 977. In 1110, Beirut was conquered by the military forces of the First Crusade and was organized, along with its coastal suburbs, as a fief of the Latin Kingdom of Jerusalem.

The crusaders

As a crusader outpost, it conducted a flourishing trade with Genoa and other Italian cities; strategically, however, its position was precarious because it was subject to raids by the Druze tribesmen of the mountain hinterland. Saladin reconquered Beirut from the crusaders in 1187, but his successors lost it to them again in 1197. It was the Mamlūks who finally drove the crusaders out of the town in 1291. Under Mamlūk rule, Beirut became the principal port of call in Syria for the spice merchants of Venice.

Ottoman rule. Beirut, along with the rest of Syria, passed under Ottoman rule in 1516, shortly after the Portuguese had rounded the African continent (1498) to divert the spice trade of the East away from Syria and Egypt. The commercial importance of Beirut declined in consequence. By the 17th century, however, the city had reemerged as an exporter of Lebanese silk to Europe, mainly to Italy and France. Beirut at the time was technically part of the Ottoman province (*eyalet*) of Damascus, and after 1660 of Sidon. Between 1598 and 1633, however, and again between 1749 and 1774, it fell under the control of the Maʿn and Shihāb emirs (feudal suzerains and fiscal agents) of the Druze and Maronite mountain hinterland. From the mid-17th to the late 18th century, Maronite notables from the mountains served as French consuls in Beirut, wielding considerable local influence. During the Russo-Turkish War of 1768–74, the town suffered heavy bombardment by the Russians. Subsequently it was wrested from the Shihāb emirs by the Ottomans, and shrank into a village of about 6,000.

The growth of modern Beirut was a result of the Industrial Revolution in Europe. Factory-produced goods of the Western world began to invade the markets of Ottoman Syria, and Beirut, starting virtually from nought, stood only to profit from the modern industrial world. The occupation of Syria by the Egyptians (1832–40) under Muḥammad ʿAlī Pasha provided the needed stimulus for the town to enter on its new period of commercial growth. A brief setback came with the end of the Egyptian occupation; by 1848, however, the town had begun to outgrow its walls, and its population had increased to about 15,000. Civil wars in the mountains, culminating in a massacre of Christians by Druzes in 1860, further swelled Beirut's population, as Christian refugees moved in to settle in large numbers. Meanwhile, the pacification of the mountains under an autonomous government guaranteed by the great powers (1861–1914) stabilized the social and economic relationship between the town and its hinterland, where traditional silk production was mechanized by French and local industrial concerns. In 1886, Beirut was made the capital of a separate province (*vilâyet*) comprising the whole of coastal Syria, including Palestine. By 1900, it was a city of about 120,000.

Egyptian occupation

Meanwhile, Protestant missionaries from Great Britain, the United States, and Germany and Roman Catholic missionaries mainly from France became active in Beirut, particularly in education. In 1866, the American Protestant Mission established the Syrian Protestant College, which later became the American University of Beirut. In 1881, French Jesuit missionaries established the Université Saint-Joseph as a rival institution. Printing presses, introduced earlier by Protestant and Roman Catholic missionaries, stimulated the growth of the city's publishing industry, mainly in Arabic but also in French and English. By 1900, Beirut was in the vanguard of Arabic journalism. A class of intellectuals sought to revive the Arabic cultural heritage and become the first spokesmen of a new Arab nationalism.

Modern Beirut. Occupied by the Allies at the end of World War I, Beirut was established by the French mandatory authorities in 1920 as the capital of the State of Greater Lebanon, which in 1926 became the Lebanese Republic. The Muslims of Beirut resented the inclusion of the city in a Christian-dominated Lebanon and declared loyalty to a broader pan-Arabism than most Christians would support. The resultant conflict became endemic. The accelerated economic growth of Beirut under the French Mandate (1920–43) and after produced rapid growth of the city's population and the rise of social tensions. These tensions were increased by the influx of thousands of Palestinian refugees after 1948. The political and social tensions in Beirut and elsewhere in Lebanon, coupled with Christian–Muslim tensions, flared into open hostilities in 1958, and even more violently in 1974–76. The conflict continued to simmer, with sporadic eruptions of violence. In 1976–80, Beirut was two cities: an East Beirut dominated by the Christian militia, and a West Beirut controlled by the Syrian military forces that intervened to stop the hostilities of the 1970s as an Arab deterrent force.

Muslim–Christian tensions

The contemporary city. Under the Ottoman *vilâyet* administration and the French Mandate, the growth of Beirut was planned, but after independence in 1943 it was as haphazard as it was rapid. It is estimated that the population of the city increased tenfold between the early 1930s and early 1970s and the city's area grew to three times the size it had been in 1900. By the 1950s, few traces of the old city were left, and most of those were destroyed in the 1974–76 civil war and its aftermath.

The neighbourhoods. Street plans and block arrangements in the city and its suburbs are not consistent or uniform. In most quarters, modern high-rise buildings, walk-up apartments, slum tenements, modern villas, and traditional two-story houses with red-tiled roofs—all in varying states of repair—stand side by side. After 1974, countless houses and apartments, particularly in West Beirut, were forcibly occupied by refugees from rural areas, especially from the Shīʿī areas of South Lebanon.

The downtown area of central Beirut (the old city) was destroyed during the civil war and remains in ruins—a vacant belt between East and West Beirut that could not be reconstructed because of sporadic fighting there between Syrian Arab deterrent forces and the Christian militia. As a result, all business moved out of the area to establish new premises in the Christian and Muslim sides of the city. While few areas of Beirut were purely residential before 1974, none was by 1980. Despite frequent disruptions, the port of Beirut began functioning again in 1976, as did Beirut International Airport in the southern suburb of Khaldah.

Effects of the civil war. Between 1952 and 1975, Beirut was the hub of economic, social, intellectual, and cultural life in the Arab Middle East. In an area dominated by authoritarian or militarist regimes, the Lebanese capital was generally regarded as a haven of liberalism, though a precarious one. With its seaport and airport—coupled with Lebanon's free economic and foreign exchange system, solid gold-backed currency, banking-secrecy law, and favourable interest rates—Beirut became an established banking centre for Arab wealth, much of which was invested in construction, commercial enterprise, and industry (mostly the manufacture of textiles and shoes, food processing, and printing). Foreign banking and business firms found in Beirut an ideal base for their operations in the Arab Middle East. The "free zone" of the Beirut port was a leading entrepôt for the region. A skilled professional class provided varied sophisticated services for a pan-Arab clientele. Beirut was also a centre for tourism. The large number of daily and weekly newspapers, journals, and other periodicals, which were normally uncensored, kept the Arab world informed about regional and world developments and provided a full array of editorial opinion. Beirut's schools, colleges, and universities—the American University of Beirut, Université Saint-Joseph, Lebanese University, and Beirut Arab University—attracted students from many Arab countries. Underlying all these aspects of development, however, were a lack of consistency and organization and an undercurrent of social and political unrest that never escaped notice.

Beirut became a prominent centre for Palestinian resistance organizations after the Arab–Israeli War of 1967, and became the leading centre of the movement after the Palestinian organization in Jordan was crushed in 1970. The Lebanese government failed in repeated attempts to bring the Palestinian movement in Beirut and the rest of Lebanon under control, and in the 1970s the Lebanese capital was considered to be a base of international terrorism. Assassinations, bank robberies, and varied forms of political blackmail became regular events in the city. Arab nationalist and leftist political parties established armed militias for themselves, frequently in association with the Palestinian resistance movement; Christian Lebanese nationalist parties did the same. In the clashes that finally broke out between the two sides, the established order of Beirut was destroyed.

Political terrorism

Beirut in 1980 was no longer the hub of the Arab Middle East; no other Arab city, however, had taken its place, though some, notably Amman, in Jordan, and Manama, in Bahrain, tried to do so. Beirut, however, remained remarkably active, despite the catastrophe it suffered and the many residual problems that seemed far from being resolved. Its banks were still very much in business, as was its service sector, despite a considerable loss of trained personnel. The older universities were still by far the best in the Arab world, at least because they continued to operate freely. The press, likewise, was still the best in the Arab world and in some cases maintained standards of excellence. While East Beirut emerged with a monolithically Christian character, parts of West Beirut (particularly Ra's Bayrūt) remained cosmopolitan to some extent. The secret of the city's survival may lie in its middle-class infrastructure, unique in the Arab world. It was established by long tradition and involved large numbers of persons with diverse skills. The middle class of Beirut is basically patriotic, contrary to appearance, and blends conservatism with resilience. In the troubled state of the Middle East in the early 1980s, however, it was impossible to make a prognosis for the city. Much depends on what happens not only in Lebanon but in the area at large. (KAMAL SULEIMAN SALIBI)

Beirut's survival

1980

Aerial Sports

During 1980 several noteworthy events occurred: a father and son completed the first balloon flight across North America; the first solar-powered aircraft passed a test flight in California; the women's distance record for gliders was broken; and death claimed Jacqueline Cochran (*see* OBITUARIES), one of the greatest pilots in aviation history.

Maxie Anderson, one of three pilots aboard the "Double Eagle II" when it completed the first successful transatlantic balloon flight in 1978, made history again in 1980. He and his 23-year-old son, Kristian, guided the "Kitty Hawk" to a new record for overland flight. The 23-m (75-ft) helium-filled balloon lifted off at Fort Baker, Calif., and traveled more than 4,991 km (3,100 mi) before returning to Earth at Ste. Félicité, Que. The Andersons, who reached an altitude of 8,387.5 m (27,500 ft), braved fierce thunderstorms, 145 kph (90-mph) winds, and subzero temperatures on a voyage that Maxie Anderson called more difficult than crossing the Atlantic Ocean. The flight consumed 99 hr 54 min and ended far north of the planned destination, Kitty Hawk, N.C. A controversy arose because the balloon had not actually reached the coast, but the U.S. National Aeronautic Association ruled that the flight was an official transcontinental crossing because the two-man crew had the Atlantic in view before landing. The Balloon Federation of America endorsed the ruling. Icing conditions over Kansas forced two other Americans, John Shoecraft and Ron Ripps, to abandon their attempt to cross the U.S. in December aboard the "Super Chicken II."

The world balloon championships in Belgium were a fiasco. The first event, at Liège, was canceled for lack of funds. The second, at Brussels, was also canceled because air traffic control failed to give clearance. The third, at St. Nicholas, was confined to a 30-min and a 50-min flight because of poor weather. Gerry Turnbull (U.K.) won first place. A new women's world altitude record for Class AX-5 through AX-15 balloons was recognized by the Fédération Aéronautique Internationale. Carol Davis (U.S.) had claimed the record after reaching 9,546.5 m (31,300 ft) in New Mexico on Dec. 8, 1979.

Doris Grove (U.S.), piloting an AS-W 19 glider, covered 1,001 km (622 mi) in an out-and-return flight between Julian, Pa., and Bluefield, W.Va. She thus became the first woman to break the 1,000-km barrier. A few weeks later Cornelia Yoder (U.S.) broke Grove's record. Yoder covered 1,025 km (637 mi) flying an AS-W 19 glider between Port Matilda, Pa., and Tazewell, Va. Early in the year Karla Karel (U.K.) established three different gliding records in Australia. She first established a women's distance record of 814 km (505.8 mi) around a triangular course. Karel then glided 949.7 km (590 mi), a record for distance in a straight line. In addition, she set a women's speed record of 125.87 kph (78 mph) over a 300-km course. Her aircraft was an LS-3 glider.

In July Rich Matros (U.S.) claimed a multiplace flex-wing hang glider altitude record of 2,440 m (8,000 ft) for a flight he made in California. George Worthington (U.S.) claimed three new records. Using a single-place flex-wing hang glider, he established a distance record of 178.7 km (111 mi), and he covered a distance of 169 km (104.9 mi) in a rigid-wing hang glider. Worthington's third record was for altitude; he climbed 2,592.2 m (8,499 ft) in a single-place rigid-wing hang glider.

Jaromir Wagner of West Germany strapped himself to a small, two-engine plane and flew from his homeland to the United States in 12 days.

YVONNE HEMSEY—GAMMA/LIAISON

Aden:
see Yemen, People's Democratic Republic of

Advertising:
see Industrial Review

Aerospace Industry:
see Defense; Industrial Review; Space Exploration; Transportation

TOM ZIMBEROFF—SYGMA

The "Kitty Hawk," manned by Maxie Anderson and his son Kristian, soars over the Sierra Nevada mountains. The Andersons completed the first balloon crossing of North America in just less than 100 hours.

At the world classical parachuting championships in Kazanlak, Bulg., in August, Dirk Boyden (Belgium) won first place in men's accuracy with a perfect score. Nikolay Usmaev (U.S.S.R.) took top honours in men's style. Kathy Cox (Canada) captured first place in women's accuracy, and Aleksandra Chvatchao (U.S.S.R.) was first in women's style. The women's team accuracy competition was won by East Germany. In February Cheryl Stearns (U.S.) set women's world records of 27 consecutive daytime landings on a disk and 12 consecutive nighttime landings. Clifford Jones (U.S.) set a men's record of 26 nighttime landings on a disk. U.S. teams also set records for eight-person and four-person longest sequence jumps.

In August 32-year-old Janice Brown made history when she took the "Gossamer Penguin" aloft on a 15-min flight at Edwards Air Force Base in California. The plane, the world's first solar-powered aircraft, weighed only 28.3 kg (68 lb) and had a wingspan of 21.9 m (72 ft). It was designed by Paul MacCready, creator of the first man-powered aircraft to fly and the first such plane to cross the English Channel. The world power-plane aerobatic championships were held at Oshkosh, Wis. The U.S. won the men's team competition. In October, Jaromir Wagner of West Germany became the first to cross the Atlantic atop an airplane. Wearing a skindiver's wet suit and many layers of clothing, the Czechoslovak-born daredevil was strapped atop a plane while it flew from near Stuttgart, West Germany, to Fairfield, N.J.; there were interim stops at the Faroe Islands, Iceland, and Labrador.

(MICHAEL D. KILIAN)

Afghanistan

A people's republic in central Asia, Afghanistan is bordered by the U.S.S.R., China, Pakistan, and Iran. Area: 652,626 sq km (251,980 sq mi). Pop. (1979 prelim.): 15,540,000, including (1978 est.) Pashtoon 50%; Tadzhik 25%; Uzbek 9%; Hazara 9%. Cap. and largest city: Kabul (pop., 1979 est., 891,750). Language: Persian and Pashto. Religion: Muslim 99% (including 80% Sunni; 20% Shiʿah); Hindu, Sikh, and Jewish 1%. President of the Revolutionary Council and prime minister in 1980, Babrak Karmal.

The Soviet military intervention launched in December 1979 to contain the insurgency and stabilize the Marxist revolutionary government of Pres. Babrak Karmal (*see* BIOGRAPHIES) failed to achieve its purpose, and problems, both political and economic, multiplied during the following months. As the Soviet Union increased the strength of its force from an initial 30,000–40,000 men to an estimated 85,000 by October 1980, resentment against the Soviet military occupation rose both within and outside Afghanistan. All estimates indicated that hatred of the Soviet Union among the 15 million Afghans was near total, and the insurgency, which was originally confined to mountainous areas of the northeast and a few provinces bordering Pakistan, was spreading throughout the country. Externally, except for the Soviet bloc and some pro-Soviet members of the nonaligned movement, no nation was prepared to condone the continued Soviet military presence.

Anti-Soviet feeling among the Afghans rose to a high pitch in February, when a general strike and violent demonstrations were staged against the Soviet presence in Kabul and other major towns. The mass uprising was quelled after Afghan armed forces and Communist militia inflicted heavy casualties on the demonstrators. As cases of Soviet soldiers disappearing began to increase, the Soviet troops assumed more and more direct control of the security situation from the Afghan Army. The demonstrations were repeated at the end of April, this time staged by students from Kabul University and other educational institutions. The April demonstrations, which occurred during the anniversary celebrations of the Saur (April) Revolution

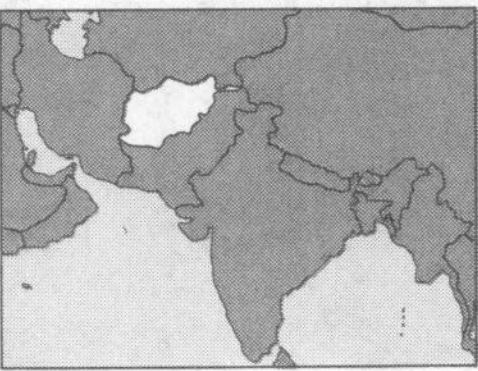

Afghanistan

launched by former president Nur Mohammad Taraki on April 27, 1978, resulted in the brutal killings of more than 50 students.

The Soviet Union announced a token withdrawal of one of its divisions in June, but this failed to placate the Afghans. Despite intense propaganda by President Karmal, Afghan state organs, and the Soviet government to the effect that the Soviet presence had a "limited" purpose and the troops would pull out as soon as peace was restored, the Karmal regime was finding itself more and more isolated from the people. Except for a small percentage consisting of ruling People's Democratic Party cadres, bureaucrats, and intellectuals, no section of the population would accept the government's thesis: that all the country's ills either were caused by saboteurs and agents from Pakistan and the U.S. or resulted from the tyrannical measures adopted by the short-lived regime of Karmal's predecessor, former president Hafizullah Amin. Increasingly, President Karmal was finding himself in a dilemma, because the very Soviet troops who were arousing such resistance from his countrymen were the only force preventing the collapse of his government. During an extended visit to Moscow that began on October 16, he was welcomed by Soviet Pres. Leonid Brezhnev. Their subsequent discussion and joint signature of a document in the Kremlin was seen as a formal acknowledgment of the Afghan government's puppet status.

Armed Afghan rebels gathered in strongholds along the Pakistan-Afghanistan border. From these positions they made sporadic attacks on the Soviet Army in Afghanistan.

ALAIN DEJEAN—SYGMA

The Karmal government also had to contend with large-scale desertions from the Afghan armed forces. From an estimated 80,000 at the time of the Soviet intervention, the Afghan Army's strength was down to 32,000 by June. The government launched an all-out recruiting drive and announced a series of measures to attract young people to the Army, but the result was poor. The drafting age was reduced from 22 to 20, the exemption granted to students entering the university was abolished, teachers were asked to enlist, and enhanced salaries and other benefits were announced for the new recruits. One reason for the emasculation of the Afghan Army was said to have been the Soviet decision to strip whole units of their weapons as their loyalty became suspect. Some of the deserters who took their arms with them found immediate acceptance among the rebel organizations.

At the same time Karmal, who had been installed in December 1979 by the Soviet Union at the head of a coalition of the Khalq ("masses") and Parcham ("flag") factions of the ruling party, faced increasing friction within the Revolutionary Council and other wings of the government. One of the most striking evidences of Khalq-Parcham feuding came when Karmal removed his deputy prime minister, Assadullah Sarwari, a prominent Khalqi, and three other Khalq followers from the scene by appointing them as ambassadors. Sarwari, who was once considered a potential Soviet choice to replace Karmal, was named envoy to Mongolia after a sojourn in the Soviet Union. There were reports of assassinations of Khalqis by Parchamites and vice versa, and bitter interparty fighting was said to have spread to army units and government agencies in various parts of the country. President Karmal reshuffled his Cabinet, promoting Sultan Ali Keshtmand, a trusted Parchamite colleague, to replace Sarwari as first deputy prime minister.

As rebel activities increased, travel outside Kabul became unsafe. The night curfew imposed on Kabul and other major towns soon after the Soviet forces moved in was becoming a permanent fixture. Except for the long supply line to the Soviet border in the north, the highways out of Kabul remained closed to traffic for weeks on end as rebel snipers held up convoys. The Soviets unleashed a series of offensives against the insurgents in the provinces of Paktia, Konarha, Ghazni, Herat, Qandahar, and Badakhshan in the months following the February riots. But while the Soviet sweeps managed to clear targeted valleys and mountain ranges of insurgents, the rebels returned soon after the operations were ended. A stalemate situation emerged, with the Soviets holding the large towns while the insurgents roamed the countryside but without secure footholds.

AFGHANISTAN

Education. (1978–79) Primary, pupils 942,817, teachers 29,789; secondary, pupils 92,401, teachers 4,503; vocational, pupils 12,118, teachers 889; teacher training, students 6,629, teachers 406; higher, students 12,480, teaching staff 1,062.

Finance. Monetary unit: afghani, with (Sept. 22, 1980) a free rate of 44 afghanis to U.S. $1 (105 afghanis = £1 sterling). Gold, SDR's, and foreign exchange (June 1980) U.S. $448 million. Budget (1976–77 est.): revenue 13,950,000,000 afghanis; expenditure 11,168,000,000 afghanis. Money supply (March 1980) 36,431,000,000 afghanis.

Foreign Trade. (1979–80) Imports U.S. $315 million; exports U.S. $474 million. Import sources (1977–78): U.S.S.R. 22%; Japan 21%; West Germany 6%; India 5%. Export destinations (1977–78): U.S.S.R. 37%; Pakistan 12%; U.K. 12%; India 8%; West Germany 6%. Main exports: fruits and nuts 44%; natural gas 16%; carpets 13%; cotton 9%; karakul (persian lamb) skins 5%.

Transport and Communications. Roads (1978) 18,752 km. Motor vehicles in use (1978): passenger 34,506; commercial 22,100. Air traffic (1978): 246 million passenger-km; freight 13 million net ton-km. Telephones (Jan. 1978) 31,200. Radio receivers (Dec. 1977) *c.* 823,000. Television receivers (March 1979) *c.* 20,000.

Agriculture. Production (in 000; metric tons; 1979): wheat *c.* 2,200; corn *c.* 750; rice *c.* 450; barley *c.* 400; grapes *c.* 460; cotton, lint *c.* 38; wool, clean *c.* 14. Livestock (in 000; 1978): cattle *c.* 3,866; karakul sheep (1976) *c.* 6,200; other sheep *c.* 16,400; goats *c.* 3,000; horses *c.* 392; asses *c.* 1,291; camels *c.* 290.

Industry. Production (in 000; metric tons; 1977–78): coal 173; natural gas (cu m) 2,582,000; cotton fabrics (m) 76,800; rayon fabrics (m) 29,700; nitrogenous fertilizers (nutrient content; 1978–79) 48; cement 125; electricity (kw-hr) *c.* 810,000.

The Soviet forces, using tanks, MiG jet fighters, and Mi-24 helicopter gunships, were said to have razed a number of villages. Villagers fleeing to Pakistan complained about the use of napalm bombs by the Soviet forces, but this could not be confirmed. The exodus of Afghan refugees to Pakistan continued without interruption. Outside estimates placed the number seeking shelter in Pakistan by September at over 900,000.

Attempts to bring about a peaceful solution of the Afghan crisis and Soviet withdrawal from the country were made by the Islamic Conference in Islamabad, Pak., in May, and by various nonaligned nations, especially India, which had taken a moderate stand on the issue. No headway could be made, however. Pakistan refused to have any direct talks with the Karmal regime, since this would involve recognition of the Soviet-backed government. Karmal insisted that all subversive activities against his country must stop before any international discussion on the crisis could be held. The Soviet Union announced that there would be no further withdrawals of Soviet forces until peace was restored.

The economy continued its downward slide. Production declined in all sectors, and exports dwindled to about one-third of the normal volume before the Saur Revolution. As trade with Japan and the Western countries declined, the economy was being kept alive by an increased flow of goods from the Soviet Union and Eastern Europe. The Soviet Union, which pumped in about 200,000 metric tons of food grains in 1978, was said to have increased its food shipments by at least another 50%. (GOVINDAN UNNY)

African Affairs

World inflationary pressures and rising oil prices cast a heavy shadow over the future of most African countries during 1980, threatening the continent's economic and political future as an increasing number of nations were unable to meet their international debt obligations. Political turbulence rather than greater stability characterized the continent. While there were fewer successful coups than in some recent years, a military takeover in Liberia destroyed Africa's oldest republic. The new state of Zimbabwe, replacing the old Rhodesian colony, was born in April.

The Organization of African Unity. The OAU held its 17th annual summit in July in Freetown, Sierra Leone, whose president, Siaka Stevens (*see* BIOGRAPHIES), became organization chairman for 1980–81. Zimbabwe was admitted as its 50th member state. The conflicts in the Western Sahara, Chad, South West Africa/Namibia, and South Africa dominated the debates. A majority of OAU members favoured accepting Western Sahara as an independent country, but a final decision to recognize the Saharan Arab Democratic Republic was delayed pending a final mediation effort to reach an agreement with Morocco, which remained committed to incorporating the former Spanish Sahara into its kingdom. The OAU also decided on one final mediation attempt to halt the civil war in Chad before admitting defeat and handing the problem over to the UN for international action. An ultimatum given to Western powers declared that unless they succeeded in persuading South Africa to implement the UN plan for Namibia's independence the UN Security Council would be asked to impose economic sanctions against the Pretoria regime. Proposals for tougher sanctions against South Africa over its policy of racial separation were adopted, including the idea of an international oil embargo and a total boycott of all air flights to and from that country.

The idea of establishing a Joint African Military Command capable of dealing with the continent's internal conflicts was again considered, and once more was postponed because of seemingly insuperable difficulties. Endorsement was given to the decisions of the OAU's special conference on an economic strategy for the continent, which had been worked out at an earlier conference held in Lagos, Nigeria. While importance was still given to the pursuit of a North-South dialogue, between developed and less developed nations, more emphasis was being placed on achieving closer cooperation among third world countries.

Southern Africa. The achievement of an independent Zimbabwe under a Patriotic Front government in April left South Africa as the only independent country still under white minority rule. The new regime of Robert Mugabe (*see* BIOGRAPHIES) suspended diplomatic relations with South Africa while accepting the need for continued economic links. However, a new initiative was launched to reduce the economic dependence on South Africa of its border nations, in opposition

ALAIN NOGUES—SYGMA

Sierra Leone was the site of the July summit conference of the Organization of African Unity.

to South African Prime Minister P. W. Botha's scheme for a "constellation of southern African states." For this purpose a new regional organization, the Southern African Development Coordination Conference, was formed comprising Botswana, Angola, Mozambique, Lesotho, Zimbabwe, Zambia, Tanzania, Malawi, and Swaziland.

The level of violence in South Africa rose with the increasing success of the African National Congress in infiltrating its guerrilla fighters into the urban areas to attack strategic targets. The Namibian liberation movement, the South West Africa People's Organization, also kept up its pressures on South Africa from its bases in Angola. South Africa took strong countermeasures, launching major military attacks across its own borders into Angola and Zambia, which produced international condemnation.

The Horn of Africa. International attention focused more sharply on the Red Sea and northern Indian Ocean region following the Soviet Union's military intervention in Afghanistan and the worsening crisis in the Persian Gulf area. The NATO powers, especially the U.S., embarked on a new policy of strengthening the Western military presence in the region. In June the U.S. acquired naval and air facilities in Kenya, and in August it signed an agreement with Somalia for the use of that nation's naval facilities at Berbera. Simultaneously, facilities were acquired in Egypt for the installation of Rapid Deployment Forces, and the U.S. Congress authorized a substantial expenditure to develop an air base on the Indian Ocean island of Diego Garcia.

These developments produced strong reactions from a number of African countries. The OAU unanimously supported Mauritius's claim for the return to it of Diego Garcia. Meanwhile, fighting in Ethiopia continued, especially in Eritrea, the Ogaden, Tigre, and Bale. Soviet efforts to mediate in the conflict between the Eritrean liberation movements and Ethiopia remained unsuccessful. Lieut. Col. Haile Mengistu Mariam's regime in Ethiopia charged that Somalia's Army was again involved in the fighting in the Ogaden and threatened to attack its neighbour unless Somali intervention was stopped.

Coups and Inter-African Affairs. A dozen or so coups against established regimes were attempted during the year, but only five were successful. In January head of state Mohamed Mahmoud Ould Louly was deposed in Mauritania and replaced by Premier Mohamed Khouna Ould Haidalla. Liberia's Pres. William R. Tolbert, Jr. (*see* OBITUARIES), was assassinated in April by noncommissioned officers and privates, led by Master Sgt. Samuel Doe (*see* BIOGRAPHIES), who established a new military regime under the People's Redemption Council. In May Pres. Godfrey L. Binaisa of Uganda was overthrown by a six-man military commission, which established an interim government pending arrangements to hold multiparty elections in December. The fourth successful coup was in Guinea-Bissau, where Pres. Luis Cabral was overthrown in November. Also in November Pres. Sangoulé Lamizana was ousted by the military in Upper Volta. Among the more serious but unsuccessful attempts at coups were those, in May, against Pres. Ahmed Sékou Touré of Guinea and Pres. Félix Houphouët-Boigny of Ivory Coast; against Pres. Kenneth Kaunda of Zambia in July and again in October; and against Vice-Pres. Aboud Jumbe of Zanzibar in July. Libya was involved in a number of interventions that caused its leader, Col. Muammar al-Qaddafi, to be regarded as a major troublemaker in the continent. In January he was involved in the attack on Gafsa, Tunisia, by opponents of Pres. Habib Bourguiba of Tunisia; in June he was accused by Pres. Léopold Sédar Senghor of Senegal of being involved in a coup attempt there and in October of a similar attempt against the president of The Gambia, Sir Dawda Jawara. The Gambia and Senegal both broke off diplomatic relations with Libya.

Border tensions between Egypt and Libya became sharper in June when Qaddafi called on the Egyptian Army to overthrow Pres. Anwar as-Sadat. Both Mali and Niger complained of Libyan interference in their internal affairs. However, the most blatant Libyan action was taken in Chad, where its forces occupied the capital in December in support of the regime of Pres. Goukouni Oueddei. Libya's proposed union with Syria was viewed with considerable skepticism in Africa in view of the previous failure of similar moves at union with Egypt, Tunisia, and Sudan.

Even before the November coup Guinea-Bissau's relations with neighbouring Guinea deteriorated seriously over a dispute about the limits of their offshore waters, which was related to possibilities of an oil discovery. Disagreements persisted between Kenya and Sudan, on one side, and Tanzania on the other, over the role of Pres. Julius Nyerere in Uganda. Despite these quarrels relations between African neighbours generally showed signs of improvement. For example, while Ethiopia's relations with Somalia remained troubled, those with Sudan got better.

Political Systems. The trend toward a greater liberalization of government noted in recent years continued during 1980. The outstanding achievement was the success of the multiparty elections in Zimbabwe that ended 15 years of an embittering civil war. For the first time since the revolution in Zanzibar in 1964 the islanders were given an opportunity in January of electing their government. Zanzibaris also participated in the elections in Tanzania in October, where popular discontent was effectively demonstrated by the defeat of about half the former National Assemblymen, although President Nyerere himself was reelected. The Ivory Coast relaxed the tight control of its ruling party by allowing villagers to nominate their own candidates for Parliament instead of having to vote for party appointees. Botswana effected a harmonious transition after the death in July of its charismatic president, Sir Seretse Khama (*see* OBITUARIES), who was replaced by the former vice-president, Quett Masire (*see* BIOGRAPHIES).

Notwithstanding its economic and security problems, Uganda held a tightly contested election in December in which former president Milton Obote emerged as victor. The turbulent democracy of the continent's most populous state, Nigeria, made significant progress during the first year after the Army's withdrawal from the government; and though the restoration of civilian rule in Ghana was not without its problems, Pres. Hilla Limann's regime weathered the attacks made by his political opponents.

External Relations. Although international involvement in the continent's affairs showed little sign of declining, the impact of external forces was less sharp than in recent years. Cuba, especially, appeared to favour reducing its military presence, now estimated at perhaps 35,000 troops, mostly in Angola and Ethiopia. The Soviet Union, though still heavily engaged in Ethiopia, did not significantly increase its African role. East Germany remained the most active Eastern European country, particularly in providing military assistance. Through exchanges of high-level visits China continued to maintain an active presence.

Relations with most Western countries remained generally friendly but were troubled by African grievances about the failure of the North-South dialogue and the lack of progress over changes in South Africa and Namibia. The buildup of U.S. forces in the Indian Ocean and Red Sea was another source of friction. Only three African countries (Angola, Ethiopia, and Mozambique) voted against the UN General Assembly resolution condemning the Soviet intervention in Afghanistan. Although 24 African countries accepted invitations to participate in the Olympic Games in Moscow, 17 boycotted them. Twenty-five African nations were represented at the Franco-African summit conference held in Nice in May; most supported the initiative to launch a Commonwealth *á la française* presented by President Senghor (who retired at year's end). (*See* Special Report.) Pope John Paul II visited Congo, Zaire, Kenya, Ghana, Upper Volta, and Ivory Coast.

Social and Economic Conditions. A grave warning that Africa faced extremely bleak prospects as it moved toward the year 2000 was given by Adebayo Adedeji, executive secretary of the Economic Commission for Africa. He added that the 1980s were likely to be particularly turbulent. With the exception of Africa's half-dozen oil-producing states, the continent was doubly hit by the international economic crisis—first by the higher costs of oil imports and second by the higher costs of importing capital goods and food from the developed nations, which included their own higher oil costs in the price of their exports. The latest round of oil price increases meant, for example, that Ghana would have to use 65% of its total foreign exchange earnings to pay for its oil imports alone, while Tanzania would have to devote 60% similarly. Consequently, few African countries could service their foreign debts. A UN Food and Agriculture Organization report showed that 29 less developed countries, mostly African, were suffering from acute food shortages in 1980, as compared with 16 in 1979. Maurice Williams, director of the UN-sponsored World Food Council, described Africa as "the world's hungriest continent." Nearly half the world's refugee population of four million was to be found in Africa, which meant that roughly one out of every 200 Africans was a displaced person.

The second Lomé Convention, between the European Economic Community (EEC) and 58 (later 60) countries from Africa, the Caribbean, and the Pacific (ACP), came into force on March 1. Off to a bad start in the cold economic climate, Lomé II nevertheless brought some benefits to its ACP signatories in the operation of its complex trading and financial support system. But later the ACP countries sought further concessions from the EEC.

(COLIN LEGUM)

See also Dependent States; articles on the various political units.

THE CONTINUING FRENCH ROLE IN AFRICA

by Colin Legum

During the post-colonial period, France has played a larger and possibly more influential role in Africa than any other major power. While the Soviets, Americans, East Germans, and Cubans ship more arms to the continent, none can match the effectiveness of France's continuous military, political, and economic involvement during the two decades since most of its African colonies became independent in 1960.

France has been successful in maintaining its high profile in Africa for two main reasons. The first is that most of its policies are endorsed, and even encouraged, by a group of prominent African leaders, headed by the two *grands hommes,* Félix Houphouët-Boigny of Ivory Coast and Léopold Sédar Senghor of Senegal. France, therefore, seldom runs the risk of finding itself without loyal African friends to defend its policies.

The second reason for the apparent success of French policy is that when France abandoned direct colonial rule it introduced a new pattern of relationships between the metropolis and the Francophone community. The net result has been to make the former territories almost as dependent on Paris as before for economic, technical, and military aid. For example, all Francophone territories are required to belong to the franc currency zone under conditions that finely integrate their central banking systems with France's; only a few have successfully avoided

Colin Legum is associate editor of The Observer, *London, and editor of* Africa Contemporary Record. *He has written and edited numerous books on African political affairs.*

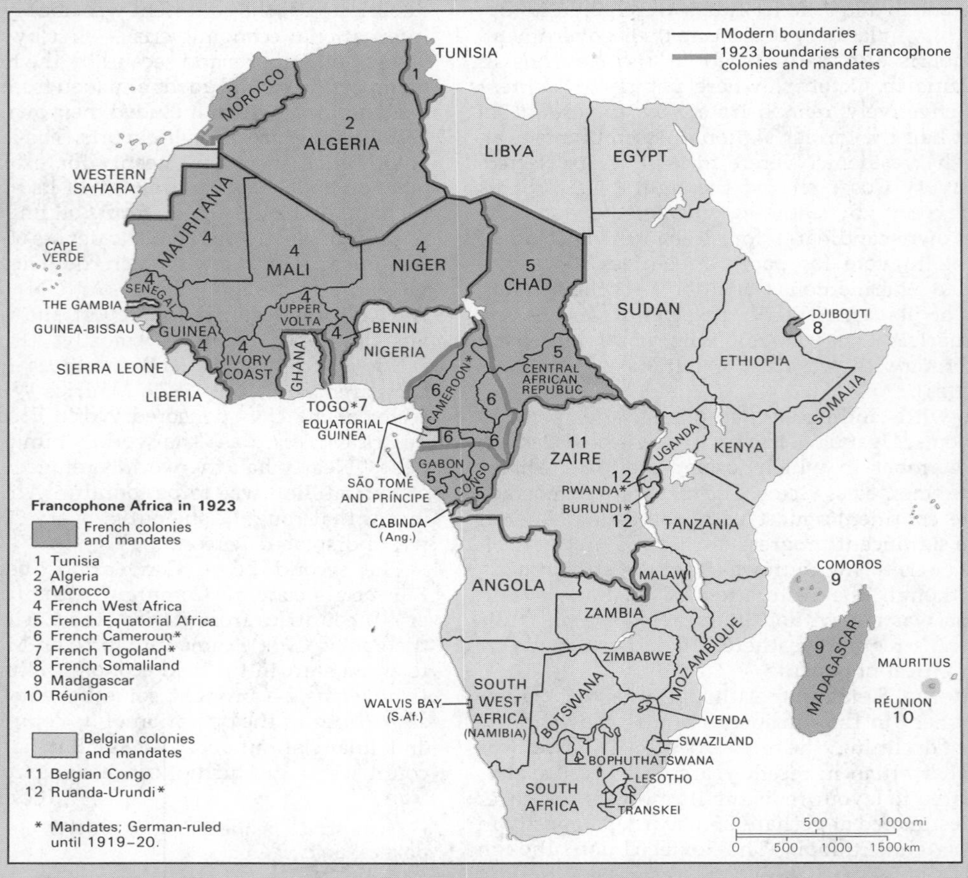

JACQUES PAVLOVSKY—SYGMA

A French captain teaches a Mauritanian soldier how to operate a mortar used in the protection of an iron ore mine at Zouirat (Zouerate) from Polisario Front guerrilla attacks.

this obligation. A plethora of economic and political institutions link the different parts of Francophone Africa to each other and to Paris. French policy allows for a wide variety of political systems in the countries it supports, provided only that their regimes do not adopt policies that undermine basic French interests.

De Gaulle's Precept. France, under Gen. Charles de Gaulle, set an exemplary lesson for African leaders who defy Paris on important issues. In 1958 Guinea was cut off without a sou because Pres. Sékou Touré opted for complete independence rather than falling in with the wishes of Paris. That estrangement was to last 20 years before the Guinea leader found it necessary to mend his fences with France. It was de Gaulle who set the policy, followed by all his successors, of being generous to France's friends in Africa while paternalistically punishing its enemies—or holding the threat of punishment over them. At the same time, Paris has courted and flattered Africa's leaders. They are encouraged to visit the metropolis frequently, and they are assured of red carpet treatment.

Alone among the Western powers, France's African policy remains the preserve of its president. One of the most influential men in de Gaulle's personal office was Jacques Foccart, who, besides a less publicized role in French intelligence, headed the general secretariat for African affairs, a department directly responsible to the presidency, during 1961–74. Under Valéry Giscard d'Estaing, the secretariat ceased to exist in name, but René Journiac (*see* OBITUARIES) replaced Foccart as a scarcely less influential confidential adviser on African affairs. When Journiac died in an air crash in February 1980, the Paris newspaper *Libération* wrote "Journiac watched over Africa like Richelieu over France."

France gives such high priority to its African connections for three main reasons. The first is the unparalleled French interest in expanding the role of the French language and culture throughout the world—an interest that has given rise to accusations of "cultural imperialism." The policy of consolidating and expanding French cultural influence extends from Quebec Province in Canada to Upper Volta to wherever French is spoken by a sizable part of the population, including such former non-French colonies as Seychelles, Mauritius, Zaire, Rwanda, and Burundi. Paris actively promotes this policy through annual Franco-African summit meetings, initiated by Pres. Georges Pompidou in 1973. The 1980 summit, held in Nice, adopted a plan of President Senghor's to launch a Francophone Commonwealth, closely modeled on the Commonwealth of Nations.

Aid and Trade. A second major determinant of France's African policy is promotion of its own trade. France has jealously sought to preserve the largely monopolistic economic interests built up in colonial times. This it does through the machinery of the franc zone and by a network of economic and political institutions. Entry by other trading powers into Francophone Africa is not easy. French economic and technical aid to Africa is extremely generous (the Ministry of Cooperation budget for 1980 was increased by 23% to about U.S. $1 billion), but its trade advantages are even greater. Almost 70% of France's trade lies within its former colonial empire. It is able to avoid a trade deficit only because of its substantial surplus earnings from Africa. Between 50 and 60% of all imports by Francophone African countries originate from France.

French business interests control half of Ivory Coast's modern sector, 65% of Gabon's, 55% of Cameroon's, and 57% of Senegal's. What is espe-

KEYSTONE

French Pres. Valéry Giscard d'Estaing (second from left) held a press conference with Pres. Léopold Sédar Senghor of Senegal (second from right) and Pres. Juvénal Habyarimana of Rwanda (right) to discuss continuing Franco-African affairs.

cially important to France is that its purchase of strategic minerals, such as uranium, is financed through the franc zone arrangements and so avoids the problem of diverting foreign exchange earnings. France is also anxious to expand its markets beyond the original French Community; hence its close involvement in assisting regimes such as that of Pres. Mobuto Sese Seko in Zaire. About 150,000 French nationals live in black Africa, most of them engaged in commerce.

A third major reason accounting for France's interest in Africa is its driving national ambition to play a major independent role in world affairs. Its alliance with Francophone Africa is seen as adding to its international stature.

"Africa's Gendarmerie." These three determinants of its foreign policy have led France to play a major interventionist role in the African continent, earning it the sobriquet of "Africa's gendarmerie." It still maintains defense agreements with a number of African countries and has military bases in Senegal, Gabon, Djibouti, Réunion, and Mayotte. Over 7,000 French troops of the Strategic Command (ground and air) are kept in Africa; the French Navy has the strongest contingent of ships in the Red Sea and Indian Ocean of any NATO power.

These forces have been used to help prevent the overthrow of strongly pro-French regimes in Senegal, Ivory Coast, and Gabon. They helped put down a rebellion in Cameroon and were engaged for some 12 years in vain attempts to defend a succession of regimes in Chad. French military aid has also gone to help Morocco and Mauritania in their struggle over the Western Sahara and to assist Pres. Habib Bourguiba's regime in Tunisia in the aftermath of an attack early in 1980 emanating from Libyan-supported opposition forces. France took the initiative in coming to the rescue of President Mobutu at the time of the two invasions of Zaire's Shaba Province in 1977–78. In 1979 French troops were directly involved in securing the overthrow of the tyrannical Emperor Bokassa I of the renamed Central African Republic (although he had enjoyed close French support up to the moment of his last disgrace).

President Giscard strongly denies that these military enterprises deserve to be described as interventionism. He prefers to call them "acts of solidarity," with France intervening only when it is invited to do so by a legitimate government and in support of its friends. France's reputation of standing by its friends is an important element in explaining the loyalty felt by many African regimes for Paris.

In 1979 President Giscard began to promote a new element in France's African policy: what he calls a "trilogue" between Europe, Africa, and the oil-producing Arab countries. This policy envisages developing Africa's economic resources by matching European technical skills with Arab finance.

French policy has many critics in Africa—not least in the Francophone countries where a younger generation of the modernizing elite is increasingly critical of the privileged position enjoyed by French business interests and of the role played by French advisers in key government departments. France's attempts to set up a so-called Pan-African Security Force after the Shaba invasions were widely resented by many African leaders, as were its extensive arms deals with South Africa. However, as long as there remain a large number of influential African leaders who feel closely identified with the concepts of *francophonie,* who enjoy generous economic aid, and who can depend on the support of French troops in case of trouble, France is likely to be able to continue to develop its ambitious role as a major political and economic power in the African continent.

Agriculture and Food Supplies

World food supplies tightened in 1980 as world food output failed to recover from the decline experienced in 1979, largely because of poor grain harvests in both the United States and the Soviet Union. Although the buildup in world cereal stocks in earlier years made it possible to cover the production shortfalls of the last two years, such stocks were drawn down to unusually low levels that made world food security and market stability heavily dependent upon harvests around the world in 1981. The suspension of U.S. grain sales to the Soviet Union early in 1980 placed food and agricultural policy in the middle of the political arena. Attempts to stabilize commodity markets and assure acceptable returns to producers were intensified during the year, and several new or revised international commodity agreements were concluded. Although a new expanded international food-aid convention was finally adopted, little if any progress was made in the negotiation of a new wheat trade convention—the focal point of international efforts to promote world food security and market stability for the last several years.

Production Indexes. Total agricultural and food production in the world (excluding China) failed to increase in 1980 for the second year in a row, according to preliminary indexes prepared by the Economics, Statistics, and Cooperatives Service of the U.S. Department of Agriculture (USDA). Farm output fell about 2.5% in the developed countries, as a nearly 6.5% reduction in U.S. production because of drought—together with smaller output in Japan and Oceania—failed to offset completely the substantial gains in Canada and Western Europe. Agricultural production climbed about 2.4% in the less developed countries, but it hardly rose at all in the centrally planned economies (U.S.S.R. and Eastern Europe) because of smaller Eastern European production. Chinese agricultural production (not covered by the USDA indexes) also appeared to have remained unchanged in 1980.

The increase of about 2.4% in food production in the less developed countries reflected larger harvests in all regions except East Asia, where losses in South Korea pulled down the regional average. Food production declined approximately 1% in the centrally planned countries.

Measured on a per capita basis, world food production fell more than 1.5%, with the developed countries declining more than 2% and the centrally planned nations close to 1.5%. Rapid population growth cut the growth in per capita food production in the less developed countries to less than 0.5%, with both East Asia and Africa registering losses. Per capita output in Africa remained about 15% below that of a decade earlier.

The United Nations Food and Agriculture Organization (FAO) in mid-October 1980 listed 29 countries that were affected by abnormal food shortages as a result of poor crops, the effects of strife, or difficult economic situations. The list rose to 22 in Africa, fell to 4 in Asia, and totaled 3 in Latin America. The year was notable for the recovery in Bangladesh that caused that nation to be dropped from the list and also for the substantial

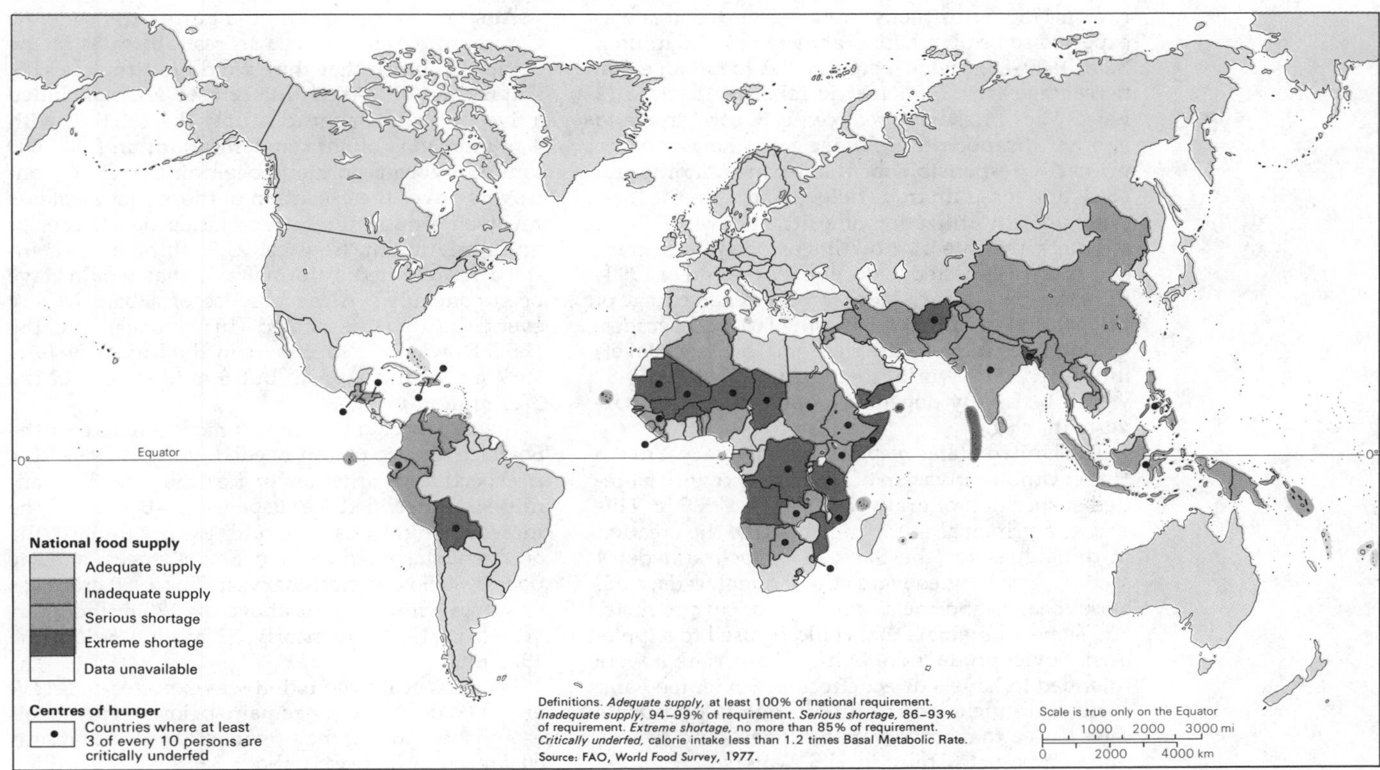

Definitions. *Adequate supply,* at least 100% of national requirement. *Inadequate supply,* 94–99% of requirement. *Serious shortage,* 86–93% of requirement. *Extreme shortage,* no more than 85% of requirement. *Critically underfed,* calorie intake less than 1.2 times Basal Metabolic Rate.

Source: FAO, World Food Survey, 1977.

Table I. Indexes of World Agricultural and Food Production (excluding China)

1969–71 = 100

Region or country	Total agricultural production						Total food production						Per capita food production					
	1975	1976	1977	1978	1979	1980[1]	1975	1976	1977	1978	1979	1980[1]	1975	1976	1977	1978	1979	1980[1]
Developed countries	108	109	113	116	119	116	109	109	113	117	119	117	104	104	107	110	111	108
United States	110	113	118	118	124	116	110	113	117	119	125	117	106	107	111	112	116	108
Canada	104	113	117	120	113	116	106	117	119	122	120	118	99	108	108	109	106	103
Western Europe	109	107	109	115	118	122	109	107	109	116	117	122	105	103	105	111	113	117
Japan	104	100	109	109	110	103	104	100	109	109	110	103	97	92	100	99	99	92
Oceania	111	113	111	121	114	106	117	122	119	130	121	111	108	109	106	115	105	96
South Africa	110	113	122	125	123	125	113	116	124	127	124	127	99	99	104	104	99	99
Less developed countries	115	117	121	126	125	128	116	119	123	127	126	129	103	103	104	105	102	101
East Asia	121	127	132	137	140	140	122	129	133	139	142	141	108	113	114	116	116	113
Indonesia	119	121	123	132	134	141	120	122	125	133	135	142	107	107	107	112	111	115
Philippines	125	130	132	136	135	141	125	132	134	137	137	143	110	113	112	112	109	111
South Korea	129	146	159	164	172	147	128	145	157	163	171	147	117	130	139	142	147	124
Thailand	118	119	117	137	131	140	123	126	122	143	131	141	107	108	102	117	105	111
South Asia	112	109	119	123	118	121	113	111	120	124	118	122	101	97	103	104	97	98
Bangladesh	110	103	113	115	111	124	114	105	116	116	111	129	101	91	97	95	88	100
India	113	110	119	125	118	122	113	111	120	125	117	121	102	98	104	106	98	99
Pakistan	101	106	118	114	129	136	106	116	126	123	133	141	91	97	102	97	101	105
West Asia	124	136	135	141	137	142	125	137	136	143	139	145	109	117	112	115	109	110
Iran	142	154	152	161	149	136	145	158	155	165	153	140	127	135	129	133	120	106
Turkey	118	127	128	131	128	137	119	126	127	132	129	138	105	109	108	109	104	108
Africa	107	108	106	109	110	112	108	110	108	110	111	113	94	93	88	88	86	85
Egypt	107	109	108	113	116	117	115	117	116	119	121	123	103	102	99	99	99	97
Ethiopia	82	78	75	69	74	70	76	73	69	63	68	64	67	62	57	52	54	50
Nigeria	108	110	110	112	113	115	108	110	110	112	113	115	93	92	89	88	86	85
Latin America	119	121	127	132	135	138	120	126	130	135	138	142	105	107	107	108	109	109
Mexico	121	118	123	130	127	135	126	122	125	133	130	140	106	99	98	101	95	99
Argentina	109	119	122	137	140	127	109	120	122	137	142	128	102	111	111	123	126	111
Brazil	127	127	138	136	144	156	129	142	148	143	150	166	112	121	122	115	117	126
Centrally planned countries	109	118	118	125	119	120	108	117	117	125	118	117	104	112	110	117	109	108
U.S.S.R.	105	116	116	124	117	119	103	115	114	123	114	115	98	109	106	115	105	105
Eastern Europe	117	121	121	126	123	121	117	121	122	127	124	122	114	116	116	121	117	114
World	111	114	117	122	121	121	111	114	117	122	121	121	101	103	103	106	103	101

[1]Preliminary.
Source: U.S. Department of Agriculture, Economics, Statistics, and Cooperatives Service, December 1980.

improvement in the critical conditions in Cambodia, where a major international relief operation was undertaken in the face of continuing military and political conflict. The worsening food situation in parts of Africa resulted in the calling of a special conference by the FAO director general in November, at which time donor countries substantially increased their pledges for African food aid.

Grains. World grain production was expected (in November) to decline for the second year in a row in 1980–81. Although total harvested area was expected to be about 1.5% above the 712.6 million ha of 1979–80, yields were forecast to fall an equal percentage from 1.96 metric tons per hectare (1 ha=2.5 ac). A sharply reduced U.S. corn crop and another disappointing Soviet grain harvest were primarily responsible for the decline. Another record high for grain trade helped maintain the level of total grain utilization at a little above 1979–80, although the rate of growth slowed. World grain stocks were expected to decline by the end of 1980–81 to the lowest level – measured as a percentage of utilization – recorded during the last two decades. Grain prices were on the rise, and low stock levels indicated that world food security in 1981–82 would be highly dependent upon successful harvests in 1981.

The United States responded on January 4 to the Soviet Union's invasion of Afghanistan with a limited suspension of grain sales to the U.S.S.R. This had as a principal economic objective the creation of difficulties for the Soviet livestock and dairy sectors. Also banned were other animal feeds, such as soybeans, and meat, poultry, dairy products, and some animal fats that could be used to supplement Soviet production. Other measures that were intended to have a direct effect on Soviet food and agriculture included the prohibition of phosphate sales – used to manufacture fertilizer – and restrictions on Soviet fishing in U.S. waters.

The suspension was not applied to the not-yet-shipped balance of the 8 million tons of wheat and coarse grains that the U.S. was committed to supply under a five-year agreement between the two countries. The ban did apply to sales beyond the 8 million tons that had not yet been shipped. The USDA estimated that the suspension affected 13 million tons of U.S. corn, 4 million tons of wheat, and about 1.3 million tons of soybeans and soybean meal, as well as some other commodities.

Australia, Canada, and the European Economic Community (EEC) agreed to restrain sales to the Soviet Union so that they would not replace U.S. shipments, but Argentina refused and concluded a five-year agreement to supply the U.S.S.R. with 4 million tons of corn and sorghum and 500,000 tons of soybeans annually beginning in 1981. Controversy over the execution of those commitments revolved around the interpretation of whether or not a sale might "replace" U.S. shipments or instead represented a normal sale that would have been concluded in the absence of a ban. In any event the USDA estimated (in October) that the U.S.S.R. was able to import in the July 1979–June 1980 marketing year all but 6 million tons of the 37.5 million-ton goal.

It was expected to be much more difficult for the Soviet Union to obtain needed grain in 1980–81 – irrespective of whether or not the new U.S. administration ended the suspension – because of the increased tightness of world grain supplies, the apparent sharp reduction of Soviet stocks, and the poor 1980 Soviet grain harvest. The 1980 crop was less than 4 million tons above the 173 million harvested in 1979 and nearly 55 million below the 1978 total.

World wheat production was expected to recover in 1980–81 but to remain below trend levels established during the previous 20 years. Harvested area was increased about 3.5% to 234 million ha, but yields were slightly below the 1.85 tons per hectare recorded in 1979–80. Production shortfalls in Australia, China, and India were more than offset by a recovery in Eastern European output, a larger U.S. harvest, and scattered increases elsewhere. The Soviet wheat crop totaled only 90 million tons, equal to the 1979–80 crop but about 31 million tons below the record high in 1978–79.

Utilization of wheat was expected to decline about 1.5% in 1980–81, largely because of reduced production in China and India and an estimated 11-million-ton decline in total Soviet wheat use that resulted from an even larger reduction in wheat fed to livestock there. In the Soviet Union the use of wheat for livestock feed usually exceeds, or at least equals, its use for human food. China was expected to increase its wheat imports about 4.2 million tons, to 13 million, in 1980–81 and the Soviet Union to increase imports about 2 million, to 14 million tons. India, however, was expected to avoid importing wheat because of greater availability of domestic barley and rice. Increased wheat exports by the U.S., the EEC, and a scattering of other smaller countries were expected to more than offset reduced exports by the other major suppliers, particularly Australia. China was likely to remain a major wheat importer over the next few years. The U.S. and China signed an agreement on October 22 that called for private U.S. traders to export between 6 million and 9 million tons of wheat and corn each calendar year during 1981–84, of which 80–85% would be wheat, with the option to buy more after further notification. That agreement and others signed by China with Canada, Australia, Argentina, and France suggested that the five countries would supply China about 12 million–17 million tons annually over the next several years.

All of the expected drawdown in world wheat stocks in 1980–81 was expected to occur outside the U.S. U.S. wheat stocks remained at about the 25-million-ton level that they reached at the end of 1978–79, compared with the lows of 9 million–12 million in 1973–74 and 1974–75. Wheat stocks in Canada, Australia, and Argentina were expected to total only 11 million tons, about one-half that at the end of 1978–79 and about equal to the lows reached in the early and mid-1970s.

Wheat prices reflected the movement in world stock levels. After world wheat stocks rose from 17.6% of consumption in 1974 to 26% in 1976, the U.S. export price for wheat fell from a record level of $4.90 per bushel in 1974 to $2.81 in 1977. In mid-November 1980, wheat stood at $5.15 per bushel, compared with $4.32 a year earlier.

The expected recovery in rice production in 1980–81 (calendar 1981) was almost exactly matched by a 9-million-ton recovery in Indian production. Output was also expected to be up in Indonesia, Bangladesh, Thailand, Vietnam, and the U.S.; the largest declines were anticipated for Japan, Korea, and China. The increase in produc-

Table II. World Cereal Supply and Distribution
In 000,000 metric tons

	1978–79	1979–80	1980–81[1]
Production			
Wheat	448	420	428
Coarse grains	747	727	705
Rice, milled	260	253	262
Total	1,455	1,400	1,395
Utilization			
Wheat	430	442	435
Coarse grains	742	729	739
Rice, milled	255	256	261
Total	1,427	1,427	1,435
Exports			
Wheat	72	85	90
Coarse grains	90	100	103
Rice, milled	12	13	13
Total	174	198	206
Ending stocks			
Wheat	102	79	72
Coarse grains	89	87	54
Rice, milled	28	24	25
Total	219	190	151
Stocks as % utilization			
Wheat	23.6%	18.0%	16.6%
Coarse grains	12.0%	12.0%	7.3%
Rice, milled	10.8%	9.4%	9.6%
Total	15.3%	13.4%	10.5%

[1]Preliminary.
Source: USDA, Foreign Agricultural Service, November 1980.

UPI

In Kansas a prolonged drought in 1980 destroyed thousands of acres of corn.

UPI

Corn from the record 1979 Iowa harvest was poured into railroad cars for shipment. Some of the corn would go to China in a deal announced by U.S. Pres. Jimmy Carter in October 1980.

tion was expected to permit some increase in consumption and a small buildup in world rice stocks.

The forecast 3% decline in world coarse-grain production in 1980–81 was almost entirely the result of damage to the U.S. corn crop from drought, which resulted in a coarse-grain harvest there that was 42 million tons smaller than in 1979–80. Output of coarse grains in the rest of the world rose 20 million tons, to about 513 million, largely because of production increases in Argentina, the U.S.S.R., Canada, and Western Europe; output was expected to be down in Australia and South Africa.

Utilization of coarse grain was expected to increase only a little more than 1% but was forecast to exceed production by 34 million tons. Total coarse-grain utilization was expected to fall in the U.S. and Eastern Europe. Soviet coarse-grain imports were expected to total about 16.5 million tons in 1980–81, after nearly doubling to 18.5 million in 1979–80. Eastern Europe's imports were expected to total about 10.4 million tons, somewhat smaller than a year earlier.

After setbacks resulting from reduced production in East Africa and India in 1979–80, the consumption of coarse grains for food in less developed countries was expected to resume rising thanks to recovered production there. The less developed nations accounted for almost one-half of the 794 million tons of coarse grain used directly for food in 1979–80.

The nearly 40% drawdown in world stocks of coarse grains—33 million tons—was absorbed almost entirely by U.S. stock reduction. World stocks of coarse grains were expected to be so low by the end of 1980–81 that it would be unlikely that they could be drawn down much further. In mid-November the U.S. export price for corn was $3.76 per bushel, compared with $2.70 a year earlier.

Table III. World Cassava Production[1]
In 000,000 metric tons

Region	1978	1979[2]	1980[3]
Far East	46.7	41.9	43.5
China	3.2	3.4	3.6
India	5.7	6.1	6.1
Indonesia	12.9	13.1	13.1
Thailand	18.4	12.5	13.5
Africa	42.8	44.9	46.3
Nigeria	11.0	11.5	12.0
Zaire	10.9	12.0	12.4
Latin America	31.7	30.9	30.7
Brazil	25.4	24.9	24.5
Total	121.2	117.7	120.5

[1]Root equivalent.
[2]Preliminary figures.
[3]Forecast.
Source: FAO, *Food Outlook*, July 1980.

Cassava. World cassava production was forecast (in July) by the FAO to rise more than 2% in 1980 to the caloric energy equivalent of about 40 million tons of grain. In addition to larger plantings in Nigeria and Zaire, increased production was being stimulated in Angola, Mozambique, and Tanzania by price supports and credit policies. Thailand's recovery from the 1979 drought and favourable government policies in China and the Philippines contributed to increased output in East Asia. Latin-American production was expected to continue to decline, as Brazil shifted land out of cassava into other crops.

World exports of cassava were forecast to decline in 1980 by about 9% from the 5.4 million tons shipped in 1979, after a 20% decline from 1978. Thailand accounted for nearly four-fifths of world cassava exports. EEC imports were expected to fall about 1.2 million tons from the 5.5 million imported in 1979.

Protein Meal and Vegetable Oil. Although world output of oilseeds was expected to fall about 8.2% in 1980–81 from the 174.9 million tons produced in 1979–80, world supplies of soybean and other protein meals and vegetable oils were expected to be little changed from 1979–80 because of a substantial drawdown of stocks of oilseeds for crushing in 1980–81. A 17.3-million-ton decline in U.S. oilseed production from the 72.8 million harvested in 1979–80 was largely responsible for the fall in production; U.S. soybean area and yields were both reduced by the severe drought. Production of oilseeds outside the U.S. was expected to increase about 3% because of increased soybean plantings in China and South America, expanded cotton acreage in the U.S.S.R. and China, and improved cotton yields in the U.S.S.R. and India. The 1980–81 soybean crush was expected to exceed the 73.4 million tons in 1978–79 by about 1.4%.

The growth in world utilization of protein meals was expected to slow in 1980–81, rising only a little above that in 1979–80 because of climbing oilseed prices, the slower expansion of livestock herds, and dampened demand for livestock products because of sluggish economic growth throughout the

World Production and Trade of Principal Grains (in 000 metric tons)

	Wheat			Barley			Oats			Rye			Corn (Maize)			Rice		
	Production		Imports − Exports +	Production		Imports − Exports +	Production		Imports − Exports +	Production		Imports − Exports +	Production		Imports − Exports +	Production		Imports − Exports +
	1961–65 average	1979	1976–79 average	1961–65 average	1979	1976–79 average	1961–65 average	1979	1976–79 average	1961–65 average	1979	1976–79 average	1961–65 average	1979	1976–79 average	1961–65 average	1979	1976–79 average
World total	254576	425478	−67432[1] +68039[1]	98474	172175	−13597[1] +13732[1]	47775	42909	−1480[1] +1468[1]	33849	23705	−653[1] +635[1]	216429	394231	−61401[1] +62618[1]	254711	379814	−9876[1] +9869[1]
Algeria	1254	c1200	−1277	476	c400	−c254	28	c80	−6[1] +2[1]	—	—		4	c5[2]	−138	7	c2[2]	−12[1] +1[1]
Argentina	7541	7800	+3673	679	329	+45	676	536	+158	422	209	+2[1]	4984	8700	+5091	193	326	−2[1] +112
Australia	8222	16100	+9148	978	3657	+1821	1172	1492	+322	11	c18	−2[1]	176	168	−2[1] +11	136	692	−1[1] +276
Austria	704	850	−6 +133	563	1129	−16 +14	322	273	−14	393	278	+7[1]	197	1347	−26 +1[1]	—	—	−44
Bangladesh	37	343[2]	−1490	15	c20[2]	−1[1]	—	—	−1[1]	—	—	—	4	c2	—	15048	19355	−370
Belgium	826	c985	−908 +514[3]	485	c770	−1272[3] +483[3]	389	c120	−74[3] +11[3]	120	64	−18[3] +7[3]	2	37[2]	−2272[3] +902[3]	—	—	−202[3] +53[3]
Brazil	574	2924	−3510	26	145[2]	−25	20	58	−30	17	14	—	10112	16309	−697 +716	6123	7589	−198 +171
Bulgaria	2213	c3000	−203 +281	694	c1600	−91 +15[1]	141	c60	—	58	c20	−1[1]	1601	c3300	−296 +86	37	c50[2]	−10[1] +1[1]
Burma	38	94[2]	—	—	—	—	—	—	—	—	—	—	58	c75[2]	+8[1]	7786	c10000	+560
Canada	15364	17746	+12756	3860	8460	+3655	6075	2978	+229	319	525	+212	1073	4963	−647 +252	—	—	−82
Chile	1082	995	−852	74	112	+10	89	150	−1[1] +2[1]	7	9	—	204	489	−138	85	105[2]	−6 +14[1]
China	22200	c70000	−c6845	14200	c20000	−c357 +c1	c1600	c1000	−c5[1]	c1500	c1800[2]	—	c22500	c40000	−c2540 +c70	c86000	c180000	−c50 +c1390
Colombia	118	38[2]	−376	106	122	−78	—	2	−9[1]	—	—	—	826	870	−64	576	1932	−7[1] +87
Czechoslovakia	1779	c4400	−460	1556	c3300	−c115 +c70	792	c400	+4[1]	897	c500	+1[1]	474	c600	−763	—	—	−76
Denmark	535	573	−25 +170	3506	6680	−145 +654	713	144	−34 +4[1]	380	245	−3[1] +96	—	—	−262	—	—	−12 +1
Egypt	1459	1856	−3409	137	122	−1[1]	—	—	—	—	—	—	1913	2938	−568	1845	2507	−2[1] +168
Ethiopia	540	449	−113	628	c732	−3[1]	5	c11	—	—	—	—	743	c1067	—	—	—	−2[1]
Finland	448	208	−98 +63	400	1650	−2[1] +132	828	1283	+31	141	77	−6[1]	—	—	−5[1]	—	—	−13
France	12495	19393	−380 +6724	6594	11238	−176 +1536	2583	1675	−1[1] +198	367	360	−3[1] +76	2760	10293	−984 +1614	120	45[2]	−251 +39
Germany, East	1357	c3226	−c994 +58[1]	1291	c3635	−c795	850	c400	−c54[1]	1741	c1720	−c62 +15[1]	3	c2	−1591	—	—	−41[1]
Germany, West	4607	7971	−1397 +743	3462	8157	−1477 +292	2185	2999	−308 +29	3031	2105	−95 +121	55	655	−3099 +260	—	—	−175 +51
Greece	1765	c2410	+116	248	869	−45	143	c90	—	19	c5	—	239	627	−933	88	c94	+17[1]
Hungary	2020	3706	−21[1] +656	970	710	−141 +3[1]	108	94	−8	271	95	−1[1] +4[1]	3350	c7400	−138 +392	36	c51[2]	−27
India	11191	34982	−c1840 +c450	2590	2121	+10[1]	—	—	−1[1]	—	—	—	4593	c5000	−5[1]	52733	c69000	−c148 +c138
Indonesia	—	—	−865	—	—	—	—	—	−1[1]	—	—	—	2804	3200	−57 +8	12396	26350	−1767
Iran	2873	c5000	−c1134	792	c900	−c364	—	—	—	—	—	—	24	60[2]	−c271	851	c1212	−c382
Iraq	849	c1492	−c834	851	c872	−147	—	—	—	—	—	−2[1]	2	c85[2]	−c52	142	c284	−267
Ireland	343	260	−184 +15	575	c1512	−50 +c160	357	c103	−12 +1[1]	1	c1	—	—	—	−c244	—	—	−3
Italy	8857	9140	−2985 +35	276	809	−1350 +1[1]	545	438	+1[1]	87	37	−3	3633	6260	−3922 +7	612	1014	−167 +414
Japan	1332	c440	−5748	1380	c375	−1626	145	c20	−167	2	c1	−84	96	c11[2]	−9848	16444	15600	−35 +121
Kenya	122	108	−c56 +2[1]	15	35[2]	—	2	c7	—	—	—	—	1110	c1800	+61	14	42[2]	−4[1]
Korea, South	170	36[2]	−1777	1148	1508	−109	—	—	—	18	5	—	26	138	−1707	4809	8051	−187 +18
Malaysia	—	—	−450	—	—	—	—	—	−5[1]	—	—	−1[1]	8	c35[2]	−402 +1[1]	1140	c2161	−285
Mexico	1672	2272	−530 +17	175	505	−34 +17[1]	76	63	−2[1]	—	—	—	7369	9255	−1470	314	489	+19[1]
Morocco	1516	1796	−c1346	1514	1888	−13[1]	18	6	—	2	c2	—	405	312	−59	20	c27[2]	−2[1]
Netherlands, The	606	836	−1443 +701	390	288	−354 +199	421	109	−52 +74	312	49	−48 +13	—	c5	−4027 +1487	—	—	−172 +99
New Zealand	248	327	−37 +5[1]	98	355	+c43	34	57	—	—	c1	—	16	216	+c33	—	—	−6[1]
Nigeria	16	c21[2]	−827	—	—	—	—	—	—	—	—	—	997	c1500	−52	207	c1000	−413
Norway	19	80[2]	−318 +1[1]	440	c647	−56	126	c357	+18	3	c9	−50	—	—	−78	—	—	−7
Pakistan	4153	9944	−1246	118	129	+13[1]	—	—	—	—	—	—	514	846	—	1824	4953	+973
Peru	150	c95	−746	185	c175	−23	4	c1	−5[1]	1	c1	—	490	c600	−192 +2[1]	324	545	−48
Philippines	—	—	−695	—	—	—	—	—	−3[1]	—	—	—	1305	3300	−96	3957	c7000	−33 +57
Poland	2988	4220	−2537 +15[1]	1368	3785	−1898 +24[1]	2641	2199	−75 +2[1]	7466	5233	−c185 +7[1]	20	c400[2]	−1850	—	—	−85
Portugal	562	233	−559	61	36	−c22[1] +3[1]	87	66	−5[1]	177	113	−7	617	456	−1577	167	c135	−72
Romania	4321	4684	−c582 +c1050	415	2037	−c95 +10[1]	154	c59	−c23[1]	95	c40	—	5853	12380	−c395 +c790	40	c55[2]	−c54
South Africa	834	2220	−1[1] +c118	40	99[2]	+c16	107	84	+c17	10	6	—	5248	8240	−37[1] +2119	2	c3	−109 +1[1]
Spain	4365	4118	−200 +5[1]	1959	6150	−88 +86[1]	447	443	+1[1]	385	215	−2[1]	1101	2237	−4068 +2[1]	386	427	+51
Sweden	909	1113	−18 +615	1167	2550	−3[1] +160	1304	1646	−7 +135	142	198	+106	—	—	−32	—	—	−23
Switzerland	355	417	−357	102	c220	−429	40	52	−148	52	45	−17	14	101	−251	—	—	−25
Syria	1093	1319	−c99 +2[1]	649	395	+64[1]	2	2	—	—	—	—	7	c66[2]	−c37	1	—	−86
Thailand	—	—	−c107	—	—	—	—	—	—	—	—	—	816	c3300	+1918	11267	15640	+2348
Turkey	8585	17631	−5[1] +800	3447	5217	+112	495	371	—	734	620	+35	950	1358	—	222	280[2]	−27
U.S.S.R.	64207	90100	−c6616 +c1256	20318	c46000	−c894 +c527	6052	c14000	−c137 +c14	15093	c8100	−c45	13122	c8400	−c11225 +c152	390	c2400	−c389 +c12
United Kingdom	3520	7140	−3337 +165	6670	9550	−553 +884	1541	535	−46 +6	21	24	−24 +1[1]	—	2[2]	−3588 +31	—	—	−205 +54
United States	33040	58289	−16 +29460	8676	8238	−160 +1006	13848	7757	−17 +120	828	624	−6 +2[1]	95561	197208	−49 +48773	3084	6199	−1[1] +2238
Uruguay	465	c380	−37[1] +32[1]	28	52[2]	−10[1] +c4	66	c60	−4[1] +1[1]	—	—	—	148	71	−1 +10[1]	67	248	+116
Venezuela	1	c1	c765	—	—	—	—	—	−c8	—	—	—	477	848	−551	136	c653	−33[1] +55
Yugoslavia	3599	4512	−451 +30[1]	557	631	+3[1]	343	283	−1[1] +4[1]	169	81	−3[1]	5618	10082	−300 +243	23	c30[2]	−16[1]

Note: (—) indicates quantity nil or negligible. (c) indicates provisional or estimated. [1]1976–78 average. [2]1978. [3]Belgium-Luxembourg economic union.

Sources: *FAO Monthly Bulletin of Statistics; FAO Production Yearbook 1978; FAO Trade Yearbook 1978.*

(M. C. MacDONALD)

world. Soybean meal use was expected to decline sharply in the U.S., primarily because of reduced pork production and lower feeding rates per animal. World soybean meal consumption was forecast to increase about 0.8% in 1980–81. EEC use of protein meal was expected to be about the same as in 1979–80 despite a somewhat less than 2% expansion in livestock output; soybean prices were rising there relative to corn, resulting in the substitution of other feedstuffs for soybean meal.

World trade in soybeans and soybean meal was expected to increase slightly in 1980 despite a forecast decline in exports of these products in 1980–81; their value was expected to rise because of higher prices. Brazilian exports were forecast to increase, assuming a larger Brazilian soybean harvest in the spring of 1981. The rapid growth in Chinese soybean imports in 1979–80 was not expected to be maintained in 1980–81, but Soviet import demand for soybeans could increase and meal imports could almost double.

World use of edible fats and oils was expected to increase slightly in 1980–81, with food use of vegetable oils increasing at least 3.5%. Consumption of soybean oil was expected to exceed the 12.4 million tons of 1979–80 by 6%. World trade in vegetable oils was expected to decline slightly, although Soviet soybean-oil imports might increase fourfold because of the expanding use of vegetable oils and reduced production of sunflower seeds.

Prices for oilseeds and protein meal rose strongly in 1980–81. The price for soybeans peaked at almost $9 per bushel in November, but holders of soybeans reduced their inventories when short-term interest rates, which determine holding costs, climbed above 20%; the price then fell to $7. Good prospects for Southern Hemisphere crops to be harvested in the spring of 1981 and reduced Soviet buying also helped dampen prices. Vegetable oil supplies were more plentiful than meal, with the result that oil prices lagged behind those for meal. Ending stocks of soybeans in 1980–81 were expected to be almost 25% below the 18.3 million tons at the end of 1979–80 but about 24% above the 1978–79 level.

Table IV. World Oilseed Products and Selected Crops
In 000,000 metric tons

Region and product	1978–79	1979–80	1980–81
Selected Northern Hemisphere crops			
U.S. soybeans	50.9	61.7	48.3
Chinese soybeans	8.3	8.3	8.7
U.S. sunflower seed	1.8	3.5	2.0
U.S.S.R. sunflower seed	5.3	5.4	4.5
U.S. cottonseed	3.9	5.2	4.0
U.S.S.R. cottonseed	4.8	4.5	5.3
Chinese cottonseed	4.3	4.4	4.8
Canadian rapeseed	3.5	3.4	2.5
Indian peanuts	6.4	5.8	6.0
Selected Southern Hemisphere crops			
Brazilian soybeans	10.2	15.0	15.2
Argentine soybeans	3.7	3.4	3.9
Malay palm oil	1.9	2.0	2.2
World production[1]			
Total fats and oils	54.2	58.0	56.1
Edible vegetable oils	37.1	40.8	39.1
High protein meals[2]	83.6	96.1	86.2

[1]Processing potential from crops in year indicated.
[2]44% soybean-meal equivalent.
Source: USDA, Foreign Agricultural Service, December 1980.

Meat. Although world meat production was leveling off in the last half of 1980, total output was expected (in October) to exceed the 1979 level of 138 million tons by 1%, according to FAO estimates. Beef and veal production had been declining for the past three years, but increases in pork and poultry offset the reduction.

OWEN FRANKEN—SYGMA

Dead cattle littered the parched earth in Texas in August 1980 after that state's worst drought in 50 years.

Production of beef and veal in the major importing regions (U.S., Canada, EEC, and Japan) was expected barely to exceed the 18.1 million tons (carcass weight) in 1979 because all but Canada recorded very small increases, according to the USDA. But output in the major exporting countries (Australia, New Zealand, Central America, Mexico, Argentina, and Uruguay)—except for Mexico—was forecast to be down about 7.2% from the 7.2 million tons in 1979. Cattle herds in 1980 were in an expansion phase, and most were expected to be larger at the beginning of 1981 than a year earlier. An expansion would permit larger production in 1981, although some producers might decide that it would be more profitable to defer slaughter and continue to build herds in anticipation of future profits. Rising feed prices tend to favour slaughter, while reduced demand because of sluggish economic growth favours herd building.

Net imports of beef and veal by the major traditional importing countries were expected to decline by almost 28% from 1.2 million tons in 1979. Net U.S. imports fell 13%, while Canadian imports also decreased. The EEC, a traditional importer, continued as a net exporter of chilled and frozen beef in 1980, becoming, after Australia and Argentina, the world's third largest exporter of beef. EEC domestic beef prices were supported at more than double the international prices, causing supplies to exceed demand and leading to a buildup of substantial surplus stocks that were disposed of at highly subsidized prices on export markets. Such stocks totaled 211,000 tons as of September 1; export refunds, storage, and other measures to support livestock prices were expected to cost the EEC taxpayers the equivalent of almost $2 billion in 1980. Exports of beef and veal by the traditional major exporters were forecast to decline almost one-fourth from 2.4 million tons in 1979.

Pork output was expected to increase strongly throughout the world in 1980. Production in the major importing regions was likely to exceed the 18.2 million tons in 1979 by about 4.6%. Rapid increases in pork supplies together with dampened consumer demand because of slow economic growth weakened pork prices in some countries, leading to a cutback in the breeding of pigs that was expected to reduce pork output in major producing regions in 1981.

The expansion of world poultry production in 1980 was likely to continue in 1981. Although poultry producers faced similar conditions to those met by pork producers, strong import demand from the Middle East and the U.S.S.R. buoyed prices, and an expansion of poultry-producing capacity was under way in the Middle East.

Dairy Products. Production of fluid milk in 36 major producing countries was expected (in September) to increase about 1.1% in 1980 over that in 1979. Most of the increase resulted from improved yields per animal, although output fell in the U.S.S.R. because of poor feed supplies. Most of the impact of higher feed prices throughout the world was expected to be felt in 1981. EEC production was again expected to increase 2.5% despite efforts to reduce milk surpluses and encourage conversion of dairy enterprises to beef production by a doubling of the 1% producer co-responsibility tax; such an increase was expected to trigger the imposition of a supplementary producer tax in 1981. An expansion of the U.S. dairy herd contributed to the rise in U.S. output.

Butter production in the major producing countries was expected to be unchanged in 1980 at 6.1 million tons, while consumption would decline 2.9% from 5.8 million tons in 1979; stocks were

Table V. World Milk Production[1]
In 000,000 metric tons

Region	1978	1979[2]	1980[3]
North America	69.6	70.7	72.3
United States	55.2	56.1	57.8
South America	18.6	18.1	18.8
Brazil	10.5	10.1	10.5
Western Europe	131.4	134.5	137.6
EEC	107.7	110.5	113.3
France	32.2	33.4	35.0
Germany, West	23.3	23.9	24.6
United Kingdom	15.9	15.9	16.4
Other Western Europe	23.7	24.0	24.3
Eastern Europe and U.S.S.R.	132.7	131.2	129.7
Poland	17.5	17.4	17.2
U.S.S.R.	94.9	93.3	91.5
India	25.0	25.7	25.2
Australia and New Zealand[4]	11.7	12.2	12.3
China, Japan, South Africa	15.3	15.9	16.3
Total	404.3	408.3	412.2

[1]Based on 36 major producing countries; production is very small or data are not available in most less developed countries.
[2]Preliminary.
[3]Forecast.
[4]Year ending June 30 for Australia and May 31 for New Zealand.
Source: USDA, Foreign Agricultural Service, October 1980.

UPI

Cattle had to be hoisted to safety by helicopter after ranches near Castle Rock, Washington, were inundated by mud following the Mt. St. Helens volcanic eruption in March.

forecast to increase nearly 8% above the 784,000 tons in 1979. The U.S. accounted for almost all the increase in stocks as the result of a nearly 12% increase in output. Soviet production was expected to decline 5% from 1.4 million tons in 1979.

Output of cheese in the major producing countries was forecast to reach 9 million tons in 1980, 2.9% above that in 1979, as cheese producers continued to maintain their large share of milk use relative to other products. Consumption of cheese in 1980 increased about 2.1% to 8.6 million tons and seemed likely to rise again in 1981 as consumers responded to rising prices for red meat.

Output of nonfat dry milk was expected to rise 3.3% over the 4.1 million tons produced in 1979, with the U.S. and the EEC accounting for most of the increase, but consumption was also down sharply in those regions. Stocks increased about 5% to 800,000 tons, with the U.S. (301,000 tons) surpassing the EEC (240,000 tons) as the largest holder. World stocks had reached between 1.3 million and 2.3 million tons in 1976–79.

Sugar. Although world production of centrifugal sugar was expected to recover in 1980–81 from the sharply reduced level of 1979–80, consumption was likely to remain at about that year's 90-million-ton level. With consumption exceeding production, stocks were expected to be down for the second year in a row, to about 21 million tons by the end of 1980–81; this would be the lowest level since 1973–74. This reduction of stocks was likely to push world sugar prices higher in early 1981. World sugar prices exceeded 40 cents per pound in early November, before falling back to about 30 cents in December.

The sugar crop in the U.S.S.R. suffered from

poor weather conditions at several times in the growing cycle, suggesting further heavy sugar imports (4.1 million tons in 1979, 17% of world trade). However, the Cuban sugar industry—the normal Soviet source of imports—was experiencing severe disease and management problems.

Brazil's expansion of sugarcane plantings was largely responsible for a substantial increase in sugar production, despite a 20% increase to 4,070,000,000 litres in the authorization for manufacture of alcohol from sugarcane in 1980–81. That country—which suspended export sales of sugar in mid-September to maintain a sugar reserve for possible conversion into alcohol for use as automobile fuel—was capable of exporting more sugar should prices go higher but indicated that it might have to divert cane to alcohol production should the Iran-Iraq war cut off petroleum supplies. Rising production of sugarcane also raised the issue of competition between sugarcane and food crops for land in Brazil that could intensify if, as contemplated, other agricultural commodities such as cassava were brought into use as a raw material for alcohol production.

For most of the first two years of the International Sugar Agreement (ISA) the indicator price remained below the agreement's lower boundary of 11 cents per pound. Then in late 1979, upon word of a poor 1979–80 sugar crop, the price climbed within the ISA price band. It remained there only a few months before rising above the 21 cents per pound ceiling. In early 1980 the price dipped below 21 cents, but shortly thereafter resumed its rise to levels well above the ceiling. As the price passed through all the trigger points of the agreement, all quotas were suspended, all reserve stocks were released, and all restrictions removed as to origin or destination of sugar sales.

The governing council of the ISA had considered the establishment of a new price band at its November 1979 meeting but then deferred its decision until March 1980, when the floor and ceiling prices were each increased by one cent. In November the council again raised these prices by one cent each to 13–23 cents. Exporters had sought a greater increase, while importers had opposed any at all. Trigger points were also changed; thus, restrictions on imports from nonmembers were to be reimposed should the price fall below 21 cents, and the restitution of export quotas would become optional at 17 cents and mandatory at 16 cents.

Table VI. World Production of Centrifugal (Freed from Liquid) Sugar

In 000,000 metric tons raw value

Region	1978–79	1979–80	1980–81
North America and Caribbean	19.7	17.7	17.9
United States	5.6	5.2	5.4
Cuba	7.5	6.4	6.0
Mexico	3.1	2.8	2.9
South America	12.4	11.6	13.3
Brazil	7.7	7.0	8.2
Europe	20.1	20.4	19.4
Western Europe	14.6	14.8	14.5
EEC	12.2	12.8	12.4
Eastern Europe	5.5	5.6	4.8
U.S.S.R.	9.3	7.8	7.0
Africa	6.3	6.5	6.3
South Africa	2.2	2.2	1.7
Asia	19.7	17.1	19.4
China	2.7	2.8	2.8
India	7.1	5.2	6.9
Philippines	2.3	2.3	2.4
Thailand	1.9	1.1	1.4
Oceania	3.3	3.5	3.8
Australia	3.0	3.0	3.3
World	90.8	84.6	87.1

Source: USDA, Foreign Agricultural Service, December 1980.

The adoption by the U.S. of the necessary legislation in April made it possible to implement the ISA Stock Financing Fund on July 1. The fund was intended to be a source of loans to exporting members to help finance the stocks that they were required to hold should the world price fall below 17 cents per pound. A fee of 50 cents per metric ton (0.023 cents per pound) was imposed on all sugar traded by ISA members through the free market.

The present ISA would expire at the end of 1982, and current supply-demand conditions were shaping the issues that would likely be raised during the negotiations for a new agreement. For instance, recent production problems in Cuba had reduced that country's export potential; the ISA provided that a country must maintain exports at a level consistent with the basic export quota assigned to it or have the quota reduced and the shortfall distributed among other exporters. The allocation and adjustment of an individual country's export quotas had required difficult and lengthy negotiations under the current ISA. Another issue that might be pursued before the expiration of the ISA was that of membership for the EEC. In July the EEC Commission indicated that it would seek a mandate to negotiate membership in the ISA. The EEC had been cool to membership in the past.

Coffee. World coffee production was forecast to about equal that in 1979–80, while exportable production (harvested production less domestic consumption in producing countries) was expected to fall about 400,000 bags (60 kg each) to 60.2 million bags. Stocks in producing countries were expected to reach unusually low levels, but because of stock building in consuming countries, only an 8% reduction in world stocks from the 24.6 million bags was expected at the end of 1979–80.

The International Coffee Organization's com-

POPPERFOTO/UPI

French farmers demonstrated in London in April because British authorities would not allow French milk to be brought into Britain. The farmers claimed that the denial was a violation of EEC regulations.

posite price (1976 agreement) fell to $1.16 per pound in November, down 37% from May, when a freeze was anticipated in Brazil, and 40% from a year earlier. Prices were weakened partly by anticipation of a recovery of 5 million–8 million bags in the 1981–82 Brazilian crop and the liquidation of some 1.5 million–2 million bags of coffee by Pancafe, the trading arm of the eight-member Bogotá Group of Latin-American Coffee Exporters. The Pancafe decision to end market operations was announced during negotiation of a new International Coffee Agreement (ICA). U.S. representatives had insisted that such an action was necessary to obtain U.S. congressional adoption of legislation to implement U.S. participation in the ICA. U.S. implementing legislation was signed into law on December 24.

Representatives of major coffee-producing and consuming countries meeting in London agreed on

Table VII. World Green Coffee Production
In 000 60-kg bags

Region	1978–79	1979–80	1980–81[1]
North and Central America	16,046	14,566	14,943
Costa Rica	1,749	1,507	1,880
El Salvador	3,186	2,530	2,100
Guatemala	2,827	2,647	2,600
Mexico	4,141	3,610	3,700
South America	36,824	38,240	37,870
Brazil	20,000	22,000	21,500
Colombia	12,600	12,300	12,400
Ecuador	1,822	1,474	1,485
Africa	17,414	18,056	17,926
Cameroon	1,627	1,600	1,500
Ethiopia	3,142	2,963	3,100
Ivory Coast	4,667	3,917	4,166
Uganda	1,615	2,200	2,500
Asia and Oceania	8,147	9,240	9,357
India	1,949	2,411	2,300
Indonesia	4,586	5,024	5,239
Total	78,431	80,102	80,096

[1]Preliminary.
Source: USDA, Foreign Agricultural Service, October 1980.

October 3 to a new package of measures under the ICA designed to maintain the composite export price of green coffee within a $1.15–$1.55 per pound band. The agreement established an initial global export quota of approximately 57.4 million bags for the 1980–81 marketing year, which shortly thereafter was increased to 58.3 million bags when the Philippines joined the pact; about 56 million bags under the quota were allocated to members entitled to basic export quotas and 2.3 million to exporting members exempt from basic quotas. The basic export quotas for individual countries were based on historical levels of coffee exports during 1976–77 and 1977–78 (weighted 70%) and stock levels (weighted 30%), modified by provisions for reallocating quota shortfalls among exporting members.

As the ICA 20-day moving-average indicator price falls below or rises above agreed-upon trigger-price levels (or remains below or above certain triggers for 20 days), the global quota is either cut or expanded by 1.4-million-bag increments with the reduction or increase distributed proportionately among exporting members. Because the indicator was below $1.35 per pound when the agreement became effective, the initial global quota was reduced immediately from 58.3 million to 56.9 million bags. Another 1.4-million reduction was triggered November 19 when the indicator price fell below $1.20 per pound and another seemed imminent if the price remained below $1.20 for 20 consecutive days. That would leave one more cut of 1.4 million bags possible if the price then fell below $1.15, but that could not be done until 1981 because the ICA permits only two such adjustments in one quarter.

Cocoa. World cocoa consumption in 1980–81 was expected to be less than output for the fourth year in a row, resulting in both a further buildup in stocks and a softening of prices. Increased production in Brazil and Malaysia was expected to slightly more than offset less favourable growing conditions in Africa and result in another record crop in 1980–81. Cocoa bean grindings were expected to increase about 2% in 1980–81 to about 1,480,000 tons. Demand for cocoa was dampened by continued use of cocoa substitutes and extenders, high prices for sugar used in cocoa products, and the economic slowdown in consuming countries that curtailed purchasing power. Prices for cocoa beans continued to fall from the peak yearly average of $1.72 per pound in 1977 to an average of $1.44 in 1979 and $1.18 during the first ten months of 1980 (93.7 cents in November).

Cocoa supplies were likely to be ample, relative to prospective demand, during the next several years, according to USDA commodity analysts. High prices for cocoa in the mid- and late 1970s stimulated new plantings, particularly in the Ivory Coast, Brazil, and Malaysia. But high prices also led manufacturers of cocoa products to seek cocoa substitutes and extenders and to shift to production of more nonchocolate items.

A conference convened by UNCTAD (United Nations Conference on Trade and Development) in Geneva reached agreement on a new International Cocoa Agreement (ICCA), the objective of which was to stabilize world cocoa prices within a $1.10–$1.50 per pound band in much the same manner as the ICA through the use of export quotas and buffer stocks. Earlier agreements (beginning in October 1973) had price bands of 23–32 cents, 29.5–38.5 cents, and (since October 1976) 39–55 cents, but cocoa prices remained well above the price ranges and export quotas and buffer stock actions were never used.

The future of the agreement remained in doubt, however, because neither the Ivory Coast—which accounted for an average of about 22% of world cocoa exports in 1978 and 1979—nor the United States—which averaged nearly 18% of total im-

Table VIII. World Cocoa Bean Production
In 000 metric tons

Region	1978–79	1979–80	1980–81[1]
North and Central America	97	88	95
South America	459	443	483
Brazil	314	290	325
Ecuador	88	97	96
Africa	877	1,005	971
Cameroon	107	122	120
Ghana	265	295	280
Ivory Coast	312	360	360
Nigeria	139	175	160
Asia and Oceania	68	77	85
Malaysia	28	34	40
Total	1,501	1,613	1,634

[1]Forecast.
Source: USDA, Foreign Agricultural Service, November 1980.

UPI

Maine farmers in March dumped their own potatoes on highways at the Canada border crossing to protest U.S. importation of Canadian potatoes.

ports—had accepted it. The U.S was not a member of the International Cocoa Organization but had participated in ICCA negotiations.

Tea. World tea production was forecast to increase about 2.5% in 1980. Exports of tea were expected to exceed the 795,700 tons shipped in 1979 by about 3.3%. The largest gains were expected to be made by China, India, and Kenya, while substantial reductions were forecast for Bangladesh and Sri Lanka. India was the largest tea exporter (24% of the 1980 world total), followed by Sri Lanka (23%), China (13%), and Kenya (11%). Imports were likely to be up in the U.K. and the U.S. World tea prices had remained relatively stable since 1978, reflecting a well-balanced supply-demand situation. The London auction price for all teas averaged $2.28 per kilogram during 1980, compared with $2.16 in 1979 and $2.19 in 1978.

Representatives of tea-producing nations continued their exploration of a framework for an international tea agreement under the auspices of UNCTAD. Examination by producers of global and national export quotas in relation to possible agreed-upon price objectives and buffer stock operations were based on producer concerns that tea prices were low relative to other commodities and that higher returns were necessary to enable them to meet rising production costs.

Table IX. World Tea Production
In 000 metric tons

Region	1978	1979	1980[1]
Asia and Oceania	1,518	1,520	1,569
China	268	277	285
India	571	550	580
Japan	105	100	104
Sri Lanka	199	206	200
Turkey	86	100	110
U.S.S.R.	111	115	110
Africa	197	200	194
Kenya	93	99	90
South America	43	48	50
Total	1,758	1,768	1,813

[1]Forecast.
Source: USDA, Foreign Agricultural Service, October 1980.

Production of tea seemed likely to continue increasing during the 1980s but at a decreasing rate, according to the USDA's Foreign Agricultural Service. Availability of land for tea was decreasing, and so there would have to be greater use of fertilizers, pesticides, and high-yielding varieties to provide larger crops. Although tea faced increased competition from other beverages such as coffee and soft drinks, it remained the least expensive and most popular beverage in the less developed countries. The availability of tea for export relative to import demand might tighten. For example, tea consumption in India had increased to the point where that country had become the largest consumer as well as exporter; by 1980 the tea industry had stagnated in Sri Lanka, where consumption was also rising; China consumed two-thirds of its own output and, along with most Asian countries, had little potential for expansion of production; and political strife blunted the expansion of tea production in several African nations.

Cotton. World cotton production was forecast to decline about 3% below 1979–80 output because of a 23% reduction in the U.S. harvest caused by severe drought. Production was expected to rise about 3% outside the U.S., where the area planted to cotton was 2% higher.

Although world utilization of cotton was expected to fall about 1% from that in 1979–80, it still exceeded production in 1980–81 by about 1.2 million bales (480 lb or 216 kg each). Slower world economic growth and higher cotton prices resulting from the tighter supply situation were depressing the demand for textile products and for cotton

Table X. World Cotton Production
In 000,000 480-lb bales

Region	1978	1979	1980
North and Central America	14.1	17.3	14.0
Mexico	1.6	1.5	1.5
United States	10.9	14.6	11.2
South America	4.7	4.9	5.1
Brazil	2.3	2.6	2.7
Europe	0.9	0.8	0.8
U.S.S.R.	12.3	13.1	13.8
Africa	5.0	5.3	5.4
Egypt	2.0	2.2	2.2
Asia	22.8	23.5	24.3
China	10.0	10.1	10.5
India	6.3	6.1	6.3
Pakistan	2.1	3.4	3.4
Turkey	2.2	2.2	2.2
Oceania	0.2	0.4	0.4
Total	60.0	65.6	63.8

Source: USDA, Foreign Agricultural Service, June and November 1980.

use in the U.S., in several major cotton-importing nations in Western Europe, and in most countries in Asia, except China. World trade in cotton in 1980–81 was expected to decline about 2.4 million bales from the 22.7 million in 1979–80, with U.S. exports down about 38% from 9.2 million bales in 1979–80, mostly because of reduced supplies. The U.S.S.R., Turkey, and Pakistan were expected to increase their cotton exports.

The Outlook "A" Index (average of five lowest priced of ten selected growths, cost, insurance, and freight, northern Europe) began to rise in late 1979, peaked at 97 cents per pound in February 1980, fell back to about 84 cents in June, and then rose to almost $1.01 in September. World cotton stocks were expected to fall about 5% from the 21.5 million bales at the beginning of 1980–81 to the lowest level since the early 1960s.

INTERNATIONAL FOOD SECURITY

Grain Reserves. Since the World Food Conference of 1974, the negotiation of an agreement to establish an international system of nationally held grain reserves had been the centrepiece of international efforts to improve world food security and to stabilize world grain markets. A 67-nation, UN-sponsored negotiating conference adjourned in February 1979 after failing to agree upon a proposed new Wheat Trade Convention (WTC) as part of an international grains agreement.

Although the conference had been able to agree upon a framework that included specific national obligations to take specific actions when a price indicator reached specified trigger points—such as the acquisition or release of stocks and consultations on measures designed to affect the production and utilization of grain—it could not reach a consensus on several important specifics. They included: the precise price points at which consultation, accumulation and release of stocks, or additional measures would be triggered; the volume of total stocks, as well as individual stockholding obligations; and special provisions to assist less developed countries in implementing their reserve stock obligations.

The UN conference did agree to recommend extension of the 1971 International Wheat Agreement (IWA) to the International Wheat Council (IWC), the governing body of the IWA. In March 1979 the IWC extended the IWA until June 30, 1981. Although the IWA had no economic articles, it did provide a consultative mechanism and supporting secretariat—the IWC—that would be useful to future negotiations of a WTC. Considerably fewer na-

During the year U.S. Department of Agriculture scientists advised farmers to leave crop stubble in their fields rather than plowing it. The scientists maintained that the stubble helps retain moisture in the soil and thus prevents erosion.

SCIENCE AND EDUCATION ADMINISTRATION—USDA

UPI

U.S. Ambassador to China Leonard Woodcock (left) and Chinese Minister of Foreign Trade Li Qiang signed a grain agreement in October under which the U.S. would sell to China between six million and nine million metric tons of grain each year from 1981 to 1984.

tions belonged to the IWA than attended the UN conference, with the large exporting and importing nations accounting for a much larger proportion of the IWA membership.

The IWC met in November 1979 and concluded that there was little prospect of successfully negotiating, in the foreseeable future, a new WTC along the lines that had evolved during the earlier negotiations. It established a Special Committee to discuss the outline of an alternative approach to be developed by the IWC secretariat.

The new approach, endorsed by the Special Committee in June 1980, gave much more emphasis to consultations and flexibility by nations in interpreting and implementing their commitments under a new pact than did the previous one. It had been concerned with more rigid national commitments, such as the acquisition or release of reserve stocks at specific trigger-price points. The Committee indicated that the earlier approach may have been overambitious and that governments had shown themselves unwilling to take risks involved in venturing quickly into untested arrangements. It suggested that the world wheat market had become so unpredictable and volatile that a rigid and elaborate system could not adequately deal with future contingencies.

The new approach was reported to contain little in the way of automatic responses. Trigger-price points and associated automatic actions and consultations were eliminated, but consideration was being given to the mandatory convening of the IWC should the price indicator move abruptly.

The Special Committee's report was to provide the basis for the negotiations for a new WTC, which had been expected to begin in the IWC in November. But when the IWC met again in November, it decided that further work and consultations were required and requested the secretariat to report back to it in a special session in early March 1981. The potential change in the direction of U.S. policy with the inauguration of a new U.S. administration presumably also influenced the postponement.

U.S. Wheat Reserve. When the U.S. government suspended grain sales to the Soviet Union, it acquired four million tons of wheat intended for shipment to that country which it promised U.S. farmers to isolate from the market in order to avoid depressing prices. It also promised to seek congressional approval for the establishment of an emergency wheat reserve to help meet U.S. commitments to provide emergency food aid to the less developed countries. A similar proposal introduced in March 1979 had died in committee in the 95th Congress, but the 96th approved the Food Security Wheat Reserve Act of 1980 and it became law in December.

The new law directs the president of the U.S. to establish a government-held wheat reserve of up to four million tons to be used "solely for emergency humanitarian food needs in developing countries" when U.S. wheat supplies are so short that wheat would not otherwise be available under Public Law 480—the U.S. food aid program. However, up to 300,000 tons of the reserve may be used in any year for unexpected disasters abroad whether or not U.S. wheat is in short supply. Releases from the reserve must take place via the PL 480 program, and replenishment through market purchases may be financed only by congressional appropriation. The authority for the reserve would terminate Sept. 30, 1985. The new reserve was in addition to the already established U.S. farmer-owned domestic grain reserve program.

Food Financing Facility. The Executive Board of the International Monetary Fund (IMF) discussed proposals in December for the establishment of a loan facility to assist less developed countries in meeting sharp short-term increases in their food import bills. These increases would result from domestic crop failures or steep price rises for imported cereals.

At least three approaches were considered: (1) an amendment of the IMF's existing Compensatory Financing Facility (CFF)—designed to finance temporary shortfalls in export earnings with five-year loans—that would permit countries to treat increased food import costs as "negative export earnings" in determining their eligibility for loans under their existing CFF quotas; (2) a "second window" into the CFF that would determine loan eligibility as above but would make loans available beyond those authorized by their regular quotas; and (3) a separate scheme that would calculate eligibility for loans in terms of increased cereal import costs without regard to a country's export earnings. The IMF's managing director strongly supported the creation of an IMF food financing facility, and a proposal could be presented for decision by May 1981.

Food Aid. Donor members of the Food Aid Committee, established by the 1971 Food Aid Convention (FAC), met in March 1980 to conclude negotiations for a new FAC, which became effective on July 1. It raised the minimum total contributions from the equivalent of 4.2 million tons of wheat to 7.6 million tons and encouraged participants and potential new members to reach the 10-million-ton food-aid target agreed upon at the World Food Conference in 1974.

Contributions were to take the form of gifts, either in grain or cash; sales in exchange for the currency of the aid-receiving country; or long-term credit sales at below-market interest rates. Pledges were expressed in terms of volume—important in times of rising prices—and represented minimum commitments. For instance, U.S. food aid shipments meeting FAC criteria totaled 5.3 million tons in fiscal 1979, when the U.S. commitment was only 1,890,000 tons. As of the end of 1980 the FAC had not been able to attract contributions from OPEC (Organization of Petroleum Exporting Countries).

Total shipments of food aid in cereals fell from the equivalent of 9,574,000 tons in 1978–79 to 8,984,000 tons in 1979–80, but commitments totaled 9,885,000 tons according to FAO estimates. U.S. shipments were about one million tons smaller in 1979–80 than the 6.2 million in 1978–79; based on the level of funds appropriated for food aid for 1980–81, U.S. commitments would again total close to 6.2 million tons. The EEC was the next largest donor, with 1,386,000 tons in 1979–80.

The FAO estimated that the proportion of cereals imported into the low-income countries covered by food aid declined from 37% in 1976–77 and 1977–78 to 32% in 1978–79 and 27% in 1979–80.

Contributions to the International Emergency Food Reserve (IEFR) administered by the World Food Program increased from 330,000 tons (U.S. share=125,000 tons) valued at $80.7 million (U.S. =$31.8 million) in 1979 to an estimated 427,000 tons (U.S.=172,000) valued at $140.8 million (U.S. =$72.5 million) in 1980. The IEFR had become operational in 1976 and was accepted by some nations as an interim voluntary measure to help deal with emergencies in the absence of both a new FAC and WTC.

Annual contributions by the end of 1980 had fallen short of the IEFR's 500,000-ton goal. The prolonged delay in negotiating a new WTC gave added impetus to efforts by the less developed countries to make the IEFR a legally binding convention and to increase the resources devoted to it.

SCIENCE AND EDUCATION ADMINISTRATION—USDA

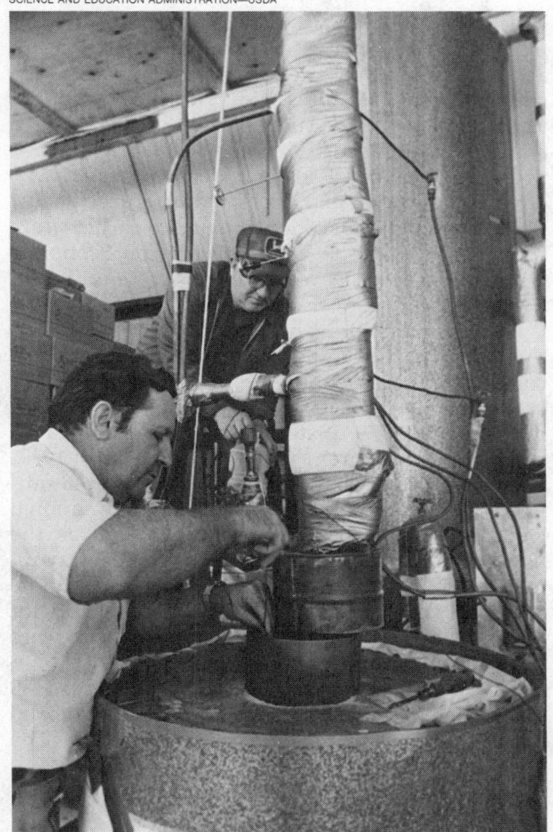

A technician adjusts an experimental still in Peoria, Illinois, designed to produce alcohol fuel from farm products. The still was powered by solar energy.

Table XI. Pledges to Food Aid Convention
In 000 metric tons

Country	1980	1971
Argentina	35	23
Australia	400	225
Austria	20	0
Canada	600	495
EEC and its member nations	1,650	1,287
Finland	20	14
Japan	300	225
Norway	30	0
Sweden	40	35
Switzerland	27	32
United States	4,470	1,890
Total	7,592	4,226

Table XII. Official Commitments of External Assistance to Agriculture in the Less Developed Countries[1]
In $000,000

Commitments	Average 1975–76	1977	1978	Preliminary 1979
Total				
Multilateral	3,062	4,028	5,264	5,116
Bilateral	2,278	3,113	3,824	4,493
Current prices	5,340	7,141	9,088	9,609
1975 prices	5,340	6,551	7,270	6,720
Concessional				
Multilateral	1,413	1,633	2,401	2,566
Bilateral	1,929	2,933	3,451	4,176
Current prices	3,342	4,566	5,852	6,742
1975 prices	3,342	4,189	4,682	4,715
Non-concessional				
Multilateral	1,649	2,395	2,863	2,550
Bilateral	350	180	373	317
Current prices	1,999	2,575	3,236	2,867
1975 prices	1,999	2,362	2,589	2,005

[1]Excludes commitments by centrally planned countries.
Sources: OECD and FAO, November 1980.

FOREIGN ASSISTANCE TO AGRICULTURE. Official commitments of external assistance to agriculture—broadly defined to include rural infrastructure, agro-industries, fertilizer production, and regional river basin projects—were almost 6% higher in 1979 than in 1978 in current prices but almost 8% lower if deflated by the 1975 UN price index for exports of manufactured goods. Revised estimates of commitments for earlier years by the FAO and the Organization for Economic Cooperation and Development (OECD) indicated that they were higher than previously believed.

Commitments on concessional terms (allowing the recipient advantages not offered in normal commercial transactions) were increasing steadily, while nonconcessional assistance apparently declined in 1979. External technical assistance grants to agriculture reached $977 million in 1979, compared with $817 million in 1978 and $648 million in 1977. The World Bank and the International Development Association (IDA), as well as the Arab and OPEC multilateral institutions, contributed less to agriculture in 1979 than during the previous year, but IFAD (International Fund for Agricultural Development) commitments were substantially larger.

The U.S. Congress was unable by the end of 1980 to complete action on a Senate-passed bill authorizing $3.2 billion for replenishment of the IDA. The agency might have to suspend its lending activities in 1981 if the U.S. contribution was not authorized by March 1, 1981, particularly if other contributors held to an agreement that pledges do not become effective until 80% of the agreed target is pledged. (The U.S. portion was 27% of the total.)

OECD and OPEC countries endorsed in December a target of $1.5 billion for the replenishment of IFAD during the 1981–83 period, with $1,270,000,000 from new funds ($230 million in old funds remained to be committed). The OECD countries pledged $650 million, but the OPEC nations indicated that their offer might come sometime after a January 1981 meeting of the OPEC Special Fund.

(RICHARD M. KENNEDY)

See also Environment; Fisheries; Food Processing; Gardening; Industrial Review: *Alcoholic Beverages; Textiles; Tobacco.*

[451.B.1.c; 534.E; 731; 10/37.C]

Albania

Albania

A people's republic in the western Balkan Peninsula, Albania is on the Adriatic Sea, bordered by Greece and Yugoslavia. Area: 28,748 sq km (11,100 sq mi). Pop. (1980 est.): 2,734,000. Cap. and largest city: Tirana (pop., 1976 est., 192,300). Language: Albanian. Religion: officially atheist; historically Muslim, Orthodox, and Roman Catholic communities. First secretary of the Albanian (Communist) Party of Labour in 1980, Enver Hoxha; chairman of the Presidium of the People's Assembly (president), Haxhi Leshi; chairman of the Council of Ministers (premier), Mehmet Shehu.

Albania and Yugoslavia concluded a five-year trade agreement, which was drafted by the Albanian minister of foreign trade, Nedin Hoxha, on his visit to Belgrade in July 1980. It was the first time in 30 years that an Albanian minister had been the guest of the Yugoslav government. For some years relations between the two countries had been improving, apart from accusations of oppression of the Albanian minority in Yugoslavia, and the new agreement gave evidence of their wish to extend economic cooperation. It was hoped that trade between them would increase from a current U.S. $70 million to $110 million in 1981.

Speaking in Tirana on Nov. 18, 1979, Hoxha had proclaimed that Albania had no wish to restore diplomatic relations with the U.S.S.R. and the U.S. but would resume them with the U.K. if the British government shipped back the estimated £15 million of Albanian gold it held (according to British sources the value of this gold amounted to £8 million).

On April 26, 1980, Mehmet Shehu was relieved of his duties as minister of defense and was succeeded by Kadri Hazbiu, until then minister of the interior. The latter post was then entrusted to Fecor Shehu.

(K. M. SMOGORZEWSKI)

ALBANIA

Education. (1973–74) Primary, pupils 569,600, teachers 22,686; secondary, pupils 32,900, teachers (1971–72) 1,318; vocational and teacher training, pupils 69,700, teachers (1971–72) 1,712; higher (1971–72), students 28,668, teaching staff 1,153.

Finance. Monetary unit: lek, with (June 30, 1980) an official exchange rate of 3.3 leks to U.S. $1 (7.8 leks = £1 sterling) and a noncommercial rate of 7 leks to U.S. $1 (16.5 leks = £1 sterling). Budget (1979 est.): revenue 7.8 billion leks; expenditure 7.7 billion leks.

Foreign Trade. (1964; latest available) Imports 490.6 million leks; exports 299.6 million leks. Import sources: China 63%; Czechoslovakia 10%; Poland 8%. Export destinations: China 40%; Czechoslovakia 19%; East Germany 10%; Poland 10%. Main exports: fuels, minerals, and metals (including crude oil, bitumen, chrome ore, iron ore, and copper) 54%; foodstuffs (including vegetables and fruit) 23%; raw materials (including tobacco and wool) 17%.

Transport and Communications. Roads (1971) 5,500 km. Motor vehicles in use (1970): passenger *c.* 3,500; commercial (including buses) *c.* 11,200. Railways: (1979) 330 km; traffic (1971) 291 million passenger-km, freight 188 million net ton-km. Shipping (1979): merchant vessels 100 gross tons and over 20; gross tonnage 56,127. Shipping traffic (1975): goods loaded *c.* 2.8 million metric tons, unloaded *c.* 760,000 metric tons. Telephones (Dec. 1965) 13,991. Radio receivers (Dec. 1977) 200,000. Television receivers (Dec. 1977) 4,500.

Agriculture. Production (in 000; metric tons; 1978): corn *c.* 300; wheat *c.* 370; oats *c.* 28; potatoes *c.* 132; sugar, raw value *c.* 20; sunflower seed *c.* 25; olives *c.* 55; grapes *c.* 57; tobacco *c.* 14; cotton, lint *c.* 7. Livestock (in 000; 1978): sheep *c.* 1,163; cattle *c.* 472; pigs *c.* 120; goats *c.* 665; poultry *c.* 2,350.

Industry. Production (in 000; metric tons; 1977): crude oil *c.* 2,600; lignite *c.* 1,000; petroleum products *c.* 2,500; chrome ore (oxide content) *c.* 370; copper ore (metal content) *c.* 10; nickel ore (metal content) *c.* 7; fertilizers (nutrient content) *c.* 80; cement *c.* 800; electricity (kw-hr) *c.* 2,150,000.

Algeria

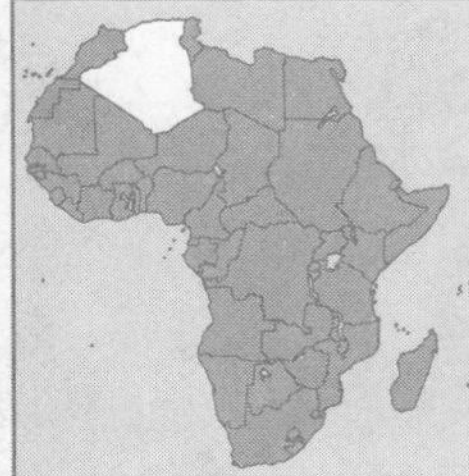

Algeria

A republic on the north coast of Africa, Algeria is bounded by Morocco, Western (Spanish) Sahara, Mauritania, Mali, Niger, Libya, and Tunisia. Area: 2,381,741 sq km (919,595 sq mi). Pop. (1979 est.): 19,129,000. Cap. and largest city: Algiers (pop., 1977 est., 1.8 million). Language: Arabic,

Aircraft:
see Aerial Sports; Defense; Industrial Review; Transportation

Air Forces:
see Defense

Alcoholic Beverages:
see Industrial Review

ALGERIA

Education. (1978–79) Primary, pupils 2,972,242, teachers 80,853; secondary, pupils 821,168, teachers 30,614; vocational, pupils 11,904, teachers 1,021; teacher training, students 11,219, teachers 986; higher (universities only), students 51,510, teaching staff 6,421.

Finance. Monetary unit: dinar, with (Sept. 22, 1980) a free rate of 3.82 dinars to U.S. $1 (8.26 dinars = £1 sterling). Gold, SDR's, and foreign exchange (June 1980) U.S. $3,482,000,000. Budget (1979 est.): revenue 36.9 billion dinars; expenditure 20.6 billion dinars (excludes 16.3 billion dinars development expenditure). Money supply (Dec. 1979) 71,421,000,000 dinars.

Foreign Trade. (1978) Imports 33,840,000,000 dinars; exports (1979) 31,556,000,000 dinars. Import sources: France 18%; West Germany 18%; Italy 11%; Japan 9%; U.S. 7%; Spain 5%. Export destinations (1978): U.S. 51%; West Germany 14%; France 11%; Italy 7%. Main exports: crude oil 87%; petroleum products 5%.

Transport and Communications. Roads (1976) 78,500 km. Motor vehicles in use (1977): passenger 333,600; commercial (including buses) 168,900. Railways: (1977) 3,918 km; traffic (1978) 1,452,000,000 passenger-km, freight 2,016,000,000 net ton-km. Air traffic (1978): 1,795,000,000 passenger-km; freight *c.* 12.1 million net ton-km. Shipping (1979): merchant vessels 100 gross tons and over 132; gross tonnage 1,258,081. Shipping traffic (1978): goods loaded 49,840,000 metric tons, unloaded 13.5 million metric tons. Telephones (Jan. 1978) 297,700. Radio receivers (Dec. 1976) 3 million. Television receivers (Dec. 1977) 560,000.

Agriculture. Production (in 000; metric tons; 1979): wheat *c.* 1,200; barley *c.* 400; oats *c.* 80; potatoes *c.* 477; tomatoes *c.* 190; onions *c.* 92; dates 208; oranges 297; mandarin oranges and tangerines *c.* 144; watermelons (1978) *c.* 145; olives *c.* 180; wine *c.* 200. Livestock (in 000; 1978): sheep *c.* 10,535; goats *c.* 2,519; cattle *c.* 1,166; asses *c.* 499; horses *c.* 147; camels *c.* 147; chickens *c.* 17,572.

Industry. Production (in 000; metric tons; 1978): iron ore (53–55% metal content) 3,040; phosphate rock (1977) 721; crude oil (1979) 50,114; natural gas (cu m; 1979) *c.* 9,700,000; petroleum products (1977) *c.* 4,220; fertilizers (nutrient content; 1978–79) nitrogenous *c.* 42, phosphate *c.* 97; cement 2,700; crude steel (1977) 213; electricity (excluding most industrial production; kw-hr) *c.* 4,700,000.

Berber, French. Religion: Muslim 99%; Roman Catholic 0.3%. President in 1980, Col. Chadli Bendjedid; premier, Mohamed Ben Ahmed Abdelghani.

At the end of April 1980, in Kabylie (the mountain region east of Algiers where most Berbers live), riots occurred after riot police were sent in to end a general strike in Tizi-Ouzou. The incidents began when a lecture on ancient Kabyle poetry was banned in March, and they spread to Algiers, Oran, Batna, and Setif. They mirrored the frustration of Algeria's Berber minority of some three million to four million, arising from decisions by the National Liberation Front (FLN) Central Committee in January and May to make Arabic the sole official language. The government made minor concessions, but not on the central issue. Pres. Chadli Bendjedid used the riots to secure his power base within the FLN and the government after the FLN's June congress. Severe criticism of party organization had been voiced after the Kabylie incidents, and the president was given complete powers to reshape it.

At its end-of-December 1979–Jan. 1, 1980, meeting the FLN decided to curtail dependence on foreign aid in order to reduce Algeria's foreign debt, currently U.S. $19 billion. Oil and gas exports were also to be reduced, to conserve stocks, while oil prices were increased until by June the price for crude oil stood at $40 per barrel, including a $3 exploration surcharge. The government also intended to create parity between gas and oil prices. The El Paso Co. of Houston, Texas, would not accept an increase in gas prices to $6 per million British thermal units, but a compromise saw rises between $3 and $4. Similar increases were negotiated with other major customers.

UPI

The town of El Asnam, Algeria, was almost totally leveled when an earthquake struck on October 10. An estimated 4,000 persons were killed.

The 1980–84 five-year plan, announced in June after a two-year delay, still favoured industry, which was to receive 38.6% of total investment. Agriculture, despite its current crisis—with 40% of arable land uncultivated—received only 6% of the $104 billion available.

The struggle in the western Sahara against Morocco by the Popular Front for the Liberation of Saguia el Hamra and Río de Oro (Polisario Front) continued to receive wholehearted Algerian support. Algeria also maintained links with Libya; new commercial agreements were signed at the fourth summit meeting between the two countries. The Libyan link created embarrassment when, in late January, the Tunisian town of Gafsa was attacked by Libyan-backed guerrillas, who entered the country from Algerian territory. The crisis subsided when Bendjedid visited Tunis in March.

In discussions within the Organization of Petroleum Exporting Countries, Algeria wanted to link oil prices to third world inflation rather than to the lower rate in the developed world. Algeria improved relations with France, signing agreements in late September over immigrant repatriation and social security matters.

At year's end Algeria acted as go-between in negotiations over release of the U.S. hostages being held in Iran. Ahmed Ben Bella, Algeria's first president, was freed in October after 15 years' detention. On October 10 an earthquake wrecked the town of El Asnam, 160 km (100 mi) southwest of Algiers. An estimated 4,000 people died and more than 300,000 in the area were made homeless.

(GEORGE JOFFÉ)

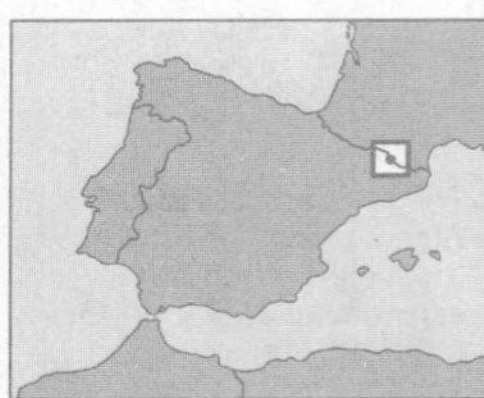

Andorra

Andorra

An independent co-principality of Europe, Andorra is in the Pyrenees Mountains between Spain and France. Area: 464 sq km (179 sq mi). Pop. (1980 est.): 35,000. Cap.: Andorra la Vella (commune pop., 1975 est., 10,900). Language: Catalan (official), French, Spanish. Religion: predominantly Roman Catholic. Co-princes: the president of the French Republic and the bishop of Urgel, Spain, represented by their *veguers* (provosts) and *batlles* (prosecutors). An elected Council General of 28 members elects the first syndic; in 1980, Estanislau Sangrà Font.

No constitutional changes were introduced in Andorra in 1980. Neither of the co-princes was eager to back the demand of a clamorous minority that the seven parishes of the Pyrenean valleys be transformed into a parliamentary democracy.

Tourism, which after World War II had replaced smuggling as the principal source of Andorra's income, continued to prosper, with five million people visiting the principality every year. Winter sports, mainly skiing, were concentrated at Soldeu and Encamp.

Andorra's population rose to 35,000, including about 10,000 native Andorrans, 18,000 Spaniards (mainly Catalans), 5,000 French (mainly Catalan-speaking from the département of Pyrénées-Orientales), and 2,000 citizens of other countries or stateless persons.

(K. M. SMOGORZEWSKI)

ANDORRA

Education. (1975–76) Primary (including preprimary), pupils 3,802, teachers (1974–75) 142; secondary, pupils 1,753, teachers (1974–75) 120.

Finance and Trade. Monetary units: French franc and Spanish peseta. Budget (1979 est.) balanced at 3,209,000,000 pesetas. Foreign trade: imports from France (1978) Fr 584,846,000 (U.S. $129.6 million), from Spain (1979) 8,568,945,000 pesetas (U.S. $127.7 million); exports to France (1978) Fr 16,008,000 (U.S. $3.5 million), to Spain (1979) 269,730,000 pesetas (U.S. $4 million). Tourism (1977) 6.7 million visitors.

Communications. Telephones (1978) 10,400. Radio receivers (1977) 7,000. Television receivers (1977) 3,000.

Agriculture. Production: cereals, potatoes, tobacco, wool. Livestock (in 000; 1978): sheep *c.* 12; cattle *c.* 4.

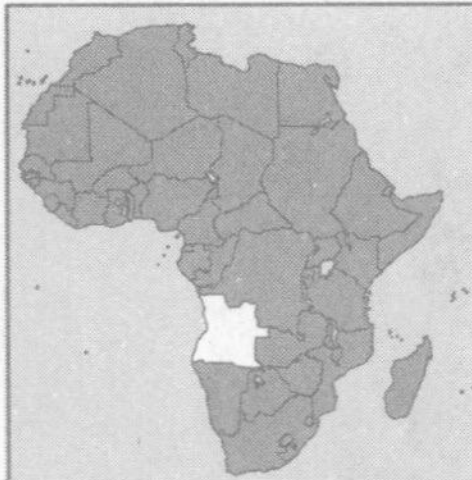

Angola

Angola

Located on the west coast of southern Africa, Angola is bounded by Zaire, Zambia, South West Africa/Namibia, and the Atlantic Ocean. The small exclave of Cabinda, a province of Angola, is bounded by the Congo and Zaire. Area: 1,246,700 sq km (481,353 sq mi). Pop. (1980 est.): 6,759,000. Cap. and largest city: Luanda (pop., 1970, 480,600). Language: Bantu languages (predominant), Portuguese (official), and some Khoisan dialects. Religion: traditional beliefs 45%; Roman Catholicism 43%; Protestantism 12%. President in 1980, José Eduardo dos Santos.

A large Soviet military mission visited Luanda in January 1980 and, coincidentally, the ruling party, the Popular Movement for the Liberation of Angola (MPLA), undertook a purge of all elements

ANGOLA

Education. (1977) Primary, pupils 1,026,291, teachers 25,000; secondary and vocational, pupils 105,868, teachers (1972–73) 4,393; teacher training (1972–73), students 3,388, teachers 330; higher (university only), students 1,109, teaching staff (1972–73) 273.

Finance and Trade. Monetary unit: kwanza, with a free rate (Sept. 22, 1980) of 29.27 kwanzas to U.S. $1 (70.35 kwanzas = £1 sterling). Budget (1974 est.): revenue 23,540,000,000 kwanzas; expenditure 19,475,000,000 kwanzas. Foreign trade (1974): imports 15,853,000,000 kwanzas; exports 31,215,000,000 kwanzas. Import sources: Portugal 22%; West Germany 13%; U.S. 10%; South Africa 10%; U.K. 7%; France 7%; Italy 5%; Japan 5%. Export destinations: U.S. 38%; Portugal 27%; Canada 8%; Japan 6%. Main exports: crude oil 48%; coffee 20%; diamonds 8%.

Transport and Communications. Roads (1974) 72,323 km. Motor vehicles in use (1976): passenger 146,863; commercial (including buses) 39,270. Railways: (1976) *c.* 3,000 km; traffic (1974) 418 million passenger-km, freight 5,461,000,000 net ton-km. Air traffic (1978): 270 million passenger-km; freight *c.* 14 million net ton-km. Shipping (1979): merchant vessels 100 gross tons and over 32; gross tonnage 64,312. Shipping traffic (1975): goods loaded 15,990,000 metric tons, unloaded 2,850,000 metric tons. Telephones (Jan. 1978) 29,800. Radio receivers (Dec. 1977) 118,000.

Agriculture. Production (in 000; metric tons; 1979): corn *c.* 300; cassava (1978) *c.* 1,700; sweet potatoes (1978) *c.* 170; dry beans *c.* 55; bananas *c.* 300; citrus fruit (1978) *c.* 80; palm kernels *c.* 12; palm oil *c.* 40; coffee *c.* 60; cotton, lint *c.* 11; sisal *c.* 20; fish catch (1978) 119; timber (cu m; 1978) *c.* 8,367. Livestock (in 000; 1978): cattle *c.* 3,070; sheep *c.* 215; goats *c.* 925; pigs *c.* 370.

Industry. Production (in 000; metric tons; 1977): cement *c.* 650; diamonds (metric carats) 353; crude oil (1979) *c.* 6,700; petroleum products *c.* 920; electricity (kw-hr) *c.* 1,360,000.

American Literature:
see Literature

Anglican Communion:
see Religion

UPI

South African troops raided a SWAPO headquarters in southern Angola in full force in June.

disagreeing with the Marxist party line. Pres. José Eduardo dos Santos also pledged total support for the independence struggle of the peoples of Zimbabwe, Namibia, and South Africa.

Backed by large quantities of Soviet military aid and encouraged by the improved efficiency of its troops—resulting from training by Soviet and Cuban military advisers—the government had launched a vigorous operation against Jonas Savimbi's National Union for the Total Independence of Angola (UNITA) at the end of 1979. By April 1980 severe losses had been inflicted on the guerrillas. UNITA suffered another blow when Zaire's Pres. Mobutu Sese Seko, in a gesture of friendship to the Angolan government, refused the use of bases in Zaire to Savimbi's forces. Savimbi's hopes were further undermined when South Africa, disappointed by his lack of success, reduced the level of its assistance. UNITA's disruptive activities continued in 1980, but on a greatly reduced scale.

On August 10 UNITA saboteurs damaged oil storage tanks in the port of Lobito at the Atlantic end of the Benguela Railway. This raid, UNITA claimed, was carried out as a reprisal for the executions, earlier in the month, of 16 of its members found guilty of waging a bombing campaign in Luanda. A fortnight later, however, nine more rebels were executed after having been found guilty of similar bomb outrages. The government also claimed that as a result of its military successes large numbers of Savimbi's supporters, emaciated from lack of food and weak from disease, were returning to the settled areas and creating a serious problem for the local authorities.

With guerrilla activity reduced, the government was able to concentrate its attention on the enormous task of economic reconstruction. Increasing oil revenue gave hope that capital might become available to revive the country's industries and agriculture. At the same time, foreign investors were beginning to be tempted by the foreign investment law of June 1979, which allowed repatriation of profits, and by the growing political stability.

In April Angola was represented at an economic summit conference in Lusaka, Zambia, where leaders of several central and southern African states met to map plans for reducing their economic dependence on South Africa. One important aspect of this campaign was the need to provide an adequate, independent system of transport and communications. With this end in view, it was agreed to set up a southern African regional transport and communications commission, backed by capital administered initially by the African Development Bank. Unfortunately for Angola, the important Benguela Railway was still subject—though less frequently—to disruption by UNITA.

In an attempt to improve efficiency, the president reorganized his Cabinet in July. Col. Pedro Maria Tonha was appointed minister of defense, and a Ministry of State Security was created with Kundi Paihama, formerly minister of the interior, as its head. There were also changes in the portfolios of health, labour, and social security, and Augusto Teixeira de Matos was appointed deputy minister of finance in charge of the budget.

The National People's Assembly of 203 MPLA members replaced the Council of the Revolution. It was chosen by a popularly elected electoral college and held its first session on November 11.

South Africa continued to harass bases occupied by forces of the South West Africa People's Organization (SWAPO) inside Angola. Late in June a strong force of South African troops established a temporary base across the Angolan border from Namibia. There was another raid in July, in which a number of Angolan troops and SWAPO guerrillas were killed.

(KENNETH INGHAM)

Antarctica

During 1979–80 the 13 Antarctic Treaty nations plus West and East Germany completed an agreement for the conservation and management of Antarctica's living marine resources. Initialed in Canberra, Australia, in May and signed in September, the agreement applies to the entire ecosystem—all the living resources—south of the Antarctic Convergence. It would enter into force following ratification by 8 of the 15 nations. A permanent commission would be established in Hobart, Tasmania, to monitor compliance.

Cooperative International Activities. Several large international research projects were conducted. In the Ellsworth Mountains 35 scientists from six nations completed a two-year program of geologic investigations in one season. The helicopter-supported scientists were based in the southern Heritage Range. Cooperative research continued in the International Antarctic Glaciological Project (IAGP), in POLEX-South, and in the Ross Ice Shelf Project (RISP).

The U.S. conducted an Antarctic Treaty inspection of six bases, the tenth inspection by treaty nations since the treaty was signed in 1959.

National Programs. ARGENTINA. A full program of scientific research was conducted in Earth, atmospheric, and biologic sciences at nine bases and camps under the direction of the Argentine Antarctic Institute. The new icebreaker "Almirante Irizar" visited Argentina's bases in the Antarctic Peninsula.

AUSTRALIA. Plans were laid for a significant increase in Antarctic work, especially in the development of marine resources in the waters between Australia and Antarctica. A research ship was to be built to free Australia from the problems involved in chartering.

CHILE. Routine scientific operations continued at Chilean bases in Antarctica. The proposed expansion of Chile's Antarctic program had not yet occurred, primarily because of financial constraints.

FRANCE. Nine automatic weather stations were set up in East Antarctica to measure the 250–300-km-per-hour (155–185-mph) katabatic, or downslope, winds present in the coastal zone. Glaciologic investigations continued at Dome C, and iceberg drift studies continued with the placement of radio transmitters on icebergs located by French, Soviet, and U.S. ships.

JAPAN. The 21st Japanese Antarctic Research Expedition worked at Syowa and Mizuko stations. A new earthquake-recording system was installed, and the geologic surveys of the Yamato and Belgica Mountains and the Prince Olav Coast continued. More than 3,000 additional meteorites were collected from ice-covered areas.

NEW ZEALAND. More than 150 men and women worked at Scott Base, Vanda Station, and remote field sites in the Dry Valleys, the Ellsworth Mountains, and the Ohio Range of the Horlick Mountains. At the latter site, geologists found the first freshwater shellfish fossils in the Transantarctic Mountains. Renovation of Scott Base continued. A violent earthquake hit the base on Macquarie Island in the sub-Antarctic, but no expedition members were injured and damage was light.

POLAND. Environmental studies were stressed at Arctowski Station on King George Island. Primary emphasis was directed toward the presence of detergents, DDT, and petroleum in the aquatic food chain in Admiralty Bay.

SOUTH AFRICA. A new research station, SANAE III, was completed to replace the nine-year-old base now buried under snow and ice. Two geologic traverses were made to Grunehogna, a substation at Ahlmann Ridge, 215 km (135 mi) in the interior.

UNITED KINGDOM. Heavy ice conditions prevented relief of the base on Signey Island. Seven men would spend a second winter in Antarctica. A Twin Otter aircraft crashed at Halley Station, killing Miles Mosley, the station leader. A hot-water drill made a hole through the 194-m (636-ft)-thick George VI Ice Shelf at Rothera Base, and instruments were emplaced for oceanographic measurements. The "John Biscoe" returned to Antarctic service and successfully reached James Ross Island in the Weddell Sea to establish a depot for future research. The Offshore Biological Program (OBP) was inaugurated. The British Trans Globe Expedition established winter quarters at Borga Base in Antarctica, some 290 km (180 mi) inland; the three-man expedition planned to cross Antarctica along the Greenwich meridian.

U.S.S.R. The Soviet Union inaugurated an air route from Moscow to Molodezhnaya in February 1980 after a compressed snow runway was completed. The route would significantly reduce the transit time for scientists and other workers traveling from Leningrad and Moscow to Antarctica. A site for the eighth permanent Soviet base in Antarctica was selected on the Ronne Ice Shelf near the base of the Antarctic Peninsula. Numerous gravimetric and magnetic flights were undertaken between the Ronne Ice Shelf and the Ellsworth Mountains, and extensive glaciologic research was conducted in East Antarctica during several over-ice traverses. The Soviet resupply ship "Olenik" burned while en route to Antarctica, causing several casualties. Geologists discovered a deep trench 272 km (169 mi) long in the Weddell Sea and under the Filchner Ice Shelf. Scientists believe it is related to the breakup of the ancient supercontinent of Gondwanaland.

UNITED STATES. The major U.S. effort in Antarctica was concentrated in the Ellsworth Mountains. Although initially delayed by bad weather and search efforts for the Air New Zealand DC-10 that crashed in 1979, the two-year scientific program was completed in one season. Fossil plants and fauna 500 million years old were discovered; they had been deposited when Antarctica was located only 5° from the Equator. Shallow ice cores were drilled at the Soviet Union's Vostok Station, and a hot-water drill was used to make 37 holes at Dome C for seismic measurements of the ice cover. Marine geology surveys in and near the Ross Sea revealed several submarine canyons, the largest of which was 1,000 m (3,280 ft) deep and 100 km (60 mi) long.

Renovation of McMurdo Station continued, rocket-launching facilities were built at Siple Station, and the Amundsen-Scott South Pole Station began under-snow operations after five years of drift finally covered the geodesic dome over the station. Special airlift flights were made to Australia's Casey Station and to Molodezhnaya and Vostok stations. About 300 scientists and about 750 support personnel were involved in the U.S. Antarctic Research Program.

WEST GERMANY. The Alfred Wegener Polar Research Institute was established at Bremerhaven to coordinate a national Antarctic research program. In Antarctica, West Germany used the Norwegian icebreaker "Polarsirkel" to search out a location at 50° W longitude on the Ronne Ice Shelf for a permanent research station, to be built in 1980–81. A second expedition, Ganovex 79, did geologic surveys and mapping in North Victoria Land, and a third expedition took geophysical measurements of the continental shelf in the Ross and Bellingshausen seas.

OTHER NATIONS. Two scientists from China, working under a cooperative scientific agreement, visited McMurdo Station en route to Australia's Casey Station. The geologist and oceanographer were the first scientists from China to work in Antarctica. Norway sent no formal expedition to Antarctica, but several Norwegian scientists worked with other national expeditions. South Korea sent a research ship to Antarctic waters to survey krill and fish resources. Belgium did not field an expedition.

Tourism. Commercial airline flights over Antarctica continued after the crash of the Air New Zealand DC-10 that killed 257 persons in November 1979. The "Lindblad Explorer" canceled three cruises after running aground off Wiencke Island while under charter to a film company. The "World Discovery" made two 24-day cruises without incident. (PETER J. ANDERSON)

Anthropology

In 1976 a new fossil early human skull was recovered from the Ngaloba beds at Laetoli in northern Tanzania. This skull, first reported in 1980, served to focus attention on the problem of the first appearance of *Homo sapiens.* The Ngaloba skull is that of a male who was between 18 and 30 years of age at the time of his death and who lived at the very end of the Middle Pleistocene period, about 120,000 years ago. It is particularly interesting because it shows a mixture of characteristics linking it both to the earlier *Homo erectus* phase of human evolution and to modern *Homo sapiens.* The long, low contour of this skull and its large browridge, heavy face, angled occipital region, and exceptionally thick bone are all characteristics found in *Homo erectus.* However, the general expansion of the braincase, particularly in the parietal region, is a characteristic of modern *Homo sapiens.*

Fully modern populations of *Homo sapiens* are known from Europe, Africa, and Asia from the period beginning about 40,000 years ago. Among these are the Cro-Magnon population from Europe, the Niah skull from Borneo, and the Fishhoek skull from South Africa. Recent analysis also suggests that modern human populations may have been present in North America at this time. Although there is considerable controversy over the accuracy of the dating, early ages have been suggested for three skulls from southern California: the Del Mar skull (48,000 years ago), the La Jolla skull (44,000 years ago), and the Los Angeles skull (23,000 years ago).

One of the major unanswered questions is the course of evolution that led to the appearance of fully modern *Homo sapiens* from *Homo erectus* ancestors. *Homo erectus* first appears in Africa and Java in the Early Pleistocene period, prior to 1.5 million years ago, and is known throughout the early part of the Middle Pleistocene from these areas as well as from China and Europe. These *Homo erectus* fossils have considerably smaller brain sizes than do later representatives of this species. The large-brained Ngaloba skull is consistent with this trend toward enlargement of the brain and suggests that at least some of the features characterizing modern *Homo sapiens* result from the continued expansion of the brain.

However, there are a number of factors that argue against the appearance of modern *Homo sapiens* merely as the result of a gradual increase in brain size in the *Homo erectus* ancestors. Other African early human skulls have been found that are of the same general age as Ngaloba but are diverse in form. A skull found in 1973 at Lake Ndutu in Tanzania, which may be considerably older than Ngaloba, has the same expansion in the parietal region of the skull together with a much more modern vertical forehead. A longer-known skull, Kabwe, from Broken Hill in Zambia, which may be 125,000 years old, lacks the modern parietal expansion as well as the vertical forehead. This skull is similar in form to two other African skulls of the same general age, Saldanha from South Africa and Bodo D'Ar from Ethiopia.

The skull of Omo II, found in southern Ethiopia and estimated to be about 130,000 years old, was believed by scientists to represent an early form of *Homo erectus.*

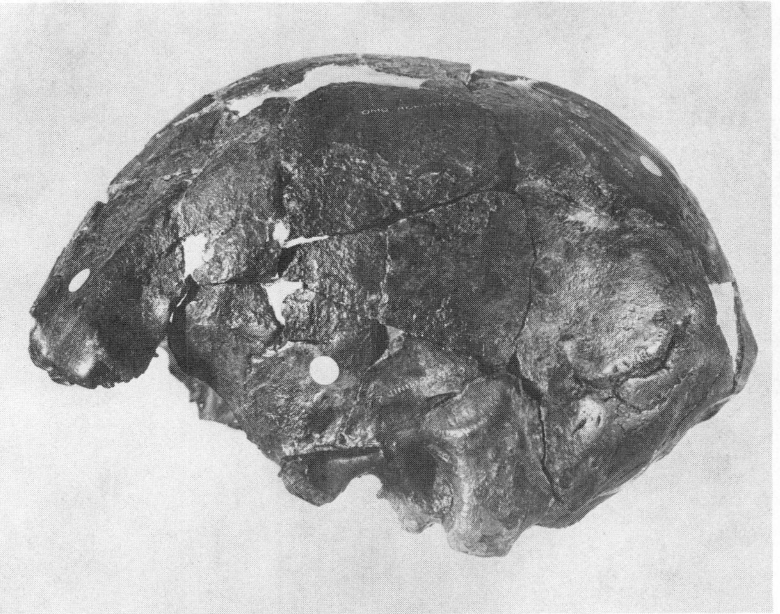

COURTESY, PROFESSOR M. H. DAY, ST. THOMAS'S HOSPITAL MEDICAL SCHOOL, LONDON

This variation in skull form is also apparent in two skulls found in 1967, which come from the Kibish formation in southern Ethiopia. Although these skulls are about the same age (130,000 years old) and both are robust in form, Omo I is very modern in its contour while the other, Omo II, is similar in form to more archaic populations.

Understanding of the emergence of *Homo sapiens* from *Homo erectus* ancestors is complicated not only by this diversity of skeletal material from Africa but also by the diversity of later Middle and Late Pleistocene fossil material from other areas of the world. In Europe the Steinheim skull from Germany (about 250,000 years old) and the Swanscomb skull from England (also about 250,000 years old) show many modern features, while the Arago material from Spain is strongly reminiscent of more archaic populations. In Java the Solo population of 11 skulls, which may be early Upper Pleistocene in age, are very similar to *Homo erectus* in form.

A particular problem facing anthropologists is the position of Neanderthal Man in human evolution. Neanderthal Man is a type of early human being who lived, primarily in Europe, from about 90,000 years ago to about 40,000 years ago. It has the same robusticity of skull form as the earlier African hominids, but it also has unique features of the face and postcranial skeleton. These have led many anthropologists to consider it as representing an extinct race of human beings that occupied Europe during the early advances of the last glacial period.

The idea that there were at least two very distinct racial types of human beings in this period is confirmed by the presence of much more gracile and modern skulls from the Near Eastern area, in particular the Jebel Qafzeh and Skhūl remains from Israel. Most anthropologists believe that these Near Eastern fossils represent the parent population of modern Europeans. However, Europe and the Near East comprise a relatively restricted area of the world. Understanding of recent human evolution is marred by an unfortunate absence of fossils recording the appearance of *Homo sapiens* in other areas.

A skull found in Tanzania was determined by scientists to be a possible link between early *Homo erectus* and modern *Homo sapiens.* The skull is about 120,000 years old.

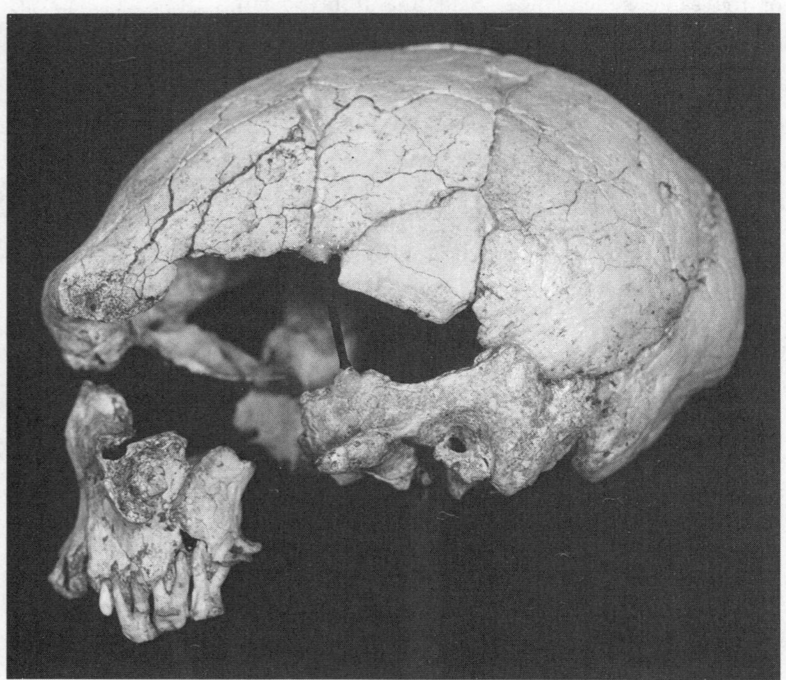

COURTESY, PROFESSOR M. H. DAY, ST. THOMAS'S HOSPITAL MEDICAL SCHOOL, LONDON

Late in 1979 an extremely interesting skull was reported from Cossack in Western Australia. This is a skull of a male who was about 40 years of age at death and who may have lived as recently as 6,500 years ago. It is important because, at this late date, it shows features that are very different from contemporaneous populations elsewhere in the world. The skull is long, the forehead slopes sharply backward, the face is large with the jawbones jutting beyond the upper face, the supraorbital margins are well developed, and the bone making up the skull is very thick. In form, this skull is similar to other robust craniums from southeastern Australia, which range in age from 13,000 years ago at Kow Swamp to 6,000 years ago at Mossgiel. At the same time, other skulls found in southeastern Australia are more lightly built and range in age from 26,000 years ago at Lake Mungo to 13,000 years ago at Keilor to 6,000 years ago at Green Gully. These two groups of fossils clearly show that there was greater variation in human skull form in Australia at this time than there is between any of the modern races of human beings today.

It has been suggested that these two different Australian populations may have entered Australia via two different migration routes as early as 40,000 years ago. The gracile group, similar in form to the Niah skull from Borneo and the later Upper Cave skulls from Zhoukoudian (Chou-k'ou-tien) in China, may have come via Indochina, Borneo, and New Guinea. The robust group, which shows many similarities with the Solo population from Java, may have come to Australia via Timor.

If this idea proves correct, it points to the conclusion that, prior to about 40,000 years ago, there was greater variation among human populations throughout the world than there is today. Besides the distinction between Neanderthal Man and the more modern Near Eastern populations, there is the distinction between the robust southern Asian parent population of the Cossack and other Australian robust craniums and the more gracile northern Asian parent population of the second Australian group.

These are all pieces in the puzzle of human evolution. The lightly built skulls from the Late Pleistocene of the Near East, Africa, Europe, China, and Borneo are virtually identical to those of modern humans. However, the evolutionary connection between these fossils, Neanderthal Man, and the parent population of the robust early Australians is not yet clear. In addition, the specific relationship between the late Middle Pleistocene fossils, such as Ngaloba, Ndutu, Kabwe, Steinheim, Swanscomb, and Arago, and the diverse Late Pleistocene populations is largely unknown.

(LESLIE C. AIELLO)

See also Archaeology.

[411; 10/36.B]

Archaeology

Eastern Hemisphere. Archaeologists with field programs in southwestern Asia understandably had a nervous year in 1980. Essentially, nothing could be done in Iran, and there were rumours that the remains of one important and well-known site, dated far earlier than the beginnings of Islam, were being bulldozed away. In the autumn the Iran-Iraq war made excavations impossible in Iraq as well, and conditions for fieldwork were not exactly propitious in Lebanon and Syria.

As usual, there were caprices. Earlier in the year, the Iraqi antiquity authorities had demanded the return of all excavated antiquities, whether or not these had come from bona fide excavations and thus had been legally "divided" between the government's antiquity service and the excavators. When war came, bombs fell near the Baghdad museum. Workmen near Cairo, doing restoration on the Sphinx, overzealously began dismantling the beast's left front paw and were hurriedly made to desist. During the past few years, there had been much publicity and a movie (*In Search of Noah's Ark*) purporting that wood found on Mt. Ararat, in Turkey, came from the remains of the biblical Ark. By 1980 specimens of the wood had been assayed by the carbon-14 method in five different and highly reputable laboratories; the age determinations, far too late for Noah, clustered about AD 600 to 800, with only one earlier, at AD 270.

The journal *Science* published a welcome and well-reasoned analysis of the current state of the Ebla controversy. Unfortunately, the reputed implications of the great find of cuneiform tablets from this north Syrian site of *c.* 2500 BC were vastly overpublicized before the tablets had been adequately translated.

During the year an excellent new journal appeared: *Atlal: The Journal of Saudi Arabian Archaeology*, edited by Abdullah H. Masry. The year also marked the centenary of the Archaeological Institute of America.

Pleistocene Prehistory. There was news that Chinese archaeologists had resumed work at the cave where Peking man was found in the 1920s. New age determinations of *c.* 460,000 BP (before present), stone tools, and a new skull were reported. In central Spain a joint Spanish-U.S. expedition resumed work at the important Acheulean site of Ambrona, and A. Ronen continued excavation at the Tabun cave on Mt. Carmel in northern Israel. The useful new journal *Early Man News* indicated much activity by Soviet prehistorians on such well-known paleolithic sites as Kostenki and Borshevo, as well as on sites in the Ukraine and about the Caucasus.

Excavations in the Wadi Kubbaniya, Egypt, yielded—along with Upper Paleolithic flint tools of *c.* 18,000–19,000 BP—several grains of barley, one or two of which were said to have dimensions resembling those of domestic varieties. If, indeed, the cultivation of barley did take place, it apparently did not persist. Two excellent Upper Paleolithic cave sequences were under excavation in the Cantabrian region of northern Spain. At La Riera a sequence from Aurignacian (+21,000 BP) through Asturian (8500 BP) yielded very good evidence for the study of changing subsistence patterns through time. At El Juyo, which is entirely Magdalenian (14,000 BP), excavators encountered the remains of a remarkable stone shrine with human and animal faces.

Near East. In Egypt the remains of a very ruined (evidently purposefully) pyramid of the son of the pharoah Khufu was under excavation. The son, Djedefre, reigned only briefly and came to an unknown end. It was hoped that his remains might be encountered. A Tel-Aviv University excavation at Tell Aphek in Israel recovered an important group of cuneiform letters. Work by a joint U.S.-Israeli team at Tell el-Hesi went forward, with special attention to 3rd-millennium-BC structures. In Jerusalem, Hebrew University archaeologists believed they might have encountered the palace-fortress of either King David or King Solomon.

In Syria the British worked again at Tell Nebi-Mend/Qadech. At a small nearby mound, Arjoune, they did test excavations that yielded traces of a seasonally occupied settlement of the 5th millennium BC, with painted pottery of the Halafian and Amouq D styles. Before hostilities began in Iraq, both local and foreign archaeologists (from seven countries) continued salvage work in the Hamrin Basin, which would soon be flooded behind a new dam. In that area, at Tell Razuk, a joint Chicago-Copenhagen team completed the clearance of a remarkable vaulted mud-brick building of 3000 BC. Such an early example of vaulting had not been encountered before.

In northern Yemen, where almost no modern archaeology had been done, Raymond Tindel of the Oriental Institute, Chicago, undertook a surface survey and encountered remains of the Himyarite kingdom of about 100 BC. In Pakistan antecedents of the Indus Valley civilization were encountered at a village site, Mehrgarb, in Baluchistan. The excavations yielded the remains of rectilinear mud-brick houses, pottery and clay figurines, and evidence for domesticated plants and animals.

In Turkey also there was salvage archaeology to be done before the pools behind two new dams on the Euphrates were completed. French, British, Dutch, West German, U.S., and Turkish teams were at work, and much new information, from paleolithic to early Islamic times, was being recovered. Outside the salvage area, the work of the Italians at Arslantepe included important new clearance on public buildings of about 3000 BC. A joint Istanbul-Chicago universities team, with architects from Karlsruhe (West Germany) University, continued the broad exposure of an early village site (*c.* 7000 BC) at Cayonu, north of Diyarbakir. In Turkish Thrace, Mehmet Ozdogan, on a National Geographic Society grant, undertook an important surface survey in this archaeologically little known southwestern Asian-southeastern European contact zone.

Greco-Roman Regions. Investigations on sites

of Greco-Roman age and contact included the underwater ruins of palaces claimed to be those of Cleopatra and Mark Antony in Alexandria Harbour, Egypt. At Quseir al-Qadim, a small Egyptian port on the Red Sea, Roman and early Islamic remains with important implications for the history of trade were uncovered. Another port, Caesarea in northern Israel, was being studied by means of submersible vacuum cleaners and scuba divers. In Cyprus new architectural clearances were made on the sanctuary of Apollo Hylates near the ancient city of Kourion. The international salvage effort at Carthage, in Tunisia, was in its final stages. As a comment on the vast reach of Roman influence, at least in attenuated form, potsherds of roulette decorated pottery—well identified as *c.* AD 0 to 200 Romano-Indian from finds on the Madras coast—were found in northwest Java.

In Greece itself, the work of the various foreign institutes proceeded, and a Royal Ontario Museum excavation at a port town in southern Crete continued. In Rome there was increased concern over the destructive effect on the monuments of air pollution and the September 1979 earthquake tremors. Within Rome an ingenious example of archaeological investigation was going forward. Using earth drillings and test pits in a variety of central city building basements, Edmund Buchner (president of the German Archaeological Institute) was well advanced in the recovery and plotting of the grid pattern of the emperor Augustus's great sundial; originally, the peak of a transported Egyptian obelisk had cast the critical shadow on the grid in a city square. New excavations at Herculaneum hinted that many residents did die during the Vesuvius eruption that also buried Pompeii. Hitherto, few skeletons had been found there. There were reports of serious damage to the Pompeii ruins in the November earthquake.

AFRICA AND ASIA. *Early Man News* contained Thurstan Shaw's excellent summary of Late Stone Age finds in West Africa. From China came word that a new type of characteristic pottery found in southeast coastal China—a black or red, shell- or fingernail-impressed ware—had been identified for the time range of about 6,000 years ago. The key collection was made on the island of Quemoy. Australian investigators established that New Guinea became inhabited by 50,000 years ago and that both wet and dry systems of horticulture were already in use by 9,000 years ago. Some of the smaller Melanesian islands were not inhabited until later, but by 3,000 years ago exotic materials had already reached islands as much as 3,000 km (1,850 mi) away. (ROBERT J. BRAIDWOOD)

What archaeologists are calling the earliest known monumental building, discovered in Turkey in the 1960s, was determined by radiocarbon analysis to have been built about 7500 BC.

COURTESY, UNIVERSITY OF CHICAGO

Western Hemisphere. Inspections and in-depth studies of little-known areas in the New World, including urban centres, produced many of the year's most important archaeological insights. In the U.S., Canada, and Latin America, much of the work was mandated by laws requiring archaeological survey and planning related to construction projects. As a result, archaeological evidence that could not have been projected from the available records was turning up in both rural and urban settings. Archaeologists were also beginning to pay more attention to material from the historic period.

NORTH AMERICA. Using careful documentary detective work and well-placed deep cores, Allan Pastron and Jack Pritchett of Archaeotech, Inc., identified and exposed the well-preserved wooden hulls of two 19th-century ships in San Francisco. The first, the "Lydia," discovered during an Environmental Protection Agency-funded survey for a proposed sewer line, was one of the last whalers. The second, the "Levi," named after the corporate property under which it was found, appears to represent one of three surviving examples of this type of vessel. During the gold rush it was beached as a store ship and later filled and used to raise the ground above the bay. Both hulls were found buried between 1.5 and 10.5 m (5 and 35 ft) below the modern surface.

On the opposite coast, Ralph Solecki of Columbia University found a unique Revolutionary War period military artifact while monitoring a sewer line cut from the docks to the water's edge in Brooklyn, N.Y. The deep construction trench exposed a line of 18th-century dock supports, and a heavily battered brass artifact was found protruding from the muck. Identified as a plaque from the cap of one of the German mercenaries who fought for the British in the Revolutionary War, it represents the first material evidence of Hessian maneuvers in Brooklyn.

In South Dakota a 4.5-m (15-ft)-deep mass grave, containing 500 bodies and dating to between AD 900 and 1400, was exposed during a severe inbank erosion of the Missouri River and excavated by Thomas Emerson of the University of South Dakota Archaeological Laboratory. Knife cuts on the skulls suggested that scalping was practiced in precolonial times. Interruptions in the growth rings on bones indicated both malnutrition and the likelihood of drought conditions in this late prehistoric period. The predominance of male skeletons suggests that the massacre was selective; women and girls were probably taken as captives. This picture of drought and intergroup conflict was quite different from the pre-contact perfection previously assumed by some scholars.

An 18-m (60-ft)-deep gorge near the Mexican border in California, exposed by Tropical Storm Kathleen in 1976, made possible a find that rekindled the debate over the antiquity of man in the New World. The more conservative and accepted position had been that fluted points dating to *c.* 12,000 BP are the earliest traces of human activity in the hemisphere. Morlin Childers and Herbert Munsell of the Imperial Valley College Museum, Imperial, Calif., found what appear to be humanly made stone tools in a location and geologic context suggesting a date between 50,000 and 100,000 BP, although the antiquity of the find had yet to be tested by laboratory methods.

New archaeological work on the coast of Labrador brought to light the activities of 16th-century Basque whaling expeditions. In 1977, while studying Spanish archives, Canadian government researcher Selma Barkam identified references to a number of Basque settlements as well as a sunken ship along the coast of Labrador. A land survey team from Parks Canada and Memorial University used Barkam's research to identify walls and a collapsed ceramic tiled structure. Concentrations of imported European clay, used in fire pits for boiling blubber, were found at the site. An underwater team of archaeologists identified and then documented the sunken remains of the Basque ship, the "San Juan," which sank in 1565.

MESOAMERICA. Recent work by Norman Hammond and others of Rutgers (N.J.) University had uncovered traces of a very early Maya farming village, dating to 2500 BC, at Cuello in coastal Belize. No earlier antecedents of Maya cultures were known, however, and archaeologists commonly assumed that the earliest Mayan sites would reflect preagricultural small hunting and gathering bands. In 1979, however, a survey of coastal Belize by Richard MacNeish of the Peabody Foundation discovered 60 pre-Maya sites suggesting five recognizable phases of cultural change between 9000 and 2500 BC. The record of stone tools, large site size, and food remains indicates that, although these Maya precursors did not practice agriculture, they were living in large coastal villages, on a protein-rich diet of oysters, lobsters, and crabs, by 4200 BC. The nomadic image of preagricultural Maya was further weakened by a 1980 report by Kenneth L. Brown of the University of Houston, Texas. His initial analysis of 117 recently identified Paleo-Indian and Archaic (*c.* 6000–2500 BC) sites in the Quiche basin of highland Guatemala shows a diversity of resources, tool forms, and possibly sedentary existence by late Archaic times.

Perhaps the most exciting archaeological revelation in Mesoamerica was provided by advanced remote-sensing technology. Until recently, many scholars had agreed that the ancient Maya lived in their jungle environment by the intensive use of shifting, slash-and-burn agriculture. From radar pictures taken in a 1978 aerial radar survey by the Jet Propulsion Laboratory of Pasadena, Calif., Richard Adams of Cambridge University and T. Patrick Culbert were able to detect an extensive network of canals and field systems under the forest near the Pasión River in Guatemala. When checked on the ground, these faint radar images were documented as 3-m (10-ft)-wide and 0.6-m (2-ft)-deep ditches from which the rich sediments were scooped to raised agricultural plots, much like those in the surviving Aztec floating garden in Mexico City. This clearly suggests that Maya civilization was dependent on intensive irrigation agriculture and that many of the so-called Maya "temples" may have been administrative buildings necessary to oversee the construction and maintenance of the elaborate canal system.

UPI

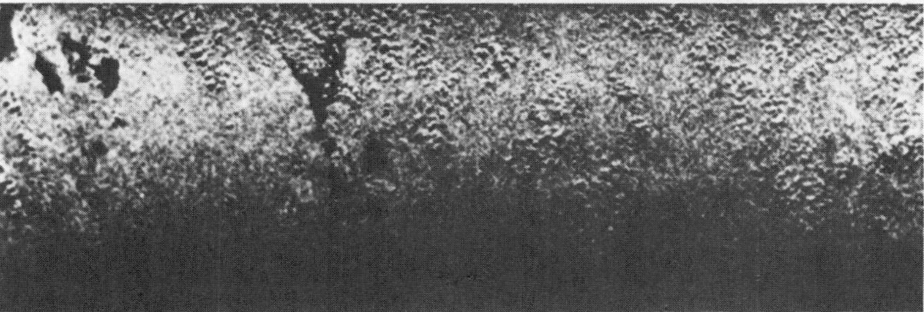

An elaborate radar system developed for use in space exploration discovered on Earth an intricate network of irrigation canals in the forests of Guatemala and Belize. The canals were believed to be 1,000 years old.

SOUTH AMERICA AND THE CARIBBEAN. During the 1960s and through the mid-1970s, South American scholars generally thought that the large towns and cities in the northern coastal desert of Peru had emerged relatively late, around AD 800, as a result of the expansion of the pre-Inca Huari empire out of the southern sierra and coastal areas. However, field excavations conducted in the Viru Valley by Curtiss T. Brennan, currently with the Institute of Andean Studies, Berkeley, Calif., documented the presence of a large town or urban centre belonging to the localized Salinar culture. The site of Cerro Arena, firmly dated to *c.* 400–150 BC, occupies the length of a 3-km (1.9-mi)-long ridge and contains over 2,000 structures. Brennan was able to identify three classes of architecture, ranging from elite administrative and ceremonial clusters to smaller and humbler groups of residences. The concentration, sheer numbers, and clearly stratified architectural patterns argue for the presence of indigenous urbanism in the north coast nearly 1,000 years before conquest by the Huari empire.

Excavations by Terrence Greider of the University of Texas in the little-known Andean Valley of Pallasca, 800 km (500 mi) north and 160 km (100 mi) inland from the coastal capital of Lima, revealed what may be the earliest and largest temple complex yet known in Peru. The La Calgada site contains the remains of two large preceramic temples and a cluster of dwellings dated by carbon-14 to between 1800 and 2400 BC. The ancient inhabitants practiced agriculture and lived in sturdy, thatched structures with stone foundations. This site also produced what may be the earliest multicoloured, dyed textiles yet identified in South America.

In San Juan, Puerto Rico, the ongoing restoration of the 1521 Dominican chapel of San José revealed some startling historic and prehistoric insights. To help the architects, archaeologist Jesús Figueroa was called in to probe the subsurface structure details of the church. While cutting through the altar area, Figueroa discovered a series of burial crypts, one of which contained the remains of the grandson of Juan Ponce de León. Deeper excavation produced prehistoric deposits containing red-on-white painted ceramics associated with carbon and shell samples, which dated between 100 and 200 BC. These ceramics, characterized by widemouthed, trumpet-like flaring bowls, represent the first in situ discovery of this style and the oldest dated ceramics from the Caribbean. (JOEL W. GROSSMAN)

See also Anthropology.
[723.G.8.e; 10/41.B.2.a.ii]

Architecture

Architectural projects are rarely completed within the time span of a single year, and it is therefore frequently difficult to isolate the most significant buildings or major trends from a single year's output. The time elapsed between publication of the first design for a major project and the completion of the final building may be as long as a decade and is rarely less than several years. Thus, as the 1980s opened, it was possible to look back over the previous decade and analyze certain trends which had their roots in the 1970s and which seemed destined to set the architectural scene for the decade ahead.

The newest and highest building in Singapore, the 52-story building of the Oversea-Chinese Banking Corporation was designed by BEP Akitek in conjunction with I. M. Pei & Partners.

COURTESY, I. M. PEI & PARTNERS, NEW YORK

The major stylistic trend seemed to be toward a new neoclassicism with an emphasis on geometric form and purity of hard-edged outline. This represented a move away from buildings designed organically from the inside out, where form is dictated by plan and site and usage. Rather, architects seemed to be moving toward the choice of symbolic "pure" forms such as cubes, cylinders, and triangles, and these forms were then allowed to dictate the arrangement of interiors.

Public and Commercial Buildings. In New York City plans were finally agreed upon, after years of controversy, for the new Exposition and Convention Center designed by I. M. Pei & Partners in association with Lewis, Turner Partnership. The design appeared to be a series of rectangular and cubic forms made of reflective glass on a steel space frame. Contrasting areas of opaque and translucent glass varied the exteriors. The building would eventually cover a site of five city blocks, above the rail yards of the Penn Central between 11th and 12th avenues and 34th to 39th streets. The structure would offer the largest exhibition space ever contained within a single building. Designs showed a 46,450-sq m (500,000-sq ft) exhibition hall adjacent to a skylighted central hall defined by a dramatic 40-m (130-ft)-high interior space. Pei described his design as inspired by the Grand Palais in Paris, a vast 19th-century exhibition hall of steel and glass.

Architects Marvin DeWinter Associates chose a right isosceles triangle as the shape for the Gerald R. Ford Presidential Museum in Grand Rapids, Mich. The two-story building, which borders the Grand River, was scheduled for completion in the winter of 1980–81 with formal dedication planned for July 4, 1981. The main design feature was on the long side of the triangular building, where a 90-m (300-ft)-long glass wall recessed under an overhang faced the river. The mirrored glass would reflect the river. The two other sides of the building were of thick concrete, intended partly to insulate the museum from noise generated by a nearby freeway.

The Luckman Partnership was successful in a limited competition for the gateway to the Long Beach, Calif., Oceangate development project. Symbolism and geometry were again dominant inspirations in the design. The complex consisted of twin semicylindrical towers separated by an open area framing a view of the harbour and the "Queen Mary" ocean liner. The two towers were not identical; the north tower featured a continuing curved facade of reflective glass, but the south tower had an undulating surface of steel panels and reflective glass designed to prevent sun glare and take maximum advantage of the spectacular harbour views. The two towers were joined by a translucent glass canopy. Completion of the project was planned for late 1981.

The geometric theme of the Merck, Sharp & Dohme headquarters at West Point, Pa., was a series of three three-story square elements set at 45-degree angles and connected at diagonally op-

Archery:
see Target Sports

posed corners. Designed by Marcel Breuer Associates of New York, it provided 10,870 sq m (117,000 sq ft) of accommodation. Completion was expected to be in mid-1981.

The newest and highest building in Singapore, the 52-story Oversea-Chinese Banking Corp. headquarters, was based on a rectangular plan with protruding solid semicircular service cores at each short end. The reinforced-concrete structure, accommodating 83,600 sq m (900,000 sq ft) of office floor area and six stories of parking, was supported on steel piles and featured windows grouped into blocks on the long sides. Architects were BEP Akitek (Singapore) with I. M. Pei & Partners as design consultants. Singapore was gradually being transformed through urban renewal from an old small-scale city to a high-rise megalopolis, and the design was considered symbolic of the new international city.

Right angles and diagonals, the square, and the triangle are central to the "field theory" of architect Walter Netsch of Skidmore, Owings & Merrill. This strict geometric formula was the rationale behind his design for the Miami University Art Museum in Oxford, Ohio. Based on a series of geometric forms in increasing volumes, with emphatic use of diagonals, it combined the square and the triangle to develop a series of exhibition galleries in proportionate sizes, the smaller ones for display of prints and drawings and the bigger for such larger-scale works as sculptures.

Office buildings too made use of geometry. In a new block for the financial district of Miami, Fla., Donald C. Smith of Skidmore, Owings & Merrill used a "butterfly" plan as the basis for a 19-story building to be clad in reflective glass. The building was essentially a simple rectangular block with a deep indentation in the front designed to increase the available waterfront views. The silver glass curtain wall would be framed with structural members of black anodized aluminum, creating an elegant and sophisticated effect.

Simple rectangular forms predominated in the design of the highly praised shopping centre for Milton Keynes in England, which opened in 1980. The centre, designed by architects of the Milton Keynes Development Corp., won two major awards, the European Steel Award and a 1980 Royal Institute of British Architects (RIBA) prize. The pyramidal elevation of the main front was reminiscent both of classical design and of Art Deco. Reflective and clear glass were widely used, and the arcades let in daylight in contrast to many pedestrian shopping malls of the last decade. The simple and clearly organized forms were praised as combining the best of functional design with the excitement and variety of technological gloss. It was certainly the best British example of the genre to date.

The Atheneum, New Harmony, Ind., by Richard Meier & Partners was also an exercise in geometric organization, this time in the well-known Neo-Modernist genre of which Meier was a leading exponent. The building, which houses a visitors' orientation centre, owes much to the International Style of the 1920s and 1930s with its contrast of solid volumes and open spaces, flat white surfaces, lack of ornament, and shiplike staircases and railings. The steel frame is clad in

COURTESY, RICHARD MEIER & PARTNERS; PHOTO, EZRA STOLLER © 1979 ESTO

The Atheneum in New Harmony, Indiana, designed by Richard Meier & Partners, features large flat white surfaces and external ramps.

A winner of two major awards was this shopping centre in Milton Keynes, England. The centre won the European Steel Award and the Royal Institute of British Architects Award.

COURTESY, JUNG/BRANNEN ASSOCIATES INC.; PHOTO, ©PETER VANDERWARKER

Part of the Chamber of Commerce building in Boston was converted into offices by Jung/Brannen Associates Inc. The offices featured white surfaces and oak trimming.

white porcelain panels. Ramps provide access on both exterior and interior, and the building in its parklike setting provides much sculptural interest. The facade is defined by a projecting triangular volume at one end and the open space of staircases balancing this at the opposite end. Though the plan itself is almost a square, the main facade incorporates both a curve and an angle. It is a superb example of geometry as a generator of form.

Energy Conservation. The need to conserve energy remained a major topic of concern for architects in 1980. The U.S. Department of Energy proposed a new set of standards that posed increasingly complex problems for architects and engineers. Pres. Jimmy Carter's administration submitted a proposal to Congress for tax incentives to encourage the use of passive solar heating and cooling in both houses and nonresidential buildings. Under the proposals the builders of suitable buildings would qualify for a tax credit.

Incentives to encourage efficient energy use in buildings were also announced in Britain, when the Department of the Environment gave a grant of £50,000 to the RIBA and the Chartered Institution of Building Services to promote mid-career educational courses for architects and to make more technical information available on the subject. The Commission of the European Communities awarded prizes of some $38,000 in a competition for houses that used passive solar designs which best responded to local climatic conditions.

Careful consideration was given to energy conservation in the design by Davis, Brody and Associates of the new biochemistry laboratory for Princeton University. It has four distinct elevations, each responding to a different environmental factor. Large areas of glass were used on the east and west walls, where maximum daylight was required. On the south wall, where the intensity of the Sun was greatest, the glazed areas were small, and the north facade was nearly blank.

In the quest for designs that made economical use of energy, common sense and good design practice remained foremost. Many design features, such as atriums, courts, skylights, sun-control devices, and window patterns were inspired by energy considerations.

Restoration and Renovation. "Recycling" of historic buildings continued to provide interesting results. One of the most highly praised of such projects in 1980 was the restoration by architects of the Greater London Council's Historic Buildings Division of the Central Market in London's Covent Garden. The original market building, in a Greek Revival idiom, was built about 1830 to designs by Charles Fowler. Two cast-iron roofs were added in 1874 and 1889 and now cover the two interior courts. The building was vacated when the market moved south of the River Thames in 1974. It was restored to house a variety of stalls, restaurants, shops, pubs, and boutiques on two levels. An undoubted architectural success, the project would be studied to determine whether it would be equally successful in economic terms. If it was, a similar development might come to fruition for Billingsgate Market, London's wholesale fish market soon destined to vacate its historic site, where Chrysalis Associates and Ove Arup were commissioned to design a commercial project.

Jung/Brannen Associates Inc. converted part of the old Boston Chamber of Commerce building into architects' offices. The original granite structure, incorporating a dramatic rotunda 23 m (75 ft) in diameter, dates from 1890–92 and was designed by Shepley, Rutan & Coolidge. The new offices made use of white surfaces and oak trimming, blending them successfully with the historic original.

In Newark, N.J., a health and fitness club—the New Jersey Bell Medical and Aerobic Fitness Facility—was created in a building that was formerly a garage used for the repair of vehicles. The rectangular space was redesigned using mirrored walls and aluminum ceiling cladding to create the illusion of space. Architects were the Grad Partnership, with Ronald H. Schmidt project partner.

Hotels, Embassies. Hyatt Hotels unveiled designs to renovate the 60-year-old Hotel Texas in Fort Worth, Texas, and unite it with the new six-story atrium of the Hyatt Regency. Such atriums had become something of a Hyatt Regency trademark, and the Fort Worth example would feature pools, streams, and an 8-m (26-ft)-high waterfall. Designers of the project were JPJ Architects.

Construction of the first modern hotel in China began in October 1980 with completion scheduled for two years later. The design for the Great Wall of Beijing Hotel in Beijing (Peking) by architects Beckett International of California featured three wings of rooms radiating from a central core. A five-story, pyramid-shaped atrium would be incorporated with landscaping, fountains, pools, and a tea garden. The $78 million project would ultimately provide 1,000 guest rooms.

Beckett International was also the architect for a proposed new Mass Communications Center for Seoul, South Korea, work on which was scheduled to begin in 1981. Designs for the centre, which would house newspaper, television, and radio operations, featured 65,000 sq m (700,000 sq ft) of space with a 21 story office tower surrounded by a low-rise block at its base.

There was a flurry of diplomatic architectural activity in Washington, D.C., with designs for five new chanceries at International Center unveiled for Bahrain, Ghana, Israel, Kuwait, and Yemen (San'a'), each designed by a different U.S. architect. The International Center would eventually accommodate 14 chanceries. Those for Bulgaria, Jordan, Libya, Nigeria, and the United Arab Emirates were already in the planning stages. Each of the buildings was designed to combine harmoniously elements of architecture characteristic of the country represented with a style appropriate to Washington.

Ghana's chancery by Brown & Wright resembled in plan a traditional palace of a Ghanaian chief. Native Ghanaian plants would adorn the balconies. The design by The Architects Collaborative for the Bahrain chancery revealed a small building featuring a domed atrium with fountain and an arcaded porte cochere. Skidmore, Owings & Merrill produced designs for the Kuwait chancery in which two-thirds of the total accommodation was below ground. The most traditional of the designs was that for the chancery of Yemen (San'a') by the Georgetown Design Group (architect Mokhless al-Harri). It featured a limestone building with granite ornamentation and windows with semicircular tops containing stained glass. Brick and granite were the materials for the Israeli chancery, which also featured deep arched windows with balconies and parapets overlooking a daylighted atrium. Architects were Cohen and Haft, Holtz Kerxton & Associates.

Also in Washington, the newly completed embassy of New Zealand featured brick walls to enable it to harmonize with the neighbouring Lutyens-designed British embassy. Architects Warren & Mahoney of Christchurch, N.Z., employed a variation of shallow-arched windows and brick piers reminiscent of 19th-century industrial architecture. The lower two floors were windowless and housed a parking area. Curved wings emphasized a central entry area, which inside reflected traditional New Zealand construction with heavy timber trusses, brick arches, and a glazed roof. A conservatory for New Zealand plant life was also incorporated.

Awards. In an effort to improve the quality of federal architecture in the U.S., Sen. Daniel Moynihan (Dem., N.Y.) presented a bill to Congress proposing that a post of federal "supervising architect" be created. The federal government employed such an architect until 1939, attached to the Department of the Treasury, to oversee standards. The bill also suggested the adoption of a "Statement of Principles of Architectural Excellence for Public Buildings." Among the proposals was a requirement for design competitions for major projects. Reactions to the proposals were initially favourable.

The American Institute of Architects presented its annual awards in June. Among the winners were the Rouse Co. for its restoration of the historic Faneuil Hall Market Place in Boston; Cyril M. Harris, architectural acoustician, teacher, and lexicographer; *Progressive Architecture* magazine for its annual design awards program; M. Paul Friedberg, landscape architect and urban designer; and Lady Bird Johnson, for her efforts to promote national beautification and natural preservation.

The 1980 Pritzker Architectural Prize was awarded to Luis Barragán, a Mexican landscape architect whose most famous work was the 1940s design of El Pedregal, a residential complex in Mexico City set among gardens carved out of volcanic terrain. His designs were praised for their romantic evocation of Mexico's past and future.

The RIBA Gold Medal for 1980 was awarded to James Stirling (*see* BIOGRAPHIES). His early major works included the pioneering "brutalist" University of Leicester Engineering Building, the History Faculty Library for the University of Cambridge, and the Olivetti Training School, Haslemere. More recently he carried out projects in West Germany and the U.S. (SANDRA MILLIKIN)

See also Engineering Projects; Historic Preservation; Industrial Review.
[626.A.1–5; 626.C]

ANTHONY HATHAWAY

The new embassy of New Zealand, in Washington, D.C., made of brick, glass, and wood in balanced proportions, was by architects Warren & Mahoney of Christchurch, New Zealand.

Arctic Regions

Oil and Gas. According to the Atlantic Richfield Co. (ARCO) at the end of June 1980, the third anniversary of the trans-Alaska pipeline, more than 1,260,000,000 bbl of oil had been transported from the Prudhoe Bay oil fields. Other statistics showed that the oil had been loaded onto 1,670 tankers at the Valdez, Alaska, terminal for shipment to markets and that the production rate of 1.5 million bbl per day comprised 17% of total U.S. domestic oil production. Between 1970 and 1980 about $15 billion had been invested to develop the Prudhoe field, including the pipeline costs and the costs of the tankers carrying the oil. Earlier in the year the Alaska Oil and Gas Conservation Commission reported that proven oil reserves in the Prudhoe Bay field amounted to 8,400,000,000 bbl as of January 1. The same report also indicated that the total value of Alaskan oil and gas production in 1979 was $5,585,129,000, a 200% increase over 1978. Of this amount, $1.7 billion went as revenue to the state of Alaska.

During the summer and fall Alaskans began to receive some of the oil wealth earned by taxes and royalties collected from the production of oil and gas. The state distributed this wealth to its residents by refunding 1979 and 1980 state income taxes and by means of dividends on money earned by the fund. The journal *Alaska* reported that projections showed that the state would have at least a $1 billion surplus in its general fund during 1980 and a balance of $184 billion by the year 2000.

In July ARCO released a study summarizing field observations made between 1969 and 1978. They indicated that the development of the Prudhoe Bay oil field and the building of the trans-Alaska pipeline had not caused major changes in the wildlife population in the area.

Throughout the pipeline operating period about 425 million hl (1,500,000,000 cu ft) per day of natural gas were brought to the surface with the produced oil. A small portion was used in the operations of the pipeline, but most—enough to provide power for a city the size of Anchorage, Alaska, for 33 years—was returned to the Prudhoe Bay reservoir because of the absence of a natural-gas pipeline to markets in the south.

In April *Alaska* reported that the U.S. federal government no longer believed that state of Alaska funds were needed to ensure construction of the estimated $23 billion Alaska Highway gas pipeline. According to the report, if agreement could be reached on the respective roles of the government and private sectors, construction could begin in 1982 and the line could be completed in the winter of 1984–85.

In a significant step forward for the construction of the pipeline, the Canadian government in July granted approval to Foothills Pipe Lines (Yukon) Ltd. to proceed with construction of about 2,400 km (1,500 mi), or 30% of the total project, which was designed to move gas from Prudhoe Bay in Alaska through Canada to markets in the United States.

In July the first sale of natural gas from the Canadian Arctic Islands, worth more than $4 billion during the life of the project, was announced by the Arctic Pilot Project, a consortium led by Petro-Canada. The sales agreements, scheduled to begin in 1983, called for Arctic Islands gas to be shipped by tanker to eastern Canada, thus freeing gas in western Canada for export to the United States.

Greenland Eskimos, claiming that the $1.5 billion project would destroy the environment and the sources of their traditional fishing and sealing economy, objected to the initial shipping routes proposed. Their opposition forced Petro-Canada to move the tanker routes away from the Greenland coast toward the centre of the 480-km (300-mi)-wide Davis Strait.

In March it was announced that the world's most northerly weather station was in operation at Malloch Dome on Ellef Ringnes Island in the Canadian Arctic Islands. The unmanned station, using a satellite communications system, was established to gather meteorologic data to assist in the design and operation of a liquefied natural gas port facility at Ellef Ringnes Island.

For the fifth consecutive year Canadian government approval was given to Dome Petroleum Ltd. to resume offshore exploration drilling in the Beaufort Sea. Total expenditures of $200 million were planned for 1980 and included the drilling of five new wells.

In May *Canada Weekly* reported the biggest natural gas discovery to date in the Canadian Arctic Islands, just south of King Christian Island. A gas flow of 2.3 million hl (8.2 million cu ft) per day was reported from a drilling operation that was conducted from an ice platform in about 240 m (800 ft) of water.

Eskimos. "Nunavut," an Eskimo word meaning "Our Land," was the name of a proposed new province covering most of the area above the tree line in Canada. The approximately 17,000 Eskimos living there made specific proposals regarding political and administrative changes that would eventually result in full provincial status for the area. The idea appeared to gain momentum during the year among the Eskimos, who were demanding greater local control over all social, economic, and land-use activities. The Canadian government was reluctant to approve the plan, however, because of the oil, gas, and other resource developments taking place in the region that might conflict with the traditional Eskimo way of life.

Arctic natives from Greenland, Canada, and Alaska met in Godthab, Greenland, late in June at the second Inuit Circumpolar Conference to develop and promote a comprehensive policy. The conference considered a charter to establish a permanent organization and addressed itself to the Arctic aspects of such matters as culture, development, education, and health.

In January a federal judge ordered the U.S. Department of the Interior to halt its more than $1 billion sale of oil and gas leases in Alaska's Beaufort Sea because such development could threaten bowhead whales, an endangered species, during their migration through the sea. The International

Whaling Commission established a quota for the Alaskan Eskimo harvesting of bowhead whales. There was serious disagreement between the Eskimos and the commission over the appropriate harvesting level for the whales when the international commission established a quota of 18 whales landed or 26 struck, while the Eskimos established a quota of 45 whales. In 1980, 15 whales were reported taken and 26 were struck on their spring migration through the Bering Sea and the Arctic Ocean.

Research. In March the U.S. government notified Alaska that the Naval Arctic Research Laboratory at Point Barrow would be placed on "caretaker" status at the end of the year. One of the largest and longest operating Arctic research stations, it was shut down because it lacked the $8 million a year needed to maintain operations and because much of the information it had furnished could now be obtained from satellites and from ground stations located in Prudhoe Bay and Fairbanks.

The Committee for High Arctic Research Liaison and Information Exchange outlined research undertakings during the year by a variety of agencies from Denmark, Sweden, the U.S., and Canada. Among the larger projects were FRAM II, a U.S. oceanographic expedition carrying out a series of experiments in the eastern Arctic; the Canadian Polar Continental Shelf Project, which supported numerous projects primarily in the Arctic Islands; measurement of the Greenland ice sheet by the U.S. Army Cold Regions Research and Engineering Laboratory; and an expedition to the northernmost point of Greenland by the Swedish icebreaker "YMER," commemorating the centenary of A. E. Nordenskiöld's 1878–80 navigation through the Northeast Passage.

(KENNETH DE LA BARRE)

See also Environment.

Argentina

Argentina

The federal republic of Argentina occupies the southeastern section of South America and is bounded by Chile, Bolivia, Paraguay, Brazil, Uruguay, and the Atlantic Ocean. It is the second-largest Latin-American country, after Brazil, with an area of 2,758,829 sq km (1,065,189 sq mi). Pop. (1980 est.): 27,064,000. Cap. and largest city: Buenos Aires (pop., 1980 est., 2,985,000). Language: Spanish. Religion: Roman Catholic 92%. President in 1980, Lieut. Gen. Jorge Rafael Videla.

The military junta headed by Pres. Jorge Rafael Videla in October 1980 nominated Gen. Roberto Viola as military president to assume office in March 1981 for a three-year term. The junta published its guidelines for the policies to be carried out during 1981–84. They included continuation of the current economic policy, reduction in the size of the public sector, development of labour union legislation, creation of a responsible political system, and the defense of national security.

The question of the reinstatement of a civilian government remained unclear. The minister of the interior, Gen. Albano Harguindeguy, suggested that the nation could be returned to civilian rule in 1984 if the junta succeeded in its antileftist campaign. Two basic conditions had been established by the armed forces for the restoration of a civilian government. The first one, published in a document at the end of 1979, was the institutionalization of the armed forces' participation in government. The second was made clear by General Viola in April 1980 and established that there should be "no revision of what had happened during the fight against terrorism." In the somewhat blunter words of the minister of the interior, "no victorious army was ever asked to explain its behaviour during a war."

Yet the government continued to face pressure both locally and abroad to explain the disappearance of thousands of people in recent years. Reports issued by several international organizations concluded that the missing people must be presumed dead. The U.S. government report on human rights, published on February 5, indicated that after 1976 the Argentine security forces embarked on a widespread countercampaign of violence against elements of society considered subversive and that there was evidence of torture, arbitrary arrest, invasion of homes, and suspension of political freedom by those forces.

This report agreed in general terms with that produced by the Inter-American Commission on Human Rights, which visited the country in September 1979. The report of this commission, which had been established by the Organization of American States, was published in Argentina on April 18, 1980. The government of Argentina answered it publicly by stating that it was neither objective nor balanced. A mission of the New York City Bar Association that visited Argentina in 1979 reported the number of disappearances as 10,000, and Amnesty International increased that figure to 15,000–20,000.

The government response to the international reports was not aimed at clarifying the situation of those who were missing but at explaining the necessity of all actions committed in pursuit of victory during the "war." But on August 14 there was a public demonstration organized by the Madres de Plaza de Mayo (Mothers of the Plaza de Mayo), a group including relatives of those who had disappeared. The 1980 Nobel Peace Prize, awarded to Adolfo Pérez Esquivel (*see* NOBEL PRIZES), an Argentine sculptor and leader of a Christian peace movement in Latin America, was accepted by Pérez in the name of the missing persons.

On the external front the government refused on January 10 to participate in imposing the grain embargo against the Soviet Union organized by the U.S. In consequence, the U.S.S.R. became an important commercial partner for Argentina in 1980 as a purchaser of beef and grains. Unlike the Western press, the Soviet Union adopted a low profile on the human rights situation in Argentina. Pres. João Baptista de Oliveira Figueiredo of Brazil and President Videla exchanged visits in May and August, respectively, and various agreements were signed covering nuclear and scientific cooperation, the construction of a bridge on the Iguaçu River, and some hydroelectric developments.

Areas:
see Demography; *see also the individual country articles*

WIDE WORLD

Gen. Roberto Viola (right) was nominated as military president of Argentina, to take office in 1981, succeeding the junta headed by Pres. Jorge Rafael Videla (left).

The territorial conflict with Chile about the Beagle Channel was still under Vatican mediation, and Pope John Paul II was to call for a final meeting before making a recommendation for solving the dispute. Relations with the U.S. were not good during 1980. After the Argentine rejection of the grain embargo against the Soviet Union, there were some signs of improvement when a mission headed by U.S. Deputy Secretary of Commerce Luther Hodges, Jr., visited the country, and the Export-Import Bank announced preliminary loan commitments for the Yacyreta hydroelectric project. However, an announced visit by the U.S. assistant secretary of state for inter-American affairs, William Bowdler, in late July was canceled following Argentina's recognition of the military junta in Bolivia. Suggestions that its government was involved in the Bolivian coup were rejected by Argentina, but President Videla made explicit his sympathies with the new Bolivian government, and a U.S. $50 million credit was to be granted to that country.

The government introduced new legislation on union organization aimed at reducing the labour movement's powers; further moves in that direction included the removal of all government contributions to the unions. Progress was made on Argentina's four planned nuclear power stations, and agreements with West German and Swiss firms to set up major components were completed in May and June, respectively.

Against the background of the collapse of several banks and of an overvalued peso, José Martínez de Hoz, the economy minister, announced income tax cuts and the extension of credit to businesses, to be balanced by an increase in the value-added tax from 16 to 20%. A slowed rate of economic growth was expected for 1980 (8.5% in 1979) because of the effects of bad weather on agriculture and an anti-inflationary policy that adversely affected the industrial sector. Price increases showed signs of slowing down; an inflation rate of about 100% was expected, compared with 139.7% in 1979.

(CHRISTINE MELLOR)

ARGENTINA

Education. (1977) Primary, pupils 3,680,185, teachers 199,384; secondary, pupils 441,907, teachers 60,199; vocational, pupils 846,200, teachers 113,515; higher, students 619,950, teaching staff 39,970.

Finance. Monetary unit: peso, with (Sept. 22, 1980) a free rate of 1,920 pesos to U.S. $1 (4,616 pesos = £1 sterling). Gold, SDR's, and foreign exchange (May 1980) U.S. $8,469,000,000. Budget (1979 est.) balanced at 20,482,000,000,000 pesos. Gross national product (1975) 1,310,700,000,000 pesos. Money supply (March 1980) 20,712,000,000,000 pesos. Cost of living (Buenos Aires; 1975 = 100; June 1980) 20,966.

Foreign Trade. (1978) Imports 3,087,500,000,000 pesos; exports 5,070,900,000,000 pesos. Import sources: U.S. 19%; West Germany 11%; Brazil 9%; Italy 8%; Japan 7%; Chile 5%. Export destinations: The Netherlands 10%; Brazil 9%; U.S. 9%; Italy 8%; West Germany 6%; U.S.S.R. 6%; Japan 6%; Spain 5%. Main exports: meat 12%; corn 9%; oilseeds and nuts 9%; machinery and transport equipment 8%; textile fibres 6%; animal and vegetable oils 6%; animal fodder 5%.

Transport and Communications. Roads (1978) 207,630 km. Motor vehicles in use (1978): passenger 2,866,000; commercial (including buses) 1,244,000. Railways (1978): 34,600 km; traffic 11,242,000,000 passenger-km, freight 10,310,000,000 net ton-km. Air traffic (1978): 5,370,000,000 passenger-km; freight 128.6 million net ton-km. Shipping (1979): merchant vessels 100 gross tons and over 495; gross tonnage 2,343,671. Shipping traffic (1978): goods loaded 23,352,000 metric tons, unloaded 8,375,000 metric tons. Telephones (Jan. 1978) 2,584,800. Radio receivers (Dec. 1977) 10 million. Television receivers (Dec. 1977) 4.6 million.

Agriculture. Production (in 000; metric tons; 1979): wheat 7,800; corn 8,700; sorghum 6,200; millet 310; barley 329; oats 536; rice 326; potatoes 1,694; sugar, raw value *c.* 1,381; linseed 816; soybeans *c.* 3,700; sunflower seed *c.* 1,430; tomatoes 570; oranges 697; lemons 275; apples 972; wine *c.* 2,516; tobacco 68; cotton, lint *c.* 140; cheese *c.* 240; wool, clean 93; beef and veal 3,092; fish catch (1978) 537; quebracho extract (1978) 115. Livestock (in 000; June 1979): cattle *c.* 60,174; sheep *c.* 35,400; pigs *c.* 3,650; goats *c.* 3,000; horses (1978) *c.* 2,700; chickens *c.* 32,000.

Industry. Fuel and power (in 000; metric tons; 1979): crude oil 24,268; natural gas (cu m) 8,720,000; coal 727; electricity (excluding most industrial production; kw-hr) 33,096,000. Production (in 000; metric tons; 1979): cement 6,701; crude steel 2,987; cotton yarn 92; man-made fibres 65; petroleum products (1977) *c.* 23,060; plastics and resins 172; sulfuric acid 279; newsprint 101; other paper (1977) 766; passenger cars (including assembly; units) 190; commercial vehicles (including assembly; units) 63. Merchant vessels launched (100 gross tons and over; 1979) 45,700 gross tons.

Art Exhibitions

For several years it had been said that the days of large, lavish loan exhibitions of works of art were past, but some major shows of the "old" order were mounted in 1980, notwithstanding the ever increasing costs of transportation and insurance coupled with the problems posed by economic recession. "The Avant-Garde in Russia, 1910–1930: New Perspectives" was an example of this genre. Shown at the Los Angeles County Museum of Art, it was the first major exhibition ever devoted to this subject in a museum in the U.S. The huge exhibition of more than 450 works by 40 artists covered all aspects of art and the decorative arts, including many distinctive and individual areas, culminating in Suprematism (which reached its definitive form in the paintings of K. Malevich) and Constructivism. All the exhibits were drawn from non-Communist sources, essential since material of this kind was now considered anti-Soviet. The art of this period in Russia represented one of the great art movements of the 20th century and was an art of ideas and form. Works by El Lissitzky and V. Tatlin were among those shown. The exhibition was due to travel from Los Angeles to the Hirchhorn Museum and Sculpture Gallery, Washington, D.C.

"Post-Impressionism—Cross-Currents in European Painting" was another vast and varied exhibition with something to interest all visitors from the hedonistic to the academic. Mounted at the Royal Academy of Art in London in the winter, and moved, with some changes, to the National Gallery of Art, Washington, D.C., in May 1980, it afforded an opportunity to study the complex interrelationships that existed in the fine arts in France, Germany, Britain, The Netherlands, Belgium, Italy, and Scandinavia from about 1880. The subtitle was a more accurate reflection of the scope of the show, since the Postimpressionists themselves represented only a small sector of the artists on display. The show was really a comprehensive survey of European modern art of the period 1880 to 1905. High points included an entire wall of Gauguins, some splendid works by Van Gogh, and the Pointillists, including Seurat. In most rooms the artists were grouped by nationality rather than style. Multiple visits would have been required for the visitor wishing to absorb fully all the visual material in this enormous show.

Also ambitious in scope and size was the Arts Council of Great Britain's exhibition devoted to the 1930s, mounted in late autumn of 1979. "British Art and Design Before the War" was an attempt to place visual arts, architecture, and design into a social and historical context that included material relating to science and engineering, press photographs of society events, and items referring to various leftist organizations. This was arguably less successful than the display of objects themselves, which included items inspired by the Arts and Crafts Movement, Jazz Style, International Style, and Avant Garde Modern Movement furniture and textiles. The display of textiles, always difficult to show, was particularly imaginative; here they were hung vertically, falling in folds as if they were curtains.

COURTESY, THE MUSEUM OF MODERN ART, NEW YORK; PHOTO, LEONARDO LE GRAND

Crowds were large at the exhibit "Pablo Picasso: A Retrospective" shown at New York City's Museum of Modern Art from May to September.

"Hommage à Monet" at the Grand Palais, Paris, from February to May 1980 was another "modern movement" retrospective and brought together the artist's best works from all periods of his life. Examples came from as far afield as the U.S. and the U.S.S.R. The selection was careful and thus not too overwhelming. An important retrospective devoted to the work of Eugène Viollet-le-Duc, the 19th-century French "Gothic Revival" architect, restorer, painter, and theorist, was seen at the Grand Palais from February to May. At the same time, the École des Beaux-Arts held a smaller show chronicling the artist's visit to Italy. The exhibition, organized to mark the centenary of his death in 1879, reassessed his importance and influence.

The Grand Palais was the venue for a show of Picasso's works, later to be housed in the new Musée Picasso, scheduled to open in 1981. This legacy, which had taken some six years to sort out, included paintings, sketches, sculpture, and prints which the artist had retained for his own collection throughout his life. The show was seen from October 1979 to January 1980.

Many of these works were shown at the Walker Art Center, Minneapolis, Minn., before going on to become part of the immense "Pablo Picasso: A Retrospective," which opened at the Museum of Modern Art in New York City in May. Filling all of MOMA's gallery space, the Picasso show included almost 1,000 items, illustrating the many media in which Picasso had worked and ranging from his early conventional paintings through many periods and styles to works done in old age. The cumulative impact on the viewer was overwhelming, confirming the artist's unique and seminal position in 20th-century art. The exhibition had been assembled by William Rubin, director of MOMA's department of painting and sculpture, and Dominique Bozo, future curator of the Musée Picasso. It would probably never be duplicated, since many of the works, finally freed from the legal entanglements surrounding Picasso's estate,

Armies:
see Defense

Art:
see Architecture; Art Exhibitions; Art Sales; Dance; Literature; Museums; Theatre

were destined for permanent disposition elsewhere. "Guernica," the huge antiwar mural housed at MOMA for many years, was to go to Spain in accordance with the artist's wishes.

Twentieth-century art was also the theme of "Abstraction: Towards a New Art—Painting 1910–20" at the Tate Gallery, London, in the spring. Its professed aim was to explain abstract art by elucidating the problem of abstraction itself. Although the approach was a scholarly one, the works were allowed to speak for themselves, and it was clear how, as artists freed their perception from the visible world, many varied forms of abstraction emerged, such as Cubism, De Stijl, Suprematism, Vorticism, and Futurism. Emphasis was on three major figures of the decade: Malevich, Mondrian, and Kandinsky. Key items were lent from collections in Munich, West Germany, Paris, The Netherlands, and New York City.

Another important 20th-century art movement was Surrealism, and the work of its most famous exponent, Salvador Dali, was shown at the Tate Gallery in 1980 in what was said to be the first major exhibition of the artist's work in Britain. The exhibition had been seen previously at the Centre National d'Art et de Culture Georges Pompidou (the Beaubourg) in Paris. Describing Dali's art in *Apollo*, James Burr wrote: "His greatest achievement is to give reality and substance to the elusive nightmare horror of subconscious fantasies that molest us in dreams."

A series of exhibitions was mounted in Florence, Italy, by the Council of Europe as its 16th Exhibition of Art, Science, and Culture. The subject of this ambitious series was "Florence and the Tuscany of the Medici in Sixteenth-Century Europe." A section entitled "The Primacy of Design" presented a wide survey of examples of the draftsman's art, including works by Michelangelo, Leonardo da Vinci, Pontormo, Bronzino, and Cellini. Another fascinating section, entitled "The Medici as Collectors," was exhibited in the Palazzo Vecchio. In the church of Santo Stefano al Ponte, "Religious Life in Florence in the Sixteenth Century," arranged by the archbishop of Florence, took as its theme Florentine religion after Savonarola. "Power and Space" dealt with fortifications, building, and urbanism, while "The Princely Stage," devoted to theatres of the court, revealed details of some spectacular performances. Other exhibitions included "The Rebirth of Science" and "Astrology, Magic, and Alchemy." Though the group of exhibitions centred on Florence, complementary regional exhibitions were shown throughout Tuscany.

In Austria a number of exhibitions were organized to celebrate the bicentenary of the death of Empress Maria Theresa. They included "Maria Theresia und ihre Zeit" at the Schönbrunn Palace; "Maria Theresia als Königin von Ungarn" at Halbthürn Castle, Burgenland; and "Österreich zur Zeit Kaiser Josephs II" at Melk Abbey. The show at Halbthürn, the smallest of the group, included many hitherto unexhibited objects from Hungary, Czechoslovakia, and Yugoslavia, together with treasures from the Esterhazy Archives in Eisenstadt. All the shows combined politics, art, history, and literature to give a picture of the times. Melk Abbey was beautifully and expensively restored for the occasion.

A show at the Pierpont Morgan Library in New York City from December 1979 to March 1980, "William and Mary and Their House," was an exhibition of trophies from the Dutch Royal Collections from the time of William the Silent to Queen Juliana but focusing on King William and Queen Mary of England. The highlights of the show were opulent items of silver furniture. The bicentenary of the death in 1779 of the most famous actor of 18th-century England, David Garrick, was celebrated in an exhibition at the British Library in London, opened in 1979. The show illustrated Garrick's career as an actor and manager with costumes, mezzotints, engravings, and other items. The centrepiece was a marble sculpture of Garrick by Louis-François Roubilliac.

"The Art of Hollywood," sponsored by a televi-

(Below) Life-size terracotta figures of men and horses were part of a display entitled "Treasures from the Bronze Age of China." It toured cities in the U.S. during the year. (Right) The massive bronze cauldron weighs 82 kilograms (181 pounds) and dates back to approximately 1030 BC.

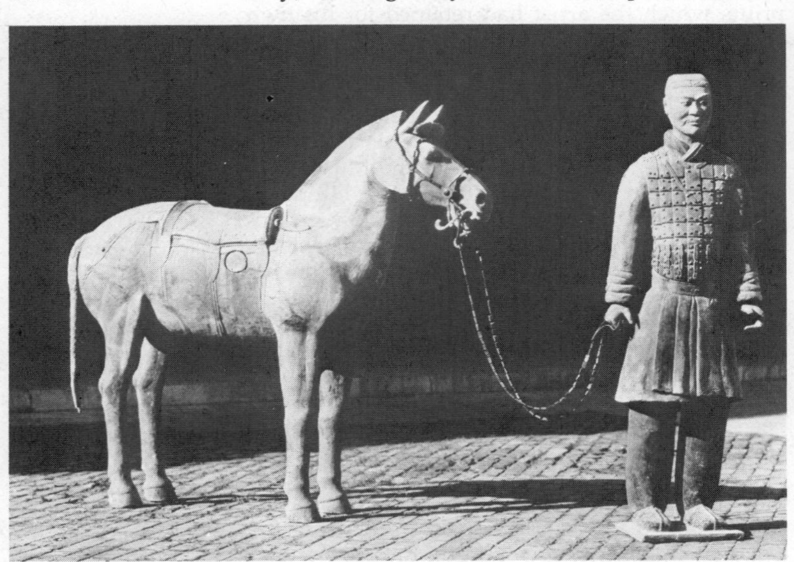

COURTESY, THE METROPOLITAN MUSEUM OF ART; PHOTOS, SETH JOEL

sion company and exhibited at the Victoria and Albert Museum, London, from October 1979 to January 1980, featured many early designs for pictures, some from the beginning of the 20th century. Enjoyable and flamboyant, it was entered through an "Alhambra" foyer and included a model of an early "picture palace," complete with cardboard silhouettes of an audience in cloches and boaters.

"The Vikings," at the British Museum from February to July and later shown at the Metropolitan Museum of Art in New York City, included objects illustrating every aspect of the Viking world. Items showing fashions, jewelry, trade, coinage, and the emergence of Christianity were included, many lent from Scandinavian museums. They ranged from gilt bronze jewelry of great delicacy and finesse to impressive examples of monumental sculpture.

In the U.S., as always, American themes were popular for major exhibitions. "American Light: The Luminist Movement (1850–1870)," mounted by the National Gallery of Art, Washington, D.C., included a vast selection of American landscape paintings including works by Frederic E. Church and John F. Kensett. In all, there were 250 paintings, 40 drawings, and 24 photographs, most of them by relatively unknown artists. A retrospective exhibition of the American painter Edward Hopper, at the Whitney Museum in New York City, included little-known early works in the "French" style as well as the characteristic Realist paintings of the artist's later years. "A Man of Genius—The Art of Washington Allston" celebrated the 200th anniversary of the birth of this important 19th-century American artist who spent the years from 1811 to 1818 in England. Organized by the Museum of Fine Arts, Boston, it later traveled to the Pennsylvania Academy of Fine Arts in Philadelphia. It was the first major exhibition devoted to this artist in 30 years.

"In Praise of America: 1650–1830" was the title of an exhibition at the National Gallery of Art in Washington, devoted entirely to American decorative art. It was the first such exhibition the gallery had held and was on view in the East Wing from February to July. Eighty pieces were chosen to illustrate the best in American design during the first 200 years of the country's history. Included were chairs, sofas, chests, mirrors, clocks, glass, silver, brass, and copper. Each piece was displayed as a separate "rarity," and no attempt was made to create ensembles.

The work of Andrew Wyeth (b. 1917), celebrated for his images of American country life painstakingly observed and exquisitely executed, was shown at the Royal Academy, London, in the first major exhibition of Wyeth's work to be seen in Europe. A large one-man show devoted to his work had been mounted in New York City in 1967 at the Whitney Museum. The 60 tempera, watercolour, and dry brush paintings on display afforded English gallery-goers an opportunity to assess the artist's merits in an international context.

The Yale Center for British Art held the first large showing in the U.S. of works by the English Camden Town Group, including paintings by H. Gilman and Spencer Gore. The work of this early 20th-century group of painters was little known in the U.S. Also at Yale, the University Art Gallery showed a collection of American paintings and decorative objects from the Francis P. Garvan collection. The collection included about 10,000 pieces of silver, furniture, pewter, ceramics, textiles, glass, paintings, prints, and sculpture.

THE TIMES, LONDON

David Hockney poses beside one of his works included in an exhibit entitled "Travels with Pen, Pencil, and Ink," at the Tate Gallery in London in July.

A number of shows devoted to sculpture were worthy of note. "The Romantics to Rodin: French Nineteenth-Century Sculpture from North American Collections" was organized for the Los Angeles County Museum of Art and traveled to the Minneapolis Institute of Arts. Many pieces dusted off for the show had previously languished in museum cellars and storerooms. Works by Auguste Clessinger, Gustave Doré, and J.-P. Dantan were especially notable. "Twentieth-Century Sculptors and Their Drawings: Selections from the Hirschhorn Museum and Sculpture Garden," an interesting show organized as a circulating exhibition by the Smithsonian Institution Traveling Exhibition Service, included works by Barbara Hepworth, Archipenko, and Matisse.

"Forgotten Medieval Sculpture" was the title of an exhibition of several hundred pieces of medieval sculpture formerly stored in the choir gallery of Norwich Cathedral, England, and shown to the public at the Sainsbury Centre, Norwich, in the spring. Included were some delicate 12th-century capitals from the original chapter house, cloisters, and infirmary, since either rebuilt or destroyed. Large pieces of 14th-century reliefs from the Ethelbert Gate, removed when the gate was restored in 1864, were on display, as were drawings, manuscripts, and photographs to help put the material in context. After the exhibition closed, it was planned to show the sculpture permanently at Norwich Cathedral.

The first comprehensive exhibition to be devoted to the work of the 18th-century French artist Jean-Honoré Fragonard since 1921 was staged in Japan at the National Museum of Western Art, Tokyo, and later at the Municipal Museum, Kyoto. The 90 oils and 73 drawings, assembled and cataloged by English art historian Denys Sutton, allowed a fresh assessment of this major artist. Over 200,000 visitors saw the show, and those unable to visit Japan could console themselves with the excellent catalog in which every oil was illustrated in colour.

An exhibition devoted to 71 drawings by Ingres was shown at the Victoria and Albert Museum. Most of the drawings were on loan from the Musée Ingres, Montauban, France. Included were portraits, landscapes, and studies for history paintings. The finest works were undoubtedly the 20 portrait drawings, which ranged over a 70-year period and included a study of the artist's father done as a boy, as well as two of his mother, one in middle age and one showing her as an old lady. Organized by the Arts Council of Great Britain, the exhibition was small in scale but broad in scope.

An exhibition devoted to the work of the English artist Stanley Spencer at the Royal Academy, London, comprised 260 paintings and drawings and 16 murals, removed for the first time since their installation at the Oratory of All Souls, Burghclere, Hampshire. Portraits and landscapes predominated. An exhibition of work by the artist William Nicholson organized by the Arts Council emphasized his skill at sensitive landscape rendition and fine portraiture. The show traveled to Cambridge, Stoke on Trent, Bristol, and Bradford.

The Tate Gallery showed 99 paintings and 53 drawings, many from collections abroad, by the 18th-century English artist Thomas Gainsborough. The fine portraits and landscapes were a visual delight. "Turner in Yorkshire" was a loan exhibition shown at the York City Art Gallery and organized in conjunction with the York Festival. Among the items shown was a set of watercolours, later engraved to illustrate Thomas Whitaker's *History of Richmondshire* (1823). Turner drew a number of patrons from Yorkshire, and many of his paintings and watercolours depict Yorkshire buildings and landscapes. (SANDRA MILLIKIN)

[613.D.1.b]

A Salvador Dali retrospective went on display at the Beaubourg (Pompidou Centre) in Paris in January.

KEYSTONE

Art Sales

Market Trends. The 1979–80 season was a contradictory mix of exceptionally high prices for items of special distinction and rarity and a sharp recession for everything else. A new auction record price for any work of art, $6.4 million, was achieved by Turner's painting "Juliet and Her Nurse" in New York City in May. Yet by the end of the season it was common for 20 to 50% of the items offered in a sale to go unsold. The market was depressed in the autumn of 1979, but prices picked up in the first three months of 1980. In April the recession returned in earnest.

Increased activity in the U.S. was a feature of the season. Sotheby's auction turnover in New York City exceeded that in London, while Christie's—comparative newcomers in the U.S.—doubled their New York turnover to £49 million, compared with £83 million in the U.K. Peter Wilson's retirement as chairman of Sotheby's in February marked the end of an era. Sotheby's was transformed under his chairmanship from an auction room with a £6 million turnover to an international combine with a turnover of £180 million. He was succeeded by the earl of Westmorland.

The application of British law to art auctions remained an area of controversy. The legality of Sotheby's and Christie's buyers' premium was to be challenged in the courts in 1981. The legality of dealers' bidding in partnership was also challenged. Three world-class dealers, Agnew, Artemis, and Eugene Thaw, purchased an Algardi marble portrait bust in partnership for £165,000 (including premium) at a Christie's auction in September 1979. Their application for a license to export the bust to the Metropolitan Museum of Art in New York for £265,000 was held up by the reviewing committee on exports, which said it should not be exported and the price should be reduced to £200,000. Next it was suggested that the dealers had broken the Auction (Bidding Agreement) Act, 1927. The case was referred to the director of public prosecutions but remained unresolved at the end of the year.

Works of Art. The biggest auction event of 1980 was the sale in New York, in May, of Impressionist and modern paintings from the Garbisch and Ford collections. Christie's offered ten superb paintings from the collection of Henry Ford II, and Sotheby's 41 paintings from that of Col. and Mrs. Edgar William Garbisch. Huge prices resulted: $3 million for Picasso's "Saltimbanque Seated with Arms Crossed" of 1923 (to the Bridgestone Museum, Japan); $5.2 million for van Gogh's "Le Jardin du poète, Arles" of 1888; $3.9 million for Cézanne's "Paysan en blouse bleue" of 1895–97 (to

WIDE WORLD

A Turner painting, "Juliet and Her Nurse," brought a world auction record of $6.4 million for a single painting at a sale at Sotheby Parke Bernet in New York City in May.

the Kimbell Art Museum, Texas); $2.9 million for Gauguin's "La Plage au Pouldu" of 1889.

A panoramic 19th-century American painting, "Icebergs" by Frederick Edwin Church, achieved the third highest price ever recorded at $2.5 million in October 1979, but it slipped to eighth place after the Ford and Garbisch sales. Dirck Bouts's "Resurrection" was briefly the second most expensive after fetching £1.7 million on April 16, 1980. On May 29 the Turner captured first place, and on July 11 Rubens's vast historical painting "Samson and Delilah" moved into third when it was bought for £2,530,000 by the National Gallery (London).

Prices for American paintings exceeded expectations: Martin Johnson Heade's "Rio de Janeiro Harbour" made £70,000; Albert Bierstadt's "Indian Encampment, Late Afternoon," $300,000; Charles Marion Russell's "The War Party," $250,000; Childe Hassam's "October Sundown, Newport," $205,000; one of Edward Hicks's "Peaceable Kingdoms," $270,000; Thomas Moran's "Children of the Mountain," $650,000; and Remington's "Apache Scout," $320,000.

The house sale at the Garbisches' Maryland home established new auction records for American applied arts. A Chippendale block- and shell-carved Cuban mahogany desk brought a record for American furniture at $250,000; a carved and painted American eagle, a record for this genre at $39,000; and a William Fitz mahogany brass dial clock of *c.* 1770, a record for a shelf clock at $36,000. A flood of images depressed prices in New York's summer photography sales, but U.S. collectors still bid record prices for rarities; a self-portrait daguerreotype of Albert Sands Southworth fetched $36,000. Art Nouveau moved into a new price bracket when a Tiffany spiderweb leaded glass, mosaic, and bronze table lamp sold for $360,000 in New York in March.

In November 1979 Ader et Picard offered the first part of the Ernest Le Veel collection of Japanese prints in Paris. The 186 lots made Fr 4,418,000, with an album of 41 Hokusai plates bringing Fr 1,450,000. The collection of 91 icons bought by George R. Hann from Soviet museums in the 1930s made $2.8 million in New York in April 1980. A 16th-century Moscow school "Ascension" made an auction record price for an icon at $170,000. The collection of Greek vases formed in Italy by the 2nd marquess of Northampton was sold in London in July for £1,340,180. A 6th-century BC vase of superb quality, known as the Northampton vase, brought £190,000.

Among items of special distinction, an Assyrian gypsum relief of a winged human-headed deity sold for £240,000 in December 1979. A Limoges enamel casket believed to have been commissioned in the 1190s to hold the remains of Thomas Becket brought £420,000. In February 1980 eight English scarlet lacquer chairs, *c.* 1740, made $290,000, a record auction price for English furniture. In March a grand piano inlaid and painted to the design of the 19th-century painter Alma-Tadema sold for $390,000.

The new strength of the Italian market was underlined in May when a "Last Judgment" painting by G. B. Tiepolo made a public auction record

Vincent van Gogh's "Le Jardin du poète, Arles" brought $5.2 million when it was put up for sale at Christie's in New York City in May.

COURTESY, CHRISTIE'S, NEW YORK

KEYSTONE

England's Royal Asiatic Society was enriched by £850,000 with the sale of this 14th-century Persian illustrated manuscript at Sotheby's in London in July.

price for the artist at 260 million lire in Florence, and again in June when an Italian painting, "Idillio Primaverile" (1901) by Pellizza da Volpedo, sold in London for a record £165,000. Notable in the field of primitive art were a 14th-century Benin bronze head of an Oba sold for £200,000 and a carved wooden drum from the Austral Islands sold for £190,000. In June a Rembrandt drawing, "Joseph Recounting His Dreams," made £190,000, and a bronze statuette of a male nude, believed—though not proven—to have been cast from a wax or clay model by Michelangelo, brought £120,000.

Books. Book sales followed the pattern of other collecting fields, with a few rarities selling for higher prices than ever before. Autographs and modern first editions were particularly affected by the recession, and the market for 19th-century travel books about the Middle East, a former boom area, dwindled.

In the major Paris auction by Ader et Picard of books from the collection formed by Francis Kettaneh, a Lebanese-born businessman and bibliophile, an early 15th-century illuminated manuscript of Laurent de Premierfait's translation of Boccaccio sold for Fr 3.8 million. An exceptionally fine first folio of Shakespeare's plays made Fr 2.6 million. An illustrated Persian manuscript of 1314, Rashid ad-Din's "World History," was sold for £850,000 by the Royal Asiatic Society.

A first edition of William Harvey's famous work of 1628 on the circulation of the blood, *De Motu Cordis*, fetched £88,000 in November 1979. In December a single vellum page dating from the early 11th century and containing the farm accounts of Ely Abbey in Anglo-Saxon sold for £59,800. A group of Brontë letters and manuscripts was sold in New York for $183,200 in March 1980. The Brontë Society paid $90,000 to secure a series of 30 letters from Charlotte to a close friend.

In April a 49-volume set of Gould's bird books, which had formerly belonged to Pierpont Morgan, made $400,000 in New York. In the same month a previously unknown 16th-century atlas that had once belonged to the Doria family in Genoa sold for £140,000 at Sotheby's. The sale of books and manuscripts from the library of Arthur A. Houghton in June was another high point. Private correspondence and personal papers of Samuel Pepys dating from 1679 to 1703 were sold for £100,000, and the same price was paid for the final manuscript draft of Gilbert White's *The Natural History of Selborne*, first published in 1789. In July, at a sale of Tennyson papers, the most complete surviving manuscript of his poem "In Memoriam" was bought by the Tennyson Research Centre in Lincoln for £100,000. (GERALDINE NORMAN)

A new record price for American furniture was established when $250,000 was paid for this Chippendale desk at an auction in Maryland.

COURTESY, ©1980 SOTHEBY PARKE BERNET INC., NEW YORK

Association Football: *see* Football

Astronautics: *see* Space Exploration

Astronomy

Solar System. Probably the most spectacular visual excitement in astronomy during 1980 resulted from the continuing unmanned exploration of the planets. While earlier satellites concentrated on studies of Venus and Mars, the recent Pioneer 11 (renamed Pioneer Saturn) and the Voyager 1 and 2 satellites vastly improved views and knowledge of Saturn and Jupiter, revealing novel features of their moons, magnetic fields, and ring systems.

The number of moons belonging to these two planetary titans has been increasing steadily throughout the past decade. Pioneer 11 discovered a 13th or possibly 14th moon of Saturn; Voyager 1 raised the number to 15. Even more startling, it appears that two of the moons share a single orbit. The latter observation was made by ground-based observers at the Pic du Midi Observatory in France.

Pioneer 11 and Voyager 1 each returned hundreds of photographs of Saturn. Along with the three new moons, they revealed a huge encircling cloud of neutral hydrogen gas and a complex system of major and minor rings, two of which appear to be interwoven in a braided pattern and one of which consists of icy boulders averaging about 1 m (3 ft) in diameter. Also provided was the first direct measurement of the planet's magnetic field, which has a strength about 20% that of the Earth's equatorial magnetic field.

When Voyagers 1 and 2 raced past Jupiter in 1979, they revealed the presence of a 14th moon. Later, Stephen P. Synnott of the Jet Propulsion Laboratory in Pasadena, Calif., discovered a 15th moon while studying photographs from the two probes in order to determine the orbit of the 14th. A mere 80 km (50 mi) across, the new moon actually appears to lie within the newly discovered ring system of Jupiter. Designated 1979J2, it was the second to be found by examining Voyager photographs.

While spacecraft directly study Jupiter and Saturn, it will be many years (or decades) before man reaches directly to the outermost planet in the solar system, Pluto. Nevertheless, scientists at Palomar Mountain Observatory in California, using the 5-m (200-in) telescope and employing the new technique of speckle interferometry, were able to make a reliable determination of the size of Pluto. They found it to be 3,600 km (2,230 mi) in diameter. By combining this measurement with the mass determination made using the 1979 discovery of Charon, the lone moon of Pluto, the scientists found the planet's density to be nearly ten times less than that of the Earth.

Though it is rare for man to go out in the solar system, it is even more rare for the solar system to come to us. Nonetheless, Luis W. Alvarez of the University of California at Berkeley suggested that about 65 million years ago, at the end of the Cretaceous Period, an Apollo asteroid smashed into the Earth's atmosphere and was subsequently responsible for the termination of many life forms on Earth, including the dinosaurs. The theory is based on the discovery of large concentrations of the rare earth element iridium in rocks from the Gubbio Valley in Italy and from regions around Copenhagen in Denmark. The 25-fold increase in the trace element corresponds precisely with the Cretaceous-Tertiary boundary. This element, while rarely found on the surface of the Earth, is abundant in extraterrestrial (meteoritic) material. The hypothesized meteorite impact would have produced an explosion equivalent to 100 million megatons, polluting the atmosphere with dust for the succeeding decade and drastically changing the conditions for life on Earth. Alvarez and his group concluded that the impact of an asteroid of only 10 km (6 mi) in diameter, about the size of the moons of Mars, would suffice to explain the excess of iridium and absence of dinosaurs.

Finally, what may well turn out to be the most

WIDE WORLD

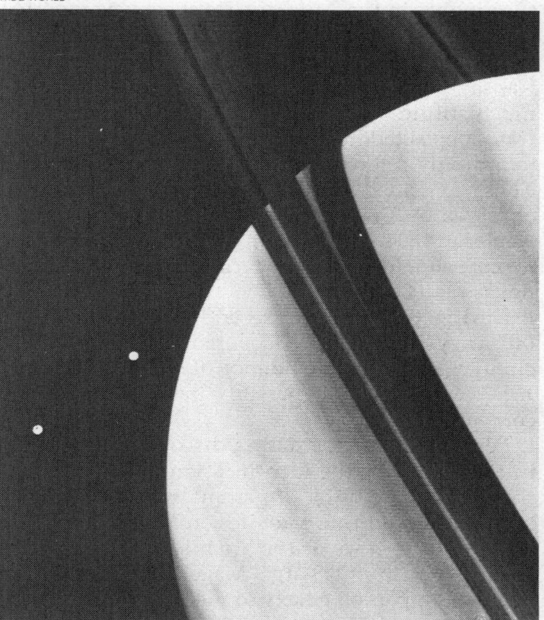

Fine detail of Saturn's ring structure is revealed in this photo taken of the planet and its moons Tethys and Dione by Voyager 1 from a distance of 13 million kilometres (8 million miles).

important discovery in the Solar System during the past year was the first reliable report of the variability of the solar luminosity. Using detectors aboard the Solar Maximum Mission satellite, scientists detected a variation in the total solar energy output by about 0.1% over a period of several months. Though corresponding to a change of only about 10K (compared with a solar temperature of about 5,700K), the existence of such a change over such a short time implies the possibility of even larger, long-term changes in solar luminosity, an effect that may well have profound influence on the Earth's weather.

Supernovas and Neutron Stars. Supernovas are thought to represent the explosive death of stars. Though theory suggests that such stellar violence should give rise to an expanding shell with a dense, rapidly rotating neutron star at its centre, only two such supernova-neutron star associations had been found by 1980: the famous Crab Nebula, remnant of a supernova that occurred in AD 1054, and the Vela Supernova, which occurred about 10,000 years ago. In 1980 G. Garmire and L. Tuohy (California Institute of Technology) reported a third such association in the southern supernova remnant RCW 103 by observing a soft (low-temperature) X-ray source within it. According to the X-ray photographs made by the orbiting Einstein X-ray Observatory, other supernova remnants, including those left behind by supernovas occurring in our Galaxy during the past 2,000 years, left behind no obvious hot neutron stars at their centres. This led astronomers to conclude either that such objects cool much faster than they had previously believed, or that supernovas only rarely make neutron stars.

In a remarkable piece of astrophysical and geophysical collaboration, the record of some of those

Earth Perihelion and Aphelion, 1981

January 2	Perihelion, 147,104,000 km (91,406,000 mi) from the Sun
July 3	Aphelion, 152,105,000 km (94,514,000 mi) from the Sun

Equinoxes and Solstices, 1981

March 20	Vernal equinox, 17:03[1]
June 21	Summer solstice, 11:45[1]
Sept. 23	Autumnal equinox, 03:05[1]
Dec. 21	Winter solstice, 22:51[1]

Eclipses, 1981

Jan. 20	Moon, penumbral (begins 05:35[1]), beginning visible in E Pacific O., N. America, S. America, NW Africa, W Europe, Atlantic O., Arctic; end visible NW S. America, N. America, Arctic, Pacific O., E Australia, New Zealand, and E Asia.
Feb. 4–5	Sun, annular (begins 19:27[1]), visible in Australia except W, New Zealand, Antarctica, W of S. America.
July 17	Moon, partial (begins 02:05[1]), beginning visible in E S. Pacific O., S. America, N. America except NW, Africa except NE, SW Europe, Atlantic O., and Antarctica; end visible in New Zealand, E Pacific O., N. America except N, S. America, NW Africa, Atlantic O., and Antarctica.
July 31	Sun, total (begins 01:11[1]), visible in E Europe, Asia except extreme S; Hawaii, NW N. America, and Arctic.

[1] Universal time.
Source: *The Astronomical Almanac for the Year 1981* (1979).

supernovas in the Antarctic ice sheet was reported by Robert T. Rood and Craig L. Sarazin (University of Virginia), Edward J. Zeller (University of Kansas), and Bruce C. Parker (Virginia Polytechnic Institute). In analyzing the atmospheric nitrates deposited in ice over the past 800 years, they found only a few unusually high concentrations. These coincided with the dates of the supernovas observed by Tycho Brahe in 1572 and by Johannes Kepler in 1604. The authors predicted that a deeper ice core should lead to the record of the great supernovas of 1006 and 1054.

During the year the second and third binary pulsar systems were discovered. The latter had a circular orbit, gave evidence of some low-energy X-ray emission, and possibly had a red star as a companion.

Perhaps the most exciting discovery of the year in this field was the identification of the origin of the spectacular burst of gamma rays detected by both Soviet and U.S. satellites on March 5, 1979. It was found to have arisen from a supernova remnant, N49, in the Large Magellenic Cloud, the nearby companion galaxy to the Milky Way. At its great distance the source had to have had a brief luminosity of 100 billion suns, brighter than the entire energy output for the Milky Way galaxy. While the precise origin of the gamma rays was unclear, an association with a neutron star in the relatively young (10,000 years old) supernova remnant seemed the most likely explanation.

Historical Astronomy. Though astronomers generally perceive themselves as forward looking, the act of observing the universe always forces them to look back in time: an event observed "now" on the Sun, in fact, occurred about eight minutes ago, and the time increases with the distance from the Earth. Observations made by early astronomers may themselves provide a kind of time machine for studying the evolution of the universe.

Supernovas occur rarely; none has been observed in our Galaxy since the invention of the telescope, or so astronomers had thought. However, by studying records of the time, William B. Ashworth, Jr., of the University of Missouri presented convincing evidence that the supernova that gave rise to the strongest radio source in the sky, Cassiopeia A, occurred in 1680. By combining this date with the date derived by extrapolating back the present expansion rate of the supernova remnant, K. Brecher (Boston University) and I. Wasserman (Cornell University) were able to derive the mass of a supernova for the first time, finding it to be about ten times the mass of the Sun.

Charles T. Kowal (California Institute of Technology) and Stillman Drake (University of Toronto) reported a sighting of the planet Neptune in 1613 by Galileo, more than two centuries before its "discovery" in 1846. It has allowed a more precise evaluation of the orbital parameters of the planet and the perturbations acting upon it.

Cosmology. The most distant objects known are the quasars, strong sources of radio, optical, and X-ray radiation, mainly lying at the very edge of the visible universe. There are perhaps a few hundred well-studied quasars spread throughout the entire sky, so that it was a great surprise in 1979 when two quasars were found to lie a mere six arc seconds from one another. Despite the similarity in their optical spectra, the two objects were considered by many astronomers to be distinct entities that chance had brought together. In 1980, however, a group at the California Institute of Technology working with the optical telescopes of the Mount Wilson and Palomar observatories was able to obtain detailed spectra of the individual objects. Meanwhile, Alan Stockton of the Univer-

An image-enhanced photo released in August shows a bleak and windswept landscape on the surface of Mars. The photo was taken by equipment on board Viking Lander 1.

UPI

sity of Hawaii was able to get clear photographs of the two quasars. After image processing it became clear that the system consisted of a single quasar with an elliptical galaxy lying nearly in the line of sight between the Earth and the quasar. The intervening galaxy acted as a lens—in fact, a gravitational lens—bending light to form two images of the single quasar.

The likelihood of finding such a fortuitous alignment is not great, and so astronomers began arguing that it was not surprising that just one such system had ever been found. Then in June 1980 a group headed by Ray Weymann of the University of Arizona reported the discovery of a second gravitational lensing system involving not two but three distinct quasar images. Though the presumed foreground spiral galaxy had not been detected by the end of the year, the discovery of this second example added further strength to the gravitational lens interpretation of these sets of multiple quasar images and lent additional weight to the validity of Einstein's general theory of relativity, which predicts these effects by analogy with the gravitational bending of light by the Sun.

A radio astronomy group from Bonn (West Germany) University headed by W. Reich reported what appears to be the largest object in the universe. Assuming its red shift correctly indicates the distance to this particular quasar, called 3C345, the object is 78 million light-years in diameter. (KENNETH BRECHER)

See also Earth Sciences; Space Exploration.
[131.A.3; 131.B.3; 131.D.2; 131.E.2; 132.A.3; 132.B.5.d; 132.D.3.a; 133.A.1; 133.B.3; 133.C.3.a,b,e]

Australia

A federal parliamentary state and a member of the Commonwealth of Nations, Australia occupies the smallest continent and, with the island state of Tasmania, is the sixth largest country in the world. Area: 7,682,300 sq km (2,966,200 sq mi). Pop. (1980 est.): 14,518,200. Cap.: Canberra (metro. pop., 1980 est., 241,300). Largest city: Sydney (metro. pop., 1980 est., 3,193,300). Language: English. Religion (1976): Church of England 28%; Roman Catholic 26%; Methodist 7%; Presbyterian 7%. Queen, Elizabeth II; governor-general in 1980, Sir Zelman Cowen; prime minister, Malcolm Fraser.

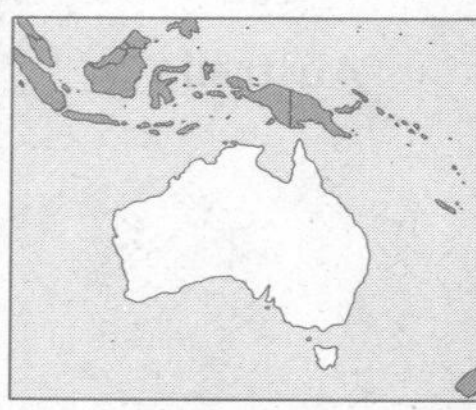

Australia

Domestic Affairs. Although public opinion polls put the issue of taxation at the top of the list of voters' priorities in the election year of 1980, both political parties ignored the taxation question and preferred to concentrate their energies elsewhere. The Australian Labor Party (ALP) claimed that it was necessary above all else to stimulate the economy, while the Liberal-National Country Party government based its electoral strategy upon the deteriorating international situation, of which the crisis in Iran and the Soviet invasion of Afghanistan were the main features. In connection with this outlook, defense expenditure in the August budget was boosted by 17.7% to A$3,541,000,000. Prime Minister Malcolm Fraser described the new strategic situation after the Soviet move into Afghanistan as being the most serious threat to world peace since World War II. Fraser wholeheartedly supported U.S. Pres. Jimmy Carter's line on Afghanistan, and Australian primary producers were prevented from replacing with Australian grain the grain lost to the U.S.S.R. as a result of the U.S. embargo. No new contracts with the Soviet Union were signed, and primary produce exports were confined to the record levels at which they stood in 1979.

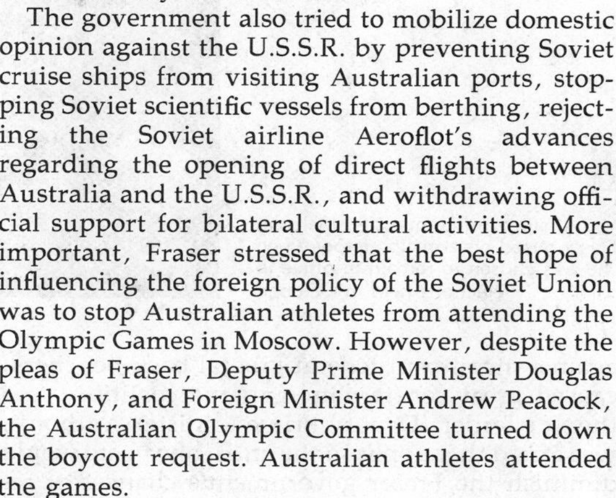

The government also tried to mobilize domestic opinion against the U.S.S.R. by preventing Soviet cruise ships from visiting Australian ports, stopping Soviet scientific vessels from berthing, rejecting the Soviet airline Aeroflot's advances regarding the opening of direct flights between Australia and the U.S.S.R., and withdrawing official support for bilateral cultural activities. More important, Fraser stressed that the best hope of influencing the foreign policy of the Soviet Union was to stop Australian athletes from attending the Olympic Games in Moscow. However, despite the pleas of Fraser, Deputy Prime Minister Douglas Anthony, and Foreign Minister Andrew Peacock, the Australian Olympic Committee turned down the boycott request. Australian athletes attended the games.

The ALP, for its part, hoped to counter the charisma and dominant personality of Fraser by opposing him with a triumvirate: federal parliamentary leader William Hayden, New South Wales Premier Neville Wran, and Robert J. Hawke, president of the Australian Council of Trade Unions. The party hoped that the comparative lack of experience and political power of Hayden would be balanced by the proven record of Wran, who took over the presidency of the party, and the fierce directness of Hawke, who gave up his labour union career to contest a seat at the election.

Despite their efforts the parties approached the elections in a shaky state as splits and discord in Queensland spilled over to affect the prospects of both. The National Executive of the ALP intervened in Queensland, dismissing in March the major party bodies and functionaries there and replacing them with an interim committee to resolve problems within the state branch. ALP leader Hayden declared that although things were bad, they would get much worse unless the party acted to reform the Queensland branch and make it more effective.

Queensland was also the site for a deepening rift between the two coalition government parties, the National Country Party (NCP) and the Liberal Party. The dispute spilled over into the federal arena when the Queensland premier, Johannes Bjelke-Petersen, steered through the NCP conference the selection of his wife, ahead of two sitting members of the federal Senate, on the party ticket. Bjelke-Petersen said that the decision to put his wife at the top of the ticket was forced on him by the political chicanery of the Liberals, who were opposing incumbent Nationals in the state Parliament and who had chosen to run a separate Senate ticket in the federal elections. Bjelke-Petersen's decision, which involved running NCP candidates

Athletics:
see articles on the various sports

UPI

A happy prime minister, Malcolm Fraser raised his arms in victory when he was chosen to remain in office in elections held in October.

against incumbent federal Liberal back-benchers, caused great consternation in the coalition, and the NCP leader, Deputy Prime Minister Anthony, was afraid that a split in the anti-Labor vote would diminish the Fraser government's chances of reelection.

Both government and opposition parties were embarrassed by controversy surrounding individual party members. The coalition was rocked when a senior NCP member, Ian Sinclair, resigned and was charged with forgery, intending to defraud, and making false statements in connection with the annual returns of three funeral companies of which he was a director and from which his father had misappropriated funds. Sinclair was found not guilty, and Fraser, who was delighted by the verdict, reinstated him to the ministry. The ALP was severely damaged after one of the members of the New South Wales Legislative Council, Peter Baldwin, was savagely beaten in a feud between rival factions in Sydney inner-city party branches, and other party members were arrested on criminal charges involving conspiracy, fraud, and forgery.

In the period leading up to the federal election on October 18, Fraser made the management of the economy a leading theme of his campaign. Hayden, for the ALP, promised income tax cuts in a package of measures to benefit average families, to be financed partly by a resource rent tax on mining companies. The third party, the Australian Democrats, led by Don Chipp, who had resigned from the government coalition in 1977, hoped to exert influence by holding the balance of power in the Senate. Its platform included opposition to uranium mining and export.

The election saw Fraser's government returned to office with a reduced majority. In the House of Representatives the Liberal Party won 54 (67 in 1977) seats and the NPC 20 (19), giving their coalition 74 (86), as against the ALP's 51 (38); the Democrats won no seat. In the Senate, the Liberals secured 28 (30) seats, the NPC 3 (5), the ALP 27 (26), the Democrats 5 (2), and independent 1 (1). Thus the government lost control of the Senate.

On November 2 Fraser announced a Cabinet reshuffle. Six ministers, one of whom had previously announced his retirement, were dropped and five new ones brought in, the Cabinet's membership being reduced from 27 to 26. Andrew Peacock, former foreign minister who wanted a domestic post, was made minister for industrial relations, exchanging portfolios with Tony Street. Sen. Dame Margaret Guilfoyle replaced Eric Robinson as finance minister. Fred Chaney, formerly minister of aboriginal affairs, became minister for social security. Vic Garland, a minister who had asked to be dropped, was appointed Australian high commissioner in London.

Foreign Affairs. Foreign Minister Peacock was seldom out of the news headlines in 1980. In July he was reported to have threatened to resign over the Australian government's recognition of the Pol Pot government in Cambodia. Peacock disagreed with Prime Minister Fraser, and in a bitter dispute offered to resign when Fraser refused to allow recognition of the Pol Pot regime to be withdrawn. Although Fraser declined to accept Peacock's resignation offer and Peacock himself refused to discuss Cabinet matters, the president of the Victoria branch of the Liberal Party, Richard Alston, supported Peacock's stand. Alston, who was also chairman of the Australian Council for Overseas Aid, said that recognition of Pol Pot was hampering Australian relief operations in Cambodia, insofar as the brutal Pol Pot regime was diverting relief supplies intended for needy women and children to its own troops. Fraser was unmoved by this criticism, believing that the Australian government ought not to do anything that might imply approval of the Vietnamese intervention against Pol Pot in Cambodia.

Australia faced diplomatic problems over Indonesia and the New Hebrides. In Indonesia Radio Australia's representative was asked to leave because the Indonesian government believed the overseas service of Radio Australia had been persistently broadcasting news items unfavourable to the Indonesian government. The separatist movement, which disrupted normal life in the Anglo-

French condominium of the New Hebrides on the eve of its independence as the republic of Vanuatu, was also a problem for Australia. Australia attached the highest importance to the peaceful and orderly transition of the condominium to independence under its elected government and viewed with deep concern the breakdown of law and order on the island of Espíritu Santo. When, on May 28, supporters of a secessionist group caused extensive damage to government offices in Santo town and obstructed the police, the Australian government called upon the British and French authorities to ensure the maintenance of law and order and the protection of Australian citizens in the New Hebrides. The Australian government emphasized the importance it attached to the achievement of independence for a united and stable New Hebrides.

Although 200 British and French troops were flown to the New Hebrides and independence was granted as scheduled, it was left to troops from Papua New Guinea, with 20 Australians in a noncombatant role, to reoccupy Espíritu Santo; a French resident official previously had warned dissidents on the island that they faced the possibility of being massacred by Australian troops. The Australian foreign minister was outraged by this incorrect and provocative observation and protested to the French Foreign Ministry in the strongest terms.

Heidrun Giersche, a ballerina with the Berlin Komische Oper ballet, was granted political asylum in Australia in April. Giersche left the company after it had finished its Australian tour. It took only 24 hours for Foreign Minister Peacock to accept her application on the grounds that she would suffer persecution should she return to East Germany. Critics accused Peacock of grandstanding during an election year.

The Economy. Unemployment, strikes, the 35-hour week, the role of the Conciliation and Arbitration Commission, and inflation were the chief economic issues in 1980. By June, the end of the financial year, Commonwealth Employment Service figures showed 427,429 Australians unemployed. Although the June figures revealed that the number of unemployed had declined 3,360 compared with the end of May, the general picture was that of continuing deterioration. The government drew some comfort from the short-term decline in unemployment, but opposition spokesman M. Young stated in August that there were 24 unemployed people competing for every job vacancy. On the average the unemployed were out of work for 29 weeks, but for those aged 45–54 years, 44 weeks of unemployment was normal; many of these people, said Young, had given up hope of ever finding a job and joined the growing army of hidden unemployed.

Higher gasoline prices pushed Australia's inflation rate to 10.7% for 1979–80, the highest in almost three years. In the second quarter of 1980 higher fuel and transport costs contributed to a cost-of-living rise of 2.8%, the largest increase for a corresponding period since 1975. The inflation rate had risen steadily from the end of 1978, when it stood at 7.8%, following the government's decision to introduce its policy of pricing domestically produced oil at parity with prevailing world rates. Fraser acknowledged that his oil pricing policy was unpopular but reaffirmed the government's intention to maintain it in order to meet Australia's future needs. The closing of the General Motors Holden (GMH) plant at Pagewood, Sydney, threw 1,200 workers in New South Wales into confusion. GMH closed the Pagewood plant as part of its plan to centralize production of its cars in more modern factories in Victoria and South Australia.

The Conciliation and Arbitration Commission was the centre of controversy during a year of strikes, disputes, and the unprecedented demand, from the Amalgamated Metal Workers Union, for a 35-hour workweek for its members. The commission's own problems centred on a decision of one of its members. Justice James F. Staples granted a wage increase to wool storemen and packers, only to have the wool brokers appeal to the full bench. His decision was overturned, and immediately the wool storemen went on an 11-week strike, holding up the export of wool worth A$500 million. The strike was settled in a compromise decision, but Staples publicly criticized the commission, accusing the members of casting aside the accepted guidelines for deciding such cases. Eight deputy

AUSTRALIA

Education. (1979) Primary, pupils 1,884,753, teachers 90,667; secondary, pupils 1,102,178, teachers 84,529; vocational (1978), pupils 45,193, teachers 13,104; teacher training (1978), students 46,136, teachers 2,870; higher, students 182,224, teaching staff 22,140.

Finance. Monetary unit: Australian dollar, with (Sept. 22, 1980) a free rate of A$0.86 to U.S. $1 (A$2.06 = £1 sterling). Gold, SDR's, and foreign exchange (June 1980) U.S. $2,179,000,000. Budget (1979 actual): revenue A$27,208,000,000; expenditure A$30,410,000,000. Gross national product (1979) A$106.7 billion. Money supply (June 1980) A$14,846,000,000. Cost of living (1975 = 100; April–June 1980) 164.

Foreign Trade. (1979) Imports A$16,316,000,000; exports A$16,713,000,000. Import sources: U.S. 23%; Japan 16%; U.K. 11%; West Germany 7%. Export destinations: Japan 28%; U.S. 12%; New Zealand 5%. Main exports: coal 10%; wool 10%; beef 9%; wheat 9%; nonferrous metals 6%; iron ore 6%; alumina 5%. Tourism (1978): visitors *c.* 631,000; gross receipts U.S. $393 million.

Transport and Communications. Roads (1974) 837,866 km. Motor vehicles in use (1978): passenger 5,642,000; commercial (including buses) 1.4 million. Railways: (government; 1978) 40,133 km; freight traffic (1976–77) 32,030,000,000 net ton-km. Air traffic (1978): 20,993,000,000 passenger-km; freight 501.5 million net ton-km. Shipping (1979): merchant vessels 100 gross tons and over 457; gross tonnage 1,651,747. Shipping traffic (1977–78): goods loaded 166,333,000 metric tons, unloaded 26,717,000 metric tons. Telephones (June 1978) 6,179,000. Radio receivers (Dec. 1977) 14.6 million. Television licenses (Dec. 1977) 5,020,000.

Agriculture. Production (in 000; metric tons; 1979): wheat 16,100; barley 3,657; oats 1,492; corn 168; rice 692; sorghum 1,127; potatoes 800; sugar, raw value 2,980; tomatoes *c.* 152; apples 335; oranges *c.* 379; pineapples 134; wine *c.* 385; sunflower seed *c.* 203; wool, clean *c.* 482; milk 5,818; butter 105; cheese 142; beef and veal 2,018; mutton and lamb 491. Livestock (in 000; March 1979): sheep 134,361; cattle 27,107; pigs 2,268; horses (1978) *c.* 445; chickens 43,731.

Industry. Fuel and power (in 000; metric tons; 1979): coal 83,141; lignite 32,590; crude oil 21,665; natural gas (cu m) 8,390,000; manufactured gas (including some natural gas; cu m) 14,830,000; electricity (kw-hr) 93,700,000. Production (in 000; metric tons; 1979): iron ore (64% metal content) 91,690; bauxite 25,680; pig iron 7,811; crude steel 8,131; aluminum 270; copper 138; lead 215; tin 5.4; zinc 305; nickel concentrates (metal content; 1977–78) 87; uranium (1977) 0.4; gold (troy oz) 677; silver (troy oz) 26,920; sulfuric acid 2,073; fertilizers (nutrient content; 1978–79) nitrogenous *c.* 207, phosphate *c.* 847; plastics and resins 677; cement 5,242; newsprint 212; other paper (1976–77) 1,020; cotton yarn 22; wool yarn 21; passenger cars (including assembly; units) 403; commercial vehicles (including assembly; units) 55. Dwelling units completed (1979) 122,700.

WIDE WORLD

Members of Australia's Olympic team appeared jubilant after the Australian Olympic Federation voted to send the team to the Summer Olympic Games in Moscow over the objections of Prime Minister Malcolm Fraser.

presidents of the Conciliation and Arbitration Commission then wrote to the president, Sir John Moore, claiming that Staples's attack was an unprecedented breach of a fundamental convention and threatened the appeal structure of the commission. As a result Moore moved against Staples, removing his authority to sit as an individual judge in industrial disputes.

A serious dispute also took place between the government and the miners over the government's determination to tax subsidized housing. In the central Queensland coal-mining town of Blackwater the federal treasurer, John Howard, was met by a violent demonstration. Howard, with Deputy Prime Minister Anthony (also minister for trade and resources), had gone to Blackwater to explain the government's policies on the relevant Section 26E of the Income Tax Act. The miners remained adamant that they would not end their six-week-old strike, which by August had cost the major mining companies A$150 million in lost revenue. The strike was finally settled by a compromise agreement reached in September.

The Western Australian government also faced a revolt against its plans to drill for oil on sacred Aborigine sites at Noonkanbah. The Australian Council of Trade Unions formed a picket line in an attempt to prevent a convoy of trucks from reaching the Noonkanbah area, but the line was broken and the demonstrators were ousted. The government took steps to tighten safeguards on the movement of uranium after it was discovered that a worker had stolen two tons of uranium oxide from the Mary Kathleen uranium mine near Mount Isa, Queensland.

In August the committee headed by Rupert Myers released its *Report on Technological Change*. The four-volume, 1,500-page report, which had taken 20 months to produce, sparked a bitter debate. The main conclusion of the committee was that Australian industry would have to embrace technological change if the country was to be competitive in the international economy and if Australians were to realize the nation's full potential. The committee considered the effects of technological change in Australia in the recent past, but it was unable to find evidence that the current high unemployment was attributable to technological change and concluded that unemployment in 1980 was more readily explicable by reference to general economic conditions. On the other hand, the committee conceded that technological change would lead to fewer jobs in the future, especially among the unskilled, whose work was more readily adapted to automation than was that of people undertaking more intellectual tasks. The Fraser government accepted the Myers report, and while it prepared to devise "social safety nets" for those either unemployed or underemployed through no fault of their own, it remained optimistic that the technology of the future had a job-creating capacity.

Federal Treasurer Howard delivered the 1980–81 budget in August, after a federal police inquiry had begun into the circumstances of the premature leaking of budget information to the press. The budget was based on a continued deflationary strategy, and Howard expected it would result in the first domestic surplus since 1973–74. Apart from the big boost to defense expenditure already referred to, there was no change from the tone of earlier years as the government continued to stress the need to help the private sector expand. In his budget speech Howard strongly defended the oil import parity pricing policy, insisting that by making Australians pay world market prices for a scarce resource, Australia's capacity to withstand world energy problems had been improved. He maintained that such projects as the Rundle, Queensland, shale oil enterprise, which could perhaps involve the largest resource investment in Australian history, could not have been contemplated without the government's crude-oil pricing policy. (A. R. G. GRIFFITHS)

See also Dependent States.

POLITICS AND THE MEDIA, AUSTRALIAN STYLE

by A. R. G. Griffiths

Australian public opinion has long been perturbed by the power of the media to influence election results. Constitutional safeguards demand that on the eve of a general election no electioneering material is broadcast or televised, allowing the voters a brief respite to make up their minds on the issues involved. No such embargo applies to printed matter, however, and election results in Australia have often been altered by the printing, on the very morning of the polls, of new information about the candidates or issues.

Since ownership of the communications industry is highly concentrated in Australia, the danger of partisan editorial views is greater than in many other industrial democracies. This situation was recognized by all the political parties, Parliament, and the judiciary. Despite the attempts of the lawmakers and the judges to enforce a more pluralistic press ownership, the concentration of control continued to grow in 1980, and Parliament and many members of the general public were uneasy about the potentially capricious roles of the rival kingmakers. The problem had been attacked first in 1965, when Sir Robert Menzies, then prime minister, amended the Broadcasting and Television Act, inserting in Section 92 a clause designed to prevent takeover of broadcasting and television companies by share transactions on the stock exchange.

The Murdoch Raids. In 1980 the problem surfaced again when Rupert Murdoch (owner of newspapers in the U.S. and U.K. as well as in Australia) tried to augment his television network by the acquisition of Ansett Transport Industries shares. Ansett was an Australian giant. It had the monopoly on half of the nation's domestic airline schedules (under a policy that divided routes and profits down the middle between the government and private enterprise) and held, in addition, a diverse business portfolio including television stations in Melbourne and Brisbane.

A. R. G. Griffiths is a senior lecturer in history at the Flinders University of South Australia. He is the author of Contemporary Australia *(1977).*

To the Australian public the maneuvers for control of Ansett involved more than a bizarre game of Monopoly. A takeover by Murdoch—or, indeed, by a rival press group led by John Fairfax or Kerry Packer—was popularly represented as a danger to civil liberty, insofar as it gave too much power to determine cultural norms to one individual. The Victorian Labor Party was loudest in describing these perils, although its secretary, R. D. Hogg, was careful to point out that the quarrel was not with Rupert Murdoch personally but against the idea that press and other media power should be so concentrated. Indeed, the Murdoch press had supported Gough Whitlam in the election of 1972, and Murdoch newspaper editorials had helped put the Australian Labor Party (ALP) in office. By 1980, however, the Victorian branch of the ALP, expressing its plans appropriately in a sporting metaphor, said that it was not likely to get "a free kick" from Murdoch and thus decided to challenge his license application before the Australian Broadcasting Tribunal. The party claimed that Section 92 barred Murdoch from control of a Melbourne television network. When the chairman of the tribunal, Bruce Gyngell, refused to give the ALP what it considered to be fair treatment in the hearings, the party appealed to the High Court; the latter ruled that the tribunal had not made a serious effort to come to grips with the central issue of whether it was proper for a company to gain control of a television station by means of buying shares on the stock exchange. Gyngell immediately resigned from the tribunal, only to be appointed to an equally sensitive communications role as director-designate of the Independent and Multi-Cultural Broadcasting Corporation (IMBC), which the government planned to establish.

Multicultural Media? The debate over Murdoch's interests was part of the wide spectrum of controversy surrounding the media in 1980. A public inquiry into the Australian Broadcasting Commission (ABC) unearthed considerable discontent with programming, editorial content, and lack of responsiveness to public opinion. Ethnic communities fought long and bitter struggles to establish an ethnic television service that would transmit television programs in Greek, Italian, Serbo-Croatian, Polish, and all the other minority languages that had been given increased status through the establishment of ethnic community radio stations.

In the face of a backlash from English-speaking Australians, who said that they would not expect to hear Australian accents and programs on Italian television, Malcolm Fraser's government attempted to press ahead with its proposed IMBC. The government hoped to get migrant votes in the upcoming election by opening up the new service, which had been an election promise in 1977, but its efforts were frustrated by Parliament and the media owners. The legislation to set up multicultural television was blocked in the Senate on May 22, 1980, when four government senators voted with the opposition to refer the legislation to a Senate Standing Committee on Education and Arts. In response, the government bowed to Senate pressure and dropped the idea of launching the IMBC in October, preferring instead to begin multicultural television broadcasting through the Special Broadcasting Service.

The Public Broadcasting Association (PBA) of Australia, which had supported the establishment of the multicultural service, then became worried by the lack of plans for the equitable time sharing of public programs with the proposed English-dubbed ethnic television services. The PBA asked for eight hours of prime viewing each week from January 1981 on television channels in Sydney and Melbourne and complained that the government had not yet revealed its plans for public television.

In the middle of the crisis, the minister primarily responsible for communications issues, A. A. Staley, minister of posts and telecommunications, quit politics. Staley and Prime Minister Fraser did not agree on the way in which the Murdoch takeover was being handled, and thereafter Staley found it difficult to gain support for his policies. For Staley, freedom of expression and diversity of thought were more important than Fraser's sensitivity to Rupert Murdoch's needs in an election year. Staley was closely identified with Fraser's rise to leadership in the Liberal Party, having been among his strongest supporters. However, Staley's decision to leave politics seemed not to be caused by personal matters. Rather, the handling of the posts and telecommunications portfolio had become increasingly difficult in 1980, with Staley the focus of attacks on a wide range of issues: the multicultural broadcasting commission, the ABC inquiry, and the construction of a domestic satellite. In regard to the latter, Staley did not want to involve private enterprise in the administration of the satellite, preferring to keep it in the hands of his department.

The Press and the October Election. In September Prime Minister Fraser announced the election date of October 18 and, as had been predicted, the Liberal and Country Party government prepared itself for a short campaign in which the electronic media would be utilized in preference to the press. However, before the ink was dry on the policy speeches, the Australian Broadcasting Tribunal delivered what was described in the *National Times* as "the most amazing and far-reaching decision in Australian broadcasting history." The tribunal stopped the Murdoch group's attempt to buy Channel 10 in Melbourne but declined at first to give reasons for its decision and thus prevented an immediate appeal. Within three hours of the decision, Fraser broadcast on national radio that he hoped that the tribunal would give its reasons quickly so that the Murdoch group could decide on its avenue of appeal. He also made a significant defense of Murdoch's editorial line, saying that Murdoch had the best interests of Australia at heart. Bill Hayden, leader of the ALP, commented that he was glad that the Broadcasting and Television Act had been defended. Toward the end of the campaign, the tribunal announced that "the public interest" would not have been served by a Murdoch takeover.

To serve the public interest, all the morning daily newspapers, having been much criticized for their partiality in earlier elections, criticized both leaders with equal ferocity and bitterly complained that most party election statements were unsubstantiated or question-begging. Fraser was stigmatized as a "music hall prime minister" because of the way in which his policy speech was presented in front of a specially invited audience of his faithful supporters, all of whom applauded and moaned at the appropriate moments.

But as the campaign progressed, the press began to influence the eventual outcome by commissioning and publishing a series of public opinion surveys, the first of which indicated a victory for the ALP. The most influential polls were published in the Australian *Financial Review,* the weekly *Bulletin* magazine, and the major daily newspapers of Melbourne and Sydney, the *Melbourne Age* and the *Sydney Morning Herald*. The *Age* and the *Morning Herald* both predicted an ALP win with about 57.4% of the electorate to the government's 42.6%. The *Bulletin* agreed that the ALP would have a clear victory, while the *Financial Review* put the ALP ahead in the marginal seats. At that stage of the campaign the surveys themselves became a political issue. The snowball effect of publishing antigovernment public opinion results was much commented on by both Hayden and Fraser.

During the campaign accredited journalists traveled around Australia with Fraser and Hayden. The latter, after a week in the company of journalists, said that when he had been with them a few days he found that they were "not the pack of bastards I thought you were—you're a worse pack of bastards." His remarks on the journalists were dismissed as a friendly joke, but he was in deadly earnest when he complained about the media proprietors. On October 9 Hayden claimed that Murdoch had thrown himself into the task of supporting Fraser and had abused the enormous power of communications available to the media. Hayden believed that the *Australian* newspaper had whipped up fear and hysteria by concentrating on one ALP proposal—to conduct an inquiry into wealth in Australia. Hayden described the *Australian*'s attack (in which it was argued that a new ALP government would use its power to pry into private bank accounts and taxation returns) as "lacking all ethical decency" and "extremist misrepresentation."

One week before the election Fraser examined the results of the newspaper opinion polls. As a result he dropped his emphasis on studio television performances and talk-back radio programs and began a closer, more personal style of electioneering. He went on handshake walks in cities and towns, hoping that in what was described as "the theatre of confrontation" such walks would provide incidents where he could exert his "strong leader" image. This change of direction was successful. Although there were demonstrations against both Hayden and Fraser, Hayden dropped his walks among the people so as to avoid being a divisive influence and the tide turned in Fraser's favour.

The election results showed that ALP optimism was misplaced, and Fraser's coalition was returned to government with a handsome though reduced majority. The media played a great part in mobilizing public opinion during the campaign, and Hayden recognized this by pledging that he would appoint a royal commission to investigate media ownership should he be elected. Such an outcome was not to be, however, and one of the Fraser government's first problems in its new term of office was how to help the Murdoch group succeed in overturning the broadcasting tribunal's findings that the public interest would be better served if media ownership were not so concentrated in Australia while at the same time preserving the ethical standards of a free press.

COURTESY, AUSTRALIAN CONSULATE-GENERAL OF CHICAGO; PHOTO, KEN FIRESTONE

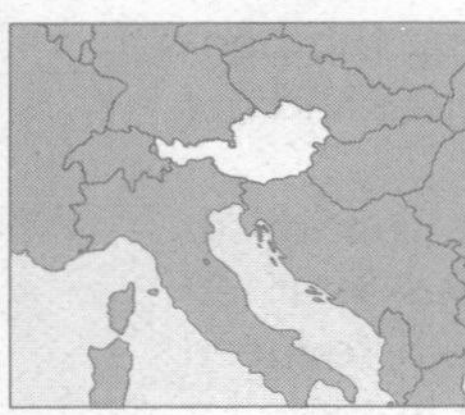

Austria

Austria

A republic of central Europe, Austria is bounded by West Germany, Czechoslovakia, Hungary, Yugoslavia, Italy, Switzerland, and Liechtenstein. Area: 83,853 sq km (32,376 sq mi). Pop (1980 est.): 7,481,600. Cap. and largest city: Vienna (pop., 1978 est., 1,580,600). Language: German. Religion (1978): Roman Catholic 88%. President in 1980, Rudolf Kirchschläger; chancellor, Bruno Kreisky.

Federal Pres. Rudolf Kirchschläger was confirmed in office for a second six-year term in Austria's May 1980 presidential election. In elections to the parliaments of four provinces in September and October 1979, the Austrian People's Party (ÖVP) had gained a seat from the Socialist Party of Austria (SPÖ) in both Tirol and Upper Austria, but there were no changes in Carinthia or Vorarlberg. A by-election in Tirol in September 1980 resulted in the ÖVP losing its additional seat to the Austrian Freedom Party (FPÖ). In Vorarlberg a citizens' initiative seeking greater autonomy for the province within the Austrian federal structure was approved by more than 60% of the voters in a June 15 provincial referendum.

In Cabinet changes effective Nov. 2, 1979, Herbert Salcher replaced Ingrid Leodolter as minister for health and the environment; trade union leader Karl Sekanina replaced Josef Moser as minister for construction; and four new state secretaries, all women, were appointed. This raised the number of women in the government to 6 out of a total of 22 ministers and state secretaries.

A 1978 referendum had narrowly rejected the bringing into operation of the Zwentendorf nuclear power station (Austria's first), but the nuclear issue continued to arouse controversy. A further referendum was sought by both supporters and opponents of nuclear power, and as a first step toward this a "popular initiative" in November calling for Zwentendorf's admission to service secured some 422,000 votes. This opened the way to an eventual repeal of the antinuclear legislation passed in 1978.

Vienna's new 2,100-bed general hospital, under construction since 1960, was at the centre of a financial and political scandal during 1980. Investigations revealing serious deficiencies in design and construction, spiraling costs, and evidence of extensive bribery led to a number of arrests. Allega-

AUSTRIA

Education. (1979–80) Primary, pupils 434,432, teachers 26,369; secondary, pupils 612,982, teachers 50,549; vocational, pupils 395,401, teachers 18,488; teacher training, students 5,471, teachers 742; higher, students 122,189, teaching staff 12,543.

Finance. Monetary unit: schilling, with (Sept. 22, 1980) a free rate of 12.76 schillings to U.S. $1 (30.67 schillings = £1 sterling). Gold, SDR's, and foreign exchange (June 1980) U.S. $4,705,000,000. Budget (1978 actual): revenue 170,890,000,000 schillings; expenditure 205,310,000,000 schillings. Gross national product (1979) 906,480,000,000 schillings. Money supply (April 1980) 139,140,000,000 schillings. Cost of living (1975 = 100; June 1980) 129.7.

Foreign Trade. (1979) Imports 269,910,000,000 schillings; exports 206,280,000,000 schillings. Import sources: EEC 65% (West Germany 42%, Italy 9%); Switzerland 5%. Export destinations: EEC 54% (West Germany 30%, Italy 10%); Switzerland 7%. Main exports: machinery 23%; iron and steel 11%; chemicals 8%; textile yarns and fabrics 6%; timber 5%; metal manufactures 5%; paper and board 5%. Tourism (1978): visitors 12,254,000; gross receipts U.S. $4,716,000,000.

Transport and Communications. Roads (1978) 106,642 km (including 884 km expressways). Motor vehicles in use (1978): passenger 2,040,268; commercial 163,387. Railways: (1977) 6,492 km; traffic (1978) 7,310,000,000 passenger-km, freight (1979) 10,567,000,000 net ton-km. Air traffic (1979): 1,086,100,000 passenger-km; freight 14,475,000 net ton-km. Navigable inland waterways in regular use (1978) 358 km. Shipping (1979): merchant vessels 100 gross tons and over 13; gross tonnage 81,437. Telephones (Dec. 1977) 2,443,400. Radio licenses (Dec. 1977) 2,068,000. Television licenses (Dec. 1977) 2,027,000.

Agriculture. Production (in 000; metric tons; 1979): wheat 850; barley 1,129; rye 278; oats 273; corn 1,347; potatoes 1,494; sugar, raw value *c.* 397; apples 326; wine 277; meat *c.* 607; timber (cu m; 1978) 13,121. Livestock (in 000; Dec. 1978): cattle 2,594; sheep 192; pigs 4,007; chickens 14,938.

Industry. Fuel and power (in 000; metric tons; 1979): lignite 2,741; crude oil 1,727; natural gas (cu m) 2,090,000; manufactured gas (cu m) 685,000; electricity (kw-hr) 40,463,000 (66% hydroelectric in 1977). Production (in 000; metric tons; 1979): iron ore (31% metal content) 3,200; pig iron 3,703; crude steel 5,421; magnesite (1978) 982; aluminum 136; copper 30; zinc 24; cement 5,615; newsprint 171; other paper (1978) 1,046; petroleum products (1978) 9,126; plastics and resins 439; fertilizers (nutrient content; 1978–79) nitrogenous *c.* 295, phosphate *c.* 104; man-made fibres (1977) 129.

The first meeting between U.S. Secretary of State Edmund Muskie (centre right) and Soviet Foreign Minister Andrey Gromyko (centre left) took place in Vienna in May. They both were attending the 25th anniversary of Austria's liberation from Allied occupation. UN Secretary-General Kurt Waldheim (right) also attended the meeting.

ALAIN MINGAM-UDO SCHREIBER—GAMMA/LIAISON

tions of bribes being paid into party funds and of the involvement of the vice-chancellor and finance minister, Hannes Androsch, led Chancellor Bruno Kreisky to take drastic action. He made his continuance as chancellor conditional upon his party's acceptance of a code of ethics imposing greater controls over politicians' business interests. Androsch, seemingly the main target, agreed to give up his tax consultancy firm (which allegedly had links with the hospital project) and to submit to closer supervision of his ministry. On December 11 Androsch resigned (as of Jan. 31, 1981) to direct the Creditanstalt bank.

Kreisky continued his personal diplomacy aimed at furthering a peaceful settlement of the Middle East conflict. In February he had talks with Palestine Liberation Organization (PLO) leader Yasir Arafat in Riyadh, Saudi Arabia, and in March the PLO was accorded de facto diplomatic recognition when Ghasi Hussain became its accredited representative in Austria. Differences between Iran and Iraq had repercussions in Austria in July when, following a bomb explosion believed to have been meant for the Iranian embassy in Vienna, two Iraqi diplomats were expelled. The Austrian ambassador to Colombia was among a number of diplomats seized as hostages by left-wing guerrillas at the embassy of the Dominican Republic in Bogotá in February, but he was released after being held for nine days.

In August the government vetoed the export by Steyr-Daimler-Puch AG of 200 tanks, worth some 2 billion schillings, to Chile. The decision, taken following strong public opposition to the deal and a refusal by railway union members to handle transportation of the tanks, was based on humanitarian grounds. The transaction was deemed a technical violation of Austria's policy of neutrality because of fears that Chile might use the tanks for purposes other than national defense.

During 1980 the Austrian economy remained one of the most stable in Europe, with a growth rate of 3–4% and an inflation rate around 6%.

(ELFRIEDE DIRNBACHER)

Bahamas, The

A member of the Commonwealth of Nations, The Bahamas comprises an archipelago of about 700 islands in the North Atlantic Ocean just southeast of the United States. Area: 13,864 sq km (5,353 sq mi). Pop. (1979 est.): 232,000. Cap. and largest city: Nassau (urban area pop., 1978 est., 133,300). Language: English (official). Religion (1970): Baptist 28.8%; Anglican 22.7%; Roman Catholic 22.5%; Methodist 7.3%; Saints of God and Church of God 6%; others and no religion 12.7%. Queen, Elizabeth II; governor-general in 1980, Sir Gerald Cash; prime minister, Lynden O. Pindling.

In announcing The Bahamas' record U.S. $298.4 million 1980 budget, Finance Minister Arthur D. Hanna indicated that the government was embarking on a "social revolution" over the next decade that would provide increased assistance with housing, health, and land for the less well-off and also restrict the holding of land by aliens. The move proved popular with Bahamians but created uncertainty in the minds of some residents who were not citizens.

In May the government, which in matters of foreign policy continued to maintain a low profile, was faced with a major crisis following the sinking of a Bahamian coast guard vessel by Cuban military aircraft. The incident, in which four Bahamians were killed, occurred after the Bahamian vessel seized two Cuban fishing craft for illegally fishing in Bahamian waters. Cuba subsequently apologized and paid compensation.

The Bahamas continued to suffer from pressures created by an influx of illegal Haitian refugees. In May Prime Minister Lynden Pindling indicated that the 25,000 illegal immigrants were creating an impossible burden on finances and health services. By the latter part of the year the Bahamian government had begun to fly some of the illegal immigrants back to Haiti.

(DAVID A. JESSOP)

BAHAMAS, THE

Education. (1976–77) Primary, pupils 37,697, teachers (state only; 1976–77) 768; secondary, pupils 24,495, teachers (state only; 1976–77) 649; vocational (1975–76), pupils 1,823, teachers 92; teacher training (1975–76), students 731, teachers 21; higher (College of the Bahamas; 1976–77), students *c.* 3,000.

Finance and Trade. Monetary unit: Bahamian dollar, with (Sept. 22, 1980) an official rate of B$1 to U.S. $1 (free rate of B$ 2.4 = £1 sterling). Budget (1979 actual): revenue B$204 million; expenditure B$205 million. Cost of living (1975 = 100; April 1980) 136. Foreign trade (1979): imports B$3,948,600,000; exports B$3,508,300,000. Import sources (1977): U.S. 35%; Saudi Arabia 24%; Iran 10%; Nigeria 9%; Libya 7%; Angola 5%. Export destinations (1977): U.S. 81%; Saudi Arabia 10%. Main exports: crude oil and petroleum products 95%. Tourism: visitors (excludes cruise passengers; 1977) 943,000; gross receipts U.S. $372 million.

Transport and Communications. Shipping (1979): merchant vessels 100 gross tons and over 91; gross tonnage 120,581. Telephones (Jan. 1978) 61,800. Radio receivers (Dec. 1977) 97,000. Television receivers (Dec. 1977) *c.* 30,000.

The Bahamas

Bahrain

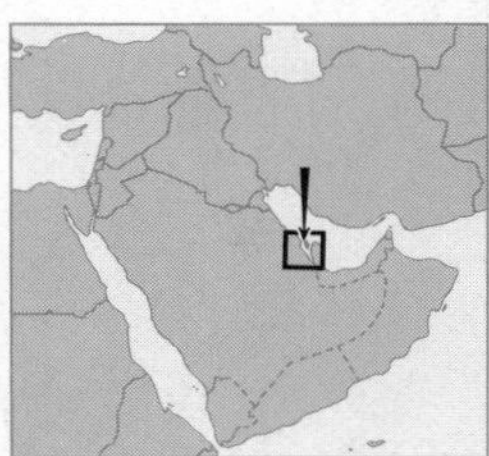

Bahrain

An independent monarchy (emirate), Bahrain consists of a group of islands in the Persian Gulf, lying between the Qatar Peninsula and Saudi Arabia. Total area: 669 sq km (258 sq mi). Pop. (1980 est.): 383,000. Cap.: Manama (pop., 1980 est., 150,000). Language: Arabic (official), Persian. Religion (1980): Muslim 95%, of which 50% are Shi'ah Muslim; Christian 4%; others 1%. Emir in 1980, Isa ibn Sulman al-Khalifah; prime minister, Khalifah ibn Sulman al-Khalifah.

Sectarian unrest among the Shi'ah Muslims, who comprise half of Bahrain's native population, continued in 1980 but on a lesser scale than in 1979. Opposition and demands for an Islamic republic on the Iranian model were concentrated in the villages of northwestern Bahrain. The government, encouraged by the absence of any official backing from Iran for the "export" of its Islamic revolution, followed a policy of allowing orderly religious demonstrations but acted to break up disturbances that threatened the peace.

Arab Gulf governments showed support for

Automobile Industry: see Industrial Review; Transportation

Automobile Racing: see Motor Sports

Aviation: see Defense; Transportation

Badminton: see Racket Games

KEYSTONE

French President Valéry Giscard d'Estaing was greeted by an honour guard when he visited Bahrain in March.

Bahrain. Kuwait and Saudi Arabia announced participation in a U.S. $400 million joint petrochemicals project; Iraq joined a $300 million iron-pelletization project; Abu Dhabi provided funds for power and water projects; and, most important, the government of Saudi Arabia reaffirmed its commitment to a $1 billion road bridge between Bahrain and the mainland. Bids for the bridge were received from 16 international construction consortia in July. In continuation of Bahrain's policy of offering the island as a service centre for the Gulf, banks from Japan, the Philippines, and France were permitted to open offshore banking units (OBU's) or representative offices, bringing the total number of OBU's to 58 by July.

(JOHN WHELAN)

BAHRAIN

Education. (1978–79) Primary, pupils 47,825, teachers 2,774; secondary, pupils 20,487, teachers 850; vocational, pupils 2,263, teachers 173; teacher training, students 102, teachers 18; higher, students 3,944, teaching staff 114.

Finance and Trade. Monetary unit: Bahrain dinar, with (Sept. 22, 1980) a free rate of 0.376 dinar to U.S. $1 (0.904 dinar = £1 sterling). Gold, SDR's, and foreign exchange (June 1980) U.S. $804 million. Budget (1979 est.) balanced at 280 million dinars. Foreign trade: imports (1978) 792.3 million dinars; exports (1979) 920.1 million dinars. Import sources: Saudi Arabia 43%; U.K. 11%; Japan 8%; U.S. 7%; West Germany 5%. Export destinations (1978): Japan 18%; United Arab Emirates 15%; Saudi Arabia 6%; Singapore 7%; Australia 5%. Main exports: petroleum products 84%; aluminum 5%.

Industry. Production (in 000; metric tons; 1977): aluminum 121; crude oil (1979) 2,497; natural gas (cu m) 2,370,000; petroleum products 12,730; electricity (kw-hr) 896,000.

Bangladesh

Bangladesh

An independent republic and member of the Commonwealth of Nations, Bangladesh is bordered by India on the west, north, and east, by Burma in the southeast, and by the Bay of Bengal in the south. Area: 143,998 sq km (55,598 sq mi). Pop. (1980 est.): 88,678,000. Cap. and largest city: Dacca (pop., 1979 est., 2.5 million). Language: Bengali. Religion: Muslim 85%, with Hindu, Christian, and Buddhist minorities. President in 1980, Maj. Gen. Ziaur Rahman; prime minister, Shah Azizur Rahman.

In 1980 Pres. Ziaur Rahman, who completed five years in office in November, made several trips abroad seeking external assistance to prop up his country's sagging economy. The tours produced no tangible results, although Zia was promised help by government leaders in Washington, London, Paris, and Tokyo if specific projects could be drawn up. In May the Bangladesh Aid Consortium, meeting in Paris, decided to allocate U.S. $1.3 billion in assistance for the fiscal year 1980–81. Of the total, $700 million was for project assistance, $350 million was in commodity aid, and the rest was in food aid. Finance Minister Saifur Rahman described the amount as falling far short of the $2.9 billion expected from the consortium countries in the first year of the second five-year plan, launched in July.

The draft five-year plan provided for a development outlay of 255,970,000,000 taka, three-quar-

BANGLADESH

Education. (1978) Primary, pupils 8,312,011, teachers 187,078; secondary, pupils (1977) 2,213,068, teachers (1976) 98,965; vocational, pupils (1976) 11,475, teachers (1973) 331; teacher training, students 9,070, teachers (1973) 631; higher (1976), students 158,604, teaching staff 13,503.

Finance. Monetary unit: taka, with (Sept. 22, 1980) a free rate of 15 taka to U.S. $1 (36.05 taka = £1 sterling). Gold, SDR's, and foreign exchange (June 1980) U.S. $253 million. Budget (1979–80 est.): revenue 18,121,000,000 taka; expenditure 11,939,000,000 taka (excludes development budget 20.7 billion taka). Gross domestic product (1978–79) 148,030,000,000 taka. Money supply (April 1980) 17,105,000,000 taka. Cost of living (1975 = 100; May 1980) 142.2.

Foreign Trade. (1979) Imports 31,647,000,000 taka; exports 10,033,000,000 taka. Import sources (1977–78): Japan 14%; U.S. 14%; U.K. 6%; Canada 5%; Singapore 5%; West Germany 5%. Export destinations (1977–78): U.S. 13%; Pakistan 8%; U.S.S.R. 7%; U.K. 6%; Mozambique 5%. Main exports (1978–79): jute products 45%; jute 23%; leather 13%; tea 6%; fish 6%.

Transport and Communications. Roads (1978) 6,240 km. Motor vehicles in use (1977): passenger 22,900; commercial 9,960. Railways: (1978) 2,874 km; traffic (1977–78) 3,585,000,000 passenger-km, freight 595 million net ton-km. Air traffic (1978): 577 million passenger-km; freight *c.* 15 million net ton-km. Navigable waterways (1978) *c.* 8,000 km. Shipping (1979): merchant vessels 100 gross tons and over 152; gross tonnage 298,524. Shipping traffic (1978–79): goods loaded 1,022,000 metric tons, unloaded 5,216,000 metric tons. Telephones (Jan. 1978) 89,200. Radio receivers (Dec. 1977) 500,000. Television receivers (Dec. 1977) 36,000.

Agriculture. Production (in 000; metric tons; 1979): rice 19,355; wheat (1978) 343; potatoes 909; sweet potatoes (1978) 783; sugar, raw value (1978) *c.* 580; onions *c.* 156; mangoes 214; bananas *c.* 600; pineapples *c.* 143; tea *c.* 39; tobacco 44; jute 996; meat *c.* 308; fish catch (1978) 640; timber (cu m; 1978) *c.* 10,300. Livestock (in 000; 1979): cattle *c.* 31,741; buffaloes 1,529; sheep 1,061; goats *c.* 11,000; chickens 70,158.

Industry. Production (in 000; metric tons; 1979): cement 306; crude steel (1978–79) 124; natural gas (cu m) 1,217,000; petroleum products (1978–79) 959; fertilizers (nutrient content; 1978–79) nitrogenous 126, phosphate 24%; jute fabrics (1978–79) 509; cotton yarn 45; newsprint 36; other paper (1978–79) 39; electricity (kw-hr; 1978) *c.* 2,400,000.

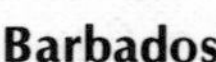

UPI

U.S. Pres. Jimmy Carter entertained Pres. Ziaur Rahman of Bangladesh in the White House when Zia visited the U.S. in August.

ters of which was earmarked for the public sector, and sought a growth rate of 7.2%, compared with the current 4.9%. Its main thrust was to reduce poverty by boosting agricultural production.

Despite World Bank aid totaling $1,274,000,000 since 1972, mainly for agricultural development, output of food grains and of jute, the major foreign exchange earner, failed to improve. The nation had barely recovered from the drought of 1978–79 when floods over vast areas took a heavy toll in lives and damaged crops. The shortfall in food grains was estimated at three million metric tons. By the end of August nearly half the country's 144,000 sq km had been flooded; about 20 million people in 14 of the 21 districts were said to have been directly affected, and approximately 5 million were homeless. The jute industry was also hard hit by lower prices and lack of demand in the international market, forcing the government to abolish the minimum support price to the farmer.

In April President Zia dropped eight of his ministers, including five of Cabinet rank, prominent among them M. N. Huda (finance) and Abdur Rahman Biswas (jute). Huda was later appointed adviser to the president. Of the new ministers, eight had the rank of minister of state and the rest that of deputy minister. Earlier, in January, Zia had sacked Deputy Prime Minister Moudud Ahmed and the minister for jute, Nur Mohammed Khan.

Mounting economic problems led to a wave of strikes and agitation in various parts of the country, the most serious being a stoppage by about 500,000 lower-grade government employees demanding higher wages. Zia accused the pro-Moscow Communist Party of Bangladesh of fomenting trouble and arrested its top leaders. Reports of an attempted coup in June, when Zia was visiting London, were quickly denied by the government. Parliament was told that some army officers were behaving in an undisciplined manner and distributing pamphlets.

An insurgency problem developed in the Chittagong Hill Tracts area, where Chakma Buddhists attacked the police and armed forces in an effort to block government plans for large-scale resettlement of Muslims in the Hill Tracts region. The Shanti Bahini guerrilla force of the Chakam tribals was officially blamed for the ambush killing of 100 soldiers and policemen in the first half of the year.

Zia's visit to Beijing (Peking) in July produced two agreements: for the opening of an air link between the two capitals and for a Chinese development loan of $44 million. Relations with India were slightly strained, as many issues evaded solution despite several rounds of talks. The irritants included the sharing of the Ganges waters and the demarcation of maritime and land boundaries, complicated by the emergence of new islands in the Bay of Bengal. (GOVINDAN UNNY)

Barbados

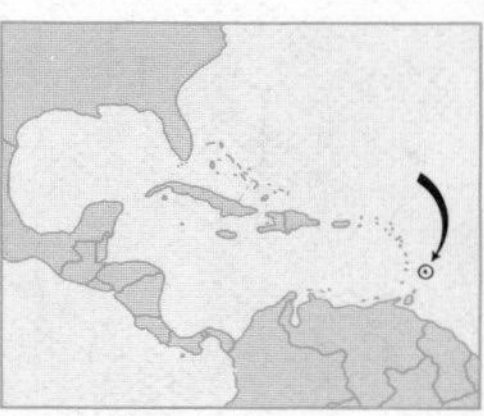

Barbados

The parliamentary state of Barbados is a member of the Commonwealth of Nations and occupies the most easterly island in the southern Caribbean Sea. Area: 430 sq km (166 sq mi). Pop. (1980 prelim.): 249,000; 91% Negro, 4% white, 4% mixed. Cap. and largest city: Bridgetown (pop., 1980 prelim., 7,600). Language: English. Religion: Anglican 53%; Methodist 9%; Roman Catholic 4%; Moravian 2%. Queen, Elizabeth II; governor-general in 1980, Sir Deighton Lisle Ward; prime minister, J. M. G. Adams.

At 7% Barbados' economic growth in 1979 was the highest in the region, though preliminary figures for 1980 indicated that this high level was unlikely to continue. Growth in tourist arrivals fell (up 6.9% in the winter of 1979–80, compared with 9% for 1978–79); increased consumer expenditure led to stricter credit controls; inflation (16% in 1979) grew; and energy prices increased. Even so, the island did not suffer as much from these problems as many of its neighbours.

During a visit to China, Prime Minister Tom Adams and External Affairs Minister Henry Forde signed trade and technical agreements that indicated Barbados did not endorse a heightened Cuban or Soviet presence in the region. Technical cooperation agreements with Trinidad were put

BARBADOS

Education. (1977–78) Primary, pupils 34,324, teachers 1,227; secondary and vocational, pupils 30,021, teachers 1,517; higher (university only), students 1,140, teaching staff (1971–72) 70.

Finance and Trade. Monetary unit: Barbados dollar, with (Sept. 22, 1980) an official rate of Bar$2 to U.S. $1 (free rate of Bar$4.81 = £1 sterling). Budget (1978–79 est.): revenue Bar$265,302,000; expenditure Bar$301,910,000. Cost of living (1975 = 100; May 1980) 165.2. Foreign trade (1978): imports Bar$628.7 million; exports Bar$261.2 million. Import sources: U.S. 29%; U.K. 18%; Trinidad and Tobago 9%; Canada 7%. Export destinations: U.S. 26%; U.K. 12%; Trinidad and Tobago 12%; Canada 5%. Main exports (1977): sugar 26%; clothing 19%; petroleum products 13%; electrical apparatus 9%; chemicals 6%. Tourism (1978): visitors 317,000; gross receipts U.S. $136 million.

Agriculture. Production (in 000; metric tons; 1978): sweet potatoes *c.* 4; corn *c.* 2; sugar, raw value *c.* 104.

Balance of Payments:
see Economy, World

Ballet:
see Dance

Ballooning:
see Aerial Sports

Banking:
see Economy, World

Baptist Churches:
see Religion

into effect. Barbados continued to act as a catalyst for a joint coast guard and fisheries protection service embracing St. Lucia and St. Vincent. Preparations were made to prospect for offshore oil and gas, and legislation establishing Barbados as an offshore banking centre was introduced.

Politically, the ruling Barbados Labour Party appeared to recover support after introducing a notably concessionary budget. The opposition Democratic Labour Party remained divided.

(DAVID A. JESSOP)

Baseball

After a threatened strike by players was averted during spring training, major league baseball proceeded on schedule in 1980. When it was all over, the Philadelphia Phillies had captured the first World Series championship in their 97-year history.

World Series. On October 21 in Philadelphia, the Phillies defeated the Kansas City Royals 4–1 to win the 77th World Series, four games to two, and atone for years of frustration and disappointment. "We were called a lot of bad things, and as much as it hurt to hear them and read them, it was tough to argue because we always were supposed to win and never did," said Philadelphia third baseman Mike Schmidt. "When they handed out courage, it always seemed like they handed out more to other teams than us, that others did things to us that we were supposed to do to them. But this year, things were different."

Schmidt's two-run single in the third inning of the sixth game was the key hit in the Phillies' Series-winning victory before an ecstatic home crowd of 65,838. Schmidt batted .381 for the Series, knocked in seven runs, and was named most valuable player.

The favoured Royals jumped to a 4–0 lead in the first game of the Series on October 14 at Philadelphia, but the Phillies rallied to win 7–6. Likewise, one night later, the Royals were ahead 4–2 entering the bottom half of the eighth inning. But the Phillies roughed up Kansas City's best relief pitcher, Dan Quisenberry, to win 6–4.

When the Series moved to Kansas City on October 17, the Royals came to life. They won the third game 4–3 in ten innings, and then rode Willie Aikens's third and fourth home runs of the Series to a 5–3 triumph October 18. But in the pivotal fifth game the Phillies staged another of their comebacks, scoring two runs in the ninth inning for a 4–3 conquest on October 19. To ensure that victory, Tug McGraw (*see* BIOGRAPHIES), Philadelphia's leading relief pitcher, had to survive a bases-loaded situation in the ninth inning.

Two evenings later veteran Philadelphia left-hander Steve Carlton hurled seven strong innings to achieve his second win of the Series, with help from McGraw, and the city was immersed in a loving celebration of its baseball team, culminated by a parade which, according to estimates, was viewed by more than a million citizens. The Series was the first ever contested solely on artificial turf and also was the first involving two rookie managers, Dallas Green of Philadelphia and Jim Frey of Kansas City.

Play-offs. Many observers deemed the World Series anticlimactic because of the dramatic nature of the play-offs that determined the league pennant winners. The Phillies had to endure a grueling best-of-five series with the Houston Astros before claiming their first National League title since 1950. On October 7 in Philadelphia the Phillies beat the Astros 3–1, but the Astros triumphed 7–4 in 10 innings the next night and then 1–0 in 11 innings at Houston on October 10. But the redoubtable Phillies tied the play-offs at two victories each by winning 5–3 in ten innings on October 11, and then rebounded from a 5–2 deficit

Mike Schmidt of the Phillies was the hero of the World Series when Philadelphia defeated the Kansas City Royals 4 games to 2 to win its first World Series.

WIDE WORLD

WIDE WORLD

A standout performer of the Kansas City Royals in the World Series was third baseman George Brett, who batted .375.

the next night to prevail 8–7 in ten innings for the pennant. As the play-offs progressed the tension rose, and Philadelphia's Pete Rose called it "the most incredible series I've ever seen or been involved in." The Phillies had won East Division championships in 1976, 1977, and 1978 but each time had failed to win the pennant.

Similarly, the Royals had been West Division champions in the American League for 1976, 1977, and 1978, only to lose the pennant each time to the New York Yankees. But in 1980 the Royals exacted a measure of revenge by sweeping the Yankees in three games during the American League play-offs. The Royals won at home 7–2 on October 8 and 3–2 on October 9. Then in New York on October 10 Royal third baseman George Brett (*see* BIOGRAPHIES) smashed a dramatic three-run, seventh-inning homer off New York's fireballing relief pitcher Rich Gossage to give the Royals a 4–2 conquest. The Royals, an expansion team formed in 1968, thus achieved their first pennant.

Regular Season. While the Royals coasted to their division crown, the Yankees, Phillies, and Astros all laboured through arduous races. The Astros led the National League West by three games with three games to go in 1980. They lost all three of those contests by one run to the Los Angeles Dodgers, who tied Houston for first place after the regular schedule of 162 games was completed. That forced a divisional play-off in Los Angeles on October 6, and the Astros arose to defeat the Dodgers 7–1 for their first division crown. The Astros, a light-hitting team, managed only 75 home runs but benefited from having the league's leading pitching staff. J. R. Richard, the most dominant member of that staff, was felled in mid-season by a blood disorder that resulted in clots. At the year's end his future in baseball remained in doubt.

The Phillies, who were 6 games out of first place with 55 to go, enjoyed a splendid closing month of the season to win the National League East by one game. They were tied with the Montreal Expos entering the final three-game series of the regular schedule at Montreal. The Phillies won the first match 2–1 and then clinched the division title on October 4 with a 6–4 triumph on Schmidt's two-run homer.

The Yankees accumulated a seemingly insurmountable lead during the first half of the season, but then the defending American League champion Baltimore Orioles made a charge. However, the Yankees stood firm and won the division by three games over the Orioles, who were runners-up despite a sparkling 100–62 record. From August 27 until the season's end Baltimore was 26–12, yet it lost 2½ games in the standings during that period. The Yankees, under rookie manager Dick Howser, established an American League attendance record of 2,627,417.

The Royals never were challenged. Despite a lukewarm spell in the closing stages of the season they finished 14 games ahead of surprising Oakland. Brett, however, kept matters interesting by chasing the coveted .400 batting mark. He stayed close to it for much of the summer and several times passed it but eventually fell back and finished with a still-exemplary .390 average, the best in baseball since Ted Williams of the Boston Red Sox hit .406 in 1941. Bill Buckner, a first baseman for the Chicago Cubs, won the National

Final Major League Standings, 1980

American League

East Division

Club	W.	L.	Pct.	G.B.	N.Y.	Balt.	Mil.	Bos.	Det.	Clev.	Tor.	Cal.	Chi.	K.C.	Min.	Oak.	Sea.	Tex.
New York	103	59	.636	...	...	6	8	10	8	8	10	10	7	4	8	8	9	7
Baltimore	100	62	.617	3	7	...	7	8	10	6	11	10	6	6	10	7	6	6
Milwaukee	86	76	.531	17	5	6	...	7	6	10	5	6	7	6	7	7	9	5
Boston	83	77	.519	19	3	5	6	...	8	7	7	9	6	5	6	9	7	5
Detroit	84	78	.519	19	5	3	7	5	...	10	9	7	10	2	6	6	10	4
Cleveland	79	81	.494	23	5	7	3	6	3	...	8	6	7	5	9	6	8	6
Toronto	67	95	.414	36	3	2	8	6	4	5	...	9	7	3	5	4	6	5

West Division

Club	W.	L.	Pct.	G.B.	K.C.	Oak.	Min.	Tex.	Chi.	Cal.	Sea.	Balt.	Bos.	Clev.	Det.	Mil.	N.Y.	Tor.
Kansas City	97	65	.599	...	...	6	5	10	8	8	7	6	7	7	10	6	8	9
Oakland	83	79	.512	14	7	...	7	7	7	10	8	5	3	6	6	5	4	8
Minnesota	77	84	.478	19½	8	6	...	9	8	6	7	2	6	3	6	5	4	7
Texas	76	85	.472	20½	3	6	3	...	7	2	9	6	7	6	8	7	5	7
Chicago	70	90	.438	26	5	6	5	6	...	10	6	6	4	5	2	5	5	5
California	65	95	.406	31	5	3	7	11	3	...	11	2	3	4	5	6	2	3
Seattle	59	103	.364	38	6	5	6	4	7	2	...	6	5	4	2	3	3	6

Tie games—Seattle *v.* Detroit and Texas *v.* Chicago (2).

National League

East Division

Club	W.	L.	Pct.	G.B.	Phil.	Mon.	Pitt.	St.L.	N.Y.	Chi.	Atl.	Cin.	Hou.	L.A.	S.D.	S.F.
Philadelphia	91	71	.562	...	...	9	7	9	12	13	7	5	9	6	8	6
Montreal	90	72	.556	1	9	...	6	12	10	12	7	9	7	1	10	7
Pittsburgh	83	79	.512	8	11	12	...	10	8	10	1	6	5	6	6	8
St. Louis	74	88	.457	17	9	6	8	...	9	9	6	7	5	5	5	5
New York	67	95	.414	24	6	8	10	9	...	8	9	4	4	5	1	3
Chicago	64	98	.395	27	5	6	8	9	10	...	4	7	1	5	4	5

West Division

Club	W.	L.	Pct.	G.B.	Hou.	L.A.	Cin.	Atl.	S.F.	S.D.	Chi.	Mon.	N.Y.	Phil.	Pitt.	St.L.
*Houston	92	70	.568	...	...	8	10	11	11	11	11	5	8	3	7	7
*Los Angeles	92	70	.568	...	10	...	9	7	13	9	7	11	7	6	6	7
Cincinnati	89	73	.549	3	8	9	...	16	7	15	5	3	8	7	6	5
Atlanta	81	80	.503	10½	7	11	2	...	11	12	8	5	3	5	11	6
San Francisco	75	86	.466	16½	7	5	11	6	...	8	7	5	9	6	4	7
San Diego	73	89	.451	19	7	9	3	6	10	...	8	2	11	4	6	7

*Houston defeated Los Angeles, 7-1, in play-off for West Division championship.

Tie game—San Diego *v.* Cincinnati.

League batting title with .324, while Schmidt led the league with 48 home runs and 121 runs batted in. Carlton paced the league in wins with 24 (he lost 9) and strikeouts with 286, while Chicago's Bruce Sutter once again topped relief pitchers with 28 saves.

Brett was not the only Kansas City player to excel offensively. Teammate Willie Wilson, a disappointment in the World Series, had 230 hits and became only the second switch-hitter in history to get 100 hits from either side of the plate. Cecil Cooper of the Milwaukee Brewers led the American League in runs batted in with 122, while teammate Ben Oglivie tied Reggie Jackson of the Yankees for the home-run leadership with 41. Baltimore's Steve Stone (25–7), New York's Tommy John (22–9), and Oakland's Mike Norris (22–9) were the top starting pitchers, while Quisenberry and Gossage each totaled 33 saves in relief. Oakland's Rickey Henderson stole 100 bases, breaking the American League record of the legendary Ty Cobb. Only two other players, Maury Wills and Lou Brock in the National League, ever had stolen 100 or more bases in one season.

Brett and Schmidt were voted most valuable players in their leagues, while the Cy Young awards for best pitchers went to Stone in the American League and Carlton in the National. Rookies of the year were relief pitcher Steve Howe of the Dodgers in the National League and outfielder Joe Charboneau of the Cleveland Indians in the American. Billy Martin of Oakland was the American League manager of the year, and Bill Virdon of Houston won the honour in the National.

The midsummer All-Star Game in Los Angeles had a familiar result. The National League defeated the American League 4–2 for its 9th consecutive victory and 17th in the last 18 contests. Ken Griffey of the Cincinnati Reds had two hits, including a home run, and was named most valuable player.

(ROBERT WILLIAM VERDI)

The Taiwan Little League team trampled the Canadian entry 23–0 in a Little League World Series game held in Williamsport, Pennsylvania, in August.

WIDE WORLD

Japan. The Hiroshima Toyo Carp beat the Kintetsu Buffaloes of Osaka four games to three in the best-of-seven Japan Series to win the national championship for the second straight year. The most valuable player of the series was Jim Lyttle, who slammed three home runs scoring six runners for Hiroshima.

During the regular season in the Central League the Toyo Carp won the 1980 pennant behind manager Takeshi Koba's cool-headed management as well as powerful batting by outfielder Koji Yamamoto and infielder Sachio Kinugasa, and pitching by Kazuo Yamane, Hiroaki Fukushi, Manabu Kitabeppu, and relief specialist Yutaka Enatsu. The Carp had previously won the championship in 1975 and 1979.

In other Central League affairs Shigeo Nagashima, 44-year-old manager of the Yomiuri Giants of Tokyo, resigned on October 21 on the grounds that he had failed to win the pennant for three consecutive years. On November 4 Sadaharu Oh of the Giants, one of the greatest batters in Japanese baseball history, announced his retirement as a player at the age of 40 but planned to serve as an assistant manager during the next season.

The news of the resignation of Nagashima and retirement of Oh surprised many. As a player, Nagashima received five most valuable player awards, two home-run titles, and six leading hitter honours. Oh obtained 9 most valuable player awards, 15 home-run championships, 5 leading batter titles, 13 runs-batted-in awards, and 2 triple crowns. He hit 868 home runs during his 22-year career. Kenichi Yazawa of the Chunichi Dragons of Nagoya won the Central League batting championship with .369, his second title since 1976. Both home-run and runs-batted-in titles were gained by Koji Yamamoto of the Carp with 44 and 112, respectively. He also was named the league's most valuable player.

In the Pacific League the Kintetsu Buffaloes of Osaka, winners of the season's second half, beat the first-half champion Lotte Orions of Kawasaki 3–0 in the play-off series to win the league championship for the second straight year. In the first and second games fine pitching enabled the Buffaloes to stop the powerful batting of the Orions. In the third game the Buffaloes made ten hits including four home runs to win 13–4.

Leon Lee of the Orions won the league's leading hitter honour with .358, while Charles Manuel of the Buffaloes won both the home-run title with 48 and the runs-batted-in championship with 129. The most valuable player award went to pitcher Isamu Kida of the Nippon Ham Fighters, who had 22 wins against 8 losses and an earned run average of 2.28. Kida was the first rookie to win the award.

(RYUSAKU HASEGAWA)

Basketball

United States. PROFESSIONAL. If Earvin Johnson was "Magic" in college basketball, he bordered on the miraculous as a professional. The eager rookie's mile-wide grin and remarkable ability delighted fans and filled arenas throughout the United States during the 1979–80 season, adding up to the National Basketball Association's most successful year since the New York Knicks packed Madison Square Garden in the early 1970s. Dropping out of Michigan State University after leading the Spartans to the 1979 National Collegiate Athletic Association (NCAA) championship, Johnson completed a rare double by sparking the Los Angeles Lakers to the 1980–81 NBA crown.

"New Faces of 1980" was a hit show from coast to coast because forward Larry Bird also made a sensational NBA debut for the Boston Celtics, outpolling Johnson for rookie of the year honours. Bird, of Indiana State, and Johnson had first collided in the 1979 collegiate final, with Johnson's team winning even though Bird was named college player of the year.

Bird did not get a chance to even the score with Johnson in an NBA final play-off confrontation. The Philadelphia 76ers beat the Celtics in the Eastern Conference showdown before losing to the Lakers in a lively six-game championship round. The perfect Hollywood finish should have taken place on the Lakers' home court in suburban Inglewood, Calif., but Johnson, who was voted the series' most valuable player, wrote his own script. With 7-ft 2-in centre Kareem Abdul-Jabbar (voted NBA most valuable player) out of action after severely spraining an ankle, the 20-year-old rookie took personal charge of the final game, played in Philadelphia. The 6-ft 8-in Johnson played forward and centre as well as guard, scoring 42 points and demoralizing the 76ers with all-around brilliance.

Overlooked in the Magic show was the demise of the defending champion Seattle SuperSonics in a welter of controversy and conflict. As it had been for every NBA champion since the 1968–69 season, the strain of repeating was too much for the Sonics, who began unraveling late in the season. The bickering rose to a crescendo while they were being eliminated by the Lakers in the Western Conference finals. In the meantime the 76ers were ousting Boston in the East to reach the finals. But despite spectacular contributions from Julius (Dr. J) Erving and backboard-shattering Darryl Dawkins, the 76ers were no match for Los Angeles.

At its meeting in February the NBA admitted Dallas, bringing league membership to 23 teams. Orderly expansion would have called for two new franchises, providing a balanced circuit of two six-team divisions in the Eastern and Western conferences, but no other city was willing to meet the $12 million price tag.

The move did force long-overdue realignment, however, Dallas forming a Texas trio (with Houston and San Antonio) in the Midwest Division along with Kansas City, Denver, and Utah. Chicago and Milwaukee shifted to the Central Division, making the Mississippi River the dividing line between East and West and providing a sense of geographic reality overlooked by the football and baseball major leagues.

Perhaps the most disturbing development of the year was the growing realization that drug use among NBA players was widespread. The death of Utah's Terry Furlow in a car crash and the arrest of Atlanta's Eddie Johnson for alleged narcotics

SARA KRULWICH—THE NEW YORK TIMES

Earvin "Magic" Johnson (centre) was a standout performer for the Los Angeles Lakers as they won the 1980–81 NBA title.

possession triggered speculation that perhaps as many as 75% of the athletes used cocaine. Belatedly reacting to the crisis, the NBA formed a study committee, and Commissioner Larry O'Brien hinted that lifetime suspension awaited convicted drug users.

In women's professional competition, Pearl Moore led the New York Stars to the Women's Basketball League title. The Stars defeated the Iowa Cornets three games to one in the championship series.

College. It seemed anticlimactic when Louisville struggled past UCLA 59–54 to win the 1980 NCAA tournament at Indianapolis, ending the Bruins' bid for their 11th basketball championship. This was the first time that UCLA had lost an NCAA final, but there was ample consolation. Rebounding from a shaky 1979–80 start under new coach Larry Brown, the Bruins came together with a rush at tournament time.

The target of strong criticism earlier, Brown suddenly found himself being compared to the retired coach John Wooden, who had produced many national champions for UCLA. Brown explained that his underclassmen-laden team needed experience, and they got it by knocking pretourney favourite DePaul out of the running in a second-round upset.

But nothing could stem the Louisville tide, powered by brilliant 6-ft 4-in guard Darrell Griffith (*see* Biographies). The Cardinals capped a 33–3 campaign by erasing a late deficit to beat UCLA behind Griffith's 23 points. Two Big Ten teams, Purdue and Iowa, also made the prestigious final four but had to settle for the third-place game, won by Purdue 75–58.

As further proof of the Big Ten's growing bas-

WIDE WORLD

The Soviet's star centre, Iuliyana Semenova, towered over her Hungarian opponents as the Soviet team won the Women's Amateur Basketball championship played in Varna, Bulgaria, in May.

ketball dominance, Minnesota and Illinois reached the semifinals of the National Invitational Tournament. Minnesota won that contest, but Virginia's awesome 7-ft 4-in freshman centre, Ralph Sampson, piled up 15 points and the same number of rebounds to beat the Gophers 58–55 in the NIT final. Sampson then surprised the sports world by turning down a multimillion-dollar offer from the Boston Celtics to stay in school. Illinois defeated Nevada-Las Vegas to take the third-place NIT trophy.

Louisville's Griffith, centre Joe Barry Carroll of Purdue, and forward Mark Aguirre of DePaul were the standout college performers, earning unanimous selection to All-America teams. Votes for the other two first-team berths were widely scattered.

An unprecedented triple triumph was achieved by tiny North Park College of Chicago in NCAA Division III competition. Behind slender 6-ft 10-in centre Michael Harper, the Vikings swept to their third straight national championship, outscoring Upsala (N.J.) College 83–76 in the final.

In women's competition Old Dominion of Virginia coasted to its second AIAW (Association of Intercollegiate Athletics for Women) crown in a row, brushing aside Tennessee 68–53 despite 26 turnovers. Inge Nissen scored 20 points to win the tournament's most valuable player honours. Her Old Dominion teammate, Nancy Lieberman (*see* BIOGRAPHIES), was supreme in the backcourt, cementing her position as the nation's best collegiate woman guard. (ROBERT G. LOGAN)

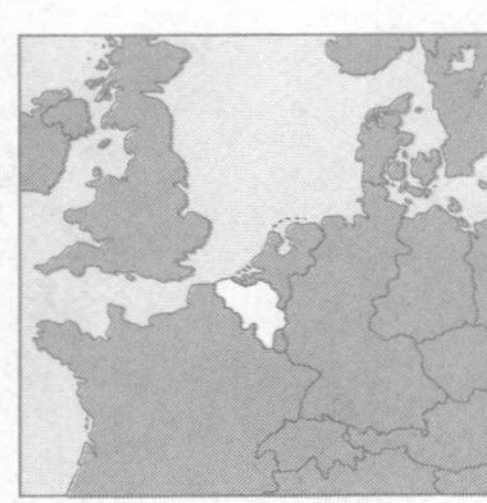

Belgium

World Amateur. Twelve men's and six women's teams competed in the Olympic Games at Moscow, but unfortunately they did not truly represent the strength of world basketball. The Olympic boycott absentees included Argentina,

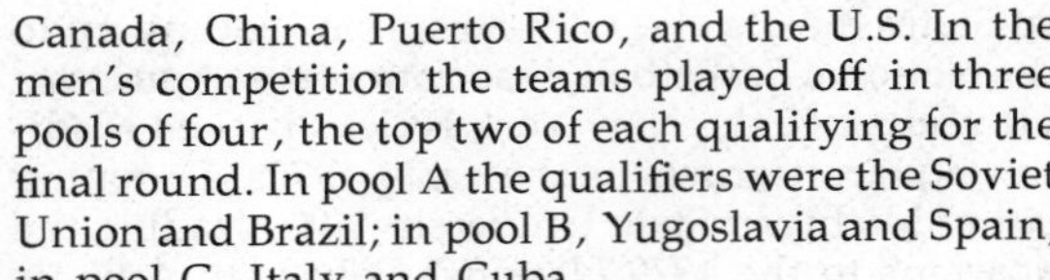

Canada, China, Puerto Rico, and the U.S. In the men's competition the teams played off in three pools of four, the top two of each qualifying for the final round. In pool A the qualifiers were the Soviet Union and Brazil; in pool B, Yugoslavia and Spain; in pool C, Italy and Cuba.

In the final round the only question seemed to be who would be the victor in the anticipated final match between the Soviet Union and Yugoslavia. Yugoslavia did its part and notched up four straight wins. This, together with its win over Spain in their pool game—results in the pool games were carried forward—gained Yugoslavia a maximum of ten points and first place. Meanwhile, the Soviet Union was in trouble. It beat Spain but was surprisingly beaten by Italy and on the following day lost to Yugoslavia. The Soviets still had a chance to finish second; if Brazil could beat Yugoslavia, the U.S.S.R. and Brazil would tie for second place and on points average the Soviet Union would be placed second. The Brazil-Yugoslavia match was tense and exciting, Yugoslavia winning by a point. In the final Yugoslavia defeated Italy 86–77, and in the play-off for third place the Soviet Union beat Spain 117–94. Final standings were, in order of finish: Yugoslavia, Italy, the Soviet Union, Spain, Brazil, and Cuba.

The women's competition was organized differently. The six teams in the final round played a round-robin tournament, after which the four with the best records played one another for the medals. The six teams were the gold medalists from the previous Olympics, the Soviet Union, plus the five best teams from the world qualifying tournament held in Varna, Bulg., on May 5–15. The five additional qualifiers were Bulgaria, Cuba, Italy, the U.S., and Yugoslavia. The U.S. team withdrew and was replaced by Hungary. The Soviet team, with its significant height advantage, won all its games and retained the title. The real competition took place between Bulgaria, Yugoslavia, and Hungary for second place. Bulgaria won the vital games against Yugoslavia (81–79) and Hungary (90–75) to gain the right to play against the Soviet Union in the final. The result was a foregone conclusion, the Soviet Union cantering home to a 104–73 win. In the Yugoslavia-Hungary play-off for the bronze medal Yugoslavia scraped home to a 68–65 win. Final standings were: the Soviet Union, Bulgaria, Yugoslavia, Hungary, Cuba, and Italy.

See also Track and Field Sports: *Special Report*.

(K. K. MITCHELL)

Belgium

A constitutional monarchy on the North Sea coast of Europe, the Benelux country of Belgium is bordered by The Netherlands, West Germany, Luxembourg, and France. Area: 30,521 sq km (11,784 sq mi). Pop. (1980 est.): 9,855,100. Cap. and largest urban area: Brussels (pop., 1980 est., commune 144,000). Language: Dutch, French, and German. Religion: predominantly Roman Catholic. King, Baudouin I; prime minister in 1980, Wilfried Martens.

Belgium's 150th anniversary celebrations in 1980 were marked by a major, albeit not yet decisive, step toward the long-promised regionalization. After two aborted attempts, Parliament approved two bills (made law on August 8 and 9, respectively) reorganizing the country's structure on the basis of three regions: Flanders, Wallonia, and Brussels. A solution for the Brussels region, where the French- and Dutch-speaking communities live side by side, was left pending.

Disagreement among the Social Christians, the Socialists, and the Front Démocratique des Francophones (FDF; Brussels federalists) had arisen over the second and third phases of the proposed reform of the state structure, and the FDF's insistence on equal status for the Brussels region led to the resignation of the FDF ministers from the government early in the year. This forced Prime Minister Wilfried Martens to bring the Liberals into the coalition in order to obtain the two-thirds majority in Parliament required for constitutional change. After a slight reshuffle of the Cabinet on January 23, the Martens government (his second) carried on with its former program. However, Flemish Social Christian senators demanded that technical guarantees be granted to Flemish members of the future Brussels regional council. Despite an appeal by the prime minister before the vote, several Social Christian senators remained adamant. Lacking a two-thirds majority, Martens's government resigned on April 9.

Martens was then invited by King Baudouin to form a new Cabinet. The Socialists accepted the presence of the Liberals in order to obtain the two-thirds majority. The third Martens government of May 18 thus brought together the three traditional parties. The Liberal (PRL and PVV) proposals providing for tax reductions for married couples and drastic cuts in public expenditure were accepted. With the Liberals in the majority, the two main bills dealing with the state reform passed after protracted debates. Tension between the communities persisted in two communes with special facilities for the minority language group. Violence erupted repeatedly at Voeren (Fourons), and in Comines (Komen) a request for a Flemish school was ignored by local authorities, forcing the government to step in.

Despite growing unemployment and warnings by employers that a 38-hour week would further jeopardize the competitive position of Belgian industries, the trade unions held to their demands, refusing to countenance any infringement of social benefits. To reduce the deficit of the social security system, the first Martens government had suggested measures that doctors regarded as a step toward socialized medicine. A national doctors' strike had been called in November 1979 but was suspended during the January political crisis.

With a BFr 82 billion deficit in current spending in 1980, the government planned a BFr 90 billion deficit for 1981. A 2% levy on contributions by civil servants toward a pension fund was proposed, but the government rescinded the measure in the face of strong trade union opposition. First to denounce this decision was Karel Van Miert, the Flemish Socialist chairman, even

UPI

Internal strife continued to plague Belgium in March. Flemish demonstrators waged a pitched battle with police at Voeren (Fourons).

BELGIUM

Education. (1979–80) Primary, pupils 877,138, teachers 48,423; secondary, pupils 562,610; vocational, pupils 228,-248; secondary and vocational, teachers (1967–68) 88,030; higher, pupils 164,459, teaching staff (universities only; 1976–77) *c.* 5,000.

Finance. Monetary unit: Belgian franc, with (Sept. 22, 1980) a free commercial rate of BFr 29 to U.S. $1 (BFr 69.7 = £1 sterling) and a free financial rate of BFr 29.1 to U.S. $1 (BFr 69.95 = £1 sterling). Gold, SDR's, and foreign exchange (June 1980) U.S. $9,097,000,000. Budget (1979 actual): revenue BFr 954.7 billion; expenditure BFr 1,166,-500,000,000. Gross national product (1979) BFr 3,293,000,-000,000. Money supply (March 1980) BFr 771.7 billion. Cost of living (1975 = 100; June 1980) 134.7.

Foreign Trade. (Belgium-Luxembourg economic union; 1979) Imports BFr 1,769,500,000,000; exports BFr 1,648,-100,000,000. Import sources: EEC 67% (West Germany 22%, The Netherlands 17%, France 16%, U.K. 8%); U.S. 7%. Export destinations: EEC 73% (West Germany 23%, France 19%, The Netherlands 16%, U.K. 8%, Italy 5%). Main exports: chemicals 12%; motor vehicles 12%; iron and steel 11%; machinery 11%; food 8%; petroleum products 6%; textile yarns and fabrics 6%; precious stones 6%. Tourism (1978) gross receipts (Belgium-Luxembourg) U.S. $1,249,000,000.

Transport and Communications. Roads (1978) 125,765 km (including 1,128 km expressways). Motor vehicles in use (1978): passenger 2,973,400; commercial 247,-454. Railways: (1978) 4,046 km; traffic 7,136,000,000 passenger-km, freight 7,312,000,000 net ton-km. Air traffic (1979): 4,819,000,000 passenger-km; freight 411.1 million net ton-km. Navigable inland waterways in regular use (1978) 1,518 km. Shipping (1979): merchant vessels 100 gross tons and over 276; gross tonnage 1,788,538. Shipping traffic (1978): goods loaded 37,701,000 metric tons, unloaded 58,694,000 metric tons. Telephones (Jan. 1978) 3,100,100. Radio licenses (Dec. 1978) 4,211,900. Television licenses (Dec. 1978) 2,866,450.

Agriculture. Production (in 000; metric tons; 1979): wheat *c.* 985; barley *c.* 770; oats *c.* 120; potatoes *c.* 1,560; tomatoes *c.* 120; apples *c.* 260; sugar, raw value *c.* 970; milk *c.* 3,840; pork *c.* 710; beef and veal *c.* 270; fish catch (1978) 51. Livestock (in 000; Dec. 1978): cattle 2,870; pigs 4,992; sheep 91; horses 40; chickens 30,328.

Industry. Fuel and power (in 000; 1979): coal (metric tons) 6,130; manufactured gas (cu m) 2,285,000; electricity (kw-hr) 52,254,000. Production (in 000; metric tons; 1979): pig iron 10,777; crude steel 13,444; copper 520; lead 113; tin 4.7; zinc 262; sulfuric acid 2,298; plastics and resins 1,969; fertilizers (nutrient content; 1978–79) nitrogenous *c.* 750, phosphate *c.* 530; cement 7,704; newsprint 99; other paper 728; cotton yarn 50; cotton fabrics 52; wool yarn 76; woolen fabrics 31. Merchant vessels launched (100 gross tons and over; 1979) 126,000 gross tons.

Beer:
see Industrial Review

though it had been approved by all the Socialist ministers. Van Miert also consistently found fault with defense policy, opposing in particular the installation of cruise missiles on Belgian territory and the extra funds required to cover the armed forces' higher fuel costs. Lack of funds prevented Belgian participation in NATO maneuvers. Another Van Miert target was Belgian policy toward Zaire and its continued support of Mobutu Sese Seko's regime.

Disagreement over measures to finance the social security system led to the fall of Martens's third government on October 4. His fourth, composed of Social Christians and Socialists, took office October 22. (JAN R. ENGELS)

Benin

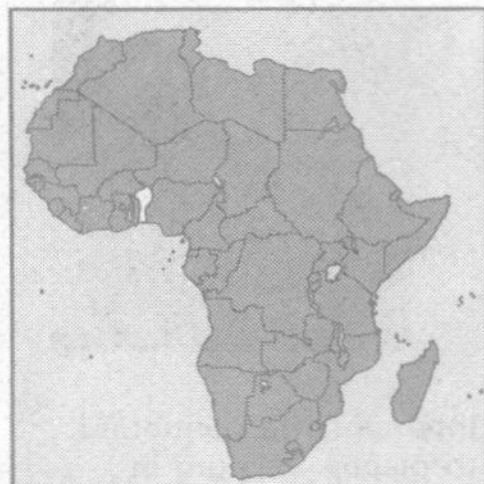

Benin

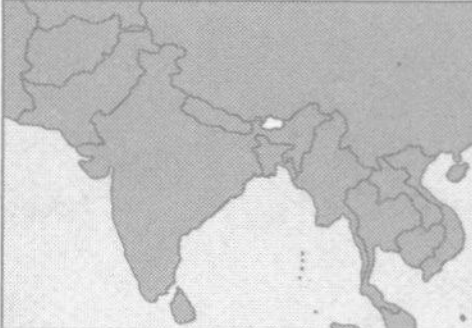

Bhutan

A republic of West Africa, Benin is located north of the Gulf of Guinea and is bounded by Togo, Upper Volta, Niger, and Nigeria. Area: 112,600 sq km (43,475 sq mi). Pop. (1979 prelim.): 3,338,000, mainly Dahomean and allied tribes. Cap.: Porto-Novo (pop., 1979 prelim., 132,000). Largest city: Cotonou (pop., 1979 prelim., 327,600). Language: French and local dialects. Religion: mainly animist, with Christian and Muslim minorities. President in 1980, Col. Ahmed Kerekou.

The elections of Nov. 20, 1979, for the 336 seats of the Revolutionary National Assembly, which replaced the National Revolution Council on Feb. 4, 1980, left the internal development of Benin proceeding along revolutionary Socialist lines. Abroad, relations with France were cool. Benin had condemned France's intervention in the Central African Republic in September 1979 and continued to accuse it of implication in the coup attempted against Benin's regime by its opponents from Gabon in 1977. Two French nationals, employees of a Swiss concern in litigation with the Benin government, had been detained in Cotonou without trial since April 1979. When the Organization of African Unity decided in May 1980 to send an inter-African force to Chad to relieve the French forces there, Benin signified its willingness to provide a contingent.

Paul Hazoume, oldest of Benin writers in French, died at Cotonou in April at the age of 90. He had been an unsuccessful candidate for the presidency of the republic in 1968.

On September 28 Pres. Mathieu Kerekou was formally converted to Islam in Libya in the presence of Libya's chief of state, Col. Muammar al-Qaddafi, and changed his first name to Ahmed. A major cooperation agreement between Libya and Benin was signed before Kerekou's return to Benin. (PHILIPPE DECRAENE)

BENIN

Education. (1978) Primary, pupils 338,949, teachers 6,048; secondary, pupils 55,654, teachers 1,215; vocational (1977), pupils 454, teachers (1975) 150; teacher training (1977), students 172, teachers (1975) 10; higher, students 2,641, teaching staff (1975) 153.

Finance. Monetary unit: CFA franc, with (Sept. 22, 1980) a parity of CFA Fr 50 to the French franc and a free rate of CFA Fr 210 to U.S. $1 (CFA Fr 504 = £1 sterling). Budget (1978 est.) balanced at CFA Fr 23,210,000,000.

Foreign Trade. (1978) Imports CFA Fr 60,210,000,000; exports CFA Fr 5,780,000,000. Import sources (1977): France 23%; U.K. 13%; West Germany 8%; The Netherlands 6%; U.S. 6%; Japan 5%. Export destinations: The Netherlands 28%; Japan 27%; France 24%. Main exports: cotton 36%; cocoa 30%; palm kernel oil 12%.

Agriculture. Production (in 000; metric tons; 1979): sorghum *c.* 70; corn (1978) *c.* 250; cassava (1978) *c.* 600; yams (1978) *c.* 590; dry beans *c.* 35; peanuts *c.* 64; palm kernels *c.* 70; palm oil *c.* 28; coffee *c.* 1; cotton, lint *c.* 7; fish catch (1978) *c.* 25. Livestock (in 000; 1978): cattle *c.* 730; sheep *c.* 850; goats *c.* 850; pigs *c.* 370.

Bhutan

A monarchy situated in the eastern Himalayas, Bhutan is bounded by China and India. Area: 46,100 sq km (17,800 sq mi). Pop. (1980 est.): 1,298,000, including Bhutia 60%, Nepalese 25%, and 15% tribal peoples. Official cap.: Thimphu (pop., approximately 10,000). Administrative cap.: Paro (population unavailable). Language: Dzongkha (official). Religion: approximately 75% Buddhist, 25% Hindu. Druk gyalpo (king) in 1980, Jigme Singye Wangchuk.

King Jigme Singye Wangchuk visited New Delhi, India, on Feb. 22–25, 1980, to counter reports of Bhutan's restiveness over the 1949 treaty whereby Bhutan would be guided by India in foreign affairs. The two sides agreed that the treaty served the common interests of Bhutan and India. Any border disputes between Bhutan and China, particularly over grazing rights, would be settled by negotiations.

After presenting his credentials on February 8, Om Pradhan, Bhutan's new representative at the UN, stated that its own troops would defend Bhutan; that there were no Indian troops there; that Bhutan sought friendly relations with all regional states and was particularly close to India, which gave economic aid; and that the dispute between China and India was believed to pose no threat to Bhutan.

India underwrote much of the cost of Bhutan's development program, notably of the Chukha hydroelectric project in the Wangchu Basin. The Rs 1,430,000,000 project (scheduled for completion by 1984) would have a capacity of 336 Mw; this would meet Bhutan's anticipated power requirements and provide a surplus for transmission to power-starved northeastern India. A Royal Bhutan Airline was projected to promote tourism, a new source of revenue (about Rs 4 million in 1979). (GOVINDAN UNNY)

BHUTAN

Education. (1979) Primary, pupils 28,913, teachers 655; secondary, pupils 2,019, teachers 439; vocational, pupils 259, teachers 23; teacher training, pupils 117, teachers 36; higher, pupils 419, teaching staff 36.

Finance and Trade. Monetary unit: ngultrum, at par with the Indian rupee (which is also in use), with (Sept. 22, 1980) a free rate of 7.69 ngultrums to U.S. $1 (18.49 ngultrums = £1 sterling). Budget (total; 1978–79): revenue 93 million ngultrums; expenditure 192 million ngultrums. Foreign trade (1979): imports *c.* $1.6 million; exports *c.* $750,000. Most external trade is with India. Main exports: timber, fruit and vegetables, cardamom.

Belize:
see Dependent States

Bicycling:
see Cycling

Billiard Games

Billiards. International three-cushion billiards received a boost in 1980 when the 35th world championships were followed by a world team tournament two weeks later. The world championships took place in Buenos Aires, Arg., May 5–13. Twelve players from nine countries included 43-year-old defending champion Raymond Ceulemans of Belgium, Yoshio Yoshihara and Nobuaki Kobayashi of Japan, Dieter Muller of West Germany, Christ Van der Smissen of The Netherlands, Luis Doyharzabal and Luis Martínez of Argentina, Galo Legarda of Ecuador, and Gabriel Fernández of Mexico. George Ashby of Illinois and Harry Sims of California represented the United States, and Muhammad al-Machak of Egypt completed the roster.

In the first round of the tournament temperatures in the building ranged from 50° to 80° F (10° to 27° C), hampering the players considerably. Only Van der Smissen played well, leading the contest with 60 points in 55 innings. By the end of the second day Ceulemans was showing his championship style with what proved to be the tournament highs of 35 and 39 innings for a 1.538 average. At the end of the eighth and final day, he had retained his title with a 1.460 average and high run of 15, compared with a 1.217 for runner-up Yoshihara.

Contestants for the world team tournament, held in Belgium two weeks later, consisted of four-person teams from Belgium and Japan, and a European group consisting of players from Austria, West Germany, France, and The Netherlands. By the eighth and final day the Belgian team, led by Ceulemans, had won the contest with 1,493 points. The European team finished second with 1,367 points, and Japan trailed with 1,294.

Pocket Billiards. Forty-eight of the nation's finest eight-ball teams gathered in Colorado Springs, Colo., for the Billiard Congress of America's All-American League championships during the first week of June. Representing the best of some 40 leagues and 7,000 players, the finalists promised formidable competition for the defending champions, the Tam O'Shanters Men of Colorado Springs and the Wheel-Inn Ladies of Billings, Mont. The two defending champions dominated the first three days of play. Under the captaincy of Charles Shootman, the Tams took every match handily, one by 115–0. In the final and deciding contest the Folsoms of Sacramento, Calif., were leading at the halfway point, but in the last game Shootman, playing a masterful series of stymies, defeated his opponent, Mike Whiting, to retain the crown for the Tams.

In the women's division the Wheel-Inn Ladies looked equally formidable. Only 2 of their 16 opponents appeared to have any chance, the Achilles Heel five from the California State Pool League and Burt's Girls from Colorado Springs. Led by Barbara Campbell, Burt's Girls gained momentum as the tourney progressed, and in the semifinals they defeated the California entry. On the final night, with the stands filled with their hometown followers, they faced the defending champions. The match seesawed back and forth, with the challengers ahead by 13 points, as the final contest began. The Wheel-Inns needed to win to force the match into a play-off, but they could not do so as the methodical play of Kathy Miao won the crown for herself and her teammates, Sherry Maldy, Patti Murphy, Vickie Gallimore, Shereen Strong, and Campbell.

In November the Billiard Congress of America national (singles) eight-ball championships were held in Columbus, Ohio. The maximum of 192 finalists were in attendance, all but the defending champions having earned their positions by winning local qualifying events. In the four-day tournament 1979 champion Jimmy Reid was eliminated at the halfway mark, but mother-to-be Gloria Walker, undefeated as the final match between herself and Billie Billing of Brooklyn, N.Y., got under way, appeared likely to become the first

BILLIARD CONGRESS OF AMERICA

Charlie Shootman, captain of the Tam O'Shanters of Colorado Springs, Colorado, sank the final eight ball that won the BCA All-American League championship for his team for the second straight year.

national champion to retain her title. Playing carefully, Walker won the first game, but then alternated wins with Billing until the score stood at four each. In the final game the table changed hands several times, as both players failed to run the balls. The outcome seemed settled when Billing missed a shot. Walker had to sink the eight ball, but was distracted by a difficult lie and failed to call the pocket for which she was shooting. The resulting foul cost her game, match, and title.

In the men's division the final match brought together two newcomers, Mike Massey of Chattanooga, Tenn., and Nick Varner of Owensboro, Ky. As the match progressed, each man revealed exceptional skill at escaping the stymies set up by the other. The last game in the "race to seven" (games won) began with the contestants tied at six each. With the table almost cleared Varner appeared to be the certain winner, needing only a fairly simple shot to grasp the title. He missed. Now Massey suddenly appeared to be the odds-on winner. Sinking his remaining balls, he shot at the eight ball, only to have it hang on the lip of the corner pocket. The reprieved and unbelieving Varner came back to the table to tap the ball in and accept the crown. (ROBERT E. GOODWIN)

[452.B.4.h.v]

Bolivia

Bolivia

A landlocked republic in central South America, Bolivia is bordered by Brazil, Paraguay, Argentina, Chile, and Peru. Area: 1,098,581 sq km (424,-165 sq mi). Pop. (1980 est.): 5,570,100, of whom more than 50% are Indian. Judicial cap.: Sucre (pop., 1979, 66,300). Administrative cap. and largest city: La Paz (pop., 1979, 696,800). Language: Spanish 78%, Quechua 15%, Aymara 7%. Religion (1978 est.): Roman Catholic 93.8%. Presidents in 1980, Lydia Gueiler Tejada until July 17 and, from July 18, Maj. Gen. Luis García Meza Tejada.

In July 1980 yet another military coup aborted the democratic process in Bolivia. On January 13 Congress had resolved that general and presidential elections would be held at midyear. Lydia Gueiler Tejada was confirmed in her post as interim president and was to govern with the support of the centre-right Movimiento Nacionalista Revolucionario (MNR), led by former president Víctor Paz Estenssoro, until a new president could be elected. During the early part of the year a steep rise in prices as a result of the 19% devaluation of the peso in November 1979 led to a series of strikes. Although rents and prices for the most important basic foods in the local diet were frozen and the urban minimum wage was increased to 3,500 pesos a month plus a compensatory lump-sum payment to lower-paid workers, the central labour union organization claimed much higher wages were needed and called a series of crippling strikes

BOLIVIA

Education. (1976) Primary, pupils 922,850, teachers (1975) 38,737; secondary, vocational, and teacher training, pupils 128,081, teachers (1975) 7,143; higher, students 51,-585, teaching staff (universities only) 2,307.

Finance. Monetary unit: peso boliviano, with (Sept. 22, 1980) a free rate of 24.93 pesos to U.S. $1 (59.93 pesos = £1 sterling). Gold, SDR's, and foreign exchange (June 1980) U.S. $179 million. Budget (1979 actual): revenue 8,384,000,000 pesos; expenditure 15,036,000,000 pesos. Gross national product (1979) 99,508,000,000 pesos. Money supply (April 1980) 10,830,000,000 pesos. Cost of living (La Paz; 1975 = 100; June 1980) 222.9.

Foreign Trade. (1979) Imports U.S. $1,011,000,000; exports U.S. $777 million. Import sources (1978): U.S. 28%; Japan 16%; Argentina 11%; Brazil 9%; West Germany 9%. Export destinations (1978): U.S. 31%; Argentina 17%; U.K. 12%; West Germany 5%. Main exports: tin 51%; natural gas 14%; silver 8%; crude oil 6%; zinc 5%; tungsten 5%.

Transport and Communications. Roads (1976) 38,085 km. Motor vehicles in use (1977): passenger 34,300; commercial (including buses) 25,400. Railways: (1979) 3,887 km; traffic (1977) 395 million passenger-km, freight 579 million net ton-km. Air traffic (1978): 700 million passenger-km; freight 43.3 million net ton-km. Telephones (Jan. 1978) 101,500. Radio receivers (Dec. 1977) 440,000. Television receivers (Dec. 1977) 49,000.

Agriculture. Production (in 000; metric tons; 1979): barley 62; corn (1978) 331; rice (1978) 89; cassava (1978) 306; potatoes *c.* 800; sugar, raw value (1978) *c.* 270; bananas *c.* 245; oranges *c.* 81; coffee *c.* 30; cotton, lint *c.* 14; rubber *c.* 5. Livestock (in 000; 1978): cattle 3,772; sheep 8,462; goats 2,946; pigs 1,351; horses *c.* 380; asses *c.* 760.

Industry. Production (in 000; metric tons; 1978): cement 252; crude oil (1979) 1,330; natural gas (cu m) 1,820,-000; petroleum products (1977) *c.* 1,180; electricity (kw-hr) *c.* 1,150,000; tin 16; lead ore 18; antimony 14; tungsten (oxide content) 3.2; zinc 59; copper 3.3; silver (troy oz) *c.* 6,000.

Tanks prowled the streets of La Paz after a coup staged by the Army in July. Maj. Gen. Luis García Meza Tejada became the new Bolivian chief of state.

MICHEL PHILIPPOT—SYGMA

Biographies:
see People of the Year

Biological Sciences:
see Life Sciences

Birth Statistics:
see Demography

Boating:
see Rowing; Sailing; Water Sports

Bobsledding:
see Winter Sports

in the banking, transport, and agricultural sectors.

Despite violence from the right, elections were held as planned on June 29. With 90% of the votes counted, Hernán Siles Zuazo of the left-wing Unidad Democrática y Popular (UDP) led, followed by Paz Estenssoro. The presidential election was to be decided by a joint session of Congress on August 4, as no candidate had obtained half of the overall poll. However, the newly appointed Army commander, Maj. Gen. Luis García Meza Tejada (*see* BIOGRAPHIES), led a coup on July 17, deposing interim president Gueiler and setting aside the election result. A military junta took over the government and arrested and reportedly tortured leaders of the political parties and labour unions. At the same time, all university teachers and magistrates were dismissed, and a state of siege was declared. The U.S. cut off all economic and military assistance and recalled its ambassador, while Bolivia's Andean Group partners (Colombia, Ecuador, Peru, and Venezuela) protested against the annulment of the elections; Ecuador broke off diplomatic relations. The U.K. canceled its £19 million mining assistance program (the largest British aid scheme in the area), and West Germany and Belgium reduced their aid. Meanwhile, Argentina, Brazil, Uruguay, Paraguay, Chile, Taiwan, Israel, and South Africa recognized the regime. Argentina granted food and financial assistance; there were reports that Argentine advisers had assisted in planning and executing the coup. The U.S. Department of State alleged that some of Bolivia's new rulers were connected with the nation's flourishing traffic in cocaine, which further damaged the regime's credibility.

Economic performance in 1980 declined from its low 1979 level. Petroleum production fell by 8% to less than 30,000 bbl a day, necessitating higher imports of crude oil from Argentina. The eventual supply of Bolivian natural gas to Uruguay and Chile was discussed. (MICHAEL WOOLLER)

Botswana

A landlocked republic of southern Africa and a member of the Commonwealth of Nations, Botswana is bounded by South Africa, a part of Bophuthatswana, South West Africa/Namibia, Zambia, and Zimbabwe. Area: 576,000 sq km (222,000 sq mi). Pop. (1980 est.): 819,000, almost 99% African. Cap. and largest city: Gaborone (pop., 1979 est., 49,600). Language: English (official) and Setswana. Religion: Christian 60%; animist. Presidents in 1980, Sir Seretse Khama until July 13 and, from July 18, Quett Masire.

The death of Pres. Sir Seretse Khama (*see* OBITUARIES) on July 13 left Botswana without the founding figure who had led the nation since it achieved independence in 1966. He was succeeded by the vice-president, Quett Masire (*see* BIOGRAPHIES), following a secret ballot on July 18. President Masire appointed Lenyeletse M. Seretse as vice-president and Peter S. Mmusi to take over the portfolio of finance and development planning, previously held by Masire himself.

BOTSWANA

Education. (1979) Primary, pupils 156,664, teachers 4,870; secondary, pupils 16,736, teachers 778; vocational, pupils 2,106, teachers 224; teacher training, students 696, teachers 52; higher, students 1,052, teaching staff 129.

Finance and Trade. Monetary unit: pula, with (Sept. 22, 1980) a free rate of 0.77 pula to U.S. $1 (1.85 pula = £1 sterling). Budget (1979–80 actual): revenue 166.4 million pula; expenditure 197.2 million pula. Foreign trade (1979): imports 410.5 million pula (85% from South Africa in 1978); exports 353.1 million pula (51% to Europe, 28% to U.S., 14% to South Africa in 1978). Main exports: diamonds 52%; meat and products 20%; copper-nickel ore 17%.

Agriculture. Production (in 000; metric tons; 1978): sorghum *c.* 45; corn *c.* 45; millet *c.* 5; peanuts *c.* 7; beef and veal *c.* 41. Livestock (in 000; 1978): cattle *c.* 3,000; sheep *c.* 440; goats *c.* 1,150; chickens *c.* 600.

Industry. Production (in 000; metric tons; 1978): coal 315; diamonds (metric carats; 1977) 2,660; copper ore (metal content) *c.* 15; nickel ore (metal content) *c.* 16; electricity (kw-hr) 408,000.

Botswana

Another event of great significance to Botswana was Zimbabwe's independence on April 18. This released energies that had been concentrated upon Zimbabwe for years, allowing refugees to return there and ending cross-border raids while at the same time opening alternative options of trade and communications with South Africa.

In 1979 drought and foot-and-mouth disease affected meat production, but revenue from mining, especially diamonds, accounted for 51% of the nation's total and was substantially above 1978. Major government expenditures were scheduled for road building and investment in the new diamond mine at Jwaneng. At Khale a satellite tracking station for telephone communications went into operation. (GUY ARNOLD)

Bowling

Tenpin Bowling. WORLD. In December 1979 a total of 321 bowlers from 30 nations competed in the ninth world bowling championships of the Fédération Internationale des Quilleurs (FIQ) at Manila, Philippines. For the first time the Philippines became top nation in the championships with four first-place gold medals and one second-place silver. Especially notable was Lita de la Rosa of the Philippines. She had already won the Bowling World Cup, recognized as the most important annual singles event, in Bogotá, Colombia, in 1978. Now in Manila she also won the gold medal in individual masters all-events. No individual had ever won both titles before. In addition, she won the singles, teamed up with Bong Coo (Phil.) to win the doubles, and, with Bong Coo and Nellie Castillo (Phil.), finished second in the trios event.

In the men's world championships Gerry Bugden (England) became the reigning king, beating Philippe Dubois (France), winner of the 1979 World Cup, in the masters all-events, with a score of 379–372 in the two-game grand final. In the opening matches of the tournament Bugden defeated Finland's 19-year-old Mikko Kaartinen 195–192 and then Malaysia's J. B. Koo 201–181 to earn his shot at the top-seeded Dubois. In the five-man event Australia won its first world title,

Bonds:
see Stock Exchanges

Books:
see Art Sales; Literature; Publishing

Bophuthatswana:
see South Africa

Botanical Gardens:
see Zoos and Botanical Gardens

Botany:
see Life Sciences

Lita de la Rosa of the Philippines won first place in a world bowling championship match held in Manila.

rolling 5,892 to leave Great Britain in second place (5,793). Another nation won its first world title in the three-man event, as Malaysia scored 3,582 to edge out the U.S. (3,564). A second gold medal was won for Australia by its doubles partners, Eric Thompson and Ronald Powell, who totaled 2,460. The runner-up was a pair from South Korea, who won their nation's first bowling medals; the U.S. pair finished third. The men's singles was won by Ollie Ongtawco (Phil.) with 1,278; Rogelio Felice of Venezuela finished second at 1,265, and Michio Matsubara of Japan placed third.

In the women's world championships Lita de la Rosa won the six-game singles (1,220); in the final masters all-events matches she first defeated Yvonne Nilsson of Sweden 224–200, and then in the grand final, over two games, she beat Daniela Gruber of West Germany 416–331. The U.S. won the gold medals in the five-woman and three-woman events, with 5,667 and 3,419, respectively. The runners-up were West Germany (5,577) and the Philippines (3,331). The women's doubles was won by Bong Coo and Lita de la Rosa, with a total score of 2,348. Second place was won by Finland. (YRJÖ SARAHETE)

UNITED STATES. The American Bowling Congress tournament has been dominated by U.S. bowlers throughout its 77-year history, but this reign almost was interrupted in the 1980 meet at Louisville, Ky. Mats Karlsson of Stockholm took the lead in the Regular Division all-events standings on the sixth day of the tournament with a nine-game total of 2,073, and his score remained the best until the next to last day of the 80-day spectacle. Then Steve Fehr from Cincinnati, Ohio, totaled 2,076 to win the all-events honour.

Other ABC Regular Division winners included: team, Stroh's Beer, Detroit, 3,115; singles, Mike Eaton, Grand Rapids, Mich., 782; doubles, Ron Thacker and Bob Bures, Cleveland, Ohio, 1,378.

In the Women's International Bowling Congress (WIBC) tournament in Seattle, Wash., the biggest surprise occurred in Division I singles, where Cheri Mason of Lansing, Ill., bowled the highest series of her life, 651, to win the championship. The best previous score that the 24-year-old Mason had rolled was 457. Other Division I champions included: team, Walker's Body Shop, Aurora, Ill., 2,703; doubles, Katherine Alexander and Marie Fouche, Los Angeles, 1,176; all-events, Verida Morris, Del City, Okla., 1,711. The professional Open Division winners were: team, All Japan, Tokyo, 3,014; singles, Betty Morris, Stockton, Calif., 674; doubles, Carole Lee, Hempstead, N.Y., and Dawn Raddatz, East Northport, N.Y., 1,247; all-events, Cheryl Robinson, Van Nuys, Calif., 1,848. Donna Adamek of Duarte, Calif., won the WIBC Queens tournament for the second successive year, defeating Cheryl Robinson 213–165 in the title game.

For the first time in many years there was no dominant figure among the male professionals. Mark Roth, the Professional Bowlers Association (PBA) bowler of the year in 1977–78–79, did not win a PBA tournament until October, although many strong performances had placed him second in the late season prize standings with $93,000. Wayne Webb of Rehoboth, Mass., led with $98,-000.

Neil Burton, little known younger brother of long-time professional star Nelson Burton, Jr., won the ABC Masters tournament. In a one-game semifinal match Neil defeated his brother 205–191, and in the title game he defeated Roth 204–192 to take the $25,000 first prize.

Duckpins. In the U.S. championship tournament the winners in the men's division were: team, Adams Five, Alexandria, Va., 2,089; singles, Jim Dion, Westport, Mass., 597; doubles, Doug Gosewisch and Kent Schwartz, Glen Burnie, Md., 989. Champions in the women's division included: singles, Brenda Wachtell, Hagerstown, Md., 500; doubles, Dawn Healey and Bonnie Myers, Baltimore, Md., 875. No women's team event was held. (JOHN J. ARCHIBALD)

Lawn Bowls. In January 1980 the fourth world lawn bowls championships were staged at Frankston, Melbourne, Australia. David Bryant (England) won the singles with Australia's John Snell second. Australia's Alf Sandercock and Peter Rheuben won the pairs; England's Jim Hobday, Tony Allcock, and Bryant the triples; and Hong Kong the fours, from Scotland. At the world indoor championships at Coatbridge, Scotland, Bryant won the singles.

In 1980 England abolished the distinction between amateur and professional bowlers. The English Indoor Bowling Association moved first, authorizing payment of cash as of April 26, and Bryant collected £2,000 for winning the Teletext Tournament at the Sole Bay Indoor Club, Southwold, Suffolk. The English Bowling Association also accepted open bowls at the start of the 1980 outdoor season. It remained to be seen what response the International Bowling Board, not scheduled to meet until 1982, would make. In the meantime many British bowlers were expected to preserve their amateur status for the 1982 Commonwealth Games. On August 22 the English Professional Bowlers and Coaches Association was formed, with Bryant as president.

(C. M. JONES)

Brazil

A federal republic in eastern South America, Brazil is bounded by the Atlantic Ocean and all the countries of South America except Ecuador and Chile. Area: 8,512,000 sq km (3,286,500 sq mi). Pop (1980 est.): 123,032,000. Principal cities (pop., 1979 est.): Brasília (cap.; federal district) 978,600; São Paulo 11,859,900; Rio de Janeiro 9,473,400. Language: Portuguese. Religion: Roman Catholic 90.3%. President in 1980, Gen. João Baptista de Oliveira Figueiredo.

Domestic Affairs. After his inauguration in 1979, Pres. João Baptista de Oliveira Figueiredo found himself confronted with a rash of labour strikes that threatened to thwart his efforts to abate inflation and to continue the democratization process initiated by his predecessor. The most serious strike, beginning in March 1979, was that of 160,000 metalworkers in the highly industrialized suburbs of São Paulo. Among their demands, the strikers asked for a 78% increase in wages. This demand was considered excessive at a time when the authorities were desperately trying to control inflation, said to be running at the rate of 65% a year. Government troops seized the metalworkers' union headquarters and arrested some 1,600 workers and supporters of the strike. The situation became tense, and bloodshed seemed imminent.

At this time some of the opposition political leaders visited the authorities, the religious leaders, and the strikers, urging them to accept an accommodation. President Figueiredo was ready to accept a compromise. Eventually, an arrangement was reached under which the strike was postponed for a 45-day negotiating period. An agreement was eventually reached, but labour troubles continued among the São Paulo metalworkers throughout 1979 and 1980.

Edgar Moura—Gamma/Liaison

Brazil

Many thousands of São Paulo's striking metalworkers met daily at the São Bernardo football stadium before the government closed it down and arrested the union's leaders.

On Aug. 22, 1979, Congress approved a bill granting amnesty and restoring political rights to all who had lost them since the national amnesty of 1961, except for those convicted of acts of terrorism, assault, kidnapping, or similar crimes. President Figueiredo signed the measure into law six days later.

In October 1979 Figueiredo sent a bill to Con-

WARREN HOGE—THE NEW YORK TIMES

Thousands of prospectors descended on Serra Pelada, near Marabá in the Brazilian Amazon, to exploit newly discovered gold deposits found there. The use of pickaxes and shovels is unchanged from 18th-century practices.

Boxing:
see Combat Sports

gress providing for the reform of the nation's system of political parties, including the extinction of the two existing parties and establishment of new ones. The bill was bitterly criticized by many, and more than 500 amendments were introduced in Congress. Eventually, on Nov. 22, 1979, the new Party Reform Bill was passed, and it was signed by the president a few days later. Political leaders were to have eight months to organize their parties under detailed regulations published by the Superior Electoral Tribunal in February 1980. Five new political groupings were eventually formed: the Social Democratic Party (PDS), backing the government; the Brazilian Democratic Movement Party (PMDB), liberal, mostly composed of members from the old opposition party; the Popular Party (PP), mildly conservative; the Brazilian Labour Party (PTB), with elements from the old Labour Party; and the Party of the Workers (PT), of more independent labour tendencies.

BRAZIL

Education. (1977) Primary, pupils (est.) 20,340,577, teachers (est.) 994,031; secondary, vocational, and teacher training, pupils 2,391,465, teachers 168,451; higher, students 1,159,046, teaching staff 95,758.

Finance. Monetary unit: cruzeiro, with a free rate (Sept. 22, 1980) of 56.44 cruzeiros to U.S. $1 (135.65 cruzeiros = £1 sterling). Gold, SDR's, and foreign exchange (April 1980) U.S. $6,695,000,000. Budget (1979 actual): revenue 509,843,000,000 cruzeiros; expenditure 507,547,000,000 cruzeiros. Gross national product (1979) 5,358,400,000,000 cruzeiros. Money supply (March 1980) 792,890,000,000 cruzeiros. Cost of living (São Paulo; 1975 = 100; May 1980) 713.1.

Foreign Trade. (1979) Imports *c.* 508 billion cruzeiros; exports 393,531,000,000 cruzeiros. Import sources: U.S. 18%; Iraq 14%; Saudi Arabia 10%; West Germany 7%; Japan 6%; Argentina 5%. Export destinations (1978): U.S. 23%; West Germany 8%; The Netherlands 6%; Japan 5%. Main exports (1978): coffee 18%; soybeans and products 12%; machinery 9%; cocoa 7%; iron ore 6%.

Transport and Communications. Roads (1978) 1,544,684 km. Motor vehicles in use (1978): passenger 7,704,100; commercial 884,200. Railways: (1976) 30,300 km; traffic (1977) 11,699,000,000 passenger-km, freight 60,721,000,000 net ton-km. Air traffic (1978): 12,544,000,000 passenger-km; freight 591.9 million net ton-km. Shipping (1979): merchant vessels 100 gross tons and over 585; gross tonnage 4,007,498. Shipping traffic (1978): goods loaded 87,517,000 metric tons, unloaded 69,790,000 metric tons. Telephones (Dec. 1977) 4,708,000. Radio receivers (Dec. 1975) 16,980,000. Television receivers (Dec. 1977) 11 million.

Agriculture. Production (in 000; metric tons; 1979): wheat *c.* 2,924; corn 16,309; rice 7,589; cassava (1978) 25,358; potatoes 2,149; sweet potatoes (1978) *c.* 1,930; sugar, raw value *c.* 7,200; tomatoes *c.* 1,500; dry beans 2,187; soybeans *c.* 10,700; coffee 1,272; cocoa 298; bananas *c.* 6,424; oranges 9,882; cotton, lint 575; sisal *c.* 210; tobacco 409; rubber *c.* 29; beef and veal *c.* 2,106; pork *c.* 850; fish catch (1978) *c.* 858; timber (cu m; 1978) *c.* 160,464. Livestock (in 000; 1979): cattle *c.* 90,000; pigs *c.* 36,000; sheep *c.* 18,000; goats *c.* 7,400; horses (1978) *c.* 6,000; chickens *c.* 320,000.

Industry. Fuel and power (in 000; metric tons; 1979): crude oil 8,309; coal *c.* 4,640; natural gas (cu m) *c.* 2,490,000; manufactured gas (cu m; 1978) *c.* 500,000; electricity (kw-hr) 122,840,000 (93% hydroelectric in 1977). Production (in 000; metric tons; 1979): cement 24,871; pig iron (1978) 10,010; crude steel 13,762; iron ore (68% metal content) 59,676; bauxite (1978) *c.* 1,400; manganese ore (metal content; 1977) *c.* 900; gold (troy oz; 1978) *c.* 400; wood pulp (1977) 1,649; paper (1977) 2,253; fertilizers (nutrient content; 1978–79) nitrogenous *c.* 273, phosphate *c.* 1,186; passenger cars (including assembly; units) 553; commercial vehicles (units) 574. Merchant vessels launched (100 gross tons and over; 1979) 665,000 gross tons.

Brazilian Literature: *see* Literature

Bridge: *see* Contract Bridge

Bridges: *see* Engineering Projects

British Commonwealth: *see* Commonwealth of Nations; *articles on the various member states*

Brunei: *see* Dependent States

Buddhism: *see* Religion

Building and Construction Industry: *see* Engineering Projects; Industrial Review

In his message to Congress in March 1980, Figueiredo declared himself willing to discuss all political problems with opposition leaders, including the postponing of the municipal elections scheduled for Nov. 15, 1980. On September 5 Congress voted to postpone the elections for two years, over the protests of opposition party members. This extended the terms of about 44,000 municipal officeholders until 1982.

The Economy. Since the inception of his administration, President Figueiredo had insisted that the struggle against inflation was the most important problem facing the nation. Unexpected increases in the price of imported oil, the paralyzing effect of the labour strikes, the drought in the northeastern states, the frosts that destroyed the crops of many coffee plantations during mid-1979, and above all the financing of Brazil's huge foreign debt of U.S. $55 billion had brought the country to a precarious situation economically. In a speech to the National Council of Economic Development, the president declared that the country would have to adopt a "war economy" to face the situation. By August 1979 the annual inflation rate was estimated at 58%.

In August 1979 Antônio Delfim Netto, an experienced economist who had served in important capacities during previous administrations, was appointed minister of planning, with broad powers to carry into effect stringent economic policies adopted by the administration. These included the control of prices. On Dec. 7, 1979, the president announced a new set of economic measures, including cutting many government subsidies to private industry and some to agriculture, reducing unnecessary government regulation of the private sector, and devaluing the exchange rate of the cruzeiro by 30%. It was expected that the new measures would result in a temporary increase in the inflation rate, but that they also would help to increase exports and decrease imports. At the end of 1979 inflation was running at the rate of 77.2%.

Because the rising cost of imported oil contributed most to inflation, the administration took steps to cut down such imports by promoting the use of alcohol distilled from sugarcane, cassava, and other tropical plants as an automotive fuel. By 1981 about 18% of Brazil's new automobiles were to be built with engines adapted to burning pure alcohol.

Foreign Affairs. In May 1980 President Figueiredo visited Buenos Aires at the invitation of Pres. Rafael Videla of Argentina. The visit was the first by a Brazilian head of state to Argentina in 40 years. Agreements were signed for increased cooperation between the two nations, marking a decisive thaw in their previously cool economic relations.

Pope John Paul II arrived in Brasília on June 30, 1980, for a 12-day visit. On his arrival the pope called upon the Brazilian people "to build an exemplary society" overcoming "inequalities with justice and harmony." The visit was considered a great success. It had been scheduled to coincide with the closing of a national conference of the Brazilian bishops, held in the northeastern city of Fortaleza. (RAUL D'EÇA)

Bulgaria

A people's republic of Europe, Bulgaria is situated on the eastern Balkan Peninsula along the Black Sea, bordered by Romania, Yugoslavia, Greece, and Turkey. Area: 110,912 sq km (42,823 sq mi). Pop. (1979 est.): 8,805,500, including 85.3% Bulgarians (but excluding some 210,000 Macedonians classified as Bulgarian according to official statistics), 8.5% Turks, 2.6% Gypsies, and 2.5% Macedonians. Cap. and largest city: Sofia (pop., 1979 est., 1,031,600). Language: chiefly Bulgarian. Religion: official sources classify 35.5% of the population as religious, although this figure is suspect since the regime promotes atheism. Of those who practice religion, it is estimated that 85% are Bulgarian Orthodox, 13% Muslim, 0.8% Jewish, 0.7% Roman Catholic, and 0.5% Protestant, Gregorian-Armenian, and others. First secretary of the Bulgarian Communist Party and chairman of the State Council in 1980, Todor Zhivkov; chairman of the Council of Ministers (premier), Stanko Todorov.

During 1980 preparations for the launching of a Soviet-Bulgarian spacecraft named Bulgaria 1300 neared completion. The launching into Earth orbit was planned for 1981, when Bulgaria would celebrate 1,300 years of statehood. (In 681 the first Bulgar state, founded south of the Danube by Khan Asparukh, was officially recognized by the Byzantine emperor Constantine IV.)

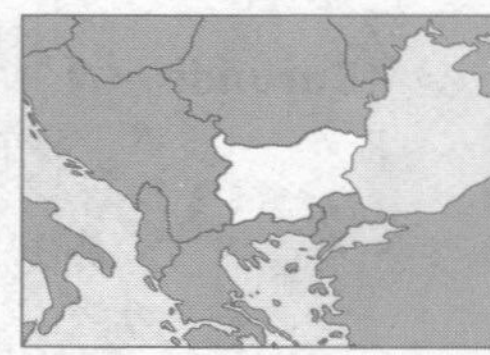

Bulgaria

On June 3–7, 1980, a Bulgarian delegation led by the Communist Party first secretary and head of state, Todor Zhivkov, paid an official visit to Romania. Among the various agreements signed by Zhivkov and Romanian Pres. Nicolae Ceausescu, probably the most important was the protocol on diversion of the Danube River as the first stage of building the Turnu Magurele-Nikopol hydroelectric complex. The diversion was necessary because of the difference in height between the Bulgarian and Romanian banks of the Danube at the selected site. Preliminary agreements concerning the project had been signed in Sofia in 1972 and 1977.

Zhivkov visited Soviet Pres. Leonid Brezhnev on Aug. 7, 1980. A joint communiqué stated that the meeting took place in "an atmosphere of cordiality and was marked by complete identity of views on all the questions discussed."

Legislation was enacted in March to allow joint enterprises to be set up in Bulgaria by Bulgarian and foreign firms. Previously, such enterprises had been permissible only in third countries.

(K. M. SMOGORZEWSKI)

BULGARIA

Education. (1978–79) Primary, pupils 973,007, teachers 49,958; secondary, pupils 102,872, teachers 7,585; vocational, pupils 268,257, teachers 19,220; higher, students 115,125, teaching staff 15,578.

Finance. Monetary unit: lev, with (Sept. 22, 1980) a free exchange rate of 0.84 lev to U.S. $1 (2.03 lev = £1 sterling). Budget (1979 est.): revenue 10,873,000,000 leva; expenditure 10,853,000,000 leva.

Foreign Trade. (1979) Imports 7,306,000,000 leva; exports 7,675,000,000 leva. Main import sources: U.S.S.R. 59%; East Germany 7%. Main export destinations: U.S.S.R. 52%; East Germany 6%. Main exports (1978): machinery 35%; tobacco and cigarettes 9%; transport equipment 9%; chemicals 7%; fruit and vegetables 7%; iron and steel 5%; wines and spirits 5%. Tourism: visitors (1978) 4,867,000; gross receipts (1975) U.S. $230 million.

Transport and Communications. Roads (1976) 36,091 km (including 20 km expressways). Motor vehicles in use (1976): passenger *c.* 218,000; commercial (including buses) *c.* 47,000. Railways: (1978) 4,341 km; traffic (1979) 6,850,000,000 passenger-km, freight 17,653,000,000 net ton-km. Air traffic (1978): 610 million passenger-km; freight *c.* 8.4 million net ton-km. Navigable inland waterways (1973) 471 km. Shipping (1979): merchant vessels 100 gross tons and over 191; gross tonnage 1,150,299. Telephones (Jan. 1978) 946,023. Radio licenses (Dec. 1977) 2,235,000. Television licenses (Dec. 1977) 1,584,000.

Agriculture. Production (in 000; metric tons; 1979): wheat *c.* 3,000; corn *c.* 3,300; barley *c.* 1,600; potatoes *c.* 400; sunflower seed *c.* 400; tomatoes *c.* 870; grapes *c.* 1,200; apples *c.* 320; tobacco *c.* 110; meat *c.* 646. Livestock (in 000; Jan. 1979): sheep 10,105; cattle 1,763; goats 374; pigs 3,772; horses (1978) 126; asses (1978) 330; chickens 38,331.

Industry. Fuel and power (in 000; metric tons; 1979): lignite 27,920; coal 280; crude oil (1978) 250; natural gas (cu m; 1977) 10,000; electricity (kw-hr) 32,474,000. Production (in 000; metric tons; 1979): iron ore (33% metal content) 2,100; manganese ore (metal content; 1977) 11; copper ore (metal content; 1977) 57; lead ore (metal content; 1978) 117; zinc ore (1977) 87; pig iron 1,450; crude steel 2,483; cement 5,402; sulfuric acid 998; nitric acid (1977) 892; soda ash (1978) 1,294; fertilizers (nutrient content; 1978) nitrogenous 685, phosphate 283; cotton yarn 85; cotton fabrics (m) 347,000; wool yarn 34; woolen fabrics (m) 34,000. Merchant vessels launched (100 gross tons and over; 1979) 171,000 gross tons.

Burma

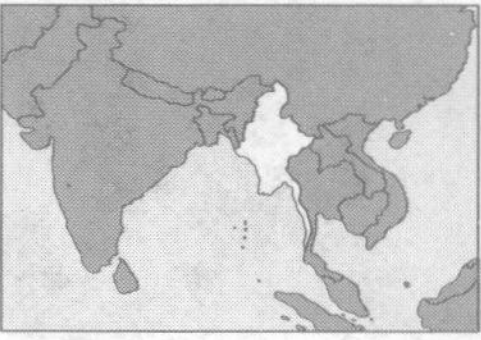

Burma

A republic of Southeast Asia, Burma is bordered by Bangladesh, India, China, Laos, Thailand, the Bay of Bengal, and the Andaman Sea. Area: 676,577 sq km (261,288 sq mi). Pop. (1980 est.): 35,289,000. Cap. and largest city: Rangoon (pop., 1980 est., 2,186,000). Language: Burmese. Religion (1977): Buddhist 80%. Chairman of the State Council in 1980, U Ne Win; prime minister, U Maung Maung Kha.

Attempts in 1980 by such neighbours as Thailand and Singapore to persuade Burma to join the Association of Southeast Asian Nations (ASEAN) were not successful, as Pres. U Ne Win preferred to maintain his completely neutral policy. Singapore's Deputy Prime Minister Sinnathamby Rajaratnam and Thai Prime Minister Prem Tinsulanond held talks in Rangoon seeking support against what they called the "growing belligerency and expansionism" of Vietnam. While sympathizing with the plight of Cambodia, Ne Win believed ASEAN was developing into an anti-Communist bastion and to join it would compromise Burma's independent foreign policy.

After the 1979 anticorruption drive among members of the ruling Burma Socialist Program Party (BSPP) Central Committee, Ne Win introduced improved retirement benefits for elected representatives. He held the view that BSPP officials would be less corruptible if their future was assured.

Except for Japan, which continued to provide assistance in agriculture and oil exploration, aid from advanced countries was slow in coming. One bright aspect of the economy was a slight surplus

BURMA

Education. (1978–79) Primary, pupils 3,731,160, teachers 84,593; secondary, pupils 924,739, teachers 31,433; vocational, pupils 9,576, teachers 786; teacher training, students 5,163, teachers 367; higher, students 112,671, teaching staff 3,922.

Finance. Monetary unit: kyat, with (Sept. 22, 1980) a free rate of 6.71 kyats to U.S. $1 (16.12 kyats = £1 sterling). Gold, SDR's, and foreign exchange (June 1980) U.S. $281 million. Budget (1977–78 est.): revenue 19,172,000,000 kyats; expenditure 20,886,000,000 kyats.

Foreign Trade. (1979) Imports 2,116,000,000 kyats; exports 2,548,800,000 kyats. Import sources (1977): Japan 25%; Singapore 12%; U.K. 8%; West Germany 7%; South Korea 6%; China 6%; U.S. 6%. Export destinations (1977): Singapore 15%; Indonesia 14%; Bangladesh 14%; Sri Lanka 10%; Japan 9%; Hong Kong 6%; Mauritius 5%. Main exports: rice 36%; teak 27%; fruits and vegetables *c.* 7%.

Transport and Communications. Roads (1977) 22,402 km. Motor vehicles in use (1977): passenger 38,600; commercial (including buses) 41,300. Railways: (1978) 4,473 km; traffic (1978–79) 3,665,000,000 passenger-km, freight 492 million net ton-km. Air traffic (1978): 185 million passenger-km; freight 1.4 million net ton-km. Shipping (1979): merchant vessels 100 gross tons and over 78; gross tonnage 64,400. Telephones (Jan. 1978) 32,600. Radio licenses (Dec. 1977) 693,000.

Agriculture. Production (in 000; metric tons; 1979): rice *c.* 10,000; dry beans *c.* 185; onions 106; plantains (1978) *c.* 448; sesame seed *c.* 110; peanuts *c.* 455; cotton, lint *c.* 16; jute *c.* 85; tobacco *c.* 51; rubber *c.* 15; fish catch (1978) 540; timber (cu m; 1978) 3,976. Livestock (in 000; March 1979): cattle *c.* 7,560; buffalo *c.* 1,750; pigs *c.* 2,200; goats *c.* 575; sheep *c.* 215; chickens *c.* 17,100.

Industry. Production (in 000; metric tons; 1979): crude oil *c.* 1,540; electricity (excluding most industrial production; kw-hr) *c.* 1,050,000; cement *c.* 360; lead concentrates (metal content; 1978–79) 5.2; zinc concentrates (metal content) 5.5; tin concentrates (metal content) 0.7; tungsten concentrates (oxide content) *c.* 0.6; nitrogenous fertilizers (nutrient content; 1978–79) 58; cotton yarn 14.

of 50,000 metric tons in rice output, achieved by better utilization of the U.S. $34 million aid provided by the International Development Association.

The amnesty offered in late May to former Burmese leaders who had fled abroad was accepted by U Nu, former prime minister, who left central India for Rangoon in July to be a Buddhist monk. The campaign against insurgent groups was assisted when both Indian and Chinese authorities tightened border security and denied sanctuary to Burmese rebels. (GOVINDAN UNNY)

Burundi

Burundi

A republic of eastern Africa, Burundi is bordered by Zaire, Rwanda, and Tanzania. Area: 27,834 sq km (10,747 sq mi). Pop. (1979 census): 4,110,000, mainly Hutu, Tutsi, and Twa. Cap. and largest city: Bujumbura (pop., 1979 census, 151,000). Language: Rundi and French. Religion: Roman Catholic 53%; animist 38%; Protestant 7%; Muslim 2%. President in 1980, Col. Jean-Baptiste Bagaza.

In 1980 there were further signs that under Pres. Jean-Baptiste Bagaza the country was moving away from the ethnicism and political intrigues that had characterized life during the previous regime. The year 1979 ended with the first national congress of the Union for National Progess (UPRONA), the only legal political party; it chose Bagaza as sole presidential candidate. The Central Committee took over power from the Supreme Revolutionary Council of army officers, some of

BURUNDI

Education. (1977–78) Primary, pupils 142,234, teachers 4,379; secondary, pupils 6,663, teachers 425; vocational, pupils 1,694, teachers (1975–76) 192; teacher training, students 6,031, teachers 209; higher, students 1,447, teaching staff (1975–76) 223.

Finance. Monetary unit: Burundi franc, with (Sept. 22, 1980) an official rate of BurFr 90 to U.S. $1 (free rate of BurFr 216.2 = £1 sterling). Gold, SDR's, and foreign exchange (June 1980) U.S. $103.9 million. Budget (1979 actual): revenue BurFr 11,881,200,000; expenditure BurFr 11,797,200,000.

Foreign Trade. (1979) Imports BurFr 13,721,000,000; exports BurFr 9,438,000,000. Import sources (1978): Belgium-Luxembourg 23%; West Germany 10%; France 9%; Japan 7%; Iran 7%; Kenya 7%. Export destinations: U.S. 47%; China 6%. Main exports (1978): coffee 86%; cotton 6%.

Agriculture. Production (in 000; metric tons; 1979): sorghum *c.* 110; corn *c.* 140; cassava (1978) *c.* 936; potatoes (1978) *c.* 230; sweet potatoes (1978) *c.* 912; dry beans *c.* 165; bananas *c.* 967; coffee *c.* 24; tea *c.* 2; cotton, lint *c.* 2. Livestock (in 000; Dec. 1977): cattle *c.* 808; sheep *c.* 324; goats *c.* 578; pigs *c.* 49.

whom were included in the Central Committee. The 650 congress delegates discussed the efforts of Bagaza and his government to promote national reconciliation and develop the state through communal farming.

Bold economic reforms were initiated during the year, including the abolition of serfdom and the nationalization of all land. Agriculture accounted for 95% of economic activity, and major customers for Burundi's exports were the U.S., West Germany, Belgium-Luxembourg, France, and Rwanda. At the end of 1979 a European Investment Bank loan for 500,000 units of account was provided for studies of industrial, mining, and tourist projects. The International Monetary Fund also provided a loan of 2,392,000 SDR's following a decline in Burundi's coffee exports, their value having dropped one-third in 1979. (GUY ARNOLD)

Cambodia

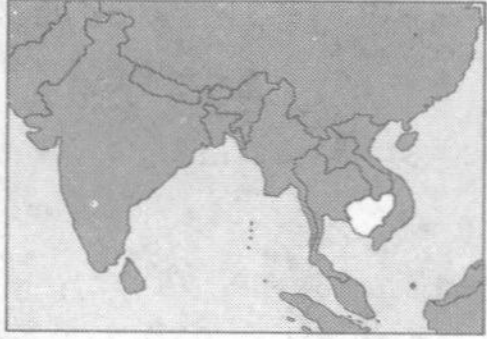

Cambodia

A republic of Southeast Asia, Cambodia (officially Kampuchea) is the southwest part of the Indochinese Peninsula, on the Gulf of Thailand, bordered by Vietnam, Laos, and Thailand. Area: 181,035 sq km (69,898 sq mi). Pop. (1979 est.): between 4.5 million and 5 million according to official figures. It is estimated to comprise: Khmer 93%; Vietnamese 4%; Chinese 3%. Cap.: Phnom Penh (urban area pop., 1979 est., 270,000). Language: Khmer (official) and French. Religion: Buddhist. President of the People's Revolutionary Council in 1980, Heng Samrin.

In 1980, a year after Hanoi-backed guerrillas headed by Heng Samrin overturned Cambodia's first Communist regime led by Pol Pot, events in the country remained centred around the legitimacy of the government. The ousted Pol Pot won another recognition vote at the UN in October, helped by an unprecedented lobbying campaign by the non-Communist countries of Southeast Asia, which resolutely opposed Vietnam's invasion of Cambodia in 1978–79. Phnom Penh said it would consider any UN decision on the matter "null and void." Vietnam for its part maintained

SIPA PRESS/BLACK STAR

Massive relief shipments of grain piled up in warehouses at the Cambodian port of Kompong Som while authorities struggled to deliver it to the needy interior of the country.

that events in Cambodia were "irreversible" and that its troops would be withdrawn from the country only after the "threat" posed by China to both Vietnam and Cambodia was over.

The Heng Samrin side scored a major point when India recognized it in July. The Indian move was criticized by Southeast Asian countries. Nonetheless, there was a growing awareness among those voting for Pol Pot that the fallen regime's genocidal record during the three and a half years it was in power would eventually prove its undoing. The regime's leaders led a drive to present a new profile. Pol Pot himself remained out of sight, the limelight moving to Premier Khieu Samphan and Foreign Minister Ieng Sary.

In August Khieu Samphan invited foreign journalists to a jungle hideout and announced a change in his group's political line: survival, not socialism, was to be the new goal. He admitted serious errors in the past. Said Ieng Sary: "People are still a bit afraid of us, but we tell them we are nationalists before we are Communists."

The change of tune did not seem to satisfy the Association of Southeast Asian Nations (ASEAN), which was spearheading the campaign to keep Heng Samrin at bay. Unofficially, some ASEAN members started looking for a "third force," tainted neither by the Pol Pot atrocities nor by Hanoi's patronage. By September there was open campaigning for the Khmer People's National Liberation Front (KPNLF) led by former Cambodian premier Son Sann, considered by some as a viable non-Communist resistance movement. Rapidly gaining influence in the crowded Cambodian refugee camps on the Thai side of the frontier, the KPNLF turned down strong suggestions from Thailand and China that it coordinate its anti-Vietnamese work with that of the Pol Pot forces. Subsequently, there were suggestions that Cambodia's charismatic former head of state, Prince Norodom Sihanouk, be persuaded to join up with the KPNLF. But Front sources indicated that the prince would be welcome only as a figurehead.

All internal developments in Cambodia re-

CAMBODIA

Education. (1978–79) 350,000 pupils, 7,500 teachers, 1,333 schools (figures are for Vietnamese-controlled areas of Cambodia).

Finance. Monetary unit: riel, with (Sept. 22, 1980) a nominal free rate of 1,200 riels to U.S. $1 (2,884 riels = £1 sterling). Budget (1974 est.): revenue 23 billion riels; expenditure 71 billion riels.

Foreign Trade. (1975) Imports *c.* U.S. $117 million; exports *c.* U.S. $17 million. Import sources (1973): U.S. *c.* 69%; Thailand *c.* 11%; Singapore *c.* 5%; Japan *c.* 5%. Export destinations (1973): Hong Kong *c.* 23%; Japan *c.* 22%; Malaysia *c.* 18%; France *c.* 12%; Spain *c.* 10%. Main export (1973): rubber 93%.

Transport and Communications. Roads (1976) *c.* 11,000 km. Motor vehicles in use: passenger (1972) 27,200; commercial (including buses; 1973) 11,000. Railways: (1977) *c.* 612 km; traffic (1973) 54,070,000 passenger-km, freight 9,780,000 net ton-km. Air traffic (1977): 42 million passenger-km; freight 400,000 net ton-km. Inland waterways (including Mekong River; 1977) *c.* 1,400 km. Telephones (Dec. 1975) 71,000. Radio receivers (Dec. 1975) 110,000. Television receivers (Dec. 1977) 35,000.

Agriculture. Production (in 000; metric tons; 1979): rice *c.* 1,000; corn *c.* 80; bananas *c.* 50; oranges *c.* 30; dry beans *c.* 20; rubber *c.* 15; tobacco *c.* 4; jute (1978) *c.* 4. Livestock (in 000; 1979): cattle *c.* 700; buffalo *c.* 460; pigs *c.* 500.

mained overshadowed by the fighting, though it was confined to the eastern and northeastern border areas. There were reports of widespread famine conditions despite the arrival of massive international aid. At one point, the UN's World Food Program was shipping 32,000 tons of food each month, with an additional 16,000 tons a month for the refugees in Thailand. The Phnom Penh regime took a strong line on the management of international relief that poured into the region. It said the aid material was used to prop up Pol Pot's group and to attract famine-threatened Cambodian peasants to the Thai border, where large numbers were armed and sent back to their country to destabilize the government. Some international relief officials lent credence to such allegations.

In April there were reports that Vice-Pres. Pen Sovan, and not Pres. Heng Samrin, was the real strong man in Phnom Penh. Pen Sovan, aged 44, who was also defense minister, was a Vietnamese-trained Communist. He was considered likely to emerge officially as the main political leader if it was decided to replace the ruling Kampuchean United Front for National Salvation.

(T. J. S. GEORGE)

Cameroon

Cameroon

A republic of west Africa on the Gulf of Guinea, Cameroon borders on Nigeria, Chad, the Central African Republic, the Congo, Gabon, and Equatorial Guinea. Area: 465,054 sq km (179,558 sq mi). Pop. (1980 est.): 8,444,000. Cap.: Yaoundé (pop., 1976, 313,700). Largest city: Douala (pop., 1976, 458,400). Language: English and French (official), Bantu, Sudanic. Religion: mainly ani-

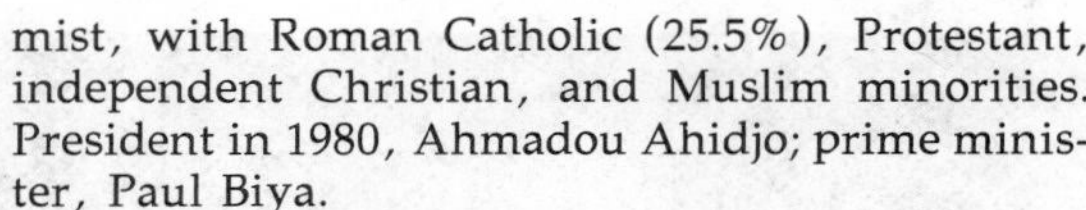

mist, with Roman Catholic (25.5%), Protestant, independent Christian, and Muslim minorities. President in 1980, Ahmadou Ahidjo; prime minister, Paul Biya.

On April 5, 1980, Ahmadou Ahidjo was reelected president of the republic for the fifth consecutive time since 1960. Opening the third congress of Cameroon's single political party at Bafoussam on February 13, he vigorously attacked the denunciation made by Amnesty International on February 9 of the conditions under which 200 political opponents of the regime were being detained.

Concerned at the deterioration of conditions in Chad, Ahidjo had discussions on the subject with France's Pres. Valéry Giscard d'Estaing in Paris. The large influx of refugees from Chad into Kousseri on the Chari River opposite N'Djamena created not only serious difficulties of food supply for the government but also, it was thought, a real risk of bringing destabilization to Cameroon.

Cameroon had high hopes of exploiting its petroleum reserves successfully. National production rose from 800,000 metric tons in 1978 to more than 3 million metric tons in 1980.

(PHILIPPE DECRAENE)

CAMEROON

Education. (1978–79) Primary, pupils 1,254,065, teachers 25,248; secondary, pupils 147,073, teachers 5,112; vocational, pupils 45,051, teachers 1,804; teacher training, students 1,677, teachers 168; higher, students (1977–78 est.) 10,001, teaching staff (1977–78) 439.

Finance. Monetary unit: CFA franc, with (Sept. 22, 1980) a parity of CFA Fr 50 to the French franc and a free rate of CFA Fr 210 to U.S. $1 (CFA Fr 504 = £1 sterling). Budget (total; 1979–80 est.) balanced at CFA Fr 186 billion.

Foreign Trade. (1979) Imports CFA Fr 271 billion; exports CFA Fr 237 billion. Import sources (1978): France 42%; West Germany 8%; Japan 6%; U.S. 5%; Italy 5%; U.K. 5%. Export destinations (1978): France 32%; The Netherlands 26%; West Germany 7%; Italy 7%; U.S. 5%. Main exports: coffee 26%; cocoa 17%; timber 7%.

Transport and Communications. Roads (1975) 43,500 km. Motor vehicles in use (1976): passenger 59,500; commercial (including buses) 51,200. Railways: (1978) *c.* 1,320 km; traffic (1979) 384 million passenger-km, freight 864 million net ton-km. Shipping (1979): merchant vessels 100 gross tons and over 32; gross tonnage 38,580. Telephones (June 1973) 22,000. Radio receivers (Dec. 1977) 240,000.

Agriculture. Production (in 000; metric tons; 1979): corn *c.* 480; millet *c.* 390; sweet potatoes (1978) *c.* 160; cassava (1978) *c.* 830; bananas *c.* 110; plantains (1978) *c.* 1,050; peanuts *c.* 285; coffee *c.* 112; cocoa *c.* 115; palm kernels *c.* 45; palm oil *c.* 80; rubber *c.* 16; cotton, lint *c.* 26; timber (cu m; 1978) *c.* 9,392. Livestock (in 000; 1978): cattle *c.* 2,972; pigs *c.* 789; sheep *c.* 2,155; goats *c.* 1,636; chickens *c.* 9,620.

Industry. Production (in 000; metric tons): cement (1977) 278; aluminum (1978) 48; electricity (kw-hr; 1979) 1,320,000.

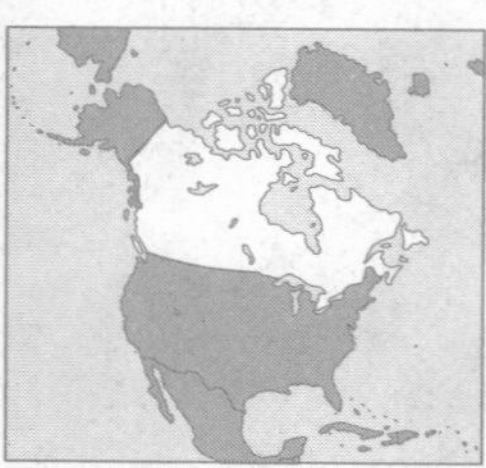

Canada

Canada

Canada is a federal parliamentary state and member of the Commonwealth of Nations covering North America north of conterminous United States and east of Alaska. Area: 9,976,139 sq km (3,851,809 sq mi). Pop. (1980 est.): 23,869,700, including (1971) British 44.6%; French 28.7%; other European 23%; Indian and Eskimo 1.4%. Cap.: Ottawa (metro pop., 1979 est., 738,600). Largest cities: Toronto (metro pop., 1979 est., 2,864,700); Montreal (metro pop., 1979 est., 2,818,300). Language (mother tongue; 1976): English 61%; French 26%; others 13%. Religion (1971): Roman Catholic 46%; Protestant 42%. Queen, Elizabeth II; governor-general in 1980, Edward R. Schreyer; prime ministers, C. Joseph Clark and, from March 3, Pierre Elliott Trudeau.

Domestic Affairs. Pierre Elliott Trudeau (*see* BIOGRAPHIES) triumphantly returned as prime minister of Canada early in 1980, after having been out of office for nine months. Beginning his 12th year in power and heartened by the resounding defeat of separatism in the Quebec referendum of May 20, the 60-year-old Trudeau dramatically introduced a new plan to resolve the long-standing dispute between the federal government and the provinces over a procedure for amending Canada's constitution and to entrench a charter of basic human rights in the document. In asserting a unilateral federal role in revising the constitution, Trudeau aroused the angry opposition of a majority of the provinces. His initiative represented the culmination of his public career, the purpose for which he had entered Canadian political life a decade and a half before.

The Liberals returned to power following a short and often inept Progressive Conservative administration under Joseph ("Joe") Clark, an Alberta MP who had led the party since 1976. After 16 years in

EVANS—GAMMA/LIAISON

Former Canadian prime minister Pierre Trudeau was greeted warmly by his supporters when he campaigned for reelection. He was returned to office on February 18.

opposition, the minority Conservative government moved slowly in taking up the reins of office. It waited almost six months before calling Parliament, spending the interim in reorganizing the federal administration. It also clung to election promises even when the country clearly did not favour the measures.

In the course of the election campaign, Clark had promised to move the Canadian embassy in Israel from Tel Aviv to Jerusalem. This action had to be abandoned, as did a plan to "privatize" the state-owned oil company, Petro-Canada. The government failed to introduce a promised $2 billion cut in personal taxes or to bring down rising interest rates. Its downfall, in December 1979, came on its first budget, which contained a proposal to impose an 18-cents-a-gallon tax on gasoline and to allow Canadian oil prices to move upward toward the world price. The opposition parties combined to defeat the budget, forcing Clark to call a general election for February 18.

During the campaign it became apparent that the Clark government had lost the confidence of the electorate. The 40-year-old prime minister was perceived as well meaning but lacking in authority. His victory the previous May had benefited from a large protest vote against Trudeau and the Liberals, but he had not managed to turn that sentiment into positive support for his new government. In the media he suffered in comparison with the experienced Trudeau. The latter had been persuaded by his party to lead it through another election even though he had announced his wish to resign as leader just before the budget defeat.

The voting on February 18 revealed a modest Liberal gain in the Atlantic provinces, a virtual sweep of Quebec, where the formerly significant Social Credit movement was wiped out, and a 20-seat gain in the vital central province of Ontario. The Conservatives held two-thirds of the seats in the west, but these were not sufficient to give them more than 103 members in the 282-seat House of Commons. Four Conservative Cabinet ministers went down to defeat. The Liberals won 147 seats, a solid majority, and the third party, the socialist New Democrats (NPD), collected 32 seats in Ontario and the west. The Liberals won 44% of the popular vote while the Conservatives, at 33%, fell 3% below their 1979 showing.

Election Results, Feb. 18, 1980
(1979 results in parentheses)

Area	Liberals	Progressive Conservatives	New Democratic Party
Atlantic region (Nfld., N.S., N.B., P.E.I.) 32 (32)	19 (12)	13 (18)	0 (2)
Quebec 75 (75)	74* (67)	1 (2)	0 (0)
Ontario 95 (95)	52 (32)	38 (57)	5 (6)
West (Man., Sask., Alta., B.C.) 77 (77)	2 (3)	49 (57)	26 (17)
North (N.W.T., Yukon) 3 (3)	0 (0)	2 (2)	1 (1)
Total 282	147*(114)	103 (136)	32 (26)

* Includes a deferred election on March 24. The Social Credit Party, which won 6 seats in Quebec in 1979, failed to return a member in 1980.

Trudeau returned to power on March 3, ending the Clark government's 272 days in office. It was Trudeau's fourth electoral victory, putting him in an unchallenged position in national politics. He chose two of his closest colleagues for key positions in his Cabinet: Allan MacEachen as minister of finance and deputy prime minister and Marc Lalonde as minister of energy. Seventeen former ministers were included, 5 were dropped, and 14 new ones were named. The lack of Liberal members from western Canada obliged Trudeau to appoint three senators to the Cabinet to represent the region. For the first time in Canada's history, a woman, Jeanne Sauvé (*see* BIOGRAPHIES), was named speaker of the House of Commons.

Trudeau's strength was enhanced by the results of the referendum on Quebec's independence on May 20. The goal of Premier René Lévesque and his Parti Québécois government ever since their advent to office in 1976, the independence option was termed "sovereignty-association." The concept envisaged Quebec enacting its own laws, collecting taxes from its people, and establishing

WIDE WORLD

Jeanne Sauvé was escorted to the rostrum by former prime minister Joe Clark (left) and Prime Minister Pierre Trudeau when she became the first woman speaker of the Canadian House of Commons.

relations with foreign countries. Simultaneously, it would form an economic union with the rest of Canada based on a common currency. In the referendum the Lévesque government did not ask directly for approval of the new status but sought authority to negotiate it with the rest of Canada. A second referendum was promised before the decisive step to separation was taken.

After a bitterly fought campaign in which Trudeau, federal ministers, and provincial premiers took part, the Quebec electorate rejected the plan. The "No" forces won 59.6% of the popular vote with 2,172,000 votes. Even among French-speaking residents, a small majority voted "No" to separation. The rejection was a deep disappointment to Lévesque, who vowed, however, to accept its consequences by continuing to work within the federal system. A provincial election would be required in 1981, and the PQ seemed intent on securing a new mandate through having provided good government rather than because it advocated Quebec's independence.

The process of creating a "renewed federalism" began immediately after May 20. Trudeau called the ten provincial premiers to meet him in Ottawa on June 9 and presented them with a list of priority items for constitutional reform. These ranged from a charter of human rights, including minority language protection, to broad powers affecting the economy and institutional changes such as a reconstructed Supreme Court. Expanded to 12 subjects, the list was discussed in a series of federal-provincial meetings, some among officials, others among ministers, over the summer. These led up to a summit conference of first ministers in Ottawa, September 8–13.

By this time it was apparent that wide differences existed between Ottawa and the provinces over what should be done to reform the constitution. Quebec's concerns over cultural and linguistic identity were supplemented by the Western provinces' demand for control over natural resources and by Newfoundland's claim that it possessed jurisdiction over offshore Atlantic resources. The long-standing quarrel between Ottawa and Alberta over energy pricing and revenue

CANADA

Education. (1979–80 prelim.) Primary, pupils 3,364,213; secondary, pupils 1,794,882; primary and secondary, teachers 266,302; higher, students 611,520, teaching staff 52,409.

Finance. Monetary unit: Canadian dollar, with (Sept. 22, 1980) a free rate of Can$1.17 to U.S. $1 (Can$2.80 = £1 sterling). Gold, SDR's, and foreign exchange (June 1980) U.S. $4,307,000,000. Budget (1979–80 actual): revenue Can$49,310,000,000; expenditure Can$56,380,000,000. Gross national product (1979) Can$260.3 billion. Money supply (May 1980) Can$31,130,000,000. Cost of living (1975 = 100; June 1980) 151.6

Foreign Trade. (1979) Imports Can$66,544,000,000; exports Can$68,134,000,000. Import sources: U.S. 73%; Japan 3%. Export destinations: U.S. 68%; Japan 6%. Main exports: motor vehicles 17%; machinery 10%; timber 6%; metal ores 6%; crude oil and products 6%; natural gas 5%; chemicals 5%; newsprint 5%; wood-pulp 5%; cereals 5%; nonferrous metals 5%. Tourism (1978): visitors 12,745,000; gross receipts U.S. $1,722,000,000.

Transport and Communications. Roads (1976) 884,273 km. Motor vehicles in use (1977): passenger 9,554,300; commercial 2,442,300. Railways (1978): 67,889 km; traffic 3,070,000,000 passenger-km, freight 215,350,000,000 net ton-km. Air traffic (1978): 29,276,000,000 passenger-km; freight 675.8 million net ton-km. Shipping (1979): merchant vessels 100 gross tons and over 1,290; gross tonnage 3,015,752. Shipping traffic (includes Great Lakes and St. Lawrence traffic; 1978): goods loaded 116,522,000 metric tons, unloaded 61,788,000 metric tons. Telephones (Jan. 1978) 14,506,000. Radio receivers (Dec. 1977) 24.3 million. Television receivers (Dec. 1977) 10 million.

Agriculture. Production (in 000; metric tons; 1979): wheat 17,746; barley 8,460; oats 2,978; rye 525; corn 4,963; potatoes 2,706; tomatoes c. 486; apples 437; rapeseed 3,561; linseed 836; soybeans 629; tobacco 86; beef and veal 955; pork 745; fish catch (1978) 1,407; timber (cu m; 1978) 156,139. Livestock (in 000; Dec. 1978): cattle 12,328; sheep 430; pigs 8,025; horses (1977) c. 350; chickens 81,883.

Industry. Labour force (June 1979) 11,424,000. Unemployment (Dec. 1979) 7%. Index of industrial production (1975 = 100; 1979) 120. Fuel and power (in 000; metric tons; 1979): coal 28,003; lignite 5,011; crude oil 73,243; natural gas (cu m) 81,760,000; electricity (kw-hr) 352,249,000 (70% hydroelectric and 8% nuclear in 1977). Metal and mineral production (in 000; metric tons; 1979): iron ore (shipments; 61% metal content) 59,706; crude steel 16,078; copper ore (metal content) 634; nickel ore (metal content; 1978) 130; zinc ore (metal content) 1,204; lead ore (metal content) 342; aluminum (exports; 1978) 1,048; uranium ore (metal content; 1978) 9.4; asbestos (1978) 1,380; gold (troy oz) 1,600; silver (troy oz) 39,000. Other production (in 000; metric tons; 1979): cement 11,000; wood pulp (1978) 19,013; newsprint 8,757; other paper and paperboard (1977) 3,986; sulfuric acid (1978) 3,260; plastics and resins (1978) 710; synthetic rubber 282; fertilizers (nutrient value; 1978–79) nitrogenous c. 1,674, phosphate c. 660, potash c. 6,387; passenger cars (units) 988; commercial vehicles (units) 644. Dwelling units completed (1979) 226,000. Merchant vessels launched (100 gross tons and over; 1979) 177,000 gross tons.

sharing, which had not been resolved despite personal negotiations between Trudeau and Alberta Premier Peter Lougheed, introduced further strains into the discussions. Thus the first ministers moved from a consideration of what might have pleased Quebec to a discussion of the claims of all the provinces.

After four days of fruitless argument, the premiers presented a list of demands representing each other's final positions. It did not include the entrenched charter of rights or the provisions for the free movement of labour, capital, and goods that Trudeau desired to strengthen Canada as an economic union. He and the federal ministers rejected the provincial consensus, and the conference dissolved in recriminations and forebodings.

As Parliament prepared to resume after the summer recess, Trudeau took a dramatic step. On October 2 he announced to the nation that he would ask the Commons and Senate to approve a resolution requesting the British Parliament to transfer the authority to amend Canada's constitution to Canada. Although a sovereign state, Canada had never possessed the power to amend its own constitution, an anomaly resulting from the inability of the provinces and the federal government to agree on an amending formula. Thus in the past the British Parliament has legally approved changes in the constitution on the request of the Parliament of Canada. Trudeau proposed to correct this situation by making the constitution a Canadian act (patriation). At the same time, he declared his desire to entrench in the act "a package for the people"—a charter of human rights and freedoms binding on the provinces as well as the federal government.

When Parliament met on October 6, Trudeau introduced his constitutional changes. The Conservatives immediately opposed them as a unilateral measure that violated the federal principle, while the NDP gave them qualified support. At a meeting of the provinces in Toronto on October 14, five provinces ranging from British Columbia to Newfoundland announced they would take the constitutional changes to court. This would be done by preparing a reference question which would be submitted to one of the provincial appeal courts. Trudeau pressed on with his plan to send his resolution to a joint Commons-Senate committee, hoping to have it endorsed so that the new Canadian constitution could be proclaimed on the country's next national day, July 1, 1981. It was a bold stroke on the success of which Trudeau's place in Canada's history would be based. (*See* Special Report.)

Jules Léger, governor-general of Canada from 1974 to 1979, died November 22. Jean Lesage, who as premier of Quebec (1960–66) presided over sweeping changes in that province's government, died December 11. (*See* OBITUARIES.)

The Economy. The economy faltered in 1980, showing a decline of 1.7% in real gross national product for the first half of the year. The GNP in current dollars was expected to reach $281.4 billion for the year, an inflation-swollen figure that masked the slowest growth rate in a quarter of a century. The recession turned on weaknesses in consumer demand and such negative forces as high interest rates and a decline in sales to the U.S. Inflation, at a rate of 10.7% in August, was somewhat higher than in 1979, while unemployment, running at a seasonally adjusted rate of 7.4% in September, remained about the same.

On March 10 the Bank of Canada announced the move to a floating bank rate, to be set in relation to the interest yield at the weekly auction of 91-day federal government treasury bills. After climbing to over 16% in April, the rate began to decline, standing at 13.9% in late November. The Canadian dollar fluctuated between 84 and 87 cents (U.S.) during the year.

Economic planning in 1980 was hindered by the continuing inability of the federal government to work out an acceptable oil-pricing agreement with Alberta, the chief producing province. The Clark administration was close to achieving such an agreement when it fell, having accepted Alberta's contention that Canadian oil prices must be allowed to rise slowly to near world levels. The Trudeau government refused to follow this policy,

JEAN-PIERRE LAFFONT—SYGMA

Signs of the times were these two banners on neighbouring houses in Quebec as Quebecers decided whether to vote for independence from Canada. The "No" vote won by a margin of 3–2 in an election on May 20.

believing that domestic prices should be based on production and replacement costs in Canada. At stake also were the division of oil and gas revenues and the federal government's imperative need to recover a larger share to support its subsidy for higher-cost imported oil needed in the east.

Finance Minister MacEachen presented his long-awaited budget, along with an energy program, on October 28. They went directly to the heart of the oil-pricing issue by establishing a regular series of increases between 1980 and 1984. Over this period, Canadian oil prices would not be allowed to climb above 85% of world or U.S. prices. The burden of the oil import subsidy would be transferred to consumers through a refinery tax. Ottawa would take a larger share of oil revenues and would work toward achieving Canadian control of the petroleum industry. Through new restrictions and Petro-Canada's purchase of foreign-owned oil companies, it was hoped that there would be 50% Canadian ownership of the industry by 1990. (The current proportion was less than 30%.) Lougheed rejected the federal plan and declared he would cut Alberta's production of oil by 15%, or 180,000 bbl a day, over the next nine months. Further work on new oil sands plants would be deferred, and MacEachen's tax on natural gas would be challenged in the courts. The prospect of further negotiation between Ottawa and Alberta seemed likely.

With over 8,000 jobs at risk, the Canadian provincial governments extended aid to the hard-pressed Chrysler Corp. on May 10. Ottawa agreed to $200 million in loan guarantees to Chrysler Canada, while Ontario gave the company $10 million toward financing a research centre at Windsor to test aluminum and plastic parts for automobiles. In return, the Canadian subsidiary of Chrysler promised to maintain employment levels in Canada at 9% of Chrysler's labour force in the U.S.

Foreign Affairs. Canada's disapproval of the Soviet intervention in Afghanistan was strongly shown in 1980. Ottawa agreed to hold wheat sales to the Soviet Union to the traditional level of slightly more than 3 million metric tons. Lifting of the commitment was announced on July 24 following conversations between Trudeau and U.S. Pres. Jimmy Carter at the Venice (Italy) economic summit meeting. Canada dropped out of the embargo in November but said it would not try to replace U.S. grain being withheld. A Canadian boycott of the Olympic Games in Moscow, first announced by the Clark administration, was confirmed by the Trudeau government on April 22.

Canadian actions against Iran were more symbolic than real, since Canadian-Iranian trade was negligible. Nevertheless, on May 22 imports and exports and banking deals were cut off to protest the taking of U.S. hostages at the U.S. embassy in Teheran on Nov. 4, 1979. A more spectacular act was the Canadian initiative in hiding six U.S. diplomats in the Iranian capital for almost three months and then removing them to safety through the use of false Canadian passports. Canada's ambassador to Iran, Kenneth Taylor (*see* BIOGRAPHIES), the architect of the Canadian rescue operation, was honoured by the U.S. Congress and given the Order of Canada.

Strains occurred between the two North American nations in 1980. Canada complained of the failure of the U.S. Senate to approve the 1979 treaty setting quotas for fish stocks in shared Atlantic coastal waters. The agreement also referred the disputed maritime boundary across the Gulf of Maine to international arbitration. The Senate felt the treaty was too generous to Canadian fishermen.

Acid rain was another Canadian concern, especially after President Carter introduced an energy bill into Congress requiring 50 power plants in the eastern U.S. to use coal instead of oil for fuel. A memorandum of intent was signed on August 5, providing for work groups to begin a study of air quality and for more vigorous enforcement of current antipollution standards.

President Carter's failure to visit Canada during his first term, making him the first U.S. president in recent years not to do so, disappointed Canadians. The most positive note struck in the bilateral field involved Congress' action to clear away the last roadblocks to the Alaskan Highway natural gas pipeline across western Canada and Canada's decision, on July 17, to allow the southern arm of the line to be started ahead of the main project. To run 850 km (530 mi) and cost $1.6 billion, the "prebuild portion" would deliver Canadian gas to the U.S. market by 1981.

After three years of evaluation, the Trudeau government announced on April 10 that it would buy 137 F-18A Hornet fighter aircraft from the McDonnell Douglas Corp. for defense needs in North America and Western Europe. The contract, which amounted to $2.7 billion for the planes and another $2 billion for spare parts and missiles, called for delivery of the last planes by 1989. Under the arrangement, some of the components would be built in Canada. Another U.S. aircraft, the long-range Aurora patrol plane (an updated U.S. Navy Orion) built by the Lockheed Corp., began to arrive in Canada in May under a procurement program worked out in 1976. (D. M. L. FARR)

A billboard in Detroit expressed the gratitude of Americans for Canada's help in smuggling six U.S. diplomats out of Iran in January.

WIDE WORLD

Canada: Special Report

CANADA'S CONSTITUTIONAL DILEMMA

by Peter Ward

Disagreement over the future shape of Canada kindled a blaze of discord in 1980, pitting eight of the nation's ten provinces against the federal government and constituting a threat to Canadian union almost as dangerous as the rise of the separatist movement in Quebec. Only Ontario, Canada's most populous province, and New Brunswick backed Prime Minister Pierre Elliott Trudeau in his effort to finally give Canada its own constitution. Trudeau was seeking to rewrite the rules of Canadian confederation unilaterally, and he accused the dissenting provinces of petty regionalism. The provinces, on the other hand, were clamouring against what they saw as a blatant federal power grab.

The British North America Act. Canada does not have its own constitution. The British North America Act, passed by the British Parliament in 1867 to establish the Canadian confederation, apportioned powers between the federal and provincial governments and set up a governmental structure for Canada based on the British parliamentary model. The Canadian Parliament has a House of Commons and a Senate, equivalent to Britain's House of Lords, with a specific number of seats allocated to each province; the senators are appointed by the government in power. Each province also has a legislature, with powers specified in the BNA Act. Legal systems were also specified. For criminal matters, all of Canada is under British-style common law. In civil law, the British common law pertains in all the provinces except Quebec, which has a codified system in the French style. The BNA Act can be amended only by the British Parliament, which in practice has not done so except at Canada's request. Customarily, such requests were made only when Ottawa and all the provincial governments were in agreement.

Periodically in Canadian history, the federal and provincial governments have struggled to reach agreement on a formula for revoking the BNA Act, so that Canada could write its own constitution. The latest series of meetings on the constitution began in 1967, Canada's centennial year, under the impetus of the populist nationalist movement coming to the fore in Quebec. Trudeau, who was then federal justice minister, won national political recognition during the 1967 talks. He gained the leadership of the Liberal Party largely on the strength of his performance at that conference.

Peter Ward operates Ward News Services Canada in the Parliamentary Press Gallery, Ottawa.

CANADIAN PRESS

A September conference signaled yet another skirmish in the continuing battle over the creation of a Canadian constitution.

As prime minister beginning in 1968, Trudeau continued the push for constitutional reform. In 1971 his hopes foundered when Quebec's government rejected an agreement reached by the premiers at Victoria, B.C. Trudeau made another try at achieving constitutional agreement in the mid-'70s, but that, too, failed. Defeated in the May 1979 election, Trudeau intended to retire but reversed his plans when Joe Clark's short-lived Conservative government fell unexpectedly in December. Following the Liberal victory in February 1980, Trudeau set out to win his constitutional goals on the strength of his parliamentary majority—acting unilaterally if necessary. This would involve Canada's Parliament asking Britain's to pass legislation "patriating" (giving Canada sole authority over) the Canadian constitution without first obtaining the approval of the provinces.

The constitution and the danger that Quebec might separate from Canada had always been Trudeau's major themes, and the perception that he could deal with the Quebec problem was one of his political strong points. His writings before he entered federal politics in 1965 played on the dual themes of necessary political reform for Quebec and Quebec's future place within Canada. He maintained that Quebec would be foolish to separate from Canada. By remaining within the confederation, it could have a share of the whole rich nation. Trudeau suggested that Quebec could wield half the influence in Canada.

The Trudeau theme was repeated by federalists throughout the spring of 1980, as Quebec prepared for a referendum in which René Lévesque's separatist government sought authority to negotiate independence. The vote was lost by the separatists, with almost 60% of those going to the polls opting to stay within Canada. In Trudeau's view, constitutional reform was now even more urgent, because the federalists had won the Quebec referendum at least in part on the basis of a promise of such reform, although it is likely that the federalists would have won in any case.

Quebec separatists claim that the French language and culture can be preserved only by building a wall of protection around the province, making it a Francophone island in predominantly English-speaking North America. Trudeau wants language rights for French-speaking Canadians enshrined in a Canadian constitution that would require all provinces to provide French services and education wherever numbers warrant. Such a document would give French-speaking Canadians economic and cultural mobility throughout Canada. The quid pro quo would be similar rights for English-speaking Canadians in Quebec, which has strict language laws limiting the use of English in education and business.

Clash with the Provinces. Trudeau wants a made-in-Canada constitution with a charter of human rights, including language rights. It is an aim that gives rise to a cultural clash with many of the provinces. Trudeau is a lawyer of the Quebec bar, trained in codified law in the continental tradition. Codified law assigns specific rights to individuals, and in theory they have no others. In British common law, citizens have all rights except those specifically withdrawn by law.

The philosophical clash between Trudeau and most of the English-speaking provinces is thus based to some degree on the difference between the British tradition of an unwritten constitution and customary law developed through judicial precedents and the more structured French approach, which reduces all matters of law to a written constitution and written legal codes. Adding to the nervousness of the dissenting provinces is the fact that in Canada members of the judiciary, with a few minor exceptions, are appointed by the central government. With a written bill of rights, their powers would be enhanced.

The conflict is also pragmatic: a battle between the two central provinces of Ontario and Quebec, which seek to maintain their traditional domination of the Canadian confederation, and the smaller and less populous provinces, many of which are enjoying or anticipating economic booms based on energy resources. In the west, Alberta, Saskatchewan, and British Columbia all have oil and/or natural gas. On the eastern seaboard, Newfoundland, with significant offshore oil and gas discoveries, is eagerly awaiting an energy bonanza.

Under existing Canadian laws, jurisdiction over resources is a provincial matter. Revenue from oil and natural gas has meant billions to the three western provinces, enabling them to enjoy budgets that are nearly in balance or actually in surplus. Newfoundland, traditionally a poor province, is confident that energy resources will make balanced budgets possible within a few years. Meanwhile, the federal government has been sliding deeper into debt each year. Trudeau's intention is to move into the resources field for revenue by taxing energy, thus switching the flow of several billion dollars from provincial to federal coffers.

Energy and the Constitution. None of the energy-producing provinces likes the current federal policy of holding the price of oil and natural gas in Canada below world prices, yet it was Clark's attempt to hike the price of gasoline that helped win the election for Trudeau in February 1980. Canadian domestic oil prices are roughly half the world price. Canada sells $4.5 billion in natural gas annually to the U.S. at double the price in the domestic Canadian market. Lower energy prices benefit the industrial provinces of Ontario and Quebec but cost the energy-producing provinces billions in lost revenue. Canada imports 420,000 bbl of foreign crude daily at world prices for use in eastern Canada and subsidizes the cost from federal tax revenue to maintain a national fixed price. That subsidy could cost almost $3 billion in fiscal 1980–81.

The energy-producing provinces view this policy as being unfairly designed to aid industry in Ontario and Quebec. Trudeau's moves to take even more energy revenue away from the producing provinces are seen by those provinces as a centralist attempt to halt the rapid shift westward of Canada's economic centre of gravity. The centralist-dominated government, on the other hand, reasons that the rapid increase in energy prices worldwide bears no

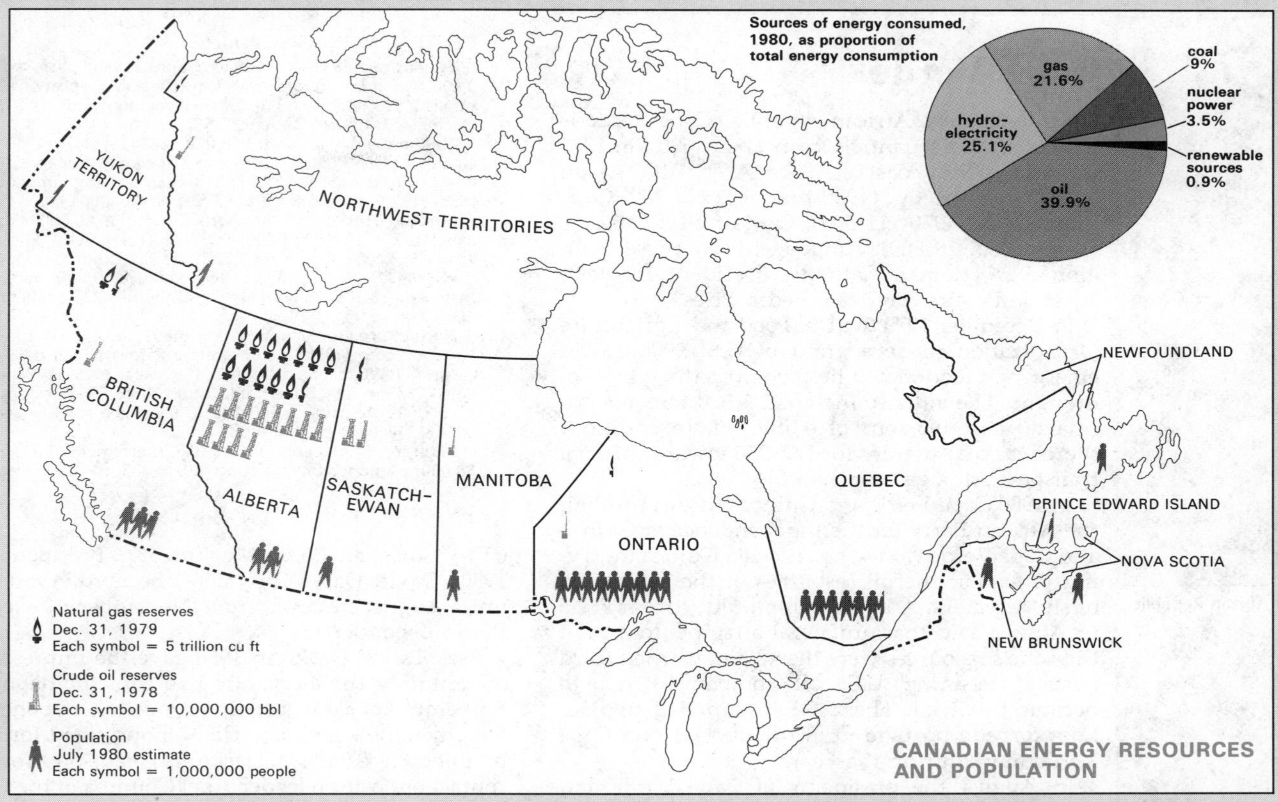

relation to production costs. In the eyes of Ontario and Quebec, increased provincial energy revenue is a windfall resulting from unnatural international conditions. Newfoundland is on the side of the energy-producing provinces because Trudeau refuses to concede to that province jurisdiction over offshore hydrocarbon discoveries.

Trudeau's position is made more difficult by the fact that, in the February 1980 election, the Liberals failed to elect a single member from the three western provinces with energy resources and elected only two in Manitoba. His majority government is based on massive support from Ontario and Quebec which together hold 170 seats in the House of Commons out of a total of 282.

Trudeau's formula for replacing the British North America Act with a made-in-Canada constitution was placed before the Canadian Parliament on Oct. 6, 1980. It made no mention of changes in the division of federal–provincial powers except for the introduction of a bill of rights, including language rights, and the creation of a system for amending the constitution. Language rights involve education, which is currently under provincial jurisdiction.

As for the amending procedure, for two years after patriation, the traditional unanimous agreement of all the provinces and the federal government would be required for any amendment. At the same time, unanimous agreement would be sought on a new amending formula, and Trudeau plans intensive constitutional meetings with the provinces during the two-year period. Lacking such agreement, a referendum would be held on any method approved by eight provinces (one of which would have to be Quebec) representing 80% of the population; an alternative method could also be offered by Ottawa. If no eight-province proposal was put forward, a modified Victoria formula would go into effect automatically. (The Victoria formula, so-called from the 1971 constitutional conference in Victoria, where it emerged, would require approval of any proposed amendment by a majority of provinces including Ontario, Quebec, two western provinces, and two Atlantic provinces.) This gives Ontario and Quebec, which between them contain slightly more than half of Canada's population, an effective veto. Both Alberta and British Columbia insist that they will not accept a veto by Ontario or Quebec unless they, too, hold veto power.

The stage is thus set in Canada for lengthy and bitter constitutional warfare, involving the courts, where federal unilateral moves are to be challenged, and the political arena, where feelings are so strong that the three wealthy western provinces may threaten separation. It may well be the stormiest period in Canadian history since the Riel Rebellion, which raged intermittently in western Canada for some 15 years a century ago.

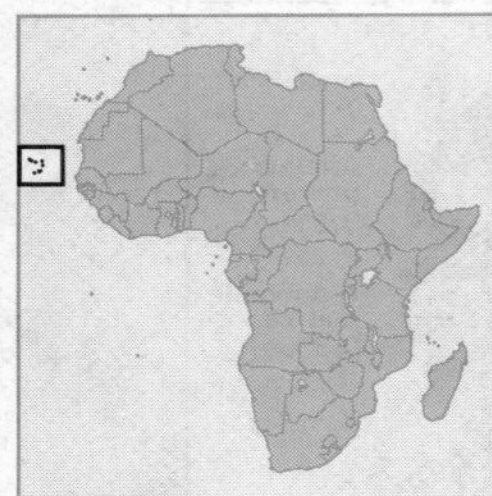

Cape Verde

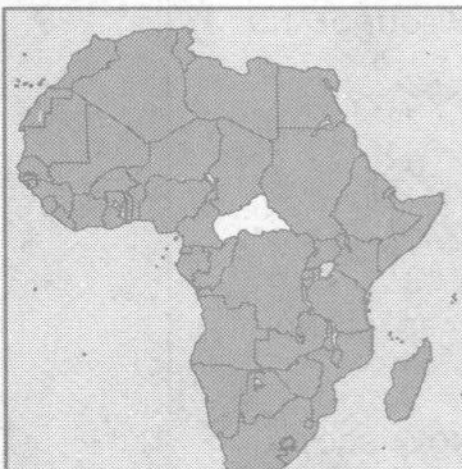

Central African Republic

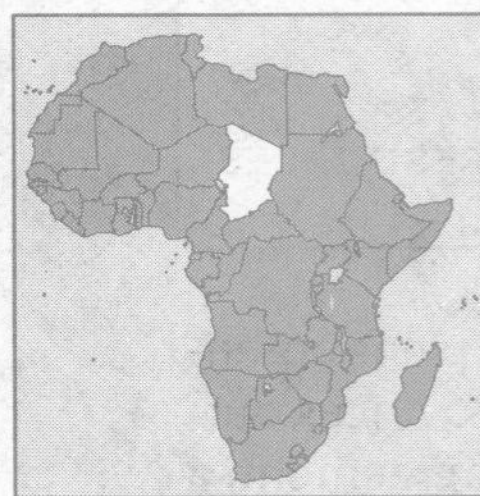

Chad

Canadian Literature: *see* Literature

Canoeing: *see* Water Sports

Catholic Church: *see* Religion

Cave Exploration: *see* Speleology

Census Data: *see* Demography; *see also the individual country articles*

Central America: *see* Latin-American Affairs; *articles on the various countries*

Ceramics: *see* Materials Sciences

Ceylon: *see* Sri Lanka

Cape Verde

An independent African republic, Cape Verde is located in the Atlantic Ocean about 620 km (385 mi) off the west coast of Africa. Area: 4,033 sq km (1,557 sq mi). Pop. (1980 prelim.): 296,100. Cap.: Praia (pop., 1970, 21,500). Largest city: Mindelo (pop., 1970, 28,800). Language: Portuguese. Religion: 91% Roman Catholic. President in 1980, Aristide Pereira; premier, Pedro Pires.

In December 1979 the UN Food and Agriculture Organization made a grant of U.S. $908,000 in emergency food aid to help combat the effects of drought. The aid also included 2,500 tons of corn (maize) and 190 tons of edible oil. In addition, there was a cash grant for $67,250 toward internal transport, storage, and handling.

In 1980 Cape Verde and Guinea-Bissau, through the African Party for the Independence of Guinea and Cape Verde (PAIGC), criticized Guinea for trying to exploit the oil resources of their disputed offshore waters. A PAIGC communiqué from Praia in August said that unilateral attempts to exploit the zone's resources were illegal and warned third parties (meaning U.S. oil companies) not to become involved. The U.S.S.R. supplied two 38-knot torpedo boats to form the nucleus of a Cape Verde navy during the year.

In August the presidents of Cape Verde and Guinea-Bissau met in Cape Verde to discuss constitutional changes, and in September preliminary negotiations on a four-year economic coordination plan were concluded. However, relations cooled after the coup in Guinea-Bissau in November. On September 5 the Cape Verde National Assembly approved a new constitution. Cape Verde was defined as a "sovereign, democratic, unitary, anticolonialist, and anti-imperialist republic." The PAIGC, the only legal party, was established as the "leading force of society." (GUY ARNOLD)

CAPE VERDE

Education. (1978–79) Primary, pupils 46,539, teachers 1,431; secondary, pupils 6,607, teachers 220; vocational, pupils 474, teachers (1977–78) 43; teacher training (1977–78), pupils 198, teachers (1976–77) 32.

Finance and Trade. Monetary unit: Cape Verde escudo, with (Sept. 22, 1980) a free rate of 36.41 escudos to U.S. $1 (87.50 escudos = £1 sterling). Budget (total; 1978 est.) balanced at 2,472,000,000 escudos. Foreign trade (1976): imports 911.4 million escudos; exports 48,030,000 escudos (excluding transit trade). Import sources: Portugal 58%; The Netherlands 5%. Export destinations: Portugal 63%; Angola 14%; Zaire 5%; U.K. 5%. Main exports: fish 29% (including shellfish 16%); bananas 19%; salt 9%.

Transport. Shipping traffic (1977): goods loaded 27,000 metric tons, unloaded 195,000 metric tons.

Central African Republic

The landlocked Central African Republic is bounded by Chad, the Sudan, the Congo, Zaire, and Cameroon. Area: 623,000 sq km (240,542 sq mi). Pop. (1980 est.): 2,362,400. Cap. and largest city: Bangui (pop., 1979 est., 362,700). Language: French (official), local dialects. Religion: animist 60%; Christian 35%; Muslim 5%. President in 1980, David Dacko; premiers, Bernard Ayandho until August 22 and, from November 12, Jean-Pierre Lebouder.

CENTRAL AFRICAN REPUBLIC

Education. (1977–78) Primary, pupils 238,605, teachers 3,690; secondary, pupils 46,084, teachers 462; vocational, pupils 2,523, teachers 118; teacher training, students 51, teachers 12; higher, students 7,547, teaching staff 405.

Finance. Monetary unit: CFA franc, with (Sept. 22, 1980) a parity of CFA Fr 50 to the French franc and a free rate of CFA Fr 210 to U.S. $1 (CFA Fr 504 = £1 sterling). Budget (total; 1980 est.) balanced at CFA Fr 25,447,000,000.

Foreign Trade. (1978) Imports CFA Fr 12,776,000,000; exports CFA Fr 16,182,000,000. Import sources (1977): France 55%; West Germany 7%; Japan 5%. Export destinations (1977): France 63%; Belgium-Luxembourg 16%. Main exports (1977): coffee 41%; diamonds 23%; timber 18%; cotton 9%.

Agriculture. Production (in 000; metric tons; 1979): millet *c.* 40; corn (1978) *c.* 30; sweet potatoes (1978) *c.* 62; cassava (1978) *c.* 940; peanuts *c.* 126; bananas *c.* 75; plantains (1978) *c.* 62; coffee *c.* 14; cotton, lint *c.* 20. Livestock (in 000; 1978): cattle *c.* 660; pigs *c.* 64; sheep *c.* 79; goats *c.* 588; chickens *c.* 1,308.

Industry. Production (in 000; 1977): electricity (kw-hr) 58,000; diamonds (metric carats; 1976) 405; cotton fabrics (m) 4,000.

Pres. David Dacko in 1980 gave the impression of resuming the autocratic habits of the deposed Emperor Bokassa. Leading political opponents were detained without trial, among them former premier Ange Patassé. Dacko also made no effort to contact opposition leader Abel Goumba of the Oubangian Patriotic Front, who was in exile in Benin. In February some members of the old regime were sentenced to death, but a number of sentences were quashed when François Guéret, minister of justice, was dismissed in March. Further death sentences scheduled for September were not carried out.

In March Dacko created the single-party Central African Democratic Union with the agreement of France, which reaffirmed its support for him. Dacko dissolved his government on July 9 and dismissed Vice-Pres. Henri Maïdou and Premier Bernard Ayandho in August. Their dismissals were concessions to public opinion but did not restore confidence. Meanwhile, public finances were in ruin, and French forces were the regime's chief support. (PHILIPPE DECRAENE)

Chad

A landlocked republic of central Africa, Chad is bounded by Libya, the Sudan, the Central African Republic, Cameroon, Nigeria, and Niger. Area: 1,284,000 sq km (495,755 sq mi). Pop. (1980 est.): 4,504,400, including Saras, other Africans, and Arabs. Cap. and largest city: N'Djamena (pop., 1979 est., 303,000). Language: French (official). Religion: Muslim 45%; animist 45%; Christian 10%. President in 1980, Goukouni Oueddei.

Civil war broke out again in Chad on March 21–22, 1980. During most of the year, in the northern two-thirds of the country, there was a confrontation between the Armed Forces of the North (FAN) of Hissen Habré and the Popular Armed Forces (FAP) of Pres. Goukouni Oueddei, who ex-

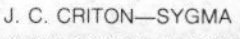
J. C. CRITON—SYGMA

Marcel Beaux (centre), French ambassador to Chad, tried but failed on March 27 to mediate in the civil war raging in that country.

ercised only nominal power as head of the Transitional Government of National Union (GUNT). In the south the Chadian Armed Forces (FAT) of Col. Wadal Abdelkadar Kamougue, vice-president of GUNT, practically constituted an autonomous state; they possessed Chad's only major resources, cotton and sugarcane, and established Moundou as their capital. Eight other factions were also active.

On March 24 the 1,100-strong French garrison force at N'Djamena began to evacuate European civilians, while Kamougue called upon Libya for aid, without success. Hundreds died in the capital in the fighting, and an estimated 70,000 refugees fled to Cameroon across the Chari River. On April 27 France announced the withdrawal of its forces, which began in May and was completed on May 17.

All attempts at a negotiated settlement of the conflict broke down, in spite of the efforts of several African presidents, notably Gen. Gnassingbe Eyadema of Togo and Omar Bongo of Gabon. The April economic conference of the Organization of African Unity (OAU) at Lagos, Nigeria, favoured sending an inter-African force to Chad but could do nothing to bring the fighting to an end. The Franco-African conference, held in Nice, France, in May, was attended by 26 nations but would not examine the problem officially.

In June Habré's forces won control of Faya-Largeau and scored successes in the north, while Oueddei signed a treaty with Libya. In July the crisis in Chad was discussed at the OAU summit conference at Freetown, Sierra Leone. In early November there were reports that Libyan forces had crossed the border, and on December 8 Libyan troops, with tanks and air cover, began a push toward N'Djamena. The capital was taken over, in Oueddei's name, by mid-December, and the fall of Habré's stronghold of Abéché was announced by the government a few days later. An emergency meeting of the OAU's ad hoc committee on Chad was held late in December, but no communiqué was issued. (PHILIPPE DECRAENE)

CHAD

Education. (1976–77) Primary, pupils 229,191, teachers *c.* 2,620; secondary, pupils 18,382, teachers 590; vocational, pupils 649, teachers (1965–66) 30; teacher training, students 549, teachers (1973–74) 26; higher, students 758, teaching staff 62.

Finance. Monetary unit: CFA franc, with (Sept. 22, 1980) a parity of CFA Fr 50 to the French franc and a free rate of CFA Fr 210 to U.S. $1 (CFA Fr 504 = £1 sterling). Budget (total; 1978 est.) balanced at CFA Fr 17,084,000,000.

Foreign Trade. (1976) Imports CFA Fr 28,111,000,000; exports CFA Fr 14,861,000,000. Import sources (1975): France 37%; Nigeria 10%; The Netherlands 7%; U.S. 6%; U.K. 5%; Cameroon 5%. Export destinations (1975): Nigeria 20%; France 7%; Congo 5%. Main exports (1975): cotton 69%; meat 6%.

Agriculture. Production (in 000; metric tons; 1979): millet *c.* 580; sweet potatoes (1978) *c.* 34; cassava (1978) *c.* 175; peanuts *c.* 85; beans, dry *c.* 40; dates *c.* 25; mangoes *c.* 29; cotton, lint *c.* 43; meat *c.* 50; fish catch (1978) *c.* 115. Livestock (in 000; 1978): horses *c.* 154; asses *c.* 271; camels *c.* 405; cattle *c.* 4,012; sheep *c.* 2,254; goats *c.* 2,254.

Chemistry

Synthesis of a factor involved in asthmatic attacks, a new theory of human colour vision, and evidence of the effect of gravity on chemical reactions made headlines during the past year. Chemists also pondered the nature of Jupiter's Great Red Spot and debated the most vigorous analytical controversy in several decades about the ash from the eruption of Mt. St. Helens.

Organic Chemistry. By 1980 computers were assuming a wide range of tasks in chemical research, from interpreting experimental results and calculating expected properties of compounds to predicting products of reactions and helping environmental scientists assess likely toxicological and environmental effects of newly synthesized chemicals. They also played a valuable role in the work of Frederick Sanger of the University of Cambridge in England, Walter Gilbert at Harvard University, and Paul Berg of Stanford University, who shared the 1980 Nobel Prize for Chemistry

Chemical Industry: *see* Industrial Review

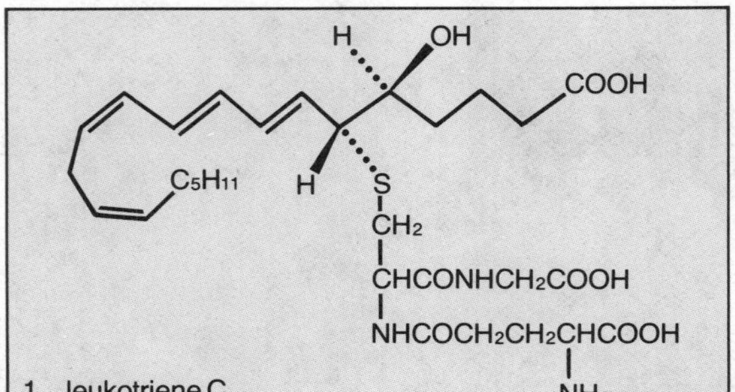

1 leukotriene C

(*see* NOBEL PRIZES). Their studies on the sequences of the chemical units known as nucleotides, which make up the RNA and DNA present in the cells of living organisms, relied heavily on computerized analysis of experimental results. Only by knowing nucleotide sequences could DNA from one organism be combined with that of another, by means of gene splicing, to produce recombinant DNA. Microorganisms could thus be turned into tiny biochemical factories to synthesize gene products foreign to their nature. Using this technique, commerical genetic engineering companies began production of several important human proteins for pharmaceutical use. Sanger, Gilbert, and Berg were certain to be remembered for their contributions to an imminent biotechnological revolution. (*See* LIFE SCIENCES: *Special Report.*)

Perhaps the most exciting laboratory synthesis of the past year was that of leukotriene C (1) by Elias J. Corey and his co-workers at Harvard in collaboration with Bengt I. Samuelsson and Sven Hammerstrom of the Karolinska Institutet in Stockholm. Leukotriene C, a biologically powerful natural product of the body, is well known for its role in the lungs during asthma attacks. Elucidation of its structure could lead to the design of drugs for treating asthmatic diseases. Other chemists added to the list laboratory-made antibiotics with the synthesis of (+)-thienamycin, lasalocid A, and a new group of drugs, known as penems, that are related to penicillins and cephalosporins.

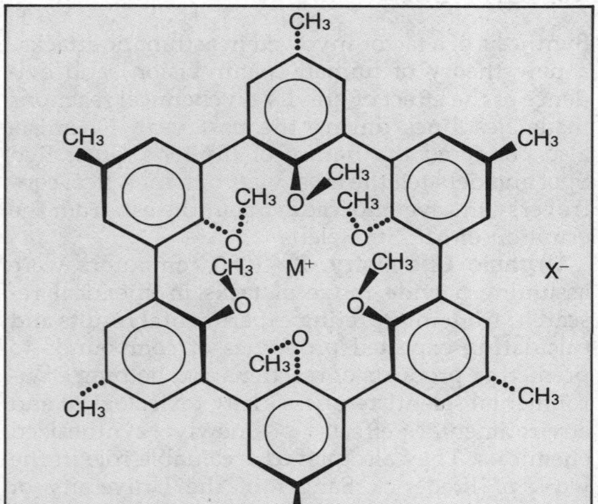

2 a spherand
(M^+ denotes trapped metal ion; X^-, its associated anion)

Other interesting syntheses included those of the anticancer compound streptonigrin, a complex compound nicknamed LICAM-C that proved extraordinarily successful in removing plutonium from living tissue, and enviroxime, an antiviral agent that might ultimately lead to a cure for the common cold.

Among structurally novel compounds produced during the past year were structures dubbed spherands (2). Spherands are ligands, or coordinating molecules, which contain spherical cavities that can incorporate certain ions but reject others. Donald J. Cram and his team from the University of California at Los Angeles were tailoring spherands of different sizes to provide a means of improving separation techniques.

Physical Chemistry. The study of chemical reactions, the properties of liquids, and the electronic structures of large molecules were being dominated increasingly by computers. In one instance, Robert Langridge and his collaborators at the University of California at San Francisco developed a computer program for illustrating in colour the shapes and structures of such complex molecules as proteins and DNA.

Lasers found their way into more chemistry laboratories, but interest in laser-induced photolysis declined because, contrary to earlier expectations, far fewer compounds were found to give breakdown products that differed according to the kind of light—laser or conventional—used to initiate the reaction. Other photochemical research continued to attract attention. James J. Turner and co-workers at the University of Nottingham, England, broke new ground with their photolysis studies of compounds in liquid xenon. Xenon had been used previously as an inert solid matrix near absolute zero (−273° C) for trapping chemical entities that would be unstable at normal temperatures. Turner's method provided a means for studying the kinetics of the decomposition and reaction of unstable molecules.

Work to emulate photosynthesis included attempts to generate hydrogen and oxygen from water using visible light and soluble catalysts. A ruthenium catalyst-based system developed by Michael Grätzel and his co-workers at the Federal Polytechnic Institute in Lausanne, Switz., showed much promise.

News was also made when Koji Nakanishi of Columbia University in New York City and Barry Honig of the University of Illinois, Urbana, provided a chemical model of how the human eye perceives colours. It had been known that a key molecule in the retina, 11-*cis*-retinal, which is bound to complex proteins called opsins, carries a light-absorbing group that constitutes the basis of colour recognition, but not how that group could be "tuned" to absorb more than one colour. The researchers offered evidence that minute differences in the positioning of electrical charges on the various opsins subtly affect the colour-absorption spectrum of retinal.

There were several notable studies of chemical reactions. Perhaps the study that caused greatest excitement—and skepticism—was that of Ralph Dougherty of Florida State University, whose experiments to synthesize a compound called isophorone oxide in a spinning tube led him to conclude that gravity was affecting the yields of right- and left-handed products. He also suggested that prebiotic gravitational fields on the Earth created the predominance of the left-handed amino acids found in plants and animals. Also interesting was a study by James P. Ferris and Robert Benson of Rensselaer Polytechnic Institute, Troy, New York, of the kinetics of of phosphine photolysis. One aim was to understand the nature of the Great Red Spot on Jupiter, thought to be due to the light-induced breakdown of phosphine in the upper atmosphere to red phosphorus.

Inorganic Chemistry. One spin-off from the development of techniques for pharmaceuticals and other biologically active compounds has been the discovery of improved organometallic reagents. The chemical selectivity of the metal in these compounds often gives quicker, more specific reactions that yield fewer by-products. Certain organometallic compounds are electrochromic; that is, they change colour in the presence of an electric field. One of these, a new neodymium compound, looked to be a promising candidate for colour imaging and graphic displays.

Bioinorganic chemists persisted in their search for inorganic compounds that model substances found in nature to gain a better understanding of how enzymes and proteins work. X-ray studies helped further unravel the structure of nitrogenase, the enzyme of certain bacteria and other primitive organisms that reduces atmospheric nitrogen to ammonia during the process of nitrogen fixation. While the results told researchers a good deal about the positions of the iron, molybdenum, and sulfur atoms in nitrogenase, much work had to be done before the mechanism for nitrogen binding at the active site could be clarified. In related work, Mark H. Emptage and colleagues at the University of Wisconsin, Madison, together with Charles D. Stout of the University of Pittsburgh, Pa., characterized new cluster compounds in an iron-sulfur protein from a nitrogen-fixing bacterium, *Azotobacter vinelandii.* One contains a cluster of three iron atoms linked by three sulfur atoms in a six-membered ring, and another contains four iron atoms at the tetrahedral corners of a cube.

Cluster chemistry, while still one of the newer branches of inorganic chemistry, maintained its momentum with the synthesis of many new compounds. Apart from providing information about the bonding interactions between metal atoms, clusters can give scientists a better understanding of what happens at the surfaces of bulk metal catalysts. F. Albert Cotton of Texas A&M University, College Station, continued to explore multiple bonding in clusters and reported tungsten compounds with very short metal-to-metal quadruple bonds, while Earl L. Muetterties of the University of California at Berkeley explored the chemical reactions of metal carbide clusters. Very few inorganic compounds were known that can be separated into right- and left- handed forms known as enantiomers, but cluster chemistry led to the synthesis and resolution of cluster enantiomers based on a carbonyl compound with a central tetrahedron having molybdenum, cobalt, iron, and sulfur as corners (3). Other optically active inorganic compounds could result from this work.

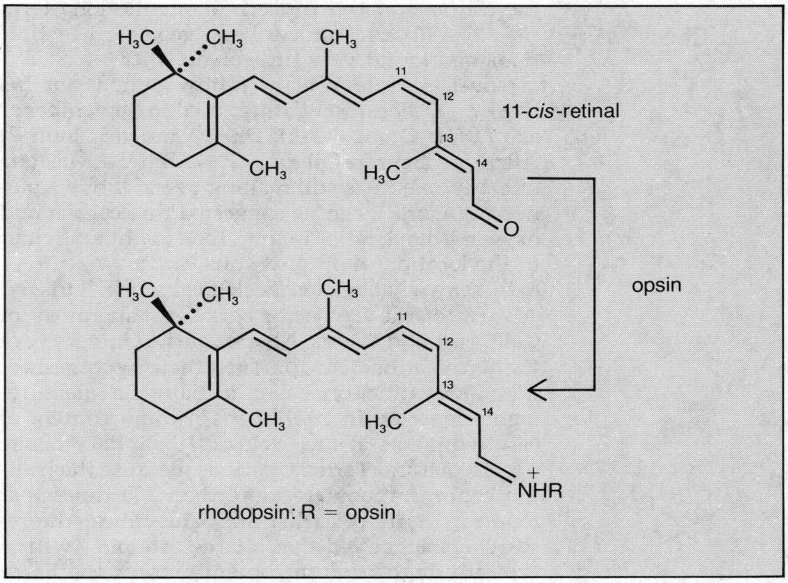

In the visual pigment rhodopsin, 11-*cis*-retinal is linked to the protein opsin by means of a light-absorbing group, or chromophore. Recently chemists learned that the portion of the chromophore most sensitive to "tuning" of its wavelength absorption characteristics lies between the carbon atom at position 12 and the nitrogen atom (N). They also found that wavelength regulation is controlled by the electrostatic interaction of sites along this region with a nearby negative charge located on the opsin.

Analytical Chemistry. As computers expanded their niche in other branches of chemistry, the microprocessor became a standard component of new analytical equipment that offered greater productivity, improved accuracy, and reduced costs. Similarly, the laser served as an integral element of an ever widening range of existing spectroscopic techniques and the cornerstone of several new ones. During the year G. Samuel Hurst of the Oak Ridge (Tenn.) National Laboratory refined his four-year-old technique of resonance ionization spectroscopy, in which a laser is tuned to the resonant frequency of a specific kind of atom in order to remove an electron. This electron can then be detected to indicate the presence of the atom from which it came. Other scientists were working to apply Hurst's technique to the detection of trace amounts of transuranic isotopes (elements with an atomic number above 92) in nuclear wastes by measuring the noble gases xenon and krypton in their fission products.

Despite the sophistication of analytical techniques and the availability of methods that could measure unbelievably small traces of particular elements, a vigorous controversy broke out concerning the analysis of volcanic ash from the May eruption of Mt. St. Helens in Washington state. Some five months later, the controversy was unresolved: state occupational-health laboratories had detected an average silica content of 4–6% in

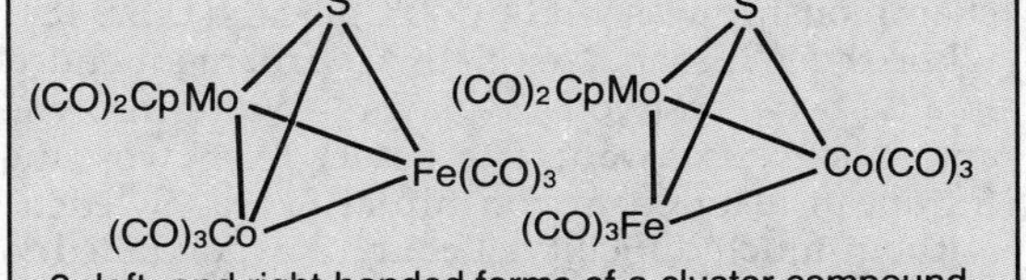

3 left- and right-handed forms of a cluster compound

the ash and voiced concern about the long-term risks of silicosis, while several geological institutions had found very little or no silica.

Nobel laureate Willard Libby, famous for his work on radiocarbon dating, died in September at age 71 (*see* OBITUARIES). During the year John R. Allan of Chevron Oil Field Research Co. was one of many scientists still making use of Libby's pioneering work when he suggested that carbon and oxygen isotope ratios in limestone might give clues to the location of oil reservoirs.

In somewhat related geological work, Luis W. Alvarez of the Lawrence Berkeley Laboratory in California and Walter Alvarez at the University of California at Berkeley pursued their hypothesis of dinosaur extinction based initially on measurements reported in 1979 of the iridium content of clay sediments at the geological boundary of the Cretaceous and Tertiary periods. Because the iridium concentrations are more than 100 times that found in strata of earlier and later times, the researchers suggested that a large asteroid—with a typically high iridium content—struck the Earth some 65 million years ago, producing a crater perhaps 145 km (90 mi) in diameter and ejecting sufficient dust into the atmosphere to reduce drastically the amount of sunlight reaching the Earth's surface for as long as five years. This dust screen virtually stopped photosynthesis, forced food chains to collapse, and caused the extinction of a wide variety of life at the end of the Cretaceous. (GORDON WILKINSON)

See also Materials Sciences; Nobel Prizes.
[122.A.6.; 122.D–E; 123.G–H; 322.C; 339.C; 422.K.5.b]

Chess

World champion Anatoly Karpov demonstrated his magnificent tournament powers by winning first prize in November 1979 at the very strong Tilburg (Neth.) grand master tournament. Two former world champions, Boris Spassky and Vassily Smyslov, came well below him. The Romanian grand master Florin Gheorghiu won a strong tournament at Novi Sad in Yugoslavia. First prize in another well-contested tournament at Vrsac went to the British grand master Michael Stean. The national championship of Czechoslovakia at Trencianske Teplice was also an international tournament and was won by the Czechoslovak grand master Jan Smejkal.

In December 1979 the Danish grand master Bent Larsen won first prize in the Clarin tournament at Buenos Aires, Arg. The Soviet championship went to a veteran grand master, Yefim Geller. The Hastings international tournament, held over the turn of the year, resulted in a tie between the Swedish grand master Ulf Andersson and the English grand master John Nunn. The European junior championship was won by V. Chernin (U.S.S.R.), while the Wijk aan Zee (Neth.) tournament ended in a tie between two U.S. players, Walter Browne and Yasser Seirawan. The Soviet team won the European team championship at Skara, Sweden, without much difficulty. Though Karpov failed to win a single game in the event, he was awarded the Oscar Prize for his achievements over the whole year. Earlier, he won first prize at a very strong quadrangular tournament at Bad Kissingen, West Germany. A knockout tournament held on BBC television was won, surprisingly, by the West German grand master Lothar Schmid, even though Viktor Korchnoi was competing.

The Candidates quarterfinal matches for the world championship were played in March 1980. Lev Polugaievsky beat Mikhail Tal (both U.S.S.R.); Korchnoi (Switz.) beat Tigran Petrosian (U.S.S.R.); Lajos Portisch (Hung.) beat Spassky; and Robert Hübner (West Germany) beat Andreas Adorjan (Hung.). Later in the year Korchnoi beat Polugaievsky and Hübner beat Portisch in the semifinals. The two finalists in the women's Candidates matches were Nana Joseliani and Marta Litinskaya. Joseliani beat the former world champion, Nona Gaprindashvili, in the semifinals.

In March the young Soviet grand master Aleksandr Belyavsky won first prize at a tournament in Bucharest, Rom. Britain won an Olympiad among the European Economic Community countries held in West Berlin. A strongly contested Swiss system tournament at Lone Pine, Calif., in April was won by the Israeli grand master Roman Dzindzihashvili, ahead of 22 other grand masters. First prize in one of the strongest tournaments ever held in London, the Phillips and Drew Kings grand master tournament, was shared among Andersson, Korchnoi, and Anthony Miles (England). The very young Garry Kasparov (U.S.S.R.) won first prize at an international tournament at Baku, U.S.S.R., in May and thereby gained the grand master title. In Yugoslavia Karpov scored

Sicilian Defense, Tilburg, Neth., 1980

White A. Karpov	Black B. Spassky	White A. Karpov	Black B. Spassky
1 P–K4	P–QB4	19 P–N4 (1)	R–N4
2 N–KB3	P–K3	20 KR–K1 ch	K–Q2
3 P–Q4	PxP	21 P–QB4	RxB
4 NxP	N–KB3	22 PxR	B–N4 (m)
5 N–QB3	P–Q3	23 P–B4	Q–B3
6 P–KN4 (a)	P–KR3	24 PxP (n)	Q–R8 ch
7 P–KR4 (b)	N–B3 (c)	25 K–B2	QxP ch
8 R–KN1	P–Q4 (d)	26 K–Q3	QxQ ch (o)
9 B–QN5 (e)	B–Q2	27 RxQ	BxP
10 PxP	NxQP	28 R–QR2	PxP
11 QNxN	PxN	29 RxP	P–R4
12 B–K3 (f)	B–K2 (g)	30 K–Q4	P–R5
13 Q–Q2	BxRP (h)	31 KxP	R–QN1
14 0–0–0	B–B3 (i)	32 P–KB6	PxP
15 N–B5	BxN	33 RxP	B–N6
16 PxB	P–R3 (j)	34 RxP ch	K–Q1
17 BxN ch	PxB	35 R–B8 ch	resigns
18 B–B5	R–QN1 (k)		

(a) An interesting and dangerous attack introduced by the great Estonian master Paul Keres, and one which Karpov has used with much success. (b) Varying from his previous practice when—against Ulf Andersson, for instance—he played 7 P–N5. (c) The alternative, which seems better, is to proceed with his king-side development by 7 ..., B–K2. (d) This is the correct procedure: to strike back in the centre against a flank attack. (e) Certainly the best move here; after the immediate exchange 9 PxP, NxP; 10 QNxN, QxN, Black even has the better game. (f) Rightly not bothering to protect his Rook's Pawn; if instead 12 P–N5, PxP; 13 PxP, R–R5, and Black again has the advantage. (g) If 12 ..., QxP; 13 Q–Q2, B–K2; 14 0–0–0, 0–0; 15 N–B5, with a winning attack for White. (h) A risky capture; preferable seems 13 ..., NxN; 14 BxB ch, QxB. (i) White has a strong attack after 14 ..., NxN; 15 BxB ch, QxB; 16 BxN, 0–0; 17 R–R1. (j) A safer line would be to return the pawn by 16 ..., Q–Q2. (k) Black has to make a difficult choice here; after, for example, 18 ..., Q–Q2; 19 Q–Q3, White's attack persists. (l) A strong and courageous move characteristic of the world champion's middle-game play. (m) In his notes to the game in "64," Karpov singles out this move as a mistake and says that 22 ..., Q–QN1 was correct. (n) And not 24 PxB, Q–R8 ch; 25 K–B2, QxP ch; 26 K–B1, Q–R8 ch; 27 K–B2, Q–R5 ch; 28 K–B1, R–QN1; when Black wins. (o) This leads to a hopeless ending; but 26 ..., QxP ch; 27 K–B2 merely loses a piece for Black; also hopeless is 26 ..., Q–N6 ch; 27 Q–B3, Q–N4 ch;28 Q–B4, B–B3; 29 R–QN1.

KEYSTONE

A new development in the chess world was the introduction of hexagonal chess. The first European championship in this new game was held in London in August.

another outstanding success at the very strong international tournament at Bugojno, and Stean won first prize at Smederevska Palanka. The U.S. championship at Greenville, Pa., in June resulted in a triple tie among Browne, Larry Christiansen, and Larry Evans. There was another triple tie among Miles, Petrosian, and Geller at the Las Palmas tournament in Spain. Karpov won first prize at the IBM tournament in Amsterdam in the summer but lost one game, to the Hungarian grand master Zoltan Ribli.

The U.S.S.R. was very successful in the world of junior chess in late summer: Valery Salov won the under-17 world championship at Le Havre, France; the U.S.S.R. won the world title in the youth (under 26) tournament at Mexico City; and Kasparov won the junior world championship at Dortmund, West Germany. There was a tie for the British championship at Brighton between Nunn and William Hartston. Dzindzihashvili won another Swiss system tournament, this time organized by the Continental Association in New York City. The U.S. Open at Atlanta, Ga., resulted in a tie between Gheorghiu and the international master John Fedorowicz. The Rubinstein Memorial tournament, held at Polanica Zdroj, Poland, was won by the Soviet grand master Oleg Romanishin. Karpov repeated his previous year's success at Tilburg, where he won first prize in an immensely powerful tournament, though he did lose a game to Larsen.

After some failures, Larsen won the Clarin grand master tournament at Buenos Aires, ahead of Karpov, who lost two games. Anthony Miles was first in a strong tournament at Vrbas, Yugos. Belyavsky and Spassky tied for first place at a strong tournament in Baden, Austria. The U.S.S.R. regained its world team championship in the Olympiad at Malta that ran from November 20 to December 6; Hungary was second and Yugoslavia third. A record 81 countries entered the event. (HARRY GOLOMBEK)

Chile

Chile

A republic extending along the southern Pacific coast of South America, Chile has an area of 756,626 sq km (292,135 sq mi), not including its Antarctic claim. It is bounded by Argentina, Bolivia, and Peru. Pop. (1980 est.): 11,104,300. Cap. and largest city: Santiago (metro. pop., 1980 est., 3,853,300). Language: Spanish. Religion: predominantly Roman Catholic. President in 1980, Maj. Gen. Augusto Pinochet Ugarte.

On Sept. 11, 1980, the seventh anniversary of the military coup that overthrew Pres. Salvador Allende's government, Chile's new constitution was submitted to a national plebiscite. Pres. Augusto Pinochet received 67.5% of the votes cast, giving him an additional eight-year term of office and an option to serve a subsequent eight-year term after that, although he stated that he would

CHILE

Education. (1979) Primary, pupils 2,235,861, teachers 72,352; secondary, pupils 358,127, teachers 19,746; vocational, pupils 178,301, teachers 11,029; higher, students 167,546, teaching staff (1974) 22,211.

Finance. Monetary unit: peso, with (Sept. 22, 1980) an official rate of 39 pesos to U.S. $1 (free rate of 93.74 pesos = £1 sterling). Gold, SDR's, and foreign exchange (June 1980) U.S. $2,668,000,000. Budget (1978 est.): revenue 183,264,000,000 pesos; expenditure 175,102,000,000 pesos. Gross national product (1977) 313,377,000,000 pesos. Money supply (Dec. 1979) 47,434,000,000 pesos. Cost of living (Santiago; 1975 = 100; June 1980) 1,490.

Foreign Trade. (1979) Imports U.S. $4,218,000,000; exports U.S. $3,763,000,000. Import sources: U.S. 23%; Brazil 9%; Iran 8%; Japan 8%; West Germany 6%. Export destinations: West Germany 16%; Japan 11%; U.S. 11%; Brazil 10%; Argentina 7%; U.K. 6%; Italy 5%. Main exports: copper 48%; metal ores *c.* 10%.

Transport and Communications. Roads (1978) 75,420 km. Motor vehicles in use (1978): passenger 328,000; commercial 176,300. Railways: (1976) 10,819 km; traffic (1979) 2,211,000,000 passenger-km, freight 2,491,000,000 net ton-km. Air traffic (1978): 1,472,000,000 passenger-km; freight 105.2 million net ton-km. Shipping (1979): merchant vessels 100 gross tons and over 154; gross tonnage 536,616. Telephones (Jan. 1978) 483,200. Radio receivers (Dec. 1977) 2 million. Television receivers (Dec. 1976) 710,000.

Agriculture. Production (in 000; metric tons; 1979): wheat 995; barley 112; oats 150; corn 489; potatoes 770; rapeseed *c.* 65; dry beans 116; tomatoes *c.* 150; sugar, raw value *c.* 100; apples 175; wine 561; wool, clean *c.* 10; beef and veal 164; fish catch (1978) 1,698; timber (cu m; 1978) 9,697. Livestock (in 000; 1979): cattle 3,607; sheep (1978) 5,729; goats (1978) *c.* 600; pigs 1,028; horses *c.* 450; poultry (1978) *c.* 20,000.

Industry. Production (in 000; metric tons; 1979): coal 880; crude oil (1978) 840; natural gas (cu m; 1978) 6,167,000; petroleum products (1977) 4,181; electricity (kw-hr) 10,940,000; iron ore (61% metal content) 11,048; pig iron (1978) 540; crude steel (ingots; 1978) 590; copper ore (metal content) 1,067; copper 674; nitrate of soda (1978) 530; manganese ore (metal content; 1978) 5.5; sulfur (1977) 32; iodine (1978) 1.9; molybdenum concentrates (metal content; 1978) 13.2; gold (troy oz; 1978) 102; silver (troy oz; 1978) 8,210; cement *c.* 1,330; nitrogenous fertilizers (1978–79) 89; newsprint 132; other paper (1977) 164; fish meal (1977) 244.

WIDE WORLD

Soldiers guarded the polling places as Chileans went to vote in September on ratifying a new constitution. The constitution won endorsement.

not do this. The Cabinet resigned in December to permit the president to reshuffle the government. The new constitution considerably extended previous plans for a return to constitutional government over a transition period of five years. There were objections regarding electoral procedures from leaders of opposition parties, especially the Christian Democrats.

Important labour legislation passed during 1979 produced labour unrest in 1980. An unsuccessful strike by 10,000 mine and smelter workers during January 19–31 shut down the El Teniente copper mine, which was producing about one-third of Chile's copper; strikers rejected a 9% wage increase and protested against the new labour laws. The most notable features of the new labour code were that labour union affiliation and the payment of union dues were made voluntary; collective bargaining was allowed, although negotiations were restricted to the individual plant or company level; labour agreements had to be for a term of at least two years and were legally binding; and strikes were permitted but only if approved by secret ballot and only for a period of up to 60 days after which workers would be assumed to have dismissed themselves. The government intended that these measures should be used to hold wage increases in line with individual plant productivity and to reduce inflationary wage agreements. However, certain unions saw in this legislation a method of reducing the strength and influence of the unions and their political supporters.

During early 1980 Chile continued to widen its sphere of international relations as it had done in 1979. In February Great Britain restored diplomatic relations with Chile after a five-year break and in July ended its embargo on arms sales to Chile. However, Chile did not meet with equal success in relations with the Far East. In March the refusal of Pres. Ferdinand E. Marcos of the Philippines to meet President Pinochet caused the last-minute cancellation of a trip to Asia, including the Philippines. This caused the forced resignation on March 26 of Foreign Minister Hernán Cubillos, who was replaced by René Rojas Galdames, previously ambassador to Spain. But on April 2 Pinochet accepted the Philippine explanation that a plot to assassinate the Chilean president had suddenly been uncovered.

Within Latin America, Chile's diplomatic position improved. The threat of war with Argentina over the islands of Picton, Lennox, and Nueva, south of the Beagle Channel, had subsided with the signing of the Montevideo Agreement in January 1979. Territorial disputes with both Bolivia and Peru also lapsed, given the fact that both countries were suffering from internal problems.

Repression continued during 1980 although there were signs of political liberalization. In February the government implemented laws that would banish its opponents into internal exile for up to three months or place "disruptive elements" under house arrest. The state of emergency was extended on March 8 for a further six months, after the lifting of the state of siege. Nevertheless, unrest continued, and Lieut. Col. Roger Vergara Campos, director of Chile's army intelligence school, was assassinated in Santiago on July 15 by four men, who escaped. It was announced officially that 20 police detectives would be tried for kidnapping and torture. Because of the actions of his subordinates, Gen. Ernesto Baeza, head of the Criminal Investigation Department, resigned on August 11.

Main economic indicators implied that Chile had made remarkable economic progress since 1973. In the period 1976–79 the gross domestic product (GDP) growth rate averaged 8%, reaching 8.5% in 1979, as compared with 1974, when the GDP fell by 12%. Inflation increased by 38.9% in 1979, with rates of 27% forecast for 1980; this compared with a rate of 600% in 1973. The balance of payments showed a surplus of U.S. $1,048,000,000, a marked reversal of the $112 million deficit registered in 1973.

As a result, foreign investors returned to Chile, although projects were mainly concentrated in the mining sector. Of the 346 projects that had been approved since 1974, 14 mining enterprises accounted for approximately 90% of total investment. Also, in line with the government's free market economic policies, many state-owned enterprises held by Corfo (the state development agency) had been sold by late 1980. In all, 400 companies had been returned to the private sector at a total purchase price of some $800 million. However, Chile's economic achievements were gained at some cost; real wages fell from 1972 levels, and there was marked unemployment, around 14% in 1980. (CHRISTINE MELLOR)

China

The most populous country in the world and the third largest in area, China is bounded by the U.S.S.R., Mongolia, North Korea, Vietnam, Laos, Burma, India, Bhutan, Nepal, Pakistan, and Afghanistan and also by the Sea of Japan, the Yellow Sea, and the East and South China seas. From 1949 the country has been divided into the People's Republic of China (Communist) on the mainland and on Hainan and other islands, and the Republic of China (Nationalist) on Taiwan. (*See* TAIWAN.) Area: 9,561,000 sq km (3,691,521 sq mi), including Tibet and excluding Taiwan. Population of the People's Republic (1980 est.): 971 million. Capital: Beijing (Peking; metro. pop., 1980 est., 9,029,000). Largest city: Shanghai (metro. pop., 1979 est., 11 million). Language: Chinese (varieties of the Beijing dialect predominate). Chairman of the Permanent Standing Committee of the National People's Congress (nominal chief of state) in 1980, Ye Jianying (Yeh Chien-ying); chairman of the Communist Party, Hua Guofeng (Hua Kuo-feng); premiers, Hua Guofeng and, from September 10, Zhao Ziyang (Chao Tzu-yang).

In 1980 the new pragmatic leadership of the Chinese Communist Party, under the guidance of Vice-Chairman Deng Xiaoping (Teng Hsiao-p'ing), consolidated its power, streamlining the party's ideology and structure and shaping domestic and foreign policies. Hua Guofeng (Hua Kuo-feng), the handpicked successor of Mao Zedong (Mao Tse-tung), remained chairman of the party but was replaced as premier by Zhao Ziyang (Chao Tzu-yang; *see* BIOGRAPHIES). Hua's power continued to dwindle in direct proportion to the rise of Deng.

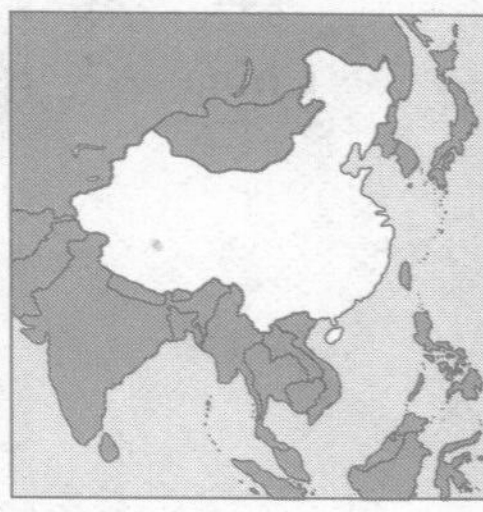
China

During the 30 years of Communist rule in China, Deng had twice fallen from power only to rise again, most recently after the death of Mao. The 11th Communist Party congress in 1977 had reinstated Deng in all his high posts, and he had become the dominant figure in the political system. The new leadership under Deng made economic growth and modernization China's highest priority, rather than ideological purity. The government adopted a new policy of opening the door to Western ideas and lifted the restrictions on a wide variety of foreign and traditional Chinese literature, as well as on religious observance. Because China lacked capital, technology, and cadres with modern scientific and technological know-how, the original ten-year plan of heavy industrial development introduced by Hua proved to be unrealistic. Instead, three years (1979–81) were being devoted to readjusting, reconstructing, consoli-

CHINA

Education. (1979–80) Primary, pupils 146,630,000, teachers (1964–65) *c.* 2.6 million; secondary, pupils 59,050,000; vocational, pupils 1,199,000; higher, students 1,020,000.

Finance. Monetary unit: yuan, with (Sept. 22, 1980) a market rate of 1.46 yuan to U.S. $1 (3.51 yuan = £1 sterling). International reserves (Dec. 1978 est.) U.S. $4.5 billion. Budget (1979 est.): revenue 129 billion yuan; expenditure 112 billion yuan. Total industrial and agricultural output (1979) 617.5 billion yuan. Gross national product (1978 est.) U.S. $425 billion.

Foreign Trade. (1979) Imports 24.3 billion yuan; exports 21.2 billion yuan. Import sources: Japan 26%; U.S. 12%; West Germany 11%; Australia 6%. Export destinations: Hong Kong 20%; Japan 20%; North Korea *c.* 5%. Main exports: light manufactures 45% (including textiles and clothing *c.* 25%); heavy industrial products 32% (including crude oil *c.* 20%); agricultural produce 23%.

Transport and Communications. Roads (1978) 890,000 km. Motor vehicles in use (1976): passenger *c.* 50,000; commercial 1,044,000. Railways: (1978) 50,000 km; traffic (1979) 121,400,000,000 passenger-km, freight 558,800,000,000 net ton-km. Air traffic (1979): *c.* 3,500,000,000 passenger-km; freight (1979) 123.4 million net ton-km. Inland waterways (including Chang Jiang [Yangtze River]; 1978) 136,000 km. Shipping (1979): merchant vessels 100 gross tons and over 846; gross tonnage 6,336,747. Telephones (Dec. 1977) *c.* 5 million. Radio receivers (Dec. 1977) *c.* 45 million. Television receivers (Dec. 1977) *c.* 1 million.

Agriculture. Production (in 000; metric tons; 1979): rice *c.* 180,000; corn *c.* 40,000; wheat *c.* 70,000; barley *c.* 20,000; millet *c.* 11,000; sorghum *c.* 11,000; potatoes 14,000; dry peas *c.* 50,000; soybeans *c.* 13,300; peanuts 2,822; rapeseed 2,402; sugar, raw value *c.* 3,000; tobacco *c.* 1,000; tea 277; cotton, lint 2,207; jute 1,089; cow's milk *c.* 5,200; beef, pork, and mutton 10,624; fish catch 4,305; timber (cu m) 54,390. Livestock (in 000; 1979): horses *c.* 6,500; asses *c.* 11,500; cattle 71,346; buffaloes *c.* 30,000; sheep *c.* 103,000; goats *c.* 80,000; pigs 319,705; chickens *c.* 1,375,000.

Industry. Fuel and power (in 000; metric tons; 1979): coal (including lignite) 635,000; crude oil 106,150; natural gas (cu m) 14,510,000; electricity (kw-hr) 281,950,000. Production (in 000; metric tons; 1979): iron ore (metal content) *c.* 42,000; pig iron 36,730; crude steel 34,480; bauxite *c.* 2,400; aluminum *c.* 400; copper *c.* 300; lead *c.* 300; zinc *c.* 300; magnesite *c.* 1,000; manganese ore *c.* 300; tungsten concentrates (oxide content) *c.* 12; cement 73,900; sulfuric acid 7,000; plastics 793; fertilizers (nutrient content) nitrogenous 8,821, phosphate 1,817; soda ash 1,486; caustic soda 1,826; cotton yarn 2,630; cotton fabrics (sq m) 11,430,000; man-made fibres 326; paper 4,930; motor vehicles (units) 186.

XINHUA NEWS AGENCY/UPI

China's new premier, Zhao Ziyang (right), succeeded Hua Guofeng in September.

dating, and improving the economy, mainly by giving priority to agriculture and light industry. Finally, under the new leadership with its emphasis on collective responsibility, steps were taken toward giving China a government of laws rather than of men.

Domestic Affairs. The third plenum of the 11th party congress in 1978 had rehabilitated practically all the victims of the Cultural Revolution, restored many of them to high posts, and embarked on the program of Four Modernizations: agriculture, industry, science and technology, and national defense. The following year the fourth plenum affirmed these changes and elected a dozen more rehabilitated leaders to the party Central Committee. The fifth plenum in February 1980 further revamped the party hierarchy by appointing more close associates of Deng to key posts and eliminating any remaining Politburo members opposed to his policies.

Deng outlined China's major tasks for the 1980s as economic development and growth, opposition to Soviet hegemonism, and solving the problem of reunification of China and Taiwan. Unprecedentedly but realistically, he considered world peace and not world revolution as the main aim of Chinese Communist policy. Moreover, he emphasized that the number one priority was the program of Four Modernizations, and he would not allow the movement for human rights to interfere with the modernization drive. In an effort to win popular support, the new leadership had instituted a policy of liberation of thought. However, the demands and demonstrations for democracy and a better standard of living proved too much for the leadership to tolerate, and by 1979 it had begun to suppress dissenters. Deng proposed that the provision of art. 45 of the 1978 constitution granting Sida (Ssu Ta; literally, the "four bigs"), the four freedoms and rights (speaking out freely; airing views fully; holding great debates; and writing big-character posters), be deleted because these rights had "consistently been abused." The fifth plenum endorsed Deng's recommendation to propose deletion of art. 45 to the National People's Congress (NPC; the nominal legislature).

As part of the political shakeup, the fifth plenum ousted four Politburo members, Wang Dongxing (Wang Tung-hsing), Ji Dengkui (Chi Teng-k'uei), Wu De (Wu Te), and Chen Xilian (Ch'en Hsi-lien), who were closely identified with Mao's policies. Two younger men known as favourites of Deng, Hu Yaobang (Hu Yao-pang; *see* BIOGRAPHIES) and Zhao, were elected to the powerful standing committee of the Politburo, and Hu was made general secretary of the Central Committee. As such, he was in charge of the party secretariat, reestablished by the fifth plenum to run the party on a day-to-day basis. One of the most dramatic events of the fifth plenum was the complete rehabilitation of the late Liu Shaoqi (Liu Shao-ch'i), China's former president who had been purged in 1968. But glorification of Liu carried an implicit criticism of Mao's ideology and position, since he had been the man most responsible for Liu's downfall. While most of Mao's policies had been repudiated in fact, the party still needed his name and authority to keep it united. Consequently, in a compromise formula, the fifth plenum's resolution on Liu's rehabilitation made the late defense minister Lin Biao (Lin Piao) and the "gang of four" (Mao's widow, Jiang Qing [Chiang Ch'ing], and three leaders of the Cultural Revolution) the scapegoats. It also asserted that Liu's restoration demonstrated "the party's determination to restore the true qualities of Mao Zedong Thought. . . ."

In an interview given on June 4, about three months before the third session of the fifth NPC, Deng confirmed his plans to resign as senior vice-premier and retire from his party and government posts by 1985 in order to make way for younger men. Opposing the system of lifelong tenure in office, he suggested that top officers of the party and government be limited to two terms. The suggestions appeared to be directed at Hua, who in 1976 had become both party chairman and premier. Hua was not seen in public after November, and there were widespread reports that he would be replaced as party leader by Hu.

On the eve of the NPC, the third session of the fifth Chinese People's Political Consultative Conference (CPPCC), a diverse front group, was convened. With 1,712 of its 2,055 members in attendance, it met from August 28 to September 12 for the purpose of displaying unified national support for policies and measures formally adopted by the NPC. For the first time in almost two decades, the sessions of the NPC and the CPPCC were open to diplomats. Just ten days before the NPC began, portraits of Marx, Engels, Lenin, Stalin, and Mao were being removed from Tian An Men (T'ien An Men) Square in Beijing (Peking).

The 12-day session of the NPC, attended by 3,255 appointed delegates, was marked by a greater sense of openness and realism than in previous years. In his opening address, 82-year-old Marshal Ye Jianying (Yeh Chien-ying), the nominal head of state, said that the Congress would elect a new premier and other ministers "in the prime of life" and urged the delegates to remedy the overconcentration of power in a few leaders who occupied too many posts.

Following Ye's speech, various officials outlined China's new economic and financial policies, designed to make profit incentives and local accountability the driving forces behind economic growth. Vice-Premier Yao Yilin (Yao I-lin), the head of the State Planning Ministry, declared that free enterprise, factory autonomy, local decision making, and competition would be expanded. Peng Zhen (P'eng Chen), the former mayor of Beijing, introduced several new bills on taxes, marriage, and nationality and a constitutional amendment to outlaw wall posters; he stated that a graduated income tax would be imposed for the first time, but it would affect only about 20 Chinese and was aimed mainly at foreigners. Finance Minister Wang Bingqian (Wang Ping-ch'ien) reported that the government had a deficit of U.S. $11.3 billion in 1979, that $14,470,000,000 had been spent on defense, and that the budget would not be balanced for at least two years.

In a two-hour report to the NPC on September 7, Chairman Hua formally announced that, in accordance with the party's policy against officials holding high posts in both party and government, he would relinquish the premiership to Zhao. Seven aging vice-premiers, including Deng at 76, also resigned to make way for younger and technically qualified leaders. Ye had been widely expected to retire as well, and the postponement of his resignation caused considerable speculation. It was thought to reflect the Army's displeasure over its low priority in China's modernization program and over the attacks on some of Mao's policies. In his first speech as premier, Zhao called for blending "regulation through planning with regulation by the market" and stated that workers should get a greater opportunity to participate in management. On Zhao's recommendation, the NPC appointed three vice-premiers, including Huang Hua, foreign minister since 1976. Congress

Chinese leaders and a great throng of people attended a memorial service on May 17 for former head of state Liu Shaoqi. The importance of the event was centred on the fact that Liu had been a critic of the late Mao Zedong.

NEW CHINA PICTURES/EASTFOTO

closed the session by adopting a resolution on the revision of the constitution and four new laws, including the abolition of the right to put up "big character wall posters."

The trials of the gang of four, who had been under arrest for four years, and six followers of Lin Biao (including five members of the military) lasted from November 20 to December 29. The charges included persecuting officials, attempting to overthrow the state, and plotting to murder Mao. Jiang, who repeatedly disrupted the proceedings, claimed she had acted entirely at Mao's behest. A verdict was expected early in 1981.

The Economy. China's economy, founded on the Soviet model of public ownership of the means of production under centralized state control, was undergoing significant changes. In addition to the rearrangement of production priorities, a number of significant reforms were introduced in 1980. The economic structure and management were being decentralized by giving more authority and responsibility to managers in agricultural communes and industrial plants. New material incentives and bonus systems were introduced. Rural markets selling peasants' homegrown products and the surplus produce of communes were revived. Individually owned shops closed during the Cultural Revolution were gradually being restored, and self-employed peddlers and craftsmen began to reappear. Increasingly, the Chinese economy was combining political authoritarianism with a capitalist posture.

The Statute of Joint Venture was promulgated in July, and subsequently the Commission for Foreign Investment was established to facilitate the formation of joint ventures with foreign concerns and the transfer of capital and technology from abroad. Negotiations between the Chinese authorities and various foreign governmental financial and industrial institutions, both public and private, resulted in agreements to undertake joint ventures involving billions of dollars. The effect on trade was apparent. China's total trade rose 28% in 1979 to $29,570,000,000, with imports exceeding exports by $2 billion. In the first half of 1980, however, exports rose 35% to $8.4 billion while imports increased only 7.8%, to $8,270,000,000.

According to a report of the Chinese Statistical Bureau, 1979 grain production amounted to 332,-115,000 tons, an increase of 27,365,000 tons, or 9%, over 1978. Because of droughts in the north and floods on the middle Chang Jiang (Yangtze) plain, 1980 grain output was expected to fall below that of 1979, necessitating increased imports. Official figures indicated that output in several key industries had risen over 1978 levels: steel production increased 8.5%, from 31,780,000 to 34,480,000 tons; coal rose 2.8%, from 618 million to 635 million tons; and electric power reached 282,000,000,-000 kw-hr, a gain of 9.9%. Much larger gains, amounting to 25% or more, were made in light industries producing consumer items such as television sets, cameras, and wristwatches.

Foreign Affairs. In the spring China replaced Taiwan in the International Monetary Fund and the World Bank. Through 1980 relations between Beijing and Washington progressed rather smoothly, with exchanges of political, communications, economic, educational, and cultural missions as well as the significant July meeting of U.S. Pres. Jimmy Carter and Chairman Hua in Japan. On the other hand, the 30-year Sino-Soviet alliance expired on April 11 without any fanfare. Beijing joined Washington in denouncing the Soviet invasion of Afghanistan and indicated concern over any prospective Soviet moves against Pakistan and Iran. In January the Soviet Union lashed back at critics of its intervention in Afghanistan, attacking the Chinese as "active accomplices and allies" of imperialism.

About a week after the expiration of the Sino-Soviet treaty, a new Chinese ambassador, Yang Shouzheng (Yang Shou-cheng), arrived in Moscow, ending an 11-month hiatus. However, nor-

Free enterprise in China was demonstrated by this food stall which was doing a thriving business in Lhasa, Tibet.

LIU QIANGANG—NEW CHINA PICTURES/EASTFOTO

WIDE WORLD

U.S. Defense Secretary Harold Brown (left) held talks in January with Chinese Premier Hua Guofeng (right) during a visit to Beijing.

malization talks with Moscow stalled in May over the issue of Soviet support of Vietnam's invasion of Cambodia. In early June China and the Soviet Union signed a trade agreement, but the Soviet role in China's economy had declined sharply compared with the roles of Japan, the U.S., and Western Europe.

High-level talks on the border dispute between Beijing and Hanoi came to nothing because the Vietnamese refused to discuss their occupation of Cambodia. In March, Khieu Samphan, premier of the Khmer Rouge government deposed by the Vietnamese forces, made an official visit to Beijing to seek material and political assistance. Vietnamese strikes into Thailand in June in pursuit of Cambodian rebels brought sharp protests from China and the U.S. and a flow of U.S. arms to Thailand. Both China and the U.S. supported the Khmer Rouge regime's right to hold Cambodia's seat in the UN. (*See* CAMBODIA; VIETNAM.)

Despite the ideological gulf between Washington and Beijing, their global interests in resisting Soviet expansionism seemed to coincide. On January 5, immediately after the Soviet invasion of Afghanistan, U.S. Secretary of Defense Harold Brown arrived in Beijing for an eight-day tour of important industrial and military establishments. During the visit, he informed the Chinese government that the U.S. was prepared to sell China a ground station for satellite reception and certain categories of equipment having possible military use that were on the banned list for the Soviet Union. On January 24 the U.S. Congress overwhelmingly approved a most-favoured-nation trade agreement with China.

Returning Brown's visit, Geng Biao (Keng Piao), vice-premier for security and secretary-general of the Military Affairs Commission of the Communist Party, arrived in the U.S. on May 25 for a two-week tour. At the conclusion of three days of talks with Geng, Brown announced on May 29 that Washington had authorized U.S. firms to sell China a wide variety of nonlethal military equipment, including transport aircraft, air defense radar, and transport helicopters. In March the U.S. and China signed an accord providing for U.S. government assistance in designing and building major hydroelectric and flood-control projects in China and in training Chinese engineers in the U.S. In June the U.S. Export-Import Bank for the first time extended government credit to China, amounting to nearly $70 million for construction of a steel mill near Shanghai. These aid projects led to a number of business deals with U.S. companies and encouraged Sino-U.S. joint ventures. U.S. trade with China had doubled, to over $2.3 billion, between 1978 and 1979.

Beijing expressed considerable concern over a suggestion by Republican presidential candidate Ronald Reagan that the U.S. should restore official government relations with Taiwan while maintaining diplomatic relations with Beijing. During a visit to China in early July, Robert Byrd, the U.S. Senate majority leader, assured Chinese leaders that his country would continue to recognize the Beijing government no matter who won the November presidential election, and George Bush, Reagan's running mate, made a special trip to China in August to clarify the Republican Party's position on China. After Reagan's election in November, Beijing expressed hope that normalization of relations between the U.S. and China would continue.

In early September William J. Percy, U.S. undersecretary of defense for research and engineering, led a high-level Pentagon delegation on an official mission to China to broaden contacts between the defense establishments of the two countries. In mid-September a high-level Chinese delegation led by Vice-Premier Bo Yibo (Po I-po) arrived in Washington to meet U.S. officials at the first formal session of the Sino-American Joint Economic Committee. President Carter and Vice-Premier Bo signed four major agreements on September 17, governing civil aviation, shipping, consulates, and textile trade.

Hua visited Japan in late May, returning the visit to China by Japanese Prime Minister Masayoshi Ohira in December 1979. He was the first head of a Chinese government to visit Japan in some 2,000 years. In a joint communiqué issued on May 29, the leaders of the two countries expressed concern over conflicts and tensions in the Asia-Pacific and Middle East regions and affirmed the importance of continued expansion of trade and economic exchange and cooperation. Hua returned to Tokyo on July 8 to attend a memorial service for Ohira, who had died on June 12. President Carter also attended the service and his special meeting with Hua afterward demonstrated Washington's desire to affirm and increase its friendship with the two leading Asian countries. (HUNG-TI CHU)

Colombia

Colombia

A republic in northwestern South America, Colombia is bordered by Panama, Venezuela, Brazil, Peru, and Ecuador and has coasts on both the Caribbean Sea and the Pacific Ocean. Area: 1,138,-914 sq km (439,737 sq mi). Pop. (1980 est.): 27,326,500. Cap. and largest city: Bogotá (pop., 1980 est., 4,293,900). Language: Spanish. Religion: Roman Catholic (96%). President in 1980, Julio César Turbay Ayala.

Colombia's midterm (*mitaca*) municipal and local elections were held in March 1980, the ruling Liberal Party gaining about 1.8 million of the votes and the Conservative Party 1.1 million. Although the elections passed without incident in spite of problems caused by the occupation of the Dominican Republic's embassy by guerrillas, 72% of the electorate abstained from voting, apparently indicative of dissatisfaction with political arrangements.

Political power was still fairly evenly divided between the Liberals and Conservatives, and the two parties acted in unison to pass legislative and judicial reforms through Congress, effectively strengthening the political system. Against Colombia's background of continuing economic and political discontent, increasing violence, and the problems brought about by the drug trade, there was no likelihood in 1980 that the state of siege imposed in 1976 or the security statute of September 1978 would be repealed.

On February 27 the Dominican Republic embassy in Bogotá was occupied by members of the left-wing M-19 guerrilla organization, marking the start of a two-month siege; 57 hostages were taken, including the ambassadors of Austria, Brazil, Costa Rica, Dominican Republic, Egypt, Guatemala, Haiti, Israel, Mexico, Switzerland, the U.S., Uruguay, and Venezuela. On April 27 the siege was ended upon payment of a ransom thought to amount to some $2.5 million and the promise of an investigation of the human rights situation in Colombia by the Inter-American Human Rights Commission. As part of the negotiations Pres. Julio Turbay Ayala appointed a team of lawyers to find a method of speeding up the trial of 219 of the M-19 guerrillas, against whom proceedings had begun at the end of 1979. On April 1 a report was issued by Amnesty International, which had been prepared in January by a three-member team. The report recommended that the state of siege continuously enforced for most of the previous 30 years should be lifted and that the trial of civilians by military courts should cease, and it stated that cases of torture were evident in Colombia. Left-wing terrorists hijacked a domestic airliner in Colombia on December 15 and flew it with 65 passengers to Havana, Cuba.

It was expected that Colombia would become a member of the General Agreement on Tariffs and Trade (GATT) early in 1981. A protocol for Colombia's accession to GATT was signed on April 17 and was ratified by the Colombian House, but the Senate had not approved it by year's end.

The economy performed well during 1979 with a gross domestic product growth rate of 5.5%, although this did not compare favourably with 1978, when a rate of 8.8% was achieved. The main economic problem was inflation, which rose by 29.8%, as opposed to 17.8% during 1978. The external sector remained strong, with a balance of

Ambassadorial hostages seized in the Dominican Republic embassy in Bogotá in February listened as the Venezuelan ambassador, Virgilio Lovera (left), talked to them under the watchful eye of an armed captor.

GAMMA/LIAISON

COLOMBIA

Education. (1977) Primary, pupils 4,160,527, teachers 128,494; secondary, pupils 1,187,148, teachers 56,402; vocational, pupils 348,590, teachers 18,316; teacher training, students 80,373, teachers 5,024; higher (1978), students 290,624, teaching staff 27,384.

Finance. Monetary unit: peso, with (Sept. 22, 1980) a free rate of 48.14 pesos to U.S. $1 (115.70 pesos = £1 sterling). Gold, SDR's, and foreign exchange (June 1980) U.S. $4,207,000,000. Budget (1979 actual): revenue 114,580,000,000 pesos; expenditure 108,595,000,000 pesos. Gross national product (1978) 884,360,000,000 pesos. Money supply (Jan. 1980) 161,510,000,000 pesos. Cost of living (Bogotá; 1975 = 100; June 1980) 298.8.

Foreign Trade. Imports (1979): U.S. $3,365,000,000; exports U.S. $3,380,900,000. Import sources (1977): U.S. 35%; Japan 10%; West Germany 8%; Venezuela 5%. Export destinations (1977): U.S. 29%; West Germany 20%; Venezuela 9%; The Netherlands 5%. Main exports (1977): coffee 62%; cotton 5%. Tourism (1977): visitors 623,000; gross receipts U.S. $201 million.

Transport and Communications. Roads (1978) 53,852 km. Motor vehicles in use (1978): passenger 453,400; commercial 82,600. Railways (1978): 2,912 km; traffic 342 million passenger-km, freight 1,232,000,000 net ton-km. Air traffic (1978): 3,786,000,000 passenger-km; freight 210.5 million net ton-km. Shipping (1979): merchant vessels 100 gross tons and over 65; gross tonnage 291,702. Telephones (Jan. 1978) 1,396,600. Radio receivers (Dec. 1977) 2,930,000. Television receivers (Dec. 1977) 1,850,000.

Agriculture. Production (in 000; metric tons; 1979): corn 870; rice 1,932; barley 122; sorghum 473; potatoes 2,066; cassava (1978) 2,200; soybeans 169; onions 278; tomatoes 243; bananas *c.* 1,300; sugar, raw value 1,113; palm oil *c.* 66; coffee *c.* 712; tobacco 68; cotton, lint *c.* 108; beef and veal *c.* 598; timber (cu m; 1978) *c.* 24,083. Livestock (in 000; Dec. 1978): cattle 26,137; sheep 2,357; pigs 1,916; goats 639; horses (1977) 1,588; chickens *c.* 32,800.

Industry. Production (in 000; metric tons; 1978): crude oil 6,760; natural gas (cu m; 1977) *c.* 2 million; coal (1977) *c.* 3,800; electricity (kw-hr; 1978) *c.* 18.4 million; iron ore (metal content) 454; crude steel (1979) 233; gold (troy oz) 243; emeralds (carats; 1973) 109; salt (1977) 614; cement 4,152; caustic soda (1979) 25; fertilizers (nutrient content; 1978–79) nitrogenous 66, phosphate *c.* 50; paper (1977) 281.

payments surplus of U.S. $1 billion and an increase in international reserves to $4 billion. In March the government published a draft of its Plan de Integracion Nacional, covering the 1979–82 period. The plan called for public investment to amount to 1,034,000,000 pesos, of which 36% would be spent on the electricity, transport, and communications sectors. (CHRISTINE MELLOR)

Combat Sports

Boxing. Larry Holmes (U.S.) successfully defended the World Boxing Council (WBC) championship four times in 1980, stopping Lorenzo Zanon (Italy) in six rounds, Leroy Jones (U.S.) in eight, Scott LeDoux (U.S.) in seven, and Muhammad Ali (U.S.) in ten. Ali came out of retirement in an attempt to become champion for the fourth time, facing Holmes in Las Vegas, Nev. Ali, 38, had not boxed for two years. He could not recapture the brilliant form of the past, and Angelo Dundee, his trainer, retired him at the end of the tenth round. It was the first time in 60 professional contests that Ali had failed to go the full distance. Holmes remained undefeated in 36 professional contests. Ali turned in his Nevada boxing license.

The World Boxing Association (WBA) heavyweight championship changed hands when Mike Weaver (U.S.) knocked out John Tate (U.S.) in the 15th round. It was Tate's first defeat as a professional. Weaver retained the crown by stopping Gerrie Coetzee (South Africa) in 13 rounds in Bophuthatswana.

The WBC introduced a new weight division, cruiserweight, with a maximum weight of 182 lb (82.6 kg). Marvin Camel (U.S.) became the first WBC cruiserweight champion, outpointing Mate Parlov (Yugos.), but he later lost to Carlos "Sugar" de León (Puerto Rico). The new division was not recognized by the WBA, European Boxing Union, or British Boxing Board of Control. Among the light-heavyweights, Matthew Saad Muhammad (U.S.) remained WBC champion, stopping John Conteh (England), Louis Pergaud (Cameroon), and Alvaro "Yaqui" Lopez (U.S.). Eddie Gregory (U.S.) won the WBA title, defeating Marvin Johnson. Gregory later changed his name to Eddie Mustafa Muhammad and retained the championship by beating Jerry Martin (U.S.).

The middleweights remained the only division with one undisputed champion accepted by both the WBC and WBA. The title changed hands twice. Alan Minter (England) won it from Vito Antuofermo (U.S.) and then stopped Antuofermo in a return bout. But he later lost the title to Marvin Hagler (U.S.) in three rounds. Maurice Hope (England) successfully defended his WBC junior middleweight title against Carlos Herrera (Arg.).

The welterweight division provided good contests. Sugar Ray Leonard (U.S.), a former Olympic champion, won the WBC championship, stopping Wilfredo Benítez (Puerto Rico) in the 15th round. Leonard successfully defended his title by knocking out Dave Green (England) in four rounds. Then in a hard-fought battle Roberto Durán (Panama), former lightweight champion, captured the title by outpointing Leonard. But in November Leonard regained his crown. Durán withdrew from the fight in the eighth round, claiming he was suffering from stomach cramps. José Pipino Cuevas (Mexico) lost the WBA championship to Thomas Hearns (U.S.), who successfully defended the title against Luis Primera (Venezuela). Saoul Mamby (U.S.) took the WBC light-welterweight title from Sang Hyun Kim (South Korea). Aaron Pryor (U.S.) won the WBA crown, knocking out Antonio Cervantes (Colombia).

Jim Watt (Scotland) retained the WBC lightweight title by defeating Charlie Nash (Northern Ireland), Howard Davis (U.S.), and Sean O'Grady (U.S.). The WBA lightweight crown changed hands when Hilmer Kenty (U.S.) stopped Ernesto España (Venezuela). Kenty successfully defended the title by defeating Yong Oh Ho (South Korea). Alexis Argüello (Nicaragua) retained the WBC junior lightweight title with wins against Bobby Chacon (U.S.), Ruben Castillo (U.S.), and Rolando Navarette (Philippines) but gave up the championship to move up into the lightweight division. Rafael "Bazooka" Limón later took the title. Yasutsune Uehara (Japan) won the WBA title from Sam Serrano (Puerto Rico) and successfully defended it against Leonel Hernández (Venezuela).

Eusebio Pedroza (Panama) retained the WBA featherweight championship, beating Shig "Spi-

Chinese Literature: see Literature

Christian Church (Disciples of Christ): see Religion

Christianity: see Religion

Churches of Christ: see Religion

Church Membership: see Religion

Church of England: see Religion

Cinema: see Motion Pictures

Cities: see Environment

Clothing see Fashion and Dress

Coal: see Energy

Coins: see Philately and Numismatics

Colleges see Education

Colonies: see Dependent States

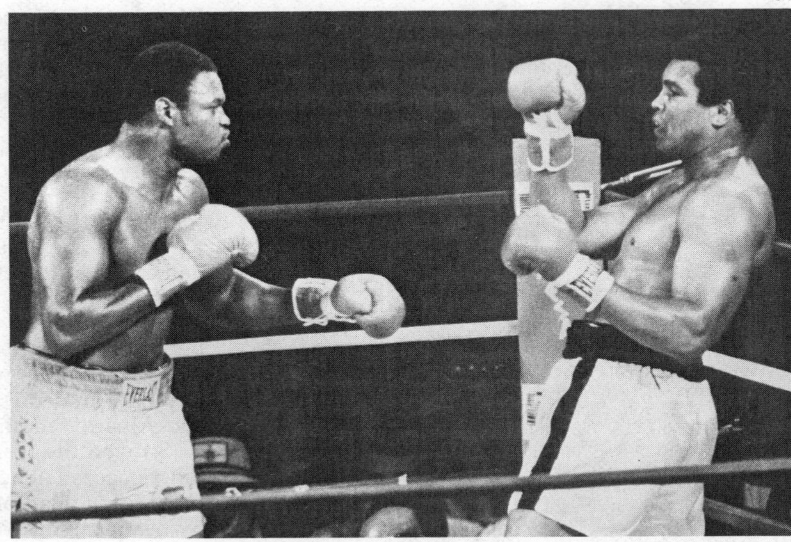

UPI

Former heavyweight boxing champion Muhammad Ali (right) was defeated by World Boxing Council heavyweight champion Larry Holmes in a fight in Las Vegas, Nevada, in October.

der" Nemoto (Japan), Johnny Aba (Papua New Guinea), Kim So Wong (South Korea), and Rocky Lockridge (U.S.). But Salvador Sánchez (Mexico) became the new WBC champion, stopping Danny López (U.S.) in López's tenth defense. Wilfredo Gómez (Puerto Rico) recorded his 11th consecutive WBC junior featherweight title win by defeating Ruben Valdez (Colombia). Gómez also beat Nick Perez (U.S.) and Derrick Holmes (U.S.). Sergio Palma (Argentina) became new WBA champion when he beat Leo Randolph (U.S.). Lupe Pintor (Mexico) retained the WBC bantamweight title by defeating Alberto Sandoval (U.S.), drawing with Eijiro Murata (Japan), and knocking out Johnny Owen (Wales) in 12 rounds. Tragically, Owen never regained consciousness and died 45 days later. Pintor later defeated Alberto Davila (U.S.). Jeff Chandler (U.S.) beat Julian Solis (Puerto Rico) to become the new WBA champion.

The WBC introduced yet another division, the super flyweight, in 1980. Rafael Orono (Venezuela) became its first champion. Shoji Oguma (Japan) became new WBC flyweight champion, defeating Chang-Hee Park (Korea). Tae-Shik Kim (South Korea) won the WBA crown from Luis Ibarra (Panama) but later lost it to Peter Mathelbula (South Africa).

In Europe John L. Gardner (England) won the heavyweight title vacated by Lorenzo Zanon (Italy), stopping Rudi Gauwe (Belgium); he later defeated Zanon. Kevin Finnegan (England) won the middleweight title from Gratien Tonna (France), retained it in a draw with Georg Steinherr (West Germany), but lost it to Matteo Salvemini (Italy) who lost it to Tony Sibson (England). Marijan Benes (Yugos.) retained his junior middleweight title. Giuseppe Martinese (Italy) won the vacant junior welterweight title, beating Clinton McKenzie (England). Charlie Nash surrendered the lightweight crown to challenge Watt for the WBC title. Francisco León (Spain) became the new champion. Carlos Hernández (Spain) won the junior lightweight title from Rodolfo Sánchez (Spain) and successfully defended it against Salvatore Liscapade

Table I. Boxing Champions
as of Dec. 31, 1980

Division	World	Europe	Commonwealth	Britain
Heavyweight	Larry Holmes, U.S.* Mike Weaver, U.S.†	John L. Gardner, England	vacant	vacant
Cruiserweight	Carlos de León (Puerto Rico)*	...	...	...
Light heavyweight	Matthew Saad Muhammad, U.S.* Eddie Mustafa Muhammad, U.S.†	Rudi Koopmans, The Netherlands	Lottie Mwale, Zambia	Bunny Johnson, England
Middleweight	Marvin Hagler, U.S.	Tony Sibson, England	Tony Sibson, England	vacant
Junior middleweight	Maurice Hope, England* Ayub Kalule, Uganda†	Marijan Benes, Yugoslavia	Kenny Bristol, Guyana	Pat Thomas, Wales
Welterweight	Sugar Ray Leonard, U.S.* Thomas Hearns, U.S.†	Jørgen Hansen, Denmark	Clyde Gray, Canada	Colin Jones, Wales
Junior welterweight	Saoul Mamby, U.S.* Aaron Pryor, U.S.†	Giuseppe Martinese, Italy	Obisia Nwankpa, Nigeria	Clinton McKenzie, England
Lightweight	Jim Watt, Scotland* Hilmer Kenty, U.S.†	Francisco León, Spain	Hogan Jimoh, Nigeria	Ray Cattouse, England
Junior lightweight	Rafael "Bazooka" Limón* Yasutsune Uehara, Japan†	Carlos Hernández, Spain	Johnny Aba, Papua New Guinea	...
Featherweight	Salvador Sánchez, Mexico* Eusebio Pedroza, Panama†	Roberto Castañón, Spain	Pat Ford, Guyana	Pat Cowdell, England
Junior featherweight	Wilfredo Gómez, Puerto Rico* Sergio Palma, Argentina†	...	...	...
Bantamweight	Lupe Pintor, Mexico* Jeff Chandler, U.S.†	Valerio Nati, Italy	vacant	vacant
Super flyweight	Rafael Orono, Venezuela*	...	...	...
Flyweight	Shoji Oguma, Japan* Peter Mathelbula, South Africa†	Charlie Magri, England	Steven Muchoki, Kenya	Charlie Magri, England
Junior flyweight	Hilario Zapata, Panama* Yoko Gushiken, Japan†	...	...	...

*World Boxing Council champion. †World Boxing Association champion.

UPI

Sugar Ray Leonard pounded Roberto Durán with a hard right during the sixth round of their welterweight championship fight in New Orleans in November. Durán later abandoned the fight, yielding the title to Leonard.

and Aristide Pizzo (both of Italy). Roberto Castañón (Spain) retained the featherweight crown, beating four challengers. With Johnny Owen dead, the bantamweight titles of Europe, Britain, and the Commonwealth became vacant, but Valerio Nati (Italy) beat Juan Francisco Rodríguez (Spain) to assume the European title. For the results of the boxing matches in the Olympic Games, *see* TRACK AND FIELD SPORTS: *Special Report.*

(FRANK BUTLER)

Wrestling. With the United States boycotting the Olympic Games, the Soviet Union dominated the wrestling events at the games held at Moscow. (*See* TRACK AND FIELD SPORTS: *Special Report.*) However, in the World Cup competition the U.S. broke the Soviet domination by defeating the U.S.S.R. 37 to 33, while Canada finished third with 15 points. Other top teams were Japan with 11 points and Africa with 4.

In the U.S. National Collegiate Athletic Association championships the University of Iowa won its third straight championship. Oklahoma State finished second and Iowa State third.

(MARVIN G. HESS)

Fencing. An unexpected resurgence by France as a top world power provided the highlight in fencing for the 1980 Olympic Games in Moscow.

Table II. World Cup Wrestling Champions

Weight class	Winner
48 kg (105.5 lb)	Bob Weaver, U.S.
52 kg (114.5 lb)	Gene Mills, U.S.
57 kg (125.5 lb)	Sergei Beloglazov, U.S.S.R.
62 kg (136.5 lb)	Victor Alekseyev, U.S.S.R.
68 kg (149.5 lb)	Dave Shultz, U.S.
74 kg (163 lb)	Lee Kemp, U.S.
82 kg (180.5 lb)	John Peterson, U.S.
90 kg (198 lb)	Ben Peterson, U.S.
100 kg (220 lb)	Ivan Yarygin, U.S.S.R.
100+ kg	Jimmy Jackson, U.S.

The French, held to one title in the world championships a year earlier in Melbourne, Australia, captured three of the team events as well as an individual crown in women's foil. The boycott of the Olympic Games by such nations as the U.S., Canada, Japan, and Switzerland, among others, did not dim the bright showing by the French in the bouts held in Moscow's huge Central Army Sports Complex.

Pascale Trinquet gave France its only individual title by winning women's foil—the only weapon with which women compete. The French also scored in men's team foil and épée and in women's team foil. Pascal Jolyot added a medal with a runner-up finish in individual foil, while Philippe Riboud, a world champion a year earlier, was third in individual épée.

Disappointed by its showing in the Olympics was the host Soviet Union. In contrast to the six of eight gold medals gained in the world title games a year earlier, the U.S.S.R. emerged with three gold medals. Vladimir Smirnov captured the men's individual foil after a fence-off with two rivals, while the other Soviet triumphs were scored by Viktor Krovopuskov in men's sabre and by the three-man unit in team sabre. Sweden continued to show strength with the épée. Johann Harmenberg, a two-time world champion, captured his first Olympic crown by defeating Hungary's Imre Kolzonay. Hungary, always a strong threat internationally, showed more balance than in recent years by gaining two silver and three bronze medals. Poland emerged with a second in team épée and thirds in men's team foil and women's individual foil.

The competition was marred by a bizarre accident. Vladimir Lapitsky of the U.S.S.R. sustained a pierced shoulder and chest from a broken foil while he was competing against Poland's Adam

Robak. Lapitsky subsequently recovered and was fencing again by the year's end.

(MICHAEL E. STRAUSS)

Judo. Europeans completely dominated judo events in the 1980 Moscow Olympics by winning all the gold medals; Japan, which won three of the six gold medals in 1976, boycotted the Games. Dietmar Lorenz of East Germany captured the coveted open-weights title. France produced two winners: superheavyweight Angelo Parisi and flyweight Thierry Rey. Robert Van de Walle of Belgium took the heavyweight crown, and Juerg Roethlisberger of Switzerland the middleweight title. Neither country had ever won a gold medal in judo. The light-middleweight title went to Shota Khabareli of the U.S.S.R. and the lightweight to Enzio Gamba of Italy, the first Italian to win an Olympic gold medal in judo.

In Japan, Yasuhiro Yamashita became the first Japanese ever to win the All-Japan championship four times in a row. The 23-year-old Tokai University graduate student pinned Sumio Endo, a 28-year-old Tokyo policeman, with *yokoshiho-gatame* in a repeat performance of their 1979 clash. Although Yamashita also won the over-95-kg title in the 13th All-Japan Weight Class Championships in Fukuoka, he fractured his left ankle in a bout with Endo. A seven-man Japanese team won six golds and a bronze in the second Canada Cup International of Judo, with Isao Matsui capturing the over-95-kg class by defeating Olympic gold medalist Van de Walle.

Karate. The world championships, held in Madrid in late November, were dominated by Japan which won a total of 11 medals. These included four gold medals, two in *kumite* (free fighting) and two in *kana* (prescribed forms). Hsiao Murase continued his winning ways in Japan, capturing the karate open competition in the 35th National Athletic Meet in September for the third consecutive year; the All-Tokyo Tournament in August; and the Shibuya (Tokyo) Ward Tourney. Murase also finished third in the open class in Madrid. But the two-time Wado-kai champion was defeated by Zenichi Ono in the All-Japan Wado-kai Championships for the second time in the past three years. It was Ono's third Wado-kai title. He also won the open class in the Tohoku (Northern Japan) Tournament on June 1 and a silver medal in the 60–65 kg class in Madrid. In the National Japan Karate Association Tournament in June, Toshiro Mori outpunched Fujikiyo Omura to win the Shotokan title, reversing the 1979 results. It marked the second time Mori took first place. Tochigi Prefecture's A team won its fourth straight, and sixth overall, title in the 19th All-Japan Bogutsuki (protective equipment) Karate Championships on May 17–18 in Tokyo. Ryoichi Fukuda outscored 127 others to win individual honours. In the only full-contact tournament, Keiji Sanpei reversed a defeat the previous year by winning the National Kyokushin-kai Championships in November. He edged Makoto Nakamura in a long, bruising final on the basis of *tamishiwara,* breaking three more boards than his opponent. *Karateka* from Canada, Denmark, and Sweden were among the 200 athletes who participated in the sixth All-Japan Goju-kai Championships during August in Aichi Prefecture. Masatatsu of Kyoto won first place with *chudan-geri* (center kick) to add to his All-Kyoto Tourney title. In other key tournaments, Toshio Aoki gained his second title in September during the 20th National Shito-kai Championships in Osaka, and Osamu Jinmon won the title in the Shishu-kai National and International Goodwill Tournament in Tokyo.

Sumo. *Yokozuna* (grand champion) Kitanoumi continued to rule the roost in sumo in 1980, winning three of the six annual 15-day tournaments and extending his *yusho* (tournament championship) victory total to 20. His dream is to surpass former *yokozuna* Taiho's all-time modern record of 32 tourney titles. Kitanoumi, as expected, was named *rikishi* (wrestler) of the year for the sixth straight time; he compiled the best annual total of 77 wins and 19 losses. The other three *yokozuna* won one *basho* (tournament) each. Mienoumi, who retired at the start of the Kyushu *basho* in November, won his third title in January. He was able to complete only two *basho* during the year. He also took longer (97 *basho*) than any other *rikishi* in history to reach the rank of *yokozuna,* and then held the top rank for a briefer period (16 months, 8 *basho*). Other *basho* victors in 1980 were Wakanohana, who won his fourth title in September, and Wajima, who triumphed in November. Mienoumi's 1980 record was 30–18–42, Wakanohana was 72–18, and Wajima 48–20–22. Masuiyama was promoted to the second-highest rank of *ozeki* after the Hatsu *basho* in January, making him and his father the only father-son *ozeki* pair in sumo history. Full-blooded Hawaiian Takamiyama completed his 16th year in professional sumo by setting three new all-time records: 88 consecutive *basho* in the Makunouchi Division (highest of six divisions), and 1,170 total (as well as consecutive) bouts in Makunouchi. Jesse Kuhaulua, who became a naturalized Japanese citizen and changed his name to Daigoro Watanabe, became the heaviest *rikishi* in history at 198.9 kg (438 lb).

In tournament action, 32-year-old Mienoumi surprised everyone by chalking up his third tourney title with a perfect 15–0 record in the Hatsu *basho* in January. *Yokozuna* Kitanoumi and *sekiwake* (second [junior] champion) Masuiyama tied for second with identical 12–3 marks. In the Haru *basho* in March, 27-year-old Kitanoumi began a string of three consecutive victories with a 13–2 record, closely followed by Wakanohana who finished 12–3, and Wajima who scored 11–4. Kitanoumi lost only one bout in the Natsu *basho* in May and registered his second straight *yusho* with a 14–1 mark. Wakanohana once again had to be content with second place, tying No. 10 *maegashira* (a senior grade) Tochihikari with a 12–3 record. Kitanoumi completely dominated the action in the Nagoya *basho* in July by scoring *zensho yusho* (a perfect 15–0 victory). No. 12 *maegashira* Takanosato astonished the experts by grabbing runner-up honours with a 12–3 record, while *sekiwake* Asashio (the only two-time college champion and two-time amateur champion) scored an unprecedented first by winning the *shukun-sho* (outstanding performance award) for the third straight time

WIDE WORLD

Valentina Sidorova of the U.S.S.R. (right) outpointed Sweden's Kerstin Palm in round one of women's foil competition in July in the Moscow Olympic Games.

for his upset victories over *yokozuna*. Wakanohana's first *yusho* of the year, which was also his fourth overall title, followed a 14–1 performance in the Aki *basho* in September. Kitanoumi and Wajima finished out of the money with identical 11–4 marks. In the final tournament of the year, the Kyushu *basho, yokozuna* Wajima, nearing retirement at age 33, captured the title with a brilliant 14–1 record. Wakanohana beat out Kitanoumi for second place with a 13–2 mark; Kita was 12–3.

Kendo. Mitsutoshi Toyama, a 26-year-old schoolteacher from Miyazaki Prefecture, outlasted defending champion Hironori Yamada in the 28th All-Japan Championships. After the two had battled to a draw in the ten-minute final, Toyama surprised the 32-year-old policeman from Kumamoto Prefecture by leaping in with his bamboo sword and scoring a *men* (helmut) strike shortly after the start of the three-minute extension.

The national men's team competition on May 3 in Osaka was won by the Kagoshima Prefecture team, which included the 1979 all-Japan champion, Eiji Sueno. He also finished third in the All-Japan Police Championships at the Nippon Budokan in Tokyo on May 13. Kiyonori Nishikawa took first place with *men* and *do* (side) strikes. Kanae Yano, a Tokyo policewoman, won the national women's championship on May 3 in Osaka. Kimihiro Ishimoto of Chuo University won the men's title in the 28th All-Japan College Championships, while Yaoi Uchida of Tsukuba University took first place in the women's competition. In the fourth Meiji-mura Tournament held in that historic village on March 23, Kenjiro Oka of Tokyo emerged the winner. Meanwhile, 71-year-old Noboru Shigeoka of Kagoshima Prefecture was finally promoted to 9th *dan* after holding the 8th degree for 20 years. (ANDREW M. ADAMS)

Commonwealth of Nations

After the 1979 upheavals, 1980 proved to be a stabilizing period for the Commonwealth of Nations, a process in which the return to power of Indira Gandhi (*see* BIOGRAPHIES) in India played its part. At the same time, however, wars, terrorist activities, and the Soviet intervention in Afghanistan deeply affected Commonwealth Muslims (70 million in India alone), as well as Asian and African refugees, many of whom the Commonwealth sheltered.

Zimbabwe Rhodesia's independence was proclaimed on April 18, when Zimbabwe became the 43rd member of the Commonwealth. The new nation's prime minister, Robert Mugabe (*see* BIOGRAPHIES), at first retained coexistence with South Africa (ties between the two were broken in July), while the attempt at the nine-nation summit conference in Lusaka, Zambia, to counter South Africa's economic domination of the area only revealed the region's continued economic dependence on it (South Africa's trade with the nine shot up by 50% in the first half of 1980). Commonwealth concern with regionalism centred on the Organization of African Unity, with its first economic summit in Lagos, Nigeria, and its costly 17th summit conference in Freetown, Sierra Leone, on July 1–4. Also in Africa, Botswana was shaken by Sir Seretse Khama's death (*see* OBITUARIES) in July.

In a historic Association of Southeast Asian Nations meeting, Singapore and Malaysia, the latter the cornerstone of anti-Communism in Southeast Asia, led the conference in accusing Vietnam of aggression and brought Australia, Canada, New Zealand, the U.S., and Japan into the conference. Papua New Guinea, given observer status, moved to the right in March when Sir Julius Chan (*see* BIOGRAPHIES) replaced Michael Somare as prime minister and set a course of planned capitalism, helped greatly by Australia. Papua New Guinea and Fiji acted as dominant partners in the South Pacific Forum, blocking French and U.S. association, demanding the development of a Pacific power bloc, and asking for more international aid. The Anglo-French condominium of the New Hebrides gained independence as Vanuatu on July 30—the Commonwealth's 44th member. Early in September a Commonwealth heads of government regional meeting (Asia and the Pacific) was held in New Delhi, India; 16 nations from the region attended to discuss economic cooperation. A compromise statement issued at the conference criticized the Soviet Union and Vietnam for their incursions into Afghanistan and Cambodia, respectively.

The 12-nation Caribbean Community, faced with Cuban ideology and refugees, sought to create a community of interests. Fear of overt U.S. intervention was felt after that nation's government proclaimed the U.S. a Caribbean nation and promised aid to any area threatened by the U.S.S.R. The election of Valerie McComie of Barbados as assistant secretary-general of the Organization of American States forged new links

Comecon:
see Economy, World

Commerce:
see Economy, World

Commodity Futures:
see Stock Exchanges

Common Market:
see Economy, World; European Unity

MACBRIDE—SIPA PRESS/BLACK STAR

Britain's Prince Charles and Lord Soames watched as the British flag was lowered on April 18 signifying Zimbabwe's independence.

between Latin America and the Commonwealth.

The Commonwealth Development Corporation showed a record year for 1979 with new commitments valued at £82.7 million (£59.2 million in 1978). Total projects were reckoned at £449 million, acting as a catalyst to private investment of at least £2,000 million. British government aid to less developed countries, largely Commonwealth, was cut in 1980 to £782 million from £974 million in 1979. India remained the chief recipient, followed by Bangladesh, Zambia, and Kenya; an extra £75 million was allowed for Zimbabwe. After a vigorous 146 years of existence, the crown agents, representing the interests of Commonwealth nations in the U.K., were legally incorporated on Jan. 1, 1980. In 1979 the corporation administered U.K. grants and loans of £367 million and managed funds of £2,000 million for more than 100 countries. Its engineering service in 18 countries worked on projects worth £223 million. (MOLLY MORTIMER)

See also articles on the various political units.
[972.A.1.a]

Comoros

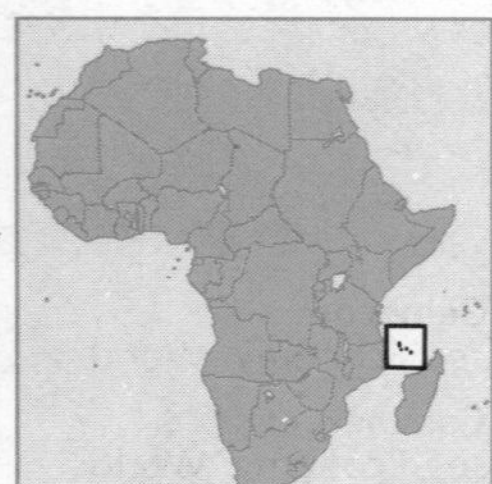

Comoros

Communications: *see* Industrial Review; Television and Radio

An island state lying in the Indian Ocean off the east coast of Africa between Mozambique and Madagascar, the Comoros in 1980 administratively comprised three main islands, Grande Comore (Ngazídja), Moheli (Mohali), and Anjouan (Dzouani); the fourth island of the archipelago, Mayotte, continued to be a de facto dependency of France. Area: 1,792 sq km (692 sq mi). Pop. (1980 est., excluding Mayotte): 300,200. Cap. and largest city: Moroni (pop., 1977 est., 16,000), on Grande Comore. Language: Comorian (which is allied to Swahili), Arabic, and French. Religion: Islam (official). President in 1980, Ahmed Abdallah; premier, Salim Ben Ali.

Pres. Ahmed Abdallah found himself much at odds with his Comoro citizens in 1980. There were strikes on Grande Comore in February; the government was dissolved on July 7, and in a new Cabinet Salim Ben Ali was reappointed as premier; Said Ali Kemel resigned his post as ambassador to France in July because of his disagreement with the government. There were disturbances on Anjouan in August, and the population demanded the dismissal of its governor, Nassus Abdallah, eldest son of the president. There were also increasingly frequent violations of human rights as a result of the imprisonment without trial of many opponents of the government.

Relations with France remained satisfactory but were complicated by two issues: the desire of the Comorans to recover the island of Mayotte, still a French dependency, and the claim, officially formulated by President Abdallah during a private visit to Paris, to the French-administered archipelago of the Glorieuses. (PHILIPPE DECRAENE)

COMOROS

Education. (Excluding Mayotte; 1978–79) Primary, pupils 49,940, teachers 934; secondary, pupils 8,932, teachers 499; teacher training, students 45, teachers 3.

Finance and Trade. Monetary unit: CFA franc, with (Sept. 22, 1980) a parity of CFA Fr 50 to the French franc and a free rate of CFA Fr 210 to U.S. $1 (CFA Fr 504 = £1 sterling). Budget (1979 est.) balanced at *c.* CFA Fr 3.2 billion. Foreign trade (1977): imports CFA Fr 4,055,000,000; exports CFA Fr 2,205,000,000. Import sources: France *c.* 41%; Madagascar *c.* 20%; Pakistan 8%; Kenya *c.* 5%; China 5%. Export destinations: France 65%; U.S. 21%; Madagascar 5%. Main exports: vanilla 49%; essential oils 27%; cloves 13%; copra 6%.

Computers

As the computer became more commonplace during 1980—a familiar sight in banks, libraries, travel agencies, even pharmacies—few people remained untouched by the dawning of the "information age." This new era, the so-called post-industrial society, held out the promise of unparalleled access to knowledge of all kinds.

Business. As the cost per unit of computing power continued to drop (an average of 15% a year), spokesmen for data processing technology boasted that similar progress in the automobile industry would have resulted in 1980 Rolls-Royces selling for $70 apiece. The remarkable decline in the price of computer hardware, making it possible for businesses of all sizes and even individuals to own a computer, remained primarily attributable to the chip, a sliver of silicon containing the computer's complicated integrated circuitry.

Surprisingly, then, one of the few serious problems facing the computer industry in 1980 concerned those very chips: demand simply far outstripped supply. The world market for semiconductor circuits reached $10 billion, and industry officials predicted that figure would more than double within five years as the chips continued to find new uses in a variety of consumer products and industrial processes.

A problem for U.S. manufacturers was a possible Japanese invasion of U.S. computer markets. The Japanese computer companies—benefiting from government-subsidized research and development—could offer customers a level of technology fully comparable to that of their U.S. counterparts. The crucial difference lay in software, the programmed instructions that tell the computer what to do. As the decade opened, U.S. companies were still enjoying a clear edge in computer software.

Without question the most aggressive U.S. company in fending off the Japanese invasion was IBM Corp. The giant U.S. computer maker, long dominant in the general-purpose (mainframe) portion of the industry, steadily increased its interest in minicomputers (a Japanese strength) and in creating a network of interrelated information devices (the "office of the future"). The increasing preference for distributed data processing, in which smaller computers and a multitude of terminals replace the single large central processor, forced IBM to reorient its approach to the market.

Other mainframe manufacturers discovered that the road to survival lay in software specialization. As a consequence Sperry Univac developed units specifically designed for governmental applications, while NCR concentrated on meeting the computer needs of retailers. Burroughs Corp., Honeywell Inc., and Control Data Corp. similarly sought out niches of the $10 billion mainframe market, and all participated in the 15–20% growth rate that segment of the computer market enjoyed.

The minicomputers, however, remained the fastest growing segment of the computer hardware industry. Expected to grow at an annual rate of more than 30% a year through the 1980s, the minicomputer industry looked to Digital Equipment Corp. as its leader. Not about to miss out in this segment of the market, IBM introduced the 5120 Computing System, a typewriter-size machine offering the computing power of a unit that 20 years before would have required a 6 by 9 m (20 by 30 ft) room. Other minicomputer manufacturers increasingly turned their attention to superminis, powerful but compact units that filled the gap between traditional mainframes and minicomputers.

Technology. As computer makers increasingly recognized the need to produce integrated information systems for the office of the future, they bent their energies toward creating systems of "smart machines." Xerox Corp., for example, introduced a single terminal that offered both word processing and a limited amount of data processing.

More importantly, the company announced its plans to design the Ethernet communications network, a system designed to link various kinds of electronic equipment within an office and to similar equipment in other offices. A single cable would connect computers, word-processing machines, photocopying machines, etc., so that any bit of information (such as a business letter) entered into any piece of office hardware could be transmitted to any other piece of hardware in that office or another office in the same communications network. The result is electronic mail—the ability to beam a message electronically from one office to another.

Close at hand was the advent of the videodisc to store computerized data. Better than magnetic tape in its ability to store great quantities of data, to store data for longer periods of time, to provide specific information faster, and to do all this at a much lower cost, the videodisc contains tiny pits (each one about 1/100 the diameter of a human hair) of digital information. A laser can both read the data from a recorded disc and encode information (create pits) on a blank disc.

Probably the most important achievement in recent computer technology has been the creation of the Josephson-effect computer switch. This switch, consisting of wires thinner than any ever

All sorts of computerized information is beginning to appear on the dashboards of late-model cars.

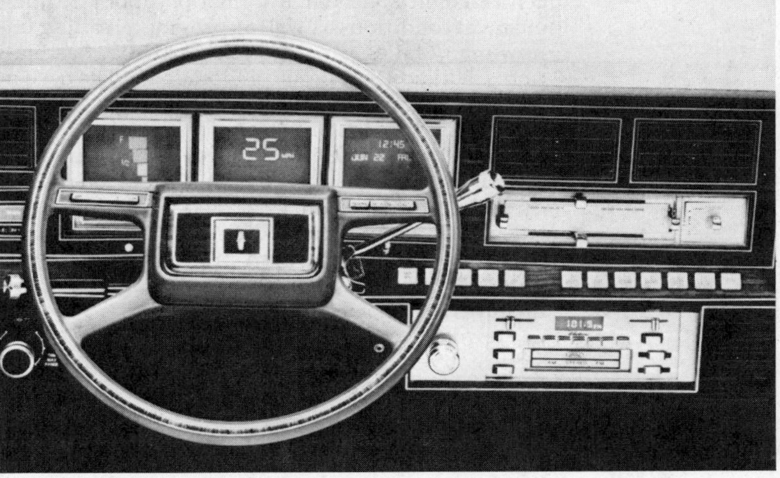

FORD MOTOR CO.

BOB SHERMAN—CAMERA 5

Canadians who wished to were enabled during the year to sign up with Viewdata, a system that made it possible for ordinary television sets to become computer terminals by means of a hookup over telephone lines.

created by man before (1/20,000 of a millimetre or 1/500,000 of an inch wide) is fashioned from metal-like materials that normally are poor conductors of electricity but which become superconductors when cooled with liquid helium to a temperature near absolute zero. In its supercool, superconducting state the material offers almost no resistance to electricity and generates very little heat, enabling the circuitry to be fabricated much closer together than present circuits without the danger of overheating. The shorter distances the electronic signals must travel thereby create the possibility of an ultrapowerful computer capable of functioning between 10 and 100 times faster than machines presently relying on semiconductor chips. The first Josephson-effect computer could be developed before 1985.

Applications. While predicting that the age of electronic equipment on automobiles was just starting, carmakers equipped 1980 vehicles with a variety of computer-related gear. The Lincoln Mark VI featured a dashboard with three microcomputers: a bar-chart fuel gauge, a digital speedometer, and a message centre. The message centre could spell out information about 36 mechanical conditions as well as provide a reading on how many miles remained to a particular destination. Cadillac's Seville and Eldorado models used a chip to determine fuel consumption, on both an average and an instantaneous basis.

For 1981 General Motors planned to include a computerized emission-control system on every car, while Ford and Chrysler models would also be laden with chip-controlled devices. And by 1983 the automakers might even provide talking computers to tell owners what was wrong with their malfunctioning cars.

Viewdata, a system in which ordinary television receivers are transformed into computer terminals via a telephone hookup between the sets and a large computerized information bank, was launched on a pilot basis in Canada. The system allowed 1,000 Canadian homes and offices to view on their TV screens a wide variety of information, including airline schedules, stock market listings, and news bulletins.

Concerns. While no one could reasonably deny the labour-saving achievements that computers had wrought, some critics voiced concern over the unresolved potential for harm associated with the "information age" at hand. Clearly, a major shift had already begun in the relationship of people to their work. On the positive side the computer terminal freed individuals from specific work sites. For example, secretaries equipped with word-processing machines could work as effectively in their homes as in an office. On the negative side electronic systems in the office of the future and computerized robots in factories would certainly take jobs from unskilled and semiskilled workers.

Although an old problem, computer crime was still far from under control. Only 1% of all computer crime during 1980 was even detected, and—because many companies refused to acknowledge that they had been victimized—only 1 in 22,000 perpetrators was successfully prosecuted. The result was a loss of between $100 million and $300 million a year to the government, banks, brokerage houses, and other businesses heavily dependent upon computers. Federal legislation designed to halt computer crime was first introduced in 1977 but had not yet won approval.

Of far greater importance than either computer crime or impending automation was the spectre of an accidental nuclear holocaust being triggered by a computer malfunction. Twice in four days (June 3 and 6) a computer led U.S. Air Force officials to believe that Soviet missiles had been fired at the U.S. The countdown toward nuclear retaliation proceeded for several minutes before the electronic error was recognized. The Pentagon promised that there would be no more false alarms, but military officials had given the same assurances following a similar incident the preceding autumn.

(JEROLD L. KELLMAN)

[735.D.; 10/23.A.6–7]

Congo

A people's republic of equatorial Africa, the Congo is bounded by Gabon, Cameroon, the Central African Republic, Zaire, Angola, and the Atlantic Ocean. Area: 342,000 sq km (132,047 sq mi). Pop. (1980 est.): 1,537,000, mainly Bantu. Cap. and largest city: Brazzaville (pop., 1977 est., 310,000). Language: French (official) and Bantu dialects. Religion (1977 est.): Roman Catholic 40.5%; Protestant 9.6%; Muslim 2.9%; animist 47%. President in 1980, Col. Denis Sassou-Nguesso; premier, Col. Louis Sylvain Ngoma.

In 1980 two paradoxical events took place in Brazzaville, capital of the Congo, at a time when Pres. Denis Sassou-Nguesso's government was continually proclaiming its adherence to scientific socialism and militant anticolonialism. On May 5 Pope John Paul II visited Brazzaville on his way from Zaire to Kenya, and on October 3 the centenary of the foundation of Brazzaville by the explorer Pierre Savorgnan de Brazza was celebrated in the presence of an important assemblage of former governors and colonial administrators.

In foreign affairs the government, while maintaining excellent relations with France, attempted to hold a balance between China, to which Sassou-Nguesso paid an official visit in July, and the Soviet Union, to which the Congo was linked by many agreements. The Congo attended a conference in Togo in October that attempted—without success—to end the civil war in Chad. With regard to the economy, the Congo continued to develop its oil production (about three million metric tons annually). (PHILIPPE DECRAENE)

CONGO

Education. (1977–78) Primary, pupils 345,736, teachers 6,675; secondary, pupils 127,210, teachers 2,883; vocational, pupils 11,123, teachers 606; teacher training (1975–76), students 705, teachers 34; higher, students 3,642, teaching staff (1975–76) 165.

Finance. Monetary unit: CFA franc, with (Sept. 22, 1980) a parity of CFA Fr 50 to the French franc and a free rate of CFA Fr 210 to U.S. $1 (CFA Fr 504 = £1 sterling). Budget (1978–79 est.) balanced at CFA Fr 60,249,000,000.

Foreign Trade. (1978) Imports CFA Fr 58,860,000,000; exports CFA Fr 31,160,000,000. Import sources (1977): France 49%; West Germany 6%; U.S. 5%. Export destinations (1977): Italy 30%; France 12%; U.S. 7%; Spain 7%; The Bahamas 6%. Main exports (1977): crude oil 54%; timber 13%; food 9%; chemical fertilizer 7%; manganese ore 5%.

Transport and Communications. Roads (all-weather; 1977) 8,246 km. Motor vehicles in use (1977): passenger 13,250; commercial 3,700. Railways: (1977) 803 km; traffic (1978) 301 million passenger-km, freight 487 million net ton-km. Air traffic (including apportionment of Air Afrique; 1978): 171 million passenger-km; freight 15.9 million net ton-km. Telephones (Jan. 1978) 13,400. Radio receivers (Dec. 1977) 88,000. Television receivers (Dec. 1977) 3,500.

Agriculture. Production (in 000; metric tons; 1978): cassava 532; sweet potatoes *c.* 24; peanuts *c.* 18; sugar, raw value *c.* 27; bananas *c.* 25; plantains 33; coffee *c.* 3; cocoa *c.* 4; palm oil *c.* 5; tobacco *c.* 1. Livestock (in 000; 1978): cattle 70; sheep 66; goats 119; pigs 49; chickens *c.* 1,000.

Industry. Production (in 000; metric tons; 1977): cement 45; crude oil (1979) 2,600; lead concentrates (metal content) 2.4; zinc ore (metal content) 4.7; potash fertilizers (nutrient content; 1977–78) *c.* 81; electricity (kw-hr) *c.* 118,000.

Consumerism

Consumers the world over continued to voice dissatisfaction with the quality and performance of products and services—often with good reason. For example, of the 62,000 formal complaints made to Australian government consumer agencies in 1979, it appeared that fully 95% justified attention and further action. Belgium's first free information centre for consumers, Test Achats, reported receiving requests for advice from more than 40,000 consumers in its first year. The French Union Féderale des Consommateurs (UFC) introduced a new advertisement column in its monthly magazine to evaluate the frequency and magnitude of individual complaints.

International Cooperation. The first attempt at a comprehensive analysis of consumer law in the European Economic Community (EEC), *Consumer Legislation in the EEC Countries* (1980), prepared on behalf of the Commission of the European Communities' Consumer Protection Service, suggested that the EEC still had far to go before it achieved any standard of harmonization or regulation in consumer law. The report concluded that equality through law for all consumers might lead to unequal treatment for those groups unable to use modern instruments of consumer policy, such as information and law enforcement.

A major concern of consumer groups and nongovernmental and international organizations continued to be infant formula. In May the World Health Assembly unanimously adopted a resolution on infant and child feeding, including a mandate to draft a marketing and advertising code for infant formulas and breast-milk substitutes. The World Health Organization/UNICEF saw the substitution of artificial feeding for breast-feeding as a major public health problem because of the hygienic and economic hazards of artificial feeding in poverty areas.

The president of the International Organization of Consumers Unions (IOCU) called the campaign on infant formula the first worldwide campaign by consumer groups. IOCU looked on the promotion of infant formula as but one of many examples of irresponsible market practices on the part of companies operating in less developed countries. Multinationals tended to observe lower standards of advertising and promotion in less developed countries than in advanced ones, and products developed with regard to the living standards and needs of developed countries might well be inappropriate in less developed areas.

Advertising, codes of practices, and multinational corporations were among the subjects discussed at a seminar organized by IOCU on "The Law and the Consumer." More than 150 delegates from 26 countries attended the weeklong meeting in Hong Kong, which also looked at complaint handling, consumer education, lobbying, and product safety and responsibility. A follow-up to this meeting was the Association of Southeast Asian Nations' consumer protection seminar in the Philippines in early October. Aims of the semi-

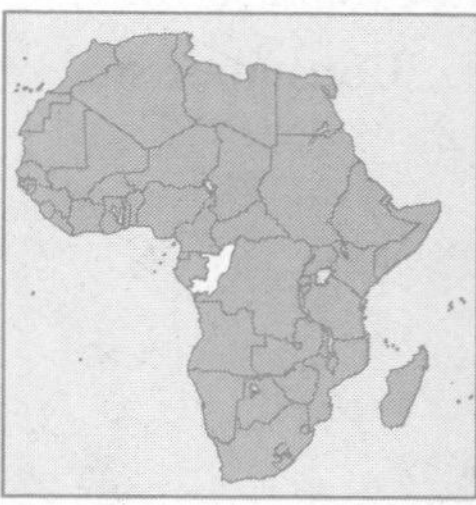
Congo

Congregational Churches: *see* Religion

Conservation: *see* Environment

Construction Industry: *see* Engineering Projects; Industrial Review nar included education of representatives of governments and nongovernmental organizations in aspects of consumer protection and the establishment of a framework for cooperation among governments and consumer organizations in the area.

National Policies. National governments and consumer bodies continued to attack consumer problems in various ways. In Australia the Trade Practices Commission warned four breakfast food companies that they faced prosecution unless they changed their (misleading) advertising, which asserted that the products in question had weight-reducing properties and contained "higher" protein and "extra" fibre. The Australian Consumers' Association called for an improved food-labeling system and made a submission to the working party of the National Health and Medical Research Council about televised food advertisements directed at children. In France the UFC revealed the extent to which breeders of calves used hormones and advised consumers to boycott the purchase of veal, sales of which subsequently dropped by some 50%.

National consumer legislation was also varied. The Belgian government proceeded with plans to ban full-page tobacco advertisements. In Canada fireworks were brought under the Hazardous Products Act. Regulations on the use, packaging, and marking of asbestos came into force in Denmark, which also introduced new provisions dealing with the delivery, price, faulty performance, and sale by sample of goods (excluding property). In West Germany a revised act against unfair competition enabled consumers to have their money refunded when goods were sold under a false description. From the beginning of the year, Swiss law demanded that all food packages give full information on the composition of the contents.

In the U.S. the Federal Trade Commission (FTC), in an August report, recommended the adoption of new trade rules for the consumer-finance industry. Under the proposed rules, creditors would be allowed to seize, after a default, only those household items bought under a defaulted credit contract. Also, a creditor would have to give the borrower credit for the fair retail market value of any item that was repossessed if the creditor attempted to collect money still owed.

The economic situation in 1980 caused an increase in the number of personal bankruptcies. Over 300,000 Americans appeared in bankruptcy courts, compared with the previous record of 120,000 set in 1975. Recent changes in federal law made bankruptcy easier. The Federal Bankruptcy Reform Act of 1978, which went into effect at the end of 1979, permitted a bankrupt individual to retain $7,500 in equity on a house, $15,000 if a joint income tax return was filed, $1,200 on a car, and other holdings. It also allowed debtors to consolidate obligations and pay them over a three-year period. With court approval, a debtor could develop a repayment program "in good faith," commensurate with his ability to pay.

In May Pres. Jimmy Carter signed legislation needed to keep the FTC in operation. The bill included a provision allowing Congress to intervene, veto, and nullify regulations of the commission. It also limited the commission's power to investigate several industries, although it did not bar the FTC from regulating any industry other than agricultural cooperatives, trademarks, and the insurance and funeral industries.

Procter & Gamble, the leading national advertiser in the U.S., agreed to spend a portion of its advertising budget, beginning in October 1980, on a campaign to discourage women from using its Rely tampons. The company voluntarily withdrew the product from retail shelves after a report issued by the Food and Drug Administration (FDA) linked tampon use with toxic-shock syndrome. (*See* HEALTH AND DISEASE.) The FTC reported that the Ford Motor Co. was placing advertisements in national magazines telling owners of its 1979 and 1980 models about major engine and transmission problems and informing them that Ford would pay for all or part of the repair cost after warranties expired.

The U.S. Supreme Court overturned a lower-court ruling that real estate firms and local realty boards were not in violation of the Sherman Act when they agreed on a fixed commission fee. The case resulted from a class-action suit brought in 1975 on behalf of all New Orleans, La., homeowners who had used brokers to sell property during the preceding four years. The real estate industry argued that the work of real estate brokers was local in nature and outside the reach of federal antitrust laws. However, the Supreme Court unanimously adopted a broad view of business activity and denied the industry's claim. This ruling would have a substantial effect on commission practices. A recent California law required all real estate listing agreements to include a notice informing the homeowner that brokers' fees are not fixed by law and are negotiable.

A bill was signed by President Carter in October deregulating the moving industry. Consumer groups and movers of household goods supported the legislation, which allowed more competition, reduced government paperwork, and permitted more rate freedom. Moving companies would no longer be required to give customers estimates of their charges, but if they made estimates, certain requirements had to be met. The customer would be allowed to delay payment for final charges exceeding 110% of the estimate; companies would be allowed to increase or decrease rates by 10% without Interstate Commerce Commission approval; and customers would be allowed to go to an arbitration board instead of the courts to settle disputes. Adding weight to a load to increase the price would become a federal crime. Movers were required to notify customers whenever the pickup or delivery date could not be met, and misleading advertising was prohibited.

The FDA entered into an agreement with pharmaceutical firms manufacturing common tranquilizers requiring these firms to inform physicians that antianxiety drugs should not be recommended to alleviate everyday stress.

(ISOLA VAN DEN HOVEN; EDWARD MARK MAZZE)

See also Economy, World; Industrial Review: *Advertising*.

[532.B.3; 534.H.5; 534.K]

WHERE DOES THE BUCK STOP?

by David C. Beckwith

For ten weeks in early 1980, a parade of ranking officials and engineers from the Ford Motor Co. marched in and out of the tiny county courthouse in Winamac, Ind. Their corporation was in the dock on three counts of reckless homicide, the first corporation so charged in U.S. history.

The case arose from the fiery deaths of three local teenage girls when the gas tank of their Ford Pinto exploded in a 1978 accident. After four days of deliberations, the jury on March 13 acquitted Ford of the charges, leaving the lesson to be drawn from the episode in sharp dispute. But the case was clearly a noteworthy, if tangential and tentative, step in a product liability revolution that has markedly altered the U.S. commercial landscape over the past two decades.

Who Bears Responsibility? Prior to the recent developments, an accident victim could collect for his injuries only if he could prove the manufacturer was totally at fault. A factory worker maimed by a complicated machine, or the unwitting victim of a poorly tested drug, often could rely only on personal insurance or workmen's compensation money. That led to serious inequities and finally prompted lawyers and courts to redistribute the risks. Their rationale was aptly stated by the California Supreme Court in *Greenman* v. *Yuba Power Products,* the 1963 case considered the Lexington and Concord of the product liability revolution: "The costs of injuries resulting from defective products [should be] borne by the manufacturers that put such products on the market rather than by the injured persons who are powerless to protect themselves."

This raises fundamental, difficult questions about the rights of citizens in a free society to take responsibility for their actions. Should a drill press operator, paid by the amount he produces, be allowed to use a faster, more dangerous machine and then be compensated when he is injured? Should a consumer who buys a cheap tire be able to sue the manufacturer when it blows out and injury results? If the solutions had been hammered out in legislatures, with policy questions dispassionately considered, the changes might have been orderly and predictable. In the U.S., however, society's toughest problems are often decided in a courtroom—where each jury has leeway to determine the law in its case—and the answers are apt to be contradictory, confusing, and erratic.

David C. Beckwith is editor of the Legal Times of Washington, *Washington, D.C.*

WIDE WORLD

Three teenage girls were killed in an accident on Aug. 10, 1978, when the gas tank of their Ford Pinto exploded. The Ford Motor Co., defendant in the case, was acquitted of reckless homicide in March 1980 after a four-day jury deliberation.

Prior to a landmark 1916 case against the Buick Motor Co., the victim of a defective product could sue only the person who sold it to him. Following that decision, however, the courts made manufacturers responsible for their negligent conduct to all who might be foreseen as using their product. The courts also gradually developed a theory of "implied warranty of fitness," which required all parties in the distribution chain to act with due care.

The Liability Explosion. The Greenman case, over a cutting saw accident in a workshop, introduced a far more radical change. It clearly held that the maker of a defective product could be held liable under tort law, not merely for a breach of contract. The distinction is important. No longer does the obligation of a manufacturer depend in any way on his agreement, and no longer do the tricky escape clauses of sales law apply. The victim can also claim exemplary or punitive damages if he proves the defendant was reckless.

As it happened, at the very moment that the California decision was announced, experts were rewriting the *Restatement of Torts,* the legal fraternity's bible in that area. They quickly folded the Greenman ruling into their text, and within a few years, tort liability for purveyors of defective products was almost universally accepted.

The initial product liability cases in tort involved defects in construction or breach of an express warranty—a pin in a candy bar, a shatterproof bottle that shattered—all relatively easy liability questions. But imaginative plaintiffs' lawyers quickly pushed the idea further, into the murkier areas of defect in design and duty to warn. If a man is crushed when he rolls his automobile, should the car manufacturer be held liable because he failed to design a stronger roof support? The common desk stapler has no shield mechanism and no warning; should an individual who staples his hand be allowed to sue? According to Victor Schwartz, a torts law expert, "True strict liability would mean that the injured plaintiff would win every time."

With courts around the country deciding such matters on a case-by-case basis, the incidence of huge judgments started to soar in the late 1970s. In one well-publicized case, for example, an Oklahoma man bought commercial glue that plainly demanded cross ventilation and open windows during use. But there were no windows in his workroom, and a jury later awarded him $600,000 for burns he suffered when the glue fumes exploded. With that type of horror story as background, insurance carriers panicked and raised premiums by an average 300% in the mid-1970s. The country had muddled itself into a product liability crisis.

Task Force Findings. Although individual states set their own tort law, the nationwide situation prompted the federal government to set up a task force study group in 1976. The inquiry revealed that virtually all sides of the controversy had made exaggerated and misleading claims. Plaintiffs' lawyers, for example, had claimed that the occasional million-dollar judgments were not significant factors in the crisis, but the study found the tort judgments had spurred insurance companies into "panic pricing." Insurance industry ads suggested that a million product liability claims were being filed annually; the study put the number at 60,000 to 70,000.

The report also questioned several underlying assumptions of the revolution. The Greenman decision noted that manufacturers were much better able to absorb increased costs and spread the risk through liability insurance than were individual accident victims. But some smaller companies could not afford increased premiums and stopped buying insurance. Thanks to group insurance and social security, an individual accident victim might well be covered for his losses while the producer company was not. The task force eventually recommended that groups of manufacturers be allowed to band together to insure themselves, exempt from state insurance regulation. A risk retention bill, to be considered by Congress early in 1981, would permit just that. It also suggested a model state statute, which was gradually gaining acceptance at year's end.

The model act holds manufacturers liable for violations of their own promises: if a drug is advertised as non-habit-forming and a user becomes addicted, then the drug company must pay. It also holds manufacturers responsible for construction defects, errors in production that do not meet their own standards. These can be forecast statistically, covered by insurance, and included in the cost of the product. In the twilight area of design defects, the model act recommends a negligence standard: at the time of manufacture, did the company take care to ascertain all forseeable risks and the reasonable cost of reducing them? If so, the company is not negligent.

In the 1970s the federal government set up several agencies—the Consumer Product Safety Commission, the Occupational Safety and Health Administration, and the National Highway Transportation Safety Administration, among others—designed to protect workers and consumers through regulation. Unfortunately, there has been little progress in coordinating the agency-drawn regulations with court-made product liability law. For example, should a manufacturer be relieved of liability if his lawn mower meets the specifications of an appropriate agency but causes an accident anyway? The answer, even under the model code, is no.

An Expensive Road to Safety. Even before the criminal trial in Indiana, Ford had been hit with more than a dozen civil verdicts—including a record $125 million punitive damage award in California—for deaths and injuries that occurred when the Pinto's poorly protected gas tank ruptured in rear-end collisions. The Indiana prosecutors attempted to transform the company's cost-cutting decisions (a $6.65 part would have shielded the tank) into a criminal act. Ford faced only a $30,000 fine if convicted, but a guilty verdict would have weakened the company's position in pending civil actions dramatically. Ford Motor Co. executives were, therefore, more than willing to spend over $1 million defending the Winamac case.

Ford also designed better-protected tanks into future cars. But even if the threat of civil suits prompts manufacturers and employers to promote safety, as the plaintiffs' lawyers suggest, it may be an overly expensive way to accomplish a worthy goal. Insurance industry statistics indicate that of every dollar paid to an accident victim, 38 cents goes to his attorney. An additional 42 cents is paid out by insurance companies to defend the case.

Schwartz, who headed the federal product liability study, cautions that his group's suggested reforms may merely amount to pouring new wine into old bottles. "What we may really need," he says, "is a new compensation system—one that gets the money to the accident victims without these middlemen going to court."

Contract Bridge

The outstanding event of 1980 was the Sixth Team Olympiad, which attracted a record entry of 58 countries. Instead of all entrants playing one another in a round-robin tournament, the field was divided into two qualifying pools with four teams to qualify from each for the semifinals. Egypt and Suriname were instructed by their respective governments not to play against South Africa, against which both found themselves scheduled. Both countries failed to appear at the table against South Africa and were suspended from participation in World Bridge Federation (WBF) events for three years (they were, however, permitted to continue in this tournament).

Europe won four of the eight qualifying places with Denmark, France, Norway, and The Netherlands, which played host to the event in Valkenburg. The remaining qualifiers were Indonesia, Taiwan, the U.S., and defending champion Brazil.

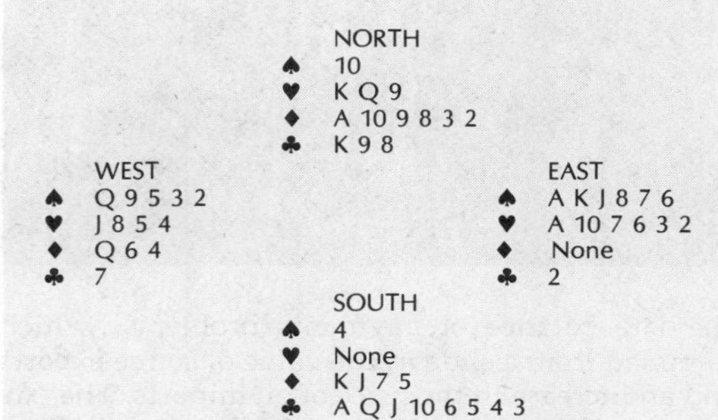

Dealer, West. Game All.

In the Open Room the optimum contract was reached:

West	North	East	South
M. Perron	I. Rubin	M. Lebel	P. Soloway
Pass	1 ♦	1 ♠	2 ♣
4 ♠	Pass	5 ♣	6 ♣
Pass	Pass	6 ♠	Double
Pass	Pass	Pass	

Lebel for France, with his "softly, softly" approach on the East hand, ended where he wanted to be, in six spades, which he could make if he found a lucky heart fit and which prevented his opponents from making a minor suit slam. After a diamond lead six spades was one down to give the U.S. a score of 200.

At the other table the action was even livelier:

West	North	East	South
B. Wolff	C. Mari	B. Hamman	P. Chemla
Pass	1 ♦	2 ♦	2 ♥
4 ♠	4 no trumps	5 ♠	6 ♣
Pass	6 ♦	6 ♠	7 ♦
Pass	Pass	Double	Pass
Pass	Pass		

Hamman's overcall of two diamonds was conventional and indicated strength in both major suits. Chemla indicated slam possibilities with his bid of two hearts, a cue bid of opponents' suit that normally would show first-round control of hearts and a powerful diamond fit. When Hamman bid five spades, he was probably hoping to be pushed into six. Chemla decided to avoid the greater loss by bidding one more himself.

Had Hamman led a spade, the U.S. would have scored a further 200 for a gain of nine match points on the deal. With such a freak deal he opted for the ace of hearts and declarer had no difficulty in locating the queen of diamonds to make his contract for a score of 2,330. France gained 19 match points on the board, when, with a different lead, the U.S. would have scored 9. France won the championship by a score of 131–111.

The semifinals were played in two pools of four with the U.S. and France emerging as winners to dispute an 80-board final, one that was effectively decided by the play of a single card.

The winners, France, were represented by Paul Chemla and Christian Mari, Michel Lebel and Michel Perron, Henri Svarc and Philippe Soulet, with Pierre Schmeil as the nonplaying captain; the U.S. by Bobby Wolff and Bob Hamman, Ira Rubin and Paul Soloway, Mike Passell and Fred Hamilton, with Ira Corn as nonplaying captain.

The U.S. won the Women's Olympic title, with Italy and Great Britain as the silver and bronze medalists. Norway and The Netherlands were joint bronze medalists in the Open series. The successful U.S. team included Jacqui Mitchell and Gail Moss, Dorothy Truscott and Emma Jean Hawes, Mary Jane Farrell and Marilyn Johnson, with Ruth McConnel as nonplaying captain.

For the WBF there were other causes for satisfaction. Egypt and Israel met for the first time at the bridge table, with the Israelis prevailing by the relatively narrow margin of 13–7, and China became a member. Formerly, bridge in China, as in the Soviet Union, had been regarded as a decadent pursuit; by 1980 it was fast becoming a popular intellectual game. In early 1979, after a 30-year ban, the All China Sports Federation formed the All China Contract Bridge Association.

China would compete against Taiwan if required to do so, but the WBF decreed that Taiwan would participate in the name of the Bridge Association of Taiwan. The entry of China into the international bridge scene was a personal triumph for WBF Pres. Jaime Ortiz-Patino, whose visit to Beijing (Peking) set the wheels in motion.

(HAROLD FRANKLIN)

Costa Rica

Costa Rica

A Central American republic, Costa Rica lies between Nicaragua and Panama and has coastlines on the Caribbean Sea and the Pacific Ocean. Area: 50,898 sq km (19,652 sq mi). Pop. (1980 est.): 2,232,000, including white and mestizo 98%. Cap. and largest city: San José (metro. pop., 1980 est., 637,000). Language: Spanish. Religion: predominantly Roman Catholic. President in 1980, Rodrigo Carazo Odio.

Political problems disturbed Costa Rica's stability in 1980, especially with regard to labour relations. These largely stemmed from increases in the cost of living; although the minimum wage was increased by 10.8% in 1980, this did not compensate for inflation, officially stated as running at 9.6% but actually at 18.5% according to the labour unions. Labour disputes included the Standard Fruit banana workers' strike, which ended on Jan. 17, 1980.

Costa Rica offered asylum during the year to up to 300 Cuban refugees, and plane flights from Havana began on April 16. On July 25 Costa Rica guaranteed asylum to more than 200 peasants from

Cosmetics: see Fashion and Dress

MICHEL PHILIPPOT—SYGMA

These Cuban refugees were among the first to arrive in Costa Rica in April from the Peruvian embassy in Havana after Cuban authorities removed armed guards from that embassy's gates.

violence-wracked El Salvador and flew them to San José.

Costa Rica's negotiations with the International Monetary Fund (IMF) resulted in a move taken to alleviate balance of payments problems, which stemmed from a slide in the value of coffee exports and an increase in the price of oil imports. The IMF was to make available its Special Drawing Rights, but only on condition of cuts in public expenditure, increased taxation, and control of money supply growth. The gross domestic product rose 5.9% in 1979 but slowed during 1980 as a result of lower coffee prices and controlled public expenditure. In August Mexico and Venezuela guaranteed Costa Rica oil under special financial arrangements. (CHRISTINE MELLOR)

COSTA RICA

Education. (1977) Primary, pupils 367,026, teachers 12,500; secondary and vocational, pupils 121,202, teachers 5,915; higher, students 38,629, teaching staff (1973) 1,967.

Finance. Monetary unit: colón, with (Sept. 22, 1980) an official rate of 8.57 colones to U.S. $1 (free rate of 20.60 colones = £1 sterling). Gold, SDR's, and foreign exchange (June 1980) U.S. $108.3 million. Budget (1979 actual): revenue 4,344,000,000 colones; expenditure 6,653,900,000 colones. Gross national product (1979) 33,013,000,000 colones. Money supply (May 1980) 6,141,000,000 colones. Cost of living (San José; 1975 = 100; May 1980) 143.9.

Foreign Trade. (1979) Imports 12,072,000,000 colones; exports 7,923,000,000 colones. Import sources (1978): U.S. 32%; Japan 13%; Guatemala 6%; West Germany 5%; El Salvador 5%; Nicaragua 5%. Export destinations (1978): U.S. 32%; West Germany 14%; Guatemala 7%; El Salvador 6%; Nicaragua 5%; The Netherlands 5%. Main exports: coffee 34%; bananas 18%; beef 9%. Tourism (1978): visitors 340,000; gross receipts U.S. $71 million.

Transport and Communications. Roads (1976) 25,339 km (including 665 km of Pan-American Highway). Motor vehicles in use (1975): passenger 59,800; commercial (including buses) 42,700. Railways: (1978) 881 km; traffic (main only; 1974) 81 million passenger-km, freight 14 million net ton-km. Air traffic (1978): 360 million passenger-km; freight 19.1 million net ton-km. Telephones (Jan. 1978) 145,100. Radio receivers (Dec. 1977) *c.* 400,000. Television receivers (Dec. 1977) *c.* 160,000.

Agriculture. Production (in 000; metric tons; 1979): sorghum 67; corn (1978) *c.* 95; rice (1978) 195; potatoes (1978) *c.* 25; bananas 1,078; oranges *c.* 74; sugar, raw value (1978) *c.* 191; coffee 97; cocoa 11; palm oil *c.* 25. Livestock (in 000; 1978): cattle *c.* 2,002; horses *c.* 111; pigs *c.* 215; chickens *c.* 5,500.

Industry. Production (in 000; metric tons; 1977): petroleum products *c.* 320; cement 398; nitrogenous fertilizers (1978–79) *c.* 33; electricity (kw-hr; 1979) 1,940,000 (76% hydroelectric in 1977).

Cost of Living:
see Economy, World

Council for Mutual Economic Assistance:
see Economy, World

Court Games

Handball. Naty Alvarado of Los Angeles won his third United States Handball Association (USHA) national open singles title by defeating Fred Lewis of Tucson, Ariz., 21–13, 18–21, 11–3 at the Tucson Athletic Club. Alvarado's win capped a fine season during which he won six of nine tournaments on the $100,000 Spalding professional handball tour. His earlier victories were at Denver, Colo., Albuquerque, N.M., Phoenix, Ariz., Dayton, Ohio, and Quebec City.

In the USHA's open doubles competition Skip McDowell and Harry Robertson of Long Beach, Calif., defeated Vern Roberts and Dave Dohman of Chicago 21–10, 14–21, 11–1. In masters play for men 40 and over Pat Kirby of Shannon Town, Ireland, defeated Rene Zamorano of Tucson 21–13, 21–1, while Bill Kennedy and Tom Natale of New York City topped Mike Dau and Joe Bukant of Lake Forest, Ill., 21–16, 21–10 for the doubles championship. Jack Briscoe of St. Louis, Mo., won the golden masters singles (50 years and over), defeating Del Mora of Los Angeles 21–11, 21–15, while Arnie Aguilar and Mora defeated Ken Schneider and Bob Peters of Chicago 19–21, 21–9, 11–7 for the golden masters doubles championship. In super masters singles for men 60 and over Steve Subak of Minneapolis, Minn., defeated Ralph Stapper of Portland, Ore., 21–19, 21–5 for the title. Rosie Bellini of New York City defeated Allison Roberts of Cincinnati, Ohio, 21–8, 21–5 for the women's championship.

Lake Forest (Ill.) College captured its seventh USHA intercollegiate title by winning the open doubles title and finishing second in the A singles. Fran Harvey and Chris Roberts of Lake Forest won the doubles by defeating Don Robie and Ed Novak of Memphis (Tenn.) State University 21–5, 21–3. Steve King from California State at Long Beach defeated Bob Martin of Lake Forest 21–10, 21–15 for the A singles title, and Robert Laarhoven from Memphis State defeated Al Del Toro of the U.S. Air Force Academy 21–12, 21–16 for the B singles title.

(TERRY CHARLES MUCK)

Volleyball. During 1980 volleyball enjoyed a full schedule of competition, highlighted by the Olympic Games. Some of the lustre was taken from the Olympics, however, as several highly ranked teams boycotted the Moscow event because of the Soviet invasion of Afghanistan.

Long before the Games, the Olympic dream of U.S. volleyball teams had been crushed, for the men on the courts and for the women at the highest political level. The U.S. men finished fourth at the final Olympic qualification tournament in Sofia, Bulg., the last week of January. Qualifying for the Olympics were the first two teams in this event, Bulgaria and Romania. Later in the year the U.S. decided to boycott the Games, so the women's team, having qualified for the Olympics during the 1979 season, had its dream of Olympic participation for the first time since 1968 shattered.

Following the lead of the U.S. in boycotting the Olympics were the men's teams of China and Algeria and the women's teams of China and Japan. On the women's side this removed from the competition three of the five top teams in the world, leaving only the Soviet Union and Cuba. The Chinese men were replaced by Czechoslovakia, and Libya replaced Algeria. For the women Brazil, Bulgaria, and Hungary were the replacements for China, the U.S., and Japan.

Both the Soviet men and the Soviet women captured gold medals at the Olympic Games. The Bulgarian men captured the silver medal, with the bronze being awarded to Romania. Poland finished fourth, Brazil fifth, Yugoslavia sixth, Cuba seventh, Czechoslovakia eighth, Italy ninth, and Libya tenth. In the women's competition East Germany took the silver and Bulgaria the bronze. They were followed, in order, by Hungary, Cuba, Peru, Brazil, and Romania. (*See also* TRACK AND FIELD SPORTS: *Special Report.*)

Because the central focus of the international volleyball calendar was the Olympic Games, there were few other significant tournaments. Most

Naty Alvarado (left), 1980 national handball champion, drops low on a shot off the backwall in a match against Vern Roberts.

TERRY MUCK–UNITED STATES HANDBALL ASSOCIATION

important from the point of view of the U.S. was women's competition against China, Japan, and East Germany. Visiting the U.S. in April, the East Germans were defeated in six of seven contests with the U.S. Olympic team. During a seven-stop tour in China the U.S. Olympic team came up empty-handed, although the scores sometimes were close. In Japan the U.S. women won the annual All Cities Tournament and also defeated the Japanese Olympic team.

(ALBERT M. MONACO, JR.)

Jai Alai. Four players from Miami, Fla., dominated the 1980 U.S. amateur finals, held in that city in January. The frontcourt championships were won by Dwayne Owens, 19, and 26-year-old Bobby Hirsh. The backcourt honours went to Jimmy Ryder, 19, and Fred Benjamin, 19. These players led throughout the four 25-point round-robin quinellas that determined the championships. Afterward, all four received professional contracts, the first year every amateur champion was so rewarded. Owens and Ryder signed to play at the Miami fronton. Benjamin went to Hartford, Conn., while Hirsh began his professional career at Dania, Fla.

Several important events occurred in professional jai alai during 1980. The Florida legislature approved summer jai alai competition for southern Florida. Consequently, the Miami fronton opened its doors on July 3 for its first summer season in its 55-year history. The season was scheduled to run until November 1. (ROBERT H. GROSSBERG)

Cricket

International contests were a highlight of cricket competition in 1979–80. Australia staged a series of tests and one-day matches with England and the West Indies; England played a jubilee test against India in Bombay; India and Pakistan played a six-match series; Australia visited India and Pakistan; the West Indies went to New Zealand; and England was at home to the West Indies and played a centenary match at Lord's, London, against Australia.

Top Australian batsman Kim Hughes smashes the ball to the boundary at Lord's for an automatic four runs during the aborted centenary test match against England.

KEYSTONE

India's series victory against Australia was its first ever against that opponent. S. M. Gavaskar (captain) and G. R. Viswanath were India's leading batsmen, and three others made centuries. K. J. Hughes captained Australia, and he, A. R. Border, and G. N. Yallop were their team's best batsmen. India's bowling was led by Kapil Dev, D. R. Doshi, and S. Yadav, and for Australia G. Dymock was outstanding.

India and Pakistan played their first series in India in 18 years, and India won. Indian batsmen Gavaskar and D. B. Vengsarkar made 100s, and Dev took 11 wickets in one test and 9 in another and scored 69 and 84. For Pakistan Mudassar Nazar was the only centurion, and Javed Miandad and Wasim Raja were the most successful batsmen. Imram Khan was Pakistan's best bowler though injured in mid-series. Sikander Bakht (fast medium) took eight wickets in one match and five each in two more.

Australia, even with all its ex-Packer players back, was overwhelmed by the West Indies. The West Indian fast bowling battery of A. M. E. Roberts, M. E. Holding, J. Garner, and C. E. H. Croft carried all before them. I. V. A. Richards was a superb batsman, and C. H. Lloyd (captain) and A. I. Kallicharran both made 100s. G. S. Chappell (captain), Hughes, and B. M. Laird batted bravely for Australia, and D. K. Lillee and Dymock bowled their hearts out.

Australia nevertheless had a successful series against England. Captain Chappell and Lillee were outstanding, and their presence made all the difference to Australia. Chappell made one century and 98 not out, while others who batted well included Hughes, Border, I. M. Chappell, and Laird. Lillee twice took six wickets in a match and was supported by L. S. Pascoe. I. T. Botham was England's outstanding allrounder, taking 11 wickets in the first match and making 119 not out in the third. G. Boycott and G. A. Gooch were a good opening pair for England, and the captain, J. M. Brearley, batted doggedly in the middle order. In the second match D. I. Gower made a brilliant 98 not out.

In a triangular series of one-day matches played concurrently with the tests in Australia, England kept Australia out of the two finals but then lost both to the West Indies, by two runs and by eight wickets. England (296 and 98 for no wickets) won the jubilee match against India (242 and 149) at Bombay by ten wickets. Botham took 13 wickets and made a superb 114, and wicketkeeper R. W. Taylor set a world record of ten catches.

The West Indies, tired after the Australian triumphs, cut a sorry figure in a three-match series in New Zealand, losing the first and tying the other two. For New Zealand R. J. Hadlee made 51 and took 11 wickets in the winning test, and followed with 103 in the second. G. B. Troup took ten wickets in the third test, and B. L. Cairns six for 85 in the second. G. P. Howarth (captain) and B. A. Edgar both made centuries, while L. G. Rowe, Kallicharran, and C. G. Greenidge all did well for the West Indies. Garner took six for 56 in the third test.

Against Pakistan Australia lost the only test

Test Series Results, October 1979–September 1980

Test	Host country and its scores		Visiting country and its scores		Result
1st	India	425	Australia	390 and 212	Match drawn
2nd	India	457 for 5 wkt dec	Australia	333 and 77 for 3 wkt	Match drawn
3rd	India	271 and 311	Australia	304 and 125	India won by 153 runs
4th	India	510 for 7 wkt dec	Australia	298 and 413	Match drawn
5th	India	347 and 200 for 4 wkt	Australia	442 and 151 for 6 wkt dec	Match drawn
6th	India	458 for 8 wkt dec	Australia	160 and 198	India won by an innings and 100 runs
1st	India	416	Pakistan	431 for 9 wkt dec and 108 for 2 wkt	Match drawn
2nd	India	126 and 364 for 6 wkt	Pakistan	273 and 242	Match drawn
3rd	India	334 and 160	Pakistan	173 and 190	India won by 131 runs
4th	India	162 and 193 for 2 wkt	Pakistan	249	Match drawn
5th	India	430 and 78 for 0 wkt	Pakistan	272 and 233	India won by 10 wkt
6th	India	331 and 205	Pakistan	272 for 4 wkt dec and 179 for 6 wkt	Match drawn
1st	Australia	268 and 448 for 6 wkt dec	West Indies	441 and 40 for 3 wkt	Match drawn
2nd	Australia	156 and 259	West Indies	397 and 22 for 0 wkt	West Indies won by 10 wkt
3rd	Australia	203 and 165	West Indies	328 and 448	West Indies won by 408 runs
1st	Australia	244 and 337	England	228 and 215	Australia won by 138 runs
2nd	Australia	145 and 219 for 4 wkt	England	123 and 237	Australia won by 6 wkt
3rd	Australia	477 and 103 for 2 wkt	England	306 and 273	Australia won by 8 wkt
1st	New Zealand	249 and 104 for 9 wkt	West Indies	140 and 212	New Zealand won by 1 wkt
2nd	New Zealand	460	West Indies	228 and 477 for 5 wkt	Match drawn
3rd	New Zealand	305 and 73 for 4 wkt	West Indies	220 and 264 for 9 wkt dec	Match drawn
1st	Pakistan	292 and 76 for 3 wkt	Australia	225 and 140	Pakistan won by 7 wkt
2nd	Pakistan	382 for 2 wkt	Australia	617	Match drawn
3rd	Pakistan	420 for 9 wkt dec	Australia	407 for 7 wkt dec and 391 for 8 wkt	Match drawn
1st	England	263 and 252	West Indies	308 and 209 for 8 wkt	West Indies won by 2 wkt
2nd	England	269 and 133 for 2 wkt	West Indies	518	Match drawn
3rd	England	150 and 391 for 7 wkt	West Indies	260	Match drawn
4th	England	370 and 209 for 9 wkt	West Indies	265	Match drawn
5th	England	143 and 227 for 6 wkt	West Indies	245	Match drawn

match finished. Slow bowlers Iqbal Qasim and Tausif Ahmed shared 18 wickets in the winning test, and for Australia spinner R. J. Bright took ten on a slow pitch. In the second test Greg Chappell (235), Yallop (172), Miandad (106 not out), and Taslim Arif (210 not out) made the most runs. In the third Border made 150 not out and 153, and Majid Khan a brilliant 110 not out.

By winning an exciting first test, the West Indies won the series against England, the other four tests being drawn because of rain and bad light. Centurions for the West Indies were Richards, Haynes, and Lloyd, and for England, Gooch and P. Willey. Garner, Holding, and Roberts for the West Indies and R. G. D. Willis, Botham, and G. R. Dilley were the most effective bowlers. Botham, in his first season as captain, was far below his best owing to persistent back trouble. B. C. Rose headed the English batting averages, and Boycott and Gooch were a stalwart opening pair. Gooch's 123 in the second test was the innings of the summer, and Willey's 100 not out in the fourth, where Willis helped him put on 117 for the last wicket, prevented the West Indies from winning.

England played a centenary test at Lord's against Australia, but bad weather prevented a finish. Brilliant batting by Hughes (117 and 84 not out), a sturdy 112 by G. M. Wood, and attractive strokeplay by Chappell and Border gave Australia the whip hand over moderate English bowling, and England (205 and 244 for 3 wickets) made no effort to win the match after two Australian declarations (at 385 for 5 wickets and 189 for 4 wickets).

South African batsmen A. J. Lamb, K. C. Wessels, and P. N. Kirsten dominated the English county championship, and South African fast-medium bowler V. van der Bijl also played a big part as Middlesex won, with Surrey a close second. R. D. Jackman (Surrey) took 121 wickets. Middlesex also beat Surrey in the Gillette Cup final by seven wickets. Warwickshire won the John Player League from Somerset and Middlesex, and Northamptonshire beat Essex in the Benson and Hedges final by six runs.

In Australia Victoria won the Sheffield Shield. In New Zealand Northern Districts won the Shell Trophy. In South Africa Transvaal won the Castle Currie Cup and the President's Cup, and Natal B the Castle Bowl. In the West Indies Barbados won the Shell Shield for the sixth successive year.

(REX ALSTON)

Crime and Law Enforcement

Violent Crime. TERRORISM. In a year marked by a resurgence of right-wing violence, Europe's bloodiest act of terrorism since World War II occurred on Aug. 2, 1980, when a massive bomb exploded at a railway station in Bologna, Italy, leaving a reported 79 persons dead and more than 160 injured. The atrocity was believed to have been perpetrated by a neofascist group. Only hours before, a judge in Bologna had indicted eight right-wing extremists for the 1974 bombing of a passenger train in which 12 persons were killed.

Right-wing extremists were also believed responsible for one of the worst terrorist attacks in West German history when, on September 26, a bomb exploded at closing time at Munich's crowded Oktoberfest, killing 13 and injuring more than 200. Among the dead was a young member of a neo-Nazi organization suspected of planting the high-explosive device. Neo-Nazis claimed respon-

BERTRAND LAFORET—GAMMA

Thousands of people attended the mass funeral of those killed in the terrorist bombing of a railroad station on August 2 in Bologna, Italy. A reported 79 persons were killed and more than 160 persons were injured.

sibility for a series of attacks on Jewish targets in France during the year, culminating in a powerful bomb explosion outside a Paris synagogue on October 3, which killed four persons and injured at least nine others. Following the explosion, members of all the major French political parties joined in a massive public demonstration in Paris held to denounce the growing wave of anti-Semitic violence in France.

Paris was also the site of attacks by assassins acting on behalf of various parties in the Middle East. Former Iranian prime minister Shahpur Bakhtiar narrowly escaped death in mid-July when his suburban Paris apartment was stormed by gunmen posing as reporters. Days later a gunman succeeded in killing former Syrian premier Salah ad-Din Bitar (*see* Obituaries), an opponent of Pres. Hafez al-Assad, at his Paris office. Elsewhere, several opponents of Libyan leader Col. Muammar al-Qaddafi were slain in separate incidents in London, Bonn, Rome, and various other cities.

In Latin America, where politically motivated violence reached epidemic proportions, the outspoken archbishop of San Salvador, Oscar Arnulfo Romero (*see* Obituaries), was mortally wounded in March by a lone gunman as he officiated at mass. It was widely suspected that rightists in El Salvador had ordered the assassination in an attempt to foment chaos that could lead to a right-wing military takeover. In September the exiled former dictator of Nicaragua, Anastasio Somoza Debayle (*see* Obituaries), and two companions were killed in an ambush in Asunción, Paraguay. A leftist Argentine guerrilla group, thought to be acting in association with Nicaraguan revolutionaries, was believed responsible.

Past acts of violence were recalled for North Americans during the year. In New York Cathlyn Wilkerson, once one of the most hunted fugitives in the U.S., surrendered to authorities in July. Wilkerson, a member of the radical Weatherman group which was responsible for a series of bombings in the late 1960s, had been on the run for ten years following an explosion in a Manhattan town house that police said was being used as a bomb factory. Another '60s figure, Abbie Hoffman of the Yippies (Youth International Party), also surrendered to authorities in New York; Hoffman had been underground since 1974 when he jumped bail after being charged with selling cocaine. In December Bernadine Dohrn surrendered to authorities in Chicago, where she was wanted on charges stemming from the Weather Underground's "Days of Rage" disturbances in 1969.

In Canada Nigel Barry Hamer was charged in July with the kidnapping of British Trade Commissioner James Cross on Oct. 5, 1970, an act that marked the beginning of that country's most serious peacetime crisis. The Cross kidnapping, and that of Quebec Minister of Labour Pierre Laporte by members of Le Front de Libération du Québec, had prompted the Canadian government to invoke the War Measures Act, suspending the civil liberties of many Canadians. Laporte was murdered, but Cross had been released unharmed.

Murder and Other Violence. Blacks were victims of murderous attacks in a number of U.S. states. In the most notorious incident, in May, Vernon Jordan, president of the National Urban League, was seriously wounded by a rifle bullet as he left an automobile driven by a white woman in the parking lot of a Fort Wayne, Ind., motel. The shooting appeared to have been carried out by a single expert marksman. A yearlong series of racial sniper attacks claimed at least ten lives in five states. In August, for instance, two black youths were shot to death by a high-powered rifle as they jogged with two white women in Salt Lake City, Utah. In Buffalo, N.Y., six black males were killed during six weeks in September and October, and in Atlanta, Ga., 11 black children were murdered over 16 months and four others were reported missing. In late October Joseph Paul Franklin, a white drifter with racist views, was indicted in connection with the Salt Lake City sniper attacks. Fears had been expressed that at least some of the crimes might be linked in a racially motivated conspiracy, although Jordan himself discounted this view.

A wave of airplane hijackings reminiscent of the late 1960s plagued U.S. airlines. In one week during August, six planes were diverted to Cuba, three of them in one day. In most cases the hijackers were recent refugees from Cuba who for one reason or another wished to return. While U.S. authorities strengthened security procedures, the Cuban government announced, in September, that the hijackers faced "drastic penal measures" and possible extradition back to the U.S.

Recalling the old film *Phantom of the Opera,* a bizarre slaying occurred in New York City's Metropolitan Opera House in July. Helen Hagnes, a member of the orchestra's violin section, disappeared during a break in a performance by the Berlin Ballet and was found dead the next morning, having been stripped, bound, gagged, and thrown down an airshaft. Following an intensive police manhunt, Craig Crimmins, a stagehand, was charged in late August with murder and attempted rape. Crimmins reportedly was apprehended after a ballerina supplied police with a description of the alleged killer while under hypnosis.

In March, in Chicago, John Wayne Gacy was convicted of 33 murders—more than any other killer in U.S. history—and sentenced to death. The bodies of 28 boys and young men had been discovered in the crawl space of Gacy's suburban home; another body was under the garage, and 4 were found in a nearby river. Gacy, who had described his crimes to police, had pleaded not guilty by reason of mental illness.

Joy Adamson (*see* OBITUARIES), author of the best-selling book *Born Free,* was killed in a remote Kenyan game reserve in January. Her death was at first attributed to mauling by a lion, but subsequently an African herdsman, Paul Wakwaro Ekai, a former employee of Adamson, was arrested and charged with her murder. On December 9 John Lennon (*see* OBITUARIES), a member of the Beatles rock group that had gained worldwide popularity in the 1960s, was shot and killed in front of his New York City apartment building. Charged with the crime was Mark David Chapman, a rock music enthusiast with a history of mental instability.

In the newly independent African nation of Zimbabwe, Edgar Tekere, a prominent member of Prime Minister Robert Mugabe's ruling Zimbabwe African National Union, was tried for killing a white farmer. The court found that he and a bodyguard had committed the murder, but he was freed under a law, passed by the previous white minority regime, that protected ministers acting "in good faith" to suppress terrorism. In Saudi Arabia the largest mass execution in the country's history occurred in January when 63 persons were beheaded in eight cities. Those executed were Muslim fundamentalists who had seized and held the Grand Mosque at Mecca late in 1979.

Nonviolent Crime. POLITICAL CRIME. In February press leaks resulted in the premature disclosure of a controversial FBI undercover operation code-named Abscam (for Abdul-scam, named for the fake company Abdul Enterprises Ltd., used as a front for the operation). In the course of Abscam, FBI agents, posing as wealthy Arabs or their representatives, tried to entice members of Congress and other officials into taking bribes. Indictments against 19 persons, 7 of them members of Congress, followed, and the first Abscam trial began in August. After several weeks of testimony that included videotapes of the bribe offer and acceptance, the four defendants, one of whom was Rep. Michael Myers (Dem., Pa.), were found guilty. Subsequently, the U.S. House of Representatives expelled Myers, the first expulsion of a congressman on corruption charges and the first on any ground since the Civil War. Later, Representatives John Jenrette (Dem., S.C.), John M. Murphy (Dem., N.Y.), and Frank Thompson, Jr. (Dem., N.J.), were also found guilty, and trials of other Abscam defendants were continuing or pending. (*See* LAW.)

Following a lengthy and highly publicized trial, Bert Lance, former presidential adviser and director of the Office of Management and Budget, was

UPI

An extortionist's bomb ripped through Harvey's $20 million hotel-casino at Lake Tahoe, Nevada, in August, causing damages estimated at about $3 million.

WIDE WORLD

On October 2, Michael Myers (centre right) became the first congressman to be expelled from the U.S. House of Representatives on corruption charges because of a conviction in the FBI's Abscam investigation.

acquitted in Atlanta on April 30 on nine counts of bank fraud. The jury remained deadlocked on three other counts of banking violations. Less fortunate was former Maryland governor Marvin Mandel, who lost his bid in the U.S. Supreme Court to avoid a four-year prison sentence; Mandel was convicted of bribery and racketeering in 1977.

WHITE COLLAR CRIME AND THEFT. The question of a manufacturer's criminal responsibility for injuries produced by a defective product was raised in the Winamac, Ind., trial of the Ford Motor Co. on charges of reckless homicide. The charges, the first of their type ever brought against an automaker, arose from an accident in 1978 when the gas tank of a Ford Pinto exploded after the car was hit from the rear, killing three teenage girls. The prosecution alleged that design faults, known to Ford but not corrected, led to the girls' deaths. The giant automaker was acquitted and later paid the parents of the three girls a total of $22,500 in exchange for a promise not to proceed with civil suits against the company. (*See* CONSUMERISM: *Special Report.*)

In the Soviet Union a "great caviar scam" was reportedly uncovered following months of investigation. The scam allegedly involved the diversion of tons of state-produced caviar to clandestine packing plants, where it was sealed in cans marked "smoked herring." Sold at herring prices to an unnamed Western European company, the caviar was repacked and resold for enormous profits, some of which were deposited in Swiss bank accounts for Soviet officials. While Soviet authorities refused to comment about the scandal, Western sources claimed that a number of senior bureaucrats, including a former minister of fisheries, were among the suspects.

The sinking of the oil tanker "Salem" off West Africa in January drew attention to maritime frauds. The "Salem," which had left Kuwait with a cargo of light crude oil bound for Italy, sank following a series of mysterious explosions. It was alleged that the cargo had been sold secretly in South Africa, after which the vessel was deliberately scuttled. Lloyd's of London, which was involved in the disputed multimillion-dollar insurance claim, estimated that more than 100 cargo ships were intentionally sunk in 1979 alone.

The soaring price of oil sparked a dramatic increase in the theft of oil products in the U.S. and elsewhere. In Houston, Texas, for example, law enforcement agencies uncovered a $12 million-a-year oil theft ring. Seventeen suspects were arrested in July when the U.S. Coast Guard and other authorities surrounded two oil barges, anchored in the Houston Ship Channel, as they began the illegal transfer of their cargo. The boom in world prices of other commodities, especially gold and silver, also prompted a rash of crime. Police in the U.S. reported that burglars had begun to ignore such items as television and stereo sets in favour of silverware and gold jewelry. The "snatch and run" theft of gold chains from wearers' necks became commonplace; New York City transit authorities recorded nearly 2,000 such thefts on the city's subways during the first eight months of the year.

The theft of art works continued to increase. While the Paris-based international police organization Interpol said worldwide official figures were impossible to obtain, authorities did not dispute reports that more than 40,000 works of art changed hands illegally each year. In France alone, more than 8,000 works of art were stolen during 1979; less than 10% of them were recovered.

Law Enforcement. The FBI's *Uniform Crime Reports* recorded a 9% rise in serious crime in the U.S. during 1979, the largest increase since 1975; violent crimes rose 11% and property offenses almost 9%. These discouraging statistics came at a time when the U.S. Congress seemed likely to slash federal government spending on such criminal justice agencies as the Office of Justice Assistance, Research, and Statistics. The cut was prompted in large part by dissatisfaction over the agencies' ineffectiveness in solving the crime problem.

A report released in May by the U.S. General Accounting Office (GAO) criticized the FBI's "quality over quantity" policy, first announced in 1975. That policy required concentration of FBI resources on high-level organized and white collar crime cases, while leaving most other cases to state and local enforcement agencies. According to the GAO, over two-thirds of the $30.3 million spent by the FBI to investigate property crimes in fiscal 1978 was devoted to nonquality cases, more than 90% of which did not lead to prosecution. Among "quality cases" that did result in prosecution was the FBI's Operation Unirac (for union racketeering). Beginning in 1975, this massive four-year effort involved hundreds of agents in a crackdown on labour racketeering in major U.S. ports. Among the 116 persons indicted as a result were 56 members or associates of the International Longshoremen's Association and 43 individuals associated with management.

After more than two years of delay, two former senior FBI officials were convicted in November on charges that they had approved illegal breakins, wiretaps, and mail openings in the early 1970s. In Canada a royal commission continued to investigate allegations of illegal breakins, wiretaps, and other misconduct on the part of the Royal Canadian Mounted Police during the same period. A report was expected in early 1981.

In September the International Association of Chiefs of Police, a professional organization with a membership extending to more than 60 nations, resolved that police should "use deadly force in cases where an officer has reasonable belief to fear for his or another's life or safety and/or in the cases consistent with laws applying within their jurisdiction." The resolution did not meet with the approval of the U.S.-based National Organization of Black Law Enforcement Executives, which felt that police departments should only sanction the use of deadly force in "defense of life" situations. On average, at least one citizen a day was killed by police in the U.S., and while many of the fatalities were unavoidable, some provoked bitterness and violence, especially among minority groups. Rioting in May in Liberty City, a black suburb of Miami, Fla., followed the acquittal of four white former police officers on charges stemming from the 1979 beating death of a black businessman.

In one of Britain's worst riots in many years, blacks vented their anger against police in the city of Bristol in April. The riot, which left at least 25 persons injured, including a number of police, followed a police raid on a cafe frequented mainly by unemployed blacks. Black youths in a number of British cities maintained that they were continually harrassed by the police. A recruiting drive aimed at getting more minority group members into British police forces met with little success.

The continuing attempts by members of the European Economic Community to encourage cooperation among their respective police forces suffered a serious setback toward year's end, when it became known that a number of French police officers belonged to neo-Nazi organizations. French police intelligence appeared to have been most affected by right-wing penetration. As an embarrassed French government made no effort to deny the charges, police units trying to track down right-wing terrorists were forced to compile new dossiers without the assistance of their own intelligence division. (DUNCAN CHAPPELL)

See also Prisons and Penology.
[522.C.6; 543.A.5; 552.C and F; 737.B; 10/36.C.5.a]

Cuba

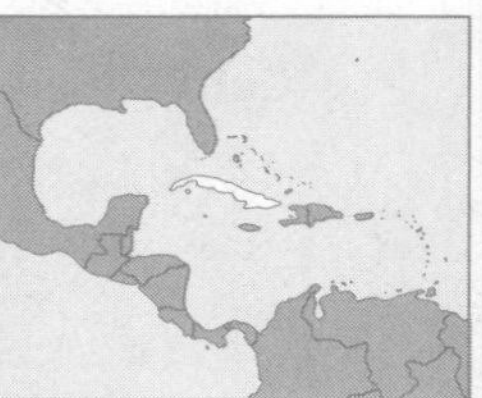
Cuba

The socialist republic of Cuba occupies the largest island in the Greater Antilles of the West Indies. Area: 110,922 sq km (42,827 sq mi), including several thousand small islands and cays. Pop. (1979 est.): 9,738,600, including (1953) white 72.8%; mestizo 14.5%; Negro 12.4%. Cap. and largest city: Havana (pop., 1979 est., 1,998,100). Language: Spanish. Religion: Roman Catholic (42%). President of the Councils of State and Ministers in 1980, Fidel Castro Ruz.

In major governmental changes announced on Jan. 11, 1980, 11 ministers were dismissed from office, and Pres. Fidel Castro himself took on the portfolios of defense, interior, public health, and culture. Managers of state enterprises were given more immediate powers for the imposition of work discipline, as well as greater freedom in hiring and firing. The first wage adjustment in 15 years was announced in March and became effective in July. It tied wages to productivity, allowed "responsibility" payments, and gave special consideration to pilots, doctors, nurses, and teachers in rural areas. To curtail black market activities, smallholders were permitted to sell their excess food in Havana. At the same time, licenses were issued to craftsmen wishing to set up their own businesses.

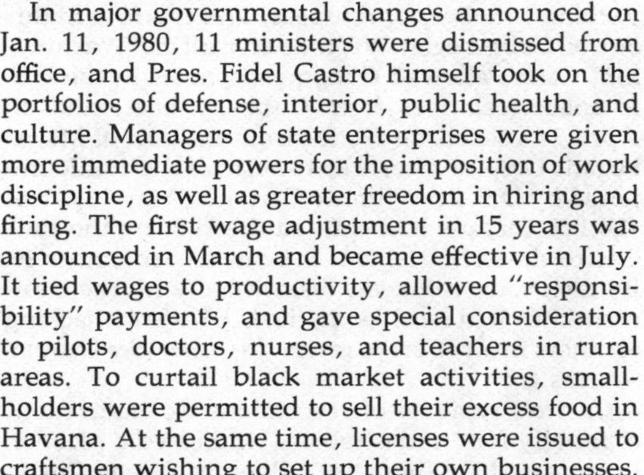

During the early months of 1980, increasing numbers of Cubans wanting to leave the country

CUBA

Education. (1978–79) Primary, pupils 1,626,386, teachers 77,605; secondary, pupils 759,288, teachers 58,136; vocational, pupils 198,261, teachers 14,630; teacher training, students 116,737, teachers 5,811; higher, students 133,014, teaching staff 10,139.

Finance. Monetary unit: peso, with (Sept. 22, 1980) a free rate of 0.70 peso to U.S. $1 (1.68 pesos = £1 sterling). Budget (1979 est.): revenue 7,619,000,000 pesos; expenditure 7,614,000,000 pesos. Gross national product (1978 est.) U.S. $7.9 billion.

Foreign Trade. (1978) Imports 3,558,000,000 pesos; exports 3,417,000,000 pesos. Import sources (1977): U.S.S.R. 54%; Japan 8%; Canada 6%;Spain 5%. Export destinations (1977): U.S.S.R. 71%. Main exports (1976): sugar 87%; nickel and copper ores 6%.

Transport and Communications. Roads (1978) *c.* 31,200 km. Motor vehicles in use (1976): passenger 80,000; commercial (including buses) 40,000. Railways (1978): 14,766 km; traffic 1,572,000,000 passenger-km, freight 1,870,000,000 net ton-km. Air traffic (1978): 1,089,000,000 passenger-km; freight *c.* 11 million net ton-km. Shipping (1979): merchant vessels 100 gross tons and over 341; gross tonnage 852,604. Telephones (Jan. 1978) 321,000. Radio receivers (Dec. 1977) 1,895,000. Television receivers (Dec. 1977) 800,000.

Agriculture. Production (in 000; metric tons; 1979): rice *c.* 500; cassava (1978) *c.* 270; sweet potatoes (1978) *c.* 258; tomatoes *c.* 241; sugar, raw value *c.* 7,992; bananas *c.* 142; oranges *c.* 190; coffee *c.* 27; tobacco *c.* 30; jute *c.* 5; beef and veal *c.* 151; fish catch (1978) 213. Livestock (in 000; 1979): cattle *c.* 5,844; pigs *c.* 1,846; sheep *c.* 356; goats *c.* 99; horses (1978) *c.* 818; chickens *c.* 20,755.

Industry. Production (in 000; metric tons; 1977): crude oil *c.* 150; natural gas (cu m) 17,800; petroleum products *c.* 6,340; electricity (kw-hr) *c.* 7,700,000; copper ore (metal content; 1978) 2.9; chrome ore (oxide content) *c.* 10; nickel ore (metal content) 37; salt 129; paper *c.* 123; sulfuric acid (1978) 347; fertilizers (nutrient content; 1978–79) nitrogenous *c.* 34, phosphate *c.* 13; cement (1978) 2,710; crude steel 341; cotton yarn (1978) 24; cotton fabrics (sq m) 149,000.

Crops:
see Agriculture and Food Supplies

sought asylum in foreign embassies, particularly those of Peru and Venezuela. On April 1 a Cuban guard was accidentally killed when six Cubans forced their way into the Peruvian embassy. Three days later the Cuban guards were withdrawn from the embassy, and the government permitted all who so wished to apply to leave the country. An estimated 10,000 would-be emigrants, most of them motivated by a desire to escape Cuba's economic ills, crowded into the Peruvian embassy compound during the following days.

By April 16 the U.S., Canada, Argentina, Brazil, Costa Rica, Ecuador, Peru, Belgium, Spain, Sweden, and West Germany had offered to take varying numbers of refugees, and the first flights out of Cuba began. Without consulting Washington, Castro allowed Cuban expatriates in the U.S. to collect relatives from Cuba by boat, and on April 21 a seaborne exodus from the port of Mariel began. Despite measures to restrict the traffic imposed by U.S. Pres. Jimmy Carter on May 14, some 120,000 Cubans had entered the U.S. by the time Castro closed Mariel to U.S. boats on September 26. By then some refugees, dissatisfied with the treatment they had received in the U.S., were hijacking airliners in an effort to return to Cuba. (*See* UNITED STATES.)

Castro's removal of restrictions on emigration, especially for "undesirables," indicated a reaction to increased U.S. hostility following alleged Cuban involvement in the disorders in El Salvador. Tension eased in May, but Castro insisted that any negotiations with the U.S. should encompass lifting of the trade embargo, closing of the Guantánamo naval base, and cessation of U.S. reconnaissance overflights. In late October, in what was described as a good-will gesture, Castro pardoned 33 Americans being held in Cuban jails, many of them hijackers. Thirty chose to return to the U.S., including five who were facing federal criminal charges.

During a visit to Cuba in August, Pres. José López Portillo of Mexico backed Castro's demands for U.S. concessions. Also affirmed during the meeting was support for the independence of Belize. On trade, Cuba would continue to sell sugar to Mexico (a first consignment of 400,000 metric tons was sold in 1980) but would not take advantage of low interest rates on Mexican and Venezuelan oil, since it preferred to buy oil from the U.S.S.R. Cuba's approval of the Soviet invasion of Afghanistan jeopardized its chairmanship of the nonaligned movement. Opposition from nonaligned countries prompted Cuba in January to withdraw its candidacy for the vacant Latin-American seat on the UN Security Council and to support Mexico's successful candidacy.

The sinking of a Bahamian patrol vessel by Cuban MiG fighters on May 10 (for which Cuba subsequently paid compensation) aroused fears of a more aggressive Caribbean policy. Cuban involvement in the Caribbean and Central America continued to be one of the major obstacles to improved relations with the U.S. Aid was being given to Grenada, El Salvador, and Nicaragua (to the latter in the form of doctors and teachers). Cuba also continued to provide aid to 14 African countries. Estimates at the end of 1979 put the total personnel involved at 45,000, ranging from limited numbers of security advisers in some countries to 25,500 military and civilian personnel in Angola. Several thousand military instructors and civilian advisers were said to be in Yemen (Aden).

In May Cuba and the Soviet Union reached agreement in Moscow on cooperation in the construction of a nuclear research station in Cuba. On June 1, during a visit by Erich Honecker, the East German Communist Party leader and premier, a

Thousands of Cubans invaded the Peruvian embassy in Havana in April and demanded political asylum. An emergency meeting, called by the Peruvian government, of Andean Group nations resulted in other countries offering to take in the refugees. However, President Castro intervened and eventually most of the refugees fled to the U.S. by boat.

EFE-SIPA PRESS/BLACK STAR

Curling:
see Winter Sports

WIDE WORLD

Leftist guerrillas, who call themselves the M-19 group, were given asylum in April in Havana after they had held diplomats hostage in the Dominican Republic embassy in Bogotá, Colombia, for 61 days.

25-year accord, including scientific and technical cooperation, was signed. Three new sugar mills were to be built in Cuba with the aid of a U.S. $20 million loan from the International Investment Bank of the Soviet-bloc Council for Mutual Economic Assistance (Comecon). However, to reduce its dependence on Comecon, Cuba signed a five-year agreement, to begin in 1981, to double its trade with Japan. Cuba was also negotiating economic and technical agreements with Finland (for oil and gas exploration technology), the U.K. (for sugar industry equipment), France, and West Germany.

Economic growth, at around 3%, was lower in 1980 than in previous years. In July, when the 1981–85 five-year plan was announced, Castro declared that austerity would continue, since Cuba had been unable to raise the loans it needed on the international market. Cane rust and bad weather limited the sugar crop to 6.7 million metric tons (compared with 7,990,000 in 1979). However, with the price of sugar more than double 1979 levels, Cuba's export earnings increased. The tobacco crop, severely affected by blue mold, produced only 5,000 of the forecast 45,000 tons. Tobacco factories had to be closed, and black tobacco was imported from Colombia. (JOHN B. H. BOX)

Cycling

Two new cycling championships were added to the 1980 world competition in France, but the amateur program there was reduced by the six events already contested at the Olympic Games. A feature of the championships was the prominence of English-speaking competitors. The U.S. took two titles, the women's sprint going to Suzan Novarra-Reber and the individual road race to Beth Heiden, an Olympic speed-skating bronze medalist. Danny Clark (Australia) won the new Keirin professional championship, a partially paced sprint race of Japanese origin, and his young amateur compatriot Gary Sutton scored top points in the 50-km race. Only three weeks after turning professional, Tony Doyle (Great Britain) dominated the field in the 5,000-m pursuit.

An outstanding championship performance was that of Bernard Hinault, who scored the first French victory in 18 years in the professional road race. Hinault's triumph was an effective reply to those who said he had ruined his career by an imprudent early-season program.

Soviet road riders won a number of the pre-Olympic events, their successes including Yuri Barinov's victory in the Warsaw–Berlin–Prague Peace Race and Ivan Mitchtenko's in the "Milk Race" Tour of Britain ahead of three compatriots. The Soviet riders were expected to continue their domination after the Olympics by again taking the honours in the Tour de l'Avenir—the amateur Tour de France—which Olympic champion Sergey Sukhoruchenkov won in 1978 and 1979. But they were well beaten by Alfonso Florez of Colombia, who said he found the Alpine passes easier to climb than many in South America.

Of the six titles contested in the Olympics, only the 4,000-m individual pursuit was not won by the U.S.S.R. or East Germany. Many world records

Sergey Sukhoruchenkov, a Soviet cyclist, raised his arms in victory as he won the 189-kilometre road race in the Moscow Olympic Games. His time of 4 hours, 48.2 minutes brought the U.S.S.R. its first gold in the individual road race since 1960.

WIDE WORLD

WIDE WORLD

Beth Heiden of the U.S. sprints low to win the world women's amateur road-race cycling championship title. Swedish cyclist Tuulikki Jahre came in second; third place went to Amanda Jones of Great Britain.

were broken on the Krylatskoye covered velodrome, built for the Games at a cost of some $45 million. Outstanding was the 1 min 2.95 sec recorded by Lothar Thoms (East Germany) in the 1,000-m time trial. (*See also* TRACK AND FIELD SPORTS: *Special Report.*) (J. B. WADLEY)

1980 Cycling Champions

Event	Winner	Country
WORLD AMATEUR CHAMPIONS—TRACK		
Men		
Tandem sprint	Y. Kucirek and P. Martinek	Czechoslovakia
50-km points	G. Sutton	Australia
50-km motor-paced	G. Mineboo	The Netherlands
Women		
Sprint	S. Novarra-Reber	U.S.
Individual pursuit	N. Kibardina	U.S.S.R.
WORLD PROFESSIONAL CHAMPIONS—TRACK		
Sprint	K. Nakano	Japan
Individual pursuit	A. Doyle	Great Britain
50-km points	C. Tourné	Belgium
One-hour motor-paced	W. Peffgen	West Germany
Keirin	D. Clark	Australia
WORLD AMATEUR CHAMPION—ROAD		
Women		
Individual road race	B. Heiden	U.S.
WORLD PROFESSIONAL CHAMPION—ROAD		
Individual road race	B. Hinault	France
WORLD CHAMPIONS—CYCLO-CROSS		
Amateur	F. Saladin	Switzerland
Professional	R. Liboton	Belgium
MAJOR PROFESSIONAL ROAD-RACE WINNERS		
Het Volk	J. Bruyere	Belgium
Milan-San Remo	P. Gavazzi	Italy
Paris-Roubaix	F. Moser	Italy
Amstel Gold Race	J. Raas	The Netherlands
Flèche Wallonne	G. Saronni	Italy
Liège-Bastogne-Liège	B. Hinault	France
Tour of Flanders	M. Pollentier	Belgium
Grande Prix of Frankfurt	G. Baronchelli	Italy
Bordeaux-Paris	H. Van Springel	Belgium
Autumn Grand Prix	D. Willems	Belgium
Paris-Brussels	P. Gavazzi	Italy
Tour of Lombardy	A. de Wolf	Belgium
Grand Prix des Nations time trial	J-L. Vandenbroucke	Belgium
Tour de France	J. Zoetemelk	The Netherlands
Tour of Italy	B. Hinault	France
Tour of Spain	F. Ruperez	Spain
Tour of Switzerland	D. Willems	Belgium
Dunkirk Four-day	J-L. Vandenbroucke	Belgium
Dauphiné-Libéré	J. Van de Velde	The Netherlands
Tour of Britain*	I. Mitchtenko	U.S.S.R.
Warsaw-Berlin-Prague*	Y. Barinov	U.S.S.R.
Tour de l'Avenir*	A. Florez	Colombia

*Amateur.

Cyprus

Cyprus

An island republic and a member of the Commonwealth of Nations, Cyprus is in the eastern Mediterranean. Area: 9,251 sq km (3,572 sq mi). Pop. (1979 est.): 621,000, including Greeks 82%; Turks 18%. Cap. and largest city: Nicosia (pop., 1978 est., 160,000). All these population figures should be considered unreliable, as they do not take into account the extensive internal migration or the recent and reportedly extensive Turkish immigration and Greek emigration, for which authoritative data are not available. Language: Greek and Turkish. Religion: Greek Orthodox 77%; Muslim 18%. President in 1980, Spyros Kyprianou.

Life in Cyprus remained conditioned by the Turkish invasion and internal disruption of 1974, and 1980 saw a continuation of attempts to reunite the Greek and Turkish communities. Responsibility for that difficult task lay with the UN. Its peacekeeping force of almost 2,500 troops still patrolled the buffer zone across the island.

After a year of deadlock, UN special envoy Javier Pérez de Cuellar paid a surprise visit to the island in June in an effort to persuade both sides to return to the negotiating table. His attempt failed, but the new UN local representative, Hugo Gobbi of Argentina, subsequently succeeded, and weekly meetings began on September 16. Gobbi said progress toward an eventual settlement would be slow and cautioned against overoptimism.

Taking a keen interest in the problem was Libya. Col. Muammar al-Qaddafi offered to act as host to a summit in Tripoli to help work out a peace formula. The offer was made unnecessary when the talks commenced, but Libya's interest was maintained by its eagerness to construct a radio station in Cyprus to beam programs of a cultural, educational, and religious nature to the Arab world. Fearing that such a station would upset those moderate Arab states with which the island had considerable trade, the Cypriots decided against the

CYPRUS

Education. Greek schools (1979–80): primary, pupils 50,579, teachers 2,191; secondary, pupils 42,357, teachers 2,374; vocational, pupils 5,840, teachers 511; teacher training, students 91, teachers 14; higher, students 1,431, teaching staff 145. Turkish schools (1976–77): primary, pupils 18,220, teachers 593; secondary, pupils 10,504, teachers 514; vocational, pupils 811, teachers 134; teacher training, students 68, teachers 4.

Finance. Monetary unit: Cyprus pound, with (Sept. 22, 1980) a free rate of C£0.34 to U.S. $1 (C£0.83 = £1 sterling). The Turkish lira is also in use in North Cyprus (Turkish Federated State). Gold, SDR's, and foreign exchange (June 1980) U.S. $293 million. Budget (1979 est.): revenue C£115.2 million; expenditure C£99 million. Excludes budget of Turkish Federated State (1979–80 est.): balanced at 2,348,000,000 Turkish liras.

Foreign Trade. (South only; 1979) Imports C£358 million; exports C£161 million. Import sources: U.K. 17%; Italy 12%; West Germany 8%; Greece 7%; Iraq 7%; U.S. 5%; Japan 5%; France 5%. Export destinations: U.K. 25%; Lebanon 9%; Saudi Arabia 7%; Syria 7%; Libya 5%. Main exports: clothing 13%; potatoes 8%; cement 6%; cigarettes 5%; wine and spirits 5%; citrus fruit 5%; footwear 5%. Tourism (South; 1978): visitors 217,000, gross receipts U.S. $33 million; (North; 1977): visitors from Turkey 147,000.

Transport and Communications. Roads (1978) 9,866 km. Motor vehicles in use (1978): passenger 79,000; commercial 17,200. Air traffic (1979): 688 million passenger-km; freight 26.7 million net ton-km. Shipping (1979): merchant vessels 100 gross tons and over 762; gross tonnage 2,355,543. Telephones (Jan. 1978) 82,800. Radio receivers (Dec. 1977) 212,000. Television licenses (Dec. 1977) 68,000.

Agriculture. Production (in 000; metric tons; 1979): barley 81; wheat (1978) 43; potatoes (1978) *c.* 250; grapes *c.* 195; oranges *c.* 100; grapefruit (1978) *c.* 65; lemons *c.* 22; olives *c.* 16. Livestock (in 000; 1978): sheep *c.* 495; cattle *c.* 38; pigs *c.* 200; goats *c.* 450.

Industry. Production (in 000; metric tons; 1978): asbestos *c.* 29; iron pyrites (exports) 122; copper ore (exports; metal content) *c.* 4.7; chromium ore (oxide content) *c.* 4.1; petroleum products (1977) *c.* 415; cement (1979) 1,155; electricity (kw-hr; 1979) 977,000.

idea, even though the Libyans were offering relatively vast sums of money.

Dominating economic life in both the Greek and Turkish sectors were the rising cost of oil products and the bleak world financial picture. Fuel prices soared and, particularly in the government-controlled south, there was a noticeable increase in the number of industrial stoppages as workers pressed for higher wages. The situation was made even worse by revelations during the summer that the massive cooperative movement, the source of employment for many Cypriots, was in dire financial straits. The government injected several million pounds to maintain the organization, and courts of inquiry were set up to investigate charges of mismanagement.

Politically, 1980 was marked by the split within the ruling Democratic Party. Alecos Michaelides, leader of the House of Representatives and acting vice-president of the republic, resigned in mid-October to set up his own party, the New Democratic Movement. Four other parliamentary deputies from Pres. Spyros Kyprianou's party also quit to join him. This had been preceded by a major Cabinet reshuffle on September 10, in which seven ministers were replaced by technocrats. The political turmoil made elections in the autumn appear certain, but technical difficulties with the electoral list made it necessary to postpone them until the spring of 1981. (CHRIS DRAKE)

Czechoslovakia

Czechoslovakia

A federal socialist republic of central Europe, Czechoslovakia lies between Poland, the U.S.S.R., Hungary, Austria, and East and West Germany. Area: 127,881 sq km (49,375 sq mi). Pop. (1980 est.): 15,309,000, including (1979 est.) Czech 64%; Slovak 30%. Cap. and largest city: Prague (pop., 1979 est., 1,188,600). Language: Czech and Slovak (official). General secretary of the Communist Party of Czechoslovakia and president in 1980, Gustav Husak; federal premier, Lubomir Strougal.

The economy and its troubles dominated Czechoslovak concerns in 1980, to the virtual exclusion of other issues. The problem was much the same as before—stagnation. Both the planning mechanism and the capacity of the economy were weak in relation to expectations. Possibly the most revealing figures were those published at the beginning of 1980 about plan fulfillment for the previous year. The category used as the equivalent of gross national product per capita—net material product growth—had fallen to 2.7%, while the other key indicator, increase in real wages, registered a mere 0.6%.

The difficulties had been evident by the end of 1979, when economic planners declared that the plans prepared by individual enterprises were unworkable. They would have placed impossible demands on labour supplies, resulted in lower exports, and would have done little to increase productivity. In fact, 1979 proved to be a generally poor year. Severe winter conditions in the early months resulted in particularly high demand for scarce energy resources, and inclement weather at harvest time led to a shortfall in cereals of 19% (as against the plan target). Industrial production rose

UPI

Pres. Gustav Husak of Czechoslovakia takes the oath of office after his reelection in May.

by a mere 3.7% and labour productivity by only 2.9%.

By 1980 the Czechoslovak economy was suffering from chronic tensions: between cost and output, investment outlays and returns, export targets and capacity, agricultural output and food consumption, supply and demand in consumer goods. The solution adopted was, for all practical purposes, an austerity program under another name. Real wages would remain at the 1979 level, and any increase in the standard of living would come through higher social benefits. The broader strategy adopted by the Czechoslovak Communist Party was outlined in March. It was given the title "Measures to Improve the System of Planned Management of the Economy."

The "Measures," as they came to be known, basically consisted of a set of rather conservative ideas. Thus, planning would emphasize the five-year period instead of the annual plan; there would be more intensive preparation of plans; supply and demand would be improved at all levels (national, ministerial, enterprise); and contractual relationships between enterprises would be more strictly enforced. As for labour, supplies of which had almost completely dried up, bonuses would be paid for high performance and penalties would be imposed for poor quality. There would be stricter control over management than before. In fact, the "Measures" amounted to little more than a codification of existing practice. They offered more exhortation and ideological mobilization but not the remotest suggestion of any structural change in the planning mechanism or of anything resembling the reintroduction of market concepts. Even the Polish concept of the early 1970s, modernization through imports from the West, was rejected.

The announcement of the "Measures" was followed in March by a full Central Committee session devoted to ideology. This confirmed the strategy of exhortation and harangues as the instrument for mobilizing the energies of the population. In later months, however, one significant innovation did surface. There was to be much stricter scrutiny of managers, and party members were expected to observe a much higher level of discipline. Several party leaders, including the general secretary, Gustav Husak, warned that far higher quality was expected from managers, and severe warnings were issued against those caught violating socialist norms, the code name for corruption.

The party took a significant step in this direction by introducing a so-called assessment of its *nomenklatura,* the list of posts and of individuals who were to fill them at the instructions of the party. The *nomenklatura* system had promoted stability, but at the cost of innovation and risk-taking. About 80,000 posts in Czechoslovakia were part of the *nomenklatura.* The exchange of party cards, usually used as a means of ridding the party of deadwood, was employed in 1980 to revitalize the membership rather than as a purge. Only about 13,000 members, less than 1%, were purged, but each member was subjected to grilling by his party committee; managers reportedly were given particularly intensive scrutiny. The total membership of the party was reported as 1,530,000, or 10% of the adult population; 45% were workers, much the same as in other Eastern European countries.

There was little change of any significance at the top, and the equilibrium of forces in the leadership remained undisturbed. Despite rumours that Husak, a conservative, might make way for a hard-line successor, he was reelected in May as president of Czechoslovakia for a five-year term. In August and September, however, it became evident that the Czechoslovak leadership was considerably worried by developments in neighbouring Poland. The struggle to establish autonomous trade unions was interpreted as a reversion to the Czechoslovak reforms of 1968 and condemned as a dangerous step. An ultra-hard-line politician, Vasil Bilak, issued barely veiled warnings of possible "fraternal assistance" against what he regarded as close to counterrevolution. In October the Czechoslovak authorities followed East Germany in closing off the border with Poland and ending free travel, presumably to prevent the "contagion" from spreading.

Intensive harassment of Czechoslovak dissidents, signaled with the trial of six members of

CZECHOSLOVAKIA

Education. (1978–79) Primary, pupils 1,878,000, teachers 91,876; secondary, pupils 133,067, teachers 8,481; vocational (1977–78), pupils 199,885, teachers 15,932; teacher training (1977–78), pupils 11,111, teachers 745; higher, students 183,632, teaching staff 17,738.

Finance. Monetary unit: koruna, with (Sept. 22, 1980) a commercial rate of 5.25 koruny to U.S. $1 (12.65 koruny = £1 sterling) and a tourist rate of 9 koruny to U.S. $1 (21.61 koruny = £1 sterling). Budget (1978 est.): revenue 286.3 billion koruny; expenditure 283.9 billion koruny. Net material product (1978) U.S. $432 billion koruny.

Foreign Trade. (1979) Imports 75,760,000,000 koruny; exports 70,156,000,000 koruny. Import sources: U.S.S.R. 35%; East Germany 11%; Poland 8%; West Germany 6%; Hungary 6%. Export destinations: U.S.S.R. 36%; East Germany 10%; Poland 8%; West Germany 6%; Hungary 6%. Main exports (1978): machinery 40%; iron and steel 9%; motor vehicles 9%; textiles 5%; chemicals 5%.

Transport and Communications. Roads (1974) 145,455 km (including 79 km expressways). Motor vehicles in use (1978): passenger 1,836,000; commercial 308,500. Railways (1978): 13,166 km (including 2,900 km electrified); traffic 18,640,000,000 passenger-km, freight (1979) 73,020,000,000 net ton-km. Air traffic (1979): 1,735,000,000 passenger-km; freight 18,043,000 net ton-km. Navigable inland waterways (1978) *c.* 480 km. Shipping (1979): merchant vessels 100 gross tons and over 17; gross tonnage 154,819. Telephones (Dec. 1978) 2,981,000. Radio licenses (Dec. 1978) 3,778,000. Television licenses (Dec. 1978) 4,048,000.

Agriculture. Production (in 000; metric tons; 1978): wheat *c.* 4,400; barley *c.* 3,300; oats *c.* 400; rye *c.* 500; corn *c.* 600; potatoes *c.* 4,000; sugar, raw value *c.* 930; apples *c.* 170; beef and veal *c.* 385; pork *c.* 870; timber (cu m; 1978) 18,055. Livestock (in 000; Jan. 1979): cattle 4,887; pigs 7,601; sheep 865; chickens 45,191.

Industry. Index of industrial production (1975 = 100; 1979) 121. Fuel and power (in 000; metric tons; 1979): coal 28,462; brown coal 96,510; crude oil 110; petroleum products (1977) 16,480; natural gas (cu m) *c.* 800,000; manufactured gas (cu m) 7,850,000; electricity (kw-hr) 67,897,000. Production (in 000; metric tons; 1979): iron ore (26% metal content) 2,014; pig iron 9,705; crude steel 14,864; magnesite (1975) 2,885; cement 10,258; sulfuric acid 1,253; plastics and resins 853; caustic soda 310; fertilizers (nutrient content; 1978) nitrogenous 625, phosphate *c.* 367; cotton yarn 134; cotton fabrics (m) 608,600; woolen fabrics (m) 59,000; man-made fibres 132; paper (1978) 865; passenger cars (units) 182; commercial vehicles (units) *c.* 88. Dwelling units completed (1979) 121,000.

VONS (the Committee for the Defense of the Unjustly Persecuted) in October 1979, was maintained. Throughout 1980 there was a steady stream of reports of arrests, beatings, house searches, and other forms of intimidation. Despite this, the opposition Charter 77 movement remained in being and active. (GEORGE SCHÖPFLIN)

Dance

The American Ballet Theatre (ABT), as it celebrated its 40th anniversary, changed directors. Lucia Chase and Oliver Smith, co-directors since 1945 (Chase had been ABT's principal patroness and guiding force since its inception), relinquished their joint post to Mikhail Baryshnikov. The anniversary was highlighted by a gala performance at New York City's Metropolitan Opera House (staged by Donald Saddler, an ABT alumnus) that brought together alumni of every generation in excerpts from past roles (Irina Baronova and Anton Dolin in a scene from *Bluebeard*, Alicia Alonso and Igor Youskevitch dancing together again), in bows, or on a screen in still photographs spanning four decades.

During the year ABT paid tribute to its longtime creative artists with programs focused exclusively on the works of Antony Tudor, Agnes de Mille, and Jerome Robbins and on those with designs by Oliver Smith. The major new offering, costing more than $500,000, was a full-length production of the Marius Petipa classic *La Bayadère*, staged by Natalia Makarova with scenery by Pier-Luigi Samaritani, costumes by Theoni Aldredge, and with the traditional score by Ludwig Minkus. Other ABT novelties included several pas de deux: *Rendez-Vous* (choreography by Stephen-Jan Hoff), *Le Retour* (John Meehan), and *Fantaisie Serieuse* (Lorca Massine). Daniel Levans's *Concert Waltzes* was added to the repertory. Among revivals was Tudor's *Dark Elegies* (1937; the first ballet to music of Mahler). The first ABT season under Baryshnikov's direction began on December 10 at the Kennedy Center for the Performing Arts, in Washington, D.C. New to the repertory were George Balanchine's *Prodigal Son*; Sir Frederick Ashton's *Les Rendezvous*; a new *Raymonda* (divertissements from Acts I and II) based on the Petipa ballet, staged by Baryshnikov with scenery and costumes by Santo Loquasto and with the music of Glazunov; and *Pas d'Esclave*, a pas de deux (from Act I of *Le Corsaire*), staged by Baryshnikov.

The New York City Ballet (NYCB) featured the world premiere of *Robert Schumann's "Davidsbündlertänze"* by Balanchine. In addition to this major new work, the NYCB presented Balanchine's *Ballade* (to music of Fauré), Robbins's *Rondo* (Mozart), and Peter Martins's *Lille Suite* (Carl Nielsen), all new; a newly revised *Suite of Dances* (from Robbins's *Dybbuk Variations* to music of Leonard Bernstein); the company's first production of Robbins's *Fancy Free*, an ABT staple; the New York premiere of Balanchine's *Walpurgis Nacht Ballet* (from the 1975 Paris Opéra Ballet production of *Faust*); and a revised *Le Bourgeois Gentilhomme* by Balanchine (first produced by the New York City Opera). Jacques d'Amboise celebrated 30 years of dancing with the NYCB. The School of American Ballet, the official school of the NYCB, presented its 15th annual workshop program of new ballets and repertory items. The opening night of the spring season at the New York State Theater was designated by Balanchine as a benefit to raise funds to purchase bulletproof vests for the New York City police; $37,000 was realized.

The Joffrey Ballet, recovering from a period of financial difficulty, returned to its home theatre, the New York City Center, for its first repertory season in two years. The fall engagement included such novelties as a new ballet by Robert Joffrey himself, *Postcards* to music of Erik Satie; *Relache*, a 1920s ballet-cinema concept of Jean Borlin restaged by Moses Pendleton; *Celebration* and *Epode* (dedicated to the ballerina Felia Doubrovska), both by Gerald Arpino; *Night* by the modern dance choreographer Laura Dean; *Helena*, choreographed by Choo San Goh; the first Joffrey staging of Jiri Kylian's *Return to the Strange Land*; and Ashton's *Illuminations*.

Productions by the Eliot Feld Ballet included *Anatomic Balm, Scenes for the Theater*, and *Circa*. The Pennsylvania Ballet presented Choo San Goh's *Celestial Images*, and Ballet Repertory Company offered Richard Englund's *Romeo and Juliet*. Ballet West, founded by Willam Christensen and directed by Bruce Marks, made its New York debut in a repertory that featured *Sanctus* (Marks-Fanshawe). The San Francisco Ballet offered the world

MARTHA SWOPE

Peter Martins and Heather Watts of the New York City Ballet dance in *Robert Schumann's "Davidsbündlertänze"* by George Balanchine.

Dams:
see Engineering Projects

premiere of Michael Smuin's *The Tempest* of Shakespeare, and the Pittsburgh Ballet Theater featured an August Bournonville program that included a production of *La Ventana* staged by the Royal Danish Ballet's Kirsten Ralov. Other U.S. national-regional companies with headquarters outside New York City opened festival engagements at the Brooklyn Academy of Music in a "Ballet America" series and at Brooklyn College's "Tribute to American Dance." The Boston Ballet had a New York season in which it offered Pierre Lacotte's reconstruction of Philippe Taglioni's *La Sylphide* (1836) with Rudolf Nureyev appearing as the star at all performances. There were also performances by Ballet Hispanico, the Puerto Rican Dance Theater, and U.S. Terpsichore. The Dance Theatre of Harlem added two traditional classics to its repertory: *Swan Lake* (Act II) and divertissements from *Paquita*. The Hartford (Conn.) Ballet, in its first repertory season in its home city, featured the new *Mulheres* choreographed by director Michael Uthoff.

Edward Villella was appointed artistic coordinator of the Eglevsky Ballet. In Chicago Maria Tallchief established a 20-member ballet troupe. Four new ballet companies were launched. Makarova and Company, headed by ballerina Natalia Makarova, made its debut in a Broadway engagement that featured stagings of divertissements from *Paquita* and *Raymonda*, *Sonata No. 5* of Maurice Béjart, Lorca Massine's *Vendetta*, *Ondine* (Barry Moreland), and *Studies* (Maya Murdma). Star dancers, in addition to Makarova, included Cynthia Gregory, Anthony Dowell, and Peter Schaufuss. For its Broadway debut, the Contemporary Ballet Company offered *Night and Day* (William Whitener), *Yerma* (Domy Reiter-Soffer), and *Juice* (Margo Sappington), with casts composed of well-known dancers from such companies as ABT and Joffrey. Two groups came into being to honour the centenary of Anna Pavlova's birth with reconstructions of dances associated with her: The Pavlova Celebration, with Starr Danias dancing the Pavlova roles; and Tribute to Pavlova, featuring Ann Marie de Angelo.

Foreign troupes visiting America included the full Royal Danish Ballet, appearing in its 1979 all-Bournonville centenary repertory at the International Dance Festival of Stars in Chicago. The Berlin Ballet featured Valery Panov's *The Idiot*, with Panov, Galina Panova, Eva Evdokimova, and guest star Nureyev, along with Nureyev's staging of *The Nutcracker*. The Ballet National de Marseille, directed by Roland Petit, made its U.S. debut in Petit ballets, among them *Marcel Proust Remembered*. Others visitors were the Royal Winnipeg Ballet, the Beijing (Peking) Opera (absent from America for 50 years), and the new Munich Dance Project.

The Martha Graham Dance Company returned to the Metropolitan Opera House in a repertory that featured Graham's new *Frescoes* (initially created for the Metropolitan Museum of Art), a new version of *Judith*, a revived and revised *Episodes* (originally created in collaboration with Balanchine and the NYCB), and the evening-long *Clytemnestra*, with Nureyev in the principal male role. Other modern dance events included productions of new works by the Alvin Ailey American Dance Theater (*Phases* by Ailey, *Later That Day* by Kathryn Posin, *Inside* by Ulysses Dove); Nikolais Dance Theater (*Count-Down* by Nikolais); Paul Taylor Dance Company in its 25th anniversary year (*Le Sacre du Printemps—The Rehearsal* by Taylor); Phyllis Lamhut (a full-length *Passing*); Merce Cunningham (*Fractions*, *Inlets*, *Duets*); and Twyla Tharp and Dancers in a three-week Broadway season (*When We Were Very Young* by Tharp).

Paul Draper, at 70, created *Tap in Three Movements* for the American Dance Machine, a company specializing in preserving great dances from Broadway musicals. The art of mime experienced a resurgence with a mime series sponsored by the Dance Theater Workshop at the American Theater Laboratory in New York City. The Spoleto Festival U.S.A. in Charleston, S.C., featured a dance gala based on Shakespeare themes including José Limón's *The Moor's Pavane* (with Soviet defector Aleksandr Godunov dancing the Othello role for the first time) and the world premiere of *The Bloody Crown*, choreographed by Ivan Tenorio and with Alicia Alonso as Lady Macbeth.

The annual *Dance Magazine* awards went to Ruth Page, Patricia McBride, and Paul Taylor and the Capezio Dance Award, to Walter Terry. Agnes de Mille was honoured with a Kennedy Center Arts Award. Lucia Chase received the presidential Medal of Freedom. (WALTER TERRY)

After a Royal Ballet season without guest stars—a policy designed to give more opportunities to resident dancers—the company, directed by Norman Morrice, began to welcome back some visitors to London's Covent Garden in the summer of 1980. Among them were Makarova, who for the

MARTHA SWOPE

Natalia Makarova staged and starred in a new version of Marius Petipa's *La Bayadère* when the American Ballet Theatre opened its 40th anniversary season.

first time danced Natalia Petrovna, the Turgenev heroine of Ashton's *A Month in the Country* (1976), and Baryshnikov. It was for Baryshnikov that Ashton created *Rhapsody*, his first major new ballet in four years, premiered on August 4 at a gala to celebrate the 80th birthday of Queen Elizabeth the queen mother, to whom it was dedicated. Set to Rachmaninoff's Paganini Rhapsody for piano and orchestra, the lighthearted bravura work also featured Lesley Collier.

Other new works were concerned with more serious matters, notably Kenneth MacMillan's *Gloria* (music by Poulenc), a lament and a thanksgiving for the victims of World War I, and *Adieu* (Panufnik) by David Bintley, a member of Sadler's Wells Royal Ballet and, at 22, the youngest choreographer to create a work for the Covent Garden company. In November the company presented the premiere of a ballet by Glen Tetley, to the music of Benjamin Britten's *Serenade* for tenor, horn, and strings, plus its first production of *Dark Elegies*; this work had been revived a month earlier by Ballet Rambert, for which it was originally created.

Sadler's Wells Royal Ballet, directed by Peter Wright, toured the Far East for the first time, visiting six countries in six weeks. Its new productions at home included Ronald Hynd's two-act *Papillon* (Offenbach), first created for the Houston (Texas) Ballet, and the grand pas from Petipa's 19th-century *Paquita* (Minkus), staged by the Russian-Canadian ballerina Galina Samsova, who became a new company principal. Two premieres reflected a prolific year for choreographer Bintley, whose *Homage to Chopin* was followed eight months later by *Polonia* (both to Panufnik music). Another young company dancer, Michael Corder, showed budding talent as the choreographer of *Day into Night* (Martinu).

London Festival Ballet, celebrating its 30th anniversary, kept up its standards in John Field's first season as artistic director, despite a heavy financial burden. The repertory edged toward the contemporary with Tetley's *Sphinx* (Martinu), first created for ABT; Geoffrey Cauley's new *Metamorphoses* (Richard Strauss); and Barry Moreland's new *Journey to Avalon* (Maxwell Davies), based on the Arthurian legends. Peter Darrell's *Chéri* for the Scottish Ballet at the Edinburgh Festival took its story from the French writer Colette, with original music by David Earl, a South African composer; Samsova was joined in the lead by Patrick Bissell. Colette herself was the central character in Domy Reiter-Soffer's *Paradise Gained* (Milhaud), a somewhat breathless biographical epic for the Irish Ballet company.

The Edinburgh Festival also brought the European debut of the Australian Dance Theatre, a company based at Adelaide and reorganized three years earlier under the direction of ex-Rambert dancer Jonathan Taylor. The regular repertory of short works by himself and other company dancers, together with Britain's Morrice and Christopher Bruce, made a more rewarding impression than did *Wildstars*, a two-part disco-style extravaganza with taped pop music.

London was host for the first time to Belgium's Royal Ballet of Flanders, directed by Jeanne Brabants, which performed a classically oriented repertory stronger on dancing than on choreography, and to the Zürich (Switz.) Opera Ballet, directed by Patricia Neary. Neary effectively supported Nureyev in his own production of the three-act *Don Quixote* (Minkus). Bella Lewitzky's modern dance company from the U.S. West Coast introduced itself to Britain almost unannounced (at Torquay) and was much admired by those who caught it. Béjart's Ballet of the 20th Century from Brussels aroused the usual controversy over its artistic merits during a short London visit.

Both London Contemporary Dance Theatre and Ballet Rambert undertook major tours of other European countries as well as Britain. The Rambert company premiered works by Richard Al-

UPI

The visiting Berlin Ballet presented its North American premiere of Valery Panov's *The Idiot* at the Metropolitan Opera House in New York City in July. In photo, Rudolf Nureyev, who danced the title role of Prince Myshkin, presents Jennifer Anne Coen with a flower.

AGIP/PICTORIAL PARADE

Dominique Khalfouni and Peter Schaufuss dance in a scene from Roland Petit's *Phantom of the Opera,* staged in Paris.

ston, newly appointed resident choreographer. It was left without a director from July, when John Chesworth parted from it after 29 years as dancer, choreographer, and, for the last seven, director; as of year's end, no successor had been named. Directorial changes elsewhere brought Jens Graff to the Norwegian National Ballet, Oscar Araiz to Geneva (Switz.), and Egon Madsen to Frankfurt and Edmund Gleede to Munich in West Germany. In Vienna a two-year extension with the State Opera Ballet was accepted by Gerhard Brunner, who had planned to leave.

West Germany's Stuttgart Ballet followed British and U.S. companies to China for performances at Beijing and Shanghai; at home it premiered Rosemary Helliwell's *The Window* (to the music of John McCabe's *Chagall Windows*) and William Forsythe's *After Ten* (Boris Blacher). Forsythe and Helliwell, together with Hamburg's John Neumeier, were also represented by new works for Munich's Ballet Week. At Frankfurt departing ballet director Fred Howald joined theatre director Michel Beretti in *Lélio* (Berlioz), which was described as "theatrical actions for dancers, singers, chorus, orchestra, and an actor."

International politics affected dance when the French government called off a planned Paris visit by Moscow's Bolshoi Ballet because of the Afghanistan crisis. Roland Petit staged a full-length *Phantom of the Opera* (Marcel Landowski) at Paris, and U.S. choreographer Douglas Dunn provided a new *Pulcinella* for the Paris Opéra Ballet in an "Homage to Stravinsky" program. This was the theme of the Paris Autumn Festival and its associated International Dance Festival, and it was reinforced by the visit of the NYCB on one leg of a European tour that also included Copenhagen and West Berlin. Other Paris visitors included Twyla Tharp and Dancers from New York.

Politics also affected dance in Italy, where Rome Opera director Luca di Schiena confessed he had not anticipated "complications" over a new *Swan Lake* production when he invited the Bolshoi Ballet director, Yury Grigorovich, to stage it and Nureyev to dance in it. Ballerina Carla Fracci, who left La Scala, Milan, to protest the lack of what she called "serious professional behaviour" toward the dance, won a Callas-sized success at Rome in *Giselle* with Nureyev. Milan, however, welcomed U.S. choreographer Louis Falco, who led the premiere of his *Eagle's Nest* (Michael Kamen) with Luciana Savignano. This production shared a program with Birgit Cullberg's *Miss Julie* (1950), starring the peripatetic Nureyev with Anna Razzi. She, in turn, joined ABT's Sallie Wilson, who choreographed *The Prince of the Pagodas* as a joint production by the Genoa Opera and Venice's Teatro La Fenice. It was set to the original Britten music, virtually unperformed in Britain since the lack of success attending John Cranko's first (1957) version for the Royal Ballet.

The Dutch National Ballet celebrated Rudi van Dantzig's 25 years as a choreographer with a program including his first ballet, *Night Island*, and *Monument for a Dead Boy* (1965), a tragedy of homosexuality regarded as a classic of its genre. The same company premiered Hans van Manen's *Einlage* (Johann Strauss) and Toer van Schayk's *Pyrrhic Dances III* (Berg). The modern-oriented Netherlands Dance Theatre, under Czechoslovak-born Jiri Kylian, introduced a Tetley premiere, *Summer's End*, set to the Second Symphony of Henri Dutilleux.

Deaths during the year included those of British photographer and designer Sir Cecil Beaton, who designed several Ashton ballets from *Apparitions* (1936) to *Marguerite and Armand* (1963), as well as Balanchine's *Swan Lake* for the NYCB (1951); Margaret Morris, British pioneer of modern dance and inventor of Margaret Morris Movement, a technique used for medical therapy as well as creative dance; and Arnold Haskell, director of the Royal Ballet School from 1947 to 1964. (*See* OBITUARIES.)

(NOËL GOODWIN)

See also Music; Theatre.

[652]

Danish Literature:
see Literature

Deaths:
see Demography; *see also obituaries of prominent persons who died in 1980 listed under* People of the Year

Defense

The year 1980 marked the real start of the "new cold war"—the end of détente and arms control. Two events symbolized this change. In January the Soviets transformed their December 1979 invasion of Afghanistan into a permanent occupation by 100,000 Soviet troops supporting a puppet government, although various Afghan resistance groups continued to wage guerrilla warfare against the Soviet invaders. Then, on November 4, the U.S. elections produced a Republican landslide, putting in power conservative hard-liners pledged to build up U.S. defenses and counter Soviet power. The Republican candidate, Ronald Reagan, became president-elect, and the GOP gained control of the U.S. Senate.

It was impossible to overestimate the importance of these changes, which marked the end of the U.S. loss of self-confidence that had been a legacy of the Vietnam war. Moreover, the new president and the new Republican senators had won by substantial majorities, and Reagan had chalked up a massive majority in the Electoral College. While defense policy was not the only issue at stake, the results showed that the U.S. public was ready to reject détente and arms control, which had been the policy not only of Pres. Jimmy Carter but also of his Republican predecessors, Gerald Ford and Richard Nixon, and of their secretary of state, Henry Kissinger. The symbols of détente, the strategic arms limitations talks agreements of 1972 and 1979 (SALT I and II), were headed for the scrap heap, and the scene was set for a U.S. attempt to contain the Soviets on a scale not seen since 1947.

The decisive point in the change in U.S.-Soviet relations from cooperation to confrontation was the Afghanistan invasion. The change came at a time when the "arc of crisis," from Afghanistan to Turkey, was the scene of fierce fighting over some 3,200 km (2,000 mi). (*See* Special Report.) The Soviet occupation had neutralized the Afghanistan armed forces, turning a pro-Soviet force into a largely anti-Soviet one. But the invasion also put 100,000 troops within striking distance of Pakistan and Iran. Soviet attacks on Afghan refugee camps and guerrilla bases in Pakistan were increasing, posing a danger that the conflict would expand. This danger would increase if, as was likely, the Reagan administration provided military assistance to the Afghan resistance and massively increased military aid to Pakistan.

On the western border of Afghanistan and Pakistan, Iran continued to resist the Iraqi invasion that had started on September 22. Iraq had seized control of most of Khuzestan, with its valuable oil fields, and Iran had suffered considerable losses. Further, Iran's economy was disintegrating. The Iran-Iraq war had also destroyed the assumptions on which the 1978 Camp David accords between Egypt and Israel had been based.

Instability had even spread to Eastern Europe, where the Polish trade unions had challenged the authority of the Polish Communist Party, gaining concessions the Soviet Union would find very difficult to accept. There were fears of Soviet military intervention to enforce the Brezhnev Doctrine, as had happened in Czechoslovakia in 1968, though the Poles would probably meet force with force. The Chinese, now de facto U.S. and NATO allies, saw these events as confirming their prediction that war with the Soviets was inevitable. Equally pessimistically, West Germany's Chancellor Helmut Schmidt likened 1980 to the summer of 1914, when World War I started. If not like August 1914, when the armies met, 1980 certainly looked like July 1914, when the moves that made war inevitable were taking place.

UNITED STATES

President Carter had kept U.S. defense spending relatively low in real terms, at 5.2% of gross national product (GNP), although inflation raised the dollar amount to $142.7 billion for fiscal 1981. His successor would thus have to request large increases to make up for cumulative defects in U.S. forces caused by underfunding. The forces totaled 2,050,000 (150,000 women), all volunteers, and were insufficient to meet U.S. defense commitments. Moreover, recruitment and retention, especially of skilled personnel, were inadequate, compromising the performance of many units, particularly in the Navy. Reintroduction of the draft was a real possibility, certainly if U.S. forces were involved in even a minor conflict. President Carter's introduction of preliminary draft registration in the summer met relatively little opposition.

Strategic forces were slowly being modernized to maintain the U.S. deterrent. The 1,000 Minuteman II and III intercontinental ballistic missiles (ICBM's) in fixed silos were based on designs 15 and 10 years old, respectively, and the 54 Titans were even older. Development of the new MX mobile ICBM continued to be plagued by technical, political, and cost problems. A total of 200 MX's were planned, each with ten Mark 12A 370-kiloton multiple independently targeted reentry vehicles (MIRV); the Mark 12A was also being fitted to Minuteman III, reducing its circular error probability (CEP; a measure of accuracy) from 275 to 185 m (900 to 600 ft). MX was to be deployed on a shell-game principle, with more silos than missiles and with the missiles moving between silos in trucks on specially constructed roads, thus reducing the likelihood of a successful Soviet strike against them. (*See* schematic drawing.) The basing mode had been changed from an oval road or racetrack system to straight roads so as to take up less land and cut costs, which were expected to rise from $35 billion to $50 billion in 1980 dollars. There were also political problems in securing acceptance of the MX from the states where it was scheduled for deployment. The two states originally designated, Nevada and Utah, were insisting that at least two other states accept MX. The opposition was reminiscent of the 1969 antiballistic missile (ABM) debate, with the difference that the people in the MX deployment areas were mostly conservatives who favoured a strong defense.

Other strategic force changes included deployment of the first of 11 giant Ohio-class ballistic missile submarines (SSBN's), each with 24 Trident

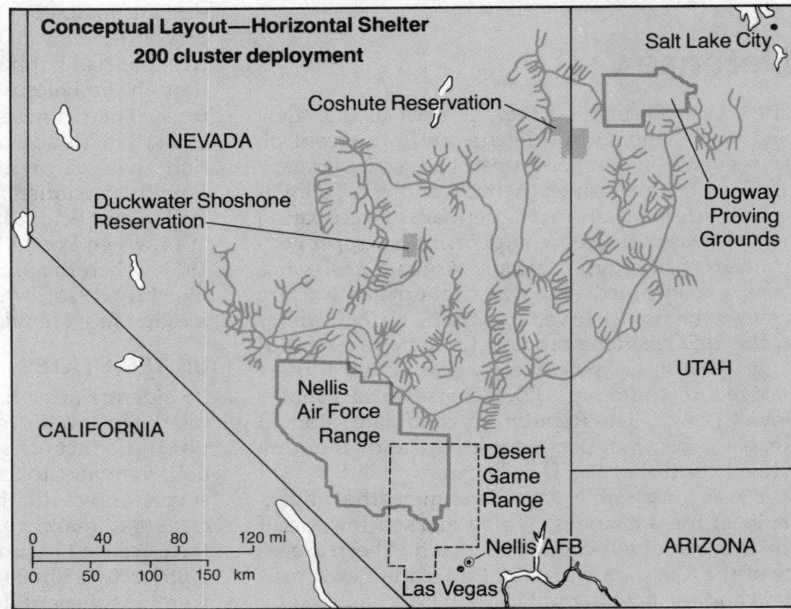

The proposed MX missile project in Utah and Nevada would utilize a series of arteries and grids in order to conceal the precise location of ICBM missiles.

C-4 submarine-launched ballistic missiles (SLBM's; 7,400-km [4,600-mi] range, 8 × 100-kiloton MIRV). They would replace the ten older Washington- and Allen-class SSBN's with Polaris SLBM's, six of which would be converted to nuclear attack submarines (SSN's) by 1981. The 31 Lafayette-class SSBN's were being retrofitted with the Trident C-4, replacing the Poseidon C-3 SLBM (4,600 km [2,860-mi] range, 10 × 50-kiloton MIRV), but they could not take the larger, follow-on Trident D-5 (11,100-km [6,900-mi] range, 14 × 150-kiloton MIRV/MARV [maneuverable reentry vehicle]). The ancient B-52 bomber force, dating from 1956–62, was being upgraded with 3,418 air-launched cruise missiles (ALCM's), specifically the Boeing AGM-86A (4,000-km [2,500-mi] range, one W-80 200-kiloton warhead), to be carried in the 241 B-52G/H's. President Carter revised U.S. doctrine to accept the idea of deliberately targeting the Soviet Communist Party leadership and control apparatus, a theoretical change that still had to be translated into practice and would need larger U.S. nuclear forces.

In general purpose forces, manpower shortages were compounded by obsolete equipment. New equipment was being introduced, but the attempt to make quality substitute for quantity often led to its being too complicated for reliability. The U.S. Army's new M-1 Abrams tank, with 120-mm gun, was criticized on these grounds; the 152 Abramses supplemented 8,905 M-60 medium tanks dating from 1959 and 1,825 even earlier M-48's. Similarly, the M-2 infantry fighting vehicle (IFV) and M-3 cavalry fighting vehicle (CFV) were supplementing the 22,000 M-577, M-114, and M-113 armoured personnel carriers (APC's). The Army of 774,000 personnel was composed of four armoured, six mechanized, four infantry, one airmobile, and one airborne divisions, with, respectively, 18,900, 18,500, and 16,500 personnel plus 324 or 216 tanks. Of these, one mechanized and one airborne division formed the Strategic Reserve in the U.S., where reinforcements for Europe were also based (two armoured, three mechanized, two infantry, and one airmobile divisions). Overseas deployment, largely in NATO-Europe, totaled 206,400 troops, mostly in the 7th Army in West Germany (196,200 troops, 3,000 tanks). Other major deployments were a twice-normal-size infantry division (30,400 troops) in South Korea, where U.S. troop reductions were no longer being considered, and an understrength infantry division in Hawaii. Reserves, totaling 535,000, included a 345,500-strong Army National Guard and Army Reserves of 190,000.

The 528,000-strong Navy had 173 major combat vessels and 74 SSN's. The core of the fleet remained its 14 aircraft carriers; 3 were nuclear-powered and one more was building, but the remaining 11 were elderly. Each carrier had one air wing of 24 new F-14A Tomcats or older F-4J Phantoms, plus 24 A-7E Corsair and 10 A-6E Intruder fighter-bombers as well as reconnaissance, early-warning, antisubmarine, tanker, and other specialized aircraft. The problems of U.S. forces were dramatized in the abortive April attempt to rescue the U.S. hostages in Teheran. In a major humiliation to a country known for its technologically advanced forces, only eight helicopters were available, and three broke down, forcing cancellation. Nonetheless, the Navy remained the most powerful single fleet in the world, with its 8 nuclear- and 17 conventionally powered guided weapons (GW) cruisers, 37 GW and 43 gun/antisubmarine warfare (ASW) destroyers, and 13 GW and 59 gun frigates. New ship types included Ticonderoga-class GW cruisers (1 building and 15 more planned) for fleet air defense, Spruance-class destroyers (30 in service and 5 building), and 7 Perry-class frigates.

The Air Force of 555,100 personnel had 3,700 combat aircraft. New types included 360 F-15 Eagle and 72 lighter F-16 fighter/fighter-bombers, plus 216 A-10 Thunderbolt close-support aircraft. Among older aircraft were 868 F-4 Phantom fighter-bombers and 282 F-111A/D/E/F medium bombers, plus 65 FB-111A's used as strategic bombers.

Formation of a rapid deployment force (RDF) had been announced, but it was only a reorganization of existing forces with improved logistic support. The RDF was based on the 189,000-strong Marine Corps, with its 575 medium tanks, 950 LVTP-7 APC's, 144 F-4N/S fighters, and 80 A-4M, 60 A-6A/E, and 78 vertical/short takeoff and landing (V/STOL) AV-8A Harrier fighter-bombers.

U.S.S.R.

Soviet defense expenditure remained high, estimated at 11 to 18% of GNP ($165 billion) or more. Regardless of détente, the percentage of GNP remained the same as it had been nearly 20 years earlier. Soviet manpower totaled 3,658,000, with equipment that was now comparable—if not superior—in quality to that of the U.S. and NATO-Europe. The cumulative effect of this buildup, while the U.S. and its allies were holding expenditures down, was destabilizing.

In strategic forces, over half the Soviet ICBM's were less than ten years old; 308 SS-18 heavy ICBM's had replaced the SS-9, and 150 SS-17s had replaced the SS-11 light ICBM (580 remaining). Deployment of the SS-20 variable/intermediate-range ballistic missile (V/IRBM), replacing the SS-4/5 medium/intermediate-range ballistic missile (M/IRBM), had accelerated to one every five days from one every seven days. Withdrawn ICBM's and IRBM's were being placed in storage, since Soviet launch silos were designed for reloading. A new generation of ICBM's was under development.

The Soviets' SLBM/SSBN forces totaled 955 SLBM's in 71 SSBN's, exceeding their 1972 SALT I limits of 950 SLBM's on 62 modern SSBN's. These figures excluded 48 SLBM's on 16 diesel submarines, as well as four Yankee-I-class SSBN's with 64 SLBM's, reportedly being converted to SSN's although this was unlikely since they were relatively new. Four new Delta-I SSBN's, each with 12 SS-N-8 SLBM's (8,000-km [5,000-mi] range, 1 × 1–2-megaton warhead), became operational. The 19 Delta-I-class SSBN's were smaller than the 4 Delta-II SSBN's (16 SS-N-8 SLBM's) and 10 Delta-III SSBN's (16 SS-N-18s, 8,000-km [5,000-mi] range, 3 × 1–2-megaton MIRV), though the one Yankee-II-class SSBN had 12 SLBM's (the experimental SS-NX-17; 5,000-km [3,100-mi] range, 1 × 1-megaton warhead, or MIRV). The giant (perhaps 24 SLBM's, 18,000 tons) Typhoon-class SSBN was building.

The Long-Range Air Force remained oriented to theatre operations against Western Europe and China. In SALT II terms, it had only 156 elderly heavy bombers, 113 Tu-95 Bear A/B's and 43 Mya-4 Bisons, first deployed in 1956. The newer medium/heavy Backfire bomber was deployed in two models, 15 Tu-26 Backfire A's and 60 Tu-22M Backfire B's (plus 70 in the Naval Air Force), with ranges of 7,000 to 8,000 km (4,350 to 5,000 mi). Longer-range versions were under development, as were anti-air-launched cruise missile/ballistic missile (ALCM/ALBM) carrier interceptors and new strategic bomber(s). The Long-Range Air Force also had 318 Tu-16 Badgers and 125 Tu-22 Blinders, soon to be replaced by Backfires.

The Soviet Army remained the most powerful in the world, with 1,825,000 men, 50,000 tanks, 62,000 armoured fighting vehicles (AFV's), and 20,000 artillery pieces forming 46 tank, 119 motor rifle (mechanized), and 8 airborne divisions. Older T-54/55 and T-62/64 tanks were being replaced by the T-72, and the PT-76 light tank and BTR-50P mechanized infantry combat vehicle (MICV) were both being replaced by the BMP MICV. This emphasized the Soviet belief in MICV's which, unlike older APC's, could operate as combined light tanks, antitank guided weapons (ATGW) carriers, and personnel carriers. Soviet deployment remained roughly constant numerically, with 30 divisions (15 tank) in central and eastern Europe, including 2 tank divisions (22,000 men and 670 tanks) in Poland. The one tank division withdrawn, with much publicity, from East Germany in 1979 had been compensated by increases in other Soviet units in that country. There were 67 divisions (23 tank, 6 airborne) in the European U.S.S.R. military districts; 6 (1 tank) in the central U.S.S.R.; 24 (1 tank, 2 airborne) in the southern U.S.S.R.; and 46 (6 tank) facing China. Besides the forces in Eastern Europe, overseas deployment included 85,000-100,000 in Afghanistan, 7,500 in Cuba, 4,000 in Vietnam, 2,500 in Syria, and forces of 1,000 to 1,800 men each in Ethiopia, Iraq, Libya, Mali, and Yemen (Aden). Soviet divisions were smaller than in NATO, with 11,000 men and 335 tanks in armoured, 14,000 men and 266 tanks in mechanized, and 7,000 men in airborne divisions.

The Soviet invasion of Afghanistan appeared to have started as a quick in-and-out intervention by one or two airborne divisions. It failed, and Soviet forces were built up to at least five mechanized and one airborne divisions (77,000 men and 1,330 tanks, plus support personnel) with a massive airlift, maintained without lessening Soviet troop concentrations against Europe and China. The Soviets also gained useful mobilization and combat experience. Initial difficulties in conducting antiguerrilla operations in mountainous terrain appeared to have been overcome. The main Soviet weapon was the armed helicopter, particularly the large Mi-24 Hind. There was evidence that chemical weapons were being used, although this was illegal under international law.

The 475,000-strong Air Force had used its Military Transport Aviation branch, with 1,550 aircraft, to airlift Soviet forces to Afghanistan. Most Soviet strike aircraft were new models with ranges of 1,100 to 1,600 km (680 to 1,000 mi) and weapons loads of 900–5,000 kg (2,000–11,000 lb), such as the 640 Su-17/20 Fitter C/D's, 370 Su-19/24 Fencers, and 400 MiG-27 Flogger D's. There were also 165 older Su-7 Fitter A's, 1,000 MiG-21 Fishbed J/K/L/N's, and 60 Yak-28 Brewer A/B/C's. Fighter aircraft in the Tactical Air Force included 850 MiG-21 Fishbed C/D/F's and 900 MiG-23 Flogger B's. Most fighters were in the 550,000-strong Air Defense Force, with 2,600 aircraft, including 600 MiG-23 Flogger B's, 330 MiG-25 Foxbat A's, 430 Su-9/11 Fishpot B/C's, 800 Su-15 Flagon D/E/F's, 135 Tu-28P Fiddlers, and 320 Yak-28P Firebars. Supplementing these were 12,000 surface-to-air missiles (SAM's) at 1,200 sites, with 10,000 launchers. En-

Approximate Strengths of Regular Armed Forces of the World

Country	Military personnel in 000s			Warships[1]			Jet aircraft[3]			
	Army	Navy	Air Force	Aircraft carriers/ cruisers	Submarines[2]	Destroyers/ frigates	Bombers and fighter-bombers	Fighters/ reconnaissance	Tanks[4]	Defense expenditure as % of GNP
I. NATO										
Belgium	63.0	4.4	20.5	—	—	4 FFG	90 FB	34, 18 R	396	3.5[5]
Canada	12.7	5.3	15.3	—	3	4 DDG, 19 FF	—	120	114	1.7
Denmark	21.0	6.2	7.8	—	6 C	3 FFG	52 FB	40, 16 R	320	2.0[5]
France[6]	321.3	70.0	103.5	2 CV, 1 CVH	21, 5 SSBN	20 DDG, 11 FFG, 13 FF	33 SB, 291 FB	135, 45 R	1,220	3.9
Germany, West	335.2	36.5	106.0	—	24 C	7 DDG, 4 DD, 6 FF	427 FB	60, 90 R	3,826	3.3
Greece	140.0	17.0	24.5	—	10	12 DD, 4 FF	140 FB	81, 26 R	1,320	. . .
Italy	253.0	42.0	71.0	1 CVH, 2 CAH	9	4 DDG, 2 DD, 4 FFG, 6 FF	162 FB	72, 30 R	1,595	2.4
Luxembourg	0.6	—	—	—	—	—	—	—	—	1.0[5]
Netherlands, The	75.0	16.5	19.0	—	6	2 DDG, 5 DD, 9 FFG	125 FB	18, 18 R	808	3.4
Norway	18.0	9.0	10.0	—	15 C	5 FFG	72 FB	16, 12 R	116	3.1
Portugal	37.0	13.0	9.5	—	3	17 FF	40 FB	—	57	4.0
Turkey	470.0	45.0	52.0	—	14	12 DD, 2 FF	192 FB	50, 48 R	3,500	. . .
United Kingdom	167.2	72.2[7]	89.7	2 CVH, 1 CVV, 1 CAH	16, 11 SSN, 4 SSBN	12 DDG, 53 FFG, 17 FF	48 SB, 60 B, 129 FB	112, 54 R	900	4.9
United States	963.0[7]	528.0	555.1	3 CVN, 11 CV, 8 CGN, 17 CG, 5 LHA, 7 LPH, 14 LPD, 33 LSD/T	7, 74 SSN, 41 SSBN	37 DDG, 43 DD, 13 FFG, 59 FF	338 SB, 347 B, 2,100 FB	800, 283 R	10,900	5.2
II. WARSAW PACT										
Bulgaria	105.0	10.0	34.0	—	4	2 FF	64 FB	116, 24 R	1,900	2.1
Czechoslovakia	140.0	—	55.0	—	—	—	164 FB	252, 55 R	3,600	2.8
Germany, East	108.0	16.0	38.0	—	—	2 FF	47 FB	300	2,600	6.3
Hungary	72.0	—	21.0	—	—	—	20 FB	150	1,310	2.1
Poland	210.0	22.5	85.0	—	4	1 DDG	220 FB	400, 81 R	3,500	2.4
Romania	140.0	10.5	34.0	—	—	—	70 FB	240, 18 R	1,700	1.4
U.S.S.R.	1,825.0	433.0[7]	1,455.0[8]	2 CVV, 2 CVH, 25 CG, 12 CA	143, 46 SSN, 71 SSBN, 16 SSB, 45 SSGN, 23 SSG	39 DDG, 36 DD, 63 FFG, 110 FF	156 SB, 880 B, 2,750 FB	3,350, 709 R	50,000	11–18
III. OTHER EUROPEAN										
Albania	30.0	3.0	8.0	—	3	—	—	100	100	. . .
Austria	46.0	—	4.3	—	—	—	34 FB	—	220	1.3
Finland	34.4	2.5	3.0	—	—	1 FF	43 FB	—	200	1.4
Ireland	13.4	0.8	0.6	—	—	—	—	—	—	1.6
Spain	255.0	49.0[7]	38.0	1 CV	8	11 DD, 9 FFG, 7 FF	29 FB	86, 32 R	750	2.9
Sweden[9]	44.5/751.0	11.8	9.8	—	14	6 DDG	150 FB	240, 60 R	600	3.3
Switzerland[9]	15.0/580.0	—	3.5/45.0	—	—	—	319 FB	32, 26 R	800	1.9
Yugoslavia	190.0	30.0[7]	44.0	—	6	—	142 FB	126, 40 R	2,150	. . .
IV. MIDDLE EAST AND MEDITERRANEAN; SUB-SAHARAN AFRICA; LATIN AMERICA[10]										
Algeria	90.0	4.0	7.0	—	—	—	24 B, 110 FB	90, 10 R	600	1.9
Egypt	320.0	20.0	27.0	—	10	4 DDG, 1 DD	23 B, 293 FB	45	1,600	13.2
Iran[11]	150.0	20.0	70.0	—	—	3 DDG, 4 FFG	354 FB	77, 14 R	1,735	. . .
Iraq[11]	200.0	4.2	38.0	—	—	—	22 B, 195 FB	115	2,750	10.9
Israel[9]	135.0/375.0	6.6/10.0	28.0/37.0	—	3	—	465 FB	18 R	3,050	31.1
Jordan	60.0	0.2	7.0	—	—	—	24 FB	24	610	. . .
Lebanon[12]	22.2	0.2	0.5	—	—	—	6 FB	9	—	. . .
Libya[13]	45.0	4.0	4.0	—	3	1 FFG	17 B, 140 FB	105, 25 R	2,400	. . .
Morocco	105.0	4.5	7.0	—	—	—	68 FB	—	180	6.0
Saudi Arabia	31.0	1.5	14.5	—	—	—	65 FB	17	380	15.0
Sudan	65.0	1.5	1.5	—	—	—	36 FB	—	130	. . .
Syria	200.0	2.5	45.0	—	—	2 FF	170 FB	225	2,920	22.1
United Arab Emirates	23.5	0.9	0.7	—	—	—	9 FB	32	—	. . .
Yemen, North	30.0	0.6	1.5	—	—	—	—	49	870	. . .
Yemen, South[13]	22.0	0.5	1.3	—	—	—	12 B, 59 FB	40	375	. . .
Angola[14]	30.0	1.0	1.5	—	—	—	—	29	235	. . .
Ethiopia[15]	225.0	1.5	3.0	—	—	1 FF	94 FB	—	640	. . .

tering service was the SA-10, a long-range SAM with a large nuclear warhead and significant capabilities against long-range cruise missiles (LRCM's) and ballistic missiles. This supplemented the 64 ABM-1 Galosh ABM's. Airborne warning and control system (AWACS) aircraft and MiG-25 interceptors using look-down, shoot-down air-to-air missiles (AAM's) were under intensive development.

Soviet naval forces continued to improve. Naval strength totaled 433,000 personnel, 289 major surface combat ships, and 257 cruise missile and attack submarines. A full-size aircraft carrier was building, as were several 25,000-ton nuclear-powered Kirov-class battle/heavy cruisers. The two Kiev-class carriers (two more building) were really combination cruiser/carriers, with 14 Yak-36 Forger A/B VTOL aircraft and 16 Ka-25 Hormone A/B helicopters, the latter also carried by the two Moskva-class ASW helicopter carriers. Modern cruisers included 17 ASW (7 Kara and 10 Kresta-II) and 8 GW (4 Kresta-I and 4 Kynda) ships. Using the Western reclassification of Soviet destroyers and frigates on U.S. Navy lines, the Soviets had 75 destroyers (39 GW and 36 gun) and 173 frigates (63 GW and 110 gun). The Soviets had long stressed sea-launched cruise missiles (SLCM's) to destroy opposing aircraft carriers and for standoff attacks on convoys and ports. Their standard SLCM since 1962, the SS-N-3 Shaddock (450-km [280-mi] range, kiloton-range warhead), was being replaced by the SS-N-9 (280-km [175-mi] range) and SS-N-12 (ranges 1,000 and 3,700 km [620 and 2,300 mi], with two warheads, probably kiloton range). These were deployed on Kiev carriers, GW cruisers, 45 nuclear cruise-missile submarines (each with 8 SLCM's), and 23 diesel submarines (each with 4 SLCM's). The Naval Air Force had 70 Tu-22M Backfire B bombers with AS-4 Kitchen air-to-surface missiles (ASM's) for antishipping strikes. These would eventually replace the 320 medium bombers (Tu-16s and Tu-22s) in this role.

Country	Military personnel in 000s			Warships[1]			Jet aircraft[3]		Tanks[4]	Defense expenditure as % of GNP
	Army	Navy	Air Force	Aircraft carriers/ cruisers	Submarines[2]	Destroyers/ frigates	Bombers and fighter-bombers	Fighters/ recon-naissance		
Mozambique[16]	22.8	0.7	0.8	—	—	—	36 FB	—	350	. . .
Nigeria	130.0	8.0	8.0	—	—	1 FF	21 FB	—	64	. . .
Somalia	60.0	0.5	1.0	—	—	—	3 B, 11 FB	7	140	. . .
South Africa[9]	71.0/404.5	4.7	10.3	—	3	3 FF	15 B, 36 FB	32	310	3.9
Tanzania	50.0	0.8	1.0	—	—	—	—	19	20	. . .
Zaire	18.5	1.0	1.0	—	—	—	—	10	—	. . .
Zimbabwe	12.0–50.0	—	1.5	—	—	—	7 B, 13 FB	—	—	. . .
Argentina	85.0	35.0[7]	19.5	1 CV, 1 CA	4	4 DDG, 4 DD	11 B, 164 FB	24	200	. . .
Brazil	182.7	47.0[7]	42.8	1 CV	8	4 DDG, 8 DD, 6 FFG	38 FB	17	60	. . .
Chile	53.0	24.0[7]	11.0	3 CA	3	2 DDG, 4 DD, 2 FFG, 3 FF	34 FB	8	70	. . .
Colombia	53.0	9.0[7]	3.8	—	2	3 DD	—	18	—	. . .
Cuba	180.0	10.0	16.0	—	3	—	40 FB	128	600	. . .
Mexico	83.0	20.0[7]	4.0	—	—	2 DD, 5 FF	14 FB	—	—	. . .
Peru	75.0	10.5	10.0	1 CG, 2 CA	8	2 DDG, 5 DD, 2 FFG	32 B, 47 FB	—	310	. . .
V. FAR EAST AND OCEANIA[10]										
Afghanistan[17]	32.0	—	8.0	—	—	—	30 B, 104 FB	35	800	. . .
Australia	32.0	16.9	22.0	1 CV	6	3 DDG, 8 FFG	20 B, 54 FB	13 R	90	2.8
Bangladesh	65.0	4.0	3.0	—	—	2 FF	27 FB	—	30	. . .
Burma	159.0	7.0	7.5	—	—	2 FF	—	—	. . .	. . .
China	3,600.0	360.0	490.0	—	97, 2 SSN, 1 SSB	12 DDG, 12 FFG 5 FF	550 B, 500 FB	3,900, 130 R	11,000	9.0
India	944.0	47.0	113.0	1 CV	8	8 FFG, 21 FF	60 B, 274 FB	252, 18 R	2,120	3.9
Indonesia	181.0	35.8[7]	25.0	—	4	7 FF	32 FB	—	—	3.4
Japan	155.0	42.0	44.0	—	14	19 DDG, 14 DD, 11 FFG, 4 FF	62 FB	280, 14 R	740	0.9
Korea, North	600.0	31.0	47.0	—	16	4 FF	85 B, 360 FB	170	2,500	11.2
Korea, South	520.0	48.0[7]	32.6	—	—	10 DD, 7 FF	330 FB	12 R	860	5.5
Laos	46.0	1.7	8.0	—	—	—	—	10	—	. . .
Malaysia	54.0	6.0	6.0	—	—	2 FF	17 FB	—	—	. . .
New Zealand	5.6	2.7	4.2	—	—	4 FFG	13 FB	—	—	2.1
Pakistan	408.0	13.0	17.6	—	6	6 DD, 1 FF	11 B, 235 FB	10 R	1,000	. . .
Philippines	70.0	26.0[7]	16.8	—	—	2 FF	40 FB	—	—	. . .
Singapore	35.0	3.0	4.0	—	—	—	67 FB	21	—	. . .
Taiwan	341.0[7]	30.2	67.0	—	2	7 DD, 15 DDG, 9 FF	—	353, 8 R	200	. . .
Thailand	155.5	32.2[7]	43.1	—	—	4 FF	30 FB	—	34	4.3
Vietnam[18]	1,000.0	4.0	25.0	—	—	3 FF	10 B, 295 FB	180	1,900	. . .

Note: Data exclude paramilitary, security, and irregular forces. Naval data exclude vessels of less than 100 tons standard displacement. Figures are for July 1980.
[1] Aircraft carrier (CV); helicopter carrier (CVH); medium (V/STOL aircraft) carrier (CVV); general purpose amphibious assault ship (LHA); amphibious transport dock (LPD); amphibious assault ship (helicopter) (LPH); dock/tank landing ship (LSD/T); heavy cruiser (CA); guided missile cruiser (CG); helicopter cruiser (CAH); destroyer (DD); guided missile destroyer (DDG); frigate (FF); guided missile frigate (FFG); N denotes nuclear powered.
[2] Nuclear submarine (SSN); ballistic missile submarine (SSB); guided (cruise) missile submarine (SSG); coastal (C); N denotes nuclear powered.
[3] Bombers (B), fighter-bombers (FB), strategic bombers (SB), reconnaissance fighters (R); data exclude light strike/counter-insurgency (COIN) aircraft.
[4] Main battle tanks (MBT), medium and heavy, 31 tons and over.
[5] Gross domestic product.
[6] French forces were withdrawn from NATO in 1966, but France remains a member of NATO.
[7] Includes marines.
[8] Figure includes the Strategic Rocket Forces (385,000) and the Air Defense Force (550,000), both separate services, plus the Long-Range Air Force (45,000).
[9] Second figure is fully mobilized strength.
[10] Sections IV and V list only those states with significant military forces.
[11] Iranian figures refer to pre-revolutionary situation. Iraqi figures before Iran-Iraq war. War losses uncertain.
[12] Figures approximate, given Lebanon's civil war and division.
[13] Some aircraft flown by Soviet pilots.
[14] Plus 19,000 Cubans and 2,500 East Germans serving with Angolan forces.
[15] Ethiopia also has 16,500 Cuban plus other Soviet bloc troops.
[16] Plus Cuban, Warsaw Pact, and Chinese advisers and technicians in Mozambique.
[17] Figures approximate, given Soviet invasion of Afghanistan. Exclude Soviet occupation forces (75,000–100,000).
[18] Figures include Vietnamese occupation forces in Cambodia (200,000) and Laos (40,000).

Sources: International Institute for Strategic Studies, 18 Adam Street, London, *The Military Balance 1980–81, Strategic Survey 1979.*

WARSAW PACT

The continuing unrest in Poland emphasized political uncertainties over the military value of the Soviet Union's Warsaw Pact allies. If, in the event of a Soviet invasion of Western Europe, they fought on the Soviet side, they would be a powerful reinforcement, but the Soviets could not be sure they would do so.

Militarily, the main Pact members were Czechoslovakia, with an army of 140,000 personnel and 3,600 medium tanks and a 55,000-strong air force with 164 fighter-bombers and 252 interceptors; East Germany, with a 108,000-strong army, 2,600 to 3,200 medium tanks, and a 38,000-strong air force with 47 fighter-bombers and 300 interceptors; Hungary, with a 72,000-strong army, 1,310 tanks, and a 21,000-strong air force with 150 interceptors and 20 fighter-bombers. The Polish forces, the largest in the Pact after the Soviet Union, included an army of 210,000 with 3,500 tanks, an air force of 85,000 with 220 fighter-bombers and 400 interceptors, and a largely coastal navy of 22,500. Romania, nominally a Pact member, was fiercely nationalistic and had no Soviet troops on its soil. Its Army of 140,000 had 1,700 tanks and the Air Force of 34,000 had 70 fighter-bombers and 240 interceptors. Bulgaria, like Romania, was basically a Balkan power. Its 105,000-strong army had 1,900 tanks, and the 34,000-man air force had 64 fighter-bombers and 116 interceptors.

All Pact equipment was Soviet—giving the Pact (unlike NATO) the two immense advantages of standardization and interoperability—and was under Soviet command. Older T-54/55 tanks were slowly being replaced by the newer T-62 and T-72. The Soviets had confined the Pact air forces to a largely air defense role, presumably to avoid the risk of fighter-bombers being used against the Soviets if rebellion occurred. The MiG-17 fighter-bombers were really obsolete and were being replaced by the MiG-23, plus some Su-7s and Su-20s. The standard interceptor was the MiG-21/21U.

UPI

The "Michigan," the second Trident-class nuclear-powered submarine for the U.S. Navy, was launched on April 26. A third submarine, still under construction, is in the background.

Pact defense expenditure was kept low—an estimated 2.8% of GNP for Czechoslovakia; 2.1% for Hungary; 2.4% for Poland; and 1.4% for Romania. East Germany's 6.3% was an exception. The Pact forces were powerful but politically unreliable. The Soviets had used their own troops to quell the liberation movement in Czechoslovakia in 1968 and the 1956 Hungarian revolt. In 1956 Poland had threatened to fight the Soviets unless some reforms were allowed, while in any Pact conflict with NATO, East German forces would be fighting fellow Germans. As the Polish situation emphasized, the Soviets still controlled Eastern Europe by virtue of military occupation.

NATO

Attention within the alliance remained focused on the balance of theatre nuclear forces (TNF). The Warsaw Pact was increasing its already significant superiority over NATO and would enjoy a TNF advantage of at least three to one in arriving warheads until NATO began to deploy new long-range TNF in 1983–84. The NATO allies had agreed to this deployment on Dec. 12, 1979, but only after one of the most divisive debates in the alliance's history. Britain and West Germany had insisted that modernized long-range TNF were vital, while The Netherlands and other smaller members argued that modernization would foreclose the chances of theatre nuclear arms control. Initially, the U.S. was divided between the Pentagon, arguing for long-range TNF, and the Arms Control and Disarmament Agency and President Carter, who favoured arms control. The U.S. eventually backed TNF modernization, but only after Belgium and The Netherlands were allowed to accept it in principle while deferring acceptance in practice.

The new NATO TNF comprised 108 Pershing II IRBM's, all in West Germany, plus 464 long-range ground-launched cruise missiles (GLCM's) in groups of four per launcher. Of the 116 GLCM launchers, 24 were to be in West Germany, 40 in Britain, 28 in Italy, 12 in Belgium, and 12 in The Netherlands. This geographic distribution met the West German principle of nonsingularity: that one other NATO member who did not have nuclear weapons—that is, not Britain or France—must accept GLCM's. By the end of 1980, it was still unclear whether the long-range TNF modernization decision would stand, although the U.S. was now committed to it.

NATO's 1978 long-term defense program was beginning to remedy some of the alliance's worst military defects, but many members, including West Germany, still had not implemented their promised 3% increase in real defense spending. This unwillingness to devote adequate resources to defense was NATO's major problem, since there were no cheap shortcuts, economic or political, for repairing the gap between NATO and Warsaw Pact capabilities. This discrepancy had been cumulative, over nearly 20 years, and had been underestimated until 1978. In addition, NATO had relied too much on its qualitative superiority—now nonexistent—to offset the Pact's numerical advantage and superior reinforcement capabilities during the first month of fighting.

On the crucial Central Front, ready forces were 27 NATO divisions (to 46 Pact divisions), 7,000 NATO main battle tanks (to 19,500 for the Pact), and 2,300 NATO tactical aircraft (to 4,000 Pact aircraft). These forces were insufficient to implement NATO's doctrine of flexible response: a conventional defense phase followed by the use of tactical, and then strategic, nuclear weapons against the Soviet Union. NATO could follow this scenario with forces inferior to those of the Pact, but not as inferior as they had become. In a crisis, the Soviet Union might not be deterred from attacking NATO forces if it believed these could be defeated in a lightning war and if U.S. and NATO nuclear forces seemed inadequate to implement the nuclear part of NATO strategy. Estimates were that NATO could offer a conventional defense for only two to ten days before NATO TNF would have to be used. The increasing fear of Soviet expansion, even—or especially—if motivated by insecurity, was causing political concern over NATO's military inferiority not seen since the height of the cold war.

UNITED KINGDOM

Despite Britain's economic problems, its defense spending remained high, totaling 4.9% of GNP ($23.7 billion). The decision to modernize Britain's independent nuclear deterrent by purchasing Trident I C-4 SLBM's from the U.S. was the nation's most important defense action in more than a decade. It demonstrated anxiety over the increasing Soviet threat to NATO-Europe, as well as doubts about the continued credibility of the U.S. nuclear guarantee of Western Europe.

Surprisingly and generously, the Carter administration made Trident available on the same basis as the Polaris SLBM's supplied under the 1962 Nassau agreement. Britain would purchase enough Trident SLBM's for four or perhaps five new SSBN's, each with 16 missiles equipped with British multiple reentry vehicles (MRV). A British Trident SLBM force would be much more powerful than Polaris, since each Trident could carry 8 × 100-kiloton MIRV over 7,400 km (4,600 mi) and could penetrate existing and future defenses. Polaris, with a smaller payload and shorter range, might not be able to get through after 1990. Modernized and augmented British nuclear forces would also enhance the credibility of the nuclear portion of NATO's flexible response strategy because they could be released by a NATO-Europe power without U.S. approval.

The British also announced plans to buy a new main battle tank. The Army, the only NATO-Europe all-volunteer force, had 167,250 personnel and 900 Chieftain main battle tanks, geared to European defense. Reinforcement capabilities for the British Army of the Rhine (BAOR), totaling 55,000 personnel, were tested in September in the U.K.'s biggest postwar exercise, Operation Crusader 80. Reinforcement would involve the Royal Air Force, with 89,714 personnel and 713 combat aircraft, and the Royal Navy, with 72,240 personnel and 70 major surface combat vessels, plus 11 nuclear and 16 diesel submarines.

The RAF was receiving the first of 165 Tornado F-2 air defense multirole combat aircraft, developed with West Germany and Italy, and had 48 Harrier GR-3 V/STOL fighter-ground attack aircraft. These would replace 48 obsolete Vulcan B-2 and 60 Buccaneer S-2A/B bombers and would supplement the 24 Lightning F-6/F-3 interceptors—being increased to 36—and the 72 Jaguar GR-1 FGA's. The first of four through-deck minicarriers ordered by the Royal Navy, the 16,000-ton "Invincible," was operational. It carried five Sea Harrier V/STOL aircraft and nine Sea King helicopters, similar to the forces on the two ASW commando carriers. Other naval units included 12 GW destroyers and 51 general purpose frigates.

FRANCE

French forces totaled 494,730 personnel, and the defense budget of $20,220,000,000 constituted 3.9% of GNP. Like the British, the French were modernizing their independent nuclear forces, tactical as well as strategic. Long-range plans called for development of mobile IRBM's and new tactical systems, including the option of enhanced radiation weapons (neutron bombs). The MSBS M-4 SLBM (4,000-km [2,500-mi] range, 6 × 200-kiloton MIRV) was scheduled for deployment in 1985–86, replacing the MSBS M-20 (3,000-km [1,860-mi]

WIDE WORLD

Soviet "Guild" surface-to-air missiles were among the weapons displayed in the Revolution Day parade held in Moscow in November.

range, one-megaton warhead) on the five operational SSBN's. A sixth SSBN was building and more were planned. The SSBS S-3 IRBM (3,000-km [1,860-mi] range, 1 × 150-kiloton warhead) was replacing the 18 SSBS S-2s in fixed silos.

Unlike the U.K., France had emphasized a wide range of tactical nuclear delivery systems, including the Pluton short-range ballistic missile (SRBM; 120-km [75-mi] range, 1 × 15–25-kiloton warhead), to be supplemented by the Hades SRBM, 30 Mirage IIIE and 40–45 Jaguar fighter-bombers (2,400/1,600-km [1,500/1,000-mi] ranges, 1 × 15–25-kiloton AN-52 nuclear weapons), plus 12 Super-Étendard carrier fighters (1,500-km [930-mi] range, 1 × 15–25-kiloton bomb). There were also 33 Mirage IVA strategic bombers (3,200-km [2,000-mi] range, 2 × megaton-range bombs). Supporting these was the 103,460-strong Air Force with 460 combat aircraft. It comprised the Tactical Air Force, with 75 Mirage III, 30 Mirage 5F, and 75 Jaguar A fighter-bombers, and the Air Defense Command with 30 Mirage IIIC and 105 Mirage F-1C fighters. New aircraft on order included 20 Mirage F-1B, 40 F-1R, and 50 Mirage 2000 fighter/strike aircraft.

The Army of 331,320 personnel remained weak in armour, with only 1,220 AMX-30 medium and 1,050 AMX-13 light tanks, plus about 2,200 MICV's. Of these, 47,000 troops were deployed in three armoured divisions in West Germany but were not under NATO command, although France remained a member of NATO. Most of the remainder were deployed in support of West Germany, in accord with the evolving French doctrine of extended deterrence. Under this doctrine, the defense of France with conventional and nuclear weapons was considered to start at or near the eastern border of West Germany. French overseas deployment remained significant, totaling about 18,000 including 3,500 in Djibouti. With the Iran-Iraq war, these took on added importance, as did the French Navy's Indian Ocean squadron of destroyers and frigates. The Navy had 69,950 personnel and 48 major surface combat vessels, including two Clemenceau-class medium attack carriers, each with 40 aircraft; one helicopter carrier; and one command cruiser. The 20 GW destroyers carried the Exocet surface-to-surface missile (SSM), Malafon ASW/SSM's, and Masurca and Crotale SAM's, while the 24 frigates included 11 GW ships. The 21 submarines were all diesel.

A Sea Sparrow III surface-to-air missile takes off from a U.S. Navy ship during NATO exercises in September.

UPI

WEST GERMANY

At 3.3% of GNP ($25,120,000,000), West Germany's defense spending was relatively low, given that its economy was the most prosperous in NATO-Europe. Thus its November decision not to meet its NATO commitment to increase defense spending was surprising, and the U.S. continued to press Chancellor Schmidt's government to fulfill its obligation. West German forces, the most powerful in NATO-Europe, totaled 495,000, including the Army with 335,200 personnel armed with 1,289 M-48A2/A4 and 2,437 Leopard 1 tanks. The Leopard 2, a completely different, much more powerful tank, was being deployed; 1,700 were on order, along with 786 TP2-1 APC's. The Field Army had been reorganized into three corps with six armoured, four armoured infantry, one mountain, and one airborne divisions. Division and brigade size followed U.S. practice (17,000–17,500 and 4,500–5,000 men, respectively).

The Air Force had 106,000 personnel with 561 combat aircraft, including 144 elderly F-104G Starfighters (and 97 Navy Starfighters) and 120 F-4F Phantom fighter-bombers. The 126 G-91R3 light attack fighters were being replaced by 126 AlphaJet fighter-bombers. On order were 125 Tornado multirole combat aircraft. The coast defense Navy of 36,500 personnel had 60 fast attack craft as well as 7 modern GW destroyers.

DISARMAMENT AND ARMS CONTROL

The year 1980 marked the end of arms control as it had been known since 1963. The failure was symbolized by President Carter's shelving of SALT II ratification. The U.S. Senate had continued the ratification debate until January 1980, when the president asked that the treaty be withdrawn from consideration in light of the Soviet incursion into Afghanistan. Even before this, however, its fate was in doubt, since many senators believed it did nothing for strategic arms control and was politically inappropriate. Thus SALT II was dying before Reagan's victory; afterward, SALT II was dead.

Reagan, the new Republican majority in the Senate, the new majority leader Sen. Howard Baker (Rep., Tenn.), and their advisers all saw SALT II as symbolic of a fatally misguided concept: that détente and arms control could serve as a substitute for defense policy and needed new weapons. NATO-Europe had echoed this same idea, manifested in the belief that theatre nuclear arms control could be achieved through a TALT I (tactical arms limitation talks) that would limit TNF and make modernization unnecessary. With SALT II eliminated, the way was clear for a massive expansion of U.S. strategic nuclear forces to counterbalance the Soviet bid for strategic superiority. The U.S. arms control bureaucracy, notably the Arms Con-

A Sea Harrier was launched from the British carrier "Invincible" during exercises in November. The "Invincible" is the largest warship to be built for the Royal Navy in 25 years.

trol and Disarmament Agency, faced elimination or possible absorption into the Pentagon.

Along with SALT II, the SALT I limitations, unilaterally extended by the Carter administration and exceeded by the Soviet Union, faced the scrap heap. So too might the 1972 ABM treaty, limiting ABM's to 100 launchers each for the U.S. and the U.S.S.R. Reagan's advisers believed that it had never really limited Soviet ABM's and that the U.S. now needed ABM's for point defense of its vulnerable ICBM force. The ABM treaty could be abrogated or renegotiated out of existence at the scheduled 1982 ABM review conference.

Even before the election, the future of both Soviet-U.S. arms control and multilateral arms control had been in serious doubt. The SALT process might survive if scrapping it proved politically expensive for the U.S. administration and if the Soviets did not withdraw, but SALT itself would not produce arms control. There was no chance of serious negotiations on theatre nuclear weapons—TALT was stillborn—or on limits on Soviet and NATO TNF modernization. Of the wide-ranging arms-control initiatives undertaken by President Carter, virtually nothing was left. Only two negotiations were continuing at the end of 1980—on a comprehensive nuclear test ban treaty and on a ban on chemical weapons—and neither had any hope of success.

The Soviet Union was already in violation of two important arms control agreements—which they had accepted—limiting chemical and biological weapons. A 1972 convention banned the production and stockpiling of biological weapons, but U.S. intelligence sources traced an anthrax outbreak at Sverdlovsk in 1980 (admitted by the Soviets) to the accidental release of anthrax spores from a plant manufacturing biological warfare agents. Similarly, asphyxiating—and probably nerve—gases were being used in Afghanistan in violation of the 1925 Geneva chemical warfare protocol.

Three multilateral arms-control negotiations were left. The Geneva Conference of the Committee on Disarmament, involving 40 states, was so large that it had become a meaningless propaganda forum. The Vienna negotiations between NATO and the Warsaw Pact on mutual and balanced force reductions (MBFR), under way since 1973, had produced no progress and could not do so. However, scrapping them would be unpopular with NATO-Europe. The Final Act of the 1975 Conference on Security and Cooperation in Europe (CSCE; the Helsinki accords) had included symbolic "confidence-building measures," and the 1980 Madrid review conference on CSCE had been expected to extend them, but the hard-line Soviet approach taken after the U.S. election made this impossible. Indeed, flagrant Soviet violations of the CSCE provisions meant the 1980 review conference might be the last. Precisely because existing arms-control negotiations and agreements were being terminated, the 1978 French proposal for a conference on disarmament in Europe was increasingly popular in NATO-Europe, which wanted to salvage as much as possible of arms control and détente. A European disarmament conference seemed the best way of doing so.

SOUTHEAST AND EAST ASIA AND AUSTRALIA

With massive Soviet support, Vietnam had proved that the domino theory was correct, certainly insofar as Indochina was concerned. Having overrun the South in 1975, after the U.S. withdrawal, Vietnam had become a regional great power with armed forces of 1,029,000 personnel. The Army of one million had 38 infantry and 1 armoured divisions (8,000–10,000 men), 1,500 Soviet main battle tanks (T-34/85s, T-54/55s, T-62s, and Type 59s), plus 400 captured U.S. M-47/48 tanks. The 25,000-strong Air Force had 485 combat aircraft, including 90 MiG-17s, 60 MiG-19s, and 60 Su-7/20 Soviet/Chinese fighter-bombers, 25 captured U.S. F-5A's and 60 A-37B FGA's, and 180 MiG-21F/PF interceptors. These forces were the second largest in the region, exceeded only by China's, and after 30 years of combat were extremely efficient. Vietnam had occupied Cambodia since December 1978, with 21 divisions (about 200,000 men), although resistance continued from the left-wing Khmer Rouge (some 20,000–30,000 strong) and the right-wing Khmer Serai (10,000). Vietnam also controlled Laos, where 40,000 troops were stationed.

China had tried to check Vietnam's expansionism with a punitive invasion in 1979 followed by withdrawal, but this had had little or no effect on Vietnamese policy. There were signs that China might repeat its invasion, perhaps occupying key North Vietnamese centres near the border. China's forces were adequate for this and for assistance to the Afghan rebels. Numerically the Chinese armed forces were the largest in the world, at 4,450,000 personnel, but they were desperately in need of modern equipment for armoured and air warfare. The Army of 3.6 million had only 11,000 elderly Soviet and Chinese Type 59 main battle tanks. The 490,000-strong Air Force had 5,200 combat aircraft, again relatively obsolete types, including 450 B-5 and 100 Tu-2 medium/light bombers, 500 F-2 and A-5 fighter-bombers, and 3,900 F-4/5/6/7 fighters; plus the new F-12s. The coastal defense Navy had 360,000 personnel but only 38 major surface combat ships, none larger than a destroyer, and 97 diesel attack submarines, plus 1 ballistic missile submarine and 2 SSN's.

Even China's nuclear deterrent forces were weak. A new ICBM, the CSS-4 (13,000-km [8,100-mi] range, 1 × 5–10-megaton warhead), had been tested, but China had only 4 CSS-3 ICBM's (6,000–7,000-km [3,700–4,350-mi] range, 1 × 1–3-megaton warhead), 65 to 85 CSS-2 IRBM's, and 50 CSS-1 MRBM's (2,500/1,800-km [1,550/1,120-mi] ranges and 1 × 3–5-megaton/15-kiloton warheads, respectively). China's TNF, mostly F-9 fighter-bombers, were numerous enough to be adequate. Influential Reagan advisers had suggested before the election that the U.S. should help modernize China's nuclear forces.

The other significant military balance in the region was between North Korea and South Korea plus Japan. North Korean forces totaled 678,000, including a 600,000-strong army with 2,500 tanks, mostly Soviet T-54/55/62s, and an air force of 47,000 with 615 combat aircraft, including 340 MiG-15/17/19 fighter-bombers and 120 MiG-21 interceptors. Against this, South Korea had total forces of 600,600 personnel. They were outnumbered in armour and aircraft. The 520,000-strong Army had 800 M-47/48 tanks, and the Air Force of 32,600 had 362 combat aircraft, mostly fighter-bombers, including 220 F-5A/B/E/F's and 60 F-4D/E's. North Korea's defense spending amounted to 11.2% of GNP (estimated at $1.3 billion) against South Korea's 5.5% of GNP ($3,460,000,000).

Japan's defense spending remained so low, at 0.9% of GNP ($8,960,000,000), that the Reagan administration was expected to insist it be increased. Its armed forces amounted to a minimal self-defense force of 155,000 personnel (1 mechanized and 12 infantry divisions) with 540 Type 61 and 200 Type 74 medium tanks. The 42,000-strong Navy had 33 destroyers, mostly GW ships, and 11 ASW frigates, while the Air Force had 44,000 men and 356 combat aircraft, including 150 F-10FDJ Starfighters and 130 F-4EJ Phantoms; 92 F-15J/DJ Eagle fighters were on order.

In the southern Pacific, Australia maintained volunteer armed forces of 71,011 personnel costing 2.8% of GNP ($3.9 billion). These comprised a 32,010-strong army with 90 Leopard AS-1 tanks, a 16,930-strong navy with 1 aircraft carrier, 3 ASW GW destroyers, and 2 FFG-7 GW frigates, and an air force of 22,071 with 115 combat aircraft, including 20 F-111C medium bombers and 48 Mirage IIIO fighter-bombers, some deployed in Malaysia/Singapore. Australia's smaller neighbour, New Zealand, spent 2.1% of GNP ($358.4 million) for token armed forces of 12,640 personnel with four frigates.

Taiwan seemed secure. Its armed forces totaled 438,200 personnel with 200 main battle tanks and 388 combat aircraft. Defense spending amounted to $1,750,000,000.

AFRICA SOUTH OF THE SAHARA

A major source of conflict was removed by the resolution of the Zimbabwe (Rhodesia) guerrilla war with Britain's grant of independence to Zimbabwe. This left two major sources of instability: the Soviet-sponsored Cuban and Warsaw Pact forces in Africa, and the hostility of the black African states toward South Africa. In late 1980 the focus had switched to the Soviet's direct and surrogate presence in the continent, the importance of which was underlined by the Iran-Iraq war. Reagan's foreign policy advisers believed that the U.S. could drive the Soviets out of Africa, and indeed the Soviet-controlled forces were at the end of long and vulnerable supply lines. Indigenous African forces remained extremely weak and could not resist properly trained and equipped forces. Hence the disproportionate political gains gleaned by the Soviets from the 19,000 Cubans in Angola and 16,500 in Ethiopia, under Soviet commanders and supported by Soviet and Warsaw Pact air cover. Soviet gains had been relatively easy but could equally easily be lost.

South Africa's relative security underlined the gap between sophisticated military forces and those in most of Africa. The South African forces totaled only 85,050 personnel (404,500 on mobilization) with 310 main battle tanks, 32 Mirage F-1AZ fighters, and 36 Mirage III/F-1 fighter-bombers. But South Africa retained control of South West Africa/Namibia and could look forward to receiving favourable treatment from the Reagan administration because of its fiercely anti-Soviet stance.

The episode of South Africa's possible nuclear test in 1978 remained unsolved. Intensive U.S. investigations had produced two incompatible interpretations of the very ambiguous evidence. Either the Vela reconnaissance satellites had reported what looked like a nuclear test but was not, or a cleverly planned clandestine nuclear test had been conducted in an area near Antarctica where U.S. satellite reconnaissance coverage was known to be poor. Such a test could have been conducted by South Africa, by Israel, or by the two in collaboration. Both could manufacture nuclear weapons, both needed them, and neither would want to admit to being a nuclear weapons power. (ROBIN RANGER)

See also Space Exploration.
[535.B.5.e.ii; 544.B.5-6; 736]

Defense: Special Report

CONFLICT IN THE CRESCENT

by Robin Ranger

Iraq's invasion of Iran on Sept. 22, 1980, fulfilled predictions that the late Shah Mohammad Reza Pahlavi's loss of power would lead to instability in the Persian Gulf. Since the Gulf provided most of the West's oil supplies, the implications of the fighting, still in progress at the end of the year, were serious.

The Tottering Balance. The Iraqi intention had been to seize control of Khuzestan Province and with it a large part of Iran's oil wealth. This would bolster Iraqi Pres. Saddam Hussein's domestically shaky regime, increase Iraq's already considerable oil wealth, and give it the advantage in a struggle for supremacy with Iran dating from the 3rd century. More recent disputes had included Iran's 1969 abrogation of the 1937 Shatt al-Arab treaty, concerning the waterway at the mouth of the Tigris which both countries claimed. Iran had also seized, in 1971, the islands of Abu Musa and Greater and Lesser Tunb, controlling the Strait of Hormuz and hence all oil tanker traffic to and from the Gulf. Furthermore, Iraq blamed Iran for the prolonged Kurdish rebellion in northern Iraq. The rebellion had died down following a 1975 Iraqi-Iranian agreement and the subsequent withdrawal of Iranian support, but it flared up again with the collapse of the shah's government.

Power here, as elsewhere in the Middle East, ultimately meant military power. The U.S. had recognized this in supporting the shah. For 35 years he had functioned as the policeman of the Gulf, with Iranian forces backed up by those of the U.S. and U.K. Whatever criticisms could be made of his domestic policies, the shah had provided stability in an unstable area of vital interest to the West. In retrospect, U.S. Pres. Jimmy Carter's withdrawal of U.S. support in 1979 was clearly a major mistake.

Iran's forces had been superior to those of Iraq or of any other Gulf power, but they depended on U.S. and U.K. technical personnel to operate their sophisticated weapons systems, including the most modern aircraft and tanks. In 1980 Iran's armed forces totaled 240,000, with an Army of 150,000, 875 British Chieftain heavy tanks, 400 M-47/48 and 460 M-60A1 tanks, 325 M-113 and 500 BTR-40/50/60/152 armoured personnel carriers (APC's), and over 1,000 guns and howitzers. The 70,000-strong Air Force had 445 combat aircraft, including 77 F-14A Tomcat air superiority fighters and 188 F-4D/E Phantom and 166 F-5E/F Tiger fighter-bombers. Although only 20,000 strong, the Navy dominated the Gulf, with 3 guided weapon (GW) destroyers, 4 GW frigates, 9 fast attack craft with missiles, and 14 hovercraft.

The political and religious revolution of 1979, coupled with the withdrawal of Western technical assistance, gravely weakened these forces, though by less than Iraq had calculated. The revolution also meant that Iran, led by the fanatic Ayatollah Ruhollah Khomeini, had become a source of instability. Iraq's forces were roughly equal to Iran's on paper and, Iraq hoped, superior in practice. They totaled 242,250, with an Army of 200,000, 2,500 T-54/55/62 main battle tanks, some 2,500 armoured fighting vehicles, including BMP mechanized infantry combat vehicles and BTR-50/60/152 APC's, and 800 guns/howitzers. The 38,000-strong Air Force had 332 combat aircraft, including 12 Tu-22 Blinder bombers, 10 Il-28 light bombers, and 80 MiG-23B, 40 Su-7B, 60 Su-20, and 15 Hunter FB-59/FR-10 fighter-bombers, plus 115 MiG-21 interceptors and about 275 helicopters. The small Navy of 4,250 was a coastal defense force. Iraqi forces were Soviet-equipped and trained.

The War that Stalled. The Iraqi plan of campaign, reportedly based on old British plans, apparently called for a limited frontal attack to pin down Iranian forces in the Abadan-Khorramshahr area, with the main thrust passing east of these cities, cutting them off from Iran. They could then be taken at leisure. Subsidiary attacks would be launched against the air bases at Ahvaz (the provincial capital) and Dezful, some 150 and 300 km (90/180 mi) to the north, to put them out of action. They might be taken later. This would give Iran control of Khuzestan's oil fields and of its military bases. Iran would have to accept Iraq's conquests or attempt difficult and costly counterattacks that were unlikely to succeed.

As the map of the war zone shows, the road and rail networks in the area are extremely limited, with one north-south rail link running through Dezful and Ahvaz to Khorramshahr. Moreover, the mountain ranges would channel Iranian counterattacks along the coastal area, on the Shiraz-Ahvaz/Khorramshahr axis, or some 150 km (90 mi) to the north, on the Isfahan-Dezful axis. Once the rainy season started in November, transportation would become

---

Robin Ranger is an associate professor in the Department of Political Science, St. Francis Xavier University, Antigonish, Nova Scotia, and a Department of National Defence Fellow in Strategic Studies.

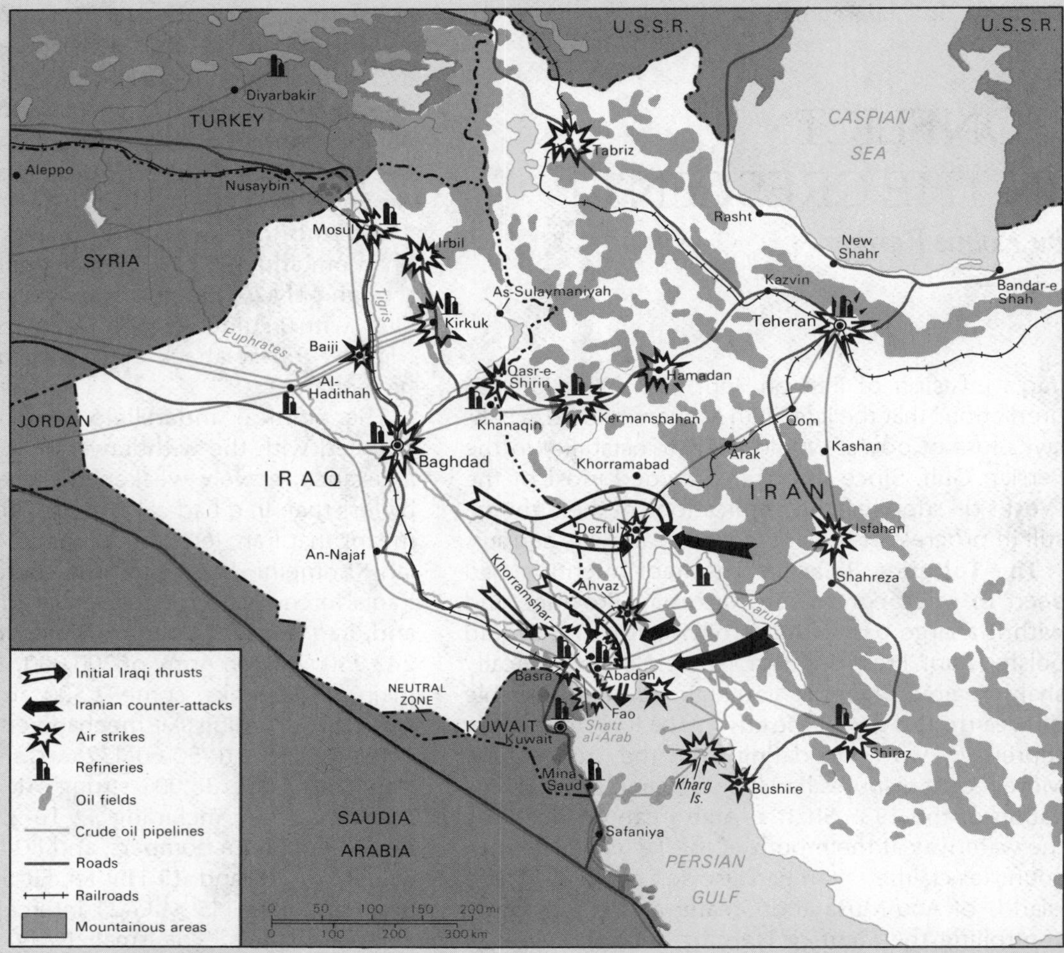

even more difficult. This plan utilized a major tactical element of blitzkrieg, the use of a successful offensive to seize key positions which the defender would have to counterattack at a disadvantage.

The Iraqi plan proved difficult to execute, although it might ultimately succeed. Secrecy and confusion made it difficult for outsiders to determine more than the general course of the fighting, but, basically, the Iraqi blitzkrieg had run into heavier and more sustained Iranian resistance than anticipated. It was also conducted at less than lightning speed. Instead of a massive armoured advance along the main axis of attack to the coast, which could have been reached in days by first-rate armoured forces, the Iraqis advanced slowly and steadily, using heavy artillery to clear the way for armour and infantry. It was not until mid-October that Abadan was surrounded, and Iraq still did not control it in early December. Control of Khorramshahr was still disputed. Iranian counterattacks enabled supplies to get through to the defenders. Iranian defenders were also holding out in Susangerd, a border town on the approaches to Ahvaz, which remained in Iranian hands, as did Dezful.

The Iraq-Iran war took such a different course from the short, intense Arab-Israeli wars because neither Iraq nor Iran was able to mount the kind of large-scale armoured warfare at which the Israelis excelled. Instead, both had adopted what were basically set-piece infantry tactics, more like the Arab side in the Arab-Israeli wars but even more cautious. In this kind of fighting, where—or once—both sides are evenly matched, it is difficult to achieve a decisive breakthrough. Unless cities can be cut off and starved out, it is impossible to take them without very heavy casualties, and not always possible then. Significantly, neither Iraq nor Iran seemed to have suffered heavy casualties in terms of killed, wounded, or captured soldiers or civilians. The air strikes by each side had caused spectacular fires in oil installations but otherwise had little effect. As the conflict continued, the military machines of both sides began to run down, with battle damage and attrition taking their toll. Thus, Iraq appeared to have lost 30 to 50 fighters and fighter-bombers to Iran's 60 to 100 planes. So, by December, the war had settled down to an infantry and artillery conflict, reminiscent of World War I albeit at a less intense level.

BALANCE OF POWER

Military personnel (active) — each symbol = 100,000
Bombers and fighter-bombers — each symbol = 100
Tanks — each symbol = 500

Country	Military personnel	Bombers and fighter-bombers	Tanks
Afghanistan			
Iran			
Iraq			
Israel			
Jordan			
Pakistan			
Saudi Arabia			
Syria			
Turkey			
Yemen (Aden)			

For actual figures and explanatory notes, see table in *Defense*.

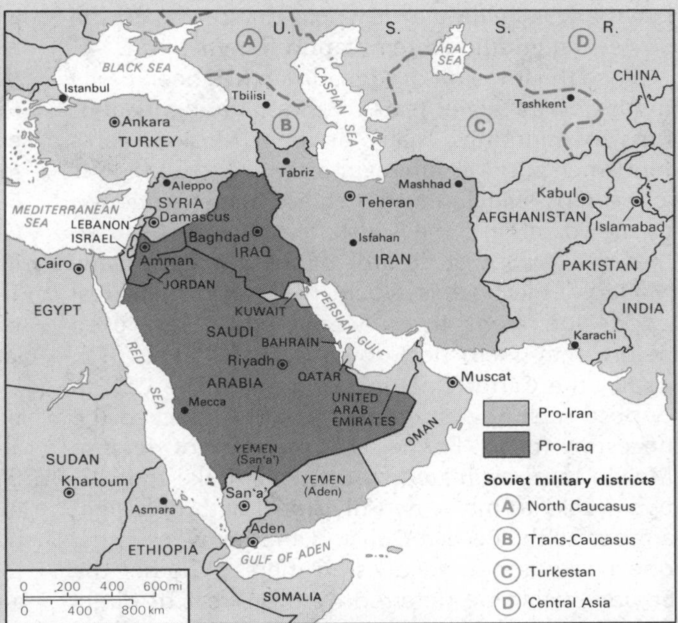

Ironically, the war could have a stabilizing effect by countering the impression that lightning victories were the rule in modern warfare, particularly if the attacker chose the right moment. This had increased the pressures to strike first, or to preempt, in a crisis, as in the 1967 and 1973 Arab-Israeli wars. The war also showed that although sophisticated equipment could be transferred to less developed countries and their forces given extensive training, without the necessary level of technological education they could not operate at full efficiency.

Unfortunately for the West, the Soviet Union possessed sophisticated equipment, the skilled personnel to operate it, and the will to use it. The Soviets showed this in their invasion of Afghanistan, and the interaction of this with the Iran-Iraq war was profoundly destabilizing.

The Widening Crisis. The Soviets' Afghanistan operation had underlined their capability for rapid, ruthless, military intervention on a scale that neither indigenous nor Western forces could counter. In Afghanistan, the Soviets had put five divisions in place within two weeks; it had taken them three weeks (November-December 1977) to put 20,000 men (Cuban, Warsaw Pact, and Soviet personnel) into Ethiopia, over a much greater distance. In both cases, the West had failed to use force to stop or push back the Soviet intervention, nor had it imposed any significant nonmilitary penalties on the Soviet Union. Hence fears that the Soviets would use force again, to protect their newly conquered Afghanistan territory or to seize Iranian oil fields.

The new balance of military forces in the so-called arc of crisis, stretching from Pakistan through Turkey, and in the Arab world was extremely favourable to the Soviets. These new opportunities for intervention coincided with their increasing difficulties in meeting their oil needs from domestic production. Pakistan itself bordered on India, Afghanistan, and Iran. India was friendly to the Soviets and had long-standing disputes with Pakistan and would probably attack Pakistan if the Soviets did so. India's armed forces totaled 1,104,000—the third largest in Asia—with a 944,000-strong Army, about 2,000 tanks (T-54/55 and Vijayanta), plus 700 Soviet T-72 main battle tanks on order. The Air Force of 113,000 had 630 combat aircraft, including 274 fighter-bombers (a roughly equal mix of Su-7BM/U's, Hunter F-56/56A's, and HF-24 Marut 1/1T's) and 252 MiG-21 fighters (all models). The Navy of 47,000 included one old aircraft carrier and 29 frigates.

Pakistan's forces had been weakened by cutbacks in U.S. supplies and were deployed for defense against India, not against Soviet strikes from Afghanistan. Numerically, its forces were large, totaling 438,600, but with old equipment. The Army of 408,000 had 250 M-47/48 and 700 T-59 tanks. The 17,600-strong Air Force had 256 combat aircraft, but modern aircraft comprised only 17 Mirage IIIEP and 38 Mirage 5PA/DP fighter-bombers. Pakistan's alliance with China might deter an Indian attack, but it could also expand a limited Soviet-Pakistan clash into one involving India and China. Pakistan's potential for becoming a nuclear power was considerable though uncertain. It could be within a few months of manufacturing a nuclear device or some years away. The Soviet troops on its border increased Pakistan's incentives to go nuclear, but the possibility that it would do so offered the Soviets an additional temptation to strike at it.

Since the invasion of Afghanistan had been partly motivated by Soviet fears of unrest among its non-Russian minorities, many of them Muslim, Iran's fundamentalist Muslim regime could also be seen as a threat to Soviet interests. Iran had been partitioned by the Soviets and the British from 1941 to 1946, so the idea of Soviet control of Iran was not new. Militarily, the Soviets would have faced little real opposition from Iran's weakened forces, even before they were tied down by Iraq's attack. On paper, the Carter Doctrine committed the U.S. to oppose such Soviet intervention, but it lacked the necessary forces. Former U.S. secretary of defense Melvin Laird estimated that it would take the U.S. two weeks to move two divisions, with only light armour, to the Persian Gulf and another week to get one heavy armoured division there. Whether the Soviets would be deterred by the threat of direct fighting with the U.S. was, unfortunately, not clear.

The Middle East and Turkey. Within the Middle East, the balance of power—or, rather, its absence—favoured the Soviets. In the Gulf area, as the regional balance-of-power map indicates, there were no large military forces. Even Saudi Arabia's armed forces totaled only 47,000, with 380 tanks, 15 Lightning F-53 fighters, and 65 F-5E Tiger fighter-bombers, plus 45 U.S. F-15 Eagle fighters on order.

With Egypt's shift to an alliance with the U.S., the Arab-Israeli balance had become more favourable to Israel. But, as tensions between Syria and Jordan showed, the balance remained unstable. Syria remained the most powerful anti-Israeli state, with armed forces of 247,500, including a 200,000-strong army with 2,200 T-54/55, 600 T-62, and 120 T-72 tanks and a 45,000-strong air force with 395 combat aircraft. These included 60 MiG-17, 20 Su-7, and 30 Su-20 fighter-bombers, 60 MiG-23 fighter-bomber/interceptors, and 200 MiG-21PF/MF and 25 MiG-25 interceptors. Against Syria, Jordan could deploy armed forces of 67,200 with 300 M-47/48 and 295 Centurion tanks and 48 F-5E/F interceptor/fighter-bombers.

Israel's defense spending remained proportionately one of the highest in the world, at 31.1% of gross national product ($5.2 billion). Its armed forces totaled 169,600 but could be increased on mobilization to 400,000 within 24 hours. The Army of 135,000 (375,000 on mobilization) had 3,050 tanks, including 1,000 Centurions, 650 M-48s, 810 M-60s, and 400 captured T-54/55s and 150 T-62s; the Israeli Merkava I/II was being introduced. The 28,000 (37,000 on mobilization)-strong Air Force had 481 combat aircraft, including 25 F/TF-15 Eagles, 130 F-4E Phantoms, 30 Mirage IIICJ/BJ and 80 Kfir-C2 fighter-bomber/interceptors, and 200 A-4E/H/M/N Skyhawk fighter-bombers.

Egypt's armed forces, totaling 367,000, were suffering from shortages of spare parts for Soviet equipment. The Air Force of 27,000 was converting to Western types. Operational aircraft included 35 F-4E Phantom, 46 Mirage IIIEE/DE, 50 MiG-21, 40 Chinese F-6, 60 Su-7BM, 18 Su-20, and 14 Mirage 5 fighter-bombers, plus 45 MiG-21MF/U interceptors. The Army of 320,000 had 850 T-54/55 and 750 T-62 tanks. Egyptian Pres. Anwar as-Sadat remained isolated in the Arab world, especially after allowing the U.S. to station forces in Egypt and train there. Relations with his unstable neighbour, Col. Muammar al-Qaddafi of Libya, were so poor that the idea of an Egyptian liberation of the Libyan population reemerged. Libya's armed forces totaled only 53,000 but they were well equipped, with 2,400 T-54/55/62/72 tanks. The Air Force of 4,000, with 287 combat aircraft, included Soviet, Pakistani, and Palestinian pilots flying 17 Tu-22 Blinder A bombers, 50 MiG-23 Flogger E, 35 MiG-25 Foxbat A, and 20 MiG-21 interceptors, and 40 Mirage IIIB/E fighter-bombers.

At the western end of the arc of crisis stood Turkey, the NATO member linking the Middle East to Europe and sharing borders with the Soviet Union, Iran, Iraq, and Syria. Turkish armed forces were large, totaling 567,000, with 3,000 M-47 and 500 M-48 tanks for the 470,000-strong Army. The Air Force of 52,000 had 290 combat aircraft, including 70 F-4E, 46 F-5A/B, 50 F-100C/D/F, and 26 F/TF-104G fighter-bombers and 20 F-5A/B and 30 F-104S interceptors.

The New Balkan Wars? Overall, the arc of crisis had thus been gravely destabilized by the weakening of Iran and by the Soviet invasion of Afghanistan. The occupation of Afghanistan and the Iraqi invasion of Iran emphasized the fragility of the balances of power built up since 1945. This instability could create temptations for the Soviets, as well as fears that it might affect their large Muslim population.

The Soviet force deployments in the military districts shown on the balance-of-power map are formidable relative to the opposition they would face if they were used. Yet this actually underestimates Soviet military power in the region. These forces could be reinforced within days and were qualitatively far superior to their opponents in air power, armour, artillery, and logistic support. Given that their military forces were the Soviets' greatest asset and that they would be, relatively, strongest from 1980 to 1984, the Soviet leadership could be tempted to use them. The arc of crisis thus bore an uncomfortable resemblance to the Balkans before 1914: an unstable area where local conflicts and external intervention provided a potentially explosive combination.

Demography

According to new UN population projections to the year 2000, developed countries would have low growth rates with modest population increases, while less developed countries would experience high rates. The populations of less developed countries would double, on average, in 35 years and, in some cases, in 20 years. Africa was expected to experience the most rapid growth, followed by Latin America and South and East Asia. Northern America and the Soviet Union would have moderate population increases, and Europe would grow much more slowly.

At the same time, it was observed that the recent trend in the global population growth rate had been downward. According to the International Demographic Data Center of the U.S. Census Bureau, the global growth rate fell from 2.1% in 1965–70 to 1.7% in 1975–79. The decline was characteristic for all areas except Africa. There was speculation that the global growth curve would level off by 2080, when the world's population would have risen from the current 4,500,000,000 persons to an estimated 11,000,000,000 or more. In 1980 China achieved a population of an estimated 1,000,000,000 persons. Countries with over 200 million were (in millions): India (676), the Soviet Union (266), and the U.S. (223).

Birth Statistics. Births and birthrates increased in the U.S. in 1979; the rise resulted from an increase in the number of women of childbearing age, as well as in the rate of childbearing. The estimated number of live births, 3,473,000, was higher than in any of the preceding seven years. The birthrate also rose, to 15.8 per 1,000 population, compared with 15.3 in 1978. The trend continued into 1980; the birthrate for the first six months was 15.6, as against 15.2 for the corresponding period in 1979. The fertility rate in 1979 was 68 live births per 1,000 women 15–44 years of age, 2% above 1978.

Final data for 1978 showed a white birthrate of 14.2 live births per 1,000 population, compared with 14.4 in 1977, and a black birthrate of 21.6, compared with 21.7 in 1977. Fertility rates also dropped; for whites, the rate of live births per 1,000 women of childbearing age was 62.7 in 1978 and 64 in 1977; for blacks, it was 88.6 in 1978 and 89.8 in 1977. Birthrates declined for all birth orders, and especially for higher order births. From 1970 to 1978 rates for mothers having their fifth birth fell by 61% and for the eighth, by 72%.

Births to unmarried women continued to increase in 1978, but at a slower rate. There were an estimated 543,900 live births to unmarried mothers in 1978, 5.5% more than in 1977. About half were to women under 20. Some 233,600 births occurred to white unmarried mothers and 293,400 to black unmarried mothers. The ratio of out-of-wedlock childbearing (the number of births to unmarried women per 1,000 total live births) rose to 87 for white women and 532 for black women.

The total fertility rate, a measure of the number of children women would have during their lifetime if current fertility rates remained constant, showed a decline in the U.S. in 1978, from 1,826.3 children per 1,000 women in 1977 to 1,800.2. This would indicate an average of 1.8 children per woman (1.7 for whites and 2.3 for blacks). The estimated total fertility rate for the world was 3.8 children per woman, with the rate in the more developed countries around 2 and in the less developed countries about 4.4. Countries with rates under 2 are considered to be below replacement levels and theoretically will decline in population, while those over 2.5 are above replacement levels and could grow considerably. The total fertility rate in northern Europe was 1.8 children per woman, while in Kenya it was 8.

The World Fertility Survey, begun in 1972, reported that fertility in both developed and less developed countries had declined. In the latter areas, a growing preference for smaller families (especially in Asia and Latin America), increased family planning, and modernizing influences—along with education and urbanization—were seen as factors. In some developed countries deaths exceeded births; fertility rates were below replacement levels in Austria, Belgium, Denmark, England, Finland, France, East Germany, West Germany, Italy, The Netherlands, Norway, Sweden, and Switzerland.

Because of the age composition of the U.S., the population was expected to double in about 99 years, despite current fertility rates. Natural increase, the excess of births over deaths, added some 1,567,000 to the population in 1979. The rate was 7 per 1,000 population and contrasts signifi-

continued on page 297

Table I. Birthrates and Death Rates per 1,000 Population and Infant Mortality per 1,000 Live Births in Selected Countries, 1979[1]

Country	Birth-rate	Death rate	Infant mortality	Country	Birth-rate	Death rate	Infant mortality
Africa				Ireland[4]	21.1	10.0	14.9
Algeria	39.1	8.0	20.5	Italy	11.8	9.4	15.3
Egypt	41.0	11.0	85.3[2]	Poland	19.5	9.2	22.5[4]
Gabon[3]	31.4	23.2	229.0	Spain	16.1	7.8	15.1[4]
Ghana[3]	48.6	19.1	156.0	Sweden	11.6	11.0	7.3
Kenya[3]	50.5	14.0	. . .	Switzerland	11.6	9.0	8.6[4]
Libya[2]	45.1	5.9	46.6	United Kingdom	13.1	12.1	13.3[4]
Mauritius	27.8	7.3	33.9	North America			
Nigeria[3]	50.3	19.7	. . .	Canada	15.0	7.2	12.0[4]
South Africa[3]	37.7	11.5	. . .	Costa Rica[4]	31.8	4.1	22.3
Zaire[3]	46.8	20.7	104.0	Dominican Republic	32.4	4.4	37.2[4]
Zambia[3]	47.5	14.9	122.0	El Salvador	39.2	7.4	53.0
Asia				Grenada	24.5	6.8	15.4
Bangladesh	45.0	17.6	13.2	Mexico[4]	34.0	6.0	44.1
China	21.7	8.7	50.0	Nicaragua	43.3	12.2	121.0
India	35.0	13.6	108.0	Panama	28.0	4.4	24.9
Indonesia	35.9	14.6	122.0	United States	15.8	8.7	13.0
Israel	24.6	6.9	16.0	Oceania			
Japan	14.3	5.9	8.0	Australia	15.5	6.9	12.2[4]
Kuwait[2]	41.5	4.8	39.1	New Caledonia[4]	26.5	6.7	30.2
Pakistan	45.7	14.2	106.0	New Zealand	16.9	8.2	13.8[4]
Philippines	34.6	8.4	64.0	Papua New Guinea	42.1	15.0	114.0
Singapore	17.3	5.3	13.2	Vanuatu	45.0	47.0	. . .
Turkey	33.0	11.0	125.0[3]	South America			
Vietnam	40.1	17.1	130.0	Argentina[4]	25.2	8.9	40.8
Yemen (San'a')[3]	48.7	19.8	. . .	Brazil[3]	37.1	8.8	170.0
Europe				Chile[4]	21.4	6.7	40.1
Austria	11.4	12.2	14.8	Ecuador[4]	29.5	7.1	72.1[5]
Czechoslovakia	17.8	11.5	18.7	French Guiana[2]	24.5	7.6	32.8
France	14.1	10.2	9.8	Peru	41.0[3]	13.6[3]	70.3[6]
Germany, East	14.0	13.9	13.0	Uruguay[2]	20.4	10.0	48.5
Germany, West	9.5	11.6	14.7[4]	Venezuela	35.9	5.5	33.7
Hungary	15.0	12.8	23.7	U.S.S.R.	18.3	10.1	27.7[7]

[1] Registered births and deaths only.
[2] 1977.
[3] 1970–75.
[4] 1978.
[5] 1976.
[6] 1972.
[7] 1974.

Sources: United Nations, *Population and Vital Statistics Report;* Economic and Social Commission for Asia and the Pacific, *Population Program News;* various national publications.

Table II. World Populations and Areas[1]

Country	AREA AND POPULATION: MIDYEAR 1979 Area in sq km	Total population	Persons per sq km	POPULATION AT MOST RECENT CENSUS Date of census	Total population	% Male	% Female	% Urban	Age distribution (%)[2] 0–14	15–29	30–44	45–59	60–74	75+
AFRICA														
Algeria	2,381,741	19,129,000	8.0	1977	17,422,000	49.7	50.3	40.6	47.9	25.4	12.7	8.2	4.5	1.3
Angola	1,246,700	6,601,000	5.3	1970	5,620,001	52.1	47.9	14.2	41.7	23.2	17.0	7.4	3.8	1.0
Benin	112,600	3,338,000	29.6	1979	3,338,240	47.9	52.1	14.2	49.0		—39.4—		—11.6—	
Botswana	576,000	791,000	1.4	1971	584,644	45.7	54.3	8.4	46.3	21.5	12.7	9.0	5.0	1.5
British Indian Ocean Territory	60	...	...	1971	110	...	...	...	...	...	...	...	...	...
Burundi	27,834	4,011,000	144.1	1979	4,011,000	...	...	...	...	...	...	...	...	...
Cameroon	465,054	8,248,000	17.7	1976	7,663,246	49.0	51.0	28.5	43.4		—48.3—		—8.3—	
Cape Verde	4,033	296,000	73.4	1980	296,093	...	...	...	...	...	...	...	...	...
Central African Republic	624,977	2,362,000	3.8	1975	2,088,000	...	...	34.8	...	...	...	...	...	...
Chad	1,284,000	4,417,000	3.4	1975	4,029,917	47.7	52.3	16.0	40.6	28.3	17.2	9.5	—4.4—	
Comoros[3]	1,792	280,000	156.3	1966	244,905	49.2	50.8	13.5	44.1	23.6	15.7	8.7	4.2	3.8
Congo	342,000	1,498,000	4.4	1974	1,300,120	48.5	51.5	37.8	...	...	...	...	...	...
Djibouti	23,000	315,000	13.7	1960–61	81,200	...	...	57.4	...	...	...	...	...	...
Egypt	997,667	41,065,000	41.2	1976	38,228,180	51.0	49.0	43.9	31.6		—65.5—		—2.9—	
Equatorial Guinea	28,051	330,000	11.8	1965	254,684	50.0	50.0	47.6	...	...	...	...	...	...
Ethiopia	1,221,900	30,421,000	24.9	1970	24,068,800	50.7	49.3	9.7	43.5	27.0	16.3	8.8	3.7	0.7
French Southern and Antarctic Lands	7,366	...	...	...	...	...	...	...	...	...	...	...	...	...
Gabon	267,667	1,356,000	5.1	1970	950,009	47.9	52.1	31.8	35.4	19.1	22.3	16.4	—6.5—	
Gambia, The	10,690	585,000	54.7	1973	493,499	51.0	49.0	15.0	41.3	—44.1—		—14.6—		
Ghana	238,533	11,100,000	46.5	1970	8,559,313	49.6	50.4	28.9	46.9	24.4	15.8	7.5	3.8	1.6
Guinea	245,857	4,887,000	19.9	1972	5,143,284	...	...	...	43.1			—56.9—		
Guinea-Bissau	36,125	777,000	21.5	1979	777,214	48.2	51.8	...	...	...	...	...	...	...
Ivory Coast	322,463	7,920,000	24.6	1975	6,671,827	52.0	48.0	31.8	44.6			—55.4—		
Kenya	580,367	15,322,000	26.4	1979	15,322,000	...	...	12.6	53.5			—46.5—		
Lesotho	30,355	1,309,000	43.1	1976	1,216,815	51.7	48.3	...	...	...	...	...	...	...
Liberia	97,790	1,802,000	18.4	1974	1,503,368	50.5	49.5	29.1	40.9	26.7	17.7	8.8	4.6	1.3
Libya	1,749,000	3,132,000	1.8	1973	2,249,237	53.0	47.0	59.8	44.3	22.2	15.4	8.2	4.0	1.6
Madagascar	587,041	8,511,000	14.5	1974–75	7,568,600	49.5	50.5	16.4	44.2	26.3	14.4	9.8	4.2	1.1
Malawi	118,484	5,817,000	49.1	1977	5,561,821	48.1	51.9	8.3	...	...	...	...	...	...
Mali	1,240,142	6,465,000	5.2	1976	6,035,272	49.1	50.9	16.7	47.3	22.2	17.2	8.8	—3.8—	
Mauritania	1,030,700	1,588,000	1.5	1976–77	1,419,939	...	...	21.9	...	...	...	...	...	...
Mauritius	2,040	941,000	461.3	1972	826,199	50.0	50.0	42.9	40.3	28.6	14.5	11.0	4.9	0.7
Mayotte	378	47,000	124.3	1978	47,246	49.9	50.1	53.3	50.2	23.4	13.9	7.0	3.8	1.7
Morocco	458,730	19,470,000	42.4	1971	15,379,259	50.1	49.9	35.4	46.2	22.4	16.0	8.3	5.3	1.8
Mozambique	799,380	12,062,000	15.1	1970	8,168,933	49.4	50.6	3.2	45.3	22.5	19.1	9.1	3.8	0.3
Niger	1,186,408	5,352,000	4.5	1977	5,098,657	49.3	50.7	11.8	...	...	...	...	...	...
Nigeria	923,800	100,075,000	108.3	1973	...	...	...	...	...	...	...	...	...	...
Réunion	2,512	489,000	194.7	1974	476,675	48.5	51.5	43.0	42.6	25.8	15.6	10.0	4.8	1.2
Rwanda	26,338	4,945,000	187.7	1978	4,819,317	48.8	51.2	4.3	60.0—			—40.0—		
St. Helena & Ascension Islands	412	7,000	17.7	1976	5,866	52.0	48.0	29.4	34.2	27.7	16.3	10.8	8.4	2.6
São Tomé & Príncipe	964	84,000	87.1	1970	73,631	50.3	49.7	25.0	...	...	...	...	...	...
Senegal	196,722	5,518,000	28.0	1976	4,907,507	49.2	50.8	29.6	42.5	27.3	17.2	8.6	3.7	0.1
Seychelles	443	63,000	141.5	1977	61,898	50.4	49.6	37.1	39.7	26.3	14.0	10.8	6.9	2.2
Sierra Leone	71,740	3,305,000	46.1	1974	2,729,479	54.1	45.9	...	36.7	27.2	19.4	9.0	—7.6—	
Somalia	638,000	3,542,000	5.6	1975	3,253,024	...	...	15.0	...	...	...	...	...	...
South Africa	1,133,759	23,772,000	21.0	1980	23,771,970	...	...	...	...	...	...	...	...	...
Bophuthatswana[4]	40,430	1,273,000	31.5	1970	880,312	46.9	53.1	14.2	44.7	26.4	12.5	—13.5—		1.3
Transkei[4]	41,002	2,484,000	60.6	1970	1,745,992	41.2	58.8	3.2	46.4	22.8	14.1	—15.3—		1.2
Venda[4]	7,184	358,000	49.8	1970	265,129	38.8	61.2	0.2	48.1	22.7	13.7	6.4	7.6	1.5
South West Africa/Namibia	824,268	1,325,000	1.6	1970	763,630	50.8	49.2	24.9	...	...	...	...	...	...
Sudan	2,503,890	17,865,000	7.1	1973	14,819,000[5]	50.4	49.6	...	46.7		—48.4—		—4.9—	
Swaziland	17,364	530,000	30.5	1976	494,534	45.6	54.4	15.2	47.7	25.2	13.7	7.9	3.7	1.7
Tanzania	945,050	17,982,000	19.0	1978	17,551,925	49.2	50.8	...	...	...	...	...	...	...
Togo	56,785	2,472,000	43.5	1970	1,953,778	48.1	51.9	...	49.8	21.5	15.1	8.0	3.6	2.0
Tunisia	154,530	6,367,000	41.2	1975	5,588,209	50.8	49.2	49.0	43.7	25.6	14.7	10.0	4.9	0.9
Uganda	241,139	12,600,000	52.2	1980	12,600,000	...	...	...	...	...	...	...	...	...
Upper Volta	274,200	6,728,000	24.5	1975	5,638,203	50.2	49.8	9.0	47.4	21.1	16.1	9.3	—6.1—	
Western Sahara	266,769	165,000	0.6	1970	76,425	57.5	42.5	45.3	42.9	27.2	16.3	7.4	4.4	1.8
Zaire	2,344,885	25,561,000	10.9	1976	25,568,640	48.5	51.5	...	—52.8—			—47.2—		
Zambia	752,614	5,649,000	7.5	1969	4,056,995	49.0	51.0	29.4	46.3	24.0	16.6	9.4	3.0	0.7
Zimbabwe	390,580	7,140,000	18.3	1969	5,099,350	50.3	49.7	16.8	47.2	25.4	15.7	8.4	—3.3—	
Total AFRICA	30,202,305	481,844,000	15.9											
ANTARCTICA total	14,244,900	[6]	—	—	—	—	—	—	—	—	—	—	—	—
ASIA														
Afghanistan	652,626	15,540,000[7]	23.8	1979	15,540,000[7]	51.5	48.5	9.8	...	...	...	...	...	...
Bahrain	669	292,000	436.5	1971	216,078	53.8	46.2	78.1	44.3	25.3	16.9	9.0	3.7	0.8
Bangladesh	143,998	86,643,000	601.7	1974	76,398,000	51.6	48.4	...	45.3	26.9	15.6	8.3	—3.9—	
Bhutan	46,100	1,269,000	27.5	1969	931,514	...	...	...	...	...	...	...	...	...
Brunei	5,765	213,000	36.9	1971	136,256	53.4	46.6	63.6	43.4	28.0	15.7	8.1	3.9	0.9
Burma	676,577	34,361,000	50.8	1973	28,885,867	49.7	50.3	...	40.5		—53.4—		—6.0—	
Cambodia	181,035	4,500,000	24.9	1962	5,728,771	50.0	50.0	10.3	43.8	24.9	16.8	9.8	4.1	0.6
China	9,561,000	945,018,000	98.8	1953	574,205,940	51.8	48.2	13.3	35.9	25.1	18.8	12.9	6.3	1.0
Cyprus	9,251	621,000	67.1	1976	612,851	...	...	...	...	...	...	...	...	...
Hong Kong	1,050	4,900,000	4,666.7	1976	4,420,390	51.0	49.0	...	30.0	30.2	15.4	14.9	7.3	1.7
India	3,287,782	650,982,000	198.0	1971	548,159,652	51.8	48.2	19.9	41.9	24.1	17.8	10.2	4.9	1.1
Indonesia	1,919,558	139,376,000	72.6	1971	119,817,706[8]	49.3	50.7	17.5	44.0	23.9	18.6	9.1	3.8	0.7
Iran	1,648,000	36,938,000	22.4	1976	33,708,744	51.5	48.5	47.0	44.5	25.2	14.8	10.1	3.8	1.0
Iraq	437,522	12,767,000	29.2	1977	12,029,700	51.7	48.3	...	...	...	...	...	...	...
Israel	20,700	3,784,000	182.8	1972	3,147,683	50.3	49.7	85.3	32.6	26.9	15.6	13.6	9.2	2.0
Japan	377,643	115,920,000	307.0	1975	111,939,643	49.2	50.8	75.9	24.3	24.9	23.1	15.9	9.2	2.5
Jordan	95,396	2,152,300	22.6	1979	2,152,273	52.3	47.7	60.0	—	—	—	—	—	—

Table II. World Populations and Areas[1] *(Continued)*

Country	AREA AND POPULATION: MIDYEAR 1979			POPULATION AT MOST RECENT CENSUS											
	Area in sq km	Total population	Persons per sq km	Date of census	Total population	% Male	% Female	% Urban	Age distribution (%)[2] 0–14	15–29	30–44	45–59	60–74	75+
Korea, North	121,929	17,498,000	143.5	—	—	—	—	—	—	—	—	—	—	—
Korea, South	98,966	37,605,000	380.0	1975	34,678,972	50.0	50.0	48.4	38.0	28.2	17.9	10.2	4.6	1.0
Kuwait	16,918	1,272,000	75.2	1975	994,837	54.7	45.3	85.9	31.3	60.0	43.0	16.8	—9.0—	
Laos	236,800	3,633,000	15.3	—	—	—	—	—	—	—	—	—	—	—
Lebanon	10,230	3,254,000	318.1	1970	2,126,325	50.8	49.2	60.1	42.6	23.8	16.7	9.1	—7.7—	
Macau	16	277,000	17,331.3	1970	248,636	51.4	48.6	100.0	37.6	28.9	15.0	11.3	5.9	1.1
Malaysia	329,747	13,297,000	40.3	1970	10,319,324	50.4	49.6	38.9	44.9	25.5	15.1	9.1	4.3	1.0
Maldives	298	145,000	486.6	1978	143,046	52.6	47.4	20.7	...	...	...	...	...	...
Mongolia	1,565,000	1,595,000	1.0	1979	1,595,000	...	...	...	...	...	...	...	...	...
Nepal	145,391	13,713,000	94.3	1971	11,555,983	49.7	50.3	13.8	40.5	25.5	18.7	9.7	—5.6—	
Oman	300,000	864,000	2.9	—	—	—	—	—	—	—	—	—	—	—
Pakistan	796,095	79,838,000	100.3	1972	65,309,340	53.3	46.7	25.4	44.0	23.2	16.6	9.3	5.4	1.5
Philippines	300,000	47,719,000	159.1	1975	42,070,660	50.6	49.4	31.6	44.0	28.0	14.9	8.4	3.9	0.8
Qatar	11,400	210,000	18.4	—	—	—	—	—	—	—	—	—	—	—
Saudi Arabia	2,240,000	8,112,000	3.6	1974	7,012,642	...	...	...	...	...	...	...	...	...
Singapore	616	2,363,000	3,836.0	1970	2,074,507	51.2	48.8	100.0	38.8	28.1	16.9	10.5	4.9	0.8
Sri Lanka	65,610	14,471,000	220.6	1971	12,689,897	51.3	48.7	22.4	39.3	27.8	15.9	10.5	5.2	1.3
Syria	185,180	8,368,000	45.2	1970	6,304,685	51.3	48.7	43.5	49.3	22.4	14.3	7.5	4.8	1.7
Taiwan	36,002	17,313,000	480.9	1975	16,206,183	51.8	48.2	...	36.7	29.8	16.4	11.7	4.6	0.8
Thailand	542,373	46,114,000	85.0	1977	44,035,129	50.4	49.6	...	...	...	...	...	...	...
Turkey	779,452	44,236,000	56.8	1975	40,347,719	50.1	49.9	41.8	39.8	26.8	16.1	9.4	5.8	1.3
United Arab Emirates	83,600	877,000	10.5	1975	655,973	...	...	...	...	...	...	...	...	...
Vietnam	329,465	52,742,000	160.0	1979	52,741,766	...	...	...	...	...	...	...	...	...
Yemen (Aden)	338,100	1,838,000	5.4	1973	1,590,275	49.5	50.4	33.3	47.3	20.8	15.8	8.6	—6.6—	
Yemen (San'a')	200,000	5,785,000	28.9	1975	5,237,893	47.6	52.4	8.2	47.0	20.0	17.0	10.0	4.5	1.5
Total ASIA[9,10]	44,646,990	2,547,558,000	57.1											
EUROPE														
Albania	28,748	2,671,000	92.2	1975	2,430,000	51.5	49.5	34.4	...	...	...	...	...	...
Andorra	464	30,000	64.7	1975	26,558	...	...	...	...	...	...	...	...	...
Austria	83,853	7,502,000	89.5	1971	7,456,403	47.0	53.0	51.9	24.4	20.5	18.3	16.5	15.5	4.8
Belgium	30,521	9,842,000	322.5	1970	9,650,944	48.9	51.1	...	23.5	21.0	19.4	17.1	14.4	4.6
Bulgaria	110,912	8,806,000	79.4	1975	8,727,771	49.9	50.1	58.0	21.8	22.4	20.6	18.8	13.0	3.4
Channel Islands	194	132,000	680.4	1971	126,363	48.5	51.5	...	21.8	21.4	18.4	18.1	14.9	5.3
Czechoslovakia	127,881	15,184,000	118.7	1970	14,344,987	48.7	51.3	55.5	23.1	24.8	18.4	16.7	13.6	3.4
Denmark	43,075	5,116,000	118.8	1976	5,072,516	49.5	50.5	82.6	22.4	22.5	19.4	16.8	13.8	5.1
Faeroe Islands	1,399	43,000	30.7	1970	38,612	52.2	47.8	27.8	31.8	23.0	16.5	16.0	9.4	3.4
Finland	337,032	4,764,000	14.1	1978	4,758,088	48.4	51.6	59.7	20.8	25.2	21.0	16.8	12.4	3.8
France	544,000	53,383,000	98.1	1975	52,655,802	48.9	51.1	70.0	22.6	24.4	17.8	16.2	13.3	5.6
Germany, East	108,328	16,751,000	154.6	1971	17,068,318	46.1	53.9	73.8	23.3	19.9	20.1	14.7	16.9	5.1
Germany, West	248,667	61,328,000	246.6	1970	60,650,599	47.6	52.4	...	23.2	21.3	19.7	16.6	15.0	4.2
Gibraltar	6	32,000	5,333.3	1970	26,833	48.1	51.9	91.9	22.9	22.7	21.1	18.7	11.2	3.4
Greece	131,990	9,360,000	70.9	1971	8,768,641	49.8	50.2	53.2	24.9	20.4	21.9	16.5	12.5	3.8
Hungary	93,032	10,699,000	115.0	1970	10,322,099	48.5	51.5	45.2	21.1	23.6	20.5	17.7	13.6	3.5
Iceland	103,000	224,000	2.2	1970	204,930	50.6	49.4	...	32.3	25.1	16.4	13.7	9.0	3.5
Ireland	70,283	3,368,000	47.9	1979	3,368,217	50.3	49.7	...	...	...	...	...	...	...
Isle of Man	572	64,000	111.9	1976	61,723	47.5	52.5	51.8	20.5	19.1	15.6	17.3	20.2	7.3
Italy	301,263	56,828,000	188.7	1971	54,136,547	48.9	51.1	...	24.4	21.2	20.7	17.0	12.8	3.9
Jan Mayen	373	—	—	1973	37	...	...	—	...	...	...	...	...	...
Liechtenstein	160	26,000	162.5	1970	21,350	49.7	50.3	...	27.9	27.1	18.6	14.5	9.3	2.6
Luxembourg	2,586	362,000	140.0	1970	339,841	49.0	51.0	68.4	22.1	20.5	21.4	17.5	14.6	3.9
Malta	320	347,000	1,084.4	1967	314,216	47.9	52.1	94.3	29.8	25.9	17.6	13.8	10.2	2.7
Monaco	1.9	25,000	13,157.9	1975	25,029	45.2	54.8	100.0	12.9	17.5	18.4	20.9	21.2	9.1
Netherlands, The	41,160	14,013,000	340.5	1971	13,060,115	49.9	50.1	54.9	27.2	24.6	17.9	15.6	10.9	3.7
Norway	323,895	4,074,000	12.6	1970	3,874,133	49.7	50.3	42.4	24.4	22.5	16.0	18.8	13.5	4.8
Poland	312,677	35,049,000	112.1	1974	33,635,900	48.5	51.5	54.1	24.3	27.5	19.0	15.3	11.1	2.7
Portugal	91,632	9,820,000	107.2	1970	8,663,252	47.4	52.6	37.2	28.4	21.9	19.0	16.2	11.2	3.3
Romania	237,500	21,953,000	92.4	1977	21,657,569	49.3	50.7	47.8	25.7	23.7	19.6	17.2	10.9	3.0
San Marino	61	21,000	344.3	1976	19,149	50.4	49.6	...	24.4	23.0	19.9	17.4	11.4	3.9
Spain	504,750	37,551,000	74.4	1970	34,032,801	48.9	51.1	54.7	27.8	22.0	19.9	16.1	10.8	3.4
Svalbard	62,050	—	—	1974	3,472	...	...	...	...	...	...	...	...	...
Sweden	449,964	8,297,000	18.4	1975	8,208,544	49.7	50.3	82.7	20.7	21.3	18.8	18.1	15.4	5.7
Switzerland	41,293	6,330,000	153.3	1970	6,269,783	49.3	50.7	52.0	23.4	23.7	20.2	16.3	12.5	3.9
United Kingdom	244,035	55,901,000	229.1	1971	55,515,602	48.5	51.5	76.9	24.1	21.0	17.6	18.3	14.3	4.7
Vatican City	.44	1,000	2,272.7	—	—	—	—	—	—	—	—	—	—	—
Yugoslavia	255,804	22,083,000	86.3	1971	20,522,972	49.1	50.9	38.6	27.2	24.6	22.7	13.5	9.8	2.2
Total EUROPE[10]	10,504,482	677,044,000	64.5											
NORTH AMERICA														
Anguilla	91	7,000	76.9	1974	6,519	...	...	...	...	...	...	...	...	...
Antigua	440	75,000	170.5	1970	64,794	47.2	52.8	33.7	44.0	24.2	12.0	11.7	—8.0—	
Bahamas, The	13,864	232,000	16.7	1970	168,812	49.6	50.4	71.4	43.6	24.3	16.8	9.8	4.4	1.1
Barbados	430	254,000	583.7	1980	248,983	47.6	52.4	...	29.9	32.6	14.1	11.9	10.4	3.4
Belize	22,965	141,000	6.4	1970	119,934	50.6	49.4	54.4	49.3	22.5	13.0	8.7	5.0	1.5
Bermuda	46	59,000	1,282.6	1970	52,330	50.2	49.8	6.9	30.0	25.8	20.5	14.4	7.7	2.0
British Virgin Islands	153	13,000	85	1970	10,484	53.0	47.0	21.9	39.0	29.1	14.7	10.0	5.1	1.9
Canada	9,976,139	23,690,000	2.4	1976	22,992,604	49.8	50.2	75.5	25.6	28.3	18.4	15.1	9.3	3.3
Cayman Islands	264	17,000	64.4	1979	16,677	...	...	...	...	...	...	...	...	...
Costa Rica	50,898	2,193,000	43.1	1973	1,871,780	50.1	49.9	40.6	43.3	27.0	14.2	8.4	4.4	2.7
Cuba	110,922	9,739,000	87.8	1970	8,569,121	51.3	48.7	60.3	27.0	25.0	16.9	12.1	6.8	2.2
Dominica	772	79,000	102.3	1970	69,549	47.4	52.6	46.2	49.1	21.2	11.2	10.0	6.3	2.2
Dominican Republic	48,442	5,275,000	108.9	1970	4,006,405	50.4	49.6	40.0	47.2	24.8	15.2	7.8	3.8	1.2
El Salvador	21,041	4,435,000	210.8	1971	3,554,648	49.6	50.4	39.4	46.2	25.1	15.2	8.2	4.3	1.0
Greenland	2,175,600	49,000	.02	1976	49,630	54.1	45.9	74.7	...	...	...	...	...	...
Grenada	344	98,000	284.9	1970	92,775	46.2	53.8	25.3	47.1	23.0	11.6	9.4	6.6	2.2
Guadeloupe	1,705	319,000	187.1	1974	324,500	...	...	41.9	41.2	22.8	14.3	10.4	5.3	1.7
Guatemala	108,889	7,046,000	64.7	1973	5,160,221	50.0	50.0	33.6	45.1	26.7	15.1	8.3	—4.8—	

Table II. World Populations and Areas[1] *(Continued)*

Country	AREA AND POPULATION: MIDYEAR 1979 Area in sq km	Total population	Persons per sq km	POPULATION AT MOST RECENT CENSUS Date of census	Total population	% Male	% Female	% Urban	Age distribution (%)[2] 0–14	15–29	30–44	45–59	60–74	75+
Haiti	27,750	4,920,000	177.3	1971	4,329,991	48.2	51.8	20.4	41.5	25.8	16.5	9.5	5.0	1.7
Honduras	112,088	3,564,000	31.8	1974	2,656,948	49.5	50.5	37.5	48.1	25.8	13.9	7.8	3.6	0.9
Jamaica	10,991	2,162,000	196.7	1970	1,797,401	48.7	51.3	41.4	37.5	25.1	15.2	12.4	7.5	2.3
Martinique	1,079	312,000	289.2	1974	324,832	48.2	51.8	55.6	39.5	25.0	14.2	11.8	7.3	2.2
Mexico	1,972,546	67,676,000	34.3	1980	67,405,700	49.2	50.8	...	...	...	...	...	...	...
Montserrat	102	11,000	107.8	1970	11,458	46.9	53.1	31.7	37.9	20.6	9.8	12.1	10.7	8.9
Netherlands Antilles	993	260,000	261.8	1972	223,196	48.8	51.2	...	38.0	26.7	16.7	10.3	6.4	1.8
Nicaragua	128,875	2,481,000	19.3	1971	1,877,972	48.3	51.7	48.0	48.1	25.6	14.1	7.4	3.6	1.1
Panama	77,082	1,785,000	23.2	1980	1,830,175	...	...	...	...	...	...	...	...	...
Puerto Rico	8,897	3,410,000	383.3	1980	3,187,566	...	...	...	...	...	...	...	...	...
St. Christopher-Nevis (-Anguilla)[11]	269	50,000	185.9	1970	44,884	46.8	53.2	31.7	37.9	20.6	9.8	12.1	10.7	8.9
St. Lucia	623	130,000	208.7	1970	99,806	47.2	52.8	36.9	49.6	21.3	11.6	9.8	5.5	2.2
St. Pierre & Miquelon	242	6,000	24.8	1974	5,840	49.4	50.6	...	33.8	24.7	18.0	12.9	—10.5—	
St. Vincent & the Grenadines	389	97,000	249.4	1970	86,314	47.3	52.7	...	51.2	21.7	11.0	8.8	—7.2—	
Trinidad and Tobago	5,128	1,156,000	225.4	1970	931,071	49.4	50.6	...	42.1	26.2	14.2	10.8	—6.8—	
Turks and Caicos Islands	500	7,000	14.0	1970	5,558	47.4	52.6	—	47.1	20.4	12.6	11.1	7.0	2.5
United States	9,363,123	220,584,000	23.5	1970	203,211,926	48.7	51.3	73.5	28.6	24.0	17.0	16.3	10.4	3.7
Virgin Islands (U.S.)	345	105,000	304.4	1980	95,214	60.5	39.5	18.3	40.6	36.2	24.9	12.9	4.8	1.6
Total NORTH AMERICA	24,244,027	362,437,000	14.9											
OCEANIA														
American Samoa	199	31,000	155.8	1980	32,395	...	...	...	...	...	...	...	...	...
Australia	7,682,300	14,418,000	1.9	1976	13,915,500	50.0	50.0	86.0	27.2	25.5	18.3	15.7	9.8	3.2
Canton and Enderbury Islands	70	—	—	1970	0	—	—	—	—	—	—	—	—	—
Christmas Island	135	3,000	22.2	1971	2,691	64.4	35.6	0	30.8	34.6	22.0	10.8	1.4	0.4
Cocos Islands	14	1,000	71.4	1971	618	49.0	51.0	0	27.3	38.6	21.8	8.9	3.3	0.2
Cook Islands	241	18,000	74.7	1976	18,128	51.3	48.7	...	49.8	22.1	12.9	9.2	4.9	1.1
Fiji	18,272	624,000	34.1	1976	588,068	50.5	49.5	37.2	41.1	29.8	16.2	8.8	3.3	0.8
French Polynesia	4,182	150,000	35.9	1977	137,382	52.5	47.5	39.7	42.0	27.2	17.0	8.9	4.0	0.8
Guam	549	116,000	211.3	1970	84,996	55.7	44.3	25.5	39.7	29.1	19.3	8.9	2.5	0.5
Johnston Island	3	1,000	333.3	1970	1,007	...	...	0	...	...	...	...	...	...
Kiribati	713	56,000	78.5	1978	56,452	...	...	...	...	...	...	...	...	...
Midway Islands	5	2,000	400.0	1970	2,220	...	...	0	...	...	...	...	...	...
Nauru	21	8,000	381.0	1977	7,254	52.1	47.9	0	44.2	33.1	11.4	8.5	—2.8—	
New Caledonia	19,079	137,000	7.2	1976	133,233	52.0	48.0	42.1	38.6	26.3	18.6	10.4	4.9	1.2
New Zealand	269,057	3,106,000	11.5	1976	3,129,383	49.9	50.1	83.0	29.1	26.0	17.3	14.5	10.0	3.1
Niue Island	259	4,000	15.4	1976	3,843	50.2	49.8	24.8	46.2	23.8	13.6	7.9	5.8	2.6
Norfolk Island	35	2,000	57.1	1971	1,683	49.0	51.0	0	25.2	20.7	19.7	18.9	12.5	2.9
Pacific Islands, Trust Territory of the	1,880	132,000	70.2	1973	114,973	51.7	48.3	43.9	46.2	25.8	12.7	9.1	—5.9—	
Papua New Guinea	462,840	3,078,000	6.6	1971	2,489,935	52.0	48.0	11.1	45.2	24.5	17.4	9.9	1.4	1.9
Pitcairn Island	4	65	16.2	1979	61	...	...	0	...	...	...	...	...	...
Solomon Islands	27,556	221,000	8.0	1976	196,823	52.2	47.8	...	47.8	24.1	14.5	8.4	3.6	1.3
Tokelau	10	2,000	200.0	1976	1,575	...	...	...	...	...	...	...	...	...
Tonga	750	95,000	126.7	1976	90,085	51.1	48.9	20.3	44.2	26.0	14.7	9.5	4.0	1.6
Tuvalu	26	7,000	269.2	1979	7,357	...	...	...	...	...	...	...	...	...
Vanuatu	11,870	106,000	8.9	1979	110,028	53.1	46.9	...	45.1	27.4	14.9	7.7	3.3	1.6
Wake Island	8	2,000	250.0	1970	1,647	...	...	...	...	...	...	...	...	...
Wallis and Futuna	255	9,000	35.3	1976	9,192	50.0	50.0	...	46.6	23.6	14.0	9.9	5.1	0.8
Western Samoa	2,849	155,000	54.4	1976	151,983	51.7	48.3	21.1	48.2	26.0	12.6	8.7	3.5	1.0
Total OCEANIA	8,503,182	22,484,000	2.6											
SOUTH AMERICA														
Argentina	2,758,829	26,730,000	9.7	1970	23,390,050	49.7	50.3	80.4	29.3	24.6	19.9	15.4	8.6	2.2
Bolivia	1,098,581	5,425,000	4.9	1976	4,613,486	49.1	50.9	41.7	41.5	27.0	15.4	9.8	4.6	1.7
Brazil	8,511,965	119,670,000	14.1	1970	93,139,037	49.7	50.3	55.9	42.5	26.7	16.3	9.4	—5.1—	
Chile	756,626	10,917,000	14.4	1970	8,884,768	48.8	51.2	75.1	39.0	25.5	16.6	10.4	5.6	2.9
Colombia	1,138,914	26,587,000	23.3	1973	22,551,811	48.6	51.4	63.6	44.1	27.3	14.9	8.5	4.1	1.0
Ecuador	281,334	8,047,000	28.6	1974	6,521,710	50.1	49.9	41.3	44.6	26.5	14.7	8.4	4.6	1.3
Falkland Islands	16,265	2,000	0.1	1972	1,957	55.2	44.8	44.7	26.7	22.4	—51.9—			
French Guiana	89,000	69,000	0.8	1974	55,125	52.1	47.9	76.5	37.9	27.7	16.7	10.7	5.5	1.5
Guyana	215,000	865,000	4.0	1970	699,848	49.7	50.3	33.3	47.1	25.1	13.4	9.0	4.4	1.0
Paraguay	406,752	2,974,000	7.3	1972	2,357,955	49.6	50.4	37.4	44.7	25.6	14.4	9.2	4.6	1.5
Peru	1,285,215	17,291,000	13.5	1972	13,538,208	50.0	50.0	59.6	43.9	25.8	15.6	8.7	—5.9—	
Suriname	181,455	381,000	2.1	1971	384,903	50.0	50.0	...	45.7	—54.3—				
Uruguay	176,215	2,905,000	16.5	1975	2,782,000	49.0	51.0	83.0	27.0	22.6	19.2	16.9	10.8	3.5
Venezuela	899,180	13,515,000	15.0	1971	10,721,522	50.1	49.9	73.1	45.0	26.9	14.9	8.5	3.7	1.0
Total SOUTH AMERICA	17,815,338	235,378,000	13.2											
U.S.S.R.[10]	22,402,000	264,108,000	11.8	1979	262,400,000	...	...	62.3	...	...	...	...	...	...
in Asia[10]	16,831,000	69,044,000	4.1											
in Europe[10]	5,571,000	195,064,000	35.0											
TOTAL WORLD[12]	150,161,224	4,326,745,000	31.8											

[1]Any presentation of population data must include data of varying reliability. This table provides published and unpublished data about the latest census (or comparable demographic survey) and the most recent or reliable midyear 1979 population estimates for the countries of the world. Census figures are only a body of estimates and samples of varying reliability whose quality depends on the completeness of the enumeration. Some countries tabulate only persons actually present, while others include those legally resident, but actually outside the country, on census day. Population estimates are subject to continual correction and revision; their reliability depends on: number of years elapsed since a census control was established, completeness of birth and death registration, international migration data, etc.
[2]Data for persons of unknown age excluded, so percentages may not add to 100.0.
[3]Excludes Mayotte, shown separately.
[4]Transkei received its independence from South Africa on Oct 26, 1976; Bophuthatswana on Dec. 6, 1977; Venda on Sept. 13, 1979. All are Bantu homeland states whose independence is not internationally recognized.
[5]Sudan census excludes three southern autonomous provinces.
[6]May reach a total of 2,000 persons of all nationalities during the summer.
[7]Excludes nomadic population.
[8]Includes 1970 census for Portuguese Timor, now part of Indonesia.
[9]Includes 18,130 sq km of Iraq-Saudi Arabia neutral zone.
[10]Asia and Europe continent totals include corresponding portions of U.S.S.R.
[11]Excludes Anguilla, shown separately.
[12]Area of Antarctica excluded in calculating world density.

continued from page 293

cantly with some other areas: 29 per 1,000 in Africa, 26 in Latin America, and 18 in Asia. China, with a rate of natural increase of 12 per 1,000 population, had announced a policy of encouraging one-child families and set a goal of zero population growth by the year 2000.

Death Statistics. The provisional count of deaths in the U.S. in 1979 was 1,906,000, and the rate of 8.7 deaths per 1,000 population was a record low. In 1970 the death rate had been 9.5 per 1,000.

The world death rate in 1979 was estimated at 11, but there were vast differences between countries, with rates ranging from 6 in Iceland to 25 in Ethiopia.

The 15 leading causes of death in the U.S. in 1979 were:

Cause of death	Estimated rate per 100,000 population
1. Diseases of the heart	331.3
2. Malignant neoplasms	183.5
3. Cerebrovascular diseases	76.9
4. Accidents	47.9
5. Chronic obstructive pulmonary diseases	22.7
6. Pneumonia and influenza	20.0
7. Diabetes mellitus	15.0
8. Chronic liver disease and cirrhosis	13.6
9. Atherosclerosis	13.0
10. Suicide	12.6
11. Homicide and legal intervention	10.5
12. Conditions in the perinatal period	10.4
13. Nephritis, nephrotic syndrome, and nephrosis	7.3
14. Congenital anomalies	6.1
15. Septicemia	3.8

Changes in some of the cause-of-death classifications occurred in 1979 as a result of the adoption of the ninth revision of the World Health Organization's International Classification of Diseases (ICD). Some terms were changed; for example, "Chronic obstructive pulmonary diseases" is an extension of the former category "Bronchitis, emphysema, and asthma." Because it is more inclusive, this became the fifth leading cause, whereas "Bronchitis, etc." had ranked 11th. The three major causes of death, heart disease, cancer, and stroke, accounted for 68% of all deaths.

Age-adjusted death rates for 1978 reveal a significant increase in influenza and pneumonia resulting from the influenza outbreak of that year. There were also increases over 1977 in deaths from motor vehicle accidents, nephritis and nephrosis, and septicemia. Between 1968 and 1978 there were important declines in several leading causes: diseases of the heart (−23%), cerebrovascular diseases (−37%), influenza and pneumonia (−43%), diabetes mellitus (−29%), cirrhosis of the liver (−10%), atherosclerosis (−38%), and bronchitis, emphysema, and asthma (−47%). In the same period, death rates rose for cancer (+4%), suicide (+10%), homicide (+16%), and septicemia (+117%).

Expectation of Life. Life expectancy at birth in 1979 was 73.8 years for the total U.S. population, a half year more than in 1978 and the highest average ever attained in the U.S. For white women it was 78.3 years; for white men, 70.6; for nonwhite women, 74.5; and for nonwhite men, 65.5. The nonwhite group had made considerable gains in recent years, and the difference between white and nonwhite had narrowed. In 1960 life expectancy for whites exceeded nonwhites by 7 years; in 1979 the difference was 4.5 years. White/nonwhite sex differentials also decreased significantly. In 1960 white men might live an average 6.3 more years than nonwhite men and white women 7.8 more years than nonwhite women; by 1979 the differentials had fallen to 5.1 years and 3.8 years, respectively.

Infant and Maternal Mortality. There were about 45,000 deaths of infants under one year of age in the U.S. in 1979, with a rate of 13 infant deaths per 1,000 live births. This rate was 4.4% lower than that for 1978 and reflected a substantial decline in deaths during the first month of life. The neonatal rate (deaths under 28 days per 1,000 live births in the same period) fell from 9.5 in 1978 to 8.8 in 1979. The infant mortality rate was a new U.S. low.

Table III. Life Expectancy at Birth, in Years, for Selected Countries[1]

Country	Period	Male	Female
Africa			
Burundi	1975–80	43.3	45.3
Egypt	1975–80	53.6	56.1
Ivory Coast	1975–80	44.4	47.6
Kenya	1979[2]	47.0	51.0
Nigeria	1975–80	45.9	49.2
Swaziland	1975–80	44.3	47.5
Asia			
Hong Kong	1979[2]	70.0	76.7
India	1976–80	53.8	52.6
Indonesia	1975–80	48.7	51.3
Israel[3]	1978[2]	69.1	72.0
Japan	1978[2]	73.3	78.6
Kuwait	1975–80	67.3	71.6
Pakistan	1975–80	51.9	51.7
Taiwan	1978[2]	69.2	71.6
Thailand	1975–80	57.6	63.0
Europe			
Albania	1975–80	68.0	70.7
Austria	1975–80	68.3	75.3
Belgium	1975–80	68.5	75.3
Bulgaria	1974–76	68.7	73.9
Czechoslovakia	1976[2]	67.0	74.0
Denmark	1977–78	71.5	77.5
Finland	1977[2]	67.9	76.7
France	1976[2]	69.2	77.2
Germany, East	1977[2]	69.0	74.9
Germany, West	1976–78	69.0	75.6
Greece	1975–80	70.8	75.0
Hungary	1975–80	66.8	72.7
Iceland	1975–80	73.1	79.3
Ireland	1975–80	69.8	74.8
Italy	1978[2]	67.0	73.1
Netherlands, The	1977[2]	72.0	78.4
Norway	1976–77	72.1	78.4
Poland	1975–76	67.3	75.0
Portugal	1975–80	66.2	72.3
Romania	1975–77	67.5	72.1
Spain	1975[2]	70.4	76.2
Sweden	1974–78	72.2	78.1
Switzerland	1975–80	71.7	77.9
United Kingdom	1974–76	69.6	75.8
Yugoslavia	1976[2]	67.3	72.1
North America			
Canada	1975–80	70.1	77.0
Costa Rica	1975–80	67.5	71.9
Cuba	1975–80	70.2	73.5
Martinique	1975–80	66.6	72.0
Mexico	1975–80	63.6	67.4
Panama	1975–80	67.5	71.9
Puerto Rico	1975–80	69.6	76.5
Trinidad and Tobago	1975–80	65.9	72.0
United States	1978[2]	69.5	77.2
Oceania			
Australia	1975–80	70.1	76.3
New Zealand	1975–80	69.8	75.9
South America			
Argentina	1975–80	66.1	72.9
Brazil	1975–80	60.7	66.7
Chile	1975–80	62.4	69.0
Peru	1975–80	55.1	58.0
Suriname	1975–80	64.8	69.8
Uruguay	1975–80	66.3	72.8
Venezuela	1975–80	64.6	68.3
U.S.S.R.	1971–72[2]	64.0	74.0

[1] Projection.
[2] Actual.
[3] Jewish population only.

Sources: United Nations, *World Population Trends and Prospects by Country, 1950–2000: Summary report of the 1978 assessment;* official country sources.

FRED R. CONRAD—THE NEW YORK TIMES

Census takers went from door to door in the South Bronx, New York, during the 1980 U.S. official census survey.

Detailed data for 1978 show that the mortality rate for white infants was 12 per 1,000 live births, while that for black infants was 21. The leading causes of infant death were congenital anomalies, immaturity, respiratory disease syndrome, asphyxia of the newborn, and hyaline membrane disease. In white-nonwhite comparisons, the greatest difference related to immature births; the death rate for nonwhite babies from this cause was over 2½ times that for white babies. Infant mortality is difficult to measure in less developed countries, but UN and other estimates showed rates of over 200 for Afghanistan, Angola, and The Gambia.

There were an estimated 270 maternal deaths associated with childbearing in the U.S. in 1979, with a maternal mortality rate of 7.8 deaths per 100,000 live births. This represented a 19% decline from 1978.

Marriage and Divorce Statistics. An estimated 2,317,000 marriages occurred in the U.S. in 1979, an increase of 3% over 1978 and the fourth consecutive annual increase. It was also the largest annual number of marriages ever recorded, exceeding the previous record high of 2,291,045 in 1946. The marriage rate was 10.5 per 1,000 population. Final statistics for 1978 placed the number of marriages at 2,282,272; of these, 37,462 were nonlicensed California marriages, included for the first time. However, since records of these marriages are sealed and no other information is available, they are excluded from detailed tabulations on marriage characteristics. The average age at first marriage continued to rise, to 21.4 years for brides and 23.2 years for grooms in 1978, compared with 20.5 and 22.4 years, respectively, in 1972. Remarriages accounted for about one-third of all marriages.

There were, provisionally, 1,170,000 divorces in 1979, 4% more than in the previous year and the highest number ever estimated for the U.S. The divorce rate was 5.3 divorces per 1,000 population, up 2% from 1978 and more than 33% above the rate in 1970. The trend continued into 1980, with divorces increasing 2% from January through June. The median duration of marriage ending in divorce was 6.6 years in 1977 and 1978, slightly above the 6.5 years in 1974–76. The average age at time of divorce was 32 for husbands and 29.7 for wives. The number of children under 18 involved in divorce in 1978 was 1,147,000, the largest number ever recorded in the U.S.

Censuses and Surveys. The UN Statistical Office reported that the 1980 World Population and Housing Census Program, covering 1975–84, would have involved 195 countries or areas by the end of the period. The most ambitious project was the China census of 1981.

In the U.S. concern over possible population undercounts in the April 1980 census resulted in many legal actions against the Census Bureau, particularly by cities where population declines had been reported. (ANDERS S. LUNDE)

[338.F.5.b; 525.A; 10/36.C.5.d]

Denmark

A constitutional monarchy of north central Europe lying between the North and Baltic seas, Denmark includes the Jutland Peninsula and 100 inhabited islands in the Kattegat and Skagerrak straits. Area (excluding Faeroe Islands and Greenland): 43,075 sq km (16,631 sq mi). Pop. (1980 est.): 5,126,500. Cap. and largest city: Copenhagen (pop., 1980 est., 658,300). Language: Danish. Religion: predominantly Lutheran. Queen, Margrethe II; prime minister in 1980, Anker Jørgensen.

The economy dominated Danish politics in 1980. The balance of payments situation continued to deteriorate, and the foreign debt was expected to reach 100 billion kroner during 1981. The budget was unbalanced, and the public sector was still growing disproportionately in comparison with industry and other activities in the private sector. Unemployment figures were rising, reaching 150,000 in October and forecast to reach 250,000 in 1981. Employment figures had never been so high, but growth was mostly in the public sector and not in producing industries. Although exports were rising, imports rose even more rapidly. The budget review, published on Oct. 9, 1980, showed a deficit of more than 15 billion kroner, nearly 3 billion kroner more than the forecast of three months earlier. The forecast for 1981 spoke of a deficit of more than 18 billion kroner.

The deficit in the balance of payments was expected to reach 25 billion kroner in 1984 unless "adjustments" proposed by the government and its supporting parties were carried through. In this case, the 1984 deficit might be brought down to some 10 billion kroner, but at a cost of some 240,000–350,000 unemployed. Under an "economic crisis" bill introduced in May 1980, the government undertook various measures, some in the face of vehement protest when vested interests were at-

DENMARK

Education. (1978–79) Primary, pupils 461,839, teachers 53,401; secondary, pupils 290,499, teachers 58,957; vocational, pupils 95,124, teachers (1974–75) 5,290; teacher training, students 9,065, teachers 502; higher, students 108,591, teaching staff 6,713.

Finance. Monetary unit: Danish krone, with (Sept. 22, 1980) a free rate of 5.59 kroner to U.S. $1 (13.43 kroner = £1 sterling). Gold, SDR's, and foreign exchange (June 1980) U.S. $2,569,000,000. Budget (1979 est.): revenue 93,270,000,000 kroner; expenditure 109,098,000,000 kroner. Gross national product (1979) 341,680,000,000 kroner. Money supply (April 1980) 70,780,000,000 kroner. Cost of living (1975 = 100; June 1980) 163.1.

Foreign Trade. (1979) Imports 97,155,000,000 kroner; exports 77,266,000,000 kroner. Import sources: EEC 50% (West Germany 20%, U.K. 12%, The Netherlands 6%, France 5%); Sweden 13%; U.S. 5%. Export destinations: EEC 49% (West Germany 18%, U.K. 15%, Italy 5%, France 5%); Sweden 13%; Norway 6%; U.S. 5%. Main exports: machinery 20%; meat 15%; chemicals 7%; dairy products 5%; fish 5%. Tourism: visitors (1976) 16,232,000; gross receipts (1978) U.S. $1,125,000,000.

Transport and Communications. Roads (1978) 67,523 km (including 464 km expressways). Motor vehicles in use (1978): passenger 1,477,300; commercial 269,000. Railways: (1977) 2,498 km; traffic (1977–78) 3,080,000,000 passenger-km, freight (1976–77) 1,921,000,000 net ton-km. Air traffic (including apportionment of international operations of Scandinavian Airlines System; 1979): 3,050,000,000 passenger-km; freight 132.4 million net ton-km. Shipping (1979): merchant vessels 100 gross tons and over 1,315; gross tonnage 5,524,416. Shipping traffic (1978): goods loaded 8,249,000 metric tons, unloaded 34,518,000 metric tons. Telephones (including Faeroe Islands and Greenland; Jan. 1978) 2,743,800. Radio licenses (Dec. 1978) 1,868,200. Television licenses (Dec. 1978) 1,771,600.

Agriculture. Production (in 000; metric tons; 1979): wheat 573; barley 6,680; oats 144; rye 245; potatoes 852; rutabagas (1977) 1,238; sugar, raw value 457; apples *c.* 125; rapeseed *c.* 91; butter 131; cheese 189; pork *c.* 900; beef and veal 245; fish catch (1978) 1,745. Livestock (in 000; July 1979): cattle 3,034; pigs 9,357; sheep (1978) *c.* 56; chickens (1978) *c.* 14,773.

Industry. Production (in 000; metric tons; 1979): crude steel 803; cement 2,410; fertilizers (nutrient content; 1978–79) nitrogenous 121, phosphate 106; plastics and resins (1976) 145; crude oil 450; petroleum products (1977) 7,774; manufactured gas (cu m) 316,000; electricity (kw-hr) 20,482,000. Merchant vessels launched (100 gross tons and over; 1979) 199,000 gross tons.

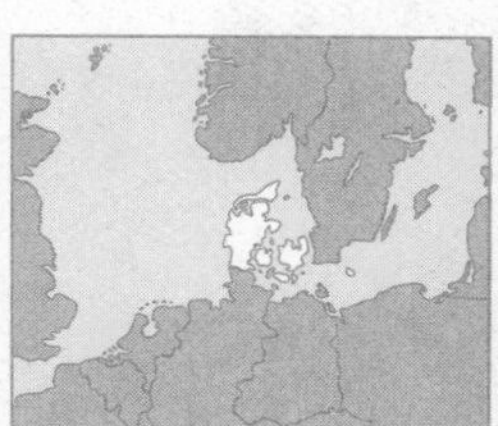

Denmark

WIDE WORLD

Leila Khaled (right), a representative of the PLO who had twice been involved in airplane hijackings, led a walkout as Jihan as-Sadat, wife of Egyptian Pres. Anwar as-Sadat, went on the rostrum to speak in Copenhagen at the World Conference of the UN Decade for Women in July.

tacked. The value-added tax was raised to 22%, taxes on gasoline, fuel oil, and electricity were increased, and adjustments in direct taxation were made, giving Denmark the highest direct taxation in the world.

Oil and other kinds of imported energy posed a big problem for Denmark, which obtained only about 5% of its supplies from indigenous sources such as North Sea oil. A natural-gas grid was under construction, and it was expected that Danish oil production would grow in future years, thus helping to arrest the deterioration in Denmark's terms of trade. The government sought to alter the terms under which the Danish consortium was working in the country's North Sea sector. Such modification was not easily undertaken, however, because the concession, granted in 1962, was to run for 50 years.

Prime Minister Anker Jørgensen, heading a minority Social Democratic government formed after the election of October 1979, succeeded in making "arrangements" with the Radical Liberals, the Christian People's Party, and the Centre Democrats. Together, these parties in 1980 could muster a narrow majority of 90 seats out of the Folketing's (parliament's) 179. The parties in this coalition were not closely united, and Jørgensen often found himself in precarious situations.

The opposition, of both right and left, was critical of the prime minister's customary review of the state of the country at the opening of the October parliamentary session. The government and its supporting parties were blamed for Denmark's parlous economic prospects. From the left claims were voiced on behalf of "economic democracy"—compulsory profit sharing and similar measures—while support for the exporting industries was castigated as "support for capitalism" and "taking from the poor and giving to the rich." It was agreed that the foreign debt must be brought down but that low-income groups should not be affected.

Defense was another difficult matter. Defense expenditure had been accepted by a substantial majority, but the Radical Liberals, previously participants in the existing defense arrangement, opted out of it. The government spoke of a "zero-solution," which meant that Denmark should avoid its NATO obligations to increase defense expenditure by 3%. The Conservatives and Liberal Democrats protested, and it seemed as though the broad majority upholding Danish defense policy within NATO might be jeopardized.

(STENER AARSDAL)

See also Dependent States.

Dependent States

In 1980 two dependent states, Zimbabwe (Rhodesia) in Africa and the New Hebrides (renamed Vanuatu) in the Pacific, were granted independence. (*See* ZIMBABWE; VANUATU.)

Europe and the Atlantic. In Denmark's Faeroe Islands the Landsting (parliament) was dissolved on Sept. 23, 1980, having failed to complete its four-year term for the first time since home rule was instituted in 1948. Interparty disagreements over the proposed operation of a winter service by a state-owned passenger and freight ferry had caused the dissolution. The ensuing elections of November 8 showed a swing to the right; the four conservative parties together won 19 seats out of 32 in the Landsting to end 18 years of Social Democratic government. Paulli Ellefsen, leader of the Unionist Party which supported closer ties with Denmark, formed a coalition government. In Greenland a home rule (*hjemmestyre*) movement was active, although Denmark continued to devolve an increasing number of functions to the island. Within a year or so, Greenlanders were to take over the Royal Greenland Trading Company, the organization responsible for all supplies to the island.

In February the Gibraltar Labour Party Association for the Advancement of Civil Rights, led by Chief Minister Sir Joshua Hassan (8 seats), again won a majority in Gibraltar's 15-seat House of Assembly. This meant continuance of a cautious ap-

Puerto Ricans lined the funeral route in San Juan to bid farewell on May 2 to their patriarch, Luis Muñoz Marín, who had served as governor from 1948 to 1964.

UPI

Dentistry:
see Health and Disease

SYNDICATION INTERNATIONAL/PHOTO TRENDS

Illegal parking can bring the 9,000 motor vehicles on tiny Gibraltar to a halt. In an attempt to cut down on violations, traffic officers send cars to a permanent parking place.

proach to the question of relations with Spain. Talks between British and Spanish foreign ministers during the year brought no solution to the question of Gibraltar's future.

The Falkland Islands were visited in late November by Nicholas Ridley, minister of state at the British Foreign and Commonwealth Office, who held discussions with the islanders on a resolution of the dispute with Argentina about their status. Action on the much-needed extension of the airstrip was refused, and action on the South Atlantic Fisheries Report was slow. Inclusion of the Falklands in the May agreement at Canberra, Australia, on Antarctic marine resources and a proposed 200-mi exclusive economic zone for the islands offered an indirect guarantee of livelihood to the islanders.

An agreement between Canada and the French overseas département of Saint-Pierre and Miquelon for delimitation of an exclusive economic zone was in the course of negotiation during the year. In July a proposed law prolonged by 18 months the term of office of the general councillors of the archipelago in order to bring the dates of renewal of the General Council into line with those in force in the National Assembly in Paris. On an official visit to Saint-Pierre, Paul Dijoud, French secretary of state for overseas départements and territories, emphasized that the status of the archipelago as a département of France was irreversible but capable of modification.

In the Azores, Portugal's last Atlantic possession, the Phoenix Foundation was showing interest in a possible future for the islands as an independent tax haven. The U.S.-based libertarian group had been involved in the insurrection led by Jimmy Stevens (*see* BIOGRAPHIES) in the New Hebrides.

The future of the Antarctic remained in doubt, confused by overlapping and unrecognized claims of sovereignty and by the approaching possibility of exploitation of the continent. (*See* ANTARCTICA.)

Caribbean. By far the most important development affecting any Caribbean dependency in 1980 related to the British dependency of Belize. Following an overwhelming surprise victory for the ruling People's United Party in late 1979, a major international initiative was begun to attempt to solve the dependency's outstanding border dispute with neighbouring Guatemala and thus clear the way for independence. Meetings between British, Guatemalan, and Belizean ministers and officials continued throughout 1980 in London, Bermuda, Belize, Guatemala City, and New York City. During the course of these discussions, it was made clear that under no circumstances would Belize cede any land to Guatemala. Britain, however, indicated that it was prepared to make economic concessions in return for Guatemala's giving up its claim to a part of Belize. By the latter part of the year, the discussions had entered a critical phase, given added impetus by the deteriorating political situation in Guatemala. Early in December the British government informed Belize that a constitutional conference looking toward independence would begin no later than February 1981.

The other remaining British dependencies and the two Caribbean associated states of Antigua and St. Kitts-Nevis continued to be concerned mainly

continued on page 305

ANTARCTIC

Claims on the continent of Antarctica and all islands south of 60° S remain in status quo according to the Antarctic Treaty, to which 19 nations are signatory. Formal claims within the treaty area include the following: Australian Antarctic Territory, the mainland portion of French Southern and Antarctic Lands (Terre Adélie), Ross Dependency claimed by New Zealand, Queen Maud Land and Peter I Island claimed by Norway, and British Antarctic Territory, some parts of which are claimed by Argentina and Chile. No claims have been recognized as final under international law.

AUSTRALIA

CHRISTMAS ISLAND

Christmas Island, an external territory, is situated in the Indian Ocean 1,410 km NW of Australia. Area: 135 sq km (52 sq mi). Pop. (1979 est.): 3,300. Main settlement: Flying Fish Cove and the Settlement (pop., 1978 est., 1,400).

COCOS (KEELING) ISLANDS

Cocos (Keeling) Islands is an external territory located in the Indian Ocean 3,685 km W of Darwin, Australia. Area: 14 sq km (5.5 sq mi). Pop. (1979 est.): 392.

NORFOLK ISLAND

Norfolk Island, an external territory, is located in the Pacific Ocean 1,720 km NE of Sydney, Australia. Area: 35 sq km (13 sq mi). Pop. (1979 est.): 2,200. Cap. (de facto): Kingston.

DENMARK

FAEROE ISLANDS

The Faeroes, an integral part of the Danish realm, are a self-governing group of islands in the North Atlantic about 580 km W of Norway. Area: 1,399 sq km (540 sq mi). Pop. (1979 est.): 42,800. Cap.: Thorshavn (pop., 1977 census, 11,600).

Education. (1979–80) Primary, pupils 6,025; secondary, pupils 2,597; primary and secondary, teachers (1977–78) 466; vocational, pupils (1978–79) 1,304, teachers (1966–67) 88; teacher training, students 113, teachers (1966–67) 12; higher, students 49.

Finance and Trade. Monetary unit: Faeroese krone, at par with the Danish krone, with (Sept. 22, 1980) a free rate of 5.59 kroner to U.S. $1 (13.43 kroner = £1 sterling). Budget (1978–79 est.): revenue 439,929,000 kroner; expenditure 439,457,000 kroner. Foreign trade (1978): imports 1,013,000,000 kroner; exports 775 million kroner. Import sources: Denmark 69%; Norway 13%; Sweden 5%. Export destinations: Denmark 23%; U.S. 20%; U.K. 13%; Spain 9%; Italy 9%; France 8%; W. Germany 7%. Main exports: fish 82%; fish meal 8%.

Transport. Shipping (1979): merchant vessels 100 gross tons and over 183; gross tonnage 63,293.

Agriculture and Industry. Fish catch (1978) 318,000 metric tons. Livestock (in 000; 1978): sheep *c.* 71; cattle *c.* 2. Electricity production (1977–78) 122 million kw-hr (39% hydroelectric).

GREENLAND (Kalâtdlit-Nunât)

An integral part of the Danish realm, Greenland, the largest island in the world, lies mostly within the Arctic Circle. Area: 2,175,600 sq km (840,000 sq mi), 84% of which is covered by ice cap. Pop. (1979 est.): 49,300. Cap.: Godthaab (Nûk; pop., 1979 est., 8,800).

Education. (1979–80) Primary, pupils 8,695; secondary, pupils 3,566; primary and secondary, teachers 744; vocational, pupils 866, teachers 53; teacher training, students 100, teachers 27; higher, students 450.

Finance and Trade. Monetary unit: Danish krone. Budget (1977 est.): revenue 128 million kroner; expenditure 100 million kroner. Foreign trade (1978): imports 987 million kroner; exports 559 million kroner. Import sources: Denmark 79%; U.K. 5%. Export destinations: Denmark 46%; U.S. 15%; Finland 14%; France 13%; West Germany 7%. Main exports: fish 53%; zinc ore 23%; lead ore 14%.

Agriculture. Fish catch (1978) 68,000 metric tons. Livestock (in 000; 1978): sheep 17; reindeer 2.

Industry. Production (in 000; metric tons; 1977): lead ore (metal content) 34; zinc ore (metal content) 83; electricity (kw-hr) *c.* 144,000.

FRANCE

FRENCH GUIANA

French Guiana is an overseas département situated between Brazil and Suriname on the northeast coast of South America. Area: 90,000 sq km (34,750 sq mi). Pop. (1980 est.): 64,400. Cap.: Cayenne (pop., 1978 est., 32,900).

Education. (1977–78) Primary, pupils 10,838, teachers 600; secondary and vocational, pupils 5,834, teachers (1975–76) 338; teacher training, students 39.

Finance and Trade. Monetary unit: French (metropolitan) franc, with (Sept. 22, 1980) a free rate of Fr 4.19 to U.S. $1 (Fr 10.08 = £1 sterling). Budget (total; 1977 est.) balanced at Fr 196 million. Foreign trade (1979): imports Fr 1,067,070,000; exports Fr 70,530,000. Import sources (1978): France 70%; Trinidad and Tobago 10%. Export destinations (1978): France 38%; U.S. 19%; Venezuela 11%; Martinique 10%. Main exports (1978): timber 25%; shrimp 22%; storage tanks 11%; coffee 10%; electrical equipment 6%.

FRENCH POLYNESIA

An overseas territory, French Polynesia consists of islands scattered over a large area of the south central Pacific Ocean. Area of inhabited islands: 4,182 sq km (1,615 sq mi). Pop. (1980 est.): 155,000. Cap.: Papeete, Tahiti (pop., 1977, 65,600).

Education. (1979–80) Primary, pupils 38,964, teachers 1,687; secondary, pupils 9,613, teachers 610; vocational, pupils 2,757, teachers 214; teacher training, students 225, teachers 20.

Finance and Trade. Monetary unit: CFP franc, with (Sept. 22, 1980) a parity of CFP Fr 18.18 to the French franc and a free rate of CFP Fr 73 to U.S. $1 (CFP Fr 175 = £1 sterling). Budget (1978) balanced at CFP Fr 13.5 billion. Foreign trade (1978): imports CFP Fr 33,070,000,000 (52% from France, 18% from U.S., 5% from West Germany); exports CFP Fr 2,973,000,000 (83% to France, 7% to Italy). Main exports: nuclear material *c.* 65%; coconut oil 11%. Tourism (1977): visitors 92,000; gross receipts U.S. $51 million.

GUADELOUPE

The overseas département of Guadeloupe, together with its dependencies, is in the eastern Caribbean between Antigua to the north and Dominica to the south. Area: 1,705 sq km (658 sq mi). Pop. (1979 est.): 319,000. Cap.: Basse-Terre (pop., 1977 est., 15,800).

Education. (1977–78) Primary, pupils 56,567, teachers (1975–76) 2,018; secondary, vocational, and teacher training, pupils 47,138; teachers (1975–76) 2,147; higher (1976–77), students 1,400.

Finance and Trade. Monetary unit: French (metropolitan) franc. Budget (total; 1977 est.) balanced at Fr 1,199,000,000. Cost of living (Basse-Terre; 1975 = 100; April 1980) 157. Foreign trade (1979): imports Fr 2,539,730,000 (73% from France in 1978); exports Fr 482,090,000 (88% to France, 9% to Martinique in 1978). Main exports (1978): bananas 56%; sugar 26%; wheat meal and flour 5%.

MARTINIQUE

The Caribbean island of Martinique, an overseas département, lies 39 km N of St. Lucia and about 50 km SE of Dominica. Area: 1,079 sq km (417 sq mi). Pop. (1979 est.): 311,900. Cap.: Fort-de-France (pop., 1974, 98,800).

Education. (1979–80) Primary, pupils 70,406, teachers 3,345; secondary and vocational, pupils 49,929, teachers 2,993; teacher training (1976–77), students 1,364, teachers 14; higher, students 1,475, teaching staff 77.

Finance and Trade. Monetary unit: French (metropolitan) franc. Budget (1977 est.): revenue Fr 594 million; expenditure Fr 531 million. Cost of living (Fort-de-France; 1975 = 100; Dec. 1979) 156. Foreign trade (1979): imports Fr 2,879,000,000; exports Fr 567 million. Import sources (1978): France 59%; Venezuela 8%. Export destinations (1978): France 59%; Guadeloupe 22%; Italy 14%. Main exports (1978): bananas 58%; petroleum products 18%; rum 8%.

MAYOTTE

An African island dependency of France that was formerly a part of the Comoros, Mayotte lies in the Indian Ocean off the east coast of Africa. Area: 378 sq km (146 sq mi). Pop. (1978): 47,200. Cap.: Dzaoudzi (pop., 1978, 4,100).

Education. (1978–79) Primary, pupils 7,253, teachers 187; secondary, pupils 667, teachers 29; vocational, pupils 62.

Finance and Trade. Monetary unit: French (metropolitan) franc. Budget (1978 est.) balanced at Fr 35 million. Foreign trade: imports (1976) Fr 12 million; exports (1978) Fr 6.5 million. Import sources: Réunion 27%; France 23%, Madagascar 14%; Pakistan 14%; Kenya 8%. Export destinations (1976): France 92%; Madagascar 6%. Main exports (1976): ylang-ylang 74%; vanilla 11%; coffee 9%; copra 6%.

NEW CALEDONIA

The overseas territory of New Caledonia, together with its dependencies, is in the South Pacific 1,210 km E of Australia. Area: 19,079 sq km (7,366 sq mi). Pop. (1980 est.): 139,600. Cap.: Nouméa (pop., 1976, 56,100).

Education. (1979–80) Primary, pupils 33,939, teachers 1,450; secondary, pupils 8,660, teachers 557; vocational, pupils 3,038, teachers 275; higher, students 396, teaching staff 53.

Finance and Trade. Monetary unit: CFP franc. Budget (1979 est.) balanced at CFP Fr 17,163,000,000. Foreign trade (1979): imports CFP Fr 27,791,000,000; exports CFP Fr 29,131,000,000. Import sources (1977): France 39%; Bahrain 14%; Australia 10%; U.S. 5%. Export destinations (1977): France 50%; Japan 29%; U.S. 16%. Main exports (1977): ferromanganese 43%; nickel ores 26%; nickel 26%.

RÉUNION

The overseas département of Réunion is located in the Indian Ocean about 720 km E of Madagascar and 180 km SW of Mauritius. Area: 2,512 sq km (970 sq mi). Pop. (1979 est.): 493,300. Cap.: Saint-Denis (pop., 1978 est., 111,900).

Education. (1979–80) Primary, pupils 128,007, teachers 4,392; secondary, pupils 62,406, teachers 3,111; teacher training (1973–74), students 319, teachers 22; higher, students 1,786, teaching staff 63.

Finance and Trade. Monetary unit: French (metropolitan) franc. Budget (1978 est.) balanced at Fr 3,573,000,000. Cost of living (Saint-Denis; 1975 = 100; March 1980) 152.9. Foreign trade (1979): imports Fr 3,305,010,000; exports Fr 549,130,000. Import sources (1978): France 66%; South Africa 5%. Export destinations (1978): France 78%; U.K. 15%. Main exports (1978): sugar 81%; essential oils 6%.

SAINT PIERRE AND MIQUELON

The self-governing overseas département of Saint Pierre and Miquelon is located about 20 km off the south coast of Newfoundland. Area: 242 sq km (93 sq mi). Pop. (1980 est.): 6,300. Cap.: Saint Pierre, Saint Pierre.

Education. (1980–81) Primary, pupils 738, teachers 59; secondary, pupils 527; vocational, pupils 221; secondary and vocational, teachers 61.

Finance and Trade. Monetary unit: French (metropolitan) franc. Budget (1977 est.) balanced at Fr 32 million. Foreign trade (1978): imports Fr 134 million; exports Fr 17.8 million. Import sources (1976): Canada 64%; France 27%. Export destinations (1976): ship's bunkers and stores 53%; Canada 30%; U.S. 13%. Main exports (1974): petroleum products 53%; cattle 30%; fish 12%.

WALLIS AND FUTUNA

Wallis and Futuna, an overseas territory, lies in the South Pacific west of Western Samoa. Area: 255 sq km (98 sq mi). Pop. (1979 est.): 9,000. Cap.: Mata Utu, Uvea (pop., 1976, 558).

NETHERLANDS, THE

NETHERLANDS ANTILLES

The Netherlands Antilles, a self-governing integral part of the Netherlands realm, consists of an island group near the Venezuelan coast and another group to the north near St. Kitts-Nevis-Anguilla. Area: 993 sq km (383 sq mi). Pop. (1979 est.): 246,500. Cap.: Willemstad, Curaçao (pop., 1970 est., 50,000).

Education. (1973–74) Primary, pupils 38,170, teachers 1,492; secondary and vocational, pupils 12,104, teachers 631; higher (university only), students *c.* 150, teaching staff *c.* 15.

Finance. Monetary unit: Netherlands Antilles guilder or florin, with (Sept. 22, 1980) a par value of 1.80 Netherlands Antilles guilders to U.S. $1 (free rate of 4.30 Netherlands Antilles guilders = £1 sterling). Budget (1977): revenue 501 million Netherlands Antilles guilders; expenditure 552 million Netherlands Antilles guilders. Cost of living (Aruba, Bonaire, and Curaçao; 1975 = 100; Nov. 1979) 139.9.

Foreign Trade. (1977) Imports 5,630,000,000 Netherlands Antilles guilders; exports 4,762,000,000 Netherlands Antilles guilders. Import sources: Venezuela 61%; Nigeria 11%; U.S. 8%. Export destinations: U.S. 49%; Nigeria 11%; Ecuador 5%. Main exports: petroleum products 89%; crude oil 7%. Tourism (1977): visitors 396,000; gross receipts U.S. $207 million.

Transport and Communications. Roads (1972) 1,150 km. Motor vehicles in use (1975): passenger 50,136; commercial 5,650. Shipping traffic (1976): goods loaded *c.* 31.1 million metric tons, unloaded *c.* 38 million metric tons. Telephones (Jan. 1978) 49,600. Radio receivers (Dec. 1977) 175,000. Television receivers (Dec. 1977) *c.* 38,000.

Industry. Production (in 000; metric tons; 1977): petroleum products *c.* 26,140; phosphate rock 79; salt 400; electricity (kw-hr) *c.* 1,650,000.

NEW ZEALAND

COOK ISLANDS

The self-governing territory of the Cook Islands consists of several islands in the southern Pacific Ocean scattered over an area of about 2.2 million sq km. Area: 241 sq km (93 sq mi). Pop. (1978 est.): 19,600. Seat of government: Rarotonga Island (pop., 1976, 9,800).

Education. (1977) Primary, pupils 4,962; secondary, pupils 2,210; primary and secondary, teachers (1975) 360; teacher training, students 48.

Finance and Trade. Monetary unit: Cook Islands dollar, at par with the New Zealand dollar, with (Sept. 22, 1980) a free rate of CI$1.02 to U.S. $1 (CI$2.45 = £1 sterling). Budget (1978–79 est.): revenue CI$13,849,000; expenditure CI$15,034,000. Foreign trade (1977): imports CI$17,497,000 (67% from New Zealand, 10% from Japan, 5% from U.S.); exports CI$2,386,000 (99% to New Zealand). Main exports: fruit juice 36%; clothing 24%; fruit and fruit preserves 19%; oilseeds 10%.

NIUE

The self-governing territory of Niue is situated in the Pacific Ocean about 2,400 km NE of New Zealand. Area: 259 sq km (100 sq mi). Pop. (1980 est.): 3,300. Capital: Alofi (pop., 1979, 960).

Education. (1976) Primary, pupils 1,038, teachers (1975) 65; secondary, pupils 286, teachers 22.

Finance and Trade. Monetary unit: New Zealand dollar. Budget (1977–78): revenue NZ$3,140,000 (excluding New Zealand subsidy of NZ$2.8 million); expenditure NZ$6,310,000. Foreign trade (1977): imports NZ$2,109,000 (83% from New Zealand); exports NZ$255,000 (92% to New Zealand). Main exports: fruit and vegetables 49%; copra 31%; sugar and honey 5%.

TOKELAU

The territory of Tokelau lies in the South Pacific about 1,130 km N of Niue and 3,380 km NE of New Zealand. Area: 10 sq km (4 sq mi). Pop. (1980 est.): 1,600.

NORWAY

JAN MAYEN

The island of Jan Mayen, a Norwegian dependency, lies within the Arctic Circle between Greenland and northern Norway. Area: 373 sq km (144 sq mi). Pop. (1973 est.): 37.

SVALBARD

A group of islands and a Norwegian dependency, Svalbard is located within the Arctic Circle to the north of Norway. Area: 62,050 sq km (23,957 sq mi). Pop. (1978 est.): 3,500.

PORTUGAL

MACAU

The overseas territory of Macau is situated on the mainland coast of China 60 km W of Hong Kong. Area: 16 sq km (6 sq mi). Pop. (1979 est.): 277,300.

Education. (1978–79) Primary, pupils 23,847, teachers 754; secondary, pupils 11,863, teachers 601; vocational, pupils 3,667, teachers 156; teacher training, students 36, teachers 6.

Finance and Trade. Monetary unit: patacá, with (Sept. 22, 1980) a free rate of 5.28 patacás to U.S. $1 (12.70 patacás = £1 sterling). Budget (1978 est.) balanced at 195 million patacás. Foreign trade (1979): imports 1,817,900,000 patacás; exports 2,014,300,000 patacás. Import sources: Hong Kong 51%; China 29%. Export destinations: U.S. 23%; West Germany 17%; France 16%; Hong Kong 13%; U.K. 8%; Italy 5%. Main exports: clothing and textiles 87%.

Transport. Shipping traffic (1978): goods loaded 647,000 metric tons, unloaded 456,000 metric tons.

SOUTH WEST AFRICA/NAMIBIA

South West Africa has been a UN territory since 1966, when the General Assembly terminated South Africa's mandate over the country, renamed Namibia by the UN. South Africa considers the UN resolution illegal. Area: 824,268 sq km (318,251 sq mi). Pop. (1979 est.): 961,500. National cap.: Windhoek (pop., 1975 est., 77,400). Summer cap.: Swakopmund (pop., 1975 est., 13,700).

Education. (1978) Primary, secondary, and vocational, pupils 173,316, teachers 5,388.

Finance and Trade. Monetary unit: South African rand, with (Sept. 22, 1980) a free rate of R 0.75 to U.S. $1 (R 1.81 = £1 sterling). Budget (total; 1978–79 est.): revenue R 378 million; expenditure R 374 million. Foreign trade (included in the South African customs union; 1978 est.): imports *c.* R 500 million (*c.* 80% from South Africa in 1972); exports *c.* R 850 million (*c.* 50% to South Africa in 1972). Main exports: diamonds *c.* 50%; uranium *c.* 25%; cattle and meat *c.* 10%; karakul pelts *c.* 5%; fish *c.* 5%.

Agriculture. Production (in 000; metric tons; 1978): corn *c.* 15; millet *c.* 20; beef and veal *c.* 101; sheep and goat meat *c.* 25; fish catch *c.* 418. Livestock (in 000; 1978): cattle *c.* 2,950; sheep *c.* 5,130; goats *c.* 2,100; horses *c.* 44; asses *c.* 65.

Industry. Production (in 000; metric tons; 1977): copper ore (metal content) 50; lead ore (metal content) 41; zinc ore (metal content) 38; tin concentrates (metal content) 0.8; vanadium ore (metal content) 0.8; uranium (1977) 2.8; diamonds (metric carats) 2,001; salt *c.* 220; electricity (kw-hr; 1963) 188,000.

UNITED KINGDOM

ANGUILLA

Formally a part of the associated state of St. Kitts-Nevis-Anguilla, the island of Anguilla comprises a separate administrative entity, having received a constitution separating its government from that of St. Kitts-Nevis-Anguilla in 1976. Area: 91 sq km (35 sq mi). Pop. (1977 est.): 6,500.

Education. (1979) Primary, pupils 1,610, teachers 68; secondary, pupils 450, teachers 20.

Finance and Trade. Monetary unit: East Caribbean dollar, with (Sept. 22, 1980) an official rate of ECar$2.70 to U.S. $1 (free rate of ECar$6.48 = £1 sterling). Budget (1978 est.) balanced at ECar$4.3 million (including U.K. grant of ECar$1.3 million). Foreign trade (included with St. Kitts–Nevis; 1976 est.) exports *c.* ECar$1 million. Main export destinations: Trinidad and Tobago *c.* 40%; Puerto Rico *c.* 30%; Guadeloupe *c.* 14%; U.S. Virgin Islands *c.* 10%. Main exports: salt *c.* 40%; lobster *c.* 36%; livestock *c.* 14%.

ANTIGUA

The associated state of Antigua, with its dependencies Barbuda and Redonda, lies in the eastern Caribbean approximately 60 km N of Guadeloupe. Area: 440 sq km (170 sq mi). Pop. (1979 est.): 75,000. Cap.: Saint John's (pop., 1974 est., 23,500).

Education. (1976–77) Primary, pupils 13,285, teachers 477; secondary, pupils 6,458, teachers 271; vocational, pupils 153, teachers 21; teacher training, students 89, teachers 9.

Finance and Trade. Monetary unit: East Caribbean dollar. Budget (1979–80 est.) balanced at ECar$75 million. Foreign trade (1977 est.): imports ECar$110 million; exports ECar$35 million. Import sources (1975): U.K. 19%; U.S. 19%; Trinidad and Tobago 11%; The Bahamas 11%; Venezuela 9%; Iran 7%; Canada 5%. Export destinations (1975): bunkers 57%; U.S. 10%; Guyana 5%. Main export (1975): petroleum products 87%.

BELIZE

Belize, a self-governing colony, is situated on the Caribbean coast of Central America, bounded on the north and northwest by Mexico and by Guatemala on the remainder of the west and south. Area: 22,965 sq km (8,867 sq mi). Pop. (1980 est.): 140,600. Cap.: Belmopan (pop., 1980 est., 4,500).

Education. (1978–79) Primary, pupils 34,149, teachers (1977–78) 1,226; secondary, pupils 5,913, teachers (1977–78) 358; vocational, pupils 477; higher, students 580, teaching staff (1977–78) 20.

Finance and Trade. Monetary unit: Belize dollar, with (Sept. 22, 1980) an official rate of Bel$2 = U.S. $1 (free rate of Bel$4.81 = £1 sterling). Budget (1978 est.): revenue Bel$53.3 million; expenditure Bel$42.8 million. Foreign trade (1977): imports Bel$180.2 million; exports Bel$124.2 million. Import sources: U.S. 42%; U.K. 15%. Export destinations: U.S. 47%; U.K. 44%. Main exports: sugar 38%; clothing 15%; fish 5%.

BERMUDA

The colony of Bermuda lies in the western Atlantic about 920 km E of Cape Hatteras, North Carolina. Area: 46 sq km (18 sq mi). Pop. (1980 est.): 57,700. Cap.: Hamilton, Great Bermuda (pop., 1973 est., 3,000).

Education. (1977–78) Primary, pupils 6,466, teachers 319; secondary, pupils 5,269, teachers 404; vocational (1974–75), pupils 510, teachers 49.

Finance and Trade. Monetary unit: Bermuda dollar, at par with the U.S. dollar (free rate, at Sept. 22, 1980, of Ber$2.40 = £1 sterling). Budget (1979–80 est.): revenue Ber$95.2 million; expenditure Ber$95.1 million. Foreign trade (1979): imports Ber$234 million; exports Ber$31.3 million. Import sources: U.S. 49%; Netherlands Antilles 16%; U.K. 12%; Canada 6%. Export destinations: bunkers 51%; U.S. 14%; Spain 9%; Netherlands Antilles 5%. Main exports: petroleum products 55%; drugs and medicines 24%; aircraft supplies 5%. Tourism (1978): visitors 551,000; gross receipts U.S. $195 million.

Transport. Roads (1979) *c.* 240 km. Motor vehicles in use (1976): passenger 12,700; commercial (including buses) 2,500. Shipping (1979): merchant vessels 100 gross tons and over 112; gross tonnage 1,726,672.

BRITISH INDIAN OCEAN TERRITORY

Located in the western Indian Ocean, this colony consists of the islands of the Chagos Archipelago. Area: 60 sq km (23 sq mi). No permanent civilian population remains. Administrative headquarters: Victoria, Seychelles.

BRITISH VIRGIN ISLANDS

The colony of the British Virgin Islands is located in the Caribbean to the east of the U.S. Virgin Islands. Area: 153 sq km (59 sq mi). Pop. (1979 est.): 13,000. Cap.: Road Town, Tortola (pop., 1973 est., 3,500).

Education. (1975–76) Primary, pupils 2,251, teachers 123; secondary and vocational, pupils 821, teachers 48.

Finance and Trade. Monetary unit: U.S. dollar (free rate, at Sept. 20, 1980, of U.S. $2.40 = £1 sterling). Budget (1979 est.): revenue U.S. $9,359,000; expenditure U.S. $8,374,000. Foreign trade (1978): imports U.S. $14.3 million; exports U.S. $100,000. Import sources (1976): U.S. 28%; Puerto Rico 24%; U.K. 15%; U.S. Virgin Islands 12%; Trinidad and Tobago 11%. Export destinations (1974):

U.S. Virgin Islands 53%; Anguilla 22%; St. Martin (Guadeloupe) 9%; U.K. 5%. Main exports (mainly reexports; 1974): motor vehicles 16%; timber 14%; beverages 10%; fish 7%; iron and steel 6%; machinery 6%.

BRUNEI

Brunei, a protected sultanate, is located on the north coast of the island of Borneo, surrounded on its landward side by the Malaysian state of Sarawak. Area: 5,765 sq km (2,226 sq mi). Pop. (1979 est.): 213,000. Cap.: Bandar Seri Begawan (pop., 1978 est., 70,000).

Education. (1978) Primary, pupils 33,053, teachers (1977) 1,824; secondary, pupils 15,571, teachers (1977) 936; vocational, pupils 306, teachers (1977) 68; teacher training, students 533, teachers (1977) 61.

Finance and Trade. Monetary unit: Brunei dollar, with (Sept. 22, 1980) a free rate of Br$2.11 to U.S. $1 (Br$5.06 = £1 sterling). Budget (1979 est.): revenue Br$1.9 billion; expenditure Br$1 million. Foreign trade (1979): imports Br$862,080,000; exports Br$5,796,490,000. Import sources (1978): Japan 24%; Singapore 22%; U.S. 15%; U.K. 11%; Malaysia 5%. Export destinations: Japan 74%; U.S. 9%; Singapore 5%; South Africa 5%. Main exports: crude oil 62%; natural gas 31%.

Agriculture. Production (in 000; metric tons; 1978): rice *c.* 7; cassava *c.* 3; bananas *c.* 2; pineapples *c.* 2. Livestock (in 000; 1978): buffalo *c.* 13; cattle *c.* 3; pigs *c.* 13; chickens *c.* 994.

Industry. Production (in 000; 1978): crude oil (metric tons) 10,960; natural gas (cu m) 10,043,000; petroleum products (metric tons; 1977) 65; electricity (kw-hr; 1977) *c.* 312,000.

CAYMAN ISLANDS

The colony of the Cayman Islands lies in the Caribbean about 270 km NW of Jamaica. Area: 264 sq km (102 sq mi). Pop. (1979 prelim.): 16,700. Cap.: George Town, Grand Cayman (pop., 1980 prelim., 7,600).

Education. (1978–79) Primary, pupils 2,280, teachers 109; secondary, pupils 1,482, teachers 115; vocational, pupils 19, teachers 8.

Finance and Trade. Monetary unit: Cayman Islands dollar, with (Sept. 22, 1980) an official rate of Cayl$0.83 to U.S. $1 (free rate of Cayl$2 = £1 sterling). Budget (1978 est.): revenue Cayl$16.2 million; expenditure Cayl$13,149,000. Foreign trade (1978): imports Cayl$42 million; exports Cayl$2,-860,000,000. Most trade is with the U.S. (about two-thirds) and Jamaica. Main export (1976): turtle products 98%. Tourism (1978): visitors 77,400; gross receipts U.S. $22 million.

Shipping. (1979) Merchant vessels 100 gross tons and over 152; gross tonnage 229,973.

FALKLAND ISLANDS

The colony of the Falkland Islands and dependencies is situated in the South Atlantic about 800 km NE of Cape Horn. Area: 16,265 sq km (6,280 sq mi). Pop. (1979 est.): 1,800. Cap.: Stanley (pop., 1978 est., 1,100).

Education. (1979–80) Primary, pupils 144, teachers 9; secondary, pupils 98, teachers 9.

Finance and Trade. Monetary unit: Falkland Island pound, at par with the pound sterling, with (Sept. 22, 1980) a free rate of U.S. $2.40 = Fl£1. Budget (excluding dependencies; 1979–80 est.): revenue Fl£1,965,000; expenditure Fl£1,936,000. Foreign trade (1977): imports Fl£1,491,000 (83% from U.K. in 1974); exports Fl£1,974,000 (93% to U.K. in 1971). Main export: wool 83%.

GIBRALTAR

Gibraltar, a self-governing colony, is a small peninsula that juts into the Mediterranean from southwestern Spain. Area: 5.80 sq km (2.25 sq mi). Pop. (1980 est.): 29,800.

Education. (1979–80) Primary, pupils 2,705, teachers 147; secondary, pupils 1,771, teachers 128; vocational, pupils 40, teachers 23.

Finance and Trade. Monetary unit: Gibraltar pound, at par with the pound sterling. Budget (1977–78 est.): revenue Gib£18,662,000; expenditure Gib£21,662,000. Foreign trade (1978): imports Gib£39,442,000 (61% from U.K.); reexports Gib£11,863,000 (31% to EEC, 16% to U.K. in 1971). Main reexports: petroleum products 73%; tobacco and manufactures 19%; wines and spirits 6%. Tourism (1977) 54,000 visitors.

Transport. Ships entered (1977) vessels totaling 19,948,000 net registered tons; goods loaded 11,000 metric tons, unloaded 284,000 metric tons.

GUERNSEY

Located 50 km W of Normandy, France, Guernsey, together with its small island dependencies, is a crown dependency. Area: 78 sq km (30 sq mi). Pop. (1976): 54,400. Cap.: St. Peter Port (pop., 1976, 17,000).

Education. (1979) Primary and secondary, pupils 7,774, teachers (1977–78) 457.

Finance and Trade. Monetary unit: Guernsey pound, at par with the pound sterling. Budget (1978): revenue £31,141,000; expenditure £26,042,000. Foreign trade included with the United Kingdom. Main exports (1978): manufactures *c.* 45%; tomatoes *c.* 38%; flowers *c.* 16%. Tourism (1978) 332,000 visitors.

HONG KONG

The colony of Hong Kong lies on the southeastern coast of China about 60 km E of Macau and 130 km SE of Canton. Area: 1,050 sq km (405 sq mi). Pop. (1980 est.): 5,067,900. Cap.: Victoria (pop., 1976, 501,700).

Education. (1978–79) Primary, pupils 553,530, teachers 18,321; secondary, pupils 441,785; vocational, pupils 11,761; secondary and vocational, teachers 15,064; higher, students 25,231, teaching staff 2,643.

Finance. Monetary unit: Hong Kong dollar, with (Sept. 22, 1980) a free rate of HK$4.97 to U.S. $1 (HK$11.94 = £1 sterling). Budget (1979–80 est.): revenue HK$13.8 billion; expenditure HK$12.4 billion.

Foreign Trade. (1979) Imports HK$85,837,-000,000; exports HK$75,934,000,000. Import sources: Japan 23%; China 18%; U.S. 12%; Taiwan 7%; Singapore 6%; U.K. 5%. Export destinations: U.S. 27%; West Germany 9%; U.K. 8%; Japan 7%. Main exports: clothing 28%; textile yarns and fabrics 9%; watches and clocks 7%; plastic toys and dolls 7%; telecommunications apparatus 6%; nonelectrical machinery 5%. Tourism (1978): visitors 2,-055,000; gross receipts U.S. $1,009,000,000.

Transport and Communications. Roads (1978) 1,110 km. Motor vehicles in use (1978): passenger 151,400; commercial 49,000. Railways (1979): 50 km; traffic 402 million passenger-km, freight 66 million net ton-km. Shipping (1979): merchant vessels 100 gross tons and over 177; gross tonnage 1,-469,623. Shipping traffic (1979): goods loaded 7,712,000 metric tons, unloaded 22,598,000 metric tons. Telephones (Dec. 1978) *c.* 1,380,000. Radio receivers (Dec. 1977) 2,510,000. Television receivers (Dec. 1977) 871,000.

ISLE OF MAN

The Isle of Man, a crown dependency, lies in the Irish Sea approximately 55 km from both Northern Ireland and the coast of northwestern England. Area: 572 sq km (221 sq mi). Pop. (1980 est.): 64,-000. Cap.: Douglas (pop., 1976, 20,300).

Education. (1978–79) Primary, pupils 5,890; secondary, pupils 5,158; vocational, pupils 3,044.

Finance and Trade. Monetary unit: Isle of Man pound, at par with the pound sterling. Budget (1979–80 est.) balanced at £64 million. Foreign trade included with the United Kingdom. Main exports: fish, lamb and mutton, livestock, potatoes. Tourism (1979) 627,000 visitors.

JERSEY

The island of Jersey, a crown dependency, is located about 30 km W of Normandy, France. Area: 117 sq km (45 sq mi). Pop. (1976): 71,000. Cap.: St. Helier (pop., 1976, 25,100).

Education. (1977–78) Primary, pupils 6,914; secondary, pupils 5,450; primary and secondary (1976–77), teachers 670.

Finance. Monetary unit: Jersey pound, at par with the pound sterling. Budget (1978): revenue £73,156,000; expenditure £57,837,000.

Foreign Trade. (1979) Imports £225,567,000 (76% from U.K.); exports £84,010,000 (64% to U.K.). Main exports: fruit and vegetables 17%; motor vehicles 13%; telecommunications apparatus 10%; tea 6%; aircraft 6%; jewelry 6%; knitted fabrics 6%; musical instruments 5%; clothing 5%. Tourism (1978): visitors 790,000; gross receipts U.S. $179 million.

MONTSERRAT

The colony of Montserrat is located in the Caribbean between Antigua, 43 km NE, and Guadeloupe, 60 km SE. Area: 102 sq km (40 sq mi). Pop. (1979 est.): 11,200. Cap.: Plymouth (pop., 1974 est., 3,000).

Education. (1977–78) Primary, pupils 2,164, teachers 110; secondary, pupils 811, teachers (1976–77) 48; vocational, pupils 56, teachers 8.

Finance and Trade. Monetary unit: East Caribbean dollar. Budget (1979 est.): revenue ECar$11,348,000 (including U.K. aid of ECar$1,-672,000); expenditure ECar$10,090,000. Foreign trade (1978): imports ECar$26,927,000; exports ECar$1,921,000. Import sources: U.K. 33%; U.S. 23%; Trinidad and Tobago 9%; Canada 5%. Export destinations: U.S. 54%; Trinidad and Tobago 7%; Antigua 5%. Main exports (domestic only): postage stamps 31%; electronic apparatus 30%; food 15%; sand 8%; fishhooks 6%.

PITCAIRN ISLAND

The colony of Pitcairn Island is in the central South Pacific, 5,150 km NE of New Zealand and 2,170 km SE of Tahiti. Area: 4.53 sq km (1.75 sq mi). Pop. (1980 est.): 63, all of whom live in the de facto capital, Adamstown.

ST. HELENA

The colony of St. Helena, including its dependencies of Ascension Island and the Tristan da Cunha island group, is spread over a wide area of the Atlantic off the southwestern coast of Africa. Area: 412 sq km (159 sq mi). Pop. (1979 est.): 7,300. Cap.: Jamestown (pop., 1978 est., 1,500).

Education. (1978–79) Primary, pupils 831, teachers (1977–78) 42; secondary, pupils 561, teachers (1977–78) 38; vocational, pupils 16, teachers (1977–78) 3; teacher training, students 6, teachers (1975–76) 2.

Finance and Trade. Monetary unit: St Helena pound, at par with the pound sterling which is also used. Budget (1977–78 est.): revenue St.H£2,-245,000; expenditure St.H£2.2 million. Foreign trade (1977–78): imports St.H£1,758,000 (52% from U.K., 36% from South Africa, 5% from Ghana in 1976–77); exports nil.

ST. KITTS-NEVIS-ANGUILLA

This associated state consists of the islands of St. Kitts and Nevis (Anguilla received a separate constitution in 1976). Area: 269 sq km (104 sq mi). Pop. (1978 est.): 49,800. Cap.: Basseterre, St. Kitts (pop., 1975 est., 16,800).

Education. (1978–79) Primary, pupils 8,890, teachers 344; secondary, pupils 5,021, teachers 274; vocational, pupils 160, teachers 33; higher, students 61, teaching staff 39.

Finance and Trade. Monetary unit: East Caribbean dollar. Budget (1978 est.): revenue ECar$27 million; expenditure ECar$30 million. Foreign trade (1977): imports ECar$59.1 million; exports ECar$40.5 million. Import sources (1975): U.S. 29%; U.K. 20%; Trinidad and Tobago 10%; Canada 7%; The Netherlands 5%; Japan 5%. Export destinations (1975): U.S. 51%; U.K. 42%. Main exports (1975): sugar 61%; television sets and parts 34%.

TURKS AND CAICOS ISLANDS

The colony of the Turks and Caicos Islands is situated in the Atlantic southeast of The Bahamas. Area: 500 sq km (193 sq mi). Pop. (1977 est.): 7,100. Seat of government: Grand Turk Island (pop., 1977 est., 2,900).

Education. (1978–79) Primary, pupils 1,849, teachers 90; secondary, pupils 708, teachers 38.

Finance and Trade. Monetary unit: U.S. dollar. Budget (1979–80 est.): revenue $6,496,000; expenditure $5,420,000. Foreign trade (1978): imports $7,083,000; exports $1,704,000. Main exports: conch meat 49%; crayfish 47%.

UNITED STATES

AMERICAN SAMOA

Located to the east of Western Samoa in the South Pacific, the unincorporated territory of American

Samoa is approximately 2,600 km NE of the northern tip of New Zealand. Area: 199 sq km (77 sq mi). Pop. (1980 prelim.): 32,400. Cap.: Pago Pago (pop., 1980 est., 2,600).

Education. (1979–80) Primary, pupils 6,680, teachers 355; secondary, pupils 2,911, teachers 175; vocational, pupils 45, teachers 4; teacher training, pupils 256, teachers 6; higher, students 472, teaching staff 54.

Finance and Trade. Monetary unit: U.S. dollar. Budget (1978 est.) balanced at $45.5 million (including U.S. federal grants of $35 million). Foreign trade (1976–77): imports (excluding fish for canneries) $55 million (73% from U.S., 11% from Japan, 5% from New Zealand); exports $82 million (99% to U.S.). Main export: canned tuna 90%.

GUAM

Guam, an organized unincorporated territory, is located in the Pacific Ocean about 9,700 km SW of San Francisco and 2,400 km E of Manila. Area: 549 sq km (212 sq mi). Pop. (1980 est.): 120,000. Cap.: Agana (pop., 1974 est., 2,500).

Education. (1977–78) Primary, pupils 24,303, teachers 1,186; secondary and vocational, pupils 6,083, teachers 509; higher, students 4,343, teaching staff (1971–72) *c.* 140.

Finance and Trade. Monetary unit: U.S. dollar. Budget (1976–77 est.): revenue $250.3 million; expenditure $204.2 million. Foreign trade (1975–76): imports $268 million (32% from U.S., 5% from Japan); exports $25 million (35% to Taiwan, 25% to U.S. Trust Territories, 21% to U.S.). Main exports: petroleum products, copra, watches, scrap metal. Tourism: visitors (1977) 246,000; gross receipts (1973) U.S. $90 million.

Agriculture and Industry. Production (in 000; metric tons; 1978): copra *c.* 1; eggs *c.* 2; fish catch 0.3; petroleum products (1977) *c.* 1,329; electricity (kw-hr; 1977) *c.* 1,058,000.

PUERTO RICO

Puerto Rico, a self-governing associated commonwealth, lies about 1,400 km SE of the Florida coast. Area: 8,897 sq km (3,435 sq mi). Pop. (1980 prelim.): 3,187,600. Cap.: San Juan (pop., 1980 prelim., mun., 433,000).

Education. (1979–80) Primary, pupils 432,012, teachers 15,308; secondary, pupils 341,716, teachers 13,676; vocational (1978–79), pupils 57,863, teachers 2,600; higher, students 130,105, teaching staff 3,300.

Finance. Monetary unit: U.S dollar. Budget (1977–78 actual): revenue $3,375,000,000; expenditure $2,963,000,000. Gross domestic product (1978–79) $12,447,000,000. Cost of living (1975 = 100; March 1980) 128.3.

Foreign Trade. (1978–79) Imports $6,556,000,000 (71% from U.S., 8% from Venezuela); exports $4,768,000,000 (88% to U.S.). Main exports (1974–75): chemicals 25%; petroleum products 14%; clothing 11%; machinery 11%; fish 8%. Tourism (1978–79): visitors 1,662,000; gross receipts $565 million.

Transport and Communications. Roads (paved; 1978) 12,343 km. Motor vehicles in use (1978): passenger 793,800; commercial 135,900. Railways (1977) 96 km. Telephones (Jan. 1978) 560,700. Radio receivers (Dec. 1976) 1,765,000. Television receivers (Dec. 1977) 535,000.

Agriculture. Production (in 000; metric tons; 1979): sugar, raw value 174; pineapples 39; bananas 113; oranges 32; coffee *c.* 12; tobacco (1978) 2; milk 442; meat (1978) 69; fish catch (1978) 78. Livestock (in 000; Jan. 1979): cattle 532; pigs 246; chickens 6,568.

Industry. Production (in 000; metric tons; 1979): cement 1,327; beer (hl) 736; rum (hl; 1977) *c.* 600; petroleum products (1976) 11,567; electricity (kw-hr) 13,681,000.

TRUST TERRITORY OF THE PACIFIC ISLANDS

The Trust Territory islands, numbering more than 2,000, are scattered over 7,750,000 sq km in the Pacific Ocean from 720 km E of the Philippines to just west of the International Date Line. Separate administrative actions within the Trust Territory have, since 1978, created four new administrative entities that are to form the framework for local government upon cessation of the UN trusteeship, scheduled in early 1981: the Commonwealth of the Northern Marianas (1978); the Federated States of Micronesia (Yap, Ponape, Kosrae, and Truk; 1979); the Marshall Islands (1979); and the Republic of Palau (early 1981). The government of the Trust Territory will not, however, cease to exist until the UN permits its dissolution, subject to referendums. Area: 1,880 sq km (726 sq mi). Pop. (1980 est.): 136,800. Seat of government: Saipan Island (pop., 1973 census, 12,400).

Education. (Including Northern Marianas; 1978–79) Primary, pupils 31,297, teachers 1,485; secondary, pupils 7,990, teachers 509; vocational (1976–77), pupils 257, teachers (1973–74) 13; higher, students 581.

Finance and Trade. Monetary unit: U.S. dollar. Budget (including Northern Marianas; 1976–77 rev. est.): revenue $99.4 million (including U.S. grant of $84.9 million); expenditure $98.6 million. Foreign trade (including Northern Marianas; 1976–77): imports $44 million (35% from U.S., *c.* 25% from Japan, 6% from Australia); exports $10.9 million (54% to Japan in 1972). Main exports: coconut products 54%; fish 32%.

VIRGIN ISLANDS

The Virgin Islands of the United States is an organized unincorporated territory located about 60 km E of Puerto Rico. Area: 345 sq km (133 sq mi). Pop. (1980 prelim.): 95,200. Cap.: Charlotte Amalie, St. Thomas (pop., 1980 prelim., 11,700).

Education. (1979–80) Primary, pupils 20,191, teachers 861; secondary, pupils 12,134, teachers 612; vocational, pupils 3,738, teachers 103; higher, students 584, teaching staff 86.

Finance. Monetary unit: U.S. dollar. Budget (1977–78 est.): revenue $123.4 million; expenditure $123 million.

Foreign Trade. (1978) Imports $3,149,000,000; exports $2,542,300,000. Import sources: Iran 46%; U.S. *c.* 12%; Libya 11%; Nigeria 9%; United Arab Emirates 8%; Angola 6%. Export destinations: U.S. 92%. Main export (1975): petroleum products 92%. Tourism (1978): visitors 1.3 million; gross receipts U.S. $241 million.

continued from page 301

about the serious effect of increasing energy prices on their fragile economies. In Antigua a general election in April returned the ruling Antigua Labour Party (ALP), under the leadership of the veteran Caribbean politician Vere Bird, Sr., to a further five-year term of office. The ALP increased its overall number of seats to 13, as against the opposition Progressive Labour Movement's 3. During the year the island took the first steps toward achieving independence, and a full constitutional conference was held in London during December. Antigua's island ward of Barbuda continued to express a desire to secede, but the government was only prepared to allow it substantial autonomy. The ruling United Bermuda Party was returned to power in an election in Bermuda in December, but with a reduced majority (22 seats in the 40-seat House of Assembly, as compared with 25 before the election).

In St. Kitts-Nevis a snap general election was called by Prime Minister Lee Moore in February. The upshot was formation of a coalition between the opposition People's Action Movement (PAM), which took three of St. Kitts's seven seats, and the secessionist Nevis Reformation Party, which won both the Nevis seats. The resulting government, under the premiership of Kennedy Simmonds, indicated that it would provide substantial aid to Nevis and would delay independence (originally planned by the Labour Party for June 1980) until the island was economically prepared for such a move. During the year the new government set forth its broad centre-right political philosophy and was publicly critical of the socialist tendencies of Grenada. As the year progressed, it encountered difficulties with the opposition Labour-dominated sugar industry, which continued to be the mainstay of the island's economy. All claims to Anguilla were given up, and Simmonds made it clear that he had no objection to the British government's passing legislation to make the island a dependency. By year's end moves to effect this had begun. In a general election on Anguilla, the opposition Anguilla United Movement led by Ronald Webster won by six seats to one.

In early 1980, after complex discussions in London, the Turks and Caicos Islands indicated that it would seek full independence by mid-1982 in return for aid amounting to £12 million. But at year's end—and just prior to general elections—the ruling People's Democratic Movement qualified this by indicating it would do so only after a referendum. Club Méditerannée announced plans to construct a major resort complex on the islands. The British Virgin Islands underwent a change of government in 1980. Few policy changes were introduced, however, and the islands were content to retain their dependent status. An agreement for oil exploration was signed with Mobil Oil in August.

The French government indicated increasing

concern about growing nationalism in the French départements of Martinique, Guadeloupe, and French Guiana, which was finding vent in strikes and attacks on metropolitan French citizens living there. The unrest stemmed from a decision to reduce salaries in the public sector to Paris levels and from the high rate of unemployment. The départements' independence movements continued to attract growing support.

In the November 4 election for governor of Puerto Rico, the pro-statehood incumbent, Carlos Romero Barceló, narrowly defeated Rafael Hernández Colón, an advocate of continued status for the island as a commonwealth associated with the U.S. The outcome was not determined for several weeks, during which a ballot by ballot recount was held. Eleven suspected members of a pro-independence terrorist group, the Armed Forces of National Liberation (FALN), were arrested in April in Evanston, Ill., near Chicago. All were subsequently convicted on various state charges, and in December ten were indicted by a federal grand jury on charges arising from 28 bombings. Among them was Carlos Torres, believed to be a top FALN leader, who before his arrest was ranked first on the FBI's most wanted list. An FBI spokesman estimated membership in the group at 25 to 35.

Africa. The outstanding event in Africa in 1980 was the achievement of independence on April 18 by Zimbabwe, formerly the British colony of Southern Rhodesia but known as Rhodesia since its unilateral declaration of independence in 1965. The only dependent territory now remaining on the continent of Africa was South West Africa/Namibia, whose future independence was the subject of prolonged discussion between the South African government and the UN. Meanwhile, the country's elected multiracial Constituent Assembly, in which the Democratic Turnhalle Alliance had an absolute majority, was not recognized by the South West Africa People's Organization. SWAPO's guerrilla wing, based in Angola, was in armed conflict with South Africa for mastery of the territory. (*See* SOUTH AFRICA.)

Morocco still claimed Western Sahara (formerly two Spanish territories), but the Popular Front for the Liberation of Saguia el Hamra and Río de Oro (Polisario Front) maintained its struggle for independence as the Saharan Arab Democratic Republic. The Front was materially aided by Algeria and Libya, supported by a majority of states (26) in the Organization of African Unity (OAU), and recognized by Portugal. In September the OAU came up with a Saharan peace plan calling, among other things, for a cease-fire by December, a UN peacekeeping force, and a referendum, but with no effect.

Indian Ocean. In the Comoros Philippe Kessler replaced Jean Rigotard as the French government's representative on Mayotte, the island still attached to France by its own choice. In September Dijoud, on a tour of the Indian Ocean, appealed to the people of Mayotte to seek a formula for increasing cooperation with the rest of the Comoro Islands, independent since 1975. His speech was ill received by Mayotte's officials but well understood by the militants of the Parti pour le Rassemblement Démocratique des Mahoris, which supported Mayotte's return to the Comoro fold.

France still had some weight in the balance of power in the Indian Ocean. It held the territories of Réunion, Mayotte, the Glorieuses Islands, and Tromelin, as against Soviet control of Aden and Socotra and the U.S. bases on Diego Garcia Island and at Berbera in Somalia. However, Mauritius claimed Diego Garcia, the Glorieuses were claimed by both Madagascar and the Comoros, and the other French islands, Juan da Nova, Europa, and Tromelin, were claimed by Madagascar.

Pacific. With the independence of the British-French condominium of the New Hebrides as the Republic of Vanuatu in July 1980, attention turned to the political status of France's remaining dependencies. Pro-independence leaders in New Caledonia, who had the support of most of the indigenous Melanesians or "Kanaks," argued that France was encouraging secessionist movements in Vanuatu in an attempt to "destabilize" the French Pacific and discourage demands for self-determination in New Caledonia. Tension had developed in January after a police inspector killed a 22-year-old Melanesian in a street incident in a suburb of Nouméa. Protest strikes and demonstrations followed, while in Paris the opposition in the National Assembly attempted to carry a motion of censure against the government. In May Dijoud visited Nouméa and secured approval of land reform by the territory's assembly. Pro-independence leader Yann Uregei sought support for his cause from the South Pacific Forum, which met in Kiribati in July. In September militants of the Union Calédonienne demanded "Kanaka independence tomorrow."

Gaston Flosse, a longtime Gaullist representative of French Polynesia in the French National Assembly, surprised political allies and opponents with his call for complete autonomy in association with France to replace the existing heavily qualified system of self-government. French officials were also embarrassed when the 1979 convictions of Charlie Ching and his associates for terrorist activities were overturned on technical grounds. A retrial, probably to take place in France, was ordered. In the wake of a further series of underground nuclear tests at Muroroa Atoll, there were allegations that France had developed a neutron bomb. The overseas territory of Wallis and Futuna signed an agreement with Tonga to delimit its exclusive economic zone in the Pacific.

The Cook Islands, a self-governing territory of New Zealand, continued to feel the effects of the dismissal in 1978 of the former head of government, Sir Albert Henry, and several of his colleagues on charges of electoral bribery and corruption. Henry himself was stripped of his knighthood by Queen Elizabeth II. A court ruled that it could not hear a defamation action for NZ$225,000 that his sister, Marguerite Story, the former speaker in the House of Assembly, brought against the government-owned *Cook Islands News*. Meanwhile, the government of Tom Davis continued to withdraw from the involvement in many aspects of the local economy that it had inherited from Henry's administration.

Disasters:
see page 56

Disciples of Christ:
see Religion

Diseases:
see Health and Disease

Divorce:
see Demography

The Cook Islands Development Bank was restructured to earn eligibility for loans from the Asian Development Bank and other agencies. North Korea paid a $100,000 fee in respect of fishing rights in the 200-mi exclusive economic zone, but the country still required a special NZ$400,000 grant from New Zealand in addition to the NZ$6,250,000 already allocated for the financial year. Controversial cancer chemotherapist Milan Brych, barred from practice in New Zealand before going to the Cook Islands, was arrested for fraudulent practice in the U.S., where he had established a clinic after the Cook Islands, in turn, excluded him. In neighbouring Niue, also self-governing in free association with New Zealand, an outbreak of dengue fever affected 15% of the population but resulted in few deaths.

Norfolk Islanders were again in disagreement with Australian authorities. In a referendum, they rejected the Australian-imposed preferential voting for the Assembly in favour of a simple plurality system. Australian plans to upgrade the airfield to allow an increase in tourism were opposed by many islanders (especially the descendants of Pitcairners) on environmental, health, and other grounds.

Further steps toward termination of the Trust Territory of the Pacific were taken when the U.S. reached agreements on a form of free association with the Federated States of Micronesia, the Marshall Islands, and the Republic of Palau. (The Northern Mariana Islands had opted for commonwealth status.) The agreements would have to be approved by the U.S. Congress and by the islanders in referenda before being submitted to the UN for dissolution of the trust. In October the U.S. secured membership in the South Pacific Commission for the Northern Marianas, the Marshall Islands, and the Federated States of Micronesia and the federated states were given observer status at the South Pacific Forum. American Samoa and the Northern Marianas protested to Japan over proposals to dump nuclear wastes near Micronesian waters. Eniwetok Atoll, made uninhabitable by nuclear tests 22 years earlier, was declared decontaminated, and its people were given an option to return.

East Asia. On October 23, in a move to prevent further illegal immigration, the citizens of Hong Kong were required to obtain identity cards and be registered as residents. It was made illegal for an industrialist to employ any person without an identity card. An estimated 450,000 of Hong Kong's population of approximately 5 million had arrived, legally or illegally, from China since January 1975. Gen. Melo Egidio, governor of Macau, Portugal's sole remaining overseas territory, visited China and secured approval for an airport and a road to China. Proposals were made by reformist members of the Legislative Assembly to give that body more responsibility for administration and make it less subordinate to Portuguese officials.

(PHILIPPE DECRAENE; DAVID A. JESSOP; BARRIE MACDONALD; MOLLY MORTIMER)

See also African Affairs; Commonwealth of Nations; United Nations.

Djibouti

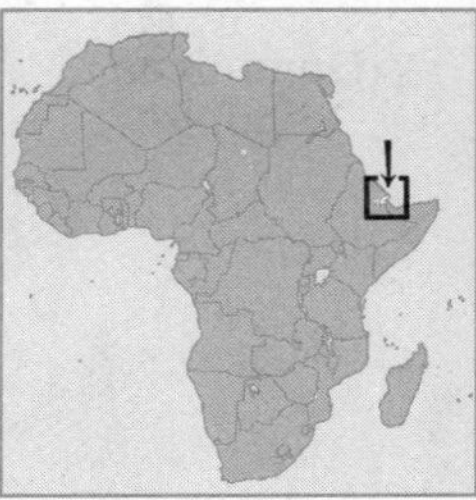

Djibouti

An independent republic in northeastern Africa, Djibouti is bordered by Ethiopia, Somalia, and the Gulf of Aden. Area: 23,000 sq km (8,900 sq mi). Pop. (1980 est., excluding refugees): 315,000, most of whom are Cushitic Afars or Somali Issas; there are smaller Arabic and European communities. Capital: Djibouti (pop., 1978 est., 160,000). Language: Arabic and French (official); Saho-Afar and Somali are spoken in their respective communities. Religion: predominantly Muslim. President in 1980, Hassan Gouled Aptidon; premier, Barkat Gourat Hamadou.

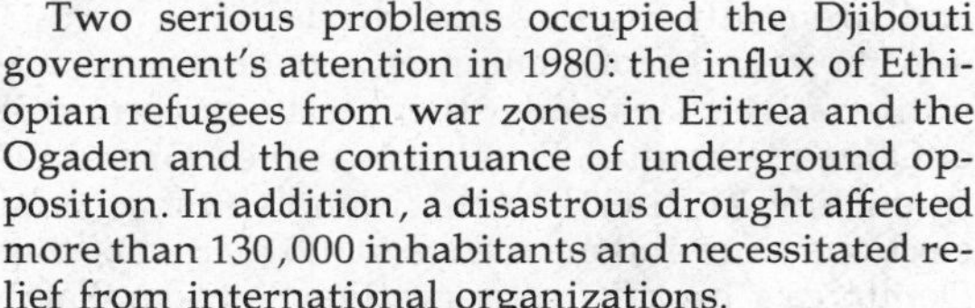

Two serious problems occupied the Djibouti government's attention in 1980: the influx of Ethiopian refugees from war zones in Eritrea and the Ogaden and the continuance of underground opposition. In addition, a disastrous drought affected more than 130,000 inhabitants and necessitated relief from international organizations.

Between 30,000 and 40,000 refugees were temporarily settled on Djibouti territory and represented some 10% of the country's population. A national office for their assistance worked in liaison with the UN High Commissioner for Refugees, but the refugees still represented a crushing financial burden that could be met only with massive external aid.

Pres. Hassan Gouled Aptidon visited France in June, when cooperation agreements were signed to complete those made at Djibouti's independence in 1977. Five hundred French technicians and administrators served in the country, in addition to some 4,000 French troops stationed there.

Several dozen individuals were being held in custody without trial. More than once, the Afar community complained of discriminatory actions by the Issa community and notified Amnesty International, which then alerted the Djibouti government. (PHILIPPE DECRAENE)

DJIBOUTI

Education. (1978–79) Primary, pupils 13,011, teachers (1975–76) 268; secondary and vocational, pupils 3,408, teachers (1975–76) 144; teacher training (1975–76), students 36, teachers 4.

Finance. Monetary unit: Djibouti franc, with (Sept. 22, 1980) a par value of DjFr 178.16 to U.S. $1 (free rate of DjFr 428 = £1 sterling). Budget (1979 est.) balanced at DjFr 10,929,000,000.

Foreign Trade. (1977) Imports DjFr 18,506,000,000; exports DjFr 3,381,000,000. Import sources: France 55%; U.K. 6%; Japan 6%; Ethiopia 5%. Export destinations (1973): France 84%. Main exports (most trade is transit): cattle *c.* 7%.

Dominica

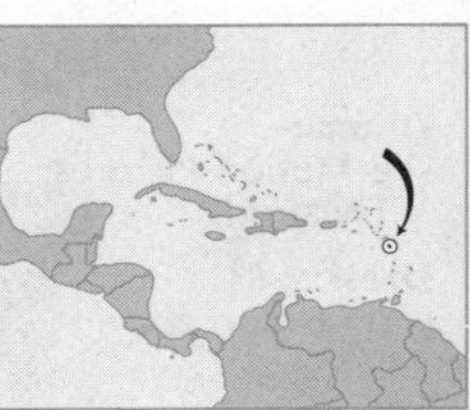

Dominica

A republic within the Commonwealth of Nations, Dominica, an island of the Lesser Antilles in the Caribbean Sea, lies between Guadeloupe to the north and Martinique to the south. Area: 772 sq km (300 sq mi). Pop. (1980 est.): 90,300. Cap. Roseau (pop., 1978 est., 16,800). Presidents in 1980, Jen-

DOMINICA

Education. (1978–79) Primary, pupils 15,220, teachers 423; secondary, pupils 9,814, teachers 299; vocational, pupils 400, teachers 21; higher, students 154, teachers 8.

Finance and Trade. Monetary unit: East Caribbean dollar, with (Sept. 22, 1980) an official rate of ECar$2.70 to U.S. $1 (free rate of ECar$6.48 = £1 sterling). Budget (1976–77 est.): revenue ECar$21,554,000; expenditure ECar$28,611,000. Foreign trade (1978): imports ECar$76.8 million; exports ECar$42.3 million. Import sources (1977): U.K. 26%; U.S. 13%; Trinidad and Tobago 9%; St. Lucia 9%; Canada 7%. Export destinations (1977): U.K. 69%; Barbados 5%. Main exports (1977): bananas 58%; essential oils and fats 12%; coconut oil 6%.

ner Armour (acting) and, from February 25, Aurelius Marie; prime ministers, Oliver Seraphin and, from July 21, Eugenia Charles.

After months of mounting economic and administrative chaos under the interim government of Oliver Seraphine, Dominicans opted for stability on July 21, 1980, in the island's first general elections since independence in 1978. In choosing Dominica's broadly conservative Freedom Party by 17 seats to 4, the island's voters also provided the Caribbean's first female prime minister, Eugenia Charles (*see* BIOGRAPHIES). Charles voiced her government's intention to reduce unemployment and increase foreign trade.

Before the election there had been accusations that much of the money designated for relief of the devastation caused by Hurricane David in 1979 had been misappropriated. A three-man investigatory team was set up by the new government to look into the matter. During the year the existence of an agreement between the Seraphine government and the U.S.-based, Iranian-linked Inter-Continental Development Corp. was revealed. Under pressure from the U.S. government, implementation of the agreement was halted when it became known that the corporation had been allowed to issue Dominican passports.

Relations between Dominica and its neighbours remained cordial. The new government appeared to be closer to centrist Barbados in its foreign relations and critical of the governments of Grenada and Cuba. (DAVID A. JESSOP)

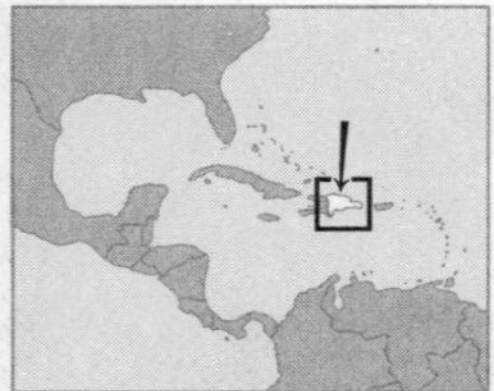

Dominican Republic

Dominican Republic

Covering the eastern two-thirds of the Caribbean island of Hispaniola, the Dominican Republic is separated from Haiti, which occupies the western third, by a rugged mountain range. Area: 48,442 sq km (18,704 sq mi). Pop. (1980 est.): 5.4 million, including mulatto 75%; white 15%; Negro 10%. Cap. and largest city: Santo Domingo (pop., 1979 est., 1,103,400). Language: Spanish. Religion: mainly Roman Catholic (95%), with Protestant and Jewish minorities. President in 1980, Antonio Guzmán Fernández.

During 1980 the Partido Revolucionario Dominicano criticized Pres. Antonio Guzmán Fernández for not implementing its policies before the 1982 elections. Strikes and violence occurred as the economy worsened and the cost of living rose. Taxation and electricity and gasoline charges were raised (gasoline by 30%), state sector wages were frozen, and the availability of foreign currency was curtailed in a financial package introduced in May.

DOMINICAN REPUBLIC

Education. (1976–77) Primary, pupils 867,592, teachers (1975–76) 17,932; secondary, pupils 136,570, teachers 4,417; vocational, pupils 5,326, teachers 299; teacher training, students 1,353, teachers 49; higher, students 42,395, teaching staff 429.

Finance. Monetary unit: peso, at parity with the U.S. dollar, with a free rate (Sept. 22, 1980) of 2.40 pesos to £1 sterling. Gold, SDR's, and foreign exchange (June 1980) U.S. $172 million. Budget (1979 actual): revenue 690.1 million pesos; expenditure 897.9 million pesos. Gross domestic product (1978) 4,695,600,000 pesos. Money supply (May 1980) 696.2 million pesos. Cost of living (Santo Domingo; 1975 = 100; March 1980) 156.1.

Foreign Trade. (1979) Imports 1,216,500,000 pesos; exports 866.2 million pesos. Import sources: U.S. 42%; Venezuela 18%; Netherlands Antilles 7%; Japan 7%. Export destinations: U.S. 53%; Switzerland 15%; Puerto Rico 6%; Venezuela 6%; The Netherlands 5%. Main exports: sugar 27%; coffee 18%; gold and alloys 15%; ferronickel 14%; cocoa 8%; tobacco 6%.

Transport and Communications. Roads (1975) 11,844 km. Motor vehicles in use (1977): passenger 82,700; commercial 39,500. Railways (1977) *c.* 590 km. Telephones (Jan. 1978) 139,400. Radio receivers (Dec. 1977) 210,000. Television receivers (Dec. 1976) 160,000.

Agriculture. Production (in 000; metric tons; 1979): rice 243; sweet potatoes (1978) *c.* 85; cassava (1978) *c.* 185; sugar, raw value *c.* 1,220; dry beans *c.* 33; tomatoes 156; peanuts *c.* 63; oranges *c.* 71; avocados (1978) *c.* 135; mangoes *c.* 170; bananas *c.* 290; plantains (1978) *c.* 610; cocoa *c.* 30; coffee *c.* 41; tobacco *c.* 48. Livestock (in 000; June 1978): cattle 2,651; sheep 22; pigs *c.* 810; goats 289; horses 197; chickens *c.* 7,800.

Industry. Production (in 000; metric tons; 1978): cement 777; bauxite 558; nickel ore 14; gold (troy oz) 336; silver (troy oz) 1,844; petroleum products (1977) *c.* 1,190; electricity (kw-hr) *c.* 2,780,000.

Sugarcane rust, heavy rain, and labour and transport difficulties reduced the 1980 sugar crop. Agriculture had not fully recovered from the two hurricanes of 1979, and coffee output also fell. In September Gulf and Western Industries and the government settled their dispute over $64.5 million made by the company's futures market speculations during the 1974–75 sugar boom. The company agreed to set up a 39 million peso nonprofit corporation for the economic and social development of the eastern region, where most of the sugar was grown. In July several hundred Haitian sugarcane labourers, kept starving in a barbedwire compound before being sent back to Haiti after the harvest, rioted. They were brought under control by soldiers, but protests against this harsh system were renewed. (SARAH CAMERON)

Drama:
see Motion Pictures; Theatre

Dress:
see Fashion and Dress

Earthquakes:
see Earth Sciences

Earth Sciences

GEOLOGY AND GEOCHEMISTRY

Following its devastating explosive eruption on May 18, Mt. St. Helens in the Cascade Range of Washington state became the focus of intensive scientific and socioeconomic studies. Early warnings by the U.S. Geological Survey that the volcano had the potential for disastrous eruption probably kept the death toll much lower than it might have been. The massive damage to nearby human development raised serious concern about the future monitoring of Mt. St. Helens and other active volcanoes in the U.S. The hazard is real. There have been six recorded eruptions of Mt. St. Helens since AD 1700. Of the 15 active volcanoes in the Cascade Range, six have erupted since 1800.

Continued detailed analysis of the activities and effects of Mt. St. Helens together with recent studies on the geology and tectonic setting made this one of the best documented cases of volcanic activity. The research would assist geologists in making more precise predictions in the future. One of the geochemical techniques used for monitoring and predicting the activity of a volcano is to measure the emission rates and composition of the gas emerging from the vent in major plumes and minor fumaroles. Since the May 18 eruption of Mt. St. Helens gas emission varied from hundreds to thousands of tons per day. It was established that the rates of emission of carbon dioxide and sulfur dioxide varied significantly before and after an eruption. Attempts were being made to correlate the emission ratio of these gases with events in order to develop a useful predictive tool. (See *Geophysics*, below.)

The volcanoes of the Cascade Range were formed as a consequence of subduction, or sinking, of the Pacific lithospheric plate beneath the North American continent. The oceanic crust atop the sinking plate was formed millions of years ago by the eruption of basaltic lava at a mid-oceanic ridge. The overlying ocean water penetrated deeply into the hot crust, causing hydration and many other chemical reactions before emerging as submarine hot springs. Later, when this crust was carried down below the continental mass, it was heated and experienced dehydration and melting reactions. As aqueous solutions and magmas rose through the overlying mantle and continental crust, they became involved in further reactions, including additional melting. The end product has been the eruption of volcanoes characterized by especially large volumes of gases. The theory of plate tectonics has been very successful in tying together such diverse phenomena as submarine hot springs at mid-oceanic ridges and explosive eruptions at volcanic island arcs and continental margins.

Recent calculations indicated that it requires only about eight million years to circulate a volume of water equivalent to the Earth's oceans through the submarine hot springs system. The reaction between water and ocean crust plays a critical role in the chemical budget of the oceans. Sulfate ions from seawater become reduced to sulfides during circulation and reaction, leading to the emission of hydrogen sulfide, which feeds the bacteria that in turn are the basis of the animal communities that thrive near hydrothermal vents.

Calculations related to subduction suggested that sinking of the partially hydrated oceanic crust may transport a mass of water the size of the oceans into the mantle in about 1,000,000,000 years. It had been assumed that the return flow to the ocean system was efficiently maintained by volcanic activity. Some recent estimates, however, hinted that the differentiation of the mantle into crust, oceans, and atmosphere may already have reversed. The rate of subduction of crust and hydrosphere may exceed that of the return flow, and both continental crust and ocean may be diminishing in volume. Although there were many uncertainties in these calculations, they were being reduced by new discoveries and the refinement of geochemical instruments.

The study of variations in the natural isotopic composition of the element neodymium has been pursued only in recent years, and as of 1980 only a few laboratories with high-precision solid-source mass spectrometers were capable of this research. Nevertheless, it was becoming a standard geochemical technique, providing otherwise inaccessible information for use in combination with more well established rubidium-strontium and uranium-lead analyses. A major advantage of the neodymium-samarium system over the latter ones is its independence of the effects of metamorphism and weathering. Because neodymium and samarium are rare-earth elements, with effectively identical chemical properties, their proportions do not change in metamorphic reactions. The system was providing new insights into cosmochemistry, geochronology, and the evolution of the Earth's crust and mantle.

The Earth has evolved two distinct reservoirs of rare-earth elements: the mantle and the continental crust. A fuller understanding of the complementary nature of these two reservoirs and their time-dependent changes has become possible as a result of studies of neodymium isotopes. The ratios of the isotopes have proved to be powerful geochemical tracers for interpretation of the sources of lavas, whether they be from mantle, crust, or mixed sources. Mass calculations are consistent with a model in which more than half the mantle has been depleted by partial melting and formation of the crust. The simplest interpretation is that the deeper half of the mantle is still essentially undifferentiated. The results constrain the possible convective regimes that have existed in the mantle and indicate that convection in the upper mantle must be decoupled effectively from the lower mantle. It appears that crustal materials formed during the first 1,000,000,000 years of the Earth's history were mixed back into the mantle but that the crust has grown since then. This conclusion contrasts with the estimate that the crust presently may be decreasing in volume.

Emerging as a separate field since about 1970 has been the comparative planetology of the Earth, Moon, and other planets and satellites. Such study has provided insight into the varied compositions and histories of these bodies for incorporation into a comprehensive hypothesis for the origin and evolution of the Earth and solar system. Direct studies of the geology and geochemistry of the Moon and its rock samples brought back by U.S. astronauts were being followed by remote-sensing studies of other planetary bodies.

Measurement of more than 93% of the topography of Venus by a radar mapper aboard the Pioneer Venus spacecraft provided intriguing contrasts with the topography of the Earth, Moon, and Mars. The mapping identified two large con-

PHOTOS, © 1980 VERN HODGSON

First moments of the May 18 eruption of Mt. St. Helens (above and facing page, top) were captured on film by amateur photographer Vern Hodgson from a distance of 24 kilometres (15 miles).

tinent-sized features, which rise above a relatively flat rolling plain covering about 60% of the surface, as well as basins below the mean radius of the planet (6,050 km, or 3,750 mi), which occupy only 16% of the surface. Only 8% of the masses above the plain are true highlands, rising to altitudes of 10.8 km (6.7 mi). The deepest point is within a rift valley three kilometres (about two miles) below average mean surface level. One highlands region appeared to be a group of large shield volcanoes. In the mid-1970s the Soviet Union's Venera 9 and Venera 10 landers recorded gamma rays corresponding to the composition of radioactive elements in basalt, a finding consistent with the volcanic interpretation of the topography. Venera 8 found a granitic composition for one region of the plains. There appeared to be no indication in the Venusian topography of the operation of global tectonics.

During the 1970s interpretation of the topography and internal dynamics of the Earth in terms of global tectonics under the aegis of the International Geodynamics Project revolutionized scientific understanding of Earth processes. As a consequence the International Union of Geodesy and Geophysics (IUGG) and the International Union of Geological Sciences (IUGS) planned for a continuing cooperative program in the 1980s. The centennial of the International Geological Congress was celebrated at its 26th Congress in Paris during July. The Congress Council approved a document submitted by a steering committee of IUGG and IUGS: "Dynamics and Evolution of the Lithosphere: the Framework for Earth Resources and the Reduction of Hazards." The principal focus of the new ten-year program would be the continental crust. A major objective, as indicated by the title, would be to apply the theory of plate tectonics to human needs. (PETER JOHN WYLLIE)

[133.C.1.b; 212.D.4; 213.A.2; 213.D.2; 214.C.9; 241.A; 241.F–G]

GEOPHYSICS

A "great" earthquake is defined as one having a magnitude of 8.0 or greater. Between late 1979 and late 1980 at least one such shock occurred, of magnitude 8.1, on Sept. 12, 1979, in the West Irian region of Indonesia resulting in the deaths of 15 persons. Another, which first was measured at magnitude 8 and later downgraded to 6.9, occurred on July 17, 1980, in the Santa Cruz Islands. Several other shocks of lesser magnitude caused fatalities or were of special interest. On Dec. 12, 1979, at least 600 persons were killed and 20,000 injured in Colombia and Ecuador by a shock of magnitude 7.9. On Jan. 1, 1980, a magnitude 6.9 earthquake in the Azores killed at least 56 and injured more than 400, and on July 29, 1980, 150 people were killed and many injured in the western Nepal-India border region by an earthquake of magnitude 6.6.

The most devastating earthquakes of 1980 occurred late in the year. On October 10 a shock of magnitude 7.7 and a second of 6.5 destroyed as much as 80% of the town of El Asnam in Algeria; early death toll estimates ran as high as 20,000 but later figures were closer to 4,000. On November 23 and 24 a broad region of southern Italy experienced a series of shocks that peaked at magnitude 6.9, causing several thousand deaths, countless injuries, and widespread damage to homes and other structures.

California experienced notable activity in late 1979 and 1980 with a large earthquake on the Mexico-California border, shocks near Livermore in the San Francisco Bay area, and an extensive swarm near the California-Nevada border. The first of these, at magnitude 6.8, was the largest to have occurred in the Imperial Valley since 1940. The region was very well instrumented, and among the excellent records produced was an astonishing ground acceleration at one station of 1.74 times the acceleration of gravity. The California-

Nevada border activity was anticipated by Alan Ryall and his colleagues from the University of Nevada. Acting accordingly, the group instrumented the region heavily prior to the swarm. The ensuing events included two magnitude 6 shocks on May 25, followed by a third shock on May 27 and by more than 100 aftershocks of magnitude 4 or greater.

By far the most spectacular and important geophysical event of the year was the eruption of Mt. St. Helens in May 1980. Mt. St. Helens is one of more than a dozen volcanic peaks in the Cascade Range of the U.S. Pacific Northwest. Prior to March 27 the last of them to act up was Mt. Lassen in California, which erupted for several years beginning in 1914.

Mt. St. Helens is a composite volcano made up of alternate layers of lava and ash, the residues of previous activity. Its last active period began in 1830 and continued until 1857. The current episode can be dated from the recording on March 20 of a magnitude 4.1 earthquake 3½ km west of the sum-

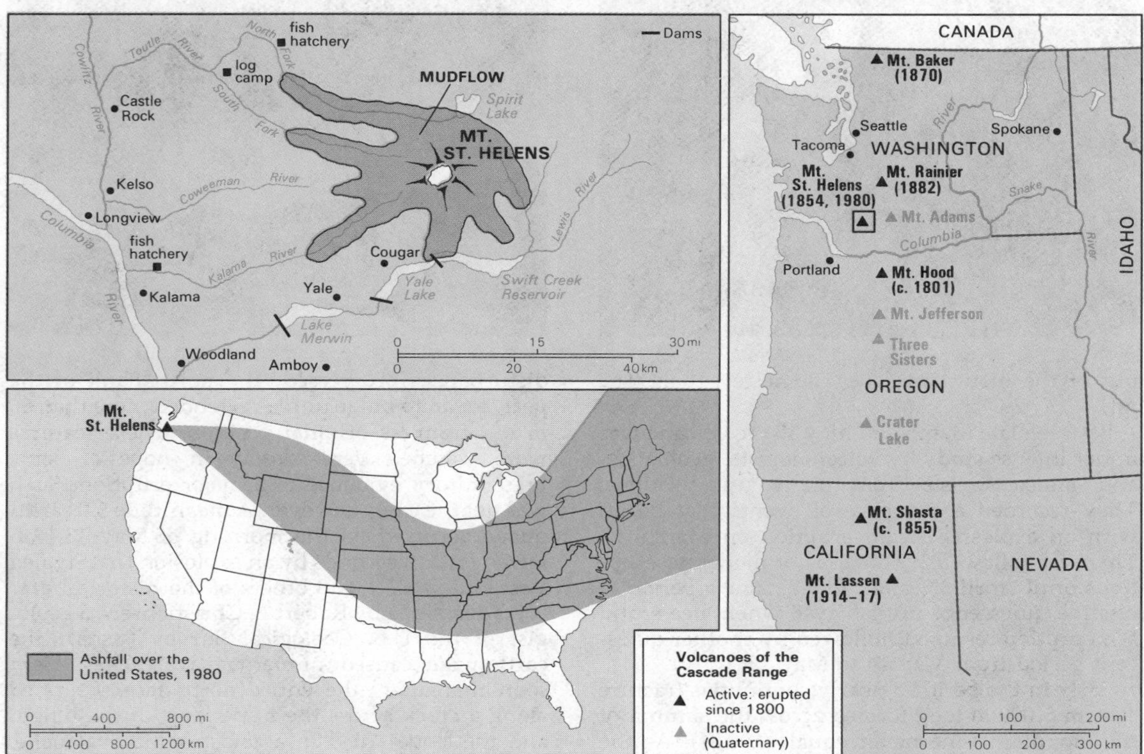

(TOP) WERTH © LONGVIEW DAILY NEWS—WOODFIN CAMP; (BOTTOM) PHOTOS, WIDE WORLD

Mt. St. Helens's blast of May 18 set nearby rivers steaming from hot debris hurled through the air (top) and flattened thousands of acres of timber (right). At Richland, Washington, 210 kilometres (130 miles) away, a boiling cloud of volcanic ash filled the sky (far right).

mit of the mountain (one kilometre equals 0.62 mi).

Between late March and May 18 the volcano was under intense study by volcanologists, geologists, and meteorologists from many organizations. They recorded a sequence of events that began with an explosive steam eruption on March 27. This was followed by a series of moderate eruptions until April 23, after which came a period of relative quiescence until May 8 when steam and ash eruption resumed, followed by another quiescent period from May 14 to May 18.

Early in the period a nearly continuous fracture system 5,000 m long formed across the summit of the mountain (one meter equals 3.28 ft). As the disturbances progressed, the north flank of the peak began to bulge until it extended more than 80 m out from its original position. These features were watched very closely in hope of some premonitory evidence of a major eruption. Such was not the case, however. A magnitude 5.0 earthquake occurred on the morning of May 18, followed within seconds by an explosion that rivaled Vesuvius, Pelée, and others of the historical era.

As described by Robert L. Christiansen, a geologist of the U.S. Geological Survey (USGS), the earthquake caused numerous avalanches. Very soon thereafter, the entire north face separated along a crack across the upper part of the bulge, and the slope failed in a catastrophic avalanche.

Within seconds a large lateral air blast carrying ash and stony fragments in a devastating wave overtook the avalanche. The blast expanded over a width of 30 km east to west and outward more than 20 km from the summit. Everything in a path ten kilometres wide was destroyed, and beyond this the forest was flattened for several kilometres on each side.

The first of four components of the eruption was the directed blast, which swept over ridges and flowed down valleys, depositing significant quantities of ash. Although it was hot, it did not char fallen or buried trees. The second component was a combined pyroclastic flow and landslide that carried the remnants of the north flank uplift across the lower slopes and about 27 km down the Toutle River valley, burying it to depths as great as 55 m. Large quantities of mud, logs, and other debris clogged several valleys around Mt. St. Helens and rendered some shipping lanes impassible in the Columbia River. The third component was a pyroclastic flow of pumice, funneled northward through the breach formed by the destruction of the north flank bulge. This flow dammed the outlet of Spirit Lake, trapping a large quantity of water. Before the lateral blast had reached its full extension, the fourth component, a vertical column, began to rise so rapidly that within ten minutes it had reached an altitude of more than 6,000 m. This column continued for nine hours, produced major ash falls as far east as central Montana, and eventually circled the globe with ash that caused hazy skies and red sunsets. The combination of these events literally blew the top off of the mountain and formed an amphitheatre 1.5 × 3 km in extent where the volcanic cone had been.

After a period of decreasing activity a second major eruption occurred on May 25. Following that date the eruptive activity continued but at a decreased level and, as expected, a volcanic dome formed in the crater due to magmatic action. Although the prognosis for future activity was varied and controversial, the historic evidence indicated that the active period for Mt. St. Helens was likely to continue for some time. As of early October, 34 persons including USGS geologist David A. Johnston, who was manning an outpost eight kilometres north-northwest of the mountain, were killed by the blast or resulting mud flows, and 32 persons were listed as missing. The damage was estimated to be in excess of $2 billion.

(RUTLAGE J. BRAZEE)

[212.D.4; 213.B]

HYDROLOGY

The most spectacular geologic event in the U.S. during 1980 was the May 18 eruption of Mt. St. Helens in southwestern Washington state (see *Geophysics,* above). Its major hydrologic effects were massive debris flows, pyroclastic mudflows, and flooding in the upper reaches of the Toutle River on the north, west, and east slopes of the volcano. Runoff from melted glaciers and snow and possibly some outflow from Spirit Lake caused widespread flooding in the Toutle and lower Cowlitz rivers. Massive volumes of sediment were transported during the flood on the Toutle River, which picked up thousands of logs and destroyed most of the local bridges. About 30 million cu m (25,000 ac-ft) of sediment moved into the lower Cowlitz River. Much of it was deposited, reducing channel capacity by about 85% and significantly increasing flood potential. Sediment that moved through the Cowlitz into the Columbia River blocked shipping lanes for several days.

The Council on Environmental Quality and the U.S. Department of State released a report titled "The Global 2000 Report to the President: Entering the 21st Century," which included a hydrologic forecast as well as projections of global population, availability and use of natural resources, and environmental trends. Many of the report findings were based on a projection of world population growth from 4,500,000,000 in 1980 to more than 6,000,000,000 in the year 2000. According to the forecast, the world's forested lands would continue to be depleted because of the conversion of forest to agricultural use and the demand for firewood and other wood products. In addition, deforestation would aggravate water shortages; intensify flooding, soil erosion, and siltation of reservoirs; and accelerate deterioration of water quality. Population growth would cause water demands to double from the 1971 level, and competition for water resources would intensify conflicts.

Evidence continued to accumulate that the acidity of atmospheric deposition, popularly known as "acid rain," was affecting lakes and streams in the northeastern U.S. and southeastern Canada. The acid-producing agents were sulfurous and nitrous oxides created by burning fossil fuels. Most of these gases were entering the air over large popu-

UPI

State highway official inspects damage to the Greenville overpass near Livermore, California, where a moderately severe earthquake on January 24 dropped the left part of the roadbed more than a foot.

lation centres, and indeed acidity was highest in samples of rain from Pennsylvania and New York. Many lakes in the Adirondacks were so acid that fish could not spawn. The U.S. and Canadian governments were combining efforts to measure the extent of acid precipitation, locate sources of acid-producing materials, and gain a better understanding of their effects.

A record-breaking summer heat wave in 1980 caused high rates of water loss to the atmosphere in much of the midcontinental and southeastern U.S. High flows from spring rains and high groundwater levels, however, prevented streamflow from reaching record lows except in parts of northern Minnesota and eastern North Carolina. Water was rationed in much of the country during the heat wave, primarily because of inadequate distribution rather than inadequate supplies.

U.S. hydrologists expressed growing concern about the future availability and quality of groundwater as a source of drinking water. Increasing evidence showed that this resource, once considered pollutant-free, was locally contaminated nationwide and that contamination at some sites posed a major health threat. The news media also focused on this concern with reports on groundwater contamination from hazardous wastes and with nationwide coverage of the Love Canal problem in New York (*see* ENVIRONMENT: *Industrial Wastes*). (JOHN E. MOORE)

[222.A.2.b; 222.D]

METEOROLOGY

Among activities of general meteorological interest during 1980 were continuing efforts to extend the time range of weather forecasts; refinements in techniques for finding, tracking, and warning of tornadoes, hurricanes, and severe local storms; and renewed field testing of designs for rainmaking and other weather modification. Although progress was reported in some sectors, there were no major breakthroughs.

Hurricane Allen, the first Atlantic tropical storm in the 1980 series, was one of the most violent ever reported. Loss of life from the August storm after it reached the U.S. was minimal because efficient warning services permitted evacuation and precautionary property protection. In Jamaica, Haiti, and elsewhere in the West Indies where advance warnings were incomplete and communication often poor, losses were very heavy. Total casualties were uncertain because of bodies hidden in mud slides and debris, but early counts of the dead approached 300.

Prolonged drought and oppressive hot weather plagued large regions of the U.S. during the summer. Although anomalies in rainfall and temperature occur every year somewhere on the Earth, the Gulf states, Midwest, and much of the eastern U.S. experienced many successive weeks between June and September during which rainfall was slight or even entirely absent. In parts of Texas, Oklahoma, and other states the daily maximum temperature exceeded 38° C (100° F) for longer than a month and in many places for longer than two months. Many official temperature records were broken. Damage to crops and related business and industry was disastrous, and effects on international markets and world economy were decisive in many significant plans and programs. Across the Atlantic the persistent drought in fringe areas of the Sahara Desert continued, causing thousands of starvation casualties among native tribes that tried to subsist on marginal rainfall.

Traditionally climate has been viewed as rather stable and unchanging during recent centuries. Climatology was mostly a descriptive science and tended to express its subject in terms of averages. Efforts by research experts some 40 years earlier to develop a dynamic climatology languished. But recent findings and growing concern about changes, either in progress or impending, in the vital constituents of the atmosphere have renewed emphasis on studies of the stratosphere and its protective ozone layer; of the increase in chlorofluorocarbons and other industrial contaminants, some of which may persist 30 years or more in the upper layers of the atmosphere; and of the increase in carbon dioxide produced by worldwide combustion of fuels. To encourage and support major new programs in climatological research the U.N. World Meteorological Organization and leading research institutions in the U.S. and U.S.S.R. organized special working groups in 1980.

The volcanic eruptions of Mt. St. Helens in Washington state during the spring and summer aroused apprehension over their possible influence on climate and weather. Remembering the historic "year without a summer," which apparently resulted from a worldwide blanket of contaminants thrown into the atmosphere by volcanic explosions in the East Indies and Southeast Asia in 1813–16, public alarm arose after the Mt. St. Helens eruption in May and subsequent drought in the U.S. Abnormal weather elsewhere added to the alarm. But geophysicists explained that no lasting effects on weather were to be expected. Only a temporary local increase in clouds and rainfall downwind from the volcano were seen.

(F. W. REICHELDERFER)

[224.B.2.c.ii; 224.B.3.b; 224.C.1.c; 224.D.2.c.iii]

California youngsters begin cleanup efforts in the wake of storms, mud slides, and flooding during mid-February that claimed several lives and caused extensive property damage in a four-county region.

UPI

OCEANOGRAPHY

From March to June of 1980 an 18-m (60-ft) double-hulled sailing canoe, a replica of the sailing canoes believed to have been used by Polynesian navigators during ancient transpacific migrations, traveled the 4,000 km (2,500 mi) from Hawaii to Tahiti and back again. A unique feature of this voyage was the employment of two methods of navigation. One method was the traditional one: a Hawaiian navigator decided on a course to be steered and recorded his estimates of the canoe's position. The other method was very modern: the canoe carried a location system tracked by satellite.

This system had been developed originally to track freely drifting buoys as they are carried by ocean currents. A number of buoys were tracked in this manner over long distances in the past several years. In 1979 and 1980 several clusters of buoys were deployed in the tropics. One such cluster, initially placed 600 km (370 mi) north of the Equator near Fanning Island in the Pacific, drifted eastward in the equatorial countercurrent for more than 4,000 km (13,000 mi); some buoys in the cluster finally left the current toward the north at about the longitude of the tip of Baja California. These results showed that the equatorial countercurrent, a narrow eastward flow only a few hundred kilometres wide and sandwiched between generally west-flowing water, is in fact a single unbroken current.

The equatorial countercurrent and tropical circulation in general are of particular interest because of the manner in which the tropical ocean and atmosphere interact to create large-scale changes in ocean and atmospheric climate. The buoy-tracking experiment was a part of a much larger observational study of tropical circulation that continued during 1980. This study involved deployment of moored current meters and temperature recorders in equatorial waters and measurement of near-surface temperatures by means of expendable sensors that are dropped from an aircraft and then return data via a thin copper wire as they fall. It also made use of island tide gauges, which can measure a small nontidal rise and fall that serves as a simple yet useful indicator of the strength of tropical ocean currents.

For a number of years during the International Decade of Ocean Exploration (1970–1980), investigators tracked freely drifting floats in the northwestern Atlantic Ocean by listening to acoustic beacons attached to each float. The floats are ballasted to drift at depths of 1,000–2,000 m (3,300–6,600 ft), and the underwater sound emitted by their beacons may be heard several thousand kilometres away. During the year tracks of these floats were combined with traditional measurements of temperature and salinity to demonstrate the existence of a new feature of deep ocean circulation. One of the floats had become trapped in a small but rapidly rotating lens of subsurface water. Measurements of the temperature, salinity, and oxygen content of this lens revealed that it must have originated many thousands of kilometres away in the eastern Atlantic. A number of similar features were subsequently identified. If they prove commonplace in the deep sea, they may be an important carrier of heat, nutrients, dissolved substances, and pollutants from one place in the ocean to another. An intriguing question was why these small features are not torn apart by ocean currents of large scale.

The passenger ship "Titanic," which sank off Cape Race, Newfoundland, on April 15, 1912, after colliding with an iceberg, was the object of an undersea search carried out during the summer of 1980. Recent developments in high-resolution undersea acoustic imaging, whereby pictures of underwater structures are formed using beams of sound rather than of light, made the search feasible. The complex relief of the seafloor in this region, combined with weather that worsened toward the end of the ship time available, kept the expedition from definitive success. At one point sonar images of the proper dimensions were obtained (the "Titanic" was 269 m, or 883 ft, long), but they turned out to be a submarine ledge rather than the wreck. Further studies were planned for 1981; promising sonar images would be followed up with magnetometer lowerings (to distinguish the steel hull from rock formations) and finally camera lowerings.

The study of the ocean by remote sensing from satellites continued to occupy researchers during 1980. Of special importance were continuing efforts to combine traditional hydrographic measurements of subsurface temperature and salinity with very recent satellite altimeter measurements of the slope of the sea surface in order to provide a composite picture of ocean circulation. The traditional measurements have been able to show how water at one depth moved relative to that at another but could not provide the actual flow. Sea level slope, on the other hand, responds primarily to near-surface flows. The combination thus allows deep flows to be determined relative to satellite-measured surface flows, but only if the two kinds of measurements are properly merged. Techniques originally developed by seismologists for using seismograms to study the interior of the Earth turned out to be applicable to this problem as well. The resulting progress constitutes an important step toward satellite monitoring of the global ocean circulation.

Another important achievement was progress in eliminating atmospheric effects from satellite images of the ocean. Such atmospheric features as high clouds are clearly not oceanic, but such others as near-surface layers of moist air may be mistaken for oceanic features. Their removal is essential for proper imagery interpretation. Following application of recently developed methods for subtracting such atmospheric effects, images from the Nimbus 7 coastal zone colour scanner showed very subtle variations in water colour. These were believed to reflect variations in the concentration of phytoplankton and thus to have the potential of making possible oceanwide surveys of this fundamental food source for all higher forms of life in the sea.

(MYRL C. HENDERSHOTT)

[223.A and C; 738.B; 738.C.3.d]

See also Disasters; Energy; Life Sciences; Mining and Quarrying; Space Exploration; Speleology.

Eastern European Literature: *see* Literature

Eastern Non-Chalcedonian Churches: *see* Religion

Eastern Orthodox Churches: *see* Religion

Ecology: *see* Environment; Life Sciences

Economy, World

During 1980 the principal features of the world economy were a slowdown in the tempo of economic growth, a strengthening of inflationary pressures, and some instability in foreign exchange markets. In general the response of governments was to tighten fiscal and monetary policies in an attempt to promote price stability. Nevertheless, in late 1980 prices were still rising at unacceptably high rates in most countries, and there were no suggestions of an early and significant upturn in the tempo of economic activity. Taking the year as a whole, the volume of gross national product (GNP) for the developed non-Communist nations was estimated to have risen by 1–2%, compared with gains of 3.4% in 1979 and 3.9% in 1978. Almost every country seemed to do worse than in 1979; as usual, Japan greatly outperformed the field with a growth of about 5%, whereas the United Kingdom—subject to a stiff dose of radical monetarism—was heading for a drop in GNP of about 2.5%. As discussed in the individual country sections, the United States did somewhat better than was expected at the start of the year, although the estimated outcome of a 0.5% decline compared unfavourably with the 2.3% gain of the previous year.

The main deflationary influences were the rapid rise in oil prices during much of 1979 and a general movement toward tighter fiscal and monetary policies. To a large extent the second was a direct consequence of the first; higher oil prices led to an acceleration in inflation by late 1979, which gave rise to more restrictive policies in most countries. Therefore, although economic activity was remarkably buoyant at the start of the year, higher energy costs coupled with deflationary measures had an increasingly powerful impact from the first quarter onward. Inflation, however, continued on a steady upward curve, forcing some governments to take further deflationary steps. Thus, the U.S. administration announced a wide range of tough monetary measures in March, the effect of which was to push up the federal funds rate (the rate banks charge each other for overnight loans) to a peak of 20% in April. Similarly, Japan's discount rate was increased on two occasions in February/March by a total of 2.75%, and even in West Germany, where the inflation rate was only 6% in the spring, interest rates were raised in February and again in May.

Not surprisingly, economic growth during the second quarter fell well below the level of the preceding three months in most of the large developed countries in the Organization for Economic Cooperation and Development (OECD). By the middle of the year, however, inflationary pressures were also exhibiting some tentative signs of leveling out. Thus, in the U.K. the annual increase in retail prices fell from 21.8% in April to 16.9% in July, and, partly in response to this, the Bank of England announced a 1% drop in the minimum lending rate. This, however, had little effect on the level of economic activity since at 16% the rate was judged to be a major obstacle to growth. Japanese wholesale prices in the late summer also indicated a potential change in the rising trend, which was followed by a 1% drop (to 8%) in the discount rate. There was also some relaxation in U.S. monetary policy in the summer (in July the Federal Reserve Board's discount rate, the rate it charges its member banks, stood at 10%, as against 13% in April), although this was more of a reaction to the unduly harsh package adopted in March than to a noticeable leveling out of inflation.

Table I. Real Changes in Gross National Products of Selected OECD Countries

% change, seasonally adjusted at annual rates

Country	Average 1966–67 to 1976–77	Change from previous year 1978	1979	1980*
Canada	4.7	3.4	2.9	0.25
France	4.6	3.3	3.2	2.00
Germany, West	3.6	3.5	4.4	2.00
Italy	3.9	2.6	5.0	3.50
Japan	7.8	6.0	5.9	5.50
United Kingdom	2.1	3.5	1.7	−2.25
United States	2.8	4.4	2.3	−1.00
Total major countries	4.1	4.2	3.5	1.00
Australia	4.6	1.7	4.6	2.50
Austria	4.6	1.5	2.2	1.75
Belgium	4.5	2.5	3.3	1.50
Denmark	3.6	1.3	3.5	−0.50
Finland	4.4	1.4	6.5	6.00
Greece	6.0	6.2	3.8	1.00
Ireland	4.3	6.1	3.1	1.25
Netherlands, The	4.4	2.4	2.6	0.25
New Zealand	2.9	−1.9	−0.4	1.00
Norway	4.6	3.3	3.1	4.25
Spain	3.2	2.5	1.0	1.25
Sweden	2.4	2.4	3.8	3.00
Switzerland	2.1	0.2	0.8	1.00
Total OECD countries	4.3	3.9	4.6	−0.25

*Estimate.
Source: Adapted from OECD, *Economic Outlook*, July 1980.

CHART 1

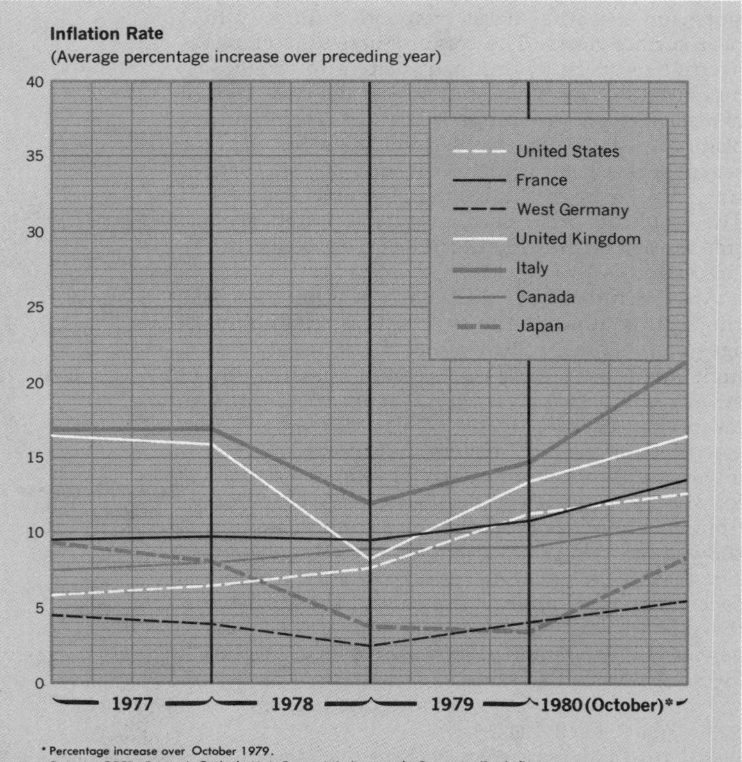

* Percentage increase over October 1979.
Sources: OECD, *Economic Outlook*, *Main Economic Indicators*; the *Economist*, *Key Indicators*.

FABIAN—SYGMA

The leaders of Japan, Canada, West Germany, France, the United States, Great Britain, and Italy held an economic summit conference in Venice, Italy, June 22–23.

U.S. monetary policy assumed a somewhat more restrictive stance in the autumn with the discount rate rising to 12% after the presidential election. This, however, was the exception rather than the rule worldwide because most countries refrained from tightening their monetary policies. In fact, in the U.K. there was a further drop of 2% in the minimum lending rate (to 14%) in November although this was accompanied by fresh fiscal curbs.

On the basis of statistics available in late 1980, it seemed that inflation in the OECD area as a whole would be a couple of percentage points lower in the second half of the year than in the preceding six months. Nevertheless, the increase for the entire year promised to be approximately 13%, with the U.K. and Italy leading the field with about 17 and 25%, respectively, and West Germany and Japan bringing up the rear with rises of 5 and 8%, respectively. This was a generally unsatisfactory performance, one that was bought only at the expense of a reduction in growth and an increase in the level of unemployment. With the exception of Japan and West Germany, unemployment rates rose rapidly in most countries, and in late 1980 the indications were that the year-end figure would exceed the 5.1% registered 12 months earlier.

The recession appeared to have had a strong influence on most components of domestic demand. The only exception to this seemed to have been government consumption, which was heading for a gain of about 2% in volume terms, the same as in the previous year. This is a telling comment on the general inability of governments to cut back their vast bureaucracies built up in recent years. Consumer expenditure, affected by pressures on wages, higher inflation, increased unemployment, and future uncertainties, suffered almost everywhere; the growth rate for the year was estimated at slightly more than 1%, which represented a substantial fall from the 3.5% gain achieved in the preceding year. Tough monetary policies and weak demand also took their toll on private (and public) investment; the OECD countries appeared to have recorded a fall of nearly 1%, compared with a gain of some 4% in 1979.

On the external front the volume growth of imports weakened almost everywhere under the impact of the recession, and the latest figures suggested that the gain for the whole year could be less than 1%, as against some 7% registered in 1979. Export growth, however, was only approximately 2% below the previous year's figure of 6.5%. Nevertheless, because of the massive increase in oil prices all Western countries with the exception of the U.K. faced a deterioration in their current account balances; France, West Germany, Japan, and Italy fared particularly badly, and in the U.S. the deficit of $800 million in 1979 seemed likely to rise to $8 billion during 1980. Taking the OECD area as a whole, the current account deficit was heading for $90 billion–$100 billion in 1980, approximately three times as large as in the previous year.

As far as exchange rates were concerned, sterling was the star performer with a rise of some 7% in its effective rate. In Japan there was a strong downward movement in the early part of the year, but as a result of a rapid improvement thereafter the rate was stronger in late 1980. The effective value of the U.S. dollar drifted downward throughout most of the year; by late 1980 it stood at about 90, compared with 93 in the opening months of the year.

Non-oil less developed countries suffered from both the rise in oil prices and the weakness in demand in developed nations in 1979 and 1980. In 1979 the aggregate growth of the gross domestic product (GDP) of those countries was 4.7%; the information in late 1980 suggested lower levels of activity coupled with an acceleration in inflation and larger external payments deficits. The financial position of oil-producing less developed countries improved as a result of the higher oil prices, although because of the sluggishness of world demand, political instability in Iran, and the Iran-Iraq war, the GDP of these nations was unlikely to have grown faster than the 2.9% registered in 1979.

NATIONAL ECONOMIC POLICIES

Developed Market Economies. UNITED STATES. The volatile and unpredictable nature of economic activity in the United States during 1980 foxed policymakers and economic forecasters alike. The previous year had closed on a surprisingly strong note when an unexpected consumer rally buoyed up the economy and postponed the recession that had been widely forecast since the summer. The slowdown in the opening quarter of 1980 signaled that the recession was imminent, and indeed the dramatic 10% crash in the real GNP during the second quarter confirmed the worst. A continuing decline though at a slower pace seemed inevitable for the remainder of 1980. However, no sooner had the economic forecasts been adjusted to take account of the second-quarter slump than a number of signs emerged suggesting that the recession might be over before it had hardly begun. These and subsequent signs were eventually confirmed by an astonishing 1.2% rebound by the real GNP in the third quarter. After that the economy displayed considerable resilience, with industrial production turning up, housing starting to recover, and consumer expenditure rising. All this led to expectations of 5–6% real GNP growth in the final quarter. Thus, the year as a whole was likely to show a marginal fall in the real GNP, confounding midyear estimates of a decline of 2–3%.

The erratic behaviour of the economy could be attributed to some extent to the shifting monetary policies of the authorities. During the year monetary policy assumed a tougher anti-inflation posture, and the revised targets of the Federal Reserve Board (Fed) for money supply growth during 1980 were unmistakably more restrictive than in the past. During the opening months of the year money and credit grew rapidly in response to worsening inflationary expectations, which encouraged borrowers to bring forward their credit demands. This appeared to apply to the business community as well as to consumers. To head off a possible new inflationary spiral, the Fed responded aggressively by raising the discount rates, by keeping credit tight, and by allowing the federal funds rate to rise by nearly 4% to more than 15%. Despite the further application of the monetary brakes, demand for credit remained high and inflation continued to point upward. The government then felt compelled to act, and Pres. Jimmy Carter proposed a five-point counterinflation program on March 14. Apart from a tighter fiscal policy, wage and price recommendations, and higher taxes on imported oil, it outlined a set of tough monetary measures. These included a 3% surcharge on the discount rate (for large borrowers), higher reserve

Table II. Percentage Changes in Consumer Prices in Selected OECD Countries

Country	Average 1961–70	Average 1971–76	1977	1978	1979	Latest month* 1980
Canada	2.7	7.4	8.0	9.0	9.1	10.7
France	4.0	9.0	9.4	9.1	10.8	13.6
Germany, West	2.7	5.9	3.7	2.7	4.1	5.5
Italy	3.9	12.2	17.0	12.1	14.8	21.7
Japan	5.8	11.1	8.1	3.8	3.6	8.4
United Kingdom	4.1	13.6	15.9	8.3	13.4	16.5
United States	2.8	6.6	6.5	7.7	11.3	12.7
Australia	2.5	10.8	12.3	7.9	9.1	10.7
Austria	3.6	7.3	5.5	3.6	3.7	7.3
Belgium	3.0	8.5	7.1	4.5	4.5	6.3
Denmark	5.9	9.2	11.1	10.0	9.6	9.3
Finland	5.0	12.1	12.2	7.8	7.5	12.3
Greece	2.1	12.5	12.1	12.6	19.0	24.5
Iceland	11.9	26.0	29.9	44.9	44.1	57.7
Ireland	4.8	14.0	13.6	7.6	13.3	18.8
Luxembourg	2.6	7.6	6.7	3.1	4.5	6.4
Netherlands, The	4.1	8.7	6.4	4.1	4.2	7.0
New Zealand	3.8	11.3	14.3	12.0	13.8	17.9
Norway	4.5	8.5	9.1	8.1	4.8	11.4
Portugal	3.9	16.0	27.2	22.6	23.6	16.0
Spain	6.0	13.0	24.5	19.8	15.7	15.2
Sweden	4.0	8.3	11.4	10.0	7.2	12.0
Switzerland	3.3	6.7	1.3	1.1	3.6	4.2
Turkey	5.9	18.4	26.0	61.9	63.5	N/A
Total OECD countries	3.4	8.6	8.7	7.7	9.9	12.4

*Twelve-month rate of change.
Sources: OECD, *Economic Outlook*, July 1980; OECD, *Main Economic Indicators*; The Economist, *Key Indicators*.

CHART 2

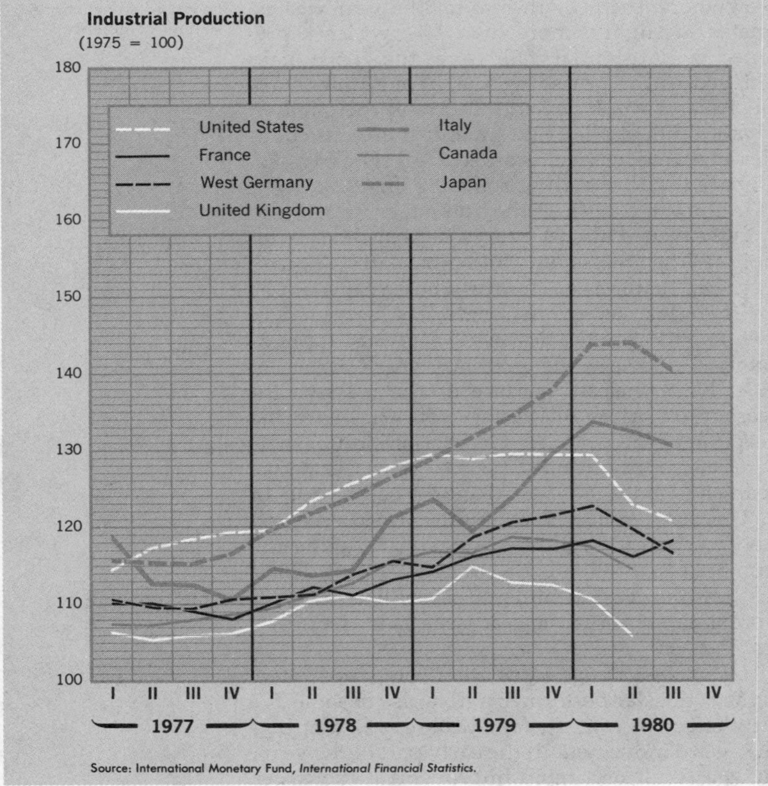

Source: International Monetary Fund, *International Financial Statistics*.

Table III. Total Employment in Selected Countries
(1975=100)

Country	1976	1977	1978	1979	1980 First quarter	1980 Second quarter
Australia	101	102	102	104	105	106
Canada	102	104	107	112	110	115
France	99	99	97	96	96	96
Germany, West	99	99	100	101	101	101
Italy	101	102	102	103	103	104
Japan	101	102	104	105	105	107
Sweden	101	101	101	103	103	...
United Kingdom	99	100	100	100	99	...
United States	103	107	111	114	114	114

Source: OECD, *Main Economic Indicators.*

requirements for banks, and special deposit requirements for certain types of credit such as credit cards, personal loans, and overdrafts. Interest rates raced up immediately after these measures, and by April both the prime rate (charged by banks to their best customers) and the federal funds rate reached a peak of 20%.

With hindsight it is clear that this "spring offensive" was an overkill because the economy was on the downswing anyway. The severity of the credit squeeze coupled with the punitive interest rates shook business and consumer confidence and could have been partly responsible for the rapid evaporation of demand that caused the record fall in activity rates during the spring and summer. As the justification for the tight credit squeeze ended, the Fed moved to ease the credit restrictions and reduced the federal funds rate to enable interest rates to fall. Fall they did with a vengeance. Within a space of three months the prime rate fell by 9 points to 11%, and the federal funds rate was more than halved to 9%. (*See* Special Report.)

Coincidental with the fall in interest rates, an economic upswing began, accompanied by a steep rise in the money supply. Although there was not a parallel movement in the rate of inflation, the underlying rate was still uncomfortably high for that stage of the recovery cycle and remained highly vulnerable to an acceleration in activity. Judging that a quick action now could nip in the bud the latest monetary surge, the Fed reverted to a more restrictive posture and engineered a rise in interest rates. Yet the monetary aggregates failed to respond and inflation remained menacingly high, perhaps suggesting that the short, sharp experience of the spring provided only a very temporary correction.

In order to restore credibility to its anti-inflation policy, at the risk of a confrontation with the president in the crucial period before the elections, the Fed persevered with its tight policy, causing interest rates to edge higher still. Once the elections were out of the way, it moved forward aggressively, raising the discount rate to 12%, and reimposed a 2% surcharge on large borrowers. The federal funds rate reached 17¾%, and the commercial banks in a series of moves raised their prime rates to 18½%. This fueled speculation that the 20% prime rates experienced in the spring could be equaled or even surpassed, and the prime rate did, in fact, reach a record 21½% in December. Thus, in a space of fewer than nine months, the emphasis again shifted to a tight-money policy at the expense of weakening economic growth; meanwhile, the interest rates rode an amazing roller coaster.

The tight monetary policy was by and large accompanied by a mildly restrictive fiscal policy. The budget for the fiscal year 1980 (from October 1979 to October 1980) envisioned a deficit of $29 billion. This was seen as a natural progression toward a balanced budget in fiscal 1981, which was one of the early objectives of President Carter. However, as higher inflation and the economic slowdown caused increases in government spending (higher unemployment benefit payments, for instance), the actual deficit seemed likely to exceed $60 billion. But even at that level, because of the fiscal drag caused by inflation, the additional deficit was unlikely to have totally neutralized the restrictive influence. Fiscal 1981 seemed to be heading the same way. In January 1980 the proposed deficit was $15 billion, but by July it had risen to $30 billion and, just before the fiscal year started, it stood at $45 billion.

As a consequence of the economic slowdown, the unemployment situation deteriorated rapidly. On a seasonally adjusted basis it stood at just over six million in December 1979. During the spring it hovered between 6.3 million and 6.4 million before dramatically rising to 7.2 million in April and to more than 8 million the following month. Such a rapid increase left economists searching for a credible explanation and the shell-shocked administration trying to invent a noninflationary, quick-acting fiscal stimulus. Fortunately, as the economy miraculously pulled out of the free fall of the spring, unemployment plateaued at about 8.1 million or 7.6% of the labour force. With economic activity relatively buoyant in the closing months of the year, a significant deterioration was considered unlikely.

After all the heat generated by the counterinflationary policies, it would have been astonishing if no progress was made toward controlling inflation. The previous year had closed with strong inflationary pressures. The 12-month increase of 13.3% in December 1979 represented the highest price rise since the removal of World War II controls in 1946. In each of the first three months of 1980 consumer prices rose by 1.4%, equivalent to an annual rate of 18%. Most of this resulted from high increases in energy prices (mainly oil) and in housing prices. A moderation was much in evidence during the second quarter, with monthly increases of just over 1%. Consumer goods prices (in particular automobiles as the rebates were removed) and capital equipment goods prices did most of the rising in the second quarter. At 7% on an annual basis, the rate of increase continued to moderate during the third quarter. Had it not been for a drought that adversely affected food prices in the summer, the improvement could have been better still. During the closing months of the year, however, the inflation rate leaped up again. Once the latest upsurge caused by high food prices and high interest rates worked its way through the economy, the downward drift was likely to restart early in 1981.

Some of the gains seen in the current account during 1979 were eroded during the year under review. Weak overseas demand and the improvement in the external value of the dollar suppressed export volumes. Imports, on the other hand, rose rapidly in value terms, reflecting the higher oil prices. However, energy conservation measures together with the deceleration of the domestic economy reduced the demand for imported oil and other imports. Such volume reductions were instrumental in containing the rise in the balance of trade deficit to about $36 billion ($29 billion in 1979).

UNITED KINGDOM. The year 1980 was the first full one subject to the radical monetarist policies of the government of Prime Minister Margaret Thatcher. It was a year during which public expenditure was to be cut heavily but was not; a period in which monetary growth was to be restrained but remained out of control; and a year in which industry was expected to benefit from a diversion of resources from the public to the private sector but instead recorded a decline of some 6–7% in output. It was also a year in which unemployment rose to unprecedented levels and in which many observers began to question not only the government's interpretation of the monetarist approach but also some of the basic tenets of the policy itself. As a result the year ended on a note of gloom and uncertainty; gloom because of the steadily deepening recession, uncertainty because of the apparent absence of any coherent strategy to retrieve the situation.

CHART 3

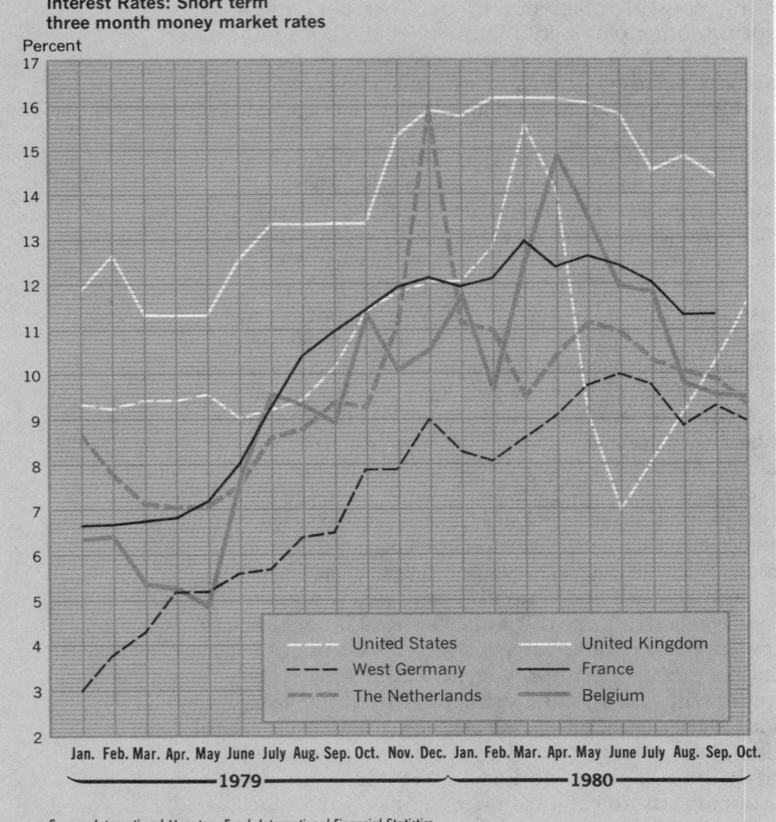

Source: International Monetary Fund, *International Financial Statistics*.

As in 1979 the principal thrust of official policy was a reduction in public expenditure and a slowdown in the rate of monetary growth coupled with a reduction in the tax burden on the private sector. As in 1979 these objectives were not achieved, but, unlike 1979, the argument that progress was frustrated by the legacy of the previous government was no longer a credible position. Despite a very high Bank of England minimum lending rate of 17% and an increasingly sluggish tempo of economic growth, the money supply grew considerably in excess of official targets during the early months of the year. The public sector borrowing requirement also remained high, and this led the chancellor of the Exchequer to announce further reductions in government spending and the continuation of the high interest rate policy in his March budget. By the middle of the year, however, the strategy was seen to be an almost total failure because of the inability to control spending and the effect of the deepening recession on tax revenues and social security payments. Thus, government borrowing continued at a high level, and the growth in the money supply was roughly double the official target of 7–11%. In the meantime, however, the high minimum lending rate was beginning to have an increasingly serious effect on industry. It underpinned the already overvalued sterling, which, together with the high level of domestic inflation, had a damaging effect on export competitiveness. This, in turn, led to a deterioration in industry's financial position, and the problems were then further aggravated by the high cost of borrowing.

At the same time the level of economic activity was beginning to suffer from a growing weakness in domestic consumption. This was partly the result of the inevitable layoffs caused by the slump in exports. However, another important reason was the strength of imports, also attributable to the strong pound, as well as the government's failure to bring about a redistribution of resources in favour of the private sector. Thus, although the March budget featured a range of income-tax concessions, the effect was largely offset by increases in indirect taxation. By the middle of the year, therefore, the economy was characterized by a combination of very high interest rates and a monetary growth that was out of control, a depressed level of demand both at home and abroad, a steadily falling industrial output, a growing number of bankruptcies, and a rapid rise in unemployment. In the second quarter of the year industrial output had declined nearly 8% from the same period of 1979; gross domestic product fell 2%, and the unemployment rate in June rose to 6.4%, compared with 5% 12 months earlier.

The government's reaction to this situation was to offer the same prescription as before on the grounds that, unpleasant as it might be in the short term, the policy could not be relaxed until there was evidence of a slowdown in monetary growth. As a result the British economy continued on a downward spiral during the third quarter of the year without any appreciable slowdown in the growth of the money supply. By September industrial output had declined nearly 10% from a year earlier, the rate of unemployment was 7.8%, and the broadly defined money supply continued to rise.

By November, however, the authorities were forced to modify their position. This took the form of a new package of measures by the chancellor of the Exchequer. The main features of this were a reduction in the minimum lending rate from 16 to 14%, a substantial increase in direct taxation in the form of a rise in employees' National Insurance contributions, a further attempt to cut public spending to make up for the failures of the past, and an increase in taxes through higher levies on North Sea oil profits. Although this went some way toward industry's demands for a substantial reduction in the cost of borrowing, it could not be regarded as a change of strategy. In particular, it provided little hope for a significant upturn in the level of economic activity in the short term, and as the year drew to a close, it was clear that—whatever the benefits in the long run—government policies would ensure that 1981 would be another year of economic recession and rising unemployment.

The two areas in which it could be argued that the policy had had some positive effect were those of prices and wage settlements. The year had started with a strong inflationary bias with the result that retail price inflation rose from 18.4% in January to 21.9% by May. However, from then on the trend began to change, and by October the 12-month increase was back to 15.4%. The government presented this development as a testimonial for its monetarist policy, although others argued that it was simply the traditional response to falling commodity prices and a severe economic recession. Achievements on the earnings front at the end of 1980 were more difficult to quantify. Up until June, mainly because of the large wage settlements conceded earlier, the index of average earnings was rising at an annual rate of about 21%. In July, however, the rate declined to about 17%; the August figure pointed to a further loss of buoyancy. Coupled with the latest settlements announced but not yet reflected in the figures, it suggested that by late autumn the trend of wage inflation was on a downward trend.

In the external sector attention was focused on sterling, which remained strong throughout the year. In fact, underpinned by North Sea oil and high interest rates, the exchange rate was on a generally and, at times, rapidly rising curve; the weighted effective rate rose from 70.3 in December 1979 to 77.8 by the end of November 1980. Similarly, the rate against the dollar, which averaged $2.229 in December 1979, was fluctuating at around the $2.35 mark 12 months later. One other reason for the strength of sterling was the improvement in the external payments balance. Although the higher exchange rate had a damaging effect on Britain's export effort, this was offset by the benefit from the North Sea and the effect of the slump on imports. As a result, during the first half of the year the trade deficit amounted to only £933 million, compared with £2,127 million in the corresponding period of 1979. During the third quarter the trade accounts yielded a surplus, of £693 million, for the first time in several years. Some of this improvement was offset by a reduction in Britain's traditional invisibles surplus, largely on account of an outflow of North Sea oil profits. Nevertheless, the current account for the first nine months of 1980 yielded a surplus of £688 million, compared with a deficit of £1,229 million in the first three quarters of the preceding year.

Japan. During most of 1980 the Japanese economy recorded satisfactory growth, and by the late autumn it was expected that the GDP for the whole year would register a volume gain of some 4.5%. Although this was not quite up to the 5.9% improvement recorded in 1979, once again it was expected to top the achievements of most comparable OECD countries. During 1980 the principal concern of the authorities was not so much the tempo of economic growth as the trend of prices, the external position of the yen, and the external payments balance. This situation required fine tuning rather than any dramatic new policy initiatives, an approach that was also justified by considerable political uncertainty that accompanied a change of government.

Halfway through 1979 the stance of official policy shifted in favour of combating inflation rather than boosting growth. Nevertheless, the tempo of economic activity remained firm in the opening months of 1980, with GDP recording an annual gain of 7.6% during January–March. During this period, however, there was also a notable weakening in the external value of the yen, largely as a result of the heavy external deficit recorded in 1979 and Japan's low interest rates relative to those of the U.S., the U.K., and other major OECD countries. Although this provided a strong boost to volume exports, it also had an adverse effect on the cost of imported raw materials, which play a larger than average role in Japanese domestic price indexes. Aggravated by a rise of approximately 50% in gas and electricity charges, wholesale prices in April were 24% higher than they had been 12 months previously, whereas in December 1979 prices had risen only 17.5% above the December 1978 rate.

This acceleration came about despite a fairly restrictive budget adopted for the 1980 fiscal year. It provided for only a 10.3% rise in general expenditures (the lowest figure for 20 years) and a decrease in the real value of public works-related spending. Not surprisingly, therefore, the government felt obliged to take some further measures; it raised the discount rate by 1% in February and by another 1.75% to 9% in March and introduced a number of measures designed to restrict the expansion of credit.

The package was conceived as both an anti-inflationary and yen-boosting scheme and was accompanied by a $5 billion "swap" arrangement with the U.S. Treasury to provide some support for the yen if that proved necessary. Combined with a subsequent decline in U.S. interest rates, the scheme was more successful in bolstering the currency than in cutting back the rate of inflation. In fact, from April onward the yen gained rapidly, and by June it had made up for all the decline recorded since August 1979.

In the meantime, however, the government's

restrictive fiscal policy and a low wage award of about 7% were beginning to have a noticeable effect on the strength of both public demand and private consumption. This caused domestic demand to lose much of its previous buoyancy, and it was only the strong rise in the volume of exports, resulting from the weakness of the yen in the early part of the year, that ensured a gain in GDP of 2.5% (annual basis) during the April–June period. Despite the weakness of demand, consumer prices continued to advance at a rapid rate, with the annual increase moving from 5.5% in December 1979 to 7.2% in March 1980 and 8.3% three months later. Nevertheless, under the impact of the stronger yen, coupled with a weakening in the world price of some commodities and increasingly sluggish stock (inventory)-building activities, the trend of wholesale prices began to look healthier. Thus, between May and June the appropriate index rose by less than 1% for the first time in several months. There was a further improvement in July, which failed to record any increase, and although the subsequent month registered a gain of some 0.6%, on a 12-month basis the advance had declined to 14.8%.

Therefore, by the middle of the year the situation appeared to be significantly different from that faced in January. Economic growth was considerably weaker, the yen had regained its previous strength, and the outlook for inflation appeared to be getting better rather than worse. At the same time, the external payments situation, which was characterized by heavy deficits in the early months of the year, was improving rapidly under the impact of a better trade performance. Although there remained some doubt about the extent of the transformation in the underlying trend of the economy, the new Liberal-Democratic government—facing strong pressure from the business community—took some modestly expansionist measures in August and September. Toward the end of August the discount rate was cut by 1% to 8%. This, however, failed to satisfy business, and even some senior economic officials called for a further reduction. Nevertheless, the Bank of Japan expressed strong opposition to any further interest rate relaxation in the absence of more evidence that the underlying inflationary pressures were firmly under control. Under the circumstances the government settled for a somewhat vague program, expansionary in general intent but containing few specifically expansionary measures. The most tangible of these was the proposal to boost expenditures related to public works in the October–December quarter, as well as the promise of some measures to encourage the building of private houses. Much more vague were the undertakings to promote private investment and to pursue a "flexible" monetary policy.

The volume of exports was on a rising curve for most of the year, which not only boosted domestic economic growth but, together with the improvement in the exchange rate from the second quarter, contributed to a gradual improvement in the external payments situation. Thus, whereas the first five months of 1980 recorded an average monthly trade deficit of $840 million, the subsequent three months yielded an average monthly surplus of nearly $200 million. This modest improvement, however, could not do more than make a dent in the traditionally large invisibles deficit, with the result that in late 1980 the current account was still heading for a considerably larger negative balance than the $8,643,000,000 recorded in 1979. Furthermore, although exports continued to register strong volume increases, there were renewed fears of friction with the country's major trading partners over the extent of Japanese competition in sensitive areas such as electronics, steel, and automobiles. There were also some anxieties about the effect of the stronger yen and overseas competitiveness, although the government's view appeared to be that a rate of 215–225 yen against the U.S. dollar was about right in terms of export competitiveness as well as domestic price considerations.

WEST GERMANY. The main feature of the West German economy during 1980 was the surprising pace of the downturn in the second half of the year. The strong growth achieved in 1979 (GNP up by 4.5%) was carried into the first quarter of 1980, enabling output to surge to 5.6% above its level a year earlier. By the second quarter the increase over 1979 had plummeted to 1.6%, as demand weakened under the weight of the higher oil prices and the government's tight monetary policy. The downturn continued during the summer, with the economy registering a 1.5% fall from its first-half level. The year as a whole was not expected to show more than a 2% growth over 1979, less than half of the previous year's growth rate.

The pattern of industrial output reflected the overall economic developments quite closely. Buoyed by fairly full order books at the beginning of the year, industrial production surged ahead by 4.3%. The gains were widespread, although the automobile industry did not share in them. As demand weakened and new orders declined in the spring, so did industrial output—by no less than 3%. The second half of the year remained flat but would have declined further if it had not been for the surprising strength of business fixed investment demand. Given the lack of new orders with no prospect of an early recovery, it is not surprising that an economic institute's business climate index, which peaked in the third quarter of 1979 and was edging downward in the early months of 1980, suddenly plunged in the summer to depths not seen since mid-1974. The gloom of businessmen was mirrored by surveys of consumer intentions, which showed a distinct preference for savings at the expense of consumption.

The improvement in unemployment during 1979 also went into reverse during 1980. From a seasonal peak of one million unemployed in January, the number of people out of work declined until May to reach 767,000. The rate of improvement was slower than the policymakers had been hoping, however, and came to an abrupt end in June when the jobless rate went up, the first June rise in five years. By October it approached the 900,000 mark, confirming a labour shakeout in most sectors. A figure of one million by the winter appeared to be inescapable as those who had recently lost their jobs joined new entrants into the labour force in search of the rapidly dwindling vacancies.

Encouraged by the previous year's remarkable achievement in holding inflation at about 4%, the authorities set a target of 4.5% for 1980. Under the impact of higher import prices (mainly oil), coupled with a steady depreciation in the value of the Deutsche Mark (DM) against the dollar (and pound sterling), the inflation rate rose sharply early in the year to reach a level of 6% in May. The developing slack in the economy, coupled with the restrictive policies of the Bundesbank, ensured that the inflationary upsurge was short-lived. The monthly rises after the summer were comparatively small, enabling the 1980 average to be kept down to 5.5%. While this was a full percentage point above the target, the consistent downward trend meant that West Germany had brought its inflation under control from a peak rate of less than half the OECD average.

Unlike the achievement with inflation, the correction of the current account deficit proved to be more elusive. The sharply deteriorating terms of trade cut the trade balance so that it fell far short of the usual deficit on invisibles and transfer payments. Based on the performance of the first nine months, a current account deficit of at least DM 27 billion appeared certain. This was the second year in a row that West Germany had faced a large current account deficit, and it was partly responsible for the weakness of the currency.

The aim of the policymakers in West Germany during 1980 was to limit the impact of the oil price rises and strive for a stable fiscal and monetary framework in order to provide a sound base for noninflationary growth when the world pulled out of the current recession. With direct controls over prices, wages, imports, and subsidies having been ruled out, a tight monetary policy and a neutral fiscal stance were the instruments chosen to reinforce the market forces. Having gotten money supply under firm control toward the end of 1979, the Bundesbank signaled its determination in the fight against inflation by setting slightly lower targets for the growth of central money stock. While the authorities suspected that the strong demand for credit in the opening months and the accelerating inflation were both temporary features, they chose not to take any chances.

High interest rates in the U.S. were causing larger capital outflows from West Germany at a time when the outlook for the current account deficit was gloomy. The value of the mark was depreciating too, adding to the cost of imports. This, in turn, fueled the inflation rate. Therefore, the discount rate was raised to 7% (highest since 1974) alongside a 1.5% rise (to 8.5%) in the Lombard rate. By April the money supply growth rate was still not to the Bundesbank's liking, and another round of higher interest rates was introduced effective from May. The discount rate at 7.5% and the Lombard rate at 9.5% stood at ten-year highs. These measures were accompanied by a new development in West Germany, the lifting of restrictions to attract capital inflows. The Bundesbank's tight monetary stance and the downturn in the economy finally were effective by summer. Money supply growth decelerated sharply, and in the autumn it became clear that it was expanding below the lower end of the range and restricting the economy too much. Meanwhile, the Bundesbank eased its tight grip somewhat by sporadically injecting modest amounts of liquidity into the banking system. But the worsening balance of payments position kept the interest rates artificially high.

As the measures taken in 1978 and 1979 had the desired effect of reducing unemployment and propping up economic growth, the authorities judged it appropriate not to take further stimulatory measures during 1980. The volume of public consumption was planned to expand slightly less than the previous year. Similarly, the general government deficit was projected to show a small decrease. In spite of the weakness in demand during the second half of the year, with unemployment rising and elections looming in October, the government remained cautious and consistently argued that a few percentage points of growth foregone would be a worthwhile price to pay to ensure that inflation remained under control and equilibrium was restored to the balance of payments.

CHART 4

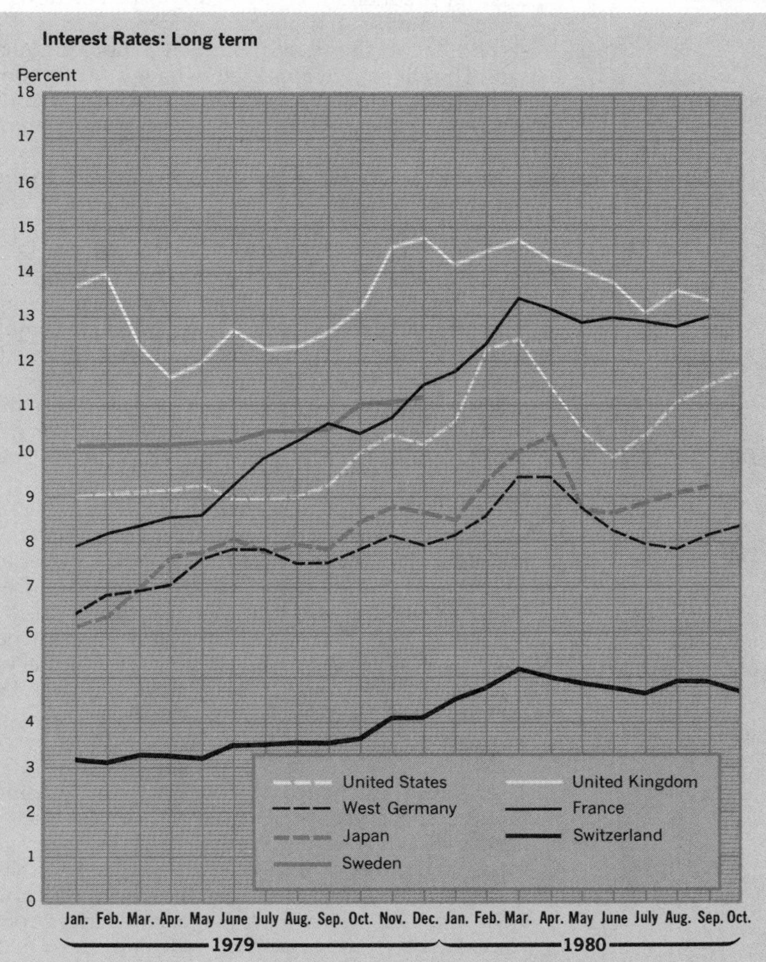

Source: International Monetary Fund, *International Financial Statistics*.

France. The French economy during 1980 showed a deviation from the fairly stable trend established during the previous three years. Although economic policy, broadly speaking, remained unchanged from the guidelines established by the Barre Plan in 1976, the weakening international economic environment and higher oil prices played a major role in the deceleration of the economy. Thanks to an unexpectedly rapid expansion in demand and output in the second half of 1979, the GDP for the year as a whole rose 3.25% in real terms. This buoyant trend was still much in evidence during the opening quarter of 1980. After March the growth rate slowed down, however, leading to a downward adjustment of the official growth rate forecasts from 2.5 to 2%. In comparison to the 3.5% average that had been achieved since 1976, this represented a significant deterioration, but viewed in the wider context of OECD economic performance as a whole, it was a fairly respectable achievement.

Underpinned by moderately strong consumer demand, which was to some extent a reaction to anticipated higher inflation in the second half of 1980, industrial production started the year on a fairly strong note. The momentum was lost during the second quarter, however, and the index of industrial production fell by nearly 3%. The downward production trend was in evidence during the second half of the year, though at a more gradual rate. The slowdown appeared to have affected consumer goods industries harder and earlier than it did those industries engaged in the production of semifinished goods.

Not surprisingly, given the growing slack in the economy, unemployment increased. During the spring the rate of increase for the seasonally adjusted number of unemployed was of the order of 18% on an annual basis; the number of those out of work rose to nearly 1.5 million in April. Following a better than expected seasonal improvement during the summer, the upward climb was resumed. Beyond the immediate recession, the French unemployment problem was likely to be more intractable than in most other OECD countries on account of the rapidly growing work force and improving trend of productivity.

As in other industrialized countries, accelerating inflation was the other dominant feature of the economy. The rate of increase was at its fastest in the opening quarter of the year as the oil price rises of 1979 were still working their way through the economy. This coincided with buoyant demand conditions. Consequently, during the January–April period consumer prices jumped at an annual rate of 17.2%. As the economy slowed down in the summer so did the inflation rate, registering a 12.5% increase during the quarter ended in July. The improvement continued into the closing months of the year, but, predictably, the rate of deceleration leveled out. Nevertheless, the average inflation for the year was likely to have been in the region of 13%, compared with 10.7% in 1979 and 9.3% the year before that. Higher oil prices continued to play havoc with the trade balance in 1980 as in 1979. Based on the performance of the first ten months, the trade deficit was heading toward Fr 55 billion (Fr 10 billion in 1979). More discouragingly, the traditional surplus on invisibles would have been too small to make up for it. The current account on this basis was likely to show a record deficit of Fr 25 billion.

During 1980 economic policy in France remained faithful to the strategy adopted in 1976. The aims of the 1976 Barre Plan were reduction in the inflation rate, reduction of state intervention (and hence budget deficits), encouragement of a more competitive industrial climate, and protection of the balance of payments position. Within this framework the counterinflation program was ostensibly given higher priority. To this end monetary policy was tightened appreciably during 1980. At first glance this might not appear to be the case because the money supply growth rate set for 1980 (11%) was identical to the previous year's target. However, as the actual expansion of the money supply at 13.5% overshot the 1979 target by a significant margin, the year opened with increased liquidity in the system. Thus, by implication, the unchanged targets were more restrictive. French monetary control techniques rely heavily on restrictions on the amount of bank credit rather than on movements of interest rates, and so steps were taken early in the year to eliminate the special status of credit for purchasing houses and to bring those loans under the overall credit growth ceiling of the banks. To curb the demand for consumer installment purchase credits, compulsory down payments were reintroduced. Partly as a result of these restrictive policies and partly because of higher interest rates abroad, French interest rates rose noticeably in the spring, when the call money rate reached 13.5% before it marginally and temporarily eased in the summer.

The fiscal stance of the government could be described as broadly neutral, but if the budgetary drift of the previous years continued, it was thought likely to have a mildly net expansionary effect. The 1980 budget envisaged an overall deficit of Fr 29.4 billion, which is larger than the previous year's budgeted deficit (Fr 15 billion) but less than the actual figure (Fr 37 billion). In line with this less restrictive fiscal policy, the official estimates for government borrowing envisaged an increase to approximately Fr 30 billion–Fr 32 billion, or 1.1% of the GDP, compared with 0.8% in 1979.

Thus, as a result of the recession, living standards registered a slight fall for the first time since 1976. Because the campaign for the spring 1981 presidential elections had begun, this represented a dilemma. The government tried to resolve it by publicly resisting the calls to reflate the economy. While Premier Raymond Barre adopted the slogan "severity works," in practice he adopted a pragmatic and flexible approach that tried to contain the inflationary forces and protect the balance of payments without plunging the economy into a severe recession.

Developing Countries. The widespread economic slowdown, accelerating inflation, and widening balance of payments deficits experienced by the industrialized world also affected the developing countries. In fact, the second oil crisis had a disproportionately adverse effect on some of the less developed countries, in particular those with a burgeoning industrial base. And yet the global growth rates achieved by the developing nations continued the trend in evidence since 1976 and exceeded those of the industrialized countries. According to World Bank estimates during 1979 (the latest year for which data were available), the former group achieved an expansion of 4.6% in real GNP, compared with a 3.3% growth registered by the latter. As the slowdown in the industrialized countries was part of an earlier trend, the deceleration was less marked than that seen in the developing economies. During 1980 the problems of the developing countries intensified, leading to weaker growth, higher inflation, and larger payment deficits.

PRODUCTION. The non-oil developing countries as a whole registered a 4.7% growth rate in 1979, representing a slight deceleration over the previous two years. Although this might appear to be a reasonably good performance given the difficult external environment, because of the rapid population expansion in those nations there was little improvement in per capita income levels. Apart from a recovery in agriculture from the extremely adverse weather conditions experienced in 1979 in southern Asia (mainly India), there was no significant improvement during 1980. The economies of these countries suffered from a sharp deterioration in their terms of trade. As a result of high oil prices and higher inflation in the industrialized world, the cost of their imports rose sharply without a corresponding increase in their exports. On the contrary, the world recession weakened the demand for their export products, which in turn depressed the prices.

Although the average growth figures were somewhat disappointing, at least one subgroup managed to achieve a fairly strong advance. This consisted of a dozen or so small-scale oil producers, which, thanks to export earnings from oil, showed a 7% increase in real GDP, compared with an average of 4% for the non-oil developing countries. Another subgroup among the low-income countries did particularly poorly and showed no growth at all. This subgroup was dominated by India where, because of adverse weather conditions, agriculture was badly affected and in turn held back total output. If India is excluded, the remaining countries achieved a small (about 2%) real growth, but this was insufficient to provide any per capita gain.

A similar pattern could be seen geographically. In Africa, where most of the low-income countries are located, growth was very weak. Similarly, Asia witnessed below-average growth rates, though if one excludes India a vast improvement in their aggregate performance emerges. The regions with the fastest growth record were the Middle East and Western Hemisphere. The former benefited from the rapid expansion of the neighbouring oil-producing countries, while the latter experienced a cyclical recovery in countries such as Argentina and Brazil.

Thanks to higher oil prices, the major oil-exporting countries improved their financial position. However, because of restrained demand policies and the static volume of oil production, the GDP of this group, at 2.9% in 1979, was barely above the previous year's level. Output in Iran was badly affected by the revolution during 1979 and was likely to have weakened further during 1980, partly as a consequence of the war with Iraq. By contrast, an improvement of demand conditions among the other major oil-exporting countries was likely to have resulted in a faster growth in the real GDP levels.

Table IV. Changes in Output in the Developing Countries, 1967–79

% changes in real GNP or GDP

Area	Annual average 1967–72	Change from preceding year 1975	1976	1977	1978	1979
Major oil exporting countries*	9.0	−0.3	12.1	6.2	2.7	2.9
Non-oil developing countries	5.9	4.4	5.5	5.1	5.0	4.7
Africa	5.0	2.9	4.9	1.7	2.7	2.6
Asia	4.9	6.5	6.2	6.8	6.9	3.5
Europe†	6.8	4.4	7.5	5.7	4.0	3.5
Middle East	6.4	8.8	1.8	6.8	6.3	7.9
Western Hemisphere	6.8	3.0	4.7	4.4	4.7	6.3

*Algeria, Indonesia, Iran, Iraq, Kuwait, Libya, Nigeria, Oman, Qatar, Saudi Arabia, United Arab Emirates, and Venezuela.
†Cyprus, Greece, Malta, Portugal, Romania, Turkey, and Yugoslavia.
Source: Adapted from the International Monetary Fund, *Annual Report 1980.*

Table V. Changes in Consumer Prices in the Developing Countries, 1967–79

In %

Area	Annual average 1967–72	Change from preceding year 1975	1976	1977	1978	1979
Major oil exporting countries*	8.0	18.8	16.6	15.4	9.7	11.0
Non-oil developing countries	9.3	27.9	24.0	27.0	23.4	29.1
Africa	4.5	15.1	13.2	16.9	14.8	20.3
Asia	5.5	10.6	0.1	7.8	5.9	10.3
Europe†	7.9	14.9	12.4	16.1	22.3	28.7
Middle East	3.9	23.4	20.7	18.7	21.0	26.6
Western Hemisphere	13.3	52.0	55.1	51.1	41.7	48.7

*Algeria, Indonesia, Iran, Iraq, Kuwait, Libya, Nigeria, Oman, Qatar, Saudi Arabia, United Arab Emirates, and Venezuela.
†Cyprus, Greece, Malta, Portugal, Romania, Turkey, and Yugoslavia.
Source: Adapted from the International Monetary Fund, *Annual Report* 1980.

CONSUMER PRICES. The non-oil developing countries, like the developed world, suffered from accelerating inflation. For the entire group the average inflation rate during 1979 was 30%, compared with 24% in 1978. In 1980 inflation seemed certain to have climbed to higher levels. The main culprits were, of course, the higher oil prices and costs of imports from the industrialized countries. According to the International Monetary Fund (IMF), the failure to tighten fiscal and monetary policies in order to offset the inflationary pressures was also partly to blame for the acceleration in the rate of inflation.

Although the three-year moderation in the inflation rate of the major oil-exporting countries came to an end in 1979, those nations succeeded in avoiding a rapid resurgence of inflation. The inflation rate was approximately one-third that of the non-oil group and only 1.3% above the previous year. Some relaxation in financial policies was in evidence during 1980, however. This could be taken as a sure sign of higher inflation rates during that year.

Table VI. Industrial Production in Eastern Europe
1975 = 100

Country	1976	1977	1978	1979
Bulgaria	107	114	122	...
Czechoslovakia	106	112	117	121
East Germany	106	111	116	...
Hungary	105	112	117	120
Poland	110	117	122	126
Romania	...	...	...	...
U.S.S.R.	105	111	116	120

Source: UN, *Monthly Bulletin of Statistics.*

Table VII. Foreign Trade of Eastern Europe
In $000,000

	Exports			Imports		
Country	1977	1978	1979	1977	1978	1979
Bulgaria	6,329	7,448	8,869	6,329	7,617	8,514
Czechoslovakia	10,818	12,322	13,198	11,149	12,560	14,262
East Germany	12,024	13,267	15,063	14,334	14,572	16,214
Hungary	5,832	6,350	7,938	6,522	7,898	8,674
Poland	12,336	13,361	16,233	14,674	15,121	17,488
Romania	7,021	8,077	9,724	7,018	8,910	10,916
U.S.S.R.	45,161	52,176	64,762	40,817	50,546	57,773

Centrally Planned Economies. The 34th plenary session of the Council for Mutual Economic Assistance (CMEA or Comecon) was held in Prague, Czech., June 17–19, 1980. The CMEA makes recommendations, but it is up to the governments of member countries to implement them. It is worth remembering, however, that the existence of the CMEA is based on political rather than economic considerations and that the main political force behind it is the Soviet Union.

The 1980 meeting was chaired by the host country's premier, Lubomir Strougal, and was attended by the premiers of the Soviet Union, Bulgaria, East Germany, Hungary, Mongolia, Poland, Romania, and Vietnam and by the vice-president of Cuba. These are the ten full member countries of CMEA. Yugoslavia, represented at the conference by the vice-president of the Council of State, had "limited participation status," while Afghanistan, Angola, Ethiopia, Laos, Mozambique, and Yemen (Aden) had observer status.

After three days of deliberations a communiqué was issued that called for increased efforts for cooperation and for coordination of economic planning by member countries. At the same time three multilateral agreements were concluded. The first dealt with specialization and cooperation in the production of computer technology products; the second concerned the joint effort aimed at speeding up the development of science and technology in Cuba; and the third dealt with cooperation on deep-drilling technology for crude oil.

The most important of these agreements was the one concerning the production of computer technology. It was envisioned that during the next five-year period, 1981–85, joint production of new computer technology would be double that of the preceding five years and reach the overall value of 15 billion rubles. In spite of these three agreements and in spite of the fact that the 1980 session was held at the prime ministerial level, it was clear that the session failed to agree on any major problems facing the member countries. These included shortages of energy and food and the inability to adjust member countries' economies to the rapidly changing world economy.

Aleksey N. Kosygin (then Soviet premier; *see* OBITUARIES) said in the opening speech to the session that Soviet oil deliveries to other CMEA countries would remain in the next five-year period "at the high level attained in 1980." This statement in fact put an end to the hopes of some member countries for large increases in deliveries of Soviet oil. The 1980 level of Soviet oil deliveries was not high in comparison with the growing demand for oil in the CMEA member countries. It was generally estimated that Eastern European countries would have to increase their imports of oil by 3–5% a year during the next five years in order to satisfy demand. Kosygin's statement provoked a sharp reply from the Romanian premier, Ilie Verdet. He stated that the question of coordination of plans had not been solved, which meant that the requirements of the member countries for energy and raw materials had not been fully taken into consideration. Verdet called for increased cooperation in the fields of energy and raw materials. This problem, he said, should be discussed at the highest possible level.

Verdet's speech was not published in Prague but was reported by Radio Bucharest. It was ironic that the premier of the country that was known to be opposed to any attempt at integration within CMEA should advocate a deepening of cooperation, and it illustrated the growing dependence of the Romanian economy on the Soviet market and on Soviet supplies of oil. This was not only a problem for Romania. In spite of the assurances in 1979 by Kosygin, who said at the 33rd CMEA session that the Soviet bloc had "avoided the heavy blows suffered by the capitalist economies as a result of the energy crisis," shortages of energy were an important factor in all major CMEA countries.

The final communiqué in Prague stated that member countries agreed to pay greater attention to cooperation in the rational use of energy and

Table VIII. Output of Basic Industrial Products in Eastern Europe, 1978
In 000 metric tons except for natural gas and electric power

Country	Anthracite (hard coal)	Lignite (brown coal)	Natural gas (000,000 cu m)	Crude petroleum	Electric power (000,000 kw-hr)	Steel	Sulfuric acid	Cement
Bulgaria	273	25,531	32	...	31,486	2,470	974	5,149
Czechoslovakia	28,290	94,879	1,151	117	69,097	15,294	1,195	10,204
East Germany	85	253,264	...	...	96,963	6,976	971	12,521
Hungary	2,954	22,716	7,333	2,200	25,542	3,877	680	4,764
Poland	192,622	41,005	7,617	363	115,557	19,251	3,172	21,651
Romania	7,418	21,845	33,690	13,724	64,255	11,779	1,655	13,892
U.S.S.R.	501,536	162,871	346,872	571,531	1,201,900	151,453	22,411	126,956

Source: CMEA, *Statistical Yearbook, 1979.*

raw materials. A signed agreement on co-production of deep-drilling equipment might indicate that in the future CMEA member countries would be expected to invest in oil extraction within the Soviet Union.

On the last day of the session the CMEA Committee for Cooperation in Planning held its meeting. At this meeting, the basic sectors of mutual planning for 1981–85 were approved. The committee also considered the draft agreement of cooperation in agricultural production and citrus fruit processing in Cuba as well as problems of cooperation in the construction of an iron-ore mine in the Soviet Union and the supply of ferrous materials from the U.S.S.R. to other CMEA countries.

The 1980 events in Poland illustrated the economic and social instability of the CMEA. The dismal performance of the Polish economy, which was at least partly caused by errors in planning and the overall inefficiency of centralized management, brought the country to the verge of economic bankruptcy. It seemed that none of Poland's major economic problems could be solved through interaction with the CMEA. These problems, including shortages of basic foods and consumer goods, general inefficiency of industry, lack of infrastructure, and weakness of transport, were shared by many other CMEA countries including the Soviet Union. It was also true that not only Poland but many other countries belonging to the CMEA were strongly affected by the world economic recession. Yet the Eastern bloc as a whole improved its trade performance with the non-Communist countries. While in 1978 the CMEA countries registered a deficit of $5 billion in trade with market economy countries, in 1979 this deficit was turned into a surplus of almost $2 billion. This was largely due, however, to the Soviet export of oil and its increase in price. Another reason was the substantial cut in imports of Western machinery and industrial equipment.

In 1980 the CMEA renewed its efforts to establish direct relations with the European Economic Community (EEC). Negotiations between the two were conducted in Geneva in March, July, and October, but they produced no practical results. The main reason for the stalemate was the fact that the CMEA secretariat insisted that it should negotiate with the EEC Commission on an equal footing, while the Commission maintained that the CMEA as an organization had nothing to compare with the power conferred on the Commission by its members. The Commission insisted, therefore, that agreements would have to be negotiated bilaterally between the EEC and the member nations of the CMEA. The first agreement of this kind was signed with Romania, while Poland appealed directly to the EEC for supplies of food.

INTERNATIONAL TRADE

The expansion of world trade was severely affected by the aftermath of the increase in oil prices that began in 1979. All oil-importing countries found their external balances deteriorating because of this increase, and in the major industrialized countries there was a general movement into either recession or much slower growth. Demand for imports by those countries from the less developed nations declined as a result, further worsening the payments problems of those already facing higher oil import bills. Commodity markets in general weakened, especially in metals. Problems in recession-hit industries in the major economies led to renewed calls for imposition of protectionist measures, both against other developed nations such as Japan and against the developing economies.

Table IX. Soviet Trade with Eastern European Countries

In 000,000 rubles, current prices

Country	Exports			Imports		
	1977	1978	1979	1977	1978	1979
Bulgaria	2,658.7	3,144.4	3,312.7	2,494.6	2,997.4	3,173.7
Czechoslovakia	2,680.4	3,002.0	3,362.9	2,436.9	3,058.6	3,183.4
East Germany	3,661.2	3,982.0	4,216.5	3,066.2	3,711.2	3,917.0
Hungary	2,066.5	2,396.4	2,741.3	2,872.1	3,600.0	3,717.5
Poland	3,195.9	3,449.6	3,837.5	1,021.9	979.0	1,067.8
Romania	1,003.5	971.3	1,077.8	...	2,429.9	2,413.8

Source: U.S.S.R. Foreign Trade Statistics/Moscow, 1977/2079.

Table X. Soviet Crude Petroleum and Products Supplied to Eastern Europe

In 000 metric tons

Country	1974	1975	1976	1978	1979
Bulgaria	10,855	11,553	11,868	12,402	13,350
Czechoslovakia	14,836	15,965	17,233	18,462	19,100
East Germany	14,424	14,952	16,766	17,880	18,620
Hungary	6,729	7,535	8,435	10,230	9,070
Poland	11,855	13,271	14,073	15,452	14,700

Source: U.S.S.R. Foreign Trade Statistics/Moscow, 1977/2079.

The increase in OPEC oil prices that began in 1979 resulted in a doubling of oil prices between January of that year and January 1980. In the first half of 1980 prices continued to rise, by a further 15%, but thereafter the pressure for further rises slackened. Even so, the effect on the trade balances of the oil-importing countries was extremely unfavourable; the overall OECD trade balance was estimated to have worsened by over $90 billion between 1978 and 1980, while that of the non-oil less developed countries moved some $15 billion further into the red over the same period. The OPEC countries achieved a corresponding increase in their combined trade balance of $140 billion.

In the industrialized countries the oil price increase brought on a resurgence of inflationary pressures, and their governments were not inclined to try to offset its deflationary effects. Most preferred to accept lower economic activity and increased unemployment and to attempt to dampen inflation immediately. This stance led to reduced growth in economic activity, and in the case of the U.S. and the U.K. to an actual decline in GDP. Lower demand for imports was the result, both for oil from OPEC and for non-oil imports from the rest of the world. The less developed countries thus suffered a further blow to their external accounts; demand for their exports fell, and in the case of many commodities this translated into both lower volumes exported and lower prices. They were, therefore, once more caught in the twin difficulties of lower export receipts and higher import costs; the problems were not eased by the fact that heavy borrowing on the international markets had left many of them with large repayments of interest and capital to make, adding to their external financing difficulties.

Overall, world trade was estimated to have risen by some 3–4% in 1980, a decline from the 5.5% growth estimated to have occurred in 1979. Trade in manufactures continued to increase about 5% as in 1979, but oil trade fell markedly. This was partially a response to lower world economic growth but also resulted from the high levels of oil inventories built up during 1979 by the OECD countries. Once fears of supply problems were dispelled, and following the relatively mild winter in the U.S. and Western Europe, the level of inventories began to be reduced. This caused the volume of production of OPEC oil to fall by as much as 8%. Trade in primary commodities in 1980 also was considerably below the previous year's level with little prospect of relief during 1981.

The major importing area in the world, the OECD, probably imported only 1–2% more in 1980 than in 1979, a considerable fall from the 8% growth in volume during 1979. In the seven major economies the growth of imports was probably even lower. Imports in the U.S. and Japan were likely to have declined for the year, and the U.K. may have experienced no change in import volumes. Export volumes, on the other hand, may have grown at the 6% rate experienced in 1979.

However, there was a recovery of export growth to the OPEC area, with a 20% increase in volume in 1980, compared with the near 13% decline the previous year. Exports to the rest of the world grew at a slower rate than in the previous year, reflecting the difficulties that the less developed countries and the centrally planned economies were also having in meeting the increased oil costs.

The effect of higher oil prices was revealed in terms of trade for the OECD area. Export prices for the industrialized countries were some 14% higher than in 1979, but they were outweighed by the 65% increase in oil import prices which helped to push overall import prices up by about 25%. Therefore, despite the fact that export volumes grew considerably in excess of import volumes, the result in actual value terms was that the OECD trade balance overall continued to move into severe deficit. From a small surplus in 1978, the area reported an overall $40 billion deficit in 1979, and this was expected to be more than doubled in 1980.

Table XI. Current Balances of Payments

In $000,000,000

Country	1974	1975	1976	1977	1978	1979	1980*
Canada	−1.5	−4.7	−3.9	−4.1	−4.6	−4.4	−6
France	−5.8	+0.1	−5.9	−3.0	+3.8	+1.5	−10
Germany, West	+9.9	+3.6	+3.6	+4.4	+8.8	−5.6	−18
Italy	−8.0	−0.6	−2.9	+2.5	+6.4	+5.1	−8
Japan	−4.7	−0.7	+3.7	+10.9	+17.6	−8.8	−16
United Kingdom	−7.7	−3.7	−1.5	−0.4	+1.2	−3.9	+5
United States	+2.2	+18.3	+4.5	−14.1	+14.3	−0.8	−4
OECD total	−27.6	+2.0	−16.8	−23.8	+11.3	−36.3	−98
Other developed countries	−3.8	−4.9	−2.8	−1.7	−0.4	−0.4	+1
Centrally planned economies*	−0.4	−6.9	−2.2	+1.8	+1.1	+5.0	+14
Oil exporting countries*	+58.6	+48.1	+45.7	+45.3	+22.2	+77.9	+142
Other less developed countries*	−26.8	−38.3	−23.9	−21.6	−34.2	−46.2	−59
at 1975 prices†							
OECD total	−31.0	+2.0	−16.8	−21.8	+9.0	−25.4	−62
Other developed countries	−4.3	−4.9	−2.8	−1.6	−0.3	−0.3	+1
Centrally planned economies*	−0.4	−6.9	−2.2	+1.7	+0.9	+3.5	+9
Oil exporting countries*	+65.8	+48.1	+45.7	+41.6	+17.8	+54.5	+90
Other less developed countries*	−30.1	−38.3	−23.9	−19.8	−27.4	−32.3	−37

*Estimate.
†In terms of export prices of manufactured goods.
Sources: International Monetary Fund, *International Financial Statistics*; UN, *Monthly Bulletin of Statistics*; national sources.

Industrialized Nations. The only favourable aspect of this deterioration was that it mostly affected the seven major economies. Of the overall deterioration of some $90 billion, the big seven sustained $70 billion. These countries are by their very size those best able to accommodate and to finance such external difficulties. As of the end of 1980, however, there seemed little likelihood of a repeat of the 1975 experience, when the sharp recession pushed the big seven countries from the oil-induced deficit in 1974 back into a small surplus in 1975. The U.S. was suffering less than the other six countries in terms of its external deficit because it had already gone into a slump. Oil imports fell by more than 10% in volume, and other imports dropped in real terms. Export growth continued to perform well in the first half of 1980, but the gradually widening world recession helped to push down that expansion in the second half of the year. Overall, therefore, the trade balance in real terms improved, but the adverse effects of the terms of trade shift probably pushed the trade account further into deficit in value terms. The surplus on invisibles helped to reduce this, and the current account deficit was, relative to GDP, the lowest among the major economies.

For Japan the second oil shock brought considerable difficulties initially, but these were being overcome. During 1979 exports and imports were still feeling the effects of the rapid appreciation of the yen during 1977–78. That rise was wiped out through a continued fall in the yen's value through 1979 and into 1980, when it reached a low point of approximately 260 yen to U.S. $1 in April. During that period the Japanese economy had to suffer not only an increase in oil prices in dollar terms but also one that was rising even further in yen terms. Prices for other commodities of which Japan was a major importer, such as wood and metals, also rose strongly, adding to the nation's difficulties. Import price inflation reached a peak of 82% in early 1980 and then abated as oil prices steadied, commodity prices weakened, and the yen strengthened. But Japan's terms of trade were still badly affected, more than in any other major economy. To offset this degeneration in price terms would require a considerable turnaround in volume terms, and though the Japanese were not totally successful in this, their efforts were remarkable. Export volume growth appeared to be about 15–20% in 1980, while import volumes at best remained constant and probably fell. It is little wonder, therefore, that in September the current account was in surplus for the first time in 15 months. There was still considerable ground to make up, however. The trade balance in 1979 was in deficit by $1.8 billion, and indications were that this would be repeated in 1980—a far cry from the $24.5 billion surplus in 1978.

The West German economy was perhaps best

WIDE WORLD

Pressman's in London was only one of many dealers in precious metals to witness an increase in over-the-counter sales of gold.

able to sustain the effects of the second oil shock. But while its growth was higher and inflation and unemployment were lower than in many of its neighbours, the nation's trade surplus was much reduced and the current account moved into enormous deficit. The 1980 deficit was likely to have been of the order of $15 billion, a rise of more than $9 billion over 1979 and a deterioration of some $24 billion since 1978. Much of that (some $18 billion) was accounted for by the increased cost of oil imports. Despite a reduction in oil import volumes, energy imports in 1980 represented 20% of the total. Exports performed relatively well in the Western European markets, with the weakness of the mark helping competitiveness. But the seemingly perennial trade surplus with the U.S. moved into deficit, and the trade position with Japan also deteriorated.

France's trade account moved into deficit in 1979, and the process continued during 1980. Part of this could be ascribed to the increase in oil prices, but even in real terms the trade performance was poor. Exports were unlikely to have risen more than 2% in volume terms, while import volumes increased by about 6%. Taken with the adverse movement in the terms of trade, it was of little surprise, therefore, that the trade deficit was of the order of $12 billion–$15 billion. Although the French surplus on invisibles account was substantial and increasing, it could not compensate for such a severe deterioration in trade, and the current account stayed in considerable deficit.

The British economy suffered the inflationary effects of the oil price rise but was able to benefit from the increased value of its North Sea oil production. Despite the fact that its energy self-sufficiency enabled it to reduce oil imports greatly and to export considerable quantities of oil, the trade account performed disappointingly. The general lack of competitiveness of British exports did not help, especially as the pound continued to remain strong and moved up against the dollar and most of the other major currencies. This led to a continuing increase of imports of manufactured goods, despite the fall in total import volumes that resulted from the decline in overall activity in the U.K.

In Italy the current account remained in surplus in 1979 despite the economy's dependence on imported oil for 68% of its energy requirements. That surplus disappeared in the first half of 1980, although it reappeared in the summer months as invisibles credits reached their seasonal peak. Lack of competitiveness affected export volume growth, although a reasonably buoyant domestic economy kept import growth moving upward. Thus, the trade deficit widened to almost $10 billion, while the current account slumped into a $7 billion deficit.

Canadian export growth was particularly dependent upon U.S. demand, and that resulted in a poor showing in 1980. Export volume fell overall and at a faster pace than import volume. The latter declined because of a sluggish economy, although lack of domestic competitiveness and a boost in demand for imported machinery helped to reduce the decline. As the invisibles deficit probably worsened slightly, the current account was expected to have moved further into deficit, to perhaps $5.5 billion.

The other developed nations faced an increase in their trade and current deficits totaling some $17 billion. Norway's increasing production of oil and gas helped to push it back into current account surplus. Conversely, even the Swiss found it impossible to prevent oil costs from pushing their seemingly permanent current surplus into deficit, while Spain's hard-won current surplus also evaporated.

Developing Countries. For the oil-exporting nations the overall trade surplus for 1980 appeared to have been approximately $180 billion, though a considerable deficit on invisibles reduced the current account to a still enormous surplus of $115 billion. Although oil export growth fell, the effect of the terms of trade was sufficiently large to allow a near 20% increase in import volumes. This partly reflected the recovery from the decline in OPEC imports in 1979, much of which resulted from the cutback from Iran. The improvement in current balances was particularly marked for the "capital surplus" or "low absorbing" oil exporters, such as Saudi Arabia, the United Arab Emirates, Kuwait, and Libya. With significant oil production and small populations, these countries have difficulty in spending all of their oil revenues and have been in current account surplus since 1973. For the other "high absorbing" oil exporting countries, such as Nigeria, Venezuela, and Indonesia, their large populations relative to their oil revenues have in the past led to current account deficits for the group as a whole. In 1980 this group provided a buoyant market for non-OPEC exporters, with imports estimated to have risen by 25%.

The non-oil developing countries registered a considerable overall current account deficit, with estimates ranging from $50 billion to $60 billion in 1980. Not only did their oil imports more than double in price during 1979–80 but the growth of their export trade was adversely affected by the economic slowdown in the developed countries. Export volumes (up 3–5% in 1980) probably just about kept pace with import volume growth, but the situation in the second half of the year was one of sluggish or negative export growth. Prices of many commodities turned downward in the course of the year, further reducing export receipts. The problem would be less acute if these nations were not already heavily in debt, and in many cases lenders (particularly the commercial banks) seemed unlikely to lend further funds to a country in balance of payments difficulties. Brazil, for example, experienced difficulty in obtaining external financing, though at $2 billion–$3 billion its estimated current account deficit was not particularly large. South Korea would probably not have difficulty in funding its increased current deficit despite doubts about its external competitiveness and its internal political troubles. Rather, it was such small economies as the Sudan and potentially politically unstable countries that might face problems.

Centrally Planned Economies. The overall current account deficit for the nations with centrally planned economies was estimated at $12 billion during 1980. Though the oil price rise had perhaps less substantial effects on these economies than on the other less developed nations, it did have repercussions on world trade that severely affected the demand for their exports. High world inflation also affected the prices of their imports.

More significant for the development of East-West trade, however, was the imposition of embargoes by the U.S. and the Western nations on trade with the U.S.S.R. Launched in the wake of the Soviet Union's intervention in Afghanistan, the ban included sales by the U.S. of grain and high-technology equipment to the U.S.S.R. Other Western countries followed the lead of the U.S. to a greater or lesser extent. The embargo on grain exports was not popular with the U.S. farming community, which believed that higher prices could be achieved for its grain from selling to the U.S.S.R. than from sales to the U.S. government. Also, the Soviet Union was able to make up most of the shortfall in grain supplies through alternative sources. Similarly, high-technology equipment was available from other Western sources; the French and Japanese, for example, were accused of breaking the embargo. Indeed, with export markets difficult to find, many of the partners of the U.S. were questioning the value of the embargo.

Commodities. The outlook for commodities became bleaker in general during 1980. Most products suffered declines in prices as the year went on, though in many cases this reflected a return from the more speculative levels that prices reached in the aftermath of the Soviet Union's intervention in Afghanistan and the Iran-U.S. conflict over the embassy hostages. As the prospects of global conflict lessened, so did the factors holding up prices. Even the Iran-Iraq war did little to arouse renewed speculative activity.

Probably the best performing commodity in 1980 was sugar, which reached prices last attained five years previously. The major factor was heavy buying by the U.S.S.R. on the world market, together with speculation that lower harvests in the Communist bloc would produce a large shortfall in supply in the 1980–81 season.

At the other extreme, cocoa prices fell to a five-year low, and it remained to be seen if the new International Cocoa Agreement would come into operation and, if so, whether it could successfully intervene in the market. The old agreement expired in March 1980, but at the year's end the new agreement had not yet been ratified by the U.S., the biggest importer, or by the Ivory Coast, the biggest exporter. Without the latter's ratification the new agreement would not be credible. If ratification was achieved, there would be $230 million to finance a buffer stock plus further funds from a levy on world cocoa trade.

Coffee prices also declined during 1980, with the level of world demand falling below capacity. Despite the efforts of the Latin-American exporters to support prices through their Pancafé intervention agency, the price of coffee declined to about $1.20 per pound, the lowest since 1975. The International Coffee Agreement was revived with a price floor of $1.15 per pound and with powers to reduce ex-

Table XII. Foreign Investment by Major Countries

In $000,000,000

Country	1973	1974	1975	1976	1977	1978	1979	1980*
Long-term capital flows								
Germany, West	+4.9	−2.4	−7.4	−0.6	−5.6	−1.4	+5.7	+1.1
Japan	−9.8	−3.9	−0.3	−1.0	−3.2	−12.4	−12.6	+1.1
United Kingdom	+2.0	+6.7	+2.2	+3.0	+6.9	−4.6	−6.9	−8.2
United States	−7.7	−6.8	−19.9	−18.0	−15.4	−12.4*	−21.5*	−10.0
Total	−10.6	−6.4	−25.5	−16.5	+17.3	−30.7	−35.3	−16.0
Net interest, dividends, and profits								
Germany, West	+0.6	+0.4	+1.0	+1.3	+0.2	+2.3	+2.4	+1.9
Japan	+0.5	−0.5	−0.3	−0.2	+0.1	+0.9	+2.0	+0.8
United Kingdom	+3.1	+3.3	+1.7	+2.4	+0.1	+1.0	+0.6	−0.8
United States	+12.2	+15.5	+12.8	+16.0	+18.0	+20.9	+32.5	+34.5
Total	+16.3	+18.8	+15.2	+19.4	+18.4	+25.1	+37.5	+36.4

*Estimate.
Source: National sources.

port quotas if the price fell below $1.35 per pound, powers that were subsequently put into operation.

The other major commodity agreement, on rubber, remained provisional and required ratification by the U.S. before becoming definitive. In 1980 prices for rubber rose sharply in the aftermath of Afghanistan but then fell back rapidly as speculative activity diminished.

Metals prices also rose at the beginning of the year but then declined. Copper rose in price in July with a shortfall in supplies because of strikes in the U.S. copper industry and at a major Peruvian smelter. The U.S. strike lasted about four months, and a small shortfall in supply thus appeared in the second half of the year. With the settlement of the strike, however, the expectation of a substantial world surplus led to sharp drops in prices to levels of the previous year. Lead prices also fell and in late 1980 reached less than 50% of the peak level of mid-1979. Zinc remained fairly stable, reflecting a general balance in world supply and demand, although it too suffered from speculative price rises early in 1980. Tin prices fell, reflecting a surplus of production over demand and thus increasing world stocks. (EIU)

INTERNATIONAL EXCHANGE AND PAYMENTS

In 1980 as in 1979 the effects of the rise in the price of oil dominated international payments, both trade and capital. That the rise continued through a second year was an important contrast to 1974–75, when the initial increase was followed by several years of relative stability. Governments, therefore, needed to change their policies from their initial responses, which had been suitable to a possibly temporary difficulty, to ones that could meet the medium-term consequences. On the domestic side these included inflation and changes in the structure of output and distribution of income; on the international, larger and more persistent deficits than in the past needed to be accepted and financed. By the end of the year there had been little progress on these problems.

In the developed countries one short-term remedy used in 1979, which was less popular in 1980, was the attempt to reduce import costs by raising exchange rates through competitive increases in interest rates. It is possible that the relatively quick completion of the February–March round of interest-rate and relative exchange-rate movements finally convinced the major countries that none of them was prepared to accept a large fall in its exchange rate; further rounds were thereby discouraged. By the summer there was also pressure from the IMF against interest-rate competition. No country, however, reversed its priorities sufficiently to be willing to lead interest rates downward, and domestic monetary policies also discouraged any declines. The policy that succeeded this in some countries, that of restraining the growth of deficits by restricting growth, was, however, likely to come under increasing pressure from two sides if oil prices continued to rise: it would prove difficult to prevent growth indefinitely; and, when the rising oil price continually raises import costs, restraint slows the growth of deficits but does not cure them.

CHART 5

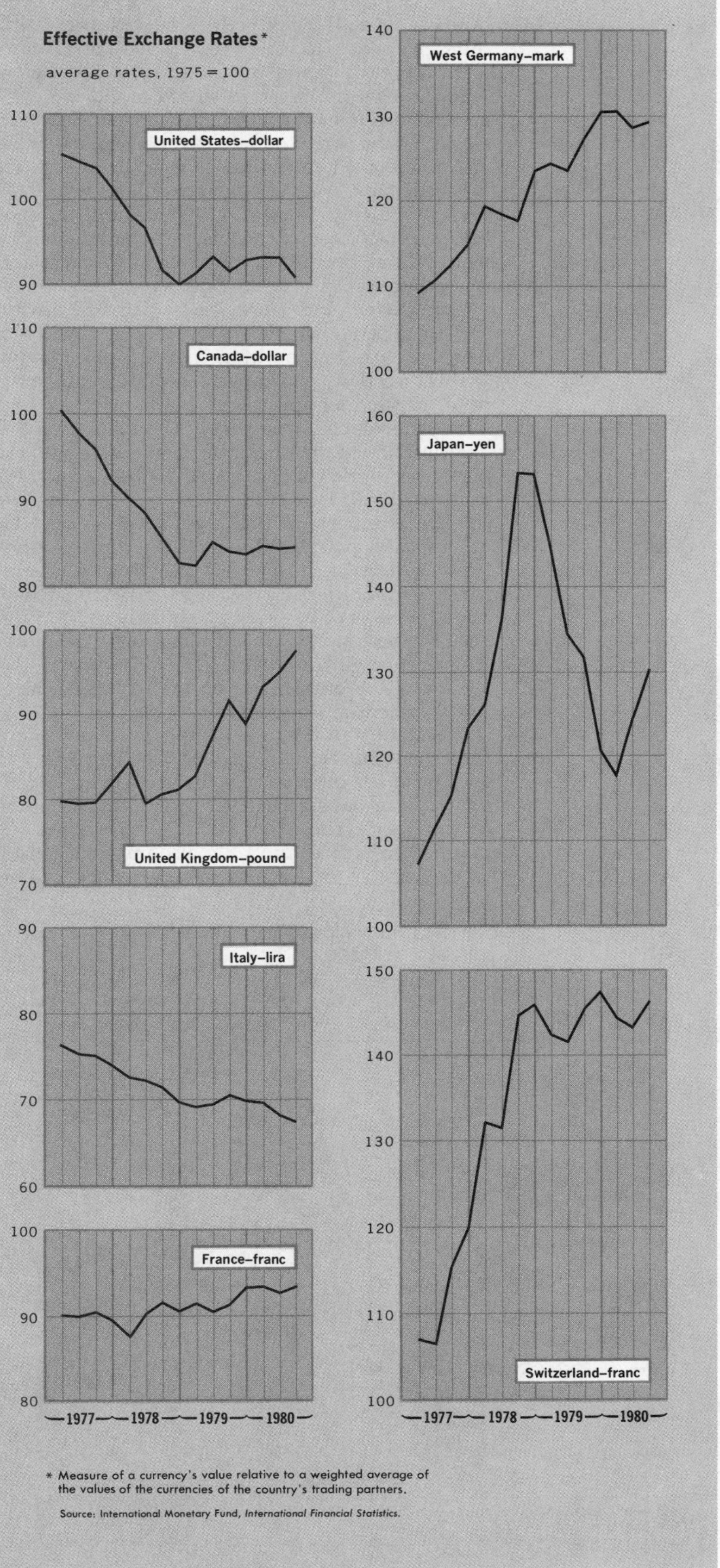

* Measure of a currency's value relative to a weighted average of the values of the currencies of the country's trading partners.

Source: International Monetary Fund, *International Financial Statistics*.

The less developed countries previously combined slowing their growth rates with increasing their borrowing to meet their higher costs. Many were approaching the limit on the first even before 1980. In 1980 the more advanced found the commercial loan markets closing to them because their existing debts were so high and, particularly if the real price of oil continued to rise, because there was little hope that their current deficits would fall back as quickly as after 1974–75. Continuing to borrow thus seemed unwise, to both potential lenders and borrowers. Increasingly, therefore, they were forced into the position of the less advanced developing countries, which had always had to depend principally on official sources of finance. With some developed nations also moving in this direction, this implied a vast increase in the need for such lending.

The developed countries suffered a massive deterioration in their balance of payments with the rest of the world, of perhaps $60 billion, much the same as in 1979 after allowing for inflation. The smaller countries, which together accounted for only about a quarter of the total developed-nations trade, suffered a third of this change, and France, West Germany, and Italy were all estimated to have had falls of between $10 billion and $15 billion. By these standards the changes for the North American countries were relatively small. The U.K. was the only major nation to have a large improvement and move into surplus.

The change in the total for the developed countries was almost exactly matched by the rise in the surplus of the oil exporters. Even allowing for inflation, this was significantly higher than after the first oil price rise. The balance of the centrally planned economies probably also improved in total because of oil exports by the Soviet Union, while that of the less developed countries that were not major oil exporters continued to deteriorate.

For some countries changes in balances on services and other payments not directly tied to trade in goods were important. For both the U.S. and Canada such payments accounted for most of the changes in their balances. In its seventh successive year of deficit and high borrowing, Canada again underwent an increase in its interest payments. Partly for temporary reasons (the change in ownership of a petroleum company branch), U.S. income from interest payments grew much less than in 1979; other increases in nontrade income were not sufficient to offset increased payments so that, unusually, the net U.S. surplus on services fell. Although about $10 billion of the increase in the West German deficit could be explained by trade in goods, payments on both travel and contributions to the EEC continued to increase the deficit, and there may have been a small decline in income from interest payments. Japan also experienced a fall in such income; this may, however, have been offset by the ending of various special arrangements made to reduce its surpluses in earlier years, and there appeared to had been some improvement on the transport account. For the first time since data had been recorded, the U.K. had a deficit on net interest payments in 1980 because of the rapidly growing earnings by oil companies from outside the nation on oil production in the North Sea. Britain was only prevented from suffering a reduction in its total surplus on service and transfer payments by the increase in the value of the pound; this offset a fall in the sterling value of the income.

The most striking result for the developed countries as a group was their virtually unchanged net balance on nontrade current income. This suggested that increased payments of interest on their own borrowing to meet their deficits must have balanced any increase in their exports of services to the oil exporters and in their income from interest payments from the non-oil less developed countries. There was a similar stagnation of net income from 1973 to 1975.

With large imbalances for all the major countries and groups of countries, the nature and direction of capital flows took on an increasing importance. The major suppliers of long-term capital had already reduced the growth of capital exports in 1979, when West Germany's balance turned positive; in 1980 preliminary estimates indicated that there was a sharp fall because of declines for Japan and the U.S. In the U.K. there was little change, although there was some early repayment of official borrowing as the current account moved into surplus. U.S. direct investment abroad appeared to decline while foreign investment in U.S. securities rose.

During the year Japan relaxed its restrictions on payments of interest to foreigners and began to encourage borrowing abroad; it also relaxed its restrictions on direct investment in Japan. There was a decrease in lending abroad and an increase in investment in Japanese securities from abroad (much of the latter probably from the oil export-

Table XIII. Financing of Deficits

In $000,000,000

Areas and principal borrowers	Use of official reserves*		Use of IMF credit		International loans and bond issues		World Bank
	1979	1980†	1979	1980†	1979	1980†	1980‡
OECD	−14.9	−29.3	−3.1	−0.1	54.1	44.4	0.7
Canada	+0.7	−0.1	—	—	4.9	4.7	—
Denmark	−0.1	+0.1	—	—	1.9	2.3	—
France	−8.3	−10.1	—	—	4.8	3.4	—
Italy	−7.1	−6.1	−1.1	—	3.8	4.8	—
Japan	+12.9	−3.6	—	—	4.2	2.6	—
Spain	−3.1	+0.1	−0.5	—	4.3	3.4	—
Sweden	+0.8	−0.3	—	—	3.0	3.3	—
Turkey	+0.1	−0.4	—	+0.5	3.2	—	0.6
United Kingdom	−3.7	−1.8	−1.3	−0.2	3.2	2.7	—
United States	−0.8	−4.1	—	—	7.4	6.3	—
Other developed countries	+1.0	−0.4	−0.2	+0.1	3.3	2.3	0.3
Yugoslavia	+1.1	+0.3	+0.2	+0.3	1.7	1.0	0.3
Centrally planned economies	−0.1	+0.1	—	+0.1	6.9	2.0	0.3
China	—	—	—	—	3.1	0.4	—
Oil exporting countries	−14.5	−18.7	—	—	9.0	5.4	1.3
Algeria	−0.7	−1.1	—	—	2.0	0.3	0.1
Nigeria	−3.7	−3.7	—	—	1.2	0.2	0.3
Venezuela	−1.2	−0.5	—	—	3.0	2.5	—
Other less developed countries	−9.6	−1.0	+0.4	+0.8	33.8	17.9	8.8
Argentina	−4.4	+0.2	—	—	2.5	2.0	0.2
Brazil	+2.9	+2.8	—	—	7.2	2.8	0.7
India	−1.0	+0.4	—	+0.3	0.1	0.1	1.7
Mexico	−0.2	−0.3	−0.2	−0.1	10.8	4.3	0.3
Philippines	−0.5	−0.2	+0.1	+0.2	2.0	1.0	0.4
South Korea	−0.8	−0.5	−0.1	+0.5	2.7	1.2	0.5
International agencies	—	—	—	—	8.6	5.5	—
Total	−38.1	−49.3	−3.0	+0.8	115.6	77.4	11.5

†First three quarters. *Denotes fall, *i.e.,* use of reserves in financing.
‡Year ending June 30, 1980.
Sources: International Monetary Fund, *International Financial Statistics*; World Bank, *Annual Report 1980*; OECD, *Financial Statistics Monthly*.

ers), but as this probably did little more than bring the long-term account into balance, further measures were necessary to finance the current deficit. There was some decline in reserves, mainly in the first part of the year before the long-term capital account turned favourable. This happened after about August, when there was an improvement in the current balance. Much of the financing, therefore, must have been in short-term forms, some of it foreign official holdings, as Japan relaxed its opposition to the yen's becoming a reserve currency.

West Germany, faced like Japan with the new problem of a growing deficit, reacted in a similar fashion by relaxing its controls on foreign holdings of securities and discouraging lending abroad. This was not sufficient, however, to obtain more than a rough balance on long-term capital in the first half of the year, although there may have been some inflow in the second half. In addition, there was a large outflow of private short-term capital in the first half. West Germany also, therefore, had to switch from opposition to tolerance, if not active support, of the mark's role as a reserve currency, with the foreign official inflows that this implies. In addition, West Germany turned to official borrowing, obtaining loans of $2,750,000,000 from Saudi Arabia.

Among the smaller OECD countries, Switzerland also encouraged the use of the Swiss franc as a reserve currency by removing restrictions on foreign investments and deposits, but most of the other nations used borrowing on the international capital markets. Total borrowing (bank loans and bond issues) fell sharply in 1980, but for the OECD countries borrowing remained at the 1979 level during the first half and started to rise in the third quarter. Many of the individual countries that were major borrowers in the past remained among the highest in 1980, including Canada, France, Italy, and Spain. A clear exception, however, was Turkey, which found itself in difficulties over repayments. It was forced to turn to official borrowing, securing loans from the IMF and the World Bank. In order to forestall similar situations for its members, the EEC set up a facility for joint borrowing from the OPEC countries to permit loans by the EEC itself to its individual members, possibly with policy conditions similar to those usually required by the IMF.

Borrowing by the centrally planned economies fell sharply in the first half of 1980; about half the decline could be explained by the large loan to China in 1979, but there were also reductions for the other countries. Although Poland had the most difficulty in making repayments and increasing its borrowing, the continuing deficits and slow growth of the other centrally planned economies also reduced their ability to borrow, and some were arranging direct lines of credit from Western governments by the end of 1980. Borrowing by the oil exporters, especially Algeria and Nigeria, was lower than in 1979, though Venezuela remained a major borrower.

Loans to the non-oil less developed countries declined from $34 billion in 1979 to $18 billion in the first three quarters of 1980 (equivalent to an annual rate of only $24 billion). Part of the reduction could be explained by reduced borrowing by Mexico, which was increasing its oil output. It was also true that borrowing in 1979 exceeded immediate needs for many of these countries; they took advantage of available funds to increase their reserves with the intention of using them in 1980. There was also an abnormal amount of refinancing in 1980 (five years after the first major round of borrowing). New borrowing in the first quarter of 1980 was further depressed by the high level of interest rates. There was also growing evidence that some countries could no longer obtain loans sufficient to finance their deficits. Borrowing by the Philippines and South Korea fell; the largest decline was for Brazil, which was also forced to accept much-increased risk premiums and shorter terms on its loans.

Use of IMF credit began to increase about the middle of the year, with India and South Korea accounting for most of the rise. A loan of $1.7 billion to Pakistan was announced at the end of the year, and India and possibly Brazil were expected to apply for loans. But although the IMF increased the formal limits on the amount a country could borrow and extended the potential period of loans (to up to eight years from two to three, indicating its recognition that the problem was medium-term), the amount available to it was not very large and could not permit an increase in its lending of more than $5 billion–$10 billion a year. This was much less than would be needed even to replace past levels of commercial borrowing by a single country such as Brazil. For this reason it was proposed that the IMF itself borrow, either directly from the oil exporters or on the international market, in order to relend. The amounts proposed would be small, about as much as from its own resources. The IMF did take one preliminary step toward borrowing, simplifying its currency unit, the SDR, from an average of 16 to an average of 5 currencies.

West Germany raised its interest rate in February and again in May to defend the value of the mark and joined France and the U.S. in opposing depreciation of their currencies. West Germany also used reserves to support the mark in the spring, but there were no further attempts among those countries to raise their exchange rates. The general level of interest rates, however, remained much higher than in the past. After fluctuating in the first half of the year, the effective (average) exchange rates of the U.S. and the continental European countries steadied in the second. There were no large changes from the 1979 averages. The pound and the yen, however, rose during most of the year. For Japan this merely reversed part of the fall during 1979, but the pound returned to a level not held since 1975. The rise in the yen did follow a large rise in interest rates in the spring, but there was also an improvement in its current balance in the second half of the year. The rise in the pound also accompanied an improving current balance along with vastly improved expectations about the future balance as the price of oil rose. Relative trade balances thus returned to being important determinants of exchange-rate movements, as they had been before 1979. (SHEILA A. B. PAGE)

Economy, World: Special Report

THE 1980 CREDIT CRUNCH

by Jane Bryant Quinn and Virginia Wilson

On March 14, 1980, the United States launched its first peacetime credit controls of the modern era. The experiment was short-lived. Controls were eased after only ten weeks and abandoned entirely within four months. The Federal Reserve Board, which administered the program, had only the most general regulations on the books, and the controlled institutions had barely begun to object.

The controls "worked" in that the amount of business and consumer credit outstanding fell abruptly. But in retrospect it appears that the economy was already heading into recession. Rather than being called upon to contain a credit explosion, the controls merely hastened a decline. Economic historians would find this episode an ambiguous addition to the long-standing debate over whether government controls can, effectively, replace market forces in an economy.

The Urge to Act. In the weeks leading up to the imposition of controls, a feeling of impending disaster hung over much of the financial community. Consumer prices were running at an 18% annual rate. Consumer debt, as a percentage of personal income, ticked up in February, after three months of decline. Interest rates jumped three percentage points in less than a month. The prime lending rate touched 18%. Billions of dollars were being lost in bond values, and seers gloomily predicted the collapse of major savings and loan associations.

The high passions of the 1980 presidential race exaggerated the political reactions to events. The fiscal 1981 budget proposed by Pres. Jimmy Carter in January, $15.8 billion in deficit, was thought insufficiently tight for dealing effectively with resurgent inflation. Critics on the right demanded a balanced budget; critics on the left thundered for wage/price controls. It was thought that only a recession could dampen the inflation emergency—yet more and more economists were predicting faster growth ahead.

Against this emotional, political, and economic background, President Carter launched his selective credit controls, plus some other proposals for tamping down the economy. The controls demanded the following: (1) Banks should not allow 1980 loan volume to grow more rapidly than 6 to 9%. (2) Certain consumer lenders should deposit, in a non-interest-bearing account at the Federal Reserve, the equivalent of 15% of any credit outstanding above the level existing on March 14 (the base level was modified later, to account for seasonal variations). This rule covered loans against bank credit cards, travel and entertainment cards, overdraft checking, retail charge accounts, unsecured personal loans, and some secured loans. (3) Money-market mutual funds should deposit 15% of their assets, over a base amount, in a non-interest-bearing account at the Federal Reserve. This move lowered the interest rate that money funds could pay on savings. It was hoped that this would stanch the flow of savings deposits out of savings and loan associations and into the funds. (4) A 3% surcharge was added to the then 13% discount rate at which large banks borrowed from the Federal Reserve Bank. (5) Reserve requirements were raised on certain bank liabilities, which had the effect of reducing the funds available for lending. (6) Ceilings were put on the interest rates payable by bank holding companies on certain debt instruments of $100,000 or less, thus curbing their ability to raise lendable funds.

Banks were advised that the Federal Reserve would smile on institutions that continued to lend money to home buyers, small businesses, and farmers while restricting credit for commodity speculation and corporate takeovers. Certain secured consumer loans were specifically exempted, among them loans for home buying, home improvements, autos, furniture, and appliances. These exemptions were made because the building and auto industries were already deep into recession.

A Perceived Emergency. Federal Reserve Board Chairman Paul Volcker was not enthusiastic about controls. The previous October 6 he had announced a credit-tightening program to "curb speculative excesses . . . and thereby . . . dampen inflationary forces." He had raised the discount rate to 12%, raised bank reserves, and announced that, henceforth, the Fed would place greater emphasis on controlling the amount of money that banks had to lend than on controlling interest rates. The latter policy is consistent with a more controlled growth in the supply of money, but it allows wider swings in interest rates as demand for credit rises and falls.

Jane Bryant Quinn is contributing editor of Newsweek *magazine, personal finance columnist of the* Washington Post, *and business correspondent of the "CBS Morning News"; she is the author of* Everyone's Money Book *(1979). Virginia Wilson is a research associate at* Newsweek.

MACNELLY—RICHMOND NEWS LEADER

The October moves were expected to cap the current inflation cycle and bring on recession. By January and February, however, the Fed's policies were widely perceived as ineffective. The very actions that raised interest rates also raised inflation, because of the way rising mortgage rates are counted in the consumer price index. Adding to the general panic of early 1980 was the fear, in financial circles, that inflation had grown strong enough to overwhelm all the weapons that the Fed could bring against it.

But a cool look backward supports the case that the Federal Reserve's actions were, in fact, already working. From October 1979 to January 1980, the growth in consumer installment loans plunged at the sharpest rate in recent history. Real retail sales, adjusted for inflation, peaked in September and started down. Retail sales in current dollars turned down just prior to the imposition of controls. Banks were already raising the cost of credit, and retailers were applying tougher yardsticks in granting new credit. It is arguable that the economy was, at that point, on the way down, with or without credit controls. But in the face of a perceived emergency, it was considered too risky to wait. The president chose the path of controls, and they undoubtedly sped the pace of decline.

Results of the Crunch. Consumer credit immediately grew even scarcer and more expensive. Many retailers raised monthly payments, changed the method of computing interest so as to raise the effective cost of credit, and made charge accounts harder to get. Many banks reduced credit lines on overdraft checking accounts and added fees for credit cards; some stopped issuing cards entirely. On the business side, some banks grew cautious about new loans to corporations (although businesses that had obtained credit lines in anticipation of controls were not denied access). Other banks—for example, those in booming cities in the Southwest—appear to have gone on lending to business as usual, on the grounds that their loans were for productive, not speculative, purposes.

The amount of consumer installment credit outstanding fell by an annual rate of almost 6.3% in April, 10% in May, and 7.8% in June. Business loans also fell. The economy plunged sharply in the second quarter (but revived in the third).

On May 6 the Federal Reserve rescinded the three percentage-point surcharge on the discount rate. On May 22 it cut in half the 15% deposits, in non-interest-bearing accounts, required of lenders and money-market funds. On July 3 the Fed announced that controls would be phased out entirely.

On the consumer side, however, the effects of credit controls lingered on. Retailers and other lenders, who had for some time found their credit programs only marginally profitable, kept the cost of credit up. Fees for bank cards stayed in place, as did higher monthly payments on many charge accounts. Credit became more widely available, but at a higher price. High inflation had been gradually raising the price of consumer credit in any event, but selective credit controls hastened the trend.

Ecuador

Ecuador

A republic on the west coast of South America, Ecuador is bounded by Colombia, Peru, and the Pacific Ocean. Area: 281,334 sq km (108,624 sq mi), including the Galápagos Islands (7,976 sq km), which is an insular province. Pop. (1980 est.): 8,354,000. Cap.: Quito (pop., 1980 est., 807,665). Largest city: Guayaquil (pop., 1980 est., 1,116,280). Language: Spanish, but Indians speak Quechuan and Jivaroan. Religion: predominantly Roman Catholic. President in 1980, Jaime Roldós Aguilera.

Differences of opinion between Pres. Jaime Roldós Aguilera and the president of Congress, Assad Bucaram, reached such a pitch that Roldós called on Congress to convene in extraordinary sessions to discuss constitutional changes giving him more power. When Congress vetoed his bill, on April 10, 1980, he threatened to call a national plebiscite and resign if he lost. By mid-May he had been persuaded to change his mind, however, and a multiparty commission was set up to study constitutional reforms, including the possible creation of a senate.

In August Congress showed its support for Roldós by electing his candidate, Raúl Baca Carbo, as its leader. Yet the president still faced economic and political problems. Party leaders were critical of the government's performance, but popular support for Roldós was strong, despite severe price rises and inflation of about 15%. The bus and truck drivers went on strike in July to protest the rise in the cost of living, but they received only nominal support.

A national development plan for 1980–84 called for investment of 370,572,000,000 sucres, two-thirds from the public sector and one-third from the private. The plan aimed to achieve a growth rate of 6.5% a year, consolidate democracy, promote social justice, and develop the economy with emphasis on agriculture and food production. The economy showed growth in 1980, with oil exports ensuring a trade surplus and rising international reserves. Increased oil exploration succeeded in raising reserves in the jungle region by over 3,000,000,000 bbl. (SARAH CAMERON)

ECUADOR

Education. (1979–80) Primary, pupils 1,427,627, teachers 39,747; secondary (1978–79), pupils 435,056, teachers 24,120; vocational (1978–79), pupils 52,250, teachers 5,951; teacher training (1977–78), pupils 2,911, teachers 189; higher, students 274,968, teaching staff 11,998.

Finance. Monetary unit: sucre, with (Sept. 22, 1980) an official rate of 25 sucres to U.S. $1 (free rate of 60.21 sucres = £1 sterling). Gold, SDR's, and foreign exchange (June 1980) U.S. $924 million. Budget (1979 actual): revenue 23,085,000,000 sucres; expenditure 24,693,000,000 sucres. Gross national product (1979) 214,990,000,000 sucres. Money supply (May 1980) 44,011,000,000 sucres. Cost of living (Quito; 1975 = 100; June 1980) 173.

Foreign Trade. (1979) Imports U.S. $1,951,000,000; exports U.S. $1,975,000,000. Import sources (1978): U.S. 35%; Japan 12%; West Germany 10%; Italy 5%. Export destinations (1978): U.S. 45%; Panama 13%; West Germany 5%; Colombia 5%; Chile 5%. Main exports (1978): crude oil 35%; coffee 19%; cocoa and products 17%; bananas 11%; fish and products 6%.

Transport and Communications. Roads (1973) 21,490 km (including 1,392 km of Pan-American Highway). Motor vehicles in use (1975): passenger 51,300; commercial (including buses) 77,200. Railways: (1977) 965 km; traffic (1978) 65 million passenger-km, freight 34 million net ton-km. Air traffic (1978): 676 million passenger-km; freight 13.2 million net ton-km. Telephones (Jan. 1978) 222,000. Radio receivers (Dec. 1971) *c.* 1.7 million. Television receivers (Dec. 1978) *c.* 400,000.

Agriculture. Production (in 000; metric tons; 1979): rice 303; corn (1978) *c.* 200; potatoes *c.* 545; cassava (1978) *c.* 230; sugar, raw value *c.* 382; bananas *c.* 2,391; pineapples *c.* 120; oranges *c.* 500; coffee *c.* 120; cocoa *c.* 79; fish catch (1978) *c.* 475. Livestock (in 000; 1978): cattle *c.* 2,874; sheep *c.* 2,198; pigs *c.* 3,150; horses *c.* 293; chickens 23,328.

Industry. Production (in 000; metric tons; 1978): cement 1,000; crude oil (1979) 10,898; natural gas (cu m) 35,028; petroleum products *c.* 4,050; electricity (kw-hr; 1977) *c.* 2,145,000; gold (troy oz; 1977) 8; silver (troy oz; 1977) 57.

Ecumenical Movement:
see Religion

Education

The deepening world recession in 1980 had a depressing effect on educational systems, particularly in the West. Most governments took steps to reduce public expenditure and with it spending on education at all levels. This was notably so in the U.K. whose government, headed by Margaret Thatcher (a former minister of education), pursued a tight monetary policy. Constraint was also severe in Sweden, where the government announced a cut of 6.3 billion kronor. Especially hard hit were peripheral areas such as adult education and educational radio centres.

The biggest single element in educational spending is teachers' salaries, and where governments attempted to restrain salaries there were reports of militant action. In the U.K. the teachers' organizations obtained an increase in salary of over 30%, largely as the result of an exercise comparing teachers' salaries with those of other occupations. The government reluctantly agreed to the increase, thus avoiding strike action, but warned that in 1981 any increase would be in single figures despite double digit inflation. Official teachers' strikes over pay in Italy had the effect of paralyzing end-of-year assessments of students in the summer of 1980. Israel's 60,000 teachers threatened to strike over the government's failure to implement the Efzioni Commission report, which was said to support pay increases of 35 to 60%.

The growing political power of teachers' unions in the U.S. was apparent at the Democratic national convention, where 433 delegates and alternates belonging to the National Education Association (NEA) formed the largest single bloc. (By contrast, only 18 NEA members were delegates or alternates to the Republican convention.) The NEA enthusiastically backed Pres. Jimmy Carter's bid for renomination, while the rival American Federation of Teachers (AFT) initially backed Sen. Ted Kennedy, switching to Carter only when Kennedy withdrew from contention. The NEA had never endorsed a presidential candidate before 1976, when it also backed Carter, but with 1.8 million members and representation in every congressional district, it had become an active and influential force in the nation's electoral process. The smaller

AFT had long been active in politics and had working relationships with other member unions of the AFL-CIO.

Fulfilling one of the campaign promises that had brought him NEA support in 1976, President Carter in 1979 had signed into law a bill creating the U.S. Department of Education (ED), which officially came into existence in 1980. Headed by a former federal judge, Shirley M. Hufstedler, the new department included some 6,000 employees, most of them transferred from the Office of Education in the former Department of Health, Education, and Welfare, and had a budget of $14 billion. Eventually, 11,000 persons in the Defense Department's overseas dependents schools would also become part of ED. Conservatives generally opposed the new department, in large measure because they saw it as a threat to local control of schools, and during the presidential campaign Ronald Reagan, the ultimately successful Republican candidate, supported its elimination.

In China there were signs of measurable improvement following the depredations of the Cultural Revolution. It was clear by early 1980 that the change from previous policies had become firmly established, and a plan was delineated that would take China up to 1985. According to the minister of education, Jiang Nanxiang (Chiang Nan-hsiang), the first objective was to make education universal, compulsory, and free. The second was to extend the system so that pupils in the towns would have six years in primary school and six years in secondary school, while in the countryside a further three years would be added to the current six years of schooling. The third priority was to alter the structure of secondary education so as to emphasize vocational training, with individual schools concentrating, for example, on agriculture or commerce. This latter policy harked back to the system in effect before the Cultural Revolution, which was associated with the name of the late former president Liu Shaoqi (Liu Shao-ch'i). Liu, probably the single most important victim of the "gang of four," was rehabilitated early in 1980. Evidently, it was Liu's thought, rather than Mao's, that—for the present at least—was shaping China's educational system.

In 1980 China had 920,000 primary schools with 146 million pupils, ranging in age from 6 or 7 to 11. The population dropped sharply in the secondary schools, to 59 million pupils aged 11 to 16 (or 10 to 15) in 140,000 schools. Almost all the secondary schools were in the cities. There were only 636 institutions of higher education containing just over a million students. By way of comparison, in the U.S. 3,540 per 10,000 of the population received higher education of some kind, while in China the figure was only 9 per 10,000. In an attempt to close this gap, the Chinese created what they called "key" schools and universities. In 1980 there were 6,000 key primary schools, 7,000 key secondaries, and 89 key universities. Resources were being concentrated in this small number of institutions with the intention that they should become pacesetters for the rest.

By contrast, India saw little progress in its educational system, despite the many promises made by the newly victorious Congress Party and the federal education minister, B. Shankaranand. Indira Gandhi's new government had inherited from the previous Janata Party administration a three-tier pattern of education (ten years in school, two years in higher secondary education or junior college, and three years at university). Not surprisingly, since it was devised during Gandhi's earlier period in office, the federal minister announced that this pattern would remain unchanged. However, more stress was to be placed on "national

DAN F. CONNOLLY—TIME, INC.

A third-grade student at a Houston, Texas, elementary school writes out her lesson in Spanish during a bilingual science class.

integration," making young people aware of their social responsibilities and helping in the battle against traditional problems such as the caste system. The Janata administration had also launched a massive adult literacy program, but it seemed to have more or less ground to a halt amid squabbling over waste and misappropriation of funds.

The percentage of illiterates in the world continued to fall, but the actual number of illiterates was growing because of the overall increase in population. At the biennial conference of the International Reading Association—a largely North American-dominated body—in Manila, a Swedish reading expert, Eve Malmquist, contended that 50% of the 6- to 12-year-olds in the world were unlikely ever to go to school. She also said there were signs that reading standards in developed countries, such as Sweden, were dropping and that imbalances between developed and less developed countries were widening. As evidence of the latter, she cited figures showing that Asia, with 56% of the world's population, produced only 20% of the world's books, while Latin America and Africa produced only 2% each.

There were growing doubts about the success of literacy drives in countries thought to have made rapid progress. A report published by the International Labour Office, *International Migration and Development in the Arab Region,* claimed that the literacy rates in Oman and the United Arab Emirates were only 20 and 14%, respectively. The problem was not confined to less developed areas. For example, a research report suggested that about one in three Italians was functionally illiterate, though official estimates placed the number of illiterates at no more than 2.5 million. State Statistical Office figures showed that only about 23% of the population remained in school throughout the prescribed 6- to 14-year age range. But the situation in less developed countries was far worse, as was evidenced at the eighth education conference of Commonwealth countries, held in the summer of 1980 in Colombo, Sri Lanka. Discussions of the rising cost of education dominated the proceedings, and it was clear to observers that the long-standing goal of universal primary education was becoming increasingly difficult for some countries to achieve.

In Western Europe the nine ministers of education of the European Economic Community (EEC) finally held a joint meeting in Brussels in June, the first since 1976. The Danes had consistently opposed such a meeting on the grounds that it was not provided for in the Treaty of Rome. The results were fairly innocuous. The ministers pressed for more "mobility" of students; a little progress was made on the mutual recognition of degrees and a common policy on fees; and it was agreed that European studies courses should be encouraged and that language teaching should be promoted. More significant was the establishment in September of an information network within the EEC called Eurydice. Its objective was to provide a feedback and general information service to member countries on such topics as the transition from school to work, the learning of foreign languages, and education of migrants.

Primary and Secondary Education. Public school enrollments in the U.S. continued to decline, a trend that was expected to continue until the mid-1980s. Meanwhile, teacher supply and demand were relatively in balance. The number of persons entering teacher-preparation programs had fallen enough to eliminate surpluses in several grade levels and subjects.

Busing for purposes of racial desegregation remained a live issue in U.S. education. During the year the largest court-ordered busing scheme in the quarter of a century since the landmark desegregation decision in *Brown* v. *Board of Education of Topeka* got under way in the nation's second-largest school district. Los Angeles had appealed to state courts and finally to the U.S. Supreme Court to block the plan, but on the day before school opened, a Supreme Court justice refused to intervene on the grounds that the normal flow of state appeals had not been exhausted. Only 27% of the children in the Los Angeles public schools were white, and the district covered a huge area of 1,840 sq km (710 sq mi). Limited busing during the preceeding two years had not succeeded in accomplishing desegregation, and meanwhile an

Members of a high school football team welcome black students being bused to their school on the first day of court-ordered desegregation in St. Louis, Missouri.

WIDE WORLD

estimated 50,000 white students had left the system. Under the new plan, some 80,000–100,000 students were being bused. In a first-of-a-kind suit, the California attorney general claimed that forcing children to attend the Los Angeles schools constituted cruel and unjust punishment. Relief was demanded, though no specific action was requested.

The largest busing plan for a city and its suburbs would affect 60% of Delaware's public school students. In a new, court-created school district that included Wilmington and 11 nearby districts, students would go to schools other than their nearest neighbourhood school for at least three years. Twice during the year the Supreme Court rejected appeals by school boards for relief from busing. Specific desegregation actions occurred in Cleveland, Ohio (where more than half the students were being bused); Dallas, Texas (which had lost increasing numbers of white students); Chicago (which agreed to develop its own plan after the Justice Department threatened to sue the system); Birmingham, Ala. (which agreed to a limited busing and magnet school plan and some school closings to increase desegregation); and Houston, Texas, and 22 suburban districts. Federal officials said they were studying the largely white suburban schools to see how they related to Chicago's situation.

Despite this activity, many civil rights advocates feared a backlash against what opponents referred to as "forced busing." In its post-election "lame duck" session, the Senate passed a bill—attached as a rider to an appropriations bill—designed to prohibit the Justice Department from using appropriated funds to pursue cases that would result in court-ordered busing. A similar measure was passed by the House. Faced with the threat of a presidential veto, Senate and House conferees dropped the provision from the bill. However, opponents of busing planned to bring up the matter again in the 97th Congress, which would be considerably more conservative. Sen. Strom Thurmond (Rep., S.C.), who would be chairman of the Senate Judiciary Committee, stated that he planned to seek legislation removing educational matters from the federal courts' jurisdiction.

Shortly before its fall recess, Congress adopted an amendment to another funding bill preventing the Department of Education from enforcing far-reaching federal requirements for bilingual education until June 1981. The plan would have required children to be taught basic subjects in their native tongue until they had mastered English. In its 1974 decision on the subject, the Supreme Court had mandated assistance for the estimated 3.5 million non-English-speaking students in the U.S. but had left the specific procedures up to local districts.

Other matters pertaining to education were before the courts during the year. The Supreme Court indicated that it would review the right of school districts to limit black enrollment in order to discourage whites from moving away. A federal judge upset a 1975 Texas law that excluded the children of illegal immigrants from the public schools unless the parents paid tuition; Texas officials claimed that the ruling would add 40,000–140,000 students to the state's school systems. Modifying a 1971 court order that the Internal Revenue Service lift tax exemptions for segregated private schools, a U.S. district judge ruled that privately operated schools must prove they do not discriminate against minorities if they want to retain their tax-exempt status. A federal appeals judge held that the principal of a church-related school had exceeded his constitutional rights when he expelled a white student for dating a black fellow student.

WHITE HOUSE PHOTO

Beverly Bimes, a teacher from St. Louis, Missouri, was congratulated at a White House ceremony by Pres. Jimmy Carter on being elected 1980 National Teacher of the Year. The annual event is sponsored by the Encyclopaedia Britannica companies, *Good Housekeeping* magazine, and the Council of Chief State School Officers.

North Carolina became the first state to implement its plan for minimal competency testing before high school graduation. Since 1976, 38 states had set dates after which they would require such tests statewide. Each state determined which competencies were to be included and the required level necessary for passing from grade to grade or for graduation. Those who failed were given remedial work until they could pass.

Criticism of the Scholastic Aptitude Test (SAT), widely used for college entrance, continued to mount, as opponents charged that it was an inadequate predictor of college potential, was inaccurately graded, and was surrounded with excessive secrecy. In an effort to counter its critics, the publisher decided to publish old tests to help students prepare for the current edition. The College Entrance Examination Board said it would make it possible for students to double-check the scored sheets. The publisher also began to provide information on how the tests are constructed and pledged to continue efforts to remove any disadvantage that minority students and females might experience.

In West Germany education became an issue in the federal elections in October. The Social Democrats, who were ultimately successful, supported comprehensive (nonselective) schools while the Christian Democrats opposed them. In fact, only some 300,000 pupils—2.5% of the total—attended the 300 comprehensive schools or *Gesamtschulen*, located chiefly in Länder controlled by Social Democrats. The issue of the education of foreign workers' children was more or less sidestepped by the politicians, though Turkish children, in par-

World Education

Most recent official data

Country	1st level (primary)			General 2nd level (secondary)			Vocational 2nd level			3rd level (higher)			Literacy	
	Students (full-time)	Teachers (full-time)	Total schools	Students (full-time)	Teachers (full-time)	Total schools	Students (full-time)	Teachers (full-time)	Total schools	Students (full-time)	Teachers (full-time)	Total schools	% of population	Over age
Afghanistan	942,817	29,789	3,417	92,401	4,530	318	12,118	889	26	19,109	1,468	20	8.0	15
Albania	569,600	22,686	1,347	32,900	1,318	46	69,700[1]	1,712[1]	85[1]	28,668	1,158	5	71.0	9
Algeria	2,972,242	80,853	8,209	821,168	30,614	939	23,123[1]	2,007[1]	52[1]	51,510	6,421	15	26.4	15
Angola	1,026,291	25,000	5,585	109,456[1,2]	4,723[1,2]	177	...	...	...	1,109	273	1	30.0	...
Argentina	3,680,185	199,384	20,538	441,907	60,199	1,674	846,200	113,515	3,718	619,950[1]	39,970[1]	412[1]	92.6	15
Australia	1,884,753	90,667	7,337	1,102,178	84,529	2,256	45,193	13,104	1,159	182,224[1]	22,140[1]	90	...	...
Austria	434,432	26,369	3,466	612,982	50,549	2,023	400,872[1]	19,230[1]	1,146[1]	122,189	12,543	37	98.0	15
Bangladesh	8,312,011	182,800	40,445	2,213,068	98,965	9,304	20,545[1]	962[1]	122[1]	158,604	13,503	700	22.2	15
Bolivia	922,850	38,737	...	128,081[1,2]	7,143[1,2]	...	...	...	...	51,585	2,307	16	39.8	15
Botswana	156,664	4,870	377	16,736	778	35	2,802[1]	276[1]	25[1]	1,052	129	1	18.4	15
Brazil	20,340,577	994,031	186,424	2,391,465[1,2]	168,451[1,2]	9,323	...	...	...	1,159,046	95,758	860	79.8	15
Brunei	34,360	1,824	172	15,204	936	27	949[1]	145[1]	4[1]	...	...	...	64.0	15
Bulgaria	973,007	49,958	...	102,872	7,585	...	268,257[1]	19,220[1]	407[1]	115,125	15,578	...	91.4	8
Burma	3,731,160	84,593	21,999	924,739	31,433	1,848	14,739[1]	1,153[1]	58[1]	112,671	3,922	19	68.3	8
Cambodia	350,000[3]	7,500[3]	1,333[3]	...	...	...	...	...	...	...	...	...	36.1	...
Cameroon	1,254,065	25,248	4,721	147,073	5,112	301	46,728[1]	3,192[1]	164[1]	10,001	439	10	12.0	...
Canada	3,364,213	266,302[3]	...	1,794,882	...	...	...	...	...	611,520	52,409	235	95.6	14
Chile	2,235,861	72,352	4,120	358,127	19,746	525	178,301[1]	11,029[1]	234[1]	167,546	22,211	8	90.7	15
China	146,630,000	2,600,000	900,000	59,050,000	...	160,000	1,199,000[1]	...	2,000[1]	1,020,000	...	598	95.0	15
Colombia	4,160,527	128,494	32,230	1,187,148	56,402	3,252	428,963[1]	23,340[1]	932[1]	290,624	27,384	70	98.5	15
Congo	345,736	6,675	...	127,210	2,883	...	11,828[1]	640	...	3,642	165	2	28.8	...
Costa Rica	367,026	12,500	...	121,202[2]	5,915[2]	...	...	...	...	38,629	1,967	5	84.7	15
Cuba	1,626,386	77,605	13,310	759,288	58,136	1,024	314,998[1]	20,441[1]	462[1]	133,014	10,139	28	98	15
Czechoslovakia	1,878,000	91,876	8,860	133,067	8,481	339	210,996[1]	16,677[1]	585[1]	183,632	17,738	36	99.5	15
Denmark	461,839	53,401	2,234	290,499	58,957	2,558	104,189[1]	5,792[1]	162[1]	108,591	6,713	385	100	15
Dominican Republic	867,592	17,932	5,487	136,570	4,417	175	6,679[1]	348[1]	20[1]	42,395	429	6	67.3	15
Ecuador	1,427,627	39,747	10,655	435,056	24,120	990	55,161[1]	6,140[1]	221[1]	274,968	11,998	30	79.0	18
Egypt	4,211,345	132,728	10,297	1,935,088	59,729	2,402	474,017[1]	42,896[1]	448[1]	518,630	...	12	43.4	10
El Salvador	858,811	16,563	...	73,967[1,2]	2,869[1,2]	...	1,069[4]	25[4]	...	31,351	2,015	...	49.0	15
Fiji	131,100	4,209	644	34,493	1,662	124	2,543[1]	242[1]	31[1]	1,448	150	1	79.0	15
Finland	422,638	25,096	4,299	343,759	19,430	1,051	100,438[1]	13,102[1]	541[1]	122,427	5,787	20	100	15
France	5,405,056	197,227	54,229	3,844,733	235,715	7,382	1,269,489[1]	77,328[1]	3,801[1]	1,041,916	17,646	82	100	7
Germany, East	2,485,386[3]	167,424[3]	5,599[3]	...	...	...	...	...	...	294,553	36,013	287	100	15
Germany, West	3,273,734	430,979[3]	22,966[3]	6,015,360	...	...	526,469[1]	31,467[1]	4,913[1]	1,103,071	120,224	3,079	99	15
Greece	933,535	34,687	9,695	579,771	24,295	2,160	124,728[1]	...	1,957[1]	123,429	6,718	155	86.0	15
Guatemala	709,018	21,060	6,010	145,770[1,2]	8,604[1,2]	493	...	...	...	29,234	1,934	5	47.0	15
Honduras	528,138	14,369	5,088	76,776[2]	2,771[2]	...	...	...	...	21,227	96	2	46.0	15
Hong Kong	553,530	18,321	882	441,785	15,064[2]	399	11,761	...	26	25,231	2,643	20	80.9	15
Hungary	1,127,900	73,469	4,214	341,700[2]	73,469[2]	282[2]	...	...	...	103,500	13,597	48	98.2	15
India	72,947,804	1,276,446	477,037	26,435,894	1,581,263	141,600	421,028[1]	15,558[1]	2,045[1]	4,296,242	232,903	9,805	34.2	15
Indonesia	22,389,796	709,511	114,741	3,380,458	212,405	14,204	1,089,460[1]	78,492[1]	3,879[1]	304,025	21,802	639	63.9	15
Iran	4,403,106	167,457	40,197	2,370,341	84,092	7,667	314,135[1]	12,303[1]	950[1]	175,675	13,952	244	36.2	15
Iraq	2,459,870	87,148	10,560	781,766	25,254	1,579	68,674[1]	4,212[1]	155[1]	89,197	5,207	62	40.0	15
Ireland	564,323	19,129	3,561	285,326	17,482	832	7,348[1]	203[1]	70[1]	37,156	3,578	63	100	15
Israel	645,095	35,066	2,041	84,416	6,220	368	78,743[1]	8,517[1]	359[1]	87,724	13,981	54	93.4	15
Italy	4,584,300	278,044	31,524	3,545,298	309,933	11,903	1,687,949[1]	148,296[1]	4,911[1]	756,922	43,120	67	93.9	15
Ivory Coast	894,184	17,044	2,697	144,605	3,423	...	22,437[1]	620[1]	...	20,087	368	...	20.0	15
Japan	11,629,121	459,553	24,876	9,498,087[1,2]	487,467[1,2]	15,875[1,2]	...	...	...	2,220,364	207,177	1,016	100.0	15
Jordan	448,411	13,898	1,095	238,763	11,267	1,333	9,880[1]	641[1]	44[1]	27,526	1,178	15	60.0	15
Kenya	2,977,000	89,773	8,896	377,000[1,2]	13,368[1,2]	1,486[1,2]	...	...	...	5,000	892	20	40.0	15
Korea, South	5,658,002	119,064	6,487	3,404,602	82,338	2,922	764,187[1]	23,468[1]	605[1]	539,601	20,510	224	88.5	13
Kuwait	145,626	7,722	224	167,253	14,032	281	3,461[1]	582[1]	6[1]	12,391	1,020	5	59.6	15
Laos	487,000	14,218	5,893	72,600	2,494	...	7,814[1]	591[1]	...	1,684	152	3	60	...
Lebanon	497,723	32,901[3]	2,319	167,578	...	1,241	7,133[1]	1,059[1]	159	50,803	2,313	13	88.0	15
Lesotho	228,523	4,233	1,075	17,732	621	60	1,780[1]	142[1]	11	847	95	9	56.5	15
Liberia	129,776	7,360[3]	843	108,077	...	275	1,173[1]	119[1]	6	2,694	190	3	21.5	15
Libya	574,770	26,182	2,150	194,866	12,792	861	30,420[1]	2,455[1]	106	17,174	1,922	19	52.4	15
Luxembourg	32,436	1,998	...	8,558	1,801[2]	15	15,816[1]	...	42	302	172	2	100.0	15
Malawi	675,740	11,115	2,371	15,079	707	61	2,641[1]	179[1]	13	1,179	128	4	16.5	15
Malaysia	1,957,722	63,228	6,370	1,012,282	37,063	1,179	16,153	1,106	82	47,624	4,568	23	60.8	10
Mali	291,966	8,280	...	8,915	540[2]	...	4,578[1]	126[4]	...	4,216	450	...	2.2	...
Mauritius	138,352	6,537	252	80,939	2,787	142	1,392[1]	115[1]	10	311	83	1	61.6	12
Mexico	13,307,333	306,173	62,511	3,024,000	174,338	8,449	478,830[1]	33,567[1]	2,688[1]	610,840	52,294	223	86.7	15
Morocco	1,925,187	50,829	2,236	650,796	40,507	644	26,223	...	...	76,054	...	19	22.2	...
Mozambique	1,500,000	...	...	80,000	...	...	...	...	...	906	164	...	7.0	...
Nepal	769,049	23,395	...	285,154	11,630	...	23,643[1]	809[1]	...	24,297	1,756	...	12.5	15
Netherlands, The	1,500,530	63,302	9,629	820,634	53,354	1,530	556,250[1]	46,000[1]	1,838[1]	269,050	27,800	369	100.0	15
New Zealand	517,190	20,822	2,569	230,128	13,390	396	6,286	2,073	21	55,008	3,532	15	100.0	15
Nicaragua	378,640	9,986	2,402	80,254	3,145[2]	198	18,620[1]	...	81[1]	23,737	1,052	8	57.0	15
Nigeria	11,457,772	287,040	35,323	1,159,404	19,409	2,959	249,469[1]	20,529[1]	357[1]	101,210	5,019	13	25.0	15
Norway	396,939	21,212	3,021	264,134	23,405[2]	1,419[2]	94,857	...	...	60,406	5,742	134	100.0	15
Pakistan	6,170,000	135,300	53,162	1,860,000	109,200	8,204	46,361[1]	3,558[1]	406[1]	316,500	18,304	554	26.7	10
Panama	372,823	13,730	2,283	96,305	4,042	84	41,511[1]	2,160[1]	114[1]	37,885	1,796	2	81.3	15
Papua New Guinea	277,301	8,872	1,994	34,626	1,299	94	12,233[1]	680[1]	107[1]	9,804	1,235	46	32.1	10
Paraguay	493,231	17,525	2,799	101,126[2]	9,663[2]	...	...	...	...	20,496	1,945	...	79.7	15
Peru	3,126,000	77,844	20,126	1,090,200[2]	37,383[2]	1,537	...	...	329	233,420	13,468	58	71.6	15
Philippines	7,992,406	256,370	33,180	1,887,469	80,192[2]	2,445	969,952	...	284	969,952	31,783	...	76.4	15
Poland	4,217,200	196,400	13,717	450,100	23,100	1,260	1,941,800[1]	76,800[1]	10,937[1]	485,200	52,300	90	97.8	15
Portugal	1,284,862	67,051	13,448	417,112	13,272	458	90,784[1]	9,590[1]	223[1]	84,911	8,198	267	71.0	...
Puerto Rico	432,012	15,308	1,725	142,836	6,051	203	57,863	2,600	84	130,105	3,300	27	90.5	14
Romania	3,423,135	150,415	14,587	1,044,135	51,217	934	175,152[1]	4,077[1]	831[1]	190,560	14,227	134	100.0	15
Rwanda	515,712	8,161	1,606	13,799[2]	820[2]	56	...	...	62[1]	975	184	4	23.0	15
Saudi Arabia	726,063	38,077	2,711	237,854	16,458	749	20,599[1]	2,065[1]	78	32,729	2,966	20	5.2	...
Senegal	346,585	8,186	...	78,384	1,758	...	14,090[1]	820[1]	124	8,892	412	...	45.6	6
Singapore	297,873	11,052	351	176,521	8,418	135	14,060[1]	945[1]	16[1]	15,684	1,068	4	77.9	10
South Africa	4,370,474	167,797[1,2,3]	17,173[1,3]	1,183,540	...	...	33,517	...	176	218,321	15,803	67	89.0	...
Soviet Union	34,200,000	2,625,000	147,000	10,200,000	...	...	4,672,000	230,000	4,357	5,185,100	345,000	870	99.7	10
Spain	6,668,066	213,386	203,023	999,479	59,375	2,342	455,943	30,762	1,971	643,272	33,581	114	90.1	15
Sri Lanka	1,975,749	138,488[3]	3,834	1,159,967	...	5,501	8,897[1]	1,771[1]	25	15,426	2,000	...	78.1	10
Sudan	1,302,040	34,988	4,440	313,093	13,792	1,075	13,157[1]	1,090	1,069	24,109	1,963	20	20.0	9
Sweden	686,111	38,689	4,923	575,190[1,2]	62,964[1,2]	...	...	...	...	157,350	...	...	100.0	15
Syria	1,375,922	45,254	7,435	540,169	28,759	1,230	35,182[1]	3,865[1]	21[1]	96,040	...	3	46.6	10
Taiwan	2,244,362	68,696	2,394	1,585,341[2]	68,190[2]	995[2]	...	...	...	329,603	16,129	101	85.9	15
Tanzania	1,954,320	38,199	...	57,143	2,930	...	10,716[1]	801[1]	...	2,534	553	...	...	...
Thailand	6,848,121	283,204	3,721[3]	1,503,646	66,965	...	244,277[1]	34,934[1]	270[1]	169,639	29,667	129	85.7	10
Togo	421,436	7,251	1,199	88,409	2,030	112	7,006[1]	347[1]	23	2,777	236	2	10.5	...
Tunisia	1,004,144	25,593	2,469	156,082	10,836[1,2]	202	74,737[1]	...	...	26,781	3,471	...	32.2	10
Turkey	5,454,356	184,123	43,221	2,028,476	40,351	4,684	468,571[1]	17,693[1]	2,619[1]	312,871	18,391	...	54.7	6
Uganda	1,139,413[5]	32,554[5]	4,022	59,882[5]	2,126[5]	198	10,765[1,5]	644[1,5]	44[1]	5,148[5]	681[5]	4	32.0	15
United Kingdom	5,535,082	241,607	27,098	4,785,520	290,359	5,801	553,128	85,544	802	319,859	44,981	106	100.0	15
United States	31,600,000[6]	1,343,000[6]	...	15,300,000[1,2]	1,117,000[1,2]	...	...	...	...	11,500,000	820,000	...	98.8	14
Uruguay	345,739	13,788	2,307	141,731	13,980	261	46,268[1]	4,541[1]	104	39,927	2,149	1	90.5	15
Venezuela	2,204,074	94,218[6]	...	710,434[1,2]	46,964[1,2]	...	...	...	...	247,518	19,787	...	83.4	...
Western Samoa	42,073	1,458	153	9,719	458	39	473[1]	41[1]	4	194	67	6	98.3	10
Yugoslavia	1,427,769	57,335	13,119	1,912,231	56,013[1,2]	...	501,557[1]	...	...	285,431	18,178	349	84.9	10
Zaire	3,818,934	80,481	...	458,776	14,483[1,2]	...	184,899[1]	...	...	21,021	2,550	...	15.0	15
Zambia	964,475	19,089	2,777	88,842	3,539	124	6,422[1]	749[1]	14	8,783	412	15	40.7	15
Zimbabwe	832,603	18,715	2,559	72,814	3,334	177	6,041[1]	615[1]	29[1]	4,563	483	11	45.0	15

[1]Includes teacher training. [2]Includes vocational. [3]Data for primary include secondary. [4]Teacher training only. [5]Public schools only. [6]Includes preprimary education.

ticular, presented a problem since they formed a large proportion of the child population in some inner city areas.

In France, as well, comprehensive schools (known as *collèges uniques*) were the centre of some controversy. According to the reforms of the previous minister of education, René Haby, the unstreamed secondary school should have become the norm by 1980, but teachers complained that in reality there was little difference and most schools remained streamed. Despite financial constraints, the French continued with Europe's most important school microcomputer program. The plan envisioned 10,000 microcomputers in upper secondary schools (*lycées*) by 1986, or one terminal unit per 70 pupils.

The most important curricular development in the U.K. was the publication of *A Framework for the School Curriculum* by the Department of Education and Science. Its main emphasis was on a "common core" of traditional subjects such as English and mathematics. This reflected the Conservative Party's long-standing concern with standards in language and arithmetic. Most teachers and administrators reacted fairly sharply, insisting that the curriculum should not be too narrowly defined. There was a suspicion, reinforced at the annual conference of the Conservative Party, that the "common core" was really a device to reduce spending.

In the Soviet Union some unusually candid criticism of the content of the secondary-school curriculum was voiced by Vsevolod N. Stoletov, president of the Academy of Pedagogical Sciences. He complained that much teaching was too academic and that, to provide better motivation for pupils, there should be a shift to more technical education and, in particular, to trade schools. In Cambodia, where there had been no schooling for ten years, it was reported that some 900,000 children had registered for primary education, although only 5,000 of the 20,000 teachers in the schools had had any training. Mexico began to provide boarding schools for primary-school children in rural areas, the object being to stem the movement of population into the overcrowded cities. A modest start was made in the first year with some 33 schools and 7,500 children.

Higher Education. Retrenchment—or, at best, readjustment—in higher education in Europe generally took one of two forms: a straight cut in expenditure (for example, The Netherlands cut spending by £10 million, mainly through salary reductions and layoffs); or the weeding out of "eternal" students and frequent repeaters of courses and the elimination of less socially necessary courses. Thus, the Dutch minister of education, Arie Pais, set about reducing the university course from six years to four and undertook to revise the lottery system used to decide who could enroll in oversubscribed courses. In West Germany, where the student population was expected to rise to almost 1.3 million by 1988 because of high birthrates in the early 1960s, entry to subjects like medicine, with a restricted number of places, began to be determined by aptitude tests.

In France Alice Saunier-Séïté, the minister for higher education, embarked on draconian measures to prune postgraduate courses in sociology and courses in education and psychology in the third and fourth years of undergraduate school. This was particularly hard on smaller universities like Limoges, Rouen, and Avignon. There were widespread protests that eventually involved confrontation between university presidents and Premier Raymond Barre, but few concessions were made to the universities. In Italy the widespread scandal of "part-time professors," who drew large salaries for giving only one or two lectures a week while holding other, highly remunerative jobs, rumbled on without resolution.

The U.S. Congress started to curtail funds for college students, with the aim of saving an estimated $3 billion within the next five years. Benefiting from federal aid that was approved were students eligible for federally guaranteed loans, black institutions and others serving disadvantaged students, and college libraries and projects dealing with language and adult education.

The cost of sending a student to a four-year college in the U.S. reached an average of $6,000 annually, an increase of $500 over the preceding year. According to the College Scholarship Service, the cost of four years of college was higher than the median yearly income of all U.S. families and was likely to increase. Alexander Astin's annual survey predicted that college costs would reach $20,000 per year if increases continued at the same rate as in 1970–80. Families were responsible for about 56% of all college expenses. Some $14 billion was available in student aid, with 17% from government loans, 57% from government grants, and 7% from state aid programs. The final 19% came from private sources.

The Carnegie Council on Policy Studies in Higher Education predicted a 5–15% drop in college and university enrollments. In its final report, the council, which began its work in 1967, said that students might, in fact, benefit from this development as colleges began to recruit, counsel, assist, teach, and grade more actively and conscientiously and as grading and course planning became more student centred. The times might be difficult for staffs and administrations, however, and a decline in quality and capability was likely. The group's chairman, Clark Kerr, thought the several hundred liberal arts colleges that recruit locally were most likely to suffer from declining enrollments. Although the council projected a decrease in students in the traditional college age range of 18–24, it did suggest that increased numbers of older students, women, and minorities might help to balance that decline. A further conjecture was that the current retention rate might improve.

College graduates in 1980 were not severely affected by the recession. Jobs were available across the board, and majors in certain fields were eagerly sought. These included engineering, computer science, business, health science, and retailing. After several lean years, jobs for public school teachers were more plentiful. The "baby boom" generation had now entered the job market, so fewer new graduates were looking for work.

Some 300 black studies programs had survived

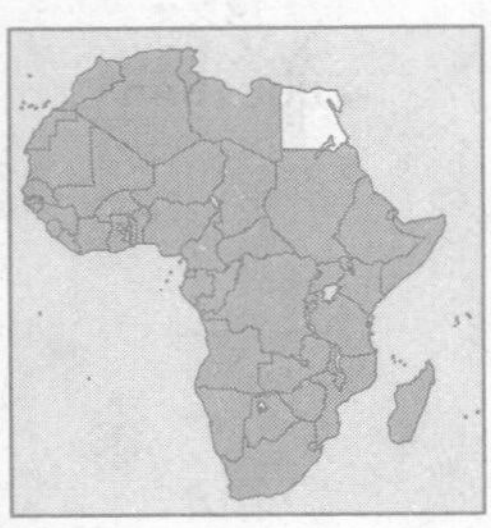

Egypt

the cutbacks of recent years, a drop of almost 200 since the peak years of the 1960s. Supporters claimed that black studies were useful to blacks and to an increasing number of whites. They also believed that the existence of such programs influenced other academic departments to include information about the history and culture of blacks, other minorities, and women.

The courts rejected attempts by several states and institutions to refuse university admission to Iranian students or to discourage them from enrolling by charging exceptional tuition. The efforts to exclude Iranians came in response to tensions that arose during the long months when Americans were held hostage in Iran. Some courts attempted to determine the extent to which foreign students are protected by the U.S. Constitution, but the Supreme Court had never clearly ruled on the matter.

Research. The third edition of the World Bank's *Education Sector Policy Paper*, published in April, contained heartening evidence of the effects education could have on production and productivity. In a study of 20 less developed countries, the social rates of return on primary education were found to be significantly positive. The rate of return was significantly higher for primary education than for secondary or higher education, and the report noted that "Arguments of economic efficiency, along with arguments of equity, support continued investment in primary education."

At the same time, surveys in Ireland and Great Britain showed that little progress had been made in increasing social mobility through education. The children of semiskilled and unskilled workers were seriously underrepresented in Irish universities. These social classes constituted one-seventh of the population, but only 634 of the student population of 37,000 had a working-class background. A major study published in January, sponsored by the Oxford Social Mobility Project in Great Britain and covering a period of some 40 years, showed that inequalities of educational opportunity had remained remarkably stable. Children of the "service class" were about three times more likely to obtain the kind of selective secondary schooling that could lead to higher education than working-class children.

A U.S. study sponsored by the National Association of Elementary School Principals and the Institute for Development of Educational Activities indicated that children living with only one parent have many more academic and discipline problems than those with two parents in the home. The 20% of schoolchildren living with one parent had lower academic achievement and were more likely to be late, to be expelled, and to become dropouts.

The University of Michigan Institute for Social Research found that the pattern of drug use had changed significantly since 1970, when users tended to be of college age. More young people were using more and stronger marijuana at an earlier age and with increased frequency. Use was common in high schools and frequent even in the elementary grades. One in nine high school students reported using marijuana daily, and 60% of seniors had tried the drug. According to the National Institute on Drug Abuse, short-term effects of pot include impaired memory, thinking, reading comprehension, and verbal and arithmetic problem solving, all important factors in learning.

(JOEL L. BURDIN; TUDOR DAVID)

See also Libraries; Motion Pictures; Museums.

Egypt

A republic of northeast Africa, Egypt is bounded by Israel, Sudan, Libya, the Mediterranean Sea, and the Red Sea. Area: 997,667 sq km (385,201 sq mi). Pop. (1979 est.): 41,065,000. Cap. and largest city: Cairo (pop., 1979 est., 5,423,000). Language: Arabic. Religion (1976): Muslim 94%, according to official figures; non-Muslims, however, may be undercounted. President in 1980, Anwar as-Sadat; prime ministers, Mustafa Khalil and, from May 15, Sadat.

Foreign Affairs. Pres. Anwar as-Sadat continued to be isolated in 1980 from the rest of the Arab community as he pursued his policy of accommodating Israel. Sadat seemed intent on respecting the agreed-upon deadline of May 26 for talks with Israel on Palestinian autonomy, but the date passed without substantive progress. The talks were broken off by the Egyptians because of the Israeli government bill presented in the Knesset annexing the whole of East Jerusalem. Kamal Hassan Ali, deputy prime minister for defense and foreign affairs, subsequently said Egypt would tear up the Camp David agreement unless a settlement was reached soon after the U.S. presidential election in November. Sadat had always maintained that the U.S. "holds all the cards" in the Middle East conflict. It was his intention in signing the 1978 Camp David agreement that the U.S. should become an active broker in the Israeli-Egyptian negotiations. Given the inertia gripping the U.S. administration in the pre-election period, the lack of progress in 1980 appeared explicable. Yet even moderate Arab rulers such as the sultan of Oman, who initially supported the Sadat peace initiative, were puzzled by the lack of progress on fundamental issues concerning the Palestinians.

Egypt was obliged to break off all remaining diplomatic links with the members of the Arab Steadfastness Front—Algeria, Libya, Syria, Yemen (Aden), and the Palestine Liberation Organization—on April 16 in protest against decisions by the hard-line states to tighten sanctions against Egypt. The nuisance nature of these decisions was distressing to the Egyptian leadership. More serious in their view, however, was the line taken by oil-rich Arab states such as Saudi Arabia and Kuwait in cutting economic aid, even though this aid was only a small proportion of Egypt's total requirements.

The Iran-Iraq war produced an appeal by President Sadat to Washington to speed up the supply of promised military hardware, including advanced interceptors for the Air Force. The U.S. expressed its support for the Sadat government by sending a military force of 1,400 men to Egypt for the first overseas exercises of the newly formed Rapid Deployment Force. Economic assistance

WIDE WORLD

Egyptian Foreign Minister Kamal Hassan Ali (left) met with Israeli Ambassador to Egypt Eliahu Ben-Elissar at the Israeli embassy in Cairo, which opened in February.

of $715 million a year made Egypt one of the biggest U.S. Agency for International Development (AID) operations anywhere in the world. In addition, the World Bank provided substantial assistance to Egypt's economy at the prompting of the U.S. administration. The U.S. agreed in principle to supply Egypt with some of its most advanced military equipment, including F-16 fighter aircraft. The military supply package included personnel carriers, Hawk antiaircraft missiles, and Chrysler M-60A3 tanks. Since Egypt's military arsenal consisted largely of aging Soviet equipment, the pressure on Sadat from his generals to rearm from U.S. sources was acute. A pan-Arab venture to build weapons and munitions factories in Egypt, headed by a Saudi, had collapsed in the aftermath of the Camp David agreement.

The stabilization of Egypt's relations with its powerful and well-armed neighbour may have had some limited beneficial effects. Ambassadors were exchanged by them in February for the first time. Israel's Foreign Minister Yitzhak Shamir (*see* BIOGRAPHIES) was in Cairo on September 9 at the invitation of the minister of state for foreign affairs, Boutros Boutros Ghali, to discuss strictly bilateral issues. The prospect of some further economic cooperation with the Israelis also seemed likely, although the first steps, including the establishment of air services between the two capitals, were hesitant. It was agreed to open the Sinai border to overland trade in December. Other Arab governments reacted angrily to the two countries' ties by extending the Arab boycott of Israel to any Egyptian entity perceived as trading in or with Tel Aviv.

Domestic Affairs. President Sadat decided in May to become his own prime minister and attempted to streamline his Cabinet. (He had taken similar actions just before the 1973 war.) Six deputy prime ministers were appointed who were to form an inner Cabinet. The most powerful man in this group was undoubtedly Defense Minister Kamal Hassan Ali, who in addition to having responsibility for defense took on foreign affairs and the task of overseeing information. The appointment of Planning Minister Abdel-Razzaq Abdel-Majid as economic czar was intriguing. He was given the task of overseeing planning, economy, trade, and supply. The concentration of all these roles into one job had been sought unsuccessfully by the former deputy prime minister for the economy, Abdel-Moneim al-Qaisouni, in June 1978.

Oil revenues for 1980 were expected to reach about U.S. $2.1 billion, as against $1.6 billion in 1979. To a great extent, they were the reason for economic recovery. Possibly as a side effect of the generally favourable Western response to Sadat's peace with Israel, there was no shortage of help for the Egyptian economy or reluctance on the part of foreign investors from the West to take advantage of the country's "open door" policies. Indeed, the health of the economy was a factor in delaying agreement with the International Monetary Fund (IMF) on an extended standby credit. Abdel-Majid said on July 9: "If we sign an agreement with the fund for us to draw on it, our balance of payments will have to be in deficit, but we have a surplus of well over $400 million."

There were signs that the IMF's medicine—which included such conditions as higher taxation and a harder line with unprofitable public-sector companies—was politically difficult for the government to swallow. In August the government was obliged to make $546 million available for food subsidies—something the IMF disapproved of—but this was followed by the politically sensitive decision to ban meat sales for one month.

Domestic opposition to President Sadat tended to become inflamed over such issues as food shortages, as evidenced by the bread riots in early 1977 that nearly toppled the government. Sadat's popularity depended on his ability to provide Egyptians with the benefits of peace, which Egyptians saw in terms of a higher standard of living. With the remittances of Egyptian workers overseas stabilized at about $2 billion a year, the only large sources of revenue other than oil were from the Suez Canal, $700 million a year, and tourism, about $650 million a year. The Suez Canal was opened to supertankers in December.

Sectarian violence increased in 1980, partly because of the Islamic fundamentalism that had swept through Muslim countries in the wake of the Iranian revolution. There were serious distur-

EGYPT

Education. (1977–78) Primary, pupils 4,211,345, teachers 132,728; secondary, pupils 1,935,088, teachers 59,729; vocational, pupils 437,495, teachers 39,816; teacher training, students 36,522, teachers 3,080; higher, students 518,630, teaching staff (1976–77) 19,507.

Finance. Monetary unit: Egyptian pound, with (Sept. 22, 1980) an official rate of E£0.70 to U.S. $1 (free rate of E£1.68 = £1 sterling). Gold, SDR's, and foreign exchange (June 1980) U.S. $1,118,000,000. Budget (1979 est.) revenue E£10,249 million; expenditure E£12,929 million. Gross national product (1977) E£7,139 million. Money supply (June 1980) E£5,008.4 million. Cost of living (1975 = 100; April 1980) 183.

Foreign Trade. (1979) Imports E£2,686 million; exports E£1,288 million. Import sources: U.S. 18%; West Germany 11%; Italy 8%; France 8%; U.K. 7%; Japan 5%. Export destinations: Italy 27%; U.S.S.R. 8%; The Netherlands 8%; West Germany 5%; U.K. 5%; Japan 5%. Main exports: crude oil 31%; cotton 21%; cotton yarn and fabrics 13%; petroleum products 11%; fruit and vegetables 7%; aluminum 5%.

Transport and Communications. Roads (1979) 28,910 km. Motor vehicles in use (1979): passenger 379,000; commercial (including buses) 114,700. Railways: (1979) 4,832 km; traffic (1976) 8,748,000,000 passenger-km, freight 2,201,000,000 net ton-km. Air traffic (1978): 2,324,000,000 passenger-km, freight 25.8 million net ton-km. Shipping (1979): merchant vessels 100 gross tons and over 243; gross tonnage 541,721. Telephones (Jan. 1975) 503,200. Radio receivers (Dec. 1977) 5,275,000. Television receivers (Dec. 1977) 1 million.

Agriculture. Production (in 000; metric tons; 1979): wheat 1,856; barley 122; millet 635; corn 2,937; rice 2,507; potatoes *c.* 977; sugar, raw value *c.* 690; tomatoes 2,421; onions *c.* 536; dry broad beans (1978) 215; watermelons (1978) *c.* 1,282; dates *c.* 416; oranges *c.* 868; grapes *c.* 270; cotton, lint *c.* 470; cheese *c.* 239; beef and buffalo meat *c.* 243. Livestock (in 000; 1979): cattle 1,954; buffalo 2,321; sheep 1,679; goats 1,427; asses 1,672; camels 105; chickens 27,292.

Industry. Production (in 000; metric tons; 1978): cement 3,033; iron ore (50% metal content) 1,540; crude oil (1979) 26,570; natural gas (cu m; 1977) 1,466,000; petroleum products 10,990; sulfuric acid 235; fertilizers (nutrient content; 1978–79) nitrogenous 216, phosphate 87; salt (1977) 701; cotton yarn 212; cotton fabrics (m) 728,000; electricity (kw-hr; 1977) *c.* 13,000,000.

bances in the Upper Egypt towns of Asyut and Minya in April in which several people were killed. Relations between Sadat's government and the Coptic hierarchy were strained, and allegations of religious persecution were exchanged. There was also a challenge to the government from prominent Egyptians associated with the late president Gamal Abdel Nasser. Their first open letter protested against the treaty with Israel. Liberals were also alienated by a referendum carried out in May, in which Sadat successfully sought changes in the 1971 constitution giving him, among other things, an unlimited number of terms of office. The vote for Sadat was 99%. In March Sadat offered asylum to the exiled shah of Iran, who died in a Cairo hospital in July (*see* OBITUARIES). In November, however, Sadat recognized the Teheran regime.

The Economy. The budget for fiscal 1980, beginning on July 1, aimed for 10.8% growth in gross domestic product during the year, to the equivalent of $21 billion at constant prices. The investment budget was an ambitious $4,607,000,000, with a further $1,225,000,000 to be invested in the private sector. Infrastructure and housing formed the largest part of the public-sector allocation (22%), followed by agriculture and food processing (20%) and transport and communications (17%). The government hoped to create 462,000 jobs during the year, raising the total work force to 11,406,000. Among major projects planned were the Cairo metro underground railway and telephone system improvements being carried out with French, West German, and Austrian help. As part of its policy of opening the door to friendly countries, Egypt accepted help from the Chinese for a freshwater fish-farming scheme at Ismailia, which also involved assistance from the International Finance Corporation. A consortium of Japanese companies was helping with a steelmaking plant at Al-Dikheila near Alexandria.

The interest of international banks in the resilience of the economy sharpened as the balance of payments position improved. In September five leading Egyptian banks were said to be negotiating with Crédit Lyonnais of France to set up a bank in Paris. This was seen in international banking circles as a possible indication that Egypt planned to have recourse to international capital markets.

(JOHN WHELAN)

El Salvador

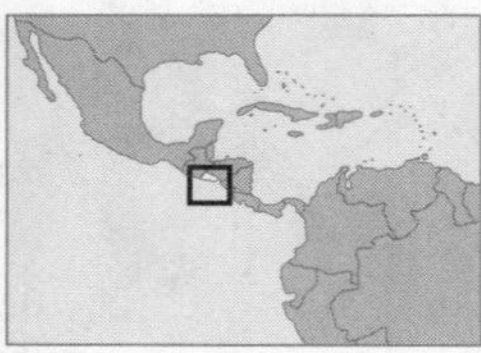

El Salvador

A republic on the Pacific coast of Central America and the smallest country on the isthmus, El Salvador is bounded on the west by Guatemala and on the north and east by Honduras. Area: 21,041 sq km (8,124 sq mi). Pop. (1980 est.): 4,801,000. Cap. and largest city: San Salvador (pop., 1980 est., 433,000). Language: Spanish. Religion: Roman Catholic (1976) 91.1%. In 1980 the country was governed by a civilian-military junta; president from December 13, José Napoleón Duarte.

Following the military coup of Oct. 15, 1979, the government seemed about to disintegrate as it failed to halt both extreme right-wing acts of violence and left-wing activity. The country moved closer to civil war with the assassination of Archbishop Oscar Romero (*see* OBITUARIES) on March 24, thought to be the work of right-wing factions. Between January and the end of June some 4,000 civilians had been reported killed.

For most of the year Col. Jaime Abdul Gutiérez and Col. Adolfo Arnoldo Majano Ramos were the dominant forces in the junta, although there were a number of personnel changes. The junta, supported only by the Christian Democratic Party (itself divided by its left wing's secession to form the Social Democratic Party), was opposed to both right and left. On January 10 three major left-wing factions and their armed wings united to form the Frente Democrático Revolucionario.

Guerrilla kidnappings of businessmen and embassy occupations continued, and several countries closed their diplomatic missions. In May the junta survived an abortive right-wing military coup mainly because of previous U.S. threats to withdraw its support from a right-wing regime. The U.S. government supported the existing government because of its declared commitment to land reform and human rights. However, although the junta did carry out agrarian reform and nationalized the banking sector, its popular support remained narrow.

PATRICK CHAUVEL—SYGMA

An injured Salvadoran is taken to shelter after an explosion erupted at the funeral of murdered Archbishop Oscar Arnulfo Romero in San Salvador in March. The consequent panic and violence caused some 30 deaths; 400 people were injured.

In late November six leading leftists were killed; a rightist "death squad" claimed responsibility, though leftists insisted the junta was involved. A bomb explosion injured several mourners, and at least 11 persons were killed as fighting broke out in the capital. In December the U.S. interrupted its aid program for two weeks after the murder of three American nuns and a lay worker. On December 13 José Napoleón Duarte, a member of the junta, was sworn in as president; Majano had been ousted a few days earlier. The start of a major leftist offensive was reported at year's end.

In October a peace treaty was signed with Honduras. (CHRISTINE MELLOR)

EL SALVADOR

Education. (1978) Primary, pupils 858,811, teachers (1976) 16,563; secondary and vocational, pupils 72,898, teachers (1975) 2,844; teacher training (1977), students 1,069, teachers (1975) 25; higher, students 31,351, teaching staff (1976) 2,015.

Finance. Monetary unit: colón, with (Sept. 22, 1980) a par value of 2.50 colones to U.S. $1 (free rate of 6 colones = £1 sterling). Gold, SDR's, and foreign exchange (June 1980) U.S. $102 million. Budget (1980 est.) balanced at 1,676,000,000 colones. Gross national product (1978) 7,610,000,000 colones. Money supply (June 1980) 1,447,600,000 colones. Cost of living (1975 = 100; June 1980) 186.

Foreign Trade. (1979) Imports 2,570,000,000 colones; exports 2,795,700,000 colones. Import sources (1978): U.S. 31%; Guatemala 15%; Japan 12%; Venezuela 8%; West Germany 5%; Costa Rica 5%. Export destinations (1978): U.S. 23%; West Germany 18%; Guatemala 17%; The Netherlands 10%; Costa Rica 7%; Japan 6%. Main exports: coffee 61%; cotton 8%.

Transport and Communications. Roads (1974) 10,972 km (including 625 km of Pan-American Highway). Motor vehicles in use (1977): passenger 70,100; commercial (including buses) 35,500. Railways (1978) 602 km. Air traffic (1978): 231 million passenger-km; freight *c.* 28 million net ton-km. Telephones (Jan. 1978) 70,400. Radio receivers (1977) 1,415,000. Television receivers (1977) 148,000.

Agriculture. Production (in 000; metric tons; 1979): corn *c.* 521; sorghum *c.* 177; dry beans *c.* 43; sugar, raw value 277; bananas (1978) *c.* 53; oranges *c.* 95; coffee *c.* 180; cotton, lint 72. Livestock (in 000; 1978): cattle 1,333; pigs *c.* 435; horses *c.* 88; chickens *c.* 5,141.

Industry. Production (in 000; metric tons; 1977): cement 334; petroleum products 715; fertilizers (nutrient content; 1978–79) nitrogenous 24, phosphate 4; cotton yarn 6.4; electricity (kw-hr; 1978) *c.* 1,480,000.

Energy

Developments in energy in 1980 were dominated by changing circumstances in the international oil market. During the first half of the year the members of the Organization of Petroleum Exporting Countries (OPEC) continued their practice of repeatedly raising the price of oil in leapfrog fashion, having failed to agree on a uniform pricing scheme at their 1979 year-end meeting. Meetings in May and June were only partially successful in achieving agreement, and the leapfrogging continued. At the same time, however, the demand for oil products was softening, the result of a mild winter in the Northern Hemisphere and worldwide conservation in the face of the high prices. At their meeting in December the OPEC members increased price ceilings for a barrel of crude oil by $4 and set a maximum price of $41 per barrel.

By midyear it was apparent that there was a growing imbalance between production and consumption. Stocks of crude oil and oil products were reaching extraordinarily high levels throughout the world, and sales of OPEC oil began to be made below the official prices even as price increases were being announced. The imbalance continued to worsen during the summer, and by summer's end prices of crude oil and oil products had declined, refineries had cut production to record low levels in the United States, and world stocks had reached all-time highs.

Industry Developments. Thus, when the Iraq-Iran war erupted at the end of September, cutting off imports from both countries, the world oil market absorbed the shock with scarcely a tremor. There was no panic buying such as followed the interruption of exports from Iran during that country's revolution. With storage tanks brimming and continued softness in demand, it was clear to all that oil-importing countries could withstand many months of the loss of supply from the two warring countries. Saudi Arabia, moreover, announced it would increase its production for an

Eire:
see Ireland

Electrical Industries:
see Energy; Industrial Review

Electronics:
see Computers; Industrial Review

Employment:
see Economy, World

EFE/PHOTO TRENDS

A new facility for the industrial use of solar energy at Getafe, near Madrid, was opened by the energy ministers of Spain and West Germany.

indefinite period, and other producing countries made special arrangements to take care of the needs of those importing nations that had been heavily dependent on Iraqi oil. Nevertheless, as the war dragged on beyond the few weeks military experts had expected, the spot market began to show increasing nervousness.

Other noteworthy events in oil during the year occurred in all phases of the industry. In March the Mexican national oil company finally capped the Ixtoc 1 well in the Bay of Campeche which had blown out of control in June 1979. During the ensuing ten months the well gushed more than three million barrels of oil into the waters of the Gulf of Mexico, making it the largest oil spill in history. In August the United Kingdom became self-sufficient in oil for the first time, the result of increasing production from the North Sea and a decline in consumption. The U.S.S.R. announced the achievement of a world record drilling depth of 10,000 m (1 m = 3.3 ft) in a well on the Kola Peninsula, near the Barents Sea west of Murmansk. A final payment by Saudi Arabia in March completed the takeover by that nation of the Arabian American Oil Co., which had been responsible for all oil production and refining there since the initial discovery of oil in the 1930s.

The first large oil discovery off the east coast of North America suggested the possible existence of a major new oil province. The Hibernia field, discovered by a well drilled in the Atlantic Ocean some 300 km (1 km = 0.62 mi) southeast of St. John's, Newfoundland, was estimated to contain at least 1,000,000,000 bbl. Across the continent a significant discovery was made in the Beaufort Sea, 16 km northeast of the giant Prudhoe Bay field (which produced its one billionth barrel in January) on the north coast of Alaska. Two wells were drilled from a gravel island one-quarter kilometre from shore and confirmed the expectation that other oil fields would be found near the Prudhoe Bay deposit.

Among events in natural gas were two affecting supplies to the U.S. and some significant new discoveries. In January imports of natural gas from Mexico began under a new agreement between U.S. companies and the Mexican government. The agreement replaced an earlier one reached in 1977 but vetoed at that time by the U.S. Department of Energy on the grounds that the price was too high. The initial price under the new agreement was 40% higher than the vetoed price. In Canada construction began on a portion of the Alaska Highway gas pipeline, intended eventually to carry gas from the Prudhoe Bay field and the Mackenzie River delta via a western leg to a delivery point near San Francisco and via an eastern leg to one near Chicago. The portion on which work was started was the Canadian segment of the western leg, to carry Alberta gas to San Francisco.

In October the Canadian government announced a new energy program designed to insulate domestic energy prices from the world oil prices set by OPEC and to bring Canadian subsidiaries of foreign oil companies under Canadian control through their purchase by the Canadian national oil company. The immediate result of the announcement was to sharpen the already intense controversy between the central government and the provinces (especially the western ones) over the allocation of political power. An unrelated announcement in the same month marked the entry of Canada into the liquefied natural gas business; beginning in 1985 such gas would be exported to Japan for use in Japanese power plants.

Initial tests of a gas discovery in the North Sea indicated that it was by far the largest gas field yet found in that oil and gas region and perhaps one of the largest in the world. The discovery was made 110 km off the Norwegian coast in 330 m of water. Continued exploration in the Baltimore Canyon area in the Atlantic Ocean off New Jersey resulted in further promising indications that were tantalizingly short of solid commercial practicability; gas was found in two more wells, adding to the initial discovery made in 1978. Further drilling was necessary, however, to determine whether the size of the reserves warranted investment in production facilities.

The successful laying of a pipeline on the floor of the Mediterranean Sea between Tunisia and Sicily marked completion of the first portion of a 2,500-km pipeline to carry gas from Algeria to Minerbio, near Bologna in northern Italy. Initial operation of the full line, the world's first intercontinental pipeline, was planned to begin in 1982.

Construction began in Australia on the world's first ship to be fueled by natural gas. Taking advantage of the abundant gas supply in the state of South Australia, the ship was designed to carry limestone from Adelaide 80 km across Gulf St. Vincent and to return each night to Adelaide to have its storage cylinders recharged.

The long-term effect of the accident at the Three Mile Island (Pa.) reactor on the future of nuclear power in the U.S. continued to be uncertain. In late February, 11 months after the accident, the Nuclear Regulatory Commission issued the first start-up license for a new nuclear unit to be awarded since the accident. In September voters in Maine defeated by a decisive margin the first referendum proposal to shut down an operating nuclear reactor. On the other hand, several nuclear plants proposed or under construction were canceled or postponed during the year, and no new orders were placed. Elsewhere in the world, Swedish voters turned down a proposal to dismantle that country's operating reactors, voting instead to go ahead with plans to double the number of reactors from 6 to 12. The Soviet Union put into operation a 600-Mw fast breeder reactor, the world's largest.

An extraordinarily severe, prolonged, and widespread heat wave during the summer drove electricity demand in the U.S. to record high levels, which the electric utilities, with ample reserve capacity, were able to meet with only minor problems. The shape of things to come in the electric utility industry was heralded in the announcement by a large utility in California that it intended to produce 30% of its output in 1990 from renewable resources, especially solar energy. In Canada the James Bay hydroelectric power complex generated its first power. Begun in 1972, it comprised a mammoth construction project that rearranged the flow of several rivers on the eastern shore of James Bay in Quebec. When completed in 1985, the project would have generating capacity that would make it one of the largest in the world.

Government Policies. Energy legislation and policy made headlines repeatedly throughout the year. In his state of the union address to the U.S. Congress in January, Pres. Jimmy Carter called dependence on foreign oil "a clear and present danger" to national security and announced that he would limit oil imports to a maximum of 8.2 million bbl a day. Although net imports remained below that figure during the first quarter, in March the president used his authority to impose a fee of $4.62 per barrel on imports of crude oil and $4.20 per barrel on imports of gasoline. The action proved to be highly controversial, opponents labeling it a means of raising government revenues under the guise of discouraging imports. Opposition was, in fact, sufficient to result in congressional resolutions that removed the president's authority for the action. Although the legislation was vetoed, both houses overrode the veto in June, the first time in 28 years that a president had sustained a veto defeat from a Congress controlled by his own party.

Carter had mixed success with three key pieces of legislation to further his energy program. In April he signed a bill imposing a "windfall profits" tax on domestically produced oil, which he described as "the keystone" of a national energy policy. Under the new law domestic producers of crude oil were taxed at a rate of 30–70% of the difference between the selling price and various specified base prices. Proceeds from the new tax went into a special account to be used for reducing income taxes, assistance to those with low incomes, and energy and transportation programs in proportions of 60, 25, and 15%, respectively. The tax was to be in effect for ten years and was expected to result in estimated revenues of $227 billion. Other provisions of the act contained new and expanded tax benefits for individuals and businesses that save energy or produce it, including subsidization of alcohol fuels.

A second measure was defeated. In June the House of Representatives rejected a bill to establish an Energy Mobilization Board that would cut red tape and speed the approval of major new energy projects such as synthetic fuels plants and pipelines. A few days later, however, the third measure, creating a Synthetic Fuels Corporation to bring a commercial synthetic fuels industry into being, was signed by President Carter. The act also provided that the corporation render similar assistance in the development of commercial energy from biomass, solar energy, and other renewable energy resources. The new agency did not get staffed until late in the year; in the meantime the U.S. Department of Energy continued its support of research and development of synthetic fuels. In July it awarded $200 million to approximately 100 companies for work on coal, oil shale, and other sources. Also in July the second largest experimental plant to convert coal into oil went into operation, and West Germany and Japan signed agreements to participate in a U.S.-sponsored commercial demonstration of synthetic fuel production from coal.

Under the Emergency Energy Conservation Act of 1979, President Carter was required to submit a standby gasoline rationing plan to Congress, with the provision that it could go into effect unless Congress did not approve it. The vote on disapproval came in July and narrowly failed. The plan thereby became available, to be called upon in the event of a supply emergency equal to a shortfall in gasoline of 20% or more.

On the international scene, in June the leaders of the seven major industrial nations of the non-Communist world met in Venice, Italy, at an "economic summit." They pledged to "break the existing link between economic growth and consumption of oil" through conservation; to increase the use of coal and nuclear energy in the medium term; and to place greater reliance on synthetic fuels, solar energy, and other renewable energy sources over the long term. Evidence that the international shift to coal was already under way was afforded by a massive backup that occurred during the year at U.S. coal-export facilities in the Norfolk, Va., area. So great was the demand that ships waited for more than a month to be loaded.

In March Venezuela and the U.S. signed an agreement providing for technical and scientific cooperation between the two countries on energy development projects, the first arrangement of its kind between the U.S. and a less developed country. In August Mexico and Venezuela announced a program of cooperation to ease the crushing financial burden of oil imports on nine poor countries of Central America and the Caribbean. Under the plan these nations would pay Mexico and Venezuela the world price for all the oil they needed, but 30% of the payments would be returned as low-interest loans. Also in August the World Bank announced a program to nearly double its lending to less developed countries in order to aid them in maximizing their production of energy from domestic sources. (BRUCE C. NETSCHERT)

COAL

The most comprehensive review ever made of world coal prospects, entitled *Coal: Bridge to the Future,* was published in May 1980. The result of a 16-nation World Coal Study (WOCOL), its major conclusions were: (1) Coal is capable of supplying a large proportion of future energy needs. It now supplies 25% of the world's energy. Economically recoverable reserves are many times those of oil and gas. (2) Coal will have to supply between one-half and two-thirds of the additional energy needed by the world in the next 20 years; production will have to increase up to threefold. This calls for immediate action by all involved—governments, producers, transporters, traders, consumers. (3) Coal can be mined, moved, and used in ways that conform to high standards of health, safety, and environmental protection. (4) Advances in combustion, gasification, and liquefaction will greatly widen the scope for use in the 1990s and beyond. (5) Capital for the expansion can be raised in the capital markets.

In general, world trends in 1979 seemed to justify the optimism of the WOCOL review, but critics urged more study on the problems of substituting coal for oil and gas, including logistic difficulties and the political implications of large growth in the international coal trade. World anthracite and bituminous coal production in 1979 was 2,779,498,000 metric tons, 6.2% above that of 1978 and continuing the upward trend of output of recent years. World lignite production was 978,446,000 metric tons, 71.6% of it coming from Europe where the largest contributor was East Germany with 26.1% of world output. (All production figures given below are in metric tons.)

Table I. Anthracite and Bituminous Coal Production by Major Geographic Regions, 1979

In 000,000 metric tons

	Tonnage	% of total
North America	734.46	26.4
South America	12.54	0.5
Europe (excluding U.S.S.R.)	490.83	17.6
U.S.S.R.	495.00	17.8
Asia	853.25	30.7
Africa	108.43	3.9
Oceania	84.99	3.1
Total	2,779.50	100.0

Table II. Largest Coal-Producing Countries, 1979

In 000,000 metric tons

	Tonnage
United States	703.7
China	663.2
U.S.S.R.	495.0
Poland	201.0
United Kingdom	121.7
South Africa	103.4
India	103.3
West Germany	93.3
Australia	83.1
North Korea	35.0
Czechoslovakia	28.5
Canada	28.0
France	18.6
South Korea	18.1

Source: *Coal International.*

NORTH AMERICA. The combined 1979 total of 734,460,000 tons for the U.S., Canada, and Mexico was 15% larger than in the previous year. The U.S. continued to expand its coal-mining capacity despite "regulatory obstacles" both to mine development and to the use of coal. Established deep mining in the East tended to stay at the same level. A major study of future coal traffic on the Great Lakes urged immediate improvement of coal-loading and unloading facilities as part of improving coal transport systems on the lakes. WOCOL estimated that the U.S. would produce possibly up to 1,883,000,000 tons in the year 2000 out of a world total of 6,780,000,000 tons.

CHINA. In 1979 China had an output of 663 million tons of coal, which supplied over 70% of its energy consumption. However, output was reported as raw coal, while other producers give figures for marketable coal. A later revised official figure was 635.6 million tons of coal ready for the market, and this might well be a more comparable figure. Modern technology was being introduced from abroad to speed construction of new mines. National coal dressing capacity was expected to double by 1985, and the proportion of coal cleaned was due to jump from the current 17% to 30% of the total. Further aims were to export coal, coke, and gasified and liquefied coal. A $1 billion loan was requested for priority projects, eight of which were coal mines.

U.S.S.R. Adjusted hard coal production was estimated at 495 million tons in 1979, down 1.3% from 1978. (Combined raw coal and lignite was 719 million tons, also a decline from the previous year.) The coal decline was attributed to serious mining problems due to deteriorating conditions in deep mining, particularly in the Donets Basin, and the failure of new productive capacity to become operational. The future outlook was to develop new production by exploiting the huge resources of Siberia. Rail transport, currently overburdened in moving eastern coals to the west, was being upgraded, but a report by the U.S. Central Intelligence Agency expressed some doubt about whether the large-scale projects for additional movement of coal would be sufficient for the intended production. Up to 1985 about two-thirds of the increase was due to come from expanded surface mining at Ekibastuz and Kuznetsk.

EUROPEAN ECONOMIC COMMUNITY. Hard coal production in 1979 showed little change, at 238,668,000 tons, from earlier years. Compared with the previous year, output in West Germany rose 3.5%, but there were declines in the U.K., Belgium, and France. Nevertheless, there was a sharp increase in 1979 in coal consumption, and the EEC Commission was optimistic about future demand, expecting it to rise from 305 million tons in 1980 to 580 million in the year 2000. Of the latter total, 400 million tons were expected to be taken by power stations and 90 million by the steel industry. EEC production was scheduled to rise from 243.5 million tons in 1980 to 300 million in the year 2000, but imports would also increase from 65.7 million tons to 280 million over the same period; 25 million tons were expected to be used for five gasification and liquefaction plants by the end of the century.

POLAND. Output in 1979 rose to 201 million tons, from 192,620,000 in 1978, and Poland remained the fourth largest coal producer in the world. One-fifth of the coal was exported—mainly steam coals, accounting for about half of all world steam coal exports. They went to both Eastern and Western Europe, Japan, South America, and elsewhere. Production had grown rapidly in recent years and was planned to rise to 240 million tons by 1985.

AFRICA. The continental production of 108,430,000 tons was dominated by that from South Africa, 103.4 million tons; 2.3 million tons came from Zimbabwe and 2.7 million from other countries. South Africa's output was expected to grow rapidly to 50% over current levels by 1984 and double the current level by the 1990s. Coal exports were currently limited to 26 million tons a year, but it was expected that when extra facilities became available in 1983 export capacity would rise to 44 million tons a year. In the eastern Transvaal the world's largest coal liquefaction project was being developed. More than 7 million tons were mined in South Africa in 1979 for liquefaction plants; by the mid-1980s, when three such plants were to be in full production, the requirement was expected to be 32 million tons.

INDIA. Already a major producer of coal, India had ambitious expansion plans. Output of 103.3 million tons in 1979 was planned to increase to 150 million in 1982–83. In earlier plans performance had been considerable but had fallen short of goals. This was attributed to deficiencies in electric power supplies, shortages of explosives, and strikes. In all these areas the government took explicit action to deal with the difficulties by ensuring supplies and raising wages. India imported 1 million tons of premium quality metallurgical coals annually.

AUSTRALIA. Output continued to grow, reaching 83.1 million tons in 1979. Exports rose to 40.3 million tons, 4.2% more than in 1978. The main recipient was Japan, which took two-thirds of all the exports, most of it coking coal. The EEC took 18.3%, the largest single importer being the U.K. with 2,450,000 tons. Other countries importing more than 1 million tons were France, Italy, South Korea, and Taiwan.

JAPAN. With its own production in 1979 only 17,640,000 tons, slightly lower than in the previous year, Japan's chief significance was as an importer of coal. Australia supplied almost half of the imports; overall, imports of coal rose considerably (12.2% over 1978) to 58,550,000 tons in 1979. Other major suppliers in order of quantity were the U.S., Canada, South Africa, U.S.S.R., China, and Poland, with further quantities of less than 500,000 tons each coming from Vietnam, West Germany, North Korea, New Zealand, Mozambique, Indonesia, and India. The imports included about 1 million tons of anthracite.

(ISRAEL BERKOVITCH)

ELECTRICITY

Average annual electricity consumption per head of population is a reliable indicator of a country's standard of living. It had been regarded as axiomatic that consumption increased at an annual rate that resulted in its doubling every ten years, and all forecasts for future demand were based on this figure. However, during the decade 1969–79 electricity demand in the U.K.—typical of a great portion of the industrialized Western world—increased by only about 25%, and at the end of 1980 consumption was actually less than in 1979. Current estimates indicated a future growth rate of only 1% per annum, and a program of power station closings was announced. This was a reflection of the world trade recession, increases in unemployment, and decreases in industrial production. In the U.K., where the electricity supply industry is state-owned, the decline in consumption was accentuated by government action that forced the industry to raise its prices to consumers and to limit capital expenditure; this led in turn to a shortage of orders for manufacturers of electrical equipment.

Throughout the industrialized West there was an emphasis on economy and a widespread demand for greater efficiency in the production and application of electric power. Environmentalists were active in most countries, and various antinuclear power campaigns continued unabated. In Sweden, with 80% of Europe's known uranium reserves but minor indigenous energy resources apart from waterpower, a referendum took place to decide present and future nuclear policy. The majority of voters proved to be in favour of a program to increase the number of nuclear stations from the 6 currently in operation (supplying nearly 26% of Sweden's electricity) to 12 under strict public control, but there was a considerable minority in favour of closing down all nuclear plants and scrapping any form of nuclear power program. In Austria the result of a 1978 referendum had prevented the 700-Mw nuclear station at Zwentendorf from being brought into operation. This was followed by a legislative ban on the use of nuclear energy. However, the issue was put to the vote again in 1980, as a result of which the way was opened for repeal of the legislation. In many other countries of the nonsocialist world there was a large, vocal, organized opposition to nuclear energy, and the previous year's Three Mile Island incident was still being cited as an example of the potential hazards of nuclear power.

Although the advanced gas-cooled reactors (AGR's) previously favoured in the U.K. had proved to be reasonably satisfactory and demonstrated operating costs lower than those of coal-fired or oil-fired stations, the British government decided to adopt U.S.-design pressurized water reactors (PWR's) for some future nuclear installations. This aroused opposition not only from the antinuclear lobby (the Three Mile Island reactor was a PWR) but also from many engineers who argued that it would be preferable to adopt the Canadian Candu design. The latter was similar in many ways to the British steam-generating heavy water design, which was claimed to be eminently suitable for medium-size nuclear stations but was ultimately abandoned.

The general decrease in electricity demand resulted in some slowing down of nuclear development. The total installed nuclear capacity of the Western world at the end of 1979 was 111,000 Mw. Capacity was estimated to reach 362,000 Mw by the end of 1990; the estimate included nuclear

THE NEW YORK TIMES

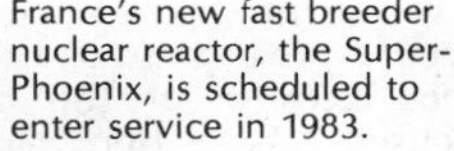
France's new fast breeder nuclear reactor, the Super-Phoenix, is scheduled to enter service in 1983.

Table III. Installed Capacity and Production of Electric Power in Selected Countries, 1977–78

	Hydroelectric power		Total electric power	
	Operating plants			
Country	Installed capacity (000 kw)	Production (000,000 kw-hr)	Installed capacity (000 kw)	Production (000,000 kw-hr)
World	...	...	...	7,209,682
Algeria	330[1]	500[1]	1,200	4,704[1]
Argentina[2]	1,945	5,771	10,073	28,884[1]
Australia	5,539[1]	13,714	20,560[1]	88,524
Austria	7,630	24,871	11,620	38,064
Bangladesh	110	530	1,560	1,908[1]
Barbados	—	—	101[1]	264[1]
Belgium[2]	459	453	18,129	50,844
Brazil	19,038	92,943	22,637	112,572
Bulgaria[2]	1,868	3,529	7,082	31,788
Burma	189	732	444	984[1]
Cameroon	—	—	...	1,308
Canada[2]	40,087	220,150	69,060	335,712
Chad	—	—	23[1]	62[1]
Chile	1,474	6,502	2,906	10,164
Colombia	2,370	10,350	3,650	16,260[1]
Congo	17[1]	68[1]	34[1]	118[1, 3]
Costa Rica	239	1,344	440	1,932
Czechoslovakia[2]	1,803	4,375	15,117	69,060
Denmark	8	22	6,453	20,784
Dominican Republic	150[1]	81[1]	900	2,671[3]
Egypt	2,445[1]	8,800[1]	3,994	13,000[3]
El Salvador[4]	243[1]	528[1]	491	1,476
Ethiopia	206	368	320	682[3]
Finland[2]	2,390	11,967	9,065	33,984
France[2]	18,416	77,297	52,451	226,692
Gabon	—	10	85[1]	324[1]
Germany, East[2]	748	1,249	17,218	95,952
Germany, West[2]	6,313	17,588	79,131	353,424
Ghana	792	4,248	900	4,300[3]
Greece	1,415[1]	1,923	4,804	21,048
Guatemala	105[1]	310	400	1,291[3]
Hong Kong	—	—	2,971[1]	9,120[1]
Hungary	40	148	5,196	25,416
Iceland[4]	492[1]	2,520	629	2,616[1]
India[2]	9,353	37,176	25,063	101,004[1]
Iran	850[1]	4,000	5,200	18,000[3]
Ireland	511[1]	1,019[1]	2,433[1]	9,984
Israel	—	—	2,420	11,892
Italy[2, 4]	15,278	52,726	42,583	175,044
Ivory Coast	224[1]	222[1]	502[1]	1,416[1]
Jamaica	15[1]	100[1]	700	1,416
Japan[2, 4]	26,099	76,373	122,349	563,988
Kenya	173	749	356	1,116
Korea, South[2]	711[1]	1,393	6,338	31,512[1]
Kuwait	40[1]	...	1,470[1]	6,996[1]
Lebanon	246	800	608	1,600[3]
Libya	—	—	800[1]	1,548[1]
Luxembourg	...	...	1,157	1,392
Madagascar	40	181[1]	95	366[3]
Malawi	67	297	111	276[1]
Malaysia	350	1,011	1,360	8,196
Mauritius	25	60	150	336
Mexico[4]	4,794	19,076	13,765	55,200
Morocco	396[1]	1,342[1]	980	3,588[1]
Mozambique	934[1]	4,490	1,213	4,940[3]
Netherlands, The[2]	—	—	15,716	61,596
New Zealand[4]	3,617[1]	14,589	5,366[1]	21,348[1]
Nigeria	420[1]	2,575[1]	960	4,848
Norway	17,408	72,292	17,560	81,108
Panama[2]	166[1]	400[1]	511	1,260[1]
Papua New Guinea	88[1]	285	280	1,122[3]
Philippines	1,160	4,850	3,600	12,528
Poland	797	2,394	21,288	115,560
Portugal	2,580	9,683	3,930	13,932
Romania	2,984	9,258	13,632	64,260
Senegal	—	—	130[1]	455[3]
Singapore	—	—	1,400[1]	5,892[1]
South Africa	535[1]	1,952	16,405	84,768
Spain[2]	13,096	40,741	27,444	99,540
Sri Lanka	335	1,248	421	1,452
Suriname	...	1,215	390	1,421[3]
Sweden[2]	12,965	53,524	25,108	92,904
Switzerland[2]	10,594	36,290	12,200	42,348
Syria	—	—	940	2,700
Thailand	930[1]	4,270[1]	2,820	13,200
Togo	2	4	24	64[3]
Tunisia	29[1]	30[1]	532	1,788[1]
Turkey	1,873	8,592	4,728	21,600
U.S.S.R.[2]	45,219	147,014	237,805	1,200,000
U.K.[2]	2,451	5,232	72,671	287,688
U.S.[2, 4]	68,933	223,934	576,206	2,285,880
Yugoslavia	5,226	24,354	10,601	51,240
Zaire	1,159	4,015	1,217	4,100[3]
Zambia	1,438	8,544	1,710	7,884
Zimbabwe	...	...	...	4,524

[1] Public sector only. [2] Includes nuclear (installed capacity in 000 kw): Argentina 370; Belgium 1,666; Bulgaria 880; Canada 3,466; Czechoslovakia 127; Finland 420; France 4,599; East Germany 950; West Germany 6,271; India 640; Italy 552; Japan 8,007; South Korea 564; The Netherlands 531; Panama 10; Spain 1,120; Sweden 3,742; Switzerland 1,006; U.S.S.R. 7,315; U.K. 5,890; U.S. 49,882. Includes nuclear (production in 000,000 kw-hr): Argentina 1,638; Belgium 11,939; Bulgaria 5,884; Canada 24,580; Czechoslovakia 114; Finland 2,505; France 17,986; East Germany 5,205; West Germany 36,059; India 3,450; Italy 3,385; Japan 31,659; South Korea 71; The Netherlands 3,710; Spain 6,525; Sweden 19,913; Switzerland 7,728; U.S.S.R. 34,826; U.K. 41,021; U.S. 250,883. [3] 1977 figure. [4] Includes geothermal (installed capacity in 000 kw): El Salvador 60; Iceland 3; Italy 398; Japan 77; Mexico 75; New Zealand 192; U.S. 599. Includes geothermal (production in 000,000 kw-hr): El Salvador 400; Iceland 16; Italy 2,501; Japan 579; Mexico 600; New Zealand 1,276; U.S. 3,582.

Sources: United Nations, *Statistical Yearbook, 1978; Monthly Bulletin of Statistics.*

Electrical Power Production of Selected Countries, 1979

By source

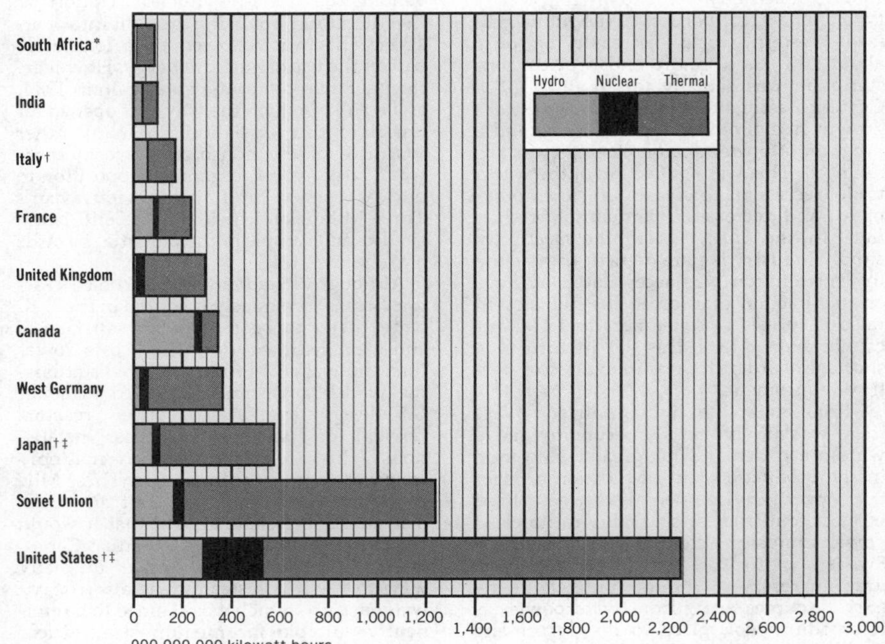

000,000,000 kilowatt-hours

*Includes Botswana, Lesotho, South West Africa/Namibia, Swaziland.

†Includes geothermal.

‡Not including industrial plants' net generation.

Source: United Nations, *Monthly Bulletin of Statistics.*

installations in Brazil, India, Mexico, South Africa, South Korea, and Taiwan and was about 17% less than that of a year earlier.

One effect of antinuclear campaigns, coupled with those against pollution and for energy conservation, was to concentrate public attention on electricity production and consumption. In the U.S. this led to intensive research into the use of electric vehicles for transportation in congested urban areas. In the U.K. electric vehicles had always been fairly common, mainly because of their extensive use for daily house-to-house deliveries of milk. The British electricity supply industry was now trying to popularize the wide use of battery-powered passenger vehicles in large cities.

Public pressure also resulted in experimental windmill installations in the U.S. and the U.K. In addition to these measures, various European countries were devoting greater attention to combined heat and power projects and even to the possibility of using household and other refuse as power-station fuel. Such schemes were already standard practice in many British industries, and London's Battersea power station had supplied heating to a residential area in Westminster across the River Thames for many years. However, where large power stations were situated a long way from populous areas, the problems associated with utilizing their waste heat were probably too great to meet the demands of conservationists.

A new windmill design, the Giromill, went into operation generating electricity in August in Colorado.

UPI

Nuclear power was not the only target of various protest groups. The Norwegian government shelved a number of hydroelectric projects until after the 1981 elections because of the controversy they aroused. Opposition came mainly from reindeer owners, farmers, and salmon fishermen, who saw the projected installations as benefiting only industrial enterprises and the more populous areas.

At one time electrical development in the third world was largely in the form of hydroelectric power, but the high capital cost and the comparatively low cost of oil made thermal stations more attractive. The recent increases in oil prices reversed the situation, and the World Bank reported that over the next ten years hydroelectric capacity in the less developed world would double from 100,000 Mw to 201,300 Mw. Nuclear capacity was expected to increase tenfold, but the capacity of nuclear stations in the third world as of 1980 was only 3,400 Mw and hydroelectric plants would provide 40% of capacity.

Because of its vast area, huge population, and long political isolation, China had not been regarded as part of the less developed world, but trade recession in the West and the search for markets drew attention to market opportunities there for Western electrical equipment manufacturers as China expanded its electrical industry. As of 1980 the average annual consumption of electricity per head in China was 160 kw-hr, only 4% of that in Western countries. The installed generating capacity of 90,000 Mw was only 1.8 times that of Great Britain's Central Electricity Generating Board (CEGB), which supplied England and Wales, with a population of some 49 million, compared with China's estimated 1,000,000,000. In this context the scope for electrical development in China was virtually limitless, and it started from a much more developed technical base than had that of the U.S.S.R. more than 50 years earlier.

Electrical development had always tended to ignore national boundaries. Electricity enterprises throughout Europe cooperated freely, and transmission networks with a common supply frequency allowed transfers of power between countries, irrespective of political considerations. The European "electricity pool" could now be fed as easily from a nuclear power station in the Ural Mountains of the Soviet Union as from a pumped-storage station in Wales.

The current energy crisis and industrial recession delayed some electrical developments but speeded up others. Some developments were hindered by what most engineers would probably consider ill-advised antinuclear and other protest groups attempting to divert research efforts from immediate problems such as safety and nuclear waste disposal to long-term objectives such as wind, solar, wave, and geothermal power. One immediate problem was the development of the fast breeder nuclear reactor, on which there was worldwide cooperation. At an international conference in Switzerland in October 1979, reports from Europe, Japan, the U.S., and the U.S.S.R. dealing with the fast breeder reactor programs of individual countries were discussed in detail. It was generally agreed that there was a complete identity of interests, that there was a possibility of standardizing some components, and that international collaboration was essential in solving all the problems associated with establishing such reactors as the natural successors to existing systems.

Until recently there had appeared to be little prospect of the early practical application of magnetohydrodynamic generation (MHD), the extraction of electricity from an intensely hot ionized gas stream. In Britain the CEGB abandoned research on MHD some years ago, but research still continued in the U.S.S.R., where it was announced that construction had begun on the first full-scale power station to employ the system. It was stated that the station, of 500-Mw capacity, would produce half its output from the MHD generator and the remainder by a stress steam turbine, giving an overall efficiency of about 50%, as against 40% in the best of conventional stations.

(JAMES F. AMOR)

NATURAL GAS

World proven gas reserves, excluding probable and possible reserves, on Jan. 1, 1980, were estimated at 73,848,000,000,000 cu m (73,848 billion cu m or bcm), a slight increase over the 1979 estimate of 68,854 bcm and almost double the figure ten years previously, 38,099 bcm in 1970. Proven reserves at the beginning of 1980 would be sufficient for 50 years of production at the rate of commercial output achieved in 1979.

In 1979 world natural gas production for commercial use, apart from gas flared or reinjected, was 1,489 bcm, an increase of 4.1% over 1978. In addition, 189 bcm were flared, equivalent to 10.4% of gross production. The three largest gas-producing countries were again the U.S. with 558 bcm, the U.S.S.R. with 407 bcm, and The Netherlands with 93 bcm. Saudi Arabia flared 38 bcm, roughly six times as much as it produced commercially.

Perhaps the most significant development during 1980 was the demand for higher prices for gas in international trade. The Organization of Petroleum Exporting Countries (OPEC) showed an increasing interest in gas pricing, with some of its members calling for gas to be priced at parity with crude oil. Since OPEC members had approximately 31.8% of the world's proven gas reserves, this move, if successful, could be as important for gas as their determination of prices had been for oil. Major gas exporters outside OPEC, such as Norway, also began to press for higher prices. Gas from the Norwegian Ula field was sold to West German companies at a price equivalent to that of crude oil, but another potential purchaser of Norwegian gas, Britain, was resisting the introduction of crude parity pricing.

Algeria, a member of OPEC and one of the leading exporters of liquefied natural gas (LNG), claimed early in 1980 that it was receiving far too low a price for its LNG relative to the price of crude oil. Algeria attempted to double the price of LNG to about $6.11 per million British thermal units (Btu), and to underline its determination suspended deliveries to Gaz de France and the U.S. company El Paso. Deliveries to France were resumed when the French agreed to pay an interim price of over $3, but the U.S. still resisted crude parity, attempting to reach a compromise of about $4.60. Algeria also reneged on its contract to sell LNG to The Netherlands and West Germany starting in 1984, canceling plans for construction of the necessary liquefaction plant. Algeria now seemed more interested in exporting gas by pipeline, rather than as LNG. The Trans-Mediterranean Gas Pipeline, from Algeria through Tunisia to Italy, would carry 12.36 bcm a year when completed, and Algeria had plans for further pipelines to Italy and to Spain.

As well as being a potential importer of Algerian gas, The Netherlands was also a major exporter of its own gas, supplying 41% of Western European demand. The Dutch successfully renegotiated their contracts with utilities in West Germany, France, Belgium, Italy, and Switzerland, winning a 15% rise in the basic price of their gas exports. More important, their customers accepted that gas prices should be more closely linked to the price of heating oil, which had been rising faster than that of gas.

Another major supplier of gas to Western Europe, the U.S.S.R., began negotiations with a consortium led by the West German company Ruhrgas for additional supplies of 40 bcm a year from western Siberia. The U.S.S.R. also offered to supply gas to Sweden and endorsed the idea of a gas pipeline from eastern Siberia to Canada and the U.S. Talks on the resumption of gas supplies from Iran to the U.S.S.R. broke down after Iran demanded a price five times higher than was paid before the Iranian revolution.

Japanese companies continued to show interest in increasing LNG imports. Agreements were reached covering additional supplies from Indonesia and Malaysia, and it appeared that development of the Western Australian North West Shelf project was to begin, with half the gas production earmarked for export as LNG to Japan. Bangladesh proposed to produce LNG if sufficient gas reserves could be proved, and Japan, the U.S., and Greece were all reported to have expressed an interest in the project. Progress on Nigeria's Bonny LNG project was stalled pending agreement with customers in the U.S. or Europe to take supplies in addition to those already agreed upon with an European group.

Some progress was made with the Arctic Pilot Project to ship LNG from Melville Island in the Canadian Arctic in icebreaker LNG carriers. A group of U.S. gas distributors agreed to purchase gas from western Canada in quantities equivalent to the LNG landed in eastern Canada. In addition the Canadian government approved the construction of a pipeline from the Alberta gas fields to Calgary and then in two branches to the U.S. border. The pipeline was ultimately to be linked to the Alaska Highway gas pipeline, supplying gas from Alaska through Canada to the U.S.

Among the year's discoveries, further exploration of the North West Dome off the coast of Qatar was reported to have revealed the existence of one of the world's largest gas fields. Norway confirmed a major offshore discovery in North Sea block 3½. Discoveries were announced by Exxon Corp. and the Tenneco and Texaco groups in the Baltimore Canyon 160 km (100 mi) off the coast of New Jersey, but additional wells would have to be drilled to determine whether gas was present in sufficient quantities to justify the cost of bringing it ashore. Other offshore discoveries included six in the Italian Adriatic, one off Ghana, another northwest of Bombay, India, and a further success off the east coast of Thailand, where commercial production was expected to start about 1983. Drilling to a deeper level than usual gave West Germany's gas reserves an unexpected boost. A field with reserves estimated at 19 bcm was found at a depth of 5,000 m (16,400 ft) in Lower Saxony, which could add 10% to the country's proven reserves. (RICHARD J. CASSIDY)

PETROLEUM

Once again the spotlight in the international oil scene in 1980 was on prices. Between December 1978 and December 1979 crude oil prices on average doubled, varying from 73% in Indonesia to 122% in Iran. By June 1980 the same figures were 132 and 175%, respectively. In the same period the "marker" crude, Saudi Arabian light, went from $12.70 a barrel to $30 a barrel in October. In December 1980 this figure reached $32. At Algiers in June and in Vienna in September the OPEC ministers were unable to agree on a unified pricing system, but in December in Indonesia they increased price ceilings for a barrel of crude oil by $4 and set a maximum price of $41 per barrel. The combined oil revenues of OPEC increased to almost $200 billion in 1979, some 72% higher than in 1978. The surplus was estimated at $60 billion.

Just as it seemed that the pressure on prices was easing and the spot market was fairly inactive, war broke out between Iraq and Iran on September 22. Each side inflicted heavy damage on the oil installations of the other, with the Abadan refinery in Iran as the main casualty. Approximately 4 million bbl of oil a day were taken out of supply, although this was partly made up by extra production elsewhere, particularly in Saudi Arabia. The repercussions of the war, including the breaking off of diplomatic relations between Saudi Arabia and Libya and the boycott of the Arab summit meeting of late November in Amman, Jordan, by several Arab League members, strained relations within OPEC.

Attempts by President Carter to obtain legislation that would reduce oil imports were not completely successful, but direct crude oil imports into the U.S. declined by 5.1% in the first quarter of 1980, and drilling reached record levels. Most other industrial countries were trying to curb oil consumption with varying success. In India Assam was wracked by internal political protests that severely curtailed domestic supplies of oil in the northeast, cutting production by 35%. The dangers of oil exploration were tragically demonstrated in late March when the "Alexander Kielland," a semisubmersible drilling rig used as a floating hotel platform, capsized in the Norwegian sector of the North Sea and 123 people perished, the worst offshore disaster to date.

In the first half of 1980 world oil production was substantially unchanged, with declines in OPEC production being offset by increases elsewhere, including Mexico, the largest at 29.9%, the United Kingdom,

Ecuador, Peru, Argentina, and Alaska, where production was averaging 1,533,000 bbl a day. Iranian production declined to 1,896,000 bbl a day.

Reserves. There was a little increase in the total world "published proved" reserves at the end of 1979, a total of 649,200,000,000 bbl, compared with 649,000,000,000 bbl a year earlier. There was a small rise in the Western Hemisphere share at 15% (12.9% the year before) and a slight decrease in the Middle East share to 55.7% (56.9%). The Chinese share again remained the same at 3%, but the U.S. at 5%, Western Europe at 3.6%, the U.S.S.R. at 10.3%, and Africa at 8.8% all showed minor decreases. At the end of 1979 the ratio of reserves to production was 28:1 (188:1 for coal and 51:1 for natural gas).

Production. World oil production increased by 4.1% in 1979, the same increase as in the decade 1969–79; this compared with a 2.3% rise in the five years 1974–79. Output in 1979 averaged 65,710,000 bbl a day, as against 63,085,000 the previous year. Most countries showed increased production, but there were declines in the U.S., Trinidad, Austria, Turkey, West Germany, Iran, Sharjah, Dubai, Oman, Algeria, Gabon, Indonesia, and Eastern Europe. Of these Iran at 40.2%, Sharjah with 36.4%, and Trinidad at 7.3% experienced the greatest falls. OPEC production rose 3.3% to 47.9% of the total at 31,285,000 bbl a day. Western Hemisphere production was 26.4% of the total at 17,565,000 bbl a day, of which the U.S. share was 8,535,000 bbl, Venezuela's was 2,425,000 bbl, and Mexico's 1,620,000 bbl. Mexican production rose 22% over the previous year.

The Middle East's share of world production, 33.4% at 21,795,000 bbl a day, was a modest increase of 1.7% over the previous year. Iraq had the largest increase, 32.7%, for a total of 3,450,000 bbl a day, followed by the Neutral Zone, 21.3% at 560,000 bbl a day, Kuwait, 17.6% at 2,285,000 bbl a day, and Saudi Arabia 14.5%. Saudi production of 9,510,000 bbl a day was only exceeded among single producing countries by the U.S.S.R., at 11,870,000 bbl a day; the Soviet Union's increase was 2.4% over 1978. African production at 6,670,000 bbl a day, 10.1% of the world total, increased by 7.2% over the previous year, with Nigerian production at 2.3 million bbl a day, 3.5% of the world total, showing a large increase of 20.2%. The largest increase was registered in Western European production, 29.3% over 1978, at 2,365,000 bbl a day for 3.6% of the world total. U.K. production of 1.6 million bbl a day rose 46.1%.

There was great variation in the productivity of producing wells. For example, in 1979 production per producing well in the U.S. was 20 bbl daily, whereas in the U.S.S.R. it was 150, in Latin America 160, Western Europe 320, Africa 1,520, and in the Middle East 5,500.

Consumption. Throughout the world there was a small increase of 1.2% in consumption in 1979 to 64,125,000 bbl a day. The increase was only 0.2%, 51,280,000 bbl a day, if the U.S.S.R., Eastern Europe, and China are excluded. Consumption declined in the U.S., the major consuming country, by 2.9% to 27.7% of the world total at 17,930,000 bbl a day; this compared with an average annual increase in the U.S. of 2% from 1974 to 1979. Total Western Hemisphere consumption declined by 1.1% to 24,220,000 bbl a day, 37.4% of the total, but Canada was up by 3.5%, at 1,895,000 bbl a day, as was Latin America, 5.2% at 4,395,000 bbl a day.

Western European consumption rose 1.5% to 23% of the total at 14,870,000 bbl a day, with Yugoslavia up 7%, Sweden 6.3%, Finland 6%, Ireland 4%, and Portugal 4.2%. Decreased consumption occurred in Switzerland 4.1%, Turkey 0.8%, and France 0.7%. The major consuming countries in Western Europe in 1979 were West Germany, the world's fourth largest consumer, 3,045,000 bbl a day; France, 2,430,000 bbl a day; Italy, 2,045,000 bbl a day; and the U.K., 1,935,000 bbl a day.

Elsewhere, Southeast Asian consumption rose 10.9% to 3.7% of the total; China increased by 7.5% to 2.9% of the total; and the U.S.S.R., the second largest consumer, rose by 5.2% to 14.5% of the total, at 8,925,000 bbl a day. Japan, the third largest consumer at 5,495,000 bbl a day, was up by 1%. Excluding the U.S.S.R., Eastern Europe, and China, the division of world consumption was middle distillates, 15,560,000 bbl a day; gasolines, 15,240,000 bbl a day; fuel oil 12,895,000 bbl a day; and the remainder 7,585,000 bbl a day. In the U.S. transportation represented 50% of consumption.

Refining. Between 1969 and 1979 world refining capacity increased at an average annual rate of 5.6%; between 1974 and 1979 it was 3.4%, and in 1979 it rose 2.2% over 1978 to a total of 80,370,000 bbl a day. In North America, with 24.7% of the total capacity, the U.S. capacity, the highest in the world at 21.8%, rose, while Canadian capacity fell by 1.1%. Western Hemisphere capacity increased by 1.5% to 35.9% of the total, 28,985,000 bbl a day. Capacity declined in Western Europe by 1.2% to 25.7% of the total, 20,555,000 bbl a day; Spanish capacity increased by 7.3%, but the United Kingdom was down by 2.1%, West Germany 1.5%, Belgium 0.9%, and France 0.8%. Middle Eastern capacity rose 6.5% to 4.5% of the total, 3.6 million bbl a day, with capacity in Iraq increasing by 22.8%. African capacity increased 28%, but Japanese capacity, at 6.6% of the total, did not change appreciably. In the U.S.S.R., Eastern Europe, and China capacity increased by 4.6% to 18.5% of the total, 14,659,000 bbl a day.

Tankers. There was an insignificant reduction of 0.6% in the size of the world tanker fleet at the end of 1979 to 327.9 million long tons deadweight (dw). The fleets of the United Kingdom, Norway, Liberia, the U.S.S.R., Eastern Europe, and China fell, while those of Greece, Panama, the U.S., Japan, and France increased. Liberia continued to own the largest share of world tonnage, 31.3% at 102.5 million long tons dw, down slightly from the 103.4 million long tons dw of 1978. As in 1978, the U.K. with a 7.6% share and Norway with 7.4% followed Liberia.

Voyages from the Middle East again continued to be the source of most tanker movements, 74.5%, with Western Europe and North and West Africa the principal destination, at 36.5%, followed by Japan with 12.5%. Interarea total oil movements in 1979 rose 4.2% over 1978 to 35,350,000 bbl a day. At the end of 1979 approximately 16.5 million long tons dw were on order, of which 6.7 million long tons dw were for vessels of 65 million–125 million long tons dw. The deliveries of new tankers, totaling 7 million long tons dw, were the lowest in ten years. (R. W. FERRIER)

See also Engineering Projects; Industrial Review; Mining and Quarrying; Transportation.
[214.C.4; 721; 724.B.2; 724.C.1–2; 737.A.5]

The Louisiana Offshore Oil Port, the first U.S. deepwater port to receive supertankers, was scheduled to be fully operational in 1981.

THE NEW YORK TIMES

Engineering Projects

Bridges. Two interesting, but totally different, bridges were structurally completed during 1980: the Humber Bridge in England and the Reichsbrücke (Imperial Bridge) in Vienna. The Humber Bridge, the 1,410-m (1 m = 3.3 ft) main span of which was the longest in the world, was a suspension bridge across the Humber estuary on the east coast of England, built to encourage regional development by shortening by more than 80 km (50 mi) the distance between the principal towns north and south of the river. The designers, Freeman Fox & Partners, used the same, though augmented, principles that they had introduced for the Severn Bridge (main span 988 m) in England and then enhanced for the Bosporus Bridge (1,074 m) in Turkey.

The crucial design factor for all long-span bridges, if there is to be any attempt to achieve an aesthetically satisfying form, is not the traffic load but the need to counter oscillation of the bridge deck under conditions of sustained wind loading. (The classic illustration of the problem was the failure in 1940 of the Tacoma [Wash.] Narrows Bridge, which broke its back as it shook itself to destruction.) The standard solution in long-span suspension bridges has been a deep truss girder, which, suspended from the main cables, carries the road surface. Truss girders were used in the Golden Gate (Calif.), Mackinac (Mich.), and Verrazano-Narrows (New York City) bridges, the three longest spans in the U.S.

For the Severn Bridge, completed in 1966, the designers substituted an aerodynamically shaped box girder for the truss girder, and this new design was subsequently employed on the Bosporus and the Humber bridges. Many advantages followed. The depth of the box girder at Humber was only 4.5 m as against 10 m or more for the truss girder, thereby generating a structure of great elegance. Second, the required strength and stiffness of the deck were obtained with much less steel; the Humber Bridge required only 4 metric tons per metre of traffic lane, as against 7.7 tons for the Golden Gate and 5.8 tons for Verrazano. This smaller steel requirement led to a reduced capital cost, and maintenance of the box girder was easier than for a truss. Together, these advantages made some fixed river crossings viable that otherwise would be ignored for reasons of cost.

The Imperial Bridge across the Danube in the centre of Vienna was a different construction. It replaced the old Reichsbrücke suspension bridge that collapsed in 1976 when the foundations were washed away by floodwater. The new bridge had a ten-span prestressed box-girder superstructure; the two main spans (169.6 m and 150 m long) crossed the Danube itself, the remainder of the bridge crossing a new flood relief channel being excavated. It was particularly noteworthy for the large number of facilities incorporated. Besides a six-lane highway on the top side of the box girders, each box contained a subway track, and where the bridge crossed the island between the Danube and the flood channel a subway station 200 m long was housed; between the two boxes a service duct contained electric power and telephone cables and water and gas mains. Along the outside of the boxes, below the overhang carrying the outer lanes of the highways, cantilevered brackets provided a footpath for pedestrians along one side of the bridge and a cycle track along the other side. It was an exceedingly complex, highly stressed structure with steel reinforcement up to three times more dense than was commonly required. It was also, by common consent, elegant and attractive in appearance.

In Japan a large number of long-span bridges were planned or already under construction, in-

FREDDIE MANSFIELD—CAMERA PRESS/PHOTO TRENDS

Construction of a multi-bridge crossing that will link the Japanese islands of Honshu and Shikoku proceeded during the year.

cluding cable-stayed girder structures, with spans of up to 450 m, along the shorelines of Tokyo, Osaka, and the other major cities in an effort to relieve the ever increasing traffic density. Work on the ambitious Honshu-Shikoku multibridge crossing was advancing with all six bridges on the central route under construction.

The most severe problem currently facing the designer of big bridges was how to get the bridge built. It was becoming increasingly difficult to obtain sufficient experienced staff and skilled men willing to work on the exposed site of a major bridge. A partial solution was increased off-site fabrication and assembly of large sections under conditions like those in a factory, the final site work being done by small, carefully selected teams with well-trained supervisors.

The vulnerability of bridges to impact by ships that had strayed off course was tragically demonstrated in May when a cargo vessel rammed the Sunshine Skyway Bridge over Tampa Bay, Fla., in a gale, with heavy loss of life. (*See* Disasters.)

(DAVID FISHER)

Buildings. The world recession had some effect on the rate of building in 1980, and there was a notable slowdown in construction in the Middle East. Two spectacular structural failures were the collapse in May of a considerable part of Berlin's prestigious Congress Hall (built in 1957 as a U.S. contribution to that year's international building exhibition, Interbau 57) and that in September of an unfired lining inside a 275-m-high chimney at the Matla power station in South Africa, one of the tallest multiflue chimneys in the world.

On the positive side there were continued developments in a number of fields, including the use of several different structural materials. Steel was still the dominant material for the very tallest buildings, and the giant 110-story, 443-m-high Sears Tower in Chicago remained the world's tallest structure of that type. It was designed using the bundled tube concept developed by Fazlur Kahn of the architectural firm Skidmore Owings & Merrill. Steel was also the material used in the largest-span roofs, where clear spans of over 200 m were achieved.

Particularly interesting developments occurred in the field of large span-braced dome structures, such as the recently completed stadium at Split in Yugoslavia. The seating areas of the stadium were covered by two double-layer, part-spherical space frames that were crescent-shaped in plan. These roofs had an overall dimension of 215 m and were supported only along the outer edge, which also lay on the circular perimeter of the stadium. The frameworks were built using a system of steel tubes and "ball" joints with screwed connections.

A number of manufacturers offered systems for building braced domes and other forms of braced structures. One of these was being used in the construction of the Spaceship Earth dome at Walt Disney's Epcot City project in the U.S. When completed, this building would appear as a 53.5-m-diameter silver-clad ball supported just off the ground on three sloping legs; display areas would be contained at several levels inside the dome. In Canada a developer was considering the feasibility of an aluminum-framed braced dome to enclose a controlled environment for combined residential, recreational, and shopping facilities. The structure would have a span of 300 m and a maximum height of 60 m. It remained to be seen whether such an enclosure was a commercially or socially viable proposition.

Five people were injured when parts of the roof of West Berlin's Congress Hall, built in 1957, collapsed in May because of structural failures.

WIDE WORLD

Reinforced concrete continued to be the principal construction material for foundations and for many heavy and medium-height structures. In spite of its weight compared with that of steel, it was also making inroads into the area of earthquake-resistant designs of medium to tall multistory buildings. This was because of a tendency toward a preference for stiffer structures and also because of advances in design techniques for improving the ductility of reinforced-concrete frames and shear walls, thereby increasing their resilience to cyclic loading. While structural steel was most economical for the tallest full-scale buildings, concrete was favoured for towers. The world's two tallest free-standing structures, the recently completed CN Tower in Toronto and the earlier Moscow tower, were both constructed of reinforced concrete.

Ferrocement, the steel-mesh-reinforced cement mortar invented by Italian engineer-architect Pier Luigi Nervi (d. 1979) and originally used in boatbuilding, hangars, and other utility buildings, was the material chosen to construct five domes up to 16 m in diameter for a mosque in Amman, Jordan, completed in 1980. These onion-shaped ribbed domes had a shell thickness of only 25 mm and were externally finished in graduated shades of blue mosaic. Although the method of construction was labour intensive, significant savings in materials and formwork were demonstrated over traditional reinforced-concrete shell methods of construction.

Timber continued to be predominantly used in the building of houses, where its use was increasing at the expense of some other materials. Mounting energy costs highlighted the good insulation properties of timber and the ease with which additional insulation could be incorporated into timber-wall construction. Timber was also used for the construction of low-rise commercial buildings, and internal framing with clear spans up to 7.5 m could be achieved. Specially laminated timber has applications in large-span beams, portal frames, and in the construction of braced domes. A notable

Major World Dams Under Construction in 1980[1]

Name of dam	River	Country	Type[2]	Height (m)	Length of crest (m)	Volume content (000 cu m)	Gross reservoir capacity (000 cu m)
Amaluza	Paute	Ecuador	A	170	410	1,157	120,000
Atatürk	Euphrates	Turkey	E, R	179	1,700	75,000	80,000,000
Baishan	Songhuajiang	China	G	150	670	1,630	6,215,000
Boruca	Terraba	Costa Rica	E, R	267	700	43,000	14,960,000
Canales	Genil	Spain	E, R	156	340	4,733	7,070,000
Chicoasen	Grijalva	Mexico	E, R	245	584	14,500	1,680,000
Dabaklamm	Dorferbach	Austria	A	220	350	950	235,000
Dongjiang	Laishui	China	A	157	438	1,389	8,120,000
Dry Creek	Dry Creek	U.S.	E	110	915	23,000	310,000
El Cajon	Humuya	Honduras	A	226	382	1,480	5,650,000
Emborcacao	Paranaíba	Brazil	E, R	158	1,500	24,000	17,600,000
Finstertal	Nederbach	Austria	E, R	150	652	4,518	60,000
Grand Maison	Eau d'Olle	France	E, R	155	550	12,000	200,000
Guri (Raúl Leoni)	Caroní	Venezuela	E, R, G	162	9,404	77,846	139,000,000
Inguri	Inguri	U.S.S.R.	A	272	680	3,880	1,100,000
Itaipú	Paraná	Brazil/Paraguay	E, R, G	185	7,900	27,000	29,000,000
Itaparica	São Francisco	Brazil	E, R	135	4,500	29,750	70,500,000
Itumbiara	Paranaíba	Brazil	E, G	106	6,262	35,600	17,000,000
Karakaya	Euphrates	Turkey	A, G	180	420	2,000	9,580,000
Kenyir	Trengganu	Malaysia	E, R	150	900	16,000	14,000,000
Kishau	Tons	India	E, R	253	360	NA	2,400,000
La Grande No. 2	La Grande	Canada	E, R	160	2,835	23,000	61,720,000
La Grande No. 3	La Grande	Canada	E, R	100	3,855	22,187	60,020,000
La Grande No. 4	La Grande	Canada	E, R	125	7,243	20,000	19,390,000
Lakhwar	Yamuna	India	G	192	440	2,000	580,000
Lunyangxia	Huanghe	China	G	172	342	1,300	24,700,000
Mihoesti	Aries	Romania	E, R	242	242	180	6,000
Naramata	Naramata	Japan	E, R	154	587	11,600	90,000
Nurek	Vakhsh	U.S.S.R.	E	300	704	58,901	10,500,000
Oosterschelde	Vense Gat Oosterschelde	The Netherlands	E	45	9,000	70,000	2,900,000
Oymapinar	Manavgat	Turkey	A	185	360	575	310,000
Revelstoke	Columbia	Canada	E, R, G	162	1,615	8,900	5,310,000
Rogun	Vakhsh	U.S.S.R.	E	325	660	75,500	11,600,000
Salvajina	Cauca	Colombia	E, R	154	360	3,500	773,000
São Felix	Tocantins	Brazil	E, R	160	1,950	34,000	50,600,000
Sayano-Shushensk	Yenisei	U.S.S.R.	A	242	1,068	9,117	31,300,000
Sterkfontein	Nuwejaarspruit	South Africa	E	89	3,050	15,500	2,660,000
Tehri	Bhagirathi	India	E, R	261	570	25,200	3,539,000
Thomson	Thomson	Australia	E, R	165	1,275	12,500	1,100,000
Tokuyama	Ibi	Japan	E, R	161	420	10,600	660,000
Tucurui	Tocantins	Brazil	E, G	85	5,294	36,375	43,000,000
Upper Wainganga	Wainganga	India	E	43	181	NA	50,700,000
Ust-Ilim	Angara	U.S.S.R.	E, G	105	3,565	8,702	59,300,000
Wujiangdu	Wujiang	China	G	165	368	1,930	2,300,000
Yacambu	Yacambu	Venezuela	E	158	107	3,000	427,000
Yacyreta-Apipe	Paraná	Paraguay/Argentina	E, G	33	69,600	61,200	21,000,000
Zillergründl	Ziller	Austria	A	180	505	980	90,000
Major World Dams Completed in 1979 and 1980[1]							
Agua Vermelha	Grande	Brazil	E, G	90	3,990	19,640	11,000,000
Dartmouth	Mitta-Mitta	Australia	R	180	670	14,100	4,000,000
Foz do Areia	Iguaçu	Brazil	E, R, G	153	830	13,700	7,320,000
Gura Apelor Retezat	Ruil Mare	Romania	E, R	168	460	9,000	225,000
Hasan Ugurlu	Yesilirmak	Turkey	E, R	175	435	9,042	1,078,000
Las Portas	Camba	Spain	A	152	484	747	162,000
Sobradinho	São Francisco	Brazil	E, R, G	43	3,900	13,200	34,200,000
Tedorigawa	Tedori	Japan	E, R	153	420	10,120	231,000

[1]Having a height exceeding 150 m (492 ft); or having a total volume content exceeding 15 million cu m (19.6 million cu yd); or forming a reservoir exceeding 14,800 × 10^6 cu m capacity (12 million ac-ft).
[2]Type of dam: E = earth; R = rockfill; A = arch; G = gravity.
NA = not available.

(T. W. MERMEL)

example of the latter was the 153-m-diameter "ensphere" covering a sports hall at the University of Arizona. This consisted of a network of laminated members with a timber deck and was in 1980 the world's largest-span timber dome.

(GEOFFREY M. PINFOLD)

Dams. By virtue of their sheer scale, large dams rank as arguably the most impressive and enduring of civil engineering works. The apparent massive simplicity of a dam is, however, deceptive in the extreme. The integration of geotechnical, structural, hydrologic, and economic factors into a balanced design requires a blending of scientific analysis and engineering judgment such as to render dam construction one of the most challenging and at the same time most satisfying areas of engineering endeavour.

In an era of ever increasing world population and of diminishing fuel supplies, the significance of dams in terms of energy production was growing steadily. Consequently, dam construction continued at a high level in 1980 despite the recession prevailing in most countries. In some countries, indeed, there was a discernible increase in dam building, particularly in relation to hydroelectric projects. This trend was largely attributable to concern over rising costs of fuel oil and also to those doubts that persisted with respect to widespread exploitation of nuclear power. In addition to a reappraisal of possible large-scale developments, circumstances stimulated a new interest in small-scale or so-called mini-hydro projects. As regards previously unexploited hydroelectric potential, it was instructive to observe that even in Spain, where installed hydroelectric capacity had grown from 2,000 Mw to 14,000 Mw since 1960, it was estimated that only some 50% of the economically viable hydroelectric potential had been harnessed.

Developments in dam design and construction were governed by two factors. First, every dam site is unique in terms of the prevailing geotechnical and hydrologic conditions and, consequently, every major dam is effectively a prototype. Second, the dam engineer is of necessity conservative in outlook, advance in dam engineering being by progressive evolution rather than by revolution. Proven analytical and construction techniques were steadily refined in the context of developments in the many related disciplines. Particularly important among the latter was progress in geotechnical engineering, a circumstance explained by the fundamental importance of the foundation to the effectiveness of any dam and further by the predominance of earthfill and/or rockfill embankment dams. That the historical emphasis on embankments, probably 80% of all dams, would increase was, in turn, attributable to their adaptability to less favourable sites and also to the plant-intensive and, therefore, low-cost nature of their construction process.

Continued development of established finite element methods (FEM) of analysis gave dam engineers their most powerful design tool, particular areas of application in recent years being with respect to predicting the influence of seismic shock within a dam or with regard to improving understanding of the complex internal strain and deformation pattern in the body of a dam. The contribution made not only to the analysis of new projects but also to assessing the structural competence and safety of existing structures was a significant one.

Looking ahead, advances in concrete dam construction techniques were likely to be based on speeding up the process through the use of variants of concrete, such as rolled dry lean concrete (RDLC), that were suited to large-scale mechanization. In the field of embankment dam construction, it was likely that the use of asphaltic or, in some cases, plastic membranes to provide the impermeable element of the structure would progress rapidly. As an example of the asphaltic membrane approach, the 56-m-high Megget Dam currently under construction in the U.K. was of particular interest. In this instance the membrane was central and was being raised in parallel with the rockfill shoulders of the dam. A further area of development might lie in perfecting methods of construction that would not necessarily require expensive river diversion works.

(A. I. B. MOFFAT)

Roads. Highway activities during 1980 followed a discernible pattern; in the industrialized nations, where the networks of main highways had been in service for a number of years, relatively little construction of new highways was carried out. Instead, highway authorities implemented intensive maintenance and reconstruction programs to protect the existing systems. In the less developed countries attention was divided between the construction of international road links and the planning and building of feeder roads to connect isolated agricultural and rural areas with the more populated areas.

Worldwide inflation and the shortage of highway materials continued to hamper road building. In the U.S. the cost of highway construction in 1980 was three times higher than in 1967. The nation's interstate highway system of more than 68,000 km (42,000 mi), which in 1980 was 93% complete, was showing signs of deterioration, especially in the sections built in the late 1950s. Federal funds were made available to the individual states to pay for resurfacing, restoration, and rehabilitation of those roads. Total expenditure for all roads and streets in the U.S. by all units of government in 1979 (the last available figure) was estimated at $35.7 billion.

In Canada much attention was being given to pavement recycling, in which worn-out road material is planed from the road surface and remixed for future use. Canada might soon have a second Trans-Canada Highway, the 4,800 km (3,000-mi) Yellowhead Highway, which runs from Portage-la-Prairie in Manitoba through Saskatoon and Edmonton to northern British Columbia. Designation as a Trans-Canada Highway would make it eligible for a federal-provincial upgrading and maintenance program.

Connection of the long-awaited Darien Gap in the Pan-American Highway system took a step forward with the formation of a special liaison committee by the presidents of Colombia and Panama to study the financial, technical, social, and medical considerations involved. In Argentina

KEYSTONE

The first of six huge half-moon steel gates arrived in London in July on the barge "Grand Turtle." The gates will be erected across the Thames at Woolwich to help keep the river from flooding.

a 74-km (46-mi) network of expressways (motorways) was under construction to relieve congestion and reduce the high accident rate in Buenos Aires. Paving was expected to be completed soon on National Route 3, which extended from Buenos Aires along the coast of Patagonia to Tierra del Fuego.

Five major trans-African highway projects were in progress: the Mombasa–Lagos Trans-African Highway, the Dakar–N'Djamena Trans-Sahelian Highway, the Lagos–Nouakchott Trans-West African Highway, the Cairo–Gabarone Trans-East African Highway, and the Algiers to Lagos Trans-Sahara Highway. Other significant road links in Africa, completed in 1980, included the 1,200-km (750-mi) Khartoum–Port Sudan road.

In the Middle East Saudi Arabia's massive road-building program was proceeding in high gear. The 64-km (40-mi) four-lane divided highway from Jidda to Mecca was opened to traffic in 1980, as was the 50-km (30-mi) Rastanura–Jubail highway. Construction was under way on the 90-km (55-mi) ring road around the capital of Riyadh.

China was initiating its nationwide road-building program with a 160-km (100-mi) highway from Beijing (Peking) to Tianjin (Tientsin). In Australia a major project was the $4.3 million repair of 755 km (470 mi) of the vital north-south highway between South Australia and the Northern Territory, damaged by flooding.

In the U.K. motorway construction was slowing down. Only 105 km (65 mi) of motorway were opened in 1980, for a total in service of 2,589 km (1,605 mi). Although they represented only 0.7% of the U.K.'s road network, these expressways carried more than 10% of its traffic. The Beaune–Mulhouse Autoroute, connecting the French and West German expressway networks, was opened by French Pres. Valéry Giscard d'Estaing in September, while the N2 in Switzerland and the A5 in West Germany were linked at the border in June.

Design was begun on the Trans European Motorway, which was to start in Gdansk, in Poland, and pass through ten countries to Adriatic, Aegean, and Black Sea border crossings. More than 250 km (155 mi) of the motorway from Prague to Brno and Bratislava in Czechoslovakia were completed in 1980, with the balance to be opened in 1981. (HUGH M. GILLESPIE)

Tunnels. Large-diameter tunneling shields were making records in 1980. In Tokyo the largest slurry mole in the world commenced work on a 1,000-m-long tunnel forming part of a 22-km extension to the Tokyo Rapid Transit System (1 km= 0.62 mi; 1 mm=0.04 in). The slurry machine was 10.3 m in diameter and weighed 780 metric tons; backup equipment included a primary and secondary crusher system that reduced all rock size down to 500 mm prior to pumping. Advances up to 9,100 mm were achieved in 40 minutes. In Egypt the 11.8-m-diameter mechanical shield completed the driving of the Ahmed Hamdi Tunnel under the Suez Canal 14 km north of Port Tewfik. The total drive of 1,460 m including the road deck was completed in record-breaking time from January 1979 to April 1980, representing an average weekly drivage of 25 m. In Switzerland another large shield with an outside diameter of 11.46 m and equipped with four road headers continued driving the Rosenberg Tunnel at St. Gall. A novel feature in the driving of this tunnel was a dust-suppression system that eliminated the need for special ventilation ducting.

Also in Switzerland, the 16.3-km-long St. Gotthard tunnel, the world's longest road tunnel, was opened to traffic after an 11-year construction period. The 12.87-km-long Fréjus road tunnel connecting France and Italy was also opened to traffic, after 6 years of construction. A feature of the tunnel driving was the successful use of rock bolts to provide temporary support in highly laminated rock. Progress on the 80-km Bolmen water tunnel in Sweden slowed owing to unforeseen ground problems, and estimated completion was set back by six years to 1990. Excessive groundwater caused problems in the construction of the new Helsinki (Fin.) subway, the first section of which was due for completion in 1983. In the U.K. the second Dartford tunnel beneath the Thames estuary 25 km east of London was opened to traffic.

Normally, a distance of one diameter is preferred between parallel tunnels. At Atlanta, Ga., however, in the construction of twin 6.25-m-diameter subway tunnels at a depth of 17 m below the surface, separation was reduced to one-quarter of a diameter. Steel liner plates were used, and the final surface settlement was 380 mm. In Chicago work continued on what was probably the world's largest tunneling job. More than 200 km of tunnel were being driven 50 m below ground level to solve the city's sewage and floodwater problems, and 12 tunneling machines, the largest 10.8 m in diameter, were in use.

A major event in 1980 was the opening of Hong Kong's first underground railway. Creating a world record for subway construction work, the first 16 km were completed in 4½ years, according to schedule and, it was claimed, within the original budget. In Rome 14.6 km of the new subway were also opened to traffic in 1980. More than 80 cities throughout the world were planning new subway systems, 19 of them in West Germany, which was becoming a world leader in the application of the new Austrian tunneling method employing spray concrete.

The technology of cutting rock with high-pressure water jets received a boost when Japanese engineers announced a system combining drill and blast methods with the formation of presplitting slots using fine water jets under a pressure of 4,000 kg per sq cm (50,000 lb per sq in). It was claimed that costs were reduced and a much more accurate control over blasting obtained. Swedish engineers also introduced a practical form of water cannon for splitting boulders. (DAVID A. HARRIES)

Environment

In a year when economic recession and high unemployment occupied most people's thoughts, environmental issues may have seemed less important than they had in the 1970s. Nevertheless, some valuable achievements in international environmental cooperation were realized in 1980. Popular opposition to nuclear power, now affecting virtually all countries, continued to dominate the voluntary environmental movement. Governments may have been more concerned about violence in declining urban areas that resulted from tensions built up during years of neglect.

England:
see United Kingdom

English Literature:
see Literature

Entertainment:
see Dance; Motion Pictures; Music; Television and Radio; Theatre

Entomology:
see Life Sciences

INTERNATIONAL COOPERATION

World Conservation Strategy. What might prove to be the most important environmental document to date was published in March. Produced by the International Union for Conservation of Nature and Natural Resources (IUCN) and the UN Environment Program (UNEP), with assistance from the World Wildlife Fund, the World Conservation Strategy was launched at impressive ceremonies in many countries. The document sought to identify principal areas of environmental concern and to propose development strategies that would minimize environmental damage and conserve resources.

UN Environment Program. The success of the Mediterranean Action Plan led to serious studies of other seas that might be helped in similar ways. UNEP supported studies of the Gulf of Guinea (West Africa), the Caribbean, the Red Sea, the seas of East Asia, the sea off Kuwait, and the southern Pacific. A meeting held at Caracas, Venezuela, January 28–February 1, reviewed a draft action plan for the Caribbean, prepared by UNEP and the UN Economic Commission for Latin America. The plan was approved by representatives of 35 countries.

The eighth session of the UNEP governing council was held in Nairobi, Kenya, in April. Executive Director Mostafa Tolba complained that more than U.S. $1 million pledged to UNEP by member states remained unpaid at the end of 1979, and the shortage of funds threatened to hamper program activities. Tolba went on to propose that UNEP programs be balanced to reflect equally the needs of less developed and developed countries and then listed the most serious environmental problems of the 1980s. These included the rate at which tropical forests were being cleared, desertification, the loss or degradation of fish breeding grounds, the extinction of species, and pollution. He also warned that expansion of the use of biomass fuels might lead to competition for land.

World Environment Day, observed on June 5, received extensive press coverage in many countries. Much of it was based on an information pack produced in several languages and distributed by UNEP.

Development Aid. *Banking on the Biosphere*, a report prepared by the International Institute for Environment and Development (IIED), examined the role of the major development agencies and banks in environmental protection. Following its publication, a group of those institutions met in New York to sign a brief environmental policy declaration. The African, Caribbean, Inter-American, and Asian Development banks, the World Bank, the European Development Fund, the Organization of American States, and the Arab Bank for Economic Development in Africa pledged themselves to reaffirm their support for the principles and recommendations of the 1972 UN Conference on the Human Environment. The document was also signed on behalf of the UN Development Program and UNEP. Its seven resolutions included the training of environmental experts in less developed countries.

In another IIED study, conducted for it by the

U.S. Natural Resources Defense Fund, the U.S. Agency for International Development (AID) was criticized for lack of technical staff to supervise its environmental policies. The study had been commissioned by AID to examine the environmental policies of bilateral aid agencies in Canada, West Germany, The Netherlands, Sweden, Britain, and the U.S.

European Economic Community. Control of air and water pollution, control of dangerous chemicals, management of waste, and the introduction of environment impact assessments were listed as priority objectives in a progress report submitted by the European Commission to a meeting of EEC environmental ministers held in Luxembourg on June 30. The proposal for environmental impact assessments of all major development projects was forwarded to member governments. While the ministers agreed on measures to control transfrontier air pollution, they could not agree on water pollution measures or on the so-called Seveso Directive, which aimed to reduce the likelihood of major industrial accidents. In September the Commission issued a draft directive designed to limit exposure to microwave radiation.

Marine Environment. The ninth session of the Third UN Conference on the Law of the Sea opened in Geneva on July 28. Despite fears that conference decisions might be preempted by legislation in the U.S. and other industrial countries permitting seabed mineral exploitation, the session ended with broad agreement. It was expected that a draft treaty would be prepared for signing at a final session, to be held in 1981 in Caracas.

The Royal Geographical Society and the International Arctic Committee held a two-day meeting in London on March 11–12 at which scientists from 20 countries discussed threats to the Arctic environment. Although the Arctic Ocean is largely landlocked, the one large pathway into it brings waters from the coasts of North America and western Europe and thus threatens to channel pollutants into the region. The aim of the meeting was to identify risks as a first step toward securing for the Arctic the same degree of protection that had been afforded to the Antarctic.

The Helsinki Convention on the Protection of the Marine Environment of the Baltic Sea, signed by seven countries, came into force on May 13. At the end of the first meeting of the Helsinki Commission, on May 8, it was stated that the condition of the Baltic was improving. The first aim of the commission would be to halt the discharge of polychlorinated biphenyls, and later mercury, into the sea. From Jan. 1, 1981, tankers of more than 20,000 metric tons and chemical carriers of more than 1,600 tons would have to report their entrance into the Baltic and their subsequent positions. The Soviet government announced that as of 1985 no more untreated sewage would be discharged into the sea from Leningrad.

On February 11 Peter Thacher, UNEP deputy executive director, told a meeting of the 17 signatories of the 1976 Barcelona Convention that only 35% of the $3.2 million promised for the Mediterranean Action Plan had been received. Several countries paid immediately, and the program continued. UNEP proposed an increased budget of $4.5 million for 1981. The third protocol to the Barcelona Convention was signed in Athens on May 17 by Cyprus, France, Greece, Italy, Lebanon, Libya, Malta, Monaco, Morocco, Spain, and Tunisia, and later by Algeria, Turkey, and Yugoslavia. Egypt and Syria were expected to sign, leaving only Albania undecided among all the Mediterranean states. The protocol dealt with pollution from land sources and pledged signatories to improve the quality of rivers, to regulate sewage discharges, and to control industrial pollutants, divided into "black list" and "gray list" categories according to their toxicity. Early in July, for the first time in several years, it was reported that all Mediterranean beaches were safe for bathing.

The institution responsible for monitoring pollution in the Red Sea, the Arab League Educational, Cultural, and Scientific Organization (ALECSO), based in Tunis and working closely with UNEP, UNESCO, IUCN, and the Intergovernmental Maritime Consultative Organization, issued a report in March. While existing pollution levels were not yet critical, the Red Sea was threatened by domestic sewage, industrial wastes, dredging, and oil. Furthermore, nuclear desalination plants in Saudi Arabia and the mining of metalliferous muds could increase pollution dramatically. ALECSO planned to establish five new research and monitoring stations.

LONDON DAILY EXPRESS/PICTORIAL PARADE

A fireman on England's Isle of Wight dressed like a spaceman to inspect this dead whale. It was washed ashore along with drums and canisters believed to contain deadly arsenic trichloride which spilled out of the wrecked Greek freighter "Aeolian Sky" that sank off Dorset, England, in November 1979.

UPI

Demonstrators were driven away by police as they attempted to occupy the Seabrook, New Hampshire, nuclear site in May.

At Canberra, Australia, in September the original signatories to the Antarctic Treaty, plus East and West Germany and Poland, signed an agreement to conserve the marine life of Antarctica. Catch quotas for 1981–82 were established at the 32nd annual meeting of the International Whaling Commission at Brighton, England, in July. (See *Wildlife Conservation,* below.)

Atmospheric Pollution. On Nov. 16, 1979, the U.S., Canada, and every European country except Albania, Cyprus, and Malta signed an 18-article draft convention on the control of sulfur dioxide. It was planned to extend control to other long-range pollutants at a later date. The signing followed a meeting organized by the UN Economic Commission for Europe, which began on November 13 in Geneva. On Aug. 5, 1980, the U.S. and Canada signed a separate temporary agreement covering emissions of sulfur and nitrogen oxides.

In *Chlorofluorocarbons and Their Effect on the Stratosphere,* published in October 1979 by the U.K. Department of the Environment, British scientists argued that the evidence did not warrant a ban on the use of these chemicals. In November 1979, however, the U.S. National Academy of Sciences disagreed. Its *Report of the Panel on Stratospheric Chemistry* maintained that depletion of the ozone layer from this cause might be twice as severe as had been estimated in its 1976 report. It called for a worldwide ban on all nonessential uses of chlorofluorocarbons. The Netherlands government said in February 1980 it would ban their use as aerosol propellants from the end of 1981, and in January the EEC environment ministers agreed to reduce usage to one-third the 1979 level by 1982.

NATIONAL DEVELOPMENTS

"Ecopolitics." Environmentalist political parties, formed to contest elections in the U.S., France, West Germany, and the U.K., had little expectation of securing a large popular vote, but they hoped to keep environmental issues before the public. The U.S. Citizens Party was formed in August 1979. In April 1980 it nominated Barry Commoner as its presidential candidate while offering a program of mildly socialist environmental improvement. In France Brice Lalonde, founder and leader of Réseau des Amis de la Terre ("Friends of the Earth"), the largest French environmental organization, was chosen to contest the 1981 presidential election.

In West Germany the national environmentalist Green Party fought its first election in March in Baden-Württemberg, where it won a few seats, as it had done previously in Bremen, before going on to fight the federal election in October. The party congress held in Saarbrücken on March 22–23 left it dominated by its own left wing—immediately nicknamed the "red Greens." At one time it appeared that the party might draw sufficient votes from Helmut Schmidt to give Franz-Josef Strauss the chancellorship, but its campaign was weakened by internal dissent. At the time of the federal election it had about 17,000 members.

The British Ecology Party increased its membership from 1,000 at the time of the May 1979 general election to 6,000 at the time of its 1980 annual conference, held in Cardiff on September 20–21. It saw as its main task the forging of a coherent political stance that would establish its electoral credibility.

Urban Problems. In September the UN International Conference on Population and the Urban Future was held in Rome—itself heavily polluted by "acid rain" that was damaging monuments. Forming a background to the discussions were UN forecasts of a global urban population of about three billion by the end of the century. A Campaign for Urban Renaissance was launched by the Council of Europe at a meeting of planning ministers held in London on October 21–22. During his visit to Brazil in July, Pope John Paul II visited the *favela* (shantytown) of Alagados and pleaded for help for its desperately poor inhabitants.

Urban problems were never absent from the news for long, and no country seemed immune. In March Dutch police mounted a massive paramilitary operation to remove barricades set up in Amsterdam by squatters occupying an empty house that was to be taken over by the municipality. Earlier, unsuccessful attempts to dislodge the squatters had sparked violent rioting. The investiture of Queen Beatrix of The Netherlands on April 30 was marred by further violence, and police used water cannons and tear gas to disperse demonstrators. On June 14 the queen visited Lekkerkerk, a town in which 871 people had been relocated because their homes were built on ground contaminated with toxic industrial wastes.

In April the St. Paul's area of Bristol, England, was the scene of disturbances in which mainly nonwhite residents fought with police. In May racial riots in Tampa and Miami, Fla., left more than 15 people dead. The riots followed the acquittal of four white former policemen charged with having beaten a black businessman to death. Order was restored, but in July several incidents—each minor in itself—led to further rioting in Miami. Looting and fighting lasted for two nights and a day. (*See* RACE RELATIONS.)

Even traditionally placid cities were affected. Two days of demonstrations and street fighting in the deprived Nørrebro district of Copenhagen ended on April 30. The disturbances had started as a protest against the demolition of a recreational area to make way for an apartment block. Litter bins were used as incendiary bombs, eight buses were formed into a barricade, and thousands of people fought 500 police. On September 9 the Zürich (Switz.) City Council approved the purchase of a new water cannon for riot control. Violence broke out on October 4, in Lausanne and Bern as well as Zürich, as young people demanded youth centres. There were no serious injuries, but about 80 people were arrested in Zürich and Lausanne.

Nuclear Power. Popular opposition to and official concern about nuclear power spread to virtually every country. Even in the U.S.S.R., which was fully committed to nuclear power expansion, leading academicians were expressing doubts about safety.

UNITED STATES. In February the city of Missoula, Mont., banned all shipments of nuclear materials within its limits. On May 24 about 1,000 demonstrators began a three-day attempt to occupy the Seabrook, N.H., nuclear site. In a September referendum, however, Maine voters rejected by three to two a proposal that would have closed Maine Yankee, the state's only nuclear power sta-

HENRI BUREAU—SYGMA

Local residents helped firemen and soldiers clean oil from beaches on the Brittany coast after the supertanker "Tanio" broke in half in the English Channel during a storm, leaking 3,000 tons of oil into the ocean.

tion. In his budget request to Congress, presented at the beginning of February, U.S. Pres. Jimmy Carter confirmed his intention to halt construction at the Clinch River, Tenn., site of what would have been the country's first fast breeder reactor. At the same time, he proposed other broad cuts in fast breeder development, in line with his decision to postpone the introduction of fast breeders indefinitely.

In January scientists from the Hershey Medical Center of Pennsylvania State University surveyed 1,000 people living within ten miles of the Three Mile Island (Pa.) nuclear plant, shut down following an accident in 1979. Nearly half reported physical symptoms of stress, and almost 13% of those living within five miles of the plant had become antinuclear activists. In April state health officials denied that the rate of infant mortality had increased since the accident. Following an unsuccessful attempt to enter the containment dome of the damaged reactor, it proved necessary to vent some krypton-85 in order to equalize pressures inside and outside the building. Venting began at 8 AM on June 29, and the dome was entered successfully on July 23. The operation posed no risk, but thousands of people left the area. In September the Nuclear Regulatory Commission issued a preliminary environmental impact assessment showing that decontamination and repair would take seven years but would pose no risk to human health or to the environment.

Early in August the Committee on the Biological Effects of Ionizing Radiation of the U.S. National Academy of Sciences issued a report, commissioned by the Environmental Protection Agency (EPA), suggesting that the health risks from low levels of exposure might be less than had been thought. Called BEIR III to distinguish it from a 1972 report on the subject and from its own first draft, issued in 1979, the report favoured the hypothesis that at low levels the relationship between exposure and damage is quadratic; that is, the damage increases as the square of the exposure.

World's 25 Most Populous Urban Areas[1]

Rank	City and Country	City proper Population	City proper Year	Metropolitan area Population	Metropolitan area Year
1	Tokyo, Japan	8,179,300	1980 estimate	28,331,000	1979 estimate
2	Osaka, Japan	2,682,221	1979 estimate	17,071,000	1979 estimate
3	New York City, U.S.	7,224,000	1980 estimate	16,707,200	1979 estimate
4	Mexico City, Mexico	9,191,300	1979 estimate	14,750,200	1979 estimate
5	London, U.K.	6,918,000	1978 estimate	12,289,400	1978 estimate
6	São Paolo, Brazil	8,732,000	1980 estimate	11,859,900	1979 estimate
7	Beijing, China	...	...	11,400,000[2]	1979 estimate
8	Los Angeles, U.S.	2,863,400	1979 estimate	10,978,300	1979 estimate
9	Buenos Aires, Argentina	2,985,000	1980 estimate	10,891,000	1980 estimate
10	Ruhr, West Germany[3]	...	...	10,278,000	1975 estimate
11	Shanghai, China	5,700,000	1970 estimate	10,000,000[2]	1978 estimate
12	Paris, France	2,102,900	1979 estimate	9,878,600	1978 estimate
13	Nagoya, Japan	2,135,000	1980 estimate	9,614,000	1980 estimate
14	Rio de Janiero, Brazil	5,539,100	1980 estimate	9,473,400	1979 estimate
15	Calcutta, India	3,148,700	1971 census	8,827,000	1980 estimate
16	Cairo, Egypt	5,423,000	1979 estimate	8,539,000	1979 estimate
17	Bombay, India	...	...	8,343,000[2]	1980 estimate
18	Seoul, South Korea	...	...	8,114,000[2]	1979 estimate
19	Moscow, U.S.S.R.	7,914,000	1980 estimate	8,100,000	1980 estimate
20	Chicago, U.S.	3,060,800	1979 estimate	7,673,300	1979 estimate
21	Jakarta, Indonesia	6,178,500	1980 estimate	6,397,300	1980 estimate
22	Manila, Philippines	1,479,100	1975 census	5,900,600	1979 estimate
23	Philadelphia, U.S.	1,757,400	1979 estimate	5,597,600	1979 estimate
24	Karachi, Pakistan	3,500,000	1972 census	5,005,000	1980 estimate
25	Bangkok, Thailand	3,112,000	1979 estimate	4,999,500	1979 estimate

[1] Ranked by population of metropolitan area.
[2] Municipality or other civil division within which a city proper may not be distinguished.
[3] A so-called industrial conurbation within which a single central city is not distinguished.

According to this thesis, a linear, one-for-one, relationship occurs only at fairly high exposure levels. The implication was that permitted exposure levels might be raised somewhat without risk.

WESTERN EUROPE. Swedish voters went to the polls on March 23 to take part in a referendum on the future of nuclear power. Of the three choices offered to them, one was moderately pronuclear; the second required the 12 existing and planned reactors to be used for the whole of their lifetimes but for no more to be built; and the third called for the phasing out of existing reactors over a ten-year period. The result showed the strength of Swedish antinuclear opinion. The pronuclear option won only 18.7% of the vote, 39.3% voted for the second option, and the avowedly antinuclear alternative received 38.7%. In Austria, where a 1978 referendum had blocked activation of the country's first nuclear power plant, at Zwentendorf, the issue was again put to the vote in November 1980; a "popular initiative" supporting the plant's use opened the way to repeal of antinuclear legislation passed in 1978.

In January the Danish government postponed indefinitely a decision on the introduction of nuclear power. The reasons given were the difficulty of finding suitable sites in a small, densely populated country and the lack of a satisfactory solution to the problem of waste storage. In Finland the largest demonstration since the Vietnam war era was held in March, when 5,000 people marched through Helsinki to show their solidarity with Swedish antinuclear groups and to oppose the building of a Soviet-designed 1,000-Mw plant. Also in March, 150 members of an antinuclear group padlocked all the gates to the Borssele nuclear plant in The Netherlands, preventing entry for 20 hours; 29 demonstrators chained themselves to the gates and were arrested.

An all-party parliamentary commission appointed by the West German Bundestag in 1978 to advise on the future of nuclear power reported in August 1980. It recommended that a final decision be delayed until 1990, but that meanwhile reactors should be built as needed, provided attention was paid to energy conservation and the development of coal and renewable energy sources.

In France a public inquiry began in January into the plan to build a 5,200-Mw nuclear plant on the Pointe du Raz, near Plogoff in Britanny. It soon became the focus of daily demonstrations, sometimes involving thousands of people. Usually, they were timed to coincide with the movement of the vans carrying documents to and from the parking area where the mobile inquiry was held, the local council having refused use of the town hall. The area was filled regularly with manure and garbage, missiles were thrown at riot police and troops, who replied with tear gas, and on February 29 seven demonstrators were arrested. Their trial led to a demonstration outside the courthouse by 40,000 people, who taunted the 1,500 police when the demonstrators were set free. On April 17 the commissioners found in favour of the proposal. An environmental group, Rhône Alpes, said it would form a syndicate, with 30,000 subscribers, which would buy up all the land at the site to

DAVE FORNELL—SYGMA

A Titan II missile exploded in its silo in Damascus, Arkansas, in September. The warhead was catapulted about 200 yards from the silo.

prevent its sale to the electricity authority. The Gravelines I and Tricastin I reactors were started in mid-February; the previous year small cracks had been found in the base plates of the primary circuit heat exchangers. On April 16 the Cap de la Hague reprocessing plant lost all power for an hour when a fire in a transformer room damaged the main and auxiliary circuits. There was no radioactive release.

There was an upsurge in antinuclear activity in the U.K. during the year. In January the results of a public opinion poll commissioned by 17 Scottish antinuclear groups, together with the Scottish National Party and the Ecology Party, revealed serious disquiet about nuclear power in Scotland. The aim was to measure opinion about the proposed Torness station, to be built on the East Lothian coast. Of those questioned, 34% opposed the scheme, 40% were undecided, and only 26% were clearly in favour. Almost one-third of the sample believed nuclear power to be necessary, but only 10% thought its development should be given priority over that of other energy sources; 66% opposed storing nuclear waste in Scotland, 14% were in favour, and 11% were undecided. A survey by National Opinion Polls, published early in August, showed that two out of three people in Britain opposed the building of more nuclear power stations.

In February a public inquiry opened at Ayr in Scotland to consider an appeal by the U.K. Atomic Energy Authority (UKAEA) against the refusal of the Kyle and Carrick District Council to permit test drilling of hard granite in the Galloway hills as part of a study of possible sites for nuclear waste storage. The Scottish Conservation Society, one of the principal objectors, organized its own rival hearing to coincide with the official one. No official decision on the test drilling program had been made by year's end. A similar inquiry, necessitated by the Northumberland County Council's refusal to authorize test borings in the Cheviot Hills, opened at Newcastle upon Tyne in October, amid lively demonstrations by protest groups.

The environmental organization Greenpeace used its converted trawler "Rainbow Warrior" to obstruct the "Pacific Swan," which was carrying spent light-water reactor fuel from Japan to France's Cap de la Hague reprocessing plant. On January 23 Greenpeace claimed a victory when the "Pacific Swan" was diverted to Barrow-in-Furness and the British Windscale plant. The Greenpeace policy of harrassing ships was forbidden by a High Court order when, on the following day, attempts were made to prevent "Pacific Swan" from unloading its cargo. On February 5 Greenpeace lost its appeal against the order, and on the same day the "Rainbow Warrior" was told to leave Cherbourg harbour. It went to Guernsey, but on the night of February 11 it returned to wait just outside French territorial waters to intercept the "Pacific Swan" as it sailed south. On March 2 "Rainbow Warrior" sailed for Cumbria and a demonstration against another waste carrier, "Pacific Fisher." This led to a prosecution for defying the High Court order, and on May 15 three Greenpeace directors were each fined £100 and Greenpeace Ltd. was fined £500.

This was not the only clash between British antinuclear protesters and the law. On July 8, 20 to 30 demonstrators erected scaffolding across a railway line in Gloucestershire and halted a train carrying nuclear waste from Didcot, Oxfordshire, to Sharpness, where it was to be loaded onto a ship and dumped at sea. Seven people were arrested and fined a total of £2,560.

In October the National Union of Students announced its support for Students Against Nuclear

Energy (SANE). Later in the month a rally organized by the Campaign for Nuclear Disarmament drew 50,000 supporters of various antinuclear and environmentalist groups to London's Trafalgar Square to hear speeches by politicians and other public figures.

EASTERN EUROPE. In November 1979 the Mecklenberg Synod of the Evangelical Lutheran Church called for a public discussion of the dangers of nuclear power. Although East Germany was committed to the expansion of nuclear energy, Western observers believed the call reflected a growing concern among the public.

In its Document 22, the Czechoslovak Charter 77 movement claimed in November 1978 that two accidents, on Jan. 5, 1976, and Feb. 24, 1977, had released radioactive coolant into the atmosphere and into a nearby stream. Two workers had been killed and others irradiated, and the Jaslovske Bohunice power station had been closed permanently. The authorities admitted the accidents, but as late as July 1980 they maintained that the station was working normally. In August Prague Radio announced that in fact the station had been closed some years earlier as a result of damage caused by a serious defect. The Charter 77 movement called for a moratorium on nuclear power until questions of safety were resolved, but the government remained fully committed to nuclear power.

In November 1979 the Yugoslav government decided to site its second nuclear power station at Prevlaka, near Zagreb, on the Sava River. This followed protests from inhabitants of the area near the island of Vir off the Dalmatian coast, the site originally selected.

PACIFIC OCEAN. Plans to dump U.S. and Japanese low-level nuclear wastes in the deep trench between Midway Island and Palmyra Atoll were opposed strongly by South Sea Islanders. The Yap Legislative Council filed a protest with the UN Trusteeship Council, and on August 2 representatives of the Mariana Islands, led by Mayor Francisco Diaz of Saipan Island, lodged a protest note with the Japanese government. They warned that if waste were dumped they would impose a 200-mi fishing limit, thus excluding Japanese vessels from traditional fishing grounds.

Fire fighters attempted to put out a fire in April after an explosion in an abandoned waterfront warehouse of stored chemicals in Elizabeth, New Jersey. Toxic gases spread rapidly, causing the closing of local schools and those in nearby Linden, New Jersey, and Staten Island, New York.

UPI

Oil Pollution. Following an explosion and fire on February 23, the Greek tanker "Irene Serenade," with 100,000 metric tons of crude oil on board, sank early the following morning in the Bay of Pylos, Greece. Beaches around the bay were heavily polluted, and slicks moved down the coast, threatening other resorts. The Niger River delta was polluted by 30,000 tons of crude oil after a well a mile from Sangana, Nigeria, blew out on January 17. The 30,000 to 50,000 people in nearby coastal villages were heavily dependent on fishing, and many left as their food supply, as well as their drinking water, became contaminated.

The tanker "Tanio" broke in half during heavy storms off the English Channel on March 7. The forward section, containing 11,000 tons of oil, sank, but the stern section, with 13,000 tons, was towed to Le Havre. Three thousand tons of oil were released when the ship broke up, and oil leaked from the sunken section at the rate of about seven tons a day, polluting 60 mi of Britanny beaches. Eventually the sunken section was sealed, and in June work began to pump out its cargo.

A 17-mi-long slick from Saudi Arabian wells at Ras Tannurah reached the coast of Bahrain on August 29; 600 soldiers were mobilized to deal with it. Streams and rivers near Marseilles, France, were contaminated on August 9 when about 35,000 cu ft of oil escaped from a leak in a pipeline supplying refineries in eastern France, West Germany, and Switzerland. The flow was stopped quickly, but not before considerable damage had been done.

In March Mexican officials announced that the Ixtoc 1 oil well in the Gulf of Mexico had finally been capped. Since the well blew up in June 1979, it had spilled an estimated 3 million bbl of crude oil into the Gulf, almost twice as much as in any previous spill.

Industrial Wastes. On May 17 the EPA said 36 people from the part of Niagara Falls, N.Y., close to the Love Canal toxic waste dump had been examined and chromosome damage had been found in 11. Some 239 families close to the dump had been evacuated in 1978, and these people lived just outside the deserted area. The tests were intended to provide evidence for the government's case against Hooker Chemicals and Plastics Corp., the company that deposited the wastes, and to determine whether evacuation of a further 710 households was necessary. Having decided that it was, the government offered financial assistance to the families to help them move elsewhere for six months, but by early July only 499 families had accepted. The news of the chromosome damage angered local people, and on May 19 they locked two federal officials in an office for five hours.

In June Sen. Edward Kennedy (Dem., Mass.) warned that as many as 1.6 million Americans might be living close to toxic waste dumps. The EPA estimated that there were 30,000 such dumps, of which it had discovered 645, including 108 that were seriously dangerous to human health. The warning was supported in September by the U.S. surgeon general, Julius Richmond, who reported to Congress that "toxic chemicals are adding to the disease burden of the U.S. in a significant, although not as yet precisely defined way." His report supported President Carter's plan to create a "superfund," partly financed by fees on the oil and chemical industries, to pay for toxic waste treatment and oil spill cleanups. The measure was passed by Congress late in the fall, but with oil spills omitted and with somewhat weaker liability provisions against dumpers than the administration had wanted.

Toxic wastes were said to be polluting U.S. waters. In January the Los Angeles Department of Water began testing tap water for traces of trichloroethylene, a suspected carcinogen, after 10 to 11 parts per billion of the substance had been found in three wells. The Council on Environmental Quality stated on February 19 that two-thirds of all U.S. lakes might be seriously contaminated by toxic industrial wastes and that groundwater contamination was becoming serious. In some lakes and rivers fish were inedible, and four million acres of shellfish waters had been closed because of pollution. To increase the efficiency of pollution control while reducing its cost, the EPA introduced the "bubble concept." This would allow companies to count several waste discharges as a single source and reduce their combined emissions to acceptable limits.

The EEC issued a draft environmental directive early in the year calling for a reduction in the amount of mercury discharged into water by particular industries. Even before the draft was discussed by the environment ministers in Luxembourg in June, the British had attacked it. *Water Pollution: Mercury*, the 38th report of the House of Lords Select Committee on the European Communities, pointed out that the directive did not distinguish among industries, or between solid and soluble mercury, and failed to indicate whether it aimed for some absolute standard.

In October 1979 the U.S. Department of Housing and Urban Development had reported its findings that lead in the blood of New York children came predominantly from lead additives. In Britain a Department of Health and Social Security working party found food and drink to be the more important sources, but its conclusions were challenged in an analysis issued in November by the Conservation Society. In the January 1980 issue of its magazine *Which?*, the Consumers' Association called for grants to replace lead plumbing that, it said, provided more than two million British homes with water containing more lead than the EEC-recommended maximum. The parents of two

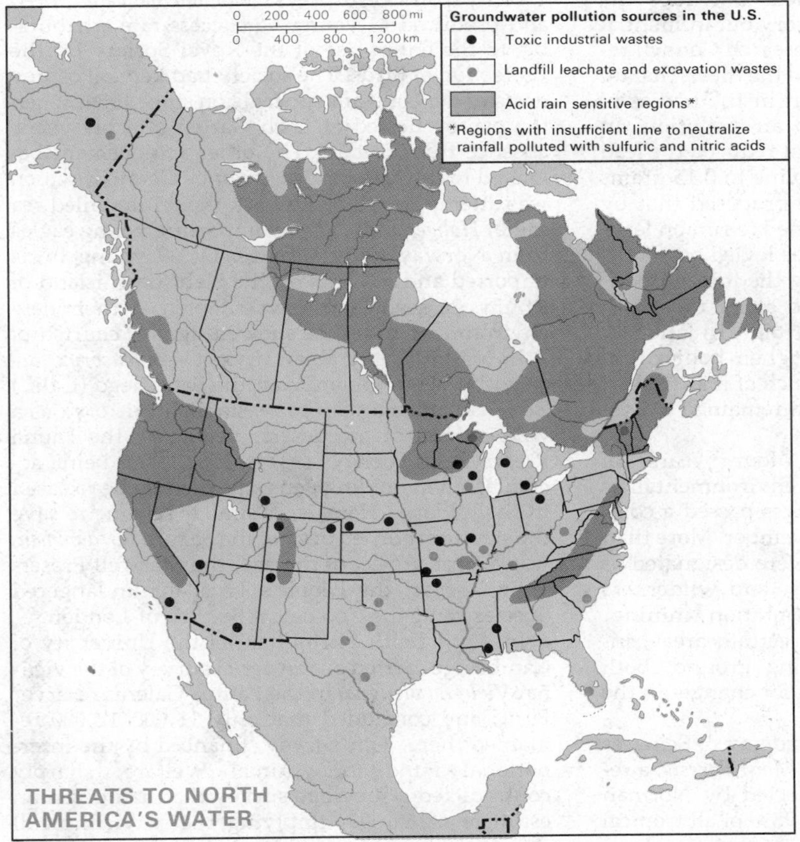

WIDE WORLD

Volunteers check airlifted burro as part of efforts led by the Fund for Animals to relocate some of the animals from the Grand Canyon in Arizona. The U.S. National Park Service had found the canyon's wild burro herds, which were descendants of prospectors' burros, to be a growing threat to the landscape and native wildlife.

London children allegedly injured by atmospheric lead won a county court suit against BP Oil Ltd. and Shell U.K. Ltd., but on May 2 the judgment was reversed on appeal. The court ruled that since the companies did not add more than the permitted amount of lead to their gasoline, they could not be held to blame.

In Australia, where the federal government sought to increase the amount of lead added to gasoline in order to save fuel, the state government of New South Wales continued to reduce the amounts it permitted. The advisory but influential National Health and Medical Research Council reported in January that it accepted the thesis that up to 20% of the total lead burden in the bodies of urban Australians was due to air pollution. In January the Swedish government reduced the lead permitted in regular grade gasoline to 0.15 grams per litre. An official committee proposed that by 1983 new Swedish cars be designed to run on lead-free fuel and that a penalty tax be levied on leaded fuel to discourage its use during the interim period. More than 2,000 birds died along the north shore of the Mersey Estuary, Britain, in January, and tissue analysis showed that their bodies contained large amounts of lead, much of it as trialkyl lead. The source of the pollution remained a mystery.

Land Conservation. After four years of acrimonious debate between environmentalists and developers, the U.S. Congress passed a compromise Alaska lands bill in November. More than 42 million ha (104 million ac) were designated as national parks, wildlife refuges, and wilderness areas. At the same time, oil exploration, mining, and logging were permitted in certain areas, including a vital caribou breeding ground. Both sides indicated they would push for changes in the next session of Congress.

In April the U.S. National Academy of Sciences published *Conversion of Tropical Moist Forests*, a report based largely on data collected by Norman Myers, in which it warned that 95% of all tropical forest might disappear in 25 to 30 years. In July the Interagency Task Force, in a report prepared for President Carter, proposed the use of bilateral development assistance and environmental assessment of projects as tools the U.S. could use to help conserve forests. (MICHAEL ALLABY)

WILDLIFE CONSERVATION

Attempts to reestablish two birds of prey in Scotland made progress during the spring of 1980. Twenty pairs of ospreys, *Pandion haliaetus*, bred and produced 41 young—a success rate attributable to the enterprise of the Royal Society for the Protection of Birds. The society had kept all osprey nests under constant supervision since 1959, when the osprey nested at Loch Garten after 49 years' absence from Britain. The other achievement belonged to the Nature Conservancy Council, which was attempting to bring back the white-tailed sea eagle, *Haliaetus albicilla*, by importing young eagles from Norway under license. Of 29 young birds imported and released on the Hebridean island of Rhum, 26 seemed to have adapted to their new environment and some showed signs of courtship.

In March five Arabian oryx, *Oryx leucoryx*, arrived by air in Oman from the San Diego (Calif.) Zoo, as part of a plan to reestablish this oryx as a wild animal of the desert, begun by the Fauna Preservation Society (FPS) in 1962. After being acclimatized in holding pens, they would be released in the Jiddat al-Harasis. A similar scheme to save the scimitar-horned oryx of the Sahara, *O. dammah*, was a joint project of the FPS, the Marwell Preservation Trust, the People's Trust for Endangered Species, and the Zoological Society of London.

In April Keith Eltringham of the University of Cambridge carried out an aerial survey of the vicuña, *Vicugna vicugna*, in the Pampa Galeras reserve, Peru, and concluded that only 11,000–12,000 remained there. This survey, financed by the International Fund for Animal Welfare, sharply contradicted a previous survey that had given an estimate of 40,000, implying that a vicuña cull might be desirable to protect the habitat from overgrazing. Five new vicuña reserves were established by Bolivia.

An educational van, supplied by the FPS Mountain Gorilla Fund with the aid of the People's Trust for Endangered Species and equipped by the World Wildlife Fund (WWF) project team at Slimbridge, England, arrived in Rwanda in May. The van, designed as a mobile audiovisual centre, was put into immediate use showing films and slides of Rwanda wildlife—especially the gorilla—throughout the republic. Bill Weber and Amy Vedder, both of the University of Wisconsin, contributed instruction in ecology and conservation and prepared a booklet, *Rwanda Heritage,* for distribution to secondary school pupils.

In May delegates of the original 12 Antarctic Treaty powers (Argentina, Australia, Belgium, Britain, Chile, France, Japan, New Zealand, Norway, South Africa, the U.S.S.R., and the U.S.), together with East and West Germany and Poland, agreed on a Convention on the Conservation of Antarctic Living Marine Resources (formally signed in September). The chief subject of discussion was the conservation and exploitation of the krill, *Euphausia superba,* a tiny shrimp-like animal that abounds in the seas around the Antarctic continent. Krill forms the major food supply of five species of whale, as well as birds, fish, and other animals, but has only recently been exploited directly by humans for food and as a fertilizer. (*See* ANTARCTICA.)

The International Whaling Commission (IWC), meeting in Brighton in July, reduced by 13% the overall quota of all species of whale to be taken annually and prohibited the use of the cruel nonexplosive harpoon on whales larger than the minke, or lesser rorqual. However, the IWC again failed to follow the recommendation of the 1972 UN environmental conference in Stockholm, which was to impose a ten-year moratorium on all commercial whaling. The commission also ignored scientific advice by allowing a quota of 1,190 sperm whales to be taken in the Pacific and by allotting the U.S. a quota of 17 bowhead whales for the Alaska Eskimos. Eventually, arguments arose as to whether the smaller members of the order Cetacea (whales, dolphins, and porpoises) were truly whales and therefore within the jurisdiction of the IWC. Altogether, the meeting achieved little from either a conservationist or a humanitarian point of view.

In June two eminent conservationists, Sir Peter Scott of Great Britain and George Schaller of the U.S., visited the 200,000-ha (494,000-ac) Wolung (Wolong) reserve in Sichuan (Szechwan), western China, to investigate the possibility of setting up a research station for the protection of the giant panda. The panda was being threatened by the reduction of the high altitude bamboo forest, which provides its food supply. Even in 1973, its numbers were believed to have fallen below 1,000. The Wolung, established in 1975, was the largest of ten reserves protecting the giant panda. Immediately after the conservationists' visit, a protocol confirming the establishment of the research station was signed.

In July the FPS enlarged its scope and changed its name to the Fauna and Flora Preservation Society (FFPS), thus recognizing the intimate relationship between animals and their food supply. It was the first international society to offer membership to those interested in plant as well as animal preservation. With the accession of Japan as the 17th party to the Convention on International Trade in Endangered Species of Wild Fauna and Flora (CITES), the initiative taken by the IUCN in 1960 achieved general recognition. All the major wildlife-importing countries and a large majority of exporting countries had ratified CITES. Difficulties of enforcement remained, however, not only because of practical difficulties, such as identification of species by customs officers, but also because what was essentially a conservation measure had acquired political overtones.

A report in *The Times* of London on September 4 traced the fate of the tiger since 1911, when its population totaled about 30,000. Deprived of its habitat by forest destruction, shot (sometimes poisoned to avoid pelt damage) to meet the demands of fashion, and slaughtered by "package" tourists who had been almost guaranteed a trophy, the tiger was reduced in numbers to less than 2,000. In 1969, however, the tiger was declared an endangered species. Subsequently, shooting was banned, and the Indian government, helped by the WWF, set up effective tiger reserves. By 1980 tiger numbers had reached about 3,000, and there were grounds for faith in the survival of this splendid animal.

In October the Shell Oil Co., in conjunction with the Royal Society for the Prevention of Cruelty to Animals (RSPCA), provided a Mobile Reception Unit at a cost of £35,000 so that immediate first-aid treatment could be given whenever a large batch of seabirds was caught in an oil slick off the British coast. The affected birds would be taken to the RSPCA cleansing centre, Little Creche, Somerset, for complete treatment and release. In spite of the best treatment, however, the true success rate —the number of cleaned birds able to reestablish themselves in the wild—probably remained low.

(C. L. BOYLE)

See also Agriculture and Food Supplies; Energy; Fisheries; Historic Preservation; Life Sciences; Transportation.
[355.D; 525.A.3.g and B.4.f.i; 534.C.2.a; 724.A; 737.C.1]

Equatorial Guinea

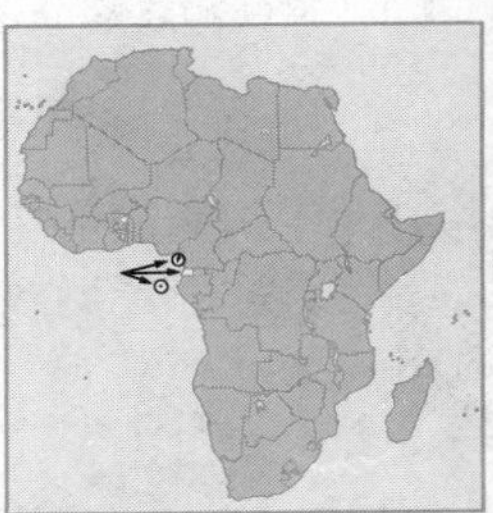
Equatorial Guinea

The African republic of Equatorial Guinea consists of Río Muni, which is bordered by Cameroon on the north, Gabon on the east and south, and the Atlantic Ocean on the west; and the offshore islands of Bioko and Pagalu. Area: 28,051 sq km (10,831 sq mi). Pop. (1980 est.): 330,200. Cap. and largest city: Malabo, on Bioko (pop., 1974 est., 25,000). Language: Spanish. President of the Supreme Military Council in 1980, Lieut. Col. Teodoro Obiang Nguema Mbasogo.

The rehabilitation of the government and the economy after the ousting of Pres. Francisco Macías Nguema in 1979 occupied Equatorial Guinea during 1980. In late 1979 normal relations had

Epidemics:
see Health and Disease

Episcopal Church:
see Religion

been resumed with Spain, which agreed to send military advisers. Following a visit by Vice-Pres. Salvador Ela, Spain also agreed on an economic and technical aid package covering communications, a food program, health, education, the exploitation of fish, wood, and cocoa resources, assistance with banking, and a U.S. $19 million loan. France, competing with Spain, offered a $2,-250,000 aid package.

The new government was anxious to establish the extent of its territorial waters in order to grant exploration concessions to oil companies. Equatorial Guinea and Morocco sought ways to strengthen relations between themselves, and Morocco offered assistance. Meanwhile, Spanish settlers who had fled the country but wished to return to their plantations were permitted to do so if they had investment plans. The government did not renew the treaty of cooperation with the U.S.S.R. (which lapsed at the end of 1979), and in February the Soviet fishing fleet was withdrawn from the island of Luba. During the year, aid was provided by the European Economic Community, the World Food Plan, and the International Monetary Fund.

(GUY ARNOLD)

EQUATORIAL GUINEA

Education. (1973–74) Primary, pupils 35,977, teachers 630; secondary (1975–76), pupils 3,984, teachers 115; vocational (1975–76), pupils 370, teachers 29; teacher training (1975–76), students 169, teachers 21.

Finance and Trade. Monetary unit: ekuele, with (Sept. 22, 1980) a par value of 2 ekuele to 1 Spanish peseta (free rate of 147 ekuele = U.S. $1; 353 ekuele = £1 sterling). Budget (1970): revenue 709.4 million ekuele; expenditure 589.3 million ekuele (excludes capital expenditure of 650.7 million ekuele). Foreign trade (1976): imports *c.* 930 million ekuele (80% from Spain in 1970); exports *c.* 2.9 billion ekuele (91% to Spain in 1970). Main exports (1975): cocoa *c.* 60%; coffee *c.* 30%.

Agriculture. Production (in 000; metric tons; 1979): sweet potatoes *c.* 33; cassava *c.* 52; bananas *c.* 16; cocoa *c.* 5; coffee *c.* 6; palm kernels *c.* 3; palm oil *c.* 5. Livestock (in 000; 1978): sheep *c.* 33; cattle *c.* 4; pigs *c.* 8; goats *c.* 8; chickens *c.* 84.

Equestrian Sports

Thoroughbred Racing and Steeplechasing. UNITED STATES AND CANADA. Among the highlights of the 1980 Thoroughbred racing season were the victory of Genuine Risk in the Kentucky Derby and the triumphs by Spectacular Bid in nine starts, all stakes races. Mrs. Bertram R. Firestone's Genuine Risk was not only the second filly to win the Kentucky Derby (Regret won in 1915) but she also was the only filly ever to compete in all of the Triple Crown events. She finished second to Codex in a controversial Preakness, in which winning jockey Angel Cordero, Jr., was charged with forcing her to run wide on the final turn; and she was runner-up to Temperence Hill in the Belmont Stakes. In another confrontation with males, the stout filly finished third to Plugged Nickle and Colonel Moran in the Wood Memorial. Her other major victory besides the Kentucky Derby came in the campaign-ending Ruffian Handicap against older fillies and mares.

Despite her unique record, Genuine Risk did not go unchallenged before being named the season's three-year-old filly champion and Eclipse Award winner. Bold'N Determined won 8 stakes races in 12 starts, including the Fantasy, Kentucky Oaks, Coaching Club American Oaks, Maskette, and Spinster. In the Maskette, the only meeting between the two, Bold'N Determined defeated Genuine Risk by a nose while conceding her four pounds (1 lb = 0.45 kg). Another leading three-year-old filly was Love Sign, which won 8 of 11 races including the Alabama and the Beldame.

Hawksworth Farm's four-year-old Spectacular Bid earned a third consecutive Eclipse Award as champion of his division and for the first time also was crowned horse of the year in the annual poll sponsored by the Thoroughbred Racing Associations, the National Turf Writers Association, and the *Daily Racing Form.* Spectacular Bid won six stakes races in California, including the Charles H. Strub and Santa Anita handicaps; the Washington Park at Arlington Park; the Amory L. Haskell at Monmouth Park; and the Woodward in a walkover at Belmont Park that climaxed a bizarre series of events in the Triple Crown of handicap races. This consists of the Marlboro, the Woodward, and the Jockey Club Gold Cup. Sponsors of the Marlboro were dismayed when Spectacular Bid's owners rejected their horse's 136-lb weight assignment, 4 lb more than his previous high and 13 lb more than the weight assigned rival Winter's Tale. The owners preferred to await the Woodward and the Jockey Club Gold Cup, both weight-for-age stakes. Winter's Tale won the Marlboro easily. The Woodward became a walkover for Spectacular Bid when a leg injury sidelined Winter's Tale for the season and the only two other entrants, Temperence Hill and Dr. Patches, were scratched. Two weeks later, only minutes before post time, Spectacular Bid himself was scratched from the race because of a leg problem, and Temperence Hill won the Jockey Club Gold Cup to clinch the championship of the three-year-old colt or gelding division. Spectacular Bid retired with earnings of $2,781,607 to surpass the all-time record of $2,393,818 established by Affirmed the previous year. The Woodward marked the first walkover on the flat in the U.S. since Coaltown won the Edward Burke Handicap at Havre de Grace in 1949.

Temperence Hill, owned by Loblolly Stable, also numbered the Belmont and Travers among his eight victories. The late-running colt, which began the season without a victory, had 1980 earnings of $1,130,452, tops for all Thoroughbreds. Until Temperence Hill achieved his late-season heroics, there was no clear-cut leader in the three-year-old division. Superbity, Plugged Nickle, Codex, Rumbo, and Rockhill Native all had their moments of apparent superiority.

Other Eclipse Award winners were SKS Stable's Lord Avie in the two-year-old colt or gelding division; Ryehill Farm's Heavenly Cause, two-year-old filly; Frank Stronach and Nelson Bunker Hunt's Glorious Song, older filly or mare; Dotsam Stable's John Henry, male turf horse; Peter Brant and Joseph Allen's Just A Game II, female turf horse; John M. Schiff's Plugged Nickle, sprinter; and Mrs. Lewis Murdock's Zaccio, steeplechaser.

UPI

Genuine Risk, ridden by Jacinto Vasquez, became the first filly to win the Kentucky Derby since 1915.

Trainer Bud Delp, owners Mr. and Mrs. Bertram Firestone, jockey Chris McCarron, apprentice jockey Frank Lovato, Jr., and breeder Mrs. Henry D. Paxson also won Eclipse Awards. Delp, whose extensive stable included Spectacular Bid, sent to the post in 1980 horses that earned more than $2 million. He ended a four-year domination of the trainer award by Laz Barrera. Mrs. Paxson, owner of a 200-ha (500-ac) farm near Buckingham, Pa., bred winners of more than $850,000 in purses. Among her five stakes winners was Heavenly Ade, first in the Delaware Handicap.

In the Triple Crown races for Canadian-foaled three-year-olds, sponsored by the Ontario Jockey Club, Driving Home won the Queen's Plate, Allan Blue was victor in the Prince of Wales Stakes, and Ben Fab triumphed in the Breeder's Stakes. Par Excellance won the Canadian Oaks and Great Neck the Canadian International.

(JOSEPH C. AGRELLA)

Europe and Australia. Berkshire trainer Dick Hern and his regular rider, Willie Carson, dominated the 1980 flat-racing season in England. Hern was the leading trainer for the third time, winning a record £831,964 first-prize money. He won the Irish Guinness Oaks with Shoot a Line and two races in France. Carson was champion jockey for the fourth time. Paradoxically, the meeting at Epsom was both the high point and a disaster for them. On June 4 they won with Henbit in the Derby, and three days later they took the Oaks with Bireme. However, Henbit broke a bone in his off fore during the final furlong and had to struggle to beat Master Willie and Rankin. Bireme also suffered an injury. Bireme was retired immediately, but Henbit might yet race again.

Hern's Shoot a Line won five of six, including the Yorkshire Oaks and her Irish triumph. Hern also trained the best English four-year-old, Ela-Mana-Mou, unbeaten in four races at home with victories over Hello Gorgeous in the Coral Eclipse and Mrs Penny in the King George VI and Queen Elizabeth Diamond Stakes. Ela-Mana-Mou was favoured to win the Prix de l'Arc de Triomphe at Longchamp, Paris, on October 5 but found the French-trained Detroit and Argument too good. Le Moss again proved himself the best distance runner in Europe with his victory in the Ascot Gold Cup and other cup wins.

Detroit was one of the best of an exceptional group of fillies on both sides of the English Channel. Her only defeat in six races in 1980 was in the Prix Vermeille, in which she was an unlucky third to Mrs Penny from England and Little Bonny from Ireland. Mrs Penny also carried off the top French summer race for fillies, the Prix de Diane de Revlon. British jockey Carson rode the 54–1 outsider, Policeman, to victory in the Prix du Jockey Club—French Derby—on June 8. Pat Eddery (Arc), Lester Piggott (Diane, Forêt, and Abbaye), John Matthias (Vermeille), and Greville Starkey (Grand Criterium) were other British jockeys to win Group One races in France. English-trained horses won more than £1.1 million abroad, counting Ireland, where Tyrnavos scored a surprise victory in the Irish Sweeps Derby.

French horses gained only one success in Britain, with Scorpio in the Hardwicke Stakes. They should have had another, but Nureyev was disqualified after passing the post first in the Two Thousand Guineas. The race was awarded to Known Fact. Both Nureyev and Known Fact were sick after this race, but Known Fact won at Goodwood, Doncaster, and in the Queen Elizabeth II Stakes at Ascot, in which he got the better of a stern battle with 1979's champion miler, Kris.

The Irish-trained Cairn Rouge took the Champion Stakes, gaining revenge on Master Willie for defeat in the Benson & Hedges Gold Cup. Cairn Rouge, who joined Ela-Mana-Mou in making Pitcairn (currently in Japan) the top Anglo-Irish sire, also won the Irish One Thousand Guineas and Ascot's Coronation Stakes. Third in the Champion Stakes was the French colt Nadjar, winner of the Prix d'Ispahan and Prix Jacques le Marois.

Although the French enjoyed little luck in England or Ireland, they made an impact in North America at the end of the year as Anifa, Argument, and Kilijaro all won major stakes races. Kilijaro won four French races in a period of 34 days during August and September, including the Prix du Moulin. Her winning streak came to an end in the Prix de la Forêt, in which she was beaten by Moorestyle. This brilliant colt won all five of his races in England, including the William Hill July Cup, and the Forêt and Abbaye in France.

Anifa, Henbit, Known Fact, Mrs Penny, and Nureyev were all purchased in the U.S. So, too, among the two-year-olds, was the colt that was the advance Guineas and Derby favourite for 1981, the Canadian-bred and Irish-trained Storm Bird. He won all four of his races against moderate opposition in Ireland but proved his merit when beating To-Agori-Mou in the William Hill Dewhurst stakes. The pair finished eight lengths ahead of the Prix de la Salamandre winner, Miswaki. Recitation won the Grand Critérium from Critique, who was trained, like Storm Bird, by Vincent O'Brien.

Robert Sangster, owner of both Detroit and Storm Bird, also won Australia's most celebrated race, the Melbourne Cup, with Beldale Ball, a colt that raced in England in 1978–79 but, once again, one that was bought in the U.S. Kingston Town, the Australian champion three-year-old in the 1979–80 season, was injured and had to miss the Melbourne Cup.

In the 1979–80 National Hunt (NH) season in Britain, U.S. owner Redmond Stewart and amateur rider Charles Fenwick took the Grand National Steeplechase with the 40–1 Ben Nevis. Only 4 of the 30 runners completed the course. Tied Cottage won the Cheltenham Gold Cup for Ireland but was disqualified when a trace of caffeine was found in his urine sample, and the race was awarded to Master Smudge. Sea Pigeon won his first champion hurdle, and J. J. O'Neill, who rode him, went on to win his second NH jockey championship. The King George VI steeplechase was won by Silver Buck and the Whitbread Gold Cup by Royal Mail.

(ROBERT W. CARTER)

Harness Racing. New world records in speed, earnings, and yearling sales prices were established in the U.S. in 1980. Three-year-old champion Niatross won the pacing Triple Crown, established world records on half-mile tracks (1 min 54.8 sec) when winning the Little Brown Jug, and became the first pacer to beat 1 min 50 sec, in a 1-min 49.2-sec time trial. His earnings after the Messenger were $1,825,556.

Toy Poodle and Guiding Beam set a world mile record for three-year-old fillies with 1 min 53.8 sec and also jointly held the season's half-mile track records. French Chef set a new world mark of 1 min 54 sec for two-year-olds. The fastest aged pacer was Pats Gypsy, at 1 min 54 sec. The $2,011,000 Woodrow Wilson pace for two-year-olds went to Land Grant in the richest-ever harness race.

Classical Way set a new world trotting record of 1 min 55.4 sec in a time trial; the Hambletonian went to Burgomeister. The International Trot at Roosevelt was won by Classical Way from the New Zealand mare Petite Evander and the French horse Idéal du Gazeau. J. Simpson, Jr., drove the winning U.S. entry.

Lord Module won the New Zealand Cup (November 1979) and Game Adios the New Zealand Derby. Delightful Lady captured the $100,000 Auckland Cup, and in the Northern Derby at Auckland Armbro Wings won from Armalight and Dictatorship. Armalight won the New Zealand Oaks, the D. B. Flying Fillies Stake, and the North Island Oaks. Lord Module set a New Zealand record with a time trial of 1 min 54.9 sec; a $600,000 offer for the pacer was later refused.

In Australia Sydney's Miracle Mile went to New Zealand's Locarno, and Koala King won the Inter-

Conrad Homfeld of the U.S. cleared this hurdle to take first place in the Fédération Équestre Internationale World Cup held in Baltimore, Maryland, in April.

ENRICO FERORELLI—"SPORTS ILLUSTRATED" © 1980 TIME INC.

Dominion Pacer championships from Locarno and Pure Steel. The $40,000 Spring Cup was won by Gammalite and the Carousel by Matong Way. In the 1980 New South Wales Sires Stakes, the fillies' section was won by Shape Up, and Black Trick won the colts' section. Greentree Helen won the Oaks. In a match in Perth top-money-winner Pure Steel beat the previously undefeated Satinover for a side wager of $10,000. Action Advice won the New South Wales Pacers' Derby, while Under A Cloud took the Victorian version, San Simeon the Australian and Western Australia events, Quambys Pride the Queensland Derby, and Gammalite the South Australian Derby. The Australian champion Paleface Adios notched his 100th race win in February, and his earnings topped the $500,000 mark. San Simeon achieved 21 consecutive wins in Western Australia.

In trotting in Europe the $280,000 Prix d'Amérique at Vincennes was won by the ten-year-old Éléazar, which went on to win the $125,000 Prix de France. The Italian Premio d'Europa was won by Mustard from Borgoplin and Gentile, while Song and Dance Man set a new Italian record of 1 min 57.8 sec over 1,600 m at Modena. The $60,000 Premio Lotteria final went to Hillion Brillouard. In Finland Billy The Kid won the Derby in a record 2 min 6 sec, and Ejakval won the $60,000 European Grand Circuit. At Jarlsberg, Sweden, locally owned Valuable Donut won the 50,000 kronor Grand International Trot and Dan Holmbo the Scandinavian Grand Prix. Mustard remained the glamour horse of Sweden. Idéal du Gazeau ($250,000 in two months) won the European Grand Prix at Gelsenkirchen, West Germany.

(NOEL SIMPSON)

Show Jumping. The world's leading equestrian nations boycotted the 1980 Olympic Games in Moscow, where the host nation won all three team gold medals in show jumping, the three-day event, and dressage. (*See* TRACK AND FIELD SPORTS: *Special Report*.) The International Equestrian Federation staged alternative Olympic competitions at Goodwood, England (dressage), at Rotterdam, Neth. (show jumping), and at Fontainebleau, France (three-day event). West Germany, represented by Uwe Schulten-Baumer with Slibovitz, Reiner Klimke's Ahlerich, and Uwe Sauer's Hurtentraum, won the team gold medals at Goodwood. Switzerland won the silver medals, and Denmark the bronze. The individual gold went to Christine Stuckelberger from Switzerland with Granat, while the silver medal went to Slibovitz and the bronze to Ahlerich. In Rotterdam the Canadian team of M. Vaillancourt with Chivas, M. Laskin with Damurez, Ian Miller with Brother Sam, and Jim Elder with Volunteer won the gold medals. The U.K. took the silver medals and Austria the bronze. Individually, the show jumping gold medal went to Hugo Simon with Gladstone (Austria), the silver to John Whitaker and Ryan's Son (U.K.), and the bronze to Melanie Smith and Calypso (U.S.).

France won at Fontainebleau, represented by J. Pons with Ensorcelleuse, J.-Y. Touzaint with Flipper, T. Touzaint with Gribouille, and A. Bigot with Gamin du Bois. West Germany won the sil-

Major Thoroughbred Race Winners, 1980

Race	Won by	Jockey	Owner
United States			
Acorn	Bold 'N Determined	E. Delahoussaye	Saron Stable
Alabama	Love Sign	R. Hernandez	Stephen C. Clark Jr.
Amory L. Haskell	Spectacular Bid	W. Shoemaker	Hawksworth Farm
Arlington-Washington Futurity	Well Decorated	L. Pincay, Jr.	Herbert Allen
Belmont	Temperence Hill	E. Maple	Loblolly Stable
Blue Grass	Rockhill Native	J. Oldham	Harry A. Oak
Brooklyn	Winter's Tale	J. Fell	Rokeby Stable
Californian	Spectacular Bid	W. Shoemaker	Hawksworth Farm
Champagne	Lord Avie	J. Velasquez	SKS Stable
Charles H. Strub	Spectacular Bid	W. Shoemaker	Hawksworth Farm
Coaching Club American Oaks	Bold 'N Determined	E. Delahoussaye	Saron Stable
Delaware Handicap	Heavenly Ade	J. D. Bailey	Mrs. Henry D. Paxson
Delaware Oaks	Bishop's Ring	M. Pino	Bayard Sharp
Flamingo	Superbity	J. Vasquez	Frances A. Genter
Florida Derby	Plugged Nickle	B. Thornburg	John M. Schiff
Frizette	Heavenly Cause	L. Pincay, Jr.	Ryehill Farm
Futurity	Tap Shoes	R. Hernandez	Leone J. Peters, Arthur Hancock III
Gulfstream Park	Private Account	J. Fell	Ogden Phipps
Hollywood Derby	Codex	E. Delahoussaye	Tartan Stable
Hollywood Gold Cup	Go West Young Man	E. Delahoussaye	Wild Plum Farm
Hollywood Oaks	Princess Karenda	D. Pierce	Shell Medall, Angelo Mazza, Donald Miller, Mario Mory, Joseph Olla
Hopeful	Tap Shoes	R. Hernandez	Leone J. Peters, Arthur J. Hancock III
Jockey Club Gold Cup	Temperence Hill	E. Maple	Loblolly Stable
Kentucky Derby	Genuine Risk	J. Vasquez	Mrs. Bertram R. Firestone
Kentucky Oaks	Bold 'N Determined	E. Delahoussaye	Saron Stable
Ladies	Plankton	C. Asmussen	Frederick Tesher, lessee
Laurel Futurity	Cure the Blues	R. Turcotte	Bertram Firestone
Marlboro Cup	Winter's Tale	J. Fell	Rokeby Stable
Matron	Prayers 'n Promises	A. Cordero, Jr.	Daniel M. Galbreath
Metropolitan	Czaravich	L. Pincay, Jr.	William L. Reynolds
Monmouth Invitational	Thanks to Tony	C. Lopez	Sui Generis Stable
Norfolk (2 divisions)	High Counsel	L. Gilligan	Nelson Bunker Hunt
	Sir Dancer	F. Olivares	George Arakelian Farm
Oak Tree Invitational	John Henry	L. Pincay, Jr.	Dotsam Stable
Preakness	Codex	A. Cordero, Jr.	Tartan Stable
Ruffian	Genuine Risk	J. Vasquez	Mrs. Bertram R. Firestone
San Juan Capistrano Invitational	John Henry	D. McHargue	Dotsam Stable
Santa Anita Derby	Codex	P. Valenzuela	Tartan Stable
Santa Anita	Spectacular Bid	W. Shoemaker	Hawksworth Farm
Santa Susana	Bold 'N Determined	E. Delahoussaye	Saron Stable
Sapling	Travelling Music	C. Perret	Elberon Farm
Selima	Heavenly Cause	L. Pincay, Jr.	Ryehill Farm
Sorority	Fancy Naskra	L. Snyder	Jim Thomas
Spinaway	Prayers'n Promises	A. Cordero, Jr.	Daniel M. Galbreath
Spinster	Bold 'N Determined	E. Delahoussaye	Saron Stable
Suburban	Winter's Tale	J. Fell	Rokeby Stable
Swaps	First Albert	F. Mena	Mrs. Carmen S. Barrera
Top Flight	Glorious Song	J. Velasquez	Frank Stronach, Nelson Bunker Hunt
Travers	Temperence Hill	E. Maple	Loblolly Stable
Turf Classic	Anifa	A. Gibert	Buckram Oak Farm
United Nations	Lyphard's Wish	A. Cordero, Jr.	Wildenstein Stable
Vanity	It's in the Air	L. Pincay, Jr.	Harbor View Farm
Washington, D.C., International	Argument	L. Piggott	Bruce McNall, Berry Gordy
Widener	Private Account	J. Fell	Ogden Phipps
Wood Memorial	Plugged Nickle	B. Thornburg	John M. Schiff
Woodward	Spectacular Bid	W. Shoemaker	Hawksworth Farm
Yellow Ribbon	Kilijaro	A. LeQueux	Serge Fradkoff
Young America	Lord Avie	J. Velasquez	SKS Stable
England			
One Thousand Guineas	Quick as Lightning	B. Rouse	O. Phipps
Two Thousand Guineas	Known Fact	W. Carson	K. Abdulla
Derby	Henbit	W. Carson	Mme. E. Plesch
Oaks	Bireme	W. Carson	R. Hollingsworth
St. Leger	Light Cavalry	J. Mercer	H. J. Joel
Coronation Cup	Sea Chimes	L. Piggott	J. Thursby
Ascot Gold Cup	Le Moss	J. Mercer	C. d'Alessio
Eclipse Stakes	Ela-Mana-Mou	W. Carson	S. Weinstock
King George VI and Queen Elizabeth Diamond Stakes	Ela-Mana-Mou	W. Carson	S. Weinstock
Sussex Stakes	Posse	P. Eddery	O. Phipps
Benson & Hedges Gold Cup	Master Willie	P. Waldron	W. Barnett
Champion Stakes	Cairn Rouge	A. Murray	D. Brady
France			
Poule d'Essai des Poulains	In Fijar	G. Doleuze	M. Fustok
Poule d'Essai des Pouliches	Aryenne	M. Philipperon	D. Volkert
Prix du Jockey Club	Policeman	W. Carson	F. Tinsley
Prix de Diane de Revlon	Mrs. Penny	L. Piggott	E. Kronfeld
Prix Royal-Oak	Gold River	F. Head	J. Wertheimer
Prix Ganay	Le Marmot	P. Paquet	R. Shafer
Prix Lupin	Belgio	M. Philipperon	H. Boccara
Grand Prix de Paris	Valiant Heart	A. Gibert	A. Michel
Grand Prix de Saint-Cloud	Dunette	G. Doleuze	Mrs. P. Love
Prix Vermeille	Mrs. Penny	J. Matthias	E. Kronfeld
Prix de l'Arc de Triomphe	Detroit	P. Eddery	R. Sangster
Ireland			
Irish Two Thousand Guineas	Nikoli	C. Roche	Lord Iveagh
Irish One Thousand Guineas	Cairn Rouge	A. Murray	D. Brady
Irish Guinness Oaks	Shoot a Line	W. Carson	R. A. Budgett
Irish Sweeps Derby	Tyrnavos	A. Murray	G. Cambanis
Irish St. Leger	Gonzales	R. Carroll	R. Sangster
Italy			
Derby Italiano	Garrido	M. Depalmas	Razza Dormello-Olgiata
Gran Premio del Jockey Club	Pawiment	O. Gervai	Gestüt Moritzberg
West Germany			
Deutsches Derby	Navarino	D. Richardson	H. Einschütz
Grosser Preis von Baden	Nebos	L. Mäder	Countess Batthyany
Grosser Preis von Berlin	Nebos	L. Mäder	Countess Batthyany
Preis von Europa	Pawiment	O. Gervai	Gestüt Moritzberg

Niatross, believed to be the best Standardbred horse in the history of harness racing, raced to victory with his driver, Clint Galbraith. Niatross clinched the Triple Crown of pacing on October 11 by winning the Messenger Stakes at Roosevelt Raceway in Long Island, New York.

ver medals and Australia the bronze. Nils Haagensen and Monaco of Denmark won the individual gold from Jimmy Wofford on Carawich (U.S.) and Torrance Watkins on Poltroon (U.S.).

(PAMELA MACGREGOR-MORRIS)

Polo. Dominating world polo in 1980, Argentina with its 40-goal "machine" of the Harriott and Heguy brothers crushed the U.S. in the Cup of the Americas. At Buenos Aires, Argentina won 18–6 and 16–6, while at Retama, Texas, Argentina won 1–8 and 10–6. In the Michelob World Cup at Palm Beach, Fla., the Nigerian-sponsored team of Hallal beat favoured Retama 13–8. Hallal consisted of J. Hipwood (England), G. Pieres and G. Tanoira (Argentina), and A. Herrera (Mexico).

In the Coronation Cup in England a Rest of the World team (J. Sieber, A. Herrera, J. Crotto, and J. Mackey) defeated England (J. Horswell, P. Withers, J. Hipwood, and H. Hipwood) 6–5 in a thrilling contest. In the supporting Silver Jubilee Cup England II beat France 5–3.

In the new European Polo Championship the gold medal went to the European Polo Academy; the silver to England's representative, Hurlingham I; and the bronze to Spain. The British Open championship was won by Stowell Park, which defeated Cowdray Park in the final 10–7. The Brazil National Open was won by Rio Pardo and the Argentine Open Championship by Coronel Zuarez. The West German Gold Cup was taken by La Ruana, while the champion of Australia was Kooralbyn with wins in the Australian Open, Gold Cup, and $5,500 Master tournament.

(COLIN J. CROSS)

[452.B.4.h.xvii; 452.B.4.h.xxi; 452.B.5.e]

Ethiopia

Ethiopia

A socialist state in northeastern Africa, Ethiopia is bordered by Somalia, Djibouti, Kenya, the Sudan, and the Red Sea. Area: 1,221,900 sq km (471,800 sq mi). Pop. (1980 est.): 31,065,300. Cap. and largest city: Addis Ababa (pop., 1980 est., 1,277,159). Language: Amharic (official) and other tongues. Religion: Ethiopian Orthodox and Muslim, with various minorities. Head of state and chairman of the Provisional Military Administrative Council in 1980, Lieut. Col. Mengistu Haile Mariam.

Political activity during 1980 focused on strengthening the organizational infrastructure for development. The Commission to Organize the Party of the Working People of Ethiopia (COPWE) was created on Dec. 18, 1979, and COPWE's first congress took place in June 1980 with some 1,500 regional representatives participating. A seven-member Executive Committee and a 93-member Central Committee were announced, both chaired by the head of state, Lieut. Col. Mengistu Haile Mariam. At a press conference in September, Mariam stated: "The struggle [for the formation of the party] is not a struggle with civilian/military implications, but a class struggle . . . the date will not be distant before the formation of the party." He added, "Since it is motivated by a single program, the need for a multiparty system does not arise. The Ethiopian Revolution tolerates no reactionary class posture and will have no place for a multiparty system."

In July the number of popular organizations increased with formation of the Revolutionary Ethiopia Women's Association and a Youth Association. Professional associations for writers, journalists, artists, and teachers were also formed, and the "Tatek" Military Camp near Addis Ababa was training production cadres who assisted in the establishment of cooperatives in agriculture and industry. Over 3,000 service cooperatives and nearly 400 production cooperatives were set up.

Economic measures were accompanied by strong action to improve cultural, health, and educational facilities. The National Literacy Campaign was awarded a UNESCO prize for meritorious work in literacy in 1980. Seven million participants were enrolled, and over four million had already moved on to postliteracy instruction. The target for eradication of urban illiteracy was May 1981, and the target for total eradication was 1987. A National Children's Commission had been established during the UN Year of the Child (1979); a children's village for 5,000 orphans was created in the Rift Valley Lakes region, and over 350 kindergartens were initiated. Since the revolution, the number of children attending formal school had doubled. The

University of Addis Ababa awarded its first post-graduate degrees during the year.

Thirty percent of the population now had access to basic health services, as compared with 15–20% at the time of the revolution. Ethiopia was declared free of smallpox in December 1979, and a nationwide campaign for the control of tuberculosis was launched in 1980. One significant result of the nationalization of rural and urban lands and the creation of Peasant and Urban Dwellers Associations was the virtual end of migration from rural to urban areas and its associated problems. The annual population growth rate of Addis Ababa had declined from 5 to 3%.

The program for economic and cultural development, initiated in October 1978, moved into its third phase, having achieved an economic growth rate of 5.3% during 1979–80. During the first two phases, existing enterprises had become more efficient and administration had developed: the National Revolutionary Development Campaign and Central Planning Supreme Council structured administrative planning; the Ministry of State Farms created regional agricultural development corporations; ministries for domestic and foreign trade and a National Building Construction Authority were established; the two government commercial banks were merged; and import-export concerns were nationalized under the Maritime and Transit Services Corporation.

A total of 6,350,000 ha (15,875,000 ac) was reported under cultivation, with an output, in spite of bad weather conditions in some regions, of just under 5.6 million metric tons in 1979. Industrial output grew by 35% during 1978 but by only 11.3% in 1979 as capacity was reached. The third development phase would include a higher level of industrial investment. External trade achieved a high rate of growth in 1979–80 (28.3%), exceeding the planned target by 16%.

The national truck fleet had more than tripled since the revolution, but transport remained a problem in terms of both vehicles and the limited road structure. However, the Ethiopian Roads Authority had built 2,035 km (1,264 mi) of rural and feeder roads since the revolution (double the work achieved in the previous 23 years). During 1980 the Cuban government donated road-building equipment worth 10 million birr. The maintained road network was around 13,000 km (8,000 mi). Ethiopian Airlines had recently increased its fleet by two Boeing 727 planes. International services now covered 28 cities on three continents.

Dissident groups in the north remained. The town of Nakfa in Eritrea Province was a rebel focus, and there was guerrilla activity in the Tigre region. Antigovernment activity by Somali-supported groups continued in the south. There was also a Somali Army attack in March, and five major assaults took place between May 27 and July 17 in the Uardare, Wel-Wel, Oubatale, and Shebele areas, well within Ethiopia's Ogaden region. Ethiopia reported a mechanized force of 14,000 supported by three infantry brigades. It claimed 3,326 enemy dead and wounded in these engagements, and the capture of equipment of NATO origin and food supplies intended for drought relief. Ethiopia made official protests to the UN and the Organization of African Unity (OAU). Two further major Somali raids between September 18 and October 9 into the El Kere region of Bale Province were repulsed with heavy losses.

WIDE WORLD

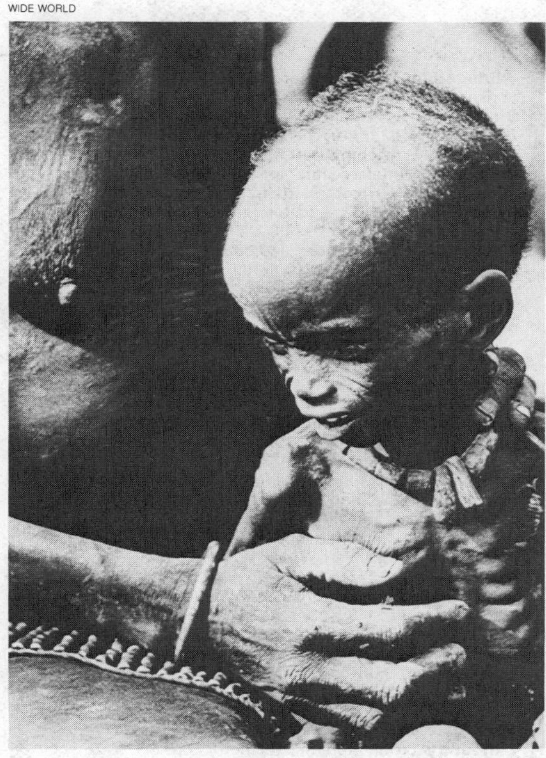

Starving drought victims in Ethiopia sought help at relief organization camps.

In August the OAU Good Offices Committee, in a six-point resolution, called for the strict application of the 1964 Cairo summit resolution on inviolability of frontiers and the recognition of the Ogaden as an integral part of Ethiopia. In July, following on-the-spot investigations by a UN interagency team, the UN Economic and Social Council recommended a grant of 1.5 billion birr for relief in the area. In May the UN High Commissioner for Refugees had expressed admiration for the steps taken by the Ethiopian government to care for refugees.

External relations during 1979–80 reflected Ethiopia's association with Eastern Europe and Cuba and the government's desire to strengthen relations with its neighbours. High-level visitors included the East German head of state, Erich Honecker, in November 1979, Soviet Deputy Minister of Defense Adm. Sergey Gorshkov in July 1980, and the Hungarian head of state, Pal Losonczi, in September. Mengistu visited Bulgaria and the Soviet Union during the year. U.S. Ambassador Frederic L. Chapin was recalled to Washington at the request of the Ethiopian government in July.

At the same time, Ethiopia maintained an unaligned posture, and in September Mengistu stated his government's willingness to accept all aid for development projects on the basis of "equality and mutual respect." Ethiopia received substantial assistance from the European Economic Community (EEC) under the Lomé agreements and

ETHIOPIA

Education. Primary, pupils (1976–77) 1,176,636; secondary and vocational, pupils 281,450; primary, secondary, and vocational, teachers 33,252; teacher training (1973–74), students 3,126, teachers 194; higher (1977–78), students 10,824, teaching staff 476.

Finance. Monetary unit: birr, with (Sept. 22, 1980) a par value of 2.07 birr to U.S. $1 (free rate of 4.98 birr = £1 sterling). Gold, SDR's, and foreign exchange (June 1980) U.S. $156 million. Budget (1977–78 est.): revenue 1,399,000,000 birr; expenditure 1,149,000,000 birr. Money supply (April 1980) 1,461,000,000 birr. Cost of living (Addis Ababa; 1975 = 100; June 1980) 211.2.

Foreign Trade. (1979) Imports 1,149, 200,000 birr; exports 877.6 million birr. Import sources (1978): Japan 15%; Italy 13%; West Germany 12%; Iran 10%; U.K. 8%; U.S. 5%. Export destinations (1978): U.S. 29%; Saudi Arabia 11%; West Germany 9%; Yugoslavia 9%; Japan 7%; Italy 5%. Main exports: coffee 69%; hides and skins 16%.

Transport and Communications. Roads (1979) 37,291 km. Motor vehicles in use (1979): passenger 38,400; commercial 10,600. Railways: (1977) 988 km; traffic (including Djibouti traffic of Djibouti-Addis Ababa line, excluding Eritrea; 1976) 132 million passenger-km, freight 260 million net ton-km. Air traffic (1979): 548 million passenger-km; freight 23.5 million net ton-km. Telephones (Jan. 1978) 78,700. Radio receivers (Dec. 1977) 215,000. Television receivers (Dec. 1977) 25,000.

Agriculture. Production (in 000; metric tons; 1979): barley *c.* 732; wheat 449; corn *c.* 1,067; millet *c.* 191; sorghum 680; potatoes (1978) *c.* 185; sugar, raw value (1978) *c.* 170; sesame seed *c.* 46; chick-peas 77; dry peas *c.* 124; dry broad beans (1978) *c.* 273; bananas *c.* 66; coffee *c.* 194; cotton *c.* 25. Livestock (in 000; 1979): cattle *c.* 25,900; sheep *c.* 23,234; goats *c.* 17,120; horses *c.* 1,530; mules *c.* 1,446; asses *c.* 3,885; camels *c.* 966; poultry *c.* 52,956.

Industry. Production (in 000; metric tons; 1975–76): cement 100; petroleum products (1977) *c.* 530; cotton yarn (1977) 22; cotton fabrics (sq m) 81,000; electricity (kw-hr; 1976–77) *c.* 682,000.

from international agencies and Western countries, notably Sweden. Social assistance included agreements with East Germany for a textile mill and a cement factory, a country loan program from the Soviet Union, and technical assistance from Cuba in the fields of livestock, health, and education, together with agreements for the supply of cement, fertilizers, and tires.

Relations with Sudan improved. A joint border commission was established, and in March Sudan Vice-Pres. Gen. Abdel Magid Khalil visited Addis Ababa. In May an Ethiopian delegation to Khartoum signed a trade agreement and cultural protocol. In September a Sudanese military delegation visited Addis Ababa.

Similar diplomatic activity strengthened relations with Yemen (Aden; South Yemen) and Djibouti. Mengistu visited South Yemen in November 1979 and again in June 1980. In April Ethiopia signed an accord with the Yemen (San'a') on the freedom of the Indian Ocean. Good relations with Kenya continued. In April a joint communiqué on Somali aggression was published, and later a development agreement facilitated the EEC-financed study program for the development of the southern rangelands.

Ethiopian athletes at the Moscow Olympic Games won two gold medals and two bronze, notably through the performance of Miruts Yifter in the 10,000 m and 5,000 m. On August 17 Ras Imru Haile Selassie, oldest surviving member of the Shewan dynasty, died at the age of 87. Known for his liberal views, he had been named prime minister by the leaders of the 1960 coup d'etat.

European Economic Community:
see Economy, World; European Unity

European Unity

The year 1980 demonstrated that, in practice, it was easier for the nine member states of the European Economic Community (EEC) to align policies regarding the outside world than to make progress toward internal unity. Internally, 1980 would be remembered for the bitter and protracted dispute over the Community's budget. The refusal of the European Parliament to endorse the draft 1980 budget—because it was held to favour farm spending at the expense of other policies—meant that the Community had to be financed on an emergency basis. It was not until July, amid fears that the financial crisis could lead to collapse of the common agricultural policy, that the European Parliament in Strasbourg finally allowed a slightly amended 1980 budget to enter into force.

Serious as this first major dispute between two major EEC institutions—the European Parliament and the Council of Ministers—proved to be, it was overshadowed by another budgetary dispute. This arose out of the British government's growing dissatisfaction with the imbalance in its payments to and receipts from the EEC budget. Successive Labour and Conservative governments had raised the issue over the previous two years, but no solution had been found. There were suggestions that, unless Britain's annual net budget contributions were reduced, the U.K. government would unilaterally suspend part or all of its budget payments.

At the European Council (the summit meeting of EEC heads of government) in Luxembourg at the end of April, no acceptable compromise was reached. British Prime Minister Margaret Thatcher (*see* BIOGRAPHIES) made it clear that, in the absence of a satisfactory solution to Britain's problem, the U.K. government would not be able to agree to the annual spring farm price increases. In effect, the budget issue became linked with a number of controversial matters including farm prices, fishing policy, and energy policy. It took another month of detailed negotiations to achieve a compromise solution, on May 30. EEC foreign ministers meeting in Brussels agreed on a formula guaranteeing a substantial reduction in Britain's expected net contribution to the EEC budget for 1980, 1981, and 1982. This was to take the form of an increased rebate on gross budget payments by the U.K. and programs of special Common Market spending in Britain itself. At the same time, Britain agreed to a new round of farm price increases, as had been demanded by France and a number of other member states. All parties set themselves the target of concluding agreements on other matters, including fishing policy, energy policy, and a new system for marketing lamb and mutton in the Common Market.

The agreement removed much of the tension from relations between Britain and other member states and from Anglo-French relations in particular. But in September new disagreements emerged about the precise way in which the May compromise should be honoured. It appeared that a final solution might have to await agreement on the level of 1981 EEC farm prices—a subject of acute domestic political importance in France, where Pres. Valéry Giscard d'Estaing would fight for reelection in May 1981.

The May agreement did remove the budget wrangle from the agenda of the European summit held in Venice in June, shortly before the Western economic summit there, which also involved the governments of Britain, France, Italy, and West Germany. Venice 1, as the European Council session became known, was dominated by discussion of major world and foreign policy issues including Afghanistan, Iran, and the Middle East.

The Soviet invasion of Afghanistan at the end of 1979 and the continuing imprisonment of the U.S. embassy hostages in Iran were two issues that arose early in 1980 to challenge the coordination of foreign policy among EEC governments. Although common policy declarations of condemnation and unity were readily forthcoming at successive meetings of Community foreign ministers, it proved more difficult to agree on what action the EEC should take. In spite of U.S. pressure, most EEC governments were reluctant to levy economic sanctions against the Soviet Union. Some minor restrictions on agricultural exports were eventually imposed, but the Nine were sharply divided over the U.S.-led campaign for a boycott of the Moscow Olympic Games. In the end, only West Germany refused to send a team to the Games, although most other governments refused to accord full official status to their athletes. Nor were relations with the U.S. helped by the reluctance of the European Community governments to impose comprehensive trade sanctions against Iran. At a meeting of foreign ministers in Naples during May, the Nine agreed on very partial sanctions against Iran, which were later amended by the British Parliament. At the December meeting of the European Council in Luxembourg, however, the Nine—without naming the Soviet Union or specifying any measures they might take—issued a strong statement of concern over the situation in Poland. The labour unrest and the threat of Soviet intervention in that country largely dominated the Council's deliberations.

The priority given to political cooperation among the EEC governments was a striking feature of 1980. The desire to have the European Community act as a major force in world affairs was amply illustrated with regard to the Middle East. The Venice EEC summit issued a major policy declaration on the Arab-Israeli conflict which went further than before in recognizing the rights of the Palestinian people to self-determination and the necessity, at some future stage, of associating the Palestine Liberation Organization in wider peace negotiations. The EEC leaders also hinted that, after sponsoring a fact-finding mission among interested governments in the region, they would launch some kind of Middle East diplomatic "initiative." Israel's reaction was predictably hostile, but the U.S. was also markedly cool. Spokesmen in Washington went so far as to say that the U.S. would veto any moves in the UN Security Council that cut across the objectives of the 1978 Camp David negotiations between Egypt, Israel, and the U.S. Arab governments were skeptical.

By the time of the Western summit in Venice, the U.S. stand had softened. It became clear that the EEC countries had no intention of putting forward any new resolution on the rights of the Palestinians before the U.S. presidential election in the fall. During August the president of the Council of Ministers, Gaston Thorn (*see* BIOGRAPHIES), foreign minister of Luxembourg, toured nine Middle Eastern countries to discuss whether there was a basis for future enlargement of the peacemaking process. In September the EEC foreign ministers decided that the initial reaction was sufficiently

OLIPHANT © 1980 WASHINGTON STAR

British Prime Minister Margaret Thatcher and foreign minister Lord Carrington (right) attend the EEC summit conference at Luxembourg in April.

encouraging to persist with the fact-finding stage of the initiative. Thorn made it clear that the Nine reserved the right to play a full part as possible sponsors of some new Middle East peace process.

The apparent determination of the European Community to pursue its own policy on the Middle East once again posed questions about the future of the Atlantic alliance. All the EEC governments stressed their desire for the closest possible association with the U.S., but in the course of 1980 doubts were expressed about the stability of U.S. leadership of the alliance. Relations with Washington were not made any easier by a proliferation of trade disputes, many of which were a direct consequence of the serious deterioration in the world economy. There were problems between the U.S. and the EEC over European steel exports and U.S. exports of textiles and chemicals.

The European Community was also involved in difficult negotiations with a number of third world countries over the terms under which they would be free to export into the EEC and with the Japanese government about that country's formidable trade surplus with the Common Market. The EEC resisted any general slide into trade protectionism during 1980, but with unemployment in EEC countries rising to more than nine million in the later months of the year, there were fears for the future of Europe's trading relations with other developed countries. Meanwhile, as was made clear at the Venice summit, the European leaders maintained their stand that any general relaxation of monetary and economic policy to reduce unemployment would not be expedient while inflation remained a serious concern.

Unemployment, recession, and the massive budgetary problems of the European Community were also causes for concern in view of the prospective enlargement of the EEC. Greece was to become the tenth member state on Jan. 1, 1981, and negotiations on applications for membership began to get under way with Spain and Portugal. Spanish entry and the competitive threat to French Mediterranean farmers became a major political issue in France. Speeches by French Premier Raymond Barre suggested that France wanted the EEC to "go slow" in the negotiations with Spain until more progress had been made in solving the European Community's many internal economic, budgetary, and agricultural problems.

The other member states insisted that the talks with Spain and Portugal proceed according to the agreed negotiating timetable, but by October Spain had accepted the prospect of delay until some months after its entry date provisionally fixed for Jan. 1, 1983. The Ten (as they would be in 1981) intended to open a major long-term review of the Community's budget system and the future of farm spending in particular. The cost of farm policy, and especially unwanted food surpluses, represented the biggest single burden on the EEC budget. Given the fixed limit to EEC revenues, there were fears that the Community budget would simply run out of money sometime in 1981.

There was some surprise in February when Turkey announced its intention to apply for full membership in the EEC by the end of 1980. This was reiterated at a meeting in Brussels in May, when the government of Suleyman Demirel secured a number of improvements in its long-standing association agreement with the EEC. However, the matter was thrown into doubt following the army coup d'etat in Turkey in September. The EEC decided not to suspend the association agreement or economic aid.

July marked the first full year's operations of the directly elected European Parliament. It was a year of mixed fortunes for the new institution. On the one hand, the Parliament attracted considerable publicity for its determined—but, in the end, unsuccessful—attempt to force radical changes in the EEC budget, on which agreement was not reached by the end of the year. On the other hand, as the year progressed the limited nature of its powers and influence became more and more apparent. There was a general desire among members to move the seat of the Parliament from Strasbourg to Brussels (where its committees met). However, the French government continued to champion Strasbourg as the Parliament's home.

West German Chancellor Helmut Schmidt (left) and French Pres. Valéry Giscard d'Estaing met in the grand ballroom of the Élysée Palace in Paris in February to discuss the Soviet Union's invasion of Afghanistan.

KEYSTONE

At the end of 1980 the Commission, the executive body of the European Communities, completed its four-year term of office. Gaston Thorn replaced the former British Cabinet minister Roy Jenkins as president. The new Commission would be 14 strong (to allow one Greek commissioner), but few of the recommendations on reform of the Commission and other European institutions recommended in two major reports published in 1980 seemed likely to be implemented soon. The new Commission would face an urgent need for a common fisheries policy, talks on which broke down in December. In spite of the attention given to energy following successive increases in oil prices, a common energy policy still eluded the Community.

Once again, other European bodies such as the Council of Europe, representing the parliaments of all Western European countries, the Western European Union, representing the parliaments of NATO member states, and the European Free Trade Association (EFTA) were somewhat overshadowed by the European Community. However, EFTA celebrated its 20th anniversary.

European members of NATO were divided over the decision by NATO to produce and deploy some 600 cruise and Pershing nuclear missiles in response to the buildup of Warsaw Pact nuclear forces. Norway and Denmark refused to accept any nuclear weapons on their soil, while Belgium and The Netherlands delayed decisions about cruise missile deployment until their governments could judge the progress of U.S.-Soviet talks on European theatre nuclear disarmament, overoptimistically planned for late 1980. (JOHN PALMER)

See also Defense; Economy, World.
[534.F.3.b.IV; 971.D.7]

Fashion and Dress

Walking sleeping bags paced the city streets in the winter of 1979–80, in dizzying colours such as hot pink, canary yellow, and cornflower blue. The nylon, down-filled garments, quilted and stitched in large squares or horizontal sections, became a new classic in Paris, London, New York, and Rome. Warm, light in weight, and inexpensive, they were seen in all lengths from the hip-hitting waistcoat to the just-above-ankle, full-length model.

For those with fatter clothes budgets, there was the belted, fur-lined, poplin raincoat with a very large, flat-on-the-shoulder, notched collar in fur to match the lining. To balance the bulk of the wide shoulder line and collar, the silhouette was topped with a narrow-brimmed soft hat, in drab tweed with tiny tone-on-tone design or in plain putty-coloured poplin to match the coat. Hats were definitely in.

Under the coat, there was no great fashion change. The straight and narrow skirt with surprise slits alternated with the soft wrap style—with a rounded hem flap instead of the previous square one—or the model with all-around pleats stitched to hip level. The alternative was pants, teamed with knit tops in plain jersey or with big knits, all in the season's colour, deep purple. Silk blouses with narrow fluting at the neckline and cuffs provided a dressier note.

Boots were still much worn, though they were shorter and with lower heels. Many women preferred sensible, hardy shoes with opaque hose, often black. Black hose were prominent for evening wear as well, teamed with black pumps to complete the all-black look provided by black velvet, jet, and transparent black lace or chiffon. With a sudden jolt, hemlines moved up in the spring to knee level, above or below according to age group. The results were mixed.

The newest trend in suits for spring was the bicoloured effect, strongest when carried out in black and white. All-around white braid trimming or piping outlined the hip-skimming, collarless black jacket. Top-gathered sleeves or padding widened the shoulder line, and skirts were straight and easy. Black and white journeyed through summer, with particularly vibrating prints seen in London and Milan—designs that undulated with every body movement, bold horizontal or diagonal stripes, and many other references to Op and kinetic art.

The everyday city costume for summer was the cotton jersey T-shirt dress with fancy striping combining two or three colours. In some cases the ribbed hemline introduced a low bubble effect, to be developed in the fall. Some models were abridged to mid-thigh, and opaque hose in plain white or pastels took over from black. Low, rounded necklines gave a 1950s flavour.

Seersucker, with its blistered, crinkled surface, was the choice for blazers, shorts, bermudas, pants, jumpsuits, and narrow skirts with seam slits. Easy to wash, it was ideal in the season's

DUSTIN PITTMAN—WWD

Trend-setter Perry Ellis fashioned pastel linen into a new suit silhouette for spring—exaggerated shoulders on a short-sleeved, cropped jacket over a strapless handknit sweater. The soft, full trousers are hemmed at midcalf.

Evangelical Churches:
see Religion

Exhibitions:
see Art Exhibitions; Museums; Photography

Faeroe Islands:
see Dependent States

Falkland Islands:
see Dependent States

Farming:
see Agriculture and Food Supplies

UPI

STAFFORD/ARNAUD

Yves Saint-Laurent's latest fantasy approach to fashion was inspired by tribal textiles (left). Kenzo (right) paired two gray wools for his suit, broadcloth for the jacket and flannel for the trousers, cut wide and a little shorter. The flat shoe returned in a variety of casual and dressy styles.

favourite soft pastels, principally pink and evanescent mauves straight from a Monet summer garden. For full summer it was the all-white look, except for shoes. Plain pumps and sandals with narrow straps drew attention with their technicolour shades and ultrahigh, spiky heels. Bright red was the favourite eye-catcher for open-toed, multistrapped sandals, particularly when worn with the new baggy pants chopped off above the ankle.

There was definitely a new cut for pants. Though second-skin, seam-splitting jeans were still plentiful, the new trousers—also in denim but more often in plain white cotton—were baggy around the hips and straight in the leg. They actually moved away from the body when the wearer walked. Jumpsuits adopted the same cropped, wide-legged cut and were newest at mid-calf level. Tops were either squared off with wide shoulder straps, pinafore style, or in shirt form and worn open to the waist over a separate brassière top. A newcomer was the flight suit with bagginess at thigh level, then pared down around the leg. Some were in striped cotton seersucker for day; some in silk crêpe de Chine for evening, prettiest with a V-neck and short sleeves.

The year's real fashion news was in accessories. With ankles cleared, shoes became very important. In contrast to the spiky-heeled sandals were flat-heeled ballerinas in gold or silver kid or in plain leather studded with gold nails, both types for day wear. Low-heeled pumps, again in kaleidoscopic colours, or jet-embroidered court pumps gave a new balance to evening clothes and silk trousers. But the shape that took the younger set by storm was the flat-heeled Chinese cloth shoe with an ankle strap, made in China. The same shape, but made in Europe, was carried over for autumn in leather, bright red velvet, and satin with an embroidered motif in the front. Ranking after shoes as trend setters were mini-size bags with long, narrow shoulder straps, varying in shape from soft purses or pouches to stiff, round, camembert boxes and fat sausages.

As the fad for disco music gave way to country and western, cowboys and Indians were everywhere. Young Hiawathas, male and female, sported wide leather fringe trimming on every available hem or yoke. Fringed moccasins added to the total Indian look, as did beaded headbands over hair parted in the middle with a plait on either side. But the hairstyle that swept all before it throughout the summer was the corn-row look, launched by film star Bo Derek in the motion picture *10*. To tiny plaited strands of hair hanging straight down from all over the scalp were added all kinds of finery, such as coloured beads and shells. More jingle was provided by bracelets, purchased by the dozen and worn in equal numbers on both wrists.

If swimming on European beaches was topless when not totally in the nude, after-swimming was dressed up. The one-piece suit made a comeback. It might shimmer with lurex or gray mercury straight from *Moonraker* and other James Bond films, or it might be decked up with ruffles and embroidery, suitable to wear with a skirt for an evening dance. In either case, it was unlikely to survive a dip in the pool.

As winter approached, the broader shoulder line was emphasized on mannish topcoats with thick padding and on belted models with jutting tippets, fringed scarves piled up on top, or tiered capes. The "preppie" look, reminiscent of '50s college styles, brought a resurgence of plaids for kilts and straight dresses, with an eye-catcher on the hem to draw attention to the new display of leg. The black and white story continued with white silk blouses ruffled at the collar and cuffs and a great deal of black velvet—suits with puffed sleeves, knickers, and plumed page boy berets—black stockings, of course, and black pumps.

Black and white called for dramatic makeup: no more of that healthy bloom, but a white foundation, Japanese style. Powder was a must. "With glints of mother of pearl," said Helena Rubinstein; "Smokey hues on eyelids," said Revlon, instead of blues and greens; and "Titian red for lips," insisted Estée Lauder, whose colours were inspired by Venetian palaces. But copper and fuchsia were also in evidence, blended to match the soft shades of the clothes. Shorter and simpler hairstyles did away with the fuss of the summer. A favourite was the boyish cut with a heavy fringe over the eyes, enhanced by an occasional streak of gold for a very special evening. (THELMA SWEETINBURGH)

Men's Fashions. In a year that saw the menswear industry in the throes of a worldwide recession, it was perhaps surprising and somewhat ironic that there should have been more and bigger menswear trade shows than ever. The well-established shows in London, Paris, and Cologne were all more international, with more exhibitors and more visitors from more countries. A new fair—the World Congress of Menswear, to be staged in Dallas, Texas—was scheduled for February 1981.

Not so surprising was the effect that the depressed economy had on men's fashions. Seldom had there been such unanimity, with London, Paris, Cologne, and New York all speaking with one voice to announce the "British look," described by a New Yorker in Paris as "sophisticated English clothing with English details." Throughout the year, both fabrics and fashions were described as the "new-look British classics." Dior named the fashionable patterns for menswear in the 1980s as very British—pin and chalk stripes, houndstooth and herringbone suitings, with a return of the Scottish glen plaid for sports clothes.

At the beginning of the year, the West German Men's Fashion Institute said: "The next suit fashion will be elegant and English in inspiration." By year's end the forecast had become fact. The sober city suit and the conventional sports jacket with contrasting trousers were being shown in classic cloths and safe styling, a little lighter then previously in weight and colour. Nothing was exaggerated; every detail was traditional. Shirts were in softer colours, many in pure cotton or in cotton-polyester blends. The polka-dot tie, sometimes with a matching handkerchief, and diagonal patterned ties were also back in fashion. There was a revival of the double-breasted blazer. Summer-weight jackets in alpaca and lightweight worsteds

The well-bred, well-tailored British look was typified in this suit by Austin Reed. The single-breasted, two-button style was cut in a striped worsted without affectation or exaggeration.

AUSTIN REED, LONDON

in tartan designs were popular, as were two-piece suits in hairline-striped cotton and cotton-polyester cloths. The traditional three-quarter-length overcoat returned for winter.

In a year when men's fashion generally stood still or looked backward, what little forward movement there was came in clothes for leisure and pleasure: blousons in a variety of fabrics, both knitted and woven; track suits for jogging; and the inevitable jackets and jeans in true blue and faded denim. (STANLEY H. COSTIN)

See also Industrial Review: *Furs*.
[451.B.2.b and d.1; 629.C.1]

Field Hockey and Lacrosse

Field Hockey. At the Olympic Games in Moscow in July 1980 India won the gold medal for men's field hockey, and the same prize for women was taken by Zimbabwe. Silver medals were won by Spain for men and Czechoslovakia for women, while the U.S.S.R. gained both bronze medals.

Pakistan retained the Champions Trophy at Karachi, with West Germany finishing second and Australia third of the seven competitors. In March the Hockey Association's tournament was held at Lord's and the Crystal Palace, London, where England defeated Ireland.

Pakistan visited Kenya and won all seven international matches there; Kenya had already tied a four-match series with Zimbabwe in that country. Pakistan also won a four-nation tournament in Kuala Lumpur, Malaysia, with Australia second, India third, and Malaysia fourth. At Liège, Belgium, Wales won a four-nation event, beating France, Belgium, and Scotland. On an artificial surface at Cologne, West Germany, The Netherlands triumphed over West Germany, Poland, and Spain.

In June England lost twice to The Netherlands, at Utrecht and Amstelveen, and Scotland defeated Ireland at Aberdeen. In September Scotland and Ireland met twice in Northern Ireland, Scotland winning the first match and Ireland the second. Meanwhile, England had beaten Zimbabwe at Norwich and later tied with Australia at Dulwich College, London, where it also defeated Canada; Wales tied with Canada and lost to Australia. In October England played two matches against Ireland in Dublin, winning the first and tying the second. The home countries' matches ended with England defeating Wales in Cardiff in November.

Indoors, Scotland won the home countries title and finished third at the European championships at Zürich, Switz., in March. West Germany won the gold and The Netherlands the silver.

In women's hockey England defeated Ireland in Dublin in March to win the "triple crown" (having also triumphed over Scotland and Wales) and later won a tournament at Rotterdam by beating the world-champion The Netherlands and the U.S. The women's team of Great Britain and Northern Ireland took part in a tournament at Cologne, where West Germany finished first, The Netherlands second, and Britain third.

(SYDNEY E. FRISKIN)

Fencing:
see Combat Sports

JOHN IAOCONO—"SPORTS ILLUSTRATED" © 1980 TIME INC.

It took a second overtime period during the NCAA lacrosse championship game in Ithaca, New York, in June for Johns Hopkins University to finally defeat the University of Virginia 9–8.

Lacrosse. MEN. Administrators of international lacrosse were concerned in 1980 with planning for the 1982 world championship to be held near Baltimore, Md. In 1980 visits at both senior and junior levels between lacrosse-playing countries became more numerous. The U.S. was represented at the Box Lacrosse Festival in Vancouver, B.C. In the National Collegiate Athletic Association championship, Johns Hopkins University of Baltimore, Md., was again the winner, with the University of Virginia runner-up. The North beat the South 9–8 in extra time. The outstanding player award went to Brendan Schneck, a midfield player from Johns Hopkins. The Long Island Athletic Club was the champion club team in the U.S.

In Australia there was no international competition in 1980. Victoria beat South Australia 16–15, and the champion teams in each state league were Williamstown in Victoria, East Torrens in South Australia, and East Freemantle in Western Australia. Best Australian player was R. Turnball of Western Australia.

Visits were made by English county and club teams to the U.S.; at the junior level three teams visited the U.S., and two U.S. teams were received in Britain. The English club championship (Iroquois Cup) was won by South Manchester and Wythenshawe, which defeated Oxford University. South Manchester and Wythenshawe also won the North of England senior flags by defeating Old Hulmeians. Cheshire won the county championship and Sheffield University the University Cup. Cheadle won the Northern League title, while Oxford University headed the Southern League and also won the South of England senior flags.

(CHARLES DENNIS COPPOCK)

WOMEN. International attention in the 1979–80 season was focused on the England squad's tour to the U.S. in April 1980 for a series of three test matches. The U.S. team was determined to avenge its defeat by England in 1979. The tour proved controversial, highlighting the many differences

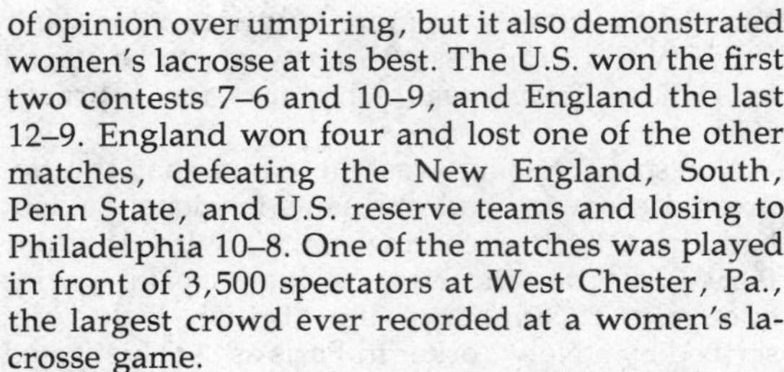

of opinion over umpiring, but it also demonstrated women's lacrosse at its best. The U.S. won the first two contests 7–6 and 10–9, and England the last 12–9. England won four and lost one of the other matches, defeating the New England, South, Penn State, and U.S. reserve teams and losing to Philadelphia 10–8. One of the matches was played in front of 3,500 spectators at West Chester, Pa., the largest crowd ever recorded at a women's lacrosse game.

In Britain Surrey defeated its old rival Middlesex to become counties champion. Despite tough opposition South held onto its territorial reserves title, but the North toppled the South to win the territorial championship. Wirral Wanderers became the first northern club since 1970 to win the National Clubs and Colleges Tournament. England dominated matches in Britain with wins over Scotland 13–2, Wales 11–3, a Celtic Select 7–4, and its own reserves 6–3. Players in Scotland and Wales were preparing for the first Celtic tour to the U.S. in 1981.

(MARGARET-LOUISE FRAWLEY)

Fiji

An independent parliamentary state and member of the Commonwealth of Nations, Fiji is an island group in the South Pacific Ocean, about 3,200 km E of Australia and 5,200 km S of Hawaii. Area: 18,272 sq km (7,055 sq mi), with two major islands, Viti Levu (10,388 sq km) and Vanua Levu (5,535 sq km), and several hundred smaller islands. Pop. (1979 est.): 619,000, including 50.1% Indian, 44.6% Fijian. Cap. and largest city: Suva (pop., 1976 census, 63,600). Language: English, Fijian, and Hindi. Religion: Christian and Hindu. Queen, Elizabeth II; governor-general in 1980, Ratu Sir George Cakobau; prime minister, Ratu Sir Kamisese Mara.

In December 1979 Prime Minister Sir Kamisese

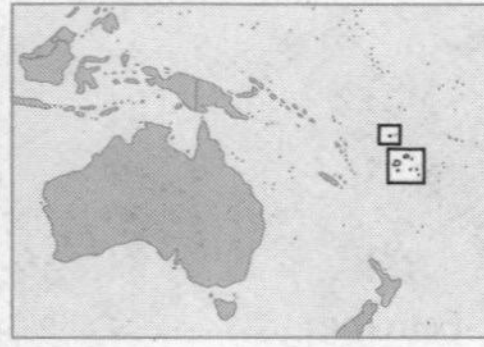

Fiji

FIJI

Education. (1978) Primary, pupils 131,100, teachers (1977) 4,209; secondary, pupils 34,493, teachers (1977) 1,662; vocational, pupils 1,930, teachers (1977) 177; teacher training, students 613, teachers (1977) 65; higher (1979), students 1,448, teaching staff 150.

Finance and Trade. Monetary unit: Fiji dollar, with (Sept. 22, 1980) a free rate of F$0.80 to U.S. $1 (F$1.92 = £1 sterling). Budget (1980 est.): revenue F$219.4 million; expenditure F$223.5 million. Foreign trade (1979): imports F$392,820,000; exports F$215,040,000. Import sources: Australia 34%; New Zealand 15%; Japan 14%; U.K. 9%; U.S. 6%; Singapore 5%. Export destinations: U.K. 37%; U.S. 15%; New Zealand 10%; Australia 9%. Main exports (1978): sugar 53%; petroleum products 15%; fish 9%; coconut oil 5%. Tourism (1978): visitors 184,000; gross receipts U.S. $102 million.

Transport and Communications. Roads (1977) 2,960 km. Motor vehicles in use (1978): passenger 20,500; commercial (including buses) 18,100. Railways (1978) 869 km. Shipping traffic (1979): goods loaded 784,000 metric tons, unloaded 823,000 metric tons. Telephones (Jan. 1979) 47,500. Radio receivers (Dec. 1977) 308,000.

Agriculture. Production (in 000; metric tons; 1979): sugar, raw value 474; rice (1978) 29; cassava (1978) *c.* 92; copra 22. Livestock (in 000; Sept. 1978): cattle *c.* 164; pigs *c.* 16; goats *c.* 55; horses *c.* 37; chickens *c.* 855.

Industry. Production (in 000; 1978): cement (metric tons) 88; gold (troy oz) 28; electricity (kw-hr; 1977) *c.* 290,000.

Mara, during a trip to the Middle East, reaffirmed Fiji's support for Israel's right to exist as a nation (Fiji also supported a Palestinian homeland) and visited the 650-strong Fiji contingent in the UN Interim Force in Lebanon (where a member of the contingent was killed in April 1980). Fiji also sent 24 men to serve with the Commonwealth Force in Zimbabwe. At the July 1980 meeting of the South Pacific Forum in Kiribati, Fiji refused to sign the South Pacific Regional Trade and Cooperation Agreement because of disputes over access to Australian and New Zealand markets for timber and citrus exports, respectively.

In March Pres. Augusto Pinochet of Chile cut short a brief visit to Fiji when his presence aroused widespread opposition and demonstrations. After China carried out missile tests in the Pacific to the northwest of Fiji in May without first consulting the island states, Fiji's protest drew an apology from Chairman Hua Guofeng (Hua Kuo-feng).

(BARRIE MACDONALD)

Finland

The republic of Finland is bordered on the north by Norway, on the west by Sweden and the Gulf of Bothnia, on the south by the Gulf of Finland, and on the east by the U.S.S.R. Area: 337,032 sq km (130,129 sq mi). Pop. (1980 est.): 4,771,300. Cap. and largest city: Helsinki (pop., 1980 est., 483,700). Language: Finnish, Swedish. Religion (1978): Lutheran 97.7%; Orthodox 1.3%. President in 1980, Urho Kaleva Kekkonen; prime minister, Mauno Koivisto.

Sharing as it does an 800-mi frontier with the U.S.S.R., Finland was quietly apprehensive about the deterioration in international relations in 1980. As Pres. Urho Kekkonen celebrated his 80th birthday on September 3, the overwhelming conviction was that the policy he personified – restraint and reconciliation with the Soviet Union – had been vindicated once more. In May he was awarded an International Lenin Peace Prize, and in July he paid an unofficial visit to the Olympic Games in Moscow.

Finland abstained in the UN vote on the Soviet intervention in Afghanistan. While this contrasted starkly with the condemnatory stance of other neutral countries, it accorded with Finland's consistent policy of not siding in great power conflicts. Addressing Parliament on February 5, Kekkonen stated: "What has happened outside Europe must not spoil the results achieved here." Finnish acceptance of a divisible form of détente differed markedly from the "global" view expressed by Pres. Valéry Giscard d'Estaing during his visit on June 2–3, the first ever paid to Finland by a French chief of state.

Finland was a factor in Soviet propaganda against NATO plans to deploy medium-range missiles in Western Europe and prestock military equipment in Norway for possible use by U.S. Marines. Through the press, the Kremlin appeared to extend Finland's obligations under its treaty with the U.S.S.R. to interception of cruise missiles, as well as more orthodox defense against NATO.

KEYSTONE

King Olav of Norway (left) was met by Pres. Urho Kekkonen upon his arrival for an official four-day visit to Helsinki in October.

Apart from the ouster of Johannes Virolainen as Centre Party chairman and his replacement by Foreign Minister Paavo Väyrynen, the domestic political scene was placid. The "low profile" centre-left coalition led by Social Democrat Mauno

FINLAND

Education. (1977–78) Primary, pupils 422,638, teachers 25,096; secondary, pupils 343,759, teachers 19,430; vocational, pupils 93,916, teachers 12,337; teacher training, students 690, teachers 71; higher, students 122,427, teaching staff 5,787.

Finance. Monetary unit: markka, with (Sept. 22, 1980) a free rate of 3.65 markkaa to U.S. $1 (8.76 markkaa = £1 sterling). Gold, SDR's, and foreign exchange (June 1980) U.S. $2,022,000,000. Budget (1980 est.): revenue 48,890,-000,000 markkaa; expenditure 48,888,000,000 markkaa. Gross national product (1979) 157,640,000,000 markkaa. Money supply (April 1980) 13,397,000,000 markkaa. Cost of living (1975 = 100; June 1980) 165.3.

Foreign Trade. (1979) Imports 44,222,000,000 markkaa; exports 43,430,000,000 markkaa. Import sources: U.S.S.R. 19%; Sweden 14%; West Germany 13%; U.K. 9%; U.S. 5%. Export destinations: Sweden 16%; U.S.S.R. 14%; U.K. 13%; West Germany 11%; Norway 5%. Main exports: paper 23%; machinery 12%; timber 10%; wood pulp 6%; ships 6%; iron and steel 5%; clothing 5%; chemicals 5%.

Transport and Communications. Roads (1979) 74,684 km (including 200 km expressways). Motor vehicles in use (1979): passenger 1,169,500; commercial 143,100. Railways: (1978) 6,079 km; traffic (1979) 3,020,000,000 passenger-km, freight 7,366,000,000 net ton-km. Air traffic (1979): 1,981,000,000 passenger-km; freight 46 million net ton-km. Navigable inland waterways (1978) 6,675 km. Shipping (1979): merchant vessels 100 gross tons and over 344; gross tonnage 2,508,764. Telephones (Jan. 1979) 2,-127,400. Radio recievers (Dec. 1978) *c.* 2.5 million. Television receivers (Dec. 1976) 1,893,000.

Agriculture. Production (in 000; metric tons; 1979): wheat 208; barley 1,650; oats 1,283; rye 77; potatoes 674; sugar, raw value (1978) *c.* 102; rapeseed 46; butter 74; cheese *c.* 67; eggs 75; meat (1978) 277; fish catch (1978) 128; timber (cu m; 1978) 37,250. Livestock (in 000; June 1979): cattle 1,736; sheep 113; pigs 1,289; reindeer (1978) 177; horses 22; poultry 9,227.

Industry. Production (in 000; metric tons; 1979): pig iron 2,037; crude steel 2,464; iron ore (66% metal content) 772; cement 1,750; sulfuric acid 1,022; petroleum products (1978) *c.* 10,300; plywood (cu m; 1978) 450; cellulose (1978) 3,393; wood pulp (1977) mechanical 1,774, chemical 3,472; newsprint 1,332; other paper and board (1978) 3,953; electricity (kw-hr) 37,490,000; manufactured gas (cu m) 24,000.

Finland

Koivisto—the first Finnish political figure in many years who could match President Kekkonen's ability to command popular support—survived minor crises over agricultural prices and the budget. The first signs appeared of a battle over the eventual succession to Kekkonen. Local elections in October produced no spectacular swings. Former prime minister Rafael Paasio died in March (*see* OBITUARIES).

For the second successive year, Finland seemed likely to attain the highest growth rate in the Organization for Economic Cooperation and Development region: official predictions were for a 6% increase in gross domestic product, following the 6.5% recorded in 1979. For the second time in half a year, the markka was revalued by 2% on March 25, 1980. However, the trade balance, comfortably in surplus until mid-1979, plunged into the red, owing to soaring energy import prices and purchases to shore up domestic industry. Trimmed to an annual 7–8% in 1978–79, inflation appeared set to touch 13%, signaling a loss of competitive edge over most other industrialized countries. In August unemployment reached 3.7%, the lowest rate in four years, but it was feared that the spread of the international recession would make this a fleeting achievement. Industrial relations remained touchy, as was shown by the collapse of the centralized incomes formula and a round of springtime strikes by merchant seamen, icebreaker crews, and salaried staff in industry.

While four-fifths of Finland's trade was with the West, commercial arrangements with the U.S.S.R. —the source of two-thirds of its oil supplies—acquired enhanced importance. A 7% increase in the annual Soviet oil quota would take place during the course of the 1981–85 trade agreement. To pay for crude petroleum, the Finns were stepping up their exports; a deal signed with the Soviet Union on July 3 totaled 2.4 billion markkaa (U.S. $650 million) and included nine multipurpose Arctic ships. President Kekkonen paid an official visit to the U.S.S.R. in the fall, and discussions were held regarding extension of the bilateral economic development program for five years beyond 1990, its original expiration date. (DONALD FIELDS)

Fisheries

With 93 coastal nations claiming a 200-mi exclusive economic zone in 1980, nations whose fishing industries had been based on the exploitation of fishing grounds adjacent to other countries had two choices: they could cut their losses and sell off the costly ships designed to fish such "distant waters," or they could apply for fishing licenses while attempting to negotiate bilateral agreements with the coastal states concerned.

For Britain, whose distant-water fisheries had been based on Iceland, Norway, and Newfoundland, there was little choice. Iceland had closed its grounds to all foreign vessels, and Canada's stock-recovery plans had cut foreign fishing to a point where it had become uneconomic for Britain. One after another, Britain's multimillion-dollar super-trawlers were being sold off to Africa, Australia, and South America, though a few owners tried desperately to stay solvent on west-coast mackerel. From a 1974 fleet of 489 vessels, the total in 1980 had fallen to 146, many of which had been laid up. Countries with control over their fishing grounds, such as Canada, South Africa, and Iceland, benefited from the restrictions imposed by their governments. Catch rates began to rise and stocks to recover from years of overfishing. In Iceland and Canada, however, investment in new vessels, combined with better catches, had brought about a surplus of the more popular species such as cod, depressing prices in European markets and causing hardship to fishermen already hard-hit by high fuel costs and interest rates.

In the third world, the more technologically advanced countries were investing in new fishing vessels. Ghana had ordered four 56-m (185-ft) tuna boats and large purse seiner-trawlers from Norwegian shipyards at a cost of $40 million, while six big fishing vessels had been ordered by Nigeria. The Danes were building trawlers for Uruguay, which expected to double its catch to a new high of 200,000 tons, mostly hake destined for export. Many less developed nations found themselves with newly acquired fish resources which they lacked the means to exploit or even to assess. The UN Food and Agriculture Organization (FAO), assuming a special responsibility for such nations, proposed to set up a computer-based system of resource calculation that would match data on fish-catching power with availability of fish resources. At a conference on small-scale fisheries, held in Japan, FAO's Menachem Ben Yami introduced the concept of community fisheries centres, which would enable practical aid to be integrated into primitive fishing communities at village level.

On several occasions FAO spokesmen warned that fishing was a resource exploited close to its limit. But if world fish production was to keep up with the growth in demand, it would have to increase by 44 million metric tons over the next 20 years. Half of this amount could be obtained by better management of existing resources. Some 5 million metric tons were lost annually by discarding undervalued species and 6 million through premature spoilage in hot climates. The Asian Bank estimated that sufficient investment could produce an additional 20 million metric tons a year, much of it from fish farming. The FAO believed the day was near when small fish abounding in tropical waters would be used to feed people, not to provide fish meal.

There were second thoughts on krill. Trawlers in Antarctic waters found that heavier catches choked trawls, and the catch suffered massive weight loss through compression in the net. Furthermore, in marketing trials only the Soviet Union reported good consumer reaction. The maximum allowable catch without environmental risk was estimated at 2.5 million metric tons a year. As krill lost some of its attraction, another unexploited fish resource was suggested, namely, the tropical species *Elagatis bipinnulata*, or rainbow runner.

Britain, France, and Spain witnessed mass demonstrations by fishermen. The main factor was fuel costs, which had outpaced the price of fish even when fuel subsidies were provided. Within the European Economic Community (EEC) fishing nations, no common policy on fuel subsidies or other "hidden" subsidies existed. Cries of "unfair competition" were raised in Britain when fish landed by EEC "partners" sold at 15% below prices required to maintain the home fleet. In Scotland fishermen refused to go to sea and lose money, and in the south there were protests in Parliament. Eventually, £15 million was distributed, pending agreement on the EEC common fisheries policy, promised for early 1981. (Accord was reached in September on fish conservation measures and, in October, on a standardized system for recording and reporting the size and nature of catches.)

In France, where fishermen received the highest direct fuel subsidies within the EEC (but also paid high social security contributions), frustration flared into protests and demonstrations. Fishermen from Normandy set up stalls in Paris street markets and sold fish at below retail prices. There were also demonstrations in the Channel ports, culminating in the much-publicized blockading of car-ferry and commercial ports for more than a week in August. The deep-sea fishermen's union was fighting against a reduction of crews from 22 men to 18 or 20, depending on the size of the trawler. The small-boat fishermen, who bore the brunt of the battle, wanted cheaper fuel, better fish prices, and reduced social security contributions. Eventually, the need for cash forced the fishermen back to sea, their public image somewhat tarnished.

In a limited area such as the EEC, a reduction of the fleets would increase each boat's share of the available catch. This was accomplished more readily by threats of bankruptcy than by retraining schemes and subsidies for scrapping, as was demonstrated by the rapid contraction of the big trawler fleets of Britain, France, and West Germany. The applications by Spain, Portugal, and Greece to join the EEC did little to encourage fleet reduction in those countries. There were fears of a "Spanish Armada" of 17,000 vessels in EEC waters, though the Spaniards insisted that few, if any, additional Spanish vessels were available for diversion to the area.

Table I. Whaling: 1978–79 Season (Antarctic); 1978 Season (Outside the Antarctic)
Number of whales caught

Area and country	Fin whale	Sei/ Bryde's whale	Hump-back whale	Minke whale	Sperm whale	Total	Percentage assigned under quota agreement[1]
Antarctic pelagic (open sea)							
Japan	–	–	–	2,733	18	2,751	33.1
U.S.S.R.	–	–	–	2,733	2,286	5,019	59.8
Brazil	–	–	–	–	–	–	7.1
Total	–	–	–	5,466	2,304	7,770	100.0
Outside the Antarctic[2]							
Japan	–	376	–	22	2,525	2,923	
U.S.S.R.	–	221	–	–	4,281	4,684[3]	
Peru	–	300	–	–	–	300	
Australia	–	–	–	–	679	679	
Iceland	236	14	–	–	141	391	
Greenland	5	–	20	–	–	25	
Others	409	86	12	690	488	1,685	
Total	650	997	32	712	8,114	10,687[3]	

[1]Antarctic only.
[2]Excluding small whales.
[3]Including 182 gray whales.
Source: The Committee for Whaling Statistics, *International Whaling Statistics*.

When China opened its books to FAO observers, it was found that past estimates of its annual catch had been 2 million metric tons higher than the true figures, which were 3.4 million metric tons of marine fish and 1.2 million metric tons of freshwater fish. But the annual catch of Taiwan had risen to nearly 1 million metric tons, and farmed fish and shellfish production was up 11.7% to 183,000 metric tons. Furthermore, a $220 million fleet-expansion program was announced that would add ten 500-ton purse seiners and 50 new trawlers to the Taiwanese fleet. In Vietnam trawlers donated by Norway as part of a fisheries aid program were found to be in use as naval auxiliaries and were accused of firing on refugees. Norwegian aid worth $20 million was promptly withdrawn.

For the first time, Norway's population was eat-

KEYSTONE

Striking French fishermen formed a blockade at the harbour entrance at Boulogne, France, in August. The fishermen were protesting high fuel costs.

GEORGE TAMES—THE NEW YORK TIMES

Vice-Admiral Robert H. Scarborough (right), acting commandant of the Coast Guard, shows Transportation Secretary Neil Goldschmidt where Soviet fishing operations in U.S. waters would be curtailed in reaction to the Soviet invasion of Afghanistan.

ing more meat than fish. Perhaps this was no bad thing, since the cod quota Norway had set for its fleet was still low, and the Atlanto-Scandinavian herring stocks still showed no sign of recovery. Norway's herring purse seine fleet had been reduced and was now catching capelin for the fish-meal plants. Ships from EEC countries fishing for cod and haddock were banned from Norwegian waters as of December 2.

In Peru the needs of the expanding food fishery conflicted with the ailing fish-meal industry. Anchoveta shoals again failed to live up to expectations. In 1979 fishing had been halted at 3.4 million metric tons, and processors were accusing the fish-meal plants of using food fish to maintain production. It was hoped that by the end of 1980 the national catch—once the world's biggest, at 10 million metric tons—would be divided equally between food fish and fish meal; fish-meal production, other than from fish waste, was to be phased out in a further 18 months. In neighbouring Chile, a future catch of 7 million metric tons was forecast (1978: 1,850,000 metric tons). A $120 million, five-year expansion plan included 50 new processing plants to boost production of canned, smoked, frozen, and salted fish. In the south, the giant Japanese fishing company Nippon Suisan was to invest $15 million in increasing production at Chile's Puerto Montt plant to 100 tons a day.

The Pacific tuna fishery was still in trouble. U.S. tuna purse seiners continued to complain of restrictions resulting from the limitation on porpoise kill imposed to satisfy the environmentalist lobby. Costa Rica arrested U.S. vessels found in its 200-mi zone, despite the U.S. claim that ocean-ranging tuna was not subject to such limitation. The U.S. was still building superseiners for this fishery, and the 67-m (221-ft) "El Rifle," which entered service in January, was one of 22 in the pipeline. The U.S. tuna catch in the Pacific amounted to 66% of the total 370,000 metric tons taken by a 17-nation fleet.

Farther north, the Canadian Pacific salmon season was a disappointment, variously blamed on too many boats, the Mt. St. Helens volcanic eruptions, too much logging activity, and a natural cycle. The Pacific herring roe fishery also encountered trouble when the Japanese market on which it relied raised retail prices steeply, with disastrous effects on demand. Canadian forecasts were speaking of doubled seafood exports by 1985, with a possible target of $2 billion.

Construction began in France on a 15-m (50-ft) fishing boat for use with both motor and sail. Trawl nets were improved to decrease water resistance and promote fuel economy, and new, simpler ways of baiting hooks automatically would encourage a return to the low-fuel-demand longline fishery. In the richer countries, fuel costs now represented 25% of operating costs. In low-wage areas, this figure jumped to 50% and discouraged investment in new vessels.

At the International Whaling Commission's 1980 meeting, in Brighton, England, yet another proposal for a moratorium on commercial whaling, supported by France, The Netherlands, the U.S., and the U.K., was defeated by the whaling nations—Japan, Iceland, South Africa, Spain, Chile, South Korea, and the U.S.S.R. However, the overall quota for all whale species to be taken in the 1981–82 season was reduced by 13% as compared with the previous year. (*See* ENVIRONMENT.)

(H. S. NOEL)

See also Food Processing.
[731.D.2.a]

Floods
see Earth Sciences; Engineering Projects

Table II. World Fisheries, 1978[1]
In 000 metric tons

Country	Catch		Trade	
	Total	Freshwater	Imports	Exports
Japan	10,752.2	268.7	923.0	745.0
U.S.S.R.	8,929.8	887.0	79.6	516.2
China	4,660.0	1,260.0	...	...
United States	3,511.7	265.8	1,073.1	350.7
Peru	3,364.8	9.8	0.3	607.3
Norway	2.647.1	1.2	41.9	660.3
India	2,367.9	904.4	0.3	78.0
South Korea	2,350.8	24.5	53.0	469.7
Thailand	2,264.0	146.5	22.4	235.1
Denmark	1,745.5	19.5	204.3	600.1
Chile	1,698.5	...	0.9	356.0
Indonesia	1,655.0	416.1	15.6	48.4
North Korea	1,600.0	...	...	...
Iceland	1,579.0	0.5	1.8	478.8
Philippines	1,558.4	204.7	44.5	24.1
Canada	1,406.8	128.9	83.6	479.4
Spain	1,379.9	19.4	200.6	200.1
United Kingdom	1,027.3	1.1	668.1	372.3
Vietnam	1,013.5	176.3	3.2	4.3
Brazil	858.0	130.8	66.2	21.1
France	795.6	2.5	468.5	134.2
Mexico	752.5	15.5	51.4	49.3
Bangladesh	640.0	540.0	...	5.5
South Africa	627.9	0.1	22.7	103.0
Poland	571.4	25.9	188.8	90.0
Malaysia	566.0	3.8	134.1	117.5
Burma	540.5	144.4	...	0.2
Argentina	537.3	10.4	9.7	190.0
Nigeria	518.6	246.0	63.1	3.6
Ecuador	475.5	...	...	92.5
South West Africa/ Namibia	417.5	...	...	...
West Germany	411.9	15.8	759.8	180.1
Italy	402.0	26.3	362.0	84.8
Senegal	345.8	5.5	9.2	57.3
Netherlands, The	324.4	2.2	329.1	274.3
Faeroe Islands	318.1	...	0.1	118.0
Pakistan	293.0	40.0	0.3	28.1
Morocco	292.2	0.6	0.1	82.7
Tanzania	287.1	234.2	5.2	0.4
Ghana	264.0	51.0	76.6	2.2
Portugal	254.5	0.1	79.5	52.4
Cuba	213.2	2.3	96.2	21.0
East Germany	198.4	20.7	102.0	...
Oman	198.0	0	...	...
Sweden	190.2	13.1	169.8	63.1
Other	5,573.6	...	...	...
World	72,379.5	7,250.5 [2]	8,368.3 [2]	8,988.4 [2]

[1] Excludes whaling.
[2] Includes unspecified amounts in Other category.
Source: United Nations Food and Agriculture Organization, *Yearbook of Fishery Statistics*, vol. 46 and 47.

Food Processing

Consumers in many countries were becoming increasingly bewildered by the conflicting official and semiofficial pronouncements of experts concerning the presumed effects of foods and food additives on health. The U.S. National Academy of Sciences (NAS) issued a report stating that healthy Americans need not cut their fat or cholesterol intake, and it challenged the previous conclusions of the Senate Select Committee on Nutrition and Human Needs that high cholesterol and fat intakes were responsible for heart disease and other chronic illnesses. However, the American Heart Association strongly disagreed with the NAS, while the American Medical Association counseled moderation. (*See* HEALTH AND DISEASE.)

Several U.S. scientists named excessive milk consumption as a major cause of juvenile delinquency. A British dental publication drew attention to the dangers of tooth erosion from the acids present in various fruit juices and carbonated beverages. A British royal commission said consumers should be less particular about the appearance of fruit and vegetables and recommended a change in the law "with the aim of reducing pressures on food processors to produce absolutely pest-free products." An Australian consumer organization asserted that Australians should reduce their daily energy intake by 1,000 calories to avoid obesity and the accompanying risks of high blood pressure, heart disease, and diabetes; it also criticized various foods for containing excessive fat. The British government criticized a university report on agricultural strategy that implied the existence of adverse dietary trends, and it emphasized that "the relationship of food to health is not sufficiently understood to provide the kind of nutritional blueprint this approach would require."

Processing and Packaging. A U.S. manufacturer of dehydrated onions successfully harnessed geothermal energy for use in the manufacturing process, and a British supermarket chain achieved an annual saving of £2,000 per store by installing heat reclamation units to recycle the heat generated by refrigeration systems. U.S. scientists claimed that a preservation process in which foods were exposed to a mixture of carbon monoxide and sulfur dioxide prior to aseptic packaging reduced energy usage by 80%. In a U.S. process for cooking meat, said to provide 70% energy savings, the meat is packed into plastic bags which are exposed

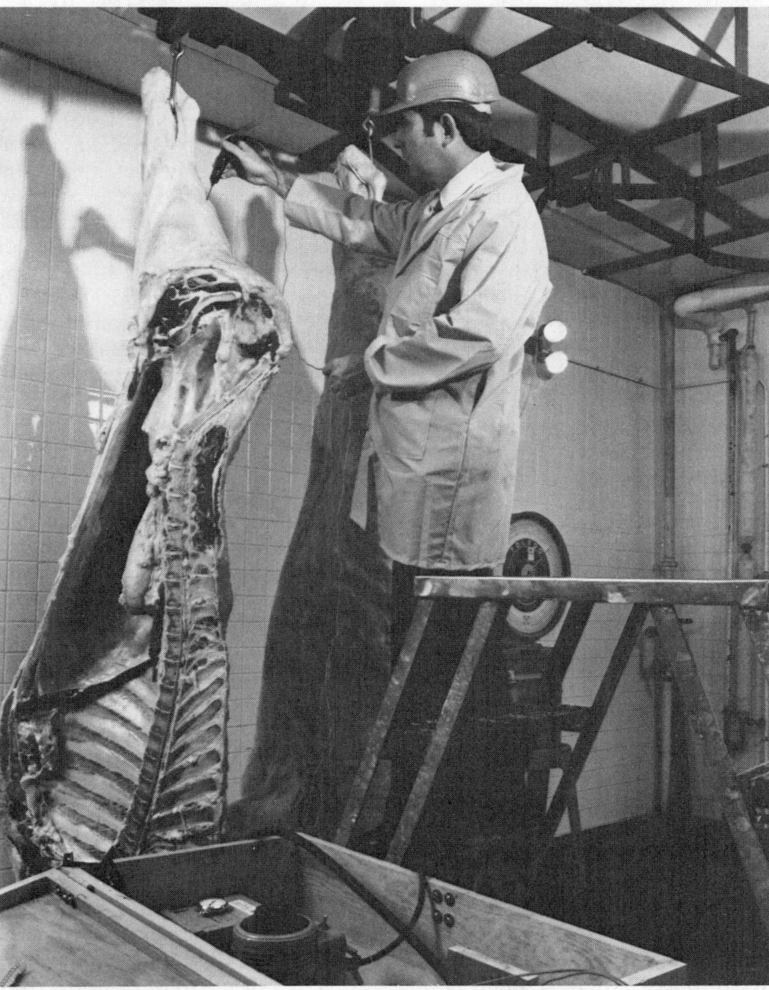

SCIENCE AND EDUCATION ADMINISTRATION—USDA

Technologists at the USDA's Science and Education Administration in Beltsville, Maryland, discovered that if electric shock is applied to beef soon after slaughter, the meat is more tender and weight loss in cooking is decreased.

to powerful jets of recirculating hot water, thereby greatly increasing heat transfer.

Considerable interest was shown in a U.S. process that made it possible to freeze foods without hardening. It was claimed that the method could revolutionize frozen-food production. According to reports, it maintains texture, permits refreezing, and conserves energy. A Swiss company developed an ingenious double-walled plastic bag which, upon inflation, closes around a frozen food and keeps it frozen for several hours.

Suppliers of packaging materials were blamed by British food manufacturers for the presence of contamination, which had resulted in a number of prosecutions. A pie manufacturer reported that 300 out of 6,000 containers examined contained foreign matter.

Fruit and Vegetable Products. The British Tropical Products Institute assisted various countries in food development. Nepal was aided in ginger and turmeric processing, the Philippines in canned coconut production, Sudan in sorghum storage, Tanzania in cereal processing and vegetable and oilseed distribution, Ghana in cocoa fermentation, and Mexico in corn (maize) storage.

In view of the declining consumption of fresh potatoes, there was much international interest in potato processing. Research in The Netherlands involved the manufacture of french fries (chips) and potato chips (crisps), peeled, canned, and dried potatoes, potato croquettes, and other products. Canadians developed a freeze-thaw process for the production of potato granules, and U.S. workers produced potato puree in flake form. A West German company prepared a protein isolate from potato juice. Improved methods of peeling and deep frying and the use of potato flour in bread and noodles were investigated in Taiwan. Research in the U.S.S.R. included storage conditions for potatoes and potato puree; the use of ionized air to improve potato shelf life; and a method for reducing waste by boiling, freezing, and thawing whole potatoes and then removing the skin from the pulp in a current of hot air.

The biology, cultivation, and food uses of edible fungi were studied in the U.S., as well as in Japan and several other Asian countries. The culture of fungi under water was also investigated. Research on the cultivation and food uses of various types of fresh- and salt-water algae was carried out in Thailand. Soviet workers studied the use of peat as a raw material for the microbial production of protein, fats, and vitamins.

Dairy Products. Earlier work on the ultrafiltration of milk and whey began to bear fruit in New Zealand and Europe. West German technologists reported savings in the manufacture of cheese attributable to increased yield and more consistent quality. A Swedish firm developed a continuous process incorporating ultrafiltration for the manufacture of all types of soft cheese. Australian scientists reported that cream from ultrafiltered milk had superior whipping properties.

Whey proteins from ultrafiltered whey became commercially available. They had excellent nutritional properties and good functional characteristics as a substitute for egg white. Progress was

MITRO-TO VIMA, ATHENS/ROTHCO

made in the utilization of lactose, which constitutes about 5% of whey, and its enzymatic conversion to a glucose-galactose syrup for sweetening proved attractive. Other processes studied included whey conversion to biomass by yeast fermentation and an anaerobic fermentation process to produce methane as a fuel for creamery boilers. U.S. scientists developed two novel processes for the conversion of whey into ruminant feed; in one the lactose was reacted with urea, and in the other it was fermented to lactic acid and converted to ammonium lactate. The latter process was approved by the Food and Drug Administration, and a plant was commissioned to produce 100 tons daily.

Meat, Unconventional Protein, and Seafood. British scientists developed a system for predicting carcass characteristics and meat quality by assessing the hormone profile of the live animal. An investigation of excessive blood splash in lambs at slaughter led to the discovery of plants containing anticoagulants which are present in certain pastures. Danish scientists demonstrated a relationship between blood groups of pigs and meat quality, and they also developed a method for the better utilization of blood from slaughter for eating purposes. Normally only the plasma is used in meat products and the red cells are discarded, although these contain three-quarters of the blood protein. In the new process, the hemoglobin is broken down enzymatically, the precipitated pigment is removed, and the residual protein hydrolysate is dried for use.

A survey of the bacteriological quality of ground meat in British retail stores showed no difference between supermarkets, retail-chain butchers, and small family butchers. Numbers of bacteria were of the same order as in similar surveys carried out in the U.S. and Canada.

Little progress was made in achieving public acceptance of vegetable protein products and meat analogues, and a number of manufacturers abandoned production. However, the British Committee on the Medical Aspects of Food Policy proposed that the permitted level of 10% vegetable protein in school meals and for institutional feeding might be raised to 30%. It was estimated that this could save about £10 million annually.

Considerable study was devoted to the improved utilization of existing marine resources and to aquaculture. A Swiss company reported on the great potential of many unexploited species, such as lantern fish and deep-sea red crabs, and of underexploited species like squid and octopus, which contain 17–20% protein and only 1–1.5% fat. The need for improved methods of fish filleting was emphasized, since currently used systems wasted more than 50% of the flesh. A process was developed for the better utilization of fish trimmings by isolating a fish protein and spinning it for use as a meat extender.

Abalone were successfully raised from spawn, and a formula diet was developed with a view to the commercial raising of lobsters. Swedish scientists developed a new trout-breeding system that produced 0.5-kg (1-lb) fish from spawn in less than a year. A proposal for whale farming involved capturing pregnant blue whales and raising the young on fertilized atolls.

New Foods. Conservative eating habits made it difficult to introduce really novel products, as was demonstrated by the failure of vegetable protein foods in the face of obvious need. Many so-called new foods were merely traditional foods of one country introduced in areas where they were unfamiliar. Thus the Japanese "discovery" of Western foods was reported to have created an immense demand for such products as American fried chicken, hamburgers, British roast beef, Turkish kebabs, French bouillabaisse, and Spanish paella. "Health consciousness" contributed not only to a proliferation of new types of fermented milk products, including a line of low-acid yogurts for babies, but also to the introduction into Western countries of koumiss and kefir, previously little known outside Asia and Eastern Europe.

Philippine nutritionists proposed the use of termites and some 50 kinds of worms (mainly maggots) as a basis for burgers and omelets. In an attempt to popularize such unexploited resources, the fare at a wildlife conference in South Africa consisted of puff adders, mopani worms, elephant biltong (jerky), and hippopotamus pie. An Anglo-American fungus-derived protein food received approval in the U.K. Another novel development was a Japanese product prepared from *Paramecium,* a microscopic protozoan common in stagnant ponds. The appearance in Western Europe of products made from combinations of insect larvae and worms with eggs and rice was reported to be due mainly to the demands of expatriates. According to an Australian report, cattle gallstones were in demand in Southeast Asia as a flavouring.

Increased demand for foods rich in dietary fibre led to numerous new formulations such as bran soups and special pastries. A preparation of soybean bran was developed in Japan, and a British company introduced a similar product. Other new products included a soufflé dessert (British) prepared from eggs, cream, and fruit and said to be superior to the homemade product; a snack food consisting of crisp potato balls with a fluffy centre (British); a smoked and matured sausage spread made from krill fermented with a lactobacillus (West German); and aseptically packaged cane sugar juice (China). (H. B. HAWLEY)

See also Agriculture and Food Supplies; Fisheries; Health and Disease; Industrial Review: *Alcoholic Beverages.*
[451.B.1.c.ii; 731.E–H]

Football

Association Football (Soccer). During 1980 one nasty fringe aspect of the game crowded upon another, as bribery took over the spotlight from the usual crowd hooliganism and violence. Regrettably, it was not confined to one country, though Italy had the greatest incidence of "fixing" matches. The scandal in Italy broke during the latter part of March 1980, and on May 18 the Italian Football Federation passed sentences on the famous AC Milan and Lazio clubs and on several well-known players. Milan and Lazio were relegated to the second division with life suspensions for Milan's president, Felice Colombo, and Lazio's goalkeeper, Massimo Cacciatori. Other players involved were given various sentences, including the national striker Paolo Rossi, who received a three-year ban.

In Greece, Switzerland, and Spain attempts to affect the results of games for reasons other than betting brought sentences on club officials and players, while in Yugoslavia two games crucial to relegation and promotion issues were abandoned when the referees were attacked by players. In Spain players of Betis, Seville, were offered $10,-

England's Nottingham Forest soccer team (dark jerseys) defeated West Germany's SV Hamburg team 1–0 to retain the European Champion's Cup in a tournament held in Madrid on May 28.

ALAIN GAVILLET—A.S.L./PICTORIAL PARADE

000 to tie in San Sebastian against Real Sociedad and $20,000 to win. Either result would help Real Madrid win the title, which they duly did for the 20th time. In Greece the president of Iraklis was jailed for three years after attempting to "buy" the cup semifinal against PAOK. Ironically, Iraklis won the match on its own merits after the errant official had been imprisoned.

EUROPEAN CHAMPIONSHIP. West Germany regained the title it had lost to Czechoslovakia four years previously by defeating Belgium 2–1 in the final in Rome on June 22, watched by some 47,000 spectators in the Olympic Stadium and millions more on television. The victory was the 19th consecutive unbeaten game for Jupp Derwall since he took over the national team from Helmut Schön. While the championship matches as a whole produced few goals and much sterile, safety-first football, the final, with Belgium contributing plenty of flair, was entertaining. The West Germans produced their fair share of skill beginning in the first half when the giant Hamburg striker, Horst Hrubesch, scored after ten minutes following a neat interpassing move between Klaus Allofs and Bern Schuster. The West Germans pressed to increase their advantage, and Belgium's Jean-Marie Pfaff produced fine saves to confine the score to that single goal at the halftime break. Some 20 minutes into the second half, after veteran Wilfred Van Moer had started to find gaps in the West German rear guard, the Belgians tied the score; René Van der Eycken scored from a penalty awarded when François Van der Elst was tripped by Ulrich Stielike. Both sides then went flat out for the winning goal, and the West Germans achieved it in the final seconds, when, from a corner by Karl-Heinz Rummenigge, Hrubesch headed home. Czechoslovakia took the consolation prize against Italy, winning 9–8 on penalty shots.

Giorgio Chinaglia of the New York Cosmos raised his arms in victory after scoring a record-breaking sixth goal during a playoff game on August 31.

UPI

Table I. Association Football Major Tournaments

Event	Winner	Country
European Championship	West Germany	
European Super Cup	Nottingham Forest	England
European Champions' Cup	Nottingham Forest	England
European Cup-Winners' Cup	Valencia	Spain
UEFA Cup	Eintracht Frankfurt	West Germany
Libadores Cup (South American Champions' Cup)	Nacional	Uruguay

Table II. Association Football National Champions

Nation	League winners	Cup winners
Albania	Dynamo Tirana	Partizan Tirana
Austria	Austria WAC	Austria WAC
Belgium	FC Bruges	Waterschei
Bulgaria	CSKA Sofia	Slavia Sofia
Cyprus	Apoel	Omonia
Czechoslovakia	Banik Ostrava	Sparta Prague
Denmark	Esbjerg	Hvidovre
England	Liverpool	West Ham
Finland	OPS Oulun	Ilves
France	Nantes	Monaco
Germany, East	Dynamo Berlin	Carl Zeiss Jena
Germany, West	Bayern Munich	Fortuna Düsseldorf
Greece	Olympiakos	Kastoria
Hungary	Vasas Budapest	Diösygyör
Iceland	IBV Vestmann	Fram
Ireland	Limerick	Waterford
Italy	Inter-Milan	AS Roma
Luxembourg	Jeunesse Esch	Sporta Luxembourg
Malta	Valetta	Hibernians
Netherlands, The	Ajax	Feyenoord
Northern Ireland	Linfield	Linfield
Norway	Viking Stavangar	Viking Stavangar
Poland	Szombierki Bytom	Legia Warsaw
Portugal	Sporting Lisbon	Benfica
Romania	Univ. Craiova	Poli. Timisoara
Scotland	Aberdeen	Celtic
Spain	Real Madrid	Real Madrid
Sweden	Halmstadt	FC Malmö
Switzerland	FC Basel	FC Sion
Turkey	Trabzonspor	Altay Izmir
U.S.S.R.	Moscow Spartak	Dynamo Tbilisi
U.S.	New York Cosmos	
Wales		Newport
Yugoslavia	Red Star Belgrade	Dynamo Zagreb

The earlier rounds of the competition were marred by some crowd hooliganism, particularly in the England versus Belgium match in Turin, Italy. The English fans—many the worse for drink—started reacting to the taunts of some equally mindless Italian youths and began brawling. Police broke up the fighting with tear gas, which drifted over the field and held up play for several minutes. Many arrests were made by the local riot police.

EUROPEAN CHAMPIONS' CUP. Nottingham Forest of England retained the premier European trophy for clubs by defeating SV Hamburg of West Germany 1–0 in Madrid on May 28. This was the same score by which the English team had won the giant cup a year earlier. In 1980 the only goal of the game was scored by Scottish winger John Robertson after some 20 minutes of play in the Bernabeu Stadium, and for the rest of the game Hamburg, well primed by Kevin Keegan, Peter Nogly, and Felix Magath, forced the champions into defensive tactics. Indeed, some superb saves by Peter Shilton from Casper Memering, Nogly, and Keegan were needed to stop the West Germans. The all-important goal stemmed from a pass by Frank Gray to Gary Mills, who flicked the ball on to Robertson. The Scot temporarily lost possession after rounding Manny Kaltz, but Garry Birtles returned it and Robertson shot in off the far post. As a spectacle the match was several degrees below par, with Nottingham Forest forced by Hamburg to be ultra-defensive.

European Cup-Winners' Cup. Valencia beat Arsenal of England to keep the trophy in Spain for another year, winning a 5–4 penalty shootout in Brussels on May 14 after the teams were scoreless at the end of two hours of play. After the goalkeepers of each side, Carlos Pereira and Arsenal's Pat Jennings, had blocked the first penalty shot of a nerve-racking session in the Heysel Stadium, each side scored its next four. Ricardo Arias scored the fifth for Valencia, beating Jennings; then Graham Rix stepped up and shot too close to Pereira. The Spanish goalkeeper blocked the shot, and the cup belonged to Valencia for the next 12 months. Though the penalty method is laid down in the rules, it seemed far from the ideal way to settle such an important tournament.

uefa Cup. Eintracht Frankfurt made sure the uefa Cup stayed in West Germany when they beat defending champion Borussia Mönchengladbach on the away goals rule over two legs. (This applied to all rounds of the competition and in essence meant that in the event of a tie on aggregate, goals scored in the away leg counted double.)

In the first leg at Mönchengladbach, Eintracht twice took the lead with goals by Harald Karger and the veteran West German international competitor, Bernd Hölzenbein. But Borussia struck back with scores by Christian Kulik and Lothar Matthäus, and then, with two minutes to go, Kulik headed a goal to win for Borussia 3–2. In the return at Eintracht's Wald Stadium a fortnight later on May 21, a brilliant save by Eintracht's Jurgen Pahl on a rebound shot by Borussia's Ewald Lienen kept the score 0–0. Then Eintracht coach Friedel Rausch sent in Freddy Schaub with some ten minutes to play, and he soon repaid that confidence by scoring the decisive goal to give Eintracht its first trophy in Europe in 20 years of attempts.

U.K. Home International Championship. Northern Ireland won the U.K. home international title for the first time since 1964, when it shared the championship with England and Scotland, and the first time outright since 1914. The Ulstermen started off on the right foot by beating Scotland 1–0 on the opening day of the tournament in Belfast on May 16. The following day Wales did them a favour by defeating England 4–1 at Wrexham. In so doing the Welsh recorded their biggest victory in more than 100 years against the English. Three days later at Wembley, London, England with a reshaped team was held by Northern Ireland to a 1–1 draw. To nip ahead of Wales on the following Friday at Ninian Park, Cardiff, was all that Northern Ireland had to do to clinch the title, and this they did 1–0. England and Scotland renewed their old rivalry at Hampden Park, Glasgow, 24 hours later, and England scored twice to win.

North American Soccer League. The New York Cosmos regained the North American Soccer League championship when they defeated the Fort Lauderdale Strikers 3–0 in the Soccer Bowl at Washington, D.C., before some 50,000 spectators on September 21. The two key factors in the final were the injury to the Strikers' West German ace scorer Gerd Müller, five minutes before the half-time break, and the goal by the Cosmos' Julio Cesar Romero early in the second half. Vladislav Bogicevic slipped a free kick to the colourful Giorgio Chinaglia—he once arrived for a training session by helicopter—and the Italian's shot bounced off the Strikers' defensive wall and came back to Romero, who then beat Striker goalie Jan Van Beveren. From that point the Cosmos were in command, and Chinaglia scored twice more to seal their victory. Ricky Davis and Wim Rijsbergen set up Chinaglia's first score, and the second came with two minutes left in the game when Roberto Cabanas's shot rebounded from the Strikers' defense. Despite the near-100° F (38° C) temperature, both sides gave an all-action display.

(Trevor Williamson)

Rugby. Rugby Union. The outstanding events of 1979–80 were the victories achieved by New Zealand in its test series against the British Isles and England's feat of winning the home international championship, the triple crown, and the grand slam. Another highlight of the season was the first official tour to Britain by the Romanian national team.

The Romanians' visit to Wales in September and October 1979 comprised five games, including an international against a Wales XV. The Romanians won their first four games and only narrowly lost the international, 13–12, at Cardiff. During the same period Canada made a six-match tour of Britain and France, the chief contests being against

CENTRAL PRESS/PICTORIAL PARADE

England's rugby team (light jerseys) achieved an impressive 24–9 victory against Ireland in the Rugby International at Twickenham in January.

France B, which the Canadians won 14–4 at Lille, and against France A, which they lost 34–15 in Paris. Also in October 1979, Australia visited Argentina for the first time, playing seven games. Argentina won the first of the two international matches 24–13, but the Australians won the second 17–12, both at Buenos Aires.

The All Blacks from New Zealand played ten matches on a tour of England and Scotland in October and November. They won all their games except the one against the North of England, which beat them 21–9 at Otley. Victories included triumphs over Scotland (20–6) at Murrayfield and over England (10–9) at Twickenham. The New Zealanders then played a game in Italy, beating the Italian national team 18–12 at Rovigo.

The South African Barbarians traveled to the U.K. in October 1979, the first multiracial team from that nation to play in Britain. Of their seven matches they won four and tied one.

In the home international championship England won an unshared title for the first time since 1963, the triple crown for the first time since 1960, and the grand slam for the first time since 1957. The hat trick of tries (touchdowns) achieved by John Carleton, the England right-wing three-quarter, in his team's 30–18 defeat of Scotland was the first for England since H. P. Jacob's against France at Twickenham in 1924.

England's captain, Bill Beaumont, was appointed captain of the Lions for their 18-match tour of South Africa in May, June, and July 1980. The coach was Noel Murphy of Ireland and the manager Syd Millar, also of Ireland. The Lions won all their 14 games outside the test series, which the Springboks won 3–1. The Springboks won the first three tests 26–22 at Cape Town, 26–19 at Bloemfontein, and 12–10 at Port Elizabeth, but the Lions won the fourth 17–13 at Pretoria. The Lions' overall tour record was played 18, won 15, lost 3, points for 401, points against 244.

Australia gained its biggest victory ever over New Zealand by winning the last match of their three-game test series 26–10 at Sydney Cricket Ground in July 1980. This result gave Australia the series: they had won 13–9 at Sydney and lost 12–9 at Brisbane. The crowd for the third test, 48,698, was the largest ever to watch a Rugby Union game in Australia.

RUGBY LEAGUE. The triangular tournament was won by England, which beat Wales 26–9 at Hull and France 4–2 at Narbonne. In the other match France beat Wales 21–7 at Widnes. In an under-24 international, Great Britain beat France 14–2 at Leigh. An attempt was made to start professional Rugby League in the south of England by the formation of a club at the Fulham soccer ground.

(DAVID FROST)

U.S. Football. PROFESSIONAL. The Oakland Raiders of the American Football Conference (AFC) became the first wild-card team to win the championship of U.S. professional football when they defeated the Philadelphia Eagles 27–10 in the Super Bowl at New Orleans, La., on Jan. 25, 1981. The game's most valuable player was Raider quarterback Jim Plunkett, who passed for all three of his team's touchdowns, two to wide receiver Cliff Branch and one to running back Kenny King. The pass to King and his subsequent run covered 80 yd, a Super Bowl record. Also outstanding for the Raiders were linebacker Rod Martin, who set a Super Bowl record by intercepting three passes, and the Raider offensive line, which gave Plunkett excellent protection throughout the game.

For Plunkett and the team as a whole the game was a fitting climax to a remarkable comeback season. Plunkett, the 1970 Heisman Trophy winner who began his pro career with several successful seasons with the New England Patriots, had been cast off by both that team and San Francisco and started the year on the Raider bench. But when first-string quarterback Dan Pastorini broke his leg in the fifth game, Plunkett took over. At that time the Raiders had a 2–3 record and seemed unlikely to make the play-offs. But Plunkett led them to an 11–5 regular-season mark and to play-off victories over Houston, Cleveland, and San Diego.

In the conference championship games the Raiders scored three touchdowns in the first quarter and then held on to beat the San Diego Chargers 34–27. The Eagles played tough defensive football to defeat Dallas 20–7 for their first National Conference (NFC) title.

The Pittsburgh Steelers failed to become the National Football League's (NFL's) first team to make nine consecutive play-off appearances and win three Super Bowls in a row. Their overwhelming injuries peaked in a week when 35 players needed medical attention. But the 9–7 Steelers had considerable company in their fall from grace. Half of the ten play-off teams in 1979 missed the 1980 Super Bowl tournament. The others were Miami, Denver, Chicago, and Tampa Bay, which fell the furthest by finishing 5–10–1 after playing for the NFC championship in 1979. Los Angeles and Houston, the 1979 semifinalists with Pittsburgh and Tampa Bay, were the first two teams eliminated from the 1980 tournament.

San Diego was the only team to win its division a second year in a row, and Philadelphia was the only other division winner that had been in the 1979 play-offs. The other four division winners were Cleveland, champion of Pittsburgh's AFC Central for the first time since 1971; Atlanta, ending Los Angeles' NFL-record string of seven consecutive championships in the NFC West; Buffalo, which leaped from fourth place the previous year in the AFC East, and Minnesota in the NFC Central. San Diego won the AFC West, and Philadelphia the NFC East.

Oakland was the fifth 1980 play-off team that had missed the 1979 tournament, qualifying as an AFC wild-card team with Houston. Oakland and Houston actually tied the AFC division winners with 11–5 won-lost records, but the NFL's tiebreaker rules denied them championships on the basis of conference records or net points in division games. Dallas also settled for wild-card status after tying Philadelphia at 12–4. Los Angeles, the other NFC wild-card, finished 11–5, one game behind Atlanta.

Detroit's improvement, from 2–14 in 1979 to 9–7, was the year's biggest. Atlanta rose from 6–10 to 12–4 and Buffalo from 7–9 to 11–5. Buffalo won

Table III. NFL Final Standings and Play-offs, 1980

AMERICAN CONFERENCE			
Eastern Division	W	L	T
*Buffalo	11	5	0
New England	10	6	0
Miami	8	8	0
Baltimore	7	9	0
Jets	4	12	0
Central Division			
*Cleveland	11	5	0
*Houston	11	5	0
Pittsburgh	9	7	0
Cincinnati	6	10	0
Western Division			
*San Diego	11	5	0
*Oakland	11	5	0
Denver	8	8	0
Kansas City	8	8	0
Seattle	4	12	0
NATIONAL CONFERENCE			
Eastern Division			
*Philadelphia	12	4	0
*Dallas	12	4	0
Washington	6	10	0
St. Louis	5	11	0
Giants	4	12	0
Central Division			
*Minnesota	9	7	0
Detroit	9	7	0
Chicago	7	9	0
Green Bay	5	10	1
Tampa Bay	5	10	1
Western Division			
*Atlanta	12	4	0
*Los Angeles	11	5	0
San Francisco	6	10	0
New Orleans	1	15	0

*Qualified for play-offs.

Play-offs

Wild-card round
Dallas 34, Los Angeles 13
Oakland 27, Houston 7

American semifinals
Oakland 14, Cleveland 12
San Diego 20, Buffalo 14

National semifinals
Dallas 30, Atlanta 27
Philadelphia 31, Minnesota 16

American finals
Oakland 34, San Diego 27

National finals
Philadelphia 20, Dallas 7

Super Bowl
Oakland 27, Philadelphia 10

its first divisional title since 1966 and made its first play-off appearance since 1974. Cleveland gained the play-offs for the first time since 1972.

The NFL continued its trend toward more passing, passing yards gained, total yards gained, and scoring, as it marked the three highest-scoring weekends in its history. San Diego best exemplified the trend, which had been spurred by rules that made it harder to rush the passer and cover receivers. San Diego quarterback Dan Fouts set NFL records with 4,715 passing yards and at least 300 yd in eight games, and he led the league with 8.01 yd per pass. As a team the Chargers set records with 372 first downs, 6,410 total yards (400.6 per game), and 4,531 net passing yards (283.2 per game).

San Diego's Kellen Winslow led the league with 89 catches, an NFL record for tight ends. Teammates John Jefferson and Charlie Joiner were second and third in the AFC, and Jefferson led the NFL with 1,340 receiving yards. Brian Sipe (*see* BIOGRAPHIES) of Cleveland joined Fouts and Joe Namath as the only NFL passers ever to gain at least 4,000 yd in a season. Sipe led the NFL in efficiency rating. His 30 touchdown passes tied Fouts for the AFC lead, and his .025 percentage of passes intercepted was the NFL's lowest.

In his third season Earl Campbell of Houston won his third NFL rushing championship with 1,934 yd, the second highest total in NFL history. Although injuries kept him out of one entire game and two halves, Campbell set records with 373 carries and four 200-yd games.

But popular coach O. A. "Bum" Phillips was fired after Houston's play-off defeat against Oakland because critics said his offense lacked imagination. The only coach to lose his job during the season was Dick Nolan of New Orleans, which lost a record 15 of 16 games.

Lester Hayes of the Raiders led the league with 13 interceptions. Buffalo's defensive yield of 256.3 yd per game led the league, and it trailed only Washington in stopping the pass.

Buffalo halfback Joe Cribbs was the AFC's only rookie all-star, but other rookie running backs included Billy Sims of Detroit, who led the league with 16 touchdowns and ranked fifth in rushing; Curtis Dickey of Baltimore, who tied Jefferson and Campbell with an AFC-leading 13 touchdowns; and Earl Cooper, whose 83 catches beat San Francisco teammate Dwight Clark by one for the NFC lead. The .645 pass-completion record of second-year San Francisco quarterback Joe Montana was the NFL's best.

Los Angeles led the league with 174.9 rushing yards per game despite losing two injured halfbacks. Dallas led the NFL with 454 points, as Danny White capably replaced retired quarterback Roger Staubach. The Eagles led the league in total defense, allowing 277.7 yd per game and limiting 10 of 16 opponents to fewer than 100 yd rushing. They allowed a league-low of 222 points. Also for the Eagles, Ron Jaworski had the NFC's best passer-efficiency rating, but Harold Carmichael's streak of receptions in 127 consecutive games ended, leaving St. Louis's Mel Gray with the NFL's longest at 105.

WIDE WORLD

Oakland Raider quarterback Jim Plunkett fades back to pass in the first quarter of the Super Bowl in New Orleans, Louisiana, on January 25, 1981. Voted the game's most valuable player, Plunkett passed for three touchdowns to lead his team to a 27–10 victory.

Atlanta had a nine-game winning streak, the league's longest. Steve Bartkowski led the league with 31 touchdown passes, and the Falcons had the NFL's best rushing pair, William Andrews and Lynn Cain, who gained 2,222 yd. Minnesota clinched its 11th division title in 13 years. Its 230.5 passing yards per game led the conference.

New England (10–6) led the AFC in scoring with 441 points and had league leaders John Smith with 129 points, Horace Ivory with a 27.6-yd kickoff return average, and Stanley Morgan with a 22.5-yd average per reception. Other league leaders were Kansas City's J. T. Smith with a 14.5-yd punt return average, and the New York Giants' Dave Jennings with a 44.8-yd punting average.

Walter Payton of 7–9 Chicago won his fifth consecutive NFC rushing championship with 1,460 yd and became the NFL's fifth-ranked all-time rusher. He was ejected from a game after one of many incorrect officiating calls that resulted in increased insistence that the NFL use televised replays as officiating aids.

COLLEGE. The University of Georgia was the only undefeated major college team and clinched a national championship with a 17–10 victory over Notre Dame in the Sugar Bowl at New Orleans on New Year's Day 1981. Georgia, which finished with a 12–0 record and won the Southeast Conference, was led by running back Herschel Walker, whose 1,616 yd rushing were the most ever gained by a freshman. Walker's third-place finish in the Heisman Trophy voting also was the best ever for a freshman. Walker, who ranked fourth in rushing, was first in rushing touchdowns with 15.

South Carolina running back George Rogers won the Heisman, which honours the best college player, and Pittsburgh defensive end Hugh Green finished second. Green won the Lombardi Trophy for linemen, and his teammate, offensive tackle Mark May, won the similar Outland Trophy. Sec-

WIDE WORLD

Georgia's Scott Woerner (right) intercepts a pass thrown to Notre Dame's Pete Holohan during the Sugar Bowl, which Georgia won 17–10.

ond-ranked Pittsburgh finished 11–1 and led the major colleges' Division I-A of the National Collegiate Athletic Association with per-game defensive averages of 65.3 yd rushing and 205.5 total yards. Big Eight champion Oklahoma finished 10–2 with an 18–17 Orange Bowl victory against Florida State and set college records by running for 758 yd and gaining 875 total yards against Colorado on October 4. The third-ranked Sooners' offense ranked second in rushing, third in total offense, fourth in scoring, and first in yardage per pass attempt with 11.8. Florida State was ranked fifth with a 10–2 record. The Seminoles allowed only 7.7 points per game, the best among major teams.

Big Ten champion Michigan (10–2, ranked fourth) allowed only nine points in its last five games, including a 23–6 Rose Bowl victory against Washington. Washington won the Pacific Ten championship without requiring the help of conference sanctions against five schools declared ineligible for academic violations. Rounding out the top ten were 10–2 Alabama, which defeated 10–2 Southwest Conference champion Baylor 30–2 in the Cotton Bowl; 10–2 Nebraska; 10–2 Penn State; 9–2–1 Notre Dame; and 11–1 North Carolina, the Atlantic Coast Conference champion.

But the college season was punctuated by passing. Major college teams had their biggest increase in passing yardage and pass-run ration since separate offensive and defensive platoons were allowed in 1965, and they set all-time records of 50% of passes completed and 4.65 yd per offensive play. Jim McMahon, Brigham Young's junior quarterback, had the best passing totals in college football history. He set records with 4,571 passing yards, 4,627 total yards, 47 touchdown passes, 53 touchdowns produced, 10.27 yd per pass attempt, and 176.9 passing efficiency points, which gave him a bigger margin over the second-ranked passer than No. 2 had over No. 22. Brigham Young, the Western Athletic Conference champion, led the country with 46.7 points and 535 yd per game, and its 409.8 passing yards per game broke the old record by 35.6 yd. Tight end Clay Brown led the country with 15 touchdown catches.

Close behind McMahon was senior Neil Lomax of Portland (Ore.) State in the smaller colleges' Division I-AA. He passed for 4,094 yd and set career records with 13,220 passing yards, 13,345 total yards, 106 touchdown passes, and 120 touchdowns produced. He threw eight touchdown passes in his team's 105–0 victory against Delaware State. Portland State won other games 93–7 and 75–0. Other record-setting passers were Dave Wilson of Illinois with 621 yd in one game, Mark Herrmann of Purdue with 9,188 yd in a Division I-A career, and Joe Adams of Tennessee State with 81 touchdowns in a Division I-A career.

Rogers was the rushing leader with 1,781 yd, but Nebraska won the team rushing title with Jarvis Redwine's national high of 7.2 yd per carry. Nebraska also ranked second offensively in total yards and scoring, second in points allowed, and third in yards allowed. Amos Lawrence of North Carolina became the second player to run for 1,000 yd four seasons in a row.

The 1980 game of the 111-year-old Princeton-Rutgers series, college football's oldest, was won by Rutgers, 44–13. Yale won the Ivy League by defeating Harvard 14–0. Navy broke its series tie with Army by winning 33–6.

Canadian Football. Edmonton won its third consecutive Grey Cup with a 48–10 victory against Hamilton in the Canadian Football League championship game Nov. 23, 1980. Hamilton had led the Eastern Conference with only an 8–7–1 won-lost-tied record, while Edmonton topped the Western Conference at 13–3. Edmonton quarterback Warren Moon was selected the Grey Cup game's top offensive player after completing 21 of 33 passes for 398 yd and three touchdowns. Linebacker Dale Potter was named the game's top defensive player and top native Canadian.

Other Edmonton stars were receiver Tom Scott, who led the CFL with 13 touchdowns and 1,245 yd on his 73 catches and caught 12 for 174 yd and three touchdowns in the Grey Cup game; CFL scoring leader Dave Cutler with 158 points; linebacker Danny Ray Kepley, voted the CFL's best defensive player; tackle Mike Wilson, the league's top lineman; and Ed Jones, who tied Saskatchewan's Ken McEachern with a league-high ten interceptions.

Dieter Brock of 10–6 Winnipeg won the Schenley Award as the CFL's most outstanding player. Brock set CFL records with 304 completions in 514 passing attempts, and he led the league with 4,252 passing yards, 28 touchdown passes, and a .023 interception percentage. Among his teammates, Mike Holmes led the league with 79 catches, and running back William Miller was rookie of the year. Gerry Dattilio of Montreal, who led Eastern Conference quarterbacks, was named outstanding Canadian. James Sykes of Calgary led with 1,263 yd rushing. (KEVIN M. LAMB)

France

A republic of Western Europe, France is bounded by the English Channel, Belgium, Luxembourg, West Germany, Switzerland, Italy, the Mediterranean Sea, Monaco, Spain, Andorra, and the Atlantic Ocean. Area: 544,000 sq km (210,040 sq mi), including Corsica. Pop. (1980 est.): 53,752,000. Cap. and largest city: Paris (pop., 1979 est., 2,102,900). Language: French. Religion: predominantly Roman Catholic. President in 1980, Valéry Giscard d'Estaing; premier, Raymond Barre.

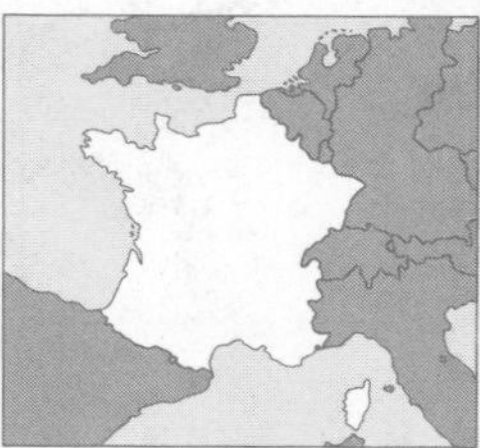

France

Domestic Affairs. In 1980 the main focus of attention in French political circles was the forthcoming presidential election in the spring of 1981. In the meantime there was further deterioration in the economic and social situation because of rising inflation and unemployment, threats to oil supplies, and increased racial violence. A solitary glimmer of peace and serenity was provided by the visit of Pope John Paul II.

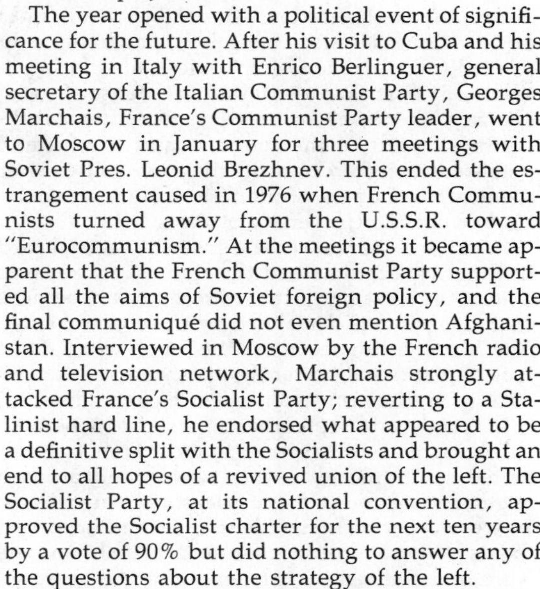

The year opened with a political event of significance for the future. After his visit to Cuba and his meeting in Italy with Enrico Berlinguer, general secretary of the Italian Communist Party, Georges Marchais, France's Communist Party leader, went to Moscow in January for three meetings with Soviet Pres. Leonid Brezhnev. This ended the estrangement caused in 1976 when French Communists turned away from the U.S.S.R. toward "Eurocommunism." At the meetings it became apparent that the French Communist Party supported all the aims of Soviet foreign policy, and the final communiqué did not even mention Afghanistan. Interviewed in Moscow by the French radio and television network, Marchais strongly attacked France's Socialist Party; reverting to a Stalinist hard line, he endorsed what appeared to be a definitive split with the Socialists and brought an end to all hopes of a revived union of the left. The Socialist Party, at its national convention, approved the Socialist charter for the next ten years by a vote of 90% but did nothing to answer any of the questions about the strategy of the left.

Social unrest began in March with a gathering in Paris of thousands of primary-school teachers from all parts of the country. Eventually, all branches of public education, from nursery

WIDE WORLD

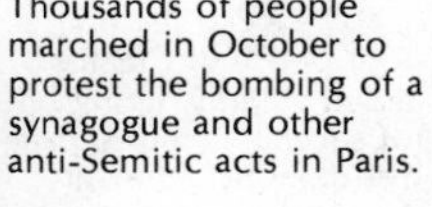

Thousands of people marched in October to protest the bombing of a synagogue and other anti-Semitic acts in Paris.

Foreign Aid: *see* Economy, World

Foreign Exchange: *see* Economy, World

schools to universities, were seriously disrupted by strikes.

On May 1, despite interunion conflicts, numerous marches of workers took place throughout the country in an atmosphere of calm. In Paris about 50,000 people took part. Later, 900 sweepers from the Paris metro (subway) struck for five weeks for higher wages and improved working conditions; they were followed by their colleagues in the railways and the postal order division of the post office. But major industries were not involved.

Both the Confédération Général du Travail (CGT) and the Confédération Française Démocratique du Travail (CFDT) trade union bodies called for a national day of strikes on May 13 in defense of social security. There was a massive response from workers in all parts of the country, and the turmoil persisted to some extent in the universities after the death of a demonstrator (though he was not a student) at the University of Paris VII.

A strike of workers in the state electricity board in June, called to defend the right to strike, was among the most significant in recent years because of the power cuts demanded by the CGT and CFDT. The board estimated that 54% of its work force took part and that power supplies were reduced by 50% with disastrous consequences for industry.

In August and September the strike of fishermen in Boulogne, which spread to most French ports, halted sea traffic for several weeks and aroused anger among tourists and pleasure-boat owners. There were violent incidents at Cherbourg and Calais, where several thousand British tourists were immobilized by barriers composed of trawlers, the crews of which were demanding maintenance of employment levels and compensation for fuel price rises. The Navy intervened in Fos, near Marseille, and Antifer, near Le Havre, to allow tankers to get through, and there were fierce confrontations with water hoses and tear gas, after which the blockade in most ports was lifted.

At a general meeting of 699 fishermen, 399 voted to resume work, adopting the line proposed by the CFDT in preference to that of the CGT and thus ending the most serious crisis in the history of an industry that gave employment directly to 25,000 people and indirectly to more than 100,000. Speaking in Nantes, Édmond Maire (CFDT) denounced "the total alignment of the CGT with the sectarian policy of the Communist Party," which was read as a confirmation of the undeclared war between Maire and Georges Séguy of the CGT, as well as of the disunity of the left.

In contrast to this turmoil, the visit of Pope John Paul II to France from May 30 to June 2 was a healing interlude that aroused extraordinary fervour. Constantly stressing the preeminence of man in a consumer society, the pontiff brought calm to troubled minds. Arriving at Orly Airport, the pope was greeted in Paris on the Champs-Elysées by Pres. Valéry Giscard d'Estaing (with whom he later had a private talk), and crowds attended his appearances at gatherings and church masses. The working session with the French bishops, during which John Paul II gave an uncompromising review of the situation of religion in France, was the most important event of the trip. It was followed by an enthusiastic vigil with young people at the Parc des Princes and a stop at the Sacré-Coeur church. Before he ended his visit at Lisieux, the pope spoke of the role of culture and education at the UNESCO headquarters in Paris: "Yes, the future of mankind does depend on culture; yes, the peace of the world does depend on the primacy of the spirit."

Unfortunately, calls for peace did not prevent a renewal of violence. In Neuilly in July Shahpur Bakhtiar, Iran's last prime minister under the for-

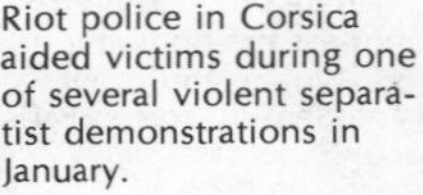

Riot police in Corsica aided victims during one of several violent separatist demonstrations in January.

WIDE WORLD

AGIP/PICTORIAL PARADE

Prime Minister Margaret Thatcher of Great Britain was the guest of Pres. Valéry Giscard d'Estaing when she visited France in September.

mer shah, escaped assassination, but a policeman and a woman were killed. A few days later Salah al-Bitar (*see* OBITUARIES), former Syrian premier and co-founder of the Ba'ath Party, was assassinated in Paris. During the previous two years there had been 12 deaths in France in the course of such settlements of accounts between rival factions from the Middle East.

Following a series of anti-Semitic attacks in September directed against buildings in Paris belonging to the Jewish community, the violence reached a peak in October with the bombing of a synagogue on the Rue Copernic near the Place Victor Hugo. The explosion of plastic explosive killed four people, caused many serious injuries, and inflicted much damage. There was some uncertainty about the perpetrators of the crime, who might have been neo-Nazis or left-wing revolutionaries. In any event there was a wave of universal indignation in France, where the outrage was compared with those in Antwerp, Bologna, and Munich.

A demonstration in Paris, organized by the mouvement contre le racisme et pour l'amitié entre les peuples, an antiracist movement, was joined by some 200,000 people who marched in a four-hour procession. To the trade unions and left-wing parties that took part were added parliamentarians and groups from the Jewish community. While demonstrations were also taking place outside Paris, President Giscard made a statement in the Council of Ministers that amounted to an appeal for the unity of the French people: "Let us together reject the hideous seeds of intolerance, terrorism, and racism."

In the political field the elections to the Senate, which were held on September 28 for one-third of the seats in the upper house, made little basic change in the composition of that chamber. The 98 seats to be filled were evenly divided between 49 reelected members and 49 new ones, among them 20 Socialists, 12 from the Union pour la Démocratie Française (UDF), and 9 from the Rassemblement pour la République (RPR). In addition, the election demonstrated (and served to accentuate further) the deterioration in relations between the Socialists and the Communists. The Communist Party's decision not to withdraw its candidates in the second round in several départements did not prevent the Socialist Party from making a noticeable gain (21 outgoing members against 30 newly or reelected). But the left wing as a whole did not advance as much as it might have hoped on the basis of its successes in earlier cantonal and municipal elections.

In view of the presidential election to be held in the spring of 1981, Premier Raymond Barre's third government team was not subject to any major changes. However, it did become more closely allied to President Giscard, though without any modification of its internal political balance. The posts of three secretaries of state were abolished: those of Marcel Cavaille in the Ministry of Housing, as a result of his resignation after electoral defeat, and those of Jacques Pelletier (education) and Marc Becam (interior) after their election as senators for Aisne and for Finistère, respectively. Nonetheless, some undoubted "Giscardiens" were promoted: Yvon Bourges, elected to the Senate, was replaced in the Ministry of Defense by Joël Le Theule, a specialist on military matters; he, in turn, was succeeded as minister of transport by Daniel Hoeffel, while Robert Galley, minister for cooperation, also elected to the Senate, retained his post. At the same time, Jean-François Deniau, minister for foreign trade, ceded that post to Michel Cointat, RPR deputy for Ille-et-Vilaine, and became minister-delegate to the premier in charge of administrative reform. After Le Theule's death in December, Galley took over defense in addition to his cooperation post.

According to the president this government was to remain in office until the spring of 1981 "except in the event of changes in personal circumstances." But its task would be a daunting one, with inflation rates expected to reach 13–14% for 1980, unemployment rising to 1.5 million, and a considerable balance of trade deficit. At the end of October the government raised its third loan for the year (Fr 10 billion over six years at a record rate of 13.8%, making a total of Fr 30 billion since Jan. 1, 1980); but it was able to predict that the budgetary deficit for the year, expected to reach between Fr 30 billion and Fr 35 billion, would be almost covered by long-term, nonmonetary resources, thus helping to reduce inflation.

Any predictions concerning the presidential elections seemed premature, since most of the major political parties with the exception of the Communists had postponed their choice of candidate until early 1981. The Bokassa affair (the assertion by the former emperor of the Central African Empire that he had given diamonds to Giscard, his wife, and his cousins, an allegation denied by the president); the polemic on the attitude of Michel Poniatowski (*see* BIOGRAPHIES), former minister of the interior, over the assassination of Jean de Broglie; and the queries surrounding the circumstances under which Communist leader Marchais was resident in Germany during World War II gave a foretaste of the low punches that were certain to be thrown by the contestants once the campaign got under way.

Foreign Affairs. The main guidelines of the government's policies were the preservation of détente between East and West, despite the taking of the U.S. hostages in Iran, the Soviet intervention in Afghanistan, and the boycott by many nations of the Olympic Games in Moscow; the ensuring of oil imports at a satisfactory level, despite the Iran-Iraq war; and the advance of a united Europe.

A sign of the times was the ten-day visit of President Giscard to the Persian Gulf and Jordan in March; included in his itinerary were Kuwait, Bahrain, Qatar, the United Arab Emirates, and Saudi Arabia. The trip filled a gap in French foreign relations. As early as 1967, first Gen. Charles de Gaulle and then Georges Pompidou had set in motion a French rapprochement with the Arab nations at the expense of Israel. But Giscard was the first French president to pay official visits to North Africa, Egypt, Saudi Arabia, and the Gulf states—a vital region that supplied France with 70% of its oil. In October, en route to Beijing (Peking) to reinforce French relations with China, he again held talks in Abu Dhabi with Sheikh Zaid ibn Sultan an-Nahayan, president of the United Arab Emirates, who promised additional oil exports to France amounting to 2.5 million metric tons a year. However, this visit raised questions about the direction of diplomatic action that appeared to give precedence to commercial interests over other aspects of foreign policy, in particular when it was taken together with Giscard's January visit to India, coinciding with Indira Gandhi's return to power and resulting in the signing of eight agreements on bilateral cooperation; with the official visit to Paris in April of Venezuelan Pres. Luís Herrera Campins and its links to the energy crisis; with that of Mexican Pres. José López Portillo in May; and finally with the sale in October of naval arms worth Fr 14.4 billion to Saudi Arabia after nearly 2½ years of negotiation.

In the quite different field of détente, the important meeting in Warsaw in May between Giscard, Brezhnev, and Edward Gierek, preceding Giscard's visit to Finland, confirmed France's desire to carry on the East-West dialogue despite the tension that had arisen in relations between the Soviet Union and the U.S. On the other hand, in June at the meeting in Venice of the leaders of the seven main industrialized countries of the non-Communist world (U.S., Canada, Britain, West Germany, France, Italy, and Japan), U.S. Pres. Jimmy Carter did not hesitate to warn the U.S.'s allies against "Soviet expansionism."

However, it was in the strengthening of Europe under the impetus of Giscard that the year's most spectacular progress was made. On May 30 the nine member nations of the EEC (France, West Germany, Belgium, The Netherlands, Luxembourg, Italy, the U.K., Denmark, and Ireland) reached agreement on reducing Britain's contribution to the organization's budget. Following the 17th meeting of the European Council in Venice on June 12 and 13, Giscard welcomed the fact that the Council (the heads of government of the EEC nations) had "regained its status and its character," adding: "Europe is steadily emerging as one of the

FRANCE

Education. (1979–80) Primary, pupils 5,405,056, teachers (1978–79) 197,229; secondary, pupils 3,844,733; teachers (1978–79) 235,715; vocational, pupils 1,253,666, teachers (1978–79) 100,973; teacher training, students 15,823, teachers (1978–79) 2,582; higher (universities only), students 859,646, teaching staff (1978–79) 41,978.

Finance. Monetary unit: franc, with (Sept. 22, 1980) a free rate of Fr 4.19 to U.S. $1 (Fr 10.08 = £1 sterling). Gold, SDR's, and foreign exchange (June 1980) U.S. $29,535,000,000. Budget (1980 est.): revenue Fr 494 billion; expenditure Fr 525 billion. Gross national product (1978) Fr 2,135,100,000,000. Money supply (May 1980) Fr 598.1 billion. Cost of living (1975 = 100; June 1980) 162.8.

Foreign Trade. (1979) Imports Fr 454,690,-000,000; exports Fr 427,950,000,000. Import sources: EEC 50% (West Germany 18%, Italy 10%, Belgium-Luxembourg 9%, The Netherlands 6%, U.K. 6%); U.S. 8%; Saudi Arabia 5%. Export destinations: EEC 53% (West Germany 17%, Italy 11%, Belgium-Luxembourg 10%, U.K. 8%, The Netherlands 5%); U.S. 5%. Main exports: machinery 19%; motor vehicles 13%; chemicals 12%; food 11%; iron and steel 7%. Tourism (1978): visitors 26,846,000; gross receipts U.S. $5,903,000,000.

Transport and Communications. Roads (1979) 802,896 km (including 4,896 km expressways; excluding *c.* 700,000 km rural roads). Motor vehicles in use (1979): passenger 18,440,000; commercial 2,364,000. Railways: (1978) 34,096 km; traffic (1979) 52,250,000,000 passenger-km, freight 70,681,-000,000 net ton-km. Air traffic (1979): 32,782,000,-000 passenger-km; freight 2,031,300,000 net ton-km. Navigable inland waterways in regular use (1978) 6,-658 km; freight traffic 11,594,000,000 ton-km. Shipping (1979): merchant vessels 100 gross tons and over 1,247; gross tonnage 11,945,837. Telephones (Jan. 1978) 17,519,000. Radio licenses (Dec. 1976) 17,441,000. Television licenses (Dec. 1977) 14,903,-000.

Agriculture. Production (in 000; metric tons; 1979): wheat 19,393; barley 11,238; oats 1,675; rye 360; corn 10,293; potatoes 7,139; sorghum 340; sugar, raw value 4,305; rapeseed 480; tomatoes 825; cauliflowers 425; carrots (1978) 518; green peas (1978) 515; apples 2,950; peaches (1978) 465; wine 8,456; tobacco 52; milk 31,800; butter *c.* 566; cheese *c.* 1,044; beef and veal 1,810; pork 1,830; fish catch (1978) 796; timber (cu m; 1978) 30,339. Livestock (in 000; Dec. 1978): cattle 23,510; sheep *c.* 11,543; pigs *c.* 11,745; horses (1978) *c.* 375; chickens 178,785.

Industry. Index of production (1975 = 100; 1979) 117. Fuel and power (in 000; 1979): coal (metric tons) 18,617; electricity (kw-hr) 241,124,000; natural gas (cu m) 7,760,000; manufactured gas (cu m; 1977) 6,040,000. Production (in 000; metric tons; 1979): iron ore (30% metal content) 31,665; pig iron 20,383; crude steel 23,361; bauxite 1,960; aluminum 574; lead 152; zinc 266; cement 28,826; cotton yarn 220; cotton fabrics 159; wool yarn 138; man-made fibres 313; sulfuric acid 4,908; petroleum products (1978) *c.* 110,400; fertilizers (nutrient content; 1978–79) nitrogenous *c.* 1,781, phosphate *c.* 1,459, potash *c.* 1,831; passenger cars (units) 3,732; commercial vehicles (units) 468. Merchant shipping launched (100 gross tons and over; 1979) 728,000 gross tons.

independent elements which have their own responsibility in the interplay of the major forces in the world."

This atmosphere surrounded the fifth annual Franco-British summit, held in Paris in September. After a year of domestic strife, this summit, particularly in comparison with that held in London in November 1979, seemed to mark a reconciliation. "The entente cordiale is in good heart," U.K. Prime Minister Margaret Thatcher concluded, though this did not mean that differences of opinion over Europe had been eliminated. The discussions were concerned rather with a "joint reflection" on major world problems. "Restoring Europe to its place" was also the central theme of Giscard's meeting in West Germany with Chancellor Helmut Schmidt, in July. *The Times* of London remarked on that occasion that the Franco-German rapprochement was one of those permanent changes in historical relationships that only a cataclysm could undo. (JEAN KNECHT)

See also Dependent States.

Gabon

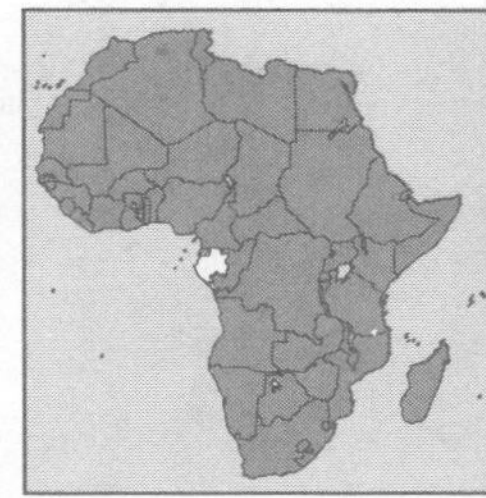

Gabon

A republic of western equatorial Africa, Gabon is bounded by Equatorial Guinea, Cameroon, the Congo, and the Atlantic Ocean. Area: 267,667 sq km (103,347 sq mi). Pop. (1978 est.): 1,300,200. Cap. and largest city: Libreville (pop., 1978 est., 225,200). Language: French and Bantu dialects. Religion: traditional tribal beliefs; Christian minority. President in 1980, Omar Bongo; premier, Léon Mébiame.

Reelected on Dec. 30, 1979, by 99.85% of votes cast, Omar Bongo entered upon his third term as president of Gabon. Legislative elections were held in February 1980 for candidates proposed by the Gabonese Democratic Party, and a Cabinet reorganization followed. The nation's financial situation was considerably improved after the near-disastrous expense of acting as host to the Organization of African Unity's 1977 summit meeting in Libreville. Gabon's CFA Fr 575 billion debt at the end of 1977 had fallen to CFA Fr 365 billion in 1980.

Relations with France were strengthened. Robert Galley, France's minister of cooperation, paid a visit to Gabon in May; combined Franco-Gabonese military maneuvers were held in June; the centenary of the founding of Francaville by the French explorer Pierre Savorgnan de Brazza was celebrated in July; and Bongo visited France officially at the end of September.

Bongo was disturbed by the deteriorating situations in neighbouring Congo, Central African Republic, and Chad. He tried on several occasions to secure a peaceful settlement to the civil war in Chad, and he made the Central African Republic a CFA Fr 1 billion loan. (PHILIPPE DECRAENE)

GABON

Education. (1978–79) Primary, pupils 141,569, teachers 3,088; secondary, pupils 20,344, teachers 1,000; vocational, pupils 3,405, teachers 256; teacher training, students 2,008, teachers 108; higher, students 1,247, teaching staff 235.

Finance. Monetary unit: CFA franc, with (Sept. 22, 1980) a parity of CFA Fr 50 to the French franc (free rate of CFA Fr 210 = U.S. $1; CFA Fr 504 = £1 sterling). Budget (1980 est.) balanced at CFA Fr 313.7 billion.

Foreign Trade. Imports (1978) *c.* CFA Fr 139 billion; exports (1979) CFA Fr 368 billion. Import sources: France 55%; U.S. 6%. Export destinations (1978): France 25%; U.S. 20%; Argentina 11%; Brazil 8%; Gibraltar 8%; West Germany 6%; Chile 5%. Main exports (1978): crude oil 72%; manganese ore 10%; uranium and thorium ores 8%; timber 6%.

Transport and Communications. Roads (1979) 7,082 km. Motor vehicles in use (1976): passenger *c.* 17,400; commercial (including buses) *c.* 12,700. Railways (1979) *c.* 185 km. Air traffic (1978): 87 million passenger-km; freight 700,000 net ton-km. Telephones (Dec. 1973) 11,000. Radio receivers (Dec. 1977) 95,000. Television receivers (Dec. 1977) 9,000.

Agriculture. Production (in 000; metric tons; 1978): cassava *c.* 107; corn 9; peanuts 6; bananas *c.* 8; plantains *c.* 63; palm oil *c.* 1; coffee *c.* 1; cocoa *c.* 4; timber (cu m) *c.* 2,289. Livestock (in 000; 1978): cattle 3; pigs *c.* 6; sheep 96; goats 89.

Industry. Production (in 000; metric tons; 1978): uranium 1; crude oil (1979) 10,786; natural gas (cu m) 56,200; manganese ore (metal content) *c.* 840; petroleum products *c.* 1,340; electricity (kw-hr) 436,000.

Gambia, The

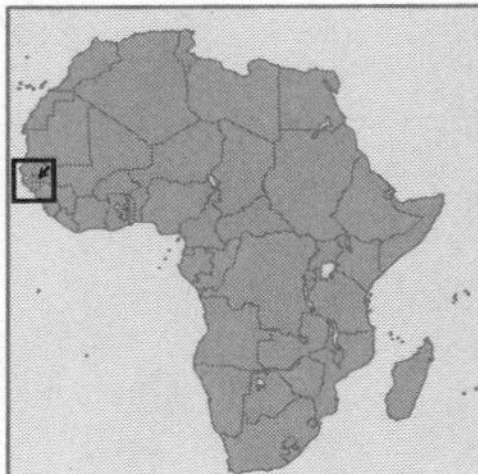

The Gambia

A small republic and member of the Commonwealth of Nations, The Gambia extends from the Atlantic Ocean along the lower Gambia River in West Africa and is surrounded by Senegal. Area: 10,690 sq km (4,127 sq mi). Pop. (1980 est.): 601,000, including (1973) Malinke 37.7%; Fulani 16.2%; Wolof 14%; Dyola 8.5%; Soninke 7.8%; others 15.8%. Cap. and largest city: Banjul (pop., 1980 est., 47,700). Language: English (official). Religion: predominantly Muslim. President in 1980, Sir Dawda Jawara.

At the beginning of September 1980 rainfall was below average, and 1979 had been a bad year for agriculture, producing a fall in gross domestic product for 1979–80. Peanut (groundnut) production was the lowest in 12 years. Despite this, average earnings were higher and the inflation rate, one of the lowest in the world, was kept down for the fourth successive year. The Gambia's economy in 1980 was adversely affected not only by drought (necessitating external aid) but also by oil price rises and unfavourable terms of trade. It was against this background that Minister of Finance Alhaji Mohamadu Cadi Cham presented the budget in June.

Major development projects attracted interna-

GAMBIA, THE

Education. (1978–79) Primary, pupils 32,196, teachers 1,241; secondary, pupils 7,464, teachers 416; vocational (1977–78), pupils 401, teachers 34; teacher training (1977–78), students 193, teachers 15.

Finance. Monetary unit: dalasi, with (Sept. 22, 1980) a free rate of 1.66 dalasis to U.S. $1 (par value of 4 dalasis = £1 sterling). Budget (1979–80 est.): revenue 76,531,000 dalasis; expenditure 72,495,000 dalasis.

Foreign Trade. (1979) Imports 265,510,000 dalasis; exports 109,820,000 dalasis. Import sources (1977–78): U.K. 26%; China *c.* 10%; France 8%; West Germany 7%; U.S. 6%. Export destinations (1977–78): U.K. 41%; France 27%; Switzerland 15%; The Netherlands 9%; Portugal 7%; West Germany 5%. Main exports: peanuts and by-products 71%.

French-Canadian Literature: *see* Literature

French Guiana: *see* Dependent States

French Literature: *see* Literature

Friends, Religious Society of: *see* Religion

Fuel and Power: *see* Energy

Furniture Industry: *see* Industrial Review

Furs: *see* Industrial Review

tional backing. A $250 million contract, partly financed by the African Development Bank and the World Bank, was awarded to a French consortium for a range of construction jobs in the country.

The Gambia maintained close relations with Senegal. In November some 150 Senegalese troops were sent to The Gambia after Banjul accused Libya of threatening invasion and broke off diplomatic relations with that country. At the end of October a Libyan-supported coup attempt was crushed with the aid of Senegalese troops.

(GUY ARNOLD)

Gambling

Despite the recession, gambling revenues in the United States rose in 1980, especially during the early part of the year. Gross taxable revenue in the Nevada casinos increased 15.4% during the first six months of the year compared with the same period in 1979. Atlantic City, N.J., opened its fourth legal casino, the Brighton, in August, and during the remainder of that month the new enterprise won $4.9 million. A new daily game in Illinois pushed state lottery revenues to more than $93 million for the 12 months ended June 30, a 43% increase over the previous year. In 1979 the states gained $1.9 billion from gambling, up from $509 million in 1970. Late in 1980, however, casinos in Nevada were reporting declines.

Gambling continued during 1980 to be one of the major leisure activities in the U.K. During 1979 nearly £12,000 million was bet, principally on horse and dog racing, football pools, bingo, slot machines, lotteries, and in casinos. The most popular form of gambling in terms of the number of participants was football (soccer) pool betting, on which approximately 15 million people staked some £320 million. In cash terms the overall increase in the level of betting over the previous year was broadly in line with the level of inflation, but this varied from one form of gambling to another, with casinos showing the greatest growth.

Among the highlights of the year were several record payoffs. On October 2 a Chilean won $1.7 million at the casino in Baden-Baden, West Germany, when his number 17 came up three times in a row. This was the largest payoff by a West German casino to a single player. A week earlier a U.S. record was set when a man bet $777,000 on three rolls of the dice at the Horseshoe Club in Las Vegas, Nev., and walked away with winnings of $1.5 million. In Canada on October 31 a man won $1,907,452.70 in the Ontario lottery, the largest tax-free lottery prize in North America. On a $2 wager in which he correctly chose the winners of the second through seventh horse races at Hollywood Park in California, a bettor won $305,668.

Illegal activities involving gambling continued to give cause for concern to the law enforcement authorities during 1980. One large public company was held to have been guilty of malpractices in the conduct of its London casinos, and all of the firm's London clubs were subsequently closed. Police action also resulted in charges being preferred against a number of persons employed in the casinos owned by another public company, and objections were lodged against the renewal of gaming licenses for all its London and provincial clubs.

In the U.S. a bomb set by extortionists demanding $3 million exploded in August in Harvey's Resort Hotel casino at Stateline, Nev., causing considerable damage to the 11-story building. No one was killed or injured because time had been

Casino gambling, which accounts for more than half the bets placed each year, has prompted the opening of four new chapters of Gamblers Anonymous in New Jersey.

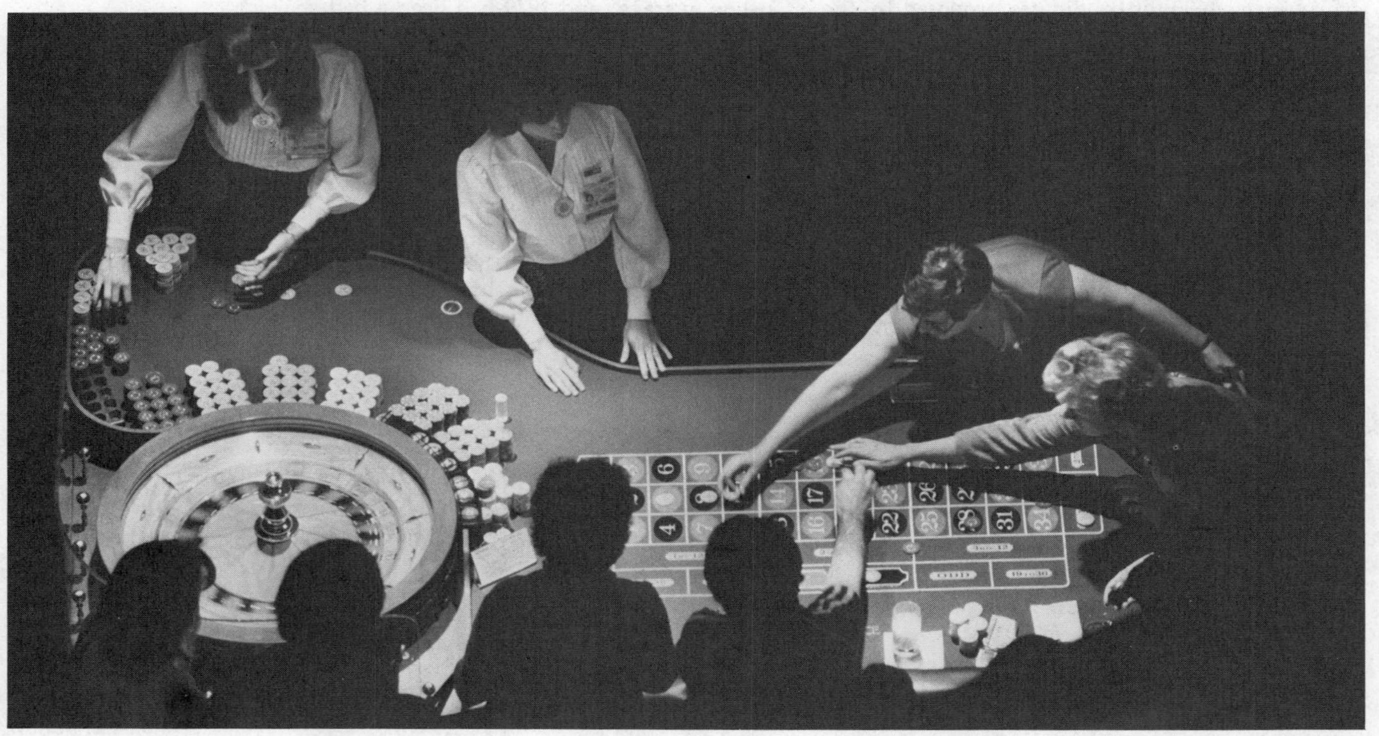

GERALD S. WILLIAMS—PHILADELPHIA INQUIRER

WIDE WORLD

Pennsylvania's acting attorney general, Harvey Bartle III (left), announced on September 19 that a scandal had been uncovered in the Pennsylvania lottery. Six persons were implicated as conspirators in an attempt to rig the winning numbers.

allowed to evacuate all those in Harvey's and nearby. In Pennsylvania on September 19 the television announcer who conducted the state's daily lottery along with a lottery official and four other persons were charged by a grand jury with conspiring to rig a lottery drawing, thereby fraudulently winning more than $1 million. Also during the year the federal government successfully prosecuted cases of horse-race fixing in New York, Massachusetts, and Pennsylvania.

(DAVID R. CALHOUN; GBGB)

See also Equestrian Sports.

Games and Toys

Following the avalanche of first-generation microprocessor-based games and toys that arrived on the market in 1979, toy merchants in all parts of the world found themselves with unusually high inventories at the beginning of 1980. Prior to the 1979 Christmas season there had been widespread overstocking by retailers, and when this was followed by a drastic downturn in consumer spending, many toy manufacturers found themselves caught between investment in new technology and the world slump in trade.

In the U.S. retail sales of electronic toys were estimated at $500 million in 1979, representing about 10% of the total U.S. toy market. Optimists predicted that this figure would increase by 50% in 1980, and at the New York Toy Fair in February more than 300 electronic items were offered to trade buyers. However, increased competition, even though it resulted in substantial reductions

Game Playing

"It's constant decision-making, a funneling effect of everything you've done before." It satisfies "the need to escape from the ever-more unpleasant reality." "It is very definitely antireligious . . . it leaves them so open to Satanic spirits." "It's all a part of the irresponsibility that college undergraduates normally have, and it shouldn't be begrudged them."

The observers were not addressing drug addiction, sensitivity enhancement seminars, or conversion to an exotic religious cult. They were talking about playing games. The first three statements referred to Dungeons and Dragons, a role-playing adventure guided by rule books and the roll of special dice. The fourth came from a Stanford University student who had been waging a night-long computer-programming battle called Wheel Wars.

Games that emphasize fantasy and conflict or that pit one's mental abilities against an electronic computer have become extremely popular with adults and children alike. Among the more recent best sellers is Simon, a computerized memory game that razzes and rewards its human opponent with lights and sound. The continually swelling ranks of war gamers support annual conventions and a spate of periodicals. Requests for the most popular of the fantasy games, Dungeons and Dragons (D&D), are keeping games shops and campus bookstores depleted and grossing an annual $2.5 million for the inventor, a former shoe repairman from Wisconsin.

Persons of high intelligence have not proved immune to the lure of game playing, although they may invent their own kinds. One of the most arcane is played on U.S. campuses by "subcultures" of bright computer-science undergraduates who call themselves hackers. For solitary entertainment, these young adults spend long hours hacking—inconsequentially toying with complex programs—at the terminals of university computers. Together, they fight Wheel Wars, using ruthless strategies to frustrate opponents' tinkering with their programs or even to block opponents' access to terminals.

Do games actually sharpen wits and nourish the imagination? Or are they intellectual "black holes" that absorb one's time and talents and return nothing? Some former Wheel Wars players consider themselves lucky to have escaped with their sanity. Do their experiences foreshadow a newly emerging form of aberrant behaviour, comparable to alcoholism or compulsive gambling?

Anyone asking such questions must also consider the true purpose of human play. As one ex-hacker concluded: "To me, as one matures, the highest forms of play cease to be consumptive and begin to be productive. . . . there is nothing wrong with consumptive play in an appropriate setting and appropriate circumstances. Middle-aged adults enjoy Great America. . . . nonetheless, I don't believe it is the highest form of play that they should be capable of."

(CHARLES M. CEGIELSKI)

MARIO RUIZ

Toy industry officials expected the total sales of electronic games to reach about $750 million in 1980.

in the prices of handheld microprocessor-based games and other electronic toys, did not persuade buyers to loosen their purse strings.

U.S. observers of the toy trade saw 1980 as a "back-to-basics" year. Consumers were reported to have spent more time in their homes, a result of which was improved demand for staple games such as Monopoly and Scrabble; against the normal pattern, retailers were selling board games well during the summer season.

The spectre that had haunted the toy industry in recent years was the decline in the birthrate in the Western world, and while this had halted in a number of countries, there remained for the toy manufacturer an equally serious problem arising from the comparatively early maturing of children's tastes. This shortening of the period during which children were the recipients of toys resulted in the preschool sector of the industry currently accounting for about 50% of the world toy market. It was significant that such companies as Fisher-Price and Lego, which specialized in preschool toys, were the ones less seriously affected by the world depression.

The boom in roller skates that had begun in the U.S. in 1979 moved across the Atlantic in 1980, and skates were one of the few bright spots in European sales during the summer months. In general, however, the consumer emphasis shifted to the traditional staple items, especially those with a low price tag. An example in the U.K. was the success achieved by one manufacturer, Thomas Salter Ltd., in selling £750,000 worth of rub-on colour transfers.

A fad that grew to major proportions in the U.S. during the year was the riding of mechanical bulls. More than 400 of these $7,000 devices were installed in country and western bars and nightclubs throughout the nation, drawing large crowds and testing the skills of would-be cowboys with bucking action that increased in violence on a scale of one to ten. The original model was in Gilley's Club in Pasadena, Texas, which was popularized in the movie *Urban Cowboy*.

It was a difficult year for the leading British toy manufacturers, especially those whose production was geared to a high percentage of export business. Apart from high interest rates, particularly onerous for an industry whose products are heavily committed to the Christmas sales period, the increasing strength of the pound seriously affected the profitability of many firms. At the beginning of the year Lesney Products Ltd. announced a loss for 1979 of £3.6 million, increased to £6 million by mid-1980. Early in the year Europe's largest toy company, Dunbee-Combex-Marx Ltd., revealed a deficit of £18 million. This failure was in the main due to the fact that the company came to grief in the U.S., where it had acquired subsidiaries that it failed to integrate.

Far East toy manufacturers continued to dominate the export field, particularly with electronic and radio-controlled items. But there was a growing awareness, especially in Hong Kong, that there would be a slowing down of demand in their best markets, the U.S. and Europe. To compensate for this, extra efforts were made to sell toys in the Middle East and South America, which met with some success.

A further step toward an international safety standard for toys was taken by the International Committee of Toy Industries at a meeting held in Paris in the spring of 1980. There the final text of a voluntary standard was agreed to by toy manufacturers in the U.S., the U.K., France, West Germany, Italy, Spain, Japan, Hong Kong, South Korea, Canada, and Australia. The standard was in three parts, covering mechanical and physical hazards, flammability, and the chemical properties of toys. (THEODORE V. THOMAS)

Gardening

The National Herb Garden at the National Arboretum in Washington, D.C., was opened to the public on June 13, 1980. A gift of the Herb Society of America, with matching funds provided by Congress, the two-acre garden contained some 7,000 carefully selected herbal plants in a series of gardens. A historic rose garden featured intensely fragrant wild roses, many of which came from Europe. The specialty gardens included an American Indian garden with plants used by Indians of eastern North America as sources of medicines, dyes, poisons, food, and craft materials.

The U.S. Department of Agriculture (USDA) put new rules into effect to prevent spread of the gypsy moth. The new approach would concentrate manpower and funds in heavily infested areas. High-risk areas for 1980 included all of Rhode Island and portions of Maine, New Hampshire, Vermont, Massachusetts, Connecticut, New York, New Jersey, Pennsylvania, and Michigan. Articles moving from high-risk areas to or through unregulated areas had to be inspected, treated if necessary, and certified pest free. At least nine species of parasitic flies and wasps were being used by the USDA to fight the gypsy moth. Some of these also attack other destructive caterpillars.

The development by pests of resistance to pesticides, the increasing cost of these chemicals, plus their pollution of the environment and possible implication in human disease, drew attention to the need for combined biologic and chemical methods of pest and disease control. The trend was toward "supervised" control in which the level of infestation was carefully assessed prior to the application of a spray program, and monitoring continued throughout the season. In England about 2,500 ha (6,750 ac) of commercial orchards were being monitored, chiefly by growers, and this had brought about an average 35% reduction in the number of insecticide applications. In warmer areas of Europe, a reduction of over 50% had been achieved.

Three roses were 1981 All-America award winners: Bing Crosby, a slightly fragrant hybrid tea with medium-ripe-persimmon orange flowers in the spring and reddish-orange flowers in the fall, hybridized by Ollie Weeks of Ontario, Calif.; White Lightnin', a grandiflora with pure white, ruffled flowers of intense fragrance, sometimes edged with a light pink blush, hybridized by Herbert C. Swim of southern California; and Marina, a large-flowered, slightly fragrant floribunda, hybridized by Reimer Kordes of Sparrieshoop, West Germany.

In the U.K. the Royal National Rose Society's Henry Edland medal for most fragrant rose went to Pristine, an ivory-pink hybrid tea from Jackson & Perkins. Margaret Merril (Harkness), winner of the Edland medal in 1978, received the Certificate of Fragrance at The Hague, Neth. The Golden Rose at West Flanders, Belg., went to a hybrid tea, Meialzonite (Meilland), and the Golden Rose at Orléans, France, to a floribunda, Patricia

PHOTOS, GEORGE TAMES—THE NEW YORK TIMES

The National Herb Garden (top), containing some 7,000 herbal plants, was opened to the public on June 13 in Washington, D.C. (Bottom) Trellised walkways, trees, and shrubs divide the area into individual gardens.

KEYSTONE

Claude Monet's garden, the subject of a number of his paintings, fell into disrepair after his death in 1926. Painstakingly restored to its former splendour by the Académie des Beaux-Arts, the garden was opened to the public in May.

German Democratic Republic

(Kordes). Another floribunda, Farouche (Meilland), won the Golden Rose at Geneva, Switz.

Gypsy, a hybrid pepper (Petoseed Co., Saticoy, Ga.), Apricot Brandy, a Celosia plumosa (T. Sakara & Co., Yokohama, Japan), and Blitz, a dwarf hybrid impatiens (Sluis & Groot BV, Enkhuizen, Neth.), were named 1981 award winners by All-America Selections.

Most textbooks state that when trees are pruned all branches must be cut flush with the trunk, but this was disputed by Alex L. Shigo, chief scientist of the USDA Forestry Sciences Laboratory, Durham, N.H. "We have learned that the collar that forms at the base of the branch should not be cut," he said. "This is extremely important. The cut should be made as close as possible to the collar, but the collar should not be removed."

R. B. Taylorson, botanist at the USDA Agricultural Research Center, Beltsville, Md., found that if most weed seeds can be forced to germinate at once and are killed with herbicides before a crop is planted, weed problems can be brought under control for many years. Using ethanol, he forced several annual weedy grasses and a few broadleaf weeds to germinate before their time. USDA plant pathologists George Papavizas and Jack Lewis found that turning the soil to a depth of 20 to 25 cm (8 to 10 in) was effective in combating *Rhizoctonia,* a fungus that attacks beans, radishes, sugarbeets, tomatoes, and other crops.

Government-controlled tests for purity and performance of cultivars demand that they be demonstrably distinct from each other. The price is the loss of old kinds, and, with them, the store of genetic variation accumulated over centuries. To correct this the National Vegetable Research Station in England set up a gene bank. The aim was to store a litre of seed of at least 9,000 vegetable cultivars, plus 3,000 of the more exotic tropical kinds already being stored at centres in Asia.

China and the U.S. began a cooperative effort to save valuable germ plasm. In the spring a team of U.S. scientists toured Chinese farms and experiment stations collecting seed or live specimens, and in the fall five U.S. botanists participated in a plant-collecting expedition sponsored by the Botanical Society of America and the Institute of Botany of the Chinese Academy of Sciences. Collections were to be shared by scientific institutions in the two countries, and specimens brought to the U.S., after checking for disease and insects, would be sent to four regional stations for propagation, evaluation, distribution, and maintenance.

(J. G. SCOTT MARSHALL; TOM STEVENSON)

See also Agriculture and Food Supplies; Environment; Life Sciences.
[355.C.2–3; 731.B.1]

Garment Industry: *see* Fashion and Dress

Gas Industry: *see* Energy

Gemstones: *see* Industrial Review

Genetics: *see* Life Sciences

Geochemistry: *see* Earth Sciences

Geology: *see* Earth Sciences

Geophysics: *see* Earth Sciences

German Democratic Republic

A country of central Europe, Germany was partitioned after World War II into the Federal Republic of Germany (Bundesrepublik Deutschland; West Germany) and the German Democratic Republic (Deutsche Demokratische Republik; East Germany), with a special provisional regime for Berlin. East Germany is bordered by the Baltic Sea, Poland, Czechoslovakia, and West Germany. Area: 108,325 sq km (41,825 sq mi). Pop. (1980 est.): 16,740,300. Cap. and largest city: East Berlin (pop., 1979 est., 1,333,900). Language: German. Religion (1969 est.): Protestant 80%; Roman Catholic 10%. General secretary of the Socialist Unity (Communist) Party and chairman of the Council of State in 1980, Erich Honecker; chairman of the Council of Ministers (premier), Willi Stoph.

Early in 1980 it seemed that the East German

GERMAN DEMOCRATIC REPUBLIC

Education. (1978–79) Primary, secondary, and vocational, pupils 2,485,386, teachers 167,424; higher, students 294,553, teaching staff (1977–78) 36,013.

Finance. Monetary unit: Mark of Deutsche Demokratische Republik, with (Sept. 22, 1980) a free rate of M 1.81 to U.S. $1 (M 4.34 = £1 sterling). Budget (1978 est.): revenue M 132,612,000,000; expenditure M 132,103,000,000. Net material product (at 1975 prices; 1978) M 161.1 billion.

Foreign Trade. (1978) Imports M 50,712,000,000; exports M 46,168,000,000. Import sources: U.S.S.R. *c.* 36%; Czechoslovakia *c.* 9%; Poland *c.* 8%; West Germany *c.* 7%; Hungary *c.* 6%. Export destinations: U.S.S.R. *c.* 36%; Czechoslovakia *c.* 10%; Poland *c.* 9%; Hungary *c.* 7%; West Germany *c.* 6%. Main exports: machinery and transport equipment 55%; durable consumer goods 15%; chemicals *c.* 10%; fuels and metals *c.* 10%.

Transport and Communications. Roads (1978) *c.* 119,000 km (including 1,655 km autobahns). Motor vehicles in use (1978): passenger 2,392,300; commercial 226,700. Railways (1978): 14,199 km (including 1,514 km electrified); traffic 22,320,000,000 passenger-km, freight 58,920,000,000 net ton-km. Air traffic (1978): 1,802,000,000 passenger-km; freight 62.3 million net ton-km. Navigable inland waterways in regular use (1978) 2,538 km; goods traffic 2,265,000,000 ton-km. Shipping (1979): merchant vessels 100 gross tons and over 453; gross tonnage 1,552,148. Telephones (Dec. 1978) 2,967,600. Radio licenses (Dec. 1978) 6,289,000. Television licenses (Dec. 1978) 5,540,000.

Agriculture. Production (in 000; metric tons; 1979): wheat *c.* 3,226; barley *c.* 3,635; rye *c.* 1,720; oats *c.* 400; potatoes *c.* 12,540; sugar, raw value *c.* 720; cabbages (1978) *c.* 540; rapeseed *c.* 232; apples *c.* 341; pork *c.* 1,124; beef and veal *c.* 380; fish catch (1978) 198. Livestock (in 000; Dec. 1978): cattle 5,572; sheep 1,965; pigs 11,734; goats 29; poultry 50,240.

Industry. Production (in 000; metric tons; 1978): lignite 253,264; electricity (kw-hr) 95,963,000; iron ore (39% metal content) 80; pig iron 2,560; crude steel 6,976; cement 12,521; sulfuric acid 971; petroleum products (1977) 18,893; fertilizers (nutrient content) nitrogenous 892, phosphate 413, potash 3,323; synthetic rubber 155; man-made fibres (1977) 286; passenger cars (units) 171.

government was just as concerned as West Germany that the freeze in relations between the superpowers following the Soviet invasion of Afghanistan should have as little effect as possible on links between the two German states. But the East German attitude changed later in the year with the outbreak of unrest in neighbouring Poland. *Abgrenzung,* withdrawal into the shell, again became the guiding principle of East German foreign policy. On October 13 the authorities greatly increased the minimum amount of money that had to be exchanged at the border by visitors from the West, and in subsequent weeks the number of visitors to East Berlin and East Germany had been cut by about 60%. This was a blow at the very heart of the West German government's *Deutschlandpolitik,* aimed at increasing contacts between the people of a divided nation.

In 1979 approximately 8.1 million visits were paid by West Berliners and West Germans to East Germany and East Berlin. This traffic exposed East Germany to Western influences. But it was calculated in East Berlin that the risks involved were outweighed by the advantages of economic ties with West Germany. Evidently, the risks in 1980 became too great. The normally mild-mannered East German Communist leader, Erich Honecker, did not dispel Western fears that the Soviet Union and its allies might intervene militarily in Poland. In a speech in Gera on October 12, he said Poland belonged inseparably to the socialist world.

This was not the first time that East Germany had raised the price of admission to Western visitors. It did so in 1973 but backed down a year later after West Germany had refused to extend an agreement on favourable credit terms. Under the current agreement, to expire at the end of 1981, East Germany was granted a yearly interest-free overdraft of up to DM 850 million (U.S. $452 million) on its trading account with West Germany. This generous concession, known as the swing, also benefited West Germany because it helped the East Germans pay for West German goods. The East German authorities explained their decision to raise the admission fees by pointing out that the value of the currencies of the capitalist countries had fallen in the past six years, while the purchasing power of their mark had risen. Moreover, the East Germans claimed that there was widespread speculation with their currency.

In late October East Germany announced the temporary suspension of visa-free travel to and from Poland, a clear sign of its increasing nervousness at the possible spread of the "Polish disease," and in early December its border with Poland was declared a "restricted area" closed to the West. The government also announced that the experiment with summer (daylight savings) time in 1980 was not to be continued in 1981. The time switch, it appeared, saved less energy than expected. West Germany had long resisted the European Economic Community's efforts to arrange a common summer time throughout the EEC, mainly to avoid being on a different time from East Germany. But West Germany did not plan to abandon summer time. There would now be difficulties in timetabling intra-German traffic, and the time difference would be most keenly felt in Berlin.

Nevertheless, the East German government was anxious to maintain close economic ties with West Germany. The East Germans needed export surpluses and loans. Honecker was intensely disappointed that the West German chancellor, Helmut Schmidt, postponed the trip he was to have made to East Germany in August, for the meeting would have strengthened his case that the two German nations had equal status and thus opened his way to meetings with other Western leaders.

SVEN SIMON/KATHERINE YOUNG

During the year the U.S.S.R. removed some of its troops stationed in East Germany.

As it was, Honecker visited Austria in November, his first official visit to a Western country.

The East German government renewed its efforts to persuade West Germany to recognize a separate East German nationality. Only in that event would East Germany consider lowering the age at which its people were allowed to visit the West. The West German government again refused to consider the matter.

A strike by some 600 West Berlin employees of the East German railway system for several weeks in September succeeded in paralyzing West Berlin's S-Bahn—the overhead railway—and in provoking an embarrassing political crisis. Freight and passenger traffic between West Germany and West Berlin was halted for a time, and rail traffic between Paris and Moscow, which normally passes through Berlin, was also brought to a standstill. The strikers demanded higher pay, better social benefits, and, imitating the Polish strikers, the free election of representatives to the East German government-controlled trade union confederation. Some 3,500 West Berliners worked for the East German railway, and they had a good case. They earned an average 25% less than their counterparts working for the West German railways. Their jobs were threatened by a program to make the system more efficient; their pensions were poor; and, if they were taken ill, they had to go to a hospital in East Berlin. The East German authorities showed little sympathy for the strikers' demands. (NORMAN CROSSLAND)

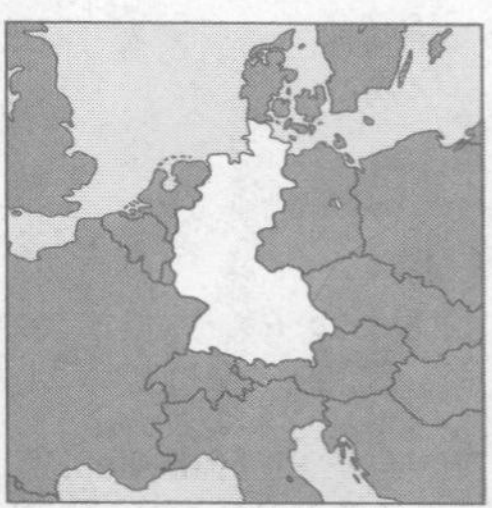

Federal Republic of Germany

Germany, Federal Republic of

A country of central Europe, Germany was partitioned after World War II into the Federal Republic of Germany (Bundesrepublik Deutschland; West Germany) and the German Democratic Republic (Deutsche Demokratische Republik; East Germany), with a special provisional regime for Berlin. West Germany is bordered by Denmark, The Netherlands, Belgium, Luxembourg, France, Switzerland, Austria, Czechoslovakia, East Germany, and the North Sea. Area: 248,667 sq km (96,011 sq mi). Pop. (1980 est.): 61,439,300. Provisional cap.: Bonn (pop., 1980 est., 286,200). Largest city: Hamburg (pop., 1980 est., 1,653,000). (West Berlin, which is an enclave within East Germany, had a population of 1,902,200 in 1980.) Language: German. Religion (1970): Protestant 49%; Roman Catholic 44.6%; Jewish 0.05%. President in 1980, Karl Carstens; chancellor, Helmut Schmidt.

In the federal election on Oct. 5, 1980, the coalition government led by Chancellor Helmut Schmidt (*see* BIOGRAPHIES) was confirmed in power with a substantially increased majority. Real economic growth was expected to reach about 2% in 1980 as compared with 4.4% in 1979.

Domestic Affairs. The electorate voted on October 5 for moderation. Franz-Josef Strauss, the chancellor candidate of the opposition, composed of the Christian Democratic Union (CDU) and the Bavarian Christian Social Union (CSU), lost because most voters considered him too far right of centre. The Free Democrats (FDP), junior partners in the coalition, achieved their success essentially as the guardians of centrism, a counterweight to the left wing of the Social Democratic Party (SPD).

For the federal chancellor, Helmut Schmidt, it was an impressive personal victory, even though his Social Democratic Party's performance was disappointing. Schmidt fought the election as the head of a coalition that had sworn to stick together, and the 11-year-old alliance emerged with a majority of 45 seats, as compared with 10 in the previous Bundestag (lower house of the federal Parliament).

Schmidt clearly had a higher popularity rating than his party. The CDU, less so than the CSU, suffered a mass desertion of traditional supporters, but these voters went to the FDP rather than to the SPD. It was estimated that at least a quarter of the FDP's 10.6% share of the total vote came from the CDU. Not surprisingly, the defections were heaviest in the Protestant north, where the candidacy of Strauss was particularly unpopular. In the country as a whole the CDU's vote fell by 4.1%, but the figures in the northern states of Lower Saxony and Schleswig-Holstein were 5.9 and 5.2%, respectively. A good many electors cast their second votes (each elector had two votes—one to choose a local constituency representative and the other in support of a party) for the FDP to ensure that it was returned to the Bundestag and thereby would continue the coalition. The quiet, factual campaign of the FDP leader, Hans-Dietrich Genscher, the foreign minister, won him considerable support. The FDP's success robbed Schmidt's party of its goal of achieving a majority in the Bundestag. The Social Democrat vote of 42.9% was only 0.3% above its 1976 result.

Although the FDP was content with its previous representation in the Cabinet—four ministers in key posts—the party made it clear that it would now wish to exert greater influence. Only once in the history of the Federal Republic had a party succeeded in winning an absolute majority, the CDU-CSU in 1957. At all other times a coalition had been necessary. As long as the FDP stayed in harness with Schmidt's party, there was little chance of a change.

In the days of Konrad Adenauer the CDU tended to benefit electorally at times of world tension. In 1980 Schmidt also reaped this bonus. The chancellor made détente, relations with Eastern Europe (the *Ostpolitik*), and foreign policy generally the main issues of his campaign. In the appalling event of war in central Europe, he said, West Germany would be hit first—and hardest. He claimed that the Eastern treaties, concluded in the early 1970s with the Soviet Union, Poland, and East Germany, had created a more relaxed situation, brought the two German states closer together, and enabled many thousands of ethnic Germans to leave Eastern Europe and settle in the West. Strauss accepted that the West had to live in peace with Eastern Europe and to trade with the Communist countries, but, he added, West Germany must not make any moral or intellectual concessions to the Communist system in East Germany or elsewhere

German Literature: *see* Literature

in Eastern Europe. He and some of his colleagues alleged that a "Moscow fraction" in Schmidt's party was determining the course of Social Democratic policy.

Strauss introduced some domestic issues into the campaign, initially with success. His attack on the high level of the national debt forced the SPD onto the defensive, but in a country with a still enviable low rate of inflation and with unemployment, though rising slowly, less of a burden than elsewhere, it was hard to persuade the well-heeled West Germans that they were on the road to economic ruin.

Negotiations between the Social Democrats and Free Democrats on the government's program for the new four-year term were mainly concerned with money. The 1981 budget was to grow by a mere 4.1%, and severe limitations were imposed on further state borrowing. Taxes on gasoline and spirits were to go up in April 1981, and all government departments were to cut spending. Defense expenditure could not be increased by 3% in real terms in 1981, as agreed upon by West Germany and the U.S. in 1978. It seemed that the U.S.'s most important European ally would be prepared to step up defense spending in that year by not more than 2%. The government said that if it stuck to the 3% target it would have to cut back heavily on social welfare with the risk of causing domestic unrest.

An automatic increase of 3%, the government argued, would not necessarily improve the strike power or defensive capability of the armed forces. But it was admitted that the delivery of vital new weapons systems to the forces, such as the Tornado multi-role combat aircraft and the Leopard II tank, would be slowed down. The U.S. insisted not only that West Germany stick to its target but also requested the Germans to make a hefty financial contribution toward stocking up supply bases for a possible reinforcement of U.S. troops in an emergency. The revised defense budget proposed in December called for an increase in real defense spending of 2.2%. Responding to criticism from U.S. Secretary of Defense Harold Brown, the West German government said it would try to reach the 3% goal in 1982.

The election in North Rhine-Westphalia on May 11 resulted in an overall majority for the SPD. But its coalition partner, the FDP, failed to poll the minimum 5% of the total votes needed to win seats, a shock that stimulated the FDP to campaign vigorously in the federal election. Similarly, in the state election in the Saarland on April 27 the SPD increased its share of the vote by 3.6% and won 24 seats. West Berlin excluded, this was the sixth successive state election in which the CDU lost support and the SPD gained ground. The CDU's vote fell by more than 5%, giving it 23 seats, 2 fewer than in the previous assembly. The FDP just about held its own by polling 6.9% and winning four seats. But the SPD, though emerging strongest, had to stay in opposition, the Saarland being the only state governed by a CDU–FDP coalition.

West Germany's environmentalists—the Green Party—looked more challenging as a movement with vague ideals than as a fledgling party with a program. They won six seats in the Baden-Württemberg state election on March 16 but then narrowly avoided a split at their party conference in Saarbrücken. A majority of the 800 delegates called for disbandment of NATO and the Warsaw Pact and creation of a demilitarized zone throughout Europe, with West Germany to make an exemplary unilateral start on disarmament. In the federal election the Greens gained only 1.5% of the vote.

SVEN SIMON/KATHERINE YOUNG

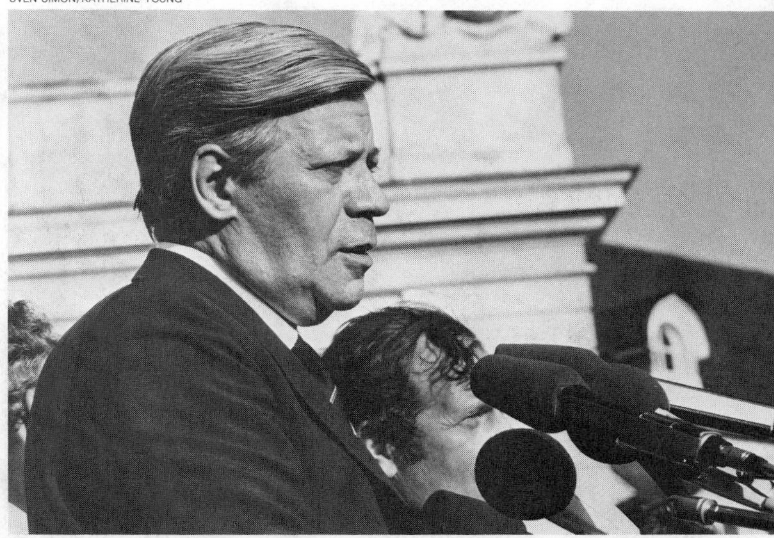

Chancellor Helmut Schmidt of West Germany scored an election triumph in October when his coalition party increased its majority from 10 to 45 seats in the lower house of Parliament.

Some clever rewording of resolutions on two major issues, the stationing of medium-range nuclear missiles in Western Europe and the further development of nuclear energy, enabled the SPD leadership to avoid a serious clash with the left at the party's conference in Essen, June 9–10. To suit the party's left wing, a resolution calling for the negotiation of a SALT III agreement to achieve a balance of nuclear forces was tailored to state that the purpose of negotiations would be to make the stationing of further medium-range nuclear missiles in Western Europe superfluous. The antinuclear energy lobby also got its views written into the party's election program; the conference decided that the option for nuclear power must remain open but that the option to abandon its development must be opened too.

The federal government found it necessary during the year to build a dike against the rising tide of foreigners seeking political asylum in West Germany. Approximately 150,000 applications were lodged by the end of 1980, ten times as many as in 1977. Fewer than 10% of them were approved, because most were not fleeing from political persecution but from unemployment and poverty. Well over half of them were Turks, and the rest included large numbers from Pakistan, India, Ethiopia, Afghanistan, and Vietnam, many having paid fees to unscrupulous agents at home for misleading advice. A fundamental reform of the asylum laws was postponed to the next Bundestag, but preliminary deterrent measures were rushed through: applicants would not be given work permits, at least for the first year of their stay in West Germany, nor would they receive children's allowances.

The security authorities had been bracing themselves for a terrorist attack during the autumn elec-

VLADIMIR MUSAELYAN—TASS/SOVFOTO

Pres. Leonid I. Brezhnev (left) and Premier Aleksey N. Kosygin (centre) of the U.S.S.R. greeted West German Chancellor Helmut Schmidt when he arrived in Moscow for talks in June.

tion campaign. But when it came, in the shape of a bomb that killed 13 people and injured more than 200 at the Munich Oktoberfest on September 26, it came, unexpectedly, from the extreme right. The bomb was planted by Gundolf Köhler, who was killed in the blast, but he was believed not to have acted alone. Köhler had been connected with an extreme right-wing group called Wehrsportgruppe Hoffmann. This "military sport group," led by commercial artist Karl-Heinz Hoffmann, had about 400 active members. Wearing military uniforms and heavily armed, they had been around Bavaria since the early 1970s but were thought harmless. The group was banned by the federal minister of the interior, Gerhart Baum, in January. Hoffmann and five of his supporters were arrested after the Munich explosion, but were released without suggestion of complicity.

German right-wing extremism in 1980 was disunited but increasingly militant. Some two million foreign workers in West Germany (plus dependents) and the influx of foreigners asking for political asylum fostered the distrust and fear of outsiders on which the extreme right fed. In 1980 five explosions were caused on property owned or occupied by Jews or foreigners. In August two Vietnamese were killed in an explosion at a hostel for "boat people" refugees in Hamburg.

The fight against left-wing terrorism met with considerable success, with the number of such terrorists on the "most wanted" list being reduced to 15. The improved efficiency of the federal criminal investigation department, its close collaboration with foreign police forces, and the removal of bureaucratic obstacles to cooperation between the security forces of the Länder (states) led to arrests and the discovery of hiding places. It had been assumed that the ringleaders of left-wing terrorist groups were out of the country, possibly in the Middle East. This assumption was proved wrong on July 25 when two terrorists were killed in a car crash near Ludwigsburg.

Pope John Paul II visited West Germany, November 15–19, the first papal visit to the land of the Reformation for nearly 200 years. The event raised a good deal of theological dust. Unflattering references to Martin Luther in a booklet published by the German Roman Catholic bishops caused offense among Protestants. And there was some bitter comment about St. Albert the Great (*c.* 1200–1280), at whose tomb in Cologne the pope paid homage. A Catholic woman theologian denounced St. Albert as a woman hater and a persecutor of Jews.

Foreign Affairs. West Germany supported U.S. policy in the Afghanistan and Iran crises with great reluctance and to the accompaniment of a chorus of criticism of U.S. Pres. Jimmy Carter. In regard to the Olympic Games in Moscow, West Germany held that it was up to the Soviet Union

GERMANY, FEDERAL REPUBLIC OF

Education. (1978–79) Primary, pupils 3,273,784; secondary, pupils 6,015,360; primary and secondary, teachers 430,979; vocational, pupils 526,469, teachers 31,467; higher, students 1,103,071, teaching staff 120,224.

Finance. Monetary unit: Deutsche Mark, with (Sept. 22, 1980) a free rate of DM 1.81 to U.S. $1 (DM 4.34 = £1 sterling). Gold, SDR's, and foreign exchange (June 1980) U.S. $53,867,000,000. Budget (federal; 1979 actual): revenue DM 186,780,000,000; expenditure DM 212,850,000,000. Gross national product (1979) DM 1,395,000,000,000. Money supply (June 1980) DM 226.6 billion. Cost of living (1975 = 100; June 1980) 122.4.

Foreign Trade. (1979) Imports DM 292,160,000,000; exports DM 314,620,000,000. Import sources: EEC 49% (The Netherlands 12%, France 11%, Italy 9%, Belgium-Luxembourg 8%, U.K. 6%); U.S. 7%. Export destinations: EEC 48% (France 13%, The Netherlands 10%, Belgium-Luxembourg 8%, Italy 8%, U.K. 7%); U.S. 7%; Austria 5%; Switzerland 5%. Main exports: machinery 28%; motor vehicles 15%; chemicals 13%; iron and steel 6%; textiles and clothing 5%. Tourism (1978): visitors 8,663,000; gross receipts U.S. $4,813,000,000.

Transport and Communications. Roads (1979) 482,000 km (including 7,292 km autobahns). Motor vehicles in use (1979): passenger 22,613,500; commercial 1,421,600. Railways: (1978) 31,700 km (including 10,984 km electrified); traffic (1979) 40,662,000,000 passenger-km, freight 66,159,000,000 net ton-km. Air traffic (1979): 19,843,000,000 passenger-km; freight 1,585,668,000 net ton-km. Navigable inland waterways in regular use (1978) 4,395 km; freight traffic 51,486,000,000 ton-km. Shipping (1979): merchant vessels 100 gross tons and over 1,926; gross tonnage 8,562,780. Shipping traffic (1979): goods loaded 35,540,000 metric tons, unloaded 120,980,000 metric tons. Telephones (1978) 24,743,000. Radio licenses (1978) 20,724,000. Television licenses (1978) 19,019,000.

Agriculture. Production (in 000; metric tons; 1979): wheat 7,971; barley 8,157; oats 2,999; rye 2,105; potatoes 8,747; sugar, raw value *c.* 3,333; apples 1,951; wine *c.* 714; cow's milk *c.* 24,000; butter *c.* 567; cheese 732; beef and veal *c.* 1,480; pork 2,688; fish catch (1978) 412. Livestock (in 000; Dec. 1978): cattle 15,007; pigs 22,641; sheep 1,136; horses used in agriculture (1978) 371; chickens 87,629.

Industry. Index of production (1975 = 100; 1979) 119. Unemployment (1979) 3.8%. Fuel and power (in 000; metric tons; 1979): coal 86,921; lignite 130,579; crude oil 4,774; coke (1978) 26,237; electricity (kw-hr) 374,219,000; natural gas (cu m) 20,660,000; manufactured gas (cu m) 13,120,000. Production (in 000; metric tons; 1979): iron ore (32% metal content) 1,648; pig iron 35,351; crude steel 46,042; aluminum 1,165; copper 376; lead 299; zinc 487; cement 35,460; sulfuric acid 5,040; newsprint 600; cotton yarn 161; woven cotton fabrics 160; wool yarn 56; man-made fibres 911; petroleum products (1978) *c.* 91,400; fertilizers (1978–79) nitrogenous 1,273, phosphate 696, potash 2,540; synthetic rubber 444; plastics and resins 7,230; passenger cars (units) 3,936; commercial vehicles (units) 324. Merchant vessels launched (100 gross tons and over; 1979) 374,000 gross tons. New dwelling units completed (1979) 283,000.

"to create the conditions which will enable teams from all countries to take part," which meant that Soviet troops must first pull out of Afghanistan. Not until April 23, when the Soviets had failed to do so, did the federal government grudgingly recommend a boycott of the Games.

West Germany was still less inclined to impose economic sanctions against Iran, because it considered that such a move would drive the Iranians into the arms of the Soviet Union and also that sanctions would be ineffective in securing the release of the U.S. hostages in Iran. But early in April Schmidt's government became the leading advocate of joint sanctions by the European Economic Community. Two main considerations prompted the government to change its mind. It feared that unless President Carter got European support for sanctions he would take military action against Iran, with unforeseeable consequences. Second, the government was persuaded that unless it backed the U.S. actively relations with the U.S. would suffer.

During the year West Germany played a leading role in arranging a big international aid package for Turkey in order to strengthen NATO's southern flank. And it also undertook to place further restrictions on the export of high-technology equipment to the Soviet Union.

On June 30 Schmidt visited Moscow for talks with the Soviet leader, Leonid Brezhnev. The chancellor's public condemnation of the Soviet invasion of Afghanistan was tough enough to be censored by *Pravda*. Reporting to the Bundestag, Schmidt said that the differences between his government and the Soviet leaders on the Afghanistan issue were not bridged in the Moscow talks but that Brezhnev had offered to open talks with the U.S. on a limitation of nuclear forces in Europe.

The chancellor's strategy was to prevent the deterioration in East-West relations from seriously affecting his policy of détente in central Europe. Throughout the Polish crisis West Germany pursued a policy of noninterference and, indeed, strove to restore stability to Poland by administering powerful injections of hard currency. On October 10 an agreement was signed to grant Poland DM 1.2 billion (U.S. $663 million) credit. This assistance had an overriding motive—to deter the Soviet Union and, for that matter, East Germany from military intervention in Poland.

But the unrest in Poland, unlike the invasion of Afghanistan, did not leave the *Ostpolitik* unscathed. In August the Polish leader Edward Gierek canceled a planned meeting with Schmidt at the chancellor's home near Hamburg. And the chancellor postponed a trip to East Germany to see that nation's leader, Erich Honecker. Subsequently, intra-German relations suffered serious setbacks. (NORMAN CROSSLAND)

Ghana

A republic of West Africa and member of the Commonwealth of Nations, Ghana is on the Gulf of Guinea and is bordered by Ivory Coast, Upper Volta, and Togo. Area: 238,533 sq km (92,098 sq mi). Pop. (1980 est.): 11.4 million. Cap. and largest city: Accra (pop., 1975 est., 716,600). Language: English (official); local Sudanic dialects: Akan 43.3%, Mole-Dagbani 12.8%, Ewe 14.5%, and Ga-Adange 9.4%. Religion: Christian 43%; Muslim 16%; animist 38%. President in 1980, Hilla Limann.

The first year of civilian rule under Pres. Hilla Limann, passed on Sept. 24, 1980, had witnessed slow progress. Parliament was active and there was opposition within it, although it was policy to play down the idea of political confrontation.

Ghana's problems were economic—to restore international confidence and obtain investment. World cocoa prices were depressed, and cocoa provided 60% of foreign exchange; 58% of the cocoa trees needed replacing. (In 1978–79 Ivory Coast had passed Ghana as the world's leading cocoa producer.) The government introduced a two-year crash program to make the country self-sufficient in food. Ghana had rich agricultural potential, but only 11% of its arable land was cultivated and only 5% was producing food. There was unrest; numerous strikes occurred in 1980, as well as a foiled military plot and mutiny in March. In a three-day tribal fight in northern Ghana in April, occasioned by the attempt to install a new chief of the Wa tribe, 26 people were killed.

Diplomatic relations with Libya were broken in November because of the activities of the Libyan embassy staff. (GUY ARNOLD)

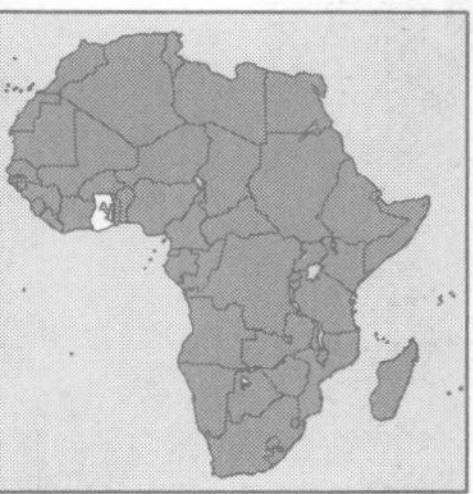
Ghana

GHANA

Education. (1977–78) Primary, pupils 1,245,853, teachers (1976–77) 41,407; secondary, pupils 568,947, teachers (1976–77) 25,081; vocational, pupils 12,382, teachers 990; teacher training, students 3,631, teachers 955; higher (1975–76), students 9,079, teaching staff 1,103.

Finance. Monetary unit: cedi, with (Sept. 22, 1980) a free rate of 2.74 cedis to U.S. $1 (6.59 cedis = £1 sterling). Gold, SDR's, and foreign exchange (June 1980) U.S. $375 million. Budget (1978–79 est.): revenue 3.2 billion cedis; expenditure 2.9 billion cedis. Gross national product (1976) 6,478,000,000 cedis. Money supply (May 1980) 5,223,100,000 cedis. Cost of living (Accra; 1975 = 100; May 1980) 1,274.

Foreign Trade. (1978) Imports *c.* 910,000,000 cedis; exports *c.* 810 million cedis. Import sources: U.K. *c.* 18%; Nigeria *c.* 13%; West Germany *c.* 12%; U.S. *c.* 10%; Switzerland *c.* 6%; Italy *c.* 5%. Export destinations: U.S. *c.* 16%; U.K. *c.* 15%; U.S.S.R. *c.* 11%; The Netherlands *c.* 9%; West Germany *c.* 9%; Japan *c.* 8%. Main exports (1976): cocoa 67%; aluminum 12%; timber 9%.

Transport and Communications. Roads (1979) 32,200 km. Motor vehicles in use (1978): passenger 33,000; commercial (including buses) 27,000. Railways: (1978) 953 km; traffic (1974) 521 million passenger-km, freight 312 million net ton-km. Air traffic (1978): 319 million passenger-km; freight 3.3 million net ton-km. Shipping (1979): merchant vessels 100 gross tons and over 95; gross tonnage 196,976. Telephones (Jan. 1978) 66,400. Radio receivers (Dec. 1977) 1,095,000. Television receivers (Dec. 1977) 40,000.

Agriculture. Production (in 000; metric tons; 1979): corn *c.* 380; cassava (1978) *c.* 1,850; taro (1978) *c.* 1,500; yams (1978) *c.* 800; millet *c.* 130; sorghum *c.* 200; tomatoes *c.* 113; peanuts *c.* 90; oranges *c.* 155; cocoa *c.* 270; palm oil *c.* 15; meat (1978) *c.* 80; fish catch (1978) 264; timber (cu m; 1978) *c.* 13,060. Livestock (in 000; 1978): cattle *c.* 900; sheep *c.* 1,600; pigs *c.* 390; goats *c.* 1,900; chickens *c.* 11,000.

Industry. Production (in 000; metric tons; 1978): bauxite 252; petroleum products *c.* 1,100; gold (troy oz) 457; diamonds (metric carats; 1977) 2,300; manganese ore (metal content; 1977) *c.* 107; electricity (kw-hr; 1977) *c.* 4,300,000.

Golf

Although Jack Nicklaus confounded those who thought that his conquering years were over by winning the U.S. Open and the Professional Golfers' Association (PGA) championships, Tom Watson qualified as player of the year for the fourth successive season. With official winnings of $530,-808, Watson became the first golfer to win more than $500,000 in one year and only the third, behind Nicklaus and Lee Trevino, to pass the $2 million mark in career earnings. Watson's most notable victories were the British Open for the third time and the World Series, but Trevino denied him success in the Vardon Trophy for best average number of strokes per round, which Watson had won the previous three years. Trevino's average was 69.73, fractionally better than Watson's and the lowest in 25 years. It was the fifth time that Trevino had won the Vardon, a number equaled only by Billy Casper, and crowned the most profitable season of his career. He won $385,-814 in the U.S. as well as considerable sums in Europe, where he finished second to Watson in the British Open.

In his 19 years as a professional Nicklaus could rarely have played with greater mastery and control than at Baltusrol in Springfield, N.J., and at Oak Hill in Rochester, N.Y. After the leanest year of his career in 1979, even the most responsible critics wondered whether his ambition and interest in competition, and the nerve essential for winning great championships, had finally declined. There was talk, which increasingly irritated Nicklaus, that his retirement was near.

When Nicklaus tied for 33rd in the Masters at Augusta, Ga., the fears of his friends seemed to be confirmed. Experiments to improve his play seemed to be fruitless, and so two months later the whole golf world was astonished when he and Tom Weiskopf tore Baltusrol apart with 63s in the opening round of the U.S. Open. The course, judged by the competitors as one of the fairest in many years, encouraged attacking rather than defensive golf. With a final score of 272, Nicklaus beat his own Open record set on the same course in 1967 by three strokes. It was his fourth U.S. Open victory, equaling the record of Willie Anderson, Bobby Jones, and Ben Hogan, and none was achieved in more commanding fashion.

Throughout the championship Nicklaus played with Isao Aoki of Japan, who kept the pressure on him until the very end. Aoki's unorthodox swing and method of putting with the toe of the club in the air had fascinated watchers. With a round to go, he and Nicklaus were tied, and, as Watson, Lon Hinkle, and Keith Fergus, who tied for third, just failed to set a telling pace, Aoki was the last threat. He remained so until Nicklaus scored a birdie on the 71st hole, but Aoki finished only two behind and also broke the old record. Both players won an extra $50,000 each, offered by *Golf Magazine* for breaking the record.

The one sour note of the Open was the failure of Severiano Ballesteros (*see* BIOGRAPHIES) to read correctly his starting time for the second day. He arrived on the first tee minutes late and was disqualified, a pathetic anticlimax to the glory he had achieved by becoming the youngest player and the first from Europe to win the Masters. The attack and flair of the Spaniard's golf and his handsome looks had made Ballesteros a favourite with galleries the world over. His victory at Augusta was one of the most masterful in the history of that event. An opening round of 66 gave him a share of the lead with David Graham of Australia, and when he followed with 69 and 68 the rest of the field fell far behind. Two errors cost Ballesteros strokes, but not until Gibby Gilbert and Hubert Green finished strongly when they had no real chance of winning was a U.S. golfer remotely in contention. Many had thought Ballesteros lucky to win the British Open the previous year when his drives were all over the place, but he showed at Augusta that he had control when necessary; his approach shots were a joy to see, and he putted beautifully. Jack Newton of Australia sustained his challenge bravely and shared second place with Gilbert.

After an opening 75 it was unlikely that Ballesteros could have challenged Nicklaus and Aoki at Baltusrol, and he also never quite assembled his game to its finest pitch in defending the British Open. On the other hand, Watson and Trevino gave swift notice of their intentions at Muirfield, Scotland, with rounds of 68 on an opening day beset with cold and heavy rain. Ideally, the fairest of British championship links should have played fast and firm, but the rain changed all that and

A tense Jack Nicklaus watched his final putt roll into the hole on the 18th green to win the U.S. Open in June for his fourth Open victory.

FRED R. CONRAD—THE NEW YORK TIMES

Gibraltar:
see Dependent States

Glass Manufacture:
see Industrial Review

Gliding:
see Aerial Sports

made it into a target exercise. On the second morning Horacio Carbonetti of Argentina scored a 64, but 78s on either side of it caused him to miss the cut for the final day. In the third round, Watson went to work with a superb 64, while Trevino, who had appeared to be in great form on the course where he had won in 1972, was taking 71. Aoki's magic returned for one round, but his 63 could not compensate for a moderate start. The previous evening Nicklaus had lost some impetus with a disappointing finish when a 65 seemed probable. An untidy start the next day left him too far behind, and when in the bitter grayness of the last afternoon Trevino missed early shots, Watson was left in almost total command. Never did he seem likely to falter, and for once there was no stirring climax for the record crowds. His total of 271, four lower than Trevino's, had only twice been beaten, by himself and Nicklaus in their historic encounter at Turnberry in 1977. Ben Crenshaw, second the previous two years, finished third and so his frustration continued. Nicklaus shared fourth place with Carl Mason, the leading British player.

A relaxed, confident Nicklaus mastered everyone in the PGA championship at Oak Hill. Gone were the tension and anxiety that haunted him at Baltusrol, and a third-round 66 swept him ahead. The only faint challenges came first from Lon Hinkle and finally from Andy Bean, but with 274 Nicklaus won by seven strokes. It was his fifth PGA victory, equaling the record of Walter Hagen, and his 19th major championship as a professional. Of contemporary competitors, Player with nine, Trevino with five, and Watson with four were nearest to him.

As if determined not to be outdone, Watson stormed home in the World Series of Golf at Akron, Ohio, with three rounds of 65 and one 75. Ray Floyd, Jerry Pate, Trevino, and Hale Irwin gave chase, but Watson, playing with enormous confidence, yielded nothing. Nicklaus injured his back in practice before the last round and had to withdraw, but at that point he was six strokes behind. Even he could not have caught Watson, whose golf throughout the year was wonderfully consistent, his swing superbly balanced and strong, and his putting often lethal.

Trevino was Watson's match in day-to-day consistency, rarely out of contention and winning three U.S. tournaments. Like Nicklaus he was 40, but several younger players, notably Bean, Crenshaw, Craig Stadler, Curtis Strange, and George Burns, continued to make impressive progress.

For the second successive year Sandy Lyle of the U.K., aged 22, headed the Order of Merit, based on official winnings for the European tour. In the last official event he overtook Greg Norman of Australia and Ballesteros. Lyle won £43,346, but Norman avenged his defeat the following week. In the Suntory world match play championship at Wentworth, England, he beat Lyle by one hole after a magnificent 36-hole final. A remarkable feature of the closing weeks of the season was the form of Bernhardt Langer, aged 23, from Munich, West Germany. His victory in the Dunlop Masters with a record score for the tournament of 270 was the first by a West German golfer in a major event.

UPI

Amy Alcott sports the U.S. Open trophy on her head after winning the championship for the first time.

The U.S. dominated amateur international competition. In the World Team championship Hal Sutton, Jay Sigel, Jim Holtgrieve, and Bob Tway retained the Eisenhower Trophy, finishing 27 strokes ahead of South Africa. Taiwan placed third another nine strokes behind, with Japan fourth. The team of Great Britain and Ireland owed a share of fifth place with Australia almost entirely to Ronan Rafferty, the Irish champion, who was only 16. His total of 286, two under par, was the fourth lowest individual score. The overwhelming U.S. victory was due in great measure to Sutton, whose total of 276 beat Nicklaus's record for the championship, set in 1960, by one stroke. Sutton was the outstanding amateur of the year. In the 36-hole final of the U.S. championship he beat Bob Lewis 9 and 8, and he also won the North and South, Northeastern, and Western titles.

Sigel was unable to defend the British Amateur championship at Porthcawl in South Wales. The U.S. entry was not strong, and the main challenge from overseas came from South Africans, of whom Keith Suddards lost 4 and 3 in the final to Duncan Evans, the first Welshman to win the championship.

In women's professional golf Amy Alcott won the U.S. Open at Nashville, Tenn., by nine strokes. Her total of 280 was also a record for the championship. Hollis Stacy, champion in 1977 and 1978, was second. On the tour the most successful players apart from Alcott were Beth Daniel—who, in only her second year as a professional, became the first player ever to win in one year over $200,-

000 in official prize money; Donna Caponi Young; Nancy Lopez-Melton, leading money winner the previous two years; and JoAnne Carner. Daniel was the leading money winner in 1980 with a total of $231,000, and under the Ladies' Professional Golfers' Association's points system she was woman player of the year.

Juli Simpson Inkster, the U.S. women's amateur champion, Patti Rizzo, her victim in the final, and Carol Semple gained a comfortable victory in the world championship at Pinehurst, N.C. Semple was a member of the U.S. team led by Nancy Roth Syms, which won a commanding victory in the Curtis Cup match at St. Pierre in Wales. The British and Irish did not win a single match until after the contest had been decided in favour of the Americans. In the British Amateur championship which followed at Woodhall Spa, Anne Quast Sander, who won the first of her three U.S. championships in 1958, beat Liv Wollin of Sweden 2 and 1 in the final. (P. A. WARD-THOMAS)

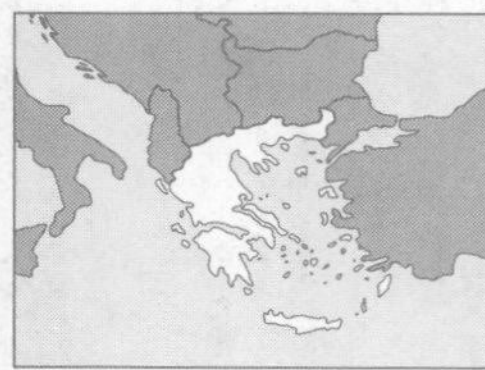
Greece

Greece

A republic of Europe, Greece occupies the southern part of the Balkan Peninsula. Area: 131,990 sq km (50,962 sq mi), of which the mainland accounts for 107,194 sq km. Pop. (1980 est.): 9,308,200. Cap. and largest city: Athens (pop., 1971, 867,000). Language: Greek. Religion: Orthodox. Presidents in 1980, Konstantinos Tsatsos and, from May 15, Konstantinos Karamanlis; prime ministers, Karamanlis and, from May 9, Georgios Rallis.

The election of Prime Minister Konstantinos Karamanlis as president of the republic on May 5 and the military reintegration of Greece into the NATO alliance on October 20 were the most significant events of 1980. Both were expected to have long-lasting effects on the country's internal situation and its external relations.

The withdrawal of Karamanlis from day-to-day politics enhanced the electoral chances of the main opposition party, the Panhellenic Socialist Movement (Pasok) led by Andreas Papandreou. Not only did Pasok no longer need to fear this formidable opponent, but the reassuring presence of Karamanlis at the top might also encourage hesitant voters to opt for political change. The possibility that the anti-Western Pasok might come to power influenced the speed with which Greece returned to the integrated military structure of NATO, from which it had withdrawn in 1974 in protest against the Turkish invasion of Cyprus. From 1978 Turkey had blocked Greece's reinstatement, demanding a share of NATO operational jurisdiction in the Aegean.

Karamanlis was elected president by the Greek Parliament with 183 votes, 3 above the three-fifths majority required on the third ballot. Pasok (93 members in Parliament) refused to vote on the grounds that Parliament, elected in 1977, no longer reflected the current will of the electorate. Pasok accepted the legality of Karamanlis's election, however. Three days afterward, the parliamentary group of the ruling New Democracy Party met and, in accordance with the democratic procedures adopted in 1979, elected a new leader. The choice went to the moderate foreign minister, Georgios Rallis (*see* BIOGRAPHIES), who received 88 votes to 84 for Defense Minister Evangelos Averoff-Tossizza, representing the party's conservative wing. Rallis was appointed prime minister the next day, May 9.

The Rallis Cabinet, which took over on May 10, consisted largely of ministers who had served on the Karamanlis team. A few changes suggested readjustments in the unpopular anti-inflationary policies adopted earlier in the year. The new government also took a tougher stand on the question of NATO reintegration. The U.S. was informed that the continued presence of the important U.S. military bases in Greece depended on the early readmission of Greece to NATO's military wing. The Greek threat coincided with a worsening situation in the Middle East and the Persian Gulf area and came just as Turkey's new military leaders were eager to eliminate any distractions on their western flank. In these circumstances, Gen. Bernard Rogers, NATO supreme allied commander, Europe, was able to induce both sides, separately,

Great Britain:
see United Kingdom

Greek Orthodox Church:
see Religion

Greenland:
see Dependent States

GREECE

Education. (1977–78) Primary, pupils 933,535, teachers 34,687; secondary, pupils 579,771, teachers 24,295; vocational, pupils 124,728; higher, students 123,429, teaching staff 6,718.

Finance. Monetary unit: drachma, with (Sept. 22, 1980) a free rate of 42.87 drachmas to U.S. $1 (103.03 drachmas = £1 sterling). Gold, SDR's, and foreign exchange (June 1980) U.S. $1,007,000,000. Budget (1979 actual): revenue 306,240,000,000 drachmas; expenditure 365,620,000,000 drachmas. Gross national product (1979) 1,464,800,000,000 drachmas. Money supply (Dec. 1979) 265,440,000,000 drachmas. Cost of living (1975 = 100; June 1980) 214.5.

Foreign Trade. (1979) Imports 356,820,000,000 drachmas; exports 144,240,000,000 drachmas. Import sources: EEC 44% (West Germany 16%, Italy 9%, France 6%, U.K. 6%); Japan 9%; Saudi Arabia 6%; U.S. 5%. Export destinations: EEC 49% (West Germany 19%, Italy 10%, The Netherlands 6%, France 6%, U.K. 5%); U.S. 6%; Saudi Arabia 5%. Main exports: fruit and vegetables 17%; petroleum products 12%; textile yarns and fabrics 10%; clothing 8%; iron and steel 6%; tobacco 5%; cement 5%; nonferrous metals 5%. Tourism (1978): visitors 4,532,000; gross receipts U.S. $1,326,000,000.

Transport and Communications. Roads (1979) 37,013 km (including 91 km expressways). Motor vehicles in use (1979): passenger 839,300; commercial 351,100. Railways (1978): 2,479 km; traffic 1,460,000,000 passenger-km, freight 840 million net ton-km. Air traffic (1979): 4,630,000,000 passenger-km; freight 67,953,000 net ton-km. Shipping (1979): merchant vessels 100 gross tons and over 3,827; gross tonnage 37,352,597. Telephones (Dec. 1978) 2,473,000. Radio receivers (Dec. 1978) 3.3 million. Television receivers (Dec. 1978) *c.* 1.5 million.

Agriculture. Production (in 000; metric tons; 1979): wheat *c.* 2,410; barley 869; oats *c.* 90; corn 627; rice *c.* 94; potatoes *c.* 963; sugar, raw value (1978) 326; tomatoes *c.* 1,669; onions *c.* 138; watermelons (1978) *c.* 600; apples 280; oranges *c.* 400; lemons *c.* 165; peaches (1978) *c.* 356; olives *c.* 1,060; olive oil 239; wine *c.* 449; raisins 136; tobacco *c.* 127; cotton, lint 130. Livestock (in 000; Dec. 1978): sheep 8,024; cattle 973; goats *c.* 4,473; pigs *c.* 830; horses *c.* 138; asses *c.* 267; chickens *c.* 29,651.

Industry. Production (in 000; metric tons; 1979): lignite 23,395; electricity (kw-hr) 20,649,000; petroleum products (1978) *c.* 11,600; iron ore (43% metal content) 1,835; bauxite 2,756; aluminum 140; magnesite (1978) 1,065; cement 12,064; sulfuric acid 1,062; fertilizers (1978–79) nitrogenous 311, phosphate 201; cotton yarn 114. Merchant vessels launched (100 gross tons and over; 1979) 26,000 gross tons.

KEYSTONE

Former Greek prime minister Konstantinos Karamanlis (hand on Bible) was sworn into office as president on May 15 while the new prime minister, Georgios Rallis (centre), looked on.

to agree to negotiate their contested jurisdiction of the Aegean after Greece had rejoined the alliance. The breakthrough was achieved on October 17, and on October 20 NATO approved Greece's return under a formula that was kept secret but that satisfied the Greeks more than the Turks.

The return of Greece to NATO touched off hostile demonstrations in Athens and other major cities. Many Greeks openly mistrusted the Western alliance, the end result of years of opposition propaganda laying the blame for the seven-year dictatorship in Greece and the Turkish invasion of Cyprus on the U.S. and NATO. The Rallis government, however, went to Parliament and won a vote of confidence by 182 votes to 20. Pasok's deputies again abstained on the grounds that Parliament was not representative.

Hopes that the September military takeover in Turkey would ease the resolution of Greek-Turkish differences led to a resumption on October 5 of the bilateral dialogue on the Aegean continental shelf and its airspace. A unilateral Turkish gesture of February 22 had led to the resumption of civil aviation flights across the Aegean, which had been interrupted for six years. The military reintegration of Greece into NATO opened the way for a revision of the U.S.-Greek agreement on U.S. military bases. The new agreement would regulate the status of the U.S. installations as well as the kind of U.S. military assistance Greece would receive. The main Greek concern was that the balance of power between Greece and Turkey not be disturbed.

External affairs were dominated by concern over reentry into NATO, the more so after the Soviet invasion of Afghanistan. Greece did not boycott the Moscow Olympics, however. Its position was that politics and sports should not be mixed. In addition, it did not wish to jeopardize Karamanlis's January proposal that a permanent home for the Olympic Games be constructed at ancient Olympia.

Karamanlis continued to cultivate his personal plan for détente in the Balkans. To this end, he paid his first state visits as president to Romania (September), Bulgaria (October), and Yugoslavia (November). But in light of the international situation, the new government was fixing its sights more firmly on Western Europe—the more so since Greece would become a full member of the European Economic Community (EEC) on Jan. 1, 1981.

One cause for concern in connection with EEC membership was that the Greek economy was already experiencing some balance of payments difficulties, and the inflation rate threatened to match the 25% leap of 1979. A gentleman's agreement with Greek importers for "self-restraint" held the Greek imports bill (already overloaded with soaring oil costs) in check. Internal economic adjustments in the second half of the year led to increased bank deposits, a slight slowing of the inflation rate, and the elimination of some state subsidies. However, productive investment continued to lag, despite generous incentives, and for the first time in recent years there was a marked increase in unemployment. A strike of electricity workers in late October led to power cuts in Athens, and on October 31 teachers, civil servants, civil aviation workers, and utility workers began a 48-hour strike. On November 6 the government granted the trade unions' demand for a five-day workweek, to be introduced on Jan. 1, 1981, but a 24-hour general strike for higher pay began on November 10. (MARIO MODIANO)

Grenada

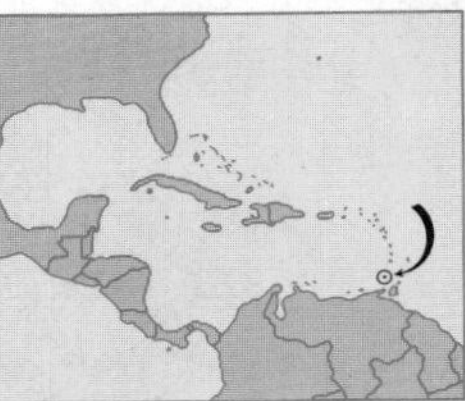

Grenada

A parliamentary state within the Commonwealth of Nations, Grenada, with its dependency, the Southern Grenadines, is the southernmost of the Windward Islands of the Caribbean Sea, 161 km N of Trinidad. Area: 345 sq km (133 sq mi). Pop. (1980 est.): 110,100, including Negro 84%, mixed 11%, white 1%, and East Indian 3%. Cap.: Saint George's (pop., 1978, 30,813). Language: English.

GRENADA

Education. (1978–79) Primary, pupils 24,106, teachers 814; secondary, pupils 6,498, teachers 275; vocational, pupils 384, teachers 28; teacher training, students 450, teachers 29; higher, students 700, teaching staff 137.

Finance and Trade. Monetary unit: East Caribbean dollar, with (Sept. 22, 1980) a par value of ECar$2.70 to U.S. $1 (free rate of ECar$6.48 = £1 sterling). Budget (1978 est.) balanced at ECar$75 million. Foreign trade (1978): imports ECar$122.8 million; exports ECar$58.5 million. Import sources (1975): U.K. 25%; Trinidad and Tobago *c.* 20%; Canada 9%; U.S. 8%. Export destinations: U.K. 40%; West Germany 17%; Belgium-Luxembourg 16%; The Netherlands 11%. Main exports: cocoa 46%; nutmeg 21%; bananas 18%. Tourism (excluding cruise passengers; 1978): visitors 32,300; gross receipts *c.* U.S. $10 million.

Religion: Christian (Roman Catholic 64%; Anglican 22%; Methodist 2%; Seventh-day Adventist 3%). Queen, Elizabeth II; governor-general in 1980, Sir Paul Scoon; prime minister, Maurice Bishop.

Throughout 1980 Grenada's People's Revolutionary Government (PRG) pursued three separate but related policies. Domestically, emphasis was placed on creating employment in agriculture and related industries and on improving education and public-sector management. The PRG sought close relations with its Caribbean neighbours, but overtures to Trinidad were rebuffed. Internationally, closer relations developed with Cuba, Eastern Europe, and Canada, but relations with the U.S. remained at a low ebb.

The island maintained its mixed economy. Work was begun on a U.S. $40 million international jet airport near Saint George's, with external assistance. In April Finance Minister Bernard Coard announced that the economy was in a much healthier state, that unemployment had fallen, and that the tourist industry was to be developed to close the trade gap, which in 1979 amounted to $54.3 million. In mid-June a bomb exploded beneath a platform on which virtually the entire government was sitting. The officials escaped, but two children and an adult were killed.

(DAVID A. JESSOP)

Guatemala

Guatemala

A republic of Central America, Guatemala is bounded by Mexico, Belize, Honduras, El Salvador, the Caribbean Sea, and the Pacific Ocean. Area: 108,889 sq km (42,042 sq mi). Pop. (1980 est.): 7,262,000. Cap. and largest city: Guatemala City (pop., 1980 est., 1,004,000). Language: Spanish, with some Indian dialects. Religion: Roman Catholic (1976) 88%. President in 1980, Fernando Romeo Lucas García.

The political situation in Guatemala in 1980 continued to deteriorate as polarization between left and right increased. There were occasional acts of violence, causing human rights organizations to protest. The chief victims of right-wing extremist groups were trade union and student leaders and key members of the United Revolutionary Front (FUR), the principal social democratic opposition group. In May formation of the Patriotic Liberation Front unified the left-wing opposition.

On January 31 a group of Indian peasants from the Quiché region occupied the Spanish embassy in a protest against repression; police stormed the buildings, and during the raid a gasoline bomb was thrown that resulted in a fire that took 39 lives. Because the police intervention had occurred against the wishes of the ambassador, Spain severed diplomatic relations on February 1.

In September Vice-Pres. Francisco Villagrán Kramer resigned, charging right-wing elements in the government with adopting a policy of violation of human rights. In February he had withdrawn a resignation he had previously tendered.

No agreement was negotiated regarding Guatemala's claim to parts of the neighbouring British colony of Belize. Britain maintained a military presence in Belize, while Guatemala's foreign minister, Rafael Castillo Valdez, reiterated on November 13 that Guatemala would never permit the unilateral independence of the colony.

(CHRISTINE MELLOR)

Rescue workers removed the bodies of 39 Quiche Indians and their hostages after a fire engulfed the Spanish embassy in Guatemala in January. Demonstrators had seized the embassy to protest Guatemalan government policies.

SYGMA

GUATEMALA

Education. (1978) Primary, pupils 709,018, teachers 21,060; secondary, vocational, and teacher training, pupils 145,770, teachers 8,604; higher (1977), students 29,234, teaching staff (1976) 1,934.

Finance. Monetary unit: quetzal, at par with the U.S. dollar (free rate, at Sept. 22, 1980, of 2.40 quetzales to £1 sterling). Gold, SDR's, and foreign exchange (June 1980) U.S. $681 million. Budget (1979 actual): revenue 682 million quetzales; expenditure 850 million quetzales. Gross national product (1978) 6,145,000,000 quetzales. Money supply (June 1980) 939 million quetzales. Cost of living (1975 = 100; June 1980) 166.6.

Foreign Trade. (1978) Imports 1,285,600,000 quetzales; exports 1,089,400,000 quetzales. Import sources: U.S. 30%; Japan 11%; El Salvador 9%; West Germany 8%; Venezuela 7%. Export destinations: U.S. 29%; West Germany 12%; El Salvador 11%; Japan 7%; Costa Rica 6%; The Netherlands 5%; Italy 5%. Main exports: coffee 46%; cotton 13%; chemicals *c.* 8%; textile yarns and fabrics *c.* 5%.

Transport and Communications. Roads (1979) 17,278 km. Motor vehicles in use (1978): passenger 156,400; commercial (including buses) 56,000. Railways: (1977) 1,828 km; freight traffic (1976) 117 million net ton-km. Air traffic (1979): 190 million passenger-km; freight 7.6 million net ton-km. Telephones (Jan. 1979) 70,600. Radio licenses (Dec. 1978) *c.* 280,000. Television receivers (Dec. 1977) 150,000.

Agriculture. Production (in 000; metric tons; 1979): corn *c.* 850; sugar, raw value *c.* 376; tomatoes *c.* 81; dry beans *c.* 85; bananas *c.* 560; coffee *c.* 169; cotton, lint *c.* 146; tobacco *c.* 8. Livestock (in 000; 1978): sheep 600; cattle *c.* 2,417; pigs 704; chickens 13,545.

Industry. Production (in 000; metric tons; 1978): cement 531; petroleum products (1977) *c.* 720; electricity (kw-hr) 1,484,000.

Guinea

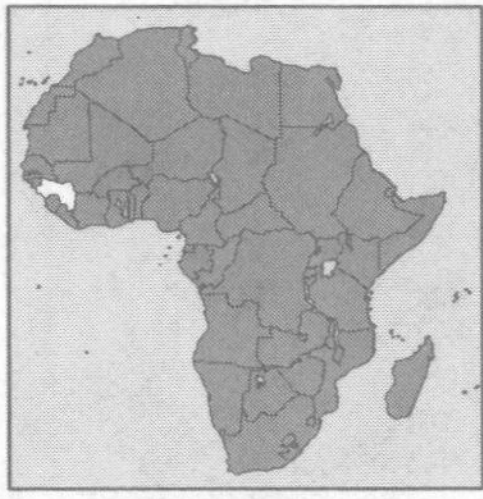
Guinea

A republic on the west coast of Africa, Guinea is bounded by Guinea-Bissau, Senegal, Mali, Ivory Coast, Liberia, and Sierra Leone. Area: 245,857 sq km (94,926 sq mi). Pop. (1980 UN est.): 5,014,000. Cap. and largest city: Conakry (pop., 1980 est., 763,000). Language: French (official). Religion: mostly Muslim. President in 1980, Ahmed Sékou Touré; premier, Louis Lansana Beavogui.

Pres. Ahmed Sékou Touré escaped assassination in Conakry on May 14, 1980. Numerous arrests and a thorough purge of the Army and the Guinea Democratic Party (the sole party) were undertaken afterward. The incident took place just at a time when the regime had initiated a policy of liberalization, freeing a number of political prisoners and organizing legislative elections in January. In the elections, a new national assembly of 210 members was elected from the one-party list.

The rapprochement with France (achieved in December 1978) was maintained effectively. In February 1980 Gen. Lansama Diane, minister of the armed forces, visited France officially. However, Guinea did not participate in the Franco-African conference held in Nice in April, and President Sékou Touré's official visit to France was postponed several times and had not taken place by the end of the year.

In the field of inter-African relations, Guinea joined the Gambia River Development Organization in June and the Mano River Union in October, took part in the inter-African force replacing the French forces in Chad, and engaged in a frontier dispute with Guinea-Bissau. This last was a particularly thorny problem, bearing upon a disputed maritime zone that was thought to lie over major petroleum resources. (PHILIPPE DECRAENE)

GUINEA

Education. (1971–72) Primary, pupils 169,132, teachers 4,698; secondary, pupils 65,210, teachers (1970–71) 2,360; vocational (1970–71), pupils 2,013, teachers 150; teacher training (1970–71), students 1,478, teachers 275; higher (1970–71), students 1,974, teachers (1965–66) 95.

Finance. Monetary unit: syli, with (Sept. 22, 1980) a free rate of 18.60 sylis to U.S. $1 (44.71 sylis = £1 sterling). Budget (total; 1979 est.) balanced at 11,250,000,000 sylis.

Foreign Trade. (1977) Imports *c.* 6.6 billion sylis; exports *c.* 6,630,000,000 sylis. Import sources: France *c.* 20%; U.S.S.R. *c.* 11%; U.S. *c.* 6%; Italy *c.* 6%. Export destinations: U.S. *c.* 18%; France *c.* 13%; West Germany *c.* 12%; U.S.S.R. *c.* 12%; Spain *c.* 12%; Canada *c.* 7%; Italy *c.* 7%. Main exports (1975–76): bauxite *c.* 57%; alumina *c.* 31%.

Guinea-Bissau

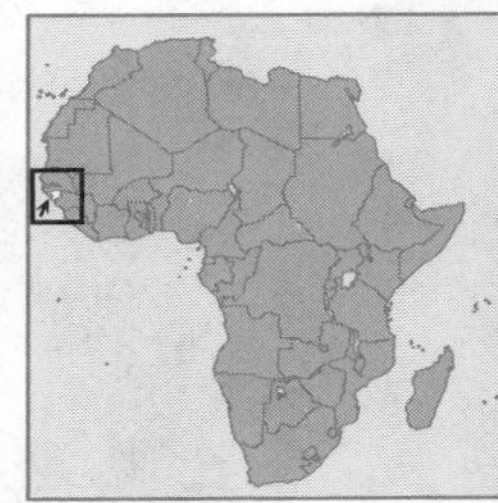
Guinea-Bissau

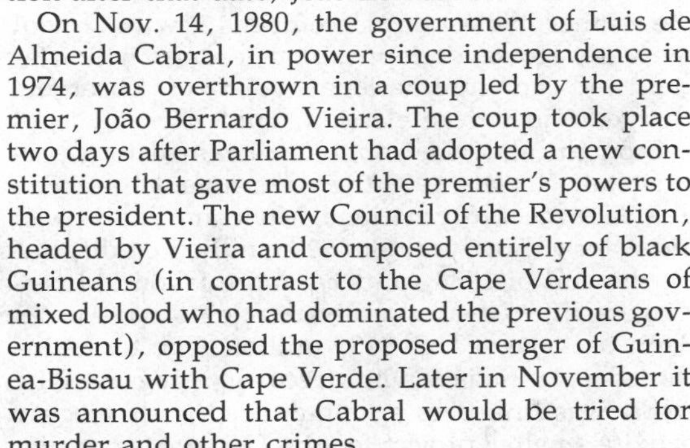

An independent African republic, Guinea-Bissau has an Atlantic coastline on the west and borders Senegal on the north and Guinea on the east and south. Area: 36,125 sq km (13,948 sq mi). Pop. (1979) 777,200. Cap. and largest city: Bissau (metro. area pop., 1979, 109,500). President to Nov. 14, 1980, Luis de Almeida Cabral; premier, to November 14 and president of the Council of the Revolution after that date, João Bernardo Vieira.

On Nov. 14, 1980, the government of Luis de Almeida Cabral, in power since independence in 1974, was overthrown in a coup led by the premier, João Bernardo Vieira. The coup took place two days after Parliament had adopted a new constitution that gave most of the premier's powers to the president. The new Council of the Revolution, headed by Vieira and composed entirely of black Guineans (in contrast to the Cape Verdeans of mixed blood who had dominated the previous government), opposed the proposed merger of Guinea-Bissau with Cape Verde. Later in November it was announced that Cabral would be tried for murder and other crimes.

Prior to the coup a boundary dispute with neighbouring Guinea had flared when Guinea decided to prospect for oil in disputed waters. In July Guinea-Bissau moved troops to the border and put its Air Force on alert. The Guinea foreign minister

GUINEA-BISSAU

Education. (1977–78) Primary, pupils 93,256, teachers 2,620; secondary, pupils 4,612; vocational, pupils 76; teacher training, students 284; secondary, vocational, and teacher training, teachers 540.

Finance and Trade. Monetary unit: Guinea-Bissau peso, with (Sept. 20, 1980) a free rate of 33.16 pesos to U.S. $1 (79.70 pesos = £1 sterling). Budget (1979 est.): revenue 890 million pesos; expenditure 1,474,000,000 pesos. Foreign trade (1978): imports 1,726,000,000 pesos; exports 423 million pesos. Import sources: Portugal 21%; West Germany 11%; Sweden 11%; U.S.S.R. 9%; Italy 7%; France 5%. Export destinations: Angola 35%; Spain 18%; Portugal 18%; Guinea 5%. Main exports (1977): peanuts 60%; fish 19%; copra 12%.

Agriculture. Production (in 000; metric tons; 1978): rice *c.* 60; plantains *c.* 25; peanuts *c.* 35; palm kernels *c.* 12; palm oil *c.* 5; copra *c.* 5; timber (cu m) *c.* 516. Livestock (in 000; 1978): cattle *c.* 262; pigs *c.* 174; sheep *c.* 72; goats *c.* 182.

Guiana: *see* Dependent States; Guyana; Suriname

visited Bissau in an attempt to defuse the situation. The disputed area, off the Bijagós Archipelago between Guinea-Bissau and Cape Verde, had been annexed unilaterally by Guinea in 1962.

(GUY ARNOLD)

Guyana

Guyana

A republic and member of the Commonwealth of Nations, Guyana is situated between Venezuela, Brazil, and Suriname on the Atlantic Ocean. Area: 215,000 sq km (83,000 sq mi). Pop. (1980 est.): 884,000, including (1970) East Indian 51.8%; African 31.2%; mixed 10.3%; Amerindian 4.9%. Cap. and largest city: Georgetown (pop., 1970, 63,200). Language: English (official). Religion (1970): Hindu 37%; Protestant 32%; Roman Catholic 13%. Presidents in 1980, Arthur Chung and, from October 6, Forbes Burnham; prime ministers, Forbes Burnham and, from October 6, Ptolemy Reid.

In June 1980 Walter Rodney, one of the Caribbean's leading historians and a member of the opposition Working People's Alliance (WPA), died after a bomb blast. Throughout the year opposition groups alleged violent intimidation by government supporters. Under the long-awaited new socialist constitution, Prime Minister Forbes Burnham on October 6 became executive president, with wide powers. Burnham was declared the winner in elections December 15, with 76% of the vote. However, opposition leader Cheddi Jagan and an international team of observers charged widespread election fraud.

Economically, the republic remained in a parlous state. In late 1979 the government had been unable to meet International Monetary Fund (IMF) terms for a three-year Guy$206 million credit, but by the end of 1980, under a more favourable arrangement, Guyana received a joint IMF-World Bank package of U.S. $133 million. The terms included a planned economic recovery program. The credit was linked to a long-desired hydroelectric bauxite smelter project for the Upper Mazaruni.

(DAVID A. JESSOP)

GUYANA

Education. (1977–78) Primary, pupils 166,239, teachers 6,172; secondary, pupils 75,144, teachers 2,505; vocational, pupils 3,756, teachers 68; teacher training, pupils 990, teachers 102; higher (university only; 1979), students 1,889, teaching staff (1976–77) 172.

Finance. Monetary unit: Guyanan dollar, with (Sept. 22, 1980) a par value of Guy$2.55 to U.S. $1 (free rate of Guy$6.13 = £1 sterling). Budget (total; 1978 est.): revenue Guy$484 million; expenditure Guy$568 million.

Foreign Trade. Imports (1978) Guy$664 million; exports (1979) Guy$743 million. Import sources: Trinidad and Tobago 27%; U.S. 23%; U.K. 22%. Export destinations (1978): U.K. 30%; U.S. 20%; Trinidad and Tobago 7%; Canada 7%; Norway 6%; Jamaica 5%. Main exports (1978): bauxite 33%; sugar 32%; rice 13%; alumina 10%.

Agriculture. Production (in 000; metric tons; 1979): rice 244; sugar, raw value *c.* 316; bananas and plantains *c.* 25; oranges (1978) *c.* 12; copra *c.* 3. Livestock (in 000; 1978): cattle *c.* 270; sheep *c.* 112; goats *c.* 66; pigs *c.* 135; chickens *c.* 11,500.

Industry. Production (in 000; 1978): bauxite (metric tons) 3,013; alumina (metric tons; 1976) 247; diamonds (metric carats) *c.* 36; electricity (kw-hr) 405,000.

Gymnastics and Weight Lifting

Gymnastics. Soviet athletes dominated the 1980 Olympic competitions, but spectators could hardly forget that world class gymnasts from Japan and the U.S. did not participate because their respective Olympic committees voted to boycott the Games in Moscow. When the final event was over, gymnasts from the U.S.S.R. had won both team titles, four of the seven gold medals awarded to men, and three of the six gold medals given to women. The latter included one first-place tie. Aleksandr Dityatin, who placed first in the all-around and on the rings, finished second on the parallel bars, the horizontal bar, the side horse, and in the vault; he also won a bronze medal in the floor exercise. Counting the first-place gold medal given to members of the Soviet men's team, Dityatin garnered an unprecedented eight medals during the 1980 Olympiad. Gold medals were also won by Roland Bruckner (East Germany) in the floor exercise, by Stoyan Deltchev (Bulg.) on the horizontal bar, and by Aleksandr Tkachyov (U.S.S.R.) on the parallel bars. Nikolay Andrianov (U.S.S.R.), the star of the 1976 Olympic Games, retained his title in the vault. And Zoltan Magyar (Hung.), world champion on the side horse, repeated his 1976 Olympic victory by winning a gold medal with an outstanding performance. Dityatin became the first male gymnast to receive a perfect score of ten from Olympic judges. He received the mark for his execution of the vault in the all-around. During that same competition, tens were also awarded to Deltchev on the rings, to Tkachyov on the horizontal bar, and to Magyar and Michael Nikolay (East Germany) on the side horse. Both the male and female gymnasts took advantage of a new rule to earn bonus points by introducing risk, originality, and virtuosity into their optional exercises.

The women's team competition was a replay of the 1976 Montreal Games: the U.S.S.R. team took the gold medal, Romania the silver, and East Germany the bronze. In individual events, however, new names appeared. Yelena Davydova (U.S.S.R.) finished first in the demanding all-around; Nadia Comaneci (Rom.) and 15-year-old Maxi Gnauck (East Germany) tied for second. Comaneci, however, retained her Olympic title on the balance beam but failed to place on the uneven bars. Gnauck won that event and Natalya Shaposhnikova (U.S.S.R.) the vault. Two gold and two bronze medals were awarded in the floor exercise. Nelli Kim (U.S.S.R.) and Comaneci tied for first place with scores of 19.875, and Shaposhnikova and Gnauck shared third-place honours with identical 19.825 scores.

The U.S. had developed its most versatile gymnasts in history, but its national Olympic committee had voted 1,604–797 to accede to Pres. Jimmy Carter's request and boycott the Moscow Games. Bart Conner, Kurt Thomas, and James Hartung had already gained recognition as world-class athletes. Kathy Johnson was generally considered the most polished U.S. female gymnast, followed by Marcia Frederick. The future, however, seemed brightest for Tracee Talavera, Amy Koopman, and Julianne McNamara.

Weight Lifting. The results of the 1980 Olympic competitions were somewhat unusual inasmuch as not a single medal winner at the previous Olympics won honours at Moscow. Even the great Vasily Alekseyev, world champion in the 110-kg-plus class, was eliminated after failing to snatch 180 kg in three attempts. For the first time a 100-kg class was sanctioned by the Olympic committee, thereby raising the total number of gold, silver, and bronze medals to ten each. Soviet athletes won five first-place medals and the Bulgarians two; gold medals were also won by a Cuban, a Czechoslovak, and a Hungarian. During the competitions, six world records and seven Olympic records fell, and Alekseyev's Olympic record of 440 kg was equaled by Sultan Rakhmanov (U.S.S.R.). A remarkable performance was also given by Yurik Vardanyan (U.S.S.R.), who set a world record in the 82.5-kg class by lifting a combined total of 400 kg in the snatch and in the clean and jerk. Neither of the gold medal winners in the next two heavier weight classes was able to match Vardanyan's performance. Though Kanybek Osmanoliev (U.S.S.R.) was awarded the gold medal in the 52-kg class, three others also broke the old Olympic record by lifting 245 kg. The three medals, therefore, were awarded on the basis of the athletes' relative body weight. Daniel Nuñez (Cuba) set a world record in the 56-kg category with a combined lift of 275 kg. Viktor Mazin (U.S.S.R.) surpassed the previous Olympic record in the 60-kg class with a lift of 290 kg. Yanko Rusev (Bulg.), gold medal winner in the 67.5-kg class, set a world record of 342.5 kg. Assen Zlatev (Bulg.), competing in the 75-kg class, established a new world mark of 360 kg. Yurik Vardanyan (U.S.S.R.) broke the world record in the 82.5-kg class with a combined total of 400 kg. Peter Baczako (Hung.) could not match either the Olympic or world record, but he won a gold medal in the 90-kg class by lifting 377.5 kg. In the new 100-kg class, Ota Zaremba (Czech.) established an Olympic record by lifting 395 kg. Leonid Taranenko (U.S.S.R.) raised the world record in the 110-kg class from 422 to 422.5 kg. (CHARLES ROBERT PAUL, JR.)

See also Track and Field Sports: *Special Report.*
[452.B.4.f.]

WIDE WORLD

Winner of the 1980 American Cup gymnastics championship was Kurt Thomas. He scored a perfect 10 on the horizontal bars in the competition in March.

WIDE WORLD

Leonid Taranenko (U.S.S.R.) hoisted a total of 422.5 kg to set a new world and Olympic record in the 110-kg weight-lifting class at the Moscow Olympics in June.

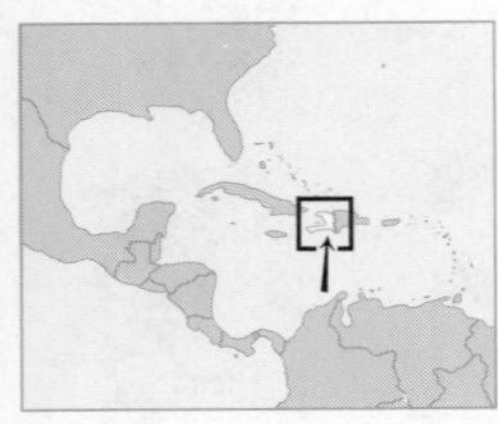

Haiti

Haiti

The Republic of Haiti occupies the western one-third of the Caribbean island of Hispaniola, which it shares with the Dominican Republic. Area: 27,-750 sq km (10,715 sq mi). Pop. (1979 est.): 4,919,-700, of whom 95% are Negro. Cap. and largest city: Port-au-Prince (pop., 1978 est., 745,800). Language: French (official) and Creole. Religion: Roman Catholic; Voodoo practiced in rural areas. President in 1980, Jean-Claude Duvalier.

Haitian Pres. Jean-Claude Duvalier's marriage to Michèle Bennett in May 1980 reduced the influence of the hard-liners surrounding his mother, Simone Duvalier. Several ministerial changes were reportedly made to soften international criticism of the regime, which had grown following the arrival of 2,300 Haitian "boat people" in Florida in January–March. Some (limited) press freedom was permitted, and in September death sentences of four alleged saboteurs were commuted. In late November, however, there was an abrupt turnaround as journalists, human rights activists, and other opponents of the regime were arrested in a widespread crackdown on dissent.

The economy made modest progress in 1979, with the growth rate of 2% (1978, 3.5%) resulting mainly from an increase in farm output and a strengthening of the external sector following improved terms of trade and increased inflows of loans and grants. But it was estimated that Hurricane Allen, which swept across southern Haiti in August 1980 and destroyed most of the main export crop, coffee, had cut gross domestic product by one-fifth. The planning ministry began preparation of a five-year development plan for 1981–85. Reynolds Haitian Mines signed a new four-year contract in August to mine bauxite ore; the government was to receive 55 cents a ton.

(ROBIN CHAPMAN)

HAITI

Education. (1977–78) Primary, pupils 508,605, teachers 11,706; secondary, pupils 56,078, teachers (1976–77) 3,324; vocational (1975–76), pupils 5,356, teachers 474; teacher training (1975–76), students 2,690, teaching staff 308; higher (university only; 1975–76), students 2,505, teaching staff 308.

Finance. Monetary unit: gourde, with (Sept. 22, 1980) a par value of 5 gourdes to U.S. $1 (free rate of 12.02 gourdes = £1 sterling). Gold, SDR's, and foreign exchange (March 1980) U.S. $45 million. Budget (1978–79 est.) balanced at 473 million gourdes. Cost of living (Port-au-Prince; 1975 = 100; March 1980) 145.3.

Foreign Trade. (1978) Imports 1,103,400,000 gourdes; exports 760.3 million gourdes. Import sources: U.S. 45%; Netherlands Antilles 10%; Japan 9%; Canada 8%; West Germany 5%. Export destinations: U.S. 59%; France 13%; Italy 7%; Belgium-Luxembourg 6%. Main exports (1977): coffee 44%; bauxite 12%; toys and sports goods 10%.

Transport and Communications. Roads (1978) *c.* 4,-000 km. Motor vehicles in use (1977): passenger 15,600; commercial (including buses) 8,800. Railways (1978) *c.* 250 km. Telephones (Jan. 1977) 17,800. Radio receivers (Dec. 1977) 98,000. Television receivers (Dec. 1977) 14,000.

Agriculture. Production (in 000; metric tons; 1978): rice *c.* 95; corn *c.* 250; sorghum 180; sweet potatoes *c.* 96; cassava *c.* 148; sugar, raw value *c.* 51; dry beans 37; bananas *c.* 52; plantains *c.* 198; mangoes *c.* 290; coffee *c.* 40; sisal *c.* 13. Livestock (in 000; 1978): cattle *c.* 900; pigs *c.* 2,000; goats *c.* 1,200; sheep *c.* 85; horses *c.* 400.

Industry. Production (in 000; metric tons; 1978): cement 250; bauxite (exports) 630; electricity (kw-hr) 246,-000.

Marooned for more than a month on a small Bahamian island, some 100 Haitian refugees were forcibly returned to their homeland in November.

MIAMI HERALD/BLACK STAR

Health and Disease

General Developments. Choice of the 1980 Nobel prizewinners for chemistry and for physiology or medicine reflected the importance of two emerging subfields of medical science. The Prize for Chemistry, shared by Frederick Sanger of Great Britain and Paul Berg and Walter Gilbert of the U.S., honoured them for work fundamental to the progress of genetic engineering, whereby bacteria, for example, can be programmed to synthesize human proteins and other extremely desirable molecules. Some fruits of their basic research also made news during the year. The Swiss firm Biogen, a commercial genetic engineering company, began producing human interferon from bacteria that had been endowed with the appropriate gene. Other firms were experimenting with interferon manufacture using similar techniques, and a commercial start was made on the bacterial manufacture of human insulin. (*See* LIFE SCIENCES: *Special Report.*)

The Prize for Physiology or Medicine was shared by George Snell and Baruj Benacerraf of the U.S. and Jean Dausset of France. Their work revealed much of the genetic basis of the immunological mechanism responsible for the rejection of grafted organs. Although interest in organ transplants remained high, the most important aspect of their work was the light it shed on the inheritance of resistance to disease and of susceptibility to such common and disabling ailments as rheumatoid arthritis, multiple sclerosis, and diabetes, in which the body's defenses appear to turn against certain of its own tissues. (*See* NOBEL PRIZES.)

The possibility of the bulk manufacture of interferon by bacteria was particularly welcome in view of a recent renewal of interest in this natural substance, which is produced when viruses invade cells. Apart from its possible use in the treatment of viral infections (which, unlike bacterial infections, do not respond to antibiotics) trials of interferon as an anticancer drug took place during the year. Although some encouraging responses were noted, early results were inconclusive, largely because the small quantities of interferon available and the high cost made adequate trials impossible. Press reports of the very limited experiments that did take place raised false hopes among many cancer sufferers and brought strong protests from some doctors who felt that accounts of such "advances" should be confined to the pages of the medical press until firm conclusions are reached.

In a first for transplant research, a team at Washington University School of Medicine, St. Louis, Mo., transplanted insulin-producing pancreatic islets from one animal species to another (rat to mouse). Previously, islet cells and pancreas glands had been transplanted only between animals of the same inbred strain and, later, between animals of different strains of the same species. The ultimate goal of such research is to allow successful transplantation of animal or human islets into human diabetics.

JIM POZARIK—GAMMA/LIAISON

Tampons underwent scientific testing after they were found to be associated with toxic shock syndrome, a rare disease that can be fatal.

An attempt at human genetic engineering caused adverse comment and sparked off an investigation. Martin Cline and co-workers of the University of California at Los Angeles (UCLA) treated two women suffering from thalassemia, an ultimately fatal condition in which, owing to a genetic defect, the sufferer is unable to manufacture normal hemoglobin and so develops a progressive anemia. Cline made a laboratory culture of cells containing the gene that initiates the production of normal hemoglobin and then introduced these genes into bone marrow cells (which give rise to the red blood cells) taken from his patients. He then returned the marrow cells to their original owners in the hope that the cells would survive and multiply and give rise to normal red cells. The experiments were performed in Italy and Israel in July, just a few days before a UCLA committee turned down his request for permission to attempt a similar experiment in California. In October Cline revealed what he had done, reporting that both patients were alive and well but not whether they had responded to the treatment. Some critics immediately accused Cline of evading U.S. regulations in order to conduct work that had not yet reached a stage in which human subjects were justified. Cline denied the charge and replied that he was dealing with patients doomed to an early death for whom no other treatment was available.

In January a plan to establish the first test-tube baby clinic in the U.S. and involving several physicians from the Johns Hopkins University School of Medicine in Baltimore, Md., was approved by Virginia health authorities. The clinic would employ techniques largely developed by British gynecologist Patrick Steptoe and physiologist Robert Edwards whereby a woman rendered sterile by a blockage of her fallopian tubes can have eggs removed from her ovaries by a minor surgical operation. The eggs are then fertilized in the

Handball:
see Court Games

Harness Racing:
see Equestrian Sports

laboratory by her husband's sperm and finally planted in the woman's womb. As of late 1980 the success rate was poor although the technique did work, as evidenced by the world's first test-tube baby born in England in 1978. When the plan for the clinic was announced, the Virginia Society for Human Life called it "an infamous day in the administration of public health." In the U.K. Steptoe resigned his post as a National Health Service specialist and partnered Edwards in establishing a private clinic for test-tube babies in a former country mansion near Cambridge.

In October investigators at the U.S. National Institute of Child Health and Human Development announced the result of a 2½-year study that seemed to offer a far simpler technique for overcoming infertility caused by blocked fallopian tubes. Working with female monkeys whose tubes had been artificially obstructed, they removed ripe eggs from the ovaries by a simple abdominal operation and returned them to the tubes beyond the point of blockage. The eggs were then fertilized during ordinary mating. Eggs are normally fertilized during their passage down the tubes from the ovary to the womb, where conditions (including a proper mixture of hormones) are ideal for the activity of both egg and sperm. When test-tube fertilization is attempted, these conditions must be imitated as far as possible in the laboratory, a complication that accounted in part for the technique's limited success.

Some infertility is due to the presence of antibodies to sperm in one of the partners of a marriage, according to a report in the *New England Journal of Medicine.* Antibodies are specialized molecules that attack, for example, bacteria and viruses against which the body has mounted defenses following inocculation or previous infection. It had long been suspected, but not proven, that some people develop antibodies to spermatozoa. A group of researchers in Pennsylvania used sophisticated radioimmunoassay techniques to demonstrate that sperm antibodies indeed were present in 7% of men and 13% of women in a group of 614 people with otherwise unexplained infertility.

Enthusiasm for oral contraceptives continued to decline. Figures published during the year showed that in the U.S. prescriptions for the Pill had dropped from 64 million in 1975 to 49 million in 1978, whereas prescriptions for diaphragms had risen by 140% over the same period. Although medical opinion remained divided concerning the comparative risks and benefits of oral contraceptives, several reports supported the generally accepted view that alternative methods should be recommended to older women, particularly those who smoke cigarettes, since both age and smoking notoriously increase the risk of undesirable side effects, notably blood clots.

The tripling in cesarean deliveries in the U.S. during the 1970s was cited by a task force of the National Institutes of Health in recommending that women who previously had delivered by cesarean section be given an opportunity to choose vaginal delivery for subsequent babies. It declared invalid the old dictum "once a cesarean, always a cesarean." Use of the low segment transverse incision has greatly reduced the possibility of rupture of the uterine scar during later vaginal delivery.

Having previously warned women to limit smoking and drinking while pregnant, the U.S. Food and Drug Administration (FDA) added caffeine to the list. An FDA study on pregnant rats fed caffeine in doses equivalent to 12–24 cups of strong coffee a day produced offspring with missing toes or parts of toes. In animals whose mothers received the equivalent of two cups a day, skeletal growth was delayed. The coffee industry said the FDA warning was premature and lacked evidence from human studies. Rats metabolize caffeine differently than do humans, the industry claimed.

A report by the Food and Nutrition Board (FNB), an agency that recommends dietary standards for the U.S., clashed with dietary guidelines issued earlier in the year by the U.S. Public Health Service and the Department of Agriculture. Whereas the federal government had urged the general public to reduce intake of saturated fats and cholesterol as a means of lowering risk from heart disease, the FNB, an arm of the National Research Council of the National Academy of Sciences, said that it could find no clear-cut cause-and-effect relationship between heart disease and the consumption of such high-cholesterol foods as fatty meat, eggs, and dairy products. In fact it found no valid reason for healthy adults to decrease dietary cholesterol. The American Heart Association, a 20-year advocate of reducing caloric intake due to fat from 40 to 30%, criticized the FNB findings.

Controversy also beset the field of cancer research. New guidelines for screening tests issued by the American Cancer Society (ACS) recommended generally less frequent routine exams for symptom-free patients. A Pap smear test for cervical cancer need be taken only once every three years instead of annually as had been recommended by the ACS for the last two decades. Dissenting, the American College of Obstetricians and Gynecologists called the advice a disservice to women. An ACS recommendation against annual X-ray screening for lung cancer in cigarette smokers older than 40 was attacked by the Johns Hopkins School of Medicine and the Mayo Clinic.

Reserpine, a drug widely used to control high blood pressure, can cause cancer in animals and may pose a similar risk in humans, the National Cancer Institute (NCI) reported. But it also noted that patients requiring reserpine would have a greater health risk from stroke and related problems if they did not take it. In 1980 an estimated one million Americans used reserpine.

Three studies of humans, including one by the NCI that involved 9,000 persons, found only a minimal risk of cancer occurring from consuming products containing saccharin, an artificial sweetener. The conclusion differed from a 1977 Canadian study in laboratory animals that showed an overall 20% greater risk of bladder cancer for saccharin users. Two other artificial sweeteners, cyclamate and aspartame, again were denied approval by the FDA for human use in the U.S.

Fears that sodium nitrite, a preservative for processed foods, may cause lymphatic cancer were allayed by the FDA. Plans by the government to phase out use of the chemical were shelved after reexamination of 50,000 slides of tissue taken from rats during the original nitrite studies showed insufficient evidence of cancer. Sodium nitrite is widely used in bacon, hot dogs, and sausages to prevent growth of bacteria that cause botulism.

An encouraging sign in the disappointingly slow battle against cancer was seen in a paper published in the British medical journal *Lancet* in October. Four British workers showed that, in a study involving some 16,000 men, cancer was more than twice as common among those with a low level of vitamin A in their body fluids. In an appropriately cautious fashion the authors suggested that a diet high in vitamin A, present in such foods as dairy products and fresh vegetables, might provide protection against the second largest cause of death in the Western world.

A newly recognized and sometimes fatal disease that most often affects women under age 30 during their menstrual periods was linked by the U.S. Center for Disease Control to the use of tampons. Known as toxic-shock syndrome, the condition starts with a high fever, vomiting, and diarrhea. Within days, blood pressure drops sharply, bringing on a potentially fatal shock. The incidence of the disease was low: two or three cases in every 100,000 of the 50 million women using tampons. The relationship between tampons and infection was not clearly understood. Some authorities speculated that the bacterium *Staphyloccocus aureus* may have undergone a mutational change, producing a toxin for which the body has no defenses. Tampons may encourage vaginal propagation of the germ, which then may enter tissue through abrasions in the vaginal lining.

Physicians at the Johns Hopkins School of Medicine and Sinai Hospital in Baltimore announced development of a 250-g (9-oz), battery-powered surgical implant that fits in the abdomen of heart patients to deliver automatic bursts of lifesaving electric shock when cardiac arrest or irregular rhythm occurs. The miniature defibrillator, about the size of a package of cigarettes, monitors the regularity of heart rhythms. If irregularity occurs, it waits 15 seconds for the heart to regulate itself and then delivers its stimulus.

Mayo Clinic in Rochester, Minn., announced development of an X-ray scanner that can show human organs, heartbeats, and blood flow in three dimensions. A refinement of computed tomography, it can also detect coronary artery disease, diagnose complex congenital heart defects, assess heart muscle damage after a heart attack, and identify small cancerous lung tumours more reliably.

A new vaccine for hepatitis B proved 92% effective in U.S. tests in immunizing a high-risk group of 549 male volunteers. The results were matched against a control group of 534 men who received placebos.

Regulation and Legal Matters. In June, by a 5–4 vote, the U.S. Supreme Court ruled in effect that Congress has the right to limit Medicaid payment for abortions to women in danger of death and to victims of rape or incest. The decision came in response to a challenge to the so-called Hyde amendment, which since 1976 had denied unlimited federal funding for abortions. As a result of the amendment Medicaid-funded abortions had dropped from 300,000 a year before 1976 to less than 2,000 in 1979.

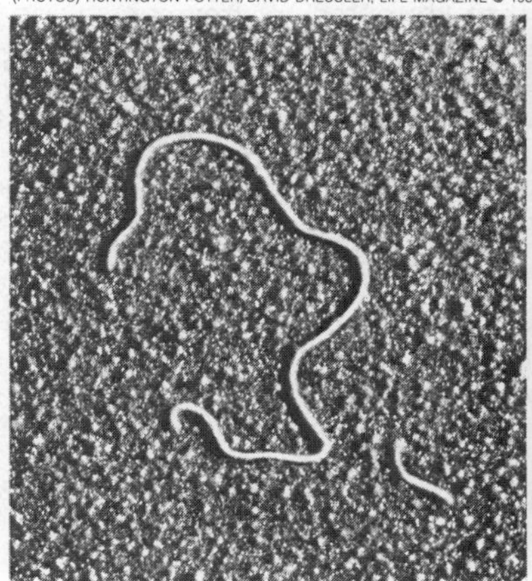

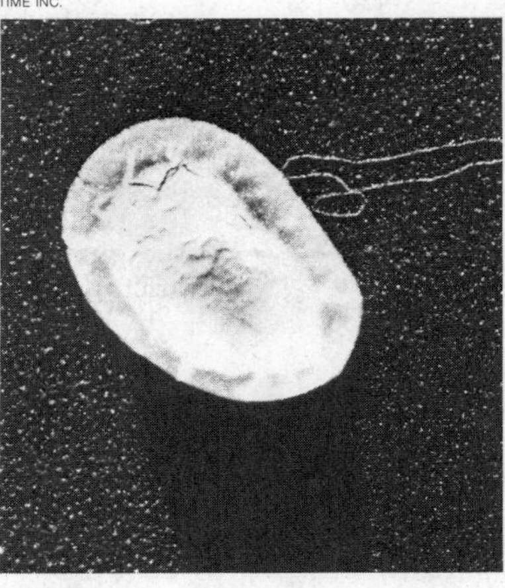

Photomicrographs depict stages in the recombinant DNA technique that forms the basis of commercial efforts to synthesize human proteins and other gene products in bacteria. First a circular bit of bacterial DNA called a plasmid is cut with a special enzyme (left), and a foreign gene (short DNA fragment in lower right corner) is inserted into the opening to form a hybrid, or recombinant, plasmid. This new molecule is then introduced into a suitable bacterial host (right), thereby endowing it with the ability to manufacture, or express, a gene product foreign to its nature.

In May a U.S. judge ordered the retrial of a case concerning a boy born with congenital defects after his mother had taken Bendectin (called Debendox in the U.K.), a morning-sickness suppressant, during her pregnancy. In the original hearing the jury decided that Bendectin had not been shown beyond a doubt to be the cause of the boy's deformity but awarded the parents $20,000 to cover their medical expenses. Both sides—the parents and Richardson-Merrell, the manufacturers—claimed that the result vindicated their opposing points of view, but the appeals judge held that the verdict was unsatisfactory in law, since either Bendectin was the cause of the boy's defects, in which case the parents were entitled to damages, or it was not, in which case the parents were entitled to nothing. The original verdict prompted some British politicians to demand that the drug be banned in the U.K., but the country's official Committee of Safety on Medicines decided that there were insufficient grounds for its withdrawal.

The case typified the difficulties surrounding attempts to fix the responsibiltiy for medical mishaps. It also drew attention to the need for codifying the legal relationship between consumers and suppliers of medical aid, so that victims of malpractice are fairly compensated in a way that does not frighten doctors, drug manufacturers, and others from undertaking innovations because of the risk of crippling lawsuits.

U.S. distribution of tetrahydrocannabinol (THC), the active ingredient of marijuana, was approved for cancer patients suffering uncontrollable nausea and vomiting as a result of treatment with anticancer drugs. Authorized to prescribe THC were doctors licensed by the NCI and the Drug Enforcement Administration. Approval of THC as an experimental drug, however, did not change its status as an illegal substance.

In the first code revision in 23 years, the American Medical Association (AMA) approved association with "talents of other health professionals." The revision was expected to relieve the AMA of some of the legal pressure imposed by several antitrust suits charging the organization with conspiracy to prevent chiropractors from practicing their profession for the public good. The new code permitted physicians to refer patients to chiropractors. It also deleted references to patient solicitation, including a ban on advertising by physicians. The ban had been the basis of a suit by the Federal Trade Commission against the AMA charging that the policy discouraged competitive pricing.

In Britain a major controversy followed a decision by Exit, the Society for the Right to Die with Dignity, to publish a booklet entitled *A Guide to Self-Deliverance,* which details five methods of painless suicide. In late 1980 there was doubt as to whether publication would go ahead and, if it did, whether those responsible would be guilty of an offense against British law, which no longer carried the act of suicide in its criminal code but which still made it a crime to aid or abet a suicide. The Exit action was an expression of a growing concern about the ability of doctors to prolong life beyond the point of tolerable living.

Economic Aspects. In May U.S. Pres. Jimmy Carter formally inaugurated the Department of Health and Human Services (HHS), a successor to the Department of Health, Education, and Welfare. Subsequently the HHS announced a two-year program to assess new medical technologies on the basis of their "social consequences" to determine if they should be funded under Medicare and Medicaid. The first assessment would cover heart transplants. Other heroic but expensive medical procedures would be studied later.

After being rebuffed by Congress in 1979, President Carter again placed legislative control of hospital costs among his highest legislative priorities in 1980. No congressional action, however, was taken on his proposal. As a means to curb inflation and to meet the problems of surplus hospital beds in the nation, President Carter signed an order blocking the building or expansion of federal hospitals except for those urgently needed.

A report to the secretary of Health and Human Services forecast an oversupply of physicians in the U.S. by 1990. The report was compiled by the Graduate Medical Education National Advisory Committee, an influential body in controlling the number of medical school graduates. The committee foresaw 536,000 physicians in 1990, compared with a national requirement of 466,000. Recommendations included decreasing U.S. medical school enrollment by 17% while promoting increases in minority enrollment, restricting entry of students from foreign medical schools, and maintaining the current level of nonphysician trainees in the health care field.

The FDA estimated that about 30% of the 178 million diagnostic X-ray procedures performed in the U.S. in 1979 were medically unnecessary and cost consumers an extra $2 billion in health care outlays. In rebuttal the American College of Radiology, an association of physicians specializing in radiological diagnosis and therapy, said the estimate lacked statistical support.

(DONALD W. GOULD; ARTHUR J. SNIDER)

[421.B.2.d; 422.G.2.c; 423.C.2.k; 424.B.1.a; 424.H.1.a; 424.I; 425.C.2.a and d; 425.J]

MENTAL HEALTH

Fundamental understanding of the roots of mental illness and advances in treatment continued to be discouragingly slow, and 1980 provided only scant cause for expectation that the pattern would soon change.

Schizophrenia, the most commonly diagnosed mental disease, affects about 1% of all adults worldwide, but its cause is still unknown. This ignorance has not been due to any lack of interest in the disease among psychiatrists and medical scientists, for an unending stream of papers in learned journals has advanced a plethora of theories and findings inculpating everything from white bread or an unhappy home life to genetically mediated faults in brain chemistry as possible factors in the disease. Although most of these theories have enjoyed short popularity and then faded from view, evidence amassed during the past two years seemed to support the idea that schizophrenia may be a delayed response to a virus infection.

In October five U.S. researchers published a paper in the British journal *Lancet* that apparently implicated cytomegalovirus (CMV) in the disease. This virus is one of several that infect most people at some time or other but usually without apparent ill effect. It was known, however, that certain viruses can linger in tissues for years, sometimes causing damage long after the original infection, when other factors happen to be favourable. The U.S. study showed that 60 schizophrenic patients, compared with 26 controls, had a high concentration of antibodies to CMV in the cerebrospinal fluid, the fluid that bathes the brain and spinal cord. These results extended findings published in 1979 by investigators in the U.K. that likewise had linked schizophrenia with evidence of past viral infection.

The presence of specific antibodies gave evidence of a past infection by the organism concerned and thus suggested a connection between CMV and the disease. The study did not explain why CMV should cause mental disorder in only a small proportion of the people that it infects, although there was growing evidence that abnormal or occasional responses to viral infections may be a factor in several diseases of hitherto unknown origin, including multiple sclerosis and at least some forms of cancer. Nevertheless, it did add some weight to the belief that schizophrenia is due to an organic disorder of the brain and is not (as some psychiatrists maintained) simply the response of a normal mind to abnormal pressures. Should an infective cause for schizophrenia be firmly established, prevention by means of immunization against the responsible virus might become possible.

Suspicion that the prevalence of mental disease and disorder is exaggerated was bolstered by a report in *Science Indications,* compiled by the U.S. National Science Foundation, which showed that mental health professionals in the U.S. have contributed more than three-fourths of the world's articles on psychological topics. This figure is markedly disproportionate to the country's size and overall research effort, since that nation produces only 40–50% of the world's writings on earth sciences and space sciences, clinical medicine, biology, and mathematics. It could be suggested that the incidence within a community of reported disorders of the mind bears a direct relationship to the magnitude of the professional effort devoted to their study and treatment.

In July the U.S. Food and Drug Administration (FDA) ordered that the popular tranquilizers Valium and Librium and other drugs of the same class (benzodiazepines) must carry warning labels stating that they should not be prescribed for "anxiety or tension associated with the stress of everyday life." This move was seen as a first step toward curbing the present excessive use of these agents. Jere E. Goyan, head of the FDA, conceded that the drugs are useful for patients facing a sudden crisis and for handling specific mental illnesses but stressed that their use should not become a casual, daily habit.

In the autumn a paper appearing in the *American Journal of Psychiatry* went so far as to suggest that major tranquilizers, or antipsychotic drugs—*e.g.*, Largactil, Stelazine, and Serenace—which have been used in vast quantities for more than a quarter of a century and which have greatly reduced the need for prolonged hospital treatment of schizophrenics and other grossly disturbed patients, should be employed only when essential, such as for the control of violence and then only in small doses and for brief periods. This recommendation reflected a growing concern about the severe side effects that frequently accompany prolonged therapy with these drugs. The most serious of these, so-called tardive (persistent) dyskinesia, takes the form of uncontrollable, involuntary movements of the tongue, lips, hands, and even the entire body, which can be both physically and socially disabling. The effects of these drugs on muscular activity were first recognized more than 20 years in the past, but only recently did it become apparent just how frequently they accompany long-term therapy, perhaps troubling more than half of those under treatment for at least ten years. (DONALD W. GOULD)

[438.D.1.a; 438.D.4.a.1]

DENTISTRY

To elevate the level of oral health in the U.S. the American Dental Association (ADA) during 1980 continued to focus attention on its multifaceted "access program" launched a year earlier. A chief goal for the coming decade, the program sought to bring comprehensive dental health care to five poorly served population groups: the elderly, the handicapped, the poor, remote-area residents, and the worker without dental insurance. At its annual session in October the ADA resolved to encourage state dental societies to develop access programs that provide reduced-fee comprehensive dental care to elderly persons who are indigent. Further, the ADA intensified its work in Congress to have dental care included under Medicare. The ADA was also helping the National Foundation of Dentistry for the Handicapped in its efforts to provide dental care to increasing numbers of handicapped individuals across the country.

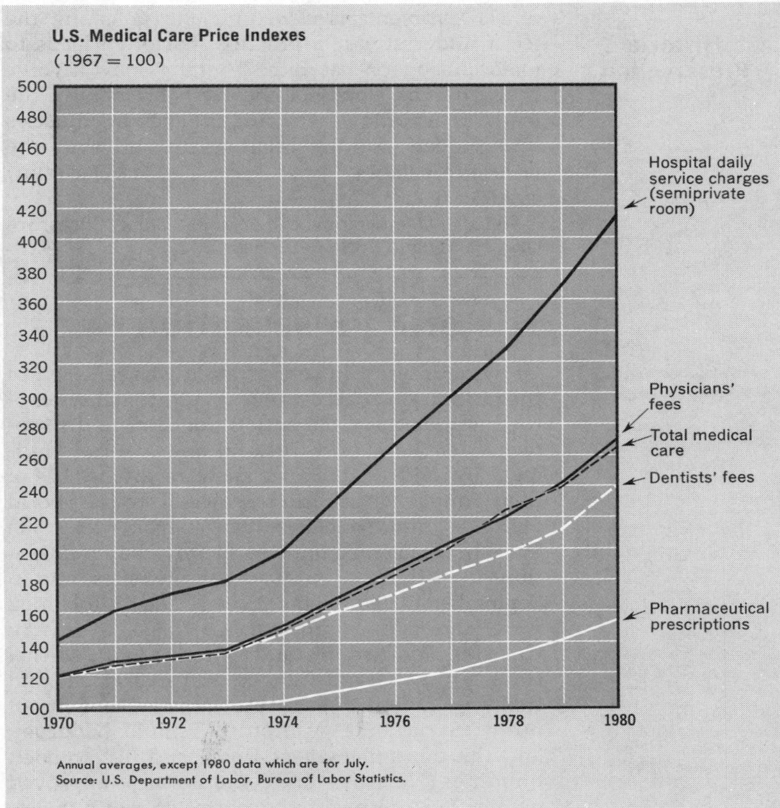

William H. Bowen and colleagues at the National Institute of Dental Research in Bethesda, Md., developed a new animal test to measure the ability of certain foods to cause cavities. By feeding rats their essential nutrition through tubes routed directly into the stomach and test foods on a programmed feeder, they found it possible to determine the cariogenicity (decay-producing ability) of many substances. Results showed that certain nonsugary snack foods and lightly sugared breakfast cereals may have the same decay-producing potential as more heavily sugared counterparts. For example, the potato chips used in the experiment demonstrated modest decay-producing potential. "Potato chips are frequently promoted as noncariogenic snacks," the investigators noted. "It may be necessary, on the basis of our results, to reevaluate this opinion." The study also reaffirmed findings of other investigations that chocolate and caramel are less cariogenic than sucrose (table sugar). In addition it suggested that the cookies used in the study are more cariogenic than sucrose and encourage the proliferation of decay-causing bacteria.

Millions of adults who suffer from severe facial pain, backaches, or dizzy spells may be unaware that dental treatment can help them, reported New York City dentist Harold Gelb. Many of the same individuals also suffer from crooked jaws, lopsided faces, and deformed lips. Gelb pointed out that these problems frequently are caused by a misalignment of the temporomandibular joint (TMJ), a location in front of the ear at which the lower jaw hinges. One of the most common causes of TMJ problems is clenching and gnashing the teeth under stress, a practice that often leads to malocclusion or bat bite. Therapy may involve changing the slopes of the teeth or making the teeth higher or lower to bring the chewing muscles into proper working relationship and thus the jaws into balance. (LOU JOSEPH)

[422.E.1.a.ii; 10/35.C.1]

See also Demography; Life Sciences; Nobel Prizes; Social Security and Welfare Services.

Historic Preservation

Growing interest in conservation was reflected in the ratification or acceptance by additional states of the International Convention Concerning the Protection of the World Cultural and Natural Heritage. By mid-1980, 53 states were giving 1% of their annual contribution to UNESCO to the World Heritage Fund. At its meeting in October 1979, the World Heritage Committee approved 45 nominations to its list of cultural and natural sites, and in September 1980 a further 25 were added. Included were the site of ancient Carthage (Tunisia); Chartres Cathedral and Mont Saint-Michel (France); the Grand Canyon and Everglades and Redwood national parks (U.S.); the ancient city of Bosra (Syria); the Aphrodite Temple (Cyprus); and the mining town of Røros and old wooden buildings (Norway). The committee also approved listing the Auschwitz concentration camp in Poland as a "unique site" but decided to restrict the inscription of other sites of a similar nature.

The first and, in many respects, the largest international conservation campaign, to preserve man's cultural heritage in Egyptian and Sudanese Nubia, came to an end in 1980, 20 years after it was launched. On March 10 a ceremony was held to mark completion of the transfer of the Ptolemaic and Roman temples of Philae to the neighbouring island of Agilkia farther up the Nile. The campaign had been marked by the dismantling and reassembly of other outstanding monuments, such as the temples of Abu Simbel, also carried out with the aid of international contributions. A number of smaller structures were saved by the governments of Egypt, Sudan, and other states through bilateral assistance projects. International contributions amounted to nearly $34 million.

A major salvage program based on the example of the Nubian project was under way in India following the construction of a dam on the Krishna River near Hyderabad. The most important temple in the area to be flooded, the 7th-century Kudavalli Sangameswaram, was completely dismantled, and the stones were moved to a site 15 mi away, above the level of the lake to be formed by the dam. Projects for the rescue of a group of 26 other temples were planned, all financed largely by the central government with some participation by the state of Andhra Pradesh.

In Venice contracts worth $6.6 million were negotiated for the installation of modern sewerage systems in the Venetian area, and specialized systems for historic Venice and the nearby island of Giudecca were under study. The municipality also placed a $3.6 million contract for additional water supplies; this would permit the further closing of artesian wells, the use of which had contributed to subsidence. Private committees completed the restoration of the Basilica dell' Assunta on the island

The temple of Isis now stands fully restored on the island of Agilkia, Egypt. It was dismantled and transferred stone by stone from its former site on Philae, flooded by the Aswan High Dam. The temple was originally built in the 3rd century BC.

MICHELE DA SILVA—CAMERA PRESS

Hebrew Literature:
see Literature

Highways:
see Engineering Projects; Transportation

Hinduism:
see Religion

Hockey:
see Field Hockey and Lacrosse; Ice Hockey

Holland:
see Netherlands, The

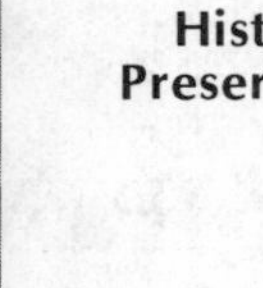

KEYSTONE

The Covent Garden central market in London was officially reopened in June as a shopping centre. It contains many shops, art galleries, and restaurants.

of Torcello. The Church of SS. Maria e Donato on Murano was reopened to the public after major restoration work on the building and its famed mosaic pavement. In southern Italy fears were expressed that the Pompeii ruins had been damaged by the November 23 earthquake.

The government of Sri Lanka launched a campaign in January 1980 for the restoration of Buddhist monuments in the roughly triangular area formed by the former capital cities of Anuradhapura, Polonnaruva, and Kandy. Within this area are such outstanding sites as Sigiriya (with its mural paintings), giant stupas, and colossal statues of Buddha. Another campaign launched during the year was for the preservation of sites in Malta. These included the Hal Saflieni Hypogeum (late Neolithic), which comprises a series of subterranean rooms carved out of the limestone rock; Vilhena Palace and the bastions of the former capital city of Mdina; Ft. St. Elmo, built by the Knights of the Order of Malta; and the Citadelle on Gozo.

In the U.S. one of the more interesting developments was the award of grants, amounting to $5 million, by the Heritage Conservation and Recreation Service of the Department of the Interior for the preservation of the nation's maritime heritage. Included were the barque "Elissa," to be restored by the Historic Galveston (Texas) Foundation; the "Falls of Clyde," a four-masted, full-rigged ship in Honolulu; various small craft of historic interest; a lighthouse in Navesink, N.J.; and support for the preservation of objects recovered by submarine archaelogists from the Civil War ship "Monitor," the first ship to have cannons mounted in a revolving turret.

In many European cities derelict buildings and quarters of historic interest were being renovated. In Edinburgh the city council, the biggest owner of empty, derelict historic buildings (purchased for road and redevelopment schemes that were not realized), turned several over to the Cockburn Conservation Trust for restoration and adaption to meet contemporary needs. Eighteenth-century terrace houses on Candlemaker Row, for example, were renovated at a cost of about £80,000 and then sold at a profit. In London the former central market in Covent Garden, restored as a shopping centre after several years of controversy over redevelopment plans, was officially reopened in June. Establishment of a £15 million National Heritage Memorial Fund was announced in April. However, British conservationists were concerned over bureaucratic delays in the listing of historic buildings, which in some cases was rendered moot by demolition. (HIROSHI DAIFUKU)

See also Architecture; Environment; Museums.

Abandoned grain silos that previously stored oats were converted at a cost of $8 million into the Quaker Square Hilton hotel in Akron, Ohio.

MARCY NIGHSWANDER—THE NEW YORK TIMES

EMPTYING THE ATTIC

by Kyle Husfloen

Collecting, as a pastime, is not new. Its roots are as old as recorded history. But until fairly recently, collecting tended to be far removed from the everyday life of ordinary people, a rather exclusive hobby suitable for those with leisure time and surplus income that they could afford to spend extravagantly.

As the 20th century draws to a close, it is apparent that this situation has changed dramatically. No longer are the wealthy the only ones with time and resources to search out works of art or antiques, whether to satisfy some personal aesthetic taste or to meet the need for ostentatious display. Since the early 1960s there has been an astounding growth of collector interest at all levels of society. Furthermore, this interest has spread beyond the field of antiques to include the much broader area of what are loosely described as collectibles.

Collectibles and Antiques. For all that it is a commonly used term, "collectible" is difficult to define precisely. In general, a collectible can be any artifact from the recent past that, when first produced, was a mundane item used in the course of daily homelife and/or commerce. "Antiques," on the other hand, are more historic pieces and by legal definition are at least 100 years old. With age, they have developed a certain aura of exclusivity.

It should be pointed out that the two terms often overlap, and strict interpretation is open to debate. Many pieces well under 100 years of age are sold as antiques. Using current market values as a guideline can also be misleading, since many collectibles will sell for much more than truly antique pieces. For example, an 18th-century handwritten American land deed, an antique in the strictest sense and certainly an intriguing historic relic, may sell on the collecting market for a fraction of the cost of a rare piece of Depression-era glass, mass-produced in the 1920s and '30s. Age alone cannot be used to judge desirability and demand in the current market.

Another popular collecting field relates to "collectors' items." Again, interpretation of the term may be open to debate, but for purposes of discussion, collectors' items may be said to encompass the new and very recently made products, such as limited edition plates, that have been and are being produced to appeal directly to the collecting mania. They are ready-made collectibles, marketed as having all the best qualities of true antiques and collectibles but without any age criteria.

Milk Bottle Madness and Other Phenomena. Clearly, collecting is a well-established and pervasive phenomenon, but what lies behind its incredible popularity? What conscious or subconscious motives drive millions to search out and accumulate a myriad of artifacts, many with seemingly little intrinsic value? Items ranging from milk bottles to Christmas seals are being collected, and each collectible has its own dedicated core of enthusiastic and well-informed aficionados. What is the magic lure that compels such pursuits?

Probably the major motivation is a desire for self-expression and personal fulfillment. In a computerized age, it seems increasingly difficult to find a creative outlet for one's energies. How can a person express his or her individuality while still remaining within the bounds of accepted social behaviour? Collecting is one way.

In the 1950s, when Marion I. Levy picked up his first apple parer at a "your choice 50¢" table in a local flea market, he was amused by the Rube Goldberg aspect of the strange apparatus. Although that first parer was purchased only as a curiosity, Levy became fascinated by the mechanical ingenuity that had gone into devising this 19th-century utensil. Pursuing his interest, he discovered that parers had been produced in a wide variety of shapes and styles. By 1980 Levy had acquired a significant collection of unusual old parers; he had done extensive research into their history and development and had become a leading authority on the subject Meanwhile, as other collectors entered the field, many of those 50-cent apple parers were bringing prices in the $25 to $50 range.

Other reasons for collecting, related to the need for personal self-expression, are nostalgia and individual aesthetics.

Many people, young and old alike, have found the hectic pace of modern life bewildering and frustrating. They seek to recapture a bit of their own past or some fragment of a bygone era that they have heard or read about. "The Good Old Days" seem to offer a respite from atomic age pressures, whether the "Good Old Days" in question are the 1920s or the 1950s. Hence, many devotees have found a pleasurable obsession in preserving the everyday items made obsolete by modern technology and economics. Take, for example, the more than 200

Kyle D. Husfloen is editor of The Antique Trader Weekly. *He is the editor of* The Antique Trader Weekly Book of Collectible Dolls *and the author of numerous articles on antiques and collectibles.*

COLLECTION OF RON VILLANI; PHOTO, BILL ARSENAULT

members of MOO (Milkbottles Only Organization). Glass milk bottles are a thing of the past, but the members of this collecting group have taken up the task of preserving them and studying their history and evolution. To disseminate information on this collectible, MOO even publishes a monthly newsletter, *The Milking Parlor*.

Perhaps it was nostalgia that led John C. Tibbitts to begin collecting old dog-license tags. His involvement began when, as a comic gift, he prepared a mounted plaque displaying the tags of his former pet. Soon, however, he became entranced by the various sizes and shapes of these bits of metal, and before long he was advertising for tags in a national collectors' publication. This led to the discovery that he was not alone. The International Society of Animal License Collectors (ISALC) was already in operation, with over 100 members scattered around the United States. Dog-license tags date back at least to the mid-19th century, and all the latest research information and data on new discoveries are presented in the club's newsletter, *Paw Prints*. For serious collectors like Tibbitts, dog-license tags have a number of virtues. They are abundant, easy to display and maintain, and relatively inexpensive. Recent dog tags sell for less than 50 cents apiece, though more unusual and scarce ones from the 19th century can bring $15 or more.

It was aesthetic appeal that attracted Marian D. Kealey to old eyewash baths (commonly called eyecups). When her father brought one home from a bottle-digging expedition at a garbage dump, Kealey was captivated by the way the old glass refracted light. Hunting for more examples, she, too, discovered that she was not alone in her pursuit. There had even been a monthly newsletter for collectors—the *Eye Wash News*—but it had ceased publication in 1975 though it had more than 150 subscribers. As Kealey continued her search, she delved into historical research, eventually publishing a feature article on the subject in a national collectors' magazine.

The Profit Motive. One final factor that has played an undeniable part in the rapid growth of the collecting hobby is investment potential.

For many years, fine antiques have been touted as prime investments, rivaling blue chip stocks. However, few people have the interest or the financial means to consider seriously, for example, the purchase of an 18th-century American highboy at around $100,000. On the other hand, many a collector who has concentrated on less expensive antiques or some of the newer collectibles has witnessed a great financial appreciation for a collection started only a few years earlier.

Although investment-minded persons often ask, "What is a good collectible investment that is sure to appreciate in the future?", most dedicated collectors put such considerations near the bottom of their list of reasons for collecting. To collect anything, one should first find it personally appealing. For most people, collecting is an expression of individual interests and desires. Mass media promotion has certainly tended to stress the investment aspect, and in today's unsteady economy this may be natural. But those for whom it is a primary concern cannot truly be classified as "collectors."

In the end, then, it is apparent that there can be no simple answers to what is collectible and why people collect. Every facet of the collecting hobby has expanded tremendously in recent years and will undoubtedly continue to do so. Citizens of the 21st century may well consider, among their "unalienable rights," "Life, Liberty and the pursuit . . ." of collectibles.

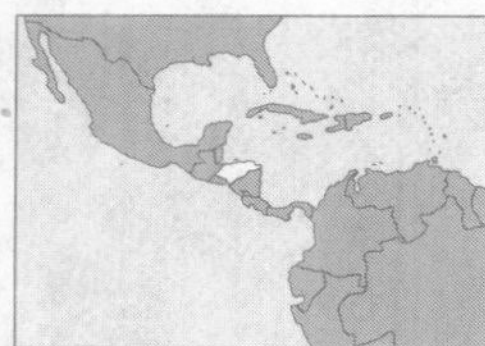

Honduras

Hungary

Honduras

A republic of Central America, Honduras is bounded by Nicaragua, El Salvador, Guatemala, the Caribbean Sea, and the Pacific Ocean. Area: 112,088 sq km (43,277 sq mi). Pop. (1980 est.): 3,691,000, including 90% mestizo. Cap. and largest city: Tegucigalpa (pop., 1977 est., 316,800). Language: Spanish; some Indian dialects. Religion: Roman Catholic. President of a three-man military junta in 1980, Gen. Policarpo Paz García until July 20; after July 20 Honduras was governed by the Constituent Assembly, though Paz remained provisional president.

On April 20, 1980, elections for a 71-member Constituent Assembly were held. The Liberal Party unexpectedly gained 52% of the votes but not a clear majority in the assembly, and the Innovation and Unity Party (PINU) held the balance of power with 3.5%; the National Party, linked with the armed forces, had 44.5%. Some three-quarters of the electorate voted, despite an abstention campaign by the left-wing Honduran Patriotic Front, a grouping of about 50 organizations ineligible to take part in the campaign.

The U.S. encouraged civilian rule in Honduras, doubling its economic aid for 1980 to $45 million. It also allocated $3.9 million in military aid, to create in Honduras a buffer state between Nicaragua, El Salvador, and Guatemala.

Honduras's relations with Nicaragua underwent a period of strain at the end of 1979, due to the use of the border area by former members of Nicaragua's National Guard. However, during 1980 diplomatic relations, severed in mid-1979, were resumed. In October Honduras and El Salvador agreed on a treaty ending the state of war that had lasted since the so-called Soccer War of 1969; a mechanism was established for settling the boundary dispute arising from the war, and diplomatic relations were reestablished.

The nation's gross domestic product grew by 6.7% in 1979, a decline from 8.9% in 1978. Based on the official cost-of-living index, inflation grew by 8.5%, although the actual rate was nearer to 14%. (CHRISTINE MELLOR)

HONDURAS

Education. (1978) Primary, pupils 528,138, teachers 14,369; secondary and vocational, pupils 108,852, teachers 2,771; teacher training, students 1,831, teachers 128; higher (university only), students 18,933, teaching staff 931.

Finance. Monetary unit: lempira, with (Sept. 22, 1980) a par value of 2 lempiras to U.S. $1 (free rate of 4.81 lempiras = £1 sterling). Gold, SDR's, and foreign exchange (June 1980) U.S. $229 million. Budget (1979 actual): revenue 655.9 million lempiras; expenditure 735.1 million lempiras. Gross national product (1979) 4,114,000,000 lempiras. Money supply (June 1980) 562.7 million lempiras. Cost of living (Tegucigalpa; 1975 = 100; April 1980) 153.9.

Foreign Trade. (1979) Imports 1,663,900,000 lempiras; exports 1,465,000,000 lempiras. Import sources (1978): U.S. 42%; Japan 9%; Guatemala 6%; Venezuela 6%. Export destinations (1978): U.S. 57%; West Germany 13%; The Netherlands 5%. Main exports: bananas 27%; coffee 27%; beef 8%; metal ores *c.* 6%; timber 6%.

Transport and Communications. Roads (1978) 8,308 km. Motor vehicles in use (1978): passenger 15,900; commercial (including buses) 27,700. Railways (1978) *c.* 1,780 km. Air traffic (1978): 324 million passenger-km; freight 3.8 million net ton-km. Shipping (1979): merchant vessels 100 gross tons and over 99; gross tonnage 193,256. Telephones (Dec. 1976) 19,000. Radio receivers (Dec. 1977) 163,000. Television receivers (Dec. 1977) 48,000.

Agriculture. Production (in 000; metric tons; 1979): corn *c.* 368; sorghum *c.* 36; sugar, raw value (1978) *c.* 128; dry beans *c.* 20; bananas *c.* 1,300; plantains (1978) *c.* 100; oranges *c.* 27; pineapples *c.* 32; palm oil *c.* 11; coffee *c.* 75; cotton, lint (1978) *c.* 9; tobacco *c.* 7; beef and veal (1978) *c.* 51; timber (cu m; 1978) *c.* 4,175. Livestock (in 000; 1978): cattle *c.* 1,700; pigs *c.* 530; horses *c.* 290; chickens *c.* 8,200.

Industry. Production (in 000; metric tons; 1978): cement 274; petroleum products (1977) *c.* 530; lead ore (metal content) *c.* 20; zinc ore (metal content) *c.* 20; electricity (kw-hr; 1977) *c.* 701,000.

Hungary

A people's republic of central Europe, Hungary is bordered by Czechoslovakia, the U.S.S.R., Romania, Yugoslavia, and Austria. Area: 93,033 sq km (35,920 sq mi). Pop. (1980 prelim.): 10,710,000, including (1970) Hungarian 95.8%; German 2.1%. Cap. and largest city: Budapest (pop., 1980 prelim., 2,060,000). Language (1970): Magyar 95.8%. Religion (1970): Roman Catholic about 60%, most of the remainder Protestant or atheist. First secretary of the Hungarian Socialist Workers' (Communist) Party in 1980, Janos Kadar; chairman of the

HUNGARY

Education. (1979–80) Primary, pupils 1,127,900, teachers 73,469; secondary, pupils 341,700, teachers 15,168; higher, students 103,500, teaching staff 13,597.

Finance. Monetary unit: forint, with (Sept. 22, 1980) a commercial free rate of 31.75 forints to U.S. $1 (76.31 forints = £1 sterling) and a noncommercial (tourist) rate of 22.80 forints to U.S. $1 (54.78 forints = £1 sterling). Budget (1979 est.): revenue 407.2 billion forints; expenditure 410.8 billion forints. Net material product (1978) 517.6 billion forints.

Foreign Trade. (1979) Imports 308,906,000,000 forints; exports 282,129,000,000 forints. Import sources: U.S.S.R. 29%; West Germany 12%; East Germany 7%; Czechoslovakia 5%; Austria 5%. Export destinations: U.S.S.R. 28%; West Germany 10%; East Germany 8%; Czechoslovakia 7%; Italy 5%; Poland 5%. Main exports: machinery 23%; motor vehicles 10%; chemicals 9%; meat and meat preparations 6%; iron and steel 5%; fruit and vegetables 5%.

Transport and Communications. Roads (1979) 87,426 km (including 192 km expressways). Motor vehicles in use (1979): passenger 913,400; commercial 151,700. Railways: (1978) 8,001 km; traffic (1979) 12,440,000,000 passenger-km, freight 24,069,000,000 net ton-km. Air traffic (1978): 761 million passenger-km; freight 5.9 million net ton-km. Inland waterways in regular use (1978) 1,302 km. Telephones (Jan. 1978) 1,103,800. Radio licenses (Dec. 1978) 2,590,000. Television licenses (Dec. 1978) 2,633,000.

Agriculture. Production (in 000; metric tons; 1979): corn *c.* 7,400; wheat 3,706; barley 710; rye 95; potatoes *c.* 1,500; sugar, raw value *c.* 511; cabbages (1978) *c.* 250; tomatoes *c.* 500; onions *c.* 130; sunflower seed *c.* 400; rapeseed *c.* 110; green peas (1978) *c.* 253; plums (1978) *c.* 159; apples *c.* 980; wine *c.* 530; tobacco *c.* 23; milk *c.* 2,392; beef and veal *c.* 140; pork *c.* 880. Livestock (in 000; Dec. 1978): cattle 1,966; pigs 8,011; sheep 2,864; horses 134; chickens 62,857.

Industry. Index of production (1975 = 100; 1979) 120. Production (in 000; metric tons; 1979): coal 3,003; lignite 22,658; crude oil 2,030; natural gas (cu m) *c.* 6,500,000; electricity (kw-hr) 24,518,000; iron ore (24% metal content) 532; pig iron 2,375; crude steel 3,877; bauxite 2,976; aluminum 72; cement 4,858; petroleum products (1978) *c.* 10,400; sulfuric acid 588; fertilizers (1978) nitrogenous 612, phosphate *c.* 239; cotton yarn 61; man-made fibres 27; commercial vehicles (units) 16.

Hong Kong:
see Dependent States

Horse Racing:
see Equestrian Sports; Gambling

Horticulture:
see Gardening

Hospitals:
see Health and Disease

Hydroelectric Power:
see Energy; Engineering Projects

Hydrology:
see Earth Sciences

Presidential Council (chief of state), Pal Losonczi; president of the Council of Ministers (premier), Gyorgy Lazar.

The 12th Congress of the Hungarian Socialist Workers' Party was held in Budapest, March 24–27, 1980. The main theme was a frank appraisal of the nation's achievements and shortcomings since the 11th congress five years earlier. Addressing the 767 delegates, Hungarian Communist Party leader Janos Kadar said: "We cannot isolate ourselves from the world economy, but by improving our work we can cushion its unfavourable impact considerably." The congress elected a new 127-member Central Committee that included 32 new faces. The Central Committee in turn named the new Politburo, which consisted of 13 members instead of the previous 15. Five of Kadar's oldest associates—Istavan Huszar, Jeno Fock, Antal Apro, Bela Biszku, and Dezso Nemez—left that key party body, and three younger men were promoted to be full Politburo members: Ferenc Havasi, 51, party secretary in charge of the economy since 1978; Mihaly Korom, 53, with a career in military security; and Lajos Mehes, 53, first secretary of the Budapest party organization. Kadar was reelected the party's first secretary.

At the general election of June 8 a new Parliament of 352 members was elected by 7,462,953 votes from candidates proposed by the Patriotic People's Front (54,070 votes against). More than 100 members were nonparty. In 15 constituencies there were two candidates instead of one; in two of those neither candidate received over 50% of the votes and by-elections were held.

The new Parliament on June 27 reelected Antal Apro as its president. The new members, one in three of whom had been elected for the first time, chose the country's Presidential Council consisting of the president of the republic, two vice-presidents, one secretary, and 17 members. Pal Losonczi was reelected president and Gyorgy Lazar again was named premier. The Parliament approved the new government (Council of Ministers) comprising four (no longer six) deputy premiers and 17 ministers, including three new ones: Istvan Hetenyi, 54, minister of finance; Istvan Horvath, 45, minister of the interior; and Jeno Vancsa, 52, minister of agriculture and food.

A two-day parliamentary debate on the country's economic situation ended on September 26. The planners had predicted that by 1980 real income would increase by 25% over 1975, but it rose by only 6%. Some 40% of Hungary's national income came from exports, about two-fifths to the U.S.S.R. and other Comecon countries. Of the balance West Germany was chief customer. Hungary's hard-currency exports of U.S. $3.4 billion in 1979 were $500 million below its imports. At the end of 1979 its debt to Western commercial banks amounted to $7.3 billion, and interest payments were approximately $800 million. To reduce its debts Hungary had to increase exports and reduce imports. In this regard 1980 started encouragingly: exports to the non-Communist world in the first six months increased by a fifth over 1979, while imports were slightly lower.

Closing the debate on the national economy, Kadar spoke of events in Poland: "Hungary wishes to see Poland strong and considers that the Poles, under the leadership of their party, are capable of solving their problems alone." Sandor Gaspar, a member of the Politburo and secretary-general of the Council of Trade Unions, admitted in October that there had been "stoppages in some Hungarian plants due to the incorrect attitude of management."

On July 24 Soviet leader Leonid Brezhnev and Kadar met in the Crimea. In the same month Veselin Djuranovic, president of the Federal Executive Council of Yugoslavia, visited Hungary officially. Laszlo Cardinal Lekai, archbishop of Esztergom and primate of Hungary, visited England from July 3 to 8 as guest of the archbishop of Canterbury. On September 29 Kadar received in Budapest Agostino Cardinal Casaroli, the Vatican secretary of state. (K. M. SMOGORZEWSKI)

Ice Hockey

North American. After four years in the grip of the heretofore invincible Montreal Canadiens, the Stanley Cup finally found a new home, gracing Long Island for the first time in the hands of the eight-year-old New York Islanders, one of the youngest teams ever to win the National Hockey League (NHL) championship. Having made it to the semifinals four times and the quarterfinals once, the Islanders believed they were ready for the finals. They soon proved that they were by winning the Cup on home ice in Nassau Coliseum

WIDE WORLD

Bobby Clarke (16) of the Philadelphia Flyers checks Bob Bourne of the New York Islanders in a Stanley Cup championship game in May at Nassau Coliseum in Uniondale, N.Y. The Islanders won the championship by beating the Flyers four games to two.

against the Philadelphia Flyers four games to two in the best-of-seven series.

The series included two overtime games, the first contest and the last. Denis Potvin's goal decided the opening contest in favour of New York, while Bobby Nystrom, the Islanders' 27-year-old right wing, scored in the final game to win the Cup.

In a year of youth that saw the emergence of 19-year-old Wayne Gretzky, the centre known as "the Great Gretzky," one of the game's finest players and certainly its most durable retired. Gordie Howe, 52 years old, announced his retirement a second time, the first having come in 1971 after 25 years with the Detroit Red Wings. Howe had returned to hockey in 1973 to play with his sons Mark and Marty on the New England (now Hartford) Whalers in the newly formed World Hockey Association (WHA). He completed his career with 11 NHL records including most regular season games, 1,767, most goals, 801, and most 30-goal years, 14.

During the 1979–80 season the WHA merged with the NHL, ending the long interleague war that had escalated player salaries into six figures. In the first year of the merger the four former WHA teams, Hartford, Quebec, Edmonton, and Winnipeg, fared poorly. Hartford had the most respectable record, finishing with 73 points, while Winnipeg had the worst with 51.

But some of the WHA players did very well, most notably Gretzky, the dazzling centre for Edmonton whom the NHL would not consider a rookie because of his year of play in the WHA. But the young player picked up two major awards, the Hart Trophy as the league's most valuable player and the Lady Byng Trophy as the most gentlemanly player, making him the most youthful double award winner in NHL history.

The rookie of the year was Raymond Bourque of the Boston Bruins, a brilliant defenseman who reminded some Bruin fans of their former idol, Bobby Orr. The league's best defenseman was Larry Robinson, who helped shore up a Montreal team missing its retired goalie, Ken Dryden. Bryan Trottier of the Islanders won the Conn Smythe Trophy as the play-offs' most valuable player.

U.S. goalie Jim Craig kissed the gold medal he won during the XIII Olympic Winter Games at Lake Placid, N.Y., in February. The U.S. ice hockey team won the gold medal for the first time since 1960.

WIDE WORLD

Although it was a relatively quiet year for violent on-ice incidents, there were fisticuffs in the stands of New York's Madison Square Garden during the winter when the Boston Bruins jumped over the rail to collar some fans who, they said, had grabbed their sticks and cut one player, Stan Jonathan, with the blade. The fans in turn sued the Bruins, and the matter was in litigation at the year's end. Players were better protected on the ice because of a new rule making helmets mandatory for all newcomers to the league and requiring all veteran players to wear them unless the player signed an insurance waiver.

The biggest trade of the year was the one that sent massive defenseman Barry Beck, the presumed cornerstone of the Colorado Rockies, to the New York Rangers for Pat Hickey, Lucien DeBlois, Mike McEwen, Dean Turner, and Bob Crawford. The Rangers did not improve noticeably through that trade alone, and the Rockies finished the season tied with Winnipeg for the lowest point total in the league, 51. After the season the Rockies found a new coach, Bill MacMillan, formerly with the Islander organization, to replace Don Cherry. The Rangers also acquired a new coach, replacing Fred Shero with Herb Brooks, coach of the U.S. Olympic team. Brooks was not immediately available because of other commitments, and in the interim his place was filled by Craig Patrick, his Olympic assistant and the Rangers' operations director.

There was also trouble in Toronto with a rift between management and players resulting in the dispatching of Lanny McDonald to Colorado. After the season Mike Palmateer, Toronto's goalie, went to the Washington Capitals for Robert Picard, a young defenseman.

The greatest hockey triumph of the year was enjoyed by the players of the U.S. team that won the gold medal in the Olympic Games (*see* below). After their victory 12 of the Olympians signed with NHL teams. The sweetest season belonged to Ken Morrow, a defenseman who joined the New York Islanders after the Olympics and went on to add the Stanley Cup to his Olympic medal.

In the minor leagues the Hershey Bears defeated New Brunswick for the American League championship, while the Salt Lake City Golden Eagles defeated the Fort Worth Texans in the Central League final. The Erie Blades were the Eastern League champions, and the Kalamazoo Wings took the International Hockey League title.

(ROBIN CATHY HERMAN)

European and International. No world championship was contested in the 1979–80 season because of the Olympic Winter Games. The titles could not be won concurrently because the Olympic amateur rules excluded professionals, who are eligible for world championship teams.

The U.S. team won the Olympic competition for the first time since 1960, suggesting a likelier North American parity with the Soviet and

Table I. NHL Final Standings, 1979–80

	Won	Lost	Tied	Goals	Goals against	Pts.
JAMES NORRIS DIVISION						
Montreal	47	20	13	328	240	107
Los Angeles	30	36	14	290	313	74
Pittsburgh	30	37	13	251	303	73
Hartford	27	34	19	303	312	73
Detroit	26	43	11	268	306	63
CHARLES F. ADAMS DIVISION						
Buffalo	47	17	16	318	201	110
Boston	46	21	13	310	234	105
Minnesota	36	28	16	311	253	88
Toronto	35	40	5	304	327	75
Quebec	25	44	11	248	313	61
LESTER PATRICK DIVISION						
Philadelphia	48	12	20	327	254	116
Islanders (N.Y.)	39	28	13	281	247	91
Rangers (N.Y.)	38	32	10	308	284	86
Atlanta	35	32	13	282	269	83
Washington	27	40	13	261	293	67
CONN SMYTHE DIVISION						
Chicago	34	27	19	241	250	87
St. Louis	34	34	12	266	278	80
Vancouver	27	37	16	256	281	70
Edmonton	28	39	13	301	322	69
Winnipeg	20	49	11	214	314	51
Colorado	19	48	13	234	308	51

Table II. Olympic Games Ice Hockey Competition, 1980

	Won	Lost	Tied	Goals	Goals against	Pts.
RED QUALIFYING DIVISION						
U.S.S.R.	5	0	0	51	11	10
Finland	3	2	0	26	18	6
Canada	3	2	0	28	12	6
Poland	2	3	0	15	23	4
Netherlands, The	1	3	1	16	43	3
Japan	0	4	1	7	36	1
BLUE QUALIFYING DIVISION						
Sweden	4	0	1	26	7	9
United States	4	0	1	25	10	9
Czechoslovakia	3	2	0	34	16	6
Romania	1	3	1	13	29	3
West Germany	1	4	0	21	30	2
Norway	0	4	1	9	36	1
MEDAL PLAY-OFFS ROUND						
United States	2	0	1	10	7	5
U.S.S.R.	2	1	0	16	8	4
Sweden	0	1	2	7	14	2
Finland	0	2	1	7	11	1

Czechoslovak teams in future international competitions. The chance to put this to an early test was thwarted by the cancellation of a Canada Cup tournament to have been held in Canada in September, a consequence of the year's strained international relations. The Olympic competition was thus the season's only serious yardstick by which to measure the relative merits of North American competition against the might of Eastern Europe. The crucial U.S. defeat of the U.S.S.R. by a score of 4–3 gave the sport a tremendous boost at the international level.

It was not just the result of the tournament but its manner of achievement that captured the imagination. The final score was on the board with ten minutes left—probably the longest ten minutes in the lives of the host nation's players and supporters. Despite all the skill of the fast-skating Soviet forwards, a tight and resolute U.S. defense held out. During the final two minutes the Americans' play became a little ragged, and their coach observed afterward: "Somehow, we managed to calm them down." But nothing could quell the high-spirited spectators as they witnessed the Soviets' first defeat in any Olympic ice hockey game in 12 years. A refusal to wilt under pressure and an ability to produce the best play during the final periods of matches were the hallmarks of a U.S. team that improved remarkably as the tournament progressed.

Making its first Olympic hockey appearance since 1968, Canada, a nation possessing the world's best professionals, entered a strictly amateur team of collegiate players based in Calgary, Alta., and lacking international experience. Even so, they won sixth place. Although level on points with Finland and with a superior goal difference in its qualifying section, Canada failed to make the last four because Finland had won the match played between the two.

Jim Craig (*see* BIOGRAPHIES) of the U.S. proved the outstanding goalkeeper in the series, conceding only 15 goals during 7 games. The three highest point scorers were all Czechoslovak forwards—Milan Novy (7 goals and 8 assists), Peter Stastny (7 goals and 7 assists), and Jaroslav Pouzar (8 goals and 5 assists), figures that emphasized their team's defensive frailty.

A special tournament contested by ten nations not represented in the Olympic competition was held during March in Ljubljana, Yugos. Switzerland won, scoring five victories and a draw with the host country. East Germany was runner-up, followed by Yugoslavia, Austria, Italy, Hungary, France, China, Denmark, and Bulgaria.

The annual senior international tournament for the Izvestia Cup, in Moscow in December 1979, was won by the U.S.S.R. for a tenth time. Czechoslovakia, Finland, and Sweden followed in that order. The world junior (under 21) championship in Helsinki, Fin., was won by the U.S.S.R. for a fifth successive time, with Finland runner-up and Sweden third, followed by Czechoslovakia, Canada, West Germany, the U.S., and Switzerland.

(HOWARD BASS)

See also Winter Sports: *Special Report*.

Iceland

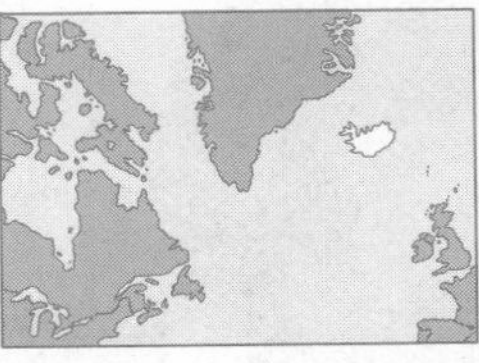

Iceland

Iceland is an island republic in the North Atlantic Ocean, near the Arctic Circle. Area: 103,000 sq km (39,769 sq mi). Pop. (1980 est.): 226,700. Cap. and largest city: Reykjavik (pop., 1980 est., 83,500). Language: Icelandic. Religion: 97% Lutheran. Presidents in 1980, Kristján Eldjárn and, from August 1, Vigdís Finnbogadóttir; prime ministers, Benedikt Gröndal and, from February 8, Gunnar Thoroddsen.

The election of Vigdís Finnbogadóttir (*see* BIOGRAPHIES) as president of Iceland on June 30, 1980, brought to office the first elected woman chief of state in the world. After an intense election campaign that concentrated chiefly on personalities rather than issues, she obtained a narrow plurality of the popular vote, 33.6%, in a field of four candidates, the others all being men. Her closest rival was Gudlaugur Thorvaldsson, the chief state labour mediator, who got 32.1% of the vote.

On February 8 a new government took office from the previous Social Democrat minority caretaker regime. The new government was formed under the leadership of Independence Party Vice-Chairman Gunnar Thoroddsen, who broke away

Ice Skating: *see* Winter Sports

ICELAND

Education. (1976–77) Primary and secondary, pupils 44,565, teachers (including part-time) 6,181; vocational, pupils 7,956, teachers 626; teacher training, pupils 210, teachers 30; higher, students 4,035, teaching staff 575.

Finance. Monetary unit: króna, with (Sept. 22, 1980) a free rate of 508 krónur to U.S. $1 (1,220 krónur = £1 sterling). Gold, SDR's, and foreign exchange (June 1980) U.S. $131 million. Budget (1979 est.): revenue 209 billion krónur; expenditure 202.3 billion krónur. Gross national product (1979) 841 billion krónur. Money supply (June 1980) 76,960,000,000 krónur. Cost of living (Reykjavik; 1975 = 100; May 1980) 531.3.

Foreign Trade. (1979) Imports 291,310,000,000 krónur; exports 278,560,000,000 krónur. Import sources: U.S.S.R. 11%; U.K. 11%; West Germany 11%; Denmark 9%; Norway 8%; The Netherlands 8%; Sweden 8%; U.S. 7%. Export destinations: U.S. 28%; U.K. 19%; West Germany 8%. Main exports: fish and products 75%; aluminum 13%.

Transport and Communications. Roads (1979) 11,649 km. Motor vehicles in use (1978): passenger 75,700; commercial 7,400. There are no railways. Air traffic (1978): 2,117,000,000 passenger-km; freight 37.1 million net ton-km. Shipping (1979): merchant vessels 100 gross tons and over 388; gross tonnage 180,442. Telephones (Dec. 1977) 95,500. Radio licenses (Dec. 1977) 65,000. Television receivers (Dec. 1977) 56,000.

Agriculture. Production (in 000; metric tons; 1979): potatoes 6; hay *c.* 315; turnips 0.3; milk 132; mutton and lamb 16; fish catch 1,641. Livestock (in 000; Dec. 1979): cattle 57; sheep 797; horses 50; poultry 394.

Industry. Production (in 000; 1979): electricity (public supply only; kw-hr) 2,906,000; aluminum (exports; metric tons) 76.

from his own party along with four other members of Parliament of that party. They joined forces with the Progressive Party and the Peoples' Alliance to form a left-of-centre government that was committed to fight inflation with a gradualist approach. The new government tacitly agreed not to raise the issue of leaving NATO, which had long been an integral part of leftist government platforms. The split in the Independence Party, traditionally right of centre, was considered politically significant.

The economy performed poorly during 1980. Real growth in gross domestic product was approximately 1.5%, but a decline in the terms of trade more than offset this gain, largely because of higher oil prices. Taking this into account, real gross national income was thought to have fallen by about 1%. Unemployment was nevertheless virtually absent. Efforts to fight inflation failed; it continued at a rate of 50–60% a year. The current account of the balance of payments was in moderate deficit in 1980, of the order of U.S. $100 million.

The country's main airline, Icelandic Airlines, a privately owned company and an important part of the local economy, was beset with heavy operational losses during the year, due to intense competition on its transatlantic routes. In the fall it was evident that it would have to give up its transatlantic service unless it received government assistance. The Icelandic and Luxembourg authorities agreed to give it an operational subsidy to continue its service on its main route from Luxembourg over Iceland to the U.S.

Iceland's dispute with Norway over fishing rights around the latter's Jan Mayen Island ended with an agreement reached between the two governments in early May. The agreement contained a broadly stated but definite recognition by Norway of Iceland's 200-mi exclusive economic zone in the direction toward Jan Mayen. It also settled division of the important capelin fish catch between the two countries, though in somewhat vague terms; Norway was accorded 15% of the total catch each year during 1980–84.

There was fairly frequent and intense volcanic activity in Iceland during the year. Four intense but brief eruptions were recorded. On August 17 at Mt. Hekla, the country's best-known volcano, a 6-km (3.7-mi)-long fissure began to emit large volumes of ash but relatively little lava. The other three eruptions were all in the Lake Myvatn area in the north, beginning on March 16, July 10, and October 25. All yielded only moderate lava outflows. The eruptions were far enough from human habitation not to endanger human life, but they did do considerable damage to grazing land, and the Lake Myvatn eruptions once again disrupted the exploitation of a nearby geothermal field, where drilling efforts had been under way for several years. (BJÖRN MATTHÍASSON)

India

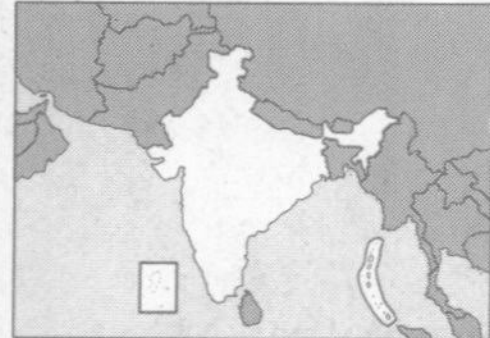
India

A federal republic of southern Asia and a member of the Commonwealth of Nations, India is situated on a peninsula extending into the Indian Ocean with the Arabian Sea to the west and the Bay of Bengal to the east. It is bounded (east to west) by Burma, Bangladesh, China, Bhutan, Nepal, and Pakistan; Sri Lanka lies just off its southern tip in the Indian Ocean. Area: 3,287,782 sq km (1,269,420 sq mi), including the Pakistani-controlled section of Jammu and Kashmir. Pop. (1979 est.): 650,982,000; Indo-Aryans and Dravidians are dominant, with Mongoloid, Negroid, and Australoid admixtures. Cap.: New Delhi (pop., 1971, 301,800). Largest cities: Calcutta (metro pop., 1977 est., 8,297,000) and Greater Bombay (metro pop., 1977 est., 7,605,000). Language: Hindi and English (official). Religion (1971): Hindu 83%; Muslim 11%; Christian 3%; Sikh 2%; Buddhist 0.7%. President in 1980, N. Sanjiva Reddy; prime ministers, Charan Singh and, from January 14, Indira Gandhi.

In 1980 Indira Gandhi (*see* BIOGRAPHIES) won back power but lost her son and closest political confidant, Sanjay Gandhi (*see* OBITUARIES). Voting took place for the Lok Sabha (lower house of Parliament) in the first week of January, resulting in a spectacular victory for Mrs. Gandhi. Of the 525 seats being contested (in a house of 542) Mrs. Gandhi's Congress (I) Party secured 351 seats, Lok Dal 41, Communist Party of India (Marxist) (CPI [M]) 35, Janata 32, Dravida Munnetra Kazhagam (DMK) 16, Congress (U) 13, Communist Party of India 10, and others 27. Indira Gandhi personally won in two constituencies, Medak in Andhra Pradesh and Rae Bareli in Uttar Pradesh (from which she later resigned). Sanjay Gandhi won in Amethi. Prominent opposition winners included Charan Singh, Jagjivan Ram, and A. B. Vajpayee. Among the losers was Raj Narain. Another former prime minister, Morarji Desai, did not run for office. With no opposition group winning more than 10%

of the seats, no leader of the opposition was designated.

Mrs. Gandhi was sworn in on January 14 with a Cabinet of 14: Zail Singh, home affairs; P. V. Narasimha Rao, external affairs; R. Venkataraman, finance; Kamalpati Tripathi, railways; Rao Birendra Singh, agriculture; A. B. A. Ghani Khan Chaudhri, energy; Pranab Mukherjee, commerce; P. Shiv Shankar, law and company affairs; P. C. Sethi, works and housing; B. Shankaranand, education and health; A. P. Sharma, shipping and transport; J. B. Patnaik, tourism and civil aviation; Bhisma Narain Singh, parliamentary affairs; and V. P. Sathe, information and broadcasting. Mrs. Gandhi retained the defense portfolio. Seven ministers of state were also named. When the Lok Sabha met, Bal Ram Jakhar was elected speaker. The first decision of the new Parliament was to extend the statutory reservation of seats in Parliament for scheduled castes and tribes by ten more years.

Among the immediate consequences of the "Indira tempest" were that in the state of Haryana the chief minister, Bhajan Lal, crossed over to the Congress (I) with 37 legislators, and in Karnataka the Devaraj Urs Cabinet resigned and R. Gundu Rao of Congress (I) formed the government. Kerala, where elections to the state assembly took place, gave a majority to the left democratic front, and CPI(M)'s E. K. Nayanar assumed chief ministership. In Manipur a four-party coalition under Dorendra Singh (Congress [I]) took office. Of the union territories that voted, Arunachal Pradesh emerged with a Congress (I) ministry and Pondicherry with a Congress (I)-DMK coalition. In Goa a Congress (U) candidate became chief minister.

Emulating the example set by the Janata government in 1977, the Congress (I) regime dissolved assemblies in nine states and called for midterm elections. Polling took place at the end of May. Congress (I) won a majority in the following eight states (names of chief ministers in parentheses): Bihar with 167 seats out of 324 (Jagannath Mishra); Gujarat with 140 seats out of 182 (Madhav Singh Solanki); Madhya Pradesh 246 out of 320 (Arjun Singh); Maharashtra 186 out of 288 (A. R. Antulay); Orissa 117 out of 147 (J. B. Patnaik); Punjab 63 out of 117 (Darbara Singh); Rajasthan 183 out of 200 (J. N. Pahadia); and Uttar Pradesh 306 out of 425 (V. P. Singh). In Tamil Nadu an alliance led by the All-India Anna DMK captured 162 seats out of 234, and M. G. Ramachandran once again formed the government.

Soon after this second victory, tragedy struck. Sanjay Gandhi, formidable leader of the youth wing of Congress (I), was killed in an airplane crash in New Delhi on June 23. His death was widely regarded as having a profound effect on the course of national politics.

The Janata Party, which had broken into two the previous year, split further after being routed in the parliamentary elections. A separate Bharatiya Janata Party came into being in April. Jagjivan Ram, the party's former leader, drifted away to join Congress (U). Raj Narain, parting company with Lok Dal, formed the Janata Party (Secular). Congress (I) was not immune from trouble. H. N. Bahuguna resigned. In Andhra Pradesh the chief minister, Channa Reddy, made way for T. Anjiah.

LAURENT MAOUS—GAMMA/LIAISON

Indira Gandhi received congratulations from supporters after her Congress (I) Party won more than a two-thirds majority in the lower house of India's Parliament during elections in January. She later resumed her former post as that country's prime minister.

Mrs. Gandhi enlarged her council of ministers in installments and filled the vacancies of persons who had left to head state governments. Among those inducted into the Cabinet were C. M. Stephen (communications), N. D. Tiwari (planning and labour), Kedar Pandey (irrigation), Veerendra Patil (petroleum and chemicals at first and shipping and transport later), V. C. Shukla (civil supplies), and S. B. Chavan (education). Ministers were added at the junior level also. On November 1 the central council of ministers consisted of 20 Cabinet members, 21 ministers of state, and 10 deputy ministers. Even so there were complaints that such key portfolios as defense and steel did not have full-time ministers. Biennial elections were held for the Rajya Sabha (upper house of Parliament) in July. Congress (I) and its allies just managed to secure a majority. In November, 15 by-elections to state assemblies were held and Congress (I) won ten.

The political impasse in Assam dragged on through most of the year, with students there insisting that all foreigners who had come into that state after 1951 should be detected, deleted (from the voters list), and deported. Schools and colleges remained closed and offices worked fitfully. A government headed by Anwara Taimor was installed by Mrs. Gandhi on December 6, but the basic problem of the immigrants, mostly Bengalis from Bangladesh, remained unresolved.

Caste clashes occurred in Bihar and Uttar Pradesh, and a tribal outburst in Tripura resulted in an estimated 550 deaths in June. Virulent religious riots broke out in Moradabad and Aligarh in August.

After Mrs. Gandhi's victory the various legal cases against her, her son, and colleagues were

INDIA

Education. (1978–79) Primary, pupils 72,947,804, teachers 1,276,446; secondary, pupils 26,435,894, teachers 1,581,263; vocational, pupils 318,956, teachers (1970–71) 14,024; teacher training, pupils 102,072, teachers (1970–71) 1,534; higher, students 4,296,242, teaching staff (1974–75) 232,903.

Finance. Monetary unit: rupee, with (Sept. 22, 1980) a free rate of Rs 7.69 to U.S. $1 (Rs 18.49 = £1 sterling). Gold, SDR's, and foreign exchange (June 1980) U.S. $7,474,000,000. Budget (1979–80 est.): revenue Rs 112,093,000,000; expenditure Rs 113,963,000,000. Gross domestic product (1978–79) Rs 963.4 billion. Money supply (April 1980) Rs 240.1 billion. Cost of living (1975 = 100; June 1980) 120.2.

Foreign Trade. (1979) Imports Rs 71,524,000,000; exports Rs 56,435,000,000. Import sources (1978–79): U.S. 11%; West Germany 9%; Iraq 9%; U.K. 8%; Japan 8%; U.S.S.R. 7%; Belgium-Luxembourg 5%; Iran 5%. Export destinations (1977–78): U.S. 13%; U.S.S.R. 12%; U.K. 10%; Japan 9%; West Germany 5%. Main exports (1977–78): textile yarns and fabrics 14%; tea 10%; diamonds 10%; clothing 6%; iron and steel 5%.

Transport and Communications. Roads (1976) 1,374,989 km. Motor vehicles in use: passenger (1977) 805,355; commercial (1976) 385,804. Railways: (1979) 60,775 km; traffic (1978–79) 192,900,000,000 passenger-km, freight 153,950,000,000 net ton-km. Air traffic (1979): 8,030,000,000 passenger-km; freight 301.2 million net ton-km. Shipping (1979): merchant vessels 100 gross tons and over 601; gross tonnage 5,854,285. Telephones (March 1978) 2,247,200. Radio licenses (Dec. 1977) 20,503,000. Television licenses (Dec. 1977) 627,000.

Agriculture. Production (in 000; metric tons; 1979): wheat 34,982; rice *c.* 69,000; barley 2,121; corn *c.* 5,000; millet *c.* 8,500; sorghum *c.* 10,000; potatoes 10,125; cassava (1978) 6,493; sugar, raw value 6,400; sugar, noncentrifugal (1978) *c.* 8,537; chick-peas 5,835; mangoes *c.* 9,300; bananas *c.* 3,900; cottonseed *c.* 2,440; rapeseed 1,877; sesame seed *c.* 500; linseed 514; peanuts *c.* 5,800; tea *c.* 550; tobacco 451; cotton, lint *c.* 1,220; jute (including substitutes) *c.* 1,170; meat *c.* 865; fish catch (1978) 2,368. Livestock (in 000; 1979): cattle *c.* 181,849; sheep *c.* 41,000; pigs *c.* 9,900; buffalo *c.* 60,650; goats *c.* 71,000; poultry *c.* 145,000.

Industry. Production (in 000; metric tons; 1979): coal 103,454; lignite 3,263; crude oil 12,825; natural gas (cu m) 1,890,000; iron ore (63% metal content) 38,773; pig iron 8,937; crude steel 9,994; bauxite 1,920; aluminum 212; gold (troy oz; 1978) 84; manganese ore (metal content; 1978) 560; cement 18,249; cotton yarn 950; woven cotton fabrics (m; 1978) 7,320,000; man-made fibres 188; petroleum products (1978) 23,768; sulfuric acid 2,228; caustic soda 567; electricity (excluding most industrial production; kw-hr) 106,060,000; passenger cars (units) 42; commercial vehicles (units) 59.

withdrawn. The judge of the special court trying one of the cases declared that his court did not have jurisdiction. A major judicial decision during the year was the judgment of a five-member bench of the Supreme Court. It struck down section 55 of the Constitution 42 Amendment Act, which had given unlimited power to Parliament to amend the constitution. The court also held as void section 4, which had allowed Parliament to pass legislation that curbed fundamental rights. The preventive detention bill that had been promulgated by the Charan Singh government in October 1979 was enacted into law on September 22 as a National Security Ordinance to legalize preventive detention for up to 12 months.

A major technological achievement of 1980 was the launching of the Rohini satellite with the help of India's own launch vehicle at Sriharikota in July. Republic Day awards, which the Janata government had abolished, were revived. Mother Teresa, a Roman Catholic nun who worked with the poor in Calcutta, was given the nation's highest civilian honour, Bharat Ratna (Star of India). The death occurred in June of V. V. Giri (*see* OBITUARIES), a former national president. Assassinated during the year was the head of the Nirankari religious sect, Baba Gurbachan Singh.

The Economy. Drought and power shortages in the first half of the year (with an estimated decline of 15 million metric tons in grain production and a fall in industrial growth) spurred inflation. The rate slowed down only after August with its encouraging monsoon rains. At the end of October the wholesale price index stood at 263.8 (1970–71 = 100), 18.1% higher than a year earlier.

Major decisions were taken to improve production and railway movement. Port congestion eased. The reconstituted Planning Commission prepared the outline of a sixth five-year plan (1980–85) involving a public outlay of Rs 950 billion to achieve an overall growth rate of 5.5%. The union government's budget, presented on June 18, provided incentives for savings. Revenue receipts for 1980–81 were estimated at Rs 123,560,000,000 (including Rs 2,230,000,000 from new taxation) and disbursements at Rs 133 billion. Amendments to industrial policy were announced in July by means of which production capacities were permitted to be enlarged and restrictions against large plants relaxed. Another major economic event during the year was the nationalization of six banks.

Foreign Affairs. Indira Gandhi's return signaled resumption of her well-understood policies. One of her first statements was to deplore the entry of foreign troops into Afghanistan and to emphasize the need for a solution through discussions. In July India announced recognition of the Heng Samrin government of Cambodia. A large number of foreign dignitaries came to India, some to mend fences and some to reestablish lost links. Among them were the presidents of Bangladesh, France, Bulgaria, Zaire, Cyprus, and Zambia; the kings of Nepal and Bhutan; the prime ministers of Vietnam, Yugoslavia, Denmark, and Mauritius; the chancellor of Austria; foreign ministers Andrey Gromyko of the Soviet Union and Lord Carrington of Great Britain; and Yasser Arafat of the PLO.

Mrs. Gandhi visited Tanzania and attended the Zimbabwe independence celebrations in April and the funeral of President Tito of Yugoslavia. In Salisbury she had talks with Pres. Mohammad Zia-ul-Haq of Pakistan and in Belgrade with Soviet Pres. Leonid Brezhnev, Prime Minister Margaret Thatcher of Great Britain, Chancellor Helmut Schmidt of West Germany, and Premier Hua Guofeng (Hua Kuo-feng) of China. A regional conference of Commonwealth heads of government was held in New Delhi in September. The Iraq–Iran fighting placed a heavy burden on India in terms of oil supplies.

There was satisfaction that the U.S. government kept its obligation by sending to India the first installment of uranium fuel for the Tarapur nuclear power plant. The hope was expressed that Indo-U.S. relations would continue to be cordial during the presidency of Ronald Reagan. President Brezhnev visited New Delhi in December and Prince Charles of Great Britain in November.

(H. Y. SHARADA PRASAD)

Indonesia

A republic of Southeast Asia, Indonesia consists of the major islands of Sumatra, Java, Kalimantan (Indonesian Borneo), Celebes, and Irian Jaya (West New Guinea) and approximately 3,000 smaller islands and islets. Area: 1,919,558 sq km (741,145 sq mi). Pop. (1980 est.): 142,178,800. Area and population figures include former Portuguese Timor. Cap. and largest city: Jakarta (pop., 1980 est., 6,397,300). Language: Bahasa Indonesia (official); Javanese; Sundanese; Madurese. Religion: mainly Muslim; some Christian, Buddhist, and Hindu. President in 1980, Suharto.

In 1980, for the first time since President Suharto formally assumed power following an abortive Communist coup in 1965, political opposition to his stewardship crystallized as Indonesia moved toward national elections scheduled for 1982. In foreign affairs, however, the Suharto government continued to command a broad spectrum of support as Indonesia denounced the occupation of Afghanistan by Soviet troops and the Vietnamese occupation of Cambodia. The economic situation, meanwhile, was brightened by a bumper rice crop.

The most important political development of 1980 was the emergence in May of a growing opposition to Suharto's quasi-military government amid indications that the president planned to run for reelection to a fourth five-year term. Fifty of the nation's prominent political, religious, and military figures joined in submitting a petition to Parliament which they described as "an expression of concern." The Group of 50, as they were called, included two former prime ministers, Islamic and Christian leaders, a former defense minister, students, and intellectuals. The opposition also expressed dismay at the widespread graft that continued both in and out of government despite Suharto's repeated promises to stamp out corruption. Also, they claimed that despite the government's annual development plans the country's poor were getting poorer as the rich grew richer. A long-term objective of the opposition appeared to be to get the Army out of government.

In November the political situation took a new turn when the government suggested that a move on the part of the increasingly restive Parliament to convene a special session would be considered by the armed forces as "constitutionally subversive." According to a spokesman for the internal security establishment, the phrase "constitutional subversion" included any effort to amend the present constitution, even under articles provided in the constitution for such amendments. This definition of subversion surprised the government's opposition and puzzled Suharto's supporters. Thus, for example, a constitutional amendment barring more than two terms for the presidency would be interpreted as an act of treason, although art. 37 of the constitution provided for amendments to the charter by a two-thirds majority of the People's Consultative Assembly.

In foreign affairs Indonesia's relations with the Communist powers grew more distant during the year. In the spring, Indonesia provided a temporary refuge for more than 50,000 "boat people" fleeing Vietnam. At the same time, three years of negotiations between Vietnam and Indonesia over their contiguous sea frontier reached an impasse. Vietnam had laid claim to the Natuna Islands, a small group in the South China Sea that had been historically Indonesian. There were unconfirmed reports during the year of an exchange of fire between Vietnamese and Indonesian patrol boats near the Natunas, where Indonesia was drilling for offshore oil. In 1980 Indonesia's armed forces staged their biggest field maneuvers in history. Indonesia also participated in the Islamic Conference of foreign ministers that condemned the Soviet invasion and occupation of Afghanistan and joined in a conference of the Association of Southeast Asian Nations (ASEAN) that called upon Vietnam to withdraw its estimated 200,000 troops from Cambodia.

In the economic realm an abundance of rice posed a serious storage problem as production of the crop soared to 20 million tons, more than one million tons above the government's estimate. The improving economic outlook was strengthened by a growth rate in the gross national product of 6.5% and an easing of the annual inflation rate to below 20%. (ARNOLD C. BRACKMAN)

INDONESIA

Education. (1978) Primary, pupils 22,389,796, teachers 709,511; secondary, pupils 3,380,458, teachers 212,405; vocational, pupils 877,129, teachers 64,486; teacher training, students 212,331, teachers 14,006; higher, students (1977) 304,025, teaching staff 21,802.

Finance. Monetary unit: rupiah, with (Sept. 22, 1980) a free rate of 623 rupiah to U.S. $1 (1,498 rupiah = £1 sterling). Gold, SDR's, and foreign exchange (June 1980) U.S. $5,467,000,000. Budget (1979–80 rev. est.): revenue 5,440,000,000,000 rupiah (excluding foreign aid of 1,493,000,000,000 rupiah); expenditure (total) 6,934,000,000,000 rupiah. Gross national product (1978) 20,942,000,000,000 rupiah. Money supply (March 1980) 3,720,200,000,000 rupiah. Cost of living (Jakarta; 1975 = 100; June 1980) 213.2.

Foreign Trade. (1979) Imports U.S. $7,202,000,000; exports U.S. $15,590,000,000. Import sources: Japan 29%; U.S. 14%; Singapore 7%; West Germany 6%; Taiwan 6%; Saudi Arabia 5%. Export destinations: Japan 46%; U.S. 20%; Singapore 13%. Main exports: crude oil 52%; timber 12%; natural gas 8%; food 8%; rubber 6%; petroleum products 5%.

Transport and Communications. Roads (1977) *c.* 123,000 km. Motor vehicles in use (1978): passenger 532,300; commercial 331,700. Railways: (1977) *c.* 6,800 km; traffic (1978) 4,458,000,000 passenger-km, freight 980 million net ton-km. Air traffic (1978): 4,480,000,000 passenger-km; freight 66.1 million net ton-km. Shipping (1979): merchant vessels 100 gross tons and over 1,122; gross tonnage 1,309,911. Telephones (Jan. 1978) 324,500. Radio licenses (Dec. 1977) 5,250,000. Television receivers (Dec. 1977) 1 million.

Agriculture. Production (in 000; metric tons; 1979): rice 26,350; corn 3,200; cassava (1978) *c.* 12,488; sweet potatoes (1978) *c.* 2,460; sugar, raw value 1,325; bananas *c.* 2,905; tea 93; copra *c.* 950; soybeans 674; palm oil 610; peanuts 697; coffee 267; tobacco 89; rubber 851; fish catch (1978) 1,655. Livestock (in 000; 1979): cattle *c.* 6,453; buffalo *c.* 2,312; pigs *c.* 2,925; sheep *c.* 3,611; goats *c.* 8,051; horses (1978) 647; chickens *c.* 99,179.

Industry. Production (in 000; metric tons; 1979): crude oil 78,321; natural gas (cu m) 28,120,000; petroleum products (1978) *c.* 23,400; coal 278; tin concentrates (metal content) 30; bauxite 1,052; cement (1978) 3,650; electricity (excluding most industrial production; kw-hr; 1977) *c.* 4,380,000.

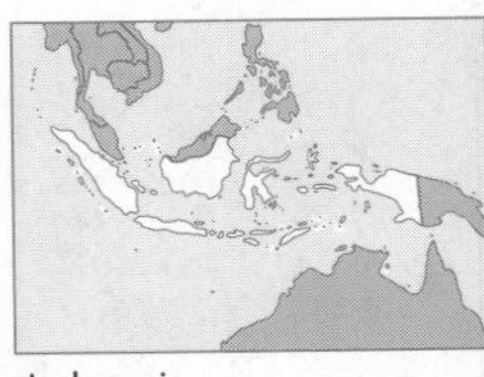

Indonesia

Industrial Relations

The strongest general influence on industrial relations in 1980 was the continuing harsh economic climate, which was made more difficult by the additional substantial rise in oil prices. In many countries unemployment remained high and dismissals were common as firms—in some cases almost whole industries—sought to adjust to lower levels of production. Employment was clearly the top priority for labour union negotiators, in terms both of pressing governments to take measures to preserve or create jobs and of persuading firms to retain existing workers. Wage negotiations tended to be considerably affected by economic constraints, and increases were usually moderate. In some countries, however, large increases continued to be common, notably where prices were rising particularly rapidly. Some workers achieved modest gains in regard to vacations or working hours.

Britain and Ireland. Both economic and political forces were at work in shaping British industrial relations developments in 1980. In relation to employers, union energies were mainly devoted to trying to reduce the rather numerous plant closings and maintaining workers' purchasing power. Nonetheless, unemployment continued to grow, and though the prevailing level of money wage increases remained high, a number of important wage claims were settled at below the rate of inflation. The year started with a major strike over wages in the nationalized steel industry, long noted for good industrial relations but now unprofitable and undergoing contraction. The dispute ended after 13 weeks, following the report of a court of inquiry, with a compromise.

Politically, the Conservative Party administration that came to power in 1979 demonstrated considerable firmness of purpose in seeking to reshape British industrial relations. First, the government made clear its belief in free collective bargaining and its unwillingness to intervene in industrial disputes. Second, in the Employment Act 1980 it modified a number of aspects of legislation, among other things dealing with the closed shop, secondary action, union recognition, and procedures for dealing with disputed dismissals. The act discontinued arrangements for hearing claims based on prevailing pay levels and introduced facilities making public funds available, when requested, for secret ballots to be used in relation to strikes, election of union officers, changes in union rules, and union mergers. The Employment Act was regarded as not going far enough by a substantial group of Conservatives and as being unfair and undesirable by the unions.

In Ireland a *Second National Understanding for Economic and Social Development* was approved in October. It covered action promised by the government on economic and social issues and an agreement on pay policy between the Irish Congress of Trade Unions and the employers' organizations participating in the standing Employer-Labour Conference.

United States. Recession in general, and the problems of structural adjustment in particular, were prominent in the background to U.S. industrial relations in 1980. Wage agreements, including the always-important steel agreement, were generally moderate. An unusual event was the appointment of Douglas Fraser, president of the United Auto Workers' union, to the board of directors of the Chrysler Corp., after the union had agreed to a modest settlement in its bargaining with the ailing firm. In October, after many years of union effort including much litigation and a highly publicized consumer boycott, the major—and notably antiunion—textile company, J. P. Stevens Inc., conceded union bargaining rights in a number of its plants.

Following its 1977 withdrawal from the International Labour Organization (ILO), in protest against its "politicization," the U.S. in 1980 decided to rejoin the organization. ILO Director General Francis Blanchard said that the U.S. decision reinforced the ILO's capability for action at a time when the world faced pressing problems in the labour field.

Continental Western Europe. Apart from employment, working time was an important issue in French industrial relations during 1980. In April Pierre Giraudet, appointed to review the subject after central negotiations had broken down, proposed a gradual and flexible movement toward 1,816 hours a year (1,770 for those engaged in arduous work) and also adjustments concerning vacations and overtime by 1983. A subsequent offer by the employers was rejected, though negotiations were resumed later in the year. As part of the government's policy to enhance workers' involvement in their jobs, a measure was put forward which became law in October. The new law provided an option for firms to distribute specially created share capital to their workers with some financial backing from the state. During the year there was a widening of the ideological rift between France's two major trade union organizations, the Communist-led Confédération Générale du Travail and the left-wing Confédération Française Démocratique du Travail.

Italian industrial relations opened the year on a positive note, with an agreement between the three trade union centres (central organizations) for voluntary regulation of strikes in certain essential public services. Another imaginative initiative was a decree worked out by the government and unions in July for a central solidarity fund financed by a 0.5% levy on the pay of all employees, the fund to be used to promote new investment. This plan foundered, however, on account of political opposition.

The dialogue between unions and government on economic policies continued, with agreement reached on a range of fiscal and social security adjustments. Most attention centred on the major dispute that followed the Fiat automobile company's plan, announced in May, to lay off 78,000 workers for periods of seven days—and later a proposal to dismiss over 14,000 workers. Following mediation by Italy's minister of labour, agreement was reached in October on the basis that some 23,000 workers would be put on state-subsidized layoff, staggered over an extended period.

In Sweden, as negotiations on wage claims broke down in both the private and the public sector, strikes and lockouts were called until ultimately almost one million workers were involved. Work was resumed on the basis of a proposal by mediators on May 11. The conflict was one of the most serious, in terms of time lost, in Swedish history. Apart from the general dispute, the dockworkers' union (not affiliated to the manual workers' trade union centre) struck for more than four weeks to secure a separate agreement and higher increases than those obtained by the general settlement; this they failed to achieve. The reasons for such conflicts occurring in a country long renowned for disposing of disputes without recourse to strikes were many and complex. Some observers spoke of the end of the Swedish model of industrial relations, but, in fact, the disputes demonstrated the strength of Swedish collective bargaining as well as its vulnerability.

Two legal matters aroused particular interest in West Germany. One, concerning the use of the lockout weapon, produced a test case ruling that held the lockout to be constitutional but laid down a number of qualifications for its use. The other concerned the desire of the important Mannesmann Co. to reorganize its activities in a manner that would have the effect of changing its obligations in terms of West Germany's codetermination legislation, a law passed in 1976 that gave workers in large companies seats on corporate boards. This was strongly contested by the metalworkers' union.

On January 10 the Dutch government introduced a two-month wage freeze, later extended by another month. The government then obtained powers to control wage increases until the end of the year, during which time limited raises only were to be permitted. In Norway a two-year framework agreement was concluded in April following intervention by the state mediator. Moderate pay increases reflected government willingness to cut income taxes and improve social security benefits. A particularly interesting feature of the agreement was a formula providing special benefits for low-income groups. Normally one of the most industrially peaceful countries, Norway was troubled in 1980 by strikes of workers engaged on North Sea oil production, who walked out for improved pay and conditions.

Spain continued the steady development of its industrial relations system in 1980 with a second framework agreement, to run for two years, between the central employers' organization and the important trade union centre, the Unión General de Trabajadores. A workers' protection act, dealing with individual rights, representation in the business enterprise, and collective bargaining, was promulgated in March.

Eastern Europe. The basic model of the Communist industrial relations system, as developed in the Soviet Union, alloted the unions the joint task of protecting the interests of their members and, as an organ of the state, playing a part in the formulation and attainment of production plans. The system provided machinery for dealing with workers' grievances, but it was considered that because industry was socially owned workers pressing grievances by means of strikes were really striking against themselves. No need was seen for other than the officially constituted trade unions, nor for strikes, in a planned socialist economy. Strikes had nevertheless occurred, and there had occasionally been attempts to form independent trade unions. But no departure from the basic model had taken place until the developments in 1980 in Poland.

KEYSTONE

Police tried to prevent demonstrations by striking British steelworkers from moving into the town centre of Sheerness on February 20. The workers were demanding more pay.

Following a government decision to raise some meat prices, a wave of strikes for wage increases occurred. These rapidly developed into a movement for a package of demands, including free trade unions and recognition of the right to strike, the strikers making it clear that their concept of independent unions was not in conflict with the Polish political structure. At the end of August an agreement was reached that met most of the workers' demands. Though many obstacles were to be encountered in adapting to this new concept of trade unionism and worker unrest continued, a historic precedent had been set. (*See* POLAND.)

Latin America. On April 1 strikes broke out in Brazil's metalworking industry, for the third successive year, in support of a package of demands concerning wages, job security, and dispute procedures. The government took action against the unions concerned and their leaders, and work was resumed on May 11. In July Pope John Paul II, during his visit to Brazil, called for improved income distribution, working conditions, and social security. (R. O. CLARKE)

The views expressed in this article are the author's own and should not be attributed to any organization with which he may be connected.

See also Economy, World; Industrial Review.
[521.B.3; 534.C.1.q; 552.D.3. and F.3.b.ii]

WHEN PUBLIC SERVANTS STRIKE

by Richard Whittingham

In the early part of the 19th century they were called "turn-outs," signifying that workers were "discharging" themselves from their jobs because of a labour dispute. Since then they have come to be known as strikes, work stoppages, walkouts, and, the ultimate euphemism, stabilization periods. Whatever the name, they have always been controversial. Forces on either side of the issue have argued the relative merits and demerits of strikes, their morality or immorality, legality or illegality.

They are a part of the struggle between employer and employee, one that has been going on for a long time. In fact, the first labour dispute, according to the *Guinness Book of World Records,* goes all the way back to 1153 BC, when workers in Thebes, Egypt, formally expressed discontent with their working conditions. And the first strike historically recorded was one engineered by a Greek orchestra leader named Aristos, who led his troupers off the job in Rome in 309 BC. In the United States strikes can be traced to Colonial days.

First Organized Strikes. Organized strikes, the kind most usual today, are, however, a product of the 19th century. The first call for an industry-wide strike in the United States occurred in 1806 when 200 Philadelphia shoemakers walked off the job. They asked for a sympathy strike by all other shoemakers in the then very small U.S. (they did not get it). Not until 1877 was a nationwide strike successfully launched. It took place when the Pennsylvania and the Baltimore and Ohio railroads announced a wage cut for employees. The workers went on strike and forced the closing of the yards at Martinsburg, W.Va. At the same time word of the strike spread quickly and so did the sympathy of the people for the strikers. Soon all railroad traffic in Pennsylvania was virtually shut down, and then the strike spread to New York, Chicago, St. Louis, and other large cities. Strikers met strikebreakers, and blood flowed. U.S. Pres. Rutherford B. Hayes referred to it as an "insurrection." Police, state militia, and federal troops were called out to quell the rioting in many different parts of the country. Strikes had suddenly taken on a new and frightening guise.

Danger and violence became an integral part of strikes, causing them to become even more controversial. In 1886, at the infamous Haymarket Square bombing in Chicago, 7 policemen were killed and 60 others were seriously injured as they attempted to disperse a crowd of people. The crowd had gathered in the square to protest the killing on the previous day of six people in a clash between strikers, strikebreakers, and police at a riotous strike of the McCormick Harvesting Machine Co., which had been called to promote an eight-hour workday. Six years later a strike was held at the Carnegie Steel Co. in Homestead, Pa. When Henry Clay Frick closed down the company and laid off the work force because they wanted a union, the tension built to an explosive climax. Eventually, thousands of workers and their supporters, armed with everything from guns to clubs, warred with hundreds of heavily armed Pinkerton guards who had been hired by Frick. In the end 16 people were dead and 60 others were seriously wounded. In the Pullman strike of 1894, a national railroad dispute, 34 were killed and hundreds injured as workers clashed with federal and state troops.

The labour-management trail was indeed a bloody one, and the conflict did not calm down until the New Deal days of U.S. Pres. Franklin D. Roosevelt. By that time strikes as a tactic of labour had assumed, if not respectability, at least a modicum of acceptance. The two sides came to the realization that they could still loathe each other but did not have to kill or maim while maintaining that feeling.

Strikes in the Public Sector. By the time World War II had come and gone, strikes were commonplace events. In fact, in 1950 the U.S. Department of Labor recorded a total of 4,843 work stoppages which involved 2,410,000 workers and the loss of 38.8 million man-days. But those statistics reflected the actions of only part of the work force. No one in the 1950s raised an eyebrow when the mine workers, auto workers, steelworkers, railroad employees, longshoremen, or factory and construction workers went out on strike. But other branches of the work force—schoolteachers, police officers, firefighters, municipal transit drivers, sanitation workers, those who, if they did not perform their jobs, could disastrously affect everyone else's health and safety—were not expected to walk off the job. And, at that time, they did not.

This situation changed during the late 1960s and the 1970s. Suddenly, government employees in many different occupations were not only threaten-

---

Richard Whittingham has written on many subjects. His books include Martial Justice, The Chicago Bears, *and* Joe D.

WIDE WORLD

After contract negotiations broke down in February, approximately 4,000 firefighters in Chicago walked off their jobs.

ing to strike, they were actually walking out. School systems were shut down and people in such cities as New York and Chicago had no way to get to work—or anywhere else for that matter. Sanitation workers refused to pick up the garbage, and the fear of pestilence accompanied the other assaults on the ordinary citizen's senses as the garbage piled up and rotted in the streets of large cities.

In New Orleans in 1979, at an exceptionally propitious time, just before Mardi Gras, the city's police went on strike. By doing so they in effect destroyed the gala Mardi Gras celebration—no one would come into a lawless city—and it cost the city an estimated 250 million tourist dollars. In addition, the state police and the National Guard called in to protect the city added another $100,000 a day to the city's accounts payable.

The cry went up that *that* kind of strike was not just controversial, it was illegal. The citizens were left unprotected; anarchy could reign and crime run rampant; those who were called in as replacements to protect the city were simply not trained for such duties. It was illegal, people argued, for such workers as police officers to walk off and leave the taxpaying citizenry stranded and unprotected.

In Kansas City, Mo., discontented firefighters staged a slowdown first. Then extraordinary numbers began calling in sick, and others refused to work overtime to fill out the manpower quota necessary for running the fire stations. Finally, the city won a court order to get the firefighters back to work. Most ignored it. The city fired 42 of the strikers and suspended 300 others. Firefighters demonstrated outside and inside the courthouse. Contempt of court charges flew around, and jail sentences were first imposed and then suspended; those who were fired were eventually reinstated. While all this was going on, the city had its share of fires and they were put out—perhaps not as effectively as they could have been but without any disaster taking place.

In Chicago the same situation developed but on a magnified scale. There, in February 1980, approximately 4,000 firefighters walked off the job. Off-duty police officers, sanitation workers, fire department trainees, and a potpourri of others were called into service. The number of trained personnel in a given firehouse was often no more than 10% of normal, and the city lived in constant fear of fires raging out of control and of people dying in the streets or in their apartments because paramedic teams or ambulances would not be available.

The strike wore on for weeks. Neither side—the city and its mayor and the firefighters and their union president—would budge in its demands. Before it was over, the union leader ended up in jail, a poll showed that fully 71% of Chicagoans were against the strike, a federal judge drew up a back-to-work order, and the mayor threatened to fire all those firefighters who did not get back to their jobs. Negotiations continued, and the firefighters stayed off the job, ignoring the mayor and the courts. But the strike finally was settled. No one went to jail except the union president, and he was out quickly once it was all over. The furor died down and then disappeared.

Is Any Strike Illegal? The foregoing discussion raises one fundamental question: Is any strike illegal? Do workers in certain jobs have fewer rights than those in less sensitive occupations? For example, can a steelworker strike while a police officer cannot? The law may say yes, but it is often not enforced. Binding arbitration, many say, is the answer, but that, like back-to-work orders and injunctions, may turn out to be just one more thing for strikers to ignore.

The strike that Rutherford B. Hayes said was an "insurrection" was not. The strikes described today as "illegal" apparently are not. Which leaves everyone wondering—will this issue be resolved like those in the early days of labour disputes, those that just gradually crept into respectability, or will it take some dreadful catastrophe, arising because there is no one available to put out a fire or control crime, to force the issue to a conclusion?

Industrial Review

The year 1979 was a relatively good one for manufacturing. World output rose by 5%; the rise in the industrial countries was not quite as great, but the less industrialized nations achieved a growth rate of more than 7%. For the first time the information in the accompanying statistical tables is based on the year 1975, as compiled by the Statistical Office of the United Nations. A comparison of the importance of the various areas in 1975 with their 1970 positions indicates that manufacturing in the less industrialized countries increased markedly during that period, from 74 to 98 out of 1,000, and that it declined in the centrally planned countries (excluding China), from 287 to 257 (chiefly the U.S.S.R., down from 207 to 178). The industrial countries' position hardly changed, up from 639 to 645, but within the total the share of the United States fell from 272 to 215, while those of Japan and almost every Western European country rose (the exceptions being the United Kingdom and Yugoslavia).

Manufacturing activity continued to advance in the early months of 1980 in the industrial countries, but recessionary tendencies affected production adversely during the spring in North America and somewhat later in Western Europe and Japan. Thus, output in the industrial market economies was expected to be only marginally higher in 1980 than in the previous year. The recession was also expected to reduce the growth rate of manufacturing in the centrally planned economies and in the less industrialized countries.

The most noteworthy feature of 1979 was the upsurge in investment activity. In the advanced nations gross fixed investment in new buildings, plant machinery, and vehicles rose 4¼% in real terms; this was well above the long-term trend of 3% annually in the ten years ended in 1978. In contrast, both private and public consumption increased at a rate about 1% below the long-term trend figure.

The pattern of demand was reflected in the performance of the different branches of manufacturing. The heavy industries—metals, engineering products, building materials—were growing faster than light industries which concentrated mainly on consumer goods. Quite a number of industries increased their output in the less developed countries at about twice the rate they achieved in the industrialized nations; these included metals, metal products, chemicals, food, paper, and wood products. The clothing-footwear industries in the advanced countries continued to

Table I. Index Numbers of Production, Employment, and Productivity in Manufacturing Industries
1975 = 100

Area	Relative importance[1] 1975	Relative importance[1] 1979	Production 1978	Production 1979	Employment 1978	Employment 1979	Productivity[2] 1978	Productivity[2] 1979
World[3]	1,000	1,000	118	124	...	...	...	...
Industrial countries	868	861	118	123	...	...	...	...
Less industrialized countries	132	139	122	131	...	...	...	...
North America[4]	315	333	126	131	...	...	...	...
Canada	27	26	117	121	101	104	116	116
United States	288	307	126	132	112	114	113	116
Latin America[5]	74	73	114	123	...	...	...	...
Mexico	12	12	116	127	...	...	...	...
Asia[6]	159	174	126	136	...	...	...	...
India	11	11	124	124	...	...	...	...
Japan	109	117	123	133	97	97	127	137
Pakistan[7]	2	2	110	114[11]	...	...	...	...
Europe[8]	416	389	112	116	...	...	...	...
Austria	8	8	113	120	97	97	116	124
Belgium	14	13	111	118	...	...	...	...
Denmark	6	6	115	120	100	101	115	119
Finland	6	5	102	111	94	97	109	114
France	80	75	113	117	96	95	118	123
Germany, West	115	110	113	119	99	100	114	119
Greece	3	3	121	128	115	118	105	108
Ireland	1	1	129	138	112	114[11]	115	121
Italy	43	43	116	124	104	104	112	119
Netherlands, The	16	15	111	113	92	...	121	...
Norway	6	5	97	99	96	93	101	106
Portugal	4	4	126	134	...	...	...	...
Spain	24	22	114	114	86	...	133	...
Sweden	17	14	94	100	89	89	106	112
Switzerland	13	11	107	109	93	92	115	118
United Kingdom	50	42	104	104	97	96	107	108
Yugoslavia	11	12	124	134	113	117	110	115
Rest of the world[9]	36	30	100	104	...	...	...	...
Australia	15	13	102	108[11]	94	95	109	114
South Africa	7	6	98	104[11]	99	101	99	103[11]
Centrally planned economies[10]	...	...	121	127	...	...	...	...

[1]The 1975 weights are those applied by the UN Statistical Office; those for 1978 were estimated on the basis of the changes in manufacturing output since 1970 in the various countries.
[2]This is 100 times the production index divided by the employment index, giving a rough indication of changes in output per person employed.
[3]Excluding Albania, Bulgaria, China, Czechoslovakia, East Germany, Hungary, Mongolia, North Korea, Poland, Romania, the U.S.S.R., and Vietnam.
[4]Canada and the United States.
[5]South and Central America (including Mexico) and the Caribbean islands.
[6]Asian Middle East and East and Southeast Asia, including Japan.
[7]Years beginning July 1.
[8]Excluding Albania, Bulgaria, Czechoslovakia, East Germany, Hungary, Poland, Romania, and the U.S.S.R.
[9]Africa and Oceania.
[10]These are not included in the above world total and consist of the countries listed in note 8 above.
[11]Estimate.

Table II. Pattern of Output, 1976–79
Percent change from previous year

	World[1]				Developed countries				Less developed countries				Centrally planned economies			
	1976	1977	1978	1979	1976	1977	1978	1979	1976	1977	1978	1979	1976	1977	1978	1979
All manufacturing	9	5	4	5	9	4	4	5	7	6	7	7	7	7	6	5
Heavy industries	10	5	5	6	10	4	5	5	8	8	7	10	8	8	7	6
Base metals	9	0	5	5	9	0	5	4	6	8	9	9	5	4	4	4
Metal products	9	5	5	6	9	5	5	5	8	4	8	10	10	9	8	8
Building materials, etc.	9	4	5	5	9	4	5	5	9	7	7	7	6	5	5	2
Chemicals	12	9	3	7	13	9	2	6	9	13	6	10	8	7	6	4
Light industries	8	4	2	4	8	4	1	4	6	4	6	5	4	5	4	4
Food, drink, tobacco	5	3	4	4	5	3	3	3	7	6	7	6	1	5	3	3
Textiles	8	−1	1	4	8	−1	0	4	5	0	4	5	5	4	4	3
Clothing, footwear	9	1	0	1	10	2	0	0	5	−1	3	3	6	4	4	4
Wood products	9	3	2	3	10	3	2	3	3	6	2	5	5	5	4	2
Paper, printing	9	3	5	5	10	3	4	5	9	3	7	10	6	5	4	−2

[1]Excluding centrally planned economies.
Source: UN, *Monthly Bulletin of Statistics.*

Table III. Output per Hour Worked in Manufacturing
1975=100

Country	1973	1974	1975	1976	1977	1978	1979
France	100	103	100	112	115	121	128
Germany, West	94[1]	96[1]	100	107	111	114	119
Italy	102[1]	106[1]	100[1]	109[1]	108	111	122
Japan	102	104	100	110	115	124	134
U.K.	100	101	100	105	105	106	108
U.S.	96	98	100	106	108	110	113

[1]Not strictly comparable with earlier years.
Source: National Institute, *Economic Review.*

Table IV. Manufacturing Production in the U.S.S.R. and Eastern Europe[1]
1975=100

Country	1976	1977	1978	1979
Bulgaria[2]	107	114	122	133[3]
Czechoslovakia	106	112	117	122
Germany, East[2]	106	111	116	120[3]
Hungary	105	112	117	121
Poland	110	117	123	124
U.S.S.R.	105	111	116	120

[1]Romania not available.
[2]All industries.
[3]Estimate.
Source: UN, *Monthly Bulletin of Statistics.*

stagnate, in contrast to their progress elsewhere in the world.

The growth rates of the U.S. and West German manufacturing industries were about 5%, but Japan's was much higher (8%) and some European countries also advanced faster: Finland 9%, Italy 7%, Austria, Belgium, and Sweden 6%. By contrast, industry in the U.K. and Spain was stagnating. The somewhat less advanced countries on the periphery of Europe also progressed rapidly (Ireland 7%, Portugal and Greece 6%, Yugoslavia 8%). Among the less developed countries growth rates were high in Brazil (7%), Argentina (11%), Mexico (9%), South Korea (12%), and Singapore (14%); there was no advance, however, in the largest of them, India.

Industrial activity started to slow down in the fourth quarter of 1979 in the industrial countries. This was mainly due to a decline in investment, concentrated in the U.S. (housing) and Japan (all types), but even so the rise in investment was considerably faster in the advanced areas than that of output, especially in Japan and West Germany. Among the major industries the motor industry, particularly in continental Europe and Japan, as well as the aircraft industry benefited from this trend, along with those sectors producing investment goods.

Lively international trade in manufactured goods also contributed to stimulating output. Despite adverse conditions affecting some trade flows (such as the collapse of trade with Iran following the revolution, the steep fall in Nigerian imports, and the virtual stagnation during the year as a whole in imports into the U.S.), trade in manufactures rose at a rate well above the average since the boom year of 1973.

As measured by output per hour worked in manufacturing, among the main industrial countries productivity rose fastest during 1979 in Italy (10%) and Japan (8%). The productivity gain in West Germany and France was about 5%, while in the U.S. it was just under 3%; the slowest growth among the large countries was recorded in the United Kingdom. This and stagnating output reflected the difficulties of British industry.

Among the centrally planned economies Bulgaria's manufacturing industry progressed the most rapidly (9%) and that of Poland the most slowly (1%). In the other countries of Eastern Europe, as well as in the U.S.S.R., the rate of growth was 3–4%. (G. F. RAY)

Increased foreign demand for Japanese cars, such as these Toyotas being shipped abroad, deprived the faltering U.S. auto industry of vitally needed sales in 1980.

J. P. LAFFONT—SYGMA

ADVERTISING

A new opportunity for U.S. advertising opened up in June 1980 when the Federal Communications Commission (FCC) took a first step toward deregulating radio stations. By diluting the clear-channel spectrum currently held by 25 AM radio stations, the FCC paved the way for creation of more than 100 new nighttime AM stations. The FCC limited the reach of the 25 stations by protecting them from interference only within a radius of 750 mi (1,200 km) from their transmitters. This allowed for the additional stations, each with a ten-mile (16-km) broadcast radius. At the same time, the FCC eliminated broadcaster guidelines dictating the amount of nonentertainment programming and the number of commercial minutes per hour.

Each year the magazine *Advertising Age* names the 100 largest national advertisers of the previous year. In 1979 the top five included Procter & Gamble, General Foods, Sears, Roebuck, General Motors, and Philip Morris. The 100 leading advertisers increased their advertising spending in 1979 to $11.7 billion, a 13.6% increase over 1978. Together, they accounted for more than half the total advertising expenditures in newspapers, magazines, network and spot television, farm publications, network and spot radio, and outdoor. The U.S. government was in the number 28 position, spending more than $140 million, a 14% increase over 1978.

In October 1980 a federal appeals court upheld a finding of the Federal Trade Commission (FTC) that the American Medical Association (AMA) could not interfere with physicians' attempts to advertise. Physicians would now be allowed to advertise their fees and services, but the court did agree that the AMA could issue ethical guidelines concerning false and deceptive advertising.

The U.S. Treasury Department removed some advertising and merchandising restrictions on the alcoholic beverage industry that had been in existence since the 1930s. The changes would permit distillers to spend more for in-store signs and product displays and for reimbursement of retailers for handling coupons. No limit was placed on the number of indoor signs provided they had no value other than as advertising. Under the new rules, a distiller could place up to $100 worth of promotional displays per brand with a retailer at any one time. The Treasury Department was also considering proposals for comparative advertising in this industry.

Sex as a dominant theme in marketing returned to television with a series of controversial ads for designer jeans. The message presented was that the buyer could achieve status and attract the opposite sex by wearing tight jeans emblazoned with a designer's name. Newcomers in this industry were spending as much as 15% of their sales revenue on advertising, compared with 2% for the largest U.S. jeans manufacturer, Levi Strauss. A study by the Television Bureau of Advertising indicated that in the first six months of 1980 the 15 leading television advertisers of ready-to-wear apparel spent $28.7 million on TV commercials, an increase of 160% over 1979. Designer jeans companies spent about $15.5 million during this period, compared with $1.9 million in 1979.

The U.S. boycott of the Olympic Games in Moscow cost NBC $100 million, approximately 85% of which was covered by insurance from Lloyd's of London. By the time the boycott was announced, NBC had already paid for thousands of souvenirs, including T-shirts, duffel bags, and warm-up suits inscribed "NBC Moscow 1980," and had paid the Soviet Union most of the $87 million for production facilities and services and television rights. NBC also had to come up with 152 hours of programming to fill the time alloted for the Games.

"It appeals to greed, lust, pride, sloth and envy, but we're overlooking gluttony and avarice."

SIDNEY HARRIS

The U.S. Department of Justice filed suit in July against the National Association of Broadcasters' television code, charging that it unfairly controls the marketplace by restricting the amount of advertising time available to manufacturers and retailers.

An all-sports radio network inaugurated in late 1980 gave charter advertisers exclusive rights for their product categories. Commercials were slotted into sportscasts that went on the air every half hour, all-night talk shows, and two-and-one-half minute tapes of memorable moments in sports. A cooperative newspaper buying service introduced in 1980 gave advertisers an opportunity to place one order for co-op ads in 62 of the top 100 metropolitan markets. The service handled insertion orders to the newspapers, shipped the advertising materials, accepted the billings, audited the claims, and paid the papers. Advertisements placed by manufacturers included the names of local dealers or retailers where the product could be purchased.

The performers' strike that delayed the scheduled September opening of the prime-time television season created no serious financial problems for the three major television networks. The networks were able to use repeat programming, and many advertisers continued to spend large amounts during the fall. Automakers, for example, could not postpone advertising of their new models.

A weekly 60-minute talk show devoted exclusively to advertisements began to appear on 350 cable television systems in September, with an audience of three million homes. The show was cosponsored by 40 advertisers at $3,500 per ten-minute slot. Each show was devoted to the products of five advertisers, and viewers were given an opportunity to place immediate orders by calling a toll-free telephone number. Advertisers used the program to sample viewer reaction to new products or new concepts.

Bristol-Myers signed a ten-year, $25 million advertising contract with the Cable News Network (CNN), a 24-hour, all-news cable television service that made its debut in June.

The first product from China advertised on national television in the U.S. was Tsingtao, a beer sold in the northeastern part of the country. A broadcast media monitoring group was established by consumer advocate Ralph Nader to make sure that commercials were honest and to rebut programs favourable only to big business.

(EDWARD MARK MAZZE)

AEROSPACE

At a time when Europe and the U.S. were experiencing major recessions, their aerospace industries weathered the storm, and record sales were almost commonplace. The airlines, on the other hand, caught between competition that forced them to lower fares and steeply rising inflation and fuel costs, ran into great difficulties, and few made a profit.

Trade figures continued to emphasize the importance of aerospace in the industrialized and the less developed countries, both as a source of revenue and as a catalyst for developing nonaeronautical technology. In 1979 Boeing Co., with orders for 479 new aircraft, headed *Fortune* magazine's list of the top 50 exporting U.S. firms, and McDonnell Douglas Corp., Lockheed Corp., and Northrop Corp. were also among the first 11. Signs were that this preeminence would be repeated in 1980.

In the U.K. aerospace was one of the few industries actually growing and was even recruiting labour; figures compiled by the Society of British Aerospace Companies showed that U.K. companies had turned in record sales figures and in some cases were unable to cope with the demand. Japan's industry, too, though small by Western standards, was quietly but swiftly expanding and was beginning to be viewed with concern by some U.S. and European firms.

The supersonic Concorde remained the most prestigious commercial aircraft, although its star was increasingly eclipsed by noise, route shortages, and crippling fuel costs. Braniff, which had begun a service using the Concorde between London and Paris and Dallas-Fort Worth, Texas, shelved the arrangement owing to high fuel costs. British Airways in a major economy drive also dropped one of its Concorde services, that to Singapore. Meanwhile, the U.S. government increased funding of an advanced supersonic transport in order to keep open U.S. options for a 1990s design.

Sales of wide-body jets—the Boeing 747, Lockheed L-1011 TriStar, and Airbus Industrie A300—continued to be strong, though passenger resistance to the McDonnell Douglas DC-10 was clearly marked. This was due to three major disasters in 1979: an accident in Chicago in May which killed 274 people; a crash in Mexico City in October killing 73; and the loss of a sightseeing DC-10 on the Antarctic ice cap with all 257 aboard in November. Decisions by Singapore Airlines and Thai Airlines to sell their DC-10s as being unsuitable for their routes cast further doubts on the aircraft's credibility.

Sales of new-generation airliners to replace the aging Boeing 707s and Douglas DC-8s proceeded slowly, the 200/210-seat Boeing 767 vying with the identically sized Airbus Industrie A310. U.S. operators bought the 767 and European ones the A310. Meanwhile, sales of the smaller, 170-seat Boeing 757 remained static, encouraging McDonnell Douglas to relaunch yet again its Advanced Technology Medium Range 170-seat product, this time as the slightly more definitive DC-XX 180-seater. By November 1980 there were only four 757 customers—Eastern Airlines, British Airways, and two newcomers, Aloha and Transbrasil; Delta Air Lines was reportedly also negotiating an order for approximately 50 of the planes.

But if the manufacturing industry thrived, the airlines did not. The revenues carefully hoarded since the 1974 fuel crisis to buy the new equipment that would put them on a faster road to recovery vanished as the airlines sought desperately to keep themselves in the black. Virtually all airlines found themselves in this situation, and predictions voiced at the annual meeting of the International Air Transport Association in October were gloomy. Some observers attributed airline misfortunes to the 1978 U.S. Airline Deregulation Act, but a number of the larger operators put the blame on inflation and, more importantly, their skyrocketing fuel bills. During the year the British government emerged as a proponent of free trade, as evinced by its approval of no fewer than four operators to service the London–Hong Kong route. It was also sympathetic toward the gathering tide of criticism against the mostly nationalized European trunk airlines for alleged gross overcharging, and there was talk of bringing some cases to the European Court of Justice for possible violation of European Economic Community (EEC) rules.

Deregulation did severely curtail airline services between many smaller terminals in the U.S., and the burden of providing such service fell largely to the so-called third-level airlines. The growing importance of this segment of the industry emerged at the annual National Business Aircraft Association meeting at Kansas City; it became evident there that while U.S. industry was providing a fine range of aircraft seating up to 15 people it had nothing to offer the suddenly large and growing market for commuter planes carrying between 15 and 20 passengers. This sector was currently being supplied by Canada, Brazil, and the U.K.

A significant military event was the disastrous U.S. attempt in April to secure the release of the U.S. hostages held since the previous November in Iran. An ambitious plan involving airlift by C-130 Hercules transport aircraft and RH-53 assault helicopters failed at the very earliest stage when three of the eight helicopters were unable to continue the mission because of technical failures or sandstorms.

The Hanover (West Germany) Air Show in May provided an opportunity to show off ideas for the proposed British-West German-French European Combat Aircraft (ECA). The ECA would replace the British and French Jaguars and the West German Phantoms. But this project was likely to remain stalled while governments thrashed out costs; the West Germans made no secret of their dissatisfaction with the alarming increases in costs for the British-West German-Italian Tornado multirole combat aircraft since it was launched in 1970. In the U.S. discussion about a new manned bomber was gaining momentum as the threat from the U.S.S.R.'s new aircraft fleets became more clearly defined. The new U.S. plane might turn out to be the so-called stealth bomber, the existence of which was leaked to the press during the year, apparently to show that the government had the interests of the defense community at heart.

(MICHAEL WILSON)

ALCOHOLIC BEVERAGES

Beer. Estimated world beer production in 1979 was 875 million hectolitres (hl), an increase of 40 million hl over the previous year. The U.S. easily retained its position as the largest producer; its output of 215,346,000 hl was 13.2% above the final figure for 1978. There was a resurgence of bars as places to drink beer, reflected in an increase of 11% in the proportion of U.S. beer sold on draft. West Germany remained the second-largest producer with 91,623,000 hl, almost unchanged from the previous year. The U.K. retained third place with 67,416,000 hl, compared with 66,416,000 hl in 1978.

Although figures were still incomplete, malting barley production in Europe in 1980 appeared poor except in the U.K. U.S. malting-quality barley was expected to be in ample supply. In many countries there had been an unwelcome rise in nitrogen levels, causing a drop in yield of beer from

The many tourists at the Moët-Hennessy winery in the Napa Valley, California, are one indication of the growing popularity of wines in the United States.

DAVID POWERS—BUSINESS WEEK

Table V. Estimated Consumption of Beer in Selected Countries
In litres[1] per capita

Country	1977	1978	1979
West Germany	148.7	145.6	145.1
Czechoslovakia	134.3	129.0	139.7
East Germany	127.0	130.0	134.3
Australia[2]	136.2	137.6	134.2
Belgium[3]	130.1	125.5	126.0
Ireland	126.2	131.8	122.7
United Kingdom	119.5	121.3	122.1
Denmark	116.32	116.89	120.28
New Zealand	122.5	127.4	118.7
Luxembourg	127.0	119.0	112.0
Austria	103.1	100.9	103.9
United States	85.9	88.7	92.0
Hungary	80.6	86.0	86
Netherlands, The	83.9	85.18	84.95
Canada[4]	85.1	86.1	84.2
Switzerland	68.3	68.0	68.2
Bulgaria	54	56	59
Finland	55.3	54.96	56.18
Spain	46.9	52.1	53.7
Venezuela	50	50	. . .
Sweden	53.6	48.9	48.2
Norway	45.47	46.04	45.88
France	46.21	45.26	45.6
Colombia	40	42.8	43.6
Japan	36.0	37.8	38.9

[1] One litre = 1.0567 U.S. quart = 0.8799 imperial quart.
[2] Years ending June 30.
[3] Excluding so-called household beer.
[4] Years ending March 31.

Table VI. Estimated Consumption of Potable Distilled Spirits in Selected Countries
In litres[1] of 100% pure spirit per capita

Country	1977	1978	1979
Luxembourg	4.7	5.5	5.8
Poland	5.8	5.6	5.5
Hungary	4.62	4.61	4.50
East Germany	3.7	3.9	4
Czechoslovakia	3.48	3.60	3.5
Canada[2]	3.42	3.45	3.49
Netherlands, The	2.90	3.01	3.41
West Germany	2.92	3.00	3.37
U.S.S.R.	3.3	3.3	3.3
United States	3.14	3.15	3.15
Sweden	2.97	2.99	3.03
Belgium	2.10	2.38	3.00
Spain	3	3	3
Finland	2.99	2.82	2.75
Yugoslavia	2.6	2.7	2.6
France[3]	2.5	2.5	2.5
Iceland	2.46	2.25	2.35
Romania	2.1	2.2	2.3
New Zealand	2.00	2.00	2.28
Ireland	2.16	2.36	2.25
Switzerland	1.88	2.00	2.00
Bulgaria	2	2	2
Italy	2.0	2.1	2
Cyprus	1.8	1.9	1.9
United Kingdom	1.42	1.72	1.89

[1] One litre = 1.0567 U.S. quart = 0.8799 imperial quart.
[2] Years ending March 31.
[3] Including aperitifs.

Table VII. Estimated Consumption of Wine in Selected Countries
In litres[1] per capita

Country	1977	1978	1979
France[2]	102.10	96.29	92.61
Italy	93.5	91.0	90
Portugal	97.0	91.3	86
Argentina	87	82	77
Spain	65.0	70.0	70
Chile	52.30	47.70	46.56
Switzerland[3]	44.9	45.9	46.2
Greece	39.6	42.0	41.0
Luxembourg	49.3	42.7	39.4
Austria	36.1	35.0	35.8
Hungary	34.0	33.8	35
Romania	30.0	33.1	35
Yugoslavia	27.9	27.5	. . .
Uruguay	25.0	25.0	. . .
West Germany	23.8	24.4	24.3
Bulgaria	22	22	. . .
Belgium	17.5	17.8	20.4
Czechoslovakia	17.2	17.5	17.5
Australia[4]	13.7	14.3	16.5
U.S.S.R.	13.3	14.0	14
Denmark	11.67	12.22	13.87
Netherlands, The	11.73	12.18	11.96
New Zealand	9.4	11.5	11.3
Poland	9.1	9.3	9.8
Sweden	9.50	9.06	9.43
Cyprus	7.8	8.8	9.0

[1] One litre = 1.0567 U.S. quart = 0.8799 imperial quart.
[2] Excluding cider (*c.* 20 litres per capita annually).
[3] Excluding cider (*c.* 5.35 litres per capita 1978–79).
[4] Years ending June 30.

Source: Produktschap voor Gedistilleerde Dranken, *Hoeveel alcoholhoudende dranken worden er in de wereld gedronken?*

a given tonnage of grain. Much winter-sown barley was in the high-nitrogen bracket.

Promising research on "genetic engineering" in yeast was being carried on in the U.S., the object being to provide yeasts of completely predictable character that would give equally predictable results with grain of known characteristics. Elsewhere, as in the U.K., this objective was achieved by maintaining a yeast bank of thousands of strains, each with a known fermenting pattern, so that brewers could match their yeast strains. There was international interest in the now-patented extraction of hops by means of liquid carbon dioxide. This method obviates the presence of solvent in the extract, and the carbon dioxide is converted back to gas and exhausted at the end of the process.

At a brewing conference in Harrogate, England, delegates from many countries heard how British brewers had cut their fuel needs by 10% over all production stages. (ARTHUR T. E. BINSTED)

Spirits. World recession had a strong effect on the spirits market. In the U.K. retail sales of spirits were down some 16% in January–November 1980 compared with a year earlier. Part of the blame could be attached to the steadily increasing wine market, but the main reason was consumer resistance to spiraling prices. Scotch whisky still accounted for more than 50% of the U.K. market, but vodka overtook gin, a clear indication that the worldwide trend to white spirits like vodka, white rum, and tequila was continuing.

Vodka now held a 21% share of the total U.S. spirits market, compared with only 11% in 1967. Vodka's gains had been largely at the expense of U.S. domestic whiskey, which had fallen by 20% in the past decade to a market share of around 27%. Scotch whisky had also lost ground in the U.S. over the past decade, after peaking in 1971 with a 14.2% share; imports of Scotch fell from 36 million proof gallons in 1971 to 30 million proof gallons in 1979. Apart from vodka, the trend was to variety with brandy, tequila, and cocktails showing significant progress.

The U.K. had become the most important export market for cognac despite a wrangle within the EEC over alleged tax discrimination against Scotch whisky in France. An EEC judgment expected soon could have far-reaching consequences, because Denmark, Italy, and the U.K., among others, were accused of similar tax discrimination against imported drink products. Another important development was the move by some Scotch distillers and trade unions to limit bulk exports of Scotch to Japan, where it was used to produce cheap blends.

The year brought renewed attacks on the drinks industry. The French government launched a concentrated "sensible drinking" campaign, and many countries clamped down heavily on advertising or introduced warning labels. (ANTONY C. WARNER)

Wine. World production of wine for 1980 was estimated at 338 million hl. It exceeded the big harvests of 1970, 1975, and 1976 but was below those of 1974 and 1979 (1979, at 378.2 million hl, was the largest ever recorded). The decline in production was due to the weather conditions encountered by the major producing countries, particularly in western Europe and the Mediterranean: a mild winter was followed by a cold, wet summer that affected growth and fruiting.

In France the vintage totaled less than 70 million hl, 18% below the exceptional 1979 harvest. The shortfall was especially marked in the quality regions. Bordeaux was 30% below 1979; Burgundy was below average; in Alsace cold and rain seriously reduced the harvest; and in Champagne the harvest was down to almost one-third of 1979. But the Côtes-du-Rhône region produced the same quantity as in 1979, while some other areas registered small gains.

In Italy production also fell but only by 7.5%. Piedmont, Friuli-Venezia-Giulia, Lombardy, and Tuscany were about 10% down from 1979. The decline was less in other regions. Spain, which had its greatest harvest in 1979 (50 million hl), fell back in 1980 to some 37 million hl. However, quality and alcohol content were high.

West Germany, which did not have a high output in 1979 (8 million hl), harvested even less in 1980 because of bad weather. The U.S.S.R. produced an estimated 32 million hl, 4% above 1979. Portugal produced 12 million hl, Romania 8 million, Yugoslavia 6.5 million, and Greece 6 million.

In the U.S. production continued to expand, to about 16 million hl (14 million in California). Production advanced a little in 1980 after steadying in 1979. Argentina harvested 24 million hl in 1980, the world's fifth-largest output. Australian estimated wine production in 1980 was 4,140,000 hl.

In sum, the world's 1980 wine harvest was a large one, above the high five-year average for 1975–79. It was distributed as follows: Europe (including the U.S.S.R.) 270 million hl (80%), South America 33 million hl (10%), North America 17 million hl (5%), and other countries 18 million hl (5%). (P. FRIDAS)

AUTOMOBILES

Chrysler Corp. in 1980 once again was the focus of attention in the automobile industry. The huge losses experienced in 1979 that compelled the firm to seek $1.5 billion in government loan guarantees in order to survive continued to mount, and by year's end it appeared that further help would be needed. But unlike 1979, when Chrysler alone was ailing, it soon became obvious that its domestic competition in the U.S. was far from healthy either.

While Chrysler took advantage of the loan guarantees to help finance bringing new products to market, its rivals were having their own troubles. In the first six months of 1980 the four U.S. automakers, General Motors Corp., Ford Motor Co., Chrysler, and American Motors Corp., posted a combined loss of $1.9 billion, the first time in industry history that losses topped the $1 billion mark. By the third quarter of the year the red ink spread, and combined losses topped the $3.5 billion mark. In the third quarter Ford reported a $595 million loss, highest ever for any three-month period in auto industry history. For the first nine months it lost a record $1,230,000,000.

A combination of factors affected the auto industry. Among them were the switch by consumers to more fuel-efficient but less profitable small cars, high interest rates that hindered both the dealers who had to finance the purchase of cars for inventory and consumers trying to obtain loans, and the huge multibillion-dollar expense associated with bringing the new, smaller cars to market.

In the 1980 model year, which ran from Oct. 1, 1979, to Sept. 30, 1980, U.S. domestic auto sales fell 22.4% to 6,787,846 from 8,758,064 in the 1979 model year. GM sales declined 17.4% to 4,228,231 from 5,119,078 the previous year; Ford sales fell 34.1% to 1,556,771 from 2,363,117; and Chrysler was down 34.2% to 649,043 from 986,649. For the first time since 1962 Chrysler sales dropped below the 900,000 mark.

American Motors sales rose 11.9% to 163,502 from 146,078 a year earlier, the first year-to-year sales gain for AMC since 1974. Volkswagen sales of its subcompact Rabbit, built in Pennsylvania, rose 32.9% to 190,299 from 143,144.

Though its sales were down sharply, GM experienced a sharp rise in market share during the 1980 model year. Its share of domestic sales rose to 62.3% from 58.4% in 1979; Ford fell to 22.9% from 27%; and Chrysler's share declined to 9.6% from 11.3%. AMC's market share rose to 2.4% from 1.7%, and Volkswagen increased to 2.8% from 1.6%.

Sales in the U.S. by domestic automakers faltered, but manufacturers from other nations had a field day. Sales rose so rapidly that both the United Auto Workers and Ford petitioned the International Trade Commission to set restrictions on the number of foreign cars that could be sold in the U.S. A decade earlier imported automobiles were accounting for sales of about 1.2 million annually, or one out of every ten cars sold in the U.S. By 1980 this figure had risen to more than 2 million, or one out of every four cars sold in the U.S. Nearly 80% of these foreign-made cars carried a Japanese nameplate.

Other than imports, one often-cited reason for sales problems was price. In the fall of 1978 when the 1979 models were introduced, the average base price of a U.S.-made car was $5,666. In the fall of 1979 when the 1980 models were brought out, the average base had risen to $6,731. In the fall of 1980 as the 1981 models were introduced, the average base price had skyrocketed to $7,856. Industry leaders adopted a trend in the 1980 model year of boosting prices every three months to keep up with inflation. As 1981 got under way, they said that they would continue that practice.

The industry maintained that a partial offset to the higher prices was the improved fuel economy of the new models. One reason for the better mileage was that the federal government raised its fuel economy standards in the fall of 1980 for the 1981 model year. For the 1981 model year the government's Environmental Protection Agency required each automaker to obtain an average of 22 mi per gallon (mpg) from its fleet of cars, up from an average of 20 mpg in the 1980 model year. In releasing its annual mileage ratings on cars, the EPA announced that the mileage champion was a Volkswagen Rabbit model powered by a four-cylinder diesel engine. It was rated at 42 mpg in city driving. The highest rated gasoline-powered car was a new mini model from Toyota, called Starlet, which averaged 39 mpg in the city.

Though the Rabbit diesel was made in the U.S., EPA rankings referred to it as an import because about 50% of its parts and components were still sourced in West Germany. U.S. cars did fare well in the EPA ratings, however. The Chevrolet Chevette, Ford Escort, and Mercury Lynx all were rated at 30 mpg for city driving, and the Dodge Omni and Plymouth Horizon came in at 28 mpg.

Along with the new mileage ratings came a lengthy list of new cars for 1981. The most talked about were the so-called K-body compacts from Chrysler. These were the cars the automaker said would turn the corporation around and the reason it needed federal loan guarantees. These cars, the Dodge Aries and Plymouth Reliant, replaced the Dodge Aspen and Plymouth Volare. They were built on 99.6-in (253-cm) wheelbases, slightly less than the 104-in (264-cm) wheelbase on the General Motors compact X-body cars that were brought out 1½ years earlier. The K-cars were offered in two-door, four-door, and wagon models, the only front-wheel drive compact wagons on the market. Their fuel economy of 25 mpg topped the EPA list for midsize cars.

The first day the K-cars went on sale, October 2, sales totaled 5,011 units, a Chrysler record that topped the 4,119 new Plymouth Belvidere and Dodge Coronet models sold on the first day of the 1965 model year. Chrysler also brought out a new Imperial luxury two-door sedan, resurrecting a name last used in 1975. The $18,311 luxury model featured a "bustle back" rear end similar to that on the 1980 Cadillac.

At Ford the emphasis was on cars that would compete against the imports. The firm brought out the Ford Escort and Mercury Lynx, successors to the Ford Pinto and Mercury Bobcat. Both were built on a 94.2-in (239-cm) wheelbase, were 165 in (419 cm) long overall, and featured front-wheel drive. They were offered in two-door hatchback and four-door wagon versions. Ford said that it would introduce sporty two-passenger versions of each car later in the model year, the Escort EXP and Lynx LN-7.

General Motors restyled its so-called A-Special cars, the intermediate Chevrolet Monte Carlo, Buick Regal, Oldsmobile Cutlass Supreme, and Pontiac Grand Prix. The restyling concentrated on lower, sloping front ends and raised deck lids in back, a move aimed at changing the appearance while improving aerodynamics, the ability to slice through air with minimum drag.

The big news from GM was reserved for mid-1981 when it would bring out its own subcompact, front-wheel drive competitors to the imports, dubbed the J-cars. The Escort-size models would be available in two-door coupe, hatchback, four-door sedan, and wagon models.

At American Motors new for 1981 were the subcompact Eagle SX/4 and Kammback models. The firm also made the 2.5-litre four-cylinder engine it purchases from GM

Lee Iacocca, chairman of the Chrysler Corp., unveiled the Plymouth Reliant, one of a new line of compact cars for which the firm obtained federal loan guarantees.

UPI

standard in all Eagle models. That move gave both the compact and subcompact Eagles 22-mpg city fuel economy ratings, a considerable improvement over the 16-mpg fuel economy rating on the compact 1980 Eagle, which had a 258-cu in, six-cylinder engine as standard. AMC also began marketing the Renault 18i luxury sedan, a high-mileage (24 mpg city) subcompact.

In addition to cars, men made news in 1980. Henry Ford II, who had been slowly relinquishing his duties as head of Ford Motor Co., stepped down as chairman on March 13. Philip Caldwell, vice-chairman and president, was named to succeed him, the first time a non-Ford family member would run the company. In a somewhat surprising move Donald Petersen, who had headed Ford's overseas operations, was named president. William Bourke, head of North American Automotive Operations, had been expected to be named to that post. Bourke resigned from Ford.

At General Motors Roger Smith, an executive vice-president, was named to succeed Thomas Murphy as chairman when Murphy retired on Dec. 31, 1980. F. James McDonald, another executive vice-president, was named to succeed E. M. "Pete" Estes as GM president when Estes retired on Jan. 31, 1981.

Non-U.S. automakers introduced several new cars in 1980. At Toyota a new mini-compact Starlet (90.6-in [230-cm] wheelbase) was brought out that boasted city driving fuel economy of 39 mpg, tops on the EPA chart for gasoline-driven cars. The engine had four cylinders and a five-speed manual transmission.

Datsun put new sheet metal on its luxury 810 model, but perhaps its best innovation was a miniature recording system in the dashboard in which a female voice warned motorists who left their car lights on to "Please, turn off your lights."

Mazda introduced a newly styled GLC model that for the first time had been converted to front-wheel drive. Subaru stayed with basically the same models but added an on-demand four-wheel drive system coupled with a dual-range transmission. By switching a lever, motorists could go from front-wheel drive to four-wheel drive.

Imports made other news when Honda confirmed that it would begin building a new Accord model in Marysville, Ohio, starting in 1982 for the 1983 model year. The company said that it was running out of production capacity in Japan and was forced to enter the market in the U.S. with an assembly plant. Nissan (Datsun) said that it would build a plant near Nashville, Tenn., to produce Datsun pickup trucks beginning in late 1983. Volkswagen, which already had an assembly plant in Westmoreland, Pa., announced that a second plant would be built in Sterling Heights, Mich., and probably would be producing trucks in late 1982.

Renault made news by increasing its equity interest in AMC. In 1978 Renault purchased 4.7% of AMC's common stock for $150 million. In October 1980 it reached an agreement with AMC to invest an additional $200 million in return for a 49.9% stock interest in AMC within two years. Under terms of the agreement Renault could purchase more than a 50% interest by exercising certain stock warrants.

Among other major developments during 1980, Ford was ruled innocent of reckless homicide charges in a Winamac, Ind., trial involving the deaths of three teenage girls who died when their subcompact Ford Pinto was struck in the rear and the Pinto's gas tank exploded. (*See* LAW: *Special Report.*)

(JAMES L. MATEJA)

BUILDING AND CONSTRUCTION

The sharp five-year rise in the value of new construction in the U.S. ended in 1980. On a seasonally adjusted annual rate basis, the value of new construction put in place in June 1980 was $216,318,000,000. For 1979 as a whole, the figure was $228,950,000,000. Throughout 1979 and in January 1980, the monthly value of construction, with few exceptions, had continued its upward climb. Even during the next three months, the value of construction was higher than in the corresponding months of 1979. By May, however, the downturn, which had been anticipated throughout 1979, had begun. Despite the high level of activity during the first quarter, it appeared that much lower monthly levels during the last half would pull total outlays for 1980 below those of the preceding year. The downturn was caused by the continuing inflationary spiral in construction costs and the resumption in the upward movement of interest rates.

A somewhat different picture emerged when adjustment was made for inflation. In constant (1972) dollars, outlays for new construction totaled $97,229,000,000 in 1975 and $114,698,000,000 in 1979. On this basis, outlays in 1979 were actually lower than in 1978. Since it appeared that expenditures in constant dollars in 1980 would be lower than in 1979, it could be said that, in terms of real value, the rise was not as sharp as the value in inflated dollars would indicate and the downward trend began in 1979.

During the 1970s dollar outlays for residential construction in the U.S. ranged from 35 to 45% of total expenditure for all building construction. In 1979 the value of residential buildings put in place was $99,030,000,000, but in July 1980 the value of residential construction on a seasonally adjusted annual rate basis was $75,838,000,000. It was expected that total outlays for residential construction for 1980 would be considerably below those in 1979, with an even greater decline in terms of constant dollars. The data were reinforced by U.S. Department of Commerce figures on the number of housing units started. In 1978, the peak year of the 1975–79 period, the number of housing units started exceeded two million. In 1979 the number of units started was down by 274,000 units, and preliminary information for 1980 indicated another substantial drop—to approximately one million units or only half the number started in 1978.

In July 1980 the Construction Composite Cost Index of the Department of Commerce was 220.5 (1972 = 100). A downturn occurred in hardwood and softwood prices, but most other items continued the inflationary spiral that had existed throughout the 1970s. The average sales price of new houses sold in the U.S. in May 1980 was $73,400, compared with an average of $71,800 in 1979 and $42,600 in 1975.

In Canada construction activity continued the decline that was evident in 1979. The general outlook was that business conditions would continue to deteriorate as a result of the developing recession in the U.S. Lower levels of productivity and rising labour costs continued to exert upward pressures on prices, and inflation remained a major national economic problem. The prospect was that 1980 prices would rise by 10% and 1981 prices by 9%. Given these conditions, the outlook for building and construction was not good.

In Western Europe the outlook for build-

The first of the Ford Motor Company's "World Cars" rolled off the assembly line in August. The Escort was a replacement for the Pinto.

UPI

DAVID WOO—THE NEW YORK TIMES

Construction of single-family houses began among the high-rise buildings of Dallas, Texas. The project is an effort to redevelop the inner city.

ing and construction was mixed. The West German construction industry had experienced a vigorous upturn in 1978 and 1979, but in 1980 it was returning to a lower level of activity. The expectation, however, was that investment demand in building and machinery would be relatively strong through the year. In Great Britain a drop in housing investments, both public and private, in 1979 was the major cause of a decline in new building. It was projected that new housing investment would probably continue to fall in both 1980 and 1981. Orders for new public buildings were low throughout 1979, and public investment policy was expected to contribute to a continuing downward trend. With some exceptions, building and construction elsewhere in Western Europe remained at very low levels.

In Japan economic growth of 6% in 1979 had been stimulated by expenditure on public works and publicly financed housing. In 1980 and 1981 the growth rate of the economy was expected to be around 4.5%, with the major stimulus provided by investment in plant and equipment and consumer expenditures.

(CARTER C. OSTERBIND)

CHEMICALS

The chemical industries in the developed countries throughout the world registered substantial gains in 1979 and continued to grow through the first quarter of 1980. In the second quarter, however, the pace faltered. By the end of the third quarter it appeared that the worst of the recession had passed in some countries, but in others there seemed to be no real hope for improvement before 1981.

In the U.S. the chemical industry recorded shipments valued at $149,181,000,000 in 1979 according to the U.S. Department of Commerce. That was 18% higher than the $126,445,000,000 shipped in 1978. A large portion of the increase represented higher prices, as the U.S. Department of Labor's index of producer prices for chemicals rose from an average of 225.6 (1967 = 100) in 1978 to 264 in 1979. But some of the growth was also caused by increased production. The Federal Reserve Board's index of industrial production for chemicals went up 6.6%, from 197.4 (1967 = 100) in 1978 to 210.4 in 1979.

Chemical exports continued to make an important contribution to U.S. trade. In 1979 they amounted to $17,306,000,000 according to figures compiled by the Department of Commerce. Chemical imports for the year totaled $7,485,000,000, yielding a favourable balance of chemical trade of $9,821,000,000, 58.6% above the $6,193,000,000 figure for 1978.

U.S. chemical production declined sharply in the second quarter of 1980, although inflation disguised the extent of the fall. Among the key indicators, however, the index of chemical production dropped each month during the first half of the year, reaching 191.7 (preliminary) in June. This was below the average for all of 1978.

Propelled by high prices for oil and other forms of energy, chemical prices moved up sharply during the first half of 1980. The U.S. Department of Labor's index of producer prices, which averaged 292.3 in December 1979, rose each month in the first half of 1980 to 327.3 in June. As a result, the value of chemical shipments climbed to $81.8 billion in the first half of 1980, 10.5% higher than in the same period of 1979.

By the fourth quarter of 1980 many chemical managers believed that the recession had bottomed out and that business would improve during 1981. Respondents to a survey said that they planned to invest $14,550,000,000 in capital expansion during 1981, as compared with a $12,050,000,000 estimated expenditure in 1980.

The chemical industry in the Soviet Union was having trouble meeting production targets. The country's 1976–80 five-year plan had called for chemical production increases of 12–13% per year. By the middle of 1980, however, it was clear that the actual growth would be less than half that rate. Soviet chemical industry minister Leonid Kostandov said that his ministry had commissioned only 186 chemical facilities in 1979, of 354 that were scheduled. The hard 1978–79 winter was partly to blame, but the minister said that his ministry was also at fault. During the third quarter of 1980 performance improved somewhat. Mineral fertilizer production rose 11% to 70.4 million metric tons for the first eight months. Sulfuric acid production for the same period increased 3% to 111 million metric tons, while man-made fibre output rose 6% to 791,000 metric tons.

Japanese chemical companies were weathering the economic storms of 1980 better than those in other industrialized countries. Chemical sales in 1979 rose more than 15% to over $70 billion. Chemical exports helped the country's trade position, with net exports of $1.3 billion realized on total chemical exports of $6.9 billion. Japan's Ministry of International Trade and Industry surveyed 343 of the nation's chemical companies and found that they planned to spend $2.3 billion on capital expenditures in 1980, 10% more than in 1979, which was, in turn, 42% higher than the outlay in 1978.

Early in 1980 Japan was looking forward to a 10% growth in chemicals, but the recession that struck in the second quarter made such a gain unlikely. One company reported that sales of some products dropped 40–50% in May. The country's chemical makers reacted quickly to the lowered demand, however. With the concurrence of the government, the industry cut production of ethylene by 24% in the third quarter and that of synthetic resins by 20–30% in the same period.

West German chemical sales, according to figures published in 1980 by the Organization for Economic Cooperation and Development, totaled $44,055,000,000 in 1978, as compared with $37,150,000,000 in 1977. Early estimates were that they increased at least 15% in 1979. The first quarter of 1980 revealed sales increases of 20%, but a slowdown took hold in the second quarter. Toward the end of the year it appeared that West German chemical sales' volume would be 1–2% below that in 1979.

But because prices rose approximately 8%, the expectation was that the full year 1980 would show a nominal sales increase of 6%.

The United Kingdom's chemical sales were estimated at $29,795,000,000 in 1978 by the OECD, an 18% boost over the $25,245,000,000 in 1977. Modest hopes for a 1980 increase were shattered by the worldwide chemical recession. The British Chemical Industries Association said late in the year that production for the first five months of 1980 was down 10% and that sales in June and July were "very depressed." It believed that chemical production for 1980 as a whole would be 6% lower than in 1979. (DONALD P. BURKE)

ELECTRICAL

The slowdown in the construction of electrical generating stations throughout the world was a major cause for declining growth rates in the electrical equipment manufacturing industries in all industrialized countries; France, with its massive nuclear power station building program, was an exception. In West Germany no power station contracts had been placed since 1975. A similar situation prevailed in Britain, and construction orders in the U.S. were virtually at a standstill. U.S. nuclear plant suppliers were working at less than 10% of capacity, and fossil-fueled power station equipment manufacturers at 40% below capacity.

One U.S. firm that withstood the pressure of low orders from utilities was General Electric Co. (GE), which had learned some hard lessons from aggressive international competition in the mid-1970s as imports of innovative and low-cost electrical products from Japan and Europe flooded the U.S. market. By the first quarter of 1975 GE's earnings had dropped 39%, but by diversifying and investing in research and development, it outperformed the U.S. gross national product in 1979. The firm's sales rose by 14% (to $22,460,000,000) over 1978, while profits ($1,409,000,000) were up 15%. Investment in research and development in 1979 was 20% higher than the 1978 record of $521 million. Also in 1979, GE spent $1,240,000,000 on plant and equipment (18% above 1978) to provide for the growth of its high-technology businesses and to improve productivity.

The persistent failure of Westinghouse Electric Corp. to meet its export goals resulted in a reorganization in 1979 of its international business approach. The corporation's need for a reorientation toward export markets was shown clearly by the decline in net sales in volume terms, although in dollar values, neglecting the effects of inflation, sales rose from $6.7 billion in 1978 to $7.3 billion in 1979. This compared with 1979 sales of about $7 billion achieved by Britain's General Electric Co. (no relation to GE), which hoped to team up with Westinghouse to build pressurized water reactor power stations in Britain.

Following the fall in value of the Swiss franc in 1979, Swiss electrical equipment manufacturers became more competitive in world markets. Results from Sulzer for the first three months of 1980 showed a 30% increase in sales over the same period in 1979. Exports of French electrical products were said to represent 45% of the total turnover of French manufacturers. France also claimed to be third in the 1979 export league table with 14% of the world market, after the West Germany (22%) and the U.S. (18%) and followed by Japan (13.5%). However, the Organization for Economic Cooperation and Development placed Japan third and France fourth.

British exports increased in value by 7.5% in 1979, while imports increased by 28.4%. This poor performance was partly explained by a long bitter strike in the engineering industries in the latter half of the year. In the year ended March 1980 the General Electric Co.'s exports totaled $1,932,000,000. In West Germany the ailing AEG-Telefunken suffered the breakup of part of its empire following an $800 million rescue by a consortium of banks at the end of 1979. The company was expected to lose $300 million in 1980 but go into the black thereafter. Since the mid-1970s electrical imports into West Germany had been accelerating at an annual rate of 10–20%, according to the manufacturers' association.

Among innovations in 1980, a large induction motor with an aluminum alloy winding was developed by Allmänna Svenska Elektriska Aktiebolaget in Sweden. The use of high-tensile aluminum was unusual, but the manufacturer said that the motor had a large heat capacity and low current density. Weight was reduced by 40% and space requirements by 15%. Metallic materials with a noncrystalline atomic structure typical of glass were developed in the U.S. by Allied Chemicals. These metals were not only strong, ductile, and corrosion-resistant but also had low magnetic hysteresis, allowing them to achieve dramatic cuts in energy losses when applied in transformers. (T. C. J. COGLE)

FURNITURE

Recession and the drying up of consumer credit caused a drop in U.S. home furnishings shipments in 1980. Since furniture requires a considerable dollar outlay and most sales are made on credit, the Carter administration's measures to curb credit buying, announced in March, caused a steep decline in retail furniture sales that lasted through August. Many consumers mistakenly believed that credit sales had been suspended and that they could buy furniture only for cash. Another depressing factor was the decline in housing starts, which slowed to a rate of less than one million (annual basis) in the second quarter.

Sales from retail stores fell to $18,380,000,000 from a 1979 level of $18,596,000,000, a drop of 1.2%. In constant dollars, however (removing the effects of inflation), the drop amounted to 8.7%. The second quarter was the worst, according to the National Association of Furniture Manufacturers. By the fourth quarter, retail sales were back to 1979 levels. Furniture continued to be a good buy compared with other consumer durables. The wholesale price index for all commodities (1967 = 100) was 269.8, but in the first half of 1980, furniture and household durables stood at 186.7.

Manufacturers' shipments fell 21% between July 1979 and July 1980. Wood furniture was down 12%, upholstered furniture 25%, tables 1%, recliners 34%, and summer and casual furniture 30%. Only metal dinette furniture showed an increase, with shipments up 36%. Because the recession was anticipated, both manufacturing and retail inventory levels were low when the credit crunch hit. This lessened the number of business failures that might otherwise have occurred. Even so, a dozen major manufacturers were forced into Chapter 11 bankruptcy proceedings.

An increase in the production of smaller-scale furniture and the introduction of more multipurpose pieces were stimulated by smaller room sizes and changing life-styles. There were chairs that converted into beds, small tables that extended into dining size, Victorian sofas that became beds, and modular wall units that hid TV and stereo equipment. Many pieces were designed to serve in either the bedroom or the living or "family" room (now referred to as the "great room") or in a combined living/dining area. Oak was by far the most popular furniture wood, followed by pecan, maple, elm, pine, and cherry. Brass beds and other metal furniture continued to grow in popularity, and there was a boomlet in unfinished or ready-to-finish furniture.

One effect of the 1980 recession was a growth of "quick-ship" programs. Previously, consumers had to wait 60 to 180 days for delivery from conventional retail stores. As a result of competitive pressures, many manufacturers were delivering upholstered furniture within 30 days and wood furniture within 60 to 90 days.

The declining value of the dollar on world markets caused a surge in the export of U.S.-made furniture, mostly to Europe. No official figures were available, but a level of $350 million was estimated.

(ROBERT A. SPELMAN)

FURS

The international fur industry encountered somewhat more difficulty in 1980 than it had for almost a decade. The problems were mostly economics-related and occurred despite the fact that more leading fashion designers were featuring furs in their collections than ever before. In the U.S. and Canada, recession fears and soaring interest rates early in the year caused most retailers to be extremely conservative in their purchases. This, in turn, forced North American pelt merchants and garment manufacturers to plan cautiously. Europeans dominated the purchasing of skins, at least for the first five months. West German and Italian buyers were not quite so conservative as their North American counterparts, but the overall result was that many skin prices came down sharply from 1979's high levels, especially for such long-haired varieties as raccoon, fox, coyote, and lynx.

Despite economic problems, retail business proved better than expected, with many furriers finding themselves insufficiently prepared for the fall upswing. Figures were incomplete, but indications were that total sales were at least equal to 1979, both in the U.S. and in major European countries. Japan also had a good year, as did Hong Kong. From a business standpoint, however, 1980 was not a good profit year for most furriers, squeezed between higher costs and intense competition at the selling end. Natural forces also took a toll. Extreme heat, drought, and floods caused heavy losses among U.S. herds of wild and ranched animals, and the eruptions of Mt. St. Helens in Washington state destroyed many animals and their habitats.

The year witnessed the emergence of South Korea and Hong Kong as important manufacturing centres for all price ranges of fur garments. Hong Kong's shipments, mostly to Japan, were expected to be substantially higher than the approximately $150 million recorded in 1979. The first Worldwide Furbearer Conference drew some 200 international delegates to a nine-day session in Frostburg, Md. The result would be a two-volume compendium that was expected to have considerable influence on decisions regarding animal management. (SANDY PARKER)

GEMSTONES

During 1980, at Sotheby's auction in New York City, a 6.15-carat ruby sold for $78,700 per carat. At Christie's auction a different 4.57-carat ruby brought $21,000 per carat. Another auction gem, a 10.77-carat diamond of the highest quality, went for almost $67,500 per carat. News of such prices continued to stimulate investment fever in the gemstone industry. The idea of selling gems for investment purposes, originally triggered by rapidly rising gem prices, was finally accepted as both legitimate and lucrative by the industry. As a result investment pressure drove the wholesale price of top-quality (D, flawless) diamonds in one year from $39,000 to $53,000 per carat.

Investment shock hit the gemstone industry strongly in October when Thomas McKinnon Securities Inc. filed for registration with the Securities and Exchange Commission for the Thomson Diamond Trust. The idea of a gem investment organization was not new, but the large size, heavy funding, and impeccable status of the Thomson firm served notice of changes to come. Such activities could siphon large numbers of high-quality diamonds off the market into investment portfolios, and any large-scale liquidation of diamonds in such portfolios could be disruptive to price stability.

For diamonds as a whole, the year's sales were good except for large diamonds. Smaller stones of 0.25, 0.33, and 0.5 carat sold well, and prices were very strong on top-colour diamonds of less than the best quality. The Central Selling Organisation in London made adjustments to steady prices across the entire range of qualities.

The coloured gem market was still expanding. The constantly increasing sophistication and education of buyers put the greatest pressure on supplies of the highest quality gems. Very good tourmalines and aquamarines were selling at extraordinarily high prices, and significant price rises occurred for tanzanite and green garnet.

Zale Corp., the world's largest retail jeweler, sold its 130-carat Light of Peace diamond to produce an after-tax profit of $6.2 million and donated its 318.44-carat black opal, the Dark Jubilee—valued at $650,000—to the Smithsonian Institution. The Smithsonian also received a superb 182-carat star sapphire from the estate of the late Mary Pickford. (PAUL E. DESAUTELS)

GLASS

Although the general economic situation in 1980 was not conducive to startling increases in production and sales, there were a number of innovations in methods of production and new products. A Belgian glass company introduced a granulated foamed glass for use as an insulating agent against both sound and heat. The material was light and fire-resistant and could be used either by itself or as a filler with other materials. Chance-Pilkington of the U.K. developed a glass powder called Crystona that could be used as a replacement for plaster of paris in the field of orthopedics. The same company's optical division carried out work that could bring about a 30% cut in production costs for certain types of optical fibres. British Insulated Callender's Cables Ltd. developed a system for incorporating an optical fibre inside an overhead power cable that would enable the electricity grid to be used for general communications.

In the field of flat glass, the Battelle Laboratory in Switzerland developed a form of fire-resistant glazing consisting of layers of glass laminated with an inorganic compound that swells out when exposed to heat. Pilkington Brothers Ltd. negotiated with the Chinese government concerning the possibility of licensing the production of float glass in China, the only leading nation not already using the process.

Sales of glass containers for carbonated beverages more than held their own against plastic materials, although the trend was toward larger bottles (1½ litres and over) for which plastics were perhaps more suitable. In spite of this, the recession caused an overall reduction in sales, and layoffs became inevitable. Under these conditions, the container industry concentrated on maintaining its share of the packaging market. Manufacturing techniques were improved, and increased speed of production and better quality of product were apparent. There were further developments in weight reduction and in strengthening glass containers by surface treatment or protective plastic coating. Wide-mouth containers were introduced for such beverages as wine and Coca-Cola. The 1½-litre soft-drink bottles that had been banned in Canada on safety grounds were reintroduced, with the proviso that they must be coated with a plastic material.

The EEC Commission prepared a draft directive dealing with conservation of energy which required that emphasis be placed on returnable containers and recycling of glass and other packaging materials. Throughout the Western world, glass recycling schemes gained momentum. Within the EEC alone, it was estimated that 1,250,000 metric tons of glass had been recycled. In the U.K. the Bottle Bank scheme was enlarged and now encompassed many local authorities, with one collection point at Buckingham Palace. Britain's first purpose-built glass recycling plant, capable of processing 50,000 metric tons of glass a year, was opened in Alloa, Scotland, at a cost approaching £500,000.

With the British pound strong, the U.K. glass industry was adversely affected by imports of domestic glassware and particularly crystal glass from Eastern Europe; imports of these products rose by some 30–40%. The glass container industry also continued to suffer from imports, although to a lesser degree than in previous years. (MARTHA H. MINA)

INSURANCE

As the 1980s began, private insurance in the West continued to grow at a faster pace than GNP. Annual insurance premium

The Corning Museum of Glass in Corning, New York, which opened in June, displays nearly 20,000 glass artifacts.

COURTESY, THE CORNING MUSEUM OF GLASS, CORNING, NEW YORK

volume of more than $400 billion in 1980 amounted to nearly 5% of GNP. The leading insurance countries were the U.S., Japan, West Germany, the U.K., France, and Canada, in that order. By region, North America's share of the market remained sizable, but it had declined from 63% in 1970 to less than one-half as insurance in Europe and Japan developed rapidly.

In the U.K. the decade ended with a year of higher profits on a record total premium income in excess of £13,000 million. Loss experience in U.K. general insurance was deteriorating, however, as was true almost everywhere in the world. Lloyd's of London entered 1980 with a new high of nearly 19,000 underwriting members. Results announced in 1980, with a three-year reporting lag, showed global profits of £120 million on £1,700 million in premiums, but the next year's results were expected to be less favourable. In 1980 a £123 million settlement for defective plastic coating in three U.S.-built methane carriers represented the largest shipping loss ever experienced by Lloyd's. The destruction in January of the unsprinklered British Aerospace spare parts depot at Weybridge, Surrey, cost £70 million, a record for a single-fire loss in Britain. Under the Insurance Brokers' Act, soon to take full effect, persons and firms would have to be approved by the Insurance Brokers' Registration Council and codes of practice established for agents.

Life insurance in force in the U.S. totaled approximately $4 trillion in 1980, and total premium income of U.S. life insurance approached $100 billion. The largest gains were in health insurance premiums and annuity receipts, which together accounted for more than half the total. Increases in life insurance premiums were slipping below the 7–10% of recent years. Lower-premium term life insurance purchases exceeded those of the traditional whole-life permanent contracts. Two-thirds of new life insurance protection was still purchased on an individual basis, as opposed to group life insurance purchases issued primarily through employers. The average insured family had about $50,000 of life insurance. New contracts, such as "adjustable life" policies that permit changes in protection or premiums, were gaining favour.

Declines in mortality and higher investment income combined to keep the annual gain from operations at more than 13%. Policy loans increased, particularly for some insurers, but remained relatively stable at less than 10% of assets. Bonds, mortgages, and stocks were the largest components of life insurer assets, in that order. Total assets exceeded $430 billion.

Pension plans covered by life insurers continued their rapid growth; 25 million persons were included in such plans, and reserves had more than tripled during the preceding decade. The Employee Retirement Income Security Act, with its liberalized tax incentives for individual retirement accounts (IRA's) and Keogh plans for the self-employed, had created substantial new marketing opportunities. Two variable-annuity companies joined the ranks of the top 50 life insurers during 1980.

U.S. property and liability insurance sales topped $100 billion during 1980. Underwriting deficits (premiums less losses and expenses) during the first two quarters amounted to $1.5 billion, but total earnings after taxes and including investment income totaled $3.3 billion, or almost 8% of earned premiums. Policyholders' surplus (assets less liabilities) rose to a total of $50 billion.

The most discussed loss of 1980 was the eruption of Mt. St. Helens in Washington state. Insured losses exceeded $14 million, but tens of thousands of additional claims were pending. Determination of coverage was complicated by lack of precedents and the fact that newer property insurance contracts exclude earth movement rather than volcanic eruption. Large-loss fires, involving more than $500,000 in direct damages, exceeded $1 billion in the U.S. for the first time. The two largest losses, totaling more than $100 million, involved crude oil tankers at refineries. A fortunate veer away from population centres kept insured property losses from Hurricane Allen to about $50 million. Losses resulting from riots in Miami, Fla., exceeded $100 million, and claims of $77 million were filed for the disappearance in space of the Satcom III communications satellite. On a broader scale, arson fire losses continued to plague insurers, with estimated total costs amounting to $15 billion annually.

Consumers in all 50 states were now protected against insurer insolvency by property-casualty insurance guaranty funds. The New York Insurance Exchange, a Lloyd's-type operation for placing larger risks, opened in March. Automobile insurance claims decreased slightly, although the average cost of accidents rose 12% and rates increased 3%. Product liability suits rose more than 25%. (*See* LAW: *Special Report*.) (DAVID L. BICKELHAUPT)

IRON AND STEEL

As expected, 1979 proved to be a year of relative recovery in terms of tonnage produced throughout the world, total output reaching a new record of 747 million metric tons. Late in the year, however, it became plain that there would be renewed recession in 1980. The decline, probably to about the 1974 output level of 710 million metric tons, was severe, especially in some major producing regions. Steel consumption fell dramatically in North America early in the year, and capacity utilization rates in the U.S. fell to the exceptionally low level of 50% during the summer; however, a modest recovery began in the fall. In Europe, in contrast, demand held up fairly well for some months (during which period a strike at British Steel Corporation disabled a substantial proportion of the U.K. national output), but plunged after midyear.

Few Western countries escaped the renewed recession. Spain, which had developed quickly in recent years and appeared to withstand the testing experiences of the later 1970s, felt its adverse effects. New producing countries such as Brazil, Venezuela, and South Korea continued to advance, but most of the traditional steelmakers encountered reduced demand levels. A notable exception was Australia, where the decline in steel output during the year was entirely due to production restraints, including the effect of strikes on raw material supplies.

The 1974–75 recession had a severe impact on steel finances and policies; the 1980 experience, coming after five years of generally poor business, invoked even more radical responses in some of the main producing areas. Steel trade policy in the U.S. was dominated for much of the year by the antidumping case brought in March by U.S. Steel Corp. against several major EEC exporters and by the responses that this move evoked, especially on the part of the U.S. administration. (Dumping is the selling of goods to other nations at less than the domestic market price.) U.S. Steel claimed that the trigger price system, introduced in February 1978 to identify quickly imports against which antidumping procedures would be justified, had been weakly administered—an allegation that a subsequent report of the U.S. General Accounting Office tended to endorse. U.S. domestic producers were also angered by the decision of the government not to raise trigger price levels for the second quarter of 1980.

As soon as the antidumping case was brought the U.S. government suspended the trigger price system, as it had long threatened to do in such circumstances, and a protracted process of bargaining began involving U.S. Steel, the government, the European Community Commission, and some EEC national governments. The issue, which contained within it the seeds of a potential general trade war, was resolved in late September, when U.S. Steel agreed to withdraw the case in return for concessions by the U.S. government in the areas of company taxation and environmental control requirements, together with the restoration of trigger prices as of October 21 at levels about 12% higher than at the time of their suspension in the spring. The government agreed also to investigate the import situation with a view to remedial action if import surges, measured by defined criteria, should occur.

Within the EEC the sharp fall in demand in the summer put such pressure on the Davignon Plan market support measures, in operation in their comprehensive form since the beginning of 1978, that the voluntary cooperation on which they depended collapsed. Market disorder ensued, and prices for most products, especially in West Germany, fell dramatically to exceptionally low levels. In these circumstances the European Community Commission proposed, for the first time in the existence of the European Coal and Steel Community (ECSC), that "manifest crisis" be declared under Article 58 of the Paris Treaty, empowering the Commission to issue compulsory output quotas for all companies and to impose financial penalties for breaches.

After considerable argument in the Council of Ministers and concessions to West Germany—which alone opposed the move in principle and in detail—the manifest crisis regime was introduced on October 31 retroactive to the beginning of the month. This represented a radical and bold departure by the ECSC institutions, putting to the test the credibility and effectiveness of their ultimate powers in regard to steel production. Only when the compulsory quota regime ended in mid-1981

STEVE ILKO—THE NEW YORK TIMES

United States Steel Corp. closed two unprofitable plants in Youngstown, Ohio.

Table VIII. World Production of Crude Steel
In 000 metric tons

Country	1975	1976	1977	1978	1979	1980 Year to date	1980 No. of months	Percent change 1980/79
World	645,430	676,360	675,430	717,230	747,524	*		
U.S.S.R.	141,330	144,810	146,660	151,440	149,000	75,900	6	+ 1.4
U.S.	105,820	116,120	113,700	124,310	123,280	73,690	9	− 22.6
Japan	102,310	107,400	102,410	102,110	111,750	85,070	9	+ 2.1
West Germany	40,410	42,410	38,980	41,250	46,040	33,950	9	− 2.5
China†	26,000	21,000	23,700	31,780	34,430	*		
Italy	21,870	23,460	23,340	24,280	24,250	20,190	9	+ 14.4
France	21,530	23,230	22,090	22,840	23,360	18,260	9	+ 8.7
United Kingdom	19,770	22,340	20,470	20,370	21,550	8,300	9	− 48.9
Poland	15,010	15,640	17,840	19,250	19,200	10,030	6	+ 6.2
Czechoslovakia	14,320	14,690	15,050	15,290	14,800	7,450	6	− 2.1
Canada	13,030	13,290	13,630	14,900	16,080	11,880	9	− 0.3
Belgium	11,580	12,150	11,260	12,600	13,440	9,820	9	− 3.9
Spain	11,100	10,980	11,170	11,340	12,250	9,370	9	+ 4.4
Romania	9,550	10,970	11,460	11,780	12,910	*		
Brazil	8,390	9,250	11,250	12,210	13,890	11,330	9	+ 10.8
India	7,990	9,360	10,010	10,100	10,130	7,130	9	− 5.7
Australia	7,870	7,790	7,340	7,600	8,120	5,680	9	− 5.1
South Africa	6,830	7,110	7,300	7,900	8,880	6,840	9	+ 3.8
East Germany	6,480	6,740	6,850	6,980	6,960	*		
Sweden	5,610	5,140	3,970	4,330	4,730	3,150	9	− 6.5
Mexico	5,270	5,300	5,600	6,710	7,010	5,200	9	− 1.8
The Netherlands	4,820	5,180	4,920	5,580	5,810	4,180	9	− 4.9
Luxembourg	4,620	4,570	4,330	4,790	4,950	3,630	9	− 1.7
Austria	4,070	4,480	4,090	4,340	4,920	3,580	9	− 2.3
Hungary	3,670	3,650	3,720	3,880	3,900	1,700	6	− 11.4
Yugoslavia	2,920	2,750	3,180	3,460	3,540	2,720	9	+ 5.4
North Korea†	2,900	3,000	4,000	5,080	5,300	*		
Bulgaria	2,270	2,460	2,590	2,470	2,390	1,200	6	− 5.6
Argentina	2,210	2,410	2,680	2,780	3,200	2,140	9	− 10.7
South Korea	1,990	3,520	4,350	4,970	7,610	6,430	9	+ 16.0
Turkey	1,700	1,970	1,900	2,170	2,400	1,690	9	− 7.6
Finland	1,620	1,650	2,200	2,330	2,460	1,850	9	+ 3.5
Venezuela	1,060	940	800	860	1,510	1,450	9	+ 40.5
Taiwan	1,010	1,630	1,770	3,430	4,250	3,090	9	− 3.2
Greece	670	720	760	940	1,000	*		
Iran	550	550	1,830†	1,300†	1,430†	*		

*1980 figures not yet available. †Estimated.
Sources: International Iron and Steel Institute; British Steel Corporation.

Table IX. World Production of Pig Iron and Blast Furnace Ferroalloys
In 000 metric tons

Country	1975	1976	1977	1978	1979
World	468,460	484,230	480,760	498,150	519,770
U.S.S.R.	102,970	105,380	107,370	110,700	109,000
Japan	86,880	86,580	85,890	78,590	83,830
U.S.	72,510	78,810	73,780	79,540	78,900
West Germany*	30,070	31,850	28,980	30,160	35,180
China†	22,000	18,000	20,000	26,000	28,000
France*	17,920	19,020	18,260	18,500	19,410
United Kingdom	11,940	13,870	12,270	11,470	12,930
Italy	11,410	11,630	11,410	11,340	11,330
Canada	9,310	10,030	9,660	10,340	11,080
Czechoslovakia	9,290	9,480	9,720	9,940	9,530
Belgium	9,070	9,870	8,910	10,130	10,780
India	8,440	9,780	9,800	9,270	8,770
Poland*	7,750	8,040	9,650	11,240	11,100
Australia	7,510	7,310	6,730	7,280	7,760
Brazil	7,050	8,170	9,380	10,040	11,590
Spain	6,840	6,630	6,640	6,250	6,510
Romania	6,600	7,650*	7,780	8,160	8,880
South Africa	5,210	5,850	5,810	5,900	7,020
The Netherlands	3,970	4,270	3,920	4,610	4,810
Luxembourg	3,890	3,760	3,570	3,720	3,800
Sweden	3,310	2,950	2,330	2,360	2,910
Austria	3,060	3,320	2,970	3,080	3,700
North Korea†	2,900	3,000	4,000	5,000	5,000
East Germany	2,460	2,530	2,630	2,560	2,390
Hungary	2,220	2,220	2,320	2,330	2,370
Mexico	2,050	2,330	3,000	3,510	3,490
Yugoslavia	2,000	1,920	1,930	2,080	2,370
Bulgaria	1,510	1,550	1,610	1,490	1,450
Finland	1,370	1,330	1,760	1,860	2,040
Turkey	1,340	1,680	1,620	1,710	2,300
South Korea	1,190	2,010	2,430	2,740	5,050
Argentina	1,030	1,280	1,100	1,440	1,110
Norway	640	650	500	550	650

*Including ferroalloys.
†Estimated.
Source: International Iron and Steel Institute.

would it be possible to assess its success in restoring order to the market and rescuing companies from their grave financial situation. The Community would maintain the voluntary principle in the trade field, but in renegotiating for 1981 the import restraint arrangements with major non-ECSC steel-exporting countries, it would seek to reduce the permitted tonnages in line broadly with the production cutback imposed internally.

In other parts of the world the business situation and official responses to it developed less dramatically. The Japanese steel industry experienced a decline in demand as the year advanced, and production was expected to reach only 111 million metric tons for the year, virtually unchanged from 1979. In Eastern Europe output generally continued to advance, but there were setbacks in some countries, including the U.S.S.R. Moreover, the strikes in Poland in late summer seemed certain to result in some decline in output there for the year as a whole. (TREVOR J. MACDONALD)

MACHINERY AND MACHINE TOOLS

Orders for machine tools in the United States were expected to exceed $5 billion in 1980. Shipments were expected to total more than $4.5 billion, and the backlog of unfilled orders late in the year stood at approximately $5.5 billion. About 12% of the nation's shipments were to customers in other nations, with the balance being used domestically. Metal-cutting machine tools, which include milling machines, lathes, drill presses, and other machines used to shape the workpiece by chip-removal techniques, accounted for approximately 78% of shipments, with the balance being metal-forming tools such as punch presses, bending machines, and shears.

According to figures of the U.S. Department of Commerce, the machine-tool industry in the U.S. consisted of approximately 1,300 firms, mostly small in size, with two-thirds of them employing fewer than 20 people. It was estimated that only about ten firms employed more than 1,000 people. Total industry employment was approximately 100,000.

Recent concerns about productivity growth in the U.S. resulted in increased interest in upgrading the machine tools installed in U.S. manufacturing plants. The U.S. Bureau of Labor Statistics reported that productivity in the manufacturing sector of the U.S. economy dropped from the second quarter of 1979 to the second quarter of 1980 by 1.4%. Even more alarming was the report that productivity in the manufacturing sector fell 4.5% from the first quarter of 1980 to the second quarter. In assessing the reasons for this decline, a recent study noted that more than 50% of productivity growth can be ascribed to the use of improved technology; however, approximately 34% of the machine tools installed in U.S. metalworking plants were more than 20 years old and only about 31% were less than 10 years old. By contrast, 60% of the machine tools installed in Japan were less than 10 years old, as were 42% of those installed in Italy. Reports indicated that 54% of the machine tools installed in the U.S.S.R. were also less than 10 years old.

An exhibition of new machine-tool technology was held in September in Chicago. International in scope, the show included exhibits from the U.S. and 32 other countries. Equipment on display had an estimated value in excess of $100 million and included items as diminutive as disposable cutter inserts used for machining of metal parts and as large as complex computer-controlled flexible manufacturing systems incorporating multiple machine tools and utilizing robotized transporters for conveying workpieces and tooling from machine to machine. The machine tools on display featured increased cutting speeds and forming rates, capability for improved surface finish on workpieces, and more extensive use of automation compared with exhibits of previous years. The increasing use of robots for work loading and unloading was in wide evidence. (JOHN B. DEAM)

MICROELECTRONICS

The performance of microelectronic products continued to improve at a rapid pace during 1980. This increase was especially evident in products utilizing metal oxide semiconductors (MOS). In MOS, as the dimensions are reduced, not only is there an increase in performance but there is also a decrease in area. A further development was the emergence of the complementary metal oxide semiconductor (CMOS) as the probable high-growth process for the 1980s. The advantages of the CMOS, which combines p-type and n-type MOS's, include very low power, a wide operating voltage range, and a high level of radiation resistance. These advantages seemed likely to result in CMOS becoming the dominant technology in memories, microprocessors, and logic in the late 1980s.

The consumption of memories was growing at approximately 50% per year in terms of the number of bits. This was accompanied by a reduction in the price per bit of 25% per year, with a matching increase in speed of 20% per year.

The microprocessor revolution continued with the extensive use of the 8-bit combined with rapid growth of the 16-bit and the emergence of the 32-bit product. In the 1980s the 16-bit was expected to be the dominant product because of the ease of programming and the relatively low cost of software for this product. Microprocessors were used for many purposes, but as of 1980 had not been extensively employed in the home. Four-bit microprocessors for simple appliance control had been used, but not any high-performance 8-bit and 16-bit products. The reason for the lack of use in the home was a combination of the cost of software and the expertise required.

The major challenge in the 1980s in microelectronics was the escalating cost of software as the performance of the hardware increased. The challenge of the decade would be to reduce the software cost by incorporating it into the microelectronic product itself. A critical requirement was to incorporate the operating system into the semiconductor chip itself. For this to be accomplished, there would have to be a high level of standardization of operating systems.

The initial attempt to develop a standard operating system was Unix, produced by AT&T. The Unix operating system in C language and/or combined with a high-level language such as Pascal could trigger the large investments necessary to incorporate the operating system into the semiconductor. This goal was expected to be accomplished during the late 1980s. The transition of incorporating the applications software into firmware, a computer program used so often that it is stored in a read-only memory, was expected to be relatively easy.

With these accomplishments, the micro-

Western Electric announced the development of a unique laser system that was capable of repairing costly high-density computer memory chips.

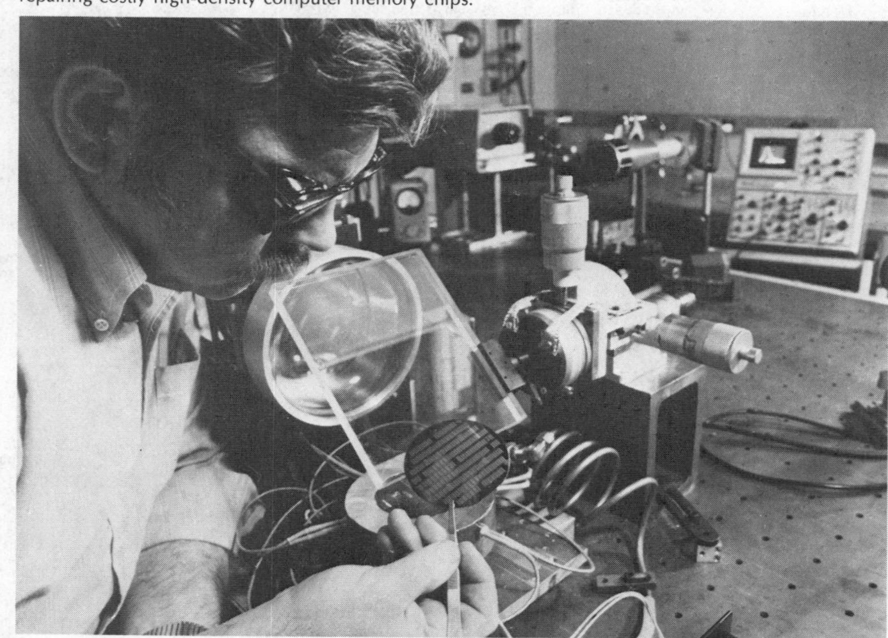

AUTHENTICATED NEWS INTERNATIONAL

electronic revolution was expected to reach the home by the mid-1980s. The home communications centre would be tied to either the television set or the telephone or both. This would allow programming to be performed in an English or near-English language.

An area that microelectronics was affecting significantly in 1980 was the automobile industry with its emphasis on reducing pollution and energy consumption. The precise fuel-mixture control available through the use of microprocessors with associated memories was generating a large market in automobiles. In addition to fuel-mixture and pollution controls, microelectronics was soon expected to be used for braking systems.

A noteworthy trend in microelectronics was the increasing sophistication in the equipment required to make the products. This, combined with an increase in the development cost of new products to the $50 million–$100 million range, was making the industry capital-intensive. The probable result was that, while in 1980 there were approximately 100 companies participating in the production of main-line microelectronics, by 1990 this number was expected to decrease to approximately 20.

(HANDEL H. JONES)

NUCLEAR INDUSTRY

The International Nuclear Fuel Cycle Evaluation (INFCE) program initiated by U.S. Pres. Jimmy Carter in 1977 concluded its investigation of the potential influence of wider use of plutonium-fueled nuclear power on the proliferation of nuclear weapons and held its final plenary conference in Vienna in February 1980. The work directed attention to those areas where research was most needed to improve safeguards but in general produced only a broad consensus. INFCE stressed the need for political solutions to proliferation problems. The industry was urged to help by participating in new institutional measures such as a world bank of plutonium and greater collaboration in sensitive and costly areas such as uranium enrichment and spent fuel reprocessing.

Third-world projects announced or developed during the year included the Indonesian Energy Agency's plans for a 30–40-Mw research reactor and for a 600-Mw power-producing heavy water reactor. A new design of small (200–400 Mw) reactors for export to less developed countries, announced by Kraftwerk Union in West Germany, was examined by a Kenyan delegation. Israel was considering plans for its first nuclear power plant proposed for the Negev region, either at Halutsa or at Nizzanim. Pakistan's Atomic Energy Commission announced that the country's second nuclear power station was to be built at Chashma at an estimated cost of $800 million over six years, half of which would be in foreign exchange. The country was also planning its own reprocessing plant for spent reactor fuel.

China announced a 300-Mw pressurized-water reactor (PWR) development program in addition to a prototype 125-Mw heavy-water reactor. Meanwhile, it was to share output from a plant in Hong Kong. The Philippines' project, held up by delays in the issuing of an export license to Westinghouse Electric Corp., began to move again with the U.S. Nuclear Regulatory Commission's (NRC's) decision in May to limit health, safety, and environmental regulations to the U.S. and "global commons" such as Antarctica and the oceans. Prime Minister Indira Gandhi confirmed her intention to develop India's program despite difficulties experienced in procuring fuel and heavy water. A new 470-Mw project and plans for a second reprocessing plant, to be situated at Kalpakkam, were announced. Despite continued opposition by the NRC, President Carter approved the sale of low-enriched uranium fuel for the Tarapur plant. India was one of the countries pursuing the development of fast reactors, and a 15-Mw unit was under construction at Kalpakkam with French collaboration.

France asked Britain for a £50 million entry fee to the European fast reactor "club" of France, Italy, West Germany, and the Benelux countries, and the U.K. Atomic Energy Authority awaited government consent to begin detailed negotiations. The most advanced fast reactor in the U.S., the $647 million Fast Flux Test Facility, sustained a chain reaction early in the year, and the world's largest fast reactor to go into full operation to date, the Soviet Union's 600-Mw BN-600, was put into operation at Beloyarsk.

The accident at Three Mile Island in Pennsylvania in March 1979 continued to delay most projects in the U.S. during 1980, while the various measures proposed by the Kemeny Commission were put into effect. The new Institute of Nuclear Power Operations (INPO) formed a 15-member advisory council to coordinate the training of power station operators. The NRC itself was reorganized in line with the Kemeny recommendations for a single administrator, with the previous five-member commission retaining its collegial responsibility for rule making and licensing.

Japan concluded agreements with Bechtel Power Corp. of the U.S. on a share of boiling-water-reactor (BWR) technology and with General Atomic Co. on an exchange of high-temperature gas-cooled reactor technology. A new company was formed to build and operate the country's second spent-fuel reprocessing plant. The first plant, at Tokai, resumed operation after a 15-month shutdown for repair work. Another new firm, the Japan Nuclear Fuel Service Co., was to undertake high-level waste-handling and storage studies as well as a joint study with the U.S. on a Pacific Basin fuel storage facility.

The British nuclear industry began its long-awaited reorganization with the appointment of a chairman to head a single-tiered National Nuclear Corporation. The letter of intent to build the first PWR in Britain at Sizewell was issued to the corporation. This reactor, built to a Westinghouse design, was to be the subject of a public inquiry toward the end of 1981. The government also announced plans for a new nuclear construction program in which one 1,500-Mw nuclear power station would be begun each year for ten years at a cost of some £10,000 million–£12,000 million (at 1979 prices). Work also began on the Heysham B and Torness advanced gas-cooled reactor stations.

France continued to supply highly enriched uranium fuel for the Iraqi 70-Mw (thermal) research reactor of the Osiris type, in the face of criticism from abroad, when the Iraqis refused to use the low-en-

KEYSTONE

Thousands of Britons marched in London to protest the use of nuclear energy.

riched "Caramel" fuel being developed for such reactors in France. The research centre housing the reactor was attacked by the Iranian Air Force during the conflict later in the year, but the reactor was not damaged. Framatome announced a $443 million order to supply two 900-Mw reactors to South Korea.

In West Germany a parliamentary commission of inquiry decided to postpone any final decision on the future development of nuclear power and in the meantime to continue with "moderate use." Delays to Italy's nuclear program continued. The 850-Mw BWR unit at Caorso reached full power in February, three years late after protracted revisions of safety requirements, but the two 1,000-Mw units at Montalto di Castro were still only at an early stage of construction. Spain revived its nuclear power program under a new energy plan, and increased expenditures on the Trillo 2, Vandellos 2, and Cofrentes plants were authorized.

The Soviet deputy minister for electric power development announced in the spring that by the end of 1980 the total installed nuclear capacity of the U.S.S.R. would be 18,000 Mw (out of a total capacity of 290,000 Mw). The nuclear share was to be increased to 90,000 Mw over the next ten years, he said. Czechoslovakia planned to make Soviet-type PWR's, of 1,000 Mw, as well as the 440-Mw units currently under construction, for plants throughout the Eastern-bloc countries.

According to statistics of world (excluding Eastern-bloc countries) nuclear capacity released in 1980, seven new reactors were commissioned in 1979. The total number of reactors (over 150 Mw) in service at the beginning of 1980 was 177, with a total generating capacity of 116,419.5 Mw; they included 77 PWR's (59,674 Mw), 53 BWR's (37,295 Mw), 12 pressurized heavy-water reactors (6,304.2 Mw), and 26 Magnox (8,515.3 Mw). (RICHARD A. KNOX)

PAINTS AND VARNISHES

In common with other sectors of the chemical industry, paint manufacturers experienced sharply changing conditions during 1980. Early in the year raw material prices were rising steeply as higher oil prices showed their effects downstream. Then the general recession began to bite, and falling demand led to shorter workweeks and plant closings. By the third quarter, U.K. paint sales were down 6% by volume from the previous year and falling. The home market in France was down 1%, but the Dutch industry was running about 4% ahead of 1979. U.S. paint makers were expecting to consolidate the gains made during the 1970s, when sales rose by more than 30% overall to over 1,000,000,000 gal worth more than $7 billion.

West Germany remained the largest European producer of paints, with sales rising 3% by volume to 1,330,000 tons. France, Italy, and the U.K. were closely bunched in second place, followed by Spain and The Netherlands. The Dutch, however, maintained their second place in terms of exports.

RALPH CRANE, LIFE MAGAZINE © 1980 TIME INC.

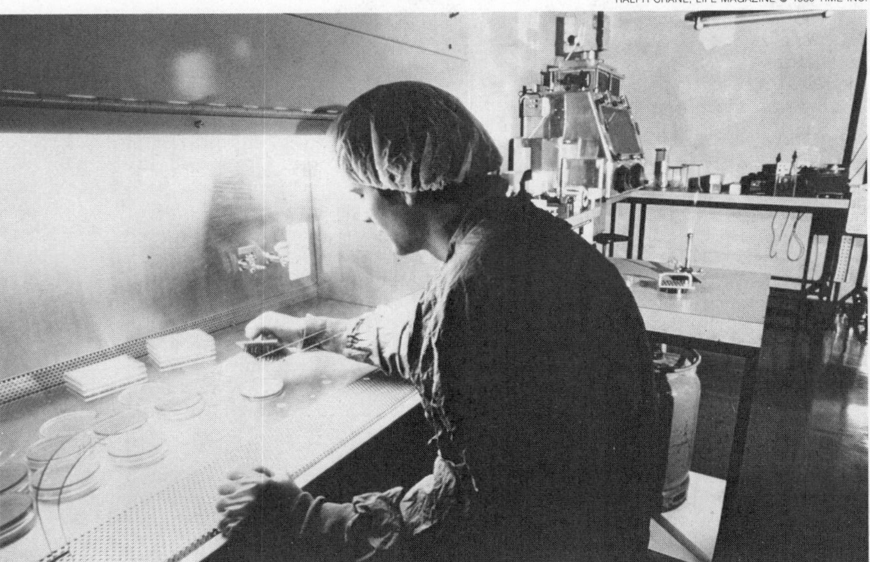

Scientists at the University of Zürich, Switzerland, were first to produce gene-spliced interferon. This natural protein has killed viruses in laboratory-grown human cells.

A notable growth area in North America and Europe was thermosetting powder coatings. Despite strong competition from other coatings "friendly to the environment," it was expected that powders would grow by 11–12% a year in the EEC alone and would account for about 6% of the relevant markets by 1990. The main outlets for the epoxy-polyester powder coatings were expected to be automotive components, domestic appliances, and pipelines. Another bright spot was paints for the refinishing of vehicles. In the U.K. this led Imperial Chemical Industries Ltd., the biggest paint company, to announce a multimillion-pound investment program intended to raise its share of the refinish products market from 30 to 40%. To cope with the variety of colours used on different manufacturers' vehicles, most paint suppliers developed sophisticated computerized systems for matching.

U.S. paint manufacturers were still grappling with the demands of a host of regulatory bodies, headed by the Environmental Protection Agency. New controls on waste disposal came on top of stringent restrictions on solvent emissions. International standards bodies continued to take a close interest in the paint industry. Among subjects under discussion were the surface preparation of steel before painting, test methods for powder coatings, and safe paints for toys. The European committee of paintmakers' associations lodged a strong protest with the EEC over repeated delays in updating the EEC paints directive concerning safety labeling. (LIONEL BILEFIELD)

PHARMACEUTICALS

Persistent complaints by drug manufacturers that U.S. Food and Drug Administration demands for safety and efficacy data on new drugs had caused a "drug lag" were given some legitimacy in 1980 when the General Accounting Office, the investigatory arm of Congress, concluded that such a lag did indeed exist. In a comprehensive report that required two years to complete, the GAO found that of 14 drugs approved by the FDA between July 1975 and February 1978 and classified by that agency as "important," 13 were available in other industrialized countries from two months to 12 years prior to their approval for marketing in the U.S.

The 13 drugs included some significant therapeutic advances. Propranolol, approved seven years earlier in Britain than in the U.S., is an important drug for hypertension. Sodium valproate, put on the market in France 11 years before it appeared in the U.S., was described as the greatest advance in treating epilepsy in 40 years. Metaproterenal, a drug for treating asthma, reached the U.S. market 11 years after its introduction abroad. Andriamysin, effective against some forms of cancer, won FDA approval four years after its first use in Europe.

Another major development was the sudden spurt of announcements concerning drugs derived from gene-splicing research with DNA. Following the U.S. Supreme Court's June 1980 ruling authorizing patent protection for new life forms created in the laboratory, the U.S. Patent Office was able to begin processing a backlog of 100 applications for such patents, most of them in the drug field. The companies concerned included not only giant multinationals, such as Eli Lilly, Searle, Hoffmann-La Roche, and Schering-Plough, but also new names like Genentech, Biogen, Genex, and Cetus (all research companies doing DNA research for drug companies). The major investment in research and new plant suggested that drugs derived from gene-spliced organisms might well constitute the pharmaceutical industry's major new-product activity during the next two decades. (*See* LIFE SCIENCES: *Special Report.*)

For over-the-counter (OTC) drugs, an adverse federal court decision regarding Category III (need more proof of efficacy or safety) ingredients and products appeared to force the FDA to set a reasonable time limit for either taking a drug out of production or validating its safety and/or efficacy before issuance of the final monographs that are part of the OTC drug review. The

FDA attempted to set such time limits but was thwarted by aerosol antiperspirants, which were said by the FDA to require two-year primate inhalation studies to validate safety.

The basic economic health of both the OTC and prescription drug sectors of the industry continued to be good, with sales gains exceeding the inflation rate.

(DONALD A. DAVIS)

PLASTICS

At the beginning of 1980, activity in the plastics industry was at a level generally regarded as artificially high. Disruption in world oil markets touched off by the Iranian revolution had caused the cost of petrochemical feedstocks to skyrocket. Anxious to build up their stocks before costs rose still further, the plastics processors and, beyond them, the end users of their products kept buying. The materials suppliers, for their part, seized the opportunity of restoring their profit margins, and polymer prices rose to unprecedented levels.

When the collapse did take place, at the end of March, it was far more sudden and severe than had been expected or experienced previously. In Europe demand for virtually all plastics materials dropped by up to one-third almost overnight as it became evident that, with oil supplies at least temporarily adequate, petrochemical prices had stopped rising.

In the shock of the downturn, most manufacturers initially responded by slashing prices in an effort to maintain volume production and market share, abandoning any prior resolve to preserve price discipline. Had they decided to reduce their own stocks by shutting down plant either temporarily or permanently—which many were later forced to do—the results for the year might have been less appalling. As it was, prices of the major plastics fell by perhaps 20–25% over the year, and even so production capacity was being utilized at less than economic rates.

European manufacturers had an additional problem in the form of growing imports of low-priced materials from the U.S., made possible because government control of oil and gas cost gave U.S. producers access to petrochemical feedstocks priced well below world levels. During 1980 tonnages of polypropylene and polyvinyl chloride (PVC) imported into Europe from the U.S. more than doubled, and shipments of low-density polyethylene increased at an even greater rate. Late in the year some European producers were reported to be selling plastics polymers for less than they had had to pay for the corresponding monomers.

Overall plastics consumption (disregarding stock factors) was thought to have been down about 5% from 1979 in the major manufacturing countries, and little recovery was expected during 1981. However, there was some feeling that the worst might be over. Many believed that by year's end the destocking effect, which had contributed so much to the speed and extent of the downturn, had worked itself through the purchasing chain. Also, although oil and feedstock prices showed some signs of hardening in the fall, they remained generally low. Some plastics producers felt sufficiently confident to attempt to raise their prices again.

For all the gloom of the immediate situation, there was no suggestion that either plastics usage or innovation was in decline. However, a switch in emphasis was detectable in the industry's unremitting expenditure on research and development. New "wonder plastics" were no longer the target. Instead, efforts were increasingly directed toward extending the utility of existing plastics through such means as better use of fillers, foaming techniques, and polymer orientation to improve properties. The part played by composite materials, in which plastics are used as reinforcements in other materials, became steadily more important. One prediction was that by the end of the century the majority of plastics would be used in composite form.

Above all, there was a growing belief that plastics were now too valuable to be used in any but the most economical ways. Recycling at last began to emerge as a practical actuality, with considerable tonnages of plastics being processed into new products in some countries, notably France and The Netherlands.

(ROBIN C. PENFOLD)

PRINTING

The printing industry largely escaped the threat of recession in 1980. Order books of suppliers of equipment and materials remained full, and plans were made to expand production. The biggest investment was by Harris Corp. Heidelberg of West Germany announced plans for investment amounting to DM 100 million and was described by the *Frankfurter Allgemeine Zeitung* as the country's most profitable engineering operation. Cerutti of Italy and some West German companies set up manufacturing facilities in the U.S.

Innovations included a Dutch method to check ink density on sheet or web while presses were running at full speed. MAN-Roland and Heidelberg ink-control systems, introduced to repro and platemaking houses, gave the printer presetting data based on density measurements to ensure rapid and secure makeready and reduce wastage. Harris presented Presfax, a system pioneered at Pacific Press. Within a few years, the U.S. manufacturers claimed, most small presses engaged in quality printing would have presetting and premakeready systems that permitted almost continuous running and reduced spoilage.

Harris reported 140 installations of its M-110 eight-page web-offset press. Komori introduced an A-size version, and Didde-Glaser introduced a four-page commercial colour press. A successful drive into the North American market was made by Mitsubishi of Japan. Tokyo Kikai Seisakusho sold the first lightweight newspaper press to the U.S. to print from photopolymer plates. The press weighed 30% less and used up to 60% less energy than conventional models.

The major U.S. and continental European telephone-book plants ordered a substantial number of new directory presses. More Cameron belt presses for book production went to Egypt and to Europe, where France and Italy were the main users. Chambon introduced a new variable-format web-offset press for books. Creuzot-Loire in France presented its new Club commercial press and sold several machines in Europe. MAN-Roland's Uniman newspaper press concept proved successful. More than half the machines went to third world countries.

By midyear silver markets had become less volatile, and some film manufacturers were able to reduce prices, though not to earlier levels. Process Shizai in Japan found a low-cost means of nonsilver, water-developed material production for negative and positive working. Coulter installed a nonsilver proofing system at Bauer in West Germany. In Japan Fuji formulated a high-sensitivity coating for offset plates compatible with fine resolution laser exposure at high speed. Water-development offset plates were launched; Aqualith from Polychrome, now Japanese-owned, joined 3M's Hydrolith. Toppan of Japan developed a microfilm-to-platemaking system for book production.

Israeli Sci-Tex Response 300 systems were being linked directly to electronic gravure cylinder-engraving machines in the U.S., Belgium, and Japan. In West Germany Grüner & Jahr started implementing a "repronik" department to store digitally all picture and text information for direct output via electronic cylinder engravers. Crosfield Electronics of the U.K. installed a Lasergravure system, and Optronics announced a digital text and storage system. Crossfield cooperated with LogEtronics in "total system" development.

At the year's major prestige event, Comprint International in Copenhagen, about 400 delegates from the world's leading printing and publishing companies agreed that print was here to stay and would live happily with the new electronic media.

(W. PINCUS JASPERT)

RUBBER

The decrease in U.S. car sales had a tremendous effect on almost all tire-producing rubber companies during 1980. Production of cars during the fourth quarter of the year was expected to be the lowest in 20 years, with a concomitant effect on original-equipment tire sales.

The use of radial tires as original equipment on virtually all cars and the increasing percentage of radial tires purchased as replacements brought about marked changes in the tire industry. Of ten tire-manufacturing plants closed during the year, with a loss of about 20,000 jobs, nine made only bias ply tires. The only one with significant radial tire production was Firestone's Salinas, Calif., plant, one of six plants closed by that company.

Europe was encountering similar problems. Predictions were that overall tire production in Europe would be down 20% by 1985 as a result of economic and market factors. In Asia, on the other hand, South Korea had been increasing its rubber-manufacturing potential by about 20% per year. Malaysian investors acquired 20% of Dunlop's stock, and this could lead to tire production in Malaysia on a much larger scale. The principal raw materials, natural rubber, oil for the production of synthetic rubber, and carbon black, were all available in the area.

President Carter ordered the National

Table X. Natural Rubber Production

In 000 metric tons

Country	1977	1978	1979
Malaysia	1,613	1,607	1,617
Indonesia	835	900	851
Thailand	431	467	498
Sri Lanka	146	156	155
India	152	133	140[1]
Liberia	70	89	75
Nigeria	59	58	60
Philippines	58	54	55[1]
Vietnam	42	46	48[1]
China	30[1]	35[1]	38[1]
Others	140[1]	139[1]	141[1]
Total	3,576[1]	3,684[1]	3,678[1]

[1] Estimate, or includes estimate.
Source: Food and Agriculture Organization of the United Nations, *Monthly Bulletin of Statistics*.

Table XI. Synthetic Rubber Production

In 000 metric tons

Country	1976	1977	1978
United States	2,425	2,528	2,473
Japan	941	971	1,029
France	437	479	492
Germany, West	373	414	407
United Kingdom	320	329	294
Netherlands, The	247	240	223
Italy[1]	250	240	250
Canada	210	238	248
Brazil	164	188	206
Germany, East	145	150[1]	155[1]
Belgium[1]	115	125	130[1]
Romania	95	136	140[1]
Poland	117	119	126
Mexico	69	78[1]	80[1]
Spain	79	77	79[1]
Korea	35	43	62
Czechoslovakia	57	59	60[1]
Australia	42	44	44
Argentina[1]	45	36	36
South Africa	35	27	32
Others	1,829[1]	2,038[1]	2,154[1]
Total	8,030[1]	8,500[1]	8,720[1]

[1] Estimate, or includes estimate.
Source: The Secretariat of the International Rubber Study Group, *Rubber Statistical Bulletin*.

Highway Traffic Safety Administration to examine the Uniform Tire Quality Grading Standards, together with various other governmental regulations, to determine their cost-benefit ratio. Maryland passed a law prohibiting the sale of new cars without a spare tire, although it did not forbid the use of temporary spares. To meet EPA standards, the rubber industry increased spending for pollution control by 136% in 1980 as compared with 1979. The average for all U.S. industry was 23%.

In April EPA released its recommended practice for measuring tire rolling resistance and grade labeling of tires for fuel efficiency. It chose the basic Society of Automotive Engineers 67-in- (170-cm-) diameter wheel dynamometer test. Grade labeling of all passenger tires for rolling resistance and fuel economy was expected to be mandatory in the near future. Potentially important savings in fuel could be realized by lowering rolling resistance.

Natural rubber was just one of the raw materials used in rubber manufacture to show a marked increase in price during the year. On Oct. 1, 1979, the New York spot price was 68 cents per pound for smoked sheets, and on Oct. 1, 1980, it was 79 cents, a 16% increase. The price of the most widely used synthetic rubber rose from 50 cents per pound to 60 cents, an increase of 20% resulting from cost increases for oil-derived raw materials.

MARCY NIGHSWANDER—THE NEW YORK TIMES

Research chemists continued to experiment with the production of rubber from a desert plant, guayule, which grows in the United States.

World production of natural rubber in 1979 was estimated at 3,855,000 metric tons, an increase of 140,000 tons over 1978. Production for 1980 was estimated at 3,850,000 metric tons, essentially the same as in 1979, an increase of 435,000 tons over 1978 production.

The U.S. continued to be the largest single buyer of natural rubber, purchasing 735,731 metric tons in 1979. World consumption of natural rubber latex (dry basis) was estimated at 291,000 metric tons. Statistics on world consumption of synthetic latices were incomplete, but U.S. consumption was 149,983 metric tons (dry basis) of the styrene-butadiene type. Consumption of both natural and synthetic rubber worldwide was estimated at 12,970,000 metric tons for 1979.

Reclaimed rubber production in 1979 was equal to or slightly above that of 1978, according to industry estimates. Rubber manufacturers were trying to increase the use not only of reclaim but also of ground scrap in rubber compounds.

Extraction and use of rubber from guayule was making rapid progress. The guayule bush, native to northern Mexico and the southwestern U.S., was a source of polyisoprene identical to the natural rubber molecule. In addition to encouraging guayule production, Mexico planned to achieve self-sufficiency in natural rubber production. The climate of southern Mexico is ideal for rubber tree cultivation.

Workers at the Cleveland (Ohio) University Hospital's department of orthopedics and the Lord Manufacturing Co. combined an elastomer (Hexsyn), originally developed by Goodyear, with titanium metal parts to make a vastly improved artificial finger joint for persons with diseased or damaged hands. (JAMES R. BEATTY)

SHIPBUILDING

Orders placed for new ships in the first half of 1980 confirmed that the market had begun to recover from the acute shortage of new contracts and massive overcapacity that had characterized 1979. After a dramatic reduction from a total of 61 million tons deadweight (dw) at mid-1978 to 53 million tons dw a year later, the world order book recovered enough in 1980 to reach 67 million tons dw or 32 million gross registered tons (grt).

The breakdown of the total world order book for new tonnage showed bulk carriers leading with 12.5 million grt, tankers second at 10 million grt, and general cargo types third at 5 million grt; the remaining 4.5 million grt consisted of fishing vessels and craft for offshore service and supply duties. In terms of tankers, bulk carriers, and dry cargo ships on order, Japan maintained a large lead with orders totaling just over 26 million tons dw. South Korea was in second place with 4,230,000 tons dw. The types of ships dominating the new order market were tankers in the 70,000–90,000-tons-dw class, Panamax (suitable for the dimensions of the locks in the Panama Canal) bulk carriers, and product and chemical carriers. The market showed particular interest in the 70,000-ton tankers because of their flexibility and effectiveness in operation.

The general feeling that despite the full order books held by the Japanese shipyards there would be at least two or three lean years ahead for the industry found support in Scandinavia and Western Europe. The only hope for the employment of certain sections of shipyard staff was the fitting of equipment to wash crude oil to several hundred tankers already in service and the installation of inert gas systems. Another source of work was the replacing of the steam turbines of certain vessels by diesel engines that burned less oil fuel, but although the number of such conversion orders approached 40, there was no concerted rush by owners to begin this work.

The interest in repairs was reflected by the provision of additional facilities to handle such work in various parts of the world. Taiwanese ship repairers were installing two new dry docks to accommodate up to

KEYSTONE

The first of a new line of commercial ships utilizing both conventional power and sails was launched in Tokyo in September.

30,000-ton and 75,000-ton ships, respectively. The state-owned Sembawang shipyard at Singapore was scheduled to take delivery in 1981 of a 150,000-ton-dw floating dock as part of a major plan to increase facilities, and the Tuas repair yard at Singapore also invested in a new dry dock, to be ready in 1982, that would take vessels of up to 330,000 tons dw. Ship repair yards in Greece hoped to benefit from the expected increase in the tonnage of tankers passing through the Suez Canal as a result of the increased draft now available in the waterway (up to 16 m [53 ft]), and they also expected to increase their share of the market when Greece entered the European Economic Community in 1981. Malta's new dry dock, built with Chinese assistance and designed for vessels of up to 300,000 tons dw, was expected to be in service by the end of 1981, but it was doubtful that it would be profitable. Plans to build a repair yard at Algiers were deferred because Arab investors appeared to have concluded that there would be a surplus of repair capacity in the Mediterranean area.

Although U.S. shipyards had orders for just over 1.5 million grt of shipping at mid-1980 and were at that time sixth on the list of ten top shipbuilders in terms of tonnage on order, builders needed new orders if heavy layoffs were to be avoided. Much depended upon the implementation of a long-range Maritime Administration program to rebuild the U.S.-flag dry bulk fleet and the immediate commencement of the subsidized construction of five new dry bulk cargo ships of about 40,000 tons dw each. In the U.K. the state-owned British Shipbuilders reached its target of 45 ships three months ahead of schedule, but the manufacturer was not yet able to operate profitably even though the merchant shipbuilding workforce was reduced to only 20,000. In November the government raised the allowable debt of British Shipbuilders for 1980–81 from £120 million to £185 million.

(W. D. EWART)

TELECOMMUNICATIONS

New Earth satellite developments and fibre optics applications were the leaders in communications technology in 1980. Meanwhile, the regulatory problems of the communications industry remained unsolved, and giant AT&T provided new services remarkably like data distribution and processing, further blurring the distinction between communications and computing.

Satellites. As more Earth satellites joined those already in space, legal questions about their orbits and frequency assignments continued to be debated. Much of this effort took place under the jurisdiction of the UN-sponsored World Administrative Radio Conference (WARC), which finished several months of discussion at the end of 1979. WARC is a general meeting occurring once every 20 years, although smaller, more specialized meetings are held in the interim. Its purpose is to divide up frequencies and satellite orbits to avoid electrical and physical interference. WARC left most questions of how to allocate old,

Table XII. Countries Having More than 100,000 Telephones

Telephones in service, 1979

Country	Number of telephones	Percentage increase over 1969	Telephones per 100 population	Country	Number of telephones	Percentage increase over 1969	Telephones per 100 population
Algeria	346,447	104.8	1.9	Kuwait	176,466	204.4	13.9
Argentina	2,659,949	66.3	10.0	Lebanon	321,500	...	11.2
Australia	6,266,290	84.7	43.7	Luxembourg	191,303	81.3	53.5
Austria	2,617,634	110.6	34.0	Malaysia	439,161	160.1	3.2
Belgium	3,270,882	77.1	33.2	Mexico	4,140,271	252.4	6.0
Bolivia	125,800	235.0	2.6	Morocco	216,500	40.9	1.2
Brazil	5,733,367	267.4	4.6	Netherlands, The	6,340,084	117.3	45.4
Bulgaria	1,032,106	172.9	11.7	New Zealand	1,762,130	52.5	56.1
Canada	15,059,428	70.7	63.5	Nigeria	135,876	66.8	0.3
Chile	531,143	70.2	4.8	Norway	1,636,491	58.0	40.2
Colombia	1,444,972	151.4	5.7	Pakistan	357,962	85.0	0.5
Costa Rica	175,444	211.8	8.3	Panama	163,930	124.9	8.9
Cuba	...	...	...	Peru[1]	402,459	143.7	2.6
Czechoslovakia	2,981,197	66.6	19.7	Philippines	593,127	145.6	1.2
Denmark	2,935,124	93.3	56.5	Poland	3,095,303	87.5	8.9
Dominican Republic	152,093	278.6	3.0	Portugal	1,253,530	91.8	12.7
Ecuador	239,620	154.1	3.1	Puerto Rico	604,271	127.0	19.3
Egypt	486,143	...	1.2	Romania	...	...	...
Finland	2,127,392	110.8	44.7	Saudi Arabia	196,565	...	2.5
France	19,870,006	164.8	37.3	Singapore	540,209	296.4	22.9
Germany, East	2,956,390	55.9	17.7	South Africa	2,456,329	75.7	10.0
Germany, West	24,743,467	120.0	40.3	Spain	10,311,423	176.9	28.0
Greece	2,487,495	226.6	26.5	Sweden	6,160,359	49.9	74.4
Hong Kong	1,382,214	224.1	29.2	Switzerland	4,292,005	59.8	68.2
Hungary	1,142,597	67.0	10.7	Syria	211,738	104.2	2.5
India	2,423,762	129.3	0.4	Taiwan	2,099,310	649.2	12.3
Indonesia	392,563	115.3	0.2	Thailand[1]	409,471	257.9	0.9
Iran	...	...	...	Tunisia	158,422	129.9	2.6
Iraq	...	...	...	Turkey	1,578,586	249.4	3.7
Ireland	554,000	106.2	16.8	U.S.S.R.	20,943,670	111.5	7.9
Israel	1,028,087	156.1	27.5	United Kingdom	24,934,670	93.3	44.6
Italy	17,080,870	120.3	30.1	United States	168,994,000	54.7	77.0
Jamaica	117,807	76.8	5.8	Uruguay	269,734	30.6	9.6
Japan	52,937,204	157.9	45.8	Venezuela	920,252	166.2	6.2
Kenya	156,303	116.3	1.1	Yugoslavia	1,732,558	215.6	7.6
Korea, South	2,387,336	387.3	6.6	Zimbabwe	205,981	68.7	3.0

[1]1978.
Sources: American Telephone and Telegraph Company, *The World's Telephones, 1970; 1979.*

still unassigned frequencies and new frequencies in the 14-gH range still unsettled. Also unsolved was the problem of the Western Hemisphere, which was fast running out of synchronous-orbit parking spaces for satellites over North America.

Among satellites launched by the National Aeronautics and Space Administration in 1980, the Solar Maximum Mission (SMM) satellite was designed to watch for the solar flares that would be peaking over the next few years. These bursts of electromagnetic noise can all but wipe out military and commercial communications, and early warning is vital to minimizing and compensating for outages. Theoretically, the satellite could be picked up by the space shuttle in 1982 or 1983 and refurbished for use, saving millions of dollars over the cost of launching a completely new satellite. However, the shuttle's timetable continued to slip. (*See* SPACE EXPLORATION.) Communications satellites planned to be launched by the shuttle were switched to the tried and true launch-rocket approach, among them the 14-gH digital technology satellite launched in November by Satellite Business Systems Corp. and geared to office and factory communications.

Fibre Optics. The application of fibre optic technology to practical systems in 1980 was led by AT&T, which started development of a 983-km (611-mi) system to link Boston, New York, Philadelphia, and Washington by a laser-powered light-wave system. The largest system announced so far, it would ultimately connect 19 of Bell's electronic digital switches. The all-digital system would let Bell carry voice, video, and data signals. It was the strongest evidence yet of Bell's commitment to a future all-digital network making extensive use of fibre-optic technology.

Looking even further ahead, Bell tested equipment with an eye to laying a fibre-optic cable 6,500 km (4,000 mi) under the Atlantic to Europe. The system would be powered by laser diodes operating at a 1.3-micrometer wavelength. At this longer wavelength—0.8 micrometers had been used heretofore—cable attenuation is lower, and far fewer costly amplifiers would be needed as compared with electrical, coaxial cable systems. Each amplifier would have an operating laser and three standbys, giving the system a mean time between failures of eight years. The digital amplifiers could carry 4,032 conversations per fibre, compared with 200 for copper systems.

Information Systems. Computer-controlled communications services became more available, again spearheaded by AT&T. The Bell Telephone Co. of Pennsylvania offered a service delivering voice messages to other subscribers in the network, a form of electronic mail in which the sender specifies phone number, message, and delivery time. Some form of this service would also be offered by Bell's Advanced Communications Service, though software and organizational problems continued to plague it in 1980. Xerox Corp.'s XTEN, a system with similar goals but with microwave transmission for local distribution, was also troubled. Questions were raised about the size of the market and the capital needed.

Home information systems and computer-controlled telephony were only a few of the products and services that AT&T might offer through a new unregulated subsidiary formally announced in 1980. This was Bell's answer to how it would compete in unregulated markets without having the financial and technical support of its regulated operations. However, federal agencies and Bell's competitors would no doubt have much to say about the new organization as it became clearly defined.

(HARVEY J. HINDIN)

TEXTILES

Throughout the world the textile industry continued to experience an exceptional depression in sales, forcing the closing of companies in Europe, the U.S., and Asia. The troubles in the oil-producing countries of the Persian Gulf added to the general depression and suggested that worse was to follow, since rising oil prices must inevitably lead to more expensive oil-based fibres and higher energy costs. The less developed nations of Africa were building plants to make textiles from their own raw cotton, and as these come on stream, the arrival of their low-priced products on world markets was certain to increase pressure on the textile industries of the industrialized countries.

Many current technological developments were directed toward high-speed production with sophisticated machinery. The best hope for industries in the developed countries seemed to lie in the manufacture of products of very high quality or in those "engineered" for specific end uses to satisfy the most stringent demands. Automation enabled many mills to be left running overnight or through a weekend, untended, thus eliminating expensive labour costs. A development known as multiphase weaving, in which a number of yarns can be taken across the loom simultaneously, was expected to speed production considerably.

In spinning a number of new processes competed with classical ring spinning, including a development known as the "floating ring," in which the ring is allowed to rotate as it floats on a cushion of air. This enabled more rapid spinning than was possible with the classical technique. The use of foamed compounds rather than liquids in the wet processing trades, permitting a lighter application of moisture to achieve much the same effects, raised expectations of reduced energy consumption in subsequent drying and/or curing.

(PETER LENNOX-KERR)

Wool. The year opened with an earlier upward trend in textile production still evident, though this covered sharp variations among different countries. As recession spread, production rates, and thus usage of wool, deteriorated patchily, but wool tended to gain ground, if only gradually, at the expense of other fibres, notably man-made fibres where oversupply was substantial. World production of wool in the 1980–81 season was estimated by the Commonwealth Secretariat at 1,584,000 metric tons clean, compared with 1,579,000 tons in 1979–80.

Wool prices fluctuated only modestly. Reserve price support by grower organizations assisted stability, with sales from stocks relieving shortages. Reserve prices generally were raised at the beginning of the 1980–81 season to compensate partially for inflation. High financing costs led to relatively low commercial stocks, which tended to accentuate seasonal price changes.

As the year closed, the wool market maintained strength without large accumulations of stock. Prospects of lower supplies in the first half of 1981 made price strength more likely, despite the recession. This strength was more evident in merinos than in crossbreds, partly because of drought in Australia and South Africa and partly because of the effect of recession on some of the larger crossbred-using sectors.

(H. M. F. MALLETT)

Space satellite engineers at British Aerospace in Stevenage, Hertfordshire, prepare a maritime satellite to be used for communication at sea.

KEYSTONE

Cotton. For the first time in more than a decade, output and consumption of raw cotton were roughly in balance during the 1979–80 season. Although the area harvested was smaller than in 1978–79, yields reached a new peak, resulting in a record production of nearly 66 million bales, 5.5 million bales more than in the previous season. At around 22 million bales, carry-over stocks at the beginning of August 1980 were similar to those of a year earlier, but the distribution among countries had changed considerably. In the U.S., for instance, stocks of just over 3 million bales were 800,000 bales below the preceding year, while in the U.S.S.R., China, and Eastern Europe output reached 23.4 million bales, against 22.4 million bales the year before. Notable gains were also achieved in Australia, Colombia, Paraguay, and Tanzania.

Textile activity in several major producing and consuming areas was adversely affected by the slowdown in business. However, given the improved situation in the third world, consumption in the 1979–80 season was expected to exceed the previous record of 63.5 million bales by at least 2 million bales.

The average price of raw cotton in Liverpool during 1979–80 rose steadily from the low point of around 77 cents per pound to nearly 84 cents by the end of 1979. After touching 98 cents in February 1980, it declined to 83 cents in June, but by the end of the season it had moved up to nearly 93 cents, reaching 100 cents by the end of August and a peak of 103.8 cents in early September. Prospects for the 1980–81 crop included increased acreage planted to raw cotton in most Northern Hemisphere countries. (ARTHUR TATTERSALL)

Silk. The Japanese silk industry spent an anxious year watching the Custody Corporation stock rise from 4,500 to 7,500 tons and wondering how long a government pledged to economy would—or could—continue purchases of surplus production. On the death of Prime Minister Masayoshi Ohira in June, prices plummeted overnight, reflecting fears that a new government might view the silk subsidy as a ready target; they reverted to normal only with the election of Zenko Suzuki in July. Although domestic cocoon production had fallen and imports were more rigidly controlled, the liquidation of accumulated stocks—given the apparently irreversible trend away from the kimono—seemed far away. A promotional campaign was frustrated by the high prices engendered by the policy of isolation, but hopes of creating new outlets were still vigorously pursued.

In July 1979 China had raised the price for 3A 20/22 denier to 49.20 yuan, announcing at the same time a price of 51.70 yuan for 1980. This was adhered to strictly, and Western merchants, gaining confidence from such stability, placed business for shipment many months ahead. Demand remained fairly steady until the summer, when a strange apathy befell the market. Holders began to view their forward commitments with some misgivings, especially in view of the current high interest rates, but it was hoped that recovery would not be long delayed. (PETER W. GADDUM)

Man-Made Fibres. Fibre producers were turning their attention to new and comparatively expensive fibres with special properties. A range of hollow fibres made from all manner of polymers was under development in all the technically advanced countries, including Eastern Europe. Their immediate application was as filter media for dialysis equipment, but their potential could reach far beyond such specific use.

Electrets were being developed in The Netherlands and the U.S. and probably in other countries. These fibres, having very strong and almost permanent electrostatic charges, could be used as filter media for removing solid matter from smoke or other fumes. Polymer scientists sought new synthetic polymers with much greater strength and/or improved heat resistance. The aramids made in the U.S. offered greater weight-for-weight strength than steel. One application for the new fibres was as an alternative to asbestos in the clutch plates of high-performance cars, and they were also used in cordage to anchor drilling platforms exactly over the boreholes of oil wells in the North Sea. These and other developments underlined a trend among manufacturers to diversify into areas where small quantities of high-priced specialities could be made profitably. (PETER LENNOX-KERR)

TOBACCO

Tobacco growers and manufacturers were reconciled to zero growth of consumption in the advanced countries, but they were comforted by increasing demand in the 58% of the world where the connection between smoking and health was not yet a live issue. As well as consuming more (largely because their populations were rising more rapidly than those of North America, Western Europe, and Japan), the less developed countries were advancing in importance as both suppliers and consumers of tobacco. At the same time, the share of world production and trade held by traditional tobacco countries such as the U.S. was falling.

During 1960–64 the U.S. had about 40% of world trade in flue-cured tobacco, the type most traded internationally and the foundation of major U.S. and European cigarette blends. Currently, this market share was a thin 19%. Indeed, the U.S. was now importing so much cheap foreign tobacco that U.S. growers were asking where the manufacturers' loyalties lay.

The total needs of consuming countries were being met more easily as techniques for making more cigarettes from each kilogram of raw tobacco, already widely exploited in the advanced countries, moved into the less developed world as well. The result was that the current world increase in tobacco products consumption of around 1.5% per year was being satisfied by almost static raw material purchases. Already there was an overproduction crisis in oriental leaf.

This potential imbalance of supply and demand could quiet the debate in less developed countries as to whether farmland should be used to grow tobacco instead of food. If world demand for cigarette tobacco started to fall (as demand for cigar and pipe tobaccos had done already), the dominant anxiety of countries from the Philippines to Malawi and Thailand to Paraguay would be about falling returns for what was, in many cases, their most lucrative cash crop. The surprise of 1980 was the failure of the end of sanctions against Zimbabwe (formerly Rhodesia) to trigger a tobacco boom there. The world was not short of the type of leaf Zimbabwe produces, so there was no rush of rejoicing buyers to the Salisbury auction sales.

Cigarette export trade, dominantly from the U.S., Britain, and West Germany, was the most buoyant feature of the international tobacco scene during the year. This reflected the magic of international brand names and the dynamic growth of duty-free trade, which now involved well over 25,000,000,000 cigarettes a year. In domestic markets, sales of cigars and of pipe tobacco were declining the world over, although there was a miniboom in the choicest, costliest cigars.

New restraints on manufacturers emerged during 1980, with more countries restricting tobacco advertising and requiring "tar" and nicotine levels to be declared on cigarette packs. In all the advanced countries, cigarette companies were progressively reducing the "tar" and nicotine content of their products without seeming to satisfy their critics. Where the antitobacco campaign had been most vigorous, activists were having some success in making smoking less respectable.

(MICHAEL F. BARFORD)

TOURISM

International tourist arrivals in 1980 were estimated at 280 million–290 million (excluding some 600 million excursionist arrivals), and receipts of the destination countries at $89 billion (excluding international fares and domestic tourism). Among source countries, West Germany continued to lead, with about 28 million departures and over $20 billion spent abroad in 1980. The U.S. remained the second most impor-

Table XIII. Major Tourism Earners and Spenders in 1979
In $000,000

Major spenders	Expenditure
West Germany	$17,952
United States	9,413
France	5,193
Japan	4,810
United Kingdom	4,497
Netherlands, The	4,084
Belgium/Luxembourg	2,969
Austria	2,966
Canada	2,710
Switzerland	2,030
Sweden	1,750
Denmark	1,542
Italy	1,507
Mexico	1,200
Norway	1,154
Major earners	**Receipts**
United States	8,335
Italy	8,185
France	6,826
Spain	6,484
United Kingdom	5,942
West Germany	5,741
Austria	5,571
Switzerland	2,568
Canada	2,017
Greece	1,663
Belgium/Luxembourg	1,629
Netherlands, The	1,325
Mexico	1,320
Denmark	1,312
Hong Kong	1,270

Source: World Tourism Organization.

tant source (24 million departures, primarily to Canada and Mexico); there was some increase in travel by Americans to the U.K. in the first half of 1980, following a drop of 11% in 1979, and to Austria, but travel to other European countries declined. France, with about 16 million departures, was the third major source of international tourists, and U.K. departures were at a level similar to that of France. Japanese tourism slowed in 1980, as did outgoing tourism from Canada, The Netherlands, and the Scandinavian countries. Relative to population, Austria continued to lead in terms of tourism expenditure abroad (about $400 per capita), while Switzerland led in tourist departures abroad (averaging about 1.5 per resident per year).

The countries of the Organization for Economic Cooperation and Development continued to be the leading sources and destinations of international tourism, spending about $4 billion more than the $62 billion they received in 1979. The less developed countries apparently expanded their share as sources and destinations; most notably, Mexico's incoming tourism grew by 14% in 1979.

The U.S. remained a leading destination ($8.3 billion tourism receipts, 260 million tourist nights in 1979). It registered considerable increases in tourism from Europe in 1980, due to reduced transatlantic fares and favourable prices of tourism services resulting from the weakness of the dollar. Florida, which had been primarily a winter resort for Americans, attracted many summer tourists, especially from the U.K.

Data for 1980 indicated increased competition for international tourists—by destinations, carriers, tour operators, and travel agents. The 1979–80 winter season in Europe was generally successful, but the summer and autumn seasons were affected by accelerated inflation, unemployment, and tighter credit, and the outlook for the winter season was problematic. Tourism to West Germany shot up (by about 10%) following a slight increase in 1979; the decennial Oberammergau Passion Play (May–September 1980) attracted large numbers of tourists, many of whom continued their pilgrimage by visiting Rome or Jerusalem. Austria reported an 8% increase, following an 11% decrease in 1979. Latin America celebrated its "Tourism Year," with increases recorded in Brazil (40%) and Colombia (16%). The Caribbean also gained in popularity. In the Far East Japan reported a 23% growth in tourist arrivals, Thailand 26%, Singapore 10%, and Hong Kong 3%, while decreases were recorded for South Korea and Taiwan, following increases in 1979. Australia expected a 20% increase in arrivals.

Political events affected tourism in many countries in 1980. Philippine terrorists tried to disrupt the conference of the American Society of Travel Agents in Manila in October. In Spain bombing incidents on the Costa Blanca and Costa del Sol, combined with steep price rises, caused a decline in tourism from many countries. Other Mediterranean destinations enjoyed increases, especially Portugal (up 50% following a rise of 34% in 1979), Cyprus and Malta (up 20%), Italy (up 7%), and Tunisia (up 6%). Tourism in Egypt (up 16%) and Israel (up 8%) was assisted by the opening of direct air and land links between the two countries in early 1980. Greece, where tourism had grown 16% in 1979, reported a drop in the first half of 1980, as did Yugoslavia. In France striking fishermen blocked the return of British vacationers through the Channel ports in August. The strikes in Poland, the change of regime in Turkey, and election violence in Jamaica also affected tourism in those countries. The U.S.S.R. had hoped for 300,000 foreign visitors for the Moscow Olympic Games, but the partial boycott cut Western tourism considerably.

Airlines had a difficult year. In addition to greatly increased fuel and other costs and heavy competition among scheduled carriers and charter operators, the deregulation of traffic from, to, and in the U.S. added uncertainty and risks. Tourists were often able to enjoy reduced fares in 1980 (especially over the North Atlantic and to the Far East), but most carriers belonging to the International Air Transport Association recorded losses. Unprofitable routes were being cut, while business tourists were demanding better services for the higher fares they paid. All in all, the future of air tourism was a source of concern.

There was a continual search for novelty. Inclusive tours to China were becoming established, and round-the-world flights were now available beginning at $2,299. New "adventure" tours were offered, for example, a version of Charles Darwin's "Beagle" voyage. Vacations to Transylvania in Romania were promoted with the slogan "Dracula—the Truth and the Legend." Massive investments continued to be made in the development of new resorts and the modernization of old plant, taking into account the need for fuel economy and labour saving. Petrodollars were an important source of financing, accompanied by the growth in tourism from Arab countries, now a major source of revenue for many resorts. In parallel with the building of giant and luxury hotels and greater use of private aircraft and yachts, demand increased for facilities for popular tourism, spurred by the growth of camping, backpacking, and youth hostels. Self-catering holidays and time-sharing or condominium projects were increasing in importance.

(RAPHAEL R. BARON)

WOOD PRODUCTS

The future of forest resources was discussed in three significant reports published in 1980. One was the *Global 2000 Report to the President.* Compiled by experts from 11 U.S. government agencies, it projected that worldwide population and deforestation trends would shrink the amount of commercial wood available per capita from the present 80 cu m (2,840 cu ft) to 40 cu m (1,420 cu ft) by the year 2000. The report indicated that by that time some 40% of the remaining forest cover in the less developed countries could be gone.

The second report was *An Assessment of the Forest and Range Land Situation in the United States.* Issued every five years by the U.S. Forest Service, it concluded that domestic U.S. timber being produced was below potential yield and that demand for forest products was rising faster than supply. The *Assessment* projected a 107% increase in demand for timber by the year 2030 over national consumption figures for 1976.

The third was the U.S. forest products industry's *Forest Productivity Report,* published by the Forest Industries Council. Issued following four years of study, this report described specific opportunities for increasing the timber-producing capacity of public, private, and industry-owned lands in the U.S. as a way of meeting the rising demand for wood and paper.

Use of U.S. national forest lands for timber supply and other purposes was debated in Congress in 1980. Several bills were introduced to carry out recommendations of a Forest Service study of 62 million ac (25 million ha) of roadless national forest. The study had recommended which unroaded areas should be categorized for use—such as timber production, recreation, grazing, or multiple purposes—and which for statutory wilderness, where no roads or shelters can be built. Legislation was passed on few of the lands in question, leaving most of these areas unusable either for production or for most forms of recreation until another Congress resolved the matter.

Construction is the most important market for lumber, and a decline in construction in the 1980 recession caused U.S. lumber shipments overall to drop about 15% from 1979 levels. Total production of lumber in the U.S. in 1980 was estimated at 31,100,000,000 board feet (37,000,000,000 in 1979). About 80% of this was softwood, such as fir and pine, which is used extensively in construction.

U.S. production of hardwood (such as oak and walnut) was buoyed by strong export levels in 1980. Particularly important markets were Japan and Europe. Demand in the U.S. for hardwood used in furniture declined, and decreased shipment of goods due to the slowed economy lowered demand for pallets made from hardwood. Production of hardwood flooring was about 80% of normal levels, and this combined with strong exports produced a modest 2.7% gain for U.S. hardwood output over 1979.

Markets for paper and paperboard were slightly improved in 1980. This was largely due to demand for consumer-oriented paper products not seriously affected by changes in the economy. Because of inflation the dollar value of shipments of these materials rose 11% over 1979, although the total volume shipped was less. Total U.S. paper and paperboard production in 1980 was 63 million tons, 1.5 million tons less than in 1979.

A new wood product that gained wider use in 1980 was structural particleboard. This is a composite product made from compressed and bonded wood scraps. Structural particleboard can be cut, sawn, and substituted for many types of conventional structural lumber. This product is an example of new technology applied to extend the potential of the available forest resource base.

(TAIT TRUSSELL)

See also Agriculture and Food Supplies; Computers; Consumerism; Economy, World; Energy; Food Processing; Games and Toys; Industrial Relations; Materials Sciences; Mining and Quarrying; Photography; Television and Radio; Transportation.

Iran

An Islamic republic of western Asia, Iran is bounded by the U.S.S.R., Afghanistan, Pakistan, Iraq, and Turkey and the Caspian Sea, the Arabian Sea, and the Persian Gulf. Area: 1,648,000 sq km (636,000 sq mi). Pop. (1980 est.): 37,694,900. Cap. and largest city: Teheran (pop., 1976, 4,530,200). Language: Persian. Religion (1976): Muslim 99%; Christian, Jewish, and Zoroastrian minorities. President from Feb. 4, 1980, Abolhassan Bani-Sadr; prime minister from August 12, Mohammad Ali Raja'i.

In 1980 the Islamic Republic came under increasing stress. Ayatollah Ruhollah Khomeini suffered a worsening heart condition from early January and was forced to move from Qom to Teheran. Despite his illness, he was Iran's sole centre of power and the final arbiter in political matters. Elections for the presidency took place on January 25. In the face of opposition from the Revolutionary Council, Abolhassan Bani-Sadr (*see* BIOGRAPHIES) was elected with 75% of the votes. There was only a 50% turnout at the polls.

General elections for the Iranian Majlis (parliament), set up under the constitution approved on Dec. 2–3, 1979, began in March. In a low turnout, the Islamic Republican Party (IRP) was returned as the majority group, with additional support from the Religious Strugglers Party and the Religious Coalition Party. Second-round voting was postponed until May in 23 constituencies as a result of a lack of security, mainly in peripheral areas dominated by ethnic minorities. The parliamentary elections gave the religious establishment under the ayatollahs Mohammad Hossein Beheshti (*see* BIOGRAPHIES) and Hashemi Rafsanjani a stranglehold on the constitutional organs of government and eclipsed the secular movements led by Bani-Sadr.

The Majlis met on May 28, with the IRP holding 60% of the seats and only 20% falling to the president's side. After a prolonged conflict, Mohammad Ali Raja'i (*see* BIOGRAPHIES) was appointed prime minister in August. He was seen as a mere secular front for the IRP's religious interests. Of the 20 Cabinet ministers appointed by Raja'i, Bani-Sadr ultimately refused to accept 6. Meanwhile, the Muslim fundamentalists sought to erode the positions of all secular groups. The Teheran headquarters of the leftist Muhajeddin-i Khalq Party was attacked in April and June, and many members of the National Front were isolated from the mainstream of political life. The Communist Tudeh ("Masses") Party supported the revolutionary model favoured by Khomeini and Beheshti and offered to share in government, though it received little encouragement.

Fearing that their religious freedom and cultural identities were threatened by the government's Shi'ah fundamentalist policies, all major groups in the border areas rose against the activities of the regime in Teheran. Early in 1980 the Kurds of western Iran put forward claims for increased self-determination. Fighting between groups of Kurds and the Islamic Militia took place in Sanandaj, Mahabad, and Kamyaran, and a combined force made up of militiamen and the regular Iranian Army attacked Sanandaj in April. After some six weeks of fighting, Sanandaj fell to the government in mid-May, at a cost of 1,500 lives. Thereafter, the government held control of most major towns in Kurdistan, but the countryside was firmly in the hands of various Kurdish factions. Following the Iraqi invasion of southern Iran in September, the Kurdish Democratic Party and most other Kurdish groups declared their support for the Iranian government but gave tacit backing to the Iraqis. By the end of 1980 Kurdistan remained largely outside the control of the central government, though divisions among the Kurds precluded the emergence of an integrated movement.

The Arabs of Khuzestan, the Turkmen of the Caspian Plain region, and the Baluch were all engaged during the year in elaborating their claims for greater local autonomy. In Khuzestan Arab guerrilla groups, with no little backing from Iraq, sustained a prolonged campaign of sabotage against oil pipelines, government offices, and communications facilities. Heavy-handed reprisals against the Arab community engendered further regional dislike of the government, although—contrary to Iraqi expectations—the Iraqi invasion of Khuzestan brought no general rebellion. Elsewhere the simmering unrest was held down only by the Militia and the regular Army, a factor that deeply inhibited the armed forces' freedom of action in the face of the Iraqi invasion.

KALARI—SYGMA

Prime Minister Mohammad Ali Raja'i addresses the Majlis after his election on August 11. His appointment was seen as a defeat for Pres. Abolhassan Bani-Sadr, who had opposed him.

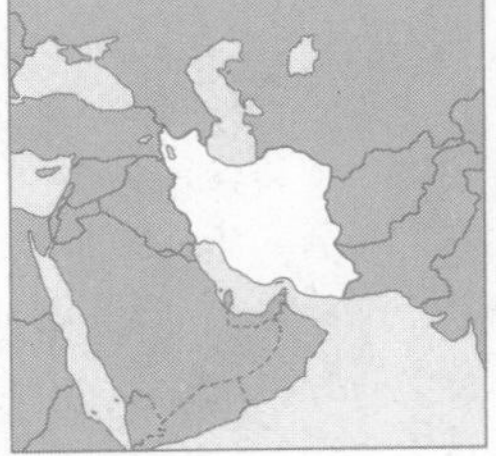

Iran

Information Science and Technology: *see* Computers; Industrial Review

Insurance: *see* Industrial Review

International Bank for Reconstruction and Development: *see* Economy, World

International Law: *see* Law

International Monetary Fund: *see* Economy, World

Investment: *see* Economy, World; Stock Exchanges

UPI

Smoke clouds obscured the landscape on October 16 after Iraqi soldiers set fire to a pipeline belonging to Iran's huge oil refinery in Abadan.

IRAN

Education. (1978–79) Primary, pupils 4,403,106, teachers (1976–77) 167,457; secondary, pupils 2,370,341, teachers (1976–77) 84,092; vocational, pupils 256,303, teachers (1976–77) 10,041; teacher training, students 57,832, teachers (1976–77) 2,262; higher, students 175,675, teaching staff (1976–77) 13,952.

Finance. Monetary unit: rial, with (Sept. 22, 1980) a free rate of 70.09 rials to U.S. $1 (168.46 rials = £1 sterling). Gold, SDR's, and foreign exchange (April 1980) U.S. $16,122,000,000. Budget (1978–79 actual): revenue 1,612,000,000,000 rials; expenditure 2,092,000,000,000 rials. Gross national product (1977–78) 5,347,600,000,000 rials. Money supply (Feb. 1980) 1,732,700,000,000 rials. Cost of living (1975 = 100; June 1980) 216.

Foreign Trade. (1979) Imports 686.3 billion rials; exports 1,399,700,000,000 rials. Import sources: West Germany *c.* 17%; U.S. *c.* 13%; Japan *c.* 12%; U.K. *c.* 6%; France *c.* 5%; Italy *c.* 5%. Export destinations: Japan *c.* 19%; U.S. *c.* 14%; West Germany *c.* 11%; U.S. Virgin Islands *c.* 6%; India *c.* 6%; The Bahamas *c.* 5%; France *c.* 5%. Main exports: crude oil 88%; petroleum products 8%.

Transport and Communications. Roads (1979) 49,700 km. Motor vehicles in use (1977): passenger 932,700; commercial 204,000. Railways: (1979) 4,604 km; traffic (1976) 3,511,000,000 passenger-km, freight 4,627,000,000 net ton-km. Air traffic (1978): 4,655,000,000 passenger-km; freight *c.* 89 million net ton-km. Shipping (1979): merchant vessels 100 gross tons and over 219; gross tonnage 1,207,372. Telephones (Jan. 1978) 828,600. Radio receivers (Dec. 1977) 2,125,000. Television receivers (Dec. 1977) 1.9 million.

Agriculture. Production (in 000; metric tons; 1979): wheat *c.* 5,000; barley *c.* 900; rice *c.* 1,212; potatoes *c.* 688; sugar, raw value *c.* 630; onions *c.* 262; tomatoes *c.* 306; watermelons (1978) *c.* 913; melons (1978) *c.* 460; dates *c.* 392; grapes *c.* 924; apples *c.* 453; soybeans *c.* 150; tea *c.* 20; tobacco *c.* 15; cotton, lint *c.* 110. Livestock (in 000; 1979): cattle *c.* 7,600; sheep *c.* 33,700; goats *c.* 13,500; horses *c.* 350; asses *c.* 1,800; chickens *c.* 67,500.

Industry. Production (in 000; metric tons; 1976–77): cement 6,100; coal *c.* 900; crude oil (1979) 148,937; natural gas (cu m; 1979) 14,483,000; petroleum products (1977) *c.* 36,680; lead concentrates (metal content; 1977–78) 40; chromium ore (oxide content; 1977–78) *c.* 80; electricity (kw-hr; 1977) *c.* 18,000,000.

The threat posed by the export of the revolution to Shiʿah groups in other Middle Eastern states contributed to Iran's increasing isolation during 1980. A declaration by Ayatollah Hossein Ali Montazeri in February that the revolution should be exported and specific Iranian intervention among Shiʿah communities in Iraq, Kuwait, and Bahrain aroused fears in the Arab states. In Iraq the attempted assassination of the deputy prime minister, Tareq Aziz, in April by a guerrilla group claiming allegiance to Ayatollah Khomeini set in motion a border confrontation that culminated in the Iraqi decision to attack. In early September Iraq made four demands on Iran as conditions for normal relations. Iran was to withdraw from the islands of Abu Musa and Greater and Lesser Tunb, to renegotiate the agreement of March 1975 signed by the two sides in Algiers, to grant autonomy to the Iranian Arabs of Khuzestan, and to undertake not to interfere in the internal affairs of Arab states. Iran declined to accept these terms, and on September 17 Iraq officially abrogated the Algiers agreement and claimed the Shatt al-Arab waterway.

Iraqi troops had already entered Kurdistan, and on September 22 they pushed into Khuzestan, though neither side declared war. Iranian air strikes at Baghdad, Basra, and the Kirkuk area followed an Iraqi bombing raid on Teheran, but the battle on the ground in Khuzestan became the main theatre of operations. By December the Iraqi offensive had been halted, and fighting was limited largely to artillery exchanges from heavily entrenched positions around the Shatt al-Arab waterway. (*See* DEFENSE: *Special Report.*)

Damage to Iran from the war included cessation of oil exports via Kharg Island, destruction of the

Abadan refinery, reduction in crude oil output in Khuzestan, closure of some domestic pipeline systems, and disruption of output at the Teheran and Tabriz refineries. Outside the petroleum sector, Iran suffered losses in the petrochemical plants at Abadan, Kharg, and Bandar Khomeini. The iron and steel industry in Ahvaz was also badly hit, and the general cargo ports of Khorramshahr and Bandar Khomeini were brought to a standstill. Large numbers of refugees, possibly up to one million persons in all, were displaced in the fighting. International attempts to end the conflict through the good offices of the UN and the Islamic Conference failed. The Iranian government announced that it would not break off the struggle until all Iraqis had been expelled from Iranian soil and the regime in Baghdad overthrown.

Relations with the international community were overshadowed by the crisis over the U.S. embassy hostages. UN Secretary-General Kurt Waldheim visited Teheran in January to negotiate their release, and a UN commission of inquiry went to Teheran in February. On April 24–25 the U.S., using transport aircraft and helicopters, made an abortive military raid into Iran. The Socialist International visited Teheran in May. But it was not until November 2 that the Majlis approved conditions for release of the hostages and negotiations began in earnest, with Algeria acting as intermediary. (*See* United States.)

Little progress was made during 1980 in resuscitating the economy. Oil production fell from 2,632,000 bbl a day in the first quarter of the year to 1,565,000 bbl in the second and 1.4 million bbl in the third. After the outbreak of war with Iraq, only minor quantities of oil were produced, mainly from the eastern oil field areas. The value of oil exports fell off sharply even before the war, from U.S. $4.9 billion in the first quarter to $4.2 billion in the second and to extremely low levels in the third, as Iranian prices became unacceptably high in a declining oil market. The war effectively reduced exports to some 150,000–200,000 bbl a day from the Lavan and Sirri terminals in the eastern Gulf.

Political confusion and preoccupation with intergroup rivalries precluded serious concern with the development of agriculture and industry. A proposed land reform designed to encourage small peasant-farmer agriculture had only a limited effect. Of 2.8 million tons of wheat consumed, 1.2 million tons were imported. Industrial enterprise remained inhibited by lack of confidence on the part of the private sector and the inactivity of the state. The Bandar Khomeini petrochemical plant, to be built by Mitsui of Japan at a cost of some $3.5 billion, remained incomplete, an early victim of the war. Iranian financial strength waned as revenues fell, the U.S. retained its freeze on Iranian assets of some $8 billion, and imports surged. Inflation was believed to be approaching 100% by the year's end. An 11-man economic mobilization committee was set up to manage the economy after September 1980.

The former shah, Mohammad Reza Pahlavi (*see* Obituaries), died in Cairo on July 27.

(KEITH S. MCLACHLAN)

Iraq

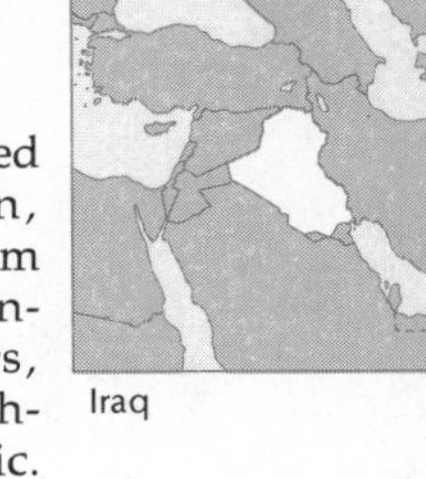

Iraq

A republic of southwestern Asia, Iraq is bounded by Turkey, Iran, Kuwait, Saudi Arabia, Jordan, Syria, and the Persian Gulf. Area: 437,522 sq km (168,928 sq mi). Pop. (1979 est.): 12,767,000, including Arabs, Kurds, Turks, Aramaic-speakers, Iranians, and others. Cap. and largest city: Baghdad (pop., 1977, 3,205,600). Language: Arabic. Religion: mainly Muslim, some Christian. President in 1980, Saddam Hussein at-Takriti.

Iraq's declaration on Sept. 17, 1980, making void its agreement with the late shah of Iran over passage in the Shatt al-Arab waterway, was the signal for the rapid escalation of border skirmishes into all-out war. Iran rejected Iraq's claim to the waterway, and on September 22 Iraqi jet aircraft mounted the first major strike of the war—an attack on ten Iranian airfields. By mid-November, with the port of Khorramshahr effectively in Iraqi hands and the vital oil-refining complex of Abadan surrounded, there was still no early end to the fighting in sight. The strength of Iranian resistance surprised many observers in the early stages of the war. The morale of Iran's revolutionary forces, inspired by the religious leader Ayatollah Ruhollah Khomeini, was high. Iran also possessed superior weapons, mainly its U.S.-supplied Phantom jets. By contrast, Iraq, supplied by the Soviet Union with T-62 and T-72 tanks and MiG-23 aircraft, seemed reluctant to commit them to battle.

With both Iraqi Pres. Saddam Hussein at-Takriti

IRAQ

Education. (1978–79) Primary, pupils 2,459,870, teachers 87,148; secondary, pupils 781,766, teachers 25,254; vocational, pupils 48,186, teachers 3,273; teacher training, students 20,488, teachers 939; higher, students 89,197, teaching staff 5,207.

Finance. Monetary unit: Iraqi dinar, with (Sept. 22, 1980) a par value of 0.295 dinar to U.S. $1 (free rate of 0.705 dinar = £1 sterling). Budget (total; 1980 est.) balanced at 14,103,000,000 dinars. Gross domestic product (1977) 5,692,000,000 dinars. Cost of living (1975 = 100; Sept. 1979) 148.4.

Foreign Trade. (1979) Imports *c.* 2,225,000,000 dinars; exports 6,350,000,000 dinars. Import sources: Japan *c.* 18%; West Germany *c.* 13%; France *c.* 9%; Italy *c.* 8%; U.K. *c.* 5%; U.S. *c.* 5%. Export destinations: France *c.* 16%; Italy *c.* 14%; Brazil *c.* 9%; Japan *c.* 9%. Main export: crude oil 99%.

Transport and Communications. Roads (1975) 9,692 km. Motor vehicles in use (1977): passenger 150,400; commercial (including buses) 74,500. Railways: (1975) 1,990 km; traffic (1976) 797 million passenger-km, freight 2,254,000,000 net ton-km. Air traffic (1978): 1,334,000,000 passenger-km; freight 41.4 million net ton-km. Shipping (1979): merchant vessels 100 gross tons and over 123; gross tonnage 1,328,256. Telephones (Jan. 1978) 319,600. Radio receivers (Dec. 1977) 2 million. Television receivers (Dec. 1977) 475,000.

Agriculture. Production (in 000; metric tons; 1979): wheat *c.* 1,492; barley *c.* 872; rice *c.* 284; cucumbers (1978) *c.* 111; watermelons (1978) *c.* 613; onions *c.* 75; tomatoes *c.* 449; dates (1978) *c.* 581; grapes *c.* 426; tobacco *c.* 12; cotton, lint *c.* 10. Livestock (in 000; 1979): cattle *c.* 2,740; sheep *c.* 11,576; goats *c.* 3,640; camels *c.* 235; asses *c.* 450.

Industry. Production (in 000; metric tons; 1978): cement *c.* 2,500; crude oil (1979) 168,575; natural gas (cu m; 1977) 1,580,000; petroleum products *c.* 6,400; electricity (excluding most industrial production; kw-hr; 1977) 5,000,000.

UPI

After Iraqi troops captured a military outpost near Khorramshahr, Iran, in September, two soldiers posed triumphantly near a portrait of Ayatollah Khomeini.

and Khomeini refusing to compromise, prospects for mediation looked bleak. Early attempts under the auspices of the Islamic Conference failed. Iraq's objectives in the war seemed to be threefold: to assert sovereignty over the Shatt al-Arab waterway controlling access to the Iraqi port of Basra; to damage the revolutionary government in Teheran by striking at vital installations; and to destabilize southwest Iran, where many of the population were Arabic-speaking, by supporting the resistance movement seeking to create an autonomous republic in Khuzestan.

Fears that the war would spread into other Gulf countries or involve a preemptive strike on the Strait of Hormuz failed to materialize. The U.S., France, and Britain stepped up their naval forces in the Arabian Sea and the Indian Ocean, but Hussein's strategy was clearly to keep the dispute localized. In the rhetoric manufactured by Baghdad after war had erupted, an Iraqi claim to the Iranian-occupied islands of Abu Musa and Greater and Lesser Tunb at the entrance to the Gulf was asserted. There appeared to be little likelihood of fighting on Iran's southeast flank, however. Shipping passing through the strait navigated Omani waters, and provided it kept to the southern shores of the Gulf, it could avoid the area designated by Iran as a war zone. In early August, before the war, Hussein made an unscheduled visit to Riyadh, Saudi Arabia, for a meeting with King Khalid. No communiqué was issued after the meeting, but on the outbreak of war the Saudi government made clear its neutrality. (*See* DEFENSE: *Special Report.*)

On the outbreak of hostilities, Iraq declared force majeure (circumstances that could not be controlled) on its oil contracts. Before the war Iraq was the second-largest Arab oil producer, after Saudi Arabia, yielding 3.5 million bbl a day of which 2.8 million bbl were exported. By 1985 refining capacity was expected to be 620,000 bbl a day, but Iranian strikes on refining installations were jeopardizing this target. With U.S. $17 billion allocated for development in 1980, Iraq was a fertile field for Western business, second only to Saudi Arabia among Arab countries. Industrialized nations, notably France, Spain, Italy, West Germany, Britain, and Brazil, were understandably eager to improve relations.

Iraq's main Arab trading partner was Jordan; King Hussein declared immediate support for President Hussein when hostilities began and allowed transit of Iraq-bound goods through the Jordanian port of Aqaba. As part of an attempt to offer leadership in the Arab world, Iraq pursued a generous foreign aid policy, although it stopped short of "oil gifts" to less developed countries. The Iraqi Fund for External Development was a conduit for such aid, which on a bilateral basis in 1980 provided U.S. $70 million for Tanzania, Kenya, and Madagascar and £104 million for India, as well as loans to Vietnam and Pakistan.

Strength in external relations and oil wealth enabled President Hussein to take an independent line. He criticized the Soviet intervention in Afghanistan as "unjustified," despite the existing Iraqi friendship treaty with Moscow. At home the separatism of the Kurdish minority was curbed and potential opposition from within the ruling Baʿath Party removed. Early in 1980 Hussein announced what he called the "Arab charter." This appealed for the rejection of foreign influence, better economic collaboration, a peaceful solution to "inter-Arab" quarrels, and, above all, solidarity among Arab states. In 1982 Hussein was scheduled to chair the summit meeting of nonaligned nations in Baghdad. Among his quarrels with other Arab states, Hussein had criticized Yemen (Aden) for allegedly harbouring Iraqi Communists.

Despite difficulties being faced in late 1980 by many contractors, new projects were still being tendered in Baghdad, including the $2 billion Mosul dam civil works. The Japanese in particular were expected to suffer if hostilities became prolonged, since in 1979 Japanese contractors earned more than $2 billion in Iraq in officially reported contracts alone. Trade relations with Britain were expected to improve after the release on November 3 of a British businessman jailed for a year for alleged espionage. (JOHN WHELAN)

Ireland

Separated from Great Britain by the North Channel, the Irish Sea, and St. George's Channel, the Republic of Ireland shares its island with Northern Ireland to the northeast. Area: 70,283 sq km (27,136 sq mi), or 84% of the island. Pop. (1979): 3,368,200. Cap. and largest city: Dublin (pop., 1979, 544,600). Language (1971): mostly English; 28% speak English and Irish or Irish only. Religion: 94% Roman Catholic. President in 1980, Patrick J. Hillery; prime minister, Charles J. Haughey.

Charles J. Haughey (*see* BIOGRAPHIES) succeeded Jack Lynch as prime minister on Dec. 11, 1979, and his efforts to create confidence in his economic and Northern Ireland policies dominated domestic affairs throughout 1980. He was faced with major problems. In common with other Western economies, but more vulnerable because of its dependence on overseas markets and its openness to foreign competition, Ireland faced a year of high inflation, steadily rising unemployment, and low growth and low investment as a result of high interest rates. In addition, industrial unrest, which had led to a record number of workdays lost during 1979, continued to cause major strikes in 1980. One of these closed the national airline at the peak of the tourist season, in June; another, of gasoline (petrol)-tanker drivers, led to a gasoline famine in August and September which was only resolved after the Army had been called in to distribute fuel to gasoline stations.

Further economic aggravation derived from an appalling summer that ruined crops and left many farmers ruined as well. Encouraged by excellent earnings over the previous two or three years resulting from the European Economic Community's common agricultural policy, many of them had invested heavily. During 1980 farming costs rose by 20%, incomes fell by 27%, and special relief measures had to be introduced by the government in the autumn. Though the Irish pound (punt) maintained its standing against other European currencies, its fall against sterling, which drove it below 90p in March and below 80p by November, had a further demoralizing effect on the economy, as well as crippling trade.

At the end of January the Supreme Court ruled that it was unconstitutional to discriminate, in any laws, against married couples. The immediate effect of this was manifest in obligatory tax benefits in the budget, introduced on February 27. The budget also made substantial cuts in direct taxation, cutting "pay as you earn" (PAYE) rates and widening tax brackets. Prime Minister Haughey promised action against industrial unrest, but no legislation was introduced. A national wages deal negotiated in the autumn provided a generous raise of more than 15% over a 15-month period and paid no more than lip service to no-strike provisions.

In a marked, but very general, departure from previous policies on Northern Ireland under Jack Lynch and the coalition government of Liam Cosgrave, Haughey turned away from any attempted solution in a Northern Ireland context and sought a Dublin-London basis for moving forward. He initiated this approach at the conference of his ruling Fianna Fail Party on February 17, when he invited Margaret Thatcher's government to join his own in "a joint effort" on Northern Ireland. On May 21 he went to London for his first meeting with the British prime minister, where he repeated the offer. A joint communiqué issued after the meeting referred to the "new and closer cooperation" and the "unique relationship" between Britain and the Republic of Ireland but did not encourage any belief in a joint initiative.

The Dublin government did increase antiterrorist activity by the police, as well as investment in training and equipment. There were substantial finds of arms and explosives, but there was also more violence; two police officers, John Morley and Henry Byrne, were shot dead by bank robbers in Roscommon in July, and Detective Garda Quaid was shot dead in Wexford on October 13. Slight embarrassment was caused to the government when a supporter, Sile de Valera, speaking from a platform being shared with Haughey, attacked Prime Minister Thatcher and spoke out in favour of the Northern Ireland campaign for political pris-

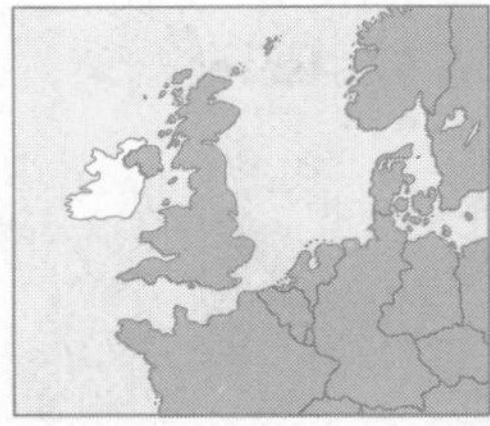
Ireland

IRELAND

Education. (1978–79) Primary, pupils 564,323, teachers 19,129; secondary, pupils 285,326, teachers 17,482; vocational, pupils 7,348, teachers 203; higher, students 37,156, teaching staff 3,578.

Finance. Monetary unit: Irish pound (punt), with (Sept. 22, 1980) a free rate of I£0.48 to U.S. $1 (I£1.15 = £1 sterling). Gold, SDR's, and foreign exchange (June 1980) U.S. $2,247,000,000. Budget (1979 actual): revenue £2,484 million; expenditure £3,539 million. Gross national product (1979) £7,200 million. Money supply (June 1980) £1,442 million. Cost of living (1975 = 100; May 1980) 192.2.

Foreign Trade. (1979) Imports £4,815.7 million; exports £3,498.5 million. Import sources: EEC 72% (U.K. 50%, West Germany 7%, France 5%); U.S. 9%. Export destinations: EEC 77% (U.K. 46%, West Germany 9%, France 8%, Belgium-Luxembourg 6%, The Netherlands 5%); U.S. 5%. Main exports: machinery 14%; chemicals 13%; beef and veal 10%; dairy products 9%; textiles and clothing 8%. Tourism (1978): visitors 1,678,000; gross receipts U.S. $462 million.

Transport and Communications. Roads (1977) 92,294 km. Motor vehicles in use (1979): passenger 682,960; commercial 61,540. Railways: (1978) 2,007 km; traffic (1979) 1,007,000,000 passenger-km, freight 559 million net ton-km. Air traffic (1979): 2,220,000,000 passenger-km; freight 100.3 million net ton-km. Shipping (1979): merchant vessels 100 gross tons and over 118; gross tonnage 200,714. Telephones (Dec. 1978) 544,000. Radio receivers (Dec. 1976) 949,000. Television licenses (Dec. 1978) 607,550.

Agriculture. Production (in 000; metric tons; 1979): barley *c.* 1,512; wheat 260; oats *c.* 103; potatoes *c.* 1,060; sugar, raw value *c.* 210; cabbages (1978) *c.* 182; cow's milk *c.* 4,871; butter 122; cheese *c.* 58; beef and veal *c.* 378; pork *c.* 145; fish catch (1978) 108. Livestock (in 000; June 1979): cattle 7,178; sheep 3,376; pigs *c.* 1,154; horses *c.* 78; chickens *c.* 8,500.

Industry. Production (in 000; metric tons; 1979): cement 2,067; coal 57; petroleum products (1978) *c.* 2,370; electricity (kw-hr) 11,015,000; manufactured gas (cu m) 300,000; beer (hl; 1976–77) 4,400; wool fabrics (sq m) 3,000; rayon, etc., fabrics (sq m; 1976) 16,700; fertilizers (nutrient content; 1978–79): nitrogenous 63, phosphate 50.

oner status for members of paramilitary organizations convicted of offenses. Haughey and Prime Minister Thatcher met again in December in Dublin, but the discussions failed to produce any concrete results.

Prime Minister Haughey faced a tangible challenge with the by-election in Donegal, the northernmost county in the republic, occasioned by the death of Joseph Brennan, speaker of the Dail (parliament). Haughey fought a highly personalized campaign, flying by helicopter to the north five weekends in a row. The seat was won by the government in spite of economic adversity—or possibly as a result of the spending of large sums of money on "improvements" in the county.

On November 1 legislation on contraceptives came into force, requiring that they be prescribed by doctors and supplied by pharmacists. Many doctors and pharmacists declined to provide them on moral grounds, and there was widespread uncertainty over what legal action would be taken against the very large numbers of people who, either privately or as organizers of family planning clinics, were in violation of the law. The conservatism of this legislation was echoed by a government decision not to enter all-party negotiations on divorce, which was banned under the constitution. As indicators of the toleration level that would exist in a united Ireland, these developments did not augur well for the new prime minister's Northern Ireland policy, but since his eyes were directed toward London rather than Belfast it did not greatly matter.

A new Protestant primate of Ireland, John Ward Armstrong, previously bishop of Cashel and Ossory, was elected unanimously. In Tipperary, a few miles from Thurles at a place called Derrynaflane, a highly significant early Christian archaeological find was made in March. Consisting of a magnificent 8th-century chalice, a paten, and a wine strainer, all of Irish design, it was discovered with the aid of a metal detector. (MAVIS ARNOLD)

See also United Kingdom.

Israel

Israel

A republic of the Middle East, Israel is bounded by Lebanon, Syria, Jordan, Egypt, and the Mediterranean Sea. Area (not including territory occupied in the June 1967 war): 20,700 sq km (7,992 sq mi). Pop. (1980 est.): 3,877,700. Cap. and largest city: Jerusalem (pop., 1980 est., 398,200). Language: Hebrew and Arabic. Religion: predominantly Jewish (1979 est., 84%), with Muslim, Christian, and other minorities. President in 1980, Yitzhak Navon; prime minister, Menachem Begin.

Israel in 1980 appeared, especially to its almost 3½ million Jewish citizens, as a society that was beleaguered from both within and without. Isolated at the UN, the nation had lost count of, and interest in, the seemingly endless resolutions passed by the General Assembly and the Security Council that condemned one aspect or another of Israeli policy and practice. The nation was beset likewise by its erstwhile friends of the third world and by its Arab neighbours. The Soviet Union and most of the Eastern European countries displayed unmitigated hostility toward Israel and its representatives, while in the West the European Economic Community adopted a position that the Israeli government considered inimical to its interests. (*See* EUROPEAN UNITY.) Even the United States, a constant pillar of support for Israel throughout its history, was moving away, under Pres. Jimmy Carter, from the kind of backing Israel had been accustomed to receive.

WIDE WORLD

In ceremonies marking the transfer of Sinai territory from Israel to Egypt, the Egyptian flag was raised at a military airfield near Bir Gafgafa in January.

There was still great admiration and trust for Egyptian Pres. Anwar as-Sadat and belief in his good intentions. But there was also a degree of uneasiness about the future once Sadat was no longer at the helm in Egypt. Thus, there seemed in 1980 no one to whom Israel could turn as an automatic ally and friend. It was as if the nation had been contained behind a moat filled with oil and petrodollars and by the powerful interests associated with them. The political and psychological boycott of Israel was almost total.

It was a situation that called for the harnessing of all the country's political, economic, and psychological resources. Instead, however, there was an ever widening gulf between the coalition government of Prime Minister Menachem Begin and the popular mood. As the government's parliamentary majorities began to shrink, the credibility of some of its coalition partners was eroded to the point of nonexistence.

Ireland, Northern:
see United Kingdom

Iron and Steel Industry:
see Industrial Review

Islam:
see Religion

This was especially true of the Democratic Movement for Change, led by former army chief of staff Yigael Yadin. When he had joined the Begin government as deputy prime minister, he had commanded a parliamentary group of 15 members and a substantial plurality among voters. Indeed, it had been Yadin's intervention in the election of 1977 that had been the principal factor in enabling Begin's Likud coalition to defeat the Labour Alignment. But every public opinion poll during the year showed with increasing emphasis that the voters who had defected to Yadin in 1977 had returned to the Labour Party in 1980.

On a personal level, Begin also experienced difficulties. One of his most impressive Cabinet members, Moshe Dayan, had resigned as foreign minister in October 1979; then in May 1980 Ezer Weizman, the minister of defense and the architect of Begin's election victory in 1977, resigned amid much public recrimination. In Dayan's case the dispute had concerned the government's policy in relation to the Palestinians and the occupied territories. For Weizman the disagreement centred on cuts in the defense budget that had been proposed by Finance Minister Yigael Hurwitz and supported by Begin. Weizman objected to the cuts on the grounds that they would adversely affect Israel's independent defensive capacity. Against the background of Israel's international isolation, Weizman argued that defense was of greater importance than inflation and that other means, even if politically unpopular, would have to be found to reduce government expenditures.

It was significant that Begin could not persuade either of his two closest colleagues, both considered to be hard-liners—Yitzhak Shamir (*see* BIOGRAPHIES), who had become foreign minister in March, or the chairman of the Knesset Defense and Foreign Affairs Committee, Moshe Arens—to accept the defense portfolio. Begin himself kept the post and by year's end still had not resolved the question of cutting defense expenditure. The last days of the year were marked by particular tension as Hurwitz threatened to resign and take his faction out of the governing coalition unless his proposed budget cuts were enacted. This could have precipitated the fall of the government, but on December 21 Begin finally agreed to Hurwitz's conditions. On November 19 the government survived the latest in a series of no-confidence votes. Subsequently, Weizman, who had voted against the government, was expelled from Begin's Herut Party, leaving the government without a parliamentary majority. The possibility that elections, due in November 1981, might be moved up to the spring seemed increasingly likely.

It was with an eye to the forthcoming elections that the government supported a bill, introduced in the Knesset (parliament) in May by an ultranationalist, that affirmed Jerusalem as the capital of Israel. Eventually, this created considerable difficulty for Israel in its international relations and consolidated opposition to it on this issue. It also illustrated the extent to which, in current Middle Eastern affairs, form may be far more important than substance, something that the Begin administration, to its cost, had notably failed to appreciate.

Jerusalem, at least that part of Jerusalem held by Israel at that time, had become the de facto capital of Israel in December 1949. This brought some protests from the U.K., France, and the U.S. However, in practice the status of Jerusalem was accepted without being formally recognized by the major

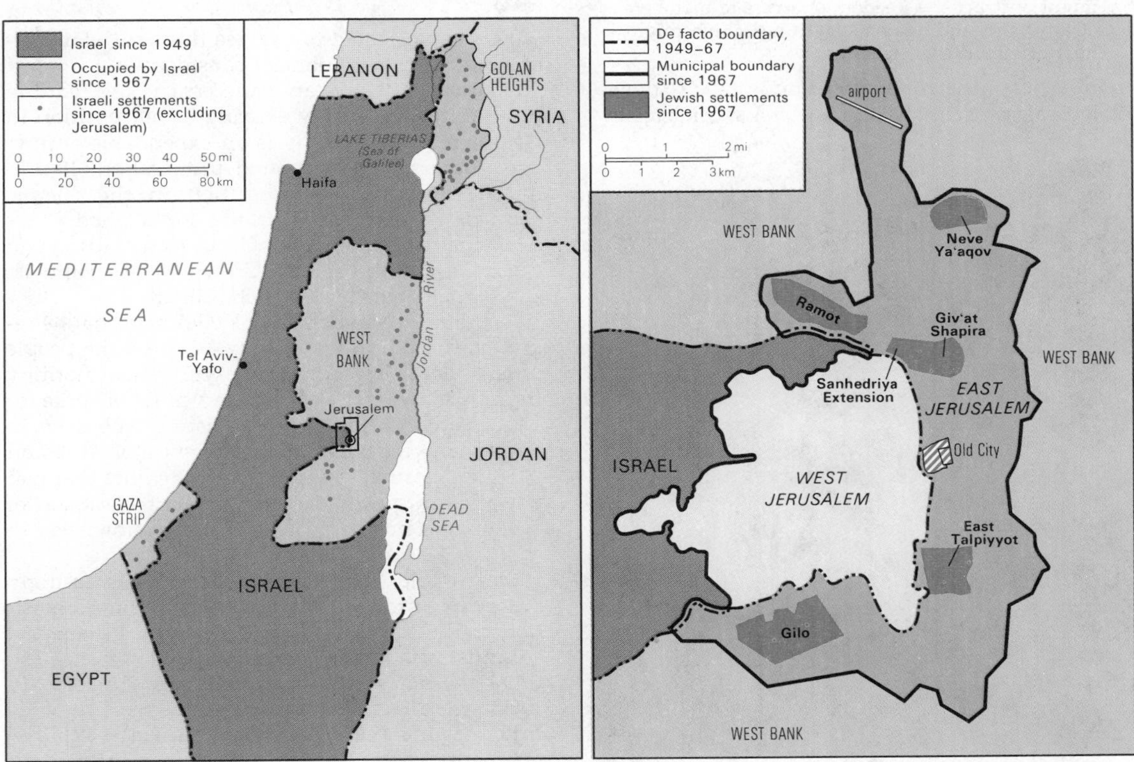

Western powers. This situation remained unchanged when Israel formally annexed East Jerusalem in June 1967, thereby reuniting the city.

In the Camp David discussions with President Carter and President Sadat—and in the negotiations concerning the autonomy of the Palestinian Arabs on the West Bank—it had been agreed to leave the Jerusalem question to the end. However, on June 30 the UN Security Council, reacting to the bill, passed a resolution declaring Israel's position in East Jerusalem to be devoid of legal basis and calling on Israel to withdraw from that part of the city and dismantle all settlements established since 1967. To the surprise of many Israelis, a somewhat differently worded resolution restating the Arab character of East Jerusalem was passed about the same time by Egypt's National Assembly. This was echoed in other Arab capitals.

The Begin government had had a choice of carrying on with Jerusalem as Israel's de facto capital and waiting for a suitable time when its status could be formalized or defying its critics with a formal declaration by the Knesset confirming Israel's annexation of East Jerusalem. The bill deprived the government of this choice and forced it to decide on formalizing the city's status immediately. On July 30 the Knesset approved by a large majority, which included many leading members of the opposition Labour Party, an amended version of the "Jerusalem Basic Law." It consisted of four articles:

> Article 1: Integral and United Jerusalem is the capital of Israel. Article 2: Jerusalem is the seat of the Presidency, the Cabinet and of the Knesset and the Supreme Court. Article 3: The Holy Places will be protected against desecration, against anything that might be offensive to them or which might obstruct the freedom of access to members of any faith and against anything which might hurt or offend their feelings.

In Article 4 the government undertook to develop Jerusalem and make it prosper. A special agency would be delegated to oversee this and would receive preferential financial consideration.

Palestinian Mayor Bassam as-Shaka of Nablus lost both legs when his car was bombed in June. Unknown Jewish underground groups, who claimed responsibility, said other Palestinian nationalists were also targeted.

UPI

Politically, it was an unnecessary law, adding nothing to the already existing Israeli position in Jerusalem. Some saw it as an expendable annoyance; others as a calculated provocation. It produced a furor of denunciation in the Islamic countries. Conferences calling for a jihad (holy war) against Israel were held in Iran, Libya, and Morocco; Saudi Arabia's Crown Prince Fahd issued a personal call for such a jihad.

Jerusalem's Mayor Teddy Kollek said that he regretted the bill in its entirety. "I think the people of Jerusalem, Jew and Arab, will benefit nothing from this law." However, it served its purpose for Israel's adversaries. Several existing embassies in Jerusalem were withdrawn as a result of Arab and Islamic pressures. Western governments that had not given a second thought to the transaction of diplomatic business in Jerusalem now had a change of heart.

Meanwhile, Israel had become increasingly preoccupied toward the year's end with the position of the economy and the future of the Begin administration. The economy suffered from high inflation, but the figures quoted—up to 200% in 1980—were largely meaningless because they resulted from a network of index-linked prices. Assessments varied, but one leading authority put

ISRAEL

Education. (1979–80) Primary, pupils 645,095, teachers 35,066; secondary, pupils 84,416, teachers 6,220; vocational, pupils 78,743, teachers 8,517; higher, students 87,724, teaching staff (1974–75) 13,981.

Finance. Monetary unit: shekel (which replaced the former pound in 1980 at 10 old pounds = 1 shekel), with (Sept. 22, 1980) a free rate of 5.76 shekels to U.S. $1 (13.85 shekels = £1 sterling). Gold, SDR's, and foreign exchange (June 1980) U.S. $3,470,000,000. Budget (1978–79 actual): revenue 12,593,000,000 shekels; expenditure 16,202,000,000 shekels. Gross national product (1979) 43,340,000,000 shekels. Money supply (May 1980) 4,558,000,000 shekels. Cost of living (1975 = 100; June 1980) 1,024.

Foreign Trade. (1979) Imports 21,855,000,000 shekels (including 2,849,000,000 shekels military goods); exports 11,582,000,000 shekels. Import sources: U.S. 20%; West Germany 10%; Switzerland 9%; U.K. 9%; Italy 5%; France 5%. Export destinations: U.S. 16%; West Germany 9%; U.K. 9%; Hong Kong 5%; Belgium-Luxembourg 5%; Japan 5%; France 5%; Switzerland 5%. Main exports: diamonds 32%; chemicals 13%; metal manufactures 7%; machinery 6%; citrus fruit 6%; aircraft 5%. Tourism (1978): visitors 1,013,469; gross receipts U.S. $596 million.

Transport and Communications. Roads (1978) 11,891 km. Motor vehicles in use (1979): passenger 403,000; commercial 86,770. Railways: (1977) 823 km; traffic (1978) 221 million passenger-km, freight 636 million net ton-km. Air traffic (1979): 5,440,000,000 passenger-km; freight 290.4 million net ton-km. Shipping (1979): merchant vessels 100 gross tons and over 57; gross tonnage 435,394. Telephones (Dec. 1978) 1,035,000. Radio receivers (Dec. 1977) 750,000. Television licenses (Dec. 1976) 475,000.

Agriculture. Production (in 000; metric tons; 1979): wheat 128; potatoes 208; watermelons (1978) *c.* 94; tomatoes 225; onions 57; oranges 941; grapefruit 503; grapes 69; apples 123; olives 8; bananas 61; cotton, lint 75; cheese *c.* 54; poultry meat *c.* 182; fish catch (1978) 26. Livestock (in 000; 1978): cattle 347; sheep 220; goats 146; pigs *c.* 91; camels 11; chickens *c.* 25,000.

Industry. Production (in 000; metric tons; 1979): cement 1,919; crude oil 20; natural gas (cu m) 54,000; phosphate rock (1978) 1,723; petroleum products (1977) *c.* 6,990; sulfuric acid 225; fertilizers (nutrient content; 1978–79) nitrogenous 73, phosphate 53, potash 653; paper (1978) 101; electricity (kw-hr) 12,433,000. New dwelling units completed (1979) 30,200.

the actual rate of inflation in real terms as low as 20%, slightly higher than that in Britain.

In general, economic and social conditions were not as critical as they had been in the winter of 1966–67 when there had been 100,000 unemployed, when emigration exceeded immigration, when there were real food shortages in some development towns, and when the morale of the country was at its lowest ebb. Six months later, in June 1967, Israel fought its most successful war, and the economy then began to expand as never before.

In February 1980 the government introduced the shekel in place of the Israeli pound, with ten old pounds making a new shekel. The change made no visible difference to the economy.

There was one other development of major significance during the last days of the year. It had been assumed that the Begin government, though unpopular, would probably be returned to power in a spring 1981 election. This was because the only alternative to Begin, the Labour Alignment, had been so fundamentally divided that it had been unable to muster an alternative and united administration.

Therefore, when the Labour Party convention met in Tel Aviv in December, it was assumed that it would present a sad spectacle of divided counsels and divided leaders. It turned out otherwise. The party chairman, Shimon Peres, a protégé of Israel's first prime minister, David Ben-Gurion, was reelected chairman with a 70% majority vote. By the end of the convention Peres had emerged as the undisputed leader who was accepted also by the minority. For months the public opinion polls had indicated a landslide Labour victory in 1981 provided the party could resolve its leadership differences. The unity displayed at the convention made it seem likely that Labour might emerge from an election with a clear majority for the first time since the establishment of Israel.

Thus there was an alternative government in being, something that Begin had not had to consider since he gained power in 1977. The immediate effect was to cause the ruling Likud to change course away from seeking a spring election and in favour of holding on at all costs until November 1981, in the hope that Labour's popularity might erode. But as the year ended, the increasing fragility of Begin's coalition made this appear unlikely.

(JON KIMCHE)

See also Middle Eastern Affairs.

Italy

A republic of southern Europe, Italy occupies the Apennine Peninsula, Sicily, Sardinia, and a number of smaller islands. On the north it borders France, Switzerland, Austria, and Yugoslavia. Area: 301,263 sq km (116,318 sq mi). Pop. (1980 est.): 56,999,000. Cap. and largest city: Rome (pop., 1980 est., 2,911,700). Language: Italian. Religion: predominantly Roman Catholic. President in 1980, Alessandro Pertini; premiers, Francesco Cossiga and, from October 18, Arnaldo Forlani.

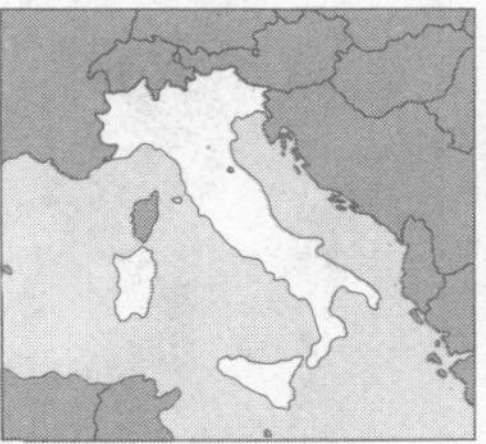
Italy

Italy in 1980 suffered its worst natural disaster in more than 70 years when an earthquake struck a large area of the south on November 23. It killed more than 3,000 people, injured nearly 8,000, and caused millions of dollars worth of damage. The nation also suffered from political terrorism by both left- and right-wing extremists. In a bomb incident at Bologna in August, 76 people died and about 200 were injured. It was Western Europe's worst single terrorist attack since World War II. In politics the return of the Socialist Party to government after an absence of six years was the most significant development.

Domestic Affairs. The earthquake that hit the south of Italy had its epicentre in the mountains of Irpinia, east of Naples. Dozens of mountain villages in the predominantly poor region were destroyed, and an area the size of Belgium was devastated. The relief operation was slow to get under way, and hundreds of victims trapped alive under the rubble of their homes died because of the failure to move in quickly with heavy lifting equipment and special detection devices. More than 250,000 people were made homeless by the tremor, the most destructive in Italy since the earthquake that destroyed the cities of Reggio di Calabria and Messina in 1908. Relief supplies were sent from all over the world, but there was widespread criticism of the lack of a proper civil defense organization to deal with what, in an area prone to earthquakes, was a foreseeable catastrophe. Judicial proceedings began against the builders and architects of hundreds of modern apartment buildings that had been erected without observing the antiearthquake building regulations and that collapsed as a result of the quake.

Naples suffered extensive damage. Hundreds of buildings were declared unsafe for habitation, and government plans to evacuate the homeless to requisitioned vacation homes along the coast failed when earthquake victims refused to move away from their livelihoods and neighbourhood facilities. The ruins of Pompeii and Herculaneum suffered considerable damage, and hundreds of churches, convents, castles, and historic monuments in the provinces of Avellino, Irpinia, and Basilicata were seriously damaged or destroyed.

Despite progress by the authorities in the battle against terrorism, which included the arrest of hundreds of suspects and the cooperation of several key terrorist figures with police in exchange for promises of leniency when they came to trial, 1980 was Italy's worst year for terrorist murders. The indiscriminate massacre at the Bologna railway station caused by a bomb placed in a waiting room shocked the nation. A state funeral was held for the victims, but most families chose private burial ceremonies—a sign of the lack of confidence in the government by ordinary Italians. Responsibility for the bomb was pinned upon neofascists. Aldo Semerari, a well-known Rome psychologist who had appeared as an expert witness in countless criminal trials, was arrested and charged with conspiracy in organizing the attack.

A long series of victims of the Red Brigades and the Front Line, the two main left-wing terrorist organizations, included Gen. Enrico Galvaligi of northern Italy's antiterrorism police force, Mario

UPI

Arnaldo Forlani (left) takes the oath during ceremonies in Rome to become the new Italian premier after Francesco Cossiga resigned from that office on September 27.

Amato, a leading investigator into neofascist terrorist crime, and one of Italy's leading journalists, Walter Tobagi of the Milan newspaper *Corriere della Sera.*

The Red Brigades directed a campaign against Italy's antiquated prison system. They kidnapped a Rome judge, Giovanni D'Urso, staged a prison revolt at the maximum security jail at Trani in southern Italy, and murdered several senior prison officials. In December Marco Donat-Cattin, the son of a former Christian Democrat minister, was arrested by French police in Paris on instructions from the Italian government. He was wanted by Italian police on charges of armed subversion and was suspected of being a leading member of the Front Line. Earlier in the year the Italian press reported that Premier Francesco Cossiga had tipped off Donat-Cattin's father that a security net was tightening around his son. A full-scale parliamentary investigation into allegations of misconduct by the premier was held, but Cossiga was cleared by a majority vote.

Two new governments were formed during the year, bringing to 40 the number of administrations that had held office in Italy since World War II. But there was no basic change in the direction of policy by the ruling Christian Democrats, who took comfort in an almost 2% drop in the Communist vote in local elections held on June 8–9. One disturbing development, however, was the increasing number of spoiled and blank votes and abstentions. More than seven million Italians entitled to vote in the elections failed to cast a valid vote, reflecting growing disillusionment with the political system. Voting is compulsory in Italy.

On October 18 Arnaldo Forlani (*see* BIOGRAPHIES) took office as premier at the head of one of the broadest-based coalitions since World War II, one that included Christian Democrats, Socialists, Social Democrats, and Republicans. The agreement by the two Socialist parties, which had split in 1947, to work together again was a significant development. The agreement in April by the Socialists to return to government in a coalition with the Christian Democrats, after an absence of six years, marked a move back toward the centre-left type of coalition that governed Italy during the 1960s and early 1970s.

The earthquake in southern Italy and the bombing in Bologna were not the only disasters in the nation in 1980. A plane crash killed 81 people on June 27, and 12 people were killed and over 100 injured in a railway accident in southern Italy on November 21. The plane crash—a DC-9 on a regular flight over the Mediterranean Sea from Bologna to Palermo in Sicily—was not satisfactorily explained.

Kidnap crime continued unabated, and more than U.S. $10 million was paid in ransoms. Police reported 46 kidnappings during the year, a slight decrease from 1979. On January 16 police in Milan intercepted a consignment of drugs that was the largest ever seized in Western Europe, 36 kg (80 lb) of pure heroin destined for the U.S. market. The consignment was disguised as a shipment of long-playing records.

Foreign Affairs. Italy's presidency of the European Economic Community from January to June 1980 was interrupted by a government crisis in Rome that caused the postponement of an EEC

ITALY

Education. (1978–79) Primary, pupils 4,584,300, teachers 278,044; secondary, pupils 3,545,298, teachers 309,933; vocational, pupils 1,469,987, teachers 128,239; teacher training, students 217,962, teachers 20,057; higher, students 777,768, teaching staff (1977–78) 43,120.

Finance. Monetary unit: lira, with (Sept. 22, 1980) a free rate of 856 lire to U.S. $1 (2,056 lire = £1 sterling). Gold, SDR's, and foreign exchange (June 1980) U.S. $23,590,000,000. Budget (1979 actual): revenue 64,042,000,000,000 lire; expenditure 90,659,000,000,000 lire. Gross national product (1979) 269,241,000,000,000 lire. Money supply (April 1980) 148,498,000,000,000 lire. Cost of living (1975 = 100; June 1980) 209.8.

Foreign Trade. (1979) Imports 64,653,000,000,000 lire; exports 59,926,000,000,000 lire. Import sources: EEC 44% (West Germany 17%, France 14%); U.S. 7%; Saudi Arabia 5%. Export destinations: EEC 49% (West Germany 19%, France 15%, U.K. 7%, The Netherlands 5%); U.S. 6%. Main exports: machinery 21%; motor vehicles 8%; chemicals 8%; textile yarns and fabrics 6%; clothing 6%; petroleum products 6%; food 6%; iron and steel 5%; footwear 5%. Tourism (1978): visitors 19,192,600; gross receipts U.S. $6,285,000,000.

Transport and Communications. Roads (1979) 293,346 km (including 5,822 km expressways). Motor vehicles in use (1979): passenger *c.* 17.6 million; commercial *c.* 1,383,000. Railways: (1976) 19,923 km; traffic (1979) 39,820,000,000 passenger-km, freight 17,690,000,000 net ton-km. Air traffic (1978): 13,336,000,000 passenger-km; freight *c.* 510 million net ton-km. Shipping (1979): merchant vessels 100 gross tons and over 1,711: gross tonnage 11,694,872. Telephones (Dec. 1978) 17,088,000. Radio receivers (Dec. 1978) 13,401,000. Television licenses (Dec. 1978) 12,868,000.

Agriculture. Production (in 000; metric tons; 1979): wheat 9,140; corn 6,260; barley 809; oats 438; rice 1,014; potatoes 2,967; sugar, raw value *c.* 1,695; cabbages (1978) 603; cauliflowers 595; onions 540; tomatoes 4,294; grapes 11,730; wine 7,968; olives *c.* 2,400; oranges 1,690; mandarin oranges and tangerines 337; lemons 844; apples 1,800; pears (1978) 1,140; peaches (1978) 1,150; tobacco 113; cheese *c.* 578; beef and veal 1,060; pork 950; fish catch (1978) 402. Livestock (in 000; Dec. 1978): cattle *c.* 8,556; sheep *c.* 8,736; pigs *c.* 9,790; goats *c.* 960; poultry *c.* 121,328.

Industry. Index of production (1975 = 100; 1979) 124. Unemployment (1979) 7.7%. Fuel and power (in 000; metric tons; 1979): lignite (1978) *c.* 1,868; crude oil 1,630; natural gas (cu m; 1978) 13,702,000; manufactured gas (cu m) 3,320,000; electricity (kw-hr) 180,522,000. Production (in 000; metric tons; 1979): iron ore (44% metal content) 218; pig iron 11,612; crude steel 24,389; aluminum 266; zinc 203; cement 39,720; cotton yarn 170; man-made fibres 407; fertilizers (nutrient content; 1978–79) nitrogenous 1,442, phosphate 544, potash 135; sulfuric acid 2,967; plastics and resins 2,562; petroleum products *c.* 114,500; passenger cars (units) 1,484; commercial vehicles (units) 151. Merchant vessels launched (100 gross tons and over; 1979) 148,000 gross tons. New dwelling units completed (1979) 136,990.

summit meeting in Brussels in March. Heads of government of the EEC met in Venice in June.

Pres. Alessandro Pertini paid a state visit to China in September. He had to cut short his tour because of the outbreak of the second government crisis during the year. Great Britain's Queen Elizabeth II paid a state visit to Italy from October 14 to 20, after which she was received by Pope John Paul II at the Vatican. She visited Rome and Genoa and afterward sailed in the royal yacht "Britannia" from Naples to Palermo.

Italian Communist Party leader Enrico Berlinguer paid a visit to China in April, during which he reestablished official relations between the Italian and Chinese parties that had been severed for 15 years. He refused to attend a Soviet-sponsored meeting of European Communist parties held in Paris during the same month. The Italian Communists strongly condemned Soviet intervention in Afghanistan and defended the independent Polish trade union movement. In August a war of words broke out between Italy's Communist Party organ, *L'Unita,* and the official Soviet Communist Party newspaper, *Pravda,* over Berlinguer's statement that in case of Soviet aggression Italian Communists would fight against the Soviet Army.

A joint venture was signed in September between Italy's state-owned Alfa-Romeo Automobile Co. and the Japanese manufacturer Nissan for the establishment near Naples of a factory for the assembly of a new Italo-Japanese compact car. This was strongly criticized in the Italian press because it would allow the Japanese into Italy's large domestic automobile market.

Givaudan, a wholly-owned subsidiary of the Swiss-based pharmaceutical multinational Hoffmann-La Roche, paid out over $100 million in compensation to Italy for damage caused by a chemical factory explosion at Seveso near Milan in July 1976. Decontamination work in the Seveso area continued in 1980, and the long-term medical effects on those exposed to the toxic chemical defoliant dioxin remained unknown.

The Economy. The fall of the Cossiga government in September was caused by a parliamentary defeat on a package of economic measures aimed at combating the rise in both unemployment and inflation. The bank rate rose to an all-time high of 16½%, and one of the most severe credit squeezes ever imposed in Italy was put into effect to prevent international speculation against the lira. The increasing cost of oil placed a growing burden on Italy's balance of payments, while the rate of inflation rose to 21%.

A month-long strike took place in Italy's biggest private industry, the Fiat automobile group. Pickets prevented workers from entering the factories. The strike came to an abrupt end in mid-October, however, after an unprecedented demonstration occurred in the industrial city of Turin. Tens of thousands of workers from both Fiat and other industries affected by the strike demonstrated in favour of the right to work. More than 23,000 Fiat workers had been laid off temporarily, but they received almost full pay under a government unemployment compensation plan.

(DAVID DOUGLAS WILLEY)

Ivory Coast

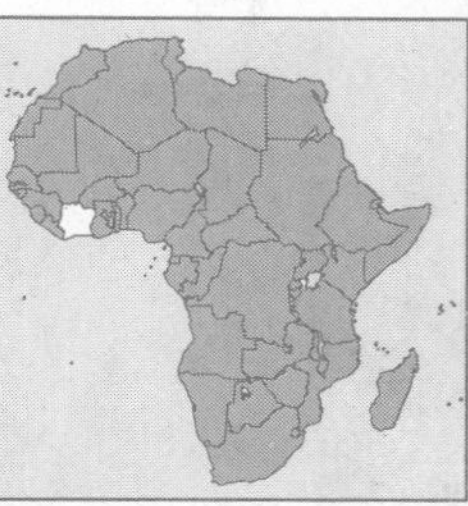

Ivory Coast

A republic on the Gulf of Guinea, the Ivory Coast is bounded by Liberia, Guinea, Mali, Upper Volta, and Ghana. Area: 322,463 sq km (124,504 sq mi). Pop (1980 est.): 8,245,000. Cap. and largest city: Abidjan (pop., 1980 est., 1,011,000). Language: French (official) and local dialects (Akan 41%, Kru 17%, Voltaic 16%, Malinke 15%, Southern Mande 10%). Religion: animist 65%; Muslim 23%; Christian 12%. President in 1980, Félix Houphouët-Boigny.

Pres. Félix Houphouët-Boigny was elected head of state for a fifth successive five-year term on Oct. 12, 1980, by 99.99% of votes cast for his sole candidacy. In the elections for the National Assembly in November, 80% of the deputies elected were new. The Democratic Party of the Ivory Coast at its congress at Abidjan in late September decided to abolish the post of secretary-general, thereby eclipsing the "crown prince," Philippe Yacé, president of the Assembly and secretary-general of the party. The membership of the party's political bureau was reduced from 70 to 32 and that of the directing committee from 201 to 100. An executive committee of nine members would assist the president, who still wielded complete power and refused to settle his succession.

Ex-emperor Bokassa and relations with France aroused concern during the year. Bokassa, ruler of the former Central African Empire, had been granted asylum in the Ivory Coast in 1979. Now his revelations (notably of his gift of diamonds to the French president) to the French satirical weekly *Le Canard Enchaîné* showed an embarrassing laxity on the part of the government of the Ivory Coast and soured its relations with France.

Ivory Coast's economy continued to expand. Among French African countries, it was a leading

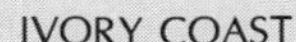

IVORY COAST

Education. (1977–78) Primary, pupils 894,184, teachers (1976–77) 17,044; secondary, pupils 144,605, teachers (1976–77) 3,423; vocational, pupils 22,437, teachers (1974–75) 620; higher, students 20,087, teaching staff (1973–74) 368.

Finance. Monetary unit: CFA franc, with (Sept. 22, 1980) a parity of CFA Fr 50 to the French franc (free rate of CFA Fr 210 = U.S. $1; CFA Fr 504 = £1 sterling). Gold, SDR's, and foreign exchange (May 1980) U.S. $20 million. Budget (1979 est.) balanced at CFA Fr 277.4 billion. Money supply (March 1980) CFA Fr 465,210,000,000. Cost of living (Abidjan; 1975 = 100; May 1980) 215.7.

Foreign Trade. (1979) Imports CFA Fr 528,850,000,000; exports CFA Fr 534,850,000,000. Import sources: France 37%; U.S. 7%; Japan 6%; West Germany 5%; Venezuela 5%. Export destinations: France 24%; The Netherlands 17%; U.S. 10%; Italy 8%; West Germany 6%. Main exports: coffee 31%; cocoa and products 28%; timber 16%.

Agriculture. Production (in 000; metric tons; 1979): rice *c.* 445; corn (1978) *c.* 325; millet *c.* 50; yams (1978) *c.* 1,700; cassava (1978) *c.* 700; peanuts *c.* 52; bananas *c.* 200; plantains (1978) *c.* 800; pineapples *c.* 315; palm kernels *c.* 32; palm oil *c.* 158; coffee *c.* 275; cocoa 312; cotton, lint *c.* 47; rubber *c.* 19; fish catch (1978) 79; timber (cu m; 1978) 10,397. Livestock (in 000; 1978): cattle *c.* 680; sheep *c.* 1,100; goats *c.* 1,150; pigs *c.* 250; poultry *c.* 10,000.

Industry. Production (in 000; metric tons; 1978): petroleum products 1,551; cement (1977) 875; cotton yarn *c.* 7; diamonds (metric carats; 1977) 41; electricity (kw-hr) 1,420,000.

Italian Literature: *see* Literature

producer of cocoa, coffee, bananas, rice, and sugar and the only one with foreign trade valued above Fr 10 billion. In March, however, a conference held at Yamoussoukro failed to establish a common front of cocoa-producing countries in preparation for negotiations in London for an international cocoa agreement. (PHILIPPE DECRAENE)

Jamaica

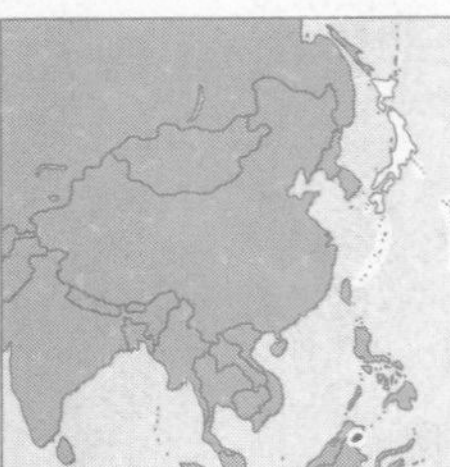
Japan

Jamaica

A parliamentary state within the Commonwealth of Nations, Jamaica is an island in the Caribbean Sea about 145 km (90 mi) S of Cuba. Area: 10,991 sq km (4,244 sq mi). Pop. (1980 est.): 2,192,000, predominantly African and Afro-European, but including European, Chinese, Afro-Chinese, East Indian, Afro-East Indian, and others. Cap. and largest city: Kingston (metro pop., 1978 est., 643,-800). Language: English. Religion: Christian, with Anglicans and Baptists in the majority. Queen, Elizabeth II; governor-general in 1980, Florizel Glasspole; prime ministers, Michael Manley and, from November 1, Edward Seaga.

Jamaicans decisively rejected the People's National Party (PNP) government led by Prime Minister Michael Manley at elections on Oct. 30, 1980. Winning by 51 seats to 9, the Jamaica Labour Party, led by Edward Seaga (*see* BIOGRAPHIES), pledged to restore the island's run-down economy by seeking assistance from the International Monetary Fund (IMF) and other Western aid donors and by creating a climate in which private enterprise could flourish.

Jamaicans rejected the PNP government because of a decline in their standard of living; a belief that the PNP government was associated with godlessness and Communism; a traditional desire to change government after two terms; and an ever increasing level of violence (at least 600 people were reported as murdered for political reasons during the first nine months of 1980). Internationally, Seaga promised a less strident foreign policy but indicated that he would not break relations with Cuba, though he demanded the recall of the Cuban ambassador.

The election was occasioned by a decision of the Manley government to break with the IMF. Unable to satisfy both the PNP and the IMF, or to meet earlier loans, Manley decided to seek funds bilaterally from nonaligned nations.

In spite of new bauxite arrangements that would bring $1 billion in investment to Jamaica over four years, unemployment stood at 31.5%. Hurricane Allen killed eight people, made 4,000 homeless, and caused $160 million in damage in August.

(DAVID A. JESSOP)

Newly elected Jamaican Prime Minister Edward Seaga was hoisted triumphantly by supporters after he defeated Michael Manley in elections held in October. Manley had served as prime minister since 1972.

UPI

JAMAICA

Education. (1976–77) Primary, pupils 367,625, teachers 9,889; secondary, pupils 220,566, teachers 9,828; vocational, pupils 5,175, teachers 340; higher, students (1978–79) 8,497, teaching staff (1973–74) 638.

Finance. Monetary unit: Jamaican dollar, with (Sept. 22, 1980) a par value of Jam$1.78 to U.S. $1 (free rate of Jam$4.29 = £1 sterling). Gold, SDR's, and foreign exchange (June 1980) U.S. $123 million. Budget (1978 actual): revenue Jam$854.1 million; expenditure Jam$1,-428,400,000.

Foreign Trade. (1979) Imports Jam$1,786,000,000; exports Jam$1,363,300,000. Import sources (1978): U.S. 37%; Venezuela 16%; U.K. 10%; Canada 6%; Netherlands Antilles 6%. Export destinations (1978): U.S. 38%; U.K. 24%; Norway 8%; Canada 8%. Main exports: alumina 49%; bauxite 19%; sugar 7%. Tourism (1978): visitors 533,-000; gross receipts U.S. $159 million.

Agriculture. Production (in 000; metric tons; 1979): sugar, raw value *c.* 273; bananas *c.* 152; oranges *c.* 19; grapefruit *c.* 19; sweet potatoes (1978) *c.* 21; yams (1978) *c.* 130; cassava (1978) *c.* 30; corn (1978) *c.* 10; copra *c.* 7. Livestock (in 000; 1978): cattle *c.* 285; goats *c.* 350; pigs *c.* 245; poultry *c.* 4,000.

Industry. Production (in 000; metric tons; 1979): bauxite 11,574; alumina (1978) 2,145; cement (1978) 298; gypsum (1978) 137; petroleum products (1978) 724; electricity (kw-hr; 1978) *c.* 2,100,000.

Japan

A constitutional monarchy in the northwestern Pacific Ocean, Japan is an archipelago composed of four major islands (Hokkaido, Honshu, Kyushu, and Shikoku), the Ryukyus (including Okinawa), and minor adjacent islands. Area: 377,643 sq km (145,809 sq mi). Pop. (1980 est.): 116,960,000. Cap. and largest city: Tokyo (pop., 1980 est., 8,179,300). Language: Japanese. Religion: primarily Shinto and Buddhist; Christian 0.8%. Emperor, Hirohito; prime ministers in 1980, Masayoshi Ohira to June 12 and, from July 17, Zenko Suzuki.

Domestic Affairs. The year 1980 saw an unexpected turnabout in the fortunes of the majority Liberal-Democratic Party (LDP), which had dominated Japanese politics in the postwar era. At the beginning of the year, as a result of the general election in October 1979, the LDP held a slim majority (258 of 511 seats) in the lower house of the Diet, the House of Representatives (it held 124 of 252 seats in the upper House of Councillors). In mid-May a nationwide survey conducted by Kyodo News Service revealed that 64% of the respondents did not support the Ohira government. Over half of those interviewed cited domestic issues, particularly concern with inflation.

On May 16 a vote of no confidence against the Ohira Cabinet, sponsored by the Japan Socialist Party (JSP), passed the lower house because 69 LDP members belonging to anti-Ohira factions absented themselves from the floor. On May 19, just seven months after the previous election, Prime Minister Masayoshi Ohira (*see* OBITUARIES) dissolved the lower house and set a general election to coincide with the triennial poll for the House of Councillors. Campaigning for the first such joint election in Japan's history officially got under way on May 30, but without the LDP leader. On May 31 Ohira was hospitalized for extreme fatigue and on June 12 the prime minister died, the victim of a heart attack. Chief Cabinet Secretary Masayoshi Ito became acting prime minister, and the incumbent Cabinet continued as a caretaker government until a special Diet session could be called following the June elections.

The unprecedented double election on June 22 attracted a high voter turnout (74.57%). Ohira's untimely death served to unify the LDP factions, so the LDP, alone among the major parties, increased its share of the popular vote (47.9%). This was translated into a comfortable majority of 284 seats in the lower house (two conservative independents raised the LDP's effective strength to 286). The JSP retained its 107-seat total. Remaining seats were distributed among the Komeito (33); Democratic Socialists (DSP; 32); Japan Communists (JCP; 29); minor parties and independents (24). With 69 successful candidates, the LDP increased its total in the upper house to 135 seats (JSP 47; Komeito 26; JCP 12; DSP 12; minor parties and independents 19; vacancies 1).

On July 15 a dark horse, Zenko Suzuki (*see* BIOGRAPHIES), 69, was selected to succeed Ohira as president of the LDP, and on July 17 he was elected Japan's 15th postwar prime minister in a special session of the Diet. A skilled mediator, Suzuki set about unifying rival LDP factions. For his Cabinet he selected powerful LDP faction leaders—Yasuhiro Nakasone (Administrative Management Agency), Toshio Komoto (Economic Planning Agency), and Masayoshi Ito (foreign affairs)—as well as younger, reformist party members. The latter included Michio Watanabe (finance), Rokusuke Tanaka (international trade and industry), and Kiichi Miyazawa (chief cabinet secretary).

Suzuki inherited a series of unfolding scandals. In October 1979 personnel of the Kokusai Denshin Denwa (KDD), Japan's privately owned overseas telecommunications service, had been caught in the act of smuggling expensive accessories while going through customs at the New Tokyo International Airport at Narita. Early in 1980 two KDD employees committed suicide and left notes stating that they had been made scapegoats by Yoichi Sato, former head of the KDD president's office. Sato was arrested on February 24 and was charged with embezzling 15 million yen from the KDD to buy influence from Diet members and to impress foreign customers. A former official and a serving section chief of the Ministry of Posts and Telecommunications were arrested on March 18 on bribery charges. On April 5 the Tokyo Metropolitan Police Department arrested Manabu Itano, former president of the KDD, who had resigned in November 1979, and charged him with misappropriation of 17 million yen from expense accounts. The KDD case dragged on through the courts for the remainder of the year.

Meanwhile, on September 19, Health and Welfare Minister Kunikichi Saito resigned "to take political and moral responsibility" for receiving some 13 million yen in political donations from a hospital director under fire for alleged malpractice. Suzuki named a former foreign minister, Sunao Sonoda, to succeed Saito.

As the public opinion polls revealed, the major economic problem faced by the Suzuki government was inflation. In February wholesale prices rose 2.6%, the sharpest month-to-month increase since the oil crisis of 1973–74. A central bank official stated that the price situation had reached "crisis proportions." On February 19 the Bank of Japan raised the official discount rate by a full percentage point to 7.25% per year. Nonetheless, the nationwide consumer price index (CPI) stood at 134.4 (1975 = 100) in March, 8% higher than a year earlier. In August the Tokyo CPI declined 0.2% from its July peak, but it still stood at 138.4.

In late January the government had submitted to the Diet a budget for fiscal 1980 (April 1, 1980–March 31, 1981). It called for outlays of 42,589,000,000,000 yen in the general account, up 10.3% over 1979 but the smallest increase in expenditures in 21 years. A revenue shortfall of 14,270,000,000,000 yen was to be covered by sale of bonds. In September Economic Planning chief Komoto announced that the target for economic growth in fiscal 1981 would be 5.5%. Japan's gross national product (GNP) for fiscal 1979–80 was running at a level of 224,800,000,000,000 yen.

Recession was not evenly felt throughout Japanese industry. In July the nation's automobile production reached an all-time monthly high of 1,039,770 units. Of particular significance for Japanese-U.S. trade, Toyota Motor Sales reported

ULYSSE GOSSET—SYGMA

On June 12 Japanese Prime Minister Masayoshi Ohira died following a heart attack. Representatives of 112 nations attended his funeral ceremony at the Budokan Hall in Tokyo on July 9.

Jai Alai:
see Court Games

WIDE WORLD

Zenko Suzuki, president of the Liberal-Democratic Party, was named the new prime minister of Japan after a vote in the Diet on July 17.

3,130,392 cars sold in fiscal 1979, including 1,502,491 exported (an increase of 19.8%). Honda Motor Co. reported its consolidated net sales for the year ended March 31 at 1,307,700,000,000 yen.

On May 7 the Defense Agency disclosed details of a controversial plan for procuring modern weapons systems. The agency envisaged increasing the annual defense budget from the current 0.9% of GNP to a full 1%, at a cost of about U.S. $6.5 billion between fiscal 1980 and 1984. In remarks before the Diet, Justice Minister Seisuke Okuno supported revision of the constitution, in apparent reference to the celebrated art. 9, which renounces war. Opposition parties, labour unions, and citizens' groups criticized Okuno, and on September 3 Secretary-General Yoshio Sakurauchi of the LDP said Okuno had expressed a personal opinion and had "gone to extremes as a state minister." Thus, although public opinion increasingly favoured enlarging Japan's Self-Defense Forces (SDF), the defense issue remained a delicate one.

Foreign Affairs. Sharp increases in the price of imported crude oil led to a record $13.9 billion balance of payments deficit on current account for fiscal 1979 (ended March 31, 1980). This represented a deterioration of $25.7 billion from the $11.8 billion surplus in fiscal 1978. As a result, the U.S. dollar soared to a 30-month high in Tokyo on April 1 (253.65 yen = U.S. $1), and Japan's foreign exchange reserves fell below $20 billion at the end of March. (Later, in July, the balance of payments returned to the black.)

Strident demands by Americans that Japan reduce its exports of automobiles to the U.S. obscured Japan's softening balance of payments position. On February 13 in Tokyo, Douglas Fraser, president of the United Auto Workers, urged Japan to restrict exports under an orderly marketing agreement. "You have to entertain a sense of urgency about this problem," Fraser said. "The impact of the tremendous flow of cars to the U.S. is having serious consequences on the American economy and employment of auto workers." Fraser told Ohira that he wanted to avoid import quotas. Honda decided in January to build an assembly plant in Ohio that would produce 10,000 cars a month. Toyota Motor Co. commissioned two U.S. institutes and a Japanese group to study the possibility of building assembly facilities in the U.S., and Nissan Motor Co. announced plans to build small trucks there. In Washington in July, Eiji Toyoda (*see* BIOGRAPHIES), president of Toyota, stated that his firm envisaged a joint venture with Ford for co-production of 20,000 small cars a month in the U.S. On August 21 Tokyo asked Washington to postpone or reduce import tariffs on Japanese truck cab-chassis units. Foreign Minister Ito, in Washington on September 19, assured

JAPAN

Education. (1979–80) Primary, pupils 11,629,121, teachers 459,553; secondary and vocational, pupils 9,498,087, teachers 487,467; higher, students 2,220,364, teaching staff 207,199.

Finance. Monetary unit: yen, with (Sept. 22, 1980) a free rate of 215 yen to U.S. $1 (516 yen = £1 sterling). Gold, SDR's, and foreign exchange (June 1980) U.S. $23.1 billion. Budget (1979–80 est.) balanced at 38,600,000,000,000 yen. Gross national product (1979) 221,583,000,000,000 yen. Money supply (June 1980) 68,130,000,000,000 yen. Cost of living (1975 = 100; June 1980) 137.8.

Foreign Trade. (1979) Imports 24,245,000,000,000 yen; exports 22,532,000,000,000 yen. Import sources: U.S. 18%; Saudi Arabia 11%; Indonesia 8%; Australia 6%; Iran 5%. Export destinations: U.S. 26%; South Korea 6%. Main exports: machinery 27% (telecommunications apparatus 5%); motor vehicles 22%; iron and steel 16%; chemicals 8%; instruments 8%; textiles 5%.

Transport and Communications. Roads (1979) 1,106,161 km (including 2,430 km expressways). Motor vehicles in use (1979): passenger 22,667,300; commercial 13,325,800. Railways (1979): 26,849 km; traffic 299,593,000,000 passenger-km, freight 43,140,000,000 net ton-km. Air traffic (1979): 29,278,000,000 passenger-km; freight 1,569,000,000 net ton-km. Shipping (1979): merchant vessels 100 gross tons and over 9,981; gross tonnage 39,992,925. Telephones (1978) 50,625,600. Radio receivers (1977) 64,979,000. Television licenses (1978) 28,394,000.

Agriculture. Production (in 000; metric tons; 1979): rice *c.* 15,600; wheat *c.* 440; barley *c.* 375; potatoes *c.* 3,400; sweet potatoes (1978) *c.* 1,400; sugar, raw value *c.* 700; onions *c.* 1,120; tomatoes *c.* 960; cabbages (1978) *c.* 3,985; cucumbers (1978) *c.* 1,100; aubergines (1978) *c.* 675; watermelons (1978) *c.* 1,223; apples *c.* 840; pears (1978) 557; oranges *c.* 370; mandarin oranges and tangerines *c.* 3,500; grapes *c.* 350; tea *c.* 106; tobacco *c.* 169; milk *c.* 6,450; eggs *c.* 1,990; pork *c.* 1,400; timber (cu m; 1978) 32,659; fish catch (1978) 10,752. Livestock (in 000; Feb. 1979): cattle *c.* 4,120; sheep *c.* 11; pigs *c.* 9,491; goats *c.* 80; chickens *c.* 306,820.

Industry. Index of production (1975 = 100; 1979) 133. Fuel and power (in 000; metric tons; 1979): coal 17,644; crude oil 483; natural gas (cu m) 2,690,000; manufactured gas (cu m) 7,240,000; electricity (kwhr; 1978–79) 500,870,000. Production (in 000; metric tons; 1979): iron ore (54% metal content) 459; pig iron 85,830; crude steel 111,748; aluminum 1,010; copper 984; petroleum products *c.* 217,700; cement 87,803; cotton yarn 508; woven cotton fabrics (sq m) 2,340,000; newsprint 2,565; man-made fibres 1,850; sulfuric acid 6,581; caustic soda 3,021; plastics and resins 6,964; fertilizers (nutrient content; 1978–79) nitrogenous 1,457, phosphate 707; cameras (35 mm; units) 10,194; wristwatches (units) 59,575; radio receivers (units) 13,910; television receivers (units) 13,577; passenger cars (units) 6,176; commercial vehicles (units) 3,470; motorcycles (units) 4,476. Merchant vessels launched (100 gross tons and over; 1979) 4,249,000 gross tons.

U.S. congressional leaders that Japan's auto exports were likely to fall off in the last quarter of the year.

Meanwhile, the dialogue between Tokyo and Washington was concerned with longer-range issues. In Tokyo in July for Ohira's official funeral, U.S. Pres. Jimmy Carter told Japanese media that the thing to remember was not the trade problem but "the resolution we have to resolve problems working together." On January 14 U.S. Defense Secretary Harold Brown, stopping in Tokyo on his way home from China, had expressed the hope that Japan would increase its defense expenditures, taking into account the current international situation. In Washington on May 1, Ohira had assured Carter of Japan's cooperation in solving the problem of the U.S. hostages being held in Iran and the issue of the Soviet presence in Afghanistan. In a May 11 report to the Diet on his trip to North America and Europe, Ohira called on Iran and the U.S.S.R. to solve the hostage and Afghan crises peacefully.

President Carter used his trip to Tokyo to meet with Chinese Premier Hua Guofeng (Hua Kuofeng). In a rather pointed statement, President Carter called for sharing by the U.S., China, and Japan of "long-range strategic concerns to minimize the threat of a Soviet military buildup."

Tokyo watched the U.S. presidential campaign closely in an effort to estimate its effects on Asia. In August George Bush, the Republican vice-presidential candidate, visited Tokyo, where he told Prime Minister Suzuki that a Republican administration would continue to recognize the importance of U.S.–Japanese relations. Later in the month, former U.S. president Gerald Ford, in Tokyo to mark the 20th anniversary of the conclusion of the revised U.S.–Japan security treaty, reassured the Japanese press that Ronald Reagan, if elected president, would support existing relations between the U.S. and China. Some of Reagan's campaign rhetoric had led Beijing (Peking) to think otherwise.

Meanwhile, Beijing was being represented in Tokyo on the highest level. In late May Premier Hua had visited Japan and had tacitly concurred with Ohira's comment that Japan should increase its defense expenditures, following national consensus and taking financial difficulties into consideration. In the presence of the two prime ministers, Foreign Minister Saburo Okita and his Chinese counterpart, Huang Hua, signed a Sino-Japanese scientific and technological treaty. On June 1, at the conclusion of his state visit, Hua lashed out at comments in the U.S.S.R. that his stay was "an attempt to heighten anti-Soviet tendencies in Tokyo's policy." In Tokyo again for the Ohira funeral, Hua stated that the Chinese would remember forever Ohira's efforts to strengthen bilateral friendship. Hua added that his nation would continue its efforts to promote closer relations among Japan, the U.S., the nations of Western Europe, and the third world.

In his annual policy speech to the Diet on January 25, Ohira set the tone for Japanese-Soviet relations during the year. He condemned the Soviet invasion of Afghanistan and stated that Japan would press for immediate withdrawal. On February 19 Chairman Kenji Miyamoto of the JCP admitted that when he had talked with Soviet Pres. Leonid Brezhnev in Moscow the previous December, he had received no hint of the imminent incursion into Afghanistan. Although Miyamoto condemned the Socialists for joining "conservative forces" on the issue, he did say that Soviet troops should be withdrawn. Under government pressure, Katsuji Shibata, president of Japan's Olympic Committee, announced on May 24 "with a heavy heart" that his group had voted to boycott the Summer Games in Moscow because of the Afghanistan situation. Returning from the Venice (Italy) summit meeting of advanced industrial powers in June, Okita reported that leaders of the seven nations involved had agreed on a condemnation of the Soviet intervention.

In his January policy speech, Ohira had labeled as "an extremely regrettable situation" the Soviet military buildup on the southernmost of the Kuril Islands, northeast of Hokkaido, which were claimed by Japan. Later, a White Paper on defense listed Moscow's deployment of medium-range SS-20 missiles and Backfire bombers in the region and tanks, heavy artillery, and troops on Shikotan in the Kurils, with these forces reinforced by the Soviet Pacific Fleet. The paper admitted that Japan's SDF was inadequate to meet the threat. On September 16, in an address to the UN General Assembly, Foreign Minister Ito called on the U.S.S.R. to return Japan's "northern territories."

The quarrel between Tokyo and Moscow had been further exacerbated by the indictment, on February 8, of retired SDF Gen. Yukihisa Miyanaga and two serving officers in an espionage case. The Tokyo public prosecutor charged the trio with passing military intelligence concerning China to Col. Yuri Kozlov of the Soviet embassy. Both the army chief of staff and the director general of the SDF lost their posts over the incident.

On September 17 Foreign Minister Ito warned the new South Korean regime of Pres. Chun Doo Hwan in Seoul that Japan's policy toward his country might be changed because of the death sentence handed down against former opposition leader Kim Dae Jung. Numerous Japanese groups expressed deep concern over the fate of Kim, who had been kidnapped from a Tokyo hotel in 1973 by the South Korean government.

(ARDATH W. BURKS)

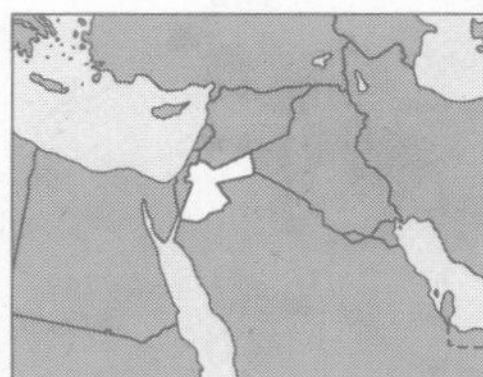
Jordan

Jordan

A constitutional monarchy in southwest Asia, Jordan is bounded by Syria, Iraq, Saudi Arabia, and Israel. Area (including territory occupied by Israel in the June 1967 war): 95,396 sq km (36,833 sq mi). Pop. (excluding Israeli-occupied West Bank, 1979 prelim.): 2,152,300. Cap. and largest city: Amman (pop., 1979 prelim., 684,600). Language: Arabic. Religion (1973 est.): Muslim 95%; Christian 5%. King, Hussein I; prime ministers in 1980, Sharif Abdul Hamid Sharaf to July 3, Qassim ar-Rimawi, and, from August 28, Mudar Badran.

Jordan surprised political observers in 1980 by its staunch support during the Iran-Iraq war for

Japanese Literature: see Literature

Jazz: see Music

Jehovah's Witnesses: see Religion

Jewish Literature: see Literature

Iraqi Pres. Saddam Hussein at-Takriti. King Hussein said on October 5 that military support for Iraq was possible, although an immediate U.S. reaction warning him against taking military action appeared to rule this out. However, the use of Aqaba as a supply route for war materials to Iraq appeared to have been amply proved by Western newsmen.

During 1980 three men acted as prime minister. The death of Sharif Abdul Hamid Sharaf on July 3 was a blow to the king. He was succeeded as caretaker by Qassim ar-Rimawi, a Palestinian and formerly deputy prime minister and agriculture minister. Hussein decided in August to reappoint Mudar Badran, the longest serving prime minister in Jordan's modern history, possibly because he felt a non-Palestinian could help heal a widening breach with Syria produced by Jordan's friendship with Iraq and by Syria's accusations that Jordan was assisting the opposition Muslim Brotherhood in Damascus and other centres. In November Syria boycotted an Arab League meeting in Amman and massed troops on the Jordanian border. Jordan responded by sending its own troops to the border area, but after a tense period the confrontation ended when Syria and then Jordan pulled back their forces. (*See also* SYRIA.)

Hussein's tough mandate to Badran was to end Israel's occupation of Arab territory, including Jerusalem. His Cabinet also included a new ministry (replacing a government bureau)—Occupied Territories Affairs. The royal mandate also stated that Jordan should encourage the European Economic Community to develop a Middle East policy based on "high principles, right, and justice."

The economy was handicapped by huge capital expenditure on major projects such as the Dead Sea potash works and the Aqaba phosphate fertilizer factory, but within five to six years the revenues from such investment might help to close the trade gap. In 1979 exports were a record 120.9 million Jordanian dinars, equivalent to U.S. $404.3 million, but imports were 585.6 million dinars, equivalent then to $1,554,800,000. Crude oil imports from Saudi Arabia made up 11% of the total import bill. Jordan offered in addition to its capital goods needs a small but growing market for consumer goods and manufactured items.

Meeting human needs was to be one of the main aims of the 1981–85 five-year plan, possibly at the expense of heavy industrial investment. In late 1980 government committees were still at the stage of establishing costs and listing priorities. Jordan was unlikely to lose its free-market status for foreign contractors, with the government broadly committed to a liberal policy on repatriation of profits made by foreign companies.

Jordan's relationship with the U.S. appeared to be improving in June, when King Hussein met U.S. Pres. Jimmy Carter. The U.S. administration appeared to have at last accepted Jordan's fundamental opposition to the Camp David accords between Israel and Egypt. Carter apparently wanted the monarch's support for a broader peace initiative he wished to undertake provided he was reelected president. This factor appeared to be a major determinant of Jordan's relationship with the U.S.

Jordan's acceptability to Western financial markets was shown in mid-1980 by the successful syndication of a $150 million loan for the government. Alia, the Royal Jordanian Airline, raised credits for aircraft finance from both the U.S. Export-Import Bank and the U.K.'s Export Credits Guarantee Department. Inflation was 13.6% in the 12 months

JORDAN

Education. (1979–80) Primary, pupils 448,411, teachers 13,898; secondary, pupils 238,763, teachers 11,267; vocational, pupils 9,880, teachers 641; higher, students 27,526, teaching staff 1,178.

Finance. Monetary unit: Jordanian dinar, with (Sept. 22, 1980) a free rate of 0.29 dinar to U.S. $1 (0.69 dinar = £1 sterling). Gold, SDR's, and foreign exchange (June 1980) U.S. $1,245,000,000. Budget (1979 actual): revenue 377 million dinars (including foreign aid and loans of 195 million dinars); expenditure 496 million dinars. Gross national product (1979) 853.2 million dinars. Money supply (June 1980) 532,240,000 dinars. Cost of living (1975 = 100; June 1980) 172.9.

Foreign Trade. (1979) Imports 589,520,000 dinars; exports 120,920,000 dinars. Import sources: Saudi Arabia 13%; West Germany 12%; U.K. 8%; U.S. 7%; Italy 7%; Japan 6%; France 5%. Export destinations: Saudi Arabia 23%; Iraq 15%; Syria 15%; India 7%; Kuwait 5%; Turkey 5%. Main exports: phosphates 22%; vegetables 14%; fruit 8%; chemicals *c.* 7%; machinery 5%; aircraft 5%. Tourism (1978): visitors 1,184,000; gross receipts (1977) U.S. $180 million.

Transport and Communications. Roads (excluding West Bank; 1979) 5,927 km. Motor vehicles in use (1979): passenger 79,400; commercial 27,900. Railways (1978) *c.* 618 km. Air traffic (1979): 2,135,000,000 passenger-km; freight 67.7 million net ton-km. Telephones (Jan. 1978) 53,100. Radio receivers (Dec. 1977) 532,000. Television licenses (Dec. 1977) 165,000.

Agriculture. Production (in 000; metric tons; 1978): wheat *c.* 54; barley *c.* 15; tomatoes 209; aubergines *c.* 43; watermelons *c.* 20; olives 31; oranges *c.* 6; lemons *c.* 9; grapes *c.* 22. Livestock (in 000; 1978): cattle *c.* 36; goats *c.* 490; sheep *c.* 838; camels *c.* 19; asses *c.* 50; chickens *c.* 4,646.

Industry. Production (in 000; metric tons; 1977): phosphate rock 2,320; petroleum products *c.* 1,390; cement 553; electricity (kw-hr; 1977) 601,000.

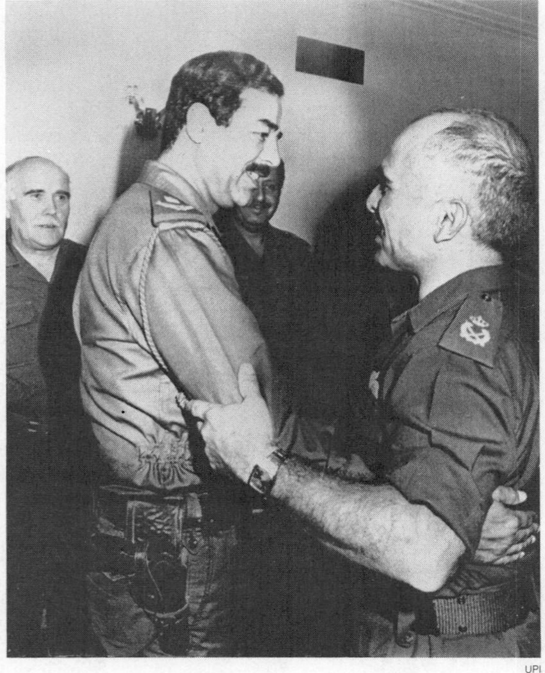

Pres. Saddam Hussein at-Takriti (left) of Iraq greeted Jordan's King Hussein on the latter's visit to Iraq in October.

UPI

ended June 1980, and the domestic economy was fairly liquid, particularly because of the continuing high level of expatriate remittances from Jordanians resident in the Persian Gulf area. The relationship with Iraq produced a gift of $100 million in August for "development and programs to build national strength." (JOHN WHELAN)

See also Middle Eastern Affairs.

Kenya

An African republic and a member of the Commonwealth of Nations, Kenya is bordered on the north by Sudan and Ethiopia, east by Somalia, south by Tanzania, and west by Uganda. Area: 580,367 sq km (224,081 sq mi), including 11,230 sq km of inland water. Pop. (1979 prelim.): 15,322,000, including (1969) African 98.1%; Asian 1.5%. Cap. and largest city: Nairobi (pop., 1979 prelim., 835,000). Language: Swahili (official) and English. Religion: Protestant 32.6%; Roman Catholic 17.4%; Muslim 24%; other, mostly indigenous, 26%. President in 1980, Daniel arap Moi.

With disagreements over division of the assets of the East African Community still unresolved, nothing of consequence emerged from the meeting of East African heads of state attended by Pres. Daniel arap Moi in Arusha, Tanzania, on Jan. 2, 1980. Recurrent hopes that a solution might be found to the dispute between Kenya and Tanzania that had led to the closing of the frontier between the two countries also proved vain. Visits by President Moi to West Germany, Britain, and the U.S. in February had a happier outcome in the form of offers of food aid and help with the country's balance of payments. On the debit side were restraints on industrial output resulting from cuts in the electricity supply during February and March, made necessary by the exceptionally low rainfall.

In March Pres. Godfrey L. Binaisa of Uganda visited Kenya, raising speculation that disillusionment with Tanzania's continuing role in Uganda might lead to some rapprochement between Uganda and Kenya. Binaisa's overthrow in May put an end to such ideas, and in September, following a border incursion, Kenya stopped rail and road movement of Uganda's coffee. A meeting of the foreign ministers of Kenya and Ethiopia in Mombasa in April led to an agreement between the two countries to monitor Somali military activities on their respective borders. During a visit in August, the French deputy foreign minister, Olivier Stirn, gave an assurance of French assistance in the event of any aggression on the part of Somalia.

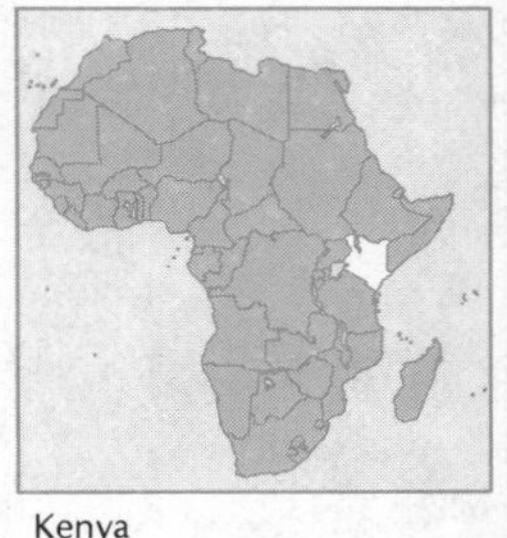

Kenya

Pope John Paul II visited Kenya in May during his tour of the African continent. Also in May, ministers of the African, Caribbean, and Pacific countries met ministers of the European Economic Community (EEC) in Nairobi. Kenya was among a number of countries pressing for restoration of their sugar quotas, since Kenya's own output of sugar was now showing a hopeful surplus.

In his budget speech in June, the minister for finance, Vice-Pres. Mwai Kibaki, said there must be restraints on public spending, but he also announced increased incentives for exporters. (In May the president had urged Kenyans to work harder to increase production and warned that stern action would be taken against illegal strikers.) At the same time, minimum wages were to be raised substantially for the first time since 1977.

In spite of help from the U.S., basic foods remained in short supply. Special famine relief arrangements were made to assist the people of the northwest, which had been severely affected by drought and by the unrest along the Uganda-Kenya border. Supplies of food from the EEC helped to reduce the sufferings of these people, but the July rains came too late to enable them to take full advantage of the season for planting crops. Meanwhile, the price of petroleum products soared. The president's visit to several Middle Eastern countries produced no tangible help.

In June President Moi made changes in his Cabinet, the most significant being the appointment of Charles Njonjo, one of the most influential men in the country, to the new Ministry of Home and

CAMERAPIX/KEYSTONE

Pres. Julius Nyerere (hands together) of Tanzania and Pres. Daniel arap Moi of Kenya (centre) were entertained by native dancers in January when Nyerere visited Kenya to attend a meeting of East African heads of state.

Journalism:
see Publishing

Judaism:
see Religion

Judo:
see Combat Sports

Kampuchea:
see Cambodia

Karate:
see Combat Sports

Kashmir:
see India; Pakistan

Kendo:
see Combat Sports

KENYA

Education. (1978) Primary, pupils 2,977,000, teachers (1977) 89,773; secondary and vocational, pupils 368,000, teachers (1977) 12,696; teacher training, students 9,000, teachers (1977) 672; higher, students 5,000, teachers (1977) 892.

Finance. Monetary unit: Kenyan shilling, with (Sept. 22, 1980) a free rate of KShs 7.25 to U.S. $1 (KShs 17.42 = £1 sterling). Gold, SDR's, and foreign exchange (June 1980) U.S. $580 million. Budget (1978–79 actual): revenue KShs 10,376,000,000; expenditure KShs 12,954,000,000. Gross national product (1979) KShs 43,887,000,000. Cost of living (Nairobi; 1975 = 100; June 1980) 183.5.

Foreign Trade. (1979) Imports KShs 12,227,000,000; exports KShs 8,256,000,000. Import sources: U.K. 23%; West Germany 11%; Saudi Arabia 8%; Japan 8%; U.S. 6%; Qatar 5%. Export destinations: West Germany 15%; U.K. 14%; Uganda 9%; aircraft and ship stores 8%; Italy 6%. Main exports: coffee 29%; petroleum products 20%; tea 16%; fruit and vegetables 6%; chemicals 5%. Tourism (1978): visitors 360,620; gross receipts U.S. $158 million.

Transport and Communications. Roads (1979) 51,368 km. Motor vehicles in use (1978): passenger 191,989; commercial (including buses) 34,200. Railways: (1978) 2,038 km; freight traffic (1977) 3,538,000,000 net ton-km. Air traffic (1978): 884 million passenger-km; freight *c.* 25 million ton-km. Telephones (Jan. 1978) 143,800. Radio receivers (Dec. 1977) 525,000. Television receivers (Dec. 1977) 60,000.

Agriculture. Production (in 000; metric tons; 1979): corn *c.* 1,800; wheat 108; millet *c.* 110; potatoes *c.* 360; sweet potatoes (1978) *c.* 330; cassava (1978) *c.* 620; sugar, raw value (1978) *c.* 203; bananas *c.* 130; coffee *c.* 75; tea *c.* 99; sisal *c.* 36; cotton, lint *c.* 11; fish catch (1978) 43. Livestock (in 000; 1978): cattle *c.* 9,960; sheep *c.* 3,980; pigs *c.* 65; goats 4,415; camels *c.* 574; chickens *c.* 17,100.

Industry. Production (in 000; metric tons; 1977): cement 1,144; soda ash (1976) 102; petroleum products (1978) *c.* 2,800; electricity (kw-hr) *c.* 1,120,000.

Constitutional Affairs. In April Njonjo had retired from the office of attorney general, which he had held with considerable effect since Kenya's independence in 1963, and almost immediately afterward he had been returned unopposed to Parliament. There was speculation about the significance of the change, but Njonjo insisted that his retirement as attorney general was the natural outcome of his having reached the age of 60.

In August one of China's vice-premiers, Ji Pengfei (Chi P'eng-fei), visited Nairobi. President Moi visited Beijing (Peking) in September.

(KENNETH INGHAM)

Kiribati

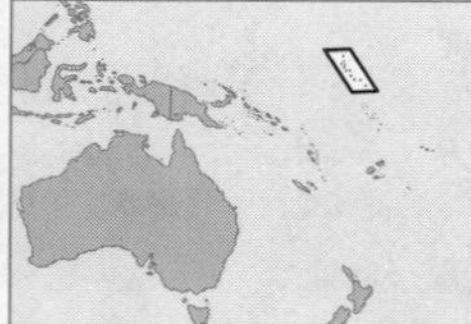

Kiribati

An independent republic in the western Pacific Ocean and member of the Commonwealth of Nations, Kiribati comprises the former Gilbert Islands, Ocean Island (Banaba), the Line Islands, and the Phoenix Islands. Area: 713 sq km (275 sq mi). Pop. (1979 est.): 56,000, including Micronesian 91%, Polynesian 4%, other indigenous 4%, others 1%. Cap.: Bairiki (pop., 1973, 1,800) on Tarawa atoll (pop., 1973, 17,100). Language: English (official). Religion (1973): Roman Catholic 48%; Protestant 45%. President (*beriti-tenti*) in 1980, Ieremia Tabai.

In 1980 Kiribati first felt the full effects of the cessation of phosphate mining at Banaba, where machinery was nevertheless maintained pending a redevelopment survey. Revenue from fishing agreements and from the sale of Christmas Island fish to Nauru and lobsters to Hawaii could not offset the loss of phosphate revenue and the depressed copra prices, and British aid was needed to balance the budget.

KIRIBATI

Education. (1978) Primary, pupils 13,481, teachers 429; secondary, pupils 1,357, teachers 92; vocational, pupils 1,176, teachers (1977) 28; teacher training, students (1979) 114, teachers (1978) 15.

Finance and Trade. Monetary unit: Australian dollar, with (Sept. 22, 1980) a free rate of A$0.86 to U.S. $1 (A$2.06 = £1 sterling). Budget (1977 est): revenue A$11,-771,000; expenditure A$9,724,000. Foreign trade (including Tuvalu; 1978): imports A$14,115,000; exports: A$21,396,000. Import sources: Australia 58%; U.K. 8%; New Zealand 8%; Japan 7%; U.S. 6%. Export destinations (1977): Australia 57%; New Zealand 29%, U.K. 13%. Main exports: phosphates 88%; copra 12%.

Industry. Production (in 000; 1977): phosphate rock (metric tons) 425; electricity (kw-hr) *c.* 5,000.

The multimillion-dollar project to build a causeway between Betio and Bairiki on South Tarawa was halted by engineering and financial problems; the matter was taken to court. In midyear government workers struck over back pay and pensions.

In July, on the first anniversary of its independence, Kiribati was host to the South Pacific Forum, which admitted Vanuatu (formerly New Hebrides) to membership and called upon Britain and France to quell the secessionist threat to that country's independence. The Forum agreed on the South Pacific Regional Trade and Cooperation Agreement, which would allow unrestricted and nonreciprocal access to Australian and New Zealand markets for many island products, and condemned U.S. plans to deposit nuclear wastes in the Pacific Ocean. (BARRIE MACDONALD)

Korea

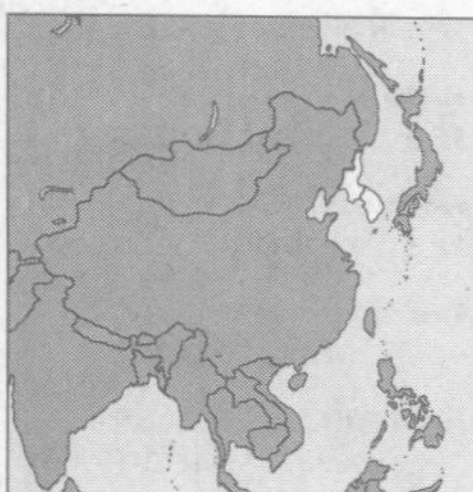

Korea

A country of eastern Asia, Korea is bounded by China, the Sea of Japan, the Korea Strait, and the Yellow Sea. It is divided into two parts roughly at the 38th parallel.

For both Koreas 1980 was a year of big changes at the top. The military took over South Korea again, while preparations seemed complete in North Korea to transfer power from father to son. Relations between the two halves hit a new low in September when the North suspended reunification talks in Panmunjom and cut off its hot-line telephone links with the South. North Korea called new southern boss Chun Doo Hwan (*see* BIOGRAPHIES) "more vicious than the late Park Chung Hee." Calls from the South for a resumption of talks went unheeded. Nor was there any response to a proposal by South Korea that the prime ministers of the two countries meet in November. There were reports, however, that the North could agree to a meeting as part of its drive to strengthen the image of Kim Il Sung's son as its future leader.

Republic of Korea (South Korea). Area: 98,966 sq km (38,211 sq mi). Pop. (1980 est.): 38,197,000. Cap. and largest city: Seoul (pop., 1979 est., 8,114,-000). Language: Korean. Religion (1978): Buddhist 47.2%; Christian 17.6%; Confucian 13.1%; Tonghak (Chondokyo) 2.3%; other 19.8%. Presidents in 1980, Choi Kyu Hah, Park Choong Hoon (acting) from August 16, and, from August 27, Chun Doo Hwan; prime ministers, Shin Hyon Hwak until May 20, Park Choong Hoon (acting) from May 21, and, from September 2, Nam Duck Woo.

South Korea opened the year with a promise of liberalization; Pres. Choi Kyu Hah announced an amnesty to restore the civil rights of 687 former opponents of the assassinated president Gen. Park Chung Hee. The move generated considerable enthusiasm among politicians and new hopes among students. As the two groups turned to political activism, however, the mood changed—and the country slipped swiftly into stern military rule as before.

The process began in March with student unrest in Seoul; activists expelled by the late Park's regime and readmitted by Choi's agitated for the removal of Park's soldiers from the universities. The agitation expanded to include demands for political reform. By May major disturbances engulfed several universities despite the closing by the Martial Law Command of the National Assembly and the headquarters of both major political parties.

What was widely described as an armed rebellion developed in Kwangju, approximately 266 km (165 mi) south of Seoul. Armed students and other rioters captured the city, gutted one radio and television station, occupied government buildings, and demanded an end to martial law. Troops laid siege to the city and eventually mounted a full-scale military assault to beat the protesters into submission on May 27. According to official estimates 144 civilians were killed along with 22 soldiers and 4 policemen. Some 800 rebels were arrested, while at least 200 armed students escaped. Damage from the Kwangju uprising was estimated at U.S. $45 million.

The protest demonstrations proved counterproductive. Even before the climactic eruption of violence in Kwangju, the military had decided to do away with the civilian trappings of government. After an emergency Cabinet session on May 17, the military took control of the country, extending martial law, banning all political activity, and closing all universities and colleges. On May 20 President Choi's Cabinet, headed by Premier Shin Hyon Hwak, resigned.

Already political power had passed to the standing committee of the Special Committee for National Security Measures. Military officers were in the majority of those appointed to the standing committee, headed by strong man Lieut. Gen. Chun Doo Hwan. On August 27, a few days after he announced his formal retirement from the Army, Chun was elected president of South Korea with 2,524 of the 2,525 electoral college votes cast. One vote was invalid. There was no other candidate.

At his inaugural ceremony on September 1, Chun said that a new constitution and a new government on the basis of free elections would be installed in the first half of 1981. Although he defined his goal as a "democratic welfare state," he noted that democracy was not indigenous to Korea. In general, Chun was expected to follow nationalistic policies such as the "koreanization" of society and a move away from Western value systems.

On May 21 the president appointed a Cabinet headed by Prime Minister Park Choong Hoon, to be replaced by Nam Duck Woo and a 20-member Cabinet on September 2. But real power remained with an "inner circle" of close advisers, all generals. The president said there would be no place for "professional politicians" in the new Korea.

As if to ensure that, all influential political figures quickly came under pressure. A "purification" drive was launched against "corruptors of power" and "social agitators," among them several leading members of the former Park regime. One of them, Democratic Republican Party boss Kim Jong Pil, retired from public life after handing over to the government $36 million worth of corruptly earned assets to avoid prosecution.

The most celebrated case concerned the country's best-known opposition figure, Kim Dae Jung. He was arrested as the student demonstrations swept into the Kwangju region, his birthplace and stronghold. He was put on trial on charges of incit-

FRANÇOIS LOCHON—GAMMA/LIAISON

Students protested against the continuation of martial law in Kwangju, South Korea. Rioting citizens filled the streets for ten days until, on May 27, the Army attacked to regain control of the city.

UPI

Pres. Chun Doo Hwan gave the oath of office to members of his new Cabinet on September 3. Key positions were retained by military men close to the president.

ing students and of collaboration with Communists. On September 17, after a 29-day trial, a military court found him guilty of antistate activities and sentenced him to death by hanging. The verdict triggered a worldwide uproar. Japan in particular publicly put pressure on the Chun government to avert an execution; at one point, it threatened to cut off economic relations that were crucial to South Korea. Seoul objected strongly to the pressure tactics, maintaining that due process of the country's laws would be carried out. By the year's end there was no indication as to whether or not Kim would be hanged.

At the end of September the president released a draft constitution to replace the existing Park-devised Yushin (Revitalizing) Constitution. He also called for new elections for president and Parliament before June 30, 1981. The new constitution reduced the powers of the president in favour of Parliament and limited him to a single seven-year term. On October 22 the nation's voters overwhelmingly approved the draft constitution in a referendum. Five days later the government officially promulgated the document, thereby ushering in the Fifth Republic.

The year's political upheaval cast a shadow on the economy, with trade losses pointing to a current account deficit of $5,560,000,000 for 1980, as against the previous year's $4 billion. The government estimated that the country would need $7 billion in foreign capital annually for the next two years. In September it announced a budget for 1981

KOREA: Republic

Education. (1980) Primary, pupils 5,658,002, teachers 119,064; secondary, pupils 3,404,602, teachers 82,338; vocational, students 764,187, teachers 23,468; higher, students 539,601, teaching staff 20,510.

Finance. Monetary unit: won, with (Sept. 22, 1980) a free rate of 601 won to U.S. $1 (1,445 won = £1 sterling). Gold, SDR's, and foreign exchange (May 1980) U.S. $5,553,000,000. Budget (1979 actual): revenue 6,242,100,000,000 won; expenditure 5,933,600,000,000 won. Gross national product (1979) 29,554,000,000,000 won. Money supply (June 1980) 2,960,000,000,000 won. Cost of living (1975 = 100; June 1980) 219.8.

Foreign Trade. (1979) Imports 9,844,100,000,000 won; exports 7,286,600,000,000 won. Import sources: Japan 33%; U.S. 23%; Saudi Arabia 8%; Kuwait 6%. Export destinations: U.S. 29%; Japan 22%; West Germany 6%; Saudi Arabia 5%. Main exports (1978): clothing 20%; textile yarns and fabrics 12%; electrical machinery and equipment 10%; ships 6%; footwear 5%; fish 5%; iron and steel 5%. Tourism (1978): visitors 1,079,000; gross receipts U.S. $408 million.

Transport and Communications. Roads (1977) 45,663 km (including 1,224 km expressways). Motor vehicles in use (1978): passenger 184,900; commercial 162,000. Railways (1979): 5,788 km; traffic *c.* 21,500,000,000 passenger-km, freight 10,840,000,000 net ton-km. Air traffic (1978): 6,838,000,000 passenger-km; freight 503 million net ton-km. Shipping (1979): merchant vessels 100 gross tons and over 1,287; gross tonnage 3,952,946. Telephones (Jan. 1978) 1,978,400. Radio receivers (Dec. 1977) 14,574,000. Television receivers (Dec. 1978) 5,133,000.

Agriculture. Production (in 000; metric tons; 1979): rice 8,051; barley 1,508; potatoes 356; sweet potatoes (1978) *c.* 1,621; soybeans 257; cabbages (1978) *c.* 977; watermelons (1978) *c.* 192; onions 393; apples 444; oranges *c.* 108; tobacco 123; fish catch (1978) 2,351. Livestock (in 000; Dec. 1978): cattle 1,624; pigs 1,719; goats 244; chickens 40,753.

Industry. Production (in 000; metric tons; 1979): coal 18,209; iron ore (56% metal content) 458; pig iron 5,174; crude steel 5,200; cement 16,429; tungsten concentrates (oxide content; 1978) 3.3; zinc concentrates 62; gold (troy oz; 1978) 26; silver (troy oz; 1978) 2,070; sulfuric acid 1,645; fertilizers (nutrient content; 1978–79) nitrogenous 751, phosphate 389; petroleum products *c.* 25,900; man-made fibres (1978) 467; electricity (excluding most industrial production; kw-hr) 35,601,000; radio receivers (units; 1978) 4,768; television receivers (units; 1978) 4,826. Merchant vessels launched (100 gross tons and over; 1979) 441,000.

KOREA: People's Democratic Republic

Education. (1976–77) Primary, pupils 2,561,674; secondary and vocational, pupils *c.* 2 million; primary, secondary, and vocational, teachers *c.* 100,000; higher, students *c.* 100,000.

Finance and Trade. Monetary unit: won, with (Sept. 22, 1980) a nominal exchange rate of 0.86 won to U.S. $1 (2.06 won = £1 sterling). Budget (1979 est.) balanced at 17,301,000,000 won. Foreign trade (approximate; 1979): imports *c.* 1.8 billion won; exports *c.* 1.9 billion won. Import sources: China *c.* 40%; U.S.S.R. *c.* 20%; Japan *c.* 17%. Export destinations: China *c.* 30%; Saudia Arabia *c.* 21%; U.S.S.R. *c.* 21%; Japan *c.* 7%. Main exports (1975): lead and ore *c.* 30%; zinc and ore *c.* 20%; magnesite *c.* 15%; rice *c.* 6%; cement *c.* 5%; coal *c.* 5%; fish *c.* 5%.

Agriculture. Production (in 000; metric tons; 1979): rice *c.* 4,800; corn *c.* 1,950; barley *c.* 380; millet *c.* 440; potatoes *c.* 1,500; sweet potatoes (1978) *c.* 365; soybeans *c.* 330; apples *c.* 440; tobacco *c.* 43; fish catch (1978) *c.* 1,600. Livestock (in 000; 1978): cattle *c.* 900; pigs *c.* 1,900; sheep *c.* 280; goats *c.* 220; chickens *c.* 17,750.

Industry. Production (in 000; metric tons; 1977): coal *c.* 45,100; iron ore (metal content) *c.* 3,800; pig iron *c.* 3,100; steel *c.* 3,100; lead *c.* 70; zinc *c.* 136; magnesite *c.* 1,500; silver (troy oz) *c.* 1,600; tungsten concentrates (oxide content) *c.* 2.7; cement *c.* 7,000; electricity (kw-hr; 1973) *c.* 20,000,000.

totaling $12.2 billion, up 29.9% from 1980. The gross national product was projected to increase by 5.5% in 1981.

Democratic People's Republic of Korea (North Korea). Area: 121,929 sq km (47,077 sq mi). Pop. (1980 est.): 17,914,000. Cap.: Pyongyang (metro. pop., 1976 est., 1.5 million). Language: Korean. Religion: Buddhist; Confucian; Tonghak (Chondokyo). General secretary of the Central Committee of the Workers' (Communist) Party of Korea and president in 1980, Marshal Kim Il Sung; chairman of the Council of Ministers (premier), Li Jong Ok.

Preparation for a leadership change and what looked like an economic policy shift dominated North Korean events during 1980. The highlight of the year was a party congress in October, the first in ten years. In his speech there, Pres. Kim Il Sung proposed direct talks with the U.S. to forge an agreement that would replace the cease-fire pact ending the Korean War in 1953. He wanted the U.S. to withdraw its 30,400 troops from South Korea and then have the two Koreas form a confederation as "the most realistic and reasonable way" to reunify the peninsula. He also declared that his government was ready to establish friendly relations with capitalistic countries as long as they were not hostile to his nation.

One of the chief purposes of the congress, however, was expected to be the nomination of Kim's 40-year-old son, Kim Chong Il, as the new party chief and thus the successor to his father as supreme leader of the nation. No official announcements were made, but Kim Chong Il headed a committee appointed by the congress to restructure the all-powerful party Central Committee. He was already secretary of the Central Committee and referred to as "Beloved Leader." He was not formally declared heir apparent, but the congress nevertheless made him the country's second most influential personage by appointing him to three powerful posts: second rank in the party's secretariat, after his father; fourth member of a newly created Standing Committee of the party Politburo; and third-ranking member of the Military Affairs Committee.

The congress also confirmed North Korea's intentions to boost trade substantially by expanding its contacts with other nations. Preliminary contacts had apparently been made with Japan, for in July the Japanese had established an East Asia Study Group. Although all Communist nations in the region as well as Taiwan were included in the scope of the group, Japanese sources unofficially indicated that the focus would be on North Korea. With all the industrial and trading giants in Japan actively backing the group, it was suggested that the Japanese were getting ready to "underwrite" the North Korean economy. The 1980 North Korean budget announced in April totaled $20,730,-000,000, 14.5% of which was earmarked for defense.

In October North Korea made headlines by supplying ammunition and medical stores to Iran, which was at war with Iraq. According to diplomatic analysis, the motivation was hard-currency earnings rather than ideology. (T. J. S. GEORGE)

Kuwait

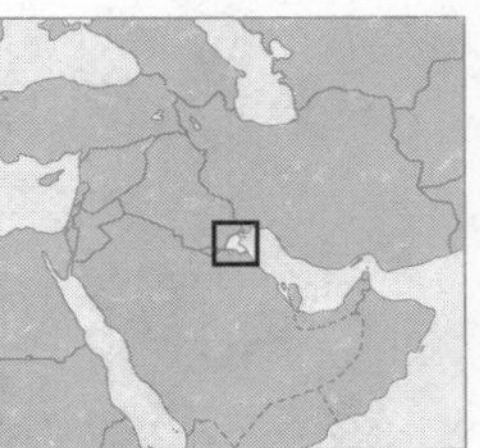
Kuwait

An independent constitutional monarchy (emirate), Kuwait is on the northwestern coast of the Persian Gulf between Iraq and Saudi Arabia. Area: 16,918 sq km (6,532 sq mi). Pop. (1980 prelim.): 1,355,800. Cap.: Kuwait City (pop., 1980 prelim., 60,400). Largest city: Hawalli (pop., 1980 prelim., 152,300). Language: Arabic. Religion (1975): Muslim 94.9% (of which Sunni 85%; Shi'ah 15%); Christian 4.5%. Emir, Sheikh Jabir al-Ahmad al-Jabir as-Sabah; prime minister in 1980, Crown Prince Sheikh Saad al-Abdullah as-Salim as-Sabah.

Kuwait adopted a policy of studied neutrality during the Iraq-Iran war, opening its hospitals to the wounded of both sides. Thousands of refugees from Iraq passed through Kuwait in the first days of the fighting. Kuwait's ports provided an alternative to Iraq's blocked Basra and Umm Qasr ports; they had been so used even before war broke out, to relieve congestion.

Parliamentary elections were promised for February 1981, and women were likely to get the vote for the first time. The decision to revive the National Assembly (suspended in 1976) caused some surprise, since during 1980 several politically motivated crimes were committed. Kuwait had cut off official aid to Egypt when that country signed a bilateral peace with Israel, but commercial links were maintained. Elsewhere, Kuwait invested in petrochemicals ventures, but instead of simply exporting capital, Kuwait sent management as well. At the annual World Bank-International Monetary Fund meeting in September, Kuwait and Saudi Arabia lobbied strongly for observer status to be granted to the Palestine Liberation Organization.

Oil production decreased from 2 million bbl a day to 1.5 million bbl on April 1, and the possibility of cuts was raised. Oil minister Sheikh Ali Khalifah as-Sabah stressed that Kuwait would drop allowable production only if other members

KUWAIT

Education. (1979–80) Primary, pupils 145,626, teachers 7,722; secondary, pupils 167,253, teachers 14,032; vocational, pupils 2,022, teachers 313; teacher training, pupils 1,439, teachers 269; higher (1977–78), students 12,391, teaching staff 1,020.

Finance. Monetary unit: Kuwaiti dinar, with (Sept. 22, 1980) a free rate of 0.27 dinar to U.S. $1 (0.64 dinar = £1 sterling). Gold, SDR's, and foreign exchange (June 1980) U.S. $3,368,000,000. Budget (1979–80 est.): revenue 3,241,000,000 dinars; expenditure 2,250,000,000 dinars. Gross national product (1979–80) 6,431,000,000 dinars. Money supply (June 1980) 793 million dinars. Cost of living (1975 = 100; Feb. 1980) 138.

Foreign Trade. (1979) Imports 1,439,000,000 dinars; exports 4,959,100,000 dinars. Import sources (1978): Japan 19%; U.S. 13%; U.K. 10%; West Germany 9%; Italy 6%. Export destinations (1978): Japan 25%; Italy 9%; The Netherlands 9%; U.K. 9%; South Korea 7%. Main exports: crude oil 76%; petroleum products 16%.

Transport. Roads (1978) 2,400 km. Motor vehicles in use (1979): passenger 363,300; commercial 125,400. Air traffic (1979): 1,810,000,000 passenger-km; freight 63.2 million net ton-km. Shipping (1979): merchant vessels 100 gross tons and over 270; gross tonnage 2,428,200.

Industry. Production (in 000; metric tons; 1978): petroleum products *c.* 18,050; crude oil (1979) *c.* 126,000; natural gas (cu m) 6,450,000; electricity (kw-hr) 7,000,000.

French Pres. Valéry Giscard d'Estaing (right) traveled to Kuwait in March to meet with Sheikh Jabir al-Ahmad al-Jabir as-Sabah (left), the emir of Kuwait.

of the Organization of Petroleum Exporting Countries agreed. Kuwait's importance as a financial centre complementing Bahrain in the lower Gulf was confirmed when, in late 1980, the government allowed the Kuwait dinar bond market (shut down in 1979) to reopen.

(JOHN WHELAN)

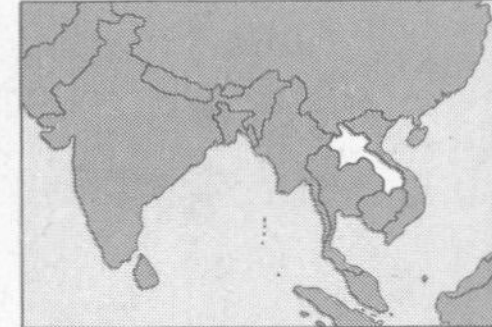

Laos

Laos

A landlocked people's republic of Southeast Asia, Laos is bounded by China, Vietnam, Cambodia, Thailand, and Burma. Area: 236,800 sq km (91,400 sq mi). Pop. (1980 est.): 3,721,000. Cap. and largest city: Vientiane (pop., 1978 est., 200,000). Language: Lao (official); French and English. Religion: Buddhist; tribal. President in 1980, Prince Souphanouvong; premier, Kaysone Phomvihan.

Except for a monetary upheaval at the beginning of the year, Laos remained a dutiful and inconspicuous member of the three-nation Indochina grouping throughout 1980. Political developments were dominated by two conferences of Laotian, Cambodian, and Vietnamese foreign ministers, in Phnom Penh, Cambodia, in January and in Vientiane in July. The Vientiane meeting took place in the shadow of stiff opposition from the Association of Southeast Asian Nations to Indochina's Communist thrust under Vietnamese leadership. The conference affirmed the militant solidarity of the three countries.

Despite the official trumpeting of "complete identity of views" with Vietnam, independent sources continued to talk of popular resentment against the Vietnamese in Laos. According to Thai estimates, there were at least 40,000 Vietnamese soldiers and 100 civilian advisers who controlled all important matters in the country. By late October it was estimated that several thousand Laotians, including government officials, had been arrested during the year for "anti-Vietnamese attitudes"; some had been released. Various official and technical missions shuttled between Vientiane and Hanoi during the year. In July Laos signed a new protocol with the Soviet Union to cover road and bridge construction, marking a significant break with the past when China was in sole charge of road works in northern Laos.

Relations with Thailand remained at a low ebb, especially after a border incident in June in which a Thai naval officer was killed. Failing to get an apology from Vientiane, Thailand closed the 1,200-km (745-mi) frontier along the Mekong River. As on previous occasions, the closure caused serious food and fuel shortages in landlocked Laos, forcing Vietnam to fill the gap as best it could. Even before the blockade, the economy appeared to be in serious difficulty. Worried by what Sisana Sisane, minister of information, called stagnation on the all-important agricultural front, the government introduced major monetary and tax reforms in December 1979. The old kip currency was called in and a new kip introduced. Initially the new kip was worth 100 old kips, which made 1 new kip equal to U.S. 25 cents. A week later it was devalued to the rate of 16 to the dollar.

The reform was to be in preparation for the country's first five-year plan, due to begin in 1981. The authorities seemed concerned enough to suggest that they would henceforth be cautious in pushing agricultural cooperatives and would encourage mixed economy on the industrial front. Some basic economic programs were pursued with assistance from international agencies. The UN Development Program and the Asian Development Bank helped to finance a $8.2 million agricultural support facilities project. In May the World Bank's International Development Association provided a concessionary credit of $13.4 million.

(T. J. S. GEORGE)

LAOS

Education. (1978–79) Primary, pupils 487,000, teachers (1977–78) 14,218; secondary, pupils 72,600, teachers (1977–78) 2,494; vocational, pupils 1,623, teachers 205; teacher training, students 6,191, teachers 386; higher, students 1,684, teaching staff (1974–75) 152.

Finance. Monetary unit: new kip, with (Sept. 22, 1980) a par value of 10 new kip to U.S. $1 (free rate of 24 new kip = £1 sterling); the new kip replaced the former [liberation] kip in December 1979 at 100 old kip = 1 new kip. Budget (1978 est.): revenue 463 million new kip (including foreign aid of 310 million new kip); expenditure 494 million new kip.

Foreign Trade. (1979) Imports *c.* U.S. $75 million; exports *c.* U.S. $20 million. Import sources (1974): Thailand 49%; Japan 19%; France 7%; West Germany 7%; U.S. 5%. Export destinations (1974): Thailand 73%; Malaysia 11%; Hong Kong 10%. Main exports (1974): timber 81%; tin 11%.

Transport and Communications. Roads (1978) *c.* 8,000 km. Motor vehicles in use (1974): passenger 14,100; commercial (including buses) 2,500. Air traffic (1978): *c.* 6 million passenger-km; freight *c.* 100,000 net ton-km. Inland waterways (total; 1978) *c.* 4,600 km. Telephones (Dec. 1973) 5,000. Radio licenses (Dec. 1977) 200,000.

Agriculture. Production (in 000; metric tons; 1978): rice *c.* 796; corn *c.* 30; onions *c.* 30; melons *c.* 22; oranges *c.* 19; pineapples *c.* 29; coffee *c.* 2; tobacco *c.* 4; cotton, lint *c.* 3; timber (cu m) 3,318. Livestock (in 000; 1979): cattle *c.* 551; buffalo *c.* 1,372; pigs *c.* 1,642; chickens (1978) *c.* 17,672.

Industry. Production (1977): tin concentrates (metal content) 600 metric tons; electricity (excluding most industrial production) *c.* 250 million kw-hr.

Labour Unions:
see Industrial Relations

Lacrosse:
see Field Hockey and Lacrosse

Latin-American Affairs

The most important event in Latin-American relations in 1980 was the replacement of the Latin American Free Trade Association (LAFTA) by the Latin American Integration Association (LAIA) following three negotiating conferences during the year. On August 12 the foreign ministers of the 11 member countries of LAFTA (Argentina, Brazil, Chile, Colombia, Bolivia, Ecuador, Peru, Venezuela, Paraguay, Uruguay, and Mexico) signed a treaty in Montevideo, Uruguay, to set up LAIA.

The treaty was a flexible one, designed to take into account the differing levels of economic development of its members. Three categories of comparative development were created so that the countries under each of the categories would obtain a different tariff treatment. At the head of the group were to be the most developed countries, Argentina, Brazil, and Mexico; the second level would be occupied by Chile, Colombia, Peru, Uruguay, and Venezuela; and the third by Bolivia, Ecuador, and Paraguay. All the tariff concessions agreed under the aegis of LAFTA between 1960 and 1980 would be renegotiated by the end of 1981.

The treaty also provided for regional and partial agreements, and a significant role was reserved to the private sector in the initiation of agreements. The three main institutions of LAFTA, the Council of Foreign Ministers, the Conference, and the Secretariat, were to continue more or less in the same form for LAIA, with a secretary-general elected for a three-year period.

Many qualified commentators felt that LAIA was too vague to be successful, and a trend was observed during the year favouring the negotiation of bilateral agreements between countries as the best means of promoting trade. An example of this was the drawing up in October by the authorities of Uruguay and Argentina of a list of about 500 noncompetitive products upon which tariffs and other trade restrictions would be eliminated immediately for Uruguayan exports to Argentina and gradually for trade in the opposite direction. Products to be subject to free-trade conditions would be expanded to 1,000 over a two-year period, including vegetable oils, timber, textiles, building materials, hydrocarbons, corn, and wheat.

Political difficulties assumed critical proportions during 1980 among the member countries of the Andean Group (Bolivia, Colombia, Ecuador, Peru, and Venezuela), and economic proposals consequently received less attention. Dissension was created by the military coup d'etat in Bolivia on July 17, when that country was about to return to constitutional rule. The other four members of the Group condemned the coup, and Ecuador broke off diplomatic relations with Bolivia. Venezuela called for a coordinated effort against the new regime by both the Andean Group and the Organization of American States (OAS) and suspended its financial assistance to Bolivia. By October Bolivia appeared to be reconsidering its membership in the Group and arriving at an accommodation with Argentina, Chile, and Uruguay. But later Bolivia denied its intention to leave the Group. Its representatives attended the meeting of the Commission (the Andean Group's main decision-making body) in Lima, Peru, on October 13 and also a presidential summit conference of member countries in Santa Marta, Colombia, on December 17.

The new Peruvian government was also reviewing certain aspects of the Andean Pact (Fernando Belaúnde Terry of Acción Popular took office as president on July 28 following the impressive victory of his party in the presidential and legislative elections on May 18; these had brought 12 years of military rule to an end). The pact's preoccupation with political affairs was criticized by the Belaúnde administration, which maintained that greater emphasis should be given to economic matters. One of Peru's new policies was to give more encouragement to the entry of foreign investment, and this was expected to contravene the tight restrictions imposed on the latter under Decisions 24

In April Thomas Farer (arm outstretched), U.S. chairman of the Inter-American Human Rights Commission of the Organization of American States, and Andrés Aguilar Mawdsley (right) of Venezuela conferred in Bogotá with guerrillas holding hostages at the Dominican Republic embassy. All hostages were later released unharmed.

WIDE WORLD

and 103 of the Commission. There was also criticism by the four other members of the Group of Peru's decision to lower the maximum import duties to 60%.

There was squabbling over the Andean Group's industrial development programs. A series of meetings attempted to expedite negotiations on the six agreements to be decided upon by the end of 1980 (steel, fertilizers, pharmaceuticals, chemicals, electronics, and communications). The motor-vehicle program, approved in September 1977, was expected to be renegotiated to reflect changes, especially technological ones, in the world vehicle industry. The trade liberalization program made steady progress, and the automatic tariff elimination process begun in 1971 was 75% complete at the beginning of 1980. Trade within the region increased significantly as a result, rising from U.S. $79 million in 1970 to approximately $1.2 billion in 1979.

There were attempts to revive the Central American Common Market (CACM) during the year; the CACM included Costa Rica, El Salvador, Guatemala, Honduras, and Nicaragua. At a meeting in Managua, Nicaragua, on July 4–5, the economic integration ministers of the member countries agreed on the drafting of a new document to replace the 1960 General Treaty. They urged the governments of Guatemala, Costa Rica, and Honduras to put into effect bilateral payment mechanisms that would alleviate the intrazonal trade deficits of Nicaragua and El Salvador. The ministers agreed to establish the Central American Maritime Transport Commission (Cocatran), with headquarters in Managua, and to strengthen relations with other regional trade associations and also with the Dominican Republic and Panama. A draft resolution supported by Costa Rica, Nicaragua, El Salvador, and Honduras called for a common protective tariff ranging from 35 to 100%, as compared with the existing multiple-tariff system whereby in some cases duties could exceed 300%. Prospects for the reinvigoration of the CACM were improved by the signature in Lima on October 30 of a peace treaty between El Salvador and Honduras, which ended a state of hostility lasting 11 years. The two countries were to negotiate over the next five years to settle their border disputes.

In August the Inter-American Development Bank (IDB) put into effect an increase of $9,750,000,000 in the bank's resources; it included "callable" capital of $8 billion and $1,750,000,000 for the Fund for Special Operations. The rise was accepted in principle by all member countries. The bank granted loans of about $2.2 billion in 1980 as against $2,030,000,000 in 1979, despite the fact that 19 loans totaling $700 million were frozen between October 1979 and April 1980, principally as a result of delays by the U.S. in making some contributions available. Portugal became the 16th extraregional full member of the IDB on March 25.

Pres. João Baptista de Oliveira Figueiredo of Brazil paid a number of state visits to neighbouring countries during the year as part of Brazil's drive to improve its relations in Latin America and to increase exports to the area. He went to Argentina in May, and the visit ended a 15-year period of cool relations between the two countries; the improvement was made possible by an agreement on the large hydroelectric plants that both countries were building in conjunction with Paraguay on the Paraná River. During Figueiredo's stay in Argentina agreements were signed concerning cooperation between the two nations in the peaceful use of nuclear energy, joint exploitation of the hydroelectric potential of the Uruguay River, and the delivery by Argentina to Brazil of natural gas at the rate of about ten million cubic feet a day. Pres. Jorge Rafael Videla of Argentina paid a return visit to Brazil in August. The most important pact signed then concerned nuclear power, with agreements by Argentina to supply 240 tons of uranium for the Brazilian reactor program and by Brazil to supply nuclear technology. The two countries also agreed on a joint feasibility study for a gas pipeline. Figueiredo also visited Paraguay in April and Chile in September.

Other important developments in Latin-American external relations included a trade agreement between Argentina and the U.S.S.R. in July providing for the purchase by the latter of 20 million tons of corn and sorghum and 2.5 million tons of soybeans over five years. During the first half of 1980 the Soviet Union became the biggest purchaser of Argentine grain, receiving more than 50% of Argentina's total grain shipments during that period. Late in July the presidents of Mexico and Venezuela (the region's two largest oil producers) signed an agreement providing for the joint supply of 160,000 bbl a day of crude petroleum at about $32 a barrel to Barbados, Costa Rica, El Salvador, Guatemala, Honduras, Jamaica, Nicaragua, Panama, and the Dominican Republic; this represented the overall consumption of those countries. A total of 30% of the payments was to be returned in the form of five-year loans at 4% interest. The agreement was to be renewed annually and could be extended to other consumer countries. Papal arbitration continued on the Beagle Channel dispute between Chile and Argentina throughout the year.

The IDB reported that the gross national product of the region grew by 6.1% in 1979 to reach $420.7 billion in 1978 U.S. dollars ($396.3 billion in 1978). Income per head in 1979 was $1,244, a rise of 65% from the 1960 level. At the end of 1979 Latin America's crude oil output amounted to almost 2,000,000,000 bbl, 15% higher than in 1978; it accounted for 6% of the world's total. Agriculture's contribution to the area's gross domestic product fell from 15.7% in 1960 to 10.5% in 1979. The region's share of world trade declined from 7.2% in 1960–62 to 5% in 1977–79. (ROBIN CHAPMAN)

See also Feature Article: *Ferment in Central America*; articles on the various political units.
[971.D.8; 974]

Latin-American Literature:
see Literature

Latter-day Saints:
see Religion

Law

Court Decisions. As in previous years, the most important judicial decisions handed down by the many courts of the world in 1980 emanated from the U.S. Supreme Court. This was hardly surprising, given that courts play a somewhat more important role in common law (English-speaking) jurisdictions than in civil law countries, that the U.S. vests tremendous powers in its courts, and that the Supreme Court is uniquely powerful within that arrangement. Nevertheless, a number of important cases were decided in the civil law countries and in England.

WOMEN'S RIGHTS. Two important cases concerning the alleged constitutional duty of the federal government and the states in the U.S. to fund abortions were decided by the Supreme Court. Title XIX of the Social Security Act established a program, known as Medicaid, under which the federal government undertakes to reimburse partially the cost incurred by the states in providing medical treatment to needy persons. In 1976 Congress enacted the "Hyde amendment," which prohibited the federal government from reimbursing states for medical charges incurred in the performance of abortions, except where the life of the mother would be endangered if the fetus were carried to term and in cases of promptly reported rape or incest. As a result, a number of states passed laws prohibiting medical assistance payments for abortions for which no reimbursement could be claimed from the federal government.

These state laws and the Hyde amendment itself came under constitutional attack in two companion cases. In *Harris* v. *McRae* the Supreme Court sustained the constitutionality of the Hyde amendment. In *Williams* v. *Zbaraz* it sustained the constitutionality of an Illinois statute prohibiting medical assistance payments for all abortions except those necessary for preserving the mother's life. In both decisions the court was divided 5–4.

Two other U.S. Supreme Court cases involving women's rights were noteworthy. *Trammel* v. *United States* did away with an old rule that spouses are absolutely barred from testifying against one another in suits brought in federal courts. The court held that the spousal privilege is personal to the witness. Henceforth, husband and wife could testify against one another if they saw fit to do so, though neither could be compelled to do so over his or her assertion of the privilege. In *Diamond* v. *Chakrabarty* the U.S. Supreme Court held that human-made microorganisms are patentable under federal patent statutes. To some specialists the case seemed to be a narrow one involving only a construction of the patent laws, but it generated enormous publicity and considerable debate in groups involved with women's rights, religion, the family, and similar concerns. (*See* LIFE SCIENCES: *Special Report*.)

Two important decisions involving women's rights were handed down by the West German Federal Constitutional Court. In the first, the court sustained the constitutionality of a divorce law that came into effect in 1977. Under that law, divorce may be granted on the sole ground of breakdown of the marriage, including separation for three years. Under this ground no consent to the divorce is necessary. In addition, the law establishes new criteria for maintenance to the financially weaker party. Eighty complaints were made, all by men, contending that the law violated Art. 6(1) of the Basic Law guaranteeing protection of marriage and the family and that it discriminated against men. The court rejected these contentions. A second case involved 3(2) of the Basic Law which guarantees "equal treatment." In 1943 legislation was passed allowing female employees one day off each month to attend to household duties. The case involved a contention that this discriminated against male employees. The court agreed, holding that the 1943 statute should be liberally construed to cover both men and women.

GENERAL ELECTRIC RESEARCH AND DEVELOPMENT CENTER

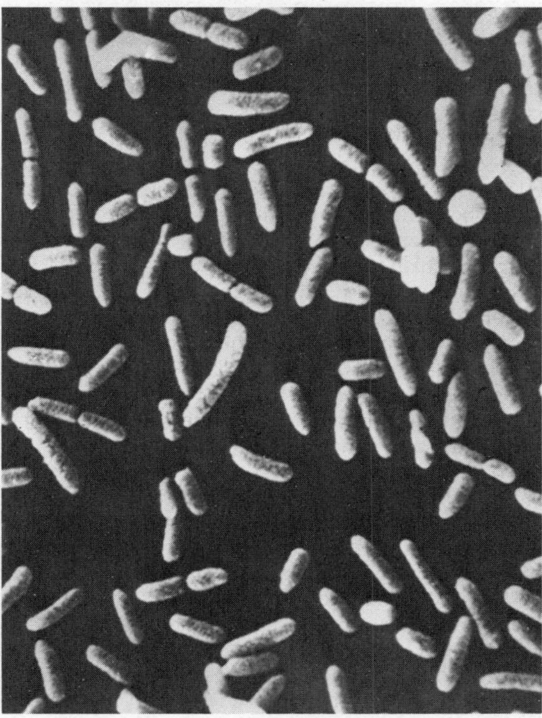

Oil-eating bacteria were the subject of a U.S. Supreme Court ruling that new life forms created in the laboratory can be patented.

English law does not require that men and women be paid the same wages or salaries for similar or identical work, but when the U.K. became a member of the European Economic Community (EEC), it agreed to be bound by certain EEC rules. During the year the U.K. Court of Appeal referred two matters involving the equal-pay question to the European Court of Justice for preliminary rulings. In *Macarthys Ltd.* v. *Smith*, the court held that a female employee was entitled to the same pay her male predecessor had been receiving when he left the job, four months before she took it over. In *Jenkins* v. *Kingsgate*, a female part-time worker complained that a pay differential between full- and part-time workers involved sex discrimination, in contravention of Art. 119 of the EEC Treaty, because part-time workers are mainly women. The case was still pending at year's end.

FREEDOM OF SPEECH AND INFORMATION. In the view of many U.S. constitutional scholars, the most important case decided by the U.S. Supreme Court during the year was *Richmond Newspapers* v. *Virginia*, holding that the press and public have a constitutional right of access to criminal trials in most situations. The case involved the trial of the defendant on murder charges for the fourth time. The first trial had resulted in a conviction that had been reversed by the Supreme Court of Virginia, and the second and third were declared mistrials. The defendant contended that his right to a fair trial was impaired, or potentially impaired, by the presence of the press, and he moved that the court have the courtroom closed for the fourth trial. The prosecution had no objection, and the judge granted the motion without making any finding of facts to support the closure. The next day a newspaper sought a hearing on the closure order, and the judge reaffirmed his decision. Subsequently, the defendant was acquitted. Nevertheless, the newspaper appealed. The Supreme Court held that the case was not moot on account of the acquittal and it ruled that the trial court had acted incorrectly in excluding the press. "Absent an overriding interest articulated in findings," Chief Justice Warren Burger opined, "the trial of a criminal case must be open to the public."

The U.K. Court of Appeal handed down an equally important decision concerning the right of a reporter or the press to refuse to disclose sources of information. In *British Steel Corporation* v. *Granada Television, Ltd.*, the court developed an elaborate balancing-of-the-interests test to determine the circumstances under which the press would be required to disclose its sources. It held that no disclosure would be ordered unless the person seeking it proved: (1) that there had been wrongdoing by the informant (*e.g.*, that the information had been obtained through breach of confidence, theft, etc.); (2) that justice required the identity of the informant to be made known (*e.g.*, to protect innocent persons); and (3) that disclosure of the informant was necessary to the remedy sought (*e.g.*, that the situation was one where monetary damages would not suffice as an adequate remedy). Even where these three elements have been established, the court will not order disclosure without considering the interest of the public in having its press and media basically free to acquire information of public concern. However, the contention that there is an absolute, constitutional right of "press secrecy" was rejected.

In July sheriff's deputies raided an Idaho television station in search of videotapes that could help identify rioting prison inmates. President Carter, on October 14, signed into law an act of Congress prohibiting such unannounced searches of newsrooms by federal, state, or local law-enforcement authorities.

DAVID FRAZIER—THE NEW YORK TIMES

In *PruneYard Shopping Center* v. *Robins*, the U.S. Supreme Court held that the state of California could, by its constitution, require the owner of a private shopping centre to allow distribution of literature on its property. The court distinguished its holding from that of *Lloyd* v. *Tanner* (1972), in which it rejected the contention that the U.S. Constitution gave individuals such a right.

RACE RELATIONS. The "minority business enterprise" provision of the Public Works Employment Act enacted by the U.S. Congress in 1977 provides that at least 10% of federal funds allocated for public works projects must be used to procure services or supplies from businesses owned by minority group members, defined as U.S. citizens who are "Negroes, Spanish-speaking, Orientals, Indians, Eskimos, and Aleuts." This provision came under constitutional attack on the ground that it denied nonminority groups the equal protection of the laws, as guaranteed by the 14th Amendment. The Supreme Court rejected this attack in *Fullilove* v. *Klutznick*. Although the members of the court constituting the majority in this case were unable to agree on the exact rationale for the decision, the case seemed to rest on the idea that it was constitutional for Congress to allocate public funds on a basis designed to remedy the present effects of past discrimination.

In *City of Mobile* v. *Bolden*, the U.S. Supreme Court upheld the system of government established by the city of Mobile, Ala., which consisted of three commissioners elected at large. A group of black citizens of Mobile challenged the constitutionality of this system on the ground that it discriminated against blacks, who made up 35% of the city's population. A majority of the court held that the Constitution does not require proportional representation as an imperative of political organization.

CRIMINAL LAW. In *People* v. *Barraza*, the California Supreme Court announced an objective test for the defense of entrapment to a criminal charge, namely, whether the acts or promises of the agent provocateur are apt to induce a normally honest and law-abiding person to commit a crime by furnishing him with a motive other than criminal intent or by making commission of the crime unusually attractive. The case attracted interest because of the so-called Abscam affair. FBI agents masquerading as Arabs or representatives of Arabs seeking political favours had met with various governmental officials, and videotapes had been made of the meetings. As a result, a number of congressmen, one senator, and several local officials were indicted, and some were convicted. One defense made in some of the cases was "entrapment," commonly defined as "the inducement of one to commit a crime not contemplated by him, for the mere purpose of instituting criminal prosecution against him."

The FBI maintained that no entrapment was involved because the agents were never the first to suggest bribes or to solicit anyone to participate in discussions with them. At year's end, a federal district court sitting in Philadelphia held that Abscam involved entrapment and overturned a guilty verdict against two local politicians. U.S. legal scholars, along with a number of indicted politicians, were eagerly awaiting final word on the subject from the U.S. Supreme Court.

(WILLIAM D. HAWKLAND)

International Law. The clear and dramatic theme in 1980 was an insistent attack on the central core of international law, namely, respect for diplomatic officers and respect for territorial sovereignty. Although the most publicized violation of diplomatic immunity involved the U.S. hostages in Teheran, Iran, dozens of other instances occurred. (*See* Special Report.)

At the same time, diplomats themselves shared in the lawlessness. The diplomatic corps in London committed some 56 nonmotoring offenses during 1979. In 1980 diplomatic luggage bound for the Moroccan embassy in London was found to contain more than 600 lb of cannabis. In several capitals assassination attempts or threats of assassination were traced to "embassy staff."

TERRITORIAL SOVEREIGNTY. A peace treaty officially ending the 1969 "Soccer War" between Honduras and El Salvador was signed October 30. Meanwhile, the desert war in the Western Sahara between Morocco and the Polisario Front continued. In December 1979 Soviet forces invaded Afghanistan, and the towns, but not the countryside, remained under Soviet occupation throughout the year. In the autumn of 1980 Iraqi troops attacked Iran, originally in order to gain control of the disputed Shatt al-Arab waterway, although the war was extended later to include more general objectives. (*See* DEFENSE: *Special Report.*)

The borders of neutrals were violated by temporary incursions into Thailand by Vietnamese troops in Cambodia and into Pakistan by Soviet forces in Afghanistan. In Lebanon the UN peacekeeping forces were involved in military action when Lebanese militia directly attacked the Irish battalion of the UN force and killed two Irish soldiers. The annual violation of Norwegian waters by unknown submarines was accompanied in 1980 by a similar incursion into Swedish waters off Stockholm. This submarine was briefly sighted and identified as Soviet; it stayed so long that orders were given to disable it with depth charges, but it departed before the order could be carried out.

The Soviet invasion of Afghanistan gave rise to allegations that dumdum bullets, germ warfare, and poison gas were being used (Afghanistan was not a signatory to the 1925 Geneva Protocol on Poison Gas). It was also claimed that Soviet nerve gas had been shipped to northern Eritrea for use by Ethiopia against the Eritrean independence movement. In October the UN concluded a conference in Geneva to restrict the use of fragmentation bombs, napalm, land mines, booby traps, and other "excessively injurious" conventional weapons that kill massively and indiscriminately or cause unnecessary pain.

Peaceful violations of territorial sovereignty also occurred. Two French customs officials carried out investigations in Switzerland to collect information about the accounts of French citizens in Swiss banks. Similarly, French employees in Luxembourg banks were requested to pass to the French authorities information about tax frauds by French citizens. Claims of long-arm jurisdiction by U.S. courts and agencies led to a strengthening of defensive legislation by France, Italy, Australia, and, especially, the U.K. The U.K. Protection of Trading Interests Act provided for attaching the assets of a successful plaintiff in cases where unacceptable extraterritorial jurisdiction was exercised by a foreign court or in order to recover the excess element in multiple or penal damages awarded by such a court.

INTERNATIONAL ORGANIZATION. In Latin America the Andean Group agreed in late 1979 to establish an Andean parliament and a Council of Ministers of Foreign Affairs; the first meeting of the Andean Assembly was held the following month. In January 1980 the 21st Inter-American Conference exhorted member governments of the Latin American Free Trade Association (LAFTA), the Caribbean Community, and the Central American Common Market to consider establishing a judicial organ to resolve disputes connected with development and integration along the lines of the European Court of Justice. Later in the year LAFTA was replaced by the new Latin American Integration Association. (*See* LATIN-AMERICAN AFFAIRS.)

At its 20th meeting in October 1980 in Port Moresby, Papua New Guinea, the South Pacific Conference took in four new members, newly independent Vanuatu (the former Anglo-French condominium of the New Hebrides) and the three U.S. trust territories of the Northern Marianas, the Marshall Islands, and the Federated States of Micronesia, bringing the total membership to 14 states and 14 dependent territories; much of the discussion was devoted to the need for regional political organization. The more politically oriented South Pacific Forum, with 13 sovereign states as members, agreed in July to sign the South Pacific-Australia-New Zealand Regional Trade Agreement, making many exports of island products to Australia and New Zealand duty free.

The Eskimo populations of Alaska, Canada, and Greenland attended the second Inuit Circumpolar Conference and agreed to set up their own international organization to protect the rights, interests, cultural unity, and civilization of the inhabitants of the Arctic polar region. The most dramatic event in Africa was the end of the long struggle over the former British colony of Southern Rhodesia. In April 1980 it was recognized by the imperial power, the U.K., and by the rest of the world as the independent nation of Zimbabwe. (*See* ZIM-

BABWE.) The dispute between South Africa and the UN over the independence of South West Africa/Namibia remained unresolved. (*See* SOUTH AFRICA.) In September the governments of Syria and Libya agreed to merge their two countries into a single political, military, and economic unit.

There were no major changes in other international organizations, except for the return of the U.S. to the International Labour Organization. There was continued serious discussion within Switzerland about possible membership in the UN. Greek accession to the EEC was set for Jan. 1, 1981, and a timetable was agreed for Portuguese accession negotiations leading to membership in 1983. Spanish accession negotiations were subjected to politico-economic difficulties, and Turkey again postponed applying for membership. However, the possibility of Swedish and Norwegian membership was being openly discussed in the press and political circles, largely stimulated by the EEC measures taken to protect its ailing steel industry.

MARITIME AFFAIRS. The UN Conference on the Law of the Sea (UNCLOS), holding its usual two meetings, reached a high degree of agreement, and there was a strong probability that the final conventions would be ready for signature in 1981. A sense of urgency had been generated following enactment by the U.S. and West Germany of legislation that could regulate and therefore encourage commercial activities on the ocean floor if UNCLOS failed to produce its own regime.

The flow of bilateral treaties settling maritime boundaries seemed to be slowing, but in two cases the creation of 200-mi exclusive economic zones (EEZ's) had legally controversial aspects. In March Indonesia created an EEZ around the whole archipelago, thus anticipating settlement of a long-standing disagreement among international lawyers on whether this was compatible with international law and freedom of the seas. Indonesia did say it was willing to negotiate with neighbouring countries that had overlapping claims. Bangladesh used a baseline joining points off its coast at a depth of ten fathoms for establishment of its EEZ, a criterion that clearly departed from existing international law. In the direction of liberalization, Denmark and Sweden reached an agreement whereby each state would limit its territorial waters in the straits so that there would be a section of open sea approximately six miles wide on each side of the centreline where ships could pass without leaving international waters.

Important conservation conventions included the Antarctic Living Marine Resources Convention and the protocol for the Protection of the Mediterranean Sea against Pollution from Land-based Sources. (*See* ANTARCTICA; ENVIRONMENT.) The Beagle Channel dispute between Argentina and Chile was still unresolved after several months of quiet diplomacy by a papal mediator. A more original question arose in connection with attempts to salvage precious metals from a Russian naval vessel that sank in Japanese waters in 1905 during the Russo-Japanese War. The Soviet government claimed property in the ship and its contents while Japan insisted they were spoils of war. The property status of sunken vessels had arisen with increasing frequency as marine archaeology developed and recovery technology improved.

LAWMAKING. As the trend toward legislative treaties on matters of private law continued to accelerate, a new legal form had been developed: the nonbinding code or guidelines. This was the form adopted for the UN Restrictive Business Practices Code, adopted in April, and the draft code on the transfer of technology, which continued to be discussed within the UN Conference on Trade and Development. It was also used by the Organization for Economic Cooperation and Development for its text guidelines on the potential effect of chemicals and on the protection of privacy in transborder flows of personal data. The privacy aspect of data processing was also the subject of a Council of Europe convention that was adopted in September.

The UN adopted conventions on contracts for the international sale of goods, international multimodal transport of goods, and elimination of discrimination against women. The Council of Europe concluded a convention on the custody of children, and the EEC a convention on conflict of laws in contractual obligations. The Strasbourg Convention on Unification of Certain Points of Law on Patents came into force, as did the Vienna Trade Marks Registration Treaty and the Budapest Treaty on International Recognition of the Deposit of Micro-organisms for the Purpose of Patent Procedures. UNESCO and the World Intellectual Property Organization jointly adopted a convention on avoidance of double taxation of copyright royalties.

In the field of public law, important new conventions included those on physical protection of nuclear material (International Atomic Energy Authority), on the duties of law-enforcement officials (UN General Assembly), and on the Moon (UN). The Vienna Convention on the Law of Treaties came into force. Work was begun in the UN on a draft convention against torture.

INTERNATIONAL COURT OF JUSTICE. The International Court of Justice delivered a highly publicized decision concerning the legality and consequences to be attached to the seizure of U.S. embassy personnel by Iran. The court held that the seizure was wrongful and violated duties owed by Iran to the U.S. It ordered Iran to release the hostages immediately and turn over the embassy premises to a third party country for protection. It also ruled that no member of the U.S. diplomatic or consular staff could be subjected to any form of legal action by Iran or be required to participate in any proceedings as a witness. Finally, it decreed that Iran pay reparations for injuries caused by its wrongful acts of seizure. The Iranian government refused to participate in the case or to abide by the decision. The court also continued with proceedings in a dispute between Tunisia and Libya and a request for an advisory opinion relating to the regional office of the World Health Organization currently located in Egypt.

(NEVILLE MARCH HUNNINGS)

See also Crime and Law Enforcement; Prisons and Penology; United Nations.

Law Enforcement:
see Crime and Law Enforcement

Lawn Bowls:
see Bowling

Lawn Tennis:
see Tennis

Law: Special Report

DIPLOMATS UNDER SIEGE

by Richard L. Clutterbuck

Twenty-six embassies or consulates were illegally occupied in 1979, and another 12 in the first half of 1980. Violation of embassies and of the immunity of diplomats is nothing new, but the pattern has changed. Between 1968 and 1975 there were 52 incidents in which diplomats or consuls were kidnapped, but most of the victims were taken to secret hideouts. Now they are more often held in their own embassies. The new pattern, though more hazardous for the terrorists, attracts more publicity—which is usually their primary aim.

New Targets for Terrorism. This pattern began in 1973 when Palestinian terrorists seized the Saudi embassy in Khartoum, Sudan, and held six diplomats hostage. Their demands included the release of terrorists imprisoned in various countries, and when these were not met, one Belgian and two U.S. diplomats were killed. The Sudanese government arrested and convicted the terrorists but, in response to pressure from other Arab countries, released them within a year.

When terrorists took over the Japanese embassy in Kuwait in 1974, they were given safe conduct to Aden and a ransom of $6 million. In 1975 the West German embassy in Stockholm was seized by German terrorists, but this time both the governments involved stood firm, despite the murder of two hostages, and all the terrorists were killed or captured. Later that year, however, when terrorists seized 11 OPEC (Organization of Petroleum Exporting Countries) oil ministers in Vienna, the governments concerned agreed to give way, and it is believed that a huge ransom was paid. The terrorists all went free, and subsequently the plague has grown worse.

The seizure of the U.S. embassy in Teheran by Iranian militants in November 1979 created a new dimension. There is no evidence that Iran's revolutionary leader, the Ayatollah Ruhollah Khomeini, gave it prior authorization. He did approve it after the fact, however, taking full responsibility for holding some 60 diplomats and a number of other hostages (later reduced to 52). Though there have been cases of governments conniving with mobs that attacked or burned embassies (*e.g.*, the U.S. embassy in Libya in 1979), Khomeini became the first national leader in modern times to put his own authority behind the prolonged detention of an accredited embassy staff.

In February 1980 in Bogotá, Colombia, 25 students of the M-19 Movement ran across the road from the university and seized the Dominican embassy, where a reception was in progress. One terrorist was shot dead by a security guard, but no one else died. After prolonged negotiations, the 57 hostages, including 14 ambassadors, were released. The terrorists were given safe conduct and a $2.5 million ransom, paid by local businessmen who raised some or all of it from the ambassadors' parent countries.

On April 30, 1980, six terrorists belonging to the Arab minority in Iran seized the Iranian embassy in London. The subsequent siege and rescue are described below. Five of the six died, but they got the publicity they wanted for their cause.

Rules of the Game. Whether from a big country or a small one, embassy personnel are as helpless as children entrusted to the care of a neighbour if their host decides to incarcerate them or threaten them with murder. Accordingly, over the centuries, rules have evolved governing their rights and responsibilities. Most nations that exchange ambassadors are parties to the Vienna Convention. Under it, the host government accepts responsibility for protecting the embassy (Art. 22), the diplomatic staffs (Art. 29), and their residences (Art. 30). Diplomats, while enjoying diplomatic immunity, are required to respect the laws of the host country and must not interfere in its internal affairs (Art. 41).

Some embassies, notably those of certain Arab countries, have flagrantly abused their privileges. Diplomatic bags have been used to smuggle in weapons. In Paris in 1978, Iraqi embassy guards shot a French policeman dead in the street outside the embassy. In 1980 several Libyans opposed to Muammar al-Qaddafi were murdered in London, and Libyan diplomats openly admitted their participation. It has been alleged that the Iraqi embassy in London supported the terrorists who seized the Iranian embassy. Neither this kind of abuse, however, nor allegations that an embassy is being used for subversion or spying can justify the host country in violating it or conniving at its violation. The lawful remedy is to withdraw immunities from individual diplomats or suspend diplomatic relations.

The parent government is responsible for security within its own embassy gates. Though it does not

---

Richard L. Clutterbuck is senior lecturer in politics at the University of Exeter and former chief army instructor at the Royal College of Defence Studies, London. His books include Living with Terrorism; Guerrillas and Terrorists; *and* Kidnap and Ransom.

UPI

Elite British Army commandos performed a daring rescue mission in May to free 19 hostages being held by Iranian Arab terrorists in the Iranian embassy in London.

have extraterritorial rights, an embassy is outside the jurisdiction of the host country, whose policemen, guards, or soldiers can enter only if invited. The parent government can place its own armed security guards inside the gates, but a handful of guards cannot keep out a mob, especially if the host country's security forces are either participating or conniving with the attackers.

Outside the embassy, diplomatic staffs in high-risk countries should avoid offering targets for terrorists, observing sensible security precautions in their homes, being discreet about their movements, and avoiding predictable times and routes. They can carry arms and employ armed bodyguards but have a moral duty to observe local law. Escorts or guards outside the diplomat's own car or home should be provided by the host country.

When Precautions Fail. If a host country fails by neglect to provide proper protection for an embassy or its staff, the parent country has no right to intervene, but if the host government willfully participates in or connives at an attack or occupation, this can be regarded as an act of war. The parent government can then justify reply by warlike means, though this may not be wise, as was illustrated by the abortive U.S. rescue mission in Iran in April 1980. The Israeli rescue of hijacked airline passengers at Entebbe, Uganda, in 1976 did prove that operations of this type can be feasible, even in defiance of the local government, but in that case the hostages were at an airfield where the commandos could land and take off again quickly.

Normally, however, such rescues must be executed by the host country, as in the case of the Iranian embassy in London in May 1980. This incident illustrates many of the problems involved. Iranian security inside the embassy was woefully inadequate. The British had one policeman with a pistol under his coat at the door. The six terrorists posed as bona fide visitors but carried concealed weapons. Once inside, they seized 26 hostages, including the policeman. In response to his "panic button" signal, the first police reinforcements were at the door within three minutes, and a seige was mounted.

No one had been seriously hurt, and the negotiators played for time. This seemed to work well at first, and after six days of negotiation, five hostages had been released. At that point, however, the terrorists lost patience. Realizing that the British and Iranian governments were not going to make concessions, they shot a hostage in cold blood and threatened to shoot another every 45 minutes. The British Army's Special Air Services (SAS) rescue squad then went in, with the agreement of the Iranian government. During the next few seconds the terrorists sprayed the hostages with machine-gun fire, killing one more before the SAS reached the room and rescued the other 19. All the terrorists were killed except one who pretended to be a hostage, and he was subsequently arrested.

Several such rescues have been carried out, though not often from embassies. Dutch Marines rescued hostages from a train and a school in 1977 and from a government office in 1978, and the German GSG9 squad freed hijacked passengers from an aircraft at Mogadishu, Somalia, in 1977. The Dutch Marines and the GSG9 have much in common with the SAS. The selection and training of that force for an embassy rescue indicate what is required.

The SAS is an elite British Army regiment. Only experienced soldiers are considered for selection. Of those tested, only one in five is chosen, and only a small number of those accepted by the regiment are picked for the rescue squad. They train intensively, and if any man's reactions or skill at arms falter in the smallest degree, he is replaced. They train with live ammunition, with one of their own comrades acting as the hostage, surrounded by figure targets representing the terrorists. They must break in and put lethal shots into every target within a few seconds without hitting the hostage. The resulting confidence and precision were proved in London when the moment came.

Such a force may well provide the best deterrent against of diplomatic violations. It is ironic that in this case the diplomats rescued were Khomeini's.

Lebanon

A republic of the Middle East, Lebanon is bounded by Syria, Israel, and the Mediterranean Sea. Area: 10,230 sq km (3,950 sq mi). Pop. (1980 est.): 3,161,-000. Cap. and largest city: Beirut (metro. pop., 1975 est., 1,172,000). The populations of both Lebanon and its capital city, Beirut, are thought to have declined since the outbreak of civil war in 1974, but reliable figures are not available. Languages: Arabic predominates; Armenian-, Kurdish-, and French-speaking minorities. Religion: available estimates show Christians comprising variously from 40 to 55% of the population and Muslims from 45 to 60%; there is a Druze minority. President in 1980, Elias Sarkis; prime ministers, Selim al-Hoss and, from October 25, Shafiq al-Wazzan.

Lebanon continued to suffer in 1980 from a breakdown of government control in the south and from Israeli armed incursions. Polarization into zones controlled by warring factions of Christians and by Palestinian commandos aided by left-wing allies and Muslim extremists was more evident. The resignation of Prime Minister Selim al-Hoss was accepted in July, but his differences of view with Pres. Elias Sarkis prolonged the finding of a replacement government. On October 25 one was formed by Shafiq al-Wazzan (*see* BIOGRAPHIES), a former justice minister who took the premiership and the interior ministry. However, there was little enthusiasm for the Cabinet of 22, only 5 of whom had served under Selim al-Hoss. Two ministers resigned almost immediately, and four more Cabinet members, all Shi'ah Muslims, resigned early in December.

In 1981 Lebanon was to receive $22 million worth of foreign military sales from the U.S. in a three-year program to restore the Lebanese Army. The Army in 1980 was not strong enough to de-

LEBANON

Education. (1972–73) Primary, pupils 497,723; secondary, pupils 167,578; primary and secondary, teachers 32,-901; vocational, pupils 3,898, teachers (1970–71) 508; teacher training, students 3,235, teachers (1971–72) 551; higher, students 50,803, teaching staff 2,313.

Finance. Monetary unit: Lebanese pound, with (Sept. 22, 1980) a free rate of L£3.42 to U.S. $1 (L£8.22 = £1 sterling). Gold and foreign exchange (June 1980) U.S. $2,-283,000,000. Budget (1980 est.): revenue L£3,572 million; expenditure L£4,939 million.

Foreign Trade. (1979) Imports *c.* L£7,248 million; exports *c.* L£2,285 million. Import sources (1977): Switzerland 15%; France 13%; Italy 8%; West Germany 8%; U.S. 7%; U.K. 5%. Export destinations (1977): Saudi Arabia 33%; Kuwait 14%; Syria 13%; United Arab Emirates 8%; Qatar 5%. Main exports (1977): financial papers and stamps 21%; food, drink, and tobacco 17%; chemicals 11%; machinery 9%; metals 8%; textiles and clothing 7%.

Transport and Communications. Roads (1978) *c.* 7,-100 km. Motor vehicles in use (1978): passenger 282,400; commercial 28,600. Railways: (1978) 417 km; traffic (1974) 2 million passenger-km, freight 42 million net ton-km. Air traffic (1979): 1,505,000,000 passenger-km; freight 594.1 million net ton-km. Shipping (1979): vessels 100 gross tons and over 185; gross tonnage 260,125. Telephones (Dec. 1978) 231,000. Radio receivers (Dec. 1976) 1.6 million. Television receivers (Dec. 1977) 450,000.

Agriculture. Production (in 000; metric tons; 1979): potatoes *c.* 110; wheat *c.* 40; tomatoes (1978) *c.* 75; grapes *c.* 135; olives *c.* 15; bananas (1978) *c.* 33; oranges *c.* 225; lemons *c.* 65; apples *c.* 135; tobacco *c.* 5. Livestock (in 000; 1978): cattle *c.* 84; goats *c.* 330; sheep *c.* 240; chickens *c.* 8,047.

Industry. Production (in 000; metric tons; 1977): cement 1,172; petroleum products (1978) *c.* 1,820; electricity (kw-hr) 1,839,000.

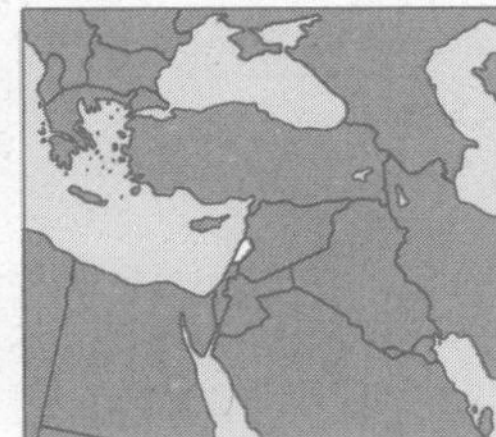

Lebanon

fend against Israeli attacks without the help of Syrian troops, who were serving with the Arab Deterrent Force (ADF), and the UN Interim Force in Lebanon (UNIFIL), monitoring Israeli attacks on the south. The Lebanese government told the UN in October that UN observers had been subject to "continued harassment" by the Israelis, particularly near the village of al-Aadeisse.

During the first nine months of 1980 approximately 1,800 people were killed, some 1,500 for

Palestinian guerrillas search through debris following an Israeli attack on a PLO base near Sarafand on April 18.

WIDE WORLD

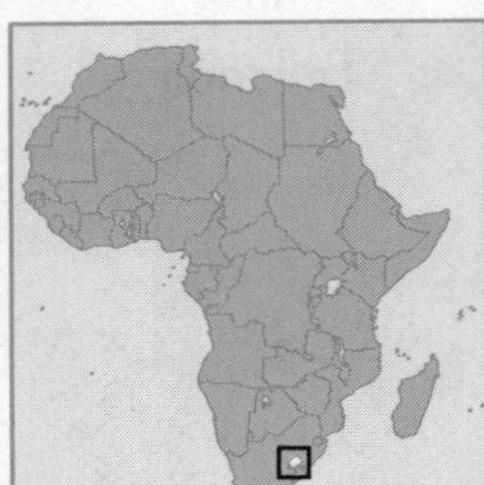

Lesotho

Liberia

political reasons; about 1,700 were wounded. The killings caused right-wing political leaders to increase their efforts to establish "alternative administrations." Responsibility for the deaths of five people on August 24 in Reyfoun northeast of Beirut was claimed by the "Marada free revolutionaries." The Marada Brigade was the militia of the Franjiya family, involved in a long feud with its Maronite Christian rightist allies, the Phalangists. Palestinian guerrillas were reported in August to have acquired Soviet-made radar and electronic surveillance equipment. In late December a large Syrian force was deployed in an effort to end factional fighting in Zahle.

About 25 Palestinians and Lebanese died in an attack on August 19 by some 600 Israeli soldiers on Palestinian camps north of the Litani River. The attack was the heaviest incursion into southern Lebanon in two years.

On October 20 the president of the Reconstruction and Development Council, Muhammad Atallah, said that only $153 million of the U.S. $400 million pledged for 1980 at an Arab summit in Tunisia in November 1979 had arrived. Lebanon was paralyzed by this financial restraint, Atallah said, because its plans were drafted on the basis of the money's arrival. In July the Cabinet had approved a $295.6 million reconstruction and development program financed by summit aid, almost half of which was for the south. A draft budget for 1981 totaling $1,515,100,000, slightly more than for 1980, was also dependent on summit aid.

The Lebanese economy showed its resilience. Exports in the first six months of 1980 totaled $515 million, a 48% rise over the corresponding period of 1979. Building materials accounted for 29%. Reexports (of imported goods) were also up 30% over 1979, with most going to Saudi Arabia (54% of the total, valued at $155.7 million). Success was achieved under difficult operating conditions by the national carrier, Middle East Airlines, which made a record profit in 1979 of $15.1 million.

As many as 500,000 Lebanese, including 30–40% of all industrial workers, had left the country since 1975 to seek work abroad, mainly in Saudi Arabia and nations on the Persian Gulf. Remittances from this source of $100 million a month helped to keep the balance of payments in surplus despite record trade deficits. (JOHN WHELAN)

Lesotho

A constitutional monarchy of southern Africa and a member of the Commonwealth of Nations, Lesotho forms an enclave within the republic of South Africa, bordering the Republic of Transkei to the southeast. Area: 30,352 sq km (11,716 sq mi). Pop. (1978 est.): 1,318,000. Cap. and largest city: Maseru (pop., 1976 prelim., 14,700). Language: English and Southern Sotho (official). Religion: Roman Catholic 38.7%; Lesotho Evangelical Church 24.3%; Anglican 10.4%; other Christian 8.4%; non-Christian 18.2%. Chief of state in 1980, King Moshoeshoe II; prime minister, Chief Leabua Jonathan.

On Jan. 19, 1980, Lesotho issued its new currency, the loti (plural, maloti), backed by South Africa's rand, and launched the Lesotho Monetary Authority. The budget showed growth in construction and improved performance in industry and commerce. Exports rose 13% to 28 million maloti due to increased diamond production. Drought was causing a 40% decline in food production in 1980, however, and imports were valued at 328 million maloti. The main economic problem remained employment: 10,000 new jobs a year were needed. Lesotho attended the nine-nation economic summit in Lusaka, Zambia, on April 1.

West Germany planned to establish a satellite station, to replace the high-frequency link with Nairobi, which would be operational by the end of 1981. A delegation visited Kuwait and Saudi Arabia to negotiate assistance with oil supplies. Work was to commence at the end of 1980 on the international airport, with Arab aid.

On February 1 Lesotho established diplomatic relations with the Soviet Union. Chief Leabua Jonathan and South African Prime Minister P. W. Botha met on August 1 in an effort to improve the poor relations between the two countries.

(GUY ARNOLD)

LESOTHO

Education. (1978) Primary, pupils 228,523, teachers (1976) 4,233; secondary, pupils 17,732, teachers (1976) 621; vocational, pupils 945, teachers (1976) 103; teacher training, students 835, teachers (1976) 39; higher (university), students 847, teaching staff (1976) 95.

Finance and Trade. Monetary unit: loti (plural maloti), at par with the South African rand, with (Sept. 22, 1980) a free rate of 0.75 loti to U.S. $1 (1.81 maloti = £1 sterling). Budget (1978–79 est.): revenue 77,443,000 maloti; expenditure 50,532,000 maloti (excludes development expenditure of 87.7 million maloti). Foreign trade (1977): imports 199.4 million maloti; exports 12.2 million maloti. Main exports: wool 21%; mohair 16%; diamonds 10%. Most trade is with South Africa.

Agriculture. Production (in 000; metric tons; 1978): corn *c.* 100; wheat *c.* 60; sorghum 59; dry peas *c.* 5; wool *c.* 1.3. Livestock (in 000; 1978): cattle *c.* 620; goats *c.* 925; sheep *c.* 1,720.

Liberia

A republic on the west coast of Africa, Liberia is bordered by Sierra Leone, Guinea, and Ivory Coast. Area: 97,790 sq km (37,757 sq mi). Pop. (1980 est.): 1,863,000. Cap. and largest city: Monrovia (pop., 1978 est., 229,300). Language: English (official) and tribal dialects. Religion: mainly animist. President until April 12, 1980, William R. Tolbert, Jr.; head of state and chairman of the People's Redemption Council from April 12, Master Sgt. Samuel K. Doe.

The Tolbert regime in Liberia was destroyed in a coup by the People's Redemption Council (PRC) led by Master Sgt. Samuel K. Doe (*see* BIOGRAPHIES) on April 12, 1980, bringing to an end more than a century of political dominance in Liberia by the True Whig Party. In events leading up to the coup, Pres. William R. Tolbert, Jr. (*see* OBITUARIES), had had leaders of the opposition, the recently formed People's Progressive Party (PPP), arrested following the call of PPP leader Gabriel

SIPA PRESS/BLACK STAR

At the order of the People's Redemption Council, 13 members of the deposed civilian government were executed by Liberian soldiers.

Baccus Matthews on March 7 for a general strike to bring down the government. Tolbert and 27 others were shot on the day of the coup; PPP members were released and four given Cabinet posts, Matthews becoming foreign minister.

Tolbert had tried various reform measures, but the nation's economy was deteriorating with the fall in demand for iron ore; also, Liberia's acting as host for the Organization of African Unity (OAU) summit conference in 1979 had cost the nation about $95 million. Measures announced by the PRC immediately after the coup were: minimum wages of $200 a month; the pay of army privates to be doubled; a price freeze; and the release of political prisoners.

Lawlessness, with elements of the Army out of control, characterized the first months after the coup. About one thousand people were rounded up and imprisoned, but half were quickly released. A military tribunal tried those accused of treason, and 13 officials, including eminent politicians—Reginald Townsend (former leader of the True Whig Party), Cecil Dennis (foreign minister), Joseph Chesson (justice), and Frank Tolbert (former president of the Senate and elder brother of the president)—were executed.

After five months there was no formal African recognition of the regime; Liberia was refused admittance to the OAU economic summit in Nigeria in April, nor did Doe attend the OAU summit in Sierra Leone in July. However, by the end of July relations with African countries were returning to normal. At home there were growing demands for the PRC to fulfill its promises of free education and cheap rice. (GUY ARNOLD)

LIBERIA

Education. (1978) Primary, pupils 129,776; secondary, pupils 108,077; primary and secondary, teachers 7,360; vocational (1976), pupils 1,236, teachers 63; teacher training (1976), students 444, teachers 40; higher, students 3,089, teaching staff *c.* 190.

Finance. Monetary unit: Liberian dollar, at par with the U.S. dollar, with a free rate (Sept. 22, 1980) of L$2.40 = £1 sterling. Budget (total; 1978–79 actual): revenue L$204 million; expenditure L$447 million.

Foreign Trade. (1979) Imports L$506,450,000; exports L$536,560,000. Import sources (1978): U.S. 25%; West Germany 11%; U.K. 7%; Saudi Arabia 6%; France 5%; The Netherlands 5%. Export destinations (1978): U.S. 28%; West Germany 22%; Italy 11%; France 10%; Belgium-Luxembourg 8%; The Netherlands 6%; Spain 5%. Main exports (1978): iron ore 56%; rubber 14%; diamonds 6%; coffee 5%.

Transport and Communications. Roads (1977) 11,218 km. Motor vehicles in use (1978): passenger 20,100; commercial (including buses) 13,800. Railways (1978) 493 km. Shipping (1979): merchant vessels 100 gross tons and over 2,466 (mostly owned by U.S. and other foreign interests); gross tonnage 81,528,175. Telephones (Jan. 1978) 8,420. Radio receivers (Dec. 1977) 274,000. Television receivers (Dec. 1977) 10,000.

Agriculture. Production (in 000; metric tons; 1979): rice *c.* 260; cassava (1978) *c.* 272; bananas *c.* 69; palm kernels *c.* 8; palm oil *c.* 28; rubber *c.* 75; cocoa *c.* 4; coffee *c.* 10. Livestock (in 000; 1978): cattle *c.* 37; sheep *c.* 185; goats *c.* 185; pigs *c.* 98.

Industry. Production (in 000; metric tons; 1978): petroleum products *c.* 550; cement *c.* 100; iron ore (68% metal content; 1979) 19,870; diamonds (metric carats; 1977) 326; electricity (kw-hr; 1977) *c.* 887,000.

Libraries

In 1980 the world recession reduced the growth of libraries that had been so marked during the preceding two decades. In France, for example, no new Bibliothèques Centrales de Prêt were created, and the number of "classified" municipal libraries remained static. Of particular concern to France's public librarians was the lack of progress on the promised public library legislation announced by the government in January 1979. It appeared that the project would be delayed pending reorganization of the communes.

The China Society of Libraries announced its formation at a meeting held in Taiyuan (T'ai-yüan), the capital of Shanxi (Shansi) Province.

The society's newly elected president called for the establishment of a countrywide library network to keep pace with China's modernization efforts. It was also reported that a new building to house the Beijing (Peking) Library, China's largest, was to be built in one of the city's western suburbs. Construction was scheduled to begin in 1981, with completion in 1985. The library, with 10.2 million books, was currently housed in a palace-type structure near Beihai (Pei-hai) Park in the centre of the city. In the new building, computers and other electronic equipment would be used in the catalog service. China now had 1,651 public libraries with 183.6 million books.

The new National Library of Mexico building was completed during 1980. In Trinidad and Tobago there was further progress in planning for the new National Library and Information Service. In West Germany controversy continued over the prestige building of the Staatsbibliothek Preussischer Kulturbesitz. One of the major topics of the year concerned working conditions in libraries, including the effect of new media and technology, and several sessions of the 70th annual conference of academic librarians in Wuppertal were devoted to this theme. The newly formed Deutsches Bibliotheksinstitut announced a reorganization of its list of publications; many of its former series would be replaced with one series, "dbi-materialien."

In East Germany the Bibliotheksverband der DDR emphasized cooperation among all types of libraries and between libraries and other institutions, with particular reference to the recommendations of the Communist Party and the next five-year plan (1981–85). Stress was laid on the furtherance of scientific and technical progress through adult education and on the importance of educating the younger generations in the use of libraries.

In the U.K. work progressed on the new British Reference Library, to be situated in Euston Road, London. Since 40% of the library's first stage was to be below ground, a great deal of excavation was required. The complete scheme would provide 200,000 sq m (2,152,800 sq ft) of library accommodation and would house some 3,500 reader places.

Internationally, the subjects most discussed during the year were Universal Bibliographic Control (UBC) and Universal Availability of Publications (UAP). The UBC program of the International Federation of Library Associations (IFLA), which was accepted by UNESCO and endorsed by national libraries and bibliographic organizations, aimed to promote the exchange of compatible bibliographic records. The IFLA International Office for UBC was responsible for coordinating the work of national bibliographic agencies in this respect.

At the heart of the UBC program was the production of a series of International Standard Bibliographic Descriptions (ISBD's). A general standard (ISBD [G]) was first produced in 1977, and within that framework others had been published covering specific types of publications. In 1980 two more appeared, one for antiquarian books and one for printed music, and work on one for component parts was well advanced.

IFLA's UAP program, which had as its ultimate aim the availability to all of all published documents, continued to be developed as a major element of IFLA's Medium Term Program. Current activity included studies of availability from publishers and booksellers and the acquisition, interlending, and retention policies and procedures of libraries, at both the national and the international level. These studies would form basic material for the joint IFLA-UNESCO International Congress on UAP, to be held in May 1982.

Since IFLA adopted new statutes in 1976, it had made positive moves toward giving more emphasis to countries outside Europe and North America and especially to library associations from less developed countries. Thus the 1980 conference, held for the first time in a less developed country—Manila, Philippines—was a milestone in IFLA's history. Because of travel costs, the number of librarians from Europe and North America was reduced, but this was largely made up by librarians from the Pacific region and particularly from the Philippines. (GODFREY THOMPSON)

In January 1980 the U.S. library press hailed Pres. Jimmy Carter's Nov. 16, 1979, address to the White House Conference on Library and Information Services, where librarians and interested citizens shaped 25 resolutions designed to democratize access to information resources. A follow-up conference was held September 15–17 in Minneapolis, Minn., but the defeats of Carter and other friends of libraries in the November 4 elections clouded earlier optimism. In September a gubernatorial veto in California denied beleaguered public libraries $18 million in relief, and a referendum lowering taxes in Massachusetts would diminish library revenues there. Other major proposals reducing library tax revenues were voted down, however.

As of 1980, some 2,200 libraries shared almost 7 million cataloging records in the OCLC, Inc., cooperative online network, and the Research Libraries Information Network had 22 members by November. Online and video technology were key topics at the American Library Association's (ALA's) annual conference, June 28–July 4 in New York City. ALA-accredited library schools with "information" in their names had increased from 10% in 1970 to 34% in 1980, indicating the shift in curriculum. The American Association of School Librarians held the nation's first national conference in this subfield, in Louisville, Ky., September 25–28. Libraries prepared for broad adoption Jan. 1, 1981, of a new and controversial *Anglo-American Cataloguing Rules, Second Edition.* The Library of Congress dedicated its $160 million, 196,250-sq-m (2,112,492-sq-ft) James Madison Memorial Building, the largest U.S. library structure.

(ARTHUR PLOTNIK)

[441.C.2.d; 613.D.1.a; 735.H]

Libya

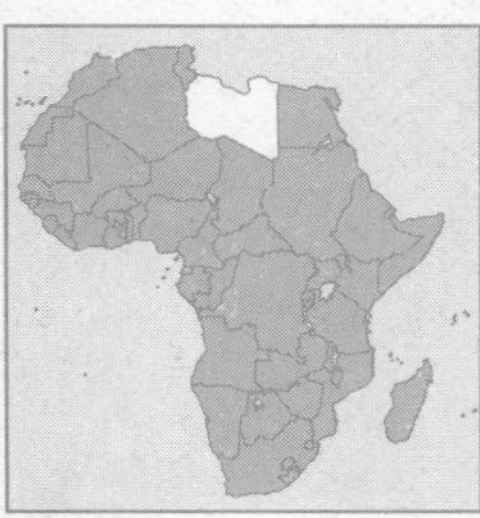
Libya

A socialist country on the north coast of Africa, Libya is bounded by the Mediterranean Sea, Egypt, the Sudan, Tunisia, Algeria, Niger, and Chad. Area: 1,749,000 sq km (675,000 sq mi). Pop.

LIBYA

Education. (1977–78) Primary, pupils 574,770, teachers 26,182; secondary, pupils 194,866, teachers 12,792; vocational, pupils 5,548, teachers 375; teacher training, students 24,153, teachers 1,968; higher, students 17,174, teaching staff 1,922.

Finance. Monetary unit: Libyan dinar, with (Sept. 22, 1980) a par value of 0.296 dinar to U.S. $1 (free rate of 0.712 dinar = £1 sterling). Gold, SDR's, and foreign exchange (June 1980) U.S. $10,863,000,000. Budget (administrative; 1979 est.) balanced at 770,000,000 dinars (excludes development expenditure of 1,573,000,000 dinars). Gross national product (1978) 5,407,000,000 dinars. Money supply (Dec. 1978) 1,687,800,000 dinars. Cost of living (Tripoli; 1975 = 100; Jan.–March 1979) 159.8.

Foreign Trade. (1979) Imports (fob) *c.* 2,217,000,000 dinars; exports 4,510,400,000 dinars. Import sources (1978): Italy 24%; West Germany 13%; France 8%; Japan 7%; U.K. 7%; U.S. 6%. Export destinations (1978): U.S. 41%; Italy 22%; West Germany 11%; Spain 6%; France 5%. Main export: crude oil 99.9%.

Transport and Communications. Roads (including tracks; 1976) *c.* 20,000 km (including 8,700 km surfaced). Motor vehicles in use (1977): passenger 386,000; commercial (including buses) 181,600. Air traffic (1978): 832 million passenger-km; freight *c.* 9.2 million net ton-km. Shipping (1979): vessels 100 gross tons and over 84; gross tonnage 885,247. Shipping traffic: goods loaded (1977) 92,892,000 metric tons, unloaded (1976) 8,451,000 metric tons. Telephones (Dec. 1974) 102,000. Radio licenses (Dec. 1977) 125,000. Television receivers (Dec. 1978) *c.* 155,000.

Agriculture. Production (in 000; metric tons; 1979): barley *c.* 200; wheat (1978) *c.* 98; potatoes (1978) *c.* 90; watermelons (1978) *c.* 150; tomatoes *c.* 232; onions *c.* 59; oranges *c.* 32; olives *c.* 100; dates *c.* 83. Livestock (in 000; 1978): sheep *c.* 4,680; goats *c.* 2,100; cattle *c.* 200; camels *c.* 75; asses *c.* 73.

Industry. Production (in 000; metric tons; 1979): crude oil 99,280; petroleum products (1978) *c.* 6,070; natural gas (cu m; 1977) 6,055,000; electricity (Tripolitania; excluding most industrial production; kw-hr) *c.* 1,600,000.

(1980 est.): 3,250,000. Cap. and largest city: Tripoli (pop., 1980 est., 994,000). Language: Arabic. Religion: predominantly Muslim. Chief of state in 1980, Col. Muammar al-Qaddafi; secretary-general of the General People's Congress, Abdul Ati al-Obeidi.

Despite Col. Muammar al-Qaddafi's Third International Theory of elected popular committees, Libya remained a centrally directed state organized through centrally appointed revolutionary committees. Qaddafi claimed that one of these, acting without authorization, had urged young Libyans overseas to execute Libyan nationals opposed to the regime who refused to return to Libya by June 11, 1980. Killings took place in Rome (four), Athens (one), Bonn (one), London (two), and Milan, Italy (one). France, the U.K., the U.S., and West Germany took action to regulate the activities of the Libyan People's Bureaus representing Libya in their respective capitals. On June 11 Qaddafi waived the death penalty except for those condemned by a revolutionary court and exiles collaborating with Israel, Egypt, and the U.S.

Libya started 1980 as an ally of Malta and the Palestine Liberation Organization (PLO) and a member of the Steadfastness Front with Algeria, Syria, Yemen (Aden), and the PLO. In oil affairs Libya was aligned with the countries that wanted prices raised and therefore opposed Saudi Arabia. Libya cut oil production more than once during the year. Qaddafi was a would-be friend of Iran, but he found it difficult to consummate the friendship. The Iranians could not accept the disappearance at the end of a 1978 visit to Libya of Imam Moussa-Sadr, a Lebanese Shiʿah Muslim leader.

WIDE WORLD

In September, Libyan leader Muammar al-Qaddafi (far right) celebrated the 11th anniversary of the military coup that brought him to power. Syrian President Hafez al-Assad (centre, shaking hands) attended the celebration in Lebanon.

At the end of 1979 Libyan revolutionary committees seized PLO offices in Tripoli and organized Palestinian revolutionary committees, turning these against the PLO leadership. PLO/Libyan relations were broken off around the beginning of the year, although the Palestinian struggle remained a theme of the Libyan leader. The relationship with Malta was terminated on August 28 when the Maltese government expelled a Libyan military advisory team after a Libyan naval vessel harassed a Maltese-licensed oil rig drilling in an area claimed by Libya. Relations with Tunisia improved steadily in the second half of 1980, a significant shift after the disturbances in Gafsa in January, which Tunisia blamed on Libya. Support for King Hassan's opponents in Morocco continued. Involvement in the Chad civil war expanded in December when Libyan troops occupied that country's capital.

On September 10 Libya and Syria agreed to form an "organic union." As a friend of Syria and so an enemy of Iraq, Qaddafi could logically sympathize with Iran in the Iraq-Iran war, but the war exacerbated relations between Libya and Saudi Arabia (assisting Iraq). Qaddafi called for a jihad (holy war) to liberate Mecca, and Saudi Arabia terminated diplomatic relations on October 28. Egypt remained the enduring enemy.

Libya's economy continued to expand, with oil revenues totaling over U.S. $18 billion. The interest in Libya shown by U.S. Pres. Jimmy Carter's brother, Billy (*see* BIOGRAPHIES), was exploited by the president's political enemies during the U.S. electoral campaign, but the affair soon died away.

(J. A. ALLAN)

Liechtenstein

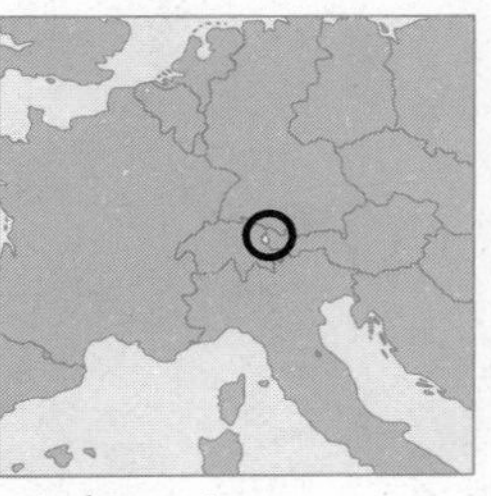
Liechtenstein

A constitutional monarchy between Switzerland and Austria, Liechtenstein is united with Switzerland by a customs and monetary union. Area: 160 sq km (62 sq mi). Pop. (1979 est.): 25,800. Cap. and

LIECHTENSTEIN

Education. (1980–81) Primary, pupils 1,960, teachers 95; secondary, pupils 1,790, teachers 93.

Finance and Trade. Monetary unit: Swiss franc, with (Sept. 22, 1980) a free rate of SFr 1.66 to U.S. $1 (SFr 3.98 = £1 sterling). Budget (1979 est.): revenue SFr 203,604,000; expenditure SFr 200,819,000. Exports (1978) SFr 680.6 million. Export destinations: Switzerland 37%; EEC 31%; EFTA (other than Switzerland) 7%. Main exports: metal manufactures, chemicals, instruments, furniture, pottery. Tourism (1978) 73,431 visitors.

largest city: Vaduz (pop., 1979 est., 4,900). Language: German. Religion (1979): Roman Catholic 88%. Sovereign prince, Francis Joseph II; chief of government in 1980, Hans Brunhart.

Citizens of Liechtenstein poured into the streets of Vaduz to meet their Olympic champion, slalom and downhill skier Hanni Wenzel, on her return from the February 1980 Winter Olympics in Lake Placid, N.Y. Hanni and her brother Andreas placed Liechtenstein sixth in the final gold medal table, ahead of such winter sports giants as Finland, Norway, Switzerland, and Canada. The Wenzels (*see* BIOGRAPHIES) also won the men's and women's World Cup skiing championships in March—the first family to win both cups.

On May 2 Queen Elizabeth II of Great Britain and the duke of Edinburgh arrived in Vaduz on a two-day visit and were welcomed by Prince Francis Joseph, a distant cousin of the duke.

In June the tax laws were tightened to require businesses to be audited and entered in a public register. The number of foreign concerns using Liechtenstein as a tax haven was not expected to fall significantly, however.

(K. M. SMOGORZEWSKI)

Life Sciences

Experiments involving the engineering of primitive life remained a focus of attention in 1980, but the kind of attention varied according to the recency of the experiment. The primordial one, conducted by nature, originated life on Earth, and a major task of paleobiologists has been to trace as far into the past as possible the sequence and timing of life's beginnings. In June a team of U.S. and Australian investigators headed by J. William Schopf of the University of California at Los Angeles announced its discovery of what it felt to be convincing evidence of structurally preserved microfossils in Australian rock dated at 3,500,000,000 years. The structures take the form of filaments that were interpreted to be chains of bacterial cells. Microfossils resembling blue-green algae (cyanobacteria) and dated at 3,400,000,000 years had been recovered in 1977 from sediments in Africa, but evidence that they had once been living organisms was not conclusive. Prior to the Australian find, the oldest microfossils of organisms for which there was generally undisputed evidence were dated at 2,300,000,000 years.

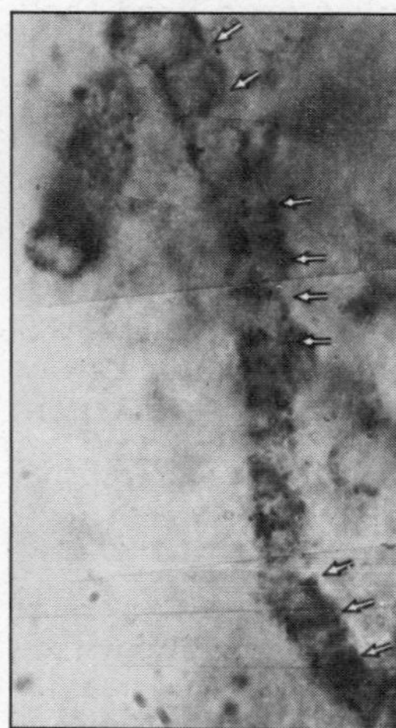

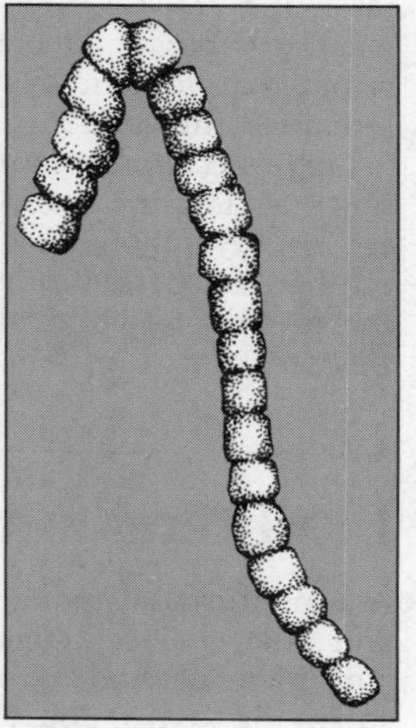

Highly magnified thin section of Australian rock dated at 3,500,000,000 years contains what scientists believe to be fossil bacterial cells. Arrows indicate apparent cell walls within the filamentous structure.

WIDE WORLD

Contemporary engineering experiments, conducted by scientists in several countries and primarily centred on genetic manipulation of bacterial life, were receiving increased attention from legal and business sectors as, in the words of one molecular biologist, "suddenly our discoveries are worth money." On June 16 the U.S. Supreme Court ruled 5 to 4 in favour of Ananda Chakrabarty, a microbiologist who since 1972 had sought to patent a bacterium that he had endowed with additional genetic material to improve its ability to degrade oil slicks. The ruling, which made laboratory-developed microorganisms patentable, was expected to clear the way for the U.S. Patent Office to begin processing the more than 100 outstanding applications that had been filed by genetic engineering firms, pharmaceutical companies, and other organizations to protect their investments.

The court's decision was narrow in the sense that it addressed only the statutory question of whether in formulating the current patent laws the U.S. Congress had intended in any way to exclude inventions that are alive. In so doing it interpreted the laboratory-contrived microorganism as a "manufacture" and not a "hitherto unknown natural phenomenon," but it did not attempt to distinguish between the living and the nonliving or to make judgments on the potential dangers of creating new life forms. Observers favourable to the decision felt that it had given deserved recognition to the rapidly advancing field of biotechnology but were undecided about its practical importance, particularly in what way, if any, the decision would affect rulings on patent applications that were seeking to protect for their discoverers some of the basic techniques of recombinant DNA technology, or gene splicing. Critics of the ruling pointed out that the ability to patent life forms might inhibit the free flow of scientific information by encouraging secrecy. Another fear was that patenting, and thereby profit seeking, would increase the use of engineered life forms throughout the world and the consequent risk of environmental mishap. (*See* Special Report.)

(CHARLES M. CEGIELSKI)

[312.A.1–4]

ZOOLOGY

Among reports published in 1980 that dealt with ancient animal life appeared one of an unusual finding by University of California scientists headed by E. M. Prager. Using immunological techniques, they succeeded in detecting a common protein, serum albumin, in muscle sampled from a mammoth frozen perhaps as long as 40,000 years and accidentally discovered in 1977. Furthermore, even though the mammoth albumin had undergone postmortem changes, it was shown to be quite similar to that of living Indian and African elephants. Previous attempts to study proteins from the remains of extinct animals had been unsuccessful.

Yet another study in evolutionary zoology provided the first evidence of the ability of carnivorous dinosaurs to swim. More than 40 footprints were found in the fossilized mud of an ancient Connecticut lake bottom. From their size and shape W. P. Coombs, Jr., of Western New England College, Springfield, Mass., argued that the tracks were probably made by indigenous species of large carnivorous dinosaurs as they floated in the water and pushed themselves along with their toes. The evidence indicates that these animals were able to pursue their prey, herbivorous dinosaurs, into the water.

A new method of dating ancient life was described by M. Ikeya and T. Miki of Yamaguchi University in Japan. They used electron spin resonance (ESR) spectroscopy, a technique that detects the presence of unpaired electrons in a substance by its behaviour in a magnetic field. The ESR signal of interest results from radiation-induced changes in the crystalline structure of fossil bones and provides a measure of the total dose of natural radiation received. The investigators called this age-dependent dose the "archaeological dose." They found a good correspondence between the ages of samples determined from ESR spectroscopy and from established methods. They felt that ESR would be of particular value because samples do not have to be ground up or heated for analysis.

Of benefit to marine zoology was the discovery of a deep-sea species of mollusk that lacks a gut, in contrast with other known mollusks. Marine-dwelling pogonophorans, commonly called beard-worms, heretofore had been regarded as the only phylum of free-living (nonparasitic) animals that lack an internal digestive system. However, R. G. B. Reid of the University of Victoria, B.C., and F. R. Bernard of the Pacific Biological Station, Nanaimo, B.C., recently described a bivalve, a species of *Solemya,* that has no alimentary tract. This species is from the northeastern Pacific Ocean. The scientists concluded that it feeds by absorbing dissolved organic molecules through its gills (ctenidia). Other members of this genus have a greatly reduced gut, and *S. borealis,* another species, may also completely lack a gut. That such comparatively large animals lack a gut is contrary to expectation; one explanation is that dissolved nutrients from pulp mills might be their nutrient source. This suggestion, however, does not explain how they evolved.

Marine biologists have estimated that at least 90% of mid-water animals are capable of emitting light. Of interest is whether in each kind of animal the light is produced by specialized animal tissue or by symbiotic bacteria. This question was approached by Gary Leisman and co-workers at the Scripps Institution of Oceanography in California, who developed a method for detecting bacterial luciferase, the enzyme involved in light production by bacteria. This particular variety of luciferase is not present in animal cells; thus, its presence is an indicator of light-producing bacteria. The investigators found that the light organs of several marine organisms which they examined had this enzyme, suggesting that bacteria are the source of their light.

Another study involved a role for bioluminescence in animal camouflage. R. E. Young and F. M. Mencher of the University of Hawaii found that at least two species of squid change the colour, intensity, and angular distribution of their emitted light when they migrate downward to colder water at night. This colour change apparently makes them more difficult to see from below against the dim light from the surface and thus protects them from predators lying deeper than themselves. This discovery offers an interesting example of the fusion of protective coloration with bioluminescence.

Robert Silberglied and Annette Aiello of the Smithsonian Tropical Research Institute, Panama, found that some insects apparently achieve camouflage from predators by becoming wet. Although the body surface of most insects resists wetting, several species of neotropical bark bugs were found to become coated with a thin film of water during rain showers. Wetting of the bugs produced approximately the same drop in reflectance as wetting of the bark of the trees on which they live, resulting in a continued visible "match" between animal and background. Thus, whereas wetting of the bark alone would reduce the protective value of insect coloration, parallel changes in reflectance of both bark and insect produced by wetting preserves the camouflage.

Among reports that studied the special senses was one involving elephant hearing. Rickye Heffner and Henry Heffner of the University of Kansas at Parsons were interested in testing whether the well-established inverse relationship between the high-frequency hearing limit and the functional interaural distance (the distance between the two ears divided by the speed of sound) is valid for large animals. They chose two adolescent female Indian elephants for their study. The elephants were found to have a hearing range from 17 hertz to 10.5 kilohertz, just what one would expect on the basis of the functional interaural distance. As of 1980 this relationship had been examined in studies of 32 mammalian genera, ranging from mouse and bat to elephant and killer whale. Cumulatively these studies indicate that as much as 80% of the variance in the upper limit is related to the functional interaural distance alone. Humans fall at the appropriate point on the curve, with a high-frequency hearing limit of about 20 kilohertz.

In 1978 E. S. Savage-Rumbaugh and co-workers of the Yerkes Regional Primate Research Center in Georgia described the first observation of symbolic communication between two nonhuman primates (chimpanzees). Two years later another study, conducted by Robert Epstein, Robert P. Lanza,

Life Insurance:
see Industrial Review

(TOP) WALTER P. COOMBS; (BOTTOM) ADAPTED FROM "SWIMMING ABILITY OF CARNIVOROUS DINOSAURS," W. P. COOMBS, SCIENCE, VOL. 207, NO. 4436, PP. 1198–1199, MARCH 14, 1980; ART BY MATTHEW HYMAN

More than 40 unusual footprints found in fossilized mud of an ancient lake bottom in Connecticut were interpreted as the first evidence of swimming by large carnivorous dinosaurs. Photos show central toe impressions and flanking claw streaks apparently made by the left feet of two species of dinosaur. Sketch reconstructs a hypothetical swimming posture for *Megalosaurus,* a dinosaur known to have lived in the region about 180 million years ago, when the tracks were made.

and B. F. Skinner of Harvard University, extended this result to the pigeon. After two birds were taught to recognize letter and word symbols, one pigeon was given the opportunity to use the symbols to communicate information about hidden colours to another pigeon in order for both to obtain food. Furthermore, the two pigeons had a prolonged and natural "conversation" without any urging from the experimenters. These results, although suggesting that even some nonprimate animals are able to communicate symbolically with one another, also support behavioural interpretations of such activity, which explain these apparent exchanges of information in terms of simple concepts of reinforced learning.

Several studies in the burgeoning field of toxicology were of zoological importance. For example, it was learned that red cochineal dye (carminic acid), produced by cochineal insects, acts as a deterrent to ant feeding. Thomas Eisner and co-workers at Cornell University, Ithaca, N.Y., also described a caterpillar, *Laetilia coccidivora,* that uses the carminic acid from cochineal insects on which it feeds for defensive purposes of its own.

A second study explored the resistance of the poison-dart frog to its own toxin, batrachotoxin, which is present in its skin. J. W. Daly of the National Institutes of Health, Bethesda, Md., led a group of three others in this study, which showed that although this frog has high levels of the toxin, its own nerves and muscles are resistant to it. The toxin acts by blocking sodium conductance channels. The frog's resistance, however, is specific. It still is sensitive to other agents that affect sodium conductance, but the frog does not encounter these naturally.

A novel pathway of vertebrate anaerobic metabolism was described in goldfish by E. A. Shoubridge and P. W. Hochachka of the University of British Columbia. They found that during short periods of anoxia (the absence of oxygen), goldfish produce carbon dioxide but do not accumulate lactic acid in their tissues to the large degree expected. Lactic acid is produced during anoxia, but it is then largely metabolized to ethanol. The appropriate enzyme for this reaction (alcohol dehydrogenase) was found to be present in the muscles. The two investigators felt that ethanol production is preferable to lactic acid accumulation because ethanol is less acidic than lactic acid and thus less likely to produce a metabolic acidosis. Fish are characterized by relatively poor buffering power; *i.e.,* their ability to maintain a fairly constant level of acidity despite small outside tendencies to change that level. Previous reports had shown that ethanol is indeed produced by microbial fermentation in the human intestinal tract, but the present case was interesting in representing a situation in which a vertebrate has the capacity to form ethanol in its own tissues.

(RONALD R. NOVALES)

[242.B.2.b.xiii; 313.G.4.a.ii; 321.B.6.c; 323.E; 333.B.1.b.v; 336.A.4.a]

Entomology. Some 2,000 scientists gathered in August 1980 at the 16th International Congress of Entomology in Kyoto, Japan, to discuss their latest research. Rice entomologists throughout Asia reported serious crop losses due to the brown plant hopper (BPH), *Nilaparvata lugens,* which breeds in paddy fields and causes "hopper burn." Swarms of hoppers were carried over the ocean on wet, southwest monsoonal winds and had annually invaded the Philippines and Japan.

It was generally agreed that the BPH invasions had begun with intensified rice growing, which involves the use of high-yield varieties and close planting and permits growing more crops per year—often under irrigation. But P. E. Kenmore and co-workers at the International Rice Research Institute, Manila, disputed claims that BPH swarms are an inevitable result of intensive production per se. They reported that BPH was adequately controlled by natural enemies in plots untreated with insecticides and blamed widespread misuse of insecticides for destroying beneficial insects. Gustave Mathys of the European and Mediterranean Plant Protection Organization, Paris, pointed out that farmers were generally afraid to abandon routine spraying and to start difficult pest-population evaluations. He stressed that simple procedures for deciding when to use pesticides were essential if rational strategies of pest management were to be widely adopted.

For some pests, forewarning of outbreaks can be obtained using traps baited with sex pheromones (chemical attractants), and there have been claims of successful control of pests by releasing sufficient pheromone to disrupt mating. Nevertheless, not all insects have proved susceptible to disruption of their pheromonal communication. Both C. J. Den Otter of the State University of Groningen, Neth., and Kazuo Nakamura of the National Institute of Agricultural Science, Yatabe, Japan, reported that many sex pheromones are formed of a bouquet of compounds, each playing a different role in the sequence of behaviour leading to copulation. V. Buda of the Lithuanian S.S.R. Academy of Sciences suggested that because these components are emitted at different concentrations and because insects have differing sensitivities to them, an insect flying into the plume of odour carried by the wind perceives first one, then another, and so on, of a structured sequence of behavioural messages. Buda suggested that the insect may therefore be able to distinguish a true source of pheromone from a somewhat different, artificial one. Moreover, R. T. Carde of Michigan State University pointed out that insects use visual and tactile as well as chemical cues in finding a mate.

There is a widely held belief among entomologists that insects and plants "co-evolved"; *i.e.*, that plants speciated under pressure of feeding by insects, the various daughter species having a variety of defenses against insects, and that, in response, insects also speciated, developing a corresponding variety of countermeasures to the plants' defenses. According to Tibor Jermy of the Research Institute for Plant Protection, Budapest, Hung., this hypothesis would require that related species of plants be attacked by related species of insects, for as each plant speciated, it should stimulate a corresponding speciation especially of those insects already specialized to feed on the ancestral plant. Yet, in reality, among those insects that have a restricted range of food plants, related species tend to feed on plants that are quite unrelated. Jermy suggested, therefore, that speciation of plants was not due to attack by insects and that insects had no particular difficulty in countering the specific defenses (if any) of plants. Instead he proposed a "sequential evolution" of insects: their speciation had indeed followed that of plants, but mainly because the plants had presented the insects with an increasing variety of easily recognizable markers of different kinds of environment, to which different species of insects had variously become particularly well adapted.

Jermy's hypothesis was supported in part by Elizabeth Bernays of the Centre for Overseas Pest Research, London. The acridids (locusts and grasshoppers) on which she worked had originated in the Carboniferous Period (between 345 million and 280 million years ago) when most plants appeared to have been loaded with highly toxic, condensed tannins. Insects that eat plants containing such chemicals require special adaptation of their digestive system. Two bursts of speciation of acridids had occurred subsequently, one coinciding with speciation of the grasses. On both occasions, however, the new species of plants apparently had been less, not more, toxic to acridids, because those acridids specialized to feed on a narrow range of modern plants have less elaborate detoxifying systems than forms that feed on a wider variety of plants.

When a toad strikes at a cockroach, on about one of every two occasions the insect will turn away at the last instant and escape. Jeffrey M. Camhi and Mark Plumrose of Cornell University, Ithaca, N.Y., found that sight is not necessarily involved, and in an ingenious series of experiments they showed that wind detectors are responsible—in the form of fine hairs that hang from the cerci (antenna-like structures at the rear of the roach's abdomen). How the insect distinguishes the puff of air caused by the toad's strike from the many other environmental air currents is apparently by sensitivity to a critical acceleration of the air. The toad's tongue was found to reach its target zone in 48 milliseconds, causing the air ahead to accelerate at 600 millimetres (two feet) per square second. The cockroach takes at least 44 milliseconds to respond, just fast enough for a 50% escape rate.

(PETER W. MILES)

[312.D; 321.B.9.c.i; 731.A.5]

Ornithology. Oropendolas, which are black birds with yellow tails, live in a wide area of Central and South America. They build hanging flask-shaped nests in palms and other tall spreading trees. Cowbirds, brood parasites that lay their eggs in the nests of oropendolas, are common around oropendola colonies. Oropendolas often, but not always, nest in trees inhabited by bees or wasps. The relationship between the oropendolas, cowbirds, and insects is bewilderingly complex.

Colonies of oropendolas are either nondiscriminators or discriminators of cowbird eggs; that is, oropendola hosts either accept the cowbird egg in the nest or reject it and throw it out. Colonies that are discriminators live in trees that have wasp or bee nests in them, while colonies that nest in trees without such insect nests are nondiscriminators. None of these observations made much sense until it was discovered that oropendola chicks are likely to be infested by botfly larvae. Botflies of the genus *Philornis* enter the bird's long flasklike nests and lay their eggs directly on the chicks. When the eggs hatch, the maggots feed on the tissues of the chick and usually cause its health to decline; eventually the chick dies. Botflies are a major cause of death among oropendola chicks.

Following this discovery a number of correlations emerged. Flypaper traps placed near oropendola colonies with bees or wasps in the tree showed that the social insects keep their surrounding "air-space" free of botflies. On the other hand, flypapers set in trees that contained oropendola colonies, but no bees or wasps, caught innumerable botflies. When Neal Smith, the investigating scientist, examined the nestlings in these latter colonies he made an especially exciting discovery. If the oropendola chick had a cowbird nest mate, it was nine times less likely to have a botfly infection than if the parasitic bird was not present.

It was found that the cowbird is very precocious compared with its host. Its eggs need five to seven days less incubation than host eggs, and the young cowbird is already covered in down when it hatches. Its eyes open within 48 hours, compared with six to nine days for the host chick. These adaptations presumably enhance the competitiveness of the brood parasite, making the cowbird stronger and better able to cheat its oropendola nest mates. They also superbly outfit it for the role of nest botfly eradicator. As soon as its eyes open, the cowbird chick snaps aggressively at intruding objects including botfly adults, eggs, and larvae. The young cowbird thus defends itself against botflies, incidentally defending its unrelated nest mates as well. Smith titled his description of this phenomenon "the advantage of being parasitized."

The advantage is indeed striking. During a four-year population study Smith showed that if botflies are prevalent in a colony the chance of an oropendola chick successfully fledging is about three times greater if its nest mates include a cowbird. For the oropendola, being parasitized is a definite help if no bees or wasps are present. Thus birds in trees without wasps or bees do not reject the cowbird eggs.

In compiling a catalogue of the seabird colonies of Alaska the U.S. Fish and Wildlife Service counted more than 22 million birds, from which it was deduced that some 40 million must exist in all. This population is easily the largest of marine birds in the Northern Hemisphere. Annual variations in the yield of guano from bird islands off the coast of South Africa provide a reliable yearly estimate of bird population sizes in that region. Also, fluctuations in these yields are correlated with changes in the abundance of the fish (mostly pilchards) on which the cormorants, gannets, and penguins feed. Thus guano yields are of value as indicators of fish stocks.

New fossils of giant, flightless penguinlike birds were found in late Oligocene and early Miocene rocks in Japan and in the western U.S. These birds belong to an extinct family called the Plotopteridae, which lived about 26 million years ago. They are not related to penguins and previously had been known only from a single fragment of bone from California. The hind limb and pelvic bones of these fossils are similar to those of living anhingas (snakebirds), but the wing is paddlelike and thus remarkably convergent toward that of penguins. Both the Plotopteridae and species of giant penguin became extinct by the middle Miocene (about 16 million years ago), possibly because of competition from seals and dolphins.

The white-winged guan, thought extinct for a century, was rediscovered in the dry forests of northwestern Peru. A few hundred birds were estimated to exist. Guans are large, gregarious, arboreal birds that feed on fruit and leaves and are confined to Central and South America.

(JEFFERY BOSWALL)

[313.J.6; 352.B.2.b.ii]

MARINE BIOLOGY

In northwestern Europe during the 1960s a decline of herring stocks occurred about the time an outburst in populations of gadoid fish (cod and related species) was also recorded. It was tempting to assume that the two events were related, but research suggested that an association would be difficult to substantiate, particularly until it was known how fish populations stabilize themselves.

Multivariate analysis of 40 years of data on the oyster (*Crassostrea virginica*) fishery in Chesapeake Bay revealed that variations in the density of spat (free-swimming young oysters) and in seedings can explain 56% of the variation in annual harvest. Remarkably, this finding would allow reasonable predictions to be made of oyster harvests as far ahead as four years.

An overview of the final Cepex (Controlled Ecosystem Pollution Experiment) project was published, appraising work carried out in British Columbia. The experiment involved the study of planktonic ecosystems in large polyethylene cylinders measuring 9.5 m (31 ft) in diameter and 23.5 m (77 ft) deep, which were suspended in the sea. Attempts were made to compare the structure and efficiency of food chains based on diatoms or flagellates as primary producers. Diatoms and flagellates were successfully established in separate enclosures, but copepod crustaceans feeding on these were rapidly eliminated by large numbers of ctenophores (comb jellies). Despite shortcomings, such enclosures may still have value in hypothesis testing in marine ecology; they provide an intermediate level of study between laboratory experiments and observations of natural populations.

In nature, when a diatom-based food chain changes to a flagellate-based one, troublesome "blooms" may arise, resulting in oxygen depletion owing to eutrophication or in toxic conditions. It was suggested that a switch from diatoms to flagellates might be related to the limiting effects of silica, which is required for diatom growth. If so, then regions of high natural silica input should be less prone to troublesome blooms. Also, since blooms often occur where nutrient-rich sewage is discharged, the addition of silica, if feasible, might alleviate eutrophication.

The maintenance of culture collections of single-celled marine algae is an expensive and time-consuming routine procedure for marine scientists, but new techniques of storage in liquid nitrogen were being successfully developed. Moreover, algae grown at 4° C (39° F) for four weeks were found to develop improved resistance to freezing storage. The temperature-reduced metabolic growth of active cells evidently causes modification of the cell membranes, an effect that increases resistance to freezing injury.

Echinoderms may form extremely dense feeding aggregations that have a dramatic effect on the environment, as typified by the starfish *Acanthaster* on coral reefs and the sea urchin *Strongylocentrotus* on kelp beds. Near the Virgin Islands the starfish *Oreaster reticulatus* was found to have a similar effect on soft bottom sediments, which are turned over twice in 24 hours by the feeding activity of the animal during spawning aggregations.

On coral reefs, fish may adopt very specialized strategies for feeding. In a simple case, wrasses (genus *Halichoeres*) follow goatfish (*Parupeneus*), whose feeding activities provide food for the wrasses. More complex examples studied in the Red Sea include predatory species that hide behind harmless species to approach a potential prey (riding behaviour) or that mimic harmless species, in which guise they are able to approach prey unrecognized (aggressive mimicry).

A long-debated question concerning cnidarians (*e.g.*, corals, sea anemones, and jellyfish) is whether the cnidoblasts, or stinging cells, used for defense and food capture are connected to the nervous system. French work suggested that in some of these animals the defensive cnidoblasts are typical receptor/effector systems independent of the nervous system, whereas cnidoblasts associated with predatory feeding are connected with and controlled by the nervous system.

Opportunities to study living *Nautilus* are rare, but a specimen of this ancient group of cephalopod mollusks was kept alive for nine months in the Monaco Aquarium after being caught near New Caledonia. Its breathing and swimming movements revealed greater sophistication of control than assumed hitherto.

Iron is incorporated into the radular teeth of mollusks, where it is responsible for tooth hardness. Other metals were shown to be of similar importance in the polychaete worms. Zinc and copper are used in the mineralization of the powerful jaws of nereids and glycerids respectively.

(ERNEST NAYLOR)

[312.C.3.b; 313.G.2.c; 313.G.4.a.ii–iii; 313.I.1.b; 354.B.2 and 5]

BOTANY

Photosynthesis is perhaps the most important process carried out by plants. It occurs within the chloroplasts of plant cells and can be divided into two phases. During the first, or light-requiring, phase solar energy is converted into chemical energy, which is then used in the second, or light-independent, phase to reduce carbon dioxide (CO_2) to form carbohydrates or other products. Concomitant with the conversion of light energy into chemical energy is the evolution of oxygen. Although many of the biochemical events of the light-requiring phase have been elucidated, very little is known about those leading to oxygen evolution. Recently a manganese-containing protein was isolated from the inner membranes (thylakoids) of spinach chloroplasts. Artificial membranes prepared by mixing phospholipids with thylakoid membranes devoid of the manganese-containing protein showed no measurable oxygen evolution. When the manganese-containing protein was added to the membrane system, however, oxygen was evolved suggesting that this protein was required for oxygen evolution.

With important exceptions the majority of chloroplasts studied to date have been shown to use the Calvin-Benson pathway, a sequence of biochemical reactions by means of which carbon from atmospheric CO_2 is fixed, or incorporated, into 3-phosphoglycerate. In a recent study guard cells (the bean-shaped cells that control pore size in plant leaves) and extracts of guard cell protoplasts of the vetch *Vicia faba* were assayed for three enzymes that are unique to the Calvin-Benson pathway: ribulosebiphosphate carboxylase, phosphoribulokinase, and glyceraldehyde-phosphate dehydrogenase. No enzyme activity or only insignificant levels of activity were detected. In addition, it was found that guard cells of tobacco leaves (*Nicotiana glauca*) also lacked another metabolic enzyme, ribulose-biphosphate carboxylase. Thus, guard cell chloroplasts of *Vicia* and tobacco—both plants that use the Calvin-Benson pathway (C_3 plants)—are deficient in the pathway. This discovery raised an important, as yet unanswered question. If they cannot fix CO_2, what is the function of guard cell chloroplasts?

Photosynthesis in C_3 plants is accompanied by photorespiration, an energetically wasteful process that results in decreased productivity. If photorespiration somehow could be reduced or eliminated, an increase in photosynthetic productivity should result. During the past year investigators working with *Arabidopsis thaliana*, an herb of the mustard family, isolated mutant plants lacking serine-glyoxylate aminotransferase, one of the enzymes of the photorespiratory pathway. The mutants were capable of living and exhibited normal rates of photosynthesis when photorespiration was suppressed. Under conditions that promoted photorespiration (normal atmospheric conditions), however, photosynthesis in the mutants occurred at greatly reduced rates; the mutants were unable to live. It was expected that continued research would yield mutants with reduced photorespiration but with the capacity to carry out photosynthesis at normal rates under atmospheric conditions. Such mutants might prove useful in developing crop plants with increased photosynthetic productivity.

In the flowering plants, chloroplasts and another kind of intracellular body, the mitochondria, exhibit maternal inheritance. This phenomenon has been ascribed to the physical exclusion of these organelles from the cells that give rise to the sperm (generative cells) carried in pollen. That organelle exclusion may not be the sole factor involved in maternal inheritance had been indicated by the results of earlier work with haploid albino (unpigmented) plantlets of rice, barley, and wheat. The plantlets were grown directly from uninucleate pollen; *i.e.*, pollen in an early developmental stage in which each grain contains only one nucleus. Because formation of the generative cell occurs only after the uninucleate stage, the albino condition of the plantlets could not be due to the exclusion of chloroplasts from the generative cell. It was suggested, therefore, that the chloroplasts were present but somehow altered, prior to formation of the generative cell, in a way that gave rise to an unpigmented plant. Evidence in support of organelle alteration was provided by a recent ultrastructural study. Leaf cells of albino rice plantlets derived from uninucleate pollen were found to contain modified chloroplasts and mitochondria. The chloroplasts lacked the usual elaborate internal membrane network; the mitochondria were consistently united into aggregates. Furthermore, an investigation of pollen development in *Hosta* showed that altered chloroplasts and mitochondria were already present in microspore mother cells, the cells that eventually give rise to pollen grains.

In addition to chloroplasts, another structural characteristic of most plant cells is the cell wall. It had been assumed that the cell wall does not exert a discriminating effect as to what kinds of molecules can penetrate it. Contrary to this assumption, it was recently determined by means of a solute-exclusion technique that the only molecules that can permeate the cell walls of living higher plants (root hair cells of radish, cotton fibres, cultured sycamore maple cells, and certain leaf cells of cocklebur and *Commelina*) have diameters no greater than 35–52Å (one angstrom, Å, is a hundred-millionth of a centimetre). Thus, the diameter of the pores present in the cell wall must place a restriction on the size of molecules that can permeate the wall. (LIVIJA KENT)

[322.A; 331.B.2.b; 336.D.2; 337.C; 338.D.2.a]

MOLECULAR BIOLOGY

Vitamin K and Blood Clotting. Nutrients can be divided into two categories, macronutrients and micronutrients. The former are required in relatively large amounts because they serve as fuels or as raw materials from which the body substance is synthesized. Carbohydrates, fats, and proteins are the familiar macronutrients. Micronutrients, in contrast, are needed in much smaller amounts because they usually serve in a catalytic fashion, facilitating essential reactions without being consumed. Some of the micronutrients are mineral substances, such as iron, copper, manganese, molybdenum, or selenium; others are organic molecules, such as thiamine, pyridoxine, or riboflavin. Organic micronutrients are called vitamins because the first of these to be well studied, thiamine, is chemically an amine and it was recognized as being vital—whence the original term vitamine.

Since vitamins are dietary essentials, any deficiency must be expected to give rise to symptoms. The existence of diseases caused by dietary deficiency and curable by dietary augmentation led to discovery of most of the known vitamins. In this way beriberi led to thiamine (vitamin B_1), scurvy to ascorbic acid (vitamin C), and pellagra to pyridoxine (vitamin B_6). Once the existence of vitamins was appreciated, investigators tried to discover new vitamins by constructing diets made up only of known and chemically defined components. If such well-defined diets failed to support normal growth of young laboratory animals, one could suspect the existence of an undiscovered vitamin, and if some supplement to the diet restored normal growth, one could hope to isolate the new vitamin from that supplement.

In the late 1920s Danish biochemist Henrik Dam was following this strategy when he noted that chicks on a defined diet developed a bleeding disease. Their blood had lost its normal ability to clot, and they died of internal hemorrhage. Such dietary supplements as alfalfa, hemp seed, or hog liver cured the disease and Dam named the new substance vitamin K, in which K stands for *Koagulation.* Vitamin K was found to be fat-soluble and so could be concentrated from natural sources by extraction in ether. Fish meal was discovered to be an excellent source of vitamin K, the more so if the meal was slightly putrid. This observation indicated that bacteria could synthesize vitamin K; in fact, in many animals the vitamin is adequately supplied by resident bacteria in the gut. Numerous bacteria were tested and found to contain vitamin K, with *Mycobacterium tuberculosis* a particularly rich source.

In the 1930s U.S. biochemist R. J. Anderson described the substance phthiocol, from *M. tuberculosis.* Subsequently another American, H. J. Almquist, purified vitamin K from dried alfalfa and suspected that it might be related to phthiocol, so he obtained phthiocol from Anderson and found that it did exhibit vitamin K activity. With this clue, the chemical structure of vitamin K was soon established. (*See* Figure 1.)

These compounds are derivatives of naphthoquinone; the methyl group on position 2 is essential for activity, whereas the substituent on position 3 is dispensable. There is, in fact, a family of vitamin K forms with R groups of different chain length. Even menadione, which entirely lacks the R group, is fully active.

Hemorrhagic problems are encountered occasionally in newborn infants because vitamin K is not readily transmitted from mother to fetus. Because this vitamin is not soluble in water, its absorption from the gut depends upon the emulsifying action of bile; biliary obstruction thus also leads to vitamin K deficiency and to a hemorrhagic tendency. For years the availability of vitamin K in pure form has allowed modern medicine to control these problems easily but without a fundamental grasp of how vitamin K exerts its effect on blood clotting.

Blood is a remarkable tissue. Under ordinary circumstances it must remain fluid so that it can be pumped throughout the body. In the event of minor injury it must solidify so that its loss from breached blood vessels will be minimal. Yet it must not clot inside intact blood vessels, because such clotting would plug the vessels and impede the flow of blood. As might be expected for a mechanism that must be at once responsive to environmental changes and yet under exquisite control, blood clotting is very complex.

Collagen is a fibrous protein that lends physical strength to tissues. It is abundant in the walls of blood vessels and in most other tissues. Yet circulating blood is not exposed to collagen, because it is not part of the inner lining of the blood vessels. Injury to a vessel will expose blood to the collagen in the vessel wall. Small bodies in the blood, the blood platelets, adhere strongly to collagen. Moreover, contact with collagen causes the platelets to release serotonin and adenosine diphosphate, substances that then cause platelets to adhere to each

Figure 1

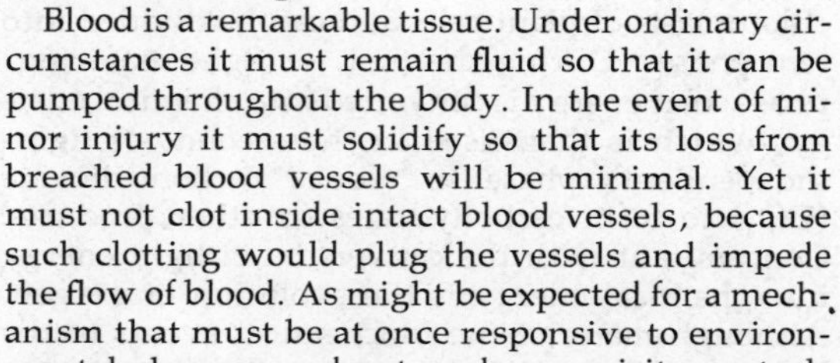

phthiocol | vitamin K

other. Injury thus quickly causes the blood platelets to form a platelet plug that will itself impede further blood loss. At the same time a remarkable cascade of reactions is initiated in which one protein, upon activation, activates the next, which in turn activates yet another. The essence of these activations is the cleavage of a peptide bond, the bond that holds together the individual amino acids in a protein chain. Such cleavage trims one or more stretches of amino acids from an inactive proenzyme, converting it into an active enzyme, which can then cleave a bond on the next proenzyme in the series. The power of such multistep cascades of reactions is that amplification is achieved at each step, resulting in a very great amplification overall. Hence, a small triggering event can cause a large end result.

Clotting can be initiated either by a lipoprotein substance released from injured tissues or, as described above, by exposure of one of the members of the clotting cascade to collagen or to activated platelets. The penultimate member of the clotting cascade is a protein called prothrombin. Its activated form, thrombin, cleaves several bonds in the ultimate member of the cascade, called fibrinogen, to yield fibrin. Fibrin reinforces the platelet plug by spontaneously self-associating into a fibrous network, which is then strengthened by the formation of cross-links by means of the action of an enzyme called a transglutaminase. Thrombin, which converts fibrinogen to fibrin, also activates the transglutaminase.

Several of the components of the clotting cascade bind calcium ions, and this bound calcium is essential for clotting to proceed. Indeed, one of the simplest ways to prevent drawn blood from clotting is to tie up all of the available calcium with chelating agents, such as citrate or EDTA, which have a strong affinity for metal ions in solution. Vitamin K deficiency results in a decrease of normal prothrombin and a concomitant increase in a protein that is actually the precursor of prothrombin. One may call this precursor preprothrombin. There are ten units, or residues, of the amino acid glutamic acid in the amino acid sequence of one end of preprothrombin. During the conversion of preprothrombin to prothrombin, these residues are converted to γ-carboxyglutamate residues. The structures in Figure 2 indicate how the latter residues can bind calcium ions (Ca^{2+}) while the former (as glutamate) cannot.

Figure 2

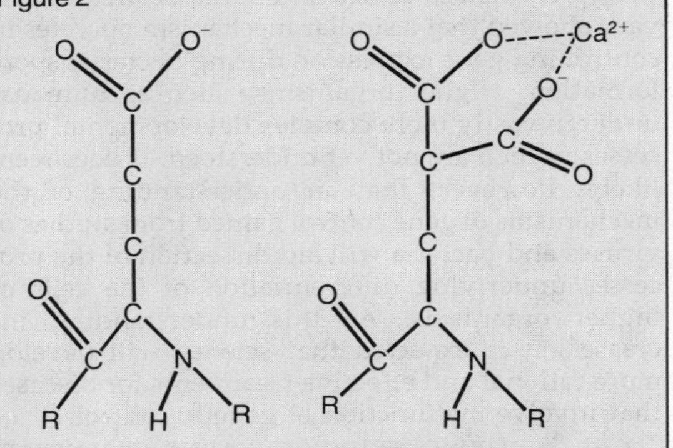

glutamate residue

γ-carboxyglutamate residue chelating calcium ion

Scientists only recently have begun to understand in detail the importance of vitamin K in normal blood clotting. Vitamin K was found to be an essential participant in the specific chemical reaction, called carboxylation, that converts particular glutamate residues in preprothrombin into γ-carboxyglutamate residues in prothrombin. It is these γ-carboxyglutamate residues that impart to prothrombin the ability to bind calcium and thus to participate in the clotting cascade. In fact, prothrombin is not the only one of the components of the cascade that contains γ-carboxyglutamate; there are three others as well, and in each case this peculiar amino acid is essential for activity.

Appreciation of the role of vitamin K in the γ-carboxylation of glutamate residues has led also to an understanding of the mechanism of action of the clotting-inhibitor drugs dicumarol and warfarin. The former was discovered as the cause of a hemorrhagic disease of cattle brought on by ingestion of fermented sweet clover, while the latter was synthesized as a water-soluble, more effective analogue of dicumarol. These compounds were found to prevent the vitamin-K-dependent γ-carboxylation reaction, presumably by competing with vitamin K for binding to enzymes involved in this reaction.

Evolution proceeds by stepwise modification of existing structures. A useful device, once hit upon, in time will be exploited to serve multiple functions. One might expect, therefore, that the ability of γ-carboxyglutamate to bind calcium is used in tissues other than blood and for purposes other than clotting. Indeed, the second most abundant protein of bone, after collagen, is osteocalcin, and it is rich in γ-carboxyglutamate residues. Its presence must have something to do with controlling the mineralization of bone. Proteins with γ-carboxyglutamate residues have been noted in several other tissues. In developing chicken embryos, for example, the transport of calcium from the shell of the egg to the developing bones of the chick is vitamin-K-dependent and therefore γ-carboxyglutamate-dependent.

Vitamin-K-dependent carboxylation is itself a fascinating process in that it is totally different from other carboxylation reactions already so well studied in living systems. The process is known to require the reduced form of vitamin K plus molecular oxygen and appears to involve two intermediates of vitamin K. Warfarin appears to inhibit the enzyme that reduces one of these intermediates back to vitamin K, and warfarin-resistant rats, which have evolved because of the widespread use of warfarin as a rat poison, have a warfarin-resistant form of this enzyme. Clearly, enormous progress has been made since the first observation of a bleeding disease of chicks fed a diet deficient in vitamin K. Henrik Dam himself would be well pleased with this progress.

Regulation of Gene Expression. Genes are composed of DNA, a long double-stranded molecule, each strand of which is a linear polymer of four components, the deoxyribonucleotides. The information in DNA resides in the specific sequence of these four components, much as the information on this page resides in the specific sequence of letters, spaces, and punctuation marks. One strand of DNA is complementary to the other, such that the sequence in one strand specifies that in the other. A gene is a segment of DNA that codes for the synthesis of a specific protein.

The gene is decoded in a two-step process involving transcription into RNA and translation of this RNA into a protein. During transcription one of the DNA strands of the gene directs the assembly of a complementary strand of RNA. The RNA molecule is similar to DNA; its components, however, are ribonucleotides rather than deoxyribonucleotides and contain the sugar ribose in place of the related sugar 2-deoxyribose. During translation this strand of RNA, called messenger RNA, then directs the synthesis of a particular protein. Thus, the sequence of deoxyribonucleotides in the DNA specifies the sequence of ribonucleotides in RNA which, in turn, specifies the sequence of amino acids in the protein.

A single cell may need to make different proteins at different times in its life cycle, and in an animal at any time, cells of different tissues need to make different proteins. It is thus clear that the decoding of genes must be a carefully regulated process. The mechanisms by which this regulation is achieved constitute the essence of cell growth and development and have been widely investigated.

From studies of bacteria and of the viruses that infect them, molecular biologists know that the extent of decoding of a gene is regulated at the level of transcription. If more of the protein specified by a given gene is needed, its transcription into RNA will be repeated more frequently. The enzyme RNA polymerase, which carries out the transcription of genes, binds onto a specific recognition site on the DNA adjacent to the gene and then progresses along the length of the gene while producing the complementary strand of RNA. When the RNA polymerase reaches the end of the gene it encounters a termination sequence that causes it to release the newly synthesized RNA and to dissociate from the DNA. It can go through this cycle of events many times.

There are at least two ways in which this action of RNA polymerase is regulated. In bacteria specific proteins, called repressors, can block transcription. These repressor proteins can bind to specific sites on the DNA, adjacent to the sites onto which RNA polymerase first binds. If the repressor protein is so bound, the action prevents the binding of the RNA polymerase and hence blocks transcription of the adjacent gene. The repressor protein is sensitive to conditions in the cell in a way that leads to adaptive responses to environmental changes. For example, if a bacterium encounters the sugar galactose, it needs an enzyme to metabolize it but should not waste its resources making that enzyme in the absence of this sugar. The repressor, which ordinarily blocks transcription of the gene for this enzyme, can recognize and bind galactose; once having bound galactose, it will no longer bind to the DNA. Galactose thus "de-represses" the synthesis of the enzyme needed for its own metabolic utilization—an exquisitely apt response.

There is also a second, entirely different means of controlling transcription. It involves not repressors that block access to the DNA but rather changes in the RNA polymerase. This enzyme is actually made up of two functionally distinct protein subunits. One, the core polymerase, is the seat of enzymatic activity. The other, the specificity factor, imparts the ability to recognize the sites on DNA at which transcription should begin. Appreciation of the regulatory role of these specificity factors is due largely to recent investigations by Janice Pero at Harvard University, Audrey Stevens of Oak Ridge (Tenn.) National Laboratory, E. P. Geiduschek at the University of California at San Diego, Helen Whiteley at the University of Washington, and their co-workers.

Pero studied a virus, called SP01, that infects the common soil bacterium *Bacillus subtilis.* The DNA of SP01 is a linear double-stranded molecule containing 100 genes. After the virus gains entry into *B. subtilis,* these genes are expressed sequentially in groups. One group, expressed early in the course of the infection, are called early genes. Their expression is followed by expression of the middle genes and, in turn, by expression of the late genes. The protein specified by one early gene (number 28) is needed for expression of the middle genes, and two proteins specified by middle genes (33 and 34) are needed for expression of the late genes.

The RNA polymerase of the host bacterium binds to the recognition site preceding the SP01 early genes and transcribes them. As the protein specified by gene 28 accumulates, it displaces the original specificity factor from the RNA polymerase of the bacterial host, causing the polymerase to bind to the recognition site preceding the middle genes and to transcribe them. As the proteins specified by genes 33 and 34 accumulate, they displace the gene 28 protein and again change the specificity of the RNA polymerase so that it binds to the recognition site preceding the late genes and transcribes them. In this manner the sequence of expression of the SP01 genes is elegantly controlled without the use of repressors. The nucleotide sequences of the recognition sites preceding the early and the middle groups of SP01 genes were determined; they are, as expected, very different.

The clever device of controlling the sequence of gene expression by displacing the specificity subunit of RNA polymerase is apparently used by many organisms other than the virus SP01. For example, Richard Losick and his associates at Harvard showed that a similar mechanism operates in controlling gene expression during bacterial spore formation. Higher organisms, such as humans, undergo vastly more complex developmental processes, which are not yet understood. It does seem likely, however, that an understanding of the mechanisms of gene control gained from studies of viruses and bacteria will aid dissection of the processes underlying differentiation of the cells of higher organisms. As this understanding increases, it is expected that science will develop more rational and effective treatments for diseases that involve malfunction of genetic control.

(IRWIN FRIDOVICH; ARNO GREENLEAF)

[313.B; 321.B.3 and 5; 321.B.8.c; 336.B.3.b–c; 339.C.1–3]

See also Earth Sciences; Environment.

THE BUSINESS OF NEW LIFE

by Nicholas Wade

On June 16, 1980, the U.S. Supreme Court ruled that "a live human-made micro-organism is patentable subject matter"; in other words, that bacteria and similar organisms may be patented if they have been altered in the laboratory by processes of genetic manipulation. This long-awaited decision marked the commercial debut of genetic engineering, a technology likely to become increasingly visible throughout the decade. Some observers consider that genetic engineering will become the characteristic new technology of the 1980s just as microelectronics was of the 1970s.

The ruling of the Supreme Court concerns a patent application filed in 1972 by General Electric Co. for a form of *Pseudomonas* bacterium, which had been genetically engineered to improve its ability to digest oil slicks. The inventor, Ananda Chakrabarty, later of the University of Illinois, used well established techniques of bacterial genetics to introduce additonal genes into the organism.

Medical Applications of Gene Splicing. In 1973 a new and unprecedently powerful method for manipulating DNA, the genetic material of all life, was discovered by Stanley Cohen of Stanford University and Herbert Boyer of the University of California at San Francisco. Called recombinant DNA technology, or gene splicing, the technique makes it possible to cut out precisely defined segments of DNA from one organism and splice them into the genome, or gene set, of another. Though developed as a tool of pure research, which its inventors at first did not even think to patent, gene splicing was soon recognized as possessing an extraordinary potential wealth of practical applications. In theory it is a general way of tailoring the properties of living organisms in almost any desired manner. The first commercial applications of gene splicing, however, have been much more specific. They consist broadly of genetically programming bacteria to manufacture human protein products of medical importance.

Nicholas Wade is a member of the News and Comment staff, Science *magazine, Washington, D.C. His books include* The Ultimate Experiment *and* The Nobel Duel *(forthcoming).*

The three products on which greatest headway has been made are insulin, interferon, and growth hormone. Insulin traditionally has been extracted from pig and cattle glands, but that source of supply will not always be enough. In addition, because animal insulin differs slightly from the human variety, it may have undesirable side effects in the diabetic patient. In the gene-splicing approach the DNA sequences for the two separate protein chains of human insulin are first obtained by chemical synthesis in the laboratory. Each synthetic DNA molecule is then inserted into its own carrier, a natural ring-shaped DNA molecule known as a plasmid, and each plasmid is introduced into a separate bacterium. Each bacterium, with its new gene, is allowed to divide repeatedly into a colony of identical daughter cells known as a clone, and the cloned bacteria are then stimulated to produce the protein product of the inserted gene. Finally the two protein chains are united chemically to produce the intact insulin molecule. The gene-splicing method of making human insulin was developed commercially by Genentech, Inc., of San Francisco for the pharmaceutical company Eli Lilly. Clinical trials of the insulin began in London in July 1980, the first step toward obtaining approval of the drug by the U.S. Food and Drug Administration.

Genentech also developed a gene-splicing method for producing human interferon, the body's natural antiviral substance, which is also believed—though not yet proved—to be of possible use against cancer. Although the method is similar to that for insulin, only one gene is involved, and because the gene for interferon is as yet too large a piece of DNA to be synthesized in the laboratory, it has been obtained by ingenious techniques from cells that naturally produce copious amounts of interferon.

A third project near commercial realization in 1980 was the bacterial production of human growth hormone, needed for treating dwarfism. The substance at present is obtained from cadavers since animal varieties do not work in humans. Other products that have been made by gene-spliced bacteria include somatostatin, a brain hormone that controls the pituitary gland's release of growth hormone, and thymosin alpha-1, a hormone from the thymus that seems to stimulate the immune response.

It would probably be 1981 at the earliest before the first gene-spliced product reached the general market. The first such product to be sold in any market was a scientific specialty item, DNA ligase, an enzyme used by researchers and marketed in 1975 by New England BioLabs of Beverly, Mass.

Financial Interest. The new technology was taken up by the business world slowly at first, but recently with gathering momentum. As is often the case with radical innovations, it has been small companies that have pioneered the first applications. Genentech, the most successful of the new enterprises, was founded in 1976 by Robert Swanson, a 28-year-old investment banker with a bachelor's degree in chemistry, and by Boyer. Genentech's main rivals include Cetus, a microbiology company founded in California in 1972 that quickly added gene splicing to its repertoire; Biogen, a Geneva-based venture with both U.S. and European scientists on its board of directors; and Genex, located in Maryland.

In an effort to raise private capital, the officers and backers of these four small companies have vigorously spread word in industrial and financial circles about the potential of gene splicing. They seem to have succeeded beyond their expectations. By September 1979 the four small companies had a total paper value of more than $225 million, and by May 1980 the total value had more than doubled to $500 million. U.S. investors include such large oil companies as Standard Oil of California and Standard Oil of Indiana, which together with National Distillers own most of Cetus. Lubrizol Corp. holds some 25% of Genentech, and Koppers Co. is a major backer of Genex. The four companies at present operate mostly under contract to produce particular products. For example, Genentech, under contract to Hoffmann-La Roche, is engaged in a race to produce interferon with the rival partnership of Biogen and the drug firm Schering-Plough.

Genentech recently took the step of offering a share of its equity to the public. So eager were investors to buy its stock that the offering on October 14 was a historic occasion on Wall Street. Within 20 minutes of trading, the shares, initially $35 each, shot to $89 and closed the day at $71.25. The closing valuation gave Genentech a theoretical worth of $529 million, almost a tenth the value of Du Pont, even though Genentech did not have a single product on the market.

The lead of the four small companies in trying to develop commercial applications of gene splicing has been followed at a more sedate pace by the large pharmaceutical houses and chemical corporations, several of which have begun setting up in-house research teams in genetic engineering. Basic research knowledge, however, is still the limiting factor in applying the technique, and the advantage presently rests with the small companies, which by establishing attractive managerial and stock ownership roles have formed special relationships with leading academic scientists. Nevertheless, as gene splicing eventually becomes a commoner art, advantage may pass to those with large marketing resources, such as the drug companies, or with special expertise in fermentation technology, such as the Japanese. On the other hand Genentech, like Xerox or IBM before it, may grow with and dominate the industry it is pioneering.

The Commercial Future. Less spectacular than the production of medically important proteins but of considerable commercial significance will be the use of recombinant DNA to improve or vary all processes in which microorganisms are used. These range from brewing and cheese-making to manufacture of antibiotics and the biological synthesis of ethanol for use in gasohol. Another application that may come to fruition in the near future is the genetic modification of plants. Plants are susceptible to such manipulation because a whole plant can be propagated from a single cell, a characteristic that allows plants to be cloned like bacteria. When more is known about plant genetics, it should be possible to introduce genes that confer such desirable properties as disease resistance and high yield.

The increasingly evident power of the new technique inevitably raises questions of how and in what form it could become directly applicable to human beings. It is possible to envisage treatments for such genetic diseases as sickle-cell anemia, caused by an error in the gene for hemoglobin. Patients might be able to have all the blood-forming cells in their bone marrow replaced by new cells into which the correct version of the hemoglobin gene had been inserted.

Such a procedure, if and when it becomes possible, would benefit only the afflicted individuals and not their children, since the reproductive cells would not be affected. To make a permanent genetic change it would be necessary to intervene directly in the human reproductive process, perhaps using gene-splicing techniques in combination with newly developed procedures for test-tube conception. With increased knowledge it may become technically possible to repair genetic defects and eventually even to improve any desired human quality that is under genetic control. Whether such intervention will prove ethically acceptable, however, is a matter for which even the most advanced technology alone has no answer.

Literature

The 1980 Nobel Prize for Literature was awarded to the Polish-born, U.S.-domiciled poet Czeslaw Milosz. (*See* NOBEL PRIZES.) The Swedish Academy's choice drew attention once again to the difficulty of its task in surveying writing throughout the world to decide what should be counted as "world literature" in order to award the prize—worth $210,000 in 1980. The choice of Odysseus Elytis as the previous year's Nobel Prize winner had won little favour in the English-speaking world; this Greek poet's work, sympathetic to socialist ideals, was not much discussed or praised during 1980, as independent, unofficial work from Communist Europe attracted more interest. Milosz, however, was not unknown to English speakers, and his award was not resented—though it drew the usual mutterings of "what about Graham Greene?" from Britain.

Peter Lennon of *The Sunday Times* (London) asked the Swedish judges if they had chosen Milosz for political reasons. He was reminded that the Nobel Prize is awarded for *idealistic* literature. On those grounds Oscar Wilde might have been awarded the prize for his essay "The Soul of Man Under Socialism" but hardly for his well-wrought comedy *The Importance of Being Earnest*. British Nobel Prize winners had not included Thomas Hardy, D. H. Lawrence, or Graham Greene, but they had included such political "idealists" as Winston Churchill, John Galsworthy, Rudyard Kipling, and Bertrand Russell.

Lennon asked the judges about third world writers, especially those from the former British Empire. One judge said that "good Indian writers in Hindi are not up to the international standards we must maintain. . . I don't think they are capable of developing in a global way. . . . These countries have a cultural tradition that it is not possible for us to evaluate. . . . It is true we are not up to the task. But who is? Do you think the English would do it better?" This refreshing argument illustrated the growing sense of dissatisfaction about the assessment of international literature. Hegemony is accorded to European languages—particularly English—and other languages and cultures have their literature assessed by a European measuring rod.

Czeslaw Milosz

CAMERA PRESS/PHOTO TRENDS

ENGLISH

United Kingdom. About 45,000 books were published in the U.K. during 1980—too many, it was suggested by Michael Sissons in *The London Review of Books* and by Derwent May broadcasting on the BBC's World Service. In the difficult economic circumstances, said May, the 350 principal British publishers were struggling to find best-sellers, with big names, exotic pictures, and glamorous titles. The booksellers, said Sissons, could not keep up with the overproduction and duplication of titles. The public libraries were not permitted to buy as many of the more literary books as they would like. Publishers expended energy on promoting only the chosen few on their lists, those they regarded as potential best-sellers. Other books, however well reviewed, were not promoted. Sometimes they were sold at a very high price—"playing the institutional market for a safe minimum sale." Sissons called this "privishing," rather than "publishing." He hoped for fewer publishers, choosing books with greater care and avoiding duplication.

Nevertheless, British publishers offered an impressive list of good novels by important writers, often breaking new ground. The three literary journals set up in 1979, when the *Times Literary Supplement* (*TLS*) was in difficulties, were still flourishing. (Indeed, the *TLS* was in danger again in 1980, thanks to the financial difficulties of Times Newspapers Ltd.) The reviews had plenty of books of literary merit to assess. They became perhaps a touch less insular, more "geopolitical," encouraged by the idiosyncratic literary section of the *New Statesman*.

British literary concern with the world outside often seemed limited to the old imperial "sphere of interest." Attention was paid to biographies of Indian statesmen, written by Indians—in excellent English, from an English point of view. Ved Mehta's *Mamaji*, an account of traditional family life in India, was no less appealing than the documentary work of the two Trinidadian novelists, Vidiadhar and Shiva Naipaul, reporting on the sorrows of the third world. Books by Africans, about Uganda and other African upheavals since independence, were also welcomed. A Kenyan, Ali Mazrui, had been invited to broadcast to the nation in the BBC's important Reith Lectures; but when they were published, as *The African Condition*, they were severely criticized.

Efforts were made to grapple with continental Europe. The writings of Antonio Gramsci, the Italian Marxist, attracted more and more discussion. German literature began to seem more interesting, in the wake of German art and "the new German cinema." A certain regret is apparent in *The German Idea (1800–1860)*, by Rosemary Ashton, for the Victorian days when Germany had a real influence on English literature. (The Schlegel-Tieck Prize for English translation from the German went to Janet Seligman for her version of *The English House*, by Hermann Muthesius.) French critical theory made a breakthrough, with discussions of the development of Structuralism and "Deconstruction"; but English readers were more at home with the English and American critics reviewed in Philip French's book *Three Honest Men*—F. R. Leavis, Lionel Trilling, and Edmund Wilson. This book was accompanied by William Walsh's biography of Leavis and by Wilson's memoir of the 1930s.

British and American fears for the common language of their literatures were expressed in a collection of more than 60 essays, *The State of the Language*, edited by Leonard Michaels and Christopher Ricks. The essayists dealt with many examples of the modernization and, sometimes, deterioration of the English language and, thus, its literature. The importance of the Book of Common Prayer was remembered, with fears for its replacement by new forms of worship. *The Alternative Service Book 1980* of the Church of England was presented to the queen by the archbishops—welcomed by the clergy, dismaying to the world of literature.

FICTION. Several established novelists surprised their admirers. Graham Greene published a grim little novel, *Doctor Fischer of Geneva or the Bomb Party*, about a murderous millionaire. He also republished his film reviews in *The Pleasure-Dome* and presented a new farce, *For Whom the Bell Chimes*, at a Leicester theatre; it is a play designed for acting, preferably by Hollywood clowns, with no pretension to literary merit. He then published a book about his travels in Africa, Asia, and the Americas and the relationship between his experiences and his fiction; it was called *Ways of Escape*.

Kingsley Amis published a collection of his short stories, very strong on Army life, and a fine novel, *Russian Hide and Seek*, with a military background. A serious and sensitive fantasy about Britain under Soviet occupation, it appealed more to left-wing critics than to the conventional anti-Communists. But it was too subtle to be popular.

The contest for the £10,000 Booker Prize was more exciting than usual, enlivened by an element of secrecy and surprise. The principal contenders were senior, ambitious novelists, Anthony Burgess and William Golding, both of whom offered historical novels about cruelty and homosexuality. Burgess's *Earthly Powers* is almost a history of the public disasters of the 20th century, narrated by a very old, very brilliant, homosexual novelist, resembling W. Somerset Maugham. Golding's *Rites of Passage* tells of a 19th-century voyage, in which a clergyman dies of shame after sexual involvement with sailors; the strange anecdote bore a universal significance and seriousness, which helped Golding to win the Booker Prize.

William Golding

A. CLIFTON—CAMERA PRESS

Doris Lessing, once a realistic narrator of erotic life and political commitment, offered in *The Marriages Between Zones Three, Four and Five* an essay in metaphysical science fiction. Angus Wilson, too, moved into the world of symbolic fantasy with *Setting the World on Fire*, the tale of two brothers who represent the Apollonian and the Dionysian philosophies of life. Margaret Drabble's *The Middle Ground* is a disquisition on a middle-class, middle-aged woman, with no effort to supply a plot: it was more like a French *roman-fleuve*.

Traditional British realism was well represented by Stanley Middleton with *In A Strange Land*, about a provincial composer, and by Stan Barstow with *A Brother's Tale*, about a provincial English master and a football hero. The scholarly and humorous David Lodge wrote *How Far Can You Go?* about the changing attitudes of British Roman Catholics in recent years, for which he received two of the annual Whitbred Awards for Literature: the fiction category award and a special prize for the year's best book. Iris Murdoch's *Nuns and Soldiers* continued her series of philosophical fables about the nature of love in all its variety. C. P. Snow died during the year, and so did Olivia Manning (see OBITUARIES). But Manning managed to complete her Levant trilogy with *The Sum of Things*—a successor to her admired Balkan trilogy.

Simon Raven exhumed a mischievous novel from his youth, *An Inch of Fortune*, long suppressed for fear of libel action; the characters include lightly disguised versions of the duke and duchess of Windsor. Virago, a feminist publishing house, reissued a number of good, half-forgotten novels by women, including F. M. Mayor's *The Third Miss Symons* (1913), Rebecca West's *Harriett Hume* (1929), and Stevie Smith's *Over the Frontier* (1938). Antonia White, whose novels Virago republished in 1978–79, died in April 1980 (see OBITUARIES). Another rediscovery was a previously unpublished novel by John Cowper Powys, *After My Fashion*; it deals with life in rural England and New York City just after World War I, and among the characters is a thinly disguised portrait of Isadora Duncan. Powys's reputation continued to grow, on both sides of the Atlantic, and several other of his books were reprinted, accompanied by critical studies.

Also set in post-World War I rural England was J. L. Carr's novel *A Month in the Country*, a nostalgic, mysterious tale centring on a medieval church in Yorkshire; it received *The Guardian* Fiction Prize for 1980. Ted Harriott won the 1980 David Higham Prize for *Keep on Running*, his first novel, about an ex-Nazi fugitive. The judges remarked on the high standard of the "first novels" of 1980, which had been rather overshadowed by the ambitious work of already celebrated writers. Altogether, 1980 was a good year for fiction.

LETTERS, LIVES. The most popular collection of letters was Mark Amory's edition of *The Letters of Evelyn Waugh*. This witty, pious, melancholy, and eccentric novelist was recognized as a serious writer and mysterious human being; his correspondence helped to interpret the mystery. Among other admired letters and diaries were those of Virginia Woolf and John Masefield, Henry James and Cardinal Newman, and William Cowper and Lord Byron. A modern diary—so modern as to cause embarrassment—was that of Barbara Castle, Labour politician and former Cabinet minister. Castle's lively account of governmental action and discussion, day-by-day, attracted as much attention and dismay as the diaries of her late colleague Richard Crossman, another Labour politician and journalist.

From the same stable came Michael Foot (*see* BIOGRAPHIES), recently elected leader of the Labour Party. He had just published an excellent book of essays, *Debts of Honour*, a set of profiles in praise (and defense) of some of his favourite people —great men and women of the past and celebrities among his contemporaries. With both categories he was clearly emulating William Hazlitt, a model to many now that essay writing was once more in fashion. The essays of the late Colin MacInnes, a half-Australian novelist, reporter, and social investigator, also had something of Hazlitt's flavour. So did the essays of Kenneth Tynan (*see* OBITUARIES). An influential theatre critic and dramaturge, identified with dandyism, left-wing politics, and sexual "liberation," Tynan gently expressed his provocative views, for the last time, in his book of profiles, *Show People*.

Among the literary biographies, those of two poets, W. H. Auden and C. Day-Lewis, attracted much critical attention though neither won universal praise. More familiar subjects for biography were George Orwell, the eccentric, left-wing anti-Communist, and Sidney Smith, the witty left-wing clergyman. Bernard Crick's biography of Orwell was received with interest and argument, while Alan Bell's life of Smith was welcomed with general delight.

In the world of popular scholarship, Richard Jenkyns scored highly with *The Victorians and Ancient Greece*. It has long been recognized that to understand the great Victorian writers and artists one must know their prayer books, their hymns, and their Bible. Richard Jenkyns reminded readers that such is also true of the ancient Greeks, and he did so with wit and learning.

POETRY. It was a year of many anthologies. The new *Oxford Book of Contemporary Verse* was edited by D. J. Enright, with a preface supporting the ideals of the poetic school known as "The November," skeptical, neat, and unromantic. A new book, called *The Movement*, was offered by a young poet, Blake Morrison. With his own poems, Morrison was one of the winners of the Eric Gregory Prize.

Charles Tomlinson offered an important anthology, the *Oxford Book of Verse in English Translation*. Geoffrey Grigson edited the *Oxford Book of Satirical Verse*, overlapping slightly with Gavin Ewart's *Penguin Book of Light Verse*. Valentine Cunningham broke new ground with the *Penguin Book of Spanish Civil War Verse*. However, most of the better poems in it were already well-known, and the new discoveries were less interesting than had been hoped. (D. A. N. JONES)

United States. FICTION. New dislocations in the forms of fiction became manifest in the U.S. in 1980. Haunted by nostalgic visions of some other time and some other place, the American novel developed more fragmentary styles barely concealing intuitions of death and touched by a deep sense

© THOMAS VICTOR

E. L. Doctorow

of the absurdity, the recalcitrance, of experience. Novels designed as labyrinthine quests leading nowhere traced chronicles and sagas to the abysmal centre of our century or earlier ones. Many novels dealt with the crippling excesses of consciousness in a world devoid of moral values, recalling the "literature of exhaustion" so pervasive in the 1960s.

Only partially filled with the historical fuel that energized *The Book of Daniel* (1971) and *Ragtime* (1975), E. L. Doctorow's *Loon Lake* was an artful but lifeless picaresque novel that followed the crossing paths in 1936 of a very young vagabond and a somewhat older failed poet, both of whom love a tormented beauty and both of whom wind up under the wing of a great tycoon at his Loon Lake estate in the Adirondacks. A fable-like scenario with capitalism's great hand corrupting or exploiting or destroying (the poet flies off into oblivion with the tycoon's aviatrix wife)—rife with free associations, annotated poems, arbitrary disjunctions and timewarps, and dreadful oh-wow-heavy pronouncements: "You are thinking it is a dream. It is no dream. It is the account in helpless linear translation of the unending love of our simultaneous but disynchronous lives."

The American Indian's heritage has perhaps suffered from overexposure in recent fiction, but Dee Brown (*Bury My Heart at Wounded Knee*) combined his sure grasp of history's sweep with a sharp foreground focus to produce the best of the lot—a lean, incident-rich 18th- and 19th-century saga, *Creek Mary's Blood*. The immediacy is supplied by two front-and-centre 1905 narrators: a white Washington, D.C., newspaperman who has trekked out to Montana to track down a legend of his native Georgia, and Dane, a 91-year-old Indian who gives the reporter the story he came for about his grandmother, Creek Mary Kingsley, and her descendants. The result is a robust work that rolls from East to West with inexorable energy.

Erica Jong's *Fanny*, a "mock-eighteenth-century novel" from a truly female viewpoint, based loosely on Henry Fielding's *Tom Jones*, is soaked in stale 1970s-chic platitudes that narrator-heroine Fanny is forced to spout smugly at every opportunity. After many rococo-erotic adventures, there are expected final revelations about secret paternities and inherited fortunes. Within the austere severity of her pre-Civil War New England setting Judith Rossner—as in *Looking for Mr. Goodbar*—pierced the central passion and terror of the victim in *Emmeline*, a tale about seduction, out-of-wedlock childbirth, and abandonment, with a Greek-tragedy wallop at the finale.

In the genre of pop-saga, James Michener proffered *The Covenant*, employing his familiar approach: tracing a region's history through a few families, with a soapy mix of celebrity cameo and didacticism. This time he began with prehistoric Bushmen crossing the desert in search of water and ended in present-day South Africa with the central dynasties involved in diamond-mining and racial conflicts. *Bellefleur* is another myth-epic family chronicle, Joyce Carol Oates-style—which means a dark household full of lust, ghosts, disappearances, mystical animals, religious conversions, and ghoulish leaps of Oatesian imagination—all in the Adirondacks.

Thomas Berger returned to middle-class America with *Neighbors*, a comic nightmare-book that has the naked, joyful aggression found only in those old slapstick vaudeville routines—the ones where somebody keeps getting hit on the head with a bladder. The somebody here is Earl Keese, 49 and fattish, an ordinary fellow living with his wife Enid in outer suburbia; their neighbours provide the bladder. A fantasia on middle-class paranoia and a lesson in how a comic master can make the same joke over and over and get a big laugh every time—a harrowing and hilarious triumph.

The theme of *The Second Coming*, Walker Percy's fifth novel, is tightly bound to the theme of his other four: Why is a person nowadays "two percent of himself"? The answer, always elusive, is clothed in fictional riches that are almost humbling: the spookily precise descriptions of odd physical sensations; the satire on the dead modern South; the rage and the Kierkegaardian comic curiosity—a tour de force by America's cool Dostoevsky. Another comic masterpiece, finally published more than ten years after its writing, was John Kennedy Toole's (1937–69) *A Confederacy of Dunces*, starring Ignatius Reilly, virgin and lute player, rhetorical wreck *in excellsis*, who was once a graduate student—but the trauma of a ride on a Greyhound Scenicruiser to Baton Rouge for a teaching-job interview has sworn him off work forever.

Judith Rossner

© THOMAS VICTOR

A number of impressive first novels of high-geared sensibility commanded serious attention. *Blackbird Days*, by Ken Chowder, is a glossy, often fey work, dazzling in its virtuosity and frazzling in its mannerisms—a Harper-Saxton Award winner. The three grown Bard brothers, unlike each other except for the contiguities of family knowledge, are just about guaranteed to miss each other's sense when they get together—though helplessly aware of one another's pain. *Household Words* was Joan Silber's first effort in American fiction's fastest growing subgenre: the novel of Woman Coping, a sad epigrammatic story about a woman who, groomed for a life of agreeable minutiae and "normal" family occasions, is immobilized and splintered by ravaging forces she cannot control.

In pop fiction several works were provocative in one way or another. *Who's on First* proved to be William F. Buckley, Jr.'s most serious espionage tale yet. Again featuring CIA agent Blackford Oakes, it manages to make a winning spy diversion out of clean plotting, Buckley barbs, and even an inkling of a moral dilemma. Cannily crafted *The Key to Rebecca*, Ken Follett's new World War II thriller, recycles the same basic scenario—now in 1942 Cairo instead of 1944 England—that made *Eye of the Needle* such a winner. Again the central figure is a Nazi spy with secrets that could change history. The ultimate appeal of *Princess Daisy*, by Judith Krantz, as in *Scruples*, lies in descriptions of high-priced food, trendy outfits (big scenes of deciding what to wear), assorted orgasms, and the advertising/public relations world—a big, fat, messy success.

Notable major short-story collections included *The Collected Stories of Eudora Welty*, a testament to Welty's masterly evocation of the old South, her genius with dialogue, and her control of brilliant and startling metaphor. *High Crimes and Misdemeanors* features mystical and adventurous stories, some airy, some ponderous, by Joanne Greenberg, the author of *I Never Promised You a Rose Garden*. In *Side Effects* Woody Allen is at his most impressive self, blending parody, nonstop one-liners, and earthy absurdity in a fine work not just from America's surest humorist but also from a story writer of wise, expanding gifts.

HISTORY, BIOGRAPHY, AND BELLES LETTRES. The long-awaited first installment of Henry Kissinger's *White House Years* finally arrived, and, advertising hype aside, it *was* an event, garnering the American Book Award for History. Beginning with the call from Richard Nixon in 1968—ironically, while Kissinger was lunching with Nelson Rockefeller—that brought him into national prominence and ending with the signing of the Paris accords on Vietnam in 1972, this volume inevitably centres on the Vietnam war, with side trips to Moscow and China. One of the great documents in the history of political statecraft and manipulation, it shows us a Kissinger who knew how to institutionalize his power and who, in the end, outmaneuvered even Richard Nixon. Only a man for whom values are ideology and power is truth could claim that "Cambodia was *not* a moral issue."

In the current explosion of economic panaceas, Ronald Muller offered *Revitalizing America*, a firmly grounded scheme to straighten out the U.S. economy that argues for the enhancement of productivity through worker control of the workplace and the establishment of such "quasi-public" corporations as a development bank to finance experimental industrial projects. *Future Shock* author Alvin Toffler was busy accommodating himself to the future in *The Third Wave*. According to Toffler, the first two were the Agricultural and Industrial revolutions; now we are on the threshold of the "Third Wave"—the Technological Revolution, which will introduce floating cities utilizing oil "grown" in the sea, "flextime" working arrangements, international geopolitical associations, and "participatory government" via computer console.

In *Human Nature and History*, an eloquent defense of historical processes as movers and shapers of mankind, Kenneth Bock added yet another voice to the swelling chorus opposed to sociobiology. His point was that change does occur and is often radical, producing differences in human behaviour in one or two generations that have little to do with biological genes or natural selection. On the practical side of social change, Gay Talese may have indeed spent nine years pondering the "social and sexual trends of the entire nation"; but the contents of *Thy Neighbor's Wife* are largely determined by which of Talese's subjects were willing to Tell All, thus putting disproportionate emphasis on just a few sexual case histories.

Woman as Subject continued to attract solid inquiry. In *Women and the American Labor Movement*, Philip S. Foner carefully and exhaustively chronicled women in the trade union movement from World War I to the present; *At Odds*, by Carl Degler, is a major and largely successful attempt to integrate the history of the family with that of women's push for equal rights from the American Revolution to the present; and in *Powers of the Weak*, Elizabeth Janeway placed important feminist concerns within general social theory by trenchantly arguing that the growth in awareness of the condition of women has already begun to erode the legitimation of power in society, which is the first step toward a new social contract.

In the important domain of New Journalism, Bob Woodward and Scott Armstrong scored impressively with *The Brethren: Inside the Supreme Court*, wherein more than 170 former law clerks—and at least some of the justices—break the U.S. Supreme Court's traditional silence. The result is a searing account of the court's inner workings and dirty linen from 1969 to 1975 that shows the chief justice to be a legal featherweight and featherbrain and quite possibly a scoundrel, that exposes other justices to ridicule and contempt, and that casts doubt on the highest court as a judicious arbiter of anything.

Thomas Berger

The major literary biography of the year was *Walt Whitman*, by Justin Kaplan, exploring the "rational line of development that led from the journalist-loafer to the incomparable poet." Rich in period colour and demonstrating rangy intellectual grasp, the book shows Whitman influenced by radical Quaker oratory, Manhattan's urban rhythms, sunny Emerson, demonic Carlyle, dark Poe, grand opera, "animal magnetism," phrenology, Egyptology, the Bible, and, above all: "In the city he explored democracy, and in democracy he explored himself."

Lyndon: An Oral Biography, by Merle Miller, offers the lowdown on Lyndon Johnson as hundreds knew him: a crackling projection of his personality and modus operandi, with the former president coming through as a super-Harry Truman, a Kohinoor-in-the-rough. There are no apologies about Johnson's personal excesses—the tall tales and outright lies, the vulgarity, the dalliances, even the brutal humiliation of loyal aides. Familiar are LBJ's shrewd, enormously successful domestic triumphs: the lasting good he did for the poor and for blacks. Also noteworthy was Ronald Steel's *Walter*

Lippmann and the American Century, a conscientious, even eloquent intellectual biography of the Harvard University *wunderkind* who often applied Freudian thought and moral philosophy to political punditry and who became "without doubt the nation's greatest journalist."

Other offerings included two brassy autobiographies of Hollywood doyennes, deliciously scandalized. In *Swanson on Swanson,* glittery "Queen of the Silents" Gloria Swanson told eye-popping all—in a life studded with clips of art, finance, finagling in the movies' salad days, the highs and lows of six marriages, and steamy affairs with Big Names—all now gone but hardly forgotten. Kiss and tell . . . and tell . . . and tell . . . is the motif of Shelley Winters's *Shelley,* an immense, munchy autobiography of spats and amours through the mid-1950s—prime popcorn for Hollywood appetites. Her roster of bedmates seems to include every major actor at first, but then her standards lowered: "I tried to say 'I don't sleep with anybody on the first date,' but my Italian wasn't up to it."

Among the notable belletristic offerings were: *On Language* by double-duty *New York Times* columnist and "libertarian language activist" William Safire, a browser's delight filled with jaunty enthusiasm for puns ("anomie-tooism"), neologisms ("eggsy"—the female version of macho), and the latest jargon in show-biz, drug-pushing, real estate, and espionage—a must for language lovers of all persuasions; and Mary McCarthy's *Ideas and the Novel,* an insightful defense of the novel as "idea-carrier."

Poetry. Among the poetic offerings the most noteworthy collections were James Merrill's *Scripts for the Pageant,* Lucille Clifton's *Two-Headed Woman,* James Schuyler's *The Morning of the Poem,* and James McMichael's *Four Good Things.*

(FREDERICK S. PLOTKIN)

Canada. Along with some long-established writers, several comparative newcomers brought out new books in 1980. Hugh MacLennan's latest work, *Voices in Time,* places the events of the Hitler era against those of a contemporary Canadian society of the next century in order to illuminate yet a third period of time, the 1980s, when a nuclear holocaust wipes out civilization. *Joshua Then and Now,* by Mordecai Richler, describes a man's search for the truth about himself and his generation as he wanders from Montreal to London to Ibiza to Hollywood and back again. Albert Johnson, the object of one of the Mounties' most-publicized manhunts, has been brought to desperate, hunted life by Rudy Wiebe in *The Mad Trapper.*

In a class by itself was the posthumously published *Hear Us O Lord from Heaven Thy Dwelling Place and Lunar Caustic,* by Malcolm Lowry, an evocative exploration of two of the most influential themes in Lowry's writing, his love of nature and the sea and the horrors of the alcoholism he endured. Helen Weinzweig garnered both critical and popular acclaim with her *Basic Black with Pearls,* in which a middle-aged woman's assignations with her (supposed?) lover lead her on a kind of mythic treasure hunt to discover the personal significance of her Jewish heritage, her marriage, and the power of illusion over all. In another novel devoted to religious and social themes, *The Third Temptation,* Charles Templeton demonstrates how piety and publicity, wealth and unworldliness battle in the heart of a popular evangelist and profoundly affect the outcome of his confrontation with a newspaper publisher who is determined to destroy him.

Although apparently based on a real event, Richard B. Wright's *Final Things* becomes a true story of its own as it investigates the rape-murder of a young boy and probes the sources, innocent and otherwise, of this grisly event. Other fine novels produced during the year included *Happenstance,* by Carol Shields; Jan Drabek's *The Lister Legacy;* George Bowering's *Burning Water;* and an ironic description of relations between the U.S. and Canada, David McFadden's *A Trip Around Lake Erie.*

Among first novels were the winner of the $50,000 Seal Book's First Novel Award for 1980, *Odd's End,* by Tim Wynne-Jones; *The Suicide Murders,* by Howard Engel, introducing Benny Cooperman, private eye; and *The Charcoal Burners,* by Susan Musgrave (better known for several volumes of poetry), in which a young woman increasingly loses the will to act through a growing involvement in visions of oblivion. Another poet who turned to fiction was Ralph Gustafson with his collection of short stories, *The Vivid Air.* Other collections showing that the art of the short story was very much alive were those of Hugh Hood, *None Genuine Without this Signature;* Don Bailey, *Making Up,* a further excursion into the meaning of imprisonment both physical and spiritual; and Roderick Haig-Brown, *Woods and River Tales,* 18 stories about people pioneering in the British Columbia wilderness.

Mordecai Richler

In 1980 as in other years there was a bumper crop of poetry books, from both established poets and their younger peers. Highlights included *Collected Poems, Volume 1 (1940–55)* by Raymond Souster, the first of a projected four-volume collection; Ralph Gustafson's *Landscape with Rain,* lyrical expositions on the nature of things and men; Tom Wayman's *Living on the Ground: Tom Wayman Country,* which included "Garrison," the poem that won first prize in the U.S. Bicentennial poetry competition; *In Search of Living Things,* by Gail Fox, in which she ventures far into the interior of new lands; and *A Long Apprenticeship,* by Fred Cogswell, in which, with typical modesty and humour, the author attempts to account for himself.

Other poets celebrating new books in 1980 were Dorothy Farmiloe with *Words for My Weeping Daughter,* in which she extends, in both detail and understanding, the perception of life in the northern Canadian bush established in her previous work, *Elk Lake Diary: Poems;* Andrew Suknaski with *Montage for an Interstellar Cry,* in which both words and images are played with in a long collage of urban life; and Anne Szumigalski with *A Game of Angels,* a display of verbal high-wire walking above the chasm where the real and the unreal contend. (ELIZABETH WOODS)

FRENCH

France. Early in the year the deaths of Jean-Paul Sartre and Roland Barthes (*see* OBITUARIES) deprived France of two dominant figures in post-World War II intellectual life. Their speculative approach to the problems of the human condition and even their paramount concern for language, which were so characteristically "French," were less evident in a society coming to mistrust intellectualism and finding expression in the visual media. A character in Alain Jouffroy's novel *L'Indiscrétion faite à Charlotte,* comparing the 1970s with the two previous decades, remarks that "it is as if intelligence had suffered a breakdown," adding that "history is happening somewhere else." Many writers, looking elsewhere, saw only incoherence and brutal ironies of the kind that opens Jean-Edern Hallier's *Fin de siècle,* when a plane bringing medical aid to Cambodia collides with another lifting out refugees. The characters in novels by Raymond Jean (*Photo souvenir*) and Claude Bonjean (*Le Jour où Baader*) also emerged against a background of recent world events, from which their creators drew a similarly bleak message.

The sense of importance in politics was specifically related by many to the failure of the left since May 1968. Only the feminist movement had made tangible progress, and the liberation of women was shown as a hopeful challenge to masculine authority. In Jouffroy's novel Charlotte does achieve personal and sexual freedom but eventually, after a terrorist attack, leaves France until men "can no longer be assassinated there by untraceable killers." Paul Savatier's *L'Homme au gerfaut* is a submissive bank clerk who violates the very social canons he represents in an unsuccessful attempt to prove himself worthy of a woman who has been the victim of male egotism. The problem of adjustment to freer relationships and the violence this could provoke was the theme of Claude Mourthe's *Le Temps des fugues.*

POPPERFOTO/UPI

Marguerite Yourcenar

These novels by men testified to the impact of women's changing place in society, and the election of Marguerite Yourcenar (*see* BIOGRAPHIES) to the French Academy marked the storming of another bastion of privilege. Male chauvinism was pilloried by Christine Arnothy, who won the Prix Interallié with *Toutes les chances plus une,* and Madeleine Chapsal (*Un Homme infidèle*). Though set early in the century, Catherine Rihoit's *Les Abîmes du coeur* carries a contemporary message of woman's liberation from bourgeois oppression, and Dorothée Letessier found an authentic working-class voice for the heroine of *Le Voyage à Paimpol.*

However positive such changes might be, there was an underlying malaise. Even the socially integrated narrator of Luc Estang's *Les déicides* discovers that religion offers at best an ambiguous answer, while for those like the homosexual in Yves Navarre's *Le Jardin d'acclimatation,* the year's Prix Goncourt winner, orthodox society and the family would go to any lengths in defense of conventional behaviour and to enforce conformity. Bernard Waller, though adopting a very different literary technique in *La Patience,* also focused on the struggle to preserve integrity in an intrusive world.

Linguistic experiment and baroque fantasy were less prominent than in previous years. However, the Prix Renaudot went to Danièle Sallenave for *Les Portes de Gubbio,* a distinguished experimental novel, and there was evidence of continued vitality among veterans, and even precursors, of the New Novel: Nathalie Sarraute published *L'Usage de la parole;* Marguerite Duras, *L'Homme assis dans le couloir;* Robert Pinget, *L'Apocryphe;* and Samuel Beckett, *Compagnie.* Among other established writers who added to their reputations with new works were Françoise Mallet-Joris, whose *Dickie-*

Roi gives a sympathetic picture of the world of rock music; Romain Gary (*see* OBITUARIES) with *Les Cerfs-volants*; Vladimir Volkoff, continuing his series *Les Humeurs de la mer*; and Jean Cayrol, whose collection *Exposés au soleil* illustrates his idea of the short story fixing the elusive moment with "the rapidity of a holdup." Pierre-Jean Remy, prolific as ever, chose an operatic setting for *Pandora* and *Salue pour moi le monde*, and André Stil attacked medical malpractice in *Le Médecin de charme*.

René Fallet's *La Soupe aux choux* reached the best-seller lists, as did Henri Troyat's *Viou*. The success of novels like these, concerning childhood and peasant life, as well as the continuing popularity of the historical novel, suggested that the public, rather than reading about contemporary society, would prefer to regress to earlier, less perplexing times. Some historical novels achieved real literary distinction, notably Florence Delay's *L'Insuccès de la fête*, describing the mishaps that befall a 16th-century ceremonial masque, but the majority of such works unashamedly indulged sentimentality and escapism.

While the status of imaginative literature seemed to be suffering a decline, factual writing, in particular historiography, was booming, perhaps because it complemented rather than rivaled the work of television. French historians enjoyed great international prestige, and, as Emmanuel Le Roy Ladurie told a conference of French and British scholars at Loches in July, they were recognized leaders in the field of demographic history. The patient research needed for such work and the fascinating insights it can provide were illustrated by Jean Delay in *Avant Mémoire*, a study of his mother's family and its social connections from the 16th century onward, which shows the development of the Parisian bourgeoisie.

Yves Navarre

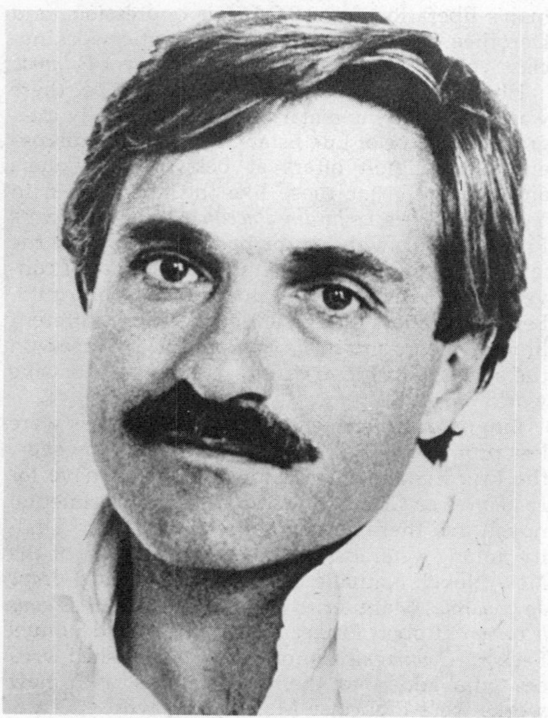

POPPERFOTO/UPI

Aragon published a collection of literary essays, *Le Mentir-vrai*, and there were new volumes of poetry from Pierre Emmanuel (*Duel*), Dennis Roche (*Dépôts de savoir et de technique*), and Guillevic (*Autres*). Guillevic discussed his career, in particular his Breton upbringing, in *Vivre en poésie*, and the much-loved writer Maurice Genevoix (*see* OBITUARIES), who died during the year, recalled a distant childhood in *30,000 jours*.

(ROBIN BUSS)

Canada. To select only three or four works from the entire body of French-Canadian literature published in 1980 is to run the risk of making a bad choice or perhaps of leading the reader into error. But because the following selection represents a range of response, it seems preferable to a purely enumerative list of works.

Quand la voile faseille, by Noël Audet, is a narrative (or, as the author states, the tale of tales) composed of four stories, three of which are set in a small village on the Gaspé Peninsula and the fourth in an urban setting. Whether their milieu is rural or urban, Audet's characters are fully drawn and are passionate about the sea, earth, sex, language—in short, about all aspects of life. The text of their story is written as the narrative of a storyteller whose tale "plays" back and forth between real and fictional worlds, gracefully intermingling both for the reader's delight. Carefully written, *Quand la voile faseille* is made up of parentheses (gusts of wind), which foretell the narrative or temporarily delay it to allow for new illumination.

One either likes or dislikes Victor-Lévy Beaulieu. In either case it must be recognized that his journeys to his most profound interior depths have enabled him to shatter certain myths and, through the discovery of this interior universe, to reaffirm the power of the writer. *Una/Un roman/illustré par deux petites filles* pursues the dialectic begun in the author's preceding novels, using this time as intermediary Una, a seven-year-old girl who is at once an endearing and an unsettling character. Una is enamoured of her father but finds him too involved in his own reveries to listen to hers. The world that Una describes is a world torn asunder, where the erotic, the obsessive, the violent, and the fantastic intermingle, recalling *Les Grand-pères* and *Un rêve québécois*. But however harsh this little girl's world, there is something appealing about it, something more poignant than is found in Beaulieu's other works.

Thanks to Nicole Deschamps, who worked on it for many years, there finally appeared a complete edition of Louis Hémon's celebrated novel *Maria Chapdelaine* built upon the author's original manuscript. For the first time in more than 60 years one is able to read Hémon's actual text, which recounts the dispossession of a people and their resignation and mute acceptance of colonization as their fate.

(ROBERT SAINT-AMOUR)

GERMAN

Günter Grass's novel-essay *Kopfgeburten*, subtitled "The Germans are dying out," imagines a youngish couple, moderately left-wing, agonizing over whether to have a child; in view of the population explosion, concern over nuclear power, and increasing intolerance both on the right and on the left, it is not a decision to be taken lightly in a world in which "nothing looks more artificial than nature." Grass is a relative optimist, but his preoccupations are shared by other, much gloomier writers.

For Martin Walser West Germany appeared preoccupied with the rush to accumulate property. His Chekhovian *Das Schwanenhaus* describes the competition among a group of provincial real-estate agents to secure the contract to sell a great fin-de-siècle mansion. But present-day Germans do not share the vision of their property-conscious forefathers; the buyer at once has the house demolished to make way for apartment buildings. Hermann Kinder's bitter satire of university life, *Vom Schweinemut der Zeit*, shows contemporary West German economic and political pressures forcing staff and students into sullen opportunism.

Across the border in Switzerland things were little better, according to Otto F. Walter, whose *Wie wird zu Gras* describes the discrimination practiced against people who demonstrate against nuclear power stations. But the most comprehensively negative attack on the contemporary scene was Botho Strauss's highly regarded *Rumor*, in which society has become simply "noise" and today's generation is characterized by physical and psychological decay. The concomitant stultification of personal relations is the subject of Nicolas Born's *Die Fälschung*. Born, who died early in 1980, set his novel in Beirut, Lebanon, during the 1975–76 civil war; his journalist-hero finds it impossible to convey the horrors of the fighting to a sensation-hungry readership, but his relationships with wife and mistress are equally "forgeries."

Other writers suggested historical causes for the malaise. Peter Renz's *Vorläufige Beruhigung* contrasts the current retreat into complacency and opportunism with the revolutionary optimism of 1968. In a more popular vein Arno Surminski's *Fremdes Land* goes back to the mid-1950s, a time when one could still hope for a better future but when German rearmament was already indicating that hopes might be dupes. This novel touches on the most prominent topic of the year—the generation conflict. Autobiographical novels by Peter Härtling, Brigitte Schwaiger, Ruth Rehmann, and, most notably, Christoph Meckel (*Suchbild über meinen Vater*) all are variations on a theme: the father as authoritarian personality, the man who at least tacitly had supported the Nazis, had given his children a filtered version of the past, and had created a materially prosperous but morally bankrupt Germany.

The remoter past is treated in Thomas Valentin's *Grabbes letzter Sommer*, concerning the last months of a 19th-century dramatist; in Hans Dieter Baroth's *Streuselkuchen in Ickern*, the story of a family of Ruhr miners from 1900 to the present; and, most impressively, in Alfred Andersch's (*see* OBITUARIES) posthumous *Der Vater eines Mörders*, an account of an earlier generation conflict, this time between headmaster and pupil (Andersch himself). The twist to the Andersch story is that the headmaster is the father of Heinrich Himmler, later the head of Hitler's SS.

ARCHIV DIOGENES VERLAG, ZÜRICH

Hermann Kinder

Various escapes from the present situation were examined. Adolf Muschg's *Baijun* analyzes personal tensions within a trade mission to post-Mao China, a land that can no longer be viewed as Utopia now that it is introducing a modicum of capitalism. Peter Handke turned to mysticism in *Die Lehre der Sainte-Victoire*, an account of a pilgrimage to Paul Cézanne's magic mountain. Sarah Kirsch, too, in her lyrical *La Pagerie*, finds refuge in southern France, but history frequently interrupts her idyll. The absurdist line is pursued in an entertaining collection of short pieces, *Wenn Adolf Hitler den Krieg nicht gewonnen hötte*, by Helmut Heissenbüttel, whose method consists of leading the reader up the garden path.

Among many anthologies of lyric poetry were Ernst Jandl's *Der gelbe Hund*, Johanna Moosdorf's *Sieben Jahr sieben Tag*, and contributions from three exiles from East Germany: Roger Loewig's *Ein Vogel bin ich ohne Flügel*, Thomas Brasch's *Der Schöne 27. September*, and Günter Kunert's *Abtötungsverfahren*.

East Germany welcomed publication of the third volume of Erwin Strittmatter's *Der Wundertäter*, in which Büdner becomes a writer but loses his party membership. Strittmatter continued to be entertainingly robust in depicting the conflict between individualism and party dogma in the early 1950s. Uwe Saeger's unusual and highly interesting *Nöhr* is a psychological study of an individual's search for identity, not only in the social and political sphere but also on the personal, even sexual, level, told in flashbacks and with a decidedly open ending. That the generation problem was not confined to the West was shown by Hedda Zinner's *Katja*, with the significant difference that here it is the parents' exclusive preoccupation with revealing the horrors of Nazism that causes their daughter to revolt. Jurij Brězan's collection of short pieces, *Der*

Brautschmuck, was enthusiastically received, as were Stephan Hermlin's autobiographical *Abendlicht* and Maxie Wander's posthumous *Tagebücher und Briefe.* (J. H. REID)

SCANDINAVIAN

Danish. A recent development in Danish fiction was the emergence of "worker writers," apparently numbering some 50 in all. Unsophisticated but often dynamic, they introduced new themes into Danish prose. John M. Pedersen's *Stedsegrønt* is a lively description of factory life, workers' home lives, and political attitudes and activities. In *Johnny og fremtiden* (1979), John Nehm told of a boy's three apprenticeships, while his *De frigjorte* (1979) centres on unemployment.

Women writers were also prominent. In *Lone,* Herdis Møllehave presented her controversial views on marriage and family life, while in *Den første sne,* Vibeke Grønfeldt took a disillusioned look at young people in the provinces seeking contact. Dorrit Willumsen's *Manden som påskud* describes a man's significance for three women: his wife, his mistress, and his daughter. A contrast was Martha Christensen's *Borgmesteren sover* (1979), in which power and responsibility undermine a man and lead him increasingly to dominate his wife.

Among long-established writers, Klaus Rifbjerg wrote *Voksdugshjertet* (1979), showing how a girl brought up to respect tradition and convention subsequently begins to question them. Willy-August Linnemann broke new ground in *Slesvigsk legende* (1979), about an apparent miracle that is exploited by society in general and politicians in particular.

Among some interesting essays, Elsa Gress's *Fanden til forskel* (1979) restates her humanist principles, while in *Læsehest med æselører* (1979) Johannes Møllehave, reputedly the Danish writer with the highest sales, presented personal views on Danish authors of the past. Thorkild Bjørnvig reflected on children in the modern world in *Barnet og dyret i industrisamfundet.* In *Fra billedmagerens værksted,* William Heinesen celebrated his 80th birthday with a series of short essays to accompany a selection of his paintings, drawings, and collages; his literary brilliance undiminished, he now showed the world what the Faeroese had long known—that he was also an artist of note.

Klaus Rifbjerg reasserted his position as a highly inventive poet in the modernist vein in *Livsfrisen,* while in *Spøgelseslege* (1979) Henrik Nordbrandt showed an equal virtuosity in some rather sombre poems reflecting his feelings on returning to Denmark from the Mediterranean.

(W. GLYN JONES)

Norwegian. Finn Carling cut deep into the problems of modern man in his novel *Brevene,* a collection of letters triggered by the eccentric behaviour of a middle-aged married woman who finds fulfillment in helping outcasts and, as a result, is certified as insane by her nearest of kin. Rolf Sagen's *Finne seg ei grein* deals humorously with painful school experiences. School and puberty are also central in Finn Havrevold's *Velkommen hjem.* In Nils Werenskiold's *Hvem var Cecilie Meyer?* a man in his 50s tries to establish the real truth about his deceased former mistress.

The historical novel continued to flourish. Asbjørn Øksendal's *Slaget ved Svolder* describes the short rule of Olav Trygvesson (995–1000). Vera Henriksen in *Kongespeil* gave a picture of the 11th-century king Harald Hardråde as seen through the eyes of his son and widow. Ragnhild Magerøy's *Den lange vandringen* and Sissel Lange-Nielsen's *Gralen* are set in 12th- and 13th-century Europe. Edvard Hoem's *Fjerne Berlin* shows reactions in Norway to social upheavals in Europe at the end of World War I.

The thriller came to the fore with several outstanding contributions. Jon Michelet's *Hvit som snø* moves in the drug world of the Norwegian capital and is written in a racy style, making full use of colloquial language and slang. *Forræderen,* by Fredrik Skagen, wittily follows the fate of a young scientist, co-discoverer of a deadly microbe, caught in the espionage activities of the U.S. and Soviet embassies in Oslo. *Mord i Stortinget,* by Andreas Norland, makes excellent use of the Norwegian Parliament as a backdrop, and the same author moved the action to the executive branch of government in *Finansministeren er myrdet.*

Novels with a strong lyrical touch were Jon Peter Rolie's *Siste eventyr,* in which the characters of a novel within the novel, written to ease the pending death of a young girl, merge with the characters of the frame story; Arild Borgen's *Alle biler kjører forbi,* about a middle-aged woman's longing for physical human contact; and Tor Åge Brigsvaerd's poetic retelling of Cretan myths, *Minotauros.* Impressive short stories were contributed by Kjell Haug in *Nattsvermere,* Karin Sveen in *Døtre,* and Odd Winger in *Byen.*

At 82, the poet Ernst Orvil in *Nær nok* remained the master of playful usage of words. Harald Sverdrup successfully sought the big perspective in the small detail in *Fugleskremsel,* while Marie Takvam in *Falle og reise seg att* was at her best in love poems. (TORBJØRN STØVERUD)

Swedish. P. C. Jersild's *En levande själ* was the year's comic, moving, and disturbing masterpiece. Its hero is a human brain living in solution in a laboratory aquarium. In the hospital the brain's owner had been given the option of dying or having the rest of his body amputated; he chose the latter, retaining all the characteristics of a human personality, including a romantic attachment to the girl laboratory assistant. As a physician turned full-time novelist, Jersild was uniquely qualified to explore the ethical and psychological frontiers of medical science. In *Orden som fängslar oss,* the psychiatrist Irene Matthis wrote about a young male schizophrenic patient, Rune, who was also the subject of film director Marianne Ahrne's novel *Äppelblom och ruiner;* thus, a double perspective was provided on a deeply disturbed but nonetheless authentic view of the world.

With his 18th-century ocean voyage in *Speranza,* Sven Delblanc created an allegory of monolithic totalitarian beliefs tempting the unheroic modern individual. Per Gunner Evander published two novels, *Se mig i mitt friska öga* and *Ängslans boningar,* both of which illustrate his talent for investing everyday reality with symbolic significance. Åke Leijonhufvud's *Förförarens nya dagbok* charts a male-chauvinist seducer's downfall. Ernst Brunner's first novel, *Känneru brorsan?*, highlights with great linguistic vitality a young man's existential dilemmas, and another first novel, Gunnar Pettersson's *Nattsvärmaren,* dramatizes the disillusionment of a young member of an ultra-left-wing group. A father's attempts to contact his dead son through the mediation of an ancient sea god turn Tore Zetterholm's *Oannes* into science fiction. Bunny Ragnerstam examined the role of sports as a career ladder for a working-class boy in *En svensk tragedi: uppkomlingen,* while Lars Ardelius concluded his trilogy on Sweden's recent past with *Provryttare,* a social panorama of the years 1909–38.

Lars Forssell's sombre poems in *Stenar* voice the problem of pain and evil. Ylva Eggehorn's poems *Hjärtats Knytnävsslag* affirm God's love in religious and secular settings, while in *Threnos* Tobias Berggren spoke, with greater simplicity than previously, of death in life. By the same token the erstwhile rebel Bengt Emil Johnson moved toward expressive lucidity with his collection *Vinterminne.*

(KARIN PETHERICK)

ITALIAN

While the year's fiction seemed to confirm the recent trend toward a rediscovery of individual subjectivity and self-analysis, the constant interest of both Italian writers and readers in social and political themes was reasserted by the remarkable growth and popularity of the essay, a genre hitherto reserved almost exclusively for the intelligentsia. This was undoubtedly the most significant single development of the year, which saw some of Italy's finest imaginative writers engaged in producing new essays or in collecting and republishing their old ones. *Nero su nero,* by Leonardo Sciascia, is a public diary consisting of pieces of varying length and covering events and themes of the last ten years: the book of a great moralist. Alberto Arbasino's *Un paese senza* is a remorseless and bitter diatribe on the 1970s in Italy, a brilliant essay written in a sparkling language and bursting with intelligence. The conflict between political and literary commitments is discussed in Alberto Moravia's *Impegno controvoglia,* a collection of the novelist's political writings from 1943 to 1979 covering a variety of topics from Stalinism to Italian terrorism. Partly on the same subject is Italo Calvino's *Una pietra sopra,* including all his essays (some previously unpublished) on literature and society from 1955 to 1978.

Notable additions to the analysis of the phenomenon of terrorism were *Il caso 7 aprile,* by Giorgio Bocca, a controversial research into the "grand inquisition" that followed the assassination of Aldo Moro by the Red Brigades, and *Storie italiane di violenza e terrorismo,* by Giampaolo Pansa, 30 true stories of terror outlining the growth of the Italian "myth of insurrection." Finally, and in categories of their own, were Giorgio Amendola's *Un'isola,* the memoirs of the late Communist leader from 1931 to 1939, and Giovanni Macchia's *L'angelo della notte,* a superb study of Marcel Proust's *À la recherche du temps perdu.*

© LUTFI ÖZKÖK

Alberto Moravia

By comparison, the year's fiction, though abundant and generally of acceptable quality, looked less impressive as a whole. Alberto Bevilacqua's *La festa parmigiana* is a Fellinian gallery of bizarre characters and figurines, from royalty and great artists to peasants and humble artisans, a collage of tales and quotations on the history of Parma, which the narrator revisits after many years of absence to recognize its bewitching magnetism but also his irreparable estrangement from it. Memory novels also included Gina Lagorio's elegiac *Fuori scena,* in which the protagonist returns to the Langhe to exorcise the myth or sickness of her youth; Vittorio Gorresio's *La vita ingenua,* covering the author's life and that of his family in Cuneo from his childhood to the post-World War II period; Lalla Romano's *Una giovinezza inventata,* set in the 1920s in Turin; and Nantas Salvalaggio's *Rio dei pensieri,* set in Venice, where the dimension of the revisited past is enriched by the present drama of a middle-aged man faced with an empty future. However, the best in this category was Francesca Sanvitale's *Madre e figlia,* a marvelously rich, subtle, and intelligent narrative in which past and present continually merge and interchange.

Among the few novels concerned with terrorism was Carlo Bernari's *Il giorno degli assassini,* a thriller in which the investigator is baffled by the apparent gratuitousness of the multiple crimes he is investigating. The apocalyptic/neohistorical line is continued by Manlio Cancogni's picaresque *Nostra Signora della speranza* and, to some extent by Elio Bartolini's metaphorical *La linea dell'arciduca,* in which the construction of a railway line in Friuli, planned first by the Austrians, then by the Fascists, and later by the Christian Democrat government, never comes to fruition until it is replaced by the quick and quiet building of a menacing NATO missile base.

Turning to poetry, it was a quiet though not a disappointing year. At opposite ends of the lyrical spectrum new collections appeared by two masters of the genre: the mythico-historical "poema" *Moses* by Piero Bigongiari and the technically brilliant potpourri in verse, *Stracciafoglio*, by Edoardo Sanguineti. Also well praised were Antonio Porta's *Passi passaggi* and Maurizio Cucchi's *Le meraviglie dell'acqua*, but perhaps more immediately appealing was Ugo Reale's *Il cerchio d'ombra*, unpretentious poetry that discreetly and yet deeply strikes at the heart of modern man's spiritual malaise.

(LINO PERTILE)

SPANISH

Spain. The prestigious Miguel de Cervantes Prize was won at the end of 1980 by Juan Carlos Onetti, an exile from Uruguay living in Spain. The prize, presented by the Ministry of Culture, is worth 10 million pesetas. Onetti announced that he was surprised that Hispanic-Americans continued to be so honoured in Spain. The Premios Nacionales de Literatura were given in 1980 to the philologist Alonso Zamora Vicente for his narrative *Mesa, sobremesa* and to Andrés Amorós, in the essay field, for *Introduccion a la literatura*. The Premios de la Crítica are given for work in the four official languages of Spain. In Castilian the winners were Onetti for his novel *Dejemos hablar al viento* and Luis Rosales for his book of poetry *Diario de una resurrección*. In Catalan the narrative prize went to Josep Pla for *Notes de capvesprol* and the poetry award to Miquel Martí i Pol for *Estimada Marta*. In Galician (Gallego) the winners were Alvaro Cunqueiro for the narrative *Os outros ferantes* and Eduardo Moreiras for his verse *O libro dos mortos*. In Basque the prize for narrative went to José Agustín Arrieta for *Abuztuaren 15 Bazkalondoa* and for poetry to Juan Mari Lekuona for *Ilargiaren eskolan*.

Late in 1979 a little noted Premio Nacional—in the essay category—was awarded to Fernando Sánchez Dragó for his historical narrative *Gárgoris y Habidis: Historia mágica de España*. A gargantuan work in four large volumes, the "history" proved to be one of the most discussed and widely read titles in 1980. The author, who had been jailed as a Communist under Francisco Franco, had become a furious anti-Communist, and he wrote in a complicated and ornate style. His treatment of Spanish identity through the ages was said to have "proved that national narcissism remained in fine form" (in the words of the critic Fernando Corujedo).

Other notable books included a new work, *Astrolabio*, by the gifted poet Antonio Colinas. Leopoldo Azancot added to his reputation with *La novia judía*. An important book of criticism was Ignacio Soldevila's *La novela desde 1936*.

(ANTHONY KERRIGAN)

Latin America. Literature in Spanish America during the year reflected a considerable amount of worthwhile creation but few superb works with international impact. The renowned writers Carlos Fuentes, José Donoso, and Octavio Paz published books in 1980 that were relatively minor contributions to their total work. A major novel by Guillermo Cabrera Infante appeared in late 1979.

Cabrera Infante's extensive *La Habana para un Infante Difunto* deals with sexuality in the humorous fashion that has been the author's trademark. As a first-person narrative set in Havana during the 1940s and 1950s, it also presents questions concerning the relationship between autobiography and fiction. The novel was well received by critics upon its publication and marked a maturation in Cabrera Infante's fiction.

Donoso's short novel, *La misteriosa desaparición de la marquesita de Loria*, also deals with sexuality, but the Chilean writer's treatment is erotic and decadent. The protagonist who experiences these perverse pleasures is a Nicaraguan diplomat's daughter living in Spain. Five other Chilean novelists published novels in late 1979: Adolfo Couve, Gustavo Frías, Antonio Montero, Carlos Morand, and Ximena Sepúlveda. Couve's *La lección de pintura* deals with an adolescent's life in the provinces of Chile. *El mundo de Maxó*, by Frías, describes the frivolity and reflections of a protagonist who is both a playboy and self-styled philosopher. Using traditional narrative techniques, Montero describes the traditions of the landed aristocracy in *Asunto de familia*. Morand's *Ohtumba* develops a series of human relationships centred on the Chilean protagonist who is a professor at a U.S. university. *El cuarto reino*, by Sepúlveda, relates the psychological experience of a protagonist who discusses her problems with a psychoanalyst.

Carlos Fuentes's *Una familia lejana* is a short mystery novel with elements characteristic of his previous work: multiple identities, an emphasis on universal human relationships, and the presence of metafiction. The renowned poet Octavio Paz published a bilingual volume of poetry, *Air Born/Hijos del aire*, in collaboration with Charles Tomlinson. An important Mexican novel published in late 1979 was Vicente Leñero's *El Evangelio de Lucas Gavilán*. Leñero sets the scene in contempo-

Carlos Fuentes

NEAL BOENZI—THE NEW YORK TIMES

rary Mexico and writes a parallel to the structure of St. Luke's Gospel. It is primarily a novel about social justice. Other notable novels appearing in Mexico in late 1979 were José Joaquín Blanco's *La vida es larga y además no importa,* Marta Robles's *Memorias de la libertad,* Julieta Campos's *El miedo de perder a Eurídice,* and Miguel Alvarez Acosta's *La frontera plural.* María Luisa Puga published her second novel (1980), the imaginative and utopian *Cuando el aire es azul.*

Literary production in Colombia was not as vigorous as in recent years. Mario Escobar Velásquez published a fine novel in late 1979, *Cuando pasé el ánima.* Amparo María Suárez's first novel, *Santificar al diablo,* an imaginative and successful work, at times recalls the style of Colombian author Gabriel García Márquez. Jaime Enrique Ardila also published his first novel, *El cadáver de papá.* Several books of short stories appeared in Colombia. Eduardo Pachón Padilla compiled a valuable two-volume anthology covering the Colombian short story from 1820 to the present, *El cuento colombiano. Todos estábamos a la espera,* a posthumous volume of stories by Alvaro Cepeda Samudio, was published by Plaza y Janés. Two novelists published volumes of stories: Alblaucía Angel, *¡Oh gloria inmarcesible!,* and Pedro Gómez Valderrama, *Más arriba del reino.*

The Casa de las Américas prize for novels was awarded to Osvaldo Jorge Salazar (Peru) for *La ópera de los fantasmas.* Other prizewinners were Raúl Pérez Torres of Ecuador for *En la noche y en la niebla* (short stories) and Eduardo Langagne of Mexico for *Donde habita el cangrejo* (poetry). Two prizes were given during the year for theatre: Colombia's Enrique Buenaventura for *Historia de una bala de plata* and Felipe Santander of Mexico for *El extensionista.* In Venezuela Denzil Romero was awarded the Premio Municipal (de Caracas) de Literatura for his volume of stories *El invencionero.* The Chilean novelist and folklore specialist Juan Uribe was awarded the Premio Nacional Ricardo Latcham in Chile. One of the most important literary events was a symposium held in Bloomington, Ind. (September 1980), "La Novela en Español, Hoy," organized by the critic José Miguel Oviedo and attended by Mario Vargas Llosa, Carlos Fuentes, and Juan Goytisolo.

(RAYMOND L. WILLIAMS)

PORTUGUESE

Portugal. The novel continued to offer a wide field for literary experimentation. In *Levantado do Chão,* José Saramago made a brave and successful attempt to break the form and the narrative codes of neorealism. The action of his novel is located in Alentejo, a southern province of Portugal, where the land reform that dispossessed absentee landowners of large estates took place in 1975. The reform was later contained and eroded by a powerful offensive from the constitutional governments. Saramago captures effectively the mood of three successive generations of peasants leading up to that period. Rural poverty, the nomadism of the peasants, their guile and disillusion, as well as their struggles and longing for a plot of land where they might be able to love, sweat, and die in peace, are described in a nonlinear fashion that adds to the subtlety of a tale that is teeming with life. By mocking the providential devices of the novel and adopting the apparently loose form of oral digression, the author undermines also the individual mythology that attributes to sudden quirks of fate all changes in life. Yet the light that shines through the last scenes of the narrative heralds no easy hope; Saramago abhors the conventions of an ending, relying mainly on the psychological complexity of his characters to illuminate the human predicament in history.

A similar awareness of the potentialities of language, now elevated to a level of refined quest, was to be found in Mário Cláudio's *Estâncias.* The poems in this book show a dense metaphorical allusiveness very much in the tradition of Ezra Pound's *Cantos.* By exploring an essential cosmic imagery, which soon follows multiple cultural directions, Cláudio retains, nevertheless, a verbal discipline that leads into an exorcism of the newly established poetical diction in order to make the reader feel that poetry can be made out of the most uncongenial material. Cláudio's vision of the world was culturally ecumenical and superseded to a large extent the surrealist ambition, still present in Mário Cesariny de Vasconcelos's *Primavera Autónoma das Estradas.* There are in this work some brilliant passages, to the credit of a poet who was one of the most powerful voices of Portuguese surrealism.

(L. S. REBELO)

Brazil. In *Farda Fardão Camisola de Dormir,* Jorge Amado describes the politics and intrigues surrounding an election to the Academia Brasileira de Letras during World War II. Critics of this best-seller related these fictional characters to an actual, recent election to the organization. Fernando Sabino's *O grande mentecapto* presents a new picaresque Brazilian antihero, Geraldo Viramundo. Viramundo's 33-year life span in Minas Gerais State

Nélida Piñon

only occasionally verges on reality. Luis Jardim's novel *O ajudante de mentiroso* also dealt with a picaresque hero. The multitalented Chico Anísio described Cleofas, the protagonist of his hilarious *O telefone amarelo,* as a consultant and adviser to Jimmy Carter, Roberto Carlos, and Princess Grace, among others. The death of the distinguished novelist José Américo de Almeida occurred in May.

Rubem Fonseca's collection of short fiction, *O Cobrador,* returns to his theme of contemporary social-class conflicts ending in bloody violence. The character in the title story ("The Getter") decides "to get" everything established society has always denied him through the use of his guns, knives, and explosives. Another view of modern Brazilian life appears in Nélida Piñon's quite original collection of stories, *O calor das coisas.* Some of her characters debate the quality of life and wonder about the recent past's significance for the future. A similar concern preoccupied Ivan Ângelo in *A casa de vidro.* The title story ("The Glass House") is a fine metaphorical narration of Brazilian political life in the 1970s. Edilberto Coutinho was awarded the Cuban Casa de las Américas Prize for his yet unpublished collection, *Maracanã, Adeus.*

In July the poet Vinícius de Moraes died; tributes to him came from all sectors of the international cultural community. Carlos Drummond de Andrade's *Esquecer para lembrar* was the third volume of his poetic autobiography; it was the year's most successful collection of verse. New poems by Mário Chamie, Astrid Cabral, Liane dos Santos, and Tarik de Sousa, a well-known music critic, also appeared. The complete poems of Dante de Milano and Paulo Mendes Campos were published, as was a new anthology of Afonso Félix de Sousa's works.

Nelson Rodrigues's newest drama, *Os 7 gatinhos,* made a powerful social and moral statement about lives at the subsistence level. Abdias do Nascimento's drama *Sortilégio, II* once again raised the question of black identity in Brazil. His theories about the status of many aspects of black Brazilian and world culture were collected in *O Quilombismo.* Heloísa Buarque de Holanda organized a series of volumes on Brazilian culture as it has evolved since the mid-1960s. (IRWIN STERN)

RUSSIAN

Soviet Literature. Many of the year's publications were timed to coincide with memorable dates and events. One of the most interesting of the many works connected with the 110th anniversary of Lenin's birth was a series of five books from the Khudozhestvennaya Literatura publishers: *Lenin on Literature and Art; Vladimir Lenin in the Poetry of the Peoples of the World; Lenin in the Poetry of the Peoples of the U.S.S.R.; Stories and Essays About Lenin;* and *Writers' Reminiscences of Lenin.* These comprised a fundamental body of work covering the full range of Lenin's writings and speeches on literature and art along with the best that had been written about him in memoirs and other literature.

Among important literary dates commemorated was the centenary of the birth of Aleksandr Blok (1880–1921), much of whose poetry was republished during the year. The most important project was a new six-volume edition of his collected

TASS/SOVFOTO

Mikhail Sholokhov

works. Blok's lyrical poetry and his well-known poem "The Twelve" were also published in other languages of the U.S.S.R.—Ukrainian, Belorussian, Kazakh, Latvian, Lithuanian, Moldavian, and Estonian. Numerous works about the poet included the two-volume literary memoirs *Blok in the Reminiscences of Contemporaries.*

Another centenary was that of the birth of Aleksandr Grin (1880–1932). Grin was an outstanding writer who created a world that was fantastic and romantic but at the same time real, and his books were especially popular among young people. One of the largest of the jubilee publications was his collected works in six volumes, in an edition of 600,000.

Mikhail Sholokhov, holder of Nobel, Lenin, and U.S.S.R. state prizes, celebrated his 75th birthday in 1980 and was awarded the Order of Lenin. Of the books on Sholokhov published during the year, especially noteworthy were Vasily Litvinov's *Mikhail Sholokhov* and Victor Gura's fundamental work of literary research entitled *How "And Quiet Flows the Don" Was Written: The History of the Novel.* A new eight-volume edition of Sholokhov's collected works also appeared.

The Great Patriotic War (World War II) continued to be a leading theme in Soviet literature. A new novella by Belorussian writer Ales Adamovich, *The Punitive Squads,* published early in the year in the magazine *Druzhba Narodov,* continued the artistic and philosophical exposure of Fascism. Vyacheslav Kondratiev, who made his literary debut in 1979 with the story "Sashka," contributed several stories, which, like the first, conveyed sincerity and authenticity in portraying people's wartime emotions and behaviour.

Among the many works by non-Russian Soviet writers published during the year was the novel

The Conscience by Uzbek writer Adyl Yakubov. The Georgian writer Nodar Dumbadze, whose most recent novel, *The Law of Eternity*, was concerned with contemporary life in the republic, was awarded a 1980 Lenin Prize. The death occurred in February of the literary historian Vasily Katanyan (*see* OBITUARIES). (MAYA Y. ISKOLDSKAYA)

Expatriate Russian Literature. In a year more notable for the continuing exodus of the Soviet Union's best writers than for any literary successes, the satirical novelist Vladimir Voinovich was the latest victim of KGB persecution to emigrate, arriving in Munich, West Germany, at the end of December. He had been preceded a few weeks earlier by Vasily Aksyonov, one of the 23 authors represented in the *Metropol* almanac, and Lev Kopelev, on whom Aleksandr Solzhenitsyn modeled a leading character in *Cancer Ward*.

Best known for his *The Life and Extraordinary Adventures of Private Ivan Chonkin*—a latter-day, Soviet good soldier Schweik—and *The Ivankiad*, Voinovich recently published a book of short stories called *In Plain Russian*. His troubles with officialdom started in 1968, when he signed a letter demanding a fair trial for Aleksandr Ginsburg and Yury Galanskov, who was to die in a labour camp a few years later. His writings banned, Voinovich was expelled from the Writers' Union in 1974. Early in 1980 it was suggested to him by the authorities that he ought to emigrate.

After several months during which the authorities played a cat-and-mouse game with him, Voinovich, who suffered a heart attack in August, wrote a brave, exasperated letter to his tormentors. "It is long past time," he wrote, "for you to understand, if only from our country's history, that the more you torment a writer, the longer his books shall live and outlive not only himself, but his persecutors as well." Two months later, Voinovich was finally allowed to leave the country with his wife and daughter.

He left behind a dwindling, though still surprisingly large, number of writers willing to risk persecution as they tried to expand the boundaries of contemporary Soviet literature. In a long dispatch from Moscow on December 21, Michael Binyon, Moscow correspondent of *The Times* (London), wrote: "One by one the new wave of writers and artists who made their name. . . in the intellectual ferment of the early 1960s have fallen foul of an increasingly strident artistic orthodoxy, been. . . harassed by the KGB. . . and forced to emigrate to the West."

Another of their number, the once popular novelist Georgy Vladimov (author of *Faithful Ruslan*), had had experiences similar to those of Voinovich. Like Voinovich, he suffered a heart attack, and he was expected to emigrate shortly.

Following the example of the authors behind *Metropol*, in early December seven young, less well-known writers tried to set up a private club for uncensored experimental writing. Their attempt was promptly squashed by the authorities.

The most interesting books to appear abroad—apart from *In Plain Russian*—were *The Radiant Future*, Aleksandr Zinoviev's follow-up to *The Yawning Heights*, and *The Institute of Fools* by Victor Nekipelov, sentenced in June 1980 to seven years in a labour camp and five in internal exile.

Andrey Amalrik, whose *Will the Soviet Union Survive Until 1984?* attracted worldwide attention in the early 1970s, died November 11 in an automobile accident in Spain (*see* OBITUARIES). (GEORGE THEINER)

EASTERN EUROPEAN LITERATURE

The award of the 1980 Nobel Prize for Literature to the Polish poet, translator, and literary critic Czeslaw Milosz, who had been living in exile since 1951, drew attention to the unnatural situation prevailing in the author's homeland. His work had been banned there for almost 30 years and could appear only in the *samizdat* editions produced under extremely difficult conditions by the unofficial publishing house NOWA. Milosz, who taught at the University of California in Berkeley, was now at last to be published in Poland officially. (*See* NOBEL PRIZES.)

The director of NOWA, Miroslaw Chojecki, was arrested in March on the fabricated charge of "stealing a duplicator." At his trial in June he was given a suspended 18-month prison sentence, but as a result of the relaxation brought about by the strikes during the summer, he was able to travel to Stockholm in December to be present at the Nobel Prize ceremony. He then visited London and Paris before returning home to attend a court hearing on his appeal against his sentence.

With him in Stockholm was Stanislaw Baranczak, poet and editor of the highly popular, unofficial literary journal *Zapis*, 14 issues of which had appeared to date. It was brought out by NOWA in Warsaw and then printed in London by *Index on Censorship*. Unable to travel for the past five years, Baranczak previously had been refused permission to attend an International Poetry Festival in Rotterdam, Neth., and prevented from taking up a visiting professorship at Harvard. Two novels by Tadeusz Konwicki, both published in *Zapis*—*Kompleks polski* ("The Polish Complex," *Zapis* 3) and *Mala apokalipsa* ("Minor Apocalypse," *Zapis* 10)—aroused considerable interest in the West. The rights were sold to publishers in several Western countries.

One of Czechoslovakia's major poets, Vladimir Holan, died in March at the age of 74. Since he started writing in the '20s, he had published over 30 collections of verse, his best-known work being perhaps *A Night with Hamlet*, published originally in the early 1960s and in English in 1979. A Prague publishing house was continuing work on his collected poems. Milan Kundera, a leading Czechoslovak novelist living in exile in Paris, published his latest novel, *The Book of Laughter and Forgetting*. John Leonard described it in the *New York Times* as "a masterwork," putting Kundera in the "demonic company" of Günter Grass and García Marquez. The book, wrote Leonard, "calls itself a novel, although it is part fairy tale, part literary criticism, part political tract, part musicology and part autobiography."

Ivan Klima was one of the many Czechoslovak writers whose work had not appeared in Prague since the 1968 invasion, except in the pages of the unofficial Edice Petlice (Padlock Publications). His long short story "Ve středu ráno" ("On Wednesday Morning"), from the volume *Má veselá jitra* ("My Happy Mornings"), was published in Norway in 1980 under the title *Karpene* ("The Carp"). Attractively produced in a special, illustrated Christmas gift edition, the book also included an interesting article by Frantisek Janouch on Edice Petlice and other unofficial literary series and magazines. Their typewritten volumes not only kept Czechoslovak literature alive despite official disapproval, but in one case at least they induced the authorities to sanction the appearance of a long-silenced author. Having had his work published only in Petlice since 1968, Czechoslovakia's best-loved poet, Jaroslav Seifert, was to be made available again to a wider readership.

Protest, the latest one-act play by Vaclav Havel, written shortly before his arrest in 1978, was performed at the London National Theatre in February 1980. It had also been seen at the Orange Tree Theatre in Richmond and—in Michael Kustow's National Theatre production—at the ICA in June, when the Writers Guild of Great Britain gave a benefit performance in support of the playwright and his friends, now serving terms in Czechoslovak jails.

The East German writer Manfred Bartz became the first victim of the tough censorship law passed in June 1979 when he was arrested for distributing unpublished texts in East Berlin. The official East German attitude to literature was spelled out by the party secretary responsible for cultural matters, Kurt Hager, in a speech at the Arts Academy in December 1980. Criticizing the "false ideological standpoint" of some (unspecified) East German writers, he declared, "Laments, pessimism and world-weariness will not help our society to move forward." (GEORGE THEINER)

JEWISH

Hebrew. During 1980 three interesting programs were developed in Israel to promote interest in Hebrew literature. The Institute for the Translation of Hebrew Literature published English translations of recent works, including plays by H. Levin and Y. Sobol, and it planned the regular publication of bibliographies of Hebrew literature in translation. Second, the Ministry of Education and Culture sponsored an outreach program that brought prominent writers into contact with 11th- and 12th-grade students to discuss the writers' works and their role in Israeli culture. Third, a Laboratory on Teaching Literature was dedicated at Haifa University's School of Education.

Promising new literary periodicals appeared in 1980. They included *Mahbarot*, edited by Y. Kenaz; *Rosh*, a poetry journal edited by O. Bartena; and *Hazerem hehadash*, founded by a group of young ex-soldiers.

Significant poetry collections included a long-awaited volume by Natan Sach, *Tsfonit mizrahit*. Prose works included the science-fiction novel *Tsavu'a be Kurundi* by David Melamed, a rising religious writer; *Ets hatut*, a first novel by Aryeh Semo; and a joint volume by three leading young poets, R. Somek, E. Bekher, and P. Banai. The journal *Akhshav* published a special two-volume issue on the 1948 generation of Israeli writers.

Critical works included two volumes on Hebrew fiction by Dan Miron; collected articles on Kahana-Carmon by A. Balaban; H. Schirmann's studies in medieval Hebrew literature; and an anthology of medieval Hebrew love poetry by Dan Pagis. Also published were anthologies of Egyptian short stories (*Al hahof shemineged*) and Egyptian poetry (*Mavet ve'ahava*) in Hebrew translation.

(WARREN BARGAD)

Yiddish. Moshe Altman, the 90-year-old author of significant interwar novels, continued to publish his *Notes of an Ancient*. His small collection *At the Window* discusses the still-unappreciated role of Yiddish in Jewish life. Hersh Remenik, the 75-year-old literary critic, published *Problems of Contemporary Soviet Yiddish Literature*. Its inclusion of Yiddish writers outside the U.S.S.R. reflected the more open orientation of his recent writing.

The 50th anniversary of the founding of Young Vilna was celebrated with published evaluations and memoirs. This literary group produced such major contemporary writers as Chaim Grade, Abraham Sutzkever, and Elchanon Vogler.

Books 5 and 6 of Elya Schechtman's epic novel *Erev* describe the tragic fate of his heroes during the civil war period in the Ukraine (1918–20). *And Still It Turns*, a brilliant novel by Nathan Zabare (1908–75), was published in Moscow in 1980. Dealing with the life of Jews in southern France at the beginning of the 13th century, it illuminates links between Arab and Jewish philosophers and rationalists against the medieval social-political background.

Romanian Yiddish writing remained at a high level. The third volume of the literary almanac *Bukareshter shriftn* appeared. Volf Tambur's novel *Autumn with Sun* comments on current conditions in Europe. Iso Schapira's *Alef Is an Eagle* and Chaim Goldenstein's *The Silent Century* discuss Jewish participation in the Spanish Civil War and World War II. Itik Svart Kara's *Young Years and ... Not So Young* reminisces about Yiddish writers in Romania. Iulian Schwartz's *Portraits and Essays* analyzes the spectrum of Jewish creativity.

Yekhiel Granatshteyn's *Alien Forest, Native Earth* retells the experience of one man who survives through the intervention of a Polish Gentile supervisor. *Landscape of Fate*, a selection of poems published by Switzerland's only Yiddish writer, Leyzer Aichenrand, shows the influence of modernist European poetry. Binem Heller's *The Promised Word* reveals a new departure in his literary quest, the search for God.

(THOMAS E. BIRD; ELIAS SCHULMAN)

CHINESE

China. Chinese literature flourished in 1980, demonstrating both vitality and diversity. Fostering this development were the further downgrading of rigid Maoist ideology, the continued relaxation of government control over art and literature, and the encouragement given to creative activity by the Communist Party, as well as more extensive exposure to Western literary works and influences. Few writers seemed to have been deterred by such recent events as the conviction of certain dissident activists, the constitutional revision to curb some freedoms, and the emphasis, voiced by literary authorities, on the writer's responsibility for the social effects of his writing. On the contrary, they continued to experiment with new forms, techniques, and themes. The "literature of the wounded" (*shang-hen wen-xue*), which revealed the tragic effects of the Cultural Revolution—a very popular theme until recently—was replaced by a new realistic literature portraying China's social conditions and political reality.

Though there was still considerable supervision of creative writing and publishing activities, writers ventured into many formerly "forbidden zones." One was the exposure of privileges enjoyed by high officials and their families, best represented by *If I Were Real*, a play by Sha Yexin (Sha Yeh-hsin) and others, which depicts with humour the privileges enjoyed by a young man who pretends to be the son of a high official. Another example was the story "A Bunch of Letters" by Bai Hua (Pai Hua), which also exposes the dark side of Communist society. Dozens of plays and works of fiction savagely lampooned officials who were corrupt or incompetent. Among the best was Liu Binyan's (Liu Pin-yen's) "Between Men and Phantoms," a powerful exposure of corruption, inefficiency, and incompetence. The personal hardships caused by political turmoil became another popular theme, exemplified by Wang Jing's (Wang Ching's) play *Recorded in Society's Files*. "When One Reaches Middle Age," a story by Chen Rong (Ch'en Jung), reveals the suffering of Chinese intellectuals and professionals under Communist rule. Also notable was Wang Meng's innovative story "The Butterfly." Most of these works portray real human beings rather than stereotypes, and their authors even boldly attribute the social evils they expose to Communist institutions.

Taiwan. In contrast to the lively literary scene in China, Taiwan produced only a small number of notable works in 1980. The persecution of political dissidents, some of whom were also active writers, may have contributed to this phenomenon. But, like their counterparts on the mainland, Taiwanese authors by and large continued their emphasis on realistic literature. A few experimented with new themes, styles, and techniques, a good example being Wang Wen-hsing's ambitious novel *The Man Against the Sea*. While fiction remained the most popular genre, works by poets such as Cheng Ch'ou-yü and Yü Kuang-chung and prose writers like P'an Ch'i-chün also had some appreciative readers.

Important achievements were also made by native Taiwanese writers. *The Cloud*, a novelette by Ch'en Ying-chen that offers a penetrating analysis of relations between the island's capitalists and labourers, was widely regarded as one of the best examples of Taiwan's "native-soil" literature. A few promising young writers emerged, among them Sung Tse-lai, Ku Meng-jen, and, in particular, Chiang Hsiao-yün, whose novel *The Marriage Road* attracted wide attention.

(WINSTON L. Y. YANG; NATHAN MAO)

JAPANESE

The Japanese literary scene was comparatively quiet in 1980. There were neither sensational literary controversies nor flamboyant best-sellers. The most noteworthy events were the deaths of three writers—Gyo Kambayashi, septuagenarian novelist who wrote sensitive vignettes of first-person narrative known as the "I novel" for about a half century; Tetsutaro Kawakami, prominent literary critic; and Masaaki Tachihara, whose prolific career was cut short by cancer.

Other significant events included the refusal of two novelists to accept literary awards. Ayako Sono's *Dirty Hand of God* deals with the morality of an obstetrician whose main practice is abortion. When this novel was chosen by the jury of Award for Women Writers, Sono refused to accept it so that she could retain her "peace of mind." Actually, this recognition came somewhat late to Sono, who already had several remarkable novels to her credit. The second refusal was by novelist Kyojin Onishi, whose *Divine Comedy* took him more than 20 years to finish. Onishi, a staunch leftist, wanted nothing to do with a "literary award with an individual's name on it" (such as the Tanizaki Prize or the Akutagawa Prize).

Several works of literary merit appeared during the year. Shusaku Endo, author of *Silence*, wrote *Samurai*, an impressive historical novel. The hero is a 17th-century samurai of the Sendai clan who visits Mexico, Spain, and Italy just as Japan is about to adopt its policy of national isolation. He is sent as chief of a foreign "trade mission" by his feudal lord, and it takes him seven years to finish the journey. As far as practical achievements are concerned, the samurai's efforts are futile, but his conversion to Christianity, originally intended to smooth trade negotiations, is followed by a genuine conversion. Endo was successful at tracing this subtle spiritual change.

Endo was given the Noma Award, while the Tanizaki Award went to Taeko Kono for her *One Year's Idyll*, which proved to be another psychological tour de force. The heroine is suffering from a mysterious disease that could be fatally contagious for her male companion. So she abstains from sexual intercourse for one year. The book had little external action, but on the psychoerotic level it was surprisingly dramatic and arresting. In Taeko Tomioka's *Full of Plum Blossoms in the Three Thousand Worlds*, the central characters are based on the founders of a new religious sect in modern Japan. The vigorous emergence of various popular sects has been a remarkable phenomenon in the modern history of Japan, and Tomioka's evocation of charismatic personalities was highly effective.

There were also achievements in the short story—the traditional forte of Japanese writers. Tatsuo Nagai's *Autumn and Other Pieces*, Tetsuro Miura's *Wild Geese in Winter*, and Tan Onuma's *Turtledove* display remarkable sensitivity. As for literary criticism, Hajime Shinoda's *Contemporary Novel*, Takasuke Shibusawa's *Ariake Kambara*, and Shin Shimaoka's *Sakutaro Hagiwara* were outstanding.

(SHOICHI SAEKI)

See also Art Sales; Libraries; Nobel Prizes; Publishing. [621]

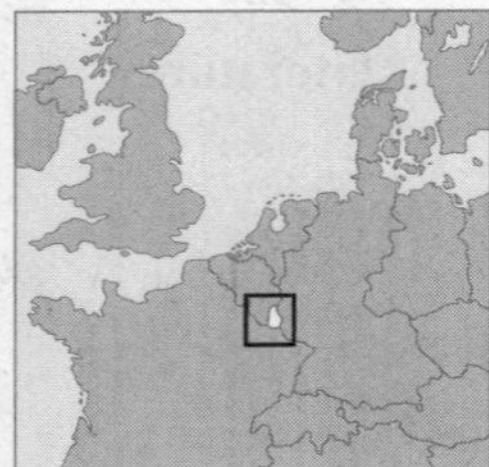
Luxembourg

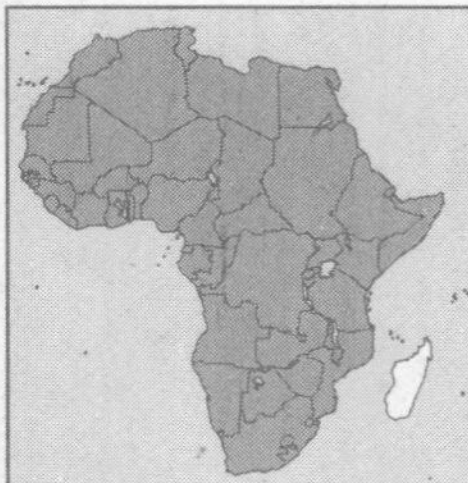
Madagascar

Luxembourg

A constitutional monarchy, the Benelux country of Luxembourg is bounded on the east by West Germany, on the south by France, and on the west and north by Belgium. Area: 2,586 sq km (999 sq mi). Pop. (1980 est.): 363,700. Cap. and largest city: Luxembourg (pop., 1978 est., 79,600). Language: French, German, Luxembourgian. Religion: Roman Catholic 95%. Grand duke, Jean; prime minister in 1980, Pierre Werner.

The prime ministers of The Netherlands, Belgium, and Luxembourg, meeting at The Hague on June 22, 1980, nominated Gaston Thorn (*see* BIOGRAPHIES), Luxembourg's foreign minister, as the next president of the European Economic Community's Commission, to succeed Roy Jenkins (U.K.) in January 1981.

Thorn's position would be delicate in the debate as to which city should be the permanent seat of the European Assembly. The Socialists, the largest party group, considered that the current practice of holding committee meetings in Brussels and plenary sessions in Strasbourg, while the Secretariat was based in Luxembourg, was nonsensical and costly. They believed that Brussels should be the single seat of all the European Assembly's institutions. The French, who had constructed a spacious building in Strasbourg, insisted that the Alsatian capital city, lying on the frontier between France and West Germany, was predestined to be the Assembly's seat.

Luxembourg, which in March had completed a special Assembly hall at a cost of $70 million, rejected both Brussels and Strasbourg. In April, Pierre Werner, Luxembourg's prime minister, warned Simone Veil, president of the European Assembly, that his government would take the issue to the European Court of Justice if any attempt were made to relocate the Assembly Secretariat. (K. M. SMOGORZEWSKI)

LUXEMBOURG

Education. (1978–79) Primary, pupils 32,436, teachers 1,998; secondary, pupils 8,558; vocational, pupils 15,697; secondary and vocational teachers (1975–76) 1,801; teacher training, students 119, higher (1977–78), students 302, teaching staff 172.

Finance. Monetary unit: Luxembourg franc, at par with the Belgian franc, with (Sept. 22, 1980) a free rate of LFr 29 to U.S. $1 (LFr 69.70 = £1 sterling). Budget (1980 est.): revenue LFr 45,361,000,000; expenditure LFr 45,549,000,000. Gross domestic product (1978) LFr 106,570,000,000. Cost of living (1975 = 100; June 1980) 133.9.

Foreign Trade: *see* BELGIUM.

Transport and Communications. Roads (1979) 5,079 km (including 44 km expressways). Motor vehicles in use (1979): passenger 164,100; commercial 10,700. Railways: (1978) 270 km; traffic (1979) 298 million passenger-km, freight 714 million net ton-km. Air traffic (1978): 190 million passenger-km; freight 300,000 net ton-km. Telephones (Jan. 1978) 185,500. Radio receivers (Dec. 1977) 180,000. Television receivers (Dec. 1977) 88,000.

Agriculture. Production (in 000; metric tons; 1978): barley 76; wheat 29; oats 25; potatoes 40; wine *c.* 7. Livestock (in 000; May 1978): cattle 216; pigs 90; poultry 163.

Industry. Production (in 000; metric tons; 1979): iron ore (29% metal content) 632; pig iron 3,802; crude steel 4,949; electricity (kw-hr) 1,339,000.

Livestock:
see Agriculture and Food Supplies

Lumber:
see Industrial Review

Lutheran Churches:
see Religion

Macau:
see Dependent States

Machinery and Machine Tools:
see Industrial Review

Madagascar

Madagascar occupies the island of the same name and minor adjacent islands in the Indian Ocean off the southeast coast of Africa. Area: 587,041 sq km (226,658 sq mi). Pop. (1980 est.): 8,742,000. Cap. and largest city: Antananarivo (pop., 1976 est., 468,000). Language: Malagasy (national) and French (official). Religion: animist 54%; Roman Catholic 21%; Protestant 18%; Muslim 7%. President in 1980, Didier Ratsiraka; prime minister, Lieut. Col. Désiré Rakotoarijaona.

During a private visit to France in August 1980, following a "ten-day holiday" in the Soviet Union, Malagasy Pres. Didier Ratsiraka discussed with French Pres. Valéry Giscard d'Estaing the project of a peace conference for the Indian Ocean region. The French president gave a favourable response to the proposal in spite of the cloud cast over Franco-Malagasy relations by the territorial demands of the Madagascar government. Madagascar claimed sovereignty over the Glorieuses Archipelago (claimed also by the Comoros) and over the other French islands scattered over the Indian Ocean and the Mozambique Channel.

In April the government received Georges Marchais, secretary-general of the French Communist Party, in Antananarivo on an official visit. Ratsiraka confirmed in May that he had undertaken major purchases of arms in the Soviet Union. In September a five-year cultural cooperation agreement with Cuba was concluded in Havana.

On the domestic scene, the president severely criticized the operation of the nation's socialist en-

MADAGASCAR

Education. (1978) Primary, pupils 1,311,000, teachers 23,937; secondary, pupils (1976) 114,468, teachers (1975) 5,088; vocational, pupils (1976) 7,000, teachers (1973) 879; teacher training (1973), students 993, teachers 63; higher (1976), students 10,976, teaching staff 692.

Finance. Monetary unit: Malagasy franc, at par with the CFA franc, with (Sept. 22, 1980) a parity of MalFr 50 to the French franc (free rates of MalFr 210 = U.S. $1 and MalFr 504 = £1 sterling). Gold, SDR's, and foreign exchange (May 1980) U.S. $9.2 million. Budget (1978 rev. est.): revenue MalFr 101.1 billion; expenditure MalFr 124.4 billion.

Foreign Trade. (1979) Imports MalFr 152,960,000,000; exports MalFr 83,830,000,000. Import sources (1978): France 35%; West Germany 14%; China 6%; Iraq 6%; Japan 5%. Export destinations (1978): U.S. 25%; France 23%; Indonesia 14%; West Germany 8%; Spain 5%. Main exports (1976): coffee 43%; cloves and clove oil 9%; vanilla 7%; petroleum products 7%.

Transport and Communications. Roads (1976) 27,507 km. Motor vehicles in use (1977): passenger 57,400; commercial (including buses) 52,300. Railways (1978): 1,035 km; traffic 296 million passenger-km, freight 211 million net ton-km. Air traffic (1978): 296 million passenger-km; freight 7.4 million net ton-km. Shipping (1979): merchant vessels 100 gross tons and over 51; gross tonnage 55,508. Telephones (Jan. 1978) 28,700. Radio receivers (Dec. 1977) 1,020,000. Television receivers (Dec. 1977) 12,000.

Agriculture. Production (in 000; metric tons; 1979): rice 2,327; corn (1978) *c.* 100; cassava (1978) 1,322; sweet potatoes (1978) *c.* 333; potatoes (1978) 137; mangoes *c.* 143; dry beans *c.* 44; bananas *c.* 278; oranges *c.* 83; pineapples *c.* 53; peanuts *c.* 30; sugar, raw value (1978) *c.* 115; coffee *c.* 43; cotton *c.* 16; tobacco *c.* 4; sisal *c.* 25; beef and veal *c.* 117; fish catch (1978) 55. Livestock (in 000; Dec. 1978): cattle *c.* 8,744; sheep *c.* 607; pigs *c.* 580; goats (1977) *c.* 1,500; chickens (1977) *c.* 13,900.

terprises in January. During the next month he announced that a plot to assassinate him named "D6 × 80" (which, according to him, signified the last six months of 1980) had been exposed. In December there were disturbances in Antananarivo, and some 40 persons, mainly unemployed youths, were reportedly arrested for looting. (PHILIPPE DECRAENE)

Malawi

A republic and member of the Commonwealth of Nations in east central Africa, Malawi is bounded by Tanzania, Mozambique, and Zambia. Area: 118,484 sq km (45,747 sq mi). Pop. (1979 est.): 5,817,000. Cap.: Lilongwe (pop., 1977 prelim. census, 102,900). Largest city: Blantyre (pop., 1977 prelim. census, 222,200). Language: English (official) and Chichewa (national). Religion: Christian 33%; remainder, predominantly traditional beliefs. President in 1980, Hastings Kamuzu Banda.

On Jan. 1, 1980, Pres. Hastings Kamuzu Banda announced changes in his Cabinet, including the transfer of Lewis Chimango from the Ministry of Health to the Ministry of Finance. The former finance minister, Edward Bwinali, became minister for the southern region and chairman of the southern region Malawi Congress Party. At the same time John Twaibu Sangala, who had been appointed minister of local government in November 1979, was given the additional portfolio of community development. In February 1980 President Banda flew to South Africa, where he underwent an operation and spent a period of convalescence.

The steady growth in recent years in the production of the country's main export crops continued into 1980, though the benefits were to some extent offset by weakening world prices for some items. Further restraints upon economic growth resulted from the imposition of controls on the supply of credit and also on imports, particularly of capital goods, which had risen sharply in 1979. These measures were particularly necessary because of the continuing increase in the price of oil; thus the foreign exchange stemming from the employment of more than 20,000 Malawian workers in South Africa was a welcome contribution to the campaign against inflation. (KENNETH INGHAM)

MALAWI

Education. (1977–78) Primary, pupils 675,740, teachers 11,115; secondary, pupils 15,079, teachers 707; vocational (1975–76), pupils 1,208, teachers 89; teacher training, students 1,433, teachers 90; higher (1976–77), students 1,179, teaching staff 128.

Finance. Monetary unit: kwacha, with (Sept. 22, 1980) a free rate of 0.79 kwacha to U.S. $1 (1.91 kwacha = £1 sterling). Gold, SDR's, and foreign exchange (June 1980) U.S. $90.3 million. Budget (1979 actual): revenue 156 million kwacha; expenditure 246 million kwacha.

Foreign Trade. (1979) Imports 326 million kwacha; exports 189.8 million kwacha. Import sources (1978): South Africa 38%; U.K. 20%; Japan 10%; U.S. 5%. Export destinations (1978): U.K. 46%; The Netherlands 9%; West Germany 7%; U.S. 6%; South Africa 5%. Main exports: tobacco 55%; tea 16%; sugar 12%; peanuts 5%.

Transport and Communications. Roads (main; 1979) 10,557 km. Motor vehicles in use (1979): passenger 12,800; commercial 11,903. Railways (1979): 679 km; traffic (1979) 84 million passenger-km, freight 244 million net ton-km. Air traffic (1978): 138.5 million passenger-km; freight 7.2 million net ton-km. Telephones (Jan. 1978) 22,600. Radio receivers (Dec. 1976) 130,000.

Agriculture. Production (in 000; metric tons; 1979): corn *c.* 1,200; cassava (1978) *c.* 90; sorghum *c.* 110; sugar, raw value (1978) *c.* 136; peanuts *c.* 170; tea 29; tobacco 64; cotton, lint (1978) *c.* 8. Livestock (in 000; 1978): cattle 760; sheep *c.* 88; goats *c.* 818; pigs *c.* 274; poultry *c.* 8,242.

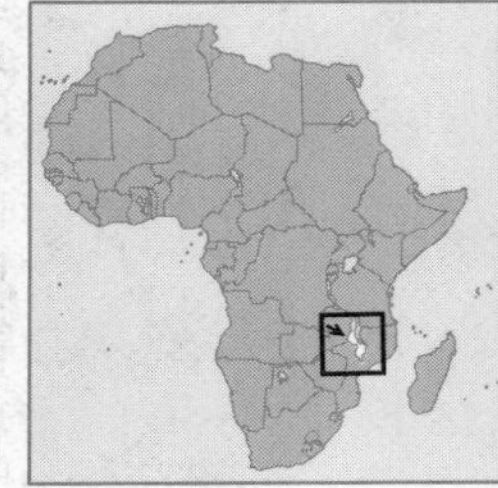
Malawi

PRANAY B. GUPTE—THE NEW YORK TIMES

In an open market in Malawi home-grown produce is sold or traded. Malawi is remarkable among the nations of black Africa as its crops feed the country with surplus to export.

Magazines:
see Publishing

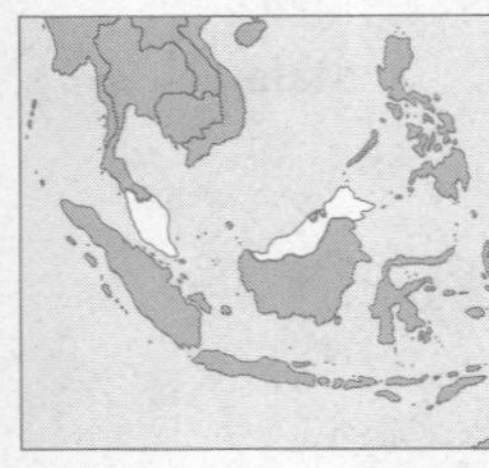
Malaysia

Malaysia

A federation within the Commonwealth of Nations comprising the 11 states of the former Federation of Malaya, Sabah, Sarawak, and the federal territory of Kuala Lumpur, Malaysia is a federal constitutional monarchy situated in Southeast Asia at the southern end of the Malay Peninsula (excluding Singapore) and on the northern part of the island of Borneo. Area: 329,747 sq km (127,316 sq mi). Pop. (1980 est.): 13,923,215, including (1980 est.) Malays 47.1%, Chinese 32.7%, Indians 9.6%, and Dayaks 3.7%. Cap. and largest city: Kuala Lumpur (metro pop., 1980 UN est., 1,081,000). Language: Malay (official). Religion: Malays are Muslim; Indians mainly Hindu; Chinese mainly Buddhist, Confucian, and Taoist; indigenous population of Sabah and Sarawak (est.), 47% animist, 38% Muslim, and 15% Christian. Supreme head of state in 1980, with the title of *yang dipertuan agong,* Tuanku Sultan Haji Ahmad Shah al-Musta'in Billah ibni al-Marhum Sultan Abu Bakar Ri'ayatuddin al-Mu'adzam Shah; prime minister, Datuk Hussein bin Onn.

Police using tear gas dispersed a massive demonstration in January 1980 by more than 10,000 rice farmers who had assembled in Alor Setar, capital of the state of Kedah. At issue was strong resentment of the government's policy of giving the farmers nonnegotiable subsidy coupons in place of supplementary cash payments for the purchase of rice. Ninety-two arrests were made, and a 24-hour curfew was imposed on the town. Despite this violent expression of opposition to government policy, Safirol Hashim from the United Malays National Organization (UMNO)—senior party in the ruling National Front coalition—narrowly won a by-election in April in Bukit Raya, Kedah, against a Party Islam candidate.

Internal opposition within UMNO was indicated in July when Datuk Harun Idris, former chief minister of the state of Selangor and serving a prison sentence for corruption and criminal breach of trust, challenged his nephew, Hadji Suhaimi Kamaruddin, for the leadership of the youth wing of the organization. Although he failed to win the election, he secured 42% of the votes cast.

Prime Minister Datuk Hussein bin Onn assumed the defense portfolio after a Cabinet reshuffle in September. At the meeting of regional Commonwealth heads of government held earlier in the month in India, he had linked Soviet and Vietnamese occupations of Afghanistan and Cambodia, respectively, as a common threat in Asia. Malaysia's growing concern with external defense was reflected by the allocation of more than 20% of its budget expenditure for 1981 to its armed forces.

In March Lim Choon Wong, who had been convicted of murdering the chief of police of the state of Perak in 1975, was executed. This was followed by several other executions of men convicted under the Internal Security Act of illegal possession of firearms, despite appeals from the International Commission of Jurists and the Malaysian Bar Council. In April a controversial Trade Union Ordinance (Amendment) Bill was passed by Parliament after the sweeping powers allocated to the minister of labour and manpower, including subordination of the role of the courts, had been withdrawn.

One of the world's largest natural-gas fields was discovered off the coast of the state of Trengganu in the South China Sea in March. The economic life of the field was estimated at 70 years. In September Malaysian business interests were revealed to be engaged in buying shares in the U.K. firm Dunlop Holdings Ltd.

Tengku Ahmad Rithauddeen traveled to Hanoi in January, the first visit to that city by a foreign minister of a member of the Association of Southeast Asian Nations (ASEAN) since the Vietnamese invasion of Cambodia. He arrived with a mandate for dialogue but failed to induce any measure of compromise on the part of his hosts over their occupation of Cambodia. A return visit to Kuala Lumpur in May by Rithauddeen's Vietnamese counterpart, Nguyen Co Thach, gave some indication of greater flexibility. But a Vietnamese armed incursion into Thailand in June put an end to the prospect of a continuing dialogue. Datuk Hussein bin Onn described the intrusion as a dangerous

MALAYSIA

Education. *Peninsular Malaysia.* (1978) Primary, pupils 1,637,143, teachers 52,492; secondary, pupils 877,815, teachers 32,149; vocational, pupils 15,547, teachers (1977) 1,043; higher (1977), students 46,527, teaching staff 4,506. *Sabah.* (1977) Primary, pupils 127,555, teachers 5,032; secondary, pupils 57,029, teachers 2,104; vocational (1976), pupils 300, teachers 35. *Sarawak.* (1977) Primary, pupils 193,024, teachers 5,704; secondary, pupils 77,438, teachers 2,810; vocational (1974), pupils 306, teachers 28; higher, students (1976) 1,097, teaching staff (1974) 62.

Finance. Monetary unit: ringgit, with (Sept. 22, 1980) a free rate of 2.12 ringgits to U.S. $1 (5.09 ringgits = £1 sterling). Gold, SDR's, and foreign exchange (June 1980) U.S. $4,337,000,000. Budget (1979 est.): revenue 9,049,000,000 ringgits; expenditure 8,709,000,000 ringgits. Gross national product (1979) 42,420,000,000 ringgits. Money supply (June 1980) 9,119,000,000 ringgits. Cost of living (Peninsular Malaysia; 1975 = 100; March 1980) 122.2.

Foreign Trade. (1979) Imports 17,161,000,000 ringgits; exports 24,219,000,000 ringgits. Import sources: Japan 22%; U.S. 15%; Singapore 9%; U.K. 6%; Australia 6%; West Germany 6%. Export destinations: Japan 23%; Singapore 17%; U.S. 17%; The Netherlands 6%. Main exports: rubber 19%; crude oil 17%; timber 17%; palm oil 10%; tin 10%; thermionic valves and tubes 8%.

Transport and Communications. Roads (1979) *c.* 29,800 km. Motor vehicles in use (1977): passenger 572,100; commercial (including buses) 196,200. Railways: (1977) 2,375 km; traffic (including Singapore; 1978) 1,270,000,000 passenger-km, freight 1,294,000,000 net ton-km. Air traffic (1979): 2,638,000,000 passenger-km; freight 73.2 million net ton-km. Shipping (1979): merchant vessels 100 gross tons and over 196; gross tonnage 620,894. Telephones (Jan. 1978) 374,700. Radio receivers (Dec. 1977) 1.5 million. Television receivers (Dec. 1977) 665,000.

Agriculture. Production (in 000; metric tons; 1979): rice *c.* 2,161; rubber 1,617; copra *c.* 210; palm oil 2,184; tea 3; bananas *c.* 450; pineapples 206; pepper (Sarawak only; 1978) 31; tobacco *c.* 8; meat (1978) *c.* 148; fish catch (1978) 685; timber (cu m; 1978) 38,449. Livestock (in 000; Dec. 1977): cattle 428; buffalo 211; pigs 1,186; goats 332; sheep 52; chickens *c.* 47,500.

Industry. Production (in 000; metric tons; 1979): tin concentrates (metal content) 63; bauxite 386; cement (1978) 2,196; iron ore (56% metal content) 350; crude oil (1978) 10,320; petroleum products (Sarawak only) 705; electricity (kw-hr; 1978) 8,202,000.

and irresponsible act when he addressed the opening session of the 13th ASEAN ministerial meeting held that month in Kuala Lumpur.

A significant improvement was indicated in relations between Malaysia and Brunei when Sultan Muda Hassanal Bolkiah Mu'izzaddin Waddaulah and his father, Sir Omar Ali Saifuddin, attended the installation in July of Tuanku Ahmad Shah as the seventh king of the federation. It was the first visit to Malaysia by members of Brunei's ruling family in nearly two decades. (MICHAEL LEIFER)

Maldives

Maldives, a republic in the Indian Ocean consisting of about two thousand small islands, lies southwest of the southern tip of India. Area: 298 sq km (115 sq mi). Pop. (1980): 145,000. Cap.: Male (pop., 1978, 29,600). Language: Divehi. Religion: Muslim. President in 1980, Maumoon Abdul Gayoom.

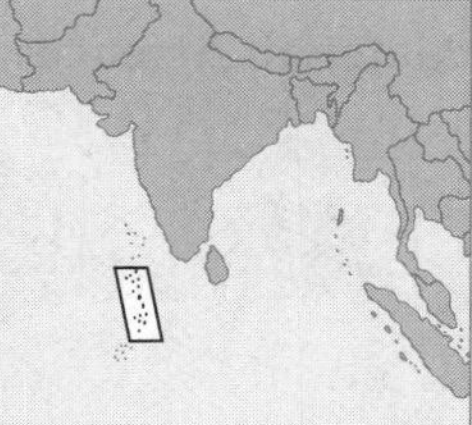
Maldives

Since Pres. Maumoon Abdul Gayoom took over the Maldives in 1978, the pace of change had accelerated. In 1980 Gayoom was establishing a national monetary authority and a statistics bureau. Direct taxes on tourist operations were introduced. In 1979, 33,000 tourists visited the islands, and 40,000 were forecast for 1980. A second tourist centre was projected for Gan Island, and the airport at Hulule was being expanded so that it could take 747s from Europe and the Middle East; currently it was being used only by 737s from India and Sri Lanka.

The fishing fleet, fishing mainly for skipjack tuna, was being mechanized, and cold storage facilities were being introduced. Fish accounted for a third of the gross national product and employed between 40 and 50% of the working population. It was planned to expand Male's harbour and to enable Radio Maldives to reach all the islands.

Gayoom insisted he would not lease Gan to a superpower. Rapprochement with Britain in 1979 and better relations with Sri Lanka were a boost to development since the islands were dependent upon aid. Britain resumed its aid program.

The Maldives were admitted to the International Fund for Agricultural Development in January 1980. A World Bank report on the economic prospects of the Maldives was published in April. In the same month, Gayoom reported an attempted coup by supporters of former president Ibrahim Nasir. Public demonstrations in favour of Gayoom were held. (GUY ARNOLD)

MALDIVES

Education. (1978) Primary, pupils 8,749, teachers 179; secondary, pupils 3,652, teachers 105; vocational, students 32, teachers 8.

Finance and Trade. Monetary unit: Maldivian rupee, with (June 30, 1980) a free rate of MRs 7.55 to U.S. $1 (MRs 17.80 = £1 sterling). Budget (1979): revenue MRs 15.2 million; expenditure MRs 39 million. Foreign trade (1978): imports MRs 51.4 million; exports MRs 16.8 million. Main import sources: Japan, U.K., Thailand, India, Sri Lanka. Main export destinations: Japan, Thailand, Sri Lanka. Main exports: fresh fish 65%; dried fish 29%.

Mali

A republic of West Africa, Mali is bordered by Algeria, Niger, Upper Volta, Ivory Coast, Guinea, Senegal, and Mauritania. Area: 1,240,142 sq km (478,832 sq mi). Pop. (1980 est.): 6,646,000. Cap. and largest city: Bamako (pop., 1980 est., 440,000). Language: French (official); Hamito-Semitic and various tribal dialects. Religion: Muslim 65%; Christian 5%; animist 30%. President in 1980, Gen. Moussa Traoré.

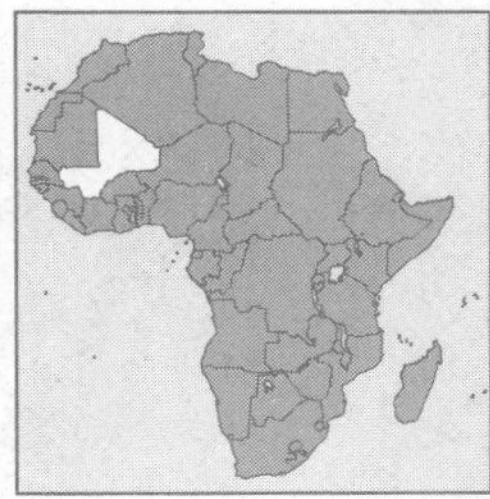
Mali

Mali was beset in 1980 by mounting violence among students and an economy heading for disaster. In March an official of a student union was tortured to death by police, and the students and pupils, in their five-month-old struggle against the authorities, won open public support. Several hundred militants were interrogated and imprisoned under brutal conditions or drafted into the Army. Amnesty International and other organizations denounced the developments in Bamako. At the end of March the government announced the release of the detainees, but repression continued to be the norm.

In a speech on September 22, the 20th anniversary of independence, Pres. Moussa Traoré said the goals of the five-year plan (1974–79) had not been met, except for cotton production. In April and November he visited Paris to seek more aid to combat drought in the Sahel region. Bad management of public enterprises crippled Mali's budget, and only direct aid from France enabled civil servants' salaries to be paid. (PHILIPPE DECRAENE)

MALI

Education. (1976–77) Primary, pupils 291,966, teachers 8,280; secondary, pupils 8,915; vocational, pupils 2,609; secondary and vocational, teachers 540; teacher training, students (1975–76) 1,969, teachers (1974–75) 126; higher (1977–78), students 4,216, teaching staff 450.

Finance. Monetary unit: Mali franc, with (Sept. 22, 1980) a par value of MFr 100 to the French franc and a free rate of MFr 419 to U.S. $1 (MFr 1,008 = £1 sterling). Budget (1980 est.) balanced at MFr 78 billion.

Foreign Trade. (1978) Imports MFr 91.3 billion; exports MFr 42.5 billion. Import sources (1976): France 40%; Ivory Coast 14%; Senegal 10%; China 7%; West Germany 6%. Export destinations (1976): France 31%; Ivory Coast 13%; West Germany 11%; China 10%; U.K. 9%; Senegal 6%. Main exports (1976): cotton 50%; livestock 13%; peanuts 12%; cereals 6%.

Agriculture. Production (in 000; metric tons; 1979): millet and sorghum *c.* 744; rice 177; corn *c.* 60; peanuts 179; sweet potatoes (1978) *c.* 37; cassava (1978) *c.* 40; cottonseed *c.* 80; cotton, lint *c.* 48; beef and veal (1978) *c.* 45; mutton and goat meat (1978) *c.* 34; fish catch *c.* 100. Livestock (in 000; 1978): cattle *c.* 4,263; sheep *c.* 5,849; goats *c.* 5,629; camels *c.* 198; horses *c.* 170; asses *c.* 459.

Malta

The Republic of Malta, a member of the Commonwealth of Nations, comprises the islands of Malta, Gozo, and Comino in the Mediterranean Sea between Sicily and Tunisia. Area: 320 sq km (124 sq mi), including Malta, Gozo, and Comino. Pop. (1980 est.): 343,700. Cap.: Valletta (pop., 1979 est., 14,000). Largest city: Sliema (pop., 1979 est., 20,-

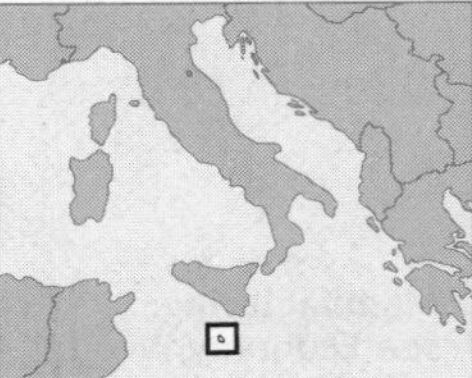
Malta

MALTA

Education. (1977–78) Primary, pupils 31,363, teachers 1,503; secondary, pupils 24,524, teachers 1,777; vocational, pupils 4,398, teachers 459; higher, students 1,099, teaching staff 198.

Finance. Monetary unit: Maltese pound, with (Sept. 22, 1980) a free rate of M£0.34 = U.S. $1 (M£0.81 = £1 sterling). Gold, SDR's, and foreign exchange (June 1980) U.S. $1,022,000,000. Budget (1980 est.): revenue M£142 million; expenditure M£164 million.

Foreign Trade. (1979) Imports M£271,960,000; exports M£152,170,000. Import sources: Italy 22%; U.K. 21%; West Germany 14%; U.S. 6%; France 5%. Export destinations: West Germany 34%; U.K. 20%; Libya 8%; The Netherlands 6%; Belgium-Luxembourg 5%; ship and aircraft stores 5%. Main exports: clothing 42%; machinery 6%. Tourism: visitors (1978) 478,000; gross receipts (1977) U.S. $81 million.

Transport and Communications. Roads (1978) 1,266 km. Motor vehicles in use (1978): passenger 64,200; commercial 13,300. There are no railways. Air traffic (1979): 589 million passenger-km; freight 5.4 million net ton-km. Shipping (1979): merchant vessels 100 gross tons and over 47; gross tonnage 116,299. Shipping traffic (1978): goods loaded 162,000 metric tons, unloaded 1,060,000 metric tons. Telephones (Dec. 1978) 71,030. Radio receivers (Dec. 1977) 85,000. Television licenses (Dec. 1978) 67,400.

100). Language: Maltese and English. Religion: mainly Roman Catholic. President in 1980, Anton Buttigieg; prime minister, Dom Mintoff.

In 1980 the close friendship that Malta had developed with Libya after Dom Mintoff became prime minister in 1971 suffered a severe setback. The Libyan government had signed an agreement in May 1976 accepting referral of the question of delimitation of the continental shelf to the International Court of Justice. However, it had failed to ratify the agreement in spite of repeated requests to do so by Malta.

Consequently, at Malta's behest, in mid-1980 Texaco Inc. started drilling operations on the shelf 109 km (68 mi) southeast of Malta. In August operations were suspended when Libyan warships threatened to use force against the Italian drilling rig being used by Texaco. The Malta government immediately expelled from the island all Libyan military personnel and appealed to the UN Security Council. A month later Italy and Malta signed an agreement guaranteeing the neutrality of Malta and laying the basis for financial, economic, and technical assistance from Italy.

In November UN Secretary-General Kurt Waldheim stated that, as a result of a mission by a special UN representative, Libya was taking steps to ratify the 1976 agreement and that the continental shelf dispute would then be brought before the International Court of Justice.

An estimated revenue of M£194 million in the budget for 1981 was expected to exceed expenditure by M£5 million. Former prime minister G. Borg Olivier died in October 1980 (*see* OBITUARIES).

(ALBERT GANADO)

Manufacturing:
see Economy, World; Industrial Review

Marine Biology:
see Life Sciences

Materials Sciences

Ceramics. The year 1980 was notable primarily for advances in ceramics to meet continuing environmental protection and energy conservation goals. The search continued for an acceptable ceramic substitute for asbestos, a recognized health hazard for asbestos workers and their families. Medical research in the 1970s had showed so conclusively the ties between asbestos and various diseases that its future use was certain to decrease. In fact, standards set by the Occupational Safety and Health Administration in the U.S. for allowable asbestos fibre levels in the atmosphere were so restrictive that many manufacturers began discontinuing asbestos products.

Unfortunately, asbestos was proving difficult to replace. It provides excellent thermal insulation in continuous use to 540° C (1,000° F) and in intermittent use to 980° C (1,800° F). It is also inexpensive, extremely tough and wear-resistant, and relatively inert to the attack of most chemicals. Glass and ceramic fibres or mineral wool fibres, often interwoven with aramid fibre, were being used to form fabrics for personnel protection that offered good insulation and wear properties. Nevertheless, it had been difficult to replace asbestos-cement building boards for use in fire walls and heat shields where a rigid structural material is needed. Recently, however, machinable calcium silicate boards were shown to be an excellent substitute for asbestos-cement boards in many of these applications. Asbestos millboard and rollboard had been even more difficult than asbestos-cement boards to replace, but silicate fibre boards, which are somewhat flexible and compressible, were recently introduced to replace asbestos in even these applications.

Because heating ceramics to develop their desirable service properties is especially energy intensive, techniques that allow preparation of ceramics at lower temperatures are of economic importance. In the sol-gel process, solutions of organometallics or organometallics and metal salts are first treated to form a gel and then dehydrated to form very reactive noncrystalline powders or monolithic porous objects. The energy required for their densification is generally much less than that for coarser ceramic powders, and there have been indications of improved properties as well. Investigators at the U.S. Naval Research Laboratory studied this process as a means of forming high-strength single-phase and composite ceramics with exceptionally uniform, fine microstructures.

The sol-gel process was also receiving special attention for glass production. Researchers at the Westinghouse Research and Development Center, Pittsburgh, Pa., used organometallics, particularly alkoxides, to form gels that could be dried and then heat-treated at 300° to 500° C (570° to 930° F) to produce glasses that would require much higher temperatures for conventional melt processing. They designed their gels specifically to contain polymer groups that react to form the bridging oxygen bonds present in oxide glasses. These gels, therefore, do not break down to powders when heated but instead form transparent glasses. Battelle-Columbus (Ohio) Laboratories and the National Aeronautics and Space Administration were also studying sol-gel formation of glasses, particularly as a containerless process for manufacturing very high-purity optical fibres in future space experiments. Initially attractive for their energy efficiency, these sol-gel processes might also lead to

UNITED TECHNOLOGIES RESEARCH CENTER AND NASA, LANGLEY

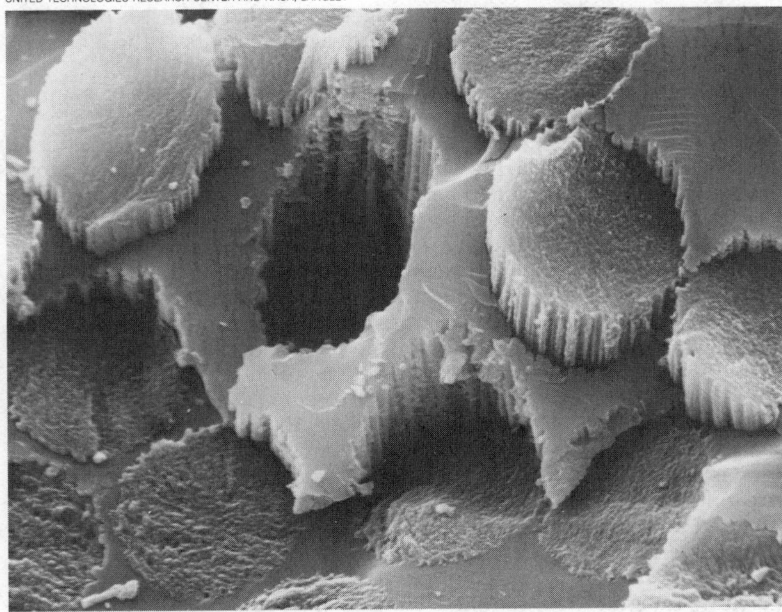

Structure of a glass-fibre composite material is shown magnified 3,000 times in a scanning electron microscope. Rough, column-shaped graphite fibres can be seen embedded in a smooth glass matrix. Stability, low density, and good mechanical properties at high temperature made such composites attractive for aerospace applications.

radically new materials that, because of instability, could not be processed at all at higher temperatures.

The use of silicon nitride and silicon carbide in diesel and turbine engines to permit more efficient operation at increasingly high temperatures has been a goal of much recent research. The ASEA High Pressure Laboratory in Sweden announced recently that it had succeeded in using hot isostatic pressing to fabricate from silicon nitride a complete turbine wheel with a solid hub and thin blades with trailing edges only 0.3 mm (0.01 in) thick. This ability to economically produce high-density complex silicon nitride shapes with close tolerances and good surface finishes was a major step forward in ASEA's program with United Turbine of Sweden. In the U.S. the Carborundum Co. worked closely with U.S., European, and Japanese automakers in developing sintered silicon carbide parts for diesel engines. They also recently announced considerable progress on lightweight silicon carbide turbocharger rotors that minimize the inertial lag in turbocharger response. One of their rotors under joint development with Volkswagen passed its first design milestone: operation at 120,000 rpm. (NORMAN M. TALLAN)

[721.B.2.d.iii; 724.C.5]

Metallurgy. The major concerns in metallurgy in 1980 were essentially the same as those of the previous few years: energy savings, scarce and unduly expensive metals, pollution control, and high production costs. Efforts to use energy more efficiently could be divided into two quite different categories—those directed toward reducing the energy represented in the finished metal and those involved with supplying metals and processes to meet such energy-related needs as reduced weight in transportation and improved erosion and corrosion resistance of material for synthetic fuel plants.

Because many metallurgical operations require high temperature, energy savings as high as 50% are possible by using waste heat and the energy in such by-products as blast furnace exhaust gas. For example, one large Japanese steel mill was operating a 20-Mw (million-watt) electric generator on waste heat and using the lower temperature exhaust from it and other sources for heating.

Changes in sources of energy were also being made. In one instance a Japanese steel mill stopped injecting 30 kg (66 lb) of oil per ton of pig iron into a blast furnace, replacing it with 70 kg (154 lb) of coke per ton; they also used the increased waste heat. Use of direct reduction of iron ore without melting, although energy efficient, was being hindered in the U.S. because of uncertainty of the natural gas supply. By contrast, many new metallurgical plants that used the direct reduction process were under construction in the less developed countries because of more reliable energy supplies. Brazil's rapidly growing steel industry was based to a large extent on direct reduction with natural gas.

Other attempts to reduce the energy consumed in product manufacture included a new hot-rolling mill in the U.S. that used 35% less energy than a conventional mill to produce aluminum sheet for rolling into foil. In a process called roll casting liquid metal is fed to the rolls and freezes to form a plate one centimetre (0.4 in) thick before emerging. Then, without further surface treatment or reheating, the plate is rolled to a thickness of 0.114 cm (0.045 in) and coiled. In another example, changing the composition of an electroplating bath at a U.S. plant to allow a reduction in operating temperature of 11° C (20° F) with little loss of efficiency appreciably reduced the 40% of plant energy use that went into bath heating. Because the cooler bath produced less evaporation, air pollution was reduced and composition control was made easier.

Recycling is a great energy saver. Steel from scrap requires only about a third of the energy needed to produce it from ore, and secondary aluminum requires about 1/22 of the energy needed for virgin metal production. Recycling also was proving an important method of reducing dependence on imported metal and holding down metal prices that were high for political reasons. In the late 1970s the U.S. was dependent on imports for more than half its consumption of 18 metals and for more than 90% of three—cobalt, chromium, and manganese—supplies of which were seriously threatened by political unrest.

In addition to recycling, other steps were available to help avoid possibly serious supply problems, such as that experienced with cobalt. One possibility, direct substitution, often involves a tedious search for a new alloy or a satisfactory nonmetal. Another, the use of presently uneconomic domestic sources, would require new extraction methods. A third approach works at reducing required quantities of expensive metals by employing surface coatings. Ion implantation is one of the more recently developed surface treatments. Ions of the scarce coat metal are accelerated to high velocity in an electric field. Aimed as a beam at a base metal target, the ions penetrate a short distance into the base metal to form a thin, integral alloy layer. (DONALD F. CLIFTON)
[725.B]

See also Industrial Review: *Glass; Iron and Steel; Machinery and Machine Tools;* Mining and Quarrying.

Mathematics

The major achievement of mathematics research in 1980 was the complete classification of the finite simple groups, the basic building blocks of a major part of modern algebra. Close cooperation among several mathematicians in different institutions finally completed a project begun in the early 1900s. This classification, comprising more than 5,000 journal pages of detailed proofs, is one of the great mathematical achievements of the 20th century.

Eleven-year-old Sheng Ke Gon of China astonished mathematicians by beating electronic calculators in solving complicated mathematical problems.

UPI

Groups are abstract representations of symmetry. They were introduced into mathematics in the 19th century in the study of solutions of equations. During the 20th century the notion of a group came to permeate virtually all of mathematics as a primitive yet powerful expression of symmetry. In addition, it became one of the major tools of the natural sciences. In physics group theory underlies the classification of elementary particles. In chemistry it provides a system for defining the structure of crystals. In the life sciences group theory contributed key elements to the search for the structure of the DNA molecule.

Simple groups are the primitive elements of group theory. As all matter above the atomic level can be constituted from the basic elements, so all finite groups can be formed as combinations of simple groups. And as chemists of the last century sought to order the elements in a periodic table, so mathematicians of this century have searched for a complete classification of simple groups. About 1900 all finite simple groups less than size (or order) 2,000 were known. By 1963 the classification had been completed as high as order 20,000, and by 1975 it had been completed through order 1,000,000. But it took five more years for mathematicians to prove that the classification pattern revealed by these earlier studies really was true for all finite simple groups.

Most simple groups belong to one of three major families: cyclic groups, alternating groups, and groups of "Lie type." Cyclic groups consist of cyclic permutations of a prime number of objects; for example, the rotations in 72° increments of a regular pentagon. Alternating groups consist of even permutations—those permutations that are formed by interchanging the positions of two objects an even number of times. For example, the 60 total rotational symmetries of a regular icosahedron, a 20-sided solid figure, form an alternating group. The groups of Lie type include 16 subfamilies, each associated with a particular family of continuous groups introduced at the end of the 19th century by the Norwegian mathematician Sophus Lie in his study of the solutions to differential equations.

Unfortunately some simple groups do not belong to these families nor, apparently, to any family. These simple groups are called sporadic. Although five sporadic groups were discovered at the end of the 19th century by French mathematician Émile Mathieu, from then until 1966 every other simple group that was discovered belonged to one of the three major families—cyclic, alternating, or Lie type.

Things changed in 1964 when Walter Feit of Yale University and John Thompson of the University of Cambridge verified a conjecture, first made more than 50 years earlier by British mathematician William Burnside, that apart from the cyclic groups all finite simple groups have an even number of elements. Their proof of this fundamental property required an unprecedented 250 journal pages and was full of new methods and insights into the classification problem. Their work launched an intensive effort to complete the classification program, an effort that was just concluded during the past year.

The Feit-Thompson methods enabled mathematicians to examine very large groups. As a consequence several group theorists discovered new sporadic groups. Ultimately 26 sporadic groups were proved to exist. The last to be confirmed is one called the Monster since it has about 8×10^{53} elements. Although it had been known for some time that the existence of the Monster was consistent with all known theory, it was not until early in 1980 that the Monster was actually constructed. Robert L. Griess, Jr., of the University of Michigan found it by showing that it is a group of rotations in a high-dimensional Euclidean space.

This discovery spurred others to complete the general classification work. The final results were obtained in the summer by Michael Aschbacher of the California Institute of Technology, Pasadena, and Daniel Gorenstein of Rutgers University, New Brunswick, N.J. Using Griess's discovery and other methods, Aschbacher and Gorenstein quickly tied up the loose ends in this century-long effort to provide a complete classification of the fundamental building blocks of group theory.

(LYNN ARTHUR STEEN)

Mauritania

The Islamic Republic of Mauritania is on the Atlantic coast of West Africa, adjoining Western Sahara, Algeria, Mali, and Senegal. Area: 1,030,700 sq km (398,000 sq mi). Pop. (1980 est.): 1,634,000. Cap.: Nouakchott (pop., 1977, 135,000). (Data above refer to Mauritania as constituted prior to the purported division of Spanish Sahara between Mauritania and Morocco.) Language: Arabic, French. Religion: Muslim. Chiefs of state in 1980, Lieut. Col. Mohamed Mahmoud Ould Louly and, from January 4, Lieut. Col. Mohamed Khouna Ould Haidalla; premier, Lieutenant Colonel Haidalla.

On Jan. 4, 1980, Mauritania underwent another palace revolution when Lieut. Col. Mohamed Khouna Ould Haidalla (*see* BIOGRAPHIES) removed Lieut. Col. Mohamed Mahmoud Ould Louly as chief of state and took over his functions, including the presidency of the Military Committee for National Salvation. In April several members of the black community seeking complete equality with the Islamic population were arrested. On July 5 the government officially abolished slavery. As in Iran, Islam in Mauritania was uncompromising, and in February Islamic jurisprudence was adopted. On September 18 a public execution and mutilations were held for the first time. On December 12 Haidalla announced the creation of a new

MAURITANIA

Education. (1978–79) Primary, pupils 82,408, teachers (1977–78) 1,765; secondary, pupils 11,957, teachers (1977–78) 389; vocational and higher, pupils 1,500, teachers (1973–74) 117.

Finance. Monetary unit: ouguiya, with (Sept. 22, 1980) a free rate of 41.29 ouguiya = U.S. $1 (99.25 ouguiya = £1 sterling). Gold, SDR's, and foreign exchange (May 1980) U.S. $124.7 million. Budget (1979 est.) balanced at 10,726,000,000 ouguiya.

Foreign Trade. (1979) Imports 11,870,000,000 ouguiya; exports 6,733,000,000 ouguiya. Import sources: France *c.* 30%; Senegal *c.* 16%; Spain *c.* 9%; Belgium-Luxembourg *c.* 7%; The Netherlands *c.* 6%; West Germany *c.* 5%. Export destinations: France *c.* 27%; Italy *c.* 18%; West Germany *c.* 13%; Japan *c.* 12%; Belgium-Luxembourg *c.* 11%; U.K. *c.* 7%; Spain *c.* 7%. Main exports: iron ore 90%; fish 9%.

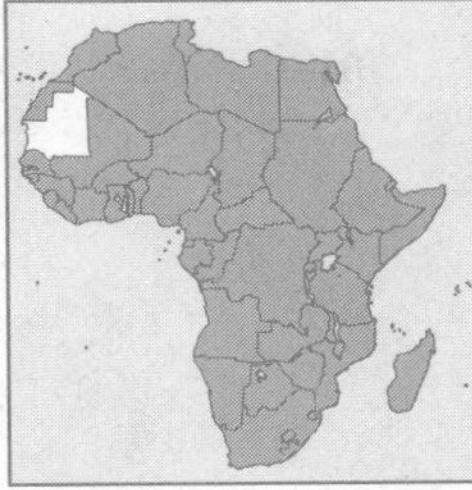

Mauritania

UPI

Sidi Ould Matalla, who was accused of murder, faced a firing squad on September 18 after the restoration of Islamic law on Mauritania.

civilian government, which would function under the guidance of the military, and a new constitution, to be submitted to public debate and referendum, was announced December 15.

Mauritania was said to have agreed to relinquish the southern part of the Western Sahara to the Saharan Arab Democratic Republic (SADR). The repatriation of French troops from Mauritania was completed in May. In June Mauritania supported recognition of the SADR by the Organization of African Unity. Relations with Morocco deteriorated, and Moroccan aircraft attacked military positions in Mauritania. (PHILIPPE DECRAENE)

Mauritius

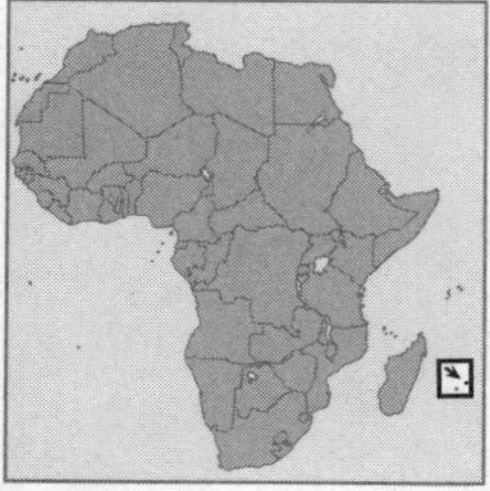

Mauritius

The parliamentary state of Mauritius, a member of the Commonwealth of Nations, lies about 800 km E of Madagascar in the Indian Ocean; it includes the island dependencies of Rodrigues, Agalega, and Cargados Carajos. Area: 2,040 sq km (787.5 sq mi). Pop. (1980 est.): 995,000, including (1977) Indian 69.3%; Creole (mixed French and African) 28%; others 2.7%. Cap. and largest city: Port Louis (pop., 1980 est., 155,000). Language: English (official); French has official standing for certain legislative and judicial purposes, and Creole is the lingua franca. Religion (1974 est.): Hindu 51%; Christian 30%; Muslim 16%; Buddhist 3%. Queen, Elizabeth II; governor-general in 1980, Sir Dayendranath Burrenchobay; prime minister, Sir Seewoosagur Ramgoolam.

Mauritius in 1980 faced an uneasy future. The economy was weakening after the boom years for sugar in the early 1970s; imports were rising faster than exports; and the government, with only a slender majority, could not take strong measures. The leading sugar estates were joining together to produce beef and milk. Cyclone Claudette, which struck on Dec. 23, 1979, left 6 dead and 4,000 homeless and damaged 30% of the 1980 sugar crop.

The government faced a crisis of expectations, the result in part of making free education available up to university level. The target of 76,000 new jobs per year, set in the second five-year plan (ended 1980), was not met.

The Organization of African Unity summit meeting in Freetown, Sierra Leone, in July supported the Mauritian claims to Diego Garcia Island. Prime Minister Sir Seewoosagur Ramgoolam, visiting Delhi, India, on October 27, reiterated his demands that Britain and the U.S. return Diego Garcia to Mauritius. In June Mauritius had also officially claimed sovereignty over Tromelin Island in the Indian Ocean, a claim disputed by France since 1976 and by Madagascar. (GUY ARNOLD)

MAURITIUS

Education. (1978) Primary, pupils 133,432, teachers 6,352; secondary, pupils 80,479, teachers 2,769; vocational, pupils 1,051, teachers 91; teacher training, students 341, teachers 24; higher, students 311, teaching staff 83.

Finance and Trade. Monetary unit: Mauritian rupee, with (Sept. 22, 1980) a free rate of MauRs 7.53 to U.S. $1 (MauRs 18.10 = £1 sterling). Gold, SDR's, and foreign exchange (June 1980) U.S. $38.2 million. Budget (1979–80 est.): revenue MauRs 1,638,000,000; expenditure MauRs 1,809,000,000. Foreign trade (1979): imports MauRs 3,575,300,000; exports MauRs 2,378,300,000. Import sources (1978): U.K. 15%; South Africa 12%; France 11%; Japan 6%; Australia 6%; China 5%; Bahrain 5%. Export destinations (1978): U.K. 65%; U.S. 8%; France 7%; Belgium-Luxembourg 5%. Main exports (1978): sugar 67%; clothing 16%. Tourism (1978): visitors 108,000; gross receipts U.S. $38 million.

Agriculture. Production (in 000; metric tons; 1979): sugar, raw value *c.* 700; bananas (1978) *c.* 8; tea *c.* 5; tobacco *c.* 1; milk (1978) *c.* 23. Livestock (in 000; 1978): cattle *c.* 58; pigs *c.* 6; sheep *c.* 4; goats *c.* 69; chickens *c.* 1,300.

Medicine:
see Health and Disease

Mental Health:
see Health and Disease

Merchant Marine:
see Transportation

Metallurgy:
see Materials Sciences

Metals:
see Industrial Review; Materials Sciences; Mining and Quarrying

Meteorology:
see Earth Sciences

Methodist Churches:
see Religion

Microbiology:
see Life Sciences

Microelectronics:
see Computers; Industrial Review

Mexico

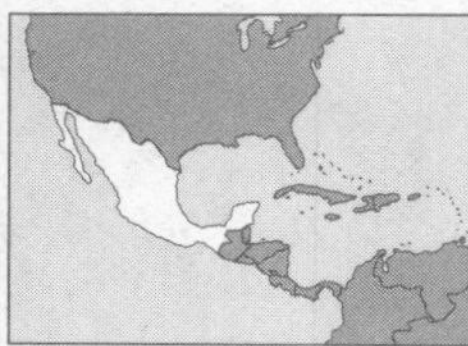

Mexico

A federal republic of Middle America, Mexico is bounded by the Pacific Ocean, the Gulf of Mexico, the U.S., Belize, and Guatemala. Area: 1,972,546 sq km (761,604 sq mi). Pop. (1980 prelim.): 67,405,700, including about 55% mestizo and 29% Indian. Cap. and largest city: Mexico City (pop., federal district, 1979 est., 9,191,300; metro. area, 1979 est., 14.7 million). Language: Spanish. Religion: predominantly Roman Catholic. President in 1980, José López Portillo.

In 1980 much of Mexico's domestic and foreign activity was tied to oil development. An oil-for-bauxite contract signed with Jamaica in February exchanged 10,000 bbl a day of Mexican petroleum for 420,000 metric tons of alumina a year and 10% of the shares in Jamaica's South Manchester alumina plant. In April nearly U.S. $1 billion was obtained in loans from Canada, West Germany, and France. Pres. José López Portillo visited those countries and Sweden in May. An oil supply contract for 50,000 bbl a day was signed with Canada, to be increased to a maximum of 100,000 bbl a day, and industrial, agricultural, and mining assistance was agreed upon. Canadian Prime Minister Pierre Trudeau supported the Mexican opposition to a North American Common Market, which was based on Mexico's wish to remain in control of its energy resources. A 100,000-bbl-a-day contract was signed with France, which also agreed to foster cooperation in the prospecting and development of uranium. Sweden in November signed a contract for 170,000 bbl of oil a day from 1981, at which time India also was expected to receive 100,000 bbl a day.

In July and August President López Portillo visited Cuba, Brazil, Nicaragua, Panama, Venezuela, and Costa Rica. In Cuba a communiqué was issued deploring the U.S. blockade of Cuba and the occupation by the U.S. Navy of the base at Guantánamo in Cuba. Mexico and Cuba signed a tourism agreement and a nonintervention treaty. An agreement was signed on August 3 with Venezuela to fulfill oil-import requirements for Central America and the Caribbean on favourable terms.

The Ixtoc well, which had blown out in June 1979, was sealed in March, having discharged about 3 million bbl of oil into the Gulf of Mexico. A gas explosion at the Giraldas oil well in August set off a fire, with a loss of 54,000 bbl a day of crude. In August Mexico and the U.S. signed a cooperation agreement to provide joint action in the future on oil slicks that affected both nations.

UPI

Pres. Rodrigo Carazo Odio (right) of Costa Rica greeted Pres. José López Portillo of Mexico on his visit to Costa Rica in August.

In his annual address to the nation on September 1, President López Portillo stated that Mexico's proven petroleum reserves totaled 60,100,000,000 bbl (oil equivalent), probable reserves 38,000,000,000 bbl, and potential reserves 250,000,000,000 bbl. Current output was about 2,300,000,000 bbl a day, making Mexico the fifth largest oil producer in the world.

Relations with the U.S. were strained in 1980. Mexico linked the exceptionally severe droughts that caused electricity shortages in July and heavy crop losses with U.S. weather experiments to divert hurricanes and stated that in the future permission would be required before such experiments could be carried out over its territory. The cost of nine million metric tons of food imports to make up for the losses was put at 50 billion pesos for 1980. Food supply treaties were signed with the U.S. in January and September for a total of 7,220,000 metric tons, and an additional 1,780,000 metric tons were obtained from Argentina to replenish the reserve stocks.

A further source of dispute with the U.S. was the "tuna war." Mexico announced on July 7 that boats fishing within 200 mi of the coast without permission would be detained. Three U.S. tuna-boat crews were arrested and fined, which led to the U.S. banning all imports of tuna from Mexico and also to some fishing concessions being canceled. On December 28 Mexico announced that it was terminating all fishing agreements with the U.S.

Relations with Argentina were also strained because the Argentine government refused to grant safe-conducts to three Peronists; in March the Mexican ambassador was recalled. At home, fighting broke out in May between 60 families of land-settlers and 600 Indians near Yajalon, Chiapas state, and 46 people were killed. There were other land occupations, and the 50,000-strong Confederación Nacional de Campesinos took over 150,000 ha (370,000 ac) of land.

Toward the end of October a severe earthquake registering 6.7 on the Richter scale with its epicentre at Huajuapan de León struck across the state of Oaxaca in the southeast up to Mexico City. The quake destroyed or damaged 300 villages, knocked down three buildings in Mexico City, killed at least 65 people, and left 6,000 homeless.

(BARBARA WIJNGAARD)

Middle Eastern Affairs

The onset of all-out war between Iraq and Iran on Sept. 22, 1980, thrust Persian Gulf security into the centre of Middle Eastern affairs. At the Arab League summit in Amman, Jordan, on November 25–27 Arab disunity crystallized, with Syria, Libya, Algeria, Yemen (Aden), Lebanon, and the Palestine Liberation Organization (PLO) boycotting the meeting. This left the Arab world divided into the Steadfastness Front led by Syria and the more moderate states led by Iraq and Saudi Arabia.

The Gulf Crisis. In December 1980 the best that could be predicted was a de facto cease-fire in the Iran-Iraq war, which had begun with the crossing of the disputed Shatt al-Arab waterway by Iraqi forces. Iraqi Pres. Saddam Hussein at-Takriti, who gambled on toppling Iran "in days," was by December resigned to a long campaign. (*See* DEFENSE: *Special Report*.) Diplomats in neighbouring

MEXICO

Education. (1977–78) Primary, pupils 13,307,333, teachers 306,173; secondary, pupils 3,024,000, teachers 174,338; vocational, pupils 321,818, teachers 23,081; teacher training, students 157,012, teachers 10,486; higher, students 610,840, teaching staff 52,294.

Finance. Monetary unit: peso, with (Sept. 22, 1980) a free rate of 22.90 pesos to U.S. $1 (55.05 pesos = £1 sterling). Gold, SDR's, and foreign exchange (April 1980) U.S. $2,389,000,000. Budget (1979 actual): revenue 342 billion pesos; expenditure 435 billion pesos. Gross domestic product (1979) 2,733,800,000,000 pesos. Money supply (Sept. 1979) 276,120,000,000 pesos. Cost of living (1975 = 100; June 1980) 256.6.

Foreign Trade. (1979) Imports 275,650,000,000 pesos; exports 204,860,000,000 pesos. Import sources: U.S. 63%; Japan 7%; West Germany 6%. Export destinations: U.S. 69%; Spain 5%. Main exports (1978): crude oil 31%; machinery and transport equipment 10%; coffee 7%; chemicals 5%; cotton 5%. Tourism (1978): visitors 3,637,000; gross receipts U.S. $537 million.

Transport and Communications. Roads (1979) 212,409 km (including 1,062 km expressways). Motor vehicles in use (1979): passenger 3,695,970; commercial 1,406,260. Railways (1978): 20,288 km; traffic 4,800,000,000 passenger-km, freight 36,410,000,000 net ton-km. Air traffic (1978): 10,027,000,000 passenger-km; freight *c.* 110 million net ton-km. Shipping (1979): merchant vessels 100 gross tons and over 349; gross tonnage 914,898. Telephones (Jan. 1978) 3,712,400. Radio receivers (Dec. 1978) 17,514,000. Television receivers (Dec. 1977) 5,480,000.

Agriculture. Production (in 000; metric tons; 1979): corn 9,255; wheat 2,272; barley 505; sorghum 3,902; rice 489; potatoes 727; sugar, raw value *c.* 3,060; dry beans 1,056; soybeans 701; tomatoes 1,082; bananas 1,929; oranges 3,240; lemons 465; cottonseed *c.* 540; coffee 228; tobacco *c.* 76; cotton, lint 336; beef and veal *c.* 585; pork *c.* 430; fish catch (1978) 725. Livestock (in 000; Dec. 1978): cattle 29,920; sheep 7,850; pigs 12,578; goats 8,103; horses 6,479; mules 3,239; asses 3,245; chickens *c.* 150,000.

Industry. Production (in 000; metric tons; 1979): crude oil 74,110; coal (1977) 6,610; natural gas (cu m) *c.* 21,300,000; electricity (kw-hr) 59,410,000; cement 15,150; iron ore (metal content) 3,991; pig iron 4,933; crude steel 6,949; sulfur (1978) 1,818; petroleum products *c.* 43,400; sulfuric acid 2,064; fertilizers (nutrient content; 1978–79) nitrogenous 593, phosphate 227; aluminum 43; copper 83; lead 158; zinc 156; manganese ore (metal content; 1978) 188; gold (troy oz) 202; silver (troy oz) 50,770; woven cotton fabrics 68; man-made fibres (1977) 192; radio receivers (units; 1977) 976; television receivers (units; 1977) 699; passenger cars (units) 297; commercial vehicles (units) 122.

Gulf countries were predicting ten years of instability in the region as a result of the conflict. Small nations such as Bahrain, whose Shiʿah populations were numerous, could also expect continuing domestic tension because of the pro-Iranian sympathies of these populations. (The Shiʿah branch of Islam is dominant in Iran, in contrast to the Sunni majority in most neighbouring countries.)

On a visit to India in December, Soviet Pres. Leonid Brezhnev, who was eager to stem the growth of U.S. power in the Gulf, proposed a plan for an international effort to ensure peace in the area. He called on the U.S., China, Japan, and Western European countries to accept "mutual obligations" to promote peace in the region. The obligations would prevent deployment of nuclear weapons and the establishment of bases in the Gulf and "adjacent islands." Outside countries would pledge not to use their military forces or to block trade and would respect Gulf countries' control over their own natural resources.

The Brezhnev proposal was rebuffed by most Gulf states, although they agreed with the Soviet "guarantee" of their right to control their hydrocarbon resources. The plan was immediately seen as a statement directed against U.S. moves to negotiate "access rights" that would allow it to use bases in three countries around the Gulf. Of these, Oman at the gateway to the strategic Strait of Hormuz was the most important. At Masirah Island in southern Oman the U.S. was embarking in late 1980 on a major refurbishment of an old Royal Air Force staging airstrip and was locating a regional command centre there. The incoming Republican administration of U.S. president-elect Ronald Reagan was thought likely to continue Pres. Jimmy Carter's policy of stationing a rapid deployment force capability near the Gulf.

The Soviet intervention in Afghanistan in December 1979 produced a climate of acceptance of a U.S. presence near the Gulf. Saudi Arabia and the Gulf states of Bahrain, Qatar, and the United Arab Emirates (UAE), all of which had semimonarchical systems of government, showed themselves willing to enter into closer relations with Washington. There were moves in 1980 toward an integrated missile defense system for the Gulf nations based on the Hawk missile, which was made in the U.S. The U.S. was clearly motivated in its friendship for the conservative Gulf states by the need to preserve the oil supply from the area. That this was reciprocated, despite Saudi differences with the U.S. over the wider Middle East peace question, was shown in September when the Saudis requested—and immediately received—four Boeing airborne warning and control systems (AWACS) aircraft.

Instability in the Gulf was a deep concern of the West, aware that 60% of its oil flowed through the Strait of Hormuz. Even Iran was prepared to allay Western fears in the early days of its war with Iraq by denying that any plan existed to cut off oil supplies through the strait. The loss of Iraqi crude oil, while not an immediate blow to the world oil market, was sure to be felt by early 1981. Limited exports of Iraqi crude were possible through the Banias terminal in Syria, although Iraq's political relationship with Syria remained frigid after the collapse of abortive unity proposals of 1979.

Egypt, Israel, and Palestine. With Egypt contemplating a second year of isolation from the Arab camp, there were fears in Cairo in late 1980 that the Reagan administration would feel none of the personal commitment exhibited by President Carter in regard to the peace question. Vice-Pres. Hosni Mubarak of Egypt, who visited the U.S. in early December, specifically warned that for Reagan to give up the framework for peace established during the Carter administration by the Camp David accords would be a serious blow to Egyptian Pres. Anwar as-Sadat. But in mid-December Reagan assured Egypt that his administration would uphold the agreements.

During his campaign for the presidency, Reagan had hinted that he saw hope in "the Jordanian option." This would mean involving Jordan's King

Delegates to the Islamic Conference, meeting in Islamabad, Pakistan, in January, condemned the Soviet invasion of Afghanistan and called for the Soviets' "immediate and unconditional withdrawal" from that country.

DEJEAN—SYGMA

KEYSTONE

Refugees from Afghanistan poured into the border town of Peshawar, Pakistan, in February after the Soviet invasion of their country.

Hussein in talks about the future of the Israeli-occupied West Bank (of the Jordan River) and the Gaza Strip and, to some extent, having Hussein negotiate on behalf of the absent Palestinians. It was apparently a cornerstone of Reagan's policy that the Palestinians were to be excluded from talks about their future. There were signs of increasing dissension within Israeli Prime Minister Menachem Begin's government, raising the possibility of the return to power of the Labour Party, generally perceived as being more flexible in its approach to the Palestinian question. The Egyptians were scheduled to receive $1.6 billion in economic aid from the U.S. in fiscal 1981, a heavy proportion of which would be in the form of strategic grants, and it had seemed that Reagan might have chosen to bargain with Egypt over it. That the Republicans were not altogether united on the Middle East was suggested when the incoming chairman of the Senate Foreign Relations Committee, Sen. Charles Percy of Illinois, was quoted as having told Brezhnev that he favoured a Palestinian state, even one led by the PLO chairman, Yasir Arafat. Later, however, Percy was at pains to explain that he favoured a "Palestinian entity" in federation with Jordan and that he opposed direct negotiations with the PLO until it renounced terrorism and publicly recognized Israel's right to exist in peace as a sovereign nation.

The question of PLO participation in the peace process became a part of European Economic Community (EEC) policy. On June 13 the EEC, in what was being called the Venice declaration, called for the PLO to be associated with the negotiations. In July 1981 the EEC and the PLO were expected to have a full ministerial conference. The announcement of this was made on November 13 and the possible site for the meeting was London. The diplomatic preliminaries to this decision included a meeting between the chairman of the EEC Council of Ministers, Gaston Thorn (*see* BIOGRAPHIES), and Arafat in Beirut, Lebanon, on August 4.

The need for a fresh initiative became apparent to EEC heads of government after the failure of Palestinian autonomy negotiations between Egypt and Israel in July. Israeli Interior Minister Josel Burg, who headed the Israeli team during talks in the U.S., said that Israel would not yield over the status of Jerusalem. On July 30 the Israeli Knesset (parliament) approved a bill that declared all Jerusalem, including East Jerusalem, to be the united capital of Israel. Egypt reacted quickly with a declaration saying that this move violated the Camp David agreements. A UN resolution of June 30, sponsored by 39 members of the Islamic Conference and by Egypt, said all measures that altered the geographic, demographic, and historic character and status of Jerusalem were null and void and must be rescinded. The Israeli declaration about Jerusalem angered a number of Arab nations, and Saudi Arabia's strong man, Crown Prince Fahd, called for a jihad (holy war) against Israel. Although the call was supported by many Arab countries, the possibility of united Arab action on Palestine looked remote.

Moves were started in the Knesset in October to introduce a bill annexing the Golan Heights, captured from Syria in the June 1967 war. Members of the Knesset said that they believed Syria's treaty with the Soviet Union and Jordan's support for Iraq in the war strengthened the case for annexation. Geula Cohen, who was leading the lobby for annexation, had also sponsored the bill about Jerusalem. Meanwhile, the situation on the West Bank showed every sign of worsening, with violent student demonstrations continuing.

Arab Disunity. The Arab League, which moved its headquarters from Cairo to Tunis in mid-1979 after Egypt's suspension, suffered acutely from Arab disunity. Its secretary-general, Chedli Klibis of Tunisia, whose nomination had been opposed by a number of states including Iraq, saw months of preparation for a coherent policy of Arab national development swept away in a few minutes at the Arab summit in November. The Iraqi team suggested that its own proposals for a "decade of Arab joint development" be translated immediately into action with the backing of a new $5 billion fund. According to the Iraqi plan, per capita income in Arab countries was to be raised by 13.5% a year, and a fund of between $1 billion and $1.5 billion a year was proposed to meet this goal. Simple arithmetic showed that much more would be needed, but such was the calibre of the Iraqi plan that was suddenly added to the summit's agenda on the opening day. A scaled-down version of it emerged two days later as the summit's most important economic conclusion.

Iraq's war with Iran angered Syria, Algeria, Libya, Lebanon, Yemen (Aden), and the PLO, all of which boycotted the summit. Lebanon allied itself somewhat uneasily with this group because of its dependence on Syrian military aid.

Syria's quarrel with Jordan, which escalated sharply after the Amman summit, cooled after Saudi Arabia offered mediation. Syrian Pres. Hafez al-Assad accused Jordan of backing the Muslim Brotherhood, an extremist Islamic organization responsible for assassinations in Syria. On December 11 Jordan's information minister, Adnan Abu Odeh, said that Syria had begun withdrawing troops from the border with Jordan. Observers suggested that the main result of the crisis was to intensify Israel's fears for its security. By the year's end the Arab cause and, in particular, the ideal of joint Arab action concerning Jerusalem appeared as remote as ever.

Arab International Finance. Increased joint Arab action in international forums such as the International Monetary Fund (IMF) and the World Bank seemed certain in 1981. As the region neared 1981, its major characteristic was oil wealth. Arab banks and Arab money could be expected to play a vital role in the world economy. On Jan. 27, 1981, the Arab Banking Corporation (ABC), with an authorized capital of $1 billion, was scheduled to hold a formal opening in Bahrain and announce plans to make itself one of the world's top 20 wholesale banks, only five years after the Bahraini authorities had embarked on a plan to make their nation a significant world financial centre midway between Japan and Europe. The arrival of 15 Japanese financial institutions in 1980 in Bahrain made it the Middle East's leading financial centre.

At the World Bank-IMF annual meeting in October the Arab oil producers used their financial muscle for political ends. Kuwait and Saudi Arabia withheld participation from loans to the World Bank because of a disagreement over observer status for the PLO at the meeting. At the time this made little difference to the World Bank's ability to extend credits, but Kuwait and Saudi Arabia were signaling their ability to make such exercises difficult. (JOHN WHELAN)

See also Feature Article: *Danger Signals from the Arc of Crisis;* Energy; articles on the various political units.
[978.B]

Migration, International

The U.S. continued to be the single most important destination for migrants from around the globe. The privations endured by some would-be immigrants ended in tragedy. In July 1980 as many as 13 illegal Salvadoran immigrants died of heat exhaustion in the Sonora Desert of Arizona, and 106 Haitians, shipwrecked on a tiny Caribbean islet en route to Florida in the fall, spent weeks with almost no food and water before being forcibly returned to Haiti.

Legitimate arrivals under the immigration laws numbered 400,000, in addition to 230,000 refugees, during the year ended in September. The average yearly number of immigrants to the U.S. had risen spectacularly after 1950, from 63,938 in the 1930s and 85,661 in the 1940s, to 249,927 in the '50s, 321,375 in the '60s, and 430,628 in the '70s. The ethnic composition and source areas of this flow had also changed markedly. Asia and Latin America now provided 82% of immigrants and Europe 12%; in 1965 the respective figures were 47 and 39%.

Canada's economic slowdown made the admission of immigrants in the "independent" category of the Immigration Act more difficult. Of some 100,000 immigrants in 1979, 42% joined immediate family members and 25% were admitted under the act's refugee or humanitarian sections. Provisional estimates for the first quarter of 1980 showed a total of 32,526 immigrants. The U.K. and Ireland

U.S. border patrol on horseback and helicopter continue to round up illegal Mexican aliens. As many as 1,000 Mexicans attempt to cross the border each day.

WIDE WORLD

WIDE WORLD

Two of 31 illegal immigrants from El Salvador are supported by their U.S. rescuers after they were found near death in the Arizona desert. At least 13 of the group died of thirst.

together were still the largest single source of permanent-residence immigrants, followed by the U.S. (1,757). Immigrants from all countries in Europe were provisionally estimated at 8,497; by comparison, 1,271 people emigrated from the West Indies.

M. J. R. MacKellar, Australia's minister for immigration and ethnic affairs, pointed out on Nov. 12, 1979, that the wartime Australian Cabinet's goal of a population of 25 million by the end of the century would not be reached by any means "short of mass net immigration of at least a quarter of a million people a year." Current demographic trends suggested the figure would be no more than 18 million to 19 million. Accordingly, the Australian government announced in August 1980 that spending on assisted-passenger schemes would be more than doubled (to just over £2,439 million).

On July 15 Hong Kong's commissioner to Britain, Dennis Bray, estimated that legal and illegal immigration to the colony from China in 1979 amounted to 200,000, representing an annual population growth rate of 6%. China's foreign minister, Huang Hua, visiting London on October 1–2, agreed to restrict illegal emigration. Besides intensified patrols by the Hong Kong military and police, new stringent measures included spot checks to control population movements. From October 30 everyone aged 15 and over had to carry an identity card or face a fine of HK$1,000, and from November employers hiring workers without identity cards were liable to fines of HK$50,000 and a year's imprisonment.

White emigration from Zimbabwe continued in 1980. The figure for August was nearly 2,000, the highest monthly total since November 1978, when 2,057 left. Totals for June and July were 1,238 and 1,644, respectively, and even these were undercounted by about 25%, since many did not complete emigration formalities for financial reasons. Immigration to Zimbabwe fluctuated around 500 per month.

West Germany's federal statistics office estimated on June 3 that the country's population had risen in 1979 for the first time in six years. The increase of 118,000 was attributable to foreign immigrants, who now accounted for 7% of the population. Migrant workers in the European Economic Community as a whole appeared to have remained stable at some six million.

On Oct. 15, 1980, a British Home Office attempt to prevent the Commission for Racial Equality (CRE) from making an investigation into the immigration service under provisions of the Race Relations Act 1976 was rejected by the High Court. David Lane, CRE chairman, reportedly said the investigation would not challenge overall immigration policy but merely "arrangements made for its application, particularly from the point of view of nondiscrimination." Changes in British immi-

Immigration and Naturalization in the United States

Year ended Sept. 30, 1978

Country or region	Total immigrants admitted	Quota immigrants	Nonquota immigrants: Total	Nonquota immigrants: Family—U.S. citizens	Aliens naturalized
Africa	11,524	7,749	3,775	3,499	3,194
Asia[1]	249,776	106,579	143,197	45,064	65,401
China[2]	21,315	15,875	5,440	4,942	11,303
Hong Kong	5,158	3,992	1,166	1,038	...
India	20,753	18,880	1,873	1,605	6,477
Iran	5,861	3,484	2,377	2,316	1,132
Iraq	2,188	1,876	312	307	672
Israel	3,276	2,079	1,197	1,099	1,419
Japan	4,010	1,973	2,037	1,730	1,533
Jordan	3,483	2,756	727	696	1,566
Korea, South	29,288	18,823	10,465	9,148	12,575
Lebanon	4,556	3,755	801	759	1,212
Philippines	37,216	19,141	18,075	16,921	20,218
Thailand	3,574	1,971	1,603	1,304	1,303
Vietnam	88,543	2,265	86,278	470	1,594
Europe[3]	73,198	48,429	24,769	22,213	47,633
Germany, West	6,739	1,736	5,003	4,511	4,278
Greece	7,035	4,780	2,255	2,123	5,758
Italy	7,415	5,089	2,326	2,130	8,180
Poland	5,050	3,646	1,404	1,322	2,962
Portugal	10,445	9,232	1,213	1,105	3,599
Spain	2,297	1,092	1,205	887	991
U.S.S.R.	5,161	4,874	287	246	613
United Kingdom	14,245	8,750	5,495	4,909	9,118
Yugoslavia	2,621	1,943	678	640	2,881
North America	220,778	144,514	76,264	43,636	45,389
Canada	16,863	10,825	6,038	5,258	3,594
Cuba	29,754	1,564	28,190	442	16,053
Dominican Republic	19,458	16,422	3,036	2,754	2,504
El Salvador	5,826	4,571	1,255	1,211	695
Haiti	6,470	5,348	1,122	1,081	2,273
Jamaica	19,265	16,471	2,794	2,649	6,459
Mexico	92,367	66,962	25,405	22,260	8,662
Trinidad & Tobago	5,973	4,973	1,000	937	1,258
Oceania	4,402	2,686	1,716	1,525	692
South America	41,764	31,147	10,617	9,882	10,777
Argentina	3,732	2,829	903	811	1,730
Colombia	11,032	7,768	3,264	3,094	2,663
Ecuador	5,732	4,380	1,352	1,263	1,257
Guyana	7,614	6,821	793	755	1,415
Peru	5,243	3,628	1,615	1,523	1,261
Total, including others	601,442	341,104	260,338	125,819	173,535

Note: Immigrants listed by country of birth; aliens naturalized by country of former allegiance.
[1]Includes Turkey. [2]Taiwan and People's Republic. [3]Includes U.S.S.R.
Source: U.S. Department of Justice, Immigration and Naturalization Service, 1978 Annual Report.

gration rules, as of March 1, affected all categories of immigrants but particularly husbands and fiancés seeking admission. The targets for further restriction were people from the Indian subcontinent, among whom marriages were customarily arranged. Fictional arranged marriages continued to be used to secure entry to the U.K., despite the Immigration Act 1971. Immigrants to the U.K. accepted for settlement, both Commonwealth citizens and foreign nationals, numbered 69,671 in 1979 (72,331 in 1978). (STUART BENTLEY)

See also Refugees.
[525.A.1.c]

Mining and Quarrying

Mining and quarrying in the United States in 1980 were adversely affected by depressed business conditions, which in the case of the steel industry caused extensive shutdowns and curtailment of iron mining in the Great Lakes and other areas. A long copper strike was experienced from midyear into the fourth quarter. Although exploration for uranium continued, plans for building new mines and concentrators were deferred.

On June 30 U.S. Pres. Jimmy Carter signed the synthetic fuels bill, which allotted $25 billion to accelerate development of the synthetic fuels industry. About $20 billion was to go to the new Synthetic Fuels Corporation, which was to provide loans, loan guarantees, and other financial incentives to encourage production of synthetic fuels from unconventional sources.

The ninth session of the UN Conference on the Law of the Sea at Geneva made progress on substantive issues so that a treaty seemed possible in 1981. In the U.S. President Carter signed the Deep Seabed Hard Mineral Resources Act, providing an interim regulatory procedure for ocean mining activities conducted by U.S. nationals.

There were many reasons for increased U.S. coal production, including conservation of petroleum and problems with nuclear energy, but as of 1980 the potential for growth was not being fulfilled. Eastern and Middle Western coals were burdened with regulations and high sulfur, and expansion in the West was hampered by insufficient transportation facilities. The difficulties were expected to be overcome, but no great leap forward was seen in the immediate future. The U.S. Department of Energy released 1985–95 coal production goals as follows: 1985, 873.3 million tons per year; 1990, 1,247,000,000 tons per year; and 1995, 1,558,000,000 tons per year.

As of July 31 copper workers in most U.S. firms were on strike following the expiration of wage contracts. At issue were wages and cost-of-living adjustments, the latter appearing to be more of a problem. After nearly 3½ months, five companies had returned to work and six were still negotiating on either wages or noneconomic issues.

A U.S. congressional subcommittee, after a three-week tour of Zaire, Zimbabwe, and South Africa, came to the conclusion that the U.S. should pay more attention to those countries because of U.S. dependence on them for strategic and critical materials. For example, together they possess 86% of the world's platinum group metals reserves, 53% of the manganese, 64% of the vanadium, 95% of the chromium, and 52% of the cobalt. The U.S. imports heavily from the three countries for its supplies of those metals.

Industry Developments. Atlantic Richfield Co. announced at the end of September that its Montana copper unit would close down the copper smelter at Anaconda and the refinery at Great Falls because it would be too expensive to make modifications to meet environmental regulations. The Anaconda smelter produced about 14% of U.S. primary production. In July the Montana Board of Health had adopted air quality standards that were as strict as—or in some instances stricter than—those set by the federal government.

Placer Services Corp., a subsidiary of St. Joe Minerals Corp., planned to begin gold dredging in 1981 near Marysville, Calif. This would be a renewal of activity in a long-dormant placer mining area. Placer expected to extract 622 kg (1,368 lb) of gold per year for seven years by deeper dredging than had been practiced previously and was rehabilitating two dredges at a cost of $10.4 million.

A significant gold discovery was made in Napa County, Calif., by Homestake Mining Co. The deposit, which could be worked by surface methods, was expected to yield 100,000 oz of gold per year for ten years. The mine and concentrator were scheduled to be operating by 1984.

A new gold mine, to be in operation in 1982, was planned near Whitehall, Mont., by Placer Amex Corp. Freeport Minerals Co. and FMC Corp. held groundbreaking ceremonies at the Jerrett Canyon mine near Elko, Nev., in June. Production there was to begin in 1981 with a capacity of 180,000–200,000 oz per year.

Standard Oil Co. (Indiana) planned to spend more than $300 million in the next three years to develop the Cyprus Thompson Creek molybdenum mine in Custer County, Idaho. The operation was to consist of an open-pit mine and concentrator, anticipated to be operational in 1983. The deposit contained reserves of 181 million tons of ore averaging 0.18% molybdenum disulfide.

The New Jersey Zinc Co. ceased production of zinc metal at Palmerton, Pa., at the end of 1980 but planned to continue to produce zinc oxide. The old pyrometallurgical plant had environmental and energy problems that were aggravated by competition from imported metal. It had accounted for 22% of U.S. primary zinc smelting capacity.

St. Joe Lead Co. was building a new lead mine near Viburnum, Mo., that would increase the company's production capacity by 20%, to a total of 5.4 million tons per year. The Viburnum mill was to be modernized and expanded 50% to treat the ore. The project, to be operational in 1983, was expected to cost $25 million. It reflected St. Joe's belief that lead-acid storage batteries would find widespread use in electric vehicles and in utility load leveling.

Considerable activity in tungsten was taking place in Nevada. General Electric Co., through its wholly owned mining subsidiary, Utah Interna-

BRISBANE COURIER MAIL

Staged protests against plans to expand mining and oil drilling and a dispute with miners over tax-subsidized housing vexed Australian leaders during the year.

tional Inc., was sinking a new shaft in an old mining area near Imlay and building a conversion plant to make tungsten trioxide at a cost of $50 million. The project, to be in operation in 1982, was designed to have a capacity of 91,000 tons per year of the trioxide. Near Fallon, NRD Mining Ltd. rehabilitated an old mine and mill at a cost of $1.5 million and produced its first concentrate early in 1980. Phillips Petroleum Co. was also exploring tungsten deposits in Nevada.

The scene of greatest mine development during the year was Chile, where nominal production of one million tons per year of copper was to be increased 50% by 1990. The Chilean Copper Corporation accounted for about 850,000 tons annually, nearly all from four big mines: Chuquicamata, El Teniente, Salvador, and Rio Blanco. These mines were being expanded by the government company in order to maintain capacity as the copper content of the ore diminished in the years ahead. The big new mines were to be in the private sector, however, and would require a combined investment of several billion dollars. Chile possesses about 20% of the world's known copper reserves and supplies 13% of the world market.

Zambia, another of the world's great copper-producing countries, had problems with productivity during the year. The result was a 2% decline in production to an annual rate of 360,000 tons per year of copper. The nation's main problem was a shortage of skilled workers.

Technological Developments. A new rock-drilling technique was successfully field tested by Sandia Laboratories of Albuquerque, N.M. In normal drilling, when the drill bit becomes dull it is necessary to pull the string of drill rods out of the hole to change the bit. The deeper the hole, the longer this bit changing operation takes. With the new technique drillers can cycle new cutting surfaces into place without pulling the drill string from the hole. The bit consists of diamond-studded cutting links mounted on a chain carried on the leading drill rod.

The U.S. Bureau of Mines appropriated money to test a new mining technique in St. Johns County, Fla., that has environmental advantages. Instead of the strip-mining technique usual for extracting phosphate, boreholes are drilled into the phosphate beds. A high-pressure water-jet device placed at the bottom of the borehole is used to slurry the mineral-bearing sediments, which are then pumped to the surface. The mineral is recovered and the water recycled to the mining process. The tests were being run by Flow Industries Inc. on the property of Agrico Chemical Co.

In the U.K. the Safety in Mines Research Establishment developed a safety helmet that provides protection for the head, eyes, and lungs in a single comfortable unit that can be worn by the miner under normal working conditions. A small axial fan, powered by the cap lamp battery, is mounted on the rear of the helmet. It draws air through coarse and fine air filters fitted to the top of the helmet, leading clean air inside the full face visor. This type of helmet is a big step forward in protecting miners from inhaling harmful dust.

A novel alluvial mining machine was jointly developed by Alluvial Dredges, Ltd., in Paisley, Scotland, and Ellicott Machine Corp., Baltimore, Md. Known as the Dragon Wheel Miner, this mineral dredging and treatment system uses a bucket wheel to excavate material and discharge it through a submerged pump into a customized treatment plant. The machine was designed to have lower first cost, greater flexibility, and greater depth range for onshore and marine-type deposits than other dredging machines. Hydraulic drive and underwater operation of the bucket wheel plus a submerged pump module permit lighter weight construction of the support structure, as compared with a bucketline dredge; the module itself was designed to minimize moving parts, thus increasing reliability and reducing downtime and maintenance costs. (JOHN V. BEALL)

Production. The overall mining production index, as calculated by the United Nations (*see* Table), showed growth of only about 2.6% during 1979 but rose nearly 2.1% in the first quarter of

1980 alone. This spurt in 1980 was, rather surprisingly, led by the developed market economies, which for several years had seen their industries overshadowed by the growing importance of the less developed and Communist (centrally planned) countries. Though metals still ran far behind energy-related mineral extraction during the late 1970s and early 1980s, the expansion of production in nonmetals was increasingly a factor in the continued health of the industry.

Public policy on matters such as energy, investment, taxation, and environmental control was a particularly evident constraint on mining development during 1979 and 1980. Inflexible tax laws limited mining production in Bolivia and artificially raised market prices in Jamaica. Public controls were imposed on energy supplies, especially on electrical power for the U.S. aluminum industry in the Pacific Northwest and, elsewhere in the world, on diesel oil and coal. Environmental controls were instituted to improve working conditions in mines and to lessen environmental pollution near smelters; for example, sulfur dioxide emission controls were imposed by the Ontario provincial government.

Despite these problems, many production records were set during 1979 and 1980: for individual mines (Palabora's world record in South Africa for rock mined in a single day [521,433 tons], U.S. Steel's Minntac mine's U.S. record for annual ore production [56,088,067 tons]); for nations (Australian bauxite, annual; U.S. refined lead, annual); and for total world industry for a given commodity (refined copper, annual; refined lead, annual).

In the U.S. the value of mining output in 1979 rose 15% over 1978, totaling about $23.5 billion (valued at some $225 billion after processing of these same materials). Of a group of 34 metal commodities for which the U.S. Bureau of Mines maintained statistics, 23 showed an increase in production levels; the greatest growth was achieved by secondary (recovered) mercury (up 73%), platinum-group metals (up 25%), and zinc slab (refined; up 25%). The greatest declines were noted in uranium for nonenergy purposes (off 30%) and secondary tin (down 18%). Of a group of 30 nonmetallic mineral commodities, 19 showed growth during 1979, although neither growth nor decline was characterized by large swings in production levels, the largest changes from the preceding year being bromine (up 12%) and diatomite (up 10%).

Indexes of Production, Mining, and Mineral Commodities

(1975=100)

	1975	1976	1977	1978	1979	1980 I	1980 II
Mining (total)							
World[1]	100.0	107.9	113.2	112.1	115.0	117.4	...
Centrally planned economies[2]	100.0	104.4	108.4	111.9	114.0	117.7	116.8
Developed market economies[3]	100.0	103.0	108.7	112.7	119.8	127.1	124.8
Less developed market economies[4]	100.0	111.9	117.3	111.9	112.6	111.9	...
Coal							
World[1]	100.0	101.5	102.6	101.8	106.5	109.4	...
Centrally planned economies[2]	100.0	102.1	104.2	105.8	107.5	106.9	108.2
Developed market economies[3]	100.0	100.9	101.2	98.6	105.7	110.7	112.1
Less developed market economies[4]	100.0	104.1	106.2	107.6	107.9	118.2	...
Petroleum							
World[1]	100.0	109.9	116.1	115.3	117.4	119.7	...
Centrally planned economies[2]	100.0	106.9	112.2	118.2	121.6	127.7	126.2
Developed market economies[3]	100.0	104.2	115.4	126.1	134.4	148.4	139.4
Less developed market economies[4]	100.0	111.9	117.0	112.1	112.3	110.9	...
Metals							
World[1]	100.0	102.4	103.7	101.5	104.4	108.1	...
Centrally planned economies[2]	100.0	101.7	102.9	103.6	102.5	105.2	104.2
Developed market economies[3]	100.0	101.8	101.7	98.0	101.7	103.5	105.5
Less developed market economies[4]	100.0	103.9	107.6	105.9	110.2	118.2	...
Manufacturing (total)	100.0	108.2	113.3	118.9	124.8	126.9	...

[1] Excluding Albania, China, North Korea, Vietnam.
[2] Bulgaria, Czechoslovakia, East Germany, Hungary, Poland, Romania, U.S.S.R.
[3] North America, Europe (except centrally planned), Australia, Israel, Japan, New Zealand, South Africa.
[4] Caribbean, Central and South America, Africa (except South Africa), Asian Middle East, East and Southeast Asia (except Israel and Japan).
Source: UN, *Monthly Bulletin of Statistics* (November 1980).

Aluminum. World mine production of bauxite, the primary ore of aluminum, rose strongly during 1979 to an estimated 86,814,000 metric tons, an increase of about 7.1% over the 81,029,000 tons in 1978. Australia produced more than twice as much as the two next largest producers: Australia produced 27,583,000 tons, Guinea, an estimated 12.5 million tons, and Jamaica 11,365,000 tons. The middle rank of producers (3 to 5 million tons) was little changed, comprising Suriname, the Soviet Union, Yugoslavia, Hungary, and Greece. Output of alumina (aluminum oxide, the concentrated intermediate stage in the production of aluminum metal) rose by 4.8% from 29,552,000 tons in 1978 to an estimated 30,976,000 tons in 1979. The major producer continued to be Australia, which achieved a 9.4% gain and reached 7,416,000 tons; the United States also showed a strong gain, about 8.2%, with its total production rising to 6,450,000 tons. Among other producers, only the Soviet Union and Jamaica exceeded 2 million tons. Production of aluminum metal in 1979 was believed to have achieved a relatively weak gain, about 3%, to a world total of 15,979,000. The U.S. still accounted for more than 30%, although production was severely restricted in the Pacific Northwest by power reductions originating in drought conditions and (in 1980) disruptions following the eruption of Mt. St. Helens.

Antimony. Production in 1979 gained 7.5% over 1978, recovering about half of the 15% decline between 1977 and 1978; the 1979 total was estimated at 71,894 metric tons. The major producers were unchanged, Bolivia leading with 12,877 tons. China was believed to follow, with about 12,000 tons, followed by South Africa, with 11,614 tons; the Soviet Union was fourth with some 7,000 tons.

Cement. World production of cement in 1979 declined slightly (about 1%) from 1978, from 711 million metric tons to an estimated 705 million tons. The world leader was the Soviet Union, with some 123 million tons, nearly a sixth of the world total but representing about a 4.8% decline against 1978; the second leading producer was Japan with 87,804,000, representing a moderate 3.4% growth over 1978. The U.S. was third at 81,894,000 tons, followed by Italy at 39.6 million tons, West Germany at 35,659,000 tons, Spain at 28,060,000 tons, Brazil at 24,880,000, and India at 18,260,000. Strongest among the concerns of the U.S. domestic industry was the conversion of manufacturing facilities to use of coal and coke; during the seven-year period ended in 1979 U.S. capacity using those fuels rose from 41 to 75%, with many other technological changes made in production facilities to maximize energy savings.

Chromite. World mine production of chromite, the principal ore of chromium, was estimated to have risen by a strong 5.8% in 1979 to a world total of some 9,524,000 metric tons, as against 9 million during 1978. South Africa was the leading producer at 3,297,000 tons; the Soviet Union followed with an estimated 2,350,000 tons. These two countries accounted for about 60% of world production, and the increasing frequency of South African proposals with regard to strategic and diplomatic use of this fact during 1979 and 1980 made Western strategic planners uncomfortable. Elsewhere, smaller chromium producers continued to expand capacity and deliveries: Albania, the third-leading producer at about 1.1 million tons (of increasingly poorer quality ore, however), the Philippines at 560,000 tons, and Zimbabwe at 542,000.

Copper. World mine production of copper was estimated by the Intergovernmental Council of Copper Exporting States (CIPEC) to have remained virtually unchanged in 1979 as against 1978, total production reaching 7,890,000 metric tons in 1979. The major producer was the U.S., at 1,456,000 metric tons, representing about 24% of total world production. The only other producers who exceeded one million tons were the Soviet Union, an estimated 1,140,000 tons, and Chile, 1,068,000 tons. The next rank of producers included only Canada, 644,000 tons, and Zambia, 588,000 tons. The only substantive changes in production levels were a Zambian decline of 8.6% and a U.S. gain of 7.2%. CIPEC members accounted for about 32% of world production and about 42% of Western production. Blister smelter production amounted to some 8,141,000 tons, virtually identical with the preceding year; major producers were the U.S. at 1,396,000 tons, the Soviet Union at an estimated 1,180,000 tons, Chile at 947,000 tons, and Japan at 921,000 tons. Refined metal producers were the same four countries; their overall production amounted to about 56% of a world total of 9,408,000 tons. World consumption of refined metal increased for the fifth year in a row, rising 3.8% to 9,960,000 tons.

WIDE WORLD

On the first day of a nationwide strike of copper workers, a striker confronts a nonunion management employee on the picket line of the Asarco Mission Mine near Tucson, Arizona.

Gold. World mine production of gold was believed on the basis of preliminary estimates by the U.S. Bureau of Mines to have risen by 2.7% during 1979, totaling 1,545 metric tons. The major producer was South Africa with 703 metric tons, representing a decline from 1978 of less than 0.5%. The Soviet Union was thought to be the second-leading producer; publication of actual levels of production had been forbidden by Soviet law since 1926, but annual levels of from 300 to 350 tons, including by-product gold from copper, lead, or zinc ores, were thought probable. Canada for the third year in a row produced 54 tons, followed by the U.S. at 36.4 tons, a decline of about 12% from 1978. A majority of producing countries showed declines in output levels, mostly slight, as producers took advantage of high world prices to mine leaner ores. Use of gold in fabrication declined 17.6% in 1979, owing primarily to the extraordinarily high price levels of the metal.

Iron. World mine production of iron ore rose by only 0.7% in 1979 as against 1978, reaching an estimated 852 million metric tons. Consumption and trade also rose during the year, reflecting continued strong demand for iron and steel. The major producer of iron ore was the Soviet Union, at 246 million tons, a slight increase over 1978 (about 29% of the world total), followed by the U.S., which regained second place in the ranks of producers from Australia (87,091,000 tons and 84,180,000 tons, respectively). The next rank of producers was led by China, with an estimated 70 million tons, Canada with 60,185,000 tons, Brazil with 59.7 million, India with 39,040,000, France with 31,966,000, South Africa with 28.4 million, and Sweden with 26,619,000 tons. Production of pig iron rose by 3.6% in 1979 based on preliminary figures, reaching 525.4 million metric tons. The major producers were the Soviet Union 112.3 million tons, Japan 83,825,000 tons, and the U.S. 78.9 million tons; there was no middle rank among the producers, but China (with 36,730,000 tons) and West Germany (35,167,000) were important.

Lead. Production of lead was estimated to have declined slightly during 1979, from 3,456,000 metric tons to 3,420,000 tons (about 1.4%). The major producer was the U.S. with 525,569 metric tons, a decline of about 0.8% from 1978. Other leading producing countries included Australia with 418,700 tons, little changed from the preceding year, Canada with 315,751 tons, Peru with 186,900, Mexico with 173,455, and Yugoslavia with 129,700. Production of refined lead declined precipitously during 1979, dropping 9.7% to a total of 3,899,600 tons, according to preliminary estimates. The major producers were the U.S. at 886,000 tons and the Soviet Union with an estimated 480,000 tons, the two together accounting for more than a third of world production. Other major producers included the U.K. at 273,900 tons, West Germany at 253,400 tons, Australia at 190,000, Canada at 184,000, and Mexico at 172,000.

Magnesium. World mine production of magnesium metal was estimated to have declined by nearly 9% during 1979 as compared with 1978; total production was thought to be just over 300,000 metric tons, of which the U.S. produced 147,228, up approximately 8.6% from the preceding year. The Soviet Union was thought to be the second-leading producer at about 72,500 tons, with Norway third, at about 45,000 tons. U.S. domestic production in 1979 equaled almost 90% of capacity at the year's end, and expansion of existing facilities was already well under way in 1980 with the March announcement of a 35,000-ton expansion of a facility at Gabb, Nev., and the mid-1980 announcement by AMAX of a 17,000-ton expansion of a newly purchased facility at Great Salt Lake in Utah (most magnesium is produced from natural brines).

Manganese. World production of manganese rose by about 3.4% in 1979 according to preliminary data, reaching a total of about 21.7 million metric tons; the Soviet Union was thought to be the world's largest producer at about 8.6 million metric tons annually, but reliable figures were not available. The second-leading country, South Africa, produced about 5 million tons, up somewhat after a 14.4% decline in 1978. The remaining major producers included Gabon, which reached a record high 2,305,000 tons (exports) after two consecutive years of decline; India at 1,690,000; Australia at about 1.4 million; and Brazil at 1.2 million.

Mercury. Worldwide production of mercury was estimated to be virtually unchanged in 1979 from the preceding year at about 190,000 flasks of 34.5 kg (76 lb) each. According to estimates, the leader continued to be the Soviet Union at about 60,000 flasks, followed by Spain at 35,000; the U.S. at 29,343, representing a strong 21% gain over 1978; Algeria at 25,000; and Mexico at 15,000. Despite continuing environmental concerns in the late 1970s and early 1980s, the efforts by mercury producers to stabilize their world market by limiting sales appeared by 1980 to have shown some success.

Molybdenum. World mine production of molybdenum in terms of contained metal rose 2.8% in 1979, according to preliminary figures from the U.S. Bureau of Mines, to an estimated 103,000 metric tons. The U.S., the leading producer with about 63% of the world total, showed a strong 9.2% gain, reaching a total of 65,306 tons; among smaller producers, Canada yielded second place to Chile (11,187 and 13,560 tons, respectively); the Soviet Union was fourth with an estimated 10,200 tons.

Nickel. World mine production of nickel was estimated to have risen by about 6% during 1979 as against 1978 but was still about 14% below production levels only two years earlier. Virtually all of the difference was attributable to low production levels in Canada, which continued to place second to the Soviet Union (approximately 131,579 and 150,000 metric tons, respectively). Canadian production was at about 56% of 1977 levels, primarily because of continued labour actions at Sudbury, Ont. Other producers included New Caledonia at 81,200, some 23% below 1977 production levels but up 23% over 1978, and Australia at 74,000; Cuba, Norway, and Indonesia were all in the 36,000 to 37,000 range. Smelter production of nickel followed a pattern similar to mine production, showing a small (3.6%) gain over 1978 but still falling well below production levels of 1976 and 1977. Total production in 1979 was 653,100 metric tons; the leader was thought to be the Soviet Union at an estimated 172,000 tons, followed by Japan with 101,600 tons, based entirely on imported supplies, and Canada with 68,400 (about 40% of total production in 1977).

Platinum-Group Metals. Production of the platinum-group metals (platinum, iridium, palladium, osmium, rhodium, and ruthenium) was estimated to have risen by about 5.2% during 1979, mainly on the basis of a strong performance by South Africa, which increased its production by an estimated 340,000 troy ounces in 1979 to a total of 3.2 million oz, or about 48% of a total world production of 6,660,000 oz. The Soviet Union was thought to have attained a similar level of production, but hard data were not available. Canada, the only other important producer, obtained virtually all of its output as a by-product of nickel refining and, as a result of drastically reduced production of that metal, managed only 185,000 oz, about 40% of 1977 production levels.

Silver. World mine production of silver was very nearly identical in 1979 with that of 1978, at about 343.6 million troy ounces. The major producer was Mexico, with 49.4 million oz, followed by the Soviet Union with an estimated 46 million oz, Peru with 42.6 million oz, Canada with 38,068,000 oz, the U.S. with 38,055,000 oz, Australia with 25 million, and Poland with 23 million. Future strength in Mexican production seemed assured for many years by the continued development of silver prospects in 1980.

Tin. World mine production of tin was estimated to have risen slightly (1.1%) during 1979 as compared with 1978, attaining a total of approximately 247,000 metric tons; major producers were Malaysia at 63,000 tons, slightly above 1978 levels; Thailand at 39,840 (up 32%); the Soviet Union at approximately 34,000; Bolivia at about 30,000; Indonesia at 29,440; and China at about 22,000. With the exception of Thailand, no major changes in production levels were visible, as most producers, especially members of the Fifth International Tin Agreement, tried with some success to stabilize their market. Production of tin metal at smelters rose minutely (0.6%) during 1979; the major producer was Malaysia at 73,070 tons, almost 40% of the world total of 178,000 tons; the Soviet Union was probably second.

Titanium. World production of titanium concentrates of ilmenite and leucoxine were estimated to have declined slightly during 1979, off about 0.3% to a total of some 3,491,000 metric tons. Major producers were Australia (32.7%), Norway (23.5%), and the U.S. (16.6%). Rutile concentrates, however, showed strong growth (almost 20%), with gains by all major producing countries. Australian production rose 7.9% to 277,000 tons, and South Africa more than doubled its total to 42,000 tons.

Tungsten. World production of tungsten declined a slight 0.9% during 1979 to 45,018 metric tons. The leading producers were China and the Soviet Union (9,800 and 8,600 tons, respectively); the largest non-Communist producers were Australia with 3,133 tons and the U.S. with 3,013 tons. Consumption in the U.S., the world's leading consumer, rose nearly 15% during 1979, led by a 19% increase in tungsten carbide for cutting tools.

Zinc. According to preliminary estimated data from the U.S. Bureau of Mines, zinc mine production declined by about 2.4% during 1979 from 5,879,000 metric tons in 1978 to 5,740,000 tons in 1979. Zinc production in the Soviet Union was about 1,020,000 metric tons; other leading mine producers were Canada at 1,148,000 tons and Australia at 483,000 tons. World smelter production rose in 1979 to an estimated 6,437,300 tons. Leading producers were the Soviet Union (16.9%), Japan (12.3%), Canada (9%), and the U.S. (8.2%). (WILLIAM A. CLEVELAND)

See also Earth Sciences; Energy; Industrial Review: *Gemstones; Iron and Steel;* Materials Sciences.

[724.B.1; 724.C.3]

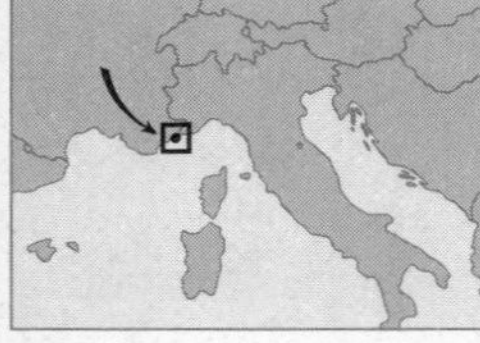
Monaco

Monaco

A sovereign principality on the northern Mediterranean coast, Monaco is bounded on land by the French département of Alpes-Maritimes. Area: 1.90 sq km (0.73 sq mi). Pop. (1979 est.): 25,000. Language: French. Religion: predominantly Roman Catholic. Chief of state, Prince Rainier III; minister of state in 1980, André Saint-Mleux.

MONACO

Education. (1977–78) Primary, pupils 1,467; secondary, pupils 1,386; vocational, pupils 644; primary, secondary, and vocational, teachers (1976–77) 357.

Finance and Trade. Monetary unit: French franc, with (Sept. 22, 1980) a free rate of Fr 4.19 to U.S. $1 (Fr 10.08 = £1 sterling). Budget (1978 est.): revenue Fr 671 million; expenditure Fr 518 million. Foreign trade included with France. Tourism (1978) 224,000 visitors.

In July 1980 an act passed by Monaco's National Council and signed by Prince Rainier III laid down conditions and restrictions so severe as to make strikes in the principality impracticable. As a last resort a strike could be forbidden on political grounds by the minister of state, who, by the treaty governing Franco-Monegasque relations, is always a French civil servant.

A favoured centre for international conferences, Monte Carlo was host to the tenth World Congress of Thanatologists (specialists in the study of death) in April 1980. It was announced in March that the first World Assembly of Oceanographic Arts and Sciences would take place there in April 1981.

The marriage of Princess Caroline, daughter of Prince Rainier and Princess Grace, to Philippe Junot, celebrated on June 28, 1978, ended in divorce in October 1980. Earlier, on January 10, a Paris court had ordered the French magazine *Photo* to pay Princess Caroline Fr 80,000 damages for publishing without permission photographs in which she appeared topless. (K. M. SMOGORZEWSKI)

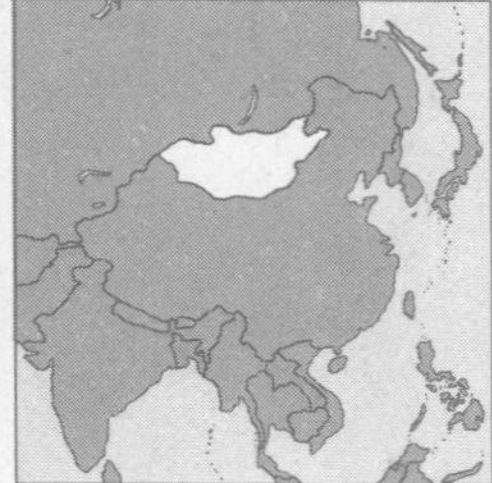
Mongolia

Mongolia

A people's republic of Asia lying between the U.S.S.R. and China, Mongolia occupies the geographic area known as Outer Mongolia. Area: 1,565,000 sq km (604,000 sq mi). Pop. (1979 census): 1,594,800. Cap. and largest city: Ulan Bator (pop., 1979, 403,000). Language: Khalkha Mongolian. Religion: Lamaistic Buddhism. First secretary of the Mongolian People's Revolutionary (Communist) Party in 1980 and chairman of the Presidium of the Great People's Hural, Yumzhagiyen Tsedenbal; chairman of the Council of Ministers (premier), Zhambyn Batmunkh.

The Soviet leader Leonid Brezhnev received Chairman Yumzhagiyen Tsedenbal of Mongolia at Oreanda in the Crimea on Aug. 18, 1980. The two leaders noted that economic relations between

MONGOLIA

Education. (1979) Primary and secondary, pupils 366,900; vocational, pupils 19,600; primary, secondary, and vocational, teachers (1977) 13,500; higher, students 19,700, teaching staff (1977) 1,000.

Finance. Monetary unit: tugrik, with (Sept. 22, 1980) a nominal exchange rate of 2.85 tugriks to U.S. $1 (6.85 tugriks = £1 sterling). Budget (1980 est.): revenue 4,070,000,000 tugriks; expenditure 4,058,000,000 tugriks.

Foreign Trade. (1979) Imports *c.* U.S. $1,010,000,000; exports *c.* U.S. $330 million. Import sources: U.S.S.R. *c.* 90%. Export destinations: U.S.S.R. *c.* 82%; Czechoslovakia *c.* 5%. Main exports (1975): livestock 27%; meat 19%; wool 16%.

Transport and Communications. Roads (1978) *c.* 75,000 km (including *c.* 9,000 km main roads). Railways: (1978) 1,710 km; traffic (1977) 227 million passenger-km, freight 2,542,000,000 net ton-km. Telephones (Dec. 1978) 35,800. Radio receivers (Dec. 1978) 140,300. Television receivers (Dec. 1978) *c.* 40,800.

Agriculture. Production (in 000; metric tons; 1979): wheat *c.* 400; oats *c.* 40; barley *c.* 65; potatoes (1978) *c.* 64; milk (1978) *c.* 238; beef and veal (1978) *c.* 65; mutton and goat meat (1978) *c.* 106; wool *c.* 12. Livestock (in 000; Dec. 1977): sheep 13,430; goats 4,411; cattle 2,388; horses 2,104; camels *c.* 615.

Industry. Production (in 000; metric tons; 1979): coal and lignite *c.* 4,108; fluorspar *c.* 530; cement 185; electricity (kw-hr; 1978) 1,156,000.

their countries were developing successfully. In the period 1981–85 Soviet-Mongolian trade would increase by 50%, as compared with the five-year period 1976–80. In 1980 more than 90% of Mongolia's imports came from the U.S.S.R. Brezhnev and Tsedenbal also discussed international issues, particularly Asian problems. They agreed that there was an intensification of activities by forces hostile to the cause of Asian peoples' freedom.

On November 26 Andrey Gromyko and Mangalyn Dugersuren, foreign ministers of the U.S.S.R. and Mongolia, respectively, signed an agreement on the regime of the Soviet-Mongolian border and on cooperation and mutual assistance in border matters. (K. M. SMOGORZEWSKI)

Morocco

A constitutional monarchy of northwestern Africa, on the Atlantic Ocean and the Mediterranean Sea, Morocco is bordered by Algeria and Western Sahara. Area: 458,730 sq km (177,117 sq mi). Pop. (1979 est.): 19,470,000. Cap.: Rabat (pop., 1979 est., 768,500). Largest city: Casablanca (pop., 1979 est., 2,220,600). (Data above refer to Morocco as constituted prior to the purported division of Spanish Sahara between Morocco and Mauritania and the subsequent Moroccan occupation of the Mauritanian zone [1979]). Language: Arabic (official); with Berber, French, and Spanish minorities. Religion: Muslim. King, Hassan II; prime minister in 1980, Maati Bouabid.

In the Western Sahara the Popular Front for Liberation of Saguia el Hamra and Rio de Oro (Polisario Front) achieved spectacular military successes in southern Morocco—in the Zag and Assa region in March, at Tan-Tan in September, around Akka in August and September, and around Zak in October—and claimed success at Rous Lekhyalat in late December. Morocco, however, claimed success in the Ouarkziz region in June and September. Portugal recognized the Front on July 26 in order to obtain the release of Portuguese fishermen. Morocco pressured Mauritania to prevent it from recognizing the Front's government-in-exile, the Saharan Arab Democratic Republic (SADR), after the August release by the Front of 45 Mauritanian prisoners.

At the summit of the Organization of African Unity (OAU) at Freetown, Sierra Leone, in July, the Polisario Front had majority support from 26 African states, but the issue was referred to a committee. In an impartial communiqué this group called for a referendum and cease-fire in September. The U.S. approved the sale of 50 military aircraft to Morocco in February and of another 25 in August. King Hassan sought support for his Sahara policy during visits to Iraq, the Persian Gulf states, and Saudi Arabia in February and to Europe in April. In April, however, a Dutch contract for the reconstruction of El Ayoun port was canceled as a result of parliamentary pressure in The Netherlands. In July Morocco announced an end of phosphate sales to countries that recognized the SADR, and diplomatic relations with Cuba and Libya were broken off.

The war posed strains on the economy, despite support from the Saudis and the Gulf states. Foreign debt rose to U.S. $5 billion, and the trade deficit increased by 12% despite a 52% rise in exports. The government announced a new energy policy in April, involving an expenditure of $42 million on domestic development in order to cut oil import bills. Oil and gas were found at Essaouira and gas at Mechra Bel Ksiri. Phosphate exports generated 72% of export earnings from minerals, which in turn were 45% of total export revenue in 1979. Tourism increased by 9% in 1979. However, the economy grew by only 3%. In September King Hassan announced a 30% cut in rents for selected social groups, and in August a $400 million improvement plan for Casablanca was unveiled. Strikes in early 1980 resulted in arrests. However, some political prisoners, including the poet Abdellatif Laabi, were later released.

Constitutional changes were approved by two nationwide referenda. On May 23 the royal coming-of-age was reduced to 16 from 18, to ease the crown prince's accession to the throne should the king abdicate or die. Then, on May 30, the life of each Parliament was extended from four years to six. Queen Elizabeth II visited Morocco in late October. (GEORGE JOFFÉ)

MOROCCO

Education. (1978–79) Primary, pupils 1,925,187, teachers 50,829; secondary, pupils 650,796, teachers 40,507; vocational, pupils 14,985; teacher training, students 11,238, teachers (1976–77) 443; higher, students 76,054, teaching staff (1975–76) 1,642.

Finance. Monetary unit: dirham, with (Sept. 22, 1980) a free rate of 3.80 dirhams to U.S. $1 (9.12 dirhams = £1 sterling). Gold, SDR's, and foreign exchange (June 1980) U.S. $291 million. Budget (total; 1979 est.): revenue 19.6 billion dirhams; expenditure 21.6 billion dirhams. Gross national product (1979) 59,820,000,000 dirhams. Money supply (June 1980) 24,258,000,000 dirhams. Cost of living (1975 = 100; June 1980) 155.9.

Foreign Trade. (1979) Imports 14,328,000,000 dirhams; exports 7,287,000,000 dirhams. Main import sources: France 28%; Spain 9%; Iraq 9%; West Germany 6%; Italy 6%; U.S. 6%. Main export destinations: France 27%; West Germany 11%; Spain 6%; The Netherlands 6%; Italy 5%; Belgium-Luxembourg 5%. Main exports: phosphates 29%; oranges, clementines, etc. 11%; vegetables 9%; nonferrous metal ores 7%; phosphoric acid 7%; fish 5%; clothing 5%; textile yarns and fabrics 5%. Tourism: visitors (1978) 1,377,510; gross receipts (1977) U.S. $375 million.

Transport and Communications. Roads (1976) 26,702 km. Motor vehicles in use (1976): passenger 347,400; commercial 121,600. Railways: (1976) 1,756 km; traffic (1977) 835 million passenger-km, freight 3,474,000,000 net ton-km. Air traffic (1978): 1,951,000,000 passenger-km; freight 23.2 million net ton-km. Shipping (1979): merchant vessels 100 gross tons and over 131; gross tonnage 364,364. Telephones (Jan. 1978) 210,000. Radio receivers (Dec. 1977) 1.6 million. Television licenses (Dec. 1977) 597,000.

Agriculture. Production (in 000; metric tons; 1979): wheat 1,796; barley 1,888; corn 312; potatoes *c.* 200; sugar, raw value *c.* 353; tomatoes *c.* 413; grapes *c.* 240; oranges *c.* 606; mandarin oranges and tangerines 229; olives *c.* 390; dates *c.* 102; fish catch (1978) 292. Livestock (in 000; 1979): sheep *c.* 13,500; goats *c.* 5,650; cattle (1978) *c.* 3,620; horses *c.* 320; mules *c.* 384; asses *c.* 1,200; camels *c.* 220; poultry *c.* 22,000.

Industry. Production (in 000; metric tons; 1979): coal 720; crude oil *c.* 48; petroleum products (1978) *c.* 2,780; electricity (excluding most industrial production; kw-hr) *c.* 4,320,000; cement 3,274; iron ore (55–60% metal content) 53; phosphate rock (1978) 19,278; manganese ore (metal content; 1978) 65; lead concentrates (metal content) 165; copper concentrates (metal content) 24; zinc concentrates (metal content) 14.

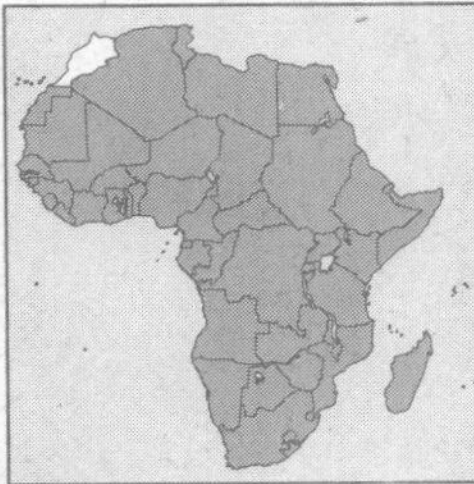

Morocco

Missiles:
see Defense

Molecular Biology:
see Life Sciences

Monetary Policy:
see Economy, World

Money and Banking:
see Economy, World

Mormons:
see Religion

Motion Pictures

English-Speaking Cinema. UNITED STATES. The outstanding phenomenon of 1979–80 was the extravagant escalation of Hollywood film budgets, out of scale even to current inflation rates. Such films as *Star Trek,* Michael Cimino's *Heaven's Gate* (briefly shown, but withdrawn for reediting), *Flash Gordon, 1941,* and *The Blues Brothers* all topped $30 million; $20 million came to seem a quite unremarkable budget. With such astronomical expenditures it became increasingly difficult for films to move into profit. Among those films of this "megabuck" class that did manage to earn back their cost was the major box-office success of the year, Irvin Kershner's *The Empire Strikes Back,* a sequel to *Star Wars.*

At the other end of the scale, some of the most successful films of the year in commercial terms were comparatively cheaply made horror films, for which there appeared to be a growing vogue among teenage moviegoers. Some of the more notable of these were John Carpenter's *The Fog,* Brian De Palma's *Dressed to Kill,* and Charles Kaufman's *Mother's Day.*

At a different level again there seemed to be a vogue for films more or less based on fact. William Friedkin's *Cruising* was based on the memoirs of a policeman who had posed as a practicing homosexual in order to trace a killer preying on homosexuals. Stuart Rosenberg's *Brubaker* was based on the memoirs of a reforming prison warden. Martin Scorsese's *Raging Bull* was the story of Jake La Motta, the 1940s middleweight boxing champion. Even *Urban Cowboy,* a vehicle for the popular star John Travolta, took as its setting the real and raucous background of working-class leisure activities in and near the Texas oil fields.

Even the backstage musical seemed to acquire a new realistic tendency. The English-born Michael Apted enjoyed a major box-office success with *Coal Miner's Daughter,* a re-creation of the life of country and western singer Loretta Lynn, played by Sissy Spacek (*see* BIOGRAPHIES), set in locations in Tennessee and Kentucky.

In *The Empire Strikes Back,* Luke Skywalker (played by Mark Hamill, left) meets the evil Darth Vader (David Prowse) in a "lightsabre" duel. This movie is the second in a projected series that was touched off by *Star Wars.*

PHOTO TRENDS

Bob Fosse's *All That Jazz,* released late in 1979, was rather an exercise in autobiography, a spectacular musical and fantastic metamorphosis of Fosse's personal history of excessive work, marital problems, and breakdown of health. Alan Parker, the British director, created his musical, *Fame,* in the setting of New York's School of Performing Arts, following the five-year development of the students, their professional progress, and their private problems.

Among established Hollywood directors, the veteran Samuel Fuller fulfilled an old ambition with his panoramic view of World War II seen through the eyes of a small and expert fighting detachment, *The Big Red One.* Lewis Carlino's *The Great Santini* was an effective drama of a military man's family life. Hal Ashby achieved a major success with his delicate transposition of Jerzy Kosinski's *Being There.* The film contained one of the last and best performances by Peter Sellers (*see* OBITUARIES) as a man whose life and ignorance have been so perfectly sheltered until middle age that a society used only to smart media talk supposes he must be some sort of genius and natural candidate for the presidency.

It was a year of debuts. Woody Allen's script collaborator, Marshall Brickman, turned director with *Simon,* a modern morality cast as farce, which poked fun at the pretensions of science fiction, fake intelligentsia, and other topical targets. David Lynch directed his first major film, *The Elephant Man,* a successful portrayal of a man grotesquely deformed at birth. The actor James Caan directed *Hide in Plain Sight,* a sympathetic and low-key story of a father trying to gain possession of his children from their feckless mother and her criminal husband. Robert Redford's first film as director, *Ordinary People,* was a similarly human subject, the effects upon his family of a disturbed youth's suicidal urges resulting from the accidental drowning death of his brother. Already well established as a director, another star, Clint Eastwood, made a disarmingly modest and self-effacing light comedy, *Bronco Billy,* in which he played a somewhat fraudulent Western-style star of a small traveling circus. Robert Altman turned to comedy with *Popeye,* featuring Robin Williams as the comic-strip character. Two popular singers also made their film debuts, Dolly Parton as an angry secretary in *Nine to Five* and Neil Diamond in a remake of *The Jazz Singer.*

In healthy contrast to the escalating costs of conventional commercial film production, there was marked activity in the production of imaginative, independently produced, low-budget films, often financed by grants from public arts funds. Richard Pearce's *Heartland,* based on Elinore Stewart's real-life reminiscences of the hardships of Wyoming homestead life in 1910, was supported by a grant from the National Endowment for the Humanities. Victor Nunez's *Gal Young 'Un* was partly supported by the National Endowment for the Arts and the Florida Arts Council and cooperatively involved the whole Florida community where it was filmed.

At a different level, and under somewhat more

UPI

In *Urban Cowboy,* Madolyn Smith and John Travolta watch the competition while Travolta prepares to ride a mechanical bull. The screenplay was written by Aaron Latham (from his story in *Esquire*) and director James Bridges.

conventional commercial conditions, two outstanding low-budget films of the year were Joan Micklin Silver's *Head over Heels,* the story of an out-of-skew love affair, and Henry Jaglom's sharp slapstick farce, *Sitting Ducks,* about the adventures of a couple of petty crooks and their unlikely mistresses of the moment.

The same area of low-budget, independent production produced three outstanding works of investigative documentary: John Lowenthal's reexamination of the evidence in *The Trials of Alger Hiss*; Allan Francovitch's inquiry into the history of the CIA's overseas activities in *On Company Business*; and John Harvey's *We Are the Guinea Pigs,* concerning the Three Mile Island nuclear accident. Made on minimal resources, Ira Wohl's *Best Boy,* a sensitive study of his own cousin, a retarded 52-year-old, and the special problems of the man's aged parents, won the year's Oscar as best documentary feature.

Several notable Hollywood veterans died during 1980, including the directors Alfred Hitchcock, Lewis Milestone, and Raoul Walsh; producer Dore Schary; the writer Donald Ogden Stewart; three archetypal stars of the 1930s, Mae West, Jimmy Durante, and George Raft, suavest of gangsters; and tough-guy action star Steve McQueen (*see* OBITUARIES).

At the annual awards ceremony of the U.S. Academy of Motion Picture Arts and Sciences, honouring works of 1979, Robert Benton's *Kramer vs. Kramer* won Oscars for best picture, best director, best actor (Dustin Hoffman), best supporting actress (Meryl Streep, *see* BIOGRAPHIES), and best screenplay based on material from another medium. The best actress was Sally Field in Martin Ritt's *Norma Rae*; the best supporting actor Melvyn Douglas in *Being There. All That Jazz* took awards for best editing, art direction, costume design, and adaptation musical score. The best foreign-language film was Volker Schlöndorff's *The Tin Drum* from West Germany.

BRITAIN. The British cinema had its share in the "megabuck movies": Stanley Kubrick's supernatural thriller *The Shining,* however, looked wholly American; while *Raise the Titanic* proved a costly and miscalculated folly. Otherwise, there was comparatively little conventional commercial production. One of the last films produced by the Rank Organisation before the announcement that it would abandon production was Nicolas Roeg's effortfully stylish thriller *Bad Timing.* Tom Clegg's *McVicar* cast the rock star Roger Daltrey as a celebrated prison-breaker. One of the best British films of the year, also a thriller, was John MacKenzie's *The Long Good Friday,* a complex but taut portrayal of the nemesis of a successful East End crook.

The makers of low-budget films attempted in several cases to analyze the "punk" generation. In *Rude Boy,* Jack Hazan and David Mingay used the same combination of fiction and documentary as in their earlier *A Bigger Splash* to study the life of a youth tagging along behind a leading punk rock group, The Clash. Julian Temple's *The Great Rock'n'Roll Swindle* created its own original amalgam of documentary and Monty Python comedy to survey the history of the Sex Pistols.

Another admirable feature debut that related popular music to social issues was Franco Rosso's *Babylon,* a lively but pessimistic portrait of black, reggae-obsessed youths in an exciting but hostile South London. Brian Gibson's debut film, *Breaking Glass,* was a more conventional treatment of the rise, exploitation, and collapse of a punk rock star, played by a striking newcomer, Hazel O'Connor.

There was a distinct upsurge of lively, small-budget, independent films. Among these were the debuts of the actor Vladek Sheybal with an ironic comedy about performers, *All About a Prima Ballerina,* and Bill Foulk's offbeat thriller, *Beastly Treatment.* In Glasgow Bill Forsyth directed *Gregory's Girl,* a sharply comic and realistic observation of the trials of young love, and Sandy Johnson directed *Never Say Die,* a short but stylish pastiche of 1940s U.S. thrillers. In Wales Karl Francis adapted a Dylan Thomas story about World War I, *The Mouse and the Woman.*

AUSTRALIA. The Australian cinema found itself at a crossroads. Having achieved, largely through imaginative public financing, an industry and a body of talent that commanded international attention, the makers of the new Australian motion pictures were divided between those who felt the future lay in aiming for an "international" (in reality, a U.S.) market, using American themes and stars, and those who felt committed to truly indigenous films. In fact, the decision appeared to be dictated by circumstances. Supposedly "international" subjects, such as Simon Wincer's *Harlequin* —mishandling the promising idea of an updated

Annual Cinema Attendance[1]

Country	Total in 000	Per capita
Albania	9,000	4.1
Algeria	45,000	2.7
Angola	3,700	0.6
Argentina	67,000	2.6
Australia	32,000	2.6
Austria	17,430	2.3
Bahrain	2,400	9.9
Barbados	1,200	5.0
Belgium	24,100	2.4
Bolivia	3,200	0.9
Brazil	209,200	1.9
Brunei	2,500	17.0
Bulgaria	112,000	12.7
Burma	222,500	8.1
Cambodia	20,000	3.0
Cameroon	6,500	1.0
Canada	81,597	3.5
Chile	10,347	1.0
Colombia	96,000	4.1
Cuba	83,100	17.1
Cyprus	6,100	9.5
Czechoslovakia	84,700	5.6
Denmark	16,900	3.3
Dominican Republic	5,200	1.2
Ecuador	38,700	5.6
Egypt	65,000	1.9
El Salvador	16,347	3.3
Finland	10,110	2.1
France	177,100	3.3
Germany, East	80,000	4.8
Germany, West	124,200	2.0
Ghana	1,000	0.1
Greece	34,200	3.7
Grenada	1,000	12.1
Guatemala	15,400	2.8
Guyana	10,400	12.9
Haiti	2,218	0.5
Hong Kong	60,200	13.3
Hungary	71,700	6.7
Iceland	2,500	11.4
India	2,260,000	3.8
Indonesia	107,500	0.7
Iraq	8,300	1.3
Ireland	38,000	13.0
Israel	22,000	6.1
Italy	280,000	4.9
Ivory Coast	10,100	1.8
Japan	165,770	1.4
Jordan	18,000	—
Kenya	9,200	0.6
Korea, South	65,000	1.8
Kuwait	4,700	4.7
Lebanon	49,700	18.0
Liberia	1,900	1.1
Libya	15,500	6.0
Luxembourg	1,100	3.2
Macau	2,272	9.1
Madagascar	2,900	0.4
Malawi	1,400	0.3
Malaysia	108,800	9.1
Mali	2,500	0.5
Malta	3,100	9.4
Martinique	2,100	6.0
Mauritius	17,500	19.3
Mexico	265,000	4.1
Mongolia	13,800	8.7
Morocco	35,800	2.0
Mozambique	3,200	0.4
Netherlands, The	28,400	1.9
New Zealand	11,900	3.8
Nicaragua	7,700	7.7
Norway	16,800	4.2
Pakistan	195,000	3.0
Panama	7,100	4.8
Philippines	318,000	7.6
Poland	116,000	3.3
Portugal	39,100	7.6
Puerto Rico	6,800	2.2
Romania	188,000	9.0
Senegal	3,800	0.7
Singapore	44,700	19.1
Somalia	4,700	1.7
South Africa	67,000	2.5
Spain	211,900	5.8
Sri Lanka	147,900	10.5
Sudan	12,000	0.8
Sweden	24,500	3.0
Switzerland	23,000	3.6
Syria	42,000	5.5
Taiwan	164,000	9.4
Tanzania	3,000	0.2
Thailand	71,000	1.7
Trinidad and Tobago	8,400	8.0
Tunisia	8,800	1.5
Turkey	246,700	6.7
Uganda	1,900	0.2
U.S.S.R.	4,155,000	16.0
United Kingdom	126,000	2.3
United States	1,133,000	5.1
Upper Volta	1,000	0.2
Venezuela	33,000	2.6
Vietnam	288,200	6.0
Yemen (Aden)	3,500	2.4
Yugoslavia	73,600	3.5
Zaire	1,600	0.1

[1] Countries having over one million annual attendance.

PHOTO TRENDS

Mary Tyler Moore and Timothy Hutton starred with Donald Sutherland in *Ordinary People*, a movie based on Judith Guest's novel of the same name.

Rasputin story—were poorly received, while the major successes of the year were films purely Australian in subject and style. Among the latter the most noteworthy was Bruce Beresford's *Breaker Morant*, a dramatized re-creation of the true story of the court-martial of three Australian soldiers serving with the British in the Boer War and the subsequent execution of two of them as scapegoats (so the film suggested) for High Command blunders. Beresford went on to make an adaptation of David Williamson's play about the behind-the-scenes of football, *The Club*. Stephen Wallace made a striking feature film debut with *Stir*, a realistic prison drama. The first feature production of the Tasmanian Film Corporation, John Honey's *Maganinnie*, was an admirable fable of coexistence, the story of a 19th-century aboriginal woman who carries off a white child and the love that grows up between them.

CANADA. Commercial production in Canada tended to U.S.-style crime and sensational subjects, with the most successful films contributing to the booming low-budget horror genre. The best of these was *The Changeling*, a ghost story of conventional form but given some style by its Hungarian-born British director, Peter Medak.

Western Europe. FRANCE. The outstanding films of the year were Alain Resnais's *Mon Oncle d'Amérique*, scripted by Jean Gruault, a wise and witty experiment in examining human relationships in terms of the behaviourist theories of the biologist Henri Laborit; and François Truffaut's attractive *Le Dernier Métro*. At once a recollection of Truffaut's own *Day for Night* and a tribute to two of his heroes, Jean Renoir and Ernst Lubitsch, the film was inspired by the recollections of the actor Jean Marais and recounted the adventures of a little Parisian theatre during the German occupation in World War II. Georges Franju's *Le Dernier Mélodrame* also took a backstage subject, the crumbling and demise of a troupe of traveling players.

Of the newer generation of directors, Bertrand Tavernier made *Death Watch*, a Franco-West German co-production, in which he imaginatively used the setting of Glasgow for a story about a television producer exploiting the supposed last days of a sick woman. Back in France Tavernier went on to make *Une Semaine de Vacances*, a likable study of a young teacher at a moment of crisis and readjustment. Maurice Pialat's *Loulou* described with warmth and humour the lives of a working-class, intermittently delinquent couple. One of the major box-office successes of the year was Bertrand Blier's *Buffet Froid*, a black comedy about some eccentric and very incompetent murderers.

WEST GERMANY. Among a fairly heterogeneous production of modestly budgeted films, often wholly or partly financed by television, the most significant of the year were all made by the young generation that had emerged in the 1970s. Werner Schröter's *Palermo oder Wolfsburg*, which won the main prize at the Berlin Film Festival in February, was a stylized tragedy about the difficulties of integration experienced by a young Italian worker who comes to the Volkswagen works at Wolfsburg. Rainer Werner Fassbinder turned back to Germany of the 1920s, for both the text and the stylistic influences, in his massive *Berlin-Alexanderplatz*, made as a 16-hour television series but reduced to more manageable length for theatrical distribution.

Alexander Kluge attacked contemporary West German complacency in *The Patriot*, recounting the often absurd adventures of a young history teacher in questioning accepted attitudes of the times. Kluge also appeared as co-director, with Volker Schlöndorff, Stefan Anst, and Alexander von Eschwege, of *Der Kandidat*, a brilliant, factual investigation of the career of Franz-Josef Strauss. Alongside a portrait of the candidate for chancellor, it provided a sweeping survey of post-World War II Germany as a whole.

ITALY. The major box-office successes of the year seemed to be farcical comedies such as Sasellano and Pepolo's *Mani de Veluto*, a Cinderella story about a millionaire industrialist and a beautiful lady pickpocket; Steno's *La Patata Bollente*, a politico-sexual farce; or Bruno Corbucci's *Angencia Ricardo Finzi. . .Practicamente Detective*. Among films of more considerable artistic interest, Ettore Scola's *La Terrazza*, probing the disillusionment of 1970s intelligentsia, had perhaps the greatest success. A co-production with France, Marco Bellocchio's *Salto nel Vuoto* used the relationship of a middle-aged and slightly eccentric sister and brother to investigate the role of the family in Catholic society. Federico Fellini's *La Città delle Donne* proved a grave disappointment, a heavy-handed and humourless nightmare of the sex war. Marco Ferreri's *Chiedo Asilo*, on the contrary, was uncharacteristically genial, an odd, gentle picture about an eccentric male kindergarten teacher.

SCANDINAVIA. In Sweden the actor Erland Josephson made his debut as director with *The Marmalade Revolution*, in which he himself played a man rebelling against drab middle-class conformism. The year's production was also notable for two superior children's films, Marie Louise de Geer Bergenstrahle's *Not for Children* and Astrid Lindgren's *You're Out of Your Mind Maggie*. Stig Borkman, a Swedish director working in Denmark, made *Inside Women*, a perceptive study of the crisis of a woman on the point of leaving her husband for a lover. A Finnish-Swedish co-production, *The Raven's Dance,* using techniques of dramatized documentary to describe the encroachment of civilization on the natural order of life in a remote northern area of Finland, represented a striking debut for its director, Markku Lehmuskallio.

Eastern Europe. U.S.S.R. The major revelation of the year was the latest film of Andrey Tarkovsky, *The Stalker,* a mysterious and mystical allegory about a group of men in a chaotic and ruinous near future who explore an unknown, forbidden, and ultimately unexplained "Zone." Two other Soviet directors whose work was of consistent high interest also produced new films during the year. Nikita Mikhalkov made a lively adaptation of Ivan Goncharov's *Platonov.* Aleksandr Mitta's *The Crew* showed allegiance to U.S. models in its portrayal of the various members of the crew of a Soviet airliner, though its dramatic catastrophe—the aircraft goes to the aid of an unidentified third-world country ravaged by an earthquake—was strictly loyal to prevailing home ideologies.

POLAND. The Polish cinema, which for a year or so had been vividly reflecting the social dissatisfaction that reached a head in the strikes during the summer, continued to echo the prevailing social malaise. Krzysztof Zanussi's *The Constant Factor* described a hero who attempts to discover a constant standard of morality in society and is finally penalized for his refusal to conform to the prevailing corruption around him. Another Zanussi film, *The Contract,* used what was superficially a form of absurdist comedy—about a disastrous wedding party—as a criticism of various attitudes of complacency, cynicism, and corruption within the socialist scheme. Andrzej Wajda's *The Conductor* (with John Gielgud in the title role) examined attitudes of provincialism and lack of national confidence through a story about a great Polish expatriate artist and the effect of his return to his homeland. Kazimierz Kutz's *Beads from One Rosary* seemed to echo the spirit and aspirations of the Polish strikers in its simple tale of an individualistic miner who resolutely refuses to leave his old home for the "ideal" new apartment offered him in his retirement.

HUNGARY. The outstanding film of the year was Istvan Szabo's *Confidence,* a story of two people forced by wartime circumstances to pose as man and wife and the impossibility in those conditions of establishing mutual trust. Elsewhere, an interest in neodocumentary themes and styles was still evident. Istvan Darday, founder of a school favouring the use of nonactors and improvisation, made *Stratagem,* about the struggles of one woman to bring to fruition a project for an old people's home in the face of bureaucratic opposition. Janos Rosza's *Sunday Parents* used more conventional narrative style in its touching story of a lonely girl in an institution for teenagers. Already Hungary's most exportable director, Marta Meszaros heightened the exportability of her films by starring in them foreign actresses of box-office appeal: in *On the Move,* Delphine Seyrig; in *The Inheritors,* Isabelle Huppert.

CZECHOSLOVAKIA. Juraj Jakubisko, a Slovak director best known for his wild and lyrical pre-1968 film *The Deserter and the Nomads,* broke a long silence with *Build a House, Plant a Tree,* a subdued film about an individualist who comes to a rural community. Another notable director of the 1960s, Jaromil Jires, also reemerged with a low-key film, *The Rabbit Case,* about a distinguished lawyer who retires to the country and discovers among less sophisticated people some human truths new to him. The major box-office hit of the year, however, was Jiri Kreikik's *Divine Emma,* a drama about a famous Bohemian diva who was convicted of espionage during World War I.

EAST GERMANY. There was a sense of renewal and unaccustomed lightness in new films from East Germany. In Konrad Wolf's *Solo Sunny,* socialist society was quite critically viewed from the unusual perspective of a girl who has progressed from orphanage and factory to become a pop singer. A former student of Wolf's, Evelyn Schmidt, also dealt with the problems of a solitary girl—the orphaned illegitimate child of a man with offspring by both wife and mistress—in *Seitensprung,* a noteworthy debut.

YUGOSLAVIA. The most notable of a group of young talents currently coming to the fore in Yugoslavia appeared to be Goran Paskaljevic, whose *Special Treatment* used a story of doctor and patients in a clinic for alcoholics as a metaphor for all kinds of paternalistic authoritarianism; and Karpo Godina, who made a considerable impact with *The Raft of the Medusa,* set in the early 1920s and taking a wry view of revolutionary ardour.

Asia. JAPAN. Japan could claim the most important film of the year—perhaps, indeed, of many years: the greatest living Japanese director, Akira Kurosawa, made a triumphant comeback with *Kagemusha,* a tragedy which, as international critics concurred, achieved a Shakespearean elevation. The story tells of a feudal clan chieftain who uses a double on the battlefield. The leader is killed, and the double—a former thief—takes his place, aspires to his courage and nobility, but is finally discovered and banished from the clan.

JEAN PAGLIUSO—SYGMA

Shelley Duvall and Robin Williams brought the comic-strip characters Olive Oyl and Popeye to life in a film directed by Robert Altman.

PHOTO TRENDS

The Tin Drum, adapted from the novel by Günter Grass and directed by Volker Schlöndorff, won the U.S. Academy Award for best foreign-language film of 1979.

Made with U.S. financing, the film achieved almost unprecedented visual spectacle.

HONG KONG. Among the proliferation of martial-arts films, a new Asian superstar had emerged in Jackie Chan (local name, Sing Lung), a young man of charm and athletic prowess. During 1980 Chan made his debut as director with *The Young Master* and followed the lead of the late Bruce Lee in making a U.S. martial-arts film, *The Big Brawl.* An unexpected box-office success was obtained by Edwin Kong's intelligent compilation film about the rise of Japanese militarism, *Rising Sun.*

INDIA. Among India's vast and ever growing number of commercial films, directors of individual talent continued to produce original work. Mrinal Sen directed *And Quiet Rolls the Day,* mainly set in the shabby flat of an impoverished family in Calcutta. When the eldest daughter and breadwinner fails to return home at night, the resulting anxiety exposes tensions and breaches in the outwardly serene family life. G. Aravindan's *Kummatty (The Bogeyman)* confirmed a highly individual gift for showing magic and reality existing side by side. The film told of children turned into animals by a wandering charlatan and the adventures of one little boy who fails to be restored to human form. Satyajit Ray, the great Bengali director, also produced a children's film, a fantasy with music, *The Kingdom of Diamonds.*

Tatsuya Nakadai (right) plays a dual role in Akira Kurosawa's *Kagemusha* ("Shadow Warrior"). The Japanese film won top honours at the Cannes Film Festival.

PHOTO TRENDS

Africa and the Middle East. AFRICA. There was little discernible indigenous activity in black Africa (but *see* BIOGRAPHIES: *Ousmane Sembene*). In Mozambique the Brazilian expatriate director Ruy Guerra staged a dramatic reconstruction of a notable massacre, 20 years earlier, of protesting villagers by the Portuguese colonial authorities in *Mueda—Memoria e Massacre.* In South Africa Ross Devenish directed an Athol Fugard script (his third collaboration with the distinguished playwright), *Marigolds in August.*

IRAN. Against all odds, films continued to emerge from Iran. The most notable was Bahram Beyzai's *The Ballad of Tara,* a fantasy of high visual quality about a girl confronted by a mysterious, perhaps ghostly, army.

IRAQ. Of Iraq's total production of seven feature films by the end of 1980, Jaisal Alyassiry had made three. His newest, *The Sniper,* was a highly contemporary and committed study of a young man so unbalanced by the general atmosphere of Beirut that he is turned into a compulsive killer.

ISRAEL. Daniel Wachsmann's *Transit* marked a breakthrough in Israeli cinema by its willingness to deal realistically with contemporary social issues. The film focused on the problem of Israel's German-born population, immigrants from the 1930s who in general still found integration into Israeli society more difficult than did others.

(DAVID ROBINSON)

Nontheatrical Motion Pictures. Two U.S. student films captured many awards throughout the world during the year. *Cabbages and Kings,* a 12-minute animated film by a group of students at the University of Southern California, Los Angeles, was honoured at international film festivals in Austria, Australia, France, New Zealand, and Portugal. Written and directed by Tim Landry, it is about the humbling of a haughty princess. The other noteworthy winner was *One,* a New York University student film. Robert Just was director, screenwriter, and editor, and Mark Tarnawsky was producer of the tale about a little boy's encounter with a street mime as he learns the power of imagination. The film won honours in Austria, Canada, Malta, and Portugal.

For its first prize, the International Film Producers Association chose *Survival Run,* a sensitive short subject about a blind runner directed by Robert Charlton for Magus Films of San Francisco.

An all-black film, written by Ernest Gaines, was the top winner of the American Film Festival. *The Sky Is Gray* is a short story of a young, poor black boy in the 1940s moving from childhood to manhood in Louisiana. An Australian film, *Frontline,* took the Grierson Award at the same festival. David Bradbury, a young cameraman, made the documentary about a fellow countryman, Neil Davis, who spent 11 years in Vietnam and Cambodia. (THOMAS W. HOPE)

See also Photography; Television and Radio.
[623; 735.G.2]

Motor Sports

Grand Prix Racing. The 1980 season of international Formula One racing continued, under the same technical rules as before. The Formula One Constructors Association was at times in conflict with the ruling Fédération Internationale du Sport Automobile (FISA), causing the Spanish Grand Prix result to be disallowed. The drivers' world championship was won by Australian-born Alan Jones, driving for the Saudi-Williams team.

The season opened at Buenos Aires with the Argentine Grand Prix, the winner being Jones, from Nelson Piquet of Brazil in a Brabham and Keke Rosberg (Fin.) in a new Fittapaldi. Jones opened in the form he was to maintain, making best lap at a speed of 194.527 kph. At São Paulo, Brazil, also in January, René Arnoux (France) gained his first grand prix victory in a turbocharged Renault over the Interlagos course. Arnoux made fastest lap, at 192.421 kph. Elio De Angelis (Italy) was second for Lotus, and third place went to Jones. The teams moved to Kyalami for the South African Grand Prix a month later, and there Renault was unassailable with Arnoux finishing first after achieving a fastest lap at 201.96 kph. Had not Jean-Pierre Jabouille (France) had a tire burst near the finish, the race would have been a walkover for the turbocharged, Michelin-shod Renaults. Even so it was a great French occasion, with Jacques Laffite's (France) Ligier second and Didier Pironi's (France) Ligier third.

The U.S. fielded the next race. At Long Beach, Calif., Piquet took the U.S. West Grand Prix, with fastest lap at 146.601 kph, Italian Riccardo Patrese's Arrows finishing second and Brazilian Emerson Fittipaldi's Fittipaldi third. The European racing began at Zolder with the Belgian Grand Prix in May, won by Pironi, although Laffite (Ligier) made best lap time at 189.703 kph. Jones finished second and Carlos Reutemann of Argentina, in a Williams, third. The Monaco race was a victory for Reutemann's Williams, which also had the fastest lap, 136.393 kph, under damp conditions. Laffite was second and Piquet third.

Formula One Grand Prix Race Results, 1980

Race	Driver	Car	Average speed
Argentine	A. Jones	Williams FW07B 4	183.443 kph
Brazilian	R. Arnoux	Renault RE21	189.933 kph
South African	R. Arnoux	Renault RE21	198.25 kph
U.S. West	N. Piquet	Brabham Bt49 06	142.385 kph
Belgian	D. Pironi	Ligier JS11 15 04	186.402 kph
Monaco	C. Reutemann	Williams FWO7B 5	136.393 kph
Spanish	A. Jones	Williams FWO7B 7	153.997 kph
French	A. Jones	Williams FWO7B 7	203.016 kph
British	A. Jones	Williams FWO7B 7	202.279 kph
German	J. Lafitte	Ligier JS11 15 03	220.826 kph
Austrian	J.-P. Jabouille	Renault RE23	223.196 kph
Dutch	N. Piquet	Brabham BT49 7	186.995 kph
Italian	N. Piquet	Brabham BT49 9	183.440 kph
Canadian	A. Jones	Williams FWO7 9	173.188 kph
U.S. East	A. Jones	Williams FWO7 9	203.494 kph

WORLD DRIVERS' CHAMPIONSHIP: Jones, 67 pt; Piquet, 54 pt; Reutemann, 42 pt (not counting Spanish Grand Prix).
CONSTRUCTORS' WORLD CHAMPIONSHIP: Williams-Cosworth-Ford, 120 pt; Ligier-Cosworth-Ford, 66 pt; Brabham-Cosworth-Ford, 55 pt.

A sorry dispute as to which organization should run the Spanish Grand Prix at Jarama made the race illegal in the eyes of Jean-Marie Balestre, president of the FISA, a verdict confirmed at a meeting of the governing Fédération Internationale de l'Automobile. So Jones had a hollow victory (and made best lap, at 157.994 kph) over Jochen Mass (West Germany) in an Arrows and De Angelis in a Lotus. The French Grand Prix, run over the Paul Ricard circuit, was won by Jones, who set a lap record of 206.171 kph.

In the British Grand Prix at Brands Hatch, Jones gained another victory for the Williams team, but

KEYSTONE

Alan Jones of Australia and his Formula One racing car clinched the Argentine Grand Prix title at Buenos Aires in January.

Motorboating: *see* Water Sports

Motor Industry: *see* Industrial Review

EFE/PHOTO TRENDS

Kenny Roberts of the U.S. leaned low on a curve during the Spanish Grand Prix for motorcycles at the two-mile Jarama Circuit near Madrid in May. Roberts was the winner of the 500-cc event.

only after Pironi had set a new lap record of 209.239 kph for Ligier. Pironi had tire trouble, however, and it was Piquet in a Brabham who placed second, ahead of Reutemann. There were many changes of fortune at Hockenheim during the German Grand Prix, the winner being Laffite's Ligier from Reutemann's Williams. Jones again drove brilliantly, but after making a lap record of 225.245 kph his Williams suffered from tire trouble, and he finished third.

In the Austrian Grand Prix at Zeltweg, Jabouille in the yellow turbocharged Renault beat Jones for first place. Finishing third was Reutemann. Arnoux set a new lap record in the other Renault, at 231.197 kph. In the Dutch Grand Prix at Zandvoort, Piquet won in a close finish with Arnoux, and Laffite placed third.

At Imola for the Italian Grand Prix, Piquet was troubled by a sticking throttle in the Ford engine of his Brabham, and Jones had braking problems. Piquet eventually won, thereby gaining a one-point championship lead over Jones. The latter, however, left no doubt about the championship at the Canadian Grand Prix, but it was a dramatic moment when his Williams brushed with Piquet's Parmalet-Brabham at the rush away from the starting grid. The race was restarted, with Piquet now using his spare car, but the engine failed while it was in the lead, two laps from the finish, and all Jones had to do was drive carefully to win the race and clinch the world championship. Reutemann finished second, ahead of Pironi, who was penalized for jumping the start signal but who had the fastest lap, at 185.90 kph.

Jones was to demonstrate that he was unquestionably a great champion at the last race of the season, the U.S. East Grand Prix, in which, after being shunted off at the first corner, he fought back to win and also set a new lap record of 208.115 kph for the Watkins Glen, N.Y., circuit. Again his teammate Reutemann followed him home, the Williams cars now dubbed Saudi-Leylands but still using Cosworth-Ford engines and Goodyear tires. As in Canada, Pironi's Ligier-Gitanes placed third. Overall, it was a relatively good grand prix season, though marked by political quarrels and a number of accidents, none of them fatal.

Rallying. Many leading manufacturers supported rallying, mostly with rather specialized cars. A dozen events constituted the world championship series. Of these, the Swedish was won by an Opel Ascona. Fiat 131 Abarths placed first and third in the Monte Carlo Rally, and Fiat also won the Portuguese rally. The tough Kenya Safari rally went to Datsun, with Ford scoring in the Acropolis and Fiat in the Coadasur and in the Rally of the 1,000 Lakes. The difficult New Zealand Motogard was a victory for Datsun, and the San Remo event was taken by a Fiat 131 Arbarth. A Porsche 911SC took the Tour de Corse, and before the two final rounds had been contested, the manufacturers' world championship had been secured by Fiat and the driver's world championship by the West German Fiat driver Walter Rohrl. The European champion was Antonio Zanini. The popular Royal Automobile Club (RAC) Lombard Rally was won by a Talbot-Sunbeam-Lotus, driven by Henri Toivenen of Finland.

(WILLIAM C. BODDY)

U.S. Racing. The marriage of convenience between CART (Championship Auto Racing Team) and USAC (United States Auto Club) broke down in midyear. The result was that spectator attendance, which seemed to be making a comeback despite the general economic conditions, sagged again. Johnny Rutherford, the Indianapolis 500 winner, was recognized as season champion by both organizations.

Rutherford won the Indianapolis 500 rather handily with an average speed of 230.008 kph (142.862 mph). He also won the pole position at

309.532 kph (192.256 mph). His margin of victory over second-place Tom Sneva was 29.58 sec as only 4 of the starting 33 finished the full 200 laps around the 2½-mi course. Rutherford's share of the $1,502,425 purse was $318,019.

Sneva, who started last, and third-place Gary Bettenhausen, who started next to last, earned $128,944 and $86,944, respectively. Fourth was Gordon Johncock and fifth was 1979 winner Rick Mears. It was Rutherford's third Indianapolis triumph, his other victories being in 1974 and 1976. Bobby Unser won the other two Triple Crown events, at Pocono in Pennsylvania and at Ontario, Calif.

In other USAC championships, Rich Vogler won the sprint car title easily from Steve Chassey but fought veteran Mel Kenyon to the final race in the midget division before taking that title as well. The USAC/SCCA (Sports Car Club of America) Mini-Indianapolis champ was Peter Kuhn, while Gary Bettenhausen was the dirt-car king, and Joe Ruttman won the stock-car title.

The National Association for Stock Car Auto Racing (NASCAR) weathered the economic storm somewhat better than USAC, thanks to a season-long race for the Winston Cup crown. In the end it came down to a contest between the veteran Cale Yarborough and young Dale Earnhardt. Yarborough had won the Atlanta 500 and the American 500 at Rockingham to draw within 29 points of Earnhardt. But at the Ontario 500, last race of the season, he finished third while Earnhardt placed fifth to win the Winston Cup by only 19 points. Earnhardt had 5 Winston victories and 14 other finishes among the top 5 drivers in 31 races. Yarborough had six victories and the same number of top five finishes. Third for the season was Benny Parsons; Richard Petty was fourth.

Buddy Baker won the pole position and the Daytona 500 to begin the Winston Cup season's classics. But he won again only in the spring Talladega (Ala.) race. Among the most interesting victories was that by Neil Bonnett at Pocono. He purposely weaved down Pocono's main straight to block would-be passers. Veteran Bobby Allison scored four victories during the season, including the Daytona Firecracker 400.

This was the final year of "big" stock cars for NASCAR. For 1981 wheelbases would be downsized five inches to 110.

John Fitzpatrick of Great Britain, driving a Porsche 935 Turbo, won the Sebring, Fla., Grand Prix en route to the GT championship of the International Motor Sports Association (IMSA). His co-driver was car owner Dick Barbour of San Diego, Calif. Winners of the 24 Hours of Daytona were Germans Volkert Merl, Reinhold Joest, and Rolf Stommelin. Patrick Tambay of France easily won the SCCA Citicorp Can Am series. The revised Trans-Am title went to John Bauer in a Porsche 911SC. (ROBERT J. FENDELL)

Motorcycles. Riding a Yamaha, Kenny Roberts of the U.S. was 500-cc world champion for the third successive time in 1980, strongly challenged by Randy Mamola (U.S.), riding for Suzuki. Eugenio Lazzarini (Iprem) of Italy won the 50-cc class, Paulo Bianchi (MBA) of Italy the 125-cc, T. Anton Mang (Kawasaki) of West Germany the 250-cc, and Jon Ekerold (Yamaha) of South Africa the 350-cc. Jock Taylor (Scotland) and Benga Johansson (Sweden) won the sidecar world championship on a Yamaha.

In Tourist Trophy (TT) races, New Zealander Graeme Crosby (Suzuki) was world champion in Formula One, Charlie Williams (Yamaha) in Formula Two, and Ron Haslam (Honda) in Formula Three. Joey Dunlop of the U.K. (Yamaha) won the Classic TT race. Taylor and Johansson won the Isle of Man sidecar TT. In long-distance racing, the French Honda-Minolta team of Marc Fontan and Hervé Moineau won the world endurance championship. France lost three riders: Olivier Chevallier, Patrick Pons, and Jean-Bernard Peyre.

Motocross world champions were Belgians André Malherbe (Honda), 500-cc; Georges Jobe (Suzuki), 250-cc; and Harry Everts (Suzuki), 125-cc. Belgian teams also won the Trophée des Nations in Italy and the Moto Cross des Nations in England. The 1980 speedway world champion was Michael Lee (Britain), and Britain won the world team cup event in Poland. (CYRIL J. AYTON)

See also Water Sports.
[452.B.4.c]

Mountaineering

The Chinese Mountaineering Association announced in September 1979 that eight mountain groups were to be made available for foreign expeditions—Everest and Xixabangma in Tibet; Muztagata, Kongur, Kongur Tiubie, and Bogda Ola in Xinjiang (Sinkiang) Uygur Autonomous Region; Gongga in Sichuan (Szechwan) Province; and Anyemaqen in Qinghai (Tsinghai) Province—under conditions similiar to those in countries such as Nepal. The cost for servicing such expeditions was extremely high; for example, the budget for the 1980 Japanese Alpine Club expedition to Ever-

(From top to bottom) John Mitchell and Alexander Wilson of Scotland and Patrick Parsons of England posed triumphantly after their successful climb up the northwest face of the 6,250-metre (20,500-foot) Mt. Phabrang in the Himalayas in October.

PRESS ASSOCIATION

est exceeded 400 million yen, more than U.S. $2 million. This expedition climbed the mountain in May 1980 by the north col-northeast ridge route pioneered by prewar British expeditions and completed by Chinese-Tibetan expeditions, probably first in 1960 and certainly in 1975. The Japanese went on to make a direct route up the north face, finishing via the Hornbein couloir on the American west route. This was the seventh separate route up the mountain.

Later the Italian Reinhold Messner (*see* BIOGRAPHIES) repeated the north col-northeast ridge route. His ascent to the summit and return to an advanced base camp at 6,450 m (21,300 ft) took three days. The first fully solo ascent was made during the monsoon without oxygen.

On the Nepalese side of Everest, a West German expedition ascended the normal route by the south col after the monsoon in 1979. Of the summit party of four (of whom one was a woman—the fourth woman to climb the mountain—and two were Sherpas), only the Sherpas survived. Early in 1980 a Polish expedition repeated the south col route, the first winter ascent of Everest, and later made a new route (the sixth) by the south pillar, between the south col and southwest face routes.

Much was made in the press of the discovery by a Chinese climber (since killed) of the body of a so-far unidentified climber high on Everest during a Japanese reconnaissance of the Tibetan side. It was perhaps the same body found by Chinese climbers near the north col in 1960, which may have been that of the Briton Maurice Wilson who attempted the mountain alone in 1934.

Elsewhere in the Himalayas after the 1979 monsoon, first ascents were made of Nuptse north face (British), Makalu II east ridge from north col (West Germans), Gaurishankar south summit by southwest ridge (British-Swiss), Annapurna III southwest ridge (British), and Ganesh II (Japanese-Nepalese, by north face). Before the monsoon in 1980 first ascents were made of Kanchenjunga north face direct (Japanese), Dhaulagiri I east face (British-French-Polish), Ganesh V (Japanese-Nepalese), Fang (Austrians), Baruntse east ridge (Spanish), and Lamjung Himal north ridge (new route by Japanese). (JOHN NEILL)

Mozambique

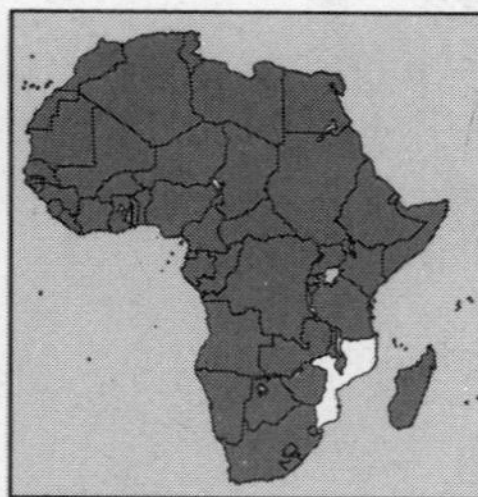
Mozambique

An independent African state, the People's Republic of Mozambique is located on the southeast coast of Africa, bounded by the Indian Ocean, Tanzania, Malawi, Zambia, Zimbabwe, South Africa, and Swaziland. Area: 799,380 sq km (308,642 sq mi). Pop. (1980 est.): 12,375,000. Cap. and largest city: Maputo (pop., 1980 est., 750,000). Language: Portuguese (official); Bantu languages predominate. Religion: traditional beliefs 65%, Christian about 21%, Muslim 10%, with Hindu, Buddhist, and Jewish minorities. President in 1980, Samora Machel.

The frontier with Zimbabwe Rhodesia was officially reopened on Jan. 12, 1980, marking the first stage in a new relationship between the two countries, which had been effectively at war for several years. Ten weeks later Lord Soames, governor of Zimbabwe Rhodesia, visited Mozambique at the invitation of Pres. Samora Machel, who had made an important behind-the-scenes contribution to the negotiations leading to Zimbabwe's constitutional settlement.

The invitation to Lord Soames and the discussion that took place between him and the president reflected the growing willingness of the government of Mozambique to contemplate some return to free enterprise and to closer relations with Western countries. In February a group of businessmen representing a number of multinational companies had visited Mozambique and had held discussions with Machel and some of his ministers. The president, while reasserting his commitment to a socialist program, had taken the opportunity to emphasize the benefits Mozambique could derive from the technology and expertise of multinational organizations, the activities of which could be controlled without preventing the companies from making adequate profits. In fact, joint enterprises involving Mozambican and foreign participants had already been launched. As a result of Soames's visit, it was hoped that there might be further foreign involvement in the development of Mozambique's economy. Soames himself suggested that the European Economic Community (EEC) might assist in rehabilitating the railway system, and there were discussions about the possibility of Mozambique becoming a member of the Lomé Convention. This possibility was also discussed at the Southern Africa Development Conference held in Maputo in November.

In an important speech on March 18, President Machel publicly criticized members of his administration and leaders of the Frelimo party for their corruption and inefficiency and dismissed three of his ministers as part of a drive against

MOZAMBIQUE

Education. (1978) Primary, pupils 1.5 million; secondary, pupils 80,000; higher (1976–77), students 906, teaching staff 164.

Finance and Trade. Monetary unit: metical (new currency, introduced in June 1980 to replace the former escudo at par), with (Sept. 22, 1980) a free rate of 28 meticals to U.S. $1 (68 meticals = £1 sterling). Budget (1978 est.): revenue 10,042,000,000 meticals; expenditure 12,642,000,000 meticals. Foreign trade (1977): imports 10,568,000,000 meticals; exports 4,909,000,000 meticals. Import sources: South Africa 20%; West Germany 15%; Portugal 10%; Iraq 9%; U.K. 7%; Japan 5%. Export destinations: U.S. 27%; Portugal 16%; U.K. 7%; South Africa 7%; The Netherlands 6%; Japan 5%. Main exports: cashew nuts 30%; textiles 9%; tea 8%; cotton 6%; sugar 5%.

Transport and Communications. Roads (1974) 39,173 km. Motor vehicles in use (1977): passenger 107,900; commercial (including buses) 24,700. Railways: (1979) 3,933 km; traffic (1975) 210 million passenger-km, freight (1974) 2,180,000,000 net ton-km. Air traffic (1978): 433 million passenger-km; freight 6.7 million net ton-km. Telephones (Jan. 1977) 52,300. Radio licenses (Dec. 1977) 230,000. Television receivers (Dec. 1977) 1,200.

Agriculture. Production (in 000; metric tons; 1979): corn *c.* 350; sorghum *c.* 180; cassava (1978) *c.* 2,450; peanuts *c.* 80; sugar, raw value *c.* 200; copra *c.* 75; bananas *c.* 65; cashew nuts (1978) *c.* 150; tea *c.* 16; cotton, lint *c.* 28; sisal *c.* 18. Livestock (in 000; 1978): cattle *c.* 1,370; sheep *c.* 100; goats *c.* 325; pigs *c.* 105; chickens *c.* 17,000.

Industry. Production (in 000; metric tons; 1977): coal *c.* 450; petroleum products (1978) 357; bauxite *c.* 5; cement *c.* 220; electricity (kw-hr) *c.* 4,940,000.

corruption started in January. The next day he announced the abolition of "people's shops" and said that their services would be provided by small private businesses. This encouraged many who had suffered in silence from bureaucratic inefficiency to give voice to their criticisms, but it did not indicate a fundamental change in political direction. A socialist state was still the goal, but Machel appeared to have accepted that rigid socialist policies must be modified when this would achieve greater efficiency. On June 16–18 Mozambique changed its currency from the escudo to the metical, at the same value.

Toward the end of May discussions took place between senior defense officers from Mozambique and Zimbabwe with a view to providing mutual assistance. Mozambique was anxious for Zimbabwe's aid in dealing with the remnants of the Mozambican National Resistance (MNR) guerrillas, who continued to operate in the Manica, Sofala, and Tete provinces and who were thought to have a base in Zimbabwe. Although the activities of the guerrillas were crippled by a prolonged Mozambican offensive against them in June, a considerable military force still had to be deployed to keep them in check. Relations with South Africa remained steady in spite of verbal recriminations over the support that each claimed the other was giving to its enemies. The significant economic links between the two countries exerted a more important influence upon their relations than did arguments over assistance given to guerrillas.

(KENNETH INGHAM)

Museums

United States. Museum activity in the U.S. only partially reflected the problems of world inflation. Both the intense pace of exhibition schedules and the pervasive funding campaigns for future construction and general museum support indicated the unaltered importance of the museum in the nation's cultural life.

On the West Coast the Seattle (Wash.) Art Museum began a $23 million campaign for new construction, while in Los Angeles the newly organized Museum of Modern Art was given $2 million by its founding trustees to launch a $10 million endowment program. Also, the Los Angeles County Museum of Art announced that it planned to build a new gallery to house the Armand Hammer Daumier collection, the world's largest such archive collection. The Ahmanson Foundation offered the County Museum $4.5 million to fund additional construction for the Ahmanson Gallery.

In the South the High Museum in Atlanta, Ga., was given $7.5 million by an anonymous donor as a challenge grant toward the estimated $15 million cost of proposed new facilities. A new $25 million cultural complex in Miami, Fla., was to include, at a cost of $3.5 million, the Center for the Fine Arts, a 1,850-sq-m (20,000-sq-ft) exhibition area with no permanent collection. Voters in Dallas, Texas, reacted to a carefully planned press campaign and approved the funding of a new Dallas Museum of Fine Arts; $24.8 million would be the public share of the $40 million building.

In the East the Virginia Museum of the Fine Arts in Richmond received 200 works from Mr. and Mrs. Paul Mellon and $2.2 million toward a $10 million building to house both that collection and the 1,500 Art Nouveau and Art Deco objects donated by Sydney and Frances Lewis. A nationwide campaign, the White House Preservation Fund, was begun to establish a permanent endowment of $25 million to provide the finest U.S. art and antiques to furnish the White House. This would make the White House a major museum and break

On June 11 the Metropolitan Museum of Art in New York City opened its new American Wing. A series of period rooms, such as the Baltimore Room (left) and an enclosed sculpture garden court (right), were highlights of the new structure, which was built around the old American Wing.

(LEFT) THE METROPOLITAN MUSEUM OF ART; PHOTO, RICHARD CHEEK; (RIGHT) THE METROPOLITAN MUSEUM OF ART; PHOTO, HENRY GROSKINSKY

COURTESY, CORNING MUSEUM OF GLASS, CORNING, NEW YORK

On June 1 the Corning Museum of Glass in Corning, New York, opened its new building designed by architect Gunnar Birkerts.

its traditional dependence upon private and temporary donations for decor. In New York City the Museum of Modern Art presented a $40 million bond issue, offered by the Trust for Cultural Resources, to fund gallery expansion, including a new skyscraper tower on its grounds. After five years of construction the Metropolitan Museum of Art opened its $18 million American Wing, which, when completed, would cover some 13,950 sq m (150,000 sq ft), about six times the size of the old wing.

In the Middle West the Detroit Institute of Arts moved closer toward its goal of renovation and modernization by 1985 by opening its new graphic art centre and its new ethnographic galleries. The Grand Rapids (Mich.) Art Museum was to move into greatly expanded quarters in a four-story, former governmental building. In Evanston, Ill., just north of Chicago, the Terra Museum of American Art opened. Named for its founder, who donated the museum's building and whose private collection was on permanent loan, the institution would be devoted to American art of the 19th and early 20th centuries.

Major acquisitions by U.S. museums included the purchase for a reported $1 million by the Whitney Museum of American Art in New York City of the 1958 painting "Three Flags" by Jasper Johns, one of the most expensive works by a living American artist ever bought. The Kimbell Art Museum in Fort Worth, Texas, set a record for a work of Cezanne when it paid $3.9 million for "Peasant in a Blue Smock"; and $3.7 million was paid by the Norton Simon Museum in Pasadena, Calif., for a 15th-century Flemish work, "The Resurrection" by Dieric Bouts.

Several important archaeological exhibitions were staged. The Detroit Institute of Arts offered "Treasures of Ancient Nigeria," the largest loan exhibition ever sent to the U.S. from an African nation. "The Great Bronze Age of China: An Exhibition from the People's Republic of China" opened at the Metropolitan Museum of Art and later traveled across the country. Including much recently uncovered material, it marked the first joint effort between scholars in the U.S. and China.

(JOSHUA B. KIND)

United Kingdom. The Museum of the Year award for 1980 was given to the British Museum (Natural History) in London. It was the first time in eight years that the honour had gone to a national museum, and the choice was a controversial one. The award seemed justified, however, for a museum whose new management, over the last few years, had made it into an exciting and lively place by using modern exhibition techniques to inform and educate a nonacademic public. New projects that had opened there in recent years included a section devoted to human biology, an introduction to ecology, dinosaurs and their living relatives, and man's place in evolution. An award of £2,000 went to the museum.

In June a celebration was held to mark the refitting and modernization program of the National Maritime Museum at Greenwich, London, which had taken over ten years to carry out. As a result the museum was now an important research centre for maritime history. It encompassed both arts and sciences and included a picture gallery, historic house, and centre for archaeological research.

The new London Transport Museum in Covent Garden, London, exhibited streetcars, buses, and trains, along with graphic material formerly at the Clapham Museum of British Transport. The new museum was in the building that was originally the Covent Garden flower market.

Other Nations. In Paris plans were well under way for a new museum to be devoted to the art and civilization of the 19th century. It was scheduled to open in 1983. The plans reflected the long-term museological planning of the French government, and when completed the museum would ease the overcrowding currently causing difficulties in the Jeu de Paume and the Louvre. The Jeu de Paume would in the future be used for temporary exhibitions. The new museum would complete the "Louvre-Orsay-Beaubourg" grouping, in which the Louvre would house objects from antiquity to the early 19th century; the Beaubourg (the Centre National d'Art et de Culture Georges Pompidou) most 20th-century material; and the Orsay painting, sculpture, architecture, graphics, and applied arts from most of the 19th century to the early 20th century.

The new museum would occupy the former railway station, the Gare d'Orsay, which was originally built for the 1900 Paris Universal Exhibition. The auctioneers and theatre that had occupied the premises since the railway moved were themselves being rehoused. The architects for the interior of the new museum were Colboc, Bardon, and Philippon, whose plans made full use of the natural lighting provided by the iron and glass vault of the former station.

In June the *Museums Journal* featured two museums devoted to wine—the Musée du Vin at Pauillac, near Bordeaux, France, and the Museo del Vino at Torgiano, Umbria, Italy. Both were long-established private museums founded by proprietors of famous vineyards and located within those vineyards. At the Musée du Vin visitors could enjoy looking at a series of splendid objects inspired by wine and viticulture. The Italian museum had a series of 14 rooms tracing the origins of viticulture from antiquity to modern times. There was also a fine display of medieval ceramics. Most wine-producing countries, surprisingly, lacked museums devoted to viticulture.

(SANDRA MILLIKIN)

See also Art Exhibitions; Art Sales.
[613.D.1.b]

Music

Classical. SYMPHONIC MUSIC. Zubin Mehta's work with a variable-sounding New York Philharmonic again elicited mixed opinions, the divided views of U.S. critics being reflected with striking clarity when the orchestra visited the 1980 Edinburgh International Festival. Mehta began controversially with the European premiere of Polish composer Kryzstof Penderecki's overtly simplistic Second Symphony, an enigmatic, downbeat piece based entirely on the old Austrian Christmas carol "Silent Night." His choice exasperated widespread sections of the British musical press and posed once again the question as to which direction this one-time enfant terrible of new music was taking. It must have been doubly chastening for the Philharmonic's managers to find press opinion no less scathing in its criticism of Mehta's subsequent bland, slackly managed reading of Beethoven's "Eroica" Symphony.

Elsewhere, Carlo Maria Giulini continued to reign supreme at Los Angeles, the city's Philharmonic continuing its leisurely, largely unadventurous exploration of mainstream European classics under the Italian maestro's elegant baton. If Los Angeles experienced a blending of New World brilliance with mid-European line and warmth, Sir Georg Solti's continuing directorship at Chicago found an admittedly spectacular-sounding symphony orchestra in 1979–80 moving even further from its Fritz Reiner-nurtured Viennese roots and emerging too often as a merely brash and garish instrument. In Boston Seiji Ozawa and Sir Colin Davis drew, respectively, civilized and turgid playing from a generally healthy-sounding symphony orchestra. In Philadelphia outgoing maestro Eugene Ormandy stayed long enough to commit to disc the Philadelphia Orchestra's first digitally engineered recording (an exciting account for RCA of Bela Bartok's *Concerto for Orchestra*). Eduardo Mata, a rising hopeful in RCA's checklist of house conductors, was to be found tackling Ravel, Stravinsky, and Copland with a newly impressive Dallas Symphony. It was still too early to say whether the appointment of Neville Marriner (*see* BIOGRAPHIES) as principal conductor of the Minnesota Symphony would achieve a similar renaissance there.

In the U.K. the orchestral scene was sadly dominated not by live music but by a headline-making labour dispute of a kind usually reserved for the country's strikebound automobile industry. For weeks before the season of BBC-sponsored Henry

TERRENCE MCCARTHY—THE NEW YORK TIMES

The Louise M. Davies Symphony Hall opened in September as part of a $38 million Performing Arts Center in San Francisco.

Wood Promenade concerts was due to begin at London's Royal Albert Hall, it had been touch and go as to whether Britain's national broadcasting organization would resolve its quarrel over cost-cutting and layoffs with members of the Musicians' Union. In the end a potentially magnificent first night, with BBC principal conductor Gennadi Rozhdestvensky directing Sir Edward Elgar's rarely staged oratorio *The Apostles,* was canceled along with a host of other programs.

Acrimony between the warring parties reached the breaking point with the promotion at the Wembley Conference Centre in northwest London of a widely publicized if slimly attended series of union-sponsored "pirate Proms" that featured renegade members of the BBC's leading symphony orchestra under such guest conductors as Simon Rattle and Sir Colin Davis and such top-line soloists as pianists Cristina Ortiz and Tamas Vasary. Only after weeks had been wiped off the proposed season did the "Proms" go ahead following a settlement of the dispute. Surviving highlights included first performances of Sir Michael Tippett's richly translucent *Concerto* for violin, viola, and cello and an Eleventh Symphony by the neglected English master Edmund Rubbra.

Other notable events in a season during which U.K. audience attendance slumped (a process exacerbated, promoters argued, by a newly introduced tax supplement on seat prices) were the increasingly frequent and impressive appearances by East German conductor Klaus Tennstedt with the London Philharmonic Orchestra; the celebrations surrounding the 50th birthday of the BBC Symphony Orchestra; and the adoption by the Philharmonia Orchestra under its new general manager, Christopher Bishop, of a Chicago Symphony-style subscription series. By the year's end the last move showed signs of proving a distinct success. John Williams (*see* BIOGRAPHIES), best known for composing the scores of such motion pictures as *Star Wars* and *Jaws,* succeeded the late Arthur Fiedler as conductor of the Boston Pops.

OPERA. The 1979–80 operatic season was again one of averages, new productions falling on hard times as old favourites were wheeled out for another, often feeble bite at the turnstiles. In New York City the moderate success early in the year of the Metropolitan Opera's *Don Carlo* was completely obliterated by an explosion of anger by the company's orchestra and chorus over pay scales and length of the workweek. This conflict with management led to a move unprecedented in the Met's 96-year history, the peremptory cancellation late in September by Executive Director Anthony Bliss of the entire 1980–81 season. Negotiations continued throughout the fall, however, and settlements were achieved with the orchestra, chorus, and other groups. On December 10, more than two months late, the Met opened its season with a concert of Mahler's "Resurrection" Symphony. The first opera, Alban Berg's complete *Lulu,* was given its New York premiere on December 12.

In May 1980 the Paris Opéra and La Scala, Milan, entered into a formal partnership, with shared productions and other activities envisaged. Chief promoter of this arrangement was the Opéra's new administrator-designate, Bernard Lefort, who planned to extend its range by means of an ambitious program of tours and television productions. A European highlight of the year was the staging by the Théâtre des Champs-Élysées, as part of a wide-ranging Stravinsky festival, of *The Rake's Progress* in the brilliantly successful David Hockney-designed Glyndebourne Opera production from England.

A particular pleasure in the U.K. was the revival at the 1980 Brighton Festival in Sussex (by the hitherto little-recognized New Sussex Opera) of the original small-scale version of Mussorgsky's *Boris Godunov,* an imaginative choice whose short run at the Cardner Centre at the University of Sussex garnered universal critical praise and made the more widely publicized attempts of some major professional companies seem sadly lacking in comparison. Covent Garden's Royal Opera and the English National Opera both experienced lean times in 1980, the Garden's weakness for importing big-name casts that failed to jell culminating in a particularly disappointing revival of the Götz Friedrich production of Wagner's *Der Ring des Nibelungen* and some unimpressive Verdi and Donizetti. At the English National imaginative revivals of Richard Strauss's *Arabella,* Benjamin Britten's *The Turn of the Screw, Boris Godunov,* and Puccini's *La Bohème* in the unrivaled Jean-Claud Auvray production were offset by calamitous stagings of *Fidelio* and Offenbach's *La Belle Hélène* and dull ones of *Don Giovanni* and *The Magic Flute.*

At the Bayreuth festival Patrice Chéreau's grimly avant-garde *Ring* and *Flying Dutchman* again delighted Wagnerphiles on their annual pilgrimage. Joseph Losey's feature film of Mozart's *Don Giovanni,* highly thought of and intelligently criticized elsewhere, at last reached London, only to be met with a battery of critical obtuseness from the movie reviewers. Expertly produced by Hal Prince, Stephen Sondheim's semioperatic Broadway hit *Sweeney Todd* also came to London but folded after only a short run. In October soprano Beverly Sills made her last appearance on the opera stage in a special performance in New York of the party scene from *Die Fledermaus.*

ALBUMS. If live music came under pressure during 1980, whole areas of the record industry seemed headed for oblivion. With consumer volume falling dramatically across the board, the biggest trade news came early in the year with the dismemberment and subsequent absorption into the giant Polygram empire of the once mighty London Decca house: a sad event for all its inevitability, compounded by the sudden death during the final takeover of the company's virtual founder and long-time commander, Sir Edward Lewis. Another death was that of John Culshaw (*see* OBITUARIES), another important figure in the recording industry, who was for many years connected with Decca.

Another striking trend as 1980 drew to a close, explored in depth in the British trade magazine *Classical Music* by *The Times*'s music critic Paul Griffiths, was the comparative success that small, privately owned record companies such as Chandos, Saga, Unicorn, and Nimbus were having in markets unexplored by the accountant-dominated big names. Notable also was the sharp reduction in new classical output released during the year by the two U.S. giants, RCA and Columbia CBS, the latter's ailing European operations reportedly coming under particularly close scrutiny. The U.S. classical recording industry seemed to be suffering from a dearth of imaginative leadership, with a consequent lowering of artistic standards.

Of special interest from a technical point of view was the appearance of the first widely marketed batch of digitally recorded long-playing records, digitalism being a high-technology system in which musical impulses are encoded directly onto computer tape in the studio without recourse to the supposedly "distorting" medium of analogue tape decks. By the end of the 1970s a number of small U.S. labels had already issued impressive digital material, but it was only with the entry into the ring during 1979–80 of the international names—London Decca, HMV Angel, DG, Columbia CBS, and RCA—that a by now wary public, hooked a few years previously by the false messiah of quadrophony, had a chance to sample (and marvel at) the truthfulness, clarity, and freshness achieved by a process hailed increasingly as the single most important technological breakthrough since stereo and the introduction of the Dolby noise-reduction system. This did not, however, halt the debate, fueled by steeply rising vinyl costs and higher store prices, over pressing and packaging quality. Too often, collectors believed, top-drawer classical albums at premium prices were being supplied with inferior annotation and flimsy jackets. As far as pressing quality went, Dutch, West German, and Japanese discs were again believed to be leading the field, with the U.K. ranking somewhere in the middle and France and the U.S.—the HMV subsidiaries Pathé-Marconi and Angel especially—falling heavily to the bottom of the pile.

Outstanding among the year's much-reduced output of classical albums were first recordings of Verdi's early *Stiffelio* and *Aroldo* (Philips, Columbia CBS); complete cycles of the Debussy *Melodies* and Chopin piano music, the latter from Herbert von Karajan (DG, HMV Angel); a complete set recorded "live" by the direct-cut process of the Beethoven sonatas played by English pianist Bernard Roberts (Nimbus); the Amsterdam Concertgebouw Orchestra's first recording for HMV Angel, the Brahms Double Concerto featuring soloists Itzhak Perlman and Mstislav Rostropovich and conducted by Bernard Haitink; the premier recording, by Sir Adrian Boult and the London Philharmonic, of Sir Hubert Parry's Fifth Symphony (HMV); and a reading by 78-year-old Swiss baritone Hugues Cuénod of Erik Satie's esoteric *Socrate* (Nimbus), which took first prize in the important Prix Mondiale du Disque de Montreux, held annually in Switzerland. (MOZELLE A. MOSHANSKY)

Jazz. If any review of jazz music in 1980 has about it a retrospective air, it is simply because the music itself has for some years either been marking time or, in the case of the more desperate avant-gardists, ignoring time altogether in an attempt to find fresh approaches. None of those fresh approaches has so far been particularly fruitful. Neither the abandonment of barlines, nor the use of modal structures instead of harmonic sequences, nor the reduction of those sequences to a virtual pendulum swing between two basic chords proved very satisfactory, which meant that in the meantime jazz music continued to live off its assets. Those assets, however, are unusually rich, and it would be misleading to assume that because nothing new has been particularly valuable the music is doomed to an imminent death.

In recent decades jazz has successfully evolved several styles, which have grown one out of another like the links in a chain. If the chain is now complete, or appears to have stopped extending itself for the moment, the improviser is still left with a choice between several equally attractive styles, and the selection he makes will depend less upon fashionable trends than on the vagaries of his own sensibility. There has never been any reason why several jazz styles should not flourish concurrently, and if during 1980 few sensational innovations appeared then at least there were several noteworthy revivals. As one example among many, the multi-instrumentalist Bob Wilber perfected a style with his soprano saxophone that was a remarkable facsimile of the best work of the late Johnny Hodges, while his clarinet playing evoked memories of the flawless Benny Goodman of the 1930s.

There is no reason why this type of tribute, by the present to the past, should not apply to groups as well as individuals, and it is significant in this regard that during 1981 Wilber hoped to reconstruct the repertoire and the instrumentation of the old Benny Goodman orchestra. A related case was that of the alto-saxophonist Art Pepper, a disciple of the Charlie Parker school of playing, whose *Blues for the Fisherman* proved to be one of the most popular jazz albums of 1980. (The fact that it was issued under the banner of the group's pianist, Milcho Leviev, should mislead nobody; the guiding light was Pepper's, and the curious tactic of attributing the album to one of its participants is explained by the rules attaching to exclusivity clauses in recording contracts.)

Among the year's most rewarding pleasures were Oscar Peterson's piano playing, Joe Pass's extraordinarily brilliant guitar solos, the forthright, frippery-free tenor saxophone solos of Zoot Sims, and the apparently inexhaustible youthful spirits of Dizzy Gillespie. The past vied with this brilliance, and on the tribute front there was no gesture more satisfying than the reissuing of five albums of Count Basie recordings featuring the finest work of the late Lester Young, whose influence on two generations of tenor saxophonists has been both benign and prolific.

Among the deaths in 1980, one of the saddest was that of the old Duke Ellington clarinetist Leon Albany "Barney" Bigard, who between 1928 and 1942 became an integral part of the Ellington orchestrating texture. It would probably be true to say that his work suffered after he left Ellington to become a small-group soloist, and that to be heard at its best it required the cushion of Ellington's orchestral settings. Another big-band casualty was the drummer Jimmy Crawford, remembered for the vitality of his playing with the old Jimmie Lunceford band between 1929 and 1942. The death of pianist Bill Evans came as a surprise, even though his health had appeared to be in decline for some years. Even at his best Evans tended toward a condition of invertebrate rhythmic lassitude, but in the harmonic sense he was at times a profound thinker and a keyboard exponent of great subtlety. (BENNY GREEN)

Popular. The year's most significant event was the murder of John Lennon (*see* OBITUARIES), the former Beatle, who was shot dead by a 25-year-old security guard, Mark Chapman, in New York City

Metropolitan Opera orchestra musicians picketed at Lincoln Center in New York City in October after their demands for higher wages and increased benefits were not met. A settlement was reached in time to save most of the productions planned for the season.

HOWARD HEYMAN—NEWSWEEK

on December 8. Chapman had apparently fantasized that he was Lennon, and so he wanted to kill the "imposter." Throughout the world the reaction was extraordinary, reminiscent of the aftermath of the assassination of U.S. Pres. John Kennedy rather than the death of a pop music star.

But then John Lennon was no ordinary pop star. Both in his work with the Beatles, the most popular group in the history of popular music, and in his later solo career, he had proved to be a prolific, original, and pioneering songwriter. At 40 he was just reemerging into the music business after five years of inactivity. A new album, *Double Fantasy* (on which he shared the billing with his wife, Yoko Ono), had been released two weeks before his death. It was by no means his greatest work, consisting of pleasant, mellow ballads about the pleasures of retirement and his love for his wife and son, but it showed that Lennon could still write strong songs and, above all, that he could still use the often cliché-filled medium of the popular song to express his feelings with remarkable honesty.

Honesty in his work and a sincere belief in the worth of what he was doing were two of Lennon's strongest characteristics. He could also be sardonic, passionate, bitter, funny, and idealistic. Those qualities, mixed with a love for pop music that began when he heard black U.S. rhythm and blues imports brought into Liverpool by sailors, were reflected in his unpredictable, patchy, but often brilliant work.

In his appearance, his attitudes, and his music Lennon was always changing, reflecting, from one jump ahead, the dizzy and traumatic youth revolution of the 1960s. With the Beatles Lennon went from being a tough rock and roller playing in rough clubs to an entertainer with a vast worldwide following. Then he went from respected songwriter to misunderstood semi-hippie mystic, as he threw himself into drugs and Indian religion with characteristic enthusiasm. As a soloist, in the 1970s, he staged bizarre happenings for peace and threw his energies behind a variety of causes.

It was a sad end to a bad year for the music industry, in which record sales had slumped by 30% and record companies merged, laid off staff, or cut back on their operations. It was ironic, though, that as the major companies contracted, a whole new group of independent firms ("the indies") flourished as never before. The "indies," such as Rough Trade in London or Factory and Zoo in Manchester, England, made no long-term plans for promoting artists and no long-term contracts. Instead, they signed artists for one record at a time, recording them as cheaply as possible and often dividing profits evenly with them.

WIDE WORLD

The Charlie Daniels (centre) Band won the Grammy Award for best country vocal performance by a group in February in Los Angeles for their hit "The Devil Went Down to Georgia."

The British music scene in 1980 was more fragmented than ever, and much British music seemed out of step with American taste, which appeared bland and safe in comparison. The "post-punk" era of optimistic, "do-it-yourself" music continued, with new bands springing up all over the country but with a far greater degree of musical sophistication than when punk first emerged in 1976–77. Many of the most successful bands consisted of white or multiracial groups reviving or reworking earlier black styles. Thus, The Police, one of the most popular British bands of the year, based their music around reggae rhythms. Ska, the Jamaican style that predated reggae, also continued to be an influence. The Specials, a multiracial band from Coventry, were leaders in that area, mixing cheerful ska rhythms with lyrics that blended social comment with humour.

Another revivalist form that flourished during the year was rhythm and blues. R&B—the amplified blues style that developed in Chicago during the 1940s and later became one of the basic ingredients in rock 'n' roll—had always remained a major force in popular music. But in the latest revival bands like The Blues Band (led by Paul Jones, once singer with Manfred Mann), or the younger 9 Below Zero, took their mood and inspiration from the white British bands of the mid-1960s "R&B boom," while also reinterpreting earlier R&B material. Nostalgia was also invoked by exponents of "new soul music," which echoed the great gospel-inspired black styles of the 1960s—though mostly without their power or freshness.

On a more experimental front there was a move toward all-electronic bands, with extensive use made of synthesizers. While the new ska bands tended to come from the English Midlands, many of the more experimental or electronics-influenced bands were from the north of England. Gary Numan, with his bleak, futuristic, and theatrical style, became the best-known "electronics" artist, but both The Human League, from Sheffield, and Orchestral Maneouvres In the Dark, from Liverpool, could be argued to have taken the style much further. The finest, and most commercially successful, of the new bands from the Northwest was Joy Division, whose second album, *Closer*, became the biggest seller for any "indie" label. But the future of the band was in doubt after the suicide of Ian Curtis, the band's singer, just before the album was released.

With all those revivals and experiments providing the year's most adventurous developments in British pop music, the most commercially successful style was Heavy Metal. Attacked by their critics as brash, overloud, and oversimple and for their pounding "head-banging" music, such bands as Whitesnake, Motorhead, or Australia's AC/DC sold records in enormous quantities. The "old wave" of previously established artists still soldiered on, and Cliff Richard—now 40—continued to pack concert halls and make hit singles. A great tragedy among established artists was the death of Led Zeppelin's drummer John Bonham (*see* OBITUARIES). The most expensive and spectacular shows of the year were provided by Pink Floyd, who went firmly against prevailing trends by performing their concept work *The Wall* at London's Earl's Court. This multimedia extravaganza cost the band $2 million.

On the recording front there was a new and impressive album from David Bowie, *Scary Monsters*, on which he proved himself to be still dazzlingly unpredictable but highly commercial. An unexpected move was the departure of Jon Anderson and Rick Wakeman from Yes and their replacement by Trevor Horn and Geoff Downes, who had previously made novelty pop singles under the name Buggles.

In the U.S., also, the record industry faced a slump in sales, but there was little sign of a "new wave" of styles to match the changing scene in Britain. The disco craze began to wane and punk-type groups surfaced in California, but most American pop music seemed bland and predictable. The Beach Boys' patchy performance at the Knebworth Festival and a second poorly received Christian revivalist album from Bob Dylan, called *Saved*, both marked a downturn in popularity for performers who had helped shape the music scene throughout the 1960s and '70s. Paul Simon proved to be in better form with his movie soundtrack album *One-Trick Pony*, while America's finest black artist, Stevie Wonder, returned to form with *Hotter than July*. Bruce Springsteen released his long-awaited double album, *The River*, which justified his reputation as a powerful, passionate singer, drawing on established styles from rhythm and blues to country and western. The latter achieved new heights of popularity during the year, with leading performers including Kenny Rogers (*see* BIOGRAPHIES), Emmylou Harris, and the Charlie Daniels Band. The Doobie Brothers won four of five possible Grammy awards.

(ROBIN DENSELOW)

See also Dance; Motion Pictures; Television and Radio; Theatre.
[624.D–J]

Nauru

An island republic within the Commonwealth of Nations, Nauru lies in the Pacific Ocean about 1,900 km (1,200 mi) E of New Guinea. Area: 21 sq km (8 sq mi). Pop. (1977 census): 7,254, including Nauruan 57%; Pacific Islanders 26%; Chinese 9%; European 8%. Capital: Yaren. Language: Nauruan and English. Religion (Nauruans only): Protestant 60%; Roman Catholic 33%. President in 1980, Hammer DeRobурt.

Problems over communications and phosphate supplies continued in Nauru, which celebrated its 12th anniversary in 1980. Although Air Nauru and the Nauru Pacific Shipping Line were not operating profitably, they provided indispensable services. In an attempt to become more economical, Air Nauru changed its aircraft from Fokker-VFW F28 Fellowship jets to Boeing 727s and 737s. It also diversified its routes.

The vital question to Nauruans remained what to do when the phosphate, the republic's lifeblood, ran out. In March the Nauru Phosphate Corporation estimated and reported to Parliament that supplies would last only another 13 years at the current anticipated rate of depletion. The *Nauru Post*, edited and owned in part by former president Bernard Dowiyogo, made its own calculations and reported to its readers that eight to nine years was more realistic. The *Nauru Post* criticized the nation's lack of energy conservation and of planning for the future. (A. R. G. GRIFFITHS)

NAURU

Education. (1978) Primary, pupils 1,500; secondary, pupils 600; primary and secondary, teachers 129; vocational, pupils 61, teachers 4; teacher training (1977), students 6, teacher 1.

Finance and Trade. Monetary unit: Australian dollar, with (Sept. 22, 1980) a free rate of A$0.86 to U.S. $1 (A$2.06 = £1 sterling). Budget (1978–79 est.): revenue A$40,610,000; expenditure A$33.6 million. Foreign trade (1975–76): imports A$13.8 million (*c.* 58% from Australia, *c.* 30% from The Netherlands in 1974); exports A$37.3 million (*c.* 51% to Australia, *c.* 41% to New Zealand, *c.* 5% to Japan). Main export: phosphate *c.* 100%.

Industry. Production (in 000): phosphate rock (exports; metric tons; 1976–77) 1,146; electricity (kw-hr; 1977) 26,000.

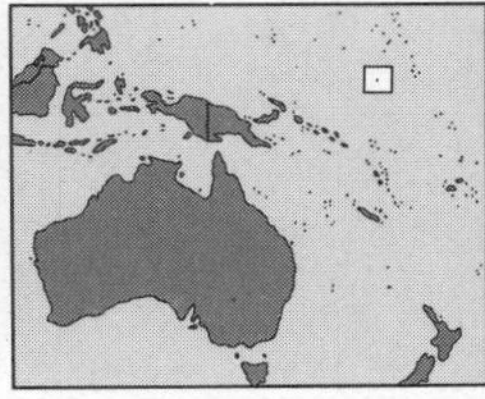
Nauru

Nepal

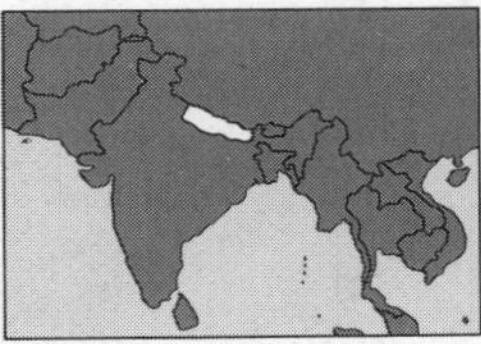
Nepal

A constitutional monarchy of Asia, Nepal is in the Himalayas between India and the Tibetan Autonomous Region of China. Area: 145,391 sq km (56,136 sq mi). Pop. (1980 est.): 14,010,000. Cap. and largest city: Kathmandu (pop., 1976 est., 171,400). Language: Nepali (official) 52.5%, also Bihari (including Maithili and Bhojpuri) 18.5%, Tamang

NEPAL

Education. (1977) Primary, pupils 769,049, teachers 23,395; secondary, pupils 285,154, teachers 11,630; vocational, pupils 20,875, teachers 594; teacher training, students 2,768, teachers 215; higher, students 24,297, teaching staff (1976) 1,756.

Finance. Monetary unit: Nepalese rupee, with (Sept. 22, 1980) a par value of NRs 12 to U.S. $1 (free rate of NRs 28.75 = £1 sterling). Gold, SDR's, and foreign exchange (June 1980) U.S. $191 million. Budget (total; 1978–79 actual): revenue NRs 1,690,000,000 (excludes foreign aid of NRs 586 million); expenditure NRs 3,115,000,000.

Foreign Trade. (1979) Imports NRs 3,053,200,000; exports NRs 1,305,700,000. Import sources (1978–79): India 55%; Japan *c.* 12%. Export destinations (1978–79): India 48%; Japan *c.* 8%; West Germany *c.* 6%; U.S. *c.* 5%. Main exports (1974–75): jute goods *c.* 33%; raw jute *c.* 13%; curio goods *c.* 11%; jute cuttings *c.* 7%. Tourism: visitors (1978) 156,000; gross receipts (1977) U.S. $2 million.

Agriculture. Production (in 000; metric tons; 1979): rice *c.* 2,500; corn *c.* 800; wheat 415; millet *c.* 140; potatoes *c.* 320; jute 45; tobacco *c.* 6; buffalo milk *c.* 475; cow's milk *c.* 220. Livestock (in 000; 1979): cattle *c.* 6,850; buffalo *c.* 4,150; pigs *c.* 350; sheep *c.* 2,360; goats *c.* 2,480; poultry *c.* 21,500.

Namibia:
see Dependent States; South Africa

NATO:
see Defense

Navies:
see Defense

4.8%, Tharu 4.3%, and Newari 3.9%. Religion (1971): Hindu 89.4%; Buddhist 7.5%. King, Birendra Bir Bikram Shah Deva; prime minister in 1980, Surya Bahadur Thapa.

In a referendum on May 2, 1980, a 54.79% majority of some 4.8 million voters elected to continue the partyless panchayat system that had superseded multiparty democracy in Nepal in 1960. An amnesty before the referendum allowed the return of critics of the regime, and B. P. Koirala, the prime minister removed in the royal coup of Dec. 15, 1960, led the movement for restoration of the multiparty system, while accepting the monarchy. Constitutional amendments making some modifications in the system of government were proclaimed by King Birendra in December.

On June 1 King Birendra reshuffled the Council of Ministers and set up a ministry for local development. He also appointed a constitutional reforms committee. On August 14 an act prohibited printing of publicity in the name of any political organization. The local administration would decide places for peaceful assembly and wall posters.

The Nepal Aid Consortium assured aid and loans at U.S. $200 million for 1980–81, the first year of the sixth development plan. Agriculture was severely affected by bad weather during most of the fifth plan period.

A devastating earthquake in late July in the western part of the country, close to the borders of India and Tibet, killed at least 150 people and destroyed villages. (GOVINDAN UNNY)

Netherlands, The

The Netherlands

A kingdom of northwest Europe on the North Sea, The Netherlands, a Benelux country, is bounded by Belgium on the south and West Germany on the east. Area: 41,160 sq km (15,892 sq mi). Pop. (1980 est.): 14,091,000. Cap. and largest city: Amsterdam (pop., 1980 est., 716,900). Seat of government: The Hague (pop., 1980 est., 456,900). Language: Dutch. Religion (1971): Roman Catholic 40.4%; Dutch Reformed 23.5%; no religion 23.6%; Reformed Churches 9.4%. Queen in 1980, Juliana and, from April 30, Beatrix; prime minister, Andreas van Agt.

A. NOGUES—SYGMA

Princess Beatrix, the eldest daughter of Queen Juliana of The Netherlands, was invested as the new queen in ceremonies held in Nieuwe Kerk (New Church) in Amsterdam on April 30.

On Jan. 31, 1980, the birthday of her daughter Princess Beatrix (*see* BIOGRAPHIES), Queen Juliana announced that she would abdicate as queen of The Netherlands in favour of the princess, after a reign of more than 30 years. On April 30, during a combined session of both houses of Parliament in the New Church in Amsterdam, Beatrix swore fidelity to the constitution and was installed as queen.

Elsewhere in Amsterdam serious riots broke out during the ceremony, involving more than 1,500 police and some 1,000 demonstrators. More than 100 police officers and 100 demonstrators were injured. This riot of predominantly young people was a sequel to earlier clashes, such as that on February 29 when a special police task force engaged housing squatters, their sympathizers, and young rioters. The police were met with smoke bombs, stones, and iron bars and withdrew; on March 3, however, supported by tanks, armoured

NETHERLANDS, THE

Education. (1978–79) Primary, pupils 1,500,530, teachers 63,302; secondary, pupils 820,634, teachers 53,354; vocational, pupils 547,373, teachers 45,000; teacher training, students 8,877, teachers 1,000; higher, students 269,050, teaching staff 27,800.

Finance. Monetary unit: guilder, with (Sept. 22, 1980) a free rate of 1.96 guilders to U.S. $1 (4.72 guilders = £1 sterling). Gold, SDR's, and foreign exchange (June 1980) U.S. $12,595,000,000. Budget (1979 actual): revenue 105.8 billion guilders; expenditure 114.3 billion guilders. Gross national product (1979) 298,270,000,000 guilders. Money supply (June 1980) 68,360,000,000 guilders. Cost of living (1975 = 100; June 1980) 133.1.

Foreign Trade. (1979) Imports 136,684,000,000 guilders; exports 127,630,000,000 guilders. Import sources: EEC 56% (West Germany 24%, Belgium-Luxembourg 12%, U.K. 8%, France 7%); U.S. 8%. Export destinations: EEC 73% (West Germany 30%, Belgium-Luxembourg 15%, France 11%, U.K. 8%, Italy 5%). Main exports: food 18%; chemicals 16%; machinery 14%; petroleum products 13%; natural gas 6%. Tourism (1978): visitors 2,683,000; gross receipts U.S. $1,254,000,000.

Transport and Communications. Roads (1977) 107,355 km (including 1,839 km expressways). Motor vehicles in use (1978): passenger 4.1 million; commercial 291,000. Railways: (1977) 2,850 km (including 1,731 km electrified); traffic (1979) 8,600,000,000 passenger-km, freight 3,334,000,000 net ton-km. Air traffic (1979): 14,012,000,000 passenger-km; freight 909.9 million net ton-km. Navigable inland waterways (1978) 4,340 km; freight traffic 34,458,000,000 ton-km. Shipping (1979): merchant vessels 100 gross tons and over 1,233; gross tonnage 5,403,350. Shipping traffic (1978): goods loaded 73,044,000 metric tons, unloaded 246,456,000 metric tons. Telephones (Jan. 1978) 5,845,900. Radio receivers (Dec. 1977) 8.5 million. Television receivers (Dec. 1977) 4.5 million.

Agriculture. Production (in 000; metric tons; 1979): wheat 836; barley 288; oats 109; rye 49; potatoes 6,277; tomatoes 395; onions 425; sugar, raw value *c.* 930; cabbages (1978) 263; cucumbers (1978) 382; carrots (1978) 180; apples 480; rapeseed 18; milk 11,562; butter *c.* 203; cheese *c.* 435; eggs *c.* 449; beef and veal *c.* 362; pork *c.* 1,100; fish catch (1978) 324. Livestock (in 000; May 1979): cattle 5,149; pigs 9,722; sheep 895; chickens 78,069.

Industry. Index of production (1975 = 100; 1979) 112. Production (in 000; metric tons; 1979): crude oil 1,316; natural gas (cu m) 82,840,000; manufactured gas (cu m) 1,050,000; electricity (kw-hr) 64,457,000; pig iron 4,813; crude steel 5,805; aluminum 259; cement 3,701; petroleum products *c.* 63,800; sulfuric acid 1,744; plastics and resins 2,013; fertilizers (nutrient content; 1978–79) nitrogenous *c.* 1,540, phosphate *c.* 405; newsprint 119. Merchant vessels launched (100 gross tons and over; 1979) 183,000 gross tons. New dwelling units (1979) 88,500.

vehicles, and water cannons, the police broke down the squatters' barricades and cleared the occupied houses.

On February 20 the minister of finance, Franciscus Andriessen, resigned because the rest of the Cabinet was unwilling to accept economy cuts of 4 billion guilders. His chief opponent, Minister of Social Affairs Willem Albeda, considered this policy unacceptable to the labour unions and the public and instead proposed cuts of 2 billion guilders. A compromise worked out by Prime Minister Andreas van Agt did not satisfy Andriessen. In May the Central Planning Office published the Central Economic Plan. The office's forecast was gloomy: increases in unemployment and in inflation, only a slight growth in production, a decline in profits, and no increase in employment in the near future. In the queen's speech on the opening of Parliament, delivered by Beatrix on September 16, the unfavourable economic situation and the increase of civil disorder received special attention. The budget, prepared by the new minister of finance, Alphons van der Stee, produced a deficit of 12.4 billion guilders, roughly 10% of expenditure.

Although the minister of foreign affairs, Christoph van der Klaauw, had declared that an oil boycott of South Africa would be impracticable, the majority of the lower house of Parliament voted in favour of that policy. A few days later the Cabinet rejected the motion. A vote of no confidence, introduced by the opposition parties, failed. Only six members of the Christian Democratic Appeal, the party of the prime minister, supported the no-confidence motion.

Because of the conflicting views of the Dutch Roman Catholic bishops, Pope John Paul II convened a special synod of Dutch bishops in Rome from January 14 to 31. Its deliberations were kept secret, only the conclusions being published. One of the issues was the question of married priests. As expected, they were to be excluded from performance of priestly functions.

At first the Cabinet was undecided in regard to boycotting the Olympic Games in Moscow, but after the Soviet government sent the Soviet dissident and Nobel laureate Andrey Sakharov into internal exile at Gorky on January 22, the Cabinet and the majority of the lower house demanded a boycott of the Games. The Dutch Olympic Committee, however, voted to go to Moscow.

In November a Chinese delegation visited The Netherlands to discuss the possibility of Dutch assistance in the building of harbours on the east coast of China. At the same time the Dutch government gave a company permission to build two submarines for Taiwan. The Chinese delegation protested against this decision and left the country at once. (DICK BOONSTRA)

See also Dependent States.

New Zealand

New Zealand, a parliamentary state and member of the Commonwealth of Nations, is in the South Pacific Ocean, separated from southeastern Australia by the Tasman Sea. The country consists of North and South islands and Stewart, Chatham, and other minor islands. Area: 269,057 sq km (103,883 sq mi). Pop. (1980 est.): 3,148,400. Cap.: Wellington (pop., 1979 est., 137,600). Largest city: Christchurch (pop., 1979 est., 171,300). Largest urban area: Auckland (pop., 1979 est., 805,900). Language: English (official), Maori. Religion (1976): Church of England 35%; Presbyterian 22%; Roman Catholic 16%. Queen, Elizabeth II; governors-general in 1980, Sir Keith Holyoake until October 25 and, from November 6, Sir David Stuart Beattie; prime minister, Robert David Muldoon.

In the face of rising inflation and unemployment, New Zealand consolidated plans to process offshore gas in such a way as to reduce one of its most expensive imports, oil, as much as possible. The plan provided for conversion of the gas to methanol, much of which would then be passed through a NZ$150 million catalyst to produce 13,000 bbl of gasoline a day, about 30% of New Zealand's needs. Some researchers preferred methanol as a final product, but the plan remained intact. It was hoped that this, together with other, supplementary plans, would make the country more than 50% self-sufficient in gasoline by 1986.

The public accounts to March 1980 showed a deficit of NZ$1,027,000,000, NZ$69 million more than provided for. The annual budget, in June, imposed heavier indirect taxes (beer, spirits, cigarettes, domestic air travel, postage) but allowed a rebate for those with low family incomes and a 4%

NEW ZEALAND

Education. (1979) Primary, pupils 517,190, teachers 20,822; secondary, pupils 230,128, teachers 13,390; vocational, pupils 6,286, teachers 2,073; higher, students 55,008, teaching staff 3,532.

Finance. Monetary unit: New Zealand dollar, with (Sept. 22, 1980) a free rate of NZ$1.02 to U.S. $1 (NZ$2.45 = £1 sterling). Gold, SDR's, and foreign exchange (June 1980) U.S. $327 million. Budget (1978–79 actual): revenue NZ$5,902,000,000; expenditure NZ$6,602,000,000. Gross national product (1978–79) NZ$17,318,000,000. Cost of living (1975 = 100; 2nd quarter 1980) 196.

Foreign Trade. (1979) Imports NZ$4,466,100,000; exports NZ$4,606,700,000. Import sources: Australia 21%; U.K. 15%; Japan 14%; U.S. 14%. Export destinations: U.S. 16%; U.K. 16%; Japan 14%; Australia 13%. Main exports: wool 18%; beef and veal 12%; lamb and mutton 11%; butter 7%. Tourism (1978): visitors 407,000; gross receipts U.S. $166 million.

Transport and Communications. Roads (1979) 93,401 km. Motor vehicles in use (1979): passenger 1,274,100; commercial 247,200. Railways (1979): 4,536 km; traffic 463 million passenger-km, freight 3,229,000,000 net ton-km. Air traffic (1979): 4,312,000,000 passenger-km; freight 152.1 million net ton-km. Shipping (1979): merchant vessels 100 gross tons and over 117; gross tonnage 258,476. Telephones (March 1979) 1,762,200. Radio receivers (Dec. 1977) 2,725,000. Television licenses (March 1979) 859,885.

Agriculture. Production (in 000; metric tons; 1979): wheat 327; barley 355; oats 57; corn 216; potatoes (1978) *c.* 245; dry peas *c.* 62; tomatoes *c.* 50; wine 42; apples 186; milk *c.* 6,361; butter 251; cheese 90; wool 229; sheepskins (1978) *c.* 104; mutton and lamb 506; beef and veal 498; fish catch (1978) 83; timber (cu m; 1978) *c.* 9,003. Livestock (in 000; Jan. 1979): cattle 8,499; sheep 62,894; pigs 503; chickens *c.* 7,400.

Industry. Production (in 000; metric tons; 1979): coal 1,739; lignite 209; crude oil (1978) 580; natural gas (cu m) 1,108,000; manufactured gas (cu m) 60,000; electricity (excluding most industrial production; kw-hr) 21,544,000; cement 751; aluminum (1977) 145; petroleum products (1977) *c.* 3,120; phosphate fertilizers (1978–79) *c.* 517; wood pulp 1,203; paper 724.

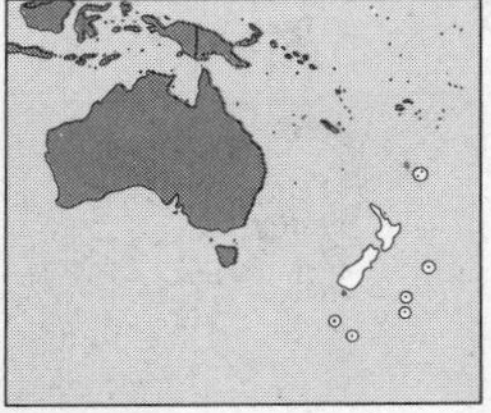
New Zealand

Netherlands Overseas Territories: *see* Dependent States

New Guinea: *see* Indonesia; Papua New Guinea

New Hebrides: *see* Vanuatu

Newspapers: *see* Publishing

general cost-of-living increase in wages. It did little to hold down inflation, which reached 18.4% for the first quarter of the year—the century's highest. Food prices, which had risen 25% in 1979, were a major component of inflation.

One of the main thrusts of the government was to restructure and modernize some obsolete domestic industries, and these plans caused increased unemployment, especially in the textile industry. The first moves toward narrowing the range of automobiles assembled inside the country provoked threats from labour unions. But the main industrial tensions resulted from government efforts to limit negotiated pay raises in the battle against inflation. Migration to other countries, mainly Australia, tapered off.

Government approval for construction of a second aluminum smelter, to process Queensland bauxite using hydroelectricity supplied at a specially negotiated fee, became controversial on economic as well as environmental grounds. The strongest critics contended that provision of more "cheap" power could be a factor in the need to build more river-dam power stations, which would be costlier than ever before.

Inflation, rising costs of commodities, and unemployment were all factors in the government's loss of a "safe" National Party seat in a by-election in September, but a new ingredient at the ballot boxes warned the government of possible trouble at the general election of 1981. A number of voters who turned against National and gave Social Credit its second member (House composition after Sept. 6, 1980: National 50, Labour 40, Social Credit 2) said that they were protesting against the manner of Prime Minister Robert Muldoon, who came through to them as arrogant and mean when retaliating against criticism. At the time of the by-election Muldoon was out of the country on one of his five different 1980 expeditions, and this increased voter hostility.

Major news stories of the year included the breaking up of a New Zealand-based drug ring operating internationally, the Rugby Union's decision to invite a South African rugby team to New Zealand after a 15-year hiatus, and the flooding of farmlands in the Otago district. Only a few New Zealanders participated in the Olympic Games at Moscow, and they had to do so without government assistance or commercial sponsorship.

The Soviet ambassador, Vsevolod Sofinsky, was expelled for allegedly supplying money to a political party, and Moscow retaliated by expelling the New Zealand representative there. Visitors included Argentina's Pres. Jorge Rafael Videla. Former Labour politician Sir Hugh Watt died in February, and sheepbreeder Sir Geoffrey Peren in July.

(JOHN A. KELLEHER)

See also Dependent States.

Nicaragua

Nicaragua

The largest country of Central America, Nicaragua is a republic bounded by Honduras, Costa Rica, the Caribbean Sea, and the Pacific Ocean. Area: 128,875 sq km (49,759 sq mi). Pop. (1980 est.): 2,-732,000. Cap. and largest city: Managua (pop., 1978 est., 517,700). Language: Spanish. Religion: Roman Catholic. In 1980 the nation was governed by a five-member Junta of the Government of National Reconstruction.

By the end of 1980 the Sandinista National Liberation Front government appeared to have turned toward the left since taking power after the civil war in 1979. Cabinet changes in December 1979 substituted fairly left-wing Sandinistas for non-Sandinista members in such posts as defense, planning, and agriculture; also, of the two non-Sandinistas appointed to the five-member junta in May in place of Alfonso Robelo and Violetta Barrios de Chamorro (who both resigned in April), Arturo Cruz was said to be more to the left than his predecessor.

People in the capital city of Managua celebrated the first anniversary of the overthrow of former president Anastasio Somoza Debayle by the Sandinista guerrillas on July 19.

OWEN FRANKEN—SYGMA

Legislative measures nationalized locally owned banks, insurance companies, and the mining industry and prohibited foreign-owned banks from accepting local currency deposits. Trade controls were introduced with the nationalization of coffee and cotton exports and with state control of seafood exports. In addition, all economic interests previously held by the Somoza family and associates were confiscated. The exiled former dictator, Anastasio Somoza Debayle, was assassinated in Asunción, Paraguay, on September 17 (*see* OBITUARIES).

In January the government outlined reconstruction measures in the national emergency and recovery program for 1980, and it was planned to regain 1978 production levels by the end of the year. The plan put forward stringent austerity measures, with a reduction in public expenditure and oil purchases, a construction program, increased exports, and a reduction in the rates of inflation and unemployment. During the 1979 civil war, it was estimated, more than 30,000 people had been killed, damage to the economy exceeded U.S. $2 billion, and the foreign debt reached $1.3 billion while reserves declined to $3 billion. Unemployment had risen to 32% of the working population, inflation at the end of December 1979 was running at around 60%, and real gross domestic product (GDP) had fallen by 26% to 1962 levels. During 1980 inflation was expected to decline to 30% and GDP to increase by 18%.

The government negotiated a debt-rescheduling program with a committee of 13 commercial banks representing the 120 debtor banks. In September a breakthrough was reached concerning $582 million in foreign debt contracted by the Somoza administration. However, an estimated $250 million in outstanding private debt remained.

(CHRISTINE MELLOR)

NICARAGUA

Education. (1978) Primary, pupils 378,640, teachers 9,986; secondary, pupils 80,254; vocational, pupils 16,567; secondary and vocational, teachers (1976–77) *c.* 3,145; teacher training, students 2,053; higher, students 23,737, teaching staff (1976) 1,052.

Finance. Monetary unit: córdoba, with (Sept. 22, 1980) a par value of 10 córdobas to U.S. $1 (free rate of 23.95 córdobas = £1 sterling). Gold, SDR's, and foreign exchange (Sept. 1979) U.S. $87 million. Budget (total; 1979 est.): revenue 3,760,000,000 córdobas; expenditure 3,409,000,000 córdobas. Gross national product (1978) 14,670,000,000 córdobas. Money supply (June 1979) 2,276,100,000 córdobas. Cost of living (Managua; 1975 = 100; Jan. 1980) 210.8.

Foreign Trade. (1978) Imports 4,187,600,000 córdobas; exports 4,538,700,000 córdobas. Import sources: U.S. 31%; Venezuela 12%; Guatemala 9%; Costa Rica 7%; Japan 7%; West Germany 5%; El Salvador 5%. Export destinations: U.S. 25%; West Germany 14%; Japan 9%; Costa Rica 9%; El Salvador 6%; China 5%; Guatemala 5%; Belgium-Luxembourg 5%. Main exports: coffee 31%; cotton 23%; meat 10%; chemicals *c.* 8%; sugar *c.* 5%.

Transport and Communications. Roads (1978) 18,197 km (including 384 km of Pan-American Highway). Motor vehicles in use (1977): passenger *c.* 38,000; commercial (including buses) *c.* 30,000. Railways: (1978) 373 km; traffic (1977) 19 million passenger-km, freight 11 million net ton-km. Air traffic (1978): 92 million passenger-km; freight 2 million net ton-km. Telephones (Jan. 1978) 55,800. Radio receivers (Dec. 1977) 600,000. Television receivers (Dec. 1977) 100,000.

Agriculture. Production (in 000; metric tons; 1979): corn *c.* 168; rice (1978) 85; sorghum *c.* 58; dry beans *c.* 54; sugar, raw value (1978) *c.* 219; bananas *c.* 160; oranges *c.* 57; cottonseed *c.* 185; coffee *c.* 53; cotton, lint *c.* 109. Livestock (in 000; 1978): cattle *c.* 2,774; pigs *c.* 710; horses *c.* 275; chickens *c.* 4,500.

Industry. Production (in 000; metric tons; 1977): petroleum products *c.* 730; cement 221; gold (exports; troy oz) 61; electricity (kw-hr) 1,180,000.

Niger

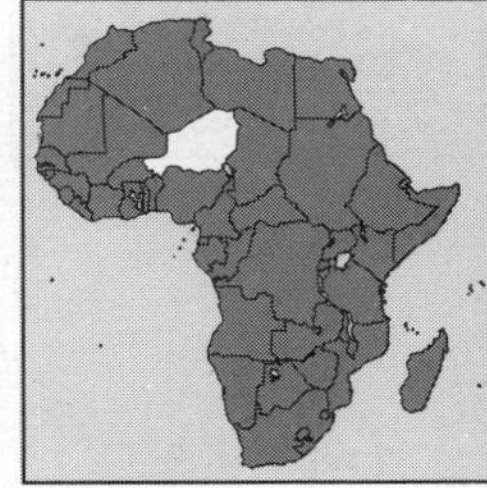

Niger

A republic of north central Africa, Niger is bounded by Algeria, Libya, Chad, Nigeria, Benin, Upper Volta, and Mali. Area: 1,186,408 sq km (458,075 sq mi). Pop. (1980 est.): 5,305,000, including (1972 est.) Hausa 53.7%; Zerma and Songhai 23.6%; Fulani 10.6%; Beriberi-Manga 9.1%; Tuareg 3%. Cap. and largest city: Niamey (pop., 1977, 225,300). Language: French (official) and Sudanic dialects. Religion: Muslim 85%; animist 14.5%; Christian 0.5%. Chief of state and president of the Supreme Military Council in 1980, Col. Seyni Kountché.

In April 1980 Pres. Seyni Kountché felt sufficiently sure of himself, at the conclusion of six years of power, to be able to extend some measure of clemency to his political adversaries. He therefore freed the former president, Hamani Diori, who had been detained after he was removed from power in the military coup of April 15, 1974. At the same time, he also released the former leader of the Sawaba opposition party, Djibo Bakary, who had been arrested in August 1975 on a charge of plotting.

Niger had become one of France's chief African sources of uranium and enjoyed excellent relations with its former colonial power. Like the French government, President Kountché was concerned about the civil war in Chad in an area neighbouring Niger's uranium deposits. He twice proposed, without success, that Chad be placed under the guardianship of the Organization of African Unity or of the UN. (PHILIPPE DECRAENE)

NIGER

Education. (1977–78) Primary, pupils 176,297, teachers 4,298; secondary, pupils 21,065, teachers 803; vocational, pupils 333, teachers 34; teacher training, students 1,225, teachers 48; higher, students 784, teaching staff 115.

Finance. Monetary unit: CFA franc, with (Sept. 22, 1980) a par value of CFA Fr 50 to the French franc (free rate of CFA Fr 210 = U.S. $1; CFA Fr 504 = £1 sterling). Gold, SDR's, and foreign exchange (May 1980) U.S. $129 million. Budget (1978–79 est.) balanced at CFA Fr 56.8 billion.

Foreign Trade. (1979) Imports *c.* CFA Fr 110 billion; exports *c.* CFA Fr 67 billion. Import sources: France *c.* 42%; U.S. 8%; U.K. *c.* 7%; Ivory Coast *c.* 7%; Libya *c.* 6%; West Germany *c.* 5%. Export destinations: France *c.* 81%; West Germany *c.* 13%. Main exports (1976): uranium 64%; livestock 15%; fruit and vegetables 9%.

Transport and Communications. Roads (1978) 7,656 km. Motor vehicles in use (1978): passenger 20,700; commercial 3,600. There are no railways. Inland waterway (Niger River; 1978) *c.* 300 km. Telephones (Jan. 1977) 8,100. Radio receivers (Dec. 1971) 150,000.

Agriculture. Production (in 000; metric tons; 1979): millet 1,246; sorghum 346; rice (1978) 34; cassava (1978) *c.* 180; onions *c.* 65; peanuts *c.* 90; goat's milk *c.* 124. Livestock (in 000; 1978): cattle 2,990; sheep 2,660; goats 6,700; camels 300.

Industry. Production (in 000; metric tons; 1977): uranium 1.6; tin concentrates (metal content) *c.* 0.1; cement 40; electricity (kw-hr) *c.* 70,000.

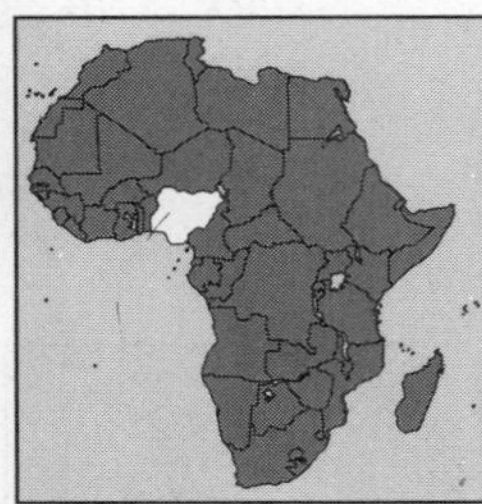
Nigeria

Nigeria

A republic and a member of the Commonwealth of Nations, Nigeria is located in Africa north of the Gulf of Guinea, bounded by Benin, Niger, Chad, and Cameroon. Area: 923,800 sq km (356,700 sq mi). Nigeria's total population is extremely uncertain; in 1979 estimates ranged from 77 million to 104 million, with official Nigerian figures falling toward the middle of that range; principal ethnic groups were Hausa 21%; Yoruba 20%; Ibo 17%; Fulani 9%. Cap.: Lagos (metro. pop., 1980 est., 4.1 million). Largest city: Ibadan (metro. pop., 1980 est., 6 million). Language: English (official), Hausa, Yoruba, and Ibo. Religion (1963): Muslim 47%; Christian 34%. President in 1980, Alhaji Shehu Shagari.

Nigeria's Pres. Alhaji Shehu Shagari, leading a minority government and faced with inflation, a weak economy, and no accepted census (necessary for revenue allocation among the country's 19 states), experienced a difficult year in 1980. The alliance of his National Party of Nigeria with Nnamdi Azikiwe's Nigerian People's Party (NPP) proved shaky, and an attempt to appoint 19 state liaison officers was not welcomed by the NPP and other parties. Action promised against corruption found an early target in the £2,330 million allegedly missing from the Nigerian National Petroleum Corporation (NNPC). Amid fears of an "oilgate" national scandal and public disorder, Shagari set up a judicial inquiry into the matter. The July 8 White Paper rejected the allegations as a hoax, but it found the affairs of the NNPC in disorder, because of lack of skilled staff and recommended sweeping reforms. The tribunal also ordered the Royal Dutch/Shell Group, Gulf Oil Corp., and Mobil Oil Corp. to repay to Nigeria over the next three to four years some 80 million bbl of crude oil, about U.S. $64 million in value. During the oil glut of 1975–78 the three firms had taken from the country proportionately more oil than allowed by their production agreements. Riots, said to have been instigated by a fanatic Muslim sect (possibly with support from Libya), were reported from Kano in late December. Just before the new year, troops were sent in to quell the disturbances.

On June 27 Shagari announced the establishment of naval and air training academies, as well as increased recruitment to the armed services. Nigeria furthermore pushed for a permanent African Defense Force at the first Organization of African Unity (OAU) economic summit, which was held in Lagos (April 28–29). Close relations with Senegal, whose president, Léopold Senghor, chaired the summit, were established during Senghor's May state visit to Lagos. At that time a permanent joint economic commission was established within the framework of the Economic Community of West African States (ECOWAS).

The summit attempted to improve sharply deteriorating food and agricultural output and establish a common market in the face of falling inter-African trade.

Despite increasing Japanese, French, and West German competition, Britain maintained the lead in Nigerian trade at 20%. High operating costs and uncertain trade regulations, as well as forced sales of holdings to Nigerian affiliates at low prices, did not encourage new development by other nations, nor did the sudden insertion of Nigerian top executives in foreign banks. Shagari's government attempted to encourage foreign investment by reducing the tax rate on business profits.

Shagari's first budget, presented to the National Assembly on March 18, gave priority to self-reliance and self-sufficiency, to the control of wages (minimum of 100 naira a month for public employees) and prices, and to stemming the migration from rural areas to cities, which was causing agricultural stagnation and, hence, increased food imports. There was a federal deficit of 1.4 billion naira in 1979, with external debts standing at about 360 million naira. Only huge oil revenues of 9.9 billion naira (83% of national revenue) made the 1975–80 development plan possible. Shagari's budget estimated 1980 revenue at 11.9 billion naira (oil accounting for 85%); state allocations totaled 2.5 billion naira and recurrent expenditures, 6.5 billion naira (20% higher than in 1979). The recurring surplus of 5.3 billion naira added to the capital budget of 7,623,000,000 naira left a deficit of 2.3 billion naira, to be financed by internal and external loans. Although 118 million naira was set aside

NIGERIA

Education. (1978–79) Primary, pupils (1979–80) 11,457,772, teachers 287,040; secondary, pupils 1,159,404, teachers (1973–74) 19,409; vocational, pupils 45,095, teachers (1973–74) 1,120; teacher training, students 204,374, teachers (1973–74) 2,360; higher, students 101,210, teaching staff (1975–76) 5,019.

Finance. Monetary unit: naira, with (Sept. 22, 1980) a free rate of 0.53 naira to U.S. $1 (1.27 naira = £1 sterling). Gold, SDR's, and foreign exchange (June 1980) U.S. $8,306,000,000. Federal budget (1979–80): revenue 8,805,000,000 naira; expenditure 9,510,000,000 naira (including 6,610,000,000 naira capital expenditure). Gross domestic product (1978–79) 28,888,000,000 naira. Money supply (May 1980) 6,187,800,000 naira. Cost of living (Lagos; 1975 = 100; Dec. 1979) 213.5.

Foreign Trade. (1979) Imports 6,609,000,000 naira; exports 10,690,000,000 naira. Import sources: U.K. *c.* 15%; West Germany *c.* 13%; Japan *c.* 9%; France *c.* 9%; The Netherlands *c.* 8%; U.S. *c.* 7%; Italy *c.* 5%. Export destinations: U.S. *c.* 47%; West Germany *c.* 12%; The Netherlands *c.* 10%; France *c.* 7%; Netherlands Antilles *c.* 7%. Main export: crude oil 94%.

Transport and Communications. Roads (1977) 105,000 km. Motor vehicles in use (1977): passenger 133,700; commercial 23,600. Railways: (1978) 3,505 km; traffic (1974–75) 785 million passenger-km, freight 972 million net ton-km. Air traffic (1978): 1,268,000,000 passenger-km; freight 10.3 million net ton-km. Shipping (1979): merchant vessels 100 gross tons and over 107; gross tonnage 382,879. Telephones (Jan. 1978) 128,400. Radio receivers (Dec. 1977) 5,250,000. Television receivers (Dec. 1977) 450,000.

Agriculture. Production (in 000; metric tons; 1979): millet *c.* 3,100; sorghum *c.* 3,785; corn *c.* 1,500; rice *c.* 1,000; sweet potatoes (1978) *c.* 202; yams (1978) *c.* 15,000; cassava (1978) *c.* 10,844; tomatoes *c.* 280; peanuts *c.* 621; palm oil *c.* 675; cocoa *c.* 180; cotton, lint 43; rubber *c.* 60; fish catch (1978) 519. Livestock (in 000; 1979): cattle *c.* 12,000; sheep *c.* 8,500; goats *c.* 24,500; pigs *c.* 1,100; poultry *c.* 110,000.

Industry. Production (in 000; metric tons; 1979): crude oil 114,511; natural gas (cu m; 1978) *c.* 540,000; cement (1978) 1,540; tin concentrates (metal content) 2.7; petroleum products (1978) 2,833; electricity (kw-hr) *c.* 5,200,000.

for Nigeria's future capital, Abuja, the largest single spending item was defense, at 466 million naira.

Oil receipts maintained their leading role among external assets, accounting for over 90% of total external payments. The discovery of uranium was to be exploited, in partnership with a French firm, by the Nigerian Uranium Mining Co., in which the government had a 60% share.

(MOLLY MORTIMER)

Norway

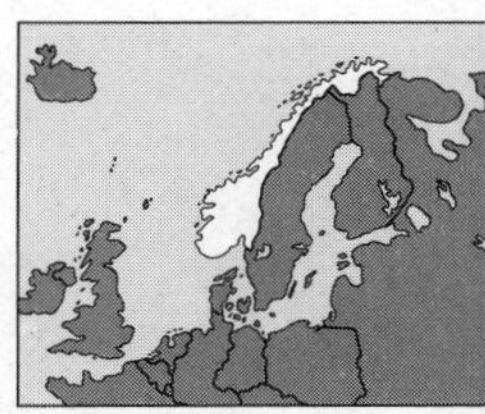

Norway

A constitutional monarchy of northern Europe, Norway is bordered by Sweden, Finland, and the U.S.S.R.; its coastlines are on the Skagerrak, the North Sea, the Norwegian Sea, and the Arctic Ocean. Area: 323,895 sq km (125,057 sq mi), excluding the Svalbard Archipelago, 62,048 sq km, and Jan Mayen Island, 373 sq km. Pop. (1980 est.): 4,082,300. Cap. and largest city: Oslo (pop., 1979 est., 457,200). Language: Norwegian. Religion: Lutheran (94%). King, Olav V; prime minister in 1980, Odvar Nordli.

The worldwide recession affected some sectors of the Norwegian economy in 1980. Foreign demand for iron ore, pellets, steel, and ferroalloys fell off. Norway's largest mining company, A/S Sydvaranger at Kirkenes, laid off its 1,000 production workers for the last two months of the year. Rising oil prices and the Iraq-Iran war lessened the demand for oil transport, forcing Norwegian tankers to lay up. Of traditional exports, only aluminum continued to do well. The main stimulus to growth came from the offshore oil and gas industry. Steeply rising oil revenues enabled the government to maintain high public spending, including subsidies to hard-hit industries.

Shipyards booked few orders for new ships but concentrated on equipment for Norway's North Sea oil and gas fields. To stay in the government's good books, the oil companies ordered equipment from Norwegian fabricators. Repair and maintenance of offshore structures provided work and, despite pockets of unemployment, Norway remained an island of prosperity.

A shadow was cast over the offshore industry in March, when the dormitory platform "Alexander Kielland" capsized in a storm with the loss of 123 lives. In the debate that followed, it emerged that safety rules were often disregarded; drilling crews worked with unqualified members, and government authorities charged with enforcing safety rules were chronically short-staffed. Some quarters urged the curbing of offshore development; in particular, environmentalists urged that exploration drilling north of the 62nd parallel should be indefinitely postponed. Checks of all floating platforms and a review of safety measures were ordered, but the decision to permit drilling in northern waters was not revoked.

The offshore industry also suffered from labour troubles during the summer. A strike by 2,000 workers on the three Norwegian producing fields —Ekofisk, Frigg, and Statfjord—was ended after two weeks when compulsory arbitration was decreed. However, a strike of 1,500 seamen operating mobile rigs continued for over a month, upsetting exploration programs. The delays may not have been entirely unwelcome to the government. To develop all viable finds at once would put an unbearable strain on the economy.

On the mainland, the principal employer and union organizations reached agreement, in April, on a countrywide "framework" for pay rises during the year. It was hailed as moderate because the general increase granted was low, although low-paid workers got more. But the cost of living rose more than expected following the end (Dec. 31, 1979) of a 15-month price and incomes freeze. Large wage claims by offshore employees affected the attitude of mainland workers in the plant-level bargaining after the general settlement, and by autumn the inflation rate was again higher than in many competing countries.

The Labour government's budget for 1981, introduced in October, would tax spending rather than earnings. It was criticized as inflationary because it permitted increased government spend-

NORWAY

Education. (1978–79) Primary, pupils 396,939, teachers 21,212; secondary, pupils 264,134; vocational, pupils 94,-857; secondary and vocational, teachers 23,405; higher, students 60,406, teaching staff 5,742.

Finance. Monetary unit: Norwegian krone, with (Sept. 22, 1980) a free rate of 4.86 kroner to U.S. $1 (11.69 kroner = £1 sterling). Gold, SDR's, and foreign exchange (June 1980) U.S. $4,977,000,000. Budget (1980 est.): revenue 72,355,000,000 kroner; expenditure 91,907,000,000 kroner. Gross national product (1979) 225,240,000,000 kroner. Money supply (May 1980) 43,150,000,000 kroner. Cost of living (1975 = 100; June 1980) 148.3.

Foreign Trade. (1979) Imports 69,333,000,000 kroner; exports 68,525,000,000 kroner. Import sources: Sweden 18%; West Germany 14%; U.K. 14%; U.S. 7%; Denmark 6%; Finland 5%. Export destinations: U.K. 36%; West Germany 14%; Sweden 11%; Denmark 6%. Main exports: crude oil 21%; natural gas 11%; ships 8%; machinery 7%; chemicals 7%; aluminum 7%; iron and steel 5%; fish 5%.

Transport and Communications. Roads (1979) 80,911 km (including 56 km expressways with more than one lane). Motor vehicles in use (1979): passenger 1,189,800; commercial 151,700. Railways: (1978) 4,241 km (including 2,440 km electrified); traffic (1979) 2,262,000,000 passenger-km, freight 3,068,000,000 net ton-km. Air traffic (including Norwegian apportionment of international operations of Scandinavian Airlines System; 1979): 3,915,-000,000 passenger-km; freight 134.9 million net ton-km. Shipping (1979): merchant vessels 100 gross tons and over 2,531; gross tonnage 22,349,337. Shipping traffic (1979): goods loaded 39,375,000 metric tons, unloaded 22,419,-000 metric tons. Telephones (Dec. 1978) 1,636,500. Radio licenses (Dec. 1977) 1,318,000. Television licenses (Dec. 1978) 1,147,198.

Agriculture. Production (in 000; metric tons; 1979): barley *c.* 647; oats *c.* 357; potatoes *c.* 426; apples *c.* 37; milk (1978) *c.* 1,844; cheese 69; beef and veal (1978) 72; pork (1978) 80; timber (cu m; 1978) 8,242; fish catch (1978) 2,647. Livestock (in 000; June 1978): cattle 954; sheep 1,-845; pigs 705; goats 72; chickens 3,758.

Industry. Fuel and power (in 000; metric tons; 1979): crude oil 18,288; coal (Svalbard mines; Norwegian operated only) 304; natural gas (cu m; 1977) 264,000; manufactured gas (cu m) 16,000; electricity (kw-hr) 88,988,000. Production (in 000; metric tons; 1979): iron ore (65% metal content) 4,251; pig iron 1,536; crude steel 922; aluminum 660; copper 21; zinc 77; cement 2,196; petroleum products (1978) *c.* 8,200; sulfuric acid 386; fertilizers (nutrient content; 1978–79) nitrogenous 444, phosphate 141; fish meal (1977) 465; wood pulp (1977) mechanical 763, chemical 863; newsprint 566; other paper (1977) 645. Merchant vessels launched (100 gross tons and over; 1979) 260,000 gross tons. New dwelling units completed (1979) 37,143.

Nobel Prizes: *see* People of the Year

ing. This was to be financed mainly by larger petroleum revenues, expected to account for nearly one-quarter of total government income in 1981.

Three government ministers resigned in October; Bjartmar Gjerde (oil and energy; replaced by Arvid Johansen); Andreas Cappelen (justice; replaced by a county governor, Oddvar Berrefjord); and Inger Louise Valle (labour; replaced by a trade union official, Harriet Andreassen). Gjerde's resignation was believed by many to reflect dissatisfaction with the indecisive leadership of Prime Minister Odvar Nordli. The ruling Labour Party was split on economic, energy, and defense policies. A bitter controversy arose over a proposal to stockpile U.S. military equipment in central Norway, said by critics to violate Norway's traditional policy of barring foreign bases on its soil in peacetime. Soviet objections to the plan were expressed at a meeting between Foreign Minister Knut Frydenlund and Soviet leaders in December.

(FAY GJESTER)

See also Dependent States.

Oman

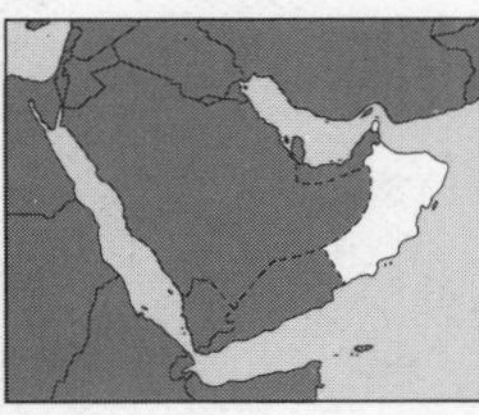

Oman

An independent sultanate, Oman occupies the southeastern part of the Arabian Peninsula and is bounded by the United Arab Emirates, Saudi Arabia, Yemen (Aden), the Gulf of Oman, and the Arabian Sea. A small part of the country lies to the north and is separated from the rest of Oman by the United Arab Emirates. Area: 300,000 sq km (120,000 sq mi). Pop. (1980 est.): 891,000; for planning purposes the government of Oman uses an estimate of 1.5 million. No census has ever been taken. Cap.: Muscat (pop., 1973 est., 15,000). Largest city: Matrah (pop., 1973 est., 18,000). Language: Arabic. Religion: Muslim (of which Ibadi 75%; Sunni 25%). Sultan and prime minister in 1980, Qabus ibn Sa'id.

Oman, guardian of the Strait of Hormuz, maintained strict neutrality in the 1980 Iran-Iraq war but was prepared to open its military bases to the West in any general war. A defense pact, with economic aid, was agreed upon with the U.S. in June.

Sultan Qabus ibn Sa'id's limited support for Egyptian Pres. Anwar as-Sadat's bilateral peace with Israel waned in view of the lack of progress on Palestinian autonomy. Oman's isolation from the rest of the Arab community was less pronounced than in 1979. The Popular Front for the Liberation of Oman, which fought a guerrilla war in the south during the early 1970s, remained an external force supported, among Arab countries, only by Yemen (Aden).

Oman's declining northern oil fields were to be supplemented in 1981 with production from the south. The country's only producing oil company, Petroleum Development Oman, promised a production level of about 350,000 bbl a day throughout the 1980s and predicted that the reserves would last 24–25 years at current production. An ambitious five-year plan was to be announced in early 1981 with state income guaranteed, because of high oil prices, at about U.S. $25 billion over the period.

(JOHN WHELAN)

OMAN

Education. (State only; 1978–79) Primary, pupils 77,974; secondary, pupils 7,963; primary and secondary, teachers 4,286; vocational, pupils 346, teachers (1977–78) 67; teacher training, students 115, teachers 16.

Finance and Trade. Monetary unit: rial Omani, with (Sept. 22, 1980) a par value of 0.345 rial to U.S. $1 (free rate of 0.827 rial = £1 sterling). Gold, SDR's, and foreign exchange (June 1980) U.S. $810 million. Budget (1979 actual): revenue 692 million rials; expenditure 650 million rials.

Foreign Trade. (1979) Imports 430.5 million rials; exports 746.7 million rials. Import sources: U.K. 17%; Japan 15%; United Arab Emirates 15%; U.S. 8%; The Netherlands 8%; West Germany 6%. Export destinations: Japan 64%; U.S. 13%; The Netherlands 7%; U.K. 6%; Norway 5%. Main export: crude oil 99.5%.

Industry. Production (in 000): crude oil (metric tons; 1979) 14,733; electricity (kw-hr; 1977) 550,000.

Pakistan

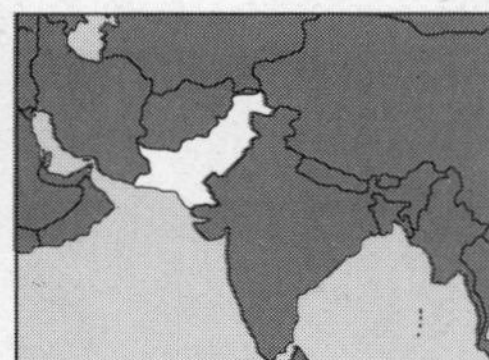

Pakistan

A federal republic, Pakistan is bordered on the south by the Arabian Sea, on the west by Afghanistan and Iran, on the north by China, and on the east by India. Area: 796,095 sq km (307,374 sq mi), excluding the Pakistani-controlled section of Jammu and Kashmir. Pop. (1980 est.): 82,441,000. Cap.: Islamabad (pop., 1972, 77,300). Largest city: Karachi (metro. area pop., 1980 est., 5,005,000). Language: Urdu and English. Religion: Muslim 97% (of which Sunni 70%; Shi'ah 30%); Hindu 1.6%; Christian 1.4%. President in 1980, Gen. Mohammad Zia-ul-Haq.

The shock wave generated by the Soviet military intervention in neighbouring Afghanistan in late 1979 gave Pres. Mohammad Zia-ul-Haq the opportunity to tighten still further the martial-law administration of Pakistan. President Zia had already placed all prominent political leaders under arrest, banned political activities, and imposed press censorship. Air Marshal Ashgar Khan was arrested, released, and rearrested three times in 1980. Begum Nusrat Bhutto and Benazir Bhutto, leaders of the Pakistan People's Party after former president Zulfikar Ali Bhutto was executed in April 1979, were put under house arrest in October 1979 but released in April 1980.

The political and economic situation had been worsening when the Afghan crisis intervened. Using the bogey of a Soviet threat to Pakistan's security, General Zia obtained promises of help from abroad. The U.S. agreed to uphold the 1959 mutual defense treaty, but a U.S. offer of $400 million in military and economic assistance over two years was rejected by Zia as "peanuts." Offers of financial assistance also came from the oil-rich Muslim countries of the Middle East, although no official figures were published. Saudi Arabia was said to have given $100 million, part of which was meant for Zia's islamization program.

Despite the rejection of the U.S. aid package, small arms and spare parts flowed into Pakistan from the U.S., and Pakistan also shopped for weapons in other Western markets. Some of these arms were being funneled into the Afghan insurgency movement through the Afghan rebels, who were finding refuge in Pakistani territory. Zia appealed to international aid agencies for assistance in caring for the growing number of Afghan refugees (over 900,000 by October). Despite denials, Pakistan did little to prevent some refugees from receiving training and arms and slipping back into Afghanistan.

President Zia organized two Islamic conferences at foreign ministers' level in which the main item on the agenda was the Afghan crisis. The first, in January, took a tough stand by deciding to withhold recognition of the Soviet-backed Babrak Karmal government unless the Soviets withdrew. The second, in May, adopted a more conciliatory approach. A three-member committee was set up to negotiate a political settlement of the crisis.

The economy showed no improvement. The growth rate for 1978–79 was 5.9%, compared with 7% in the previous year. The farming sector improved slightly, but industry suffered as investors shied away because of the unsettled political climate. The trade gap stood at over $2 billion and foreign debt liability at $7 billion. Foreign exchange reserves, which had touched $140 million, the lowest on record, in October 1979, picked up, thanks to remittances from Pakistanis in the Middle East amounting to an impressive $1.9 billion.

Relations with China were cordial, but those with India remained strained. India was suspicious of Pakistan's arms buildup and was convinced that, despite official statements to the contrary, Pakistan was going ahead with plans to manufacture a nuclear bomb. The establishment of trade and exchanges of visits and communications were welcomed by both sides, but several rounds of talks in Islamabad and New Delhi failed to make headway toward further normalization. India resented Pakistan's attempts to raise the Kashmir dispute at international forums, despite the Simla accord of 1972 in which both countries had agreed to settle the issue through bilateral talks.

PAKISTAN

Education. (1978–79) Primary, pupils 6,170,000, teachers 135,300; secondary, pupils 1,860,000, teachers 109,200; vocational, pupils 30,000, teachers 2,808; teacher training (1977–78), students 16,361, teachers 750; higher, students 316,500, teaching staff 18,340.

Finance. Monetary unit: Pakistan rupee, with (Sept. 22, 1980) a par value of PakRs 9.90 to U.S. $1 (free rate of PakRs 23.55 = £1 sterling). Gold, SDR's, and foreign exchange (June 1980) U.S. $832 million. Budget (1979–80 est.): revenue PakRs 33,220,000,000; expenditure PakRs 34,174,000,000. Gross national product (1978–79) PakRs 209,220,000,000. Money supply (June 1980) PakRs 60,980,000,000. Cost of living (1975 = 100; June 1980) 149.6.

Foreign Trade. (1979) Imports PakRs 40,118,000,000; exports PakRs 20,355,000,000. Import sources (1978–79): U.S. 16%; Japan 11%; Kuwait 6%; U.K. 6%; West Germany 6%; Saudi Arabia 5%; The Netherlands 5%. Export destinations (1978–79): Japan 10%; Hong Kong 8%; U.K. 8%; U.S. 7%; West Germany 6%; Saudi Arabia 6%. Main exports (1978–79): rice 20%; cotton fabrics 13%; cotton yarn 11%; carpets 10%; leather 7%; textile fibres 5%.

Transport and Communications. Roads (1979) 86,585 km. Motor vehicles in use (1979): passenger 130,400; commercial 35,700. Railways: (1978) 8,815 km; traffic (1978–79) 16,435,000,000 passenger-km, freight 9,401,000,000 net ton-km. Air traffic (1979): 4,993,000,000 passenger-km; freight 219.7 million net ton-km. Shipping (1979): merchant vessels 100 gross tons and over 83; gross tonnage 442,694. Telephones (June 1979) 312,200. Radio receivers (Dec. 1977) 5 million. Television receivers (Dec. 1977) 625,000.

Agriculture. Production (in 000; metric tons; 1979): wheat 9,944; corn 846; rice 4,953; millet *c.* 310; sorghum *c.* 280; potatoes *c.* 320; sugar, raw value *c.* 662; sugar, noncentrifugal (1978) *c.* 1,666; chick-peas 538; onions *c.* 330; rapeseed 248; cottonseed 1,301; mangoes *c.* 600; dates *c.* 215; oranges *c.* 540; tobacco *c.* 72; cotton, lint 577; beef and buffalo meat *c.* 341; mutton and goat meat *c.* 289; fish catch (1978) 293. Livestock (in 000; 1979): cattle 14,992; buffalo 11,306; sheep 24,185; goats 27,804; camels (1978) 819; chickens 48,872.

Industry. Production (in 000; metric tons; 1979): cement 3,146; crude oil 512; coal and lignite 1,329; natural gas (cu m) 6,706,000; petroleum products (1978) *c.* 3,680; electricity (kw-hr; 1976–77) *c.* 11,050,000; sulfuric acid 57; caustic soda 38; soda ash (1978–79) 71; nitrogenous fertilizers (nutrient content; 1978–79) 336; cotton yarn 338; woven cotton fabrics (sq m) 330,000.

WIDE WORLD

U.S. T-37 jets promised to Pakistan before the Soviet invasion of Afghanistan were shipped in March after negotiations resumed to discuss new terms of aid. The U.S. had terminated military and economic aid to Pakistan in April 1979.

Organization of African Unity: see African Affairs

Organization of American States: see Latin-American Affairs

Ornithology: see Life Sciences

Orthodox Churches: see Religion

Painting: see Art Exhibitions; Art Sales; Museums

Paints and Varnishes: see Industrial Review

In his capacity as chairman of the Islamic Conference, President Zia tried to mediate in the Iran-Iraq war by visiting Teheran and Baghdad, but without success. He also attended the UN General Assembly. (GOVINDAN UNNY)

Panama

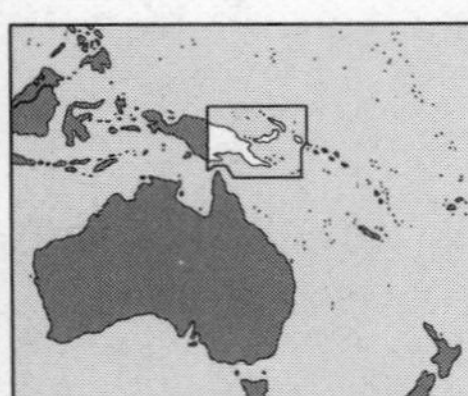

Papua New Guinea

Panama

A republic of Central America, Panama is bounded by the Caribbean Sea, Colombia, the Pacific Ocean, and Costa Rica. Area: 77,082 sq km (29,762 sq mi). Pop. (1980 prelim.): 1,830,175. Cap. and largest city: Panama City (pop., 1980 prelim., 388,-638). Language: Spanish. Religion (1978 est.): Roman Catholic 86.2%. President in 1980, Aristides Royo.

The formal transfer of the Canal Zone to Panama on Oct. 1, 1979, failed to bring the new economic and political age expected by Panamanians. Between 17 and 25% were unemployed, and all the population suffered from an inflation rate that rose from 10 to 14% during 1980. The national debt approached the U.S. $3 billion mark, and food imports grew while farmers' output declined. Panamanians reacted with strikes and riots. There were five disturbances around Christmas 1979, but violence was not confined to that period.

While the depressed economy was the basic cause of the disturbances, the presence of Mohammad Reza Pahlavi (*see* OBITUARIES), the exiled shah of Iran, provided an additional excuse. Through the personal appeal of Hamilton Jordan, U.S. Pres. Jimmy Carter's special envoy, Panama's strong man Omar Torrijos was persuaded to give the shah asylum on Contadora Island. However, the legal involvements of extradition proceedings, the quarrel over whether Panamanian or U.S. doctors should attend him, and the need for surgery finally impelled the shah to take flight to a more hospitable sanctuary in Egypt.

The pressures from Washington regarding the shah were displeasing to Panama, and there were other irritants, including the U.S. delay in naming members of the new Panama Canal Commission. Students marked the departure of the last governor of the Canal Zone with a riot. Two units of ITT, All America Cables and Radio and ITT Central America Cables and Radio, received notices that their licenses would not be renewed. To Panama's benefit, tolls on ship transits through the canal were raised nearly 30%, but the Organization of American States roundly condemned the increase. Relations with El Salvador were disturbed by the seizure of the Panamanian embassy by Salvadoran militants. In March Pres. Aristides Royo signed an agreement with Japan's prime minister for feasibility studies on a new Isthmian canal.

An election, devoid of issues and personalities, was held on Sept. 28, 1980, to fill some of the seats of the National Assembly's Executive Council. (ALMON R. WRIGHT)

PANAMA

Education. (1979) Primary, pupils 372,823, teachers 13,-730; secondary, pupils 96,305, teachers 4,042; vocational, pupils 40,807, teachers 2,121; teacher training, students 704, teachers 39; higher, students 37,885, teaching staff 1,796.

Finance. Monetary unit: balboa, at par with the U.S. dollar, with a free rate (Sept. 22, 1980) of 2.40 balboas to £1 sterling. Gold, SDR's, and foreign exchange (June 1980) U.S. $195 million. Budget (1979 est.): revenue 466 million balboas; expenditure 519 million balboas. Gross national product (1978) 2,259,400,000 balboas. Cost of living (Panama City; 1975 = 100; June 1980) 139.7.

Foreign Trade. (1979) Imports 1,185,300,000 balboas; exports 287.9 million balboas. Import sources (1978): U.S. 33%; Ecuador 15%; Panama (Colón free zone) 9%; Venezuela 6%; Japan 5%. Export destinations (1978): U.S. 44%; West Germany 12%; Panama Canal Zone 11%; Costa Rica 5%. Main exports: petroleum products 25%; bananas 23%; shrimps 15%; sugar 8%.

Transport and Communications. Roads (1978) 8,148 km. Motor vehicles in use (1977): passenger 66,900; commercial 19,500. Railways (1978) 678 km. Air traffic (1978): 392 million passenger-km; freight 3.9 million net ton-km. Shipping (1979): merchant vessels 100 gross tons and over 3,803 (mostly owned by U.S. and other foreign interests); gross tonnage 22,323,931. Telephones (Jan. 1978) 156,700. Radio receivers (Dec. 1977) 275,000. Television receivers (Dec. 1977) 206,000.

Agriculture. Production (in 000; metric tons; 1979): rice *c.* 200; corn *c.* 65; sugar, raw value (1978) *c.* 187; mangoes *c.* 26; bananas *c.* 1,000; oranges 65; coffee *c.* 6; fish catch (1978) 114. Livestock (in 000; 1978): cattle 1,396; pigs 190; horses *c.* 164; chickens *c.* 4,400.

Industry. Production (in 000; metric tons; 1977): petroleum products *c.* 2,790; cement 331; manufactured gas (cu m; 1979) 1,200; electricity (kw-hr; 1979) *c.* 1,980,000.

Papua New Guinea

Papua New Guinea is an independent parliamentary state and a member of the Commonwealth of Nations. It is situated in the southwest Pacific and comprises the eastern part of the island of New Guinea, the islands of the Bismarck, Trobriand, Woodlark, Louisiade, and D'Entrecasteaux groups, and parts of the Solomon Islands, including Bougainville. It is separated from Australia by the Torres Strait. Area: 462,840 sq km (178,704 sq

PAPUA NEW GUINEA

Education. (1979) Primary, pupils 277,301, teachers 8,-872; secondary, pupils 34,626, teachers 1,299; vocational (1976), pupils 9,575, teachers 495; teacher training (1978), students 2,658, teachers 185; higher (1978), students 9,804, teaching staff 1,235.

Finance. Monetary unit: kina, with (Sept. 22, 1980) a free rate of 0.65 kina to U.S. $1 (1.57 kinas = £1 sterling). Gold, SDR's, and foreign exchange (June 1980) U.S. $450 million. Budget (1979 est.): revenue 562 million kinas; expenditure 574 million kinas.

Foreign Trade. (1979) Imports 668.2 million kinas; exports 685.9 million kinas. Import sources (1978): Australia *c.* 47%; Japan *c.* 19%; Singapore *c.* 11%; U.S. *c.* 5%. Export destinations (1978): Japan 31%; West Germany 25%; Australia 10%; U.S. 9%; U.K. 6%. Main exports: copper concentrates 42%; coffee 18%; cocoa 9%; coconut products 9%; fish *c.* 5%.

Transport. Roads (1977) 17,241 km. Motor vehicles in use (1976): passenger 17,700; commercial (including buses) 19,200. There are no railways. Shipping (1979): merchant vessels 100 gross tons and over 75; gross tonnage 21,022.

Agriculture. Production (in 000; metric tons; 1979): bananas *c.* 900; cassava (1978) *c.* 90; taro (1978) *c.* 230; yams (1978) *c.* 180; palm oil 36; cocoa 30; coffee *c.* 52; copra 160; tea *c.* 8; rubber *c.* 4; timber (cu m; 1978) 6,186. Livestock (in 000; 1978): cattle *c.* 166; pigs *c.* 1,383; goats *c.* 15; chickens *c.* 1,145.

Industry. Production (in 000; 1977): silver (troy oz) 1,-500; copper ore (metal content; metric tons) 182; gold (troy oz; 1979) *c.* 640; electricity (kw-hr; 1977–78) 1,145,-000.

Palestine:
see Israel; Jordan

Paper and Pulp:
see Industrial Review

mi). Pop. (1979 est.): 3,078,500. Cap. and largest city: Port Moresby (pop., 1979 est., 121,600). Language: English, Hiri or Police Motu (a Melanesian pidgin), and Pisin (also called Pidgin English or Neo-Melanesian) are official, although the latter is the most widely spoken. Religion (1966): Roman Catholic 31.2%; Lutheran 27.3%; indigenous 7%. Queen, Elizabeth II; governor-general in 1980, Sir Tore Lokoloko; prime ministers, Michael T. Somare and, from March 11, Sir Julius Chan.

On March 11, 1980, Papua New Guinea's first prime minister, Michael Somare, who had led the country since it became independent in 1975, was defeated on a no-confidence motion in Parliament and resigned. He was replaced by Sir Julius Chan (*see* BIOGRAPHIES), leader of the People's Progress Party. Chan, who said that he looked forward to Somare's continued contribution to the affairs of the nation, formed a new coalition government consisting of his own party, the National Party, the Papua Besena, the United Party, and the Melanesian Alliance. The change of government was orderly and marked no break in the continuity of economic policy. Chan was at pains to emphasize that overseas investors had no cause for alarm. He also stressed that while Somare had built up "a dangerously personalized form of government," his own aim was to govern through consultation. In August, at the request of the government of newly independent Vanuatu (formerly the New Hebrides), Papua New Guinea sent troops to help suppress a revolt there. (*See* VANUATU.)

(A. R. G. GRIFFITHS)

Paraguay

A landlocked republic of South America, Paraguay is bounded by Brazil, Argentina, and Bolivia. Area: 406,752 sq km (157,048 sq mi). Pop. (1980 est.): 3,067,000. Cap. and largest city: Asunción (metro. pop., 1980 UN est., 529,000). Language: Spanish (official), though Guaraní is understood by more than 90% of the population. Religion: Roman Catholic (official). President in 1980, Gen. Alfredo Stroessner.

By 1980 Gen. Alfredo Stroessner had been in power as president of Paraguay for 26 years, and speculation about a possible successor increased in diplomatic circles, with Gen. Andrés Rodríguez, commander of the General Caballero division, seen as the most likely candidate. The new military government set up in Bolivia in July was quickly recognized by Paraguay. Relations were broken off with Nicaragua, held responsible for the assassination of its former president, Anastasio Somoza (*see* OBITUARIES), in Asunción in September.

There was a serious armed confrontation between troops and peasants in Caaguazú Department in March. Censorship of the press prevented publication of full details of the events, but the Partido Liberal Radical Auténtico, in a paid advertisement in the press, condemned the repression being carried out against peasants in the region. Some estimates put the number killed at between 20 and 50, and some sectors of the church accused the government of executing the peasants after arresting them.

The economy continued to grow, gross domestic product increasing by 9.5% in 1979. Construction continued to be the most dynamic sector, reflecting the impact of the Itaipú hydroelectric project.

(MARTA BEKERMAN DE FAINBOIM)

PARAGUAY

Education. (1978) Primary, pupils 493,231, teachers 17,525; secondary and vocational, pupils 101,126, teachers 9,663; higher, students 20,496, teaching staff 1,945.

Finance. Monetary unit: guaraní, with (Sept. 22, 1980) a par value of 126 guaranis to U.S. $1 (free rate of 302 guaranis = £1 sterling). Gold, SDR's, and foreign exchange (June 1980) U.S. $687 million. Budget (1979 actual): revenue 48,651,000,000 guaranis; expenditure 41,250,000,000 guaranis. Gross domestic product (1978) 323 billion guaranis. Money supply (Feb. 1980) 49,468,000,000 guaranis. Cost of living (Asunción; 1975 = 100; May 1980) 196.8.

Foreign Trade. (1979) Imports 65,652,000,000 guaranis; exports 37,617,000,000 guaranis. Import sources: Brazil 21%; Argentina 18%; U.S. 12%; Algeria 11%; Japan 9%; West Germany 7%; U.K. 6%. Export destinations: Argentina 17%; West Germany 15%; The Netherlands 15%; Brazil 9%; Italy 7%; Switzerland 7%; U.S. 6%; Japan 5%. Main exports: cotton 32%; soybeans 27%; timber 14%; vegetable oils 6%.

Transport and Communications. Roads (1978) *c.* 12,000 km. Motor vehicles in use (1978): passenger 29,000; commercial 9,300. Railways: (1978) 498 km; traffic (1977) 23 million passenger-km, freight 17 million net ton-km. Navigable inland waterways (including Paraguay-Paraná River system; 1978) *c.* 3,000 km. Telephones (Jan. 1977) 41,600. Radio receivers (Dec. 1977) 187,000. Television receivers (Dec. 1977) 55,000.

Agriculture. Production (in 000; metric tons; 1979): corn 585; cassava (1978) *c.* 1,763; sweet potatoes (1978) *c.* 132; soybeans 549; dry beans 58; sugar, raw value (1978) *c.* 68; tomatoes *c.* 56; oranges 247; bananas *c.* 255; palm kernels *c.* 16; tobacco *c.* 19; cottonseed *c.* 145; cotton, lint *c.* 71; beef and veal (1978) *c.* 121. Livestock (in 000; 1978): cattle *c.* 5,800; sheep *c.* 374; pigs *c.* 1,190; horses *c.* 332; chickens *c.* 10,274.

Industry. Production (in 000; metric tons; 1979): petroleum products (1977) *c.* 220; cement 135; cotton yarn (1977) 73; electricity (kw-hr) 716,000.

Paraguay

Peru

Peru

A republic on the west coast of South America, Peru is bounded by Ecuador, Colombia, Brazil, Bolivia, Chile, and the Pacific Ocean. Area: 1,285,215 sq km (496,224 sq mi). Pop. (1979 est.): 17,291,000, including approximately 52% whites and mestizos and 46% Indians. Cap. and largest city: Lima (metro. area pop., 1978 est., 4,376,100). Language: Spanish and Quechua are official; Indians also speak Aymara. Religion: Roman Catholic. President of the military government until July 28, 1980, Francisco Morales Bermúdez; president from July 28, Fernando Belaúnde Terry; prime minister from July 28, Manuel Ulloa Elías.

Fifteen political groupings contested the presidential and congressional elections of May 18, 1980, to elect the first civilian government to hold office in Peru since 1968. The elections were the first to enfranchise illiterates (13% of voters) and the first to give the vote to those between 18 and 20 years old; 63% of the electorate of 6.4 million were voting for the first time. The two front-running contestants in the presidential election were Armando Villanueva Del Campo of the Alianza

Parachuting: see Aerial Sports

Penology: see Prisons and Penology

Pentecostal Churches: see Religion

Popular Revolucionaria Americana (APRA) and ex-president Fernando Belaúnde Terry (*see* BIOGRAPHIES) of Acción Popular (AP). Although opinion polls predicted a close battle, Belaúnde won easily, with 45.4% of valid votes, a healthy surplus over the 36% required for a candidate to be declared president. On June 18 he appointed a financier, Manuel Ulloa Elías, to be prime minister.

The left-wing parties presented no serious opposition; a tentative coalition collapsed before the elections. APRA, seriously split, could offer little concerted opposition to the governing party, which, in coalition with the Partido Popular Cristiano (PPC), had a majority in both houses.

On July 28 Belaúnde took office as president of Peru, at the head of the coalition. One of his first acts was to hand back to their former owners the seven Lima daily newspapers confiscated by the military government. Preparations began for the resumption of work on the construction of the Marginal Highway in the jungle, begun during President Belaúnde's first term (1963–68). Road works were a major election promise made by Belaúnde as part of his declared intention to create full employment and increase investment. Other proposals in his economic program included raising agricultural production, developing the jungle region, reducing state participation in the economy and increasing private investment, reducing subsidies and taxes, refinancing part of the external public debt, and seeking long-term loans for financing priority development projects.

Despite the president's initiatives to review labour legislation and reduce inequalities in the distribution of income, together with a quarterly adjustment of wages and salaries in line with inflation (expected to be 55–60% in 1980), labour disputes gathered momentum. Increases in electricity rates, gasoline prices, and bus fares triggered unrest, and in the first half of September there were 30 strikes in progress. In the first municipal elections in 14 years, held in November, the AP appeared to lose some ground to the left.

The Peruvian economy, on the other hand, showed signs of continuing the upward trend begun in 1978 and 1979. The buoyancy of the export sector, an increase in construction and manufacturing activity, and higher tax collections helped the gross domestic product to show an annual growth rate of 3.7% by midyear, and there was a possibility that the official target of a 5% growth rate for 1980 would be achieved. At the end of June there was an overall balance of payments surplus of U.S. $516 million. Exports rose 39% over the first half of 1979 to $1,943,000,000 by June, while imports rose by 52% to $1,109,000,000, reflecting increased demand generated by a more buoyant economy. Of total exports, 11% were petroleum, 10% silver, and 10% copper, which showed increases of 218, 47, and 229%, respectively, over the first half of 1979. A government decision in September to cut the maximum level of duties on imported goods from 115 to 60% was expected to increase imports. (SARAH CAMERON)

PERU

Education. (1978) Primary, pupils 3,126,000, teachers 77,844; secondary and vocational, pupils 1,090,200, teachers 37,383; higher (1977), students 233,420, teaching staff 13,468.

Finance. Monetary unit: sol, with (Sept. 22, 1980) a free rate of 278 soles to U.S. $1 (667 soles = £1 sterling). Gold, SDR's, and foreign exchange (June 1980) U.S. $1,887,000,000. Budget (1979 actual): revenue 532,907,000,000 soles; expenditure 477,619,000,000 soles. Gross national product (1979) 2,909,800,000,000 soles. Money supply (March 1980) 539 billion soles. Cost of living (Lima; 1975 = 100; March 1980) 665.5.

Foreign Trade. (1979) Imports 490,850,000,000 soles; exports 805,820,000,000 soles. Import sources (1978): U.S. *c.* 32%; Venezuela *c.* 9%; West Germany *c.* 7%; Japan *c.* 6%. Export destinations (1978): U.S. 38%; Japan 12%; West Germany 5%; Yugoslavia 5%. Main exports: copper 19%; lead 8%; coffee 7%; silver 7%; fish meal 7%; zinc 5%.

Transport and Communications. Roads (1976) 56,940 km. Motor vehicles in use (1977): passenger 300,400; commercial (including buses) 166,200. Railways: (1978) 2,155 km; traffic (1976) 528 million passenger-km, freight (1977) 612 million net ton-km. Air traffic (1978): 1,470,000,000 passenger-km; freight *c.* 37.5 million net ton-km. Shipping (1979): merchant vessels 100 gross tons and over 694; gross tonnage 646,380. Telephones (Jan. 1978) 402,500. Radio receivers (Dec. 1977) 2.2 million. Television receivers (Dec. 1977) 825,000.

Agriculture. Production (in 000; metric tons; 1979): rice 545; corn *c.* 600; wheat *c.* 95; barley *c.* 175; potatoes *c.* 1,700; sweet potatoes (1978) *c.* 165; cassava (1978) *c.* 410; sugar, raw value 695; onions *c.* 170; oranges *c.* 166; lemons *c.* 86; coffee *c.* 66; cotton, lint *c.* 95; fish catch (1978) 3,365. Livestock (in 000; 1979): cattle 4,187; sheep 14,473; pigs 2,200; goats *c.* 2,000; horses (1978) *c.* 648; poultry *c.* 36,000.

Industry. Production (in 000; metric tons; 1977): cement 1,970; crude oil (1979) 9,360; natural gas (cu m) *c.* 520,000; iron ore (metal content; 1978) 1,966; pig iron 244; crude steel 379; copper (1979) 222; lead (1978) 74; zinc (1978) 67; tungsten concentrates (oxide content) *c.* 0.7; gold (troy oz) 119; silver (troy oz; 1979) *c.* 40,000; fish meal 497; petroleum products *c.* 5,780; electricity (kw-hr) 8,557,000.

Petroleum:
see Energy

Pharmaceutical Industry:
see Industrial Review

Philately and Numismatics

Stamps. A new world record price for a single stamp was established in April 1980 by Robert A. Seigel of New York City when he auctioned the only known example of the British Guiana 1856 one-cent stamp for $850,000. The buyer's identity was not disclosed. Classic stamps advanced steadily in value, but the overstretched market in the British "Seahorses" stamps of King George V reacted adversely when too many were released for sale almost simultaneously.

Sotheby Parke Bernet stamp auctions made an increasing impact on the U.S. stamp market and claimed two records: $240,000 for a mint block of four of the 1901 two-cent Pan-American Exposition stamps with inverted centres; and $240,000, again, for the only known cover with three clear impressions of the "Running Chicken" cancellation created by the postmaster of Waterbury, Conn. This identical cover was sold in 1976 for $45,000. In May, Harmers of San Francisco held a four-day sale of the Sandra Ilene West collection of German stamps in the firm's London offices and realized £1,005,443, a new record for a single-country collection. The Bavarian section made £314,843 on the first day.

Two major international exhibitions were held under the patronage of the International Philatelic Federation (FIP). LONDON 1980 took place at

Earls Court, London, in May. The three major awards presented there were: the FIP Grand Prix d'Honneur, R. B. Pracchia (Brazil) for Brazil classic issues; the Grand Prix National for the best exhibit of British stamps, "Daisy" (Switzerland); and Grand Prix International, A. Perpiña Sebria (Spain) for classic Spanish issues. In June NORWEX '80 took place in Oslo, Norway, and the major awards were: FIP Grand Prix d'Honneur, Marcel F. Décerier (France) for classic French issues; Grand Prix National, F. C. Moldenhauer (Norway) for Norway 1855–60; Grand Prix International, Isac Seligson (Luxembourg) for Luxembourg 1852–65; Prix d'Honneur Nordique (for a non-Norwegian Scandinavian collection), Holger Crafoord (Sweden) for classic Iceland; Prix d'Honneur d'Outremer, Enrique M. de Bustamente (Spain) for classic Peru.

At the British Philatelic Federation congress, held at Trinity College, Cambridge, in August, new signatories to the Roll of Distinguished Philatelists were Stig Andersen (Denmark), Tevfik Kuyas (Turkey—the first from his nation), Kenneth Pennycuick (U.K.), Gary S. Ryan (U.K.), and Arthur Salm (U.S.). The Philatelic Congress Medal went to Jack C. Simmonds of Cambridge and the Lichtenstein Medal of the Collectors Club of New York to Ronald A. G. Lee (U.K.).

New appointments included those of W. Raife Wellsted as curator of London's National Postal Museum and Douglas N. Muir as editor of the British monthly *Philatelic Magazine*.

In May the UN Postal Administration announced the discovery of forgeries of the 1954 three-cent United Nations Day stamp. They were printed by photo-offset rather than the steel engraving (recess) process used for the genuine stamps. It was the first recorded forgery of a UN stamp. There was no worldwide issue during 1980, but the U.K. and many Commonwealth territories marked the 80th birthday of Queen Elizabeth, the queen mother, by issuing special stamps.

(KENNETH F. CHAPMAN)

Coins. Coin collecting during the year was greatly influenced by the drastic changes in the prices of silver and gold bullion. After reaching highs of $50 and $880 per troy ounce, respectively, in the spring of 1980, silver and gold dropped quickly to $12 and $460. Before the decline the value of a U.S. silver dime, 1964 and earlier, had risen to about $3.50, that of a pre-1936 silver dollar to about $38.50, and that of a $20 gold coin to about $850. Many of the common-date silver and gold coins were melted and the metal reclaimed.

Continuing inflation and the purchase of rare coins as investments forced prices to new highs during the early part of 1980. However, the influence of the business recession caused some weakening in the rare coin market by midyear.

As expected, the U.S. Treasury did start to sell gold medals to the public in one-ounce and half-ounce sizes in 1980. The purchase of these pieces through the Postal Service was coordinated with the changing gold market, making transactions a bit complex. During the first two months that the medals could be ordered only about 332,000 of the 1.5 million pieces struck were sold, and the original September 30 deadline for ordering was extended to Dec. 31, 1980. The Susan B. Anthony dollar, released in 1979, continued to be unpopular, largely because its size caused it to be confused with the quarter. A "P" mint mark was placed on all coins struck at the Philadelphia Mint in 1980 except the cent.

Paper money of all kinds and numismatic books continued to increase in popularity with collectors, resulting in higher prices for both. An 1890 $1,000 U.S. "Treasury Note" reportedly sold for a record price for paper money of $100,000. At a California auction in June 1980, an 1869 *American Bond Detector* realized $3,200; a two-volume work on coinage in The Netherlands that brought $1,600 a year earlier was sold for $2,900; and an unusually fine first edition of *Heath's Counterfeit Detector* brought a record $650 for that series of books.

False collector coins continued to plague the marketplace. In addition to known false rare and expensive coins, the certification service of the

WIDE WORLD

These rare Pan-American stamps with inverted centres were sold for $240,000 in April by Sotheby Parke Bernet Stamp Auction Co. in New York City.

PHOTOS, WIDE WORLD

A new U.S. gold medallion was put up for sale in July by the Treasury Department. A one-ounce gold coin (left) was offered at $645 and a half-ounce gold coin (right) for $322.50.

American Numismatic Association in Colorado Springs, Colo., discovered counterfeits of such pieces as the 1972 doubled-die cent, 1926 $20 gold coin, and the popular 19th-century U.S.-type coins.

During the year a number of countries issued new coins of interest to collectors. Coins relating to the 1980 Olympic Games in Moscow included issues by the Soviet Union, China, Hungary, Isle of Man, Jamaica, and Western Samoa. Belgium issued a 1980 silver 500-franc coin in observance of the 150th anniversary of its independence. Canada's 1980 silver dollar portrays a polar bear on an Arctic ice floe with the northern lights above. Canada also issued a 1980 gold coin containing one-half ounce of fine gold. Another 1980 gold coin was the $200 of Australia, containing about 0.295 troy ounce of fine gold and depicting the koala.

The medal authorized by the U.S. Congress in May 1979 honouring movie actor John Wayne was released by the Mint in March 1980. Orders for the two sizes of the portrait medal, which bears no other legend than "John Wayne—American," approached 500,000, making it the most popular mint medal of all time. (GLENN B. SMEDLEY)

[452.D.2.b; 725.B.4.g]

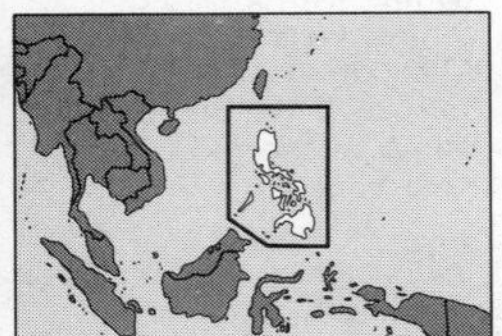
Philippines

Philippines

Situated in the western Pacific Ocean off the southeast coast of Asia, the Republic of the Philippines consists of an archipelago of about 7,100 islands. Area: 300,000 sq km (115,800 sq mi). Pop. (1980 est.): 48,358,000. Cap. and largest city: Manila (pop., metro. area, 1979 est., 5,900,600). Language: Pilipino and English are the official languages. Pilipino, the national language, is based on a local language called Tagalog and is spoken by 55.2% of the population but only by 23.8% as a mother tongue. English is spoken by 44.7% of the population but only by 0.04% as a mother tongue. Other important languages spoken as mother tongues include Cebuano 24.4%, Ilocano 11.1%, Hiligaynon 8%, Bicol 7%; and others 25.7%. Religion (1970): Roman Catholic 85%; Muslim 4.3%; Aglipayan 3.9%; Protestant 3.1%; others 2.4%. President in 1980, Ferdinand E. Marcos.

PHILIPPINES

Education. Primary (1977–78), pupils 7,992,406, teachers 256,370; secondary, pupils 1,887,469; vocational, pupils 969,952; secondary and vocational, teachers 80,192; higher, students 969,952, teaching staff (1975–76) 31,783.

Finance. Monetary unit: peso, with (Sept. 22, 1980) a free rate of 7.36 pesos to U.S. $1 (17.70 pesos = £1 sterling). Gold, SDR's, and foreign exchange (June 1980) U.S. $2,569,000,000. Budget (1979 actual): revenue 35,260,000,000 pesos; expenditure 35,749,000,000 pesos. Gross national product (1979) 217.2 billion pesos. Money supply (June 1980) 18,587,000,000 pesos. Cost of living (1975 = 100; June 1980) 170.7.

Foreign Trade. (1979) Imports 48,787,000,000 pesos; exports 33,446,000,000 pesos. Import sources: U.S. 23%; Japan 23%; Saudi Arabia 6%; Kuwait 5%. Export destinations: U.S. 30%; Japan 26%; The Netherlands 8%; West Germany 5%. Main exports (1978): coconut oil 18%; metal ores 14%; clothing 10%; fruit and vegetables 8%; electrical equipment 7%; timber 7%; sugar 6%; oilseeds 5%.

Transport and Communications. Roads (1979) 127,150 km. Motor vehicles in use (1977): passenger 440,500; commercial (including buses) 327,100. Railways: (1976) 1,069 km; traffic (1979) 485 million passenger-km, freight 34 million net ton-km. Air traffic (1978): 4,432,000,000 passenger-km; freight 126.6 million net ton-km. Shipping (1979): merchant vessels 100 gross tons and over 620; gross tonnage 1,606,019. Telephones (Jan. 1978) 567,300. Radio receivers (Dec. 1977) 1,936,000. Television receivers (Dec. 1977) 850,000.

Agriculture. Production (in 000; metric tons; 1979): rice *c.* 7,000; corn 3,300; sweet potatoes (1978) *c.* 888; cassava (1978) *c.* 1,707; sugar, raw value *c.* 2,355; bananas *c.* 2,430; pineapples *c.* 480; copra *c.* 1,910; coffee *c.* 86; tobacco *c.* 57; rubber *c.* 55; pork *c.* 386; fish catch (1978) 1,558; timber (cu m; 1978) 34,345. Livestock (in 000; March 1979): cattle *c.* 1,910; buffalo *c.* 3,018; pigs *c.* 7,300; goats *c.* 1,430; horses *c.* 340; chickens *c.* 60,000.

Industry. Production (in 000; metric tons; 1979): coal 263; cement 3,941; chrome ore (oxide content; 1977) 162; copper ore (metal content) *c.* 260; gold (troy oz) *c.* 640; silver (troy oz; 1977) 1,621; petroleum products (1978) *c.* 9,570; sulfuric acid (1977) 257; cotton yarn (1977) 31; electricity (kw-hr) *c.* 19,000,000.

A wave of terrorist bombings began in Manila on Aug. 22, 1980, as a challenge to continued martial-law rule by Pres. Ferdinand E. Marcos. Responsibility was claimed by the previously unknown April 6 Liberation Movement, named for demonstrations against Marcos that had taken place on that date in 1978. Within two months more than 30 bombs were set off. A U.S. woman tourist was killed by one on September 12, and more than 60 persons were injured. Marcos was attending a conference of the American Society of Travel Agents in Manila when a bomb went off there on October 19, but he was not hurt. After an

Former senator Gerardo Roxas (left), president of the opposition Liberal Party, and José Laurel, Jr., chairman of the Ad Hoc Committee of the Nacionalista Party in the Philippines, announced in August a new movement to try to achieve a peaceful solution to the country's internal problems.

UPI

intensive hunt, the government announced that 15 persons had been arrested and had admitted guilt. In November more than 60 people were charged in connection with 25 bombings.

A group of 72 persons, including leaders of the government before Marcos assumed power in 1972, issued on August 29 a "Covenant for Freedom." It called for an immediate end to what it termed the dictatorship of Marcos, an end to martial law, the holding of free elections, and other changes. Some Filipinos at home and in exile abroad warned, however, that these old politicians lacked the appeal to lead opposition to Marcos, and the bombings showed that new, more desperate forms of opposition were developing.

The New Society Movement headed by Marcos won the first nationwide series of local elections since 1972, held on Jan. 30, 1980. His son, Ferdinand, Jr., a 22-year-old student in the United States, was elected vice-governor of the family's home province, Ilocos Norte.

The best known opposition leader, former senator Benigno S. Aquino, Jr., was allowed to leave prison on May 8 for a heart operation in Dallas, Texas. Aquino had been under a death sentence. In leaving, he promised to "desist from commenting on our domestic political situation or engage or participate in any partisan political activity" while in the U.S. But, beginning with an August 4 speech in New York City, he started speaking out in opposition to the Marcos regime.

Aquino later met in Syria with Chairman Nur Misuari of the Moro National Liberation Front to seek a negotiated end to the Muslim separatist conflict in the southern islands. However, sporadic violence in that region continued and so did widely scattered violence from the Maoist New People's Army, which the government said was gaining strength.

Despite these problems the Philippines' economy continued to grow at a rate estimated between 4 and 5.8% for 1980. Inflation was cut from 24% in February to 13.8% in September, according to government statistics. Some businesses experienced hard times, however, and the government launched a program to help them and those workers who had lost their jobs. One measure was to set up 12 new export processing zones where Filipino workers could produce goods for export free of taxes. These would compete with similar arrangements in other Southeast Asian countries. As part of this industrial policy the government expanded development of energy resources, including geothermal, hydroelectric, and nuclear, in order to reduce dependence on imported oil. Foreign investment continued to come into the country, showing confidence in economic prospects.

(HENRY S. BRADSHER)

Photography

After more than a decade of vigorous growth as an image-making technology, a commercial enterprise, and a cultural force, photography in 1980 showed signs of leveling off, temporarily at least. It was a year of consolidation rather than innovation and of the fruition of numerous trends more than the setting of new directions. In the early months of the year the soaring cost of silver was a sharp reminder that a basic natural resource of the medium was finite. Among books, exhibitions, and auction sales, retrospective and rediscovered work drew more notice than did new talent.

Photo Equipment. Designers and manufacturers of single-lens-reflex (SLR) 35-mm cameras continued to spend much of their main effort in developing highly automated models in the medium-to-low price range. Three firms, however, introduced top-of-the-line, professional-quality cameras that attracted much attention.

Nikon's F3 embodied an attempt to combine heavy-duty construction with sophisticated state-of-the-art exposure automation. Somewhat lighter and smaller than previous models of the Nikon F series, it was an aperture-priority camera (user selects the aperture; shutter speed is chosen automatically) with stepless shutter speeds from 8 to 1/2000 sec, a liquid crystal display (LCD) exposure-information readout in the viewfinder, and a behind-the-mirror metering system. A silicon photodiode measured light that passed through thousands of microscopic holes in the reflex mirror and then was reflected downward by a secondary mirror. In the event of battery failure a backup mechanical release lever allowed mechanical shutter operation at 1/60 sec.

Nearly ten years in developing, the Pentax LX included a wide range of accessories that formed a versatile system with many professional, industrial, medical, and scientific applications. Extremely compact, the LX was an aperture-priority, automatic-exposure design using a silicon photocell recessed in the floor of the mirror chamber. The central portion of the reflex mirror was a semi-transparent beam splitter that permitted about 15% of the light to pass through to a secondary

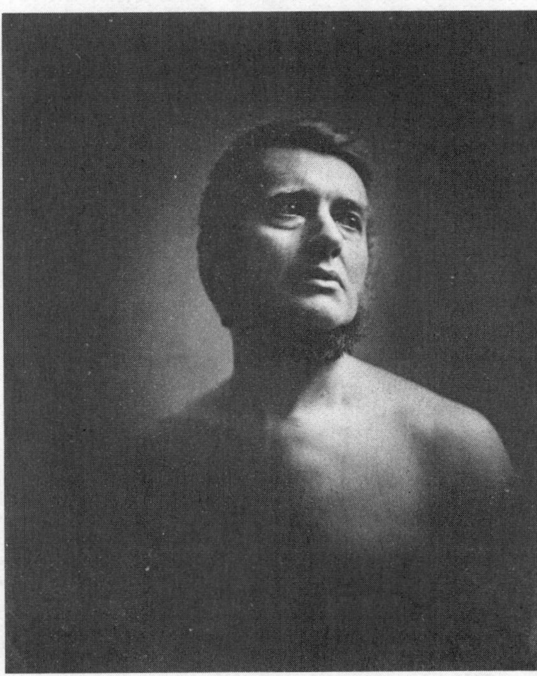

CHRISTIE'S, NEW YORK

At a photography sale in New York City in May, this "Self Portrait" by Albert Sands Southworth (*c.* 1848) fetched $36,000.

JEAN-PIERRE LAFFONT—SYGMA

Jean-Pierre Laffont's photo of children working in Egypt was part of his award-winning "Le Monde terrifiant des enfants qui traviallent."

mirror, which in turn reflected it to the photocell for measuring. Shutter speeds from a full 125 sec to 1/2000 sec were provided in the automatic mode and from 1/75 sec (its synchronization speed for electronic flash) to 1/2000 sec mechanically in the event of battery failure.

The Leica R4-MOT supplied multimode exposure automation (a choice of aperture-priority, shutter-priority, programmed, and full manual modes) plus both "spot" and averaging metering, a feature adapted from its predecessor, the Leica R3. As with the F3 and LX, the Leica R4 also used a secondary mirror behind the main reflex mirror to reflect a portion of the light downward to a photocell on the mirror chamber floor.

As the sale of 110 pocket cameras leveled off or declined, there was rekindled interest in compact 35-mm rangefinder and autofocus cameras. Many new models were introduced in 1980. In many cases only slightly larger than a conventional 110, they all offered the advantage of full-frame 35-mm format and a wide choice of 35-mm colour and black-and-white films. A built-in electronic flash was a commonplace feature, and many designers devised ways to shield the lens with an integral protective cover when the camera was not in use.

Autofocusing technology made some advances during the year. Canon introduced a new system called SST (for solid-state triangulation), the first autofocusing system in a production camera to use a CCD (charge-coupled device) for sensing light. A passive system, it employed two stationary mirrors to place a "standard" image and "reference" image of the subject on an array of 240 sensors. An integrated circuit linked with the array sought the best match between the two images—the point of sharpest focus—and drove a motorized lens-focusing system until that point was achieved. The SST system was first used in Canon's AF 514XL-S super-eight sound movie camera and later shown at the 1980 Photokina exhibition in a prototype autofocus *f*/4 35–70-mm zoom lens for 35-mm SLR cameras. Also shown in prototype at Photokina was a Ricoh autofocus lens in a K mount. Meanwhile, Honeywell, whose Visitronic module was being used in many current autofocusing compact 35-mm cameras, was developing a new CCD module that was expected to be incorporated in production cameras in the near future.

Although there were no outstanding breakthroughs in lens technology in 1980, the number and variety of lenses for SLR cameras proliferated as camera manufacturers expanded their lines and an increasing number of independent lens makers flooded the market. Manufacturers vied in producing lighter, more compact lenses at lower cost, with the emphasis on zooms that often included a close-up "macro" capacity. Several new lenses in the convenient 28–80-mm or 28–85-mm range were introduced, and at Photokina Tokina showed a prototype *f*/3.5 to *f*/4.5 35–200-mm lens, a harbinger of very extended range zooms to come.

A significant development in film technology was the application of chromogenic imaging to black-and-white emulsions with Ilford's XP-1 400 and Agfa's Vario-XL films. Chromogenic imaging, used in most modern colour print and transparency films, employs light-sensitive silver halides only to capture the image, which then is transferred during development to nonsilver coupled dyes while the silver is chemically removed. An advantage of the new Ilford and Agfa films was that their silver likewise could be retrieved and recycled. For the user they offered speeds of ASA 400 and higher, extremely fine grain, and extremely wide exposure latitude.

The market for instant photography failed to expand as rapidly as many industry analysts expected. Polaroid introduced its SX-70 Time Zero instant colour print film, which produced a developed image in about 30 to 60 seconds and yielded stronger colour saturation than previous, slower SX-70 print material.

Eastman Kodak Co. celebrated its 100th anniversary year with publicity and special promotions but, as 1980 ended, with no major new products, despite rumours of a new type of 35-mm cartridge that would automatically set the exposure system of a compatibly designed camera to the correct ASA setting.

Demonstrated in prototype form was the Nimslo 3-D camera and colour prints. The point-and-shoot camera used conventional 35-mm colour print film but had four lenses that recorded four images simultaneously. After processing, the film was turned over to a special computerized Nimslo printer that integrated the images in the form of tiny elliptical dots. The final image was printed on a plastic base surfaced with a screen of fine lenses. The print gave a three-dimensional effect without requiring special glasses.

Cultural Trends. Despite a recession and pessimistic predictions, the boom in photographic prints as collectible art objects did not go bust. At major auctions in New York City and elsewhere the trend was generally up. Landscape photographer Ansel Adams's photograph of "Moonrise, Hernandez, New Mexico," a bellwether among contemporary works, sold in a rare oversize print for $46,000. Signed prints by a growing number of living photographers were commanding $500 prices and higher. The number of serious collectors, motivated by a love of the medium, investment possibilities, or both, continued to grow.

As in 1979, many of the outstanding photographic books of the year represented the work of established or nearly forgotten photographers. Of special note was *Photographs for the Tsar*, a collection of colour images made between 1909 and 1914 by Sergei Mikhailovich Prokudin-Gorskii. A pioneer colour photographer, he was commissioned by Nicholas II to document the Romanov empire. Purchased by the Library of Congress in 1948, the remarkable black-and-white colour separation prints and negatives lay almost forgotten in the archives until recently rediscovered and reproduced in full colour. Other outstanding photographic books of the year included *Lisette Model: An Aperture Monograph*; *Artists: Portraits from Four Decades*, by Arnold Newman; and *Flowers*, by Irving Penn.

Photokina, the huge international trade and cultural photographic exhibition held every two years in Cologne, West Germany, celebrated its 30th anniversary year in 1980. The retirement was announced of L. Fritz Gruber, who had been Photokina's cultural director since its beginnings in 1950. His last exhibition, "The Imaginary Museum," was an impressive selection of nearly 500 vintage prints from museums and collections around the world.

The International Museum of Photography at George Eastman House in Rochester, N.Y., was plagued by financial and personnel problems, which led to the resignation of its director and a reduction in its staff. A financial reorganization and continued funding support from Eastman Kodak subsequently helped alleviate the crisis. A new director was appointed in October. In Great Britain, the venerable Royal Photographic Society, long located in London, moved its headquarters and collections to new facilities in Bath.

For the first time in history the Pulitzer Prize for spot news photography went to an anonymous photographer, for a photograph of the execution of Kurdish rebels in Iran. The Pulitzer for feature photography went to Erwin H. Hagler of the *Dallas Times Herald* for a colour essay on the American cowboy. The University of Missouri School of Journalism and the National Press Photographers Association presented their annual Pictures of the Year awards. Honours for Magazine Photographer of the Year went to David Burnett of Contact Press Images, who also won the top award from the World Press Photo competition. Newspaper Photographer of the Year was Bill Wax of the *Gainesville* (Fla.) *Sun*. Among others also honoured was Jean-Pierre Laffont of Sygma for his "Le monde terrifiant des enfants qui traviallent," a powerful self-assigned documentary essay.

Perhaps the most sensational and widely photographed U.S. news event of the year was the eruption in May of Mt. St. Helens in Washington state. Hundreds of amateur and professional photographers covered the catastrophe, and at least one news photographer, Reid Blackburn of the *Vancouver Columbian*, lost his life during the eruption.

(ARTHUR GOLDSMITH)

See also Motion Pictures.
[628.D; 735.G.1]

Physics

High-Energy Physics. The year 1980 marked the 49th birthday of the concept of the neutrino. This elementary particle was predicted in 1931 by Austrian physicist Wolfgang Pauli, who described it as a particle with zero rest mass, zero electric charge, and therefore a very weak tendency to interact with matter. The neutrino was necessary to explain the phenomenon of beta decay, in which a neutron in an unstable nucleus transforms into a proton by spontaneously emitting an electron. The electron must be accompanied by a neutrino for momentum and energy to be conserved. Twenty-five years later the neutrino was experimentally observed by U.S. physicists Clyde L. Cowan, Jr., and Frederick Reines in a reaction in which a neutrino is absorbed by a proton to give a neutron plus a positive electron (positron).

Despite 24 years of further investigation the neutrino was still providing physicists with many enigmas, some of which could well have a bearing on the future of the universe. By 1980 it had become generally accepted that there are more than one species of neutrino, but there was some controversy as to exactly how many. In addition it was not yet clear whether each species always maintains its separate identity or whether they all actually oscillate continuously between identities. The final quandary concerned the mass itself; physicists were not sure whether the rest mass is absolutely zero as originally thought or whether it is small but finite. From estimates based on theories about the origin of the universe, there are possibly a billion relic neutrinos for every proton and neutron in existence; hence, even a small mass for the neutrino would lead to its dominance of the mass of the universe.

Six members (plus their corresponding antiparticles) of a family of light particles called leptons were known as of 1980. One subgroup comprises the electron, the muon, and the more recently discovered tau. In addition, there is thought to be a second group of three leptons, the neutrinos, each of which is associated with one of the first group. The electron neutrino and the muon neutrino have been experimentally observed, but the tau neutrino has avoided detection to date. The possibility that neutrinos can change identities is an intriguing one and could go a long way in explaining some scientific puzzles. For example, why is the measured flux of electron neutrinos that emanate from nuclear reactions in the Sun only one-third of the value calculated by standard theory? If these neutrinos were free to oscillate between identities, then their chances of being counted by a detector on Earth sensitive only to electron neutrinos would be less than expected.

During the past year experimental proof of this possibility was sought using nuclear reactor cores as neutrino sources. One approach was to study the ratio of the products of two kinds of reactions that result when reactor-produced neutrinos, known initially to be pure electron antineutrinos, interact with the nucleus of deuterium (hydrogen-2). The value of this ratio depends on whether all of the interacting neutrinos have retained their original identity or whether some have interacted while wearing a new guise. This experiment, carried out by Reines and co-workers at the Savannah River reactor in South Carolina, produced evidence in favour of neutrino oscillations. Another group, working with the reactor at the Institut Laue-Langevin, Grenoble, France, but using a different approach, came to the opposite conclusion. The two groups planned more definitive experiments in which neutrino-induced reactions would be studied at a fixed energy but at two or more distances from the reactor core. Different neutrino flight paths would yield different electron neutrino intensities if oscillations occur.

The mass of the neutrino was under study by teams of scientists at the Institute of Theoretical and Experimental Physics in Moscow and at the University of Guelph in Ontario. The Soviet team was 99% confident that the mass lies between 14 and 46 electron volts (eV). Although the Canadian work was at an early stage, it set an upper limit of 70 eV for the neutrino mass. These values should be compared with a mass of 500,000 eV for the electron, itself a very light object.

It is generally believed that the universe started with a "big bang" and has been expanding ever since. The number of neutrinos that were created in this primordial event is "fantastiquement grand," to quote a French scientist. On the assumption that neutrinos are massless, many cosmological experts estimate that not enough mass exists in the universe to allow gravitational attraction to bring an eventual halt to the expansion. However, if neutrinos have even the feeble mass measured by the Soviet workers, universal expansion may well be arrested in the distant future and followed by a phase of contraction.

From its beginnings as the unobservable particle predicted by Pauli, the neutrino has become a key feature of astrophysics, cosmology, and theoretical physics, as well as of high-energy physics, in which beams of neutrinos are irreplaceable instruments in their own right. Many theoretical physicists would be delighted if in 50 years time two other elusive particles, the quark and the gluon, become as solidly established as the neutrino. In the early 1980s the quark, the postulated basic constituent of much of matter, and the gluon, the particle that binds quarks together, were being sought with the same determination that had accompanied the neutrino hunts decades earlier.

Low-Temperature Physics. The race for world records is not restricted to the swift and the strong. It is also a very active part of scientific research, in which the search for extremes is a necessary part of the discovery process. One topic within this province that attracted attention during the year was the attainment of ultralow temperatures. Although physicists believed that the absolute zero of temperature, zero degrees Kelvin (0 K), is an unobtainable infinity of science that can only be approached, this has not prevented a number of different groups throughout the world from pursuing ever lower temperatures.

The pioneer in modern low-temperature cooling methods is Nicholas Kurti of the Clarendon Laboratory, University of Oxford, who in the mid-1950s used an adiabatic demagnetization technique to reach temperatures below a thousandth of a degree Kelvin. For its first phase this technique involved cooling a mass of paramagnetic salt (for example, iron ammonium alum) to about 1 K using liquid helium. The salt was magnetized at constant temperature and then demagnetized while isolated from its environment. This "first-stage demagnetization" resulted in the cooling of the salt, and a copper sample to which it was linked, to a hundredth of a degree Kelvin. A second demagnetization was performed on the copper, reducing its temperature to a hundred-thousandth of a degree Kelvin. A major problem with Kurti's approach was that immediately after the low temperature was reached the sample began warming owing to inevitable heat leaks from the surroundings. Kurti illustrated the problem by pointing out that the energy required to heat his sample from a millionth to a hundredth of a degree Kelvin was equivalent to that obtained by dropping a pin a distance of two millimetres (eight-hundredths of an inch). The definition of temperature in this region requires great care because, in the copper samples used, the coupling between the spins of the conduction electrons and the atomic lattice is relatively weak; the conduction electrons can have a temperature that differs from that of the nuclei. In Kurti's experiments the nuclei reached temperatures as low as a hundred-thousandth of a degree Kelvin while the electronic temperature was a thousand times higher.

The double-stage demagnetizing technique was recently adapted and improved by groups at Jülich, West Germany; Tokyo; and Helsinki. Initial cooling was achieved by a commercially available adiabatic dilution refrigerator, which produced temperatures in the range of 15–25 mK (thousandths of a degree Kelvin). In the experiments of the first two groups the paramagnetic-salt first stage was replaced by an intermetallic compound, such as praseodymium combined with copper or nickel, which has greater cooling power than copper at 20 mK. Copper was again used for the final stage. The West German investigators managed to cool a two-kilogram (4.4-lb) copper sample to an overall temperature of 48 μK (millionths of a degree Kelvin). In addition, very careful engineering and design reduced the heat leaks to the copper sample to a minimum so that it warmed at a rate of only 2 μK per day. The Japanese achievement was roughly comparable; they cooled a 1.2-g (0.04-oz) copper sample to 50 μK, which then warmed up at "a few μK per hour." The world record, however, was taken by the Helsinki team, who used a system employing copper for both stages to obtain a temperature, for the nuclear spin system only, of 50 nK (billionths of a degree Kelvin).

Whereas these feats were pleasing simply as a demonstration of the capability of present-day science and technology, they also had a wide range of applications. Experiments at ultralow temperatures should help understanding of the superfluid behaviour of liquid helium-3 and helium-4, allow studies of possible superconducting behaviour in such strongly paramagnetic metals as palladium, and check the existence of nuclear magnetic ordering in such materials as praseodymium.

(S. B. PALMER)

See also Nobel Prizes.
[111.C.7.c; 111.H; 124.G.1; 131.E]

Poland

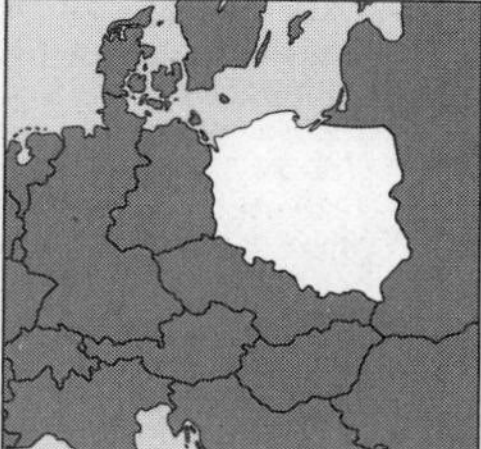
Poland

A people's republic of eastern Europe, Poland is bordered by the Baltic Sea, the U.S.S.R., Czechoslovakia, and East Germany. Area: 312,677 sq km (120,725 sq mi). Pop. (1980 est.): 35,382,000. Cap. and largest city: Warsaw (pop., 1979 est., 1,552,300). Language: Polish. Religion: predominantly Roman Catholic. First secretaries of the Polish United Workers' (Communist) Party in 1980, Edward Gierek and, from September 6, Stanislaw Kania; chairman of the Council of State, Henryk Jablonski; chairmen of the Council of Ministers (premiers), Piotr Jaroszewicz to February 15, Edward Babiuch from February 18 to August 24, and, from August 24, Jozef Pinkowski.

The year 1980 began tensely, with the Polish people facing food shortages, rationing of electric power, unsatisfactory public transport, and insufficient housing. At the eighth congress of the Polish United Workers' (Communist) Party (PUWP), held in Warsaw February 11–15, First Secretary Edward Gierek warned that the country faced higher energy and raw material prices and difficult international trading conditions.

The delegates elected the new Central Committee, which in turn elected the new Politburo of 14 members. The premier, Piotr Jaroszewicz, was dropped from the Politburo, and on February 18 the Sejm (parliament) elected Edward Babiuch as the new premier. On March 23 general elections produced the new Sejm (*see* POLITICAL PARTIES), which reelected Henryk Jablonski chairman of the Council of State.

Local strikes of industrial workers started early in the year, becoming more frequent in July when Babiuch increased meat prices. He was prepared to use force against the "antisocialist" elements but was opposed in the Politburo by Jablonski and Stanislaw Kania (*see* BIOGRAPHIES), among others. Gierek sought guidance from Soviet leader Leonid Brezhnev, who received him on July 31 and advised him to reach a compromise with the strikers. On August 14 the entire work force of 17,000 stopped production at Gdansk's Lenin shipyard.

On August 18 Gierek announced his readiness to accept sensible demands formulated by "honest" strikers. Discovering that Babiuch was planning to "promote" him to the presidency of the Council of State and assume the party leadership, Gierek on August 24 convoked the Central Committee, which expelled Babiuch and three of his supporters from the Politburo. Josef Pinkowski was nominated a full member of the Politburo and recommended to succeed Babiuch as head of government. The way was now open to negotiate with the Interfactory Strike Committee (IFSC) formed in Gdansk by Lech Walesa (*see* BIOGRAPHIES). This organization's demands included the workers'

JEAN-LOUIS ATLAN—SYGMA

Blue-collar workers in Poland went on strike in August demanding free trade unions. The Polish government later reluctantly acceded to their demands.

Pipelines: *see* Energy; Transportation

Plastics Industry: *see* Industrial Review

Poetry: *see* Literature

POLAND

Education. (1979–80) Primary, pupils 4,217,200, teachers 196,400; secondary, pupils 450,100, teachers 23,100; vocational and teacher training, pupils 1,941,800, teachers 76,800; higher (1978–79), students 485,200, teaching staff 52,300.

Finance. Monetary unit: zloty, with (Sept. 22, 1980) a commercial and tourist rate of 30.30 zlotys to U.S. $1 (72.86 zlotys = £1 sterling). Budget (total; 1979 est.): revenue 1,161,400,000,000 zlotys; expenditure 1,064,400,000,000 zlotys. Net material product (1978) 1,903,000,000,000 zlotys.

Foreign Trade. (1979) Imports 54,317,000,000 exchange zlotys; exports 50,192,000,000 exchange zlotys. Import sources: U.S.S.R. 31%; East Germany 8%; West Germany 7%; Czechoslovakia 6%. Export destinations: U.S.S.R. 35%; East Germany 7%; Czechoslovakia 7%; West Germany 7%. Main exports (1978): machinery 37%; coal 12%; transport equipment 10%; chemicals 8%; food 7%.

Transport and Communications. Roads (1979) 298,477 km (including 139 km expressways). Motor vehicles in use (1979): passenger 2,117,100; commercial 583,700. Railways: (1978) 23,975 km (including 6,496 km electrified); traffic (1979) 45,472,000,000 passenger-km, freight 135,364,000,000 net ton-km. Air traffic (1979): 2,314,000,000 passenger-km; freight 18,453,000 net ton-km. Navigable inland waterways in regular use (1978) 3,734 km. Shipping (1979): merchant vessels 100 gross tons and over 813; gross tonnage 3,580,294. Telephones (Dec. 1978) 3,095,300. Radio licenses (Dec. 1978) 8,486,000. Television licenses (Dec. 1978) 7,474,000.

Agriculture. Production (in 000; metric tons; 1979): wheat 4,220; rye 5,233; barley 3,785; oats 2,199; potatoes 49,582; sugar, raw value *c.* 1,587; rapeseed 233; cabbages (1978) *c.* 1,467; onions *c.* 446; tomatoes *c.* 164; carrots (1978) *c.* 532; cucumbers (1978) *c.* 357; apples *c.* 1,030; tobacco 70; butter *c.* 290; cheese 381; hen's eggs *c.* 499; beef and veal *c.* 730; pork *c.* 1,835; fish catch (1978) 571; timber (cu m; 1978) 21,530. Livestock (in 000; June 1979): cattle 13,036; pigs 21,224; sheep 4,221; horses (1978) *c.* 2,000; chickens (adult birds) 75,526.

Industry. Index of industrial production (1975 = 100; 1979) 125. Fuel and power (in 000; metric tons; 1979): coal 201,004; brown coal 38,110; coke (1978) 19,429; crude oil (1978) 360; natural gas (cu m) 7,330,000; manufactured gas (cu m; 1978) 7,974,000; electricity (kw-hr) 117,460,000. Production (in 000; metric tons; 1979): cement 19,180; iron ore (30% metal content; 1978) 530; pig iron 11,525; crude steel 19,219; aluminum (1978) 100; copper (1978) 332; lead (1978) 86; zinc (1978) 222; petroleum products (1977) *c.* 14,830; sulfuric acid 2,982; plastics and resins 561; fertilizers (nutrient content; 1978) nitrogenous 1,470, phosphate 1,026; cotton yarn 204; wool yarn 107; man-made fibres 231; cotton fabrics (m) 884,000; woolen fabrics (m) 123,000; passenger cars (units) 350; commercial vehicles (units) 64. Merchant vessels launched (100 gross tons and over; 1979) 489,000 gross tons. New dwelling units completed (1978) 292,000.

right to organize themselves in free trade unions. On August 31 Mieczyslaw Jagielski, first deputy premier, signed an agreement with Walesa stating that the new self-governing trade unions would "adhere to the principles defined in the Constitution of the People's Republic of Poland" and recognized "the leading role of the PUWP in the state." All the strikers' major demands were granted.

On September 1 the Kremlin sounded its disapproval of the historic compromise between the PUWP and Solidarnosc (Solidarity), as the IFSC now renamed itself. An article in *Pravda* warned Poland of "antisocialist elements" attempting to overthrow its Communist system. At a Central Committee meeting on September 5, Kania revealed that Gierek had been hospitalized after a serious heart attack. The next day Kania was elected party first secretary in his place, and the Central Committee again revamped the Politburo. As further warnings appeared in *Pravda*, the Central Committee convoked an extraordinary party congress on October 5, and the Sejm reshuffled the Council of State.

On October 24 the Warsaw District Court registered Solidarity as a legal organization. However, Walesa protested the insertion into the organization's charter of a clause stating that the union recognized the leading role of the PUWP. On October 30 Kania and Pinkowski met Brezhnev and Nikolay Tikhonov, the new Soviet premier, in Moscow. An understanding was reached on Soviet economic aid to Poland, and in a joint communiqué Brezhnev expressed the conviction that Poland would solve its problems. On October 31 Pinkowski informed Walesa that Solidarity would have free access to all state mass media. Walesa retorted that if the insertion into the union's charter was not deleted he would order a protest strike. On November 10 the Supreme Court of Poland upheld Solidarity's position, with a compromise: the PUWP clause was removed to an annex.

In November Jerzy Ozdowski, a leading Roman Catholic layman, was appointed a deputy prime minister, the first non-Communist to attain such a high government post. Major personnel changes were made in the local party structure in late November, and the Politburo was again revamped on December 2. Meanwhile, unrest continued. On December 5 leaders of the Warsaw Pact member states meeting in Moscow expressed their confidence that Poland would overcome its difficulties and pledged their support for it within the fraternal treaty membership—an allusion to the disobedience of Hungary in 1956 and Czechoslovakia in 1968. Both the Central Committee and the Roman Catholic Church urged restraint and an end to disorders. Threats of a strike by the nation's independent farmers abated, at least temporarily, when the Supreme Court on December 30 postponed a decision on legalization of a new farmers' organization, Rural Solidarity.

(K. M. SMOGORZEWSKI)

Police:
see Crime and Law Enforcement

Political Parties

The following table is a general world guide to political parties. All countries that were independent on Dec. 31, 1980, are included; there are a number for which no analysis of political activities can be given. Parties are included in most instances only if represented in parliaments (in the lower house in bicameral legislatures); the figures in the last column indicate the number of seats obtained in the last general election (figures in parentheses are those of the penultimate one). The date of the most recent election follows the name of the country.

The code letters in the affiliation column show the relative political position of the parties within each country; there is, therefore, no entry in this column for single-party states. There are obvious difficulties involved in labeling parties within the political spectrum of a given country. The key chosen is as follows: F-fascist; ER-extreme right; R-right; CR-centre right; C-centre; L-non-Marxist left; SD-social democratic; S-socialist; EL-extreme left; and K-Communist.

The percentages in the column "Voting strength" indicate proportions of the valid votes cast for the respective parties, or the number of registered voters who went to the polls in single-party states.

[541.D.2]

COUNTRY AND NAME OF PARTY	Affiliation	Voting strength (%)	Parliamentary representation
Afghanistan			
Pro-Soviet government since April 27, 1978	—	—	—
Albania (November 1978)			
Albanian Labour (Communist)	—	99.9	250 (250)
Algeria (February 1977)			
National Liberation Front	—	99.95	261
Angola (August 1980)			
Movimento Popular de Libertaçao de Angola (MPLA)	—	—	203
Argentina			
Military junta since March 24, 1976	—	—	—
Australia (November 1980)			
National Country	R	8.7	20 (19)
Liberal	C	37.5	54 (67)
Australian Labor	L	45.4	51 (38)
Other	—	1.9	0 (0)
Austria (May 1979)			
Freiheitliche Partei Österreichs	R	6.06	11 (10)
Österreichische Volkspartei	C	41.90	77 (80)
Sozialistische Partei Österreichs	SD	51.03	95 (93)
Bahamas, The (July 1977)			
Progressive Liberal Party	CR	55.0	30 (30)
Bahamian Democratic Party	L	...	5 (8)
Free National Movement	L	...	2 —
Bahrain			
Emirate, no parties	—	—	—
Bangladesh (February 1979)			
Jatiyabadi Dal (Nationalist Party)	R	49.0	207
Awami League	CR	...	40
Muslim League	C	...	20
Jatiya Samajtantrik Dal (National Socialist)	L	...	9
Others	—	...	24
Barbados (September 1976)			
Democratic Labour	C	...	7 (18)
Barbados Labour	L	...	17 (6)
Belgium (December 1978)			
Vlaams Blok	ER	...	1 (0)
Volksunie	R	...	14 (20)
Front Démocratique Francophone	R	...	10 (11)
Rassemblement Wallon	R	...	5 (4)
Parti Libéral — Flemish	CR	...	22 (17)
Parti Libéral — Wallon	CR	...	15 (16)
Parti Social-Chrétien — Flemish	C	...	57 (56)
Parti Social-Chrétien — Wallon	C	...	25 (24)
Parti Socialiste Belge — Flemish	SD	...	26 (27)
Parti Socialiste Belge — Wallon	SD	...	32 (35)
Parti Communiste	K	...	4 (2)
UDRT (Brussels anti-tax)	—	...	1 (0)
Benin (November 1979)			
People's Revolutionary Party	—	—	336
Bhutan			
A monarchy without parties	—	—	—
Bolivia			
Military junta since July 17, 1980	—	—	—
Botswana (October 1979)			
Botswana Democratic Party	C	...	29 (27)
Botswana People's Party	L	...	1 (2)
Botswana National Front	EL	...	2 (2)
Brazil (November 1978)			
Aliança Renovadora Nacional (ARENA)	CR	...	231 (199)
Movimento Democrático Brasileiro (MDB)	L	...	189 (165)
Bulgaria (May 1976)			
Fatherland Front	—	99.9	400 (400)
Bulgarian Communist Party			268
Bulgarian Agrarian Union			100
Young Communist League			19
No party affiliation			13
Burma (January 1978)			
Burma Socialist Program Party	—	99.0	464 (451)
Burundi (October 1974)			
Tutsi ethnic minority government	—	—	—
Cambodia (Kampuchea)			
Civil war since 1979	—	...	—
Cameroon (May 1978)			
Cameroonian National Union	—	99.98	120 (120)
Canada (February 1980)			
Social Credit	R	1.9	0 (6)
Progressive Conservative	CR	33.0	103 (136)
Liberal	C	43.9	147 (114)
New Democratic	L	19.8	32 (26)
Cape Verde (December 1980)			
African Party for the Independence of Guinea-Bissau and Cape Verde	—	93.0	—
Central African Republic			
Provisional military government since Sept. 26, 1979	—	...	—
Chad			
Military government since 1975	—	—	—
Chile			
Military junta since Sept. 11, 1973	—	—	—
China, People's Republic of (February 1978)			
Communist (Kungchantang) National People's Congress	—	...	3,500
Colombia (February 1978)			
Partido Conservador	R	...	86 (66)
Partido Liberal	C	...	109 (113)
Unión Nacional de Oposisión	L	...	4 (20)
Comoros (December 1974)			
Single party rule from Aug. 3, 1975	—	—	—
Congo			
Military government since Sept. 1968	—	—	—
Costa Rica (February 1978)			
Partido de Liberación Nacional	R	...	25 (27)
Partido de Unidad	C	...	27 (16)
Three left-wing parties	L	...	5 (8)
Cuba (November 1976)			
Partido Comunista Cubano	—	...	481
Cyprus (September 1976)			
Greek Zone: Pro-Makarios three-party alliance	—	...	34
Independent	—	...	1
Turkish Zone: National Unity Party	—	...	30
Communal Liberation Party	—	...	6
Populist Party	—	...	2
Republican Turkish Party	—	...	2
Czechoslovakia (October 1976)			
National Front	—	...	200
Denmark (October 1979)			
Conservative	R	12.5	22 (15)
Liberal Democratic (Venstre)	CR	12.5	23 (22)
Christian People's	CR	2.6	5 (6)
Progress (M. Glistrup)	C	11.0	20 (26)
Radical Liberal (Radikale Venstre)	C	5.4	10 (6)
Justice (Retsforbund)	C	2.6	5 (6)
Centre Democrats (E. Jakobsen)	C	3.2	6 (10)
Social Democrats	SD	38.3	69 (66)
Socialist People's	EL	5.9	11 (8)
Left Socialists	EL	3.6	6 (5)
Communist	K	1.9	0 (7)
Others	—	...	2 (2)
Djibouti (May 1977)			
Ligue Populaire Africaine pour l'Indépendance (mainly Somali)	C	...	33
Front de Libération de la Côte des Somalis	L	...	30
Dominica (July 1980)			
Freedom Party	C	...	17 (3)
Labour Party	L	...	2 (16)
Independents	—	...	2 (2)
Dominican Republic (May 1978)			
Partido Reformista	C	...	42 (86)
Partido Revolucionario	SD	...	49 ...
Others	—	...	... (5)
Ecuador (April 1979, figures incomplete)			
Partido Conservador	R	...	10
Concentración de Fuerzas Populares	C	...	30
Izquierda Democrática	L	...	14
Unión Democrática Popular	EL	...	3
Egypt (November 1976)			
Arab Socialist Union	—	...	350
El Salvador			
Provisional government since Oct. 15, 1979	—	...	—
Equatorial Guinea			
Provisional military government since Aug. 3, 1979	—	...	—
Ethiopia			
Military government since 1974	—	—	—
Fiji (September 1977)			
Alliance Party (mainly Fijian)	—	...	36 (24)
National Federation (mainly Indian)	—	...	15 (26)
Others	—	...	1 (2)
Finland (March 1979)			
National Coalition Party (Conservative)	R	21.7	47 (35)
Swedish People's	R	4.3	10 (10)
Centre Party (ex-Agrarian)	C	17.4	36 (39)
Liberal	C	3.7	4 (9)
Christian League	C	4.8	9 (9)
Rural	L	4.6	7 (2)
Social Democratic	SD	24.0	52 (54)
People's Democratic League (Communist)	K	17.9	35 (40)
Others	—	1.75	0 (2)
France (March 1978)			
Centre-Right:			
Gaullists (Rassemblement pour la République)	R	25.84	148 (185)
Giscardians (Union pour la Démocratie Française)	CR	23.18	137 (54)
Other	—	16.4	6 (36)
Union of Left:			
Parti Radical	L	2.02	10 (12)
Parti Socialiste	SD	28.46	103 (89)
Parti Communiste	K	18.83	86 (73)
Others	—	...	1 (9)
Gabon (February 1973)			
Parti Démocratique Gabonais	—	...	70
Gambia, The (April 1977)			
People's Progressive Party	C	...	29 (28)
United Party	L	...	2 (3)
German Democratic Republic (October 1976)			
National Front (Sozialistische Einheitspartei and others)	—	99.9	500 (434)
Germany, Federal Republic of (October 1980)			
Christlich-Demokratische Union	R	34.2	174 (190)
Christlich-Soziale Union	R	10.3	52 (53)
Freie Demokratische Partei	C	10.6	53 (39)
Sozialdemokratische Partei Deutschlands	SD	42.9	218 (214)
The Green (Ecology) Party		1.5	0
Ghana (June 1979)			
People's National Party	—	...	71
Popular Front Party	—	...	43
Action Congress Party	—	...	10
United National Convention	—	...	13
Social Democratic Party	—	...	3
Greece (November 1977)			
National Rally	R	6.82	5 (0)
New Democracy Party	CR	41.85	172 (215)
Democratic Centre Union	C	11.95	15 (57)
New Liberals (mainly in Crete)	C	1.08	2 (0)
Panhellenic Socialist Movement	SD	25.33	93 (15)
Left Alliance (Eurocommunist)	EL	2.72	2 (6)
Greek Communist Party (pro-Moscow)	K	9.36	11 (5)
Others	—	0.89	— (2)
Grenada			
People's Revolutionary Government since March 13, 1979	—	...	—
Guatemala (March 1978)			
Movimiento de Liberación Nacional	CR	...	20
Partido Institucional Democrático	CR	...	17
Partido Demócrata Cristiano	C	...	7
Partido Revolucionario	L	...	14
Others	—	...	3
Guinea (December 1974)			
Parti Démocratique de Guinée	—	100.0	150

COUNTRY AND NAME OF PARTY	Affiliation	Voting strength (%)	Parliamentary representation
Guinea-Bissau			
Governed by the Council of the Revolution since Nov. 14, 1980	—	—	—
Guyana (December 1980)			
People's National Congress	—	. . .	(37)
People's Progressive Party	—	. . .	(14)
Others	—	. . .	(2)
Haiti			
Presidential dictatorship since 1957	—	—	—
Honduras (April 1980)			
Partido Nacional	R	44.5	33
Partido Liberal	C	52.0	35
Partido de Innovación y Unidad	L	3.5	3
Hungary (June 1975)			
Patriotic People's Front	—	97.6	352
Iceland (December 1979)			
Independence (Conservative)	R	35.4	21 (20)
Progressive (Farmers' Party)	C	24.9	17 (12)
Social Democratic	SD	17.4	10 (14)
People's Alliance	K	19.7	11 (14)
Independent	—	. . .	1 (0)
India (January 1980)			
Congress (I) and allied parties:			
Congress (I)	C	. . .	351
Dravida Munnetra Kazhagam	R	. . .	16
Lok Dal (Janata secular)	—	. . .	41
Three smaller parties	—	. . .	7
Opposition:			
Janata (People's) Party	C	. . .	32 (295)
Congress (Urs)	C	. . .	13 (150)
Communist Party of India (Marxist)	K	. . .	35 (22)
Communist Party of India (pro-Soviet)	K	. . .	10 (7)
Anna Dravida Munnetra Kazhagam	R	. . .	2 (19)
Akali Dal (Sikh Party)	C	. . .	1 (9)
Six small parties	—	. . .	11
Independents	—	. . .	6
Indonesia (May 1977)			
Sekber Golkar (Functional Groups)	—	62.1	232 (236)
United Development Party (merger of four Islamic parties)	—	29.3	99 (94)
Partai Demokrasi Indonesia (merger of five nationalist and Christian parties)	—	8.6	29 (30)
Iran (May 1980)			
Islamic Republican Party	R	. . .	150
Islamic National Party	CR	. . .	80
Independents	—	. . .	40
Iraq			
Military and Ba'ath Party governments since 1958	—	. . .	. . .
Ireland (June 1977)			
Fianna Fail (Sons of Destiny)	C	. . .	84 (69)
Fine Gael (United Ireland)	C	. . .	43 (54)
Irish Labour Party	L	. . .	17 (19)
Sinn Fein (We Ourselves)	—	. . .	0 (0)
Others	—	. . .	4 (2)
Israel (May 1977)			
Likud	R	33.4	43 (39)
Torah Front	CR	4.8	5 (5)
National Religious	C	9.2	12 (10)
Democratic Movement for Change	C	11.6	15 —
Independent Liberal	C	1.2	1 (4)
Civil Rights Movement	L	1.2	1 (3)
Labour Alignment	SD	24.6	32 (51)
Democratic Front for Peace and Equality (pro-Soviet)	K	4.6	5 (4)
United Arab List	—	1.2	1 (3)
Others	—	8.0	5 (1)
Italy (June 1979)			
Movimento Sociale Italiano	F	5.3	30 (35)
Partito Liberale Italiano	CR	1.9	9 (5)
Democrazia Cristiana	C	38.3	262 (262)
Partito Repubblicano Italiano	C	3.0	16 (14)
Partito Social-Democratico Italiano	L	3.8	20 (15)
Partito Socialista Italiano	SD	9.8	62 (57)
Partito d'Unità Proletaria	EL	1.4	6 (6)
Partito Radicale	EL	3.4	18 (4)
Partito Comunista Italiano	K	30.4	201 (228)
Südtiroler Volkspartei	—	0.6	4 (3)
Others	—	2.1	2 (1)
Ivory Coast (October 1980)			
Parti Démocratique de la Côte d'Ivoire	—	99.9	100
Jamaica (October 1980)			
Jamaica Labour Party	L	57.0	51 (12)
People's National Party	SD	43.0	9 (48)
Japan (June 1980)			
Liberal-Democratic	R	. . .	284 (258)
Komeito (Clean Government)	CR	. . .	33 (57)
Democratic-Socialist	SD	. . .	32 (35)
Socialist	S	. . .	107 (107)
Communist	K	. . .	29 (39)
Independents and others	—	. . .	26 (25)
Jordan			
Royal government, no parties	—	—	60
Kenya (November 1979)			
Kenya African National Union (158 elected, 12 nominated, 2 ex-officio)	—	. . .	172 (158)
Kiribati (ex. Gilbert Islands, July 1979)			
House of Assembly	—	. . .	35
Korea, North (November 1977)			
Korean Workers' (Communist) Party	—	100.0	579
Korea, South (February 1973)			
Democratic Republican	CR	38.7	73
New Democratic	L	32.6	52
Democratic Unification	S	10.1	2
Independents	—	18.6	19
Kuwait			
Princely government, no parties	—	—	30
Laos, People's Democratic Republic of			
Lao People's Revolutionary Party	—	. . .	. . .
Lebanon (April 1972)			
Maronites (Roman Catholics)	—	. . .	30
Sunni Muslims	—	. . .	20
Shi'ite Muslims	—	. . .	19
Greek Orthodox	—	. . .	11
Druzes (Muslim sect)	—	. . .	6
Melchites (Greek Catholics)	—	. . .	6
Armenian Orthodox	—	. . .	4
Other Christian	—	. . .	2
Armenian Catholics	—	. . .	1
Lesotho			
Constitution suspended Jan. 30, 1970	—	—	—
Liberia			
People's Redemption Council since April 1980	—	—	—
Libya			
Military government since Sept. 1, 1969	—	—	—
Liechtenstein (February 1978)			
Vaterländische Union	CR	. . .	8 (7)
Fortschrittliche Bürgerpartei	C	. . .	7 (8)
Luxembourg (June 1979)			
Parti Chrétien Social	CR	34.5	24 (18)
Parti Libéral	C	21.3	15 (14)
Parti Ouvrier Socialiste	SD	24.3	14 (17)
Parti Social Démocratique	S	6.0	2 (5)
Parti Communiste Luxembourgeois	K	5.8	2 (5)
Independents	—	. . .	2 (0)
Madagascar (June 1977)			
Avant-garde de la Révolution Malgache	C	. . .	112
Parti du Congrès de l'Indépendance	L	. . .	16
Others	—	. . .	9
Malawi (June 1978)			
Malawi Congress Party	—	. . .	87
Malaysia (July 1978)			
Barisan Nasional	—	. . .	131 (120)
Democratic Action Party (mainly Chinese)	L	. . .	16 (9)
Party Islam	—	. . .	5 (14)
Maldives (February 1975)			
Presidential rule since 1975	—	—	—
Mali			
Military government since Nov. 19, 1968	—	—	—
Malta (September 1976)			
Nationalist Party	R	48.7	31 (27)
Labour Party	SD	51.3	34 (28)
Mauritania			
Military government since July 10, 1978	—	—	—
Mauritius (December 1976)			
Independence Party (Indian-dominated)	C	. . .	28 (39)
Parti Mauricien Social-Démocrate	L	. . .	8 (23)
Mauritius Militant Movement	K	. . .	34
Mexico (July 1979, results incomplete)			
Partido Revolucionario Institucional	CR	. . .	291
Partido Acción Nacional	C	. . .	4
Partido Auténtico de la Revolución Mexicana	L	. . .	. . .
Partido Popular Socialista	S	. . .	. . .
Partido Comunista Mexicano	K	. . .	. . .
Monaco (January 1978)			
Union Nationale et Démocratique	—	. . .	18 (17)
Mongolia (June 1977)			
Mongolian People's Revolutionary Party	—	99.99	354 (295)
Morocco (June 1977)			
Independents (pro-government)	CR	44.7	141 (159)
Popular Movement (rural)	CR	12.4	44 (60)
Istiqlal (Independence)	C	21.6	49 (8)
National Union of Popular Forces	L	14.6	16 (1)
Others	—	. . .	14 (12)
Mozambique (December 1977)			
Frente da Libertação do Moçambique (Frelimo)	—	. . .	210
Nauru (November 1977)			
Nauru Party (Dowiyogo)	—	. . .	9
Opposition Party (DeRoburt)	—	. . .	8
Independent	—	. . .	1
Nepal			
Royal government since December 1960	—	—	—
Netherlands, The (May 1977)			
Christian Democratic Appeal (Anti-Revolutionaire Partij, Christelijk-Historische Unie, and Katholieke Volkspartij)	CR	31.9	49 (48)
Boerenpartij (Farmers' Party)	CR	0.8	1 (3)
Volkspartij voor Vrijheid en Democratie	C	18.0	28 (22)
Democrats 1966	C	5.4	8 (6)
Democratische-Socialisten '70	L	0.7	1 (6)
Partij van de Arbeid	SD	33.8	53 (43)
Communistische Partij van Nederland	K	1.7	2 (7)
Seventeen other parties	—	. . .	8 (15)
New Zealand (November 1978)			
National (Conservative)	CR	39.5	51 (54)
Labour Party	L	40.5	40 (32)
Social Credit	C	16.4	1 (1)
Nicaragua			
Provisional government since July 20, 1979	—	. . .	—
Niger			
Military government since April 17, 1974	—	—	—
Nigeria (July–August 1979)			
National Party of Nigeria	—	. . .	168
Unity Party of Nigeria	—	. . .	111
Nigerian People's Party	—	. . .	79
Great Nigeria People's Party	—	. . .	48
People's Redemption Party	—	. . .	49
Norway (September 1977)			
Høyre (Conservative)	R	24.7	41 (29)
Kristelig Folkeparti	CR	12.1	22 (20)
Senterpartiet (Agrarian)	C	8.6	12 (21)
Venstre (Liberal)	C	3.2	2 (1)
New People's Party	C	1.7	0 } (2)
Party of Progress	C	1.9	0 }
Arbeiderpartiet (Labour)	SD	42.5	76 (62)
Sosialistisk Venstreparti (Socialist Left)	S	4.1	2 } (16)
Kommunistiske Parti	K	0.4	0 }
Oman			
Independent sultanate, no parties	—	—	—

COUNTRY AND NAME OF PARTY	Affiliation	Voting strength (%)	Parliamentary representation
Pakistan			
Military government since July 5, 1977	—	—	—
Panama (August 1978)			
National Union Assembly	—	...	505
Papua New Guinea (June–July 1977)			
Pangu Party	—	...	39 (22)
United Party (chief opposition)	—	...	38 (34)
People's Progress Party	—	...	18 (12)
National Party	—	...	3 (10)
Country Party	—	...	1 —
Papua Besena	—	...	5 (2)
Other	—	...	5 —
Paraguay (February 1977)			
Partido Colorado (A. Stroessner)	R	69.0	...
Opposition parties	—	31.0	...
Peru (May 1980)			
Acción Popular	—	...	98
Alianza Popular Revolucionaria Americana	—	...	58
Popular Christian Party	—	...	10
Others	—	...	14
Philippines			
Martial law since Sept. 23, 1972	—	—	—
Poland (March 1980)			
Front of National Unity	—	99.0	460 (460)
Communists			261
Peasants			113
Democrats			37
Non-party			49
Portugal (October 1980)			
Democratic Alliance	R	47.1	136 (128)
Republican and Socialist Front	SD	28.0	75 (74)
United People's Alliance	K	16.9	41 (47)
Popular Democratic Union	K	...	1 (1)
Qatar			
Independent emirate, no parties	—	—	—
Romania (March 1980)			
Social Democracy and Unity Front	—	98.5	369 (349)
Rwanda (July 1975)			
National Revolutionary Movement	—	—	—
Saint Lucia (July 1979)			
United Workers' Party	C	...	5
St. Lucia Labour Party	S	...	12
Saint Vincent and the Grenadines (December 1979)			
St. Vincent Labour Party	—	...	11
New Democratic Party	—	...	2
San Marino (May 1980)			
Communist coalition (Partito Comunista, Partito Social Democratico, Partito Socialista Unitario)		56.0	—
Christian Democrats		40.0	—
São Tomé and Príncipe (1975)			
Movimento Libertaçao	—	—	—
Saudi Arabia			
Royal government, no parties	—	—	—
Senegal (February 1978)			
Parti Socialiste	CR	82.5	83
Parti Démocratique Sénégalais	L	17.1	17
Seychelles			
People's Progressive Front (alone in power after the June 5, 1977, coup)	—	—	—
Sierra Leone (June 1978)			
All People's Congress	CR	...	85 (70)
Singapore (December 1980)			
People's Action Party	CR	75.5	75 (69)
Solomon Islands			
Independent Group	C	...	...
National Democratic Party	L	...	...
Somalia (December 1979)			
Somalian Revolutionary Socialist Party	—	...	171
South Africa (November 1977)			
Herstigte Nasionale Partij	ER	3.2	0 —
National Party	R	64.8	134 (122)
South African Party	CR	1.7	3 —
New Republic Party	C	11.8	10 —
United Party	C	—	— (41)
Progressive Federal Party	L	16.7	17 —
Progressive Reform Party	L	—	— (7)
Others	—	...	— (1)
Spain (March 1979)			
Coalición Democrática	R	5.0	9 (16)
Unión Centro Democrático	CR	34.0	168 (165)
Partido Socialista Obrero Español	SD	29.0	121 (118)
Partido Comunista Español	K	10.0	23 (20)
Catalans (two parties)	—	...	9 (13)
Basques (three parties)	—	...	12 (9)
Others	—	...	8 (9)
Sri Lanka (July 1977)			
United National Party	R	...	139 (19)
Freedom Party	C	...	8 (91)
Tamil United Liberation Front	C	...	17 (12)
Communists and others	—	...	2 (44)
Sudan (February 1978)			
Sudan Socialist Union	—	...	304
Suriname			
National Military Council since Feb. 25, 1980	—	—	—
Swaziland			
Royal government, no parties	—	—	—
Sweden (September 1979)			
Moderata Samlingspartiet	R	20.4	73 (55)
Centerpartiet	CR	18.2	64 (86)
Folkpartiet (Liberal)	C	10.6	38 (39)
Socialdemokratiska Arbetarepartiet	SD	43.5	154 (152)
Vänsterpartiet Kommunisterna	K	5.6	20 (17)
Switzerland (October 1979)			
Christian Democrats (Conservative)	R	...	44 (46)
Republican Movement / National Action (V. Ochen)	R	...	3 (6)
Evangelical People's	R	...	3 (3)
Swiss People's (ex-Middle Class)	CR	...	23 (21)
Radical Democrats (Freisinnig)	C	...	51 (47)
League of Independents	C	...	8 (11)
Liberal Democrats	L	...	8 (6)
Social Democrats	SD	...	51 (55)
Socialist Autonomous	EL	...	3 (1)
Communist (Partei der Arbeit)	K	...	3 (4)
Others	—	...	3 (0)
Syria (August 1977)			
National Progressive Front	—	...	159
Others	—	...	36
Taiwan (Republic of China)			
Nationalist (Kuomintang)	—	...	773
Tanzania (October 1980)			
Tanganyika African National Union	C	...	111 (218)
Zanzibar Afro-Shirazi (nominated)	L	...	40 (52)
Thailand (April 1979)			
Social Action Party	—	...	82
Thai Nationalist Party	—	...	38
Democratic Party	—	...	32
Thai People's Party	—	...	32
Serithan (Socialist) Party	—	...	21
Others	—	...	96
Togo (December 1979)			
Rassemblement du Peuple Togolais	—	96.0	67
Tonga (June 1972)			
Legislative Assembly (partially elected)	—	—	21
Trinidad and Tobago (September 1976)			
People's National Movement	C	...	24 (36)
Democratic Action Congress	—	...	2
United Labour Front	L	...	10
Tunisia (November 1979)			
Parti Socialiste Destourien	—	...	121 (112)
Turkey			
National Security Council since Sept. 12, 1980	—	—	—
Uganda (December 1980)			
Uganda People's Congress Party	—	...	68
Democratic Party	—	...	48
Union of Soviet Socialist Republics (March 1979)			
Communist Party of the Soviet Union	—	99.99	1,500 (767)
United Arab Emirates			
Federal government of seven emirates	—	—	—
United Kingdom (May 1979)			
Conservative	R	43.9	339 (276)
Liberal	C	13.8	11 (13)
Labour	L	36.9	268 (319)
Communist	K	...	0 (0)
Scottish National Party	—	...	2 (11)
Plaid Cymru (Welsh Nationalists)	—	...	2 (3)
Ulster Unionists (four groups)	—	...	10 (10)
Others	—	...	3 (3)
United States (November 1980)			
Republican	CR	...	192 (159)
Democratic	C	...	242 (276)
Independent		...	1 (0)
Upper Volta			
Military Committee for Recovery of National Progress since Nov. 25, 1980	—	—	—
Uruguay			
Rule by Council of State from 1973	—	—	—
Vanuatu (New Hebrides) (November 1979)			
Vanuaaku Pati	C	...	26
Others	—	...	13
Venezuela (December 1978)			
COPEI (Social Christians)	CR	...	88 (64)
Acción Democrática	L	...	88 (102)
Movimiento al Socialismo	SD	...	11 (9)
Movimiento Electoral del Pueblo	S	...	3 (8)
Movimiento Institucional Revolucionario	EL	...	4 (2)
Partido Comunista Venezuelano	K	...	1 (2)
Vietnam, Socialist Republic of (April 1976)			
Communist Party	K	...	...
Yemen, People's Democratic Republic of			
National Liberation Front	—	—	—
Yemen Arab Republic			
Military government since 1974	—	—	—
Yugoslavia (May 1978)			
Communist-controlled Federal Chamber	—	...	220
Zaire (October 1977)			
Legislative Council of the Mouvement Populaire de la Révolution	—	...	268
Zambia (December 1973)			
United National Independence Party	—	80.0	125
Zimbabwe (February–March 1980)			
Zimbabwe African National Union	—	63.0	57
Zimbabwe African People's Union	—	24.0	20
United African National Council	—	8.0	3
Rhodesian Front (Europeans)	—		20

(K. M. SMOGORZEWSKI)

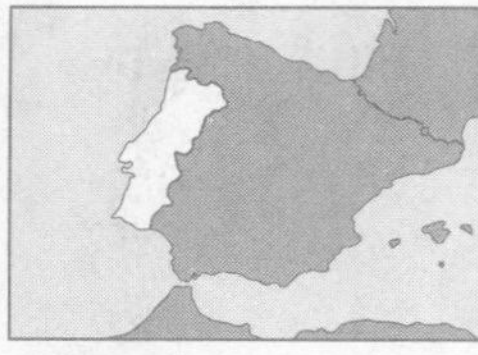

Portugal

Portugal

A republic of southwestern Europe, Portugal shares the Iberian Peninsula with Spain. Area: 91,632 sq km (35,379 sq mi), including the Azores (2,335 sq km) and Madeira (796 sq km). Pop. (1980 est.): 9,856,000, excluding about 550,000 refugees (mostly from Africa). Cap. and largest city: Lisbon (pop., 1979 est., 861,500). Language: Portuguese. Religion: Roman Catholic. President in 1980, Gen. António dos Santos Ramalho Eanes; premiers, Maria de Lurdes Pintassilgo, Francisco Sá Carneiro from January 3 to December 4, and, from December 22, Francisco Pinto Balsemão.

Pres. António Ramalho Eanes's decision to call elections in December 1979 rested on the Assembly's failure to produce a workable parliamentary majority. The new elections resulted in the emergence of the centre-right Democratic Alliance (AD) as the country's major political party, at both the national and municipal level. Nevertheless, the 1976 constitution required both general and presidential elections to be held in 1980. The new AD administration, therefore, only had ten months in office before submitting itself to the electorate again, and the administration moved to implement its manifesto with a speed uncharacteristic of Portuguese politics.

On Jan. 18, 1980, the AD won approval of its governmental program after carrying a vote of confidence in the Assembly with a majority of 15. The basic objectives of its program included: stimulating economic growth by foreign investment to help the country prepare for European Economic Community (EEC) membership in 1983; reversing the four-year decline in real wages; carrying out the 1977 agrarian reform law, which provided for the return of a sizable portion of the nation's collectively owned farmland to previous owners dispossessed by the revolution; and providing increased pensions and social security benefits. These aims were consolidated and published in the 1980 budget proposed in April. A basic principle was to open the economy to private enterprise, but the Council of the Revolution, led by President Eanes, declared as unconstitutional laws that would have permitted private banks and insurance companies to compete with nationalized firms. The government finally decided to delay its initiative until after the elections.

Portuguese farmers protested in April against the return of land to former owners. The lands had been seized in 1975 by the revolutionary government.

WIDE WORLD

The impasse focused attention on the programmed revision of the 1976 constitution. The AD government was adamant that references to the achievement of socialism be removed from the text, the Council of the Revolution abolished, and the revised document made to conform to the requirements of the EEC's 1957 Treaty of Rome. Under the existing constitution, revision required a two-thirds majority in the Assembly. The AD argued for a popular referendum to enable Parliament to alter the constitution by a simple majority.

The Republican Socialist Front (FRS), comprising the Socialist Party and smaller socialist groups, was committed to preserving the existing constitution, though it seemed prepared to cede the deletion of references to socialism and a reduced role for the Council of the Revolution. Nevertheless, art. 83 of the constitution, which stated that "all nationalizations effected since April 25, 1974, are irreversible conquests by the working classes," remained sacrosanct in FRS eyes. There was broad agreement on EEC membership and the changes required from Portugal, but this consensus was set aside during the election campaign. The left-wing parties showed themselves particularly adept at mudslinging. They concentrated on accusing the AD of having quashed a parliamentary inquiry into allegations of improper financial activities by the premier and on his unorthodox private life—Francisco Sá Carneiro (*see* OBITUARIES) campaigned with his Danish-born mistress at his side while still legally married to the Portuguese mother of his five children.

The AD preferred to concentrate on its achievements in office. It claimed to have given Portugal its most efficient government since the revolution. Early in the summer the government began to pay compensation in bonds for assets nationalized during the revolution and introduced a new system of financial and fiscal incentives for the private investor. Tax cuts and increases in the minimum monthly wage and in pensions provided electoral sweeteners. At the same time, the administration proceeded with land reform, handing back land to owners who had been illegally dispossessed and awarding the landless farming land from the official reserves.

From the start of the campaign the AD and the premier tried to undermine President Eanes's political image, accusing him not merely of ineffi-

PORTUGAL

Education. (1977–78) Primary, pupils 1,284,862, teachers 67,051; secondary, pupils 417,112, teachers 13,272; vocational, pupils 82,656, teachers 8,829; teacher training, students 8,128, teachers 761; higher, students 84,911, teaching staff 8,198.

Finance. Monetary unit: escudo, with (Sept. 22, 1980) a free rate of 49.93 escudos to U.S. $1 (120 escudos = £1 sterling). Gold, SDR's, and foreign exchange (June 1980) U.S. $1,472,000,000. Budget (1979 est.) balanced at 283,395,000,000 escudos. Gross national product (1978) 767.4 billion escudos. Money supply (May 1980) 393,790,000,000 escudos. Cost of living (Lisbon; 1975 = 100; June 1980) 264.6.

Foreign Trade. (1979) Imports 320,080,000,000 escudos; exports 170,510,000,000 escudos. Import sources: EEC 42% (West Germany 12%, U.K. 9%, France 8%, Italy 5%); U.S. 12%; Iraq 7%; Spain 6%. Export destinations: EEC 57% (U.K. 18%, West Germany 13%, France 10%, Italy 6%); U.S. 6%; Sweden 5%. Main exports: textile yarns and fabrics 16%; clothing 14%; machinery 9%; food 7%; cork and manufactures 6%; chemicals 6%; wine 6%. Tourism (1978): visitors 1,680,000; gross receipts U.S. $600 million.

Transport and Communications. Roads (1978) 50,710 km (including 66 km expressways). Motor vehicles in use (1978): passenger 970,000; commercial 57,000. Railways: (1978) 3,588 km; traffic (1979) 5,628,000,000 passenger-km, freight 884 million net ton-km. Air traffic (1979): 3,927,000,000 passenger-km; freight 122.6 million net ton-km. Shipping (1979): merchant vessels 100 gross tons and over 347; gross tonnage 1,205,478. Telephones (Dec. 1978) 1,253,500. Radio receivers (Dec. 1976) 1.6 million. Television licenses (Dec. 1978) 1,175,000.

Agriculture. Production (in 000; metric tons; 1979): wheat 233; oats 66; rye 113; corn 456; rice *c.* 135; potatoes 1,012; tomatoes *c.* 685; figs (1978) *c.* 200; apples 107; oranges *c.* 107; wine 1,150; olives 236; olive oil *c.* 41; cow's milk *c.* 695; meat *c.* 423; fish catch (1978) 255; timber (cu m; 1978) *c.* 8,110. Livestock (in 000; 1979): sheep *c.* 5,200; cattle *c.* 1,050; goats *c.* 745; pigs *c.* 2,500; poultry *c.* 17,200.

Industry. Production (in 000; metric tons; 1979): coal 181; petroleum products (1978) *c.* 5,980; manufactured gas (Lisbon; cu m) 154,000; electricity (kw-hr) 15,250,000; kaolin (1978) 74; iron ore (50% metal content) 58; crude steel 420; sulfuric acid *c.* 600; fertilizers (nutrient content; 1978–79) nitrogenous 189, phosphate 103; plastics and resins (1978) 101; cement 5,136; wood pulp (1977) 616; cork products (1977) 249; cotton yarn 101; woven cotton fabrics 54.

ciency but of being a veiled Communist. Sá Carneiro stated repeatedly that should President Eanes be reelected in the Dec. 7, 1980, polls he would resign. In April the AD put up 52-year-old Gen. António Soares Carneiro, a right-winger and veteran of the Angola war, as its presidential candidate.

In the October 5 general elections, the AD was able to increase its majority from 6 seats in the Assembly to 19. (*See* POLITICAL PARTIES.) The Socialists ceased to lose ground after their weak showing in the December 1979 elections, but a major swing against the Communist Party and those further to the left occurred. The voters might have been influenced by the Soviet invasion of Afghanistan and the party's support for the Soviet Union.

On October 8 the official campaign for the presidential election began. The first victim of the campaign was the secretary-general of the Socialist Party, Mário Soares. During the party's congress after the general elections, Soares, blamed for the party's failure to increase its share of the popular vote, resigned after failing to persuade the party to withdraw its support for the reelection of President Eanes. Soares had turned against Eanes after the president began trying to capture centrist voters from AD ranks with a moderate stance. Soares was replaced temporarily by Víctor Constancio, Portugal's brightest economist. A split then developed in the Socialist Party, with the left wing proposing Soares as a presidential candidate and the moderate majority hardening its resolve to support Eanes.

On December 4, only four days before the election, Sá Carneiro was killed when the light plane that was to take him to a Soares Carneiro rally in Oporto crashed just after takeoff in Lisbon. The election, almost overshadowed by the tragedy, resulted in an overwhelming victory for Eanes, who gained about 57% of the vote. Soares Carneiro, whose lacklustre campaign had been livened only by Sá Carneiro, obtained 40%, while the remainder went to four minor candidates. On December 22 Eanes designated as premier Francisco Pinto Balsemão, a journalist and lawyer and a close associate of Sá Carneiro. (MICHAEL WOOLLER)

See also Dependent States.

Prisons and Penology

A dangerous atmosphere of tension and unrest pervaded the prison systems of many countries. Overcrowding was often at record levels, particularly in the U.S. and the U.K. Conditions were bad for staff as well as prisoners, and both groups showed their discontent. By far the most serious disturbance of the year occurred in February at New Mexico's state penitentiary at Santa Fe, where a savage outbreak left 33 prisoners dead, many of them horribly mutilated, and five wings of the prison extensively damaged. (*See* Sidebar.)

Efforts continued to reduce prison populations by speeding up the process of bringing accused persons held in custody to trial; by dealing with as many of the less serious offenders as possible in the community; and by shortening prison sentences where these were unavoidable. Given the high cost of building new prisons, other, less expensive penal methods which produced no worse results had to be pursued whenever it was safe. The French National Assembly adopted a new draft penal code that would restrict the right of examining magistrates to detain suspects without trial, a move designed to reduce the large number of accused held in custody for long periods. However, the measure would also limit the powers of courts to pass suspended sentences. West Germany's Bundestag (federal parliament) passed a bill under which life imprisonment, which hitherto had meant just that, was reduced to a period of 15 years, provided experts were satisfied that the prisoner concerned was unlikely to commit further crimes.

In the U.K., Home Secretary William Whitelaw, faced with a prison population of 44,000, appealed to the courts to refrain from passing prison sentences for relatively minor offenses or, when this was inevitable, to impose very short ones. But if nondangerous but repeated offenders were to be dealt with in the community, many new facilities were required: accommodation for the single

Polo:
see Equestrian Sports; Water Sports

Populations:
see Demography; *see also the individual country articles*

Portuguese Literature:
see Literature

Power:
see Energy; Engineering Projects; Industrial Review

Presbyterian Churches:
see Religion

Prices:
see Economy, World

Printing:
see Industrial Review

homeless; day centres to train—or at least occupy—such people during the day; and facilities for intensive group work to deal with such problems as alcoholism.

On a theoretical level, more penologists had come to question penal systems based on the attempt to rehabilitate the offender. Instead, they favoured a return to a modified "justice model" or, as it was called in European countries, the neoclassical approach. This rejected indeterminate sentences, where release from prison depended on response to treatment, in favour of fixed sentences. Criticism of indeterminacy focused on parole, particularly in Australia, the U.S., and the U.K. Parole is a form of early conditional release from a penal institution, followed by a period of supervision during which recall to prison is possible.

The decisions of parole boards sometimes seemed inexplicable, not only to prisoners and their families but also to the staff whose opinion had been asked. There were increasing demands that parole boards make the reasons for their negative decisions known and possibly appealable. This, however, might involve disclosure of confidential views and prognoses by staff members, including psychiatrists. On the one hand, it was feared that opinions would not be expressed freely once they were no longer confidential. On the other, it was held that decisions about liberty were so fundamental that they had to be made openly.

Beyond that, some critics argued that the element of uncertainty introduced by parole virtually constituted an additional punishment; prisoners continually saw some among their number released while others in apparently similar circumstances were not. Others, however, believed that parole provided a useful flexibility, permitting consideration of new information, not available at the time of the original sentence.

What the advocates of a penal system based on the justice model wanted was punishment that, with certain exceptions, matched the seriousness of the offense. Lawbreakers guilty of similar offenses should receive the same sentence; penalties should be fixed; and, whenever possible, the victim should be compensated for harm done. Because a rehabilitative system could seem arbitrary, the main aim was fairness.

Among other reasons for the swing away from rehabilitation was the fact that penological research tended to show that no one treatment method produced significantly better results than any other. Such results were normally expressed in terms of reconviction rates. Reconviction, however, depended at least as much on the offender's life circumstances and desire, or otherwise, to commit further crimes as it did on the effect of a particular sentence.

Treatment in the community still involved the notion of rehabilitation, so difficult to apply in the harsh circumstances of a penal institution. If two offenders, both having committed similar offenses, got community service orders, for example, the type of community service would vary according to the circumstances of the individual concerned. Probation orders were often combined with a variety of confidence-building schemes, including literacy programs, and heroic efforts to

The New Mexico Riot

"I don't remember anything as bad as this" was how a National Guard officer and veteran of World War II described the Santa Fe, N.M., state penitentiary after the riot of Feb. 2–3, 1980. Thirty-three inmates died in the disturbance, most of them at the hands of fellow prisoners, and much of the prison was destroyed.

According to a report issued in June by the state attorney general, the outbreak began when several inmates, drunk on homemade liquor, overcame their guards and broke through the supposedly shatterproof windows of the prison's control centre. Once there, they were able to open electrically controlled doors throughout the prison.

Eyewitnesses reported that the inmates ran amok, setting fires and destroying equipment. Many were high on drugs taken from the pharmacy. A cellblock designed to protect prisoners at special risk was forced open, and rioters began killing suspected informants. Of the casualties, some died from drug overdose or smoke inhalation. Most, however, were murdered, and many of the bodies bore signs of torture or mutilation. During the riot approximately 700 inmates surrendered to escape the carnage. Remarkably, although 11 guards were taken hostage, none was killed.

The riot was the worst in the U.S. since the outbreak at Attica, N.Y., in 1971, when 32 inmates and 11 prison employees died. The complaints of overcrowding, poor food, and harassment by guards were much the same at Santa Fe as at Attica. Considered a model prison for 800 when it was opened in 1956, the Santa Fe penitentiary housed about 1,100 in 1980, including some regarded as mentally abnormal and very dangerous. It was also understaffed; some of the guards were barely 18 years of age and had had only a few weeks of training.

Unlike Attica, however, where most of the casualties occurred when state troopers and law enforcement officers stormed the prison, the Santa Fe riot pitted inmate against inmate. Police and National Guardsmen waited out the violence until inmate spokesmen offered to exchange the hostages for interviews with reporters. Entering the prison without meeting resistance, they found many rioters in a drugged stupor.

With much of the prison uninhabitable, half of the survivors were moved to other facilities, in some cases outside of the state. Minor disturbances continued to flare among those who remained, partly traceable to the lack of such amenities as the gymnasium, library, and kitchen, all seriously damaged or destroyed. Damage was estimated in the neighbourhood of $25 million.

(DAPHNE DAUME)

JIM NACHTWEY—BLACK STAR

wean drug-dependent offenders away from their addiction were sometimes made. All this was clearly rehabilitative.

In attempting to reduce crime, practitioners and researchers were increasingly turning to early prevention. In *Research and Criminal Policy* (1980), John Croft, head of the U.K. Home Office Research Unit, indicated five means by which such reduction had been achieved. They were: (1) proper supervision of children by their parents, or those in loco parentis (foster parents, teachers, probation officers), within the home and outside it; (2) schools where discipline was similarly firm; (3) neighbourhoods where multiple disadvantages were reduced to a minimum and opportunities for crime were limited; (4) positive community influences and example; and (5) increasing the risk of being caught.

These were large areas. More detailed research was needed, for example, on preventive work in schools, but there was already enough evidence to make further work worthwhile. Meanwhile, penological research had moved away from measuring reconviction rates and toward comparing the cost-effectiveness of different penal methods for broadly similar offenders. This is what Anne B. Dunlop did in her study of *Junior Attendance Centres* (1980).

At such centres, operated in the U.K. by the police, young offenders were deprived of two hours of highly prized leisure time on Saturday afternoons for a number of weeks. During these two hours they were given physical exercise and engaged in work of various kinds. The scheme had the additional advantage that police officers and young offenders got to know each other and could form positive relationships. Dunlop concluded

JOHN BARR—GAMMA/LIAISON

Smoke rising from one of the prison blocks (above) and a bloody cell (left) depict the vicious nature of the riot at New Mexico's state penitentiary in Santa Fe in February. After 36 hours of rioting, 33 inmates had been killed.

Profits:
see Economy, World

Protestant Churches:
see Religion

Psychiatry:
see Health and Disease

that courts might usefully and more cheaply make attendance orders for some of those young offenders whom they had, in the past, reluctantly sent to short-term penal institutions.

(HUGH J. KLARE)

See also Crime and Law Enforcement; Law.
[521.C.3.a; 543.A.5.a; 10/36.C.5.b]

Publishing

As the recession in many parts of the world deepened in 1980, there were few publishing enterprises that did not feel the effects. Some succumbed entirely, while others were absorbed by stronger rivals through takeovers and mergers that led to an ever increasing concentration of ownership. Typical of the latter was the December deal by which the French communications conglomerate Matra, in partnership with Daniel Filipacchi's *Paris-Match* group, took control of the old-established Librairie Hachette publishing house.

In London's Fleet Street, beset by its own labour-relations problems as much as by the general economic malaise, some heirs of the legendary press barons of earlier days had their backs to the wall. One of them, Lord Thomson of Fleet, second-generation owner of *The Times*, seemed about to abandon the fray.

The International Press Institute (IPI), in its *Annual Review of Press Freedom*, reported that governmental interference in the freedom of the press, far from being confined to authoritarian regimes, was on the increase in Western democracies. France was cited as one of the worst examples, with particular reference to the French government's action against *Le Monde* (*see* below). Also criticized were the U.K. (for the restraints imposed by its Official Secrets Act and other obstacles to investigative reporting), Australia, Spain, and Switzerland. Referring to recent murders of journalists in Italy, Lebanon, El Salvador, Turkey, and Zambia, the IPI concluded that journalism carried a greater risk to life than any other profession.

Editor William Rees-Mogg (centre) of *The Times* of London announced in October that the venerable newspaper would cease publication in March 1981 unless new owners could be found. The paper has long been plagued with labour problems.

POPPERFOTO/UPI

Newspapers. In 1980 the crisis whose onset many had predicted for years finally hit Fleet Street, its most potent symbol being the putting up for sale, on October 22, of *The Times* and its associated publications. The troubles of Times Newspapers Ltd. (TNL) had never been fully resolved in the wake of the 11-month suspension of publication by the group's management in 1979. The central elements of the agreement with the printing unions, concerning use of the new technology already installed, had not been carried through into detailed negotiations, while production disruptions continued despite new procedures for handling disputes. *The Sunday Times*, the leader in its market and potentially a profitable publication, suffered particularly.

Then in August a strike by journalists at *The Times*, seen by management as pursuit of a 27% pay increase over 1½ years and by the journalists as a call for an existing agreement to be honoured, caused the first stoppage of its kind in the paper's history. In November Lord Thomson, chairman of the International Thomson Organization, of which TNL formed a part, announced his decision to shut down the TNL publications in March 1981 unless buyers for all or any came forward. By the year's end such a deal within that time seemed increasingly unlikely, and although names of British and U.S. potential bidders were mentioned, the thought gained ground that a closure which would permit subsequent restaffing might be the deliberate tactic of any aspiring owner. *The Times*'s editor, William Rees-Mogg, led the exploration of ideas for involving the staff in some form of ownership syndicate, although he let it be known that he would not continue as editor after any change of hands.

TNL was not alone in its problems. On October 31 the London *Evening News*, owned by Associated Newspapers Ltd., was closed and the title merged with the *Evening Standard*, owned by the rival Express Newspapers Ltd. Such a move had long been rumoured, as both papers watched their sales slide in the face of population shifts out of town. The *New Standard*, born of the merger, was jointly owned by both organizations. In December it was the turn of the *Financial Times* to face trouble. It was not published for a week because of a pay dispute, during the course of which its management delivered warnings about the paper's long-term prospects.

Ironically, in view of the TNL decision, the quality newspaper sector maintained the remarkable all-around growth that had begun when *The Times*'s 1979 suspension ended. Both *The Times* and *The Sunday Times* and their rivals, *The Guardian*, the *Daily Telegraph*, the *Financial Times*, *The Observer*, and the *Sunday Telegraph*, demonstrated historically high sales and substantial growth even in the face of sharp price increases.

The difficulties encountered by British newspaper publishers in introducing new technology contrasted with developments elsewhere. In West Germany *Die Welt* shifted to new technology in July. The Paris-based *International Herald Tribune* launched an ambitious satellite-based system giving it faster worldwide distribution, aimed particularly at the booming markets of the Far East via Hong Kong. It was in the East itself, however, that the most spectacular advance was made. In Tokyo, on September 24, Japan's leading newspaper, the *Asahi Shimbun*, completed its move to what one foreign journalist described as a temple to technology. On that day it printed its first edition of 12 million copies, untouched by human hands from the journalists' visual display units for writing and layout to the baling and loading onto trucks for nationwide distribution.

In France there was continued concern over the activities of Robert Hersant's publishing empire. In particular, the further decline of *L'Aurore*, a newspaper associated in its early days with Georges Clemenceau and Émile Zola, was marked by its virtual merger into *Le Figaro*, with little but the mastheads to distinguish them. The year had started with two of Hersant's new projects, *Le Figaro-Dimanche* and *France-Soir-Dimanche*, being abandoned within months of their launching on grounds of production and distribution difficulties. During the year, however, the greatest interest focused on the independent *Le Monde*, despite its economic health and for reasons far outweighing the problems that its staff experienced in electing Claude Julien (*see* BIOGRAPHIES) to succeed Jacques Fauvet as editor on the latter's retirement at the end of 1982. Fauvet himself, with his legal correspondent Philippe Bouchet, took the brunt of an important case in which France's minister of justice, Alain Peyrefitte, authorized legal action against the paper for impugning the impartiality of judges.

It was widely believed that behind the prosecution was official anger at *Le Monde*'s continued reporting of the charges concerning diamonds given by Bokassa, then emperor of the Central African Empire, to French Pres. Valéry Giscard d'Estaing and people close to him. In March two of the president's cousins had been awarded token damages against the satirical weekly *Le Canard Enchaîné* and another journal because of their allegations in this connection, and the matter did not go away.

In Australia the concentration of newspaper and other media ownership, widely seen as potentially antidemocratic, was much under discussion during the country's election year. (*See* AUSTRALIA: *Special Report.*) (PETER FIDDICK)

Newspapers in the United States enjoyed one of their most prosperous years in recent memory. Total daily circulation hit a six-year high of 62,223,040, up 0.4% from the previous year, according to the 1980 *Editor & Publisher International Year Book.* Morning circulation set a record: 28,574,879, a gain of 3.3% over the previous year's all-time high. Evening circulation, however, dropped to its lowest point in two decades: 33,648,161, down 2% from the year before. The number of daily newspapers rose to 1,763, a gain of 7 for the year.

Nearly all of that gain was accounted for by the continuing trend toward morning delivery. There were 382 morning papers, 27 more than during the previous year, as compared with 1,405 evening papers, 14 fewer than a year earlier. A dozen evening papers became morning papers. Six evening papers began issuing editions around the clock,

World Daily Newspapers and Circulation, 1978–79[1]

Location	Daily newspapers	Circulation per 1,000 population
AFRICA		
Algeria	4	13
Angola	5	18
Benin	2	0.3
Botswana	1	31
Cameroon	1	2
Central African Republic	1	. . .
Chad	3	0.3
Congo	5	. . .
Egypt	10	79
Equatorial Guinea	2	. . .
Ethiopia	5	2
Gabon	2	1
Ghana	4	42
Guinea	1	2
Guinea-Bissau	1	11
Ivory Coast	2	6
Kenya	3	12
Lesotho	1	1
Liberia	2	8
Libya	2	26
Madagascar	12	. . .
Malawi	2	6
Mali	2	. . .
Mauritius	12	96
Morocco	9	21
Mozambique	2	4
Niger	1	0.2
Nigeria	21	. . .
Réunion	3	98
Senegal	1	6
Seychelles	2	58
Sierra Leone	2	. . .
Somalia	1	. . .
South Africa	23	45
Sudan	4	. . .
Tanzania	2	9
Togo	1	4
Tunisia	5	38
Uganda	1	2
Upper Volta	1	0.2
Zaire	4	3
Zambia	2	20
Zimbabwe	2	16
Total	171	
NORTH AMERICA		
Antigua	2	146
Bahamas, The	3	138
Barbados	1	101
Belize	2	43
Bermuda	1	203
Canada	117	218
Costa Rica	5	. . .
Cuba	16	. . .
Dominican Republic	10	42
El Salvador	11	54
Guadeloupe	1	56
Guatemala	9	37
Haiti	7	20
Honduras	7	52
Jamaica	3	58
Martinique	1	80
Mexico	256	. . .
Netherlands Antilles	5	206
Nicaragua	6	49
Panama	6	81
Puerto Rico	4	140
Trinidad and Tobago	3	121
United States	1,763	282
Virgin Islands (U.S.)	4	192
Total	2,244	
SOUTH AMERICA		
Argentina	176	. . .
Bolivia	14	35
Brazil	280	39
Chile	47	. . .
Colombia	40	. . .
Ecuador	29	49
French Guiana	1	21
Guyana	3	150
Paraguay	5	46
Peru	30	51
Suriname	7	74
Uruguay	30	. . .
Venezuela	54	178
Total	716	
ASIA		
Afghanistan	17	4
Bangladesh	31	5
Burma	7	10
Cambodia	17	10
China	392	. . .
Cyprus	13	127
Hong Kong	51	350
India	929	17
Indonesia	172	. . .
Iran	28	25
Iraq	5	26
Israel	25	180
Japan	180	396
Jordan	4	27
Korea, North	11	. . .
Korea, South	37	173
Kuwait	6	179
Laos	8	. . .
Lebanon	33	. . .
Macau	7	. . .
Malaysia	31	87
Mongolia	2	77
Nepal	29	. . .
Pakistan	102	. . .
Philippines	18	. . .
Saudi Arabia	12	. . .
Singapore	12	239
Sri Lanka	11	25
Syria	7	. . .
Taiwan	31	. . .
Thailand	18	42
Turkey	450	. . .
Vietnam	5	5
Yemen (Aden)	3	. . .
Yemen (San'a')	2	. . .
Total	2,706	
EUROPE		
Albania	2	48
Austria	32	336
Belgium	27	241
Bulgaria	14	250
Czechoslovakia	30	255
Denmark	49	359
Finland	55	472
France	156	182
Germany, East	39	496
Germany, West	411	404
Gibraltar	2	173
Greece	106	107
Hungary	29	223
Iceland	6	575
Ireland	10	246
Italy	78	113
Liechtenstein	2	393
Luxembourg	5	365
Malta	5	. . .
Netherlands, The	95	315
Norway	83	440
Poland	44	237
Portugal	30	70
Romania	35	145
Spain	143	116
Sweden	113	584
Switzerland	97	385
U.S.S.R.	686	396
United Kingdom	130	251
Vatican City	1	. . .
Yugoslavia	26	87
Total	2,541	
OCEANIA		
American Samoa	2	320
Australia	70	394
Cook Islands	1	40
Fiji	2	70
French Polynesia	4	98
Guam	1	165
New Caledonia	2	81
New Zealand	33	341
Niue	1	60
Papua New Guinea	1	6
Total	117	

[1] Only newspapers issued four or more times weekly are included.
Sources: UN, *Statistical Yearbook, 1978;* UNESCO, *Statistical Yearbook, 1978–79; Editor & Publisher International Year Book* (1980); *Europa Year Book 1980, A World Survey;* various country publications.

Polish workers eagerly read their country's first uncensored newspaper which began publication in August.

raising the number of such "all day" dailies to 24. (One "all day" paper shifted to morning delivery, and the rest are counted above in both morning and evening totals.)

One significant exception to the morning trend in 1980 involved the *New York Daily News*, the nation's largest metropolitan daily, with a circulation of about 1.6 million. The circulation had slid by some 500,000 since 1970, largely because the paper's traditional blue-collar readers had moved to the suburbs. To recapture that market the morning *Daily News* launched an evening edition, *Tonight*, with an initial, as yet unaudited, circulation somewhere between 100,000 and 300,000, depending on whose estimates one accepts. *Tonight*, which was aimed at a more affluent audience than the *Daily News* had ever approached, was part of a $20 million investment the *Daily News* and its parent, Chicago Tribune Co., were making to stop the circulation slide. Tribune Co. executives hoped to attract readers from Australian publisher Rupert Murdoch's evening *New York Post* (circulation 654,000), which had gained readers—though not profits—through an increasing emphasis on crime, sex, and gossip.

The *Daily News*'s owners were also hoping to pick up readers from the staid *New York Times* (circulation 915,000). *Times* officials continued to deny persistent reports that they, too, planned an afternoon edition, but they did begin printing an abridged edition of the paper in Chicago for distribution in nine Middle Western states. Mindful of the heavy financial losses the *Times* had suffered with its short-lived West Coast edition in the early 1960s, *Times* executives insisted that the Chicago operation was not a precursor to a national edition.

Unlike Britain and some other nations, the U.S. still did not have a truly national newspaper—except, perhaps, for the *Wall Street Journal* (circulation 1.8 million), which concentrated mostly on financial news. In 1980 the *Journal* became the nation's largest daily newspaper of any kind, surpassing the *New York Daily News*. The *Journal* also made one of its most radical format changes since its founding in 1889. The paper was split into two parts, thus raising the maximum number of pages in a single edition from 48 to 56 a day in a move designed largely to accommodate an increase in advertising. However, the change also gave the *Journal* more space for news, much of which it devoted to nonbusiness stories.

The most significant newspaper transaction of the year was the sale of the *Denver* (Colo.) *Post* (circulation 260,000), a leading paper in the fast-growing Rocky Mountain region, to the Times Mirror Co., a diversified communications firm known principally as owner of the *Los Angeles Times* (circulation 1,013,000). The firm had a reputation for spending generously to maintain editorial and commerical supremacy in the markets in which it competed, and the Denver paper could use plenty of both. Earlier in the year its circulation slipped behind that of the rival *Rocky Mountain News* for the first time since the *Post* was founded in 1895.

On the legal front a couple of recent setbacks for the press were in effect nullified. In *Richmond Newspapers* v. *Virginia* the U.S. Supreme Court narrowed a year-old ruling that had granted local judges the right to close certain pretrial hearings to the press; some local magistrates had misinterpreted that decision as allowing them to close all kinds of legal proceedings, including trials themselves. In *Richmond Newspapers* the court declared that the First Amendment to the U.S. Constitution requires that all criminal trials must be open to press and public except in rare cases. (*See* LAW: *Court Decisions*.) In addition, Congress passed a law requiring police officers to obtain a subpoena rather than a search warrant, under most circumstances, when trying to obtain evidence from news reporters. This stemmed from *Zurcher* v. *Stanford Daily*, a 1978 decision that allowed the police to search newsrooms as long as they had obtained a search warrant.

The *Boston Globe* won three Pulitzer Prizes in 1980, the second time that had happened in the 64-year history of the awards (the *New York Times* won three in 1978). The *Globe* won the special local reporting prize for a series on mismanagement in the local transit system; *Globe* columnist Ellen Goodman won the award for commentary; and *Globe* television critic William A. Henry III was given the criticism prize. The *Philadelphia Inquirer* won its sixth Pulitzer in a row, the general local reporting prize for its coverage of the Three Mile Island nuclear reactor accident. The prestigious Gold Medal for Public Service went to the Gannett News Service for exposing mismanagement of contributions to the Pauline Fathers, a Pennsylvania-based religious order. (The news service distributes stories to member papers of the Gannett chain.) The Pulitzer for national reporting went to Bette Orsini and Charles Stafford of the *St. Petersburg* (Fla.) *Times* for their investigation of the Church of Scientology. Joel Brinkley and Jay Mather of the *Louisville* (Ky.) *Courier-Journal* were cited

for their reporting from Cambodia. The award for editorial writing went to Robert Bartley of the *Wall Street Journal*, and the editorial cartooning prize was given to Don Wright of the *Miami* (Fla.) *News*.
(DONALD MORRISON)

Magazines. The British magazine industry showed less obvious symptoms of the recession than did the nation's newspapers, although there was little doubt that profits were harder to find. The continuing trend was toward specialization, with new markets being sought and tested, sometimes with one-shot publications capable of being used as pilots for longer term ventures. The two latest titles from EMAP National Publications Ltd., a group built up during the 1970s on the foundation of a regional newspaper business, illustrated the trend: *Greatest Hits* was to be a bimonthly, covering 25 years of pop music, and *Rail Enthusiast*, also bimonthly, would focus on modern train operations. At the same time, two quarterlies, *Alternative Cars* and *Classic Bike*, planned to become bimonthlies, while two monthlies, for motorcycle and horse enthusiasts, would be published every two weeks. Such tactics had increased the firm's magazine titles from 4 to 21 during the decade and had led to record profits, even in 1980.

Older established concerns also found cause for celebration: *The Stage* celebrated its centenary, with a star-studded Savoy Hotel reception; *The Lady*, its domestic service advertising holding up well in a more egalitarian age, was 95 years old; *Political Quarterly*, 80 years. *Spare Rib*, the feminist journal, reached its 100th edition in robust form. First-birthday celebrations held by Sir James Goldsmith for his *Now!* magazine were attended by British Prime Minister Margaret Thatcher, but sales figures, at about 135,000, were well short of the quarter million the publishers had forecast, and the weekly newsmagazine was clearly going to have to fight for its place in the market.

The giant of the industry, IPC Magazines Ltd., was hit by a lengthy journalists' dispute during the summer, with inevitable effects on sales and revenue. But it was one of the smallest, yet still familiar, groups that suffered real tragedy in August, when the announcement that Hansom Books, whose titles included *Dance and Dancers*, *Music and Musicians*, and *Plays and Players*, was being declared bankrupt was followed by the death of its founder and proprietor, Philip Dossé.
(PETER FIDDICK)

Termed the "fastest growing segment of the print industry" in the U.S., magazines expected their advertising revenues to increase by 41% from 1980 to 1982. This was the finding of "Consumer Magazines in the 1980s," a study issued by Knowledge Industry Publications. Thanks to such promises of growth, approximately 200–350 new general magazines were started in the U.S. each year. Only about one in ten got past the second issue. The success rate for the little magazine, which had about the same number of starters, was somewhat higher, although a total life expectancy of three or four years was average.

The remarkably long-lived *Atlantic Monthly* and *Harper's*, intellectual voices of the U.S. since the mid-19th century, almost ceased publication in 1980. Decreasing lack of readership and editorial focus accounted for the near disasters. Both were saved by last-minute business arrangements. In early summer *Harper's* ceased publication. A month later it started again, thanks to the MacArthur Foundation of Chicago and the Atlantic Richfield Foundation, which committed $3 million to its current and future operation. The *Atlantic Monthly* was sold to Mortimer Zuckerman, a real-estate tycoon. Rivaled only by *The New Yorker* and *Harper's* for its literary reputation, the *Atlantic* was not likely to change in content.

Museum Magazine, among the most widely publicized new efforts, offered readers a tour through the treasures of civilization in the world's 24,000 museums. Edited for the general reader, the magazine followed the format of such successful publications as *Smithsonian*, as did another new title, *Science 80*. Issued by the American Association for the Advancement of Science, the latter was an effort to capture the audience that is mildly involved with science but is not knowledgeable enough for *Scientific American*. And by late 1980 Time Inc. promised still another popular science title, *Discover*.

"Nonprofit" was a common descriptor for many specialized magazine publishing ventures, such as *Sierra*, *Mother Jones*, *Smithsonian*, and *Black Scholar*. Although this situation is rare for general, large-circulation titles, it might become more common. *Ms.* magazine found salvation in its new nonprofit status in 1979. The change allowed it to avoid higher costs by taking advantage of special postal rates and the infusion of tax-deductible grant money from outsiders. The publisher said that the opportunity was offered by the Internal Revenue Service to many publishers.

Among sales in 1980, *Us* proved no competition to *People*, and the *New York Times* finally realized

Time Inc.'s new popular science magazine, *Discover*, began publication in October.

Eudora Welty (left) accepted the National Medal for Literature from editor Toni Morrison at the first American Book Awards ceremony held May 1 in New York City.

it by selling the magazine to the MacFadden Group for about $4 million. Rupert Murdoch sold the Los Angeles-based *New West* to the owners of *Texas Monthly* for $4.5 million. *Saturday Review* went to the owner of *Financial World* for an undisclosed amount. Founded in 1924, the *Review* gained fame under long-time editor Norman Cousins, but under its last owner, 29-year-old Carll Tucker, the format was so drastically changed as to confuse readers. As a result the magazine was losing between $500,000 and $1 million a year.

(WILLIAM A. KATZ)

Books. The deepening world recession was reflected by cutbacks in public-sector funding for book purchases in many countries. This was particularly true in India, where university grants for library acquisitions were much reduced. In the U.K. the Educational Publishers Council increased its protests against the low levels at which books were being provided in primary and secondary schools. British book exports were severely hampered by a combination of high domestic interest rates, a strong pound, and continuing high levels of domestic inflation. The unusually low value of the U.S. dollar during the same period underlined the lack of competitiveness of British books in world markets. Estimates indicated that British book exports declined by approximately 10% in real terms in 1980 from the 1979 figure of £215 million. (Total sales of British books in 1979 topped £580 million, an increase of about 16% over 1978.)

The combination of rising prices with generally lower institutional book budgets (and a chronic lack of foreign exchange facilities in many less developed countries) gave impetus to the growing problem of book piracy. In 1980 serious piracy was reported from Egypt, Jordan, Syria, Iran, Pakistan, India, Malaysia, Singapore, and Hong Kong. Latin America produced examples of pirated English-language teaching materials, and legal actions against piracy were brought in Japan and West Germany. The scale of the problem was estimated at over $1 billion a year, and piracy now affected paperbacks and general books as well as textbooks and scholarly monographs. The British Publishers Association led the way in bringing the practice of piracy to the attention of governments, and the International Publishers Association decided in October to set up a system to monitor piracy, viewed as one of the most serious threats to international publishing.

The lack of growth in the international market for books and the economic pressures on publishing caused much de-stocking. As a result, remainders (books sold in bulk at greatly reduced prices) appeared in large quantities in British and other markets. Remainders made a significant impact on sales patterns, particularly of new books.

The 32nd Frankfurt (West Germany) Book Fair, held October 8–13, was attended by 5,216 publishers, an increase of about 200 over the previous year. As usual, the largest foreign contingent, 570, was from the U.K., with the U.S. close behind. The fair's theme on this occasion was publishing in black Africa, with a special exhibition devoted to books printed and published in that continent.

(ANTHONY A. READ)

Indications that book publishers were not immune to recessions became noticeable in the U.S. in 1979 and 1980. Publishers noted few and often small increases in unit sales, and much of the growth in book publishing receipts could be attributed to price increases. But hopeful signs were also evident, and such factors as increased retail book outlets, higher purchases per pupil in education, and more publisher emphasis on international sales also contributed to the increased receipts.

Total book sales in the U.S. for the first eight months of 1980 increased 11.5% to $4.3 billion from $3.9 billion, while the number of units rose 6.3%. The only category to experience a decline for the period was paperback book clubs, down 7.5% in sales and 10.9% in units. Sales of hardcover book clubs rose 10.7%. For the first eight months of 1980 sales of juvenile paperbacks increased 62.7% over 1979 to $30.9 million and those of hardcover juveniles rose 7.8% to $100.3 million. Adult trade hardcover and paperback sales also continued strong with hardcover sales up 19.1% and paperback 21.1%. Another strong performer was religious publishing, up 18.4%; college sales gained a total of 12%, and university press sales were up 11.5%. Professional and elementary-high school sales continued to struggle, however. For professional books, sales for the first eight months were up 8.2% while units declined 5.3%; elementary-high school sales for the eight months rose 4.5% and units were up 1.8%.

Final compilations of U.S. book title output in 1979, according to figures compiled by the R. R. Bowker Co., revealed an overall rise of 9.6% in the number of titles published for a total of 45,182 titles in all subject categories, including both hardcover and paperback books. The comparable total for 1978 was 41,216. Hardcover fiction output appeared to have dropped by almost 10% from 1978 to 1979. In overall title output, art books showed the highest proportionate increase, one of more than 36%; technology books rose 26%; medicine, 16.8%; and business and science, almost 10% each. Title production in sociology and economics increased more than 19%. This category was the largest, accounting for more than 17% of all 1979 titles.

The dollar value of U.S. book exports rose 17.2% for the first nine months of 1980, to $384.2 million, up from $327.9 million during the 1979 period. Quantity value rose 14.6% (1980 figures do not include sales in the music books category and thus are not exactly comparable to 1979). The dollar value of book imports rose 18.4% to $227.7 million with quantity up 6%. The above figures apply to shipments valued at $250 or more only. Among exports the biggest increase by category was in Bibles, testaments, and other religious books, which rose 42.6% to $24.1 million. Categories that fell in amount were encyclopaedias, down 10.8% to $21.4 million, and dictionaries and thesauruses, down 4.2% to $4.5 million. Among imports, a quantum leap was recorded in the toy books and colouring books category, to $7.3 million from $2.4 million in the same period a year earlier. Foreign-language books except Bibles rose 18.6% to $21.7 million; other books rose 16% to $190.4 million; and imports of Bibles and prayer books fell 2% to $4.8 million.

A total of 22 merger announcements were made in the printing and publishing field in the first half of 1980, according to W. T. Grimm & Co., a merger specialist. This number represents a 31% decline from the first six months of 1979, when 32 mergers were announced.

While members of publishers' row continued to hold discussions about the evils of mergers, a study by the Library of Congress noted that the outlook for the publishing business in the U.S. looked healthy. The report said that the growth of small publishing houses counterbalanced the recent trend toward book-company mergers and acquisitions. The report's findings supported the general position of the Association of American Publishers (AAP) that the industry was not concentrated.

In December 1980 Congress voted to exempt book publishers from an Internal Revenue Service ruling that, according to the publishers, would have forced them to destroy millions of books in their warehouses in order to avoid additional taxes.

In April 1980 Newhouse Publications acquired the Random House book-publishing subsidiary of RCA for $65 million in cash. RCA also agreed to continue to carry $5 million worth of Random House debt, which was to be paid back eventually by the book publisher. The Newhouse group owns 29 newspapers coast to coast; the Conde Nast magazines (*Vogue, Glamour, House & Garden,* and *Mademoiselle*); and a number of radio stations and cable TV systems.

Not all publishing acquisitions in 1980 involved books. Nelson Doubleday, Jr., who reputedly owns a controlling interest in the publishing company started by his grandfather, bought a controlling interest in the New York Mets baseball team; Doubleday's great-granduncle Abner reputedly invented baseball.

An interesting and unusual undercover publishing story occurred in April; ironically, it involved one of the Watergate conspirators. After a year and a half of almost total secrecy, St. Martin's Press published and distributed to its accounts more than 80,000 copies of *Will: The Autobiography of G. Gordon Liddy*. The reasons for the secrecy were twofold: to preserve the news impact of the book and also to elude any potential restraint order from anyone who might have wished to thwart shipment. Among the explosive pieces of information revealed by the convicted Watergate conspirator were his plans for assassinating journalist Jack Anderson and E. Howard Hunt.

The tough economic situation across the U.S. appeared to benefit the sales of a bumper crop of financial titles. Among the books that made it to national best-seller lists were *Free to Choose: A Personal Statement,* by Milton and Rose Friedman; *Nothing Down: How to Buy Real Estate with Little or No Money Down,* by Robert Allen; and *Crisis Investing: Opportunities and Profits in the Coming Great Depression,* by Douglas Casey.

Despite fears of the recession's adverse impact on the publishing of new talent, many firms brought out first novels in 1980. A survey by *Publishers Weekly* showed that in the fall season alone (September 1980 until January 1981), more than 110 first novels were published.

Paperback publishers during the year turned more often to books that they originated themselves rather than reprinting books a year after their appearance in hardcover. Paperback firms noted that the percentage of originals generally ranged from 40 to 50% of each month's releases. One consequence of this change was that for the first time in almost a decade there was no new record set for a reprint sale. No paperback publisher even came within shooting distance of the previous record of $3.2 million, set in 1979 when Bantam Books bought Judith Krantz's *Princess Daisy*. (DAISY G. MARYLES)

See also Literature.
[441.D; 543.A.4.e]

Qatar

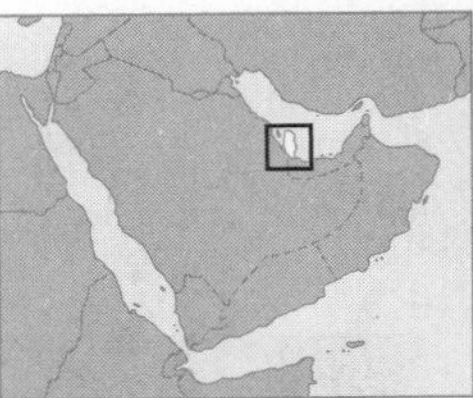
Qatar

An independent monarchy (emirate) on the west coast of the Persian Gulf, Qatar occupies a desert peninsula east of Bahrain, with Saudi Arabia and the United Arab Emirates bordering it on the south. Area: 11,400 sq km (4,400 sq mi). Pop. (1979 est.): 250,000. Capital: Doha (pop., 1979 est., 180,000). Language: Arabic. Religion: Muslim. Emir and prime minister in 1980, Sheikh Khalifah ibn Hamad ath-Thani.

Qatar's revenue, U.S. $3.8 billion in 1979, was likely to increase substantially in 1980 because of a $2 per barrel increase in the price of its crude oil that became effective at midyear. The limited capacity of the country to absorb this income led to capital flight abroad, but firm commitments were made to increase investment in domestic industry, including a high-density polyethylene plant at the industrial zone of Umm Said, 48 km (30 mi) south of Doha, and a new refinery. Crude oil production in 1980 was expected to be lower than the 506,000 bbl a day achieved in 1979 because of a government conservation program.

Puerto Rico:
see Dependent States

QATAR

Education. (1977–78) Primary, pupils 26,065, teachers 1,577; secondary, pupils 10,915, teachers 912; vocational, pupils 323, teachers 71; teacher training, students 231, teachers 56; higher (1976–77), students 910, teaching staff 118.

Finance. Monetary unit: Qatar riyal, with (Sept. 22, 1980) a free rate of 3.62 riyals to U.S. $1 (8.71 riyals = £1 sterling). Gold, SDR's, and foreign exchange (March 1980) U.S. $342 million. Budget (1980 est.): revenue 13,745,000,000 riyals; expenditure 12,174,000,000 riyals.

Foreign Trade. (1979) Imports 5,378,000,000 riyals; exports 14,125,000,000 riyals. Import sources: Japan 19%; West Germany 17%; U.K. 15%; France 10%; U.S. 9%; Italy 6%. Export destinations (1978): Japan 24%; France 18%; The Netherlands 12%; Thailand 10%; U.S. 9%; Italy 6%; Netherlands Antilles 5%. Main export: crude oil 96%.

Industry. Production (in 000; metric tons): crude oil (1979) 24,440; natural gas (cu m; 1977) 1,607,000; petroleum products (1977) 281; nitrogenous fertilizers (1978–79) 118; electricity (kw-hr; 1977) *c.* 900,000.

Although crude oil dominated the economy, providing almost all exports and 90% of government revenue, useful contributions were made by the Qatar Steel Co. (Qasco), managed by Kobe Steel of Japan, and the Qatar Fertiliser Co. (Qafco), managed by Norsk Hydro of Norway. Qatar continued to exercise a conservative monetary policy and repaid early two large loans taken out in 1977 and 1978 for financing industrial projects at Umm Said.

With a sizable minority (about 20%) of citizens of Iranian extraction, the government faced the problem of containing religious opposition sympathetic to the revolutionary regime in Iran. The authorities also felt required to act against the large number of illegal immigrants of Asian origin by passing tough sponsorship regulations to eliminate the surplus of floating labour.

(JOHN WHELAN)

Race Relations

Against the background of worldwide economic recession and high levels of unemployment in most, if not quite all, of the major advanced industrial nations, there was a resurgence in 1980 of fascist and racist political activity on a wide scale.

A burning and overturned car was one of the symbols of a riot that broke out in Miami, Florida, in May after an all-white jury acquitted four white policemen of charges of having beaten a black man to death.

WIDE WORLD

The fascists, drawing on unemployed youth and racist sentiments in general, marked the year with intimidation of minorities, terror, and brutality reminiscent of the years before World War II.

In September the political committee of the Council of Europe in Strasbourg, France, prepared a draft report tracing the increased incidence of fascism and racism in Western Europe; such a threat could become significant, the report maintained, if the only response was one of "indifference and tolerance." The report also said that it would be "premature" to claim that a major revival of fascist and racist ideology was taking place in Europe. Nevertheless, sporadic assaults and even the murder of blacks and Jews occurred in France, West Germany, Britain, and the U.S.

Britain. The National Front and the British Movement, avowedly admirers of Adolf Hitler, marched throughout the year in 13 cities and towns. Among them were South London (March 2), Lewisham (April 20), Nuneaton (August 17), and Preston (September 14). In response the Anti-Nazi League on November 10 announced the rejuvenation of its campaign, an international conference, and plans for a major youth conference to be held in 1981.

The reason for the marching by the National Front was explained in the members' internal bulletin, "Our Plans for the 1980s." After the humiliation of electoral defeats in the May local elections, members were reassured that in conditions "when the streets are beset by riots, when unemployment soars and when inflation gets even beyond the present degree of minimal control" their negative media image would be a positive asset. On the level of institutionalized racialism the London Institute of Race Relations' *Annual Report, 1979-80* noted the "increased harassment of black people at the points of entry, even further restrictions on dependants and fiancés, greater Home Office zeal in separating children from their mothers by deportation, wider and more systematic raids for 'illegal' immigrants, and continual demands from both central and local government agencies on black people to prove their right to medical treatment, housing, and welfare services before receiving them."

As William Keys, general secretary of the Society of Graphical and Allied Trades, said, introducing the equal rights committee report to the British Trades Union Congress on September 2, young black people found it even more difficult than their white contemporaries to get work: "This unemployment will exacerbate a situation which is already flammable. Many black British believe they are being made the nation's scapegoats." Government figures showed that over the 12 months to August unemployment among ethnic minorities had risen by 48%, as compared with an increase of 35% in total unemployment.

On April 2 in the St. Paul's area of Bristol 20 police in a drink and drugs raid on a café were obliged to withdraw when confronted by angry black and white youths; some shops were wrecked and a bank was set ablaze. For offenses arising out of the disturbances 12 people were put on trial in November on charges of riotous assembly; 38 cases

WIDE WORLD

(Left to right) Ku Klux Klansmen Coleman Pridmore, David Matthews, and Jerry Paul Smith celebrated after their acquittal in November in Greensboro, North Carolina, of having killed five Communist Workers Party demonstrators in November 1979.

had already been summarily dealt with by the courts. Against the opposition of the Home Office, a High Court judge, Mr. Justice Woolf, affirmed on October 14 that "Immigration clearly has a very real impact on race relations." As a result the Commission for Racial Equality was to investigate the workings of the 1971 Immigration Act. (*See* UNITED KINGDOM: *Special Report.*)

France. Four passers-by were killed and nine wounded by a bomb outside a Paris synagogue on October 3; the outlawed organization Fédération d'Action nationale et Européenne (FANE), an anti-Semitic group, claimed responsibility. This outrage, which had been preceded by machine-gun attacks on four Jewish targets on September 26, provoked a demonstration in Paris of some 200,000 on October 7 and the formation of young people into Jewish self-defense units. On September 23 the French policemen's union called for a parliamentary inquiry into neo-Nazi terrorism and cited 37 attacks in the previous three months; José Deltorn, secretary-general of the police union, told reporters that 20% of FANE's members were policemen. Pres. Valéry Giscard d'Estaing made an appeal against intolerance, terrorism, and racism.

West Germany. Six arrests were made in West Germany in September as a result of bomb attacks by the neo-Nazi "German Action Group" on February 21, April 18 and 27, June 30, and August 17 on a school, a Vietnamese refugee centre, and an Ethiopian refugee residential home. A supporter of the banned Wehrsportgruppe Hoffmann blew himself up while planting a bomb that killed 12 others and injured more than 200 at the Munich Oktoberfest on September 26. National Democratic Party political activity continued to centre on a virulent antiforeigner campaign.

Belgium. A march against racism and fascism in Brussels on October 20, estimated by organizers to number 100,000, was the biggest of its kind in many years. The demonstration anticipated a Belgian Senate inquiry into the Flemish Militant Order (Vlaamse Militanten Orde), or VMO, and its Nazi-inspired attacks on Jewish people and synagogues.

North and South America. The acquittal on May 17 of four white former Miami, Fla., police officers of charges relating to the death of a black man provoked rioting in Liberty City, a black section of Miami, and led to 14 deaths and a curfew. In August a National Urban League survey revealed that unemployment among black heads of households was almost four times that for whites; for black teenagers the unemployment rate was 40%. In November six present and former members of the Ku Klux Klan and U.S. Nazi Party were acquitted in Greensboro, N.C., on charges of murdering five members of the Communist Workers Party at an anti-Klan rally in Greensboro in 1979. A $1 million class-action lawsuit in Alabama in November asked that the Klan be barred from intimidating blacks.

A significant event of 1980 was the fourth Russell Tribunal on the Indians of the Americas, held in Rotterdam, Neth., from November 24 to 30. The Dutch organizers of the tribunal, the Workshop Indian Project Foundation, had received more than 40 documented complaints from North and South America along with others from non-Indian indigenous groups throughout the world. The proceedings were an indictment of the oppression of primitive races by whites through seizure of land and destruction of environment and way of life, in some cases almost amounting to genocide. The gravest cases were those from Brazil, which had prevented the appearance of the Xavante Indians' leader, Mario Juruna, before the tribunal. In ten years the Nambiquara in Brazil had declined from being in full control of their territory to becoming a small remnant; before the tribunal Bishop Tomás Balduino of Goiás had pleaded for the World Bank to withdraw financing from a road construction project that would remove altogether the diminished tribe from its land in Brazil's interior. Also in Brazil, the Yanomami were in misery and sickness after their land had been overrun by highway workers and commercial enterprise. The Brazilian Rio Negro Indian community and Aruak and Tukano tribes accused the Roman Catholic Church of systematically destroying their religious culture

Quakers:
see Religion

Quarrying:
see Mining and Quarrying

and freedom; the Rio Negro Indians also stated that the Brazilian authorities had banned them from using the 35 languages spoken by their community of 17,000. Peruvian Indians of the San Juan de Ondores community had twice been evicted from their land in 1980 and had had their houses burned.

Indians from the U.S. and Canada revived old wrongs and told of the theft of their land. The Western Shoshone tribe from Nevada—not among the official cases but nevertheless offered a platform—charged the U.S. government with violating the 1863 Treaty of Ruby Valley by its plan to requisition 25,900 sq km (10,000 sq mi) of Shoshone land for the MX missile system.

Southern Africa. At midnight on April 17 Zimbabwe became an independent multiracial state governed democratically for the first time in its history under the leadership of the Zimbabwe African National Union-Patriotic Front. Thus ended the rule of the white minority. A report in October showed that firms in seven of the nine countries of the European Economic Community ignored or flagrantly flouted the EEC's "Code of Conduct for European firms in South Africa."

Attacks on white domination of South Africa occurred during the year. On June 1 simultaneously coordinated attacks on oil refineries at Sasolburg in Orange Free State and 240 km (150 mi) away at Secunda, in the Transvaal, were carried out by the African National Congress. Over 1,000 farms were abandoned by their white owners fleeing from the prospect of black insurgents on the Transvaal borders with Zimbabwe and Botswana, according to Christiaan Cilliers, director of the South African agricultural union, in September. Perhaps of more lasting significance were the strikes by black industrial workers. The country's biggest strike against a single employer occurred on July 24. By July 30, 10,000 out of 14,000 workers, led by the unregistered Black Municipality Workers' Union, were on strike for higher wages in Johannesburg; observers noted that of the 748 strikes by black workers between 1973 and 1979, only one was legal. Approximately 1,100 strikers were deported to the Bantu homelands on August 1, and Joseph Mavi and Philip Dlamini, union organizers, were arrested and charged with sabotage. There were also mass school boycotts in the Cape Province during June–September by African and Coloured (mixed race) schoolchildren protesting their inferior education. Minister of Education and Training Ferdinand Hartzenberg ordered the closing of 77 schools. Rioting in Cape Town on June 17 resulted in more than 40 deaths after the police fired on young looters. (STUART BENTLEY)

[522.B]

Racket Games

Badminton. In the second world badminton championships, played from May 27 to June 1, 1980, at Jakarta, Indonesia, Rudy Hartono of the host nation defeated his compatriot Liem Swie King 15–9, 15–9 to win the men's singles. Wiharjo Verawaty of Indonesia won the women's singles by outpointing Lie Ivana of Indonesia 11–1, 11–3. Indonesia also claimed the champions of the men's doubles, Ade Chandra and Christian Hadinata, and of the mixed doubles, Hadinata and Imelda Wigoeno. The only break in the dominance of the Indonesians was the victory by Nora Perry and Jane Webster of the U.K. in the women's doubles.

The John Player All-England championships were held at Wembley, England, from March 19 to 22. Champion in the men's singles was Prakash Pacukone of India, who defeated Liem Swie King 15–3, 15–10. Lene Koppen of Denmark won the women's singles 11–2, 11–6 over Verawaty. The men's doubles competition was won by Johan Wahjudi and Tjun Tjun of Indonesia, while Perry and Gillian Gilks gained the women's doubles crown for the U.K. Perry teamed with Mike Tredgett to give Britain a championship in the mixed doubles.

In the U.S. the national championships took place at Offutt Air Force Base in Nebraska from April 16 to 19. Gary Higgins of Alhambra, Calif., defeated Chris Kinard of Pasadena, Calif., 15–5, 15–8 to win the men's singles. The women's singles champion was Cheryl Carton of San Diego, Calif., who outlasted Judianne Kelly of Costa Mesa, Calif., 11–4, 8–11, 11–8. Matt Fogarty of Duxbury, Mass., and Mike Walker of Manhattan Beach, Calif., won the men's doubles 8–15, 15–8, 15–12 from Higgins and John Britain of Redondo Beach, Calif. The women's doubles crown went to Kelly and Pam Brady of Flint, Mich., who defeated Carton and Vicki Toutz of Los Alamitos, Calif., 15–9, 15–8. Walker and Kelly won the mixed doubles 15–12, 14–18, 18–16. (C. R. ELI)

Squash Rackets. The men's World Open championship took place in October 1980 in Adelaide, Australia, and resulted in a convincing and easy win in the final for the defending champion, Geoffrey Hunt of Australia, who beat Qamar Zaman of Pakistan in three games in little over half an hour. Hunt also retained his British Open championship, winning this event (also against Zaman in the final) for the seventh time; he thus equaled the record set by Hashim Khan of Pakistan in the 1950s. The latter succeeded in winning the Open Vintage championship (over 55) for the third successive year.

The last British amateur championship (in view of the game adopting the principle of open squash) was won by Jonathan Leslie. The first British player to win this event in 11 years, he defeated Ross Norman of New Zealand in the final. The South African Open championship was won by Hunt, who beat B. Brownlee of New Zealand in the final in four games. In the European team championship, England was defeated for the first time in the championship's eight years, losing to Sweden, runner-up during the previous three years. The North American Open championship was won by Sharif Khan of Pakistan for the 12th time when he beat Michael Desaulniers (Canada) in four games. Desaulniers won the U.S. amateur championship.

In women's squash the World Open championships (both team and individual) are held triennially, and there was no competition in 1980. Vicky Hoffman of Australia won the British women's

ARTHUR SHAY PHOTO—COURTESY, NATIONAL RACKETBALL CLUB

Marty Hogan (right), here playing top contender Dave Peck, battled his way to a third straight national racquetball championship.

championship, beating Sue Cogswell of the U.K. in the final.

In the first official World Junior championships, Peter Nance of Australia beat his compatriot Chris Dittmas in four games to win the individual championship. Australia won the team event 2–1 over Pakistan. (JOHN H. HORRY)

Rackets. John Prenn retained the British amateur singles title and won the British Open championship, beating Willie Boone in both finals at Queen's Club, London, in the spring of 1980. Prenn also won the U.S. Open singles in 1980 and the European championship singles in Gibraltar in September 1979.

Boone won both the Canadian and U.S. amateur singles championships and also both those doubles with Randall Crawley. Boone and Crawley won the British amateur doubles title for the first time, beating the defending champions, Howard Angus and Andrew Milne, in the final at Queen's Club in April 1980. They also won the world invitation open doubles against the same opponents at Eton, England, in June.

Real Tennis. Howard Angus, world champion, won the singles championships at Queen's Club in April 1980 and the Marylebone Cricket Club gold racket at Lord's, London, in June, each for the 15th consecutive year. In both finals he defeated Alan Lovell. Angus also took the British Open singles championship title from Chris Ronaldson of the U.K. at Queen's Club in December 1979. Ronaldson won the first world invitation open singles from Angus at Seacourt, Hayling Island, in June 1980. Norwood Cripps (Eton College) and Lovell, who had already won the open doubles for the fourth time, beat Ronaldson and Graham Hyland of the U.S. in the world doubles final. Ronaldson won the British professional singles championship over defending champion Frank Willis in May 1980, having also won the Scottish Open singles in March.

Britain retained the Bathurst Cup, defeating the only contenders, France, 5–0 at Lord's in June. Oxford and Cambridge beat the combined U.S. universities 4–3 to retain the Van Alen Trophy at Queen's Club in July. Pierre Etchebaster, the great Basque world real tennis champion, died in April. (CHRISTINA WOOD)

Racquetball. The racquetball phenomenon, which had placed the sport among the top 20 participatory activities in the U.S. in the late 1970s, began showing signs of leveling off in 1980. High interest rates during the year severely hampered the efforts of potential racquetball club developers, thereby limiting the availability of new facilities. Yet the sport continued to gain players, with more than 10 million estimated participants.

In professional racquetball Marty Hogan captured his third consecutive championship in 1980, defeating Mike Yellen for the second consecutive year in the final match. A significant development was the formation of the Women's Professional Racquetball Association (WPRA). Representing every top woman professional player, the WPRA severed relations with the governing body of professional racquetball, the National Racquetball Club, and conducted its own series of tournaments, including its first national professional championship. This event was won by Heather McKay, who defeated Shannon Wright in the final. (CHARLES S. LEVE)

Refugees

During 1980 emergency situations calling for rapid and sustained action occupied a growing place in the daily work of the office of the United Nations High Commissioner for Refugees (UNHCR). A significant number of refugees were helped to return to their countries of origin, while thousands were either integrated locally in countries of first asylum or resettled in third countries.

Africa remained the continent with the highest number of refugees, with approximately 5 million refugees and displaced persons. The refugee case load grew in early 1980 because of events in the Ethiopia-Somalia region and continued uncertain-

Radio:
see Television and Radio

Railroads:
see Transportation

Real Tennis:
see Racket Games

Recordings:
see Music

Reformed Churches:
see Religion

MIAMI HERALD/BLACK STAR

An exhausted refugee collapsed on the beach while fellow Haitians waited for permission from local police to leave the crowded boat that landed near Miami Beach, Florida, in June.

ty in southern Africa. Refugees congregated in such urban centres as Djibouti and Khartoum, straining local resources. A continued influx gave Somalia the largest refugee problem in the world with more than 800,000 in 32 camps and (by government estimates) an equivalent number elsewhere in the country. Sudan reported 441,000 refugees in midyear and declared 1980 the "Year of the Refugee." Refugees fleeing civil strife in Chad also entered neighbouring countries, particularly Cameroon and Nigeria. Fresh influxes of refugees from Uganda reached Zaire and Sudan toward the end of the year. In Angola Namibian refugees were again subject to military attacks on their camps by South African forces. Refugees in Djibouti constituted nearly 15% of the population. In Ethiopia assistance to displaced people was hampered by their swelling numbers and by prolonged drought. Toward the end of the year UNHCR announced a new program to assist refugees returning to Ethiopia from neighbouring countries.

At the same time, solutions to several refugee problems in Africa were attained. The mutual repatriation of Zairians and Angolans continued. UNHCR coordinated the voluntary repatriation of Zimbabwean refugees. Some 33,000 were repatriated under UNHCR auspices before the national elections, mainly from Botswana (about 18,000), Mozambique (about 11,000), and Zambia (about 4,000). In addition, several thousand returned home on their own. The repatriation resumed after the independence of Zimbabwe, and by the end of July more than 51,000 persons had returned home with UNHCR's help. Tanzania announced the naturalization of some 35,000 refugees from Rwanda.

There was a further decline in the number of refugees in Latin America. During 1980 UNHCR was completing its program for the rehabilitation of former Nicaraguan refugees who had returned to their country. In the first half of 1980 about 130,000 Cubans left their country, of whom more than 110,000 were received in the U.S. Costa Rica accepted a limited number for resettlement, and the Peruvian government accepted for permanent resettlement 1,000 of the Cuban nationals who had entered the Peruvian embassy in Havana. Some 35,000 citizens left El Salvador for neighbouring countries. About 20,000 went to Honduras. Argentina accepted a number of Indochinese families, the majority of Lao origin, for resettlement.

In Southeast Asia the mass influx of Indochinese

Cuban refugees filled a hangar at Eglin Air Force Base in Florida where they were temporarily housed after having fled Havana in May.

UPI

refugees, particularly Vietnamese "boat people," decreased in the second half of the year. The U.S. raised its admission quota for Indochinese refugees to 168,000 for the year, and other nations continued to make places available. Piracy in Southeast Asian waters posed major problems, with refugees being subjected to repeated attacks on the high seas. UNHCR made a patrol boat available to the Thai Navy to help deter such attacks.

The influx in late 1979 and early 1980 of large numbers of Cambodians into Thailand (in addition to some half a million displaced along the Thai-Cambodian border) necessitated major international assistance in 1980. Some 165,000 stayed in emergency holding centres where they received care and maintenance assistance. Toward the end of the year UNHCR was able to announce a program of assistance to an estimated 300,000 Cambodian returnees in their home country.

The year also witnessed the dramatic escalation of the number of refugees fleeing from Afghanistan into Pakistan, which reached 1.2 million. UNHCR reviewed its program of assistance twice during the year, raising its eventual needs for basic food, shelter, health, education, water supplies, household items, and self-help for refugees in Pakistan projects to U.S. $99 million. During 1980 seven more nations ratified the 1951 convention and the 1967 protocol relating to the status of refugees, bringing the total number of countries acceding to these major legal instruments to 83.

Toward the end of the year plans were announced by UN Secretary-General Kurt Waldheim, in collaboration with the Organization of African Unity and UNHCR, to hold an international conference on refugees in Africa early in 1981.

(UNHCR)

See also Migration, International.

Religion

On the religious scene, the decade of the 1980s began with several strong-willed spiritual leaders asserting their authority in worldly affairs. The headlines were dominated by the names of such men as Ayatollah Ruhollah Khomeini, the religious and temporal leader of Islamic Iran; Pope John Paul II, whose vision of the mission of the Roman Catholic Church became increasingly clear as he ended the second year of his reign; and the television "superstars" in America's "electronic church," who made concerted attempts to "get out the Christian vote" in the November 4 election.

Although the temperaments and the mind-sets of these men had been shaped by vastly different religious and cultural traditions, all had certain traits in common. They were troubled by few self-doubts or doubts about the validity of their heritages, and they were unawed by the claims to superior wisdom made by the cosmopolitan elite of the secular world.

In its first issue of 1980, *Time* magazine devoted its cover story to Ayatollah Khomeini, the newsmagazine's choice as its "man of the year" for 1979, "the person who has done the most to change the news, for better or for worse." His audacious attempt to dewesternize Iran and turn that country into a theocratic Islamic state had thrown the Middle East balance of power into chaos and fueled the fervour of Islamic conservatives in other parts of the Muslim world. (See *Islam,* below.)

Meanwhile, John Paul II, the "pilgrim pope," was no more of a homebody in 1980 than he had been in 1979. In May the Polish-born pontiff was seen by millions of Africans. His messages to them contained attacks on governmental corruption, statements of support for the poor and hungry, and appeals for obedience to traditional church teachings. From May 30 to June 2, the papal entourage went to France, where modern secularism had made deep inroads into the church loyalty of baptized Catholics. Indefatigably, the pope took off on June 30 for a 12-day, 9,000-mi journey to Brazil, the world's largest Roman Catholic nation.

Many progressive Catholics had speculated that the visit to Brazil would be the supreme test to date of the pope's commitment to social justice. In a land of 123 million people, where the gap between the rich minority and the poor majority is wide, the pope deplored acts of violence and class warfare, but he also called for pastoral action "which defends the poor in the face of unjust campaigns that offend their dignity." John Paul also addressed the Brazilians in the language of symbol and gesture. At a reception for members of the church hierarchy, the spiritual leader of world Catholicism made a point of embracing and kissing Dom Helder Câmara, archbishop of Olinda and Recife, a radical who for many years had been a relentless critic of Brazil's military regimes. Similarly, after visiting a squalid squatters' colony in Rio de Janeiro, the pope appeared so moved by the poverty he saw that he removed the gold ring given to him when he was made a cardinal and gave it to the parish church.

The pope's November five-day trip to West Germany took him into divided territory for Catholics. Although the West German bishops had supported the 1979 Vatican decision that the liberal Hans Küng of the University of Tübingen "can no longer be considered a Catholic theologian," the pontiff still was under attack by theological progressives.

The tireless pontiff apparently would not rest until he personally fulfilled the biblical commandment to carry the Christian gospel to the ends of the Earth. Already announced by the Vatican were plans for a February 1981 papal pilgrimage to Japan and the Philippines and a 1982 trip to Great Britain. Meanwhile, between trips, John Paul set about getting his ecclesiastical house in order.

A strong believer in doctrinal orthodoxy and structural coherence in the life of the church, John Paul began his year by tackling one of his toughest problems: the divisions in the church in The Netherlands, where progressives had allowed several practices that offended Rome. After two and a half weeks of deliberations at a special synod, the Vatican brought the Dutch prelates into line on every major disputed issue. Although many observers predicted church leaders would have trouble enforcing the agreement, the Dutch bishops promised to back clerical celibacy, revive the tradition of individual confession, produce a more conservative catechism, and issue stricter rules governing mixed marriages.

In addition, the Vatican reaffirmed its stand on euthanasia, cracked down on "abuses" in liturgical practices that "bewilder" the faithful, and, in preparation for the autumn synod of bishops, published a 115-page document on "The Role of the Christian Family in the World Today." Besides restating familiar church beliefs on abortion, birth control by "artificial" methods, and premarital and extramarital sex, the document called upon Catholics to take a discriminating look at the women's liberation movement.

Politics was often on the pope's mind during 1980. At home and abroad, he constantly stressed that political activism was a proper role for laity but an improper one for clergy. The point was driven home in May when church authorities withdrew permission for Robert F. Drinan, a Jesuit, to run for reelection as a Democratic representative from Massachusetts. (See *Roman Catholic Church*, below.)

Ironically, as the pope was ordering Catholic priests to stay out of politics, conservative Protestant ministers on the U.S. television circuit and in large parareligious organizations were becoming more openly and actively involved in politics than ever before. At the heart of the "new Christian right" movement were such theological and political conservatives as Bill Bright, founder of the Campus Crusade for Christ, and fundamentalist television preachers like Jerry Falwell (*see* BIOGRAPHIES) of Lynchburg, Va., and James Robison of Fort Worth, Texas.

From their large television audiences, the TV preachers had acquired sources of funds and mailing lists that gave them quick access to millions of voters. The Christian zealots worked in the presidential campaign, but their main targets were liberal incumbents in carefully selected congressional contests. Their key issues were identified in the congressional "report cards" and sample ballots they distributed. Generally, they opposed the proposed Equal Rights Amendment (ERA) to the U.S. Constitution, the use of federal funds for abortions, the SALT II arms-limitation treaty, and the right of homosexual persons to teach in public schools. With equal fervour, they favoured prayer in the public schools, budget increases to "restore U.S. military superiority for national defense," and intense efforts to "stop or control pornography."

Not all evangelicals supported the "get out the Christian vote" campaigns. Kenneth Kantzer, editor of *Christianity Today* magazine, declared that the Christian gospel should not be identified with "the extreme right wing." David Hubbard, president of Fuller Theological Seminary in Pasadena, Calif., said he would "hate for evangelical Christianity to become a spiritual version of the National Rifle Association." And Billy Graham, celebrated evangelist and friend of many U.S. presidents, told reporters in September that he intended to "remain above, below or beyond the whole political fray." (*See* Special Report.)

On the ecumenical and interfaith fronts, three events stood out in 1980.

On the Greek islands of Patmos and Rhodes in late spring, official representatives of the Roman Catholic Church and Eastern Orthodoxy engaged in the first formal interchurch dialogues since the schism that had separated the two large branches of Christendom in 1054. At the end of the historic gathering, a spokesman said, "It is hoped that steps will be taken that will lead toward the restoration of full ecclesiastical communion between Eastern Orthodoxy and Roman Catholicism." (See *Roman Catholic Church; The Orthodox Church*, below.)

In late August, Anglican-Roman Catholic relations went through a period of stress when Catholic leaders surprised their Anglican counterparts by announcing that some married Episcopal clergy might be accepted for ordination as Catholic clergymen. Chiefly affected by the ruling would be dissident Episcopalians who had become disaffected in recent years by the decision of the Episcopal Church in the U.S. to ordain women as priests and its adoption of a new Book of Common Prayer. (See *Anglican Communion*, below.)

The move, regarded as precipitous and unilateral by critics in both churches, did not seem likely to undo the cordial relationship established between Pope John Paul and Robert Runcie, the new archbishop of Canterbury, when the two leaders met in Africa in May. The future of Anglican-Catholic relations would undergo a new test in 1982 when the pope visited the home of the Church of England.

On a bureaucratic level, some strains developed between U.S. Jewish leaders and officials of the National Council of Churches when the Protestant and Orthodox ecumenical agency began working on a new study document on Middle East relations. Some Jews contended that the working document reflected a pro-Palestinian bias, but intense lobbying efforts appeared to produce a tentative proposal that both sides could live with.

In the United Methodist Church, the rapidly growing influence of women ministers was reflected in the July election of Marjorie S. Matthews as the denomination's first woman bishop. In September she took over her duties as the new spiritual leader of Methodists in Wisconsin.

The expanding interest of religious leaders in biomedical ethics and other science-and-religion issues took symbolic form in May when, in a London ceremony, the £90,000 Templeton Foundation Prize for Progress in Religion was presented to Ralph Wendell Burhoe, a Unitarian-Universalist scholar whose career has been devoted to strengthening the links between science and religion. He was the first North American to receive the award.

Two historic milestones were passed in 1980. The Sunday school movement, started by Robert Raikes in England in an attempt to reach the children of the poor with the Christian gospel, celebrated its 200th birthday. Throughout the world, especially in areas where Lutheranism is strong, observances were held marking the 450th anniversary of the publication of the Augsburg Confession, the basic statement of faith for Lutherans. (See *Lutheran Churches*, below.) (ROY LARSON)

PROTESTANT CHURCHES

Anglican Communion. For Anglicans throughout the world, the high point of 1980 came early with the enthronement at Canterbury Cathedral on March 25 of Robert Runcie as the new archbishop of Canterbury. Within two months Archbishop Runcie emphasized his support for ecumenism by meeting Pope John Paul II. The two leaders, visiting Africa at the same time, took the opportunity of arranging an informal meeting at Accra, Ghana, on May 9. The announcement in August that the pope would visit England—the birthplace of Anglicanism—in 1982 was greeted with delight in most Anglican circles, although some of the more Protestant elements in the Church of England expressed reservations.

The Anglican-Roman Catholic International Commission (ARCIC) met again to complete its work on the nature of authority in the Christian church. Another encouraging ecumenical sign was the resumption in July of similar talks between the Anglican and Orthodox churches. This followed a cool period in which the Orthodox had threatened to break off the discussions became some Anglican churches were permitting the ordination of women.

The harmony was at least temporarily ruffled by the announcement in August that married Episcopal priests in the U.S. could become Roman Catholic priests and that former Episcopalians, both clergy and lay, might be allowed to retain certain aspects of their liturgy and structure. The special arrangement was made for those Episcopalians who had been deeply unhappy ever since their church ordained women and introduced a new liturgy. The move caught the Anglican Communion by surprise, but after some initial turmoil the consensus was that the arrangement would probably cause more trouble for Rome than for the Anglican Church. Vatican officials were at pains to stress that they would be dealing with individuals only, thus discounting any idea that whole congregations, with their priests, might go over to Rome and form some sort of "uniate" church within Roman Catholicism.

Anglican relations with Protestantism were less happy. The unity scheme in New Zealand collapsed when it failed by one vote to obtain the necessary majority in the Anglican General Synod. In England a covenanting scheme to bring the Church of England and four free churches closer together appeared doomed from the start.

Harassment of the tiny Episcopal Church in Iran intensified. By the end of the year the last priest had been arrested, the son of the bishop murdered, several missionaries expelled, and the bishop's secretary injured in a shooting and then held on suspicion of spying, together with another missionary and his wife. Having survived an assassination attempt in 1979, the bishop, H. Dehqani-Tafti, went into self-imposed exile.

(SUSAN YOUNG)

Baptist Churches. The positive news in the Baptist world was reflected in the 14th meeting of the Baptist World Alliance in Toronto, July 8–13, 1980, where 20,000 Baptists from 90 countries gathered for inspiration and fellowship. The keynote speaker was evangelist Billy Graham. Duke McCall, president of the Southern Baptist Seminary in Louisville, Ky., was unanimously elected to a five-year term as president, and Gerhard Claas of West Germany succeeded Robert S. Denny as general secretary. Of particular interest was a resolution passed by the women's department urging government officials in Liberia to free Victoria Tolbert, widow of William R. Tolbert, Jr., the country's recently assassinated president.

On the negative side, turmoil continued between liberals and conservatives in the 13 million-member Southern Baptist Convention, the largest Protestant denomination in the U.S. At its annual meeting in St. Louis, Mo., in June, the SBC, for the second straight year, elected as president an avowed conservative and believer in an "inerrant Bible": Bailey Smith of Del City, Okla. Opinion differed as to whether there actually was a "ten-year plan" for purging liberal scholars and teachers from Southern Baptist seminaries. However, all Southern Baptists agreed that there was a major division within the denomination which some felt could threaten the vitality of the SBC during the 1980s.

In other action, the SBC messengers (delegates) took a stand against permissive abortion, supported the Supreme Court's decision forbidding "government authored or sponsored religious exercises in public schools," went on record against the ERA, and commended the president of Baylor University in Waco, Texas, for his stand against Baylor women students posing nude for *Playboy* magazine.

Among black Baptists, the largest denomination, the National Baptist Convention, U.S.A., Inc., held its annual meeting in Birmingham, Ala., where it had been founded in 1880. In Chicago, earlier in the summer, the younger and smaller Progressive National Baptist Convention criticized ultraconservative evangelicals for not dealing with the problem of economic injustice. Forces such as the politically oriented Moral Majority and the "electronic church" were denounced as "dispensers of cheap grace and invalid, distorted witnesses of the true and full Gospel."

The American Baptist Churches in the U.S.A. (formerly the Northern Baptist Convention) joined various ecumenical organizations in fielding emergency medical teams for Cambodian relief. Chief implementer of the program would be the Thailand Baptist Missionary Fellowship, which included not only American Baptists but Swedish and Australian Baptists as well.

(NORMAN R. DE PUY)

Christian Church (Disciples of Christ). Disciples of Christ leaders from Zaire told their North American counterparts that, while a moratorium on missionaries and aid might be valid in some parts of Africa, they saw no attempt by U.S. and Canadian Disciples to dominate the Zairian church and therefore wanted assistance to continue. The "parent church" agreed to keep on giving $500,000 a year to Zaire Disciples, now a part of the unified Church of Christ in Zaire. At the same time, representatives of the Disciples in Zaire and North America agreed to seek ways to make mission a truly two-directional partnership.

The ecumenically minded Disciples completed organization of a Disciples Ecumenical Consultative Council, representing Disciples-related churches in 12 nations, to coordinate world ecumenical responses. A delegation sent to the United Church of Canada agreed to a special relationship between the two churches in light of Canadian union talks involving Disciples. In the U.S. a joint steering committee of Disciples and United Church of Christ leaders decided they would recommend by 1985 whether the two churches should enter union negotiations. (ROBERT LOUIS FRIEDLY)

Robert Runcie, the 102nd archbishop of Canterbury, was enthroned with regal pomp in March.

KEYSTONE

Churches of Christ. In 1980 the Churches of Christ focused on strengthening the family, foreign missions, and local church growth. Seminars, film series, and workshops designed to strengthen marriage and family ties were sponsored by hundreds of congregations. Churches in Stillwater, Okla., and Richland Hills in Fort Worth, Texas, constructed family centres, and many counseling centres to help with family as well as personal problems were established.

Churches of Christ in the U.S. were supporting 427 missionary families around the world. Some 745 persons were baptized during a four-week evangelistic campaign in Ghana, and one preaching tour in India resulted in 1,326 baptisms and 37 new congregations. The radio program "La Busqueda," on 53 stations throughout Mexico, led to the establishment of over 30 congregations there.

Campus ministries had doubled in the past ten years, and over the past five years baptisms had increased by 270% with retention rates of 80 to 90%. Christian education from preschool through university received great emphasis. Abilene Christian University celebrated its 75th anniversary.
(M. NORVEL YOUNG)

Church of Christ, Scientist. The denomination's June annual meeting—the first in the church's second century—centred on the Sermon on the Mount. More than 7,000 members, on hand for the Boston meeting, heard Jean Stark Hebenstreit, incoming chairman of the Christian Science Board of Directors, emphasize that: "Humanity can't afford a continued drift toward the morally bankrupt doctrine that material pleasures are the sole or chief good in life. . . ." Referring to New Testament examples, she noted that: "The Master brought the blessing of spiritual vision right into the midst of human need. That same spiritual vision of Jesus' day is central to our responsibilities in these times."

Church officers reported a slight increase in the flow of new membership applications from Africa and Latin America; a sound financial picture; modest circulation gains for the *Christian Science Monitor*; and steady growth of the endowment fund opened in 1978 to help support the newspaper. Saville R. Davis, a former *Monitor* senior editor and correspondent, was named church president to serve through May 1981.
(ALLISON W. PHINNEY)

Church of Jesus Christ of Latter-day Saints. The 150th anniversary of Mormonism's founding in a log cabin in Fayette, N.Y., on April 6, 1830, featured a General Conference, held in a restored cabin on that site and in Salt Lake City and utilizing the latest developments in satellite-linked telecasting.

By May most meetings for congregations, formerly held on Sundays and weekdays, had been consolidated into a three-hour block on Sundays. It was hoped the change would encourage the family's development as the focal point of religious instruction, help conserve energy, and enable Latter-day Saints to participate in more civic and Christian service. The April announcement of plans for the construction of seven new temples signaled a turn to greater numbers of smaller, highly functional temples. Mormon interest in family history was reflected in a nondenominational World Conference on Records sponsored by a church affiliate, the Genealogical Society of Utah, in Salt Lake City in August.

In April a university student in Logan, Utah, discovered what was believed to be the oldest Mormon document extant. The handwriting, identified as that of the church's founder, Joseph Smith, included characters Smith purportedly copied in 1828 from metallic plates before translating the Book of Mormon from those plates.

The December 1979 excommunication of dissident feminist Sonia Johnson was upheld when appealed to the First Presidency. In response to publicity over the Johnson controversy, official church opposition to passage of the ERA was reiterated and explained. A handful of Johnson sympathizers applied for excommunication, but it was clear that advocacy of ERA did not in itself constitute grounds for church discipline. In December seven dissidents announced plans to found a new church.
(LEONARD J. ARRINGTON)

Jehovah's Witnesses. An international, interracial, unincorporated "brotherhood" found in 205 countries and island groups, Jehovah's Witnesses in 1980 numbered some 2.2 million individuals. Impelled to imitate Christ's evangelizing spirit and his close adherence to a chaste and separate life, Witnesses are neutral toward and take no part in politics and worldly conflicts.

Emphasis on Bible study continued to be an outstanding characteristic of the group. Besides attending five Bible study classes each week in their 43,181 congregations, Witnesses conducted free, weekly Bible classes in over 1,250,000 private homes during the year. This resulted in the baptism of 113,779 new converts. This intensive Bible educational program was enhanced by 102 "Divine Love" district conventions held in the U.S. during the summer, with over one million in attendance.

Witnesses believe the Lord's Prayer expresses the purpose of Jehovah God and the hope of mankind, namely, that the coming of God's kingdom means the establishment of a righteous, heavenly government. This will extend its rule over all obedient mankind and will transform the Earth into an Edenic paradise.
(FREDERICK W. FRANZ)

Lutheran Churches. A major anniversary in the history of their movement was a focus of attention for the world's 70 million Lutherans in 1980. On June 25, 1530, supporters of Martin Luther formally presented a relatively brief and irenic statement of their views at an imperial diet in Bavaria. The 450th anniversary of that Augsburg Confession was marked around the Lutheran world, often in conjunction with Roman Catholics. The chief celebration was an eight-day cycle of events in Augsburg itself, which attracted about 25,000 people from more than 50 countries. Pope John Paul II sent a message in which he said that theological dialogues between Lutherans and Roman Catholics in the last decade and a half had "led us to discover anew the breadth and solidity of the foundations of our common grounding in the Christian faith." In the spring, the official international Lutheran-Roman Catholic dialogue team concluded that in large measure the "contents of the statements of the Augsburg Confession . . . can be regarded as an expression of the common faith."

Besides that with Roman Catholics, official international, regional, and national dialogue with other Christian traditions continued. In the U.S. the Lutheran-Episcopal group completed its second round of work (begun in 1976) with common statements on gospel, eucharist, scripture, justification, and apostolicity. At the beginning of the year, the U.S. Lutheran-United Methodist group's common statement on baptism was circulated. Preparatory commissions for the first international Lutheran-Eastern Orthodox conversations met in Greece and Iceland.

In North America, two of the three large Lutheran denominations held their biennial conventions. The Lutheran Church in America, meeting in Seattle, Wash., in June, approved a major statement on economic justice and decided to follow the pattern of most Lutherans and other Christians by referring to its leaders as bishops. The American Lutheran Church met in Minneapolis, Minn., in October. Union discussions continued among these two denominations and a third, small body in the U.S., as well as among their counterparts in Canada.

Efforts continued in Sweden and Norway to loosen ties between church and state in those overwhelmingly Lutheran countries. A generally though not always improving church-state climate was reported in predominantly Lutheran East Germany. World Lutheranism continued to show concern about the situation in southern Africa, especially in South West Africa/Namibia, where it is the major Christian grouping. Refugees were also a major social concern of world and U.S. Lutheranism. The influx of Cuban refugees to the U.S. prompted financial help from Lutherans in Canada, West Germany, and Australia, as well as in the U.S. The Lutheran Immigration and Refugee Service marked the resettling of its 100,000th refugee since World War II.
(TOM DORRIS)

Methodist Churches. A rally was held in Suva, Fiji, attended by 30,000 people, to launch a Methodist "Mission to the Eighties," the commencement of the World Methodist Council's (WMC's) ten-point plan for evangelism. The second event within the plan was an International Youth Conference in Truro, England, attended by 1,000 young people from 47 countries who lived for eight days in a tented "city." They produced a message to the world calling for "commitment to nonviolent means of change."

The Irish Conference called for a new initiative between Methodists and Catholics on the issues that divide the churches and cause hatred and conflict within the community. At the international level, the joint commission between the WMC and the Roman Catholic Church continued, as representatives of each church met to discuss the person and work of the Holy Spirit.

The quadrennial General Conference of the United Methodist Church of the U.S., representing some ten million members, met in Indianapolis, Ind. Much of the time was spent in legislative committees considering more than 20,000 petitions submitted by members, boards, and agencies of the church. An issue that attracted considerable publicity was the church's attitude toward homosexuality; an attempt to exclude those with a homosexual orientation from the ministry and from officeholding was successfully resisted.

At the heart of the vast mass of legislative action was a deep concern for more effective evangelism. Bishop C. Dale White reported on his visit to the U.S. hostages in Iran and called for understanding of the deep sense of outrage felt by the people of that country because of past injustice and exploitation. The conference sent a message of greeting to newly independent Zimbabwe.

The annual British Conference, held in Sheffield, also considered homosexuality. It was decided to send the revised version of the previous year's report on human sexuality, which included a controversial section on homosexual relationships, to districts and circuits for discussion. The conference agreed that the time had come to set about revising the Methodist hymnbook. Also discussed was the desirability of appointing more overseas ministers to British Methodist churches in order to improve links with other countries.

(PETER H. BOLT)

Pentecostal Churches. In a presidential election year in the U.S., there were signs that Pentecostals were entering the political arena more openly than in the past. At the call of a Pentecostal pastor, John Gimenez of Virginia Beach, Va., over 200,000 born-again Christians gathered in Washington, D.C., on April 29, 1980, for a mammoth "Washington for Jesus" rally. In August a gathering of evangelical leaders met in Dallas, Texas, in a "national briefing" for church leaders. In these meetings, Pentecostal-charismatic leaders appeared with prominent non-Pentecostal evangelicals for the first time.

The Foursquare International Convention met in April in the Angelus Temple in Los Angeles, where delegates were told of a new denominational television ministry. In February leaders of the Pentecostal Holiness Church and the Congregational Holiness Church signed an agreement of affiliation which began the process of healing a schism that had occurred in 1920. Bishop J. Floyd Williams was elected the 20th president of the National Association of Evangelicals, only the second Pentecostal to serve in this position.

In September the Assemblies of God conducted seven regional "conferences of the Holy Spirit" for the purpose of relating to the charismatic movement in the main line churches. The Assemblies of God also announced the opening of new mission fields in Luxembourg, Sudan, Morocco, and Uganda, bringing the total missions outreach of the church to 105 nations.

(VINSON SYNAN)

Presbyterian, Reformed, and Congregational Churches. The newest members of the World Alliance of Reformed Churches (WARC) were the Evangelical Reformed Church of Angola and the Presbyterian Church of Mauritius, whose admission brought the total membership to 147. The task of the WARC was to knit together the vast and scattered membership (most of the members were minority churches in their own context) while affirming a distinctive contribution to ecumenism. The continent with the largest number of member churches was Asia, with 34 in 17 countries; in Latin America 11 countries were represented by 17 members. Australasia contributed 6 members to the Alliance, from 4 countries; the U.S. and Canada had 11 member churches between them; and in Europe there were 35 member churches among 20 countries.

The ecumenical involvement of the WARC included ongoing interconfessional dialogues with the Anglicans, Baptists, Lutherans, and the Orthodox and Roman Catholic churches. The WARC's general secretary was in his second year of service

JOHNSON/BURGEE ARCHITECTS; PHOTOS, GORDON H. SCHENCK, JR.

The massive Garden Grove (California) Community Church, called the Crystal Cathedral, opened in September. Built at a cost of $18 million, it can seat up to 3,000 people.

as chairman of the Christian World Communities' Committee, where the major Christian traditions meet with the World Council of Churches (WCC) to define their respective roles in the total ecumenical movement.

Human rights and interchurch cooperation continued to stand high on the list of WARC priorities. During 1980 WARC representatives visited Taiwan and worked in various ways to support the Presbyterian Church there, which was under increasing pressure from the government of the island. At the invitation of the local member church, a joint WARC–WCC delegation went to Equatorial Guinea to observe the needs of the people and the churches. The country had been cut off from the rest of the world for over a decade, until the overthrow of the Macías Nguema regime in 1979. Relief and ongoing support were being made possible through joint WARC–WCC action. The WARC also continued its focus on women in church and society and was working out a new approach in this field.

The European member churches of the WARC met in September in Poiana Brasov, Rom. On this occasion—the first European Area Council meeting in an Eastern European country since the end of World War II—the Alliance made a gift of 10,000 Bibles to the Reformed Church of Romania. Such assemblies had previously been held in Amsterdam (1973), Torre Pellice, Italy (1967), and Zürich, Switz. (1961). Preparations continued for the WARC's next General Council, to be held in Ottawa during Aug. 17–27, 1982. (ALDO COMBA)

Religious Society of Friends. The idea that human beings are stewards responsible for God's world made Quakers natural supporters of ecological movements. For American Friends, this meant activity in the growing debate over nuclear power. In Britain, particularly, Quakers also played a vigorous part in the protest movement against nuclear arms. This was paralleled in the U.S. by the "New Call to Peacemaking," which held its second conference in October and which drew together the three "historic peace churches"—Mennonites, Brethren, and Quakers.

In Britain a group of young Friends pointed out to the Yearly Meeting in May that some of the Society's investments were with companies engaged in activities that conflicted with Friends' principles—armaments, alcohol, and, in one case, involvement in South Africa. The Yearly Meeting accepted the criticism and took steps to work out a more ethical investment policy. Through the Friends World Committee for Consultation and the Quaker UN Office, Swiss Friends (membership 124), with some success, pressed their concern over the involvement of children in military training before committees of nongovernmental organizations at the UN.

(DAVID FIRTH)

Salvation Army. Gen. Arnold Brown, world leader of 2.5 million Salvationists, observed at first hand during 1980 the combat gear of this "Army without guns" in more than 20 countries. His visits included the Army's centenary celebrations in the U.S. in June and in Australia in September.

Salvation Army refugee-aid programs were intensified, with greater emphasis placed on long-term planning and rehabilitation. While sustaining its medical program to the 40,000 refugees in Sa Kaeo camp, Thailand, the Army acquired land for the erection of a permanent building to be used as a work and community centre. Overcrowding caused by wave upon wave of refugees arriving in Hong Kong and the Philippines continued to challenge every resource at the Army's disposal, as did some 850,000 displaced persons without shelter in Zimbabwe. Early in 1980 a Salvationist presence was reestablished in Uganda.

In February Queen Elizabeth II opened the new Hope Town centre for homeless women in Whitechapel, east London, within a stone's throw of where William Booth, the Army's founder, began his salvation warfare in 1865.

(JENTY FAIRBANK)

Seventh-day Adventist Church. World membership of the Seventh-day Adventist Church reached approximately 3.5 million in 1980, with 80% of the members outside North America. At the quinquennial session of the General Conference, held April 17–26 in Dallas, the 1,815 delegates reflected the international nature of the church by electing a black from Barbados as secretary and an Australian as treasurer.

At Dallas a new Statement of Fundamental Beliefs was debated and adopted. A blue-ribbon international committee, meeting in August in response to a doctrinal challenge by a Bible teacher from Australia, expressed full support for the Statement.

Economic belt tightening was evident in the merger of church institutions and organizations, including two of the church's largest and oldest publishing houses—the Southern Publishing Association, Nashville, Tenn., and the Review and Herald Publishing Association, Washington, D.C. The Northern and Central union conferences merged into the Mid-America Union.

At the request of the emerging Marshall Islands government, the church accepted responsibility for administering hospital and medical services for the Marshall Islands.

The church's international radio program, "The Voice of Prophecy," celebrated its 50th anniversary.

(KENNETH H. WOOD)

Unitarian (Universalist) Churches. The 200th anniversary of the birth of William Ellery Channing, seminal liberal thinker and co-founder of the institutional Unitarian movement in North America, was observed throughout 1980. The year also marked the 40th anniversary of the Unitarian Universalist Service Committee.

The annual General Assembly of the Unitarian Universalist Association, meeting June 13–18, 1980, in Albuquerque, N.M., attracted 1,400 delegates and observers from 50 states and 6 Canadian provinces. General resolutions were passed dealing with abortion rights, hunger, nursing home reform, refugee assistance, human rights and war, and repressive legislation.

June D. Bell, a professor at the University of Edinburgh, was elected president of the British General Assembly of Unitarian and Free Christian Churches at its 52nd annual meeting, held in April in Hatfield, Hertfordshire. She was the sixth woman to hold that post. Issues drawing concern among British Unitarians included avenues to peace, environmental conditions, freedom of information, abortion, police accountability, and immigration inequities.

Surveys indicated that British Unitarians attend church more regularly and rate religion more highly in their daily lives than their North American counterparts. Among instrumental values, Britishers valued helpfulness and self-control while Americans placed imaginativeness and intelligence on a higher level. Both groups, however, put responsibility, loving, and broadmindedness among the top five values and, theologically, ranked salvation last.

For the first time, Unitarian Universalist congregations in North America were presenting weekly broadcasts over National Public Radio. The "Cambridge Forum" featured distinguished diplomats, authors, and scholars. In another first, more women than men were enrolled in UU seminaries.

(JOHN NICHOLLS BOOTH)

The United Church of Canada. For the first time in its 55-year history, the church elected a woman, Lois M. Wilson of Kingston, Ont., as its moderator. The election took place at the 28th General Council of the United Church held during the summer at Dalhousie University, Halifax, Nova Scotia. The theme of the council was "Affirming Our Heritage: Seeking Our Future."

Included on the agenda of the 450 lay and clergy commissioners (delegates) were reports on the church in metropolitan areas, Christian initiation, abortion, human sexuality, and ministerial salaries and pensions. A proposal to develop an international rescue team received support, as did increased pressure on world leaders for disarmament.

The church's position on abortion affirms that the taking or hurting of human life is evil; that abortion is acceptable in certain medical, economic, and social situations; that any interruption in pregnancy is less objectionable in the early stages; and that the male partner and/or other supportive persons should have a responsibility to both the woman and the fetus. The report on human sexuality, "In God's Image—Male and Female," was received as a United Church study document and would be sent to the 2,379 congregations with a request to study, along with an earlier statement on "The Permanence of Christian Marriage."

A report on agriculture and food resources expressed concern about the lack of a national food policy, the need for an understanding of the family farm, and the need to give urgent attention to the depletion of prime arable land.

(NORMAN K. VALE)

United Church of Christ. A new Coordinating Center for Women in Church and Society, led by a 32-person coordinating committee, came into existence on Jan. 1, 1980. Marilyn M. Breitling of Trenton, Ill., was named its executive head. Implementing a mandate of the church's 12th General Synod in 1979, Yvonne V. Delk was appointed full-time affirmative action officer for the church.

In 1964 the denomination's Office of Communication, long a champion of affirmative action at every level of broadcasting, had petitioned the U.S. Federal Communications Commission not to renew the license of WLBT-TV in Jackson, Miss. The church agency claimed that WLBT, an NBC affiliate and the most powerful station in the mid-South, had discriminated against blacks in hiring and had presented racist programming. The struggle ended with a victory in 1979, when WLBT's license was awarded to locally based, black-controlled TV-3. The office was currently involved in a project to monitor equal employment practices of every radio and television station in the U.S. and a campaign to defend less developed countries' right of access to international telecommunications systems.

A new manual published by the church's Office for Church Life and Leadership, *The Ministry of Volunteers in the National Settings of the United Church of Christ*, was now in use throughout the church as well as by allied religious and secular agencies.

The world missions unit of the Christian Church (Disciples of Christ) joined the United Church Board for World Ministries in the United Church's long-standing mission relationships in the Middle East. Ecumenical activity was gaining momentum, particularly in relation to the church's membership in the Consultation on Church Union, as well as the covenant with the Christian Church (Disciples of Christ). (See *Christian Church [Disciples of Christ]*, above.) (AVERY D. POST)
[827.D; 827.G.3; 827.H; 827.J.3]

ROMAN CATHOLIC CHURCH

The Roman Catholic Church in 1980 was dominated by the personality and policies of Pope John Paul II. His journeys and initiatives did not exhaust what was happening—far from it—but they provided a unifying focus for considering it.

John Paul II's main concern was for discipline, order, and a clear definition of Catholic identity. This had become apparent at the end of 1979, when two famous theologians, Hans Küng and Edward Schillebeeckx, had been called to order, and Küng's license to teach as a Catholic theologian had been withdrawn because of his sustained attacks on the doctrine of papal infallibility. In January 1980 the seven bishops of the Dutch church were called to the Vatican for a special synod. Outvoted and overawed, they went home two and a half weeks later with a set of 46 propositions that effectively put an end to the 15 years of Dutch experimentation in catechetics, ecumenism, and liturgy. The Dutch bishops were not greeted with any notable enthusiasm when they returned, so the outcome of the special synod—the first ever—remained ambivalent.

In March there was another special synod, this time of the Ukrainian Catholic Church. Here the problem was simpler. The Ukrainian church, now living mostly in exile, had been bitterly divided. One faction supported the aged major archbishop, Josyf Cardinal J. Slipyj, who believed that he should be granted the title of patriarch; the other faction was prepared to drop this claim. The purpose of the synod was to elect an assistant to Cardinal Slipyj with the right of succession. The man chosen was Msgr. Miroslav Ivan Lubachivsky, metropolitan of Philadelphia, who was known to be opposed to the patriarchate idea.

On May 2 John Paul set off on an 11-day journey to six African countries (Zaire, Congo, Kenya, Ghana, Upper Volta, and Ivory Coast). The visit was a huge success, though marred by a tragic incident in Kinshasa, Zaire, when nine people were trampled to death. Warning the African churches of the dangers of excessive or overhasty "africanization," the pope said that the traditional disciplines on marriage and clerical celibacy could not be relaxed on the grounds that they were a "European importation." He also had a political message for Africa: that the continent could solve its own problems and should stay out of superpower conflicts.

After a brief weekend (May 30–June 2) in Paris, where he addressed UNESCO, John Paul was off again on June 30 for a 12-day visit to Brazil. The crowds were bigger even than in Africa, and a fiesta mood (marred, again, by three deaths in Fortaleza) prevailed. But events elsewhere had made the visit to Brazil problematic. Catholics had played an important part in the overthrow of Pres. Anastasio Somoza Debayle in Nicaragua. It was the first instance of "liberation theology" in action, and there were several priests in the new Cabinet. The murder during mass of Archbishop Oscar Romero (*see* OBITUARIES) in El Salvador in March had served to dramatize the truth that those who "opt for the poorest" must expect to get killed. In Brazil itself the church was becoming the only rallying point for opposition to the military government. John Paul came down unambiguously on the side of the Brazilian bishops, in the name of human rights and the Christian doctrine of man. The government was exhorted to "speedy reforms." Nevertheless, the pope echoed one of his favourite themes when he said that priests should stay out of direct involvement in politics.

The same question had come up in another form in May when it was learned that Robert F. Drinan SJ, a member of the U.S. Congress from Massachusetts, had been ordered by Father Pedro Arrupe, superior general of the Jesuits, not to stand for reelection. Somewhat mystified, Drinan accepted the order. This episode was only one incident in the running conflict between the Jesuits and the pope. Earlier, John Paul had spoken darkly of "disquieting reports" that had reached him about Jesuits who had succumbed to secularization, slackness, or theological unorthodoxy. Arrupe was impelled to write a stern letter to his 27,000 Jesuits urging immediate action.

On the ecumenical front, the most notable progress was registered in relations with the 13 Orthodox churches. The Roman Catholic-Orthodox Joint Dialogue Committee held its first meeting on the Greek islands of Patmos and Rhodes during May 29–June 4. The measure of agreement was already great, the main difficulty arising from the post-schism (*i.e.*, post-1054) definitions of the Catholic Church.

The Anglican-Roman Catholic International Commission had all but completed its work, and the celebration of the 450th anniversary of the Augsburg Confession prompted John Paul to take note of how far Catholic-Lutheran relations had improved. The impression remained, however, that he was less interested in ecumenical dialogue with the churches of the Reformation than with the Orthodox churches. This impression was not dispelled when, in August, the U.S. bishops' conference announced that married Episcopal priests who had decided to leave their church be-

The Cologne Cathedral was one of the sites at which Pope John Paul II spoke on his five-day visit to West Germany in November.

REGIS BOSSU—SYGMA

cause of its decision to ordain women might be allowed to continue to exercise their priesthood within the Roman Catholic Church. (See *Anglican Communion*, above.)

The theme of social justice was dominant in John Paul's second encyclical, *Dives in Misericordia*, issued in December. The pope urged the church to work for justice but warned that justice is distorted if it is not based in mercy and love. Concern within the church over such matters as priestly celibacy, contraception, and the role of women continued to be evident. It surfaced at the National Pastoral Congress held in Liverpool, England, in May and again in November when, during the pope's five-day visit to Germany, a youth leader at an open-air mass accused the church of timidity in dealing with such matters. At the synod on the theme "The Role of the Christian Family in the Modern World," which began in Rome on September 26, U.S. and British bishops, without deviating from church doctrine on contraception, called attention to its widespread rejection by the faithful. (*See* VATICAN CITY STATE.)

(PETER HEBBLETHWAITE)

[827.C; 827.G.2; 827.J.2]

THE ORTHODOX CHURCH

A fellowship of local churches united in faith, sacraments, and canon law but without worldwide administrative unity, the Orthodox Church faced the diverse challenges of the modern world in a variety of ways. In the socialist countries of Eastern Europe, it continued to encounter antireligious propaganda and discrimination. Ecclesiastics who attempted to cross the limits imposed by law or to make statements critical of the regime were quickly silenced. This was the case with Dmitry Dudko, a Russian priest who had organized discussions and youth activities in his parish. Arrested in January 1980, he was forced to "recant" over Moscow television on June 20. Another dissident priest, Gleb Yakunin, was sentenced to five years of hard labour and five years of exile by a Moscow court. A similar sentence was given to a Romanian priest, George Calciu, in Bucharest.

Preparation for a pan-Orthodox Great Council made no significant progress in 1980, although all the autocephalous (independent) Orthodox churches continued to express their commitment to the idea. The first item on the agenda of a council would be the abnormality of overlapping ethnic jurisdictions in Western countries and the need for more unity. A statement published by the archbishop of Finland, Paul, who visited the autocephalous church in America in May, described the unwillingness of some churches to relinquish administrative control of their branches abroad, particularly in America, as the major obstacle to convening the council.

The church of Russia had relinquished its American branch in 1970. The autocephalous Orthodox Church in America, which resulted from this action, celebrated its tenth anniversary at a council in Detroit. Since its inception, it had been joined by several ethnic groups and represented the major English-speaking Orthodox body in the West. The 25th Clergy-Laity Congress of the Greek Archdiocese of America (July 1980), which is dependent on the administrative authority of the patriarch of Constantinople, also expressed commitment to unity.

The first session of a dialogue with Roman Catholicism, held at Patmos and Rhodes in Greece (May 29–June 4), approved a program of theological discussions. Some criticism was expressed concerning the composition of the Orthodox delegation, which seemed to reflect considerations of prestige rather than effectiveness. On the other hand, strong Greek voices—the Theological Faculty of Athens and the monks of Mount-Athos—protested the presence of Eastern rite Catholics (uniates) on the Roman side. Strong statements by Pope John Paul II in favour of Eastern rite Catholicism and on papal authority were unlikely to alleviate Orthodox fears in these respects. (JOHN MEYENDORFF)

EASTERN NON-CHALCEDONIAN CHURCHES

Also known as "Monophysite" (believing in one divino-human nature of Christ, and not "two natures" as defined by the Council of Chalcedon in AD 451), these churches represent a sizable part of the Christian population in the Middle East, East Africa, and India. In 1980 particular attention was focused on the Coptic Church of Egypt, with a membership that might amount to over six million faithful (although government statistics reduced the figure by half). In several areas of Egypt, Coptic churches and faithful were being harassed by Muslim extremists.

To protest what appeared to him as a government policy of condoning anti-Christian violence, Coptic Patriarch Shenuda III refused to welcome government officials at Easter celebrations and personally retired to the desert during the feast. Observers believed that the authorities were at least partially to blame insofar as they attempted to divert Islamic fervour away from Pres. Anwar as-Sadat's peace policies at the expense of the Christian minority.

(JOHN MEYENDORFF)

[827.B; 827.G.1; 827.5.1]

JUDAISM

The year saw vigorous debate on fundamental issues in U.S. Orthodox and Conservative Judaism, with alternative positions clearly outlined. For Orthodoxy the precipitating event was the publication of Charles Liebman's article "Orthodox Judaism Today" in *Midstream* (August–September 1979). Presenting Orthodoxy as a possible means of securing a stable future for Judaism in America, Liebman recommended the modes of Orthodoxy to Conservative and Reform Judaism. The first of these he referred to as compartmentalization, Orthodoxy's pattern of adopting two different sets of behaviour patterns, a religious and a secular code, side by side. The second, commitment, is the integration of the individual into the community, as contrasted with stress on individualism and self-fulfillment.

Commenting on these proposals, the sociologist Erich Rosenthal remarked, "Such an in-grown community has as little appeal to the American Jew as has the life of the Amish for the American gentile." Rosenthal further noted that the formula for Jewish survival in the 1950s and '60s was voluntary residential segregation in a high-status area, a modicum of Jewish education, and "Zionism," meaning "raised Jewish self-consciousness and identification." But, he observed, matters are by no means settled. "The search for a survival formula must go on." Liebman countered, "It is precisely Orthodoxy's compartmentalization and the partial nature of the community which makes its impingement on individuality, freedom, and personal expression tolerable."

The issue of full equality between the sexes was dramatically joined in Judaism with regard to ordaining women as rabbis for Conservative synagogues. (The Reconstructionist seminary and Hebrew Union College-Jewish Institute of Religion had long ago settled the question in favour of ordaining women.) Although initially opposed, Gerson D. Cohen, chancellor of the Jewish Theological Seminary of America (JTSA) and principal leader of Conservative Judaism, established a study commission (1977), which held hearings in many major cities. Following the arguments, which were of both a legal (*halakhic*) and a moral character, Cohen recognized the justice of women's claim to full religious equality in Conservative Judaism and supported their admission to the rabbinical school of JTSA, the training ground of a majority of Conservative rabbis (that is, members of the Rabbinical Assembly).

Cohen then referred the issue to the faculty senate of the rabbinical school. The senate, however, voted to table the question, on the grounds that "the bitter divergence of opinion threatens to inflict irreparable damage to the academic excellence of the Seminary and the pluralistic unity of the Rabbinical Assembly." The faculty further called on Cohen to convene a "committee of talmudic scholars" to study systematically "the status of women in Jewish law." This Cohen declined to do, since, in his view, the matter already had been thoroughly studied.

A solution to the crisis came three months later when Cohen sidestepped the JTSA faculty altogether and created a new program, open to women, for "a new form of ministry." This new program would, he said, "be distinct from the Rabbinical School," but it would be comparable "in duration, breadth, and depth." It would stress courses in Jewish texts as well as those in liturgy, homiletics, and pastoral counseling. "Graduates of the new program will be qualified," Cohen stated, "for a form of religious ministry presently scarce . . . in our community . . . they will be prepared to teach, preach, to guide young people, and to counsel their parents and grandparents." Thus Cohen set forth a new vision of religious leadership for U.S. Judaism. It seemed certain that women would soon become members of the Rabbinical Assembly and serve Conservative synagogues. In May 1980 the Rabbinical Assembly approved the ordination of women in principle.

While these vigorous debates took place in the U.S., equally strong differences of opinion emerged within Judaism in the state of Israel. One party, the Block of the Faithful, organized around Jewish settlements in Judea and Samaria (the West Bank), maintained that it is a religious duty to settle throughout the Land of Israel. A second group held that attaining peace and fraternal relations with the Arab world should have moral priority. Since the former group included many who maintained that preparation for the coming of the Messiah is involved in the formation of Jewish settlements in every part of the Holy Land, thus completing the restoration of Israel to Zion, the issues encompassed genuinely religious feelings and beliefs. (*See* ISRAEL.)

(JACOB NEUSNER)

[826]

BUDDHISM

There was nothing auspicious about Buddhism's entry into the 1980s. The 30-year-old World Fellowship of Buddhists reported steadily increasing activities, especially in North America and Europe, but the jubilant optimism of Asian Buddhists in the 1940s and '50s had been thoroughly chastened by the Vietnam war and other painful experiences. By the end of the 1970s many once highly placed advocates of Buddhism, such as Sirimavo Bandaranaike of Sri Lanka, U Nu of Burma, and Prince Norodom Sihanouk of Cambodia, had fallen from power. Buddhists in Indochina suffered further from the continuing upheavals in Vietnam and Cambodia and the mass exodus of refugees. In Laos the number of monks reportedly declined from 20,000 in 1976 to 1,700 in 1979. In order to survive under the Communist regime, Laotian Buddhist leaders were forced to compromise with Marxism. "We still praise Buddha in the pagoda," one spokesman said, but "we praise Marx and Lenin at political meetings."

Elsewhere in Southeast Asia, Theravada Buddhist leaders felt compelled to straighten out their own household. Early in 1980 representatives of Burma's 100,000 monks decided to establish a central governing authority to discipline the wayward and expel undesirable or bogus elements from the monastic orders. In Thailand, where Buddhism traditionally had been identified with the monarchy and the status quo, some young Buddhists were developing a new rapport with rebel elements.

Announcements from Beijing (Peking) promised a series of wide-ranging reforms in Tibet, including more economic assistance and support for indigenous cultural life. The announcements of these measures coincided with a visit to China by emissaries of the Dalai Lama, who had been living in exile in India for two decades. However, the future of Buddhism in Tibet remained uncertain. In China itself Buddhists celebrated the 1,300th anniversary of the death of Shan-tao, a patriarch of the Pure Land School.

During the 1970s Western interest in Buddhism, especially in North America, had grown steadily along three lines—ethnic-cultural, cultic, and academic. First, there was renewed interest in Buddhism among Orientals in the West who, like other ethnic groups, were seeking their cultural and religious "roots." Second, unlike the activist youth of the '60s, many young people in the '70s turned their attention inward and were attracted by a variety of Eastern cults, including Zen and Tibetan forms of Buddhist meditation. Finally, the continuing academic interest in Buddhism was reflected by the number of teachers—1,653 in 1980—providing instruction in Asian religious traditions in U.S. and Canadian colleges and universities.

(JOSEPH M. KITAGAWA)

[824]

DAVID DE VOSS—TIME, INC.

A monk grieves by a ruined Buddha near Phnom Penh in Cambodia, where once-prohibited worship was being tolerated by the new Vietnamese-backed regime.

HINDUISM

In India 1980 was marked by caste conflicts within Hinduism, by communal strife between Hinduism and Islam, and by important archaeological discoveries. The year opened with conflict in Maharashtra between caste Hindus and outcastes, or Harijans, occasioned by the state government's unsuccessful attempt to rename Marathwada University in Aurangabad after the Harijan leader B. R. Ambedkar. On Dec. 6, 1979, the 23rd anniversary of Ambedkar's death, a Harijan group, the Dalit Panthers, began satyagraha (passive resistance) at the university to force the name change. This led to weeks of violent clashes as the change was fought by caste Hindus. In another caste conflict, caste Hindus made several attacks on Harijan villages in Bihar in February in which more than 25 persons were killed. Violence between Harijans and caste Hindus also broke out in the hill region of Uttar Pradesh. Evidence indicated that the conflicts originated in the anger and frustration felt by the Harijans over their economic and social oppression.

Violence between Hindus and Muslims broke out on August 13, the last day of the Muslim holy month of Ramadan, when a stray pig wandered into a mosque at Moradabad, defiling it during the Id prayers. The incident triggered violence in Moradabad, Allahabad, and Aligarh which, over a period of weeks, left more than 200 dead and hundreds injured.

Archaeological discoveries in 1980 included the uncovering at Dwarka in Gujarat of four strata of temple construction greatly antedating the 12th–16th-century Dwarkadesh temple complex. The first temple dates from the 1st century of the Christian era, making it among the oldest known temple sites in India. A 10th-century AD temple was found at a village in Rajasthan under remarkable circumstances. A young villager reportedly learned in a dream of the existence of a temple dedicated to Shiva lying buried nearby. Villagers dug at the site and, at a depth of five metres (16½ ft), found the ruins. Archaeologists at the Institute of Advanced Studies in Simla claimed to have located sites of events related in the Indian epic the *Ramayana*. Material at the sites would date the epic as being about 2,800 years old, not the 900,000 years sometimes traditionally ascribed to it.

The Kumbh Mela was celebrated during the year. Held every three years and rotating among four holy sites, the Kumbh at Ujjain in Madhya Pradesh in 1980 brought well over a million pilgrims to the shores of the Sipra River to join with thousands of ascetics and holy men in purificatory bathing and worship. Also celebrated during the year was the 300th anniversary of the death of the semilegendary Maratha hero Shivaji, who overturned Muslim rule in Maharashtra.

(H. PATRICK SULLIVAN)

[823]

Religion

ISLAM

The 1,359th year of the Islamic era witnessed events of serious consequence to Muslims. The crisis in relations between Iran and the U.S. brought about by Iran's seizure of U.S. embassy personnel as hostages in November 1979 was followed by the Soviet occupation of Afghanistan in December and, in the following September, by the outbreak of hostilities between Iran and Iraq. While a number of Islamic congresses met during the year, some ostensibly planned for other than political purposes, their discussions and resolutions inevitably reflected political concerns. Political events also overshadowed more specifically religious developments within Muslim countries.

As for the Iran-Iraq fighting, the Shiʿah holy places in Iraq are a principal centre for all Shiʿah. The Iranian leader Ayatollah Ruhollah Khomeini had been a resident there for a number of years before the Iranian revolution. The hostilities appeared to be motivated by long-standing political differences, aggravated by refugee Iranian military officers and others currently resident in Iraq. (*See* IRAN; IRAQ.)

Meanwhile, Afghani refugees poured into Pakistan, further overburdening that country's government services. While the Soviet invasion of Afghanistan could be explained in part by political, geographic, and imperial interests, it could also be seen in part as an attempt to divert a resurgence of Islamic interests among the U.S.S.R.'s own Muslim population. (*See* AFGHANISTAN.)

In Saudi Arabia, 63 persons were beheaded in January for their part in the November 1979 attack on the Grand Mosque in Mecca. That event was never fully explained, but as an attempt to discredit and destabilize the Saudi Arabian government, the attack was as much an act of political calculation as it was an expression of religious disaffection. Syria executed five members of the Muslim Brotherhood for their involvement in an attack on a group of military cadets in Aleppo in June 1979. Syrian Pres. Hafez al-Assad and some of his close advisers were members of the Alawite sect, although the majority of the country's population was Sunni. The fundamentalist Muslim Brotherhood and the city of Aleppo had been focuses of opposition to Alawite domination and the Assad regime.

In the spring Egyptian Copts protested attacks on their churches and congregations by Muslim extremists. (See *Eastern Non-Chalcedonian Churches*, above.) Also in the spring, the killing of a teacher and a number of internecine attacks involving Muslim extremists alerted West German authorities to a growing problem among groups of Turks resident in West Berlin.

In Malaysia the minority Chinese population protested alleged discrimination by Muslims, who constituted almost 50% of the population and dominated the government. The Muslim Youth Movement of Malaysia appeared active and growing, and fundamentalist pressures there were increasing. In an attempt to pacify the Islamic fundamentalist unrest that had spurred the attack on the Grand Mosque, the Saudi Arabian government enforced Islamic prohibitions more strictly during the year, while still continuing its giant program of modernization. (REUBEN W. SMITH)
[828]

WORLD CHURCH MEMBERSHIP

Reckoning religious adherence throughout the world is a precarious exercise. Different religions and even different Christian churches vary widely in their theories and methods of counting and reporting. Some simply depend on government population figures; for others, "numbering the people" is blocked by religious law. Some faith communities number only adults or heads of families; others count children, retainers, servants. Where religious liberty obtains, some count contributors; others estimate communicants or constituents.

Procedures vary from country to country even within the same religion. Quite reliable statistics are available on the mission fields, for Buddhism, Islam, and Hinduism as well as Christianity. Where a religion has prevailed for centuries (Christianity in Europe, Hinduism in India), official figures usually report whole populations as adherents, although the rise of antireligious ideologies rebukes the casual assumption implicit in that procedure. Although Albania is the only officially atheist state, the 20th century has produced a number of governments hostile to religion in theory and/or practice. It is difficult if not impossible to get any reliable religious statistics from the peoples they control.

The traditional listing of religions, used by scholars since the study of world religions became an academic discipline, makes no provision for several religions now numerous and important—Baha'i, Cao Dai, Ch'ondokyo, Jainism, the Umbandu and Kimbandu cults in Brazil. Finally, each year brings reports of new genocides or substantial movements of refugees fleeing persecution in their native lands. The flight of millions from Uganda, Cambodia, Vietnam, and Equatorial Guinea adds uncertainty to statistics. This also holds true for movements of persons seeking better employment. Muslim Turks resident for decades as "guest workers" in West Germany change the religious complexion of that land, at least when their grandchildren begin to arrive and their "temporary" residence must be considered permanent.

The reader is therefore advised to reflect carefully upon the statistics and to refer to articles discussing the different countries and different religions when pursuing the subject in depth.

(FRANKLIN H. LITTELL)

Estimated Membership of the Principal Religions of the World

Religions	North America[1]	South America	Europe[2]	Asia[3]	Africa	Oceania[4]	World
Total Christian	237,096,500	175,114,000	342,630,400	95,987,240	128,617,000	18,058,500	997,503,640
Roman Catholic	133,489,000	162,489,000	177,087,300	55,077,000	47,024,500	4,395,500	579,562,300
Eastern Orthodox	4,750,000	516,000	55,035,600	2,428,000	13,306,000[5]	409,000	76,444,600
Protestant[6]	98,857,500	12,109,000	110,507,500	38,482,240	68,286,500[7]	13,254,000	341,496,740
Jewish	6,250,340	595,800	4,045,120	3,192,860	176,400	76,000	14,336,520
Muslim[8]	376,200	251,500	14,945,000	428,266,000	145,214,700	90,000	589,143,400
Zoroastrian	1,250	2,100	10,000	256,000	650	1,000	271,000
Shinto[9]	60,000	90,000	—	57,003,000	1,200	—	57,154,200
Taoist	16,000	10,000	—	31,260,000	—	—	31,286,000
Confucian	97,100	70,000	—	155,887,500	1,500	14,000	156,070,100
Buddhist[10]	185,250	193,200	193,000	254,241,000	20,000	35,000	254,867,450
Hindu[11]	88,500	850,000	400,000	475,073,000	1,179,800	400,000	477,991,300
Totals	244,171,140	177,176,600	362,223,520	1,501,166,600	275,211,250	18,674,500	2,578,623,610
Population[12]	369,759,000	245,067,000	750,198,000	2,557,562,000	469,361,000	22,775,000	4,414,722,000

[1] Includes Central America and the West Indies.
[2] Includes the U.S.S.R. and other countries with established Marxist ideology where religious adherence is difficult to estimate.
[3] Includes areas in which persons have traditionally enrolled in several religions, as well as mainland China with an official Marxist establishment.
[4] Includes Australia and New Zealand as well as islands of the South Pacific.
[5] Includes Coptic Christians, of restricted status in Egypt and in a precarious situation under the military junta in Ethiopia.
[6] Protestant statistics usually count "full members," that is, adults, rather than all family members or baptized infants, and are therefore not comparable to the statistics of ethnic religions or churches counting all constituents of all ages.
[7] Including many new sects and cults among African Christians.
[8] The chief base of Islam is still ethnic, although missionary work is now carried on in Europe and America (viz., "Black Muslims"). In countries where Islam is established, minority religions are frequently persecuted and accurate statistical reports are hard to come by.
[9] A Japanese ethnic religion, Shinto has declined since the Japanese emperor gave up his claim to divinity (1947). Neither does Shinto survive easily outside the homeland.
[10] Buddhism has produced several renewal movements in the last century which have gained adherents in Europe and America and other areas not formerly ethnic-Buddhist. In Asia it has made rapid gains in recent years in some areas, and under persecution it has shown greater staying power than Taoism or Confucianism. It also transplants better.
[11] Hinduism's strength in India has been enhanced by nationalism, a phenomenon also observable in Islam. Modern Hinduism has developed renewal movements that have won converts in Europe and America.
[12] United Nations, Department of International Economic and Social Affairs; data refer to midyear 1980.

(FRANKLIN H. LITTELL)

THE NEW CHRISTIAN RIGHT

by Martin E. Marty

The morning after the Nov. 4, 1980, national elections in the U.S., a cluster of forces code-named the Moral Majority took credit for having helped turn America to a more conservative course. Not only had they supported Republican candidate Ronald Reagan for the presidency and thus helped him win a landslide in the Electoral College, they also had backed a number of aspirants who defeated liberal senators and members of the House of Representatives, along with numerous candidates for statehouses and various lesser offices.

A New Force. Moral Majority was really only a code name used by the media and the public, since the cluster included other vote-seeking organizations like the Religious Roundtable and the Christian Voice. But Moral Majority was both the best-financed and the most visible of these sometimes cooperating, sometimes competing groups that made up what might more properly be called the New Christian Right. Most of the members were of traditionalist Protestant backgrounds, and almost all of them had been brought together by television evangelists, most notably the Rev. Jerry Falwell (see BIOGRAPHIES) of Virginia and the Rev. James Robison of Texas.

Two pre-election events served to give visibility to the New Christian Right. While its parties had been working behind the scenes and gathering momentum for a couple of years, they surfaced at a "Washington for Jesus" rally in the spring. Advance criticism against the overt political intentions of this evangelistic rally led the leaders to mute the political sounds and may have served to keep the hoped-for crowd of a million down to about 200,000. But from then on the media began to take the new political force seriously.

In late summer, in Texas, the leaders showed their political finesse and their increasing power by attracting thousands of pastors to a rally and training session. And with them came candidate Reagan, who endorsed them even though, for legal reasons (of separation of church and state), they were not free to endorse him, their obvious choice. A tape, made at this rally and later released, overheard the president of the Southern Baptist Convention, the largest U.S. Protestant body, announcing that God did not hear the prayers of Jews. Debate over this statement by the Rev. Bailey Smith of Del City, Okla., tended to preoccupy the media and distract from the issues that the rally organizers were bringing forward.

Most of these issues had to do with what they saw as moral decline during the presidencies of two fellow evangelical Protestants, Jimmy Carter and, before him, Gerald Ford. The new militants claimed that liberals, humanists, and leftists in religion and politics had conspired to take God out of the public schools, to teach evolution as an alternative religion, and to create a climate on television and in popular culture that was unfavourable to traditional American moral values. They extended their program to include specific issues: they would defeat the Equal Rights Amendment, abolish the Department of Education, continue to oppose the Panama Canal treaties, limit the rights of homosexuals and women

The Rev. Jerry Falwell (flanked by choir members) took his "I Love America" crusade to St. Paul, Minnesota, in September.

UPI

Martin E. Marty is Fairfax M. Cone distinguished service professor at the University of Chicago and associate editor of The Christian Century.

Some 200,000 people attended a "Washington for Jesus" rally in Washington, D.C., in April.

seeking abortions, and prevent the spread of obscene and pornographic materials and images.

The suddenness of the rise of this New Christian Right caught much of the public off guard. It was regionally strong, originating in the Sunbelt and the Midwest. Thus it was underrecognized in the Northeast, which was less familiar with the kind of Protestantism that nurtured the Moral Majority. Even after becoming aware that this force spoke for only a very small minority of the population and even a minority of evangelical, fundamentalist, and Pentecostal Protestantism, the larger public found few means to counter its effective television appeals and its highly technological use of direct mail services.

Uncertain Strength. The Moral Majority was more effective at defeating candidates in primaries —among them Rep. John Buchanan (Rep., Ala.), himself a Southern Baptist minister—than at being noticed nationally. Some of its favoured candidates, among them Rep. Richard Kelly (Rep., Fla.) and Rep. Robert Bauman (Rep., Md.), were subjects of highly publicized personal scandals, and this seemed to deprive the Moral Majority of some of its moral claims. Polls taken before the election showed that most evangelicals joined the public in repudiating the overt intrusion of ministers into partisan politics. Backlash had set in, with evangelical politicians like Sen. Mark Hatfield (Rep., Ore.) and prominent evangelical theologians protesting this intrusion.

Given these trends and countertrends, it was hard to assess the true scope and the potential of the New Christian Right. The rejection of President Carter was so massive, and the public's evident taste for any sort of change in executive and legislative ranks so consistent, that a tide was created, a tide on which the New Christian Right rode just as much as it helped form the swell. President-elect Reagan in a press conference acknowledged that he would take Moral Majoritarian interests into consideration when forming policy, but he simply included these interests with those of all other backers. Before the election he had already taken some steps that alienated the New Christian Right, and many expected that he would further disappoint these supporters as he took office.

Religion in Politics. The New Christian Right did not represent the first bold entry into politics by fundamentalists, the extreme Protestant conservatives. In *The Politics of Doomsday,* historian Erling Jorstad tells of fundamentalist support for Sen. Joseph R. McCarthy in the 1950s and for Sen. Barry Goldwater and Gov. George Wallace in the 1960s. But these pioneers lacked the instruments of television and computerized direct mail, and Dwight Eisenhower and Lyndon Johnson provided stronger rallying points to counter them than did Carter.

Nor did the New Christian Right pioneer in using religion to affect politics. Nineteenth-century evangelicals had spoken out on both sides of the abolition cause and promoted the temperance movement. But they gradually retreated into evangelism, concern for personal morality, and life in subcultural pockets. As recently as the early 1970s, the leaders who now shaped the New Christian Right had decried as ungodly the participation of more liberal religious leaders in the civil rights movement and other controversial causes. This meant that they now had to make an about-face—one which they readily acknowledged.

In the 1980 campaigns the main-line Protestants were largely silent. Roman Catholics, who shared some of the New Christian Right's viewpoint of opposition to abortion, were eclipsed by these Protestants. If there was a Jewish vote, it was concerned chiefly with matters affecting Israel. The new religious voice to be reckoned with, then, was that of militant Protestants who evoked nostalgia for a simpler "Christian America," who gained power from the resentment and rage many felt against moral change and those they claimed were responsible for it, and who offered their followers the vision of power to defeat "humanists" and liberals in church and state. They turned out to be far less powerful than they claimed to be, but far more powerful than a caught-off-guard larger public had expected them to become.

Rodeo

The Professional Rodeo Cowboys Association (PRCA) got a new all-around world champion in 1980. Paul Tierney of Rapid City, S.D., wrested the title from Tom Ferguson of Miami, Okla., who reigned as all-around champion from 1974 through 1979. Tierney was the top rodeo winner of 1980 with $105,568 in arena earnings. Rodeo championships are determined on the basis of total arena winnings, including money won at the National Finals Rodeo in Oklahoma City each December. In the course of the season Tierney also won more than $20,000 in special cash awards given by various rodeo sponsors. The 28-year-old cowboy, who was raised on a ranch near Broken Bow, Neb., competed in calf roping, steer wrestling, team roping, and steer roping.

Other PRCA champions included Bruce Ford of Kersey, Colo., with $69,392 in bareback riding; Clint Johnson of Spearfish, S.D., who earned $44,711 in saddle bronc riding; Don Gay of Mesquite, Texas, winner of $60,639 in bull riding; Roy Cooper of Durant, Okla., whose $77,027 in calf roping topped that of all other competitors; Butch Myers of Welda, Kan., with $44,708 in steer wrestling; Tee Woolman of Llano, Texas, who won $49,983 in team roping; and Guy Allen of Santa Anna, Texas, who finished first in steer roping with $20,567.

Martha Josey of Karnack, Texas, won the 1980 Women's Professional Rodeo Association (WPRA) barrel racing title with earnings of $45,883. The WPRA (formerly Girls Rodeo Association) held its rodeo finals for women at Long Beach, Calif., in November. All-around champion cowgirl for the year was Gloria Paulsen of Bakersfield, Calif., who won nearly $6,000 during the season.

The Canadian Professional Rodeo Association (formerly Canadian Rodeo Cowboys Association) all-around title went to 28-year-old Tom Eirikson of Innisfail, Alta., who competed in saddle bronc riding and calf roping. Eirikson won more than $10,000 in Canadian rodeos, including the Canadian Finals at Edmonton, Alta., in November, and competed extensively in the U.S. as well, finishing 17th in PRCA calf roping with $23,968.

COURTESY, THE PROFESSIONAL RODEO COWBOYS ASSOCIATION, INC.

Paul Tierney, of Rapid City, South Dakota, was the new all-around cowboy world champion for the year.

The finals of the International Rodeo Association were scheduled to take place in Tulsa, Okla., in January 1981. Dan Dailey of Franklin, Tenn., seemed headed for his fourth all-around championship with more than $40,000 in winnings by December 1980. In 1979 Dailey, who competed in all events, won both the all-around and saddle bronc riding titles.

The National Intercollegiate Rodeo Association (NIRA) all-around champion for 1980 was Lance Robinson, a senior from Weber State College at Ogden, Utah. Robinson also won the national titles in calf roping and steer wrestling during the college finals, which were held in June at Bozeman, Mont. The NIRA women's all-around title

WIDE WORLD

Doug Buffington of the Montana Mountain Men team took a fall the hard way during team rodeo events at the Calgary Stampede.

Rhodesia:
see Zimbabwe

Roads:
see Engineering Projects; Transportation

Rockets:
see Defense; Space Exploration

Roman Catholic Church:
see Religion

was won by Lea Erwin of the University of Central Arkansas at Pine Bluff.

Interest in all-Indian rodeo continued to grow during the year, and the fifth annual Indian National Finals Rodeo in November was attended by good crowds at Albuquerque, N.M. Felix Gilbert of Seba Delkai, Ariz., won the 1980 all-around title. (RANDALL E. WITTE)

Romania

Romania

A socialist republic on the Balkan Peninsula in southeastern Europe, Romania is bordered by the U.S.S.R., the Black Sea, Bulgaria, Yugoslavia, and Hungary. Area: 237,500 sq km (91,700 sq mi). Pop. (1979 est.): 22,048,000, including (1977) Romanian 88.1%; Hungarian 7.9%; German 1.6%. Cap. and largest city: Bucharest (pop., 1978 est., 1,858,400). Religion: Romanian Orthodox 70%; Greek Orthodox 10%. General secretary of the Romanian Communist Party, president of the republic, and president of the State Council in 1980, Nicolae Ceausescu; chairman of the Council of Ministers (premier), Ilie Verdet.

During 1980 Pres. Nicolae Ceausescu continued his courageous policy of enhancing Romania's independence and sovereignty while underscoring the Communist characteristics of his country's institutions and its membership in the Warsaw Treaty and the Council for Mutual Economic Assistance (Comecon). On November 5 in an interview for a Swedish newspaper, he boldly called for Soviet troops to be recalled from Afghanistan; at the beginning of the year he had already stood aside from the general Communist endorsement of the invasion.

In July Ceausescu paid an official visit to France. He met Soviet Pres. Leonid I. Brezhnev on August 4 in the Crimea and exchanged views. In October he visited Yugoslavia where he was received by Cvijetin Mijatovic, current president of Yugoslavia's collective presidency. A joint declaration stated that the Yugoslav-Romanian close collaboration, established by the late Yugoslav leader Marshal Tito and Ceausescu, would continue. In November Ceausescu paid state visits to Sweden, Denmark, and Norway. Among the foreign statesmen who visited Romania during the year were Lord Carrington, British foreign secretary (in March); Konstantinos Karamanlis, president of Greece (in September); and Todor Zhivkov, first secretary of the Bulgarian Communist Party and chairman of the State Council, who visited Romania in June and October to discuss the building of joint industrial complexes. Stefan Andrei, the Romanian foreign minister, met with Brezhnev in Moscow in early December.

In September Turkey sued Romania and a Greek shipping firm for U.S. $500 million in damages caused by an accident on the Marmara side of the Bosporus in November 1979. As a result of the collision of a Greek cargo vessel and the Romanian 150,000-ton tanker "Independenta," 50 Romanian

ROMANIA

Education. (1978–79) Primary, pupils 3,423,135, teachers 150,415; secondary, pupils 1,044,135, teachers 51,217; vocational, pupils 164,278, teachers 2,677; teacher training, students 10,874, teachers 1,400; higher, students 190,560, teaching staff 14,227.

Finance. Monetary unit: leu, with (Sept. 22, 1980) an official main noncommercial rate of 12 lei to U.S. $1 (free rate of 28.13 lei = £1 sterling). Budget (1980 est.) balanced at 315.9 billion lei.

Foreign Trade. (1979) Imports 48.8 billion lei; exports 43.5 billion lei. Import sources (1978): U.S.S.R. 16%; West Germany 8%; East Germany 7%; U.S. 5%; Czechoslovakia 5%; China 5%. Export destinations: U.S.S.R. 18%; West Germany 8%; East Germany 7%; Czechoslovakia 6%; Poland 5%; U.S. 5%; China 5%. Main exports (1973): machinery 9%; transport equipment 8%; petroleum products 7%; meat 7%; chemicals 7%; clothing 6%; timber 5%.

Transport and Communications. Roads (1975) *c.* 95,000 km (including 96 km expressways). Motor vehicles in use (1977): passenger *c.* 220,000; commercial *c.* 110,000. Railways: (1977) 11,127 km; traffic (1978) 22,811,000,000 passenger-km, freight 73,738,000,000 net ton-km. Air traffic (1979): 1,179,000,000 passenger-km; freight 15.2 million net ton-km. Inland waterways in regular use (1975) 1,628 km. Shipping (1979): merchant vessels 100 gross tons and over 286; gross tonnage 1,797,108. Telephones (Dec. 1978) 1.3 million. Radio licenses (Dec. 1978) 3,141,000. Television receivers (Dec. 1978) 3,409,000.

Agriculture. Production (in 000; metric tons; 1979): wheat 4,684; barley 2,037; corn 12,380; potatoes 4,134; cabbages (1978) *c.* 738; onions *c.* 424; tomatoes *c.* 1,393; sugar, raw value *c.* 650; sunflower seed 889; soybeans 376; linseed *c.* 60; plums (1978) *c.* 450; apples *c.* 490; grapes 1,486; tobacco *c.* 45; cheese *c.* 139; beef and veal *c.* 309; pork *c.* 819; timber (cu m; 1978) 20,609. Livestock (in 000; Jan. 1979): cattle *c.* 6,283; sheep 15,612; pigs 10,337; horses (1978) 550; poultry 99,725.

Industry. Fuel and power (in 000; metric tons; 1978): coal 7,420; lignite 21,840; coke 3,458; crude oil 13,724; natural gas (cu m) 28,973,000; manufactured gas (cu m) *c.* 1,300,000; electricity (kw-hr; 1979) 64,910,000. Production (in 000; metric tons; 1978): cement 13,892; bauxite 900; iron ore (26% metal content) 2,511; pig iron 8,155; crude steel 11,779; petroleum products *c.* 24,000; sulfuric acid 1,655; caustic soda 725; fertilizers (nutrient content) nitrogenous 1,723, phosphate 660; cotton yarn 175; cotton fabrics (sq m) 718,000; wool yarn 64; woolen fabrics (sq m) 123,000; man-made fibres (1977) *c.* 170; newsprint 103; other paper 521. New dwelling units completed (1977) 145,000.

In March Romanian Pres. Nicolae Ceausescu (right) was reelected chairman of the Socialist Democracy and Unity Front by a unanimous vote.

AGERPRES/AUTHENTICATED NEWS INTERNATIONAL

seamen were killed. The tanker was the first ship of that size built at the Constanta shipyard.

On March 9 a new Grand National Assembly was elected. Out of 15,631,351 citizens entitled to vote, 99.99% went to the polls and 98.52% voted for the candidates of the Socialist Democracy and Unity Front. There were 598 nominations for 369 constituencies.

On March 28–29 the Assembly reelected Ceausescu president of the republic and Ilie Verdet (his son-in-law) as premier. Verdet announced the composition of the new Council of Ministers. In addition to the premier, the new 50-member government consisted of 3 first deputy premiers (one of whom was Elena Ceausescu, the president's wife), 9 deputy premiers, 28 ministers, and 9 chairmen of special committees. The new government included only 14 ministers of the 50 in the previous government.

On October 17 the Grand National Assembly approved the national social and economic development plan for 1981. The rate of economic growth was to be lower than the 1976–80 plan average. Agricultural production in 1981 was to increase by 9% over that of 1980. Out of the total national investment of 220 billion lei in 1981, industry would take 54% and agriculture 14%. In December, in an apparent attempt to stave off domestic troubles, the government announced that it had scrapped plans to raise prices for food and consumer goods in 1981.

The event of the year was the International Congress of Historians held August 10–17 in Bucharest. The congress, the 15th of the series that started 80 years previously in Paris, assembled 2,700 historians from 60 countries. For six days in four different halls and in five languages the congress debated different great themes, generally with urbanity but sometimes not without passion.

On November 29, in a methane gas explosion at a coal mine near Petrosani, 49 miners were killed and 26 injured. (K. M. SMOGORZEWSKI)

Rowing

Twenty nations shared the honours in the 31 world-class rowing events held in 1980. The East Germans won 19 of these titles and took 4 silver and 4 bronze medals in the other events they contested. The only other country to reach double figures was the Soviet Union with a total of 22.

Although the absence of some countries from the Olympic Games in Moscow affected the quality of competition in some sports, the only notable absentees from rowing were the Hansen brothers of Norway, who had reigned supreme in double sculls for several years. Otherwise only 4 of the 23 other world-class medalists of the previous year were missing from the men's events.

East Germany won seven titles at the Olympics, and the eighth went to Pertti Karppinen of Finland, who repeated his 1976 Olympic triumph in single sculls. The Landvoigt twins did likewise in coxless pairs for East Germany. The East German crews won the coxed fours, coxless fours, and double sculls by more than 2 sec. Their winning margin in quadruple sculls was 1.66 sec and their coxed pair succeeded only by 0.81 sec. The surprise of the regatta came in the eights final, when Great Britain unexpectedly finished between East Germany and the U.S.S.R. to take the silver medal.

Racing in the six women's events was unusually close. Every winning verdict was by a margin of less than 1½ sec. Although the East German women carried off all but two of the titles, they had to race hard to do so. Soviet oarswomen held them to a 0.97-sec margin in eights and as little as 0.41 sec in quadruple sculls. The East Germans defeated Bulgaria by 1.48 sec in coxed fours but had a lead of only 0.46 sec over Poland in coxless pairs. The Soviet Union won the double sculls by 1.36 sec and finished 0.96 sec behind Romania in singles. (*See also* TRACK AND FIELD SPORTS: *Special Report.*)

KEYSTONE

The Oxford University rowing team (right) crossed the finish line only 1.8 metres (6 feet) ahead of the Cambridge team in their annual University Boat Race on the River Thames in April.

There was a shock for world rowing shortly before the Olympic Games when the International Rowing Federation banned two Soviet world medalists from all national and international regattas until the end of 1981 after random dope tests made at an early-season international regatta proved positive. The drug identified was nandrolone. It was the first doping case in the history of rowing.

Great Britain, Australia, Italy, and West Germany were the four gold medal winners in the lightweight championships held at Hazewinkel in Belgium. The U.S. won two silver medals and Spain two bronze medals. There were no competitors from Eastern European countries. In the junior championships, held at the same venue, East Germany won four of the men's titles as well as four of the women's events. The Soviet Union won twice in each category, and the seventh men's championship went to Bulgaria.

In England at the Henley Royal Regatta the U.S. won 6 of the 11 open trophies. Charles River Rowing Association won the Grand Challenge Cup (eights), Prince Philip Cup (coxed fours), and successfully partnered Dartmouth College in the Stewards' Cup (coxless fours). Yale University took the Ladies Plate (eights); the Borchelt brothers of the Potomac Boat Club triumphed in the Silver Goblets (coxless pairs); and the sixth U.S. winner was St. Paul's School, Concord, N.H., in the Princess Elizabeth Cup (eights). The Victoria City Rowing Club won the double sculls for Canada, and R. D. Ibarra of Argentina became the new holder of the Diamond Sculls. Oxford won the 126th University Boat Race in the closest finish since the dead heat in 1877, thereby reducing Cambridge's lead in the series to 68–57.

(KEITH OSBORNE)

Rwanda

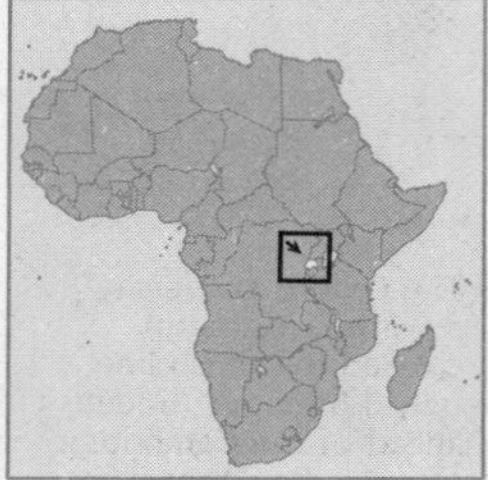

Rwanda

A republic in eastern Africa and former traditional kingdom whose origins may be traced back to the 15th century, Rwanda is bordered by Zaire, Uganda, Tanzania, and Burundi. Area: 26,338 sq km (10,169 sq mi). Pop. (1980 est.): 5,130,000, including (1970) Hutu 90%; Tutsi 9%; and Twa 1%. Cap. and largest city: Kigali (pop., 1978 census, 117,750). Language (official): French and Kinyarwanda. Religion: Roman Catholic 45%; Protestant 9%; Muslim 1%; most of the remainder are animist. President in 1980, Maj. Gen. Juvénal Habyarimana.

Rwanda continued to enjoy political stability though remaining one of the poorest economies on the continent. At the end of 1979 the International Monetary Fund provided a loan of 2,392,000 Special Drawing Rights to assist the nation in its balance of payments and to help finance economic diversification, and in January 1980 France provided aid worth Fr 14.6 million for protein food development and modernization of the Rehenger hospital.

Agriculture accounted for 77% of Rwanda's economic activity, and the problem of marketing rural produce held back development. Improving cooperatives was a major strategy; 20% of the population was involved in them, and they accounted for half the coffee, peanuts, and beans produced in some areas. In July a seminar on the role of cooperatives in community development was held in Kigali.

In April Pres. Juvénal Habyarimana attended a meeting in Mwanza, Tanzania, of the three member countries of the Kagera River Basin Organization. There it was agreed to establish direct telephone links and improve roads in the region. Tanzania promised to provide better port facilities to serve fellow members Rwanda and Burundi.

(GUY ARNOLD)

RWANDA

Education. (1978–79) Primary, pupils 515,712, teachers (1976–77) 8,161; secondary, vocational, and teacher training, pupils 13,799, teachers (1976–77) 820; higher, students 975, teaching staff (1976–77) 184.

Finance. Monetary unit: Rwanda franc, with (Sept. 22, 1980) a par value of RwFr 92.84 to U.S. $1 (free rate of RwFr 223.14 = £1 sterling). Gold, SDR's, and foreign exchange (June 1980) U.S. $176.3 million. Budget (1979 est.) balanced at RwFr 9,214,000,000.

Foreign Trade. Imports (1978) RwFr 16,618,000,000; exports (1979) RwFr 11,093,000,000. Import sources (1978): Belgium-Luxembourg 22%; Japan 12%; West Germany 11%; Kenya 10%; France 8%; Iran 7%; China 6%. Export destinations (1978): U.S. 52%; France 15%; West Germany 8%; Kenya 7%; Belgium-Luxembourg 7%. Main exports: coffee 76%; tea 10%.

Agriculture. Production (in 000; metric tons; 1979): sorghum *c.* 150; corn *c.* 72; potatoes *c.* 214; sweet potatoes (1978) *c.* 695; cassava (1978) *c.* 437; dry beans *c.* 184; dry peas *c.* 51; pumpkins (1978) *c.* 62; plantains (1978) *c.* 1,988; coffee *c.* 22; tea *c.* 7. Livestock (in 000; July 1978): cattle *c.* 610; sheep *c.* 248; goats *c.* 682; pigs *c.* 71.

Rubber:
see Industrial Review

Rugby Football:
see Football

Russia:
see Union of Soviet Socialist Republics

Russian Literature:
see Literature

Sabah:
see Malaysia

Sailing

Boats from Australia, the U.K., Sweden, and France challenged the U.S. titleholders for possession of the America's Cup in August–September 1980. Elimination series selected the challenger and defender for this cup, which the U.S. had never lost. In Dennis Conner the U.S. found a dedicated young sailor whose attention to detail could not be faulted. He built up his team on the West Coast using two 12-m boats and finally choosing "Freedom," in which he easily won the U.S. selection series. In the challengers' series the British team in "Lionheart" threw away any chance it might have had of winning by sacking skipper John Oakeley at the last minute and changing mast and sails. "Lionheart" showed only flashes of speed and was defeated by the French yacht in the capable hands of Bruno Troublé. In the other pairing the Australians beat Pelle Petterson's Swedish challenge, the Swedish yacht "Sverige" never quite having sufficient boat speed. Against the French the Australians, under Jim Hardy for the third time, had the boat speed, and an easy victory looked likely, but Bruno's team went down fighting.

The British in one of their last-minute changes had produced a new mast with a flexible top section; the Australians saw it, thought the idea was right, and quickly produced a copy. They used it in their final-round challenge against the U.S.'s "Freedom." It may have given them almost equal boat speed with "Freedom" and perhaps a little more in light winds. The Australians won one race, but Dennis Conner, master of match-race starting techniques, proved too good, and "Freedom" retained the cup for the U.S. 4–1.

In sailing competition at the 1980 Olympic Games the six gold medals were shared by five nations, Brazil winning in both the 470 and Tornado classes. Valentin Mankin piloted a Soviet boat to victory in the Star class, while Esko Rechardt of Finland triumphed in the Finn races. Boats from Denmark and Spain won the Soling and Flying Dutchman classes, respectively. (*See* TRACK AND FIELD SPORTS: *Special Report*.)

The Southern Ocean Racing Conference's annual circuit consisted of a six-race series, Jan. 26–Feb. 22, 1980. As usual the best in U.S. heavy machinery was competing. Surprisingly, Burt Keenan of the U.S. and his crew in "Acadia," based on a standard Peterson 42 hull, won the series. Dennis Conner, taking time off from his 12-m America's Cup campaign, joined the crew of Jim Kilroy's "Kialoa," which won both class and fleet honours in the race from St. Petersburg to Boca Grande and back. Overall results: (1) "Acadia" (Burt Keenan, Class C); (2) "Tatoosh" (Robert Hutton, Class B); and (3) "Forté" (Tom Tobin, Class C).

In the Ton Cup series the designer and ¼-ton

The yacht "Freedom" sailed to victory over the Australian challenger in the America's Cup races held off Newport, R. I.

WIDE WORLD

World Class Boat Champions

Class	Winner	Country
Cadet	Carlos Casrillo	Argentina
Cherub	Derek Snow	New Zealand
Enterprise	Max Francey	U.K.
Europe	Lars Christensen	Norway
Finn	Cam Lewis	U.S.
Fireball	Kim Slater	U.K.
Flying Dutchman	Terry McLaughlin	Canada
Flying 15	Barry Finlayson	New Zealand
505	Steve Benjamin	U.S.
470	David Ullman	U.S.
18-ft skiff	Iain Murray	Australia
Laser	Ed Baird	U.S.
O.K.	Poul Kirketorp	Denmark
Solo	Cor-Jan Schouten	The Netherlands
Soling	Glenn Dexter	Canada
Star	B. Binkhorst	The Netherlands
Sunfish	Cor-Van Aanholt	The Netherlands
Tempest	Rolf Bähr	West Germany
Wayfarer	Chris Kofler	Canada
Women's 420	C. Mazzaferro	Italy
Women's Laser	Lynne Jewell	U.S.
WORLD TON CUP CHAMPIONS		
1-ton	P. G. Vigliani	Italy
¾-ton	Jacques Faroux	France
½-ton	Guy Dupuy	France
Mini-ton	Mike Braney	U.S.
Micro-ton	Jean-Pierre Lostis	France

helmsman of 1979, Jacques Faroux of France, continued his winning ways with an outstanding ¾-tonner, "Maligawa." "Maligawa" showed excellent boat speed, which, combined with Faroux's mastery of tactics on the Olympic courses, won them the first four races. In the One-Ton Cup competition there was little to choose between the first six yachts. The Italian "Filo da Torcere," designed by Andrea Vallicelli, won from "Buonalena," U.S. owned and Italian designed (Fontana-Maletto-Navare).

The Observer Singlehanded Transatlantic Race was won in record time by Philip Weld (*see* BIOGRAPHIES) in his trimaran "Moxie." In August Margaret Hicks, a teacher from Southampton, England, became the first woman to make a double crossing of the Atlantic, single-handed, in a small yacht. (ADRIAN JARDINE)

Saint Lucia

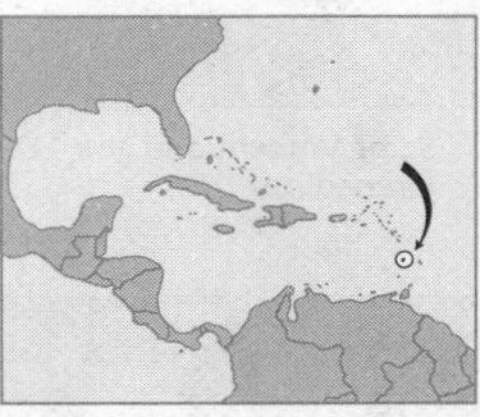

Saint Lucia

A parliamentary democracy and a member of the Commonwealth of Nations, St. Lucia, the second largest of the Windward Islands in the Eastern Caribbean, is situated 32 km (20 mi) NE of St. Vincent and 40 km (25 mi) S of Martinique. Area: 622 sq km (240 sq mi). Pop. (1979 est.): 130,000, predominantly of African descent. Cap. and largest city: Castries (pop., 1979 est., 45,000). Language: English and a local French dialect. Religion (1970): Roman Catholic 91%, Anglican 3%, Seventh-day Adventist 2%, others 4%. Queen, Elizabeth II; governors-general in 1980, Sir Allen Montgomery Lewis and, from February 22, Boswell Williams (acting); prime minister, Allan Louisy.

Early in 1980, after Deputy Prime Minister George Odlum had announced that Prime Minister Allan Louisy had gone back on his agreement to hand over the leadership of the ruling St. Lucia Labour Party after six months in office, an acrimonious public debate broke out. It centred mainly on Louisy's appointment on February 22 of Boswell Williams to succeed retiring Sir Allen Montgomery Lewis as acting governor-general. A

ST. LUCIA

Education. (1978–79) Primary, pupils 30,295, teachers 863; secondary, pupils 4,584, teachers 173; vocational, pupils 169, teachers 24; teacher training, students 125, teachers 11.

Finance and Trade. Monetary unit: East Caribbean dollar, with (Sept. 22, 1980) a par value of ECar$2.70 to U.S. $1 (free rate of ECar$6.48 = £1 sterling). Budget (1977–78 est.): revenue ECar$50,596,000; expenditure ECar$51,120,000. Foreign trade (1978): imports ECar$223.6 million; exports ECar$72.3 million. Import sources (1976): U.K. 25%; U.S. 20%; Trinidad and Tobago 15%; Canada 12%. Export destinations: U.K. 45%; Leeward and Windward Islands 17%; Trinidad and Tobago 12%; Barbados 8%; Jamaica 5%. Main exports (1977): bananas 46%; cardboard boxes 17%; coconut oil 10%; beverages 8%; clothing 6%. Tourism (including cruise passengers; 1978) 107,000 visitors.

Cabinet reshuffle in which Louisy emerged triumphant resolved differences. But, as a result, few of the government's election proposals were introduced. Yet the island remained economically buoyant until Hurricane Allen struck in August. Tourist arrivals were increasing, and new hotels were under construction. The U.S. Amerada Hess Corp. agreed to upgrade its oil transshipment facility into a full refinery; the banana industry was growing; and light manufacturing industries were being attracted.

The damage caused by Hurricane Allen was put at ECar$250 million. Sixteen persons died, and 6,000 were made homeless. The south of the island was particularly hard hit. Approximately 97% of the banana crop was destroyed, and factories in the industrial area at Vieux Fort were severely damaged. (DAVID A. JESSOP)

Saint Vincent and the Grenadines

Saint Vincent and the Grenadines

A constitutional monarchy within the Commonwealth of Nations, St. Vincent and the Grenadines (islands of the Lesser Antilles in the Caribbean Sea) lies southwest of St. Lucia and west of Barbados. Area (including Grenadines): 388 sq km (150 sq mi). Pop. (1978 est.): 117,600, predominantly of African descent. Cap. and largest city: Kingstown (pop., 1978 est., 22,800). Language: English (official). Religion (1970): Anglican 47%; Methodist 28%; Roman Catholic 13%. Queen, Elizabeth II; governor-general in 1980, Sir Sydney Gun-Munro; prime minister, Milton Cato.

Prime Minister Milton Cato's St. Vincent Labour Party government pursued a broadly conservative policy during 1980, the islands' first year of independence. The opposition remained in disarray. James Mitchell, leader of the New Democratic Party—who had lost his seat in the December 1979 general election—moderated his demands for secession of the Grenadines after being returned to Parliament in a by-election. The state of emergency proclaimed following an armed uprising on Union Island (one of the St. Vincent Grenadines) on Dec. 7, 1979, was lifted in May.

Gross domestic product was expected to rise by 5% in 1980 after recording a slight decline in 1979 because of the eruption of La Soufrière volcano.

ST. VINCENT

Education. (1977–78) Primary, pupils 25,191, teachers 1,087; secondary, pupils 5,219, teachers 284; vocational, pupils 135; teacher training, students 227; vocational and teacher training, teachers 35.

Finance and Trade. Monetary unit: East Caribbean dollar, with (Sept. 22, 1980) a par value of ECar$2.70 to U.S. $1 (free rate of ECar$6.48 = £1 sterling). Budget (1979–80 est.): revenue ECar$39.4 million; expenditure ECar$43.2 million. Foreign trade (1978): imports ECar$97.7 million; exports ECar$44.3 million. Import sources (1976): U.K. 30%; Trinidad and Tobago 20%; U.S. 9%; Canada 9%; St. Lucia 5%; Guyana 5%. Export destinations (1976): U.K. 75%; Trinidad and Tobago 13%. Main exports (1976): bananas 62%; arrowroot *c.* 12%.

Agriculture recovered from the effects of the eruption but received a further blow when Hurricane Allen destroyed 95% of the banana crop in August. Overall damage from the hurricane was put at ECar$60 million.

St. Vincent maintained a low profile internationally. Its relations with Barbados remained close as both governments pursued the establishment of a joint coast guard and fisheries protection service. St. Vincent joined the International Monetary Fund and the UN. (DAVID A. JESSOP)

San Marino

San Marino

A small republic, San Marino is an enclave in northeastern Italy, 8 km (5 mi) SW of Rimini. Area: 61 sq km (24 sq mi). Pop. (1980 est.): 21,300. Cap. and largest city: San Marino (metro. pop., 1980 est., 8,500). Language: Italian. Religion: Roman Catholic. The country is governed by two *capitani reggenti*, or co-regents, appointed every six months by a Grand and General Council. Executive power rests with three secretaries of state: foreign and political affairs, internal affairs, and economic affairs. In 1980 the positions were filled, respectively, by Giordano Bruno Reffi, Alvaro Selva, and Emilio della Balda.

Western Europe's only Communist-controlled government became more firmly so on May 25, 1980. In an election on that day the Communists, who led a three-party coalition in the republic, gained an additional 2% of the votes compared with the 1978 general election. With their allies, the Socialists and Unitary Socialists, they won 56.48% of the total vote of 11,305. The Christian Democratic opposition remained the largest single party with nearly 40% of the votes.

On Sept. 20, 1979, an agreement was concluded between the U.S.S.R. and San Marino on cooperation in culture, education, tourism, and sport. It was signed in Moscow by the Soviet deputy foreign minister, Igor Zemskov, and San Marino's secretary of state for foreign affairs, Giordano Bruno Reffi. On Dec. 3, 1979, Reffi and Stanislaw

SAN MARINO

Education. (1979–80) Primary, pupils 1,535, teachers 132; secondary, pupils 1,288, teachers (1975–76) 108.

Finance. Monetary unit: Italian lira, with (Sept. 22, 1980) a free rate of 856 lire to U.S. $1 (2,056 lire = £1 sterling); local coins are issued. Budget (1979 est.) balanced at 44,304,000,000 lire. Tourism (1978) 2,905,000 visitors.

Salvador, El:
see El Salvador

Salvation Army:
see Religion

Samoa:
see Dependent States; Western Samoa

Trepczynski, the Polish ambassador to Italy, signed at the government palace in San Marino a treaty establishing official diplomatic relations between Poland and San Marino.

On July 18, 1980, Pres. Alessandro Pertini of Italy became the first Italian head of state to receive the co-regents of San Marino (Pietro Chiaruzzi and Primo Marani, appointed in April).

(K. M. SMOGORZEWSKI)

São Tomé and Príncipe

An independent African state, the Democratic Republic of São Tomé and Príncipe comprises two main islands and several smaller islets that straddle the Equator in the Gulf of Guinea, off the west coast of Africa. Area: 964 sq km (372 sq mi), of which São Tomé, the larger island, comprises 854 sq km. Pop. (1980 est.): 85,000. Cap. and largest city: São Tomé (pop., 1977 est., 20,000). Language: Portuguese. Religion: mainly Roman Catholic. President in 1980, Manuel Pinto da Costa.

Because many of the Portuguese technicians had left the country, São Tomé and Príncipe in 1980 leaned increasingly on Cuban assistance, relying upon Cubans for 75% of skilled manpower. The islands also established direct telephone links with Angola, with which an agreement was signed on Jan. 16, 1980, for cooperation on fishing, finance, energy, and the establishment of a joint commission. Angola, Mozambique, and Guinea-Bissau offered military aid against possible aggression. After the removal of Premier Miguel Trovoada at the end of 1979, Pres. Manuel Pinto da Costa turned for help increasingly to socialist countries.

Accused of helping to plot an attempted coup, Trovoada had sought sanctuary on UN mission territory. His arrest there on Oct. 5, 1979, continued in 1980 to be the subject of international protest as a violation of international law. From March 1980 the duties of premier were carried out by the president, who was reelected head of the ruling party in May. During the year the British firm VIP Travel was asked to help develop the nation's tourist industry. Meanwhile, Japan was installing a new telephone service, and the African Development Bank in May 1980 provided a loan of U.S. $1.3 million for extensions to the nation's airport.

(GUY ARNOLD)

SÃO TOMÉ AND PRÍNCIPE

Education. (1976) Primary, pupils 14,162, teachers 527; secondary, pupils 3,012, teachers 81; vocational, pupils 155, teachers 30.

Finance and Trade. Monetary unit: dobra, with (Sept. 22, 1980) a free rate of 34.10 dobras to U.S. $1 (81.95 dobras = £1 sterling). Budget (1977 est.): revenue 180 million dobras; expenditure 454 million dobras. Foreign trade (1975): imports 288,469,000 dobras; exports 180,432,000 dobras. Import sources: Portugal 61%; Angola 13%. Export destinations: The Netherlands 52%; Portugal 33%; West Germany 8%. Main exports: cocoa *c.* 82%; copra *c.* 6%; palm kernels and nuts *c.* 5%.

São Tomé and Príncipe

Saudi Arabia

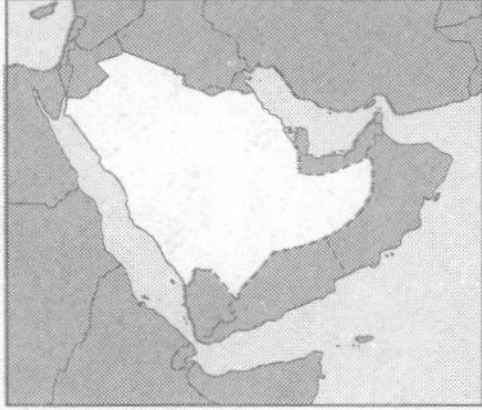
Saudi Arabia

A monarchy occupying four-fifths of the Arabian Peninsula, Saudi Arabia has an area of 2,240,000 sq km (865,000 sq mi). Pop. (1980 est.): 8,367,000. Cap. and largest city: Riyadh (pop., 1980 est., 1,044,000). Language: Arabic. Religion: Muslim, predominantly Sunni; Shiʿah minority in Eastern Province. King and prime minister in 1980, Khalid.

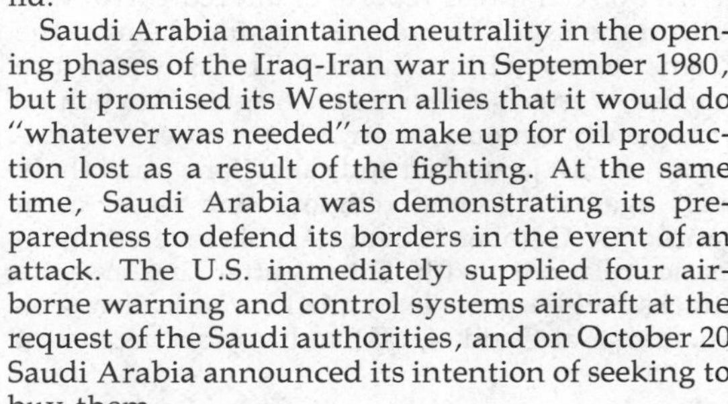

Saudi Arabia maintained neutrality in the opening phases of the Iraq-Iran war in September 1980, but it promised its Western allies that it would do "whatever was needed" to make up for oil production lost as a result of the fighting. At the same time, Saudi Arabia was demonstrating its preparedness to defend its borders in the event of an attack. The U.S. immediately supplied four airborne warning and control systems aircraft at the request of the Saudi authorities, and on October 20 Saudi Arabia announced its intention of seeking to buy them.

Washington's readiness to come to the aid of its main supplier of crude oil reintroduced a note of warmth into its relations with Riyadh, absent since 1979 when Saudi Arabia condemned Egypt's peace treaty with Israel. It made more likely a further resupplying of the Saudi forces with advanced equipment after the U.S. presidential election in November. The stalled U.S. deal over the supply of 60 McDonnell Douglas F-15 jets was expected to go through Congress after the election. In the meantime, on October 14, the Saudi authorities signed a U.S. $3.5 billion naval equipment agreement with France providing for the supply of four frigates, two supply ships, helicopters, and training.

SCHREIBER—GAMMA/LIAISON

Saudi Foreign Minister Prince Saud al-Faisal (centre) and oil minister Sheikh Ahmad Zaki Yamani (right) were under fire from more radical members at a September OPEC meeting in Vienna. Although a pricing compromise resulted, the ministers were not able to agree on long-term strategy.

U.S. confidence in the stability of Saudi Arabia had been shaken by the events following the temporary seizure of the Grand Mosque in Mecca on Nov. 20, 1979. This incident, and later trouble in the Shiʿah populated oases of the Eastern Province where the kingdom's oil was produced, led to fears of a Khomeini-style revolution against the ruling house of Saud. Saudi policy following the Mecca siege was to take limited but sharp reprisals, including imposition of the death sentence on the perpetrators of the "sacrilege" against Islam. Sixty-three of the men captured after the attack, including 41 Saudis, were executed on Jan. 9, 1980, by beheading. Subsequently, Crown Prince Fahd outlined plans for major government changes, including a consultative council of 50–70 members to complement the Council of Ministers (Cabinet). By year's end little had evolved from these promises of greater participation, but a reshuffle in the Saudi military was a direct result of the handling of the Mecca siege.al

Crown Prince Fahd, confirmed during the year as the strong man at the side of the ailing king, was critical of U.S. press reports of alleged corruption within the Saudi hierarchy, blaming them on the Zionist lobby within the U.S. The crown prince startled Western observers on August 14 when he vehemently denounced Israel's proposed "annexation" of East Jerusalem and called for a jihad (holy war) against "Zionist religious and racist arrogance." On October 28 Saudi Arabia severed diplomatic relations with Libya after intemperate attacks had been made by the Libyan leader, Col. Muammar al-Qaddafi, on Saudi Arabia because of its purchase of radar-equipped aircraft from the U.S. Saudi Arabia played an important role in defusing the border confrontation between Syria and Jordan that erupted at the end of November. After a week of intensive diplomacy, Prince Abdullah ibn Abdul Aziz, second deputy prime minister and commander of the Saudi National Guard, negotiated a formula under which both countries withdrew the troops that had been massed in the border area.

Saudi sensitivity to media criticism reached the point of open anger in April, when British television showed a dramatized version of the execution of a Saudi princess and her lover for adultery. The Cabinet decided on an unofficial embargo of British companies shortly after the program was screened, and on April 23 the British ambassador, James Craig, was asked to leave Jidda. It took a visit by British Foreign Secretary Lord Carrington on August 26 to restore relations and bring about Craig's return. Among the factors that assuaged Saudi anger was the positive line the British government took over a European Economic Community call for inclusion of the Palestinians in talks on a Middle East peace settlement.

The major domestic event of the year was the announcement in May of an ambitious third five-year development plan to cover the period up to 1985. Expenditure, equivalent to $235 billion, was much larger than the second plan's $149.5 billion. Perhaps as much as 30% of the plan's allocations were to be committed in the first year. Apart from strict adherence to Islamic social values, the guiding principle would be to ensure the development of human resources, as opposed to the emphasis on construction of infrastructure which was the focus of the second plan. The performance under the second plan was impressive: inflation had been cut to single figures and port congestion eliminated, while gross domestic product had grown at an average rate of more than 10% a year—all this despite general flatness in the hydrocarbons sector and Saudi Arabia's moderate oil pricing policies. No country could afford to ignore the trade potential posed by the Saudi plan—in 1979 more than 42% of all contracts awarded in the Middle East, excluding Israel, were in Saudi Arabia.

The Ministry of Industry was to get 26% of the total plan budget, emphasizing the kingdom's commitment to developing productive industries by capitalizing on the existence of cheap gas. The two most important industrial developments were to be at Yanbu, 400 km (250 mi) north of Jidda on the Red Sea, and at Jubail 145 km (90 mi) north of Dhahran on the Gulf coast. In addition, a number of agreements reached in 1980 made it likely that by the end of the 1980s Saudi Arabia would be a significant force on the world market for refined products (separate from crude oil), natural gas, and petrochemicals. A Greek company reached agreement with the General Petroleum and Mineral Organization (Petromin) for a $2,620,000,000 refinery at Rabigh between Jidda and Yanbu; the Saudi Basic Industries Corporation (Sabic) and a subsidiary of Shell Oil of the U.S. reached agreement on a $3 billion petrochemicals complex at Jubail; and the first of two natural gas fractionation

SAUDI ARABIA

Education. (1976–77) Primary, pupils 726,063, teachers 38,077; secondary, pupils 237,854, teachers 16,458; vocational, pupils 5,256, teachers 834; teacher training, students 15,343, teachers 1,231; higher, students 32,729, teaching staff 2,966.

Finance. Monetary unit: riyal, with (Sept. 22, 1980) a free rate of 3.30 riyals to U.S. $1 (7.94 riyals = £1 sterling). Gold, SDR's, and foreign exchange (June 1980) U.S. $19,867,000,000. Budget (1980–81 est.): revenue 265 billion riyals; expenditure 245 billion riyals. Gross national product (1977–78) 185,384,000,000 riyals. Money supply (April 1980) 56.4 billion riyals. Cost of living (1975 = 100; 1st quarter 1980) 149.

Foreign Trade. (1979) Imports (fob) *c.* 80.4 billion riyals; exports 199.4 billion riyals. Import sources (1978): U.S. 21%; Japan 15%; West Germany 11%; U.K. 7%; Italy 7%. Export destinations (1978): Japan 20%; U.S. 16%; France 11%; Italy 7%. Main exports: crude oil 94%; petroleum products 6%. Tourism (1977) gross receipts U.S. $823 million.

Transport and Communications. Roads (1978) 37,500 km. Motor vehicles in use (1978): passenger 360,500; commercial 272,200. Railways: (1979) 680 km; traffic (1974) 72 million passenger-km, freight 66 million net ton-km. Air traffic (1978): 6,771,000,000 passenger-km; freight *c.* 140 million net ton-km. Shipping (1979): merchant vessels 100 gross tons and over 172; gross tonnage 1,442,952. Telephones (Jan. 1978) 185,000. Radio receivers (Dec. 1977) 275,000. Television receivers (Dec. 1977) 300,000.

Agriculture. Production (in 000; metric tons; 1979): sorghum *c.* 100; wheat *c.* 150; barley *c.* 15; tomatoes *c.* 181; onions (1978) *c.* 50; grapes *c.* 51; dates *c.* 357. Livestock (in 000; 1978): cattle *c.* 340; sheep *c.* 2,400; goats *c.* 1,700; camels *c.* 108; asses *c.* 104; poultry *c.* 17,000.

Industry. Production (in 000; metric tons): crude oil (1979) 476,305; petroleum products (1978) *c.* 26,000; natural gas (cu m; 1977) 9,442,000; electricity (excluding most industrial production; kw-hr; 1977) *c.* 2,500,000; cement (1977) 1,292.

plants built for the Arabian-American Oil Co. (Aramco) was in full operation in late 1980.

Aramco, the main force in the Saudi hydrocarbons industry, was due to be taken over by the government in 1981. In September 1980 the chairman of Petromin, Abdul-Hadi Taher, said the U.S. shareholders in Aramco (Exxon, Mobil Oil, Standard Oil Co. of California, and Texaco) had received full compensation for nationalization in the second quarter of 1980. He declined to specify the amount, but other reports put it at between $1.5 billion and $2 billion. For the first ten months of 1980, direct sales by Petromin of the Saudi crude oil output of 9.5 million bbl a day were running at about 1,770,000 bbl a day. Oil production had been increased to 9.5 million bbl a day from 8.5 million bbl during the crisis following the fall of the shah of Iran in 1979. From October 1, output increased to 10.4 million bbl a day.

Future oil production policies were likely to be determined by constraints imposed by the Aramco gas-gathering system. This would require a minimum output level to avoid underutilization of the system, which relied on gas produced as a by-product of crude oil production. At the same time, vastly increased production would result in too much flared gas. It was also likely that Saudi Arabia would use its oil power to secure a market for its petrochemicals, though this would probably meet strong resistance from Western chemical companies. The official price of Saudi Arabia's marker crude (Arabian light) was $30.21 a barrel in the third quarter of 1980, against $28.82 a barrel in the second quarter and $27.12 a barrel in the first quarter. This continued the steadily rising trend from $14.54 a barrel in the first quarter of 1979, although Saudi policy, as stated on October 21 by the Saudi ambassador to the U.S., Faisal al-Hegelan, was still to maintain unified pricing within the context of the Organization of Petroleum Exporting Countries. A further $2 was added to the price in December.

During 1980 the process of saudization of foreign banks within the kingdom continued, with the biggest foreign bank, Citibank of the U.S., becoming the Saudi American Bank on July 11. The Saudi Arabian Monetary Agency (SAMA) acted shrewdly to maintain the value of the Saudi riyal by forestalling speculators with periodic adjustments of the value of the riyal against the dollar. There was no sign that SAMA would move to allow more banks, but at least 12 international banks were being "permitted" to maintain an unofficial presence as advisers to local businessmen.

On August 19 the world's third worst air accident to that date occurred at Riyadh airport when 301 people died on the tarmac after a Lockheed TriStar burst into flames. An official inquiry later said the cause of the fire was unknown, although butane camping stoves believed to have belonged to Muslim pilgrims were found in the wreckage. The Saudi authorities and the national airline, Saudia, took action to improve airport security. This included clamping down on a system whereby passengers could buy and sell boarding passes for congested Saudi domestic flights in the airport concourse. (JOHN WHELAN)

Senegal

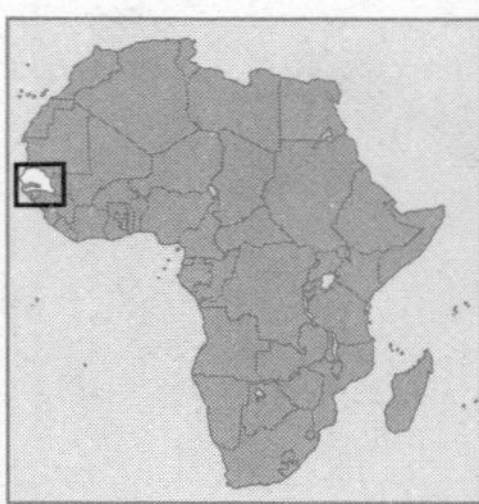
Senegal

A republic of northwestern Africa, Senegal is bounded by Mauritania, Mali, Guinea, and Guinea-Bissau and by the Atlantic Ocean. The independent nation of The Gambia forms an enclave within the country. Area: 196,722 sq km (75,955 sq mi). Pop. (1980 est.): 5,661,000. Cap. and largest city: Dakar (pop., 1978 est., 914,500). Language: French (official); Wolof 29%; Serer 17%; Peulh 17%; Diola 8%; Bambara 6%; other tribal dialects. Religion: Muslim 86%; Christian 5%; animist 9%. President in 1980, Léopold Sédar Senghor; premier, Abdou Diouf.

Léopold Sédar Senghor, Senegal's president since independence in 1960 and one of Africa's most widely known leaders, announced his resignation on Dec. 31, 1980, at the age of 74. The resignation, which had been expected, took effect at midnight, and the office passed to Premier Abdou Diouf.

Senegal experienced unrest in 1980. A school strike at Ziguinchor in January left one dead and several wounded and resulted in a student march to the centre of Dakar. Two leaders of the clandestine branch of the Parti Africain l'Indépendance were questioned in March. Also, in April there was a demonstration in Dakar by about 1,000 sympathizers of the legal opposition led by the Parti Démocratique Sénégalais.

The economic situation was serious in spite of the recovery plan of December 1979. Because of the oil price rise of 1980, only 40% of the cost of importing petroleum was covered by exports. The first stone of the Diama dam was laid, marking the start of works to control the Senegal River.

In spite of some coolness after the indefinite postponement in March of French Pres. Valéry Giscard d'Estaing's visit to Dakar, relations with France remained a cornerstone of Senegal's foreign policy. In May Senghor attended the Franco-African conference at Nice, France, and revealed his project of a French Commonwealth. Senghor visited Paris in April and August, and Diouf was received there in July. However, the close relations Senghor maintained with Socialist Party leader François Mitterrand irritated the French president. On June 28 Senegal broke off diplomatic relations with Libya, accusing the latter of interference in Senegal's affairs. (PHILIPPE DECRAENE)

SENEGAL

Education. (1977–78) Primary, pupils 346,585, teachers 8,186; secondary, pupils 78,384, teachers 1,758; vocational and teacher training, pupils 14,090, teachers 820; higher, students (1976–77) 8,892, teaching staff (1975–76) 412.

Finance and Trade. Monetary unit: CFA franc, with (Sept. 22, 1980) a par value of CFA Fr 50 to the French franc (free rate of CFA Fr 210 = U.S. $1; CFA Fr 504 = £1 sterling). Budget (total; 1977–78 est.) balanced at CFA Fr 151 billion. Foreign trade (1977): imports CFA Fr 187.5 billion; exports CFA Fr 152.9 billion. Import sources: France 40%; U.S. 8%; West Germany 6%; Italy 5%. Export destinations: France 45%; U.K. 7%; Italy 5%; Mauritania 5%. Main exports (1976): peanut oil 36%; phosphates 15%; fish and products 7%; petroleum products 5%; peanuts 11%; animal fodder 9%.

Scandinavian Literature:
see Literature

Schools:
see Education

Scotland:
see United Kingdom

Sculpture:
see Art Exhibitions; Art Sales; Museums

Securities:
see Stock Exchanges

Seismology:
see Earth Sciences

Seventh-day Adventist Church:
see Religion

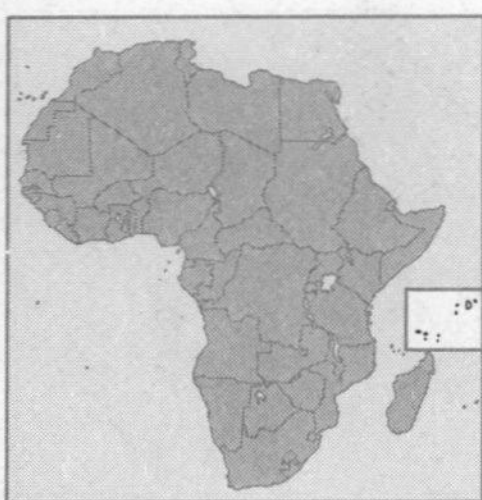

Seychelles

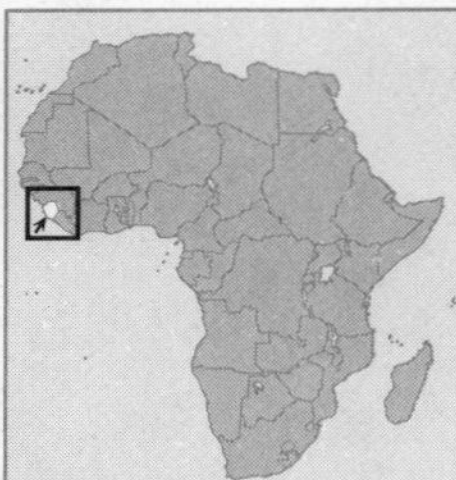

Sierra Leone

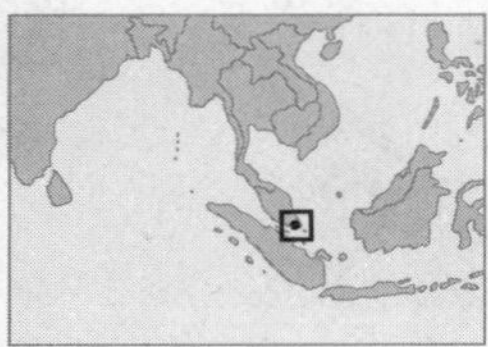

Singapore

Seychelles

A republic and a member of the Commonwealth of Nations in the Indian Ocean consisting of 89 islands, Seychelles lies 1,450 km from the coast of East Africa. Area: 443 sq km (171 sq mi), 166 sq km of which includes the islands of Farquhar, Desroches, and Aldabra. Pop. (1980 est.): 63,200, including Creole 94%, French 5%, English 1%. Cap.: Victoria, on Mahé (pop., 1977, 23,000). Language: English and French are official, creole patois is also spoken. Religion: Roman Catholic 90%; Anglican 8%. President in 1980, France-Albert René.

Presenting the 1980 budget, with expected revenue of SRs 358.7 million, Pres. France-Albert René said in January that the Seychelles had to rely less on imports, change its patterns of consumption, and export more. Meanwhile, the turnover tax (on sales of all commodities by manufacturers, wholesalers, and retailers) was doubled to 10%.

An ice plant for the fishing industry, financed by the Abu Dhabi Development Fund, was opened in July to produce ten metric tons of ice a day. Following a visit to Cochin by President René, India agreed to help the Seychelles develop marine culture of oysters, mussels, shrimps, and prawns. An Italian group was to exploit granite for export to Italy.

Work began on extending the international airport with funds from the African Development Bank. A terminal for internal traffic was planned to relieve pressure on the main building. In September, in accordance with resolutions of the Organization of African Unity, the Seychelles banned the weekly South African Airways flights to the islands. Tourism remained strong; in 1979 the 60,000 visitors equaled the entire population of the Seychelles. (GUY ARNOLD)

SEYCHELLES

Education. (1979) Primary, pupils 9,839, teachers 393; secondary, pupils 4,611, teachers 215; vocational, pupils 449, teachers 51; teacher training, students 93, teachers 22; higher (1977), students 117, teaching staff 24.

Finance and Trade. Monetary unit: Seychelles rupee, with (Sept. 22, 1980) a free rate of SRs 6.20 to U.S. $1 (SRs 14.90 = £1 sterling). Budget (1979–80 est.) balanced at SRs 359 million. Foreign trade (1979): imports SRs 561.7 million; exports SRs 198.2 million. Import sources (1978): U.K. 26%; Kenya 11%; South Africa 10%; Singapore 6%; Japan 6%. Export destinations (1978): ship and aircraft bunkers and stores 70%; Pakistan 12%; India 5%. Main exports: petroleum products 47%; ship and aircraft stores 22%; copra 17%. Tourism (1978): visitors 64,000; gross receipts U.S. $29 million.

Sierra Leone

A republic within the Commonwealth of Nations, Sierra Leone is a West African state on the Atlantic coast between Guinea and Liberia. Area: 71,740 sq km (27,699 sq mi). Pop. (1980 est.): 3,474,000, including (1963) Mende and Temne tribes 60.7%; other tribes 38.9%; non-African 0.4%. Cap. and largest city: Freetown (pop., 1974, 314,340). Language: English (official); tribal dialects. Religion: animist 54%, Muslim 40%, Christian 6%. President in 1980, Siaka Stevens.

In December 1979 the first major shipment of rutile (7,000 tons) was exported from Sierra Leone; the country was producing the mineral (an ore of titanium) at the rate of 54,000 tons a year. An agreement was made with the Swiss Austro-Mineral concern to rehabilitate the iron-ore mines at Marampa, abandoned in 1975. Major efforts were made in 1980 to improve agriculture with international and foreign loans. The program to increase rice production and thus reduce dependence on imports was stepped up; Romania supplied 200 tractors as well as technical assistance, and 83,025 ha (205,000 ac) were to be devoted to rice. Cocoa production was expanded, and there was a major fisheries development.

In the 1980–81 budget duties on liquor, tobacco, and cars were increased, and top priority was to be accorded to the Bumbuna hydroelectric project in order to lessen dependence upon imported oil. The country faced a serious trade deficit due to imports of oil, rice, and also of material for the 17th annual Organization of African Unity (OAU) summit meeting, held at Freetown, July 1–4. There, Pres. Siaka Stevens became OAU chairman for the year 1980–81. The cost to Sierra Leone was 123.1 million leones. With Liberia, Sierra Leone invited Guinea to join the Mano River Union, which it did in October. (GUY ARNOLD)

SIERRA LEONE

Education. (1976–77) Primary, pupils 218,379, teachers 6,700; secondary (1977–78), pupils 53,897, teachers 3,037; vocational, pupils 1,690, teachers 154; teacher training, students 1,269, teachers 121; higher, students 2,077, teaching staff 327.

Finance and Trade. Monetary unit: leone, with (Sept. 22, 1980) a free value of 1.01 leones to U.S. $1 (2.43 leones = £1 sterling). Budget (1979–80 est.): revenue 162.9 million leones; expenditure 156.7 million leones. Foreign trade: imports (1978) 290,840,000 leones; exports (1979) 154,630,000 leones. Import sources (1977): Nigeria 24%; U.K. 18%; U.S. 9%; Japan 7%; West Germany 6%; France 5%. Export destinations (1978): U.K. 55%; The Netherlands 24%; U.S. 9%; Switzerland 5%. Main exports (1978): diamonds 64%; coffee 14%; cocoa 7%.

Agriculture. Production (in 000; metric tons; 1979): rice *c.* 480; cassava (1978) *c.* 90; palm kernels *c.* 50; palm oil *c.* 48; coffee *c.* 6; cocoa *c.* 6; fish catch (1978) 50. Livestock (in 000; 1978): cattle *c.* 260; sheep *c.* 57; goats *c.* 165; pigs *c.* 33; chickens *c.* 3,500.

Industry. Production (in 000; metric tons; 1977): petroleum products *c.* 310; bauxite (1978) 716; diamonds (metric carats) 771; electricity (kw-hr) *c.* 200,000.

Singapore

Singapore, a republic within the Commonwealth of Nations, occupies a group of islands, the largest of which is Singapore, at the southern extremity of the Malay Peninsula. Area: 616 sq km (238 sq mi). Pop. (1980 est.): 2,390,800, including (1979) 76% Chinese, 15% Malays, and 7% Indians. Language: official languages are English, Malay, Mandarin Chinese, and Tamil. Religion: Malays are Muslim; Chinese, mainly Buddhist; Indians, mainly Hindu. President in 1980, Benjamin Henry Sheares; prime minister, Lee Kuan Yew.

Ships and Shipping:
see Industrial Review;
Transportation

SINGAPORE

Education. (1979) Primary, pupils 297,873, teachers 11,052; secondary, pupils 176,521, teachers 8,418; vocational, pupils 12,013, teachers 810; teacher training, students 2,047, teachers 135; higher, students 15,684, teaching staff 1,068.

Finance. Monetary unit: Singapore dollar, with (Sept. 22, 1980) a free rate of Sing$2.11 to U.S. $1 (Sing$5.06 = £1 sterling). Gold, SDR's, and foreign exchange (May 1980) U.S. $6,093,000,000. Budget (1979–80 est.) balanced at Sing$3,885,000,000. Gross national product (1979) Sing$19,451,000,000. Money supply (May 1980) Sing$5,824,000,000. Cost of living (1975 = 100; June 1980) 119.3.

Foreign Trade. (1979) Imports Sing$38,335,000,000; exports Sing$30,939,000,000. Import sources: Japan 17%; U.S. 14%; Malaysia 14%; Saudi Arabia 10%. Export destinations: Malaysia 14%; U.S. 14%; Japan 10%; Hong Kong 7%. Main exports: petroleum products 24%; machinery 23%; rubber 10%; ship and aircraft stores 6%; food 5%. Tourism (1978): visitors 2,047,000; gross receipts U.S. $423 million.

Transport and Communications. Roads (1979) 2,285 km. Motor vehicles in use (1979): passenger 153,700; commercial 67,200. Railways (1979) 38 km (for traffic *see* Malaysia). Air traffic (1979): 12,050,000,000 passenger-km; freight 574,240,000 net ton-km. Shipping (1979): merchant vessels 100 gross tons and over 1,031; gross tonnage 7,869,152. Shipping traffic (1979): goods loaded 31,892,000 metric tons, unloaded 49,198,000 metric tons. Telephones (Dec. 1979) 625,000. Radio licenses (Dec. 1979) 430,600. Television licenses (Dec. 1979) 371,700.

The government canceled the licenses of two Chinese-language newspapers in January for allegedly carrying "news of a prurient and permissive nature" and then withdrew the order after the proprietors promised to change editorial policies. Amnesty International published on January 31 a report of a mission to Singapore that drew attention to the widespread use of powers of detention without trial and alleged that a variety of techniques were used to induce the mental and spiritual collapse of detainees. In March a government panel concluded that there was no basis "for lurid accounts of torture and assault." Two weeks after the publication of the Amnesty International report, Lee Tze Tong, detained without trial for 16 years for alleged Communist-inspired activities, was released.

In a Cabinet reshuffle in June, Foreign Minister Sinnathamby Rajaratnam became second deputy prime minister. He was succeeded by the senior minister of state for foreign affairs, Suppiah Dhanabalan. Goh Keng Swee, first deputy prime minister, relinquished the education portfolio to Anthony Tan Keng Yam.

A visit to the Soviet Union by Prime Minister Lee Kuan Yew was postponed in August because of the illness of Soviet Premier Aleksey N. Kosygin. It was the second time in 15 months that Lee's visit had been put off. Singapore had taken a vociferous position against the Soviet Union for its support of Vietnam in Cambodia and for its invasion of Afghanistan. In March a cipher clerk in the Singapore embassy in Moscow was sentenced to ten years in prison after pleading guilty to charges of passing classified information to a female Soviet agent who was blackmailing him.

In September an open public disagreement took place between the prime minister and Australian Prime Minister Malcolm Fraser over Australia's protectionist policies against the products of the Association of Southeast Asian Nations. By contrast, there was an evident harmony over defense matters: Singapore's Skyhawk fighter-bombers were to train in eastern Australia.

In the general election, held December 23, the ruling People's Action Party won all the parliamentary seats for the fourth straight time.

(MICHAEL LEIFER)

Social Security and Welfare Services

Government-imposed austerity programs continued to keep social expenditure within tight limits in 1980 and in a few cases led to substantial cutbacks. At the same time, there were some positive innovations, generally of a minor though by no means insignificant nature.

International Developments in Social Security. The most striking cutbacks took place in the U.K., where the Conservative government succeeded in getting two social security acts onto the statute book. The first reformed the Supplementary Benefits or social assistance scheme, which was not in itself a cutback, and changed the rule regarding the annual adjustment of pensions. Previously, the government had been obliged to increase pensions in line with earnings or prices, whichever was greater; under the act, pensions were to be adjusted in line with prices only.

The Social Security (No. 2) Act 1980 made fundamental changes in various National Insurance benefits and cut the social assistance entitlement of the dependents of workers involved in trade disputes. The earnings-related supplements payable for up to six months in the case of unemployment, sickness, work injury, or widowhood were to be reduced in 1981 and abolished in 1982. At this point, short-term social security benefits in the U.K. would revert to being purely flat-rate, as had been the case up to 1966. The duty to adjust them in line with the cost of living was suspended for three years, although the government was empowered to increase them by up to 5% less than the rate of inflation each year; and from 1982 they would become taxable.

Although the Conservative Party had a long-standing commitment to abolish the retirement test, the 1980 act, for reasons of economy, tended in the opposite direction. There would no longer be compulsory uprating of the amount that pensioners could earn without having their pensions reduced. More people claiming sickness benefit would have to wait three days before receiving it. The supplementary benefit that strikers might claim for their dependents (strikers were not eligible themselves) was reduced by £12 per week, the disregard of £4 of any tax rebate payable to the claimant was abolished, and severe restrictions were placed on urgent needs payments to strikers and their families.

In France the government continued its attempt to stem the rise in the cost of medical care. Doctors' fees were held down, and legislation was passed (December 1979) empowering the government to

Skating:
see Ice Hockey; Winter Sports

Skeet Shooting:
see Target Sports

Skiing:
see Water Sports; Winter Sports

Soccer:
see Football

STAYSKAL—CHICAGO TRIBUNE/NEW YORK SYNDICATE, INC.

close hospitals or hospital departments against the wishes of the hospital management board. However, under an agreement concluded in June 1980 between the sickness insurance funds and the doctors, any doctor might choose to charge more than the standard fee, a right previously enjoyed only by doctors with special qualifications and experience. If the authorities continued to hold down the standard fee (on which sickness insurance benefits were based), many doctors might well opt to charge more than the standard fee, thus raising the amount patients themselves had to pay.

In Seychelles the final stage of a universal and comprehensive social security scheme was implemented in 1980. The scheme paid retirement and survivors' pensions, sickness and maternity benefits, funeral benefits, total and partial invalidity pensions, and work injury benefits. Health care was provided under a National Health Plan, outside the framework of social security. There were no unemployment benefits, but an Unemployment Fund was set up to finance work projects reserved for the registered unemployed.

The scheme was revolutionary in a number of respects. While all benefits were flat-rate, contributions were a proportion of income and there was no upper limit to the amount payable. Since the system covered all residents in receipt of an income (or social security benefit), contributions were payable on earnings from employment or self-employment as well as on private incomes. None of the benefits was conditional upon the payment of contributions. The criterion of social need thus wholly replaced the traditional insurance-type criteria. Other highly original features of the scheme, certainly in the context of the less developed world, were its breadth of coverage and the speed with which it was introduced.

Jordan established a scheme covering work injury, old age, invalidity, and death, which applied to 20 enterprises in the Amman area. Liberia introduced a work injury scheme covering 100,000 employees in the public and private sectors, out of a total employed population of 135,000, and announced that a scheme covering old age, invalidity, and death would be introduced in the course of the year. In Libya work injury insurance was extended to cover the self-employed, and minimum pensions for the disabled were substantially increased.

Nicaragua undertook wide-ranging reforms in its social insurance system, as well as in the field of health care. Coverage, previously limited to employees in industry, commerce, and the public sector, was to be extended to all employees and to many of the self-employed. The minimum benefit was to be raised substantially and to become payable even to people who did not satisfy the qualifying period of insurance. In the Philippines social security coverage was extended to various groups of self-employed persons with an annual income of at least 1,800 pesos. Self-employed farmers and fishermen, the majority of the country's population, remained outside the scope of social security coverage.

Finland reduced the age at which unemployed persons might opt for early retirement to 55, although the minimum age was to rise again gradually to 60. France, motivated by demographic considerations, introduced six months' paid maternity leave, instead of the normal 16 weeks, for women giving birth to their third (or subsequent) child. The Italian National Health Service began to operate, at least partially, in the course of 1980, its introduction having been postponed from 1979. In Poland the agreement concluded between the government and striking shipyard workers in Szczecin contained, in addition to the widely publicized right to set up self-governing trade unions, various items relating to social security. These included an increase in retirement pensions and a raise in family allowances to the same level as militia and army family allowances.

Partial pensions in Sweden, designed to facilitate a gradual transition from work to retirement, were extended to self-employed persons, on condition that they reduce their working hours by 50%. More flexible retirement arrangements were also introduced in the U.S.S.R., where for the first time workers might defer their pension and thereby earn additional pension rights. In addition, most workers might draw their pension while continuing to work and earn their normal salary.

(ROGER A. BEATTIE)

U.S. Developments. Social welfare issues received relatively low priority in the U.S. in 1980 in two important arenas—Congress and the presidential election campaign.

With attention focused on the economy and foreign affairs, social policy took a back seat during the campaign even though the candidates had clear philosophical differences. Republican Ronald Reagan favoured reversing the trend toward greater federal responsibility, while Pres. Jimmy Carter talked of an even greater federal role in meeting social needs.

A cautious, economy-minded Congress shied away from either new initiatives or major reforms in the social welfare field. Typical was its approach to Social Security, which produced considerable discussion about basic changes in funding and eligibility, but little action. Two minor cutbacks were enacted—a reduction of disability benefits for workers disabled after July 1, 1980, and removal of prison inmates from the ranks of those eligible to collect benefits. The 35 million Social Security recipients received an automatic 14.3% cost-of-living increase in their benefits in July. On Jan. 1, 1981, the largest single boost in payroll taxes since the inception of Social Security was to go into effect. The tax rate would rise from 6.13 to 6.65% and taxable earnings from $25,900 to $29,700.

The controversial subject of welfare reform was almost ignored in 1980. Both Carter and Reagan agreed that the system should be overhauled, but they disagreed as to how. Carter favoured a guaranteed minimum wage and more standardized benefits, while Reagan wanted to give states more authority to run the program. Congress did not even consider the matter during the year.

Congress did make one important shift in social policy. It acted to move low-income children out of foster homes and back with their real families or into new, adoptive families. Nearly half of the 500,000 children in foster care in the U.S. had been there more than two years and about 100,000 more than six years. A new law limited the money that Washington could provide to states for foster care and furnished financial aid for adoption.

Other legislation enacted by Congress included: a $41.2 billion housing and community development bill that reauthorized several programs for low-income housing but did not include apartments for middle-income families; an extension of child nutrition programs, with an increase in the cost of school lunches for middle-income children; an increase in federal spending for mental health services and expansion of those services to groups that had not been adequately served in the past, such as the elderly, severely disturbed children, and the chronically mentally ill. Other important measures were a three-year extension of revenue sharing, the no-strings grant program, providing $4.6 billion a year to local governments and $2.3 billion annually (in fiscal 1982 and 1983 only) to states; an increase in food stamp expenditures to $9.5 billion for fiscal 1980 and $9.7 billion for 1981 and enactment of several cost-saving changes. Food stamp rolls reached an all-time high of 22.1 million persons in August 1980, and the new spending ceiling made the program the largest of the three main federal welfare programs. Also enacted were a low-income energy assistance program funded at $1.8 billion annually; and renewal of the Legal Services Corporation.

One issue that did not produce its usual lengthy debate in Congress was federal funding of abortions. The centre of attention shifted to the U.S. Supreme Court, which ruled in July that poor women do not have a constitutional right to publicly funded abortions. In a 5 to 4 decision, the court upheld the so-called Hyde Amendment, which prohibits federal funding of most abortions. As a result, it was estimated that federal funds would pay for only 2,000 abortions a year, compared with about 470,000 that would be financed if there were no restrictions.

Although social issues were not uppermost among congressional or political concerns, they were the subject of consideration and study in other forums. Among the recommendations given highest priority by the White House Conference on Families were: reform of Social Security to eliminate biases against families; better health care and home care for the aging; development of alternative forms of child care; support for efforts to prevent family violence; health, education, and social services to assist pregnant teenagers and teenage parents.

The Social Security Administration reported that the U.S. was spending an increasingly smaller share of its gross national product (GNP) on social welfare. In 1976 combined federal, state, and local expenditures for social welfare, including Social Security, accounted for 20.4% of GNP; the proportion fell to 19.3% by 1978. Meanwhile, the poverty population of the U.S. remained about level. According to the Census Bureau, 25.2 million Americans lived below the poverty line ($7,412 annual income for a nonfarm family of four) in 1979. That was about 11 million fewer than in 1964, when the War on Poverty began, but most of the decline occurred during the 1960s. Between 1972 and 1979, the proportion of Americans who were poor fell only from 11.9 to 11.6%.

One possible explanation was that the real value of welfare payments had fallen in recent years because of inflation and budget-conscious legislatures. The average welfare grant for a family of four with no other income dropped from $424 a month in 1973 (measured in 1979 dollars) to $349 in 1979. Whatever reduction had occurred in the poverty ranks was primarily a result of income transfer and social welfare programs, according to a report from the National Advisory Council on Economic Policy. The council also said that the distribution of the poverty population was changing, with minorities and women comprising a greater percentage than they had a decade earlier.

Adding to the ranks of the poor were refugees, chiefly Cubans, Haitians, and Indochinese. Congress authorized grants for education and social services for the refugees, but the action was criticized as "piecemeal." (*See* REFUGEES.)

(DAVID M. MAZIE)

See also Education; Health and Disease; Industrial Review: *Insurance*.
[522.D; 535.B.3.e; 552.D.1]

Soil Conservation:
see Environment

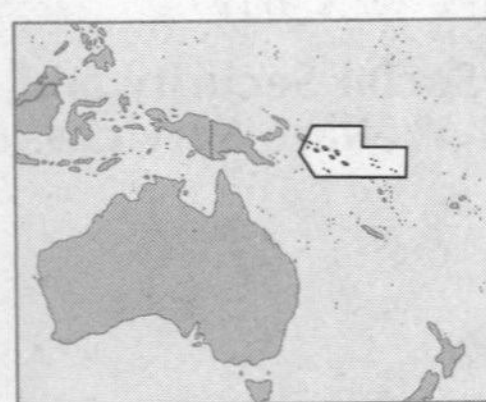

Solomon Islands

Solomon Islands

The Solomon Islands is an independent parliamentary state and member of the Commonwealth of Nations. The nation comprises a 1,450-km (900-mi) chain of islands and atolls in the western Pacific Ocean. Area: 27,556 sq km (10,640 sq mi). Pop. (1980 est.): 227,500 (Melanesian 93.8%; Polynesian 4%; Gilbertese 1.4%; others 1.3%). Cap. and largest city: Honiara (pop., 1980 est., 18,500). Language: English (official), Pidgin (lingua franca), and some 90 local languages and dialects. Religion (1976 census): Anglican 34%; Roman Catholic 19%; South Sea Evangelical 17%; other Protestant 25%; traditional 5%. Queen, Elizabeth II; governor-general in 1980, Baddeley Devesi; prime minister, Peter Kenilorea.

On Aug. 6, 1980, the Solomon Islands had its first general election since achieving independence in 1978. Two-thirds of the legislators who were seeking reelection lost their seats, among them veteran politician David Kausimae, co-leader of the People's Alliance Party. His colleague Solomon Mamaloni, a former chief minister, challenged Peter Kenilorea of the United Party for the prime ministership but was defeated by 25 votes to 5 in a ballot among the 38 members of the Assembly. In Kenilorea's new Cabinet half of the seats went to independent members.

The government sought aid for major hydroelectricity developments for Honiara and planned for an expansion of its joint fishing venture with Japanese interests. It also reached agreement with South Korea on access to its 200-mi exclusive economic zone. Aid and technical cooperation were expected to follow from the visit to China early in the year by Deputy Prime Minister Benedict Kinika. (BARRIE MACDONALD)

SOLOMON ISLANDS

Education. (1979) Primary, pupils 26,973, teachers 1,065; secondary, pupils 3,154, teachers 178; vocational, pupils 336, teachers 37; teacher training, students 129, teachers 23.

Finance and Trade. Monetary unit: Solomon Islands dollar, with (Sept. 22, 1980) a free value of SI$0.81 to U.S. $1 (SI$1.94 = £1 sterling). Budget (total; 1977): revenue SI$12.1 million (excluding SI$8.4 million U.K. aid); expenditure SI$21.8 million. Foreign trade (1978): imports SI$30.9 million; exports SI$30.6 million. Import sources: Australia 33%; Japan 13%; U.K. 10%; Singapore 10%; New Zealand 6%. Export destinations: Japan 24%; U.K. 20%; Singapore 10%; The Netherlands 10%; Western Samoa 6%; U.S. 6%. Main exports: copra 25%; timber 23%; fish 22%; palm oil 15%.

Somalia

Somalia

A republic of northeast Africa, the Somali Democratic Republic, or Somalia, is bounded by the Gulf of Aden, the Indian Ocean, Kenya, Ethiopia, and Djibouti. Area: 638,000 sq km (246,300 sq mi). Pop. (1980 est.): 3,645,000, mainly Hamitic, with Arabic and other admixtures. Cap. and largest city: Mogadishu (pop., 1980 UN est., 377,000). Language: Somali spoken by a great majority (Arabic also official). Religion: predominantly Muslim. President of the Supreme Revolutionary Council in 1980, Maj. Gen. Muhammad Siyad Barrah.

National life in Somalia in 1980 was overshadowed by what the UN High Commissioner for Refugees described as "the worst refugee problem in the world." The background to this situation was the continuing guerrilla war in the Ogaden region of Ethiopia, which was inhabited almost entirely by ethnic Somali nomadic herdsmen. While the Ethiopian forces and their Cuban allies held the towns, the countryside remained largely controlled by the secessionist Western Somali Liberation Front. Fighting flared up repeatedly during the year. Somalia denied accusations by Ethiopia that its regular army was involved while at the same time affirming its continued moral support for the people of the Ogaden and their right to self-determination.

For two years a stream of refugees from the disputed area had been entering Somalia. In 1979–80, as guerrilla activity and reprisals by the Ethiopians (including destruction of villages and livestock) increased, the stream became a flood. By mid-1980 there were 1.5 million refugees in the country, their numbers swollen by members of other ethnic groups from neighbouring Ethiopian provinces. This meant that one person in four in Somalia was now a refugee. In July 743,000 were in 26 government camps and an estimated 800,000 were scattered among the general population; 92% were women and children. The influx continued during the rest of the year.

By July the Somali government had spent some U.S. $38 million out of its own resources on relief. At first international aid was late in arriving and inadequate in amount. Malnutrition was widespread in the camps, and the general population was under stress from shortages, severe inflation, and the failure of the 1979 winter rains. In the latter part of the year, however, more aid began to

SOMALIA

Education. (1978–79) Primary, pupils 56,798, teachers 4,014; secondary, pupils 3,361, teachers 731; vocational, pupils 1,098, teachers 333; teacher training, students 902, teachers 162; higher (1977–78), students 299.

Finance. Monetary unit: Somali shilling, with (Sept. 22, 1980) a par value of 6.295 Somali shillings to U.S. $1 (free rate of 15.13 Somali shillings = £1 sterling). Gold, SDR's, and foreign exchange (May 1980) U.S. $81 million. Budget (total; 1980 est.): revenue 1,935,000,000 Somali shillings; expenditure 2,479,000,000 Somali shillings. Cost of living (Mogadishu; 1975 = 100; April 1980) 244.1.

Foreign Trade. (1979) Imports 2,480,800,000 Somali shillings; exports 667.4 million Somali shillings. Import sources (1978): Italy 30%; West Germany 11%; U.K 10%; Iraq 5%; The Netherlands 5%; Kenya 5%. Export destinations (1978): Saudi Arabia 86%; Italy 8%. Main exports (1978): livestock 83%; bananas 9%.

Transport and Communications. Roads (1973) *c.* 17,100 km. Motor vehicles in use (1972): passenger 8,000; commercial (including buses) 8,000. There are no railways. Air traffic (1978): 22 million passenger-km; freight 300,000 net ton-km. Shipping (1979): merchant vessels 100 gross tons and over 15; gross tonnage 54,895. Telephones (Jan. 1971) *c.* 5,000. Radio receivers (Dec. 1977) 75,000.

Agriculture. Production (in 000; metric tons; 1979): corn *c.* 100; sorghum *c.* 100; cassava *c.* 30; sesame seed *c.* 25; sugar, raw value (1978) *c.* 20; bananas *c.* 150; goat's milk *c.* 276. Livestock (in 000; 1978): cattle *c.* 4,000; sheep *c.* 9,900; goats *c.* 16,400; camels *c.* 5,400.

arrive, mainly from the European Economic Community, which assigned the greater part of its East African food aid to Somalia, and from the U.S.

In August, after months of negotiation, Somalia and the U.S. initialed an agreement granting the latter use of the naval base at Berbera. In return, Somalia was to receive $20 million in military and $25 million in general credits. The government gave a "firm assurance" that neither regular Somali troops nor U.S. equipment would be used in the Ogaden.

In October Pres. Muhammad Siyad Barrah declared a national state of emergency. This was necessary, he said, in order to crack down on "opportunists" who were using tribalism and corruption to threaten the stability of the state. The People's Assembly, elected for the first time in December 1979, was suspended, and power returned to the Supreme Revolutionary Council of 17 senior military officers, which had ruled from the 1969 revolution until 1976. Its tasks now included the reorganization of state agencies and countering acts of sabotage. It would be supported by district revolutionary committees, composed of party leaders and army and police officers, with power to imprison anyone contravening their directives.

(VIRGINIA R. LULING)

South Africa

The Republic. Occupying the southern tip of Africa, South Africa is bounded by South West Africa/Namibia, Botswana, Zimbabwe, Mozambique, and Swaziland and by the Atlantic and Indian oceans on the west and east. South Africa entirely surrounds Lesotho and partially surrounds the three former Bantu homelands of Transkei (independent Oct. 26, 1976), Bophuthatswana (independent Dec. 6, 1977), and Venda (independent Sept. 13, 1979), although the independence of the latter three is not recognized by the international community. Walvis Bay, part of Cape Province since 1910 but administered as part of South West Africa since 1922, was returned to the direct control of Cape Province on Sept. 1, 1977. Area (including Walvis Bay but excluding the three former homelands): 1,133,759 sq km (438,073 sq mi). Pop. (1980 prelim.): 23,772,000 (excluding the three homelands), including black (Bantu) 67%, white 19%, Coloured 11%, Asian 3%. Executive cap.: Pretoria (pop., 1980 prelim., 528,000); judical cap.: Bloemfontein (pop., 1978 est., 174,500); legislative cap.: Cape Town (pop., 1978 est., 892,200). Largest city: Johannesburg (pop., 1980 prelim., 1,536,000). Language: Afrikaans and English (official); Bantu languages predominate. Religion: mainly Christian. State president in 1980, Marais Viljoen; prime minister, P. W. Botha.

DOMESTIC AFFAIRS. Legislation enacted in 1980 abolished the 70-year-old second legislative chamber, the Senate, and replaced it with a multiracial advisory President's Council of 54 government-nominated members selected from the white, Coloured, Indian, and Chinese communities. No black representatives were included. A separate black advisory council was to be consulted by the President's Council when necessary. The noninclusion of blacks was criticized by the opposition Progressive Federal Party (PFP). The black, Coloured, and Indian organizations would not cooperate in forming the council. The government then dropped the black advisory council. The President's Council was to become operative on Jan. 1, 1981, under the chairmanship of the vice-state president—a newly created office filled by A. L. Schlebusch, former minister of justice and of the interior and chairman of the original constitutional committee. Functioning through committees, the council would advise the state president on matters referred to it or in the national interest, with the Cabinet and Parliament normally making the final decisions.

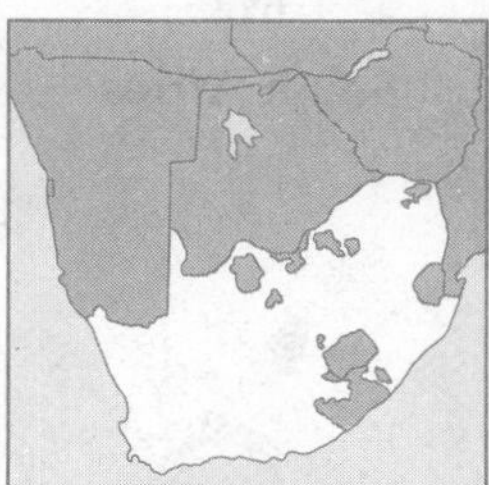
South Africa

Under the same legislation the Cabinet was enlarged from 18 to 20 and Parliament—the single-chamber Assembly—by 12 members, 4 nominated by the state president and 8 elected by the existing parties in proportion to their numbers. This change gave the ruling party 11 additional members. A further change was the disbandment of the Coloured Persons' Representative Council, not to be replaced with a nominated Coloured Persons' Council, in view of Coloured opposition. During a Cabinet reshuffle in August Magnus Malan, former chief of the Defense Force, became minister of defense, and Gerrit Viljoen, former administrator general of Namibia, was named minister of national education. By-elections followed these changes, and the small South African Party was disbanded.

The concept of a "constellation of states," envisioning the ultimate objective of a "common market" for southern Africa, was furthered by an agreement between South Africa and leaders of the three independent homelands in July to establish full regional cooperation. A multilateral bank for southern Africa was to be established and existing development corporations reorganized under a constellation committee headed by Gerhardus de Kock, governor-designate of the South African Reserve Bank. The black homelands jointly pleaded with the government to delay such moves until

JOHN RUBYTHON—GAMMA/LIAISON

Race-related riots plagued Soweto and other South African areas, despite some relaxation of apartheid initiated by Prime Minister P. W. Botha.

South Africa's internal problems—with particular reference to themselves—had been solved. The semiofficial Bureau for Economic Research, Cooperation, and Development reported that separate economies could not be created for the homelands and advocated drastic structural changes, including joint management of industrial border areas.

Policy trended toward decentralized local government within an overall confederal structure in which the homelands, as well as the urban black communities, could be accommodated. Meanwhile, the chief minister of the Ciskei, Chief Lennox Sebe, intimated that he was prepared to accept independence for the homeland subject to retention of South African citizenship rights by Ciskeians living outside the homeland and to the transfer of more land to the Ciskei. The Ciskei voted overwhelmingly for independence in a referendum held in December.

With nearly half of the Ciskeians living outside the borders of the homeland, Sebe's decision to opt for independence, even on his stated terms, drew sharp criticism from other homeland leaders such as Gatsha Buthelezi (KwaZulu), who were asserting their own claims. Prime Minister P. W. Botha said that it was not government policy to press the homelands to become independent. They had the right of self-determination while cooperating within a "constellation of states." Provisional proposals to consolidate the Ciskei, issued on October 31, provided for the addition of 100,000 ha (250,000 ac) of land to the territory and the incorporation of the century-old settlers' city of King William's Town (est. pop. 22,680, of whom 50% were white). In KwaZulu a nonofficial commission sponsored by Buthelezi's Inkatha movement was to seek cooperation and possible union between the homeland and the province of Natal.

Tentative steps were taken during the year to relax policies affecting the employment and movement of black workers in "white" urban areas and also affecting restrictions on the sharing of public facilities and racially mixed sports. There was mounting public opposition to the rigid enforcement of the Group Areas Act in such cases as the occupation by nonwhites of flats or other dwellings in "white" areas and of their removal from such areas to make way for whites. A former postmaster general, Louis Rive, was appointed coordinator of far-reaching projects to improve life in the Soweto complex near Johannesburg, with its estimated million black inhabitants. Funds were earmarked for housing, electrification, and the building of commercial and industrial centres there. It was proposed to grant black townships local government with municipal status through town or village councils.

With the acceptance of the right of black workers to join or form legally recognized trade unions, some registered unions in 1980 admitted black members. In addition to the mixed groups, several black unions sought registration under the amended industrial legislation. For the first time, representatives of black labour sat on the industrial council of the major iron, steel, engineering, and metallurgical industries. Job reservation, the long-standing barrier to the entry of black workers into skilled occupations, was practically abolished. In general, the training of badly needed black skilled workers was encouraged, but in mining, determined white trade union opposition still imposed a colour bar. A government-sponsored project entitled Manpower 2000 envisioned far-reaching developments in training and better manpower utilization of all races.

The changes raised expectations of more radical reforms. Added emphasis was given to those expectations by the publication of a judge's report on the Soweto riots of 1976 criticizing the government's role. It coincided with a wave of unrest and violence in black and Coloured communities in many parts of the country which originated primarily, as in 1976, in the admittedly inadequate system of nonwhite education. School-class boycotts in Soweto and on a larger scale in the Cape Peninsula, with the accompanying disorders, were followed by similar disturbances in other areas, including South West Africa/Namibia and some of the black homelands. As the unrest dragged on, particularly in the Eastern Cape, it gradually also involved industries and transportation services. The attempts to restore order gave rise to a growing loss of life and limb. The government blamed behind-the-scenes agitators and closed down many schools in the affected areas indefinitely. Through the Human Sciences Re-

SOUTH AFRICA

Education. (1980) Primary, pupils 4,370,474; secondary, pupils 1,183,540; vocational, pupils 33,517; primary, secondary, and vocational, teachers 167,797; higher, students 218,321, teaching staff 15,803.

Finance. Monetary unit: rand, with (Sept. 22, 1980) a free rate of R 0.75 to U.S. $1 (R 1.81 = £1 sterling). Gold, SDR's, and foreign exchange (June 1980) U.S. $1,373,000,000. Budget (1979 actual): revenue R 9,729,000,000; expenditure R 11,839,000,000. Gross national product (1979) R 46,136,000,000. Money supply (June 1980) R 6,884,000,000. Cost of living (1975 = 100; June 1980) 173.2.

Foreign Trade. (Excluding crude oil and products; 1979) Imports R 7,562,000,000; exports R 15,462,000,000. Import sources: West Germany 19%; U.K. 18%; U.S. 18%; Japan 11%; France 7%. Export destinations (excluding gold): Switzerland 16%; U.S. 15%; U.K. 10%; Japan 10%; West Germany 10%. Main exports: gold specie *c.* 39%; nonferrous metals and ores 11%; food 8%; gold coin 8%; diamonds 8%; iron and steel 7%.

Transport and Communications. Roads (1978) 185,489 km. Motor vehicles in use (1979): passenger 2,310,900; commercial 858,300. Railways: (1979) 19,910 km; freight traffic (including Namibia; 1978) 80,963,000,000 net ton-km. Air traffic (1979): 8,281,000,000 passenger-km; freight 256.6 million net ton-km. Shipping (1979): merchant vessels 100 gross tons and over 286; gross tonnage 741,469. Telephones (March 1978) 2,320,000. Radio receivers (Dec. 1977) 2.5 million. Television receivers (Dec. 1978) *c.* 1,250,000.

Agriculture. Production (in 000; metric tons; 1979): corn 8,240; wheat 2,220; sorghum 354; potatoes *c.* 750; tomatoes 265; sugar, raw value *c.* 2,100; peanuts 197; sunflower seed 315; oranges 560; grapefruit 106; pineapples *c.* 185; apples 379; grapes *c.* 1,130; tobacco 45; cotton, lint 47; wool 56; milk *c.* 2,550; meat *c.* 990; fish catch (1978) 628. Livestock (in 000; June 1979): cattle *c.* 13,200; sheep *c.* 31,500; pigs *c.* 1,500; goats *c.* 5,300; horses (1978) *c.* 225; chickens *c.* 29,000.

Industry. Index of manufacturing production (1975 = 100; 1979) 105. Fuel and power (in 000; 1978): coal (metric tons) 90,360; manufactured gas (cu m; 1977) *c.* 3,500,000; electricity (kw-hr) 84,765,000. Production (in 000; metric tons; 1978): cement 6,824; iron ore (60–65% metal content; 1979) 31,565; pig iron 7,020; crude steel (1979) 8,857; copper 152; chrome ore (oxide content; 1979) 1,450; manganese ore (metal content; 1979) 2,302; uranium (1977) 6.7; gold (troy oz; 1979) 22,610; diamonds (metric carats; 1979) 8,392; asbestos (1979) 247; petroleum products (1977) *c.* 12,690; fertilizers (nutrient content; 1978–79) nitrogenous *c.* 451, phosphate *c.* 425; newsprint 240; fish meal (including Namibia; 1977) 176.

search Council it set up a commission of inquiry into the educational system, covering all races.

In a wider context South Africa had its share of political terrorism. In a Pretoria suburb a bank was occupied and hostages were held, with a resultant loss of life. A series of explosions at Sasol oil-from-coal installations caused damage estimated at about R 6 million. Such acts of sabotage were attributed to underground political movements.

Foreign Relations. Efforts continued intermittently to reach an agreement on the future of South West Africa/Namibia in terms of an internationally accepted independence for the territory. Proposals by UN Secretary-General Kurt Waldheim for a cease-fire in the guerrilla warfare, a demilitarized zone on the Namibia-Angola border to be patrolled by a UN Transition Assistance Group (UNTAG), and a UN-supervised election for a constituent assembly were modified from time to time to meet South African objections. These centred mainly on the composition and functions of UNTAG, the location and monitoring of the South West Africa People's Organization (SWAPO) guerrilla forces during the cease-fire and transition period, and what South Africa held to be the UN's attitude of partiality toward SWAPO.

The negotiations reached a virtual deadlock in midyear. In late October a UN team headed by Brian Urquhart, undersecretary for special political affairs, arrived in Pretoria on a mission to end the stalemate and secure a final timetable for implementing the settlement proposals. The mission sounded out internal Namibian opinion and left the door open for the next move by Waldheim and the Security Council, where there were pressures for mandatory sanctions after the UN initiative failed. Meanwhile, the National Assembly in the Namibian capital of Windhoek, dominated by the Democratic Turnhalle Alliance (DTA), elected a multiparty Council of Ministers with executive powers, headed by Dirk Mudge, DTA leader. Antidiscrimination legislation was adopted, and provision was made for the introduction of compulsory military service for all races. The territory established its own defense department, subject to the South African Defense Force's remaining responsible for security as long as required. Fighting in the "operational area" continued unremittingly, with increasingly heavy losses for SWAPO in border skirmishes and in their bases farther afield.

Newly independent Zimbabwe broke off diplomatic and sports relations with South Africa but maintained economic, tourist, and other ties under special arrangements. Its prime minister, Robert Mugabe (*see* Biographies), made it clear that his sympathies lay with South African resistance movements. They would receive his support but would not be allowed to use Zimbabwe as a springboard for attacks on South Africa, he declared. Reacting against South African plans for a regional "constellation of states," Zimbabwe joined eight other southern African nations in considering steps to reduce their dependence on South Africa in trade, transport, and communications. The other countries were Angola, Botswana, Malawi, Mozambique, Swaziland, Tanzania, Zambia, and Lesotho. The same countries, with the exception of Angola and Tanzania, set up a commission to consider ways of checking the flow of migrant labour to South Africa, even though it formed an important source of revenue for them.

An exchange of visits by the prime ministers of South Africa and Taiwan cemented existing ties, and agreements were concluded on trade, technology, and culture; it was also envisioned, without formal agreements, that there would be military cooperation whenever possible. Also during the year trade and cultural links with Israel were further expanded.

On September 29 the Appeal Court set aside the conviction and sentence of six years in prison passed on Eschel Mostert Rhoodie in the Transvaal Supreme Court in October 1979 on charges of alleged fraud. Rhoodie had been the secretary of the former Department of Information, the activities of which both in and outside South Africa were the centre of investigation by government commissions and of a political storm in 1978–79.

The Economy. On March 26 the minister of finance, Owen Horwood, presented the 1980 budget—totaling R 13 billion, with 16% for defense—against a background of strong economic revival stimulated by higher gold prices and the long-term effects of the fiscal discipline of the previous years. Significant indicators were a record balance of payments surplus, increased foreign reserve holdings, buoyant state revenue and tax remissions, and more flexible credit policies. These conditions, accompanied by an appreciable improvement in South Africa's international credit standing, were maintained during the year. An overall growth rate of 7.5% was projected. New mining developments in gold, uranium, and other basic minerals were begun or planned, and there was a resurgence of industrial activity, which helped to relieve unemployment.

Negative factors in the South African economy were the serious shortage of skilled labour and the high rate of inflation, the latter aggravated by excessive liquidity and heavy consumer spending. As the cost of living rose, labour unrest and wage demands increased. Toward the end of the year a curb on liquidity was advocated by the Reserve Bank. The government planned to establish a privately managed, nonracial, small-business development corporation with state assistance. It was also proposed to allow the creation of multiracial trading zones in central city areas, free from the restrictions of racial separation.

Bophuthatswana. The republic of Bophuthatswana consists of six discontinuous, landlocked geographic units, one of which borders Botswana on the northwest; it is otherwise entirely surrounded by South Africa. Area: 40,430 sq km (15,610 sq mi). Pop. (1978 est.): 1,245,000, including 99.6% Bantu, of whom Tswana 69.8%, Northern Sotho 7.5%. Cap.: Mmabatho. Largest city: Ga-Rankuwa (pop., 1973 est., 64,200). Languages (official): Central Tswana, English, Afrikaans. Religion: predominantly Christian (Methodist, Lutheran, Anglican, and Bantu Christian churches). President in 1980, Lucas Mangope.

Legislative provision was made by South Africa to transfer to Bophuthatswana some farms bought in earlier years as a first step toward territorial consolidation. Also, the historic town of Mafeking and the surrounding area, with a population of 27,700 (including 5,400 whites), was incorporated into the republic, a significant voluntary acceptance by white residents of black rule. The town was renamed Mafikeng, a Tswana word meaning "place of stones." Consolidating the fragmented territory remained for futher interstate discussions.

Bophuthatswana attracted some R 200 million in investment capital for industrial projects, including an explosives factory in a new industrial township. A second industrial area was laid out, and a university was established for academic and advanced technical education. Loans were successfully floated in South Africa and Switzerland. A law revision commission was appointed.

Transkei. Bordering the Indian Ocean and surrounded on land by South Africa, Transkei comprises three discontinuous geographic units, two of which are landlocked. Area: 41,002 sq km (15,831 sq mi). Pop. (1978 est.): 2,178,000, including (1970) Bantu 99%, of whom 95% were Xhosa. Cap. and largest city: Umtata (pop., 1978 est., 30,000). Language: Xhosa (official); English and Sesotho may be used for official purposes as well. Religion: Christian 65.8%, of which Methodist 25.2%; non-Christian 13.8%; 20.4% unspecified. President in 1980, Kaiser Daliwonga Matanzima; prime minister, George Matanzima.

Diplomatic relations with South Africa, broken off by Transkei in 1978, were restored in March 1980. Some territorial adjustments in favour of Transkei, enacted by South Africa in February, facilitated this step. Subsidies to the republic by South Africa totaled R 572 million for the three years of independence. South Africa in 1980 considered further development aid and, in agreement with Transkei, instituted improved control of such funds. Against a background of internal political controversy and economic problems, the Transkei government sought international recognition.

Venda. The independent republic of Venda comprises two geographic units in extreme northeastern South Africa separated by a narrow corridor belonging to its eastern neighbour, the Gazankulu homeland. Area: 7,184 sq km (2,448 sq mi). Pop. (1978 est.): 357,000, including (1970) 90% Venda, 6% Shangaan, and 3% Northern Sotho. Cap.: Thohoyandou (replacing Sibasa). Largest town, Makearela (pop., 1976 est., 1,972). Language (official): Venda, English, and Afrikaans. Religion: traditional religions predominate; Christian minority. President in 1980, Patrick Mphephu.

Agriculture, Venda's major economic asset along with coal, was to be developed by a multimillion-rand consortium, it was announced in October. Remoteness from South African markets, high transport costs, and a primitive economy were the main stumbling blocks to development of the republic, and these were only partly counterbalanced by cheap labour and tax inducements offered by the Venda Development Corporation. About two-thirds of the active male population worked outside the country. There were minor boundary adjustments as a result of South African legislation in 1980. (LOUIS HOTZ)

See also Dependent States.

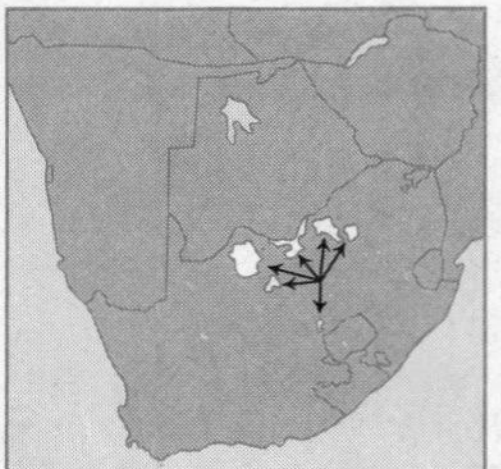
Bophuthatswana

BOPHUTHATSWANA

Education. Primary, pupils (1976) 326,826, teachers 5,329; secondary, pupils (1976) 58,930, teachers 1,568; vocational (1973), students 471, teachers 37; teacher training, students (1976) 3,035; secondary and teacher training, teachers (1973) 771; higher, students (1973) 167.

Finance and Trade. Monetary unit: South African rand, with (Sept. 22, 1980) a free rate of R 0.75 to U.S. $1 (R 1.81 = £1 sterling). Budget (1977–78) balanced at R 72 million. Foreign trade included in South Africa.

Transkei

TRANSKEI

Education. (1978) Primary, pupils 647,985, teachers 12,627; secondary, pupils 33,636, teachers 1,179; vocational, pupils 908, teachers 59; teacher training, students 3,034, teachers 126; higher, students 503, teaching staff 96.

Finance and Trade. Monetary unit: South African rand. Budget (total; 1978–79 est.): revenue R 225 million; expenditure R 328 million. Most trade is with South Africa.

Venda

VENDA

Education. (1978) Primary, pupils 107,711, teachers 2,300; secondary, pupils 23,460, teachers 555; vocational, pupils 323; teacher training, students 674.

Finance and Trade. Monetary unit: South African rand. Budget (1979–80) balanced at R 36.7 million. Most trade is with South Africa.

Southeast Asian Affairs

Defense and security remained Southeast Asia's primary preoccupation throughout 1980. Already alarmed by Vietnam's invasion of Cambodia in December 1978, members of the Association of Southeast Asian Nations (ASEAN) had their worst fears confirmed when Vietnamese troops staged a lightning military strike into Thailand in June. Its effect was summed up by Singapore Deputy Prime Minister Sinnathamby Rajaratnam when he said, "I would like publicly to thank Vietnam for what it did: it consolidated ASEAN much more than before."

Vietnamese in Cambodia. ASEAN foreign ministers gathered in Kuala Lumpur within days of the Vietnamese attack on Thailand. Their counterparts from the U.S., Canada, Japan, Australia, and New Zealand also journeyed to the Malaysian capital, demonstrating worldwide concern over the trend of events in the region. Despite earlier differences in policy approaches to Indochina, the ASEAN ministers spoke with one voice in expressing anxiety over the continued presence of Vietnamese troops in Cambodia; deploring Hanoi's failure to heed calls for a political settlement of the Cambodia conflict; noting with grave concern the growing rivalry of outside powers in the region; and calling for an international conference on Cambodia.

Although the ministers' 23-page communiqué and a separate "joint statement on the situation along the Thai-Cambodian border" proclaimed a strong ASEAN stance against Vietnam, many leaders were worried that the latter, in its isolation, would turn even more toward Moscow and get the Soviet Union embroiled yet more deeply in the region's affairs. That in turn could push ASEAN closer to China, leading to an ominous polarization in Southeast Asia.

The grim scenario received a further boost as ASEAN countries plunged as never before into a flurry of intense international lobbying to keep the Vietnam-backed Cambodian government out of Cambodia's UN seat. They succeeded, but the lobbying did not stop. There were reports of a growing recognition at ASEAN's highest echelons that the deposed Pol Pot regime, which continued to occupy the UN seat, was unworthy of support because of its record of genocide. ASEAN began promoting the idea that a non-Communist alternative should be found in Cambodia.

The Thai and Singapore prime ministers led the campaign by trying to enlist China's support for the concept. But there were no definite indications that China would give up its backing of Pol Pot. That and the refusal till the end of the year by former Cambodian head of state Prince Norodom Sihanouk to lead a third force left ASEAN leaders unsure of how the overall security problem in the region would develop.

ASEAN and U.S. Support. In line with this sense of uncertainty, a rethinking of ASEAN's relations with the big powers seemed under way. Many government leaders were of the view that the U.S. should become more involved in regional defense than had the administration of Pres. Jimmy Carter. The Philippine government made no secret of its support of Ronald Reagan in the U.S. presidential election. Even before the shift in its leadership, the U.S. had started restoring its old military presence in Thailand. By midyear U.S. Department of Defense sources indicated that military assistance to all Southeast Asian countries was being increased. From a peak of $161,750,000 in 1977, such assistance to the five ASEAN countries had declined to $106.6 million in 1979. During 1980 it picked up again and was estimated to reach a total in excess of $147 million. There was also an upswing in the sale of weapons to ASEAN countries by the U.S., their principal military supplier.

Relations with the U.S.S.R. If ASEAN countries moved closer to the U.S. during the year, there was a clear cooling off toward the Soviet Union. Singapore took the lead in projecting the view that Moscow was spearheading a new kind of imperialism with Southeast Asia as a prime target. Others did not go quite that far but nevertheless developed reservations about Soviet intentions. China fueled Southeast Asian suspicions about the U.S.S.R. by pointing to Soviet gains in Indochina. In October China's Xinhua (Hsinhua) news agency reported that the number of Tupolev TU-95 heavy bombers stationed by the Soviet Union in Vietnam's giant Cam Ranh Bay base had doubled from two to four; that the Soviet Union used the base as a takeoff point for surveillance flights over Southeast Asia; that flights of Ilyushin IL-62 transports from Vladivostok to Cam Ranh Bay had more than doubled; that "well over 20" Soviet warships were sometimes simultaneously serviced at the port; and that the aircraft carrier "Minsk" put into the port for the first time in September.

The Soviet Union for its part was clearly interested in keeping itself on the right side of Southeast Asian countries and in cautioning them against China's tactics. Describing the visit to China in November by Singapore Prime Minister Lee Kuan Yew as pointless, a Moscow commentator said: "To regard Beijing [Peking] as a kind mother who will understand the concerns of ASEAN means cherishing illusions." According to diplomatic circles, the Soviet Union wished to maintain a dialogue with Southeast Asian countries because it was worried that China might gain ground in the region through false pretenses. It was also apprehensive of the return of U.S. influence to the area.

Relations with China. With China itself, Southeast Asian countries maintained close commercial and consular relations, attracted by Beijing's pragmatic shift to economic modernization. But the view persisted that the long-term threat to the region's stability came from China. Underlying this fear was China's insistence that its relations with and support of the underground Communist groups in most Southeast Asian counties would not be affected by the state-to-state relations it was now fostering with the governments of the region. During his visit to China in November Lee Kuan Yew planned to challenge this position in a banquet speech. But his Chinese hosts persuaded him to cancel the speech and instead discuss the matter with national leader Deng Xiaoping (Teng Hsiao-p'ing) in private.

In November Indonesia's First Admiral Suwarso publicly warned that China had finalized plans to expand its naval presence off Southeast Asia, purportedly to counter the growing Soviet naval strength there and to protect its disputed claims to marine oil fields and other resources in the area. He said that such an enlargement of China's fleet would pose a security threat to ASEAN nations and increase the risk of superpower tension.

Approaches to Japan and Australia. Japan and Australia were the other outside powers that loomed large on Southeast Asia's horizon during the year. ASEAN had running arguments with both countries—with Japan because of its apparent stinginess in regard to promised aid, and with Australia over its protectionist trade and commercial policies. Lee Kuan Yew even had a public exchange of hot words with Australian Prime Minister Malcolm Fraser while they were returning from the Commonwealth regional meeting in New Delhi, India, in September. However, ASEAN countries seemed interested in moving closer to Japan and Australia through the Pacific Community concept, promoted by the latter two countries in tandem with the U.S. ASEAN representatives attended an unofficial seminar held in Canberra in February to discuss the concept.

Economic Developments. The region's relations with Europe, largely confined to trade and commerce, were consolidated in March when an ASEAN-European Economic Community cooperation agreement was signed. It was hailed as a landmark heralding a new stage of formalized arrangements with European countries on an equitable footing. The agreement, to last for five years, offered ASEAN the prospect of liberal terms for trade, investment, and technological cooperation.

Southeast and East Asia together maintained their position as the world's most dynamic growth area. While Japan, Taiwan, and Hong Kong were leaders in their fields, Southeast Asian countries contributed to the overall picture. Singapore led the region with an estimated growth rate of 8%, while Malaysia followed with 7%. Indonesia and the Philippines each registered a rate of growth of about 5%. Thailand alone was in some difficulty due to a ruinous succession of drought and flood and a crushing refugee burden.

In April the Asian Development Bank released its annual report providing final figures for 1979 for the whole of Asia. Growth rates had risen, it noted, in Singapore (9.3% from 8.6% in 1978) and Malaysia (8.1% from 7.4%). They declined in Indonesia (4.9% from 7.2%), the Philippines (5.7% from 5.8%), and Thailand (6.5% from 12%), largely because of a slowdown in agriculture. While the Asia-wide inflation rate rose to 11.6%, Indonesia recorded the highest at 21.8% followed by the Philippines at 18.8%.

ASEAN bankers took a major step toward regional industrialization in February when they approved plans to create an ASEAN Financial Corporation and an ASEAN bankers' acceptance market. The wholly ASEAN-owned corporation, with an initial capitalization of $50 million, was intended to provide capital and support services to industrial ventures catering to three or more ASEAN members. The acceptance market's aim was to promote trade within the group.

(T. J. S. GEORGE)

See also articles on the various countries.
[976.B]

Space Exploration

The year 1980 marked the 20th anniversary of the Yuri Gagarin Cosmonaut Training Centre of the U.S.S.R. During the past two decades the centre had trained more than 50 cosmonauts of the Soviet Union as well as those from Eastern European countries, France, and Cuba. The year also was the 35th anniversary of the U.S. National Aeronautics and Space Administration's (NASA's) Wallops Flight Center on Wallops Island, Va. Its first research rocket, a solid-propellant Tiamat, was launched on July 4, 1945. Two of the earliest U.S. animal experiments in space medicine, the monkeys Sam and Miss Sam, were launched in the Mercury spacecraft from the centre in 1959 and 1960.

On May 15 Erik Quistgaard assumed his duties as the new director general of the European Space Agency (ESA). A Dane, the new director general had varied experience in engineering companies in Denmark, the U.S., and Sweden. The failure of Japan's Ayame 2 communications satellite to achieve orbit in February prompted Akiyoshi Matsuura, chairman of the Japanese National Space Development Agency, to submit his resignation. Ayame 1, launched in 1979, was also lost.

Manned Flight. Clearly the most significant event in manned space flight during 1980 was the record-breaking 185 days spent aboard the Salyut 6 space station by Soviet cosmonauts Valery V. Ryumin and Leonid I. Popov. The pair returned to Earth in the Soyuz 37 spacecraft on October 11.

Ryumin had previously spent 2 days in space in 1977 and 175 days aboard the space station in 1979, giving him a total of 362 days. Neither cosmonaut evidenced any disability on medical examination at the landing site. Physicians were, however, baffled by the fact that both men had gained weight. The two men each grew an inch, but soon lost it as they adjusted to the Earth's gravity.

During their six months in space, Ryumin and Popov performed a number of scientific and technological experiments. Primary among them were the growing of various crystals in the weightless environment in an effort to produce better semiconductor materials and the production of polyurethane foam structures. Among the life science experiments were studies of the production and effect of interferon in human cells. The end of the mission brought the number of Soviet man-hours in space to 45,564, more than double the U.S. total of 22,494.

The Salyut 6, which began its fourth year in orbit on September 29, was visited by six manned spacecraft and six unmanned spacecraft between December 1979 and November 1980. Among them was an improved T model of the Soyuz spacecraft. Aboard it were Soviet cosmonauts Yury V. Malyshev and Vladimir V. Aksenov. The spacecraft had an onboard computer, an improved and simplified propulsion and maneuvering system, solar-cell power arrays, and a powerful retrorocket for soft landings. The two men tested the T-2 extensively before docking with the Salyut 6. They returned to Earth aboard it on June 9.

Manned space flight by the U.S. was nonexistent during the year, as it had been since 1975. Optimistically, however, NASA began recruiting for mission specialists and pilot astronauts. A total of 3,465 men and women applied, and 19 were selected in May. Eight were pilots, all male, and 11 were mission specialists, of whom 2 were female.

Experiments for the first operational Spacelab mission late in 1982 were selected by NASA and ESA in May. The 37 scientific experiments were in the fields of atmospheric physics and Earth observations, astronomy and solar physics, materials science and technology, space plasma physics, and the life sciences. Of the total, 13 were to be sponsored by NASA and 24 by ESA.

Japan announced that its first astronaut would engage in materials-processing experiments aboard Spacelab in 1985. China confirmed that it had astronauts and astronaut instructors undergoing active training in much the same manner as those of the U.S.S.R. and U.S. France revealed that Lieut. Col. Jean-Loup Chrétien, a test pilot, and Maj. Patrick Baudry, a jet pilot, would be its astronaut candidates for a joint space flight with the Soviets in 1982.

South West Africa: *see* Dependent States; South Africa

Soviet Literature: *see* Literature

Soviet Union: *see* Union of Soviet Socialist Republics

WIDE WORLD

Soviet cosmonauts Valery V. Ryumin (left) and Leonid I. Popov prepare for their space flight to the orbiting space station Salyut 6. They returned to Earth on October 11 after a record 185 days in space.

Launch Vehicles. The year was a frustrating one for NASA's trouble-plagued space shuttle. By the end of the year developmental costs of the program had increased by 25% in terms of fiscal year 1971 dollars, or $6.4 billion. The increase could be attributed to insufficient funding of the original program and to unexpected technological problems. In addition to troubles with the main engine of the shuttle orbiter, the problem of bonding the heat-shield tiles to the vehicle proved to be much more complicated and time-consuming than originally foreseen. There were 32,000 tiles, each of which had to be hand-bonded to the orbiter.

The decision was made as 1979 ended to incorporate an auxiliary propulsion system on the aft end of the orbiter's liquid propellant tank. The additional thrust provided by the system would permit the shuttle to lift payloads weighing between 16,000 and 19,000 kg (35,000–42,000 lb) into low-Earth orbit when launched at a 98° angle and return payloads weighing as much as 12,000 kg (26,000 lb) from such orbit. The extra capability was needed to launch the U.S. Air Force's improved KH-11 reconnaissance satellite. .The shuttle was moved to its launch site at Cape Canaveral, Florida, in December.

The usually well-informed magazine *Aviation Week & Space Technology,* in its June 16, 1980, issue made public what had long been known to the intelligence agencies of the West. The U.S.S.R. had under development a huge launch vehicle that seemed destined to play an important role in that nation's interplanetary space programs for decades to come. The vehicle was approximately 90 m (300 ft) long and 15 m (50 ft) in diameter at the base. It was designed to be capable of lifting 99,000 kg (220,000 lb) into low-Earth orbit. Also revealed in 1980 was the Soviets' two-man, reusable space shuttle to be launched by an expendable rocket.

Unmanned Satellites. As 1979 ended, West Germany and France were making plans with far-reaching consequences in the field of communications satellite technology. The two nations were organizing a joint venture to build, market, and manage a direct broadcast television satellite system. Within the next decade it might comprise 12 to 15 satellites in orbit. Two operational satellites, one each built by West Germany and France, were scheduled to be launched by the end of 1985.

Sweden announced that it would expand its national space program by designing and building the Viking magnetospheric research satellite, scheduled for launch in May 1984 aboard a French Ariane launch vehicle. Viking would be designed to study the aurora borealis.

Launched on Oct. 30, 1979, NASA's Magsat satellite proved to be a valuable scientific tool for the U.S. Geological Survey. Data from it helped compile the most accurate maps ever produced of the Earth's magnetic field. Such information is of great assistance to geologists searching for new mineral and petroleum deposits.

The successful HEAO-1 satellite completed its 17-month mission and reentered the atmosphere in January 1979. In processing the data it gathered, scientists in 1980 discovered a huge halo of superheated gas with a diameter of 1,000 light-years surrounding the Northern Cross constellation. The gas appeared to have a temperature of 2,000,000° C (3,600,000° F).

A scientific satellite designed to study the ultraviolet and X-ray radiation from the Sun during its maximum period of activity was launched on February 14. Solar Maximum Mission satellite (SMM) provided scientists with data that complemented that obtained by Skylab, which orbited during the period of the Sun's minimum activity. On May 21 SMM recorded a 40-minute solar flare, one of the largest ever detected.

Space Probes. Feb. 22, 1980, was an exceptionally clear day on Mars, and the Viking 1 orbiter probe noted it well. Photomosaics revealed two meteorologic features never before seen on the planet. One of them was a sharp, dark line, curving north and east from the volcano Arsia Mons in the Tharsis Ridge. Unsure of what it was, scientists suggested it could be either a weather front or an atmospheric shock wave. Also pictured were

Major Satellites and Space Probes Launched Oct. 1, 1979–Sept. 30, 1980

Name/country/ launch vehicle/ scientific designation	Launch date, lifetime*	Physical characteristics: Weight in kg†	Shape	Diameter in m†	Length or height in m†	Experiments	Orbital elements: Perigee in km†	Apogee in km†	Period (min)	Inclination to Equator (degrees)
Magsat/U.S./Scout/ 1979-094A	10/30/79 6/11/80	277 (611)	octagon with four panels	0.77 (2.53)	1.64 (5.38)	Measure near-Earth magnetic field and crustal anomalies of Earth	348 (216)	550 (342)	93.6	96.8
Meteor-2 (5)/U.S.S.R./A I/ 1979-095A	10/31/79	2,750 (6,063)	cylinder with two panels	1.5 (4.92)	5 (16.4)	Meteorological satellite	877 (545)	904 (562)	102.6	81.2
Intercosmos 20/U.S.S.R./C I/ 1979-096A	11/1/79	550 (1,213)	octagonal ellipsoid (probably)	1.8 (5.91)	1.5 (4.92)	International experiment concerning ocean and land resources	467 (290)	523 (325)	94.4	74
Satcom C/U.S./Delta/ 1979-101A	12/7/79	895 (1,973)	cube with two panels	1.6 (5.25)	1.2 (3.94)	Communications satellite	152 (94)	35,772 (22,228)	629.9	23.8
Soyuz-T (1)/U.S.S.R./A II/ 1979-103A	12/16/79 3/25/80	‡	sphere and cone	2.2 (7.22)	7.5 (24.61)	Unmanned test of modified Soyuz spacecraft	364 (226)	376 (234)	92	51.6
Horizon 3/U.S.S.R./D le/ 1979-105A	12/28/79	‡	cylinder with two panels	‡	‡	Communications satellite at synchronous altitude	36,240 (22,518)	36,339 (22,580)	1,461.9	0.8
Molniya-1 (46)/U.S.S.R./A IIe/ 1980-002A	1/11/80	1,000 (2,205)	cylinder with cone and six panels	1.5 (4.92)	3.4 (11.15)	Communications satellite	592 (368)	39,751 (24,700)	717.6	62.9
Fleetsatcom 3/U.S./Atlas Centaur/1980-004A	1/18/80	1,876 (4,136)	hexagonal cylinder	2.4 (7.87)	1.3 (4.27)	Communications satellite	35,743 (22,210)	35,833 (22,266)	1,436.2	2.6
NavStar 5/U.S./Atlas F/ 1980-011A	2/9/80	430 (948)	cube with two solar panels	1.2 (3.94)	1.8 (5.91)	Navigation satellite	20,143 (12,516)	20,220 (12,564)	718	53.2
SMM/U.S./Delta/ 1980-014A	2/14/80	2,316 (5,105)	octagonal box with two panels	2.3 (7.55)	4 (13.12)	Studies of the Sun in its active period	563 (350)	570 (354)	96	28.6
Ayame 2/Japan/Nu-1/ 1980-018A	2/22/80	260 (573)	cylinder	1 (3.28)	1.5 (4.92)	Experimental communications satellite	35,390 (21,990)	35,399 (21,996)	1,441.6	0.5
Progress 8/U.S.S.R./A II/ 1980-024A	3/27/80 4/26/80	7,000 (15,432)	sphere and cone-cylinder	2.2 (7.22)	8 (26.25)	Delivered supplies to Salyut 6 space station	180 (112)	260 (162)	88.8	51.6
Soyuz 35/U.S.S.R./A II/ 1980-027A	4/9/80 6/3/80	6,500 (14,330)	sphere and cylinder	2.2 (7.22)	7.5 (24.61)	Ferried crew to Salyut 6 space station	276 (171)	315 (196)	90.3	51.6
NavStar 6/U.S./Atlas Agena/ 1980-032A	4/26/80	430 (948)	cube with two solar panels	1.2 (3.94)	1.8 (5.91)	Navigation satellite	20,002 (12,429)	20,360 (12,651)	718	62.9
Progress 9/U.S.S.R./A II/ 1980-033A	4/27/80 5/22/80	7,000 (15,432)	sphere and cone	2.2 (7.22)	8 (26.25)	Ferried supplies to Salyut 6 space station	192 (119)	275 (171)	88.9	51.6
Soyuz 36/U.S.S.R./A II/ 1980-041A	5/26/80 7/31/80	6,500 (14,330)	sphere and cylinder	2.2 (7.22)	7.5 (24.61)	Ferried Soviet and Hungarian cosmonauts to Salyut 6 space station	327 (203)	340 (211)	91.2	51.6
NOAA 7/U.S./Atlas E/ 1980-043A	5/29/80	723 (1.594)	cube with three panels	1 (3.28)	1.2 (3.94)	Earth-monitoring satellite	265 (165)	1,371 (852)	103.3	92.2
Soyuz-T (2)/U.S.S.R./A II/ 1980-045A	6/5/80 6/9/80	‡	sphere and cylinder	2.3 (7.55)	7.5 (24.61)	Ferried two cosmonauts to Salyut 6 space station	194 (121)	231 (144)	88.8	51.2
Horizon 4/U.S.S.R./D le/ 1980-049A	6/14/80	‡	cylinder and two panels	2 (6.56)	5 (16.4)	Communications satellite	35,745 (22,211)	35,828 (22,262)	1,436.1	0.8
Molniya-1 (47)/U.S.S.R./A IIe/ 1980-053A	6/21/80	1,000 (2,205)	cylinder with cone and six panels	1.5 (4.92)	3.4 (11.15)	Communications satellite	633 (393)	39,682 (24,657)	717	62.8
Progress 10/U.S.S.R./A II/ 1980-055A	6/29/80 7/19/80	7,000 (15,432)	sphere and cone	2.2 (7.22)	8 (26.25)	Ferried supplies to Salyut 6 space station	206 (128)	255 (158)	89.1	51.6
Ekran/U.S.S.R./D le/ 1980-060A	7/14/80	‡	cylinder with two panels	‡	‡	Television communications satellite	35,262 (21,911)	35,681 (22,171)	1,420.1	0.4
Rohini 1/India/SLV-3/ 1980-062A	7/18/80	35 (77)	‡	‡	‡	Technical monitoring satellite	306 (190)	888 (552)	96.6	44.7
Soyuz 37/U.S.S.R./A II/ 1980-064A	7/23/80 10/11/80	6,600 (14,551)	sphere and cone	2.3 (7.55)	7.5 (24.61)	Ferried Soviet and Vietnamese cosmonauts to Salyut 6 space station	190 (118)	273 (170)	‡	51.6
Meteor-2/U.S.S.R./A II/ 1980-073A	9/9/80	2,750 (6,063)	cylinder with two panels	1.5 (4.92)	5 (16.4)	Weather satellite	868 (539)	906 (563)	102.4	81.2
GOES 4/U.S./Delta/ 1980-074A	9/9/80	243 (536)	cylinder	1.9 (6.23)	2.6 (8.53)	Weather satellite in geosynchronous orbit	1,577 (980)	49,771 (30,926)	920.5	26.5
Soyuz 38/U.S.S.R./A II/ 1980-075A	9/18/80 9/26/80	6,700 (14,771)	sphere and cone	2.3 (7.55)	7.5 (24.61)	Ferried crew of two to and from Salyut 6 space station	263 (163)	313 (194)	90.3	51.6
Progress 11/U.S.S.R./A II/ 1980-079A	9/28/80	7,000 (15,432)	sphere and cone	2.2 (7.22)	8 (26.25)	Resupply vehicle for Salyut 6 space station	193 (120)	270 (168)	88.8	51.6

*All dates are in universal time (UT).
†English units in parentheses: weight in pounds, dimensions in feet, apogee and perigee in statute miles.
‡Not available.

(MITCHELL R. SHARPE)

four small clouds near the crater Lowell. From shadows cast on the surface, scientists estimated that the largest was about 32 km (20 mi) long.

Also during the month the Soviet probe Venera 12, at a distance of 190,373,790 km (118,031,679 mi) from Earth, was commanded to turn its instruments toward Comet Bradfield. The nucleus of the comet was studied by its ultraviolet spectrometer, jointly developed by Soviet and French scientists. Spectral analyses of its data would permit quantitative estimates of such elements as hydrogen, helium, argon, and oxygen in the comet.

Evaluation of images made on March 5, 1979, and returned from Voyager 1 convinced Stephen P. Synnott of the Jet Propulsion Laboratory that Jupiter had a 15th moon. The satellite was numbered 1979 J2 and appeared to be between 70 km and 80 km (43 to 50 mi) in diameter. With a period of 16 hours it circles the planet at a distance of 151,000 km (93,000 mi) above the cloud tops and between the orbits of its sister moons Amalthea and Io. Synnott later discovered a 16th moon some 40 km (25 mi) in diameter orbiting about 56,000 km (34,800 mi) above the planet's cloud layer.

NASA

Each of the 30,922 tiles covering the U.S. space shuttle "Columbia" requires about 25 hours of work. The tiles, only part of the reason for a delayed launching, are designed to withstand 14 pounds of pressure per square inch and temperatures ranging to 1,650° C (3,000° F).

On April 2 Mars Viking Lander 2 exhausted its energy and became an artifact awaiting discovery or recovery by interplanetary archaeologists of the future. After 3.5 years of searching for evidence of Earth-type life forms on Mars, the probe finished its mission with negative results. Since landing on Mars on Sept. 3, 1976, the probe had returned to Earth more than 1,800 pictures.

The Viking Orbiter 1 was ordered silenced in August during its 1,489th orbit of Mars. Its gas supply for the stabilizing jets was exhausted. The orbiter began a slow tumble that would take it on a 75-year fall to the surface of Mars.

Radar scanning of 93% of Venus by Pioneer Venus provided scientists with the first map of the surface of that planet. Long considered Earth's sister planet, Venus proved to be nothing like the Earth. The two major terrain features were "continents," one as large as Australia and the other half the size of Africa. The highest point on Venus is Maxwell Montes, which occupies the entire eastern end of Ishtar Terra. It is 11,800 m (35,300 ft) above "sea level."

After a journey of 2,000,000,000 km (1,250,000,000 mi) and more than two years, Voyager 1 passed within 125,000 km (77,000 mi) of Saturn on November 12. Among its many remarkable discoveries were that the planet has at least 15 moons rather than 12; a complex system of major and minor rings, two of which appear to be interwoven in a braided pattern; and a huge encircling cloud of neutral hydrogen gas. After its encounter with Saturn, Voyager 1 continued on a trajectory that would eventually take it out of the Solar System.

At a meeting of ESA held in Paris on July 8 and 9, it was decided that that organization would develop a probe to study Halley's Comet. The 750-kg (1,650-lb) spacecraft would be derived from the organization's GEOS satellite and would fly through the comet in 1986. Its instrumentation would consist primarily of a camera and mass spectrometers to determine the atomic composition of the comet.

(MITCHELL R. SHARPE)

See also Astronomy; Defense; Earth Sciences; Industrial Review: *Aerospace; Telecommunications;* Television and Radio.

[738.C]

Spain

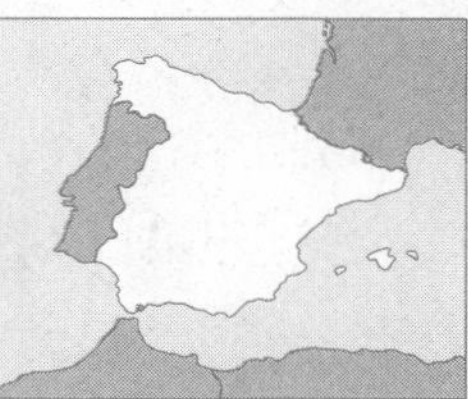

Spain

A constitutional monarchy of southwest Europe, Spain is bounded by Portugal, with which it shares the Iberian Peninsula, and by France. Area: 504,750 sq km (194,885 sq mi), including the Balearic and Canary islands. Pop. (1980 est.): 37,272,000, including the Balearics and Canaries. Cap. and largest city: Madrid (pop., 1980 est., 3,232,300). Language: Spanish. Religion: Roman Catholic. King, Juan Carlos I; premier in 1980, Adolfo Suárez González.

In 1980 political developments demanded more than their fair share of the government's energy and led to a feeling of loss of direction and lack of efficient leadership in economic matters. In March, having seen moderate nationalists safely elected to head regional parliaments in the Basque region and Catalonia (March 9 and 20, respectively), the authorities concluded that the autonomy issue was defused. Earlier, in the February 28 referendum on the issue of devolution (the delegation of powers formerly held by the central government to regional or local authorities) for Andalusia, seven of the eight Andalusian provinces voted in favour of full regional autonomy. A campaign in favour of Andalusia's demands in particular and of speeded autonomy in general was mounted, and it resulted in a decline in the government's popularity nationwide. The Partido Socialista Obrero Español (PSOE) on May 30 moved to censure the policies of the government and lost by only 14 votes. The government's majority was cut to a single vote on June 13, when it defeated an opposition proposal to change Spain's law on referenda; the proposal was aimed at clearing a legal path for reholding the referendum in the Andalusian province of Almeria, the only one of the eight that did not vote for full autonomy.

The summer recess of the Cortes (parliament) was taken up by negotiations among the factions of the governing Unión Centro Democrático (UCD) and with the regionally based parties in order to reengineer a working parliamentary majority. Premier Adolfo Suárez González announced his

SPAIN

Education. (1978–79) Primary, pupils 6,668,066, teachers 213,386; secondary, pupils 999,479, teachers 59,375; vocational, pupils 455,943, teachers 30,762; higher, students 643,272, teachers 33,581.

Finance. Monetary unit: peseta, with (Sept. 22, 1980) a free rate of 73.52 pesetas to U.S. $1 (176.70 pesetas = £1 sterling). Gold, SDR's, and foreign exchange (June 1980) U.S. $12,461,000,000. Budget (1979 actual): revenue 1,716,000,000,000 pesetas; expenditure 1,893,000,000,000 pesetas. Gross domestic product (1979) 13,222,000,000,000 pesetas. Money supply (June 1980) 3,658,000,000,000 pesetas. Cost of living (1975 = 100; June 1980) 227.5.

Foreign Trade. (1979) Imports 1,704,100,000,000 pesetas; exports 1,221,200,000,000 pesetas. Import sources: EEC 36% (West Germany 10%, France 10%, Italy 6%, U.K. 5%); U.S. 12%; Saudi Arabia 9%. Export destinations: EEC 48% (France 16%, West Germany 10%, U.K. 7%, Italy 6%); U.S. 7%. Main exports: machinery 13%; fruit and vegetables 11%; motor vehicles 10%; iron and steel 9%; chemicals 8%; textiles and clothing 5%. Tourism (1978): visitors 39,970,000; receipts U.S. $5,488,000,000.

Transport and Communications. Roads (including rural trails; 1979) 231,416 km (including 2,266 km expressways). Motor vehicles in use (1979): passenger 7,057,500; commercial 1,261,200. Railways: (1978) 15,739 km; traffic (1979) 16,609,000,000 passenger-km, freight 10,573,000,000 net ton-km. Air traffic (1979): 15,184,000,000 passenger-km; freight 404,810,000 net ton-km. Shipping (1979): merchant vessels 100 gross tons and over 2,773; gross tonnage 8,313,658. Telephones (1978) 10,311,400. Radio receivers (1976) 9.3 million. Television receivers (1976) 7,425,000.

Agriculture. Production (in 000; metric tons; 1979): wheat 4,118; barley 6,150; oats 443; rye 215; corn 2,237; rice 427; potatoes 5,437; sugar, raw value *c.* 764; tomatoes 2,050; onions 905; cabbages (1978) *c.* 527; melons (1978) 641; watermelons (1978) 440; apples 1,156; pears (1978) 445; peaches (1978) 425; oranges 1,771; mandarin oranges and tangerines 803; lemons 360; sunflower seed 500; bananas 403; olives 2,270; olive oil 469; wine 5,058; tobacco *c.* 38; cotton, lint 40; cow's milk 5,823; hen's eggs *c.* 586; meat 2,255; fish catch (1978) 1,380. Livestock (in 000; 1979): cattle *c.* 4,650; pigs 9,943; sheep *c.* 14,500; goats *c.* 2,300; horses (1978) *c.* 260; mules (1978) *c.* 269; asses (1978) *c.* 243; chickens *c.* 53,300.

Industry. Index of industrial production (1975 = 100; 1979) 115. Fuel and power (in 000; metric tons; 1979): coal 11,490; lignite 10,480; crude oil 894; manufactured gas (cu m) *c.* 1,500,000; electricity (kw-hr) 105,411,000. Production (in 000; metric tons; 1979): cement 28,051; iron ore (50% metal content) 8,479; pig iron 6,840; crude steel 12,116; aluminum (1978) 212; copper (1977) 149; zinc (1978) 168; petroleum products (1978) *c.* 47,800; sulfuric acid 2,906; fertilizers (nutrient content; 1978–79) nitrogenous *c.* 929, phosphate *c.* 493, potash 663; cotton yarn (1977) 82; wool yarn (1977) 35; man-made fibres (1978) 251; passenger cars (units) 973; commercial vehicles (units) 158. Merchant vessels launched (100 gross tons and over; 1979) 512,000 gross tons.

fifth Cabinet on September 8, including his principal critics in UCD who had lost their posts after the March 1979 elections. Suárez then sought a vote of confidence in the Cortes for a declaration of general policy. The five members of the Partido Socialista Andalusia (PSA) promised support for Suárez on his program for fully autonomous regional governments for Galicia and Andalusia and an accelerated transfer of power to the Basque and Catalan areas, thereby assuring the vote of confidence. Nevertheless, bitter confrontations occurred between Suárez and the leader of the PSOE, Felipe González, while the Basque Partido Nacionalista Vasco (PNV) ended its eight-month boycott of the Cortes and announced it would vote against the government.

Voting in the Cortes on the declaration of general policy was 180 votes in favour and 164 against, but PSA support was conditional on Suárez's fulfilling his part of the bargain on autonomy and government economic support for Andalusia. For Spain's economy Suárez promised to raise gross national product growth from near zero in 1980 to 4 or 5% by 1983. On September 30 the 1981 budget was introduced; government expenditure was to be raised by 23%. To help contain the increase in the deficit, indirect taxes were to be raised on, among other things, tobacco, gambling, and petroleum products; there was to be a freeze on civil-service recruitment and only a 12% increase in pay awarded to public-sector employees (5% below the forecast 1981 inflation).

On October 23 an agreement was signed in Madrid between the government and opposition parties. In it the administration agreed to hold a second referendum on the autonomy question in Almeria, thus allowing Andalusia to proceed to self-government, and to allow the passage of a bill to reform the referendum law (to allow a second poll on the same subject within five years). Elections for Andalusia's regional parliament would be held in 1981. Galicia voted for autonomy on December 21, but only about a fourth of those eligible actually voted. On December 31 the Cabinet voted to restore to the Basque regional government powers of taxation enjoyed before the Civil War.

The Cortes on October 29 passed a new antiterrorism law by 298 votes to 2, with 8 abstentions, in reply to mounting terrorism in the Basque provinces. Suspects might now be held incommunicado for an extra seven days beyond the previous 72-hour maximum. With unemployment zooming toward the 15% mark, the Basque terrorists chose to increase their murder campaign. In 1980 there was on average one political assassination every three days, and in November the UCD in the Basque provinces became a principal target, losing five members in a short space of time. Meanwhile, the "moderate" or political military wing of the Euzkadi ta Azkatasuna (ETA) movement also began to kill.

Faced with a real threat to civil liberties, the right and centre wings of the PSOE pressed to join the UCD in mounting an all-out offensive against terrorism. On November 2, after abstaining from the vote on the new antiterrorism bill, prominent members of the PNV joined forces for the first time with local representatives of the UCD and other major parties in San Sebastian in a demonstration against violence in the Basque country. Supporters of ETA tried to prevent the 50,000-strong march but were forced to flee when the police intervened.

In June the government announced that it would seek membership in NATO in 1981. This brought protests from the Socialists and Communists. The government argued that with Spain's treaty with the U.S. running out in 1981, Spain should take part in its own defense; NATO membership was to be conditional on the solving of the Gibraltar dispute with Great Britain. Following the signing on April 10 of the Declaration of Lisbon between Spain and Britain, the Spanish hoped to negotiate a solution.

Spain finished its first round of preliminary entry negotiations with the European Economic Community (EEC). The second, more detailed discussions were postponed from July until November, when Spain's new EEC minister, Eduardo Punset, took office. Spain accepted that the vital agricultural negotiations would be delayed but asked to borrow from the European Investment Bank in advance of its EEC membership. (*See* EUROPEAN UNITY.)

(MICHAEL WOOLLER)

Speleology

The Réseau Jean Bernard, in the French Alps, became the deepest cave in the world. Patrick Penez dived through the 40-m (131-ft)-long sump that had previously formed the end of the cave. Beyond it he followed descending passages until he was stopped by an 8-m (26-ft)-drop, the bottom of which was estimated to be 1,410 m (4,626 ft) beneath the surface. The former deepest cave, the Gouffre de la Pierre Saint-Martin (French Pyrenees), was itself extended to 1,350 m (4,429 ft) by the discovery of a higher entrance. A newly discovered Mexican cave, La Nita, was connected, via four sumps at a depth of about 1,020 m (3,346 ft), with the Sotano de San Augustin. The combined system, called Sistema Huautla, was 1,220.5 m (4,004 ft) deep and thus the third deepest in the world. In the Gouffre Berger in southeastern France cave divers from Toulon and Cavaillon reached a depth of 7 m (23 ft) in the final sump, thus increasing the overall depth to 1,148 m (3,766 ft). The Schneeloch (Austria) was extended in the same way when Belgian divers penetrated 25 m (82 ft) below the surface of the terminal sump to a total depth of 1,111 m (3,645 ft). Diving at the bottom of the French Réseau Félix Trombe gave access to 64 m (210 ft) of shafts which connected with the nearby Goueil di Her; the depth of the combined system thus became 1,018 m (3,340 ft). Potentially very important was the extension of the Scialet d'Engins to 980 m (3,215 ft). This cave is close to the Gouffre Berger, and a connection would result in an overall depth of about 1,219 m (4,000 ft).

The longest caves were also extended. Discovery of a connection between the Mammoth Cave of Kentucky and the nearby Proctor Cave resulted in a combined length of 345.25 km (214.5 mi). Connection was also reported between the two long gypsum caves in the U.S.S.R., Optimisticheskaya and Ozyornaya, giving a total of 230 km (143 mi), but this was unconfirmed.

The record length for a cave dive was set in Australia, where Hugh Morrison, Simon Jones, and Keith Dekkers dived to the end of a 2,000-m (6,562-ft)-long submerged passage in Cocklebiddy Cave. The starting point of the dive was an air-filled chamber itself reachable only by a 650-m (2,-133-ft)-dive. The European record for the longest underwater passage dived remained at 1.829 km (1.14 mi) at Keld Head in England, but Bertrand Léger achieved a longer dive in the Grotte de la Bourne (France), where he turned back at 1.68 km (1.04 mi) to make a continuous double journey of 3.36 km (2.09 mi). In Trou Madame the longest individual sump dived was 1.285 km (0.8 mi), but the divers passed through five sumps totaling 2.455 km (1.525 mi) before returning.

The dating of stalagmites recovered from 45 m (148 ft) below sea level in a Bahamas cave added to knowledge of the glacial period. These deposits must have been formed above water during the Illinoian glaciation, at which time the sea level must have been at least 42 m (138 ft) lower than at present.

(T. R. SHAW)

Sri Lanka

An Asian republic and member of the Commonwealth of Nations, Sri Lanka (Ceylon) occupies an island in the Indian Ocean off the southeast coast of peninsular India. Area: 65,610 sq km (25,332 sq mi). Pop. (1980 est.): 14,871,000, including (1977) Sinhalese about 73%; Tamil 19%; Moors 7%. Cap. and largest city: Colombo (pop., 1978 est., 624,000). Language: Sinhalese (official), Tamil, English. Religion (1971): Buddhist 67%; Hindu 18%; Christian 8%; Muslim 7%. President in 1980, Junius Richard Jayawardene; prime minister, Ranasinghe Premadasa.

In 1980 Sri Lanka welcomed foreign investment in fields lacking local capital, technology, or expertise and permitted a major role for the private sector. Protection from imports was given to some local industries. Finance Minister Ronnie de Mel sought aid in Europe and the U.S. early in the year. A 12-member Sri Lanka Aid Consortium, meeting in Paris in July, pledged more than U.S. $1 billion in new aid (a 42% increase over 1979). As a corrective measure, subsidies on most essential commodities were withdrawn early in the year. A general strike threatened to paralyze the economy, and the government proclaimed an emergency on July 16; press censorship and action against the strikers followed. The emergency was ended on August 15.

The ruling United National Party, which was swept into power in July 1977, continued to

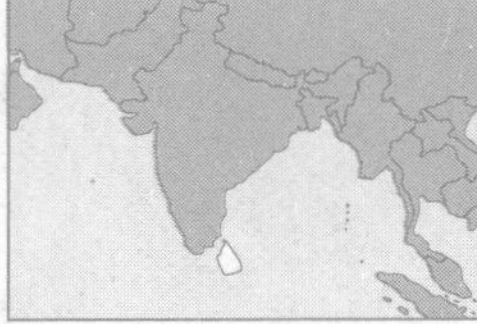
Sri Lanka

SRI LANKA

Education. (1979) Primary, pupils 1,975,749, secondary, pupils 1,159,967, primary and secondary teachers 138,488; vocational (1976), pupils 4,778, teachers 1,239; teacher training, students 4,119, teachers 532; higher (universities only; 1975), students 15,426, teaching staff 2,000.

Finance. Monetary unit: Sri Lanka rupee, with (Sept. 22, 1980) a free rate of SLRs 16.68 to U.S. $1 (SLRs 40.10 = £1 sterling). Gold, SDR's, and foreign exchange (May 1980) U.S. $404 million. Budget (1979 actual): revenue SLRs 12,730,000,000; expenditure SLRs 20,339,000,000. Gross national product (1979) SLRs 51,373,000,000. Money supply (April 1980) SLRs 8,364,000,000. Cost of living (Colombo; 1975 = 100; May 1980) 159.1.

Foreign Trade. (1979) Imports SLRs 22,828,000,000; exports SLRs 15,282,000,000. Import sources: Japan 13%; India 10%; U.K. 9%; Saudi Arabia 7%; West Germany 5%; U.S. 5%; Australia 5%; China 5%. Export destinations: U.S. 10%; U.K. 8%; Japan 7%; West Germany 6%; China 6%. Main exports: tea 37%; rubber 16%; coconut products 8%.

Transport and Communications. Roads (1978) 24,911 km. Motor vehicles in use (1978): passenger 103,800; commercial 40,550. Railways: (1977) 1,485 km; traffic (1977–78) 3,710,000,000 passenger-km, freight 246 million net ton-km. Air traffic (1978): 129 million passenger-km; freight 500,000 net ton-km. Telephones (Jan. 1978) 74,200. Radio receivers (Dec. 1977) 1 million.

Agriculture. Production (in 000; metric tons; 1979): rice 1,806; cassava (1978) *c.* 565; sweet potatoes (1978) *c.* 130; onions *c.* 59; mangoes *c.* 57; lemons *c.* 55; pineapples *c.* 78; copra *c.* 135; tea *c.* 210; coffee *c.* 13; rubber *c.* 155; fish catch (1978) 157. Livestock (in 000; June 1978): cattle 1,-542; buffalo 814; sheep 23; goats 450; pigs 41; chickens 4,912.

Industry. Production (in 000; metric tons; 1979): cement 662; salt (1978) 115; graphite (exports; 1978) 11.4; petroleum products *c.* 1,300; cotton yarn 5.7; electricity (kw-hr) 1,527,000.

Squash Rackets: *see* Racket Games

win all subsequent by-elections. On October 16 former prime minister Sirimavo Bandaranaike was expelled from Parliament and deprived of her civil rights for alleged abuses of power. Fearing possible disorders, the government had declared an emergency on October 14.

A major legislative effort in tackling the country's ethnic problems was the passage in August of the district development bill, introduced after the verdict of a presidential commission that a separate Tamil homeland could not be permitted. It provided for decentralization and the association of people of various regions through 24 elected district councils.

In international affairs Sri Lanka's policies were closer to those of the Association of Southeast Asian Nations (ASEAN) than to those of its northern neighbour, India. Sri Lanka condemned Soviet action in Afghanistan, did not accord recognition to the Heng Samrin government in Cambodia, and opposed militarization of the Indian Ocean.

(GOVINDAN UNNY)

Stock Exchanges

Most major stock market indexes throughout the world scored gains in 1980. As usual, stock price movements were generally determined by a mixture of economic developments and psychological factors.

The pace of worldwide economic activity slowed appreciably in 1980 as signs of recession surfaced in several major industrial nations. Some industrialized countries suffered milder setbacks, however, and others experienced strong growth. This divergent pattern raised investors' hopes that the world economy would avoid the synchronized cycle of recession and recovery that prevailed in 1974–75. To be sure, relatively buoyant economic activity, coupled with the unwillingness of most industrial nations to pursue aggressive deflationary policies, kept upward pressure on both short-term and long-term interest rates.

Moreover, solutions to the basic causes of persistent, high-level inflation appeared nowhere in sight despite the generally higher priority assigned to inflation than to unemployment. The cost of petroleum continued to rise in 1980, which pushed inflation higher and depressed real growth. The need to avoid social unrest prevented cuts in government spending as a means of reducing government budget deficits. The disequilibrium in international balance of payments between the debt burdens of less developed nations and the huge surpluses accumulated by the oil-exporting countries threatened the international monetary system. Thus, most industrial nations were forced to keep interest rates high so as to maintain the attractiveness of their currencies to foreigners in order to finance current account deficits, which stemmed mainly from oil imports. The high rates of interest, however, increased the risk of deepening the recession, while any substantial reduction in interest rates would likely weaken a nation's currency. In short, the global economy in 1980 experienced a high level of stagflation which seemed so deeply embedded that conventional fiscal and monetary restraints could not remove it without incurring the cost of massive unemployment and substantially lower industrial output.

Stock market psychology was basically positive throughout most of 1980. The deterioration of paper currency fostered the belief that stocks would continue to act as a hedge against future inflation. Moreover, the rapid rise in values of such tangible assets as precious metals, stamps, rare coins, and art caused stocks to become a relatively inexpensive investment alternative. In addition, increasing recognition that tangible assets failed to produce a rate of return in the form of dividends lessened their attractiveness.

Stock markets were also favourably influenced by poor and volatile bond-market performance. During the late 1970s bond investments failed to provide a total return in excess of the inflation rate, and they performed considerably below the combined capital appreciation and dividends of common stocks. The result was that many investing institutions switched from bonds to stocks in an effort to beat inflation. Corporations also learned to adjust to inflation. Not only did corporate profits hold up much better than during earlier uptrends in inflation but also the rate of increase in dividends generally grew much faster than during previous inflationary periods, thereby increasing the relative attractiveness of stocks. Also adding to the demand for equities was the widely held belief that recessions are the best time to own common stocks because, as more and more investors anticipate the return of buoyant economic and business conditions, stock prices tend to move higher. Finally, the overall strength in equity prices in 1980 mirrored the view that the worldwide trend toward political and economic conservatism could produce a salutary environment for equity investment.

The uptrend in stock prices initiated late in 1979 continued throughout 1980. Stock prices were largely influenced by the acceleration in inflation triggered in mid-1979 by the surge in the world price of oil earlier that year. Profit-taking moved the market lower before the end of February 1980, and the sell-off did not reach bottom until the end of March. Political tensions in the Middle East, mainly caused by the outbreak of war between Iran and Iraq, and uncertainties about oil supplies and oil price developments were important negative factors. The recovery in equity values in midsummer was largely propelled by an abrupt downswing in interest rates. Stock prices weakened in late summer amid fears of deepening recession and as interest rates strengthened. Most stock markets with gains for 1980 as a whole recorded their yearly high in November. At the close of the year, 11 of the world's 17 major stock price indexes were higher than at the beginning of 1980 (TABLE I).

(ROBERT H. TRIGG)

United States. Investors in the U.S. experienced a bull market as stock prices rose steadily for most of 1980 and carried many indexes to all-time highs despite a continuing recession, record high interest rates, and international political problems in the Middle East. The Dow Jones in-

Stamp Collecting:
see Philately and Numismatics

Steel Industry:
see Industrial Review

dustrial average of 30 blue-chip stocks closed the year at 963.99, up 125.25 or 14.9% from its 1979 finish at 838.74. For the first time in four years the average climbed above 1,000, when it closed at 1,000.17 on November 20. The 1980 gain was the biggest since 1976, when the average advanced 17.9%. Standard & Poor's 500-stock index, the New York Stock Exchange (NYSE) composite index of all its common stocks, the American Stock Exchange market value index, and the index of over-the-counter stocks all established historic highs in November. Standard & Poor's 500, which peaked at 140.52, ended the year at 135.52, up 25.5% for its biggest gain since 1975. The NYSE composite with a top of 81.02 on November 28 finished at 77.86, up 25.7%. The Amex Index was up 41.2%, and the over-the-counter index 33.9%.

The Dow Jones industrials displayed a roller-coaster behaviour in 1980, rising in January from a level of 870 to 890 before beginning a slide that ended in mid-April at a level of about 759.13. From mid-April there was a steady climb to a high of 960 in August, and then after much backing and filling a peak of 1,000.17 was hit in November. At the year's end the index closed at 963.99.

The increasing interest in the stock market by major financial institutions, first noted in 1979, continued during 1980 as the return of corporate money flows to the market pushed trading volume to record levels. Stocks traded on listed exchanges and over-the-counter surged to a record $1.4 trillion in market value, appreciating about $350 billion during the year despite two sharp setbacks during the market's rise. The prime (interest) rate changed more frequently in 1980 than in any previous year, as it rose from 15% at the beginning of the year to a peak of 20% in April. It declined sharply to a low of 10.5% at the end of July and then resumed a steady, rapid climb to a record 21.5% by the end of the year.

On the New York Stock Exchange the record of 8,155,915,314 shares traded, set in 1979, was eclipsed on September 25, and volume for the year totaled 11,350,000,000 shares, an increase of 39%. Average daily volume was about 44,870,000 shares, up from just under 32 million shares a day in 1979. Large blocks of 10,000 or more shares purchased by institutions were also more frequent in 1980, accounting for about 31% of NYSE volume, as compared with 27% in 1979. The average daily transaction volume in government securities alone was 18,100,000,000, up 37% from 1979.

Some of the gains on the NYSE were spectacular. For example, Shearson Loeb Rhoades, a securities brokerage firm, was up about 250%. The five most active stocks on the NYSE for 1980 were IBM with a turnover of 134 million shares, Texaco Inc. with 126 million, Mobil Oil Corp. with 103 million, AT&T with 93 million, and Gulf Oil Corp. with 88 million. As a group, automobile stocks were among the biggest losers, falling more than 15%.

Volume on the American Stock Exchange rose to a record 1,630,000,000 in 1980, a 47.8% increase over the 1,099,990,000 traded the prior year. In the over-the-counter market volume was so hectic that on some days it exceeded that on the NYSE. For the year, unlisted trading volume neared 6,700,000,000 shares, more than half the 1980 turnover on the NYSE and up more than 80% from 1979. Indicative of the "hot new issue" sentiment was the performance of Genentech Inc., which went public at $35 a share on October 14 and within hours jumped to $88.

Mutual funds did well in 1980. The Investment Company Institute, a trade group, estimated in a year-end report that mutual fund shareholders numbered more than 11 million, a record high. Aggregate assets of mutual funds doubled between 1978 and 1980 to about $138 billion. Investors bought more shares of common stock mutual funds than they redeemed in 1980, the first year in which that happened since 1971. Growth funds had a net inflow of $667.6 million in 1980. Money market funds, which invest in U.S. Department of the Treasury bills and such short-term securities as large certificates of deposit issued by banks, were particularly successful, with assets increasing from $11 billion in 1978 to $45 billion at the end of 1979 and $76 billion in 1980. Securities firms projected record profits for the year of $2.1 billion pretax, according to the Securities Industry Association. This was nearly double the 1979 pre-

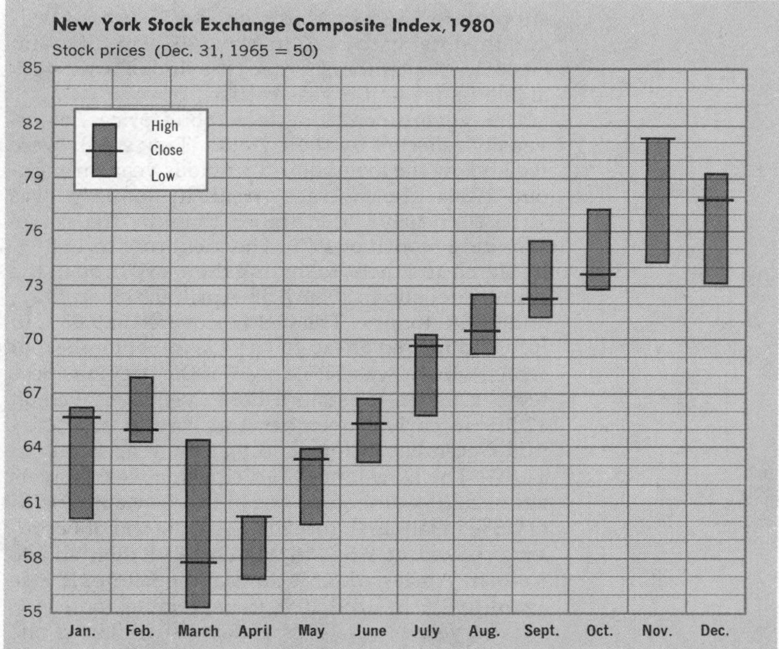

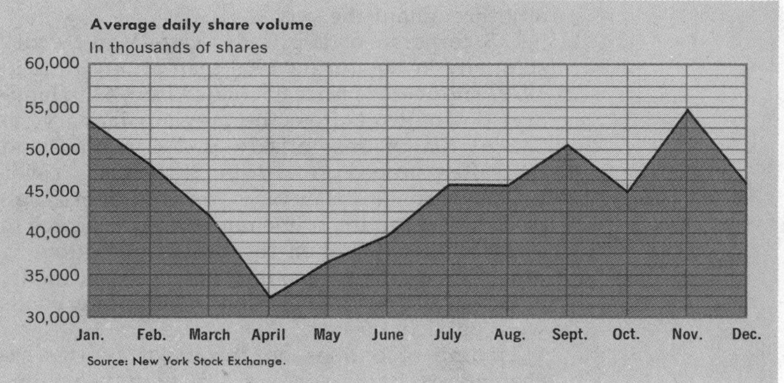

tax income of $1.1 billion. Gross revenues were $15 billion, up from $11.3 billion the previous year. Corporate underwritings were $55 billion, compared with $36.6 billion in 1979.

The Standard & Poor composite index of 500 New York Stock Exchange stocks (TABLE II) began the year at 110.87, approximately 11% above the corresponding figure for 1979, rose to 115.34 in February, dipped to 102.97 in April, and then briskly advanced to 107.69 in May, 114.55 in June, 119.83 in July, and 126.51 in September, when it was 16.4% ahead of the prior year. By the year's end the index reached a level of 135.52. The 400 stocks in the industrials sector of the index rose from 124.72 in January to 130.91 in February, then dropped during March and April before moving ahead to 120.80 in May, 128.80 in June, 135.23 in July, and 143.73 in September. Public utility stocks did not share in the buoyant market performance in 1980, as the index fluctuated within a very narrow range about the levels of the previous year. From an average of 50.26 in January, the 40 stocks fell to 45.40 by March, recovered to 50.63 in May, and showed little year-to-year change thereafter. Railroad stocks performed unusually well, climbing from 58.64 in January to 69.61 in February, slipping to 63.39 in March and to 59.46 in April, and then rising to 61.12 in May, 70.79 in July, and 80.64 in September, when the index was 44% above its level of a year earlier.

U.S. government long-term bond prices, as inversely reflected by their yields (TABLE III), were well below the levels of the previous year throughout 1980. The average yield in January was 10.03%, nearly 19% higher than in the corresponding month of 1979. The yield rose to 11.87% in March and then, following the sharp drop in the prime rate, slid to 10.83% in April, 9.82% in May, and 9.40% in June. The yield recovered at 9.83% in July and moved ahead to 10.94% in September, at which time it was 26% ahead of the previous September figure. Treasury bond yields peaked at 12.5% in early November and rose to 12.8% by mid-December before ending the year at about 11.8%. The Dow Jones Municipals, a weekly average of 20 20-year bonds, began the year with yields of 7.5% in January, rose to 9% by the end of February, peaked at 9.5% in March, and then slid to 8.6% in April and 8.5% in May and June. It rose again to 9% in July, 10% in September, and 11% by the year's end. This index also reflected the radical upward movement of interest rates generally throughout the year.

U.S. corporate bond prices (TABLE IV) were substantially lower during 1980 than at any time in 1979. The average price fluctuated from 44 in January, down 16.6% from the previous January, to 37.3 by March, rose briskly to 47.4 in June, and thereafter slipped to 41.1 in September. Yields were well above earlier years, ranging from a high of 12.96% when the prime rate peaked in March to a low of 10.58% when the prime hit bottom in June. Despite the unfavourable market conditions, a record total of $40.9 billion of corporate bonds were publicly offered.

Trading of options on the major futures exchanges rose impressively in 1980 with the volume for all contracts on the Chicago Board of Trade at 45.1 million, up 33% from 1979. The gain on the Chicago Mercantile Exchange was up 11.5% at 22 million contracts. Very high interest rates eliminated many of the small investors from the futures markets in 1980, but financial institutions did not appear to be deterred.

On March 27, later referred to as "Silver Thursday," a near collapse of silver prices shook all the markets. The great silver crash of 1980 involved the brothers Nelson Bunker Hunt (*see* BIOGRAPHIES) and W. Herbert Hunt, who appeared to have cornered the market in silver before sustaining very heavy losses. Silver prices dropped from more than $50 per ounce in January to $10.80 per ounce in late March. By acquiring control of huge amounts of silver for future delivery, largely on credit, a handful of speculators had pushed the price of silver to incredible levels during the fall and winter of 1979–80. When the commodity exchanges suddenly restricted trading and raised margins, the price dropped sharply and the collateral for billions of dollars of debt vanished.

Canada. The year 1980 was an exceptionally good one for the Canadian stock market. Share prices posted healthy gains, and both volume and value set records. On the Toronto Stock Exchange, measured by its composite index of 300 stocks, prices rose 25%, closing at 2,268.70. Volume totaled 2,110,000,000 shares, up 52% from 1979. The value of 1980 share trading on the Toronto exchange was Can$29.5 billion, 57.7% ahead of the previous record of Can$18.7 billion set in 1979 and representing 77% of the Can$38.2 billion on all exchanges. Heavy speculation in mining, oil, and gas stocks sent the market's composite index soaring 21% in the first two months of 1980. The rush, caused by hopes for offshore oil discoveries and rising metal prices, forced the exchange temporarily to curtail trading hours and boost margin rates. When interest rates began climbing, the market fell to its low of 1,670.80 on March 27.

On the Toronto exchange the best performing issues were gold mining stocks, up 67%; real estate issues, up 63%; and paper and forest shares, up 46%. The weakest were utility stocks, the index for which edged up only 2%. Canadian stocks were especially favoured because of the country's oil, gas, metal, and mining resources, the shares of which comprise more than 30% of the 300 issues in the exchange's composite index.

The low value of the Canadian dollar, a 47-year low against the U.S. dollar in November, made Canadian stocks especially attractive to foreigners. Interest rates in Canada rose sharply during the year with the Central Bank quoting 17.28% at the year's end, up from 14% a year earlier. Canada 90-day treasury bills ended the year at 17%, compared with 13.55% in 1979. The Canadian prime rate began the year at 15% and ended it at 18.25%. The long-term Canada bond average fluctuated wildly in response to U.S. interest-rate developments. From an opening of 11.1% in January, it climbed to 12% in February and 13% in March before declining to a low of 10% in July. In August it jumped to 12.5% and then rose steadily to close at 13%. (IRVING PFEFFER)

Western Europe. Three of the four largest European economies experienced higher stock markets in 1980. The two most economically powerful countries in the region, Great Britain and West Germany, showed divergent trends, with the former posting a gain of 15% and the latter a decline of 4%. Italy, on the other hand, enjoyed the largest increase in equity prices among the major world stock market indexes (+110%), while France turned in a good performance with an increase in share prices of 9%. Among the smaller countries, Sweden, Denmark, and Spain posted gains for 1980 as a whole. Counted among the countries with declines were Belgium, Norway, The Netherlands, Austria, and Switzerland.

The stock market in Great Britain reversed a two-year decline as the *Financial Times* index of 30 industrial stocks traded on the London Stock Exchange increased 15% from the end of 1979 to the end of 1980. The index reached the 1980 high on November 21, and the low was established on January 3.

Stock prices in Great Britain began 1980 on a flurry of buying despite the first national steel strike since 1926. By the end of February equity values revealed a gain of 13%. Investors' confidence was buoyed by the persistence of the U.K. government in maintaining anti-inflationary policies in the face of a pronounced recession and also by the strength of the British pound in international currency markets. Stock prices, however, began to weaken several weeks after the announcement that the British steel unions had accepted a 15½% pay boost to end their strike and also as evidence began to mount that the relatively high interest rates were choking economic activity. By the end of May nearly the entire gain in stock prices since January was wiped out.

The ensuing recovery generated momentum in July, when the Bank of England cut its minimum lending rate to 16% from the record 17% that had prevailed since the beginning of the year. Although this announcement was followed by news that industrial output had not rebounded from the steel strike and that July had witnessed the largest monthly increase in unemployment in the nation's history and the highest jobless total in Britain in the post-World War II period, the market continued its rally until mid-September. During this period 22% was added to equity values.

The market then entered a period of profit-taking that lasted four weeks and cut equity values by 8%. During the rally that followed not only was the entire loss recovered, but stock prices reached their highest levels of the year. The nearly 11% gain from October 10 to November 21 was triggered mainly by news that Britain's inflation rate (15.4% annually) had dropped for the fifth consecutive month and stood substantially below the May 1980 peak of 21.9%. However, stock prices finished the year on a sour note. The government proposed a new tax on gross revenue from North Sea oil and gas production, which raised investor concerns over whether the country could be restored to economic vigour. Troublesome, too, were the record-high interest rates in the U.S. and the turmoil in the Middle East and Poland. The decline from November 21 to the December close amounted to 8%.

In West Germany the seesaw movement of stock prices resulted in a small net loss in the leading averages. The Commerzbank index of 60 issues traded on the Frankfurt Stock Exchange fell 4% from year-end 1979 to year-end 1980. Reflecting optimistic forecasts for capital goods spending and growth in the nation's export business, stock prices experienced a broad upswing that added 8% to equity values from January 18 to February 22.

Table I. Selected Major World Stock Price Indexes*

Country	1980 range† High	1980 range† Low	Year-end close 1979	Year-end close 1980	Percent change
Australia	1,044	760	740	1,017	+37
Austria	69	66	69	67	− 3
Belgium	106	83	103	84	−18
Denmark	98	75	87	96	+10
France	120	97	103	112	+ 9
Germany, West	749	667	716	684	− 4
Hong Kong	1,655	739	879	1,474	+68
Italy	188	83	82	172	+110
Japan	7,188	6,476	6,570	7,063	+ 8
Netherlands, The	68	58	68	62	− 9
Norway	145	110	135	120	−11
Singapore	722	430	435	661	+52
South Africa	661	456	451	594	+32
Spain	111	94	100	106	+ 6
Sweden	423	335	352	423	+20
Switzerland	318	276	303	299	− 1
United Kingdom	516	407	414	475	+15

*Index numbers are rounded and limited to countries for which at least 12 months' data were available on a weekly basis.
†Based on the daily closing price.
Sources: *The Economist*, *Financial Times*, and the *New York Times*.

Table II. U.S. Stock Market Prices

Month	Railroads (10 stocks) 1980	Railroads (10 stocks) 1979	Industrials (400 stocks) 1980	Industrials (400 stocks) 1979	Public utilities (40 stocks) 1980	Public utilities (40 stocks) 1979	Composite (500 stocks) 1980	Composite (500 stocks) 1979
January	58.64	44.45	124.72	111.15	50.26	50.33	110.87	99.71
February	69.61	44.92	130.91	109.49	49.04	50.74	115.34	98.23
March	63.39	46.64	118.73	111.66	45.40	50.62	104.69	100.11
April	59.46	49.75	115.57	113.95	48.37	50.09	102.97	102.07
May	61.12	49.88	120.80	111.24	50.63	48.65	107.69	99.73
June	65.44	52.60	128.80	112.98	52.48	50.57	114.55	101.73
July	70.79	54.73	135.23	113.63	52.82	51.73	119.83	102.71
August	73.90	57.62	140.18	118.93	51.18	52.52	123.50	107.36
September	80.64	56.00	143.73	121.06	51.10	51.16	126.51	108.60
October	...	53.18	...	116.95	...	49.05	...	104.47
November	...	54.23	...	116.12	...	48.79	...	103.66
December	...	56.90	...	120.78	...	50.50	...	107.78

Sources: U.S. Department of Commerce, *Survey of Current Business;* Board of Governors of the Federal Reserve System, *Federal Reserve Bulletin.* Prices are Standard & Poor's monthly averages of daily closing prices, with 1941–43 = 10.

Table III. U.S. Government Long-Term Bond Yields

Month	Yield (%) 1980	Yield (%) 1979	Month	Yield (%) 1980	Yield (%) 1979
January	10.03	8.43	July	9.83	8.35
February	11.55	8.43	August	10.53	8.42
March	11.87	8.45	September	10.94	8.68
April	10.83	8.44	October	...	9.44
May	9.82	8.55	November	...	9.80
June	9.40	8.32	December	...	9.59

Source: U.S. Department of Commerce, *Survey of Current Business.* Yields are for U.S. Treasury bonds that are taxable and due or callable in ten years or more.

Table IV. U.S. Corporate Bond Prices and Yields
Average price in dollars per $100 bond

Month	Average 1980	Average 1979	Yield (%) 1980	Yield (%) 1979	Month	Average 1980	Average 1979	Yield (%) 1980	Yield (%) 1979
January	44.0	52.8	11.09	9.25	July	45.5	53.4	11.07	9.20
February	37.8	52.6	12.38	9.26	August	42.1	53.0	11.64	9.23
March	37.3	52.2	12.96	9.37	September	41.1	51.8	12.02	9.44
April	41.0	52.3	12.04	9.38	October	...	47.8	...	10.13
May	45.7	51.9	10.99	9.50	November	...	45.8	...	10.76
June	47.4	53.5	10.58	9.29	December	...	46.1	...	10.74

Source: U.S. Department of Commerce, *Survey of Current Business.* Average prices are based on Standard & Poor's composite index of A1 + issues. Yields are based on Moody's Aaa domestic corporate bond index.

However, the huge jump in the world price of oil since the end of 1978 caused the nation to experience its first deficit in its current international payments account since 1965 and precipitated a decline in the value of the West German mark against the U.S. dollar. That, in turn, tended to keep West Germany's oil bill painfully high since the U.S. dollar is the basic denominator of oil prices. In the ensuing selling wave, equity values dropped 11% by March 28, but the loss was erased before the end of August.

West Germany's central bank, sensitive to charges that tight money had accelerated the slowdown in the nation's economy, announced several measures to soften its restrictive monetary policy, including the lowering of bank reserve requirements. It also unveiled plans to limit monetary growth in 1981 as a means of strengthening the mark and curtailing inflation. During early December the U.S. dollar climbed above two West German marks for the first time since 1978. From October 10 to the end of 1980 stock prices fell 8%, which left year-end share prices 9% below the February high and 3% above the March lows.

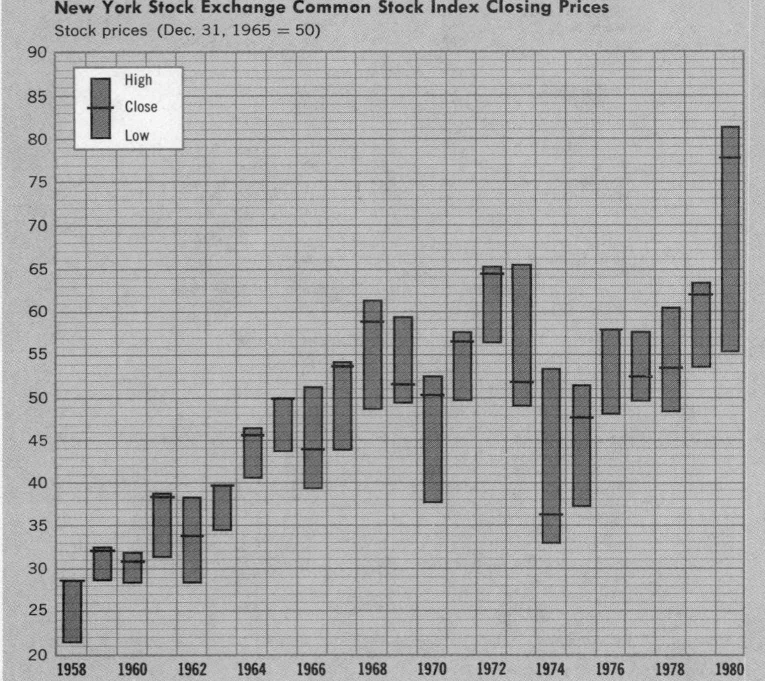

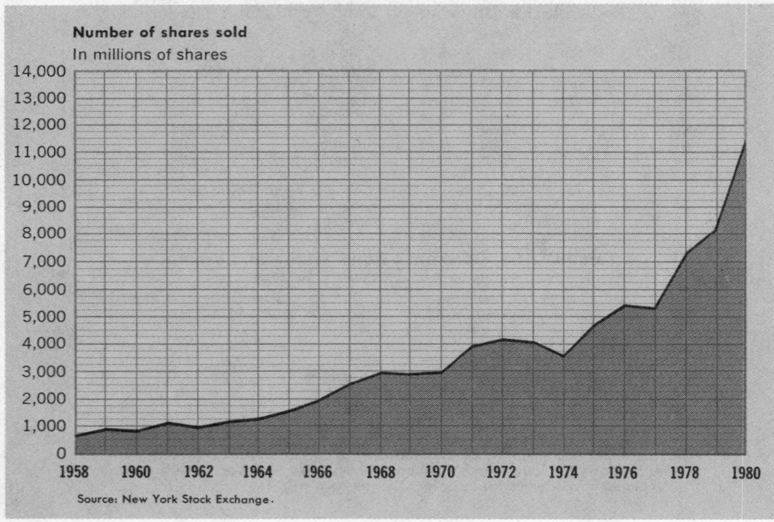

For the third consecutive year the stock market in Italy experienced higher prices. For 1980 as a whole the average rise in prices on the Milan Stock Exchange was 110%, the best performance among the major world stock price indexes. At its peak on November 4 the general index of share prices was up 129% from the beginning of the year and was 236% higher than at the end of 1977. Although part of the bull market's strength can be ascribed to a correction of the unrealistically low levels of 1977, the major thrust seemed to have come from investors who flocked to the stock market as a means of protecting savings against the highest inflation rate in Western Europe. The speculative bubble, however, seemed to burst following the devastating earthquake on November 23 in Campagnia, where many major companies had manufacturing plants. Stock prices dropped 14% from the November peak to mid-December before recovering as 1980 drew to a close.

As 1980 came to a close, industrial output in France was in a steep decline, and the government's policy of maintaining interest rates much higher than those available on the West German mark and Swiss franc in order to ensure the value of the French franc appeared to be changing. The result was that the general index of shares traded on the Paris Bourse, which had risen in almost uninterrupted fashion from the end of March through mid-November, began to collapse. From the year's high set on November 5 to the final trading day in 1980, the drop in stock prices amounted to almost 7%. Nevertheless, equity values managed to finish with a gain of 9% for the year as a whole.

The stock market in Spain reversed the long decline that had begun in April 1975. Prices on the Madrid Stock Exchange at the end of 1980 were 6% higher than at the beginning of the year. After a hesitant start, stock prices were strong from late April until the upswing topped out in October. The strength in equity markets was in part a reaction to an extremely oversold condition. Bullish sentiment also was fueled when Premier Adolfo Suárez announced the reshuffling of his Cabinet as a first step in creating a program to restore the nation's economic and political credibility.

Higher stock prices also prevailed in Sweden and Denmark. In Sweden the index of share prices traded on the Stockholm Exchange gained 20% after falling 3% in 1979. Stock prices showed a small gain during the January–July 1980 period (+6%) only to give up nearly the entire amount in August. Prices advanced in September and recorded even stronger gains over the next two months. At the end of December stock prices were at the year's highest level, 14% below the 1976 all-time high.

The pattern in Denmark was very different. After falling almost in a straight line from the beginning of January through the end of April, average share prices on the Copenhagen Stock Exchange followed an upward trend on a month-to-month basis until the beginning of November, when they again began to decline. As a result, stock prices finished the year 10% higher than at the end of 1979.

In Belgium a severe government budget deficit, the highest unemployment rate in Western Europe, and social unrest between Dutch- and French-speaking communities were the major influences on stock prices in 1980. After rising 8% in 1978 and 5% in 1979, average share prices on the Brussels Bourse finished 1980 with a loss of 18%.

Norway had outperformed all the other global exchanges in 1979, but the results in 1980 were far different. On average, the decline in equity values on the Oslo Stock Exchange was 11%. The market made anemic attempts to rally during April and May, but selling pressure built up in the summer months and again in December, causing overall stock prices to end the year some 17% below the February highs.

Other Countries. The influence of soaring inflation was especially apparent in the Hong Kong stock market. The huge gains from property speculation, created by the trend of major multinational companies to establish a presence in Hong Kong in order to compete for China's business, spilled over into the stock market. The profits accumulated by equity investors in 1978 and 1979 tended to attract investors who had stayed out of the market after it had crashed in 1973. Also, some of the money withdrawn from less politically stable areas found its way into Hong Kong. The surge in equity prices added 124% to equity values between the March lows and mid-November. At the November high the cumulative gain in the value of Hong Kong equities since the end of 1977 amounted to 310%. Shortly thereafter, the base lending fee of Hong Kong banks was raised from 14 to 16%. As the market began to react to tighter credit conditions, speculators decided to take their profits and the selling momentum accelerated. On November 24 the Hang Seng index of 33 issues suffered its biggest one-day loss (6%) since 1973. Stock prices finished the year 68% higher than in 1979 but 11% below the November highs.

The performance of the Singapore stock market was one of the best in the world. Reflecting equity trends in Hong Kong and booming economic activity due in part to China's turn toward freer world trade, prices on the Singapore Stock Exchange rose 52% for 1980.

The stock market in Australia was also a star performer in 1980. After rising 37% in 1979, prices on the Sydney Stock Exchange entered the new decade in a bullish atmosphere. The All Ordinaries Index pierced the 1,000 barrier for the first time in October. As the year ended, the Australian stock market was surprisingly strong, having finished with a net gain of 37%.

In Japan the Nikkei Dow Jones average of leading industrial shares jumped 8% in 1980 to its highest level ever recorded. This continuing strength of the Japanese bull market, which began near the end of 1977, could be attributed to the country's success in absorbing the higher costs of energy and other raw materials and to its ability to maintain the value of the yen in international currency markets.

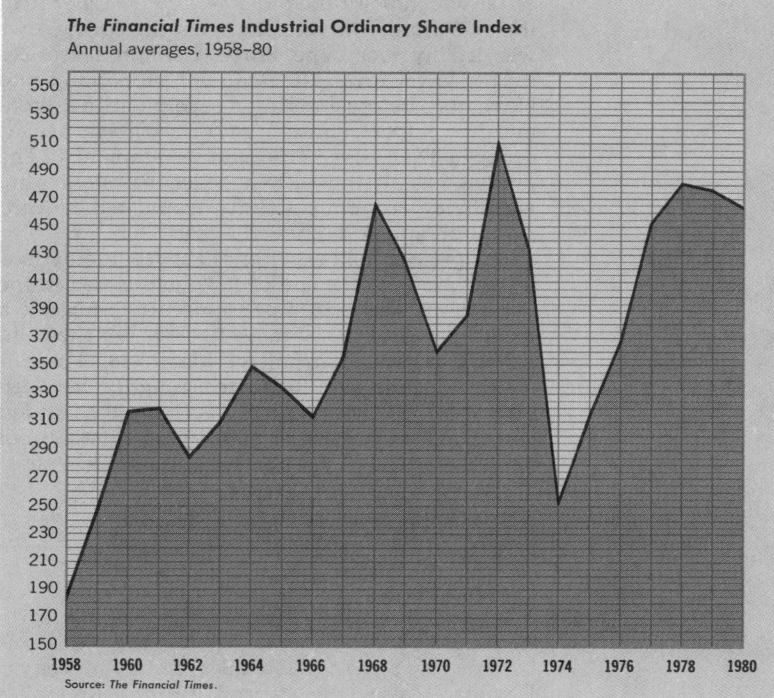

Source: *The Financial Times.*

The broad trend of stock prices in South Africa was likewise bullish. The index of industrial share prices on the Johannesburg Stock Exchange increased 32% in 1980. The gold shares index performed even better as it closed the year at 790, up 49% from its 1979 finish at 531.

Commodity Markets. Wide fluctuations characterized the international commodity markets during 1980. For the year as a whole, however, the broad trend of major world commodity price indexes showed only small gains. *The Economist*'s commodity index, which measures spot prices in terms of the U.S. dollar, climbed only 3% from the end of 1979 to mid-December 1980.

Commodity prices began 1980 on a strong uptrend in a continuation of the flight from paper currencies and search for inflation hedges that started in the summer of 1979. Political disturbances in the Middle East also added to buying pressure in commodity markets. However, prices began to fall in mid-February following the U.S. embargo on grain shipments to the Soviet Union and a steep climb in interest rates. Prices tumbled further amid worries about global recession, and the decline gathered momentum when large commodity speculators were forced to sell because of an inability to meet their brokers' calls for additional margin on money-losing positions. By mid-April *The Economist*'s index had fallen nearly 11% from the February highs, but the price decline in some individual commodities was much greater. For example, silver plunged 67% from its early 1980 peak, copper 35%, and wheat 14%.

A rebound in overall commodity prices restored all of the declines by mid-September. After a brief pause, the rally resumed and lasted until October

21, at which point the index was 13% higher than the 1979 close. The recovery from the spring lows was led by foods and fibres. Commodity prices drifted lower toward the end of October and into November before entering a severe decline. From mid-November until mid-December sugar dropped 32%, silver 30%, and soybeans 23%. The plunge was attributed to a belief that slackening worldwide economic activity would reduce consumption and to high credit costs.

The price of gold experienced sharp fluctuations during 1980. At the end of 1979 gold closed in the London market at $524 per ounce. It climbed to a record high of $850 on Jan. 21, 1980, but then slid to $474 on the morning of March 18. Thereafter, gold generally fluctuated roughly between $500 and $700. By the end of December the London gold quotation settled at $589.50 for a net gain of 12½% for 1980 as a whole. (ROBERT H. TRIGG)

See also Economy, World.
[534.D.2.g.i]

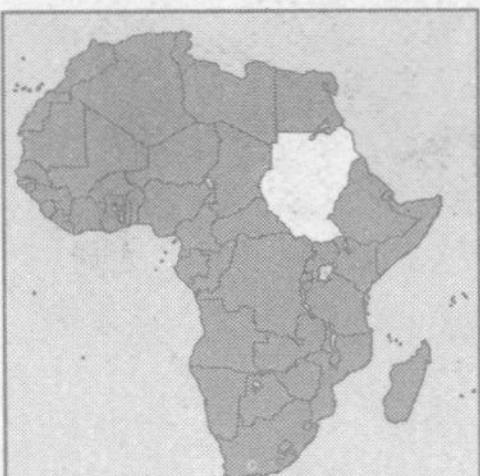
Sudan

Sudan

A republic of northeast Africa, the Sudan is bounded by Egypt, the Red Sea, Ethiopia, Kenya, Uganda, Zaire, the Central African Republic, Chad, and Libya. Area: 2,503,890 sq km (966,757 sq mi). Pop. (1980 est.): 18,371,000, including Arabs in the north and Negroes in the south. Cap. and largest city: Khartoum (pop., 1980 est., 1,621,000). Language: Arabic, various tribal languages in the south. Religion: Muslim (66%) mainly in the north; predominantly animist (29%) with Christian minority (5%) in the south. President and prime minister in 1980, Gen. Gaafar Nimeiry.

During 1980 the Sudan tried to improve its relations with some of its neighbours. Toward the end of December 1979 the Ugandan foreign minister, Otema Alimadi, visited Juba and held discussions with Gen. Joseph Lagu, president of the Executive Council of southern Sudan. His aim was to enlist Sudanese aid in the restitution of vehicles taken over the border by supporters of former Ugandan president Idi Amin when they fled from Uganda. From Juba, Alimadi went to Khartoum, where he apologized for the damage done to Sudanese embassy property in the Ugandan capital of Kampala by Tanzanian liberation forces as a reprisal for the Sudan's protest against the Tanzanian invasion of Uganda. More recently, the presence of Tanzanian troops near the Sudan–Uganda border had impeded the flow of goods to the Sudan from Kenya. Contrary to expectations, Pres. Gaafar Nimeiry did not attend the meeting of the presidents of Uganda, Tanzania, and Kenya held in Arusha, Tanzania, at the beginning of January. Nevertheless, as a result of Alimadi's visit the Sudan-Uganda border was reopened to normal traffic on January 10.

More significant for the Sudan was a visit to Khartoum by the Ethiopian head of state, Lieut. Col. Mengistu Haile Mariam, which resulted in a trade agreement and arrangements concerning refugees from the Ethiopian province of Eritrea currently in the Sudan. The divisive issue of Sudan's tolerance of arms-supply routes leading over its borders into rebel Eritrean areas was not resolved, however. In November President Nimeiry paid a return visit to Addis Ababa, which concluded with the signing of a joint declaration of friendship and cooperation. (KENNETH INGHAM)

SUDAN

Education. (1977–78) Primary, pupils 1,302,040, teachers 34,988; secondary, pupils 313,093, teachers 13,792; vocational, pupils 8,936, teachers 602; teacher training, students 4,221, teachers 488; higher, students 24,109, teaching staff (1976–77) 1,963.

Finance. Monetary unit: Sudanese pound, with (Sept. 22, 1980) a par value for a commercial rate of Sud£0.50 to U.S. $1 (free rate of Sud£1.19 = £1 sterling) and a par value for other transactions of Sud£0.80 to U.S. $1 (free rate of Sud£1.92 = £1 sterling). Gold, SDR's, and foreign exchange (June 1980) U.S. $32.8 million. Budget (1979–80 est.): revenue Sud£908 million; expenditure Sud£817 million (excludes development expenditure of *c.* Sud£285 million). Gross national product (1978) *c.* Sud£2,080 million. Money supply (June 1980) Sud£874,970,000. Cost of living (1975 = 100; March 1980) 219.6.

Foreign Trade. (1979) Imports Sud£477,320,000; exports Sud£232,670,000. Import sources (1978): U.K. 15%; West Germany 11%; U.S. 7%; France 7%; India 6%; Italy 6%; China 6%; Japan 6%; The Netherlands 6%; Belgium-Luxembourg 5%. Export destinations (1978): Italy 13%; Japan 9%; China 8%; Saudi Arabia 7%; France 6%; Yugoslavia 6%; Egypt 6%. Main exports: cotton 65%; gum arabic 8%.

Transport and Communications. Roads (1978) *c.* 50,000 km (mainly tracks; including *c.* 560 km asphalted). Motor vehicles in use (1977): passenger *c.* 55,000; commercial (including buses) *c.* 30,000. Railways: (1979) 4,786 km; freight traffic (1973–74) 2,324,000,000 net ton-km. Air traffic (1978): *c.* 600 million passenger-km; freight *c.* 11 million net ton-km. Inland navigable waterways (1978) *c.* 4,100 km. Telephones (Jan. 1978) 62,300. Radio receivers (Dec. 1977) 1.4 million. Television receivers (Dec. 1977) 100,000.

Agriculture. Production (in 000; metric tons; 1979): wheat 266; millet 370; sorghum 1,970; sesame seed *c.* 210; cottonseed *c.* 230; peanuts *c.* 1,100; sugar, raw value (1978) *c.* 229; dates *c.* 110; cotton, lint *c.* 131; cow's milk *c.* 925; beef and veal *c.* 195; mutton and goat meat *c.* 119; timber (cu m; 1978) 28,993. Livestock (in 000; 1979): cattle 17,300; sheep *c.* 17,200; goats *c.* 12,200; camels (1978) *c.* 2,904; asses (1978) *c.* 679; chickens *c.* 26,000.

Industry. Production (in 000; metric tons; 1977): petroleum products *c.* 1,210; electricity (kw-hr) *c.* 810,000; salt 92; cement *c.* 178.

Suriname

Suriname

A republic of northern South America, Suriname is bounded by Guyana, Brazil, French Guiana, and the Atlantic Ocean. Area: 181,455 sq km (70,060 sq mi). Pop. (1980 est.): 389,000, including (1971) Hindustanis 37%, Creoles 30.8%, Indonesians 15.3%, Bush Negroes 10.3%, Amerindians 2.6%. Cap. and largest city: Paramaribo (pop., 1971, 102,300). Language: Dutch (official); English and Sranan (a creole) are lingua francas; Hindi, Javanese, Chinese, and various Amerindian languages are used within individual ethnic communities. Religion: predominantly Hindu, Christian, and Muslim. Presidents in 1980, Johan Ferrier and, from August 15, Hendrick R. Chin A Sen; prime ministers, Henck Arron to February 25 and, from March 15, Hendrick R. Chin A Sen.

On Feb. 25, 1980, a group of noncommissioned army officers overthrew the government headed by Prime Minister Henck Arron and set up a Na-

Strikes:
see Industrial Relations

Sumo:
see Combat Sports

Surfing:
see Water Sports

SURINAME

Education. (1977–78) Primary, pupils 85,250, teachers 3,077; secondary, pupils 27,775, teachers 1,290; vocational, pupils 4,472, teachers 321; teacher training, students 1,874, teachers 174; higher, students 900, teaching staff 118.

Finance. Monetary unit: Suriname guilder, with (Sept. 22, 1980) a par value of 1.785 Suriname guilders to U.S. $1 (free rate of 4.30 Suriname guilders = £1 sterling). Gold, SDR's, and foreign exchange (June 1980) U.S. $188 million. Budget (1978 est.): revenue 623 million Suriname guilders; expenditure 650 million Suriname guilders.

Foreign Trade. (1977) Imports 707 million Suriname guilders; exports *c.* 551 million Suriname guilders. Import sources: U.S. 31%; The Netherlands 21%; Trinidad and Tobago 14%; Japan 7%. Export destinations: U.S. 41%; The Netherlands 24%; Norway 8%; U.K. 7%; Japan 5%. Main exports: alumina 48%; bauxite 20%; aluminum 16%; rice 6%; shrimps 5%.

Transport and Communications. Roads (1977) *c.* 2,500 km. Motor vehicles in use (1976): passenger 28,800; commercial 6,900. Railways (1977) 152 km. Navigable inland waterways (1977) *c.* 1,500 km. Telephones (Jan. 1978) 20,800. Radio receivers (Dec. 1977) 182,000. Television receivers (Dec. 1977) 39,000.

Agriculture. Production (in 000; metric tons; 1979): rice *c.* 220; oranges *c.* 10; grapefruit *c.* 7; bananas *c.* 35; palm kernels *c.* 10; sugar, raw value *c.* 12. Livestock (in 000; 1978): cattle *c.* 26; pigs *c.* 19; goats *c.* 5; chickens *c.* 1,000.

Industry. Production (in 000; metric tons; 1978): bauxite 5,025; alumina 1,316; aluminum 59; electricity (kw-hr) 1,511,000 (86% hydroelectric in 1977).

tional Military Council (NMC). In March the NMC appointed Hendrick R. Chin A Sen prime minister. The immediate motive of the coup was a conflict between Arron and the military cadre over conditions of service, but the silent support of the majority of the population indicated that discontent with the Arron government was widespread. In May an attempted invasion by a mercenary force proceeding from neighbouring French Guiana was repulsed.

There was another coup on August 13, led by one of the NMC's original leaders, Sgt. Maj. Daysi Bouterse. Two of the NMC's members were imprisoned, Pres. Johan Ferrier was dismissed, and Chin A Sen, who remained prime minister, was named president as well. Suriname's new rulers stressed the importance of nationalism, hard work, and respect for authority. Relations with The Netherlands, the former colonial power, deteriorated over the question of development aid.

(DICK BOONSTRA)

Swaziland

A landlocked monarchy of southern Africa and a member of the Commonwealth of Nations, Swaziland is bounded by South Africa and Mozambique. Area: 17,364 sq km (6,704 sq mi). Pop. (1978 est.): 544,000. Cap. and largest city: Mbabane (pop., 1976 prelim. census, 23,100). Language: English and siSwati (official). Religion: Christian 60%; animist 40%. King, Sobhuza II; prime minister in 1980, Prince Mandabala Fred Dlamini.

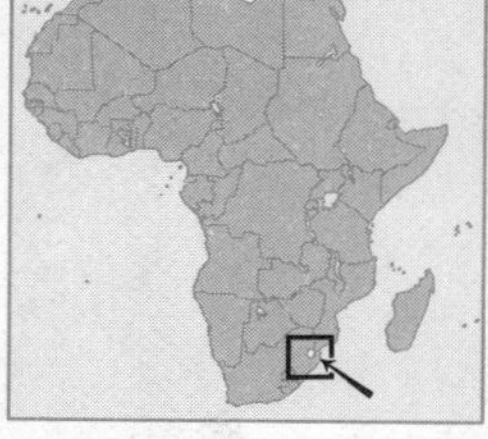
Swaziland

After the death of Maj. Gen. Maphevu Dlamini on Oct. 25, 1979, Prince Mandabala Fred Dlamini was appointed his successor as prime minister on November 23. Zimbabwe's independence in 1980 opened up for Swaziland new options and chances to lessen dependence upon South Africa. On June 4 explosions in Manzini, believed to have been caused by stored bombs of the African National Congress, killed two and drew attention to pressures on Swaziland caused by guerrilla activities against South Africa.

SWAZILAND

Education. (1979) Primary, pupils 105,607, teachers 3,016; secondary, pupils 22,091, teachers 1,158; vocational, pupils 605, teachers 57; higher, students 1,336, teaching staff 123.

Finance and Trade. Monetary unit: lilangeni (plural emalangeni), at par with the South African rand, with (Sept. 22, 1980) a free rate of 0.75 lilangeni to U.S. $1 (1.81 emalangeni = £1 sterling). Budget (1979–80 est.): revenue 115 million emalangeni; expenditure 68 million emalangeni (excludes capital expenditure of 101 million emalangeni). Foreign trade (1979): imports 295 million emalangeni; exports 188.9 million emalangeni. Export destinations (1977): U.K. 33%; South Africa 20%. Main exports (1977): sugar 37%; wood pulp 15%; asbestos 10%; iron ore 6%; citrus fruit 5%; timber 5%.

Agriculture. Production (in 000; metric tons; 1978): corn 90; rice *c.* 5; potatoes *c.* 6; sugar, raw value (1979) 255; pineapples *c.* 20; cotton, lint *c.* 6; timber (cu m) *c.* 2,572. Livestock (in 000; 1978): cattle *c.* 640; sheep *c.* 32; pigs *c.* 21; goats *c.* 260.

Industry. Production (in 000; metric tons; 1977): coal 129; iron ore (metal content; 1978) 770; asbestos 38; electricity (kw-hr) *c.* 173,000.

Swaziland and Mozambique established a joint commission for cooperation in industry, commerce, transport, and energy. Swaziland would export and import through Mozambique's port, Maputo.

Swaziland's priorities were rural development and education. The European Development Fund made a grant to help establish branches of the Institute of Development Management (already in Botswana) in Lesotho and Swaziland to train middle and senior management. A program of Rural Development Areas had been launched to raise subsistence standards and increase incomes. The nation's fast-growing tourist industry was attracting more than 200,000 visitors a year, but inflation in 1980 was at 15%, and the country also suffered from drought.

(GUY ARNOLD)

Sweden

A constitutional monarchy of northern Europe lying on the eastern side of the Scandinavian Peninsula, Sweden has common borders with Finland and Norway. Area: 449,964 sq km (173,732 sq mi). Pop. (1980 est.): 8,314,500. Cap. and largest city: Stockholm (pop., 1980 est., 649,400). Language: Swedish, with some Finnish and Lapp in the north. Religion: predominantly Lutheran. King, Carl XVI Gustaf; prime minister in 1980, Thorbjörn Fälldin.

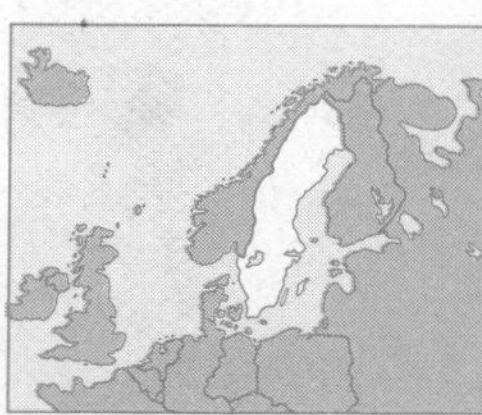
Sweden

Two events overshadowed all others in Sweden in 1980. In a national referendum on March 23, Sweden said a cautious "yes" to nuclear power. Then, in April and May, the country was shattered by the worst labour dispute in its history. After a year of discussion and contention, the referendum ended a great deal of political and economic uncertainty. But any optimism that might have been generated was wiped out just over a month later with the ending of 42 years of more or

PATRICK ZACHMANN—KATHERINE YOUNG

Swedish voters went to the polls on March 23 for a referendum on the future of nuclear power in their country. The result favoured a measured increase in nuclear power generation.

less unbroken labour peace. The dispute, which at its height saw one-quarter of the work force of four million either on strike or locked out, threw into question the much vaunted "Swedish model" of a highly centralized wage-bargaining structure.

In the referendum, 58% voted for the use of not more than 12 nuclear reactors over 25 years, while 38.7% favoured a shutdown of all reactors in 10 years. (Another 3.3% returned a special blank ballot paper indicating that they disapproved of the referendum.) After 25 years, options would be reviewed.

The labour crisis of April and May shook a nation that had become used to industrial peace. Since the Saltsjöbaden Agreement of 1938, centralized wage negotiations had always ended peacefully, but in 1980 they deadlocked almost simultaneously in the public and private sectors. On April 25, 14,000 employees in the public sector struck, and 12,000 others were locked out four days after an overtime ban by 1.2 million workers in support of a 11.3% pay increase had gone into effect. All air traffic into and out of the country was grounded, shipping and haulage were disrupted, and the Stockholm subway and Göteborg tram system were halted. Hospitals treated only emergency cases. Mail was delayed, television blacked out except for newscasts, and radio restricted to one channel.

In the private sector, on May 2, the Swedish Confederation of Trade Unions (LO) added a series of selective strikes to an overtime ban already in effect in support of an 11.3% pay increase. The Swedish Employers Confederation (SAF) responded with a lockout of 750,000 workers, originally set to last one week but later extended until May 18. Practically all industry in Sweden shut down, and 110 major stores and 60 hotels were forced to close. On May 9 the transport union stopped gasoline and oil deliveries to 80% of the country's suppliers.

Agreement was reached two days later after two government-appointed mediation commissions, one for the private and one for the public sector, presented the employers and the unions with final offers. These gave a 7.3% increase to public sector employees and 6.8% to those in private industry. Peace was restored, but the question was, for how long? The outlook for the 1981 wage round was not hopeful, as the Centre-Liberal-Conservative coalition government of Prime Minister Thorbjörn Fälldin continued to push ahead with measures designed to revive Sweden's ailing economy but strongly condemned by the labour movement.

On August 25 the first extraordinary session of the Riksdag (parliament) since World War II raised the value-added tax from 17.1 to 19% (from 20.63 to 23.46% at consumer price level), the highest in Europe. Then, on September 16, the government presented a 6.3 billion kronor package of public spending cuts. These two measures were expected to reduce the estimated budget deficit for 1981–82 by more than 7 billion kronor. There were strong protests from the Social Democratic Party, and on October 22 the government survived Sweden's first no-confidence vote by one vote.

On November 17 the automotive concern Volvo, Sweden's largest company, merged with the industrial and trading conglomerate Beijerinvest, the fifth largest company in the country. The new group would have a turnover in the 40 billion kronor range.

(CHRIS MOSEY)

SWEDEN

Education. (1978–79) Primary, pupils 686,111, teachers 38,689; secondary, vocational, and teacher training, pupils 575,190, teachers 62,964; higher, students 157,350.

Finance. Monetary unit: krona, with (Sept. 22, 1980) a free rate of 4.16 kronor to U.S. $1 (10.01 kronor = £1 sterling). Gold, SDR's, and foreign exchange (June 1980) U.S. $3,953,000,000. Budget (1979–80 est.): revenue 126,233,000,000 kronor; expenditure 159,569,000,000 kronor. Gross national product (1979) 431,140,000,000 kronor. Money supply (Dec. 1979) 65,750,000,000 kronor. Cost of living (1975 = 100; June 1980) 162.2.

Foreign Trade. (1979) Imports 122,610,000,000 kronor; exports 118,138,000,000 kronor. Import sources: West Germany 17%; U.K. 12%; U.S. 7%; Denmark 7%; Finland 6%; Norway 5%; The Netherlands 5%. Export destinations: U.K. 12%; West Germany 11%; Norway 10%; Denmark 9%; Finland 6%; U.S. 6%; France 5%; The Netherlands 5%. Main exports: machinery 26%; motor vehicles 12%; paper 10%; iron and steel 8%; chemicals 5%; wood pulp 5%; timber 5%.

Transport and Communications. Roads (1979) 129,066 km (including 850 km expressways). Motor vehicles in use (1979): passenger 2,868,300; commercial 177,900. Railways: (1978) 12,079 km (including 7,582 km electrified); traffic (1979) 5,843,000,000 passenger-km, freight 16,580,000,000 net ton-km. Air traffic (including Swedish apportionment of operations of Scandinavian Airlines System; 1979): 4,409,000,000 passenger-km; freight 197 million net ton-km. Shipping (1979): merchant vessels 100 gross tons and over 697; gross tonnage 4,636,662. Telephones (Dec. 1978) 6,181,000. Radio receivers (Dec. 1977) 8.3 million. Television licenses (Dec. 1978) 3,076,900.

Agriculture. Production (in 000; metric tons; 1979): wheat 1,113; barley 2,550; oats 1,646; rye 198; potatoes 1,182; sugar, raw value *c.* 346; rapeseed 313; apples *c.* 120; milk *c.* 3,391; butter *c.* 65; cheese *c.* 96; beef and veal *c.* 151; pork *c.* 311; fish catch (1978) 190; timber (cu m; 1978) 47,070. Livestock (in 000; June 1979): cattle *c.* 1,911; sheep (1978) *c.* 385; pigs *c.* 2,711; chickens (1978) *c.* 11,390.

Industry. Index of industrial production (1975 = 100; 1979) 99. Production (in 000; metric tons; 1979): cement 2,342; electricity (kw-hr) *c.* 92,400,000 (59% hydroelectric in 1977); iron ore (60–65% metal content) 26,618; pig iron 2,907; crude steel 4,732; aluminum (1978) 79; petroleum products *c.* 15,600; sulfuric acid 764; wood pulp (1978) 6,458; newsprint 1,484; other paper (1978) 3,071; passenger cars (units) 310. Merchant vessels launched (100 gross tons and over; 1979) 461,000 gross tons. New dwelling units completed (1979) 55,500.

Swimming

The Games of the XXII Olympiad, contested from July 19 to Aug. 3, 1980, in Moscow, failed to produce the major aquatic competition that had always been an Olympic highlight. Joining the United States in a boycott to protest the Soviet Union's invasion of Afghanistan, swimmers from Canada, West Germany, Japan, and several other nations supported their Olympic committees' ban on participation. (*See* TRACK AND FIELD SPORTS: *Special Report*.) The boycott gave the aquatic events a heavy East German and Soviet flavour. Swimmers from those two nations alone won two-thirds of all of the medals and 20 of the 26 golds.

Many new world swimming records were set during the year. Seven were by men (three by U.S. swimmers) beginning with 3 min 51.20 sec for the 400-m freestyle by the Soviet Union's Vladimir Salnikov (*see* BIOGRAPHIES) at the U.S.S.R. indoor championships in Leningrad on February 24. The women were far more prolific, as they set 14 world marks inaugurated by Tracy Caulkins of the U.S.; she lowered her 200-m individual medley time to 2 min 13.69 sec at the third annual U.S. Women's International Swimming Competition at Austin, Texas, on January 5.

The male swimmers of the Soviet Union and the East German women completely dominated all rivals at the Olympic Games. The Soviet men placed first and second in the 200-, 400-, and 1,500-m freestyle and the 400-m individual medley. It marked the first time any Soviet male swimmer had won an Olympic gold medal. Salnikov won three events and became the first man ever to break the 15-min barrier for 1,500-m freestyle, winning in 14 min 58.27 sec on July 22. The old mark was 15 min 2.40 sec, set in the 1976 Olympics by Brian Goodell of the U.S.

Surpassing their 1976 Olympic medal output of 18 medals, the East German women's team won 26 medals (11 gold, 8 silver, and 7 bronze). Led by Barbara Krause, who won three gold medals and set three individual world records in the process, the East Germans finished first, second, and third 6 times in 11 individual events. They were one-two in another, two-three in still another, and gained a lone first-place finish in two more events. In fact, only nine potential medals escaped them. Krause became the only woman ever to break 55 sec in the 100-m freestyle, swimming the distance in 54.98 sec in the preliminary competition on July 20. In the finals a day later she won the gold medal in 54.79 sec. Teammate Ines Diers achieved an incredible Olympic performance, winning five medals (two gold, two silver, and one bronze).

Sergei Kopliakov broke the listed world mark in the 200-m freestyle by swimming the distance in 1 min 49.81 sec in the Olympics on July 21. However, awaiting approval by the governing body for amateur aquatics, the Fédération Internationale de Natation Amateur, was a world record for that event of 1 min 49.16 sec by Rowdy Gaines at the U.S. indoor championships at Austin, Texas, on April 11. At the Austin competition, also on April 11, Par Arvidsson of Sweden set a world mark for the 100-m butterfly of 54.15 sec. He was to win this event later at the Olympics, though in a slower time. Mary T. Meagher lowered the women's 100-m butterfly record to 59.26 sec, also at Austin.

UPI

Tracy Caulkins set a U.S. record in the 100-metre breaststroke during the U.S. Women's International Swimming Competition in January. She also set a world record in the 200-metre individual medley.

The U.S. outdoor championships at Irvine, Calif., from July 29 to August 2 were designated as the U.S. Olympic team selection. A team was chosen to honour those athletes who would have competed in the Moscow Olympics. The championship started two days after the completion of swimming in Moscow in the hope that the competitors would swim faster than the medal winners in the Olympics. The swimmers generally failed to respond,

World Swimming Records Set in 1980

Event	Name	Country	Time
MEN			
200-m freestyle	Rowdy Gaines	U.S.	1 min 49.16 sec
400-m freestyle	Vladimir Salnikov	U.S.S.R.	3 min 51.20 sec
400-m freestyle	Peter Szmidt	Canada	3 min 50.49 sec
1,500-m freestyle	Vladimir Salnikov	U.S.S.R.	14 min 58.27 sec
100-m butterfly	Par Arvidsson	Sweden	54.15 sec
200-m butterfly	Craig Beardsley	U.S.	1 min 58.21 sec
200-m individual medley	William Barrett	U.S.	2 min 3.24 sec
WOMEN			
100-m freestyle	Barbara Krause	E. Ger.	54.98 sec
100-m freestyle	Barbara Krause	E. Ger.	54.79 sec
100-m backstroke	Rica Reinisch	E. Ger.	1 min 1.50 sec
100-m backstroke	Rica Reinisch	E. Ger.	1 min 0.86 sec
200-m backstroke	Rica Reinisch	E. Ger.	2 min 11.77 sec
100-m breaststroke	Ute Geweniger	E. Ger.	1 min 10.20 sec
100-m breaststroke	Ute Geweniger	E. Ger.	1 min 10.11 sec
100-m butterfly	Mary T. Meagher	U.S.	59.26 sec
200-m butterfly	Mary T. Meagher	U.S.	2 min 6.37 sec
200-m individual medley	Tracy Caulkins	U.S.	2 min 13.69 sec
200-m individual medley	Petra Schneider	E. Ger.	2 min 13.00 sec
400-m individual medley	Petra Schneider	E. Ger.	4 min 39.96 sec
400-m individual medley	Petra Schneider	E. Ger.	4 min 38.44 sec
400-m individual medley	Petra Schneider	E. Ger.	4 min 36.29 sec
4 × 100-m freestyle relay	East German national team (Barbara Krause, Caren Metschuck, Ines Diers, Sarina Hulsenbeck)	E. Ger.	3 min 42.71 sec
4 × 100-m medley relay	East German national team (Rica Reinisch, Ute Geweniger, Andrea Pollack, Caren Metschuck)	E. Ger.	4 min 6.67 sec

Swedish Literature: *see* Literature

EASTFOTO

Vladimir Salnikov of the Soviet Union won the gold medal in the 1,500-metre freestyle swimming event in the 1980 Olympics with a record time of 14 min 58.27 sec.

however, setting two world marks in the 200-m butterfly and one in the 200-m individual medley. On July 30 Meagher lowered her butterfly world mark by 0.64 sec, clocking 2 min 6.37 sec. A day later in the same event for men, Craig Beardsley set a world mark of 1 min 58.21 sec, and on August 1 William Barrett set a new record of 2 min 3.24 sec in the 200-m individual medley.

Canada followed the U.S. selection method at its national championships in Toronto. There, Peter Szmidt on July 16 swam the 400-m freestyle in a record 3 min 50.49 sec, lowering by 0.71 sec the record set by Salnikov in February.

In addition to Krause's records, the East German women set an additional seven world marks during the year. They included: Rica Reinisch, 100-m backstroke, 1 min 1.50 sec (preliminaries) and 1 min 0.86 sec (finals); Reinisch, 200-m backstroke, 2 min 11.77 sec; Ute Geweniger, 100-m breaststroke, 1 min 10.11 sec (preliminaries); Petra Schneider, 400-m individual medley, 4 min 36.29 sec; 400-m freestyle relay 3 min 42.71 sec; and 400-m medley relay 4 min 6.67 sec.

Diving. Unable to compete in Moscow, U.S. and Canadian divers did manage to meet the eventual Olympic medalists in a series of three international competitions during April and May in Canada, the U.S., and Mexico. Winner of the men's 3-m springboard in all three competitions was Carlos Giron of Mexico, who also won the 10-m platform in Mexico. Brian Bungum of the U.S. and Bruce Kimball of the U.S. were the winners in the 10-m platform in Canada and the U.S., respectively. In the women's events Jennifer Chandler of the U.S., Carrie Irish Finneran of the U.S., and Milagros Gonzalez of Cuba were the 3-m springboard winners. Melissa Briley of the U.S. won the 10-m platform in the U.S. and Canada, and Guadalupe Canseco of Mexico won the event in Mexico.

At the Olympics the men's gold medals went to Aleksandr Portnov of the Soviet Union in the springboard and to veteran Falk Hoffman of East Germany in the platform event. In women's competition Irina Kalinina of the Soviet Union won the springboard and Martina Jaschke of East Germany the platform. (ALBERT SCHOENFIELD)

Switzerland

A federal republic in west central Europe consisting of a confederation of 23 cantons (three of which are demi-cantons), Switzerland is bounded by West Germany, Austria, Liechtenstein, Italy, and France. Area: 41,293 sq km (15,943 sq mi). Pop. (1980 est.): 6,310,000. Cap.: Bern (pop., 1979 est., 142,900). Largest city: Zürich (pop., 1979 est., 376,400). Language (1970): German 65%; French 18%; Italian 12%; Romansh 1%. Religion (1970): Roman Catholic 49.4%; Protestant 47.7%. President in 1980, Georges-André Chevallaz.

Switzerland

By the end of 1980 Switzerland appeared to have come through the economic blizzard almost unscathed, with a high national income, low taxation, a small budget, practically full employment, and inflation below 5%. Economic activity showed growth, with the gross national product increasing by about 3%.

No parliamentary elections and no political surprises troubled 1980. Public discussion revolved around popular initiatives, referenda, and draft laws proposed by the government. In the spring a popular initiative proposing the separation of church and state at the federal level was rejected by 79% of those voting. At the same time, 86% of the people approved a constitutional amendment authorizing the government to purchase and stock in peacetime primary supplies for a potential emergency (it already had this authority in wartime).

In the fall a plebiscite involved, besides the grants of some supplementary sources of revenue to the federal government (largely at the expense of subsidies to the cantons), the heatedly controversial question of whether or not the wearing of safety belts in automobiles should be enforced by law. The results of the financial proposals were largely favourable to the federal government, but the compulsory safety belt won only narrowly. The French-speaking cantons, in contrast with most of the German-speaking, all voted massively against what they considered an inadmissible interference with individual freedom.

The growing deficit of the federal budget was of major concern and was expected to exceed SFr 1 billion in 1981. The largest item in the budget was expenditure on national defense. Against Socialist opposition it was fixed at SFr 1,550,000,000, of which SFr 1.2 billion were earmarked for the Skyguard and Rapier air defense weapons. Another concern was future energy supply. As of 1980 the country possessed sufficient stocks, but in anticipation of future needs the government was working out a comprehensive strategy and sought a new constitutional article to give it the necessary authority. The fixing of financial responsibility in case of accidents in the production of nuclear energy was discussed, and the construction of nuclear plants continued to be strongly opposed by ecology groups. In the usual rotation, Kurt Furgler was chosen president for 1981.

In foreign affairs the questions of eventual full membership in the UN and of closer commitments to the European Economic Community advanced slowly. The principle of "neutrality with solidarity" again proved more difficult to realize than to define. The Swiss preferred flexible bilateral relations and agreements with all countries to rigid systematized multilateralism or to the overriding authority of European and international lawgivers and enforcers. At the Madrid conference that opened in November to review compliance with the Final Act of the 1975 Helsinki Conference on Security and Cooperation in Europe, the Swiss delegation nevertheless played a constructive role.

Aware of the criticism leveled against it, especially by international organizations, the government sought to persuade Parliament and the people to increase the country's contribution to development aid. While the Organization for Economic Cooperation and Development aimed at a rate of 0.32% of each member's gross national product, Switzerland lagged behind with 0.19%, although private credits raised this figure to 4%. At the end of 1980 the federal Parliament approved the extension of credits of SFr 1,650,000,000 (out of government funds) for three years.

Within Switzerland the loudest critics of the established system were the youth movements, which displayed unusual violence, particularly in Zürich, in the second half of the year. In an effort to understand and conciliate rather than to punish, the government set up a federal youth commission. Nevertheless, police reaction was sometimes severe. There was criticism of the government-proposed system of centralized electronic assembly and processing of police information across cantonal boundaries. (MELANIE STAERK)

SWITZERLAND

Education. (1978–79) Primary, pupils 524,500, teachers (excluding craft teachers; 1961–62) 23,761; secondary, pupils 424,400, teachers (full time; 1961–62) 6,583; vocational, pupils 206,000; teacher training, students 9,300; higher, students 71,500, teaching staff (universities and equivalent institutions only; 1977–78) 5,911.

Finance. Monetary unit: Swiss franc, with (Sept. 22, 1980) a free rate of SFr 1.66 to U.S. $1 (SFr 3.98 = £1 sterling). Gold and foreign exchange (June 1980) U.S. $18,292,000,000. Budget (1980 est.): revenue SFr 15,045,000,000; expenditure SFr 17,342,000,000. Gross national product (1979) SFr 162.8 billion. Money supply (June 1980) SFr 69,310,000,000. Cost of living (1975 = 100; June 1980) 112.1.

Foreign Trade. (1979) Imports SFr 48.7 billion; exports SFr 44.1 billion. Import sources: EEC 69% (West Germany 29%, France 13%, Italy 10%, U.K. 8%); U.S. 6%. Export destinations: EEC 50% (West Germany 20%, France 9%, Italy 7%, U.K. 7%); U.S. 7%; Austria 5%. Main exports: machinery 31%; chemicals 20%; watches and clocks 7%; precious metals and stones 7%; textile yarns and fabrics 5%; instruments, etc (excluding watches and clocks) 5%. Tourism (1978): visitors 7,855,000; gross receipts U.S. $2,446,000,000.

Transport and Communications. Roads (1979) 63,081 km (including 764 km expressways). Motor vehicles in use (1979): passenger 2,154,300; commercial 160,600. Railways: (1977) 4,974 km (including 4,945 km electrified); traffic (1979) 8,288,000,000 passenger-km, freight (1978) *c.* 6,580,000,000 net ton-km. Air traffic (1979): 10,329,000,000 passenger-km; freight 434.3 million net ton-km. Shipping (1979): merchant vessels 100 gross tons and over 32; gross tonnage 265,336. Telephones (Dec. 1978) 4,292,000. Radio licenses (Dec. 1978) 2,172,100. Television licenses (Dec. 1978) 1,895,000.

Agriculture. Production (in 000; metric tons; 1979): wheat 417; barley *c.* 220; oats 52; corn 101; potatoes 880; rapeseed 31; apples 430; pears (1978) 113; sugar, raw value (1978) *c.* 110; wine *c.* 102; milk 3,642; butter 37; cheese 121; beef and veal 163; pork 271. Livestock (in 000; April 1979): cattle 2,038; sheep 361; pigs 2,062; chickens (1978) 6,688.

Industry. Index of industrial production (1975 = 100; 1979) 107. Production (in 000; metric tons; 1978): aluminum 79; cement 3,697; petroleum products *c.* 4,080; manmade fibres (1977) 81; cigarettes (units) 29,735,000; watches (exports; units) 36,677; manufactured gas (cu m) 51,000; electricity (kw-hr; 1979) 42,710,000.

Syria

Syria

A republic in southwestern Asia on the Mediterranean Sea, Syria is bordered by Turkey, Iraq, Jordan, Israel, and Lebanon. Area: 185,180 sq km (71,498 sq mi). Pop. (1979 est.): 8,647,000. Cap. and largest city: Damascus (pop., 1979 est., 1,156,000). Language: Arabic (official); also Kurdish, Armenian, Turkish, Circassian, and Syriac. Religion: predominantly (over 80%) Muslim. President in 1980, Gen. Hafez al-Assad; premiers, Muhammad Ali al-Halabi and, from January 9, Abdul Rauf al-Kasm.

Rapidly deteriorating relations with its neighbours dominated Syria's politics in 1980. Pres. Hafez al-Assad's regime was also shaken by the most violent civil disturbances in its ten-year existence. A union with Libya declared on September 10 appeared to be foundering by November, although it had brought quick rewards for Assad; it was reported that Libya had paid off U.S. $1 billion of Syria's weapons debt to the Soviet Union. Syria continued to drift into the Soviet camp with the signing of a friendship treaty in October. The outbreak of war between Iran and Iraq brought into the open Syria's polarization in the extreme Arab grouping, known as the Steadfastness Front. Syria led Libya, Algeria, Yemen (Aden), Lebanon, and the Palestine Liberation Organization (PLO) in a boycott of the Arab summit in Amman, Jordan, on November 25–27. Two years earlier, at the Baghdad (Iraq) summit, Syria had been pledged an annual $1.8 billion by the Arab oil-producing countries.

WIDE WORLD

Pres. Hafez al-Assad of Syria (right) was greeted by Soviet Pres. Leonid I. Brezhnev when the nations signed a 20-year treaty in October pledging cooperation.

Relations with Jordan, which had been improving in 1979 with the start of a number of joint economic ventures, slipped into tension in late 1980. Saudi mediation was necessary to defuse a border crisis. By December three Syrian divisions—at least 30,000 men—had been massed on the border, while two divisions were assembled on the Jordanian side. On December 4 Saudi Arabia's second deputy prime minister, Prince Abdullah ibn Abdul Aziz, said that President Assad had agreed to withdraw Syrian forces gradually from the border. But Jordan had apparently rejected Syria's two basic demands: that Jordan end its support for the Muslim Brotherhood in Syria and abandon its alleged plans to usurp the PLO's right to be sole representative of the Palestinians. Jordan's point of view was that King Hussein could not accept these conditions because the charges were themselves "senseless."

President Assad had cause to worry about the Muslim Brotherhood, an extreme Muslim grouping. Membership in the Brotherhood was made a capital offense in Syria on July 9. There had been violent incidents in Hamah and Aleppo in March, and individuals close to the regime had been assassinated. The security forces had some success against the Brotherhood, but by year's end it was unclear how much it had been permanently weakened.

In 1979 Syria had had ambitions for a political union with Iraq, but the project ended with the discovery in mid-1979 of a coup attempt in Iraq in which Syria was alleged to be involved. The Soviet intervention in Afghanistan in December 1979 hastened the split, with Syria defending the move and Iran, Saudi Arabia, and moderate Arab states attacking it. Contacts were still being maintained with Baghdad, however, and on December 22 the two countries reportedly agreed on the resumption of crude oil pumping from Kirkuk in Iraq to Banias in Syria.

A major cause of the unease with Syria felt in Baghdad and other capitals was the 20-year friendship and cooperation treaty with the Soviet Union, signed by Soviet Pres. Leonid Brezhnev and Assad on October 8 during the latter's visit to Moscow. The treaty stipulated that Syria and the Soviet Union would consult each other immediately should the security of either be threatened. Union with Libya proved a more difficult undertaking for Assad. Problems arose in November when Libya's leader, Col. Muammar al-Qaddafi, expressed a desire to see Syria adopt Libya's form of government by committee.

Continued economic hardship seemed likely in 1981. Economy Minister Muhammad al-Atrash said the investment budget was to be cut drastically, from S£14,000 million in 1980 to between S£8,000 million and S£10,000 million in 1981. Syria was about to embark on its fifth development plan (1981–85). It was admitted that the fourth plan had been too ambitious and had emphasized industry at the expense of agriculture. In an attempt to stop a drift to the cities investment and technical and vocational training in country areas would be stressed. (JOHN WHELAN)

SYRIA

Education. (1978–79) Primary, pupils 1,375,922, teachers 45,254; secondary, pupils 540,169, teachers 28,759; vocational, pupils 24,818, teachers 2,877; teacher training, students 10,364, teachers 988; higher, students 96,040, teaching staff (universities only; 1975–76) 1,332.

Finance. Monetary unit: Syrian pound, with (Sept. 22, 1980) a par value of S£3.925 to U.S. $1 (free rate of S£9.41 = £1 sterling). Gold, SDR's, and foreign exchange (Dec. 1979) U.S. $619 million. Budget (total; 1980 est.) balanced at S£28,903 million. Gross domestic product (1978) S£30,685 million. Money supply (Dec. 1979) S£16,010 million. Cost of living (Damascus; 1975 = 100; April 1980) 166.

Foreign Trade. (1979) Imports S£13,067 million; exports S£6,453 million. Import sources (1978): West Germany 11%; Italy 8%; France 8%; Iraq 7%; Romania 7%; Japan 5%. Export destinations (1978): West Germany 10%; France 10%; U.S.S.R. 9%; The Netherlands 9%; U.S. 9%; Italy 8%; Greece 7%; Saudi Arabia 5%. Main exports: crude oil 62%; cotton 17%.

Transport and Communications. Roads (1976) *c.* 16,339 km. Motor vehicles in use (1977): passenger 69,100; commercial 70,600. Railways: (1976) 1,672 km; traffic (1978) 322 million passenger-km, freight (1979) 449 million net ton-km. Air traffic (1978): 986 million passenger-km; freight 13.1 million net ton-km. Telephones (Jan. 1978) 193,000. Radio receivers (Dec. 1978) 1,792,000. Television receivers (Dec. 1978) 454,000.

Agriculture. Production (in 000; metric tons; 1979): wheat 1,319; barley 395; potatoes (1978) *c.* 165; pumpkins (1978) *c.* 142; cucumbers (1978) *c.* 182; tomatoes *c.* 510; onions *c.* 162; watermelons (1978) *c.* 717; melons (1978) *c.* 201; grapes *c.* 346; olives *c.* 190; cottonseed *c.* 213; cotton, lint *c.* 127. Livestock (in 000; 1979): sheep *c.* 7,563; goats *c.* 1,094; cattle (1978) *c.* 649; horses (1978) *c.* 55; asses (1978) *c.* 242; chickens *c.* 12,687.

Industry. Production (in 000; metric tons; 1977): cement 1,395; crude oil (1979) 8,939; natural gas (cu m) 474,000; petroleum products (1978) *c.* 4,300; cotton yarn 28; phosphate rock (1978) 747; electricity (kw-hr) 2,152,000.

Table Tennis

During the 1980 Summer Olympic Games in Moscow, the International Olympic Committee declined to sanction table tennis as a new Olympic sport, but it agreed to discuss the matter again at a later date.

The first World Cup competition, sponsored by the International Table Tennis Federation, was held in late August. The ITTF invited 16 of the world's top men players to compete for $36,500 at the Queen Elizabeth II Stadium in Hong Kong. Guo Yuehua (China) won the competition and the $12,500 first prize. His compatriot Li Zhenshi finished second. The next top finishers, in order, were J. Dvoracek (Czech.), M. Orlowski (Czech.), J. Hilton (England), S. Bengtsson (Sweden), T. Klampar (Hung.), and E. Boggan (U.S.).

The 12th European Championships were staged in Bern, Switz., in April. Sweden took the men's

1980 World Rankings

MEN	WOMEN
1. Seiji Ono (Japan)	1. Ge Xinai (China)
2. Guo Yuehua (China)	2. Li Song Suk (North Korea)
3. Shi Zhihao (China)	3. Zhang Deying (China)
4. Wang Huiyuan (China)	4. Qi Baoziang (China)
5. John Hilton (England)	5. Tong Ling (China)
6. Stellan Bengtsson (Sweden)	6. Pak Yung Sun (North Korea)
Tibor Klampar (Hungary)	7. Valentina Popova (U.S.S.R)
8. Li Zhenshi (China)	8. Jill Hammersley (England)
9. Xie Saike (China)	9. Zhang Li (China)
10. Jacques Secretin (France)	10. Kayoko Kawahigashi (Japan)

team title. Runner-up West Germany was followed by England, Hungary, France, and Czechoslovakia. In the men's singles final, Hilton defeated Dvoracek in straight sets. The Soviet women's team was also victorious, finishing in first place ahead of Hungary. Next in order were Romania, England, Yugoslavia, and France. In the women's singles final, Valentina Popova (U.S.S.R.) dropped the first set to Gordana Perkucin (Yugos.) but went on to win 20–22, 21–7, 23–21, 21–8. The men's doubles title went to Jacques Secretin and Patrick Birocheau (France), who defeated Dragutin Surbek and Anton Stipancic (Yugos.) 21–15, 20–22, 21–13, 21–19. Popova and Narine Antonian (U.S.S.R.) captured the women's doubles, defeating Maria Alexandru and Liana Macean-Mihut (Rom.) 21–13, 24–22, 21–19, 21–16. Czechoslovakia won the mixed doubles, but Milan Orlowski and Ilona Uhlikova needed five sets to defeat Desmond Douglas and Linda Jarvis (England) 18–21, 21–16, 18–21, 21–19, 21–13.

As expected, China totally dominated the fifth Asian Championships held in Calcutta in May. China not only won both the men's and women's team titles but monopolized the finals of the men's singles and doubles, the women's singles and doubles, and the mixed doubles. Shi Zhihao took the men's singles crown with a 21–17, 18–21, 21–11, 21–15 victory over Xie Saike. Qi Baoziang won the women's singles title by defeating Liu Yang 21–19, 12–21, 21–14, 21–17. Guo Yuehua and Xie Saike were crowned men's doubles champions. They beat Shi Zhihao and Cai Zhenhua 21–23, 21–16, 21–8, 21–10. Pak Yong Ok and Hong Gil Son (North Korea) managed to reach the women's doubles final, but they lost three straight sets to Zhang Deying and Liu Yang; the Chinese team won 21–16, 21–17, 21–15. In the mixed doubles, the two Chinese teams battled five sets before Xie Saike and Zhang Deying defeated Guo Yuehua and Liu Yang 21–14, 24–26, 15–21, 21–15, 22–20.

The European League winners for 1979–80 were Hungary in the Super Division, the U.S.S.R. in Division 1, Finland in Division 2, and Romania in Division 3. During the fourth Afro Asian and Latin American Friendship Invitational Tournament in Tokyo, China won both team titles, the men's and women's singles, and the women's doubles. Japan captured the men's doubles and the mixed doubles. The seventh Arab Championships were held in Syria. Saudi Arabia won the men's team championship and Libya the women's team title.

(ARTHUR KINGSLEY VINT)

Taiwan

Taiwan, which consists of the islands of Taiwan (Western conventional Formosa) and Quemoy and other surrounding islands, is the seat of the Republic of China (Nationalist China). It is north of the Philippines, southwest of Japan, and east of Hong Kong. The island of Taiwan has an area of 36,002 sq km (13,900 sq mi); including its 77 outlying islands (14 in the Taiwan group and 63 in the Pescadores group), the area of Taiwan totals 35,990 sq km (13,896 sq mi). Pop. (1980 est.): 17,704,200. Area and pop. exclude the Quemoy and Matsu groups, which are administered as an occupied part of Fukien Province. Their combined area is about 160 sq km; their population at the end of 1978 was 66,700. Cap. and largest city: Taipei (pop., 1980 est., 2,223,300). President in 1980, Chiang Ching-kuo; president of the Executive Yuan (premier), Sun Yun-suan.

In 1980 the international status of the Republic of China suffered a further setback when the International Monetary Fund and the World Bank voted in April and May, respectively, to replace Taiwan by the People's Republic of China. Nevertheless, Taiwan continued to prosper and to enjoy political stability and economic growth. Only about 20 countries—most of them in Central and South America—maintained formal diplomatic representation in Taipei. At the same time, trade relations were being established with more countries than ever before, including several Eastern European countries. The Nationalist regime's determination to maintain its independent status was reflected in its increased defense budget and in the statements of its leaders and people for the celebration of the 69th year of the republic. The new year was termed the year of self-reliance.

The economy of Taiwan depended largely on foreign trade. Total two-way trade reached U.S. $30,877,000,000 in 1979, with a favourable balance of $1,329,000,000. In the first half of 1980

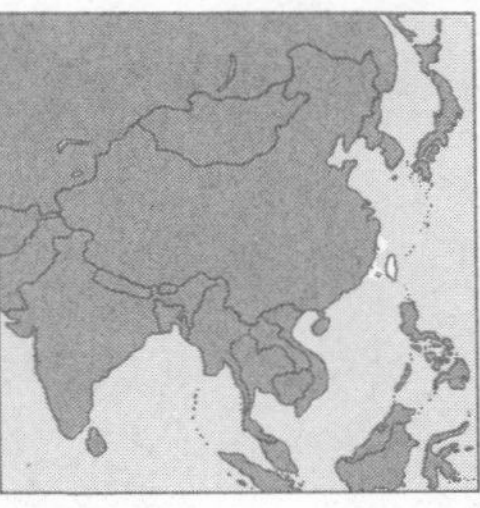

Taiwan

TAIWAN

Education. (1978–79) Primary, pupils 2,278,726, teachers 68,413; secondary and vocational, pupils 1,572,687, teachers 66,320; higher, students 317,188, teaching staff 15,452.

Finance. Monetary unit: new Taiwan dollar, with (Sept. 22, 1980) an official rate of NT$36 to U.S. $1 (free rate of NT$86.50 = £1 sterling). Gold, SDRs, and foreign exchange (Feb. 1980) U.S. $1,652,000,000. Budget (1979–80 est.) balanced at NT$194,177,000,000. Gross national product (1978) NT$889,360,000,000. Money supply (Jan. 1980) NT$254,710,000,000. Cost of living (1975 = 100; Feb. 1980) 141.8.

Foreign Trade. (1979) Imports NT$533.8 billion; exports NT$581.6 billion. Import sources: Japan 31%; U.S. 23%; Kuwait 8%; Saudi Arabia 6%. Export destinations: U.S. 35%; Japan 14%; Hong Kong 7%; West Germany 5%. Main exports: machinery 21% (including telecommunications apparatus 10%); clothing 12%; textile yarns and fabrics 10%; food 9%; footwear 6%; wood manufactures 5%; toys and sports goods 5%.

Transport and Communications. Roads (1979) 17,447 km. Motor vehicles in use (1979): passenger 340,600; commercial 201,300. Railways (1979): 3,700 km; traffic 7,327,000,000 passenger-km, freight 2,668,000,000 net ton-km. Air traffic (1978): 5,995,000,000 passenger-km; freight 678.5 million net ton-km. Shipping (1979): merchant vessels 100 gross tons and over 490; gross tonnage 2,011,311. Telephones (Dec. 1979) 1,860,600. Radio licenses (Dec. 1976) 1,493,100. Television receivers (Dec. 1978) 2,505,400.

Agriculture. Production (in 000; metric tons; 1979): rice 2,450; sweet potatoes 1,225; cassava (1978) 250; sugar, raw value 845; citrus fruit 399; bananas 227; pineapples 245; tea 27; tobacco (1978) 22; pork *c.* 670; fish catch 929. Livestock (in 000; Dec. 1979): cattle 143; pigs 5,418; goats and sheep 188; chickens 38,941.

Industry. Production (in 000; metric tons; 1979): coal 2,720; crude oil (1978) 247; natural gas (cu m; 1978) 1,841,000; electricity (kw-hr; 1978) 35,711,000; cement 11,897; crude steel (1978) 625; sulfuric acid (1978) 685; plastics and resins (1978) 625; petroleum products (1978) 14,054; cotton yarn 159; man-made fibres (1978) 540; paper and board (1978) 1,159; radio receivers (units; 1978) 9,649; television receivers (units) 5,870.

Taiwan's exports rose 29% to $9.3 billion, but it experienced its first trade deficit in four years, about $220 million. This was attributable chiefly to increasing imports of crude oil and machinery and, especially, to the rise in the price of oil. Total trade in 1980 was expected to reach $40 billion, with little or no surplus. Per capita income in 1980 rose to more than $1,800 from $1,720 in 1979, the highest in Asia after Japan.

When U.S. Pres. Jimmy Carter announced, in December 1978, his intention to recognize the Beijing (Peking) government "as the sole legal government of China," he also declared that the people of the U.S. and Taiwan would "maintain cultural, commercial and other [unofficial] relations." To this end, the U.S. established a quasi-governmental agency, the American Institute in Taiwan, and its Taiwanese counterpart, the Coordination Council for North American Affairs, was set up in New York and other major cities. After arduous negotiations, the "unofficial" U.S. and Taiwanese institutes signed an agreement on Oct. 2, 1980, granting customary privileges and immunities to each other's representatives.

During 1980 the so-called unofficial relations between the U.S. and Taiwan progressed smoothly. In January, after a year's moratorium, the U.S. Defense Department approved Taiwan's request to buy about $300 million worth of weapons, despite the usual protest from Beijing. Partly as a test of U.S. intentions toward them, the Nationalists continued to seek U.S. approval to purchase high-performance fighter planes.

Aided by large loans from the U.S. Export-Import Bank and private U.S. banks and by new investments on the part of U.S. corporations, bilateral trade with the U.S. continued to grow in spite of derecognition. In 1979 it rose 22% to $9,030,000,000, making Taiwan the eighth-ranking trade partner of the U.S. The U.S. was Taiwan's chief trade partner, followed closely by Japan. In the first six months of 1980, Taiwan's exports to the U.S. reached $3.2 billion.

While the long-standing hostility and suspicion between the rival governments on Taiwan and the mainland continued, unofficial and indirect contacts began to expand. Two-way trade through Hong Kong showed a considerable increase. Beijing ceased its campaign to isolate Taiwan economically; in April it announced that goods from Taiwan were exempt from import duty. Chinese industrial experts, scientists, scholars, and athletes from both sides met at international conferences and meetings in third countries. All this indicated some loosening-up by both sides and a reduction of tension in the Taiwan Straits.

In elections held on December 6, the ruling Kuomintang won 57 of 70 seats at stake in the Legislative Yuan. (HUNG-TI CHU)

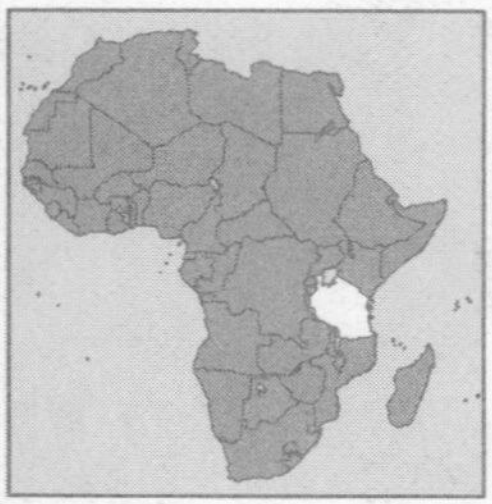

Tanzania

Tanzania

This republic, an East African member of the Commonwealth of Nations, consists of two parts: Tanganyika, on the Indian Ocean, bordered by Kenya, Uganda, Rwanda, Burundi, Zaire, Zambia, Malawi, and Mozambique; and Zanzibar, just off the coast, including Zanzibar Island, Pemba Island, and small islets. Total area of the united republic: 945,050 sq km (364,886 sq mi). Total pop. (1979 est.): 17,982,000, including 98.9% African and 0.7% Indo-Pakistani. Cap. and largest city: Dar es Salaam (pop., 1978 est., 860,000) in Tanganyika. Language: English and Swahili. Religion (1967): traditional beliefs 34.6%; Christian 30.6%; Muslim 30.5%. President in 1980, Julius Nyerere; prime ministers, Edward Moringe Sokoine and, from November 7, Cleopa David Msuya.

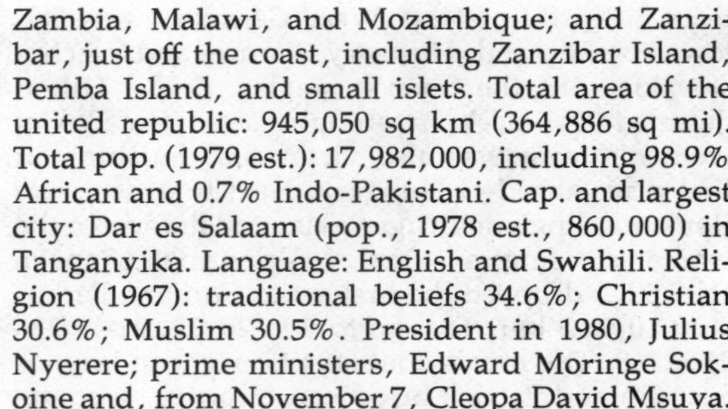

Under a new constitution and for the first time since the 1964 revolution, elections were held in Zanzibar on Jan. 7, 1980, for the National Assembly. Pressure for an end to union with mainland Tanzania continued, however, because critics of the government regarded the union as the main cause of the island's economic problems. In July, 16 people were arrested and accused of plotting to overthrow the regime, but in October Aboud Jumbe was overwhelmingly elected president of the Revolutionary Council, a post that he had previously held by nomination.

Elections in mainland Tanzania on October 26 resulted in more than half of the members of the National Assembly, including several former ministers, losing their seats. This reflected the electorate's concern about failure to solve the country's economic problems created by the high price of oil and the cost of the war in Uganda. Pres. Julius Nyerere was reelected for another five-year term.

TANZANIA

Education. (1976–77) Primary (state only), pupils 1,956,320, teachers 38,199; secondary, pupils 57,143, teachers 2,930; vocational, pupils 1,765, teachers 174; teacher training, pupils 8,951, teachers 627; higher (1977–78), students 2,534, teaching staff 533.

Finance. Monetary unit: Tanzanian shilling, with (Sept. 22, 1980) a free rate of TShs 8.03 to U.S. $1 (TShs 19.30 = £1 sterling). Gold, SDR's, and foreign exchange (June 1980) U.S. $68 million. Budget (1978–79 actual): revenue TShs 6,442,000,000; expenditure TShs 11,921,000,000. Gross national product (1979) TShs 37,583,000,000. Money supply (Dec. 1979) TShs 10,315,000,000. Cost of living (1975 = 100; 1st quarter 1980) 174.8.

Foreign Trade. (1979) Imports TShs 9,073,000,000; exports TShs 4,484,000,000. Import sources (1978): U.K. 19%; Japan 11%; West Germany 11%; The Netherlands 7%; Italy 6%. Export destinations (1978): U.K. 21%; West Germany 15%; U.S. 11%; The Netherlands 5%; Italy 5%. Main exports (1978): coffee 36%; cotton 12%; fruit and vegetables 9%; diamonds 6%; tobacco 6%; sisal 6%; tea 5%.

Transport and Communications. Roads (1978) *c.* 35,000 km. Motor vehicles in use (1977): passenger 43,600; commercial (including buses) 46,400. Railways (1978) 3,550 km. Air traffic (1978): 99 million passenger-km; freight 800,000 net ton-km. Telephones (Jan. 1978) 74,300. Radio receivers (Dec. 1977) 310,000. Television receivers (Dec. 1977) 5,000.

Agriculture. Production (in 000; metric tons; 1979): corn *c.* 900; millet *c.* 160; sorghum *c.* 240; rice *c.* 200; sweet potatoes (1978) *c.* 343; cassava (1978) *c.* 4,076; sugar, raw value (1978) *c.* 100; dry beans *c.* 149; mangoes *c.* 172; bananas *c.* 746; cashew nuts (1978) *c.* 77; coffee *c.* 49; tea *c.* 20; tobacco 22; cotton, lint *c.* 60; sisal *c.* 85; meat (1978) *c.* 194; fish catch (1978) 287; timber (cu m; 1978) 40,039. Livestock (in 000; 1979): sheep *c.* 3,000; goats *c.* 4,700; cattle (1978) *c.* 15,272; chickens *c.* 20,700.

Industry. Production (in 000; metric tons; 1977): cement 247; salt (1976) 22; diamonds (metric carats) *c.* 375; petroleum products *c.* 620; electricity (kw-hr; 1979) *c.* 734,000.

He appointed Cleopa David Msuya prime minister in succession to Edward Sokoine (who had retired because of ill health). Salim Salim, formerly Tanzania's representative at the UN, became foreign minister, and Lieut. Gen. Abdallah Twalipo, chief of the defense forces, was appointed minister of defense.

Relations with Tanzania's neighbours remained uneasy. Nyerere's criticisms of Britain's handling of the elections in Zimbabwe caused embarrassment to the eventual victor, Robert Mugabe (*see* BIOGRAPHIES). In March Tanzania began to withdraw its troops from Uganda, but unsettled conditions there made it necessary to retain half the original invading force. Nyerere agreed to this arrangement subject to wholehearted efforts being made by Uganda to restore law and order and to hold elections. Nevertheless, the continuing presence of Tanzanian troops in Uganda aroused suspicions in Kenya about Nyerere's motives, while in Uganda itself, although there was no lack of appreciation for the contribution made by Tanzania's armed forces to the country's stability, there were fears that their presence might promote the interests of Milton Obote's Uganda People's Congress Party. Nor was Tanzania's own shaky economy helped by having to pay the returned soldiers; unrest in the Army over pay led to the arrest of 30 officers in May.

A drought in the early part of the year seriously affected the output of corn, the country's staple food, and although the Ministry of Agriculture acted to avert famine, the need to use foreign currency reserves to buy corn was a further blow. Aid from various sources helped to keep the economy afloat. France assisted Tanzania, and a visit to Dar es Salaam by the French foreign minister, Jean François-Poncet, in July reflected the improvement in relations between the two countries. China also offered to assist in the rehabilitation of the Tanzam Railway. Nevertheless, in November much of Tanzania's industry had to close down for a month to preserve electricity supplies that had suffered because of the prolonged drought.

(KENNETH INGHAM)

Target Sports

Archery. As the year 1980 began, the world's leading archers were looking forward to the Summer Olympic Games, scheduled to be held in Moscow, as an opportunity to break Olympic records set in 1976. This was not to happen, however, because of troubling world events that led to a boycott of the Games by a number of nations. Thus, Olympic archery records established in 1976 remained in the record book with one exception. Keto Losaberidze of the Soviet Union set a new record at 30 m (98 ft) of 690 points out of a possible 720. The previous record was 686.

Olympic gold medal winners in 1980 were Losaberidze, with a score of 2,491 points, and, for men, Tomi Poikolainen of Finland with 2,455. A perfect score is 2,880 points. Silver medal winners were Natalia Butuzova and Boris Isachenko, both of the U.S.S.R., while bronze medals were taken by Paivi Meriluoto of Finland and Giancarlo Ferrari of Italy. Sixty-seven archers from 25 nations participated in the competition. (*See* TRACK AND FIELD SPORTS: *Special Report.*)

WIDE WORLD

The Soviet Olympic biathlon team, represented by Vladimir Alikin (centre), took the gold medal in the Winter Olympics at Lake Placid, New York.

In other competitions sanctioned by the International Archery Federation (FITA), several new records were set. For men Vladimir Esheev established a new mark at 90 m (295 ft), while Ho Jin Kim of North Korea, at 60 m (200 ft), and Olga Rogova of the U.S.S.R., at 30 m, set records for women.

(CLAYTON B. SHENK)

Shooting. Although only 38 of the 102 countries eligible participated in shooting events at the 1980 Moscow Olympic Games, three new world records were set. (*See* TRACK AND FIELD SPORTS: *Special Report.*) The U.S. Olympic Committee, which boycotted the Games, accepted an invitation to compete with the Chinese team at Beijing (Peking) with one new world record resulting. The Ladies' European Rifle and Pistol championships were held in Madrid.

TRAP AND SKEET. Thirty-three competitors from 20 countries participated in the Olympic trapshooting event. Luciano Giovannetti, a gunsmith from Pistoia, Italy, won the gold medal with a score of 198 out of a possible 200. Three shooters scored 196. After the tie was broken by shoot-off rules, Rustam Yambulatov of the U.S.S.R. won the silver medal, and Jorg Damme of East Germany the bronze. The skeet shooting drew 46 competitors from 25 countries. Five of them posted a score

World Archery Records

Event	Winner and country	Year	Record	Maximum possible
Men				
FITA	D. Pace, U.S.	1979	1,341	1,440
90 m	V. Esheev, U.S.S.R.	1980	322	360
70 m	S. Spigarelli, Italy	1978	338	360
50 m	S. Spigarelli, Italy	1976	340	360
30 m	D. Pace, U.S.	1978	356	360
Team	U.S.	1979	3,868	4,320
Women				
FITA	N. Butuzova, U.S.S.R.	1979	1,321	1,440
70 m	N. Butuzova, U.S.S.R.	1979	328	360
60 m	H. Kim, North Korea	1980	336	360
50 m	N. Butuzova, U.S.S.R.	1979	330	360
30 m	O. Rogova, U.S.S.R.	1980	352	360
Team	U.S.S.R.	1979	3,878	4,320

of 196 out of a possible 200. This tie was broken by the rule that penalizes misses in the later rounds. Hans Rasmussen of Denmark won the gold medal, while Lars-Goran Carlsson of Sweden took the silver and Roberto Castrillo of Cuba the bronze.

In the competition at Beijing the trap match was won by Terry Howard of the U.S. with a score of 192. Matt Dryke of the U.S. won the skeet matches with a 196.

Rifles. At the Olympic Games a new world record score of 1,173 was set for three-position small-bore rifles by Viktor Vlasov of the U.S.S.R. Another record mark was established by Igor Sokolov of the U.S.S.R., who fired 589 on the moving target. This score was equaled by Thomas Pfeffer of East Germany, who won the silver medal under the tie-breaking rules. The world record prone position small-bore rifle score of 599 was equaled by Karoly Varga of Hungary and Hellfried Heilfort of East Germany.

At the Beijing matches Rod Fitz-Randolph of the U.S. equaled the world-record English Match score of 599. Lones Wigger of the U.S. fired an 1,168 in the small-bore free rifle match to break by one point his own world record set in 1973. Yu Jiping of China won the moving target event with a 577.

At the Ladies European Championships at Madrid in September, a three-way tie score of 594 was broken to give E. Dingu of Albania first place in the prone rifle match. H. Helbig of East Germany finished second and H. Muller of Austria third. The three-position match was won by K. Boiko of the U.S.S.R. with a 583.

Handguns. Aleksandr Melentev of the U.S.S.R. won the gold medal in the Moscow free pistol competition with a new world record score of 581. Harald Vollmar of East Germany took the silver with a 568, while Lubtcho Diakov of Bulgaria gained the bronze with 565. In the rapid-fire pistol matches, Corneliu Ion of Romania won the gold with a 596. This score was equaled by Jurgen Wiefel of East Germany and Gerhard Petritsch of Austria, who were awarded the silver and bronze medals, respectively.

At the Beijing matches Su Zhibo of China won the free pistol event with a 571, and his compatriot Li Zhongai won the rapid-fire match with 596. Terry Anderson and Steve Collins of the U.S. both scored 595 in the latter. At the Ladies European Championships, Galina Korzun and T. Turischeva of the U.S.S.R. both scored 586 in the standard pistol match. Korzun was awarded first place in the close decision. E. Pecsi of Hungary finished third with a 582.

The U.S. rifle and pistol championships were contested during the summer at Camp Perry, Ohio. The pistol competition was won by James Pascarella of Las Cruces, N.M., with Don Nygord of La Crescenta, Calif., second and Jimmie Dorsey of Spokane, Wash., third. In the three-position small-bore rifle shooting the winner was Lones Wigger of Ft. Benning, Georgia, followed by Lance Peters of North St. Paul, Minn., and Ernest VandeZande of Ft. Benning. The prone-position small-bore rifle competition was won by VandeZande; Presley Kendall of Carlisle, Ky., finished second, and John Comley of Oklahoma City was third. For the high-power rifle the winner was Carl Bernosky of Gordon, Pa., followed by Gary Newton of Tacoma, Wash., and Robert Goller of Quantico, Va. (Robert N. Sears)

[452.B.4.e; 452.B.4.h.i]

Tariffs: see Economy, World

Taxation: see Economy, World

Telecommunications: see Industrial Review

Television and Radio

In some form television and radio service was available in all major nations in 1980. Approximately 828 million radio sets were in use, of which about 456.2 million, or 55%, were in the United States. There were about 425 million television sets, of which 169 million, or 40%, were in the U.S.

The Soviet Union, with 75 million television sets, ranked next to the U.S., according to estimates published in the 1980 *Broadcasting Yearbook*. Japan was third with 27.8 million. Other *Broadcasting* estimates included: West Germany, 20.5 million; United Kingdom, 18 million; Brazil, 16 million; France, 15 million; Italy, 12.6 million; Canada, 11 million; Spain, 8.4 million; Poland, 7 million; Mexico, 6 million; East Germany, 5.2 million; The Netherlands, 5.1 million; Australia, 5 million; and Argentina, 4.5 million.

More than 6,790 television stations were operating or under construction throughout the world in 1980. Approximately 2,200 were located in the Far East, 2,110 in Western Europe, 1,130 in the U.S., 920 in Eastern Europe, 180 in South America, 105 in Mexico, 96 in Canada, and 45 in Africa. Radio stations totaled about 15,800, mostly of the amplitude modulation (AM) type but with a growing proportion of frequency modulation (FM) stations. In the U.S. there were 9,238, of which 4,546, or 49%, were FM.

Organization of Services. Broadcasting organizations throughout the world used communications satellites to exchange news coverage of major events. Among the most widely disseminated were the U.S. Republican and Democratic presidential nominating conventions and election returns, the Winter Olympic Games in Lake Placid, N.Y., the Summer Olympics in Moscow, the fighting between Iraq and Iran beginning in September, and, until the Iranian government clamped down, events relating to the U.S. personnel held hostage in Iran.

During the year particular interest focused on the first definite plans for satellite broadcasting outside the U.S. The source of the sudden interest was an international treaty signed in 1977 under the auspices of the International Telecommunication Union that had allocated five satellite channels to practically every country in Europe, Africa, and Asia (the Americas were to discuss a similar treaty in 1982–83). After the treaty came into effect in 1979, several countries began preparing their plans, and in May 1980 France and West Germany ratified an agreement to operate twin national satellite services by 1984. Meanwhile, the European Space Agency (ESA) maintained its intentions to have a regional service in operation by 1984.

Relationships in the U.S. between many broadcasters and cable television operators became more strained—and more competitive—in 1980. The Federal Communications Commission (FCC) repealed two of the last rules limiting cable television in its use of broadcast signals: by a 4–3 vote the FCC struck down restrictions on the number of broadcast signals a cable system might carry and also removed the protection formerly granted local television stations against the use by cable systems of the syndicated programs to which the stations held exhibition rights. Broadcasters immediately appealed to the courts, arguing that they faced heavy erosion of audience and loss of program values if the decision was allowed to stand.

The FCC majority argued that its studies showed that broadcasters had suffered little or no loss of audience and had enjoyed rising profits in recent years despite large increases in the number of cable subscribers. In November the courts granted a temporary stay of the decision pending trial. At the time, according to estimates compiled by *Broadcasting* magazine, there were more than 4,200 operating cable systems in the U.S. serving some 10,200 communities, with another 1,300 or more systems approved but not yet built. *Broadcasting* estimated that the operating systems reached more than 15.1 million subscriber homes, or in excess of 44 million people.

In radio the FCC took the final step in breaking up the historic assignment of clear-channel AM stations by approving a plan that would allow up to 125 new AM stations to be built outside a 750-mi radius around existing clear-channel stations. The commission also proposed far-reaching changes that would permit the creation of scores of new FM stations.

Broadcasters—and the FCC—did get some good news. The U.S. Supreme Court refused to hear an appeal of an appellate court ruling that the FCC rather than the district court had "primary jurisdiction" in the so-called family-viewing case. In that case the district court had held that the FCC, the networks, and the National Association of Broadcasters had acted unconstitutionally when the networks set aside the first two hours of prime time—7–9 PM Eastern time—for programming deemed suitable for viewing by the entire family. The appellate court reversed the decision, and the Supreme Court's refusal to review that ruling in effect left the family-viewing plan undisturbed. In another case an eight-year-old U.S. Department of Justice suit charging the networks with monopolistic practices neared settlement when CBS and ABC agreed to substantially the same terms—mostly the imposing of restrictions on network ownership of programs—that had been accepted earlier by NBC.

The Corporation for Public Broadcasting (CPB) continued to operate in the U.S. under a system of private and public financing in which the federal government's share was budgeted at $162 million for 1981, rising to $220 million in 1983. And the Public Broadcasting Service (PBS), concentrating solely on programming as the result of a reorganization voted in 1979, offered an ambitious proposal of its own: a "momentous partnership" with the nation's performing arts and cultural institutions, in which nonprofit museums, theatres, dance and opera companies, and symphony orchestras would "invest" in public stations. It was estimated that the plan, coupled with the sale of station shares to public-TV subscribers, could generate $55 million to bring a dramatic increase in cultural programming.

In the U.K. a Broadcasting Act passed in November allocated the country's fourth UHF TV channel to the Independent Broadcasting Authority (IBA) after almost ten years of discussion. Channel Four, scheduled to start services in late 1982, had a mandate to encourage innovation and experiment. It would be financed by the Independent Television (ITV) companies, which would sell advertising time on the channel and thereby ensure a monopoly of TV advertising that in many countries had had a deleterious effect on programs.

The British home secretary announced on November 10 that he would accept applications (by December 31) for up to 12 pilot schemes for cable-TV networks for a two-year period. The licenses to be issued were fairly restrictive: feature films might not be shown in the first year after release, and advertising was not allowed. But the decision was the first step along the road to a national system of cable TV.

The British Broadcasting Corporation (BBC) announced cuts of £135 million in its budget over the next two years because of its worsening financial position. It attempted to disband several orchestras that it supported, but after vigorous negotiations and a strike by musicians it kept all but three.

In France there emerged a new wave of "radio libre," stations run not by extremists but by established political organizations. There were numerous battles between the police and station staff, and the courts passed heavy fines and prison sentences. The government's attempts to mollify the main audience for the "radios libres" by setting up a few local stations expressly aimed at young peo-

WIDE WORLD

Actors (from left) Jack Klugman, Ricardo Montalban, Loretta Swit, and Ralph Bellamy were on the picket lines in July when the Screen Actors Guild went on strike against large studios and TV networks. As a result of the strike, the TV fall season had to be rescheduled.

ple did not solve the real problem. In 1980, more than in any year since the 1974 reform, the French broadcasting organizations were seen to be out of touch with their audiences. In Spain, similarly, the government institution that had dominated broadcasting since the 1930s was increasingly criticized for excessive bureaucracy and corruption and for boring programs. Changes effected in 1980 were expected to lead to an increase in regional (such as Basque and Catalan) stations and a spread of private interests. In Australia the government appointed an inquiry board to look into the Australian Broadcasting Commission, which was to report by March 1981.

Programming. Programs made in the U.S. remained popular in many countries. They represented many forms: comedies, mysteries, Westerns, made-for-television movies, and dramatic programs comprising a limited number of episodes, known as "miniseries." Sales of U.S. programs and feature films to broadcasters overseas were estimated by *Broadcasting* at $350 million for 1979, and 1980 sales were expected to approach if not surpass that level despite a strike by actors that virtually halted production for more than two months during the summer. Among the most widely sold programs were the "Roots," "Centennial," "Holocaust," and "Rich Man, Poor Man" miniseries and such conventional series as "Dallas," "Police Woman," "Gunsmoke," "Starsky and Hutch," "Hawaii Five-O," "Happy Days," "Charlie's Angels," and "The Mary Tyler Moore Show."

A strike by the American Federation of Television and Radio Artists and the Screen Actors Guild stopped almost all U.S. program production from July 22 until October 3, forcing the three commercial television networks to delay the start of the 1980–81 prime-time season. Instead of beginning in mid-September as planned, the new schedules were introduced in stages, as new programs and new episodes of held-over series became available. In the meantime, the networks presented reruns of current hits, interspersed with a large number of specials. One of the most notable specials was NBC's "Shogun," a 12-hour, $22 million miniseries based on James Clavell's best-selling novel set in feudal Japan and starring Richard Chamberlain and Yoko Shimada (*see* BIOGRAPHIES). Shown over a five-night period starting September 15, "Shogun" became one of the highest-rated programs in television history, with an average A. C. Nielsen Co. rating of 32.6 and a 51 share of the audience. (Each rating point is equal to 1% of television homes, which in September numbered 77.8 million in the U.S.; each share point equals 1% of all homes with their TV sets turned on at the time the rating is taken.) NBC estimated that some 125 million viewers watched all or some part of "Shogun," as compared with 130 million in 1977 for "Roots," the ratings record holder for a miniseries.

Richard Chamberlain and Yoko Shimada starred in the miniseries "Shogun," which aired on NBC in September.

NBC PHOTO

In preparing for the new season, the networks dropped more than a dozen weekly series that had not maintained consistently strong ratings. These included "Galactica 1980," "The Ropers," "Angie," and "Goodtime Girls" on ABC; "Hawaii Five-O" and "Barnaby Jones" on CBS; and "Hello Larry," "The Big Show," and "United States" on NBC. In their places the networks scheduled a mixture of comedies, dramas, and magazine or information shows, including "Too Close for Comfort," "But I'm a Big Girl Now," "It's a Living," and "Those Amazing Animals" on ABC; "Ladies' Man," "Enos," and "Secrets of Midland Heights" on CBS; and "Hill Street Blues," "Flamingo Road," "Harper Valley PTA," and "Speak Up America" on NBC. *Broadcasting* estimated that, even before the 1980–81 season began to unfold, the networks were spending a combined total of $1 billion a year on prime-time programming.

Although the new season started late, there were signs that the old program-mortality rule—that two out of three new series fail to survive into a second season—was still at work. NBC decided to drop "Speak Up America" a few weeks after it started, and several other new entries were getting ratings that could prove terminal. For the week that ended November 23, only one new series ranked among the top 20 programs in the ratings: ABC's "Too Close for Comfort," a comedy, which placed ninth. The highest-rated programs of the week were "Dallas," a vastly popular "nighttime soap opera" on CBS; "The Dukes of Hazzard," a comedy drama, also on CBS; and "60 Minutes," a CBS News magazine show that was the highest rated program of the 1979–80 season.

The highest rated program of the year—and of any year since the early days of television when programs often played with little or no competition in their time periods—was the November 21 episode of "Dallas," when the identity of the culprit who had shot John Ross Ewing, the rich, ornery, wheeler-dealer star of the show played by Larry Hagman (*see* BIOGRAPHIES), was finally revealed. "Who shot J.R.?" had become a national, even international, catch-question during the summer, after his shooting in an episode at the end of the 1979–80 season. The November 21 story, in which Kristin, J.R.'s conniving sister-in-law, admitted doing the dirty deed, was watched in 53.3% of all TV homes and by 76% of all homes that had their sets turned on during that time. CBS estimated that 83 million people watched the show. The 53.3 rating exceeded the previous record for a series episode, a 45.9 rating, set Aug. 29, 1967, when "the one-armed man" was finally caught in the concluding episode of "The Fugitive." It also topped the record held by the final installment of the "Roots" miniseries, which scored a 51.1 rating and a 71 share on Jan. 30, 1977. In Britain the "Dallas" installment attracted the BBC's highest rating of the month.

Among other programs attracting attention in 1980 was "Playing for Time," a drama shown on CBS on September 30. The showing was widely protested in advance because of its casting of the actress Vanessa Redgrave, an outspoken Palestine Liberation Organization supporter, as a Jewish inmate in a Nazi death camp. The program scored a 26.2 rating and a 41 share of audience, with its viewers estimated at 41 million.

Networks and stations continued their efforts to improve programming for children, playing down violence and racial and sexual stereotypes and adding informational broadcasts and news reports designed for young audiences, especially in the Saturday-morning and Sunday schedules. During the daytime, game shows and soap operas continued to predominate. In an effort to break the mold NBC introduced a 90-minute variety program, "The David Letterman Show," but apathetic audiences led to its being cut to 60 minutes and finally canceled and replaced by game shows.

In the 32nd annual Emmy awards, the Academy of Television Arts and Sciences voted "Lou Grant" the outstanding drama series and "Taxi" the outstanding comedy series, both for the second year in a row. Ed Asner of "Lou Grant" and Barbara Bel Geddes of "Dallas" were named outstanding lead actor and actress in a dramatic series, and Richard Mulligan and Cathryn Damon, both of "Soap," best lead actor and actress in a comedy series. Johnny Carson of "The Tonight Show with Johnny Carson" received the annual special award of the Academy's governors.

Sports continued to rank among the most popular television fare and became increasingly expensive. *Broadcasting* estimated that television and radio networks and stations paid $207,241,350 for rights to broadcast college and professional football games in 1980, or about $6 million more than in 1979, and $80,225,000 to broadcast major league baseball games, an increase of almost $26 million. Philadelphia's victory over Kansas City in the sixth and final game of baseball's World Series was watched in 40% of all U.S. television homes, making it the highest rated World Series game in history. Overall, the six games had an average rating of 32.5, and NBC, which carried the Series, estimated that 140 million people—a baseball record—watched all or some of the contests.

NBC had paid $87 million for rights to cover the Summer Olympic Games in Moscow but withdrew—at a cost estimated at $16.1 million after insurance claims had been collected—because of the U.S. boycott of the Games after the Soviet invasion of Afghanistan. The Winter Olympics at Lake Placid, N.Y., however, were a boon for ABC, which had acquired the TV rights there. ABC's prime-time coverage drew ratings in the 20s and its broadcast on February 23, the day after the U.S. hockey team defeated the Soviet Union, gained an average audience of 22,050,000 homes, said to be a record for Olympics broadcasts.

News and public affairs, which normally represent about one-fourth of television programming, increased substantially as a result of coverage of state political primaries, the Republican and Democratic conventions, the ensuing campaigns for national, state, and local offices, and the election returns on November 4. Thanks to the availability of communications satellites, live coverage of regional and national events by local stations increased dramatically. As is usually the case, however, TV audiences were relatively small. Coverage of the Republican convention on ABC, CBS, and NBC had a combined rating of about 22 and a 45 share of audience; with the Democratic convention the combined rating was 27 and the share 55. On a normal evening of entertainment programming, combined network ratings were in the 50s and the share was above 80.

The only televised debate between President Carter and Ronald Reagan brought a departure from this trend. Carried on ABC, CBS, and NBC, the debate drew a 58.9 rating and an 84 share. But on election night, when all three networks were carrying the returns, the ratings dropped again. For the hours from 7 PM to 11 PM Eastern time, they averaged 46.3, with the share at 67. On the whole, however, the public's appetite for news remained strong, and two new national television news services were formed to help satisfy it, both distributed by communications satellites.

Music and news remained the basic format in radio programming. A study by *Broadcasting* found that, among the 10 highest rated stations in each of the top 50 U.S. markets, "contemporary" or currently popular music was featured by 32.2%, "beautiful music" by 15.7%, and various forms of rock music by 15%. News or news and talk were basic formats at 7.4% of the stations.

The PBS fall schedule included 11 new programs. One of the most ambitious was "Cosmos," a 13-part series with Carl Sagan, the astronomer, as host. Another was "The Body in Question," also a 13-part series, exploring mysteries of the human body. Other new entries included "From Jumpstreet," on black musical heritage; "Vikings!," tracing the travels of the Nordic sailors; "This Old House," offering information on refurbishing houses; and "Matinee at the Bijou," presenting classic films, newsreels, and old cartoons. A possible blow to PBS was the BBC's agreement to sell U.S. rights to its programming—a PBS staple for many years—to a new cable-TV network.

A British television documentary about a member of Saudi Arabia's royal family, "Death of a Princess," provoked enormous controversy not just within the medium but at the highest govern-

KEYSTONE

"Death of a Princess," a British show aired in April (also shown on U.S. public television in May), aroused angry protest from Saudi Arabia. The show dealt with the execution of a Saudi princess accused of adultery.

ment levels. The two-hour dramatized documentary told how Princess Misha'al had reportedly rejected her arranged husband, who was her cousin, in favour of another man, with the result that in 1977 she had been accused of adultery and executed. Antony Thomas, a noted British filmmaker, presented the story in the form of a search by a Westerner (himself) through the labyrinth of Arab religious and political conventions. The Saudi royal family made substantial efforts to stop the film from being shown, but Associated Television (ATV), the main backers, broadcast it as scheduled on April 9. British Foreign Secretary Lord Carrington said he regretted its showing but had no powers to intervene in such matters. On April 23 Saudi Arabia expelled the U.K. ambassador in Riyadh and halted the appointment, then in process, of a new Saudi ambassador to London. However, the atmosphere cooled over the months, and by the end of the summer diplomatic relations had returned to normal. In the U.S. PBS was urged to cancel the program, but went ahead and achieved a network-record audience.

Stricter standards for drama documentaries were imposed by the IBA, partly as a result of "Death of a Princess" but mainly because of the showing of a U.S. series, "A Man Called Intrepid," about Britain's wartime espionage activities. Col. Maurice Buckmaster, head of Britain's World War II Special Operations Executive, described the series as "a travesty of fictionalized espionage activities," and his criticisms were supported by many others who had been involved in the series' subject matter. Following talks with the IBA, the ITV companies promised to change their editorial processes to ensure stricter controls.

Several regular series of current affairs caused controversy. Among them was a "World in Action" (Granada TV) program on industrial relations in the British Steel Corporation (BSC), which used some highly confidential BSC documents. This led to a series of court cases, in which BSC asked for the name of the informer and Granada first refused to supply the name and then said that it was known only to a freelance researcher over whom they had no authority. On appeal, the House of Lords ruled that, although the use of the documents had been in the public interest, the issue of confidentiality and privacy was, in this case, of greater public interest, and they upheld BSC's position. The decision was strongly opposed by ITV and the press in general on the grounds that a journalist's ability to protect his sources was a legitimate and long-standing principle and an essential factor in the freedom of the press.

The year's drama in Britain was notable for a large number of successful adaptations of well-known novels, including Fay Weldon's adaptation of Jane Austen's *Pride and Prejudice* (BBC), Simon Raven's adaptation of Nancy Mitford's *Love in a Cold Climate* (Thames), Alan Plater's adaptation of J. B. Priestley's *The Good Companions* (YTV), and Philip Mackie's version of Emile Zola's *Thérèse Raquin* (BBC). Vera Brittain's autobiographical *A Testament of Youth* (BBC) was adapted by Elaine Morgan. London Weekend Television's (LWT's) "Why Didn't They Ask Evans?" was the first TV adaptation of a work by Agatha Christie.

In France the screening by Télévision France 1 of the hugely successful "Josephine" heralded fierce competition between the two national channels for Sunday evening and other prime times. Overall, however, audiences declined. In October all three French networks published a report on violence on television and agreed to adopt stricter standards.

In West Germany audiences also continued to decline. News and current affairs programs suffered the largest losses, surprisingly, as 1980 was an election year. The most popular programs were thrillers and quiz shows. Rainer Werner Fassbinder's $7 million version of Alfred Döblin's Expressionist novel *Berlin Alexanderplatz* was shown in 14 one-hour episodes during the autumn. The final episode, in which the protagonist, petty criminal Franz Biberkopf, is in a mental hospital, was remarkable for its dream-like sequences.

Successful Australian programs included "Water Under the Bridge," a drama series about Sydney between 1918 and 1960, and "The Last Outlaw," a four-part series about Ned Kelly, described as the best of the many narratives of the famous folk hero.

The Japanese public's increasing dissatisfaction with the broadcasters' offerings reached a climax with a series of attacks on the repetitiveness and blandness of programs. In response, the broadcasters began to experiment with new formats and more imaginative topics, with more programs being made on location and on film instead of in studios on videotape. One of the biggest projects ever seen in Japan was Japan Broadcasting Corporation's "The Silk Road," comprising 22 programs on the people, art, and trade of the old route between Europe and China.

The 1980 Prix Italia awards reflected two worldwide trends: at one extreme, bland nostalgia and, at the other, a sharply radical display of society's weaknesses and failures. The television music category winner was Britain's "A Time There Was (A Profile of Benjamin Britten)," directed by Tony Palmer for LWT's excellent "South Bank Show."

The television drama winner was the Dutch "In For Treatment," about a man who discovers he has terminal cancer. The television documentary winner was "Creggan" (Thames, U.K.), a film by Michael Whyte and Mary Holland about a housing estate in Northern Ireland. Winners of the corresponding radio categories were Norway's "The Descent," Italy's "The Witch's Baby," and France's "Questions Round Lesconil."

(RUFUS W. CRATER; JOHN HOWKINS; SOL J. TAISHOFF)

Amateur Radio. The number of amateur radio operators continued to rise in 1980. The American Radio Relay League, the leading organization of amateur ("ham") radio operators, estimated that there were 380,000 licensed operators in the U.S. as of Sept. 30, 1980, a gain of about 5% in 12 months. The number of licensed ham stations, including those operated by clubs and military recreation units, was put at about 385,000. Throughout the world there were approximately 1.2 million licensed amateur radio operators as of November 1980. Japan had about 400,000, the largest concentration in the world.

Ham operators continued to provide vital communications services when normal links were down. When earthquakes struck northern Africa and Italy, for example, networks of ham operators provided virtually the only links available for several days. (RUFUS W. CRATER; SOL J. TAISHOFF)

See also Industrial Review: *Advertising; Telecommunications;* Motion Pictures; Music.
[613.D.4.b; 735.I.4–5]

Tennis

Increasing spectator attendance and increasing earnings by the leading players were outstanding features of 1980. The U.S. Tennis Association estimated that Björn Borg (Sweden) and John McEnroe (U.S.) each earned more than $1 million during 1979 in prize money alone; the three leading women were Martina Navratilova (Czech.) $747,548, Chris Evert Lloyd (U.S.) $564,398, and Tracy Austin (U.S.) $541,676. Attendance at the French championships at a refurbished Stade Roland Garros, Paris, set a record, more than 222,000. At the Wimbledon championships in London, despite persistently wet weather, spectators numbered more than 333,000, and at the U.S. Open championships there were more than 331,000, a record. The International Tennis Federation (ITF) in 1980 named Borg and Navratilova as world champions, based on their 1979 performances. Raul Viver (Ecuador) and Mary Lou Piatek (U.S.) were designated world junior champions.

A dispute about the authority of supervisors appointed by the Men's International Professional Tennis Council (MIPTC) to officiate at all Grand Prix tournaments followed an incident during the 1980 French championships when Manuel Orantes (Spain) was defaulted for not obeying the instructions of the committee to play against Guillermo Vilas (Arg.) the day after the match was originally scheduled. The committee acted against the ruling of the supervisor, who wished Vilas to be defaulted for not appearing on court at the original time. Orantes appealed to the MIPTC, which fined the French tournament the amount of prize money Orantes would have earned had he won the match and then awarded it to the Spaniard. Feelings ran high among members of the Association of Tennis Professionals (ATP) that the supervisors' authority should be final, and there were moves to boycott the U.S. Open championships because of their refusal to allow such authority, but a compromise was reached in which the supervisors shared authority with the traditional tournament officers.

CENTRAL PRESS

Björn Borg fell to his knees after his victory over John McEnroe in the men's finals of the Wimbledon tennis championships in July.

Men's Competition. Vilas won the Australian singles for the second straight year when on January 2 in Melbourne he beat John Sadri (U.S.) 7–6, 6–3, 6–2. This was the last event in the Grand Prix for 1979. That title was won by McEnroe, winner of nine qualifying tournaments, for a bonus of $300,000. Borg won ten tournaments for second place and a bonus of $200,000. In the subsequent Masters' Tournament in Madison Square Garden, New York City, Borg beat McEnroe 6–7, 6–3, 7–6 in the semifinals. In the same round Vitas Gerulaitis (U.S.) defeated Jimmy Connors (U.S.) 7–5, 6–2. In the final Borg beat Gerulaitis 6–2, 6–2.

The eight-tournament series organized by World Championship Tennis (WCT) again maintained its own identity while being incorporated in the Grand Prix. In the eight-man WCT finals at the Reunion Arena in Dallas, Texas, in May, Connors beat McEnroe 2–6, 7–6, 6–1, 6–2 in the final.

The West German championship in Hamburg, was won by Harold Solomon (U.S.), who beat Vilas in the final 6–7, 6–2, 6–4, 2–6, 6–3. Vilas won the Italian championship in Rome, defeating Yannick Noah (France) 6–0, 6–4, 6–4. Borg won the French championship for the third successive year and for the fifth time in all, a record in both cases.

UPI

Chris Evert Lloyd displays her U.S. Open trophy after beating Hana Mandlikova for the women's singles title.

He did not lose a set in any of seven matches. In the final he beat Gerulaitis 6–4, 6–1, 6–2.

Borg also set a record in the Wimbledon championships. He won for the fifth consecutive year, a feat not achieved since the abolition of the challenge round system in 1922 required the defending champion to play all rounds. Borg beat Brian Gottfried (U.S.) in the semifinal. McEnroe won his semifinal against Connors 6–3, 3–6, 6–3, 6–4 to reach the final for the first time, but ungracious aspects of his behaviour toward line officials made him unpopular. In the final Borg beat McEnroe 1–6, 7–5, 6–3, 6–7, 8–6 after a memorable contest. McEnroe saved seven match points during the 18–16 tiebreaker in the fourth set. McEnroe's prowess earned him a standing ovation as a loser of heroic mold. With five wins in five years, Borg made his own place in the history of tennis. His total of consecutive winning matches in the singles at Wimbledon became 35. In 1976 through 1980 he won 104 out of 124 sets and 742 out of 1,217 games.

In the U.S. Open Borg reached the final after five set matches against Roscoe Tanner (U.S.) and unseeded Johan Kriek (South Africa). McEnroe reached the final after a perilous five-set semifinal against Connors, 6–4, 5–7, 0–6, 6–3, 7–6. In the final McEnroe beat Borg 7–6, 6–1, 6–7, 5–7, 6–4 to take the title for the second straight year.

In doubles competition two Australians, Peter McNamara and Paul McNamee, won their national open title at the start of the year. The French championships had unexpected winners in Victor Amaya (U.S.) and Hank Pfister (U.S.), who won the final against the revived partnership, outstanding in 1976, of Brian Gottfried and Raúl Ramírez (Mexico). McNamara and McNamee won at Wimbledon. In the final they beat another revived partnership, Bob Lutz (U.S.) and Stan Smith (U.S.). Lutz and Smith won the U.S. title, beating the defending champions, Peter Fleming (U.S.) and McEnroe, in the final. A doubles tournament endorsed by ATP at Sawgrass, Fla., in September was won by Gottfried and Ramírez against Lutz and Smith.

In the Davis Cup participants agreed upon a change in the competition format, to take effect in 1981. Zoning was abolished for the 16 leading nations, which would compete in an elimination tournament against one another. The remaining nations would maintain their zoning, American, Eastern, European "A," and European "B," with the four zone winners qualifying for promotion to the upper group in the following year. The 8 first-round losers of the top group would compete to determine which 4 would drop out of the top 16 in the following year. The 16 nations exempted from zoning for 1981 were, in draw order, West Germany, Argentina, Romania, Brazil, Great Britain, Italy, South Korea, New Zealand, Japan, Sweden, France, Australia, Switzerland, Czechoslovakia, U.S., and Mexico.

The U.S. had a brief tenure as champion nation in 1979. In February 1980 the U.S. beat Mexico in Mexico City 3–2. In March, however, Argentina beat the U.S. 4–1, José-Luis Clerc and Vilas each taking two singles against McEnroe and Gottfried. By so doing Argentina won the American Zone. Australia beat Japan and New Zealand to win the Eastern Zone. An unexpected result was a win, 3–2, by South Korea over India. South Korea then lost 5–0 to New Zealand. In the European Zone "A" Italy and Sweden were finalists. Borg was unfit and could not play for Sweden. Italy beat Sweden 4–1 in Rome. Czechoslovakia won the European Zone "B." In the semifinal round they beat France 5–0 in Prague. In the other semifinal Romania beat Great Britain 3–2 at Bristol. Because of complaints about the behaviour of Ilie Nastase in this contest, the Romanian was subsequently suspended for 18 months from Davis Cup play. Against a team thus weakened, Czechoslovakia beat Romania 4–1 in Bucharest. At the interzone stage Czechoslovakia beat Argentina 3–2 in Buenos Aires, and Italy beat Australia 3–2 in Rome. In the final at Prague, Czechoslovakia defeated Italy 4–1.

Women's Competition. Chris Evert Lloyd announced at the start of the year that she would not play again until she felt her former urge to win. Her absence proved brief. In the Colgate Series championships in Landover, Md., in January, the climax to the 1979 women's equivalent to the Grand Prix, Austin beat Evert Lloyd 6–3, 6–0. Navratilova beat Austin 6–2, 6–1 to win the tournament. A little later Austin again beat Evert Lloyd, 6–2, 6–1, in the final of the first of the Avon championship series in Cincinnati, Ohio. Evert Lloyd subsequently withdrew from the series. The ten-tournament series was dominated by Navratilova, but in the climactic event in Madison Square Garden, Austin beat Navratilova 6–2, 2–6, 6–2 in the final.

Evert Lloyd returned to competition in May, winning the Italian championship, staged in Perugia, with a final win 5–7, 6–2, 6–2 against Virginia Ruzici (Romania). She beat the same opponent 6–0, 6–3 to win the French championship in Paris, her fourth French title in five attempts.

In the Wimbledon tournament Evert Lloyd beat Navratilova, champion in 1979 and 1978, 4–6, 6–4, 6–2 in the semifinals. Evonne Goolagong Cawley

(Australia) beat Austin 6–3, 0–6, 6–4 in the other semifinal. In the final Cawley won 6–1, 7–6. She had won the title once before, in 1971.

Evert Lloyd won at Flushing Meadow to take the U.S. Open title for the fifth time in six years. In the semifinals she beat Austin 4–6, 6–1, 6–1. In the final she beat Hana Mandlikova (Czech.) 5–7, 6–1, 6–1. In her semifinal Mandlikova, aged 18, beat Andrea Jaeger (U.S.), aged 15 years 3 months, 6–1, 3–6, 7–6. With Austin 17 years old, the average age of three of the semifinalists was only 17 years 2 months.

In doubles Kathy Jordan (U.S.) and Anne Smith (U.S.) had notable success. After winning the French championship, they beat Rosemary Casals (U.S.) and Wendy Turnbull (Australia) 4–6, 7–5, 6–1 to win at Wimbledon. Pam Shriver (U.S.) and Betty Stove (Neth.) beat them in the semifinals of the U.S. Open only to lose to Billie Jean King (U.S.) and Navratilova 7–6, 7–5 in the final.

The 1980 Federation Cup, staged in May in Berlin, involved the sacrifice of women's events in the West German championships. It was won by the U.S. for the fifth consecutive year and for the ninth time out of 18. For the second consecutive year the U.S. did not lose in any round, and wins by 3–0 were made over Poland, New Zealand, the U.S.S.R., Czechoslovakia, and Australia. The U.S. team comprised Austin, Evert Lloyd, Jordan, and Casals. In the Wightman Cup the U.S. (Evert Lloyd, Jaeger, Jordan, Smith, and Casals) beat Great Britain (Virginia Wade, Sue Barker, Anne Hobbs, and Glynis Coles) 5–2 at the Royal Albert Hall, London, to record the 42nd U.S. victory in 52 contests. (LANCE TINGAY)

Thailand

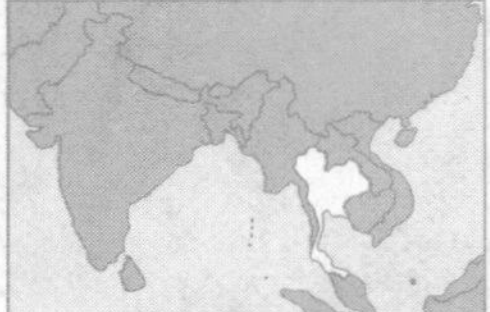

Thailand

A constitutional monarchy of Southeast Asia, Thailand is bordered by Burma, Laos, Cambodia, Malaysia, the Andaman Sea, and the Gulf of Thailand. Area: 542,373 sq km (209,411 sq mi). Pop. (1980 est.): 46,113,800. Cap. and largest city: Bangkok (pop., 1980 est., 4,999,500). Language: Thai. Religion (1970): Buddhist 95.3%; Muslim 3.8%. King, Bhumibol Adulyadej; prime ministers in 1980, Gen. Kriangsak Chamanand until February 29 and, from March 3, Gen. Prem Tinsulanond; chairman of the National Policy Council, Adm. Sa-ngad Chaloryu until November 23.

The year dawned with a rising crescendo of criticism against Prime Minister Kriangsak Chamanand's administration, primarily over economic issues. Opposition parties in Parliament planned a no-confidence motion for the end of February. There were clear indications that Kriangsak would have trouble winning the slender majority with which he had survived a similar motion in October 1979. Steep rises in the prices of domestic fuel and electricity had caused nationwide disaffection, and economic frustrations in turn sparked a higher crime rate. The prime minister was also criticized for his open-door policy toward Indochinese refugees.

Persuaded by his close supporters that he had lost the confidence of Parliament and that his clinging to office would only create tension and perhaps violence, Kriangsak resigned on February 29. Parliament thereupon elected Defense Minister Gen. Prem Tinsulanond (*see* BIOGRAPHIES) to succeed him. The 37-member Cabinet Prem introduced after two weeks of deliberations was the least military-dominated government in Thailand in recent years. Its heavy emphasis on economic policies was indicated by the appointment of highly rated banker Boonchu Rojarsthien as deputy prime minister for economic affairs.

Once the government was settled in office, security became its principal concern. Border tension with Vietnamese-dominated Cambodia and Laos persisted throughout the year, reaching a climax on June 23 when regular Vietnamese forces crossed the border and occupied three villages and two temporary refugee encampments in Thailand before they were repulsed. The Thai Foreign Ministry said that the incursion was "planned, premeditated, and carefully thought out," and Thailand played a central role in the successful attempt at the UN General Assembly in September to deny the Cambodian seat to the Vietnam-backed Heng Samrin regime. Thailand also made strenuous efforts to persuade other countries to support its stand that Vietnam must withdraw its troops from Cambodia. Prem himself toured Southeast Asia early in the year and China in October.

Despite its popularity, the government was criticized because of General Prem's retention of his army post beyond the retirement age of 60. In September Parliament adopted legislation extending Prem's tenure as army commander in chief for up to five years. Some opposition groups also tabled censure motions against the ministers of commerce and interior on charges of mismanagement. The government preempted the challenge by closing the special session of Parliament that was to debate the motions. On November 23 Adm. Sangad Chaloryu, chairman of the National Policy Council and leader of a military coup in 1976, died (*see* OBITUARIES). At the year's end he had not yet been replaced.

Besides political and defense problems, Thai-

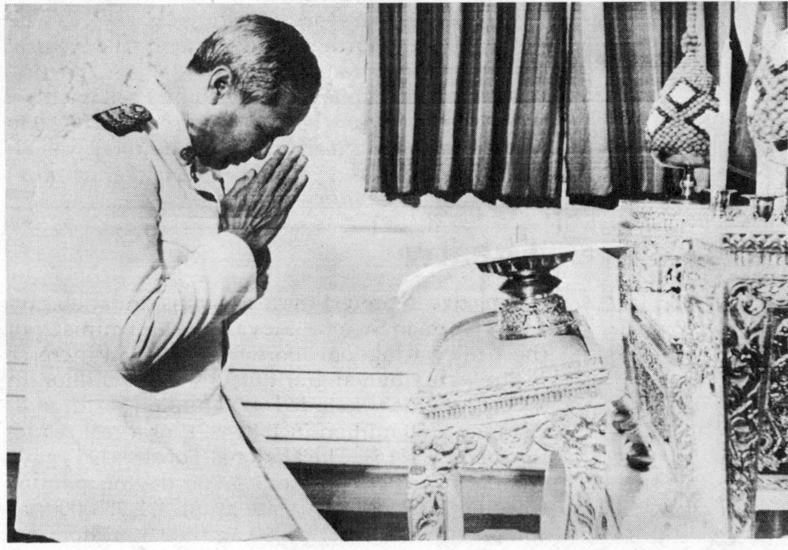

UPI

Gen. Prem Tinsulanond bows before King Bhumibol's letter notifying him of his appointment as prime minister of Thailand.

THAILAND

Education. (1978–79) Primary, pupils 6,848,121, teachers 283,204; secondary, pupils 1,503,646, teachers 66,965; vocational, pupils 221,411, teachers 28,894; teacher training, students 22,866, teachers 6,040; higher, students 169,-639, teaching staff 29,667.

Finance. Monetary unit: baht, with (Sept. 22, 1980) a free rate of 20.26 baht to U.S. $1 (48.70 baht = £1 sterling). Gold, SDR's, and foreign exchange (June 1980) U.S. $2,317,000,000. Budget (1979 actual): revenue 78,-537,000,000 baht; expenditure 91,826,000,000 baht. Gross national product (1979) 556,780,000,000 baht. Money supply (Feb. 1980) 68.8 billion baht. Cost of living (1975 = 100; June 1980) 161.3.

Foreign Trade. (1979) Imports 146,161,000,000 baht; exports 108,299,000,000 baht. Import sources (1978): Japan 31%; U.S. 14%; West Germany 6%; Saudi Arabia 6%. Export destinations (1978): Japan 20%; The Netherlands 15%; U.S. 11%; Singapore 8%; Hong Kong 5%; Malaysia 5%. Main exports: rice 14%; rubber 11%; tapioca 9%; tin 9%; corn 5%. Tourism (1978): visitors 1,454,000; gross receipts U.S. $390 million.

Transport and Communications. Roads (1979) 64,078 km. Motor vehicles in use (1979): passenger 387,300; commercial 417,200. Railways: (1979) 3,855 km; traffic (1978) 6,070,000,000 passenger-km, freight 2,650,000,000 net ton-km. Air traffic (1979): 4,683,000,000 passenger-km; freight 183.1 million net ton-km. Shipping (1979): merchant vessels 100 gross tons and over 136; gross tonnage 361,669. Telephones (Dec. 1977) 367,000. Radio receivers (Dec. 1977) 5.7 million. Television receivers (Dec. 1977) 765,000.

Agriculture. Production (in 000; metric tons; 1979): rice 15,640; corn *c.* 3,300; sweet potatoes (1978) *c.* 373; sorghum *c.* 240; cassava (1978) *c.* 13,000; dry beans *c.* 260; soybeans *c.* 125; peanuts *c.* 130; sugar, raw value *c.* 1,845; pineapples *c.* 2,000; bananas *c.* 2,082; tobacco *c.* 71; rubber *c.* 498; cotton, lint *c.* 33; jute and kenaf *c.* 370; meat *c.* 465; fish catch (1978) 2,264; timber (cu m; 1978) 21,797. Livestock (in 000; 1979): cattle *c.* 4,850; buffalo *c.* 5,500; pigs *c.* 5,386; chickens *c.* 65,324.

Industry. Production (in 000; metric tons; 1979): cement 5,243; lignite 1,356; petroleum products (1977) *c.* 7,810; tin concentrates (metal content) 40; lead concentrates 21; manganese ore (metal content; 1977) 18; sulfuric acid (1977) 48; electricity (kw-hr) 11,690,000.

land had to cope with natural disasters. In the early months, in the severest drought the country had experienced in 25 years, some 240,000 ha (600,000 ac) of rice fields were ruined, drastically cutting the second rice and sugarcane crops. Consequently, a steep decline in the country's vital rice exports was expected. Then, in the second half of the year, the country was ravaged by its worst flood in five years, affecting Bangkok as well as the lower northern region and the central plains, the traditional rice bowl.

The fiscal 1981 budget adopted by Parliament in September showed a 28% increase over 1979–80 to 140 billion baht. Nearly 20% of the total was allocated to defense. (T. J. S. GEORGE)

Theatre

The pledge to protect the arts against inflation given by Norman St. John-Stevas, the arts minister of the United Kingdom, bore fruit with an increase in the Arts Council grant of 12% (£70 million in 1980–81, which included £21 million for drama, rising to £80 million in 1981–82), or a real reduction of only 4¼%. The National Theatre (NT) gave 909 performances before 564,000 paying patrons (income £3.4 million, state grant £4,950,000, as compared with £3,190,000 and £2.3 million, respectively, for the Royal Shakespeare Company [RSC]). The NT announced annual seasons starting in 1982 in Bath, whose 175-year-old Theatre Royal was thus saved.

The RSC won most of the year's Society of West End Theatre (SWET) awards. SWET received a promotional state grant of £5,000, while the Association for Business Sponsorship of the Arts obtained £25,000. SWET opened a booth for the last-minute half-price sale of unsold theatre seats in London.

In a mid-December announcement, the Arts Council withdrew support from 41 theatre and arts organizations for financial 1981–82, saving £1.2 million. The Old Vic Theatre's touring organization, Prospect Productions, would lose its £300,-000 grant.

Subscription schemes began to catch on. The Old Vic, whose founder, Toby Robertson, resigned to make way for Timothy West, presold 60% of its seats before launching a new season with a much-criticized *Macbeth;* it starred Peter O'Toole, who resigned as associate director at the end of the year. Despite adverse notices, all performances sold out, wiping out a £200,000 deficit. Peter Gill left the Riverside to join the NT, while the Lyric at Hammersmith signed on Peter James of the Sheffield Crucible for 1982.

In West Germany Peter Palitzsch left Frankfurt. Hansgünther Heyme moved to Stuttgart, Claus Peymann to Bochum, Boy Gobert to the Berlin Schiller Theatre, and Peter Striebeck to the Thalia and Niels-Peter Rudolph to the Schauspielhaus, both in Hamburg. In Paris Jean-Louis Perinetti switched to the Théâtre de Paris, being replaced at the Chaillot by Antoine Vitez. Although Jean-Philippe Lecat, France's minister of culture, raised the arts budget by only 11.6% to Fr 300 million (6% behind the inflation rate), the drama grant rose more than 20%.

Rolf Hochhuth, the controversial German playwright living in Switzerland, replied to attacks in the right-wing press with allegations of covert censorship. Censorship and political discrimination were burning issues in many countries. Ariane Mnouchkine and Patrice Chéreau, both of France, formed the International Association for the Defense of Artists. They presented, in Munich, West Germany, a reenactment of the trial of dissidents in Prague, Czech., in 1979. The Vienna Burgtheater canceled its Moscow trip when a member of the troupe, Czechoslovak-born Pavel Landovsky, was refused a visa. The Arts Council in Britain defended the Theatre Royal, Stratford East, and the NT in London from hostile attacks on two new plays by Howard Brenton.

Great Britain and Ireland. Peter Hall's NT production of *Othello*, starring Paul Scofield, represented Britain at the European Common Market's biennial Europalia Festival in Brussels, while Peter Shaffer's (*see* BIOGRAPHIES) *Amadeus* continued to break all box-office records. At the Olivier the NT staged Brenton's new translation of Bertolt Brecht's *The Life of Galileo* in a production by John Dexter; Brenton's epic drama of *The Romans in Britain*, produced by Michael Bogdanov, which attracted much abuse for its political bias and scenes of violence; and Bogdanov's dazzling adaptation of

Hiawatha. Popular at the Lyttelton were David Storey's *Early Days*, with Ralph Richardson; Bernard Pomerance's *The Elephant Man*; Harold Pinter's *The Caretaker*, with Warren Mitchell; and Lillian Hellman's *Watch on the Rhine*, featuring Peggy Ashcroft. The Eugene O'Neill season continued with *The Iceman Cometh* and *Hughie*, at the Cottesloe, where Bill Bryden staged Arthur Miller's *The Crucible* and Athol Fugard's *A Lesson from Aloes* with its original South African cast.

With the RSC taking the SWET top awards, the Aldwych had a record season. David Edgar's nine-hour, two-part version of *Nicholas Nickleby* was named best play; and other awards for the play went to Roger Rees as best actor, David Threlfall for best supporting performance, Suzanne Bertish as best supporting actress, Trevor Nunn and John Caird for direction, and John Napier and Dermot Haynes for design. Two other SWET awards to the RSC went to Judi Dench (best actress in a revival) for her Juno in Trevor Nunn's moving re-creation of *Juno and the Paycock*, and to Willy Russell, author of *Educating Rita*, at the Warehouse, for the best comedy.

Transfers from Stratford included, at the Aldwych, *Twelfth Night*, with Cherie Lunghi as Viola and John Woodvine as Malvolio, *The Merry Wives of Windsor*, with Woodvine as Falstaff, and *Othello*, with Donald Sinden and Suzanne Bertish in the leads; and at the Warehouse, *The Caucasian Chalk Circle*, with Jane Carr as Grusha. New plays included works by Barrie Keefe, Howard Barker, Ron Hutchinson, and Peter Prince, and *No Limits to Love* by David Mercer (*see* OBITUARIES). Outstanding at the Aldwych was *The Greeks*, a three-part epic adaptation of Aeschylus, Homer, Sophocles, and Euripides, notable for Lynn Dearth's Electra and Janet Suzman's Helen. A few commercial West End shows originated in fringe or regional theatres, such as Andrew Davies's *Rose*, with Glenda Jackson (in Coventry), Ronald Harwood's *The Dresser* (in Manchester), Alan Ayckbourn's *Season's Greetings* (in Scarborough), Rodney Ackland's *Before the Party* (in Oxford), Tom Kempinski's *Duet for One*, which won Frances de la Tour the SWET award for best actress in a new play (at the Bush), Frederick Lonsdale's *The Last of Mrs. Cheyney* (at the Chichester Festival), Noël Coward's *Private Lives* (in Greenwich), Michael Frayn's *Make and Break* (at the Lyric in Hammersmith), Pinter's *The Hothouse* (in Hampstead), and the smash hit *Pal Joey* (at the Half Moon).

Among musicals *Sweeney Todd*, though a box-office failure, secured two SWET awards, as best musical and, for Denis Quilley in the title role, that for best actor in a musical. Gemma Craven won the equivalent actress award for *They're Playing Our Song*. Other musicals included *Tom-foolery, Colette, The Streets of London* (transferred from the Theatre Royal, Stratford East), *The Biograph Girl* (from Brighton), and *Oklahoma!*

At the Royal Court Jonathan Pryce won the SWET award for best actor in a revival for his portrayal of Hamlet. New plays at the Royal Court included Paul Kember's *Not Quite Jerusalem*, Sam Shepard's *Seduced*, and the 18-year-old Andrea Dunbar's *The Arbor*. Other events were Miller's *The Price* at the Shaw, Michael Frayn's *Liberty Hall* at Greenwich, Shepard's *Buried Child* at Hampstead, the return of Frank Dunlop to the Young Vic with *King Lear*, the world premiere of *Mayakovski* by East German writer Stefan Schütz at the Half Moon, Charles Marowitz's *Hedda* at the Round House, and Edward Dukes's one-man show *Jeeves Takes Charge*, which won a special SWET award for most promising newcomer.

KEYSTONE

Paul Scofield (centre) starred in London's National Theatre production of *Amadeus* by Peter Shaffer.

The Abbey Theatre, Dublin (with a grant of I£800,000), continued its Sean O'Casey season with *The Shadow of a Gunman* and *Red Roses for Me*, while *Juno and the Paycock*, starring and staged by Siobhan McKenna, also went to the English Theatre in Vienna. At the 22nd Dublin Festival were Hugh Leonard's *A Life*; new plays by Bernard Farrell, J. Graham Reid, Neil Donnelly, and Stewart Parker; and Maureen Charlton's *Nora Barnacle*, about James Joyce's wife, which created a minor theatrical scandal. Earlier, Joe Dowling had staged *Faith Healer* by Brian Friel, who joined forces with Stephen Rea to found the northern Irish "Field Day" company and launch a tour of his own highly praised historical drama *Translations*.

France, The Netherlands, Italy, and Spain. The Comédie Française (*see* SIDEBAR) began its birthday celebrations with revivals, new productions, and foreign guest visits. Of special interest were a revival of Villiers de l'Isle-Adam's feminist drama *The Revolt* at the Odéon; Ludmila Mikael's twofold triumph as Ysé in Paul Claudel's *The Midday Break* and Nina in Chekhov's *The Seagull*; and Jean-Louis Cochet's production, with Richard Strauss's music, of *The Would-be Nobleman*. Jean-Louis Barrault staged a six-hour-long revival of Claudel's *The Satin Slipper* at the d'Orsay. At the Théâtre de la Ville Jean Mercure presented *Every Good Boy Deserves Favour*, staged by Robert Dhéry. A new work by Rezvani and Dario Fo in person were both to be seen at the Théâtre de l'Est Parisien. Peter Stein's *The Oresteia* from West Berlin and Peter Brook's latest double-bill from 1979 were at the Autumn Festival.

Claude Rich's *A Winter Suit* won the 1980 Critics'

The Comédie Française

The world's oldest national theatre celebrated its 300th anniversary with a festive program scheduled to last into the middle of 1981 and with a spectacular retrospective exhibition illustrating its story and its achievements, which the French minister of culture, Jean-Philippe Lecat, opened at the Centre Pompidou in Paris. The Comédie Française was founded by Louis XIV on Aug. 18, 1680. The exhibition included the original founding document, signed by the king at Versailles on Oct. 21, 1680; the first "Act of Association" of 1681, still in force today; and the document creating the category of "sociétaires" in 1804, confirmed in the historic Moscow Decree signed by Napoleon in 1812.

The ensemble of actors, or *comédiens* in French, hence its official title, came together in 1671 at the Hôtel Guénégaud. After the death of their creator and first manager, Jean-Baptiste Poquelin, known as Molière, in 1673, they moved to their present home, the Salle Richelieu, which was rebuilt in 1786 and completely modernized in 1974–76. In the interim they also occupied premises in three other theatres, including their present second stage, the Odéon.

The plays of Molière (the ensemble's popular name is the "House of Molière"), Corneille, Racine, Regnard, Voltaire, Marivaux, Beaumarchais, Dumas, de Vigny, Hugo, Musset, and of every leading French dramatist up to Eugène Ionesco (in 1966) are the company's staple fare. Events for the tricentenary, under the management of Jacques Toja, the present administrator (a post created in 1850), were fixed by Pierre Dux, who retired in 1980; they included revivals and new productions, such as *Twelfth Night* staged by Britain's Terry Hands and Chekhov's *The Seagull* staged by Czechoslovak guest director Otomar Krejca. (OSSIA TRILLING)

and Lugné Poë's prizes; Remo Forlani's *A King's Mighty Troubles* gained the Courteline prize. On the small Montparnasse stage, Raymond Gérôme acted the solo role in *The Gospel of St. Mark*. Commercial hits were Dumas's *Kean*; the late Pascal Jardin's *Madame's Out*, with Jean-Claude Brialy; Loleh Bellon's *Heart on Hand*, with Suzanne Flon; *The Booze-Up* by Françise Dorin, with Jeanne Moreau; *Happy Easter* by Jean Poiret; and Harwood's *The Dresser*. Two novelties were the world premieres of a lost fragment by Federico García Lorca and of *Mephisto*, adapted by Mnouchkine and her Théâtre du Soleil troupe from the anti-Nazi Klaus Mann novel.

At the Holland Festival were *Every Good Boy Deserves Favour* (from Rotterdam), *The Island*, by Sweden's Pistol Theatre, and *The People*, by Tukak, Denmark-based company from Greenland. The "Europalia" of Belgian arts offered *Measure for Measure*, staged by Dinu Cernescu, at the Belgian National Theatre; two plays by Paul Willems; Otomar Krejca's *Three Sisters*; and plays by Jean Sigrid and Patrick Rogiers.

Notable in Italy were Giorgio Strehler's staging of Strindberg's *The Storm*, with Tino Carraro and Franco Graziosi, at the Milan Piccolo; Benno Besson's production of *Oedipus Tyrannus*, at Spoleto; and Tadeusz Kantor's *Wielopole, Wielopole*, at Florence. In Madrid Nuria Espert became head of Spain's National Theatre, and the rebuilt Teatro Español reopened. Lorca's *Doña Rosita* was staged by Parisian guest Jorge Lavelli and *The Threepenny Opera* by East Berlin guest Friedo Solter.

Switzerland, East and West Germany, and Austria. In Switzerland Lucerne was the first theatre to stage *The Jeweller's Shop*, by Karol Wojtyla (Pope John Paul II). Zürich's repertoire included a stage version of Ulrike Meinhof's unperformed film script (*Bambule*) at the Neumarkt, the world premiere of Ernst Jandl's poetic *From Afar* at the Winkelwiese, and a rewrite of Friedrich Dürrenmatt's *Romulus the Great* at the Schauspielhaus.

The 1980 Oberammergau Passion Play in West Germany was trimmed to placate objectors. At West Berlin's German Theatre Review, Jandl's *From Afar* (winner of the Muhlheim Prize) was the Schaubühne's entry. At the Berlin Schiller's small Schlosspark stage, the late Marie-Louise Fleisser's autobiographical *The Deep Sea Fish* was seen. Hochhuth's *The Lady Doctors* was first presented in Mannheim.

Stuttgart's first Summer Festival welcomed many foreign troupes. At its third Arena Theatre Festival, Münster staged new plays by German writers, including works by Tankred Dorst, Hans Magnus Enzensberger, Heinar Kipphardt, Horst Laube, Gerlind Reinshagen, and the proscribed East German Stafan Schütz.

In East Germany two Heiner Müller plays were staged at the East Berlin Volksbühne and Freundshaft theatres. New productions at the Deutsches Theatre were mainly revivals.

The feature of the Vienna Festival was Hans Hollmann's restaging in the Concert Hall of *The Last Days of Mankind*, by Karl Kraus, whose *The Unconquerable* of 1927 received its world premiere during the season. The Burg was the scene of Zankl's production of Arthur Schnitzler's *Comedy of Seduction*. At the Akademie were seen *The Enthusiasts* by Robert Musil and the world premiere of Horvath's *Murder in the Mohrengasse*.

Scandinavia and Eastern Europe. Sweden's 76-year-old Alf Sjöberg (*see* OBITUARIES) was fatally injured in a road accident on the eve of his last production, Molière's *School for Wives* at Stockholm's Royal Dramatic Theatre. Also staged at that theatre were Lars Noren's *Orestes* and the world premiere of *Birth on a Hard Shoulder* by Howard Barker. The Stockholm City Theatre put on Ernst Toller's *Hurrah, We're Alive!* and Etienne Glaser's rewrite of Peter Weiss's *Marat/Sade*.

East Germany's Wolfgang Pintzka directed the Norwegian premiere of Brecht's *Fear and Misery in the Third Reich* at Oslo's National Theatre. Four women were prominent at Copenhagen's Royal Theatre: Ulla Ryum for her latest play *Journey Through the Day*, Swedish guest Gunnel Lindblom for her staging of *Twelfth Night*, Lone Bastholm for that of the world premiere of P. O. Enquist's *To*

Phaedra, and Line Krogh for that of Ernst Bruun Olsen's adaptation of Holberg's *Ulysses*.

Noteworthy productions in Finland were Eugen Terttula's of Nikolay Gogol's *Diary of a Madman*, starring Tauno Manni, at the National Theatre and Jouko Turkka's of a first play by novelist Hannu Salama at the City. First prize at the Tampere Summer Festival went to Taisto-Bertil Orsman's adaptation of Molière's *Tartuffe* and Mikhail Bulgakov's *Molière* into a single play called *The Master and the Rogue*. At the biennial Rejkjavik Festival in Iceland one of the main events was Kjartan Ragnarsson's *Snow* at the National Theatre.

After staging Brecht's *Turandot* and Yury Trifonov's *The House on the Riverside* at his old Taganka Theatre, Yury Liubimov opened his ultramodern new playhouse in Moscow with a revival of *Hamlet*, starring Vladimir Vysotsky (*see* OBITUARIES), only days before the popular 42-year-old actor died. Among new plays were *Hurry To Do Good!* by Mikhail Roshchin at the Sovremennik; *The Road* by Vladimir Balyasny, adapted from Gogol's *Dead Souls*, at the Malaya Bronnaya; and *Myself a Man*, based on the Karl Marx letters, by Aleksandr Sanin, at the Yermolova.

In Warsaw the 30th anniversary of the Jewish State Theatre coincided with the death, in exile in New York, of its 80-year-old former head Ida Kaminska. Jerzy Zurek's *100 Hands, 100 Daggers*, about the nation's 1830 insurrection, won the Konrad Swinarski Prize. Kriszta Kovats sang the title role in *Evita* on Margaret Island in Budapest, the first European production after London. Also in Hungary there were new works by Istvan Csurka, Magda Szabo, Gyula Hernadi, and Tibor Cyurkovics. In Bulgaria Stefan Kostov's *Comedy Without a Title* (1938) was revived at Sofia's Tears and Laughter. (OSSIA TRILLING)

United States and Canada. Like the presidential election, the U.S. theatre in 1980 reflected the country's growing conservatism. The nation's stages were dominated by Broadway, a Broadway that was producing traditional works. Consequently, the accounting reports were rosier than the artistic ones.

For example, the trend in recent years toward reviving old musicals swelled to oppressive proportions. On Broadway there were revivals of *West Side Story*, *The Music Man*, *Camelot*, and *Brigadoon*. Audiences proved not quite the gulls they were supposed to be. Of all those shows, only *Camelot* was a real hit and that only because its star, Richard Burton, was a gilt-edged box-office attraction. None of the revivals was outstanding, and even *West Side Story* demonstrated itself to be, if a landmark in terms of dance, not really a great work. The blitz of revivals crowded out new musicals, which are the lifeblood of Broadway. Of the few that were produced, the only real hit was *Barnum*, while *A Day in Hollywood / A Night in the Ukraine* was moderately successful.

Conservatism also set the tone among dramas, but in that area it was sometimes beneficial. Audiences were demanding and getting well-made plays, unlike some of the indulgent modern dramas of recent years. Even Harold Pinter's latest, *Betrayal*, was comprehensible. Indeed, *Betrayal* was our old friend the romantic triangle. Pinter did put modern clothes on this story of a wife, her husband, and his best friend. He arranged the scenes so that the play began at the end and worked its way to the beginning. None of this, though, altered the play's basic orthodoxy.

MARTHA SWOPE

Forty-second Street, a spirited hit musical directed by Gower Champion, opened in New York City in September.

Other established playwrights with new works on Broadway included Arthur Miller (*The American Clock*), Tennessee Williams (*Clothes for a Summer Hotel*), Edward Albee (*The Lady from Dubuque*), and Howard Sackler (whose *Goodbye Fidel* was his first play since the Pulitzer Prize-winning *The Great White Hope*). All were rudely rejected. More than ever it seemed that Broadway's commercial system was inimical to artistic thriving. In other countries, though their work was criticized, such established artists were not often subjected to that kind of humiliating commercial test.

Dramas that did make a mark on the season were straightforward and effective but artistically unambitious. The British import *Whose Life Is It Anyway?* was a problem play, the problem being one's right to death. The case in point was a young man (later changed to a woman and played by Mary Tyler Moore), paralyzed in a motorcycle accident, who wanted his hospital physician to pull the plug. Because the playwright, Brian Clark, gave the fellow a marvelous black sense of humour, audiences enjoyed the play as if it were a comedy while being effectively struck by its point.

Another successful problem play during the year was Mark Medoff's *Children of a Lesser God*, dealing with a romance between a man who teaches speech to those born deaf and one of his students. This play took many of the season's prizes, including the Tony award for best play. Lanford Wilson's *Talley's Folly*, the year's Pulitzer Prize winner, was most definitely not a problem play. Rather, it was a valentine, a romance between an immigrant Jewish accountant from St. Louis and a barren young heiress of the local Missouri aristocracy. The author had for 15 years been the U.S. theatre's unsung poet of the Midwest.

MARTHA SWOPE

Children of a Lesser God, starring John Rubinstein (centre foreground) and Phyllis Frelich (to his left), opened in New York City in March and was a great success.

Suddenly, in 1980, Wilson was not only produced but produced twice. His other play, *The Fifth of July*, was related to *Talley's Folly*—they are part of a cycle. But their relationship is tenuous, and *The Fifth of July* is a talky play without the sunny warmth of *Talley's Folly*.

All these dramas, *Children of a Lesser God, Talley's Folly,* and *The Fifth of July,* originated at nonprofit institutional and regional theatres before being transferred to Broadway. Such a routing had become familiar in recent years as private producers looked to such theatres for tryouts, while the institutions in turn hoped to derive income from shares of Broadway transfers. The relationship was born of mutual economic need. Dwindling theatre interest by governmental and private foundations put the institutional theatres in economic crisis, but even so their intimacy with Broadway was unhealthy. The idea behind nonprofit regional theatre was to decentralize the U.S. stage and provide alternatives to Broadway. These institutions should be presenting what Broadway will not or can not present: classics, and unusually modern or sombre plays.

Wilson's pair originated at New York's Circle Repertory Company before being staged at the Mark Taper Forum in Los Angeles, where *Children of a Lesser God* began. Other Broadway transfers from the Mark Taper were Steve Tesich's *Division Street* and a new comedy, *I Ought To Be in Pictures*, by Neil Simon. As the most commercially successful playwright in the history of the Western theatre, Simon did not need help from theatre supported by federal tax waivers. Although one could sympathize with the financial plight of the Mark Taper Forum and other regional theatres, their production of patently commercial plays only made them seem less necessary.

Hand-holding with Broadway was not the only worrisome development for the regional theatre in 1980. Artistic directors resigned, were fired, or went unreplaced at such established places as the Guthrie Theatre in Minneapolis, Minn., the McCarter Theatre in Princeton, N.J., and the Hartford Stage Company and the Hartman Theatre Company, both in Connecticut. Even Canada's venerable Stratford (Ont.) Festival ran into leadership trouble.

Stratford's 1980 season was as ambitious and successful as ever. No fewer than 15 productions were mounted, an astounding number economically and artistically. The Shakespeare plays included *Twelfth Night, Henry V, Titus Andronicus, Much Ado About Nothing, King Lear,* and *Henry VI.* Additionally, there were productions of Chekhov (*The Seagull*), Carlo Goldoni (*The Servant of Two Masters*), and Eugene O'Neill (*Long Day's Journey into Night*). The festival presented such new plays as D. L. Coburn's *The Gin Game* and John Guare's *Bosoms and Neglect* and even a musical classic (*The Beggar's Opera*). Yet shadows fell across the season. Robin Phillips, Stratford's artistic director, had been unhappy with his board of trustees for bowing to governmental pressure on various issues. Phillips finally resigned and was replaced by John Dexter, a respected British director who was also artistic head of New York's Metropolitan Opera. Fierce Canadian nationalist reaction followed the choice of a foreigner, and the government refused to issue Dexter a work permit.

But back in New York City there was a new beginning for the most troubled institutional theatre of all, the Vivian Beaumont in Lincoln Center. It had been closed for three years, ever since Joseph Papp withdrew to concentrate on his Public Theater in downtown Manhattan. Somehow convincing the right people, Richmond Crinkley became administrator of a new Lincoln Center Theatre Company, leaving the Folger Theatre in Washington, D.C., for the job. Instead of finding an artistic director, he hired an "artistic directorate," composed of playwright Edward Albee, directors Ellis Rabb and Robin Phillips, the Romanian avant-gardist Liviu Ciulei, conductor Sarah Caldwell, and writer-comedian Woody Allen. The Beaumont reopened in the fall with a revival of Philip Barry's *The Philadelphia Story*. The new company's inaugural season was to include *Macbeth* and a new play by Allen. Whether that first season would be successful was less important than that the most visible regional theatre in the United States was now, in fact visible.

(MARTIN GOTTFRIED)

See also Dance; Music.

Togo

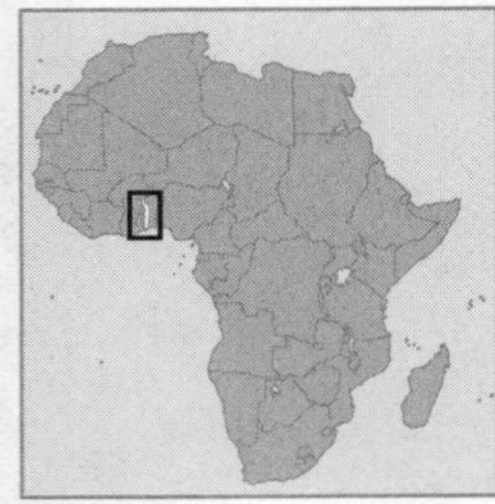

Togo

A West African republic on the Bight of Benin, Togo is bordered by Ghana, Upper Volta, and Benin. Area: 56,785 sq km (21,925 sq mi). Pop. (1980 est.): 2,699,000. Cap. and largest city: Lomé (pop., 1980 est., 283,000). Language: French (official). Religion: animist 60%; Christian 25%; Muslim 7.5%. President in 1980, Gen. Gnassingbe Eyadema.

On Dec. 30, 1979, the new constitution was approved and Gen. Gnassingbe Eyadema was reelected head of state by 99.9% of the electorate. The 67

TOGO

Education. (1977–78) Primary, pupils 421,436, teachers 7,251; secondary, pupils 88,409, teachers 2,030; vocational, pupils 6,618, teachers 326; teacher training, students 388, teachers 21; higher (1976–77), students 2,777, teaching staff (university only; 1975–76) 236.

Finance. Monetary unit: CFA franc, with (Sept. 22, 1980) a par value of CFA Fr 50 to the French franc (free rate of CFA Fr 210 to U.S. $1; CFA Fr 504 = £1 sterling). Budget (1980 est.) balanced at CFA Fr 67.3 billion.

Foreign Trade. (1978) Imports CFA Fr 100,898,000,000; exports CFA Fr 54,238,000,000. Import sources: France 34%; Switzerland 10%; U.K. 10%; West Germany 9%; The Netherlands 6%; U.S. 5%. Export destinations: The Netherlands 31%; France 14%; West Germany 8%; U.S. 8%; Yugoslavia 6%; Poland 6%. Main exports: phosphates 39%; cocoa 29%; coffee 9%.

single-list candidates for the National Assembly received 96% of the votes cast.

On Jan. 13, 1980, the 13th anniversary of his accession to power, General Eyadema proclaimed the Third Togolese Republic. As fourth-largest world producer of phosphates, Togo celebrated, at the same time, the sixth anniversary of the Togolese Phosphates Office, set up in anticipation of the nationalization of mining. Thirty-four political prisoners were set free, but this did not satisfy opponents who had taken refuge abroad, most of whom had gathered together within the Mouvement Togolais pour la Démocratie. Nevertheless, a further five political prisoners were freed in May.

In April Eyadema sought to play a part in settling the war in Chad; after flying to N'Djamena, he secured a cease-fire agreement on April 8, but it was violated almost at once. In August and October he initiated further negotiations which proved to be equally fruitless. (PHILIPPE DECRAENE)

Tonga

An independent monarchy and member of the Commonwealth of Nations, Tonga is an island group in the Pacific Ocean east of Fiji. Area: 750 sq km (290 sq mi). Pop. (1980 est.): 96,000, 98% of whom are Tongan. Cap. and largest city: Nukualofa (pop., 1976, 18,300). Language: English and Tongan. Religion (1976): Free Wesleyan 47%; Roman Catholic 16%; Free Church of Tonga 14%; Mormon 9%; Church of Tonga 9%; other 5%. King, Taufa'ahau Tupou IV; prime minister in 1980, Prince Fatafehi Tu'ipelehake.

King Taufa'ahau Tupou IV followed his state visit to New Zealand in October 1979 with another to West Germany, during which he signed agreements covering technical and financial cooperation. Early in 1980 Tonga's nurses resigned over dissatisfaction with the chief nursing officer. It was an unusual step in a country that recognized neither trade unions nor strikes. After directives for a return to work failed to produce any result, the government transferred the officer, whereupon the nurses returned to work.

Tonga's economy suffered from the downturn in copra prices that followed the high returns of 1979. Development expenditure was concentrated on an A$2 million fishing industry funded by the European Economic Community and a small industries

TONGA

Education. (1978) Primary, pupils 19,730, teachers 761; secondary, pupils 12,368, teachers 654; vocational, pupils 281, teachers 19; teacher training, students 146, teachers 14.

Finance and Trade. Monetary unit: pa'anga, with (Sept. 22, 1980) a free rate of 0.86 pa'anga to U.S. $1 (2.06 pa'anga = £1 sterling). Budget (1979–80 est.): revenue 9,474,000 pa'anga; expenditure 9,850,000 pa'anga. Foreign trade (1979): imports 26,210,000 pa'anga; exports 6,134,000 pa'anga. Import sources: New Zealand 34%; Australia 27%; U.K. 9%; Japan 8%; Fiji 5%. Export destinations: Australia 40%; New Zealand 27%; Fiji 14%. Main exports: coconut oil 31%; copra 27%; desiccated coconut 18%; bananas 5%.

Tonga

centre, funded by the Asian Development Bank, that would manufacture such items as footwear, clothing, paper products, and building supplies. Communications projects included an airstrip at Niuatoputapu and a road project on Tongatapu. At a meeting of the South Pacific Forum in Kiribati in July, Tonga became a signatory to the South Pacific Regional Trade and Cooperation Agreement, under which a wide range of island products would have privileged access to markets in Australia and New Zealand.

In September the king annulled the marriage of his second son, Prince Fatafahi, and in November he canceled the prince's rights to the throne. The marriage was recognized outside the kingdom, however, because it took place in Hawaii. Under Tongan law the prince should have sought royal approval before his marriage to Heimataura Anderson in a Christian ceremony in July and a Polynesian ceremony in August.

(BARRIE MACDONALD)

Track and Field Sports

Although diminished in scope and performance by international politics, the Olympic Games dominated a productive 1980 track and field season. Forty-one world records were broken or equaled before, during, and after the Olympics, which were held in Moscow without the presence of the United States and several other nations.

Men's International Competition. Even though the spectre of a boycott of the Olympics hung over track and field competitors from the beginning of the year, there was no apparent letup in preparation for the Games. Record breaking started on April 23, and by the time of the Olympics (July 24–August 1) no fewer than 17 new world marks had been established. Three more were recorded during the Olympics but only one after the Games despite a busy two-month schedule.

Three field events and the middle distances attracted attention before and during the Olympics. Five new records were set in the pole vault and hammer throw, while the high-jump standard was broken or equaled three times. Competition in each of the three events was climaxed with a new world record in the Olympics.

Poland's Wladyslaw Kozakiewicz began the pole vault festivities with a new record of 5.72 m (18 ft 9¼ in) on May 11. France contributed the

Theology: *see* Religion

Timber: *see* Industrial Review

Tobacco: *see* Industrial Review

Tobogganing: *see* Winter Sports

Tourism: *see* Industrial Review

Toys: *see* Games and Toys

next three records as Thierry Vigneron cleared 5.75 m (18 ft 10¼ in) on June 1 and again on June 29, while Philippe Houvion made 5.77 m (18 ft 11 in) on July 17. Kozakiewicz then won a stirring Olympic competition with his second record of the year, 5.78 m (18 ft 11½ in).

The hammer throw records were set by three Soviets. Yury Sedykh, the 1976 Olympic titlist, threw 80.38 m (263 ft 8 in) on May 16, lost his record in the same competition to Juri Tamm, who threw 80.46 m (264 ft), and regained it later that day with 80.64 m (264 ft 7 in). Then, after Sergey Litvinov upped the standard to 81.66 m (267 ft 11 in) on May 24, Sedykh had his final turn in the Olympics on July 31. On the very first throw of the meeting he reached 81.80 m (268 ft 4½ in), regaining the global mark and becoming the first two-time Olympic hammer winner in 48 years. The other two record breakers also won medals, Litvinov taking second and Tamm third.

The 1976 Olympic high-jump champion, Jacek Wszola of Poland, opened the season with a new high of 2.35 m (7 ft 8½ in) on May 25. Just a day later the mark was matched by Dietmar Mogenburg of West Germany. That record stood until the Olympics, when Gerd Wessig of East Germany became one of the least expected Olympic winners with a jump of 2.36 m (7 ft 8¾ in).

Missing from the Games, mostly because of the U.S.-inspired boycott, were three major track and field powers, the U.S., West Germany, and Kenya, along with a number of other nations. Based on previous and expected performance, about 25% of the projected medal winners were absent. The U.S. presence was missed mostly in the sprints, hurdles, and relays.

But in most other events the U.S. would have been hard pressed to provide a winner, and competition was at a high level. Particularly keen was the double battle between Britain's Sebastian Coe and Steve Ovett (*see* BIOGRAPHIES) in the 800-m and 1,500-m runs. Coe, who set world marks in the 800 m, 1,500 m, and one mile in 1979, added the 1,000-m mark with a 2-min 13.40-sec performance on July 1. But he lost his mile record in the same Oslo meet when Ovett ran the distance in 3 min 48.8 sec. Two weeks later Ovett equaled Coe's 1,500-m time of 3 min 32.1 sec.

The two Britons had not raced each other in two years, and so there was great anticipation when both entered the 800 and the 1,500 in the Olympics. Coe, the world record holder and believed to possess more natural speed, was the favourite in the 800, while Ovett, the stronger of the two, was favoured in the 1,500. But Ovett was the surprise winner in the 800, taking the lead in a long drive for the finish as Coe unexpectedly lagged at the rear of the pack. Coe made a closing rush but was unable to dent Ovett's margin and was beaten by a half second as Ovett ran 1 min 45.4 sec. Surprised and disappointed, Coe made up for the unexpected loss six days later when he won the 1,500 m handily with Ovett third behind East Germany's Jurgen Straub. It was a tactical race, and the time was a modest 3 min 38.4 sec.

With Coe and Ovett splitting victories, it was left to Miruts Yifter to become the only men's double track and field winner of the Games. The little Ethiopian, of unknown age but thought to be at least 38, won the 10,000 m in 27 min 42.7 sec and then the 5,000 m in 13 min 21 sec. He succeeded Lasse Viren of Finland as gold medalist in both events, Viren achieving no better than a fifth in the 10,000.

Joining Sedykh as the only other successful defending champion was East Germany's Waldemar Cierpinski. He took 2 hr 11 min 3 sec to become the second runner ever to win the Olympic marathon twice.

Olympic records fell in several events: the three world record events (high jump, pole vault, hammer throw) plus the 20,000-m and 50,000-m walks and the shot put. Maurizio Damilano of Italy captured the shorter walk in 1 hr 23 min 35.5 sec, while Hartwig Gauder of East Germany was the 50,000-m champion in 3 hr 49 min 24 sec. The long jump was won by Lutz Dombrowski of East Germany. His leap of 8.54 m (28 ft ¼ in) was the second longest ever and the best at low altitude. Vladimir Kiselyov of the Soviet Union established a new Olympic shot put record of 21.35 m (70 ft ½ in).

Other Olympic winners were: 100 m, Alan Wells, U.K., 10.25 sec; 200 m, Pietro Mennea, Italy, 20.19 sec; 400 m, Viktor Markin, U.S.S.R., 44.60 sec (a new European record); 3,000-m steeplechase, Bronislaw Malinowski, Poland, 8 min 9.7 sec; 110-m hurdles, Thomas Munkelt, East Germany, 13.39 sec; 400-m hurdles, Volker Beck, East Germany, 48.70 sec; 4 x 100-m relay, U.S.S.R., 38.26 sec; 4 x 400-m relay, U.S.S.R., 3 min 1.1 sec; triple jump, Jaak Uudmae, U.S.S.R., 17.35 m (56 ft 11 in); discus, Viktor Rasshchupkin, U.S.S.R., 66.64 m (218 ft 8 in); javelin, Dainis Kula,

In January Mary Decker of the United States set a women's record for the mile run in world competition in New Zealand.

UPI

U.S.S.R., 91.20 m (299 ft 2 in); and decathlon, Daley Thompson (*see* BIOGRAPHIES), U.K., 8,495 points.

The Soviet Union and East Germany dominated the medal count, winning more than half of the awards for the 24 events. The U.S.S.R. won 8 events and 15 other medals, while East Germany had 6 golds and 8 other prizes. (*See* Special Report.)

All world record action in 1980 occurred in Europe, with no new marks being set in the U.S. for the first time in 35 years. Only one U.S. athlete achieved a new world record, Edwin Moses lowering his own 400-m hurdle standard to 47.13 sec on July 3.

Ferenc Paragi of Hungary threw the javelin 96.72 m (317 ft 4 in) on April 23 to begin the parade of records. And the decathlon mark fell twice, Thompson earning 8,622 points on May 18 and Guido Kratschmer of West Germany topping that with 8,649 on June 14. Only Ovett was able to break a record in an unexpected post-Olympic letdown. He captured sole ownership of the 1,500-m prize, running the distance in 3 min 31.36 sec on August 27.

Women's International Competition. The pattern in women's participation paralleled that of the men. An early start was followed by a burst of midyear activity with the season climaxing in the Olympic Games and only a single world best achieved after the Games. Thirteen women broke 17 records in nine individual events, and three relay records were established.

Eastern Europeans dominated competition throughout the year, including the Olympics. The U.S.S.R. accounted for nine of the world records and won 7 of the 14 Olympic events. East Germany scored with eight world marks and five Olympic gold medals. All but one of the 20 records were established in Europe, mostly in the Eastern sector. The lone exception was the first new mark of the year. Mary Decker of the U.S. ran the mile in 4 min 21.68 sec in New Zealand on January 26.

The most honours were won by Nadyezhda Olizarenko of the Soviet Union. She lowered the 800-m record to 1 min 54.85 sec on June 12 and then knocked it down to 1 min 53.5 sec in winning the Olympics. Tatyana Kazankina, another Soviet middle-distance star, won in the Olympics and broke the 1,500-m standard twice, but neither record was set in the Games. A double winner in the 1976 Games, Kazankina completed a comeback after time out for motherhood. She ran 3 min 55 sec on July 6 and created the sole post-Olympic record with a 3 min 52.47 run on August 13.

Two others broke world records twice during the year. East Germany's Ilona Slupianek extended the shot put record to 22.36 m (73 ft 4¼ in) on May 2 and to 22.45 m (73 ft 8 in) on May 11, and later won the Olympics. Olga Kuragina of the Soviet Union twice bettered the pentathlon standard, first scoring 4,856 points on June 20. She raised the figure to 4,875 points on July 24 in the Olympics but despite her record-shattering performance finished only third. This unusual finish was made possible by a unique sequence of events in which the pentathlon record was broken three times in just 1.6 sec.

Kuragina was the first to finish the 800-m run, the concluding event in the pentathlon. As she crossed the line in 2 min 3.6 sec, she achieved her 4,875 record. But when Olga Rukavishnikova finished in 2 min 4.8 sec, her total was 4,937 points. Kuragina's mark had lasted only 1.2 sec. The new figure remained a record for even less time as Nadyezhda Tkachenko finished in 2 min 5.2 sec for 5,083 points.

Among the other record setters only Evelin Jahl and the East German 4 x 100-m relay team were successful in the Olympics. The foursome of Romy Muller, Barbel Eckert-Wockel, Ingrid Auerswald, and Marlies Göhr ran a record-equaling 42.09 sec on July 9, 41.85 sec on July 13, and 41.60 sec in the Olympics on August 1. Jahl of East Germany threw the discus 71.50 m (234 ft 7 in) on May 10.

Non-Olympic winners who set new world bests were Grazyna Rabsztyn of Poland, 12.36 sec for the 100-m hurdles on June 13; Karin Rossley, East Germany, 54.28 sec for the 400-m hurdles on May 17; Maria Vergova, Bulgaria, 71.80 m (235 ft 7 in) in the discus July 13; Ruth Fuchs, East Germany, 69.96 m (229 ft 6 in) in the javelin April 29; and Tatyana Biryulina, U.S.S.R., 70.08 m (229 ft 11 in) in the javelin July 12.

Non-record-breaking Olympic winners were: 100 m, Lyudmila Kondratyeva, U.S.S.R., 11.06 sec; 200 m, Barbel Eckert-Wockel, East Germany, 22.03 sec (she won also in 1976 and ran on a winning relay team each year); 400 m, Marita Koch, East Germany, 48.88 sec; 1,500 m, Kazankina, 3 min 56.6 sec; 100-m hurdles, Vera Komisova, U.S.S.R., 12.56 sec; 4 x 400-m relay, U.S.S.R., 3 min 20.2 sec; high jump, Sara Simeoni, Italy, 1.97

Alberto Salazar, who had never before run in a marathon race, won the New York marathon in record time.

UPI

m (6 ft 5½ in); long jump, Tatyana Kolpakova, U.S.S.R., 7.06 m (23 ft 2 in); shot put, Slupianek, 22.41 m (73 ft 6¼ in); discus, Jahl, 69.96 m (229 ft 6 in); javelin, Maria Colón, Cuba, 68.40 m (224 ft 5 in).

U.S. Competition. Not allowed to compete in the Olympics, U.S. athletes climaxed their season with the so-called "Olympic Trials" at Eugene, Ore., in late June. Probably partly because of the disappointment of the Olympic boycott, it was not a good year. Only Moses and Decker produced world marks, and only two national standards were bettered at the Trials; Henry Marsh ran the 3,000-m steeplechase in 8 min 15.68 sec, and Jodi Anderson long jumped 7 m (22 ft 11½ in).

Table I. World 1980 Outdoor Records—Men

Event	Competitor, country, date	Performance
1,000 m	Sebastian Coe, U.K., July 1	2 min 13.40 sec
1,500 m	Steve Ovett, U.K., July 15	3 min 32.09 sec
	Steve Ovett, U.K., August 27	3 min 31.36 sec
One mile	Steve Ovett, U.K., July 1	3 min 48.8 sec
400-m hurdles	Edwin Moses, U.S., July 3	47.13 sec
High jump	Jacek Wszola, Poland, May 25	2.35 m (7 ft 8½ in)
	Dietmar Mogenburg, West Germany, May 26	2.35 m (7 ft 8½ in)
	Gerd Wessig, East Germany, August 1	2.36 m (7 ft 8¾ in)
Pole vault	Wladyslaw Kozakiewicz, Poland, May 11	5.72 m (18 ft 9¼ in)
	Thierry Vigneron, France, June 1	5.75 m (18 ft 10¼ in)
	Thierry Vigneron, France, June 29	5.75 m (18 ft 10¼ in)
	Philippe Houvion, France, July 17	5.77 m (18 ft 11 in)
	Wladyslaw Kozakiewicz, Poland, July 30	5.78 m (18 ft 11½ in)
Hammer throw	Yury Sedykh, U.S.S.R., May 16	80.38 m (263 ft 8 in)
	Juri Tamm, U.S.S.R., May 16	80.46 m (264 ft)
	Yury Sedykh, U.S.S.R., May 16	80.64 m (264 ft 7 in)
	Sergey Litvinov, U.S.S.R., May 24	81.66 m (267 ft 11 in)
	Yury Sedykh, U.S.S.R., July 31	81.80 m (268 ft 4½ in)
Javelin	Ferenc Paragi, Hungary, April 23	96.72 m (317 ft 4 in)
Decathlon	Daley Thompson, U.K., May 18	8,622 pt
	Guido Kratschmer, West Germany, June 14	8,649 pt

Table II. World 1980 Outdoor Records—Women

Event	Competitor, country, date	Performance
800 m	Nadyezhda Olizarenko, U.S.S.R., June 12	1 min 54.85 sec
	Nadyezhda Olizarenko, U.S.S.R., July 27	1 min 53.5 sec
1,500 m	Tatyana Kazankina, U.S.S.R., July 6	3 min 55 sec
	Tatyana Kazankina, U.S.S.R., August 13	3 min 52.47 sec
One mile	Mary Decker, U.S., January 26	4 min 21.68 sec
100-m hurdles	Grazyna Rabsztyn, Poland, June 13	12.36 sec
400-m hurdles	Karin Rossley, East Germany, May 17	54.28 sec
4 x 100-m relay	East Germany, July 9	42.09 sec
	East Germany, July 13	41.85 sec
	East Germany, August 1	41.60 sec
Shot put	Ilona Slupianek, East Germany, May 2	22.36 m (73 ft 4¼ in)
	Ilona Slupianek, East Germany, May 11	22.45 m (73 ft 8 in)
Discus	Evelin Jahl, East Germany, May 10	71.50 m (234 ft 7 in)
	Maria Vergova, Bulgaria, July 13	71.80 m (235 ft 7 in)
Javelin	Ruth Fuchs, East Germany, April 29	69.96 m (229 ft 6 in)
	Tatyana Biryulina, U.S.S.R., July 12	70.08 m (229 ft 11 in)
Pentathlon	Olga Kuragina, U.S.S.R., June 20	4,856 pt
	Olga Kuragina, U.S.S.R., July 24	4,875 pt
	Olga Rukavishnikova, U.S.S.R., July 24	4,937 pt
	Nadyezhda Tkachenko, U.S.S.R., July 24	5,083 pt
Nonstandard events		
4 x 200-m relay	East Germany, August 9	1 min 28.2 sec

Decker enjoyed the best season, adding four U.S. 1,500-m records and one 3,000-m mark to her world mile figure. Her best times were 3 min 59.43 sec in the 1,500 and 8 min 38.73 sec in the 3,000. Another successful performer was discus thrower Lorna Griffin. After breaking the U.S. record four times in 1979, she did it another five times in 1980, finally reaching 63.22 m (207 ft 5 in).

Additional U.S. records for women were made by Jan Merrill with 15 min 30.6 sec for 5,000 m; Joan Benoit, 2 hr 31 min 23 sec, and Patti Lyons-Catalano, 2 hr 30 min 57 sec, in the marathon; Sandy Myers, 56.40 sec, and Esther Mahr, 56.16 sec, for the 400-m hurdles; and Louise Ritter, 1.95 m (6 ft 4¾ in) for the high jump.

U.S. males were not as productive. In addition to the steeplechase, national records were set in the 10,000 m, 27 min 29.16 sec by Craig Virgin; high jump, 2.32 m (7 ft 7¼ in) by Jeff Woodard (record equaled); and in the discus, 70.98 m (232 ft 10 in) by Mac Wilkins.

Indoors, Steve Scott set U.S. bests for one mile (3 min 53 sec) and 3,000 m (7 min 45.2 sec); Larry Myricks long jumped a world best 8.38 m (27 ft 6 in); and Ron Livers extended the triple jump to 17.07 m (56 ft). For the women, Decker lowered the world 1,500-m figure to 4 min 0.8 sec, while Ritter high jumped 1.93 m (6 ft 4¼ in) for a national best.

The University of Texas at El Paso led the way in team competition, winning the men's National Collegiate Athletic Association outdoor and indoor tournaments and becoming a power in women's track while capturing the indoor Association for Intercollegiate Athletics for Women (AIAW) title. California State at Northridge won the AIAW outdoor.

Marathon Running and Cross Country. Aside from the Olympic Games, the most notable marathons of the year were those in Boston and New York City. Bill Rodgers (*see* BIOGRAPHIES) of the U.S. won his third straight Boston crown in 2 hr 12 min 11 sec, while Jacqueline Gareau of Canada won the women's division in 2 hr 34 min 26 sec. More than 14,000 runners competed in New York on October 26 with Alberto Salazar of the University of Oregon a surprise victor in 2 hr 9 min 41 sec, the second fastest ever by an American. It was his first marathon. Norway's Grete Waitz ran her third marathon, won the New York race for the third time, and set her third world record with a time of 2 hr 25 min 42 sec. The "trials" for the nonexistent U.S. Olympic team were won by Tony Sandoval in 2 hr 10 min 19 sec.

In cross country the U.S. gained its first men's title when Craig Virgin won the International Cross Country Championships in Paris over a 12,580-m course in 37 min 2 sec. The women's winner was Waitz, covering 4,820 m in 15 min 5 sec. The men's team title went to the U.K. with the U.S. second, while the Soviet Union won the women's division from the U.K. The NCAA victors were Suleiman Nyambui and his University of Texas at El Paso teammates. Julie Shea led her teammates at North Carolina State to AIAW wins. Julie's sister, Mary, won the Athletic Congress national championships, and John Sinclair won the men's division.

(BERT NELSON)

THE POLITICIZED 1980 OLYMPICS

by Chris Brasher

Cities with names that begin with the letter "M" have spelled death and political disruption for the Olympic Games: Mexico City, 1968, when more than 200 people were killed in student demonstrations just before the Games opened; Munich, 1972, when members of the Black September Movement burst in on the Israeli quarters in the Olympic village and 17 men died; Montreal, 1976, when black Africa brought the word boycott into the Olympics; and finally Moscow in 1980, when the great nations of the world played power politics.

The Boycott. The issue in the Moscow Games had nothing to do with sport or the Olympic movement. It concerned a country, Afghanistan, which was created over a century ago by Russia and Great Britain to act as a buffer state. At the end of 1979 the Soviet Union invaded Afghanistan, thus threatening the oil of the Middle East. That is how the West saw the situation. The Soviets, on the other hand, maintained that their forces had been invited into Afghanistan by the legitimate government there to help quell a rebellion. Thus began a war of bullets in Afghanistan and a propaganda war between the East and the West.

Western leaders, most notably U.S. Pres. Jimmy Carter and British Prime Minister Margaret Thatcher, found themselves powerless to intervene militarily, and so instead they sought trade embargoes and a boycott of the Olympic Games due to open in Moscow on July 19. In theory national Olympic committees are independent of governments. Rule 26 of the Olympic Charter says: "NOC's must be autonomous and must resist all pressures of any kind whatsoever, whether of a political, religious or economic nature." In practice the national Olympic committees of the developed nations of the West proved as susceptible to political pressure as the new NOC's from emerging Africa had been in 1976. From the U.S. and Canada to New Zealand came the news that the committees were listening to the political views of their governments.

In the spring of 1980 Lord Killanin, president of the International Olympic Committee, thought that no more than 50 nations would send teams to Moscow, but eventually 81 nations took part. The counterattack against political pressure was led by the British Olympic Association, which argued that as long as the British government maintained diplomatic relations and trade links with the U.S.S.R., it was right and proper to maintain sporting links and send a team to Moscow.

Highlights of the Games. But those 81 nations that did participate did not include some of the most powerful in the world and must be compared with the 122 that went to Munich in 1972. The track and field results were affected by the absence of the U.S. team, and the swimming events were affected even more by the absence of two out of the four best swimming nations, the U.S. and Canada. Nevertheless, perhaps the two most eagerly awaited events did take place unaffected by the boycott. These were the 800-m and 1,500-m runs.

At the Olympics, the co-holders of the 1,500-m world record were to meet for the first time at that distance. Both were Englishmen: Sebastian Coe of Sheffield and Steve Ovett (*see* BIOGRAPHIES) of Brighton. The two were also matched in the 800 m. One has to go back a quarter of a century to find a parallel: the "Miracle Mile" in 1954 when Roger Bannister, the first man to run a mile in less than four minutes, was matched in the final of the Commonwealth Games against John Landy, the world record holder and only other man to have run a mile in under four minutes. But that race, won by Bannister, was before the days of worldwide television.

Now, in 1980, the world waited for Coe, the man who had broken the 800-m, 1,500-m, and one-mile world records in 1979, to race against Ovett, who in 1980 had taken the mile record from Coe and equaled his 1,500-m mark. Expert opinion was that Coe would take the 800-m gold medal and Ovett the 1,500-m prize. Ovett agreed. Just before he arrived in Moscow he said: "I've got a 50% chance of winning the 800 metres and 90% of winning the 1,500 metres. The 1,500 metres is the one that I am really prepared for. It's the one I want. Steve Ovett is a miler."

Both races turned out to be something of a disappointment. In the 800 m nobody wanted the lead and so the first lap took an ambling 54.3 seconds, a time good only for a schoolboy. Ovett was in the pack, pushing and shoving to give himself space. Coe trailed, taking no apparent interest in the proceedings. Instead, a third Englishman, Dave Warren, sprang to the front pursued by Nikolay Kirov of the

---

A gold medalist (3,000-m steeplechase) in the 1956 Olympics, Chris Brasher is sports correspondent to The Observer *and a reporter and producer for BBC Television, London. He is author of* Tokyo 1964, Mexico 1968, *and* Munich 72.

OLYMPIC CHAMPIONS, 1980 SUMMER GAMES, MOSCOW

Archery

Men's round T. Poikolainen (Finland) 2,455 pt
Women's round K. Losaberidze (U.S.S.R.) 2,491 pt

Basketball

Winning men's team Yugoslavia (beat Italy 86–77 in final)
Winning women's team U.S.S.R. (beat Bulgaria 104–73 in final)

Boxing

Light flyweight	S. Sabyrov (U.S.S.R.)	Welterweight	A. Aldama (Cuba)
Flyweight	P. Lessov (Bulgaria)	Light middleweight	A. Martinez (Cuba)
Bantamweight	J. Hernandez (Cuba)	Middleweight	J. Gomez (Cuba)
Featherweight	R. Fink (East Germany)	Light heavyweight	S. Kacar (Yugoslavia)
Lightweight	A. Herrera (Cuba)	Heavyweight	T. Stevenson (Cuba)
Light welterweight	P. Oliva (Italy)		

Canoeing

Men

500–m Canadian singles	S. Postrekhin (U.S.S.R.)	1 min 53.37 sec
500–m Canadian pairs	Hungary	1 min 43.39 sec
500–m kayak singles	V. Parfenovich (U.S.S.R.)	1 min 43.43 sec
500–m kayak pairs	U.S.S.R.	1 min 32.38 sec
1,000–m Canadian singles	L. Lubenov (Bulgaria)	4 min 12.38 sec
1,000–m Canadian pairs	Romania	3 min 47.65 sec
1,000–m kayak singles	R. Helm (East Germany)	3 min 48.77 sec
1,000–m kayak pairs	U.S.S.R.	3 min 26.72 sec
1,000–m kayak fours	East Germany	3 min 13.76 sec

Women

500–m kayak singles	B. Fischer (East Germany)	1 min 57.96 sec
500–m kayak pairs	East Germany	1 min 43.88 sec

Cycling

Sprint	L. Hesslich (East Germany)	10.75 sec (best 200 m)
1,000–m time trial	L. Thoms (East Germany)	1 min 02.955 sec*
4,000–m individual pursuit	R. Dill-Bundi (Switzerland)	4 min 35.66 sec
4,000–m team pursuit	U.S.S.R.	4 min 15.70 sec
100–km team time trial	U.S.S.R.	2 hr 01 min 21.70 sec
Individual road race	S. Sukhoruchenkov (U.S.S.R.)	4 hr 48 min 28.90 sec

Equestrian Sports

	Individual	Team
Dressage	E. Theurer (Austria) on Mon Chérie	U.S.S.R.
3-day event	F. Roman (Italy) on Rossinan	U.S.S.R.
Show jumping	J. Kowalczyk (Poland) on Artemor	U.S.S.R.

Fencing

	Individual	Team
Foil	V. Smirnov (U.S.S.R.)	France
Épée	J. Harmenberg (Sweden)	France
Sabre	V. Krovopuskov (U.S.S.R.)	U.S.S.R.
Women's foil	P. Trinquet (France)	France

Football (Soccer)

Winning team Czechoslovakia (beat East Germany 1–0 in final)

Gymnastics

	Men	Women
Combined exercises		
individual	A. Dityatin (U.S.S.R.)	Y. Davydova (U.S.S.R.)
team	U.S.S.R.	U.S.S.R.
Parallel bars	A. Tkachyov (U.S.S.R.)	–
Uneven parallel bars	–	M. Gnauck (East Germany)
Horizontal bar	S. Deltchev (Bulgaria)	–
Horse vaults	N. Andrianov (U.S.S.R.)	N. Shaposhnikova (U.S.S.R.)
Pommeled horse	Z. Magyar (Hungary)	–
Rings	A. Dityatin (U.S.S.R.)	–
Balance beam	–	N. Comaneci (Romania)
Floor exercises	R. Bruckner (East Germany)	N. Comaneci (Romania) and N. Kim (U.S.S.R.) (tie)

Handball

Winning men's team East Germany (beat U.S.S.R. 23–22 in final)
Winning women's team U.S.S.R. (beat East Germany 18–13 in final)

Hockey (Field)

Winning men's team India
Winning women's team Zimbabwe

Judo

60–kg class	T. Rey (France)	86–kg class	J. Roethlisberger (Switz.)
65–kg class	N. Solodukhin (U.S.S.R.)	95–kg class	R. Van de Walle (Belgium)
71–kg class	E. Gamba (Italy)	95–kg+ class	A. Parisi (France)
78–kg class	S. Khabareli (U.S.S.R.)	Open class	D. Lorenz (East Germany)

Modern Pentathlon

Individual	A. Starostin (U.S.S.R.)	5,568 pt
Team	U.S.S.R.	16,126 pt

Rowing

Men (2,000–m course)

Single sculls	P. Karppinen (Finland)	7 min 09.61 sec
Double sculls	East Germany	6 min 24.33 sec
Quadruple sculls	East Germany	5 min 49.81 sec
Pairs with coxswain	East Germany	7 min 02.54 sec
Pairs without coxswain	East Germany	6 min 48.01 sec
Fours with coxswain	East Germany	6 min 14.51 sec
Fours without coxswain	East Germany	6 min 08.17 sec
Eights with coxswain	East Germany	5 min 49.05 sec

Women (1,000–m course)

Single sculls	S. Toma (Romania)	3 min 40.69 sec
Double sculls	U.S.S.R.	3 min 16.27 sec
Quadruple sculls	East Germany	3 min 15.32 sec
Pairs without coxswain	East Germany	3 min 30.49 sec
Fours with coxswain	East Germany	3 min 19.27 sec
Eights with coxswain	East Germany	3 min 03.32 sec

Shooting

Free pistol	A. Melentev (U.S.S.R.)	581 pt*
Small-bore rifle (prone)	K. Varga (Hungary)	599 pt
Small-bore rifle (3-position)	V. Vlasov (U.S.S.R.)	1,173 pt*
Rapid-fire pistol	C. Ion (Romania)	596 pt
Trapshooting	L. Giovannetti (Italy)	198 pt
Skeet shooting	H. Rasmussen (Denmark)	196 pt
Moving target	I. Sokolov (U.S.S.R.)	589 pt*

*World record. †Olympic record. ‡Best Olympic performance.

Swimming and Diving

Men

100–m freestyle	J. Woithe (East Germany)	50.40 sec
200–m freestyle	S. Kopliakov (U.S.S.R.)	1 min 49.81 sec†
400–m freestyle	V. Salnikov (U.S.S.R.)	3 min 51.31 sec†
1,500–m freestyle	V. Salnikov (U.S.S.R.)	14 min 58.27 sec*
100–m backstroke	B. Baron (Sweden)	56.53 sec
200–m backstroke	S. Wladar (Hungary)	2 min 01.93 sec
100–m breaststroke	D. Goodhew (Great Britain)	1 min 03.34 sec
200–m breaststroke	R. Zulpa (U.S.S.R.)	2 min 15.85 sec
100–m butterfly	P. Arvidsson (Sweden)	54.92 sec
200–m butterfly	S. Fesenko (U.S.S.R.)	1 min 59.76 sec
400–m individual medley	A. Sidorenko (U.S.S.R.)	4 min 22.89 sec†
800–m freestyle relay	U.S.S.R.	7 min 23.50 sec
400–m medley relay	Australia	3 min 45.70 sec
Springboard diving	A. Portnov (U.S.S.R.)	905.025 pt
Platform diving	F. Hoffmann (East Germany)	835.650 pt

Women

100–m freestyle	B. Krause (East Germany)	54.79 sec*
200–m freestyle	B. Krause (East Germany)	1 min 58.33 sec†
400–m freestyle	I. Diers (East Germany)	4 min 08.76 sec†
800–m freestyle	M. Ford (Australia)	8 min 28.90 sec†
100–m backstroke	R. Reinisch (East Germany)	1 min 00.86 sec*
200–m backstroke	R. Reinisch (East Germany)	2 min 11.77 sec*
100–m breaststroke	U. Geweniger (East Germany)	1 min 10.22 sec
200–m breaststroke	L. Kachushite (U.S.S.R.)	2 min 29.54 sec†
100–m butterfly	C. Metschuck (East Germany)	1 min 00.42 sec
200–m butterfly	I. Geissler (East Germany)	2 min 10.44 sec†
400–m individual medley	P. Schneider (East Germany)	4 min 36.29 sec*
400–m freestyle relay	East Germany	3 min 42.71 sec*
400–m medley relay	East Germany	4 min 06.67 sec*
Springboard diving	I. Kalinina (U.S.S.R.)	725.910 pt
Platform diving	M. Jaschke (East Germany)	596.250 pt

Track and Field

Men

100–m dash	A. Wells (Great Britain)	10.25 sec
200–m dash	P. Mennea (Italy)	20.19 sec
400–m dash	V. Markin (U.S.S.R.)	44.60 sec
800–m run	S. Ovett (Great Britain)	1 min 45.40 sec
1,500–m run	S. Coe (Great Britain)	3 min 38.4 sec
5,000–m run	Miruts Yifter (Ethiopia)	13 min 21.0 sec
10,000–m run	Miruts Yifter (Ethiopia)	27 min 42.7 sec
Marathon	W. Cierpinski (East Germany)	2 hr 11 min 03.0 sec
110–m hurdles	T. Munkelt (East Germany)	13.39 sec
400–m hurdles	V. Beck (East Germany)	48.70 sec
3,000–m steeplechase	B. Malinowski (Poland)	8 min 09.7 sec
400–m relay	U.S.S.R.	38.26 sec
1,600–m relay	U.S.S.R.	3 min 01.1 sec
20–km walk	M. Damilano (Italy)	1 hr 23 min 35.5 sec‡
50–km walk	H. Gauder (East Germany)	3 hr 49 min 24.0 sec‡
High jump	G. Wessig (East Germany)	2.36 m*
Long jump	L. Dombrowski (East Germany)	8.54 m
Pole vault	W. Kozakiewicz (Poland)	5.78 m*
Triple jump	J. Uudmae (U.S.S.R.)	17.35 m
Shot put	V. Kiselyov (U.S.S.R.)	21.35 m†
Discus	V. Rasshchupkin (U.S.S.R.)	66.64 m
Hammer throw	Y. Sedykh (U.S.S.R.)	81.80 m*
Javelin	D. Kula (U.S.S.R.)	91.20 m
Decathlon	D. Thompson (Great Britain)	8,495 pt

Women

100–m dash	L. Kondratyeva (U.S.S.R.)	11.06 sec
200–m dash	B. Eckert-Wockel (East Germany)	22.03 sec†
400–m dash	M. Koch (East Germany)	48.88 sec†
800–m run	N. Olizarenko (U.S.S.R.)	1 min 53.5 sec*
1,500–m run	T. Kazankina (U.S.S.R.)	3 min 56.6 sec†
100–m hurdles	V. Komisova (U.S.S.R.)	12.56 sec†
400–m relay	East Germany	41.60 sec*
1,600–m relay	U.S.S.R.	3 min 20.2 sec
High jump	S. Simeoni (Italy)	1.97 m†
Long jump	T. Kolpakova (U.S.S.R.)	7.06 m†
Shot put	I. Slupianek (East Germany)	22.41 m*
Discus	E. Jahl (East Germany)	69.96 m†
Javelin	M. Colon (Cuba)	68.40 m†
Pentathlon	N. Tkachenko (U.S.S.R.)	5,083 pt*

Volleyball

Winning men's team U.S.S.R. (beat Bulgaria 3–1 in final)
Winning women's team U.S.S.R. (beat East Germany 3–1 in final)

Water Polo

Winning team U.S.S.R. (won all 5 of the final matches)

Weight Lifting

Flyweight	K. Osmanoliev (U.S.S.R.)	245.0 kg†
Bantamweight	D. Nũnez (Cuba)	275.0 kg†
Featherweight	V. Mazin (U.S.S.R.)	290.0 kg†
Lightweight	Y. Rusev (Bulgaria)	342.5 kg*
Middleweight	A. Zlatev (Bulgaria)	360.0 kg*
Light heavyweight	Y. Vardanyan (U.S.S.R.)	400.0 kg*
Middle heavyweight	P. Baczako (Hungary)	377.5 kg
(First) Heavyweight	O. Zaremba (Czechoslovakia)	395.0 kg†
(Second) Heavyweight	L. Taranenko (U.S.S.R.)	422.5 kg*
Superheavyweight	S. Rakhmanov (U.S.S.R.)	440.0 kg

Wrestling

	Freestyle	Greco-Roman
Paperweight	C. Pollio (Italy)	Z. Ushkempirov (U.S.S.R.)
Flyweight	A. Beloglazov (U.S.S.R.)	V. Blagidze (U.S.S.R.)
Bantamweight	S. Beloglazov (U.S.S.R.)	S. Serikov (U.S.S.R.)
Featherweight	M. Abushov (U.S.S.R.)	S. Migiakis (Greece)
Lightweight	S. Absaldov (U.S.S.R.)	S. Rusu (Romania)
Welterweight	V. Raitchev (Bulgaria)	F. Kocsis (Hungary)
Middleweight	I. Abilov (Bulgaria)	G. Korban (U.S.S.R.)
Light heavyweight	S. Oganesyan (U.S.S.R.)	N. Nottny (Hungary)
Heavyweight	I. Mate (U.S.S.R.)	G. Raikov (Bulgaria)
Superheavyweight	S. Andiev (U.S.S.R.)	A. Kolchinsky (U.S.S.R.)

Yachting

Finn class	E. Rechardt (Finland)
Flying Dutchman class	Spain
Soling class	Denmark
Tornado class	Brazil
470 class	Brazil
Star class	U.S.S.R.

PHOTO TRENDS/CAMERA PRESS

Steve Ovett (279) unexpectedly finished ahead of fellow Briton Sebastian Coe (254) to take the gold medal in the 800-metre race in the Summer Olympics. Coe, also unexpectedly, reversed the order in the 1,500 metre.

U.S.S.R. As they entered the final straightaway, Ovett clicked into his electrifying top gear and within five strides went to the front to stay. The time was slow: 1 min 45.0 sec, slower than in the Rome Olympics in 1960. And Coe was buried.

He knew it himself. He admitted as much when he said: "I knew that my fellow athletes believed that I had blown it in the 800 metres and there was no way back. They wished me well for the 1,500 metres, but I knew that they had already buried me and they were patting down the earth."

Few in the packed Lenin Stadium believed he could win. But as it turned out the race was made for him. Again nobody wanted the lead, and so Jurgen Straub of East Germany led the field through a leisurely 800 m in 2 min 4.9 sec. Then Straub drove for the tape 700 m away with Coe in his shadow and Ovett in Coe's shadow. The three entered the final straightaway bunched together, and everyone waited for Ovett's kick. But the pace was too fast for him, and it was Coe who surged to the front to win the gold and regain his self-respect.

In a sense justice was done because both won gold medals. Justice was certainly done when the wizened Ethiopian Miruts Yifter won both the 5,000 and 10,000 m. Yifter had looked old when he won the bronze medal in the 10,000 m in the 1972 Olympics. He looked no different in 1980; balding and deeply lined, he said that he was only 36, but that is old to be the supreme distance athlete of the world. Many people believed that he would have won two gold medals in Montreal in 1976, but he could not compete because of the African boycott. Moscow was his last chance for Olympic glory.

The Ethiopians, Yifter, Mohammed Kedir, and Tolossa Kotu, ran the 10,000 m like a cycling team race, each holding the lead for a while and then dropping back to let his countryman take over. Lasse Viren of Finland, who had won the event in 1972 and 1976, tried a heroic surge with three laps to go, but the Ethiopians packed close behind him and in the last 300 m Yifter let fly with a sprint that won him the gold medal. He gave his opponents the same medicine in the 5,000 m.

Thus, the middle- and long-distance runs were won by true champions with no "ifs" or "buts." The same could not be said about many other events; for instance, the 400-m hurdles, won by the East German Volker Beck, was without Ed Moses of the U.S., unbeaten for years at his specialty and the world record holder.

Of all the major sports, swimming suffered most from the boycott. In the absence of the U.S., the East German women won 11 out of 13 gold medals. Led by Vladimir Salnikov (*see* BIOGRAPHIES), the Soviet men won eight golds.

Women's gymnastics often turned out to be a contest between girls and women. Nelli Kim, a Soviet Asian woman, shared the floor exercises title with Nadia Comaneci of Romania (a girl in 1976; a woman in 1980), who also won the balance beam. But the other two events went to girls: the vault to Nataliya Shaposhnikova of the U.S.S.R. and the parallel bars to Maxi Gnauck of East Germany. And the overall title went to one of the most diminutive gymnasts in Moscow, the Soviet Union's Yelena Davydova. Much of the gymnastics competition was marked by rows about the judging.

These were the joyless Games. The memory of seven months of political war could not be banished, and there was tight security in Moscow. The Soviets said that it was to protect the competitors from outside interference, but to those who spent three weeks in Moscow the security seemed to be designed to prevent any contact between visitors and the Soviet people.

After the Games Lord Killanin sounded a warning for the future. As the Olympic flame died in the Lenin Stadium, he said: "I would implore the sportsmen of the world to unite in peace before a holocaust descends. Alas, sport is intertwined with politics but, and I do not mind being accused of being naive, sport and the Olympic Games must not be used for political purposes, especially when other political, diplomatic and economic means have not been tried."

Transportation

Three major considerations dominated the transport scene in 1980: the economic recession, energy, and deregulation. The recession brought the bleakest year in international aviation history and difficulties for those transport activities (*e.g.*, bulk movement of iron and steel) most closely geared to economic activity. The temporary shortage of fuel oils and the corresponding rise in prices in the early part of the year provided a reminder of the need to find alternative energy sources for the 1990s and beyond—a reminder later underlined by the outbreak of hostilities between Iraq and Iran. The liberalization of competition was spreading from the North American domestic air market and the North Atlantic to other routes (*e.g.*, London to Hong Kong) and to surface transport.

The economic recession affected not only transport use but also consumer demand for vehicles. The European and North American motor industries were badly hit, partly because of economic circumstances and partly because of the continued ascendency of the Japanese motor industry.

(DAVID BAYLISS)

AVIATION

The world airline industry faced a disastrous financial situation in 1980 as economic depression reduced traffic while fuel prices continued to cause concern. In the U.S. it was the second full year of deregulation, the relaxation of economic regulation of airlines by the government following passage of the Airline Deregulation Act of 1978.

The U.S. airlines lost more than $1 billion in the second half of 1979 and a further $475 million in the first half of 1980. The notable exception among the trunk carriers was Delta, which managed to record a significant profit. Among the regional carriers, which benefited considerably from deregulation, USAir, Air Florida, and Southwest achieved excellent results. There was an improvement later in the year, but in late December the U.S. Air Transport Association, representing almost all of the nation's scheduled carriers, estimated that the airlines' operating loss for the year would be between $150 million and $200 million. This would be the largest loss in the 42 years since the ATA began keeping records.

With losses thought likely to continue for one or two years, the main concern of the U.S. industry was financing the acquisition of new aircraft. According to the ATA, airlines needed to spend $4.4 billion per year up to 1990 on new aircraft. Actual expenditure, however, was running at less than half that figure in 1979 and at only $1 billion in the first nine months of 1980. To generate the necessary capital, a rate of return on investment of 13–15% was needed, a figure achieved in only one year of the past 20.

All U.S. trunk carriers except United and Northwest experienced a traffic decline in the first ten months of 1980 as compared with the corresponding period of 1979. Traffic, at 304,000,000,000 revenue passenger-kilometres (189,000,000,000 revenue passenger-miles) overall, was 5% below the 1979 period. Most trunk carriers' load factors were down significantly in the ten-month period—by a disastrous nine percentage points in the case of United. Braniff, following a major cutback of the extra capacity it had operated immediately following deregulation, increased its load factor marginally. Some observers believed that the instability that had followed deregulation was beginning to subside. Regional carriers in general benefited from the new regulatory environment, but it was the commuter carriers that showed the strongest growth rate. The commuters' revenue passenger-kilometres increased 35% in 1979 compared with 1978, and a further increase of at least 10% was anticipated in 1980.

Traffic of international scheduled airlines during the year was about 3% above the previous year, according to a preliminary assessment by the International Air Transport Association (IATA) in October. At the same time, it was estimated that

Airline services between Beijing and London began when the first flight from China arrived in London on November 17.

KEYSTONE

Trade, International: see Economy, World

Trade Unions: see Industrial Relations

Transkei: see South Africa

capacity had risen by 8%. IATA members' operating revenue in 1980 was forecast by the association's director general, Knut Hammarskjöld, at $23.7 billion, representing an increase of 21% over 1979. However, operating costs rose 27% to $25.1 billion, leaving the airlines with an operating loss before interest of $778 million and a loss after interest of $1.4 billion. Despite this bleak picture, Hammarskjöld believed that the industry was at the bottom of a trough and that recovery could well be evident within two to three years. Fuel costs for IATA members averaged about $1.22 per gallon in 1980, nearly three times the figure for 1978. The IATA predicted that fuel would constitute 31% of members' operating costs on international scheduled services in 1981. IATA continued its campaign against excessive increases in user charges levied by airports and air navigation authorities. In particular, the association singled out charges levied by Euro-control, the European air traffic control authority, on behalf of 11 countries and by the British Airports Authority. In September 1980 a group of airlines using London's Heathrow Airport began legal action against BAA and the British government, alleging excessive charges and monopolistic practices.

During 1980 the issue of deregulation was a matter of public debate in Europe, where air fares per kilometre were considerably higher than in the U.S. The U.K. government made some tentative deregulatory moves, notably freeing competition on the London–Hong Kong route by allowing British Caledonian, Cathay Pacific, and Laker to compete with the established British Airways (participation by Laker was not approved by the Hong Kong authorities). Other European governments showed little enthusiasm for freeing competition on intra-European routes.

Total world traffic in 1979, as recorded by the International Civil Aviation Organization, was 532,900,000,000 passenger-kilometres (331,100,000,000 passenger-miles), an increase of 9.9% over 1978. Charter traffic, included in that total, declined 5.8% to 102,200,000,000 passenger-kilometres (63,500,000,000 passenger-miles). The number of scheduled passengers in 1979 was 155 million, 10.4% more than in the preceding year.

(DAVID WOOLLEY)

SHIPPING AND PORTS

Early in 1980 the world merchant fleet stood at 675 million tons deadweight (dw) or about 413 million gross registered tons (grt), an increase of nearly 20 million tons dw compared with a year earlier. Both the tanker and the dry cargo fleets increased in total deadweight capacity, but the overall rate of growth remained well below the 9–12% prevailing in the first half of the 1970s. Liberia continued to lead the table of world fleets with 160 million tons dw of shipping, followed closely by Japan with 66 million tons dw and Greece with 63 million tons dw. The U.K. fleet was in fourth place at 45 million tons dw. More than two-thirds of the Liberian fleet consisted of tankers. Worldwide, the tonnage of vessels laid up fell to a low of 11 million tons dw; nearly 76% of this represented tankers, mostly in the over 100,000-tons-dw class.

Provisional figures showed that world seaborne trade increased by just under 5% during the year, an improvement over the low of 1.8% for the year before. Crude oil and oil products together accounted for about half the world seaborne trade. Shipments of the three other major bulk commodities, iron ore, coal, and grain, increased by 7½% in volume with shipments of iron ore (the largest bulk commodity after oil) up by more than 8½%. The increase in coal shipments was largely attributable to a recovery in steel production in Japan.

The first stage of the Suez Canal improvement project was completed. The maximum permitted draft was increased to 16 m (53 ft) and the vessel beam to 43 m (142 ft). The canal could now accept vessels of up to 150,000 tons dw fully loaded, 230,000-tonners partly loaded, and possibly 350,000 tons in ballast. Attempts by the Suez Canal Authority to increase tolls were resisted by owners of dry cargo tonnage, particularly the Japanese. There was congestion in the canal as a result of the heavy shipments of grain in transit, and owners of the larger bulk carriers had to face extra daily costs of up to $13,000 because of delays.

A massive program for the modernization of all major ports in India was introduced, with emphasis on facilities for handling containers and bulk commodities such as coal and iron ore. Plans were put in hand for the improvement of U.S. coal export facilities. A new deepwater berth to take bulk carriers of up to 100,000 tons dw was nearing completion at the port of Beilun in China's Zhejiang (Chekiang) Province. (W. D. EWART)

FREIGHT AND PIPELINES

Freight transport is closely geared to economic activity, and this was reflected in the fortunes of various sectors of the industry. Air and seaborne freight grew with international trade, but slack national economies depressed traffic in such prod-

"Get your ticket at the station for the Rock Island Line."

The last line of this famous song by Huddie Ledbetter ("Leadbelly") lost some currency in May 1980 when the 128-year-old railroad was ordered by the U.S. Interstate Commerce Commission to discontinue service on approximately 70% of its 10,500-mi route.

The venerable railroad, which had been a major hauler of grain in the Midwest, filed for bankruptcy in 1975, and in the years since then had piled up $160 million in losses.

The ICC ruled that the legendary railroad had "no realistic hope" of recovering from its poor financial condition. Pointing to deteriorated equipment and track, the ICC said that continued operation of the railroad would be unfair to the Rock's stockholders and creditors. The commission ordered the railroad to sell off approximately $400 million in property, with the money raised to be used to pay $386.6 million in creditors' claims.

World Transportation

Country	Railways: Route length in 000 km	Railways Traffic: Passenger in 000,000 pass.-km	Railways Traffic: Freight in 000,000 net ton-km	Motor transport: Road length in 000 km	Motor transport, Vehicles in use: Passenger in 000	Motor transport, Vehicles in use: Commercial in 000	Merchant shipping, Ships of 100 tons and over: Number of vessels	Merchant shipping, Ships of 100 tons and over: Gross reg. tons in 000	Air traffic: Total km flown in 000,000	Air traffic: Passenger in 000,000 pass.-km	Air traffic: Freight in 000,000 net ton-km
EUROPE											
Austria	6.5[1]	7,310	10,567	106.6	2,040.3	163.4	13	81	20.1	1,086	14.5
Belgium	4.0	7,136	7,312	125.8	2,973.4	247.5	276	1,789	53.1	4,819	411.1
Bulgaria	4.3	6,850	17,653	36.1[1]	c.218.0[1]	c.47.0[1]	191	1,150	11.0	610	c.8.4
Cyprus	—	—	—	9.9	79.0	17.2	762	2,356	7.4	688	26.7
Czechoslovakia	13.2	18,640	73,020	145.5[1]	1,836.0	308.5	17	155	28.3	1,735	18.0
Denmark	2.5[1]	3,080	1,921[1]	67.5[1]	1,477.3	269.0	1,315	5,524	40.2[2]	3,050[2]	132.4[2]
Finland	6.1	3,020	7,366	74.7	1,169.5	143.1	344	2,509	30.0	1,981	46.0
France	34.1	52,250	70,681	802.9	18,440.0	2,364.0	1,247	11,946	276.1	32,782	2,031.3
Germany, East	14.2	22,320	58,920	c.119.0	2,392.3	226.7	453	1,552	31.5	1,802	62.3
Germany, West	31.7	40,662	66,159	482.0	22,613.5	1,421.6	1,926	8,563	183.8	19,843	1,585.7
Greece	2.5	1,460	840	37.0	839.3	351.1	3,827	37,353	41.4	5,132	68.0
Hungary	8.0	12,440	24,069	87.4	913.4	151.7	23	78	13.9	761	5.9
Ireland	2.0	1,007	559	92.3[1]	683.0	61.5	118	201	21.0	2,220	100.3
Italy	19.9[1]	39,820	17,690	293.3	c.17,600.0	c.1,383.0	1,711	11,695	135.7	13,336	c.510.0
Netherlands, The	2.8[1]	8,600	3,334	107.4[1]	4,100.0	291.0	1,233	5,403	103.8	14,012	909.9
Norway	4.2	2,262	3,068	80.9	1,189.8	151.7	2,531	22,349	56.5[2]	3,915[2]	134.9[2]
Poland	24.0	45,472	135,364	298.5	2,117.1	583.7	813	3,580	32.8	2,314	18.5
Portugal	3.6	5,628	884	50.7	970.0	57.0	347	1,205	37.5	3,927	122.6
Romania	11.1[1]	22,811	73,738	c.95.0[1]	c.220.0[1]	c.110.0[1]	286	1,797	20.2	1,179	15.2
Spain	15.7	16,609	10,573	231.4	7,057.5	1,261.2	2,773	8,314	151.6	15,184	404.8
Sweden	12.1	5,843	16,580	129.1	2,868.3	177.9	697	4,637	64.2[2]	4,409[2]	197.0[2]
Switzerland	5.0[1]	8,288	c.6,580	63.1	2,154.3	160.6	32	265	92.7	10,329	434.3
U.S.S.R.	228.1	332,100	3,354,000	1,423.5	c.6,640.0	c.6,330.0	8,120	22,900	...	139,787	c.2,840.0
United Kingdom	c.18.2	30,740[3]	19,893[3]	374.2	c.14,920.0	c.1,820.0	3,211	27,951	385.7	47,004	1,247.6
Yugoslavia	9.8	10,311	25,730	127.4	1,923.9	158.0	478	2,407	33.5	2,719	28.8
ASIA											
Bangladesh	2.9	3,585	595	6.2	22.9[1]	10.0[1]	152	299	9.1	577	c.15.0
Burma	4.5	3,665	492	22.4[1]	38.6[1]	41.3[1]	78	64	5.4	185	1.4
Cambodia	c.0.6[1]	54[1]	10[1]	c.11.0[1]	27.2[1]	11.0[1]	3[1]	4[1]	0.8[1]	42[1]	0.4[1]
China	50.0	121,400	558,800	890.0	c.50.0[1]	1,044.0[1]	846	6,337	31.0	3,500	123.4
India	60.8	192,900	153,950	1,375.0	805.4[1]	385.8[1]	601	5,854	83.1	8,030	301.2
Indonesia	c.6.8[1]	4,458	980	123.0[1]	532.3	331.7	1,122	1,310	77.9	4,480	66.1
Iran	4.6	3,511[1]	4,627[1]	49.7	932.7[1]	204.0[1]	219	1,207	41.7	4,655	c.89.0
Iraq	2.0[1]	797[1]	2,254[1]	9.7[1]	150.4[1]	74.5[1]	123	1,328	16.1	1,334	41.4
Israel	0.8[1]	221	636	11.9	403.0	86.8	57	435	32.1	5,440	290.4
Japan	26.8[1]	299,593	43,140	1,106.2	22,667.3	13,325.8	9,981	39,993	324.3	29,278	1,569.0
Korea, South	5.8	c.21,500	10,840	45.7[1]	184.9	162.0	1,287	3,953	53.1	6,838	503.0
Malaysia	2.4[1]	1,270[4]	1,294[4]	c.29.8	572.1[1]	196.2[1]	196	621	30.7	2,638	73.2
Pakistan	8.8	16,435	9,401	86.6	130.4	35.7	83	443	45.4	4,993	219.7
Philippines	1.1[1]	485	34	127.1	440.5[1]	327.1[1]	620	1,606	43.7	4,432	126.6
Saudi Arabia	0.7	72[1]	66[1]	37.5	360.5	272.2	172	1,443	67.0	6,771	c.140.0
Syria	1.7[1]	322	449	c.16.3[1]	69.1[1]	70.6[1]	41	32	11.6	986	13.1
Taiwan	3.7	7,327	2,668	17.4	340.6	201.3	490	2,011	34.1	5,995	678.5
Thailand	3.9	6,070	2,650	64.1	387.3	417.2	136	362	31.9	4,683	183.1
Turkey	8.1	5,620	6,649	232.2	658.7	309.8	475	1,422	21.7	1,904	15.5
Vietnam	c.4.2[1]	...	...	c.60.0[1]	c.100.0	c.200.0	85	202	...	...	...
AFRICA											
Algeria	3.9[1]	1,452	2,016	78.5[1]	333.6[1]	168.9[1]	132	1,258	25.3	1,795	c.12.1
Congo	0.8[1]	301	487	8.2[1]	13.2[1]	3.7[1]	15	7	2.9[5]	171[5]	15.9[5]
Egypt	4.8	8,748[1]	2,201[1]	28.9	379.0	114.7	243	542	24.6	2,324	25.8
Ethiopia	1.0[1]	132[1,6]	260[1,6]	37.3	38.4	10.6	17	24	11.1	548	23.5
Gabon	0.2	...	...	7.1	c.17.4[1]	c.12.7[1]	14	77	3.1	87	0.7
Ghana	1.0	521	312	32.2	33.0	27.0	95	197	4.3	319	3.3
Ivory Coast	0.7	1,274[7]	533[7]	45.2	75.9[1]	13.7[1]	67	181	2.6[5]	186[5]	c.15.6[5]
Kenya	2.0	...	3,538[1]	51.4	192.0	34.2	21	26	12.1	884	c.25.0
Liberia	0.5	...	4,396[1]	11.2[1]	20.1	13.8	2,466	81,528	1.3	11	0.1
Libya	—	—	—	c.20.0[1]	386.0[1]	181.6[1]	84	885	9.9	832	c.9.2
Malawi	0.7	84	244	10.6	12.8	11.9	—	—	4.3	138	7.2
Morocco	1.8[1]	835[1]	3,474[1]	26.7[1]	347.4[1]	121.6[1]	131	364	24.4	1,951	23.2
Nigeria	3.5	785[1]	972[1]	105.0[1]	133.7[1]	23.6[1]	107	383	18.0	1,268	10.3
Senegal	1.0	180[1]	164[1]	13.3	65.5	4.1	86	34	2.5[5]	167[5]	15.5[5]
Somalia	—	—	—	c.17.1[1]	8.0[1]	8.0[1]	15	55	1.2	22	0.3
South Africa	19.9	...	80,963[8]	185.5	2,310.9	858.3	286	741	58.5	8,281	256.6
Sudan	4.8	...	2,324[1]	c.50.0	c.55.0[1]	c.30.0[1]	13	43	10.1	c.600	c.11.0
Tanzania	3.5	...	...	c.35.0	43.6[1]	46.4[1]	30	58	3.6	99	0.8
Tunisia	2.3	737	1,479	24.2	115.3	84.6	44	128	12.1	1,348	11.9
Uganda	1.3	...	...	27.9	26.0	5.4	1	6	...	...	...
Zaire	5.3	467[1]	2,203[1]	c.145.0	96.7[1]	87.1[1]	32	92	11.2	778	36.9
Zambia	c.2.2	320[1]	897[1]	36.4	c.104.5[1]	c.62.5[1]	1	6	10.0	544	37.1
Zimbabwe	3.5	...	6,149	c.83.0	c.180.0[1]	c.70.0[1]	—	—	5.1	241	1.9
NORTH AND CENTRAL AMERICA											
Canada	67.9	3,070	215,350	884.3[1]	9,554.3[1]	2,442.3[1]	1,290	3,016	287.8	29,276	675.8
Costa Rica	0.9	81[1]	14[1]	25.3[1]	59.8[1]	42.7[1]	25	19	6.9	360	19.1
Cuba	14.8	1,572	1,870	c.31.2	80.0[1]	40.0[1]	341	853	13.9	1,089	c.11.0
El Salvador	0.6	...	...	11.0[1]	70.1[1]	35.5[1]	5	2	7.1	231	c.28.0
Guatemala	1.8[1]	...	117[1]	17.3	156.4	56.0	6	9	4.0	190	7.6
Honduras	c.1.8	174[1]	3[1]	8.3	15.9	27.7	99	193	5.7	324	3.8
Mexico	20.3	4,800	36,410	212.4	3,696.0	1,406.3	349	915	112.2	10,027	c.110.0
Nicaragua	0.4	19[1]	11[1]	18.2	c.38.0[1]	c.30.0[1]	20	13	2.5	92	2.0
Panama	0.7	...	...	8.1	66.9[1]	19.5[1]	3,803	22,324	7.5	392	3.9
United States	320.2[1]	16,450[9]	1,252,800[9]	6,251.7	116,575.0	31,702.6	5,088	17,542	4,043.6	404,550	10,387.1
SOUTH AMERICA											
Argentina	34.6	11,242	10,310	207.6	2,866.0	1,244.0	495	2,344	76.1	5,370	128.6
Bolivia	3.9	395[1]	579[1]	38.1[1]	34.3[1]	25.4[1]	2	15	12.0	700	43.3
Brazil	30.3[1]	11,699[1]	60,721[1]	1,544.7	7,704.1	884.2	585	4,007	170.7	12,544	591.9
Chile	10.8[1]	2,211	2,491	75.4	328.0	176.3	154	537	20.9	1,472	105.2
Colombia	2.9	342	1,232	53.9	453.4	82.6	65	292	49.3	3,786	210.5
Ecuador	1.0[1]	65	34	21.5[1]	51.3[1]	77.2[1]	69	234	15.7	676	13.2
Paraguay	0.5	23	17	c.12.0	29.0	9.3	27	23	3.9	223	2.3
Peru	2.2	528[1]	612[1]	56.9[1]	300.4[1]	166.2[1]	694	646	23.9	1,470	c.37.5
Uruguay	3.0	389[1]	307[1]	25.0[1]	127.1[1]	104.2[1]	53	198	3.2	64	0.3
Venezuela	0.4	42[1]	15[1]	61.8	1,390.0	639.5	220	882	55.7	3,498	113.2
OCEANIA											
Australia	40.1[10]	...	32,030[1]	837.9[1]	5,642.0	1,400.0	457	1,652	193.0	20,993	501.5
New Zealand	4.5	463	3,229	93.4	1,274.1	247.2	117	258	49.7	4,312	152.1

Note: Data are for 1978 or 1979 unless otherwise indicated. (—) Indicates nil or negligible; (. . .) indicates not known; (c.) indicates provisional or estimated.
[1] Data given are the most recent available. [2] Including apportionment of traffic of Scandinavian Airlines System. [3] Excluding Northern Ireland. [4] Including Singapore.
[5] Including apportionment of traffic of Air Afrique. [6] Including Djibouti traffic. [7] Including Upper Volta traffic. [8] Including Namibia traffic. [9] Class 1 railways only. [10] State system only.
Sources: UN, *Statistical Yearbook 1978, Monthly Bulletin of Statistics, Annual Bulletin of Transport Statistics for Europe 1978;* Lloyd's Register of Shipping, *Statistical Tables 1979;* International Road Federation, *World Road Statistics 1975–79;* International Civil Aviation Organization, *Civil Aviation Statistics of the World 1978.* (M. C. MacDONALD)

UPI

In October the Dutch cruise ship "M.S. Prinsendam" heeled and sank off Alaska after a fire had forced 320 passengers and 150 crew members to abandon ship. All passengers and crew were rescued.

ucts as steel and chemicals, which are particularly important to the railways. In the air there was a growth in the specialist freighter fleet. The increase in roll on/roll off and piggyback operations (*e.g.*, the new service linking New York and Los Angeles) improved modal coordination. British Railways was introducing large 100-car train ferries between England and the continent.

New rail freight links opened included a 185-km (115-mi) spur from the Burlington Northern railway line to the Powder River basin coalfield in the U.S. and a 200-km (124-mi) link between Carandivo and its port, Lazaro Cardenas, in Mexico. A 70-km (43-mi) coal railway was opened in New South Wales, Australia. Most freight continued to go by road, but even within Europe rail's share (in metric ton-kilometres) varied from 5% in The Netherlands to 45% in Sweden. The road freight industry was suffering as a result of the recession. In Europe the harmonization of maximum truck weights continued to be debated. The U.K. accepted the EEC requirement for the use of tachographs, to be compulsory from Jan. 1, 1982. Dieselization of the U.S. commercial fleet increased as the older middle-weight gasoline-engine trucks were replaced.

Many major pipeline projects planned before the recession remained on paper. Apart from the basic networks for water and gas distribution and sewerage, oil products and gas trunking were still the main focus of pipeline construction activity. Networks had developed to the extent that 20% of inland freight went by pipeline in the U.S., 18% in France, 15% in the U.S.S.R., and 5% in the U.K. Among notable recent additions to the world's pipeline systems was the 71-km (44-mi) pipeline between Kudremuth and Mangalore, India, which was expected to carry about five million tons of iron ore slurry a year. A large-diameter (1.2 m [3.9 ft]), pneumatic-capsule pipeline for carrying domestic refuse was commissioned in Leningrad. Research was being carried out on the possible use of pipelines to accommodate chemical reactions between different materials (*e.g.*, the conversion of biomass to alcohol in transit). Work was also being done on mixed-use pipelines that would carry different types of commodities, for example, oil used to propel sealed capsules with dry contents.

ROADS AND TRAFFIC

Efforts were made to hasten completion of major transcontinental routes and to fill in missing links. Notable completions were the Beune to Mulhouse Motorway linking the French and West German national expressway networks and the 4.2-km (2.6-mi) Ahmed Hamidi tunnel under the Suez Canal linking Africa and Asia. Autoroute 26 connecting the North Sea coast to the south of France was opened to traffic.

Maintenance problems first seen on the U.S. Interstate System were occurring on other national networks, particularly in the U.K. Unorthodox materials were being used, both to renew existing pavements and for new construction. The Trans-Sahara Highway was being constructed of low-moisture laterite, and the world's first highway to be paved with sulfurous materials (3.3 km [2 mi] long) was completed at San Antonio, Texas. Recycling of the existing pavement (using hot-mix methods) could save up to a quarter of the cost of complete replacement; this method was used to rebuild the Edens Expressway in the Chicago area and to renew 87 km [54 mi] of U.S. highway in New Jersey. There was a reaction against road development in some parts of the third world because of concern over potential environmental and cultural disruption.

Despite economic difficulties, world road traffic continued to grow, particularly in those countries

KEYSTONE

British Rail put into service near the end of the year an Advance Passenger Train capable of achieving speeds of 250 km (155 mph). The train leans dramatically when going around corners and when at rest.

that were neither "Western rich" nor "less developed poor." In Poland, for example, the current growth rate was 13% per year. The world's road vehicle fleet reached 400 million units. U.S. manufacturers retained their dominance, but Japanese manufacturers were moving up, thanks to steady improvement in the design of their vehicles coupled with higher productivity. Efforts continued to reduce reliance on hydrocarbons for fuel. Of particular note during the year were General Motors' proposal to mass produce an electric car during the mid-'80s, the mass production of an electric light van by Diahatsu, the announcement by Gulf and Western of a breakthrough in battery technology, and the mass production (for Brazil) of alcohol-powered cars.

INTERCITY RAIL

The British Advanced Passenger Train (APT) made its inaugural run in the autumn, just 150 years after the opening of the world's first intercity railway between Manchester and Liverpool. The APT owes its very high average speed to its ability to negotiate curves at high speed as well as to its high top speed of 250 km per hour (kph; 155 mph). The fastest trains in service were still on the Japanese National Railways (JNR) Shinkhansen, with a top recorded speed of 304 kph (189 mph), but even this was relatively slow compared with the speed reached by the JNR's experimental Maglev tracked vehicle: 517 kph (321 mph) at the Miyazaki test track. The Soviets' high-speed train was put into service for the Moscow Olympics.

Other technological innovations during the year included the introduction of a computerized reservation and ticketing system on VIA Rail (Canada) and the development of a new tubular axle induction motor by British Railways, which was also developing a low-cost, lightweight "railbus" for lightly trafficked short/medium-distance services. A rail connection was provided between Zürich, Switz., and its airport, and a new high-speed line was planned to link Moscow with the Black Sea (1,140 km [708 mi]).

Electrification of main intercity railways continued. In India electrification of the Madras to Vizayawada line was completed as part of a 350 km (217 mi) per year program. Similar programs were planned in Spain, West Germany, Canada, and Australia. Most of the major passenger networks continued to need large operating subsidies. Tight financial restrictions in the U.K. led to plans to trim services and close branch lines. In the U.S. the Amtrak network appeared to have been stabilized, at least for the time being.

URBAN MASS TRANSIT

During the 1970s, 21 new rail transit systems were opened, and most of the pre-World War II systems were extended. The total route length in operation in 1980 was about 3,500 km (2,175 mi) serving 3,400 stations. Operating speeds ranged from 19 kph (12 mph) on the Budapest, Hung., system to 70 kph (43 mph) on San Francisco's Bay Area Rapid Transit; the average was 34 kph (21 mph). As of 1980 there were 90 cities with rail transit systems in operation or under construction, and this number seemed likely to top one hundred by 1990. Some 800 route-kilometres (500 route-miles) were currently under construction, and a further 1,800 (1,100) were planned.

Light rail transit (LRT) and tramway technologies were under consideration in about one hundred cities. The key difference between these two systems is that LRT uses formal railway signaling whereas vehicle separation on tramways is a matter for the driver. There were 45,000 trams (streetcars) running on 290 systems, ranging from the huge network in Leningrad to the tiny system in Bex, Switz. The first stage of the Tyne and Wear system in the U.K. opened in August.

Despite the large investment being made in urban rail systems, buses were a more important form of urban public transport and would continue to be for many years to come. Roughly 800,000 buses in the world's towns and cities carried one billion journeys each day. Bus manufacturing was more stable than in 1978–79, and the traditional major manufacturers consolidated their positions. Structural problems, possibly attributable to the highly complex federal specifications, were reported in many of the new buses purchased by the U.S. government for several U.S. bus systems.

The decline of the trolley bus seemed to have been halted as systems were introduced by such countries as Switzerland, South Africa, Brazil, and Canada that either had good electricity supplies or were excessively dependent on imported oil. Currently there were 20,000 troiley buses operating in over 200 systems, the largest being in Moscow. Perhaps the most interesting technological developments were in the field of hybrid systems (trolley/battery and trolley/diesel), which offered the prospect of greater routing flexibility and the possibility of avoiding overhead wires in sensitive and difficult areas. (DAVID BAYLISS)

See also Energy; Engineering Projects; Environment; Industrial Review: *Aerospace; Automobiles.*
[725.C.3; 734; 737.A.3]

Trinidad and Tobago

A republic and a member of the Commonwealth of Nations, Trinidad and Tobago consists of two islands off the coast of Venezuela, north of the Orinoco River delta. Area: 5,128 sq km (1,980 sq mi). Pop. (1979 est.): 1,156,100, including (1970) Negro 43%; East Indian 40%; mixed 14%. Cap. and largest city: Port-of-Spain (pop., 1976 est., 47,300). Language: English (official); Hindi, French, Spanish. Religion (1970): Christian 64%; Hindu 25%; Muslim 6%. President in 1980, Sir Ellis Clarke; prime minister, Eric Williams.

With its vast reserves of oil and natural gas, Trinidad and Tobago remained the wealthiest Caribbean nation in 1980. In January Prime Minister Eric Williams announced a record TT$5 billion budget, of which a massive TT$2,168,000,000 was to be spent on capital projects. These included a vast high-technology complex at Point Lisas, which was to comprise an ultramodern iron and steel plant; liquefied natural gas, methanol, and fertilizer plants; an aluminum smelter; and a number of related industries. By the year's end all of the projects except the aluminum smelter were well under way. However, many utilities such as water supply, electricity, and the telephone system remained in poor condition.

Politically, Williams and his ruling People's National Movement (PNM) maintained their unassailable position. In contrast, the opposition United Labour Front remained disunited and was virtually routed in local government elections. During the year a new party led by Karl Hudson-Phillips, a former PNM attorney general, emerged. Throughout the year Trinidad was plagued by a spate of bombings, fires, and attacks on prominent individuals, but the perpetrators remained unidentified. Toward the year's end Parliament agreed to allow Tobago considerable authority over its own affairs. In elections for Tobago's first House of Assembly November 24, 8 of 12 seats were won by advocates of autonomy.

Regionally, Trinidad and Tobago continued to assist some of the less developed Caribbean countries by supplying them with oil at low cost and furnishing other financial aid. The government remained critical of developments in neighbouring Grenada but generally maintained a low profile internationally. (DAVID A. JESSOP)

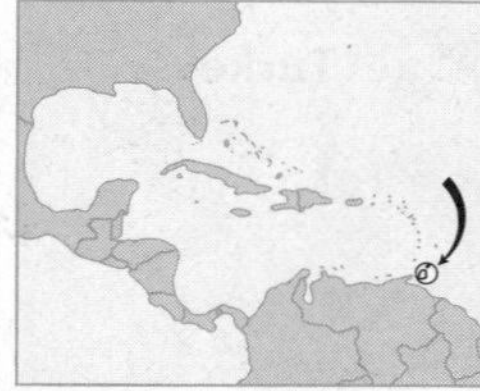
Trinidad and Tobago

TRINIDAD AND TOBAGO

Education. (1978–79) Primary, pupils 181,863, teachers (1976–77) 6,471; secondary, pupils 87,301, teachers (1976–77) 1,631; vocational, pupils 4,200, teachers (1975–76) 114; higher (1975–76), students 4,940, teaching staff *c.* 500.

Finance and Trade. Monetary unit: Trinidad and Tobago dollar, with (Sept. 22, 1980) a par value of TT$2.40 to U.S. $1 (free rate of TT$5.77 = £1 sterling). Gold, SDR's, and foreign exchange (June 1980) U.S. $1,958,000,000. Budget (1980 est.) balanced at TT$5,059,600,000. Foreign trade (1979): imports TT$4,669,500,000; exports TT$5,942,400,000. Import sources (1978): Saudi Arabia 22%; U.S. 21%; Indonesia 14%; U.K. 13%; Japan 5%. Export destinations (1978): U.S. 69%. Main exports (1978): petroleum products 48%; crude oil 41%.

Transport and Communications. Roads (1977) 7,100 km. Motor vehicles in use (1978): passenger 131,500; commercial 27,400. There are no railways in operation. Air traffic (1979): 1,261,000,000 passenger-km; freight 22.3 million net ton-km. Shipping traffic (1977): goods loaded 20,834,000 metric tons, unloaded 14,861,000 metric tons. Telephones (Jan. 1978) 74,900. Radio receivers (Dec. 1977) 275,000. Television receivers (Dec. 1977) 125,000.

Agriculture. Production (in 000; metric tons; 1979): sugar, raw value *c.* 144; rice *c.* 22; tomatoes *c.* 10; grapefruit *c.* 6; copra *c.* 7; coffee *c.* 2; cocoa *c.* 3. Livestock (in 000; 1978): cattle *c.* 75; pigs *c.* 57; goats *c.* 44; poultry *c.* 7,000.

Industry. Production (in 000; metric tons; 1979): crude oil 11,073; natural gas (cu m; 1978) *c.* 2,400,000; petroleum products *c.* 10,900; cement 217; nitrogenous fertilizers (nutrient content; 1978–79) 49; electricity (kw-hr; 1978) 1,680,000.

Tunisia

A republic of North Africa lying on the Mediterranean Sea, Tunisia is bounded by Algeria and Libya. Area: 154,530 sq km (52,664 sq mi). Pop. (1980 est.): 6,367,000. Cap. and largest city: Tunis (pop., 1975 census, city proper 550,404; 1978 est., governorate 1,030,400). Language: Arabic (official). Religion: Muslim; Jewish and Christian minorities. President in 1980, Habib Bourguiba; prime ministers, Hedi Nouira and, from April 23, Mohammed Mzali.

Pres. Habib Bourguiba, continually confronted with a watchful and active opposition, had to show both firmness and a spirit of accommodation. At the end of December 1979, Prime Minister Hedi Nouira delivered a violent attack on Islamic unity

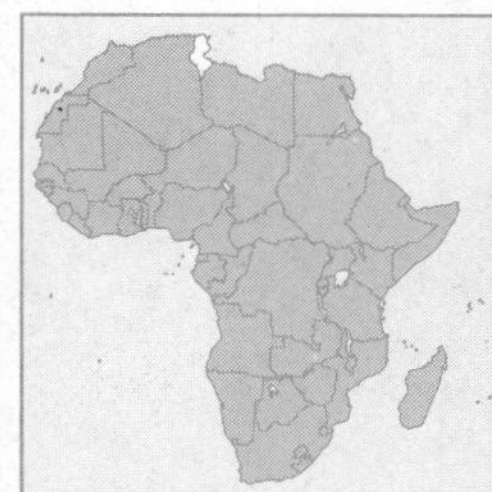
Tunisia

TUNISIA

Education. (1978–79) Primary, pupils 1,004,144, teachers 25,593; secondary, pupils 156,082; vocational, pupils 72,750; secondary and vocational, teachers 10,711; teacher training (1977–78), students 1,987, teachers 125; higher (1977–78), students 26,781, teaching staff 3,471.

Finance. Monetary unit: Tunisian dinar, with (Sept. 22, 1980) a free rate of 0.40 dinar to U.S. $1 (0.96 dinar = £1 sterling). Gold, SDR's, and foreign exchange (June 1980) U.S. $651 million. Budget (1979 est.): revenue 625 million dinars; expenditure 482 million dinars. Gross domestic product (1979) 2,838,000,000 dinars. Money supply (May 1980) 780,390,000 dinars. Cost of living (Tunis; 1975 = 100; June 1980) 139.1.

Foreign Trade. (1979) Imports 1,149,350,000 dinars; exports 716,530,000 dinars. Import sources: France 26%; Italy 13%; West Germany 10%; U.S. 6%; Greece 5%. Export destinations: Italy 20%; France 19%; Greece 16%; West Germany 10%; U.S. 9%. Main exports (1978): crude oil 37%; clothing 18%; phosphates 9%; olive oil 8%; phosphoric acid 5%. Tourism (1978): visitors 1,142,000; gross receipts U.S. $402 million.

Transport and Communications. Roads (1978) 24,168 km. Motor vehicles in use (1978): passenger 115,300; commercial 84,600. Railways: (1978) 2,257 km; traffic (1979) 737 million passenger-km, freight 1,479,000,000 net ton-km. Air traffic (1979): 1,348,000,000 passenger-km; freight 11.9 million net ton-km. Telephones (Jan. 1978) 144,100. Radio receivers (Dec. 1977) 866,000. Television receivers (Dec. 1977) 213,000.

Agriculture. Production (in 000; metric tons; 1979): wheat 680; barley 270; potatoes (1978) *c.* 105; tomatoes *c.* 300; watermelons (1978) *c.* 160; grapes *c.* 90; dates *c.* 50; olives *c.* 500; oranges *c.* 106. Livestock (in 000; 1978): sheep *c.* 3,526; cattle *c.* 810; goats *c.* 950; camels *c.* 205; poultry *c.* 15,439.

Industry. Production (in 000; metric tons; 1979): crude oil 5,507; natural gas (cu m) 330,000; cement 1,403; iron ore (53% metal content) 393; pig iron 154; crude steel 176; phosphate rock (1978) 3,712; phosphate fertilizers (1978–79) 251; petroleum products *c.* 1,400; sulfuric acid 1,262; electricity (excluding most industrial production; kw-hr) 2,080,000.

Trapshooting: *see* Target Sports

Trucking Industry: *see* Transportation

Trust Territories: *see* Dependent States

purists, and in February 1980 the government closed all university faculties. In March, however, several opponents belonging to the Mouvement des Démocrates Socialistes joined the government Parti Socialiste Destourien. In July six Marxist-Leninist students were freed, and in August trade union leaders were granted some freedom from restriction.

Hedi Nouira underwent surgery in March following a stroke and went to Nice, France, for his convalescence. Appointed "coordinator of government activity" on March 1, Mohammed Mzali became prime minister on April 23. A few days earlier Hassan Belkhodja was appointed foreign minister. There was a minor government reshuffle on December 3, in the direction of further liberalization. Restricted to living under observation, Mohammed Masmoudi, an important political personality, went on a hunger strike in July and was granted complete freedom in August.

During the night of January 26–27, the regime faced a commando attack by 50 men sent from Libya via the "Qaddafi route," generally used by the Polisario Front guerrillas of the Western Sahara. This armed group attempted to seize the mining town of Gafsa in a surprise attack. Although the Libyan government professed astonishment at being suspected of involvement in the incident, Tunisia recalled its ambassador from Tripoli and then its workers in Libya; it also exposed a Libyan scheme to implicate Algeria in the affair. After France had sent three warships into the Gulf of Gabès, the French embassy at Tripoli and the consulate at Benghazi were sacked by Libyan mobs.

After the Gafsa affair, the U.S. speeded up the delivery of arms to Tunisia. On March 10 the trial of captured Gafsa commandos began before the Court of State Security, and on March 27, 15 of them were condemned to death. When their appeal was rejected, 13 were hanged (two had been sentenced in absentia).

Before the deterioration of Tunisian-Libyan relations, Bourguiba had attempted to strengthen existing ties with Algeria and Morocco and with France. There were numerous comings and goings between Paris and Tunis. As a result of French Premier Raymond Barre's visit in October, it was decided to create a Franco-Tunisian development bank and to release, as of Jan. 1, 1981, French credits blocked in Tunis. Queen Elizabeth II visited Tunis in October. (PHILIPPE DECRAENE)

Turkey

Turkey

A republic of southeastern Europe and Asia Minor, Turkey is bounded by the Aegean Sea, the Black Sea, the U.S.S.R., Iran, Iraq, Syria, the Mediterranean Sea, Greece, and Bulgaria. Area: 779,452 sq km (300,948 sq mi), including 23,698 sq km in Europe. Pop. (1980 prelim.): 45,217,600. Cap.: Ankara (pop., 1979 est., 2,106,100). Largest city: Istanbul (pop., 1979 est., 2,882,600). Language: Turkish, Kurdish, Arabic. Religion: predominantly Muslim. President to April 6, 1980, Fahri Koruturk; acting president from April 6 to September 12, Ihsan Sabri Caglayangil; head of state from October 27, Gen. Kenan Evren; prime ministers, Suleyman Demirel and, from September 20, Bulent Ulusu.

UPI

Gen. Kenan Evren took over as Turkey's chief of state after a bloodless military coup ousted the government of Suleyman Demirel on September 12.

The minority administration formed on Nov. 12, 1979, by Suleyman Demirel, leader of the right-of-centre Justice Party, was overthrown by the armed forces in a bloodless coup on Sept. 12, 1980. In spite of an extension of martial law in February, political violence claimed some 2,000 lives, including those of Nihat Erim (*see* OBITUARIES) and other prominent figures. Muslim sectarian violence broke out between the Sunni majority and the Shi'ah minority (known in Turkey as Alevi). The armed forces suppressed leftist-led workers in Izmir in February and occupied the Black Sea coastal town of Fatsa in July, so ending a "liberated zone" run by revolutionary leftists.

Agreement among the political parties proved impossible. Demirel failed to secure an early dissolution of Parliament; the Republican People's Party (RPP) leader, Bulent Ecevit, failed to agree on an alternative coalition with Necmettin Erbakan, leader of the Islamic National Salvation Party (NSP), but, with the help of NSP votes, achieved the dismissal of Demirel's pro-Western foreign minister, Hayrettin Erkmen, on September 5. Parliament failed to elect a president of the republic to succeed Adm. Fahri Koruturk, whose term of office expired on April 6. On September 6 a rally by Erbakan's Islamic fundamentalists in Konya challenged the government and provided the immediate cause of the military takeover.

Tunnels: *see* Engineering Projects

Demirel was more effective in economic management. On January 24 he introduced new economic measures, including a one-third devaluation of the Turkish lira against the U.S. dollar, the limitation of multiple exchange rates, the abolition of price controls and of most subsidies, and the promotion of exports and of foreign investments. These and later measures found favour with Turkey's Western creditors. On April 15 the Organization for Economic Cooperation and Development pledged Turkey $1,160,000,000 in fresh aid, and on July 23 it recommended the rescheduling of Turkey's existing debts. The International Monetary Fund agreed to extend to Turkey standby credits of $1,162,500,000 over three years.

Demirel's foreign policy was pro-Western. The Soviet invasion of Afghanistan was condemned and the Olympic Games in Moscow were boycotted. On February 6 it was announced that Turkey would apply for full membership in the European Economic Community. On February 22 Turkey announced the resumption of civil air traffic with Greece. Turkish objections to the return of Greece to NATO were resolved through negotiations by October 20.

After the military takeover the foreign and economic policies of the Demirel government were continued by a National Security Council headed by the chief of the general staff, Gen. Kenan Evren, and including the services' commanders. Parliament was dissolved; political activity banned; leftist and rightist unions and associations banned; and more than 6,000 people, including party leaders, were detained. On September 21 a mainly civilian Cabinet was formed under retired Adm. Bulent Ulusu (*see* BIOGRAPHIES), who was commander of the Navy until August 8.

A constitutional instrument issued on October 27 transferred Parliament's powers to the National Security Council, General Evren officially becoming head of state. Priority was given to the struggle against terrorism, with the promise that a new democratic constitution would be submitted to a popular referendum at a later date. Terrorist incidents were fewer, the most notable being the hijacking of an airliner by Islamic fundamentalists on October 13. The crew and passengers were rescued and the terrorists arrested. Ecevit resigned from the leadership of the RPP on October 30.

(ANDREW MANGO)

TURKEY

Education. (1977–78) Primary, pupils 5,454,356, teachers 184,123; secondary, pupils 2,028,476, teachers (1973–74) 40,351; vocational, pupils 436,469, teachers (1974–75) 15,692; teacher training, students 32,102, teachers 2,001; higher, students 312,871, teaching staff 18,391.

Finance. Monetary unit: Turkish lira, with (Sept. 22, 1980) a free rate of 79.47 liras to U.S. $1 (191 liras = £1 sterling). Gold, SDR's, and foreign exchange (June 1980) U.S. $975 million. Budget (1979–80 est.): revenue 395,871,000,000 liras; expenditure 406,876,000,000 liras. Gross national product (1979) 2,103,530,000,000 liras. Money supply (Sept. 1979) 389.2 billion liras. Cost of living (1975 = 100; June 1980) 753.

Foreign Trade. (1979) Imports 178,497,000,000 liras; exports 75,743,000,000 liras. Import sources: West Germany 12%; Iraq 11%; Italy 9%; U.S. 7%; France 6%; Japan 5%; Switzerland 5%; U.K. 5%. Export destinations: West Germany 22%; Italy 10%; France 6%; U.S.S.R. 6%; Iraq 5%; Switzerland 5%. Main exports (1978): fruit and vegetables 27%; cotton 15%; textile yarns and fabrics 11%; tobacco 10%; wheat 9%. Tourism (1978): visitors 1,644,000; gross receipts U.S. $230 million.

Transport and Communications. Roads (1979) 232,162 km (including 189 km expressways). Motor vehicles in use (1979): passenger 658,700; commercial 309,800. Railways (1978): 8,139 km; traffic 5,620,000,000 passenger-km, freight 6,649,000,000 net ton-km. Air traffic (1978): 1,904,000,000 passenger-km; freight 15.5 million net ton-km. Shipping (1979): merchant vessels 100 gross tons and over 475; gross tonnage 1,421,715. Telephones (Jan. 1978) 1,379,000. Radio licenses (Dec. 1978) 4,275,000. Television licenses (Dec. 1978) 2,644,000.

Agriculture. Production (in 000; metric tons; 1979): wheat 17,631; barley 5,217; corn 1,358; rye 620; oats 371; potatoes 2,903; tomatoes 3,136; onions *c.* 1,000; sugar, raw value *c.* 1,145; sunflower seed 590; cottonseed *c.* 810; chick-peas 226; dry beans 165; cabbages (1978) *c.* 650; pumpkins (1978) *c.* 320; watermelons (1978) *c.* 4,000; cucumbers (1978) *c.* 450; oranges 703; lemons 273; apples *c.* 1,150; grapes 3,485; raisins *c.* 350; olives 411; tea 102; tobacco 245; cotton, lint 505. Livestock (in 000; Dec. 1978): cattle 14,941; sheep 43,942; buffalo 1,023; goats 18,447; horses 812; asses 1,371; chickens *c.* 49,000.

Industry. Fuel and power (in 000; metric tons; 1979): crude oil 2,884; coal 4,460; lignite 9,350; electricity (kw-hr; 1978) 21,726,000. Production (in 000; metric tons; 1979): cement 13,786; iron ore (55–60% metal content; 1978) 3,568; pig iron (1978) 736; crude steel 1,788; petroleum products (1978) *c.* 11,900; sulfuric acid 161; fertilizers (nutrient content; 1978–79) nitrogenous *c.* 269, phosphate *c.* 220; bauxite (1978) 454; chrome ore (oxide content; 1978) 236; cotton yarn (1978) *c.* 110; man-made fibres (1977) 50.

Tuvalu

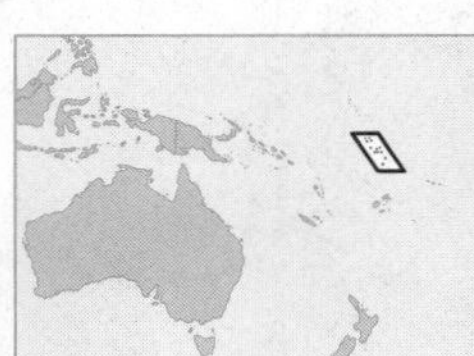
Tuvalu

A constitutional monarchy within the Commonwealth of Nations comprising nine main islands and their associated islets and reefs, Tuvalu is located in the western Pacific Ocean just south of the Equator and west of the International Date Line. Area: 26 sq km (9.5 sq mi). Pop. (1979): 7,400, mostly Polynesians. Cap.: Funafuti (pop., 1979, 2,200). Queen, Elizabeth II; governor-general in 1980, Penitala Fiatau Teo; prime minister, Toaripi Lauti.

In May the interisland passenger and freight service provided by Tuvalu's only, aging vessel was supplemented by a seaplane service linking six of Tuvalu's nine islands. Agreement was reached with Japanese interests for a tuna and bait survey in Tuvalu waters; a fishing agreement was signed with South Korea, and negotiations were under way with Taiwan (which Tuvalu recognized). The government announced that it would withdraw its controversial A$550,000 investment with U.S. real estate developer Sydney Gross and invest the funds in a new national bank to be established in partnership with Barclays Bank International Ltd. Even more controversial was another project associated with Gross—the sale to Tuvaluans of barren Texas land at inflated prices. The U.S.

TUVALU

Education. (1978) Primary, pupils 1,481, teachers (1977) 48; secondary, pupils 235, teachers (1977) 12.

Finance and Trade. Monetary unit: Australian dollar, with (Sept. 22, 1980) a free rate of A$0.86 to U.S. $1 (A$2.06 = £1 sterling). Budget (1979 est.) balanced at A$2 million (including U.K. aid of A$750,000). Foreign trade: imports (1978) A$1,572,800; exports (1979) A$237,400. Main export: copra 100%.

government made it clear that such purchases would not establish eligibility for immigration purposes and instituted an investigation.

Tuvalu protested to China over the testing in June of intercontinental ballistic missiles in the waters adjacent to the islands. In July Prime Minister Toaripi Lauti led a delegation to London to discuss future aid grants and while there was sworn in as a privy councillor. At the regional meeting of Commonwealth heads of government in New Delhi in September, he proposed the establishment of a Commonwealth pool of experts who could be sent to aid less developed countries on a short-term basis. (BARRIE MACDONALD)

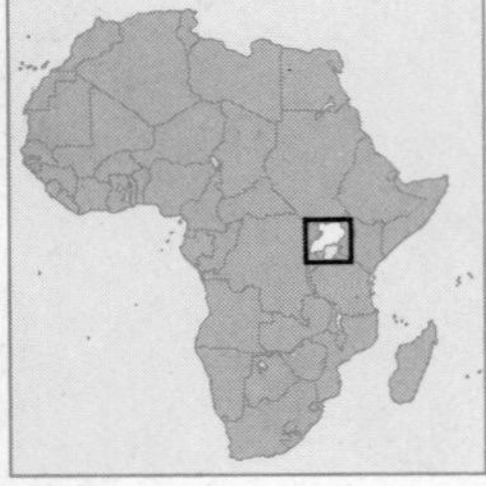

Uganda

Uganda

A republic and a member of the Commonwealth of Nations, Uganda is bounded by Sudan, Zaire, Rwanda, Tanzania, and Kenya. Area: 241,139 sq km (93,104 sq mi), including 44,081 sq km of inland water. Pop. (1980 prelim.): 12.6 million, virtually all of whom are African. Cap. and largest city: Kampala (pop., 1980 prelim., 458,000). Language: English (official), Bantu, Nilotic, Nilo-Hamitic, and Sudanic. Religion: Christian 63%, Muslim 6%, traditional beliefs. President to May 11, 1980, Godfrey L. Binaisa; chairman of the Military Commission from May 23 to December 17, Paulo Muwanga; president from December 17, Milton Obote.

In 1980 Uganda's border with the Sudan was reopened and relations between the two countries improved, but stable government remained elusive. Pres. Godfrey L. Binaisa tried unsuccessfully to encourage foreign investment to revive Uganda's export crops. In February he dismissed Paulo Muwanga, minister of the interior, for banning three newspapers reporting Uganda's lawlessness. Pres. Julius Nyerere of Tanzania threatened to withdraw his troops from Uganda if steps were not taken to restore order quickly. Kenya observed Nyerere's intervention with dismay and in March promised Uganda aid if Tanzanian troops were withdrawn. Later, clashes took place between Tanzanian troops near Kampala and some of the local population. The cost of maintaining the Tanzanian troops—£60 million in 1979–80—was also of concern to Uganda.

In April Binaisa induced the National Consultative Council to endorse his proposal that political parties should not be permitted to participate in the forthcoming elections but that candidates should stand instead as representatives of the Uganda National Liberation Front. On May 10 he dismissed Brig. David Oyite Ojok, army chief of staff and an associate of former president Milton Obote (*see* BIOGRAPHIES), charging that Uganda's new Army was looting and killing Uganda citizens. Ojok refused to accept dismissal and was supported by Muwanga, now minister of labour. Nyerere refused to intervene, and Muwanga then headed a six-man Military Commission that removed Binaisa from office on May 11. The commission appointed a new Cabinet, replacing several supporters of Binaisa with adherents of Obote and including Ojok. Otema Alimadi continued as foreign minister and announced that Uganda would remain nonaligned.

On May 27 Obote returned to Uganda and soon announced that he would lead the Uganda People's Congress in the forthcoming elections. In the north and east he was warmly welcomed, but many Buganda could not forgive him for overthrowing their traditional leader, the kabaka, in 1966; in western Uganda attitudes varied. Obote's opponents became increasingly hostile, and in June the Uganda Patriotic Movement was set up under Yoweri Museveni, vice-chairman of the Military Commission, to challenge him. Former president Yusufu Lule, expected to lead the Democratic Party, was prevented by the Military Commission from returning to Uganda because he refused to deny statements he had made at the time of his overthrow in 1979. In his place, Paul Semogerere

Former Ugandan president Milton Obote (centre) returned to his country in May after a nine-year exile in neighbouring Tanzania and was greeted by enthusiastic crowds. Obote was again installed as president in December after his party won a majority of seats in Parliament.

MOHAMED AMIN—CAMERAPIX/KEYSTONE

Unemployment:
see Economy, World; Social Security and Welfare Services

UGANDA

Education. (State aided; 1977) Primary, pupils 1,-139,413, teachers 32,554; secondary, pupils 59,882, teachers 2,126; vocational, pupils 3,819, teachers 270; teacher training, students 6,946, teachers 374; higher (1976), students 5,148, teaching staff 681.

Finance and Trade. Monetary unit: Uganda shilling, with (Sept. 22, 1980) a free rate of UShs 7.25 to U.S. $1 (UShs 17.42 = £1 sterling). Budget (1979–80 est.): revenue UShs 4,871,000,000; expenditure UShs 4,990,000,000. Foreign trade: imports (1978) UShs 1,963,000,000; exports (1979) UShs 3,182,000,000. Import sources (1977): Kenya 57%; U.K. 9%; West Germany 9%; Italy 6%. Export destinations (1977): U.S. 38%; U.K. 17%; The Netherlands 6%; France 5%. Main export: coffee 98%.

Transport and Communications. Roads (1979) 27,901 km. Motor vehicles in use (1979): passenger 26,000; commercial 5,400. Railways (1978) 1,286 km. Telephones (Jan. 1978) 48,900. Radio receivers (Dec. 1977) 250,000. Television receivers (Dec. 1977) 81,000.

Agriculture. Production (in 000; metric tons; 1979): millet *c.* 450; sorghum *c.* 400; corn *c.* 500; sweet potatoes (1978) *c.* 674; cassava (1978) *c.* 1,100; peanuts *c.* 227; dry beans *c.* 181; bananas *c.* 367; coffee *c.* 120; tea *c.* 2; cotton, lint *c.* 13; meat (1978) 148; fish catch (1978) *c.* 179; timber (cu m; 1978) *c.* 20,004. Livestock (in 000; 1978): cattle *c.* 5,320; sheep *c.* 1,068; goats *c.* 2,144; pigs *c.* 220; chickens *c.* 13,000.

Industry. Production (in 000; metric tons; 1977): cement 80; copper ore (metal content) 10.8; tungsten concentrates (oxide content) 0.14; electricity (kw-hr) 689,000.

was elected Democratic Party leader in June. Also in June Kenya called for Tanzanian troops to be withdrawn and replaced by Organization of African Unity, UN, or Commonwealth forces.

Meanwhile, famine in the northeastern district of Karamoja, due to drought and the depredations of armed bandits, brought suffering and death to thousands. For a time in July even external relief organizations had to stop work in the area because of attacks by armed gangs in search of food, while Kampala's crime rate became more serious because of the violence caused by rival political groups and by individuals.

The target date for national elections, September 30, could not be met and, later, Cabinet members opposed to the Uganda People's Congress refused to support a proposal by Muwanga regarding the number of seats in the new Parliament because it favoured areas where Obote's supporters were strong. Agreement was eventually reached, and Ugandans went to the polls on December 9–10 to vote in the first national election since 1962. Amid charges of fraud and intimidation, Obote's Uganda People's Congress won 68 of the 126 seats in Parliament to 48 for the Democratic Party. As a result Obote became the nation's president for a five-year term and was inaugurated on December 17. (KENNETH INGHAM)

Union of Soviet Socialist Republics

The Union of Soviet Socialist Republics is a federal state covering parts of eastern Europe and northern and central Asia. Area: 22,402,200 sq km (8,-649,500 sq mi). Pop. (1980 est.): 264.5 million, including (1979) Russians 52%; Ukrainians 16%; Uzbeks 5%; Belorussians 4%; Kazakhs 3%. Cap. and largest city: Moscow (pop., 1980 est., 8.1 million). Language: officially Russian, but many others are spoken. Religion: about 40 religions are represented in the U.S.S.R., the major ones being Christian denominations. General secretary of the Communist Party of the Soviet Union and chairman of the Presidium of the Supreme Soviet (president) in 1980, Leonid Ilich Brezhnev; chairmen of the Council of Ministers (premiers), Aleksey N. Kosygin and, from October 23, Nikolay A. Tikhonov.

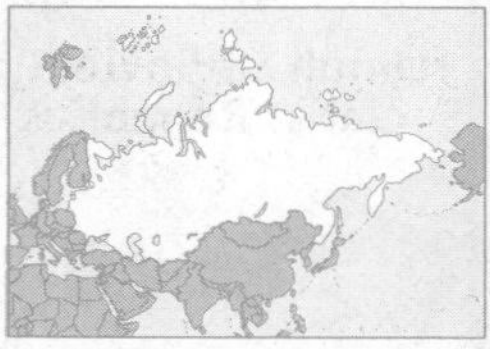

Union of Soviet Socialist Republics

Domestic Affairs. The Soviet leadership found 1980 a difficult year. The weather again was unkind and adversely affected the harvest. The summer in Moscow was extremely wet. And in addition to economic problems there were major foreign policy issues that proved very troublesome.

The major change at the top was the resignation of 76-year-old Aleksey N. Kosygin (*see* OBITUARIES) as premier in October. He was replaced by his deputy Nikolay A. Tikhonov (*see* BIOGRAPHIES), a man only one year younger than himself. Kosygin's ill health over the last four years, which ended in his death in December, had meant that Tikhonov had often headed the government. In effect he had been in charge since October 1979. The new premier worked closely with Pres. Leonid Brezhnev during the post-World War II reconstruction of the Ukrainian city of Dnepropetrovsk and had amassed great experience in the economic bureaucracy. He was made a full member of the

The Summer Olympic Games opened in Moscow on July 19 amid considerable controversy. The U.S. and numerous other nations boycotted the Games because of the Soviet invasion of Afghanistan.

SIMON—GAMMA/LIAISON

Politburo as recently as November 1979. His appointment meant that the post of premier had been downgraded. It appeared now to be a post for an economic functionary. All the members of the Politburo except one were senior to Tikhonov. Kosygin lost his seat on the Politburo, and there were veiled criticisms of his handling of the economy. Of five previous premiers who had been removed, only N. S. Khrushchev had lost his Politburo post at the same time.

The newest recruit to the Politburo was Mikhail Gorbachov, who became a full member in October 1980, at the age of 49. Central Committee secretary for agriculture since November 1978, Gorbachov was a successful party leader in the north Caucasus, a fertile agricultural region. He was faced with an even more daunting task than Tikhonov. His predecessor had lost his Politburo seat after harvest failures. Gorbachov could expect forbearance for one bad harvest but not two. Pyotr Masherov, first party secretary in Belorussia and a candidate for membership in the Politburo, was killed in an automobile accident on October 4. He was replaced by Tikhon Kiselev, who also became a candidate member of the Politburo.

The Summer Olympic Games were the year's major domestic event and were well organized. The Soviet Union carried off the largest number of gold medals. The Games were overshadowed, however, by the U.S.-led boycott, which resulted in the withdrawal from competition of many leading nations—the U.S., West Germany, and Japan, for example. (*See* TRACK AND FIELD SPORTS: *Special Report*.) The U.S. action was in response to Soviet intervention in Afghanistan. U.S. Pres. Jimmy Carter also prevented the export of 17 million metric tons of grain to the U.S.S.R. and halted sales of high-technology products such as computers and oil-drilling equipment. The embargo on the latter, however, was quietly dropped during the summer. The eight million tons provided for under the terms of the U.S.-Soviet grain agreement were delivered, but this agreement was to expire in 1981. The Soviets were able to purchase most of the shortfall in other markets but in so doing forced up the price. One U.S. source estimated that President Carter's embargo cost the U.S.S.R. an extra U.S. $1 billion. In July the U.S.S.R. signed an agreement with Argentina to purchase 4.5 million tons of forage cereals annually over the next five years.

Since the Soviet Union was unable to import all the extra fodder it needed, meat production suffered as did the output of butter, milk, and cheese. This led to considerable problems for the urban population. Meat was often unavailable in Moscow, Leningrad, and Kiev, usually the three best-provisioned cities in the nation. Many labour strikes were reported during the year, the most significant being in Gorky and Togliatti, both with large automobile plants. The Soviet authorities vehemently denied that the closing of the plants on May 8 and 9 amounted to a strike. They claimed that workers were merely celebrating Victory Day. This, however, would account for the stoppage on May 9 but not on May 8.

The stoppages were apparently caused by transport workers blocking the main highways and refusing to take workers to the plants. They were protesting against poor food supplies. Erratic distribution of available food was at the root of the problem. The railway system was unable to cope with the situation because of an acute shortage of refrigeration cars. Brezhnev had sharply criticized the shortcomings of the transport network but to little effect.

The widespread shortages of food, the poor quality of some consumer goods, and the unavailability of others led to an expansion of the black market. The government turned a blind eye to some of its activities because it was satisfying consumer needs but dealt severely with some black marketeers. For example, Yuza Kobakhidze, a Georgian, was shot for corruption. Between 1976 and 1979 he had accepted bribes amounting to 88,000 rubles from 13 citizens in return for providing them with apartments. The Georgian journal *Kommunisti* stated that this had been the "first time in 30 years" that a death sentence had been passed for bribery. Two Georgian "bandits" were executed in September. They had led a life of crime and had

U.S.S.R.

Education. (1979–80) Primary, pupils 34.2 million; secondary, pupils 10.2 million; primary and secondary, teachers 2,625,000; vocational and teacher training (1978–79), students 4,672,000, teachers 230,000; higher, students 5,185,100, teaching staff (1978–79) 345,000.

Finance. Monetary unit: ruble, with (Sept. 22, 1980) a free rate of 0.64 ruble to U.S. $1 (1.55 rubles = £1 sterling). Budget (1980 est.): revenue 284.8 billion rubles; expenditure 284.5 billion rubles.

Foreign Trade. (1980) Imports 37,883,000,000 rubles; exports 42,427,000,000 rubles. Import sources: Eastern Europe 46% (East Germany 10%, Poland 10%, Czechoslovakia 8%, Bulgaria 8%, Hungary 6%); U.S. 7%; West Germany 6%; Cuba 6%. Export destinations: Eastern Europe 44% (East Germany 10%, Poland 9%, Czechoslovakia 8%, Bulgaria 8%, Hungary 6%); West Germany 5%; Cuba 5%. Main exports: crude oil and products 34%; machinery 12%; transport equipment 6%; natural gas 5%; iron and steel 5%.

Transport and Communications. Roads (1978) 1,423,500 km. Motor vehicles in use (1977): passenger *c.* 6,640,000; commercial (including buses) *c.* 6,330,000. Railways (1978): 228,100 km (including 87,700 km industrial); traffic 332,100,000,000 passenger-km, freight (1979) 3,354,000,000,000 net ton-km. Air traffic (1978): 139,787,000,000 passenger-km; freight *c.* 2,840,000,000 net ton-km. Navigable inland waterways (1978) 142,600 km; freight traffic 243,700,000,000 ton-km. Shipping (1979): merchant vessels 100 gross tons and over 8,120; gross tonnage 22,900,201. Telephones (Jan. 1978) 19.6 million. Radio receivers (Dec. 1975) 122.5 million. Television receivers (Dec. 1979) *c.* 60 million.

Agriculture. Production (in 000; metric tons; 1979): wheat 90,100; barley *c.* 46,000; oats *c.* 14,000; rye *c.* 8,100; corn *c.* 8,400; rice *c.* 2,400; millet *c.* 1,800; potatoes 90,300; sugar, raw value *c.* 8,100; tomatoes *c.* 6,400; watermelons *c.* 3,400; apples *c.* 7,500; sunflower seed 5,370; cottonseed *c.* 5,954; linseed *c.* 300; soybeans *c.* 600; dry peas *c.* 5,400; wine 2,920; tea *c.* 105; tobacco *c.* 310; cotton, lint 2,821; flax fibres (1978) *c.* 390; wool 283; hen's eggs *c.* 3,618; milk *c.* 92,800; butter *c.* 1,409; cheese *c.* 1,495; meat *c.* 15,500; fish catch (1978) 8,930; timber (cu m; 1978) *c.* 361,400. Livestock (in 000; Jan. 1979): cattle 114,086; pigs 73,484; sheep 142,600; goats 5,504; horses (1978) *c.* 5,822; chickens *c.* 915,200.

Industry. Index of production (1975 = 100; 1979) 120. Fuel and power (in 000; metric tons; 1979): coal and lignite 719,000; crude oil 586,000; natural gas (cu m) 407,000,000; manufactured gas (cu m; 1977) 37,310,000; electricity (kw-hr) 1,239,000,000. Production (in 000; metric tons; 1979): cement 123,018; iron ore (metal content; 1977) 131,418; pig iron *c.* 123,000; steel 149,000; aluminum (1978) *c.* 2,300; copper (1978) *c.* 1,480; lead (1978) *c.* 640; zinc (1978) *c.* 1,055; magnesite (1978) *c.* 1,900; manganese ore (metal content; 1977) 2,904; tungsten concentrates (oxide content; 1978) *c.* 10; gold (troy oz) *c.* 10,000; silver (troy oz) *c.* 50,000; sulfuric acid 22,400; caustic soda (1978) 2,763; plastics and resins 3,500; fertilizers (nutrient content; 1978) nitrogenous 9,220, phosphate 5,811, potash 8,193; newsprint (1978) 1,432; other paper and board *c.* 7,300; man-made fibres 1,131; cotton fabrics (sq m) 6,970,000; woolen fabrics (sq m) 800,000; rayon and acetate fabrics (sq m) 1,700,000; passenger cars (units) 1,314; commercial vehicles (units) 859. New dwelling units completed (1978) 2,125,000.

killed one man and injured a policeman, among other things. Many officials throughout the country were found guilty of accepting bribes. A huge caviar fraud came to light in April. According to reports, about 200 officials of the Ministry of Fisheries had been arrested during the year and accused of being involved in the fraudulent export of caviar in tins marked as herring. The hunt for World War II criminals continued, and three Ukrainians were shot. Two of them were discovered in remote parts of Siberia.

Not since 1977 had Soviet dissidents been treated so harshly. In order to ensure that no demonstrations took place during the Olympic Games, a campaign was launched, beginning in 1979, to clear dissidents, beggars, and ne'er-do-wells from the streets of Moscow and other cities accommodating the Games. Many living farther away were also arrested because it had been their custom to travel to Moscow to publicize their grievances and to contact the world press. The Committee of State Security (KGB) was successful in intimidating the vast majority of dissidents and their sympathizers. Only the hard core were arrested since the political police only resorted to arrest if all other methods failed. By late summer 252 arrests had been documented. These actions, carried out despite international protests, revealed that the Kremlin had given up all hope of SALT II being ratified by the U.S. Senate. Since Soviet-U.S. relations were at a low ebb, the Politburo obviously believed that there was little more to lose.

The KGB came up with a neat solution to the problem of what to do with the dissident physicist and 1975 Nobel Peace Prize winner, Andrey Sakharov. They exiled him to Gorky and provided him with an apartment without a telephone. His wife was free to remain in Moscow. Sakharov was stripped of his Soviet decorations but remained a member of the U.S.S.R. Academy of Sciences. There was no legal foundation for the measures adopted.

About two-fifths of dissidents arrested were Christians, with Baptists figuring prominently. Orthodox Christians (a prominent figure, Father Gleb Yakunin, was sentenced by a Moscow court in August to five years at hard labour and five years of internal exile), Seventh-day Adventists (Vladimir Shelkov, 84-year-old leader sentenced in 1979 to five years at hard labour, died in a camp in January 1980, having spent 25 years of his life in prisons and camps), and Pentecostals accounted for most of the others. Representatives of national minorities who were taken into custody included Ukrainians, Lithuanians, Jews, Crimean Tatars, Estonians, Germans, and Armenians. Among the organizations that were particularly hard hit were the Helsinki Final Act monitoring groups in the Ukraine and Moscow, the Moscow Commission to Combat Political Psychiatry, the human rights journal *Chronicle of Current Events*, the Christian Committee for the Defense of the Rights of Believers, and the free interprofessional associations of workers (SMOT). Those that were weakened but too strong to be eliminated were the Lithuanian movement, which combined national and religious opposition; the Crimean Tatars; the Jewish and German emigration movements; and the main Protestant denominations. The unregistered Baptists (those who opposed making concessions to the state) especially remained active.

WIDE WORLD

Newly appointed Soviet Premier Nikolay A. Tikhonov expressed a readiness to negotiate with the West on arms control during ceremonies on November 6 marking the 63rd anniversary of the Bolshevik Revolution.

Examples of other prison sentences were: Vasil Stus, ten years of a special regime in a labour camp and five years of internal exile (Stus, a member of the Kiev Helsinki monitoring group, had already been convicted of anti-Soviet slander in 1972); Tatyana Velikanova, an editor of the *Chronicle of Current Events*, four years in a strict regime at a labour camp and five years of internal exile; Vyacheslav Chornovil, five years in a forced labour camp, having just completed a nine-year sentence of imprisonment and exile for his role in unauthorized Ukrainian publications. About 150 physicists at the European Organization for Nuclear Research (CERN) in Switzerland decided to abandon professional contacts with their Soviet counterparts in protest against the continued imprisonment of dissident physicist Yury Orlov.

The KGB also had some successes to report. Yury Stepanov, a ballet dancer who defected in January, returned to Moscow in April from the U.S.; Vyacheslav Bakhmin, who had been active in the campaign to combat political psychiatry, recanted and was set free in September, as was Viktor Kapitanchuk, a religious activist. Among well-known critics of the regime who were expelled or who left the Soviet Union during the year were Vladimir Borisov, a founder of SMOT, who had spent nine years in psychiatric hospitals; Lev Kopelev, a novelist; Vasily Aksyonov, a writer; and the satirical writer Vladimir Vornovich.

The number of Jews granted exit visas reached a peak in 1979 when about 50,000 left, but numbers began to drop thereafter. A much more restrictive policy was adopted in the wake of the U.S.-led boycott of the Olympics. If Jews found it increasingly difficult to leave the U.S.S.R., Germans and Armenians did not. The number of Armenians leaving was unprecedented, exceeding 1,000 a month by midyear. The Armenians were mostly those who were drawn to the Soviet Union after World War II when Stalin conducted a vigorous campaign to attract them to Soviet Armenia.

The Economy. The far-reaching changes in the management of the national economy announced in July 1979 appeared to have had little impact. The industrial growth target of 4.5% in 1980 was unlikely to be met because during the first nine months of the year industrial output grew only by 4%. National income was only 3.8% above that of 1979. In the important energy sector oil production rose 3%, and the target of 606 million metric tons might be achieved. Coal output declined 0.7% from the previous year. The real income of the population rose 3%. The harvest was again disappointing, only about 181 million tons, far short of the target of 235 million tons. The Soviet leadership could console itself with the knowledge that two successive bad harvests were rare. Due to the shortage of fodder, meat production declined 5% from 1979. The output of animal and vegetable fats, sausages, and tinned fruit was also below that of the previous year. Citizens were being encouraged to produce more on their private plots.

The 1976–80 plan would not be fulfilled. Growth of industrial output for the period would be about 25%, far short of the target of 36%. Average annual agricultural output over the last five years had only exceeded the 1971–75 period by 9%. Given the huge investment in agriculture (one ruble in three went into agriculture or agriculture-related industries), this was very disappointing. Since the Soviet population had risen by about 4%, the people's diet had not improved significantly.

The Soviet Union's hard currency debt dropped $1 billion to $16.2 billion in 1979. It was likely that the U.S.S.R. would again show a surplus on its hard currency trade in 1980. Soviet sales of gold plummeted during the year, and only 25 tons instead of the usual 1,400 tons had been sold by November. This revealed that earnings from oil, natural gas, and mineral exports had remained buoyant.

The Soviet Union warned its partners in the Council for Mutual Economic Assistance (CMEA, or Comecon) that it was rapidly approaching the limit of its capacity to meet their energy needs. Whereas in 1970 other Comecon countries obtained 70% of their energy needs from the Soviet Union, this figure was expected to drop to 50% in 1990. Over the period 1976–80 Comecon countries imported Soviet oil at about 40% below the world price, and this was estimated to have cost the U.S.S.R. 5 billion rubles.

Foreign Affairs. Relations with the outside world deteriorated throughout 1980. The Soviet Union came to the conclusion that nothing positive could be expected from relations with the U.S. as long as President Carter remained in office. Carter was particularly incensed by Soviet intervention in Afghanistan after the U.S. had reportedly warned Moscow five times that such a move would seriously affect détente. The zigzags in the president's foreign policy left the Soviets bewildered. They completely miscalculated U.S. and world reaction to their Afghanistan move. A UN motion in January calling for the withdrawal of foreign troops from Afghanistan was passed by 104 votes to 18, an unprecedentedly heavy defeat for Soviet diplomacy. Once in Afghanistan, the U.S.S.R. discovered that the task of subduing the Muslim rebels was much more difficult than it had imagined. The decision to intervene apparently took Ministry of Defense personnel by surprise. Pres. Babrak Karmal (*see* BIOGRAPHIES) of Afghanistan visited Moscow in October and received assurances of continuing Soviet aid.

As hopes for the ratification of SALT II faded, incomprehension about U.S. motives reigned in Moscow. The Soviets hoped that a dialogue could be started with Ronald Reagan when he entered the White House. SALT II would probably have to be renegotiated, but the U.S.S.R. was eager to reach an agreement. Andrey Gromyko, the key figure in Soviet foreign relations, knew that if relations with the U.S. were bad so were those with its allies. The revolution in Iran had not benefited the Soviet Union as much as it had expected. Moscow had expected to move closer to Iran in the wake of the anti-U.S. mood in Teheran and to benefit from the abortive U.S. move to free the hostages. But one Soviet offer of arms was publicly rejected by Teheran. The Iraqi attack on Iran further complicated the situation. Iraq had a treaty of friendship with the U.S.S.R. and continued to receive Soviet arms through the port of Aqaba. The war drew Jordan closer to Iraq, and if that continued Jordan might establish closer relations with Moscow. Syria found itself isolated and hastened to support Iran, the only other Muslim country to do so being Libya. This finally led Syria to accede in October to the Soviet wish for a treaty of friendship. Thus the Soviet position in the Middle East improved.

France's Pres. Valéry Giscard d'Estaing became the first Western head of state to meet President Brezhnev after the Soviet intervention in Afghanistan. Giscard decided to meet the Soviet leader in Warsaw in May, but Brezhnev gave nothing away, and any diplomatic gain from the meeting accrued to the Soviet side. The U.S.S.R. had further cause for gratification when the French Commu-

Human rights leader and physicist Andrey Sakharov (left) and his wife, Yelena, were prominent spectators at a trial of dissidents in the Soviet Union prior to Sakharov's arrest and exile to Gorky in January.

ZAL—SYGMA

nist Party (PCF) sided with it over Afghanistan. PCF leader Georges Marchais traveled to Moscow to heal the breach that had occurred as a result of the PCF's support for Eurocommunism. The latter phenomenon was still alive but restricted to the Italian and Spanish Communist parties. Both criticized the Soviet move into Afghanistan as did Romania, which called for withdrawal. West German Chancellor Helmut Schmidt visited Moscow on June 30–July 1 and forcibly argued Western views on Afghanistan and the need for NATO to modernize its nuclear weapons. The discussions became heated, and Brezhnev was critical of Schmidt's support for U.S. policy. After he left, Radio Moscow criticized Schmidt's "hard line attitude."

The Soviets found the year's events in Poland deeply embarrassing since the leadership was sensitive about any manifestation of worker discontent. Independent labour unions were anathema to the Communist Party of the Soviet Union. A propaganda campaign was launched, blaming the trouble in Poland on the West and accusing Western governments and labour unions of interfering in Polish internal affairs. Elements in West Germany were accused of launching a "massive anti-Polish campaign" using Nazi methods and propaganda to stir up unrest. The Soviet media on occasion accused the West of pouring "millions of dollars" into Poland to support anti-Communist groups. They served notice that the U.S.S.R. would not countenance the Polish independent union Solidarity receiving money from abroad and also did not favour Poland borrowing money from the West. Given the dire straits of the Polish economy, it was difficult to see how the country could overcome its crisis without Western aid. The Soviet Union provided some credit but was in no position to cover all needs. The new Polish Communist Party leader, Stanislaw Kania (*see* BIOGRAPHIES), won support in Moscow for his policy of trying to whittle away piecemeal the concessions forced on the party. Not all Eastern European regimes followed the U.S.S.R. in its hostility to the developments in Poland. Bulgaria, for example, contented itself with merely reprinting a few articles from the Soviet press.

Relations with China deteriorated. The border talks that began in October 1979 foundered on the rocks of Afghanistan. China then launched a campaign calling for the withdrawal of Soviet troops. In October it blamed the U.S.S.R. for an incident during which a Chinese peasant and a Soviet soldier were killed, the first official report of shooting on the Sino-Soviet border since 1969.

Soviet-Japanese relations reached a new low in November when the Soviet chairman of the U.S.S.R.-Japan Friendship Society accused the Japanese of limiting contacts between the two countries, of impeding the expansion of economic relations, and of raising a hullabaloo about a "supposed Soviet military threat." All the blame for the current frigid state of relations was placed on Japan's shoulders. The Soviet Union had become alarmed at recent developments, especially the Sino-Japanese treaty of friendship. Ongoing disputes over fishing boundaries, the Japanese boycott of the Olympics, Japan's refusal to allow a crippled Soviet submarine to be towed through its territorial waters, and the possible amendment of the Japanese constitution to permit the expansion of the armed forces all left a bitter taste in Moscow. The Soviet media regularly attacked Japan, seeing a revival of militarism and a desire to expand Japanese influence throughout the world. The U.S.S.R. now believed that Japan, China, and the U.S. had united against it in the Far East, and this was seen as an alarming development.

The second Helsinki Final Act (of the Conference on Security and Cooperation in Europe) review conference opened in Madrid in November with the Soviet Union on the defensive. Led by Leonid Ilichev, who had previously spent years negotiating with the Chinese without giving or gaining an inch, the Soviet delegation attempted to reduce significantly the amount of time devoted to examining the human rights record of the member countries but was not wholly successful. Evidently the U.S.S.R. regarded the conference as an embarrassment but had decided to attend so as not to bring détente officially to an end. Western powers attacked intervention in Afghanistan and the Soviet Union's human rights record and argued that détente, to be successful, had to cover all aspects of the Helsinki Final Act.

(MARTIN MCCAULEY)

United Arab Emirates

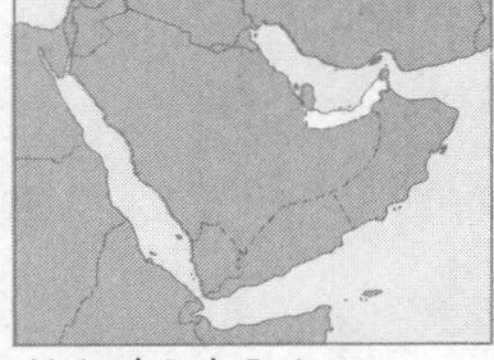
United Arab Emirates

Consisting of Abu Dhabi, Ajman, Dubai, Fujairah, Ras al-Khaimah, Sharjah, and Umm al-Qaiwain, the United Arab Emirates is located on the eastern Arabian Peninsula. Area: 83,600 sq km (32,300 sq mi). Pop. (1980 est.): 891,000, including Arab 42%, South Asian 50% (predominantly Iranian, Indian, and Pakistani), others 8% (mostly Europeans and East Asians). Cap.: Abu Dhabi town (pop., 1975, 95,000). Language: Arabic. Religion: Muslim. President in 1980, Sheikh Zaid ibn Sultan an-Nahayan; prime minister, Sheikh Rashid ibn Said al-Maktum.

Political unity in the Arab world's only working federation came under pressure in 1980, but progress was made. The most powerful emirate gov-

UNITED ARAB EMIRATES

Education. (1977–78) Primary, pupils 67,058, teachers (state only) 4,179; secondary, pupils 18,610, teachers (1976–77) 1,748; vocational, pupils 261, teachers 103; teacher training, students 34, teachers (1975–76) 8.

Finance. Monetary unit: dirham, with (Sept. 22, 1980) a free rate of 3.67 dirhams to U.S. $1 (8.82 dirhams = £1 sterling). Gold, SDR's, and foreign exchange (June 1980) U.S. $1,547,000,000. Budget (total public sector; 1979 actual): revenue 34,063,000,000 dirhams; expenditure 26,939,000,000 dirhams.

Foreign Trade. (1979) Imports 26,527,000,000 dirhams; exports 51,733,000,000 dirhams. Import sources (1978): Japan 18%; U.K. 18%; U.S. 12%; West Germany 10%; The Netherlands 5%; France 5%. Export destinations (1978): Japan 25%; France 13%; U.S. 12%; Netherlands Antilles 10%; The Netherlands 7%; Spain 5%; U.K. 5%. Main export: crude oil 94%.

Industry. Production (in 000; metric tons): crude oil (1979) 89,830; petroleum products (1977) 494; natural gas (cu m; 1977) 1,502,000; electricity (Abu Dhabi only; kw-hr; 1977) *c.* 700,000.

Unions:
see Industrial Relations

Unitarian (Universalist) Churches:
see Religion

ernments, those of Abu Dhabi and Dubai, agreed to establish a central bank into which a proportion of oil revenues would be paid. The bank's governor, appointed in mid-1980, was Sheikh Surour ibn Muhammad, a member of the Abu Dhabi ruling family. Other expressions of greater unity were the amalgamation of government departments in Ras al-Khaimah, the last emirate to join the union (1972), into the federal government and the decision by Abu Dhabi to guarantee a borrowing by Sharjah from international banks. Abu Dhabi, the federation's largest producer of crude oil, threatened cuts in production from the 1980 level of 1.3 million bbl a day because of oversupply in world markets. Social unrest among students was expressed in demonstrations over gasoline prices in February, and there was unease concerning the high proportion of Asian immigrants in the population. (JOHN WHELAN)

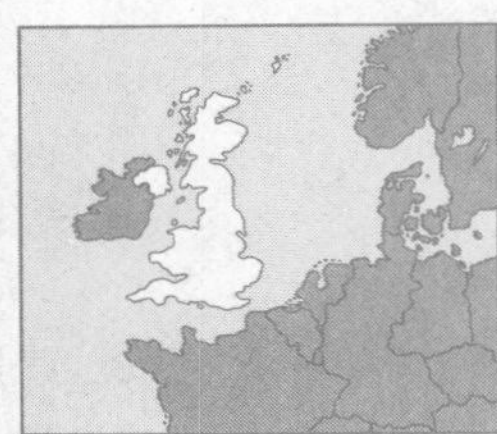

United Kingdom

United Kingdom

A constitutional monarchy in northwestern Europe and member of the Commonwealth of Nations, the United Kingdom comprises the island of Great Britain (England, Scotland, and Wales) and Northern Ireland, together with many small islands. Area: 244,035 sq km (94,222 sq mi), including 3,084 sq km of inland water but excluding the crown dependencies of the Channel Islands and Isle of Man. Pop. (1980 est.): 55,902,000. Cap. and largest city: London (Greater London pop., 1979 est., 6,877,100). Language: English; some Welsh and Gaelic also are used. Religion: mainly Protestant, with Catholic, Muslim, and Jewish minorities, in that order. Queen, Elizabeth II; prime minister in 1980, Margaret Thatcher.

In 1980 the British economy became engulfed in its deepest recession since the 1930s, and in August unemployment topped the two million mark. It continued to rise thereafter. Combating inflation, however, remained the first priority of the Conservative Party government of Prime Minister Margaret Thatcher (*see* BIOGRAPHIES), and control of the money supply continued to be the chief instrument of her economic policy.

Steelworkers from Consett, Durham, marched through London toward the House of Commons in July to protest the closure of one of Britain's steel mills.

KEYSTONE

Foreign Affairs. World events, nevertheless, impinged upon British politics, in the shadow of the Soviet invasion of Afghanistan and against the background of the drama in Iran, where more than 50 U.S. diplomats had been held hostage since Nov. 4, 1979. These twin crises complicated the government's endeavours to strike a balance between Britain's traditional friendship with the U.S. and its membership in the politically conscious European Economic Community (EEC). The Soviet invasion's Christmas and New Year holiday timing made it difficult for the Atlantic allies to coordinate their response to it. Mrs. Thatcher ordered "100% support" for U.S. Pres. Jimmy Carter when he called for economic sanctions against the Soviet Union and a boycott of the Olympic Games in Moscow. In Bonn and Paris the governments of Chancellor Helmut Schmidt and Pres. Valéry Giscard d'Estaing were unwilling to jeopardize détente between Eastern and Western Europe; they were reluctant to engage in sanctions, and France was opposed to an Olympic boycott.

Lord Carrington, the British foreign secretary, subsequently regretted that his first reaction to the crisis had been to embark upon a tour of South and Southwest Asia (he visited Turkey, Saudi Arabia, Oman, Pakistan, and India) rather than to consult his European partners. By contrast, the first move made by Schmidt and Giscard was to get together in Paris. The result, made worse by some U.S. clumsiness, was a spectacle of allied disarray that left Britain—already estranged from its European partners by the continuing quarrel about its contributions to the EEC budget—open to the traditional accusation of being a U.S. stooge. Carrington, at the meeting of the EEC foreign ministers in Rome on Feb. 19, 1980, put forward proposals (which were adopted) for the neutralization of Afghanistan matched by a withdrawal of Soviet forces. This plan established a more united approach to the crisis by the EEC.

The allies could not agree about boycotting the Olympic Games. On January 22 Thatcher had offered British sites for certain events of an alternative games, but in the end many British athletes ignored the call to boycott and competed in Moscow—although without government support. In Britain, in retaliation against the Soviet Union, a visit by the Soviet foreign minister, Andrey Gromyko, was postponed and a tour by the Red Army Chorus canceled; a five-year credit arrangement was allowed to lapse upon expiration. Britain also participated in such actions as the EEC was prepared to take collectively, although none of these (such as a grain embargo and a ban on high-technology exports) proved effective.

Great Britain and West Germany were the strongest advocates of EEC compliance with President Carter's demand for allied sanctions against

Iran. After considerable debate a limited version of the U.S.-proposed sanctions was agreed upon by the EEC on April 22. However, this proposal met with such disapproval in the British Parliament that the government decided to soften its sanctions against Iran even further.

EEC solidarity was made difficult by the festering problem of the British contribution to the EEC budget, an anomaly that in the financial year 1979–80 had resulted in Britain, as the the third poorest member of the EEC, becoming the largest net contributor to its funds. That net contribution amounted to £1,100 million and at a rancorous meeting of the European Council in Dublin on Nov. 29–30, 1979, Thatcher had demanded Britain's money back. When the European Council eventually met again in Luxembourg on April 27–28, 1980, Thatcher was offered a rebate worth about £800 million, as compared with the £350 million proposed at Dublin. Still she turned it down, partly because the arrangements did not guarantee a sufficient longer-term reduction. The matter was settled by the EEC foreign ministers at a marathon meeting in Brussels on May 29–30. A combined repayment of some £1,570 million was agreed upon for 1980 and 1981 with a firm commitment of a similar arrangement for 1982. Thatcher called it a day, and a victory.

British policy within the EEC then concentrated on the long-term reform of the common agricultural policy (from which Britain benefited little) and the structural reform of the organization's budget, which would become unavoidable when it ran out of funds sometime in 1981. Relations in Europe quickly improved although the "war" with France over British exports of lamb was not ended until September 30, and British tourists made headlines in August when they demonstrated their chauvinistic feelings toward the French after being inconvenienced by an industrial dispute affecting the Channel ports. At the highest level, however, Anglo-French relations took a turn for the better when Thatcher met Giscard in Paris on September 19. During a similar visit to West Germany in November, both she and Lord Carrington made plainer than ever before Britain's commitment to the European Community.

When the year began in Zimbabwe Rhodesia, a British Cabinet minister, Lord Soames, was already installed as governor to preside over the implementation of the so-called Lancaster House agreement of Dec. 5, 1979, to secure that country's transition to legal independence. After considerable intimidation on all sides, the agreed-upon elections took place on March 4, 1980, and resulted in the choice of a Marxist freedom fighter, Robert Mugabe (*see* BIOGRAPHIES), to head the first government of an independent Zimbabwe. The result was accepted in Britain with scarcely a murmur, and Prince Charles attended the independence ceremonies in Salisbury on April 18.

Domestic Affairs. The year 1980 began with a major industrial dispute. The strike in the nationalized steel industry was the first in that sector of the economy since the general strike in 1926. The 13-week strike (January 2–April 1) was made more difficult to resolve by interunion rivalries and a lack of confidence in the management of the British Steel Corporation (BSC). The dispute was ostensibly about pay, with the virtually bankrupt BSC's 6% annual wage increase offer adding insult to the injury of proposed closings that would do away with 52,000 jobs by August 1. The two issues, pay and jobs, became intertwined. The government, at the insistence of the secretary of state for industry, Sir Keith Joseph, refused to be drawn directly into the dispute and insisted that the BSC must live within its cash limit of £450 million; in the end the BSC reported losses for the financial year ended in March totaling £1,800 million. In September the government bailed it out temporarily with an additional aid package, bringing the total amount of aid for the financial year ending March 31, 1981, to about £970 million, and in November a major financial reconstruction was promised. Meanwhile, the strike had been settled with an annual wage increase of 15.5%, and the closings went ahead with production ceasing in Corby and Shotton steel towns. Ian MacGregor (*see* BIOGRAPHIES) was appointed to succeed Sir Charles Villiers as BSC chairman. On December 10 MacGregor announced plans for further closings with the loss of an additional 20,000 or more jobs.

The steel dispute illustrated the difficulties faced by the government in controlling the money supply and in pursuing its market-oriented policies under conditions of deepening recession. It also posed a question as to the limits to social tolerance of rapid structural adaptation in a deteriorating economic atmosphere. Sir Geoffrey Howe, chancellor of the Exchequer, used his budget on March 26 to reaffirm determination to bring down inflation by control of government borrowing and of the growth in the money supply. Extra taxes were imposed on alcohol, tobacco, and gasoline, but for the City of London and the financial commentators the budget's chief importance lay in the announcement of a medium-term financial strategy. This, for the first time, stated the government's monetary targets over a period of four years. In spite of continuing recession and inflation, the path set was a downward one; it would intensify the squeeze on the economy and seemed certain to lead to more unemployment and bankruptcies.

The government could not achieve its targets for the financial year 1980–81. The near explosion of the money supply during the summer was due in part to technical banking reasons, but more fundamental were the cost of public-sector wage settlements and the expensive consequences of the recession itself. By August unemployment figures had exceeded two million and were moving upward. In order to restore the public expenditure limits for 1981–82, the Treasury needed a further £2,000 million of net economies. The Cabinet was unable to agree on departmental cuts on such a scale, which meant that a substantial increase in taxation was required. Howe made a start in November by announcing an increase in the national insurance contribution, the government's first departure from its promises to reduce taxes.

Was this the proverbial U-turn? Did this mark the abandonment or at least the modification of the government's monetarist policies and the first

United Church of Canada: *see* Religion

United Church of Christ: *see* Religion

stage of a return to a more interventionist form of economic management? The government vehemently denied that this was so. Combating inflation remained the first priority, and at least that was coming down faster than the official forecasts had expected. Announcing measures on November 24, the chancellor reduced the minimum lending rate from 16% (to 14%) in the hope that this would help to relieve the burden of a high exchange rate on Britain's exporting industries. The exchange rate and high interest rates had been the chief causes of complaint from industry.

Further rises in unemployment reported at the time of the chancellor's November package caused a parliamentary furor. Nevertheless, there were no signs yet of abandonment by the government of its stringent monetarism or of adoption of measures to arrest or reverse recession.

The recession affected the atmosphere of industrial relations. After the round of wage increases that ended in August, earnings were ahead of inflation. In the private sector they were up by 20.6%, and in the public sector by 25.6%. The average overall increase was 22%, which compared with a 16.3% increase in prices over the same period. But from early in the year there were signs of a new moderation entering into collective bargaining. The number of working days lost through strikes was at its lowest in 14 years.

In British Leyland, fighting for its existence, workers in February rejected a management offer of a 5–10% pay increase. Management nevertheless imposed the increase in March, causing some 18,400 workers to strike for more than a week in April. Later in the year a 6.8% pay increase was at first rejected, but after a threatened strike was averted the work force accepted the increase. In the private sector there were signs of a willingness to settle for less than 10%, and the 1980–81 wages round started promisingly with two million engineering workers settling at 8.2%; the coal miners, always a key bargaining group, voted for acceptance of a 13% settlement recommended by their leaders.

As part of its attempt to bring public spending back under control, the government set a cash limit of 6% on wage increases in the public sector. The unions were in no mood for a showdown. The attempt by the Trades Union Congress (TUC) to organize a day of protest on May 14 was a failure, and members of the TUC General Council smarted increasingly at their exclusion from the inner counsels of Thatcher's government.

For the Labour Party the year was one of turmoil. The left-controlled National Executive Committee (NEC), in which Tony Benn (*see* BIOGRAPHIES) played a prominent role, kept up a running ideological and organizational battle with the party leadership under James Callaghan. A commission of inquiry into party organization, which had been specially charged with considering reforms in the method of electing the party leader, drawing up the election manifesto, and the procedure for reselecting parliamentary candidates, became the focus of a three-way power struggle. The parliamentary Labour Party insisted on preserving its independence; the trade unions, which provided 80% of the party's funds, were ready to exercise a more direct political influence; and the constituency Labour parties, predominantly leftist, wanted the conference to elect the leader and, through the NEC, to be responsible for the manifesto. At the commission of inquiry meeting held in June, Callaghan and Michael Foot (*see* BIOGRAPHIES), then deputy leader of the party and a leading left-winger, agreed to a compromise that would vest the election of the leader and the drawing up of the manifesto in an electoral college. At the Labour Party conference in Blackpool on September 29–October 3, the conference voted by a narrow margin in favour of an electoral college, although it was still unable to agree on its composition, a task referred to a special conference called for Jan. 24, 1981.

Callaghan resigned as party leader on October 15. It was generally expected that his successor would be Denis Healey, chancellor of the Exchequer throughout the Harold Wilson–Callaghan government of 1974–79. However, the position went to Foot, at 67 only a year younger than Callaghan. Foot came into the race as the man who could best unite the party, and some members of Parliament might have feared that Healey's election would be overturned by the electoral college. Foot had been a lifelong member of the Tribune Group, the left-wing backbenchers' organization, and had declined to hold office until becoming secretary of state for employment in 1974. Unlike Healey, he was broadly in sympathy with the policy decisions taken by the conference at Blackpool in favour of Britain's leaving the European Community, pursuing a policy of unilateral nuclear disarmament, and adopting a strategy of nationalization, state intervention, and trade protection in order to regenerate the economy.

The defense issue came to the fore in British politics in 1980. NATO's decision in December 1979 to deploy cruise and Pershing II missiles in Western European countries aroused new fears of becoming a Soviet target in a limited or preemptive war. The failure of the U.S. to ratify SALT II and the acceleration of the arms race by the U.S. and U.S.S.R. added to alarm. Finally, the government announced in July that it would (as expected) replace the Polaris submarine missile system with the Trident I at a cost of £5,000 million, reopening the nuclear-arms-in-Britain issue. Resentment about additional defense spending at a time of cuts in social spending drew support to the Campaign for Nuclear Disarmament, which in October, after the Labour conference had repudiated defense policies involving nuclear weapons, staged a massive rally in London.

It was a bad year for the newspaper industry. London in November became a city with only one evening paper when the *Evening News* and the *Evening Standard,* old rivals, merged to form the *New Standard*. The job loss was 1,750. More alarming still was the announcement on October 22 that unless buyers could be found for *The Times* and *The Sunday Times,* both would be closed by March 1981, at a cost of 4,000 jobs. (*See* PUBLISHING.)

The most exciting moment of the year occurred on May 5 when millions of television viewers saw

THE TIMES, LONDON

Michael Foot and his wife, Jill Craigie, greet the cameras after Foot was elected to succeed James Callaghan as head of the Labour Party.

live pictures of the spectacular relief of the Iranian embassy in London by armed and hooded commandos of the Special Air Services (SAS). The embassy had been occupied on April 30 by six terrorists who were demanding a degree of autonomy for the Arabic-speaking Khuzestan province of Iran and the release of 91 political prisoners there. The gunmen originally held 26 hostages inside the embassy, and it was when one of them was shot and thrown through the door that the commandos, swinging on ropes and discharging explosives, went in. Five terrorists and one more hostage were killed. One terrorist was captured.

Northern Ireland. The year brought little hope for Northern Ireland, where sectarian violence continued. Talks aimed at restoring a semblance of local government ("devolution") to the province came to nothing. The Rev. Ian Paisley's Democratic Unionist Party remained adamantly opposed to any form of power sharing or any attempt to achieve closer relations with Ireland. The predominantly Roman Catholic Social Democratic and Labour Party, for its part, was equally opposed to any return to local—that is, Protestant—majority rule. When the new session of Parliament opened in November, it was plain from the silence of the queen's speech that the government had shelved its hopes of legislating new constitutional arrangements. Some progress was made in reducing the number of British troops.

Despite a hunger strike begun October 27 by seven prisoners at Maze prison near Belfast, the government refused to treat convicted members of the Irish Republican Army as political prisoners. It was feared that there would be a violent reaction if any of the prisoners died, but the strike was called off December 18.

In May and December, in London and Dublin, respectively, Thatcher and Charles Haughey, prime minister of Ireland, met to discuss Northern Ireland, but no positive results emerged.

(PETER JENKINS)

See also Commonwealth of Nations; Dependent States; Ireland.

UNITED KINGDOM

Education. (1978–79) Primary, pupils 5,535,082, teachers 241,607; secondary, pupils 4,785,520, teachers 290,359; vocational, pupils 553,128, teachers 85,544; higher, students 319,859, teaching staff 44,981.

Finance. Monetary unit: pound sterling, with (Sept. 22, 1980) a free rate of £0.42 to U.S. $1 (U.S. $2.40 = £1 sterling). Gold, SDR's, and foreign exchange (June 1980) U.S. $23.2 billion. Budget (1980–81 est.): revenue £65,415 million; expenditure £73,175 million. Gross national product (1979) £188,330 million. Money supply (June 1980) £27,563 million. Cost of living (1975 = 100; June 1980) 197.1.

Foreign Trade. (1979) Imports £48,467 million; exports £42,804 million. Import sources: EEC 43% (West Germany 12%, France 8%, The Netherlands 7%, Italy 5%, Belgium-Luxembourg 5%); U.S. 10%; Switzerland 5%. Export destinations: EEC 42% (West Germany 10%, France 7%, The Netherlands 7%, Ireland 6%, Belgium-Luxembourg 6%); U.S. 9%; Switzerland 6%. Main exports: machinery 23%; chemicals 11%; petroleum and products 10%; motor vehicles 7%; diamonds 6%. Tourism (1978): visitors 11,730,000; gross receipts U.S. $4,464,000,000.

Transport and Communications. Roads (1979) 374,206 km (including 2,593 km expressways). Motor vehicles in use (1979): passenger *c.* 14,920,000; commercial *c.* 1,820,000. Railways (1978): 18,240 km; traffic (excluding Northern Ireland) 30,740,000,000 passenger-km, freight (1979) 19,893,000,000 net ton-km. Air traffic (1979): 47,004,000,000 passenger-km; freight 1,247,600,000 net ton-km. Shipping (1979): merchant vessels 100 gross tons and over 3,211; gross tonnage 27,951,342. Shipping traffic (1979): goods loaded 100,910,000 metric tons, unloaded 157,260,000 metric tons. Telephones (March 1978) 22,939,000. Radio receivers (Dec. 1977) 40 million. Television licenses (Dec. 1979) 18,268,000.

Agriculture. Production (in 000; metric tons; 1979): wheat 7,140; barley 9,550; oats 535; potatoes 6,485; sugar, raw value *c.* 1,196; cabbages *c.* 780; cauliflowers *c.* 220; green peas (1978) 494; carrots 672; apples 370; dry peas 104; tomatoes 139; onions 256; rapeseed 198; hen's eggs 823; cow's milk 16,012; butter 159; cheese 235; wool 36; beef and veal *c.* 990; mutton and lamb 227; pork 943; fish catch 770. Livestock (in 000; Dec. 1979): cattle 13,318; sheep 21,658; pigs 7,794; poultry 123,898.

Industry. Index of production (1975 = 100; 1979) 112.6. Fuel and power (in 000; metric tons; 1979): coal 122,369; crude oil 77,854; natural gas (cu m) 37,720,000; electricity (kw-hr) 299,960,000. Production (in 000; metric tons; 1979): cement 16,140; iron ore (26% metal content) 4,300; pig iron 13,000; crude steel 21,554; petroleum products 90,583; sulfuric acid 3,498; plastics and resins 3,417; fertilizers (nutrient content; 1978–79) nitrogenous 1,147, phosphate 419, potash 172; man-made fibres 596; cotton fabrics (m) 365,000; woolen fabrics (sq m) 138,000; rayon and acetate fabrics (m) 458,000; newsprint 363; television receivers (units) 2,110; passenger cars (units) 1,070; commercial vehicles (units) 408. Merchant vessels launched (100 gross tons and over; 1979) 608,000 gross tons. New dwelling units completed (1979) 242,000.

RACIAL TENSIONS IN BRITAIN

by Sheila Patterson

In post-1945 Britain the term "race" was revived in connection with large-scale immigration of nonwhites from Commonwealth countries. This virtual identification of "race" and "colour" was legitimated by policymakers in successive Race Relations Acts (1965, 1968, and 1976), a Race Relations Board, and a Commission for Racial Equality; it has been perpetuated by a rising tide of media debates about racism and racialism and the "race problem." There has also been a revival of pseudoscientific squabbles about race, intelligence, and IQ. Concurrently, systematic campaigns at international political forums have singled out "racism" as the worst form of oppression, defined "racism" as "white racism," and identified it with "colonialism" and "fascism." Some Marxist sociologists have also focused on "racism" as an ideology, to be traced to the capitalist and neocolonialist interests it is supposed to serve.

Amid such confusion a number of non-Marxist social scientists would like to dispense with the term "race" as a social category and "race relations" as a distinctive field of study and instead study ethnic relations and ethnicity, and the interaction between ethnicity and class, as only one of the social factors that influence intergroup relations. The academic debate remains unresolved.

Developments in race relations in Britain fall within the wider context of ethnic and minority-majority relations, whether the minorities are white or nonwhite, and "racialism" can be regarded as an extension of "ethnocentrism" instead of as a racist ideology in itself. Although negative stereotypes, hostility, and discriminatory behaviour vis-à-vis coloured ethnic minorities in particular exist in the majority society, their content and context is not constant but changing, and "racialist" ideas and attitudes are not the only motivations involved.

Variety of Immigrants. After World War II Great Britain experienced the largest and most variegated influx of immigrants in its history. In addition to a new wave from Ireland, it had by the late 1960s taken in up to half a million immigrants from the European continent. The largest group of postwar arrivals, however, were mostly nonwhite and from an unskilled rural background. At first these newcomers came mainly from the West Indies (about 60% from Jamaica). Just before controls were introduced, immigration from India and Pakistan began to accelerate and continued after the Commonwealth Immigrants Act 1962. By 1968 it was estimated that there were about one million "New Commonwealth" (Commonwealth countries other than Australia, Canada, and New Zealand) immigrants in Britain, including their British-born children. By 1978 the total number of persons of New Commonwealth origins (including Cypriots, Maltese, and Chinese) was estimated at 1,771,000, of whom up to 40% had been born in Britain. Persons of West Indian ethnic origin by then numbered 604,000, Pakistanis and Bangladeshis 246,000, Indians 390,000, and East African Asians 160,000.

There has been a meaningless tendency to lump all these groups together as "coloured"—and lately, even more misleadingly, as "black." Most West Indian immigrants in Britain have come from an English-speaking, Christian, British-oriented culture, albeit a rural and impoverished one. They are mobile and individualistic, resist strong intracommunal organization, and, in the early years at least, had high expectations of acceptance by the "mother country." Such acceptance has been slowed by real social differences but also by British society's general ethnocentrism and the persistence of a set of historical stereotypes about "blackness." These immigrants are, nevertheless, overall a group that can potentially be assimilated into British society.

By contrast, the major Asian groups are not "assimilating" but "pluralistic." While they differ from one another in religion, language, caste, class, and other traits, they share certain basic organizational and cultural features, and each group has its own satisfying and persistent ethnocultural identity. This also applies in the case of the East African Asians. They too are divided into several ethnic subcommunities, but they differ from Asians who migrated directly from the Indian subcontinent in that the majority had already adapted themselves and their

---

Sheila Patterson is the editor of New Community, *the journal of Britain's Commission for Racial Equality, and an honorary fellow of the Centre for Southern African Studies at the University of York. Her publications include* Colour and Culture in South Africa, Dark Strangers, *and* Immigrants in Industry.

institutions to an intermediate urban status (as merchants, traders, refugees, white-collar workers, some professionals, and artisans) in an English-speaking colonial system.

Phases of Assimilation. Despite Britain's colonial history, the bulk of the general public was unaccustomed to contact with coloured people en masse in Britain itself before 1939, and a survey in 1951 found that 50% of Britons had never met a coloured person and that most of the other 50% had done so overseas. Postwar coloured immigrants were thus seen as "dark strangers." Three decades later there could be few in Britain's major urban areas who had not encountered coloured people face-to-face in public places, at work, in the schools, or even as neighbours. The changes that thus occurred in race relations and racial ideas and attitudes fall into three broad, overlapping phases. These are:

1. "Open door" policy, 1950–61: postimperial optimism, liberal internationalism, laissez-faire voluntarism among legislators and administrators; growing unease and hostility in areas (predominantly working-class) of intensive coloured settlement (occasionally erupting into violence as in Nottingham and Notting Hill in 1958); rise of a small but vocal anti-immigration lobby.

2. "Postcolonial blues," 1960–70s: restrictionist and negative policies and legislative curbs on immigration (Commonwealth Immigrants Act 1962); growing public hostility and discriminatory practices; beginnings of pragmatic antidiscrimination and integrative action at government, academic, and local level and of immigrant accommodation in jobs and housing.

3. The 1970s: growing mainstream political consensus on strict control of "coloured" immigration as part of a dual strategy linking controls with the promotion of racial harmony and justice; bureaucratization of "the race relations industry"; growing professional initiatives for integration in schools, hospitals, welfare departments, workplaces, and so on; politicization of the race issue on the ultraright and ultraleft; emergence of a second immigrant or minority generation; and increasing ethnic group consolidation, consciousness, and expectations.

Adjustment and Establishment. After the immigration surge of 1950–60, phase 2 occurred when the receiving society felt threatened not only because of growing competition for jobs, housing, and social services but also with regard to its "community core." Such widespread feelings of insecurity and threat could be discerned behind the ugly manifestations of anti-immigrant and anticoloured feeling that characterized the massive outburst of approval of Enoch Powell's anti-immigration speech in April 1968, feelings perpetuated by the media, whose role throughout in mobilizing, not merely reflecting, public opinion on race and immigration has been crucial. More attention has been focused on the discrimination and disadvantage that immigrants have experienced than on their real progress and achievements. In employment, for instance, there was advancement into skilled, supervisory, and white-collar work for some individuals well before the Race Relations Act was extended to cover discrimination in employment and housing in 1968.

Housing presented greater problems at first than employment for the newcomers. Most early migrants, West Indian or Asian men, found cheap accommodations only in the poorest lodging houses. As they were joined by their families, they usually moved into owner-occupied dwellings, where, in turn, they rented rooms to new arrivals. Since the mid-1960s, however, there has been a move of West Indians into public housing and of Asians into owner-occupation.

By the mid-1970s the main problem for most coloured households was disadvantage rather than direct discrimination. Another factor, however, was that of choice—many, particularly Asians, preferred to remain concentrated close to jobs, specialty shops, and places of worship, and many chose to send their savings home to buy land or build a prestige house there. Successful Asians and West Indians alike, however, tended to move to "nicer" suburban areas, predominantly white.

The Second Generation. The large second generation of West Indian and Asian immigrants was subject to discrimination and disadvantage in home and school and achieved relatively poor attainment overall, partly because of language difficulties. As these adolescents pass into adult life, with higher expectations than their parents, they are facing increasing difficulties in employment in a time of economic recession, with West Indians suffering more than Asians. In contrast with the young Asians, young West Indians have reacted against their parents and the white outside world with a conspicuous black peer-group subculture and an aggressive posture that has brought them into confrontation with the police and with white neo-Nazi gangs in the same decaying urban territories.

But the continual process of adjustment points toward eventual accommodation of the immigrants and their children. The attitude of the British receiving society remains basically negative, though blanket criticism of immigrants is often tempered with approval of those who are known personally. Over the next decades, as "we" adjust to "them" and as more of "them" become "us," it should become easier to talk about a "nonracial" rather than a "multiracial" society.

United Nations

Among the year's highlights in the United Nations, observers could point to the striking progress made in fashioning a new treaty on the law of the sea, a special General Assembly session on international economic goals, and a spate of old and new political problems.

Law of the Sea. During a five-week meeting of the UN Conference on the Law of the Sea, which ended August 29, delegates in Geneva prepared an informal draft treaty incorporating the results of arduous negotiations since 1973. The most significant progress was made in devising a unique voting formula to be used by the Council, executive organ of the projected International Seabed Authority. The agreement spelled out how the Council would allocate the still-untapped mineral wealth below the deep oceans. It classified substantive issues that required decisions into three "tiers," each needing a different majority (two-thirds, three-quarters, or consensus) for approval. A special conciliation committee working with the Council president was to help promote consensus when required. The one major issue that the conferees still would have to resolve at a six- or seven-week session scheduled for New York City in March 1981 was how to settle disputes about overlapping maritime boundaries beyond the territorial seas. UN officials anticipated signing ceremonies to take place in Caracas, Venezuela, before the end of 1981.

Economic Assembly. On September 15 the General Assembly concluded a special session devoted to international economic problems. At those meetings the member nations agreed on the goals of an international development strategy for the 1980s, but they were unable to reconcile their differences about ways and means of achieving them. The agreed-upon strategy reaffirmed a long-standing UN aim to have developed states allocate, by 1985, 0.7% of their gross national product for official aid to less developed countries and to aim at a higher target (1%) as soon as possible thereafter. The Assembly also hoped that the less developed countries would increase the growth rate of their gross domestic products to an annual average of 7%.

Despite agreement on goals, West Germany, the United Kingdom, and the United States differed with the majority on how best to negotiate to achieve Assembly objectives. The majority suggested a new global conference; the three dissenting nations preferred to continue working through established specialized agencies, the International Monetary Fund, and the International Bank for Reconstruction and Development. As a result, the "North-South dialogue" between "rich and poor" countries was at a stalemate.

The Assembly's regular session, September 16–December 17, discussed the issues again. Indeed, in his inaugural address as Assembly president, Baron Rudiger von Wechmar of West Germany criticized his own country and other developed nations for failing adequately to support the economic objectives of the third world. He called it "appalling" that "rich" states were not meeting UN guidelines (West Germany was contributing under 0.35% and the U.S. 0.19%). "The need to create a new, more just and balanced international economic order is much too urgent a task to permit any substantial further delays," he said.

UPI

Mexican Ambassador Porfirio Muñoz Ledo made the acceptance speech when Mexico was elected to the UN Security Council in January.

Afghanistan. On January 7 the Security Council voted on a resolution calling on all foreign (*i.e.,* Soviet) troops to withdraw immediately and unconditionally from Afghanistan. The draft received 13 favourable votes but was not approved because of a Soviet veto. On January 9 the Council requested the General Assembly to meet in emergency special session on the problem. The Assembly met the following day and on January 14 voted 104–18–18 for the "immediate, unconditional and total withdrawal of foreign troops" from Afghanistan.

On November 20 the Assembly overwhelmingly (111–22–12) repeated its call for the U.S.S.R. to withdraw. The resolution, though similar to the earlier one in not naming the Soviet Union, was somewhat softer; it called only for "immediate" (not "immediate unconditional") withdrawal and, instead of saying that the Assembly "strongly deplores" the military intervention, it viewed the crisis merely with "grave concern."

Iran. A UN commission of inquiry, created on February 20 "to hear Iran's grievances and to allow for an early solution of the crisis between Iran and the United States," suspended work on March 11, unable to arrange to free the U.S. hostages seized on Nov. 4, 1979. On May 24 the International Court of Justice ruled unanimously that Iran "must immediately release each and every one" of the hostages and that none could be kept in Iran for trial or to participate in a trial as a witness. In addition, the court held, 12–3, that Iran was obliged to make reparations to the U.S. for its actions in seizing the U.S. embassy in Teheran.

On April 25, after learning that the U.S. had unsuccessfully attempted to rescue the hostages by military force, UN Secretary-General Kurt Waldheim called for "restraint, reason, and reinvigorated efforts to solve the problem" peacefully. Iran called the U.S. operation an act of aggression, but the U.S. defended it in a letter to the Security Council as an exercise of its inherent right of self-defense, adding that the mission was occasioned by mounting dangers to the hostages' safety.

Iran-Iraq War. On September 22 Iraq invaded Iran. Waldheim repeatedly offered his good offices to settle the conflict, and he and the Security Council tried diligently to arrange a cease-fire. Even while engaging in Security Council debate, however, the spokesmen for the two countries merely exchanged recriminations; Iran insisted that Iraq was engaged in aggression, and Iraq claimed that it was fighting to recover its own territories and because Iran had violated obligations under a 1975 treaty.

Two goodwill missions to stop the war proved fruitless, one undertaken in September by Pres. Zia-ul-Haq of Pakistan on behalf of nine Islamic states and a second in November, when, acting on Security Council instructions, Waldheim named former Swedish prime minister Olof Palme as UN mediator. Palme ended a week of talks with the parties on November 24. He reported that, although he did not expect rapid results, he anticipated that in the long run the need of both nations for development and construction would bring the war to an end.

Israeli-Arab Relations. The UN was preoccupied throughout the year with border attacks and reprisals between Israel and its Arab neighbours, with Israeli unwillingness to surrender occupied Arab territories, and with the security of the UN Interim Force in Lebanon (UNIFIL). Israel complained to the secretary-general that terrorists had crossed its border from Lebanon on the night of February 6 and that "terrorist" Palestine Liberation Organization (PLO) explosions had wounded 12 people in an Israeli town on February 11. In retaliation, Israel shelled Lebanese border villages for eight days in March, a reprisal that Lebanon protested on March 21 and 25. On April 7 Israel advised the Security Council of an "atrocity" perpetrated at one of its rural settlements by "PLO terrorists based in Lebanon" that had resulted in the deaths of an infant, a civilian, and a soldier and the wounding of 4 small children and 11 soldiers. Israel also complained of a "rash" of terrorist outrages in August. On October 27 Israel's UN delegate complained to Waldheim that the PLO had set off explosions near Jerusalem and Tel Aviv the day before that had injured 16 persons. On December 3, a few days after the PLO claimed responsibility for an attack on an Israeli bus outside the West Bank town of Nablus, Israeli forces carried out a seaborne raid against Palestinian guerrilla targets on the Lebanese coast nine miles south of Beirut, killing six persons and wounding five. Lebanon protested to the UN about the raid.

On March 21 Waldheim expressed his deep concern about exchanges of heavy fire in Lebanon, reportedly started by forces there commanded by Maj. Saad Haddad, a former career officer in the Lebanese Army, whose efforts on behalf of Lebanese Christians were supported by Israel. Israeli troops entered the UNIFIL operations area on April 9 in a separate move and withdrew on April 14. At about the same time an engagement between Muslim insurgents and UNIFIL resulted in the deaths of two Irish soldiers serving with the UN. In a unanimously agreed-upon statement issued through its president on April 18, the Security Council strongly condemned the "cold-blooded murder" of the two UNIFIL soldiers. On April 24 the Council reaffirmed UNIFIL's need to enjoy free movement in the area up to internationally recognized boundaries. It strongly deplored violations of Lebanese sovereignty, Israeli military intervention in Lebanon, all acts of violence contrary to the 1949 armistice agreements, and the provision of military assistance to the "so-called *de facto* forces." UNIFIL came under attack by PLO forces on August 12, and on September 17 the secretary-general appealed for all parties to cooperate with UNIFIL and to abstain from further acts of violence against it. On October 28 the Security Council president conveyed to Israel the Council's concern about the situation in southern Lebanon. On December 13 UNIFIL reportedly intercepted two Arab terrorist squads attempting to infiltrate Israeli lines.

Several UN bodies called throughout the year for Israel to dismantle its settlements in Arab territories occupied since 1967, including Jerusalem, and pressed the claims of Palestinians for a homeland in the Middle East. Starting on February 22, the Security Council held a series of meetings on the subject of the occupied lands, and on March 1 it unanimously called on Israel to withdraw from them. On April 30 the U.S. vetoed a Council resolution that would have affirmed the Palestinian people's right to establish an independent state in the area. U.S. delegate Donald F. McHenry (*see* BIOGRAPHIES) explained his vote by saying that, although the Palestinian issue was central, Middle East solutions had to be negotiated and could not be achieved by fiat. On May 8 and 20 the Council called on Israel to rescind its "illegal measures" expelling two Arab mayors and a judge from their posts on the West Bank. (The Council unanimously reiterated its call on December 19, and immediately thereafter the two expelled Arab mayors staged a five-day hunger strike at the UN to demonstrate "solidarity with Security Council resolutions.") Then, on June 30, the Council declared

UNITED NATIONS—KEYSTONE

U.S. Ambassador to the UN Donald F. McHenry voted in March in favour of a Security Council resolution condemning Israel for establishing settlements in occupied Arab territories. The U.S. later rescinded its vote after a storm of protest.

that Israeli measures to alter the character and status of Jerusalem had no legal validity; were a flagrant violation of the fourth Geneva Convention relating to the protection of civilians in time of war; and constituted a serious obstruction to achieving a comprehensive, just, and lasting peace. It also reaffirmed the "overriding necessity" to end the Israeli occupation. The vote was 14–0, with the U.S. abstaining on the grounds that the resolution would undercut U.S.-Israeli-Egyptian negotiations and because it failed to reiterate Israel's right to enjoy secure and recognized boundaries in lasting peace.

The General Assembly had its turn at dealing with these questions when, at the request of 90 member states, it met on July 22 in emergency special session. It reaffirmed (112–7–24) on July 29 the Palestinian people's right to establish their own independent state and called once more on Israel to withdraw unconditionally from occupied lands. It also asked the Security Council to consider imposing sanctions on Israel if it did not comply. The General Assembly adopted several anti-Israeli resolutions on December 15 when it called again (94–19–34) for Security Council sanctions; criticized (98–16–32) Security Council resolution 242 (1967) as not providing "an adequate basis" for justly solving the question of Palestine although all UN peacemaking efforts stemmed from it; rejected (86–22–40) the Camp David agreement between Egypt and Israel; and censured Israel (143–1–4) for annexing the Arab sector of Jerusalem. On December 16 the Assembly repeated (101–13–30) its call for a Palestinian state led by the PLO.

South Africa. On November 24 Waldheim reported to the Security Council that South Africa had conditionally agreed to a cease-fire that could end 15 years of guerrilla war in South West Africa/Namibia in 1981 and bring independence to the territory, which the UN considered was illegally occupied by South Africa. The report envisaged South African and Namibian leaders conferring with guerrillas of the South West Africa People's Organization (SWAPO) in January 1981 in an effort to dispel mutual mistrust. Should that meeting be successful, a cease-fire would come into effect in March and a UN peacekeeping force would patrol a demilitarized zone 50 km (31 mi) wide on either side of Namibia's northern border with Angola. An assembly would then write a constitution for an independent Namibia in October 1981.

One U.S. diplomat called the report "very much a step in the right direction," but a SWAPO observer pointed out that it "only calls for a pre-implementation conference. It is," he said, "South Africa's success, to win a stay of execution." On April 11 and June 27 the Council condemned South Africa for military operations against Zambia and Angola, respectively, which South Africa characterized as essential to protect Namibia from SWAPO incursions.

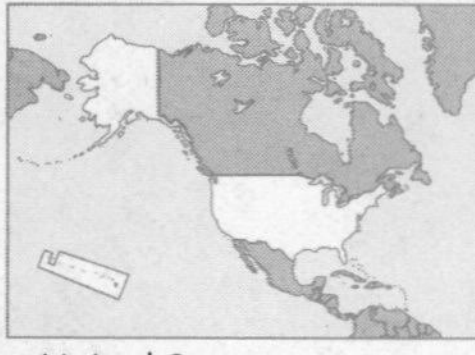
United States

Cambodia. Secretary-General Waldheim told the General Assembly on October 2 that, while UN humanitarian operations had alleviated the intense suffering of the Cambodian people, those concerned needed to renew their efforts toward achieving a political settlement that would allow

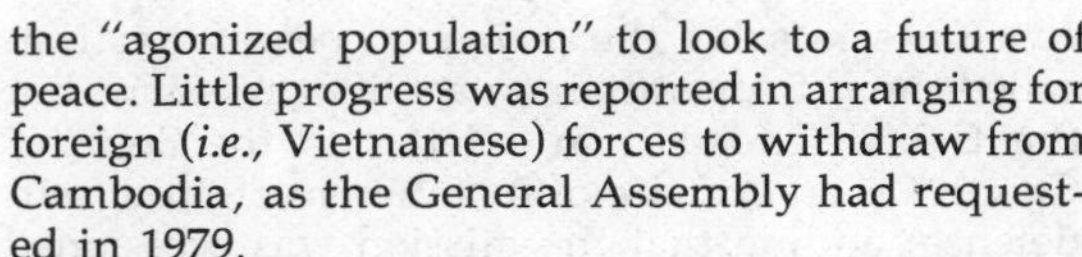

the "agonized population" to look to a future of peace. Little progress was reported in arranging for foreign (*i.e.,* Vietnamese) forces to withdraw from Cambodia, as the General Assembly had requested in 1979.

Other Matters. On November 13 the Assembly elected Panama (111–24) to the Security Council on the 23rd ballot. Costa Rica had been its leading opponent, until Panama convinced members that, because U.S. president-elect Ronald Reagan opposed the Panama Canal treaties of 1979, Panama needed the seat to defend its national interests. Ireland, Japan, Spain, and Uganda also were to begin terms on the Council in January 1981. The other members were East Germany, Mexico, Niger, Tunisia, and the Philippines, which were to serve until the end of 1981, and the permanent "big five": China, France, the U.K., U.S., and U.S.S.R.

Two vacancies occurred on the International Court of Justice with the deaths of Judges Richard Baxter (U.S.) on September 26 and Salah El Deine Tarazi (Syria) on October 4. Waldheim proposed on November 7 that the Security Council and Assembly fill the vacancies during the resumed 35th Assembly session in January 1981.

UN membership increased to 154, with the admission on September 16 of the new nation (formerly British-ruled) of St. Vincent and the Grenadines. Zimbabwe had become the 153rd UN member when it was admitted during the Assembly's special economic session on August 25. The UN had long concerned itself with the problems of Zimbabwe (formerly Southern Rhodesia), which achieved independence on April 18.

The late Ralph Bunche, former undersecretary-general and winner of the 1950 Nobel Prize for Peace for his role as UN mediator in Palestine, was honoured on September 15 at a dedication ceremony for the memorial "Peace Form One" sculpture, a 15-m (50-ft) steel obelisk by Daniel La Rue Johnson erected in a small park across the street from the UN Secretariat building in New York City.

(RICHARD N. SWIFT)

[552.B.2]

United States

The United States of America is a federal republic composed of 50 states, 49 of which are in North America and one of which consists of the Hawaiian Islands. Area: 9,363,123 sq km (3,615,122 sq mi), including 202,711 sq km of inland water but excluding the 156,192 sq km of the Great Lakes that lie within U.S. boundaries. Pop. (1980 est.): 223,239,000, including 87% white and 11.6% Negro. Language: English. Religion (1979 est.): Protestant 73.7 million; Roman Catholic 49.8 million; Jewish 5.8 million; Orthodox 3.6 million. Cap.: Washington, D.C. (pop., 1978 est., 674,000). Largest city: New York (pop., 1980 est., 7,224,000). President in 1980, Jimmy Carter.

In an election that major polling organizations had described as "too close to call," Republican Ronald Reagan overwhelmingly defeated Democrat Jimmy Carter on November 4 to become the

40th president of the United States (*see* BIOGRAPHIES). Reagan carried 44 states with a combined total of 489 electoral votes; Carter won 6 states and the District of Columbia, with 49 electoral votes. Reagan won 43.2 million popular votes, or 51% of the total; Carter won 34.9 million (41%); and independent candidate John Anderson won 5.6 million (7%). Carter's percentage of the vote dropped below his 1976 share in every state by at least two percentage points. (*See* Special Report.)

After his election Reagan began the process of choosing his Cabinet and other top aides. His most controversial selection was Alexander Haig, former supreme commander of NATO forces in Europe, as secretary of state. Haig's role as Pres. Richard Nixon's chief of staff in the last days of the Watergate crisis seemed likely to cause opposition to him in the Senate confirmation hearings. Among the other appointments were Donald Regan, chairman of Merrill Lynch & Co., as secretary of the treasury; Caspar Weinberger, a former secretary of health, education, and welfare, as secretary of defense; and William French Smith, Reagan's personal lawyer, as attorney general.

The Republicans also scored significant gains in congressional elections, capturing control of the Senate and picking up 33 additional seats in the House. The Senate lineup for the 97th Congress would be 53 Republicans and 47 Democrats. That was the largest number of Republican senators since the 71st Congress (1929–31), when the GOP had 56 seats. The Republican majority was the first since 1954 and ended the longest one-party dominance of the Senate in U.S. history.

Not only would the Senate be more Republican, it would be noticeably more conservative as well. Several pillars of Democratic liberalism went down to defeat, including John Culver of Iowa, Warren Magnuson of Washington, Birch Bayh of Indiana, Frank Church of Idaho, and George McGovern of South Dakota, the party's nominee for president in 1972.

In the House, Democrats had 243 seats, compared with 192 for the Republicans. The Democratic total included one independent, Thomas Foglietta of Pennsylvania, who was expected to caucus with the Democrats. Republicans last topped 192 House seats in 1956, when they captured 201. Before the election there had been 273 Democrats and 159 Republicans; three vacant seats had formerly been held by Democrats.

The Republicans increased their number of governorships by 4, bringing their nationwide total to 23. Democrats maintained their lead with 27. The four Republican additions all came in states west of the Mississippi River that were won by Reagan: Arkansas, Missouri, North Dakota, and Washington.

The Republicans picked up additional seats in state legislative elections across the country, giving party leaders reason to hope that the GOP would have more influence over the redrawing of congressional district boundaries in 1981. Before the November 4 election the Republicans controlled both houses of the legislatures of 11 states, and the Democrats controlled both houses in 31 states. The legislatures of seven states were under divided control. (Nebraska does not figure in such calculations because its legislature is unicameral and nonpartisan.) When the newly elected legislators took office in 1981, the Republicans would control 14 legislatures, the Democrats 28, and 7 would be divided between the parties.

As in previous countings of the nation's population, controversy over its fairness and accuracy marked the 1980 census. In a ruling handed down on September 25, U.S. District Court Judge Horace Gilmore of Detroit held that the 1980 census had undercounted the population of the nation's minorities and ordered that the figures for them be revised upward before release of the data. Subsequently an appeals court permitted release of national and state totals by year's end, but the suit, brought by Detroit and supported by dozens of other cities, remained in the courts. Preliminary data confirmed the shift in the U.S. population toward the so-called Sunbelt states of the South and Southwest.

Foreign Affairs. A reason often cited for President Carter's failure to win reelection was his inability to obtain the release of the U.S. hostages held captive in Iran since a band of Iranian militants seized the U.S. embassy in Teheran on Nov. 4, 1979. The hostage issue was Carter's main foreign-policy concern during the year.

U.S. spirits were lifted briefly on January 29, when Canada announced that six other Americans working at the U.S. embassy had been sheltered by Canadian embassy personnel after the takeover and flown out of Iran secretly the previous day. Thousands of Americans sent messages of gratitude to the Canadian government.

Iranian Pres. Abolhassan Bani-Sadr (*see* BIOGRAPHIES) announced on February 11 his nation's conditions for release of the hostages. He demanded that the U.S. acknowledge "past crimes"; recognize Iran's right to obtain extradition of the deposed shah, Mohammad Reza Pahlavi, and take control of his fortune; and promise not to interfere in Iran's internal affairs. Twelve days later a UN commission arrived in Teheran to review Iranian grievances and try to secure the hostages' release. Nothing came of this mission, and on April 7 Iranian leader Ayatollah Ruhollah Khomeini announced that the hostages would remain in the militants' custody until the Majlis (parliament), to be elected in the spring, decided their fate.

On the same day Carter severed diplomatic relations with Iran and ordered all its diplomatic personnel still in the U.S. to leave the country. He also imposed an embargo on all U.S. exports, except for food and medicine, bound for Iran. The president announced additional sanctions on April 17, banning all imports from Iran and prohibiting travel there by U.S. citizens. In addition, he made military equipment previously purchased by Iran and impounded after the embassy takeover available for sale to other nations and asked Congress for the authority to use frozen Iranian assets to pay reparations to the hostages and their families.

The most dramatic development in the hostage crisis began to unfold on the night of April 24, when eight U.S. Navy Sea Stallion helicopters took off from the U.S. aircraft carrier "Nimitz" in the

NEW REPUBLICAN SENATORS ELECTED IN 1980

WIDE WORLD

Steven Symms of Idaho

WIDE WORLD

Jim Abdnor of South Dakota

UPI

Paula Hawkins of Florida

WIDE WORLD

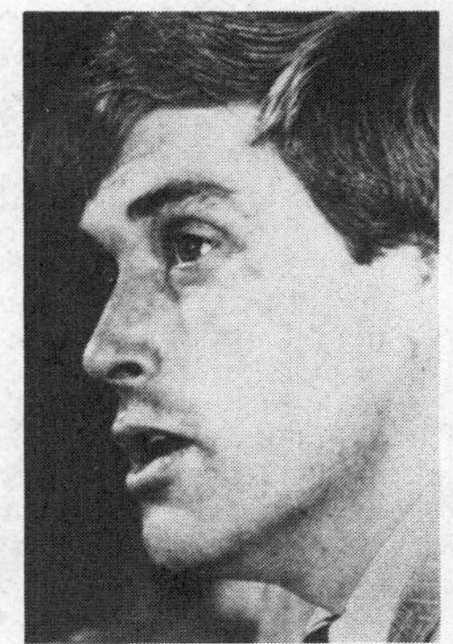

Dan Quayle of Indiana

UPI

Independent presidential candidate John B. Anderson stands with his newly announced running mate, Patrick J. Lucey, a former governor of Wisconsin. The two men garnered 7% of the popular vote in the presidential election.

Gulf of Oman and headed for a secret base in the salt desert of eastern Iran. Due to mechanical failures, only five of the helicopters finished the trip intact. Carter ordered the 180 commandos and airmen to abort the mission and return, but when one of the remaining helicopters maneuvered to refuel, it crashed into a C-130 transport plane and exploded in flames. Eight men died.

Contrary to their threats, the militants did not retaliate against the hostages. But they did claim to have moved some of them to Qom, Kerman, and other cities in order to make a repeat rescue attempt impossible. The failed mission also had repercussions in the U.S. Secretary of State Cyrus Vance, who had opposed the rescue mission from the start, resigned in protest. His successor, Sen. Edmund Muskie (Dem., Maine), was confirmed by the Senate on May 7 (*see* BIOGRAPHIES).

The abortive rescue was followed by a lull in diplomatic efforts to free the hostages which lasted through the remainder of the spring and summer. On July 11, however, Iran released hostage Richard Queen, a vice-consul, because of an undiagnosed illness that was later found to be multiple sclerosis. Then, on July 27, the shah died in Cairo.

Hope for the release of the hostages began to rise again in the waning days of the campaign. In a televised debate with Reagan on October 28, Carter reiterated that he was prepared to unfreeze Iranian assets under U.S. control and send Iran items it already had bought and paid for if the hostages were released. Five days later the Majlis endorsed a special commission's conditions for freeing the hostages. The terms were similar to those announced earlier by Khomeini: the U.S. must relinquish the property and assets of the shah, cancel all financial claims against Iran, release the frozen assets, and promise not to interfere in Iran's internal affairs.

Carter's loss to Reagan, which appeared to surprise Iranian leaders, clouded the hostage question once again. Negotiations continued, however, with Algerian diplomats acting as intermediaries between the two nations. After a visit to Iran in late November the Algerians reported that the 52 hostages "are in good health." Much of the difficulty apparently centred around the ability of the U.S. government to return the frozen Iranian assets, since various U.S. individuals and firms had brought suit in U.S. courts claiming part of this money as compensation for losses suffered in the Iranian revolution.

Hostages Freed

After 444 days, the U.S. hostages in Iran were freed on Jan. 20, 1981, the same day that Ronald Reagan took the oath of office as U.S. president. The 52 Americans were released after agreement had been reached concerning the return of Iranian assets impounded in the U.S.

Iran was not the only country in the Middle East that aroused concern in the U.S. in 1980. The nation's policymakers were deeply disturbed by the Soviet invasion and occupation of Afghanistan. In

UNITED STATES

Education. (1979–80) Primary and preprimary, pupils 31.6 million, teachers 1,343,000; secondary and vocational, pupils 15.3 million, teachers 1,117,000; higher (including teacher training colleges), students 11.5 million, teaching staff 820,000.

Finance. Monetary unit: U.S. dollar, with (Sept. 22, 1980) a free rate of U.S. $2.40 to £1 sterling. Gold, SDR's, and foreign exchange (June 1980) $23 billion. Federal budget (1980–81 est.): revenue $600 billion; expenditure $615.8 billion. Gross national product (1979) $2,368,800,000,000. Money supply (June 1980) $372 billion. Cost of living: (1975 = 100; June 1980) 153.6.

Foreign Trade. (1979) Imports $218,930,000,000; exports (excluding military aid exports of $160 million) $181,640,000,000. Import sources: Canada 18%; Japan 13%; West Germany 5%. Export destinations: Canada 18%; Japan 10%; U.K. 6%; West Germany 5%; Mexico 5%. Main exports: machinery 25%; motor vehicles 8%; chemicals 10%; cereals 8%; aircraft 5%. Tourism (1978): visitors 19.8 million; gross receipts U.S. $7,070,000,000.

Transport and Communications. Roads (1978) 6,251,692 km (including 81,700 km expressways). Motor vehicles in use (1978): passenger 116,575,000; commercial 31,702,600. Railways: (1977) 320,178 km; traffic (class I railways only; 1978) 16,450,000,000 passenger km, freight 1,252,800,000,000 net ton-km. Air traffic (1979): 404,550,000,000 passenger-km (including domestic services 325,600,000,000 passenger-km); freight 10,387,090,000 net ton-km (including domestic services 6,600,680,000 net ton-km). Inland waterways freight traffic (1977) 537,630,000,000 ton-km (including 132,410,000,000 ton-km on Great Lakes system and 287,400,000,000 ton-km on Mississippi River system). Shipping (1979): merchant vessels 100 gross tons and over 5,088; gross tonnage 17,542,220. Shipping traffic (1978): goods loaded 274,988,000 metric tons, unloaded 549,283,000 metric tons. Telephones (Dec. 1978) 169,027,000. Radio receivers (Dec. 1978) *c.* 450 million. Television receivers (Dec. 1978) *c.* 150 million.

Agriculture. Production (in 000; metric tons; 1979): corn 197,208; wheat 58,289; barley 8,238; oats 7,757; rye 624; rice 6,199; sorghum 20,684; sugar, raw value 5,059; potatoes 15,769; soybeans 61,751; dry beans 937; cabbages (1978) 1,375; lettuce (1978) *c.* 2,550; onions 1,746; tomatoes 7,663; apples 3,515; oranges 8,306; grapefruit 2,491; peaches (1978) 1,359; grapes 4,467; peanuts 1,804; sunflower seed 3,314; linseed 343; cottonseed 5,258; cotton, lint 3,163; tobacco 702; butter 447; cheese 2,067; hen's eggs 4,077; beef and veal 9,925; pork 7,008; fish catch (1978) 3,512; timber (cu m; 1978) *c.* 338,440. Livestock (in 000; Jan. 1979): cattle 110,864; sheep 12,224; pigs 60,101; horses (1978) *c.* 9,549; chickens 395,769.

Industry. Index of production (1975 = 100; 1979) 129; mining 111; manufacturing 132; electricity, gas, and water 114; construction 118. Unemployment (1979) 5.8%. Fuel and power (in 000; metric tons; 1979): coal and lignite 703,750; crude oil 419,520; natural gas (cu m) 534,600,000; manufactured gas (cu m) *c.* 23,600,000; electricity (kw-hr) *c.* 2,340,000,000. Production (in 000; metric tons; 1979): iron ore (61% metal content) 86,489; pig iron 78,960; crude steel 124,270; cement (shipments) 70,507; newsprint 3,716; other paper 50,056; petroleum products *c.* 676,000; sulfuric acid 37,874; caustic soda 11,236; plastics and resins 13,866; man-made fibres 4,200; synthetic rubber 2,534; fertilizers (including Puerto Rico; nutrient content; 1978–79) nitrogenous 10,155, phosphate 8,552, potash 2,286; passenger cars (units) 8,113; commercial vehicles (units) 2,980. Merchant vessels launched (100 gross tons and over; 1979) 706,000 gross tons. New dwelling units started (1979) 1,749,000.

UPI

Pres. Jimmy Carter (centre) announced in April that his choice for secretary of state was Maine senator Edmund Muskie (left). Secretary of State Cyrus Vance (right) had resigned because he could not support the abortive mission to rescue the American hostages in Iran.

a nationwide television address on January 4, Carter announced that 17 million metric tons of grain ordered by the Soviet Union for use in building up its livestock herds would not be delivered because of the invasion. He also suspended the sale of high-technology equipment to the U.S.S.R., severely curtailed Soviet fishing privileges in U.S. waters, and delayed the opening of new U.S. and Soviet consular facilities.

Moreover, Carter said that the U.S. would consider boycotting the 1980 Summer Olympic Games in Moscow if the Soviet Union continued its "aggressive actions" in Afghanistan. But the Soviets refused to withdraw their forces. Under strong pressure from the White House, the U.S. Olympic Committee voted 1,604 to 797 in April in favour of a resolution to boycott the Moscow Olympics. A number of other countries, including Japan and West Germany, took the same action. (*See* TRACK AND FIELD SPORTS: *Special Report*.)

The simmering border dispute between Iran and Iraq that erupted into open warfare late in September came at a time when the U.S. was moving to bolster its military presence in the Arabian Sea and Persian Gulf areas. The U.S. negotiated agreements for access to air and naval bases at Mogadishu and Berbera in Somalia, at Mombasa in Kenya, and on Masirah Island in Oman. Plans also were announced to expand the existing U.S. base on the British-owned island of Diego Garcia. Military construction bills providing funds to build the new and expanded facilities cleared Congress in mid-September. At about the same time, the U.S. massed an unprecedented number of ships and troops in the Indian Ocean. One apparent purpose of this show of naval force was to warn the Soviet Union against any attempt to send troops into Iran from neighbouring Afghanistan and thereby imperil Western access to Middle Eastern oil supplies.

The rising turmoil in the Middle East and the failure of the mission to rescue the U.S. hostages in Iran raised questions about the state of U.S. military preparedness in general. For instance, a confidential fleet readiness report that came to light late in September said that 7 of the U.S. Navy's 13 aircraft carriers were rated not ready for combat. It also stated that only 94 of the Navy's 155 air squadrons were rated combat-ready at any given time. Moreover, an article in the October 11 issue of *Foreign Report*, a newsletter published by *The Economist* in London, said that Western European officers had criticized the discipline of a U.S. Army division that had participated in a recent NATO military exercise. A confidential Army report, made public in September, revealed that while all six of the Army's combat divisions based overseas were rated combat-ready, six of the Army's ten combat divisions in the continental U.S. did not achieve this rating in December 1979.

Disturbed by reports that the all-volunteer armed forces were below par, Congress approved legislation in June providing for the registration of some four million young men aged 19 or 20 for the draft. A subsequent proclamation by Carter required all men born in 1960 and 1961 to sign up between July 21 and August 2 for any future military conscription. Although antidraft groups staged protest demonstrations across the country, Selective Service System Director Bernard Rostker said on September 4 that 93% of the men subject to draft registration had registered.

Government officials disclosed in August that Carter had adopted a new strategy for the U.S. to employ in fighting a nuclear war with the Soviet Union. Detailed in Presidential Directive 59, it gave priority to attacking military targets in the Soviet Union and lessened a previous emphasis on all-out retaliation against Soviet cities and industrial complexes. Administration officials asserted that the chance of nuclear war would decrease if U.S. forces had the capacity to initiate limited nuclear strikes against Soviet military targets. They believed that the Soviets would be less inclined to launch pinpoint nuclear attacks designed to destroy American land-based missile forces if the U.S. could deny them eventual victory in the nuclear war by similarly destroying vital Soviet military capabilities without resorting to all-out retaliation.

In a speech given in August at the Naval War College in Newport, R.I., Secretary of Defense Harold Brown said that the nuclear policy revision "is not a new strategic doctrine . . . not a radical departure from U.S. strategic policy over the last decade or so." But in a surprising statement Brown said that the U.S. land-based Minuteman nuclear missile force might already be vulnerable to a Soviet first strike. This was seen as a major reassessment of U.S. vulnerability. In his annual report on defense preparedness, Brown had predicted that the Soviets would attain the capability to destroy many or most of America's 1,000 Minuteman missiles "within a year or two." In his prepared draft for the Newport speech, in a paragraph that Brown did not read, he admitted, "That potential has been realized, or close to it."

Pentagon officials said that the new assessment of the Soviet threat to the U.S. land-based nuclear strike force came from recent intelligence reports. Brown emphasized plans to build the mobile MX missile and the cruise missile as a way of reducing the increased vulnerability to a Soviet first strike.

The question of U.S. military preparedness vis-à-vis the Soviet Union took on new urgency in December amid reports that Soviet armed forces were massing for a possible invasion of Poland. Both Carter and Reagan warned the Soviets of the grave consequences of such an attack. But U.S. and Western European officials said that there was virtually no chance of a Western military response if Poland was invaded.

Domestic Affairs. The troubled state of the nation's economy aroused widespread concern in 1980 and was generally considered a major reason for President Carter's defeat in his quest for reelection. As of October consumer prices had risen 12.6% from the previous year, as measured by the U.S. Bureau of Labor Statistics' Consumer Price Index; 7.6% of the nation's work force was unemployed; and sales of new single-family homes had declined to an annual rate of 548,000 units.

Interest rates were unusually volatile throughout the year. The prime lending rate—the interest that financial institutions charge their most creditworthy corporate customers—climbed to a record high of 20% in April. It then declined in stages to 11% in July and August before heading upward again. In mid-December it reached 21%.

These sharp fluctuations sapped the confidence of both businessmen and consumers. The automobile industry was especially hard hit. After an initial recovery at the start of the year, U.S. auto sales took a sharp turn for the worse as higher interest rates and car prices kept potential buyers out of the market. Sales volume for November was 8% below that of November 1979.

The year-end sales slump was only one of a series of adverse developments for U.S. automakers. In January President Carter signed into law a bill granting $1.5 billion in federal loan guarantees to the financially troubled Chrysler Corp. The president said that the legislation had helped preserve 200,000 jobs and had spared the government hundreds of millions of dollars in welfare, unemployment, and other benefits that would have been claimed if Chrysler had gone bankrupt.

Chrysler in October reported a third-quarter loss of $489.7 million, the company's second-largest quarterly deficit. It was the second quarterly deficit in 1980 that was much larger than the company had projected to the federal government when it requested financial assistance.

Ford Motor Co. and General Motors Corp., the two other members of the U.S. auto industry's Big Three, also experienced financial difficulties. Ford reported in late October a third-quarter loss of $595 million, the largest quarterly net loss for any U.S. corporation in history. The deficit broke the record

Hundreds of Columbia University students took to the streets of New York City in January to protest the reinstatement of draft registration, but legislation was passed by Congress in June that began the process.

MAXINE ORRIS—KEYSTONE

The 1980 U.S. Census

The editors of Britannica had planned on reporting the data from the 1980 U.S. census in this edition of the *Britannica Book of the Year.*

However, at the time this edition went to press, these data were not available in complete form. Further complications arose when various U.S. municipalities filed suits in the courts challenging the validity of the census count.

Rather than publish information that is incomplete or that may prove later to be inaccurate, the *Britannica Book of the Year,* as a book of record, has elected not to publish the detailed census information in this edition. It will publish this information as soon as it is complete and unchallenged.

We are publishing, however, in the United States Statistical Supplement on page 702, the state totals, which the Census Bureau was required by law to report to the president before Dec. 31, 1980.

set by GM a day earlier when it announced a third-quarter loss of $567 million, the company's second consecutive large quarterly deficit.

Ford and the United Auto Workers union asked the International Trade Commission for temporary protection against Japanese automobile imports while the U.S. industry was carrying out its massive conversion to small, fuel-efficient cars. But the commission turned down the request in November, saying that imports were not the major cause of injury to the domestic automakers. It held that recession, higher gasoline prices, and the shift in consumer demand to smaller cars were primarily responsible for the U.S. industry's problems.

The 96th Congress spent the first half of 1980 trying to deal with economic issues and the second half avoiding them. It was not a productive combination. Congress discovered that it could do little to alleviate the nation's fiscal troubles, while at the same time it ended up achieving little in the way of other major legislation.

Confronted by an aggressive Republican Party and concerned about its own reputation as the party of "big spenders," the Democratic-controlled Congress began the year by attempting to cut programs in order to balance the federal budget. But hopes of achieving a balance were soon dashed by the recession combined with spiraling inflation. And these new economic problems did not encourage Democrats to resume working for some of their favourite programs.

As campaign pressures mounted, Democratic leaders were forced to delay until after the election Congress's consideration of the budget and other key spending bills. With the scheduling of a lame-duck session, the Democrats hoped that the post-election climate in Washington would be more favourable for them. By the year's end, however, the Democrats found that their scheme had backfired. Instead of rewarding them for their restraint, the voters had taken from them their control of the White House and Senate and put them in a substantially weakened position in the House. Consequently, many of the top-priority bills advanced by the Carter administration and the Democratic leaders in Congress earlier in the year made little progress during the lame-duck session and died at adjournment. The lame-duck session did hold a few pleasant surprises for the Democrats. A budget was finally approved (although it included a $27.4 billion deficit), along with several regular appropriations bills. But many bills rated high on the Democrats' list of priorities died in the second session, including national health insurance, welfare reform, fair-housing legislation, a rewriting of the criminal code, a comprehensive regulatory reform bill, a youth jobs bill, an extension of unemployment benefits, and legislation establishing an Energy Mobilization Board. The pressures and cautiousness engendered by an imminent election and the stunning change in power that followed were principally responsible for the failure of so many major bills. Looking forward to their takeover of the Senate and the White House in January, Republicans were able to prevent legislative action on most of the major controversial bills during the session's final days.

UPI

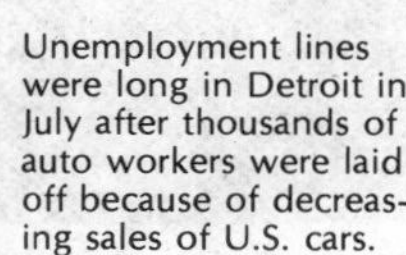

Unemployment lines were long in Detroit in July after thousands of auto workers were laid off because of decreasing sales of U.S. cars.

In perhaps the most unusual development during a year of surprises, it was the Democrats who held off last-minute action on a tax bill. In previous election years a tax cut designed by the party in power to win favour with the voters seemed almost inevitable. In 1980, however, the minority party advocated the tax cut, and the majority opposed it. Faced with a veto threat from Carter and the opposition of the Democratic leadership of both chambers, the Republicans were unable to bring a tax cut bill to a vote. But they promised to give top priority to an immediate tax cut in the next Congress.

The 96th Congress was also concerned with the continuing debate over defense spending. But unlike such debates in earlier years, this one was not over where to cut the defense budget but about how much to add to it. Both houses of Congress approved defense spending bills larger than the president had requested, the first time this had occurred during the post-Vietnam war era.

UPI

President-elect Ronald Reagan and vice-president-elect George Bush held their first news conference on November 6.

TERESA ZABALA—THE NEW YORK TIMES

A smiling President Carter triumphantly waved the Alaska lands bill after he signed it into law in December. The law created millions of acres of national parks, wildlife refuges, and wilderness areas.

What many had believed would be the major foreign policy debate of the year never materialized. On January 3 Carter asked the Senate to delay its debate on ratification of the second strategic arms limitation treaty with the Soviet Union (SALT II). It was clear that the Soviet invasion of Afghanistan had eliminated any possibility of the treaty's ratification during the session.

Perhaps the most significant energy measure to be approved during the year was Carter's windfall profits tax, which was proposed to tax a portion of the oil companies' expected profits resulting from the decontrol of oil prices. The most important environmental bill passed during the session was the Alaska lands measure. After four years of struggle between environmental and development groups, Congress settled on a bill restricting the development of 42.2 million ha (104.3 million ac) of Alaskan lands. The bill tripled the size of the state's designated wilderness areas. The lame-duck Congress handed the Carter administration one last environmental victory with the passage of a bill to set up a $1.6 billion "superfund" to clean up toxic waste dumps and chemical spills.

The most controversial event in agriculture during the year was Carter's decision to suspend most U.S. grain sales to the Soviet Union. Republicans promised to end the embargo, arguing that it placed an undue burden on farmers. Following the elections, however, the party postponed a decision on the embargo bill until 1981.

Two major transportation deregulation measures streamlined the government's regulation of the trucking and railroad industries. Both houses of Congress voted to prohibit the Department of Justice from bringing lawsuits that would require the busing of students for the purpose of school desegregation, but the provision was dropped in conference committee.

Congress's image was tarnished following reports in February that eight of its members had been implicated in an FBI "sting" operation called Abscam. Seven of them subsequently were indicted in connection with the undercover investigation, in which FBI agents posed as representatives of wealthy Arabs willing to pay for political favours. By the year's end four of the seven had been convicted and one of those, Rep. Michael Myers (Dem., Pa.), was expelled from the House. (*See* CRIME AND LAW ENFORCEMENT; LAW.) In another 1980 disciplinary action, the House censured Rep. Charles H. Wilson (Dem., Calif.) for financial misconduct.

Mt. St. Helens, a volcano in southwestern Washington state that had been dormant since 1857, erupted in 1980. A series of minor eruptions that began on March 27 culminated in a major explosion on May 18 that left 34 people dead, 32 others missing, and damage estimated at $2.7 billion. It was the first volcano to erupt in the contiguous United States since volcanic activity ceased in Mt. Lassen in northern California in 1921. (*See* EARTH SCIENCES: *Geology and Geochemistry*.)

A summer-long drought and a record-breaking heat wave caused widespread suffering in the Great Plains, the South, and the Southwest. The final toll from the heat wave was more than 1,200 deaths and approximately $12 billion in damage. Only three other summers in this century had caused more heat-related fatalities in the U.S. Crops and livestock suffered extensive damage from the combined effects of heat and drought. The hot, dry weather had little effect on the winter wheat crop but seriously damaged corn, soybean, sorghum, cotton, and spring wheat crops in the stricken areas. The price of finished, ready-for-sale food items rose 4.4% in August alone, partly because of the drought.

A massive, five-month-long boatlift known as the "freedom flotilla" brought approximately 125,000 Cuban refugees to the U.S. beginning April 21. About 80,000 of them settled in Dade County (Miami), Fla., which already had a sizable Cuban community. Other refugees were placed in makeshift camps in Florida and other states until they could find U.S. sponsors. The latest influx of Cubans, coming at a time of recession and high unemployment, aroused considerable resentment in the Miami area and elsewhere, especially when it became known that the refugees included criminals who had been released from Cuban jails and ordered to leave the country. These undesirables were blamed for outbreaks of violence in the resettlement camps.

An outburst of rioting by blacks in Miami, May 17–19, left 18 persons dead, more than 300 persons injured, about 1,250 arrested, and an estimated $100 million in damage to property. The rioting erupted only hours after an all-white jury in Tampa had acquitted four former Miami police officers who had been charged in the fatal beating of Arthur McDuffie, a black insurance executive from Miami. McDuffie had died Dec. 21, 1979, four days after having been chased down for a traffic violation. (RICHARD L. WORSNOP)

See also Dependent States.

United States: Special Report

A LANDSLIDE, NOT A MANDATE

by Stanley Cloud

In 1980 the political sword by which Jimmy Carter had lived was turned on him with a vengeance. Carter, the once-obscure Georgia governor, had run for president in 1976 as an "outsider," an untainted non-Washingtonian who pledged to come to the capital and sweep away the evils of post-Vietnam, post-Watergate America. But after four years in the Oval Office, Carter was himself swept aside by another "outsider," Republican Ronald Reagan, the conservative former governor of California, who accused Carter of being too liberal, too soft, and too incompetent for the nation's good.

When the votes were counted on November 4, Democrat Carter had carried only six states and the District of Columbia. Reagan was elected the 40th president of the United States in a 10–1 electoral-vote landslide, with a popular-vote margin of 51 to 41%. Rep. John Anderson, a Republican from Illinois who declared himself an independent candidate for president after being defeated in every GOP primary he entered, captured 7% of the vote in the general election.

Stanley W. Cloud is Assistant Managing Editor of the Washington *(D.C.)* Star.

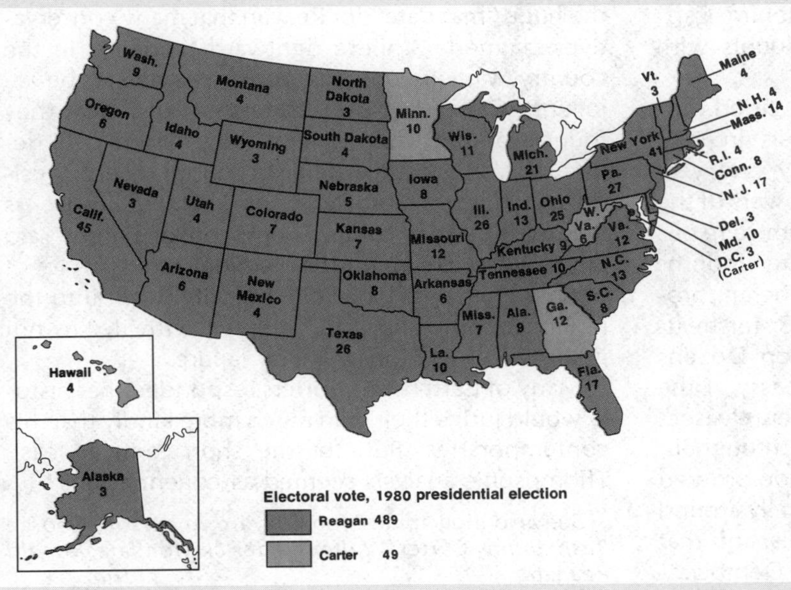

Carter thus was the first elected incumbent to be defeated for reelection as president since Herbert Hoover lost to Franklin D. Roosevelt in 1932. So quick and decisive was the verdict of the voters that Carter delivered his concession speech even before the polls had closed on the West Coast. "I promised you four years ago that I would never lie to you," the president told his supporters on election night, "so I can't stand here and say it doesn't hurt [to lose]."

Reagan, a one-time movie star and president of the Screen Actors Guild, had tried unsuccessfully for the Republican presidential nomination in 1968 and 1976. But in 1980 he overcame objections to his conservatism and age (at 69, he was the oldest president-elect in U.S. history) and made major inroads into the traditional Democratic coalition of organized labour and big-city ethnics. He carried every region of the nation, including such normally Democratic strongholds as Massachusetts, New York, and the South (where only Carter's native Georgia remained in the Democratic column).

The Long Campaign. Reagan's victory marked the end of what had probably been the longest presidential campaign ever. Reagan himself had been stumping in one forum or another for nearly four years. By late 1979 the list of Republican hopefuls had swelled to include Senators Howard Baker (Tennessee), Robert Dole (Kansas), and Lowell Weicker (Connecticut); Representatives Anderson and Philip Crane (both of Illinois); former Treasury secretary and Texas governor John Connally; and former Central Intelligence Agency director and ambassador to China George Bush.

As it developed, Reagan's most serious opposition came from Bush, whom middle-of-the-road Republicans took to be their last, best hope. Yet, despite Bush victories in the Iowa caucuses and in the Massachusetts, Pennsylvania, and Michigan primaries, it quickly became evident that Reagan, whose claim on conservative sympathies bordered on the mystical, could not be stopped.

By the time the Republican nominating convention convened in Detroit, the only real suspense surrounded the identity of Reagan's choice as his running mate. Would the conservatives' darling extend an olive branch to the party's moderates by asking one of their own to join him on the ticket? Or would he strive for ideological "purity"? The first clue came when, in one of the more bizarre episodes of recent U.S. political history, Reagan flirted with the idea of choosing former president Gerald R. Ford, whose moderate credentials were considered sound. As the complexities of having a former president in the second spot became evident, however, Reagan turned to Bush. The move may have irritated some conservatives at first, but did no lasting damage to Reagan.

Chappaquiddick and Teheran. In the meantime, Carter was on his way to renomination by the Democrats. He had been opposed during the primaries by a man who, if not himself a legend, was certainly the symbol of a legend: Sen. Edward M. Kennedy, the last surviving brother of the late Pres. John F. Kennedy. As Carter's standing in the public opinion polls plummeted in 1978 and 1979, thanks largely to his failure to solve the nation's economic woes, Kennedy was widely seen as the logical Democratic alternative. Yet when the senator from Massachusetts finally declared his candidacy late in 1979, his freewheeling brand of liberalism and his role in the famous, fatal incident at Chappaquiddick, Mass.—when the car he was driving had run off a bridge, killing a woman passenger—caused many voters to have serious doubts about him. Carter and his aides played upon those doubts with considerable skill.

The Carter camp was unquestionably aided during the primaries by the ongoing crisis in Iran, which began on Nov. 4, 1979, exactly one year before the general election. Militant followers of the Ayatollah Ruhollah Khomeini, the Muslim religious leader who had toppled the shah of Iran ten months earlier, stormed the U.S. embassy in Teheran, protesting the shah's admittance to the U.S. for treatment of an ultimately fatal cancer condition. Dozens of Americans who were inside the embassy at the time were taken hostage. Some were later released, but more than 50 remained hostages throughout 1980, despite an abortive rescue operation ordered by Carter. It is axiomatic that Americans rally around a president in times of international crisis, and that was precisely what happened during the Democratic primaries, to Kennedy's obvious and outspoken chagrin. Kennedy victories in a number of key states, including New York and California, were unable to stave off the inevitable. Carter, along with Vice-Pres. Walter Mondale, was the clear, although far from joyous, choice of the Democratic convention in New York City.

The Last Lap. The general election campaign between Carter and Reagan seemed more an exercise in shadowboxing than a serious discussion of issues that concerned the voters: double-digit inflation, rising unemployment, the crisis in Iran, the position of the U.S. vis-à-vis the Soviet Union, Carter's unpopular stands on the need for energy conservation, and doubts about his competence and that of the people around him. Reagan stressed the Communist threat abroad and the dire effects that "big government" was having on the nation's economy, but he never clearly spelled out his remedies beyond calling for a massive cut in income taxes. Meanwhile, Carter spent most of the campaign attempting to paint his opponent as an extremist who would divide the nation and tend to shoot from the hip in international relations.

After still more shadowboxing on the question of whether or not they would debate one another face-to-face, the candidates finally did meet in a nationally televised confrontation a week before the election. When they had finished, it seemed to many observers that Carter had won on "substance" while Reagan, with his easygoing diffidence and moderate tone, had dispelled fears that he was the "dangerous" fanatic portrayed by Carter. In the end, given all their obvious and long-standing frustrations with the incumbent, the voters evidently decided to take a chance on someone new.

That attitude alone, of course, would not provide the huge "mandate" for Reagan that many conservatives claimed. While a rightward tendency in the country was obvious, the voters seemed to be rejecting Carter, whose leadership qualities they found wanting, rather than calling for a radical departure from policies followed by all recent presidents, both Democratic and Republican. As Republican Gov. James Thompson of Illinois said when asked to sum up the election results: "A lot of people, the so-called silent majority, went into the polling booths and said, 'To hell with it, I'm not going to reward four years of failure.'"

Many of Carter's supporters responded that history would judge their man much more kindly than his contemporaries. But, for the short term at least, Thompson's analysis seemed as cogent as any.

See also Biographies: *John Bayard Anderson; George Bush; Jimmy Carter; Walter Frederick Mondale; Ronald Reagan.*

UNITED STATES STATISTICAL SUPPLEMENT

DEVELOPMENTS IN THE STATES IN 1980

Increasingly open adversarial dealings with the federal government plus renewed financial problems occupied the attention of state officials during 1980. The U.S. federal system displayed cracks in numerous areas, with state and national lawmakers at odds over control of lands, reduced federal assistance to states, preemption of state laws, and responsibility for dealing with national emergencies.

After two years of tax-cutting that eliminated more than $4 billion in levies, states in 1980 began raising taxes in order to compensate for high energy and borrowing costs, reduced sales and income tax receipts, and other recession by-products. Forty-two states held regular legislative sessions and 16 had special sessions during the year.

Party Strengths. Continuing their recovery from the 1974 Watergate-related debacle, Republicans added four governorships and a modest number of legislative seats during 1980 elections. The results were particularly important because these newly elected officials would be redrawing congressional and legislative district boundaries based on 1980 census results.

Of the 13 governorships contested, Republicans won 7, wresting the statehouse from Democrats in Arkansas, Missouri, North Dakota, and Washington. That put the 1981 gubernatorial lineup at 27 Democrats and 23 Republicans.

Even though the Republican national committee invested $3 million in state legislative races (the Democratic counterpart spent no funds), the GOP picked up control of only five additional chambers. For 1981 Democrats would thus control both houses of 28 legislatures, while Republicans would dominate in 14. All states would be solidly Democratic except Arizona, Colorado, Idaho, Indiana, Iowa, Kansas, Montana, New Hampshire, North Dakota, Pennsylvania, South Dakota, Utah, Vermont, and Wyoming (where Republicans had a majority in both houses); Delaware, Illinois, Maine, New York, Ohio, and Washington (where each party controlled one chamber); Alaska (where Republicans controlled the House but the Senate was tied); and Nebraska (which has a nonpartisan, unicameral legislature).

Partisan legislatures in 41 states would redraw congressional district lines, and the 1980 elections meant that Republicans would be protected in 22 of them (with control of the governorship or at least one legislative chamber). Democrats would have a free redistricting hand in 19 states and the Republicans in 3.

Government Structures and Powers. Amid signs of increasing citizen disenchantment with government and taxes, belt tightening and retrenchment marked state organization during 1980. Although the Michigan governor vetoed a similar measure, Delaware and Illinois (late in 1979) approved new "sunset" laws, bringing to 34 the number of states providing for periodic termination of state agencies unless specific reauthorization is made. Arkansas voters rejected a proposed new state constitution. Alaska, California, and Mississippi reorganized various executive departments, and Illinois voters, following a 1978 Massachusetts lead, reduced the size of the lower house of the state legislature by one-third, from 177 to 118.

Several legal rulings appeared to diminish the benefits of state political participation. The U.S. Supreme Court ruled that post-election personnel moves must be reasonably related to job performance, a decision that threatened the traditional political patronage system. The high court also expanded grounds on which citizens could sue state officials; the justices said such complaints could be brought individually for violation of any federal law, not only an infringement of a constitutional right.

Amid grumbling about the time and cost involved, 37 presidential primaries were staged by 35 states, Puerto Rico, and the District of Columbia during 1980, 7 more than in 1976. Pennsylvania and South Dakota prohibited state candidates from running in the general election after they were defeated in a primary. Voters in six southern New Jersey counties approved a resolution to secede from their state.

Government Relations. The ongoing tension between federal and state governments flared up during the year over finances and distribution of power. As a nationwide recession cut markedly into state revenue collections, the federal government proceeded with a cutoff of funding to states under general revenue sharing, countercyclical assistance, and Law Enforcement Assistance Administration (LEAA) grants; at least part of federal lawmakers' motivation was irritation over calls by 30 state legislatures for a balanced federal budget to battle inflation.

As U.S. Pres. Jimmy Carter made efforts early in the year to cut federal expenditures, he began withholding federal highway aid to states, already hard hit by a decline in maintenance funds (despite gasoline tax increases) as a result of a drop in gasoline consumption. Arkansas, Maine, New Mexico, and Vermont obtained court injunctions ordering the resumption of federal funding but not before lengthy delays had occurred.

The phasing out of the $600 million LEAA program along with the cutoff of the $1 billion antirecession aid and the $2.3 billion annual revenue share were opposed only tepidly by state officials. National Conference of State Legislatures leaders did submit alternative preferred funding cutbacks exceeding $7 billion, but most of the suggested cuts enjoyed powerful built-in federal voting constituencies. State revenue sharing was scheduled to resume in October 1981 but might be vulnerable to future budget cuts.

Smoldering resentment over federal control of lands, especially in Western states, grew in intensity during the year. Arizona, New Mexico, Utah, Washington, and Wyoming formally joined Nevada in the "Sagebrush Rebellion," approving laws calling for state takeover of unreserved land currently controlled by the federal government. About one-third of the nation's land area is owned by the U.S., 90% of it west of the Rocky Mountains. Yet the revolt appeared to be spreading eastward: Ohio became the first state to revoke its "automatic consent" statute that gave formal state approval to federal land purchases under Article I, Section 8, Clause 17 of the U.S. Constitution. The provision was originally intended to give states a veto over the construction of forts, magazines, and dockyards by the federal government, but most development-hungry states later passed the "automatic consent" laws to encourage federal dam and park expenditures.

Several state leaders predicted that federal-state tensions would worsen in future years as the nation looked to western lands for development of alternative energy sources. The governors of Nevada and Utah provided a foretaste of that conflict when they informed Congress that they opposed construction of the MX missile system in their states because of economic and environmental problems.

Some disputes were resolved amicably, however. State attorneys general lobbied Congress successfully for a $1.6 billion "superfund" to cover cleanups of chemical spills and toxic wastes. The U.S. Supreme Court settled two boundary disputes, favouring Ohio over Kentucky in one conflict and Nevada over California in another. The latter ruling allowed continued operation of four casinos in the Lake Tahoe region claimed by California, where gambling is prohibited.

The U.S. Supreme Court in December prohibited California officials from conducting an investigation into the Arkansas prison system. An escaped prisoner, fighting extradition from California to Arkansas, had alleged that penal conditions there were "cruel and inhuman."

Finances and Taxes. After two years of sizable budget surpluses and tax cuts, the effects of inflation and recession caught up with state governments during 1980, prompting cost cutting and some tax increases. That latter trend was countered by an anti-government-spending drive predicated on the success of California's Proposition 13 in 1978, which reduced property tax burdens markedly without destroying essential services as predicted by opponents.

Nonetheless, voters were reluctant to copy and extend the tax revolt blindly. Proposition 13 clones were defeated by Arizona, Nevada, Oregon, South Dakota, and Utah citizens in November balloting. The California electorate rejected an attempt by Howard Jarvis, a Proposition 13 father, to halve the state's income tax. Michigan voters rejected three major tax relief measures.

However, less drastic tax relief was approved in Arizona, Arkansas, Massachusetts, Montana, and Utah. Massachusetts voters endorsed "Proposition 2½," a measure limiting property taxes to 2.5% of property value. Delaware, Idaho, and South Carolina adopted a state revenue collection lid, bringing to 17 the number of states with a statutory spending cap. Alaska, its coffers overflowing with oil revenue, attempted to eliminate income taxes for long-time residents; when a court declared that the measure discriminated against newcomers, state voters abolished the entire tax in September.

Boosts in state gasoline taxes were the most popular revenue-raising measure, with 13 states raising the rate, some substantially. Kentucky and Massachusetts switched the tax from a flat per-gallon charge to a percentage of sales price, allowing for future increases.

New Jersey increased its corporate income tax rate. Connecticut hiked its state sales tax to 7.5%, highest in the nation; South Dakota also boosted sales taxes. Cigarette taxes were increased in Alabama and Maryland and imposed for the first time in Connecticut. Nebraska began taxing hotel-motel rooms, and Missouri abolished its inheritance tax. Sales and income tax reductions were approved in Colorado, Arizona, Illinois, and Louisiana. A survey by the Tax Foundation revealed that 16 states increased taxes during the year, raising an additional $850 million, while 7 enacted $430 million worth of tax trimming.

Figures accumulated in 1980 showed that state revenue from all sources totaled $247.1 billion during the 1979 fiscal year, an increase of 9.8% over the preceding 12 months. General revenue (excluding state liquor and state insurance trust revenue) was $208 billion, up 10%. Total state expenditures rose 10.2% to $224.3 billion, creating a surplus of $22.8 billion for the year. General expenditures, not including outlays of the liquor stores and insurance trust systems, amounted to $200.5 billion, up 11.5% for the year. Of general revenue, some 60.3% came from state taxes and licenses; 12.1% from charges and miscellaneous revenue, including educational tuition; and 27.6% from intergovernmental revenue (mostly from the federal government).

The largest state outlay was $77.7 billion for education, of which $24.8 billion went to state colleges and universities and $46.2 billion to local public schools. Other major outlays were $38.9 billion for public welfare, $21.2 billion for highways, and $15.6 billion for health and hospitals.

Ethics. The Federal Bureau of Investigation's stepped-up drive on white-collar crime resulted in the indictment of several state officials during 1980. Washington House speaker John Bagnariol and Senate majority leader Gordon Walgren, both Democrats, were accused of conspiring to legalize and control gambling in their state. Texas House speaker Billy Clayton and two associates were indicted but later found innocent on charges arising from the FBI's Brilab inquiry, an investigation of a scheme to influence health insurance contracts for state employees.

Former Louisiana administration commissioner Charles Roemer was among four persons indicted in a separate Brilab investigation. Four-term Illinois Attorney General William Scott was convicted of filing a false income-tax report in 1972; he was sentenced to 366 days in prison and resigned. The U.S. Supreme Court ruled that a state legislator does not enjoy the same immunity from criminal prosecutions as a U.S. congressman; the case was brought by Tennessee Sen. Edgar Gillock, convicted of accepting money to prevent an inmate's extradition and to introduce legislation.

Two former governors suffered major setbacks. Raymond Blanton, whose term as Tennessee governor ended abruptly in 1979 amid charges that his aides were selling prison pardons, was indicted with two associates for peddling state liquor licenses. (Other Blanton aides were indicted for perjury as 30 construction companies and executives pleaded guilty July 5 to charges of bid rigging and price fixing on major public works projects.) And former Maryland governor Marvin Mandel, like Blanton a Democrat, exhausted legal appeals and on May 19 began serving a three-year federal prison term for mail fraud and racketeering. During the year Maryland's new attorney general sued Mandel and his wife for $23,000 and 57 items of furniture Mandel allegedly removed from the governor's mansion.

Education. Testy relations with the federal government also marred developments in state education during the year. The U.S. Supreme Court ruled that Texas must pay for free public education for illegal aliens. And the new U.S. Department of Education issued proposed regulations on education of children "whose primary language is not English and who have limited proficiency in English," requiring that school districts nationwide establish bilingual education programs for them. States complained that the regulations were excessively rigid and allowed no room for innovation and experimentation.

A federal judge ruled that Ohio must help pay costs of Cleveland school desegregation because the state failed to act on what it knew was intentional segregation. The New Jersey legislature ordered a bold program of sex education for all schoolchildren from kindergarten through high school, but then backed down under pressure; the program would be optional within individual school districts and attendance could not be required, the legislature stated.

Health and Welfare. Relations between federal and state governments were further strained by squabbles over funding to alleviate several public emergencies. The eruption of Mt. St. Helens in southern Washington eventually resulted in an estimated $2.7 billion in damage. U.S. officials attempted to force state governments to pay 25% of cleanup costs, but Idaho refused.

An estimated 116,000 Cubans joined about 25,000 Haitians in fleeing to Florida during the year, creating a major burden on that state and also on Pennsylvania, Arkansas, and Wisconsin, where refugee centres were established. Although the federal government provided some emergency aid, many of the refugees landed on state-funded welfare rolls, adding to policing and resettlement costs. One of the worst heat waves in the century claimed more than 1,200 lives in 22 states, ruined crops, and prompted federal disaster aid to Arkansas, Kansas, Louisiana, Missouri, Oklahoma, and Texas.

Rhode Island lawmakers established alcoholism as a disease, with treatment eligible for health-insurance compensation. Colorado and Kentucky joined 19 states in legalizing laetrile as a cancer treatment. Nevada approved a law providing rape victims with up to $1,000 in medical care and counseling, provided that the crime is reported within three days. A federal judge declared Alabama's mental health commission had allowed "indefensible conditions" to infect state facilities and ordered the system into receivership by the state governor.

Abortion. Although court-approved cutoffs of government funding for elective abortions took effect during 1980, legislation and further litigation on the controversial subject continued unabated in the states. Tennessee became the 16th state to call for a U.S. constitutional convention to overturn the U.S. Supreme Court's 1973 decision, which struck down antiabortion statutes in several states. Louisiana, Massachusetts, Rhode Island, and South Dakota passed new restrictions, typically requiring pregnant women to sign an "informed written consent" document and wait 24 hours before receiving the abortion. New Jersey's governor vetoed a similar law.

Kentucky joined states abolishing public funding for abortions, but Michigan's governor vetoed a bill forbidding funding except when necessary to save the mother's life. Illinois attempted to prohibit abortion unless a physician deems it "necessary." Laws in Connecticut and North Dakota, prohibiting physicians from advertising abortion services and requiring informed consent and parental notice for minors, were invalidated by federal judges as infringing on the doctor-patient relationship.

Drugs. Even though 11 states had decriminalized possession of small amounts of marijuana, a hardening of attitudes toward the drug was noticeable during 1980. Kentucky's governor vetoed a legislature-approved bill that would have established a ten-year prison term for conviction of marijuana possession. Although Arizona, Colorado, Georgia, Michigan, New York, Rhode Island, and South Carolina joined 18 states allowing prescription of marijuana for treatment of cancer and glaucoma, an attempt to outlaw sale of drug paraphernalia through so-called head shops took hold nationally. Alabama, Colorado, Connecticut, Delaware, Florida, Idaho, Indiana, Louisiana, Maryland, Nebraska, New York, and Virginia passed laws shutting down the shops; similar laws were vetoed in Tennessee and declared unconstitutionally vague by federal judges in Georgia and West Virginia.

During the year Hawaii and Louisiana approved substitution of generic drugs for brand-name varieties. Reversing a short-lived trend, several states raised the legal age for consumption of alcohol: Florida, New Jersey, and Georgia to 19, Rhode Island to 20, and Illinois to 21. A Nebraska law raised the age to 19 on July 1, 1980, and to 20 on July 1, 1981.

Law and Justice. With the U.S. Supreme Court clearly unenthusiastic about its 1976 decision allowing resumption of the death penalty, the debate over capital punishment continued inconclusively during 1980. The high court voided the death law of Alabama on technical grounds, and court delays led to another year without any executions in the U.S. New Mexico and Connecticut approved new capital punishment laws, bringing to 39 the jurisdictions providing the death penalty, but New York's governor for the fourth consecutive year vetoed a death law for his state. The Massachusetts Supreme Court declared that state's capital punishment law unconstitutional. To soften criticism of the brutality of traditional execution methods, four states —Idaho, New Mexico, Oklahoma, and Texas—had provided for death by lethal injection; during the year, however, the American Medical Association house of delegates declared that physicians should not cooperate in that execution method.

New York enacted a tough one-year mandatory prison sentence for conviction of carrying a loaded, unlicensed handgun in a public place. Eight states barred police searches of newsrooms before a federal law preempted the matter, declaring the practice illegal nationwide. Police strip searches, which often victimize women stopped for minor traffic offenses, were regulated in Illinois, Iowa, and Connecticut.

Illinois and Michigan made fraud by computer a state felony. Rhode Island downgraded prostitution to a petty misdemeanour in order to speed courtroom trials. Arizona, Kansas, Kentucky, Minnesota, Missouri, and Vermont approved new laws prohibiting abuse of the aged, bringing to 24 the number of states outlawing mistreatment of the elderly.

Gambling. Despite corruption problems in two states, state-organized games of chance enjoyed a good run of luck in 1980. Voters in Arizona, Colorado, and the District of Columbia approved government-run lotteries in November, bringing to 17 the number of jurisdictions using this fund-raising method. (District voters had rejected a more ambitious referendum including jai alai and dog racing in May.) The electorate in Missouri, Texas, and West Virginia and the legislature in Tennessee all legalized nonprofit bingo and raffles during the year.

There were problems, however. The vice-chairman of the New Jersey Casino Control Commission resigned after news reports linked him to a payoff in the FBI's Abscam investigation. (*See* CRIME AND LAW ENFORCEMENT.) And six individuals were indicted in September on charges that they fixed the Pennsylvania state lottery. Officials said that the conspirators had injected a weighted substance into eight of ten table tennis balls used in the drawing while their confederates bought chances on all combinations of "4" and "6," the two unweighted balls. About $1,180,000 of the record $3.5 million payout in the resulting drawing was fraudulently collected, according to the indictment, after "666" was announced as the winning number.

Environment. With news reports highlighting economic and personal losses stemming from toxic chemical dumping at Love Canal, N.Y., legislatures in numerous states considered new measures to regulate disposal of hazardous wastes. California, Connecticut, Delaware, Louisiana, New Jersey, and Pennsylvania set up new waste-control programs; Colorado, Illinois, Kentucky, Maine, Michigan, Mississippi, North Dakota, New York, and Pennsylvania were among states markedly toughening laws controlling disposal of hazardous or toxic wastes; and all states prepared to assist in the enforcement of new waste regulations issued during 1980 by the federal Environmental Protection Agency. By the year's end, responding to excessive pollution of lakes and rivers not directly attributable to waste dumping, 32 states had set up monitoring stations for so-called acid rain, a growing national problem.

Under EPA pressure Colorado, Michigan, and Montana established automobile emission-testing programs in urban areas; California and Kentucky failed to act and at least temporarily lost nearly $900 million in EPA road and sewer funds. New York sued Hooker Chemicals and Plastics Corp., accused in the Love Canal dumping, for $635 million; the federal government had previously sued the same company for $124 million. Arizona and Colorado during the year joined other Western states in setting up a groundwater management system.

Isolated victories cheered environmentalists during the year. Michigan enacted a marshlands protection bill. California and Nevada signed amendments to their Lake Tahoe regional compact restricting development and new casino construction. Kentucky, Minnesota, and Oregon joined Colorado in setting up the "chickadee checkoff," an optional individual allocation of state income-tax refund money for protection of nongame wildlife species. And the largest conservation measure of the century—a compromise bill setting aside 104 million ac of Alaska for parks, wildlife refuges, and national conservation areas—was signed into law by President Carter in December. Neither conservationists nor development interests, however, expressed complete satisfaction with the size of this reserve and the restrictions placed on its commercial exploitation.

Energy. Sparring over nuclear plant construction continued during 1980 with decidedly mixed results. Oregon voters approved a measure to ban plant construction until safe disposal of fuel rod waste becomes practical; Missouri and South Dakota voters rejected similar proposals. Maine voters defeated a referendum that would have shut down the state's single nuclear plant. Washington approved, but Montana rejected, a plan to regulate nuclear waste disposal. Montana and Vermont voters enacted prohibitive restrictions on uranium mining. A federal judge again told California that its attempts to ban nuclear-plant construction pending waste disposal improvement were illegal because the federal government had preempted the field.

Connecticut and New York approved gross receipts taxes on oil companies doing business within their borders, but federal judges invalidated state laws prohibiting the companies from passing the costs on to their customers. Kentucky and North Dakota helped in construction of the nation's first large-scale commercial synthetic fuels plants. Late in 1979, a reluctant Massachusetts became the 50th state to allow right turns at red lights, thus avoiding a federal Department of Energy fund cutoff.

A study published during the year indicated that the benefits of oil price decontrol would hardly be spread evenly: eight states (Alaska, Texas, California, Louisiana, Oklahoma, Wyoming, New Mexico, and Kansas) stood to receive a $128 billion windfall over the next decade from increased severance taxes and other payments associated with decontrol.

Equal Rights. For the third consecutive year no additional state ratified the proposed Equal Rights Amendment (ERA) to the U.S. Constitution; the measure would fail unless three more states (for a total of 38) approved it by the June 1982 deadline. Iowa voters also rejected an equal rights amendment to their state constitution.

News for opponents of sex discrimination was not all gloomy, however. Legislators in Connecticut and Michigan outlawed sexual harassment, and a federal appellate court declared that a National Organization of Women (NOW) boycott of Missouri (which had failed to ratify the federal ERA) did not violate antitrust laws. In an unrelated development a NOW volunteer was indicted June 5 and later convicted on charges of attempting to bribe an Illinois state legislator with a $1,000 campaign contribution in return for a pro-ERA vote.

A second proposed constitutional amendment, granting District of Columbia citizens authority to elect two voting U.S. senators and a representative, also bogged down. Only two states, Maryland and Hawaii, ratified the amendment, bringing the approval total to nine. Discouraged D.C. voters approved a call for a state constitutional convention in November balloting, but most observers suggested that the statehood alternative for D.C., which would require congressional and presidential approval, also faced a dismal future.

Prisons. The most vicious prison riot in U.S. penal history took place in New Mexico's overcrowded facility at Santa Fe on February 2–3, leaving over 30 inmates dead and 89 guards and prisoners hospitalized. The rioters took over in a planned ambush on four dormitory guards and soon began maiming guards and killing each other in shockingly cruel ways. After the situation was finally brought under control, the New Mexico legislature appropriated nearly $90 million for restoration of the facility, construction of a new maximum-security prison, and various payments arising from the riot.

Inmates were also killed at prison disturbances during the year in Monroe, Wash., and Stillwater, Minn. Federal judges declared Oregon and Texas prisons unconstitutionally crowded. Kentucky officials, settling a civil suit brought by inmate representatives, agreed to spend $42 million to relieve overcrowding in state penal facilities.

Continuing a trend reflecting lack of confidence in allegedly lenient judges and parole boards, several states adopted laws requiring jail time for certain convictions. Hawaii, Massachusetts, New Mexico, and Oklahoma joined 27 other states in establishing mandatory minimum prison sentences under specified circumstances. Connecticut became the 15th state to abolish its parole board and establish fixed, determinate sentences for those convicted of crimes.

Those developments tended to lengthen terms and increase the number of prisoners. The U.S. Bureau of Justice Statistics reported in 1980 that a record 314,083 inmates were housed in U.S. prisons on a typical day in 1979, 287,850 of them in state facilities. Texas, with 26,522, and California, with 22,628, headed the list.

Consumer Protection. Although soaring market interest rates prompted numerous states to amend or cancel their usury ceilings, the federal government preempted state interest regulation during 1980, first by executive order and later by legislation. States would have until April 1983 to override the federal standards, which set relatively high interest ceilings in an attempt to avoid disruption of commercial transactions.

Connecticut, Hawaii, New Jersey, and New York joined states establishing or expanding the scope of "plain English" regulations, which required simple, understandable language in such documents as insurance forms, leases, and consumer contracts. Colorado outlawed solicitation by means of automatic-dialing telephone equipment. Fearing interruption of farm produce transportation following the bankruptcy of two major railroads, South Dakota arranged to purchase 457 mi of Milwaukee Road track; Iowa, Montana, and Wisconsin officials investigated similar purchase and operation options.

(DAVID C. BECKWITH)

AREA AND POPULATION

Area and Population of the States

State	AREA in sq mi: Total	AREA in sq mi: Inland water[1]	POPULATION (000): 1970 census[2]	POPULATION (000): 1980 census	POPULATION (000): Percent change 1970–80
Alabama	51,609	901	3,444	3,890	12.9
Alaska	589,757	20,157	303	400	32.0
Arizona	113,909	492	1,775	2,718	53.1
Arkansas	53,104	1,159	1,923	2,286	18.9
California	158,693	2,332	19,971	23,669	18.5
Colorado	104,247	481	2,210	2,889	30.7
Connecticut	5,009	147	3,032	3,108	2.5
Delaware	2,057	75	548	595	8.6
Dist. of Columbia	67	6	757	638	−15.7
Florida	58,560	4,470	6,791	9,740	43.4
Georgia	58,876	803	4,588	5,464	19.1
Hawaii	6,450	25	770	965	25.3
Idaho	83,557	880	713	944	32.4
Illinois	56,400	652	11,110	11,418	2.8
Indiana	36,291	194	5,195	5,490	5.7
Iowa	56,290	349	2,825	2,913	3.1
Kansas	82,264	477	2,249	2,363	5.1
Kentucky	40,395	745	3,221	3,661	13.7
Louisiana	48,523	3,593	3,645	4,204	15.3
Maine	33,215	2,295	994	1,125	13.2
Maryland	10,577	686	3,924	4,216	7.4
Massachusetts	8,257	431	5,689	5,737	0.8
Michigan	58,216	1,399	8,882	9,258	4.2
Minnesota	84,068	4,779	3,806	4,077	7.1
Mississippi	47,716	420	2,217	2,521	13.7
Missouri	69,686	691	4,678	4,917	5.1
Montana	147,138	1,551	694	787	13.4
Nebraska	77,227	744	1,485	1,570	5.7
Nevada	110,540	651	489	799	63.4
New Hampshire	9,304	277	738	921	24.8
New Jersey	7,836	315	7,171	7,364	2.7
New Mexico	121,666	254	1,017	1,300	27.8
New York	49,576	1,745	18,241	17,557	−3.8
North Carolina	52,586	3,788	5,084	5,874	15.5
North Dakota	70,665	1,392	618	653	5.7
Ohio	41,222	247	10,657	10,797	1.3
Oklahoma	69,919	1,137	2,559	3,025	18.2
Oregon	96,981	797	2,092	2,633	25.9
Pennsylvania	45,333	367	11,801	11,867	0.6
Rhode Island	1,214	165	950	947	−0.3
South Carolina	31,055	830	2,591	3,119	20.4
South Dakota	77,047	1,092	666	690	3.6
Tennessee	42,244	916	3,926	4,591	16.9
Texas	267,338	5,204	11,199	14,228	27.1
Utah	84,916	2,820	1,059	1,461	38.0
Vermont	9,609	342	445	511	14.8
Virginia	40,817	1,037	4,651	5,346	14.9
Washington	68,192	1,622	3,413	4,130	21.0
West Virginia	24,181	111	1,744	1,950	11.8
Wisconsin	56,154	1,690	4,418	4,705	6.5
Wyoming	97,914	711	332	471	41.8
TOTAL U.S.	3,618,467	78,444	203,302[3]	226,505[3]	11.4

[1] Excludes the Great Lakes and coastal waters.
[2] Corrected.
[3] State figures do not add to total given because of rounding.
Source: U.S. Department of Commerce, Bureau of the Census, *Current Population Reports.*

Largest Metropolitan Areas[1]

Name	Population: 1970 census[2]	Population: 1979 estimate	Percent change 1970–79	Land area in sq mi	Density per sq mi 1979
New York-Newark-Jersey City SCSA	17,494,149	16,707,208	−4.5	5,498	3,039
New York City	9,973,716	9,175,777	−8.0	1,384	6,650
Nassau-Suffolk	2,555,868	2,674,995	4.7	1,218	2,196
Newark	2,057,468	1,952,632	−5.1	1,008	1,937
Bridgeport[3]	792,814	812,679	2.5	627	1,296
New Brunswick-Perth Amboy	583,813	591,503	1.3	312	1,896
Jersey City	607,839	554,378	−8.8	47	11,795
Long Branch-Asbury Park	461,849	500,241	8.3	476	1,051
Paterson-Clifton-Passaic	460,782	445,003	−3.4	426	1,045
Los Angeles-Long Beach-Anaheim SCSA	9,980,859	9,074,635	−9.1	34,007	267
Los Angeles-Long Beach	7,041,980	7,208,583	2.4	4,069	1,772
Anaheim-Santa Ana-Garden Grove	1,421,233	1,866,052	31.3	782	2,386
Riverside-San Bernardino-Ontario	1,139,149	1,410,381	23.8	27,293	52
Oxnard-Simi Valley-Ventura	378,497	493,236	30.3	1,863	265
Chicago-Gary SCSA	7,608,122	7,673,323	0.9	4,657	1,648
Chicago	6,974,755	7,021,758	0.7	3,719	1,888
Gary-Hammond-East Chicago	633,367	651,565	2.9	938	695
Philadelphia-Wilmington-Trenton SCSA	5,627,719	5,597,632	−0.5	4,946	1,132
Philadelphia	4,824,110	4,764,996	−2.0	3,553	1,341
Wilmington	499,493	515,220	3.2	1,165	442
Trenton	304,116	317,416	4.4	228	1,392
San Francisco-Oakland-San Jose SCSA	4,425,691	4,802,046	8.5	5,390	891
San Francisco-Oakland	3,109,249	3,241,210	4.2	2,480	1,307
San Jose	1,065,313	1,254,419	17.8	1,300	965
Vallejo-Fairfield-Napa	251,129	306,427	22.0	1,610	190
Detroit-Ann Arbor SCSA	4,669,154	4,651,148	−0.4	4,627	1,005
Detroit	4,435,051	4,395,229	−0.9	3,916	1,122
Ann Arbor	234,103	255,919	9.3	711	360
Boston-Lowell-Lawrence SCSA[3]	3,848,593	3,309,460	−14.0	3,114	1,063
Washington, D.C.	2,910,111	3,011,183	3.5	2,812	1,071
Houston-Galveston SCSA	2,169,128	2,873,096	32.4	7,193	399
Houston	1,999,316	2,669,447	33.5	6,794	393
Galveston-Texas City	169,812	203,649	19.9	399	510
Cleveland-Akron-Lorain SCSA	2,999,811	2,857,698	−4.7	2,917	980
Cleveland	2,063,729	1,935,619	−6.2	1,519	1,274
Akron	679,239	655,887	−3.4	903	726
Lorain-Elyria	256,843	266,192	3.6	495	538
Dallas-Fort Worth	2,377,623	2,794,342	17.5	8,360	334
Miami-Fort Lauderdale SCSA	1,887,892	2,413,128	27.8	3,261	740
Miami	1,267,792	1,500,978	18.4	2,042	735
Fort Lauderdale-Hollywood	620,100	912,150	47.1	1,219	748
St. Louis	2,410,884	2,386,168	−1.0	4,935	484
Pittsburgh	2,401,362	2,272,542	−5.4	3,049	745
Baltimore	2,071,016	2,148,362	3.7	2,259	951
Minneapolis-St. Paul	1,965,391	2,089,467	6.3	4,647	450
Seattle-Tacoma SCSA	1,836,949	1,982,360	7.9	5,902	336
Seattle-Everett	1,424,605	1,527,804	7.2	4,226	362
Tacoma	412,344	454,556	10.2	1,676	271
Atlanta	1,595,517	1,864,689	16.9	4,326	431
San Diego	1,357,854	1,775,040	30.7	4,261	417
Cincinnati-Hamilton SCSA	1,613,414	1,645,889	2.0	2,620	628
Cincinnati	1,387,207	1,389,868	0.2	2,149	647
Hamilton-Middletown	226,207	256,021	13.2	471	544
Milwaukee-Racine SCSA	1,574,722	1,608,477	2.1	1,793	897
Milwaukee	1,403,884	1,429,791	1.9	1,456	982
Racine	170,838	178,686	4.6	337	530
Denver-Boulder	1,239,545	1,561,973	26.0	4,651	336
Tampa-St. Petersburg	1,088,549	1,444,091	32.7	2,045	706
Phoenix	971,228	1,346,053	38.6	9,155	147
Kansas City	1,273,926	1,330,042	4.4	3,341	398

[1] Standard Metropolitan Statistical Area, SMSA, unless otherwise indicated; SCSA is a Standard Consolidated Statistical Area, which may be comprised of SMSA's.
[2] Revised. [3] New England County Metropolitan Area.
Sources: U.S. Dept. of Commerce, Bureau of the Census, *Current Population Reports*; U.S. Dept. of Justice, FBI, *Uniform Crime Reports for the United States, 1979.*

Population Change

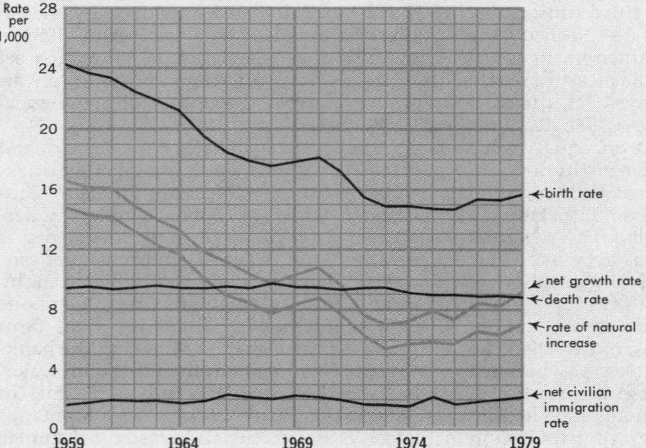

Source: U.S. Department of Commerce, Bureau of the Census, *Current Population Reports.*

Marriage and Divorce Rates

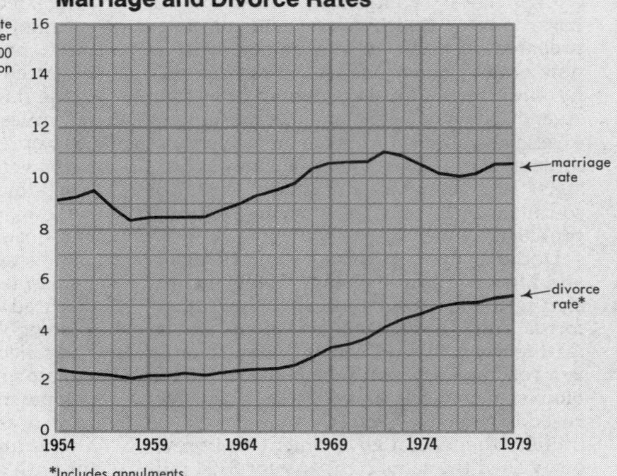

*Includes annulments.

Source: U.S. Department of Health, Education, and Welfare, Public Health Service, *Monthly Vital Statistics Report.*

Church Membership

Religious body	Total clergy	Inclusive membership
Baptist bodies		
American Baptist Association	5,700	1,500,000
American Baptist Churches in the U.S.A.	7,299	1,271,000
Baptist General Conference	1,325	126,800
Baptist Missionary Association of America	2,500	226,290
Conservative Baptist Association of America	...	225,000
Free Will Baptists	4,525	231,167
General Baptists (General Association of)	1,309	73,046
National Baptist Convention of America	28,754	2,668,799
National Baptist Convention, U.S.A., Inc.	27,500	5,500,000
National Primitive Baptist Convention	636	250,000
Primitive Baptists	...	72,000
Progressive National Baptist Convention	863	521,692
Regular Baptist Churches, General Assn. of	...	244,000
Southern Baptist Convention	56,200	13,372,757
United Free Will Baptist Church	915	100,000
Buddhist Churches of America	108	60,000
Christian and Missionary Alliance	1,640	173,986
Christian Congregation	1,169	83,199
Church of God (Anderson, Ind.)	3,018	175,113
Church of the Brethren	1,911	172,115
Church of the Nazarene	7,745	474,820
Churches of Christ—Christian Churches		
Christian Church (Disciples of Christ)	6,607	1,213,061
Christian Churches and Churches of Christ	7,689	1,054,266
Churches of Christ	...	1,600,000
Community Churches, National Council of	...	190,000
Congregational Christian Churches, Natl. Assn. of	708	100,000
Eastern churches		
American Carpatho-Russian Orth. Greek Catholic Ch.	68	100,000
Antiochian Orthodox Christian Archdiocese of N. Am.	132	152,000
Armenian Apostolic Church of America	34	125,000
Armenian Church of America, Diocese of the (incl. Calif.)	61	450,000
Bulgarian Eastern Orthodox Church	11	86,000
Coptic Orthodox Church	25	100,000
Greek Orthodox Archdiocese of N. and S. America	655	1,950,000
Orthodox Church in America	531	1,000,000
Russian Orth. Ch. in the U.S.A., Patriarchal Parishes of	60	51,500
Russian Orthodox Church Outside Russia	168	55,000
Serbian Eastern Orth. Ch. for the U.S.A. and Canada	64	65,000
Ukrainian Orthodox Church in the U.S.A.	131	87,745
Episcopal Church	12,600	2,841,350
Evangelical Covenant Church of America	770	76,092
Evangelical Free Church of America	1,218	77,592
Friends United Meeting	607	61,366
Independent Fundamental Churches of America	1,366	120,446
Jehovah's Witnesses	none	526,961
Jews	5,300	5,860,900
Latter Day Saints (Mormons)		
Church of Jesus Christ of Latter-day Saints	23,073	2,706,000
Reorganized Church of Jesus Christ of L.D.S.	16,386	188,580
Lutherans		
American Lutheran Church	6,925	2,362,685
Evangelical Lutheran Churches, Association of	532	113,942
Lutheran Church in America	7,944	2,921,090
Lutheran Church—Missouri Synod	7,211	2,623,181
Wisconsin Evangelical Lutheran Synod	1,276	404,564
Mennonite Church	2,596	98,027
Methodists		
African Methodist Episcopal Church	3,938	1,970,000
African Methodist Episcopal Zion Church	6,716	1,125,176
Christian Methodist Episcopal Church	2,259	466,718
Free Methodist Church of North America	1,637	67,394
United Methodist Church	36,066	9,563,711
Wesleyan Church	2,356	100,925
Moravian Church in America	222	53,646
North American Old Roman Catholic Church	123	69,412
Old Order Amish Church	2,140	80,250
Open Bible Standard Churches	797	60,000
Pentecostals		
Apostolic Overcoming Holy Church of God	350	75,000
Assemblies of God	22,584	1,629,014
Church of God	2,737	75,890
Church of God (Cleveland, Tenn.)	9,385	411,385
Church of God in Christ	6,000	425,000
Church of God in Christ, International	1,502	501,000
Church of God of Prophecy	2,370	227,850
Full Gospel Fellowship of Ch. and Min., Intl.	931	59,100
International Church of the Foursquare Gospel	2,690	89,215
Pentecostal Church of God	2,168	110,870
Pentecostal Holiness Church	2,899	86,103
United Pentecostal Church, International	6,063	465,000
Plymouth Brethren	400	79,000
Polish National Catholic Church of America	141	282,411
Presbyterians		
Cumberland Presbyterian Church	722	94,574
Presbyterian Church in America	668	86,885
Presbyterian Church in the U.S.	5,431	852,711
United Presbyterian Church in the U.S.A.	14,092	2,477,364
Reformed bodies		
Christian Reformed Church	990	212,700
Reformed Church in America	1,456	348,417
Roman Catholic Church	59,059	49,812,178
Salvation Army	5,165	414,659
Seventh-day Adventist Church	4,388	553,089
Triumph the Church and Kingdom of God in Christ	1,375	54,307
Unitarian Universalist Association	942	139,052
United Church of Christ	9,692	1,745,533

Table includes churches reporting a membership of 50,000 or more and represents the latest information available.
Source: National Council of Churches, *Yearbook of American and Canadian Churches*, 1981.

(CONSTANT H. JACQUET)

THE ECONOMY

Gross National Product and National Income

in billions of dollars

Item	1965[1]	1970[1]	1979	1980[2]
GROSS NATIONAL PRODUCT	688.1	982.4	2,368.8	2,521.3
By type of expenditure				
Personal consumption expenditures	430.2	618.8	1,509.8	1,626.6
Durable goods	62.8	84.9	213.0	195.7
Nondurable goods	188.6	264.7	596.9	654.1
Services	178.7	269.1	699.8	776.9
Gross private domestic investment	112.0	140.8	387.2	368.5
Fixed investment	102.5	137.0	369.0	357.1
Changes in business inventories	9.5	3.8	18.2	11.4
Net exports of goods and services	7.6	3.9	−4.6	−2.2
Exports	39.5	62.5	257.5	307.0
Imports	32.0	58.5	262.1	309.2
Government purchases of goods and services	138.4	218.9	476.4	528.3
Federal	67.3	95.6	166.6	193.3
State and local	71.1	123.2	309.8	335.0
By major type of product				
Goods output	336.6	456.2	1,030.5	1,079.2
Durable goods	133.6	170.8	423.1	414.7
Nondurable goods	203.1	285.4	607.4	664.5
Services	272.7	424.6	1,085.1	1,199.9
Structures	78.8	101.6	253.2	242.2
NATIONAL INCOME	566.0	798.4	1,924.8	2,024.6
By type of income				
Compensation of employees	396.5	609.2	1,459.2	1,567.2
Proprietors' income	56.7	65.1	130.8	120.5
Rental income of persons	17.1	18.6	26.9	27.3
Corporate profits	77.1	67.9	178.2	152.8
Net interest	18.5	37.5	129.7	156.8
By industry division[3]				
Agriculture, forestry, and fisheries	20.4	24.5	64.0	57.0
Mining and construction	35.9	51.6	132.6	141.9
Manufacturing	170.4	215.4	510.3	513.5
Nondurable goods	65.4	88.1	199.2	215.5
Durable goods	105.0	127.3	311.2	298.1
Transportation	23.1	30.3	78.4	80.2
Communications and public utilities	22.9	32.5	81.9	92.4
Wholesale and retail trade	84.7	122.2	291.4	308.3
Finance, insurance, and real estate	64.0	92.6	238.7	263.8
Services	64.1	103.3	277.9	309.4
Government and government enterprises	75.4	127.4	277.4	297.0
Other	4.7	4.6	...	...

[1] Revised. [2] Second quarter, seasonally adjusted at annual rates.
[3] Without capital consumption adjustment.
Source: U.S. Department of Commerce, Bureau of Economic Analysis, *Survey of Current Business.*

Personal Income Per Capita

State	1950	1960[1]	1970[1]	1979
Alabama	$ 880	$1,510	$2,892	$ 6,962
Alaska	2,384	2,743	4,638	11,219
Arizona	1,330	1,994	3,614	8,423
Arkansas	825	1,358	2,791	6,933
California	1,852	2,711	4,423	10,047
Colorado	1,487	2,247	3,838	9,122
Connecticut	1,875	2,838	4,871	10,129
Delaware	2,132	2,735	4,468	9,327
District of Columbia	2,221	2,823	4,644	10,570
Florida	1,281	1,965	3,698	8,546
Georgia	1,034	1,644	3,300	7,630
Hawaii	1,386	2,289	4,599	9,223
Idaho	1,295	1,811	3,243	7,571
Illinois	1,825	2,616	4,446	9,799
Indiana	1,512	2,149	3,709	8,570
Iowa	1,485	1,960	3,643	8,772
Kansas	1,443	2,084	3,725	9,233
Kentucky	981	1,576	3,076	7,390
Louisiana	1,120	1,649	3,023	7,583
Maine	1,186	1,835	3,250	7,039
Maryland	1,602	2,320	4,267	9,331
Massachusetts	1,633	2,435	4,276	8,893
Michigan	1,701	2,326	4,041	9,403
Minnesota	1,410	2,064	3,819	8,865
Mississippi	755	1,196	2,547	6,178
Missouri	1,431	2,091	3,654	8,251
Montana	1,622	1,983	3,395	7,684
Nebraska	1,490	2,009	3,657	8,684
Nevada	2,018	2,791	4,583	10,521
New Hampshire	1,323	2,160	3,720	8,351
New Jersey	1,834	2,700	4,684	9,747
New Mexico	1,177	1,814	3,045	7,560
New York	1,873	2,703	4,605	9,104
North Carolina	1,037	1,577	3,200	7,385
North Dakota	1,263	1,681	3,077	8,231
Ohio	1,620	2,322	3,949	8,715
Oklahoma	1,143	1,850	3,341	8,509
Oregon	1,620	2,194	3,677	8,938
Pennsylvania	1,541	2,239	3,879	8,558
Rhode Island	1,605	2,186	3,878	8,510
South Carolina	893	1,394	2,951	7,057
South Dakota	1,242	1,758	3,108	7,455
Tennessee	994	1,576	3,079	7,343
Texas	1,349	1,894	3,507	8,788
Utah	1,309	1,954	3,169	7,197
Vermont	1,121	1,864	3,447	7,329
Virginia	1,228	1,884	3,677	8,587
Washington	1,674	2,354	3,997	9,565
West Virginia	1,065	1,592	3,038	7,372
Wisconsin	1,477	2,178	3,712	8,484
Wyoming	1,668	2,210	3,672	9,992
United States	1,496	2,201	3,893	8,773

[1] Revised.
Source: U.S. Department of Commerce, Bureau of Economic Analysis, *Survey of Current Business.*

Average Employee Earnings

September figures

Industry	HOURLY 1979	HOURLY 1980[1]	WEEKLY 1979	WEEKLY 1980[1]
MANUFACTURING				
Durable goods				
Lumber and wood products	$6.30	$6.80	$252.63	$267.92
Furniture and fixtures	5.18	5.57	202.02	213.89
Stone, clay, and glass products	6.99	7.68	291.48	316.42
Primary metal industries	9.16	9.95	378.31	397.01
Fabricated metal products	6.95	7.60	283.56	307.04
Nonelectrical machinery	7.48	8.27	312.66	339.90
Electrical equipment and supplies	6.47	7.15	262.04	283.86
Transportation equipment	8.59	9.59	349.61	388.40
Instruments and related products	6.21	6.90	252.75	276.69
Nondurable goods				
Food and kindred products	6.32	6.93	256.59	279.28
Tobacco manufactures	6.43	7.44	252.06	280.49
Textile mill products	4.82	5.23	196.66	207.63
Apparel and related products	4.27	4.70	150.73	165.44
Paper and allied products	7.33	8.05	312.99	341.32
Printing and publishing	7.08	7.72	268.33	287.96
Chemicals and allied products	7.74	8.44	323.53	384.57
Petroleum and coal products	9.50	10.33	424.65	446.26
Rubber and plastics products	6.03	6.65	244.22	268.66
Leather and leather products	4.29	4.59	157.87	167.08
NONMANUFACTURING				
Metal mining	9.63	10.49	393.87	402.82
Coal mining	10.37	10.88	423.10	446.08
Oil and gas extraction	7.78	8.70	350.88	395.85
Contract construction	9.52	10.18	361.76	386.84
Local and suburban transportation	6.89	7.03	274.91	276.28
Electric, gas, and sanitary services	8.48	9.09	353.62	378.14
Wholesale trade	6.52	7.06	252.98	271.10
Retail trade	4.57	4.94	139.84	148.69
Hotels, tourist courts, and motels[2]	4.04	4.49	126.05	136.05
Banking	4.60	5.03	167.90	181.08

[1] Preliminary. [2] Excludes tips. Source: U.S. Dept. of Labor, Bureau of Labor Statistics, *Employment and Earnings.*

Unemployment Trends

quarterly averages, seasonally adjusted

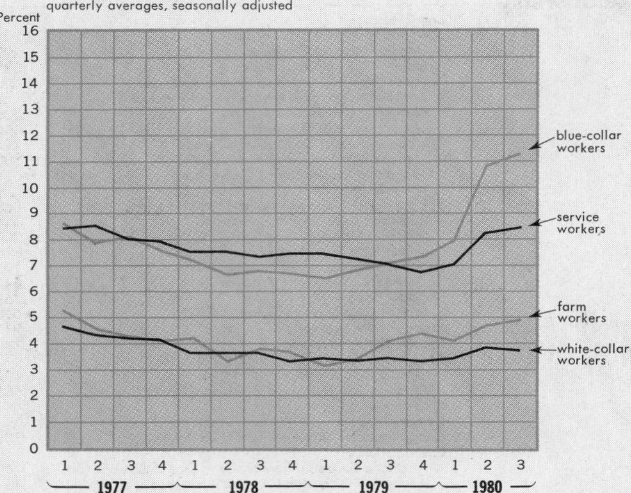

Source: U.S. Department of Labor, Bureau of Labor Statistics, *Monthly Labor Review.*

Value of Agricultural Products, with Fisheries, 1979

in thousands of dollars

State	PRINCIPAL CROPS: Corn (grain)	Hay	Soybeans	Wheat	Tobacco	Cotton (lint)	Potatoes	LIVESTOCK AND PRODUCTS: Cattle, calves	Hogs, pigs	Sheep, lambs	Milk[1]	Eggs[2]	Chickens[2]	FISHERIES[3]
Alabama	90,335	61,236	340,313	9,633	1,101	96,307	11,972	409,365	129,278	[4]	82,068	180,676	9,426	49,981
Alaska	...	2,054	...	...	...	...	978	622	218	[5]	2,301	667	79	597,034
Arizona	16,043	113,856	...	35,968	...	448,632	5,729	365,632	22,561	13,349	121,346	4,360	168	...
Arkansas	5,565	67,512	894,040	53,655	...	182,707	...	430,968	85,612	...	90,288	218,175	14,018	...
California	100,386	616,428	...	237,180	...	1,098,413	103,928	1,075,076	35,863	47,526	1,459,449	368,851	8,835	227,473
Colorado	239,395	186,528	...	245,641	...	...	40,154	1,120,273	62,428	43,351	113,038	22,046	972	...
Connecticut	...	12,600	...	...	26,678	...	2,717	13,779	1,631	176	79,013	60,344	1,748	6,900
Delaware	48,547	3,068	49,290	4,284	...	...	3,538	5,066	7,143	[4]	16,344	7,931	547	638
Florida	54,378	28,899	86,704	[4]	30,476	1,092	30,435	453,915	55,997	[4]	285,267	130,217	4,546	124,002
Georgia	297,213	60,255	364,560	20,720	142,361	45,235	...	309,898	238,559	[4]	168,998	336,213	19,480	27,738
Hawaii	...	...	...	...	...	...	...	29,127	7,551	[4]	25,350	14,007	277	10,659
Idaho	10,463	216,615	...	261,001	...	...	282,240	528,277	9,685	22,556	194,911	8,000	121	35
Illinois	3,327,296	205,247	2,320,164	220,805	...	...	1,252	625,072	1,102,633	6,619	288,222	64,207	1,952	1,024
Indiana	1,627,192	121,475	978,588	173,219	19,045	...	5,757	367,488	695,659	5,181	268,830	171,201	5,765	66
Iowa	3,820,160	380,466	1,862,760	8,791	...	...	878	1,680,796	2,265,962	12,302	453,936	67,797	3,095	818
Kansas	447,174	280,084	239,772	1,539,000	...	...	...	1,779,632	316,650	9,319	157,002	19,723	1,735	35
Kentucky	344,760	148,865	334,490	42,978	498,945	...	...	484,991	179,396	836	263,070	26,721	1,139	...
Louisiana	6,199	38,042	568,960	2,948	109	205,013	897	236,332	17,253	206	135,793	35,159	2,211	198,508
Maine	...	22,330	...	...	...	...	117,875	14,634	1,857	371	83,642	110,263	4,338	80,260
Maryland	167,879	35,148	71,610	17,083	32,525	...	794	64,529	26,698	545	192,280	19,865	1,121	36,945
Massachusetts	...	20,016	...	...	10,833	...	4,862	11,563	8,201	226	74,598	20,849	1,055	175,544
Michigan	570,000	147,571	174,552	124,894	...	...	40,979	283,790	133,106	4,651	582,498	62,125	2,504	3,555
Minnesota	1,242,300	388,290	995,792	331,308	...	...	40,883	770,878	708,613	10,690	1,035,214	89,685	1,142	1,946
Mississippi	17,732	57,915	743,125	15,088	...	428,736	[4]	315,436	52,391	[4]	103,297	94,083	7,019	33,342
Missouri	548,784	294,395	1,120,770	264,000	7,949	47,089	...	1,324,974	653,512	4,371	322,498	61,920	6,268	203
Montana	924	246,733	...	410,510	...	...	7,920	646,595	28,343	10,265	33,981	9,271	126	...
Nebraska	1,864,725	323,765	322,966	312,120	...	...	7,352	1,894,752	632,639	5,183	153,846	28,872	820	25
Nevada	...	76,362	...	6,577	...	476	13,118	121,386	1,522	4,304	22,885	77	4	...
New Hampshire	...	13,160	...	...	...	...	...	8,969	2,219	222	44,563	12,826	958	3,327
New Jersey	22,140	20,340	45,225	5,904	...	...	8,500	17,115	6,411	248	63,084	17,956	702	53,034
New Mexico	24,198	78,744	...	35,024	...	36,322	3,933	446,324	11,304	12,851	67,247	18,707	234	...
New York	151,938	296,337	3,319	23,616	...	...	56,423	202,883	17,168	1,678	1,278,276	80,104	2,804	38,966
North Carolina	372,476	38,285	290,989	30,240	869,733	13,728	14,304	175,031	331,869	194	200,790	173,788	21,066	58,454
North Dakota	49,590	225,420	32,538	949,826	...	...	51,072	529,045	44,615	6,503	95,790	2,819	79	101
Ohio	1,022,753	200,133	899,496	253,440	22,640	...	11,974	389,061	320,877	13,463	517,345	96,023	4,595	2,559
Oklahoma	23,513	219,635	43,643	844,740	...	142,771	...	1,461,511	46,895	3,180	136,639	38,899	1,335	...
Oregon	3,410	151,767	...	217,778	...	...	68,211	360,813	16,517	12,765	136,772	26,451	630	65,221
Pennsylvania	340,504	229,676	14,957	33,706	13,702	...	29,100	309,952	90,553	2,588	1,043,644	178,055	14,858	251
Rhode Island	...	1,296	...	...	...	...	4,395	534	1,318	[4]	6,620	3,577	117	36,006
South Carolina	114,016	24,408	252,984	14,028	166,553	35,052	...	116,158	70,577	[4]	70,792	77,660	3,698	25,792
South Dakota	400,710	265,153	122,587	218,466	...	...	3,609	1,143,247	284,229	38,480	179,404	16,213	363	309
Tennessee	146,661	103,122	435,051	37,613	142,983	51,517	3,077	364,113	213,178	316	258,175	48,736	2,677	...
Texas	383,670	325,791	116,162	531,300	...	1,555,840	20,540	3,466,033	128,270	62,084	454,371	153,492	6,388	160,200
Utah	4,437	108,391	...	24,054	...	...	5,590	150,829	5,341	17,219	112,812	14,438	264	...
Vermont	...	51,850	...	...	...	...	1,029	49,499	1,768	349	272,593	7,687	229	...
Virginia	148,031	99,400	91,884	25,515	158,224	62	11,944	318,426	95,132	6,910	238,726	51,880	3,070	84,632
Washington	37,997	172,130	...	460,200	...	...	114,974	309,470	13,448	2,297	342,942	49,712	1,860	115,959
West Virginia	11,585	36,701	...	1,343	2,575	...	...	81,637	10,004	3,841	44,232	10,294	470	14
Wisconsin	752,003	395,483	58,174	8,000	29,414	...	68,040	671,663	247,779	4,180	2,579,125	40,919	3,128	4,862
Wyoming	6,055	121,239	...	21,945	...	...	4,176	356,703	3,780	27,078	13,923	698	15	...
TOTAL U.S.	18,863,137	7,334,216	13,875,465	8,074,141	2,175,846	4,389,042	1,205,149	26,292,862	9,443,969	418,472	14,967,830	3,355,239	170,051	2,226,418

[1] Farm value. [2] Gross income, Dec. 1, 1978–Nov. 30, 1979. [3] Preliminary. [4] Estimates discontinued. [5] Deficit.
Sources: U.S. Department of Agriculture, Statistical Reporting Service, Crop Reporting Board, *Crop Values, Meat Animals, Milk, Poultry*; U.S. Department of Commerce, National Oceanic and Atmospheric Administration, National Marine Fisheries Service, *Fisheries of the United States, 1979.*

Income by Industrial Source, 1979

State and region	SOURCES OF PERSONAL INCOME: Total personal income	Farm income	Govt. income disbursements: Federal	Govt. income disbursements: State, local	Private nonfarm income	SOURCES OF LABOUR AND PROPRIETORS' INCOME % OF TOTAL: Total	Farms	Mining	Construction	Mfg.	Wholesale, retail trade	Finance, insurance, real estate	Transportation, communications, public util.	Service	Govt.	Other
United States	$1,930,742	$41,763	$77,340	$159,849	$1,209,719	$1,488,671	%2.8	%1.4	%6.1	%26.0	%11.2	%5.8	%7.7	%17.0	%15.9	%5.8
New England	109,504	443	2,952	8,438	69,434	81,267	0.5	0.1	4.7	31.7	15.9	6.4	6.1	20.0	14.0	0.6
Maine	7,722	99	452	625	4,514	5,689	1.7	0.1	6.0	28.4	16.2	4.2	6.4	16.8	18.9	1.3
New Hampshire	7,407	20	189	508	4,462	5,179	0.4	0.2	7.4	33.7	17.0	5.1	5.5	17.0	13.4	0.3
Vermont	3,613	125	90	304	2,221	2,739	4.6	0.5	6.3	29.6	15.1	4.3	6.6	18.4	14.4	0.2
Massachusetts	51,303	101	1,355	4,303	33,067	38,826	0.3	0.1	4.0	29.2	16.1	6.3	6.6	22.4	14.6	0.4
Rhode Island	7,906	9	261	689	4,688	5,648	0.2	0.1	4.6	33.0	15.4	5.6	4.6	19.1	16.8	0.6
Connecticut	31,553	90	605	2,008	20,484	23,187	0.4	0.2	4.8	36.3	15.4	7.9	5.5	18.0	11.3	0.2
Mideast	383,590	2,018	17,031	33,189	241,288	293,536	0.7	0.6	4.5	26.0	15.6	7.1	8.3	19.9	17.1	0.2
New York	160,662	628	3,589	15,438	102,755	122,411	0.5	0.2	3.5	23.3	16.0	9.8	9.0	21.9	15.5	0.3
New Jersey	71,461	144	1,853	5,612	42,713	50,322	0.3	0.1	5.0	29.8	17.3	5.2	8.8	18.4	14.8	0.3
Pennsylvania	100,398	862	2,669	7,176	66,644	77,351	1.1	1.8	5.5	33.8	15.0	5.0	8.0	16.9	12.7	0.2
Delaware	5,428	121	174	442	3,637	4,374	2.8	0.1	6.1	38.4	13.6	4.4	5.9	14.4	14.1	0.2
Maryland	38,706	264	3,346	3,499	19,578	26,687	1.0	0.1	6.6	17.1	17.2	5.4	6.5	20.1	25.6	0.4
District of Columbia	6,934	—	5,400	1,032	5,960	12,392	—	[1]	2.1	2.8	6.5	4.7	5.6	25.7	51.9	0.7
Great Lakes	376,443	6,988	7,314	29,373	253,879	297,554	2.3	0.8	5.5	36.9	15.6	4.8	6.9	14.7	12.3	0.2
Michigan	86,572	999	1,277	7,846	59,416	69,539	1.4	0.5	4.9	42.4	14.0	3.9	5.5	14.1	13.1	0.2
Ohio	93,517	1,000	2,116	6,676	64,962	74,754	1.3	1.1	5.4	38.6	15.4	4.3	7.1	14.7	11.8	0.3
Indiana	46,279	1,133	899	3,230	31,264	36,885	3.1	0.8	6.0	40.8	14.8	4.2	6.8	12.2	11.2	0.1
Illinois	110,032	2,168	2,469	8,249	72,382	85,268	2.5	1.0	5.7	29.6	17.5	6.4	8.1	16.4	12.6	0.2
Wisconsin	40,043	1,689	552	3,372	25,495	31,108	5.4	0.2	5.7	35.6	15.3	4.7	6.1	14.0	12.6	0.4
Plains	147,687	10,337	4,366	11,719	88,061	114,483	9.0	1.1	6.4	22.8	17.6	5.4	8.5	14.7	14.1	0.4
Minnesota	31,910	1,994	1,323	2,433	23,194	28,987	6.9	1.6	6.5	24.4	18.3	5.6	7.8	15.4	13.1	0.4
Iowa	25,455	2,107	387	2,028	14,383	18,904	11.1	0.3	6.6	26.4	17.1	5.4	6.6	13.4	12.8	0.3
Missouri	40,155	1,531	1,442	2,911	26,362	32,246	4.7	0.6	6.0	25.6	17.7	5.5	10.1	15.9	13.5	0.4
North Dakota	5,408	704	309	455	2,609	4,077	17.3	3.3	9.0	6.2	18.8	4.4	8.5	13.5	18.8	0.2
South Dakota	5,137	766	275	428	2,393	3,862	19.8	1.6	6.2	10.3	17.8	4.6	7.1	14.0	18.2	0.4
Nebraska	13,668	1,622	493	1,179	7,301	10,595	15.3	0.4	6.1	15.3	17.3	6.2	9.4	13.8	15.8	0.4
Kansas	21,873	1,616	793	1,584	11,819	15,812	10.2	2.1	6.2	22.1	16.6	5.0	15.1	13.6	15.0	0.1
Southeast	380,373	8,853	20,536	31,324	226,995	287,709	3.1	2.5	6.7	23.8	16.9	5.1	8.0	15.4	18.0	0.5
Virginia	44,628	418	5,040	3,549	23,888	32,893	1.3	1.9	6.9	19.6	15.0	4.9	7.2	16.7	26.1	0.4
West Virginia	128,751	2,166	7,035	10,820	77,858	10,580	0.5	16.9	7.2	23.8	13.8	3.1	8.6	12.0	13.9	0.2
Kentucky	26,066	784	1,198	1,935	16,047	19,965	3.9	7.4	6.7	26.0	15.0	4.0	7.7	13.3	15.7	0.3
Tennessee	32,162	532	1,621	2,672	20,976	25,800	2.1	0.8	5.7	30.0	17.2	5.0	7.1	15.3	16.6	0.2
North Carolina	41,399	1,291	1,943	3,561	26,272	33,066	3.9	0.3	5.5	32.6	16.3	4.4	6.8	13.3	16.6	0.3
South Carolina	20,690	365	1,365	1,847	12,636	16,212	2.3	0.2	6.6	33.7	14.4	4.2	6.3	12.1	19.8	0.4
Georgia	39,044	899	2,361	3,381	24,935	31,577	2.8	0.4	5.2	23.7	19.3	5.7	9.6	14.5	18.2	0.6
Florida	75,713	1,688	1,823	5,954	40,139	50,604	3.3	0.4	7.6	13.6	19.9	7.3	8.8	20.9	17.3	0.9
Alabama	26,240	567	1,620	2,333	15,769	20,287	2.8	2.1	6.1	28.7	15.3	4.5	7.4	13.2	19.5	0.4
Mississippi	15,007	801	789	1,320	8,728	11,638	6.9	1.8	6.5	26.6	15.4	4.4	7.0	12.9	18.1	0.4
Louisiana	30,467	436	968	2,491	20,061	23,956	1.8	7.8	10.2	17.0	17.7	4.7	10.3	15.6	14.4	0.5
Arkansas	15,114	1,024	504	1,120	8,482	11,130	9.2	1.0	6.5	26.8	16.0	4.4	7.9	13.1	14.6	0.5
Southwest	172,212	4,346	8,002	13,429	107,266	133,043	3.3	6.0	8.3	18.5	18.3	5.6	8.0	15.3	16.1	0.6
Oklahoma	24,607	1,166	1,297	1,763	13,610	17,836	6.5	8.7	6.2	17.5	16.7	5.0	8.1	13.7	17.2	0.4
Texas	17,585	2,421	4,938	8,544	76,614	92,517	2.6	5.7	8.4	19.9	19.0	5.7	8.2	15.3	14.6	0.6
New Mexico	9,383	366	737	1,074	4,969	7,147	5.1	9.3	7.9	7.1	15.8	4.3	8.2	16.7	25.4	0.2
Arizona	20,637	393	1,029	2,048	12,073	15,543	2.5	3.6	10.3	16.6	17.1	6.1	6.8	16.7	19.8	0.5
Rocky Mountain	52,479	1,613	3,005	4,723	32,094	41,435	3.9	5.8	8.4	15.4	17.3	5.5	8.8	15.8	18.7	0.4
Montana	6,040	229	317	605	3,288	4,439	5.2	4.5	8.0	11.0	18.5	4.7	11.0	15.9	20.8	0.4
Idaho	6,852	475	309	578	3,949	5,312	8.9	1.7	8.2	18.3	17.2	4.9	7.8	15.4	16.7	0.9
Wyoming	4,465	259	186	374	2,826	3,646	7.1	23.2	11.9	4.9	13.6	3.3	9.5	10.7	15.4	0.4
Colorado	25,285	541	1,482	2,245	15,778	20,046	2.7	4.2	7.8	16.7	17.6	6.4	8.4	17.2	18.6	0.4
Utah	9,838	110	711	921	6,251	7,992	1.4	5.5	8.5	17.6	17.5	5.0	8.9	14.9	20.4	0.3
Far West	295,541	6,955	12,272	26,197	183,311	228,734	3.0	0.6	6.6	21.7	17.1	6.4	7.2	19.7	16.8	0.9
Washington	37,552	1,111	1,921	3,387	22,809	29,227	3.8	0.3	8.7	22.4	17.4	5.5	7.1	15.7	18.2	1.2
Oregon	22,587	593	617	2,050	14,431	17,691	3.4	0.3	7.4	25.5	18.9	5.6	7.7	15.4	15.1	0.7
Nevada	7,386	75	315	615	5,002	6,006	1.2	1.5	10.2	5.5	15.5	4.9	8.1	37.2	15.5	0.4
California	228,017	5,176	9,421	20,145	141,069	175,810	2.9	0.6	6.0	21.7	17.0	6.6	7.2	20.2	16.8	1.0
Alaska	4,555	6	687	702	2,961	4,355	0.1	6.0	10.1	7.3	12.3	4.2	12.7	14.4	31.9	1.0
Hawaii	8,356	204	1,176	745	4,429	6,554	3.1	[1]	7.7	5.6	16.5	7.7	9.6	20.1	29.3	0.4

Dollar figures in millions. Percentages may not add to 100.0 because of rounding.
[1] Less than 0.05%.
Source: U.S. Department of Commerce, Bureau of Economic Analysis, *Survey of Current Business*.

Farms and Farm Income

State	Number of farms 1980 [1,2]	Land in farms 1980 in 000 acres [1,2]	CASH RECEIPTS, 1979, IN $000 [1] — Farm marketings: Total	Crops	Livestock and products
Alabama	54,000	13,100	2,053,040	770,576	1,282,464
Alaska	310	1,700 [3]	12,358	8,159	4,199
Arizona	5,700	40,400	1,765,780	911,902	853,878
Arkansas	57,000	16,800	3,161,996	1,599,901	1,562,095
California	60,000	32,300	12,589,963	8,404,724	4,185,239
Colorado	25,500	37,700	3,180,431	716,616	2,463,815
Connecticut	3,800	450	253,524	96,023	157,501
Delaware	3,000	620	357,892	121,174	236,718
Florida	35,000	13,800	3,892,905	2,897,529	995,376
Georgia	54,000	16,000	2,962,186	1,340,158	1,622,028
Hawaii	4,000	2,290	418,853	340,626	78,227
Idaho	23,500	15,500	1,860,199	956,143	904,056
Illinois	105,000	28,600	6,991,819	4,591,584	2,368,394
Indiana	88,000	16,900	3,968,782	2,372,132	1,596,650
Iowa	119,000	34,000	9,497,989	3,874,101	5,590,757
Kansas	72,000	48,200	5,885,687	2,354,749	3,530,938
Kentucky	94,000	14,300	2,055,136	1,140,977	914,159
Louisiana	34,500	10,200	1,637,895	1,110,702	527,193
Maine	8,000	1,640	442,027	139,184	302,843
Maryland	16,400	2,780	879,715	313,336	566,379
Massachusetts	5,200	650	255,719	137,838	117,881
Michigan	63,000	10,500	2,485,806	1,338,443	1,147,363
Minnesota	104,000	30,300	5,566,256	2,607,251	2,946,996
Mississippi	48,000	14,500	2,083,506	1,191,844	891,662
Missouri	117,000	32,300	4,345,416	1,787,642	2,557,774
Montana	21,500	62,000	1,371,383	571,071	800,312
Nebraska	63,000	47,800	6,021,669	2,120,481	3,895,642
Nevada	2,000	8,990	207,217	51,270	155,947
New Hampshire	3,200	580	93,154	26,001	67,153
New Jersey	7,700	990	403,024	287,803	115,221
New Mexico	11,100	46,700	1,121,375	240,325	881,050
New York	44,000	9,800	2,191,976	637,056	1,554,920
North Carolina	98,000	12,300	3,397,368	1,973,525	1,423,843
North Dakota	40,000	41,690	2,330,478	1,641,206	689,272
Ohio	96,000	16,200	3,476,122	2,083,376	1,392,746
Oklahoma	71,000	34,500	3,230,031	1,127,234	2,102,797
Oregon	30,500	18,600	1,562,064	926,263	635,801
Pennsylvania	61,000	9,000	2,576,045	792,988	1,783,057
Rhode Island	720	63	32,313	19,163	13,150
South Carolina	35,000	6,500	1,059,538	685,254	374,284
South Dakota	41,000	45,450	2,287,164	594,188	1,692,976
Tennessee	92,000	13,600	1,779,496	824,056	955,440
Texas	159,000	138,400	9,971,043	3,878,942	6,092,101
Utah	12,000	12,600	471,235	115,393	346,394
Vermont	6,300	1,740	342,510	23,129	319,381
Virginia	60,000	9,700	1,347,590	556,342	791,248
Washington	33,500	16,100	2,400,993	1,622,475	778,518
West Virginia	19,500	4,180	231,213	62,844	168,369
Wisconsin	94,000	18,600	4,267,098	739,587	3,527,511
Wyoming	7,200	35,100	681,706	96,434	677,247
TOTAL U.S.	2,309,130	1,046,713	131,458,685	62,819,720	68,638,965

[1] Preliminary. [2] Places with annual sales of agricultural products of $1,000 or more.
[3] Exclusive of grazing land leased from the U.S. Government. Alaska farmland totals about 70,000 acres.
Source: U.S. Department of Agriculture, Statistical Reporting Service and Economic Research Service.

Principal Minerals, Production and Value, 1979

State	Principal nonfuel minerals, in order of value	Value ($000)	% of U.S. total prod.	Crude Petroleum: Production (000 bbl)	Crude Petroleum: Value ($000)	Natural Gas: Production (000,000 cu ft)	Natural Gas: Value ($000)	Coal[1]: Production (000 ST)	Coal[1]: Value ($000)
Alabama	Cement, stone, lime, clays	$336,367	1.40	19,161	$286,281	85,815	$174,977	23,873	...
Alaska	Sand and gravel, stone, gold, gem stones	123,419	.51	511,335	5,493,596	220,754	114,351	706	...
Arizona	Copper, molybdenum, cement, silver	2,490,481	10.39	472	3,913	247	102	11,389	...
Arkansas	Bromine, cement, stone, sand and gravel	302,622	1.26	18,869	277,940	109,452	104,964	521	...
California	Cement, sand and gravel, boron, stone	1,769,675	7.38	352,268	4,438,577	248,206	423,191	...	...
Colorado	Molybdenum, cement, sand and gravel, vanadium	826,098	3.44	32,324	424,737	191,239	269,647	18,135	...
Connecticut	Stone, sand and gravel, feldspar, lime	69,236	.28	...	...	...	...	...	...
Delaware	Sand and gravel, magnesium compounds, clay	3,290	...	...	...	...	...	...	...
Florida	Phosphate rock, stone, cement, sand and gravel	1,269,271	5.29	47,168	616,486	50,190	78,899	...	...
Georgia	Clays, stone, cement, sand and gravel	698,690	2.91	...	...	...	...	50	...
Hawaii	Cement, stone, sand and gravel, pumice	63,904	.26	...	...	...	...	...	...
Idaho	Silver, phosphate rock, lead, zinc	437,885	1.82	...	...	...	...	...	...
Illinois	Stone, sand and gravel, cement, lime	478,405	1.99	21,793	511,978	1,585	2,949	59,507	...
Indiana	Cement, stone, sand and gravel, lime	326,086	1.36	4,715	111,085	350	369	27,502	...
Iowa	Cement, stone, sand and gravel, gypsum	277,901	1.15	...	...	...	...	724	...
Kansas	Cement, salt, stone, sand and gravel	263,392	1.09	56,995	1,253,894	797,762	603,108	857	...
Kentucky	Stone, lime, cement, sand and gravel	207,927	.86	5,514	124,506	59,520	56,365	149,836	...
Louisiana	Sulfur, salt, sand and gravel, cement	455,276	1.89	489,687	5,582,432	7,266,217	8,100,795	...	...
Maine	Sand and gravel, cement, stone, gem stones	45,910	.19	...	...	...	...	...	...
Maryland	Stone, cement, sand and gravel, clays	192,962	.80	...	...	28	29	2,717	...
Massachusetts	Stone, sand and gravel, lime, clays	92,546	.38	...	...	...	...	...	...
Michigan	Iron ore, cement, sand and gravel, magnesium compounds	1,506,476	6.28	34,862	520,832	159,731	277,932	...	...
Minnesota	Iron ore, sand and gravel, stone, lime	2,067,990	8.62	...	...	...	...	...	...
Mississippi	Sand and gravel, cement, clays, magnesium compounds	107,689	.44	37,327	520,708	144,077	230,523	...	...
Missouri	Lead, cement, stone, lime	1,159,835	4.83	91	2,216	...	...	6,487	...
Montana	Copper, silver, cement, sand and gravel	291,287	1.21	29,957	371,181	53,888	65,258	32,147	...
Nebraska	Cement, sand and gravel, stone, lime	99,181	.41	6,068	101,673	3,208	2,727	...	...
Nevada	Gold, barite sand and gravel, diatomite	238,150	.99	1,235	14,202	...	...	...	...
New Hampshire	Sand and gravel, stone, clays, gem stones	23,258	.09	...	...	...	...	...	...
New Jersey	Stone, sand and gravel, zinc, titanium concentrate	151,689	.63	...	...	...	...	...	...
New Mexico	Copper, potassium salts, molybdenum, sand and gravel	694,448	2.89	79,649	1,119,861	1,181,363	1,613,742	15,037	...
New York	Cement, stone, salt, sand and gravel	453,710	1.89	855	20,332	15,500	19,623	...	...
North Carolina	Stone, phosphate rock, sand and gravel, cement	340,411	1.42	...	...	...	...	...	...
North Dakota	Sand and gravel, salt, lime, clays	21,234	.08	30,914	371,000	18,468	23,639	14,963[6]	...
Ohio	Stone, lime, sand and gravel, cement	607,320	2.53	11,953	269,129	123,431	222,824	43,495	...
Oklahoma	Cement, stone, sand and gravel, helium	201,022	.84	143,642	2,158,526	1,835,366	2,062,951	4,782	...
Oregon	Stone, sand and gravel, cement, nickel	165,207	.68	...	...	2	4	...	...
Pennsylvania	Cement, stone, lime, sand and gravel	722,614	3.01	2,874	69,235	96,313	127,711	89,167	...
Rhode Island	Sand and gravel, stone, gem stones	7,886	.03	...	...	...	...	...	...
South Carolina	Cement, stone, sand and gravel, clays	201,711	.84	...	...	...	...	...	...
South Dakota	Gold, cement, stone, sand and gravel	148,686	.62	846	21,387	914	1,926	...	...
Tennessee	Stone, cement, sand and gravel, clays	385,744	1.60	614	12,440	941	1,600	9,303	...
Texas	Cement, sulfur, stone, sand and gravel	1,406,168	5.86	1,018,094	12,848,346	7,174,623	8,850,782	26,634[6]	...
Utah	Copper, gold, molybdenum, cement	753,384	3.14	27,728	316,376	58,605	41,961	11,834	...
Vermont	Stone, asbestos, sand and gravel, talc	54,136	.22	...	...	...	...	...	...
Virginia	Stone, cement, lime, sand and gravel	309,765	1.29	4	92	8,544	14,365	37,038	...
Washington	Cement, sand and gravel, stone, lime	224,948	.93	...	...	...	...	5,050	...
West Virginia	Stone, sand and gravel, cement, salt	118,595	.49	2,406	67,368	150,505	158,030	112,381	...
Wisconsin	Sand and gravel, stone, iron ore, lime	179,682	.74	...	...	...	...	...	...
Wyoming	Sodium carbonate, clays, iron ore, stone	590,176	2.46	131,890	1,121,063	414,416	468,290	71,823	...
TOTAL U.S.		$23,964,000	100.00	3,121,310	$39,051,332	20,471,260	$24,113,634	781,134	...

[1] Bituminous coal, unless otherwise noted. [2] Lignite only.
Sources: U.S. Department of the Interior, *Minerals Yearbook*; Department of Energy.

Services

Kind of service	Number of services 1976	Number of services 1977	Number of employees[1] 1976	Number of employees[1] 1977
Hotels and other lodging places	46,122	45,399	890,512	915,178
Hotels, tourist courts, and motels	35,147	35,109	829,157	859,001
Rooming and boarding houses	4,010	3,579	33,282	30,168
Camps and trailering parks	3,957	3,939	15,434	15,499
Sporting and recreational camps	1,844	2,267	8,990	9,749
Personal services	159,719	162,161	880,718	901,047
Laundry, cleaning, garment services	44,869	44,462	356,130	357,102
Photographic studios, portrait	5,441	6,105	28,563	32,066
Beauty shops	70,174	71,311	274,485	280,645
Barber shops	11,521	11,029	27,586	27,620
Shoe repair and hat cleaning shops	3,100	2,935	7,537	6,994
Funeral service and crematories	14,472	14,733	71,121	71,209
Miscellaneous personal services	9,692	11,023	113,062	123,563
Business services	133,804	145,005	2,126,688	2,307,384
Advertising	9,589	10,203	114,325	120,024
Credit reporting and collection	5,627	5,741	60,210	61,492
Mailing, reproduction, stenographic	11,755	12,297	93,081	95,067
Building services	22,740	23,901	383,502	408,157
Employment agencies	6,314	7,091	72,768	76,084
Temporary help supply services	3,331	3,570	233,322	293,728
Computer and data processing services	7,476	9,109	174,595	199,177
Research and development laboratories	2,004	2,013	73,189	75,929
Management and public relations	20,192	23,095	218,386	240,838
Detective and protective services	5,841	6,312	248,050	268,684
Equipment rental and leasing	10,327	11,002	80,911	85,134
Photofinishing laboratories	2,341	2,478	56,292	60,683
Auto repair, services, and garages	91,653	97,327	444,165	477,370
Automobile rentals, without drivers	7,256	7,386	73,638	76,910
Automobile parking	7,001	7,153	32,910	33,709
Automotive repair shops	69,468	73,970	282,297	305,447
Automotive services, except repair	7,520	8,374	53,073	59,473
Car washes	5,286	5,564	40,792	44,901
Miscellaneous repair services	47,874	49,483	242,767	254,140
Radio and television repair	9,112	9,079	37,674	38,114
Motion pictures	14,748	15,034	184,607	180,933
Motion picture production	3,220	3,529	52,963	55,495
Motion picture distribution	1,126	1,129	15,358	15,940
Motion picture theatres	10,289	10,217	115,752	108,862

Kind of service	Number of services 1976	Number of services 1977	Number of employees[1] 1976	Number of employees[1] 1977
Amusement and recreation services	44,903	46,842	563,380	585,304
Producers, orchestras, entertainers	6,112	6,451	63,110	67,497
Bowling and billiard establishments	7,859	7,843	102,433	106,476
Racing, including track operation	1,782	1,781	...	37,664
Public golf courses	2,127	2,153	13,879	14,733
Amusement parks	552	564	30,299	32,058
Membership sports, recreation clubs	9,009	9,415	136,465	143,652
Health services	263,576	283,274	4,089,115	4,339,178
Physicians' offices	124,122	132,546	566,495	601,354
Dentists' offices	76,359	80,588	252,295	273,980
Osteopathic physicians' offices	4,336	4,547	15,354	16,024
Chiropractors' offices	6,502	7,231	12,593	14,127
Optometrists' offices	10,132	11,013	25,016	27,514
Nursing and personal care facilities	11,790	12,316	736,309	793,769
Hospitals	5,333	5,414	2,194,141	2,283,839
Medical and dental laboratories	9,459	10,442	84,785	90,035
Outpatient care facilities	5,419	7,704	104,513	126,697
Legal services	85,758	91,942	363,088	392,481
Educational services	25,521	25,994	983,431	992,019
Elementary and secondary schools	14,007	13,461	312,374	295,441
Colleges and universities	2,317	2,438	548,118	576,196
Libraries and information centres	1,469	1,599	16,371	12,691
Correspondence and vocational schools	2,891	3,039	46,919	46,082
Social services	43,036	52,322	723,119	764,310
Residential care	5,575	7,645	149,659	172,098
Museums, botanical, zoological gardens	871	1,063	23,398	22,588
Membership organizations	135,628	137,891	1,071,128	1,100,716
Business associations	12,077	12,398	70,343	73,130
Professional organizations	3,746	3,958	36,712	36,410
Labour organizations	22,265	22,189	164,129	170,102
Civic and social organizations	33,854	34,182	270,039	266,076
Political organizations	1,371	1,137	6,286	4,160
Religious organizations	54,986	56,712	447,938	482,159
Miscellaneous services	67,554	75,257	639,767	670,425
Engineering, architectural services	29,468	32,520	345,003	369,706
Noncommercial research organizations	2,349	2,398	60,357	52,144
Accounting, auditing and bookkeeping	32,657	37,109	218,534	233,487
TOTAL[2]	1,164,782	1,233,652	13,340,684	14,059,994

[1] Mid-March pay period. [2] Includes administrative and auxiliary businesses not shown separately.
Source: U.S. Department of Commerce, Bureau of the Census, *County Business Patterns 1976* and *1977*.

Principal Manufactures, 1976

monetary figures in millions of dollars

Industry	Employees (000)	Cost of labour[1]	Cost of materials	Value of shipments	Value added by mfg.
Food and kindred products	1,536	$17,289	$128,618	$180,930	$52,760
Meat products	311	3,474	38,252	45,827	7,530
Dairy products	164	1,908	19,657	24,830	5,261
Preserved fruits and vegetables	222	2,032	10,935	17,722	6,799
Grain mill products	114	1,453	15,133	21,189	6,083
Beverages	204	2,629	12,241	21,069	8,833
Tobacco products	65	704	4,659	8,786	4,128
Textile mill products	876	7,368	22,194	36,389	14,495
Apparel and other textile products	1,271	8,563	18,150	34,758	16,860
Lumber and wood products	629	6,143	18,121	31,239	13,454
Furniture and fixtures	426	3,772	6,946	14,232	7,370
Paper and allied products	615	8,046	27,877	48,218	20,604
Printing and publishing	1,086	12,680	15,288	42,838	27,647
Chemicals and allied products	851	12,365	53,725	104,139	51,408
Industrial chemicals	251	4,032	20,237	37,296	17,513
Plastics materials and synthetics	153	2,187	10,688	17,156	6,648
Drugs	151	2,223	3,813	13,016	9,333
Soap, cleaners, and toilet goods	110	1,415	6,383	14,741	8,469
Paints, allied products	60	810	3,438	5,931	2,562
Agricultural chemicals	52	722	5,448	9,195	3,763
Petroleum and coal products	144	2,437	69,392	82,347	13,169
Rubber, misc. plastics products	627	6,742	15,885	31,765	15,950
Leather and leather products	247	1,805	3,691	7,176	3,559
Stone, clay, and glass products	599	7,086	14,056	30,635	16,773
Primary metal industries	1,106	16,975	59,932	93,002	34,182
Blast furnace, basic steel products	532	9,166	30,231	46,687	17,274
Iron, steel foundries	216	2,966	4,361	9,787	5,496
Primary nonferrous metals	59	963	6,909	9,970	2,980
Nonferrous drawing and rolling	171	2,339	13,653	18,753	5,360
Nonferrous foundries	85	951	1,653	3,389	1,738
Fabricated metal products	1,471	18,382	38,720	77,507	39,145
Ordnance and accessories	75	976	1,115	2,804	1,664
Machinery, except electrical	1,960	$26,480	$48,648	$105,525	$57,357
Engines and turbines	125	1,939	4,935	9,009	4,200
Farm and garden machinery	146	1,949	5,776	10,534	4,783
Construction and related mach.	312	4,378	10,234	19,741	9,646
Metalworking machinery	290	3,954	3,867	11,278	7,458
Special industry machinery	196	2,556	4,159	9,454	5,175
General industrial machinery	281	3,746	6,184	14,196	8,043
Service industry machines	173	2,152	5,587	10,660	5,214
Office, computing machines	229	3,277	5,664	13,723	8,102
Electric and electronic equipment	1,578	19,253	32,831	73,867	41,746
Electric distributing equip.	104	1,193	2,018	4,688	2,702
Electrical industrial apparatus	195	2,284	3,691	8,453	4,916
Household appliances	157	1,699	4,847	9,161	4,454
Electric lighting, wiring equip.	159	1,700	3,228	7,342	4,204
Radio, TV receiving equipment	90	956	3,302	5,823	2,544
Communication equipment	422	6,050	7,513	19,138	11,656
Electronic components, access.	323	3,763	5,008	12,433	7,568
Transportation equipment	1,668	26,442	85,892	141,026	55,657
Motor vehicles and equipment	797	13,019	65,343	95,381	30,948
Aircraft and parts	408	6,665	10,087	23,463	12,735
Ship, boat building, repairing	207	2,605	3,481	7,516	4,032
Railroad equipment	50	740	2,077	3,616	1,455
Guided missiles, space vehicles	142	2,723	2,347	7,142	5,027
Instruments and related products	518	6,598	8,989	25,030	16,386
Measuring, controlling devices	169	2,100	2,143	6,180	4,102
Medical instruments and supplies	111	1,248	1,892	4,766	2,956
Photographic equipment and supplies	107	1,732	2,915	8,845	6,077
Miscellaneous manufacturing industries	410	3,868	7,580	16,286	8,822
All establishments, including administrative and auxiliary	18,753	233,389	681,194	1,185,695	511,471

[1] Payroll only. Source: U.S. Department of Commerce, *Annual Survey of Manufactures 1976.*

Business Activity

Category of activity	WHOLESALING				RETAILING				SERVICES			
	1960	1965	1970	1977	1960	1965	1970	1977	1960	1965	1970	1977
Number of businesses (in 000)												
Sole proprietorships	306	265	274	307	1,548	1,554	1,689	1,862	1,966	2,208	2,507	3,303
Active partnerships	41	32	30	29	238	202	170	164	159	169	176	227
Active corporations	117	147	166	228[1]	217	288	351	417[1]	121	188	281	473[1]
Business receipts (in $000,000)												
Sole proprietorships	17,061	17,934	21,556	33,499	65,439	77,760	89,315	123,595	23,256	29,789	40,869	67,791
Active partnerships	12,712	10,879	11,325	16,624	24,787	23,244	23,546	31,983	9,281	12,442	18,791	37,788
Active corporations	130,637	171,414	234,885	572,364[1]	125,787	183,925	274,808	527,571[1]	22,106	36,547	66,460	146,817[1]
Net profit (less loss; in $000,000)												
Sole proprietorships	1,305	1,483	1,806	2,548	3,869	5,019	5,767	6,880	8,060	11,008	15,063	22,516
Active partnerships	587	548	557	755	1,612	1,654	1,603	1,870	3,056	4,402	6,189	9,245
Active corporations	2,130	3,288	4,441	15,769[1]	2,225	4,052	5,217	10,367[1]	849	1,505	1,199	4,185[1]

Data refer to accounting periods ending between July 1 of year shown and June 30 of following year. [1] 1976.
Source: U.S. Department of the Treasury, Internal Revenue Service, *Statistics of Income: Business Income Tax Returns* and *Corporation Income Tax Returns.*

Retail Sales

in millions of dollars

Kind of business	1960	1965	1970	1979
Durable goods stores[1]	70,560	94,186	114,288	308,156
Automotive group	39,579	56,884	64,966	177,714
Passenger car, other automotive dealers	37,038	53,484	59,388	161,277
Tire, battery, accessory dealers	2,541	3,400	5,578	16,437
Furniture and appliance group	10,591	13,352	17,778	41,868
Furniture, home furnishings stores	...	...	10,483	26,726
Household appliance, TV, radio stores	...	...	6,073	12,119
Building materials, hardware, farm equipment group	11,222	12,388	20,494	52,239
Lumberyards, building materials dealers	8,567	9,731	11,995	35,102
Hardware stores	2,655	2,657	3,351	8,993
Nondurable goods stores[1]	148,969	189,942	261,239	577,891
Apparel group	13,631	15,765	19,810	43,028
Men's, boys' wear stores	2,644	...	4,630	8,772
Women's apparel, accessory stores	5,295	...	7,582	15,802
Family clothing stores	...	...	3,360	9,389
Shoe stores	2,437	...	3,501	7,127
Drug and proprietary stores	7,538	9,186	13,352	27,174
Eating and drinking places	16,146	20,201	29,689	75,139
Food group	54,023	64,016	86,114	191,326
Grocery stores	48,610	...	79,756	177,703
Meat and fish markets	...	...	2,244	...
Bakeries	...	...	1,303	2,921
Gasoline service stations	17,588	20,611	27,994	71,894
General merchandise group	...	42,299	61,320	110,233
Department stores and dry goods general merchandise stores	...	...	45,000	102,319
Variety stores	...	...	6,959	7,914
Mail-order houses (department store merchandise)	...	...	3,853	5,341
Liquor stores	4,893	5,674	7,980	15,595
TOTAL	219,529	284,128	375,527	886,047

[1] Includes some kinds of business not shown separately.
Source: U.S. Department of Commerce, Bureau of the Census, *Monthly Retail Trade,* Bureau of Economic Analysis, *1975 Business Statistics.*

Sales of Merchant Wholesalers

in millions of dollars

Kind of business	1960	1965	1970	1979
Durable goods[1]	56,803	82,861	111,970	404,286
Motor vehicles, automotive equipment	7,883	12,140	19,482	76,519
Electrical goods	8,660	12,681	16,667	44,487
Furniture, home furnishings	2,910	3,777	5,199	14,055
Hardware, plumbing, heating equipment	6,422	8,413	10,858	28,875
Lumber, construction supplies	6,680	9,765	10,863	36,998
Machinery, equipment, supplies	14,287	20,561	27,638	111,843
Metals, metalwork (except scrap)	5,708	9,162	13,647	45,173
Scrap, waste materials	3,296	4,789	6,040	16,818
Nondurable goods[1]	80,477	104,470	135,029	479,048
Groceries and related products	27,661	38,068	53,411	138,635
Beer, wine, distilled alcoholic beverages	7,424	9,464	13,332	30,648
Drugs, chemicals, allied products	5,370	7,180	9,135	12,638
Tobacco, tobacco products	4,164	5,014	6,232	10,203
Dry goods, apparel	6,675	8,804	10,577	27,537
Paper, paper products	4,153	5,612	7,679	19,721
Farm products	11,683	13,711	13,987	98,252
Other nondurable goods	13,346	16,966	22,632	63,969
TOTAL	137,281	187,331	246,999	883,334

[1] Includes some kinds of business not shown separately.
Source: U.S. Dept. of Commerce, Bureau of the Census, *Monthly Wholesale Trade.*

Commercial Banks[1]

December 31, 1979

State	Number of banks	Total assets or liabilities $000,000	SELECTED ASSETS ($000,000) Loans	Investments[2]	Reserves, cash, and bank balances	SELECTED LIABILITIES ($000,000) Deposits Total	Demand	Time, savings	Capital accounts
Ala.	317	15,785	8,574	4,116	1,705	13,450	4,811	8,640	1,322
Alaska	12	1,981	1,041	484	209	1,564	679	885	180
Ariz.	22	12,153	7,568	2,183	1,370	10,347	3,733	6,570	703
Ark.	258	10,256	5,339	2,629	1,128	8,756	3,244	5,512	843
Calif.	242	219,233	126,833	22,776	45,296	177,783	44,980	77,045	9,691
Colo.	307	14,715	8,334	2,580	2,612	12,351	5,611	6,726	1,085
Conn.	65	12,945	7,468	2,293	2,329	10,803	4,366	5,923	800
Del.	18	3,484	1,687	1,080	383	2,747	1,033	1,714	252
D.C.	17	7,816	4,151	1,562	1,623	6,354	2,630	2,668	511
Fla.	577	42,185	19,515	12,132	6,117	36,166	15,354	20,699	3,168
Ga.	439	22,007	11,194	3,979	3,571	17,681	8,335	8,991	1,779
Hawaii	9	4,871	2,990	995	592	4,363	1,504	2,695	303
Idaho	27	4,609	2,677	956	565	3,904	1,243	2,661	326
Ill.	1,250	132,790	72,087	24,246	24,682	102,860	26,285	50,546	7,611
Ind.	404	30,511	16,395	7,829	3,177	25,444	7,788	17,420	2,244
Iowa	651	19,697	11,399	4,710	2,100	17,036	5,178	11,845	1,565
Kan.	616	15,289	7,941	3,969	1,703	13,164	4,601	8,563	1,245
Ky.	342	17,877	9,770	4,284	1,954	15,005	5,705	9,200	1,386
La.	262	21,811	11,121	5,532	2,661	18,543	7,216	11,250	701
Maine	41	3,222	1,931	712	358	2,748	813	1,936	239
Md.	102	15,490	9,438	2,962	1,946	12,989	4,759	7,795	1,086
Mass.	143	32,079	15,967	5,870	6,380	24,353	8,985	10,230	1,797
Mich.	371	50,201	28,724	11,471	6,120	41,232	10,963	28,835	3,493
Minn.	759	13,619	16,154	6,309	3,638	22,927	7,519	14,397	2,040
Miss.	182	10,580	5,677	2,811	1,124	9,198	3,196	6,006	787
Mo.	721	32,485	16,384	7,331	4,668	25,842	10,245	15,122	2,308
Mont.	162	4,890	2,868	1,151	481	4,321	1,363	2,958	383
Neb.	454	10,501	5,886	2,302	1,410	8,962	3,476	5,485	853
Nev.	9	3,632	2,130	810	427	3,127	1,339	1,787	274
N.H.	78	3,023	1,927	564	325	2,645	692	1,953	230
N.J.	176	34,307	18,455	9,253	3,892	28,969	10,406	18,266	2,364
N.M.	86	5,422	2,967	1,191	657	4,727	1,752	3,475	406
N.Y.	219	410,911	222,931	38,422	107,451	314,721	89,326	67,192	19,181
N.C.	82	23,526	11,796	4,858	4,287	18,865	6,806	10,161	1,632
N.D.	172	4,230	2,517	1,078	383	3,749	1,214	2,535	354
Ohio	407	52,888	27,838	13,322	7,157	41,721	13,765	26,845	4,180
Okla.	489	19,711	9,998	4,884	2,739	16,841	6,742	10,038	1,519
Ore.	75	12,339	7,257	2,093	1,799	10,104	3,443	6,534	915
Pa.	367	84,910	47,043	18,552	11,954	67,309	18,869	40,613	5,730
R.I.	14	6,245	3,850	1,190	623	4,920	1,137	3,332	384
S.C.	85	6,965	2,589	1,706	969	5,810	3,023	2,787	582
S.D.	154	4,675	2,875	1,065	453	4,184	1,185	2,999	365
Tenn.	350	22,056	12,030	4,948	2,628	18,644	6,262	12,232	1,623
Texas	1,422	102,840	51,675	21,025	18,599	85,270	33,534	44,200	7,186
Utah	74	6,334	3,691	1,061	878	5,413	1,958	3,455	452
Vt.	29	2,212	1,476	446	174	1,989	454	1,535	160
Va.	233	22,359	13,203	4,974	2,419	18,888	6,245	12,513	1,688
Wash.	100	21,350	13,450	2,397	3,225	17,365	5,877	10,270	1,320
W.Va.	235	9,484	4,979	2,813	802	8,029	2,216	5,813	827
Wis.	631	25,828	15,121	5,991	2,740	21,319	6,502	14,296	1,853
Wyo.	94	3,083	1,645	766	377	2,735	1,042	1,693	255
TOTAL[3]	14,364	1,692,078	923,860	293,923	306,602	1,363,068	430,776	659,799	103,494

[1] Detail may not add to total given due to rounding; excludes noninsured banks.
[2] Includes investment securities and trading account securities.
[3] Includes Guam and Puerto Rico bank statistics, not itemized in this table.
Source: Federal Deposit Insurance Corporation, *1979 Bank Operating Statistics.*

Life Insurance, 1979

Number of policies in 000s; value in $000,000

State	Total Number of policies	Total Value	Ordinary Number of policies	Ordinary Value	Group Number of certificates	Group Value	Industrial Number of policies	Industrial Value	Credit[1] Number of policies	Credit[1] Value
Ala.	12,498	$51,282	2,045	$25,288	1,782	$19,159	6,905	$2,837	1,766	$3,998
Alaska	570	6,193	136	2,773	249	3,210	10	3	175	207
Ariz.	5,402	36,780	1,982	21,354	1,493	12,163	169	117	1,758	3,146
Ark.	2,979	22,374	1,026	11,576	728	8,633	440	244	785	1,921
Calif.	31,481	317,557	10,772	157,679	12,398	145,347	1,917	1,364	6,394	13,167
Colo.	4,934	45,807	1,815	24,783	1,624	17,834	300	294	1,195	2,896
Conn.	5,721	55,147	2,364	25,834	1,953	27,107	259	206	1,145	2,000
Del.	2,434	16,347	470	4,551	524	10,795	220	149	1,220	852
D.C.	2,516	20,925	440	4,588	1,086	15,335	487	286	503	716
Fla.	16,544	112,718	5,392	62,448	3,642	40,286	3,767	2,593	3,743	7,391
Ga.	12,917	79,362	3,602	39,528	2,765	32,011	4,017	2,715	2,533	5,108
Hawaii	1,736	17,232	615	9,370	703	6,901	5	2	413	959
Idaho	1,326	11,071	512	6,108	472	4,069	24	12	318	882
Ill.	22,823	191,823	9,340	94,713	6,943	86,676	2,940	1,942	3,600	8,492
Ind.	10,307	80,150	4,120	40,431	2,701	34,077	1,603	997	1,883	4,645
Iowa	5,074	44,356	2,585	25,799	1,420	15,945	222	123	847	2,489
Kan.	4,303	34,660	1,882	20,793	1,160	11,414	303	172	958	2,281
Ky.	6,501	41,044	2,271	20,249	1,348	16,969	1,417	792	1,465	3,034
La.	9,922	55,489	2,111	28,046	1,780	20,949	3,919	2,273	2,112	4,221
Maine	1,881	12,774	717	6,523	662	5,351	74	51	428	849
Md.	8,011	60,043	2,916	31,267	1,892	24,727	1,678	1,003	1,525	3,046
Mass.	9,006	79,447	3,915	38,227	2,660	37,674	715	476	1,716	3,070
Mich.	16,933	154,722	5,598	56,488	5,978	89,358	1,887	1,187	3,470	7,689
Minn.	6,331	61,579	2,537	29,774	2,416	29,089	222	135	1,156	2,572
Miss.	4,051	24,674	949	12,646	991	9,321	763	475	1,348	2,432
Mo.	9,286	70,403	3,866	34,631	2,665	31,488	1,144	690	1,611	3,594
Mont.	1,138	9,432	452	5,578	365	3,092	24	11	297	751
Neb.	2,707	24,513	1,360	14,976	745	8,167	114	65	488	1,305
Nev.	1,395	11,468	296	4,629	551	5,431	10	6	538	1,402
N.H.	1,545	13,391	688	6,942	414	5,636	84	60	359	753
N.J.	12,209	123,651	5,436	58,784	3,517	59,431	1,288	1,062	1,968	4,374
N.M.	1,903	15,470	609	7,505	589	6,674	91	57	614	1,234
N.Y.	27,039	257,592	10,981	115,987	8,030	128,195	1,740	1,327	6,288	12,083
N.C.	12,548	74,320	4,131	38,271	2,377	29,163	3,268	1,865	2,772	5,021
N.D.	999	9,352	459	5,678	315	3,015	4	3	221	656
Ohio	21,017	167,927	8,175	82,275	5,531	74,236	3,173	2,091	4,138	9,325
Okla.	4,193	37,791	1,722	20,622	1,124	14,513	373	224	974	2,432
Ore.	3,454	33,281	1,219	15,983	1,353	16,018	79	42	803	1,778
Pa.	24,227	170,444	9,885	84,205	5,899	73,383	3,993	2,537	4,450	10,319
R.I.	1,952	15,266	784	7,497	716	7,132	157	100	295	537
S.C.	7,947	37,962	2,551	19,876	1,657	14,095	2,407	1,481	1,332	2,510
S.D.	1,003	9,084	523	5,765	266	2,720	4	2	210	597
Tenn.	9,810	61,051	2,768	29,323	2,568	25,237	2,360	1,383	2,114	5,018
Texas	25,119	201,776	8,539	103,697	7,254	81,761	3,308	2,094	6,018	14,224
Utah	2,212	17,326	665	8,954	949	6,959	89	40	509	1,373
Vt.	805	6,116	353	3,399	223	2,333	32	23	197	361
Va.	10,784	75,220	3,406	36,746	2,589	33,109	2,468	1,460	2,321	3,905
Wash.	5,523	53,213	1,937	26,166	2,210	24,458	156	78	1,220	2,511
W.Va.	3,388	21,041	1,029	9,316	869	9,572	569	354	921	1,799
Wis.	7,567	64,870	3,424	34,772	2,539	26,913	455	288	1,149	2,897
Wyo.	643	6,084	258	3,465	208	2,188	5	3	172	428
TOTAL U.S.	406,614	$3,222,340	145,628	$1,585,878	114,893	$1,419,418	61,658	$37,794	84,435	$179,250

[1] Life insurance on loans of ten years' or less duration.
Source: Institute of Life Insurance, *Life Insurance Fact Book '80.*

Savings and Loan Associations

Dec. 31, 1979[1]

State	Number of assns.	Total assets ($000,000)	Per capita assets
Alabama	62	$4,688	$1,244
Alaska	5	297	734
Arizona	16	5,869	2,396
Arkansas	77	4,203	1,928
California	179	109,931	4,844
Colorado	46	8,918	3,217
Connecticut	38	4,081	1,310
Delaware	18	277	476
District of Columbia	16	4,858	7,406
Florida	122	46,602	5,260
Georgia	98	10,285	2,010
Guam	2	75	649
Hawaii	9	3,757	4,106
Idaho	12	997	1,101
Illinois	381	42,600	3,794
Indiana	163	9,908	1,835
Iowa	77	6,833	2,355
Kansas	82	6,825	2,881
Kentucky	105	5,569	1,579
Louisiana	127	7,682	1,912
Maine	20	663	604
Maryland	204	9,896	2,386
Massachusetts	162	7,919	1,373
Michigan	65	16,925	1,838
Minnesota	57	10,031	2,471
Mississippi	59	2,716	1,118
Missouri	115	15,097	3,102
Montana	15	1,074	1,367
Nebraska	41	5,041	3,202
Nevada	8	2,204	3,139
New Hampshire	17	1,058	1,193
New Jersey	217	22,427	3,059
New Mexico	33	2,347	1,891
New York	122	26,630	1,509
North Carolina	201	11,188	1,996
North Dakota	11	2,230	3,395
Ohio	399	37,857	3,528
Oklahoma	54	5,413	1,872
Oregon	31	6,640	2,628
Pennsylvania	387	23,247	1,982
Puerto Rico	12	1,861	547
Rhode Island	6	761	819
South Carolina	75	5,956	2,031
South Dakota	19	1,033	1,500
Tennessee	98	6,904	1,576
Texas	312	31,468	2,352
Utah	14	3,959	2,896
Vermont	7	242	492
Virginia	85	8,859	1,705
Washington	48	9,233	2,352
West Virginia	35	1,467	781
Wisconsin	114	11,950	2,532
Wyoming	13	871	1,934
TOTAL U.S.	4,709	$579,307	$2,591

[1] Preliminary. Components do not add to totals because of differences in reporting dates and accounting systems.
Source: U.S. League of Savings Associations, *Savings and Loan Fact Book '80.*

GOVERNMENT AND POLITICS

The National Executive

December 31, 1980

Department, bureau, or office	Executive official and official title
PRESIDENT OF THE UNITED STATES [1]	Jimmy Carter
Vice-President	Walter F. Mondale
EXECUTIVE OFFICE OF THE PRESIDENT	
Assistant to the President	Zbigniew Brzezinski
	Stuart E. Eizenstat
	Hamilton Jordan
Press Secretary to the President	Joseph L. Powell
Counsel to the President	Lloyd N. Cutler
Special Assistant to the President	Louis E. Martin
Office of Management and Budget	James T. McIntyre, Jr., director
Council of Economic Advisers	Charles L. Schultze, chairman
National Security Council	[2]
Central Intelligence Agency	Adm. Stansfield Turner, director
Domestic Policy Staff	Stuart E. Eizenstat, executive director
Office of the United States Trade Representative	Reubin Askew, trade representative
Council on Environmental Quality	J. Gustave Speth, chairman
Council on Wage and Price Stability	Alfred E. Kahn, chairman
Office of Science and Technology Policy	Frank Press, director
Office of Administration	Richard Harden, director
DEPARTMENT OF STATE	Edmund S. Muskie, secretary
	Warren M. Christopher, deputy secretary
Political Affairs	David D. Newsom, undersecretary
Economic Affairs	Richard N. Cooper, undersecretary
Security Assistance, Science and Technology	Matthew Nimetz, undersecretary
Management	Ben H. Read, undersecretary
Ambassador at Large	W. Beverly Carter
	Henry D. Owen
	Elliot L. Richardson
	Victor H. Palmieri
	Gerard C. Smith
Counselor of the Department	Rozanne L. Ridgway
Permanent Mission to the Organization of American States	Gale W. McGee, permanent representative
Sinai Support Mission	Frank Maestrone, director
Mission to the United Nations	Donald F. McHenry, representative
African Affairs	Richard M. Moose, asst. secretary
European Affairs	George S. Vest, asst. secretary
East Asian and Pacific Affairs	Richard C. Holbrooke, asst. secretary
Inter-American Affairs	William G. Bowdler, asst. secretary
Near Eastern and South Asian Affairs	Harold H. Saunders, asst. secretary
International Organization Affairs	Richard L. McCall, Jr., asst. secretary
DEPARTMENT OF THE TREASURY	G. William Miller, secretary
	Robert Carswell, deputy secretary
Monetary Affairs	Robert Carswell, undersecretary (acting)
Comptroller of the Currency	John G. Heimann, comptroller
Bur. of Government Financial Operations	William Douglas, commissioner
U.S. Customs Service	Robert E. Chasen, commissioner
Bureau of Engraving and Printing	Harry R. Clements, director (acting)
Bureau of the Mint	Stella B. Hackel, director
Bureau of the Public Debt	H. J. Hintgen, commissioner
Internal Revenue Service	William E. Williams, commissioner (acting)
Office of the Treasurer	Azie Taylor Morton, treasurer
Savings Bond Division	Azie Taylor Morton, national director
U.S. Secret Service	H. Stuart Knight, director
Bureau of Alcohol, Tobacco and Firearms	G. R. Dickerson, director
Federal Law Enforcement Training Center	Arthur F. Brandstatter, director
DEPARTMENT OF DEFENSE	Harold Brown, secretary
	W. Graham Claytor, Jr., deputy secretary
Joint Chiefs of Staff	Gen. David C. Jones, USAF, chairman
Chief of Staff, Army	Gen. Edward C. Meyer, USA
Chief of Naval Operations	Adm. Thomas B. Hayward, USN
Chief of Staff, Air Force	Gen. Lew Allen, Jr., USAF
Commandant of the Marine Corps	Gen. Robert H. Barrow, USMC
Department of the Army	Clifford L. Alexander, Jr., secretary
Department of the Navy	Edward Hidalgo, secretary
Department of the Air Force	Hans M. Mark, secretary
DEPARTMENT OF JUSTICE	
Attorney General	Benjamin R. Civiletti
Solicitor General	Wade H. McCree, Jr.
Community Relations Service	Gilbert G. Pompa, director
Law Enforcement Assistance Admin.	Homer F. Broome, Jr., administrator
Antitrust Division	Sanford M. Litvack, asst. attorney general
Civil Division	Alice Daniel, asst. attorney general
Civil Rights Division	Drew S. Days III, asst. attorney general
Criminal Division	Philip B. Heymann, asst. attorney general
Land and Natural Resources Division	James W. Moorman, asst. attorney general
Tax Division	M. Carr Ferguson, asst. attorney general
Justice Management Division	Kevin D. Rooney, asst. attorney general
Federal Bureau of Investigation	William H. Webster, director
Bureau of Prisons	Norman A. Carlson, director
Immigration and Naturalization Service	David Crosland, commissioner (acting)
Drug Enforcement Administration	Peter B. Bensinger, administrator
U.S. Marshals Service	William E. Hall, director
DEPARTMENT OF THE INTERIOR	Cecil D. Andrus, secretary
	James A. Joseph, undersecretary
Fish and Wildlife and Parks	Robert L. Herbst, asst. secretary
National Park Service	Russell E. Dickenson, director
Fish and Wildlife Service	Lynn A. Greenwalt, director
Heritage Conservation and Recreation Service	Chris T. Delaporte, director
Energy and Minerals	Joan M. Davenport, asst. secretary
Office of Minerals Policy and Research Analysis	Hermann Enzer, director
Geological Survey	H. William Menard, director
Bureau of Mines	Lindsay D. Norman, director
Office of Surface Mining Reclamation and Enforcement	Walter N. Heine, director
Land and Water Resources	Guy R. Martin, asst. secretary
Bureau of Land Management	W. Frank Gregg, director
Water and Power Resources Service	R. Keith Higginson, commissioner
Indian Affairs	Thomas W. Fredricks, asst. secretary (acting)
DEPARTMENT OF AGRICULTURE	Bob Bergland, secretary
	Jim Williams, deputy secretary
Small Community and Rural Development	Alex P. Mercure, undersecretary
Rural Electrification Administration	Robert W. Feragen, administrator
Farmers Home Administration	Gordon Cavanaugh, administrator
Marketing and Transportation Services	P. R. (Bobby) Smith, asst. secretary
Agricultural Marketing Service	Barbara L. Schlei, administrator
International Affairs and Commodity Programs	Dale E. Hathaway, undersecretary
Commodity Credit Corporation	Dale E. Hathaway, president
Natural Resources and Environment	Ned Bayley, asst. secretary (acting)
Forest Service	R. Max Peterson, chief
Soil Conservation Service	Norman A. Berg, chief
Economics, Policy Analysis, and Budget	Howard W. Hjort, director
Economics and Statistics Service	Kenneth R. Farrell, administrator
Food and Consumer Services	Carol Tucker Foreman, asst. secretary
DEPARTMENT OF COMMERCE	Philip M. Klutznick, secretary
	vacancy (deputy secretary)
International Trade	Robert E. Hertstein, undersecretary
Chief Economist	Courtenay M. Slater
Bureau of the Census	Vincent P. Barabba, director
Bureau of Economic Analysis	George Jaszi, director
Productivity, Technology, and Innovation	Jordan Baruch, asst. secretary
National Bureau of Standards	Ernest Ambler, director
Patent and Trademark Office	Sidney A. Diamond, commissioner
Maritime Affairs	Samuel B. Nemirow, asst. secretary
Tourism	vacancy (asst. secretary)
National Oceanic and Atmospheric Administration	Richard A. Frank, administrator
DEPARTMENT OF LABOR	Ray Marshall, secretary
	John N. Gentry, undersecretary
Administration and Management	Alfred M. Zuck, asst. secretary
Employment and Training	Ernest G. Green, asst. secretary
Labor-Management Relations	William P. Hobgood, asst. secretary
Occupational Safety and Health	Eula Bingham, asst. secretary
Labor Statistics	Janet L. Norwood, commissioner
Mine Safety and Health	Robert B. Lagather, asst. secretary
DEPARTMENT OF HEALTH AND HUMAN SERVICES	Patricia Roberts Harris, secretary
	vacancy (undersecretary)
Office of Human Development Services	Cesar A. Perales, asst. secretary
Public Health Service	Julius B. Richmond, M.D., asst. secretary
Food and Drug Administration	Jere E. Goyan, commissioner
National Institutes of Health	Donald S. Fredrickson, director
Health Resources Administration	Karen Davis, administrator
Health Services Administration	George I. Lythcott, M.D., administrator
Center for Disease Control	William H. Foege, M.D., director
Alcohol, Drug Abuse, and Mental Health Administration	Gerald L. Klerman, administrator
Health Care Financing Administration	Howard Newman, administrator
Social Security Administration	William J. Driver, commissioner
Office of Child Support Enforcement	Stanford G. Ross, director
DEPARTMENT OF HOUSING AND URBAN DEVELOPMENT	Moon Landrieu, secretary
	Victor Marrero, undersecretary
Community Planning and Development	Robert C. Embry, Jr., asst. secretary
Federal Housing Commissioner	Lawrence B. Simons, asst. secretary
Fair Housing and Equal Opportunity	Sterling Tucker, asst. secretary
Policy Development and Research	vacancy (asst. secretary)
DEPARTMENT OF TRANSPORTATION	Neil Goldschmidt, secretary
	William Beckham, Jr., deputy secretary
United States Coast Guard	Adm. John B. Hayes, USCG, commandant
Federal Aviation Administration	Langhorne M. Bond, administrator
Federal Highway Administration	John S. Hassell, Jr., administrator
National Highway Traffic Safety Administration	Joan B. Claybrook, administrator
Federal Railroad Administration	John M. Sullivan, administrator
Urban Mass Transportation Admin.	Theodore C. Lutz, administrator
St. Lawrence Seaway Development Corp.	David W. Oberlin, administrator
Research and Special Programs Administration	Howard Dugoff, administrator
DEPARTMENT OF ENERGY	Charles W. Duncan, Jr., secretary
	Lynn R. Coleman, deputy secretary (acting)
	C. Worthington Bateman, undersecretary
Federal Energy Regulatory Commission	Charles B. Curtis, chairman
General Counsel	Eric Fygi, general counsel (acting)
Chief Financial Officer	John A. Hewitt, Jr.
DEPARTMENT OF EDUCATION	Shirley M. Hufstedler, secretary
	Steven A. Minter, undersecretary
Inspector General	James B. Thomas, Jr.
General Counsel	Betsy Levin

[1] On Nov. 4, 1980, Ronald Reagan and George Bush were elected president and vice-president, effective Jan. 20, 1981. Subsequently, Reagan nominated the following for positions in his Cabinet: Alexander M. Haig, Jr., State; Donald T. Regan, Treasury; Caspar W. Weinberger, Defense; William F. Smith, Justice; James G. Watt, Interior; John R. Block, Agriculture; Malcolm Baldrige, Commerce; Raymond J. Donovan, Labor; Richard S. Schweiker, Health; Samuel R. Pierce, Jr., Housing; Andrew L. Lewis, Jr., Transportation; James B. Edwards, Energy; Terrel H. Bell, Education. [2] Council comprised of the President of the United States and certain other members.

Senate January 1981

State, name, and party	Term expires
Ala.—Heflin, Howell (D)	1985
Denton, Jeremiah (R)	1987
Alaska—Stevens, Ted (R)	1985
Murkowski, Frank H. (R)	1987
Ariz.—Goldwater, Barry M. (R)	1987
DeConcini, Dennis (D)	1983
Ark.—Bumpers, Dale (D)	1987
Pryor, David (D)	1985
Calif.—Cranston, Alan (D)	1987
Hayakawa, S. I. (R)	1983
Colo.—Hart, Gary W. (D)	1987
Armstrong, William L. (R)	1985
Conn.—Weicker, Lowell P., Jr. (R)	1983
Dodd, Christopher J. (D)	1987
Del.—Roth, William V., Jr. (R)	1983
Biden, Joseph R., Jr. (D)	1985
Fla.—Chiles, Lawton M. (D)	1983
Hawkins, Paula (R)	1987
Ga.—Nunn, Samuel A. (D)	1985
Mattingly, Mack (R)	1987
Hawaii—Inouye, Daniel K. (D)	1987
Matsunaga, Spark M. (D)	1983
Idaho—McClure, James A. (R)	1985
Symms, Steven D. (R)	1987
Ill.—Percy, Charles H. (R)	1985
Dixon, Alan J. (D)	1987
Ind.—Lugar, Richard G. (R)	1983
Quayle, Dan (R)	1987
Iowa—Jepsen, Roger W. (R)	1985
Grassley, Charles E. (R)	1987
Kan.—Dole, Robert J. (R)	1987
Kassebaum, Nancy Landon (R)	1985
Ky.—Huddleston, Walter (D)	1985
Ford, Wendell H. (D)	1987
La.—Long, Russell B. (D)	1987
Johnston, J. Bennett, Jr. (D)	1985
Maine—Cohen, William S. (R)	1985
Mitchell, George J. (D)	1983
Md.—Mathias, Charles, Jr. (R)	1987
Sarbanes, Paul S. (D)	1983
Mass.—Kennedy, Edward M. (D)	1983
Tsongas, Paul E. (D)	1985
Mich.—Riegle, Donald W., Jr. (D)	1983
Levin, Carl (D)	1985
Minn.—Durenberger, David (R)	1983
Boschwitz, Rudy (R)	1985
Miss.—Stennis, John C. (D)	1983
Cochran, Thad (R)	1985
Mo.—Eagleton, Thomas F. (D)	1987
Danforth, John C. (R)	1983
Mont.—Melcher, John (D)	1983
Baucus, Max (D)	1985
Neb.—Zorinsky, Edward (D)	1983
Exon, J. James (D)	1985
Nev.—Cannon, Howard W. (D)	1983
Laxalt, Paul (R)	1987
N.H.—Humphrey, Gordon J. (R)	1985
Rudman, Warren (R)	1987
N.J.—Williams, Harrison A. (D)	1983
Bradley, Bill (D)	1985
N.M.—Domenici, Pete V. (R)	1985
Schmitt, Harrison H. (R)	1983
N.Y.—Moynihan, Daniel P. (D)	1983
D'Amato, Alfonse M. (R)	1987
N.C.—Helms, Jesse A. (R)	1985
East, John P. (R)	1987
N.D.—Burdick, Quentin N. (D)	1983
Andrews, Mark (R)	1987
Ohio—Glenn, John H., Jr. (D)	1987
Metzenbaum, Howard M. (D)	1983
Okla.—Boren, David L. (D)	1985
Nickles, Don (R)	1987
Ore.—Hatfield, Mark O. (R)	1985
Packwood, Robert W. (R)	1987
Pa.—Heinz, H. John, III (R)	1983
Specter, Arlen (R)	1987
R.I.—Pell, Claiborne (D)	1985
Chafee, John H. (R)	1983
S.C.—Thurmond, Strom (R)	1985
Hollings, Ernest F. (D)	1987
S.D.—Pressler, Larry (R)	1985
Abdnor, James (R)	1987
Tenn.—Baker, Howard H., Jr. (R)	1985
Sasser, James R. (D)	1983
Texas—Tower, John G. (R)	1985
Bentsen, Lloyd M. (D)	1983
Utah—Garn, Jake (R)	1987
Hatch, Orrin G. (R)	1983
Vt.—Stafford, Robert T. (R)	1983
Leahy, Patrick J. (D)	1987
Va.—Byrd, Harry F., Jr. (I)	1983
Warner, John W. (R)	1985
Wash.—Jackson, Henry M. (D)	1983
Gorton, Slade (R)	1987
W.Va.—Randolph, Jennings (D)	1985
Byrd, Robert C. (D)	1983
Wis.—Proxmire, William (D)	1983
Kasten, Robert W., Jr. (R)	1987
Wyo.—Wallop, Malcolm (R)	1983
Simpson, Alan K. (R)	1985

House of Representatives membership at the opening of the first session of the 97th Congress in January 1981

State, district, name, party

Ala.—1. Edwards, Jack (R)
2. Dickinson, William L. (R)
3. Nichols, William (D)
4. Bevill, Tom (D)
5. Flippo, Ronnie G. (D)
6. Smith, Albert L., Jr. (R)
7. Shelby, Richard C. (D)
Alaska—Young, Don (R)
Ariz.—1. Rhodes, John J. (R)
2. Udall, Morris K. (D)
3. Stump, Bob (D)
4. Rudd, Eldon D. (R)
Ark.—1. Alexander, Bill (D)
2. Bethune, Ed (R)
3. Hammerschmidt, J. P. (R)
4. Anthony, Beryl F. (D)
Calif.—1. Chappie, Eugene A. (R)
2. Clausen, Don H. (R)
3. Matsui, Robert T. (D)
4. Fazio, Vic (D)
5. Burton, John L. (D)
6. Burton, Phillip (D)
7. Miller, George, III (D)
8. Dellums, Ronald V. (D)
9. Stark, Fortney H. (D)
10. Edwards, Don (D)
11. Lantos, Tom (D)
12. McCloskey, Paul N., Jr. (R)
13. Mineta, Norman Y. (D)
14. Shumway, Norman D. (R)
15. Coelho, Tony (D)
16. Panetta, Leon E. (D)
17. Pashayan, Charles, Jr. (R)
18. Thomas, William (R)
19. Lagomarsino, Robert J. (R)
20. Goldwater, Barry M., Jr. (R)
21. Fiedler, Bobbi (R)
22. Moorhead, Carlos J. (R)
23. Beilenson, Anthony C. (D)
24. Waxman, Henry A. (D)
25. Roybal, Edward R. (D)
26. Rousselot, John H. (R)
27. Dornan, Robert K. (R)
28. Dixon, Julian C. (D)
29. Hawkins, Augustus F. (D)
30. Danielson, George E. (D)
31. Dymally, Mervyn M. (D)
32. Anderson, Glenn M. (D)
33. Grisham, Wayne (R)
34. Lungren, Daniel E. (R)
35. Dreier, David (R)
36. Brown, George E., Jr. (D)
37. Lewis, Jerry (R)
38. Patterson, Jerry M. (D)
39. Dannemeyer, W. E. (R)
40. Badham, Robert E. (R)
41. Lowery, Bill (R)
42. Hunter, Duncan L. (R)
43. Burgener, Clair W. (R)
Colo.—1. Schroeder, Patricia (D)
2. Wirth, Timothy E. (D)
3. Kogovsek, Ray (D)
4. Brown, Hank (R)
5. Kramer, Ken (R)
Conn.—1. Cotter, William R. (D)
2. Gejdenson, Samuel (D)
3. DeNardis, Lawrence J. (R)
4. McKinney, Stewart B. (R)
5. Ratchford, William R. (D)
6. Moffett, Toby (D)
Del.—Evans, Thomas, Jr. (R)
Fla.—1. Hutto, Earl D. (D)
2. Fuqua, Don (D)
3. Bennett, Charles E. (D)
4. Chappell, William, Jr. (D)
5. McCollom, Bill (R)
6. Young, C. William (R)
7. Gibbons, Sam (D)
8. Ireland, Andrew P. (D)
9. Nelson, Bill (D)
10. Bafalis, L. A. (R)
11. Mica, Dan (D)
12. Shaw, Clay (R)
13. Lehman, William (D)
14. Pepper, Claude (D)
15. Fascell, Dante B. (D)
Ga.—1. Ginn, R. B. (D)
2. Hatcher, Charles F. (D)
3. Brinkley, Jack (D)
4. Levitas, Elliott H. (D)
5. Fowler, Wyche, Jr. (D)
6. Gingrich, Newt (R)
7. McDonald, Lawrence P. (D)
8. Evans, Billy Lee (D)
9. Jenkins, Edgar L. (D)
10. Barnard, Doug (D)
Hawaii—1. Heftel, Cecil (D)
2. Akaka, Daniel (D)
Idaho—1. Craig, Larry (R)
2. Hansen, George V. (R)

State, district, name, party

Ill.—1. Washington, Harold (D)
2. Savage, Gus (D)
3. Russo, Martin A. (D)
4. Derwinski, Edward J. (R)
5. Fary, John G. (D)
6. Hyde, Henry J. (R)
7. Collins, Cardiss (D)
8. Rostenkowski, Dan (D)
9. Yates, Sidney R. (D)
10. Porter, John E. (R)
11. Annunzio, Frank (D)
12. Crane, Philip M. (R)
13. McClory, Robert (R)
14. Erlenborn, J. N. (R)
15. Corcoran, Tom (R)
16. Martin, Lynn M. (R)
17. O'Brien, G. M. (R)
18. Michel, Robert H. (R)
19. Railsback, Thomas F. (R)
20. Findley, Paul (R)
21. Madigan, E. R. (R)
22. Crane, Daniel B. (R)
23. Price, Melvin (D)
24. Simon, Paul (D)
Ind.—1. Benjamin, Adam (D)
2. Fithian, Floyd J. (D)
3. Hiler, John P. (R)
4. Coats, Daniel R. (R)
5. Hillis, Elwood H. (R)
6. Evans, David W. (D)
7. Myers, John (R)
8. Deckard, H. Joel (R)
9. Hamilton, L. H. (D)
10. Sharp, Philip R. (D)
11. Jacobs, Andrew, Jr. (D)
Iowa—1. Leach, James (R)
2. Tauke, Tom (R)
3. Evans, Cooper (R)
4. Smith, Neal (D)
5. Harkin, Tom (D)
6. Bedell, Berkley (D)
Kan.—1. Roberts, Pat (R)
2. Jeffries, Jim (R)
3. Winn, Larry, Jr. (R)
4. Glickman, Dan (D)
5. Whittaker, Robert (R)
Ky.—1. Hubbard, Carroll, Jr. (D)
2. Natcher, William H. (D)
3. Mazzoli, Romano L. (D)
4. Snyder, Gene (R)
5. Rogers, Harold (R)
6. Hopkins, Larry J. (R)
7. Perkins, Carl D. (D)
La.—1. Livingston, Bob (R)
2. Boggs, Lindy (D)
3. Tauzin, William J. (D)
4. Roemer, Buddy (D)
5. Huckaby, Jerry (D)
6. Moore, W. Henson, III (R)
7. Breaux, John B. (D)
8. Long, Gillis W. (D)
Maine—1. Emery, David F. (R)
2. Snowe, Olympia J. (R)
Md.—1. Dyson, Roy (D)
2. Long, Clarence D. (D)
3. Mikulski, Barbara A. (D)
4. Holt, Marjorie S. (R)
5. Spellman, Gladys N. (D)
6. Byron, Beverly (D)
7. Mitchell, Parren J. (D)
8. Barnes, Michael D. (D)
Mass.—1. Conte, Silvio O. (R)
2. Boland, Edward P. (D)
3. Early, Joseph D. (D)
4. Frank, Barney (D)
5. Shannon, James M. (D)
6. Mavroules, Nicholas (D)
7. Markey, Edward J. (D)
8. O'Neill, Thomas P., Jr. (D)
9. Moakley, Joe (D)
10. Heckler, Margaret (R)
11. Donnelly, Brian J. (D)
12. Studds, Gerry E. (D)
Mich.—1. Conyers, John, Jr. (D)
2. Pursell, Carl D. (R)
3. Wolpe, Howard (D)
4. Stockman, David A. (R)
5. Sawyer, Harold S. (R)
6. Dunn, Jim (R)
7. Kildee, Dale E. (D)
8. Traxler, Bob (D)
9. Vander Jagt, Guy (R)
10. Albosta, Donald J. (D)
11. Davis, Robert W. (R)
12. Bonior, David E. (D)
13. Crockett, George W. (D)
14. Hertel, Dennis M. (D)
15. Ford, William D. (D)
16. Dingell, John D. (D)
17. Brodhead, William M. (D)
18. Blanchard, James J. (D)
19. Broomfield, William S. (R)
Minn.—1. Erdahl, Arlen (R)
2. Hagedorn, Tom (R)
3. Frenzel, William (R)
4. Vento, Bruce F. (D)
5. Sabo, Martin Olav (D)
6. Weber, Vin (R)
7. Stangeland, Arlan (R)
8. Oberstar, James L. (D)
Miss.—1. Whitten, Jamie L. (D)
2. Bowen, David R. (D)

State, district, name, party

3. Montgomery, G. V. (D)
4. Hinson, Jon C. (R)
5. Lott, Trent (R)
Mo.—1. Clay, William (D)
2. Young, Robert A. (D)
3. Gephardt, Richard A. (D)
4. Skelton, Ike (D)
5. Bolling, Richard (D)
6. Coleman, E. Thomas (R)
7. Taylor, Gene (R)
8. Bailey, Wendell (R)
9. Volkmer, Harold L. (D)
10. Emerson, William (R)
Mont.—1. Williams, Pat (D)
2. Marlenee, Ron (R)
Neb.—1. Bereuter, D. K. (R)
2. Daub, Harold (R)
3. Smith, Virginia (R)
Nev.—Santini, James (D)
N.H.—1. D'Amours, Norman (D)
2. Gregg, Judd (R)
N.J.—1. Florio, James J. (D)
2. Hughes, William J. (D)
3. Howard, James J. (D)
4. Smith, Christopher (R)
5. Fenwick, Millicent (R)
6. Forsythe, Edwin B. (R)
7. Roukema, Marge (R)
8. Roe, Robert A. (D)
9. Hollenbeck, Harold C. (R)
10. Rodino, Peter W., Jr. (D)
11. Minish, Joseph G. (D)
12. Rinaldo, Matthew J. (R)
13. Courter, James A. (R)
14. Guarini, Frank J. (D)
15. Dwyer, Bernard J. (D)
N.M.—1. Lujan, Manuel, Jr. (R)
2. Skeen, Joseph (R)
N.Y.—1. Carney, William (C-R)
2. Downey, Thomas J. (D)
3. Carman, Gregory W. (R)
4. Lent, Norman F. (R)
5. McGrath, Raymond J. (R)
6. LeBoutillier, John (R)
7. Addabbo, Joseph P. (D)
8. Rosenthal, Benjamin S. (D)
9. Ferraro, Geraldine (D)
10. Biaggi, Mario (D)
11. Scheuer, James H. (D)
12. Chisholm, Shirley (D)
13. Solarz, Stephen J. (D)
14. Richmond, Frederick W. (D)
15. Zeferetti, Leo C. (D)
16. Schumer, Charles E. (D)
17. Molinari, Guy V. (R)
18. Green, S. William (R)
19. Rangel, Charles B. (D)
20. Weiss, Theodore S. (D)
21. Garcia, Robert (D)
22. Bingham, J. B. (D)
23. Peyser, Peter A. (D)
24. Ottinger, Richard L. (D)
25. Fish, Hamilton, Jr. (R)
26. Gilman, B. A. (R)
27. McHugh, Matthew F. (D)
28. Stratton, Samuel S. (D)
29. Solomon, Gerald (R)
30. Martin, David (R)
31. Mitchell, D. J. (R)
32. Wortley, George (R)
33. Lee, Gary A. (R)
34. Horton, Frank J. (R)
35. Conable, B. B., Jr. (R)
36. LaFalce, John J. (D)
37. Nowak, Henry J. (D)
38. Kemp, Jack F. (R)
39. Lundine, Stanley N. (D)
N.C.—1. Jones, Walter B. (D)
2. Fountain, L. H. (D)
3. Whitley, Charles (D)
4. Andrews, Ike F. (D)
5. Neal, Stephen L. (D)
6. Johnston, Eugene (R)
7. Rose, C. G., III (D)
8. Hefner, Bill (D)
9. Martin, James G. (R)
10. Broyhill, James T. (R)
11. Hendon, William M. (R)
N.D.—Dorgan, Byron L. (D)
Ohio—1. Gradison, Willis D. (R)
2. Luken, Thomas A. (D)
3. Hall, Tony P. (D)
4. Guyer, Tennyson (R)
5. Latta, Delbert L. (R)
6. McEwen, Robert (R)
7. Brown, Clarence J. (R)
8. Kindness, Thomas N. (R)
9. Weber, Ed (R)
10. Miller, Clarence E. (R)
11. Stanton, J. William (R)
12. Shamansky, Robert (D)
13. Pease, Donald J. (D)
14. Seiberling, John F., Jr. (D)
15. Wylie, Chalmers P. (R)
16. Regula, Ralph S. (R)
17. Ashbrook, John M. (R)
18. Applegate, Douglas (D)
19. Williams, Lyle (R)
20. Oakar, Mary Rose (D)
21. Stokes, Louis (D)
22. Eckart, Dennis E. (D)
23. Mottl, Ronald M. (D)

State, district, name, party

Okla.—1. Jones, James R. (D)
2. Synar, Mike (D)
3. Watkins, Wes (D)
4. McCurdy, Dave (D)
5. Edwards, Mickey (R)
6. English, Glenn (D)
Ore.—1. AuCoin, Les (D)
2. Smith, Denny (R)
3. Wyden, Ron (D)
4. Weaver, James (D)
Pa.—1. Foglietta, Thomas (I)
2. Gray, William H., III (D)
3. Lederer, Raymond F. (D)
4. Dougherty, C. F. (R)
5. Schulze, Richard T. (R)
6. Yatron, Gus (D)
7. Edgar, Robert W. (D)
8. Coyne, James K. (R)
9. Shuster, E. G. (R)
10. McDade, Joseph M. (R)
11. Nelligan, James (R)
12. Murtha, John P. (D)
13. Coughlin, R. L. (R)
14. Coyne, William J. (D)
15. Ritter, Donald L. (R)
16. Walker, Robert S. (R)
17. Ertel, Allen E. (D)
18. Walgren, Doug (D)
19. Goodling, William F. (R)
20. Gaydos, Joseph (D)
21. Bailey, Don (D)
22. Murphy, Austin J. (D)
23. Clinger, William F., Jr. (R)
24. Marks, Marc L. (R)
25. Atkinson, Eugene V. (D)
R.I.—1. St. Germain, Fernand (D)
2. Schneider, Claudine (R)
S.C.—1. Hartnett, Thomas F. (R)
2. Spence, Floyd D. (R)
3. Derrick, Butler C., Jr. (D)
4. Campbell, Carroll A., Jr. (R)
5. Holland, Kenneth L. (D)
6. Napier, John L. (R)
S.D.—1. Daschle, Thomas A. (D)
2. Roberts, Clint (R)
Tenn.—1. Quillen, James H. (R)
2. Duncan, John J. (R)
3. Lloyd Bouquard, Marilyn (D)
4. Gore, Albert, Jr. (D)
5. Boner, Bill (D)
6. Beard, Robin L., Jr. (R)
7. Jones, Edward (D)
8. Ford, Harold E. (D)
Texas—1. Hall, Sam B. (D)
2. Wilson, Charles (D)
3. Collins, James M. (R)
4. Hall, Ralph M. (D)
5. Mattox, Jim (D)
6. Gramm, Phil (D)
7. Archer, William R. (R)
8. Fields, Jack (R)
9. Brooks, Jack (D)
10. Pickle, J. J. (D)
11. Leath, J. Marvin (D)
12. Wright, James C., Jr. (D)
13. Hightower, Jack (D)
14. Patman, William N. (D)
15. de la Garza, E. (D)
16. White, Richard C. (D)
17. Stenholm, Charles W. (D)
18. Leland, Mickey (D)
19. Hance, Kent (D)
20. Gonzalez, Henry B. (D)
21. Loeffler, Tom (R)
22. Paul, Ron (R)
23. Kazen, Abraham, Jr. (D)
24. Frost, Martin (D)
Utah—1. Hansen, James V. (R)
2. Marriott, Dan (R)
Vt.—Jeffords, James M. (R)
Va.—1. Trible, Paul S. (R)
2. Whitehurst, G. W. (R)
3. Bliley, Thomas J. (R)
4. Daniel, Robert W. (R)
5. Daniel, Dan (D)
6. Butler, M. Caldwell (R)
7. Robinson, J. Kenneth (R)
8. Parris, Stanford E. (R)
9. Wampler, William C. (R)
10. Wolf, Frank R. (R)
Wash.—1. Pritchard, Joel (R)
2. Swift, Al (D)
3. Bonker, Don (D)
4. Morrison, Sid (R)
5. Foley, Thomas S. (D)
6. Dicks, Norman D. (D)
7. Lowry, Mike (D)
W.Va.—1. Mollohan, R. H. (D)
2. Benedict, Cleve (R)
3. Staton, Mick (R)
4. Rahall, Nick J. (D)
Wis.—1. Aspin, Leslie (D)
2. Kastenmeier, Robert W. (D)
3. Gunderson, Steven (R)
4. Zablocki, Clement J. (D)
5. Reuss, Henry S. (D)
6. Petri, Thomas E. (R)
7. Obey, David R. (D)
8. Roth, Tobias A. (R)
9. Sensenbrenner, F. J. (R)
Wyo.—Cheney, Richard (R)

Supreme Court

Chief Justice Warren Earl Burger (appointed 1969)

Associate Justices (year appointed)

William J. Brennan, Jr.	(1956)	Harry A. Blackmun	(1970)
Potter Stewart	(1958)	Lewis F. Powell, Jr.	(1972)
Byron R. White	(1962)	William H. Rehnquist	(1972)
Thurgood Marshall	(1967)	John Paul Stevens	(1975)

The Federal Administrative Budget

in millions of dollars; fiscal years ending Sept. 30

Source and function	1979	1980 estimate	1981 estimate
BUDGET RECEIPTS	$465,900	$523,800	$600,000
Individual income taxes	217,800	238,700	274,400
Corporation income taxes	65,700	72,300	71,600
Excise taxes	18,700	26,300	40,200
Social insurance taxes and contributions	141,600	162,200	187,400
Estate and gift taxes	5,400	5,800	5,900
Customs duties	7,400	7,600	8,400
Miscellaneous receipts	9,200	10,900	12,100
BUDGET EXPENDITURES	493,700	563,600	615,800
National defense	117,700	130,400	146,200
Department of Defense military functions	115,000	127,400	142,700
Atomic energy defense activities	2,500	3,000	3,400
Defense-related activities	100	50	200
International affairs	6,100	10,400	9,600
Conduct of foreign affairs	1,300	1,400	1,500
Foreign economic and financial assistance	4,700	6,000	6,200
Foreign information and exchange activities	500	500	600
International financial programs	−900	1,700	700
Military assistance	600	900	800
General science, space, and technology	5,000	5,900	6,400
Agriculture	6,200	4,600	2,800
Farm income stabilization	4,900	3,300	1,400
Agricultural research and services	1,300	1,400	1,400
Natural resources and environment	12,100	12,800	12,800
Water resources	3,900	4,200	4,100
Conservation and land management	1,900	2,300	2,200
Recreational resources	1,500	1,500	1,500
Pollution control and abatement	4,700	4,900	5,100
Other natural resources	1,300	1,400	1,500
Energy	6,900	7,800	8,100
Energy supply	4,900	5,500	4,500
Energy conservation	300	600	1,200
Commerce and housing credit	2,600	5,500	700
Mortgage credit and thrift insurance	−700	1,900	−2,800
Payment to the Postal Service	1,800	1,700	1,600
Other advancement and regulation	1,500	2,100	2,100
Transportation	17,500	19,600	20,200
Air transportation	3,400	3,800	4,000
Water transportation	2,000	2,200	2,300
Ground transportation	12,100	13,600	13,800
Other transportation	100	100	100
Community and regional development	9,500	8,500	8,800
Community development	4,000	4,500	5,000

Source and function	1979	1980 estimate	1981 estimate
Area and regional development	$3,900	$2,700	$3,000
Disaster relief and insurance	1,600	1,300	900
Education, training, employment, and social services	29,700	30,700	32,000
Elementary, secondary, and vocational education	6,700	7,300	7,800
Higher education	4,500	5,500	5,200
Research and general education aids	1,200	1,400	1,400
Training and employment	10,800	10,400	11,300
Social services	5,900	5,500	5,700
Health	49,600	56,600	62,400
Health care services	45,100	51,600	57,300
Health research and education	3,600	4,000	4,200
Consumer and occupational health and safety	900	1,000	1,000
Income security	160,200	190,900	220,000
General retirement and disability insurance	108,500	124,600	144,100
Federal employee retirement and disability	12,400	14,600	17,100
Unemployment compensation	10,700	15,600	18,800
Public assistance and other income supplements	28,600	36,100	40,100
Veterans benefits and services	19,900	20,800	21,700
Income security for veterans	10,800	11,700	13,000
Veterans education, training, and rehabilitation	2,800	2,200	1,900
Hospital and medical care for veterans	5,600	6,400	6,400
Other veterans benefits and services	600	700	700
Administration of justice	4,200	4,500	4,700
Federal law enforcement activities	2,000	2,200	2,300
Federal litigative and judicial activities	1,100	1,400	1,500
Federal correctional activities	300	300	400
Criminal justice assistance	700	600	600
General government	4,200	4,900	4,900
Legislative functions	900	1,100	1,100
Central fiscal operations	2,300	2,700	2,800
General property and records management	200	300	400
Other general government	600	700	500
General purpose fiscal assistance	8,400	8,700	9,600
Interest	52,600	63,300	67,200
Allowances for contingencies, civilian agency pay raises	—	100	2,600
Undistributed offsetting receipts	−18,500	−22,300	−25,100
Employer share, employee retirement	−5,300	−5,900	−6,200
Interest received by trust funds	−9,900	−11,500	−13,000
Rents and royalties on the Outer Continental Shelf	−3,300	−4,800	−6,000

Source: Executive Office of the President, Office of Management and Budget, *The United States Budget in Brief: Fiscal Year 1981.*

State Government Revenue, Expenditure, and Debt

1979 in thousands of dollars

	GENERAL REVENUE						GENERAL EXPENDITURE[1]					DEBT		
		State taxes												
State	Total	Total	General sales	Income[2]	Intergov-ernmental	Charges & misc.	Total	Education	Highways	Public welfare	Hospitals	Total	Issued 1979[3]	Retired 1979[3]
Ala.	3,292,500	1,747,400	547,300	463,500	1,094,200	450,900	2,246,400	782,100	339,700	433,800	279,600	1,053,400	111,100	57,600
Alaska	1,508,300	816,700	—	373,000	283,900	220,800	1,052,600	242,800	143,000	101,400	34,800	1,362,500	271,500	41,400
Ariz.	2,274,100	1,515,800	704,200	359,600	489,600	268,600	1,255,500	439,900	234,700	116,600	134,700	96,200	—	1,800
Ark.	1,798,300	994,600	346,000	312,300	644,300	159,400	1,195,300	305,400	221,700	306,100	105,700	244,300	76,800	7,200
Calif.	25,067,600	16,352,000	5,659,300	7,132,800	6,225,500	2,490,100	11,594,500	2,694,900	759,800	3,366,000	938,900	7,676,100	852,700	360,300
Colo.	2,554,400	1,440,800	515,200	569,400	675,900	437,700	1,488,300	594,900	222,100	205,100	161,900	426,200	140,000	42,600
Conn.	2,827,700	1,718,100	736,100	314,600	725,200	384,400	1,974,600	366,300	190,300	541,600	221,700	3,591,000	488,700	229,600
Del.	806,500	491,900	—	265,900	173,900	140,700	517,200	156,300	59,500	83,900	46,100	855,000	153,700	65,600
Fla.	6,298,300	4,291,000	1,947,000	314,400	1,450,100	557,300	3,564,800	738,000	644,500	621,000	543,200	2,671,000	397,500	70,500
Ga.	4,100,700	2,448,100	893,600	955,500	1,291,200	361,400	2,732,600	713,400	497,000	598,000	296,600	1,370,700	7,400	82,400
Hawaii	1,446,800	876,000	430,500	304,400	1,446,800	236,900	1,373,900	501,200	90,500	218,900	122,100	1,696,900	77,100	75,800
Idaho	831,000	466,400	129,900	182,600	831,000	117,200	542,000	131,600	99,600	94,700	45,800	220,900	77,800	7,100
Ill.	9,655,900	6,322,800	2,195,500	2,232,300	2,437,100	1,615,500	6,321,900	1,324,100	782,800	2,241,100	516,900	5,717,900	912,300	350,700
Ind.	4,230,300	2,668,600	1,310,300	720,400	930,800	631,000	2,289,300	877,700	365,300	345,600	284,000	580,500	4,000	22,500
Iowa	2,575,600	1,569,300	405,700	689,000	649,300	357,000	1,692,300	488,800	324,800	381,800	192,800	372,800	150,000	4,500
Kan.	1,961,000	1,187,700	399,100	438,900	493,400	280,000	1,374,000	393,700	246,000	310,700	175,600	459,100	70,400	33,100
Ky.	3,466,000	2,075,700	599,300	619,700	969,600	420,700	2,713,000	658,600	724,800	519,200	158,100	2,810,500	538,100	345,100
La.	4,063,100	2,240,300	676,600	454,800	1,115,100	707,700	2,584,100	628,400	405,000	541,500	333,200	2,636,900	771,600	142,300
Maine	1,071,300	554,400	197,800	153,800	369,000	147,900	733,400	135,200	128,700	217,600	50,200	695,600	102,400	108,700
Md.	4,418,500	2,647,200	699,100	1,151,200	990,700	780,700	3,010,200	644,600	350,200	647,000	326,300	3,690,200	281,400	384,800
Mass.	6,166,300	3,616,100	718,300	2,114,700	1,911,700	638,500	3,967,100	562,300	309,300	1,542,300	493,600	5,414,500	1,365,600	1,108,100
Mich.	9,746,900	6,017,700	1,702,700	2,935,500	2,444,900	1,284,300	5,938,400	1,567,200	422,700	2,122,700	672,600	2,505,500	429,800	103,700
Minn.	4,803,100	3,133,800	608,000	1,612,700	1,094,200	575,200	2,468,200	701,600	365,100	502,400	261,600	1,873,700	268,800	166,900
Miss.	2,217,300	1,196,500	603,200	251,800	772,800	248,100	1,402,000	361,900	210,900	351,600	146,700	843,100	25,000	478,700
Mo.	3,292,800	2,013,000	782,900	664,900	945,400	334,400	2,201,700	468,400	442,100	548,200	276,200	711,600	167,400	32,800
Mont.	810,800	400,600	—	177,700	300,500	109,700	541,800	120,000	124,700	85,300	49,200	147,000	15,900	5,100
Neb.	1,264,100	742,600	252,600	258,500	346,500	175,000	836,800	256,200	152,700	162,400	84,000	52,700	200	3,500
Nev.	726,900	462,600	175,700	—	188,900	75,300	452,300	103,900	105,800	55,700	36,200	374,100	86,900	7,400
N.H.	614,100	264,100	—	73,200	221,000	129,000	512,900	116,100	105,500	102,700	57,700	738,600	250,200	24,100
N.J.	6,376,500	3,729,300	1,098,100	1,298,000	1,703,000	944,200	3,788,900	799,900	357,000	768,600	427,500	5,382,500	1,189,100	667,900
N.M.	1,678,200	845,400	369,800	109,100	437,700	395,100	977,600	297,800	206,200	140,500	108,800	513,900	258,300	90,700
N.Y.	20,426,200	11,633,700	2,588,700	6,281,100	7,078,100	1,714,400	9,137,800	1,986,300	903,500	670,100	1,513,000	22,982,800	2,297,500	1,070,900
N.C.	4,811,500	2,914,900	648,300	1,251,000	1,414,100	482,500	3,044,600	820,500	569,500	545,200	376,100	1,107,400	235,600	56,500
N.D.	741,800	324,800	109,000	78,100	212,800	204,300	530,900	135,200	102,800	72,800	39,700	130,800	53,700	4,300
Ohio	7,879,700	4,619,900	1,427,000	1,373,100	2,160,700	1,099,200	4,958,000	1,389,700	582,000	1,189,500	722,200	3,745,200	496,700	160,200
Okla.	2,675,300	1,515,900	279,700	428,600	696,500	462,900	1,741,200	520,700	227,600	483,300	153,400	1,511,000	492,100	60,200
Ore.	2,683,400	1,384,500	—	973,000	778,100	520,900	1,794,600	405,000	185,900	449,700	162,700	3,808,800	768,600	68,500
Pa.	10,446,000	6,781,800	1,895,500	2,405,900	2,679,900	984,200	6,370,900	1,253,600	645,600	2,299,800	691,300	6,448,100	257,300	335,800
R.I.	1,037,600	537,800	158,200	209,400	307,200	192,600	827,600	181,500	42,900	236,400	114,100	1,177,900	454,100	127,200
S.C.	2,644,400	1,523,000	525,900	555,900	810,400	311,000	1,793,700	627,300	210,400	301,900	270,400	1,590,100	169,000	360,900
S.D.	603,500	245,500	130,500	2,900	225,300	132,700	518,400	136,100	99,400	86,200	34,500	579,800	243,100	27,200
Tenn.	3,225,500	1,843,900	942,600	212,100	1,029,300	352,300	2,240,700	646,500	369,000	526,500	220,500	1,388,600	81,400	90,500
Texas	10,100,900	5,738,400	2,185,000	2,763,700	2,521,000	1,841,500	6,170,500	1,725,900	1,230,200	1,372,000	749,400	2,316,900	259,400	137,700
Utah	1,313,700	694,900	290,000	258,800	401,900	216,900	916,800	328,500	138,200	176,600	96,000	393,100	109,600	7,300
Vt.	556,900	267,500	38,300	107,200	194,100	95,300	449,600	121,000	53,500	91,000	38,200	510,600	92,200	44,200
Va.	4,572,700	2,563,700	534,900	1,162,800	1,237,500	571,200	3,348,900	861,200	785,900	481,400	492,500	1,662,800	424,300	49,400
Wash.	4,445,000	2,718,300	1,524,800	—	1,192,700	534,000	2,826,000	988,200	465,800	553,200	188,400	1,514,800	169,800	100,100
W.Va.	1,981,500	1,150,100	562,500	242,900	613,100	227,800	1,539,200	305,200	474,300	218,000	105,700	1,636,900	328,200	66,600
Wis.	5,232,300	3,260,400	819,700	1,702,800	1,367,000	604,900	2,641,600	835,100	247,900	680,100	211,100	2,234,000	307,100	69,500
Wyo.	670,400	342,800	141,300	112,800	211,000	134,500	360,200	75,900	112,200	35,000	24,200	216,100	121,900	14,000
TOTAL	207,993,300	124,908,100	39,505,500	44,750,000	57,087,400	25,997,800	124,554,400	31,516,700	17,078,900	28,742,500	13,785,800	111,739,900	16,903,200	7,973,800

Fiscal year ending June 30, 1979, except Alabama, September 30; New York, March 31; and Texas, August 31. [1]Direct only, intergovernmental excluded. [2]Includes individual and corporation. [3]Long term only. Source: U.S. Department of Commerce, Bureau of the Census, *Governmental Finances in 1978–79.*

EDUCATION

Public Elementary and Secondary Schools

Fall 1979 estimates

State	ENROLLMENT[1]		INSTRUCTIONAL STAFF				TEACHERS' AVERAGE ANNUAL SALARIES		STUDENT-TEACHER RATIO		Expenditure per pupil
	Elementary	Secondary	Total[2]	Principals and supervisors	Teachers, elementary	Teachers, secondary	Elementary	Secondary	Elementary	Secondary	
Alabama	367,000	380,000	38,450	1,950	17,300	19,200	$12,890	$14,090	21.2	19.8	$1,472
Alaska	48,025	38,594	6,024	271	2,778	2,403	25,865	26,522	17.3	16.1	4,439
Arizona	350,000	160,500	27,410	1,060	16,900	7,400	15,300	16,000	20.7	21.7	2,102
Arkansas	241,210	211,861	26,622	1,392	11,801	12,063	12,088	12,744	20.4	17.6	1,423
California	2,761,000[3]	1,372,000[3]	196,400	9,800	105,500	71,500	18,670	19,620	26.2	19.2	1,972
Colorado	305,000	245,000	33,000	1,600	13,000	14,200	15,920	15,980	23.5	17.2	2,004
Connecticut	378,120	192,316	39,030	2,225	20,505	13,700	16,173	16,574	18.4	14.0	2,551
Delaware	50,247	53,788	6,865	373	2,624	3,353	15,923	16,367	19.1	16.0	2,456
District of Columbia	58,496	47,660	6,928	397	3,538	2,408	22,259	22,088	16.5	19.8	2,936
Florida	757,000	743,000	88,840	3,940	38,200	37,000	14,430	14,710	19.8	20.1	1,798
Georgia	638,644	434,101	54,937	2,475	32,763	19,699	13,800	14,350	19.5	22.0	1,323
Hawaii	88,848	79,545	9,418	601	4,730	3,245	20,000	19,440	18.8	24.5	1,707
Idaho	110,782	91,976	10,789	586	5,072	4,603	13,340	13,918	21.8	20.0	...
Illinois	1,379,942	683,678	122,427	7,072	72,200	37,349	16,964	18,359	19.1	18.3	2,300
Indiana	560,455	530,632	60,851	4,129	26,742	27,143	14,665	15,484	21.0	19.6	1,735
Iowa	285,740	263,760	35,150	1,350	15,200	17,000	14,470	15,530	18.8	15.5	2,376
Kansas	239,513	185,764	28,675	1,600	13,600	11,850	13,980	14,050	17.6	15.6	2,168
Kentucky	442,240	248,760	37,800	2,050	21,072	12,428	14,060	15,200	21.0	20.0	1,592
Louisiana	426,000	384,000	44,660	2,180	23,580	18,900	13,550	14,030	18.1	20.3	1,669
Maine	156,500	76,250	13,060	1,190	6,850	4,920	12,580	13,780	22.8	15.5	1,740
Maryland	385,570	392,155	48,050	3,400	19,800	22,100	17,430	17,720	19.5	17.7	2,353
Massachusetts	687,300	359,800	90,100	5,200	29,000	37,000	17,312	17,659	23.7	9.7	2,482
Michigan	989,000	940,000	93,749	6,700	41,919	38,730	18,650	19,010	23.6	24.3	...
Minnesota	379,300	399,050	48,840	2,125	20,115	23,400	16,100	17,310	18.9	17.0	2,283
Mississippi	269,080	211,420	29,838	1,705	14,798	11,802	11,646	12,168	18.2	17.9	1,549
Missouri	579,541	293,463	55,880	3,176	24,718	23,988	13,455	14,000	23.4	12.2	...
Montana	109,500	55,500	10,560	470	5,230	4,370	14,060	15,420	20.9	12.7	2,106
Nebraska	156,396	133,675	20,945	1,030	9,650	8,775	12,880	14,112	16.2	15.2	1,986
Nevada	73,500	73,500	7,440	370	3,340	3,210	16,330	16,460	22.0	22.9	1,750
New Hampshire	101,800	72,000	10,600	650	4,910	4,320	12,190	12,960	20.7	16.7	1,459
New Jersey	802,280	491,720	94,269	5,879	44,715	33,732	16,819	17,419	17.9	14.6	2,625
New Mexico	141,500	133,500	16,235	1,071	6,738	7,109	13,518	14,311	21.0	18.8	1,764
New York	1,458,500	1,511,500	194,600	13,100	79,000	92,800	19,100	19,300	18.5	16.3	2,706
North Carolina	802,224	358,829	63,351	3,910	37,677	18,140	14,201	14,669	21.3	19.8	1,686
North Dakota	56,652	60,686	8,065	360	4,286	2,909	12,959	13,416	13.2	20.9	1,638
Ohio	1,208,760	820,870	116,780	6,700	54,580	44,670	14,810	15,654	22.1	18.4	1,770
Oklahoma	322,000	263,000	36,610	2,030	17,150	15,850	12,930	13,505	18.8	16.6	1,955
Oregon	281,904	185,224	29,594	2,142	14,868	9,912	15,915	16,700	19.0	18.7	2,281
Pennsylvania	972,800	1,004,400	122,900	5,400	51,230	57,830	16,450	17,030	19.0	17.4	2,289
Rhode Island	77,106	76,988	10,750	641	5,081	4,174	17,140	18,300	15.2	18.4	2,432
South Carolina	432,000	198,000	34,350	1,910	18,270	11,750	12,610	13,521	23.6	16.8	1,508
South Dakota	88,399	45,440	9,310	490	5,220	2,950	12,040	12,410	16.9	15.4	1,712
Tennessee	522,840	342,659	47,886	2,585	25,236	15,940	13,512	13,914	20.7	21.5	1,513
Texas	1,569,314	1,295,686	179,378	12,367	81,036	77,464	13,683	14,317	19.4	16.7	1,580
Utah	191,167	141,408	15,919	831	7,526	6,674	14,555	15,455	25.4	21.2	1,518
Vermont	59,000	39,500	7,550	850	3,250	2,900	12,040	12,870	18.1	13.6	1,745
Virginia	630,300	401,103	65,760	4,560	35,000	26,200	13,490	14,740	18.0	15.3	1,791
Washington	398,449	365,548	40,820	2,995	19,445	15,600	18,473	19,330	20.5	23.4	2,125
West Virginia	232,516	155,852	24,547	1,645	11,684	9,991	13,282	14,065	19.9	15.6	...
Wisconsin	479,847	378,008	56,300	2,100	29,200	25,000	15,500	16,430	16.4	15.1	2,284
Wyoming	52,966	42,502	6,730	387	3,086	2,956	15,440	16,610	17.2	14.4	2,197
TOTAL U.S.	24,157,400	17,665,801	2,485,042	143,020	1,181,713	1,002,610	$15,661	$16,387	20.4	17.6	$2,002

[1] Kindergartens included in elementary schools; junior high schools in secondary schools. [2] Includes librarians, guidance, health and psychological personnel, and related educational workers. [3] Junior high students included in elementary figures.
Source: National Education Association Research, *Estimates of School Statistics, 1979–80*

Universities and Colleges

state statistics

State	NUMBER OF INSTITUTIONS 1979–1980		Enrollment[1,2] fall, 1979	EARNED DEGREES CONFERRED 1977–1978		
	Total	Public		Bachelor's and first professional	Master's except first professional	Doctor's
Alabama	57	36	159,784	16,100	6,948	269
Alaska	16	12	20,052	357	160	3
Arizona	25	17	188,976	9,486	4,432	403
Arkansas	34	19	74,701	6,522	2,167	108
California	263	135	1,698,668	84,274	39,960	3,642
Colorado	44	28	156,100	14,480	6,065	679
Connecticut	49	24	156,067	13,433	6,687	530
Delaware	10	6	32,308	2,997	495	75
District of Columbia	17	1	87,855	6,727	8,033	511
Florida	79	37	395,233	27,770	10,704	1,321
Georgia	73	34	178,017	16,351	8,802	563
Hawaii	12	9	47,204	3,679	1,171	129
Idaho	9	6	40,661	2,877	759	59
Illinois	155	63	612,916	43,451	22,066	1,874
Indiana	66	24	228,397	23,607	10,973	1,015
Iowa	60	22	132,599	13,199	4,062	515
Kansas	52	29	133,300	11,621	4,305	480
Kentucky	41	9	135,179	11,226	6,279	242
Louisiana	32	20	153,812	15,307	5,766	319
Maine	27	11	42,912	4,679	674	41
Maryland	54	32	218,745	16,453	6,303	578
Massachusetts	116	33	396,267	38,434	17,881	1,952
Michigan	96	45	503,839	36,279	18,159	1,338
Minnesota	65	30	193,830	18,185	5,008	501
Mississippi	45	27	100,272	8,784	3,978	269
Missouri	85	28	222,046	21,818	10,324	593
Montana	13	9	31,906	3,577	700	49
Nebraska	30	16	86,446	7,657	2,696	206
Nevada	6	5	35,935	1,543	479	18
New Hampshire	24	10	42,112	6,177	1,059	52
New Jersey	63	31	312,460	25,086	9,356	713
New Mexico	19	16	56,189	4,620	2,419	155
New York	296	82	970,168	85,209	40,706	3,399
North Carolina	126	73	269,065	23,792	7,024	742
North Dakota	16	11	31,904	3,436	584	47
Ohio	131	60	463,548	40,407	16,057	1,603
Oklahoma	44	29	152,683	12,744	4,744	390
Oregon	44	21	154,597	10,329	4,351	331
Pennsylvania	177	61	481,347	53,514	17,278	1,645
Rhode Island	13	3	64,435	6,859	1,652	188
South Carolina	60	33	131,459	11,343	4,182	198
South Dakota	19	8	31,294	3,750	782	50
Tennessee	76	23	199,654	17,801	2,224	513
Texas	149	95	676,047	52,306	20,362	1,502
Utah	14	9	90,398	8,589	2,614	357
Vermont	21	6	29,550	3,768	1,363	32
Virginia	71	39	270,559	20,709	6,901	538
Washington	49	33	303,469	16,139	4,926	453
West Virginia	28	17	81,335	7,638	2,547	117
Wisconsin	63	30	255,907	21,347	6,328	757
Wyoming	8	8	19,490	1,359	473	58
TOTAL U.S.	3,142	1,465	11,541,697	917,895	377,270	32,122

Excludes service academies. [1] Excludes non–degree-credit students. [2] Preliminary.
Source: U.S. Department of Health, Education and Welfare, National Center for Education Statistics, *Digest of Education Statistics* and *Education Directory*.

Universities and Colleges, 1979–80[1]

Selected four-year schools

Institution	Location	Year founded	Total students[2]	Total faculty[3]	Bound library volumes
ALABAMA					
Alabama A. & M. U.	Normal	1875	4,403	370	305,700
Alabama State U.	Montgomery	1874	4,754	179	150,000
Auburn U.	Auburn	1856	18,329	1,123	1,086,000
Birmingham-Southern	Birmingham	1856	1,300	88	126,000
Jacksonville State U.	Jacksonville	1883	6,717	315	415,300
Troy State U.	Troy	1887	6,489	392	201,600
Tuskegee Institute	Tuskegee Institute	1881	3,736	293	250,000
U. of Alabama	University	1831	16,919	936	1,235,000
U. of South Alabama	Mobile	1963	7,885	421	220,000
ALASKA					
U. of Alaska	Fairbanks	1917	3,756	355	500,000
ARIZONA					
Arizona State U.	Tempe	1885	37,122	1,613	1,384,300
Northern Arizona U.	Flagstaff	1899	12,094	560	1,000,000
U. of Arizona	Tucson	1885	34,559	1,774	1,364,800
ARKANSAS					
Arkansas State U.	State University	1909	7,616	350	546,000
U. of Arkansas	Fayetteville	1871	15,688	669	876,100
U. of A. at Little Rock	Little Rock	1927	10,009	436	235,200
U. of Central Arkansas	Conway	1907	5,739	299	294,000
CALIFORNIA					
California Inst. of Tech.	Pasadena	1891	1,650	352	330,000
Cal. Polytech. State U.	San Luis Obispo	1901	16,000	1,000	600,000
Cal. State Polytech. U.	Pomona	1938	12,651	687	290,000
Cal. State U., Chico	Chico	1887	13,826	970	536,400
Cal. State U., Dominguez Hills	Dominguez Hills	1960	7,896	350	250,000
Cal. State U., Fresno	Fresno	1911	16,278	830	600,000
Cal. State U., Fullerton	Fullerton	1957	21,435	1,292	500,000
Cal. State U., Hayward	Hayward	1957	10,666	443	605,000
Cal. State U., Long Beach	Long Beach	1949	29,515	1,281	681,400
Cal. State U., Los Angeles	Los Angeles	1947	22,123	1,282	700,000
Cal. State U., Northridge	Northridge	1958	28,000	1,505	550,000
Cal. State U., Sacramento	Sacramento	1947	20,419	893[4]	693,400
Golden Gate U.	San Francisco	1901	9,530	862	250,000
Humboldt State U.	Arcata	1913	7,419	500	266,000
Loyola Marymount U.	Los Angeles	1911	5,107	309	190,000
Occidental	Los Angeles	1887	1,701	123	338,000
San Francisco State U.	San Francisco	1899	24,131	1,777	500,000
San Jose State U.	San Jose	1857	26,358	1,570	700,000
Sonoma State U.	Rohnert Park	1960	5,860	392	268,700
Stanford U.	Stanford	1885	11,692	1,072	4,363,600
U. of C., Berkeley	Berkeley	1868	30,879	1,290	5,750,000
U. of C., Davis	Davis	1905	18,762	902	1,600,000
U. of C., Irvine	Irvine	1960	10,286	427	930,000
U. of C., Los Angeles	Los Angeles	1919	34,032	1,523	4,230,000
U. of C., Riverside	Riverside	1868	4,707	275	980,000
U. of C., San Diego	La Jolla	1912	11,418	604	1,370,000
U. of C., Santa Barbara	Santa Barbara	1944	15,451	538	1,370,000
U. of C., Santa Cruz	Santa Cruz	1965	6,472	242	610,000
U. of the Pacific	Stockton	1851	4,130	320	560,000
U. of San Francisco	San Francisco	1855	6,007	537	57,600
U. of Santa Clara	Santa Clara	1851	6,718	397	330,000
U. of Southern California	Los Angeles	1880	27,879	1,741	1,650,000
COLORADO					
Colorado	Colorado Springs	1874	1,942	192	290,700
Colorado School of Mines	Golden	1874	2,584	186	158,000
Colorado State U.	Fort Collins	1870	18,083	1,313	1,240,700
Metropolitan State	Denver	1963	14,464	603	351,800
U. S. Air Force Academy	USAF Academy	1954	4,544	530	500,000
U. of Colorado	Boulder	1876	21,878	1,162	1,800,000
U. of Denver	Denver	1864	8,039	497	842,800
U. of Northern Colorado	Greeley	1889	10,830	608	500,000
U. of Southern Colorado	Pueblo	1933	4,682	253	300,000
CONNECTICUT					
Central Connecticut State	New Britain	1849	12,250	719	275,600
Southern Connecticut State	New Haven	1893	11,368	692	372,100
Trinity	Hartford	1823	1,806	175	510,000
U. S. Coast Guard Acad.	New London	1876	905	113	125,000
U. of Bridgeport	Bridgeport	1927	6,805	528	311,800
U. of Connecticut	Storrs	1881	12,563	1,154	1,476,700
U. of Hartford	West Hartford	1877	10,451	707	270,000
Wesleyan U.	Middletown	1831	2,500	235	788,000
Western Connecticut State	Danbury	1903	5,656	250	150,000
Yale U.	New Haven	1701	9,000	1,500	6,692,600
DELAWARE					
Delaware State	Dover	1891	2,348	139	128,400
U. of Delaware	Newark	1833	19,258	929	1,700,000
DISTRICT OF COLUMBIA					
American U.	Washington	1893	12,495	638	502,800
Catholic U. of America	Washington	1887	7,400	533	900,000
George Washington U.	Washington	1821	21,330	3,180	867,400
Georgetown U.	Washington	1789	11,000	1,800	1,000,000
Howard U.	Washington	1867	10,813	1,908	1,012,500
FLORIDA					
Florida A. & M. U.	Tallahassee	1887	6,011	398	294,200
Florida State U.	Tallahassee	1857	22,424	1,080	1,393,200
Florida Tech. U.	Orlando	1963	10,605	397	371,800
Rollins	Winter Park	1885	3,380	156	189,500
U. of Florida	Gainesville	1853	33,200	3,022	2,153,400
U. of Miami	Coral Gables	1925	13,813	869	965,900
U. of South Florida	Tampa	1960	19,430	1,109	523,400
GEORGIA					
Atlanta U.	Atlanta	1865	1,334	156	353,500
Augusta	Augusta	1925	3,713	174	267,900
Emory U.	Atlanta	1836	7,420	1,188	1,500,000
Georgia	Milledgeville	1889	3,366	160	120,000
Georgia Inst. of Tech.	Atlanta	1885	10,688	774	850,000
Georgia Southern	Statesboro	1906	6,626	329	600,000
Georgia State U.	Atlanta	1913	21,000	668	635,700
Mercer U.	Macon	1833	2,972	150	240,000
Morehouse[5]	Atlanta	1867	1,941	121	200,000
Oglethorpe U.	Atlanta	1835	1,153	61	65,000
Spelman[6]	Atlanta	1881	1,366	117	60,000
U. of Georgia	Athens	1785	23,462	1,418	1,985,600
HAWAII					
Brigham Young U.-Hawaii	Laie	1955	1,828	116	110,000
U. of Hawaii	Honolulu	1907	20,706	1,581	1,751,100
IDAHO					
Boise State U.	Boise	1932	10,025	455	230,000
Idaho State U.	Pocatello	1901	10,689	314	340,000
U. of Idaho	Moscow	1889	7,931	749	1,050,000
ILLINOIS					
Augustana	Rock Island	1860	2,434	151	212,900
Bradley U.	Peoria	1897	5,458	420	440,000
Chicago State U.	Chicago	1869	6,998	368	229,000
Concordia Teachers	River Forest	1864	1,194	84	127,000
De Paul U.	Chicago	1898	12,857	676	343,600
Eastern Illinois U.	Charleston	1895	9,989	494	460,000
Illinois Inst. of Tech.	Chicago	1892	6,325	665	1,338,000
Illinois State U.	Normal	1857	19,717	1,042	849,000
Knox	Galesburg	1837	950	82[4]	199,200
Lake Forest	Lake Forest	1857	1,105	94	240,000
Loyola U. of Chicago	Chicago	1870	8,080	1,370	703,300
Northeastern Ill. U.	Chicago	1867	10,346	425	341,100
Northern Illinois U.	De Kalb	1895	26,064	708	1,000,000
Northwestern U.	Evanston	1851	15,429	1,670	2,714,900
Southern Illinois U.	Carbondale	1869	23,236	1,592	1,500,000
SIU at Edwardsville	Edwardsville	1957	10,475	720	740,200
U. of Chicago	Chicago	1891	7,750	1,000	4,200,000
U. of Illinois	Urbana	1867	33,684	2,771	5,582,100
U. of I. at Chicago Circle	Chicago	1965	21,001	1,272	680,000
Western Illinois U.	Macomb	1899	13,542	702	600,000
Wheaton	Wheaton	1860	2,496	199	245,200
INDIANA					
Ball State U.	Muncie	1918	18,490	925	1,006,000
Butler U.	Indianapolis	1855	3,925	280	189,300
De Pauw U.	Greencastle	1837	2,409	191	361,200
Indiana State U.	Terre Haute	1865	12,362	721	800,000
Indiana U.	Bloomington	1820	32,366	3,798	1,400,900
Purdue U.	West Lafayette	1869	31,990	4,556	1,357,800
U. of Evansville	Evansville	1854	5,180	238	230,000
U. of Notre Dame du Lac	Notre Dame	1842	8,925	712	1,419,400
Valparaiso U.	Valparaiso	1859	4,179	327	306,000
IOWA					
Coe	Cedar Rapids	1851	1,426	109	146,000
Drake U.	Des Moines	1881	6,737	382	415,000
Grinnell	Grinnell	1846	1,260	117	243,000
Iowa State U.	Ames	1858	24,268	1,737	1,290,000
U. of Iowa	Iowa City	1847	25,100	1,653	2,217,000
U. of Northern Iowa	Cedar Falls	1876	11,020	662	520,500
KANSAS					
Emporia State U.	Emporia	1863	6,411	350	46,200
Kansas State U.	Manhattan	1863	19,547	1,511	850,000
U. of Kansas	Lawrence	1866	24,466	1,296[4]	1,855,100
Wichita State U.	Wichita	1895	16,621	843	635,700
KENTUCKY					
Berea	Berea	1855	1,442	136	170,000
Eastern Kentucky U.	Richmond	1906	13,871[4]	596[4]	610,700
Kentucky State U.	Frankfort	1886	2,342	170	218,900
Murray State U.	Murray	1922	8,061	360[4]	550,000
U. of Kentucky	Lexington	1865	39,516	1,875	1,640,200
U. of Louisville	Louisville	1798	19,155	1,363	930,100
Western Kentucky U.	Bowling Green	1907	13,332	608	375,000
LOUISIANA					
Grambling State U.	Grambling	1901	3,549	219	29,200
Louisiana State U.	Baton Rouge	1860	27,236	1,185	1,546,800
Louisiana Tech. U.	Ruston	1894	10,092	425	934,700
Northeast Louisiana U.	Monroe	1931	10,037	451	412,600
Northwestern State U.	Natchitoches	1884	15,332	300	350,000
Southern U.	Baton Rouge	1880	8,404	421	388,100
Tulane U.	New Orleans	1834	5,000	540	1,200,000
U. of Southwestern La.	Lafayette	1898	13,865	575[4]	465,000
MAINE					
Bates	Lewiston	1864	1,479	328	300,000
Bowdoin	Brunswick	1794	1,375	109	575,000
Colby	Waterville	1813	1,729	130	358,100
U. of Maine, Farmington	Farmington	1864	1,967	79	86,400
U. of Maine at Orono	Orono	1865	11,262	461	544,400
U. of Southern Maine	Portland	1878	8,203	327	287,800
MARYLAND					
Goucher[6]	Towson	1885	1,087	145	191,200
Johns Hopkins U.	Baltimore	1876	7,843	645	1,849,300
Morgan State U.	Baltimore	1867	4,741	379	217,500
Towson State U.	Baltimore	1866	15,528	943	327,800
U.S. Naval Academy	Annapolis	1845	4,528	550	367,000
U. of Maryland	College Park	1807	36,905	1,942	2,000,000
MASSACHUSETTS					
Amherst	Amherst	1821	1,574	167	550,000
Boston	Chestnut Hill	1863	14,430	822	838,800
Boston U.	Boston	1869	28,165	2,255	1,280,000
Brandeis U.	Waltham	1948	3,613	775	650,000
Clark U.	Worcester	1887	4,510	196	365,000
Harvard U.	Cambridge	1636	16,132	921[4]	10,000,000
Holy Cross	Worcester	1843	2,527	215	350,000
Mass. Inst. of Tech.	Cambridge	1861	9,443	1,821	1,750,000
Mt. Holyoke[6]	South Hadley	1837	1,943	206	448,700
Northeastern U.	Boston	1898	37,472	3,043	480,000
Radcliffe[6]	Cambridge	1879	2,200	...	...
Salem State	Salem	1854	5,025	301	184,300
Simmons[6]	Boston	1899	2,963	253	150,000

Universities and Colleges (continued)

Selected four-year schools

Institution	Location	Year founded	Total students[2]	Total faculty[3]	Bound library volumes
Smith	Northampton	1871	2,651	260	880,000
Tufts U.	Medford	1852	6,766	966	530,000
U. of Lowell	Lowell	1894	14,000	825	285,000
U. of Massachusetts	Amherst	1863	24,018	1,465	1,500,000
Wellesley[6]	Wellesley	1870	2,168	288	600,000
Wheaton[6]	Norton	1834	1,208	130	250,000
Williams	Williamstown	1793	1,999	188	500,000
MICHIGAN					
Albion	Albion	1835	1,874	119	225,000
Central Michigan U.	Mt. Pleasant	1892	16,912	788	649,100
Eastern Michigan U.	Ypsilanti	1849	18,274	780	580,300
Ferris State	Big Rapids	1884	11,112	585	182,000
Hope	Holland	1866	2,464	160	181,000
Michigan State U.	East Lansing	1855	47,316	3,898	2,500,000
Michigan Tech. U.	Houghton	1885	7,865	507	484,100
Northern Michigan U.	Marquette	1899	9,335	394	347,800
U. of Detroit	Detroit	1877	6,610	598	504,000
U. of Michigan	Ann Arbor	1817	35,670	2,294[4]	5,500,000
Wayne State U.	Detroit	1868	34,341	2,400	1,750,000
Western Michigan U.	Kalamazoo	1903	20,698	1,068	753,900
MINNESOTA					
Carleton	Northfield	1866	1,862	167	260,000
Concordia	Moorhead	1891	2,625	193	248,000
Gustavus Adolphus	St. Peter	1862	2,315	207	287,000
Hamline U.	St. Paul	1854	1,802	205	175,000
Macalester	St. Paul	1874	1,728	170	250,000
Mankato State U.	Mankato	1867	11,427	580	538,400
Moorhead State U.	Moorhead	1885	6,962	284[4]	248,800
St. Catherine[6]	St. Paul	1905	2,399	208	210,000
St. Cloud State U.	St. Cloud	1869	11,591	599	477,300
St. John's U.[5]	Collegeville	1857	1,977	215	300,000
St. Olaf	Northfield	1874	3,059	277	326,500
St. Thomas	St. Paul	1885	5,281	295	200,000
U. of Minnesota	Minneapolis	1851	55,076	4,439	3,300,000
Winona State U.	Winona	1858	4,000	245	165,000
MISSISSIPPI					
Alcorn State U.	Lorman	1871	2,776	136	124,000
Jackson State U.	Jackson	1877	7,718	350	220,000
Mississippi	Clinton	1826	3,055	173	224,000
Mississippi U. for Women	Columbus	1884	2,550	191	304,100
Mississippi State U.	Mississippi State	1878	11,409	667	712,200
U. of Mississippi	University	1848	9,597	500	850,000
U. of Southern Mississippi	Hattiesburg	1910	10,222	615	630,000
MISSOURI					
Central Missouri State U.	Warrensburg	1871	9,989	477	577,400
Northeast Missouri State U.	Kirksville	1867	6,366	277	240,200
St. Louis U.	St. Louis	1818	9,538	2,136	780,200
Southeast Missouri State U.	Cape Girardeau	1873	9,135	473	250,000
Southwest Missouri State U.	Springfield	1906	14,651	633	348,700
U. of Missouri-Columbia	Columbia	1839	23,545	1,051	1,984,600
U. of Missouri-Kansas City	Kansas City	1929	10,824	544	562,800
U. of Missouri-Rolla	Rolla	1870	6,182	322	300,000
U. of Missouri-St. Louis	St. Louis	1963	11,380	540	352,000
Washington U.	St. Louis	1853	10,804	743	1,500,000
MONTANA					
Montana State U.	Bozeman	1893	10,109	743	600,000
U. of Montana	Missoula	1893	8,884	468	626,900
NEBRASKA					
Creighton U.	Omaha	1878	5,614	900	442,600
U. of Nebraska	Lincoln	1869	24,128	1,223	1,494,000
U. of Nebraska at Omaha	Omaha	1908	14,873	501	340,000
NEVADA					
U. of Nevada-Las Vegas	Las Vegas	1951	7,437	303[4]	393,200
U. of Nevada-Reno	Reno	1864	9,160	407	622,000
NEW HAMPSHIRE					
Dartmouth	Hanover	1769	4,248	297	1,000,000
U. of New Hampshire	Durham	1866	10,714	671	760,000
NEW JERSEY					
Glassboro State	Glassboro	1923	10,100	454	362,000
Jersey City State	Jersey City	1927	8,700	530	250,000
Kean Col. of N. J.	Union	1855	13,237	723	200,000
Montclair State	Upper Montclair	1908	15,576	560	318,800
Princeton U.	Princeton	1746	6,187	571	3,000,000
Rider	Lawrenceville	1865	5,726	289	327,000
Rutgers State U.	New Brunswick	1766	33,667	2,130	3,199,000
Seton Hall U.	South Orange	1856	9,902	568	300,000
Stevens Inst. of Tech.	Hoboken	1870	2,430	163	100,000
Trenton State	Trenton	1855	10,000	434	400,000
Upsala	East Orange	1893	1,570	116	145,000
William Patterson	Wayne	1855	11,774	699	283,000
NEW MEXICO					
New Mexico State U.	Las Cruces	1888	12,347	605	610,000
U. of New Mexico	Albuquerque	1889	22,405	1,364	1,000,000
NEW YORK					
Adelphi U.	Garden City	1896	11,774	885	350,800
Alfred U.	Alfred	1836	2,265	161	223,000
Canisius	Buffalo	1870	3,924	257	208,500
City U. of New York					
Bernard M. Baruch	New York	1919	13,449	776	261,200
Brooklyn	Brooklyn	1930	17,133	1,274	781,000
City	New York	1847	12,320	753	1,000,000
Herbert H. Lehman	Bronx	1931	9,248	595	365,000
Hunter	New York	1870	17,509	1,238	463,000
Queens	Flushing	1937	18,000	900	450,000
Richmond	Staten Island	1965	2,291	101	165,000
York	Jamaica	1966	3,819	169	153,500
Colgate U.	Hamilton	1819	2,550	229	330,000
Columbia U.	New York	1754	15,311	4,000	4,500,000
Barnard[6]	New York	1889	2,550	200	150,000
Teachers	New York	1887	6,107	222	450,000
Cornell U.	Ithaca	1865	16,716	1,848	4,000,000
Elmira	Elmira	1855	2,709	187	128,000
Fordham U.	Bronx	1841	14,854	675[4]	2,160,000
Hamilton	Clinton	1812	960	85	325,900
Hofstra U.	Hempstead	1935	10,989	687	847,000
Ithaca	Ithaca	1892	4,800	408	270,000
Juilliard School	New York	1905	1,000	150	50,000
Long Island U.	Greenvale	1926	7,459	789	650,000
Manhattan[5]	Bronx	1853	4,879	355	200,000
Marymount[5]	Tarrytown	1907	1,269	143	104,500
New School for Soc. Res.	New York	1919	27,000	1,500	175,000
New York U.	New York	1831	45,320	4,000	2,700,200
Niagara U.	Niagara University	1856	3,870	242	206,400
Polytechnic Inst. of N.Y.	Brooklyn	1854	4,606	217	251,500
Pratt Inst.	Brooklyn	1887	4,354	491	211,490
Rensselaer Polytech. Inst.	Troy	1824	6,309	382	300,000
Rochester Inst. of Tech.	Rochester	1829	15,134	1,063	190,800
St. Bonaventure U.	St. Bonaventure	1856	2,833	167	207,800
St. John's U.	Jamaica	1870	13,729	622	980,400
St. Lawrence U.	Canton	1856	2,277	155	290,000
State U. of N.Y. at Albany	Albany	1844	16,069	750	937,000
SUNY at Buffalo	Buffalo	1846	24,683	1,830	1,884,900
SUNY at Stony Brook	Stony Brook	1957	14,867	816	1,086,500
State U. Colleges					
Brockport	Brockport	1836	8,633	572	373,000
Buffalo	Buffalo	1867	11,909	556	408,400
Cortland	Cortland	1868	6,080	341	225,000
Fredonia	Fredonia	1867	5,262	284	313,600
Geneseo	Geneseo	1867	5,551	316	325,500
New Paltz	New Paltz	1828	7,204	391	345,800
Oneonta	Oneonta	1889	5,900	360	382,900
Oswego	Oswego	1861	7,554	722	400,000
Plattsburgh	Plattsburgh	1889	6,320	375	230,800
Potsdam	Potsdam	1816	4,652	316	300,000
Syracuse U.	Syracuse	1870	19,828	967	2,000,000
U.S. Merchant Marine Acad.	Kings Point	1943	1,142	89	100,000
U.S. Military Academy	West Point	1802	4,417	642	400,000
U. of Rochester	Rochester	1850	8,100	426	1,800,000
Vassar	Poughkeepsie	1861	2,250	221	500,000
Wagner	Staten Island	1883	2,454	187	250,000
Yeshiva U.	New York	1886	4,320	2,486	788,600
NORTH CAROLINA					
Appalachian State U.	Boone	1899	9,794	1,066	406,700
Catawba	Salisbury	1851	998	65	162,000
Davidson	Davidson	1837	1,403	107	250,000
Duke U.	Durham	1838	9,531	1,697	3,022,800
East Carolina U.	Greenville	1907	13,165	674	600,400
Lenoir-Rhyne	Hickory	1891	1,388	92	100,000
N. Carolina A. & T. St. U.	Greensboro	1891	5,407	361	288,700
N. Carolina State U.	Raleigh	1887	21,225	1,219	1,000,000
U. of N.C. at Chapel Hill	Chapel Hill	1789	21,465	2,022	2,604,400
U. of N.C. at Greensboro	Greensboro	1891	10,390	616	1,150,000
Wake Forest U.	Winston-Salem	1834	4,661	1,058	781,200
Western Carolina U.	Cullowhee	1889	6,459	340	310,300
NORTH DAKOTA					
North Dakota State U.	Fargo	1890	8,232	391[4]	343,800
U. of North Dakota	Grand Forks	1883	10,217	495	407,700
OHIO					
Antioch	Yellow Springs	1852	816	425	240,000
Bowling Green State U.	Bowling Green	1910	17,659	723	664,600
Case Western Reserve U.	Cleveland	1826	8,300	1,700	1,576,000
Cleveland State U.	Cleveland	1964	19,103	730	440,000
Denison U.	Granville	1831	2,100	182	238,000
John Carroll U.	Cleveland	1886	3,994	268	350,000
Kent State U.	Kent	1910	18,331	884	1,000,000
Kenyon	Gambier	1824	1,455	133	250,000
Marietta	Marietta	1835	1,327	111	247,900
Miami U.	Oxford	1809	17,907	751	988,000
Oberlin	Oberlin	1833	3,971	244	900,000
Ohio State U.	Columbus	1870	54,462	2,306	3,530,000
Ohio U.	Athens	1804	13,310	823	985,700
U. of Akron	Akron	1870	24,632	1,230	584,500
U. of Cincinnati	Cincinnati	1819	39,065	2,215	1,500,000
U. of Dayton	Dayton	1850	9,800	600	600,000
U. of Toledo	Toledo	1872	20,270	942	1,134,600
Wooster	Wooster	1866	1,800	145	270,600
Xavier U.	Cincinnati	1831	6,385	280	189,000
Youngstown State U.	Youngstown	1908	15,800	807	440,400
OKLAHOMA					
Central State U.	Edmond	1890	11,724	447	604,700
Oklahoma State U.	Stillwater	1890	21,904	1,488	1,200,000
U. of Oklahoma	Norman	1890	21,703	826	1,672,700
U. of Tulsa	Tulsa	1894	6,311	429	1,000,000
OREGON					
Lewis and Clark	Portland	1867	2,404	170	187,300
Oregon State U.	Corvallis	1868	17,682	1,071	854,700
Portland State U.	Portland	1955	16,841	938	574,000
Reed	Portland	1909	1,132	106	283,000
U. of Oregon	Eugene	1872	17,400	1,509	1,474,400
PENNSYLVANIA					
Allegheny	Meadville	1815	1,936	133[4]	290,000
Bryn Mawr[6]	Bryn Mawr	1885	1,784	175	550,000
Bucknell U.	Lewisburg	1846	3,261	240	395,300
Carnegie-Mellon U.	Pittsburgh	1900	5,311	428	572,800
Dickinson	Carlisle	1773	1,825	258	250,000
Drexel U.	Philadelphia	1891	11,800	475	400,000
Duquesne U.	Pittsburgh	1878	6,500	493	413,700
Edinboro State	Edinboro	1857	5,624	381	337,000
Franklin and Marshall	Lancaster	1787	2,075	126	185,000
Gettysburg	Gettysburg	1832	1,966	161	246,000
Indiana U. of Pa.	Indiana	1875	12,278	681	500,000
Juniata	Huntingdon	1876	1,301	91	200,000
Lafayette	Easton	1826	2,390	170	358,000
La Salle	Philadelphia	1863	7,661	340	350,000
Lehigh U.	Bethlehem	1865	6,276	589	680,000
Moravian	Bethlehem	1742	1,240	79	141,000
Muhlenberg	Allentown	1848	2,234	112	178,000

Institution	Location	Year founded	Total students[2]	Total faculty[3]	Bound library volumes
Pennsylvania State U.	University Park	1855	35,298	1,584	1,467,600
St. Joseph's	Philadelphia	1851	5,539	298	185,000
Slippery Rock State	Slippery Rock	1889	5,690	314	420,300
Susquehanna U.	Selinsgrove	1858	1,830	119	115,000
Swarthmore	Swarthmore	1864	1,316	140	456,000
Temple U.	Philadelphia	1884	33,593	2,572	1,600,000
U. of Pennsylvania	Philadelphia	1740	22,006	6,720	2,900,000
U. of Pittsburgh	Pittsburgh	1787	28,781	2,556	1,631,600
Ursinus	Collegeville	1869	1,912	99	140,000
Villanova U.	Villanova	1842	10,341	400	460,000
West Chester State	West Chester	1812	8,703	460	360,000
PUERTO RICO					
Inter American U.	San Juan	1912	23,296	1,042	260,000
U. of Puerto Rico	Río Piedras	1903	23,373	1,092	2,156,600
RHODE ISLAND					
Brown U.	Providence	1764	7,045	495	1,640,200
Rhode Island	Providence	1854	8,558	376	252,000
U. of Rhode Island	Kingston	1892	9,001	900	650,000
SOUTH CAROLINA					
The Citadel[5]	Charleston	1842			
Clemson U.	Clemson	1889	11,579	671	765,000
Furman U.	Greenville	1826	3,151	159	254,000
U. of South Carolina	Columbia	1801	25,992	1,192[4]	1,880,700
SOUTH DAKOTA					
South Dakota State U.	Brookings	1881	6,848	565	350,000
U. of South Dakota	Vermillion	1882	5,968	490	313,700
TENNESSEE					
Fisk U.	Nashville	1867			
Memphis State U.	Memphis	1909	20,784	932	869,700
Middle Tennessee State U.	Murfreesboro	1911	11,275	587	422,500
Tennessee State U.	Nashville	1912	10,880	450	403,800
Tennessee Tech. U.	Cookeville	1915	8,098	512	348,000
U. of Tennessee	Knoxville	1794	30,000	2,100	1,600,000
Vanderbilt U.	Nashville	1873	8,874	3,435	1,439,300
TEXAS					
Austin	Sherman	1849	1,190	107	176,200
Baylor U.	Waco	1845	9,933	903	893,000
East Texas State U.	Commerce	1889	9,282	470	550,000
Hardin-Simmons U.	Abilene	1891	1,969	119	166,000
Lamar U.	Beaumont	1923	12,800	496	430,000
North Texas State U.	Denton	1890	17,158	808	1,267,800
Prairie View A. & M.	Prairie View	1876	5,400	410[4]	195,700
Rice U.	Houston	1891	3,700	445	991,800
Sam Houston State U.	Huntsville	1879	10,601	385	617,000
Southern Methodist U.	Dallas	1911	9,100	575	1,700,000
Southwest Texas State U.	San Marcos	1899	15,400	682	564,800
Stephen F. Austin State U.	Nacogdoches	1923	10,768	540	59,500
Texas A. & I. U.	Kingsville	1925	5,426	247	400,600
Texas A. & M. U.	College Station	1876	31,331	1,615	700,000
Texas Christian U.	Fort Worth	1873	6,283	361	565,100
Texas Southern U.	Houston	1947	9,500	427	270,000
Texas Tech. U.	Lubbock	1923	23,043	1,450	1,250,000
U. of Houston	Houston	1927	30,692	1,513	1,225,900
U. of Texas at Arlington	Arlington	1895	17,201	742	635,000
U. of Texas at Austin	Austin	1881	92,296	1,909[4]	4,547,500
U. of Texas at El Paso	El Paso	1913	15,751	458	780,000
West Texas State U.	Canyon	1909	6,701	277	686,600
UTAH					
Brigham Young U.	Provo	1875	27,091	1,349	1,040,000
U. of Utah	Salt Lake City	1850	21,880	1,350	1,500,000
Utah State U.	Logan	1888	9,939	462[4]	687,700
Weber State	Ogden	1889	8,311	398	257,014
VERMONT					
Bennington	Bennington	1925	594	77	85,000
Middlebury	Middlebury	1800	1,900	168	413,900
U. of Vermont	Burlington	1791	10,990	1,119	920,000
VIRGINIA					
James Madison U.	Harrisonburg	1908	8,817	506	284,500
Old Dominion U.	Norfolk	1930	13,935	638	481,600
U. of Richmond	Richmond	1830	4,847	474	273,100
U. of Virginia	Charlottesville	1819	15,903	1,534	2,351,900
Virginia Commonwealth U.	Richmond	1838	17,096	1,210	376,900
Virginia Military Inst.[5]	Lexington	1839	1,319	135	261,100
Va. Polytech. Inst. & State U.	Blacksburg	1872	21,069	1,927	1,200,000
Washington & Lee U.[5]	Lexington	1749	1,622	178	325,700
William & Mary	Williamsburg	1693	6,465	486	836,900
WASHINGTON					
Central Washington U.	Ellensburg	1891	7,551	419	300,000
Eastern Washington U.	Cheney	1890	7,469	373	354,000
Gonzaga U.	Spokane	1887	3,351	209	235,000
U. of Washington	Seattle	1861	36,636	2,594	4,000,000
Washington State U.	Pullman	1890	16,850	805	1,190,000
Western Washington U.	Bellingham	1893	9,616	512	391,900
Whitman	Walla Walla	1859	1,165	78	284,200
WEST VIRGINIA					
Bethany	Bethany	1840			
Marshall U.	Huntington	1837	886	82	140,000
West Virginia U.	Morgantown	1867	11,884	523	339,000
			21,220	2,071	961,800
WISCONSIN					
Beloit	Beloit	1846	1,058	95	250,000
Lawrence U.	Appleton	1847	1,137	131	225,000
Marquette U.	Milwaukee	1881	11,616	906	700,000
St. Norbert	De Pere	1898	1,686	119	100,000
U. of W.-Eau Claire	Eau Claire	1916	11,054	549	405,800
U. of W.-Green Bay	Green Bay	1965	4,147	242	300,000
U. of W.-La Crosse	La Crosse	1909	7,617	359[4]	445,800
U. of W.-Madison	Madison	1848	41,349	2,345	3,700,000
U. of W.-Milwaukee	Milwaukee	1956	25,933	1,687	1,350,000
U. of W.-Oshkosh	Oshkosh	1871	10,400	667	292,200
U. of W.-Platteville	Platteville	1866	4,884	294	375,000
U. of W.-River Falls	River Falls	1874	5,339	241	190,000
U. of W.-Stevens Point	Stevens Point	1894	9,081	535	475,000
U. of W.-Stout	Menomonie	1893	7,413	337[4]	175,000
U. of W.-Superior	Superior	1896	2,323	222	211,000
U. of W.-Whitewater	Whitewater	1868	10,006	555	278,600
WYOMING					
U. of Wyoming	Laramie	1886	9,013	1,324	650,000

[1] Latest data available; coeducational unless otherwise indicated. [2] Total includes part-time students. [3] Total includes part-time or full-time equivalent faculty. [4] Total includes full-time equivalent only. [5] Men's school. [6] Women's school.

LIVING CONDITIONS

Health Personnel and Facilities

State	Physicians Dec. 31, 1978[1]	Dentists 1979	Registered Nurses[2]	Hospital facilities 1978: Hospitals	Hospital facilities 1978: Beds	Nursing homes 1978: Facilities	Nursing homes 1978: Beds
Alabama	4,554	1,314	10,235	148	25,242	204	19,246
Alaska	460	232	2,030	26	1,697	12	1,108
Arizona	4,918	1,173	12,383	78	11,339	84	6,823
Arkansas	2,610	714	5,033	96	12,650	179	16,561
California	52,194	14,052	103,385	613	114,836	3,500[2]	138,219[2]
Colorado	5,600	1,701	15,515	101	14,666	190	19,228
Connecticut	7,705	2,194	23,612	64	18,791	286	20,189
Delaware	972	265	4,389	15	4,099	27	2,484
District of Columbia	3,491	587	5,545	19	9,003	70[2]	2,873[2]
Florida	18,353	4,323	38,398	245	54,211	346	34,422
Georgia	7,259	2,167	17,423	189	31,146	278	29,768
Hawaii	1,808	599	4,117	27	3,813	148	3,315
Idaho	1,010	459	3,755	51	3,737	48	4,381
Illinois	20,628	5,999	60,806	285	75,484	557	61,487
Indiana	6,993	2,234	21,481	135	33,816	476	41,010
Iowa	3,635	1,396	17,812	141	21,613	488	33,910
Kansas	3,618	1,080	12,655	164	18,161	283	19,842
Kentucky	4,699	1,490	11,734	121	18,815	237	17,551
Louisiana	5,955	1,586	11,524	159	25,128	133	13,885
Maine	1,752	489	7,440	53	7,324	353	10,733
Maryland	10,390	2,591	22,462	85	25,210	183	19,322
Massachusetts	14,985	3,983	56,567	189	45,456	829	51,175
Michigan	14,290	4,772	46,681	244	50,661	563	60,238
Minnesota	7,676	2,429	23,638	188	31,051	495	44,350
Mississippi	2,571	763	6,288	114	16,234	96	10,162
Missouri	7,839	2,303	18,823	167	35,437	824	40,588
Montana	1,024	442	4,429	65	5,652	67	4,320
Nebraska	2,338	931	9,798	108	11,674	214	16,586
Nevada	925	340	2,564	25	3,234	29	1,686
New Hampshire	1,542	465	7,044	33	4,995	96	6,583
New Jersey	13,820	4,706	51,061	139	44,157	487	37,528
New Mexico	1,869	511	4,077	54	6,503	43	2,640
New York	47,021	12,611	125,794	368	134,425	1,027[2]	104,523[2]
North Carolina	8,428	2,175	21,366	158	33,774	722[2]	24,614[2]
North Dakota	825	312	3,653	60	5,830	79	5,080
Ohio	17,325	5,064	57,052	241	64,158	669	52,007
Oklahoma	3,650	1,192	8,698	141	17,482	222	17,223
Oregon	4,546	1,685	11,382	85	11,568	184	11,663
Pennsylvania	22,149	6,272	96,414	313	86,474	609	79,888
Rhode Island	1,967	509	6,638	21	6,700	112	7,981
South Carolina	3,873	1,130	10,187	88	16,919	161	9,427
South Dakota	723	286	3,852	70	5,676	138	8,647
Tennessee	6,808	2,034	12,051	160	31,008	245	18,461
Texas	20,143	5,757	40,372	565	79,071	966	92,574
Utah	2,225	853	4,531	41	5,084	72	4,386
Vermont	1,075	270	4,521	19	3,036	214	4,981
Virginia	8,653	2,599	23,935	135	32,138	330	21,008
Washington	6,981	2,611	21,953	127	16,138	504	34,909
West Virginia	2,565	703	7,314	80	14,170	125	6,089
Wisconsin	7,271	2,654	23,318	171	28,630	490	51,138
Wyoming	479	216	1,922	31	2,529	28	1,982
TOTAL U.S.	404,190	117,223	1,127,657	7,015	1,380,645	18,722	1,348,794

[1] Non-federal only. [2] Latest data available. Sources: *Physician Distribution and Medical Licensure in the U.S., 1978,* Dept. of Statistical Analysis, Center for Health Services Research and Development, American Medical Association, Chicago, 1980; American Dental Association, *Distribution of Dentists in the United States by State, Region, District, and County, 1979;* American Nurses' Association; American Hospital Association, *Hospital Statistics, 1979 Edition;* U.S. Dept. of Health, Education, and Welfare, Public Health Service.

Crime Rates per 100,000 Population

State or metropolitan area	VIOLENT CRIME										PROPERTY CRIME							
	Total		Murder		Rape		Robbery		Assault		Total		Burglary		Larceny		Auto theft	
	1974	1979	1974	1979	1974	1979	1974	1979	1974	1979	1974	1979	1974	1979	1974	1979	1974	1979
Alabama	372.9	413.3	15.0	13.2	22.7	27.5	99.6	109.5	235.6	263.1	2,627.2	3,830.5	1,057.9	1,287.3	1,308.7	2,223.2	260.6	320.1
Alaska	453.1	491.1	13.6	13.3	**49.3**	**71.9**	88.4	109.6	301.8	296.3	4,786.6	5,712.6	1,166.8	1,383.3	2,972.1	3,713.3	647.8	616.0
Arizona	566.7	593.0	9.6	8.9	37.5	45.7	204.2	175.7	315.5	362.6	**7,654.9**	7,264.4	**2,534.0**	1,996.6	**4,518.6**	**4,774.5**	608.3	493.3
Arkansas	316.2	366.2	11.2	9.1	23.9	27.3	80.7	74.6	200.5	255.3	2,984.4	3,254.5	1,075.2	984.3	1,743.3	2,076.5	163.9	193.8
California	610.6	811.1	9.5	13.0	40.6	53.9	252.7	333.8	307.8	410.3	6,236.2	6,657.7	2,072.0	2,186.8	3,525.5	3,732.6	638.8	738.3
Colorado	429.8	522.1	6.0	5.8	36.5	53.1	165.7	157.0	221.6	306.1	5,736.0	6,529.0	1,843.1	1,794.4	3,354.2	4,253.2	538.6	481.4
Connecticut	228.1	414.2	3.3	4.2	11.2	24.1	92.3	193.3	121.4	192.6	4,178.8	5,365.0	1,353.9	1,548.3	2,275.0	3,113.9	549.9	703.2
Delaware	443.1	537.3	10.3	5.7	17.3	27.8	127.9	129.4	287.6	374.4	5,506.5	5,988.5	1,517.8	1,527.5	3,459.9	3,965.8	528.8	495.2
Florida	677.6	833.9	14.7	12.2	36.0	51.6	275.2	249.4	351.8	520.6	6,709.7	6,854.2	2,287.3	2,154.4	3,939.5	4,267.5	482.9	432.3
Georgia	442.2	558.7	**17.8**	17.1	27.1	43.3	176.5	213.7	220.8	284.5	3,470.2	4,858.2	1,462.4	1,594.0	1,660.8	2,847.9	347.1	416.3
Hawaii	208.0	289.7	8.3	7.2	26.1	32.3	121.6	184.5	52.1	65.7	5,863.6	6,957.8	1,784.8	1,807.4	3,492.8	4,435.0	586.1	715.4
Idaho	183.4	288.7	5.6	5.4	16.0	20.6	37.9	43.3	123.8	219.4	3,899.2	3,952.0	1,001.8	1,075.0	2,683.5	2,605.2	214.0	271.8
Illinois	627.1	481.3	11.8	10.7	27.7	29.4	313.4	198.0	274.2	243.2	4,557.1	4,687.9	1,264.2	1,189.0	2,761.5	2,961.7	531.4	537.2
Indiana	293.3	338.0	8.0	8.3	23.5	31.1	134.4	132.7	127.3	165.9	4,043.6	4,263.4	1,254.6	1,169.9	2,396.0	2,660.5	393.0	433.0
Iowa	121.0	181.2	1.9	2.2	10.1	11.0	48.7	50.2	60.4	117.7	3,292.6	4,120.6	791.5	922.1	2,282.1	2,928.8	219.1	269.7
Kansas	276.3	353.6	6.9	5.5	19.7	26.4	107.8	102.3	141.9	219.4	4,024.1	4,542.2	1,268.6	1,329.8	2,516.9	2,938.9	238.6	273.5
Kentucky	234.0	248.0	10.3	9.5	17.6	20.4	92.3	92.1	113.7	126.1	2,525.7	2,935.9	830.1	909.6	1,466.8	1,770.1	228.8	256.2
Louisiana	472.7	676.3	16.0	16.9	25.2	38.6	156.3	219.4	275.1	401.4	3,343.7	4,682.4	1,045.7	1,396.8	1,956.2	2,877.7	341.7	407.9
Maine	137.5	202.5	2.9	2.8	8.7	11.9	27.9	31.8	98.1	155.9	3,462.7	4,104.8	1,318.9	1,147.9	1,946.0	2,719.1	197.7	237.9
Maryland	719.1	795.5	11.7	9.8	29.8	39.4	360.6	331.2	316.9	415.2	4,931.0	5,499.1	1,402.9	1,509.5	2,944.8	3,502.0	583.3	487.6
Massachusetts	388.7	531.3	4.4	3.7	15.6	24.8	212.4	203.2	156.3	299.6	4,994.2	5,386.7	1,549.8	1,604.6	2,078.8	2,637.1	**1,365.6**	**1,144.9**
Michigan	659.4	614.2	13.0	9.1	37.1	44.5	337.2	219.6	272.0	341.1	5,860.2	5,532.8	1,903.9	1,507.5	3,331.6	3,423.2	624.7	602.1
Minnesota	207.3	221.0	3.0	2.3	17.7	21.5	104.1	92.5	82.5	104.8	3,723.7	4,171.8	1,121.8	1,112.5	2,228.2	2,729.7	373.7	329.2
Mississippi	334.9	323.6	12.9	12.6	17.4	21.7	48.0	70.7	256.5	218.6	1,914.3	2,637.0	755.7	973.7	1,034.5	1,496.5	124.1	166.8
Missouri	452.4	527.2	9.8	11.2	26.9	33.6	216.7	210.9	199.0	271.4	4,335.6	4,412.7	1,471.3	1,446.7	2,437.3	2,555.4	427.1	410.6
Montana	162.4	224.2	4.2	4.2	12.2	20.6	35.6	33.1	110.3	166.3	3,921.4	4,236.4	887.9	803.3	2,750.5	3,121.8	283.0	311.3
Nebraska	239.6	225.9	3.6	4.1	18.9	21.5	91.0	73.5	126.2	126.8	3,104.7	3,767.2	773.8	813.5	2,053.5	2,680.7	277.5	272.9
Nevada	682.4	835.6	14.8	**17.5**	45.2	59.5	277.8	407.5	344.5	351.0	7,144.7	**7,996.0**	2,452.5	**2,820.4**	4,086.0	4,471.2	606.1	704.4
New Hampshire	91.5	139.9	3.5	2.4	8.4	17.1	25.9	28.6	53.7	91.8	3,052.5	4,438.9	820.4	1,199.0	1,973.0	2,915.0	259.0	324.9
New Jersey	403.4	501.2	6.8	6.6	19.7	27.8	216.6	250.0	160.3	216.8	4,368.3	5,319.4	1,429.4	1,601.5	2,392.2	3,021.7	546.7	696.2
New Mexico	450.4	586.0	11.3	12.4	34.8	46.9	124.6	121.0	279.6	405.6	4,762.6	5,202.5	1,583.1	1,481.5	2,873.4	3,363.8	306.1	357.2
New York	**791.6**	**917.4**	10.6	11.9	28.4	30.6	**476.3**	**529.6**	276.3	345.3	4,065.5	5,287.7	1,443.6	1,746.9	2,054.4	2,836.4	567.5	704.5
North Carolina	488.9	446.1	11.7	10.7	15.5	20.3	92.3	77.2	**369.4**	337.9	3,022.3	3,926.4	1,186.9	1,296.6	1,647.1	2,406.4	188.3	223.4
North Dakota	50.1	61.3	1.4	1.5	7.8	8.2	12.9	9.9	27.9	41.7	2,110.0	2,694.5	433.0	461.0	1,544.7	2,071.1	132.3	162.4
Ohio	364.1	457.5	8.9	8.1	23.9	31.8	191.2	194.8	140.2	222.8	3,859.3	4,672.3	1,171.8	1,287.2	2,285.1	2,946.2	402.4	438.9
Oklahoma	280.1	405.2	8.1	9.7	25.0	33.0	83.5	102.6	163.5	260.0	3,815.9	4,297.8	1,455.2	1,474.6	1,999.0	2,396.0	361.7	427.2
Oregon	367.4	545.4	5.6	4.2	32.3	44.4	130.8	130.6	198.7	366.2	5,977.3	5,827.6	1,843.2	1,609.9	3,665.5	3,831.5	468.7	386.2
Pennsylvania	315.0	333.6	6.7	6.2	17.8	21.6	159.5	152.2	131.0	153.6	2,738.5	3,161.8	927.8	934.9	1,435.0	1,837.6	375.0	389.4
Rhode Island	282.9	375.1	3.8	3.2	7.4	15.2	91.0	109.7	180.7	247.0	4,831.1	5,394.4	1,296.1	1,550.1	2,612.0	3,051.3	923.1	793.0
South Carolina	455.7	678.3	16.2	12.6	26.2	34.3	127.4	107.6	285.9	**523.8**	3,709.5	4,387.8	1,562.4	1,506.1	1,864.7	2,585.5	282.4	296.2
South Dakota	180.9	159.1	2.1	2.0	10.7	16.4	20.4	20.3	147.8	120.3	2,489.9	2,800.7	597.1	626.4	1,735.3	2,000.3	157.5	174.0
Tennessee	386.8	414.0	13.4	9.8	25.7	34.5	157.2	166.1	190.4	203.6	3,272.4	3,599.3	1,350.1	1,294.7	1,575.6	1,937.2	346.7	367.4
Texas	386.0	507.9	13.7	16.7	29.2	45.1	161.2	191.8	182.0	254.3	4,309.1	5,417.3	1,531.6	1,791.2	2,405.8	3,081.9	371.7	544.2
Utah	214.6	304.2	3.2	4.8	22.3	27.9	75.8	77.7	113.4	193.8	4,735.6	5,187.9	1,132.9	1,178.9	3,272.9	3,673.4	329.8	355.6
Vermont	75.1	184.2	3.4	1.4	12.3	22.9	13.8	28.6	45.5	131.2	2,799.6	5,115.0	1,019.4	1,577.9	1,606.6	3,200.0	173.6	337.1
Virginia	309.0	301.0	8.6	8.6	23.3	27.1	122.8	111.6	154.3	153.7	3,505.7	4,060.3	1,005.0	1,082.6	2,234.7	2,730.9	266.0	246.8
Washington	346.3	434.6	5.1	4.8	29.0	46.4	115.5	120.7	196.6	262.8	5,662.0	6,094.9	1,772.5	1,783.6	3,484.8	3,876.8	405.5	434.5
West Virginia	137.4	168.1	6.0	6.8	10.0	15.5	35.2	43.9	86.1	101.8	1,632.0	2,157.2	551.8	636.8	953.3	1,318.2	126.9	202.3
Wisconsin	140.4	166.1	3.0	3.4	11.3	16.1	66.3	60.5	59.9	86.1	3,500.7	4,221.9	836.9	949.3	2,417.8	3,005.9	246.1	266.7
Wyoming	144.6	350.9	5.0	9.1	15.3	27.6	42.6	42.2	81.6	272.0	3,505.8	4,473.1	827.3	863.8	2,464.1	3,246.0	214.5	363.3
Baltimore	1,026.1	1,088.1	16.8	13.7	35.7	43.1	543.0	470.3	430.5	561.0	5,555.1	5,928.0	1,653.8	1,652.2	3,194.6	3,705.6	706.7	570.2
Boston	475.5	648.2	5.6	4.7	18.5	25.8	282.5	290.4	168.9	327.3	5,088.2	5,647.2	1,470.8	1,619.7	1,978.4	2,608.4	**1,639.0**	**1,419.1**
Chicago	793.9	568.8	15.9	14.3	34.8	34.0	431.2	263.1	312.1	257.4	5,171.9	5,070.7	1,352.7	1,193.2	3,117.7	3,150.4	701.5	727.1
Dallas	467.2	693.9	14.5	18.3	40.8	60.2	191.2	262.3	220.7	353.2	5,889.5	7,093.8	1,963.0	2,245.1	3,446.6	4,258.4	479.9	590.3
Detroit	949.0	786.4	**20.2**	13.8	45.7	51.9	576.4	351.5	306.6	369.2	6,434.0	5,990.2	2,010.2	1,623.5	3,396.0	3,413.6	1,027.8	953.1
Houston	517.3	673.5	18.7	**30.0**	31.6	68.3	352.0	394.4	115.0	180.8	4,745.0	6,561.6	1,917.7	**2,450.0**	2,165.4	2,967.1	661.9	1,144.5
Los Angeles	890.4	1,205.1	12.9	20.0	**54.5**	**71.3**	376.3	529.2	**446.6**	**584.7**	6,101.8	6,601.2	**2,249.8**	2,387.8	2,953.6	3,156.7	898.4	1,056.7
Minneapolis	348.7	356.0	4.2	3.2	28.4	31.7	184.3	164.9	131.9	156.2	4,970.0	5,312.5	1,511.7	1,457.5	2,872.8	3,398.9	585.5	456.0
Newark	585.3	856.0	9.6	9.9	24.2	40.3	341.5	484.5	210.1	322.0	4,560.3	5,688.4	1,495.8	1,736.6	2,403.0	2,973.3	661.5	978.5
New York	**1,307.5**	**1,496.9**	16.3	19.8	42.8	44.5	**811.8**	**926.7**	436.6	506.0	4,764.6	6,308.4	1,820.7	2,216.9	2,121.5	3,012.0	822.4	1,079.5
Philadelphia	517.8	528.9	11.9	10.6	28.1	32.1	281.7	257.5	196.2	228.6	3,661.2	4,109.8	1,211.1	1,219.5	1,829.9	2,330.3	620.2	559.9
Pittsburgh	313.3	362.6	5.3	5.2	17.8	25.6	162.8	171.3	127.3	160.4	2,621.6	2,919.1	891.1	847.8	1,258.8	1,508.1	471.6	563.1
St. Louis	676.3	721.5	13.9	16.0	35.0	44.3	337.3	319.5	290.1	341.7	5,746.3	5,187.7	1,952.5	1,727.8	3,113.3	2,883.2	680.5	576.7
San Francisco	688.1	862.4	11.6	11.0	42.2	56.0	337.1	426.1	297.2	369.2	**6,789.3**	**7,355.6**	2,145.9	2,199.9	**3,946.3**	**4,424.1**	697.2	731.7
Washington, D.C.	687.2	693.0	13.4	9.3	41.0	45.3	409.1	390.6	223.7	247.7	5,253.0	5,895.3	1,403.2	1,540.4	3,303.0	3,879.5	546.8	475.4

Boldface: highest rate among states or listed metropolitan areas. Source: U.S. Department of Justice, Federal Bureau of Investigation, *Uniform Crime Reports*.

TRANSPORTATION AND TRADE

Transportation

State	Road and street mi[1] 1980	Motor vehicles in 000s, 1979[2]			Railroad mileage 1979[3]	Airports 1979[4]	Pipeline mileage 1977[5]
		Total	Auto-mobiles	Trucks and buses			
Ala.	87,136	2,863	2,105	758	4,497	156	1,660
Alaska	9,930	268	168	100	550	734	193
Ariz.	60,745	1,776	1,261	515	1,865	210	1,355
Ark.	74,666	1,502	999	503	2,749	167	3,071
Calif.	177,805	15,973	12,343	3,630	6,977	819	10,352
Colo.	88,425	2,694	2,021	673	3,413	301	2,396
Conn.	19,295	2,229	2,051	178	664	106	94
Del.	5,137	396	322	74	269	35	3
D.C.	1,101	229	212	17	52	18	[6]
Fla.	96,281	7,191	5,939	1,252	3,698	458	288
Ga.	104,014	3,789	2,975	814	5,471	283	2,024
Hawaii	3,909	548	460	88	...	54	...
Idaho	66,528	796	485	311	2,567	194	633
Ill.	134,243	7,353	6,080	1,273	11,167	891	10,914
Ind.	91,079	3,878	2,910	968	5,896	325	4,552
Iowa	111,907	2,425	1,786	639	5,805	258	4,581
Kan.	134,952	1,978	1,377	601	6,699	374	17,152
Ky.	68,952	2,648	1,834	814	3,572	112	2,444
La.	55,834	2,678	1,899	779	3,452	291	9,460
Maine	22,218	726	544	182	1,727	160	353
Md.	27,158	2,789	2,331	458	1,054	144	219
Mass.	33,618	3,744	3,295	449	1,462	137	242
Mich.	120,080	6,488	5,300	1,188	4,411	413	4,861
Minn.	129,168	2,754	2,012	742	6,983	468	2,841
Miss.	69,589	1,648	1,178	470	3,161	165	3,246
Mo.	117,907	3,238	2,406	832	5,902	374	7,142
Mont.	77,173	902	563	339	4,660	177	3,232
Neb.	96,457	1,242	858	384	4,903	319	3,317
Nev.	49,936	631	465	166	1,564	119	275
N.H.	15,654	682	583	99	617	52	190
N.J.	33,396	4,762	4,284	478	1,576	266	494
N.M.	72,026	1,048	661	387	1,964	145	6,960
N.Y.	109,277	8,350	7,335	1,015	4,582	482	1,586
N.C.	92,305	4,489	3,386	1,103	3,640	271	896
N.D.	106,321	617	360	257	5,121	221	1,773
Ohio	111,561	8,141	6,441	1,700	7,320	586	6,524
Okla.	109,771	2,542	1,715	827	3,860	292	20,710
Ore.	123,275	1,996	1,486	510	2,957	308	414
Pa.	117,480	6,898	5,793	1,105	7,248	684	8,097
R.I.	6,396	674	590	84	143	20	17
S.C.	62,086	1,984	1,541	443	2,772	127	668
S.D.	82,564	599	369	230	2,829	153	642
Tenn.	82,639	3,021	2,401	620	3,136	155	739
Texas	264,858	10,681	7,720	2,961	13,304	1,332	65,966
Utah	49,636	1,004	684	320	1,659	100	1,118
Vt.	14,032	377	305	72	384	61	177
Va.	65,141	3,516	2,996	520	3,511	256	824
Wash.	84,246	3,113	2,254	859	5,340	365	783
W.Va.	37,529	1,208	863	345	3,513	76	3,511
Wis.	106,666	2,898	2,284	614	5,653	382	926
Wyo.	35,684	436	255	181	1,985	97	7,151
TOTAL	3,917,819	154,412	120,485	33,927	188,304	14,693	227,066

[1] Includes federally controlled roads. [2] Estimated registration, excluding military. Detail may not add to totals because of rounding. [3] Class I and II line-haul only. [4] Public and Private. [5] Petroleum and products only. [6] Included with Maryland. Sources: ICC; Dept. of Transportation, FAA, FHWA; Dept. of Energy; Motor Vehicles Manufacturers Assn.

Communications Facilities

State	Post Offices Oct. 5, 1980	TELEPHONES Jan. 1, 1979		COMMERCIAL BROADCAST STATIONS, 1978			Public TV stations 1977	NEWSPAPERS Sept. 30, 1979					
				Radio				Daily		Weekly*		Sunday	
		Total	Residential	AM	FM	TV		Number	Circulation	Number	Circulation	Number	Circulation
Alabama	614	2,419,979	1,849,732	138	69	17	9	27	747,106	118	534,993	20	685,845
Alaska	189	240,000	144,000	20	6	7	4	8	102,636	13	30,560	1	53,595
Arizona	212	1,795,955	1,316,749	60	32	11	2	19	601,459	57	221,183	6	543,378
Arkansas	633	1,389,618	1,049,157	86	53	8	4	33	481,624	120	360,159	15	466,611
California	1,112	19,123,465	13,608,641	231	194	56	14	122	5,935,086	451	5,549,713	48	5,681,527
Colorado	407	2,180,695	1,546,552	70	43	11	2	28	880,030	121	490,496	9	888,409
Connecticut	245	2,583,453	1,925,792	38	23	5	4	25	923,041	55	754,390	7	716,499
Delaware	55	501,332	367,578	10	8	—	—	3	158,513	14	105,371	2	135,127
District of Columbia	1	1,069,187	512,042	7	7	5	—	2	921,591	...	...	2	1,702,094
Florida	459	7,272,155	5,397,456	200	111	31	10	52	2,557,402	142	948,152	34	2,700,832
Georgia	632	3,904,785	2,906,935	178	86	18	10	36	1,045,807	203	1,174,407	17	1,244,204
Hawaii	76	661,303	429,847	25	6	10	2	5	238,740	4	107,178	2	218,076
Idaho	259	662,359	486,866	42	16	8	3	15	207,652	59	132,399	6	172,037
Illinois	1,265	9,792,452	7,314,939	125	129	22	6	86	2,885,122	699	3,804,450	22	2,822,534
Indiana	751	4,042,963	3,099,101	86	95	19	7	78	1,640,053	183	621,242	18	1,425,460
Iowa	950	2,211,566	1,667,175	75	71	13	8	41	894,491	366	812,469	9	813,931
Kansas	687	1,859,025	1,400,561	59	40	12	2	50	632,594	244	515,863	17	477,099
Kentucky	1,221	2,215,495	1,680,910	119	86	11	14	27	767,143	143	613,257	11	1,055,124
Louisiana	530	2,729,378	2,072,435	95	61	15	3	27	852,412	103	613,371	15	807,217
Maine	492	769,565	592,796	37	28	7	5	9	287,294	33	130,214	1	202,508
Maryland	425	3,386,804	2,536,110	50	37	6	4	13	686,724	75	872,430	4	812,773
Massachusetts	424	4,472,070	3,272,607	64	38	12	3	48	2,036,162	143	994,918	9	1,514,037
Michigan	855	6,981,139	5,326,848	127	109	24	7	52	2,457,818	277	2,306,123	17	2,490,167
Minnesota	855	3,056,266	2,254,351	91	66	12	5	30	1,041,796	432	1,953,522	11	1,472,658
Mississippi	462	1,464,192	1,131,797	105	68	10	8	25	403,144	99	313,083	13	325,231
Missouri	960	3,690,599	2,772,969	111	77	23	3	52	1,639,186	281	1,610,438	18	1,517,167
Montana	363	575,509	422,148	45	21	12	—	11	196,295	73	150,057	8	191,102
Nebraska	545	1,246,659	928,091	48	31	14	9	19	492,310	207	470,826	5	391,249
Nevada	90	697,837	477,532	22	14	7	1	9	204,432	16	44,880	5	201,833
New Hampshire	239	673,049	508,742	28	17	1	5	9	194,069	24	174,720	2	75,179
New Jersey	519	6,335,199	4,722,525	38	34	5	4	28	1,729,251	199	2,032,396	15	1,486,748
New Mexico	326	813,090	567,112	55	29	9	3	20	267,204	26	193,465	13	246,226
New York	1,626	13,065,378	9,417,851	160	117	29	12	79	7,688,120	415	2,494,621	35	6,432,683
North Carolina	775	3,906,567	2,950,454	209	85	18	9	53	1,362,803	128	560,565	23	1,365,475
North Dakota	441	499,587	366,164	26	12	11	2	10	196,785	93	184,729	3	106,534
Ohio	1,081	7,784,619	5,904,732	122	130	24	12	96	3,337,020	260	1,856,642	28	2,655,178
Oklahoma	624	2,226,430	1,637,968	67	50	10	4	55	878,529	196	390,201	46	1,157,996
Oregon	346	1,884,852	1,362,558	80	33	12	4	22	685,115	95	585,424	5	604,431
Pennsylvania	1,776	9,519,098	7,225,456	178	125	25	9	104	3,912,194	232	1,652,002	16	3,271,301
Rhode Island	55	698,115	524,983	15	7	2	1	7	314,589	16	99,092	2	235,931
South Carolina	390	1,981,232	1,487,452	108	55	11	7	20	597,924	72	272,362	8	507,108
South Dakota	403	497,631	369,578	33	18	11	6	13	172,728	152	198,827	4	123,542
Tennessee	566	3,063,810	2,321,539	155	74	18	5	32	1,109,435	129	606,901	16	1,183,272
Texas	1,491	10,245,165	7,393,901	286	185	54	7	118	3,399,229	523	1,598,863	94	3,838,428
Utah	209	992,768	732,790	34	19	3	2	6	272,984	52	188,322	5	277,468
Vermont	285	348,645	254,123	19	12	2	4	8	115,420	20	59,880	3	72,716
Virginia	888	3,671,932	2,733,317	137	173	14	7	33	1,086,894	95	616,088	13	1,253,092
Washington	461	2,998,511	2,167,694	92	51	14	6	26	1,179,901	138	1,189,431	16	1,113,438
West Virginia	1,010	1,085,548	832,568	62	32	9	3	25	475,249	75	282,165	9	402,487
Wisconsin	775	3,393,369	2,524,884	101	91	17	7	37	1,243,121	250	777,116	9	910,770
Wyoming	165	346,548	244,631	30	11	4	—	10	92,813	33	97,556	3	60,458
TOTAL U.S.	30,326	169,026,948	124,742,739	4,459	2,922	720	268	1,763	62,223,040	7,954	42,347,512	720	59,114,789

*Excluding District of Columbia; data for Sept. 30, 1978. Sources: U.S. Postal Service; Federal Communications Commission; American Telephone and Telegraph Co.; The Editor & Publisher Co., Inc., *International Year Book, 1980* (Copyright 1980. All rights reserved. Used by permission.); National Newspaper Association; Corporation for Public Broadcasting.

Major Trading Partners, by Value

in millions of dollars

Country	EXPORTS 1974	EXPORTS 1979	IMPORTS 1974	IMPORTS 1979
North America	27,889	47,983	31,364	55,406
Canada	19,936[1]	33,096	21,928	38,099
Mexico	4,855	9,847	3,390	8,813
South America	7,856	13,571	8,961	13,174
Argentina	597	1,890	386	587
Brazil	3,088	3,442	1,700	3,119
Chile	452	886	310	440
Colombia	659	1,409	511	1,209
Peru	647	720	609	1,181
Venezuela	1,768	3,931	4,671	5,166
Europe	30,070	60,014	24,410	43,549
Belgium and Luxembourg	2,284	5,186	1,657	1,741
France	2,942	5,587	2,257	4,771
Germany, West	4,985	8,482	6,324	10,955
Italy	2,752	4,359	2,585	4,918
Netherlands, The	3,979	6,907	1,433	1,852
Spain	1,899	2,507	888	1,304
Sweden	908	1,513	856	1,652
Switzerland	1,150	3,660	890	2,076
United Kingdom	4,574	10,635	4,063	8,029
U.S.S.R.	609	3,607	350	872
Asia	26,240	50,204	27,437	67,121
Hong Kong	882	2,083	1,640	4,006
India	760	1,167	600	1,038
Indonesia	531	982	1,688	3,621
Iran	1,734	1,019	2,132	2,784
Israel	1,206	1,857	281	749
Japan	10,679	17,579	12,338	26,243
Korea, South	1,546	4,191	1,445	4,047
Malaysia	377	932	770	2,146
Philippines	747	1,570	1,084	1,489
Saudi Arabia	835	4,875	1,671	7,983
Singapore	988	2,331	550	1,467
Taiwan	1,427	3,271	...	...
Oceania	2,697	4,319	1,506	3,072
Australia	2,157	3,617	1,042	2,164
Africa	3,204	4,866	6,551	23,996
Algeria	315	404	1,091	4,940
Nigeria	286	632	3,286	8,162
South Africa[2]	1,160	1,423	609	2,623
TOTAL	98,596[1]	181,802[1]	100,648[1]	206,327[1]

[1] Includes shipments to or from unidentified countries. [2] Includes Namibia.
Source: U.S. Department of Commerce, Domestic and International Business Administration, *Overseas Business Reports*.

Major Commodities Traded, 1979

in millions of dollars

Item	Total[1]	Canada	American Republics	Western Europe	Far East[2]
TOTAL EXPORTS	181,802	33,096[3]	26,257	54,331	36,016
Agricultural commodities					
Grains and preparations	14,450	132	1,684	2,489	3,264
Soybeans	5,708	79	176	2,961	1,486
Cotton, including linters, wastes	2,229	85	29	276	1,374
Nonagricultural commodities					
Ores and scrap metals	2,182	328	151	1,078	525
Coal, coke, and briquettes	3,496	958	260	1,193	994
Chemicals	17,306	1,994	3,814	5,596	3,856
Machinery	45,816	8,785	8,494	13,095	7,363
Agricultural machines, tractors, parts	3,808	1,369	755	748	263
Electrical apparatus	8,634	961	1,595	2,264	2,513
Transport equipment[4]	23,588	9,294	3,130	4,238	3,190
Civilian aircraft and parts	8,823	688	936	3,002	2,543
Paper manufactures	1,967	367	461	507	283
Metal manufactures	3,431	960	734	595	345
Iron and steel mill products	2,227	550	653	260	247
Yarn, fabrics, and clothing	2,812	421	635	1,078	260
Other exports	56,590	9,143	6,036	20,965	12,828
TOTAL IMPORTS	206,327	38,099	24,782	41,684	51,156
Agricultural commodities					
Meat and preparations	2,539	169	522	218	10
Fish	2,639	595	792	390	550
Coffee	3,820	[5]	2,911	8	283
Sugar	974	26	679	1	64
Nonagricultural commodities					
Ores and scrap metal	3,247	1,116	589	140	118
Petroleum, crude	46,100	1,888	5,852	2,113	2,838
Petroleum products	9,946	591	2,969	957	606
Chemicals	7,485	2,362	405	3,448	764
Machinery	28,530	4,001	2,124	9,436	13,015
Transport equipment	25,148	8,572	351	6,220	9,850
Automobiles, new	14,813	3,705	[5]	4,437	6,671
Iron and steel mill products	6,764	901	198	2,380	3,031
Nonferrous metals	4,678	1,384	621	1,082	863
Textiles other than clothing	2,216	54	235	662	1,074
Other imports	62,241	16,440	6,534	14,629	18,090

[1] Includes areas not shown separately. [2] Includes Japan, East and South Asia.
[3] Excludes grains and oilseeds transshipped through Canada to unidentified overseas countries. [4] Excludes parts for tractors. [5] Less than $500,000.
Source: U.S. Dept. of Commerce, Domestic and International Business Administration, *Overseas Business Reports*.

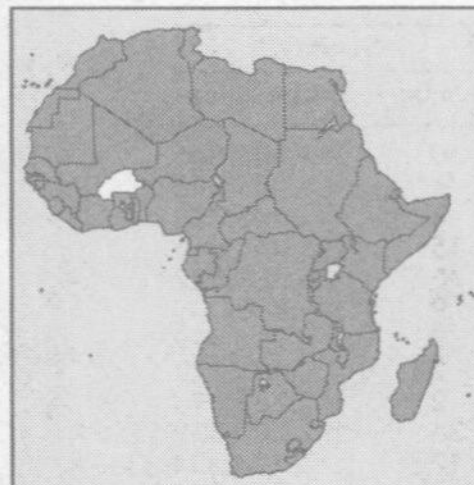

Upper Volta

Upper Volta

A republic of West Africa, Upper Volta is bordered by Mali, Niger, Benin, Togo, Ghana, and Ivory Coast. Area: 274,200 sq km (105,869 sq mi). Pop. (1980 est.): 6,908,000. Cap. and largest city: Ouagadougou (pop., 1980 est., 235,000). Language: French (official). Religion: animist 49.8%; Muslim 16.6%; Roman Catholic 8.3%. President to Nov. 25, 1980, Maj. Gen. Sangoulé Lamizana; premier to November 25, Joseph Conombo; from November 25 the country was ruled by a Military Committee of Recovery for National Progress headed by Col. Saye Zerbo.

On Nov. 25, 1980, the government of Pres. Sangoulé Lamizana was overthrown in a bloodless military coup. Lamizana, who had come to power in a coup in 1966, had returned his country to civilian rule with the forms of a pluralist democracy. The new military rulers, calling themselves the Military Committee of Recovery for National Progress, were headed by Col. Saye Zerbo, commander of armed forces in Ouagadougou. The coup was preceded by a two-month strike of teachers, supported by the opposition parties.

In May Pope John Paul II had spent six hours in Ouagadougou during his African tour.

(PHILIPPE DECRAENE)

UPPER VOLTA

Education. (1978–79) Primary, pupils 159,948, teachers 3,204; secondary, pupils 15,271, teachers 817; vocational, pupils 1,852, teachers 175; teacher training, students 495, teachers (1977–78) 33; higher (1977–78), students 1,233, teaching staff 93.

Finance. Monetary unit: CFA franc, with (Sept. 22, 1980) a par value of CFA Fr 50 to the French franc (free rate of CFA Fr 210 = U.S. $1; CFA Fr 504 = £1 sterling). Budget (1980 est.) balanced at CFA Fr 40.1 billion.

Foreign Trade. (1978) Imports CFA Fr 51,080,000,000; exports CFA Fr 9,520,000,000. Import sources (1977): France 45%; Ivory Coast 13%; U.S. 9%; West Germany 6%. Export destinations (1977): Ivory Coast 32%; Denmark 22%; The Netherlands 11%; France 7%; Taiwan 6%. Main exports (1977): cotton 40%; livestock 29%; oilseeds and nuts 14%.

Uruguay

Uruguay

A republic of South America, Uruguay is on the Atlantic Ocean and is bounded by Brazil and Argentina. Area: 176,215 sq km (68,037 sq mi). Pop. (1979 est.): 2,905,000, including (1961) white 89%; mestizo 10%. Cap. and largest city: Montevideo (pop., 1975, 1,238,100). Language: Spanish. Religion: mainly Roman Catholic. President in 1980, Aparicio Méndez.

Through most of 1980 preparations for the general election promised for 1981 continued, and in May the executive submitted to the Cabinet the draft of the projected constitution; it provided for a restricted parliamentary democracy under a Council of National Security. A Constitutional Tribunal would resolve cases of conflict between authorities and of governmental infringement of ethics. Both the Blanco and Colorado parties were legalized; to achieve the same status other parties would have to have gained 2% of the vote in the preceding election.

In September the ban on the political activities of 50 people was lifted. However, the ban continued to affect many who had been politically active. An opposition newspaper, *El Día*, called for restoration of rights for all citizens. The draft constitution was submitted to a popular referendum on November 30. It was rejected by 879,765 votes to 642,279; 80% of the electorate voted. On December 3 the government called off the general election, while still promising to restore democracy.

Economic growth trends continued in 1980, though they were affected by a slowdown of Argentina's economy. The Salto Grande hydroelectric complex was scheduled to be completed early in 1981; the 300-Mw Palmar project was under construction. Price increases slowed as a result of a programmed annual 16% cut in customs duties from Jan. 1, 1980, but industrialists feared the increased competition from abroad.

(MICHAEL WOOLLER)

URUGUAY

Education. (1976) Primary, pupils (including preprimary) 345,739, teachers 13,788; secondary, pupils 141,731, teachers *c.* 13,980; vocational, pupils 42,271, teachers *c.* 4,200; teacher training, students (1975) 3,997, teachers (1973) 341; higher, students 39,927, teaching staff 2,149.

Finance. Monetary unit: new peso, with (Sept. 22, 1980) a free rate of 9.32 new pesos to U.S. $1 (22.40 new pesos = £1 sterling). Gold, SDR's, and foreign exchange (June 1980) U.S. $649 million. Budget (1979 actual): revenue 8,424,000,000 new pesos; expenditure 8,176,000,000 new pesos. Gross national product (1979) 54,528,400,000 new pesos. Cost of living: (Montevideo; 1975 = 100; June 1980) 917.1.

Foreign Trade. (1979) Imports U.S. $1,206,300,000; exports U.S. $788.4 million. Import sources (1978): Argentina 11%; Brazil 11%; Iraq 11%; U.S. 8%; West Germany 7%; Nigeria 6%; Kuwait 5%. Export destinations (1978): Brazil 19%; U.S. 17%; West Germany 12%; The Netherlands 7%; Argentina 6%. Main exports (1978): wool 21%; clothing 16%; meat 15%; footwear 5%; leather 5%.

Transport and Communications. Roads (1977) 24,954 km. Motor vehicles in use (1976): passenger 127,100; commercial (including buses) 104,200. Railways: (1979) 3,005 km; traffic (1977) 389 million passenger-km, freight 307 million net ton-km. Air traffic (1978): 64 million passenger-km; freight 200,000 net ton-km. Shipping (1979): merchant vessels 100 gross tons and over 53; gross tonnage 198,169. Telephones (Jan. 1978) 268,000. Radio receivers (Dec. 1977) 1,625,000. Television receivers (Dec. 1977) 360,000.

Agriculture. Production (in 000; metric tons; 1979): wheat *c.* 380; corn 71; rice 248; sorghum 54; potatoes 135; sweet potatoes *c.* 85; sugar, raw value *c.* 82; linseed 31; sunflower seed 51; apples *c.* 27; oranges 44; grapes *c.* 90; wool *c.* 42; beef and veal *c.* 261. Livestock (in 000; May 1979): cattle 10,007; sheep (1978) *c.* 18,854; pigs *c.* 400; horses (1978) *c.* 520; chickens (1978) *c.* 7,537.

Industry. Production (in 000; metric tons; 1978): cement 667; petroleum products *c.* 1,900; crude steel (1977) 17; electricity (kw-hr) 2,806,000.

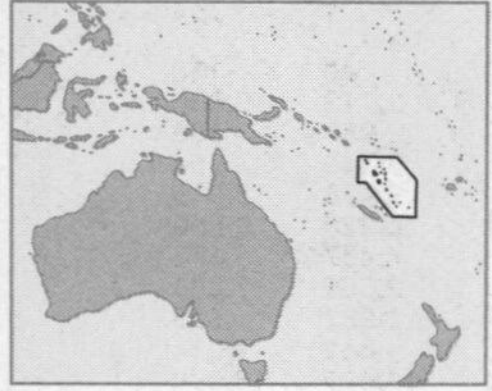

Vanuatu

Vanuatu

The republic of Vanuatu, a member of the Commonwealth of Nations, was proclaimed on July 30, 1980, when the former Anglo-French condominium of the New Hebrides was granted independence by the United Kingdom and France. The republic, whose name means "our land," comprises 12 main islands, the largest of which are

Espíritu Santo, Malekula, Efate, Ambrym, Aoba, and Tanna, and some 60 smaller ones in the southwest Pacific Ocean, forming a chain some 800 km (500 mi) in length extending southeast from the southern Solomon Islands and located about 1,100 km northeast of the Australian mainland. Area: 11,870 sq km (4,583 sq mi). Pop. (1979 prelim.): 109,425, predominantly Melanesian. Cap. and largest city: Vila, on Efate Island (pop., 1979 prelim., 14,590). Language: Bislama, a Melanesian pidgin (national); French and English (official). Religion: Presbyterian 40%, Roman Catholic 16%; Anglican 14%, other Christian 15%; Animist 15%. President in 1980, George Kalkoa; prime minister, the Rev. Walter Lini.

On July 30, 1980, the Anglo-French condominium of the New Hebrides achieved independence as the republic of Vanuatu. Comprising 66 inhabited islands with 130 languages, Vanuatu had no heritage of unity, and condominium rule had exacerbated differences. In November 1979 the Vanuaaku Party, mostly supported by English-speaking Protestant Melanesians, won 26 of the 39 seats in the Representative Assembly, defeating an alliance of "moderates"—generally French-speaking Roman Catholic Melanesians and French settlers. From that time France tried to slow the transference of power and to secure further protection for pro-French minority interests.

At the end of May several hundred Espíritu Santo secessionists, led by Jimmy Stevens (*see* BIOGRAPHIES), seized administrative centres, looted shops, and forced the evacuation of their opponents. Vanuatu had no army to oppose them, and the government, led by the Rev. Walter Lini (*see* BIOGRAPHIES), had no power over the police until independence. British and French forces landed on Santo shortly before independence but achieved little because the French government was unwilling to move against several of its nationals who were involved in the rebellion. In mid-August the colonial forces were replaced by 400 Papua New Guinea troops brought in by the Lini government under a hastily signed defense pact. Within days the rebellion had been quashed with the loss of only two lives; 110 French citizens were declared prohibited immigrants and deported while several hundred rebel citizens of Vanuatu were held and charged. In November Stevens was sentenced to 14½ years' imprisonment.

On July 4 an electoral college voted 27–12 to elect George Kalkoa as president of the new republic. He had served as deputy chief minister of the colony.

(BARRIE MACDONALD)

VANUATU

Education. (1977) Primary, pupils 21,805, teachers (1976) 595; secondary and vocational, pupils 2,051, teachers (1976) 113; teacher training (1976), students 137, teachers 12.

Finance. Monetary units: Australian dollar and Vanuatu franc, with (Sept. 22, 1980) a free rate of VFr 64 = U.S. $1 (VFr 155 = £1 sterling). Condominium budget (1978 est.): revenue VFr 1,056,000,000; expenditure VFr 1,051,000,000. British budget (1976–77 est.): revenue A$6,923,000; expenditure A$7,138,000. French budget (1976 est.): revenue VFr 1,496,000,000; expenditure VFr 1,497,000,000.

Foreign Trade. (1977) Imports VFr 3,164,000,000; exports VFr 2,525,000,000. Import sources (1975): Australia 30%; France 25%; Japan 8%; New Caledonia 7%; U.K. 5%. Export destinations (1975): France 43%; U.S. 28%; Japan 15%; New Caledonia 8%. Main exports: copra 44%; fish 42%; cocoa 7%.

Agriculture. Production (in 000; metric tons; 1978): bananas *c.* 1; copra *c.* 50; cocoa 1; fish catch *c.* 8. Livestock (in 000; 1978): cattle *c.* 92; pigs *c.* 65; chickens *c.* 137.

In a move to reunite the Catholic and Anglican churches, Pope John Paul II met with England's Queen Elizabeth on her historic visit to the Vatican in October.

UPI

Vatican City State

This independent sovereignty is surrounded by but is not part of Rome. As a state with territorial limits, it is properly distinguished from the Holy See, which constitutes the worldwide administrative and legislative body for the Roman Catholic Church. The area of Vatican City is 44 ha (108.8 ac). Pop. (1978 est.): 729. As sovereign pontiff, John Paul II is the chief of state. Vatican City is administered by a pontifical commission of five cardinals headed by the secretary of state, in 1980 Agostino Cardinal Casaroli.

Besides continuing his world travels and presiding over three synods at the Vatican in 1980, Pope John Paul II supervised renewal of the high offices of the Curia. He appointed the archbishop of Washington, D.C., William Cardinal Baum, to succeed Gabriel Cardinal Garrone, of retiring age, as head of the Congregation for Catholic Education, and Wladyslaw Cardinal Rubin replaced Paul Cardinal Philippe at the Oriental Congregation. The pope named Msgr. Paul Poupard, auxiliary of Paris and rector of its Catholic Institute, as pro-president of the Secretariat for Unbelievers (atheists) in place of Franz König, archbishop of Vienna (aged 75). Archbishop Jean Jadot, apostolic delegate at Washington, D.C., succeeded Sergio Cardinal Pignedoli (*see* OBITUARIES) as president of the Secretariat for Non-Christians.

Vatican City State

Visitors received by the pope included King Hassan II of Morocco, King Hussein I of Jordan, U.S. Pres. Jimmy Carter, and Queen Elizabeth II of Britain. The pope appealed for peace in the Middle East, and during Poland's crisis he asked for prayers for his native country. (MAX BERGERRE)

See also Religion: *Roman Catholic Church*.

Universities:
see Education

Urban Mass Transit:
see Transportation

U.S.S.R.:
see Union of Soviet Socialist Republics

Venezuela

Venezuela

A republic of northern South America, Venezuela is bounded by Colombia, Brazil, Guyana, and the Caribbean Sea. Area: 899,180 sq km (347,175 sq mi). Pop. (1980 est.): 13,913,200, including mestizo 69%; white 20%; Negro 9%; Indian 2%. Cap. and largest city: Caracas (metro area pop., 1980 est., 2,944,400). Language: Spanish. Religion: predominantly Roman Catholic. President in 1980, Luis Herrera Campins.

Opinion polls showed that in 1980 the popularity of Pres. Luis Herrera Campins plummeted. Opposition came from the business sector, which called for reduced government intervention in the economy while criticizing the government bureaucracy and its inefficiency, and also from the labour unions, which demanded a greater part in determining economic policy and company management, particularly in the public sector. Both called for an end to the recession (gross domestic product grew by only 0.7% in 1979) through a strategy designed to increase employment and raise the consumption levels of the poor.

Some improvement in growth was expected in 1980, but the rate would remain low because oil production had been reduced from an average of 2,350,000 bbl a day in 1979 to 2,140,000 bbl in 1980. The government attributed the recession to deliberate policies that it had instituted to cool the overheated economy after the expansionism of the mid-1970s and took only limited steps to stimulate the economy, specifically, by introducing financial incentives for the construction industry. At least 200 million bolivares a month were to be channeled into the mortgage banking system by the Ministry of Finance solely to finance low-cost housing.

External trade, however, continued to benefit from high oil prices, and a trade surplus of about U.S. $6.7 billion was expected in 1980, as compared with one of $3.4 billion in 1979; the nation's current account was forecast to register a surplus of $2.4 billion against a deficit of $2.1 billion the previous year. The government continued to borrow heavily on the international capital markets, principally to consolidate short-term debt contracted by state agencies, and international reserves held by the Banco Central grew steadily. A senator and former president (1974–79), Carlos Andreas Perez, was censured by the Congress in May as "politically responsible" for financial corruption involved in the purchase of the Norwegian ship "Sierra Nevada" in 1977 through a Swiss intermediary.

Venezuela continued to support neighbouring countries in 1980 and took an active role in third world matters. An economic cooperation agreement was signed with Mexico for the provision of oil to nine countries in Central America and the Caribbean; under the scheme oil would be sold at market prices, but 30% of the income would be returned as low-interest loans for the development of alternative sources of energy. Venezuela's role as political stabilizer in the region and its support for democracy and social justice were proved once again when the military took power in Bolivia in July on the eve of that country's planned return to democratically elected government. Venezuela cut off aid of $40 million to Bolivia and drew up a document with the other member countries of the Andean Group condemning the coup.

Relations with Cuba sank to an all-time low following the decision of a Venezuelan military tribunal to acquit four men (two Cuban and two Venezuelan) accused of blowing up a Cubana airliner off Barbados in 1976. As a result Cuba withdrew diplomats from Caracas in October but stopped short of breaking diplomatic relations.

As a member of the Organization of Petroleum Exporting Countries (OPEC), Venezuela again took the line of the doves, favouring small, gradual increases in the price of oil. Venezuela also pressed for the transformation and enlargement of the OPEC Special Fund into a development bank for financial aid to third world countries.

Venezuela and the European Economic Community (EEC) again expressed interest in co-financing development projects in the Caribbean, and EEC officials visited Caracas to hold discussions with Venezuelan ministers. In October the 120 members of the Group of 77 less developed countries elected Venezuela to chair the group's deliberations for 1981, in place of India.

(SARAH CAMERON)

VENEZUELA

Education. (1976–77) Primary, pupils 2,204,074, teachers (including preprimary) 94,218; secondary and vocational, pupils 690,571; teacher training, students 19,863; secondary, vocational, and teacher training, teachers 46,964; higher, students 247,518, teaching staff 19,787.

Finance. Monetary unit: bolivar, with (Sept. 22, 1980) a par value of 4.29 bolivares to U.S. $1 (free rate of 10.28 bolivares = £1 sterling). Gold, SDR's, and foreign exchange (June 1980) U.S. $7,195,000,000. Budget (1979 actual): revenue 50,027,000,000 bolivares; expenditure 46,911,000,000 bolivares. Gross national product (1979) 210 billion bolivares. Money supply (May 1980) 45,546,000,000 bolivares. Cost of living (Caracas; 1975 = 100; June 1980) 169.3.

Foreign Trade. (1979) Imports 48,932,000,000 bolivares; exports 60,776,000,000 bolivares. Import sources (1978): U.S. 41%; Japan 10%; West Germany 9%; Italy 5%. Export destinations (1978): U.S. *c.* 37%; Netherlands Antilles *c.* 20%; Canada *c.* 12%. Main exports: crude oil 59%; petroleum products 36%.

Transport and Communications. Roads (1979) 61,826 km. Motor vehicles in use (1979): passenger 1,390,000; commercial (including buses) 639,500. Railways: (1978) 444 km; traffic (1971) 42 million passenger-km, freight 15 million net ton-km. Air traffic (1978): 3,498,000,000 passenger-km; freight 113.2 million net ton-km. Shipping (1979): merchant vessels 100 gross tons and over 220; gross tonnage 882,098. Telephones (Jan. 1978) 847,300. Radio receivers (Dec. 1977) 5,273,000. Television receivers (Dec. 1977) 1,530,000.

Agriculture. Production (in 000; metric tons; 1979): corn 848; rice *c.* 653; sorghum *c.* 429; potatoes 225; cassava (1978) *c.* 380; sugar, raw value *c.* 350; tomatoes 135; sesame seed 40; bananas 967; oranges 369; coffee *c.* 61; cocoa *c.* 17; tobacco *c.* 23; cotton, lint *c.* 35; beef and veal *c.* 292. Livestock (in 000; 1979): cattle 9,963; pigs 2,099; sheep *c.* 314; goats *c.* 1,354; horses (1978) *c.* 466; asses (1978) *c.* 460; poultry *c.* 34,000.

Industry. Production (in 000; metric tons; 1979): crude oil 123,483; natural gas (cu m; 1978) *c.* 12,000,000; petroleum products (1978) *c.* 50,200; iron ore (64% metal content) 15,460; crude steel 1,506; cement (1977) 3,292; gold (troy oz; 1977) 17; diamonds (metric carats; 1977) 687; electricity (kw-hr; 1977) 23,051,000.

Venda:
see South Africa

Veterinary Science

A new virus disease was causing deaths and illness in dogs. The infection, due to a canine parvovirus (CPV), was first noticed on a small scale in 1978 and developed almost simultaneously in the U.S., the U.K., Europe, and Australia. Numerous cases were reported in 1980. In unweaned pups the disease can produce heart disease (myocarditis), while older animals suffer vomiting and diarrhea (gastroenteritis). Typically, pups in a litter affected by CPV myocarditis will start dying at approximately 3½ weeks old, and about 70% will be dead by 8 weeks. Survivors may have permanent heart damage. In older pups and young adult dogs, CPV enteritis kills some 70% of affected animals. CPV is related to the virus of panleucopenia, which causes feline infectious enteritis (FIE). FIE vaccine was used successfully to protect dogs at risk.

Two important developments were reported in studies on the reproduction of horses. Using a technique involving sophisticated microsurgery and embryo transfer, workers at the U.K. Agricultural Research Council's Animal Research Station at Cambridge produced identical twin foals, which never occur normally. Such genetically identical animals can be useful in research. An egg from a naturally mated mare is collected a few hours after fertilization, when it contains either two or four cells (blastomeres). Individual or paired cells are removed, transferred to the womb of a ewe, and allowed to develop for four days. Each "new" embryo is then transferred to the womb of a mare that is at exactly the same stage of the sexual cycle (estrus) as the natural mother. The identical twins, each in a different mare, then develop normally to birth.

Immunization is the best treatment for dogs exposed to canine parvovirus. A puzzling epidemic of the viral disease struck several areas of the U.S. during the year.

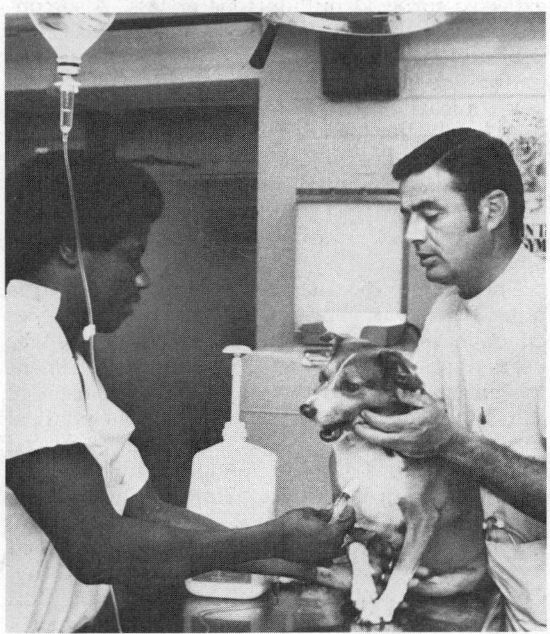

BERNARD GOTFRYD—NEWSWEEK

Related work, also involving embryo transfer and synchrcnization of the estrus cycle (by prostaglandins), resulted in the successful transfer and development to birth of a donkey embryo in a pony mare, and vice versa. This had considerable implications in the study of immunology, since it demonstrated that the maternal placental barrier can prevent rejection of a fetus of marked genetic difference.

An often symptomless cancer-like disease of cattle, enzootic bovine leukosis, is so widespread that humans may be exposed to the responsible virus by, for example, handling animals or drinking milk. Studies in the U.S., however, established that exposure does not increase the risk of cancer and that bovine leukemia does not represent a public health hazard.

Possible risks from the use of low (subtherapeutic) doses of antibiotics as growth promoters in animal feeds were still being debated. Workers in the U.K. continued to report the development of multiple resistance in microorganisms following the use in animals of new antibiotic substances. The U.S. Food and Drug Administration had proposed a ban on the addition of penicillin and tetracycline to feeds in 1977, but studies were still under way, and no final action was expected in the near future.

Certain anti-inflammatory drugs such as phenylbutazone ("bute") effectively relieve joint problems in horses' limbs, but they could mask conditions that would diminish the performance of competitive animals such as show jumpers. There was controversy as to whether their use should be banned in such animals. Veterinary opinion argued that animals could be permanently damaged if the medication enabled them to compete when they were unfit. (EDWARD BODEN)

[353.C]

Vietnam

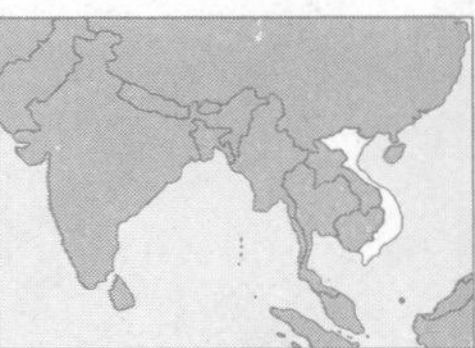

Vietnam

The Socialist Republic of Vietnam is a southeast Asian state bordered in the north by China, in the west by Laos and Cambodia, and in the south and east by the South China Sea. Area: 329,465 sq km (127,207 sq mi). Pop. (1980 est.): 52,299,000. Capitol: Hanoi (pop., 1976 est., 1,443,500). Largest city: Ho Chi Minh City (pop., 1976 est., 3,460,500). Language: Vietnamese, French, English. Religion: Buddhist, animist, Confucian, Christian (Roman Catholic), Hoa Hao and Cao Dai religious sects. Secretary-general of the Communist Party in 1980, Le Duan; presidents, Ton Duc Thang to March 30 and Nguyen Huu Tho (acting); premier, Pham Van Dong.

For Vietnam 1980 was another year of tribulation, with a war it seemed unable to bring to a close, continuing isolation from much of the world, and yet more economic setbacks. At the end of what the government had hoped would be the first peacetime development plan, the nation lay trapped under military priorities.

One million out of a national labour force of some 20 million were soldiers. Up to 200,000 troops were stationed in Cambodia opposing a Khmer Rouge force estimated at about 30,000. As many as

100,000 men were massed along the Thai-Cambodian frontier where the resistance forces, apparently with substantial assistance from China and Thailand, were at their strongest. Vietnamese operations aimed at "wiping out" the remnants of the deposed Pol Pot regime in Cambodia evidently did not gain their objective.

The most serious escalation of the fighting took place in June, when Vietnamese units struck across the Thai border into the refugee camps. Several of the camps, controlled by either the Khmer Rouge or the Free Khmers, were suspected of turning out guerrillas who would later be sent back to Cambodia. The thrust into Thailand, however, enabled Hanoi's adversaries to focus on its reputed expansionist policy. The non-Communist countries of Southeast Asia charged Hanoi with taking the first steps toward annexing Thailand. In August and again in October there were reports of Vietnamese troop movements to the Thai border. On each occasion, adversaries accused Hanoi of territorial ambitions threatening all Southeast Asia.

Although the Southeast Asian nations were not in complete agreement over the Vietnam-Cambodia problem, they all held that the first step toward any solution should be the withdrawal of Hanoi's troops from Cambodia. As Vietnam saw it, this was impossible. Therefore, its efforts to seek out a common ground with at least some Southeast Asian countries did not make much headway. Foreign Minister Nguyen Co Thach visited Malaysia in May, Indonesia in June, and Thailand more than once, but all he obtained were assurances about the need to keep the dialogue going.

Nor did the year see any improvement in Vietnam's relations with the Western powers. In November 1979 U.S. pressure had led the World Bank to announce that it would make no loans to Vietnam in 1980. U.S. opposition continued during the year with a trade embargo in which Washington's close allies were asked to join. For its part, Hanoi kept making statements that it was ready to establish full relations with the U.S. A group of prominent but unofficial Americans issued a statement calling for normalization of relations. China remained Vietnam's most implacable foe. Both sides accused each other of border violations throughout the year. In September China said that tension along its borders with Vietnam had grown so much that it was impossible to resume peace talks with Hanoi (begun in 1979 and last held in March 1980).

One result of this virtual ostracism was that Hanoi found itself moving even closer to the Soviet Union. In July party chief Le Duan and Premier Pham Van Dong led a delegation to Moscow for the first Hanoi-Moscow summit since the two countries signed their friendship treaty 20 months earlier. Apart from attaining "a complete identity of views on all questions," the two governments signed economic assistance agreements covering, in particular, energy resources on the continental shelf off southern Vietnam. (Some European countries were already engaged in offshore oil prospecting in the area at Hanoi's invitation.)

Despite the aid provided by the Soviet Union, Vietnam's economy remained in a shambles. The damage suffered during the war with China in 1979 proved too heavy to be repaired quickly, and the continuing war in Cambodia demanded all the attention and resources the nation could mobilize. With all available technical and managerial expertise going to the military, economic activity was left largely in the hands of unskilled workers and managers. In some industrial sectors 70% of the work force was female. None of the targets set by the 1976–80 state plan was achieved. In the all-important agricultural sector, the target for 1980 was 21 million tons of grain. In fact, output was expected to be 17 million tons or less. Also contributing to the shortfall were what officials called "objective" factors—a series of typhoons and alternating floods and droughts.

With fears of another attack by China dominating Hanoi's thinking, one official said in May that the thrust of the next state plan (1981–85) would be to "militarize the whole country." This was to involve a high priority for food production, less emphasis on heavy industry, and reliance on massive Soviet aid.

The leadership structure in Hanoi underwent a quiet upheaval, presumably to ensure greater effectiveness than the aging hierarchy of the war years was able to provide. A formal announcement in February marked the rise of a new cluster of stars. The most notable newcomers on the political front were Nguyen Co Thach, who replaced Nguyen Duy Trinh as foreign minister, and Nguyen Thanh Le, who took over as head of the party Central Committee's foreign affairs section. On the military front, top leadership was provided by a new defense minister, Gen. Van Tien Dung; Gen. Chu Huy Man, head of the Army's political section; and Gen. Le Trong Tan, army chief of

VIETNAM

Education. (1976–77) Primary, pupils 7,722,524, teachers 217,064; secondary, pupils 3,108,629, teachers 119,388; vocational, pupils 66,553, teachers 5,911; teacher training, pupils 25,730, teachers 2,336; higher (1977–78), students 120,125, teaching staff 13,428.

Finance. Monetary unit: dong, with (Sept. 22, 1980) a free rate of 2.17 dong to U.S. $1 (5.23 dong = £1 sterling). Budget (1979 est.) balanced at 10.5 billion dong.

Foreign Trade. (1978) Imports *c.* U.S. $1.5 billion; exports *c.* U.S. $480 million. Import sources: U.S.S.R. *c.* 30%; Japan *c.* 16%; France *c.* 7%; Italy *c.* 5%; East Germany *c.* 5%. Export destinations: U.S.S.R. *c.* 46%; Japan *c.* 10%; Hong Kong 5%. Main exports (1974): clothing *c.* 10%; fish *c.* 10%; rubber *c.* 10%; coal *c.* 5%; beverages *c.* 5%.

Transport and Communications. Roads (1977) *c.* 60,000 km. Motor vehicles in use (1976): passenger *c.* 100,000; commercial (including buses) *c.* 200,000. Railways (1977) *c.* 4,230 km. Navigable waterways (1977) *c.* 6,000 km. Telephones (South only; Dec. 1973) 47,000. Radio receivers (Dec. 1978) *c.* 5 million. Television receivers (Dec. 1978) *c.* 2 million.

Agriculture. Production (in 000; metric tons; 1979): rice *c.* 10,500; sweet potatoes (1978) *c.* 1,700; cassava (1978) *c.* 3,000; bananas *c.* 530; tea (1978) *c.* 19; coffee (1978) *c.* 15; tobacco *c.* 28; jute *c.* 53; rubber *c.* 48; pork *c.* 435; fish catch (1978) *c.* 1,010; timber (cu m; 1978) *c.* 21,288. Livestock (in 000; 1978): cattle *c.* 1,700; buffalo *c.* 2,300; pigs *c.* 9,600; chickens *c.* 57,200; ducks *c.* 36,000.

Industry. Production (in 000; metric tons; 1977): coal *c.* 6,200; cement *c.* 700; salt *c.* 375; phosphate rock *c.* 1,500; fertilizers (nutrient content; 1978–79) nitrogenous *c.* 40, phosphate *c.* 130; electricity (kw-hr) 3,473,000.

Virgin Islands:
see Dependent States

Vital Statistics:
see Demography

Volleyball:
see Court Games

Wages and Hours:
see Economy, World; Industrial Relations

Wales:
see United Kingdom

Warsaw Treaty Organization:
see Defense

Water Resources:
see Earth Sciences; Environment

staff. Trades Union Federation president Nguyen Van Linh was believed to have moved up to the post of chief political coordinator. On the other hand, Planning Chief Le Thanh Nghi and Interior Minister Tran Quoc Hoan lost their portfolios. Premier Pham Van Dong himself appeared to slip into the background amid reports that he was "getting tired." Pres. Ton Duc Thang (*see* OBITUARIES) died in March, aged 91. Late in December the National Assembly adopted a new constitution establishing a collective presidency, to consist of a Council of State headed by a chairman. The size of the council would be determined by the Assembly. However, supreme power was said to be consolidated in the hands of Le Duan and the party's secretary for organization, Le Duc Tho.

(T. J. S. GEORGE)

Water Sports

Motorboating. Dean Chenoweth of Tallahassee, Fla., was the outstanding driver of the unlimited-class hydroplane racing season. Survivor of a 200-mph crash in October 1979, he returned to competition in June and won the first five races of the 1980 season, including his third American Power Boat Association (APBA) Gold Cup on July 6 in Madison, Ind. Before losing to Bill Muncey in "Atlas Van Lines" at the Columbia Cup on July 27 in Tri-Cities, Wash., Chenoweth and the Rolls-Royce Griffon-powered "Miss Budweiser" had won a record 20 consecutive competition heats.

Chenoweth's boat lost its rudder during a qualification attempt in Seattle, Wash., on August 7, causing the craft to flip and returning him to the nearby Harborview Medical Center for the second time in ten months. With Chenoweth sidelined nursing rib and shoulder injuries, Muncey won the Seattle World Championship and the inaugural Big Mac Thunderboat Regatta in Ogallala, Neb. Lee ("Chip") Hanauer in "Squire Shop" won the Utah Governor's Cup at Ogden, Utah.

By the time of the Circus Circus Regatta on September 21 at San Diego, Calif., Chenoweth had recovered sufficiently to return in a backup hull. Victories in both of his preliminary heats gave him the points needed to clinch his third APBA national championship. Muncey won the race in "Atlas Van Lines" after qualifying at a record 140.065 mph.

Highlights of the year included a record crowd of 750,000 spectators for the Spirit of Detroit regatta on June 29 and the debuts of several innovative new boats. Ocean racer Don Aronow and shipbuilder Hal Halter entered a lightweight tunnel hull powered by a pair of turbocharged Cosworth engines. David Heerensperger returned with a new turbine-powered "Pay 'N Pak."

The 1980 offshore season saw Bill Elswick of Fort Lauderdale, Fla., sweep the major awards in his 39-ft-deep vee "Long Shot." Elswick won the Bacardi Trophy race on May 10 at Miami, Fla., the Benihana Grand Prix on July 16 at Point Pleasant, N.J., and the Le Club International on October 4 at Fort Lauderdale to earn his first APBA national championship. Elswick's victories in the Benihana and the Cowes–Torquay race off the coast of England also gave him the Harmsworth Trophy, recently returned to international competition.

Catamaran or tunnel hulls won three races. Defending national champion Betty Cook (*see* BIOGRAPHIES) of Newport Beach, Calif., won the inaugural event at New Orleans, La., in "Kaama." Joel Halpern of Tarrytown, N.Y., won the Spirit of Detroit regatta, and Michel Meynard of Concord, Mass., won the Guy Lombardo Classic off Long Island.

Lee Taylor was killed when his "U.S. Discovery II" disintegrated at 330 mph as he attempted to set a water-speed record on Lake Tahoe, Nevada.

(JOHN H. LOVE)

River Sports. At the U.S. national flat-water championships, held in August at Lake Sebago, New York, Gregory Barton took first place in all three men's single kayak events, while Terry White and David Gilman won all the two-man kayak races. Ann Turner won the single-kayak women's events and, together with Leslie Klein, took all the double-kayak women's races.

Although the U.S. flat-water team could not go to the Olympic Games, they competed in two important pre-Olympic regattas, held in Nottingham, England, and Duisburg, West Germany. The U.S. team made the finals in five events at Duisburg, an unprecedented accomplishment.

V. MOREV—TASS/SOVFOTO

Vladimir Parfenovich and Sergey Chukhrai of the U.S.S.R. won the kayak pairs (500 metre) competition in the Summer Olympic Games in Moscow.

The performances of the U.S. women, led by first-place winner Leslie Klein, were particularly outstanding.

At the flat-water competition held at the 1980 Olympic Games in Moscow, the Soviet Union's Vladimir Parfenovich won three of the four gold medals that went to his country, while East German paddlers also won four golds. The remaining three gold medals went to competitors from Hungary, Bulgaria, and Romania. (*See* TRACK AND FIELD SPORTS: *Special Report*.)

In white-water competition Chuck Stanley won the men's kayak race at the U.S. national slalom championships in July on California's Kern River. The national wildwater championships, held near Buena Vista, Colo., were won by Dan Schnurrenberger in the men's kayak event and Cathy Hearn in the women's.

The only international white-water competition in 1980 was the pre-world championships, held at Bala, Wales, in August. Shane Kelly of Ireland won the men's slalom kayak event, and Gabriele Kohllmann of East Germany was the women's champion. (ERIC LEAPER)

Water Skiing. Great Britain's Mike Hazelwood resumed his mastery of the world's best water skiers by winning the U.S. Masters invitational for the third year in a row and the Australian Moomba Masters for the fourth time in as many years. Hazelwood, who had lost his world overall title in 1979 to Joel McClintock of Canada, set a new jumping record of 195 ft in the Moomba, eclipsing by 8 ft the mark established in 1979 by John Mondor of the U.S.

Other records fell during 1980. Bob LaPoint of Castro Valley, Calif., a member of the winning U.S. team at the Pan-American Champions at Berkeley, Calif., in September, raised the slalom record to 62 buoys. Another U.S. skier, Cory Pickos of Eagle Lake, Fla., regained the tricks record from France's Patrice Martin by scoring 8,660 points in the Liz Allan Superstars meet in August.

A brother-sister combination led the open divisions in the U.S. national championships. Sixteen-year-old Carl Roberge of Orlando, Fla., won the open overall title, the youngest male skier ever to take the top nationals honour, while his sister Karin, 17, won her second consecutive open women's overall crown. Roberge also won the U.S. men's national slalom title. Pickos was the best of the tricks competitors, and LaPoint topped the jumpers. Karin Roberge again was the women's tricks winner. Cyndi Benzel of Newberry Springs, Calif., won the slalom, while Linda Giddens of Eastman, Ga., regained the national jumping title she last held in 1977. (THOMAS C. HARDMAN)

Surfing. The eighth world amateur surfing championships were held in France during September with the Federation Francaise de Surf et Skate as host. This outstanding biennial international contest crowned Mark Scott of Australia as the winner.

A milestone in amateur surfing occurred with the formation of the United States Surfing Federation. One of the first acts of the new organization was to prohibit amateur members from receiving compensation for advertising. This ruling was sure to aid professional surfers in their efforts to earn a living in the field.

The 1979 international professional championship title was undecided until the last contest, the Hawaiian Tropic World Cup. Australia's Wayne Bartholomew, Mark Richards, and Cheyne Horan, along with Dane Kealoha of Hawaii, all were in contention. In great surf conditions Mark Richards edged his opponents to take the World Cup and the professional crown. Lyne Boyer of Hawaii placed first among the professional women. (JACK C. FLANAGAN)

Water Polo. In the absence of the powerful teams from the United States and West Germany, water polo in the 1980 Olympic Games was dominated by Eastern European teams. The host team from the Soviet Union finished with a perfect final-round record of 5 wins, 0 losses, and 0 ties to capture the gold medal. Yugoslavia (3–1–1) placed second, while the 1976 Olympic winner, Hungary, took the bronze medal with a 3–2–0 record. Spain (2–3–0), Cuba (0–3–2), and The Netherlands (0–4–1) rounded out the final six. Australia surprisingly was able to win the consolation bracket to take seventh place, followed in order by Italy, Romania, Greece, Sweden, and Bulgaria. (*See* TRACK AND FIELD SPORTS: *Special Report*.)

For the first time the men's and women's senior outdoor championships of the U.S. Amateur Athletic Union were held jointly, with Stanford (Calif.) University the site. Industry Hills, led by the tournament's most valuable player, Laura Cox, went undefeated in winning the women's portion of the tournament. Commerce, FAST A, and FAST B took second, third, and fourth places. The men's competition was extremely close, but when it was all over the Concord (Calif.) Swim Club came out victorious as they narrowly defeated second place Newport A 5–4 and third place Industry Hills 5–3. Gary Figueroa and Jon Svendsen shared the James W. Lee Award as most valuable players. The University of California at Santa Barbara defeated UCLA 11–3 in the finals of the 1979 National Collegiate Athletic Association championships. (WILLIAM ENSIGN FRADY)

Western Samoa

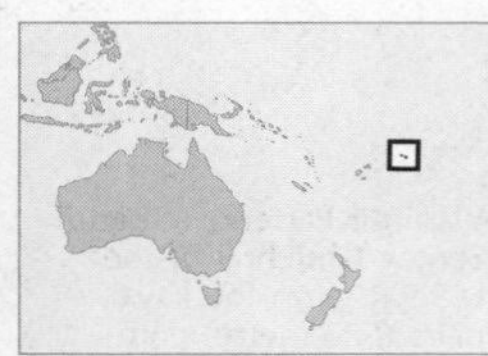

Western Samoa

A constitutional monarchy and member of the Commonwealth of Nations, Western Samoa is an island group in the South Pacific Ocean, about 2,600 km E of New Zealand and 3,500 km S of Hawaii. Area: 2,849 sq km (1,100 sq mi), with two major islands, Savai'i (1,813 sq km) and Upolu (1,036 sq km), and seven smaller islands. Pop. (1980 est.): 155,800. Cap. and largest city: Apia (pop., 1980, 33,400). Language: Samoan and English. Religion (1976): Congregational 50%; Roman Catholic 22%; Methodist 16%; others 12%. Head of state (*O le Ao o le Malo*) in 1980, Malietoa Tanumafili II; prime minister, Tupuola Taisi Tufuga Efi.

There was a sharp downturn in both prices and output of Western Samoa's agricultural products (copra, bananas, and cocoa) in 1980, following the dramatic increases that had boosted export earn-

Weather:
see Earth Sciences

Weight Lifting:
see Gymnastics and Weight Lifting

Welfare:
see Social Security and Welfare Services

WESTERN SAMOA

Education. (1979) Primary, pupils 42,073, teachers 1,458; secondary, pupils 9,719, teachers 458; vocational, pupils 252, teachers 27; teacher training, students 221, teachers 14; higher, students 194, teaching staff 67.

Finance and Trade. Monetary unit: tala, with (Sept. 22, 1980) a free rate of 0.88 tala to U.S. $1 (2.11 tala = £1 sterling). Budget (1978 est.): revenue 22.3 million tala; expenditure 19.3 million tala. Foreign trade (1979): imports 60,946,000 tala; exports 14,981,000 tala. Import sources (1978): New Zealand 33%; Japan 19%; Australia 15%; Canada 9%; Vietnam 6%. Export destinations (1978): New Zealand 35%; West Germany 21%; The Netherlands 9%; American Samoa 7%; Japan 6%; U.K. 5%. Main exports: copra 54%; cocoa 23%; fruit and vegetables *c.* 6%.

ings to record levels the previous year. Faced with a shortage of foreign exchange in midyear, the government slashed import quotas, tightened exchange controls, and deferred overseas payments. The annual inflation rate reached 16% and continued to rise.

Western Samoa's relationship with New Zealand, its former administering power, continued to be affected by the sometimes harsh treatment accorded to Samoan migrants who overstayed visitor's permits to New Zealand. Also, there was renewed controversy over the language test that Samoan students were required to pass in addition to ordinary requirements for entry to New Zealand universities.

During a state visit to China in June, Prime Minister Tupuola Taisi Tufuga Efi was assured by Chairman Hua Guofeng (Hua Kuo-feng) that China would protect the island states of the Pacific against any "hegemonist aggression" from the Soviet Union. In August Japanese officials on a mission to explain their government's proposals for the dumping of nuclear wastes in the Pacific were greeted by a strongly critical Western Samoan government and by public demonstrations condemning their proposals. (BARRIE MACDONALD)

Winter Sports

Increased worldwide coverage by the news media of major competitions on snow and ice, in addition to the best shop window of all, the Winter Olympics (*see* Special Report), considerably furthered public awareness of these sports during 1980 and undoubtedly generated greater eagerness to participate. There was keener competition among resorts bidding for future international events.

Skiing. Longer annual vacation periods in many countries and more economical winter package holidays assisted a general growth of recreational skiing at mountain resorts. Cross-country (Nordic-style) skiing continued to gather more following in North America and the European Alps. In Switzerland approximately 2,500 km (1,500 mi) of cross-country circuits were available in 250 centres. An ever widening selection of ski and après-ski wear reflected the general expansion of participation. The popularity of plastic practice slopes and grass (roller) skiing helped more enthusiasts to keep in touch with technique when and where snow was unavailable, markedly so in Great Britain, South Africa, the U.S., and West Germany.

ALPINE RACING. Although Olympic glamour could not be denied, the season's most prestigious competition was the 14th Alpine World Cup series, which rewarded consistency in events spread over four months. This time a unique family success was achieved by the Liechtenstein brother and sister Andreas and Hanni Wenzel (*see* BIOGRAPHIES), respective winners of the men's and women's titles, a proud achievement for the tiny European principality of only 25,800 residents.

Ingemar Stenmark of Sweden, foremost in both the giant slalom and slalom, finished a close second in men's competition despite his refusal to race in any downhill event. The former World Cup champion had a string of 15 giant slalom victories broken by a fall at Waterville Valley, N.H., in late February; until then he had won every World Cup giant slalom since the final race of the 1978 season. Phil Mahre of the U.S. was able to finish third in the Cup competition through sheer all-round ability without specializing. Wenzel was most noted as a slalom racer, but his considerable downhill skills helped win him the title. The best downhill skiers were Peter Müller of Switzerland and Ken Read of Canada, who, conversely to Stenmark, preferred not to race in the slaloms.

Regaining the women's title she first won in 1978, Hanni Wenzel—always stylishly efficient and unwavering in concentration—jockeyed for the leadership with her two main rivals, Annemarie Moser-Proell of Austria and Marie-Theres Nadig of Switzerland, who finished second and third, respectively. Moser-Proell, the defending champion, was eventually thwarted in her bid for a seventh success by flu and a knee injury during the latter part of the winter. She extended her record total of individual events won to 66, spanning 11 World Cup seasons. Wenzel proved best in the giant slalom and Nadig in the downhill, but the highest scorer in the slalom was Perrine Pelen of France. The concurrently decided Nations' Cup was won for the eighth successive time by Austria. Switzerland was runner-up for the sixth straight year, and the U.S. placed third.

André Arnold of Austria won the professional men's title for the third straight year on the North American circuit. His compatriot Hans Hinterseer placed second, and Lonny Vanatta of the U.S. finished third. Jocelyne Perrillat of France captured the women's crown from the defending champion, Norway's Toril Forland, who placed second. Lyndall Heyer of the U.S. finished third.

The International Ski Federation (FIS) began discussing plans to launch a new alpine combined event comprising downhill and slalom; it would be separate from and in addition to the regular downhill and slalom racing. The proposal was expected to be introduced in the 1982 world alpine championships at Schladming, Austria, and perhaps added to the 1984 Olympic schedule at Sarajevo, Yugos.

NORDIC EVENTS. Following the first official Nordic World Cup series in 1979 and with plans for a second in 1981, unofficial standings in a series of 15 major cross-country meetings in 13 countries during 1980 were registered and served as guides to the season's best performers. Juha Mieto of

Wine:
see Industrial Review

Finland was thus acknowledged as a decisive victor, with Thomas Wassberg of Sweden runner-up, and Lars-Erik Eriksen of Norway third. No comparable women's series was staged. Unofficial ratings were similarly assessed in jumping, involving 104 of the world's leading competitors. The winner was Hubert Neuper and the runner-up Armin Kogler, both Austrians, with Stanislaw Bobak from Poland in third place.

The largest entry was, as usual, for the annual Vasa race from Salen to Mora, Sweden. Approximately 12,000 skiers took part in the event commemorating the Swedish king's escape on skis from Danish soldiers in 1521. The winner was Walter Mayer of Austria. The organizers, aware that some women had already participated incognito, announced that women would be officially admitted for the first time in 1981.

A 20-km cross-country event for women was proposed by the FIS for future world and Olympic programs, which would bring the number of men's and women's Nordic races to four each. The event was expected to be included in the 1982 world Nordic championships in Oslo, Norway.

OTHER EVENTS. Professional freestyle skiing gained a new men's champion in Greg Athans of Canada, winner of the World Trophy series in North America. The runner-up was Frank Beddor of the U.S., and another Canadian, Rick Bowie, finished third. Canada's Stephanie Sloan retained the women's title, with her compatriot Lauralee Bowie runner-up; third was Hedi Garharmer from West Germany.

A world endurance record was claimed by an Italian, Ivano Marangoni. He skied 252 km (155 mi) in 24 hours at Lanzada, Italy.

Ice Skating. New indoor ice rinks were built throughout the world during 1980, especially in North America but notably also in Australia, Japan, South Africa, and southern Europe. But they were still insufficient to satisfy a mushrooming demand for facilities, a demand that Great Britain, with only 40 rinks, in particular failed to meet.

FIGURE SKATING. All four titles changed hands at the world championships on March 11–15 in Dortmund, West Germany, contested by 119 skaters from 23 countries. The men's victor, Jan Hoffmann of East Germany, was strong enough in all phases of the competition to outscore Robin Cousins, the runner-up from Great Britain. Having won the European and Olympic titles earlier in the season, Cousins narrowly failed to complete the triple crown because he was unable to trace good enough compulsory figures. His free-skating performance was the best of his career, climaxing three years of superiority in this division with a near-flawless performance that included five triple jumps; he gained maximum six marks from three of the nine judges. Charles Tickner, the 1978 champion from the U.S., finished third.

The women's victory of Anett Pötzsch was her second, her first having been in 1978. After gaining a useful points advantage in the figures, the East German elected not to take undue risks in the free skating, a policy that paid off because Linda Fratianne, the U.S. title defender, was too far behind. Despite comfortably winning the free skating in a program that included two triple jumps, Fratianne could only finish third, close behind Dagmar Lurz of West Germany.

Fans were denied what could have been a great pairs confrontation between the U.S. titleholders, Randy Gardner and Tai Babilonia, and the Soviet Olympic champions, Aleksandr Zaitsev and Irina Rodnina, because of Gardner's injured groin and Rodnina's strained shoulder. Another Soviet pair, Sergey Shakhrai and Marina Tcherkasova, won the vacant title, followed by Uwe Bewersdorff and Manuela Mager of East Germany and Stanislav Leonovich and Marina Pestova of the Soviet Union. The victory inevitably seemed hollow and the event anticlimactic, bereft of a hoped-for fascinating duel between masters of contrasting styles.

The ice dance contest ended on an excitingly high note when Andras Sallay and Krisztina Regöczy became the first Hungarian champions, overtaking the Soviet title defenders, Gennadi Karponosov and Natalia Linichuk, with a superb free dance. Andrey Minekov and Irina Moiseyeva of the U.S.S.R. finished third.

In the third world junior championships at Mégève, France, on January 16–19, Soviet skaters dominated three of the four events. Aleksandr Fadeev gained the men's title; Oleg Makarov and Larisa Selezneva the pairs; and Aleksey Soloviev and Elana Batanova the ice dance. As it had in both previous tournaments, the women's title went to a U.S. skater, Rosalyn Sumners.

A proposal by Romania to abolish compulsory figures from future championships was decisively rejected at the 38th biennial congress of the International Skating Union at Davos, Switz., on June 2–6. It was decided that as of the 1981–82 season free-skating performances in senior men's and pairs championships would be reduced from five to four-and-a-half minutes and that separate judging panels for compulsory figures and free skating would be tried.

SPEED SKATING. Attempting a fourth successive title, Eric Heiden of the U.S. (*see* BIOGRAPHIES) was unexpectedly defeated in the men's world championship at Heerenveen, Neth., on March 1–2. Hilbert van der Duim of the host country gained a narrow overall points margin over the defending champion. Tom Erik Oxholm of Norway finished third. In the four events van der Duim won the 1,500 m, Heiden the 500 m, Oxholm the 5,000 m, and Mike Woods of the U.S. the 10,000 m.

Natalia Petruseva of the U.S.S.R. became the new women's world champion at Hamar, Norway, on January 12–13, with Beth Heiden of the U.S. second and Bjørg Eva Jensen of Norway third. Petruseva was first in each of the four distances except the longest, the 3,000 m, which was won by Jensen.

The separate world sprint titles for men and women, each contested at West Allis, Wis., on February 9–10, were won, respectively, by Heiden and Karin Enke of East Germany. Each title was decided over four races, two each at 500 m and 1,000 m. Heiden was beaten only once, in one of the 500-m dashes, by his compatriot Tom Plant,

WIDE WORLD

Jan Hoffmann of East Germany captured the gold medal for figure skating at the Dortmund (West Germany) world championship matches on March 13.

who finished third overall behind Gaetan Boucher of Canada. Enke likewise was only defeated once, also in a 500 m, by Leah Poulos-Mueller of the U.S., who finished second overall, just above Beth Heiden.

Three new world men's records were established during the season. Heiden lowered the 1,000-m sprint time to 1 min 13.6 sec on January 13 at Davos, Switz., where, six days later, he covered the 1,500 m in 1 min 54.79 sec. Dmitry Ogloblin of the U.S.S.R. astonishingly bettered Heiden's Olympic time for the 10,000 m with 14 min 25.71 sec at Medeo, U.S.S.R., on March 30. The only new world women's record was in the 1,000 m, reduced to 1 min 23.01 sec on March 27 by Natalia Petruseva, also at Medeo.

The second annual short track championships for men and women, in Milan, Italy, on March 22–23, were won, respectively, by Boucher and Miyoshi Kato of Japan. Boucher also led a Canadian team to victory in the men's relay, the women's being won by Italy. These championships, designed especially for indoor rinks, had rules adapted to suit circuits necessarily smaller than those used outdoors. Subject to the success of these tournaments during an experimental period, the intention was for such competition to attain its own world championship status.

Bobsledding. With the world titles decided concurrently with those of the Olympics, the season's next most important contests were the European championships in January at St.-Moritz, Switz. Erich Scharer of Switzerland maintained his form of recent years by driving the winning four-man sled. His brother Peter was runner-up. Hans Hiltebrand, who completed a Swiss clean sweep in third place, avenged that defeat by winning the two-man title, with Erich Scharer this time third behind Bernhard Germeshausen of East Germany.

Leading riders tended to recognize the most demanding courses as those at Cortina d'Ampezzo and Cervinia, both in Italy, and St.-Moritz. The latter two are naturally frozen and Cortina is partly refrigerated; the only four courses in the world that are fully refrigerated are at Königssee and Winterberg in West Germany, Igls in Austria, and Lake Placid, N.Y. The International Bobsleigh Federation passed new legislation governing the standardization of sled designs for international competition in order to ensure a greater degree of uniformity.

Tobogganing. The installation of North America's first fully refrigerated course for luge tobogganing at Lake Placid—1,000 m long with 15 curves—promoted a wider interest in the sled sport, which was still practiced mainly in European Alpine countries. In the European luge championships, in January at Valdaora, Italy, Italian riders Karl Brunner and Maria-Luisa Rainer took the men's and women's individual titles. The men's two-seater event was won by the consistent East German veterans Hans Rinn and Norbert Hahn.

Swiss riders achieved grand slams in both the classic events for skeleton tobogganists on the Cresta Run at St.-Moritz. Marcel Melcher won the 71st Grand National over the full course, with Gian Saratz runner-up and Gianni Bibbia third. The 57th Curzon Cup over the shorter distance was won for the third straight year by Poldi Berchtold, the track recordholder. Runner-up was Franco Gansser, followed by Christian Nater.

Curling. The 22nd world curling championship for the Air Canada Silver Broom, at Moncton, N.B., on March 24–30, was won for the host country by a Saskatoon four comprising skip Rick Folk, Ron Mills, and the brothers Tom and Jim Wilson. After nine preliminary-round games without a defeat, Canada won a record 13th world title by defeating Norway 7–6 in the final. Defending champion Norway, again represented by Trondheim, was skipped by Kristian Soerum in his third successive final, aided by brothers Eigil and Harald Ramsfjell and Gunnar Meland. Switzerland finished third, followed by Sweden, the U.S., West Germany, Italy, Scotland, Denmark, and France.

Scotland, represented by a rink from Stranraer skipped by Andrew McQuistin, won the sixth world junior championship, sponsored by Uniroyal at Kitchener-Waterloo, Ont., on March 9–16. Canada, represented by Winnipeg, was runner-up among ten countries participating.

Ten nations also contested the second women's world championship, sponsored by the Royal Bank of Scotland at Perth, Scotland, on March 17–22. Canada, skipped by Marj Mitchell with her rink from Regina, Sask., beat Sweden 7–6 in the final. Switzerland, the title defender, failed to reach the play-off round in a tournament that revealed marked progress in women's playing standards. (HOWARD BASS)

See also Ice Hockey.
[452.B.4.g–h]

THE OLYMPIC WINTER GAMES

by Howard Bass

The XIII Olympic Winter Games took place Feb. 13–24, 1980, at Lake Placid, N.Y., which was also the site of the 1932 Winter Olympics. China competed for the first time among a record entry of 37 nations—equaling that at Innsbruck, Austria, in 1976—represented by 1,283 competitors (1,012 men and 271 women). Of the 38 events that were contested, the only new one was the 10-km biathlon. Athletes from 11 nations shared the gold medals, the U.S.S.R. gaining ten, East Germany nine, the U.S. six, Austria and Sweden three each, Liechtenstein two, and Finland, Great Britain, The Netherlands, Norway, and Switzerland one apiece.

The star of the alpine skiing on Whiteface Mountain was Hanni Wenzel of Liechtenstein. Her two gold medals, for slalom and giant slalom, and one silver, in the downhill, equaled the women's record set by Rosi Mittermaier of West Germany in 1976. A remarkable family achievement was completed when Hanni's brother Andreas won the silver medal in the men's giant slalom. Annemarie Moser-Proell, the Austrian genius who was twice denied a gold at Sapporo, Japan, in 1972 by Switzerland's Marie-Theres Nadig, had sweet revenge in the downhill, gaining her first Olympic victory. Nadig finished third behind Wenzel.

Ingemar Stenmark, the Swedish slalom specialist who shuns the downhill, won both the slalom and giant slalom events for men, each time reserving his better effort for the second descent. Third to Wenzel after the first giant slalom run, Stenmark next time gave his opponents no chance with a faultless dash through the gates that finally left the Liechtensteiner three-quarters of a second in arears. In the slalom Stenmark fought back from fourth to win from the U.S. runner-up, Phil Mahre, by half a second. Leonhard Stock was a surprise downhill winner for Austria, many considering him lucky to be chosen at all from a strong national squad. First during both runs, Stock left his compatriot Peter Wirnsberger trailing helplessly in his wake.

The largest number of individual honours in the Nordic skiing, on Mt. Van Hoevenberg, went to Nikolay Zimyatov, the first man to win three cross-country gold medals in one Olympics. The Soviet

---

Howard Bass, winter sports correspondent for several newspapers, is the author of many books on the subject, including This Skating Age, The Magic of Skiing, Winter Sports, *and* Success in Ice Skating.

Liechtenstein's Hanni Wenzel received gold medals for slalom and giant slalom and a silver medal in the downhill during the XIII Olympic Winter Games.

WIDE WORLD

OLYMPIC CHAMPIONS, 1980 WINTER GAMES, LAKE PLACID

Alpine Skiing		
Men		
Downhill	L. Stock (Austria)	1 min 45.50 sec
Slalom	I. Stenmark (Sweden)	1 min 44.26 sec
Giant slalom	I. Stenmark (Sweden)	2 min 40.74 sec
Women		
Downhill	A. Moser-Proell (Austria)	1 min 37.52 sec
Slalom	H. Wenzel (Liechtenstein)	1 min 25.09 sec
Giant slalom	H. Wenzel (Liechtenstein)	2 min 41.66 sec
Nordic Skiing		
Men		
15-km cross-country	T. Wassberg (Sweden)	41 min 57.63 sec
30-km cross-country	N. Zimyatov (U.S.S.R.)	1 hr 27 min 02.80 sec
50-km cross-country	N. Zimyatov (U.S.S.R.)	2 hr 27 min 24.60 sec
40-km ski relay	U.S.S.R.	1 hr 57 min 03.46 sec
70-m ski jump	A. Innauer (Austria)	266.3 pt
90-m ski jump	J. Tormanen (Finland)	271.0 pt
Nordic combined	U. Wehling (East Germany)	432.200 pt
Women		
5-km cross-country	R. Smetanina (U.S.S.R.)	15 min 06.92 sec
10-km cross-country	B. Petzold (East Germany)	30 min 31.54 sec
20-km ski relay	East Germany	1 hr 2 min 11.10 sec
Biathlon		
10 km	F. Ullrich (East Germany)	32 min 10.69 sec
20 km	A. Alyabyev (U.S.S.R.)	1 hr 8 min 16.31 sec
30-km relay	U.S.S.R.	1 hr 34 min 03.27 sec
Figure Skating		
Men	R. Cousins (U.K.)	189.48 pt
Women	A. Pötzsch (East Germany)	189.00 pt
Pairs	I. Rodnina and A. Zaitsev (U.S.S.R.)	147.26 pt
Ice dancing	N. Linichuk and G. Karponosov (U.S.S.R.)	205.48 pt
Speed Skating		
Men		
500 m	E. Heiden (U.S.)	38.03 sec*
1,000 m	E. Heiden (U.S.)	1 min 15.18 sec*
1,500 m	E. Heiden (U.S.)	1 min 55.44 sec*
5,000 m	E. Heiden (U.S.)	7 min 02.29 sec*
10,000 m	E. Heiden (U.S.)	14 min 28.13 sec*†
Women		
500 m	K. Enke (East Germany)	41.78 sec*
1,000 m	N. Petruseva (U.S.S.R.)	1 min 24.10 sec*
1,500 m	A. Borckink (Neth.)	2 min 10.95 sec*
3,000 m	B. E. Jensen (Norway)	4 min 32.13 sec*
Ice Hockey		
Winning team	U.S. (beat Finland 4–2 in final)	
Bobsledding		
Two man	Switzerland	4 min 09.36 sec
Four man	East Germany	3 min 59.92 sec
Tobogganing (Luge)		
Men (single)	B. Glass (East Germany)	2 min 54.796 sec
Men (double)	H. Rinn and N. Hahn (East Germany)	1 min 19.331 sec
Women (single)	V. Zozulya (U.S.S.R.)	2 min 36.537 sec

*Olympic record. †World record.

skier finished the 30 km with a 31-sec margin over his teammate Vasily Rochev. Third-place Ivan Lebanov gained the first medal by a Bulgarian in any Winter Olympics. In the grueling 50 km Zimyatov paced himself well to leave Juha Mieto of Finland almost three minutes behind. Mieto was again runner-up in the 15 km, this time to Thomas Wassberg of Sweden; only 0.01 sec divided them. Zimyatov completed his triple victory as last-leg racer on the winning Soviet relay team.

Barbara Petzold of East Germany ended the women's 10 km ahead of two Finns, Hilkka Riihivuori and Helena Takalo. Raisa Smetanina of the U.S.S.R. scored a victory in the 5 km with Riihivuori again second. Petzold helped the East Germans triumph in the relay, while the veteran Galina Kulakova's silver as a member of the Soviet second-place team was a record eighth medal in her fourth and final Olympics.

Jouko Tormanen caught a timely updraft from a swirling wind at Intervale when winning the 90-m ski jump for Finland, and Anton ("Toni") Innauer comfortably gained Austria's first 70-m ski jump victory. Another East German, Ulrich Wehling, gained his third straight Olympic victory in the Nordic combination, the first skier in Olympic history to win three golds for the same event. Frank Ullrich of East Germany, with better skiing than shooting, won the

Eric Heiden of the U.S. achieved five records with his five gold medals, an event unprecedented in Olympic Winter Games.

WIDE WORLD

UPI

The U.S. Olympic hockey team (black jerseys) scores the third and deciding goal against Finland to gain the gold medal. The Soviets, who placed second, failed to gain the gold medal for the first time since 1960.

10-km biathlon and finished second to Anatoly Alyabyev of the U.S.S.R. in the 20-km event. Alyabyev was also anchor man in the Soviet biathlon team victory.

The new $16 million ice arena was filled to its 8,500 capacity for the climax in each of the four figure-skating events, three of which featured close finishes. Robin Cousins continued where John Curry had left off to keep the men's title in Great Britain, defeating Jan Hoffmann of East Germany by the slenderest of margins. Hoffmann had begun the final free skating with an appreciable advantage from his compulsory figures, but Cousins whittled that away with a dazzling display of jumps and spins. Cousins was awarded 5.9 (out of a possible 6) by eight of the judges for artistic presentation.

Anett Pötzsch gained the women's title, as her U.S. arch-rival, Linda Fratianne, was unable to eliminate the lead the East German had acquired in the compulsory figures. The eagerly awaited pairs confrontation between the U.S. world champions, Randy Gardner and Tai Babilonia, and the Soviet Olympic title defenders, Aleksandr Zaitsev and Irina Rodnina, was sadly canceled because Gardner had to withdraw from competition after aggravating a groin injury. But any hollowness of the Soviets' subsequent victory was offset by the magnitude of Rodnina's personal achievement, her third gold medal in successive Olympics. The second-place pair, Sergey Shakhrai and Marina Tcherkasova, also of the U.S.S.R., were never serious challengers. Two more Soviet skaters, Gennadi Karponosov and Natalia Linichuk, gained ice dance crowns in a close contest with Andras Sallay and Krisztina Regoczy of Hungary.

One of the most outstanding individual performances in the Games was that of the U.S. speed skater Eric Heiden, the only person ever to win five gold medals in one Winter Olympics. To finish first in each of five widely varying distances within nine days and at the end break the world record for the stamina-sapping, 25-lap 10,000 m seemed like something from schoolboy fiction and was comparable to a track sprinter winning the marathon.

The women's ice speed honours were evenly distributed among an East German, Karin Enke (500 m), a Soviet, Natalia Petruseva (1,000 m), a Netherlander, Annie Borckink (1,500 m), and a Norwegian, Bjørg Eva Jensen (3,000 m). In the nine men's and women's speed skating events on the fast oval track the previous Olympic records were bettered an unprecedented 106 times.

Ice hockey, which in the early stages threatened to become a monotonous succession of Soviet victories, was suddenly transformed when the U.S. upset the U.S.S.R. 4–3—the first hockey game the Soviets had lost in Olympic competition since 1968 and only their sixth defeat in 46 games dating back to 1956. The U.S. went on to beat Finland 4–2 in the final match of the 35-game series to clinch its first Olympic ice hockey gold medal since 1960. The crucial match against the Soviet Union, which finished in second place, was a memorable thriller. Down 3–2 after 22 minutes, the U.S. scored two goals in 81 seconds, one each by Mark Johnson and Mike Eruzione.

Yemen, People's Democratic Republic of

A people's republic in the southern coastal region of the Arabian Peninsula, Yemen (Aden; South Yemen) is bordered by Yemen (San'a'), Saudi Arabia, and Oman. Area: 338,100 sq km (130,541 sq mi). Pop. (1980 est.): 1,859,000. Cap. and largest city: Aden (pop., 1980 est., 343,000). Language: Arabic. Religion: predominantly Muslim. Chairmen of the Presidium of the Supreme People's Council in 1980, Abd-al Fattah Ismail and, from April 21, Ali Nasir Muhammad Husani; prime minister, Ali Nasir Muhammad Husani.

On April 21, 1980, Prime Minister Ali Nasir Muhammad Husani took over as chief of state, replacing Abd-al Fattah Ismail, who officially resigned because of ill health. Muhammad was considered more pragmatic and less doctrinaire than his pro-Soviet predecessor and sought better relations with Saudi Arabia—which he visited in June—and Yemen (San'a'; North Yemen). A new Cabinet was formed on October 16.

The Cabinet's main preoccupation was the five-year plan, 1981–85. Priorities included improvements to Aden's refinery and existing industries. A cement works was to be built, and emphasis would be given to improving water supplies and electricity. Housing received U.S. $117.1 million, roughly half the allocation for water and electricity in the $1,244,500,000 plan.

Balance of payments projections for 1980 showed a deficit of $27.3 million, due to a projected 41% increase in import prices. Development planning and general economic policy emphasized state ownership and a comprehensive system of economic controls. Relations with North Yemen improved, and no border incidents with Oman were reported. (JOHN WHELAN)

YEMEN, PEOPLE'S DEMOCRATIC REPUBLIC OF

Education. (1976–77) Primary, pupils 206,358, teachers 9,018; secondary, pupils 54,670, teachers (1975–76) 2,071; vocational, pupils 875, teachers 68; teacher training, students 1,083, teachers 72; higher (1974–75), students 934, teaching staff 92.

Finance and Trade. Monetary unit: Yemen dinar, with (Sept. 22, 1980) a par value of 0.345 dinar to U.S. $1 (free rate of 0.83 dinar = £1 sterling). Budget (1977–78 actual): revenue 34,890,000 dinars; expenditure 47,370,000 dinars. Foreign trade: imports (1977) 187.9 million dinars; exports (1978) 76.4 million dinars. Import sources: Japan *c.* 16%; Qatar *c.* 10%; Kuwait *c.* 10%; U.K. *c.* 8%; Saudi Arabia *c.* 7%; U.S. *c.* 6%. Export destinations: Yemen (San'a') 14%; Italy 11%; United Arab Emirates 7%; China 5%. Main exports (1977): petroleum products 84%; fish 9%.

Transport. Roads (1976) 10,494 km (including 1,356 km with improved surface). Motor vehicles in use (1976): passenger 11,900; commercial (including buses) 10,500. There are no railways. Shipping traffic (1977): goods loaded 1,373,000 metric tons, unloaded 2,429,000 metric tons.

Agriculture. Production (in 000; metric tons; 1979): millet and sorghum *c.* 70; wheat *c.* 25; watermelons *c.* 55; dates *c.* 42; cotton, lint *c.* 4; fish catch (1978) 133. Livestock (in 000; 1978): cattle *c.* 107; sheep *c.* 950; goats *c.* 1,286; camels *c.* 40; chickens *c.* 1,460.

Industry. Production (in 000; metric tons; 1977): petroleum products *c.* 1,770; salt *c.* 75; electricity (kw-hr) *c.* 180,000.

Yemen Arab Republic

A republic situated in the southwestern coastal region of the Arabian Peninsula, Yemen (San'a'; North Yemen) is bounded by Yemen (Aden), Saudi Arabia, and the Red Sea. Area: 200,000 sq km (77,200 sq mi). Pop. (1980 est.): 5,212,000. Cap. and largest city: San'a' (pop., 1980 est., 210,000). Language: Arabic. Religion: Muslim. President in 1980, Col. Ali Abdullah Saleh; premiers, Abdel-Aziz Abdel-Ghani and, from October 15, Abdel Karim al-Iriani.

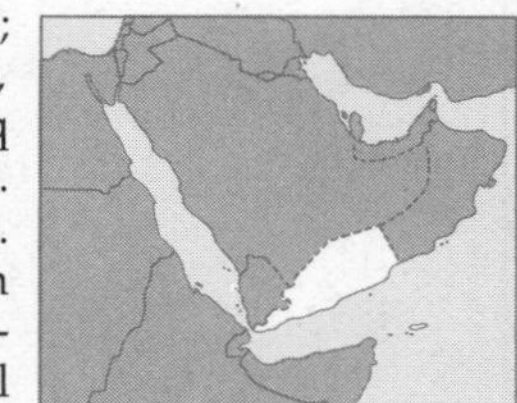
People's Democratic Republic of Yemen

Yemen Arab Republic

Pres. Ali Abdullah Saleh formed a new Cabinet on Oct. 15, 1980, under Premier Abdel Karim al-Iriani. Iriani had held the education, development, and agriculture portfolios in previous Cabinets. The former premier, Abdel-Aziz Abdel-Ghani, became second vice-president, and the job of first vice-president went to Abdel Karim al-Arashi. The president did not yield to pressure in early 1980 to cut the government's dependence on Saudi Arabia. In March an agreement was concluded with Saudi Arabia under which San'a' would refuse to accept more Soviet military advisers. Relations with Yemen (Aden; South Yemen) improved with agreements in February to unify telephone and postal charges.

Despite North Yemen's attraction for Western business, it remained under severe fiscal restraints and heavily dependent on concessionary aid and expatriate remittances. The 1979 war with South Yemen had caused the flow of remittances to stagnate, and the number of Yemenis abroad also stabilized. The government asked the International Monetary Fund for assistance in reviewing spending in the second half of 1980. From a record U.S. $425 million in 1977–78, the overall balance of payments surplus had declined to $125 million in 1978–79 and was $90 million in deficit in the first half of the 1979–80 fiscal year. Customs receipts, a principal source of revenue, had risen by only 6% a year because of inefficient collection, whereas imports had grown by 30% a year.

(JOHN WHELAN)

YEMEN ARAB REPUBLIC

Education. (1976–77) Primary, pupils 221,482, teachers (1975–76) 6,604; secondary, pupils 24,873, teachers (1975–76) *c.* 1,172; vocational, pupils 503, teachers (1975–76) 60; teacher training, students 1,650, teachers (1975–76) 113; higher, students (1977–78) 4,058, teaching staff (1973–74) 58.

Finance and Trade. Monetary unit: rial, with (Sept. 22, 1980) a par value of 4.56 rials to U.S. $1 (free rate of 10.96 rials = £1 sterling). Budget (1979–80 est.): revenue 3,013,000,000 rials; expenditure 4,384,000,000 rials. Foreign trade (1978): imports 5,855,000,000 rials; exports 31.3 million rials. Import sources: Saudi Arabia 21%; Japan 10%; France 8%; U.K. 6%; Italy 6%. Export destinations: Yemen (Aden) 48%; Saudi Arabia 22%; Djibouti 9%; Italy 9%. Main exports (1977): cotton 49%; coffee 17%; hides and skins 12%.

Agriculture. Production (in 000; metric tons; 1979): barley *c.* 60; corn *c.* 90; wheat *c.* 100; sorghum *c.* 700; potatoes (1978) *c.* 106; grapes *c.* 45; dates 67; coffee *c.* 3; tobacco (1978) 4; cotton, lint *c.* 1. Livestock (in 000; 1978): cattle *c.* 950; sheep *c.* 3,700; goats *c.* 7,800; camels *c.* 105; asses *c.* 700.

Wood Products:
see Industrial Review

World Bank:
see Economy, World

Wrestling:
see Combat Sports

Yachting:
see Sailing

Yugoslavia

Yugoslavia

A federal socialist republic, Yugoslavia is bordered by Italy, Austria, Hungary, Romania, Bulgaria, Greece, Albania, and the Adriatic Sea. Area: 255,-804 sq km (98,766 sq mi). Pop. (1980 est.): 22,328,-000. Cap. and largest city: Belgrade (pop., 1980 UN est., 976,000). Language: Serbo-Croatian, Slovenian, and Macedonian. Religion (1953): Orthodox 41%; Roman Catholic 32%; Muslim 12%. President of the republic for life and president of the League of Communists until May 4, 1980, Marshal Tito (Josip Broz); presidents of the Presidium of the League of Communists, Stevan Doronjski and, from October 20, Lazar Mojsov; presidents of the collective Presidency, Lazar Kolisevski from May 4 and, from May 15, Cvijetin Mijatovic; president of the Federal Executive Council (premier), Veselin Djuranovic.

For Yugoslavia, 1980 was the year of transition from the Tito into the post-Tito era. The collective bodies to head the nation and the Communist Party, which had been set up and were already functioning during Tito's lifetime, took over completely during his illness, which began in December 1979. After Tito's death on May 4, 1980 (*see* OBITUARIES), the president of the collective Presidency was Lazar Kolisevski until May 15, when he was succeeded by Cvijetin Mijatovic for 12 months as head of state and commander of the armed forces. World leaders attended Tito's funeral on May 8 in Belgrade. They included Soviet Pres. Leonid Brezhnev, China's Chairman Hua Guofeng (Hua Kuo-feng), West German Chancellor Helmut Schmidt, and British Prime Minister Margaret Thatcher. U.S. Pres. Jimmy Carter was criticized in the U.S. and elsewhere for not attending the funeral personally and for sending Vice-Pres. Walter Mondale instead, but he paid Yugoslavia a visit in June after the Western leaders' summit in Venice, Italy, and specifically reaffirmed U.S. support for Yugoslavia's independence and integrity.

Yugoslavia's relations with the Soviet Union became strained as a result of the Soviet invasion and occupation of Afghanistan in December 1979, which Yugoslavia condemned. Relations with the Soviet Union's closest ally, Bulgaria, also deteriorated early in 1980 over Macedonia, but they improved and in November Yugoslavia's foreign minister, Josip Vrhovec, visited Sofia. Relations with the Soviet Union also improved later in the year. In July a top-level Supreme Soviet delegation visited Yugoslavia, and in September Yugoslavia signed a long-term trade agreement with the Soviet Union that envisioned an increase in mutual trade in 1981–85 to U.S. $26 billion from $11 billion in 1976–80. The Soviet Union committed itself to ordering in that period nearly 100 ships worth $1.3 billion from Yugoslav shipyards. Relations with Albania improved despite continuing ideological debates, and the two countries signed a trade agreement in July.

In February Yugoslavia agreed to an economic cooperation pact with the European Economic Community (EEC) in Brussels. It allowed duty-free access to EEC markets for a wide range of Yugoslav goods, leaving mostly textiles, steel products, ferrous metals, and alloys still subject to tariffs. Yugoslavia was granted a $280 million credit by the EEC for the completion of its east-west highway linking Austria and Greece. To service and repay its estimated $15 billion debt, Yugoslavia was obliged to raise a number of credits and loans in the West. The Yugoslav dinar was devalued by 30% against major Western currencies in June. A partial price freeze was also introduced in June but lifted in October. The rate of inflation in 1980 averaged 30%. Shortages of various foodstuffs and consumer goods occurred.

During Tito's illness a crackdown began on political dissidents despite a marked absence of public political dissent. In January a law was passed in the federal republic of Serbia enabling the government to fire seven Marxist philosophers for criticizing the Yugoslav system. In June seven people were sentenced in Zagreb to terms ranging from 5 to 15 years for allegedly plotting sabotage.

U.S. Pres. Jimmy Carter was greeted by Yugoslavian Pres. Cvijetin Mijatovic when he made a visit to Belgrade on June 24. While there, Carter visited the grave of Marshal Tito.

CHRISTIAN VIOUJARD—GAMMA/LIAISON

YUGOSLAVIA

Education. (1978–79; revised classification) Primary, pupils 1,427,769, teachers 57,335; secondary, pupils 1,912;231; vocational, pupils 487,171; teacher training, pupils 14,386; secondary, vocational, and teacher training, teachers 56,013; higher, students 285,431, teaching staff 18,178.

Finance. Monetary unit: dinar, with (Sept. 22, 1980) a free rate of 27.46 dinars to U.S. $1 (66.01 dinars = £1 sterling). Gold, SDR's, and foreign exchange (June 1980) U.S. $968 million. Budget (1977 actual): revenue 172,920,000,000 dinars; expenditure 185,130,000,000 dinars. Gross material product (1978) 902 billion dinars. Money supply (June 1980) 402.2 billion dinars. Cost of living (1975 = 100; May 1980) 217.3.

Foreign Trade. (1979) Imports 244.4 billion dinars; exports 123.4 billion dinars. Import sources: West Germany 18%; U.S.S.R. 14%; Italy 8%; U.S. 8%; Iraq 7%; France 5%. Export destinations: U.S.S.R. 22%; Italy 11%; West Germany 9%; U.S. 6%; Czechoslovakia 5%. Main exports: machinery 20%; transport equipment 10%; chemicals 9%; food 8%; textiles 8%; nonferrous metals 5%; timber 5%. Tourism: visitors (1978) 6,385,000; gross receipts (1977) U.S. $841 million.

Transport and Communications. Roads (1978) 127,424 km (including 292 km expressways). Motor vehicles in use (1977): passenger 1,923,900; commercial 157,960. Railways: (1978) 9,762 km; traffic (1979) 10,311,000,000 passenger-km, freight 25,730,000,000 net ton-km. Air traffic (1978): 2,719,000,000 passenger-km; freight 28.8 million net ton-km. Shipping (1979): merchant vessels 100 gross tons and over 478; gross tonnage 2,407,221. Telephones (Dec. 1978) 1,733,000. Radio licenses (Dec. 1978) 4,634,000. Television licenses (Dec. 1978) 3,955,000.

Agriculture. Production (in 000; metric tons; 1979): wheat 4,512; barley 631; oats 283; corn 10,082; potatoes *c.* 2,724; sunflower seed 525; sugar, raw value *c.* 870; onions *c.* 294; tomatoes *c.* 455; cabbages (1978) 691; chillies and peppers (1978) *c.* 354; watermelons (1978) *c.* 600; plums (1978) *c.* 706; apples 434; wine 674; tobacco 57; beef and veal *c.* 330; pork *c.* 630; timber (cu m; 1978) *c.* 15,898. Livestock (in 000; Jan. 1979): cattle 5,491; sheep 7,339; pigs 7,747; horses 701; chickens 61,513.

Industry. Fuel and power (in 000; metric tons; 1979): coal 435; lignite 41,680; crude oil 4,143; natural gas (cu m) *c.* 1,860,000; manufactured gas (cu m) *c.* 240,000; electricity (kw-hr) 54,880,000. Production (in 000; metric tons; 1979): cement 9,029; iron ore (35% metal content) 4,678; pig iron 2,608; crude steel 2,320; magnesite (1977) 345; bauxite 3,012; aluminum 190; copper 137; lead 111; zinc 99; petroleum products *c.* 14,200; sulfuric acid 1,046; plastics and resins 340; cotton yarn 120; wool yarn 44; man-made fibres (1977) 97; wood pulp (1978) *c.* 610; newsprint 84; other paper (1977) 618; television receivers (units; 1978) 449; passenger cars (units) 206; commercial vehicles (units) 64. Merchant vessels launched (100 gross tons and over; 1979) 173,000 gross tons.

A group of 50 Albanians (mostly young people) was tried during the summer for alleged separatism.

In July sharp press attacks were made on Milovan Djilas, a former vice-president and for many years Yugoslavia's leading dissident, for publishing abroad articles and interviews critical of the Yugoslav system, including a "critical portrait" of Tito. Also during the year a group of Yugoslav intellectuals demanded the abolition of the article of the penal code dealing with hostile propaganda. A group of Croatian intellectuals in Zagreb demanded amnesty for all political prisoners. Two Croatian dissidents, Gen. Franjo Tudjman and writer Vlado Gotovac, were interrogated for giving interviews to Western journalists. Legal proceedings were started against them in October.

(K. F. CVIIC)

Zaire

A republic of equatorial Africa, Zaire is bounded by the Central African Republic, Sudan, Uganda, Rwanda, Burundi, Tanzania, Zambia, Angola, Congo, and the Atlantic Ocean. Area: 2,344,885 sq km (905,365 sq mi). Pop. (1979 est.): 25,560,800. Cap. and largest city: Kinshasa (pop., 1979 est., 2,242,300). Language: French; Bantu dialects. Religion: animist approximately 50%; Christian 43%. President in 1980, Mobutu Sese Seko; prime ministers, Bo-Boliko Lokonga Monse Mihambo and, from August 27, Nguza Karl-I-Bond.

With the inflation rate at 100%, the task of reviving the country's economy was one of the main concerns of Zaire's government throughout 1980. Another problem was the widespread discontent of the people, whose standard of living had declined steadily for years while a handful of the country's leaders amassed wealth. The discontent provided fertile ground for dissidents, and there were rumours that agents from countries hostile to Zaire were attempting to stir up trouble. The government acted firmly against any suspected agitators, but its repressive measures only led to further suspicion and hostility. The situation was aggravated by the low price paid for copper, the output of which had been cut drastically in 1979, and by the high cost of petroleum products.

In one respect Zaire was fortunate. A number of Western powers, fearing the further spread of Communist influence in Africa, were determined to support the regime however little they respected its policies. Representatives of the country's main creditors had met in December 1979 and agreed to recommend the rescheduling of Zaire's external public debt, which would fall due in 1980. In April 1980 the government of Zaire signed an agreement with representatives of 122 commercial bank creditors making the rescheduling proposals effective.

In January 1980 Zaire's power to draw on a standing fund set up by the International Mone-

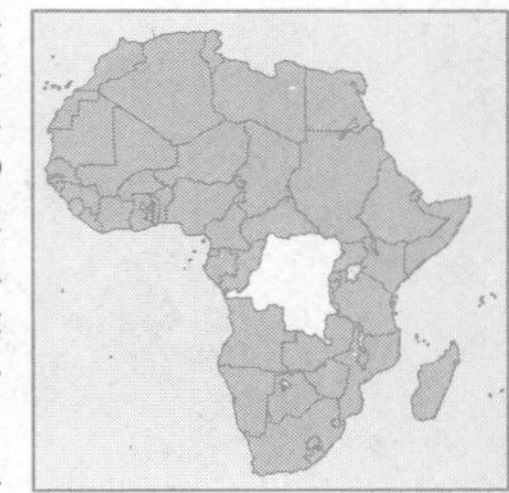

Zaire

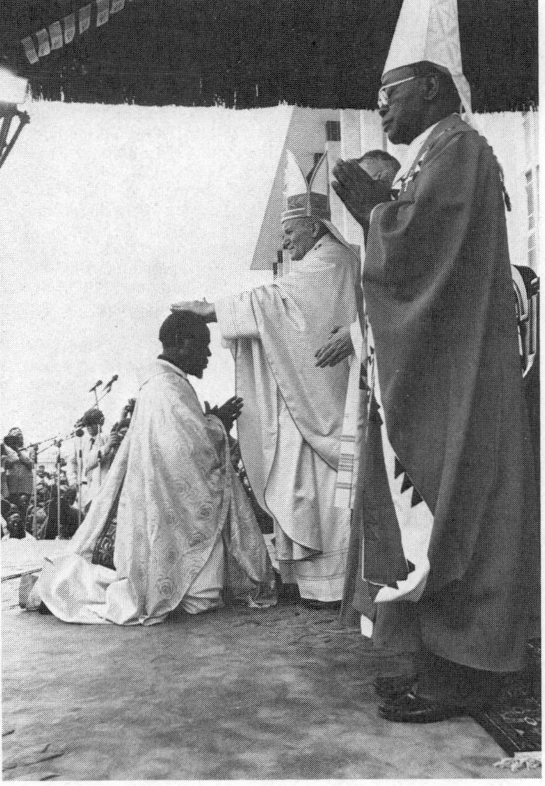

GIANSANTI-FABIAN—SYGMA

Pope John Paul II celebrated mass at the People's Palace during his visit to Zaire in May. One million people were reported in attendance.

tary Fund (IMF) was suspended when it became known that the 1979 budget deficit had seriously exceeded the limit set by the IMF. An IMF mission visited Kinshasa with the object of reviewing Zaire's economy and suggesting new criteria for the operation of the standing fund arrangement. The Consultative Group for Zaire, consisting of representatives of nine industrial countries, together with the IMF, the World Bank, and the European Economic Community, met in Paris at the end of May and decided to recommend additional aid, the nature and extent of which would be subject to further discussion. On May 20 Amnesty International published a report claiming that about 1,000 political detainees were being held in Zaire, many of them without trial. Nguza Karl-I-Bond, the foreign minister (and prime minister from August 27), declared that the report was an attempt to influence the discussions of the Consultative Group for Zaire. The evidence did not seem to support his statement, however.

In return for the various measures of assistance, the country's creditors insisted that the government take more effective measures to control the situation and restore order. On January 18 Pres. Mobuto Sese Seko announced a number of changes in his Executive Council. He himself relinquished the portfolio of national defense and veterans' affairs in favour of Lieut. Gen. Babia Zongbi Malobia, but he retained the portfolio of territorial security. Speaking on February 4, the president affirmed that as long as he lived there would be no biparty or multiparty system. At the same time, efforts were made to reform the Army with the assistance of Belgian and French advisers, together with a number of Chinese instructors. In February it was reported that Zaire had signed an agreement on military matters with Egypt aimed at an exchange of technical knowledge and reciprocal training of troops. The following month Mobutu visited Romania, where he signed a treaty of cooperation, and later in March he visited China.

None of these measures brought any immediate improvement in the conditions of the ordinary people. The cost of food remained high and jobs were scarce. Rioting in January at the Institute for Applied Technology in Kinshasa was followed by a month-long strike by students, culminating in demonstrations in April protesting the inadequate support provided for higher education. This led to closure of the National University in Kinshasa, along with several other educational centres. In the course of a visit to Zaire early in May for the consecration of several new bishops, Pope John Paul II cautioned the congregation against hasty africanization of church ceremonial. His visit was marred by the deaths of nine people and the injury of many more when huge crowds flocked to attend his celebration of mass. (KENNETH INGHAM)

ZAIRE

Education. (1977–78) Primary, pupils 3,818,934, teachers (1972–73) 80,481; secondary, pupils 458,776; vocational, pupils 84,995; teacher training, students 99,904; secondary, vocational, and teacher training, teachers (1973–74) 14,483; higher, students (1974–75) 21,021, teaching staff 2,550.

Finance. Monetary unit: zaire, with (Sept. 22, 1980) a free rate of 2.87 zaires to U.S. $1 (6.90 zaires = £1 sterling). Gold, SDR's, and foreign exchange (June 1980) U.S. $210 million. Budget (1977 actual): revenue 694 million zaires; expenditure 1,281,000,000 zaires. Gross national product (1977) 4,011,000,000 zaires. Money supply (April 1980) 2,164,700,000 zaires. Cost of living (Kinshasa; 1975 = 100; March 1980) 1,158.9.

Foreign Trade. (1979) Imports 1,046,900,000 zaires; exports 2,342,200,000 zaires. Import sources (1978): Belgium-Luxembourg *c.* 17%; France *c.* 11%; West Germany *c.* 9%; U.S. *c.* 8%. Export destinations (1978): Belgium-Luxembourg *c.* 29%; Angola *c.* 19%; U.S. *c.* 9%; U.K. *c.* 7%; France *c.* 6%; Italy *c.* 5%; West Germany *c.* 5%. Main exports: cobalt 46%; copper 36%; coffee 10%; diamonds 7%.

Transport and Communications. Roads (1979) *c.* 145,000 km. Motor vehicles in use (1977): passenger 96,700; commercial (including buses) 87,100. Railways: (1979) 5,254 km; traffic (1976) 467 million passenger-km, freight 2,203,000,000 net ton-km. Air traffic (1978): 778 million passenger-km; freight 36.9 million net ton-km. Shipping (1979): merchant vessels 100 gross tons and over 32; gross tonnage 91,784. Inland waterways (including Zaire River; 1979) *c.* 14,000 km. Telephones (Jan. 1978) 33,800. Radio receivers (Dec. 1977) 125,000. Television receivers (Dec. 1977) 8,000.

Agriculture. Production (in 000; metric tons; 1979): rice *c.* 230; corn *c.* 350; sweet potatoes (1978) *c.* 313; cassava (1978) *c.* 12,510; peanuts *c.* 310; palm kernels *c.* 70; palm oil *c.* 170; mangoes *c.* 172; pineapples *c.* 150; bananas *c.* 310; oranges *c.* 157; coffee *c.* 87; rubber *c.* 27; jute *c.* 13; cotton, lint *c.* 13; meat (1978) *c.* 178; fish catch (1978) 100; timber (cu m; 1978) *c.* 20,691. Livestock (in 000; 1978): cattle *c.* 1,144; sheep *c.* 761; goats *c.* 2,731; pigs *c.* 729; poultry *c.* 12,200.

Industry. Production (in 000; metric tons; 1978): copper ore (metal content) 481; zinc ore (metal content) 74; manganese ore (metal content; 1977) 21; cobalt ore (metal content) 13; gold (troy oz) 77; silver (troy oz) 2,900; diamonds (metric carats) 11,245; crude oil (1979) 1,027; coal 106; petroleum products 183; sulfuric acid 138; cement 468; electricity (kw-hr) *c.* 4,050,000.

Zambia

A republic and a member of the Commonwealth of Nations, Zambia is bounded by Tanzania, Malawi, Mozambique, Zimbabwe, South West Africa/Namibia, Angola, and Zaire. Area: 752,614 sq km (290,586 sq mi). Pop. (1980 est.): 6,027,000, about 99% of whom are Africans. Cap. and largest city: Lusaka (pop., 1980 est., 684,000). Language: English and Bantu. Religion: predominantly animist, with Roman Catholic (21%), Protestant, Hindu, and Muslim minorities. President in 1980, Kenneth Kaunda; prime minister, Daniel Lisulo.

Zambia

In 1980 Zambia was again forced to import corn (maize) from a variety of sources; in May Pres. Kenneth Kaunda announced a £300 million, ten-year plan to raise the country's level of food production. The achievement of independence by neighbouring Zimbabwe was celebrated, but it led to further criticism of the government, which could no longer attribute shortages to Rhodesian hostility. Although rumours of an attempt to assassinate Kaunda in February were denied, Kaunda himself admitted that he had thwarted an attempted coup in October. He imposed a curfew on most of the towns in Zambia, and this was followed by the arrest of several leading businessmen and former government officials. In a separate operation, more than 40 members of a heavily armed gang were captured after a gun battle near Lusaka. Kaunda accused South Africa of involvement, but the charge was denied.

ZAMBIA

Education. (1978) Primary, pupils 964,475, teachers (1976) 19,089; secondary, pupils 88,842, teachers (1976) 3,539; vocational, pupils (1977) 2,670, teachers (1976) 481; teacher training (1977), students 3,752, teachers 268; higher (1976), students 8,783, teaching staff 412.

Finance. Monetary unit: kwacha, with (Sept. 20, 1980) a free rate of 0.77 kwacha to U.S. $1 (1.85 kwachas = £1 sterling). Gold, SDR's, and foreign exchange (June 1980) U.S. $87 million. Budget (1978 actual): revenue 551.9 million kwachas; expenditure 636.9 million kwachas. Gross domestic product (1979) 2,566,000,000 kwachas. Cost of living (1975 = 100; March 1980) 200.1.

Foreign Trade. Imports (1978) 584,030,000 kwachas; exports (1979) 1,118,800,000 kwachas. Import sources: U.K. 25%; Saudi Arabia 14%; West Germany 11%; U.S. 8%; South Africa 7%; Sweden 5%. Export destinations (1978): Japan 20%; U.K. 14%; West Germany 12%; U.S. 11%; France 10%; Italy 9%; India 6%. Main export: copper 83%.

Transport and Communications. Roads (1979) 36,415 km. Motor vehicles in use (1977): passenger *c.* 104,500; commercial (including buses) *c.* 62,500. Railways (1978) *c.* 2,187 km (including *c.* 890 km of the 1,870-km Tanzam railway). Air traffic (1978): 544 million passenger-km; freight 37.1 million net ton-km. Telephones (Jan. 1978) 54,500. Radio receivers (Dec. 1977) 115,000. Television receivers (Dec. 1977) *c.* 50,000.

Agriculture. Production (in 000; metric tons; 1979): corn *c.* 600; cassava (1978) *c.* 173; millet *c.* 50; sorghum *c.* 30; peanuts *c.* 74; sugar, raw value *c.* 105; tobacco *c.* 4. Livestock (in 000; 1978): cattle *c.* 1,800; sheep *c.* 51; goats *c.* 300; pigs *c.* 180; poultry *c.* 14,000.

Industry. Production (in 000; metric tons; 1978): coal 650; copper ore (metal content; 1979) 724; lead ore (metal content) 16; zinc ore (metal content) 50; petroleum products (1977) *c.* 830; cement (1979) 300; electricity (kw-hr) 7,880,000.

Low prices for copper meant that reserves of foreign currency remained disastrously low. On January 23 the government nationalized stores of diesel oil and gasoline held in Zambia by five international companies. On April 1, at Lusaka, Zambia was one of nine southern African countries pledging economic cooperation and efforts to improve transport and communications.

(KENNETH INGHAM)

Zimbabwe

A republic (independent April 18, 1980) in eastern Africa and member of the Commonwealth of Nations, Zimbabwe is bounded by Zambia, Mozambique, South Africa, and Botswana. Area: 390,508 sq km (150,804 sq mi). Pop. (1980 est.): 7,360,000, of whom 96% are African and 4% white. Cap. and largest city: Salisbury (urban area pop., 1979 est., 627,000). Language: English (official) and various Bantu languages (1969 census, Shona 71%, Ndebele 15%). Religion: predominantly traditional tribal beliefs; Christian minority. President in 1980, the Rev. Canaan Banana; prime minister, Robert Mugabe.

Zimbabwe became independent at midnight on April 17, 1980, with the Rev. Canaan Banana as its first president. This was the culmination of three and a half months of intensive preparation under the direction of the British governor, Lord Soames. The cease-fire that had come into force at midnight on Dec. 28, 1979, marked the official end of the civil war in Zimbabwe Rhodesia. The soldiers of the Patriotic Front were given a week in which to assemble in camps supervised by troops of a Commonwealth monitoring force, and many thousands, though not all, responded to the governor's appeal.

ZIMBABWE

Education. (1979) Primary, pupils 832,603, teachers 18,715; secondary, pupils 72,814, teachers 3,534; vocational (including part-time), pupils 2,959, teachers 357; teacher training, students 3,082, teachers 258; higher, students 4,563, teaching staff 483.

Finance. Monetary unit: Zimbabwe dollar, with (Sept. 22, 1980) a free rate of Z$0.62 to U.S. $1 (Z$1.50 = £1 sterling). Budget (1979–80 est.): revenue Z$616 million; expenditure Z$974 million. Gross national product (1978) Z$2,297,000,000.

Foreign Trade. (1979) Imports Z$549.1 million; exports Z$684.9 million. Import sources (1965): U.K. 30%; South Africa 23%; U.S. 7%; Japan 6%. Export destinations (1965): Zambia 25%; U.K. 22%; South Africa 10%; West Germany 9%; Malawi 5%; Japan 5%. Main exports: chrome ore *c.* 13%; gold *c.* 12%; asbestos *c.* 9%; tobacco *c.* 9%; cotton *c.* 6%.

Transport and Communications. Roads (1978) *c.* 83,000 km. Motor vehicles in use (1977): passenger *c.* 180,000; commercial (including buses) *c.* 70,000. Railways: (1979) 3,470 km; freight traffic (1978–79) 6,149,000,000 net ton-km. Telephones (June 1979) 206,000. Radio licenses (June 1979) 208,000. Television licenses (June 1979) 78,100.

Agriculture. Production (in 000; metric tons; 1979): corn *c.* 1,000; millet *c.* 140; wheat *c.* 100; sugar, raw value *c.* 230; peanuts *c.* 120; tobacco *c.* 45; cotton, lint *c.* 30; beef and veal (1978) *c.* 150. Livestock (in 000; 1978): cattle *c.* 6,600; sheep *c.* 650; goats *c.* 2,050; pigs *c.* 202.

Industry. Production (in 000; metric tons; 1977): coal *c.* 2,500; cement (1979) 393; asbestos *c.* 200; chrome ore (oxide content) *c.* 300; iron ore (metal content) *c.* 325; gold (troy oz) *c.* 610; electricity (kw-hr; 1979) 4,231,000.

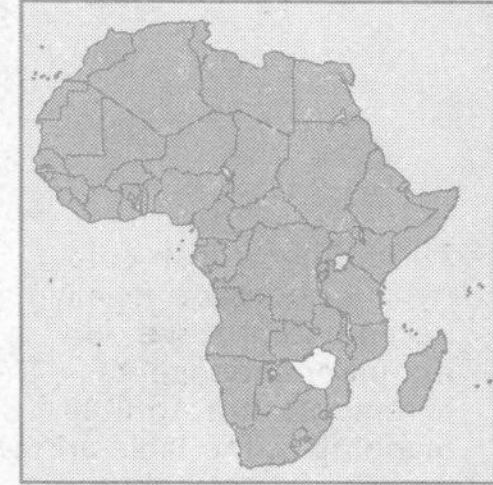
Zimbabwe

On January 13 Joshua Nkomo arrived in Salisbury from Zambia after three years in exile, and Robert Mugabe (*see* BIOGRAPHIES), leader of the Zimbabwe African National Union (ZANU), the larger section of the Patriotic Front, returned to Rhodesia from Mozambique a fortnight later. Against a background of recriminations, resulting at times in violence between the various parties that were to contest the elections at the end of February, and of criticism of the handling of the highly volatile situation by Lord Soames, a beginning was made toward repatriating an estimated 200,000 refugees from Zambia, Mozambique, Botswana, and other countries. Under the supervision of British soldiers, a start was also made toward integrating some of the former guerrillas into the existing Rhodesian Army.

When the elections took place (results completed March 4), 94% of the electorate cast their votes. Mugabe's ZANU (PF), with 63% of the total vote and 57 of the 80 seats contested by black candidates, won an overwhelming victory. Nkomo's Patriotic Front was second with 24% of the vote and 20 seats. Mugabe's victory caused apprehension among many of the white citizens, but he was at pains to reassure all sections within the country of his good intentions toward them. On March 5 he agreed to form a coalition with Nkomo's party and, after speculation as to whether he would become independent Zimbabwe's first president, Nkomo accepted the portfolio of home affairs. Only three other members of his party were given ministries, but two white ministers were appointed to Mugabe's Cabinet.

W. CAMPBELL—SYGMA

The former British colony of Rhodesia officially became Zimbabwe during independence ceremonies on April 18. Standing at the table are Prime Minister Robert Mugabe (left) and Pres. Canaan Banana.

Some whites were worried by Mugabe's insistence that he had been elected to introduce changes and that the main areas of change would be in land settlement, in the restructuring of the civil service to open opportunities for the promotion of blacks, and in the fields of health and education. Several hundred white members of the Army and police refused to serve under Mugabe, and many whites began to leave the country. On the other hand, fears that Zimbabwe would be seriously affected by Mugabe's Marxist ideology were partly allayed by his application for membership in the Lomé Convention, linking African and other less developed countries with the European Economic Community. The foreign minister, Simon Muzenda, also announced in March that Zimbabwe intended to maintain close relations with Britain. In April the minister of mines, Maurice Nyagumbo, reassured those who feared nationalization of the mines by stating the government's policy would be to encourage private ownership with a view to increasing output and profits.

The promise of good relations with Britain was reinforced by the offer of an immediate grant of £7 million by Britain as part of a £75 million grant over the next three years. There was also an offer of aid from the U.S., and in June loans totaling £80 million were secured from West Germany and France to finance a thermal power station. A month later West Germany offered aid worth £12 million for rural development. In August Mugabe visited Britain and the U.S. in an attempt to raise further loans of £146 million for the construction of roads, schools, and hospitals.

Meanwhile, the first session of Zimbabwe's Parliament opened on May 16. A statement by the minister of finance, Enos Nkala, indicated that the white community would be called on to make a major contribution to the country's reconstruction, but Mugabe urged white farmers to stay in Zimbabwe, promising them security in return for their contribution to the country's prosperity. He also stressed the need to reopen the oil pipeline, owned by the Lonrho Co., between Beira, Mozambique, and the Zimbabwean refinery in the Eastern Province.

The task of reconstruction facing Zimbabwe after years of civil war was enormous. Once an exporter of corn (maize), Zimbabwe now had to import large quantities. Finance for rehabilitation was threatened by the fall in income from the tobacco industry—the main earner of foreign currency as well as the chief employer—because of overproduction throughout the world and a consequent decline in prices. Relations between Mugabe and Nkomo were uneasy at times, and there was pressure from within the prime minister's own party for more radical measures.

The formation of the new Army was also beset by problems. The members of the two branches of the former Patriotic Front were not at ease with each other, and neither group found it easy to cooperate with the former Rhodesian Army. Erstwhile guerrillas, still in camps, were restless at the delay in reintegrating them into the life of independent Zimbabwe, and violent incidents involving armed members of the guerrilla forces became more numerous. In July Parliament agreed to extension of the state of emergency for a further six months. Lieut. Gen. Peter Walls, the former Rhodesian commander in chief, had been asked by Mugabe to stay on after independence to integrate the guerrilla forces into the Army. However, he was relieved of his post as chief of the joint high command on September 15, as a result of derogatory remarks made while on leave about the risk of civil war and the fairness of the elections, and was barred from returning to the country.

At the end of September Mugabe ordered the Army and police to act against dissidents. Army units moved into areas where armed troublemakers had been most in evidence, and in November fighting broke out in Bulawayo between members of the two guerrilla forces who had supported Mugabe and Nkomo. Order was restored only after about 50 people had been killed, some of them civilians. In July white civil servants were given assurances about the security of their appointments and promotion prospects.

Mugabe also announced that Zimbabwe would not provide a base for African National Congress guerrillas wishing to operate against South Africa. Nevertheless, the prime minister ordered closure of the South African mission in Zimbabwe because, he claimed, Pretoria was recruiting mercenaries to fight against Zimbabwe. The South African government then withdrew all senior diplomats from Salisbury. A further blow to the government came with the arrest in August of the minister of manpower, Edgar Z. Tekere, on a charge of murdering a white farmer. Tekere was acquitted on December 8 after a month-long trial. (*See* CRIME AND LAW ENFORCEMENT.)

In October the government regretfully announced its intention to introduce regulations to control the activities of visiting journalists. An example of the difficulties faced by the government was provided at the beginning of November. It was reported that Mugabe—contrary to his previous statements—had announced the government's intention to take possession of some white-owned farms without compensation because Britain had failed to fulfill its preindependence promise to pay white farmers for land needed by the government. The land thus taken would be allocated to Africans living in reserves or on less fertile land. Almost at once it was explained that the speech, delivered in Shona, had been misinterpreted and that the prime minister had only stated that it might be necessary to seize vacant and unused land if the international community did not provide the aid Zimbabwe so urgently needed.

On November 4 Zimbabwe signed the Lomé Convention. This would enable the country to draw upon aid from the EEC and to export specified quantities of sugar and beef to EEC countries on favourable terms. (KENNETH INGHAM)

Zoos and Botanical Gardens

Zoos. Two authoritative reports published in 1980, *World Conservation Strategy,* prepared by the International Union for Conservation of Nature and Natural Resources, and *Global 2000,* a study initiated by U.S. Pres. Jimmy Carter on the future of the environment, estimated that approximately 600,000 to one million species of plants and animals would become extinct by the year 2000.

Such prognostications increased awareness among zoo scientists, directors, curators, and councils of their fundamental and increasingly urgent obligation to propagate and sustain in captivity species that might otherwise disappear. Papers given at the third international conference on "Breeding Endangered Species in Captivity," held in San Diego, Calif., in November 1979, and published in the 1980 *International Zoo Yearbook,* emphasized these obligations. They also stressed some of the difficulties inherent in long-term wild-animal propagation and reintroduction schemes.

The emphasis given to various manipulative techniques, such as artificial incubation, cross-fostering between related species and individuals, artificial insemination, and semen banks, indicated the direction that research was taking. Also stressed were the needs for data collection, careful record keeping, and cooperation and coordination; these points were also underlined at the international symposium on "The Use and Practice of Wild Animal Studbooks," organized by the International Union of Directors of Zoological Gardens and held in Copenhagen in October 1979.

In mid-August the first captive birth outside China of a giant panda occurred at Chapultepec Park Zoo in Mexico City. The parents, Yin-yin and Pe-pe, had been given as young animals to the people of Mexico by China in 1975. Despite the utmost care, at eight days old the cub died, inadvertently suffocated by its mother. Among the first or rare breedings reported by zoos during 1979–80 were: yellowhead jawfish (*Opistognathus aurifrons*), San Diego, Calif.; Coahuilan box turtle (*Terrapene coahuila*), Dallas, Texas; Santa Catalina Island rattleless rattlesnake (*Crotalus catalinensis*), Fresno, Calif.; scarlet-headed blackbird (*Amblyramphus*

UPI

Three emperor penguin chicks, believed to be the first hatched outside the Antarctic, were born at the Hubbs-Sea World Research Institute in San Diego, California.

Zoology:
see Life Sciences

THE TIMES, LONDON

Baby "Bonny," a puma born at the London Zoo, is the first large cat to be conceived by artificial insemination. This technique is considered critical to the preservation of endangered species.

holosericeus), Philadelphia, Pa.; Hispaniolan conure (*Aratinga chloroptera*), Santo Domingo, Dominican Republic.

Other outstanding propagation news included the recording of the 70th cheetah birth at Whipsnade, England, and the rearing of the rare Tahitian blue lory (*Vini peruvini*) at San Diego, Calif., and in a private collection in England. Under schemes based on captive-bred stock, various species that had become rare in the wild state were reintroduced into their natural habitats. These included rhinoceros iguanas (into Dominica), Houston toads (the Houston, Texas, region), Arabian oryx (Jordan and Oman), and badgers (Norfolk, England).

Although artificial insemination had already resulted in successful births in a number of animals, two important achievements involving this technique were announced in 1980: the birth of a puma in London (to act as a prototype for further work on the rarer large cats), and of the rare Speke's gazelle in St. Louis, Mo. Late in the spring the U.S. National Zoo in Washington, D.C., artificially inseminated its giant panda Ling-Ling with sperm from its companion Hsing-Hsing, but the effort failed to produce offspring.

Recent new zoo buildings and exhibits included a magnificent walk-through aviary in Melbourne, Australia, the imaginative North American Living Museum in Tulsa, Okla., and the well-equipped veterinary hospital and pathology unit in Jersey, Channel Islands. *Great Zoos of the World* (1980), edited by Lord Zuckerman, president of the Zoological Society of London, dealt comprehensively with the history, present collections, and future policy of 24 selected zoos and included a long introduction by Lord Zuckerman on the rise of zoos and their future. (P. J. S. OLNEY)

Botanical Gardens. In many countries an increasing awareness of environmental problems led to greater efforts to preserve threatened plant life. A priority was the establishment wherever possible of nature reserves in which local flora could be given lasting shelter, allowing threatened species to be protected and propagated under scientific control until such time as they could be returned to their natural habitat. Important also was that all relevant information about such establishments' contents be made readily accessible to the visiting public.

"Botanical garden" is an elastic designation covering a heterogeneous range of institutions that vary widely as regards basic function, area of specialization, and possibilities for expansion. While new gardens were being opened in all continents, this was often done in the face of considerable difficulties in both developed and less developed countries. In the former a shortage of qualified staff was a serious problem which sometimes necessitated limiting the size and variety of collections.

In times of crisis, whether occasioned by political upheaval, energy shortages, or natural disasters such as hurricanes, floods, or drought, botanical gardens are often severely affected and need prompt assistance from other gardens. Lack of funds also threatens these "living museums," and as a rule the smaller establishments are most seriously affected, while the large, long-established, and well-known institutions are more likely to receive the support needed. In establishing new gardens an area of 20 ha (50 ac), sometimes supplemented by a number of neighbouring satellite grounds, was increasingly considered the minimum necessary to ensure viability.

An essential basis for all efforts to preserve the natural environment must be the dissemination among an ever more crowded human population of information about conservational aims and methods. Preferably, such instruction should begin at school, and in this connection current activities at the Viera y Clavijo garden at Tafira Alta, Canary Islands, were of particular interest. They included: visits to outlying schools by mobile exhibitions devoted to the islands' natural history, with filmstrips available for biology lessons; one-week courses in conservation for schoolteachers; distribution of seedlings of endemic plant species among schoolchildren for tending at home and eventual return for planting in open ground; and the award of a prize commemorating the garden's founder, E. R. Sventenius, to the group of pupils submitting the best work on a conservational theme.

The International Conference of the Technical Heads of Botanical Gardens, held in July 1980 in Zürich, Switz., gathered together representatives from 12 countries to exchange experience, study Swiss nature, and visit some of the country's other botanical gardens, at Bern, Basel, and Montreux. Besides the protection of species the main points of discussion concerned the exchange of plants among interested gardens and suggestions for obtaining cultivated plants and garden varieties to be found in certain countries. Ideas for providing gardens with sections devoted to healing herbs, fodder plants, poisonous plants, biblical plants, and enclosures with aromatic plants for the enjoyment of blind people were also discussed.

(JOHANNES APEL)

See also Environment; Gardening.

[355.C.6]

CONTRIBUTORS

Names of contributors to the Britannica Book of the Year *with the articles written by them. The arrangement is alphabetical by last name.*

AARSDAL, STENER. Economic and Political Journalist, *Borsen*, Copenhagen.
Denmark

ADAMS, ANDREW M. Free-lance Foreign Correspondent; Editor and Publisher, *Sumo World* magazine. Author of *Ninja: The Invisible Assassins; Born to Die: The Cherry Blossom Squadrons.* Co-author of *Sumo History and Yokozuna Profiles; Japan Guide and Directory to Martial Arts and Modern Sports.*
Combat Sports: *Judo; Karate; Kendo; Sumo*

AGRELLA, JOSEPH C. Correspondent, *Blood-Horse* magazine; former Turf Editor, *Chicago Sun-Times.* Co-author of *Ten Commandments for Professional Handicapping; American Race Horses.*
Equestrian Sports: *Thoroughbred Racing and Steeplechasing* (*in part*)

AIELLO, LESLIE C. Lecturer, Department of Anthropology, University College, London.
Anthropology

ALLABY, MICHAEL. Free-lance Writer and Lecturer. Author of *The Eco-Activists; Who Will Eat?; Inventing Tomorrow; World Food Resources.* Co-author of *A Blueprint for Survival; Home Farm.* Editor of *The Survival Handbook; Dictionary of the Environment.*
Environment (*in part*)

ALLAN, J. A. Lecturer in Geography, School of Oriental and African Studies, University of London.
Libya

ALSTON, REX. Broadcaster and Journalist; retired BBC Commentator. Author of *Taking the Air; Over to Rex Alston; Test Commentary; Watching Cricket.*
Cricket

AMOR, JAMES F. Formerly Assistant Press Officer, U.K. Central Electricity Generating Board.
Energy: *Electricity*

ANDERSON, PETER J. Assistant Director, Institute of Polar Studies, Ohio State University, Columbus.
Antarctic

APEL, JOHANNES. Curator, Botanic Garden, University of Hamburg. Author of *Gärtnerisch-Botanische Briefe.*
Zoos and Botanical Gardens: *Botanical Gardens*

ARCHIBALD, JOHN J. Feature Writer, *St. Louis Post-Dispatch.* Author of *Bowling for Boys and Girls.*
Bowling: *Tenpin Bowling* (*in part*); *Duckpins*

ARNOLD, GUY. Free-lance Writer. Author of *Modern Nigeria; Kenyatta and the Politics of Kenya; The Last Bunker; Britain's Oil; Aid in Africa.*
Botswana: Burundi; Cape Verde; Equatorial Guinea; Gambia, The; Ghana; Guinea-Bissau; Lesotho; Liberia; Maldives; Mauritius; Rwanda; São Tomé and Príncipe; Seychelles; Sierra Leone; Swaziland

ARNOLD, MAVIS. Free-lance Journalist, Dublin.
Biographies (*in part*); **Ireland**

ARRINGTON, LEONARD J. Church Historian, Church of Jesus Christ of Latter-day Saints. Author of *Great Basin Kingdom; An Economic History of the Latter-day Saints; Building the City of God: Community and Cooperation Among the Mormons; The Mormon Experience: A History of the Latter-day Saints.*
Religion: *Church of Jesus Christ of Latter-day Saints*

AYTON, CYRIL J. Editor, *Motorcycle Sport*, London.
Motor Sports: *Motorcycles*

BARFORD, MICHAEL F. Editor and Director, *World Tobacco*, London.
Industrial Review: *Tobacco*

BARGAD, WARREN. Milton D. Ratner Professor of Hebrew Literature, Spertus College of Judaica, Chicago. Author of *Hayim Hazaz: Novelist of Ideas; Anthology of Israeli Poetry.*
Literature: *Hebrew*

BARON, RAPHAEL R. Director of Research and Statistics, Israel Tourism Administration, Jerusalem. Author of *Seasonality in Tourism* and other analytical treatments of the subject.
Industrial Review: *Tourism*

BASS, HOWARD. Journalist and Broadcaster. Editor, *Winter Sports*, 1948–69. Winter Sports Correspondent, *Daily Telegraph* and *Sunday Telegraph*, London; *Evening Standard*, London; *Toronto Star*, Toronto; *Canadian Skater*, Ottawa; *Skating*, Boston; *Ski Racing*, Denver; *Ski*, London. Author of *The Sense in Sport; The Magic of Skiing; International Encyclopaedia of Winter Sports; Let's Go Skating.* Co-author of *Skating for Gold.*
Biographies (*in part*); **Ice Hockey:** *European and International;* **Winter Sports; Winter Sports:** *Special Report*

BAYLISS, DAVID. Chief Planner (Transportation), Greater London Council. Co-author of *Developing Patterns of Urbanization; Uses of Economics.* Advisory Editor of *Models in Urban and Regional Planning.*
Transportation (*in part*)

BEALL, JOHN V. Sales Manager, Davy McKee Corp. Author of sections 1 and 34, *Mining Engineering Handbook.* Frequent Contributor to *Mining Engineering.*
Mining and Quarrying (*in part*)

BEATTIE, ROGER A. Member of Secretariat, International Social Security Association, Geneva.
Social Security and Welfare Services (*in part*)

BEATTY, JAMES R. Research Fellow, B. F. Goodrich Research and Development Center, Brecksville, Ohio. Co-author of *Concepts in Compounding; Physical Testing of Elastomers and Polymers in Applied Polymer Science.*
Industrial Review: *Rubber*

BECKWITH, DAVID C. Editor, *Legal Times of Washington*, Washington, D.C.
Consumerism: *Special Report;* **United States Statistical Supplement:** *Developments in the States in 1980*

BENTLEY, STUART. Principal Lecturer in Sociology, Sheffield City Polytechnic, England. Co-author of *Work, Race, and Immigration.*
Migration, International; Race Relations

BERGERRE, MAX. Correspondent ANSA for Vatican Affairs, Rome.
Vatican City State

BERKOVITCH, ISRAEL. Free-lance Writer and Consultant. Author of *Coal on the Switchback; Coal: Energy and Chemical Storehouse.*
Energy: *Coal*

BICKELHAUPT, DAVID L. Professor of Insurance and Finance, College of Administrative Science, Ohio State University, Columbus. Author of *Transition to Multiple-Line Insurance Companies; General Insurance* (10th ed.).
Industrial Review: *Insurance*

BILEFIELD, LIONEL. Technical Journalist.
Industrial Review: *Paints and Varnishes*

BINSTED, ARTHUR T. E. Vice-President and former Chairman, British Bottlers' Institute, London.
Industrial Review: *Alcoholic Beverages* (*in part*)

BIRD, THOMAS E. Assistant Chairman, Jewish Studies Program, Queens College, City University of New York; Chairman (1978–79), Yiddish Section, Modern Language Association of America. Contributor to *Lexicon of Modern Yiddish Literature.*
Literature: *Yiddish* (*in part*)

BODDY, WILLIAM C. Editor, *Motor Sport.* Full Member, Guild of Motoring Writers. Author of *The History of Brooklands Motor Course; The World's Land Speed Record; Continental Sports Cars; The Bugatti Story; History of Montlhéry.*
Motor Sports: *Grand Prix Racing*

BODEN, EDWARD. Editor, *The Veterinary Record*; Executive Editor, *Research in Veterinary Science.*
Veterinary Science

BOLT, PETER H. Secretary, British Committee, World Methodist Council. Author of *A Way of Loving.*
Religion: *Methodist Churches*

BOONSTRA, DICK. Assistant Professor, Department of Political Science, Free University, Amsterdam.
Biographies (*in part*); **Netherlands, The; Suriname**

BOOTH, JOHN NICHOLLS. Lecturer and Writer; Co-founder, Japan Free Religious Association; Senior Pastor of a

number of U.S. churches. Author of *The Quest for Preaching Power; Introducing Unitarian Universalism.*
Religion: *Unitarian (Universalist) Churches*

BOSWALL, JEFFERY. Producer of Sound and Television Programs, BBC Natural History Unit, Bristol, England.
Life Sciences: *Ornithology*

BOX, JOHN B. H. Free-lance Writer and Researcher on Latin America and Iberia.
Cuba

BOYLE, C. L. Lieutenant Colonel, R.A. (retired). Chairman, Survival Service Commission, International Union for Conservation of Nature and Natural Resources, 1958–63; Secretary, Fauna Preservation Society, London, 1950–63.
Environment *(in part)*

BRACKMAN, ARNOLD C. Asian Affairs Specialist. Author of *Indonesian Communism: A History; Southeast Asia's Second Front: The Power Struggle in the Malay Archipelago; The Communist Collapse in Indonesia; The Last Emperor.*
Indonesia

BRADNOCK, ROBERT W. Lecturer in Geography with special reference to South Asia. Author of *Agricultural Change in South Asia* (forthcoming).
Feature Article: *Danger Signals from the Arc of Crisis*

BRADSHER, HENRY S. Diplomatic Correspondent, *Washington* (D.C.) *Star.*
Philippines

BRAIDWOOD, ROBERT J. Professor Emeritus of Old World Prehistory, the Oriental Institute and the Department of Anthropology, University of Chicago. Author of *Prehistoric Men; Archeologists and What They Do.*
Archaeology: *Eastern Hemisphere*

BRASHER, CHRIS. Sports Correspondent, *The Observer,* London; Reporter and Producer, BBC Television. Past Olympic Gold Medalist. Author of *Tokyo 1964; Mexico 1968; Munich 72.*
Biographies *(in part)*; **Track and Field Sports:** *Special Report*

BRAZEE, RUTLAGE J. Program Manager for Seismological Research, U.S. Nuclear Regulatory Commission, Washington, D.C.
Earth Sciences: *Geophysics*

BRECHER, KENNETH. Associate Professor of Astronomy, Boston University. Coauthor and co-editor of *Astronomy of the Ancients; High Energy Astrophysics and Its Relation to Elementary Particle Physics.*
Astronomy

BRUNO, HAL. Director of Political Coverage, ABC News, Washington, D.C.
Biographies *(in part)*

BURDIN, JOEL L. Professor of Educational Administration, the American University, Washington, D.C. Co-author of *A Reader's Guide to the Comprehensive Models for Preparing Elementary Teachers; Elementary School Curriculum and Instruction.*
Education *(in part)*

BURKE, DONALD P. Executive Editor, *Chemical Week,* New York City.
Industrial Review: *Chemicals*

BURKS, ARDATH W. Professor of Asian Studies, Rutgers University, New Brunswick, N.J. Author of *The Government of Japan; East Asia: China, Korea, Japan; Japan: Portrait of a Postindustrial Power.*
Japan

BUSS, ROBIN. Lecturer in French, Woolwich College of Further Education, London.
Biographies *(in part)*; **Literature:** *French (in part)*

BUTLER, FRANK. Sports Editor, *News of the World,* London. Author of *A History of Boxing in Britain.*
Combat Sports: *Boxing*

CALHOUN, DAVID R. Editor, Encyclopædia Britannica, Yearbooks.
Gambling *(in part)*

CALVERT, PETER. Reader in Politics, University of Southampton, England. Author of *Latin America; Mexico; The Mexicans; Emiliano Zapata.*
Feature Article: *Ferment in Central America*

CAMERON, SARAH. Economist, Lloyds Bank International Ltd., London.
Dominican Republic; Ecuador; Peru; Venezuela

CARTER, ROBERT W. Free-lance Journalist, London. Author of numerous newspaper and magazine articles.
Equestrian Sports: *Thoroughbred Racing and Steeplechasing (in part)*

CASSIDY, RICHARD J. Information Officer, British Gas Corporation. Author of *Gas: Natural Energy.*
Energy: *Natural Gas*

CASSIDY, VICTOR M. Writer and Editor, currently at work on a biography of Wyndham Lewis.
Biographies *(in part)*

CEGIELSKI, CHARLES M. Associate Editor, Encyclopædia Britannica, Yearbooks.
Games and Toys *(sidebar)*; **Life Sciences:** *Introduction*

CHAPMAN, KENNETH F. Former Editor, *Stamp Collecting* and *Philatelic Magazine;* Philatelic Correspondent, *The Times,* London. Author of *Good Stamp Collecting; Commonwealth Stamp Collecting.*
Philately and Numismatics: *Stamps*

CHAPMAN, ROBIN. Senior Economist, Lloyds Bank International Ltd., London.
Haiti; Latin-American Affairs

CHAPPELL, DUNCAN. Professor, Department of Criminology, Simon Fraser University, Vancouver, B.C. Co-author of *The Police and the Public in Australia and New Zealand.* Co-editor of *The Australian Criminal Justice System* (1st and 2nd ed.); *Violence and Criminal Justice; Forcible Rape: the Crime, the Victim and the Offender.*
Crime and Law Enforcement

CHU, HUNG-TI. Expert in Far Eastern Affairs; Former International Civil Servant and University Professor.
China; Taiwan

CLARKE, R. O. Principal Administrator, Social Affairs and Industrial Relations Division, Organization for Economic Cooperation and Development, Paris.
Industrial Relations

CLEVELAND, WILLIAM A. Geography Editor, *Encyclopædia Britannica* and Britannica Yearbooks.
Mining and Quarrying *(in part)*

CLIFTON, DONALD F. Professor of Metallurgy, University of Idaho.
Materials Sciences: *Metallurgy*

CLOUD, STANLEY W. Assistant Managing Editor, *Washington* (D.C.) *Star.*
Biographies *(in part)*; **United States:** *Special Report*

CLUTTERBUCK, RICHARD L. Senior Lecturer in Politics, University of Exeter, England. Formerly Chief Army Instructor, Royal College of Defence Studies, London. Author of *Living with Terrorism; Guerrillas and Terrorists; Kidnap and Ransom.*
Law: *Special Report*

COCKSEDGE, DAVID. Features Writer, *Athletics Monthly,* Brighton, England.
Biographies *(in part)*

COGLE, T. C. J. Editor, *Electrical Review,* London.
Industrial Review: *Electrical*

COMBA, ALDO. Executive Secretary, Department of Cooperation and Witness, World Alliance of Reformed Churches; former President, Federation of Protestant Churches in Italy. Author of *Le Parabole di Gesú.*
Religion: *Presbyterian, Reformed, and Congregational Churches*

COPPOCK, CHARLES DENNIS. Vice-President, English Lacrosse Union. Author of "Men's Lacrosse" in *The Oxford Companion to Sports and Games.*
Field Hockey and Lacrosse: *Lacrosse (in part)*

COSTIN, STANLEY H. British Correspondent, *Herrenjournal International* and *Men's Wear, Australasia.* Council of Management Member, British Men's Fashion Association Ltd. Former President, Men's Fashion Writers International.
Fashion and Dress *(in part)*

CRATER, RUFUS W. Chief Correspondent, *Broadcasting,* New York City.
Television and Radio *(in part)*

CROSS, COLIN J. Editor, *The Polo Times,* U.K. Chairman, European Polo Association.
Equestrian Sports: *Polo*

CROSSLAND, NORMAN. Bonn Correspondent, *The Economist,* London.
Biographies *(in part)*; **German Democratic Republic; Germany, Federal Republic of**

CVIIC, K. F. Leader Writer and East European Specialist, *The Economist,* London.
Yugoslavia

DAIFUKU, HIROSHI. Chief, Section for Operations and Training, Cultural Heritage Division, UNESCO, Paris.
Historic Preservation

DAUME, DAPHNE. Editor, Encyclopædia Britannica, Yearbooks.
Prisons and Penology *(sidebar)*

DAVID, TUDOR. Managing Editor, *Education,* London.
Education *(in part)*

DAVIS, DONALD A. Editor, *Drug & Cosmetic Industry,* and *Cosmetic Capers,* New York City. Contributor to *The*

Science and Technology of Aerosol Packaging; Advances in Cosmetic Technology.
Industrial Review: *Pharmaceuticals*

DEAM, JOHN B. Technical Director, National Machine Tool Builders Association, McLean, Va. Author of *The Synthesis of Common Digital Subsystems.*
Industrial Review: *Machinery and Machine Tools*

d'EÇA, RAUL. Retired from foreign service with U.S. Information Service. Co-author of *Latin American History.*
Brazil

DECRAENE, PHILIPPE. Member of editorial staff, *Le Monde,* Paris. Former Editor in Chief, *Revue française d'Études politiques africaines.* Author of *Le Panafricanisme; Tableau des Partis Politiques Africains; Lettres de l'Afrique Atlantique; L'expérience socialiste Somalienne.*
Benin; Biographies (*in part*); **Cameroon; Central African Republic; Chad; Comoros; Congo; Dependent States** (*in part*); **Djibouti; Gabon; Guinea; Ivory Coast; Madagascar; Mali; Mauritania; Niger; Senegal; Togo; Tunisia; Upper Volta**

de FAINBOIM, MARTA BEKERMAN. Economist, Lloyds Bank International Ltd., London.
Paraguay

de la BARRE, KENNETH. Staff Scientist, Arctic Institute of North America, Calgary, Montreal.
Arctic Regions

DENSELOW, ROBIN. Rock Music Critic, *The Guardian,* London. Current Affairs Producer, BBC Television. Co-author of *The Electric Muse.*
Music: *Popular*

DE PUY, NORMAN R. Pastor and Executive Minister, First Baptist Church of Dearborn, Mich. Author of *The Bible Alive; Help in Understanding Theology.*
Religion: *Baptist Churches*

DESAUTELS, PAUL E. Curator, Department of Mineral Sciences, National Museum of Natural History, Smithsonian Institution, Washington, D.C. Author of *The Mineral Kingdom; The Gem Kingdom.*
Industrial Review: *Gemstones*

DIRNBACHER, ELFRIEDE. Austrian Civil Servant.
Austria

DORRIS, TOM. Director, Lutheran News Bureau, New York City. Author of several periodical articles on religion, education, and medicine.
Religion: *Lutheran Churches*

DRAKE, CHRIS. Managing Director, *Cyprus Weekly,* Nicosia. Proprietor, East Med News Agency.
Cyprus

EIU. The Economist Intelligence Unit, London.
Economy, World (*in part*)

ELI, C. R. Secretary-Treasurer, U.S. Badminton Association.
Racket Games: *Badminton*

ENGELS, JAN R. Editor, *Vooruitgang* (Quarterly of the Belgian Party for Freedom and Progress), Brussels.
Belgium

ESZEKI, BASCO. Copy Editor, Encyclopædia Britannica; Assistant Editor, *Chicago Faces.*
Biographies (*in part*)

EWART, W. D. Editor and Director, *Fairplay International Shipping Weekly,* London. Author of *Marine Engines; Atomic Submarines; Hydrofoils and Hovercraft; Building a Ship.* Editor of *World Atlas of Shipping.*
Industrial Review: *Shipbuilding;* **Transportation** (*in part*)

FAIRBANK, JENTY. Director of Information Services, International Headquarters, The Salvation Army. Author of *William and Catherine Booth: God's Soldiers.*
Religion: *Salvation Army*

FARR, D. M. L. Professor of History and Director, Paterson Centre for International Programs, Carleton University, Ottawa. Co-author of *The Canadian Experience.*
Canada

FENDELL, ROBERT J. Auto Editor, *Science & Mechanics;* Auto Contributor, *Gentlemen's Quarterly.* Author of *The New Era Car Book and Auto Survival Guide; How to Make Your Car Last and Last.* Co-author of *Encyclopedia of Motor Racing Greats.*
Motor Sports: *U.S. Racing*

FERRIER, R. W. Group Historian and Archivist, British Petroleum Company Ltd., London.
Energy: *Petroleum*

FIDDICK, PETER. Specialist Writer, *The Guardian,* London.
Publishing: *Newspapers (in part); Magazines (in part)*

FIELDS, DONALD. Helsinki Correspondent, BBC, *The Guardian,* and *The Sunday Times,* London.
Finland

FIRTH, DAVID. Editor, *The Friend,* London; formerly Editor, *Quaker Monthly,* London.
Religion: *Religious Society of Friends*

FISHER, DAVID. Civil Engineer, Freeman Fox & Partners, London; formerly Executive Editor, *Engineering,* London.
Engineering Projects: *Bridges*

FLANAGAN, JACK C. Travel Counselor.
Water Sports: *Surfing*

FRADY, WILLIAM ENSIGN, III. Editor, *Water Polo Scoreboard,* Newport Beach, Calif.
Water Sports: *Water Polo*

FRANKLIN, HAROLD. Editor, *English Bridge Quarterly.* Bridge Correspondent, *Yorkshire Post; Yorkshire Evening Post.* Broadcaster. Author of *Best of Bridge on the Air.*
Contract Bridge

FRANZ, FREDERICK W. President, Watch Tower Bible and Tract Society of Pennsylvania.
Religion: *Jehovah's Witnesses*

FRAWLEY, MARGARET-LOUISE. Retired Press Officer, All-England Women's Lacrosse Association.
Field Hockey and Lacrosse: *Lacrosse (in part)*

FRIDAS, P. Assistant Director, International Vine and Wine Office, Paris.
Industrial Review: *Alcoholic Beverages (in part)*

FRIDOVICH, IRWIN. James B. Duke Professor of Biochemistry, Duke University Medical Center, Durham, N.C. Contributor to *Oxidase and Redox Systems; Molecular Mechanisms of Oxygen Activation.*
Life Sciences: *Molecular Biology (in part)*

FRIEDLY, ROBERT LOUIS. Executive Director, Office of Communication, Christian Church (Disciples of Christ), Indianapolis, Ind.
Religion: *Disciples of Christ*

FRISKIN, SYDNEY E. Hockey Correspondent, *The Times,* London.
Field Hockey and Lacrosse: *Field Hockey*

FROST, DAVID. Rugby Union Correspondent, *The Guardian,* London.
Football: *Rugby*

GADDUM, PETER W. Chairman, H. T. Gaddum and Company Ltd., Silk Merchants, Macclesfield, Cheshire, England. Honorary President, International Silk Association, Lyons. Author of *Silk—How and Where It Is Produced.*
Industrial Review: *Textiles (in part)*

GANADO, ALBERT. Lawyer, Malta.
Malta

GBGB. Gaming Board of Great Britain.
Gambling (*in part*)

GEORGE, T. J. S. Editor, *Asiaweek,* Hong Kong. Author of *Krishna Menon: A Biography; Lee Kuan Yew's Singapore; Revolt in Mindanao.*
Biographies (*in part*); **Cambodia; Korea; Laos; Southeast Asian Affairs; Thailand; Vietnam**

GIBNEY, FRANK. Vice-Chairman, Britannica Board of Editors. Founding president of TBS-Britannica, Tokyo.
Feature Article: *A Visit with President Sadat (sidebar)*

GILLESPIE, HUGH M. Director of Communications, International Road Federation, Washington, D.C.
Engineering Projects: *Roads*

GJESTER, FAY. Oslo Correspondent, *Financial Times,* London.
Norway

GOLDSMITH, ARTHUR. Editorial Director, *Popular Photography* and *Camera Arts,* New York City. Author of *The Photography Game; The Nude in Photography; The Camera and Its Images.* Co-author of *The Eye of Eisenstaedt.*
Photography

GOLOMBEK, HARRY. British Chess Champion, 1947, 1949, and 1955. Chess Correspondent, *The Times,* London. Author of *Penguin Handbook of the Game of Chess; A History of Chess.*
Chess

GOODWIN, NOËL. Associate Editor, *Dance & Dancers;* U.K. Dance Correspondent, *International Herald Tribune,* Paris, and *Ballet News,* New York City. Author of *A Ballet for Scotland;* editor of Royal Ballet and Royal Opera yearbooks for 1978, 1979, 1980. Contributor to the *Encyclopædia Britannica* (15th ed.).
Dance (*in part*)

GOODWIN, R. M. Free-lance Writer, London.
Biographies (*in part*)

GOODWIN, ROBERT E. Executive Director, Billiard Congress of America, Chicago; managing Director, Billiard and Bowling Institute of America.
Billiard Games

GOTTFRIED, MARTIN. Drama Critic, *Saturday Review*, New York City. Author of *A Theater Divided; Opening Nights; Broadway Musicals.*
Theatre (*in part*)

GOULD, DONALD W. Medical Writer and Broadcaster, U.K.
Health and Disease: *Overview* (*in part*); *Mental Health*

GREEN, BENNY. Record Reviewer, BBC. Author of *Blame It on My Youth; 58 Minutes to London; Jazz Decade; Drums in My Ears; Shaw's Champions.* Contributor to *Encyclopedia of Jazz.*
Music: *Jazz*

GREENLEAF, ARNO. Assistant Professor, Department of Biochemistry, Duke University Medical Center, Durham, N.C.
Life Sciences: *Molecular Biology* (*in part*)

GRIFFITHS, A. R. G. Senior Lecturer in History, Flinders University of South Australia. Author of *Contemporary Australia.*
Australia; Australia: *Special Report*; **Biographies** (*in part*); **Nauru; Papua New Guinea**

GROSSBERG, ROBERT H. Executive Director, U.S. Amateur Jai Alai Players Association, Miami, Fla.
Court Games: *Jai Alai*

GROSSMAN, JOEL W. Director, Archaeological Survey Office, Rutgers University, New Brunswick, N.J.
Archaeology: *Western Hemisphere*

HARDMAN, THOMAS C. Editor and Publisher, *The Water Skier*, American Water Ski Association. Co-author of *Let's Go Water Skiing.*
Water Sports: *Water Skiing*

HARRIES, DAVID A. Director, Tarmac International Ltd., London.
Engineering Projects: *Tunnels*

HASEGAWA, RYUSAKU. Editor, TBS-Britannica Co., Ltd., Tokyo.
Baseball (*in part*)

HAWKLAND, WILLIAM D. Chancellor and Professor of Law, Louisiana State University, Baton Rouge. Author of *Sales and Bulk Sales Under the Uniform Commercial Code; Cases on Bills and Notes; Transactional Guide of the Uniform Commercial Code; Cases on Sales and Security.*
Law: *Court Decisions*

HAWLEY, H. B. Specialist, Human Nutrition and Food Science, Switzerland.
Food Processing

HEBBLETHWAITE, PETER. Rome Correspondent, *National Catholic Reporter*, Kansas City, Mo. Author of *The Council Fathers and Atheism; Understanding the Synod; The Runaway Church; Christian-Marxist Dialogue and Beyond; The Year of Three Popes.*
Religion: *Roman Catholic Church*

HENDERSHOTT, MYRL C. Professor of Oceanography, Scripps Institution of Oceanography, La Jolla, Calif.
Earth Sciences: *Oceanography*

HERMAN, ROBIN CATHY. Reporter, *New York Times.*
Ice Hockey: *North American*

HESS, MARVIN G. Executive Vice-President, National Wrestling Coaches Association, Salt Lake City, Utah.
Combat Sports: *Wrestling*

HICKEY, GERALD C. Senior Social Analyst, Asia Bureau, Agency for International Development, U.S. Department of State. Former Research Anthropologist for the RAND Corp. in Saigon. Author of *Village in Vietnam.*
Special Preprint: *Vietnam, Socialist Republic of*

HINDIN, HARVEY J. Communications Editor, *Electronics* magazine, New York City. Author of numerous articles on electronics and mathematics.
Industrial Review: *Telecommunications*

HOPE, THOMAS W. President, Hope Reports, Inc. Rochester, N.Y. Author of *Hope Reports AV-USA; Hope Reports Education and Media; Hope Reports Perspective.*
Motion Pictures (*in part*)

HORRY, JOHN H. Former Secretary, International Squash Rackets Federation. Contributor to *The Oxford Companion to Sports and Games.*
Racket Games: *Squash Rackets*

HOTZ, LOUIS. Former Editorial Writer, *Johannesburg* (S.Af.) *Star.* Co-author and contributor to *The Jews in South Africa.*
South Africa

HOWKINS, JOHN. Editor, *InterMedia*, International Institute of Communications, London. Author of *Understanding Television; 1980 China Media Industry Report.*
Television and Radio (*in part*)

HUNNINGS, NEVILLE MARCH. Editorial Director, European Law Centre Ltd., London. Editor of *Common Market Law Reports, Commercial Laws of Europe*, and *European Commercial Cases.* Author of *Film Censors and the Law.* Co-editor of *Legal Problems of an Enlarged European Community.*
Law: *International Law*

HUSFLOEN, KYLE D. Editor, *The Antique Trader Weekly*, Dubuque, Iowa. Editor of *The Antique Trader Weekly Book of Collectible Dolls.*
Historic Preservation: *Special Report*

INGHAM, KENNETH. Professor of History, University of Bristol, England. Author of *Reformers in India; A History of East Africa.*
Angola; Kenya; Malawi; Mozambique; Sudan; Tanzania; Uganda; Zaire; Zambia; Zimbabwe

ISKOLDSKAYA, MAYA Y. Correspondent, Fiction Department, *Knizhnoye Obozreniye*, Moscow.
Literature: *Russian* (*in part*)

JACQUET, CONSTANT H. Staff Associate for Information Services, Office of Research, Evaluation and Planning, National Council of Churches. Editor of *Yearbook of American and Canadian Churches.*
United States Statistical Supplement: *Church Membership table*

JARDINE, ADRIAN. Company Director. Member, Guild of Yachting Writers.
Sailing

JASPERT, W. PINCUS. Technical Editorial Consultant. European Editor, North American Publishing Company, Philadelphia. Member, Inter-Comprint Planning Committee; Member, Society of Photographic Engineers and Scientists; Life Member, *Eurographic Press.* Author of *State of the Art.* Editor of *Encyclopaedia of Type Faces.*
Industrial Review: *Printing*

JENKINS, PETER. Policy Editor and Political Columnist, *The Guardian*, London.
United Kingdom

JESSOP, DAVID A. Editor, *Caribbean Chronicle* and *Insight.* Consultant on Caribbean affairs.
Bahamas, The; Barbados; Biographies (*in part*); **Dependent States** (*in part*); **Dominica; Grenada; Guyana; Jamaica; Saint Lucia; Saint Vincent and the Grenadines; Trinidad and Tobago**

JOFFÉ, GEORGE. Journalist and Writer on North African Affairs.
Algeria; Morocco

JONES, C. M. Consultant, *World Bowls*; Editor, *Tennis.* Member, British Society of Sports Psychology; Associate Member, British Association of National Coaches. Author of *Winning Bowls; How to Become a Champion*; numerous books on tennis. Co-author of *Tackle Bowls My Way; Bryant on Bowls.*
Bowling: *Lawn Bowls*

JONES, D. A. N. Assistant Editor, *The Listener*, London.
Literature: *Introduction; United Kingdom*

JONES, HANDEL H. Vice-President, Gnostic Concepts, Inc., Menlo Park, Calif.
Industrial Review: *Microelectronics*

JONES, W. GLYN. Professor of Scandinavian Studies, University of Newcastle upon Tyne, England. Author of *Johannes Jorgensens modne ar; Johannes Jörgensen; William Heinesen; Færo og kosmos; Danish: A Grammar and Exercises.*
Literature: *Danish*

JOSEPH, LOU. Manager of Media Relations, Bureau of Communications, American Dental Association. Author of *A Doctor Discusses Allergy: Facts and Fiction; Natural Childbirth; Diabetes; Childrens' Colds.*
Health and Disease: *Dentistry*

KATZ, WILLIAM A. Professor, School of Library Science, State University of New York, Albany. Author of *Magazines for Libraries* (3rd ed.); *Magazine Selection.*
Publishing: *Magazines* (*in part*)

KELLEHER, JOHN A. Editorial Consultant, *The Dominion*, Wellington, N.Z.
New Zealand

KELLMAN, JEROLD L. Editor in Chief, Publications International, Ltd. President

and Publisher, Writer's Guide Publications. Author of *Presidents of the United States; A Writer's Guide to Chicago-Area Publishers and Other Freelance Markets.* Contributor to *The People's Almanac.*
Computers

KENNEDY, RICHARD M. Agricultural Economist, International Economics Division of the Economics, Statistics, and Cooperatives Service, U.S. Department of Agriculture.
Agriculture and Food Supplies

KENT, LIVIJA. Associate Professor, Botany Department, University of Massachusetts.
Life Sciences: *Botany*

KERRIGAN, ANTHONY. Faculty Fellow and Translator-in-Residence, Center for the Study of Man in Contemporary Society, University of Notre Dame, Indiana. Editor and Translator of *Selected Works* of Miguel de Unamuno (7 vol.) and of works of Jorge Luis Borges. Author of *At the Front Door of the Atlantic.*
Literature: *Spanish (in part)*

KHINDARIA, BRIJ. Geneva Correspondent, *Financial Times,* London. Specialist in the work of international organizations and the role of private enterprise in development.
Feature Article: *Foundation for Survival*

KILIAN, MICHAEL D. Columnist, *Chicago Tribune;* News Commentator, WBBM Radio, Chicago. Captain, U.S. Air Force Civil Air Patrol. Author of *Who Runs Chicago?*
Aerial Sports

KILLHEFFER, JOHN V. Associate Editor, *Encyclopædia Britannica.*
Nobel Prizes *(in part)*

KIMCHE, JON. Editor, *Afro-Asian Affairs,* London. Author of *There Could Have Been Peace: The Untold Story of Why We Failed With Palestine and Again with Israel; Seven Fallen Pillars; Second Arab Awakening.*
Biographies *(in part)*; Israel

KIND, JOSHUA B. Associate Professor of Art History, Northern Illinois University, De Kalb. Author of *Rouault; Naive Art in Illinois 1830–1976.*
Museums *(in part)*

KITAGAWA, JOSEPH M. Professor of History of Religions, Divinity School, University of Chicago. Author of *Religions of the East; Religion in Japanese History.*
Religion: *Buddhism*

KLARE, HUGH J. Chairman, Gloucestershire Probation Training Committee, England. Secretary, Howard League for Penal Reform 1950–71. Author of *People in Prison.* Regular Contributor to *Justice of the Peace.*
Prisons and Penology

KNECHT, JEAN. Formerly Assistant Foreign Editor, *Le Monde,* Paris; formerly Permanent Correspondent in Washington and Vice-President of the Association de la Presse Diplomatique Française.
Biographies *(in part)*; **France**

KNOX, RICHARD A. Editor, *Nuclear Engineering International,* London. Author of *Experiments in Astronomy for Amateurs; Foundations of Astronomy.*
Industrial Review: *Nuclear Industry*

KOPPER, PHILIP. Free-lance Writer and Journalist, Washington, D.C.
Biographies *(in part)*; **Nobel Prizes** *(in part)*

KUNKLER, JULIE. Picture Editor, Encyclopædia Britannica, *Yearbook of Science and the Future.*
Biographies *(in part)*

LAMB, KEVIN M. Sports Writer, *Chicago Sun-Times.*
Biographies *(in part)*; **Football:** *U.S. Football; Canadian Football*

LARSON, ROY. Religion Editor, *Chicago Sun-Times.*
Religion: *Introduction*

LEAPER, ERIC. Executive Director, National Organization for River Sports, Colorado Springs, Colo.
Water Sports: *River Sports*

LEGUM, COLIN. Associate Editor, *The Observer;* Editor, *Middle East Contemporary Survey* and *Africa Contemporary Record,* London. Author of *Must We Lose Africa?; Congo Disaster; Pan-Africanism: A Political Guide; South Africa: Crisis for the West.*
African Affairs; African Affairs: *Special Report;* **Biographies** *(in part)*

LEIFER, MICHAEL. Reader in International Relations, London School of Economics and Political Science. Author of *Dilemmas of Statehood in Southeast Asia.*
Malaysia; Singapore

LENNOX-KERR, PETER. Editor, *High Performance Textiles;* European Editor, *Textile World.* Author of *The World Fibres Book.* Editor of *Nonwovens '71;* Publisher of *OE-Report* and *WP-Report,* New Mills, England.
Industrial Review: *Textiles (in part)*

LEVE, CHARLES S. Executive Director, National Court Clubs Association. Author of *Inside Racquetball;* Co-author of *Winning Racquetball.*
Racket Games: *Racquetball*

LITTELL, FRANKLIN H. Professor of Religion, Temple University, Philadelphia, Pa. Co-editor of *Weltkirchenlexikon;* Author of *Macmillan Atlas History of Christianity.*
Religion: *World Church Membership*

LOGAN, ROBERT G. Sportswriter, *Chicago Tribune.* Author of *The Bulls and Chicago—A Stormy Affair.*
Basketball *(in part)*

LOVE, JOHN H. Executive Director, American Power Boat Association, East Detroit, Mich. Editor, *Propeller,* a publication of the APBA.
Water Sports: *Motorboating*

LULING, VIRGINIA R. Social Anthropologist.
Somalia

LUNDE, ANDERS S. Consultant; Adjunct Professor, Department of Biostatistics, University of North Carolina. Author of *Systems of Demographic Measurement: The Single Round Retrospective Interview Survey.*
Demography

McCAULEY, MARTIN. Lecturer in Russian and Soviet Institutions, School of Slavonic and East European Studies, University of London. Author of *Khrushchev and Soviet Agriculture: The Virgin Land Programme 1953–1964; Marxism-Leninism in the German Democratic Republic; The Stalin File.* Editor of *The Russian Revolution and the Soviet State 1917–1921; Communist Power in Europe 1944–1949.*
Union of Soviet Socialist Republics

MACDONALD, BARRIE. Senior Lecturer in History, Massey University, Palmerston North, N.Z. Author of several articles on the history and politics of Pacific islands.
Biographies *(in part)*; **Dependent States** *(in part)*; **Fiji; Kiribati; Solomon Islands; Tonga; Tuvalu; Vanuatu; Western Samoa**

MacDONALD, M. C. Director, World Economics Ltd., London.
Agriculture and Food Supplies: *grain table;* **Transportation:** *table;* statistical sections of articles on the various countries

MACDONALD, TREVOR J. Manager, International Affairs, British Steel Corporation.
Industrial Review: *Iron and Steel*

MACGREGOR-MORRIS, PAMELA. Equestrian Correspondent, *The Times* and *Horse and Hound,* London. Author of books on equestrian topics.
Equestrian Sports: *Show Jumping*

McLACHLAN, KEITH S. Senior Lecturer, School of Oriental and African Studies, University of London.
Feature Article: *Danger Signals from the Arc of Crisis (in part);* **Iran**

MALLETT, H. M. F. Editor, *Wool Record Weekly Market Report,* Bradford, England.
Industrial Review: *Textiles (in part)*

MANGO, ANDREW. Orientalist and Broadcaster.
Biographies *(in part)*; **Turkey**

MAO, NATHAN K. Professor of Chinese Literature, Shippensburg (Pa.) State College. Author of *Modern Chinese Fiction; Pa Chin.*
Literature: *Chinese (in part)*

MARSHALL, J. G. SCOTT. Horticultural Consultant.
Gardening *(in part)*

MARTY, MARTIN E. Fairfax M. Cone Distinguished Service Professor, University of Chicago; Associate Editor, *The Christian Century.*
Religion: *Special Report*

MARYLES, DAISY G. Associate Editor, Bookselling and Marketing, *Publishers Weekly,* New York City.
Publishing: *Books (in part)*

MATEJA, JAMES L. Auto Editor and Financial Reporter, *Chicago Tribune.*
Industrial Review: *Automobiles*

MATTHÍASSON, BJÖRN. Economist, European Free Trade Association, Geneva.
Biographies *(in part)*; **Iceland**

MAZIE, DAVID M. Associate of Carl T. Rowan, syndicated columnist. Free-lance Writer.
Social Security and Welfare Services *(in part)*

MAZZE, EDWARD MARK. Dean and Professor of Marketing, School of Busi-

ness Administration, Temple University, Philadelphia. Author of *Personal Selling: Choice Against Chance; Introduction to Marketing: Readings in the Discipline.*
Consumerism (*in part*); **Industrial Review:** *Advertising*

MELLOR, CHRISTINE. Economist, Lloyds Bank International Ltd., London.
Argentina; Chile; Colombia; Costa Rica; El Salvador; Guatemala; Honduras; Nicaragua

MENDELSON, PAUL. Copy Editor, Encyclopædia Britannica.
Biographies (*in part*)

MERMEL, T. W. Consultant; formerly Chairman, Committee on World Register of Dams, International Commission on Large Dams. Author of *Register of Dams in the United States.*
Engineering Projects: *Dams table*

MEYENDORFF, JOHN. Professor of Church History and Patristics, St. Vladimir's Orthodox Theological Seminary; Professor of History, Fordham University, New York City. Author of *Christ in Eastern Christian Thought; Byzantine Theology; Byzantium and the Rise of Russia.*
Religion: *The Orthodox Church; Eastern Non-Chalcedonian Churches*

MILES, PETER W. Chairman, Department of Entomology, University of Adelaide, Australia.
Life Sciences: *Entomology*

MILLIKIN, SANDRA. Architectural Historian.
Architecture; Art Exhibitions; Biographies (*in part*); **Museums** (*in part*)

MINA, MARTHA H. Market Research Assistant, Glass Manufacturers' Federation, London.
Industrial Review: *Glass*

MITCHELL, K. K. Lecturer, Department of Physical Education, University of Leeds, England. Director, English Basket Ball Association.
Basketball (*in part*)

MODIANO, MARIO. Athens Correspondent, *The Times,* London.
Biographies (*in part*); **Greece**

MOFFAT, A. I. B. Senior Lecturer, Department of Civil Engineering, University of Newcastle upon Tyne, England. Editor of *Inspection, Operation and Maintenance of Existing Dams.*
Engineering Projects: *Dams*

MONACO, ALBERT M., JR. Executive Director, United States Volleyball Association, Colorado Springs, Colo.
Court Games: *Volleyball*

MOORE, JOHN E. Deputy Assistant Chief Hydrologist, Scientific Publications and Data Management, Water Resources Division, U.S. Geological Survey.
Earth Sciences: *Hydrology*

MORRISON, DONALD. Senior Editor, *Time* magazine.
Publishing: *Newspapers (in part)*

MORTIMER, MOLLY. Commonwealth Correspondent, *The Spectator,* London. Author of *Trusteeship in Practice; Kenya.*
Commonwealth of Nations; Dependent States (*in part*)

MOSEY, CHRIS. Associate Editor, *Sweden Now,* Stockholm; Swedish Correspondent, *The Observer, Daily Mail,* and *The Times Educational Supplement.* Contributor to *The Boat People.*
Sweden

MOSHANSKY, MOZELLE A. Music Journalist and Writer, *The Guardian, International Music Guide, Classical Music,* BBC Radio, Royal Philharmonic Orchestra, and Philips Records.
Biographies (*in part*); **Music:** *Classical*

MUCK, TERRY CHARLES. Editor, *Handball* magazine, Skokie, Ill.
Court Games: *Handball*

NAYLOR, ERNEST. Professor of Marine Biology, University of Liverpool; Director, Marine Biological Laboratory, Port Erin, Isle of Man. Author of *British Marine Isopods.* Co-editor, *Estuarine and Coastal Marine Science.*
Life Sciences: *Marine Biology*

NEILL, JOHN. Product Development Manager, Walker Engineering Ltd.; Consultant, Submerged Combustion Ltd. Author of Climbers' Club Guides; *Cwm Silyn and Tremadoc, Snowdon South;* Alpine Club Guide: *Selected Climbs in the Pennine Alps.*
Biographies (*in part*); **Mountaineering**

NELSON, BERT. Editor, *Track and Field News.* Author of *Little Red Book; The Decathlon Book; Olympic Track and Field; Of People and Things.*
Track and Field Sports

NETSCHERT, BRUCE C. Vice-President, National Economic Research Associates, Inc., Washington, D.C. Author of *The Future Supply of Oil and Gas.* Co-author of *Energy in the American Economy: 1850–1975.*
Energy: *World Summary*

NEUSNER, JACOB. University Professor, Brown University, Providence, R.I. Author of *Invitation to the Talmud; A History of the Mishnaic Law of Purities.*
Religion: *Judaism*

NOEL, H. S. Free-lance Journalist; formerly Managing Editor, *World Fishing,* London.
Fisheries

NORMAN, GERALDINE. Saleroom Correspondent, *The Times,* London. Author of *The Sale of Works of Art; Nineteenth Century Painters and Painting: A Dictionary;* Co-author of *The Fake's Progress.*
Art Sales

NOVALES, RONALD R. Professor of Biological Sciences, Northwestern University, Evanston, Ill. Contributor to *Handbook of Physiology; Comparative Animal Physiology; Frontiers of Hormone Research; Pigment Cell; American Zoologist.*
Life Sciences: *Zoology Overview*

OLNEY, P. J. Curator of Birds, Zoological Society of London. Editor, *International Zoo Yearbook.* Co-editor of *Birds of the Western Palearctic.*
Zoos and Botanical Gardens: *Zoos*

OSBORNE, KEITH. Editor, *Rowing, 1961–63;* Honorary Editor, *British Rowing Almanack,* 1961– . Author of *Boat Racing in Britain, 1715–1975.*
Rowing

OSTERBIND, CARTER C. Director, Gerontology Center, and Professor of Economics, University of Florida. Editor of *Income in Retirement; Migration, Mobility, and Aging;* and others.
Industrial Review: *Building and Construction*

PAGE, SHEILA A. B. Research Officer, National Institute of Economic and Social Research, London.
Economy, World (*in part*)

PALMER, JOHN. European Editor, *The Guardian,* London.
Biographies (*in part*); **European Unity**

PALMER, S. B. Senior Lecturer, Department of Applied Physics, University of Hull, England.
Physics

PARKER, SANDY. Publisher of weekly international newsletter on fur industry.
Industrial Review: *Furs*

PATTERSON, SHEILA. Honorary Research Fellow, Centre for Southern African Studies, University of York, England. Editor of *New Community,* Commission for Racial Equality.
United Kingdom: *Special Report*

PAUL, CHARLES ROBERT, JR. Director of Communications, U.S. Olympic Committee, Colorado Springs, Colo. Author of *The Olympic Games.*
Gymnastics and Weight Lifting

PENFOLD, ROBIN C. Free-lance Writer specializing in industrial topics. Editor, *Shell Polymers.* Author of *A Journalist's Guide to Plastics.*
Industrial Review: *Plastics*

PERTILE, LINO. Lecturer in Italian, University of Sussex, England.
Literature: *Italian*

PETHERICK, KARIN. Reader in Swedish, University of London.
Literature: *Swedish*

PFEFFER, IRVING. Attorney. Chairman, Pacific and General Insurance Co., Ltd. Author of *The Financing of Small Business; Perspectives on Insurance.*
Stock Exchanges (*in part*)

PHINNEY, ALLISON W. Manager, Committees on Publication, The First Church of Christ, Scientist, Boston.
Religion: *Church of Christ, Scientist*

PINFOLD, GEOFFREY M. Associate, NCL Consulting Engineers, London. Author of *Reinforced Concrete Chimneys and Towers.*
Engineering Projects: *Buildings*

PLOTKIN, FREDERICK S. Professor of English Literature and Chairman, Division of Humanities, Stern College, Yeshiva University, New York City. Author of *Milton's Inward Jerusalem; Faith and Reason; Judaism and Tragic Theology.*
Literature: *United States*

PLOTNIK, ARTHUR. Editor, *American Libraries,* American Library Association.
Libraries (*in part*)

POST, AVERY D. President, United Church of Christ, New York City.
Religion: *United Church of Christ*

PRASAD, H. Y. SHARADA. Information Adviser to the Prime Minister, New Delhi, India.
Biographies (*in part*); **India**

QUINN, JANE BRYANT. Contributing Editor, *Newsweek* magazine; Personal Finance Columnist, *Washington Post*; Business Correspondent, CBS Morning News. Author of *Everyone's Money Book.*
Economy, World: *Special Report* (*in part*)

RANGER, ROBIN. Associate Professor, Department of Political Science, St. Francis Xavier University, Antigonish, Nova Scotia; Department of National Defence Fellow in Strategic Studies (1978–79); NATO Fellow, 1980–81. Author of *Arms and Politics, 1958–1978; Arms Control in a Changing Political Context.*
Defense; Defense: *Special Report*

RAY, G. F. Senior Research Fellow, National Institute of Economic and Social Research, London; Visiting Professor, University of Surrey, Guildford, England.
Industrial Review: *Introduction*

READ, ANTHONY A. Director, Book Development Council, London.
Publishing: *Books* (*in part*)

REBELO, L. S. Lecturer, Department of Portuguese Studies, King's College, University of London.
Literature: *Portuguese* (*in part*)

REICHELDERFER, F. W. Consultant on Atmospheric Sciences; formerly Director, Weather Bureau, U.S. Department of Commerce, Washington, D.C.
Earth Sciences: *Meteorology*

REID, J. H. Senior Lecturer in German, University of Nottingham, England. Co-editor of *Renaissance and Modern Studies.* Author of *Heinrich Böll: Withdrawal and Re-emergence*; Co-author of *Critical Strategies: German Fiction in the Twentieth Century.*
Literature: *German*

RIGHTER, ROSEMARY. Development Correspondent, *The Sunday Times,* London. Author of *Whose News?: Politics, the Press and the Third World.* Co-author of *The Exploding Cities.*
Feature Article: *The Media and the Third World: A Fair Shake?*

ROBINSON, DAVID. Film Critic, *The Times,* London. Author of *Buster Keaton; The Great Funnies—A History of Screen Comedy; A History of World Cinema.*
Biographies (*in part*); **Motion Pictures** (*in part*)

RUZIC, NEIL P. President, Island for Science Inc., Beverly Shores, Ind. Author of *Where the Winds Sleep; The Case for Going to the Moon.*
Feature Article: *American Ingenuity—Does It Still Thrive?*

SADAT, ANWAR AS-. President of Egypt.
Feature Article: *The Global Views of President Sadat*

SAEKI, SHOICHI. Professor of Comparative Literature, University of Tokyo. Author of *In Search of Japanese Ego.*
Literature: *Japanese*

SAINT-AMOUR, ROBERT. Professor, Department of Literary Studies, University of Quebec at Montreal.
Literature: *French* (*in part*)

SALIBI, KAMAL SULEIMAN. Professor of History, American University of Beirut. Author of *The Modern History of Lebanon.*
Special Preprint: *Beirut*

SARAHETE, YRJÖ. General Secretary, Fédération Internationale des Quilleurs, Helsinki.
Bowling: *Tenpin Bowling* (*in part*)

SCHOENFIELD, ALBERT. Co-publisher, *Swimming World*; Vice-Chairman, U.S. Olympic Swimming Committee. U.S. Representative to FINA Technical Committee. Contributor to *The Technique of Water Polo; The History of Swimming; Competitive Swimming as I See It.*
Swimming

SCHÖPFLIN, GEORGE. Lecturer in East European Political Institutions, London School of Economics and School of Slavonic and East European Studies, University of London.
Czechoslovakia

SCHULMAN, ELIAS. Professor, Queens College, City University of New York. Author of *Israel Tsinberg, His Life and Works; A History of Yiddish Literature in America; Soviet-Yiddish Literature; Portraits and Studies.*
Literature: *Yiddish* (*in part*)

SEARS, ROBERT N. Writer, *The American Rifleman.*
Target Sports: *Shooting*

SHARPE, MITCHELL R. Science Writer; Historian, Alabama Space and Rocket Center, Huntsville. Author of *The Rocket Team; Living in Space: The Environment of the Astronaut; "It Is I, Seagull": Valentina Tereshkova, First Woman in Space; Satellites and Probes, the Development of Unmanned Spaceflight.*
Space Exploration

SHAW, T. R. Commander, Royal Navy. Associate Editor, *International Journal of Speleology.* Author of *History of Cave Science.*
Speleology

SHENK, CLAYTON B. Honorary President, U.S. National Archery Association.
Target Sports: *Archery*

SIMPSON, NOEL. Managing Director, Sydney Bloodstock Proprietary Ltd., Sydney, Australia.
Equestrian Sports: *Harness Racing*

SMEDLEY, GLENN B. Public Relations Director, American Numismatic Association.
Philately and Numismatics: *Coins*

SMITH, REUBEN W. Dean, Graduate School, and Professor of History, University of the Pacific, Stockton, Calif. Editor of *Venture of Islam* by M. G. S. Hodgson.
Religion: *Islam*

SMOGORZEWSKI, K. M. Writer on contemporary history. Founder and Editor, *Free Europe,* London. Author of *The United States and Great Britain; Poland's Access to the Sea.*
Albania; Andorra; Biographies (*in part*); **Bulgaria; Hungary; Liechtenstein; Luxembourg; Monaco; Mongolia; Poland; Political Parties; Romania; San Marino**

SNIDER, ARTHUR J. Medical Columnist, *Chicago Sun-Times.* Author of *Learning How to Live with Heart Trouble; Learning How to Live with Nervous Tension; Learning How to Live with High Blood Pressure.*
Health and Disease: *Overview* (*in part*)

SPELMAN, ROBERT A. President, Home Furnishings Services, Washington, D.C.
Industrial Review: *Furniture*

STAERK, MELANIE. Member, Swiss Press Association. Former Member, Swiss National Commission for UNESCO.
Switzerland

STEEN, LYNN ARTHUR. Professor of Mathematics, St. Olaf College, Northfield, Minn. Author of *Mathematics Today; Counterexamples in Topology; Annotated Bibliography of Expository Writing in the Mathematical Sciences.*
Mathematics

STERN, IRWIN. Assistant Professor of Portuguese, Columbia University, New York City. Author of *Júlio Dinis e o romance português (1860–1870)*; Co-editor of *Modern Iberian Literature: A Library of Literary Criticism.*
Literature: *Portuguese* (*in part*)

STEVENSON, TOM. Garden Columnist, *Washington Post*; Washington Post-Los Angeles Times News Service. Author of *Pruning Guide for Trees, Shrubs, and Vines; Lawn Guide.*
Gardening (*in part*)

STØVERUD, TORBJØRN. W. P. Ker Senior Lecturer in Norwegian, University College, London.
Literature: *Norwegian*

STRAUSS, MICHAEL. Ski and Sports Writer, *New York Times.* Author of *Ski Areas, U.S.A.*
Combat Sports: *Fencing*

SULLIVAN, H. PATRICK. Dean of the Faculty and Professor of Religion, Vassar College, Poughkeepsie, N.Y.
Religion: *Hinduism*

SWEETINBURGH, THELMA. Paris Fashion Correspondent for the British Wool Textile Industry.
Fashion and Dress (*in part*)

SWIFT, RICHARD N. Professor of Politics, New York University, New York City. Author of *International Law: Current and Classic; World Affairs and the College Curriculum.*
United Nations

SYNAN, VINSON. Assistant General Superintendent, Pentecostal Holiness Church. Author of *The Holiness-Pentecostal Movement; The Old Time Power.*
Religion: *Pentecostal Churches*

TAISHOFF, SOL J. Editor, *Broadcasting,* Washington, D.C.
Television and Radio (*in part*)

TALLAN, NORMAN M. Chief Scientist, Air Force Materials Laboratory, Wright-Patterson Air Force Base, Dayton, Ohio. Editor of *Electrical Conductivity in Ceramics and Glass.*
Materials Sciences: *Ceramics*

TATEISHI, KAY K. Tokyo Night News Editor, Associated Press.
Biographies (*in part*)

TATTERSALL, ARTHUR. Textile Trade Statistician, Manchester, England.
Industrial Review: *Textiles (in part)*

TERRY, WALTER, JR. Dance Critic, *Saturday Review* magazine, New York City. Author of *The Dance in America; Great Male Dancers of the Ballet.*
Dance *(in part)*

THEINER, GEORGE. Assistant Editor, *Index on Censorship*, London. Co-author of *The Kill Dog*; editor of *New Writing in Czechoslovakia*; translator of *Poetry of Miroslav Holub.*
Literature: *Eastern European; Russian (in part)*

THOMAS, HARFORD. Retired City and Financial Editor, *The Guardian*, London.
Biographies *(in part)*

THOMAS, THEODORE V. Free-lance Journalist and Press Consultant. Editor (1961–79), *British Toys and Hobbies.*
Games and Toys

THOMPSON, GODFREY. Director of Libraries and Art Galleries, City of London. Author of *Planning and Design of Library Buildings.*
Libraries *(in part)*

TINGAY, LANCE. Lawn Tennis Correspondent, the *Daily Telegraph*, London. Author of *100 Years of Wimbledon; Tennis, A Pictorial History.*
Tennis

TOKUOKA, TAKAO. Staff Writer, Mainichi Newspapers. Author of *Fifty Years of Light and Dark; Background of the Literature of Yukio Mishima.*
Biographies *(in part)*

TRIGG, ROBERT H. Assistant Vice-President, Economic Research, New York Stock Exchange.
Stock Exchanges *(in part)*

TRILLING, OSSIA. Vice-President, International Association of Theatre Critics (1956–77). Co-editor and Contributor, *International Theatre.* Contributor, BBC, the *Financial Times*, London.
Biographies *(in part)*; **Theatre** *(in part)*; **Theatre** *(sidebar)*

TRUSSELL, TAIT. Senior Vice-President, American Forest Institute.
Industrial Review: *Wood Products*

UNHCR. The Office of the United Nations High Commissioner for Refugees.
Refugees

UNNY, GOVINDAN. Agence France-Presse Special Correspondent for India, Nepal, and Sri Lanka.
Afghanistan; Bangladesh; Bhutan; Burma; Nepal; Pakistan; Sri Lanka

VALE, NORMAN K. Retired Director of News Services, The United Church of Canada.
Religion: *United Church of Canada*

van den HOVEN, ISOLA. Writer on Consumer Affairs, The Hague, Neth.
Consumerism *(in part)*

VERDI, ROBERT WILLIAM. Sportswriter, *Chicago Tribune.*
Baseball *(in part)*

VINT, ARTHUR KINGSLEY. Counselor, International Table Tennis Federation, East Sussex, England.
Table Tennis

WADE, NICHOLAS. Member, News and Comment Staff, *Science* magazine, Washington, D.C. Author of *The Ultimate Experiment; The Nobel Duel* (forthcoming).
Life Sciences: *Special Report*

WADLEY, J. B. Writer and Broadcaster on cycling; Cycling Correspondent, *Daily Telegraph*, London. Editor of *Guinness Guide to Bicycling.* Author of *Tour de France 1970, 1971, and 1973; Old Roads and New.*
Cycling

WARD, PETER. Owner and Operator, Ward News Service, Ottawa; Parliamentary Reporter and Commentator.
Canada: *Special Report*

WARD-THOMAS, P. A. Golf Correspondent, *Country Life*, London.
Biographies *(in part)*; **Golf**

WARNER, ANTONY C. Editor, *Drinks Marketing*, London.
Industrial Review: *Alcoholic Beverages (in part)*

WAY, DIANE LOIS. Historical Researcher, Ontario Historical Studies Series.
Biographies *(in part)*

WHELAN, JOHN. Deputy Editor and News Editor, *Middle East Economic Digest*, London.
Bahrain; Biographies *(in part)*; **Egypt; Iraq; Jordan; Kuwait; Lebanon; Middle Eastern Affairs; Oman; Qatar; Saudi Arabia; Syria; United Arab Emirates; Yemen, People's Democratic Republic of; Yemen Arab Republic**

WHITTINGHAM, RICHARD J. Free-lance Writer, Editor and Photographer, Chicago. Author of *Martial Justice; The Chicago Bears.*
Industrial Relations: *Special Report*

WIJNGAARD, BARBARA. Economist, Lloyds Bank International Ltd., London.
Mexico

WILKINSON, GORDON. Director, NPM Communications, New Product Management Group, London. Chemistry Consultant, *New Scientist*, London. Author of *Industrial Timber Preservation.*
Chemistry

WILLEY, DAVID DOUGLAS. Rome Correspondent, BBC.
Biographies *(in part)*; **Italy**

WILLIAMS, RAYMOND L. Assistant Professor of Spanish, Washington University, St. Louis, Mo. Author of *La novela colombiana contemporanea; Aproximaciones a Gustavo Álvarez Gardeazabal.*
Literature: *Spanish (in part)*

WILLIAMSON, TREVOR. Chief Sports Subeditor, *Daily Telegraph*, London.
Football: *Association Football*

WILSON, MICHAEL. Employed with Carl Byoir & Associates Ltd., London.
Industrial Review: *Aerospace*

WILSON, VIRGINIA. Research Associate, *Newsweek* magazine.
Economy, World: *Special Report (in part)*

WITTE, RANDALL E. Associate Editor, *The Western Horseman* magazine, Colorado Springs, Co.
Rodeo

WOOD, CHRISTINA. Free-lance Sportswriter.
Racket Games: *Rackets; Real Tennis*

WOOD, KENNETH H. Editor, *Adventist Review.* Author of *Meditations for Moderns; Relevant Religion*; co-author of *His Initials Were F.D.N.*
Religion: *Seventh-day Adventist Church*

WOODS, ELIZABETH. Writer. Author of *The Yellow Volkswagen; Gone; Men; The Amateur.*
Literature: *English (in part)*

WOOLLER, MICHAEL. Economist, Lloyds Bank International Ltd., London.
Bolivia; Portugal; Spain; Uruguay

WOOLLEY, DAVID. Editor, *Airports International*, London.
Transportation *(in part)*

WORSNOP, RICHARD L. Associate Editor, Editorial Research Reports, Washington, D.C.
United States

WRIGHT, ALMON R. Retired Senior Historian, U.S. Department of State.
Panama

WYLLIE, PETER JOHN. Homer J. Livingston Professor and Chairman, Department of Geological Sciences, University of Chicago. Author of *The Dynamic Earth; The Way the Earth Works.*
Earth Sciences: *Geology and Geochemistry*

YANG, WINSTON L. Y. Professor of Chinese Studies, Department of Asian Studies, Seton Hall University, South Orange, N.J. Author of *Modern Chinese Fiction; Teng Hsiao-p'ing: A Political Biography* (forthcoming).
Biographies *(in part)*; **Literature:** *Chinese (in part)*

YOUNG, M. NORVEL. Chancellor, Pepperdine University, Malibu, California; Chairman of the Board, 20th Century Christian Publishing Company. Author of *Preachers of Today; History of Colleges Connected with Churches of Christ; The Church Is Building.*
Religion: *Churches of Christ*

YOUNG, SUSAN. News Editor, *Church Times*, London.
Religion: *Anglican Communion*

Index

The black type entries are article headings in the *Book of the Year*. These black type article entries do not show page notations because they are to be found in their alphabetical position in the body of the book. They show the dates of the issues of the *Book of the Year* in which the articles appear. For example "Archaeology 81, 80, 79" indicates that the article "Archaeology" is to be found in the 1981, 1980, and 1979 *Book of the Year*.

The light type headings that are indented under black type article headings refer to material elsewhere in the text related to the subject under which they are listed. The light type headings that are not indented refer to information in the text not given a special article. Biographies and obituaries are listed as cross references to the sections "Biographies" and "Obituaries" within the article "*People of the Year*." References to illustrations are preceded by the abbreviation "il."

All headings, whether consisting of a single word or more, are treated for the purpose of alphabetization as single complete headings. Names beginning with "Mc" and "Mac" are alphabetized as "Mac"; "St." is treated as "Saint."

A

B

E

F

G

H

I

J

K

L

N

P

T

U

V

W

To extend the tradition of excellence of your Encyclopaedia Britannica educational program, you may also avail yourself of other aids for your home reference center.

Described on the next page is a companion product–the Britannica 3 bookcase–that is designed to help you and your family. It will add attractiveness and value to your home library, as it keeps it well organized.

Should you wish to order it, or to obtain further information, please write to us at

Britannica Home Library Service
Attn: Year Book Department
P. O. Box 4928
Chicago, Illinois 60680

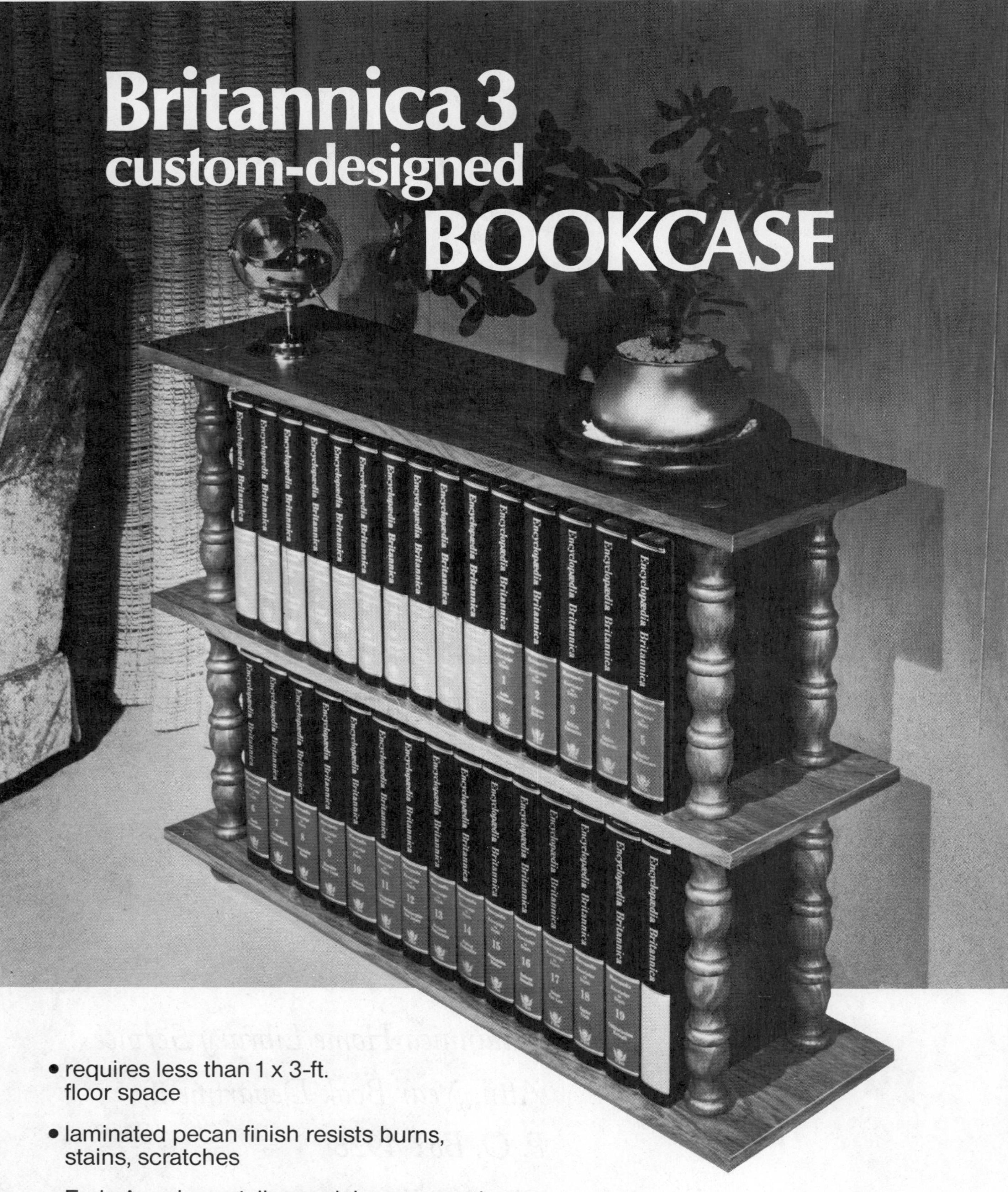

- requires less than 1 x 3-ft. floor space
- laminated pecan finish resists burns, stains, scratches
- Early American styling enriches any setting
- case size: 35¾″ wide, 9¾″ deep, 27⅝″ high

This offer available only in the United States